Koren Talmud Bavli

THE NOÉ EDITION

MOED KATAN · ḤAGIGA

Steinsaltz Center

KOREN

תלמוד בבלי

KOREN TALMUD BAVLI

THE NOÉ EDITION

מועד קטן · חגיגה

MOED KATAN · ḤAGIGA

COMMENTARY BY

Rabbi Adin Even-Israel
Steinsaltz

EDITOR-IN-CHIEF

Rabbi Dr Tzvi Hersh Weinreb

EXECUTIVE EDITOR

Rabbi Joshua Schreier

STEINSALTZ CENTER
KOREN PUBLISHERS JERUSALEM

Supported by the Matanel Foundation

The Noé Edition Koren Talmud Bavli
Volume 13: Tractate Moed Katan · Tractate Ḥagiga

Hardcover edition, ISBN 978 965 301 574 6

First Hebrew/English Edition, 2014

Koren Publishers Jerusalem Ltd.
PO Box 4044, Jerusalem 91040, ISRAEL
PO Box 8531, New Milford, CT 06776, USA
www.korenpub.com

Steinsaltz Center

Steinsaltz Center is the parent organization of institutions established by Rabbi Adin Even-Israel Steinsaltz

PO Box 45187, Jerusalem 91450 ISRAEL
Telephone: +972 2 646 0900, Fax +972 2 624 9454
www.steinsaltz-center.org

This book was published in cooperation with the Israel Institute for Talmudic Publications.

Hardcover design by Ben Gasner

Third printing, 2022

Printed in PRC

הִנֵּה יָמִים בָּאִים, נְאֻם אֲדֹנָי יֱהוִֹה, וְהִשְׁלַחְתִּי רָעָב בָּאָרֶץ,
לֹא־רָעָב לַלֶּחֶם וְלֹא־צָמָא לַמַּיִם, כִּי אִם־לִשְׁמֹעַ אֵת דִּבְרֵי יהוה.

Behold, days are coming – says the LORD God –
I will send a hunger to the land, not a hunger for bread
nor a thirst for water, but to hear the words of the LORD.

(AMOS 8:11)

The Noé edition of the Koren Talmud Bavli
with the commentary of Rabbi Adin Even-Israel Steinsaltz
is dedicated to all those who open its cover
to quench their thirst for Jewish knowledge,
in our generation of Torah renaissance.

This beautiful edition is for the young, the aged,
the novice and the savant alike,
as it unites the depth of Torah knowledge
with the best of academic scholarship.

Within its exquisite and vibrant pages,
words become worlds.

It will claim its place in the library of classics,
in the bookcases of the Beit Midrash,
the classrooms of our schools,
and in the offices of professionals and businesspeople
who carve out precious time to grapple with its timeless wisdom.

For the Student and the Scholar

DEDICATED BY LEO AND SUE NOÉ

Steinsaltz Center

Executive Director, Steinsaltz Center

Rabbi Meni Even-Israel

Managing Editor

Rabbi Jason Rappoport

Senior Content Editor

Rabbi Dr. Shalom Z. Berger

Editors

Rabbi Joshua Amaru, *Coordinating Editor*
Rabbi Yehoshua Duker
Rabbi Yonatan Shai Freedman
Raz Hartman
Gila Hock
Rabbi Adin Krohn
Catriel Lev
Rabbi Jason Lieb
Adina Luber
Rabbi Avishai Magence, *Content Curator*
Sarit Nagus
Rabbi David Sedley
Shira Shmidman
Rabbi Michael Siev
Avi Steinhart
Rabbi David Strauss
Amiel Vick

Copy Editors

Aliza Israel, *Coordinator*
Bracha Hermon
Ita Olesker
Debbie Ismailoff
Shira Finson
Ilana Sobel
Deena Nataf
Eliana Kurlantzick Yorav
Nava Wieder

Language Consultants

Dr. Stephanie E. Binder, *Greek & Latin*
Rabbi Yaakov Hoffman, *Arabic*
Dr. Shai Secunda, *Persian*
Shira Shmidman, *Aramaic*

KOREN

Design & Typesetting

Raphaël Freeman, *Design & Typography*
Dena Landowne Bailey, *Typesetting*
Rina Ben Gal, *Typesetting*
Tani Bayer, *Jacket Design*

Images

Eliahu Misgav, *Illustration & Image Acquisition*

והגדת לבנך ביום ההוא לאמר...

And you should teach your children on that day...

(FROM THE PASSOVER HAGGADA)

We dedicate this volume
with much love and gratitude
to our parents

Lotte and Lou Bravmann

We treasure the Passovers spent with you
each year leading our Seders

And we thank you
for all of the lessons you have taught us,
our children and grandchildren

Judy and Uri Kaufthal
Carol and Chuck Berlin

Contents

For the vocalized Vilna Shas layout, please open as a Hebrew book.

Haskama

Rabbi Moshe Feinstein

RABBI MOSES FEINSTEIN
455 F. D. R. DRIVE
New York N. Y. 10002
OResgon 7-1222

משה פיינשטיין
ר"ם תפארת ירושלים
בנוא יארק

ב"ה

הנה ראיתי הפירוש החשוב של הרב הגאון מוהר"ר עדין שטיינזלץ
שליט"א מעיה"ק ירושלים, על מסכתות ביצה ור"ה. באמת כבר ידוע
לי פירושו של הרה"ג הנ"ל על מסכתות מתלמוד בבלי, וכבר כתבתי
מכתב הסכמה עליהם. ובאתי בזה רק להדגיש מחוש איך שהחידושים
של הרה"ג הנ"ל, שכולל פירוש חדש על הגמרא עצמו וגם פירוש שיש
בו סיכום להלכה מהנידונים שבגמרא, נוסף לעוד כמה חלקים, הם
באמת עבודה גדולה, שיכולים להיות לתועלת לא רק לאלו שכבר
מורגלים בלמוד הגמרא, ורוצים להעמק יותר, אלא גם לאלו שמתחילים
ללמוד, להדריכם בדרכי התורה איך להבין ולהעמיק בים התלמוד.

והריני מברך להרה"ג הנ"ל שיצליחהו השי"ת בספריו אלו ושיזכה
לחבר עוד ספרים, להגדיל תורה ולהאדירה, לתפארת השם ותורתו.

ועל זה באתי על החתום לכבוד התורה ביום ז' לחודש אייר תשמ"ג.

משה פיינשטיין

משה פיינשטיין

…These new commentaries – which include a new interpretation of the Talmud, a halakhic summary of the debated issues, and various other sections – are a truly outstanding work; they can be of great benefit not only to those familiar with talmudic study who seek to deepen their understanding, but also to those who are just beginning to learn, guiding them through the pathways of the Torah and teaching them how to delve into the sea of the Talmud.

I would like to offer my blessing to this learned scholar. May the Holy One grant him success with these volumes and may he merit to write many more, to enhance the greatness of Torah, and bring glory to God and His word…

Rabbi Moshe Feinstein
New York, 7 Adar 5743

ר׳ משה פיינשטיין שליט״א
הנה ראיתי את מסכת אחת מהש״ס שנקד אותה וגם צייר צורות הצמחים וכדומה מדברים שלא ידוע לכמה אנשים הרה״ג ר׳ עדין שטיינזלץ מירושלים שליט״א וגם הוסיף שם בגליון פירושים וחידושים וניכר שהוא ת״ח וראויין לעיין בהם ת״ח ובני הישיבה וטוב גם לקנותם בבתי כנסיות ובבתי מדרשות שיש שיהיו להם לתועלת. — ועל זה באתי עה״ח ג׳ אדר ב׳ תש״ל.
נאם משה פיינשטיין
ר״מ תפארת ירושלים, ניו־יורק, ארה״ב

I have seen one tractate from the Talmud to which the great scholar Rabbi Adin Steinsaltz שליט״א has added *nikkud* (vowels) and illustrations to explain that which is unknown to many people; he has also added interpretations and innovations, and is evidently a *talmid ḥakham*. *Talmidei ḥakhamim* and yeshiva students ought to study these volumes, and synagogues and *batei midrash* would do well to purchase them, as they may find them useful.

Rabbi Moshe Feinstein
New York, Adar 5730

Haskama

Rabbi Menachem Mendel Schneerson

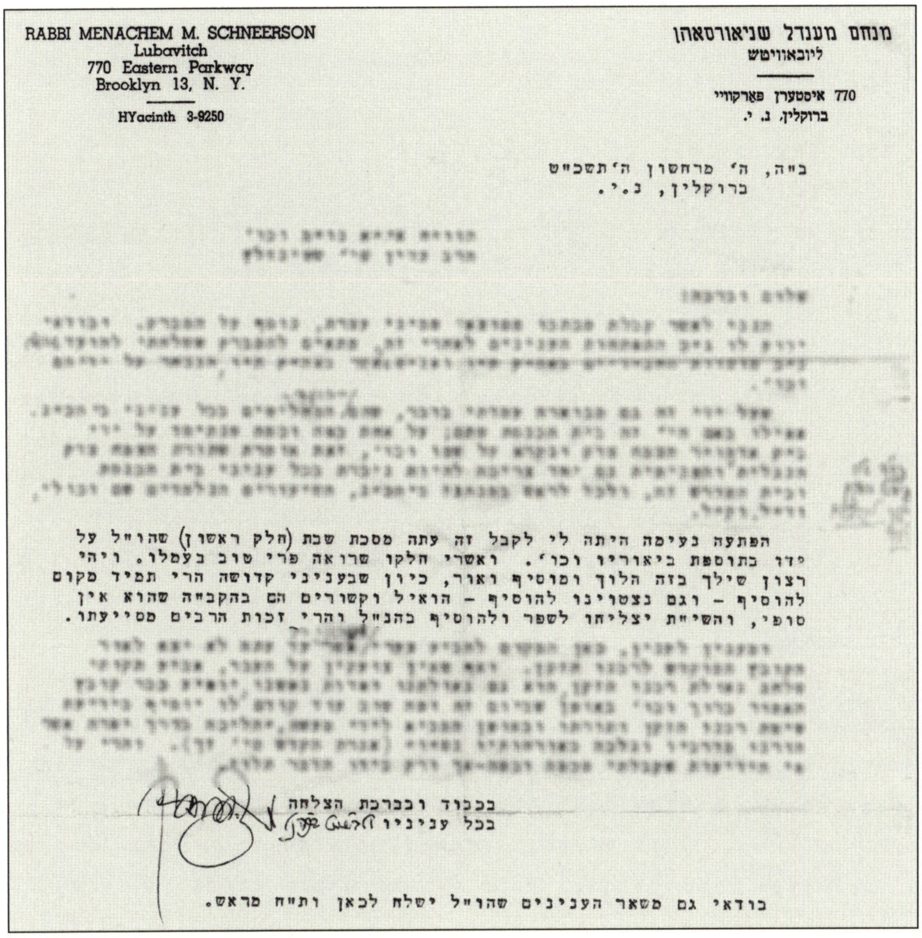

RABBI MENACHEM M. SCHNEERSON
Lubavitch
770 Eastern Parkway
Brooklyn 13, N. Y.
HYacinth 3-9250

מנחם מענדל שניאורסאהן
ליובאוויטש
770 איסטערן פארקוויי
ברוקלין, נ. י.

ב"ה, ה׳ מרחשון ה׳תשכ"ט
ברוקלין, נ.י.

הפתעה נעימה היתה לי לקבל זה עתה מסכת שבת (חלק ראשון) שהו"ל על ידו בתוספת ביאוריו וכו׳. ואשרי חלקו שרואה פרי טוב בעמלו. ויהי רצון שילך בזה הלוך ומוסיף ואור, כיון שבעניני קדושה הרי תמיד מקום להוסיף – וגם נצטוינו להוסיף – הואיל וקשורים הם בהקב"ה שהוא אין סופי, והשי"ת יצליחו לשפר ולהוסיף בהנ"ל והרי זכות הרבים מסייעתו.

בכבוד ובברכת הצלחה
בכל עניניו

בודאי גם משאר הענינים שהו"ל ישלח לכאן ותי"ח מראש.

…I have just had the pleasant surprise of receiving tractate *Shabbat* (part one), which has been published by [Rabbi Steinsaltz] along with his explanations, etc. Happy is the man who sees good fruits from his labors. May he continue in this path and increase light, for in the matters of holiness there is always room to add – and we have been commanded to add – for they are linked to the Holy One, Blessed be He, Who is infinite. And may the Holy One grant him success to improve and enhance this work, since the greater good strengthens his hand…

Rabbi Menachem Mendel Schneerson
The Lubavitcher Rebbe
Brooklyn, 5 Marḥeshvan 5729

Haskama

Rabbi Moshe Zvi Neria

מכתבו של הרב משה צבי נריה

ב"ה

"ושמעו ביום ההוא החרשים דברי ספר"
(ישעי' כט' יח')

תרגום ספרי קדמונים לשפת דורות אחרונים – היא משימתם של חכמי דור ודור. ובישראל שמצוות "ושננתם לבניך" מקיפה את כל חלקי האומה, ודאי שהיתה זאת המשימה בכל עידן ועידן.

בכל דור כך, ובדורנו אשר רבים בו הקרובים שנתרחקו וחוזרים ומתקרבים – לא כל שכן. כי רבים היום האומרים "מי ישקנו מים מבאר" התלמוד, ומועטים הם הדולים ומשקים.

ראוי אפוא להערכה מיוחדת נסיונו המבורך של הצעיר המופלא, הרב עדין שטיינזלץ, לפרש פרקי-תלמוד בהסברה מורחבת-תמציתית, אשר נוסף על הפרוש המלולי והעניני הוא מעלה גם את ההגיון של הדברים ומתרגמת אותם לשפת-המושגים של בן-דורנו.

דומה שכל הנגשים אל חומר למודי מתוך רצון להבינו – התלמיד החרוץ והמבוגר המשכיל – לא יתקלו בשום קושי בבואם ללמוד סוגיא תלמודית לפי פרוש זה. ולא עוד אלא שיש לקוות כי ההסברה ההגיונית תעמידם מיד על טוב-הטעם של דף-הגמרא, והם ימשכו יותר ויותר אל הלמוד העיוני הזה אשר טובי המוחות בישראל לנו בעומקו, ואשר ממנו פינה, ממנו יתד לבנין חיינו.

נועם ד' על המפרש הנמרץ להמשיך במפעלו, וברוכים כל העוזרים להוצאתו לאור-עולם.

ביקר אורייתא

(חתימה)

The translation of the books of our past into the language of the present – this was the task of the sages of every generation. And in Israel, where the command to "teach them repeatedly to your children" applies to all parts of the nation, it was certainly the task of every era. This is true for every generation, and in our time – when many of those who have strayed far are once again drawing near – all the more so. For many today say, "Who will let us drink from the well" of Talmud, and few are those who offer up the waters to drink.

We must, therefore, particularly commend the blessed endeavor of Rabbi Adin Steinsaltz to explain the chapters of the Talmud in this extensive yet succinct commentary, which, in addition to its literal interpretation of the text, also explicates the latter's underlying logic and translates it into the language of our generation.

It appears that all those who seek to study Talmud – the diligent student and the learned adult – will have no difficulty understanding when using this commentary. Moreover, we may hope that the logical explanation will reveal to them the beauty of the talmudic page, and they will be drawn deeper and deeper into the intellectual pursuit which has engaged the best Jewish minds, and which serves as the cornerstone of our very lives…

Rabbi Moshe Zvi Neria

 THIS HASKAMA REFERS TO THE ORIGINAL HEBREW EDITION OF THE STEINSALTZ TALMUD, UPON WHICH THIS VOLUME IS BASED

Haskama

Rabbi Mordechai Eliyahu

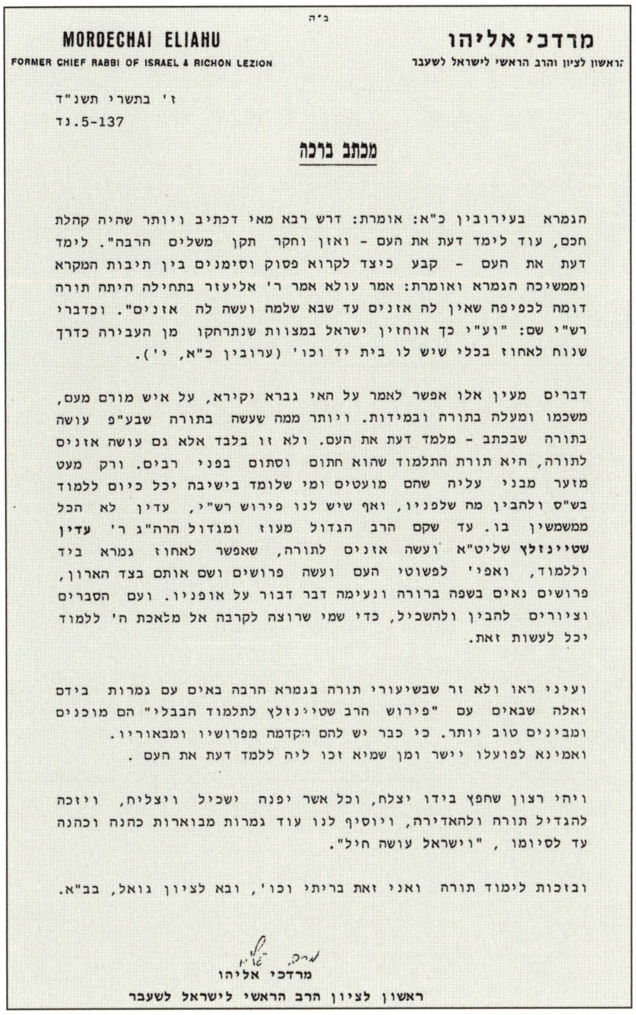

ב"ה

MORDECHAI ELIAHU
FORMER CHIEF RABBI OF ISRAEL & RICHON LEZION

מרדכי אליהו
ראשון לציון והרב הראשי לישראל לשעבר

ז' בתשרי תשנ"ד
נד.5-137

מכתב ברכה

הגמרא בעירובין כ"א: אומרת: דרש רבא מאי דכתיב ויותר שהיה קהלת חכם, עוד לימד דעת את העם - ואזן וחקר תקן משלים הרבה". לימד דעת את העם - קבע כיצד לקרוא פסוק וסימנים בין תיבות המקרא וממשיכה הגמרא ואומרת: אמר עולא אמר ר' אליעזר בתחילה היתה תורה דומה לכפיפה שאין לה אזנים עד שבא שלמה ועשה לה אזנים". וכדברי רש"י שם: "וע"י כך אוחזין ישראל במצוות שנתרחקו מן העבירה כדרך שנוח לאחוז בכלי שיש לו בית יד וכו' (ערובין כ"א, י').

דברים מעין אלו אפשר לאמר על האי גברא יקירא, על איש מורם מעם, משכמו ומעלה בתורה ובמידות. ויותר ממה שעשה בתורה שבע"פ עושה בתורה שבכתב - מלמד דעת את העם. ולא זו בלבד אלא גם עושה אזנים לתורה, היא תורת התלמוד שהוא חתום וסתום בפני רבים. ורק מעט מזער מבני עליה שהם מועטים ומי שלומד בישיבה יכל כיום ללמוד בש"ס ולהבין מה שלפניו, ואף שיש לנו פירוש רש"י, עדין לא הכל ממשמשין בו. עד שקם הרב הגדול מעוז ומגדול הרה"ג ר' **עדין שטיינזלץ** שליט"א ועשה אזנים לתורה, שאפשר לאחוז גמרא ביד וללמוד, ואפי' לפשוטי העם ועשה פרושים ושם אותם בצד הארון, פרושים נאים בשפה ברורה ונעימה דבר דבור על אופניו. ועם הסברים וציורים להבין ולהשכיל, כדי שמי שרוצה לקרבה אל מלאכת ה' ללמוד יכל לעשות זאת.

ועיני ראו ולא זר שבשיעורי תורה בגמרא הרבה באים עם גמרות בידם ואלה שבאים עם "פירוש הרב שטיינזלץ לתלמוד הבבלי" הם מוכנים ומבינים טוב יותר. כי כבר יש להם הקדמה מפרושיו ומבאוריו. ואמינא לפועלו יישר ומן שמיא זכו ליה ללמד דעת את העם .

ויהי רצון שחפץ בידו יצלח, וכל אשר יפנה ישכיל ויצליח, ויזכה להגדיל תורה ולהאדירה, ויוסיף לנו עוד גמרות מבוארות כהנה וכהנה עד לסיומו , "וישראל עושה חיל".

ובזכות לימוד תורה ואני זאת בריתי וכו', ובא לציון גואל, בב"א.

מרדכי אליהו
ראשון לציון הרב הראשי לישראל לשעבר

The Talmud in *Eruvin* 21b states: Rava continued to interpret verses homiletically. What is the meaning of the verse: "And besides being wise, Kohelet also taught the people knowledge; and he weighed, and sought out, and set in order many proverbs" (Ecclesiastes 12:9)? He explains: He taught the people knowledge; he taught it with the accentuation marks in the Torah, and explained each matter by means of another matter similar to it. And he weighed [*izen*], and sought out, and set in order many proverbs; Ulla said that Rabbi Eliezer said: At first the Torah was like a basket without handles [*oznayim*] until Solomon came and made handles for it. And as Rashi there explains: And thus were Israel able to grasp the mitzvot and distance themselves from transgressions – just as a vessel with handles is easily held, etc.

Such things may be said of this beloved and eminent man, a great sage of Torah and of virtue. And far more than he has done with the Oral Torah, he does with the Written Torah – teaching the people knowledge. And beyond that, he also affixes handles to the Torah, i.e., to the Talmud, which is obscure and difficult for many. Only the intellectual elite, which are a precious few, and those who study in yeshiva, can today learn the Talmud and understand what it says – and even though we have Rashi, still not everyone uses him. But now the great scholar Rabbi Adin Steinsaltz שליט"א has come and affixed handles to the Torah, allowing the Talmud to be held and studied, even by simple men. And he has composed a commentary alongside the text, a fine commentary in clear, comprehensible language, "a word fitly spoken" with explanations and illustrations, so that all those who seek to study the work of God can do so.

Rabbi Mordechai Eliyahu
Former Chief Rabbi of Israel, 7 Tishrei 5754

Message from Rabbi Adin Even-Israel Steinsaltz

The Talmud is the cornerstone of Jewish culture. True, our culture originated in the Bible and has branched out in directions besides the Talmud, yet the latter's influence on Jewish culture is fundamental. Perhaps because it was composed not by a single individual, but rather by hundreds and thousands of Sages in *batei midrash* in an ongoing, millennium-long process, the Talmud expresses not only the deepest themes and values of the Jewish people, but also of the Jewish spirit. As the basic study text for young and old, laymen and learned, the Talmud may be said to embody the historical trajectory of the Jewish soul. It is, therefore, best studied interactively, its subject matter coming together with the student's questions, perplexities, and innovations to form a single intricate weave. In the entire scope of Jewish culture, there is not one area that does not draw from or converse with the Talmud. The study of Talmud is thus the gate through which a Jew enters his life's path.

The *Koren Talmud Bavli* seeks to render the Talmud accessible to the millions of Jews whose mother tongue is English, allowing them to study it, approach it, and perhaps even become one with it.

This project has been carried out and assisted by several people, all of whom have worked tirelessly to turn this vision into an actual set of books to be studied. It is a joyful duty to thank the many partners in this enterprise for their various contributions. Thanks to Koren Publishers Jerusalem, both for the publication of this set and for the design of its very complex graphic layout. Thanks of a different sort are owed to the Steinsaltz Center and its director, Rabbi Menachem Even-Israel, for their determination and persistence in setting this goal and reaching it. Many thanks to the translators, editors, and proofreaders for their hard and meticulous work. Thanks to the individuals and organizations that supported this project, chief among them the Matanel Foundation and the Noé family of London. And thanks in advance to all those who will invest their time, hearts, and minds in studying these volumes – to learn, to teach, and to practice.

Rabbi Adin Even-Israel Steinsaltz
Jerusalem 5773

Acknowledgments

We are indeed privileged to dedicate this edition of the *Koren Talmud Bavli* in honor of the generous support of Leo and Sue Noé of London.

The name Noé is synonymous with philanthropy. The family's charitable endeavors span a vast range of educational projects, welfare institutions, and outreach organizations across the globe, with a particular emphasis on the "nurturing of each individual." Among so many other charitable activities, the Noés have been deeply involved with Kisharon, which provides the British Jewish community with vital support for hundreds of people with learning difficulties and their families; they provide steadfast support of SEED, which stands at the forefront of adult Jewish education in the UK, and Kemach, an organization in Israel that "helps Haredi students sustain themselves in dignity," providing both professional and vocational training for the Haredi community in Israel.

The Noés are not simply donors to institutions. They are partners. Donors think of a sum. Partners think of a cause, becoming rigorously and keenly involved, and giving of their time and energy. We are honored that they have chosen to partner with our two organizations, the Steinsaltz Center and Koren Publishers Jerusalem, enabling us to further and deepen learning among all Jews.

Leo and Sue are the proud parents and grandparents of five children and their families. The next generation has been taught by example that with life's gifts come the responsibilities to be active within and contribute to society – both Jewish and non-Jewish – as is consistent with the noblest of Jewish values.

Rabbi Adin Even-Israel Steinsaltz
Matthew Miller, Publisher
Jerusalem 5773

Introduction by the Editor-in-Chief

The vastly expanded audience of Talmud study in our generation is a phenomenon of historical proportions. The reasons for this phenomenon are many, and include the availability of a wide array of translations, commentaries, and study aids.

One outstanding example of such a work is the translation of the Talmud into modern Hebrew by Rabbi Adin Even-Israel Steinsaltz. The product of a lifetime of intense intellectual labor, this translation stands out in its uniqueness.

But what can the interested student do if he or she does not comprehend the Hebrew, even in its modern form? Where is the English speaker who wishes to access this instructive material to turn?

The *Koren Talmud Bavli* that you hold in your hand is designed to be the answer to those questions.

This work is the joint effort of Rabbi Steinsaltz himself, his closest advisory staff, and Koren Publishers Jerusalem. It is my privilege to have been designated editor-in-chief of this important project, and to have worked in close collaboration with a team of translators and copy editors, artists and graphic designers, scholars and editors.

Together we are presenting to the English-speaking world a translation that has all the merits of the original Hebrew work by Rabbi Steinsaltz, and provides assistance for the beginner of any age who seeks to obtain the necessary skills to become an adept talmudist.

This is the thirteenth volume of the project, tractates *Moed Katan* and *Ḥagiga*. It includes the entire original text, in the traditional configuration and pagination of the famed Vilna edition of the Talmud. This enables the student to follow the core text with the commentaries of Rashi, *Tosafot*, and the customary marginalia. It also provides a clear English translation in contemporary idiom, faithfully based upon the modern Hebrew edition.

At least equal to the linguistic virtues of this edition are the qualities of its graphic design. Rather than intimidate students by confronting them with a page-size block of text, we have divided the page into smaller thematic units. Thus, readers can focus their attention and absorb each discrete discussion before proceeding to the next unit. The design of each page allows for sufficient white space to ease the visual task of reading. The illustrations, one of the most innovative features of the Hebrew edition, have been substantially enhanced and reproduced in color.

The end result is a literary and artistic masterpiece. This has been achieved through the dedicated work of a large team of translators, headed by Rabbi Joshua Schreier, and through the unparalleled creative efforts of Raphaël Freeman and the gifted staff at Koren.

The group of individuals who surround Rabbi Steinsaltz and support his work deserve our thanks as well. I have come to appreciate their energy, initiative, and persistence. And I thank the indefatigable Rabbi Menachem Even-Israel, whom I cannot praise highly enough. The quality of his guidance and good counsel is surpassed only by his commitment to the dissemination and perpetuation of his father's precious teachings.

Finally, in humility, awe, and great respect, I acknowledge Rabbi Adin Even-Israel Steinsaltz. I thank him for the inspirational opportunity he has granted me to work with one of the outstanding sages of our time.

Rabbi Tzvi Hersh Weinreb
Jerusalem 5774

Preface by the Executive Editor

Toward the beginning of tractate *Pesaḥim* (3a), the Gemara questions the Mishna's use of the term *or* rather than the standard term *leil* when referring to the evening of the fourteenth of Nisan. The Gemara introduces a discussion of the value of euphemism and refraining from the use of crude language. It concludes that despite the importance of euphemism, if the euphemism comes at the expense of clarity and requires a less succinct formulation, it is preferable to speak concisely. Only when the choice is between equally concise phrases is the euphemism preferred.

In his *peirush*, Rabbi Steinsaltz's language is both concise and aesthetic. While explaining often difficult passages, he avoids the temptation to over-explain, inviting the reader to study the Talmud with him rather than doing all the thinking in the reader's place. We have attempted to follow his path in translating and editing the *Koren Talmud Bavli*.

My involvement in the production of the *Koren Talmud Bavli* has been both a privilege and a pleasure. The Steinsaltz Center, headed by Rabbi Menachem Even-Israel and devoted to the dissemination of the wide-ranging, monumental works of Rabbi Adin Even-Israel Steinsaltz, constitutes the Steinsaltz side of this partnership; Koren Publishers Jerusalem, headed by Matthew Miller, with the day-to-day management of the project in the able hands of Dena Landowne Bailey, constitutes the publishing side of this partnership. The combination of the inspiration, which is the hallmark of the Steinsaltz Center, with the creativity and professionalism for which Koren is renowned and which I experience on a daily basis, has lent the *Koren Talmud Bavli* its outstanding quality in terms of both content and form.

I would like to express my appreciation for Rabbi Dr. Tzvi Hersh Weinreb, the editor-in-chief, whose insight and guidance have been invaluable. The contribution of my friend and colleague, Rabbi Dr. Shalom Z. Berger, the senior content editor, cannot be overstated; his title does not begin to convey the excellent direction he has provided in all aspects of this project. In addition, I would like to thank Rabbi Jason Rappoport, managing editor; Rabbi Joshua Amaru, coordinating editor; and Rabbi Avishai Magence, content curator, whose tireless devotion to this project has been and continues to be crucial to the continued success of this project. The erudite and articulate men and women who serve as translators, editors, and copy editors have ensured that this project adheres to the highest standards.

There are several others whose contributions to this project cannot be overlooked. On the Steinsaltz side: Meir HaNegbi, Yacov Elbert, and Tsipora Ifrah. On the Koren side, Rabbi David Fuchs, Rabbi Hanan Benayahu, Efrat Gross, Rachel Hanstater Meghnagi, Rabbi Eliahu Misgav, and Rabbi Yinon Chen. Their assistance in all matters, large and small, is appreciated.

At the risk of being repetitious, I would like to thank Rabbi Dr. Berger for introducing me to the world of Steinsaltz. Finally, I would like to thank Rabbi Menachem Even-Israel, with whom it continues to be a pleasure to move forward in this great enterprise.

Rabbi Joshua Schreier
Jerusalem 5773

Introduction by the Publisher

The Talmud has sustained and inspired Jews for thousands of years. Throughout Jewish history, an elite cadre of scholars has absorbed its learning and passed it on to succeeding generations. The Talmud has been the fundamental text of our people.

Beginning in the 1960s, Rabbi Adin Even-Israel Steinsaltz שליט״א created a revolution in the history of Talmud study. His translation of the Talmud, first into modern Hebrew and then into other languages, as well the practical learning aids he added to the text, have enabled millions of people around the world to access and master the complexity and context of the world of Talmud.

It is thus a privilege to present the *Koren Talmud Bavli*, an English translation of the talmudic text with the brilliant elucidation of Rabbi Steinsaltz. The depth and breadth of his knowledge are unique in our time. His rootedness in the tradition and his reach into the world beyond it are inspirational.

Working with Rabbi Steinsaltz on this remarkable project has been not only an honor, but a great pleasure. Never shy to express an opinion, with wisdom and humor, Rabbi Steinsaltz sparkles in conversation, demonstrating his knowledge (both sacred and worldly), sharing his wide-ranging interests, and, above all, radiating his passion. I am grateful for the unique opportunity to work closely with him, and I wish him many more years of writing and teaching.

Our intentions in publishing this new edition of the Talmud are threefold. First, we seek to fully clarify the talmudic page to the reader – textually, intellectually, and graphically. Second, we seek to utilize today's most sophisticated technologies, both in print and electronic formats, to provide the reader with a comprehensive set of study tools. And third, we seek to help readers advance in their process of Talmud study.

To achieve these goals, the *Koren Talmud Bavli* is unique in a number of ways:

- The classic *tzurat hadaf* of Vilna, used by scholars since the 1800s, has been reset for greater clarity, and opens from the Hebrew "front" of the book. Full *nikkud* has been added to both the talmudic text and Rashi's commentary, allowing for a more fluent reading with the correct pronunciation; the commentaries of *Tosafot* have been punctuated. Upon the advice of many English-speaking teachers of Talmud, we have separated these core pages from the translation, thereby enabling the advanced student to approach the text without the distraction of the translation. This also reduces the number of volumes in the set. At the bottom of each *daf*, there is a reference to the corresponding English pages. In addition, the Vilna edition was read against other manuscripts and older print editions, so that texts which had been removed by non-Jewish censors have been restored to their rightful place.

- The English translation, which starts on the English "front" of the book, reproduces the *menukad* Talmud text alongside the English translation (in bold) and commentary and explanation (in a lighter font). The Hebrew and Aramaic text is presented in logical paragraphs. This allows for a fluent reading of the text for the non-Hebrew or non-Aramaic reader. It also allows for the Hebrew reader to refer easily to the text alongside. Where the original text features dialogue or poetry, the English text is laid out in a manner appropriate to the genre. Each page refers to the relevant *daf*.
- Critical contextual tools surround the text and translation: personality notes, providing short biographies of the Sages; language notes, explaining foreign terms borrowed from Greek, Latin, Persian, or Arabic; and background notes, giving information essential to the understanding of the text, including history, geography, botany, archaeology, zoology, astronomy, and aspects of daily life in the talmudic era.
- Halakhic summaries provide references to the authoritative legal decisions made over the centuries by the rabbis. They explain the reasons behind each halakhic decision as well as the ruling's close connection to the Talmud and its various interpreters.
- Photographs, drawings, and other illustrations have been added throughout the text – in full color in the Standard and Electronic editions, and in black and white in the Daf Yomi edition – to visually elucidate the text.

This is not an exhaustive list of features of this edition; it merely presents an overview for the English-speaking reader who may not be familiar with the "total approach" to Talmud pioneered by Rabbi Steinsaltz.

Several professionals have helped bring this vast collaborative project to fruition. My many colleagues are noted on the Acknowledgments page, and the leadership of this project has been exceptional.

RABBI MENACHEM EVEN-ISRAEL, DIRECTOR OF THE STEINSALTZ CENTER, was the driving force behind this enterprise. With enthusiasm and energy, he formed the happy alliance with Koren and established close relationships among all involved in the work.

RABBI DR. TZVI HERSH WEINREB שליט״א, EDITOR-IN-CHIEF, brought to this project his profound knowledge of Torah, intellectual literacy of Talmud, and erudition of Western literature. It is to him that the text owes its very high standard, both in form and content, and the logical manner in which the beauty of the Talmud is presented.

RABBI JOSHUA SCHREIER, EXECUTIVE EDITOR, assembled an outstanding group of scholars, translators, editors, and copy editors, whose standards and discipline enabled this project to proceed in a timely and highly professional manner.

RABBI MEIR HANEGBI, EDITOR OF THE HEBREW EDITION OF THE STEINSALTZ TALMUD, lent his invaluable assistance throughout the work process, supervising the reproduction of the Vilna pages.

RAPHAËL FREEMAN created this Talmud's unique typographic design which, true to the Koren approach, is both elegant and user friendly.

It has been an enriching experience for all of us at Koren Publishers Jerusalem to work with the Steinsaltz Center to develop and produce the *Koren Talmud Bavli*. We pray that this publication will be a source of great learning and, ultimately, greater *avodat Hashem* for all Jews.

Matthew Miller, Publisher
Koren Publishers Jerusalem
Jerusalem 5773

Introduction to **Moed Katan**

Tractate *Moed Katan*[1] deals mainly with the *halakhot* pertaining to the intermediate days of the Festival, which are often referred to as simply: The Festivals, in rabbinic literature.[2] The discussion of these *halakhot* leads to a comprehensive treatment of two other fundamental areas of *halakha*: The *halakhot* of mourning and the *halakhot* of ostracism.

Combining the *halakhot* of days of rejoicing with the *halakhot* of days of sadness in one tractate is seemingly contradictory, yet there exists a double connection between the two topics. First, there is a practical halakhic connection between these areas of *halakha*, as the labors that are prohibited on the intermediate days of the Festival are similar to the labors that are prohibited both during the period of mourning and with regard to one who is ostracized, as he must act as if he is in mourning. It is reasonable, then, to discuss these prohibitions in the same context. Second, there is an intrinsic connection between the *halakhot* of the intermediate days of the Festival and the *halakhot* of mourning in that they are derived in a parallel manner.

The essential elements of both the intermediate days of the Festival and the period of mourning are mentioned in the Torah, and some of the broader details are alluded to as well. However, they do not appear as explicit commandments or obligations, and consequently are treated in talmudic literature as rabbinic commandments[3] that are part of the oral tradition. This is the case despite the fact that they are mentioned in the written Torah and were practiced in the time of Moses. Even the Sages who maintain that these *halakhot* have a basis in Torah law agree that with regard to the specific details, the Bible delegated them to the Sages.[4] As a result, the *halakhot* discussed in this tractate are not based on the objective categories that characterize Torah law, but like most rabbinic commandments are dependent on circumstances and relative to the situation.

This means that there is a basic difference between the labor prohibitions on the intermediate days of the Festival and those on Shabbat and the first or last days of the Festival. On Shabbat and Yom Kippur, "all labor" (Exodus 20:10), i.e., all creative, physical labor as defined by the Sages, is prohibited, and similar prohibitions apply to Festivals with a few exceptions, one of which is labor performed for the purpose of food preparation. In contrast, on the intermediate days of the Festival and during the period of mourning there is no objective prohibition against labor in its usual halakhic definition. Rather, the prohibition is against work, which is defined based on the amount of effort, exertion, or professional expertise that is involved in a given activity.

Additionally, these *halakhot* of prohibited work are not absolute, as their main function is to preserve the unique nature of the day in order to ensure that it is not treated like an ordinary weekday. They therefore include certain leniencies such as, *inter alia*, in cases of incurred loss. These are not objective categories that depend on the nature of the labor, but rather they are categories that depend on the relationship between the person performing the action and the labor he needs to perform. Thus, on the intermediate days of the Festival one is permitted to do work that is specifically related to and necessary for the Festival. However, he may not treat these days as ordinary weekdays by performing labor that is unrelated to its celebration.

It is the Sages who determine the criteria of what is prohibited on these days. They take into account issues such as when does a certain labor constitute degrading the Festival by treating it as a non-sacred day, and when, due to a specific need or for the purpose of enjoyment of the Festival, is it permitted to perform that labor? These same considerations play a role in determining what is permitted during the period of mourning. These days do not have a fundamental prohibition against labor, but rather one has an obligation to direct his attention to mourning and not turn them into ordinary days of routine where he is occupied with his normal work and occupations and cannot give appropriate attention to his mourning.

As there are no comprehensive categories governing the prohibition of labor on these days, the Sages were forced to establish many isolated *halakhot* that address specific situations. The Gemara in one place calls these: Sterile *halakhot*,[5] in that each instance must be addressed separately: Does this activity involve a desecration of the Festival either due to excessive exertion or by resembling an activity performed on weekdays that would make this day seem ordinary and routine? Additional considerations include the indispensable needs of the individual and of society, and considerations such as the unrecoverable loss that will be incurred by not working on the Festival. Therefore, this tractate contains many individualized rulings which do not fit under one rubric.

Due to the fact that so many activities were permitted, the Sages wondered if it would not be better to simply cancel the prohibition of work on the intermediate days of the Festival completely. As these celebratory days did not have any specific ritual obligations, there was concern that they would turn into sole days of idleness.[6] In certain places the Sages in fact drastically limited the scope of the prohibitions of the intermediate days of the Festival.[7]

In a similar vein, the *halakhot* of mourning, despite the fact that many of them are mentioned in the Torah and books of the prophets, were never formulated as obligatory commandments. Rather, the Sages consolidated all of the traditions and early customs[8] within general parameters. The *halakhot* of mourning establish a specific and defined framework for the expression of sorrow and mourning, the role of which is to provide an opportunity to feel and recognize the extent of the loss, while at the same time limiting the flow of emotions so that they do not destabilize the progression of life. The exemption of acute mourners from all positive commandments as well as the prohibition of labor for all mourners was intended to allow them to deal with the burial of the deceased in a proper and respectful way, as well as to provide time and space for thinking about and feeling the loss of the deceased, expressing sorrow over this loss, and receiving comfort from others.

Another aspect of the *halakhot* of mourning involves the public expression of the pain and loss: The mourner is required to rend his clothes, sit on the ground, and overturn his bed. Furthermore, the mourner is required to refrain from both pleasure and expressions of human grandeur: The prohibition against taking haircuts and doing laundry is an expression of the former, and the prohibition against donning phylacteries during the first day of mourning is an example of the latter.

The *halakhot* of ostracism, which are explored in depth in this tractate, are related to the *halakhot* of mourning. Excommunication and ostracism are not simply punishments involving social isolation; they are a form of banishment that requires one to act as though in mourning. Many of these *halakhot* are derived from and connected to those of a leper, who in a certain respect is ostracized and in mourning as well.

There is another point of contact between the *halakhot* of mourning and those of the intermediate days of the Festival: When the period of mourning overlaps with Shabbat and Festivals. This raises the difficulty of the conflict between the commandments of rejoicing and delight on these days with the obligation to feel sorrow and mourning. Essentially, it was determined that the general obligations of taking delight in Shabbat and rejoicing on the Festival cancel the obligation of outward expression of personal mourning.

There are three chapters in tractate *Moed Katan*. The first two mainly discuss the *halakhot* of the intermediate days of the Festival, while the third focuses on the *halakhot* of mourning, ostracism, and excommunication. Although this division is not absolute, as the Talmud often merges the discussion of various topics, each chapter has specific topics to which the discussion therein is dedicated:

Chapter One discusses the activities that are prohibited during the course of the Festival, both those that are prohibited because they are considered work and those that would minimize the joy of the Festival.

Chapter Two deals with the details of work that is permitted on the Festival due to the financial loss that would be incurred by abstaining from this work and due to other considerations.

Chapter Three briefly addresses the *halakhot* of shaving and writing during the Festival. The main discussion, however, revolves around a comprehensive analysis of the *halakhot* of mourning and the *halakhot* of ostracism and excommunication. Additionally, this chapter takes a brief look at the related *halakhot* of leprosy.

NOTES

1. In earlier generations, this tractate was referred to only as *Moed*, but it was changed to *Moed Katan* in order to distinguish between the tractate and the order *Moed*. In many earlier sources, *Moed Katan* is referred to as *Mashkin*, its opening word.
2. The statement in the mishna that one who disparages the Festivals has no part in the World-to-Come (*Avot* 3:11) should be understood to refer to the intermediate days of the Festivals, and is a condemnation of one who acts as though they are ordinary weekdays.
3. There is a dispute among the early commentaries as to whether the *halakhot* of the intermediate days of the Festival and the *halakhot* of mourning contain an element that is based on Torah law, or if their authority is entirely by rabbinic law.
4. *Ḥagiga* 18a.
5. *Moed Katan* 12a.
6. Jerusalem Talmud, *Moed Katan* 2:3.
7. See B.M. Levin, *Compendium of Differences in Custom between the Land of Israel and Babylonia.* Jerusalem: 1942 (Hebrew).
8. Some of these are mentioned in the book of Genesis, chapters 23 and 50.

Introduction to **Perek I**

These are the appointed seasons of the Lord, which you shall proclaim to be holy convocations, to bring an offering made by fire unto the Lord, a burnt-offering, and a meal-offering, a sacrifice, and drink-offerings, each on its own day.

(Leviticus 23:37)

And on the fifteenth day of this month shall be a feast; seven days shall unleavened bread be eaten. The first day shall be a holy convocation; you shall do no manner of servile work.

(Numbers 28:17–18)

And on the fifteenth day of the seventh month you shall have a holy convocation; you shall do no manner of servile work, and you shall keep a feast unto the Lord seven days.

(Numbers 29:12)

The unique status of the intermediate days of the Festival, in that they are not full-fledged Festivals but at the same time are not ordinary weekdays, requires specific categories and halakhic definitions with regard to which activities are prohibited and which are permitted on those days. The central question clarified in this chapter is: Which labors are prohibited or permitted on the intermediate days of the Festival?

It is clear that there is no absolute prohibition against performing labor on these days, and therefore one cannot issue a blanket ban on all work during this time. On the other hand, it is necessary to maintain the special and holy nature of these days, as they are called "appointed seasons," and therefore should not be desecrated by being treated as workdays. As all agree that there are no clear principles set out in the Torah with regard to these issues, and the Bible delegated them to the Sages (*Ḥagiga* 18a), it is necessary to clarify the criteria the Sages established with regard to the work that is prohibited or permitted on the intermediate days of the Festival, while comparing them to similar areas of *halakha* such as the agricultural labors of the Sabbatical Year.

Another aspect that requires explication is how to achieve the sanctity and celebration of the intermediate days of the Festival. As these weekdays occur within a period of festivity, nested between two Festivals, the commandment: "And you shall rejoice in your feast" (Deuteronomy 16:14) applies to them as well. This principle determines which activities should be avoided during the intermediate days of the Festival due to the fact that they interfere with the holiness and celebration of the time. This is either because the activity disrupts the rejoicing of the Festival by introducing other components that distract from the essence of the day or because it contains elements of grief and mourning that are inappropriate for times of celebration.

The elucidation of these issues is the topic of this chapter.

מתני׳ מַשְׁקִין בֵּית הַשְּׁלָחִין בַּמּוֹעֵד וּבַשְּׁבִיעִית, בֵּין מִמַּעְיָן שֶׁיָּצָא בַּתְּחִילָּה, בֵּין מִמַּעְיָן שֶׁלֹּא יָצָא בַּתְּחִילָּה. אֲבָל אֵין מַשְׁקִין לֹא מִמֵּי הַגְּשָׁמִים, וְלֹא מִמֵּי הַקִּילוֹן.

MISHNA One may irrigate[N] **a field that requires irrigation**[N] on the intermediate days of **a Festival**[H] **as well as during the Sabbatical Year,**[H] **both from a newly emerged spring** that began to flow only during the Festival, **and from a spring that did not just emerge** and that has been flowing for some time. **However, one may not irrigate** a field **with rainwater** collected in a cistern, a procedure that requires excessive exertion, **or with water drawn with a shadoof** [*kilon*],[LBN] a lever used to raise water with a bucket from deep down in a well.

וְאֵין עוֹשִׂין עוּגִיּוֹת לַגְּפָנִים. רַבִּי אֶלְעָזָר בֶּן עֲזַרְיָה אוֹמֵר: אֵין עוֹשִׂין אֶת הָאַמָּה בַּתְּחִילָּה בַּמּוֹעֵד וּבַשְּׁבִיעִית. וַחֲכָמִים אוֹמְרִים: עוֹשִׂין אֶת הָאַמָּה בַּתְּחִילָּה בַּשְּׁבִיעִית, וּמְתַקְּנִין אֶת הַמְקוּלְקָלוֹת בַּמּוֹעֵד.

And one may not construct circular ditches around the bases of **grapevines** on the intermediate days of a Festival. **Rabbi Elazar ben Azarya says: One may not construct a new** water **channel during** the intermediate days of **a Festival or during the Sabbatical Year. And the Rabbis say: One may construct a new** water **channel during the Sabbatical Year**[H] **and one may repair damaged** water channels **during** the intermediate days of **a Festival.**

וּמְתַקְּנִין אֶת קִלְקוּלֵי הַמַּיִם שֶׁבִּרְשׁוּת הָרַבִּים, וְחוֹטְטִין אוֹתָן, וּמְתַקְּנִין אֶת הַדְּרָכִים וְאֶת הָרְחוֹבוֹת וְאֶת מִקְווֹת הַמַּיִם, וְעוֹשִׂין כׇּל צוֹרְכֵי הָרַבִּים, וּמְצַיְּינִין אֶת הַקְּבָרוֹת, וְיוֹצְאִין אַף עַל הַכִּלְאַיִם.

In addition to performing labor on one's own property in order to avoid financial loss, it is also permitted to perform labor on the intermediate days of a Festival for the public welfare: **One may repair damaged water** cisterns[N] **that are in the public domain, and clean them out** by removing the dirt and sediment that accumulated there; **one may repair roads, streets,**[N] **and ritual baths; and one may tend to all** other **public needs.**[H] So too, **one may mark graves** to inform the public of their ritual impurity, **and** inspectors **may even go out to** uproot **the** shoots of prohibited **diverse kinds** [*kilayim*][B] that grew in the fields during the rainy season.

LANGUAGE

Shadoof [*kilon*] – קִילוֹן: From the Greek κηλῶν, *kèlon*, a mechanical device for drawing water operated by a lever. In the Gemara, *kilon* water refers to water that is not directly accessible and can be drawn only by means of a *kilon*.

BACKGROUND

Shadoof [*kilon*] – קִילוֹן: The *kilon* was generally constructed with a long rod that served as a lever to draw water primarily from streams or irrigation canals.

Shadoof

Diverse kinds [*kilayim*] – כִּלְאַיִם: This general term refers to many types of prohibited mixtures: Mixtures of wool and linen, crossbreeding of livestock, food crops in a vineyard, and a mixture of seeds. The mishna is discussing the prohibition against planting a mixture of seeds, i.e., planting different species of crops in one area of the same field.

NOTES

One may irrigate – מַשְׁקִין: This tractate opens with the *halakhot* concerning working the land on the intermediate days of a Festival. As some Sages rendered prohibited all agricultural labor, there is consequently a novelty in the leniency presented here (*Tal Ḥayyim*).

A field that requires irrigation – בֵּית הַשְּׁלָחִין: Opinions differ as to the precise meaning of a field that requires irrigation. Some explain that it refers exclusively to a field of grain, and not to an orchard (Rif). Others say that it refers specifically to a vegetable garden (Rid; Rid the Younger). Yet others say that it is referring to both a vegetable garden and a field of grain (Ritva; Meiri). Many early authorities maintain that orchards are also included in the definition.

Shadoof [*kilon*] – קִילוֹן: Some commentaries explain *kilon* to mean a deep channel (*Arukh*; Ran). Others say that it is called *kilon* because a bucket, *kulta* in Aramaic, is used to draw water from it (Rif; *Nimmukei Yosef*; Ritva). Following Rav Hai Gaon, the Meiri explains that a *kilon* is a deep, covered channel from which water is drawn through special openings.

Damaged water cisterns – קִלְקוּלֵי הַמַּיִם: Some explain that the reference is to water cisterns that were damaged (*Talmid Rabbeinu Yeḥiel of Paris*). This also fits in with the Ra'avad's version of the text of the Gemara, in which the word *kilkulei* is spelled with two *kafs*, and, therefore is referring to ducts through which water is channeled to provide for municipal needs (see Meiri). Others explain, according to the standard text in which the word is spelled with two *kufs*, that this is referring to the sewage system through which unclean water flows (Rif; Ritva).

Streets – רְחוֹבוֹת: This term includes the city plazas where business is conducted. However, others say that it is referring to the lots behind houses where children play (*Talmid Rabbeinu Yeḥiel of Paris*).

HALAKHA

Irrigation on the intermediate days of a Festival – הַשְׁקָיָה בַּמּוֹעֵד: On the intermediate days of a Festival, one may not irrigate a field that suffices with rainwater, as the labor enhances, rather than maintains, the land. If a field requires irrigation, and one has begun to irrigate it before the Festival, one may continue to water the field on the intermediate days of a Festival. This is due to the fact that insufficient irrigation would lead to a significant loss. Even in the case of a field that requires irrigation, watering is permitted only when it does not entail excessive exertion, as in the case where one irrigates the field from a spring. One may not draw water from the spring with a bucket (*Magen Avraham*). It is also prohibited to irrigate with rainwater collected in a cistern, which must be drawn with a bucket (*Shulḥan Arukh, Oraḥ Ḥayyim* 537:1–2).

Irrigation during the Sabbatical Year – הַשְׁקָיָה בַּשְּׁבִיעִית: A field that requires irrigation may be watered during the Sabbatical Year so that the trees will not be ruined (Rambam *Sefer Zera'im, Hilkhot Shemitta VeYovel* 1:8).

Working the land during the Sabbatical Year – עֲבוֹדַת קַרְקַע בַּשְּׁבִיעִית: One is permitted to perform agricultural labor during the Sabbatical Year if it serves to preserve, rather than enhance, the trees or plants. This includes activities such as digging and repairing water channels, as will be explained in the Gemara (Rambam *Sefer Zera'im, Hilkhot Shemitta VeYovel* 1:9).

One may tend to all other public needs – עוֹשִׂין כׇּל צוֹרְכֵי הָרַבִּים: Public needs may be tended to during the intermediate days of a Festival. Therefore, one may repair roads, damaged water systems, and public ritual baths, as well as mark graves. The Rema adds that tasks that do not fulfill bodily needs, such as building a synagogue, should not be performed during the intermediate days of a Festival (*Shulḥan Arukh, Oraḥ Ḥayyim* 544:1).

גמ׳ הָשְׁתָּא יֵשׁ לוֹמַר מִמַּעְיָן שֶׁיָּצָא בַּתְּחִילָּה, דְּאָתֵי לְאִינְפּוּלֵי – מַשְׁקִין, מִמַּעְיָן שֶׁלֹּא יָצָא בַּתְּחִילָּה, דְּלָא אָתֵי לְאִינְפּוּלֵי, מִיבַּעְיָא?

GEMARA

The Gemara begins by questioning the wording of the mishna: **Now that it has been said** that on the intermediate days of a Festival **one may irrigate** a field **from a newly emerged spring,** whose walls have not yet stabilized and are **likely to collapse,**[N] necessitating laborious repairs, **is it necessary** to mention that one may irrigate a field **from a spring that did not just emerge,** whose walls have already stabilized **and are** therefore **not likely to collapse?**

אָמְרִי: אִצְטְרִיךְ; אִי תָּנָא מַעְיָן שֶׁיָּצָא בַּתְּחִילָּה – הֲוָה אָמִינָא: הָכָא הוּא דְּבֵית הַשְּׁלָחִין – אִין, בֵּית הַבַּעַל – לָא, מִשּׁוּם דְּאָתֵי לְאִינְפּוּלֵי. אֲבָל מַעְיָן שֶׁלֹּא יָצָא בַּתְּחִילָּה, דְּלָא אָתֵי לְאִינְפּוּלֵי, אֵימָא אֲפִילּוּ בֵּית הַבַּעַל נַמִי.

The Gemara answers: **They say** that **it was necessary** to mention the second case as well. For **had** the *tanna* **taught** us the *halakha* with regard to only **a newly emerged spring, I would have said** that **here,** in the case of **a field that requires irrigation, yes,** one is permitted to irrigate from such a spring, but in the case of **a field that** ordinarily **suffices with rainwater, no,** one is not permitted to do so, **because it is likely to collapse. But** with regard to **a spring that did not just emerge, that is not likely to collapse, I** might **say that** one may provide supplementary irrigation **even** in the case of **a field that** ordinarily **suffices with rainwater.**

קָא מַשְׁמַע לָן: לָא שְׁנָא מַעְיָן שֶׁיָּצָא בַּתְּחִילָּה, וְלָא שְׁנָא מַעְיָן שֶׁלֹּא יָצָא בַּתְּחִילָּה, בֵּית הַשְּׁלָחִין – אִין, בֵּית הַבַּעַל – לָא.

Therefore, the *tanna* **teaches us** that **a newly emerged spring is no different** from **a spring that did not just emerge.** In the case of **a field that requires irrigation, yes,** one may irrigate on the intermediate days of a Festival, while in the case of **a field that** ordinarily **suffices with rainwater, no,** one may not do so, even from an established spring.

וּמַאי מַשְׁמַע דְּהַאי בֵּית הַשְּׁלָחִין לִישָּׁנָא דִּצְחוּתָא הִיא? דִּכְתִיב: ״וְאַתָּה עָיֵף וְיָגֵעַ״ וּמְתַרְגְּמִינַן: וְאַתְּ מְשַׁלְהֵי וְלָאֵי.

The Gemara raises a question with regard to a linguistic issue: **And from where** may it **be inferred that this** term, *beit hashelaḥin*, a field that requires irrigation, **is a term** denoting **thirst,**[N] implying that supplementary watering is necessary? The Gemara answers: **As it is written: "And you were faint and weary"** (Deuteronomy 25:18). The term faint is referring to the thirst of the Israelites in the desert. **And,** in the standard Aramaic translation, **we translate** the verse as: **And you were thirsty** [*meshalhei*] **and weary.** The letters *ḥet* and *heh* are sometimes interchanged, and therefore the term *beit hashelaḥin* connotes a thirsty field.

וּמַאי מַשְׁמַע דְּהַאי בֵּית הַבַּעַל לִישָּׁנָא דְּמִיַּיתְבוּתָא הִיא? דִּכְתִיב: ״כִּי יִבְעַל בָּחוּר בְּתוּלָה״, וּמְתַרְגְּמִינַן: אֲרֵי כְּמָה דְּמִיתּוֹתַב עוּלֵם עִם בְּתוּלְתָא יִתְיַיתְּבוּן בְּגַוֵּיךְ בְּנָיִךְ.

And from where may it **be inferred that this** term, *beit haba'al*, a field that suffices with rainwater, **is a term denoting settlement,**[N] i.e., an established field that does not require extensive upkeep? **As it is written: "For as a young man takes to himself** [*yiv'al*] **a virgin,** so shall your sons take you to themselves" (Isaiah 62:5). **And it is translated** in the Aramaic translation: **As a young man settles down with a virgin, so shall your sons become settled within you.** Similarly, *beit haba'al* is referring to a settled field that suffices with rainwater.

מַאן תָּנָא דִּפְסֵידָא – אִין, הַרְוָוחָה – לָא, וַאֲפִילּוּ בִּמְקוֹם פְּסֵידָא מִיטְרַח נַמִי לָא טָרְחִינַן?

The Gemara begins to clarify the underlying principle of the mishna, asking: **Who is the** anonymous ***tanna***[N] of the mishna who maintains **that** labor performed to prevent a considerable **loss,** such as watering a field that requires irrigation, **yes,** it is permitted on the intermediate days of a Festival; but labor performed to increase one's **profit,** such as watering a field that ordinarily suffices with rainwater, **no,** it is not permitted? Furthermore, **even in a case** involving **loss, one may not** excessively **exert** oneself, as the *tanna* of the mishna renders prohibited all cases of watering fields with collected rainwater or with water drawn with a shadoof, even in a field that requires irrigation.

אָמַר רַב הוּנָא: רַבִּי אֱלִיעֶזֶר בֶּן יַעֲקֹב הִיא. דִּתְנַן, רַבִּי אֱלִיעֶזֶר בֶּן יַעֲקֹב אוֹמֵר: מוֹשְׁכִין אֶת הַמַּיִם מֵאִילָן לְאִילָן, וּבִלְבַד שֶׁלֹּא יַשְׁקֶה אֶת הַשָּׂדֶה כּוּלָּהּ.

Rav Huna said: It is Rabbi Eliezer ben Ya'akov, as we learned in a mishna: **Rabbi Eliezer ben Ya'akov says:** In a field filled with trees, **one may draw water** via channels **from tree to tree, provided that** in doing so **he does not water the entire field.**[N] As this field ordinarily suffices with rainwater, it is prohibited to water the entire field. Therefore, it is evident that Rabbi Eliezer ben Ya'akov renders prohibited work performed to increase profit on the intermediate days of a Festival.

NOTES

Likely to collapse – **דְּאָתֵי לְאִינְפּוּלֵי**: Most commentaries explain that if the walls of this new spring were to collapse, the field's owner would be forced to exert himself excessively on the Festival. Others add that if the walls of the irrigation channel were to collapse, the efforts that the owner had already invested would have been for naught, as he would be unable to utilize the spring (Ritva).

A term denoting thirst – **לִישָּׁנָא דִּצְחוּתָא**: Some commentaries note that the Gemara in tractate *Bava Batra* (68a) discusses the meaning of the term *beit hashelaḥin*, translated here as a field that requires irrigation, and offer various biblical sources: "Your shoots [*shelaḥayikh*] are like an orchard of pomegranates" (Song of Songs 4:13), and "Who sends [*shole'aḥ*] water upon the fields" (Job 5:10). Some explain that in the context of that tractate the Gemara seeks to demonstrate that the term *beit hashelaḥin* is referring to a specific type of field, whereas here the Gemara cites a source to indicate that any field that requires irrigation is a *beit hashelaḥin* with regard to the *halakhot* discussed in the mishna (see *Talmid Rabbeinu Yeḥiel of Paris*, Rabbi Shlomo ben HaYatom, Ritva, and Meiri).

A term denoting settlement – **לִישָּׁנָא דְּמִיַּיתְבוּתָא**: Some explain this derivation as follows: Similar to a young man who is pleased with his wife, a field referred to as a *beit haba'al* is a field whose owners are pleased with it and have no worries, as it has all the water it needs (Ran; Ritva).

Who is the *tanna* – **מַאן תָּנָא**: A parallel discussion in the Jerusalem Talmud does not reach a clear conclusion with regard to the opinion of the anonymous *tanna* of the mishna in a case of excessive exertion to avoid financial loss. There is even an opinion cited in that discussion that attributes the mishna to Rabbi Meir, who holds that one may even use a new spring to irrigate a field that is not dependent upon irrigation.

One may draw…provided that he does not water the entire field – **מוֹשְׁכִין...וּבִלְבַד שֶׁלֹּא יַשְׁקֶה אֶת הַשָּׂדֶה כּוּלָּהּ**: The commentaries dispute what type of field this is referring to. Rashi explains that the reference is to a field that suffices with rainwater. The Ra'avad and Ran maintain that it is referring to a field that requires irrigation, where there are trees but not vegetables growing.

אימור דשמעת ליה לרבי אליעזר הרווחה דלא, טירחא במקום פסידא מי שמעת ליה?

The Gemara challenges this comparison: **Say that you heard** that **Rabbi Eliezer** ben Ya'akov holds that labor performed only to increase **profit is not** permitted.[N] But **did you hear him** prohibit excessive **exertion in a case of** considerable loss? This aspect of the mishna finds no expression in the words of Rabbi Eliezer ben Ya'akov.

אלא אמר רב פפא: הא מני – רבי יהודה היא, דתניא: מעיין היוצא בתחילה משקין ממנו אפילו שדה בית הבעל, דברי רבי מאיר. רבי יהודה אומר: אין משקין אלא שדה בית השלחין שחרבה. רבי אלעזר בן עזריה אומר: לא כך ולא כך. יתר על כן אמר רבי יהודה: לא יפנה אדם אמת המים וישקה לגינתו ולחורבתו בחולו של מועד.

Rather, Rav Pappa said: In accordance with **whose** opinion **is this** mishna? **It is** in accordance with the opinion of **Rabbi Yehuda, as it is taught** in a *baraita*: **From a newly emerged spring one may irrigate even a field that** ordinarily **suffices with rainwater;** this is **the statement of Rabbi Meir. Rabbi Yehuda says: One may irrigate only a field requiring irrigation that dried up** and needs water. **Rabbi Elazar ben Azarya says: Neither the one nor the other. Furthermore, Rabbi Yehuda said:** Owing to the exertion involved, **one may not divert a water channel** from its regular path in order **to water his garden**[N] **or his ruin,** which is now being used for planting, **during the intermediate days of a Festival.**

מאי חרבה? אילימא חרבה ממש – למה לי דמשקי לה? אמר אביי: שחרבה ממעיין זה, ויצא לה מעיין אחר.

The Gemara first clarifies the case of the *baraita*: **What** does Rabbi Yehuda mean when he speaks of a field that **is dried up? If we say** that the field is **literally dried up** and the plants are already parched, **why do I need to water it? Abaye said:** It means that **the one spring** from which the field had been irrigated until now **dried up, but** in the meantime **another spring emerged.** If the field is not irrigated from this spring, it will be ruined.

רבי אלעזר בן עזריה אומר לא כך ולא כך. לא שנא חרב מעיינה ולא שנא לא חרב מעיינה, מעיין שיצא בתחילה – לא.

The Gemara explains the next clause of the *baraita*, which states: **Rabbi Elazar ben Azarya says: Neither the one nor the other.** By this he means that **it is no different** whether **the** original **spring dried up or did not dry up.** The guiding principle is: From **a newly emerged spring** one may **not** irrigate even a field that requires irrigation.

וממאי? דלמא עד כאן לא קאמר רבי יהודה בית השלחין אין, בית הבעל לא – אלא מעיין שיצא בתחילה,

In any event, Rabbi Yehuda seems to maintain an opinion that is like that of the mishna, i.e., that only a field that requires irrigation may be watered, but not a field that suffices with rainwater. And even in the case of a field that requires irrigation, excessive exertion is prohibited. The Gemara challenges this understanding: **And from where** do you conclude that the mishna reflects the opinion of Rabbi Yehuda? **Perhaps Rabbi Yehuda stated** that **a field that requires irrigation, yes,** one may irrigate it on the intermediate days of a Festival, and **a field that suffices with rainwater, no,** one may not do so, **only** with regard to **a newly emerged spring,**[N]

NOTES

Profit is not permitted – הרווחה דלא: Some read this sentence together with the next word, exertion [*tirḥa*], forming a phrase that means: Say that you heard that Rabbi Eliezer ben Ya'akov holds that labor done to increase profit without exertion is not permitted, but did you hear him prohibit labor done to prevent financial loss? Labor done in this circumstance should be permitted even if it involves exertion (see Ran). They explain that an orchard requires little water, and therefore one can profit without significant exertion by allowing the water collecting around one tree to flow to the others (*Peirush*).

Divert…to water his garden – יפנה...וישקה לגינתו: This is referring to a garden that suffices with rainwater (Rashi on Rif). However, *Tosafot* and the Ran hold that it is a field that requires irrigation.

Perhaps…Rabbi Yehuda stated a distinction…only with regard to a newly emerged spring – דלמא...לא קאמר רבי יהודה...אלא מעיין שיצא בתחילה: This is a logical assumption, as Rabbi Yehuda's statement is a continuation of a *baraita* that discusses a newly emerged spring (*Talmid Rabbeinu Yeḥiel of Paris*).

Perek **I**
Daf **2** Amud **b**

דלמא אתי לאינפולי. אבל מעיין שלא יצא בתחילה, דלא אתי לאינפולי – אפילו בית הבעל נמי.

as it is likely to collapse. But in the case of **a spring that did not just emerge, which is not likely to collapse** because its walls have already stabilized, **even a field that** ordinarily **suffices with rainwater** may be irrigated.

אם כן מתניתין אמאן תרמייה? אלא: לרבי יהודה לא שנא מעיין שיצא בתחילה ולא שנא מעיין שלא יצא בתחילה, בית השלחין – אין, בית הבעל – לא. והאי דקתני מעיין שיצא בתחילה – להודיעך כחו דרבי מאיר, דאפילו מעיין היוצא בתחילה משקין ממנו אפילו שדה הבעל.

The Gemara asks: **If** that were **so,** then **to whom,** i.e., to which *tanna*, **would you attribute** the mishna?[N] According to this interpretation, the mishna does not correspond to any opinion, while according to the previous interpretation, it corresponds to the opinion of Rabbi Yehuda. **Rather,** it must be that according to the opinion of **Rabbi Yehuda, a newly emerged spring is no different** from **a spring that did not just emerge. A field that requires irrigation, yes,** it may be irrigated, while **a field that suffices with rainwater, no,** it may not be irrigated. **And** the *baraita* opted **to teach** this dispute in the case of **a newly emerged spring** in order **to convey the far-reaching nature of** the opinion **of Rabbi Meir,** which states that **one may irrigate even from a newly emerged spring,** and **even a field that suffices with rainwater.**

NOTES

To whom would you attribute the mishna – מתניתין אמאן תרמייה: There are no other known tannaitic opinions on the topic of watering fields during the intermediate days of a Festival. Since it is difficult to assert that the mishna is an additional opinion unlike other known opinions (see Meiri), it is preferable to suggest that Rabbi Yehuda's ruling in the *baraita* is not limited to a newly emerged spring, so that his opinion, which is already quite similar to the ruling of the mishna, is entirely consistent with the mishna (see *Tosafot*).

§ אִתְּמַר, הַמְנַכֵּשׁ וְהַמַּשְׁקֶה מַיִם לְזֶרָעִים בְּשַׁבָּת, מִשּׁוּם מַאי מַתְרִינַן בֵּיהּ? רַבָּה אָמַר: מִשּׁוּם חוֹרֵשׁ; רַב יוֹסֵף אָמַר: מִשּׁוּם זוֹרֵעַ.

It was stated that the *amora'im* disputed the following question: With regard to **one who weeds or one who waters seedlings on Shabbat,**[H] **for what** prohibited labor **do we forewarn him?**[N] Judicial punishment may be administered to a sinner only if he has been forewarned by two witnesses prior to the commission of his offense. This forewarning must include the specific transgression being violated, and on Shabbat it must include the specific category of prohibited labor that the action involves. **Rabba said:** It is **due to** the prohibition against **plowing. Rav Yosef said:** It is **due to** the prohibition against **sowing.**[N]

אָמַר רַבָּה: כְּוָותִי דִּידִי מִסְתַּבְּרָא, מַה דַּרְכּוֹ שֶׁל חוֹרֵשׁ – לְרַפּוּיֵי אַרְעָא, הַאי נַמִי מְרַפּוּיֵי אַרְעָא. אָמַר רַב יוֹסֵף: כְּוָותִי דִּידִי מִסְתַּבְּרָא, מַה דַּרְכּוֹ שֶׁל זוֹרֵעַ – לְצַמּוּחֵי פֵּירָא, הָכָא נַמִי מְצַמַּח פֵּירָא.

Rabba said: According to my opinion it **is reasonable. Just as the** usual objective **of plowing is to loosen the earth,** so **too, this,** weeding or watering, **loosens the earth. Rav Yosef said: According to my** opinion, it **is reasonable. Just as the** usual objective **of sowing is to cause the fruit to grow, here too,** weeding or watering **causes the fruit to grow.**

אֲמַר לֵיהּ אַבַּיֵי לְרַבָּה: לְדִידָךְ קַשְׁיָא, וּלְרַב יוֹסֵף קַשְׁיָא. לְדִידָךְ קַשְׁיָא: מִשּׁוּם חוֹרֵשׁ אִין, מִשּׁוּם זוֹרֵעַ לָא? לְרַב יוֹסֵף קַשְׁיָא: מִשּׁוּם זוֹרֵעַ אִין, מִשּׁוּם חוֹרֵשׁ לָא?

Abaye said to Rabba: According to your opinion, it is **difficult, and according to** the opinion of **Rav Yosef,** it is **difficult.** Abaye explains: **According to your** opinion, it is **difficult:** Is it true that **for** the prohibition against **plowing, yes,** he is forewarned, but **for** the prohibition against **sowing, no,** he is not forewarned? Similarly, **according to** the opinion of **Rav Yosef, it is difficult:** Can it be that **for** the prohibition against **sowing, yes,** he is forewarned, but **for** the prohibition against **plowing, no,** he is not forewarned? Everyone should agree that weeding and watering fall under the categories of both plowing and sowing.

וְכִי תֵּימָא כָּל הֵיכָא דְּאִיכָּא תַּרְתֵּי לָא מִיחַיַּיב אֶלָּא חֲדָא, וְהָאָמַר רַב כַּהֲנָא: זוֹמֵר וְצָרִיךְ לָעֵצִים – חַיָּיב שְׁתַּיִם, אַחַת מִשּׁוּם נוֹטֵעַ וְאַחַת מִשּׁוּם קוֹצֵר.

And if you say that anywhere that there are two possible categories of prohibited labor into which a particular action might fall, **one is liable** to be punished **for only one** of them, **didn't Rav Kahana say:** If **one prunes**[B] the branches of a vine on Shabbat **and he needs the wood**[H] for firewood or any other purpose, **he is liable** to bring **two** sin-offerings? He is liable to bring **one** sin-offering **for** violating the primary category of **sowing,** as pruning vines facilitates their growth, and so it is a sub-category of sowing. **And** he is liable to bring **one** sin-offering **for** violating the primary category of **reaping,** as the essence of reaping is detaching that which one needs from the ground. Since he needs the wood that he is detaching from the vine, his action is considered reaping. Consequently, one action that incorporates two prohibited labors causes liability for both.

קַשְׁיָא.

The Gemara concludes: Indeed, it is **difficult**[N] according to both opinions.

HALAKHA

One who weeds or one who waters seedlings on Shabbat – הַמְנַכֵּשׁ וְהַמַּשְׁקֶה מַיִם לְזֶרָעִים בְּשַׁבָּת: One who weeds beneath trees in order to facilitate their growth (*Leḥem Mishne*) or who waters plants on Shabbat violates a subcategory of the prohibited labor of sowing, in accordance with the opinion of Rav Yosef (*Maggid Mishne*; Rambam *Sefer Zemanim*, *Hilkhot Shabbat* 8:1–2).

If one prunes the branches of a tree and he needs the wood – זוֹמֵר וְצָרִיךְ לָעֵצִים: If one unwittingly prunes a tree on Shabbat in a case where the pruning facilitates the growth of the tree, and he needs the wood that he prunes, he is liable to bring two sin-offerings, one for the prohibited labor of reaping and one for the prohibited labor of sowing, in accordance with the opinion of Rav Kahana (Rambam *Sefer Zemanim*, *Hilkhot Shabbat* 8:4).

NOTES

For what prohibited labor do we forewarn him – מִשּׁוּם מַאי מַתְרִינַן בֵּיהּ: Since weeding and watering plants are not explicitly mentioned in the Torah, and are also not listed among the thirty-nine primary categories of labor prohibited on Shabbat, the transgressor might think that they constitute labors prohibited merely by rabbinic decree, not by Torah law. Therefore, the name of the primary labor whose category includes weeding and watering must be mentioned in the warning (Rid; *Talmid Rabbeinu Yeḥiel of Paris*).

The dispute between Rabba and Rav Yosef – מַחְלוֹקֶת רַבָּה וְרַב יוֹסֵף: *Tosafot* explain that their dispute is whether an activity is categorized based upon the nature of the action one performs or based upon the purpose of that action. The Ritva offers a different explanation, that the dispute is whether to define the action based upon what occurs at the time of the action or based upon the eventual result.

It is difficult – קַשְׁיָא: Many delete this phrase from the text of the Gemara, because as a principle, the Gemara does not challenge the opinion of one *amora* with the opinion of another (see *Tosafot*). Some say that because Rav Kahana was the greatest Sage of his generation, and his opinions were widely accepted, his statements are considered like those of a *tanna* and there is no need to delete the phrase. Nevertheless, the Gemara did not deem Rav Kahana's statement a conclusive refutation of the opinions of Rabba and Rav Yosef, because Rabba and Rav Yosef maintain that a Festival is different from Shabbat, and one is not liable to be punished separately for the performance of each one of multiple primary categories of labor. Indeed, the Ritva cites a version of the text that indicates that the Gemara is referring to one who performs these activities on a Festival and not on Shabbat. Alternatively, according to the Rashbam (*Bava Batra* 52b), although the Gemara does challenge the opinion of one *amora* on the basis of the opinion of a more authoritative *amora*, such a challenge can never serve as a conclusive refutation of the ruling of the other *amora*.

BACKGROUND

If one prunes – זוֹמֵר: Pruning, which was performed primarily on grapevines, is done in order to strengthen the vine. A grapevine that is not pruned will not grow well the following year and will not produce good fruit. Consequently, the purpose of such pruning is to facilitate the vine's growth.

Pruned vines

אִיתִיבֵיהּ רַב יוֹסֵף לְרַבָּה: הַמְנַכֵּשׁ וְהַמְחַפֶּה לְכִלְאַיִם – לוֹקֶה. רַבִּי עֲקִיבָא אוֹמֵר: אַף הַמְקַיֵּים.

Rav Yosef raised an objection to the opinion of **Rabba** from what is taught in the following *baraita*: **One who weeds** in proximity to diverse kinds of seeds, **or covers** with earth the exposed roots of **diverse kinds,**[H] **is flogged** for transgressing the prohibition against diverse kinds, i.e., tending different species of crops in one area of the same field, as it is stated: "You shall not sow your field with two kinds of seed" (Leviticus 19:19). **Rabbi Akiva says: Even one who maintains** in his field a mixture of species[N] that he could have uprooted is flogged for violating the prohibition against diverse kinds of seeds.

בִּשְׁלָמָא לְדִידִי דְּאָמֵינָא מִשּׁוּם זוֹרֵעַ – הַיְינוּ דַּאֲסִירָא זְרִיעָה בְּכִלְאַיִם. אֶלָּא לְדִידָךְ דְּאָמְרַתְּ מִשּׁוּם חוֹרֵשׁ חֲרִישָׁה בְּכִלְאַיִם מִי אֲסִירָא?

Rav Yosef explains: **Granted, according to my** opinion, **that I say** that one who weeds on Shabbat is forewarned **for** the prohibited labor of **sowing, this is** the reason he is liable to be punished with flogging for weeding diverse seeds: **Sowing diverse kinds is prohibited. But according to you, who said** that one who weeds on Shabbat is forewarned **for plowing,** why is one liable to be flogged for weeding in proximity to diverse kinds? **Is plowing prohibited** in connection with **diverse kinds?** At the time of plowing, there is no mixture of different species of crops, so plowing cannot be prohibited in this case.

אֲמַר לֵיהּ: מִשּׁוּם מְקַיֵּים.

Rabba **said to him:** According to my opinion, one who weeds a field of diverse kinds is flogged not because he is guilty of plowing, but **for** violating the prohibition against **maintaining** a mixture of species in his field.

וְהָא מִדְּקָתָנֵי סֵיפָא: רַבִּי עֲקִיבָא אוֹמֵר אַף הַמְקַיֵּים, מִכְּלָל דְּתַנָּא קַמָּא לָאו מִשּׁוּם מְקַיֵּים הוּא!

The Gemara objects: **However, from** the fact **that it teaches in the latter clause** of the *baraita* that **Rabbi Akiva says: Even one who maintains** in his field a mixture of species is liable to be flogged, **it may be inferred that** according to **the** anonymous **first *tanna*,** the liability for weeding is **not for maintaining** diverse kinds, but for performing some other prohibited labor.

כּוּלָּהּ רַבִּי עֲקִיבָא הִיא, וּמַאי טַעַם קָאָמַר; מַאי טַעַם הַמְנַכֵּשׁ וְהַמְחַפֶּה בְּכִלְאַיִם לוֹקֶה – מִשּׁוּם מְקַיֵּים, שֶׁרַבִּי עֲקִיבָא אוֹמֵר אַף הַמְקַיֵּים.

The Gemara rejects this opinion: In fact, **the entire** *baraita* reflects the opinion of **Rabbi Akiva, and it is stated** in the style of **what is the reason.** The *baraita* should be understood as follows: **What is the reason that one who weeds and one who covers** the exposed roots of **diverse kinds** with earth **is flogged?** He is flogged **for maintaining** diverse kinds in his field, **as Rabbi Akiva says: Even one who maintains** in his field a mixture of species is flogged.

מַאי טַעְמָא דְּרַבִּי עֲקִיבָא? דְּתַנְיָא: "שָׂדְךָ לֹא תִזְרַע כִּלְאָיִם". אֵין לִי אֶלָּא זוֹרֵעַ; מְקַיֵּים מִנַּיִין?

With regard to Rabbi Akiva's opinion, the Gemara asks: **What is the reason** for **Rabbi Akiva's** opinion? How did he derive this prohibition from the verses? The Gemara answers: **As it is taught** in a *baraita*: **"You shall not sow your field with mingled seed"** (Leviticus 19:19). **I have** derived from this verse that **only sowing** diverse kinds is prohibited. **From where** is it derived that **maintaining** diverse kinds, which does not involve any positive action, is also prohibited?

תַּלְמוּד לוֹמַר: "כִּלְאַיִם שָׂדְךָ לֹא".

The verse states: "Diverse kinds, you shall not sow **your field** with mingled seed" (Leviticus 19:19).[N] The prohibition against planting different species of a crop in one area of the same field is preceded in the verse by the prohibition against cross-breeding livestock: "You shall not let your cattle gender with a diverse kind." A slight change in punctuation yields the phrase: Diverse kinds in your field, you shall not, indicating that merely preserving diverse kinds in one's field is prohibited.

תְּנַן: מַשְׁקִין בֵּית הַשְּׁלָחִין בַּמּוֹעֵד וּבַשְּׁבִיעִית.

§ The Gemara returns to the original topic of discussion: **We learned** in the mishna: **One may irrigate a field that requires irrigation on** the intermediate days of **a Festival as well as during the Sabbatical Year.**[B]

HALAKHA

One who weeds or covers with earth the exposed roots of diverse kinds – הַמְנַכֵּשׁ וְהַמְחַפֶּה לְכִלְאַיִם: It is prohibited to sow diverse kinds of seeds in Eretz Yisrael. If one sows them or performs any other action to facilitate their growth, such as weeding or covering them with earth, he is liable to receive lashes (*Shulḥan Arukh, Yoreh De'a* 297:1).

NOTES

One who maintains a mixture of species – הַמְקַיֵּים: Opinions differ as to how to interpret this category of prohibition. In several places in his commentary, Rashi interprets maintaining a mixture of species in its simple sense, as referring to one who sees diverse kinds in a vineyard but refrains from uprooting them. Many commentaries challenge this understanding, because it is a generally accepted principle that one is not flogged for a passive transgression. One is responsible for maintaining diverse kinds only if he performed some action, e.g., if he constructed a fence around the prohibited plantings (Rashi on *Avoda Zara* 64a; *Talmid Rabbeinu Yeḥiel of Paris*; Ritva). Some explain that others sowed the diverse kinds for him, and now he is tending to them and facilitating their growth (Rabbeinu Ḥananel).

Diverse kinds, you shall not sow your field with mingled seed – כִּלְאַיִם שָׂדְךָ לֹא: According to many early commentaries, the text here reads: No diverse kinds. According to this reading, the verse is being interpreted homiletically in accordance with the method of subtracting a word and interpreting what is left. In this case the word sow is left out, and the verse is understood to mean that the mere presence of diverse kinds is prohibited (Rid; Rabbi Shlomo ben HaYatom).

BACKGROUND

The Sabbatical Year – שְׁבִיעִית: The Sabbatical Year is the last year of the seven-year Sabbatical cycle. The first such cycle began after the conquest of Canaan by Joshua. It is also known as *shemitta*, literally, abandonment, or release. The *halakhot* of the Sabbatical Year are explicitly commanded in the Torah (Leviticus 25:1–7; Deuteronomy 15:1–6). Most authorities maintain that the conditions under which there is an obligation by Torah law to observe the Sabbatical Year have lapsed, and its present-day observance is by rabbinic decree. The particular regulations that apply to the Sabbatical Year fall under two main categories:

(1) All agricultural land must lie fallow. It is prohibited to work the land, except for what is necessary to keep existing crops alive. All produce that does grow is ownerless and must be left unguarded in the fields so that any creature, including wild animals and birds, can have ready access to it. So long as produce can still be found in the fields, one may keep small amounts of it in his home in order to eat it. After the last remnants of a crop have been removed from the field, that crop may no longer be kept in one's home. Produce that grew from existing plants during the Sabbatical Year may be eaten, but it may not be bought and sold in the normal manner or used for purposes other than eating. Produce that grew from seeds during the Sabbatical Year, even if it grew by itself, may not be consumed. Most understand that the prohibition against consuming produce that was grown from seeds during the Sabbatical Year is by rabbinic decree, but some authorities say it is prohibited by Torah law.

(2) All loans are canceled. All outstanding loans owed by Jews to each other are canceled on the last day of the Sabbatical Year. This does not apply to loans whose payment is not yet due on this day, nor does it apply when collection proceedings have already been initiated in court.

HALAKHA

The release of land – שְׁמִיטַת קַרְקַע: The Sabbatical Year is observed only in Eretz Yisrael. The Sages were divided as to whether it must be observed by Torah law at all times, or only when the Jubilee year is observed, or only when the Temple is standing. Some maintain that even today, the *halakhot* governing the Sabbatical Year are in effect by Torah law. Rabbi Yehuda HaNasi and Abaye do not agree with this opinion (*Kesef Mishne*). Others hold that the obligation at present is by rabbinic law (Ramban; Rashba). Some (*Sefer HaTeruma*; Rabbi Yosef Kurkus; see also *Pe'at HaShulḥan*) claim that the Rambam agrees with the opinion that at present the obligation is by rabbinic law (Rambam *Sefer Zera'im*, *Hilkhot Shemitta VeYovel* 4:25).

The release of money – שְׁמִיטַת כְּסָפִים: The Torah obligation to release money, i.e., the prohibition against collecting loans, is applicable only when the Jubilee is in effect. When the Jubilee is in effect, loans are canceled upon the conclusion of the Sabbatical Year, both in and outside of Eretz Yisrael. The obligation to release money is observed today by rabbinic law, so that the Jewish people will not forget this *halakha* (Rambam *Sefer Zera'im*, *Hilkhot Shemitta VeYovel* 9:2–3).

NOTES

When you are mandated by Torah law to release land – בִּזְמַן שֶׁאַתָּה מְשַׁמֵּט קַרְקַע: The commentaries disagree about the meaning of the release of land. According to Rashi, the Gemara is referring to the prohibition against performing agricultural labor during the Sabbatical Year. When this prohibition is not in effect, there is also no obligation to refrain from collecting loans. Other commentaries question this explanation: Why was it more obvious to Rabbi Yehuda HaNasi that the Torah prohibition against agricultural labor does not apply nowadays and less obvious that the prohibition to collect loans does not apply? Rabbeinu Ḥananel explains that the prohibition against agricultural labor became irrelevant de facto because the majority of the land in Eretz Yisrael was owned by gentiles. According to this explanation, the Gemara speaks not of the Temple period, but of a period many years after the destruction of the Temple. Rabbeinu Tam (cited in *Tosafot* on *Gittin* 36a), on the other hand, maintains that the release of land referred to here is the release of land in the Jubilee Year, when fields that have been purchased return to their original owners. This release of land no longer applied from the end of the First Temple period. The later commentaries discussed these *halakhot* at great length in connection with the present-day obligations of the Sabbatical Year (see *Ḥazon Ish*).

בִּשְׁלָמָא מוֹעֵד מִשּׁוּם טִירְחָא הוּא, וּבִמְקוֹם פְּסֵידָא שָׁרוּ רַבָּנַן. אֶלָּא שְׁבִיעִית, בֵּין לְמַאן דְּאָמַר מִשּׁוּם זוֹרֵעַ, וּבֵין לְמַאן דְּאָמַר מִשּׁוּם חוֹרֵשׁ – זְרִיעָה וַחֲרִישָׁה בִּשְׁבִיעִית מִי שָׁרֵי?!

The Gemara asks: **Granted,** with regard to the intermediate days of a **Festival,** where the prohibition against irrigation is **due to** the mandate to avoid excessive **exertion** on the Festival, **in a case of** considerable **loss, the Sages permitted** one to exert himself. **However,** during the **Sabbatical Year, both according to** the one who **said** that one who waters is liable **due to** the prohibition against **sowing, and according to the one who said** that one is liable **due to** the prohibition against **plowing, are sowing and plowing permitted during the Sabbatical Year?** How can these actions be permitted when the Torah explicitly renders prohibited working the land during the Sabbatical Year?

אָמַר אַבָּיֵי: בִּשְׁבִיעִית בַּזְּמַן הַזֶּה, וְרַבִּי הִיא. דְּתַנְיָא, רַבִּי אוֹמֵר: ״וְזֶה דְּבַר הַשְּׁמִטָּה שָׁמוֹט״ – בִּשְׁתֵּי שְׁמִיטּוֹת הַכָּתוּב מְדַבֵּר, אַחַת שְׁמִיטַּת קַרְקַע וְאַחַת שְׁמִיטַּת כְּסָפִים.

Abaye said: The mishna is referring **to the Sabbatical Year in the present time,** when its prohibitions are only by rabbinic decree, **and it is** in accordance with the opinion of **Rabbi** Yehuda HaNasi. **As it is taught** in a *baraita* that **Rabbi** Yehuda HaNasi **says:** When the verse states: **"And this is the manner of the release,** every creditor **will release** that which he has lent to his neighbor" (Deuteronomy 15:2), **the verse speaks of two releases: One is the release of land,**[H] that one must refrain from working the land, **and the other is the release of money,**[H] that one must refrain from collecting debts.

בִּזְמַן שֶׁאַתָּה מְשַׁמֵּט קַרְקַע – אַתָּה מְשַׁמֵּט כְּסָפִים, וּבִזְמַן שֶׁאִי אַתָּה מְשַׁמֵּט קַרְקַע – אִי אַתָּה מְשַׁמֵּט כְּסָפִים.

This verse equates these two releases, indicating that **when you** are mandated by Torah law to **release land,**[N] **you** must **release money, and when you** are **not** mandated to **release land, you need not release money.** This indicates that according to Rabbi Yehuda HaNasi, at the present time, the release of land is not mandated by Torah law. Therefore, observance of the Sabbatical Year is mandated only by rabbinic law, and the Sages were lenient in a case of significant loss.

רָבָא אָמַר: אֲפִילּוּ תֵּימָא רַבָּנַן, אָבוֹת אֲסַר רַחֲמָנָא,

Rava said: Even if **you say** that the mishna was taught in accordance with the opinion of **the Rabbis,** who disagree with Rabbi Yehuda HaNasi and maintain that the observance of the Sabbatical Year, even at the present time, is mandated by Torah law, one can understand the leniency in the mishna. The reason for the leniency with regard to irrigation is because only **primary categories of labor were prohibited by the Merciful One,** i.e., by Torah law,

Perek **I**
Daf **3** Amud **a**

תּוֹלָדוֹת לָא אֲסַר רַחֲמָנָא, דִּכְתִיב: ״וּבַשָּׁנָה הַשְּׁבִיעִת שַׁבַּת שַׁבָּתוֹן יִהְיֶה לָאָרֶץ שָׂדְךָ לֹא תִזְרָע״ וגו׳.

whereas **the subcategories** of labor that are derived from them, e.g., watering, **were not prohibited by the Merciful One,** i.e., by Torah law, but only by rabbinic law; and in a case of loss the Sages were lenient. The source for this distinction is **as it is written: "But in the seventh year shall be a sabbath of solemn rest for the land,** a sabbath for the Lord: **Your field you shall not sow,** and your vineyard you shall not prune. That which grows of its own accord of your harvest you shall not reap, nor gather the grapes of your undressed vines" (Leviticus 25:4–5).

מִכְּדִי, זְמִירָה בִּכְלָל זְרִיעָה, וּבְצִירָה בִּכְלָל קְצִירָה, לְמַאי הִלְכְתָא כְּתָבִינְהוּ רַחֲמָנָא?

Since pruning is included in the principal category of **sowing,** as its objective is to encourage the plant's growth, **and picking** grapes **is included in** the principal category of **reaping** grain, as both involve removal of produce from a plant, **for** the purpose of teaching **what *halakha* did the Merciful One write them?** Why did the Torah explicitly prohibit pruning and picking grapes, rather than sufficing with the general prohibitions against sowing and reaping?

לְמֵימְרָא: דְּאַהָנֵי תּוֹלָדוֹת – מִיחַיַּיב, אַאַחֲרָנְיָיתָא – לָא מִיחַיַּיב.

The Gemara answers that these were individually enumerated **to** say that only **for these subcategories**[N] of labor **is one liable** to be flogged, while **for other** subcategories of labor, i.e., watering a field, **one is not liable.**[H] Consequently, there are only four types of labor that are prohibited by Torah law during the Sabbatical Year: Sowing and its subcategory of pruning, as well as reaping and its subcategory of grape picking. All other subcategories of labor are prohibited only by rabbinic decree.

וְלָא? וְהָתַנְיָא: ״שָׂדְךָ לֹא תִזְרַע וְכַרְמְךָ לֹא תִזְמוֹר״ – אֵין לִי אֶלָּא זֵירוּעַ וְזִימּוּר. מִנַּיִן לְנִיכּוּשׁ וּלְעִידּוּר וּלְכִיסּוּחַ? תַּלְמוּד לוֹמַר: ״שָׂדְךָ לֹא״ ״כַּרְמְךָ לֹא״ – לֹא כׇּל מְלָאכָה שֶׁבְּשָׂדְךָ, וְלֹא כׇּל מְלָאכָה שֶׁבְּכַרְמְךָ.

The Gemara asks: **And** is there really **no** liability for other subcategories of labor? **Isn't it taught** in a *baraita*: **"Your field you shall not sow, and your vineyard you shall not prune"** (Leviticus 25:4). **I have** derived from here an explicit prohibition **only** against **sowing and pruning. From where** do I derive that **weeding,** i.e., uprooting weeds, **hoeing, and cutting weeds,** even without uprooting them, are also prohibited? **The verse states: "Your field** you shall **not** sow" and **"your vineyard** you shall **not** prune."[N] This wording indicates that **no labor** may be performed **in your field, and no labor** may be performed **in your vineyard.**

מִנַּיִן שֶׁאֵין מְקַרְסְמִין, וְאֵין מְזָרְדִין, וְאֵין מְפַסְּגִין בְּאִילָן? תַּלְמוּד לוֹמַר: ״שָׂדְךָ לֹא״ ״כַּרְמְךָ לֹא״ – לֹא כׇּל מְלָאכָה שֶׁבְּשָׂדְךָ וְלֹא כׇּל מְלָאכָה שֶׁבְּכַרְמְךָ.

Similarly, **from where** is it derived **that one may not prune**[N] **trees,**[N] **and one may not trim dry branches** from trees,[N] **and one** may **not cut large branches** [*mefasegin*][LN] **from trees? The verse states: "Your field** you shall **not** sow" and **"your vineyard** you shall **not** prune," thereby teaching that **no labor** may be performed **in your field, and no labor** may be performed **in your vineyard.**

מִנַּיִן שֶׁאֵין מְזַבְּלִין, וְאֵין מְפָרְקִין, וְאֵין מְאַבְּקִין, וְאֵין מְעַשְּׁנִין בְּאִילָן? תַּלְמוּד לוֹמַר: ״שָׂדְךָ לֹא״ ״כַּרְמְךָ לֹא״, כׇּל מְלָאכָה שֶׁבְּשָׂדְךָ לֹא, וְכׇל מְלָאכָה שֶׁבְּכַרְמְךָ לֹא.

Similarly, **from where** is it derived that **one** may **not fertilize** fields and vineyards, **and one may not remove stones**[N] that surround the base of a tree and impede its growth, **and one** may **not** cover exposed roots with **dust,**[N] **and one may not fumigate**[B] **a tree** in order to exterminate worms? **The verse states: "Your field** you shall not sow" and **"your vineyard** you shall **not** prune," thereby indicating that **no labor** may be performed **in your field, and no labor** may be performed **in your vineyard.**[H]

יָכוֹל לֹא יְקַשְׁקֵשׁ תַּחַת הַזֵּיתִים, וְלֹא יְעַדֵּר תַּחַת הַגְּפָנִים, וְלֹא יְמַלֵּא נְקָעִים מַיִם, וְלֹא יַעֲשֶׂה עוּגִיּוֹת לַגְּפָנִים – תַּלְמוּד לוֹמַר: ״שָׂדְךָ לֹא תִזְרָע״.

The apparent conclusion from this is that all labor in a field or a vineyard is prohibited. One **might** have thought that **one may** also **not hoe lightly under olive** trees **and one may not hoe under grapevines, and one may not fill cracks** in the ground **with water, and one may not construct circular ditches** around the bases of **grapevines** in order to collect rainwater.[H] Therefore, **the verse states: "Your field you shall not sow."**

HALAKHA

Primary categories and subcategories of prohibited labor during the Sabbatical Year – אָבוֹת וְתוֹלָדוֹת בִּשְׁבִיעִית: There is a positive mitzva to refrain from working the land and cultivating trees during the Sabbatical Year. Flogging by Torah law is administered only for sowing, pruning, reaping, and gathering, which are all explicitly enumerated in the Torah. One who performs other agricultural tasks is liable by rabbinic decree to be flogged (Rambam *Sefer Zera'im, Hilkhot Shemitta VeYovel* 1:1–3).

No labor may be performed in your field and no labor may be performed in your vineyard – כׇּל מְלָאכָה שֶׁבְּשָׂדְךָ לֹא, וְכׇל מְלָאכָה שֶׁבְּכַרְמְךָ לֹא: One who removes rocks from a field, fertilizes, grafts, plants trees, supports an unsteady tree, covers a tree's roots with dust, fumigates, or performs any similar task that facilitates the growth of plants and trees violates a positive mitzva and is liable by rabbinic decree to be flogged (Rambam *Sefer Zera'im, Hilkhot Shemitta VeYovel* 1:4).

Light hoeing and constructing circular ditches – עֲשִׂיַּית עוּגִיּוֹת וְקִשְׁקוּשׁ: One may hoe beneath grapevines in order to dig circular ditches. Similarly, one may hoe beneath an olive tree to seal cracks, but one may not hoe in order to strengthen the tree (Rambam *Sefer Zera'im, Hilkhot Shemitta VeYovel* 1:7).

LANGUAGE

Cut large branches [*mefasegin*] – מְפַסְּגִין: Some maintain that this word is the verb form of the word *pisga*, peak, and means to raise or elevate. Others suggest that it is similar to the root *p-s-k*, meaning to open and broaden, in the sense that one who cuts large branches creates more room for the remaining branches. Yet others say that the root *p-s-g* simply means to cut.

BACKGROUND

Fumigate – מְעַשְּׁנִין: Fumigation, whether it was done with plain smoke or with smoke from burning sulfur, served the same purpose as does fumigating trees in our time: To rid the tree of various types of bugs that infest its leaves and fruit.

NOTES

For these subcategories – דְּאַהָנֵי תּוֹלָדוֹת: According to the manuscript version of Rashi's commentary, the word subcategories does not appear in the Gemara. According to this version, it is possible to suggest that since pruning and picking grapes are explicitly enumerated in the Torah, they are considered primary categories. Most commentaries, however, accept the version of the text that refers to pruning and picking grapes as subcategories. They explain that the primary categories are the significant labors while the subcategories are the less significant labors (*Talmid Rabbeinu Yeḥiel of Paris*). Others explain that the terms primary categories and subcategories are employed here as they apply to the prohibited labors of Shabbat: That which is considered a primary category with regard to Shabbat is also considered a primary category with regard to the Sabbatical Year, whereas all other labors are called subcategories (Rabbi Shlomo ben HaYatom; Rashi; see also Ritva).

Your field you shall not sow and your vineyard you shall not prune – שָׂדְךָ לֹא, כַּרְמְךָ לֹא: There are several ways to understand this derivation. Rabbeinu Ḥananel explains that since it is obvious that sowing is performed in a field and pruning in a vineyard, the terms your field and your vineyard are superfluous. Therefore, they are understood to indicate that all labor in the field and the vineyard is prohibited. Others suggest that this derivation is based upon the order of words in the verse. The verse could have stated: You shall not sow your field, and: You shall not prune your vineyard. The unusual phraseology of the verse, which places the Hebrew term for the word not adjacent to the Hebrew words for field and vineyard, indicates that all labors in the field and vineyard are prohibited (*Talmid Rabbeinu Yeḥiel of Paris*). The Ritva explains that the wording of the verse itself is not the source of the *halakha*, but rather an abbreviated reference to the generalization, detail, and generalization principle that the Gemara mentions below, which is the real source of this *halakha*.

Prune – מְקַרְסְמִין: The commentaries agree that here, pruning is referring to the removal of dry branches. Rashi explains that this is merely a linguistic change from the term *zemira* mentioned in the verse, which refers exclusively to vineyards. Others say that the term used here is referring to the removal of branches in a way that is different from ordinary pruning (see *Shenot Eliyahu*).

From where is it derived that one may not prune trees – מִנַּיִן שֶׁאֵין מְקַרְסְמִין: The commentaries question why the prohibited labors derived from this verse are not listed all together. Some explain that the *tanna* of this *baraita* was taught the prohibitions listed here in separate groupings, and repeated each lesson as it had been conveyed to him (*Talmid Rabbeinu Yeḥiel of Paris*). Alternatively, the groups of prohibited labors are listed independently because they relate to different spheres of activity: Labors performed in a field, labors performed directly on a tree, and labors performed on the ground (*Talmid Rabbeinu Yeḥiel of Paris*; Ran).

Trim dry branches from trees – מְזָרְדִין: Some say that this refers to removing branches from the tree in order to allow the tree trunk to thicken (*Talmid Rabbeinu Yeḥiel of Paris*). Others explain that it is referring to cutting superfluous roots (*Peirush*).

Cut large branches – מְפַסְּגִין: Rashi and Rabbeinu Gershom Meor HaGola explain that this means supporting weak branches. Others explain that it means tying branches together in order to stimulate growth (*Peirush*; Ran). Others say that this is referring to cutting off all the tree's branches so that its trunk will grow thicker (Meiri; see *Arukh*).

Remove stones – מְפָרְקִין: Some explain that this means removing the stones that weigh down heavily on the roots of the tree (Rashi; Rabbi Shlomo ben HaYatom). Others understand that it means removing unneeded leaves from the tree (Meiri; Jerusalem Talmud).

Cover exposed roots with dust – מְאַבְּקִין: Some say this refers to removing dust from the tree (*Arukh*), whereas others say it means just the opposite, applying dust and earth to the tree (Rashi). The Meiri cites two additional explanations: Applying dust and other materials to a place where the tree suffered a cut, or sprinkling fragrant powder on the tree's fruit.

זְרִיעָה בִּכְלָל הָיְתָה. וְלָמָּה יָצְתָה – לְהַקִּישׁ אֵלֶיהָ, לוֹמַר לְךָ: מָה זְרִיעָה מְיוּחֶדֶת, עֲבוֹדָה שֶׁבַּשָּׂדֶה וְשֶׁבַּכֶּרֶם – אַף כׇּל שֶׁהִיא עֲבוֹדָה שֶׁבַּשָּׂדֶה וְשֶׁבַּכֶּרֶם!

The Gemara explains the derivation: **Sowing was included** in the general prohibition against performing agricultural labors during the Sabbatical Year, as the verse states "But in the seventh year shall be a sabbath of solemn rest for the land" (Leviticus 25:4). **Why was** sowing **singled out** and mentioned explicitly? In order **to compare** other types of labor **to it** and to **say to you: Just as sowing is unique**[N] **in that it is labor** performed both **in the field and in the vineyard, so too, any** other **labor** performed both **in the field and in the vineyard** is prohibited. However, labors performed only in the vineyard but not in the field, i.e., whose objective is merely to sustain the vines from year to year, such as the labors mentioned above, are permitted. In any case, this *baraita* indicates that many subcategories of labor are prohibited during the seventh year, and not just sowing and pruning, as Rava had stated.

מִדְּרַבָּנַן, וּקְרָא – אַסְמַכְתָּא בְּעָלְמָא.

The Gemara rejects this opinion: These labors, with the exceptions of sowing, pruning, grape picking, and reaping, are all prohibited only **by rabbinic law, and the verse** that is cited as a source from the Torah **is a mere support,** and not a bona fide source.

וְקִשְׁקוּשׁ בַּשְּׁבִיעִית מִי שָׁרֵי? וְהָא כְּתִיב: "וְהַשְּׁבִיעִית תִּשְׁמְטֶנָּה וּנְטַשְׁתָּהּ". "תִּשְׁמְטֶנָּה" – מִלְּקַשְׁקֵשׁ, "וּנְטַשְׁתָּהּ" – מִלְּסַקֵּל!

Incidental to this discussion, the Gemara asks: **Is** light **hoeing** under olive trees in fact **permitted during the Sabbatical Year? Isn't it written: "But the seventh year you shall let it rest and lie fallow"** (Exodus 23:11), and it is taught with regard to this verse: **"You shall let it rest" from light hoeing, "and lie fallow" from clearing** the field of **stones.** This indicates that light hoeing is indeed prohibited during the Sabbatical Year.

אָמַר רַב עוּקְבָא בַּר חָמָא: תְּרֵי קִשְׁקוּשֵׁי הָווּ; חַד – אַבְרוּיֵי אִילָנֵי, וְחַד – סַתּוּמֵי פִּילֵי. אַבְרוּיֵי אִילָן – אָסוּר, סַתּוּמֵי פִּילֵי – שָׁרֵי.

Rav Ukva bar Ḥama said: There are two types of light **hoeing, one** whose objective is **to strengthen** the **trees,**[N] **and another** that is intended **to seal cracks.**[N] There is a practical halakhic difference between them: Hoeing performed in order **to strengthen the tree is prohibited,** as it is similar to plowing in that it enhances the tree's growth. However, hoeing undertaken in order **to seal cracks is permitted,** as by doing so one prevents damage to the tree.

אִיתְּמַר, הַחוֹרֵשׁ בַּשְּׁבִיעִית, רַבִּי יוֹחָנָן וְרַבִּי אֶלְעָזָר. חַד אָמַר: לוֹקֶה, וְחַד אָמַר: אֵינוֹ לוֹקֶה. לֵימָא בִּדְרַבִּי אָבִין אָמַר רַבִּי אִילְעָא קָמִיפַּלְגִי, דְּאָמַר רַבִּי אָבִין אָמַר רַבִּי אִילְעָא: כׇּל מָקוֹם שֶׁנֶּאֱמַר כְּלָל בַּעֲשֵׂה, וּפְרָט בְּלֹא תַעֲשֶׂה – אֵין דָּנִין אוֹתוֹ בִּכְלָל וּפְרָט וּכְלָל.

§ **It was stated** that **Rabbi Yoḥanan and Rabbi Elazar** disagreed with regard to **one who plows during the Sabbatical Year.**[H] **One said: He is flogged** for doing so, **while the other one said: He is not flogged.** The Gemara suggests: **Let us say that they disagree with regard to** the principle that **Rabbi Avin** said that **Rabbi Ile'a said,** and one accepts this principle while the other does not. **As, Rabbi Avin said** that **Rabbi Ile'a said: Wherever a generalization is stated** in the Torah **as a positive** mitzva, **and a detail** relating to that generalization is stated **as a negative** mitzva, **one does not apply** the hermeneutical principle of **a generalization, and a detail, and a generalization,**[N] according to which the *halakha* under discussion is expanded to all cases that resemble the detail.

מַאן דְּאָמַר לוֹקֶה – לֵית לֵיהּ דְּרַבִּי אָבִין אָמַר רַבִּי אִילְעָא,

The Gemara explains: **The one who said** that one who plows during the Sabbatical Year **is flogged does not** accept the principle **that Rabbi Avin** said that **Rabbi Ile'a said.** Accordingly, he expounds the verses as follows: The verse "But in the seventh year shall be a sabbath of solemn rest for the land" (Leviticus 25:4) is a generalization stated as a positive mitzva. The continuation of the verse is "Your field you shall not sow," which is a detail stated as a negative mitzva. This is followed by another generalization: "For it shall be a year of rest for the land" (Leviticus 25:5). By applying the principle of a generalization, a detail, and a generalization, one can derive that there is a prohibition against performing any agricultural task that is similar to sowing, including plowing.

וּמַאן דְּאָמַר אֵינוֹ לוֹקֶה – אִית לֵיהּ דְּרַבִּי אָבִין!

And the one who said that **one is not flogged** for plowing **holds** in accordance with the ruling **that Rabbi Avin** stated in the name of Rabbi Ile'a. Therefore, the prohibition stated as a detail, i.e., the prohibition against sowing, is not extended to include any other labor. One who plows violates the positive command to let the land rest, but does not transgress a Torah law phrased as a negative mitzva, and therefore he is not flogged.

NOTES

Just as sowing is unique – מַה זְּרִיעָה מְיוּחֶדֶת: Rabbeinu Ḥananel and Rashi understand that any agricultural task that is not common to both a field and a vineyard is not included. Some say that the term unique is used here in the sense of significant (*Talmid Rabbeinu Yeḥiel of Paris*). Similarly, the Ran explains that the distinction is between a labor that is performed once a year and labor that needs to be performed throughout the year.

Strengthen [*avruyei*] the trees – אַבְרוּיֵי אִילָנֵי: Rabbeinu Ḥananel and most other commentaries explain that this expression stems from the Hebrew word for health [*beriut*] and is referring to performing a task that strengthens the tree. The manuscript version of Rashi's commentary explains that this expression is referring to boring holes in the soil surrounding the base of a tree. In that case, the term *avruyei* stems from the word meaning to pierce, as in the verse: "And they pierced [*uvarei*] them with their swords" (Ezekiel 23:47).

To seal cracks – סַתּוּמֵי פִּילֵי: Some explain that this is referring to sealing cracks in the tree (Rabbeinu Gershom Meor HaGola; Rabbi Shlomo ben HaYatom; see Rambam).Others say that it is referring to sealing cracks in the ground (Riaz; *Talmid Rabbeinu Yeḥiel of Paris*).

One does not apply the hermeneutical principle of a generalization, and a detail, and a generalization – אֵין דָּנִין אוֹתוֹ בִּכְלָל וּפְרָט וּכְלָל: Rabbeinu Gershom Meor HaGola explains as follows: The hermeneutical principle of a generalization, and a detail, and a generalization indicates that the *halakha* expressed in the generalization applies to any case that is somewhat similar to the case specified in the detail. However, cases where the generalizations are positive mitzvot and the detail is formulated as a prohibition, or vice versa, are treated as a generalization followed by a detail, in which case the *halakha* expressed in the generalization is limited to the specific case mentioned in the detail. See also *Tosafot HaRosh*.

HALAKHA

Plowing during the Sabbatical Year – חֲרִישָׁה בַּשְּׁבִיעִית: If one plows during the Sabbatical Year, even if his intention is to improve the land for agricultural purposes, he is not flogged. According to one opinion, if he plows for non-agricultural purposes he does not even violate a positive mitzva (*Pe'at HaShulḥan*, based upon the Jerusalem Talmud; Rambam *Sefer Zera'im, Hilkhot Shemitta VeYovel* 1:4).

לָא, דְּכוּלֵּי עָלְמָא לֵית לֵיהּ דְּרַבִּי אָבִין אָמַר רַבִּי אִילְעָא. מַאן דְּאָמַר לוֹקֶה – שַׁפִּיר.

The Gemara rejects this suggestion: **No,** one can say that **everyone** holds that the *halakha* **is not** in accordance with the principle **that Rabbi Avin** said that **Rabbi Ile'a said.** According to **the one who said he is flogged,** all is **well,** as he applies the hermeneutical principle of a generalization, a detail, and a generalization to derive a prohibition for plowing.

וּמַאן דְּאָמַר אֵינוֹ לוֹקֶה – אָמַר לָךְ: מִכְּדִי, זְמִירָה בִּכְלָל זְרִיעָה, וּבְצִירָה בִּכְלָל קְצִירָה, לְמַאי הִלְכְתָא כְּתַבִינְהוּ רַחֲמָנָא? לְמֵימַר דְּאַהָנֵי תּוֹלָדוֹת הוּא דְּמִיחַיַּיב, אַתּוֹלָדָה אַחֲרִינָא – לָא מִיחַיַּיב.

And the one who said that **he is not flogged** could have **said to you: Since pruning is** included **in** the primary category of **sowing, and** grape **picking is** included in the primary category **of reaping, for** the purpose of teaching **what** ***halakha*** **did the Merciful One write them?** They were individually enumerated **to say** that only **for these** specific **subcategories** of labor **is one liable** to be flogged, but **for** performing **other subcategories** of labor **one is not liable.** According to this opinion, the verse comes to teach that one is not liable to be flogged for performing any labor not explicitly enumerated in the Torah, including plowing.

וְלֹא? וְהָתַנְיָא: "שָׂדְךָ לֹא תִזְרָע וְכַרְמְךָ לֹא תִזְמוֹר" – אֵין לִי אֶלָּא זֵירוּעַ וְזִימּוּר. מִנַּיִן לְעִידּוּר וּלְקִישְׁקוּשׁ וּלְכִיסּוּחַ? תַּלְמוּד לוֹמַר: "שָׂדְךָ לֹא" "כַּרְמְךָ לֹא" – לֹא כָּל מְלָאכָה שֶׁבְּשָׂדְךָ, וְלֹא כָּל מְלָאכָה שֶׁבְּכַרְמְךָ.

The Gemara asks: **And** is there really **no** liability for other subcategories of labor? **Isn't it taught** in a *baraita* with regard to the verse **"Your field you shall not sow, and your vineyard you shall not prune"** that **I have** derived from here an explicit prohibition **only** against **sowing and pruning? From where** do I derive that **weeding, hoeing, and cutting weeds** are also prohibited? **The verse states: "Your field** you shall **not** sow and **your vineyard** you shall **not** prune" (Leviticus 25:4). By placing the word "not" immediately following the words "field" and "vineyard," the verse indicates that one may **not** perform **any labor that** is generally performed **in your field, and** one may **not** perform **any labor that** is generally performed **in your vineyard.**

וּמִנַּיִן שֶׁאֵין מְקַרְסְמִין וְאֵין מְזָרְדִין וְאֵין מְפַסְּגִין בְּאִילָן? תַּלְמוּד לוֹמַר: "שָׂדְךָ לֹא", "כַּרְמְךָ לֹא" – כָּל מְלָאכָה שֶׁבְּשָׂדְךָ לֹא, כָּל מְלָאכָה שֶׁבְּכַרְמְךָ לֹא.

Similarly, **from where** is it derived that **one may not prune trees, and one may not trim dry branches** from trees, **and one** may **not cut large branches from trees? The verse states: "Your field** you shall **not** sow and **your vineyard** you shall **not** prune," indicating that **any labor** that is generally performed **in your field may not** be performed during the Sabbatical Year, **and any labor** generally performed **in your vineyard may not** be performed during the Sabbatical Year.

מִנַּיִן שֶׁאֵין מְזַבְּלִין וְאֵין מְפָרְקִין וְאֵין מְעַשְּׁנִין בְּאִילָן? תַּלְמוּד לוֹמַר: "שָׂדְךָ לֹא" "כַּרְמְךָ לֹא" – כָּל מְלָאכָה שֶׁבְּשָׂדְךָ לֹא, וְכָל מְלָאכָה שֶׁבְּכַרְמְךָ לֹא.

From where is it derived that **one may not fertilize** fields and vineyards, **and one may not remove stones** from around the base of a tree that impede its growth, **and one may not fumigate a tree** in order to exterminate worms? **The verse states: "Your field** you shall **not** sow and **your vineyard** you shall **not** prune," thereby indicating that **any labor** that is generally performed **in your field may not** be performed during the Sabbatical Year, **and any labor** generally performed **in your vineyard may not** be performed during the Sabbatical Year.

יָכוֹל לֹא יְקַשְׁקֵשׁ תַּחַת הַזֵּיתִים, וְלֹא יְעַדֵּר תַּחַת הַגְּפָנִים, וְלֹא יְמַלֵּא נְקָעִים מַיִם, וְלֹא יַעֲשֶׂה עוּגִיּוֹת לַגְּפָנִים – תַּלְמוּד לוֹמַר: "שָׂדְךָ לֹא תִזְרָע".

One **might** have thought that **one may** also **not hoe** lightly **under olive** trees **and one may not hoe under grapevines, and one may not fill cracks** in the ground **with water, and one may not construct circular ditches** around the bases of **grapevines** in order to collect rainwater. Therefore, **the verse states: "Your field you shall not sow."**

זְרִיעָה בִּכְלָל הָיְתָה. וְלָמָּה יָצְתָה? לְהַקִּישׁ אֵלֶיהָ, לוֹמַר לָךְ: מַה זְּרִיעָה מְיוּחֶדֶת – עֲבוֹדָה שֶׁבַּשָּׂדֶה וְשֶׁבַּכֶּרֶם, אַף כָּל שֶׁהִיא עֲבוֹדָה שֶׁבַּשָּׂדֶה וְשֶׁבַּכֶּרֶם!

Sowing was included in the general prohibition against performing agricultural labors during the Sabbatical Year. **Why was** sowing **singled out** and mentioned explicitly? In order **to compare** other types of labor **to** it and to **say to you: Just as sowing is unique in that it is labor** performed both **in the field and in the vineyard, so too, any other labor** performed both **in the field and in the vineyard** is prohibited. However, labor performed only in the vineyard, but not in the field, i.e., whose objective is merely to sustain the vines from year to year, is permitted. In any case, this *baraita* indicates that many labors are prohibited during the seventh year, and not just sowing and pruning.

מִדְּרַבָּנָן, וּקְרָא אַסְמַכְתָּא בְּעָלְמָא.

The Gemara rejects this opinion: These labors, with the exceptions of sowing, pruning, grape picking, and reaping, are all prohibited only **by rabbinic law, and the verse** that is cited as source from the Torah **is a mere support,** and not a bona fide source.

Perek **I**
Daf **3** Amud **b**

כִּי אֲתָא רַב דִּימִי אָמַר: יָכוֹל יִלְקֶה עַל הַתּוֹסֶפֶת – וְנָסֵיב לָהּ תַּלְמוּדָא לִפְטוּרָא, וְלָא יָדַעְנָא מַאי תַּלְמוּדָא וּמַאי תּוֹסֶפֶת.

When Rav Dimi came[B] from Eretz Yisrael to Babylonia, **he stated** a tradition he had heard from the Sages in Eretz Yisrael: One **might** have thought **that one would be flogged for the addition, but a teaching states an exemption** from lashes. Rav Dimi noted: **But I do not know what teaching**[N] **or what addition** this tradition is referring to.

רַבִּי אֶלְעָזָר אָמַר: חֲרִישָׁה, וְהָכִי קָאָמַר: יָכוֹל יִלְקֶה עַל חֲרִישָׁה, דְּאָתְיָא מִכְּלָל וּפְרָט וּכְלָל, וְנָסֵיב לֵיהּ תַּלְמוּדָא לִפְטוּרָא,

The Sages disputed the meaning of this tradition. **Rabbi Elazar said:** The addition in question is **plowing** during the Sabbatical Year, for which there is no explicit prohibition in the Torah, and so it may be regarded as an addition to the labors explicitly enumerated in the Torah. **And this is what it is saying:** One **might** have thought that **one would be flogged for plowing** during the Sabbatical Year, **as it is derived by way** of the hermeneutical principle of **a generalization, and a detail, and a generalization** that teaches that plowing is prohibited. **But a teaching states an exemption** from lashes for the labor of plowing.

דְּאִם כֵּן, כָּל הָנֵי פְּרָטֵי לָמָּה לִי?

This is logical, **because if** one is flogged for plowing, **why do I** need **all these details**[N] that were enumerated in the verse, i.e., pruning and picking grapes? Rather, one must certainly conclude that these were singled out in order to teach that one is flogged only for these specific labors, but not for any other.

וְרַבִּי יוֹחָנָן אָמַר: יָמִים שֶׁהוֹסִיפוּ חֲכָמִים לִפְנֵי רֹאשׁ הַשָּׁנָה, וְהָכִי קָאָמַר: יָכוֹל יִלְקֶה עַל תּוֹסֶפֶת רֹאשׁ הַשָּׁנָה, דְּאָתְיָא מִ״בֶּחָרִישׁ וּבַקָּצִיר תִּשְׁבֹּת״, וְנָסֵיב לָהּ תַּלְמוּדָא לִפְטוּרָא, כִּדְבָעֵינַן לְמֵימַר לְקַמָּן.

And Rabbi Yoḥanan said: This addition is referring to **the** extra **days that the Sages added** to the prohibition against performing agricultural labor, **before Rosh HaShana** of the seventh year, when the Sabbatical Year formally begins. **And this is what it is saying:** One **might** have thought that **one would be flogged for** working the land during **the additional** period[N] prior to **Rosh HaShana** of the Sabbatical Year,[H] **as** this prohibition **is derived** from the verse: **"In plowing and in reaping you shall rest"** (Exodus 34:21). This seemingly superfluous verse is understood as teaching that not only is working the land prohibited during the seventh year, but plowing a field during the sixth year to prepare the land for the seventh year, and reaping what grew in the seventh year during the eighth year are also prohibited. **But a teaching states an exemption** from lashes for these actions, **as we are about to state below.**

BACKGROUND

When Rav Dimi came – כִּי אֲתָא רַב דִּימִי: Rav Dimi was one of the Sages who often traveled from Eretz Yisrael to Babylonia, primarily to transmit the Torah of Eretz Yisrael to the Torah centers of the Diaspora, although occasionally he traveled on business as well. Many questions, particularly those concerning the statements of Sages from Eretz Yisrael, remained unresolved in Babylonia until Rav Dimi would arrive and elucidate the *halakha*, the novel expression, or the unique circumstances pertaining to a particular statement that required clarification.

HALAKHA

The additional period prior to Rosh HaShana of the Sabbatical Year – תּוֹסֶפֶת רֹאשׁ הַשָּׁנָה: There is a *halakha* transmitted to Moses from Sinai that it is prohibited for one to work the land for thirty days prior to the Sabbatical Year, as doing so would prepare the land for the following year. The Sages decreed that an orchard may be plowed only until *Shavuot*, and a grain field until Passover. This is in accordance with the opinions of Rabbi Yishmael and Rabbi Shimon. However, these *halakhot* applied only while the Temple was standing. After the Temple was destroyed, working the land was permitted until Rosh HaShana, in accordance with the opinion of Rav Ashi, as stated later in the Gemara (4a). Planting fruit trees is prohibited a month prior to Rosh HaShana even today, as afterward it would appear as though they were planted during the seventh year (Rambam *Sefer Zera'im, Hilkhot Shemitta VeYovel* 3:1, 3:11).

NOTES

But I do not know what teaching – וְלָא יָדַעְנָא מַאי תַּלְמוּדָא: Even in the time of the *tanna'im* there were oral traditions that were not fully understood, and those who transmitted the traditions and other Sages attempted to accurately ascertain their meaning. In this case, the Sages of Eretz Yisrael had a tradition, or, according to some commentaries, a *baraita*, that contained an allusion that was not satisfactorily understood.

All these details – כָּל הָנֵי פְּרָטֵי: According to Rabbeinu Gershom Meor HaGola, the fact that only these labors were enumerated proves that one is not liable to receive lashes for the other labors. There is an opinion that this should be understood in accordance with the talmudic principle that no inference can be drawn from two verses that come to teach the same *halakha*. Since several labors were specified, no generalization can be inferred from them (*Talmid Rabbeinu Yeḥiel of Paris*).

One might have thought that one would be flogged for working the land during the additional period – יָכוֹל יִלְקֶה עַל הַתּוֹסֶפֶת: Rashi, cited by Ritva, explains that the reference is to lashes by rabbinic law, to which one is liable due to violating a positive mitzva. *Tosafot* maintain that due to the analogy established through the verse, all of the *halakhot* that apply to the Sabbatical Year itself apply to the additional period before the Sabbatical Year as well (see Ritva). Consequently, one is flogged by Torah law for violating a prohibition.

מַאי יָמִים שֶׁלִּפְנֵי רֹאשׁ הַשָּׁנָה? כְּדִתְנַן: עַד מָתַי חוֹרְשִׁין בִּשְׂדֵה אִילָן עֶרֶב שְׁבִיעִית? בֵּית שַׁמַּאי אוֹמְרִים: כָּל זְמַן שֶׁיָּפֶה לַפְּרִי; וּבֵית הִלֵּל אוֹמְרִים: עַד הָעֲצֶרֶת. וּקְרוֹבִין דִּבְרֵי אֵלּוּ לִהְיוֹת כְּדִבְרֵי אֵלּוּ.

The Gemara elaborates: **What** are the extra **days before Rosh HaShana? As we learned** in a mishna (*Shevi'it* 1:1): **Until when may** one **plow an orchard on the eve of the Sabbatical Year? Beit Shammai say:** One may plow **so long as** the plowing **is beneficial for the fruit** already on the trees. Once the plowing serves to benefit only the tree itself and the fruit it will produce the following year, it is prohibited. **And Beit Hillel say:** One may plow **until *Shavuot*.**[N] The mishna notes: **And the statement of these,** Beit Shammai, **is close to being like the statement of these,** Beit Hillel; i.e., in practice, there is little difference between the dates established by the two opinions.

וְעַד מָתַי חוֹרְשִׁין שְׂדֵה הַלָּבָן עֶרֶב שְׁבִיעִית? מִשֶּׁתִּכְלֶה הַלֵּחָה, וְכָל זְמַן שֶׁבְּנֵי אָדָם חוֹרְשִׁים לִיטַּע מִקְשָׁאוֹת וּמִדְלָעוֹת.

The mishna (see *Shevi'it* 2:1) additionally states: **And until when may** one **plow a white field,** i.e., a grain field, on **the eve of the Sabbatical Year?** One may plow **until the** residual **moisture** in the fields from the rain **ceases and so long as people** continue to **plow**[N] their fields in order **to plant cucumbers and gourds,**[BN] which are planted at the end of the winter.

רַבִּי שִׁמְעוֹן אוֹמֵר: אִם כֵּן – נָתַתָּה תּוֹרָה שִׁיעוּר לְכָל אֶחָד וְאֶחָד בְּיָדוֹ! אֶלָּא: בִּשְׂדֵה הַלָּבָן – עַד הַפֶּסַח, וּבִשְׂדֵה הָאִילָן – עַד הָעֲצֶרֶת. וּבֵית הִלֵּל אוֹמְרִים: עַד הַפֶּסַח.

Rabbi Shimon says: If it is so that no set time was established, then **the Torah has given an** individual **measure** of time **into the hands of each and every individual.** One may plow until a self-determined time, as he can always claim that he is plowing in order to plant during the sixth year. **Rather,** a fixed time must be established: **In a white field** one may plow **until Passover, in an orchard** one may plow **until *Shavuot*, and Beit Hillel say: Until Passover.**

וְאָמַר רַבִּי שִׁמְעוֹן בֶּן פַּזִּי אָמַר רַבִּי יְהוֹשֻׁעַ בֶּן לֵוִי מִשּׁוּם בַּר קַפָּרָא: רַבָּן גַּמְלִיאֵל וּבֵית דִּינוֹ נִמְנוּ עַל שְׁנֵי פְּרָקִים הַלָּלוּ וּבִטְּלוּם.

And Rabbi Shimon ben Pazi said that **Rabbi Yehoshua ben Levi said in the name of bar Kappara: Rabban Gamliel and his court** discussed and then **voted about the** prohibitions of **these two periods,** i.e., from Passover or *Shavuot* until Rosh HaShana, **and nullified them,** thereby permitting plowing until Rosh HaShana, the actual beginning of the Sabbatical Year.

אֲמַר לֵיהּ רַבִּי זֵירָא לְרַבִּי אַבָּהוּ, וְאָמְרִי לַהּ רֵישׁ לָקִישׁ לְרַבִּי יוֹחָנָן: רַבָּן גַּמְלִיאֵל וּבֵית דִּינוֹ הֵיכִי מָצוּ מְבַטְּלִי תַּקַּנְתָּא דְּבֵית שַׁמַּאי וּבֵית הִלֵּל? וְהָא תְּנַן: אֵין בֵּית דִּין יָכוֹל לְבַטֵּל דִּבְרֵי בֵּית דִּין חֲבֵירוֹ אֶלָּא אִם כֵּן גָּדוֹל מִמֶּנּוּ בְּחׇכְמָה וּבְמִנְיָן!

Rabbi Zeira said to Rabbi Abbahu, and some say that it was **Reish Lakish** who said **to Rabbi Yoḥanan: How could Rabban Gamliel and his court nullify an ordinance** instituted by **Beit Shammai and Beit Hillel,** who were greater authorities than they were? **Didn't we learn** in a mishna (*Eduyyot* 1:5): **A court cannot nullify the ruling of another** court **unless it surpasses it in wisdom and in number?**[HN]

״אֶשְׁתּוֹמַם כְּשָׁעָה חֲדָא״ אֲמַר לֵיהּ: אֵימוֹר כָּךְ הִתְנוּ בֵּינֵיהֶן: כׇּל הָרוֹצֶה לְבַטֵּל – יָבוֹא וִיבַטֵּל.

Rabbi Abbahu **"was astonished for a while"** (Daniel 4:16), and then **said to him: Say** that when Beit Shammai and Beit Hillel established their decree, **they stipulated among themselves: Anyone who** later **wishes to nullify** this decree **may come and nullify** it.

BACKGROUND

Plowing for cucumbers – חֲרִישָׁה לְמִקְשָׁאוֹת: Cucumbers and gourds are among the plants that grow in fields that suffice with rainwater and do not require manual irrigation. As it is difficult to plow moist soil, the time to plow the ground for these crops is after the winter rains have ceased and after the moisture has lessened, but before the earth has completely dried out.

HALAKHA

Ordinances instituted by a court – תַּקָּנוֹת בֵּית דִּין: If a court instituted an ordinance or issued a decree that gained acceptance among all the Jewish people, it remains in effect even when the reason for the ordinance or decree no longer applies. Only a court that is greater in both wisdom and number can abrogate an ordinance instituted by an earlier court. In the case of a decree issued to prevent violation of a Torah law, a later court cannot abrogate it at all (Rambam *Sefer Shofetim, Hilkhot Mamrim* 2:2).

NOTES

Beit Hillel say: One may plow until *Shavuot* – בֵּית הִלֵּל אוֹמְרִים עַד הָעֲצֶרֶת: In the Jerusalem Talmud, this dispute is included among the list of the unusual circumstances where Beit Hillel rule more stringently than Beit Shammai. The reason it is not listed in tractate *Eduyyot* along with the other disputes of this type is that occasionally, in a dry year, the latest time to plow that is beneficial for the fruit is before *Shavuot*, and Beit Hillel's ruling is more lenient. Similarly, *Talmid Rabbeinu Yeḥiel of Paris* explains that whereas for most trees the latest time to plow that is beneficial for the fruit is after *Shavuot*, for some trees it is before *Shavuot* (see *Tosafot*).

And so long as people plow – וְכָל זְמַן שֶׁבְּנֵי אָדָם חוֹרְשִׁים: Many of the medieval commentaries had a version of the text that leaves out the word: And. The difference between this version of the text and the common text, which includes the word: And, is whether these are two distinct times, or a single date with two different identifying characteristics (Ritva).

To plant cucumbers and gourds – לִיטַּע מִקְשָׁאוֹת וּמִדְלָעוֹת: The term *litta*, which generally refers to planting trees rather than vegetables or grains, is used with respect to cucumbers and gourds because they are planted in a manner similar to that of trees; each seed is planted individually. Vegetables and grains are planted by scattering many seeds at once (*Talmid Rabbeinu Yeḥiel of Paris*).

In wisdom and in number – בְּחׇכְמָה וּבְמִנְיָן: The Rambam asks: How can a court be greater in number than the Sanhedrin, which has seventy-one members? There is no court with a greater number of judges than that. The Rambam explains that the reference here is to the number of Sages who are not members of the court who accept the court's ruling. It has also been suggested that this is referring to the number of students of the judges comprising that particular court (*Talmid Rabbeinu Yeḥiel of Paris*).

דִּידְהוּ הִיא? הֲלָכָה לְמֹשֶׁה מִסִּינַי הִיא! דְּאָמַר רַבִּי אַסִי אָמַר רַבִּי יוֹחָנָן מִשּׁוּם רַבִּי נְחוּנְיָא אִישׁ בִּקְעַת בֵּית חוֹרְתָן: עֶשֶׂר נְטִיעוֹת, עֲרָבָה, וְנִיסּוּךְ הַמַּיִם – הֲלָכָה לְמֹשֶׁה מִסִּינַי.

The Gemara asks: **Is this** ordinance **theirs?** Did Beit Shammai and Beit Hillel institute the ordinance and as such have the authority to attach stipulations to it? **It is a *halakha*** transmitted **to Moses from Sinai. As Rabbi Asi said** that **Rabbi Yoḥanan said in the name of Rabbi Neḥunya from the valley of Beit Ḥortan:** The *halakha* of **ten saplings,**[HN] the *mitzva* of bringing **willow**[H] branches to the Temple on *Sukkot* and standing them up around the altar, and the *halakha* of **water libation**[HB] on *Sukkot* are all ***halakhot*** transmitted **to Moses from Sinai.** Consequently, the prohibition against plowing on the eve of the seventh year is a not a rabbinic ordinance from the Second Temple period, but rather an oral tradition dating back to Moses at Sinai.

אָמַר רַבִּי יִצְחָק: כִּי גְּמִירִי הִלְכְתָא – שְׁלֹשִׁים יוֹם לִפְנֵי רֹאשׁ הַשָּׁנָה, וְאָתוּ הָנֵי תַּקּוּן מִפֶּסַח וּמֵעֲצֶרֶת. וְאַתְנוּ בְּדִידְהוּ: כָּל הָרוֹצֶה לְבַטֵּל – יָבוֹא וִיבַטֵּל.

Rabbi Yitzḥak said: When they learned this ***halakha*** as a tradition dating back to Moses at Sinai, the prohibition applied from only **thirty days before Rosh HaShana.** Afterward, **these** Sages of Beit Shammai and Beit Hillel **came** and **instituted** lengthier periods of restriction, **from Passover and from *Shavuot*,** respectively, **but they stipulated among themselves: Anyone who** later **wishes to nullify** this decree **may come and nullify** it. Rabban Gamliel and his court were therefore able to nullify extended restrictions instituted by Beit Shammai and Beit Hillel.

וְהָנֵי הִלְכְתָא נִינְהוּ? קְרָאֵי נִינְהוּ. דִּתְנַן: ״בֶּחָרִישׁ וּבַקָּצִיר תִּשְׁבֹּת״, רַבִּי עֲקִיבָא אוֹמֵר: אֵין צָרִיךְ לוֹמַר חָרִישׁ וְקָצִיר שֶׁל שְׁבִיעִית – שֶׁהֲרֵי כְּבָר נֶאֱמַר: ״שָׂדְךָ לֹא תִזְרָע וְכַרְמְךָ לֹא תִזְמֹר״, אֶלָּא חָרִישׁ שֶׁל עֶרֶב שְׁבִיעִית

The Gemara raises another question: **Are these** prohibitions of plowing before the Sabbatical Year really ***halakhot*** transmitted to Moses from Sinai? **They are** actually prohibitions based on explicit **verses.**[N] **As we learned**[N] in a *baraita* with regard to the verse **"In plowing and in reaping you shall rest"** (Exodus 34:21)[N] that **Rabbi Akiva says: It is unnecessary** for the verse **to speak** about **plowing and reaping during the Sabbatical Year, as it was already stated:** "But in the seventh year shall be a sabbath of solemn rest for the land, a sabbath for the Lord; **your field you shall not sow, and your vineyard you shall not prune"** (Leviticus 25:4).[N] This teaches that during the seventh year all agricultural labor is prohibited. **Rather,** the verse comes to prohibit **plowing on the eve of the Sabbatical Year**

HALAKHA

Ten saplings – עֶשֶׂר נְטִיעוֹת: If ten saplings were spread out in a field that has an area of a *beit se'a*, fifty by fifty cubits, one may plow the entire field for the benefit of these saplings until Rosh HaShana of the seventh year. This is a *halakha* transmitted to Moses from Sinai (Rambam *Sefer Zera'im, Hilkhot Shemitta VeYovel* 3:5).

Willow – עֲרָבָה: According to a *halakha* transmitted to Moses from Sinai, a willow branch must be brought to the Temple on *Sukkot*. This willow branch is not the same as the one taken together with the *lulav* (Rambam *Sefer Zemanim, Hilkhot Lulav* 7:20).

Water libation – נִיסּוּךְ הַמַּיִם: According to a *halakha* transmitted to Moses from Sinai, water libations are brought on the altar on all seven days of *Sukkot* along with the wine libations, which are brought with the daily offerings every morning (Rambam *Sefer Avoda, Hilkhot Temidin UMusafin* 10:6).

BACKGROUND

Water libation – נִיסּוּךְ הַמַּיִם: During the festival of *Sukkot*, in addition to the other special offerings brought in the Temple, a water libation was poured over the altar. This libation is not mentioned explicitly in the Torah, as its source is an oral tradition transmitted to Moses from Sinai. The water libation was accompanied by great festivity and ceremony, from the time that the water was drawn from the Siloam pool until it was poured over the altar. The water libation was brought on all seven days of *Sukkot*, including Shabbat, even though it was not permitted to draw water for this offering on Shabbat.

NOTES

Ten saplings – עֶשֶׂר נְטִיעוֹת: This *halakha* states that if ten saplings are dispersed in an orchard of twenty-five hundred square cubits, the entire orchard may be plowed until Rosh HaShana of the Sabbatical Year in order to prevent the saplings from withering. Implicitly, this indicates that in other cases plowing is prohibited prior to Rosh HaShana.

The wording of this *halakha* is precise, referring specifically to saplings, which are defined in the Jerusalem Talmud, and not to mature trees. It also refers specifically to ten, because if there are fewer than ten one may plow only directly under the trees, and if there are more than ten it is not a sustainable orchard, and some of the trees will have to be uprooted due to overcrowding (*Talmid Rabbeinu Yeḥiel of Paris*). However, some commentaries dispute this latter point.

They are actually prohibitions based on explicit verses – קְרָאֵי נִינְהוּ: Most commentaries explain that this refers to the *halakha* of ten saplings. Others, however, understand that the Gemara is referring to all three *halakhot*, as according to certain Sages, each has an allusion in the Torah (see *Tosafot*; Rabbi Shlomo ben HaYatom).

As we learned *[ditnan]* – דִּתְנַן: This term generally introduces a quotation from a mishna. However, the *Mesoret HaShas* cites the Rash, who notes that the text here is different from the version of this tannaitic source as it appears in the mishna in tractate *Shevi'it* (1:4). Consequently, it would seem that this source is a *baraita* that is similar but not identical to the mishna. This is supported by the fact that when this source is cited in tractate *Rosh HaShana* (9a), it is introduced by the word *tanya*, which connotes a *baraita*. Furthermore, in all of the available manuscripts, as well as previous printings of the Talmud, the text here includes the word *tanya* rather than the word *tenan*.

In plowing and in reaping you shall rest – בֶּחָרִישׁ וּבַקָּצִיר תִּשְׁבֹּת: In context, this verse is referring to Shabbat, not to the Sabbatical Year. However, if this is the case, the verse is superfluous, as plowing and reaping are among the labors already prohibited on Shabbat (Jerusalem Talmud; see Rashi manuscript). In addition, Rashi (on *Rosh HaShana* 9a) writes that one could have derived from here that only these particular labors are prohibited on Shabbat and all others are permitted. Consequently, the verse is interpreted as referring to the Sabbatical Year rather than to Shabbat.

Your field you shall not sow, and your vineyard you shall not prune – שָׂדְךָ לֹא תִזְרָע וְכַרְמְךָ לֹא תִזְמֹר: *Tosafot* explain that the proof that reaping is prohibited is actually from the next verse: "That which grows of its own accord of your harvest you shall not reap" (Leviticus 25:5). Once it has been proven that the prohibition against reaping mentioned in the verse in Exodus must teach something beyond the prohibition during the Sabbatical Year itself, the same must be true of the prohibition against plowing mentioned in that verse. Some say that the proof is actually from another, more general verse: "Then shall the land keep a sabbath to the Lord" (Leviticus 25:2), but the Gemara cited a verse that people are more familiar with (*Talmid Rabbeinu Yeḥiel of Paris*).

שֶׁנִּכְנָס לַשְּׁבִיעִית, וְקָצִיר שֶׁל שְׁבִיעִית שֶׁיָּצָא לְמוֹצָאֵי שְׁבִיעִית.

that entered into the Sabbatical Year, i.e., plowing in the sixth year that will benefit crops growing in the seventh year, **and reaping** the crops **of the Sabbatical Year that continued into the conclusion of the Sabbatical Year,** i.e., reaping seventh-year produce that continued to grow into the eighth year.

רַבִּי יִשְׁמָעֵאל אוֹמֵר: מָה חָרִישׁ רְשׁוּת – אַף קָצִיר רְשׁוּת, יָצָא קְצִיר הָעוֹמֶר שֶׁהִיא מִצְוָה.

Rabbi Yishmael says that this verse is to be understood as referring to Shabbat and not to the Sabbatical Year, in accordance with the straightforward meaning of the verse. It teaches as follows: **Just as** only **optional plowing** is prohibited on Shabbat, as there is no instance where plowing fulfills a biblical mitzva, **so too,** only **optional reaping** is prohibited, **to the exclusion of the reaping of the *omer*[B] offering, which is a mitzva,[HN]** and consequently permitted on Shabbat. Nonetheless, the first opinion cited in the *baraita*, that of Rabbi Akiva, holds that the prohibition against plowing on the eve of the Sabbatical Year is derived from an explicit verse.

אֶלָּא אָמַר רַב נַחְמָן בַּר יִצְחָק: כִּי גְּמִירִי הִלְכְתָא – לְמִישְׁרֵי יַלְדָּה, קְרָאֵי – לְמֵיסַר זְקֵינָה.

Rather, Rav Naḥman bar Yitzḥak said: When we learned this as a ***halakha*** transmitted to Moses from Sinai, **it was to permit** plowing in the case of **young** saplings until Rosh HaShana. In contrast, **the verses** that were cited come **to prohibit** plowing in the case of **mature** and well-rooted trees thirty days before Rosh HaShana of the Sabbatical Year.

וְכֵיוָן דְּהִלְכְתָא לְמִשְׁרֵי יַלְדָּה לָאו מִמֵּילָא זְקֵינָה אֲסִירָה?

The Gemara asks: **But since the *halakha*** transmitted to Moses from Sinai comes **to permit** plowing in the case of **young** saplings until Rosh HaShana, **does it not automatically** follow that in the case of **mature** trees, plowing **is prohibited** before Rosh HaShana? Therefore, not only the allowance, but the prohibition as well was learned by tradition as a *halakha* transmitted to Moses from Sinai, and not from the verses.

אֶלָּא: הִלְכְתָא לְרַבִּי יִשְׁמָעֵאל, קְרָאֵי לְרַבִּי עֲקִיבָא.

Rather, the ***halakha*** transmitted to Moses from Sinai is the basis of the prohibition against plowing on the eve of the Sabbatical Year **according to** the opinion of **Rabbi Yishmael,** who interprets the verse as referring to Shabbat, and not to the Sabbatical Year, whereas **the verses** are the basis of the prohibition **according to the** opinion of **Rabbi Akiva.**

וְרַבִּי יוֹחָנָן אָמַר: רַבָּן גַּמְלִיאֵל וּבֵית דִּינוֹ מִדְּאוֹרָיְיתָא בַּטֵּיל לְהוּ.

The Gemara previously cited Rabbi Yitzḥak, who explained how Rabban Gamliel's court nullified the extension to the prohibition against plowing before the Sabbatical Year that had been enacted by Beit Shammai and Beit Hillel. The Gemara now cites another opinion, which holds that Rabban Gamliel's court abolished the prohibition against plowing before the Sabbatical Year entirely. **And Rabbi Yoḥanan said** that **Rabban Gamliel and his court nullified** the restrictions on working the land on the eve of the Sabbatical Year **based on** a source written **in the Torah.[N]**

BACKGROUND

Omer **– עוֹמֶר:** This term is used to refer to the measure of barley brought in the Temple on the sixteenth of Nisan, the second day of Passover. The offering was a measure of grain, one-tenth of an *epha*, that was brought irrespective of whether the sixteenth of Nisan was a Shabbat or a weekday. The *omer* consisted of newly ripe barley that was prepared as roasted flour. The barley was harvested on the night following the first day of Passover. A handful of the barley flour was burned on the altar and the rest was eaten by the priests. In addition to this meal-offering, a male sheep was sacrificed as a burnt-offering, together with a wine libation and two-tenths of an ephah of wheat flour as a meal-offering. Once the *omer* was sacrificed, grain from the new harvest could be eaten.

HALAKHA

The reaping of the *omer* offering, which is a mitzva – קְצִיר הָעוֹמֶר שֶׁהִיא מִצְוָה: The grain used for the *omer* offering must be reaped at night on the eve of the sixteenth of Nisan, whether it is a weekday or Shabbat. Only if there is no grain that was reaped at that time may one bring the *omer* offering from grain that had been reaped earlier (Rambam *Sefer Avoda, Hilkhot Temidin UMusafin* 7:6–7).

NOTES

The reaping of the *omer* offering, which is a mitzva – קְצִיר הָעוֹמֶר שֶׁהִיא מִצְוָה: According to most commentaries, Rabbi Yishmael understands the verse as referring to Shabbat, in accordance with the straightforward interpretation of the verse. The verse teaches that only optional reaping is prohibited on Shabbat, but an act of reaping that constitutes a mitzva is permitted. Harvesting barley for the *omer* offering the night before it is sacrificed is a mitzva, and it is therefore permitted on Shabbat. Others explain that even Rabbi Yishmael interprets the verse as referring to the Sabbatical Year, and the verse indicates that even during the Sabbatical Year, the *omer* may be reaped in the usual manner (Rabbeinu Gershom Meor HaGola; Rabbi Yitzḥak ben Malki Tzedek; Rav Natan *Av HaYeshiva*). Some interpret the Jerusalem Talmud to be in accordance with the latter opinion as well.

Nullified the restrictions on working the land based on a source in the Torah – מִדְּאוֹרַיְיתָא בַּטֵּיל לְהוּ: The Ritva explicates two different versions of the text in this passage. One version states that Rabban Gamliel and his court nullified the restrictions from the Torah, meaning that based on a source written in the Torah, they derived that it is permitted to work the land prior to the Sabbatical Year. A different version states that Rabban Gamliel and his court nullified the Torah prohibition, meaning that there had been a rabbinic decree to refrain from working the land in accordance with the Torah law that had been applicable during the time of the Temple, and Rabban Gamliel and his court nullified that decree.

מַאי טַעֲמָא? גָּמַר "שַׁבָּת" "שַׁבָּת" מִשַּׁבַּת בְּרֵאשִׁית, מַה לְּהַלָּן הִיא אֲסוּרָה, לְפָנֶיהָ וּלְאַחֲרֶיהָ – מוּתָּרִין, אַף כָּאן, הִיא אֲסוּרָה, לְפָנֶיהָ וּלְאַחֲרֶיהָ – מוּתָּרִין.

What is the reason? He derives it by means of a verbal analogy between the word **Shabbat** stated with regard to the Sabbatical Year in the verse: "But in the seventh year shall be a sabbath of solemn rest for the land" (Leviticus 25:4), **and** the word **Shabbat** stated with regard to the weekly Shabbat, which commemorates **the Shabbat of Creation. Just as there,** on Shabbat **itself it is prohibited** to perform labor, but **before and after** Shabbat **it is permitted, so too here,** in the case of the Sabbatical Year, during the Sabbatical Year **itself it is prohibited** to perform labor, but **before and after** the Sabbatical Year **it is permitted.**

מַתְקִיף לָהּ רַב אַשִׁי: מַאן דְּאָמַר הִלְכְתָא – אָתְיָא גְּזֵרָה שָׁוָה עָקְרָה הִלְכְתָא? וּמַאן דְּאָמַר קְרָא – אָתְיָא גְּזֵרָה שָׁוָה עָקְרָה קְרָא?!

Rav Ashi strongly objects to this: If Rabban Gamliel and his court nullified the restrictions based on a verbal analogy, then according to **the one who said** that the prohibition against plowing thirty days before Rosh HaShana of the Sabbatical Year is a ***halakha*** that was transmitted to Moses from Sinai, **can a verbal analogy**[B] **come** and **uproot a *halakha*** that was transmitted to Moses from Sinai?[N] **And** similarly, according to **the one who said** that the prohibition against plowing is derived from **a verse, can a verbal analogy come** and **uproot a verse?**

אֶלָּא אָמַר רַב אַשִׁי: רַבָּן גַּמְלִיאֵל וּבֵית דִּינוֹ סָבְרִי לָהּ כְּרַבִּי יִשְׁמָעֵאל דְּאָמַר הִלְכְתָא גְּמִירִי לָהּ, וְכִי גְּמִירִי הִלְכְתָא – בִּזְמַן שֶׁבֵּית הַמִּקְדָּשׁ קַיָּים, דּוּמְיָא דְּנִיסּוּךְ הַמַּיִם, אֲבָל בִּזְמַן שֶׁאֵין בֵּית הַמִּקְדָּשׁ קַיָּים – לֹא.

Rather, Rav Ashi said: Rabban Gamliel and his court held in accordance with the opinion of **Rabbi Yishmael, who said** that **they learned this** prohibition as a ***halakha*** transmitted to Moses from Sinai. **But they learned this *halakha*** only with regard to the time period **when the Temple is standing.** This is evidenced by the fact that it is **similar to** the other *halakha* stated along with it, that of the **water libation,**[N] which was part of the service in the Temple. **But when the Temple is not standing** this *halakha* **does not** apply, and therefore Rabban Gamliel and his court nullified the prohibition after the destruction of the Temple.

"אֲבָל לֹא מִמֵּי הַגְּשָׁמִים וּמִמֵּי הַקִּילוֹן". בִּשְׁלָמָא מֵי קִילוֹן – אִיכָּא טִירְחָא יְתֵירָא, אֶלָּא מֵי גְּשָׁמִים מַאי טִירְחָא אִיכָּא?

§ It was taught in the mishna: **However,** one **may not** irrigate a field on the intermediate days of a Festival **with rainwater** collected in a cistern **or with water drawn with a shadoof.** The Gemara asks: **Granted,** irrigating a field with **water drawn with a shadoof involves excessive effort,** and so it is prohibited on the intermediate days of a Festival. **But what excessive effort is involved** in irrigating a field **with rainwater?** Rainwater collects on its own and one merely has to channel it to where it is needed.

אָמַר רַבִּי אִילְעָא אָמַר יוֹחָנָן: גְּזֵירָה מֵי גְשָׁמִים אַטּוּ מֵי קִילוֹן. רַב אַשִׁי אָמַר: מֵי גְשָׁמִים גּוּפַיְיהוּ לִידֵי מֵי קִילוֹן אָתוּ.

Rabbi Ile'a said that Rabbi **Yoḥanan said:** A rabbinic **decree** was enacted with regard to **rainwater**[N] **due to** its similarity **to water drawn with a shadoof. Rav Ashi said: Rainwater itself will come to be** like **water drawn with a shadoof.** Once the level of the collected rainwater drops, it will become necessary to draw it with a bucket, a procedure involving excessive effort.

וְקָמִיפַּלְגִי בִּדְרַבִּי זֵירָא. דְּאָמַר רַבִּי זֵירָא אָמַר רַבָּה בַּר יִרְמְיָה אָמַר שְׁמוּאֵל: נְהָרוֹת הַמּוֹשְׁכִין מַיִם מִן הָאֲגַמִּים – מוּתָּר לְהַשְׁקוֹת מֵהֶן בְּחוּלּוֹ שֶׁל מוֹעֵד.

The Gemara comments: Rabbi Ile'a and Rav Ashi **disagree with regard to** the ruling issued by **Rabbi Zeira, as Rabbi Zeira said** that **Rabba bar Yirmeya said** that **Shmuel said:** With regard to **streams that draw water from pools** of collected water,[N] **one is permitted to irrigate** his field **from them on the intermediate days of a Festival,**[H] because the flow of water is steady.

מָר אִית לֵיהּ דְּרַבִּי זֵירָא, וּמַר לֵית לֵיהּ דְּרַבִּי זֵירָא.

One **Sage,** Rav Ashi, **is of** the opinion that the ruling is in accordance with the opinion **of Rabbi Zeira,** as he prohibits only irrigating with rainwater, because the supply might come to an end, but he does not prohibit watering from a source whose flow is steady. **And** one **Sage,** Rabbi Yoḥanan, **is not of** the opinion that the ruling is in accordance with the opinion of **Rabbi Zeira,** as he prohibits irrigating with rainwater due to its similarity to water drawn with a shadoof. This applies regardless of whether the level of the rainwater will drop, and therefore Rabbi Yoḥanan would prohibit using collected water even if a stream flows through it and it will not dry up.

BACKGROUND

Verbal analogy – **גְּזֵרָה שָׁוָה:** This is a fundamental talmudic principle of biblical exegesis that appears in all standard lists of exegetical principles. If the same word or phrase appears in two places in the Torah and a certain *halakha* is explicitly stated in one of those places, it may be inferred on the basis of the verbal analogy that the same *halakha* must apply in the other case as well. Consequently, the inferences drawn on the basis of verbal analogy rely on verbal, rather than conceptual, similarity. For example, the Torah states concerning those convicted of certain types of sorcery: "They shall be put to death; they shall stone them with stones; their blood shall be upon them" (Leviticus 20:27). Since this verse uses the expression: Their blood shall be upon them, in the context of death by stoning, the Talmud infers by verbal analogy that in all cases where this expression is used, capital punishment is to be inflicted by stoning. Generally, inferences can be drawn through verbal analogy only if the same word or phrase appears in both of the verses being compared, although a verbal analogy may occasionally be drawn even if the words being compared are not identical, provided that their meanings are similar.

NOTES

Can a verbal analogy come and uproot a *halakha* transmitted to Moses from Sinai – **אָתְיָא גְּזֵרָה שָׁוָה עָקְרָה הִלְכְתָא:** It is clear that this verbal analogy is unlike other verbal analogies, which have the force of Torah law. In this case, the Sages developed their own exposition according to the style of verbal analogy. Since a verbal analogy is authoritative only if it was transmitted to Moses from Sinai, the Sages' exposition does not have the authority to override a known *halakha* based upon a biblical verse or a *halakha* transmitted to Moses from Sinai.

It is similar to the water libation – **דּוּמְיָא דְּנִיסּוּךְ הַמַּיִם:** The Gemara could have cited the mitzva of the willow branches as a precedent, as it too was applicable only in the Temple, but the water libation was cited instead because there is no vestige of the mitzva today, even by rabbinic decree (Ritva).

A rabbinic decree was enacted with regard to rainwater – **גְּזֵירָה מֵי גְשָׁמִים:** Many explain this decree as an extension of the decree prohibiting irrigating with well water, which is gathered in one place and does not flow. The Sages extended that decree to all water that does not flow (*Tosefot Rid*; Ran; Ritva). Some say that there was one decree prohibiting all forms of rainwater, as well water is also rainwater (*Talmid Rabbeinu Yeḥiel of Paris*).

Streams that draw water from pools of collected water – **נְהָרוֹת שֶׁמּוֹשְׁכִין מַיִם מִן הָאֲגַמִּים:** The commentaries emphasize that this refers not to actual streams but to water channels. *Talmid Rabbeinu Yeḥiel of Paris* adds that since these channels are shallow, using their water does not require much exertion.

HALAKHA

Streams that draw water from pools – **נְהָרוֹת הַמּוֹשְׁכִין מַיִם מִן הָאֲגַמִּים:** On the intermediate days of a Festival one may irrigate a field from a stream that draws water from a pool, provided that there is no danger that the supply of water will cease. If it will cease, even if there is sufficient water for his field, one may not irrigate from it, due to a rabbinic decree (*Magen Avraham*). Similarly, one may irrigate a field that requires irrigation from a pool that is fed by water dripping from another field, as long as the spring that is the source of the water in the latter field continues to flow (*Shulḥan Arukh, Oraḥ Ḥayyim* 537:3).

גּוּפָא, אָמַר רַבִּי זֵירָא אָמַר רַבָּה בַּר יִרְמְיָה אָמַר שְׁמוּאֵל: נְהָרוֹת הַמּוֹשְׁכִין מַיִם מִן הָאֲגַמִּים – מוּתָּר לְהַשְׁקוֹת מֵהֶן בְּחוּלּוֹ שֶׁל מוֹעֵד.

After mentioning the statement of Rabbi Zeira in the course of the previous discussion, the Gemara examines **the matter itself. Rabbi Zeira said** that **Rabba bar Yirmeya said** that **Shmuel said:** With regard to **streams that draw water from pools** of water, **one is permitted to irrigate** his field **from them on the intermediate days of a Festival.**

אִיתִיבֵיהּ רַבִּי יִרְמְיָה לְרַבִּי זֵירָא: אֲבָל לֹא מִמֵּי גְשָׁמִים וְלֹא מִמֵּי קִילוֹן! אֲמַר לֵיהּ: יִרְמְיָה בְּרִי, הָנֵי אֲגַמִּים דְּבָבֶל – כְּמַיָּא דְּלָא פָּסְקִי דָּמוּ.

Rabbi Yirmeya raised an objection to Rabbi Zeira from what is taught in the mishna: **However, one may not** irrigate a field on the intermediate days of a Festival **with rainwater** collected in cisterns **or with water drawn with a shadoof.** This indicates that whenever there is a concern that the water might run out, it is prohibited to irrigate from this water source. Consequently, Rabbi Yirmeya wanted to know why this concern did not exist in the case of the pools of water as well. Rabbi Zeira **said to him: Yirmeya, my son,**[N] **these pools in Babylonia are like water that does not stop** flowing.[N] Therefore, there is no concern that the water level in these pools might go down to such an extent that it will become necessary to draw the water with buckets.

תָּנוּ רַבָּנַן: הַפְּסִיקוֹת וְהַבְּרֵיכוֹת שֶׁנִּתְמַלְּאוּ מַיִם מֵעֶרֶב יוֹם טוֹב – אָסוּר לְהַשְׁקוֹת מֵהֶן בְּחוּלּוֹ שֶׁל מוֹעֵד, וְאִם הָיְתָה אַמַּת הַמַּיִם עוֹבֶרֶת בֵּינֵיהֶן – מוּתָּר.

The Sages taught in a *baraita*: With regard to **temporary pools**[N] and regular **pools that were filled with water on the eve of a Festival, it is prohibited for one to irrigate** his field **from them on the intermediate days of the Festival,** lest they run out of water and he will come to exert himself and bring water from elsewhere. **But if a water channel passes between them** so that water flows from the one to the other, **it is permitted.**

אָמַר רַב פַּפָּא: וְהוּא שֶׁרוּבָּהּ שֶׁל אוֹתָהּ שָׂדֶה שׁוֹתָה מֵאוֹתָהּ אַמַּת הַמַּיִם. רַב אַשִׁי אָמַר: אַף עַל פִּי שֶׁאֵין רוּבָּהּ שֶׁל אוֹתָהּ שָׂדֶה שׁוֹתָה, כֵּיוָן דְּקָא מָשְׁכָא וְאָתְיָא – מֵימַר אָמַר: אִי לָא שָׁתְיָא לְחַד יוֹמָא – תִּשְׁתֵּי לִתְרֵי וּתְלָתָא יוֹמֵי.

Rav Pappa said: And this allowance applies only **when the majority of that field can be irrigated from that water channel,** such that most of the field can be irrigated at the same time. In this case, there is no concern that when the water runs out, he will come to exert himself and irrigate the rest of the field from another source of water. **Rav Ashi said:** It applies **even though the majority of that field cannot be irrigated** from that water channel at the same time. **Since** the channel **continuously draws** water, constantly replenishing its supply, even if it does so at a slow rate, one will **say** to himself that even **if** the entire field **cannot be irrigated** from that water channel **on a single day, it can be irrigated** from it **over** the course of **two or three days.** Accordingly, he will not find it necessary to exert himself to quickly irrigate that portion of the field that did not already receive its water.

תָּנוּ רַבָּנַן: בְּרֵיכָה שֶׁנּוֹטֶפֶת מַיִם מִשְּׂדֵה בֵּית הַשְּׁלָחִין זוֹ – מוּתָּר לְהַשְׁקוֹת מִמֶּנָּה שְׂדֵה בֵּית הַשְּׁלָחִין אַחֶרֶת.

The Sages taught in a *baraita*: With regard to **a pool** that receives **drips of water from this field that requires irrigation,** which itself receives water from a spring, **one is permitted to irrigate from** this pool **another field** situated below it **that requires irrigation.**

וְהָא עֲבִידָא דְּפָסְקָא! אָמַר רַבִּי יִרְמְיָה: וַעֲדַיִין הִיא מְטַפְטֶפֶת. אָמַר אַבָּיֵי: וְהוּא שֶׁלֹּא פָּסַק מַעְיָין רִאשׁוֹן.

The Gemara asks: **But isn't** the pool **likely to stop flowing,** which will force him to exert himself and draw water from somewhere else? **Rabbi Yirmeya said:** The case is where the upper field **is still trickling** water into the pool and does not stop. **Abaye said: And this** allowance applies only **when** the water from **the first spring** that irrigates the upper field **has not stopped** flowing. Only in that case can one rely on the water trickling from the upper field and consequently irrigating the lower field from the pool.

תַּנְיָא, רַבִּי שִׁמְעוֹן בֶּן מְנַסְיָא אוֹמֵר: שְׁתֵּי עֲרוּגוֹת זוֹ לְמַעְלָה מִזּוֹ – לֹא יַדְלֶה מִן הַתַּחְתּוֹנָה וְיַשְׁקֶה אֶת הָעֶלְיוֹנָה. יוֹתֵר עַל כֵּן אָמַר רַבִּי אֶלְעָזָר בַּר שִׁמְעוֹן: אֲפִילּוּ עֲרוּגָה אַחַת, חֶצְיָהּ נָמוּךְ וְחֶצְיָהּ גָּבוֹהַּ – לֹא יַדְלֶה מִמָּקוֹם נָמוּךְ וְיַשְׁקֶה לְמָקוֹם גָּבוֹהַּ.

It is taught in a *baraita* that **Rabbi Shimon ben Menasya says:** With regard to **two garden beds** located **one above the other, one may not draw** water **from** the channel supplying **the lower** garden bed in order **to irrigate the upper** garden bed, due to the excessive exertion involved. **Furthermore, Rabbi Elazar bar Shimon said: Even** in the case of **a single garden bed, half of which is lower and half of which is higher, one may not draw water**[H] **from the** channel supplying **the lower area to irrigate the upper area,** even though they are two parts of the same garden bed.

NOTES

Yirmeya, my son – יִרְמְיָה בְּרִי: Most commentaries explain that this is an expression of affection (see Rabbi Shlomo ben HaYatom). The Ritva explains that the word *beri* does not mean my son, but clearly, or certainly.

Like water that does not stop flowing – כְּמַיָּא דְּלָא פָּסְקִי דָּמוּ: Opinions differ as to whether water was so abundant that there was no concern that there would not be enough to water the field (*Talmid Rabbeinu Yeḥiel of Paris*) or whether the water still flowed continuously because it was fed from a spring (*Maggid Mishne*). The opinions of the halakhic authorities are similarly divided (see *Beit Yosef*).

Temporary pools [*pesikot*] – פְּסִיקוֹת: Some commentaries explain that *pesikot* are imperfectly finished channels, whereas *bereikhot* are well-constructed and finished (Rashi manuscript; Rabbeinu Yehonatan). The Meiri suggests that *bereikhot* are structures, while *pesikot* are simply trenches dug in the ground. *Talmid Rabbeinu Yeḥiel of Paris* maintains that *bereikhot* are rounded, whereas *pesikot* are squared.

HALAKHA

Drawing water – דְּלִיַּת מַיִם: One may not draw water from a channel supplying the lower portion of a garden bed even to irrigate the upper portion of that very same garden bed (*Shulḥan Arukh*, *Oraḥ Ḥayyim* 537:2).

HALAKHA

One may draw water and irrigate vegetables – מַדְלִין לְיָרָקוֹת: It is permitted to draw water and irrigate vegetables that one wishes to eat during a Festival. If one does not intend to eat the vegetables during the Festival but simply wishes to enhance their appearance, it is prohibited (*Shulḥan Arukh, Oraḥ Ḥayyim* 537:4).

NOTES

In order to eat them – כְּדֵי לְאוֹכְלָן: One may water vegetables so that they will be fresh when they are picked and eaten on the intermediate days of the Festival (*Talmid Rabbeinu Yeḥiel of Paris*; *Sefer HaMeorot*).

In order to enhance their appearance – בִּשְׁבִיל לְיַיפּוֹתָן: Some explain that this is referring to watering vegetables to cause them to grow larger so that they can be sold at a higher price after the Festival (Rashi). Rabbi Shlomo ben HaYatom explains that they would wash the vegetables in order to enhance their appearance, but because this involves extra effort and it is not necessary for the Festival, it is prohibited.

תָּנוּ רַבָּנַן: מַדְלִין לְיָרָקוֹת כְּדֵי לְאוֹכְלָן. וְאִם בִּשְׁבִיל לְיַיפּוֹתָן – אָסוּר.

The Sages taught in a *baraita*: **One may draw** water and irrigate **vegetables**[H] **in order to eat them**[N] on the intermediate days of a Festival. **But if** he does this **in order** to improve their growth and **to enhance their** appearance[N] **it is prohibited,** as he is considered to be unnecessarily exerting himself on the Festival.

רָבִינָא וְרַבָּה תּוֹסְפָאָה הָווּ קָא אָזְלִי בְּאוֹרְחָא, חָזוּ לְהַהוּא גַּבְרָא דַּהֲוָה דָּלֵי דַּוְולָא בְּחוּלָּא דְּמוֹעֲדָא. אֲמַר לֵיהּ רַבָּה תּוֹסְפָאָה לְרָבִינָא: לֵיתֵי מָר לְשַׁמְּתֵיהּ! אֲמַר לֵיהּ: וְהָתַנְיָא: מַדְלִין לְיָרָקוֹת כְּדֵי לְאוֹכְלָן! אֲמַר לֵיהּ: מִי סָבְרַתְּ מַאי מַדְלִין – מַדְלִין מַיָּא? מַאי

The Gemara relates that **Ravina and Rabba Tosefa'a**[P] **were** once **walking along the road** when **they saw a certain man that was drawing** water **with a bucket on the intermediate days of a Festival. Rabba Tosefa'a said to Ravina: Let the Master come and excommunicate him** for transgressing the words of the Sages. Ravina **said to him: But isn't it taught** in a *baraita*: **One may draw for vegetables in order to eat them,** and so he has not committed a transgression. Rabba Tosefa'a **said to him: Do you maintain** that **what is** meant by **one may draw** [*madlin*] **is** that **one may draw water** in order to irrigate the vegetables? This is not so. Rather, **what is** meant by

Perek **I**
Daf **4** Amud **b**

מַדְלִין? שַׁלּוֹפֵי. כְּדִתְנַן: הַמֵּידֵל בַּגְּפָנִים, כְּשֵׁם שֶׁהוּא מֵידֵל בְּשֶׁלּוֹ – כָּךְ הוּא מֵידֵל בְּשֶׁל עֲנִיִּים, דִּבְרֵי רַבִּי יְהוּדָה. רַבִּי מֵאִיר אוֹמֵר: בְּשֶׁלּוֹ – רַשַּׁאי, וְאֵינוֹ רַשַּׁאי בְּשֶׁל עֲנִיִּים.

one may draw is that **one may pull out**[N] some of the vegetables that are growing densely together. The *baraita* comes to teach that one is permitted to thin out a garden bed on the intermediate days of a Festival in order to eat on the Festival those that he removes, but he is prohibited to do so in order to enhance the appearance of those that remain. **As we learned** in a mishna (*Pe'a* 7:5): **One who thins out** [*meidel*] **the vines**[N] in his vineyard, **just as he may thin out his own** vines, **so too, he may thin out** the vines set aside for **the poor.**[N] Since he is doing it for the sake of the vines, he may also thin out what he leaves for the poor; this is **the statement of Rabbi Yehuda. Rabbi Meir** disagrees and **says: His own** vines **he is permitted** to thin out, **but he is not permitted** to thin out the vines set aside **for the poor.** This mishna indicates that the term *meidel* can be used to mean thinning out and does not refer only to drawing water.

אֲמַר לֵיהּ: וְהָתַנְיָא: מַדְלִין מַיִם לְיָרָקוֹת כְּדֵי לְאוֹכְלָן! אֲמַר לֵיהּ: אִי תַּנְיָא – תַּנְיָא.

Ravina **said to** Rabba Tosefa'a: **But wasn't it** explicitly **taught** in a *baraita*: **One may draw water** to irrigate **vegetables in order to eat them?** Rabba Tosefa'a **said to him: If it is taught** explicitly in a *baraita*, the *halakha* is as **it is taught,** and I retract my statement.

NOTES

One may pull out – שַׁלּוֹפֵי: This understanding of the *baraita* seems to remain valid even according to the Gemara's conclusion that the *baraita* may be understood as referring to watering (Meiri; *Sefat Emet*). Consequently, it is permitted to pick vegetables or fruit in order to eat them, even if one thereby improves the produce that remains. However, if his sole intention is to improve the remaining produce, it is prohibited to pick the produce (Meiri).

One who thins out the vines – הַמֵּידֵל בַּגְּפָנִים: The commentaries debate the meaning of this phrase. Some explain that one removes some of the grape clusters in order to allow the remaining clusters to grow better than they would if left alone (*Talmid Rabbeinu Yeḥiel of Paris*). Others understand that one trims some of the branches. Other commentaries explain that if the vines are crowded and close together, he uproots some of them (Rabbeinu Shimshon; Rabbi Yitzḥak ben Malki Tzedek; Ritva).

So too, may he thin out the vines set aside for the poor – כָּךְ הוּא מֵידֵל בְּשֶׁל עֲנִיִּים: Rashi explains that he thins out the corner [*pe'a*], the portion of the crop that must be left for the poor, or the *olelot*, the small, incompletely formed clusters of grapes that must also be left for the poor. Some write that the discussion pertains only to *pe'a* but not to *olelot* (*Talmid Rabbeinu Yeḥiel of Paris*), while others claim that it pertains only to *olelot* and not to *pe'a* (*Tosefot Rid*; Ritva).

״וְאֵין עוֹשִׂין עוּגִיּוֹת לַגְּפָנִים״. מַאי עוּגִיּוֹת? אָמַר רַב יְהוּדָה: בִּנְכֵי. תַּנְיָא נַמִּי הָכִי: אֵלּוּ הֵן עוּגִיּוֹת – בְּדִידִין שֶׁבְּעִיקְּרֵי זֵיתִים וְשֶׁבְּעִיקְּרֵי גְּפָנִים.

§ It was taught in the mishna: **And one may not construct circular ditches** [*ugiyyot*] around the bases of **grapevines**[H] on the intermediate days of a Festival. The Gemara asks: **What are *ugiyyot*?**[N] **Rav Yehuda said:** They are what are called in Aramaic *binkei*, circular ditches around vines. The Gemara notes that **this is also taught** in a *baraita*: **These are *ugiyyot*: *Bedidin*,**[L] circular ditches **around the bases of olive trees and around the bases of grapevines.**

אִינִי? וְהָא רַב יְהוּדָה שְׁרָא לִבְנֵי בַּר צִיתַאי לְמֶעֱבַד בִּנְכֵי לְכַרְמֵיהוֹן! לָא קַשְׁיָא, הָא – בַּחֲדַתֵי, הָא – בְּעַתִּיקֵי.

The Gemara asks: **Is that so?** Is it prohibited to dig circular ditches on the intermediate days of the Festival? **Didn't Rav Yehuda permit the family of bar Tzitai to construct circular ditches for their vineyards** on the intermediate days of a Festival? The Gemara answers: This is **not difficult. This** source, i.e., the mishna that renders the practice prohibited, is referring to digging **new** ditches. **That** other source, i.e., Rav Yehuda's ruling that permits the digging of such ditches, is referring to **old** ones,[N] which merely need to be cleared.

״רַבִּי אֶלְעָזָר בֶּן עֲזַרְיָה אוֹמֵר אֵין עוֹשִׂין אֶת הָאַמָּה״. בִּשְׁלָמָא מוֹעֵד – מִשּׁוּם דְּקָא טָרַח. אֶלָּא שְׁבִיעִית – מַאי טַעְמָא?

§ It was taught in the next clause of the mishna that **Rabbi Elazar ben Azarya says: One may not construct a new** water **channel** during the intermediate days of a Festival or during the Sabbatical Year. The Gemara asks: **Granted,** it is prohibited for him to do so on the intermediate days of **a Festival, because** in so doing **he** excessively **exerts himself** on the Festival. **But what is the reason** that this is prohibited during **the Sabbatical Year,** when only labors that enhance the growth of plants are prohibited?

פְּלִיגוּ בָּהּ רַבִּי זֵירָא וְרַבִּי אַבָּא בַּר מֶמֶל. חַד אָמַר: מִפְּנֵי שֶׁנִּרְאֶה כְּעוֹדֵר, וְחַד אָמַר: מִפְּנֵי שֶׁמַּכְשִׁיר אֲגַפֶּיהָ לִזְרִיעָה.

The Gemara answers: **Rabbi Zeira and Rabbi Abba bar Memel disagreed with regard to this** issue. **One** of them **said:** It is prohibited **because it appears** to others **as if he were hoeing** his field. As onlookers do not know that he is merely digging a water channel, they suspect him of working his land during the Sabbatical Year. **And** the other **one said:** It is prohibited **because he** thereby **prepares** the channel's **banks**[N] **for planting,** for when he digs out the channel, he piles the fresh soil that is fit for planting on its two banks.

מַאי בֵּינַיְיהוּ? אִיכָּא בֵּינַיְיהוּ דְּקָא אָתוּ מַיָּא בַּתְרֵיהּ. מַאן דְּאָמַר מִפְּנֵי שֶׁמַּכְשִׁיר אֲגַפֶּיהָ לִזְרִיעָה – אִיכָּא, וּמַאן דְּאָמַר מִפְּנֵי שֶׁנִּרְאֶה כְּעוֹדֵר – לֵיכָּא.

The Gemara asks: **What is** the practical halakhic difference **between them?**[N] The Gemara answers: **There is** a practical halakhic difference **between them** in a case where **water comes** into the channel immediately **after he** digs it out. According to **the one who said** that digging a water channel is prohibited **because he** thereby **prepares its banks for planting, there is** still a prohibition, as here too, he piles the fresh soil on the channel's banks. **But** according to **the one who said** it is prohibited **because it appears as if he were hoeing, there is no** prohibition here, as the immediate entry of water makes it obvious that he is digging a water channel.

וּלְמַאן דְּאָמַר מִפְּנֵי שֶׁנִּרְאֶה כְּעוֹדֵר – לֵיחוּשׁ מִפְּנֵי שֶׁמַּכְשִׁיר אֲגַפֶּיהָ לִזְרִיעָה! אֶלָּא: אִיכָּא בֵּינַיְיהוּ דְּקָא שָׁקֵיל מִינֵּיהּ וְשָׁדֵי לְבָרָאֵי. לְמַאן דְּאָמַר מִפְּנֵי שֶׁמַּכְשִׁיר אֲגַפֶּיהָ לִזְרִיעָה – לֵיכָּא, לְמַאן דְּאָמַר מִפְּנֵי שֶׁנִּרְאֶה כְּעוֹדֵר – אִיכָּא.

The Gemara asks: **But according to the one who said** that digging a water channel is prohibited **because it appears as if he were hoeing, let him be concerned that** the digger thereby **prepares** the channel's **banks for planting** and render digging prohibited in this case as well. **Rather,** the matter must be explained differently, such that **there is** a practical difference **between them** in a case **where he takes** the earth that he excavates **from** the channel **and throws** it a considerable distance **outside. According to the one who said** that it is prohibited **because he** thereby **prepares** the channel's **banks for planting, there is no** prohibition here, as he does not prepare them for planting. But **according to the one who said** it is prohibited **because it appears as if he were hoeing, there is** a prohibition here, as here too, it appears as if he were hoeing.

וּלְמַאן דְּאָמַר מִפְּנֵי שֶׁמַּכְשִׁיר אֲגַפֶּיהָ לִזְרִיעָה, לֵיחוּשׁ מִפְּנֵי שֶׁנִּרְאֶה כְּעוֹדֵר? עוֹדֵר נַמִּי, כִּי קָא שָׁקֵיל – בְּדוּכְתֵּיהּ מַנַּח לֵיהּ.

The Gemara asks: **But according to the one who said** that digging a water channel is prohibited **because he** thereby **prepares its banks for planting, let him be concerned that** the digger **appears as if he were hoeing.** The Gemara answers that this is not a concern, because it is **also** true of **one who hoes** that **when he takes** up a clump of earth, he **puts it down** again **in its place.** Consequently, since one throws the dug-up earth far away, it is immediately apparent that he is not engaged in hoeing but is rather digging a water channel.

HALAKHA

Circular ditches around the bases of grapevines – עוּגִיּוֹת לַגְּפָנִים: One may not dig circular ditches around the bases of grapevines and olive trees during the intermediate days of a Festival. It is permitted to repair old ditches if they are still somewhat recognizable (*Mishna Berura*). However, one may not render them deeper than they had been originally (*Shulḥan Arukh*, *Oraḥ Ḥayyim* 537:5, and in the comment of Rema).

NOTES

What are *ugiyyot* – מַאי עוּגִיּוֹת: There are two explanations of the source of the term *ugiyyot*. Rashi explains that it comes from the word *uga*, circle. Others connect the term to the word *igun*, waiting, as in the verse "Would you, for them, refrain [*te'agena*] from having husbands?" (Ruth 1:13). This is because water collects and stands still alongside the vines.

New and old – חֲדַתֵי וְעַתִּיקֵי: According to most commentaries, the reason why it is prohibited to dig new ditches is that digging new ditches involves excessive effort, whereas restoring old ditches does not. It has also been suggested that digging new ditches is prohibited because the walls of the ditches may collapse (*Peirush*). Some understand the passage in the opposite manner and explain that digging new ditches is permitted, whereas restoring old ones is prohibited. The reason for this is that new ditches are dug around young vines, and if they are not dug, the vines may become ruined and cause a significant loss (*ge'onim*). Alternatively, old ditches could certainly have been strengthened prior to the Festival.

Because he prepares the channel's banks – מִפְּנֵי שֶׁמַּכְשִׁיר אֲגַפֶּיהָ: The commentaries disagree about the substance of this prohibition and the reason why it is prohibited. According to Rashi, the earth that is removed from the channel is soft and fit for planting. On the other hand, in the Rambam's Commentary on the Mishna it says that the earth adjoining the channel becomes moist from the water in the channel and is therefore better fit for planting. Rashi and Rabbeinu Ḥananel explain that the reason for the prohibition is that although the individual digging the water channel does not intend to make the ground suitable for planting, the fact that he accomplishes this task classifies his activity as prohibited agricultural labor. Conversely, the Ran and the Ritva maintain that although there is no real agricultural labor being done here, it appears as if he is doing so. *Tosafot* cite both explanations.

What is the difference between them – מַאי בֵּינַיְיהוּ: Rabbi Shlomo ben HaYatom explains that the question is based upon the fact that both sides agree that the prohibition is due to the impression the activity will leave on others. A difference between the two sides that is not mentioned here is cited in the Jerusalem Talmud, and that is a case where he digs for construction purposes rather than for irrigation.

LANGUAGE

***Bedidin* – בְּדִידִין:** The *ge'onim* explain that the term *badid* refers to a kind of hoe, but the term is also applied to the ditches that are dug with that tool.

אַמֵימָר מַתְנֵי לָהּ מִפְּנֵי שֶׁנִּרְאֶה כְּעוֹדֵר, וְקַשְׁיָא לֵיהּ דְּרַבִּי אֶלְעָזָר בֶּן עֲזַרְיָה אַדְּרַבִּי אֶלְעָזָר בֶּן עֲזַרְיָה: וּמִי אָמַר רַבִּי אֶלְעָזָר בֶּן עֲזַרְיָה כָּל שֶׁנִּרְאֶה כְּעוֹדֵר אָסוּר?

Ameimar would teach this mishna as stating explicitly that Rabbi Elazar ben Azarya says that one may not dig a new water channel during the Sabbatical Year **because it appears as if he were hoeing** his field, **and he** therefore found **a difficulty between** this statement of **Rabbi Elazar ben Azarya and** another statement of **Rabbi Elazar ben Azarya.** The difficulty is as follows: **Did Rabbi Elazar ben Azarya** actually **say** that **any** action **that** causes him to **appear as if he were hoeing is prohibited?**

וּרְמִינְהִי: עוֹשֶׂה אָדָם אֶת זִבְלוֹ אוֹצָר. רַבִּי מֵאִיר אוֹסֵר עַד שֶׁיַּעֲמִיק שְׁלֹשָׁה טְפָחִים, אוֹ עַד שֶׁיַּגְבִּיהַּ שְׁלֹשָׁה טְפָחִים. הָיָה לוֹ דָּבָר מוּעָט – מוֹסִיף עָלָיו וְהוֹלֵךְ.

One may **raise a contradiction** to this assertion from a mishna (*Shevi'it* 3:3) that states: **A person** may pile **his manure** in his field during the Sabbatical Year so that it **becomes a storage** heap,[H] and there is no cause for concern that it may appear as if he were fertilizing his field. **Rabbi Meir prohibits** this **unless he deepens** the storage area for the manure **three handbreadths** below the ground **or raises** it **three handbreadths** above the surface of the ground, so that it does not appear as if he were fertilizing his field. If **he** already **had a small amount** of manure in that heap from before the Sabbatical Year, **he may continue to add to it,**[N] and there is no need for concern.

רַבִּי אֶלְעָזָר בֶּן עֲזַרְיָה אוֹסֵר עַד שֶׁיַּעֲמִיק שְׁלֹשָׁה, אוֹ עַד שֶׁיַּגְבִּיהַּ שְׁלֹשָׁה, אוֹ עַד שֶׁיִּתֵּן עַל הַסֶּלַע.

Rabbi Elazar ben Azarya prohibits piling his manure in his field **unless he deepens** the storage area for the manure **three** handbreadths below the surface of the ground, **or he raises** it **three** handbreadths **above** the surface, **or he places** it **on a rock.** In any event, it seems that according to Rabbi Elazar ben Azarya, it is permitted for him to dig a hole in the ground in order to deposit his manure there, even though he might appear to be hoeing the ground.

רַבִּי זֵירָא וְרַבִּי אַבָּא בַּר מֶמֶל, חַד אָמַר: כְּגוֹן שֶׁהֶעֱמִיק, וְחַד אָמַר: זִיבְלוֹ מוֹכִיחַ עָלָיו.

Rabbi Zeira and Rabbi Abba bar Memel both offered resolutions to this difficulty: **One** of them **said:** The case in this second mishna is one **where he** had already **deepened** the three-handbreadth pit during the sixth year. **And** the other **one said: His** pile of **manure is proof** that he intends merely to bury the manure and not to hoe the field.

״וּמְתַקְּנִין אֶת הַמְקוּלְקֶלֶת בַּמּוֹעֵד״. מַאי מְקוּלְקֶלֶת? אָמַר רַבִּי אַבָּא: שֶׁאִם הָיְתָה עֲמוּקָּה טֶפַח – מַעֲמִידָהּ עַל שִׁשָּׁה טְפָחִים.

§ It was taught in the mishna that the Rabbis say: **One may repair a damaged** water channel **during** the intermediate days of **a Festival. What is** meant by **a damaged** water channel? **Rabbi Abba said that if it was** now **a handbreadth**[B] **deep** because it had become filled with sediment, he may dredge it out until **he sets it at** its original depth of **six handbreadths.**[H]

פְּשִׁיטָא, חֲצִי טֶפַח עַל שְׁלֹשָׁה טְפָחִים, כֵּיוָן דְּלָא עָבַר מַיָּא – לָאו כְּלוּם הוּא. טְפָחַיִים עַל שְׁנֵים עָשָׂר, דְּקָא טָרַח טִירְחָא יְתֵירָא – לָא.

Based on this ruling, the Gemara clarifies several practical issues: It is **obvious** that if the channel is **half a handbreadth** deep and he wants to restore it to a depth **of three handbreadths,**[N] **since water does not flow** through a three-handbreadth-deep channel in sufficient quantity, **it is nothing** at all and it is certainly prohibited to exert oneself with work that provides insignificant benefit. So too, if the channel is **two handbreadths** deep and he wants to deepen it **to twelve handbreadths,** even though he preserves the same ratio as in Rabbi Abba's case, **since it involves excessive exertion, no,** this is also not permitted.

טְפָחַיִים עַל שִׁבְעָה מַהוּ? הָכָא חֲמִשָּׁה קָא מַעֲמִיק וְהָכָא חֲמִשָּׁה קָא מַעֲמִיק, אוֹ דִּלְמָא, כֵּיוָן דְּאִיכָּא טֶפַח יְתֵירָא – אִיכָּא טִירְחָא טְפֵי? תֵּיקוּ.

However, in a case where the channel is **two handbreadths** deep and he wants to deepen it **to seven** handbreadths, **what is** the *halakha*? The Gemara explains the two sides of the question of whether this can be compared to the case in the mishna: **Here,** in the case of dredging a one-handbreadth-deep channel to restore its depth of six handbreadths, **he deepens** the channel by **five** handbreadths, **and** similarly **here,** in the case of deepening the channel from two to seven handbreadths, **he** likewise wants to **deepen** it by **five** handbreadths, and therefore it should be permitted. **Or perhaps, since there is an extra handbreadth** of depth, then bending over to dig that additional handbreadth **involves greater effort,**[N] which is unnecessary, and so possibly it should be prohibited. The Gemara states that the dilemma **shall stand** unresolved.

HALAKHA

Storing manure during the Sabbatical Year – הַטְמָנַת זֶבֶל בַּשְּׁבִיעִית: One may gather and bury his manure during the Sabbatical Year in order to use it the following year, in accordance with the opinion of the first *tanna* of the mishna cited here (Rambam *Sefer Zera'im*, *Hilkhot Shemitta VeYovel* 2:2).

Fixing a water channel on the intermediate days of a Festival – תִּיקּוּן אַמַּת מַיִם בַּמּוֹעֵד: It is permitted to fix a blocked water channel on the intermediate days of a Festival. If it is one handbreadth deep, one may deepen it up to six handbreadths; if it is two handbreadths deep, he may deepen it to seven handbreadths, as one may be lenient with regard to matters of rabbinic law that are left unresolved in the Gemara. However, some are strict in this matter (*Nimmukei Yosef*). The *Magen Avraham* writes that if the channel is three handbreadths deep, it may not be deepened to eight handbreadths (*Shulḥan Arukh*, *Oraḥ Ḥayyim* 537:6).

NOTES

He may continue to add to it – מוֹסִיף עָלָיו וְהוֹלֵךְ: It is explained in the Jerusalem Talmud that although outsiders will not know that there was a small amount of manure in the heap from before the Sabbatical Year, this is of no consequence, as one must be concerned only about the suspicions of the local population.

Half a handbreadth to a depth of three handbreadths – חֲצִי טֶפַח עַל שְׁלֹשָׁה טְפָחִים: Rabbi Shlomo ben HaYatom presents an entirely different understanding of this passage, and claims that these dimensions refer to the width and the depth of the channel. A small channel that is half a handbreadth wide and three handbreadths deep is not useful, whereas restoring a large channel that was two handbreadths wide and twelve handbreadths deep involves excessive effort. The *Sefat Emet* explains that if the channel was originally only half a handbreadth deep, it is not regarded as a proper channel that is being deepened, but as a channel that is being dug out for the first time.

Since there is an extra handbreadth, it involves greater effort – כֵּיוָן דְּאִיכָּא טֶפַח יְתֵירָא אִיכָּא טִירְחָא טְפֵי: Rabbeinu Gershom Meor HaGola explains that the extra effort consists of the very activity of deepening of the channel, since it already has the necessary depth of six handbreadths, and further deepening is unnecessary. Others suggest that the extra effort involved refer to the need to reach lower down in order to remove the dirt from the bottom of the channel (Rabbeinu Yehonatan; Ran).

BACKGROUND

Handbreadth – טֶפַח: A handbreadth is one of the standard measures of length used in the Talmud. It is the width of a clenched fist. One handbreadth is equal to four fingerbreadths, equivalent to five times the width of the middle finger, or six times the width of the little finger. According to the measurements of Rabbi Ḥayyim Na'e, a handbreadth is 8 cm long. According to the measurements of the *Ḥazon Ish*, a handbreadth is 9.6 cm long.

אַבַּיֵי שְׁרָא לִבְנֵי בַּר הַמְדָּךְ לְשַׁחוּפֵי נַהֲרָא. רַבִּי יִרְמְיָה שְׁרָא לְהוּ לִבְנֵי סִכְוָתָא לְמִיכְרָא נַהֲרָא טְמִימָא. רַב אַשִׁי שְׁרָא לְהוּ לִבְנֵי מָתָא מְחַסְיָא לְאַקְדּוּחֵי נְהַר בּוּרְנִיץ. אָמַר: כֵּיוָן דְּשָׁתוּ מִינֵּיהּ רַבִּים – כְּרַבִּים דָּמֵי, וּתְנַן: עוֹשִׂין כׇּל צוֹרְכֵי רַבִּים.

It was related that **Abaye permitted the people of Bar Hamdakh to remove**[N] the branches of the trees from **the river** on the intermediate days of a Festival. **Rabbi Yirmeya permitted the people of Sekhavta to dredge out a river that had become blocked. Rav Ashi permitted** his townsmen, **the people of Mata Meḥasya,**[B] **to clean out the** nearby **Burnitz River.**[N] **He said: Since the public drinks from it, it is considered like a public** need, **and we learned** in the mishna that **one may tend to all** other **public needs** on the intermediate days of a Festival.[H]

״וּמְתַקְּנִין אֶת

§ It was taught in the mishna: During the intermediate days of a Festival **one may repair**

BACKGROUND

Mata Meḥasya – מָתָא מְחַסְיָא: A small town near Sura, Mata Meḥasya was the home of Rav Ashi, and the Talmud was edited there. In later times, Sura and Mata Meḥasya apparently merged, becoming a single town.

HALAKHA

Fixing rivers – תִּיקּוּן נְהָרוֹת: It is permitted to redirect a river on the intermediate days of a Festival as well as to clean out a river that had become blocked, as these tasks represent communal needs (Rambam *Sefer Zemanim*, *Hilkhot Yom Tov* 8:4).

NOTES

To remove – לְשַׁחוּפֵי: Some explain that this refers to cleaning the dirt and the rocks at the bottom of the river (Rashi manuscript). Others explain that this refers to cutting the roots or the branches of the trees that grew in the river (Rabbi Shlomo ben HaYatom).

To clean out the Burnitz River – לְאַקְדּוּחֵי נְהַר בּוּרְנִיץ: This expression is explained in various ways. Rashi explains that it is referring to clearing out the sediment in the river in order to enhance its flow. Others say that it means widening the opening of the spring or the bed of the river (Rashi manuscript; Rabbeinu Yehonatan). The Ra'avad and Meiri explain that it means redirecting the river so that it flows closer to the town. The Rambam seems to accept this interpretation as well, and he also includes digging new wells in this category.

קִילְקוּלֵי הַמַּיִם שֶׁבִּרְשׁוּת הָרַבִּים״, וכו׳. חֲטִיטָה – אִין, חֲפִירָה – לָא.

damaged water cisterns **in the public domain and** clean them out by removing the dirt and sediment that has accumulated in them. The Gemara infers: **Cleaning**[N] out the cisterns of dirt and sediment during the intermediate days of a Festival **is** indeed permitted, but **digging** a new cistern **is not** permitted.

אָמַר רַבִּי יַעֲקֹב אָמַר רַבִּי יוֹחָנָן: לֹא שָׁנוּ אֶלָּא שֶׁאֵין רַבִּים צְרִיכִין לָהֶם, אֲבָל רַבִּים צְרִיכִין לָהֶם – אֲפִילּוּ חֲפִירָה מוּתָּר.

Rabbi Ya'akov said that **Rabbi Yoḥanan said: They taught** that it is prohibited to dig new cisterns **only when the public does not need them; but if the public needs them,**[N] **even digging** new cisterns **is permitted.**

וְכִי רַבִּים צְרִיכִין לָהֶם מִי שָׁרֵי? וְהָתַנְיָא: חוֹטְטִין בּוֹרוֹת שִׁיחִין וּמְעָרוֹת שֶׁל יָחִיד, וְאֵין צָרִיךְ לוֹמַר שֶׁל רַבִּים, וְאֵין חוֹפְרִין בּוֹרוֹת שִׁיחִין וּמְעָרוֹת שֶׁל רַבִּים, וְאֵין צָרִיךְ לוֹמַר שֶׁל יָחִיד. מַאי לָאו – בְּשֶׁרַבִּים צְרִיכִין לָהֶם?

The Gemara asks: **And when the public needs them, is** digging really **permitted? But isn't it taught** in a *baraita*: **One may clean** out **cisterns, ditches, and caves of an individual** during the intermediate days of a Festival, **and, needless to say,** one may clean out those **of the public. But one may not dig** new **cisterns, ditches, or caves of the public** during the intermediate days of a Festival, **and, needless to say,** one may not dig those **of an individual. What, is it not** so that this *baraita* is referring to a case **where the public needs them,** but nevertheless digging new cisterns, ditches, and caves is prohibited?

לֹא, בְּשֶׁאֵין רַבִּים צְרִיכִין לָהֶם.

The Gemara rejects this opinion: **No,** this *baraita* is referring to a case **where the public does not need them.**

NOTES

Cleaning – חֲטִיטָה: According to Rashi and most commentaries, this refers to removing rocks and dirt that fell into cisterns in order to create room for more water. Rabbi Shlomo ben HaYatom explains that it refers to removing dirt and sand in order to clean the water in the cistern.

The public needs them – רַבִּים צְרִיכִין לָהֶם: Opinions differ as to how to define public need. The Ritva cites Rashi as explaining that this refers to a case where there is no drinking water at all. Some question this explanation, however, as in that instance even an individual would be permitted to do whatever necessary, as it would be a matter of life and death. The Ritva cites *Tosafot* as explaining that the water is not needed immediately but it will be needed after the Festival. The Ritva provides another explanation, citing the Ramban, that there is enough water for the public but they would like to have easier access to it by digging a well that is closer to where they are located.

דִּכְוָותָהּ גַּבֵּי יָחִיד – שֶׁאֵין יָחִיד צָרִיךְ לָהֶם, חֲטִיטָה מִי שָׁרֵי? וְהָתַנְיָא: בּוֹרוֹת שִׁיחִין וּמְעָרוֹת שֶׁל יָחִיד – כּוֹנְסִין מַיִם לְתוֹכָן, אֲבָל לֹא חוֹטְטִין, וְלֹא שָׁפִין אֶת סִדְקֵיהֶן. וְשֶׁל רַבִּים – חוֹטְטִין אוֹתָן וְשָׁפִין אֶת סִדְקֵיהֶן.

The Gemara raises a difficulty: It would follow that **in the corresponding** situation **with regard to** the cisterns of **an individual,** the *baraita* is referring to a case where **the individual does not need them.** But in that case, **is cleaning** them out really **permitted? Isn't it taught** in a *baraita*: **One may gather water**[N] into **the cisterns, ditches, and caves of an individual, but one may not clean** them out **or plaster their cracks; but** for those **of the public, one may** indeed **clean out and plaster their cracks?** This indicates that on the intermediate days of a Festival, unneeded cisterns belonging to an individual may not even be cleaned out.

וְאֶלָּא מַאי? בְּשֶׁיָּחִיד צָרִיךְ לָהֶם? דִּכְוָותָהּ גַּבֵּי רַבִּים – בְּשֶׁרַבִּים צְרִיכִין לָהֶם, חֲפִירָה מִי אֲסִיר? וְהָתַנְיָא: בּוֹרוֹת שִׁיחִין וּמְעָרוֹת שֶׁל יָחִיד כּוֹנְסִין מַיִם לְתוֹכָן, וְחוֹטְטִין אוֹתָן, אֲבָל לֹא שָׁפִין אֶת סִדְקֵיהֶן, וְלֹא חוֹטְטִין לְתוֹכָן, וְלֹא סָדִין אוֹתָן בְּסִיד. וְשֶׁל רַבִּים – חוֹפְרִין אוֹתָן, וְסָדִין אוֹתָן בְּסִיד.

The Gemara rejects this difficulty: **Rather,** to **what** case does the first *baraita* refer? Is it referring to a case **where the individual needs** the cisterns? If so, then **in the corresponding** situation **with regard to** cisterns of **the public,** the *baraita* would be referring to a case where **the public needs them.** But in that case, **is digging** new cisterns really **prohibited? Isn't it taught** in yet another *baraita*: **One may gather water into cisterns, ditches, and caves of an individual, and one may clean them** out, **but one may not plaster their cracks, clear** earth **into them** in order to fill in the cracks, or **lime them with lime** so that they hold water. **But** with regard to those **of the public, one may** even **dig them out and lime them with lime.** Therefore, in a case where the public needs them, it is permitted to dig out public cisterns.

אֶלָּא קַשְׁיָא הַךְ קַמַּיְיתָא! תְּרֵיץ הָכִי: חוֹטְטִין בּוֹרוֹת שֶׁל יָחִיד – בְּשֶׁיָּחִיד צָרִיךְ לָהֶם, וְאֵין צָרִיךְ לוֹמַר בְּשֶׁל רַבִּים כְּשֶׁרַבִּים צְרִיכִין לָהֶם, דַּאֲפִילּוּ חֲפִירָה מוּתָּר.

But if so, **the first** *baraita*, which states that one may not dig new cisterns even for the public, is **difficult,** as it is contradicted by this last *baraita*. The Gemara explains: **Answer** the difficulty and explain the first *baraita* **as follows: One may clean** out **cisterns,** ditches, and caves **of an individual**[H] during the intermediate days of a Festival **when the individual needs them; and needless to say,** one may clean out those **of the public**[H] **when the public needs them, as even digging** new cisterns **is permitted** when the public needs them.

וְאֵין חוֹפְרִין בּוֹרוֹת שִׁיחִין וּמְעָרוֹת שֶׁל רַבִּים בְּשֶׁאֵין רַבִּים צְרִיכִין לָהֶם, וְאֵין צָרִיךְ לוֹמַר שֶׁל יָחִיד, דְּכִי אֵין יָחִיד צָרִיךְ לָהֶם – אֲפִילּוּ חֲטִיטָה נַמִי אָסוּר.

But one may not dig cisterns, ditches and caves for the public when the public does not need them. And needless to say, one may not dig them **for an individual, as when an individual does not need** the cisterns on the intermediate days of a Festival, **even cleaning them out is prohibited.** In this way all of the seemingly contradictory sources can be reconciled.

אָמַר רַב אַשִׁי: מַתְנִיתִין נַמִי דַּיְקָא, דְּקָתָנֵי: עוֹשִׂין כׇּל צוֹרְכֵי רַבִּים. ״כׇּל״ לְאֵתוֹיֵי מַאי? לָאו לְאֵתוֹיֵי חֲפִירָה?

Rav Ashi said: The wording of **the mishna is also precise,** indicating that when there is a public need for such cisterns, they may be dug even on the intermediate days of a Festival. **As it teaches: One may tend to all** other **public needs.**[H] **What** does the word **all** come **to add** that was not stated explicitly? **Does it not** come **to add the digging** of cisterns, which is permitted?

לָא, לְאֵתוֹיֵי הָא דְּתַנְיָא: יוֹצְאִין לְקַוֵּוץ אֶת הַדְּרָכִים, וּלְתַקֵּן אֶת הָרְחוֹבוֹת וְאֶת הָאִסְטְרָטָאוֹת, וְלָמוֹד אֶת הַמִּקְוָאוֹת. וְכׇל מִקְוֶה שֶׁאֵין בּוֹ אַרְבָּעִים סְאָה מַרְגִּילִין לְתוֹכוֹ אַרְבָּעִים סְאָה.

The Gemara rejects this opinion: **No,** the word all comes **to add that which is taught** in the following *baraita*: On the intermediate days of a Festival, agents of the court **go out to clear thorns from the road, and to repair the city streets**[N] **and highways** [*isterata'ot*],[L] **and to measure the ritual baths** to ascertain that they have the requisite quantity of water. **And if any ritual bath does not contain forty** ***se'a***,[B] the minimal measure for ritual purification, **they direct** [***margilin***][L] a stream of water **into it,**[N] such that it flows over the ground before entering the bath, so as not to disqualify the water as drawn water until it holds **forty** ***se'a*** of water.

NOTES

One may gather water – כּוֹנְסִין מַיִם: The Ran explains that this is referring to collecting rainwater in vessels, which they would then empty into the cisterns. The Ritva suggests that it refers to directing water from other locations through existing channels into the cisterns. The Meiri does not distinguish between these activities and permits both.

Streets – רְחוֹבוֹת: According to most commentaries, these are streets where people congregated to engage in business. The Ran cites Rashi as explaining that the reference is to places designated for comforting mourners.

They direct a stream of water into it – מַרְגִּילִין לְתוֹכוֹ: The Ran explains that a channel was dug from a spring to allow its water to flow to the ritual bath. Others propose that they would open a spring at the bottom of the well from which the water of the ritual bath emerged (Rabbeinu Gershom Meor HaGola; Rabbeinu Yehonatan).

HALAKHA

Digging and cleaning the cisterns of an individual – חֲפִירָה וַחֲטִיטָה בְּבוֹרוֹת שֶׁל יָחִיד: It is prohibited to dig new cisterns for an individual during a Festival, even if he currently has only a minimal supply of drinking water (*Magen Avraham*). Repairing cisterns that have become damaged is permitted during the intermediate days of a Festival if the individual needs the water for use on the Festival. It is permitted to fill a cistern with water on the intermediate days of a Festival. The *Magen Avraham* adds that it is permitted to do so only by collecting water in vessels and bringing that water to the cistern; it is prohibited to transport water through a ditch, which is more strenuous (*Shulḥan Arukh*, *Oraḥ Ḥayyim* 544:2).

Public cisterns – בּוֹרוֹת הָרַבִּים: It is permitted to repair public cisterns during the intermediate days of a Festival and to clear them of stones and dirt even if the public does not need them on the Festival itself. But one may dig new cisterns only if they are needed by the public on the Festival. When the digging of public cisterns is permitted, they may be dug even if they require strenuous effort and the labor is performed publicly, and even if this labor was purposely scheduled to take place during the Festival (*Shulḥan Arukh*, *Oraḥ Ḥayyim* 544:2).

Public needs during a Festival – צָרְכֵי הָרַבִּים בַּמּוֹעֵד: One is permitted to tend to all public needs during a Festival, such as repairing and removing obstacles from roads, marking graves, and repairing ritual baths, even if one planned to do so in advance (*Mishna Berura*). The Rema writes that this leniency applies only to the physical needs of the community. Other public needs, such as building a synagogue, may not be tended to during a Festival if they require the work of a professional (*Shulḥan Arukh*, *Oraḥ Ḥayyim* 544:1, and in the comment of Rema).

LANGUAGE

Highways [*isterata'ot*] – אִסְטְרָטָאוֹת: From the Latin strata, meaning street. The Sages used this term to refer to highways or primary thoroughfares.

Direct [*margilin*] – מַרְגִּילִין: *Hargala* refers to a streaming flow, as in water flowing from place to place. It is similar to the Aramaic *ragalta*, meaning stream.

BACKGROUND

Forty *se'a* – אַרְבָּעִים סְאָה: Forty *se'a* is the equivalent of eighty *hin*, or 5,760 egg-bulks, which is the minimum quantity of water necessary for a ritual bath. The measure of forty *se'a* is the basis for all modern calculations of the various talmudic measures of volume. The Talmud states that the dimensions of a ritual bath must be three cubits by one cubit by one cubit, and that its volume must be forty *se'a*. Therefore, according to the calculation of Rav Ḥayyim Na'e, a ritual bath must contain 332 ℓ of water. According to the calculations of the Ḥazon Ish, it must contain 573 ℓ.

וּמִנַּיִן שֶׁאִם לֹא יָצְאוּ וְעָשׂוּ כׇּל אֵלּוּ, שֶׁכׇּל דָּמִים שֶׁנִּשְׁפְּכוּ שָׁם מַעֲלֶה עֲלֵיהֶם הַכָּתוּב כְּאִילּוּ הֵם שְׁפָכוּם? תַּלְמוּד לוֹמַר: ״וְהָיָה עָלֶיךָ דָּמִים״.

And from where is it derived **that if** agents of the court **did not go out and do all these** repairs, **that** with regard to **any blood that is shed there** on account of their negligence, **the verse ascribes to them** guilt **as if they had shed it? The verse states** with regard to the cities of refuge that offer protection to someone who committed inadvertent manslaughter: "That innocent blood be not shed in your land, which the Lord your God gives you for an inheritance, **and so blood be upon you**" (Deuteronomy 19:10).[N] The Gemara maintains that the mishna uses the word all to allude to the cases mentioned in this *baraita*, and not to the digging of public cisterns.

הָא – בְּהֶדְיָא קָתָנֵי לַהּ: וּמְתַקְּנִין אֶת הַדְּרָכִים, וְאֶת הָרְחוֹבוֹת, וְאֶת הַמִּקְוָאוֹת, וְעוֹשִׂין כׇּל צוֹרְכֵי רַבִּים. לְאַתוּיֵי מַאי? לָאו לְאַתוּיֵי חֲפִירָה? שְׁמַע מִינַּהּ.

The Gemara questions this: **But** these additional cases **are explicitly taught** in the mishna: **One may repair the roads, streets, and ritual baths, and one may tend to all** other **public needs. What** does this last phrase come **to add? Does it not** come to **add the digging** of cisterns needed by the public? The Gemara agrees: **Conclude from this** that the mishna means to permit the digging of new cisterns when they are needed by the public.

״מְצַיְּינִין אֶת הַקְּבָרוֹת״. אָמַר רַבִּי שִׁמְעוֹן בֶּן פָּזִי: רֶמֶז לְצִיּוּן קְבָרוֹת מִן הַתּוֹרָה מִנַּיִן? תַּלְמוּד לוֹמַר: ״וְרָאָה עֶצֶם אָדָם וּבָנָה אֶצְלוֹ צִיּוּן״.

§ It was taught in the mishna: **One may mark graves**[H] on the intermediate days of a Festival so that passersby will know to avoid them and not become ritually impure. **Rabbi Shimon ben Pazi said: Where is there an allusion in the Torah to the marking of graves?**[N] **The verse states:** "And when they that pass through shall pass through the land, **and any see a man's bone, then shall he set up a sign by it**" (Ezekiel 39:15).[N] Ezekiel prophesies that at some future time, the Jewish people will erect signs over the strewn remains of the dead so that others will know to avoid ritual impurity.

אֲמַר לֵיהּ רָבִינָא לְרַב אַשִׁי: הָא מִקַּמֵּי דְּלֵיתֵי יְחֶזְקֵאל מַאן אֲמַר? וְלִיטַעֲמִיךְ, הָא דְּאָמַר רַב חִסְדָּא: דָּבָר זֶה מִתּוֹרַת מֹשֶׁה רַבֵּינוּ לֹא לָמַדְנוּ, מִדִּבְרֵי יְחֶזְקֵאל בֶּן בּוּזִי לָמַדְנוּ: ״כׇּל בֶּן נֵכָר עֶרֶל לֵב וְעֶרֶל בָּשָׂר לֹא יָבֹא אֶל מִקְדָּשִׁי לְשָׁרְתֵנִי״,

Ravina said to Rav Ashi: Before the prophet **Ezekiel came** and alluded to this obligation, **who said** that graves must be marked? Even before the time of Ezekiel, people were careful with regard to ritual impurity. Rav Ashi responded: **And according to your reasoning,** that Ezekiel was introducing a new *halakha*, the same question can be raised with regard to **this** statement **that Rav Ḥisda said.** As Rav Ḥisda said with regard to the *halakha* that one who is uncircumcised or an apostate may not serve in the Temple: **This matter we did not learn from the Torah of Moses our teacher,** but rather, **we learned** it **from the words of** the prophet **Ezekiel ben Buzi,** who said of such individuals: **"No stranger, uncircumcised in heart, or uncircumcised in flesh, shall enter into My Sanctuary to serve Me"** (Ezekiel 44:9).

מִקַּמֵּי דְּלֵיתֵי יְחֶזְקֵאל מַאן אֲמַר? אֶלָּא: גְּמָרָא גְּמִירִי לַהּ, וַאֲתָא יְחֶזְקֵאל וְאַסְמְכַהּ אַקְּרָא. הָכָא נַמִי: גְּמָרָא גְּמִירִי לַהּ וַאֲתָא יְחֶזְקֵאל וְאַסְמְכַהּ אַקְּרָא.

Here too, one can ask: **Before Ezekiel came, who said** that such individuals cannot serve in the Temple? **Rather,** you must say that originally **they learned it as a tradition** and it was an accepted *halakha* for generations, **and then Ezekiel came and based it on a verse. Here too,** with regard to the obligation to mark graves, **they** originally **learned it as a tradition, and** then **Ezekiel came and based it on a verse.**

רַבִּי אַבָּהוּ אָמַר מֵהָכָא: ״וְטָמֵא טָמֵא יִקְרָא״ – טוּמְאָה קוֹרְאָה לוֹ, וְאוֹמֶרֶת לוֹ: פְּרוֹשׁ. וְכֵן אָמַר רַבִּי עוּזִּיאֵל בַּר בְּרֵיהּ דְּרַבִּי עוּזִּיאֵל רַבָּה: טוּמְאָה קוֹרְאָה לוֹ וְאוֹמֶרֶת לוֹ: פְּרוֹשׁ.

Rabbi Abbahu said: An allusion to the marking of graves may be derived **from here:**[N] "And the leper in whom the plague is, his clothes shall be rent, and the hair of his head shall go loose, and he shall cover his upper lip, and **shall cry: Impure, impure**" (Leviticus 13:45). This verse teaches that **impurity cries out** to the passerby **and tells him: Remove yourself.** The leper must inform others of his status so that they know not to come into contact with him and thereby maintain their ritual purity. So too, in our case, graves must be marked so that others will know to avoid them and prevent contracting ritual impurity. **And similarly, Rabbi Uzziel, grandson of Rabbi Uzziel the Great, said: Impurity cries out** to the passerby **and tells him: Remove yourself.**

וְהַאי לְהָכִי הוּא דַּאֲתָא? הַהוּא מִיבָּעֵי לֵיהּ לְכִדְתַנְיָא: ״וְטָמֵא טָמֵא יִקְרָא״ – צָרִיךְ לְהוֹדִיעַ צַעֲרוֹ לָרַבִּים, וְרַבִּים מְבַקְּשִׁין עָלָיו רַחֲמִים!

The Gemara asks: **But** with regard to **this** verse, **does it come to teach this** idea? **That** verse **is needed for that which is taught** in the following *baraita*: **"And he shall cry: Impure, impure"**; this teaches that the leper **must inform the public of his distress,**[H] **and the public will pray for mercy on his behalf.**

NOTES

And so blood be upon you – וְהָיָה עָלֶיךָ דָּמִים: Rabbeinu Ḥananel apparently had a different version of this text, reading: "As it is stated: That you bring not blood on your house" (Deuteronomy 22:8), a verse referring to the obligation to build a railing around one's roof (see *Tosafot*).

An allusion…to the marking of graves – רֶמֶז לְצִיּוּן קְבָרוֹת: The Ritva writes that the Sages understood that since marking the location of graves is so essential for the general good of the community, it would be impossible that there is no allusion to it in the Bible.

And any that see a man's bone, then shall he set up a sign by it – וְרָאָה עֶצֶם אָדָם וּבָנָה אֶצְלוֹ צִיּוּן: Many commentaries question why this is referred to as an allusion, when it would appear that the *halakha* of marking graves is presented in this verse quite explicitly. Rashi explains that this is referred to as an allusion because the verse foretells this activity but does not state that it is a mitzva. *Tosafot* explain that the verse is unclear, because it speaks about the future and not about current practice. Rabbi Shimon holds that gentile graves do not impart ritual impurity by means of a tent, and consequently this marking of graves in Ezekiel may be understood not as a way of distancing people from ritual impurity but as a way of clearing the land of corpses. Therefore, it does not provide an absolute proof for the *halakha* discussed in the Gemara (*Talmid Rabbeinu Yeḥiel of Paris*, citing Rivam).

Rabbi Abbahu said an allusion may be derived from here – רַבִּי אַבָּהוּ אָמַר מֵהָכָא: The commentaries explain that the different opinions cited in the Gemara do not disagree; each Sage simply identified the verse providing an allusion to the marking of graves that was most convincing to him. The Maharsha explains at length that there are grounds to refute each of these proofs, either because it is insufficiently clear or because a different *halakha* is derived from that particular verse.

HALAKHA

Marking graves – צִיּוּן הַקְּבָרוֹת: If one finds a grave or part of a corpse that imparts ritual impurity via a tent, he should mark it so as to prevent others from becoming impure. Court-appointed agents would go out on the intermediate days of a Festival to mark the location of graves (Rambam *Sefer Tahara, Hilkhot Tumat Met* 8:9).

Inform the public of his distress – לְהוֹדִיעַ צַעֲרוֹ לָרַבִּים: It is a mitzva for a leper to cover his head and wrap himself up as a mourner, and to inform passersby that he is ritually impure (Rambam *Sefer Tahara, Hilkhot Tumat Tzara'at* 10:6).

אִם כֵּן לִיכְתּוֹב "וְטָמֵא יִקְרָא". מַאי "וְטָמֵא טָמֵא" – שְׁמַעְתְּ מִינָּהּ תַּרְתֵּי.

The Gemara answers: **If it is so** that the verse comes to teach only one idea, **let it write: And he shall cry: Impure. What** is to be derived the repetition of **impure, impure? Learn from this** reiteration **two** ideas: First, that the leper must inform the public of his pain so that others will pray on his behalf, and second, that he must warn the public to stay away so that they avoid coming into contact with him and contracting ritual impurity.

אַבַּיֵי אָמַר מֵהָכָא: "וְלִפְנֵי עִוֵּר לֹא תִתֵּן מִכְשׁוֹל". רַב פַּפָּא אָמַר: "וְאָמַר סֹלּוּ סֹלּוּ פַּנּוּ דָרֶךְ".

Abaye said: An allusion to the marking of graves may be learned **from here,** as it is written: **"You shall not put a stumbling block before the blind"** (Leviticus 19:14). **Rav Pappa said** the obligation is alluded to in the verse: **"And He will say: Pave, pave, clear the way,**[N] take up the stumbling block out of the way of My people" (Isaiah 57:14), which indicates that roads must be cleared of all obstacles and hazards.

רַב חִינְּנָא אָמַר: "הָרִימוּ מִכְשׁוֹל מִדֶּרֶךְ עַמִּי". רַבִּי יְהוֹשֻׁעַ בְּרֵיהּ דְּרַב אִידִי אָמַר: "וְהוֹדַעְתָּ לָהֶם אֶת הַדֶּרֶךְ אֲשֶׁר יֵלְכוּ בָהּ".

Rav Ḥinnana said: This may be derived from the end of that very same verse: **"Take up the stumbling block from the way of My people"** (Isaiah 57:14). **Rabbi Yehoshua, son of Rav Idi, said:** This may be derived from the verse: **"And you shall show them the way in which they must walk"** (Exodus 18:20), i.e., you must properly repair the roads, which includes marking graves.

מָר זוּטְרָא אָמַר: "וְהִזַּרְתֶּם אֶת בְּנֵי יִשְׂרָאֵל מִטּוּמְאָתָם". רַב אַשִׁי אָמַר: "וּשְׁמַרְתֶּם אֶת מִשְׁמַרְתִּי" – עֲשׂוּ מִשְׁמֶרֶת לְמִשְׁמַרְתִּי.

Mar Zutra said that an allusion to this obligation is found in the verse **"Thus you shall separate the children of Israel from their impurity"** (Leviticus 15:31), which indicates that people must be warned to stay away from that which could cause them to become ritually impure. **Rav Ashi said** it is derived from the verse: **"And you shall keep My charge"** (Leviticus 18:30), which means that you must **establish a safeguard for My charge,** i.e., protective measures must be enacted to prevent people from transgressing *halakha*, a task that includes distancing people from ritual impurity by marking off graves, so that they not come to convey ritual impurity to *teruma* or other consecrated items.

רָבִינָא אָמַר: "וְשָׂם דֶּרֶךְ אַרְאֶנּוּ בְּיֶשַׁע אֱלֹהִים."

And finally, **Ravina said:** This obligation is alluded to by the verse **"And to him who orders his way,**[N] **I will show the salvation of God"** (Psalms 50:23), meaning that one must mark the pathways that are ritually pure and upon which it is appropriate to walk.

אָמַר רַבִּי יְהוֹשֻׁעַ בֶּן לֵוִי: כׇּל הַשָּׁם אוֹרְחוֹתָיו – זוֹכֶה וְרוֹאֶה בִּישׁוּעָתוֹ שֶׁל הַקָּדוֹשׁ בָּרוּךְ הוּא, שֶׁנֶּאֱמַר "וְשָׂם דֶּרֶךְ", אַל תִּקְרֵי "וְשָׂם" אֶלָּא "וְשָׁם דֶּרֶךְ" – אַרְאֶנּוּ בְּיֶשַׁע אֱלֹהִים.

With regard to the verse from Psalms cited above, **Rabbi Yehoshua ben Levi said: Whoever appraises his ways**[N] in this world and contemplates how to act in the most appropriate way possible **merits seeing the salvation of the Holy One, Blessed be He,**[N] **as it is stated: "And to him who orders his way." Do not read** it as *vesam*, who orders; **rather,** read it as ***vesham***, and appraises. With this reading, the verse indicates that one who appraises his ways, **him will I show the salvation of God.**

רַבִּי יַנַּאי הֲוָה לֵיהּ הַהוּא תַּלְמִידָא דְּכׇל יוֹמָא הֲוָה מַקְשֵׁי לֵיהּ, בְּשַׁבְּתָא דְּרִיגְלָא לָא הֲוָה מַקְשֵׁי לֵיהּ.

Rabbi Yannai had a certain student who would raise difficulties with his teachings **every day** as they were learning. **On Shabbat of a Festival,**[N] when the broader public would come to hear the lesson, the student **would not raise** any **difficulties,** lest Rabbi Yannai lack an immediate answer and suffer embarrassment.

NOTES

Pave, pave, clear the way – סֹלּוּ סֹלּוּ פַּנּוּ דָרֶךְ: Some commentaries explain that the words "clear the way" are understood to mean: Clear away the impurity. As the conclusion of the verse indicates, this is to be removed from the way of the Jewish people (*Peirush*).

And to him who orders [*vesam*] his way – וְשָׂם דֶּרֶךְ: Rabbeinu Gershom Meor HaGola apparently understood this as: To him who marks [*vesimen*] the way.

Whoever appraises his ways – כׇּל הַשָּׁם אוֹרְחוֹתָיו: Rashi explains that this is referring to one who calculates the reward for fulfilling a mitzva against the loss for transgressing it and avoids sin. The Meiri understands this to refer to one who conducts himself in a balanced fashion, following the golden mean, which the Rambam praises at length (see his introduction to *Avot*, known as Eight Chapters). The *Sefat Emet* explains that even when faced with two mitzvot, one evaluates which is preferable and less likely to lead to undesirable side effects.

The salvation of the Holy One, Blessed be He – יְשׁוּעָתוֹ שֶׁל הַקָּדוֹשׁ בָּרוּךְ הוּא: refers to God's salvation of the Jewish people, which is called in various places in the Bible the salvation of the Lord (Ritva).

On Shabbat of a Festival – בְּשַׁבְּתָא דְּרִיגְלָא: *Tosafot* explain that this refers to the Shabbat during a Festival. Others say that this refers to the Shabbat before a Festival, when public lectures would be delivered about the *halakhot* of the Festival (*Talmid Rabbeinu Yeḥiel of Paris*; Rabbi Shlomo ben HaYatom). This custom continues nowadays in the form of the public lectures customarily delivered on the Shabbat before Passover and before Yom Kippur. The *Iyyun Ya'akov* writes that it is customary not to raise challenging questions during these lectures, as the purpose of the lecture is for the public to come and listen attentively, absorbing the practical halakhic teachings.

קָרֵי עֲלֵיהּ: ״וְשָׂם דֶּרֶךְ אַרְאֶנּוּ בְּיֵשַׁע אֱלֹהִים.״

Rabbi Yannai **read** this verse **about him: "And to him who orders his way,**[N] **I will show the salvation of God"** (Psalms 50:23), for he considered his conduct and determined when it was inappropriate to challenge his master.

תָּנוּ רַבָּנַן: אֵין מְצַיְּינִין לֹא עַל כְּזַיִת מִן הַמֵּת, וְלֹא עַל עֶצֶם כִּשְׂעוֹרָה, וְלֹא עַל דָּבָר שֶׁאֵינוֹ מְטַמֵּא בְּאֹהֶל. אֲבָל מְצַיְּינִין עַל הַשִּׁדְרָה, וְעַל הַגּוּלְגּוֹלֶת, עַל רוֹב בִּנְיָן וְעַל רוֹב מִנְיַן הַמֵּת.

§ With regard to the *halakhot* of marking graves, **the Sages taught** the following *baraita*: The courts **do not mark**[N] the area **of an olive-bulk of a corpse; nor of a bone** that is the size of a **barleygrain-bulk; nor of any item**[N] **that** imparts impurity only through physical contact but **does not impart ritual impurity by means of a tent** to an individual or object that it overshadows, or that is overshadowed by it, or that is found together with it under the same structure. **But they do mark** the area of **the spine** of a corpse, **the skull,** or the bones that comprise **the majority of the** skeletal **structure or the majority of the number** of bones in the body.[H]

וְאֵין מְצַיְּינִין עַל הַוַּדָּאוֹת, אֲבָל מְצַיְּינִין עַל הַסְּפֵיקוֹת. וְאֵלּוּ הֵן הַסְּפֵיקוֹת: סְכָכוֹת, וּפְרָעוֹת, וּבֵית הַפְּרָס. וְאֵין מַעֲמִידִין צִיּוּן בִּמְקוֹם טוּמְאָה – שֶׁלֹּא לְהַפְסִיד אֶת הַטְּהָרוֹת, וְאֵין מַרְחִיקִין צִיּוּן מִמְּקוֹם טוּמְאָה – שֶׁלֹּא לְהַפְסִיד אֶת אֶרֶץ יִשְׂרָאֵל.

And furthermore, **they do not mark** the area **of certain** ritual impurity, i.e., a place that is known to all as ritually impure, **but they do mark** a place **of uncertain** ritual impurity. **And these are the** places of **uncertain** ritual impurity: **Overhanging boughs, protrusions, and a *beit haperas*.**[L] **And they do not erect the marker** directly **over the site of the ritual impurity, so as not to cause a loss of ritually pure** food items, as one who is carrying such food might inadvertently walk up to the site of ritual impurity and only then notice the marker, after the food has already contracted impurity. **Similarly, they do not distance the marker from the** actual **site of ritual impurity, so as not to cause a loss of Eretz Yisrael,**[N] i.e., so as not to increase the area into which individuals refrain from entering.

וּכְזַיִת מִן הַמֵּת אֵינוֹ מְטַמֵּא בְּאֹהֶל? וְהָא תְּנַן: אֵלּוּ שֶׁמְּטַמְּאִין בְּאֹהֶל – כְּזַיִת מִן הַמֵּת!

The Gemara begins to analyze this *baraita* by asking: **Is it** really **so that an olive-bulk of a corpse does not impart ritual impurity by means of a tent? But didn't we learn** in a mishna (*Oholot* 2:1): **These are** the items **that impart ritual impurity by means of a tent,** and among other items this list includes **an olive-bulk of a corpse?**

אָמַר רַב פַּפָּא: הָכָא בִּכְזַיִת מְצוּמְצָם עָסְקִינַן, דְּסוֹף סוֹף מִיחְסַר חָסַר, מוּטָב יִשָּׂרְפוּ עָלָיו תְּרוּמָה וְקָדָשִׁים לְפִי שָׁעָה, וְאַל יִשָּׂרְפוּ עָלָיו לְעוֹלָם.

Rav Pappa said: Here, we are dealing with a case **where** the piece of flesh **is exactly an olive-bulk, which,** as it decays, **will ultimately diminish** in size to less than an olive-bulk. Accordingly, **it is preferable that *teruma* and consecrated items be burned because of it for the time being,** in a case where one inadvertently encounters this impurity because it was not marked and consequently one must burn any *teruma* or consecrated items that became ritually impure, **and not be burned because of it forever** afterward. After some time the piece of flesh will be less than an olive-bulk, yet if the area is marked, people will continue to burn *teruma* or consecrated items because of it, as, due to the marking, they will assume that ritual impurity was imparted by means of a tent.

NOTES

Rabbi Yannai read this verse about him: And to him who orders his way – קָרֵי עֲלֵיהּ: וְשָׂם דֶּרֶךְ: This student appraised his ways; although he sacrificed the opportunity to clarify what he was learning and perhaps did not find out the reason behind what his teacher had said, it was more important to refrain from embarrassing him (Ritva).

The courts do not mark – אֵין מְצַיְּינִין: Some explain that it is prohibited to mark these locations lest a passerby unnecessarily burns *teruma* even after the quantity of remains has become reduced (*Talmid Rabbeinu Yeḥiel of Paris*; see *Tosafot*).

Nor of any item – וְלֹא עַל דָּבָר: This includes not only parts of a corpse that do not impart ritual impurity by means of a tent, but also other sources of impurity, e.g., a creeping animal or the carcass of an animal, which do not impart impurity by means of a tent (*Talmid Rabbeinu Yeḥiel of Paris*; Ritva).

To cause a loss of Eretz Yisrael – לְהַפְסִיד אֶת אֶרֶץ יִשְׂרָאֵל: Some explain that because it is common practice not to sow there, or according to others, because it is prohibited to do so, this would cause damage to the land (Rashi manuscript). Others say that it would cause a narrowing of the roads (Rabbi Shlomo ben HaYatom).

LANGUAGE

Beit haperas – בֵּית הַפְּרָס: Opinions are divided as to the origin of this term. Rashi and *Tosafot* explain the word *peras* to mean broken, as the field became impure when it was plowed and the bones were broken and scattered about. The Rambam apparently understands the term in the sense of spreading [*perisa*], as the impurity spreads over the entire area. Some explain the term as derived from the Greek πάρος, *paros*, meaning before, as the field is like a courtyard around the grave. Finally, some maintain that it comes from the Greek ἄπορος, *aporos*, meaning a place through which one may not pass.

HALAKHA

Marking graves – צִיּוּן קְבָרוֹת: If one finds a grave or part of a corpse that imparts ritual impurity by means of a tent, he must mark the location in order to inform others that walking there will cause them to become impure. One does not mark the location of a piece of a corpse that is precisely an olive-bulk, despite the fact that it imparts ritual impurity by means of a tent, because its size will decrease as it decomposes. The marker should be placed adjacent to the location of the corpse; it should not be placed directly over it, as it may not effectively prevent others from becoming impure. It should neither be distanced from the corpse, so as not to section off parts of Eretz Yisrael unnecessarily. Markers must be placed only in locations where it is not widely known that there is a grave (Rambam *Sefer Tahara, Hilkhot Tumat Met* 8:9).

וְאֵלּוּ הֵן הַסְּפֵיקוֹת: סְכָכוֹת וּפְרָעוֹת;

The Gemara continues to explicate the *baraita*: **And these are the** places of **uncertain** ritual impurity: **Overhanging boughs, and protrusions,**[N] and a *beit haperas*.

סְכָכוֹת – אִילָן הַמֵּיסֵךְ עַל הָאָרֶץ;

The Gemara explains: **Overhanging boughs** is referring to **a tree that hangs over the ground** next to a cemetery, and under one of its branches there might be a corpse. If there is a corpse there, the branch overhanging it creates a tent and therefore imparts ritual impurity to anyone who passes underneath it.

פְּרָעוֹת – אֲבָנִים פְּרוּעוֹת הַיּוֹצְאוֹת מִן הַגָּדֵר;

Protrusions[N] is referring to **protruding stones that jut out from a wall** and are not flush with it, under which there might be a corpse. Once again, if the stones protrude over a corpse, they create a tent and impart ritual impurity to anyone who passes underneath.

בֵּית הַפְּרָס – כִּדְתְנַן: הַחוֹרֵשׁ אֶת הַקֶּבֶר הֲרֵי הוּא עוֹשֶׂה בֵּית הַפְּרָס. וְכַמָּה הוּא עוֹשֶׂה? מְלֹא מַעֲנָה מֵאָה אַמָּה.

The definition of a ***beit haperas*** is **as we learned** elsewhere in a mishna (*Oholot* 17:1): **One who plows** a field containing **a grave,**[H] thereby raising concern that bones may have become strewn throughout the field, **renders** the field **a *beit haperas*. And how much** of the field **does he render** a *beit haperas*? **The full** length of **a furrow,** which is **a hundred cubits.**

וּבֵית הַפְּרָס מִי מְטַמֵּא בְּאֹהֶל? וְהָאָמַר רַב יְהוּדָה אָמַר שְׁמוּאֵל: מְנַפֵּחַ אָדָם בֵּית הַפְּרָס וְהוֹלֵךְ.

The Gemara asks: **Does a *beit haperas*** really **impart ritual impurity by means of a tent?**[N] **But didn't Rav Yehuda say** that **Shmuel said:** If **a person** is carrying ritually pure items or wishes to remain ritually pure so that he may consume consecrated items, yet he must cross a *beit haperas*, he **may blow upon** the earth in **the *beit haperas***[H] before each step to clear away any small bones that may have become strewn across the field **and** proceed to **walk** across the area, thereby remaining ritually pure. This indicates that there is no concern about contracting ritual impurity by means of a tent in a *beit haperas*; otherwise, it would be prohibited to cross in this way, as it is possible that in the course of blowing one may already have contracted ritual impurity by leaning over the bones or by passing over bones that are buried beneath the surface.

וְרַב יְהוּדָה בַּר אַמִּי מִשְּׁמֵיהּ דְּעוּלָּא אָמַר: בֵּית הַפְּרָס שֶׁנִּידַּשׁ טָהוֹר!

Similarly, **Rav Yehuda bar Ami said in the name of Ulla: A *beit haperas* that was trampled,**[N] i.e., a well-trodden *beit haperas*, **is ritually pure,** as passersby have certainly cleared away any bones with their feet. If a *beit haperas* were to impart ritual impurity by means of a tent, there should be a concern that the bones may have been trampled upon and buried in the ground. Both these sources prove that a *beit haperas* does not impart impurity by means of tent, posing a contradiction to the mishna.

HALAKHA

A field in which a grave was plowed – שָׂדֶה שֶׁנֶּחֱרַשׁ בּוֹ קֶבֶר: A field in which a grave was plowed is called a *beit haperas*. The Sages decreed that the area is ritually impure due to a concern that bones were scattered throughout the field. No distinction is made based on the particulars of the case, and the *halakha* applies even if the corpse was buried deep in the ground in a coffin. The field has the status of a *beit haperas* to a distance of one hundred cubits from the location of the grave (Rambam *Sefer Tahara, Hilkhot Tumat Met* 10:1).

He may blow upon the earth in the *beit haperas* – מְנַפֵּחַ אָדָם בֵּית הַפְּרָס: One who is traveling to sacrifice the Paschal lamb may blow the dirt along the path of a *beit haperas* as he travels through it. If he does not find any bones, he may slaughter and eat his Paschal lamb. Similarly, one who passes through a well-trodden *beit haperas* remains ritually pure and may offer the Paschal lamb (Rambam *Sefer Korbanot, Hilkhot Korban Pesaḥ* 6:8).

NOTES

Overhanging boughs and protrusions – סְכָכוֹת וּפְרָעוֹת: The commentaries disagree about the meaning of this phrase. Rashi explains that it refers to trees or walls adjacent to a cemetery where there is a concern that a corpse or part of a corpse may be buried beneath them. According to this interpretation, the tree or wall must be located in a private domain, as cases of questionable impurity are judged leniently in the public domain. However, some say that there is certainly a corpse buried underneath the branch or protrusion from the wall, but there is doubt as to the precise location of the corpse. Other commentaries explain that there is certainly a corpse underneath the branch or protruding stone, but the branch or stone is not wide enough to constitute a tent by Torah law. The uncertainty is about whether by rabbinic law it constitutes a tent in combination with the other branches of the tree or the other stones protruding from the same row of stones on the wall (Ramban on *Nidda* 57a, citing Ra'avad; Rabbeinu Shimshon on *Oholot* 8:2; see Ritva).

Protrusions – פְּרוּעוֹת: Some interpret this to mean large stones, as in the verse: "He shall let the locks of the hair of his head grow [*pera*]" (Numbers 6:5). *Pera* in this verse is rendered in the Aramaic translation as: Grow long (Rashi manuscript; *Talmid Rabbeinu Yeḥiel of Paris*).

Does a *beit haperas* impart ritual impurity by means of a tent – וּבֵית הַפְּרָס מִי מְטַמֵּא בְּאֹהֶל: Several commentaries had a different version of the text, according to which it is taken for granted that a *beit haperas* does not impart ritual impurity by means of a tent. The Gemara's question according to their version is: Does a *beit haperas* require marking? The ensuing discussion in the Gemara can also be understood according to this explanation (*Tosefot Rid*).

A *beit haperas* that was trampled – בֵּית הַפְּרָס שֶׁנִּידַּשׁ: The Rambam, and apparently also Rashi, rule that this is a case where an individual is on his way to sacrifice the Paschal lamb. The Sages did not impose their decree that one who walks through a *beit haperas* becomes ritually impure in a situation where it would prevent someone from fulfilling the mitzva of the Paschal lamb, which carries a punishment of *karet* for those who fail to fulfill it.

אָמַר רַב פַּפָּא: לָא קַשְׁיָא; כָּאן – בְּשָׂדֶה שֶׁאָבַד בָּהּ קֶבֶר, כָּאן – בְּשָׂדֶה שֶׁנֶּחֱרַשׁ בָּהּ קֶבֶר.

Rav Pappa said: It is **not difficult,** as a distinction can be made between different types of *beit haperas*: **Here,** where the *baraita* states that a *beit haperas* must be marked because it imparts tent impurity, it is referring to **a field in which a grave was lost,**[H] i.e., a field that was known with certainty to contain a grave, though its precise location can no longer be recalled. **There,** where it ruled that a *beit haperas* does not convey tent impurity, it is a case of **a field where a grave was plowed** and it is not at all clear whether there are bones strewn across the field. In that case ritual impurity is not imparted by means of a tent, and so it need not be marked.

וְשָׂדֶה שֶׁנֶּחֱרַשׁ בָּהּ קֶבֶר ״בֵּית הַפְּרָס״ קָרֵי לֵיהּ? אִין, וְהָתְנַן: שְׁלֹשָׁה בֵּית הַפְּרָס הֵן: שָׂדֶה שֶׁנֶּאֱבַד בָּהּ קֶבֶר, וְשָׂדֶה שֶׁנֶּחֱרַשׁ בָּהּ קֶבֶר, וּשְׂדֵה בּוֹכִין.

The Gemara asks: **But is a field where a grave was plowed called a** ***beit haperas,*** such that one must be concerned about its ritual impurity? The Gemara answers: **Yes, and so we learned** in a mishna (*Oholot* 18:2–4): **There are three** types of ***beit haperas*** through which those who eat *teruma* and consecrated items are prohibited to walk: **A field in which a grave was lost** and its precise location is no longer known, **a field in which a grave was plowed** and bones may have been scattered about, **and a weepers' field.**[HN]

מַאי שְׂדֵה בּוֹכִין? רַב יְהוֹשֻׁעַ בַּר אַבָּא מִשְּׁמֵיהּ דְּעוּלָּא אָמַר: שָׂדֶה שֶׁמַּפְטִירִין בָּהּ מֵתִים.

The Gemara asks: **What is** meant by **a weepers' field? Rav Yehoshua bar Abba said in the name of Ulla: A field where** those escorting the deceased **would take leave of the deceased,**[N] handing the corpse over to those who would perform the actual interment.

וְטַעֲמָא מַאי? אָמַר אֲבִימִי: מִשּׁוּם יֵאוּשׁ בְּעָלִים נָגְעוּ בָּהּ.

And what is the reason that one must be concerned about ritual impurity in a weepers' field? **Avimi said:** It is **due to the** possible **despair by the owners** of recovering bones[N] that the Sages **touched** upon **it.** There is a concern that in transporting the deceased from far away, a loose limb may have fallen from the corpse into the field, and unseen by those transporting the deceased, it was abandoned there. Since over time many corpses passed through this weepers' field, it is assumed that ritual impurity might be found in many places throughout the field.

וְשָׂדֶה שֶׁנֶּחֱרַשׁ בָּהּ קֶבֶר לָא בָּעֵי צִיּוּן? וְהָא תַּנְיָא: מָצָא שָׂדֶה מְצוּיֶּינֶת, וְאֵין יָדוּעַ מַה טִּיבָהּ. יֵשׁ בָּהּ אִילָנוֹת – בְּיָדוּעַ שֶׁנֶּחֱרַשׁ בָּהּ קֶבֶר; אֵין בָּהּ אִילָנוֹת – בְּיָדוּעַ שֶׁאָבַד בָּהּ קֶבֶר.

The Gemara asks: **And does a field in which a grave was plowed not require marking? But isn't it taught** in a *baraita*: **If one encountered a field that was marked**[HN] due to ritual impurity, **and** it is no longer **known what the nature of the** ritual impurity was, **if there are trees in** the field, **it is known that a grave was plowed in it,** as it is permitted for one to plant trees in such a field. **If there are no trees in** the field, **it is known that a grave was lost in it,** as it is prohibited for one to plant trees in such a field. If a field is suitable for planting trees and yet there are none, clearly it is because a grave was lost in it.

רַבִּי יְהוּדָה אוֹמֵר: עַד שֶׁיְּהֵא שָׁם זָקֵן אוֹ תַּלְמִיד, לְפִי שֶׁאֵין הַכֹּל בְּקִיאִין בַּדָּבָר!

Rabbi Yehuda says: We do not rely on these signs **unless there is an Elder or** a rabbinic **scholar** who can testify about the subject, **as not all are experts in this matter,** and perhaps the field was not plowed at all. In any case, this *baraita* teaches that a field in which a grave was plowed is also marked.

אָמַר רַב פַּפָּא: כִּי תַּנְיָא הַהִיא – בְּשָׂדֶה שֶׁאָבַד בָּהּ קֶבֶר, דְּצַיְּינוּהָ. יֵשׁ בָּהּ אִילָנוֹת – בְּיָדוּעַ שֶׁנֶּחֱרַשׁ בָּהּ קֶבֶר. אֵין בָּהּ אִילָנוֹת – בְּיָדוּעַ שֶׁאָבַד בָּהּ קֶבֶר.

The Gemara answers: **Rav Pappa said: When that** *baraita* concerning a marked field **is taught,** it is taught with regard to **a field where a grave was** certainly **lost** and **they** immediately **marked it.** However, **if there are trees in** the field, **it is known that a grave was** later **plowed in it,** i.e., it was forgotten that a grave had been lost in the field and so it was inappropriately plowed and prepared for planting. But **if there are no trees in** the field, **we know that a grave was lost in it** and it was not later plowed.

וְלֵיחוּשׁ דִּלְמָא אִילָנוֹת מִגַּוַּאי וְקֶבֶר מִבָּרָאִי!

The Gemara raises a question about this ruling: **But let us be concerned that perhaps the trees were** located **inside** the field **and the grave was** located **outside** of it, and the actual site of the grave was never plowed but simply lost? How then can one rely on the presence of trees to indicate that the grave had been plowed in the field?

HALAKHA

A field in which a grave was lost – שָׂדֶה שֶׁאָבַד בָּהּ קֶבֶר: The soil of a field in which a grave was lost imparts ritual impurity through direct contact and to those who carry the soil even without direct contact, and the field imparts ritual impurity to those who pass over it (Rambam *Sefer Tahara, Hilkhot Tumat Met* 8:1).

A weepers' field – שְׂדֵה בּוֹכִין: A field near the cemetery, where women sit and weep, is called a weepers' field. Due to the concern that perhaps a corpse has been buried there, it is prohibited to plant in this field so that people will not accustom themselves to going there. However, since there is no known source of impurity there, the soil of such a field is presumed to be ritually pure and may be used to fashion ovens for cooking consecrated food items (Rambam *Sefer Tahara, Hilkhot Tumat Met* 8:4).

A field that was marked – שָׂדֶה מְצוּיֶּינֶת: If one finds a field that was marked as ritually impure but he does not know what type of impurity the field contains, he can assume that if the field has a tree, it is presumably a field where a grave was plowed. Therefore, the field does not impart ritual impurity by means of a tent. If there is no tree, it is presumably a field where a grave was lost. Therefore, it does impart ritual impurity by means of a tent. However, this applies only if there is a local Torah scholar who knows that it is permitted to plant trees in a field where a grave was plowed and prohibited to plant trees in a field where a grave was lost. The *Kesef Mishne* notes that this is in accordance with the opinion of Rabbi Yehuda, who merely explains the opinion of the anonymous first *tanna* (Rambam *Sefer Tahara, Hilkhot Tumat Met* 10:10).

NOTES

A weepers' [*bokhin*] field – שְׂדֵה בּוֹכִין: The Rashbam's version of the text reads: A field of crypts [*kokhin*]. He explains that this refers to a field adjoining a cemetery where the deceased would be buried temporarily in a crypt until a proper grave could be prepared. The Sages were concerned about the ritual purity of this field, due to the possibility that corpses interred there had not been transferred to permanent graves.

Where those escorting the deceased would take leave of [*maftirin*] the deceased – שֶׁמַּפְטִירִין בָּהּ מֵתִים: Some commentaries explain that this refers to a field where corpses would be brought from distant locations and where the local residents would begin to attend to them. The *ge'onim* explain that it is called a weepers' field because family members from different places would assemble there to mourn their dead together. Indeed, some understand the word *maftirin* as it is used in the Jerusalem Talmud, in the sense of eulogizing the dead (see Ritva).

Due to the despair by the owners of recovering bones – מִשּׁוּם יֵאוּשׁ בְּעָלִים: According to one explanation, this means that a corpse would sometimes be brought there after it had already begun to decompose, and perhaps a body part had fallen off without being noticed. Alternatively, perhaps several corpses were brought together and one of them, possibly the corpse of an infant or stillborn child, was left behind (*Talmid Rabbeinu Yeḥiel of Paris*). The Ritva offers a completely different explanation, citing Rabbeinu Shimshon: The despair of the owners refers to the fact that once the field has been used regularly for these purposes, the original owners no longer have a right to prevent its continued use in this way by planting in the field.

If one encountered a field that was marked – מָצָא שָׂדֶה מְצוּיֶּינֶת: Most commentaries explain that finding trees in a field is the indication that there is no grave there, as it is prohibited to plant trees in a field where there is a grave whose precise location one does not know (*Tosefot Rid*; Ritva). The Ra'avad adds that when the Gemara states that the field has no trees, it means that the trees have been cut down (see Rashi, Meiri, and Ritva).

כִּדְאָמַר עוּלָּא: בְּעוֹמְדִין עַל הַגְּבוּלִין; הָכָא נַמִי: בְּעוֹמְדִין עַל הַגְּבוּלִין.

The Gemara answers: It is **as Ulla said** elsewhere. This is a case **where** the trees **are standing along the** field's **boundaries,** next to a public domain, as the grave is certainly not outside the trees in the public domain, since people do not bury a corpse in the public thoroughfare. Rather, the grave must be between the trees, and was therefore plowed. **Here too,** then, this is a case **where** the trees **are standing along the borders.**

Perek **I**
Daf **6** Amud **a**

וְדִלְמָא טוּמְאָה מִגַּוָּאי וְאִילָנוֹת מִבָּרַאי!

The Gemara asks: **But perhaps the ritual impurity was on the inside and the trees were on the outside,** and only the area between the trees was plowed, while the inner portion of the field with the grave was not plowed?

בִּמְסוּבָּכִין. וְאִיבָּעֵית אֵימָא: הָא אֲמָרַן אֵין מַרְחִיקִין צִיּוּן מִמְּקוֹם טוּמְאָה, שֶׁלֹּא לְהַפְסִיד אֶת אֶרֶץ יִשְׂרָאֵל.

The Gemara answers: The case is where the trees are **scattered**[N] throughout the entire field, so that it is likely that the entire field was plowed. **And if you wish, say** instead: This is not a concern, as **we said** earlier that **one does not distance the marker** too far **from the** actual **site of ritual impurity, so as not to cause a loss of Eretz Yisrael.** As the marker is located near the trees, presumably the trees are close to the actual site of the grave, and the site of the grave was plowed.

"רַבִּי יְהוּדָה אוֹמֵר: עַד שֶׁיְּהֵא שָׁם זָקֵן אוֹ תַּלְמִיד, לְפִי שֶׁאֵין הַכֹּל בְּקִיאִין בַּדָּבָר". אָמַר אַבָּיֵי: שְׁמַע מִינָּהּ: צוּרְבָא מֵרַבָּנַן דְּאִיכָּא בְּמָתָא – כָּל מִילֵּי דְּמָתָא עֲלֵיהּ רַמְיָא.

It is taught in the *baraita* that **Rabbi Yehuda says:** One relies on these signs **only** when **there is an Elder or** a rabbinic **scholar** who can testify about the matter, **as not all are well versed in this matter,** and perhaps the field was not plowed at all. **Abaye said: Learn from this** statement of Rabbi Yehuda that when **there is a Torah scholar in the city, all affairs of the city**[N] **are thrust upon him,** i.e., are his responsibility. Consequently, he is expected to know what has happened in the city.

אָמַר רַב יְהוּדָה: מָצָא אֶבֶן מְצוּיֶּנֶת – תַּחְתֶּיהָ טָמֵא. שְׁתַּיִם, אִם יֵשׁ סִיד בֵּינֵיהֶן – בֵּינֵיהֶן טָמֵא. וְאִם אֵין סִיד בֵּינֵיהֶן – בֵּינֵיהֶן טָהוֹר.

§ The Gemara continues its discussion of marking graves. **Rav Yehuda said: If one found** a single **marked stone,**[N] this indicates that the ground **underneath it is ritually impure.** If he found **two** marked stones,[B] the following distinction applies: **If there is lime** on the ground **between them,** this indicates that the area **between them is ritually impure** and the two stones mark the boundaries of the impure area; **and if there is no lime** on the ground **between them,** this indicates that the area **between them is ritually pure** and each stone marks a separate area of ritual impurity.[H]

NOTES

Scattered [*mesubakhin*] – בִּמְסוּבָּכִין: The Ritva explains that the trees have large branches that cover some portion of the field. This may be based upon versions of the text that read *mesukhakhin*, covered, instead of *mesubakhin*, scattered.

All affairs of the city, etc. – כָּל מִילֵּי דְּמָתָא וכו׳: Rabbi Shlomo ben HaYatom derives from here that a Torah scholar must pay attention to communal affairs, as halakhic rulings will be issued in accordance with his reports of what has taken place in his community.

A single marked stone – אֶבֶן מְצוּיֶּנֶת: Rashi explains that although one does not generally place a marker of ritual impurity directly over the source of the impurity, this is not the case with regard to a stone, as the marker is noticeable from a distance due to the height of the stone. However, it is apparent in the Jerusalem Talmud that even in the case of a stone, the marker should not be directly over the source of the impurity. Consequently, if a single stone was marked, it is assumed that the stone covers an area greater than the source of the impurity (see *Tosefot HaRosh*).

BACKGROUND

Two marked stones – שְׁתֵּי אֲבָנִים מְצוּיָּנוֹת: This refers to two stones that have lime on top of them and, at least minimally, on the sides that face each other, so that it is plausible that there was once lime between the stones that peeled off.

Two stones marked with lime

HALAKHA

Marking on stones – צִיּוּן עַל אֲבָנִים: If one finds a single marked stone, the area beneath it is ritually impure. If two stones are marked and there is lime between them, the area between them is ritually impure. If the lime is found only on the tops of the stones and there are pottery fragments between them, it is assumed that the fragments were part of a structure. This is in accordance with the versions of the text that include the word *heres* instead of *ḥoresh* (see *Tosafot*; *Kesef Mishne*). If there is no pottery between them and the lime spreads down from the tops of the stones to the area between them, the area between the stones is ritually impure. The Ra'avad writes that if the area between the stones has been plowed, it is considered ritually pure, as it is assumed that the plowing caused the lime to fall from the stones to the ground between them. This is in accordance with the version of the text found in the Vilna Talmud, which includes the word *ḥoresh* (Rambam *Sefer Tahara*, *Hilkhot Tumat Met* 8:11, and *Kesef Mishne* there).

וְאַף עַל גַּב דְּלֵיכָּא חוֹרֵשׁ? וְהָתַנְיָא: מָצָא אֶבֶן אַחַת מְצוּיֶּנֶת – תַּחְתֶּיהָ טָמֵא. שְׁתַּיִם, אִם יֵשׁ חוֹרֵשׁ בֵּינֵיהֶן – בֵּינֵיהֶן טָהוֹר; וְאִם לָאו – בֵּינֵיהֶן טָמֵא!

The Gemara asks: **And** is the area between them deemed ritually pure **even though there is no** sign of **plowing** having taken place between the stones? **But isn't it taught** otherwise in a *baraita* as follows: **If one found a single marked stone,** this indicates that the ground **underneath it is ritually impure.** If he found **two** marked stones, then the following distinction applies: **If there is** evidence of **plowing**[N] having taken place **between them,** the area **between** the two stones **is ritually pure; and if not,** the area **between them is ritually impure.**

אָמַר רַב פַּפָּא: הָכָא כְּשֶׁהַסִּיד שָׁפוּךְ עַל רָאשֵׁיהֶן וּמְרוּדֶּה לְכָאן וּלְכָאן. אִי אִיכָּא חוֹרֵשׁ בֵּינֵיהֶן – בֵּינֵיהֶן טָהוֹר, דְּאֵימוֹר מֵחֲמַת חוֹרֵשׁ הוּא דְּאִיקְּפַל. וְאִי לָא – סִיד דְּבֵינֵי בֵּינֵי הוּא, וְטָמֵא.

Rav Pappa said: The contradiction can be resolved by explaining that **here,** in the *baraita,* the case is **where the lime** used as a marker of ritual impurity **had been poured on top** of the stones, **and it is spread thinly this way and that.** In this case, **if there is** evidence of **plowing** having taken place **between** the stones, the area **between them is ritually pure, as one** can **say** that the lime **was peeled off** from the stones **due to the plowing;** originally the lime was only on top of the stones, to indicate that there is ritual impurity underneath them, but then fell into the area between them during the plowing. **But if** there is **no** evidence of a plow having passed between them, then it is most likely that **the lime was** meant to mark the ground **between** the stones, and the entire area between them **is ritually impure.**

אָמַר רַבִּי אַסִי: מֵצַר אֶחָד מְצוּיָּין – הוּא טָמֵא, וְכָל הַשָּׂדֶה כּוּלָּהּ טְהוֹרָה. שְׁנַיִם – הֵם טְמֵאִין, וְכָל הַשָּׂדֶה כּוּלָּהּ טְהוֹרָה. שְׁלֹשָׁה – הֵם טְמֵאִין, וְכָל הַשָּׂדֶה כּוּלָּהּ טְהוֹרָה. אַרְבָּעָה – הֵן טְהוֹרִין, וְכָל הַשָּׂדֶה כּוּלָּהּ טְמֵאָה.

Rabbi Asi said: If only **one border** of a field[B] **is marked,**[N] it is assumed that the border itself **is ritually impure while the entire** rest of the **field is ritually pure.** If **two** borders are marked, it is assumed that **they are** both **ritually impure while the entire** rest of the **field is ritually pure.** If **three** borders are marked, it is assumed that the three of **them are ritually impure while the entire** rest of the **field is ritually pure.** If all **four** borders are marked, the borders themselves **are ritually pure, while the entire field** enclosed by the borders **is ritually impure.**[H]

דְּאָמַר מָר: אֵין מַרְחִיקִין צִיּוּן מִמְּקוֹם טוּמְאָה, שֶׁלֹּא לְהַפְסִיד אֶת אֶרֶץ יִשְׂרָאֵל.

As the Master said in the *baraita:* **One does not distance the marker from the** actual **site of ritual impurity, so as not to cause a loss of Eretz Yisrael,** i.e., not to increase the area into which people refrain from entering. Consequently, they marked all of the borders to indicate that the entire field is ritually impure.

״וְיוֹצְאִין אַף עַל הַכִּלְאַיִם״.

§ It is taught in the mishna: And inspectors **even go out** on the intermediate days of a Festival **to** uproot **the** shoots of prohibited **diverse kinds** [*kilayim*] that grew in the fields during the rainy season.

וְאַכִּלְאַיִם בְּחוּלּוֹ שֶׁל מוֹעֵד נָפְקִינַן? וּרְמִינְהוּ: בְּאֶחָד בַּאֲדָר מַשְׁמִיעִין עַל הַשְּׁקָלִים וְעַל הַכִּלְאַיִם.

The Gemara asks: **Do they go out to** uproot **diverse kinds during the intermediate days of a Festival?** The Gemara **raises a contradiction** from another mishna (*Shekalim* 1:1), which states: **On the first of Adar** the court **issues a proclamation concerning** the collection of **the shekels,**[HB] i.e., the yearly half-shekel contribution to the Temple treasury made by each adult male for the purpose of buying communal offerings. **And** the court also issues a proclamation **with regard to** the obligation to uproot **diverse kinds**[NH] from the fields.

BACKGROUND

Borders of a field – מְצָרֵי שָׂדֶה: In many places the borders of fields were marked not only with stones, but also with areas of elevated soil, which served both to indicate precisely where the border ran and to provide an easier way to pass through the field without treading upon the cultivated areas.

Elevated ground between fields

The shekels – הַשְּׁקָלִים: All male Jews over the age of twenty were required to contribute half a shekel to the Temple annually, before the first day of the month of Nisan, which was the beginning of the new Temple year. This money was used to cover the expenses of the Temple, including purchasing communal offerings and paying for repairs to the structure of the Temple. It was also used to maintain and repair the walls of Jerusalem. From the beginning of the month of Adar, notice was served to the public that the half-shekel contributions would soon be due. Nowadays, toward the end of the Fast of Esther on the thirteenth of Adar, before the beginning of Purim, it is customary to donate charity in commemoration of the half-shekel contribution. The *halakhot* of the half-shekel contributions made to the Temple are discussed in tractate *Shekalim.*

HALAKHA

Marked borders of a field – מְצָרֵי שָׂדֶה מְצוּיָּנִים: If one finds a field with a single border marked with lime, the area beneath the border is ritually impure. The same is true if two or three borders are marked in this manner. However, if all of the field's borders are marked with lime, the area directly beneath the borders is ritually pure, and the rest of the field is ritually impure (Rambam *Sefer Tahara, Hilkhot Tumat Met* 8:11).

The court issues a proclamation concerning the collection of the shekels – מַשְׁמִיעִין עַל הַשְּׁקָלִים: On the first of Adar a public proclamation would be made concerning the contribution of half-shekels, so that all would prepare the half-shekel to be given on the fifteenth of Adar (Rambam *Sefer Zemanim, Hilkhot Shekalim* 1:9).

The court also issues a proclamation with regard to the obligation to uproot diverse kinds – מַשְׁמִיעִים עַל הַכִּלְאַיִן: On the first of Adar the court would proclaim that everyone must uproot the diverse kinds growing in his fields and gardens. On the fifteenth of Adar, agents appointed by the court would go out to ensure that this was done (Rambam *Sefer Zera'im, Hilkhot Kilayim* 2:15).

NOTES

If there is evidence of plowing – אִם יֵשׁ חוֹרֵשׁ: If there is evidence that the area between the stones has been plowed, it is assumed that the plowing caused the lime to fall from the stone, and originally the area between the stones had not been marked. Alternatively, if the area had been plowed, even if there was a corpse buried there, one who walks there remains pure. This is because a grave that has been plowed does not impart ritual impurity by way of a tent, as it is assumed that the corpse has been torn to pieces (*Peirush;* see also *Tosafot, Divrei David,* and *Sefat Emet*).

Some versions of the text read *ḥeres,* earthenware, instead of *ḥoresh,* plowing. Some suggest that according to this version, if one found fragments of pottery between the stones, it is possible that the pottery fell from the stones and caused some of the lime to fall between the stones as well (Rabbeinu Gershom Meor HaGola; Rabbi Shlomo ben HaYatom). Others suggest that the absence of pottery is a sign of virgin soil, and the presence of pottery indicates that the area has been plowed (*Peirush*). The Rambam explains that the potsherds between the stones indicate that some structure had once stood there, and this accounts for the presence of the lime.

If one border of a field is marked – מֵצַר אֶחָד מְצוּיָּין: Ordinarily, one does not mark the ritual impurity directly over the location of the source of the impurity. However, since the border of the field is elevated above the ground and therefore easily noticeable, the marking may be placed on the border, directly over the source of the impurity (Ritva).

The court also issues a proclamation with regard to the obligation to uproot diverse kinds – מַשְׁמִיעִים עַל הַכִּלְאַיִן: Some explain that the proclamation is that people should take care not to sow diverse kinds in their fields (*Talmid Rabbeinu Yeḥiel of Paris*).

בַּחֲמִשָּׁה עָשָׂר בּוֹ קוֹרִין אֶת הַמְּגִילָּה בַּכְּרַכִּים, וְיוֹצְאִין לְקַוֵּוץ אֶת הַדְּרָכִים, וּלְתַקֵּן הָרְחוֹבוֹת, וְלָמוֹד הַמִּקְוָאוֹת, וְעוֹשִׂין כׇּל צוֹרְכֵי רַבִּים, וּמְצַיְּינִין אֶת הַקְּבָרוֹת, וְיוֹצְאִין עַל הַכִּלְאַיִם!

On the fifteenth of Adar **the Megilla,** the Scroll of Esther, **is read in** the walled **cities,**[H] **and they go out to clear thorns**[N] from the **roads, to repair the** city **streets, and to measure the ritual baths** to ascertain that they have the requisite quantity of water. **And they tend to all** other **public needs, and they mark graves** with lime, **and they go out to** uproot **the** shoots of **diverse kinds.**[N] If they already went out in Adar to uproot the diverse kinds, why would they go out again on the intermediate days of the festival of Passover?

רַבִּי אֶלְעָזָר וְרַבִּי יוֹסֵי בַּר חֲנִינָא; חַד אָמַר: כָּאן – בְּבַכִּיר, כָּאן – בְּאָפִיל. וְחַד אָמַר: כָּאן – בִּזְרָעִים, כָּאן – בִּירָקוֹת.

Rabbi Elazar and Rabbi Yosei bar Ḥanina disagreed about this issue: **One said: Here,** in the mishna that states that they go out on the fifteenth of Adar, it is referring to **the early crop,** while **there,** in the mishna that states that they go out on the intermediate days of the Festival, it is referring to **the late crop,**[H] which isn't clearly recognizable until the intermediate days of Passover. **And one said: Here,** in the mishna that states that they go out on the fifteenth of Adar, it is referring to **grains** that are sown in the winter and have already grown tall by Adar, while **there,** in the mishna that states that they go out on the intermediate days of the Festival, it is referring to **vegetables,**[B] which only grow later in the season.

אָמַר רַבִּי אַסִּי אָמַר רַבִּי יוֹחָנָן: לֹא שָׁנוּ אֶלָּא שֶׁאֵין נִיצָּן נִיכָּר, אֲבָל נִיצָּן נִיכָּר – יוֹצְאִין עֲלֵיהֶן.

Rabbi Asi said that **Rabbi Yoḥanan said: They taught** that court messengers go out to uproot diverse kinds in the middle of the month of Adar **only** in a case **where the blossom was not** yet **recognizable** at an earlier date, so it was still impossible to determine whether or not the seedling was from diverse kinds of seeds. **But** if **the blossom was** already **recognizable** at an earlier date, **they go out** at that time to uproot the shoots of diverse kinds of seeds.

מַאי שְׁנָא בְּחוּלּוֹ שֶׁל מוֹעֵד דְּנָפְקִינַן? אָמַר רַבִּי יַעֲקֹב אָמַר רַבִּי יוֹחָנָן: מִשּׁוּם שְׂכַר פְּעוּלָּה, דְּמוּזְלִי גַּבָּן.

The Gemara asks: **What is different about the intermediate days of a Festival that we** specifically **go out** to uproot shoots of diverse kinds of seeds during that week? **Rabbi Ya'akov said** that **Rabbi Yoḥanan said:** It is **due to the wages** paid to the workers hired by the court to uproot the diverse kinds. On the intermediate days of the Festival it is prohibited for them to perform ordinary labor, and so **they reduce** their rates **for us,** i.e., for public works, as otherwise they would have no income at all.

אָמַר רַב זְבִיד וְאִיתֵּימָא רַב מְשַׁרְשְׁיָא: שְׁמַע מִינָּהּ כִּי יָהֲבִינַן לְהוּ שָׂכָר – מִתְּרוּמַת הַלִּשְׁכָּה יָהֲבִינַן לְהוּ. דְּאִי סָלְקָא דַּעְתָּךְ מִדִּידְהוּ יָהֲבִינַן לְהוּ – מַאי נַפְקָא לַן מִינַּיְיהוּ, כׇּל כַּמָּה דְּבָעוּ לִיתֵּן לְהוּ!

Rav Zevid said, and some say that it was **Rav Mesharshiyya** who **said: Learn from this** explanation **that when we give** the workers who uproot the diverse kinds their **wages, we give it to them from** the funds of **the collection of the** Temple treasury **chamber.**[NB] Since they are paid with consecrated money, an attempt is made to minimize the expenses. **As, if it enters your mind** that **we pay them from theirs,** i.e., the court forces the owners of the fields where the diverse kinds are found to pay the workers who uproot them, **what** benefit **would we derive from** saving the expense? **However much** the workers **desire, they should pay them.**[N]

וְעַד כַּמָּה? אָמַר רַב שְׁמוּאֵל בַּר יִצְחָק: כְּאוֹתָהּ שֶׁשָּׁנִינוּ: כׇּל סְאָה שֶׁיֵּשׁ בָּהּ

Concerning the issue of uprooting diverse kinds, the Gemara asks: **And how much**[N] of another species must be mixed in with a crop in order to be considered diverse kinds that must be uprooted by these workers? **Rav Shmuel bar Yitzḥak said:** The amount is **like that which we learned** in the mishna (*Kilayim* 2:1): **Any** ***se'a*** of seeds **that contains**

HALAKHA

Reading the Megilla in walled cities – קְרִיאַת הַמְּגִילָּה בִּכְרַכִּים: On the fifteenth of Adar, the Megilla is read in cities that were walled during the time of Joshua, son of Nun (*Shulḥan Arukh, Oraḥ Ḥayyim* 688:1).

The early crop and the late crop – בַּכִּיר וְאָפִיל: On the intermediate days of Passover, agents of the court would go out to check for diverse kinds growing in the fields. If they found more than the permitted quantity, they would declare the entire field ownerless. If the diverse kinds blossomed before Passover, the court agents would investigate the matter immediately (Rambam *Sefer Zera'im, Hilkhot Kilayim* 2:17).

NOTES

They go out to clear thorns – יוֹצְאִין לְקַוֵּוץ: These tasks were performed at that time of year in order to prepare the roads for the pilgrims who would come to Jerusalem for Passover. Similarly, they would repair the ritual baths so that the pilgrims would be able to immerse and purify themselves. They would also mark the graves so that the pilgrims would not inadvertently become ritually impure on their way to the Temple (*Talmid Rabbeinu Yeḥiel of Paris*; Rabbi Shlomo ben HaYatom).

They go out to uproot the shoots of diverse kinds – יוֹצְאִים עַל הַכִּלְאַיִם: The Gemara addresses only the question of why they would go out to uproot the shoots of diverse kinds both in Adar as well as on the intermediate days of Passover. However, there are other, additional items listed that were apparently performed twice, including marking the graves, fixing the roads, and measuring the ritual baths. It is explained in the Jerusalem Talmud that although the graves were marked in Adar, they would go out to mark them again during Passover because of the possibility that it rained in the meantime and the lime was washed away. It may be suggested that the roads also needed to be fixed again for that reason (see Rashi). Some write that the Gemara addresses only the issue of diverse kinds because the other activities assigned to the fifteenth of Adar were not immediately obligatory, and it is possible that they would not have been performed by Passover. However, the uprooting of diverse kinds, which is performed in order to prevent violating Torah law, was certainly not delayed, and so the question arises why it was done twice (*Talmid Rabbeinu Yeḥiel of Paris*). Others propose that the other tasks, e.g., repairing the roads, were performed a second time on the intermediate days of Passover for the benefit of the pilgrims returning home from Jerusalem after the Festival (Rabbi Shlomo ben HaYatom).

From the funds of the collection of the Temple treasury chamber – מִתְּרוּמַת הַלִּשְׁכָּה: *Tosafot* write that the court would stipulate that money from these funds would be dedicated to pay for various communal needs. A list of communal needs that were funded in this way is found in tractate *Shekalim* (10b). The later commentaries discuss why the Gemara says that the payment was made from the collection of the Temple treasury chamber, and not from the remains of the chamber, i.e., the money that remained in the chamber after the three collections of money were taken to use for communal offerings (see *Tosefot Yom Tov*; *Tal Ḥayyim*).

However much the workers desire, they should pay them – כׇּל כַּמָּה דְּבָעוּ לִיתֵּן לְהוּ: Since the owners of the fields have transgressed and sown or maintained diverse kinds, it would have been appropriate to hire workers to do the work necessary without taking pains to minimize the expense (Rabbi Shlomo ben HaYatom; Meiri).

And how much – וְעַד כַּמָּה: It is unclear from the Gemara whether the quantity discussed here refers to a percentage of the seeds planted or a percentage of the plants that are growing in the field. However, it is clear in the Jerusalem Talmud that the discussion refers to the percentage of the plants that are growing. Consequently, one can understand why the Gemara discusses a matter that appears to be explicit in the mishna in tractate *Kilayim* (2:1); the mishna is referring to a percentage of the seeds, and the Gemara applies the same percentage to the plants that are growing in the field (see *Tal Ḥayyim*).

BACKGROUND

Grains [*zera'im*] **and vegetables** – זְרָעִים וִירָקוֹת: Rashi explains that the term *zera'im*, which literally means seeds, refers to grains, which are sown before vegetables. The Meiri explains that it refers to all plants whose seeds are consumed, while vegetables are plants whose leaves are eaten.

The funds of the collection of the Temple treasury chamber – תְּרוּמַת הַלִּשְׁכָּה: These funds were called the collection of the Temple treasury chamber because the half-shekels donated by the Jewish people each year were kept in a specific chamber in the Temple complex. Three times a year, a priest would enter this chamber with three containers and remove some of the coins. This money was used to purchase animals for communal offerings and for other needs of the Temple. The money that remained in the chamber was used for building and maintaining communal structures in Jerusalem and for purchasing offerings to be sacrificed when no other offerings were being brought.

רוֹבַע זֶרַע מִמִּין אַחֵר – יְמַעֵט.

a quarter-*kav* or more **of seeds of a different type,**[H] i.e., one twenty-fourth of the mixture is a type of seed other than the main type, **one must reduce**[N] the other type of seeds in the mixture by uprooting the shoots.

וְהָתַנְיָא: הִתְקִינוּ שֶׁיְּהוּ מַפְקִירִין כׇּל הַשָּׂדֶה כּוּלָּהּ! לָא קַשְׁיָא: כָּאן – קוֹדֶם תַּקָּנָה, כָּאן – לְאַחַר תַּקָּנָה.

With regard to the *halakha* that inspectors must go out and uproot the shoots of diverse kinds of seeds that grew in the fields, the Gemara asks: **But isn't it taught** in a *baraita* that the Sages **ordained that they should pronounce** the crop of **the entire field** in which diverse kinds was found **ownerless,** rather than uprooting the diverse kinds? The Gemara responds: **This is not difficult. Here,** in the mishna, where it says that the inspectors go out and uproot the diverse kinds, it is referring to the time **before the** institution of the new **ordinance; there,** in the *baraita*, where it says that the entire field is pronounced ownerless, it is referring to the time **after the** institution of that **ordinance.**

דְּתַנְיָא: בָּרִאשׁוֹנָה הָיוּ עוֹקְרִין וּמַשְׁלִיכִין לִפְנֵי בְּהֶמְתָּן, וְהָיוּ בַּעֲלֵי בָתִּים שְׂמֵחִין שְׁתֵּי שְׂמָחוֹת: אַחַת – שֶׁמְּנַכְּשִׁין לָהֶם שְׂדוֹתֵיהֶן, וְאַחַת – שֶׁמַּשְׁלִיכִין לִפְנֵי בְּהֶמְתָּם.

The Gemara explains this ordinance **as it is taught** in another *baraita*: **At first,** the agents of the court **would uproot** the diverse kinds **and cast them before the livestock** belonging to the owners of the fields. However, **the property holders would rejoice for two** reasons: **One, that** the agents of the court **weeded their fields for them** when they uprooted the plants of the other type; and another **one, that they cast** the diverse kinds **before their livestock,** thereby saving them from having to feed them. Accordingly, the field owners took no steps to keep their fields free of diverse kinds of seeds.

הִתְקִינוּ שֶׁיְּהוּ עוֹקְרִין וּמַשְׁלִיכִין עַל הַדְּרָכִים. וַעֲדַיִין הָיוּ שְׂמֵחִין שִׂמְחָה גְּדוֹלָה שֶׁמְּנַכְּשִׁין שְׂדוֹתֵיהֶן. הִתְקִינוּ שֶׁיְּהוּ מַפְקִירִין כׇּל הַשָּׂדֶה כּוּלָּהּ.

The Sages, therefore, **ordained that** the agents of the court **should uproot** the diverse kinds **and cast** them **on the roads.** Yet the property holders **would still greatly rejoice that** the agents of the court **weeded their fields** free of charge. Finally, the Sages **ordained that they should pronounce** the crop of **the entire field** in which diverse kinds was found **ownerless.**[H]

מתני׳ רַבִּי אֱלִיעֶזֶר בֶּן יַעֲקֹב אוֹמֵר: מוֹשְׁכִין אֶת הַמַּיִם מֵאִילָן לְאִילָן, וּבִלְבַד שֶׁלֹּא יַשְׁקֶה אֶת כׇּל הַשָּׂדֶה. זְרָעִים שֶׁלֹּא שָׁתוּ לִפְנֵי הַמּוֹעֵד – לֹא יַשְׁקֵם בַּמּוֹעֵד. וַחֲכָמִים מַתִּירִין בָּזֶה וּבָזֶה.

MISHNA **Rabbi Eliezer ben Ya'akov**[P] **says:** In a field that is filled with trees, **one may draw water**[N] via channels **from** one **tree to** another **tree**[H] on the intermediate days of a Festival because trees are in dire need of water. **And** this is permitted **provided that** in doing so **he does not water the entire field.**[N] With regard to **plants that were not watered**[HN] **prior to the Festival, one may not water them on** the intermediate days of **the Festival** because they do not need the water. **But the Rabbis permit** watering **in this** case, i.e., trees, **and that** case, i.e., plants.

HALAKHA

The measure of diverse kinds of seeds – שִׁיעוּר כִּלְאֵי זְרָעִים: If seeds of a vegetable, grain, or legume became mixed with another of these types of seeds in a ratio of more than one to twenty-four, it is prohibited to sow the mixture until the ratio is reduced. If one sows the mixture, he is liable to flogging. The same *halakha* applies to plants of these types that grow together in a field: If one type is growing amidst another type in a ratio of at least one to twenty-four, it must be reduced (*Shulḥan Arukh, Yoreh De'a* 297:5, 8).

The action of the court concerning diverse kinds of seeds – מַעֲשֵׂה בֵּית דִּין בְּכִלְאֵי זְרָעִים: At first the agents of the court would uproot the diverse kinds and cast them from the field, but the owners of the fields found this beneficial. It was therefore ordained that if diverse kinds are found in a field, the entire crop is pronounced to be ownerless property, provided that the diverse kinds are found in a ratio of at least one to twenty-four. The agents of the court do not interfere if the field contains a lower ratio of diverse kinds (Rambam *Sefer Zera'im, Hilkhot Kilayim* 2:16).

One may draw water from tree to tree – מוֹשְׁכִין אֶת הַמַּיִם מֵאִילָן לְאִילָן: One may draw water from tree to tree provided that he does not irrigate the entire field. This is in accordance with the opinion of Rabbi Eliezer ben Ya'akov, whose opinions are always accepted as *halakha*. The Ra'avad and *Maggid Mishne* disagree about whether this refers to a field that requires irrigation or to a field that does not require irrigation. If the field was already moist, one is permitted to water it while drawing water from tree to tree, in accordance with the statement of Rav Yehuda (*Shulḥan Arukh, Oraḥ Ḥayyim* 537:7).

Plants that were not watered – זְרָעִים שֶׁלֹּא שָׁתוּ: Plants that were not watered prior to the Festival may not be watered during the Festival, in accordance with the opinion of Rabbi Eliezer ben Ya'akov (Rambam *Sefer Zemanim, Hilkhot Yom Tov* 8:4).

PERSONALITIES

Rabbi Eliezer ben Ya'akov – רַבִּי אֱלִיעֶזֶר בֶּן יַעֲקֹב: There are two *tanna'im* by this name, one who lived during the Second Temple period, and the other who was a student of Rabbi Akiva. The Gemara comments in several places that the teaching of Rabbi Eliezer ben Ya'akov measures a *kav*, but is clean, meaning that it is small in quantity but clear and complete. This indicates that his opinion is followed in almost every case. This statement appears to refer to the earlier Sage. Rabbi Eliezer ben Ya'akov merited to see the service in the Second Temple prior to its destruction. Tractate *Middot*, which relates many traditions about the physical structure of the Temple, is attributed to him.

NOTES

One must reduce – יְמַעֵט: *Tosafot* note that the mishna is referring to reducing the ratio of seeds prior to sowing them, whereas the Gemara is referring to reducing the plants growing in the field once they have already been sown. Standing behind these *halakhot* is the fact that although diverse kinds of seeds may not be eaten, it is permitted to derive benefit from them. Therefore, at first the Sages merely ordained that the diverse kinds be removed from the field, and only when they saw that their ordinance caused property holders not to heed the prohibition at all, did they begin to declare the plants and fields ownerless.

One may draw water – מוֹשְׁכִין אֶת הַמַּיִם: Some commentaries explain this to mean that they would open the water channel that brought water to one tree, allowing the water to flow from there through channels to other trees. Others understand that when a large quantity of water would collect in the circular ditch beneath one tree, they would dig a channel to allow the water to flow from there to other trees as well (Rabbeinu Yehonatan; Ran; Meiri).

And provided that he does not water the entire field – וּבִלְבַד שֶׁלֹּא יַשְׁקֶה אֶת כׇּל הַשָּׂדֶה: The commentaries differ as to the nature of this field: Rashi and the Rid understand that it refers to a field that does not require irrigation. The Ra'avad identifies it as a field that requires irrigation but has not yet been sown, and one wishes to water it now in order to prepare it for future sowing. In the Jerusalem Talmud there is a distinction between a field where the trees are close together, in which case it is certainly permitted to water the trees as well as the areas between them, and a field where the trees are very spread out, in which case all agree that it is prohibited to water all the areas between the trees. This dispute is restricted to a case where there are ten trees within an area of fifty by fifty cubits. The dispute is whether they are considered to be planted close together or spread out (see *Tosefot HaRosh*).

Plants that were not watered – זְרָעִים שֶׁלֹּא שָׁתוּ: The commentaries dispute whether the determining factor in this passage is loss of property or the effort necessary to perform the labor. Rashi and most other commentaries understand that plants that were not watered prior to the Festival will not be harmed if they are not watered during the Festival, whereas refraining from watering plants that had already been watered before the Festival would result in the complete loss of those plants. The Rambam explains that plants that were not watered prior to the Festival require a great deal of water, and this would entail excessive effort.

גמ׳ אָמַר רַב יְהוּדָה: אִם הָיְתָה שָׂדֶה מְטוּנֶּנֶת – מוּתָּר. תַּנְיָא נַמִּי הָכִי: כְּשֶׁאָמְרוּ אָסוּר לְהַשְׁקוֹתָן בַּמּוֹעֵד – לֹא אָמְרוּ אֶלָּא בִּזְרָעִים שֶׁלֹּא שָׁתוּ מִלִּפְנֵי הַמּוֹעֵד, אֲבָל זְרָעִים שֶׁשָּׁתוּ לִפְנֵי הַמּוֹעֵד – מוּתָּר לְהַשְׁקוֹתָן בַּמּוֹעֵד.

GEMARA **Rav Yehuda said: If the field was moist** [*metunenet*][LN] before the Festival but in the meantime it dried up, **it is permitted** to water the entire field even according to Rabbi Eliezer ben Ya'akov. **That** ruling **is also taught** in a *baraita*: **When they said** that **it is prohibited to water them on** the intermediate days of **a Festival, they said this only with regard to plants that were not watered** at all **before the Festival. However,** with regard to **plants that were** already **watered before the Festival** and had begun to grow, **it is permitted to water them on** the intermediate days of **the Festival** because failure to water them would lead to substantial financial loss.

וְאִם הָיְתָה שָׂדֶה מְטוּנֶּנֶת – מוּתָּר. וְאֵין מַשְׁקִין שְׂדֵה גָּרִיד בַּמּוֹעֵד. וַחֲכָמִים מַתִּירִין בָּזֶה וּבָזֶה.

And if the field was moist before the Festival, **it is permitted** to water it even if the field had not been watered prior to the Festival. **And one may not water a dry field**[N] **on** the intermediate days of **a Festival. But the Rabbis permit** watering **this and that,** i.e., plants that were not watered before the Festival and a dry field.

אֲמַר רָבִינָא: שְׁמַע מִינָּהּ, הַאי תַּרְבִּיצָא שָׁרֵי לְתַרְבּוּצֵי בְּחוּלָּא דְמוֹעֲדָא. שְׂדֵה גָּרִיד מַאי טַעְמָא? דְּאַפְלָא מְשַׁוֵּי לָהּ חָרְפָּא; הָכָא נַמִּי – אַפְלָא מְשַׁוֵּי לָהּ חָרְפָּא.

Ravina said: Learn from here that one is permitted to sprinkle a garden [*tarbitza*][LN] with water **on the intermediate days of a Festival.**[H] Ravina explains how he arrived at this conclusion: **What is the reason** that the Rabbis permit one to water **a dry field**[N] despite the fact that the plants will not die from a lack of moisture? This is because watering the field in advance **turns a late crop into an early crop.**[B] It can be understood from this that the late ripening of a crop is considered a substantial financial loss that serves as a reason to permit labor that would otherwise be prohibited on the intermediate days of a Festival. **Here too,** in the case of a garden, sprinkling it with water **turns a late crop into an early crop,** and so it is permitted on the intermediate days of a Festival.

תָּנוּ רַבָּנַן: מַרְבִּיצִין שְׂדֵה לָבָן בַּשְּׁבִיעִית, אֲבָל לֹא בַּמּוֹעֵד.

The Sages taught the following *baraita*: **One may sprinkle** water in **a field of grain during the Sabbatical Year,**[H] **but not on the** intermediate days of **a Festival.**[N]

וְהָא תַּנְיָא: מַרְבִּיצִין בֵּין בַּמּוֹעֵד בֵּין בַּשְּׁבִיעִית! אָמַר רַב הוּנָא: לָא קַשְׁיָא: הָא – רַבִּי אֱלִיעֶזֶר בֶּן יַעֲקֹב, הָא – רַבָּנַן.

The Gemara asks: **But isn't it taught** in another *baraita*: **One may sprinkle** water in a field of grain **both on** the intermediate days of **a Festival and during the Sabbatical Year? Rav Huna said: This** is **not difficult. This** *baraita* that prohibits sprinkling water in a field of grain on the intermediate days of a Festival is in accordance with the opinion of **Rabbi Eliezer ben Ya'akov,** who prohibits watering an entire field. **That** *baraita* that permits it is in accordance with the more lenient opinion of **the Rabbis.**

LANGUAGE

Moist [*metunenet*] **– מְטוּנֶּנֶת:** Some say that this word is derived from the root *tin*, which means mud in Aramaic and Arabic. By extension, this led to the formation of the root *tanan*, meaning watering or moistening. Some maintain that in this sense, *tanan* is a verb of its own. This difference in opinion concerning the etymology of the root *tanan* may have contributed to the dispute about the meaning of a field that is *metunenet*: Does it refer to clay-like soil that had been wet but then became dry, or does it refer simply to a moist field?

Garden [*tarbitza*] **– תַּרְבִּיצָא:** Some maintain that this word, which is found in various Aramaic dialects, is derived from Assyrian, and it originally referred to a sheep pen. It is used here in the borrowed sense of a yard or garden. Others say that the term *rabbatz* means to be watered, and that this may be the source of the word *tarbitza* in the sense of a garden.

HALAKHA

Sprinkling water on a field during a Festival – הַרְבָּצַת שָׂדֶה בַּמּוֹעֵד: It is permitted to sprinkle a field with water during the intermediate days of a Festival, in accordance with the opinion of Ravina. However, the Ra'avad disagrees with this ruling, as he understands that Ravina follows the opinion of the Rabbis, rather than that of Rabbi Eliezer ben Ya'akov. The *Maggid Mishne*, however, explains that here too, the Rambam rules in accordance with Rabbi Eliezer ben Ya'akov, but that he is referring to plants that may be sprinkled with water during a Festival even before they are sown, because failure to do so would result in an irretrievable loss (Rambam *Sefer Zemanim*, *Hilkhot Yom Tov* 8:3).

Sprinkling water during the Sabbatical Year – הַרְבָּצַת שָׂדֶה בַּשְּׁבִיעִית: One may sprinkle a field of grain with water during the Sabbatical Year so that the trees do not suffer damage (Rambam *Sefer Zemanim*, *Hilkhot Shemitta VeYovel* 1:8).

BACKGROUND

Turns a late crop into an early crop – אַפְלָא מְשַׁוֵּי לָהּ חָרְפָּא: A lack of water in winter crops delays the development of their root systems, resulting in a general delay in the development of the plants. This ultimately causes the crop to ripen late. Early supplemental watering is likely to significantly quicken the ripening process.

NOTES

The field was moist – הָיְתָה שָׂדֶה מְטוּנֶּנֶת: Some explain that this is referring to a field that was previously watered but has since dried up, and the owner will suffer an irretrievable loss if the field is not watered again (Rashi; Rabbeinu Gershom Meor HaGola; *Talmid Rabbeinu Yeḥiel of Paris*). Others understand that this refers to a field that is naturally moist and therefore suffices with a small amount of water, and watering it does not require substantial effort (Rabbeinu Ḥananel; Rabbi Shlomo ben HaYatom; Rambam's Commentary on the Mishna). According to Rabbeinu Yehonatan, since the field is moist on its own, the plants are regarded as having been irrigated prior to the Festival.

A dry field – שְׂדֵה גָּרִיד: The *ge'onim* explain that this is a field one intends to sow at some later point and he is watering it now in advance. Others understand that this refers to an orchard (see *Tosafot*).

Garden [*tarbitza*] **– תַּרְבִּיצָא:** Most commentaries understand that a *tarbitza* is a vegetable garden, which requires only a little bit of water for the vegetables to grow. The Ra'avad explains similarly that a *tarbitza* is a garden of ornamental and aromatic plants, located in close proximity to a house; since it is shaded by the walls of the house it needs little water. The Rid explains that it is a field of flax, which must be sprinkled with water before being sown.

What is the reason that the Rabbis permit one to water a dry field – שְׂדֵה גָּרִיד מַאי טַעְמָא: This sentence is critical to understanding the entire passage. Rashi understands these words to be a continuation of the previous statement, meaning that Ravina's opinion is in accordance with that of the Sages. On the other hand, Rabbeinu Ḥananel and the Rif interpret these words as a challenge to the previous statement: Just as Rabbi Eliezer ben Ya'akov holds that it is prohibited to water a dry field because one will thereby cause the crop to ripen earlier, the same should be true in the case of a vegetable garden. According to this explanation, since the Gemara does not respond, Ravina's opinion has been rejected.

The Sabbatical Year and the intermediate days of a Festival – שְׁבִיעִית וּמוֹעֵד: In the Jerusalem Talmud, the differences between the *halakhot* of the Sabbatical Year and those governing the intermediate days of a Festival are explained in two different ways. According to one explanation, the difference lies in the fact that during the Sabbatical Year there is no general prohibition against labor, as it is only agricultural labor that is prohibited. According to the other explanation, the differences are due to the fact that the Sabbatical Year is a much longer period of time and there are tasks that cannot be postponed for an entire year.

תַּנְיָא אִידָךְ: מַרְבִּיצִין שְׂדֵה לָבָן עֶרֶב שְׁבִיעִית כְּדֵי שֶׁיֵּצְאוּ יְרָקוֹת בַּשְּׁבִיעִית. וְלֹא עוֹד אֶלָּא שֶׁמַּרְבִּיצִין שְׂדֵה לָבָן בַּשְּׁבִיעִית כְּדֵי שֶׁיֵּצְאוּ יְרָקוֹת לְמוֹצָאֵי שְׁבִיעִית.

It is taught in another *baraita*: **One may sprinkle** water in a **white field**[N] **on the eve of the Sabbatical Year so that vegetables will sprout during the Sabbatical Year; and not only that, but one may sprinkle** water in a **field of grain even during the Sabbatical Year** itself, **so that vegetables will sprout upon the conclusion of the Sabbatical Year.** Since sprinkling water is not regarded as full-fledged agricultural labor, it is permitted as long as the sprinkling and the sprouting of the vegetables do not both occur during the Sabbatical Year itself.

מתני׳ צָדִין אֶת הָאִישׁוּת וְאֶת הָעַכְבָּרִים מִשְּׂדֵה הָאִילָן וּמִשְּׂדֵה הַלָּבָן כְּדַרְכּוֹ, בַּמּוֹעֵד וּבַשְּׁבִיעִית. וַחֲכָמִים אוֹמְרִים: מִשְּׂדֵה הָאִילָן – כְּדַרְכּוֹ, וּמִשְּׂדֵה הַלָּבָן – שֶׁלֹּא כְּדַרְכּוֹ.

MISHNA **One may trap moles** [*ishut*][B] **and mice in an orchard and in a field of grain in his** usual **manner,** i.e., as he would trap them all year round, both **on** the intermediate days of **a Festival and during the Sabbatical Year.**[N] **But the Rabbis say: In an orchard** he may trap them **in his** usual **manner, but in a field of grain,** where there is no danger of substantial financial loss, he may only trap them in a way that is **not his** usual **manner.**[N]

וּמְקָרִין אֶת הַפִּירְצָה בַּמּוֹעֵד, וּבַשְּׁבִיעִית בּוֹנֶה כְּדַרְכּוֹ.

And one may seal a breach in the wall of his garden **on the** intermediate days of **a Festival, and during the Sabbatical Year one may** even **build** a wall **in his** usual **manner,** as this is not considered an agricultural labor. Consequently, despite the fact that this benefits the garden by offering it protection, it is not prohibited during the Sabbatical Year.

גמ׳ מַאי אִישׁוּת? אָמַר רַב יְהוּדָה: בְּרִיָּה שֶׁאֵין לָהּ עֵינַיִם. אָמַר רָבָא בַּר יִשְׁמָעֵאל, וְאִיתֵּימָא רַב יֵימַר בַּר שֶׁלַמְיָא: מַאי קְרָא? ״כְּמוֹ שַׁבְּלוּל תֶּמֶס יַהֲלֹךְ נֵפֶל אֵשֶׁת בַּל חָזוּ שָׁמֶשׁ״.

GEMARA The Gemara asks: **What is** meant by the term ***ishut*? Rav Yehuda said:** An *ishut* is **a creature that has no eyes,** a rodent that digs holes in the ground and can cause damage to roots and vegetables. **Rava bar Yishmael said, and some say** that it was **Rav Yeimar bar Shelamya** who **said: What is the verse** that indicates the identity of the *ishut*? **"As a snail that melts and disappears; like the fall of a young mole** [***eshet***] **that has not seen the sun"** (Psalms 58:9). It is understood that this creature has not seen the sun because it does not have eyes.

תָּנוּ רַבָּנַן: צָדִין אֶת הָאִישׁוּת וְאֶת הָעַכְבָּרִים מִשְּׂדֵה הַלָּבָן וּמִשְּׂדֵה הָאִילָן כְּדַרְכּוֹ, וּמַחְרִיבִין חוֹרֵי נְמָלִים. כֵּיצַד מַחֲרִיבִין? רַבָּן שִׁמְעוֹן בֶּן גַּמְלִיאֵל אוֹמֵר: מֵבִיא עָפָר מֵחוֹר זֶה וְנוֹתֵן לְתוֹךְ חוֹר זֶה, וְהֵן חוֹנְקִין זֶה אֶת זֶה.

The Gemara expands upon the *halakha* recorded in the mishna. **The Sages taught** the following *baraita*: **One may trap moles and mice in a field of grain and in an orchard in his** usual **manner, and one may destroy ant holes** so that the ants will cause no damage. **How does one destroy** ant holes? **Rabban Shimon ben Gamliel says: One brings soil from this** ant **hole and places it in that** ant **hole, and** since the ants from the two nests are not familiar with each other, **they strangle each other.**[B]

אָמַר רַב יֵימַר בַּר שֶׁלַמְיָא מִשְּׁמֵיהּ דְּאַבַּיֵי: וְהוּא דְּקָאֵי בִּתְרֵי עִבְרֵי נַהֲרָא, וְהוּא דְּלֵיכָּא גִּשְׁרָא, וְהוּא דְּלֵיכָּא גַּמְלָא, וְהוּא דְּלֵיכָּא מְצְרָא.

Rav Yeimar bar Shelamya said in the name of Abaye: And this advice works only in certain circumstances: **When** the ant holes **are** located **on two** opposite **sides of a river, when there is no bridge** connecting the two sides, **when there is not** even **a plank** bridge over the water, **and when there is not** even **a rope** stretched taut across the river. If there is any connection whatsoever between the two sides of the river, the ants from the two nests are likely to recognize each other and not fight.

NOTES

A white field – שְׂדֵה לָבָן: This term generally denotes a field of grain. However, Rashi explains that it is used here in a more general sense as a reference to a field that suffices with rainwater, similar to a field of grain.

A mole during the Sabbatical Year – אִישׁוּת בַּשְּׁבִיעִית: Rabbeinu Yehonatan explains that even though the process of trapping a mole in the ground looks like digging in preparation for planting a field, which is a prohibited agricultural labor during the Sabbatical Year, the Sages did not issue a decree prohibiting one from trapping it (see *Tosafot*).

From a field of grain in an unusual manner – מִשְּׂדֵה הַלָּבָן שֶׁלֹּא כְּדַרְכּוֹ: The Rambam, in his Commentary on the Mishna, explains that a mole causes only minor damage in a grain field, and the main concern is that the mole will move into an orchard. Therefore, in a field of grain one is not permitted to trap it in the usual manner.

BACKGROUND

Moles [*ishut*] – אִישׁוּת: Based on the descriptions in the Gemara, the *ishut* is the rodent referred to in the Torah as *ḥoled*, a member of the genus *spalax*. The species most commonly found in Eretz Yisrael is the *Spalax ehrenbergi*, which is 12–25 cm long with a cylindrical body and gray fur. Its tiny eyes are covered with fur and they become atrophied to the point that the animal is blind. The mole lives in the ground and digs tunnels, forming scattered mounds with the removed soil. It eats the roots of plants and can cause serious damage to crops.

Mole

The destruction of ant holes – הַחְרָבַת חוֹרֵי נְמָלִים: Every nest of ants has a particular scent that is affected by the scent of the soil and the objects that collect in the nest, including leftover food and deceased ants. Ants excrete a liquid with a particular odor from small nodes in their chests. Ants from the same nest that are separated for some time do not recognize each other as members of the same nest. When ants from a distant nest are introduced, they begin to fight and kill each other.

עַד כַּמָּה? עַד פַּרְסָה.

Up to what distance are the ant holes considered to be adjacent such that a river is required in order to separate between them? **Up to a parasang** [*parsa*].[N]

״רַבִּי יְהוּדָה אוֹמֵר מִשְּׂדֵה הָאִילָן כְּדַרְכּוֹ, וּמִשְּׂדֵה הַלָּבָן שֶׁלֹּא כְּדַרְכּוֹ״. תָּנוּ רַבָּנַן: כֵּיצַד כְּדַרְכּוֹ? חוֹפֵר גּוּמָא, וְתוֹלֶה בָּהּ מְצוּדָה. כֵּיצַד שֶׁלֹּא כְּדַרְכּוֹ? נוֹעֵץ שַׁפּוּד, וּמַכֶּה בְּקוּרְדּוֹם, וּמְרַדֶּה הָאֲדָמָה מִתַּחְתֶּיהָ.

§ We learned in the mishna that **Rabbi Yehuda says:**[N] **In an orchard** one may trap moles and mice **in his** usual **manner, but in a field of grain,** he may trap them only in a way that is **not his** usual **manner. The Sages taught** the following *baraita*: **How** does one trap **in his** usual **manner? He digs a hole** in the ground **and hangs a trap in it. How** does one trap in a way that is **not his** usual **manner? He inserts a spit**[N] into the ground where the rodents are suspected of hiding, **strikes** it **with a spade, and removes the earth from beneath it**[B] until he finds and kills the rodents.

תַּנְיָא, רַבִּי שִׁמְעוֹן בֶּן אֶלְעָזָר אוֹמֵר: כְּשֶׁאָמְרוּ ״מִשְּׂדֵה לָבָן שֶׁלֹּא כְּדַרְכּוֹ״ – לֹא אָמְרוּ אֶלָּא בִּשְׂדֵה לָבָן הַסְּמוּכָה לָעִיר, אֲבָל בִּשְׂדֵה לָבָן הַסְּמוּכָה לִשְׂדֵה הָאִילָן – אֲפִילּוּ כְּדַרְכּוֹ, שֶׁמָּא יֵצְאוּ מִשְּׂדֵה הַלָּבָן וְיַחֲרִיבוּ אֶת הָאִילָנוֹת.

It is taught in a *baraita* that **Rabbi Shimon ben Elazar says: When they said** that one may trap moles and mice **in a field of grain** on the intermediate days of a Festival[H] only in a way that is **not his** usual **manner, they spoke only with regard to a field of grain** that is **adjacent to the city,** where the damage is limited to that field and is not extensive. **But in a field of grain** that is **adjacent to an orchard,** one may trap **even in his** usual **manner, lest** the moles and mice **leave the field of grain and destroy the trees** in the adjacent orchard, causing great damage.

״וּמְקָרִין אֶת הַפִּירְצָה בַּמּוֹעֵד״. כֵּיצַד מְקָרִין? רַב יוֹסֵף אָמַר: בְּהוּצָא וְדַפְנָא.

§ It is taught in the mishna: **And one may seal a breach** in the wall of his garden **on** the intermediate days of a **Festival.** The Gemara asks: **How does one seal** such a breach? **Rav Yosef said: With palm branches** [*hutza*][L] **and** the branches of a **bay tree** [*dafna*],[NL] which do not create a significant partition, but simply a temporary barrier.

בְּמַתְנִיתָא תָּנָא: צָר בִּצְרוֹר וְאֵינוֹ טָח בְּטִיט. אָמַר רַב חִסְדָּא: לֹא שָׁנוּ אֶלָּא כּוֹתֶל הַגִּינָּה, אֲבָל כּוֹתֶל הֶחָצֵר – בּוֹנֶה כְּדַרְכּוֹ.

It was taught in a *baraita*: **One fills** in the breach **with stone, but he does not plaster** the stones **with clay.**[H] **Rav Ḥisda said: They taught** that he may seal a breach but not build a wall in his usual manner **only** with regard to **the wall of a garden,** as no significant loss will be suffered if he delays building until after the Festival. **However,** with regard to **the wall of a courtyard,** which prevents the entry of strangers who are likely to steal from him, **he may build** a wall **in his** usual **manner** even on the intermediate days of a Festival.

לֵימָא מְסַיַּיע לֵיהּ: כּוֹתֶל הַגּוֹחֶה לִרְשׁוּת הָרַבִּים – סוֹתֵר וּבוֹנֶה כְּדַרְכּוֹ מִפְּנֵי הַסַּכָּנָה? הָתָם כְּדְקָתָנֵי טַעְמָא: מִפְּנֵי הַסַּכָּנָה.

The Gemara suggests: **Let us say that** the following *baraita* **supports** Rav Ḥisda's statement: With regard to **a wall that is leaning** [*goḥeh*][L] **toward the public domain** and is likely to fall, **one may demolish and rebuild** it **in his** usual **manner** on the intermediate days of a Festival, **due to the danger**[N] that it poses to passersby. The Gemara rejects this opinion: **There, the reason is as** the *baraita* explicitly **teaches,** i.e., it is **due to the danger** that the wall poses to passersby, and not due to the protection that it affords the courtyard.

LANGUAGE

Palm branches [*hutza*] – **הוּצָא:** This Aramaic term is similar to the Hebrew *hutz* and the Arabic خوص, *hūṣ*. It refers to a palm branch, specifically after it has hardened and become sharp.

Bay tree [*dafna*] – **דַּפְנָא:** Rashi and others identify the *dafna* with the plant known today as bay, *Laurus nobilis*. The word *dafna* comes from the Greek name for this plant, δάφνη, *daphnē*.

Leans [*goḥeh*] – **גּוֹחֶה:** This term for "leans" is similar to the Hebrew *goḥen*, which refers to a person who is leaning.

BACKGROUND

Trapping a mole – **צֵיד הָאִישׁוּת:** These two methods were common in the past. If one wished to trap the animal or kill it when it was resting in its burrow, he had to locate the tunnel between the mounds that are visible on top of the ground, and insert a trap. If one killed the mole in the second way, then removing the soil beneath the mound, as suggested here, was apparently done in order to ensure that the mole would not escape, and to remove its carcass.

HALAKHA

Trapping pests during the intermediate days of a Festival – **צֵיד מַזִּיקִים בַּמּוֹעֵד:** Moles and mice that are found in an orchard or in a field of grain near an orchard may be trapped in the usual manner on the intermediate days of a Festival. If they are found in a field of grain that is not near an orchard, they may be trapped in a manner that is different than how they are usually trapped. The Rambam rules that in a field of grain that is near an orchard, the moles may be trapped in an unusual manner, whereas in a field of grain that is not near an orchard, they may not be trapped at all, in accordance with the opinion of Rabbi Shimon ben Elazar as recorded in some versions of the Gemara (*Beit Yosef*). The halakha is that no objection is raised toward those who are lenient, as most commentaries accept the lenient opinion. However, if possible, the trapping should be done by a gentile. In a case of significant loss, it may be done by the Jew himself in an unusual manner (*Kaf HaḤayyim*; *Shulḥan Arukh*, *Oraḥ Ḥayyim* 537:13).

Sealing a breach during the intermediate days of a Festival – **גִּידּוּר פִּירְצָה בַּמּוֹעֵד:** Construction is prohibited during the intermediate days of a Festival. If the wall separating an individual from his neighbor is breached (Rema), or if the fence around one's garden is breached, one may perform simple repairs such as replacing stones without cementing them in place, or fencing the area with reeds and branches, in accordance with the statement of Rav Yosef. If a wall adjacent to the public domain falls, it may be rebuilt in the usual manner. If the wall is leaning and in danger of collapse, it may be demolished and then rebuilt in the usual manner (*Shulḥan Arukh*, *Oraḥ Ḥayyim* 540:1).

NOTES

Up to a parasang [*parsa*] – **עַד פַּרְסָה:** Most commentaries maintain that a river is needed to separate between the two ant holes only when the distance between them is less than a parasang. However, if the distance is more than a parasang, no river is necessary (Rashi manuscript; Riaz; *Talmid Rabbeinu Yeḥiel of Paris*; however, see Rashi's second explanation and *Tosafot*.)

Rabbi Yehuda says – **רַבִּי יְהוּדָה אוֹמֵר:** This is a quote from the mishna on 6b. The version of the mishna that appears in the Vilna Talmud ascribes this quote to the Rabbis rather than to Rabbi Yehuda. However, according to the version of the mishna found in *Tosafot* and several other early commentaries, the mishna ascribes this statement to Rabbi Yehuda, in accordance with the Gemara here.

He inserts a spit – **נוֹעֵץ שַׁפּוּד:** Some commentaries explain that he pierces the ground with a spit repeatedly until the mole emerges, and then he catches it in a trap (Rabbeinu Gershom Meor HaGola; Meiri; Rabbeinu Yehonatan of Lunel).

Bay tree – **דַּפְנָא:** Rav Hai Gaon explains that a *hutza* is a fence of reeds, while *dafna* refers to the poles that hold up this fence. According to this, *dafna* is derived from the word *dofen*, meaning wall (Rabbeinu Yehonatan of Lunel of Lunel; *Nimmukei Yosef*; Ran).

Due to the danger – **מִפְּנֵי הַסַּכָּנָה:** Some understand that initially, the danger was thought to mean danger of theft. Consequently, no distinction was drawn between the wall of a courtyard and a wall abutting the public domain, as this consideration applies to both. Subsequently, the Gemara understood the danger to be referring to the physical danger of the wall collapsing (*Talmid Rabbeinu Yeḥiel of Paris*).

וְאִיכָּא דְּאָמְרִי, תָּא שְׁמַע: כּוֹתֶל הַגּוֹחֶה לִרְשׁוּת הָרַבִּים – סוֹתֵר וּבוֹנֶה כְּדַרְכּוֹ מִפְּנֵי הַסַּכָּנָה. מִפְּנֵי הַסַּכָּנָה – אִין; שֶׁלֹּא מִפְּנֵי הַסַּכָּנָה – לֹא. לֵימָא תֶּיהֱוֵי תְּיוּבְתֵּיהּ דְּרַב חִסְדָּא!

And some say that this *baraita* was cited not to support Rav Ḥisda's opinion but in order to refute it, as follows: **Come** and **hear** that which is taught in a *baraita*: With regard to **a wall that is leaning toward the public domain** and is likely to fall, **one may demolish and rebuild** it **in his usual manner, due to the danger** that it poses to passersby. The Gemara explains: The *baraita* indicates that if the need to build the wall is **due to the danger** that it poses, **yes,** he is permitted to rebuild the wall, but if the reason is **not due to the danger, no,** he is not permitted to do so. **Shall we say that this is a conclusive refutation of** the opinion of **Rav Ḥisda,** who says that one may build the wall of his courtyard in his usual manner, even if no danger is present?

אָמַר לָךְ רַב חִסְדָּא: הָתָם – סוֹתֵר וּבוֹנֶה; הָכָא – בּוֹנֶה וְלֹא סוֹתֵר.

The Gemara answers: **Rav Ḥisda** could have **said to you: There,** in the case where the existing wall poses a danger, **he is** even permitted to **demolish** the wall **and build** it from scratch. **Here,** in the case of an ordinary wall enclosing a courtyard, **he is permitted to build** the breached wall in the usual manner, **but not to demolish** it.

הָתָם נַמִי לִיסְתּוֹר וְלָא לִיבְנֵי! אִם כֵּן מִימְנַע וְלֹא סוֹתֵר.

The Gemara asks: **There too,** in the case of the leaning wall, let us say that he is permitted **to demolish** it and thereby remove the danger, **but not to rebuild** it until after the Festival. The Gemara answers: **If so, he might refrain** even **from demolishing** it, as demolishing the wall would leave his courtyard unprotected. Therefore, to eliminate the danger posed by the leaning wall, he is permitted not only to demolish it, but to rebuild it as well.

אָמַר רַב אַשִׁי: מַתְנִיתִין נַמִי דַּיְקָא, דְּקָתָנֵי: וּבַשְּׁבִיעִית בּוֹנֶה כְּדַרְכּוֹ.

Rav Ashi said: The wording of **the mishna is also precise** and indicates that it is referring to the wall of a garden, as understood by Rav Ḥisda, **as it teaches: During the Sabbatical Year one may** even **build in his usual manner.**[N]

דְּהֵיכָא? אִילֵימָא דְּחָצֵר – צְרִיכָא לְמֵימַר? אֶלָּא לָאו – דְּגִינָּה, וְאַף עַל גַּב דְּמֶיחֱזֵי כְּמַאן דְּעָבֵיד נְטִירוּתָא לְפֵירֵי? שְׁמַע מִינָּהּ.

The Gemara clarifies: **Where** is the wall to which the mishna refers? **If we say** that the mishna is referring to the wall **of a courtyard, need it be said** that it may be built during the Sabbatical Year? Only agricultural labors are prohibited during the Sabbatical Year, but construction is permitted. **Rather, is it not** referring to the wall **of a garden,** and it was necessary to state that this wall may be built during the Sabbatical Year to indicate that **even though he appears as one who is building a protection for his produce,**[N] he is nevertheless permitted to do so. This proves that the mishna's discussion pertains to building the wall of a garden. The Gemara concludes: **Learn from this** that Rav **Ḥisda's interpretation is** indeed the correct understanding of the mishna.

מתני׳ רַבִּי מֵאִיר אוֹמֵר: רוֹאִין אֶת הַנְּגָעִים בַּתְּחִילָּה לְהָקֵל, אֲבָל לֹא לְהַחְמִיר. וַחֲכָמִים אוֹמְרִים: לֹא לְהָקֵל וְלֹא לְהַחְמִיר.

MISHNA When symptoms of leprosy appear, they must be examined by a priest, who determines whether or not the symptoms qualify as leprosy. **Rabbi Meir says:** A priest[N] **may initially examine** an individual showing **symptoms of leprosy**[N] **on the intermediate days of a Festival**[H] in order **to be lenient,** i.e., he may pronounce the individual to be free of leprosy, **but not** in order **to be stringent;** he may not pronounce the individual to be impure. The individual does not become ritually impure until the priest pronounces him to have leprosy, and therefore the priest may remain silent and thereby prevent causing the afflicted individual distress during the Festival. **And the Rabbis say:** The priest may **not** examine the symptoms in order **to be lenient or** in order **to be stringent.**[N]

NOTES

During the Sabbatical Year one may even build in his usual manner – **בַּשְּׁבִיעִית בּוֹנֶה כְּדַרְכּוֹ**: The Meiri cites tractate *Shevi'it* of the Jerusalem Talmud, where a distinction is drawn between the wall of a courtyard facing the public domain and a wall between two neighbors, which may not be built even during the Sabbatical Year.

Protection for his produce – **נְטִירוּתָא לְפֵירֵי**: This could have been prohibited for two reasons: First, an action performed in order to protect one's produce is considered an agricultural labor and is consequently prohibited during the Sabbatical Year. Additionally, by guarding one's produce, one transgresses the mitzva to leave the produce ownerless and available for all. The reason it is permitted to build the wall is that he can leave the doors open (Rashi manuscript; Rabbeinu Yehonatan of Lunel).

The role of the priest in determining the ritual impurity of leprosy – **הַכֹּהֵן בְּטוּמְאַת נְגָעִים**: Leprosy is unique among ritual impurities in that the ritual purity is dependent not only upon specific symptoms, but also upon the determination of a priest. If an individual, a garment, or a house, which are all subject to leprosy, are stricken with leprous symptoms, they are not ritually impure until a priest determines this to be so. Moreover, a leper does not regain his ritual purity until a priest declares that he is pure. Even an exceedingly learned Sage may not declare ritual purity and impurity; rather, he must inform a priest who pronounces the individual to be either ritually pure or impure. As no one nowadays has reliable genealogical proof of his priesthood, the *halakhot* of leprosy are no longer applicable (*Minḥat Ḥinnukh* 169).

A symptom of leprosy – **נֶגַע הַצָּרַעַת**: The primary *halakhot* of leprosy are spelled out in the Torah (Leviticus, chapters 13–14) and in tractate *Nega'im*. If an individual finds a white spot on his skin he must appear before a priest, who is authorized to determine the status of the spot. He may declare the individual to be pure or to be a confirmed leper, or he may quarantine him for seven days and then examine him further. If he is quarantined, the individual is ritually impure and most of the laws that apply to a confirmed leper apply to him. After this initial quarantine the priest inspects the individual a second time; if there has been no change, he is quarantined for an additional seven days. If after this time there still has been no change in the symptoms, the individual is declared to be pure. However, if the leprous symptoms have increased or spread after either quarantine period, the priest declares the individual a confirmed leper. When the symptoms of leprosy eventually recede, the individual again appears before the priest; if the priest determines that he has indeed been cured, the leper counts seven days before bringing various purification offerings. Although the primary principles of leprosy are well explained, there are several issues that are not discussed in the Talmud, and are subject to dispute between the medieval commentaries. Their differences of opinion on these matters impact upon their interpretations of the Gemara's discussion here.

Not to be lenient or to be stringent – **לֹא לְהָקֵל וְלֹא לְהַחְמִיר**: Most commentaries explain that the dispute between Rabbi Meir and the Rabbis hinges upon the question of whether a priest is permitted to remain silent even after examining the leprous symptoms, or if he must declare the individual ritually pure or impure. The Ran explains that according to the Rabbis, the priest's silence is irrelevant to the case under discussion; even if he does not explicitly pronounce the individual to be ritually impure, since it is clear from his silence that the symptoms do constitute leprosy, he causes the individual distress on the Festival.

HALAKHA

Examining symptoms of leprosy during the intermediate days of a Festival – **רְאִיַּת נְגָעִים בַּמּוֹעֵד**: Leprous symptoms may not be examined during a Festival, lest an individual be found to be ritually impure and his celebration of the Festival turn into mourning. This applies even to an individual at the end of his first period of quarantine, contrary to the opinion of Rava (Rambam *Sefer Zemanim*, *Hilkhot Yom Tov* 7:16, and *Maggid Mishne* there).

גמ׳ תַּנְיָא, רַבִּי מֵאִיר אוֹמֵר: רוֹאִין אֶת הַנְּגָעִים לְהָקֵל, אֲבָל לֹא לְהַחְמִיר. רַבִּי יוֹסֵי אוֹמֵר: לֹא לְהָקֵל וְלֹא לְהַחְמִיר. שֶׁאִם אַתָּה נִזְקָק לוֹ לְהָקֵל – נִזְקָק לוֹ אַף לְהַחְמִיר.

GEMARA **It is taught** in a *baraita*: **Rabbi Meir says:** A priest **may examine** an individual showing **symptoms of leprosy on the intermediate days of a Festival** in order **to be lenient, but not** in order **to be stringent. Rabbi Yosei says:** The priest **may not** examine the symptoms **to be lenient or to be stringent.** The reasoning behind Rabbi Yosei's opinion is **that if you attend to** the individual with the symptoms of leprosy **to be lenient, you must attend to him even to be stringent.** If the priest sees that the symptom is in fact leprosy, he must declare the affected person ritually impure rather than remain silent. Consequently, in order to avoid declaring that he has leprosy on the Festival, the priest should not examine him at all.

אָמַר רַבִּי: נִרְאִין דִּבְרֵי רַבִּי מֵאִיר בְּמוּסְגָּר, וְדִבְרֵי רַבִּי יוֹסֵי בְּמוּחְלָט.

Rabbi Yehuda HaNasi **said: The statement of Rabbi Meir appears** to be correct **with regard** to the case of **a quarantined** leper. In this case, the priest may reexamine him at the end of the week even on the intermediate days of a Festival, because if he declares the individual to be pure, he will cause him to rejoice, and if he declares that the individual must be quarantined for another week, his situation is no worse than it was previously. On the other hand, **the statement of Rabbi Yosei appears** to be correct **with regard to** the case of **a confirmed** leper, one who has already been declared conclusively impure by a priest. The Gemara (7b) will explain the reason for this statement.

אָמַר רָבָא: בְּטָהוֹר – כּוּלֵּי עָלְמָא לָא פְּלִיגִי דְּלָא חָזוּ לֵיהּ. בְּהֶסְגֵּר רִאשׁוֹן – דְּכוּלֵּי עָלְמָא לָא פְּלִיגִי דְּחָזֵי לֵיהּ. כִּי פְּלִיגִי

Rava said: With regard to an individual with symptoms of leprosy who is still **ritually pure,** i.e., who has not yet been examined by a priest, **everyone agrees that** the priest **does not examine him,** as his status can only worsen due to the examination. **With regard to** a suspected leper who is in his **first** week of **quarantine,**[N] **everyone agrees that** the priest **examines him,** as the priest may declare him pure if his symptoms have subsided, and even if his symptoms remained as they were, he will simply be quarantined for another week. **When they disagree**

NOTES

His first week of quarantine – הֶסְגֵּר רִאשׁוֹן: *Tosafot* ask: Why does the priest examine a leper after the first quarantine on the intermediate days of a Festival when it is certainly possible that the leprous symptoms will have spread and the priest will be forced to declare the individual a confirmed leper? *Tosafot* answer that since at the end of the first quarantine the priest may extend the quarantine for an additional week, even Rabbi Yosei, who derives from the phrase: "to pronounce it pure or to pronounce it impure" (Leviticus 13:59), that the priest is generally not permitted to be silent, agrees that in this case, the priest may remain silent. The Meiri explains that signs of confirmed leprosy are usually not found at the end of the first quarantine, and therefore the possibility that this may occur is not taken into consideration. The *Divrei David* similarly explains that the symptom may disappear, and even if it does not, it may remain as it was; since the likelihood is that the symptom will not have spread, the priest examines the leper.

בְּהֶסְגֵּר שֵׁנִי. מָר סָבַר: בְּכֹהֵן תַּלְיָא מִילְּתָא. אִי טָהוֹר – אָמַר לֵיהּ טָהוֹר; וְאִי טָמֵא – שָׁתֵיק. וּמָר סָבַר: ״לְטַהֲרוֹ אוֹ לְטַמְּאוֹ״ כְּתִיב.

it is with regard to a suspected leper who is already in his **second** week of **quarantine. One Sage,** Rabbi Meir, **holds** that **the matter depends upon** the discretion of **the priest; if he is** found ritually **pure, the priest declares him pure, and if he is** found **ritually impure, the priest** can **remain silent.** As long as the priest does not declare the affected individual ritually impure, he does not become impure. **And one Sage,** Rabbi Yosei, **holds** that since **it is written:** "This is the law of the plague of leprosy… **to pronounce it pure or to pronounce it impure**" (Leviticus 13:59), the priest is not permitted to be silent; just as he is obligated to declare him pure when that is the case, so too, he is bound to declare him impure when his symptoms indicate impurity.

אָמַר מָר, אָמַר רַבִּי: נִרְאִין דִּבְרֵי רַבִּי יוֹסֵי בְּמוּחְלָט וְדִבְרֵי רַבִּי מֵאִיר בְּמוּסְגָּר. וְהָתַנְיָא אִיפְּכָא!

The Gemara proceeds to analyze the *baraita*. **The Master said** that **Rabbi Yehuda HaNasi said: The statement of Rabbi Yosei appears** correct **with regard to a confirmed leper,**[N] **and the statement of Rabbi Meir appears** correct **with regard to a quarantined** leper. The Gemara raises an objection: **But isn't the opposite taught** in a different *baraita*, namely, that Rabbi Yosei's statement appears correct with regard to the case of a quarantined leper, while Rabbi Meir's statement appears correct with regard to the case of a confirmed leper?

NOTES

The statement of Rabbi Yosei appears correct with regard to a confirmed leper – נִרְאִין דִּבְרֵי רַבִּי יוֹסֵי בְּמוּחְלָט: The interpretation of this passage depends upon some *halakhot* pertaining to a leper's quarantine that are not entirely clear. Some commentaries hold that a quarantined leper is forbidden to engage in conjugal relations and is expelled from the Israelite camp (*Tosafot*; Rashi manuscript). According to this opinion, Rabbi Meir's statement is more convincing because no additional stringency is added with regard to his relationship with his wife or with the world at large when he is declared a confirmed leper. There are, however, those who hold that a quarantined leper is permitted to engage in conjugal relations or that he is not expelled from the Israelite camp (Rashi; see *Tosefot HaRosh* and Ritva). According to these opinions, the status of a confirmed leper is significantly more severe than that of a quarantined leper.

תַּנָּאֵי הִיא אַלִּיבָּא דְּרַבִּי, מָר סָבַר צַוְותָא דְעָלְמָא עָדִיף לֵיהּ,

The Gemara answers: **This is** a dispute between ***tanna'im*** **in accordance with** the opinion of **Rabbi** Yehuda HaNasi. **One Sage,** the author of the latter *baraita,* **holds that the company of the world** at large **is preferable to** the leper. Consequently, the priest may examine a confirmed leper during the Festival because the priest will either decide that the leper's symptoms are still present, in which case the leper's situation will be no worse than before, or the priest will declare that his symptoms have subsided, in which case the leper may reenter the community, which will bring him joy.

וּמָר סָבַר צַוְותָא דְּאִשְׁתּוֹ עֲדִיפָא לֵיהּ.

And one Sage, the author of the *baraita* (7a), **holds that the company of his wife is preferable to** the leper. Consequently, the priest may not examine a confirmed leper on the Festival, because if he declares that his symptoms have subsided, the leper will begin his seven day purification process, during which time he is prohibited from engaging in conjugal relations with his wife. Due to the distress that this causes him, it is preferable that the priest not examine him at all during the Festival.

לְמֵימְרָא דִּמוּחְלָט מוּתָּר בְּתַשְׁמִישׁ הַמִּטָּה? אִין, וְהָתַנְיָא: ״וְיָשַׁב מִחוּץ לְאׇהֳלוֹ שִׁבְעַת יָמִים״ – שֶׁיְּהֵא אָסוּר בְּתַשְׁמִישׁ הַמִּטָּה. וְאֵין אׇהֳלוֹ אֶלָּא אִשְׁתּוֹ, שֶׁנֶּאֱמַר: ״לֵךְ אֱמוֹר לָהֶם שׁוּבוּ לָכֶם לְאׇהֳלֵיכֶם.״ רַבִּי יְהוּדָה אוֹמֵר: ״שִׁבְעַת יָמִים יִסְפְּרוּ לוֹ״ – יְמֵי סְפִירוֹ, וְלֹא יְמֵי חִלּוּטוֹ.

The Gemara asks: **Is this to say that a confirmed** leper **is permitted** to engage **in conjugal relations** with his wife? The Gemara answers: **Yes, and so** too **it is taught** in a *baraita*: With regard to a leper who is counting his seven days, it is written: **"But he shall remain outside his tent seven days"** (Leviticus 14:8). This verse teaches **that** the leper **is prohibited** from engaging **in conjugal relations,** as the words **his tent** refer **only to his wife, as it is stated: "Go, say to them: Return again to your tents"** (Deuteronomy 5:27).[N] **Rabbi Yehuda says:** The verse states: "And after he is cleansed, **they shall count for him seven days"** (Ezekiel 44:26),[N] indicating that he is prohibited from having conjugal relations during **the days of his counting, but not** during **the days of his confirmed** leprosy.[H]

רַבִּי יוֹסֵי בְּרַבִּי יְהוּדָה אוֹמֵר: שִׁבְעָה יְמֵי סְפִירוֹ, קַל וָחוֹמֶר לִימֵי חִלּוּטוֹ.

Rabbi Yosei, son of Rabbi Yehuda, says: Since the verse indicates that the prohibition to engage in conjugal relations applies during **the seven days of his counting** before becoming ritually pure, it follows based on an ***a fortiori*** inference that the prohibition should also apply during **the days of his confirmed** leprosy, when his impurity is more severe.

וְאָמַר רַבִּי חִיָּיא: דַּנְתִּי לִפְנֵי רַבִּי: לִימַּדְתָּנוּ רַבֵּינוּ, יוֹתָם לֹא הָיָה לוֹ לְעוּזִּיָּהוּ אֶלָּא בִּימֵי חִלּוּטוֹ. אָמַר לוֹ: אַף אֲנִי כָּךְ אָמַרְתִּי.

And Rabbi Ḥiyya said: I deliberated this matter **before Rabbi** Yehuda HaNasi[P] and said: **Have you not taught us, our teacher,** that King **Jotham was only** born **to Uzziah,**[N] the king of Judah, **during the days of his confirmed** leprosy? This would indicate that a confirmed leper is permitted to engage in conjugal relations. Rabbi Yehuda HaNasi **said to him: I too said this;** I am also of the opinion that a confirmed leper is permitted to engage in conjugal relations, in contrast to the opinion of Rabbi Yosei, son of Rabbi Yehuda.

בְּמַאי קָמִיפַּלְגִי? רַבִּי יוֹסֵי בְּרַבִּי יְהוּדָה סָבַר: גַּלֵּי רַחֲמָנָא בִּימֵי סְפִירוֹ, וְכׇל שֶׁכֵּן בִּימֵי חִלּוּטוֹ. וּמָר סָבַר: מַאי דְּגַלֵּי – גַּלֵּי, וּמַאי דְּלָא גַּלֵּי – לָא גַּלֵּי.

The Gemara asks: **With regard to what** principle do **they disagree?** The Gemara explains that **Rabbi Yosei, son of Rabbi Yehuda, holds: The Merciful One revealed** the prohibition of conjugal relations with one's wife **during the days of his counting; and all the more so** the prohibition applies **during his days of confirmed** leprosy, when his ritual impurity is more severe. **And one Sage,** Rabbi Yehuda, **maintains: That which** the verse **revealed, it revealed, but that which it did not reveal, it did not reveal;** the prohibition is not interpreted in a way that adds an extra stringency beyond what is stated explicitly in the Torah.

לְמֵימְרָא דִּבְכֹהֵן תַּלְיָא מִילְּתָא? אִין, וְהָתַנְיָא: ״וּבְיוֹם הֵרָאוֹת בּוֹ״ – יֵשׁ יוֹם שֶׁאַתָּה רוֹאֶה בּוֹ, וְיֵשׁ יוֹם שֶׁאִי אַתָּה רוֹאֶה בּוֹ.

§ The Gemara returns to the original dispute with regard to the priest's examination of the symptoms of leprosy. **Is this to say that the matter depends upon** the discretion of **the priest,** i.e., the priest can decide whether to declare the affected person ritually pure or impure or whether to examine the leprous symptoms or not? The Gemara answers: **Yes, and so** too **it is taught** in a *baraita*: The verse states: **"But on the day it appears in him"** (Leviticus 13:14), from which it may be inferred that **there is a day when you examine** the symptoms found in **him and there is a day when you do not examine** those symptoms.

NOTES

As it is stated…Return again to your tents – שֶׁנֶּאֱמַר...שׁוּבוּ לָכֶם לְאׇהֳלֵיכֶם: The proof is from the fact that prior to the giving of the Torah, the people were told: "Prepare yourselves for the third day; do not approach a woman" (Exodus 19:15). After the giving of the Torah, this prohibition was lifted with the words: Return again to your tents (Rashi manuscript; *Talmid Rabbeinu Yeḥiel of Paris*).

They shall count for him seven days – שִׁבְעַת יָמִים יִסְפְּרוּ לוֹ: The commentaries write that it was unnecessary to cite this verse as the matter could have been derived from the verse in Leviticus. This verse is cited here only because it is mentioned later in the tractate (15b) with regard to another topic (Rashi manuscript; see *Tosafot*).

Jotham was only born to Uzziah – יוֹתָם לֹא הָיָה לוֹ לְעוּזִּיָּה: The biblical proofs for Rabbi Ḥiyya's statement are discussed at length by *Tosafot*, the *She'iltot*, and many other commentaries. The primary difficulty lies in the fact that there is no clear record as to the year in Uzziah's reign when he became a leper, and the date can be determined only indirectly. This is further complicated by the fact that several verses concerning the dates of various kings of Judah and Israel cannot be easily reconciled (see II Kings 15:1, 8, 30; I Chronicles 5:11).

Some of the contradictions can be resolved with the assumption that Uzziah was considered the king even while afflicted with leprosy, yet it was his son, Jotham, who actually ruled during this period. Most commentaries understand that Uzziah became a leper in the twenty-seventh year of his fifty-two-year reign, and therefore it stands to reason that his son Jotham, who was twenty-five when he officially ascended to the throne, was conceived when Uzziah was already a leper. In accordance with Rabbi Yosei, son of Rabbi Yehuda, it may be suggested that Uzziah was stricken with leprosy at the end of the twenty-seventh year of his reign, and Jotham was conceived shortly before then (*Tosafot*).

HALAKHA

The *halakha* of a leper with regard to conjugal relations – מְצוֹרָע בְּתַשְׁמִישׁ הַמִּטָּה: A leper is permitted to engage in conjugal relations, in accordance with the opinion of Rabbi Yehuda, as Rabbi Yehuda HaNasi and Rabbi Ḥiyya agree with his opinion (Rambam *Sefer Tahara, Hilkhot Tumat Tzara'at* 10:6, and *Kesef Mishne* there).

PERSONALITIES

Rabbi Yehuda HaNasi – רַבִּי יְהוּדָה הַנָּשִׂיא: Rabbi Yehuda HaNasi closed the period of the *tanna'im* with his arrangement of the Mishna. The son of Rabban Shimon ben Gamliel II, he lived from 135–220 CE. When he was thirty years old he was appointed *Nasi*, or prince, and his great scholarship led him to be referred to in the Talmud simply as Rabbi. Rabbi Yehuda HaNasi spoke Greek, which was the language spoken by the elite in Eretz Yisrael, and he was friendly with the Roman Emperor, Antonius. His knowledge of Hebrew was legendary, to the extent that the Sages learned the meaning of difficult words by overhearing the speech of servants who worked in his house.

According to the Gemara (*Gittin* 59a), from the time of Moses until Rabbi Yehuda HaNasi, Torah scholarship and prominent leadership were not found in a single individual. His life's work was the collection of oral traditions and opinions that he wove into the Mishna, which serves as the basis for the Talmud that is studied to this day.

His students were the Sages of the first generation of *amora'im*, including Rabbi Yoḥanan, Rabbi Ḥiyya, Rav, and bar Kappara.

מִכָּאן אָמְרוּ: חָתָן שֶׁנּוֹלַד בּוֹ נֶגַע – נוֹתְנִין לוֹ שִׁבְעַה יְמֵי הַמִּשְׁתֶּה, לוֹ וּלְבֵיתוֹ וְלִכְסוּתוֹ. וְכֵן בָּרֶגֶל, נוֹתְנִין לוֹ שִׁבְעַת יְמֵי הָרֶגֶל, דִּבְרֵי רַבִּי יְהוּדָה.

From here they stated: With regard to **a bridegroom upon whom leprous symptoms came into being,**[H] **we give him the seven days of the** wedding **feast** before the examination that determines ritual purity or impurity. This ruling applies whether the leprous symptoms appeared **upon him, upon his house, or upon his clothing. Similarly,** if the symptoms of leprosy appeared upon an individual **during a pilgrimage Festival, we give him the seven days of the Festival** in order to avoid causing him distress during that time; this is **the statement of Rabbi Yehuda.**

רַבִּי אוֹמֵר: אֵינוֹ צָרִיךְ, הֲרֵי הוּא אוֹמֵר: ״וְצִוָּה הַכֹּהֵן וּפִנּוּ אֶת הַבַּיִת״, אִם מַמְתִּינִים לוֹ לִדְבַר הָרְשׁוּת – כָּל שֶׁכֵּן לִדְבַר מִצְוָה.

Rabbi Yehuda HaNasi **says:** The ruling is correct, but **there is no need** to prove it from this verse, as a much simpler proof can be brought from a different source. **It says: "Then the priest shall command that they empty the house** before the priest goes into it to see the plague, so that all that is in the house be not made unclean" (Leviticus 14:36). **If we delay** the priest's examination of the house in order to give the owner time to remove his utensils and prevent them from contracting ritual impurity, which is merely **an optional matter, all the more so** should we delay his examination **for a matter of mitzva,** e.g., so as not to detract from the bridegroom's joy or from the joy of a Festival.

מַאי בֵּינַיְיהוּ? אָמַר אַבַּיֵי: מַשְׁמָעוּת דּוֹרְשִׁין אִיכָּא בֵּינַיְיהוּ. וְרָבָא אָמַר: דְּבַר הָרְשׁוּת אִיכָּא בֵּינַיְיהוּ.

The Gemara asks: **What is** the practical difference **between them,** whether the source of the *halakha* is one verse or another? **Abaye said:** There is no practical difference between the opinions; rather, **the interpretation of the meaning** of the verses[N] is the difference **between them,** as each has a different interpretation of the verse from which the other derived this *halakha*. **And Rava said:** There is in fact a practical difference **between them** with regard to whether or not one delays the examination of leprous symptoms found on an individual's body for **an optional matter.** Rabbi Yehuda holds that one delays the examination only for the sake of a mitzva, while Rabbi Yehuda HaNasi holds that one may delay it even for the sake of an optional matter.

וְרַבִּי יְהוּדָה: מֵהָתָם לָא גָּמְרִינַן, דְּחִידּוּשׁ הוּא,

The Gemara asks: **And** according to the opinion of **Rabbi Yehuda,** why is it not permitted to delay the priest's examination of leprous symptoms on an individual's body for an optional matter, just as with regard to leprous symptoms on one's house? The Gemara answers: **We do not learn** a halakhic principle **from there because** the *halakha* of leprosy of houses **is** itself **a novelty,**[N] a unique biblical law from which one cannot extrapolate to other cases.

HALAKHA

A bridegroom upon whom leprous symptoms came into being – חָתָן שֶׁנּוֹלַד בּוֹ נֶגַע: A bridegroom upon whom leprous symptoms have appeared is given all seven days of his wedding feast before he must be examined by a priest. The same *halakha* applies if leprous symptoms appeared on his clothes or house. Similarly, based on an *a fortiori* inference, one is given all seven days of a Festival in a case of leprosy of houses, in accordance with the opinion of Rabbi Yehuda HaNasi (Rambam *Sefer Tahara, Hilkhot Tumat Tzara'at* 9:8; see *Mishne LaMelekh*).

NOTES

The interpretation of the meaning of the verses – מַשְׁמָעוּת דּוֹרְשִׁין: This expression may be understood to mean that there is actually no halakhic difference between these two opinions, but only a difference in explaining the verses. It seems, however, that a difference with regard to the source of the *halakha* affects other exegetical interpretations of the verses in question, so that while there may be no halakhic difference in this case, there could conceivably be a halakhic difference in other cases whose *halakhot* are derived from these verses.

A novelty – חִידּוּשׁ: Many *halakhot* are derived by way of analogies, which apply exegetical inferences from the details of a particular case to other similar cases. However, when the detail is unique and has particular elements that set it apart from other areas, it is considered a novelty, which cannot be extended to other cases.

Perek **I**
Daf **8** Amud **a**

דְּהָא עֵצִים וַאֲבָנִים בְּעָלְמָא לָא מִטַּמְּאוּ, וְהָכָא מִטַּמְּאוּ.

The Gemara explains that the *halakha* of leprous symptoms on a house constitutes a novelty, **as** by Torah law, **wood and stones are generally not susceptible to ritual impurity, yet here** in the case of house leprosy **they are susceptible to ritual impurity.**

וְרַבִּי אָמַר: אִצְטְרִיךְ. דְּאִי כְּתַב רַחֲמָנָא ״וּבְיוֹם הֵרָאוֹת בּוֹ״ – הֲוָה אָמִינָא: לִדְבַר מִצְוָה – אִין, לִדְבַר הָרְשׁוּת – לָא. כְּתַב רַחֲמָנָא ״וְצִוָּה הַכֹּהֵן״.

And Rabbi Yehuda HaNasi **said: It was necessary** for the Torah to state both verses: "But on the day it appears in him" (Leviticus 13:14), as well as: "Then the priest shall command that they empty the house" (Leviticus 14:36). **As, if the Merciful One had written** only: **"But on the day it appears in him," I would have said** that **for a matter of mitzva, yes,** one may delay the priest's examination of the leprous symptoms, but **for an optional matter, no,** one may not, in accordance with the opinion of Rabbi Yehuda. Therefore **the Merciful One wrote: "Then the priest shall command,"** in order to teach that one may delay his examination even for an optional matter.

וְאִי כְּתַב רַחֲמָנָא ״וְצִוָּה הַכֹּהֵן״ – הֲוָה אָמִינָא: הָנֵי – אִין, דְּלָאו טוּמְאָה דְּגוּפֵיהּ. אֲבָל טוּמְאָה דְּגוּפֵיהּ – אֵימָא מֶיחֱזֵא חָזֵא לֵיהּ. צְרִיכָא.

And conversely, **if the Merciful One had written** only: **"Then the priest shall command,"** I **would have said** that **for these** utensils that are found in the house, **yes,** one may delay the priest's examination, as this is **not** a case of **impurity of the** individual's **body**[N] but only that of his possessions; **but** in a case of **impurity of** the individual's **body, I** would **say** that the priest **must examine it** immediately. Therefore, it is **necessary** for the Torah to state that even in this case, one may delay his examination.

אָמַר מָר: יֵשׁ יוֹם שֶׁאַתָּה רוֹאֶה בּוֹ וְיֵשׁ יוֹם שֶׁאִי אַתָּה רוֹאֶה בּוֹ.

§ The Gemara proceeds to analyze the aforementioned *baraita*. **The Master said** that as the verse states: "But on the day it appears in him," it may be inferred that **there is a day when you examine** the symptoms found in **him and there is a day when you do not examine** those symptoms.

מַאי מַשְׁמַע? אָמַר אַבָּיֵי: אִם כֵּן לִיכְתּוֹב רַחֲמָנָא ״בְּיוֹם״. מַאי ״וּבְיוֹם״? שְׁמַע מִינָּהּ: יֵשׁ יוֹם שֶׁאַתָּה רוֹאֶה בּוֹ וְיֵשׁ יוֹם שֶׁאִי אַתָּה רוֹאֶה בּוֹ.

The Gemara asks: **From where** in this verse **may it be inferred? Abaye said: If** it were **so** that the priest must always examine the symptoms immediately, **the Merciful One should have written** simply: **On the day** it appears in him. **What is** implied by the actual formulation of the verse: **"But on the day"? Learn from here,** i.e., from the seemingly superfluous word "but" at the beginning of the phrase, that this is not an absolute *halakha*, but a conditional one, depending upon other factors: **There is a day when you examine** the leprous symptoms found in **him and there is a day when you do not examine** those symptoms.

רָבָא אָמַר: כּוּלֵּהּ קְרָא יְתֵירָא הוּא. דְּאִם כֵּן לִכְתּוֹב רַחֲמָנָא ״וּבְהֵרָאוֹת״. מַאי ״וּבְיוֹם״? שְׁמַע מִינָּהּ: יֵשׁ יוֹם שֶׁאַתָּה רוֹאֶה בּוֹ, וְיֵשׁ יוֹם שֶׁאִי אַתָּה רוֹאֶה בּוֹ.

Rava offered a different explanation and **said: The entire phrase** "but on the day," **is superfluous. As, if** it were **so** that the priest must always examine the symptoms immediately, **the Merciful One should have written** simply: **And when it appears. What is** the meaning of the additional words **"but on the day"? Learn from here** that the issue is dependent upon other factors, as **there is a day when you examine** the symptoms of leprosy **in him and there is a day when you do not examine** them.

וְאַבָּיֵי: הַהוּא מִיבְּעֵי לֵיהּ: בַּיּוֹם וְלֹא בַּלַּיְלָה.

The Gemara explains: **And** according to **Abaye,** who derives the *halakha* from the word "but," why does the verse include the phrase "on the day"? **That** phrase **is necessary** in order to teach that the priest examines the symptoms of leprosy only **during the day, but not at night.**[H]

וְרָבָא, בַּיּוֹם וְלֹא בַּלַּיְלָה מְנָא לֵיהּ? נָפְקָא לֵיהּ מִ״לְּכָל מַרְאֵה עֵינֵי הַכֹּהֵן״. וְאַבָּיֵי: הַהוּא מִיבְּעֵי לֵיהּ לְמַעוּטֵי סוּמָא בְּאַחַת מֵעֵינָיו.

The Gemara asks: **And from where** does **Rava** derive the *halakha* that the examination is performed **during the day but not at night?** The Gemara answers: **He derives it from** the verse: **"As far as the priest's eyes can see"** (Leviticus 13:12), which indicates that the priest must be able to carry out a careful examination of the leprous symptoms; this cannot be done at night, when his vision is limited. **And Abaye** could say that **this** verse **is necessary to exclude** a priest who is **blind in one eye**[H] from inspecting symptoms of leprosy, as it says "eyes," in the plural.

וְרָבָא נַמִי מִיבְּעֵי לֵיהּ לְהָכִי! אִין, הָכִי נַמִי.

The Gemara asks: **But Rava also requires** this verse **to** teach **this** *halakha*, i.e., that a priest who is blind in one eye is unfit to examine symptoms of leprosy. The Gemara answers: **Yes, it is indeed so;** he agrees that this verse is the source of the *halakha* concerning a priest who is blind in one eye, and it is not the source of the *halakha* that the priest may only view leprous symptoms by day.

וְאֶלָּא בַּיּוֹם וְלֹא בַּלַּיְלָה מְנָא לֵיהּ? נָפְקָא לֵיהּ מִ״כְּנֶגַע נִרְאָה לִי בַּבָּיִת״, לִי – וְלֹא לְאוֹרִי.

If so, **from where** does Rava derive the *halakha* that a priest examines leprous symptoms **during the day but not at night?** The Gemara answers: **He derives it from** the verse that quotes a homeowner saying to a priest: **"There seems to me as it were a plague in the house"** (Leviticus 14:35), which emphasizes that the leprous symptom is seen **by me, and not by** way of **my light,** i.e., that this takes place during the day. When the next verse states that the priest comes to view the leprous symptom, it means that this also takes place by day.

NOTES

Impurity of the individual's body – **טוּמְאָה דְּגוּפֵיהּ**: Rashi seems to distinguish between ritual impurity in general and ritual impurity due to leprosy of houses, which is a novelty. The *Talmid Rabbeinu Yeḥiel of Paris* distinguishes between ritual impurity originating from one's body and ritual impurity that is contracted from external sources (see *Tal Hayyim*).

HALAKHA

Examining leprous symptoms during the day – **רְאִיַּת נְגָעִים בַּיּוֹם**: Leprous symptoms may be examined only during the day, whether to determine if the leper should be quarantined, declared a confirmed leper, or declared pure (Rambam *Sefer Tahara, Hilkhot Tumat Tzara'at* 9:6).

A blind priest – **כֹּהֵן סוּמָא**: A priest who is blind in one eye or whose eyesight has grown dim is unfit to examine leprous symptoms (Rambam *Sefer Tahara, Hilkhot Tumat Tzara'at* 9:5).

וְאַבַּיֵי: אִי מֵהָתָם הֲוָה אָמֵינָא: הָנֵי מִילֵּי – טוּמְאָה דְּלָאו דְּגוּפֵיהּ, אֲבָל טוּמְאָה דְּגוּפֵיהּ – אֲפִילּוּ לְאוֹרוֹ נַמִּי, קָא מַשְׁמַע לַן.

And why does **Abaye** require the proof that he adduces when it would seem that the verse that Rava brings offers sufficient proof? The Gemara explains: According to Abaye, **if** the source was derived **from there, I would have said** that **this** *halakha*, that one must wait until the light of day to examine the symptom, **applies** only to leprous symptoms on a house, which is **an impurity that is not** related to **the** individual's **body. However,** in a case of **impurity of the** individual's **body,** perhaps the priest may conduct his examination **even by** artificial **light,** as it is a more severe impurity. Therefore the verse **teaches us:** "But on the day," to indicate that even in the case of impurity of the body the priest may perform the examination only during the day by natural sunlight, and not by any artificial light.

מתני׳ וְעוֹד אָמַר רַבִּי מֵאִיר: מְלַקֵּט אָדָם עַצְמוֹת אָבִיו וְאִמּוֹ, מִפְּנֵי שֶׁשִּׂמְחָה הִיא לוֹ.

MISHNA **Rabbi Meir also stated** another leniency concerning the *halakhot* of the intermediate days of a Festival: **A person may gather the bones of his father and mother** from their temporary graves on the intermediate days of a Festival. In ancient times, it was customary to first bury a corpse in a temporary grave. After the flesh had decomposed, the bones would be collected, placed in a coffin, and buried in a vault together with the bones of the deceased individual's ancestors. This is permitted on the intermediate days of a Festival **because** the fact that one merited to bring the bones of his deceased parents to the graves of their ancestors **is** a source of **joy for him.**[N]

רַבִּי יוֹסֵי אוֹמֵר: אֵבֶל הוּא לוֹ.

Rabbi Yosei says: One does not gather these bones on the intermediate days of a Festival, because **it is** a source of **mourning for him.**[NH] Even though he is happy to be able to bury his parents' bones in their ancestral graves, he is still pained by the memory of their death.

לֹא יְעוֹרֵר אָדָם עַל מֵתוֹ וְלֹא יַסְפִּידֶנּוּ קוֹדֶם לָרֶגֶל שְׁלֹשִׁים יוֹם.

And all agree that **a person may not arouse** [*ye'orer*] **lamentation**[NL] **for his deceased** relative, **and he may not eulogize him** during the **thirty days before a pilgrimage Festival.**[H]

גמ׳ וּרְמִינְהוּ: הַמְלַקֵּט עַצְמוֹת אָבִיו וְאִמּוֹ – הֲרֵי זֶה מִתְאַבֵּל עֲלֵיהֶם כָּל הַיּוֹם, וְלָעֶרֶב אֵין מִתְאַבֵּל עֲלֵיהֶן. וְאָמַר רַב חִסְדָּא: אֲפִילּוּ צְרוּרִין לוֹ בִּסְדִינוֹ!

GEMARA The Gemara **raises a contradiction** to Rabbi Meir's opinion that gathering the bones of one's parents is considered an occasion of joy, based on what is taught in a *baraita*: **One who gathers the bones of his father or his mother mourns for them the entire day, but he does not mourn for them in the evening.**[H] **And Rav Ḥisda said: And even** in a case where he does not gather the bones from a temporary grave, but where **he had them bundled up in his sheet,**[N] when he buries them he mourns for them all day. This indicates that gathering one's parents' bones is an occasion of mourning rather than joy.

NOTES

The joy of gathering bones – שִׂמְחַת לִיקּוּט עֲצָמוֹת: Rashi explains that the individual is happy because he has merited burying his parents' bones in their ancestral burial plots. It is explained in the Jerusalem Talmud that his joy stems from the fact that once the flesh of the deceased has decomposed, his transgressions have been forgiven. The Ra'avya suggests that he is happy because worms are no longer consuming his parents' flesh.

It is a source of mourning for him – אֵבֶל הוּא לוֹ: Most commentaries understand that it is a sad occasion for him because he sees his parents' skeletons, but Rabbeinu Yehonatan of Lunel explains that the source of his distress is that when he sees the skeletons he is reminded of death.

A person may not arouse [*ye'orer*] lamentation – לֹא יְעוֹרֵר: The commentaries differ in their explanations of the difference between this phrase and the next. It is explained in the Jerusalem Talmud that eulogizing refers to a eulogy in memory of that individual, whereas arousing lamentation occurs when the deceased individual is mentioned during a eulogy for someone else. The *Sefer Hashlama* suggests that arousing lamentation refers to eulogizing a great deal during the period of mourning. *Talmid Rabbeinu Yeḥiel of Paris* explains that it refers to memorial services that were held on the seventh or thirtieth day of the mourning period. Alternatively, it refers to the eulogizer passing among the relatives of the deceased and urging them to participate in the eulogy.

Even where he had them bundled up in his sheet – אֲפִילּוּ צְרוּרִין בִּסְדִינוֹ: Some commentaries explain that Rav Ḥisda means to say that one who gathers the bones of his father or mother must mourn for them even if the bones were bundled up in a sheet and not visible to him (Rashi; Rabbeinu Gershom Meor HaGola). Others say that whenever he unties the sheet he is obligated to mourn for them (Commentary on *Moed Katan*). Still others say that he means that he does not mourn for them in the evening, even if the bones are bundled in a sheet and have not yet been reinterred (*Talmid Rabbeinu Yeḥiel of Paris*; *Tosafot*; Rambam; Rosh).

LANGUAGE

Arouse [*ye'orer*] lamentation – יְעוֹרֵר: This seems to be a unique usage of the verb *or*, in the sense of raising one's voice in sorrow and weeping, used specifically with regard to eulogies. The commentaries have noted the connection to the verse: "Those who are ready to arouse [*orer*] the leviathan" (Job 3:8).

HALAKHA

Gathering bones during a Festival – לִיקּוּט עֲצָמוֹת בַּמּוֹעֵד: One may not gather his parents' bones during a Festival, and certainly not the bones of other relatives, in accordance with the opinion of Rabbi Yosei, whose opinion is accepted as *halakha* when he disagrees with a colleague (*Shulḥan Arukh, Yoreh De'a* 403:4).

Eulogy before a Festival – הֶסְפֵּד קוֹדֶם הַמּוֹעֵד: During the thirty days before a Festival one may not eulogize an individual who died prior to this period. It is permitted to eulogize someone who died within this thirty-day period (Jerusalem Talmud); however, one may not eulogize another individual who died prior to this period along with the individual who died during this period. In the case of a Torah scholar who died before this time period, there are some who prohibit eulogizing him within thirty days of the Festival and some who permit it (*Mishna Berura*, citing *Peri Megadim*). With regard to this *halakha*, Rosh HaShana and Yom Kippur are not considered Festivals (*Pitḥei Teshuva*), and it is permitted to eulogize during the entire month of Elul (Ramban, citing Rav Nissim Gaon). Everything stated above is according to the majority of the halakhic authorities, who rule in accordance with the opinion of Shmuel (Rambam; Ra'avad; *Smag*; Rosh; Ritva). However, some rule in accordance with the opinion of Rav, as is the general policy in the area of ritual law (Rabbi Yitzḥak ibn Giat; *Tosafot*; Ramban), and maintain that whereas it is prohibited to pay for a eulogizer within thirty days of a Festival, it is permitted to eulogize without pay. According to this opinion, it makes no difference whether the individual being eulogized died before or during this time period. The *Shulḥan Arukh* rules in accordance with the opinion of Shmuel (*Shulḥan Arukh, Oraḥ Hayyim* 547:3; *Yoreh De'a* 347:1).

Mourning when gathering bones – אֲבֵלוּת בְּלִיקּוּט עֲצָמוֹת: One who gathers the bones of his parents must observe all the rites of mourning for the entire day, but he does not mourn for them in the evening, even if the bones are still bundled in a sheet, in accordance with the statement of Rav Ḥisda (*Shulḥan Arukh, Yoreh De'a* 403:1).

אָמַר אַבַּיֵי: אֵימָא, מִפְּנֵי שֶׁשִּׂמְחַת הָרֶגֶל עָלָיו.

Abaye said: Say that Rabbi Meir means that collecting and reinterring the bones of one's parents is permitted on the intermediate days of a Festival, not because it causes one joy, but rather **because the joy of the pilgrimage Festival is upon him.**[N] The pain of gathering the bones of his parents is overpowered by the joy of the Festival.

"וְלֹא יְעָרֵעַר עַל מֵתוֹ". מַאי לֹא יְעָרֵעַר עַל מֵתוֹ? אָמַר רַב: כַּד הָדַר סַפְדָּנָא בְּמַעְרְבָא אָמְרִי: יִבְכּוּן עִמֵּיהּ כָּל מְרִירֵי לִיבָּא.

§ It is taught in the mishna: **One may not arouse** lamentation **for his deceased** relative during the thirty days before a Festival. The Gemara asks: **What is** meant by: **One may not arouse** lamentation **for his deceased** relative? **Rav said: In the West,**[B] Eretz Yisrael, **whenever** a professional **eulogizer would circulate** and ply his trade, **they would say: Let all those of bitter heart weep with him.**[N] When they would say this, all those who had recently suffered losses would recall their pain and lament their losses.

"קוֹדֶם הָרֶגֶל שְׁלֹשִׁים יוֹם". מַאי שְׁנָא שְׁלֹשִׁים יוֹם?

It is taught in the mishna that one may not arouse lamentation or eulogize his relative for **thirty days before a pilgrimage Festival.**[N] The Gemara asks: **What is different** about **thirty days,** that it is prohibited for one to lament the dead for specifically that amount of time before the Festival?

אָמַר רַב כַּהֲנָא אָמַר רַב יְהוּדָה אָמַר רַב: מַעֲשֶׂה בְּאָדָם אֶחָד שֶׁכִּינֵּס מָעוֹת לַעֲלוֹת לָרֶגֶל, וּבָא סַפְדָּן וְעָמַד עַל פֶּתַח בֵּיתוֹ, וּנְטָלָתַן אִשְׁתּוֹ וּנְתָנָתַן לוֹ, וְנִמְנַע וְלֹא עָלָה. בְּאוֹתָהּ שָׁעָה אָמְרוּ: לֹא יְעוֹרֵר עַל מֵתוֹ, וְלֹא יַסְפִּידֶנּוּ קוֹדֶם לָרֶגֶל שְׁלֹשִׁים יוֹם.

Rav Kahana said that Rav Yehuda said that Rav said: There was an **incident** involving **a certain man who saved up money to ascend** to Jerusalem **for the pilgrimage Festival.** A professional **eulogizer came and stood at the opening to his house and** the man's **wife took** the money that he had saved **and gave it to** the eulogizer for his services. As a result, the man did not have enough money and **he refrained and did not ascend** to Jerusalem for the Festival. **At that time, they said: One may not arouse** lamentation **for his deceased** relative, **nor may** he **eulogize him** during the **thirty days before a pilgrimage Festival.**

וּשְׁמוּאֵל אָמַר:

And Shmuel said:

Perek **I**
Daf **8** Amud **b**

לְפִי שֶׁאֵין הַמֵּת מִשְׁתַּכֵּחַ מִן הַלֵּב שְׁלֹשִׁים יוֹם. מַאי בֵּינַיְיהוּ? אִיכָּא בֵּינַיְיהוּ דְּקָעָבֵיד בְּחִנָּם.

It is **because the dead is not forgotten from the heart** and put out of mind **for thirty days,** and therefore, when one laments the loss of a deceased relative within thirty days before a Festival, the pain is still remembered on the Festival. The Gemara asks: **What is** the practical difference **between** the two reasons? The practical difference **between them** is in a case **where** the eulogizer **performs** the eulogy **free** of charge.[N] In that case there is no worry that money that had been set aside for the Festival will be spent, but there is still room for concern about the lingering pain that will be felt on the Festival.

NOTES

Because the joy of the pilgrimage Festival is upon him – **מִפְּנֵי שֶׁשִּׂמְחַת הָרֶגֶל עָלָיו:** Rashi explains that the joy of the Festival overpowers his pain. Alternatively, many commentaries understand that since one does not observe the general customs of mourning on the intermediate days of a Festival, the mourning that is associated with reinterring the bones will not overpower the joy of the Festival (Rid; Rabbeinu Yehonatan of Lunel; Meiri). According to this approach, Rabbi Yosei's reasoning is that even though one does not observe the customs of mourning during the Festival, he still feels pain in his heart, and it is prohibited to cause oneself pain during a Festival.

Let all those of bitter heart weep with him – **יִבְכּוּן עִמֵּיהּ כָּל מְרִירֵי לִיבָּא:** Some explain that the eulogizer would recite these words in his eulogy and in this way he would arouse the mourners to recall their grief. Others, among them the Ritva, suggest that the eulogizer would say these words when inviting people to come hear a eulogy, or else that he would say this to advertise his expertise and encourage mourners to hire him (Ran).

Thirty days before a pilgrimage Festival – **קוֹדֶם הָרֶגֶל שְׁלֹשִׁים יוֹם:** This period was chosen because thirty days before a Festival one begins to expound the *halakhot* of that Festival. Consequently, people are reminded of the upcoming Festival and begin to prepare their finances for the expenses of the Festival (Rashi manuscript; Rashba; Ritva).

BACKGROUND

The West – **מַעַרְבָא:** In the Babylonian Talmud, Eretz Yisrael is referred to as: The West, since it is southwest of Babylonia. In later periods, the customs in Eretz Yisrael were referred to as western ones, as opposed to the eastern customs of Babylonia.

NOTES

The practical difference between them is in a case where the eulogizer performs the eulogy free of charge – **אִיכָּא בֵּינַיְיהוּ דְּקָעָבֵיד בְּחִנָּם:** The commentaries discuss other possible distinctions between the opinions of Rav and Shmuel. Rabbi Yitzḥak ibn Giat writes that according to Rav, since the concern is that one might not be able to travel to Jerusalem for the Festival, this *halakha* does not apply in the absence of the Temple. The Ramban, however, disagrees, and writes that Rav's concern applies to funds set aside for all of the Festival needs and not just the pilgrimage to Jerusalem. Rabbeinu Yehonatan of Lunel notes an additional distinction between the opinions: According to the opinion of Shmuel, that the reason is that one will be distressed during the Festival due to one's memory of the recent loss, this *halakha* does not apply if one's relative dies during the thirty day period preceding the Festival, as he will not be forgotten by the Festival in any event.

BACKGROUND

Crypts – כּוּכִין:

Ancient burial cave with crypts in Beit She'arim

A pond and a small pond – גִּיהָא וּבַר גִּיהָא: The *Arukh* explains that the pond refers to a laundry pond that is dug in the ground, and there is a smaller pond connected to it, into which goes the overflow from the larger pond.

HALAKHA

Digging graves on the intermediate days of a Festival – חֲפִירַת קְבָרִים בַּמּוֹעֵד: One may not dig a crypt or build a grave on the intermediate days of a Festival to prepare for the possibility that a corpse may need to be buried. However, if there is a corpse that actually needs to be buried, one may dig a grave for it (*Tur*). Adjusting the dimensions of a grave or crypt by making it shorter or longer is permitted on the intermediate days of a Festival (*Shulḥan Arukh, Oraḥ Hayyim* 547:11).

A laundry pond – נִבְרֶכֶת: A laundry pond may be constructed on the intermediate days of a Festival (Rambam *Sefer Zemanim, Hilkhot Yom Tov* 8:4).

מתני׳ אֵין חוֹפְרִין כּוּכִין וּקְבָרוֹת בַּמּוֹעֵד, אֲבָל מְחַנְּכִין אֶת הַכּוּכִין בַּמּוֹעֵד. וְעוֹשִׂין נִבְרֶכֶת בַּמּוֹעֵד, וְאָרוֹן עִם הַמֵּת בֶּחָצֵר. רַבִּי יְהוּדָה אוֹסֵר, אֶלָּא אִם כֵּן יֵשׁ עִמּוֹ נְסָרִים.

MISHNA One may not dig crypts[B] or graves on the intermediate days of a Festival[NH] in preparation for those who are still alive, **but one may adjust**[N] previously dug **crypts on** the intermediate days of **a Festival** in order to receive a particular corpse. **And one may** also **construct** a laundry **pond**[H] **on** the intermediate days of **a Festival** as it does not involve excessive effort. **And** one may also prepare **a coffin** if he is together **with the corpse in the** same **courtyard,** as in that case everyone knows that he is preparing the coffin for the deceased. **Rabbi Yehuda prohibits** making the coffin **unless** one **has** wooden **boards with him**[N] that had already been cut before the Festival and that need only to be attached.

גמ׳ מַאי כּוּכִין וּמַאי קְבָרוֹת? אָמַר רַב יְהוּדָה: כּוּכִין – בַּחֲפִירָה, וּקְבָרוֹת – בְּבִנְיָן. תַּנְיָא נַמִי הָכִי: אֵלּוּ הֵן כּוּכִין וְאֵלּוּ הֵן קְבָרוֹת, כּוּכִין – בַּחֲפִירָה, וּקְבָרוֹת – בְּבִנְיָן.

GEMARA The Gemara asks: **What are crypts and what are graves,** and what is the difference between them? **Rav Yehuda said: Crypts** are constructed **by digging and graves** are constructed **by building.**[N] The Gemara adds: **That is also taught** in the following *baraita*: **These are crypts and these are graves: Crypts** are constructed **by digging and graves** are constructed **by building.**

״אֲבָל מְחַנְּכִין אֶת הַכּוּכִין״. כֵּיצַד מְחַנְּכִין? אָמַר רַב יְהוּדָה: שֶׁאִם הָיָה אָרוֹךְ – מְקַצְּרוֹ. בְּמַתְנִיתָא תָּנָא: מַאֲרִיךְ בּוֹ וּמַרְחִיב בּוֹ.

It is taught in the mishna: **But one may adjust** previously dug **crypts** on the intermediate days of a Festival. The Gemara asks: **How does one adjust** a crypt? **Rav Yehuda said: If** the crypt **was long**er than the corpse, **he shortens it.** With regard to this issue it **was taught in a** ***baraita*: He lengthens** the crypt **and widens it** to make it the right size for the particular corpse.

״וְעוֹשִׂין נִבְרֶכֶת״ כו׳. מַאי נִבְרֶכֶת? אָמַר רַב יְהוּדָה: זוֹ בָּקִיעַ. וְהָתַנְיָא: הַנִּבְרֶכֶת וְהַבָּקִיעַ! אָמַר אַבַּיֵי וְאִיתֵּימָא רַב כַּהֲנָא: גִּיהָא וּבַר גִּיהָא.

It was further taught in the mishna: **And one may** also **construct a** laundry **pond**[N] on the intermediate days of a Festival. The Gemara asks: **What is a** laundry **pond? Rav Yehuda said: This is a ditch** dug in the ground for washing clothes. The Gemara raises a difficulty: **Isn't it taught** in a *baraita*: **A** laundry **pond and a** laundry **ditch,** which indicates that they are different from one another? **Abaye said, and some say** that it was **Rav Kahana** who said: **A pond and a small pond,**[B] i.e., the only difference between them is their size; a laundry pond is larger than a laundry ditch.

NOTES

Digging graves on the intermediate days of a Festival – חֲפִירַת קְבָרוֹת בַּמּוֹעֵד: The commentaries dispute the precise parameters of the mishna's statement that it is prohibited to dig graves on a Festival. It is certainly permitted to dig a grave for someone who has died and is awaiting burial. Many say that the mishna's prohibition applies to digging graves in advance for those who will die after the Festival (see Rabbeinu Hananel and Rif). Others understand that the mishna is even referring to a case of digging graves in a big city, where although it is clear that someone will die on the Festival itself, there is still no corpse awaiting burial when the grave is being prepared (Rabbeinu Yehonatan of Lunel; Ran; see Ramban).

But one may adjust – אֲבָל מְחַנְּכִין: There is an opinion in the Jerusalem Talmud that this actually refers to applying lime to the grave, while the Gemara below explains that it refers to adjusting the size of the crypts. The Ramban likens this *halakha* to the allowance to perform certain labors for the public welfare, e.g., repairing wells, on the intermediate days of a Festival: It is prohibited to dig the well or the crypt to begin with, but if it is already dug, it may be adjusted or repaired. The Ra'avad explains that it is permitted to adjust the crypts because it must be adjusted according to the dimensions of a particular corpse awaiting burial. This is in accordance with the policy that on the intermediate days of a Festival one is permitted to tend to all of the needs of a corpse awaiting burial.

Unless one has wooden boards with him – אֶלָּא אִם כֵּן יֵשׁ עִמּוֹ נְסָרִים: Some write that the reason for this is that not all people are buried in wooden coffins, and therefore it is not a disgrace to the deceased to be buried without a coffin. Consequently, when preparation of the coffin would involve excessive work on a Festival, it is prohibited (Ran).

Graves are constructed by building – קְבָרוֹת בְּבִנְיָן: Some explain that this refers to building walls for a grave that is dug into the ground, while others suggest that it refers to erecting a memorial stone on top of the grave (Rabbi Shlomo ben HaYatom).

A laundry pond [*nivrekhet*] – נִבְרֶכֶת: Many explanations have been suggested for this word. Some say that it is a ditch dug in a courtyard for collecting sewage (Rid). Others propose that it is a stone that is placed next to the laundry pond and used to assist in the laundering process (*Arukh*). Some suggest that it is a regular laundry pond for the clothes that are permitted to be laundered on the intermediate days of a Festival (*ge'onim*; Rabbeinu Hananel). Although it is generally prohibited to dig new ditches for personal use, in this case it is permitted for purposes of modesty, so that women would not have to go down to the river or some other public place to launder clothes. The mishna mentions this here in the context of burial because both have to do with digging on the Festival (Rabbeinu Yehonatan of Lunel). Many, however, connect this *nivrekhet* to burial, explaining that it is a place to wash the body (see *Tosafot*; Meiri), or a place to wash the hands of those accompanying the dead (Meiri). The Ra'avad explains that it refers to a grave dug into the ground but not surrounded by a structure; the deceased would later be transferred to a permanent grave. The Ramban understands that the *nivrekhet* is an extension to a grave that had already been dug.

״וְאָרוֹן עִם הַמֵּת בֶּחָצֵר״. תָּנֵינָא לְהָא דְּתָנוּ רַבָּנַן: עוֹשִׂין כָּל צוֹרְכֵי הַמֵּת: גּוֹזְזִין לוֹ שְׂעָרוֹ, וּמְכַבְּסִין לוֹ כְּסוּתוֹ, וְעוֹשִׂין לוֹ אָרוֹן מִנְּסָרִין הַמְנוּסָּרִין מֵעֶרֶב יוֹם טוֹב. רַבָּן שִׁמְעוֹן בֶּן גַּמְלִיאֵל אוֹמֵר: אַף מְבִיאִין עֵצִים, וּמְנַסְּרָן בְּצִינְעָא בְּתוֹךְ בֵּיתוֹ.

It was taught in the mishna: **And** one may also prepare **a coffin** on the intermediate days of a Festival if he is together **with the corpse in the** same **courtyard.** The Gemara comments: **We** already **learned this, as the Sages taught** in the following *baraita*: **One may tend to all the needs of the deceased** on the intermediate days of a Festival:[H] **One may cut** the deceased's **hair for him** if it was too long, **and one may wash his clothing,** i.e., his shrouds, **for him, and one may construct a coffin for him from boards that had** already **been cut from the eve of the Festival. Rabban Shimon ben Gamliel says: One may even bring timber and discreetly cut it** into boards **in** the privacy of **his house.**

מתני׳ אֵין נוֹשְׂאִין נָשִׁים בַּמּוֹעֵד, לֹא בְּתוּלוֹת וְלֹא אַלְמָנוֹת, וְלֹא מְיַיבְּמִין, מִפְּנֵי שֶׁשִּׂמְחָה הִיא לוֹ, אֲבָל מַחֲזִיר הוּא אֶת גְּרוּשָׁתוֹ.

MISHNA **One may not marry a woman on** the intermediate days of **a Festival, not virgins and not widows, and one may not perform levirate marriage**[B] with his sister-in-law, if his brother died childless, **because it is a joyous** occasion **for him. However, one may remarry his divorced wife** on the intermediate days of a Festival, as this is not as great a joy for him.[H]

וְעוֹשָׂה אִשָּׁה תַּכְשִׁיטֶיהָ בַּמּוֹעֵד. רַבִּי יְהוּדָה אוֹמֵר: לֹא תָּסוּד, מִפְּנֵי שֶׁנִּיווּל הוּא לָהּ. הַהֶדְיוֹט תּוֹפֵר כְּדַרְכּוֹ, וְהָאוּמָּן מַכְלִיב. וּמְסָרְגִין אֶת הַמִּטּוֹת, רַבִּי יוֹסֵי אוֹמֵר: מְמַתְּחִין.

And a woman may engage in all **her** usual **cosmetic treatments** to enhance her physical appearance **on** the intermediate days of **a Festival. Rabbi Yehuda says: She may not apply lime** to her skin **because it** is temporarily **a disgrace to her,** as she is unattractive before the lime is peeled off and will therefore be distressed during the Festival. The mishna continues: **A layman,** who is not a skilled tailor, **may sew in his** usual **manner** if necessary for the Festival, **whereas a craftsman may form** only **temporary stitches.**[H] **And one may interweave** the cords attached to the frames of **beds** upon which a mattress is placed. **Rabbi Yosei says: One may** only **tighten** the cords but not interweave them.

גמ׳ וְכִי שִׂמְחָה הִיא לוֹ מַאי הָוֵי? אָמַר רַב יְהוּדָה אָמַר שְׁמוּאֵל, וְכֵן אָמַר רַבִּי אֶלְעָזָר אָמַר רַבִּי אוֹשַׁעְיָא, וְאָמְרִי לָהּ אָמַר רַבִּי אֶלְעָזָר אָמַר רַבִּי חֲנִינָא: לְפִי שֶׁאֵין מְעָרְבִין שִׂמְחָה בְּשִׂמְחָה. רַבָּה בַּר [רַב] הוּנָא אָמַר: מִפְּנֵי שֶׁמַּנִּיחַ שִׂמְחַת הָרֶגֶל וְעוֹסֵק בְּשִׂמְחַת אִשְׁתּוֹ.

GEMARA It was taught in the mishna that one may not marry a woman on the intermediate days of a Festival, because it is a source of joy for him. The Gemara asks: **And if it is** a source of **joy for him, what of it?** Isn't there is a mitzva to rejoice on a Festival? **Rav Yehuda said** that **Shmuel said, and, so too, Rabbi Elazar said** that **Rabbi Oshaya said, and some say** that **Rabbi Elazar said** that **Rabbi Ḥanina said:** The reason that one may not get married on the intermediate days of a Festival is **because one may not mix** one **joy with** another **joy,**[N] as each requires its own celebration. **Rabba bar Rav Huna said:** The reason is **because he forsakes the rejoicing of the pilgrimage Festival and occupies** himself **with rejoicing** with **his wife.**

אֲמַר לֵיהּ אַבַּיֵי לְרַב יוֹסֵף: הָא דְּרַבָּה בַּר [רַב] הוּנָא – דְּרַב הוּא, דְּאָמַר רַב דָּנִיאֵל בַּר קְטִינָא אָמַר רַב: מִנַּיִן שֶׁאֵין נוֹשְׂאִין נָשִׁים בַּמּוֹעֵד? שֶׁנֶּאֱמַר: ״וְשָׂמַחְתָּ בְּחַגֶּךָ״, בְּחַגֶּךָ – וְלֹא בְּאִשְׁתְּךָ.

Abaye said to Rav Yosef: This statement **of Rabba bar Rav Huna is** actually a statement **of Rav, as Rav Daniel bar Ketina said that Rav said: From where** is it derived **that one may not marry a woman on** the intermediate days of **a Festival? As it is stated: "And you shall rejoice in your Festival"** (Deuteronomy 16:14). This verse emphasizes that you must rejoice **in your Festival and not in your wife.**

עוּלָּא אָמַר: מִפְּנֵי הַטּוֹרַח. רַבִּי יִצְחָק נַפָּחָא אָמַר: מִפְּנֵי בִּיטּוּל פְּרִיָּה וּרְבִיָּה.

Ulla said: The reason one may not marry on the intermediate days of a Festival is **due to the** excessive **exertion** that the wedding preparations demand, which is prohibited during the Festival. **Rabbi Yitzḥak Nappaḥa said:** The reason is **due to the neglect of** the mitzva to be **fruitful and multiply.** If it were permissible to get married during the intermediate days of a Festival, people would delay getting married until then in order to save money by avoiding the necessity of preparing separate feasts for the Festival and for the wedding. In the meantime they would neglect the mitzva of procreation.

מֵיתִיבִי: כָּל אֵלּוּ שֶׁאָמְרוּ אֲסוּרִין לִישָּׂא בַּמּוֹעֵד

The Gemara **raises an objection** from the following *baraita*: **All those whom** the Sages **said are prohibited to marry on** the intermediate days **of a Festival**

HALAKHA

The needs of the deceased on the intermediate days of a Festival – צוֹרְכֵי הַמֵּת בַּמּוֹעֵד: It is permitted to tend to all the needs of the deceased on the intermediate days of a Festival, including cutting his hair, washing his clothes, and sewing him shrouds, even when the labor is performed by a craftsman (*Mishna Berura*, citing *Peri Megadim*). Similarly, a coffin may be prepared, provided this takes place in the courtyard where the deceased is located, so that it is evident that the coffin is constructed for him. If there are no boards for the coffin, wood may be brought and discreetly cut in one's house, in accordance with the opinion of Rabban Shimon ben Gamliel. If the deceased was a well-known individual, this may be done even in a public venue (Jerusalem Talmud). In a place where there are few Jews, everyone is considered well-known (*Tosafot*; *Shulḥan Arukh, Oraḥ Hayyim* 547:10).

Marrying a woman on the intermediate days of a Festival – נְשִׂיאַת אִשָּׁה בַּמּוֹעֵד: One may not marry on the intermediate days of a Festival, regardless of whether the woman is a virgin or a widow. Levirate marriage may also not be performed on the intermediate days of a Festival. However, one is permitted to remarry a woman whom he had previously married and divorced. In this case, some are stringent and do not permit preparing a wedding feast (*Beit Yosef*). Engagement and betrothal are permitted on the intermediate days of a Festival as long as one does not prepare a feast to celebrate the occasion (*Shulḥan Arukh, Oraḥ Hayyim* 546:1–2; *Even HaEzer* 64:6).

A craftsman may form only temporary stitches – הָאוּמָּן מַכְלִיב: It is permitted for one who is not a professional tailor to sew in his usual manner on the intermediate days of a Festival. A professional tailor is permitted to sew only in the manner of an ordinary individual (*Shulḥan Arukh, Oraḥ Hayyim* 541:5).

BACKGROUND

Levirate marriage – יִבּוּם: A man whose brother died without children is obligated by Torah law to marry his deceased brother's widow or free her by means of a *ḥalitza* ceremony (see Deuteronomy 25:5–10). As long as neither levirate marriage nor *ḥalitza* has taken place, it is prohibited for her to marry another man. According to the Torah, levirate marriage is effected by the act of sexual intercourse. The Sages, however, instituted the practice of *ma'amar*, in which the deceased husband's brother betroths the widow, even though this betrothal is not effective by Torah law without intercourse. Conjugal relations consummate the marriage between the deceased's brother and the widow and she is thereafter considered his wife in all respects. A bill of divorce would be necessary to formalize a divorce between them. Nowadays, the brother-in-law is required to free his brother's widow of her obligation through *ḥalitza*, and he is not permitted to marry her through levirate marriage.

NOTES

One joy with another joy – שִׂמְחָה בְּשִׂמְחָה: According to this opinion, every cause for joy should be celebrated separately. See *Tosafot*, who discuss different types of celebrations and whether or not it is fitting for them to be observed on the intermediate days of a Festival. The Ritva writes that this is the opinion of a single authority, one of several explanations of the prohibition, and it is not accepted as *halakha*. Consequently, only weddings are prohibited on the intermediate days of a Festival, due to the excessive effort involved in preparing a wedding feast (Rav Hai Gaon; Rashi manuscript).

Perek **I**
Daf **9** Amud **a**

מוּתָּרִין לִישָּׂא עֶרֶב הָרֶגֶל. קַשְׁיָא לְכוּלְּהוּ!

are permitted to marry on the eve of the pilgrimage Festival.[H] This poses **a difficulty to all of** the opinions, as a wedding celebration ordinarily extends for seven days, and the majority of the celebration will coincide with the Festival.

לָא קַשְׁיָא; לְמַאן דְּאָמַר מִשּׁוּם שִׂמְחָה – עִיקַּר שִׂמְחָה חַד יוֹמָא הוּא.

The Gemara answers: This is **not difficult,** as this *baraita* can be reconciled with all of the opinions. **According to the one who said** that one may not get married on the intermediate days of a Festival **because of joy,** i.e., because one must not mix one joy with another, or because one may not put aside the rejoicing of the Festival and occupy himself with rejoicing with his wife, this is not difficult, as **the primary joy** of a wedding **is** only **one day,** and after that, the joy of the wedding will not affect the joy of the Festival.

לְמַאן דְּאָמַר מִשּׁוּם טִירְחָא – עִיקַּר טִירְחָא חַד יוֹמָא הוּא. לְמַאן דְּאָמַר מִשּׁוּם בִּיטּוּל פְּרִיָּה וּרְבִיָּה – לְחַד יוֹמָא לָא מַשְׁהֵי אִינִישׁ נַפְשֵׁיהּ.

And **according to the one who said** that one may not marry on the intermediate days of a Festival **due to** the excessive **exertion** that the wedding preparations demand, it is not difficult, as **the primary exertion is** only **one day.** After the wedding, excessive exertion is not required. And **according to the one who said** that the reason is **due to the neglect of** the mitzva to be **fruitful and multiply,** there is no room for concern: Since there is only **one day,** the eve of the Festival, when he can get married and save money on the feast, **a man will not delay** his wedding in order to get married then, lest some unforeseen circumstance arise that will prevent him from getting married on that day. Therefore, according to all the reasons offered, there is no need to prohibit weddings on the eve of a Festival.

וְדְאֵין מְעָרְבִין שִׂמְחָה בְּשִׂמְחָה מְנָלַן? דִּכְתִיב: ״וַיַּעַשׂ שְׁלֹמֹה בָעֵת הַהִיא אֶת הֶחָג וְכׇל יִשְׂרָאֵל עִמּוֹ קָהָל גָּדוֹל מִלְּבוֹא חֲמָת עַד נַחַל מִצְרַיִם [לִפְנֵי ה׳ אֱלֹהֵינוּ] שִׁבְעַת יָמִים וְשִׁבְעַת יָמִים אַרְבָּעָה עָשָׂר יוֹם״. וְאִם אִיתָא דִּמְעָרְבִין שִׂמְחָה בְּשִׂמְחָה – אִיבָּעֵי לֵיהּ לְמִינְטַר עַד הֶחָג, וּמֶיעֱבַד שִׁבְעָה לְהָכָא וּלְהָכָא.

§ The Gemara asks: With regard to the principle that **one may not mix** one **joy with** another **joy,**[N] **from where do we** derive it? The Gemara explains that the source is **as it is written** with regard to the dedication of the Temple: **"So Solomon held the feast at that time, and all Israel with him, a great congregation, from the entrance of Hamath to the Brook of Egypt, before the Lord our God, seven days and seven days, fourteen days"** (I Kings 8:65). **And if it is so** that **one may** in fact **mix** one **joy with** another **joy, he should have waited until the festival** of *Sukkot,* which was the second set of seven days, **and made** a feast of **seven** days **for this and for that,** i.e., for the dedication of the Temple and for the festival of *Sukkot* together. The fact that he did not do so indicates that one must not mix one joy with another.

וְדִלְמָא: מִינְטַר – לָא נָטְרִינַן, וְהֵיכָא דְּאִתְרַמֵּי – עָבְדִינַן! אִיבָּעֵי לֵיהּ לְשַׁיּוּרֵי פּוּרְתָּא.

The Gemara raises a question: **Perhaps,** however, it may be derived from here only that **we may not delay** a wedding to be on a Festival, just as King Solomon did not delay the Temple dedication to be on the Festival, but nevertheless, **where it happens** to occur that way, **we may** indeed **prepare** a feast to celebrate both occasions together. The Gemara answers: If this were permitted, Solomon **should have left a small** part of the Temple unfinished until the Festival, and thereby arranged for a joint celebration of the dedication of the Temple and the festival of *Sukkot.*

שַׁיּוּרֵי בִּנְיַן בֵּית הַמִּקְדָּשׁ לָא מְשַׁיְּירִינַן! אִיבָּעֵי לֵיהּ לְשַׁיּוּרֵי בְּאַמָּה כַּלְיָא עוֹרֵב.

The Gemara responds: **One may not leave** any part of **the building of the Temple** undone, as a mitzva should be completed as quickly as possible. The Gemara modifies its previous opinion: Solomon **should have left the cubit**-wide plates with spikes, which were designed to **eliminate the ravens,** unfinished.[B] The roof of the Temple was fitted with sharp metal spikes to deter the ravens, who were attracted by the smell of the sacrificial meat, from perching there. Although this was not considered a part of the building itself, delaying its installation would have allowed Solomon to delay the celebration of the Temple dedication.

HALAKHA

Weddings on the eve of a pilgrimage Festival – נִישּׂוּאִין בְּעֶרֶב הָרֶגֶל: It is permitted to marry a woman on the eve of a Festival, preferably in the morning (*Mishna Berura*), and to hold the wedding feast on the Festival itself. However, the *Magen Avraham* writes it is customary not to have weddings on the eve of a Festival (*Shulḥan Arukh, Oraḥ Hayyim* 546:3).

NOTES

One may not mix one joy with another joy – אֵין מְעָרְבִין שִׂמְחָה בְּשִׂמְחָה: In the Jerusalem Talmud, proof is adduced for this principle on the basis of Laban's statement to Jacob: "Fulfill her week, and we will give you this one also" (Genesis 29:27). Some note that this applies only to wedding celebrations, and therefore the proof of the Gemara here is necessary to include other celebrations (Riaf).

BACKGROUND

The cubit-wide plates with spikes to eliminate the ravens – אַמָּה כַּלְיָא עוֹרֵב: The Temple courtyards, including the priestly courtyard and the site of the altar, were not roofed. As the meat of offerings was always present there, steps had to be taken to keep away the ravens and other carnivorous birds. Since the Temple courtyards were adjacent to the Sanctuary, which due to its height was apt to become a gathering place for the ravens, spiked metal plates were placed on top of the Sanctuary to deter the ravens from landing there.

Since the muscles in the feet of birds usually tighten due to the pressure of their weight on those muscles, relatively heavy birds cannot perch on narrow places, especially sharp points. These iron spikes made it very difficult for ravens and other birds of prey to live on the roof of the Sanctuary.

Spikes on the roof of the Sanctuary

אַמָּה כַּלְיָא עוֹרֵב צוֹרֶךְ בִּנְיַן הַבַּיִת הוּא. אֶלָּא, מִדְּמַיְּיתַר קְרָא; מִכְּדֵי כְּתִיב: ״אַרְבָּעָה עָשָׂר יוֹם״, ״שִׁבְעַת יָמִים וְשִׁבְעַת יָמִים״ לָמָּה לִי? שְׁמַע מִינָּהּ: הָנֵי לְחוּד, וְהָנֵי לְחוּד.

The Gemara rejects this opinion as well: **The cubit**-wide plates with spikes to **eliminate the ravens was a necessary** element **in the building of the Temple,**[N] and consequently Solomon could not delay its construction either. **Rather,** the proof is **from the redundancy** in **the verse. Since it is written "fourteen days," why do I** need the verse to specify **"seven days and seven days"? Learn from it** that **these** seven days of celebrating the Temple dedication must **be discrete, and** similarly, **these** seven days of celebrating the Festival must **be discrete,** due to the principle that one may not mix one joy with another.

אָמַר רַבִּי פַּרְנָךְ אָמַר רַבִּי יוֹחָנָן: אוֹתָהּ שָׁנָה לֹא עָשׂוּ יִשְׂרָאֵל אֶת יוֹם הַכִּפּוּרִים, וְהָיוּ דּוֹאֲגִים וְאוֹמְרִים: שֶׁמָּא נִתְחַיְּיבוּ שׂוֹנְאֵיהֶן שֶׁל יִשְׂרָאֵל כְּלָיָיה. יָצְתָה בַּת קוֹל וְאָמְרָה לָהֶם: כּוּלְּכֶם מְזוּמָּנִין לְחַיֵּי הָעוֹלָם הַבָּא.

§ Apropos the discussion of the celebration at Solomon's dedication of the Temple, the Gemara relates that **Rabbi Parnakh said that Rabbi Yoḥanan said: That year,** the Jewish people **did not observe Yom Kippur,** as the seven-day celebration of the dedication of the Temple coincided with Yom Kippur and all seven days were celebrated with feasting. **And** the people **were worried and said: Perhaps the enemies of the Jewish people,** a euphemism for the Jewish people themselves, **have become liable to be destroyed** for the transgression of eating on Yom Kippur, which is punishable by *karet*. **A Divine Voice issued forth and said to them: All of you are designated for life in the World-to-Come.**

מַאי דְּרוּשׁ? אָמְרוּ: קַל וָחוֹמֶר; וּמַה מִּשְׁכָּן שֶׁאֵין קְדוּשָּׁתוֹ קְדוּשַּׁת עוֹלָם, וְקָרְבַּן יָחִיד – דּוֹחֶה שַׁבָּת, דְּאִיסּוּר סְקִילָה, מִקְדָּשׁ, דִּקְדוּשָּׁתוֹ קְדוּשַּׁת עוֹלָם, וְקָרְבַּן צִבּוּר, וְיוֹם הַכִּפּוּרִים דַּעֲנוּשׁ כָּרֵת – לֹא כָּל שֶׁכֵּן?!

The Gemara asks: **What derivation** led them to conclude that it was permitted for them to eat on Yom Kippur? The Gemara explains that they based their ruling on an ***a fortiori*** inference: **If** at the dedication of **the Tabernacle, whose sanctity is not a permanent sanctity,**[N] **an individual's offering,** i.e., an offering of one of the tribal princes, **overrides** the prohibition of **Shabbat,** as the princes' offerings were brought every day including Shabbat despite the attendant transgression of **a prohibition** that is punishable by **stoning;** then with regard to the dedication of **the Temple, whose sanctity is a permanent sanctity** and the offerings brought there were **communal offerings,** is it **not all the more so** clear that the dedication of the Temple overrides the prohibition of **Yom Kippur,** a violation that is **punishable by** the less severe punishment of ***karet***?

אֶלָּא אַמַּאי הָיוּ דּוֹאֲגִים? הָתָם – צוֹרֶךְ גָּבוֹהַּ; הָכָא – צוֹרֶךְ הֶדְיוֹט. הָכָא נַמִי, מִיעֲבַד – לִיעַבְדוּ, מֵיכַל לָא נֵיכְלוּ וְלָא לִישְׁתּוּ! אֵין שִׂמְחָה בְּלֹא אֲכִילָה וּשְׁתִיָּה.

The Gemara asks: **But** if they had firm basis for their behavior, **why were they worried?** The Gemara answers that one can refute this *a fortiori* inference as follows: **There,** at the dedication of the Tabernacle, Shabbat was desecrated only **for the necessities** of the Temple service to God on **High,** i.e., by sacrificing offerings. **Here,** at the dedication of the Temple, they desecrated Yom Kippur by eating and drinking, which was for **the need of common** mortals. Based on this distinction the Gemara suggests: **Here too,** at the dedication of the Temple **they should** have **performed** the rites of the sacrificial offerings and **they should not** have **eaten or drunk.** The Gemara answers: **There is no** complete **rejoicing without eating and drinking.**[N]

וּמִשְׁכָּן דְּדָחֵי שַׁבָּת מְנָלַן? אִילֵימָא מִדִּכְתִיב: ״בַּיּוֹם הָרִאשׁוֹן״ וּ״בַיּוֹם הַשְּׁבִיעִי״ – דִּלְמָא שְׁבִיעִי לְקׇרְבָּנוֹת! אָמַר רַב נַחְמָן בַּר יִצְחָק: אָמַר קְרָא: ״בְּיוֹם עַשְׁתֵּי עָשָׂר יוֹם״, מַה יּוֹם כּוּלּוֹ רָצוּף – אַף עַשְׁתֵּי עָשָׂר כּוּלָּן רְצוּפִין.

With regard to the proof itself, the Gemara asks: **And from where do we** derive that the offerings brought at the dedication of **the Tabernacle overrode Shabbat?**[N] **If we say** it is **as it is written** with regard to the offerings brought by the tribal princes: **"On the first day"** (Numbers 7:12) **and "on the seventh day"** (Numbers 7:48), this is not a conclusive proof, as **perhaps** this refers not to the seventh day of the week but to **the seventh** day of sacrificial **offerings.** Perhaps they skipped Shabbat and did not sacrifice offerings connected to the dedication of the Tabernacle on that day. **Rav Naḥman bar Yitzḥak said: The verse** also **states: "On the day of the eleventh day"** (Numbers 7:72). The repetition of the word day indicates that **just as a day is all** one **continuous** period of time, **so too, the eleven** days **were all** one **continuous** period of time, with no break in the middle, even for Shabbat.

NOTES

The cubit-wide plates with spikes to eliminate the ravens was a necessary element in the building of the Temple – **אַמָּה כַּלְיָא עוֹרֵב צוֹרֶךְ בִּנְיַן הַבַּיִת הוּא:** Some explain that this was considered a necessary element in the building of the Temple because it completed the required height of the structure (Rashi manuscript). Many have pointed out that if this was considered a part of the building, it should not have been permitted to leave it undone, and if it was not part of the building, leaving it undone should not have been sufficient cause to delay the dedication of the Temple. Some explain, based on Rashi, that this was not considered a part of the structure of the Temple, and therefore as long as the Temple was not yet functioning, it was permitted to delay installing this arrangement of spikes. Once the Temple was to start functioning, this arrangement became necessary (*Mishḥat Aharon*).

Whose sanctity is not a permanent sanctity – **אֵין קְדוּשָּׁתוֹ קְדוּשַּׁת עוֹלָם:** Some explain that the fact that the Tabernacle's sanctity was not permanent is demonstrated by the fact that when the Jewish people entered Eretz Yisrael it was permissible to sacrifice offerings on private altars rather than in the Tabernacle (Rashi manuscript). Others suggest that after the Temple was built, the Tabernacle was no longer used and was concealed, so that from the outset the Tabernacle's sanctity was planned to be only for a limited time, until the permanent Temple was to be built (Rabbi Shlomo ben HaYatom).

There is no complete rejoicing without eating and drinking – **אֵין שִׂמְחָה בְּלֹא אֲכִילָה וּשְׁתִיָּה:** An allusion to this idea can be found in the command given to the Jewish people that after they cross the Jordan, set up stones as monuments, and build the first altar in Eretz Yisrael, they must bring peace-offerings (Deuteronomy 27:7), which are partly consumed on the altar and partly consumed by the priests and by its owners. Alternatively, it can be found in the passage referring to the Temple (Deuteronomy 12:6–7), which also mentions sacrificing and eating peace-offerings (*Talmid Rabbeinu Yeḥiel of Paris*).

Overriding Shabbat to sacrifice offerings – **דְּחִיַּית שַׁבָּת לְקׇרְבָּנוֹת:** The fact that these offerings overrode Shabbat could not be proven from the daily offerings that had to be sacrificed even on Shabbat, as these daily offerings were brought at God's command, whereas the tribal princes' offerings were brought on their own initiative (Maharsha). The Ritva explains that they decided to sacrifice these offerings through divine inspiration, and their actions received divine approval. Therefore, this incident served as the historical precedent in the similar situation of the dedication of the Temple many generations later (*Ramat Shmuel*).

NOTES

Why do I need two verses – תְּרֵי קְרָאֵי לָמָּה לִי: The version of the text known to Rabbi Shlomo ben HaYatom, and perhaps also the Ritva, may not have contained the second verse cited here at all, in which case the proof is from the double usage of the word day in the first verse, with regard to the eleventh day.

And glad of heart – וְטוֹבֵי לֵב: *Talmid Rabbeinu Yeḥiel of Paris* notes that an allusion to the idea that the birth of a male child gladdens the heart may be found in what the verse says about the birth of Moses: "And she saw him that he was good" (Exodus 2:2).

וְדִלְמָא יָמִים הָרְאוּיִין! כְּתִיב קְרָא אַחֲרִינָא: "בְּיוֹם שְׁנֵים עָשָׂר יוֹם", מַה יּוֹם כּוּלּוֹ רָצוּף – אַף שְׁנֵים עָשָׂר יוֹם כּוּלָּן רְצוּפִין.

The Gemara asks: **But perhaps** this refers only to **days that are fit** for an individual's offerings, i.e., the offerings were sacrificed on eleven consecutive days that were suitable for sacrificing the offerings of an individual, but not on Shabbat. The Gemara answers: In **another verse it is written: "On the day of the twelfth day"** (Numbers 7:78), indicating that **just as a day is all** one **continuous** period of time, **so too, the twelve days were all** one **continuous** period of time.

וְדִלְמָא הָכָא נַמִי: יָמִים הָרְאוּיִין! אִם כֵּן, תְּרֵי קְרָאֵי לָמָּה לִי?

The Gemara asks again: **But perhaps here too** this is referring to **days that are fit** for sacrificing the offerings of an individual? The Gemara rejects this opinion: **If so, why do I** need **two verses,**[N] the verse with regard to the eleventh day and the verse with regard to the twelfth day, to teach the same principle? The fact that the Torah uses repetitive phraseology in both verses indicates that all the days were consecutive, without a break for Shabbat.

וּמִקְדָּשׁ דְּדוֹחֶה יוֹם הַכִּפּוּרִים מְנָלַן? אִילֵימָא מִדִּכְתִיב: "אַרְבָּעָה עָשָׂר יוֹם" – וְדִלְמָא יָמִים הָרְאוּיִין? גָּמַר "יוֹם" "יוֹם" מֵהָתָם.

The Gemara asks: **And from where do we** derive that the feasting at the time of the dedication of **the Temple overrides Yom Kippur,** so that the people did not have to fast? **If we say** it is derived **from that which is written: Fourteen days, perhaps** this is referring to **days that are fit** for feasting, to the exclusion of Yom Kippur. The Gemara answers: This is **derived** by means of a verbal analogy between the word **"day"** mentioned in this context **and** the word **"day"** mentioned **there,** with regard to the dedication of the Tabernacle. Just as there the days were consecutive, without a break for Shabbat, so too here, the days were consecutive, without a break for Yom Kippur.

יָצְתָה בַּת קוֹל וְאָמְרָה לָהֶם: כּוּלְּכֶם מְזוּמָּנִין לְחַיֵּי הָעוֹלָם הַבָּא. וּמְנָלַן דְּאַחֵיל לְהוּ? דְּתָנֵי תַּחְלִיפָא: "בַּיּוֹם הַשְּׁמִינִי שִׁלַּח אֶת הָעָם וַיְבָרֲכוּ אֶת הַמֶּלֶךְ וַיֵּלְכוּ לְאָהֳלֵיהֶם שְׂמֵחִים וְטוֹבֵי לֵב עַל כׇּל הַטּוֹבָה אֲשֶׁר עָשָׂה ה׳ לְדָוִד עַבְדּוֹ וּלְיִשְׂרָאֵל עַמּוֹ".

It was stated above that **a Divine Voice issued forth and said to them: All of you are designated for life in the World-to-Come.** The Gemara asks: **And from where do we** derive **that** God **pardoned them** for this sin? The Gemara answers: The Sage **Taḥlifa taught** in a *baraita* that the verse states: **"On the eighth day he sent the people away, and they blessed the king, and went to their tents joyful and glad of heart for all the goodness that the Lord had done for David His servant and for Israel His people"** (I Kings 8:66).

"לְאָהֳלֵיהֶם" – שֶׁהָלְכוּ וּמָצְאוּ נְשֵׁיהֶם בְּטׇהֳרָה; "שְׂמֵחִים" – שֶׁנֶּהֱנוּ מִזִּיו הַשְּׁכִינָה; "וְטוֹבֵי לֵב" – שֶׁכׇּל אֶחָד וְאֶחָד נִתְעַבְּרָה אִשְׁתּוֹ בְּבֵן זָכָר. "עַל כׇּל הַטּוֹבָה" – שֶׁיָּצְתָה בַּת קוֹל וְאָמְרָה לָהֶם: כּוּלְּכֶם מְזוּמָּנִין לְחַיֵּי הָעוֹלָם הַבָּא.

This verse may be expounded as follows: The words **"to their tents"** indicate **that they went and found their wives in** a state of **purity,** as the terms tent and house often denote one's wife. The term **"joyful"** is referring to the fact **they had enjoyed the splendor of the Divine Presence,** as there was a revelation of the Divine Presence when the offerings were sacrificed in the Temple. The phrase **"and glad of heart"**[N] refers to the fact that **each of their wives conceived a male child.** The words **"for all the goodness"** indicate **that a Divine Voice issued forth and said to them: All of you are designated for life in the World-to-Come,** which is the ultimate good.

"לְדָוִד עַבְדּוֹ וּלְיִשְׂרָאֵל עַמּוֹ". בִּשְׁלָמָא לְיִשְׂרָאֵל עַמּוֹ – דְּאַחֵיל לְהוּ עֲוֹן יוֹם הַכִּפּוּרִים. אֶלָּא לְדָוִד עַבְדּוֹ מַאי הִיא?

The aforementioned verse stated: "For all the goodness that the Lord had done **for David His servant and for Israel His people.**" The Gemara asks: **Granted,** when the verse mentions the goodness that God did **for Israel His people,** this is referring to the fact **that He pardoned them the sin of** eating on **Yom Kippur** that year; **but what is** the goodness that God performed **for David His servant?**

אָמַר רַב יְהוּדָה אָמַר רַב: בְּשָׁעָה שֶׁבִּיקֵּשׁ שְׁלֹמֹה לְהַכְנִיס אָרוֹן לְמִקְדָּשׁ דָּבְקוּ שְׁעָרִים זֶה לָזֶה. אָמַר שְׁלֹמֹה עֶשְׂרִים וְאַרְבַּע רְנָנוֹת וְלֹא נַעֲנָה. פָּתַח וְאָמַר: "שְׂאוּ שְׁעָרִים רָאשֵׁיכֶם" וגו׳ וְלֹא נַעֲנָה.

Rav Yehuda said that Rav said: When Solomon sought to bring the Ark into the Temple the gates clung together and could not be opened. **Solomon uttered twenty-four songs** of praise, **and** his prayer **was not answered. He began and said: "Lift up your heads, O you gates,** and be lifted up, you everlasting doors; and the King of glory shall come in" (Psalms 24:7), **but** once again his prayer **was not answered,** and the Temple gates remained closed.

כֵּיוָן שֶׁאָמַר: ״ה׳ אֱלֹהִים אַל תָּשֵׁב פְּנֵי מְשִׁיחֶךָ זָכְרָה לְחַסְדֵי דָּוִד עַבְדֶּךָ״ – מִיָּד נַעֲנָה. בְּאוֹתָהּ שָׁעָה נֶהֶפְכוּ פְּנֵי שׂוֹנְאֵי דָוִד כְּשׁוּלֵי קְדֵירָה וְיָדְעוּ הַכֹּל שֶׁמָּחַל לוֹ הַקָּדוֹשׁ בָּרוּךְ הוּא עַל אוֹתוֹ עָוֹן.

Once he said: "Now therefore arise, O Lord God, into your resting place, You, and the Ark of Your strength; Let your priests, O Lord God, be clothed with victory and let Your pious ones rejoice in goodness. **O Lord God, do not turn away the face of Your anointed; remember the faithful love of David Your servant"** (II Chronicles 6:41–42), **he was immediately answered. At that moment the faces of David's enemies turned** dark **like the** charred **bottom of a pot, and all knew that the Holy One, Blessed be He, forgave him for that sin** involving Bathsheba, as they saw that it was only in his merit that the gates of the Temple opened.

רַבִּי יוֹנָתָן בֶּן עַסְמַיי וְרַבִּי יְהוּדָה בֶּן גֵּרִים תָּנוּ פָּרָשַׁת נְדָרִים בֵּי רַבִּי שִׁמְעוֹן בֶּן יוֹחַי. אִיפַּטוּר מִינֵּיהּ בְּאוּרְתָּא. לְצַפְרָא הֲדוּר וְקָא מִפַּטְרִי מִינֵּיהּ. אֲמַר לְהוּ: וְלָאו אִיפַּטְרִיתוּ מִינִי בְּאוּרְתָּא?

The Gemara relates that **Rabbi Yonatan ben Asmai and Rabbi Yehuda, son of converts,**[P] **studied the portion** dealing with **oaths in the study hall of Rabbi Shimon ben Yoḥai.**[P] After completing their studies, the disciples **took leave of** their master **in the evening,** but did not yet leave the city. **In the morning they went back and took leave of him** a second time. **He said to them: Did you not** already **take leave of me** yesterday **in the evening?**

אֲמַרוּ לֵיהּ: לִמַּדְתָּנוּ רַבֵּינוּ, תַּלְמִיד שֶׁנִּפְטַר מֵרַבּוֹ וְלָן בְּאוֹתָהּ הָעִיר – צָרִיךְ לִיפָּטֵר מִמֶּנּוּ פַּעַם אַחֶרֶת, שֶׁנֶּאֱמַר: ״בַּיּוֹם הַשְּׁמִינִי שִׁלַּח אֶת הָעָם וַיְבָרֲכוּ אֶת הַמֶּלֶךְ״, וּכְתִיב: ״וּבְיוֹם עֶשְׂרִים וּשְׁלֹשָׁה לַחֹדֶשׁ הַשְּׁבִיעִי שִׁלַּח אֶת הָעָם״!

They said to him: You have taught us, our teacher,[N] that **a disciple who takes leave of his teacher**[H] **and** then **stays overnight in the same city must take leave of him an additional time, as it is stated** at the conclusion of the dedication of the Temple: **"On the eighth day he sent the people away, and they blessed the king"** (I Kings 8:66), **and** elsewhere **it is written: "And on the twenty-third day of the seventh month he sent the people away"** (II Chronicles 7:10). The eighth day in the verse is referring to the Eighth Day of Assembly, the twenty-second of the month of Tishrei, yet it says that he sent the people away on the next day, the twenty-third of the month.

אֶלָּא מִכָּאן לְתַלְמִיד הַנִּפְטָר מֵרַבּוֹ וְלָן בְּאוֹתָהּ הָעִיר – צָרִיךְ לִיפָּטֵר מִמֶּנּוּ פַּעַם אַחֶרֶת.

Rather, it can be derived **from here** that **a disciple who takes leave of his teacher and** then **stays overnight in the same city must take leave of him an additional time,** just as the Jewish people took leave of Solomon an additional time on the day after the Festival, on the twenty-third of Tishrei.

אֲמַר לֵיהּ לִבְרֵיהּ: בְּנֵי אָדָם הַלָּלוּ אֲנָשִׁים שֶׁל צוּרָה הֵם, זִיל גַּבַּיְיהוּ דְּלִיבָרְכוּךְ. אֲזַל, אַשְׁכְּחִינְהוּ דְּקָא רָמוּ קְרָאֵי אַהֲדָדֵי; כְּתִיב: ״פַּלֵּס מַעְגַּל רַגְלֶךָ וְכָל דְּרָכֶיךָ יִכֹּנוּ״, וּכְתִיב: ״אֹרַח חַיִּים פֶּן תְּפַלֵּס״!

Rabbi Shimon ben Yoḥai **said to his son: These** two **people,** Rabbi Yonatan ben Asmai and Rabbi Yehuda, son of converts, **are men of** noble **form** [*tzura*][N] i.e., wise and learned individuals; **go to them so that they will bless you. He went and found them** deep in discussion, **raising** apparent **contradictions between verses** as follows: **It is written: "Make level the path of your feet, and let all your ways be established"** (Proverbs 4:26), indicating that when one has the opportunity to perform more than one mitzva, he must evaluate which of them is most important. **And** elsewhere **it is written: "Lest you level out the path of life,"** (Proverbs 5:6),[N] indicating that one must perform each mitzva as the opportunity arises, without considering its relative importance.

לָא קַשְׁיָא: כָּאן – בְּמִצְוָה שֶׁאֶפְשָׁר לַעֲשׂוֹתָהּ עַל יְדֵי אֲחֵרִים,

They explained that it is **not difficult: Here,** in the first verse cited above, it is discussing **a mitzva that can be done by others,** and therefore one must consider what is most worthwhile for him to perform himself and what he will leave to others.

PERSONALITIES

Rabbi Yehuda, son of converts – רַבִּי יְהוּדָה בֶּן גֵּרִים: As Rashi in tractate *Shabbat* (33b) writes, this Sage's name indicates that he was the son of two converts. The passage here indicates that he was an important scholar who was shown honor even by Rabbi Shimon ben Yoḥai. Their relationship, however, had a tragic ending. Rabbi Yehuda repeated Rabbi Shimon's derogatory comments about Roman rule, and these came to the attention of the Roman authorities, who decreed a death sentence against Rabbi Shimon. Consequently, Rabbi Shimon and his son were forced into hiding for many years. When Rabbi Shimon finally emerged and saw Rabbi Yehuda, son of converts, he directed his eyes toward him, and Rabbi Yehuda died.

Rabbi Shimon ben Yoḥai – רַבִּי שִׁמְעוֹן בֶּן יוֹחַי: Rabbi Shimon ben Yoḥai was a *tanna* in the second generation following the destruction of the Second Temple. He was born in the Galilee, and according to tradition he died on *Lag BaOmer* in Meron. He was one of Rabbi Akiva's closest students, and he studied with him for thirteen years in Benei Berak.

Initially, Rabbi Shimon was not involved in the rebellion against the Romans, but the persecutions of the Romans, and their subsequent execution of Rabbi Akiva turned him against them. According to the Gemara in tractate *Shabbat* (33b), Rabbi Shimon's criticism of Roman rule in the presence of Rabbi Yehuda, son of converts, led to a death sentence being placed on him, forcing him to hide in a cave together with his son for thirteen years. According to tradition, it was during that period that he compiled kabbalistic material that became the Book of the Zohar. This is disputed by the academic world.

Among his many teachings in Jewish law and lore, the Gemara in tractate *Berakhot* (5a) quotes him as asserting: Three wonderful gifts were bestowed upon the Jewish People by God, but all are attained only by means of ordeal: Torah, Eretz Yisrael and the World-to-Come.

HALAKHA

A disciple who takes leave of his teacher – תַּלְמִיד שֶׁנִּפְטַר מֵרַבּוֹ: If a disciple takes leave of his teacher and then spends the night in the same city, he must take leave from him again the next day. This applies only if he did not inform his teacher that he would spend the night in the city; however, if he told this to him when he took leave of him the first time, he need not take leave of him again (*Shulḥan Arukh*, *Yoreh De'a* 242:16, and in the comment of Rema).

NOTES

You have taught us, our teacher – לִימַּדְתָּנוּ רַבֵּנוּ: The commentaries question why Rabbi Shimon ben Yoḥai asked his question if he himself had taught them this *halakha*. However, the *halakha* is that when a disciple cites a *halakha* before his teacher, he should always use the wording: You have taught us, our teacher, even if he heard it elsewhere (see *Shulḥan Arukh*, *Yoreh De'a* 242:23, and the comment of the Vilna Gaon).

Men of noble form [*tzura*] – אֲנָשִׁים שֶׁל צוּרָה: This expression appears in several places in the Talmud, but it may not always have the same meaning. Some explain that in tractate *Ta'anit* (15a) this expression refers to the external appearance of these individuals, which leaves an impression on others, whereas here it apparently indicates that these were people of importance, stature, and wisdom. Perhaps the word *tzura* is used here in the sense of the imprint on a coin, indicating famous and well-known people.

Lest you level out the path of life – אוֹרַח חַיִּים פֶּן תְּפַלֵּס: The most common interpretation of the Gemara is that this refers to weighing the value of one mitzva against another. However, many explain that the path of life mentioned here refers to the Torah, and that the Gemara is stating that one should not interrupt his Torah study even in order to fulfill another mitzva, unless it cannot be fulfilled by anyone else (Rashi manuscript; Ra'avad; *Talmid Rabbeinu Yeḥiel of Paris*).

NOTES

May it be God's will that you should sow and not reap – יְהֵא רַעֲוָא דְּתִזְרַע וְלָא תֶּחֱצַד: Various commentators ask: Why did Rabbi Yonatan ban Asmai and Rabbi Yehuda, son of converts, formulate their blessing in a way that made it possible to understand it as a curse? The answer is that they knew Rabbi Shimon ben Yoḥai's son would not understand what they said and he would certainly go to his father for an explanation, and his father would then bless him a second time with the same blessings (Riaf; *Paḥad Yitzḥak*; see Maharsha).

כָּאן – בְּמִצְוָה שֶׁאִי אֶפְשָׁר לַעֲשׂוֹתָהּ עַל יְדֵי אֲחֵרִים.

There, in the other verse, it is referring to **a mitzva that cannot be done by others,** and therefore, one must not consider its relative importance, but rather do it immediately.

הֲדַר יָתְבִי וְקָא מִבָּעֲיָא לְהוּ: כְּתִיב: ״יְקָרָה הִיא מִפְּנִינִים וְכָל חֲפָצֶיךָ לֹא יִשְׁווּ בָהּ״, הָא חֶפְצֵי שָׁמַיִם – יִשְׁווּ בָהּ, וּכְתִיב: ״כָּל חֲפָצִים לֹא יִשְׁווּ בָהּ״ – דַּאֲפִילּוּ חֶפְצֵי שָׁמַיִם לֹא יִשְׁווּ בָהּ!

The two scholars, Rabbi Yonatan ben Asmai and Rabbi Yehuda, son of converts, **once again sat and raised the** following **dilemma:** In one place **it is written** in praise of the Torah: **"She is more precious than rubies; and all of your desires are not to be compared to her"** (Proverbs 3:15). One can infer from here that all human desires cannot be compared to the Torah, **but the desires of Heaven,** i.e., mitzvot, **can** indeed **be compared to her. And** elsewhere **it is written:** "For wisdom is better than rubies; **and all the things that may be desired are not to be compared to it"** (Proverbs 8:11), which indicates that even mitzvot cannot be compared to the Torah.

כָּאן בְּמִצְוָה שֶׁאֶפְשָׁר לַעֲשׂוֹתָהּ עַל יְדֵי אֲחֵרִים; כָּאן – בְּמִצְוָה שֶׁאִי אֶפְשָׁר לַעֲשׂוֹתָהּ עַל יְדֵי אֲחֵרִים.

They resolved this contradiction by stating that **here,** in the second verse, it is discussing **a mitzva that can be done by others.** In that case, even mitzvot cannot be compared to the Torah, and accordingly, one who is engaged in Torah study should not interrupt his studies in order to perform another mitzva. However, **there,** in the first verse, it is discussing **a mitzva that cannot be done by others.** In that case Torah study is not more important than the mitzva, and one should interrupt his studies in order to perform the mitzva.

אֲמַרוּ לֵיהּ: מַאי בָּעֵית הָכָא? אֲמַר לְהוּ: דַּאֲמַר לִי אַבָּא: זִיל גַּבַּיְיהוּ דְּלִיבָרְכוּךְ. אֲמַרוּ לֵיהּ: יְהֵא רַעֲוָא דְּתִזְרַע וְלָא תֶּחֱצַד; תְּעַיֵּיל וְלֹא תֵּיפּוֹק; תֵּיפּוֹק וְלָא תְּעַיֵּיל; לִיחֲרוּב בֵּיתָךְ וְלֵיתוּב אוּשְׁפִּיזָךְ; לְבַלְבֵּל פְּתוֹרָךְ; וְלָא תֶּחֱזֵי שַׁתָּא חַדְתָּא.

When Rabbi Yonatan ben Asmai and Rabbi Yehuda, son of converts, noticed Rabbi Shimon ben Yoḥai's son, **they said to him: What do you want here? He said to them: Father told me: Go to them so that they should bless you. They said to him** as follows: **May it be** God's **will that you should sow and not reap,**[N] **that you should bring in and not take out, that you should take out and not bring in, that your house should be destroyed and your lodging place should be inhabited, that your table should become confused, and that you should not see a new year.**

כִּי אֲתָא לְגַבֵּי אֲבוּהּ, אֲמַר לֵיהּ: לָא מִבָּעְיָא דְּבָרוּכֵי לָא בֵּירְכָן – אֲבָל צַעוּרֵי צַעוּרָן. אֲמַר לֵיהּ: מַאי אֲמַרוּ לָךְ? הָכִי וְהָכִי אֲמַרוּ לִי. אֲמַר לֵיהּ: הָנָךְ כּוּלְּהוּ בִּרְכָתָא נִינְהוּ; תִּזְרַע וְלָא תֶּחֱצַד – תּוֹלִיד בָּנִים וְלֹא יָמוּתוּ. תְּעַיֵּיל וְלָא תֵּיפּוֹק – תְּעַיֵּיל כַּלָּתָא וְלָא לֵימוּתוּ בָּנָךְ דְּלֵיפְּקוּן. תֵּיפּוֹק וְלָא תְּעַיֵּיל – תּוֹלִיד בְּנָתָא וְלָא יָמוּתוּ גּוּבְרַיְיהוּ וְלֵיהַדְרוּ לְוָתִיךְ.

When he came back **to his father, he said to him: Not only did they not bless me, but they** even **caused me pain** with their negative words. His father **said to him: What** exactly **did they say to you?** He answered: **They said to me such and such.** Rabbi Shimon ben Yoḥai **said to** his son: **These are all blessings,** uttered in a cryptic manner, and this is what they meant: When they said that **you should sow and not reap** they meant that **you should bear sons and they should not die.** Their statement that **you should bring in and not take out** means that **you should bring in brides** for your sons **and your sons should not die, which** would cause their wives **to leave.** When they said **you should take out and not bring in** they meant that **you should have daughters and their husbands should not die,** which would cause your daughters to **return to you.**

לִיחֲרוּב בֵּיתָךְ וְלֵיתוּב אוּשְׁפִּיזָךְ – דְּהַאי עָלְמָא אוּשְׁפִּיזָךְ וְהַהִיא עָלְמָא בֵּיתָא, דִּכְתִיב: ״קִרְבָּם בָּתֵּימוֹ לְעוֹלָם״. אַל תִּקְרִי ״קִרְבָּם״ אֶלָּא ״קִבְרָם״.

When they said that **your house should be destroyed and your lodging place should be inhabited,** this should be interpreted allegorically. **As this world is** compared to **your lodging place, and the World-to-Come is** compared to **your house, as it is written: "Their inward thought [*kirbam*], is that their houses shall continue forever"** (Psalms 49:12), and the Sages said: **Do not read** it as **"their inward thought [*kirbam*]"; rather** read it as **their graves [*kivram*].** According to this reading, one's grave is considered his permanent house. The Sages gave Rabbi Shimon ben Yoḥai's son a blessing that he should dwell in his temporary home rather than his permanent home, i.e., he should live a long life.

לְבַלְבֵּל פְּתוֹרָךְ – בְּבָנֵי וּבְנָתָא. וְלָא תֶּיחֱזֵי שַׁתָּא חַדְתָּא – דְּלָא תְּמוּת אִנְתָּךְ וְלָא תִּנְסַב אִינְתְּתָא אַחֲרִיתִי.

When they said that **your table should become confused,** they meant that you should be blessed **with** many **sons and daughters,** so that there will be noise and confusion at your table. When they said that **you should not see a new year,** they meant **your wife should not die and** as a result **you should not** have to **marry another woman,** about which it says: "When a man has taken a new wife, he shall not go out to war, neither shall he be charged with any business; he shall be free at home for one year" (Deuteronomy 24:5).

רַבִּי שִׁמְעוֹן בֶּן חֲלַפְתָּא אִפַּטַר מִינֵּיהּ דְּרַב. אֲמַר לֵיהּ אֲבוּהּ: זִיל לְגַבֵּיהּ דְּלִיבָרְכָךְ. אֲמַר לֵיהּ: יְהֵא רַעֲוָא דְּלָא תְּבַיֵּישׁ וְלָא תִּתְבַּיֵּישׁ. אֲתָא גַּבֵּי אֲבוּהּ. אֲמַר לֵיהּ: מַאי אֲמַר לָךְ? אֲמַר לֵיהּ: מִילִּין בְּעָלְמָא הוּא דַּאֲמַר לִי.

Apropos a blessing with an obscure meaning, the Gemara relates: **Rabbi Shimon ben Ḥalafta took leave of Rav.**[P] **His father said to him: Go to him so that he should bless you.** When **Rabbi Shimon ben Ḥalafta** returned to him for a blessing, Rav **said to him: May it** be God's **will that you should not shame** others[N] **and that you should not feel ashamed. He came** home **to his father,** who **said to him: What did he say to you? He said to him: Mere words he said to me,** i.e., he did not say anything of significance.

– אֲמַר לֵיהּ: בֵּירְכָךְ בִּרְכָתָא דְּבִרְכָן קוּדְשָׁא בְּרִיךְ הוּא לְיִשְׂרָאֵל וּתְנָא בָּהּ, דִּכְתִיב: "וַאֲכַלְתֶּם אָכוֹל וְשָׂבוֹעַ וְהִלַּלְתֶּם" וגו' "וְלֹא יֵבוֹשׁוּ עַמִּי לְעוֹלָם וִידַעְתֶּם כִּי בְקֶרֶב יִשְׂרָאֵל אָנִי" וגו' "וְלֹא יֵבוֹשׁוּ עַמִּי לְעוֹלָם".

After Rabbi Shimon ben Ḥalafta repeated what Rav had said, his father **said to him: He blessed you with the blessing with which the Holy One, Blessed be He, blessed Israel and** then **repeated** the blessing, indicating that is a very great blessing, **as it is written: "And you shall eat in plenty, and be satisfied, and praise** the Name of the Lord your God, who has dealt wondrously with you; **and My people shall never be ashamed. And you shall know that I am in the midst of Israel,** and that I am the Lord your God, and there is none else; **and My people shall never be ashamed"** (Joel 2:26–27).

"וְעוֹשָׂה אִשָּׁה תַּכְשִׁיטֶיהָ". תָּנוּ רַבָּנַן: אֵלּוּ הֵן תַּכְשִׁיטֵי נָשִׁים: כּוֹחֶלֶת, וּפוֹקֶסֶת, וּמַעֲבִירָה סְרָק עַל פָּנֶיהָ. וְאִיכָּא דְּאָמְרִי: מַעֲבֶרֶת סְרָק עַל פָּנֶיהָ שֶׁל מַטָּה.

§ It was taught in the mishna: **And a woman may engage in** all of **her** usual **cosmetic treatments**[NH] on the intermediate days of a Festival. **The Sages taught** in a *baraita*: **These are the cosmetic treatments of women** that are permitted: **She may paint her eyelids, she may remove** unwanted **hair** [*pokeset*],[NL] **and she may put rouge on her face. And some say: She may pass a comb over her lower face,** i.e., she may remove the hair from her pubic area.

דְּבֵיתְהוּ דְּרַב חִסְדָּא מְקַשְּׁטָא בְּאַנְפֵּי כַּלָּתָהּ. יְתֵיב רַב הוּנָא בַּר חִינָּנָא קַמֵּיהּ דְּרַב חִסְדָּא, וְיָתֵיב וְקָאָמַר: לֹא שָׁנוּ אֶלָּא יַלְדָּה, אֲבָל זְקֵנָה – לֹא.

The Gemara relates that **Rav Ḥisda's wife would adorn herself** on the intermediate days of a Festival **in the presence of her daughter-in-law,**[N] i.e., when she already had a married son. **Rav Huna bar Ḥinnana sat before Rav Ḥisda,**[P] **and he sat and said: They taught only** that a woman is permitted to engage in cosmetic treatments on the intermediate days of a Festival **only** with regard to **a young woman,** as such treatments bring her joy, **but** in the case of **an old woman, no,** the treatments are not permitted, as she does not need them.

NOTES

That you should not shame others – דְּלָא תְּבַיֵּישׁ: Some explain the blessing to mean that he should become increasingly scrupulous in his observance of *halakha*, so that he not sin; in that way, he would never have to be embarrassed about his deeds. This parallels the substance of the blessing in the Bible (see Maharsha; *Iyyei HaYam*).

Some texts have *teivosh*, be shamed, instead of *tevayesh*, to shame others. According to this reading, they said the same blessing twice, just as this blessing is doubled in the Bible (Rabbeinu Gershom Meor HaGola).

A woman may engage in her cosmetic treatments – עוֹשָׂה אִשָּׁה תַּכְשִׁיטֶיהָ: Even though this may involve excessive effort, and even though it is not connected to food preparation, it is permitted, since it brings a woman enjoyment. Rabbi Shlomo ben HaYatom adds that it is permitted in order to promote peace within the household. There is also no concern that a woman will purposely delay her cosmetic treatments to the intermediate days of a Festival, as women do not commonly delay such treatments (Ritva).

She may remove unwanted hair [*pokeset*] – פּוֹקֶסֶת: This has been understood in many different ways; Some explain that the woman applies a sticky substance to her hair to keep it in place (Rashi manuscript; *Tosafot*; Rabbi Zekharya Agamati). In another reading, recorded by Rabbeinu Yehonatan of Lunel, the word is *poseket*, meaning that the woman parts her hair with a special instrument designed for this purpose (Rabbi Shlomo ben HaYatom). Alternatively, this has been understood to mean that the woman places a doughy substance on her face to remove facial hair and refine the skin.

In the presence of her daughter-in-law – בְּאַנְפֵּי כַּלָּתָהּ: Rabbi Shlomo ben HaYatom suggests that she did this in order to teach her daughter-in-law the proper way to adorn herself.

HALAKHA

A woman may engage in all of her usual cosmetic treatments – עוֹשָׂה אִשָּׁה תַּכְשִׁיטֶיהָ: A woman, even if she is unmarried (*Peri Megadim*), is permitted to engage in all of her usual cosmetic treatments on the intermediate days of a Festival. She may paint her eyelids, remove unwanted hair, and apply rouge to her face. She may also apply lime to her skin for beautification purposes, provided that she can peel it off during the Festival, in accordance with the opinion of Rabbi Yehuda. Some disagree and say that this is permitted even if she cannot remove it during the Festival, in accordance with the opinion of the Rabbis (Rabbi Yitzḥak ibn Giat; Ritva). She may also remove hair from her armpits and pubic area, by hand or with an instrument. However, she may not get a haircut, just as it is prohibited for a man to get a haircut (*Shulḥan Arukh*, *Oraḥ Hayyim* 546:5; *Peri Megadim*; Vilna Gaon).

LANGUAGE

Remove unwanted hair [*pokeset*] – פּוֹקֶסֶת: This word apparently derives from Greek, but there are several possibilities depending on how the term is understood. It may derive from φῦκος, *fukos*, red paint, meaning rouge for the face. Alternatively, it may be related to the root πέκω, *peko*, which means to comb or cut hair.

PERSONALITIES

Rav – רַב: Rav, whose full name was Rabbi Abba bar Ivu was the first, and perhaps the greatest, of the Babylonian *amora'im*. Known as Abba Arikha because of his great height, Rav established the academy in Sura that lasted for over eight hundred years, through the period of the *ge'onim*. The Gemara reports that aside from the visiting students who attended the academy only during the *yarḥei kalla* months of Adar and Elul, 1,200 full-time students learned in the academy throughout the year.

In his youth, Rav traveled with his uncle, Rabbi Ḥiyya, to Eretz Yisrael, where he studied under Rabbi Yehuda HaNasi, the redactor of the Mishna. He traveled back and forth between Eretz Yisrael and Babylonia until he settled in Babylonia in the year 219 CE. Rav's greatness is apparent not only in the large number of *amora'im* who were his students and quote him throughout the Gemara, but also by the fact that he is recognized as the last of the *tanna'im*, and is permitted to disagree with tannaitic rulings.

Rav's teachings are found throughout both the Jerusalem Talmud and the Babylonian Talmud. Among his many rulings are several that concern issues of marriage, such as his ruling that a man cannot marry a woman without first meeting her, and the requirement that underage girls cannot be married until they are old enough to state whom they want to marry. His rulings in the area of ritual law were invariably accepted, although the rulings of his colleague and adversary, Shmuel, were accepted in criminal and financial matters.

Rav's son, Rabbi Ḥiyya, followed in his father's footsteps and became a great scholar; his other son, Ivu, was a merchant.

Rav Ḥisda – רַב חִסְדָּא: One of the greatest second-generation Babylonian *amora'im*, Rav Ḥisda was one of Rav's younger students as well as being a priest. Throughout his life, Rav Ḥisda showed great affinity for the teachings of Rav, and constantly tried to learn from other statements that Rav made. After Rav's death, he remained a disciple-colleague of Rav's student, Rav Huna. Although he was poor as a youth, he became wealthy and lived most of his life in comfort. He was very generous toward his fellow man. Rav Ḥisda was devoted to his students and his children, guiding them in both spiritual and worldly matters.

אָמַר לֵיהּ: הָאֱלֹהִים! אֲפִילּוּ אִמָּךְ, וַאֲפִילּוּ אִימָּא דְּאִימָּךְ, וַאֲפִילּוּ עוֹמֶדֶת עַל קִבְרָהּ. דְּאָמְרִי אֱינָשֵׁי: בַּת שִׁיתִּין כְּבַת שִׁית, לְקָל טַבְלָא רָהֲטָא.

Rav Ḥisda **said to him: By God! Even your mother, and even your mother's mother, and even a woman** so old **that** she **is standing at** the edge of **her grave** are all permitted to adorn themselves. **As people say** in the popular adage: **A woman of sixty years, like one of six, runs at the sound of the timbrel** [*tavla*],[L] implying that women of all ages are young in spirit; since they all take pleasure in their adornments, they are allowed to adorn themselves, regardless of age.

"רַבִּי יְהוּדָה אוֹמֵר לֹא תָסוּד". תַּנְיָא, רַבִּי יְהוּדָה אוֹמֵר: אִשָּׁה לֹא תָסוּד, מִפְּנֵי שֶׁנִּיוּוּל הוּא לָהּ. וּמוֹדֶה רַבִּי יְהוּדָה בְּסִיד שֶׁיְּכוֹלָה לְקַפְּלוֹ בַּמּוֹעֵד שֶׁטּוֹפַלְתּוֹ בַּמּוֹעֵד, שֶׁאַף עַל פִּי שֶׁמְּצֵירָה הִיא עַכְשָׁיו – שְׂמֵחָה הִיא לְאַחַר זְמַן.

§ It was taught in the mishna that **Rabbi Yehuda says: She may not apply lime** to her skin **because it renders her** temporarily **unattractive** and she will be distressed during the Festival. **It is taught** in a *baraita*: **Rabbi Yehuda says: A woman may not apply lime** to her skin[N] on the intermediate days of a Festival **because it** is temporarily **a disgrace to her,** as she appears unattractive until it is peeled off. **But Rabbi Yehuda concedes that with regard to lime that she can peel off during the Festival, she may apply it on** the intermediate days of **the Festival,**[B] **as even though she is distressed now,** as the lime renders her appearance unattractive, **she will be happy afterward,** when the lime is removed and she sees the results.

וּמִי אִית לֵיהּ לְרַבִּי יְהוּדָה הַאי סְבָרָא? וְהָתְנַן,

The Gemara asks: **But does Rabbi Yehuda accept this reasoning** that it is permitted, despite the fact that it causes distress, because it will cause joy later? **Didn't we learn** elsewhere in a mishna (*Avoda Zara* 2a): On the three days before the holidays of idolaters, it is prohibited to do business with them, so as not to cause them to thank their idols for their success. Similarly, it is prohibited on these days to lend to them, to borrow from them, to repay a debt to them, or even to collect a debt from them.

רַבִּי יְהוּדָה אוֹמֵר: נִפְרָעִין מֵהֶן מִפְּנֵי שֶׁמֵּיצֵר. אָמְרוּ לוֹ: אַף עַל פִּי שֶׁמֵּיצֵר עַכְשָׁיו – שָׂמֵחַ הוּא לְאַחַר זְמַן!

Rabbi Yehuda says: One may collect a debt **from them** during this period, **due to** the fact **that** the gentile **is distressed** when he makes the payment. The Rabbis **said to him: Even though he is distressed now, he will be happy afterward,** as he is relieved of the debt, and therefore, it is prohibited to collect a debt from him during the three days before his holiday.[H] In this mishna, Rabbi Yehuda considers only the immediate distress and does not consider the joy that will be experienced after some time.

אָמַר רַב נַחְמָן בַּר יִצְחָק: הַנַּח לְהִלְכוֹת מוֹעֵד, דְּכוּלְּהוּ מֵיצַר עַכְשָׁיו וְשָׂמֵחַ לְאַחַר זְמַן נִינְהוּ.

Rav Naḥman bar Yitzḥak said: Leave aside the *halakhot* governing a Festival,[N] which cannot be compared to other areas, as **all** of the labors that are permitted on a Festival are permitted because even though **one is distressed** by them **now, he will be happy** about them **afterward.** For example, cooking and baking are permitted even though preparing food involves effort and trouble, because eating the food after it is prepared provides pleasure and enjoyment.

רָבִינָא אָמַר: גּוֹי לְעִנְיַן פֵּרָעוֹן לְעוֹלָם מֵיצַר.

Ravina said a different explanation: According to Rabbi Yehuda, **with regard to repaying** a debt, **a gentile is always distressed,** even after he repays a debt. However, in general, even Rabbi Yehuda accepts the principle of taking into account the joy that will be experienced at a later time.

LANGUAGE

Timbrel [*tavla*] – טַבְלָא: This word is found in Arabic, طبلة, *ṭabla*, and in Greek, τάβλα, *tabla*. In this context, it refers to a type of drum. See also LANGUAGE, p. 182.

NOTES

A woman may not apply lime to her skin – אִשָּׁה לֹא תָסוּד: According to one opinion cited in the Jerusalem Talmud, if the woman will remove the lime only after the Festival, all agree that it is prohibited to apply it on the Festival. The *Sefat Emet* suggests that this may be the reason that the Rambam ruled, in accordance with the opinion of Rabbi Yehuda, that it is permitted for a woman to apply lime to her skin only if she will remove it during the Festival.

Leave aside the *halakhot* governing a Festival – הַנַּח לְהִלְכוֹת מוֹעֵד: This refers to the labors that are permitted on the Festival days themselves; it is permitted for one to exert himself in preparing the meal because he derives pleasure from it in the end (Rashi; Rid; Rabbeinu Yehonatan of Lunel). The Ran, however, explains that this refers to the labors that are permitted during the intermediate days of a Festival, which also bring eventual enjoyment.

BACKGROUND

Applying lime [*tefila*] – טְפִילָה: Historically, extraneous hair, especially for women, has been considered an aesthetic blemish, and various methods have been developed to remove such hair. Even today there are people in some areas of the world who apply lime or similar materials to excess hair on their bodies to hairy areas on their bodies, although this can cause burns or other damage to sensitive skin. Applying lime to a large portion of the body at once can even be fatal, as it can block the spores of the skin. Other, less caustic, materials are used as a refining cream for the skin.

HALAKHA

Business before the holidays of idolaters – מִסְחָר לִפְנֵי אֵידֵי נׇכְרִים: On the three days preceding the holidays of idol worshippers, it is prohibited to borrow money from them, to lend money to them, to collect a debt from them, or to pay off a debt to them. However, it is permitted to collect a debt for which there is no documentation, as it is considered like rescuing money that would otherwise be lost. If the idol worshipper is powerful, one may collect a debt from him even if a document had been written. For these and other reasons, many authorities in recent generations have permitted business transactions with gentiles on their holidays (*Shulḥan Arukh*, *Yoreh De'a* 148:1).

אָמַר רַב יְהוּדָה: בְּנוֹת יִשְׂרָאֵל שֶׁהִגִּיעוּ לְפִירְקָן וְלֹא הִגִּיעוּ לַשָּׁנִים, עֲנִיּוֹת – טוֹפְלוֹת אוֹתָן בְּסִיד; עֲשִׁירוֹת – טוֹפְלוֹת אוֹתָן בְּסוֹלֶת; בְּנוֹת מְלָכִים – בְּשֶׁמֶן הַמּוֹר, שֶׁנֶּאֱמַר: ״שִׁשָּׁה חֳדָשִׁים בְּשֶׁמֶן הַמּוֹר״.

With regard to applying lime to one's body, **Rav Yehuda said: The daughters of Israel who reached** physical **maturity, but had not** yet **reached the age** of majority, i.e., girls that were less than twelve years of age, and therefore embarrassed by their precocious physical development, would seek to remove the excess hair from their bodies. **The poor** among them would **smear their** skin **with lime** in order to remove the hair. **The wealthy ones** would **smear themselves with fine flour** for this purpose, **and the daughters of kings would smear themselves with *shemen hamor*. As it is stated** with regard to the women who were brought to King Ahasuerus: **"Six months with *shemen hamor*"** (Esther 2:12).

מַאי שֶׁמֶן הַמּוֹר? רַב הוּנָא בַּר חִיָּיא אָמַר: סְטַכְּת. רַב יִרְמְיָה בַּר אַמִי אָמַר: שֶׁמֶן זַיִת שֶׁלֹּא הֵבִיא שְׁלִישׁ.

The Gemara asks: **What is *shemen hamor*? Rav Huna bar Ḥiyya said:** This is the perfume called ***setaket*.**[L] **Rav Yirmeya bar Ami said:** It is **olive oil** extracted **from** an olive **that** has **not** yet **reached one-third** of its growth; the acidic oil is effective as a depilatory.

תַּנְיָא, רַבִּי יְהוּדָה אוֹמֵר: אַנְפִּיקִינוֹן – שֶׁמֶן זַיִת שֶׁלֹּא הֵבִיא שְׁלִישׁ. וְלָמָּה סָכִין אוֹתוֹ? שֶׁמַּשִּׁיר אֶת הַשֵּׂעָר וּמְעַדֵּן אֶת הַבָּשָׂר.

It is taught in a *baraita* that **Rabbi Yehuda says:** Wherever the Mishna mentions ***anpikinon*,**[L] it is referring to **olive oil** from an olive **that has not yet reached one-third** of its growth. **And why do** women **spread it** on the body? It is due to the fact **that it removes the hair and pampers the skin.**

רַב בֵּיבָי הֲוָה לֵיהּ בְּרַתָּא, טְפַלָּהּ אֵבֶר אֵבֶר, שְׁקַל בָּהּ אַרְבַּע מְאָה זוּזֵי. הֲוָה הַהוּא גּוֹי בְּשִׁבָבוּתֵיהּ דַּהֲוָה לֵיהּ בְּרַתָּא. טְפַלָּהּ בְּחַד זִמְנָא – וּמֵתָה. אֲמַר: קְטַלָא בֵּיבָי לִבְרַתִּי. אָמַר רַב נַחְמָן: רַב בֵּיבָי דְּשָׁתֵי שִׁיכְרָא – בָּעְיָין בְּנָתֵיהּ טַפְלָא; אֲנַן דְּלָא שָׁתֵינַן שִׁיכְרָא, לָא בָּעְיָין בְּנָתִין טַפְלָא.

It was related that **Rav Beivai had a daughter,** and **he spread** lime **on her limb by limb,** which caused her hair to fall out and her skin to whiten. She became so beautiful that when marrying her off, **he took four hundred dinars for her. There was a certain gentile in his neighborhood who** also **had a daughter** and wanted to do this as well. **He spread her** entire body with lime all **at once, and she died.** That gentile **said: Beivai killed my daughter. Rav Naḥman said: Rav Beivai, who** regularly **drinks beer, his daughters require** that they be **smeared** with lime, as beer causes hair growth, **but we who do not drink beer, our daughters do not require** that they be **smeared** with lime, as they have little hair even without this treatment.

LANGUAGE

***Setaket* – סְטַכְּת:** From the Greek στακτή, *staktè*, referring to a fragrant oil that is derived from the resin of the myrrh tree, such as the *Commiphora myrrha*.

Myrrh tree

Myrrh tree resin

***Anpikinon* – אַנְפִּיקִינוֹן:** From the Greek ὀμφάκινον, *omfakinon*, oil extracted from unripe olives.

Perek **I**
Daf **10** Amud **a**

״הַהֶדְיוֹט תּוֹפֵר כְּדַרְכּוֹ״. הֵיכִי דָּמֵי הֶדְיוֹט? אָמְרִי דְּבֵי רַבִּי יַנַּאי: כָּל שֶׁאֵינוֹ יָכוֹל לְהוֹצִיא מְלֹא מַחַט בְּבַת אַחַת. רַבִּי יוֹסֵי בַּר חֲנִינָא אָמַר: כָּל שֶׁאֵינוֹ יָכוֹל לְכַוֵּין אִימְרָא בְּחֵפֶת חֲלוּקוֹ.

§ It was taught in the mishna: **A layman,** who is not a skilled tailor, may **sew in his** usual **manner** on the intermediate days of a Festival. The Gemara asks: **What are the circumstances** in which an individual is considered **a layman?** The Sages **of the school of Rabbi Yannai said: Anyone who cannot** deftly **pull a full needle** of stiches[N] through the fabric **at the same time** is considered a layman. **Rabbi Yosei bar Ḥanina said: Anyone who cannot form a straight seam on the hem** [***ḥefet***][L] **of his shirt**[N] is considered a layman.[H]

NOTES

Pull a full needle of stitches – לְהוֹצִיא מְלֹא מַחַט: Some explain that this means that he inserts a needle several times into the fabric and then pulls the needle through to complete all the stitches at once. Others say that it means that he can align these stitches in a straight line (Rashi manuscript). Another suggestion is that the act of a craftsman discussed here is mending a hole in a garment by filling it in with netlike stitches that cause the fabric to look whole (see Rabbeinu Gershom Meor HaGola; Rabbeinu Yehonatan of Lunel).

A straight seam on the hem [*ḥefet*] of his shirt – אִימְרָא בְּחֵפֶת חֲלוּקוֹ: Some explain that *ḥefet* is a heavy piece of material that would be sewn onto the edge of a shirt to protect it from wear and tear. Anyone who cannot sew its seam evenly is considered a layman (see Rashi). Others propose that this seam refers to an embroidered patch that would be sewn onto the hem of a garment (*ge'onim*; Rabbi Zekharya Agamati).

HALAKHA

Sewing on the intermediate days of a Festival – תְּפִירָה בְּחוֹל הַמּוֹעֵד: If one needs an article of clothing on the intermediate days of a Festival because he has nothing else to wear (*Arukh HaShulḥan*), he may sew in his usual manner, provided that he is a layman. If he is a professional, he must sew as a layman does, making stitches that are widely spaced and uneven. A layman is defined as one who cannot sew an even seam at the edge of his shirt or cannot pull a full needle of stitches through the fabric at one time. The Rema writes that nowadays, everyone should sew in an unusual manner on the intermediate days of a Festival. Furthermore, holding the needle in an unusual way is not sufficient; there must be a recognizable difference in the final product. The *Mishna Berura* writes that all this applies if one does the work without receiving compensation; one is prohibited to perform the labor for compensation even in the manner of a layman unless it is a situation where he will suffer an irretrievable loss if he does not perform the labor immediately (*Shulḥan Arukh*, *Oraḥ Hayyim* 541:5).

LANGUAGE

Hem [*ḥefet*] – חֵפֶת: The edge of a garment, which is folded over to ensure that the garment is the right size, or to reinforce the edge of the garment in order to prevent it from becoming frayed. It parallels the Arabic حافة, *ḥāfa*, which has the same meaning.

״וְהָאוּמָּן מַכְלִיב״. מַאי מַכְלִיב? רַבִּי יוֹחָנָן אָמַר: מַפְסִיעַ. רַבָּה בַּר שְׁמוּאֵל אָמַר: שִׁינֵּי כַּלְבְּתָא.

§ It was further taught in the mishna: **A craftsman,** however, **may form** only **temporary stitches** [***makhliv***].[LN] The Gemara asks: **What is** meant by **forming temporary stitches? Rabbi Yoḥanan said: He** does not sew all the stitches that are necessary, but rather **he skips** certain stitches in the middle (Rabbeinu Hananel). **Rabba bar Shmuel said:** He sews stitches that are like **the teeth of a dog.**[N] He does not sew all the stitches in a straight line, so that they resemble the teeth of a dog, which also are not straight.

״מְסָרְגִין אֶת הַמִּטּוֹת״. מַאי מְסָרְגִין וּמַאי מְמַתְּחִין? כִּי אֲתָא רַב דִּימִי אֲמַר: פְּלִיגִי בָּהּ רַבִּי חִיָּיא בַּר אַבָּא וְרַבִּי אַסִי, וְתַרְוַיְיהוּ מִשְּׁמֵיהּ דְּחִזְקִיָּה וְרַבִּי יוֹחָנָן; חַד אָמַר: מְסָרְגִין – שְׁתִי וָעֵרֶב, וּמְמַתְּחִין – שְׁתִי בְּלֹא עֵרֶב. וְחַד אָמַר: מְסָרְגִין שְׁתִי בְּלֹא עֵרֶב, וּמְמַתְּחִין – שֶׁאִם הָיָה רָפוּי מְמַתְּחוֹ.

§ It was also taught in the mishna: **One may interweave** the cords attached to the frame of **a bed.** Rabbi Yosei says: One may only tighten the cords. The Gemara asks: **What is** meant by **interweaving,**[B] **and what is** meant by **tightening? When Rav Dimi came** from Eretz Yisrael to Babylonia, **he said: Rabbi Ḥiyya bar Abba and Rabbi Asi disagree about** the matter, **and both of them** reported their opinions **in the name of Ḥizkiyya and Rabbi Yoḥanan. One Sage said: Interweaving** involves placing and tying the cords of the bed both **lengthwise and widthwise,** whereas **tightening** means arranging the cords only **lengthwise and not widthwise. And one** Sage **said: Interweaving** involves arranging the cords only **lengthwise and not widthwise, while tightening** means **that if** a cord **became loose, he** may **tighten it** but he may not tie any new cords.[H]

אִינִי? וְהָא תָּנֵי רַב תַּחְלִיפָא בַּר שָׁאוּל: וְשָׁוִין שֶׁאֵין מַפְשִׁילִין חֲבָלִים לְכַתְּחִלָּה. בִּשְׁלָמָא לְמַאן דְּאָמַר מְסָרְגִין שְׁתִי וָעֵרֶב, וּמְמַתְּחִין שְׁתִי בְּלֹא עֵרֶב – הַיְינוּ דְּקָתָנֵי רַב תַּחְלִיפָא בַּר שָׁאוּל: וְשָׁוִין שֶׁאֵין מַפְשִׁילִין חֲבָלִים לְכַתְּחִלָּה.

The Gemara asks: **Is that so? Didn't Rav Taḥlifa bar Shaul teach** the following *baraita*: **And** both Rabbi Meir and Rabbi Yosei **agree that one may not braid cords anew**[H] on the intermediate days of a Festival? **Granted, according to the one who said** that **interweaving** means tying the cords **lengthwise and widthwise, and tightening** means tying them only **lengthwise and not widthwise, this** explanation is consistent with **that which Rav Taḥlifa taught: And they** both **agree that one may not braid cords anew,** as even though one is permitted to arrange the cords of the bed, he is not permitted to produce new cords.

אֶלָּא לְמַאן דְּאָמַר: מְסָרְגִין – שְׁתִי בְּלֹא עֵרֶב, מְמַתְּחִין – שֶׁאִם הָיָה רָפוּי הָיָה מְמַתְּחוֹ, הַשְׁתָּא שְׁתִי וָעֵרֶב אָמְרַתְּ לָא, חֲבָלִים לְכַתְּחִלָּה מִיבָּעֲיָא! קַשְׁיָא.

However, according to the one who said that **interweaving** means tying the cords only **lengthwise and not widthwise,** while **tightening** means **that if** a cord **became loose, he** may **tighten it,** there is a difficulty. **Now that you said** that tying the cords **lengthwise and widthwise, no,** it is not permitted even though the cords are readily available, **is** it **necessary** to say that braiding **cords anew** is prohibited? The Gemara comments: Indeed **it** is **difficult.**

אֲמַר לֵיהּ רַב נַחְמָן בַּר יִצְחָק לְרַבִּי חִיָּיא בַּר אָבִין: מִי אִיכָּא לְמַאן דְּאָמַר מְסָרְגִין שְׁתִי בְּלֹא עֵרֶב? וְהָתְנַן, רַבִּי מֵאִיר אוֹמֵר: הַמִּטָּה – מִשֶּׁיְּסָרוֹג בָּהּ שְׁלֹשָׁה בָּתִּים!

Rav Naḥman bar Yitzḥak said to Rabbi Ḥiyya bar Avin: Is there one who says that interweaving means tying the cords **lengthwise, but not widthwise? Didn't we learn** in a mishna (*Kelim* 16:1) that **Rabbi Meir says: A bed** is considered a utensil and becomes susceptible to ritual impurity **from when one interweaves**[N] **three** rows of **meshes in it,** i.e., three rows lengthwise and widthwise? It is clear from here that interweaving a bed involves tying its cords lengthwise and widthwise.

אֶלָּא, כִּי אֲתָא רָבִין אֲמַר: בִּמְסָרְגִין – כּוּלֵּי עָלְמָא לָא פְּלִיגִי דִּשְׁתִי וָעֵרֶב. אֶלָּא כִּי פְּלִיגִי – בִּמְמַתְּחִין, מָר סָבַר: מְמַתְּחִין שְׁתִי בְּלֹא עֵרֶב, וּמָר סָבַר: שֶׁאִם הָיָה רָפוּי – מְמַתְּחוֹ.

Rather, when Ravin came from Eretz Yisrael to Babylonia **he stated** a different version of the tradition: **With regard to interweaving, everyone agrees** that it is referring to tying the cords of a bed **lengthwise and widthwise. When they disagree it is only about** the meaning of **tightening. One Sage holds** that **tightening** means arranging the cords only **lengthwise and not widthwise. And one Sage holds** that it means that **if** a cord **became loose, he may tighten it.**

מֵיתִיבִי: מְסָרְגִין אֶת הַמִּטָּה וְאֵין צָרִיךְ לוֹמַר שֶׁמְּמַתְּחִין, דִּבְרֵי רַבִּי מֵאִיר. רַבִּי יוֹסֵי אוֹמֵר: מְמַתְּחִין, אֲבָל לֹא מְסָרְגִין. וְיֵשׁ אוֹמְרִים: אֵין מְמַתְּחִין כָּל עִיקָּר.

The Gemara **raises an objection** from the following *baraita*: **One may interweave** the cords attached to the frame of **a bed** on the intermediate days of a Festival, **and needless to say one may tighten** those cords; **this is the statement of Rabbi Meir. Rabbi Yosei says: One may** only **tighten** the ropes **but not interweave** them. **And some say: One may not tighten** them **at all.**

LANGUAGE

Form temporary stitches [*makhliv*] – מַכְלִיב: This refers to poor-quality sewing. It has also been related to the word dog [*kelev*] or cage [*keluv*], manners of describing poor-quality stitching.

NOTES

Form temporary stitches [*makhliv*] – מַכְלִיב: In the Jerusalem Talmud there is an opinion that *makhliv* refers to sewing the stitches one by one, not in the manner of a craftsman, who sews several stitches at once. Skipping refers to sewing wide stitches as if he were taking wide steps, skipping over the space in the middle. Others say that it means sewing quickly and imprecisely (Commentary on *Moed Katan*).

The teeth of a dog – שִׁינֵּי כַּלְבְּתָא: The version of the text recorded by Rashi does not read: Teeth of a dog, but simply: Dog, which is a term for an imprecise manner of sewing (Rashi manuscript).

A bed is considered a utensil and becomes susceptible to ritual impurity from when one interweaves – הַמִּטָּה מִשֶּׁיְּסָרוֹג: The Ritva cites another explanation in the name of Rabbeinu Shimshon of Saens, that the question here relates to the time from which a cord that is tied to the bed is considered part of the bed, so that even the part that has not yet been interwoven becomes susceptible to ritual impurity.

BACKGROUND

Interweaving beds – סֵירוּג הַמִּיטוֹת: Most beds in the talmudic period had wooden frames that were mounted on legs. On top of this frame, and sometimes within the frame, cords would be tied and interwoven lengthwise and widthwise. The cushions they would use as a mattress would be placed on top. In pressing circumstances, they would use cords tied only widthwise, with firm cushioning on top.

HALAKHA

Weaving a bed – סֵירוּג מִטָּה: It is permitted to interweave the cords attached to the frame of a bed lengthwise and widthwise, and it is certainly permitted to tighten cords that have become loose. Some are stringent and say that one should not interweave the cords unless they had already been placed in their holes before the Festival (*Shulḥan Arukh, Oraḥ Hayyim* 541:2; *Mishna Berura*).

Braid cords anew – מַפְשִׁילִין חֲבָלִים לְכַתְּחִלָּה: One may not braid cords anew on the intermediate days of a Festival (*Shulḥan Arukh, Oraḥ Hayyim* 541:2).

בִּשְׁלָמָא לְמַאן דְּאָמַר מְמַתְּחִין שְׁתִי בְּלֹא עֵרֶב – הַיְינוּ דְּאָתוּ יֵשׁ אוֹמְרִים לְאִיפְּלוּגֵי. אֶלָּא לְמַאן דְּאָמַר שֶׁאִם הָיָה רָפוּי מְמַתְּחוֹ, לְיֵשׁ אוֹמְרִים מְמַתְּחוֹ נַמִּי לָא?

Granted, according to the one who said that **tightening** means tying the cords only **lengthwise and not widthwise, this is** why the opinion presented as: **Some say, comes to disagree** and says that one may not tie the cords at all, even only lengthwise. However, if the cords became loose, all agree that they may be tightened. **But according to the one who said** that tightening means **that if** a cord **became loose he** may **tighten it,** then **according to** the opinion presented here as: **Some say,** may **he not even tighten** the cords of his bed? How, then, would he be able to sleep on it?

אִין, כֵּיוָן דְּאֶפְשָׁר לְמַמְלְיֵיהּ בְּמָאנֵי – לָא טָרְחִינַן.

The Gemara answers: **Yes,** indeed, according to this opinion, it is prohibited even to tighten the cords of one's bed. **Since it is possible** for him **to fill** the depression in his bed **with clothing,** so that he can sleep there, **he** may **not exert** himself during the week of the Festival and fix the bed in a more permanent manner.

מתני׳ מַעֲמִידִין תַּנּוּר וְכִירַיִם וְרֵיחַיִם בַּמּוֹעֵד. רַבִּי יְהוּדָה אוֹמֵר: אֵין מְכַבְּשִׁין אֶת הָרֵיחַיִם בַּתְּחִילָּה.

MISHNA One may set up an oven, a stove, and a mill on the intermediate days of a **Festival.**[H] **Rabbi Yehuda says: One may not chisel millstones**[B] **for the first time** on the intermediate days of a Festival.

גמ׳ מַאי מְכַבְּשִׁין? רַב יְהוּדָה אָמַר: מְנַקֵּר רֵיחַיָא. רַב יְחִיאֵל אָמַר: בַּת עֵינָא.

GEMARA The Gemara asks: **What** is meant by **chiseling** millstones? **Rav Yehuda said: Cutting** grooves into **the millstones.** As the millstones wear down over time and become smooth, one must occasionally cut grooves into the stones so that they can grind properly. **Rav Yeḥiel said:** Cutting out **an eyehole**[N] in the upper millstone, through which the grain can pass, so that it can be ground between the two millstones.[N]

מֵיתִיבִי: מַעֲמִידִין תַּנּוּר וְכִירַיִם בַּמּוֹעֵד, וּבִלְבַד שֶׁלֹּא יִגְמוֹר מְלַאכְתָּן, דִּבְרֵי רַבִּי אֱלִיעֶזֶר. וַחֲכָמִים אוֹמְרִים: אַף יִגְמוֹר. רַבִּי יְהוּדָה אוֹמֵר מִשְּׁמוֹ: מַעֲמִידִין אֶת הַחֲדָשָׁה, וּמְכַבְּשִׁין אֶת הַיְשָׁנָה. וְיֵשׁ אוֹמְרִים: אֵין מְכַבְּשִׁין כָּל עִיקָּר.

The Gemara **raises an objection** from a *baraita*: **One may set up an oven and a stove on** the intermediate days of **a Festival, provided that he does not** fully **complete the labor;** this is **the statement of Rabbi Eliezer. But the Rabbis say: He** may **even complete** the labor. **Rabbi Yehuda says in the name of** Rabbi Eliezer: **One may set up a new** millstone **and one may chisel an old** millstone. **And some say: One may not chisel** a millstone **at all.**

בִּשְׁלָמָא לְמַאן דְּאָמַר מְכַבְּשִׁין מְנַקֵּר רֵיחַיָא – הַיְינוּ דְּמַשְׁכַּחַתְּ לַהּ בִּישָׁנָה. אֶלָּא לְמַאן דְּאָמַר בַּת עֵינָא – יְשָׁנָה, בַּת עֵינָא לָמָּה לַהּ? כְּגוֹן דְּקָא בָּעֵי לְאַרְווֹחֵי טְפֵי פּוּרְתָּא.

Granted, according to the one who said that **chiseling** a millstone means **cutting** grooves into **the millstones, this is** how **you** can **find** this activity relevant **to an old** mill. **But according to the one who said** it means cutting out **an eyehole, why does** an **old** millstone **need an eyehole** to be cut out? It must have one already. The Gemara answers: This is referring to a case **where he wants to widen** the hole **a little more.**

רַב הוּנָא שְׁמָעֵיהּ לְהַהוּא גַּבְרָא דְּקָא מְנַקֵּר רֵיחַיָא בְּחוּלָּא דְּמוֹעֲדָא, אֲמַר: מַאן הַאי? אִיתְחִיל גּוּפֵיהּ דְּקָא מַחִיל חוּלָּא דְּמוֹעֲדָא! סָבַר לַהּ כְּיֵשׁ אוֹמְרִים.

The Gemara relates that **Rav Huna** once **heard a certain man cutting** grooves into **his millstone on the intermediate days of a Festival. He said: Who is this?** May **his body be desecrated, for he desecrates the intermediate days of a Festival.** The Gemara comments: Rav Huna **holds in accordance** with the statement cited as: **Some say,** that one is not permitted to roughen his millstones at all.

דָּרַשׁ רַב חָמָא: נוֹקְרִין רֵיחַיִם בַּמּוֹעֵד. מִשּׁוּם רַבִּי מֵאִיר אָמַר: אֲפִילּוּ סוּס שֶׁרוֹכֵב עָלָיו וַחֲמוֹר שֶׁרוֹכֵב עָלָיו מוּתָּר לִיטּוֹל צִפָּרְנַיִם בְּחוּלּוֹ שֶׁל מוֹעֵד,

Rav Ḥama taught as follows: **One may cut** grooves into **millstones on** the intermediate days of **a Festival. In the name of Rabbi Meir he said: Even** with regard to **the horse that** one **rides upon and the donkey that he rides upon, he is permitted to trim** their **hooves**[N] on the intermediate days of a Festival so that they do not suffer when they walk.[H]

BACKGROUND

Chiseling millstones – מְכַבְּשִׁין אֶת הָרֵיחַיִם: The upper millstone could be constructed in various ways, depending upon the general structure of the mill. It had a hole, usually in the middle of the stone, through which the grain was poured, so that it would fall between the two millstones, which would grind it. This image also depicts the rod that would be inserted in a second hole in order to turn the millstone. Some mills also included a hole in the lower millstone that was used to connect the two millstones. In order to render the grinding more effective, grooves or holes would be cut into the millstones in order to hold the kernels in place so that they would be well ground. Over time the stones would become worn and these grooves would disappear. Consequently, it was periodically necessary to cut new grooves in order to return the mill to optimal working condition.

Millstones with eyeholes

NOTES

Eyehole – בַּת עֵינָא: Some explain that this refers to any hole in the millstone, including the hole in the upper millstone through which the grain is poured and the hole in the lower millstone into which the rod that connects the two stones is inserted.

Cutting grooves and an eyehole into the millstones – נִיקּוּר וּבַת עֵינָא: The Ra'avad writes that it is not clear which of these two rulings is a greater novelty. On the one hand, cutting an eyehole is certainly the work of a craftsman, as opposed to cutting grooves into the millstones. Conversely, the mill can be operated even without cutting grooves into the millstones, however, without an eyehole it cannot grind at all, and therefore not cutting an eyehole would cause a great deal of distress on the Festival.

To trim their hooves – לִיטּוֹל צִפָּרְנַיִם: Some write that this is done in order to prepare the hooves for horseshoes, or that this process includes attaching horseshoes. This is not clarified in the Gemara because animals were not ordinarily fitted with shoes in Babylonia, as it was unnecessary due to the soft ground there (Ran; Meiri).

HALAKHA

Setting up a mill on the intermediate days of a Festival – הַעֲמָדַת רֵיחַיִם בְּחוֹל הַמּוֹעֵד: On the intermediate days of a Festival it is permitted to cut grooves into millstones, to cut the eyehole in the upper millstone, and to set the millstones in place (*Shulḥan Arukh*, *Oraḥ Ḥayyim* 540:8).

Trimming hooves on the intermediate days of a Festival – תִּיקּוּן פַּרְסוֹת בְּחוֹל הַמּוֹעֵד: One may trim the hooves of a donkey or a horse on the intermediate days of a Festival if he needs to ride on it, provided that he did not intentionally leave this to be done on the Festival (*Shulḥan Arukh*, *Oraḥ Ḥayyim* 536:1).

BACKGROUND

Donkey that turns the millstones – חֲמָרָא דְּרֵיחַיָּא: The image depicts ancient mills found in a bakery in Pompeii. A rod was inserted into the square-shaped hole on the top part and a donkey would pull the rod around the mill, which would in turn crush the grain.

Ancient mills from a bakery in Pompeii

To groom a horse – לְסָרוֹקֵי סוּסְיָא: There are different types of combs that are used for grooming horses. Rashi explains that the Gemara here is referring to a metal comb.

Metal horse comb

To let the blood of an animal – לְמִישְׁקַל דְּמָא לִבְהֵמָה: For many generations physicians believed that bloodletting was a powerfully effective remedy, both as a cure and as a general preventative therapy for staying healthy. Bloodletting was based on an ancient system of medicine in which blood and other bodily fluids were considered to be humors, the proper balance of which was believed to maintain health. Bloodletting was the most common medical procedure performed by doctors on both humans and animals from antiquity through the late nineteenth century, a period of almost two millennia. Today it is well established that bloodletting is not effective for most diseases. The only remaining condition for which it is used is polycythemia vera, a disease in which the body produces too many red blood cells.

אֲבָל חֲמָרָא דְּרֵיחַיָּא – לָא.

However, with regard to the hooves of **a donkey** that turns the **millstones,**[B] **no,** they may not be trimmed. This is unnecessary on the intermediate days of a Festival, as one may only grind grain that one needs to use on the Festival itself, and the donkey can perform this task even if its hooves are not trimmed.

רַב יְהוּדָה שָׁרֵי לְמִישְׁקַל טוּפְרֵיהּ לַחֲמָרָא דְּרֵיחַיָּא, וּלְאוֹקוֹמֵי רֵיחַיָּא, וּלְמִיבְנֵי רֵיחַיָּא, וּלְמִיבְנֵי אַמַּת רֵיחַיָּא, וּלְמִיבְנֵי אוּרְיָא. רָבָא שָׁרֵא לְסָרוֹקֵי סוּסְיָא, וּלְמִיבְנֵי אַקַּרְפִּיטָא, וּלְמִיבְנֵי אִיצְטַבָּא.

Rav Yehuda permits one **to trim the hooves of the donkey** that turns **a mill, to set** the stones of **a mill** in their place, **to build** the base of **a mill, to construct** a water **channel** to carry water that drives **a mill,**[NH] **and to build a stable**[N] for horses on the intermediate days of a Festival. **Rava permitted** one **to groom a horse,**[HB] **to build a trough,**[NH] **and to build a bench**[H] on the intermediate days of a Festival.

רָבָא שָׁרֵא לְמִישְׁקַל דְּמָא לִבְהֵמָה בְּחוּלָּא דְמוֹעֲדָא. אֲמַר לֵיהּ אַבָּיֵי: תַּנְיָא דִּמְסַיַּיע לָךְ: מַקִּיזִין דָּם לִבְהֵמָה, וְאֵין מוֹנְעִין רְפוּאָה לִבְהֵמָה בְּחוּלּוֹ שֶׁל מוֹעֵד.

Rava also **permitted** one **to let the blood of an animal**[NB] for medical purposes **on the intermediate days of a Festival. Abaye said to him:** A *baraita* **is taught that supports you: One may let blood from an animal, and one** does **not withhold** any **medical treatment**[H] **from an animal on the intermediate days of a Festival.**

רָבָא שָׁרֵא לְכַסְכּוּסֵי קִירְמֵי. מַאי טַעְמָא? מַעֲשֵׂה הֶדְיוֹט הוּא. אָמַר רַב יִצְחָק בַּר אַמִי אָמַר רַב חִסְדָּא: קִיטּוּרֵי בִּירֵי – אָסִיר. מַאי טַעְמָא? מַעֲשֵׂה אוּמָּן הוּא.

Rava further **permitted** one **to scrub garments**[NH] as part of the laundry process. **What is the reason? It is the work of a layman** and not the work of a craftsman, which is prohibited on the intermediate days of a Festival. **Rav Yitzḥak bar Ami said that Rav Ḥisda said: Tying sleeves** to create pleats[N] **is prohibited. What is the reason? It is the work of a craftsman** and is consequently prohibited on the intermediate days of a Festival.

NOTES

A water channel to carry water that drives a mill – אַמַּת רֵיחַיָּא: Some explain that this phrase actually refers to the base on which the millstones are placed (*Talmid Rabbeinu Yeḥiel of Paris*; Commentary on *Moed Katan*).

To build a stable [*ureya*] – לְמִיבְנֵי אוּרְיָא: Some commentaries write that it would seem very surprising if it were permitted to build an entire stable for animals on the intermediate days of a Festival (*Talmid Rabbeinu Yeḥiel of Paris*). They interpret *ureya* to mean a trough, as it does in several other places in the Talmud. Alternatively, it means that one may flatten and smooth the location where the horses sleep (Rabbeinu Yehonatan of Lunel; *Talmid Rabbeinu Yeḥiel of Paris*).

To build a trough [*akarpita*] – לְמִיבְנֵי אַקַּרְפִּיטָא: Rashi and Rabbeinu Gershom Meor HaGola explain that an *akarpita* is a trough. Others understand it to be a wooden bench, unlike an *itztabba*, or regular bench, which is of stone (Rabbeinu Yehonatan of Lunel; *Sefer HaMeorot*; Ran). Some say there is no difference between an *itztabba* and an *akarpita*, and that both can be made of wood or stone (*Talmid Rabbeinu Yeḥiel of Paris*; Rabbi Shlomo ben HaYatom; Meiri). Rabbi Shlomo ben HaYatom asserts that the Gemara's next phrase, to build a bench, is meant as an explanation of this phrase.

To let the blood of an animal – לְמִישְׁקַל דְּמָא לִבְהֵמָה: Some explain that the reason for the leniency is in order to prevent an irretrievable loss (Ritva; Meiri). Some later authorities understand that the allowance is due to the pain suffered by the animal (*Keren Ora*; *Tal Ḥayyim*).

To scrub garments – לְכַסְכּוּסֵי קִירְמֵי: Rashi explains that this is scrubbing the garments by hand after washing them (Rashi manuscript). Others understand it as wetting the clothes and softening them (Rabbeinu Hananel, citing *ge'onim*). Alternatively, this means ironing the clothes (Rashi; *Talmid Rabbeinu Yeḥiel of Paris*).

Tying sleeves to create pleats – קִטּוּרֵי בִּירֵי: Most commentaries explain that this means making special pleats on sleeves that later would be sewn or tied in place; this is the work of a craftsman (Rid; *Arukh*). Some explain that it refers to making pleats in women's pants (*Talmid Rabbeinu Yeḥiel of Paris*). Rabbi Shlomo ben HaYatom understands it to mean burning spices underneath garments so that they will absorb the scent or tying the clothes in a special way before laundering them so that they will not shrink.

HALAKHA

Setting up a mill on the intermediate days of a Festival – תִּקּוּנֵי רֵיחַיִם בַּמּוֹעֵד: It is permitted to set up a mill on the intermediate days of a Festival, to construct a water channel for it, and to trim the hooves of the donkey used in the mill, in accordance with the opinion of Rav Yehuda (*Shulḥan Arukh, Oraḥ Hayyim* 540:8).

Grooming a horse – סְרִיקַת סוּס: On the intermediate days of a Festival one may groom a horse in order to beautify it (*Shulḥan Arukh, Oraḥ Hayyim* 536:2).

To build a trough – לְמִיבְנֵי אַקַּרְפִּיטָא: It is permitted to build a trough for an animal on the intermediate days of a Festival (*Shulḥan Arukh, Oraḥ Hayyim* 540:5).

To build a bench – לְמִיבְנֵי אִיצְטַבָּא: On the intermediate days of a Festival it is permitted to build a bench in a nonprofessional manner in order to be able to sit or lie down upon it (*Shulḥan Arukh, Oraḥ Hayyim* 540:6).

Medical treatment for an animal – רְפוּאַת בְּהֵמָה: One may let blood from an animal on the intermediate days of a Festival and take care of any of its health needs, even when this involves actions that are prohibited labors (*Shulḥan Arukh, Oraḥ Hayyim* 536:3).

To scrub garments – לְכַסְכּוּסֵי קִירְמֵי: It is permitted to scrub certain articles of clothing on the intermediate days of a Festival after they have been laundered in order to wear them on the Festival (*Magen Avraham*), and it is permitted to iron them in the usual manner (Rema). However, one may not iron pleats into a garment, as this is regarded as the work of a craftsman (*Shulḥan Arukh, Oraḥ Hayyim* 541:3).

אָמַר רָבָא: מַאן דְּמַתְקִיל אַרְעָא, אַדַּעְתָּא דְּבֵי דָּרֵי – שָׁרֵי; אַדַּעְתָּא דְּאַרְעָא – אֲסִיר.

§ **Rava said:** With regard to one **who clears the ground**[H] on the intermediate days of a Festival, the following distinction applies: If **his intention** is to prepare **a threshing floor,**[N] **it is permitted,** but if **his intention** is to prepare **the ground** for planting, **it is prohibited.**

הֵיכִי דָּמֵי? מוּלְיָא בְּמוּלְיָא וְנַצָּא בְּנַצָּא – אַדַּעְתָּא דְּבֵי דָּרֵי; שָׁקַל מוּלְיָא וּשְׁדָא בְּנַצָּא – אַדַּעְתָּא דְּאַרְעָא.

The Gemara asks: **What are the circumstances** of each case? The Gemara explains: If he casts earth from one **mound** [*mulya*] **onto** another **mound,**[N] **or from one furrow into** another **furrow** [*natza*], it is clear that he is doing this **with the intention of** preparing **a threshing floor,** as his sole interest is the level area in the middle and not the ground that surrounds it. However, if **he takes** earth **from a mound and casts it into a furrow,** he is presumably doing this **with the intention of** preparing **the ground** for planting, which is prohibited on the intermediate days of a Festival due to its similarity to the prohibited labor of plowing.

וְאָמַר רָבָא: הַאי מַאן דְּזָבֵי זִיבֵי אַדַּעְתָּא דְּצִיבֵי – שָׁרֵי; אַדַּעְתָּא דְּאַרְעָא – אֲסִיר. הֵיכִי דָּמֵי? שָׁקֵיל רַבְרְבֵי וְשָׁבֵיק זוּטְרֵי – אַדַּעְתָּא דְּצִיבֵי; שָׁקַל רַבְרְבֵי וְזוּטְרֵי – אַדַּעְתָּא דְּאַרְעָא.

And Rava said: With regard to **one who clears** his field from **twigs** on the intermediate days of a Festival, the following distinction applies: If **his intention** is to use **the twigs it is permitted,** but if **his intention** is to prepare **the ground** for planting, **it is prohibited.** The Gemara asks: **What are the circumstances** of each case? The Gemara explains: If **he takes the large** twigs **and leaves the small** ones, it is clear that he is doing this **with the intention of** using **the twigs.** But if **he takes** both **the large** twigs **and the small** ones, it appears as though that he is doing so **with the intention of** preparing **the ground,** and it is prohibited.[H]

וְאָמַר רָבָא: הַאי מַאן דְּפָתַח מַיָּא לְאַרְעֵיהּ, אַדַּעְתָּא דְּכַוְורֵי – שָׁרֵי; אַדַּעְתָּא דְּאַרְעָא – אֲסִיר.

And Rava further **said:** With regard to **one who opens the** gates **of a water** channel[H] running **through his land** on the intermediate days of a Festival, the following distinction applies: If **his intention** is to catch **the fish** that come along with the water, **it is permitted,** but if **his intention** is to water **the ground, it is prohibited.**

הֵיכִי דָּמֵי? פָּתַח תְּרֵי בָּבֵי, חַד מֵעִילָּאֵי וְחַד מִתַּתָּאֵי – אַדַּעְתָּא דְּכַוְורֵי; פָּתַח חַד בָּבָא – אַדַּעְתָּא דְּאַרְעָא.

The Gemara asks: **What are the circumstances** of each case? The Gemara explains: If **he opens two gates** in the water channel, **one above** his field **and one below,** so the water that flows in also flows out, it is clear that he is doing this **with the intention of** catching **fish,** as the water will flow out and only the fish will remain in the indentations in his field. But if **he opens** only **one** gate, he is presumably doing this **with the intention of** watering **the ground,** as it is evident that he wants the channel to fill and the water to overflow into the field.

וְאָמַר רָבָא: הַאי מַאן דְּפָשַׁח דִּיקְלָא אַדַּעְתָּא דְּחֵיוָתָא – שָׁרֵי; אַדַּעְתָּא דְּדִיקְלָא – אֲסִיר. הֵיכִי דָּמֵי? שָׁקֵיל כּוּלֵּיהּ מֵחַד גִּיסָא – אַדַּעְתָּא דְּחֵיוָתָא; מֵהַאי גִּיסָא וּמֵהַאי גִּיסָא – אַדַּעְתָּא דְּדִיקְלָא, וַאֲסִיר.

And Rava also **said:** With regard to **one who cuts** the branches of his **date palm** on the intermediate days of a Festival, the following distinction applies: If he does this **with the intention of feeding his animals, it is permitted,** but if he does it **with the intention of** enhancing the growth of his **date palm, it is prohibited.**[H] The Gemara asks: **What are the circumstances** of each case? The Gemara explains: If **he takes all** of the branches **from one side** of the tree, he is doing this **with the intention of** feeding the branches to **his animals,** as it is evident that he is not concerned with the damage to the date palm. However, if he takes the branches **from this side** of the tree **and** also **from the other side,** it appears as though he is doing so **with the intention of** enhancing the growth of **the date palm, and it is prohibited.**

וְאָמַר רָבָא: הָנֵי תַּמְרֵי תּוּחֲלָנֵי, מִיגְזְרִינְהוּ – שָׁרֵי; מְיָיצִינְהוּ – אֲסִיר. רַב פַּפָּא אָמַר: כֵּיוָן דְּמִתְלְעֵי – כִּפְרַקְמַטְיָא הָאָבֵד דָּמֵי, וְשָׁרֵי.

And Rava further **said: With regard to these unripe dates,**[H] **cutting them** into pieces in order to render them fit for eating **is permitted** on the intermediate days of a Festival, but **preserving them is prohibited,** as they will not be ready for use until after the Festival. **Rav Pappa said: Since they** are likely to **become infested with worms** if they are not properly attended to, **they are treated like merchandise that will be lost, and it is permitted** to preserve them on the intermediate days of a Festival.

HALAKHA

One who clears the ground – מַאן דְּמַתְקִיל אַרְעָא: It is prohibited to clear a field on the intermediate days of a Festival for the sake of plowing it. If it is evident that one is flattening the field in order to thresh grain there for the Festival, it is permitted (*Shulḥan Arukh, Oraḥ Hayyim* 537:9).

Gathering wood from a field – אִיסּוּף עֵצִים מִן הַשָּׂדֶה: One may not gather wood from a field on the intermediate days of a Festival in order to prepare the field for plowing, but it is permitted for one to do so if it is clear that he needs the wood (*Shulḥan Arukh, Oraḥ Hayyim* 537:10).

Opening the gates to a water channel running through one's field – פְּתִיחַת מַיִם לַשָּׂדֶה: It is prohibited to open the gates of a water channel running through one's field in order to water the field. However, if he does this to catch the fish that come with the water, e.g., if he opens both sides of the channel so that the water enters his field and drains from it, it is permitted (*Shulḥan Arukh, Oraḥ Hayyim* 537:8).

Cutting branches – קְצִיצַת עֲנָפִים: It is prohibited to cut the branches of a tree if one's intention is to enhance the growth of the tree, but if it is clear that he is cutting them to feed them to an animal, it is permitted (*Shulḥan Arukh, Oraḥ Hayyim* 537:11).

Unripe dates – תַּמְרֵי תּוּחֲלָנֵי: Fruit that is slightly ripened and is minimally edible may be picked on the intermediate days of a Festival in order to be eaten. If one picked them in order to eat them and there was fruit left over, and he is concerned that they will spoil, he may press them so that they not become ruined. However, he may not pick them from the outset in order to press them. In the case of a fruit that will not be available after the Festival, it is permitted even to pick them in order to press them, in accordance with the opinion of Rav Pappa (*Shulḥan Arukh, Oraḥ Hayyim* 533:3).

NOTES

If his intention is to prepare a threshing floor [*bei darei*] – אַדַּעְתָּא דְּבֵי דָּרֵי: Some explain that *bei darei* refers to a sheep pen. The continuation of the Gemara is to be understood in light of the fact that it is not necessary to flatten the entire field in order to construct a sheep pen (*Talmid Rabbeinu Yeḥiel of Paris*; *Tosefot HaRosh*).

From one mound onto another mound – מוּלְיָא בְּמוּלְיָא: Many commentaries had a different version of the text, according to which the ground is completely flattened for a threshing floor, whereas one is not as particular about this for a field (Rabbeinu Gershom Meor HaGola; Rabbeinu Yehonatan of Lunel). Conversely, some say that not only does a threshing floor not have to be entirely flat; it is actually convenient for there to be a slope (Rid; Ran). All agree that the difference is that in the first case, one flattens only part of the field, primarily the mounds and furrows, whereas in the second case one tries to render the entire field completely flat. Rabbeinu Hananel explains *mulya* and *natza* to mean soft and hard places in the ground, respectively.

וְאָמַר רָבָא: פְּרַקְמַטְיָא כׇּל שֶׁהוּא אָסוּר. אָמַר רַבִּי יוֹסֵי בַּר אָבִין: וּבְדָבָר הָאָבֵד – מוּתָּר. רָבִינָא הֲוָה לֵיהּ הַהוּא עִיסְקָא דַּהֲוָה מִזְדַּבֵּן בְּשִׁיתָּא אַלְפֵי. שָׁהֲיֵיהּ לְזַבּוּנֵיהּ בָּתַר חוּלָּא דְּמוֹעֲדָא וְזַבְּנֵיהּ בִּתְרֵיסַר אַלְפֵי.

§ And Rava also said: Any commerce[N] is prohibited on the intermediate days of a Festival. Rabbi Yosei bar Avin said: But with regard to a matter that, if left unattended, will result in significant loss,[N] it is permitted.[H] The Gemara relates that Ravina once had a joint business venture that could have been sold for six thousand dinars, but he delayed selling it until after the intermediate days of a Festival, and he sold it then for twelve thousand dinars.

רָבִינָא הֲוָה מַסֵּיק זוּזֵי בִּבְנֵי אַקְרָא דְּשַׁנְוָאתָא. אֲתָא לְקַמֵּיהּ דְּרַב אַשִׁי, אֲמַר לֵיהּ: מַהוּ לְמֵיזַל הָאִידָּנָא עֲלַיְיהוּ? אֲמַר לֵיהּ: כֵּיוָן דְּהָאִידָּנָא הוּא דְּמַשְׁכַּחַתְּ לְהוּ, בְּיוֹמֵי אַחֲרִינֵי לָא מַשְׁכַּחַתְּ לְהוּ – כִּפְרַקְמַטְיָא הָאָבֵד דָּמֵי, וְשָׁרֵי.

It is further related that Ravina had lent money to the residents of the fortress of Shanvata. He came before Rav Ashi and said to him: What is the *halakha* with regard to going to them now, on the intermediate days of the Festival, to collect my debt? Rav Ashi said to him: Since it is now that you will find them, whereas on other days you will not find them, as during the year these people would travel from place to place to earn their livelihood, this is treated like merchandise that will be lost, and it is therefore permitted.

תַּנְיָא נַמִּי גַּבֵּי עֲבוֹדָה זָרָה כִּי הַאי גַּוְונָא: הוֹלְכִין

The Gemara adds: So too, it is taught in a *baraita* with regard to idol worship like this case: One may go

NOTES

Any commerce – פְּרַקְמַטְיָא כׇּל שֶׁהוּא: Even though this seems obvious from the mishna in the next chapter, it was necessary for Rava to emphasize that this applies not only to a substantial business deal, but even to a trivial one (*Tal Hayyim*).

A matter that, if left unattended, will result in significant loss – דָּבָר הָאָבֵד: There are many different opinions about how to define a loss with regard to this *halakha*. The primary dispute is about whether the loss must be in the principal itself (*Tosafot*; see Rosh), or whether it can even be in the potential profit that one can earn (see Rashi and Ritva).

HALAKHA

Commerce on the intermediate days of a Festival – פְּרַקְמַטְיָא בַּמּוֹעֵד: It is prohibited to engage in commerce, including both selling and purchasing merchandise, on the intermediate days of a Festival. It is also prohibited to collect a loan that one had made if he needs the money for his business. The *Taz* holds that if he does not have to go to court, but merely needs to demand that the money be repaid, it is permitted. Others hold that even this is prohibited (Rabbi Akiva Eiger, citing Rosh). However, if he will not be able to find his debtor after the Festival, or if for any reason he will not be able to collect his loan, he may collect it on the intermediate days of the Festival. If he has the opportunity to make a great profit he may engage in commerce privately and then use his profits generously for the sake of the Festival (see Jerusalem Talmud; *Shulḥan Arukh*, *Oraḥ Hayyim* 539:1, and the comment of Rema).

Perek **I**
Daf **11** Amud **a**

לְיָרִיד שֶׁל גּוֹיִם, וְלוֹקְחִים בְּהֵמָה עֲבָדִים וּשְׁפָחוֹת בָּתִּים שָׂדוֹת וּכְרָמִים, וְכוֹתֵב וּמַעֲלֶה בְּעַרְכָּאוֹת שֶׁלָּהֶן, מִפְּנֵי שֶׁהוּא כְּמַצִּיל מִיָּדָן.

to a fair of pagan gentiles[H] held on a day they have designated for idol worship and buy animals, slaves, maidservants, houses, fields, and vineyards from them. And he may write the necessary deeds and confirm them in their courts [*arkaot*][LN] by verifying the signatures on the documents to prevent the sellers from appealing and retracting the sale. Although this behavior might be construed as a display of respect for the gentiles and their idols, it is nevertheless permitted because it is as if he were rescuing his property from their hands, as he would not have another opportunity to acquire these items. This indicates that time-sensitive transactions are considered like cases where one might suffer financial loss, and are permitted.

HALAKHA

A fair of pagan gentiles – יְרִיד שֶׁל גּוֹיִם: It is permitted to attend a fair of pagan gentiles and to buy animals, slaves, maidservants, houses, and fields. One may also write the necessary deeds and confirm them in the gentile courts (*Shulḥan Arukh*, *Yoreh De'a* 149:3).

LANGUAGE

Courts [*arkaot*] – עַרְכָּאוֹת: Apparently from the Greek ἀρχεῖον, *arkheyon*, which can be translated in a number of ways, including the seat of a judge, or the site of the local ruling council. Apparently this word was adopted into the Hebrew root *a-r-kh* in order to create a word that sounds like Hebrew. In talmudic parlance, *arkaot* refer to the official gentile courts, as opposed to the Jewish rabbinical courts.

NOTES

Gentile fairs and courts – יְרִידִים וְעַרְכָּאוֹת: Ordinarily, one may not do business at a fair of idol-worshipping gentiles, as the fair is held in honor of an idol, and the gentile will come to thank his god for his success. One may also not employ a gentile court, even if the laws are the same as Jewish laws on the issue at hand, as this accords honor to the pagans and detracts from the honor of the Jewish people.

רַב שְׁרָא לְחִיָּיא בַּר אַשִׁי לְמִיגְדַּל אוֹהֲרֵי בְּחוּלָּא דְמוֹעֲדָא. מַאי טַעְמָא? מַעֲשֵׂה הֶדְיוֹט הוּא. אֲבָל אִיזְלֵי – אָסוּר. מַאי טַעְמָא? מַעֲשֵׂה אוּמָּן הוּא.

It was related that **Rav permitted Ḥiyya bar Ashi to weave** simple **traps** [*oharei*][LB] **on the intermediate days of a Festival.** The Gemara explains: **What is the reason** for this? It is because **it is the work of a layman. However,** complex **nets** [*izlei*][LN] **are prohibited.**[H] **What is the reason? It is the work of a craftsman,** which is prohibited on the intermediate days of a Festival.

רַב יְהוּדָה שְׁרָא לְאַמִי תַּנּוּרָא לְמִיגְדָּל תַּנּוּרֵי, וּלְרַבָּה בַּר עַשָׁבִי לְמִיגְדָּל מְהוֹלְתָא. אִינִי? וְהָא תָּנֵי רַבָּה בַּר שְׁמוּאֵל: וְשָׁוִין שֶׁאֵין גּוֹדְלִין תַּנּוּר לְכַתְחִילָּה! לָא קַשְׁיָא: כָּאן – בִּימוֹת הַחַמָּה, כָּאן – בִּימוֹת הַגְּשָׁמִים.

It was further related that **Rav Yehuda permitted Ami the oven maker to construct ovens**[BNH] on the intermediate days of a Festival **and Rabba bar Ashabi to craft sieves.** The Gemara asks: **Is that** really **so? Didn't Rabba bar Shmuel teach** the following *baraita*: **And they** all **agree that one may not construct a new oven** on the intermediate days of a Festival. The Gemara answers that this is **not difficult: Here,** where Rav Yehuda permitted constructing an oven, he was referring **to the summer,** i.e., when the weather is hot and dry, so the oven can dry out and already be fit for use on the Festival; **there,** where the *baraita* prohibits constructing an oven, it is referring to **the rainy season,**[N] i.e., when the weather is such that the oven will not be ready for use on the Festival.

מתני׳ עוֹשִׂין מַעֲקֶה לַגַּג וְלַמִּרְפֶּסֶת מַעֲשֵׂה הֶדְיוֹט, אֲבָל לֹא מַעֲשֵׂה אוּמָּן. שָׁפִין אֶת הַסְּדָקִין וּמַעְגִּילִין אוֹתָן בְּמַעְגִּילָה בְּיָד וּבְרֶגֶל, אֲבָל לֹא בְּמַחֲלָצַיִם.

MISHNA **One may construct a railing for a roof or a balcony** if it is done in a nonprofessional manner, as **the work of a layman, but not** if it is done skillfully, as **the work of a craftsman. One may plaster the cracks**[H] in an oven **and roll over them with a roller,**[B] a wooden tool used to smooth out clay, **with a hand or a foot, but not with a presser,**[N] a tool that is specially designed for this task.

LANGUAGE

Traps [*oharei*] – אוֹהֲרֵי: This word seems to be related to the word *ḥarayot*, palm branches. *Oharei* refers to baskets that are made of palm branches and used to catch fish.

Complex nets [*izlei*] – אִיזְלֵי: This word stems from the Syriac root *azel*, which means a target. The reference is to a net woven from string by a skilled craftsman.

BACKGROUND

Traps [*oharei*] – אוֹהֲרֵי: According to the *ge'onim*, *oharei* are types of baskets made from braided palm branches that were used to catch fish or birds. The fish or bird would enter the basket on its own, and when it attempted to exit, the top of the basket would close.

Traditional fish trap

To construct ovens – לְמִיגְדָּל תַּנּוּרֵי: This term, which literally means braiding ovens, alludes to the manner in which they would construct clay ovens. First they would form a frame out of soft branches. Clay would be applied to the frame, and afterward when the oven would be heated, the branches would burn and the walls of the oven would turn hard and strong.

Roller – מַעְגִּילָה: In the talmudic era, most roofs were flat and lined with plaster, which would be reapplied each year before the rainy season. It was necessary to ensure that the surface of the roof would be smooth and at a very slight incline. The first stage in the process of smoothing the plaster was done with a roller, a large, circular piece of wood that would be rolled over the roof while the plaster was still moist. One would generally grip the roller by its handle, but it could be used without a handle as well. After this first stage was completed, the second, more precise stage would be done with a presser.

Ancient rollers found at Mount Gerizim

NOTES

Simple traps [*oharei*] and complex nets [*izlei*] – אוֹהֲרֵי וְאִיזְלֵי: There are various opinions as to the meaning of *oharei* and *izlei*. Some maintain that *oharei* are traps used to catch fish, whereas *izlei* are nets used to catch birds (Rashi). Others suggest that both are used to catch fish, but *oharei* are small nets, while *izlei* are large and intricate professional nets (Rashi on Rif; Rabbi Shlomo ben HaYatom). Yet others propose that *oharei* are fish nets made from branches, whereas *izlei* are nets woven from fabric (Rabbeinu Hananel; Ra'avad; *Talmid Rabbeinu Yeḥiel of Paris*; Ritva).

To construct [*lemigdal*] ovens – לְמִיגְדָּל תַּנּוּרֵי: Rabbeinu Yehonatan of Lunel understands that *lemigdal* is like *lemigbal*, meaning to mix [*legabel*] clay to construct an oven. Others explain that the term *lemigdal*, means to tie, as they would tie branches together to build the frame of the oven, cover the frame with clay, and then fire it in a kiln (Rashi on Rif; *Talmid Rabbeinu Yeḥiel of Paris*; Ritva; Meiri). Rabbi Shlomo ben HaYatom suggests that they made ovens by weaving together rolls of clay.

The summer and the rainy season – יְמוֹת חַמָּה וִימוֹת הַגְּשָׁמִים: Most commentaries interpret these terms as referring to Passover and Sukkot respectively. However, *Talmid Rabbeinu Yeḥiel of Paris* explains that it depends on the actual weather conditions at a given time.

A roller [*magila*] and a presser [*maḥalatzayim*] – מַעְגִּילָה וּמַחֲלָצַיִם: There are various opinions about the meaning of these terms. Some suggest that a *magila* is a roller made of wood or stone with which roofs are straightened (*Arukh*). Others propose that it is a large and heavy piece of wood that is used to even out plaster (Rabbi Shlomo ben HaYatom).

According to most commentaries, *maḥalatzayim* refers to a trowel (Rashi on Rif; Rabbeinu Yehonatan of Lunel; Rabbi Zekharya Agamati; *Talmid Rabbeinu Yeḥiel of Paris*). Others say that it is a piece of wood that is used to knock the plaster in order to even it out, which is difficult work (Meiri). The *Arukh* explains that the term *maḥalatzayim* refers to the handles of the roller.

HALAKHA

Fish traps on a Festival – רְשָׁתוֹת דָּגִים בַּמּוֹעֵד: It is permitted to produce fish traps from willow branches on the intermediate days of a Festival, as this is an ordinary, unskilled task, but one may not weave nets, as this is the work of a craftsman (*Shulḥan Arukh, Oraḥ Hayyim* 541:1).

An oven on a Festival – תַּנּוּר בַּמּוֹעֵד: It is permitted to construct earthenware ovens and stoves if there is sufficient time for them to dry and be used on the Festival. The same applies to pots and other utensils (Rema). If it is cold, it is permitted to construct an oven for heating (*Magen Avraham*) and to repair a window (*Shulḥan Arukh, Oraḥ Hayyim* 540:7; *Ḥayyei Adam*).

Fixing cracks – תִּיקּוּן סְדָקִים: It is permitted to fix cracks in the roof with one's hand or foot on the intermediate days of a Festival, but not with a craftsman's tools. If rain is leaking into the house, he may fix the roof even with tools (*Shulḥan Arukh, Oraḥ Hayyim* 540:3; *Beur Halakha*).

הַצִּיר וְהַצִּינּוֹר וְהַקּוֹרָה וְהַמַּנְעוּל וְהַמַּפְתֵּחַ שֶׁנִּשְׁבְּרוּ – מְתַקְּנָן בַּמּוֹעֵד, וּבִלְבַד שֶׁלֹּא יִתְכַּוֵּין לַעֲשׂוֹת מְלַאכְתּוֹ בַּמּוֹעֵד.

With regard to **the hinge** of a door, **and the cylinder** of the hinge, **and the** cross **beam**[N] that holds the door, **and a lock and a key that broke, one may fix them on** the intermediate days of **a Festival** as these items are essential for the Festival and their repair cannot be delayed.[H] This is permitted, **provided that he does not intend** ahead of time **to do his labor on the Festival** and delay it until that time.

וְכָל כְּבָשִׁין שֶׁהוּא יָכוֹל לֶאֱכוֹל מֵהֶן בַּמּוֹעֵד – כּוֹבְשָׁן.

And with regard to **all preserved food from which one can eat on the Festival,** since they become ready to be eaten in a short amount of time, **he** may **preserve them** on the intermediate days of a Festival.

גמ׳ הֵיכִי דָּמֵי מַעֲשֵׂה הֶדְיוֹט? רַב יוֹסֵף אָמַר: בְּהוּצָא וְדַפְנָא. בְּמַתְנִיתָא תָּנָא: צָר בִּצְרוֹר וְאֵינוֹ טָח בְּטִיט.

GEMARA The Gemara asks: **What are the circumstances** in which a railing is considered **the work of a layman? Rav Yosef said:** When it is made **with palm branches and** the branches of **bay trees,** which do not create a permanent structure. **It was taught in a *baraita*** that **he fills in** the space **with stone but he does not plaster** the stones **with clay.**

״שָׁפִין אֶת הַסְּדָקִין וּמַעְגִּילִין אוֹתָן בְּמַעְגִּילָה״. הַשְׁתָּא בְּמַעְגִּילָה אָמְרַתְּ שָׁרֵי, בְּיָד וּבְרֶגֶל מִיבַּעְיָא?! הָכִי קָאָמַר: שָׁפִין אֶת הַסְּדָקִין וּמַעְגִּילִין אוֹתָן כְּעֵין מַעְגִּילָה בְּיָד וּבְרֶגֶל, אֲבָל לֹא בְּמַחֲלָצַיִם.

It was taught in the mishna: **One may plaster the cracks** in an oven **and roll over them with a roller,** with a hand or a foot, but not with a presser. The Gemara asks: **Now** that **you said** that **it is permitted** to roll over the cracks **with a roller, is it necessary** to say that one may plaster the cracks **with a hand or a foot?** The Gemara answers that **this is what** the mishna **is saying: One may plaster the cracks** in an oven **and roll over them as if with a roller,** meaning **with a hand or a foot,**[N] **but not with a presser,** which is a craftsman's tool made especially for this.

״הַצִּיר וְהַצִּינּוֹר וְהַקּוֹרָה וְהַמַּנְעוּל וְהַמַּפְתֵּחַ שֶׁנִּשְׁבְּרוּ מְתַקְּנָן בַּמּוֹעֵד״. וּרְמִינְהִי: עַד יָמָיו הָיָה פַּטִּישׁ מַכֶּה בִּירוּשָׁלַיִם כו׳. עַד יָמָיו – אִין, מִכָּאן וְאֵילָךְ – לָא!

It was taught in the mishna: With regard to **the hinge** of a door, **and the cylinder** of the hinge, **and the** cross **beam** that holds the door, **and a lock and a key that broke, one may fix them on** the intermediate days of **a Festival.** The Gemara **raises a contradiction** to this from a different mishna (*Ma'aser Sheni* 5:15): **Until the days** of Yoḥanan the High Priest, workmen's **hammers would beat in Jerusalem** on the intermediate days of a Festival. One can deduce from this mishna that **until his days, yes,** the workmen's hammers would beat, **but from then on, no,** because Yoḥanan the High Priest banned such work. This seems to contradict the mishna here that permits fixing certain items on the intermediate days of the Festival.

לָא קַשְׁיָא; כָּאן – בְּדַנַּפָּחֵי. כָּאן – בְּדַנַּגָּרֵי.

The Gemara answers: **This** is **not difficult: There,** when it is prohibited, it is referring to the work of **smiths,** which generates a great deal of noise; **here,** where it is permitted, it is referring to the work **of carpenters,** which is much quieter.

מַתְקִיף לָהּ רַב חִסְדָּא: יֹאמְרוּ קָלָא רַבָּה – אֲסִיר, קָלָא זוּטָר – שָׁרֵי! אֶלָּא אָמַר רַב חִסְדָּא: לָא קַשְׁיָא; הָא – בְּמַגְלֵי, הָא – בַּחֲצִינֵי. רַב פָּפָּא אָמַר: כָּאן – קוֹדֶם גְּזֵירָה, כָּאן – לְאַחַר גְּזֵירָה.

Rav Ḥisda strongly objects to this: If so, people **will say** that **a loud noise is prohibited,** but **a soft noise is permitted. Rather, Rav Ḥisda said** that the apparent contradiction is **not difficult** for a different reason: **This** mishna that permits labor is referring to **sickles,** as sickles emit no noise at all; whereas **that** mishna that prohibits labor is referring to **chisels.**[N] **Rav Pappa said: Here** in the mishna it is referring to the period **before the decree** of Yoḥanan the High Priest; whereas **there** in the other mishna it is referring to the period **after the decree.**

רַב אַשִׁי אָמַר: הָא – רַבִּי יְהוּדָה, הָא – רַבִּי יוֹסֵי. דְּאָמַר רַבִּי יִצְחָק בַּר אַבְדִּימִי: מַאן תְּנָא שִׁינּוּי בַּמּוֹעֵד בְּדָבָר הָאָבֵד? דְּלָא כְּרַבִּי יוֹסֵי.

Rav Ashi said: That mishna, which prohibits this labor, was taught in accordance with the opinion of **Rabbi Yehuda;** while **this** mishna was taught in accordance with the opinion of **Rabbi Yosei. As Rabbi Yitzḥak bar Avdimi said: Who is the *tanna*** who **taught** that all labor performed **on** the intermediate days of **a Festival** must be done **with a change,** i.e., in an altered manner, even **with** regard to **a matter that will be lost** if timely action is not taken? It is **not in accordance with** the opinion of **Rabbi Yosei,** as Rabbi Yosei permits doing labor that will prevent financial loss even when it is done in the usual manner.

NOTES

The hinge [*tzir*], the cylinder [*tzinor*], and the cross beam [*kora*] – הַצִּיר וְהַצִּינּוֹר וְהַקּוֹרָה: Most commentaries understand that *tzir* refers to a hinge upon which the door swivels. Others suggest that it is the hole into which the hinge is inserted (Rid).

According to most commentaries, *tzinor* refers to the hole into which the hinge is inserted. Some explain that it is a water pipe (Rambam's Commentary on the Mishna). The *kora* is a crossbeam that reinforces the door or serves as a bolt (*Talmid Rabbeinu Yeḥiel of Paris*). Alternatively, it refers to a beam that supports the house (Rabbeinu Yehonatan of Lunel). The reason that these items may be fixed on the intermediate days of a Festival is that the lack of a functioning door is likely to cause an irretrievable loss, in accordance with the talmudic adage: An opening beckons to a thief (Rambam; Rabbeinu Yehonatan of Lunel; Riaz).

As if with a roller, with a hand or a foot – כְּעֵין מַעְגִּילָה בְּיָד וּבְרֶגֶל: For those who explain that *magila* is a kind of roller and *mahalatzayim* is a trowel, this should be understood as follows: Not only is a roller, which is a special tool used to even out a roof, prohibited; even a trowel is prohibited. One may only do the work by hand, and this is permitted even if the finished product is as smooth and beautiful as if a tool had been used. According to the *Arukh*, who explains *mahalatzayim* as the handles of the roller, this means that one is permitted to use a roller but only without the handles, by rolling it with his hand or his foot (see Meiri).

Sickles and chisels – מַגְלֵי וַחֲצִינֵי: Rashi and the Rid maintain that tools that emit almost no noise are permitted. Most commentaries understand that sickles are tools that are not made for this kind of work, as opposed to chisels, which are the tools of craftsmen (Commentary on *Moed Katan*; *Tosefot HaRosh*; Ritva).

HALAKHA

Fixing a door or a lock – תִּיקּוּן הַדֶּלֶת וּמַנְעוּלָהּ: If the hinges of a door, its lock, key, cylinder, or crossbeam break even slightly, regardless of whether they are made from wood or metal, it is permitted to repair them on the intermediate days of a Festival in the usual manner. This is true only if one does not intentionally leave the repairs to be done on the Festival (*Shulḥan Arukh*, *Oraḥ Ḥayyim* 540:4, and the comment of Rema).

אָמַר רָבִינָא: כְּמַאן מַדְלֵינַן הָאִידָּנָא קַבְיוּתָא דְּדָשָׁא בְּחוּלָּא דְּמוֹעֲדָא? כְּמַאן – כְּרַבִּי יוֹסֵי.

Ravina said: In accordance with whose opinion **do we now lift the lintel above the door**[N] in order to drive in the nails that had loosened **on the intermediate days of a Festival** in the usual manner? **In accordance with whose** opinion is this done? It is done **in accordance with** the opinion of **Rabbi Yosei,** who permits labor that will prevent financial loss even when it is done in the usual manner.

״כְּבָשִׁין שֶׁהוּא יָכוֹל לֶאֱכוֹל בַּמּוֹעֵד – כּוֹבְשָׁן״. בְּדִיתָא לְבָאי כַּוְורֵי. אָזֵיל כּוּלֵּי עָלְמָא צוּד, אַיְיתוּ כַּוְורָא. שְׁרָא לְהוּ רָבָא לְמִימְלַח מִינַּיְיהוּ.

§ It was taught in the mishna: With regard to all **preserved food from which he can eat on the Festival, he** may **preserve them** on the intermediate days of a Festival. The Gemara relates that the **Bedita** River once **overflowed,** depositing large quantities of **fish**[N] in small water deposits on the river bank on the intermediate days of a Festival. **Everyone went and trapped and brought** home **fish,**[H] and **Rava permitted them to salt** some **of** the fish.

אֲמַר לֵיהּ אַבַּיֵי: וְהָא תְּנַן: כְּבָשִׁין שֶׁהוּא יָכוֹל לֶאֱכוֹל מֵהֶן בַּמּוֹעֵד – כּוֹבְשָׁן! אֲמַר לֵיהּ: כֵּיוָן דְּמֵעִיקָּרָא אַדַּעְתָּא דַּאֲכִילָה אַיְיתִינְהוּ, וְאִי שָׁבֵיק לְהוּ פָּסְדִי – כִּפְרַקְמַטְיָא הָאָבֵד דָּמֵי, וְשָׁרֵי.

Abaye[P] **said to him: Didn't we learn** in the mishna: With regard to **all preserved food from which he can eat on the Festival, he** may **preserve them** on the intermediate days of a Festival? In this case it was impossible to eat that much fish on the Festival, and therefore preserving them should have been prohibited. Rava **said to him: Since they initially brought** these fish **with the intention of eating** them on the Festival,[N] and it only became clear afterward that they had brought too many, **and if one would leave them** without salting them **they would be ruined, they are** treated **like merchandise that will be lost, and** therefore preserving them **is permitted.**

וְאִיכָּא דְּאָמְרִי: שָׁרֵי לְהוּ רָבָא מֵיצָד, מֵיזָל, אַיְיתוּיֵי, וּמִימְלָח. אֲמַר לֵיהּ אַבַּיֵי: וְהָא אֲנַן ״כְּבָשִׁין שֶׁהוּא יָכוֹל לֶאֱכוֹל מֵהֶן כּוֹבְשָׁן״ תְּנַן!

And some say that it did not happen in this manner, rather, **Rava permitted them to trap** the fish, **to bring them** home, **and to salt** them. **Abaye said to him: Didn't we learn** in the mishna: With regard to **all preserved food from which he can eat on the Festival, he** may **preserve them** on the intermediate days of a Festival? These fish were heavily salted and consequently could not be eaten until they thoroughly dried out.

אֲמַר לֵיהּ: הָנֵי נַמִי מִיתְאַכְלִי אַגַּב אִיצְיָא. כִּי הָא דִּשְׁמוּאֵל עֲבַדוּ לֵיהּ שִׁיתִּין אִיצְיֵי, וַאֲכַל. רָבָא אִיקְּלַע לְבֵי רֵישׁ גָּלוּתָא, עָבְדִי לֵיהּ שִׁיתִּין אִיצְיֵי וַאֲכַל.

Rava **said to him: These** fish that were just salted **can also be eaten** now, **by pressing** out the salt and brine, and therefore, they too are fit to be eaten on the Festival, **as in that** case **of Shmuel,** where **they prepared** recently salted fish **for him by pressing** it **sixty times and he ate** the fish. The Gemara relates that **Rava happened** to come **to the house of the Exilarch** and **they prepared** freshly salted fish **for him by pressing** it **sixty times, and he ate** it.

NOTES

The lintel above the door – **קַבְיוּתָא דְּדָשָׁא**: The meaning of this term is in dispute. Some understand that it refers to a lintel from which nails have fallen out (Ran; see Rabbi Shlomo ben HaYatom). Others explain that it is a bolt that fell out of place and needs to be reinforced with nails (Commentary on *Moed Katan*; *Tosefot HaRosh*). There are also those who understand that it refers to the door's lock. Yet others suggest that it is the hole into which the bolt is inserted (Rabbi Shlomo ben HaYatom).

The Bedita River overflowed [*levai*], depositing large quantities of fish – **בְּדִיתָא לְבָאי כַּוְורֵי**: Some understand that the river's waters overflowed its banks and some of the fish were carried out into the neighboring fields (*Tosefot HaRosh*; Rabbi Shlomo ben HaYatom). Others interpret *levai* as the name of a place, or meaning to dry up. They explain that the river went dry or its waters were diverted, leaving fish on the river bed (Rabbeinu Gershom Meor HaGola; Rashi; Rid).

Since they initially brought these fish with the intention of eating them on the Festival – **כֵּיוָן דְּמֵעִיקָּרָא אַדַּעְתָּא דַּאֲכִילָה אַיְיתִינְהוּ**: It is clear from this discussion that it would have been prohibited to catch the fish with the intention of leaving them for after the Festival. The Ra'avad questions why this case is different than the case cited in the Jerusalem Talmud of a passing caravan that offers a unique business opportunity. The *halakha* is that it is permitted to conduct business in that case because not doing so would be considered an irretrievable loss. Here, too, the opportunity to catch these fish should be treated similarly. He answers by distinguishing between buying and selling merchandise and acquiring ownerless property; the latter can never be considered a loss. Alternatively, there is a difference between conducting business, which is prohibited only due to the exertion involved, and catching fish, which involves a prohibited labor.

HALAKHA

Fishing on the Festival – **דִּיג בַּמּוֹעֵד**: One may trap as many fish as he can on the intermediate days of a Festival and salt them all, as it is possible for him to eat them on the Festival. Likewise, it is permitted to catch them in public, as it is clear to all that it is for the Festival (*Shulḥan Arukh*, *Oraḥ Hayyim* 53:34, and the comment of Rema).

PERSONALITIES

Abaye and Rava – **אַבַּיֵי וְרָבָא**: Abaye, whose name was Naḥmani ben Kaylil, and Rava, whose name was Abba ben Yosef bar Ḥama, were among the great Sages of the fourth generation of Babylonian *amora'im*, and lived in the fourth century CE. The dialogues between Abaye and Rava recorded in the Gemara are classic examples of talmudic debate, so much so that the Gemara itself is referred to as the discussions of Abaye and Rava. Among their hundreds of disagreements, the accepted halakhic ruling follows the opinion of Abaye in only six cases.

Abaye and Rava were close friends, and their teachings often appear together in the Gemara. Abaye was orphaned at the time of his birth and raised by his paternal uncle, Rabba. Rava also studied under Rabba as a student in the academy in Pumbedita. After the death of Rabba and of Rav Yosef, Abaye was chosen to head the academy in Pumbedita, and Rava moved to Meḥoza, where he headed a yeshiva. Following Abaye's death, many of the students in Pumbedita joined Rava in Meḥoza, which had become the center of Torah study in Babylonia.

רַב אִיקְלַע לְבֵי רַב שַׁפִּיר, אַיְיתוּ לְקַמֵּיהּ הַהוּא כַּוְורָא, תִּילְתָּא בִּישׁוּלָא, תִּילְתָּא מִילְחָא, וְתִילְתָּא טַוְויָא.

Apropos eating fish in various ways, the Gemara relates that **Rav** once **happened** to come **to the house of Rav Shapir,** and **they brought before him a certain fish,** of which **one- third** was **cooked, one-third** was **salted** and made edible via pressing, and **one-third** was **broiled.**

אָמַר רַב, אָמַר לִי אַדָּא צַיָּידָא: כַּוְורָא, סָמוּךְ לְמִיסְרְחֵיהּ מַעֲלֵי. וְאָמַר רַב, אָמַר לִי אַדָּא צַיָּידָא: כַּוְורָא, טַוְויֵיא בְּאַחוּהּ, אַסּוּקֵיהּ בַּאֲבוּהּ, מֵיכְלֵי בִּבְרֵיהּ, אִשְׁתִּי עֲלֵיהּ אֲבוּהּ.

Rav said: Adda the fisherman told me that **a fish** that has sat for some time and is **close to spoiling is** at its **best.**[B] **And Rav** also **said: Adda the fisherman told me:** With regard to **a fish, broil it with its brother,** i.e., with salt, which, like fish, also comes from the sea; **place it in its father,** i.e., in water; and **eat it with its son,**[N] i.e., with fish brine which comes from it; **and drink after it its father,** i.e., water.[B]

וְאָמַר רַב, אָמַר לִי אַדָּא צַיָּידָא: כַּוְורָא תַּחְלֵי וְחַלְבָּא לִיטְעוֹן גּוּפָא וְלָא לִיטְעוֹן פּוּרְיָא. וְאָמַר רַב, אָמַר לִי אַדָּא צַיָּידָא: כַּוְורָא, תַּחְלֵי, וְחַלְבָּא – מַיָּא וְלָא שִׁיכְרָא, שִׁיכְרָא וְלָא חַמְרָא.

And in addition **Rav said: Adda the fisherman told me:** After eating **fish, cress, and milk, let the body carry them**[N] **and let not the bed carry them,** i.e., it is advisable to go for a walk after eating them, rather than immediately going to sleep. **And Rav said: Adda the fisherman told me:** After eating **fish, cress,**[N] **and milk,** it is better to drink **water and not beer,** and if he has no water, he should drink **beer and not wine,** in order to avoid harming his body.

הדרן עלך משקין בית השלחין

BACKGROUND

Close to spoiling is at its best – סָמוּךְ לְמִיסְרְחֵיהּ מַעֲלֵי: One of the ways of processing raw meat is to leave it out for an extended period of time, almost to the point of rotting. With the help of bacteria, the meat begins to decompose and the hard meat softens. This bacterial activity also adds flavor to the meat. It seems that certain fish (see *Tosafot*) were also prepared in this manner. Of course, this process can lead to food poisoning if the meat or fish are left out too long.

Ways to eat fish – דַּרְכֵי אֲכִילַת דָּגִים: The Ra'avad explains that these pieces of advice were intended to ensure that the food not be digested too quickly and that the digestive process not interfere with sleep. Therefore, one was advised not go to sleep immediately after eating. On the other hand, it was believed that alcoholic beverages, e.g., beer, and certainly wine, speed up the digestion of fats, and so, in order to prolong the feeling of satiation and the taste of the food, it was advised that one not drink such beverages after eating these foods.

NOTES

Eat it with its son – מֵיכְלֵי בִּבְרֵיהּ: Some explain that this means that it should be eaten with a sauce made from young fish, in which case the word son is even more precise (*Arukh*).

Let the body carry [*liton*] them – לִיטְעוֹן גּוּפָא: Rav Sherira Gaon explains that these foods are good for the body but increase semen, and therefore it is better not to go to sleep immediately after eating them. Some have an alternative version of the text that reads: Let the body taste [*litom*] them, which means that the tastes of these foods remain in one's mouth for a certain period of time after they are eaten, and therefore it is recommended that one let the body savor these tastes and not go to sleep immediately (Ra'avad).

Cress – תַּחְלֵי: Some explain that the reference is to a type of dates (Rabbi Shlomo ben HaYatom).

Summary of **Perek I**

Despite the fact that the Sages stated that the *halakhot* of the Festival are sterile, i.e., isolated, and may not be learned one from the other (*Moed Katan* 12a), there are clear criteria that can be used to determine which activities are prohibited or permitted on the intermediate days of the Festival.

Among the activities permitted on the intermediate days of the Festival are those that are defined as incurring financial loss, i.e., refraining from this work will cause significant loss, and therefore the Sages permitted them on the intermediate days of the Festival.

Another category of permitted activity on the intermediate days of the Festival includes labors that are not performed by craftsmen, i.e., those that do not require a specific skill, or that are not performed in the manner of the craftsmen. Additionally, an activity that is necessary for the celebration of the Festival would be permitted on the intermediate days of the Festival. In general, the Sages prohibited labors that involved significant exertion, especially those that were directly related to agricultural labor.

Because there was often a clash between the various criteria delineated above, the Sages established individualized rulings on a case by case basis. In each case, in order to determine the *halakha* they applied the principles that had been set in place.

With regard to the injunction to rejoice on the Festival, it was concluded that one should not do anything on the intermediate days of the Festival that would likely lead to distress. Thus, a priest may not examine a leper on the intermediate days of the Festival, and one may not make public eulogies during this period. Out of a similar concern for the commandment to rejoice on the Festival, the Sages prohibited marrying during this time, as this would impinge upon the preparations for the Festival as well as introduce a conflicting source of celebration.

Introduction to **Perek II**

The clarification of the conditions and considerations that permit or prohibit labor on the intermediate days of a Festival is the central topic of this chapter.

In the previous chapter the justifications for a person's performing labor on the intermediate days of a Festival were discussed. One of the most common and important dispensations to work on the intermediate days of a Festival would be for a matter for which there is a high probability that loss will occur if timely action is not taken to safeguard it. In the present chapter the discussion of various issues, with regard to which such a concern is significant, continues.

One question is: What exactly is a matter that, if left unattended, will result in meaningful loss? Would an item suffering any amount of damage or monetary loss be considered a matter that will be lost? Or perhaps only the probability of serious damage or monetary loss would permit the performance of labor on the intermediate days of a Festival.

Another fundamental question concerns employment of artifice, since a person could intentionally create circumstances that require performing labor on the intermediate days of a Festival such that, if he does not perform it at that time, it will cause a great loss. The question, therefore, is whether we operate according to the existing situation, which has been caused by artifice, in which we have a matter that will be lost that can justify performing labor, or whether we punish the perpetrator for his trickery.

Two other justifications for the performance of labor on the intermediate days of a Festival are discussed in this chapter: Performance of labor for the community and performance of labor in order to enable the laborer to have food for the days of the Festival.

מתני׳ מִי שֶׁהָפַךְ אֶת זֵיתָיו, וְאֵירְעוֹ אֵבֶל אוֹ אוֹנֶס, אוֹ שֶׁהִטְעוּהוּ פּוֹעֲלִים – טוֹעֵן קוֹרָה רִאשׁוֹנָה, וּמַנִּיחָהּ לְאַחַר הַמּוֹעֵד, דִּבְרֵי רַבִּי יְהוּדָה.

MISHNA The mishna discusses **one who had** already **turned over his olives**[BH] as part of the process of preparing them for pressing, **and mourning** for a close relative **befell him**[N] and as a result he was prohibited from engaging in work, **or** some other **unavoidable accident** occurred, **or** his **workers misled him,** promising to come but failing to do so, so that he could not press his olives before the Festival. Under these circumstances, during the intermediate days of the Festival, **he may** place the olives in the press and **load the beam**[B] with weights for the **initial** pressing of the olives and **leave it** this way **until after the Festival;** this is **the statement of Rabbi Yehuda.**

רַבִּי יוֹסֵי אוֹמֵר: זוֹלֵף וְגוֹמֵר וְגָף כְּדַרְכּוֹ.

Rabbi Yosei says: He may press the olives **and complete** the process **and** then **plug** each barrel of oil **in its** usual **manner.**[N] Since delay can entail financial loss, the Sages did not require him to alter the normal process of extracting the oil.

גמ׳ פָּתַח בְּאֵבֶל וְסַיֵּים בְּמוֹעֵד! אָמַר רַב שֵׁישָׁא בְּרֵיהּ דְּרַב אִידִי: זֹאת אוֹמֶרֶת דְּבָרִים הַמּוּתָּרִין בַּמּוֹעֵד – אֲסוּרִים בִּימֵי אֶבְלוֹ.

GEMARA The Gemara asks: The *tanna* **opens** the mishna **with** a case of **mourning and ends** it **with** the *halakhot* of the intermediate days of **the Festival,** leaving the connection between them unclear. **Rav Sheisha, son of Rav Idi, said: That is to say: Actions that are permitted on** the intermediate days of **a Festival**[N] **are prohibited during the days of one's mourning.**[H] Therefore, if a mourning period befell one before the Festival, and he could not prepare properly for the Festival due to the prohibition against performance of labor by a mourner, he is permitted to perform labor during the intermediate days of the Festival to avoid financial loss.

NOTES

Mourning befell him – אֵירְעוֹ אֵבֶל: Rashi explains that this mishna is addressing two distinct cases: The case of one whose relative died unrelated to the Festival and was therefore prohibited from completing the process of pressing his olives, etc., and a different case of one who suffered some accident that prevented him from completing the process of pressing his olives before the Festival. According to Rashi, the dispute between Rabbi Yehuda and Rabbi Yosei is with regard to the labors permitted either during the mourning period or during the intermediate days of the Festival. Other commentaries understand the mourning as occurring right before the Festival. According to that explanation, it is merely another example of an unforeseen circumstance that can interfere with preparations for the Festival, and the dispute between Rabbi Yehuda and Rabbi Yosei with regard to what one is permitted to do concerns only the intermediate days of the Festival (Ritva).

And plug each barrel of oil in its usual manner – וְגָף כְּדַרְכּוֹ: The early authorities understood the dispute between Rabbi Yehuda and Rabbi Yosei in different ways. Some maintain that they disagree with regard to whether labor is permitted during the intermediate days of a Festival in order to prevent even a moderate loss. The most valuable oil is extracted in the first press, and the loss of the oil extracted subsequently is not as substantial (Rashi; Rabbeinu Yehonatan of Lunel; Ritva). Others explain that the dispute is about the nature of the allowance to perform labor during the intermediate days of the Festival due to financial loss. Rabbi Yehuda requires that it be performed in an altered manner and Rabbi Yosei permits one to perform the labor in the usual way (Rosh).

That is to say, actions permitted on the intermediate days of a Festival, etc. – זֹאת אוֹמֶרֶת דְּבָרִים הַמּוּתָּרִין בַּמּוֹעֵד וכו׳: Rav Sheisha's point is that the allowance of labor on the intermediate days of the Festival in order to avoid financial loss does not apply in parallel to one who is in mourning. According to those who explain that the mourning period mentioned in the mishna is merely an example of circumstances interfering with preparations for the Festival, Rav Sheisha's point is derived directly from the fact that the mishna allows labor in cases of loss on the Festival. Since the loss in this case arises from the fact that one could not complete his labor beforehand because he was in mourning, it must be the case that such labors were prohibited during the mourning period (Ritva). According to Rashi's reading of the mishna, Rav Sheisha's point is derived from the fact that the mishna specifies the allowance only in the context of the Festival.

BACKGROUND

Turning over the olives – הֲפִיכַת הַזֵּיתִים: In order to extract the maximum amount of oil from olives, one must first soften them. For this purpose, they are collected into piles. The fermentation that results releases heat, which aids the softening process but necessitates that the olives be turned from time to time to prevent spoilage.

Beam – קוֹרָה: The beam of an olive press is a large, heavy pole that is placed in a hole in a wall above a basket of olives and weighted down on the other side in such a way that it presses down on the olives. The olive oil that is squeezed out is collected in a hole in the ground or in special utensils prepared for it.

Ancient olive press

HALAKHA

One who had already turned over his olives – מִי שֶׁהָפַךְ אֶת זֵיתָיו: If one had turned over his olives, or had his wine in the pit, and an unavoidable accident befell him, preventing him from finishing the task on time, or even if he began these labors because he thought he could complete them after the Festival but was in fact unable to do so, then since it is a matter that, if unattended, will result in significant loss, he may finish it as usual and line the barrels with pitch. Any labor that, if unattended, will result in significant loss is permitted on the intermediate days of the Festival (*Shulḥan Arukh*, *Oraḥ Ḥayyim* 538:1).

Festival and mourning – מוֹעֵד וְאֵבֶל: With regard to all matters that are permitted on the intermediate days of a Festival for the needs of the Festival, a mourner is prohibited from engaging in them, even through others (*Shulḥan Arukh*, *Yoreh De'a* 380:10).

רַב אַשִׁי אָמַר: לָא מִיבָּעֲיָא קָאָמַר: לָא מִיבָּעֲיָא בִּימֵי אֶבְלוֹ דְּמִדְּרַבָּנָן הוּא, וְשָׁרֵי, אֶלָּא אֲפִילּוּ בַּמּוֹעֵד, דְּאִיסּוּר מְלָאכָה מִדְּאוֹרַיְיתָא, בִּמְקוֹם פְּסֵידָא – שָׁרוּ רַבָּנַן.

Rav Ashi said that the *tanna* of the mishna **is speaking** utilizing the didactic style of: **It is not necessary,**[N] and he is teaching two separate *halakhot*, one about mourning and the other about the Festival: **It is not necessary** to state that **during the days of his mourning, when** the prohibition against labor **is rabbinic, it is permitted** to perform labor that, if delayed, could cause serious loss; **but even on the** intermediate days of the **Festival, when the prohibition against** performing **labor is by Torah law,**[N] performing such labor is permitted because **in a case of a loss the Sages permitted** it.

תַּנְיָא כְּווֹתֵיהּ דְּרַב שֵׁישָׁא בְּרֵיהּ דְּרַב אִידִי: אֵלּוּ דְּבָרִים הָעוֹשִׂין לָאָבֵל בִּימֵי אֶבְלוֹ: זֵיתָיו הֲפוּכִין – טוֹעֲנִין לוֹ, וְכַדּוֹ לָגוּף, וּפִשְׁתָּנוֹ לְהַעֲלוֹת מִן הַמִּשְׁרָה, וְצַמְרוֹ לְהַעֲלוֹת מִן הַיּוֹרָה, וּמַרְבִּיצִים שָׂדֵהוּ מִשֶּׁתַּגִּיעַ עוֹנַת הַמַּיִם שֶׁלּוֹ.

The Gemara comments: **It is taught** in a *baraita* **in accordance with** the opinion **of Rav Sheisha, son of Rav Idi: These are actions that** others **perform for the mourner during the days of his mourning:** If **his olives have** already **been turned over, they may load** them **for him** into the olive press, **and** likewise if **his cask** needs **to be plugged,** or if **his flax** needs **to be lifted out of the soaking pool**[B] where it will rot if not removed in time, **or** if **his wool** needs **to be lifted from the cauldron** into which it was placed for dyeing, they perform all these actions for him. **They** also **irrigate his field when his turn for water**[B] **arrives,** as in many places, each field would receive water in turn according to a prearranged schedule. If one does not utilize the water when his turn arrives, he loses that water. This supports Rav Sheisha's opinion that the prohibition against performing labor is waived in cases of loss only on the Festival. Under such circumstances, labor is prohibited to a mourner and in cases of loss may only be performed for him by others.

רַבִּי יְהוּדָה אוֹמֵר: אַף זוֹרְעִין לוֹ שְׂדֵה נִיר, וְשָׂדֶה הָעוֹמֶדֶת לְפִשְׁתָּן. אָמְרוּ לוֹ: אִם לֹא תִּזָּרַע בְּבַכִּיר – תִּזָּרַע בְּאָפֵל, אִם לֹא תִּזָּרַע פִּשְׁתָּן – תִּזָּרַע מִמִּין אַחֵר.

The *baraita* continues: **Rabbi Yehuda says: They also sow for him a plowed field or a field set aside for flax,**[B] where the time of sowing is critical. If the field is sown later, it will cause a loss. The Sages **said to him:** If that field **is not sown in the early** season, **it can be sown in the later** season; and similarly, **if it is not sown with flax, it can be sown with another species.** Therefore, this is not considered a great loss, and the Sages did not permit it.

רַבָּן שִׁמְעוֹן בֶּן גַּמְלִיאֵל אוֹמֵר: זֵיתָיו הֲפוּכִין וְאֵין שָׁם אוּמָּן אֶלָּא הוּא, כַּדּוֹ לָגוּף וְאֵין שָׁם אוּמָּן אֶלָּא הוּא, פִּשְׁתָּנוֹ לְהַעֲלוֹת מִן הַמִּשְׁרָה, וְצַמְרוֹ לְהַעֲלוֹת מִן הַיּוֹרָה וְאֵין שָׁם אוּמָּן אֶלָּא הוּא – הֲרֵי זֶה יַעֲשֶׂה בְּצִינְעָא.

Rabban Shimon ben Gamliel says: If **his olives have** already **been turned over and there is no skilled worker** available who knows how to press them properly **but him,** or **his cask** needs **to be plugged and there is no skilled worker** available **but him,** or **his flax** needs **to be lifted out of the soaking pool, or his wool** needs **to be lifted from the cauldron, and there is no skilled worker** available **but him, he may perform** all of these actions himself **in private.**[H]

יָתֵר עַל כֵּן אָמַר רַבָּן שִׁמְעוֹן בֶּן גַּמְלִיאֵל: אִם הָיָה אוּמָּן לָרַבִּים, וְסַפָּר וּבַלָּן לָרַבִּים, וְהִגִּיעַ עֵת הָרֶגֶל וְאֵין שָׁם אוּמָּן אֶלָּא הוּא – הֲרֵי זֶה יַעֲשֶׂה.

Rabban Shimon ben Gamliel said further: If this mourner **was a craftsman** who serves **the public,** providing a necessary service, **or a barber or a bath attendant for the public, and the time of the Festival arrived,** i.e., it was the eve of a Festival, **and there is no** other **skilled worker** available **but him,** then **he may perform** the labor even in public, as the needs of the public takes precedence over the mourning of an individual.

NOTES

Rav Ashi said that he is speaking utilizing the didactic style of: It is not necessary – רַב אַשִׁי אָמַר לָא מִיבָּעֲיָא קָאָמַר: Rav Ashi disagrees with Rav Sheisha and claims that there is an allowance for performance of labor to avoid financial loss during the mourning period as well. In fact, since the mourning period is by rabbinic law while the intermediate days of the Festival are by Torah law, one could derive the allowance with regard to the mourning period from the *halakha* pertaining to the intermediate days of the Festival *a fortiori* (Rid). According to the reading of the mishna that the mourning period occurs just before the Festival and serves as the justification for performing labor during the Festival, Rav Ashi claims that mourning can justify performing labor during the Festival even though in principle labor was permitted during the mourning period that befell him just before the Festival (Ritva).

On the intermediate days of the Festival, when the prohibition against labor is by Torah law – בַּמּוֹעֵד דְּאִיסּוּר מְלָאכָה מִדְּאוֹרַיְיתָא: Rav Ashi's statement serves as evidence for those commentaries that understand that the prohibition against performing labor during the intermediate days of a Festival is by Torah law. Those who argue that it is a rabbinic decree explain that Rav Ashi's point is that the prohibition against performing labor during the intermediate days of a Festival is more stringent than during the mourning period. This is because there is at least an intimation in the Torah to that effect with regard to Festivals, as opposed to the mourning period, where there is no such association (*Tosefot Rabbeinu Yehuda HaḤasid*).

HALAKHA

A matter relating to a mourner that, if unattended, will result in significant loss – דָּבָר הָאָבֵד לְאָבֵל: It is permitted for others to perform labor for a matter that, if unattended, will result in significant loss for a mourner. Labors prohibited on the intermediate days of a Festival because they require excessive effort or a high level of expertise may be performed for the mourner by others. Some permit the mourner himself to perform tasks that cannot be performed by others and that, if unattended, will result in significant loss (Rema, citing Ramban and Rosh). According to some opinions, it is permitted for the mourner himself to perform labor after the first three days of mourning in cases of significant loss, but he should perform such tasks only in private (*Shakh*; *Shulḥan Arukh*, *Yoreh De'a* 380:5).

BACKGROUND

Flax in a soaking pool – פִּשְׁתָּן בַּמִּשְׁרָה: After the stems of flax are reaped, they are soaked in water in order to cause the husks around the fibers to rot. The fibers are then removed from the water and beaten in order to remove unwanted material before the fibers are processed. If the flax soaks for too long, the fibers themselves might rot.

Turn for water – עוֹנַת הַמַּיִם: In Eretz Yisrael, where water was scarce and depended upon shared springs, and in Babylonia, where the water reached the fields through irrigation canals, the owners of the fields would set turns for watering. Since the success of the crop depended upon its receiving water at the appropriate time, everyone would be careful not to lose his turn.

Planting flax seed – זְרִיעַת פִּשְׁתָּן: Flax is planted during the winter, or shortly beforehand. Early planting is critical, particularly for flax grown for its fiber. This flax is made into linen, which was the main use of flax at the time of the Talmud. Flax requires cold weather for its growth, and high temperatures or dryness can cause damage both to the quality of the fibers and the oil extracted from the flax seeds.

Flax field in bloom during the spring

הָאֲרִיסִין וְהַחֲכִירִין וְהַקַּבְּלָנִין – הֲרֵי אֵלּוּ יַעֲשׂוּ אֲחֵרִים בִּשְׁבִילָן. הַחַמָּרִין הַגַּמָּלִין וְהַסַּפָּנִין – הֲרֵי אֵלּוּ לֹא יַעֲשׂוּ. וְאִם הָיוּ מוּחְכָּרִין אוֹ מוּשְׂכָּרִין אֵצֶל אֲחֵרִים – הֲרֵי אֵלּוּ יַעֲשׂוּ. שְׂכִיר יוֹם, אֲפִילּוּ בְּעִיר אַחֶרֶת – לֹא יַעֲשֶׂה. הָיְתָה מְלֶאכֶת אֲחֵרִים בְּיָדוֹ, אַף עַל פִּי שֶׁבְּקִיבּוֹלֶת לֹא יַעֲשֶׂה.

The *baraita* continues: **Tenant farmers,** who farm others' land in exchange for a certain percentage of the crop, **and leasers,**[N] who work the land in exchange for a fixed amount of the crop, **and contractors,**[N] who work the land in exchange for a set amount of money, are included amongst **those for whom others may perform** their labor when they are in mourning.[H] In contrast, **donkey drivers, camel drivers,**[H] **and sailors** are **those** for whom others **may not perform** their work during their mourning periods. **However, if they** or their animals **were leased or hired out to others, then they may perform** work, because they were hired personally and cannot be replaced without loss. **A day laborer, even** if he is **in a different city** where his mourning status is not public knowledge, **may not perform** his work.[H] If **a commission for others was his responsibility, even if it was by contract** and he was paid not by the day but upon its completion, **he may not perform** that labor.[H]

אַף עַל פִּי שֶׁבְּקִיבּוֹלֶת וְלָא מִיבַּעְיָא שֶׁאֵינָהּ קִיבּוֹלֶת?! אַדְּרַבָּה, קִיבּוֹלֶת כְּדִידֵיהּ דָּמֵי! אֶלָּא, אֵימָא: בֵּין קִיבּוֹלֶת בֵּין שֶׁאֵינָהּ קִיבּוֹלֶת לֹא יַעֲשֶׂה.

The statement in the *baraita* that one may not perform a task for others **even if it was by contract** implies that **it is not necessary** to state that if it was **not by contract** the work is prohibited to a mourner. The Gemara asks: **On the contrary,** when he works **by contract it is considered as** though it were **his** own work, since he simply receives payment for the completed task. Non-contracted labor, where he is paid for the time he works, is not viewed as his own and it is conceivable that it would be permitted during his mourning period. The Gemara concludes: **Rather,** emend the text and **say** that the *baraita* should read: If a commission for others was his responsibility, **whether by contract or not by contract, he may not perform** it.

הָיְתָה מְלַאכְתּוֹ בְּיַד אֲחֵרִים, בְּבֵיתוֹ – לֹא יַעֲשׂוּ; בְּבַיִת אַחֵר – יַעֲשׂוּ.

The *baraita* continues: If **he commissioned others** to perform **his work,**[H] then if it was **in his house they may not perform** the work, but if it was **in another house they may perform** it.

מָרְיוֹן בְּרֵיהּ דְּרָבִין וּמָר בְּרֵיהּ דְּרַב אַחָא בְּרֵיהּ דְּרָבָא הֲוָה לְהוּ הַהוּא גַּמְלָא דְּתוֹרָא בַּהֲדֵי הֲדָדֵי. אִיתְרְעָא בֵּיהּ מִילְּתָא בְּמָר בְּרֵיהּ דְּרַב אַחָא בְּרֵיהּ דְּרָבָא, וּפְסַקֵיהּ לְגַמְלֵיהּ. אֲמַר רַב אַשִׁי: גַּבְרָא רַבָּה כְּמָר בְּרֵיהּ דְּרַב אַחָא עָבֵיד הָכִי?! נְהִי דִּלְפְסֵידָא דִּידֵיהּ לָא חָיֵישׁ, אַדַּאֲחֵרִים לָא חָיֵישׁ? וְהָא תַּנְיָא: אִם הָיוּ מוּשְׂכָּרִין אוֹ מוּחְכָּרִין אֵצֶל אֲחֵרִים – הֲרֵי אֵלּוּ יַעֲשׂוּ!

The Gemara relates that **Maryon, son of Ravin, and Mar, son of Rav Aḥa, son of Rava, held a team of** two **oxen** in partnership **between them,** one ox apiece. **An event,** i.e., a death in the family, **befell Mar, son of Rav Aḥa, son of Rava, and he detached his** ox **from the team,** preventing any work from being performed by the team, because he did not want work performed with his animal during his days of mourning. **Rav Ashi said: A distinguished man like Mar, son of Rav Aḥa, is behaving this** way? **Granted, he is not concerned about his own loss,** but **is he not concerned about the loss of others,** i.e., his partner? **Isn't it taught** in the *baraita* cited above: **If they** or their animals **were hired out or leased to others, then they may perform** their work? In that case, why not allow the partner to work with the animal of Mar, son of Rav Aḥa?[NH]

וְהוּא סָבַר: אָדָם חָשׁוּב שָׁאנֵי.

The Gemara explains: **But** Mar, son of Rav Aḥa, **maintains: An important person**[N] **is different.** Even if strictly speaking something is permitted, an important person must be more rigorous with himself, so that people learn not to take the *halakha* lightly.

NOTES

Tenant farmers and leasers, etc. – הָאֲרִיסִין וְהַחֲכִירִין וכו׳: Some commentaries understand that the tenant farmers and leasers themselves are mourners (Rashi; Rabbi Shlomo ben HaYatom). However, most maintain that the reference is to the tenant farmers, leasers, and contractors of a mourner (Rif; Ra'avad; Rid; Rosh; Ramban).

And contractors – וְהַקַּבְּלָנִין: The early commentaries ask: Why mention contractors together with tenant farmers and leasers, since the contractor performs his own work for a set amount of money? Some explain that the reference is to a contractor who receives his payment from the produce of the field, and will therefore suffer a loss if the field is not worked properly (Rabbeinu Yehonatan of Lunel; Ran).

Partners, one of whom is a mourner – שׁוּתָּפִים שֶׁאֶחָד מֵהֶם אָבֵל: According to the Ra'avad, the partner who is not in mourning may not work in public but may do so in private (see Meiri). This situation is discussed at greater length in the Jerusalem Talmud.

An important person – אָדָם חָשׁוּב: This is referring to one whose actions people take into consideration and learn from. Such a person is obligated according to *halakha* to be stringent with himself even with regard to matters that are technically permitted, since gossip about him can lead to desecration of God's name (see Rabbi Shlomo ben HaYatom).

HALAKHA

A tenant farmer during his mourning period – אָרִיס בִּימֵי אֶבְלוֹ: A tenant farmer who becomes a mourner is prohibited from performing labor himself, but it is permitted for him to have the work performed by others (*Shulḥan Arukh, Yoreh De'a* 380:12).

Donkey drivers, camel drivers – הַחַמָּרִין, הַגַּמָּלִין: One who has a donkey, a boat, or the like and becomes a mourner, is prohibited from hiring it out to others during his mourning period. However, if it was hired out already and the rental period has not yet concluded, it is permitted for the arrangement to continue (Ra'avad; *Shulḥan Arukh, Yoreh De'a* 380:14).

Working in the field of a mourner – עֲבוֹדָה בִּשְׂדֵה הָאָבֵל: A day laborer may not work in the field of a mourner even in a different city (*Shulḥan Arukh, Yoreh De'a* 380:13).

A mourner commissioned to perform a task for others – אָבֵל שֶׁמְּלֶאכֶת אֲחֵרִים בְּיָדוֹ: A mourner may not perform labor for others, regardless of whether or not it is contract work. If it is a matter that, if unattended, will result in significant loss, he may have others perform it for him. Some say that even if there is no concern for loss, others may perform his work for him (*Ateret Zahav*; *Shulḥan Arukh, Yoreh De'a* 380:17).

If he commissioned others to perform his work – הָיְתָה מְלַאכְתּוֹ בְּיַד אֲחֵרִים: A contractor may perform a commission for someone who became a mourner after the onset of the contract. If the job is movable, he should not perform it in the mourner's house (*Shulḥan Arukh, Yoreh De'a* 380:18).

Partners, one of whom is a mourner – שׁוּתָּפִים שֶׁאֶחָד מֵהֶם אָבֵל: When one member of a partnership becomes a mourner, the other partners are prohibited from performing work in public, though they may continue to do so in private. If the mourner is an important person, and the partnership is associated with his name, his partners may not work even in private (*Shulḥan Arukh, Yoreh De'a* 380:21).

אָמַר שְׁמוּאֵל: מְקַבְּלֵי קִיבּוֹלֶת, בְּתוֹךְ הַתְּחוּם אָסוּר, חוּץ לַתְּחוּם – מוּתָּר.

§ **Shmuel said:** With regard to gentile **contractors,**[NH] who are paid for the completed job rather than by the day, **it is prohibited** for them to work for a Jew **within** the boundaries of **the** Shabbat **limit** on a day that it is prohibited for the Jew to work. It looks like the Jew assigned work for them to do on that day, even though they in fact make their own schedule. **Outside the** Shabbat **limit,** where Jews will not see the work being done, **it is permitted.**

אָמַר רַב פַּפָּא: וַאֲפִילּוּ חוּץ לַתְּחוּם לָא אֲמַרַן אֶלָּא דְּלֵיכָּא מָתָא דְּמִקַּרְבָא לְהָתָם, אֲבָל אִיכָּא מָתָא דְּמִקַּרְבָא לְהָתָם – אָסוּר.

Rav Pappa said: And even outside the Shabbat **limit, we said only** that it is permissible to let them work **when there is no** other **city in close proximity to there, but if there is** another **city in close proximity to there,**[N] **it is prohibited,** since the work is likely to be seen by a Jew.

אָמַר רַב מְשַׁרְשְׁיָא: וְכִי לֵיכָּא מָתָא דְּמִקַּרְבָא לְהָתָם נַמִי, לָא אֲמַרַן אֶלָּא בְּשַׁבָּתוֹת וּבְיָמִים טוֹבִים, דְּלָא שְׁכִיחִי אֱינָשֵׁי דְּאָזְלִי לְהָתָם. אֲבָל בְּחוּלּוֹ שֶׁל מוֹעֵד, דִּשְׁכִיחִי אֱינָשֵׁי דְּאָזְלִי וְאָתוּ לְהָתָם – אָסוּר.

Rav Mesharshiyya said: And even when there is no other **city in close proximity, we said** that it is permissible for gentile contractors to work for a Jew **only on *Shabbatot* and Festivals, when** Jewish **people do not routinely go there,** i.e., to the place where the work is being performed. **However, on the intermediate days of a Festival, when** Jewish **people routinely come and go from there** and see the work being done, **it is prohibited.**[H]

מָר זוּטְרָא בְּרֵיהּ דְּרַב נַחְמָן בָּנוּ לֵיהּ אַפַּדְנָא מְקַבְּלֵי קִיבּוֹלֶת חוּץ לַתְּחוּם. אִיקְּלַע רַב סָפְרָא וְרַב הוּנָא בַּר חִינָּנָא, וְלָא עָלוּ לְגַבֵּיהּ. וְאִיכָּא דְּאָמְרִי: הוּא נַמִי לָא עָל בְּגַוֵּיהּ.

The Gemara relates about **Mar Zutra, son of Rav Naḥman,** that gentile **contractors built a mansion** [*apadana*][L] **for him outside the** Shabbat **limit. Rav Safra and Rav Huna bar Ḥinnana happened** to come there, **but they did not enter it,** because it had been built on Shabbat in a prohibited manner. **And there are** those **who say: Even he,** Mar Zutra himself, **did not enter it.**[N]

וְהָאָמַר שְׁמוּאֵל: מְקַבְּלֵי קִיבּוֹלֶת, בְּתוֹךְ הַתְּחוּם – אָסוּר, חוּץ לַתְּחוּם – מוּתָּר! אָדָם חָשׁוּב שָׁאנֵי. וְאִיכָּא דְּאָמְרֵי: סִיּוּעֵי סַיַּיע בְּתִיבְנָא בַּהֲדַיְיהוּ.

The Gemara asks: **But didn't Shmuel say:** With regard to gentile **contractors, within** the boundaries of **the** Shabbat **limit, it is prohibited** to let them work on Shabbat, but **outside the** Shabbat **limit it is permitted?** The Gemara answers: **An important person is different** and must behave in a stricter manner. **And there are** those **who say: He provided them with assistance**[N] **with straw** for making the bricks. Consequently, they were not fully independent contractors, and therefore it was prohibited for them to work on Shabbat, even outside the Shabbat limit.

רַב חָמָא שְׁרָא לְהוּ לְאַבּוּנַגְרֵי דְּבֵי רֵישׁ גָּלוּתָא לְמֵיעֲבַד לְהוּ עֲבִידְתָּא בְּחוּלָּא דְּמוֹעֲדָא. אֲמַר: כֵּיוָן דַּאֲגַר לָא קָא שָׁקְלִי – שְׁרַשׁוּיֵי הוּא דְּקָא מְשַׁרְשׁוּ לֵיהּ. וְלֵית לָן בָּהּ.

The Gemara relates that **Rav Ḥama permitted the bath attendants** [*abunagrei*][NL] **of the Exilarch's house to work for them,** i.e., the Exilarch and his household, **on the intermediate days of a Festival. He said** in explanation of this leniency: **Since they do not take payment** for working during the week of the Festival, they **are** merely **conferring a favor**[N] on the Exilarch. Therefore, it is not viewed as actual labor, **and we have no** problem **with it.**[H]

NOTES

Gentile contractors – מְקַבְּלֵי קִיבּוֹלֶת: Most commentaries explain that Shmuel's extension of the prohibition against a gentile performing work for a Jew to include contract work was stated with regard to Shabbat and Festivals, as is indicated by Rav Mesharshiyya's qualification of that ruling stated later in the Gemara (Rashi; Ritva, citing Rabbeinu Yitzḥak of Dampierre). However, some explain that this *halakha* was stated with regard to a mourner and that contract work by a gentile is permitted on Shabbat and Festivals (Rabbeinu Tam).

But if there is another city in close proximity to there – אֲבָל אִיכָּא מָתָא דְּמִקַּרְבָא לְהָתָם: Rashi manuscript explains differently: If the city is nearby there is a concern lest one come to the assistance of the contractor.

Even he did not enter it – הוּא נַמִי לָא עָל בְּגַוֵּיהּ: Some ask: If he thought it was prohibited, why did he build it in the first place? They explain that he did not instruct the contractors to build at prohibited times and only discovered that they had done so after the fact (Rashi manuscript; *Nimmukei Yosef*).

He provided… assistance – סִיּוּעֵי סַיַּיע: Some early commentaries had the following version of the text: His slave provided assistance, i.e., without the master's knowledge. The early commentaries discuss whether there is an actual halakhic prohibition against having labor performed for one by a contractor on Shabbat or a Festival when he or his slave is assisting by providing material. Some say that it is merely a stringency for an important person; others claim that for a permanent structure whose construction details are widely known, it is an unequivocal halakhic prohibition (see Meiri).

Permitted the bath attendants, etc. – שְׁרָא לְהוּ לְאַבּוּנַגְרֵי וכו׳: According to most commentaries, the work performed by these bath attendants was not in itself prohibited on the intermediate days of the Festival. They derive from here that even permitted labor should not be performed for pay (see Rosh). This assumes that these workers were Jews. Others explain that these people were performing carpentry work, which is prohibited labor, and they were gentiles (Rashi; Rabbeinu Gershom Meor HaGola).

Conferring a favor, etc. – שְׁרַשׁוּיֵי הוּא וכו׳: These workers were not paid a set salary; rather, they received only collateral benefits, such as food, or small gifts (Rabbeinu Ḥananel; Rashi manuscript). One early commentary explains that these people did not receive payment at all, and they donated their labor to the Exilarch (Rabbi Shlomo ben HaYatom).

LANGUAGE

Mansion [*apadana*] – אַפַּדְנָא: This word is mentioned in the Bible (Daniel 11:45). Its origin is the Old Persian apadāna, and from there it was adopted by a number of languages. It means a palace or audience hall.

Bath attendants [*abunagrei*] – אַבּוּנַגְרֵי: The preferred reading in the better manuscripts and medieval commentaries is *avzangrei*, which apparently comes from the Middle Persian ābzan, bath, and the agent, gar, and means bath attendant.

HALAKHA

Gentile contractors – מְקַבְּלֵי קִיבּוֹלֶת: If a Jew gives a gentile contract work to build his house or work his field, if the work is performed in the city or within the Shabbat limit, the Jew must not allow the gentile to perform it on Shabbat, lest those who see suspect him of misconduct, not knowing that it is contract work. Even if his neighbors are all gentiles, it is prohibited due to concern that Jewish passersby or the members of his own household will misinterpret the situation (Rema). If the work is done beyond the Shabbat limit and there is no other city nearby in which Jews dwell, he need not prevent the gentile from working on Shabbat (*Shulḥan Arukh, Oraḥ Ḥayyim* 244:1).

The work of a gentile on the intermediate days of the Festival – עֲבוֹדַת נָכְרִי בְּחוֹל הַמּוֹעֵד: It is prohibited to allow a gentile who was contracted to build a house for a Jew to work on the intermediate days of the Festival, even if the house is beyond the Shabbat limit, in accordance with the ruling of Rav Mesharshiyya. If a house was built in this prohibited manner, it is permissible to enter the house (*Magen Avraham*; *Taz*). There is no obligation to prevent gentiles from doing contract work in the privacy of their own homes (*Shulḥan Arukh, Oraḥ Ḥayyim* 543:2).

Labor performed by others – מְלָאכָה עַל יְדֵי אֲחֵרִים: One may not hire workers to perform labor that one is permitted to do oneself on the intermediate days of the Festival, though one may work for another for free. If a worker is not paid but is only allowed to eat with the employer, it is permitted. It is permitted to perform labor, even for pay, for a matter that, if unattended, will result in significant loss (Rema), but it is preferable to be stringent and have it done for free or by a gentile (*Mishna Berura*; *Shulḥan Arukh, Oraḥ Ḥayyim* 542:1).

תָּנוּ רַבָּנַן: מְקַבְּלִין קִיבּוֹלֶת בַּמּוֹעֵד לַעֲשׂוֹתָהּ לְאַחַר הַמּוֹעֵד, וּבַמּוֹעֵד – אָסוּר. כְּלָלוֹ שֶׁל דָּבָר: כֹּל שֶׁהוּא עוֹשֶׂה – אוֹמֵר לְגוֹי וְעוֹשֶׂה; וְכָל שֶׁאֵינוֹ עוֹשֶׂה – אֵינוֹ אוֹמֵר לְגוֹי וְעוֹשֶׂה. תַּנְיָא אִידָךְ: מְקַבְּלִין קִיבּוֹלֶת בַּמּוֹעֵד לַעֲשׂוֹתָהּ לְאַחַר הַמּוֹעֵד, וּבִלְבַד שֶׁלֹּא יִמְדּוֹד וְשֶׁלֹּא יִשְׁקוֹל וְשֶׁלֹּא יִמְנֶה כְּדֶרֶךְ שֶׁהוּא עוֹשֶׂה בַּחוֹל.

The Sages taught in a *baraita*: Gentiles **may receive contract work on** the intermediate days of a **Festival** in order **to execute it after the Festival, but it is prohibited** to execute it **during the Festival** week itself. **The principle of the matter** is: **Any** action **that** a Jew **may perform** himself, **he may tell a gentile to perform, and any** action **that he may not perform** himself, **he may not tell a gentile to perform. It is taught** in **another** *baraita*: A gentile **may receive contract work on** the intermediate days of **a Festival** in order **to execute it after the Festival, provided that he does not measure, weigh, or count,** in order to plan the work, **in the** same **manner as he does on an** ordinary **weekday.**[H]

תָּנוּ רַבָּנַן: אֵין מַרְבִּיעִין בְּהֵמָה בְּחוּלּוֹ שֶׁל מוֹעֵד. כַּיּוֹצֵא בּוֹ אֵין מַרְבִּיעִין בִּבְכוֹר, וְלֹא בִּפְסוּלֵי הַמּוּקְדָּשִׁין.

The Sages taught in a *baraita*: **One may not breed an animal,** i.e., coax or compel a male to mate with a female, **on the intermediate days of a Festival,**[H] as this is similar to prohibited labor. **Similarly, one may not breed a firstborn** animal,[HNB] **nor an unfit consecrated animal.** It is prohibited to ever work these animals because of their sanctified status, and breeding them resembles working them.

תַּנְיָא אִידָךְ: אֵין מַרְבִּיעִין בְּהֵמָה בְּחוּלּוֹ שֶׁל מוֹעֵד. רַבִּי יְהוּדָה אוֹמֵר: חֲמוֹרָה שֶׁתָּבְעָה – מַרְבִּיעִין עָלֶיהָ זָכָר בִּשְׁבִיל שֶׁלֹּא תִּצְטַנֵּן. וּשְׁאָר כָּל הַבְּהֵמוֹת מַכְנִיסִין אוֹתָן לַבְּקָרוֹת.

It is taught in **another** *baraita*: **One may not breed an animal on the intermediate days of a Festival. Rabbi Yehuda says:** If **a she-donkey yearns** for a mate because she is in heat, **one may breed her with a male, lest she cool off,** i.e., lest her estrus cycle pass without her mating, which will cause a significant loss. With regard to **all other animals** that are in heat, **they are** merely **brought into corrals** in which there are males, there being no need for further human intervention.

תָּנוּ רַבָּנַן: אֵין מְדַיְּירִין לֹא בְּשַׁבָּתוֹת, וְלֹא בְּיָמִים טוֹבִים, וְלֹא בְּחוּלּוֹ שֶׁל מוֹעֵד. וְאִם בָּאוּ מֵאֲלֵיהֶן – מוּתָּר.

The Sages taught in a *baraita*: **One may not enclose** livestock in particular areas of a field, in order to fertilize that area with their manure, **on *Shabbatot*, or on Festivals, or on the intermediate days of a Festival.**[H] **But if** the animals **came on their own** to the field, **it is permitted,** and he need not remove them although he benefits from their manure.

וְאֵין מְסַיְּיעִין אוֹתָן, וְאֵין מוֹסְרִין לָהֶם שׁוֹמֵר לְנַעֵר אֶת צֹאנָם. הָיָה שְׂכִיר שַׁבָּת, שְׂכִיר חֹדֶשׁ, שְׂכִיר שָׁנָה, שְׂכִיר שָׁבוּעַ – מְסַיְּיעִין אוֹתָן, וּמוֹסְרִין לָהֶם שׁוֹמֵר לְנַעֵר אֶת צֹאנָם. רַבִּי אוֹמֵר: בְּשַׁבָּת – בְּטוֹבָה, בְּיוֹם טוֹב – בִּמְזוֹנוֹת, בַּמּוֹעֵד – בְּשָׂכָר. אָמַר רַב יוֹסֵף: הִלְכְתָא כְּרַבִּי.

The *baraita* continues: **And one may not assist** gentile shepherds in pasturing their sheep in his field so that it will be fertilized, **nor may one provide them with a shepherd to** help **herd their sheep**[N] all around the field so that it is completely fertilized. If the gentile shepherds **were hired by the week, by the month, by the year,** or **by the septennial** period, i.e., the seven years from one Sabbatical Year to the next, **one may assist them and provide them with a shepherd to herd their sheep.** Since they were hired for an extended period of time, it is not as though they were hired specifically for Shabbat or the Festival. **Rabbi** Yehuda HaNasi **says: On Shabbat** one may have the gentile pasture the sheep in one's field **as a favor,** i.e. in order to earn one's good graces, but not for pay; **on a Festival,** it is permitted even in exchange **for food;** and **on the** intermediate days of **the Festival,** it is permitted **for pay. Rav Yosef said: The *halakha* is in accordance with** the opinion of **Rabbi** Yehuda HaNasi.

HALAKHA

Allocating work on a Festival – מְסִירַת עֲבוֹדָה בַּמּוֹעֵד: It is permitted to allocate work for execution after the Festival provided one does not measure or count or weigh in the same manner as he does on an ordinary weekday. One may do so with both Jewish and gentile workers by contract or for wages (*Mishna Berura*, citing Ritva). Even if ultimately the gentile executes it on the intermediate days of the Festival, the result is permitted, since the Jew stipulated with the gentile not to do so (*Shulḥan Arukh*, *Oraḥ Ḥayyim* 543:3, and in the comment of Rema).

Breeding an animal on the Festival – הַרְבָּעַת בְּהֵמָה בַּמּוֹעֵד: One may not coax or compel an animal to mate on the Festival. Some say that if a female donkey yearns for a mate because she is in heat, it is permissible to coax her to mate (*Eliyahu Rabba*), and some prohibit it (see *Mishna Berura*; *Shulḥan Arukh*, *Oraḥ Ḥayyim* 536:3).

Breeding a firstborn – הַרְבָּעָה בִּבְכוֹר: It is prohibited to coax a firstborn or disqualified consecrated animals to mate (Rambam *Sefer Avoda*, *Hilkhot Me'ila* 1:9).

One may not enclose livestock in a field in order to fertilize the field on the Festival – אֵין מְדַיְּירִין בַּמּוֹעֵד: One may not bring sheep into a field on the intermediate days of the Festival in order to fertilize it. If a gentile brought them in, as long as the Jew does not pay for it, it is permitted even on Shabbat. On a Festival, it is permitted even if the gentile is given food. On the intermediate days of a Festival, it is permitted to pay him for this, provided it is included in payment for other work. One should not hire a gentile explicitly to enclose animals in a field, nor should one assist him or give him an assistant to herd the sheep. However, if the gentile is hired for a more extended period, it is permitted to assist him and give him an assistant to herd the sheep (*Shulḥan Arukh*, *Oraḥ Ḥayyim* 537:14).

NOTES

One may not breed a firstborn animal, etc. – אֵין מַרְבִּיעִין בִּבְכוֹר וכו׳: The early commentaries explain that this is considered labor. It is prohibited to shear or to work firstborn animals, even after they have become blemished and unfit for sacrifice. This prohibition likewise applies to any animal that was meant to be sacrificed as an offering and became unfit and was deconsecrated (see Ran). Some give an additional reason for prohibiting the breeding of these animals: These animals are meant to be consumed for their meat, and if one allows the owner to breed them he will delay slaughtering them (Rabbeinu Yehonatan of Lunel).

To herd [*lena'er*] their sheep – לְנַעֵר אֶת צֹאנָם: The standard explanation is that *lena'er* means to transfer from place to place so that the whole field be fertilized (Rambam, based on Jerusalem Talmud, tractate *Shevi'it*). Some explain that it is referring to guarding the sheep (Rashi; Rabbeinu Yehonatan of Lunel), and others explain that it involves cleansing the animals from the debris adhering to them (Commentary on *Moed Katan*; *Shibbolei HaLeket*).

BACKGROUND

A firstborn animal – בְּכוֹר: The firstborn males of cattle, sheep or goats belonging to a Jew are sacred from birth. They are the property of the priests; the owner of the herd in which the animal is born may decide to which priest to give it, at his own discretion. Unblemished animals are consecrated as offerings and, once they are sacrificed, the meat is eaten by the priests and their families (Numbers 18:17–18). If a firstborn animal acquires a physical blemish that disqualifies it from being sacrificed as an offering, it ceases to be consecrated and may be slaughtered and eaten like any other non-sacred, kosher animal. However, even after becoming blemished, it is prohibited to work the animal or shear its fleece. It is prohibited to intentionally inflict a wound on a firstborn that will cause it to be unfit for sacrifice.

The *halakhot* of firstborn animals still apply nowadays, despite the fact that it is impossible to sacrifice them as offerings in the absence of the Temple. In the present time, they may be slaughtered only if they have a disqualifying blemish. Various halakhic devices are employed to restrict the number of animals classified as consecrated firstborn.

מתני׳ וכן מי שהיה יינו בתוך הבור ואירעו אבל או אונס, או שהטעוהו – זולף וגומר וגף כדרכו, דברי רבי יוסי. רבי יהודה אומר: עושה לו לימודים בשביל שלא יחמיץ.

MISHNA **And similarly,** with regard to **one whose wine was** already **in the** collection **pit** beside the wine press and needed to be removed lest it sour, **and mourning** for some close relative **or** some other **unavoidable accident befell him, or** his workers **misled him,** promising to come but failing to do so, during the intermediate days of the Festival **he may draw off**[N] the wine **and complete** the process, **and** then **plug**[N] each barrel of wine **in its usual manner;** this is **the statement of Rabbi Yosei.**[H] **Rabbi Yehuda says: He should construct a wooden panel** to cover the collection pit **so that** the wine **will not sour.**

גמ׳ וצריכא. דאי אשמעינן קמייתא – בההיא קאמר רבי יוסי, משום דמישחא נפיש פסידיה. אבל חמרא דלא נפיש פסידיה – אימא מודי ליה לרבי יהודה. ואי אשמעינן בתרייתא – בההיא קאמר רבי יהודה, אבל בהך אימא – מודה לרבי יוסי. צריכא.

GEMARA The Gemara comments: **And** both this mishna and the previous one (11b), about the olive press, are **necessary,** as, **if** the *tanna* **teaches us** only **the first** mishna, one might say that only **in that** case **does Rabbi Yosei say** that one is permitted to complete the process, **because** in the case of **oil, the** potential **loss is considerable. However,** in the case of **wine, where the loss is not** as **considerable,** one might **say that he concedes to Rabbi Yehuda** that it must be done in an altered manner. **And if he teaches us** only **the last** mishna, one might say that only **in that** case involving wine **did Rabbi Yehuda say** that one must be stringent, **but in the other** case involving oil one might **say that he concedes to Rabbi Yosei** and is lenient. Therefore, it is **necessary** to teach both cases.

אמר רב יצחק בר אבא: מאן תנא שינוי במועד בדבר האבד? דלא כרבי יוסי. אמר רב יוסף: הלכה כרבי יוסי.

Rav Yitzhak bar Abba said: Who is the *tanna* who teaches that labor performed **during the intermediate days of the Festival** must be performed in **an altered fashion** even **with regard to a matter that,** if unattended, will result in significant **loss?** That ruling is **not** in accordance with **Rabbi Yosei's** opinion, as Rabbi Yosei permits one to perform labor that will prevent such a loss even in the usual manner. **Rav Yosef said:** The ***halakha*** is **in accordance with** the opinion of **Rabbi Yosei,**[H] and it is permitted in cases of loss to perform labor in the usual manner.

בעו מיניה מרב נחמן בר יצחק: מהו למישע חביתא דשיכרא בחולא דמועדא? אמר להו: סיני אמר: הלכה כרבי יוסי. אימור דאמר רבי יוסי בחמרא; בשיכרא מי אמר?

The students **asked of Rav Naḥman bar Yitzḥak: What is** the *halakha* with regard **to sealing a barrel**[N] **of beer during the intermediate days of the Festival?** If it is not properly sealed, the beer will leak out through the sides of the barrel. **He said to them: Sinai,**[P] i.e., Rav Yosef, **said:** The ***halakha*** **is in accordance with** the opinion of **Rabbi Yosei.** They asked: **Say that Rabbi Yosei said** that one may be lenient **about wine,** but **about beer does he say** the same thing? Beer is much cheaper than wine, and the loss would be much less significant.

חמרא טעמא מאי? משום דנפיש פסידיה; שיכרא נמי אית בה פסידא. דאמר אביי, אמרה לי אם: בר שית סאוי ושייע – מבר תמני ולא שייע.

The Gemara explains why no distinction should be made: With regard to **wine, what is the reason** that Rabbi Yosei was lenient? It is **because the loss** involved **is considerable;** with **beer as well, there is a loss** if the barrel is not properly sealed, **as Abaye said:** My foster **mother told me:** It is better to have a barrel **of six *se'a* that is sealed than** a barrel **of eight** ***se'a*** **that is not sealed,** as in the end more beer will remain in the smaller sealed barrel than in the larger unsealed one.

אמר רב חמא בר גוריא אמר רב: הלכות מועד כהלכות כותים בהלכה. למאי הלכתא? אמר רב דניאל בר קטינא אמר רב: לומר שהן עקורות, ואין למידות זו מזו.

§ **Rav Ḥama bar Gurya said** that **Rav said: The *halakhot*** **relating to** the intermediate days of **a Festival resemble the *halakhot*** **relating to the Samaritans in the *halakha*.**[N] The Gemara asks: **With regard to what** aspect of **the *halakha*** are they similar? **Rav Daniel bar Ketina said** that **Rav said:** He meant **to convey that they are sterile, and one may not learn** further *halakhot* by extrapolation **one from one another** in both of these areas of *halakha*.

NOTES

Draw off [*zolef*] – זולף: Some explain *zolef* as removing all the wine from the wine press (Rashi). Others explain it as placing the grapes in the press (Rabbi Ovadya MiBartenura). Still others explain that it means pouring water on the grapes (Rabbeinu Shlomo ben HaYatom).

And plug – וגף: The commentaries differ as to whether this is referring to sealing the barrels or constructing some sort of seal for the pit in which the wine is stored (see Rabbeinu Yehonatan of Lunel).

Sealing a barrel – למישע חביתא: Some explain that the question here is whether it is permitted to seal the cork on a barrel with plaster in its usual manner (*Tosefot Rabbeinu Yehuda HaḤasid; Tosefot HaRosh*).

Resemble the *halakhot* relating to the Samaritans in the *halakha* – כהלכות כותים בהלכה: Most commentaries understand that the *halakhot* relating to the Samaritans follow no clear principles or logic; there were areas in which the Samaritans were reliable and areas in which they were not (*Tosefot Rabbeinu Yehuda HaḤasid*). Others understand this phrase to refer to the manner in which the Samaritans interpret the Torah, which insists that only matters explicit in the Torah are binding and does not derive new *halakhot* through legal reasoning (Rabbeinu Shlomo ben HaYatom; see Ran and Ritva).

HALAKHA

Wine in a collection pit on the intermediate days of the Festival – יין בבור בחול המועד: If one had wine in his collection pit and an unavoidable accident befell him, or for some other reason he did not complete his wine processing before the Festival, since it is a matter that, if unattended, will result in significant loss, it is permitted to complete the process and plug the barrels in the usual manner. It is also permitted to do this for beer, even though the loss is not as great (*Shulḥan Arukh, Oraḥ Ḥayyim*, 538:1).

A matter that, if unattended, will result in significant loss on a Festival – דבר האבד במועד: It is permitted to perform labor on the intermediate days of the Festival for any matter that, if unattended, will result in significant loss, in accordance with Rabbi Yosei's opinion. Moreover, it is permitted even in cases of uncertainty about the loss (*Magen Avraham*). Nevertheless, one should reduce the amount of the exertion one expends as much as possible (*Shulḥan Arukh, Oraḥ Ḥayyim*, 537:1, and in the comment of Rema).

PERSONALITIES

Sinai – סיני: Sinai was the appellation for Rav Yosef, who was one of the greatest of the third-generation Babylonian *amora'im*. He was called Sinai due to his expert knowledge of *baraitot* and the oral traditions of the Torah. His colleague Rabba was called: Uprooter of mountains, in contrast, as he was known for his brilliant analysis. Rav Yosef was a disciple of Rav Yehuda and eventually headed the Pumbedita academy, where his most prominent students were Abaye and Rava. An illness caused him to forget much of his knowledge, and the Talmud often recounts how Abaye helped him recall matters that he had taught previously. At his death, he was succeeded by Abaye as head of the Pumbedita academy.

דְּאָמַר שְׁמוּאֵל: זוֹפְתִין כּוּזְתָא, וְאֵין זוֹפְתִין חָבִיתָא. רַב דִּימִי מִנְּהַרְדְּעָא אָמַר: זוֹפְתִין חָבִיתָא וְאֵין זוֹפְתִין כּוּזְתָא. מָר חָיֵישׁ לִפְסֵידָא, וּמָר חָיֵישׁ לְטִירְחָא.

The Gemara offers an example: For instance, **Shmuel said: One may seal a jug with pitch,**[N] **but one may not seal a barrel with pitch** on the intermediate days of a Festival. **Rav Dimi from Neharde'a said: One may seal a barrel with pitch,**[H] **but one may not seal** a small **jug with pitch.** Their reasoning is as follows: **This Sage,** i.e., Rav Dimi, **was** more **concerned about** possible financial **loss,** and so he permitted sealing the larger vessel, for which the potential for loss is great, but not the smaller one. **And this Sage,** i.e., Shmuel **was concerned about** unnecessary **exertion** on the Festival, and therefore he permitted sealing the smaller vessel, which requires less effort.

אָמַר אַבַּיֵי: נְקִטִינַן, הִלְכוֹת מוֹעֵד כְּהִלְכוֹת שַׁבָּת;

Abaye stated a different principle: **We have a tradition** that **the** ***halakhot*** **of** the intermediate days of **a Festival are like the** ***halakhot*** **of Shabbat:**

NOTES

One may seal a jug with pitch – זוֹפְתִין כּוּזְתָא: In the Jerusalem Talmud this dispute appears as two versions of Shmuel's opinion. The reasoning behind the two opinions is explained as follows: A barrel requires a thin layer of pitch, which is relatively easy to apply and so is permitted on the intermediate days of the Festival. The jug requires a thicker layer, and it is prohibited to apply it because of the effort required. On the other hand, the barrel is used for long-term storage, and it is prohibited to apply pitch to it on the Festival because only those labors which are for the sake of the Festival are permitted. The jug is to be used on the Festival itself, and therefore it is permitted (see *Tosefot Rabbeinu Yehuda HaḤasid*).

HALAKHA

One may seal a barrel with pitch, etc. – זוֹפְתִין חָבִיתָא וכו׳: Both a barrel and a small jug may be sealed with pitch on the intermediate days of a Festival. This is in accordance with the leniencies of both Shmuel and Rav Dimi (Rambam *Sefer Zemanim*, *Hilkhot Yom Tov* 8:14).

Perek **II**
Daf **12** Amud **b**

יֵשׁ מֵהֶן פָּטוּר אֲבָל אָסוּר, וְיֵשׁ מֵהֶן מוּתָּר לְכַתְּחִלָּה.

Some of the actions for which one is **exempt** by Torah law **are** nevertheless **prohibited,**[N] **and some of them** are **permitted** ***ab initio.***

רַב הוּנָא חֲצַדוּ לֵיהּ חֲצָדָא בְּמוֹעֲדָא. אֵיתִיבֵיהּ רַבָּה בַּר רַב הוּנָא לְרַב הוּנָא: טוֹחֲנִין קֶמַח בְּמוֹעֵד לְצוֹרֶךְ הַמּוֹעֵד, וְשֶׁלֹּא לְצוֹרֶךְ הַמּוֹעֵד – אָסוּר. דָּבָר שֶׁאָבוּד בַּמּוֹעֵד – מוּתָּר לַעֲשׂוֹתוֹ בַּמּוֹעֵד; דָּבָר שֶׁאֵינוֹ אָבוּד בַּמּוֹעֵד – אָסוּר.

§ The Gemara relates that **Rav Huna had his crop harvested for him on** the intermediate days of **a Festival. Rabba bar Rav Huna raised an objection to** his father **Rav Huna** from a *baraita*: **One may grind flour on** the intermediate days of **a Festival for the sake of the Festival, but** if it is **not for the sake of the Festival,** it is **prohibited.** With regard to **a matter that,** if unattended, will result in significant **loss on the Festival, it is permitted to perform** labor to prevent that loss **on** the intermediate days of **the Festival.** For **a matter that** will not result **in loss** if unattended during the intermediate days of **the Festival, it is prohibited** to perform labor.

בַּמֶּה דְּבָרִים אֲמוּרִים – בְּתְלוּשִׁין מִן הַקַּרְקַע, אֲבָל מְחוּבָּר לַקַּרְקַע – אֲפִילּוּ כּוּלּוֹ אָבוּד אָסוּר. וְאִם אֵין לוֹ מַה יֹּאכַל – קוֹצֵר, וּמְעַמֵּר, וְדָשׁ, וְזוֹרֶה, וּבוֹרֵר, וְטוֹחֵן, וּבִלְבַד שֶׁלֹּא יָדוּשׁ בְּפָרוֹת!

In what case **is this statement said? In the case of** crops that are already **detached from the ground, but** in the case of crops that are still **attached to the ground, even if it all will be lost,** labor **is prohibited** during the intermediate days of the a Festival. **And if one does not have anything to eat,** then **he may reap**[H] **and bind sheaves, and thresh, and winnow** the grain in the wind, **and separate** the grain from the chaff, **and grind** the grain into flour, **provided that he does not thresh with cows,**[N] the way that threshing is performed on an ordinary weekday. Why, then, did Rav Huna, who certainly had enough to eat, allow his workers to reap the field during the Festival week?

NOTES

Some of the actions for which one is exempt by Torah law are nevertheless prohibited, etc. – יֵשׁ מֵהֶן פָּטוּר אֲבָל אָסוּר וכו׳: In the context of the *halakhot* of Shabbat, the concept: Exempt but prohibited, means that one who performs a certain action is exempt from punishment or from the obligation to offer a sin-offering, but the action is still prohibited by rabbinic law (Rambam *Sefer Zemanim*, *Hilkhot Shabbat* 1:3). It is unclear how this terminology applies to the *halakhot* of the intermediate days of a Festival. Most commentaries explain that matters permitted due to loss are permitted *ab initio*, while the term: Exempt but prohibited, extends to all those actions prohibited on the intermediate days of a Festival. There is no punishment by Torah law for violating the sanctity of these days, either because the prohibition is by rabbinic law (Rambam) or because it is founded on a positive mitzva (Ra'avad). Some commentaries explain that the category: Exempt but prohibited, is referring to actions that are permitted only in private (Rashi manuscript). The Ritva understands this passage to be making simply the general point that the *halakhot* on the intermediate days of a Festival involve cases in which one action may be prohibited and a very similar one permitted. The *Sefat Emet* suggests that the Gemara uses the term: Exempt but prohibited, to indicate prohibitions that it is prohibited to circumvent by artifice.

That he does not thresh with cows – שֶׁלֹּא יָדוּשׁ בְּפָרוֹת: Despite the fact that the *halakha* is that one need not alter the manner of performing an action that is permitted due to loss, the prohibition against threshing with cows remains extant. Rashi and others explain that this is due to the public nature of the activity. Rambam holds that even according to Rabbi Yosei, who is the source of the ruling that one need not diverge from the normal manner of performing the action, any change that can be made without causing a loss should be made.

HALAKHA

Reaping on the Festival – קְצִירָה בַּמּוֹעֵד: One should not reap a field on the intermediate days of the Festival if the grain will not be ruined if it remains until after the Festival. If one has nothing to eat, then even if he could find food in the marketplace, he may perform all of the required labor in its usual manner until he has produced enough grain for the needs of his home, provided he does not thresh with cows. Some say that in places where it is not customary to thresh with cows he must effect another change (*Magen Avraham*), while others disagree (see *Mishna Berura*). And if the threshing is for the sake of the community, it is permitted to thresh in the usual manner, even with cows (Rosh, citing the Jerusalem Talmud). This *halakha* is not in accordance with Rabbi Yosei's opinion that the allowance for loss is limited to items that are detached from the earth (*Shulḥan Arukh*, *Oraḥ Ḥayyim* 537:15).

אֲמַר לֵיהּ: יְחִידָאָה הִיא, וְלָא סְבִירָא לָן כְּוָותֵיהּ. דְּתַנְיָא, כְּלָל אָמַר רַבָּן שִׁמְעוֹן בֶּן גַּמְלִיאֵל מִשּׁוּם רַבִּי יוֹסֵי: דָּבָר הַתָּלוּשׁ מִן הַקַּרְקַע, אֲפִילּוּ מִקְצָתוֹ אָבוּד – מוּתָּר. וְהַמְחוּבָּר לַקַּרְקַע – אֲפִילּוּ כּוּלּוֹ אָבוּד אָסוּר.

Rav Huna **said to** his son: The opinion expressed in this unattributed *baraita* **is an individual** opinion, **and we do not hold in accordance with it; as it is taught** in a different *baraita*: **Rabban Shimon ben Gamliel stated a principle in the name of Rabbi Yosei:** In the case of **an item that is** already **detached from the ground, even if** only **a portion of it will be lost** by not working during the Festival, **it is permitted** to perform labor to prevent the loss, **whereas** for crops **that are** still **attached to the ground, even if all of them will be lost, it is prohibited** to perform labor for them. The opinion that all labor is prohibited for crops that have not yet been harvested is the opinion of an individual authority, Rabbi Yosei, with whom the Rabbis disagree.

וְאִי רַבִּי יוֹסֵי – יָדוּשׁ נַמִי בְּפָרוֹת, הָא אֲמַר רַב יִצְחָק בַּר אַבָּא: מַאן תְּנָא שִׁינּוּי בַּמּוֹעֵד – בְּדָבָר הָאָבֵד? דְּלָא כְּרַבִּי יוֹסֵי!

The Gemara asks: **But if** the unattributed *baraita* reflects the opinion of **Rabbi Yosei,** and it is permitted to work when one has nothing to eat, **let him thresh even with cows.** Didn't **Rav Yitzḥak bar Abba say: Who** is the *tanna* who **taught** that labor performed **on** the intermediate days of **a Festival** must be done in **an altered manner** even **with regard to a matter that** will involve **a loss** if unattended? It is **not in accordance with** the opinion of **Rabbi Yosei,** as Rabbi Yosei does not require altering the manner in which one performs the labor. Why, then, does the *baraita* say that the threshing must be done in an altered manner and not with cows?

אָמַר לָךְ: הָכָא נַמִי, כֵּיוָן דְּכָל יוֹמָא לָאו בְּפָרוֹת דָּיְישִׁי – הָאִידָּנָא נַמִי לָאו שִׁינּוּי הוּא.

The Gemara rejects this argument: Rabbi Yosei could have **said to you: Here, too, since one does not always thresh with cows,** threshing without them **now** on the intermediate days of the Festival **is also not** considered threshing in **an altered manner.** The prohibition against threshing with cows is not because one must perform that labor in an altered manner but in order to avoid attracting public attention to the fact that one is working during the Festival week.

תָּנוּ רַבָּנַן: טוֹחֲנִין בַּמּוֹעֵד לְצוֹרֶךְ הַמּוֹעֵד; וְשֶׁלֹּא לְצוֹרֶךְ הַמּוֹעֵד – אָסוּר. וְאִם טָחַן וְהוֹתִיר – הֲרֵי זֶה מוּתָּר. קוֹצְצִין עֵצִים בַּמּוֹעֵד, לְצוֹרֶךְ הַמּוֹעֵד; וְשֶׁלֹּא לְצוֹרֶךְ הַמּוֹעֵד – אָסוּר. וְאִם קָצַץ וְהוֹתִיר – הֲרֵי זֶה מוּתָּר.

The Sages taught in a *baraita*: **One may grind** flour **on** the intermediate days of **a Festival for the sake of the Festival, but** if it is **not for the sake of the Festival,** it is **prohibited. And if he ground and left** some flour **over, it is permitted** for use after the Festival. Similarly, **one may cut down trees on** the intermediate days of **a Festival for the sake of the Festival, but** if it is **not for the sake of the Festival** it is **prohibited. And if he cut down** trees for the Festival **and left** some wood **over, it is permitted** for use after the Festival.[H]

מַטִּילִין שֵׁכָר בַּמּוֹעֵד לְצוֹרֶךְ הַמּוֹעֵד, וְשֶׁלֹּא לְצוֹרֶךְ הַמּוֹעֵד – אָסוּר, וְאִם הִטִּיל וְהוֹתִיר – הֲרֵי זֶה מוּתָּר. וּבִלְבַד שֶׁלֹּא יַעֲרִים.

The *baraita* continues: **One may brew beer on** the intermediate days of **a Festival for the sake of the Festival, but** if it is **not for the sake of the Festival,** it is **prohibited. And if he brewed** beer for the sake of the Festival **and left** some **over, it is permitted** for use after the Festival **provided that he does not employ an artifice,** exploiting the allowance to work on a Festival by knowingly making more than was needed.

וּרְמִינְהוּ: מַטִּילִין שֵׁכָר בַּמּוֹעֵד לְצוֹרֶךְ הַמּוֹעֵד; וְשֶׁלֹּא לְצוֹרֶךְ הַמּוֹעֵד – אָסוּר. אֶחָד שֵׁכָר תְּמָרִים, וְאֶחָד שֵׁכָר שְׂעוֹרִים. וְאַף עַל פִּי שֶׁיֵּשׁ לוֹ יָשָׁן – מַעֲרִים וְשׁוֹתֶה מִן הֶחָדָשׁ! תַּנָּאֵי הִיא; דְּתַנְיָא: אֵין מַעֲרִימִין בְּכָךְ. רַבִּי יוֹסֵי בַּר יְהוּדָה אוֹמֵר: מַעֲרִימִין.

The Gemara **raises a contradiction** from a *baraita*: **One may brew beer on** the intermediate days of **a Festival for the sake of the Festival, but** if it is **not for the sake of the Festival,** it is **prohibited.** This applies **both** to **date beer and** to **barley beer. And even though he has old** beer, **he may employ an artifice and drink from the new** beer, i.e., he may say he prefers new beer and brew a new batch, although he has enough old beer for the Festival. This statement contradicts the previous *baraita* that prohibited circumventing the prohibition against labor through artifice. The Gemara answers: **This** matter **is** a dispute between ***tanna'im*, as it is taught** in a *baraita*: **One may not employ an artifice in this regard,**[H] i.e., to circumvent the prohibition against labor during the intermediate days of a Festival. **Rabbi Yosei bar Yehuda says: One may employ an artifice.**

HALAKHA

Work that one benefits from on the Festival – מְלָאכָה שֶׁנֶּהֱנָה מִמֶּנָּה בַּמּוֹעֵד: It is permitted to grind flour for the sake of the Festival, even if one deliberately planned to do this work during the Festival week. Work not for the sake of the Festival is prohibited. If one performs labor for the sake of the Festival, he need not meticulously limit himself to what he needs for the Festival, but he should not employ an artifice to produce extra from the outset. It is permissible to brew beer and to cut wood for the sake of the Festival (*Shulḥan Arukh, Oraḥ Ḥayyim* 533:1).

Employing an artifice – הַעֲרָמָה: One who has flour or stored beer should not employ an artifice and intentionally produce new stock for the sake of the Festival. If one employed an artifice in this way, it is nevertheless permitted to benefit from it (*Magen Avraham*). However, if the new stock actually is better than the old, it is permitted to produce new stock (*Shulḥan Arukh, Oraḥ Ḥayyim* 533:1, and in the comment of Rema).

רַב חֲצַדוּ לֵיהּ חֲצָדָא בְּחוּלָּא דְּמוֹעֲדָא. שְׁמַע שְׁמוּאֵל אִיקְפַּד. לֵימָא שְׁמוּאֵל כִּיחִידָאָה סְבִירָא לֵיהּ? לָא, חֲצָדָא דְּחִיטֵּי הֲוָה, דְּלָא הֲוָה פְּסִיד.

§ The Gemara relates that **Rav had his crop harvested on the intermediate days of a Festival. Shmuel heard** about this and **was dismayed.** The Gemara asks: **Shall we say** that **Shmuel holds in accordance with the individual** opinion of Rabbi Yosei, who prohibits all labor for crops that are attached to the ground, even if inattention will result in significant loss? The Gemara answers: **No, it was a crop of wheat, which would not have been ruined** had the harvest been pushed off a week, and therefore Shmuel was offended.

וְרַב מַאי טַעְמָא עֲבֵיד הָכִי? ״אֵין לוֹ מַה יֹּאכַל״ הֲוָה. וּשְׁמוּאֵל – לָא סִיְּימוּהָ קַמֵּיהּ. אִי נַמִי: אָדָם חָשׁוּב שָׁאנֵי.

The Gemara asks: **What is the reason** that **Rav acted in this manner?** The Gemara answers: Rav is in the category of **one who does not have anything to eat,**[N] and that is why it was permitted to harvest his crops. The Gemara asks: **And** why, then, did **Shmuel** disapprove? The Gemara explains: The people who reported Rav's actions to Shmuel **did not complete** the story **for him. Alternatively, an important person** such as Rav **is different,** and Shmuel thought Rav should have been stringent even in his difficult circumstances.

רַבִּי יְהוּדָה נְשִׂיאָה נְפַק בְּחוּמְרְתָא דְּמְדוּשָׁא, וְאִשְׁתִּי מַיָּא דְּאַחֵים קַפֵּילָא אַרְמָאָה. שְׁמַע רַבִּי אַמִּי אִיקְפַּד. אֲמַר רַב יוֹסֵף: מַאי טַעְמָא אִיקְפַּד? אִי מִשּׁוּם חוּמְרְתָא דִּמְדוּשָׁא – הָא תַּנְיָא: הַשִּׁירִין הַנְּזָמִים וְהַטַּבָּעוֹת – הֲרֵי הֵן כְּכָל הַכֵּלִים הַנִּיטָּלִין בְּחָצֵר.

It was further related that **Rabbi Yehuda Nesia**[P] once **went out** on Shabbat **with a coral seal** [*ḥumreta*][L] on his ring **and drank water heated by a gentile cook. Rabbi Ami heard** about this and **was dismayed** about both things. **Rav Yosef said: What is the reason** that **he was dismayed?**[N] **If** it was **because of the coral seal, isn't** it **taught** in a *baraita*: **Bracelets, nose rings, and rings are like all** other **utensils that may be carried in a courtyard?** Therefore, Rabbi Yehuda Nesia's action conformed to *halakha*.

אִי מִשּׁוּם דְּאִישְׁתִּי מַיָּא דְּאַחֵים קַפֵּילָא אַרְמָאָה – הָא אָמַר שְׁמוּאֵל בַּר יִצְחָק אָמַר רַב: כָּל שֶׁנֶּאֱכָל כְּמוֹת שֶׁהוּא חַי – אֵין בּוֹ מִשּׁוּם בִּישּׁוּלֵי גוֹיִם! אָדָם חָשׁוּב שָׁאנֵי.

And **if** Rabbi Ami was dismayed **because** Rabbi Yehuda Nesia **drank water heated by a gentile cook** [*kapeila*],[L] **didn't Shmuel bar Yitzḥak say** that **Rav said:** With regard to **anything that is eaten raw,** like water, even if it was cooked by a gentile, **it is not subject to** the prohibition against eating **food cooked by gentiles?**[H] The Gemara resolves both difficulties: **An important person is different,** and Rabbi Ami believed that Rabbi Yehuda Nesia should have been more stringent.

אָמַר רַב חֲנַנְאֵל אָמַר רַב: קוֹצֵץ אָדָם דֶּקֶל בַּמּוֹעֵד, אַף עַל פִּי שֶׁאֵינוֹ צָרִיךְ אֶלָּא לִנְסוֹרֶת שֶׁלּוֹ. לָיֵיט עֲלָהּ אַבַּיֵי.

Rav Ḥananel said that **Rav said: A person may chop down a palm tree on** the intermediate days of **a Festival, although he needs only its sawdust.** The Gemara comments: **Abaye cursed it,** i.e., the behavior of one who exerts such effort on the Festival for so small a need.

NOTES

One who does not have anything to eat – אֵין לוֹ מַה יֹּאכַל: According to the interpretation that Rav, the owner of the field, had nothing to eat, there are those who explain that this need not mean that he had nothing at all to eat, but only that he did not have his own produce, and it was permitted for him to perform labor in order to eat from his own produce. Shmuel's objection was that as an important person, he could buy from the market rather than utilizing labor performed on the Festival (Ritva). The Meiri cites an explanation that the case here is one where the workers had nothing to eat, in which case it is permitted to hire them even for labor that is not performed to avoid loss. Shmuel's objection is that an important person should pursue a different course to aid the poor in order to avoid people misconstruing his action.

What is the reason that he was dismayed – מַאי טַעְמָא אִיקְפַּד: *Tosefot Rabbeinu Yehuda HaḤasid* explains the question as an attempt to identify the action of which Rabbi Ami disapproved. The answer is that his disapproval was specifically related to the food cooked by a gentile, about which an important person should be more careful.

PERSONALITIES

Rabbi Yehuda Nesia – רַבִּי יְהוּדָה נְשִׂיאָה: Rabbi Yehuda Nesia was the son of Rabban Gamliel, who was the son of Rabbi Yehuda HaNasi. He was called Nesia to differentiate him from his illustrious grandfather, the redactor of the Mishna. One of the earliest *amora'im* in Eretz Yisrael, he was a colleague of Rabbi Yehuda HaNasi's great students. His own students included Rabbi Yoḥanan and Reish Lakish.

Rabbi Yehuda Nesia's court enacted various decrees. It was considered the Torah center in the Jewish world, to the extent that even the great *amora* Rav deferred to its authority. Rabbi Yehuda Nesia served as *Nasi* for many years and was probably the last *Nasi* to have outstanding Torah knowledge and to serve as the head of the Sanhedrin. As a mark of great respect, he, like his grandfather, is sometimes referred to simply as Rabbi, especially in the Jerusalem Talmud. He was succeeded as *Nasi*, but not as head of the Sanhedrin, by his son, Rabban Gamliel.

LANGUAGE

Seal [*ḥumreta*] – חוּמְרְתָא: The meaning of the word here, as in many other places, is a ring. Some liken this word to the Middle Persian muhr, meaning a seal.

Cook [*kapeila*] – קַפֵּילָא: The origin of the word is the Greek κάπηλος, *kapèlos*, meaning a peddler, the owner of a small store, or the owner of a pub.

HALAKHA

Food cooked by gentiles – בִּישּׁוּלֵי גוֹיִם: Only foods that are important enough to be served at a king's table and that are not eaten raw are subject to the prohibition against eating food cooked by gentiles. The determination of what is considered fit for a king's table depends upon the time and the place. This rabbinic decree applies even when it is certain that the food contains only kosher ingredients (*Kaf HaḤayyim*; *Shulḥan Arukh, Yoreh De'a* 113:1).

רַב אַשִׁי הֲוָה לֵיהּ אָבָא בְּשְׁלָנְיָא. אֲזַל לְמִיקְצְיֵיהּ בְּחוּלָּא דְּמוֹעֲדָא. אֲמַר לֵיהּ רַב שֵׁילָא מִשְּׁלָנְיָא לְרַב אַשִׁי: מַאי דַּעֲתִיךְ? דְּקָאָמַר רַב חֲנַנְאֵל אָמַר רַב: קוֹצֵץ אָדָם דֶּקֶל בַּמּוֹעֵד אַף עַל פִּי שֶׁאֵינוֹ צָרִיךְ אֶלָּא לַנְּסוֹרֶת שֶׁלּוֹ? הָא לָיֵיט עֲלָהּ אַבַּיֵי! אֲמַר לֵיהּ: לָא שְׁמִיעַ לִי, כְּלוֹמַר: לָא סְבִירָא לִי. אִישְׁתַּמֵּיט נַרְגָּא, בָּעֵי לְמִיפְסְקֵיהּ לְשָׁקֵיהּ. שְׁבַקֵיהּ, וַהֲדַר אֲתָא.

The Gemara relates that **Rav Ashi had a forest** [*ava*][L] **in Shelaniya. He went to cut it down on the intermediate days of the Festival. Rav Sheila from Shelaniya said to Rav Ashi: What is your opinion** about what you are doing? Do you rely on **that** which **Rav Ḥananel said** that **Rav said: A person may chop down a palm tree on** the intermediate days of **a Festival even though he needs only its sawdust? Didn't Abaye curse** such behavior? Rav Ashi **said to him: I did not hear** that Abaye said that; **that is to say,** in a delicate way, **I do not hold** in accordance with his opinion. **The** iron of Rav Ashi's **ax** then **slipped** and **was about to cut off his leg. He left it,** ceasing his chopping, **and came back again**[N] to chop down the forest only after the Festival.

רַב יְהוּדָה שְׁרָא לְמִיעֲקַר כִּיתָּנָא, וּלְמִיקְטַל כְּשׁוּתָא, וּלְמִיעֲקַר שׁוּמְשְׁמִי. אֲמַר לֵיהּ אַבַּיֵי לְרַב יוֹסֵף: בִּשְׁלָמָא כִּיתָּנָא – חֲזִי לַחֲפִיפָה; כְּשׁוּתָא – חֲזִי לְשִׁיכְרָא; אֶלָּא שׁוּמְשְׁמִי לְמַאי חֲזִי? חֲזִי לְנַזְיֵי דְּאִית בְּהוּ.

The Gemara relates that **Rav Yehuda permitted uprooting flax, cutting hops, and uprooting sesame plants** on the intermediate days of a Festival. **Abaye said to Rav Yosef: Granted,** this is reasonable in the case of **flax,** which is **suitable for** use as **a cover** [*ḥafifa*][N] for various objects and therefore has a use even during the Festival, and so too **hops,** which are **suitable for** making **beer, but for what are sesame plants suitable,** since the sesame seeds require a long drying period before oil can be extracted from them? Rav Yosef said to him: **They are suitable for the seeds** [*nazyei*][N] **on them,** which can be consumed immediately.[H]

רַבִּי יַנַּאי הֲוָה לֵיהּ הַהוּא פַּרְדֵּיסָא דְּמְטָא זִמְנֵיהּ בְּחוּלָּא דְּמוֹעֲדָא, קְטָפֵיהּ. לְשָׁנָה שֶׁהֱיוּהָ כּוּלֵּי עָלְמָא לְפַרְדֵּיסַיְיהוּ לְחוּלָּא דְּמוֹעֲדָא. אַפְקְרֵיהּ רַבִּי יַנַּאי לְפַרְדֵּיסֵיהּ הַהוּא שַׁתָּא.

It was further mentioned that **Rabbi Yannai had an orchard whose time** for harvesting the fruit **arrived during the intermediate days of the Festival. He harvested it** during the Festival, as the fruit would otherwise have spoiled. **The following year, everyone delayed** the harvest of **their orchards until the intermediate days of the Festival. Rabbi Yannai declared** the earnings from **his orchard ownerless**[N] **that year,** since his harvesting of his fruit provided a misleading example for the public, causing many people to adopt an inappropriate leniency.

LANGUAGE

Forest [*ava*] – **אָבָא**: The meaning of the Aramaic word is a forest, which is similar to the Syriac *eba*.

HALAKHA

Uprooting various plants – עֲקִירַת צְמָחִים שׁוֹנִים: It is permitted to uproot flax on the intermediate days of the Festival, since it is suitable for covering food, and to harvest hops, because they are suitable to put into beer, and to uproot sesame plants, since one can use the dry seeds (*Shulḥan Arukh, Oraḥ Ḥayyim* 533:2).

NOTES

He left it and came back again – שְׁבַקֵיהּ וַהֲדַר אֲתָא: Most commentaries explain that from the time of this mishap, he ceased chopping wood on the intermediate days of a Festival. The Meiri explains that though it is technically permitted, it is inappropriate to exert oneself so strenuously for such a minor matter on the intermediate days of a Festival. Some explain that Rav Ashi never conceded the point, and though he left the forest at that time, he returned and chopped it down on the intermediate days of the Festival (Commentary on *Moed Katan*; Ritva). Similarly, Rabbi Shlomo ben HaYatom explains that though he returned home, he did not tell anyone why he did not chop the trees, so that they should not rule that it is prohibited.

Suitable for use as a cover [*ḥafifa*] – **חֲזִי לַחֲפִיפָה**: Some explain that *ḥafifa* does not mean covering but rather washing. Accordingly, the point is that the soaked flax would be used to prepare a substance used in washing one's hair (Rosh, citing Ra'avad; *Nimmukei Yosef*).

They are suitable for the seeds [*nazyei*] – **חֲזִי לְנַזְיֵי**: Rav Hai Gaon explains that the seeds, even while still moist, can be burned to provide heat; some explain in his name that the sesame stalks can be burned to provide heat (Rif). Others explain that the seeds are suitable for eating with honey (Rid; *Tosefot Rabbeinu Yehuda HaḤasid*). Yet others explain that *nazyei* are seeds that withered on the plant, from which oil can be extracted immediately (Rashi manuscript; Commentary on *Moed Katan*).

Rabbi Yannai declared the earnings from his orchard ownerless – אַפְקְרֵיהּ רַבִּי יַנַּאי לְפַרְדֵּיסֵיהּ: Some explain that Rabbi Yannai declared the orchard as ownerless for the entire coming year (Rabbeinu Shlomo ben HaYatom). Others understand that he declared the orchard completely ownerless and would not benefit from it ever again (Rabbeinu Yehonatan of Lunel). In Rabbeinu Shlomo ben HaYatom's version of the text, the Gemara adds: The Sages applied this verse to him: "They are wise to do evil" (Jeremiah 4:22), i.e., an important person must be cautious in his actions, because people imitate his leniencies but not his stringencies. Similarly, in the Jerusalem Talmud it is stated that Rabbi Yannai said: They learn from deficiency, but they do not learn from correctness.

מתני׳ מַכְנִיס אָדָם פֵּירוֹתָיו מִפְּנֵי הַגַּנָּבִים, וְשׁוֹלֶה פִּשְׁתָּנוֹ מִן הַמִּשְׁרָה בִּשְׁבִיל שֶׁלֹּא תֹּאבַד, וּבִלְבַד שֶׁלֹּא יְכַוֵּין אֶת מְלַאכְתּוֹ בַּמּוֹעֵד. וְכוּלָּן, אִם כִּוְּונוּ מְלַאכְתָּן בַּמּוֹעֵד – יֹאבְדוּ.

MISHNA **A person may bring his fruit in** from the field on the intermediate days of the Festival **because** he is concerned **about thieves, and he may draw his flax out of the soaking pool so that it is not ruined** from soaking too long in the water, **provided that he does not plan** from the outset to perform **his work on** the intermediate days of **the Festival. And** with regard to **all** of these cases, **if one planned** from the outset to perform **his labor on** the intermediate days of **the Festival,** the fruit of that labor **must be lost**[N] and no benefit may be derived from it.

גמ׳ תָּנָא: וּבִלְבַד שֶׁיַּכְנִיסֵם בִּצְנְעָא לְתוֹךְ בֵּיתוֹ.

GEMARA It is **taught** in a *baraita* that one may bring in crops out of concern for thieves, **provided that he brings them into his house discreetly.**[NH]

רַב יוֹסֵף הֲוָה לֵיהּ כְּשׁוּרֵי, עַיְילִינְהוּ בִּימָמָא.

The Gemara relates: **Rav Yosef had** wooden **beams,** which **he brought into** his house **during the day** on one of the intermediate days of a Festival.

אֲמַר לֵיהּ אַבַּיֵי, וְהָתַנְיָא: וּבִלְבַד שֶׁיַּכְנִיסֵם בִּצְנְעָא בְּתוֹךְ בֵּיתוֹ! אֲמַר לֵיהּ: צִנְעָא דְּהָנֵי – יְמָמָא הוּא. כֵּיוָן דִּבְלֵילְיָא בָּעוּ גַּבְרָא יְתֵירִי, וּבָעוּ מְדוֹכְרֵי דְּנוּרָא – אַוְושָׁא מִילְּתָא.

Abaye said to him: But isn't it taught in a *baraita*: One may bring in items **provided that he brings them into his house discreetly?** Rav Yosef **said to him: Discretion** with respect **to these** beams is moving them during **the day, since at night more people**[N] **are required, and** also **torchbearers** [*medokhrei denura*][L] **are needed,** and **the matter** would be more **noticeable.**

״וְשׁוֹלֶה פִּשְׁתָּנוֹ מִן הַמִּשְׁרָה״ כו׳. בָּעֵי מִינֵּיהּ רַבִּי יִרְמְיָה מֵרַבִּי זֵירָא: כִּוֵּין מְלַאכְתּוֹ בַּמּוֹעֵד וּמֵת, מַהוּ שֶׁיִּקְנְסוּ בָּנָיו אַחֲרָיו?

The mishna states: **And he may draw his flax out of the soaking pool** so that it is not ruined from soaking too long in the water, provided that he does not plan from the outset to do his work on the intermediate days of the Festival. And with regard to anyone, if he planned from the outset to perform his labor on the intermediate days of the Festival, the fruit of that labor must be destroyed. **Rabbi Yirmeya asked Rabbi Zeira: If one planned** from the outset to perform **his labor on** the intermediate days **of a Festival, and he died** after doing so, **what is** the *halakha*? **Should his children be penalized after him** and have to lose the products of their father's labor?

אִם תִּימְצֵי לוֹמַר

Even **if you might say** that

Perek **II**
Daf **13** Amud **a**

צָרַם אֹזֶן בְּכוֹר קְנָסוּ בְּנוֹ אַחֲרָיו – מִשּׁוּם דְּאִיסּוּרָא דְּאוֹרַיְיתָא.

in the case of **one who slit the ear of a firstborn** animal,[N] the Sages **penalized his son after him,** that is **because the prohibition is by Torah law.**[N] A firstborn animal is disqualified from sacrifice if it becomes blemished, rendering it permitted to be eaten as non-sacred meat. It is prohibited to deliberately engender a blemish in a firstborn animal, and one who does so is prohibited from eating the meat.

NOTES

If one planned to perform his labor…it must be lost – אִם כִּוְּונוּ מְלַאכְתָּן...יֹאבְדוּ: The commentaries disagree about what it means that the labor is lost. Some say that the court confiscates whatever was produced on the intermediate days of the Festival (Rambam; Rabbi Yitzḥak ibn Giat). Others say that one may not take any action to preserve the products of the illicit work, even if they will be ruined as a result (Meiri).

That he brings them into his house discreetly – שֶׁיַּכְנִיסֵם בִּצְנְעָא לְתוֹךְ בֵּיתוֹ: The Ramban wonders why the Gemara insists in this case that the crops be brought in discreetly while in other cases of potential loss one is permitted to work in public. He explains that there is a difference between cases where the loss is internal to the object, such as spoilage, and cases where the potential loss is due to some external cause, e.g., the risk of it being stolen. In the former case, insistence on discretion could be an obstacle and cause loss, and therefore it was not required. In the latter case, as long as the discretion does not interfere, it is required (Ritva).

More people – גַּבְרָא יְתֵירִי: More effort is required to find people to work at night, and therefore it is more noticeable (*Tosefot Rabbeinu Yehuda HaḤasid*).

HALAKHA

Bringing objects to a secure place – הַכְנָסַת חֲפָצִים לְמָקוֹם מִשְׁתַּמֵּר: It is permitted for one to bring fruit into a secure place for fear of thieves, but he must do so discreetly, e.g., at night. However, an action that will attract more attention at night should be accomplished during the day, and all actions are permitted in the case of potential loss (*Shulḥan Arukh, Oraḥ Ḥayyim* 538:2, and in the comment of Rema).

LANGUAGE

Torchbearers [*medokhrei denura*] – מְדוֹכְרֵי דְּנוּרָא: In the *Arukh* the phrase is *medubrei denura*. According to that version of the text, the first word derives from the root letters *d-b-r*, meaning transported, so that the meaning of the phrase *medubrei denura* would be carriers of fire, or bearers of torches.

NOTES

One who slit the ear of a firstborn animal – צָרַם אֹזֶן בְּכוֹר: Firstborn animals are sanctified from birth and must be sacrificed as an offering unless they are blemished, at which point the animal is deconsecrated and may be eaten without being sacrificed on the altar. It is prohibited to deliberately cause such a blemish, from the verse: "There shall be no blemish in it" (Leviticus 22:21), which the Sages interpreted as meaning that no blemish should be effected on it. The Sages penalized a priest who deliberately caused a blemish, and a firstborn with a purposeful blemish may not be slaughtered until another blemish occurs.

NOTES

Because the prohibition is by Torah law – מִשּׁוּם דְּאִיסּוּרָא דְּאוֹרַיְיתָא: Even according to those authorities who understand that the prohibition against labor on the intermediate days of the Festival is by Torah law, in cases of loss, labor is permitted. Even if one planned that it be done on the Festival, labor that will prevent financial loss is permitted by Torah law. However, the Sages prohibited labor in that case (Rashi manuscript; Ritva).

וְאִם תִּמְצֵי לוֹמַר: מָכַר עַבְדּוֹ לְגוֹי וּמֵת קָנְסוּ בְּנוֹ אַחֲרָיו – מִשּׁוּם דְּכׇל יוֹמָא מַפְקַע לֵיהּ מִמִּצְוֹת,

And if you might say that in the case of **one who sold his slave to a gentile**[N] and then **died** the Sages **penalized his son after him,** that is **because every day** the slave **is in the gentile's possession precludes him from** performing mitzvot. A Canaanite slave is obligated in the same mitzvot as a Jewish woman. If he is illicitly sold to a gentile and escapes, requiring the seller to compensate the gentile, the seller may not them re-enslave the slave, who is regarded as emancipated. The Sages extended this penalty to the owner's heirs as well.

הָכָא מַאי? גַּבְרָא קָנֵיס רַבָּנַן – וְהָא לֵיתֵיהּ, אוֹ דִּלְמָא: מָמוֹנָא קָנֵיס רַבָּנַן, וְהָא אִיתֵיהּ!

What, then, is the *halakha* **here,** where one planned from the outset to perform his work on the intermediate days of a Festival and then after performing the work he died? Should one say that **the Sages penalized the man** himself **and he is no longer** alive, **or perhaps the Sages imposed a penalty on the money,** such that no benefit may be derived from it, **and it** still **exists** in the hands of his heirs?

אֲמַר לֵיהּ: תְּנִיתוּהָ, שָׂדֶה שֶׁנִּתְקַוְּוצָה בַּשְּׁבִיעִית – תִּזָּרַע לְמוֹצָאֵי שְׁבִיעִית. נִטַּיְּיבָה אוֹ נִדַּיְּירָה – לֹא תִּזָּרַע לְמוֹצָאֵי שְׁבִיעִית. וְאָמַר רַבִּי יוֹסֵי בַּר חֲנִינָא: נְקִטִינַן, הֵטִיבָהּ וּמֵת – בְּנוֹ זוֹרְעָהּ. אַלְמָא: לְדִידֵיהּ – קָנְסוּ רַבָּנַן, לִבְרֵיהּ – לָא קָנְסוּ רַבָּנַן; הָכָא נַמִי: לְדִידֵיהּ – קָנְסוּ רַבָּנַן, לִבְרֵיהּ – לָא קָנְסוּ רַבָּנַן.

Rabbi Zeira **said to** Rabbi Yirmeya: **You** already **learned** the answer to your question in a mishna (*Shevi'it* 4:2): **A field whose thorns were removed**[N] **during the Sabbatical Year**[H] **may be sown in the eighth year,** as removing thorns is not full-fledged labor that renders the field prohibited; but **if it had been improved**[NH] with fertilizer, **or if had been enclosed** so that animals therein would fertilize it with their manure, **it may not be sown in the eighth year.** The Sages imposed a penalty that one not benefit from prohibited labor. **And Rabbi Yosei bar Ḥanina said: We have a tradition** that if one **improved** his field in a prohibited manner **and** then **died, his son may sow it. Apparently, the Sages penalized** only **him,** the one who acted wrongly, but **the Sages did not penalize his son. Here, too,** with regard to work performed on the intermediate days of a Festival, **the Sages penalized him,** but **the Sages did not penalize his son.**

אָמַר אַבַּיֵי: נְקִטִינַן, טִימֵּא טָהֳרוֹתָיו וּמֵת – לֹא קָנְסוּ בְּנוֹ אַחֲרָיו. מַאי טַעְמָא? הֶיזֵּק שֶׁאֵינוֹ נִיכָּר לָא שְׁמֵיהּ הֶיזֵּק. לְדִידֵיהּ – קָנְסוּ רַבָּנַן, לִבְרֵיהּ – לָא קָנְסוּ רַבָּנַן.

Abaye said: We have a tradition that if one **rendered impure** another's **ritually pure items and died** before paying, the Sages **did not penalize his son after him** and require him to pay for the damage. **What is the reason** for this? It is that **damage that is not evident,**[H] i.e., that does not involve any physical change visible to the eye, **is not considered damage** by Torah law; nevertheless, the injured party suffers a loss, and **the Sages penalized** only **him,** but **the Sages did not penalize his son.**

מתני׳ אֵין לוֹקְחִין בָּתִּים, עֲבָדִים וּבְהֵמָה אֶלָּא לְצוֹרֶךְ הַמּוֹעֵד, אוֹ לְצוֹרֶךְ הַמּוֹכֵר שֶׁאֵין לוֹ מַה יֹּאכַל.

MISHNA One may not purchase houses, slaves, and cattle on the intermediate days of a Festival **unless** it is **for the sake of the Festival, or** to provide **for the needs of the seller who does not have anything to eat.**[H]

גמ׳ בְּעָא מִינֵּיהּ רָבָא מֵרַב נַחְמָן: שְׂכַר פְּעוּלָּה שֶׁאֵין לוֹ מַה יֹּאכַל מַהוּ? אֲמַר לֵיהּ: תְּנֵינָא, אוֹ לְצוֹרֶךְ הַמּוֹכֵר שֶׁאֵין לוֹ מַה יֹּאכַל. לְאַתּוּיֵי מַאי? לָאו לְאַתּוּיֵי שְׂכַר פְּעוּלָּה? אֲמַר לֵיהּ: לָא, פָּרוּשֵׁי קָא מְפָרֵשׁ.

GEMARA Rava asked Rav Naḥman: What is the *halakha* with regard to **wages**[N] for a worker **who does not have anything to eat?** Is it permitted to provide a poor worker with work on the intermediate days of the Festival? Rav Naḥman **said to him: We learned** this in the mishna: **Or** to provide **for the needs of the seller, if he has nothing to eat. What is added by** mentioning the condition that he has nothing to eat? Does it not **add** the case of **wages** and not only the case of one selling items he owns? Rava **said to him: No,** it is merely **explaining** what is meant by the needs of the seller.

HALAKHA

A field whose thorns were removed during the Sabbatical Year – שָׂדֶה שֶׁנִּתְקַוְּוצָה בַּשְּׁבִיעִית: It is prohibited to remove thorns from one's field during the Sabbatical Year in order to prepare it for the year after. If one did so, or if one removed rocks from the field, which is also prohibited, the Sages did not penalize him, and it is permitted for him to sow it in the eighth year (Rambam *Sefer Zera'im, Hilkhot Shemitta VeYovel* 1:14).

Improved in the Sabbatical Year – נִיטַּיְּיבָה בַּשְּׁבִיעִית: One who plows his field or fertilizes it during the Sabbatical Year in order to prepare it for the next year is penalized and may not sow it in the following year. It is also prohibited for others to lease it from him in order to sow it; rather, the field should be left fallow that year. However, if he dies, his heirs are permitted to sow it (Rambam *Sefer Zera'im, Hilkhot Shemitta VeYovel* 1:13).

Damage that is not evident – הֶיזֵּק שֶׁאֵינוֹ נִיכָּר: One who causes damage to another person that is not evident, e.g., by making his ritually pure items impure or mixing forbidden wine into his wine, is exempt by Torah law; if he did so unintentionally or as a result of coercion, he need not pay for the damages. However, if he did so intentionally, the Sages penalize him such that he must pay for the damage with his superior quality land. If he died before paying, his son is not penalized. Some (*Shakh*) say that if the father stood trial and was ordered to pay the damages but died before he paid, the son is obligated to pay, and some (*Sefer Meirat Einayim*) say he is exempt (*Shulḥan Arukh, Ḥoshen Mishpat* 385:1).

Purchasing during the intermediate days of the Festival – קְנִיָּה בַּמּוֹעֵד: One may not purchase houses, stones, slaves, or animals from a Jew on the intermediate days of the Festival, except for the sake of the Festival, or to provide for the needs of the seller if he has nothing to eat, or to provide for the needs of the porter hired to transport the merchandise if he has nothing to eat. The prevailing custom permits the discreet purchase of small implements and clothes (Rema), but some (*Magen Avraham*) say it is not appropriate to do so (*Shulḥan Arukh, Oraḥ Ḥayyim* 539:12).

NOTES

Sold his slave to a gentile – מָכַר עַבְדּוֹ לְגוֹי: The Sages imposed a double penalty in this case: First, the slave is emancipated according to *halakha*, such that the owner may not enslave him even if the gentile sells him back. Second, the owner is obligated to redeem the slave from the gentile at any cost, even for much more than his worth.

A field whose thorns were removed – שָׂדֶה שֶׁנִּתְקַוְּוצָה: Many commentaries explain that this is specifically when one removes detached thorns, but actually uprooting thorns and grass from the ground during the Sabbatical Year is prohibited by Torah law (Ritva, citing Rabbeinu Ḥananel; *Tosafot*).

If it had been improved – נִיטַּיְּיבָה: Some explain this to mean that one brought in fertilizer from outside, as opposed to enclosing animals in the field to fertilize it with their manure (Rashi). Others explain, in accordance with the Jerusalem Talmud, that the improvement was that one plowed it several times to make the field more productive (Rabbeinu Ḥananel).

Wages – שְׂכַר פְּעוּלָּה: Although the mishna permitted the purchase of an item because of the seller's financial difficulties, Rava did not think he could readily extrapolate from that precedent with regard to wages, as selling does not involve labor (*Tosefot Rabbeinu Yehuda HaḤasid*).

אֵיתִיבֵיהּ אַבַּיֵי: אֵין כּוֹתְבִין שְׁטָרֵי חוֹב בַּמּוֹעֵד; וְאִם אֵינוֹ מַאֲמִינוֹ אוֹ שֶׁאֵין לוֹ מַה יֹּאכַל – הֲרֵי זֶה יִכְתּוֹב. שֶׁאֵין לוֹ מַה יֹּאכַל לְאַתּוּיֵי מַאי? לָאו לְאַתּוּיֵי שְׂכַר פְּעוּלָּה? שְׁמַע מִינָּהּ.

Abaye raised an objection from a mishna (18b): **Promissory notes may not be written on** the intermediate days of a **Festival, but if** the lender **does not trust** the borrower and is concerned that without such a note he will be unable to collect, **or if he has nothing to eat, he may write**[H] a promissory note. The Gemara elaborates: **What is added** here by the words: **If he has nothing to eat?** Are they not meant to add that a promissory note may be written for the sake of **the wages** of the scribe who draws up the document? **Conclude from it** that it is permitted to hire a worker who is in need of a livelihood[H] even for work that would otherwise be prohibited on the intermediate days of a Festival.

מוֹתִיב רַב שֵׁשֶׁת: וַחֲכָמִים אוֹמְרִים: שָׁלֹשׁ אוּמָּנִיּוֹת עוֹשִׂין מְלָאכָה בְּעַרְבֵי פְסָחִים עַד חֲצוֹת: הַחַיָּיטִין, וְהַסַּפָּרִין, וְהַכּוֹבְסִין. הַחַיָּיטִין – שֶׁכֵּן הֶדְיוֹט תּוֹפֵר כְּדַרְכּוֹ בְּחוּלּוֹ שֶׁל מוֹעֵד; הַסַּפָּרִין וְהַכּוֹבְסִין – שֶׁכֵּן הַבָּאִין מִמְּדִינַת הַיָּם וְהַיּוֹצֵא מִבֵּית הָאֲסוּרִין מוּתָּרִין לְסַפֵּר וּלְכַבֵּס בְּחוּלּוֹ שֶׁל מוֹעֵד.

Rav Sheshet raised an objection from a mishna (*Pesaḥim* 55a) that addresses the prohibition against performing labor on the eve of Passover: **And the Rabbis say:** The practitioners of only **three crafts** are permitted to **perform labor until midday on Passover eve,** and they are **the tailors, the barbers, and the launderers,** whose work is needed for the Festival.[H] The *baraita* elaborates: **The tailors** may perform labor on Passover eve, **as a layperson** is permitted to **sew in his** usual **manner during the intermediate days of the Festival.** Since similar labor is permitted during the Festival, one may be lenient on Passover eve as well. **The Barbers and the launderers** are permitted to work, **as those who arrive from overseas** or **one who leaves prison** are permitted to **cut** their **hair and wash** their clothes **on the intermediate days of the Festival** because they had no opportunity to do so prior to the Festival.

וְאִי סָלְקָא דַּעְתָּךְ שְׂכַר פְּעוּלָּה שֶׁאֵין לוֹ מַה יֹּאכַל שָׁרֵי – כָּל מְלָאכוֹת נַמִי לִישְׁתְּרוּ, דְּהָא אִיכָּא שְׂכַר פְּעוּלָּה שֶׁאֵין לוֹ מַה יֹּאכַל!

And if it enters your mind that paying **wages** to a worker **who does not have anything to eat is permitted** on the intermediate days of the Festival, then **all** other types of **labor should also be permitted** on the eve of Passover, **as there is** something similar permitted on the intermediate days of the Festival, namely, **the wages** paid to a worker **who does not have anything to eat.** Tailors are permitted to work on the eve of Passover because similar work is permitted during the intermediate days of the Festival. The payment of wages to a worker who does not have anything to eat on the Festival must be prohibited, as otherwise similar work, i.e., any work involving the payment of wages, would be permitted on the eve of Passover, which is not the case.

מַתְקִיף לַהּ רַב פָּפָּא: אֶלָּא מֵעַתָּה, בִּנְיָן לִישְׁתְּרֵי, שֶׁכֵּן כּוֹתֶל הַגּוֹהֶה לִרְשׁוּת הָרַבִּים – סוֹתֵר וּבוֹנֶה כְּדַרְכּוֹ מִפְּנֵי הַסַּכָּנָה!

Rav Pappa strongly objects to this:[N] **If that is so,** that one can derive *halakhot* in this manner, then **building** as well **should be permitted** on the eve of Passover, **as a wall that tilts toward the public domain** and is likely to fall **may be demolished and rebuilt in the usual manner** on the intermediate days of a Festival **due to the danger** posed to passersby. Since building under such circumstances is permitted on the intermediate days of a Festival, it should be permitted in general on the eve of Passover.

מַתְקִיף לַהּ רָבִינָא: אֶלָּא מֵעַתָּה, לַבְלָר לִישְׁתְּרֵי, שֶׁכֵּן כּוֹתְבִין קִידּוּשֵׁי נָשִׁים גִּיטִּין וְשׁוֹבְרִין!

Ravina also **strongly objects to this: If that is so, a scribe** [*lavlar*][L] who draws up documents **should be permitted** to do so on the eve of Passover, **as one may write betrothal deeds, bills of divorce, and receipts** on the intermediate days of a Festival.

אֶלָּא אָמַר רַב אַשִׁי: מוֹעֵד אַאַרְבָּעָה עָשָׂר קָא רָמֵית?! מוֹעֵד – מִשּׁוּם טִירְחָא הוּא, וּבִמְקוֹם פְּסֵידָא – שָׁרוּ רַבָּנַן. אַרְבָּעָה עָשָׂר – מִשּׁוּם צוֹרֶךְ יוֹם טוֹב הוּא, מִידֵּי דְּצוֹרֶךְ יוֹם טוֹב – שָׁרוּ רַבָּנַן, מִידֵּי דְּלָאו צוֹרֶךְ יוֹם טוֹב – לָא שָׁרוּ רַבָּנַן.

Rather, Rav Ashi said that Rav Sheshet's original objection has no basis: **Are you raising a contradiction** between the *halakhot* of the intermediate days of **a Festival and** the *halakhot* of **the fourteenth** day of Nisan, i.e., the eve of Passover? They are not comparable, as the prohibition against labor on each is for a different reason: Labor is prohibited on the intermediate days of **a Festival because it involves** excessive **exertion,**[N] **and in a situation of** significant **loss the Sages permitted** it. In contrast, the prohibition against labor on **the fourteenth** of Nisan **is due to the need** to prepare **for the Festival,** and especially the Paschal lamb. **Whatever is needed for the Festival,** e.g., the work of tailors and barbers, **the Sages permitted,** but **whatever is not needed for the Festival, the Sages did not permit.**

HALAKHA

Writing documents on the Festival – כְּתִיבַת שְׁטָרוֹת בַּמּוֹעֵד: It is prohibited to write promissory notes on the Festival unless the borrower needs the money (Rema) and the lender does not trust him without a document, or the scribe has nothing to eat. It is permitted to write a bill of sale on the Festival, but one may not write contracts for tenant farming or contracting that were undertaken before the Festival (*Shulḥan Arukh*, *Oraḥ Ḥayyim* 545:6, and in the comment of Rema).

Wages of a worker who does not have anything to eat – שְׂכַר פְּעוּלָּה שֶׁאֵין לוֹ מַה יֹּאכַל: It is permitted to hire a person to perform any task on the intermediate days of the Festival if that person has nothing to eat, in order to provide him a livelihood from the work. Even if he has household utensils that he could sell, he is still included in the category of one who does not have anything to eat (*Taz*, citing the *Tur*). With regard to one who has only bread and water, some say he is not considered someone with nothing to eat (*Eliyahu Rabba*), while according to others, someone who has only bread and water may work for wages during the intermediate days of the Festival (*Shulḥan Arukh*, *Oraḥ Ḥayyim* 542:2, and in the comment of Rema).

Labor on the eve of Passover – מְלָאכָה בְּעֶרֶב פֶּסַח: In a place where the custom is to work on the eve of Passover, one should not begin a new task on this day, even if he can complete it before noon. This does not apply to three types of craftsmen: Tailors, barbers, and launderers, and some replace barbers with shoemakers (*Ḥavvot Yair*, citing *Roke'aḥ*), who may begin a new task as long as they complete it by noon. Other craftsmen are only permitted to continue tasks begun before the fourteenth day of Nisan, until noon. Some (Rema) say that craftsmen of the three aforementioned types are permitted to begin a task on the fourteenth even in a place where the custom is not to work on the eve of Passover. According to that opinion, tasks of other craftsmen, if they are for the sake of the Festival, are also permitted to be continued on the fourteenth until noon. Accordingly, the custom not to work before noon on the eve of Passover applies only to other craftsmen beginning new tasks or anyone performing tasks not for the sake of the Festival (*Shulḥan Arukh*, *Oraḥ Ḥayyim* 468:5).

NOTES

Rav Pappa strongly objects to this – מַתְקִיף לַהּ רַב פָּפָּא: Some explain that the objections of Rav Pappa and Ravina are against the opinion of Rav Naḥman permitting the hiring of a worker in need of a livelihood for a wage (Rabbi Shlomo ben HaYatom). Others explain that the objections are against Rav Sheshet's inference that hiring someone who has nothing to eat during the intermediate days of the Festival must be prohibited because otherwise hiring would be permitted on the eve of Passover. They show that this argument is impossible and that the *halakhot* of the eve of Passover and of the intermediate days of a Festival are not interdependent. This understanding fits the standard printed version of the text, which reads: Rather Rav Ashi said, introducing an explanation of the *halakhot* that makes a distinction between the two.

On the intermediate days of a Festival because it involves excessive exertion – מוֹעֵד מִשּׁוּם טִירְחָא הוּא: Some infer that anyone who works in order to have enough to eat is not engaging in excessive exertion (*Nimmukei Yosef*).

LANGUAGE

Scribe [*lavlar*] – לַבְלָר: The origin of the word is the Latin librarius, meaning scribe, one who copies and writes documents.

מתני׳ אֵין מְפַנִּין מִבַּיִת לְבַיִת, אֲבָל מְפַנֶּה הוּא לַחֲצֵרוֹ. אֵין מְבִיאִין כֵּלִים מִבֵּית הָאוּמָּן. אִם חוֹשֵׁשׁ לָהֶם – מְפַנָּן לְחָצֵר אַחֶרֶת.

MISHNA **One may not move**[N] his possessions **from house to house** during the intermediate days of a Festival, **but he may move** them **to his courtyard** if that is necessary. **One may not bring** home **utensils**[N] **from the house of a craftsman** after he has completed his work, but **if one is concerned about them**[N] that if he leaves them in the craftsman's house they are likely to be stolen, **he may move them to another courtyard.**[H]

גמ׳ וְהָאָמְרַתְּ רֵישָׁא אֵין מְפַנִּין כְּלָל! אָמַר אַבַּיֵי: סֵיפָא אֲתָאן לְבַיִת שֶׁבֶּחָצֵר.

GEMARA The Gemara asks: **But didn't you say in the first clause** of the mishna that **one may not move** one's possessions **at all,** even from one house to another? How is it that the mishna then permits moving objects from one courtyard to another in the second clause? **Abaye said** in explanation: **In the latter clause we come to** the case of moving objects from **the house in his courtyard** to that same courtyard.

״וְאֵין מְבִיאִין כֵּלִים מִבֵּית הָאוּמָּן״. אָמַר רַב פַּפָּא: בָּדֵיק לָן רָבָא: תְּנַן, אֵין מְבִיאִין כֵּלִים מִבֵּית הָאוּמָּן. וּרְמִינְהוּ: מוֹלִיכִין וּמְבִיאִין כֵּלִים מִבֵּית הָאוּמָּן וְאַף עַל פִּי שֶׁאֵינָן לְצוֹרֶךְ הַמּוֹעֵד!

The mishna states: **And one may not bring** home **utensils from the house of a craftsman. Rav Pappa said: Rava tested us** with the following question: **We learned** in the mishna that **one may not bring** home **utensils from the house of a craftsman. And this raises a contradiction to** another mishna (*Pesaḥim* 55b): **One may take utensils to and bring them from the house of a craftsman, even if they are not** needed **for the sake of the Festival.**

וְשַׁנֵּינַן לֵיהּ: כָּאן – בְּאַרְבָּעָה עָשָׂר, כָּאן – בְּחוּלּוֹ שֶׁל מוֹעֵד. אִיבָּעֵית אֵימָא: הָא וְהָא בְּחוּלּוֹ שֶׁל מוֹעֵד; כָּאן – בְּמַאֲמִינוֹ, כָּאן – בְּשֶׁאֵינוֹ מַאֲמִינוֹ.

And we answered him: Here, the mishna that permits the practice is referring **to the fourteenth** of Nisan, the eve of Passover,[H] and **here,** the mishna that prohibits it, is referring **to the intermediate days of a Festival.** And **if you wish, say** another explanation: Both **this and that** refer **to the intermediate days of a Festival,** but **here,** the mishna that prohibits the practice is referring to a case **where he trusts** the craftsman and is not concerned about his utensils being lost or stolen, whereas **here,** the mishna that permits taking utensils to and from the craftsman is referring to a case **where he does not trust** the craftsman.

NOTES

One may not move – אֵין מְפַנִּין: In the Jerusalem Talmud it states that it is permitted to move objects from another house to one's own because that is a source of joy. According to the Ra'avad, the Babylonian Talmud does not dispute this. The *Maggid Mishne* disagrees and infers from the fact that the Gemara specifically mentions the case of moving items from the house to one's courtyard that it is not permitted to move them from one house to another, even if the destination is one's own house.

One may not bring home utensils – אֵין מְבִיאִין כֵּלִים: Three reasons are given for this *halakha*: Some say that it involves excessive exertion, or that people will suspect that the craftsman works on the intermediate days of the Festival (Ran). Others say that collecting an item from the craftsman is not appropriate behavior for the Festival (Ritva).

If one is concerned about them – אִם חוֹשֵׁשׁ לָהֶם: Either he fears that the craftsman's house is vulnerable to thieves, or he is concerned that the craftsman will try to cheat him by requesting payment again even though he already received it (Rashi manuscript; Rabbeinu Yehonatan of Lunel).

HALAKHA

Moving utensils on the intermediate days of a Festival – פִּינּוּי כֵּלִים בְּחוֹל הַמּוֹעֵד: One should not move items on the intermediate days of a Festival from courtyard to courtyard, through the public domain, if it is not for the sake of the Festival. It is certainly prohibited to transport one's property from one city to another (Rema). However, it is permissible to move items from one house to another in the same courtyard. If he needs to take them through an alleyway, some permit transferring from one house to an adjacent one, and some prohibit it if the alleyway is open on both sides (*Baḥ*; Vilna Gaon). If he is concerned about theft or other types of loss, it is permitted to transfer from courtyard to courtyard and even from city to city (*Shulḥan Arukh, Oraḥ Ḥayyim* 535:1, and in the comment of Rema).

Transporting utensils on the eve of Passover – הוֹלָכַת כֵּלִים בְּעֶרֶב פֶּסַח: One may take utensils to, and bring them back from, the craftsman's house all day, even those that are not for the sake of the Festival (*Shulḥan Arukh, Oraḥ Ḥayyim* 468:10).

Perek **II**
Daf **13** Amud **b**

וְהָתַנְיָא: מְבִיאִין כֵּלִים מִבֵּית הָאוּמָּן כְּגוֹן כַּד מִבֵּית הַכַּדָּר, וְכוֹס מִבֵּית הַזַּגָּג, אֲבָל לֹא צֶמֶר מִבֵּית הַצַּבָּע, וְלֹא כֵּלִים מִבֵּית הָאוּמָּן. וְאִם אֵין לוֹ מַה יֹּאכַל – נוֹתֵן לוֹ שְׂכָרוֹ, וּמַנִּיחוֹ אֶצְלוֹ. וְאִם אֵינוֹ מַאֲמִינוֹ – מַנִּיחוֹ בַּבַּיִת הַסָּמוּךְ לוֹ. וְאִם חוֹשֵׁשׁ לָהֶם שֶׁמָּא יִגָּנְבוּ – מְפַנָּן לְחָצֵר אַחֶרֶת. וְאִם אֵינוֹ מַאֲמִינוֹ – מְבִיאָן בְּצִנְעָה בְּתוֹךְ בֵּיתוֹ.

And so **it is taught** in a *baraita*: **One may bring** home **utensils from the house of a craftsman;**[H] **for example, a jug from the jug-makers house**[N] **and a cup from the glass-blower's house,** as they will be used on the Festival itself. **But** he may **not** bring home **wool from the dyer's house or utensils from the craftsman's house,** as they are not needed on the Festival. **But if** the craftsman **has nothing to eat, he may give him his wages** during the Festival week **and leave** the utensil **with him. And if he does not trust** the craftsman to properly safeguard his utensil, **he may** take the utensil from the craftsman and **leave it in a house near him. And if he is concerned about** his utensils **lest they be stolen, he may move them to another courtyard. And if he does not trust** the owner of the other courtyard, **he may bring them into his house discreetly.**

NOTES

A jug [*kad*] from the jug-maker's house – כַּד מִבֵּית הַכַּדָּר: Some have the version: A pillow [*kar*] from the house of the pillow-maker, meaning one whose craft is making pillows (Commentary on Moed Katan).

HALAKHA

One may bring home utensils from the house of a craftsman – מְבִיאִין כֵּלִים מִבֵּית הָאוּמָּן: One may bring utensils from the craftsman's house for the sake of the Festival, but not utensils that are not for the sake of the Festival, like a plow. This is the case even with a gentile craftsman (*Magen Avraham*). And if the craftsman does not have anything to eat, he should give him his wages but leave the utensils with him. And if he does not trust him, he should leave them in an adjacent house. And if he is concerned lest they be stolen there, he may relocate them to another courtyard; but he may only bring them into his house in a private manner (*Shulḥan Arukh, Oraḥ Ḥayyim* 534:3).

תַּרְצְתְּ מְבִיאִין; מוֹלִיכִין – קַשְׁיָא! דְּקָתָנֵי: אֵין מְבִיאִין, וְכׇל שֶׁכֵּן שֶׁאֵין מוֹלִיכִין! אֶלָּא: מְחַוַּורְתָּא כִּדְשַׁנְיַין מֵעִיקָּרָא.

The Gemara comments: **You have** adequately **explained** the contradiction between the *mishnayot* about whether **one may bring** home utensils from the house of a craftsman. The mishna that permits it can be understood as referring to a case where the craftsman is not to be trusted. But the mishna in *Pesaḥim* also states that **one may take** utensils to the house of a craftsman, and this is **difficult, as** the mishna above **teaches: One may not bring** home utensils from the house of a craftsman. **And** this indicates that **all the more so, one may not take** utensils from his house to that of the craftsman. **Rather, it is clear as we answered initially** that one mishna is referring to the eve of Passover and the other to the intermediate days of a Festival.

מתני׳ מְחַפִּין אֶת הַקְּצִיעוֹת בְּקַשׁ, רַבִּי יְהוּדָה אוֹמֵר: אַף מְעַבִּין. מוֹכְרֵי פֵּירוֹת, כְּסוּת וְכֵלִים – מוֹכְרִים בְּצִנְעָה לְצוֹרֶךְ הַמּוֹעֵד. הַצַּיָּידִין וְהַדָּשׁוֹשׁוֹת וְהַגָּרוֹסוֹת – עוֹשִׂין בְּצִנְעָה לְצוֹרֶךְ הַמּוֹעֵד. רַבִּי יוֹסֵי אוֹמֵר: הֵם הֶחְמִירוּ עַל עַצְמָן.

MISHNA On the intermediate days of a Festival, **figs** that were spread out to dry **may be covered with straw** to protect them from rain and dew.[H] **Rabbi Yehuda says: One may even condense**[N] the figs. **Those who sell produce, clothing, and utensils may sell** them **in private, for the sake of the Festival.**[H] **Fishermen, and groats makers** [*dashoshot*],[L] **and** bean **pounders,** who pulverize the beans, **may** ply their trades **in private for the sake of the Festival.**[H] **Rabbi Yosei says: They were stringent with themselves** to refrain from this work even with respect to what was needed for the Festival.

גמ׳ פְּלִיגִי בָּהּ רַבִּי חִיָּיא בַּר אַבָּא וְרַבִּי אַסִי, וְתַרְוַויְיהוּ מִשְּׁמֵיהּ דְּחִזְקִיָּה וְרַבִּי יוֹחָנָן. חַד אָמַר: מְחַפִּין – אַקְלוּשֵׁי; מְעַבִּין – אַסְמוּכֵי. וְחַד אָמַר: מְחַפִּין – בֵּין אַקְלוּשֵׁי בֵּין אַסְמוּכֵי; מְעַבִּין – עוֹשֶׂה אוֹתוֹ כְּמִין כְּרִי. תַּנְיָא נַמִי הָכִי: מְעַבִּין – עוֹשֶׂה אוֹתוֹ כְּמִין כְּרִי, דִּבְרֵי רַבִּי יְהוּדָה.

GEMARA **Rabbi Ḥiyya bar Abba and Rabbi Asi disagree about** the following issue, **and both of them** assert their opinions **in the name of Ḥizkiyya and Rabbi Yoḥanan. One said: Cover** the figs means to **lightly** cover them with straw, and **condense** means to spread straw over them **densely. And** the other **one said: Cover** means to spread straw over them **whether lightly or densely,** and **condense** means to amass the figs into a pile, **making it as if** it were **a pile** of grain.[N] **This is also taught** in a *baraita*: **One may condense,** i.e., amass the figs into a pile, **making it as if** it were **a pile** of grain. This is **the statement of Rabbi Yehuda.**

״מוֹכְרֵי פֵּירוֹת כְּסוּת וְכֵלִים מוֹכְרִין בְּצִנְעָה״ וכו׳. אִיבַּעְיָא לְהוּ: הֵן הֶחְמִירוּ עַל עַצְמָן – דְּלָא הָווּ עָבְדִי כְּלָל, אוֹ דִּלְמָא: דְּהָווּ עָבְדִי בְּצִנְעָה?

§ The mishna states: On the intermediate days of a Festival, **those who sell produce, clothing, and utensils may sell** them **in private,** for the sake of the Festival. Fishermen, groats makers, and bean pounders may ply their trades in private for the sake of the Festival. Rabbi Yosei says that they were stringent with themselves. The Sages were **asked:** When it says that **they were stringent with themselves,** does it mean that **that they did not work at all** on the intermediate days of a Festival, **or perhaps** it means **that they did** their work **in private,** though it is permitted to do it publicly?

NOTES

One may even condense – אַף מְעַבִּין: Some early commentaries, based on a version of the text that reads: Rabbi Yehuda says one may condense, understand that Rabbi Yehuda is more stringent than the first *tanna* and holds that one may not cover the figs, but only assemble them into a pile (Rabbeinu Yehonatan of Lunel).

Cover…and condense – מְחַפִּין...וּמְעַבִּין: In the Jerusalem Talmud the question is raised as to how an action that is permitted on Shabbat could be prohibited on the intermediate days of the Festival. It is explained that the dispute is about whether it is permitted to pick straw in order cover with it.

LANGUAGE

Groats makers [*dashoshot*] – דָּשׁוֹשׁוֹת: There are several textual variants of this word. If the word is *dashoshot*, it is from the root *d-o-sh*, meaning threshing. Some texts have *dasosot*, from the word *daisa*, meaning porridge; and some have the version *rashoshot* or *rasosot*, from the word *resisim*, meaning fragments, since they break the seeds into slivers or fragments.

HALAKHA

Covering figs spread out to dry – חִיפּוּי קְצִיעוֹת: One who had figs laid out in the field to dry and is concerned lest rain fall on them, is allowed to cover them even with a thick layer of straw. He is even allowed to uproot straw for this purpose (*Mishna Berura* citing the Jerusalem Talmud; *Shulḥan Arukh, Oraḥ Ḥayyim* 538:4).

Selling on the intermediate days of the Festival – מְכִירָה בְּחוֹל הַמּוֹעֵד: Sellers of produce, clothing, and utensils may sell discreetly for the sake of the Festival (*Shulḥan Arukh, Oraḥ Ḥayyim* 539:11).

Fishermen, and groats makers, etc. – הַצַּיָּידִין וְהַדָּשׁוֹשׁוֹת וכו׳: Any task for the sake of the Festival performed by craftsmen in their own fields must be performed discreetly. Therefore, hunters, as well as the millers and grape harvesters, who perform their tasks in order to sell immediately for the sake of the Festival, must nevertheless do so discreetly. According to the Rema, this applies to animal and bird hunters, but not fishermen, as it is obvious to all that a fisherman's catch is for immediate use (*Mishna Berura*); some authorities (*Magen Avraham*) prohibit even fishermen from selling in public (*Shulḥan Arukh, Oraḥ Ḥayyim* 533:5).

The Gemara answers based on a *baraita*. **Come and hear: Those who sell produce, clothing, and utensils may sell** them **in private, for the sake of the Festival. Rabbi Yosei says: The merchants of Tiberias**[B] **were stringent with themselves not to sell at all,** even in private. **Hunters of animals, fowlers, and fishermen may hunt** their quarry **discreetly for the sake of the Festival. Rabbi Yosei says: The hunters of Akko**[N] **were stringent with themselves not to hunt at all. Groats makers** who crack grain into groats called ***ḥilka***,[L] ***targis***,[L] **and *tisanei***,[L] **crack** the grain **in private for the sake of the Festival. Rabbi Yosei says: The groats makers of Tzippori**[B] **were stringent with themselves not to crack** grain **at all.** According to Rabbi Yosei, the stringencies involve refraining from work entirely.

תָּא שְׁמַע: מוֹכְרֵי פֵּירוֹת כְּסוּת וְכֵלִים מוֹכְרִין בְּצִנְעָה לְצוֹרֶךְ הַמּוֹעֵד. רַבִּי יוֹסֵי אוֹמֵר: תַּגָּרֵי טְבֶרְיָא הֵן הֶחְמִירוּ עַל עַצְמָן שֶׁלֹּא יְהוּ מוֹכְרִין כָּל עִיקָּר. צָדֵי חַיּוֹת וְעוֹפוֹת וְדָגִים צָדִין בְּצִנְעָה לְצוֹרֶךְ הַמּוֹעֵד. רַבִּי יוֹסֵי אוֹמֵר: צָדֵי עַכּוֹ הֵן הֶחְמִירוּ עַל עַצְמָן שֶׁלֹּא יְהוּ צָדִין כָּל עִיקָּר. דָּשׁוֹשֵׁי חִילְקָא טַרְגִּים וְטִיסָנֵי דּוֹשְׁשִׁין בְּצִנְעָה לְצוֹרֶךְ הַמּוֹעֵד. רַבִּי יוֹסֵי אוֹמֵר: דָּשׁוֹשֵׁי צִיפּוֹרִי הֵן הֶחְמִירוּ עַל עַצְמָן שֶׁלֹּא יְהוּ דּוֹשְׁשִׁין כָּל עִיקָּר.

Abaye said: The term *ḥilka* means **one** kernel that is broken **into two;** the term ***targis*** means **one** kernel that is broken **into three;** and the term ***tisanei*** means **one** grain that is broken **into four. When Rav Dimi came** from Eretz Yisrael to Babylonia, **he said:** *Ḥilka* is referring to **emmer wheat.**

אָמַר אַבַּיֵי: חִילְקָא – חֲדָא לְתַרְתֵּי; טַרְגִּים – חֲדָא לִתְלָת; טִיסָנֵי – חֲדָא לְאַרְבְּעָה. כִּי אֲתָא רַב דִּימִי אֲמַר: כּוּנְתָּא.

The Gemara **raises an objection** from a *baraita*: ***Ḥilka, targis***,[H] **and *tisanei* are** susceptible to **ritual impurity everywhere.**[N] **Granted, according to the one who said** that these are **one** grain broken **into two, into three, and into four, due to that** reason **they are** susceptible to **impurity everywhere, as they** have already **become fit** to contract ritual impurity by being rinsed with water in their processing. **But according to the one who says that *ḥilka* is emmer wheat** that has not necessarily been processed, **why is it susceptible to** ritual **impurity everywhere, since it has not** necessarily **become fit** to contract impurity by coming into contact with water?

מֵיתִיבִי: חִילְקָא טַרְגִּים וְטִיסָנֵי – טְמֵאִין בְּכָל מָקוֹם. בִּשְׁלָמָא לְמַאן דְּאָמַר חֲדָא לְתַרְתֵּי לִתְלָת וּלְאַרְבְּעָה – מִשּׁוּם הָכִי טְמֵאִין בְּכָל מָקוֹם, דְּאִתְכַּשּׁוּר. אֶלָּא לְמַאן דְּאָמַר כּוּנְתָּא – אַמַּאי טְמֵאִין בְּכָל מָקוֹם? הָא לָא אִיתְכַּשּׁוּר!

The Gemara answers: The *baraita* is referring to a case **where, for example,** the emmer wheat **was husked, since if it had not been** previously **soaked in water, it would not have been possible to husk it. And why,** according to this opinion, **is it called *ḥilka*?** It is called this **because their husks [*ḥelkayhu*] were removed.**

כְּגוֹן דְּמִיקַּלְפָן, דְּאִי לָאו דִּשְׁרָא לְהוּ בְּמַיָּא – לָא הֲוָה מִיקַּלְפָא. וְאַמַּאי קָרֵי לֵיהּ חִילְקָא? דִּשְׁקַל חֶלְקַיְהוּ.

NOTES

The hunters of Akko – צָדֵי עַכּוֹ: Mishnaic Hebrew uses the same term for hunters and fishermen. Since Akko is on the sea, it is likely that the reference is to fishermen rather than hunters of animals.

In the Jerusalem Talmud it is recounted that the fishermen of Tiberias also accepted upon themselves a stringency that they would fish in an altered manner on the intermediate days of the Festival. Some of the Sages objected to this practice, as it resulted in a shortage of fish that might mar the joy of the Festival for the entire community.

Susceptible to ritual impurity everywhere – טְמֵאִין בְּכָל מָקוֹם: Apparently, the production of these types of cracked wheat always involved them coming into contact with water. Most commentaries and halakhic authorities explain that that is why they are susceptible to impurity everywhere, as opposed to other wheat products. Some flours are not malted before grinding and are not ground with water; since the wheat has not come into contact with water, it is not susceptible to impurity in those places.

HALAKHA

***Ḥilka, targis*, etc. – חִילְקָא טַרְגִּים וכו׳:** All types of flour and grist sold in the marketplace are presumed to be susceptible to ritual impurity (Rambam *Sefer Tahara, Hilkhot Tumat Okhalin* 16:1).

LANGUAGE

***Ḥilka* – חִילְקָא:** Some think that this word derives from the Latin halica or alica, meaning grist. According to this, the explanations given for the word are attempts at finding allusions in a foreign word to the meaning of the concept that is then expressed in Hebrew or Aramaic; there are many examples of this in the Talmud.

***Targis* – טַרְגִּים:** Apparently from the Greek τράγος, *tragos*, among whose meanings are buckwheat and wheat grist.

***Tisanei* – טִיסָנֵי:** Apparently from the Greek πτισάνη, *ptisanè*, which means grist or barley grist.

BACKGROUND

Tiberias – טְבֶרְיָא: Tiberias is a town on the shore of the Sea of Galilee founded by Herod Antipas, c. 18 CE. It was apparently founded on the site of earlier settlements, and according to some opinions in the Talmud (*Megilla* 6a) Tiberias was the site of the biblical city of Rakkath. From the outset, Tiberias was a town of mixed Jewish and gentile population. The Jewish population was not distinguished for its Torah scholarship. However, after the destruction of the Temple, important Torah scholars such as ben Azzai and Rabbi Meir lived there. Its period of greatness came when the Sanhedrin moved there, c. 235 CE, and it became the seat of the Great Council, presided over by Rabbi Yehuda Nesia I. After him Rabbi Yoḥanan became its leading spiritual figure and headed the yeshiva there. From that time on, Tiberias was the Torah center of Eretz Yisrael. Most of the disciples of Rabbi Yoḥanan, particularly those who immigrated from Babylonia, lived and continued their studies there. Reish Lakish lived in Tiberias, as did Rabbi Elazar ben Pedat, Rabbi Ami, Rabbi Yirmeya, and Rabbi Yona. It is likely that most of the Jerusalem Talmud was redacted there. After the talmudic period, Tiberias remained a significant creative religious and spiritual center, and many of the works of aggadic midrash were composed there, as were many liturgical poems. During the post-talmudic era, the inhabitants of Tiberias were renowned as experts in Hebrew grammar, and the system of Hebrew vocalization used today is called Tiberian vocalization because it was formulated and established there.

Tzippori – צִיפּוֹרִי: Tzippori, or Sepphoris in Greek, was a large town in the Upper Galilee, and rivaled Tiberias as the religious capital of Galilee. During the Second Temple period it enjoyed special status among the towns of the Galilee because of its large and learned Jewish community. Among the *tanna'im* who lived there were Rabbi Yoḥanan ben Nuri, Rabbi Ḥalafta, and his famous son Rabbi Yosei. Rabbi Yehuda HaNasi moved to Tzippori toward the end of his life, and it was the seat of the Sanhedrin for about a generation. Rabbi Yehuda HaNasi's leading disciples lived in Tzippori: Rabbi Yishmael, son of Rabbi Yosei; Rabban Gamliel, son of Rabbi Yehuda HaNasi, who was later appointed *Nasi*; his brother Rabbi Shimon; Rabbi Ḥanina bar Ḥama, who was later the head of the Tzippori academy; and Rabbi Yannai. Even after the Sanhedrin moved to Tiberias, Torah scholars continued to live in Tzippori, among them the important *amora'im* of Eretz Yisrael, Rabbi Ḥanina of Tzippori and Rabbi Mana.

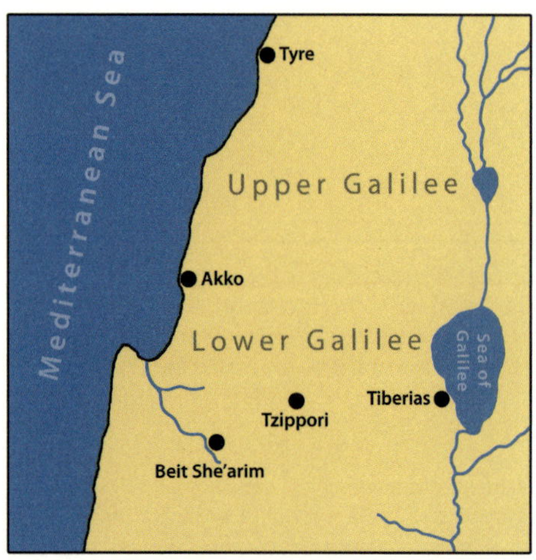

Tiberias, Tzippori, and Akko

מֵיתִיבִי: הַנּוֹדֵר מִן הַדָּגָן אָסוּר אַף בַּפּוֹל הַמִּצְרִי יָבֵשׁ, וּמוּתָּר בְּלַח, וּמוּתָּר בְּאוֹרֶז, בְּחִילְקָא וְטַרְגִּיס וְטִיסָנֵי. בִּשְׁלָמָא לְמַאן דְּאָמַר חֲדָא לְתַרְתֵּי חֲדָא לִתְלָת וַחֲדָא לְאַרְבָּעָה – שַׁפִּיר, דִּנְפַקוּ לְהוּ מִתּוֹרַת דָּגָן. אֶלָּא לְמַאן דְּאָמַר כּוּנְתָּא – דָּגָן מְעַלְיָא הוּא! קַשְׁיָא.

The Gemara **raises an objection** from a *baraita*: **One who vows to** prohibit himself **from** eating **grain** [*dagan*] **is prohibited to** partake **of even dry Egyptian beans, and** it **is permitted** for him to partake **of fresh** beans. **And** it **is permitted** for him to partake **of rice,** as well as **of** ***ḥilka*****, and** ***targeis*****, and** ***tisnei*****. Granted, according to the one who said** that these are **one** grain broken **into two, one** grain broken **into three, and one** grain broken **into four, it is fine,** as when the wheat is crushed into these **it leaves the category of grain. But according to the one who says** that *ḥilka* is **emmer wheat, it is** still a **proper grain.** The Gemara concludes: Indeed, it is **difficult.**

רַב הוּנָא שְׁרָא לְהוּ לְהַנְהוּ כְּרוּפַיָּיתָא לְמֵיזַל לְזַבּוּנֵי כִּי אוֹרְחַיְיהוּ בְּשׁוּקָא. אֵיתִיבֵיהּ רַב כַּהֲנָא: חֲנוּת פְּתוּחָה לְסְטָיו – פּוֹתֵחַ וְנוֹעֵל כְּדַרְכּוֹ;

§ The Gemara relates that **Rav Huna permitted the spice merchants** [*kerufayata*][N] **to go and sell** their products **in their usual manner in the marketplace** on the intermediate days of a Festival. **Rav Kahana raised an objection to** Rav Huna's ruling from a *baraita*: If **a store opens into a row of pillars** that runs along the street, the storekeeper **may open and close it in his usual manner** on the intermediate days of a Festival, since it is not in the public's view.

פְּתוּחָה לִרְשׁוּת הָרַבִּים – פּוֹתֵחַ אַחַת וְנוֹעֵל אַחַת; וְעֶרֶב יוֹם טוֹב הָאַחֲרוֹן שֶׁל חַג – מוֹצִיא, וּמְעַטֵּר אֶת שׁוּקֵי הָעִיר בְּפֵירוֹת בִּשְׁבִיל כְּבוֹד יוֹם טוֹב הָאַחֲרוֹן. מִפְּנֵי כְּבוֹד יוֹם טוֹב הָאַחֲרוֹן – אִין; שֶׁלֹּא מִפְּנֵי כְּבוֹד יוֹם טוֹב – לָא!

However, if it is **open to the public domain, he may open** only **one** door and must **close the other.**[H] **And on the eve of the last day of the festival** of *Sukkot*, **he may take out** his wares from the store **and adorn the markets of the city with fruit in honor of the last day of the Festival.** The Gemara infers: **For the honor of the last day of the Festival, yes,** it is permitted for him to open the store in order to give people the opportunity to prepare for the holiday, but when **not for the honor of the Festival,** i.e., during the other intermediate days of the Festival, he is **not** permitted to do so. How, then, did Rav Huna permit those spice merchants to sell as usual on the intermediate days of the Festival?

לָא קַשְׁיָא: הָא – בְּפֵירֵי, הָא – בִּתְבָלִין.

The Gemara answers: This is **not difficult: This** *baraita* that prohibits selling in the usual manner is referring **to** the sale of **fruit,** which is usually bought in large quantities and could have been purchased before the Festival; people might therefore suspect the buyer of purchasing it for use after the Festival. In contrast, **this** lenient ruling of Rav Huna is referring **to** the sale of **spices,** which is permitted[H] because people buy them only in small quantities for the sake of the Festival.

הדרן עלך מי שהפך

NOTES

Spice merchants [*kerufayata*] – **כְּרוּפַיָּיתָא:** There are several versions and explanations of this word. Many commentaries suggest that it is referring to spice merchants (Rabbeinu Gershom Meor HaGola; Rabbi Shlomo ben HaYatom; Rosh). In the Rashi manuscript, the term is explained as referring to merchants who sell cabbage, vetch, and other kinds of vegetables.

HALAKHA

Selling discreetly – מְכִירָה בִּצְנִעָה: One may sell discreetly on the intermediate days of the Festival in the following manner: If the store opens to an isolated corner or an alleyway, one may open it in its usual manner. If it is open to the public domain he must open only one door and keep the other door closed. On the eve of the concluding Festival day of *Sukkot*, and also the eve of the seventh day of Passover (*Taz*), one may sell in the usual manner and adorn the market with fruits to honor the Festival, and it is permissible to buy even for the sake of the second day of the concluding Festival (*Shulḥan Arukh, Oraḥ Ḥayyim* 539:11, and in the comment of Rema).

Permitting the spice merchants – שְׁרָא לִכְרוּפַיָּיתָא: Merchants selling spices and vegetables, as well as anything that does not keep, may sell their wares in the usual manner in public, as all know that this is for the sake of the Festival. The same applies to the perfume merchants (*Mishna Berura*; *Shulḥan Arukh, Oraḥ Ḥayyim* 539:10).

Summary of **Perek II**

The conclusive ruling on permitting labor on the intermediate days of a Festival for a matter that, if unattended, will result in significant loss, is that it is permissible to perform labor to prevent a loss of any size. Additionally, once a labor is deemed permissible it may be performed in its usual manner without any change.

Despite that, the Sages were very strict with regard to one who engages in artifice and directs his labor to the intermediate days of a Festival. In such a case, the Sages ruled that even if he incurs a great loss, the perpetrator must not perform the labor and therefore must lose everything. However, they specified that such a penalty falls only on the perpetrator himself, and not on the object, so that his heirs, if he should die, are permitted to complete the labor in such a case.

The blanket authorization to perform labor on the intermediate days of a Festival was extended to include one who has to work in order to buy food for the days of the Festival. Clearly this does not mean only in a case of a life-threatening lack of food; he is allowed to work on those days even where performing labor is for the purpose of increasing his provisions for the Festival.

In order for celebrants to honor the Festival and in order to provide for the community's needs, the Sages permitted merchants to operate stores during the intermediate days of a Festival and to sell their merchandise in their usual weekday manner, even if it is not perishable merchandise. Though in many places the residents adopted a more stringent practice, various labors are permitted on the intermediate days of a Festival as long as they are for community needs or for the sake of the Festival itself.

Introduction to **Perek III**

And the children of Israel wept for Moses in the plains of Moab thirty days; so the days of weeping in the mourning for Moses were ended.

(Deuteronomy 34:8)

And Joab sent to Tekoa, and fetched from there a wise woman, and said to her: "I pray you, feign yourself to be a mourner, and put on mourning apparel, I pray you, and do not anoint yourself with oil, but be as a woman that had a long time mourned for the dead."

(II Samuel 14:2)

Also the word of the Lord came to me, saying: "Son of man, behold, I take away from you the desire of your eyes with a stroke; yet neither will you make lamentation nor weep, nor shall your tears run down. Sigh in silence; make no mourning for the dead, bind your headwear upon yourself, and put your shoes on your feet, and do not cover your upper lip, and eat not the bread of men."

(Ezekiel 24:15–17)

Then Job arose, and rent his mantle, and shaved his head, and fell down upon the ground, and worshipped.

(Job 1:20)

And that whoever does not come within three days, according to the counsel of the princes and the elders, all his substance should be forfeited, and himself separated from the congregation of the captivity.

(Ezra 10:8)

The *mishnayot* in this chapter deal primarily with the *halakhot* of the intermediate days of the Festival. Specifically, they discuss the prohibitions of laundering, haircutting, and writing during these days. Also discussed are the various circumstances when the Sages permitted these activities for particular reasons. The Gemara brings in other topics, particularly regarding the *halakhot* of mourning and of ostracism. These *halakhot* are included here because there is a certain similarity between the seven days of rejoicing of a Festival and the seven days of mourning. Furthermore, the Gemara discusses how to behave when both a Festival and a mourning period occur at the same time.

Many of the *halakhot* of mourning, as well as those of ostracism and excommunication, are mentioned in various places in the Bible. However, they are not written as a complete, systematic description of the *halakha*. Therefore, when it comes to matters of practical *halakha* there are many unresolved issues. For example, there is a custom of tearing garments when one is in mourning, but the Bible gives no details of when, for whom, or how to tear. Concepts such as comforting mourners and overturning the beds are alluded to in the Bible, but again no halakhic details are provided, such as when or how these activities are to be performed. Even the number of days of mourning isn't fixed. The Gemara explains which of the activities mentioned in the Bible are *halakha* and obligatory on all mourners, and which are only customs of suffering that certain people took upon themselves.

There are many other, related issues and practical questions. For example, when precisely does mourning begin? What is the *halakha* in a case when someone heard of a relative's death some time later? Also, how must one act when the days of mourning occur on Shabbat or Festivals?

The *halakhot* of ostracism and excommunication are likewise only alluded to in the Bible, yet the Torah does not explicate many of their numerous practical aspects therein. For example, when and for what violations are people ostracized? For how long is someone ostracized? How should one who has been ostracized or excommunicated behave, and how should others act toward him?

These questions and others are the main topics discussed in this chapter.

Perek **III**
Daf **13** Amud **b**

מתני׳ וְאֵלּוּ מְגַלְּחִין בַּמּוֹעֵד: הַבָּא מִמְּדִינַת הַיָּם, וּמִבֵּית הַשִּׁבְיָה, וְהַיּוֹצֵא מִבֵּית הָאֲסוּרִין, וְהַמְנוּדֶּה שֶׁהִתִּירוּ לוֹ חֲכָמִים, וְכֵן מִי שֶׁנִּשְׁאַל לְחָכָם וְהוּתַּר, וְהַנָּזִיר וְהַמְּצוֹרָע מִטּוּמְאָתוֹ לְטָהֳרָתוֹ.

MISHNA **And these may shave** and cut their hair[N] **on** the intermediate days of **a Festival: One who comes from a country overseas;**[N] **and** one who is released **from a house of captivity; and one who comes out of prison** on the intermediate days of a Festival; **and one who had been ostracized** and therefore prohibited from cutting his hair, **and the Sages released him** from his decree of ostracism on the intermediate days of the Festival; **and similarly, one who** had vowed not to cut his hair and then **requested of a Sage** to dissolve his vow **and was released** from it on the intermediate days of the Festival; **and the nazirite** whose term of naziriteship ended on the intermediate days of a Festival; **and the leper**[N] who needs to purify himself on the intermediate days and must shave his entire body in order to leave **his** state of ritual **impurity**[N] and regain **his** ritual **purity.** Since these people were not able to cut their hair on the eve of the Festival, they are permitted to do so on the intermediate days of the Festival.[H]

וְאֵלּוּ מְכַבְּסִין בַּמּוֹעֵד: הַבָּא מִמְּדִינַת הַיָּם וּמִבֵּית הַשִּׁבְיָה, וְהַיּוֹצֵא מִבֵּית הָאֲסוּרִין,

And these may launder their clothes **on** the intermediate days of **a Festival: One who comes from a country overseas; and one who** is released **from a house of captivity; and one who comes out of prison** on the intermediate days of a Festival;

HALAKHA

Those who are permitted to shave and cut their hair on the intermediate days of the Festival – הַמּוּתָּרִין בְּתִגְלַחַת בַּמּוֹעֵד: Both one who came out of captivity or was freed from jail during a Festival and one who had been ostracized and was released from his decree of ostracism during a Festival are permitted to shave on the Festival (*Shulḥan Arukh Oraḥ Ḥayyim* 531:4).

NOTES

And these may shave and cut their hair – וְאֵלּוּ מְגַלְּחִין: The Ritva and *Tosafot* ask why the mishna begins with the conjunctive: And, although there is no apparent connection to the previous chapters of mishna. *Tosafot* explain the connection: The previous two chapters listed exceptional cases, where certain activities are permitted during the intermediate days of a Festival. Similarly, this mishna continues with exceptions to the prohibitions against cutting hair and laundering during the intermediate days of a Festival. The Ritva explains that this mishna continues to discuss the subject matter of the previous chapters, which is activities that are permitted during the intermediate days of a Festival because they could not have been performed earlier.

One who comes from a country overseas – הַבָּא מִמְּדִינַת הַיָּם: Some explain that this is not necessarily referring to another country but to any distant place (*Talmid Rabbeinu Yeḥiel of Paris*). The Ritva holds that anyone coming from outside the city is included in this category with regard to the intermediate days of the Festival.

The nazirite and the leper, etc. – הַנָּזִיר וְהַמְּצוֹרָע וכו׳: There is a dispute as to whether a priest may rule on a case of leprosy during the intermediate days of a Festival. The commentaries point out that according to Rabbi Meir, who holds that the priest may rule on the status of a leper, the priest may instruct the leper to shave the hair around the site of the leprosy, and the leper may shave during the intermediate days of the Festival. This case is different than the case of the leper listed in the mishna. The mishna is referring to shaving once he has completed the purification process, whereas this case is referring to shaving that is part of the process of ascertaining whether or not one is impure. This case is not included in the mishna because it is not shaving for aesthetic purposes but for a halakhic purpose (Ran, citing Rashi; see Ritva and *Melekhet HaShulḥan*).

And the leper his impurity – וְהַמְּצוֹרָע מִטּוּמְאָתוֹ: The Rambam and other early authorities had a version of the text that did not specify the leper, but read: And the one ascending from his state of ritual impurity. The Rambam writes that all who purify themselves are permitted to shave on the Festival. In the *Mishne LeMelekh* it is explained that it is not appropriate for an impure person to beautify himself with a haircut. Therefore, when he purifies himself it is considered as if he did not have time to cut his hair on the eve of the Festival (see *Dikdukei Soferim*).

Perek **III**
Daf **14** Amud **a**

וּמְנוּדֶּה שֶׁהִתִּירוּ לוֹ חֲכָמִים, וְכֵן מִי שֶׁנִּשְׁאַל לְחָכָם וְהוּתַּר.

and one who had been ostracized and the Sages released him from his decree of ostracism; **and similarly, one who** had vowed not to launder his clothes and he **requested from a Sage**[N] to dissolve his vow **and was released** from it on the intermediate days of a Festival.

NOTES

One who requested from a Sage – מִי שֶׁנִּשְׁאַל לְחָכָם: Some explain that this means that one was prohibited by his oath from washing clothes, and he changed his mind on the Festival (manuscript of Rashi; Rabbeinu Yehonatan of Lunel). Others explain that in such a case it is not permitted, and the only cases in which it is permitted are when the oath was for a specific duration that expired during the Festival, or if one did not find a Sage to permit him to do so until the Festival (Rosh and *Tosafot*, citing the Jerusalem Talmud).

מִטְפְּחוֹת הַיָּדַיִם, וּמִטְפְּחוֹת הַסַּפָּרִים, וּמִטְפְּחוֹת הַסְּפָג, הַזָּבִין וְהַזָּבוֹת וְהַנִּדּוֹת וְהַיּוֹלְדוֹת, וְכׇל הָעוֹלִין מִטּוּמְאָה לְטׇהֳרָה – הֲרֵי אֵלּוּ מוּתָּרִין. וּשְׁאָר כׇּל אָדָם אֲסוּרִין.

Hand towels;[H] **and barbers' towels,**[N] which are used to cover a person having a haircut; **and body-drying towels,** all of which get quickly soiled, may be laundered on the intermediate days of a Festival. ***Zavim,*** men suffering from an impure venereal emission; ***zavot,***[H] women who experience a flow of menstrual-type blood on three consecutive days during a time of the month when they do not expect to experience menstrual bleeding; **menstruating women; women who have** just **given birth; and all others who leave** a state of **ritual impurity for** a state of **ritual purity** on the intermediate days of the Festival, **these** people **are** all **permitted** to launder their clothes in order to purify themselves. **But all other people are prohibited** from laundering during the intermediate days of the Festival.

גמ׳ וּשְׁאָר כׇּל אָדָם מַאי טַעְמָא אֲסוּרִין?

GEMARA The Gemara asks: **What is the reason** that **all other people are prohibited** from performing these actions during the intermediate days? Why are these actions not included in the category of actions that are permitted in deference to the Festival?

כִּדְתְנַן: אַנְשֵׁי מִשְׁמָר וְאַנְשֵׁי מַעֲמָד אֲסוּרִין לְסַפֵּר וּלְכַבֵּס, וּבַחֲמִישִׁי מוּתָּרִין, מִפְּנֵי כְּבוֹד הַשַּׁבָּת.

The Gemara answers: **As we learned** in a mishna (*Taanit* 15b): Both **the members of the priestly watch**[B] whose week it is to serve in the Temple **and the members of the non-priestly watch**[HB] who accompanied the members of the watch to Jerusalem **are prohibited from cutting** their **hair**[N] **or laundering** their clothes during that week. **But on the Thursday** of that week **they are permitted**[N] to do so **in deference to Shabbat.**

וְאָמַר רַבָּה בַּר בַּר חָנָה אָמַר רַבִּי אֶלְעָזָר: מַאי טַעְמָא? כְּדֵי שֶׁלֹּא יִכָּנְסוּ לְמִשְׁמַרְתָּן כְּשֶׁהֵן מְנוּוָּלִין. הָכָא נָמֵי: כְּדֵי שֶׁלֹּא יִכָּנְסוּ לָרֶגֶל כְּשֶׁהֵן מְנוּוָּלִין.

And Rabba bar bar Ḥana said in the name of Rabbi Elazar: What is the reason that the members of the priestly and non-priestly watch are prohibited from cutting their hair and laundering their clothes? It is **in order that they not enter their watch when they are untidy.** If it were permitted for them to cut their hair and launder their clothes during the week of their watch, they would leave their haircuts and laundry until the middle of that week and begin their service in a disorderly state. **Here, too,** ordinary people are prohibited from cutting their hair or laundering their clothes on the intermediate days of a Festival, **in order that they** complete all necessary preparations beforehand and **not enter the Festival when they are untidy.**

HALAKHA

Washing hand towels, etc. – כִּבּוּס מִטְפְּחוֹת הַיָּדַיִם וכו׳: On the intermediate days of a Festival it is permitted to wash hand towels, barbers' towels, and body towels, even in public, but this is not the accepted custom (Rema). Baby clothes, such as diapers, may be washed, even several at once, based on the ruling in the Jerusalem Talmud (*Shulḥan Arukh, Oraḥ Ḥayyim* 534:1).

Zavim and *zavot*, etc. – הַזָּבִין וְהַזָּבוֹת וכו׳: *Zavim, zavot*, menstruating women, women who have given birth, and all who are purifying themselves from their ritual impurity during the Festival are permitted to wash their clothes on the intermediate days of the Festival (Rambam *Sefer Zemanim, Hilkhot Yom Tov* 7:21).

The members of the priestly watch and the members of the non-priestly watch – אַנְשֵׁי מִשְׁמָר וְאַנְשֵׁי מַעֲמָד: The members of the priestly watch and the members of the non-priestly watch are prohibited from cutting their hair and laundering their clothes during the whole week of their watch. However, on Thursday they are permitted to do so in deference to Shabbat (Rambam *Sefer Avoda, Hilkhot Kelei HaMikdash* 6:11 and *Hilkhot Biat HaMikdash* 1:12).

BACKGROUND

Priestly watch – מִשְׁמָר: The priests who served in the Temple were divided into twenty-four groups, called watches. Each watch served for one week at a time. In this manner, each watch performed the Temple service for approximately two weeks every year. During the pilgrimage Festivals, the members of all the watches went to the Temple and performed the Temple service together. Each watch received the priestly gifts that were contributed to the Temple during their week of Temple service. The watches were divided into extended patrilineal families. The priests were originally divided into watches in the time of King David. However, during the Second Temple period, many of the Jews who had been exiled to Babylonia after the destruction of the First Temple remained in Babylonia. Therefore, those priestly families who returned to Eretz Yisrael had to be divided again into twenty-four watches.

Non-priestly watch – מַעֲמָד: Each priestly watch was responsible for sacrificing the offerings for their week. Corresponding to each of these watches was a group of non-priests who constituted a non-priestly watch. The Jewish men of Eretz Yisrael were divided into twenty-four non-priestly watches, and each time a priestly watch went to Jerusalem to sacrifice offerings, part of the corresponding non-priestly watch went there as well. The remainder of the non-priestly watch stayed at home. During that week, those at home would fast each day, from Monday to Thursday, read certain portions from the Torah, and say special prayers.

NOTES

Barbers' [*sapparim*] towels – מִטְפְּחוֹת הַסַּפָּרִים: Some say that these were the towels used during the haircut for those who were permitted to have their hair cut during the Festival (Rabbi Ovadya MiBartenura). Some explain that these are the cloth covers of *sefarim*, holy books (Meiri). Others, based on a slightly different version of the text, explain that it means cloths of the *soferim*, scribes, which they place over their manuscripts to protect them from ink blots and dirt (see Meiri and Rabbeinu Yehonatan of Lunel).

The prohibition against cutting hair on the intermediate days of a Festival – אִיסּוּר תִּסְפּוֹרֶת בַּמּוֹעֵד: According to most commentaries and halakhic authorities, cutting hair is a prohibited labor (see *Tosafot*). However, there are cases of leniency for the sake of beautifying oneself, since doing so is not an exertion (*Talmid Rabbeinu Yeḥiel of Paris*). Others hold that it is considered like other necessary activities that are permitted from the outset on the intermediate days of a Festival (Ritva).

But on the Thursday they are permitted – וּבַחֲמִישִׁי מוּתָּרִין: The early and later authorities discuss the following question: Why are members of the non-priestly watch permitted to cut their hair on Thursday in deference to Shabbat, whereas cutting hair on the Thursday of the intermediate days of a Festival is prohibited? Some write that because cutting hair throughout the Festival is a prohibited labor, if others see a person cutting his hair on a Thursday they will think it is permitted during all the intermediate days and will come to be lenient on those days as well (Rid).

Haircutting and shaving is prohibited during the intermediate days and during the watch, so that people will cut their hair and shave before the Festival or watch begins. Some explain that since the priestly watch always begins on Sunday, Thursday is always at the end of the shift, and permitting haircutting or shaving on that day does not discourage people from doing so before the watch begins. However, a Festival can begin on any day of the week. Sometimes Thursday is near the beginning of the Festival, so there is concern that people will not make themselves look nice before the Festival, but wait until the Thursday to do so.

Another reason is that for the members of the watch, the prohibition against shaving was a rabbinic decree, but on the intermediate days of the Festival there is a Torah prohibition against performing labor (Meiri). The later authorities reached the same conclusion (see *Tal Ḥayyim*).

With regard to the general mitzva to cut one's hair on a Thursday when it is not a Festival, to show deference to Shabbat, some write that it is also permitted to cut one's hair on Friday (Commentary on *Moed Katan*; Ritva). Others write that it is permitted only on Thursday, but not on Friday, so as not to add extra tasks on Friday (manuscript of Rashi; see Meiri).

בָּעֵי רַבִּי זֵירָא: אָבְדָה לוֹ אֲבֵידָה עֶרֶב הָרֶגֶל, כֵּיוָן דַּאֲנִיס – מוּתָּר, אוֹ דִּלְמָא: כֵּיוָן דְּלָא מוֹכְחָא מִילְּתָא – לָא?

Rabbi Zeira asks: If one lost an item on the eve of a Festival and he was busy searching for it and had no time to cut his hair or launder his clothes before the Festival commenced, can one say that **since** he was **a victim of circumstances beyond his control,** which prevented from taking care of these matters prior to the Festival, **he is permitted** to cut his hair and launder his clothes on the intermediate days of the Festival? **Or perhaps since it is not** clearly **evident** to others that he failed to cut his hair or launder his clothes due to unavoidable circumstances, he is **not** permitted to perform these actions during the Festival week.

אָמַר אַבַּיֵי, יֹאמְרוּ: כָּל הַסְּרִיקִין אֲסוּרִין סְרִיקֵי בַּיְיתוֹס מוּתָּרִין?!

Abaye said, in answer to this question, that there is a principle of the Sages that applies here. They prohibited the baking of decorated Syrian cakes for Passover, lest people tarry in their preparation of these elaborate cakes and the cakes become leavened. When Baitos ben Zunen,[P] wished to prepare the cakes in a way that would not lead to a violation of any prohibition, the Sages nevertheless prohibited it. They explained that were they to permit him to do so, others **would say: All the** decorated **Syrian cakes are forbidden,** but **the Syrian cakes of Baitos**[L] **are permitted?** This teaches that the Sages do not permit exceptions when the reason for leniency is not clearly evident, like in the case of one who was busy looking for a lost item.

וּלְטַעְמִיךְ, הָא דְּאָמַר רַבִּי אַסִּי אָמַר רַבִּי יוֹחָנָן: כָּל מִי שֶׁאֵין לוֹ אֶלָּא חָלוּק אֶחָד – מוּתָּר לְכַבְּסוֹ בְּחוּלּוֹ שֶׁל מוֹעֵד, הָתָם נָמֵי: יֹאמְרוּ כָּל הַסְּרִיקִין אֲסוּרִין סְרִיקֵי בַּיְיתוֹס מוּתָּרִין!

Rabbi Zeira retorted: **And according to your reasoning,**[N] **that** which **Rabbi Asi said** that **Rabbi Yoḥanan said: Anyone who has only one shirt is permitted to launder it on the intermediate days of a Festival, there too,** one should apply the principle that others **will say: All the** decorated **Syrian cakes are forbidden** but **the Syrian cakes of Baitos are permitted.** There, too, it is not clearly evident that the reason for leniency is that one has only one shirt.

הָא אִתְּמַר עֲלָהּ, אָמַר מָר בַּר רַב אַשִׁי: אֵיזוֹרוֹ מוֹכִיחַ עָלָיו.

The Gemara rejects this argument: **Wasn't it** already **said about this** that **Mar, son of Rav Ashi, said: His belt is proof for him,**[N] as when he launders his only shirt he will have to wear his outer garment tied with his belt so that his body is not exposed, and everyone will understand that he has no other shirt to wear.

רַב אַשִׁי מַתְנֵי: בָּעֵי רַבִּי זֵירָא אוּמָּן שֶׁאָבְדָה לוֹ אֲבֵידָה עֶרֶב הָרֶגֶל מַהוּ? כֵּיוָן דְּאוּמָּן הוּא – מוֹכְחָא מִילְּתָא, אוֹ דִּלְמָא: כֵּיוָן דְּלָא מוֹכְחָא מִילְּתָא כִּי הָנָךְ – לֹא? תֵּיקוּ.

Rav Ashi taught a different version of this passage, as follows: **Rabbi Zeira asks:** With regard to **a craftsman who lost an item**[N] **on the eve of a Festival** and was busy searching for it, **what is** the *halakha*? Is it permitted for him to launder his clothes and cut his hair on the intermediate days of the Festival because he had been unable to do so before the Festival? The Gemara explains the two sides of the question: Can one say that **since he is a craftsman, it is** clearly **evident** why he did not launder his clothes and cut his hair before the Festival, as many people would have come to his place of work and seen that he was busy looking for his lost article? **Or perhaps since** the special circumstances **are not** as clearly **evident as in those** cases in the mishna, it is **not** permitted for him to cut his hair or launder his clothes during the intermediate days of the Festival. The dilemma **shall stand** unresolved.

PERSONALITIES

Baitos ben Zunen – בַּיְיתוֹס בֶּן זוֹנִן: Baitos was a wealthy man who lived in Lod during the time of Rabban Gamliel of Yavne. From many sources in the Talmud, it appears that he was a major importer and exporter, and he owned a great deal of land. He was apparently closely associated with the house of the *Nasi*, and he would insist that all of his actions be in accordance with the *halakha* and the opinion of Sages. Therefore, proofs for the proper *halakha* are derived from his actions. His father may have been the Zunen who was appointed by Rabban Gamliel. It is also possible that the Zunen mentioned as an important man during the days of Rabbi Yehuda HaNasi was the son of Baitos.

LANGUAGE

Baitos – בַּיְיתוֹס: From the Greek βοηθός, *Boethos*, meaning helper or assistant, like the name Ezra in Hebrew.

NOTES

And according to your reasoning, etc. – וּלְטַעְמִיךְ וכו׳: According to Rabbi Zeira's opinion, since the essence of the prohibition against cutting hair is a rabbinic decree, there is no need to add another stricture lest others misunderstand the reason behind the leniency. But according to Abaye's opinion, that even exceptional cases are included within the original decree against haircuts, why does the same principle not apply to laundering as well, such that it is prohibited even when one has only one piece of clothing (Ritva)?

His belt is proof for him – אֵיזוֹרוֹ מוֹכִיחַ עָלָיו: There are many explanations suggested for this expression. According to Rashi, one who has no clothing wraps himself in a coat and ties it with a belt (see Rabbeinu Gershom *Meor HaGola* and *Arukh*, citing Rabbis of Mainz). Rabbeinu Ḥananel explains that when others see a person who is wearing only an outer garment, they understand that he has no clothing. Some explain that the custom was to transfer the belt from one piece of clothing to another, and consequently, clothing was laundered without a belt. If others would see a person washing a piece of clothing with a belt or sending it to the launderer, they would know that he has no other clothing (manuscript of Rashi; Rashi on *Ḥullin* 108a; *Tosefot HaRosh*). Some explain that one who has no clothing wraps his waist with a cloth in order to cover himself, and all know that he has no other item of clothing (Rabbeinu Shlomo ben HaYatom). Others explain that one who has no clothing and wears a shirt alone does not tie it with a belt, so that his outer coat, which is made of wool, not scratch him (*Talmid Rabbeinu Yeḥiel of Paris*). Still others write the converse, that one who has no clothing ties his coat tightly in order to be warmed by the coat (Meiri).

A craftsman who lost an item – אוּמָּן שֶׁאָבְדָה לוֹ אֲבֵידָה: Some explain that this is referring to any craftsman whose services are needed on the eve of the Festival. People know that he is not at home because he is searching for his lost object or because he is concerned due to his loss (Rashi). Some say that this is referring specifically to a barber (Commentary on *Moed Katan*; Rabbeinu Shlomo ben HaYatom). Some add to this explanation that since a barber could cut his own hair and did not, it is clear that it was because he was concerned with something else and had no time to do so (Ran).

NOTES

One who comes from a country overseas – מִמְּדִינַת הַיָּם: Some explain that the difference between leaving for sustenance and leaving for travel applies specifically to one who leaves Eretz Yisrael, since leaving Eretz Yisrael was permitted only under duress. Since one left, despite the fact that his leaving was not entirely necessary, the Sages did not permit him to cut his hair on the intermediate days of the Festival (Ra'avad; Rabbi Yitzḥak ibn Giat; *Sefer Hashlama*; Ritva; Meiri). Others hold that it is referring to anyone leaving his home to travel.

Talmid Rabbeinu Yeḥiel of Paris explains that one who leaves for his sustenance is considered to be leaving under duress and is therefore like the others who are permitted to cut their hair during the intermediate days of the Festival. However, one who leaves for pleasure could have made sure to cut his hair on the eve of the Festival. The only disagreement pertains to the case of one who goes out to earn greater profit; the disagreement is with regard to whether this is comparable to the other cases in the mishna or not.

Some learn from the discussion in Jerusalem Talmud on this issue that Rabbi Yehuda's statement applies to leaving from any place, whereas leaving from Eretz Yisrael is always considered to be leaving without permission (Vilna Gaon).

HALAKHA

One who comes from a country overseas – מִמְּדִינַת הַיָּם: If one comes to Eretz Yisrael from overseas on the intermediate days of the Festival or on the eve of the Festival and did not have time to cut his hair beforehand, it is permitted for him to shave and cut his hair during the intermediate days, provided that he is not simply returning from a leisure travel in the Diaspora. This ruling is in accordance with the opinion of the Rabbis, following the conclusion of the Gemara (*Shulḥan Arukh*, *Oraḥ Ḥayyim* 531:4).

"מִמְּדִינַת הַיָּם". מַתְנִיתִין דְּלָא כְּרַבִּי יְהוּדָה, דְּתַנְיָא, רַבִּי יְהוּדָה אוֹמֵר: הַבָּא מִמְּדִינַת הַיָּם – לֹא יְגַלֵּחַ, מִפְּנֵי שֶׁיָּצָא שֶׁלֹּא בִּרְשׁוּת.

§ The mishna taught: One who comes **from a country overseas**[N] on the intermediate days of a Festival is permitted to cut his hair.[H] The Gemara comments: **The mishna is not in accordance with** the opinion of **Rabbi Yehuda, as it is taught** in a *baraita* that **Rabbi Yehuda says: One who comes from a country overseas** on the intermediate days of a Festival **must not shave** or cut his hair, **due to** the fact that **he left** his home **without permission.**

אָמַר רָבָא: לָשׁוּט – דִּבְרֵי הַכֹּל אָסוּר; לִמְזוֹנוֹת – דִּבְרֵי הַכֹּל מוּתָּר; לֹא נֶחְלְקוּ אֶלָּא לְהַרְוִיחָא. מָר מְדַמֵּי לֵיהּ כְּלָשׁוּט, וּמָר מְדַמֵּי לֵיהּ כִּלְמְזוֹנוֹת.

The Gemara continues to explain the definition and parameters of leaving without permission. **Rava said:** If one left Eretz Yisrael **to travel, all agree** that **it is prohibited** for him to shave during the intermediate days of the Festival because he left on his own initiative, and this is not considered an unavoidable circumstance. If he left **for** basic **sustenance,** i.e., due to financial difficulty, **all agree** that **it is permitted** for him to shave upon his return because he is regarded as having left due to circumstances beyond his control. **They disagree only** with regard to the case where he left **to** earn greater **profit,** i.e., he had enough to live on in Eretz Yisrael, but he left in order to increase his income. **One Sage,** Rabbi Yehuda, **compares him** to one who left **to travel, and the other Sage,** the Rabbis of the mishna, **compare him** to one who left **for** basic **sustenance.**

מֵיתִיבִי, אָמַר רַבִּי: נִרְאִין דִּבְרֵי רַבִּי יְהוּדָה כְּשֶׁיָּצָא שֶׁלֹּא בִּרְשׁוּת, וְדִבְרֵי חֲכָמִים כְּשֶׁיָּצָא בִּרְשׁוּת. מַאי שֶׁלֹּא בִּרְשׁוּת? אִילֵּימָא לָשׁוּט – וְהָאָמְרַתְּ דִּבְרֵי הַכֹּל אָסוּר. וְאֶלָּא לִמְזוֹנוֹת – וְהָאָמְרַתְּ דִּבְרֵי הַכֹּל מוּתָּר! אֶלָּא פְּשִׁיטָא – לְהַרְוִיחָא.

The Gemara **raises an objection** from the following *baraita*: **Rabbi** Yehuda HaNasi **said:** The **statement of Rabbi Yehuda seems** more reasonable in a case **when he left without permission, and the statement of the Rabbis** seems more reasonable **when one left with permission.** The Gemara clarifies: **What is** meant by **without permission? If we say** that it means that he left **to travel, didn't you say** that in this case **all agree** that **it is prohibited** for him to cut his hair upon his return? **Rather,** say that it means that he left **for** basic **sustenance.** But **didn't you say** that **all agree** that **it is permitted** for him to cut his hair in such a case? **Rather,** it is **obvious** that it means that he left in search of greater **profit.**

אֵימָא סֵיפָא: נִרְאִין דִּבְרֵי חֲכָמִים כְּשֶׁיָּצָא בִּרְשׁוּת. מַאי בִּרְשׁוּת? אִילֵּימָא לִמְזוֹנוֹת – הָא אָמְרַתְּ דִּבְרֵי הַכֹּל מוּתָּר. וְאֶלָּא לְהַרְוִיחָא – וְהָא אָמְרַתְּ נִרְאִין דִּבְרֵי רַבִּי יְהוּדָה בְּהָא!

Say the latter clause of the *baraita* as follows: **The statement of the Rabbis seems** more reasonable in a case **when one left with permission.** The Gemara clarifies: **What is** meant by **with permission? If we say** that he left **for** basic **sustenance, didn't you say** that **all agree** that **it is permitted** for him to cut his hair upon his return? **Rather,** say that it means that he left **for** greater **profit.** But **didn't you say** in the first clause that **the statement of Rabbi Yehuda seems** more reasonable **in this** case? Therefore, according to Rava's distinctions, there is an internal contradiction within the *baraita.*

הָכִי קָאָמַר: נִרְאִין דִּבְרֵי רַבִּי יְהוּדָה לְרַבָּנָן כְּשֶׁיָּצָא שֶׁלֹּא בִּרְשׁוּת, וּמַאי נִיהוּ – לָשׁוּט, שֶׁאֲפִילּוּ חֲכָמִים לֹא נֶחְלְקוּ עָלָיו אֶלָּא לְהַרְוִיחָא, אֲבָל לָשׁוּט – מוֹדוּ לֵיהּ. וְנִרְאִין דִּבְרֵי רַבָּנָן לְרַבִּי יְהוּדָה כְּשֶׁיָּצָא בִּרְשׁוּת, וּמַאי נִיהוּ – לִמְזוֹנוֹת, שֶׁאֲפִילּוּ רַבִּי יְהוּדָה לֹא נֶחְלַק עֲלֵיהֶם אֶלָּא לְהַרְוִיחָא, אֲבָל לִמְזוֹנוֹת – מוֹדֶה לְהוּ.

The Gemara resolves the difficulty: **This is what** Rabbi Yehuda HaNasi **is saying: The statement of Rabbi Yehuda seems** more reasonable **to the Rabbis** in the case **where one left without permission. And what is** meant by without permission? It means a case where one left **to travel, as even the Rabbis disagree with** Rabbi Yehuda **only** when one left **for** greater **profit, but** when one left **to travel they agree with** Rabbi Yehuda that it is prohibited for one to shave and cut his hair. **And the statement of the Rabbis seems** more convincing **to Rabbi Yehuda** in the case **where one left with permission. And what is** meant by with permission? It is a case where one left **for** basic **sustenance, as even Rabbi Yehuda disagrees with** the Rabbis **only** when one left **for** greater **profit, but** when he left **for** basic **sustenance** Rabbi Yehuda **concedes to them** that it is permitted for him to shave and cut his hair. Therefore, Rabbi Yehuda HaNasi's intent was not to decide between the opinions of the Rabbis and Rabbi Yehuda but to clarify their dispute.

אָמַר שְׁמוּאֵל: קָטָן הַנּוֹלָד בַּמּוֹעֵד – מוּתָּר לְגַלֵּחַ בַּמּוֹעֵד, שֶׁאֵין לְךָ בֵּית הָאֲסוּרִין גָּדוֹל מִזֶּה. בַּמּוֹעֵד – אִין, מֵעִיקָּרָא – לָא.

§ **Shmuel said:** If **a baby was born on a Festival** and he has long hair that is bothering him, **it is permitted to cut** his hair **on the** intermediate days of the **Festival, as there is no greater prison than this,** the womb of his mother, due to which his hair could not have been cut prior to the Festival. A precise reading of Shmuel's statement indicates that if the child was born **on the Festival, yes,** his hair may be cut. However, if he was born **before** the Festival, but for some reason his hair was not cut, **no,** it is not permitted to cut it on the intermediate days of the Festival because there was time to do so before the Festival.

מְתִיב רַב פִּנְחָס: כׇּל אֵלּוּ שֶׁאָמְרוּ מוּתָּר לְגַלֵּחַ בַּמּוֹעֵד – מוּתָּר לְגַלֵּחַ בִּימֵי אֶבְלוֹ. הָא אָסוּר לְגַלֵּחַ בַּמּוֹעֵד – אָסוּר לְגַלֵּחַ בִּימֵי אֶבְלוֹ.

Rav Pineḥas raised an objection from that which is taught in a *baraita*: **All of those** about **whom** the Sages **said: It is permitted to shave** and cut his hair **on** the intermediate days of the **Festival, it is** also **permitted to shave** and cut his hair **during the days of his mourning. But** from this it follows that **one who is prohibited from shaving** and cutting his hair **on** the intermediate days of **a Festival is** also **prohibited from shaving** and cutting his hair **during the days of his mourning.**

Perek **III**
Daf **14** Amud **b**

וְאִי אָמְרַתְּ קָטָן אִית בֵּיהּ פְּלוּגְתָּא – נִמְצֵאת אֲבֵילוּת נוֹהֶגֶת בְּקָטָן.

And if you say that with regard to **a baby there is a distinction** between being born before the Festival and being born on it, and in some cases it is prohibited to cut the hair of a baby, then **you find that mourning** is **practiced** even **with a minor.**

וְהָתַנְיָא: מְקָרְעִין לְקָטָן מִפְּנֵי עָגְמַת נֶפֶשׁ!

Isn't it taught in a *baraita*: **One rends** the clothes of **a minor**[H] whose relative has passed away, **due to** the desire to bring about feelings of **grief** among those who see him? However, there is no inherent requirement for the minor to observe any of the *halakhot* of mourning.

אָמַר רַב אַשִׁי, מִי קָתָנֵי: הָא אֲסוּרִין?! דִּלְמָא: יֵשׁ מֵהֶן אָסוּר, וְיֵשׁ מֵהֶן מוּתָּר.

Rav Ashi said: Is it taught explicitly in the first *baraita* cited by Rav Pineḥas that if it is prohibited for one to have a haircut during the Festival, **it is** likewise **prohibited** to have a haircut during the week of mourning? That was merely an inference. **Perhaps there are** those **among them,** i.e., those listed in the mishna, for whom it is **prohibited,** while **there are** others **among them** for whom it is **permitted,** and the *halakhot* of mourning do not apply to a baby.

אַמֵימָר, וְאִי תֵּימָא רַב שֵׁישָׁא בְּרֵיהּ דְּרַב אִידִי, מַתְנֵי הָכִי: אָמַר שְׁמוּאֵל: קָטָן מוּתָּר לְגַלְּחוֹ בַּמּוֹעֵד, לָא שְׁנָא נוֹלַד בַּמּוֹעֵד וְלָא שְׁנָא נוֹלַד מֵעִיקָּרָא.

Ameimar, and some say it was **Rav Sheisha, son of Rav Idi, taught** that statement **in this** manner. **Shmuel said:** With regard to **a baby, it is permitted to cut his** hair[H] **during the Festival.** It **is no different** whether **he was born during the Festival, and it is no different** whether **he was born beforehand.**

אָמַר רַב פִּנְחָס, אַף אֲנַן נַמִי תָּנֵינָא: כׇּל אֵלּוּ שֶׁאָמְרוּ מוּתָּר לְגַלֵּחַ בַּמּוֹעֵד – מוּתָּר לְגַלֵּחַ בִּימֵי אֶבְלוֹ. הָא אֲסוּרִין לְגַלֵּחַ בַּמּוֹעֵד – אֲסוּרִין לְגַלֵּחַ בִּימֵי אֶבְלוֹ.

Rav Pineḥas said: We, too, learn in the *baraita* a support for this statement: **All of those** about **whom** the Sages **said: It is permitted to shave** and cut his hair **on** the intermediate days of the **Festival, it is** also **permitted to shave** and cut his hair **during the days of his mourning. But** from this it follows that **one who is prohibited from shaving** and cutting his hair **on** the intermediate days of **a Festival is** also **prohibited from shaving** and cutting his hair **during the days of his mourning.**

אִי אָמְרַתְּ קָטָן אָסוּר – נִמְצֵאת אֲבֵילוּת נוֹהֶגֶת בְּקָטָן. וְתַנְיָא: מְקָרְעִין לְקָטָן מִפְּנֵי עָגְמַת נֶפֶשׁ.

If you say that with regard to **a baby it is prohibited** to cut his hair, then **you find that mourning is practiced** even **with a minor. And it was taught** in a *baraita*: **One rends** the clothes of **a minor** whose relative has passed away **due to** the desire to bring about feelings of **grief** among those who see him. However, there is no inherent requirement for the minor to observe any of the *halakhot* of mourning.

אֲמַר רַב אַשִׁי, מִי קָתָנֵי: הָא אֲסוּרִין? דִּלְמָא: יֵשׁ מֵהֶן אָסוּר וְיֵשׁ מֵהֶן מוּתָּר.

Rav Ashi said: Is it taught explicitly in the first *baraita* cited by Rav Pineḥas that if it is prohibited for one to shave during the Festival, it is likewise **prohibited** to shave during the week of mourning? That was merely an inference. **Perhaps there are** those **among them** for whom it is **prohibited,** while **there are** others **among them** for whom it is **permitted.** If so, there is no clear support from this *baraita* for Shmuel's statement.

אָבֵל אֵינוֹ נוֹהֵג אֲבֵילוּתוֹ בָּרֶגֶל, שֶׁנֶּאֱמַר: "וְשָׂמַחְתָּ בְּחַגֶּךָ".

§ **A mourner does not practice** the *halakhot* of **his mourning on a Festival, as it is stated: "And you shall rejoice in your Festival"** (Deuteronomy 16:14).

HALAKHA

One rends the clothes of a minor – מְקָרְעִין לְקָטָן: If a minor has a close relative who dies, he rends his garment in order to arouse feelings of grief in those around him (*Shulḥan Arukh*, *Yoreh De'a* 340:27).

Cutting the hair of a baby – גִּלּוּחַ שַׂעֲרוֹת קָטָן: During the intermediate days of the Festival, it is permitted for one to cut a baby's hair if it is bothering him, regardless of whether he was born before or during the Festival. This is permitted even in public (Rema; *Shulḥan Arukh*, *Oraḥ Ḥayyim* 531:6).

אִי אֲבֵילוּת דְּמֵעִיקָּרָא הוּא – אָתֵי עֲשֵׂה דְּרַבִּים, וְדָחֵי עֲשֵׂה דְּיָחִיד. וְאִי אֲבֵילוּת דְּהַשְׁתָּא הוּא – לָא אָתֵי עֲשֵׂה דְּיָחִיד וְדָחֵי עֲשֵׂה דְּרַבִּים.

The Gemara explains: **If it is a mourning** period that had already begun **at the outset** of the Festival, **the positive mitzva of** rejoicing on the Festival, which is incumbent upon **the community, comes and overrides the positive mitzva of** the **individual,**[N] i.e., the mourning. **And if the mourning** period began only **now,** i.e., the deceased died during the Festival, **the positive mitzva of the individual does not come and override the positive mitzva of the community.**

מְנוּדֶּה, מַהוּ שֶׁיִּנְהוֹג נִידּוּיוֹ בָּרֶגֶל? אָמַר רַב יוֹסֵף, תָּא שְׁמַע: דָּנִין דִּינֵי נְפָשׁוֹת, וְדִינֵי מַכּוֹת, וְדִינֵי מָמוֹנוֹת. וְאִי לָא צָיֵית דִּינָא – מְשַׁמְּתִינַן לֵיהּ.

The Gemara asks: With regard to **one who was ostracized, what is the** *halakha*? Must he **observe the practices of ostracism,** or are they overridden by the mitzva to rejoice **on the Festival? Rav Yosef said: Come** and **hear** an answer from that which is taught: During the Festival **the court judges** cases of **capital law,** cases of **lashes,** and cases of **monetary law.**[H] It is known that **if one does not listen to** and follow **the judgment,** among the possibilities of enforcement is that **we ostracize him**[N] until he accepts the verdict.

וְאִי סָלְקָא דַּעְתָּךְ אֵינוֹ נוֹהֵג נִידּוּיוֹ בָּרֶגֶל – מְשׁוּמֶּת וְאָתֵי מֵעִיקָּרָא – אָתֵי רֶגֶל דָּחֵי לֵיהּ, הַשְׁתָּא מְשַׁמְּתִינַן לֵיהּ אֲנַן?!

And if it enters your mind that one does not observe the practices of ostracism during the Festival, the following *a fortiori* argument can be made: If, for **one who has already been ostracized at the outset** of the Festival, **the Festival comes and overrides his** observance of that status, is it reasonable that **now we,** the court, should **ostracize he** who does not listen to the judgment of the court during the Festival itself? Rather, it must be that one does observe the practices of ostracism, even during the Festival.

אָמַר לֵיהּ אַבָּיֵי: וְדִלְמָא לְעִיּוּנֵי בְּדִינֵיהּ. דְּאִי לָא תֵּימָא הָכִי דִּינֵי נְפָשׁוֹת דְּקָתָנֵי, הָכָא נַמִי דְּקָטְלִין לֵיהּ?

Abaye said to him: There is no proof from here, **as perhaps** when the *baraita* states that the court judges cases, what it meant is that it **deliberates in judgment** on the Festival, but it does not actually reach a verdict. Therefore, the court never ostracizes someone during the Festival. Accordingly, there is no *a fortiori* argument proving that one observes the practices of ostracism during the Festival. **Because if you do not say so,** that the *baraita* is referring to deliberation, then in the cases of **capital law that are taught, here too, would we put someone to death** on the Festival?

וְהָא קָא מִימְנְעִי מִשִּׂמְחַת יוֹם טוֹב. דְּתַנְיָא, רַבִּי עֲקִיבָא אוֹמֵר: מִנַּיִן לְסַנְהֶדְרִין (שֶׁרָאוּ בְּאֶחָד) שֶׁהָרְגוּ אֶת הַנֶּפֶשׁ שֶׁאֵין טוֹעֲמִין כׇּל אוֹתוֹ הַיּוֹם? תַּלְמוּד לוֹמַר: ״לֹא תֹאכְלוּ עַל הַדָּם״.

But if so, the judges **would be prevented from rejoicing on the Festival, as it is taught** in a *baraita* that **Rabbi Akiva says: From where** is it derived with regard **to the Sanhedrin who put someone to death that they may not taste** any food or drink **for the entire rest of the day?**[H] **The verse states: "You shall not eat with the blood"** (Leviticus 19:26). It is not appropriate to eat during the same day that they caused bloodshed.

אֶלָּא – לְעִיּוּנֵי בְּדִינֵיהּ; הָכָא נַמִי – לְעִיּוּנֵי בְּדִינֵיהּ. אָמַר לֵיהּ: אִם כֵּן נִמְצֵאתָ מְעַנֶּה אֶת דִּינוֹ!

Rather, the statement of the *baraita*, that the court judges cases of capital law, must be referring **to deliberating in judgment** and not actually reaching a verdict. **Here too,** in cases of monetary law and of lashes, it is referring **to deliberating in judgment,** without the possibility of ostracizing anyone during the Festival. Rav Yosef said **to him: If so,** if only deliberations are conducted during the Festival, **you find a perversion of justice** by delaying **his** verdict.

אָתוּ מִצַּפְרָא וּמְעַיְּינִי בְּדִינֵיהּ, וְעָיְילִי וְאָכְלִי וְשָׁתוּ כּוּלֵּי יוֹמָא, וַהֲדַר אָתוּ בִּשְׁקִיעַת הַחַמָּה וְגָמְרִינַן לְדִינֵיהּ, וְקָטְלוּ לֵיהּ.

Rather, the judges **come in the morning** as usual **and deliberate in judgment.** They then **enter** their homes **and eat and drink all day,** i.e., as much as they desire, in order to rejoice fully on the Festival. **Then they come** back to the courthouse close to **sunset and complete his judgment,** i.e., they dispense the verdict, and if necessary, **they kill him.**[H] In this manner, they are not prevented from enjoying the Festival properly.

אָמַר אַבָּיֵי, תָּא שְׁמַע: וּמְנוּדֶּה שֶׁהִתִּירוּ לוֹ חֲכָמִים.

Abaye said: Come and **hear** another support from a *baraita*: **And** it is the case with regard to **one who is ostracized, that the Sages permitted him** to get a haircut during the intermediate days of the Festival. This indicates that one who is ostracized need not observe the practices of ostracism during the Festival.

NOTES

Overrides the positive mitzva of the individual – דָּחֵי עֲשֵׂה דְּיָחִיד: The language of the Gemara here implies that mourning is a positive mitzva by Torah law, and many halakhic authorities rule in this manner (see Rambam). They bring support from verse: "And if I had eaten the sin-offering today" (Leviticus 10:19), which is written in reference to Aaron the priest after the death of two of his sons (Rambam). Another verse states: "Make for yourself mourning, as for an only son" (Jeremiah 6:26), which implies that the mourning rituals were well established before the time of Jeremiah (Rabbeinu Gershom *Meor HaGola*; Rashi; Rid). There are also other verses that refer to mourning practices (see Ezekiel 24:17, 31:15).

However, other authorities hold that only the first day of mourning is by Torah law, and there is also a dispute with regard to the following evening (Rif on tractate *Berakhot*). The statement here that mourning is a positive mitzva of the individual is only according to the opinion of certain *tanna'im*. Rabbeinu Shlomo ben HaYatom writes that the term used by the Gemara here is referring only to the first day of the mourning period. Others write that while most of the *halakhot* of mourning are by rabbinic law, the Gemara here is referring specifically to the prohibition against haircutting, which is derived from the Torah itself in reference to Aaron and his sons (Ra'avad; *Sefer Hashlama*).

Some authorities hold that all the *halakhot* of mourning are by rabbinic law, and when the Gemara uses the term positive mitzva it means by rabbinic law. It uses shorthand rather than explaining at length that a positive mitzva incumbent upon the community by Torah law overrides a positive mitzva of an individual by rabbinic law (Rosh). Another possibility is that the positive mitzva of the community to rejoice on a Festival is also referring to a rabbinic mitzva (see *Tosafot*; *Ba'al Halakhot Gedolot*).

If one does not listen to the judgment we ostracize him – אִי לָא צָיֵית דִּינָא מְשַׁמְּתִינַן לֵיהּ: *Tosafot* question this, as normally the court would seize property as collateral and ostracize only as a last resort. However, it could be argued that ostracism is a more universal judgment, since if one does not own property, he can still be forced to listen to the court by being ostracized (*Ramat Shmuel*).

HALAKHA

Judgment during the Festival – דִּין בְּמוֹעֵד: A court may judge cases of capital or monetary law on the intermediate days of a Festival, and it may ostracize one who refuses to listen to its judgment (*Shulḥan Arukh, Oraḥ Ḥayyim* 545:10).

The fast of the Sanhedrin – צוֹם הַסַּנְהֶדְרִין: If the Sanhedrin condemns someone to death, the judges may not eat the entire day. This is derived from the verse: "You shall not eat with the blood" (Rambam *Sefer Shofetim*, *Hilkhot Sanhedrin* 13:4).

One who is liable to be put to death during the Festival – חַיָּיב מִיתָה בְּמוֹעֵד: If one is liable to be put to death by the court during the Festival, the court deliberates for the entire day, allowing the judges to eat and drink during that time. They then convict him just before sunset and put him to death (Rambam *Sefer Shofetim*, *Hilkhot Sanhedrin* 13:5).

אָמַר רָבָא: מִי קָתָנֵי שֶׁהִתִּירוּהוּ חֲכָמִים? שֶׁהִתִּירוּ לוֹ חֲכָמִים קָתָנֵי, דַּאֲזַל וּפַיְּיסֵיהּ לְבַעַל דִּינֵיהּ, וְאָתֵי קַמֵּי דְּרַבָּנַן, וְשָׁרוּ לֵיהּ.

Rava said: Is it taught in the *baraita*: **That they permitted it,** which would indicate that **the Sages** permitted all those who were ostracized to cut their hair on the intermediate days of the Festival? Rather, **it is taught: They permitted him.** This indicates that it is referring to an individual case, **where one went and appeased his** opposing **litigant and the Sages came and released him** from his decree of ostracism.

מְצוֹרָע מַהוּ שֶׁיִּנְהִיג צָרַעְתּוֹ בָּרֶגֶל? אָמַר אַבַּיֵי, תָּא שְׁמַע: וְהַנָּזִיר וְהַמְּצוֹרָע מִטּוּמְאָתוֹ לְטָהֳרָתוֹ. הָא בִּימֵי טוּמְאָתוֹ – נָהֵיג.

§ The Gemara asks a similar question: With regard to **a leper,**[B] **what is** the *halakha*? Must he **observe the practices of his leper status,** or are they overridden by the mitzva to rejoice **during the Festival?**[NH] **Abaye said: Come** and **hear** a proof from a *baraita*: **And** both **the nazirite and the leper** who transfers **from his** state of **ritual impurity to his** new state of **purity** may shave on the intermediate days of the Festival. **This** implies that if **during the days of his impurity** he must **observe** all of the ordinary practices, even during the Festival.

לָא מִיבָּעֲיָא קָאָמַר; לָא מִיבָּעֲיָא בִּימֵי טוּמְאָתוֹ דְּלָא נָהֵיג, אֲבָל לְטָהֳרָתוֹ – נִיגְזוֹר שֶׁמָּא יַשְׁהֶה קָרְבְּנוֹתָיו. קָמַשְׁמַע לָן.

The Gemara rejects this proof: The *baraita* **is speaking** employing the didactic style of: **Needless to say. Needless to say, during the days of his impurity** on the Festival, **he does not observe** the practices of ostracism. **However,** with regard to one who regains **his** state of **purity** during the intermediate days of the Festival, one might think that **we should issue a decree** that he not be permitted to shave, **lest he delay** sacrificing **his offerings** until the last day of the Festival, when it is prohibited to sacrifice offerings of an individual. Perhaps prohibiting him from shaving will prevent this possibility. Therefore, because one might have thought that shaving should be prohibited, the *baraita* **teaches us** that it is, in fact, permitted for him to shave during the intermediate days of the Festival.

אָמַר רָבָא, תָּא שְׁמַע: ״וְהַצָּרוּעַ״ – לְרַבּוֹת כֹּהֵן גָּדוֹל. וְהָא כֹּהֵן גָּדוֹל, דְּכָל הַשָּׁנָה כְּרֶגֶל לְכוּלֵּי עָלְמָא דָּמֵי, דִּתְנַן: כֹּהֵן גָּדוֹל מַקְרִיב אוֹנֵן וְאֵינוֹ אוֹכֵל. שְׁמַע מִינָּהּ: נוֹהֵג צָרַעְתּוֹ בָּרֶגֶל. שְׁמַע מִינָּהּ.

Rava said: Come and **hear** another source. The verse states: "**And the leper**[N] in whom the plague is, his clothes shall be rent" (Leviticus 13:45). The extra emphasis of the phrase: "And the leper" comes **to include the High Priest,** teaching that all the *halakhot* of the leper apply to him. **And** the status of **the High Priest** during **the entire year is like** that of **everyone on a Festival, as we learned** in a mishna (*Horayot* 12b): The **High Priest sacrifices** animals when he has the status of **an acute mourner,**[H] i.e., before the burial of a close relative who died, **but he may not eat** of the offering. **Learn from it** that a leper **practices the customs of his leprosy during the Festival.** The Gemara concludes: Indeed, **learn from it** that this is so.

אָבֵל אָסוּר בְּתִסְפּוֹרֶת, מִדְּקָאָמַר לְהוּ רַחֲמָנָא לִבְנֵי אַהֲרֹן ״רָאשֵׁיכֶם אַל תִּפְרָעוּ״ – מִכְּלָל דְּכוּלֵּי עָלְמָא אָסוּר.

§ The source for the *halakha* that **it is prohibited for a mourner to** receive **a haircut**[H] is derived **from** the fact that **the Merciful One states to the sons of Aaron: "Let not the hair of your heads go loose"** (Leviticus 10:6). It was prohibited for them to let their hair grow long during their period of mourning over the death of their brothers, Nadav and Avihu. **By inference,** it is teaching **that for everyone** else, i.e., non-priests, **it is prohibited** to cut their hair during the period of mourning.

NOTES

A leper during the Festival – מְצוֹרָע בָּרֶגֶל: Some explain that the question is whether or not all the *halakhot* of the leper should be observed on the Festival (Rashi; Rabbeinu Gershom *Meor HaGola*). However, the Rid finds this explanation difficult and explains that the only question is with regard to the rabbinic prohibitions pertaining to the leper, such as washing clothes or greeting people. However, those activities that are prohibited by Torah law, such as cutting one's hair or entering the camp, certainly remain in effect (see *Talmid Rabbeinu Yeḥiel of Paris*).

And the leper – וְהַצָּרוּעַ: Some explain that this derivation is based on the apparently superfluous letters *vav* and *heh* at the beginning of the word (Rabbeinu Shlomo ben HaYatom). Others suggest that the entire word seems to be extraneous (*Talmid Rabbeinu Yeḥiel of Paris*). Still others hold that it is not this word that is unnecessary, but the following phrase: "In whom the plague is" (see *Korban Aharon*).

HALAKHA

A leper on Shabbat and during the Festival – מְצֹרָע בְּשַׁבָּת וְיוֹם טוֹב: Even on Shabbat and Festivals, a leper observes all of his normal practices, including those that are similar to mourning (Rambam *Sefer Tahara, Hilkhot Tumat Tzara'at* 10:6).

The High Priest sacrifices as an acute mourner – כֹּהֵן גָּדוֹל מַקְרִיב אוֹנֵן: The High Priest may perform the service in the Temple, even when he is an acute mourner. However, he may not eat from consecrated meat (Rambam *Sefer Avoda, Hilkhot Biat HaMikdash* 2:6, 8).

A mourner with regard to receiving a haircut – אָבֵל בְּתִסְפּוֹרֶת: It is prohibited for a mourner to have a haircut or to shave (*Shulḥan Arukh, Yoreh De'a* 390:1).

BACKGROUND

Leprosy [*tzara'at*] – צָרַעַת: Traditionally rendered as leprosy, the term *tzara'at* used in the Torah is not necessarily identical with leprosy as defined by modern medicine. The Torah term refers to symptoms that cause severe ritual impurity. The *halakhot* governing these symptoms are detailed at length in Leviticus, chapters 13–15, and in the Mishna in tractate *Nega'im*. There can be leprosy of the skin, hair, articles of clothing, or houses.

When a symptom appears, it is examined by a priest. Only a priest is authorized to determine whether to quarantine the affected person for a certain period or to declare immediately that the symptom is, or is not, leprosy.

Leprosy is one of the primary sources of ritual impurity, and any item touched by a leper also becomes impure. While the Jews were in the desert, one afflicted with leprosy was sent out of the Israelite camp, and when the Jewish people lived in Eretz Yisrael, a leper was sent out of any walled city. The leper was obligated to live alone until his affliction was cured.

A garment affected by leprosy is burned, and a contaminated house is entirely destroyed and its rubble disposed of in a ritually impure place. A cured leper must undergo special purification rites outside the city and a purification ceremony in the Temple itself. He is obligated to bring special offerings as part of his purification.

מְנוּדִּין וּמְצוֹרָעִין מַה הֵן בְּתִסְפּוֹרֶת? תָּא שְׁמַע: מְנוּדִּין וּמְצוֹרָעִין אֲסוּרִין לְסַפֵּר וּלְכַבֵּס.

The Gemara asks: **What is the** *halakha* governing **those who are ostracized and lepers,**[N] with regard to **a haircut?** The Gemara answers: **Come** and **hear that which** was taught in a *baraita*: **Those who are ostracized**[H] **and lepers**[H] **are prohibited from cutting** their hair **and laundering** their clothes.

מְנוּדֶּה שֶׁמֵּת – בֵּית דִּין סוֹקְלִין אֶת אֲרוֹנוֹ. רַבִּי יְהוּדָה אוֹמֵר: לֹא שֶׁיַּעֲמִידוּ עָלָיו גַּל אֲבָנִים כְּגַלּוֹ שֶׁל עָכָן, אֶלָּא: בֵּית דִּין שׁוֹלְחִין וּמַנִּיחִין אֶבֶן גְּדוֹלָה עַל אֲרוֹנוֹ. לְלַמֶּדְךָ שֶׁכָּל הַמִּתְנַדֶּה וּמֵת בְּנִידּוּיוֹ בֵּית דִּין סוֹקְלִין אֶת אֲרוֹנוֹ.

It was further taught there: If **one who is ostracized dies, the court** places **stones on his coffin. Rabbi Yehuda says:** This does **not** mean **that they pile up a heap of stones over him like the heap** of stones that was placed over the grave **of Achan**[N] (see Joshua 7:26). **Rather, the court sends** its agents, **who place a large stone**[N] **on his coffin** as a symbolic gesture. This comes **to teach you** that **anyone who is ostracized and dies while in his** period of **ostracism,** without seeking to be released from it, **the court** places **stones on his coffin.**[H]

אָבֵל חַיָּיב בַּעֲטִיפַת הָרֹאשׁ. מִדְּקָאָמַר לֵיהּ רַחֲמָנָא לִיחֶזְקֵאל: ״וְלֹא תַעֲטֶה עַל שָׂפָם״ – מִכְּלָל דְּכוּלֵּי עָלְמָא מִיחַיְּיבִי.

§ The Gemara continues: **A mourner is obligated to wrap** his **head** as a sign of mourning, covering his head and face.[H] This is derived from the fact **that the Merciful One says to Ezekiel,** while he is in mourning: **"And cover not your upper lip"** (Ezekiel 24:17). God commands Ezekiel not to display outward signs of mourning, which proves **by inference that everyone** else **is obligated** to wrap their heads in this manner.

מְנוּדֶּה מַהוּ בַּעֲטִיפַת הָרֹאשׁ? אָמַר רַב יוֹסֵף, תָּא שְׁמַע: וְהֵן מִתְעַטְּפִין וְיוֹשְׁבִין כִּמְנוּדִּין וְכַאֲבֵלִים עַד שֶׁיְּרַחֲמוּ עֲלֵיהֶם מִן הַשָּׁמַיִם. אֲמַר לֵיהּ אַבָּיֵי: דִּלְמָא מְנוּדֶּה לַשָּׁמַיִם שָׁאנֵי דַּחֲמִיר.

The Gemara asks: **What is** the *halakha* governing **a person who is ostracized,** with regard to **wrapping of the head?**[NH] **Rav Yosef said: Come** and **hear** that which was taught in a *baraita* about those who were fasting for rain and whose prayers were not answered: **And they wrap themselves and sit as those who are ostracized and as mourners, until they are shown mercy from Heaven.** This implies that those who are ostracized must wrap their heads like mourners. **Abaye said to him: Perhaps one who is ostracized by Heaven is different, as that is more serious** than being ostracized by an earthly court.

מְצוֹרָע מַהוּ בַּעֲטִיפַת הָרֹאשׁ? תָּא שְׁמַע: ״וְעַל שָׂפָם יַעְטֶה״ – מִכְּלָל שֶׁחַיָּיב בַּעֲטִיפַת הָרֹאשׁ. שְׁמַע מִינַּהּ.

The Gemara continues and asks: **What is** the *halakha* in the case **of a leper** with regard to **wrapping of the head?**[H] **Come and hear** a proof based upon the verse: **"And he shall cover his upper lip"** (Leviticus 13:45), from which it may be learned **by inference that he is obligated to wrap** his **head.** The Gemara concludes: Indeed, **learn from here** that this is the case.

NOTES

Those who are ostracized and lepers – מְנוּדִּין וּמְצוֹרָעִין: The early authorities ask: Isn't it implicit in the mishna that one who is ostracized or a leper may not cut his hair? Why is it necessary to seek evidence from another source (see Rid; *Talmid Rabbeinu Yeḥiel of Paris*)? Similarly, the answers to some of the questions of the Gemara appear to be stated explicitly in the verse, e.g., the question concerning the wrapping of a leper's head.

Some suggest that perhaps the Gemara here holds in accordance with the opinion of Rabbi Akiva, that the verse there is referring to a different issue. The Ritva writes that perhaps these questions are asked because this is the style of the Gemara. In the manuscript of Rashi, this idea is taken further. It is suggested there that these questions are not actually necessary and are only mentioned to increase Torah learning. Therefore, when asking these questions, the Gemara uses a set formula to ask questions: A question is asked based on a *halakha* that applies to a mourner, and the Gemara asks if it applies to a person who was ostracized or to a leper. In order to maintain this formula, the Gemara also asks questions for which there are straightforward answers (see *Tal Ḥayyim*).

Like the heap of Achan – כְּגַלּוֹ שֶׁל עָכָן: Achan was notorious for having taken from the spoils of Jericho, which had been set aside for God. His theft led to casualties in the subsequent war against the city of Ai. Once his trespass was discovered, Achan was put to death and a pile of stones was heaped upon his grave (see Joshua 7:26).

Who place a large stone – וּמַנִּיחִין אֶבֶן גְּדוֹלָה: Rashi explains that placing the stone is meant to serve only as a reminder of the decree of ostracism (manuscript of Rashi). It is intended to publicize the matter (*Talmid Rabbeinu Yeḥiel of Paris*). According to Rabbi Shlomo ben HaYatom, this also warns others about the severity of the deceased's sin. He further explains that it is sufficient to place only one stone on the grave because when a court rules that one is to be stoned, a single large stone is first placed on his chest, and if he dies he is not stoned further. Therefore, the placement of one stone is defined as stoning by *halakha*. Based on this, the halakhic authorities understand that all those mourning customs that show respect for the deceased are not practiced in the case of one who was ostracized, and only those customs that are meant to honor the living mourners apply in such a case (see Rif).

A person who is ostracized wrapping his head – מְנוּדֶּה בַּעֲטִיפָה: Some say that an ostracized person is required to wrap his head. Abaye is merely rejecting the proof, but not the *halakha*, which is in accordance with the opinion of Rav Yosef (Rav Hai Gaon).

HALAKHA

One who has been ostracized with regard to cutting hair and laundering clothes – מְנוּדֶּה בְּתִסְפּוֹרֶת וּכְבִיסָה: One who has been ostracized may not cut his hair or launder his clothes (*Shulḥan Arukh*, *Yoreh De'a* 334:2).

A leper with regard to cutting hair and laundering clothes – מְצוֹרָע בְּתִסְפּוֹרֶת וּכְבִיסָה: A leper may not cut his hair or launder his clothes as long as he is quarantined (Rambam *Sefer Tahara*, *Hilkhot Tumat Tzara'at* 10:6).

One who is ostracized and dies – הַמִּתְנַדֶּה וּמֵת: If one who was ostracized died without having his decree of ostracism removed, then the court appoints emissaries to place a stone on his coffin. The relatives of such a person do not rend their clothes, remove their shoes, or deliver eulogies for the deceased.

This applies to those who were ostracized for committing sins; however, one who was ostracized as a penalty for not meeting his financial obligations is treated with the honor due to any other person who passed away. The reason for this is because one becomes exempt from such a penalty once he passes away (*Shulḥan Arukh*, *Yoreh De'a* 334:3).

A mourner wrapping his head – אָבֵל בַּעֲטִיפָה: A mourner is required to wrap his head in such a way that the end of a scarf or shawl covers his mouth and nose. According to the Rema, it is not customary to carry out this practice today because shawls are not ordinarily worn, and one should not be stringent (*Shulḥan Arukh*, *Yoreh De'a* 386:1).

A person who is ostracized wrapping his head – מְנוּדֶּה בַּעֲטִיפָה: One who has been ostracized is not required to wrap his head. This is because the issue is left unresolved by the Gemara, and the *halakha* generally follows the lenient opinion in unresolved issues concerning rabbinic mitzvot (*Shakh*; *Shulḥan Arukh*, *Yoreh De'a* 334:1).

A leper wrapping his head – מְצוֹרָע בַּעֲטִיפָה: A leper is required to wrap his head and cover his upper lip (Rambam *Sefer Tahara*, *Hilkhot Tumat Tzara'at* 10:6).

אָבֵל אָסוּר לְהָנִיחַ תְּפִילִּין. מִדְּקָאָמַר לֵיהּ רַחֲמָנָא לִיחֶזְקֵאל: ״פְּאֵרְךָ חֲבוֹשׁ עָלֶיךָ״ – מִכְּלָל דְּכוּלֵּי עָלְמָא אָסוּר.

§ The Gemara moves on to another *halakha*: **A mourner is prohibited from donning phylacteries.**[H] This is derived from the fact **that the Merciful One says to Ezekiel,** while he is in mourning: **"Bind your headwear [*pe'er*] upon yourself"** (Ezekiel 24:17).[N] The word *pe'er* alludes to phylacteries. Ezekiel was unique in that he was commanded to put on phylacteries while in mourning, which proves **by inference that everyone** else **is prohibited** from doing so.

מְנוּדֶּה מַהוּ בִּתְפִילִּין? תֵּיקוּ. מְצוֹרָע מַהוּ בִּתְפִילִּין? תָּא שְׁמַע: ״וְהַצָּרוּעַ״ – לְרַבּוֹת כֹּהֵן גָּדוֹל; ״בְּגָדָיו יִהְיוּ פְרֻמִים״ – שֶׁיְּהוּ מְקוֹרָעִים; ״וְרֹאשׁוֹ יִהְיֶה פָרוּעַ״ – אֵין פְּרִיעָה אֶלָּא גִּידּוּל שֵׂעָר, דִּבְרֵי רַבִּי אֱלִיעֶזֶר.

The Gemara asks: **What is** the *halakha* governing **one who is ostracized,** with regard to phylacteries? The dilemma **shall stand** unresolved. The Gemara proceeds to its next question: **What is** the *halakha* in the case of **a leper** with regard to phylacteries? The Gemara suggests: **Come** and **hear** a proof from the following *baraita*: The verse states: **"And the leper"** (Leviticus 13:45); as explained earlier, this comes **to include the High Priest** in all the *halakhot* of the leper. The verse states there: **"His garments shall be *perumim*,"** meaning **that they shall be rent.** The verse continues: **"And his head shall be *parua*,"** and this ***peria*** means **only growing the hair long;** this is **the statement of Rabbi Eliezer.**

רַבִּי עֲקִיבָא אוֹמֵר: נֶאֶמְרָה הֲוָיָיה בָּרֹאשׁ וְנֶאֶמְרָה הֲוָיָיה בַּבֶּגֶד. מָה הֲוָיָיה הָאֲמוּרָה בַּבֶּגֶד – דָּבָר שֶׁחוּץ מִגּוּפוֹ, אַף הֲוָיָיה בָּרֹאשׁ – דָּבָר שֶׁחוּץ מִגּוּפוֹ. מַאי לָאו אַתְּפִילִּין?

Rabbi Akiva says: The meaning of these terms is derived through a verbal analogy. The verse **states** a form of the verb **being, with regard to** one's **head** in the verse: "His head shall be," teaching that a leper must perform a certain action with his head. **And the verse states** a form of the verb **being with regard to** a leper's **garment,** in the verse: "His garment shall be." **Just as** the term **being stated with regard to** his **garment** is referring to **an object external to his body, so too,** the term **being** used **with regard to** his **head** is referring to **an object external to his body.** The Gemara derives from this: **What, is it not** referring to **phylacteries,** and the verse teaches that it is prohibited for a leper to wear phylacteries?

אָמַר רַב פָּפָּא: לָא, אַכּוּמְתָּא וְסוּדָרָא.

Rav Pappa said: No, there is no proof from here, as the verse may be referring **to a cap [*kumta*]**[L] **or a scarf [*sudara*],**[L] which people wear on their heads. It is possible to explain that according to Rabbi Akiva, it is prohibited for a leper to wear such headwear because it is excessive adornment.[H]

אָבֵל אָסוּר בִּשְׁאִילַת שָׁלוֹם, דְּקָאָמַר לֵיהּ רַחֲמָנָא לִיחֶזְקֵאל: ״הֵאָנֵק דֹּם״.

§ The Gemara continues: **A mourner is prohibited from greeting** others or be greeted.[H] This is derived from the fact **that the Merciful One says to Ezekiel: "Sigh in silence"** (Ezekiel 24:17),[N] implying that aside from what was absolutely essential, he was prohibited from speaking.

HALAKHA

A mourner and phylacteries – אָבֵל וּתְפִילִּין: On the first day of mourning, a mourner is prohibited from donning phylacteries, even if the deceased was buried the night before. From the second day of mourning onward, one should don phylacteries. However, different customs exist with regard to whether or not this may be done only in private (*Mishna Berura*; *Shulḥan Arukh, Oraḥ Ḥayyim* 38:5 and *Yoreh De'a* 388:1).

A leper growing his hair and rending his garments – מְצוֹרָע בִּפְרִיעָה וּבִפְרִימָה: Every leper must let his hair grow long and rend his garments, even if he is the High Priest (Rambam *Sefer Tahara, Hilkhot Tumat Tzara'at* 10:6).

A mourner with regard to greeting others – אָבֵל בִּשְׁאִילַת שָׁלוֹם: A mourner may not greet others or be greeted (*Shulḥan Arukh, Yoreh De'a* 385:1).

LANGUAGE

Cap [*kumta*] – כּוּמְתָּא: The *ge'onim* explain that this word refers to a soft hat or a beret. It is related to the Arabic كمة, *kumma*, which has the same meaning.

Scarf [*sudara*] – סוּדָרָא: From the Latin sudarium, meaning scarf or towel. Here and in other cases, this word refers to a scarf wrapped around the head, which was worn by married rabbis. Similarly, it is customary in several communities for the rabbi to wrap a special scarf around his turban.

NOTES

Bind your headwear [*pe'er*] upon yourself – פְּאֵרְךָ חֲבוֹשׁ עָלֶיךָ: In tractate *Berakhot* this conclusion is reached in a different manner. It is stated there that phylacteries are referred to as *pe'er*, literally meaning splendor, and it is not appropriate for a mourner to be crowned with such splendor. Additionally, when a mourner wears phylacteries it is disrespectful toward the mitzva of phylacteries, as the mourner is in a lowly state, and it is inappropriate that words describing God's glory rest upon him. In *Tosefot HaRosh* it is noted that these two explanations complement each other. While the *halakha* is derived from the Gemara here, the reasoning behind it is explained in tractate *Berakhot*.

Sigh in silence – הֵאָנֵק דֹּם: *Tosafot* allude to the difficulty with this proof. The Gemara has already shown that Ezekiel's mourning was an exceptional case, and ordinary mourners should do the opposite of everything he was instructed to do. If so, how is it possible to prove that a mitzva of silence stated with regard to Ezekiel also applies to other mourners?

The early authorities who address this issue answer it in several different ways. Some say that the instruction: "Sigh in silence," applies to Ezekiel and other mourners as well. Immediately afterward he was instructed: "Make no mourning for the dead" (Ezekiel 24:17), with regard to the further instructions, which were unique to him (Ra'avad; *Talmid Rabbeinu Yeḥiel of Paris*). The reason for this is because mourning is not immediately evident through a mourner's silence (*Talmid Rabbeinu Yeḥiel of Paris*).

Others suggest that God instructed Ezekiel to deviate from the common practice in this case as well. Therefore, the verse should be understood as: Sighing in silence and mourning for the dead, do not do. If this is the case, then this proof is similar to those cited for the other practices mentioned here (Rabbi Shlomo ben HaYatom; *Nimmukei Yosef*, citing Rabbi Meir HaLevi).

Tosefot HaRosh gives a simple explanation: Certainly the Merciful One was not stricter with Ezekiel than with other mourners, and therefore any stringency that applied to him certainly also applies to other mourners as well. A similar explanation appears in several places in *Tosafot*. Others explain that all these proofs are meant only as support or allusions and should not be read too carefully. Instead, the Sages relied upon traditions or made decrees on their own (*Sefer HaMe'orot*).

HALAKHA

Mourning practices during a time of drought – אֲבֵלוּת בַּעֲצִירַת גְּשָׁמִים: If there is a drought and the thirteen fasts have been carried out without rain falling, then people should begin to greet each other with less emotion, and Torah scholars should not greet each other at all (*Shulḥan Arukh, Oraḥ Ḥayyim* 575:7).

A mourner with regard to Torah study – אָבֵל בְּדִבְרֵי תוֹרָה: A mourner is prohibited from studying Torah for all seven days of mourning. This includes the Bible, Talmud, and *halakha*. He may read the prophecies that speak about catastrophes in the books of Jeremiah and Job. Similarly, he may study this third chapter of *Moed Katan* and the *halakhot* of mourning (*Pitḥei Teshuva; Arukh HaShulḥan; Shulḥan Arukh, Yoreh De'a* 384:1).

One who has been ostracized with regard to earning a livelihood and studying Torah – מְנוּדֶּה בְּפַרְנָסָה וְתוֹרָה: One who has been ostracized may study, teach, or be taught Torah. In addition, he may earn a livelihood by hiring other people to work for him or by hiring himself out to others (*Shulḥan Arukh, Yoreh De'a* 334:2).

One who has been excommunicated – מוּחְרָם: One who has been excommunicated may not teach or be taught Torah. However, he may study Torah on his own, so that he will not forget what he has learned. He may not be hired for work, and he may not hire other people to work for him. However, he may establish a small store in order to earn a minimal income (*Shulḥan Arukh, Yoreh De'a* 334:2).

A leper with regard to Torah study – מְצוֹרָע בְּדִבְרֵי תוֹרָה: Like others who are impure, a leper may study Torah (Rambam *Sefer Tahara, Hilkhot Tumat Tzara'at* 10:6).

NOTES

Ostracized and excommunicated – מְנוּדֶּה וּמוּחְרָם: Most authorities explain that these terms refer to two different levels within the same concept. One is ostracized as a warning, and if he fails to listen and have his decree of ostracism reversed then he will be excommunicated afterward. According to the Ra'avad, between excommunication and ostracism there is an intermediate level of banishment: *Shamta*.

Selling water in the valley of Aravot – זַבּוּנֵי מַיָּא בְּפַקְתָּא דַעֲרָבוֹת: Some say that this is meant to serve merely as a suggestion. Since one who is excommunicated cannot hire other people or be hired, and he may earn a livelihood only by selling his property, he is permitted to earn this small amount of income (Rabbeinu Yehonatan of Lunel). Some say that this statement teaches something novel: He is permitted to sell water in a place where it is needed. Similarly, he may earn his livelihood by providing any goods or services that are necessities (Ritva). Others suggest that he may be involved only in businesses that involve minimal interaction with other people (see *Beit Yosef*). Others say that he is permitted to work only in a place where few people are present (Rabbi Shlomo ben HaYatom).

BACKGROUND

Valley [*pakta*] of Aravot – פַּקְתָּא דַעֲרָבוֹת: The word *pakta* is another form of the word *bakta*, meaning valley or plain. From other sources, it is known that people worked and lived in such places, although they did not have sources of water. One could earn money by selling water in such places; however, one was able to earn only a small profit by doing so.

מְנוּדֶּה מַהוּ בִּשְׁאִילַת שָׁלוֹם? אָמַר רַב יוֹסֵף: תָּא שְׁמַע: וּבִשְׁאִילַת שָׁלוֹם שֶׁבֵּין אָדָם לַחֲבֵרוֹ, כִּבְנֵי אָדָם הַנְּזוּפִין לַמָּקוֹם. אֲמַר לֵיהּ אַבָּיֵי: דִּלְמָא מְנוּדֶּה לַשָּׁמַיִם שָׁאנֵי, דַּחֲמִיר.

The Gemara asks: **What is** the *halakha* governing **one who is ostracized** with regard to **greeting** others? **Rav Yosef said: Come** and **hear** a proof from a *baraita* dealing with those who were fasting for rain and whose prayers were not answered. These people were prohibited **from greeting one another, as people who are reprimanded by the Omnipresent.**[H] This indicates that those who are ostracized must not greet each other, just as mourners may not greet each other. **Abaye said to him: Perhaps one who is ostracized by Heaven is different, as that is more serious** than being ostracized by an earthly court.

מְצוֹרָע מַהוּ בִּשְׁאִילַת שָׁלוֹם? תָּא שְׁמַע: ״וְעַל שָׂפָם יַעְטֶה״ – שֶׁיְּהוּ שִׂפְתוֹתָיו מְדוּבָּקוֹת זוֹ בָּזוֹ, שֶׁיְּהֵא כִּמְנוּדֶּה וְכָאָבֵל, וְאָסוּר בִּשְׁאִילַת שָׁלוֹם. שְׁמַע מִינַּהּ.

The Gemara continues and asks: **What is** the *halakha* concerning **a leper** with regard to **greeting** others? The Gemara suggests: **Come** and **hear** a proof from the following *baraita*: The verse states: **"And he shall cover his upper lip"** (Leviticus 13:45). This means that **his lips should be stuck together, that he should be like one who is ostracized and like a mourner, and he is prohibited from greeting** others or being greeted. The Gemara concludes: Indeed, **learn from this** that this is so.

וְנִיפְשׁוֹט מִינַּהּ לִמְנוּדֶּה! אָמַר רַב אַחָא בַּר פִּנְחָס מִשְּׁמֵיהּ דְּרַב יוֹסֵף: מִי קָתָנֵי שֶׁאָסוּר? שֶׁיְּהֵא כִּמְנוּדֶּה וְכָאָבֵל [קָתָנֵי] – בְּמִילֵּי אַחֲרָנְיָיתָא, וְאָסוּר נַמִי בִּשְׁאִילַת שָׁלוֹם.

The Gemara asks: If this is the case, then **we should** also **resolve** the question asked above **with regard to one who is ostracized** and say that such a person is prohibited from offering greetings. **Rav Aḥa bar Pineḥas said in the name of Rav Yosef: Does it** explicitly **teach** that a leper **is prohibited** from greeting others, like one who is ostracized? **It teaches** only **that he should be** treated **like one who is ostracized and like a mourner,** i.e., he should be like them **with regard to other things, and** that **he is also prohibited from greeting** others. This being the case, no proof can be derived from here with regard to whether or not one who is ostracized may offer greetings.

אָבֵל אָסוּר בְּדִבְרֵי תוֹרָה, מִדְּקָאָמַר רַחֲמָנָא לִיחֶזְקֵאל ״דֹּם״.

§ The Gemara moves on to a new topic: **A mourner is prohibited** from studying **words of Torah.**[H] This prohibition is derived **from** the fact **that the Merciful One says to Ezekiel:** "Sigh in **silence**" (Ezekiel 24:17). Ezekiel was commanded to be silent and not discuss even Torah matters.

מְנוּדֶּה מַהוּ בְּדִבְרֵי תוֹרָה? אָמַר רַב יוֹסֵף, תָּא שְׁמַע: מְנוּדֶּה – שׁוֹנֶה וְשׁוֹנִין לוֹ, נִשְׂכָּר וְנִשְׂכָּרִין לוֹ.

The Gemara asks: **What is** the *halakha* concerning **one who is ostracized** with regard to speaking **words of Torah? Rav Yosef said: Come** and **hear that which** was taught in the following *baraita*: **One who is ostracized may teach** Torah to others, **and** others **may teach him** Torah. Similarly, **he may be hired** for work by others, **and** others **may be hired by him.**[H]

מוּחְרָם – לֹא שׁוֹנֶה וְלֹא שׁוֹנִין לוֹ, לֹא נִשְׂכָּר וְלֹא נִשְׂכָּרִין לוֹ. אֲבָל שׁוֹנֶה הוּא לְעַצְמוֹ שֶׁלֹּא יַפְסִיק אֶת לִמּוּדוֹ. וְעוֹשֶׂה לוֹ חֲנוּת קְטַנָּה בִּשְׁבִיל פַּרְנָסָתוֹ.

One who has been excommunicated,[NH] which is a more severe form of ostracism, **may not teach** Torah to others **and** others **may not teach him. He may not be hired** by others, **and** others **may not be hired by him. However, he may study by himself,** so **that he will not interrupt his study** entirely and forget everything he knows. **And he may build a small store for his livelihood,** so that he can earn enough money to cover his most basic needs, but not more.

וְאָמַר רַב: זַבּוּנֵי מַיָּא בְּפַקְתָּא דַעֲרָבוֹת. שְׁמַע מִינַּהּ.

And Rav said: What is the small store referred to here? This is referring to **selling water in the valley of Aravot,**[NB] where no water was to be found. One selling water there could earn a small income. The Gemara concludes: Indeed, **learn from this** *baraita* that one who is ostracized is permitted to study Torah.

מְצוֹרָע מַהוּ בְּדִבְרֵי תוֹרָה? תָּא שְׁמַע: ״וְהוֹדַעְתָּם לְבָנֶיךָ וְלִבְנֵי בָנֶיךָ יוֹם אֲשֶׁר עָמַדְתָּ לִפְנֵי ה׳ אֱלֹהֶיךָ בְּחוֹרֵב״, מָה לְהַלָּן בְּאֵימָה וּבְיִרְאָה וּבִרְתֵת וּבְזִיעָה.

The Gemara asks: **What is** the *halakha* with regard to **a leper** speaking **words of Torah?**[H] The Gemara answers: **Come** and **hear** that which is taught in a *baraita*: It is written: **"And you shall impart them to your children and your children's children; the day that you stood before the Lord your God in Horeb"** (Deuteronomy 4:9–10). **Just as there,** the revelation at Sinai was **in reverence, fear, and trembling,** so too, here, in every generation, Torah must be studied in a similar fashion.

מִכָּאן אָמְרוּ: הַזָּבִין וְהַמְּצוֹרָעִין וּבוֹעֲלֵי נִדּוֹת מוּתָּרִין לִקְרוֹת בַּתּוֹרָה וּבַנְּבִיאִים וּבַכְּתוּבִים, וְלִשְׁנוֹת בַּמִּדְרָשׁ וּבַתַּלְמוּד, בַּהֲלָכוֹת וּבָאַגָּדוֹת, וּבַעֲלֵי קְרָיִין אֲסוּרִין. שְׁמַע מִינַּהּ.

From here the Sages **stated:** ***Zavim*, lepers, and those who had intercourse with menstruating women** despite their severe ritual impurity **are permitted to read the Torah, Prophets, and Writings, and to study midrash, Talmud, *halakhot*, and *aggada*. But those who experienced a seminal emission are prohibited**[N] from doing so.[H] The reason for this distinction is that the cases of severe impurity are caused by ailment or other circumstances beyond one's control; as a result, they do not necessarily preclude a sense of reverence and awe as one studies Torah. However, a seminal emission usually occurs due to frivolity and a lack of reverence and awe, and it is therefore inappropriate for one who experiences a seminal emission to engage in matters of Torah. The Gemara concludes: Indeed, **learn from this** that a leper is permitted to study words of Torah.

אָבֵל אָסוּר בְּתִכְבּוֹסֶת, דִּכְתִיב: ״וַיִּשְׁלַח יוֹאָב תְּקוֹעָה וַיִּקַּח מִשָּׁם אִשָּׁה חֲכָמָה וַיֹּאמֶר אֵלֶיהָ הִתְאַבְּלִי נָא וְלִבְשִׁי נָא בִגְדֵי אֵבֶל וְאַל תָּסוּכִי שֶׁמֶן וְהָיִית כְּאִשָּׁה זֶה יָמִים רַבִּים מִתְאַבֶּלֶת עַל מֵת״.

§ The Gemara proceeds to discuss another issue: **A mourner is prohibited from laundering his clothes,**[NH] **as it is written: "And Joab sent to Tekoa, and fetched from there a wise woman, and said to her, I pray you, feign yourself to be a mourner, and put on now mourning apparel, and do not anoint yourself with oil, but be as a woman that had a long time mourned for the dead"** (II Samuel 14:2).

מְנוּדִּין וּמְצוֹרָעִין מַה הֵן בְּתִכְבּוֹסֶת? תָּא שְׁמַע: מְנוּדִּין וּמְצוֹרָעִין אֲסוּרִין לְסַפֵּר וּלְכַבֵּס. שְׁמַע מִינַּהּ.

The Gemara asks: **What** is the *halakha* concerning **laundering** with regard to **those who are ostracized or lepers? Come** and **hear** that which is taught in a *baraita*: **Those who are ostracized or lepers are prohibited from cutting** their hair **or laundering** their clothes. The Gemara concludes: Indeed, **learn from** here that they are prohibited from laundering their clothes.

אָבֵל חַיָּיב בִּקְרִיעָה. דְּקָאָמַר לְהוּ רַחֲמָנָא לִבְנֵי אַהֲרֹן: ״לֹא תִפְרֹמוּ״ – מִכְּלָל דְּכוּלֵּי עָלְמָא מִיחַיְּיבִי.

The Gemara continues: **A mourner is obligated to rend** his clothes.[H] This is derived from the fact **that the Merciful One says to the sons of Aaron: "Neither rend** your clothes" (Leviticus 10:6), which proves **by inference that everyone** else, all other mourners, **are obligated** to rend their clothes.

מְנוּדֶּה מַהוּ בִּקְרִיעָה? תֵּיקוּ.

The Gemara asks: **What is** the *halakha* of **rending** clothes with regard to **one who is ostracized?**[H] No answer is found, and the question **shall stand** unresolved.

מְצוֹרָע מַהוּ בִּקְרִיעָה? תָּא שְׁמַע: ״בְּגָדָיו יִהְיוּ פְרֻמִים״ – שֶׁיְּהוּ מְקוֹרָעִין. שְׁמַע מִינַּהּ.

The Gemara continues: **What is** the *halakha* concerning **a leper** with regard to **rending? Come** and **hear that which** is taught in the following *baraita*: The verse states: **"His garments shall be rent"** (Leviticus 13:45), meaning **that they shall be torn.** The Gemara concludes: Indeed, **learn from here** that this is the case.

אָבֵל חַיָּיב בִּכְפִיַּית הַמִּטָּה, דְּתָנֵי בַּר קַפָּרָא:

§ The Gemara moves to a different issue: **A mourner is obligated to overturn** his **bed,**[H] so that he sleeps on the underside of it, **as bar Kappara taught** a *baraita* that states:

NOTES

But those who experienced a seminal emission are prohibited – וּבַעֲלֵי קְרָיִין אֲסוּרִין: *Talmid Rabbeinu Yeḥiel of Paris* explains that when the Torah was given the men were instructed to separate themselves from the women. Therefore, one suffering from this type of impurity is prohibited from learning Torah. However, there was no mention of other types of impurity at the time that the Torah was given.

A mourner is prohibited from laundering his clothes – אָבֵל אָסוּר בְּתִכְבּוֹסֶת: Most commentaries explain that the proof from this verse is that the woman was instructed to wear mourner's clothes, meaning clothes that were dirty and black (Rashi; *Talmid Rabbeinu Yeḥiel of Paris*; Rabbi Shlomo ben HaYatom).

HALAKHA

One who experienced a seminal emission with regard to Torah study – בַּעַל קֶרִי בְּדִבְרֵי תוֹרָה: Ezra the Scribe decreed that one who experiences a seminal emission is prohibited from studying Torah until he has immersed. In the era of the *amora'im*, this decree was nullified, and today it is permitted for such a person to study Torah without immersing. However, it is still the custom of the pious to be strict and immerse before studying Torah (*Shulḥan Arukh, Oraḥ Ḥayyim* 88:1).

A mourner with regard to laundering clothes – אָבֵל בְּתִכְבּוֹסֶת: A mourner may not launder his clothes for all seven days of mourning (*Shulḥan Arukh, Yoreh De'a* 389:1).

A mourner with regard to rending clothes – אָבֵל בִּקְרִיעָה: Upon hearing that one of his close family members has passed away, one is required to rend his clothes (*Shulḥan Arukh, Yoreh De'a* 340:1).

One who is ostracized with regard to rending clothes – מְנוּדֶּה בִּקְרִיעָה: One who has been ostracized is not required to rend his clothes because the issue is left unresolved by the Gemara, and the ruling is generally lenient in cases of doubtful issues of *halakha* concerning rabbinic decrees (*Shakh*; *Shulḥan Arukh, Yoreh De'a* 334:1).

Overturning the bed – כְּפִיַּית הַמִּטָּה: A mourner is required to overturn his bed. However, for many generations this has no longer been the custom. The reason is either because the gentiles will view this as a practice of witchcraft or because this act is not noticeable with contemporary beds (*Tur*, citing Rosh). Some say that a mourner is required to sleep on the ground (*Shakh*), but others disagree (*Panim Meirot*). The custom today is not to be stringent with regard to this *halakha* (*Arukh HaShulḥan*; *Shulḥan Arukh, Yoreh De'a* 387:1–2).

דְּמוּת דְּיוֹקְנִי נָתַתִּי בָּהֶן, וּבַעֲוֹנוֹתֵיהֶם הֲפַכְתִּיהָ – כְּפוּ מִטּוֹתֵיהֶן עָלֶיהָ. מְנוּדֶּה וּמְצוֹרָע מַהוּ הֵן בִּכְפִיַּית הַמִּטָּה? תֵּיקוּ.

God stated: **I have placed the likeness of My image** [*deyokan*][L] **within** humans, as they were created in My image, **and owing to their sins I have overturned it,** as when this person died the Divine image in him was removed. Therefore, you must also **overturn your beds on account of this.** The Gemara asks: **What** is the *halakha* governing **one who was ostracized or a leper,** with regard to **overturning the bed?**[NH] The Gemara has no answer, and the question **shall stand** unresolved.

אָבֵל אָסוּר בַּעֲשִׂיַּית מְלָאכָה, דִּכְתִיב: ״וְהָפַכְתִּי חַגֵּיכֶם לְאֵבֶל״. מַה חַג אָסוּר בִּמְלָאכָה – אַף אָבֵל אָסוּר בִּמְלָאכָה.

§ The Gemara proceeds to the next topic: **A mourner is prohibited from performing work, as it is written: "And I will turn your Festivals into mourning"** (Amos 8:10). The Gemara infers: **Just as a Festival** is a time when it is **prohibited to work, so too, a mourner is prohibited from performing work.**[H]

מְנוּדֶּה מַהוּ בַּעֲשִׂיַּית מְלָאכָה? אָמַר רַב יוֹסֵף, תָּא שְׁמַע: כְּשֶׁאָמְרוּ אָסוּר בַּעֲשִׂיַּית מְלָאכָה – לֹא אָמְרוּ אֶלָּא בַּיּוֹם, אֲבָל בַּלַּיְלָה מוּתָּר. וְכֵן אַתָּה מוֹצֵא בִּמְנוּדֶּה וּבְאָבֵל. מַאי לָאו – אַכּוּלְּהוּ? לָא, אַשְּׁאָרָא.

The Gemara asks: **What is** the *halakha* concerning **one who was ostracized** with regard to **the performance of work? Rav Yosef said: Come** and **hear** that which is taught in the following *baraita*: **When** the Sages **said that the performance of work is prohibited** on a communal fast due to lack of rain, **they meant only** that work is prohibited **during the day** of the fast, **but during the night** of the fast **it is permitted.**[H] **And you find a similar** *halakha* **with regard to a person** who was **ostracized and** with regard to **a mourner. What, is it not with regard to all** of the prohibitions stated that the *baraita* says that they apply to one who was ostracized as well, including the prohibition to engage in work? The Gemara rejects this argument: **No,** this **is referring to the rest** of the prohibitions, but not to work.

תָּא שְׁמַע: מְנוּדֶּה שׁוֹנֶה וְשׁוֹנִין לוֹ, נִשְׂכָּר וְנִשְׂכָּרִין לוֹ. שְׁמַע מִינַּהּ. מְצוֹרָע מַהוּ בַּעֲשִׂיַּית מְלָאכָה? תֵּיקוּ.

The Gemara offers a different proof: **Come** and **hear that** which was taught in the following *baraita*: **One who is ostracized may teach Torah** to others, **and** others **may teach him** Torah. Similarly, **he may be hired** for work by others, **and** others **may be hired by him.** The Gemara concludes: **Learn from here** that it is permitted for one who is ostracized to engage in work. The Gemara asks: **What is** the *halakha* concerning **a leper,** with regard to **the performance of work?** An answer is not found, and the question **shall stand** unresolved.

אָבֵל אָסוּר בִּרְחִיצָה, דִּכְתִיב: ״וְאַל תָּסוּכִי שֶׁמֶן״, וּרְחִיצָה בִּכְלָל סִיכָה.

§ The Gemara discusses a different prohibition: **A mourner is prohibited from bathing, as it is written: "And do not anoint yourself with oil,** but be as a woman that had for a long time mourned for the dead" (II Samuel 14:2). **And bathing is included in** the category of **anointing,**[N] as both activities have a similar goal, i.e., cleanliness.

מְנוּדֶּה מַהוּ בִּרְחִיצָה? אָמַר רַב יוֹסֵף, תָּא שְׁמַע: כְּשֶׁאָמְרוּ אָסוּר בִּרְחִיצָה – לֹא אָמְרוּ אֶלָּא כׇּל גּוּפוֹ, אֲבָל פָּנָיו יָדָיו וְרַגְלָיו – מוּתָּר. וְכֵן אַתָּה מוֹצֵא בִּמְנוּדֶּה וּבְאָבֵל. מַאי לָאו אַכּוּלְּהוּ? לָא, אַשְּׁאָרָא. מְצוֹרָע מַהוּ בִּרְחִיצָה? תֵּיקוּ.

The Gemara asks: **What is** the *halakha* concerning **one who is ostracized** with regard to **bathing? Rav Yosef said: Come** and **hear that which** was taught in the following *baraita*: **When** the Sages **said that bathing is prohibited** on a communal fast, **they meant only** that a person may not wash **his entire body,** but washing **his face, his hands, and his feet is permitted. And you find a similar** *halakha* **with regard to a person who was ostracized and** with regard to **a mourner. What, is it not with regard to all** the prohibitions stated in the *baraita*, including the prohibition against bathing, that they apply also to one who is ostracized? The Gemara rejects this argument: **No,** this **is referring to the rest** of the prohibitions, but not to bathing. The Gemara asks: **What is** the *halakha* concerning **a leper** with regard to **bathing?** An answer is not found, and the question **shall stand** unresolved.

LANGUAGE

Image [*deyokan*] – דְּיוֹקָן: This word has a Greek root, and some claim that it is related to the Greek δείκανον, *deikanon*, meaning a drawn or woven image. However, the *ge'onim* understand it to mean *dio-iconin*, from the Greek εἰκών, *eikon*, meaning image or form. Together with the prefix this word is said to mean double image or copy.

NOTES

One who was ostracized or a leper with regard to overturning the bed – מְנוּדֶּה וּמְצוֹרָע...בִּכְפִיַּית הַמִּטָּה: The Ritva asks: The explanation offered for this custom in the case of a mourner does not apply to these other two groups. Therefore, why would they be required to overturn their beds? He explains that since their world has turned upside down, and they are distanced from other people, it is appropriate for them to overturn their beds.

Bathing is included in anointing – רְחִיצָה בִּכְלָל סִיכָה: This verse does not mention bathing, which makes the proof somewhat problematic. The Ritva explains that there is never a case in which anointing is prohibited and bathing is permitted. Furthermore, it is clear that the verse compares the two of them. The Rambam explains, as does the Meiri in greater detail, that the common practice was to bathe and afterward to anoint oneself with oil. Since the verse states that the woman from Tekoa was instructed not to anoint herself, she must have been prohibited from bathing as well.

HALAKHA

A leper with regard to overturning the bed – מְצוֹרָע בִּכְפִיַּית הַמִּטָּה: A leper is not required to overturn his bed. The ruling is lenient with regard to this *halakha* because the question is one of rabbinic law that is left unresolved (Rambam *Sefer Tahara*, *Hilkhot Tumat Tzara'at* 10:6).

Working while mourning – מְלָאכָה בַּאֲבֵילוּת: A mourner is prohibited from working for all seven days of the mourning period (*Shulḥan Arukh*, *Yoreh De'a* 380:1).

The final fast days for lack of rain – מִנְהַג בְּתַעֲנִיּוֹת אַחֲרוֹנוֹת שֶׁל גְּשָׁמִים: During the final stage of fast days for a drought, it is prohibited to perform work during the day, but working at night is permitted. In addition, one may not wash his entire body with hot water; however, he may wash his hands, face, and feet. It is likewise prohibited to walk with shoes in the city (*Shulḥan Arukh*, *Oraḥ Ḥayyim* 575:3).

אָבֵל אָסוּר בִּנְעִילַת הַסַּנְדָּל, מִדְּקָאָמַר לֵיהּ רַחֲמָנָא לִיחֶזְקֵאל: ״וּנְעָלֶיךָ תָּשִׂים בְּרַגְלֶיךָ״ – מִכְּלָל דְּכוּלֵּי עָלְמָא אָסוּר.

§ The Gemara moves to the next topic: **A mourner is prohibited from wearing shoes.**[H] **Since the Merciful One says to** Ezekiel with regard to how his mourning rites should differ from the accepted custom: **"And put your shoes upon your feet"** (Ezekiel 24:17), which shows **by inference that everyone** else, i.e., all other mourners, **is prohibited** from wearing shoes.

מְנוּדֶּה מַהוּ בִּנְעִילַת הַסַּנְדָּל? אָמַר רַב יוֹסֵף, תָּא שְׁמַע: כְּשֶׁאָמְרוּ אָסוּר בִּנְעִילַת הַסַּנְדָּל – לֹא אָמְרוּ אֶלָּא בָּעִיר, אֲבָל בַּדֶּרֶךְ – מוּתָּר. הָא כֵּיצַד? יָצָא לַדֶּרֶךְ – נוֹעֵל; נִכְנָס לָעִיר – חוֹלֵץ. וְכֵן אַתָּה מוֹצֵא בִּמְנוּדֶּה וּבְאָבֵל. מַאי לָאו אַכּוּלְּהוּ? לָא, אַשְּׁאָרָא.

The Gemara asks: **What is** the *halakha* concerning **one who is ostracized** with regard to **wearing shoes?**[H] **Rav Yosef said: Come** and **hear that which** is taught in the following *baraita*: **When** the Sages **said** that **wearing shoes is prohibited** on a communal fast, **they meant only** that one may not wear shoes when he is walking about **in the city, but** if he set out to travel **on the road,** wearing shoes **is permitted. How so?** When **he sets out on the road, he may put on** his shoes. But as soon as **he enters the city** once again, **he must take off** his shoes and continue barefoot. **And you find a similar** *halakha* **with regard to a person** who was **ostracized and** with regard to **a mourner. What, is it not with regard to all** of the prohibitions stated in the *baraita*, including the prohibition against wearing shoes, that they apply also to one who was ostracized? The Gemara rejects this argument: **No,** this **is referring to the rest** of the prohibitions, but not to wearing shoes.

מְצוֹרָע מַהוּ בִּנְעִילַת הַסַּנְדָּל? תֵּיקוּ.

The Gemara asks: **What is** the *halakha* concerning **a leper** with regard to **wearing shoes?**[H] No answer is found, and the question **shall stand** unresolved.

אָבֵל אָסוּר בְּתַשְׁמִישׁ הַמִּטָּה, דִּכְתִיב: ״וַיְנַחֵם דָּוִד אֵת בַּת שֶׁבַע אִשְׁתּוֹ וַיָּבֹא אֵלֶיהָ״ – מִכְּלָל דְּמֵעִיקָּרָא אָסוּר.

§ The Gemara considers another issue: **A mourner is prohibited from engaging in sexual relations,**[H] **as it is written: "And David comforted Bath-Sheba his wife, and went into her,** and lay with her" (II Samuel 12:24), after their son had died. This proves **by inference that initially,** during the period of mourning, sexual relations **were forbidden.**

מְנוּדֶּה מַהוּ בְּתַשְׁמִישׁ הַמִּטָּה? אָמַר רַב יוֹסֵף, תָּא שְׁמַע: כָּל אוֹתָן שָׁנִים שֶׁהָיוּ יִשְׂרָאֵל בַּמִּדְבָּר מְנוּדִּין הָיוּ, וְשִׁימְּשׁוּ מִטּוֹתֵיהֶן. אֲמַר לֵיהּ אַבַּיֵי: וְדִלְמָא מְנוּדֶּה לַשָּׁמַיִם שָׁאנֵי, דְּקִיל.

The Gemara asks: **What is** the *halakha* concerning **one who is ostracized** with regard to **sexual relations? Rav Yosef said: Come** and **hear that which** is taught in a *baraita*: **All those years that the Jewish people were in the wilderness they were ostracized,**[N] **and yet they engaged in sexual relations,** as there were children born to them during that period. It follows that it is permitted for one who is ostracized to engage in sexual relations. **Abaye said to him: Perhaps one who is ostracized by Heaven is different,** as **that is less serious**[N] than being ostracized by an earthly court.

קִיל?! וְהָא אָמְרַתְּ חֲמִיר! סַפּוּקֵי מְסַפְּקָא לֵיהּ, זִיל הָכָא – קָמַדְחֵי לֵיהּ, וְזִיל הָכָא – קָמַדְחֵי לֵיהּ.

The Gemara asks in astonishment: Is it **less serious? But didn't you,** Abaye, **say** elsewhere that a decree of ostracism imposed by Heaven is **more serious** than one issued by an earthly court? For this reason, Abaye rejected several proofs of Rav Yosef from the previously cited *baraita*. The Gemara answers: Abaye **is uncertain** whether a decree of ostracism imposed by Heaven is more or less serious than one imposed by an earthly court. Therefore, when **he goes in this** direction **he rejects** the argument, **and** when **he goes in that** direction **he rejects** the argument. Abaye asserts that since the issue is in doubt, no proof can be derived from ostracism issued by Heaven.

HALAKHA

A mourner with regard to wearing shoes – אָבֵל בִּנְעִילַת הַסַּנְדָּל: A mourner may not wear shoes for all seven days of the mourning period (*Shulḥan Arukh, Yoreh De'a* 380:1).

One who is ostracized with regard to wearing shoes – מְנוּדֶּה בִּנְעִילַת הַסַּנְדָּל: One who has been ostracized may not wear shoes, like a mourner, because many sources imply that one who has been ostracized is required to remove his shoes. The *Beit Yosef* explains the opinion of the Rivash, who cites the Rashba, and maintains that it is permitted for such a person to wear shoes. The common practice follows this opinion (*Shakh*; *Shulḥan Arukh, Yoreh De'a* 334:2).

A leper with regard to bathing and wearing shoes – מְצוֹרָע בִּרְחִיצָה וּבִנְעִילַת הַסַּנְדָּל: A leper is permitted to bathe and to wear shoes. The ruling is lenient with regard to these *halakhot* and other similar cases because the issue is left unresolved, and the law itself is rabbinic (Rambam *Sefer Tahara, Hilkhot Tumat Tzara'at* 10:6).

A mourner with regard to sexual relations – אָבֵל בְּתַשְׁמִישׁ: A mourner may not engage in sexual relations for all seven days of the mourning period (*Shulḥan Arukh, Yoreh De'a* 380:1).

NOTES

In the wilderness they were ostracized – בַּמִּדְבָּר מְנוּדִּין הָיוּ: The early authorities find evidence of this ostracism in that which is stated after the sin of the spies: "For every day a year, you shall bear your sins…and you shall know My displeasure" (Numbers 14:34; manuscript of Rashi). Others derive evidence of ostracism from the fact that God did not speak to Moses throughout the years following the sin of the spies until that generation had died out (Rabbi Shlomo ben HaYatom).

One who is ostracized by Heaven…that is less serious – מְנוּדֶּה לַשָּׁמַיִם...דְּקִיל: A simple explanation for this opinion is that people are generally less afraid of God than they are of other people (Commentary on *Moed Katan*). The Ra'avad explains that being ostracized by Heaven is dependent upon God, Who does not want to prevent one from observing mitzvot such as sacrificing offerings or having children. Instead He only prohibited one from activities that relate to other people. However, a court that has imposed ostracism does not make this distinction and prohibits such a person from both types of activities (*Tosefot HaRosh*).

HALAKHA

A leper with regard to sexual relations – מְצוֹרָע בְּתַשְׁמִישׁ: A quarantined leper may engage in sexual relations (Rambam *Sefer Tahara*, *Hilkhot Tumat Tzara'at* 10:6).

Sending offerings – שִׁילּוּחַ קָרְבָּנוֹת: A mourner may not send offerings for all seven days of the mourning period. Similarly, a leper may not send offerings because as long as he is unfit to enter the camp, he is also unfit to sacrifice an offering. This is the case even if he sends it with a messenger. It is unclear whether or not one who has been ostracized may send an offering; therefore, if an offering is sacrificed on his behalf it is accepted (Rambam *Sefer Avoda*, *Hilkhot Biat HaMikdash* 2:11).

BACKGROUND

Peace-offering – שְׁלָמִים: Male and female cattle or sheep may be sacrificed as peace offerings (see Leviticus, chapter 3). They are offerings of lesser holiness and may be slaughtered anywhere within the Temple courtyard. Their blood is sprinkled on the two opposite corners of the altar in such a manner that it will drip down on each of the altar's four sides. Part of each peace-offering is burned on the altar, and the breast and the right hind leg are given to the priests. The rest is eaten by one bringing the offering, with his family. They may eat of the offering anywhere in the city, on the day the animal is sacrificed and during the following night and day. With the exception of the Festival peace-offering and a few other cases, the peace-offerings were voluntary gifts. The word offering used without qualification usually means a peace-offering.

מְצוֹרָע מַהוּ בְּתַשְׁמִישׁ הַמִּטָּה? תָּא שְׁמַע, דְּתַנְיָא: "וְיָשַׁב מִחוּץ לְאָהֳלוֹ" – שֶׁיְּהֵא כִּמְנוּדֶּה וּכְאָבֵל, וְאָסוּר בְּתַשְׁמִישׁ הַמִּטָּה. וְאֵין אָהֳלוֹ אֶלָּא אִשְׁתּוֹ, שֶׁנֶּאֱמַר: "לֵךְ אֱמוֹר לָהֶם שׁוּבוּ לָכֶם לְאָהֳלֵיכֶם". שְׁמַע מִינַּהּ.

The Gemara continues: **What is the** *halakha* concerning **a leper** with regard to **sexual relations?**[H] **Come** and **hear** a proof, **as it is taught** in a *baraita*: The verse concerning a leper states: **"But he shall remain outside his tent** seven days" (Leviticus 14:8), from which it is derived **that** a leper **should be like one who is ostracized and like a mourner, and he is prohibited** from engaging **in sexual relations.** How is this derived? The **only** meaning of the term **"his tent"** is **his wife, as is stated** after the giving of the Torah: **"Go say to them, return again to your tents"** (Deuteronomy 5:27). This statement rendered it permitted for the men to once again engage in sexual relations with their wives after they had previously been prohibited to do so in anticipation of the giving of the Torah, as expressed in the verse: "Come not near a woman" (Exodus 19:15). The Gemara concludes: Indeed, **learn from this** that it is prohibited for a leper to engage in sexual relations.

וְנִיפְשׁוֹט נַמִי לִמְנוּדֶּה! אָמַר רַב הוּנָא בְּרֵיהּ דְּרַב פִּנְחָס מִשְּׁמֵיהּ דְּרַב יוֹסֵף: מִי קָתָנֵי "שֶׁאָסוּר"? שֶׁיְּהֵא כִּמְנוּדֶּה וּכְאָבֵל – בְּמִילֵּי אַחֲרָנְיָיתָא, וְאָסוּר נַמִי בְּתַשְׁמִישׁ הַמִּטָּה.

The Gemara asks: If this is the case, then **can we** also **resolve** the question raised above with regard to **one who is ostracized,** by saying that it is prohibited for such a person to engage in sexual relations? **Rav Huna, son of Rav Pineḥas, said in the name of Rav Yosef: Is it taught** that a leper **is prohibited** from engaging in sexual relations like one who is ostracized? **It states** only that **he should be** treated **like one who is ostracized and like a mourner,** i.e., he should be like them **with regard to other things, and in addition he is prohibited** from engaging in **sexual relations.** Therefore, no proof can be derived from here with regard to one who is ostracized that he, too, is prohibited from engaging in sexual relations.

אֲבָל אֵינוֹ מְשַׁלֵּחַ קׇרְבְּנוֹתָיו, דְּתַנְיָא, רַבִּי שִׁמְעוֹן אוֹמֵר: "שְׁלָמִים" – בִּזְמַן שֶׁהוּא שָׁלֵם, וְלֹא בִּזְמַן שֶׁהוּא אוֹנֵן.

§ The Gemara continues: **A mourner may not send his offerings** to the Temple,[H] **as it is taught** in a *baraita*: **Rabbi Shimon says: A peace-offering** [*shelamim*][B] is given this name also to teach us that one may sacrifice it only **at a time when he is whole** [*shalem*][N] and his mind is settled,[N] **but not at a time when he is an acute mourner,**[N] i.e., on the first day of his bereavement, when he is distressed.

מְנוּדֶּה מַהוּ שֶׁיְּשַׁלֵּחַ קׇרְבְּנוֹתָיו? אָמַר רַב יוֹסֵף, תָּא שְׁמַע: כׇּל אוֹתָן שָׁנִים שֶׁהָיוּ יִשְׂרָאֵל בַּמִּדְבָּר מְנוּדִּין הָיוּ, וְשִׁלְּחוּ קׇרְבְּנוֹתֵיהֶן. אֲמַר לֵיהּ אַבָּיֵי: וְדִלְמָא מְנוּדֶּה לַשָּׁמַיִם שָׁאנֵי, דְּקִיל.

The Gemara asks: **What is** the *halakha* concerning **one who is ostracized** with regard to **sending his offerings** to the Temple? **Rav Yosef said: Come** and **hear** a proof from that which is taught in a *baraita*: **All those years that the Jewish people were in the wilderness they were ostracized, and yet they sent their offerings.**[N] **Abaye said to him: Perhaps one who is ostracized by Heaven is different, as that is less serious** than being ostracized by an earthly court.

קִיל?! וְהָאָמְרַתְּ חָמִיר! סְפוּקֵי מְסַפְּקָא לֵיהּ, וּמַדְחֵי לֵיהּ.

The Gemara asks in astonishment: Is it **less serious? But certainly you,** Abaye, **said** elsewhere that being ostracized by Heaven is **more serious** than being ostracized by an earthly court. The Gemara offers a resolution: Abaye **is uncertain** whether being ostracized by Heaven is more or less serious than being ostracized by an earthly court, and therefore **he rejects** Rav Yosef's arguments in both directions.

NOTES

A peace-offering [*shelamim*] at a time when he is whole [*shalem*] – שְׁלָמִים בִּזְמַן שֶׁהוּא שָׁלֵם: Some say that the word *shelamim*, which is written in Hebrew in the plural, indicates that both the animal being sacrificed and the one sacrificing it must be whole [*shalem*]. In a *baraita* it is taught that this principle applies to other offerings as well, not only to peace-offerings.

At a time when he is whole and his mind is settled – בִּזְמַן שֶׁהוּא שָׁלֵם: According to Rashi, this statement indicates that his mind is whole and he is settled. Similarly, in the manuscript of Rashi it is written that this expression means he must be joyous. Others explain that such a person must not be lacking anything, and when one member of his immediate family is lacking he can no longer be considered whole (*Talmid Rabbeinu Yeḥiel of Paris*; Commentary on *Moed Katan*).

When he is an acute mourner – שֶׁהוּא אוֹנֵן: Some of the early authorities write that the prohibition against sending an offering refers specifically to an acute mourner, whose pain is very intense (Rid; Ra'avad on *Sifra*). However, the majority of the commentaries disagree, and they show from the *Tosefta* that a mourner is prohibited from sending an offering for the entire seven-day period of mourning.

They were ostracized and they sent their offerings – מְנוּדִּין הָיוּ וְשִׁלְּחוּ קׇרְבְּנוֹתֵיהֶם: *Tosafot* note that the Torah does not explicitly mention that the people sacrificed offerings during the forty years in the wilderness. Some explain that it can be assumed that they sacrificed the daily offering and the additional offerings (*Talmid Rabbeinu Yeḥiel of Paris*). Others write that because they did not eat non-consecrated meat in the desert, according to the opinion of Rabbi Yishmael, whenever the Torah mentions that they ate meat it must be referring to eating meat from peace-offerings (Rabbi Shlomo ben HaYatom; see *Turei Aven*).

מְצוֹרָע מַהוּ שֶׁיְּשַׁלַּח קׇרְבְּנוֹתָיו? תָּא שְׁמַע, דְּתַנְיָא: "וְאַחֲרֵי טׇהֳרָתוֹ" – אַחַר פְּרִישָׁתוֹ מִן הַמֵּת; "שִׁבְעַת יָמִים יִסְפְּרוּ לוֹ" – אֵלּוּ שִׁבְעַת יְמֵי סְפִירוֹ; "וּבְיוֹם בֹּאוֹ אֶל הַקּוֹדֶשׁ אֶל הֶחָצֵר הַפְּנִימִית לְשָׁרֵת בַּקּוֹדֶשׁ יַקְרִיב חַטָּאתוֹ" –

The Gemara asks: **What is** the *halakha* with regard to **a leper sending his offerings**[N] to the Temple? The Gemara answers: **Come and hear** a proof, **as it is taught** in a *baraita* with regard to a priest who became ritually impure: "And after he is purified, they shall count for him seven days" (Ezekiel 44:26). The verse should be understood as follows: **"And after he is purified"; after he has separated from** his **deceased** relative.[N] **"They shall count for him seven days"; these are the seven days of his counting**[N] before he may purify himself. **"And on the day that he goes into the Sanctuary, into the inner court, to minister in the Sanctuary, he shall sacrifice his sin**-offering, says the Lord God" (Ezekiel 44:27);

NOTES

What is the *halakha* with regard to a leper sending his offerings – מְצוֹרָע מַהוּ שֶׁיְּשַׁלַּח קׇרְבְּנוֹתָיו: The doubt in this case is not due to impurity, as other impure people are permitted to send offerings. Here, the question is whether a leper falls into the same category as a mourner, who is not considered to be whole (Rid).

After he has separated from his deceased relative – אַחַר פְּרִישָׁתוֹ מִן הַמֵּת: The reason that the Gemara does not explain this phrase according to the simple meaning of the words, i.e., that it is referring to counting after the purification of the one who became ritually impure, is because after he has become pure there is no clear reason for him to continue counting (Ra'avad) In the commentary on *Moed Katan*, it is written that this verse is referring to the High Priest. Immediately after he has left the deceased he may return to sacrificing offerings, because he is permitted to do so while he is a mourner, unlike other priests (Rid).

These are the seven days of his counting – אֵלּוּ שִׁבְעַת יְמֵי סְפִירוֹ: In the manuscript of Rashi, it is explained that since the verse is referring to these days as counting, it must be referring to the purification of a leper, whose purification process involves counting. *Talmid Rabbeinu Yeḥiel of Paris* explains slightly differently, noting that since the verse lists the days of one's counting, it must be referring to a purification process that involves counting after the impurity has passed, i.e., the purification of a leper.

זוֹ עֲשִׂירִית הָאֵיפָה שֶׁלּוֹ, דִּבְרֵי רַבִּי יְהוּדָה.

this is the meal-offering of **a tenth of an ephah** of flour, which every priest would bring on the day he began serving in the Temple. But as long as he is ritually impure, whether because he had come into contact with a corpse or due to leprosy, he may not send his offerings to the Temple; this is **the statement of Rabbi Yehuda.**

רַבִּי שִׁמְעוֹן אוֹמֵר: "בְּבֹאוֹ יַקְרִיב" – בִּזְמַן שֶׁרָאוּי לְבִיאָה רָאוּי לְהַקְרָבָה; בִּזְמַן שֶׁאֵינוֹ רָאוּי לְבִיאָה – אֵינוֹ רָאוּי לְהַקְרָבָה.

Rabbi Shimon says: The verse states: "And on the day that **he goes into** the Sanctuary, into the inner court, to minister in the Sanctuary **he shall sacrifice** his sin offering." This teaches that **when he is fit to enter**[N] the Sanctuary, **he is fit to sacrifice** an offering. But **when he is not fit to go into** the Sanctuary, i.e., when he is ritually impure, **he is not fit to sacrifice** an offering. This implies that a leper may not send his offerings to the Temple to be sacrificed on the altar, as he himself is not fit to enter the Temple.

אָמַר רָבָא: מְנָלַן דִּמְשַׁדְּרִין שְׁלִיחָא דְּבֵי דִינָא, וּמְזַמְּנִינַן לֵיהּ לְדִינָא? דִּכְתִיב: "וַיִּשְׁלַח מֹשֶׁה לִקְרֹא לְדָתָן וְלַאֲבִירָם בְּנֵי אֱלִיאָב". וּמְנָלַן דִּמְזַמְּנִינַן לְדִינָא? דִּכְתִיב: "וַיֹּאמֶר מֹשֶׁה אֶל קֹרַח אַתָּה וְכׇל עֲדָתְךָ".

§ Having discussed some of the restrictions applying to a person who was ostracized, the Gemara explains some of the basic principles relating to ostracism: **Rava said: From where do we** derive **that a court agent is sent**[N] **to summon** the defendant **to** appear before the **court** before he is ostracized? **As it is written: "And Moses sent to call Dathan and Abiram, the sons of Eliab"** (Numbers 16:12). **And from where do we** derive **that we summon** the defendant, that he himself must appear before the **court?**[H] **As it is written: "And Moses said to Korah: Be you and all your congregation** before the Lord, you and they, and Aaron, tomorrow" (Numbers 16:16).

NOTES

When he is fit to enter – בִּזְמַן שֶׁרָאוּי לְבִיאָה: Everyone agrees that this principle does not apply in all cases, since impure people may send their animals as offerings. Rather, this statement applies to those whose level of impurity is as severe as that of a leper, including, according to the Rambam, one who is impure due to contact with a corpse. This verse implies that due to the serious nature of their impurity they may not sacrifice offerings (Ritva).

From where do we derive that a court agent is sent, etc. – מְנָלַן דִּמְשַׁדְּרִין שְׁלִיחָא וכו׳: According to the version of the text used by some of the early authorities, it was Korah himself who was sent by the court to summon the rest of his congregation (see Ran).

HALAKHA

Summoning to court – הַזְמָנָה לְדִין: The court sends messengers that summon one to court on a specific day. If he does not come the first time, he is summoned a second time. If he does not come the second time, he should be summoned a third time. If he does not come at any time during that day, he is ostracized on the next day (*Shulḥan Arukh*, *Ḥoshen Mishpat* 11:1).

לְקַמֵּי גַּבְרָא רַבָּה – דִּכְתִיב: ״לִפְנֵי ה׳״. אַתְּ וּפְלָנְיָא – דִּכְתִיב: ״אַתָּה וָהֵם וְאַהֲרֹן״. דְּקָבְעִינַן זִימְנָא – דִּכְתִיב: ״מָחָר״. זִימְנָא בָּתַר זִימְנָא – דִּכְתִיב: ״קָרְאוּ שָׁם פַּרְעֹה מֶלֶךְ מִצְרַיִם שָׁאוֹן הֶעֱבִיר הַמּוֹעֵד״.

From where is it derived that the defendant must be told that he is being summoned to appear **before a great man? As it is written:** "And Moses said to Korah: Be you and all your congregation **before the Lord**" (Numbers 16:16). From where is it derived that the summons must mention the names of both parties: **You and so-and-so,** the plaintiff? **As it is written: "You, and they, and Aaron"** (Numbers 16:16). From where is it derived **that we set a date** for the court proceedings? **As it is written: "Tomorrow"** (Numbers 16:16). From where is it derived that a second **date** must be set **after** the first **date,** if the defendant did not heed the first summons? **As it is written: "They did cry there, Pharaoh,**[N] **king of Egypt is but a noise; he has passed the time appointed…** Surely as Tabor is among the mountains, and as Carmel by the sea, so shall he come" (Jeremiah 46:17). Although a time had been appointed and it had passed, it was not canceled entirely but pushed off to a later date.

וּמְנָלַן דְּאִי מִתְפַּקֵּר בִּשְׁלִיחָא דְּבֵי דִינָא, וְאָתֵי וַאֲמַר, לָא מִיתְחֲזֵי כְּלִישָּׁנָא בִּישָׁא – דִּכְתִיב: ״הַעֵינֵי הָאֲנָשִׁים הָהֵם תְּנַקֵּר״.

And from where do we derive **that if** the summoned person **behaves disrespectfully toward the agent of the court, and** the agent **comes** back **and reports** his conduct, that **this is not considered slander?**[H] **As it is written: "Will you put out the eyes of these men?"** (Numbers 16:14). Dathan and Abiram spoke these words to the messenger that Moses had sent to them, and the messenger reported them back to Moses.

וּמְנָלַן דִּמְשַׁמְּתִינַן? דִּכְתִיב: ״אוֹרוּ מֵרוֹז״. דְּהָכִי סְבָרָא דְּגַבְרָא רַבָּה, דִּכְתִיב: ״אָמַר מַלְאַךְ ה׳״. וּמְנָלַן דְּמַחַרְמִינַן? דִּכְתִיב: ״אוֹרוּ אָרוֹר״.

From do we derive **that we ostracize** one who does not obey a court summons? **As it is written: "Curse Meroz"** (Judges 5:23), who was ostracized for not coming to battle after having been summoned. From where is it derived that the ostracized person must be told **that it** was **the decision of a great man** to ostracize him? **As it is written:** "Curse Meroz, **said the messenger of the Lord**" (Judges 5:23).[N] **And from where do we** derive **that,** if he fails to mend his ways, **we excommunicate** such a person more harshly, putting him under the most severe form of excommunication? **As it is written:** "Curse Meroz… **curse bitterly** its inhabitants" (Judges 5:23), implying that one curse is followed by another, i.e., lesser ostracism is followed by harsh excommunication.

דְּאָכֵיל וְשָׁתֵי בַּהֲדֵיהּ וְקָאֵי בְּאַרְבַּע אַמּוֹת דִּידֵיהּ – דִּכְתִיב: ״יוֹשְׁבֶיהָ״. וּמְנָלַן דְּפָרְטִינַן חֶטְאֵיהּ בְּצִיבּוּרָא? דִּכְתִיב: ״כִּי לֹא בָאוּ לְעֶזְרַת ה׳״.

From where is it derived **that** the curse applies to anyone who **eats or drinks with, or stands within, four cubits of** the ostracized person?[H] **As it is written:** "Curse bitterly **its inhabitants**" (Judges 5:23), in reference to all those sitting together with Meroz. **And from where do we derive that we detail his sin in public?**[H] **As it is written:** "Curse bitterly its inhabitants, **because they did not come to the help of the Lord**" (Judges 5:23).

וְאָמַר עוּלָּא: בְּאַרְבַּע מְאָה שִׁיפּוּרֵי שַׁמְתֵּיהּ בָּרָק לְמֵרוֹז. אִיכָּא דְּאָמְרִי: גַּבְרָא רַבָּה הֲוָה. וְאִיכָּא דְּאָמְרִי: כּוֹכָבָא הֲוָה, שֶׁנֶּאֱמַר: ״מִן שָׁמַיִם נִלְחָמוּ הַכּוֹכָבִים״.

And Ulla said: Barak ostracized Meroz with the blowing of **four hundred *shofarot*** due to his failure to come. As for the identification of Meroz, **some say** that **he was a great man** and that he was ostracized because he did not join in the war effort. **And others say** that the reference is to **a star** and not a human being, and that it did not aid the Jewish people in their battle, **as it is stated: "The stars fought from heaven;** in their courses they fought against Sisera," (Judges 5:20). This star, which did not help the Jewish people, was cursed.

וּמְנָלַן דְּמַפְקָרִינַן נִכְסֵיהּ? דִּכְתִיב: ״וְכֹל אֲשֶׁר לֹא יָבוֹא לִשְׁלֹשֶׁת הַיָּמִים בַּעֲצַת הַשָּׂרִים וְהַזְּקֵנִים יָחֳרַם כָּל רְכוּשׁוֹ וְהוּא יִבָּדֵל מִקְּהַל הַגּוֹלָה״.

And from where do we derive **that** the court **may declare the property of** one who does not obey its orders **as ownerless?**[H] **As it is written: "And that whoever would not come within three days, according to the counsel of the princes and the Elders, all his substance shall be forfeited [*yaḥoram*] and himself separated from the congregation of the exiles"** (Ezra 10:8). "Shall be forfeited" is referring to excommunication.

וּמְנָלַן דְּנָצֵינַן וְלָיְיטִינַן וּמָחֵינַן וְתָלְשִׁינַן שֵׂיעָר וּמַשְׁבְּעִינַן? דִּכְתִיב: ״וָאָרִיב עִמָּם וָאֲקַלְלֵם וָאַכֶּה מֵהֶם אֲנָשִׁים וָאֶמְרְטֵם וָאַשְׁבִּיעֵם״.

And from where do we derive **that we may contend with** such a person, **and curse**[H] him, **and beat** him, **and pull out** his **hair, and** make him **take an oath** in order to prevent him from sinning? **As it is written: "And I contended with them, and cursed them, and beat some of them, and pulled out their hair, and made them take oath** by God" (Nehemiah 13:25).

NOTES

They did cry there, Pharaoh, etc. – קָרְאוּ שָׁם פַּרְעֹה וכו׳: In the manuscript of Rashi, it is explained that Jeremiah set a time for the downfall of Pharaoh, and although it did not occur at that time, it was to occur at another time. The Ritva writes that although God set a time for the downfall of Pharaoh at the hands of Nebuchadnezzar, Nebuchadnezzar arrived late. Despite this, God did not punish Nebuchadnezzar because he did eventually arrive. If so, certainly a Jew who is threatened with ostracism should be given a second chance even if he misses the first opportunity. Some explain that Pharaoh made noise in joy because he thought that the time for the war had passed, and he was informed that there would be another time for war later (Rabbeinu Yehonatan of Lunel; Ran).

Said the messenger of the Lord – אָמַר מַלְאַךְ ה׳: Most of the commentaries explain that it was Barak who served as God's messenger. However, some say that Barak was a messenger for the decree of the Lord's angel (Ran).

HALAKHA

One who shows disrespect toward the court's messenger – הַמְבַזֶּה שְׁלִיחַ בֵּית דִּין: The testimony of a court's messenger carries the weight of two witnesses, if he testifies that he was treated disrespectfully. He may tell the court what occurred, and it is not considered to be slanderous speech (Rema). The one who acted disrespectfully toward the court's messenger is ostracized (*Shulḥan Arukh*, *Ḥoshen Mishpat* 11:1 and *Yoreh De'a* 334:43).

Who eats or drinks with him, etc. – דְּאָכֵיל וְשָׁתֵי בַּהֲדֵיהּ וכו׳: When the courts see that a person is transgressing a serious prohibition and they wish to separate him from it, they may excommunicate not only the one committing the sin but even those who are eating, drinking, and standing within four cubits of him (*Shulḥan Arukh*, *Yoreh De'a* 334:9).

We detail his sin in public – פָּרְטִינַן חֶטְאֵיהּ בְּצִיבּוּרָא: A court, if it deems it appropriate, is permitted to ostracize a person who is not strictly liable for ostracism, in order to serve as a warning to others. His sin should be made public, and it should be made known that he was ostracized or excommunicated by the court (Rambam *Sefer Shofetim*, *Hilkhot Sanhedrin* 24:7).

The court may declare his property ownerless – מַפְקָרִינַן נִכְסֵיהּ: A court is permitted to declare a person's property ownerless or destroy it in order to prevent sins that are widespread at that time (*Shulḥan Arukh*, *Ḥoshen Mishpat* 2:1, and in the comment of Rema).

We may contend with and curse – נָצֵינַן וְלָיְיטִינַן: A judge is permitted to purposely antagonize the defendant when appropriate, curse, strike, pull out hair, and force a person to take an oath. Similarly, he is permitted to seize the guilty party, imprison him, and punish him with any type of punishment (Rambam *Sefer Shofetim*, *Hilkhot Sanhedrin* 24:8–9).

ומנלן דכפתינן ואסרינן ועבדינן הרדפה? דכתיב: "הן למות הן לשרושי הן לענש נכסין ולאסורין". מאי לשרושי? אמר אדא מרי אמר נחמיה בר ברוך אמר רב חייא בר אבין אמר רב יהודה: הרדפה. מאי הרדפה? אמר רב יהודה בריה דרב שמואל בר שילת משמיה דרב: מנדין לאלתר, ושונין לאחר שלשים, ומחרימין לאחר ששים.

And from where do we derive **that we may shackle** his hands and feet, **chain** him, **and apply pressure?**[N] **As it is written: "Whether it be for death, or for banishment [*lishroshi*], or for confiscation of goods, or for imprisonment"** (Ezra 7:26). The Gemara asks: **What** is the meaning of the word **"*lishroshi*,"** translated here as banishment? **Adda Mari said** that **Neḥemya bar Baruch said** that **Rav Ḥiyya bar Avin said** that **Rav Yehuda said:** This is **pressure.** Since this expression is also unclear, the Gemara asks: **What is pressure? Rav Yehuda, son of Rav Shmuel bar Sheilat, said in the name of** Rav that this term refers to the following series of actions: **They ostracize** him **immediately,** and then once **again after thirty** days, and if he still does not repent, **they excommunicate him after sixty** days.

אמר ליה רב הונא בר חיננא, הכי אמר רב חסדא: מתרין ביה שני וחמישי ושני. הני מילי – לממונא. אבל לאפקירותא – לאלתר.

Rav Huna bar Ḥinnana said to him: Rav Ḥisda said as follows: Before excommunicating a person, the court **warns him** three times, on **Monday, Thursday, and** the following **Monday.** The Gemara notes: **This applies** in a case where one ignores **a monetary judgment** that was issued against him. He is warned three times that he must repay his debt.[H] **But** in a case where one **behaves disrespectfully** toward a Torah scholar, he is **immediately** ostracized.[H]

ההוא טבחא דאיתפקר ברב טובי בר מתנה, אימנו עליה אביי ורבא ושמתוהו. לסוף אזל פייסיה לבעל דיניה. אמר אביי: היכי ליעביד? לישרי ליה – לא חל שמתא עליה תלתין יומין. לא לישרי ליה – קא בעו רבנן למיעל!

§ The Gemara relates that **a certain butcher behaved disrespectfully toward Rav Tuvi bar Mattana. Abaye and Rava were appointed** to the case **and ostracized him. In the end** the butcher **went and appeased his disputant,** Rav Tuvi. **Abaye said: What should we do** in this case? Shall **he be released** from his decree of ostracism? **His** decree of **ostracism has not** yet **been in effect for** the usual **thirty days.** On the other hand, **shall he not be released** from ostracism? But **the Sages wish to enter**[N] his shop and purchase meat, and they are presently unable to do so. What, then, is the most appropriate course of action?

אמר ליה לרב אידי בר אבין: מידי שמיע לך בהא? אמר ליה: הכי אמר רב תחליפא בר אבימי אמר שמואל: טוט אסר, וטוט שרי. אמר ליה: הני מילי – לממונא, אבל לאפקירותא – עד דחיילא שמתא עליה תלתין יומין.

He said to Rav Idi bar Avin: Have **you heard anything with regard to such** a case? Rav Idi bar Avin **said to** Abaye: **Rav Taḥlifa bar Avimi said** that **Shmuel said as follows:** A *shofar* **blast**[N] at the time of the ostracism **makes** it **binding, and a** *shofar* **blast releases** it.[H] In other words, the *shofar* should be sounded now, as it had been sounded when the decree of ostracism was pronounced, and it should be canceled, although thirty days have not passed. Abaye **said to him: This applies** in a case where one ignores **a monetary judgment** that was issued against him; **but** in a case where one **behaves disrespectfully,** there must be no release **until the** decree of **ostracism has been in effect for thirty days.**[N]

אלמא קסבר אביי: הני בי תלתא דשמיתו – לא אתו תלתא אחריני ושרו ליה.

The Gemara comments: **Apparently, Abaye maintains** that if **three** people **ostracized** one, **three others may not come and release him.** This is derived from the fact that Abaye was concerned about releasing the butcher from ostracism and did not delegate the task to someone else.

NOTES

Pressure [*hardafa*] – הרדפה: The *ge'onim* have a different version of the text, according to which the word *hardafa* refers to a method of imprisonment similar to solitary confinement. Similarly, many of the early authorities understood this term to be a separate type of punishment, different from ostracism and excommunication, such as lashes (see Rabbeinu Gershom *Me'or HaGola*), or that the quality of life of one who was admonished would be lowered through other types of persecution (Rid; see Rambam).

The Sages wish to enter – בעו רבנן למיעל: This is the text of the standard edition of the Talmud, and it is the text that Rashi follows (see Ritva). However, the manuscript of Rashi has a version that reads: To go, meaning that the Sages wished to return home and Abaye wished to keep them there until they nullified the decree of ostracism, in accordance with his opinion that three other people could nullify his decree of ostracism. This is the explanation of most commentaries, although many have a version that reads: That they wished to take leave of their teacher.

Blast [*tut*] – טוט: The word used by the Gemara here is a form of onomatopoeia and is meant to mimic the sound of the *shofar* itself. Similar words can be found in every language (Rabbeinu Shlomo ben HaYatom). According to *Tosafot* on tractate *Menaḥot*, this word is related to the term *tat*, which the Talmud explains to mean two. Here, this expression is referring to the two people who enacted the decree of ostracism, and it teaches that these two are also able to nullify it. In the manuscript of Rashi, it is explained that the numerical value of the word *tut* is twenty-four, which alludes to the twenty-four actions for which one may be ostracized.

Ostracism for thirty days – נידוי שלשים: In the Jerusalem Talmud an allusion to this time period is found in the verse: "But a whole month, until it comes out at your nostrils" (Numbers 11:20), referring to the punishment that God gave the Jewish people in the desert.

HALAKHA

Warning before ostracism – התראה לפני נידוי: When one is ostracized because he has not repaid loans, he is warned three times: On Monday, on Thursday, and on the following Monday, before he is ostracized. This ruling is in accordance with the opinion of Rav Ḥisda (*Shulḥan Arukh, Yoreh De'a* 334:1, and in the comment of the Rema).

Ostracism due to disrespect – נידוי לאפקירותא: When one is ostracized because he has shown disrespect, he is ostracized immediately. However, it is the accepted practice to first give him a warning (*Shakh*; *Shulḥan Arukh, Yoreh De'a* 334:1).

Nullifying ostracism – התרת נידוי: If one was told that he is ostracized for thirty days, his decree of ostracism may still be nullified immediately once he repays the money that he owes or once he makes amends with the one toward whom he acted disrespectfully. Some say that his decree of ostracism should be reversed after thirty days when he comes to the court after thirty days and asks for his decree of ostracism to be nullified, even if he has not repented. However, if he does not make such a request, he remains ostracized until his death. Some disagree and say that if one does not repent then he remains ostracized, and one who makes amends can have his decree of ostracism nullified only after thirty days (Rema). Others say that if he makes amends then his decree of ostracism may be nullified immediately (*Taz*; *Shulḥan Arukh, Yoreh De'a* 334:13).

דְּאִיבַּעְיָא לְהוּ: הָנֵי בֵּי תְלָתָא דְּשַׁמְּתוּהּ, מַהוּ לְמֵיתֵי תְּלָתָא אַחֲרִינֵי וְשָׁרוּ לֵיהּ? תָּא שְׁמַע: מְנוּדֶּה לָרַב – מְנוּדֶּה לַתַּלְמִיד; מְנוּדֶּה לַתַּלְמִיד – אֵינוֹ מְנוּדֶּה לָרַב.

As a dilemma was raised before the Sages: If **three** people **ostracized** someone, **what is** the *halakha* with regard to **three others coming and releasing him** from his decree of ostracism? The Gemara suggests: **Come** and **hear** a proof from that which is taught in a *baraita*: **One who was ostracized by the teacher** of Torah for having acted disrespectfully toward him **is** considered **ostracized with regard to the student,** and the latter must keep his distance from him. However, **one who was ostracized by the student is not** considered **ostracized with regard to the teacher.**[H]

מְנוּדֶּה לְעִירוֹ – מְנוּדֶּה לְעִיר אַחֶרֶת; מְנוּדֶּה לְעִיר אַחֶרֶת – אֵינוֹ מְנוּדֶּה לְעִירוֹ. מְנוּדֶּה לַנָּשִׂיא – מְנוּדֶּה לְכָל יִשְׂרָאֵל; מְנוּדֶּה לְכָל יִשְׂרָאֵל – אֵינוֹ מְנוּדֶּה לַנָּשִׂיא. רַבָּן שִׁמְעוֹן בֶּן גַּמְלִיאֵל אוֹמֵר: אֶחָד מִן הַתַּלְמִידִים שֶׁנִּידָּה וּמֵת – חֶלְקוֹ אֵינוֹ מוּפָר.

One who was ostracized by his own **city is** considered **ostracized with regard to another city.** However, **one who was ostracized by another city is not** considered **ostracized with regard to his** own **city.**[H] **One who was ostracized by the** *Nasi* of the Sanhedrin **is** considered **ostracized with regard to all the Jewish people;** but **one who was ostracized by all the Jewish people is not** considered **ostracized with regard to the** *Nasi* of the Sanhedrin.[H] **Rabban Shimon ben Gamliel says:** If **one of the students** sitting as a judge on the court **had ostracized** someone, **and he died** before releasing him from the decree of ostracism, **his portion** of the decree of ostracism **is not nullified.**

שְׁמַע מִינַּהּ תְּלָת. שְׁמַע מִינָּהּ: תַּלְמִיד שֶׁנִּידָּה לִכְבוֹדוֹ – נִידּוּיוֹ נִידּוּי. וּשְׁמַע מִינָּהּ: כָּל אֶחָד וְאֶחָד מֵיפֵר חֶלְקוֹ. וּשְׁמַע מִינָּהּ: הָנֵי בֵּי תְלָתָא דְּשַׁמְּתוּהּ – לָא אָתוּ תְּלָתָא אַחֲרִינֵי וְשָׁרוּ לֵיהּ.

The Gemara says: **Learn three** *halakhot* **from this** *baraita*. **Learn from this** that in the case of **a student who ostracizes** someone **due to** an insult to **his dignity**[H] and not because the ostracized person was guilty of some transgression, **his** decree of **ostracism is valid.** Were the case one where one was ostracized due to sin, everyone is required to respect the decree of ostracism, even the student's teacher. **And learn from this** that **each and every one** who participated in the decree of ostracism **nullifies his** own **portion**[H] of the decree of ostracism, as the *baraita* speaks of: His portion. **And learn from this** that if **three** people **ostracized** another person, **three other** people **may not come and nullify** the decree of ostracism. Were this not the case, it wouldn't matter if a certain person's portion was not nullified. His portion could be nullified by someone else.

אֲמַר אַמֵּימָר: הִלְכְתָא, הָנֵי בֵּי תְלָתָא דְּשַׁמְּתוּהּ – אָתוּ בֵּי תְלָתָא אַחֲרִינֵי וְשָׁרוּ לֵיהּ. אֲמַר לֵיהּ רַב אַשִׁי לְאַמֵּימַר: וְהָא תַּנְיָא רַבָּן שִׁמְעוֹן בֶּן גַּמְלִיאֵל אוֹמֵר: אֶחָד מִן הַתַּלְמִידִים שֶׁנִּידָּה וּמֵת – חֶלְקוֹ אֵינוֹ מוּפָר. מַאי לָאו – אֵינוֹ מוּפָר כְּלָל? לֹא, עַד דְּאָתוּ בֵּי תְלָתָא אַחֲרִינֵי וְשָׁרוּ לֵיהּ.

Ameimar[P] **said: The** *halakha* is that if **three** people **ostracize** another person, **three others may come and nullify** the decree of ostracism.[H] **Rav Ashi said to Ameimar: But isn't it taught** in a *baraita*: **Rabban Shimon ben Gamliel says:** If **one of the students had ostracized** another person, **and he died** before releasing him from the decree of ostracism, **his portion is not nullified? What, is it not** that **it is not nullified at all,** i.e., it cannot be nullified by another person? The Gemara rejects this argument: **No,** this means that the decree of ostracism remains in force **until three other people come and nullify** it.

HALAKHA

One who is ostracized by a teacher and a student – מְנוּדֶּה לָרַב וְלַתַּלְמִיד: One who has been ostracized by a teacher of Torah is also ostracized with respect to that teacher's students. However, other rabbis are not obligated to observe this ban (Rema).

If one is ostracized by a student, people who are not Torah scholars are bound by this ban, but this student's teacher and other Torah scholars are not (Rema). According to some authorities, scholars of lesser status than the student are bound by the ban (*Shakh*). In the presence of his teacher, a student may not ostracize another without permission (*Shulḥan Arukh, Yoreh De'a* 334:15).

One who is ostracized by his city and by another city – מְנוּדֶּה לְעִירוֹ וּלְעִיר אַחֶרֶת: One who has been ostracized by his city is ostracized by another city as well, even when it is bigger than his city (Rema). One who has been ostracized by another city is not ostracized by his city; however he is ostracized by other cities, since they are considered like the city from which he was originally ostracized.

This distinction applies only if one was ostracized because he acted disrespectfully. However, if one was ostracized because he did not listen to the ruling of the court or because he had sinned, then he is ostracized by his own city as well (*Shakh*). The people of his city are not required to treat him as though he were ostracized; however, he is required to observe the restrictions of ostracism on his own (*Pitḥei Teshuva*, citing *Levushei Serad*; *Shulḥan Arukh, Yoreh De'a* 334:20).

One who is ostracized by the *Nasi* of the Sanhedrin and by all the Jewish people – מְנוּדֶּה לַנָּשִׂיא וּלְיִשְׂרָאֵל: One who is ostracized by the *Nasi* of the Sanhedrin is ostracized by all Jewish people; however, one who is ostracized by the entire Jewish people is not ostracized by the *Nasi* of the Sanhedrin (*Shulḥan Arukh, Yoreh De'a* 334:21).

A student who ostracizes due to his dignity – תַּלְמִיד שֶׁנִּידָּה לִכְבוֹדוֹ: A Torah scholar is permitted to ostracize one who acts disrespectfully toward him, even if he did not explicitly show disrespect to him but intended to do so (Rema). If he showed disrespect in a manner that makes him worthy of being ostracized according to the *halakha*, then he is ostracized by everyone. However, if he showed disrespect in a different manner, he is ostracized only from people of smaller stature than that Sage (*Shulḥan Arukh, Yoreh De'a* 334:15).

Each and every one nullifies his portion – כָּל אֶחָד וְאֶחָד מֵיפֵר חֶלְקוֹ: One who has been ostracized by three people cannot have his decree of ostracism nullified by two of the three unless the third has given them permission. If many people were present when one was ostracized, all of them must participate in nullifying his decree of ostracism. All those who join in ostracizing a person must also join together in order to reverse his decree of ostracism. However, any of those involved in the ostracism may nullify his own portion by himself, and it is not necessary to gather them together, even if they were together when he was ostracized (*Shulḥan Arukh, Yoreh De'a* 334:26).

Another court may nullify ostracism – בֵּית דִּין אַחֵר הַמַּתִּיר נִידּוּי: If one was ostracized by a court of three people who have moved away, his decree of ostracism may be nullified by three other people, on condition that he has abandoned his sin. Rav Hai Gaon writes that those three must be of the same stature as the original three people, i.e., they must be as wise, as great, and of the same age (Rema). These requirements apply only if they perform the nullification within the initial period of ostracism (*Shakh*, citing Ra'avad; *Shulḥan Arukh, Yoreh De'a* 334:25).

PERSONALITIES

Ameimar – אַמֵּימָר: Ameimar was one of the great talmudic Sages of the fifth and sixth generation of Babylonian *amora'im*. Ameimar was born and raised in Neharde'a, where he studied and taught Torah, although it is likely that he studied with the Sages of Pumbedita as well. The teachings that he quotes are mainly from fifth-generation *amora'im* who were students of Abaye and Rava. It appears that he served as rabbi and religious judge in Neharde'a, where he established various rabbinic regulations. However, he also wielded influence in many other places, such as Meḥoza. The leaders of the following generation, e.g., Rav Ashi, were his students and came before him for judgment. He had at least one son, named Mar, who studied with Rav Ashi while Ameimar was still alive.

תנו רבנן: אין נידוי פחות משלשים יום, ואין נזיפה פחות משבעה ימים. ואף על פי שאין ראיה לדבר – זכר לדבר, שנאמר: "ואביה ירק ירק בפניה הלא תכלם שבעת ימים".

§ **The Sages taught** the following *baraita*: **Ostracism does not** apply **for less than** a period of **thirty days, and admonition,**[N] which is less severe than ostracism, **does not** apply **for less than** a period of **seven days.**[H] **And although there is no proof with regard to the matter,** i.e., the standard duration of admonition, there is **an allusion to the matter, as it is stated: "If her father had but spit in her face, should she not be ashamed for seven days?"** (Numbers 12:14). This implies that admonition lasts for seven days.

אמר רב חסדא: נידוי שלנו כנזיפה שלהן. ונזיפה דידהו שבעה, ותו לא? והא רבי שמעון בר רבי ובר קפרא הוו יתבי וקא גרסי, קשיא להו שמעתא. אמר ליה רבי שמעון לבר קפרא: דבר זה צריך רבי. אמר ליה בר קפרא לרבי שמעון: ומה רבי אומר בדבר זה?

Rav Ḥisda said: Our decree of **ostracism** in Babylonia has the power **of their admonition** in Eretz Yisrael. Since the authorities in Eretz Yisrael are ordained with the title Rabbi, their admonition carries more weight than a decree of ostracism issued in Babylonia. The Gemara asks: Is **their admonition** in Eretz Yisrael only **seven** days **and no more? But isn't** it related that **Rabbi Shimon, son of Rabbi** Yehuda HaNasi,[P] **and bar Kappara**[P] **were sitting and studying,** and they posed **a difficulty with** a certain ***halakha***. **Rabbi Shimon said to bar Kappara: This issue requires** my father, **Rabbi** Yehuda HaNasi, to explain it. **Bar Kappara said to Rabbi Shimon,** somewhat mockingly: **And what can** your father, **Rabbi** Yehuda HaNasi, **say**[N] **about this** issue? What can he add and teach us about it?

אזל אמר ליה לאבוה. איקפד. אתא בר קפרא לאיתחזויי ליה, אמר ליה: בר קפרא, איני מכירך מעולם. ידע דנקט מילתא בדעתיה, נהג נזיפותא בנפשיה תלתין יומין.

Rabbi Shimon **went and told his father,** Rabbi Yehuda HaNasi, what bar Kappara had said, and Rabbi Yehuda HaNasi **became angry** with him. When **bar Kappara came** at some later point **to visit,** Rabbi Yehuda HaNasi **said to him: Bar Kappara, I do not know you at all.** Bar Kappara **understood that** Rabbi Yehuda HaNasi **had taken** his **statement to heart,** i.e., was insulted. He subsequently **behaved** as if he had been **admonished,** as a self-imposed punishment, **for thirty days.**

שוב, פעם אחד גזר רבי שלא ישנו לתלמידים בשוק. מאי דרש? "חמוקי ירכיך כמו חלאים", מה ירך בסתר

Once again, on another occasion, Rabbi Yehuda HaNasi **decreed that students not be taught in the marketplace** but only in a study hall. **What** verse did he **expound** to serve as the basis for this decree? The verse states: **"Your rounded thighs are like jewels,** the work of the hands of an artist" (Song of Songs 7:2). **Just as a thigh is** ordinarily **hidden** and kept covered with clothes,

NOTES

Admonition – נְזִיפָה: The punishment of admonition is not expressed through the way others act toward the admonished person. Rather, the onus is on this person to conduct himself as if he had been admonished, like one who has been publicly shamed and who is embarrassed to show his face in public (Ra'avad).

And what can Rabbi Yehuda HaNasi say – וּמָה רַבִּי אוֹמֵר: Most commentaries who explain this statement claim that Rabbi Shimon understood that bar Kappara wished to mock him and to state: This question is challenging, and will Rabbi Yehuda HaNasi have anything to say about it? Others suggest that he was upset because bar Kappara used the title Rabbi and not the greater honorific *Rabbeinu*, meaning: Our Rabbi (Ran).

HALAKHA

Ostracism and admonition – נִידּוּי וּנְזִיפָה: Generally, ostracism lasts for thirty days, and admonition lasts for seven days. However, in Babylonia ostracism lasts for seven days and admonition lasts for only one day, in accordance with the opinion of Rav Ḥisda (*Shulḥan Arukh*, *Yoreh De'a* 334:1).

PERSONALITIES

Rabbi Shimon, son of Rabbi Yehuda HaNasi – רַבִּי שִׁמְעוֹן בַּר רַבִּי: Rabbi Shimon was the youngest son of Rabbi Yehuda HaNasi and his close student. In addition, he was especially close to Rabbi Ḥiyya, who also his close friend and partner in the silk business. In many places, it is noted that he was very meticulous about his honor, which he saw as related to the honor of the office of *Nasi*. In particular, he was careful to ensure that nothing he did would imply offense to his great father. At least one of his sayings is found in the Mishna itself, although he was actually in the transitional generation between *tanna'im* and *amora'im*. His sayings are often introduced by the word *itmar*, meaning: It was said, a term used for *amora'im*.

Rabbi Yehuda HaNasi considered Rabbi Shimon to be a great scholar. Before Rabbi Yehuda HaNasi's death, he appointed Rabbi Shimon to be the *Ḥakham*, which was the third-highest position in the Sanhedrin after the *Nasi* and the Head of the Court, although he appointed Rabbi Shimon's older brother, Rabban Gamliel, to replace him as *Nasi*.

Bar Kappara – בַּר קַפָּרָא: Bar Kappara was one of the Sages of Eretz Yisrael during the transitional generation between *tanna'im* and *amora'im*. His first name is unknown, although some say his name was Shimon. It is unclear whether he was related to Elazar HaKafar, and if so, what their relationship was. Bar Kappara was one of the more important students of Rabbi Yehuda HaNasi and a colleague of Rabbi Ḥiyya. He assembled a unique collection of *baraitot* that are introduced in the Talmud with the words: Bar Kappara teaches. His halakhic statements are mentioned many times in the Talmud. His aggadic statements and expositions appear in both the Babylonian and Jerusalem Talmud.

Bar Kappara was well known for his sharp personality and intellect. He was considered to be well-versed in the Bible, so much so that even Rabbi Yehuda HaNasi asked him about the meaning of certain verses. Because he was prone to making harsh statements, it sometimes happened that certain members of Rabbi Yehuda HaNasi's family were insulted; however, Rabbi Yehuda HaNasi himself thought very highly of bar Kappara, praised him, and was the first to offer a eulogy for him. Almost all of the first generation of *amora'im* were his students, including his nephew, Rabbi Yehuda ben Padda.

He lived, at least toward the end of his life, in the Galilee and was buried in the city of Parod.

PERSONALITIES

Rabbi Ḥiyya – רַבִּי חִיָּיא: Rabbi Ḥiyya, son of Abba, from the Babylonian city of Kafri, was one of the last of the *tanna'im*. He was a contemporary of Rabbi Yehuda HaNasi.

Rabbi Ḥiyya was born to an important family that traced its roots to King David and included many important Sages. Rabbi Ḥiyya was recognized as a leading Torah scholar even while living in Babylonia. As the Gemara attests, his efforts were credited by many with saving the Torah from oblivion. Upon moving to Eretz Yisrael, Rabbi Ḥiyya became a close friend and colleague of Rabbi Yehuda HaNasi. He also became a close friend of Rabbi Yehuda HaNasi's son, Rabbi Shimon, with whom he became partners in trade. A powerful force in his generation, he also worked closely with Rav, who was recognized as the leader of the Jewish people in Babylonia, but still learned from Rabbi Ḥiyya.

Rabbi Ḥiyya's greatest work was his *Tosefta*, a collection of oral traditions that were not included in the Mishna compiled by Rabbi Yehuda HaNasi. This collection, which was assembled with the assistance of Rabbi Ḥiyya's disciple-colleague, Rabbi Oshaya, was viewed as authoritative to the extent that the Talmud states that any *baraita* that was not found in his work should not be discussed in the study hall (*Ḥullin* 141a–b). Some hold that Rabbi Ḥiyya edited the *Tosefta* that exists today.

While it appears that Rabbi Ḥiyya was financially supported by others when he first came to Eretz Yisrael, ultimately he was a successful merchant who dealt in international business ventures, and in particular the silk trade. He had twin daughters, Pazi and Tavi, and twin sons, Yehuda and Ḥizkiya, who were leading Sages in the generation between the *tanna'im* and *amora'im*. His sons apparently took over his yeshiva in Tiberias after his passing.

NOTES

Iyya, who is calling you outside – עִיָּיא, מִי קוֹרֵא לְךָ בַּחוּץ: When Rabbi Yehuda HaNasi called Rabbi Ḥiyya by this name it was meant to show his displeasure. Rabbi Ḥiyya was unable to pronounce guttural consonants, and in his accent *ḥet* and *ayin* sounded the same. Therefore, calling him Iyya was a way of mocking his accent. In addition, Rabbi Yehuda asked: Who is calling you outside, in order to hint that he taught Torah outside (Maharsha). Others claim that he was suggesting that someone else had called him outside, as if to say: I, Rabbi Yehuda HaNasi, did not call you (Rabbi Shlomo ben HaYatom; see Rashi).

If you read, you did not read a second time – אִם קָרִיתָ לֹא שָׁנִיתָ: Some explain this expression as follows: If you have read this only one time without reviewing it, then you certainly have forgotten what you read. If you have read it a second and third time and have not forgotten it, then certainly it was not explained to you. Therefore, you do not properly understand what is written in this verse (Commentary on *Moed Katan*).

Kalla – כַּלָּה: The *kalla* is a uniquely Babylonian Jewish tradition, though it may have its early roots in Eretz Yisrael. The *kalla* is essentially a gathering of all the Sages. It took place twice a year, in Adar and in Elul, and focused on a specific tractate, which the Sages would analyze and interpret. Thousands of people would attend the days of the *kalla* [*yarḥei kalla*], which also served as an extraordinary occasion of paying homage to the Torah.

אַף דִּבְרֵי תוֹרָה בְּסֵתֶר.

so too, **the words of Torah,** which are "the work of the hands of an artist," i.e., God, must remain **hidden** in the study hall.

יָצָא רַבִּי חִיָּיא וְשָׁנָה לִשְׁנֵי בְּנֵי אֶחָיו בַּשּׁוּק, לְרַב וּלְרַבָּה בַּר בַּר חָנָה. שְׁמַע רַבִּי – אִיקְפַּד. אֲתָא רַבִּי חִיָּיא לְאִיתְחֲזוּיֵי לֵיהּ. אֲמַר לֵיהּ: עִיָּיא, מִי קוֹרֵא לְךָ בַּחוּץ? יָדַע דְּנָקֵט מִילְּתָא בְּדַעְתֵּיהּ, נְהַג נְזִיפוּתָא בְּנַפְשֵׁיהּ תְּלָתִין יוֹמִין.

Despite Rabbi Yehuda HaNasi's decree, **Rabbi Ḥiyya**[P] **went out and taught his two nephews, Rav and Rabba bar bar Ḥana, in the marketplace. Rabbi** Yehuda HaNasi **heard** what he had done and **became angry** with him. When **Rabbi Ḥiyya came** at some later date **to visit him,** Rabbi Yehuda HaNasi mockingly **said to him: Iyya, who is calling you outside?**[N] By asking this question Rabbi Yehuda HaNasi was intimating that Rabbi Ḥiyya should leave his house. Rabbi Ḥiyya **understood that** Rabbi Yehuda HaNasi **had taken the matter to heart** and was insulted, and so **he conducted** himself as if he had been **admonished,** as a self-imposed punishment, **for thirty days.**

בְּיוֹם תְּלָתִין שְׁלַח לֵיהּ: תָּא; הֲדַר שְׁלַח לֵיהּ דְּלָא לֵיתֵי.

On the thirtieth day, Rabbi Yehuda HaNasi **sent him** a message, saying: **Come** and visit me. However, **he later** reversed his opinion and **sent him** another message, telling him **not to come.**

מֵעִיקָּרָא מַאי סָבַר וּלְבַסּוֹף מַאי סָבַר? מֵעִיקָּרָא סָבַר: מִקְצָת הַיּוֹם כְּכוּלּוֹ; וּלְבַסּוֹף סָבַר: לָא אָמְרִינַן מִקְצָת הַיּוֹם כְּכוּלּוֹ.

The Gemara asks: **At the outset what did he hold, and ultimately what did he hold? Initially,** Rabbi Yehuda HaNasi **held that** the legal status of **part of the day is like** that of **an entire** day, and since the thirtieth day already begun, Rabbi Ḥiyya's time of admonition had ended. **But ultimately he held** that with regard to this issue **we do not say** that the legal status of **part of the day is like** that **of an entire** day.

לְסוֹף אֲתָא. אֲמַר לֵיהּ: אַמַּאי אָתֵית? אֲמַר לֵיהּ: דִּשְׁלַח לִי מָר דְּלֵיתֵי. וְהָא שְׁלַחִי לָךְ דְּלָא תֵּיתֵי? אֲמַר לֵיהּ: זֶה רָאִיתִי, וְזֶה – לֹא רָאִיתִי. קָרֵי עֲלֵיהּ: "בִּרְצוֹת ה׳ דַּרְכֵי אִישׁ גַּם אוֹיְבָיו יַשְׁלִים אִתּוֹ".

In the end Rabbi Ḥiyya **came** on that same day. Rabbi Yehuda HaNasi **asked him: Why have you come?** Rabbi Ḥiyya **responded: Because** you, **Master, sent** me a message that **I should come.** He said to him: **But I sent** you a second message **that you should not come. He responded: This** messenger that you sent, i.e., the first one, **I saw** him and I did as he said, **but that** messenger, i.e., the second one, **I did not see.** Rabbi Yehuda HaNasi **read** the verse **about** Rabbi Ḥiyya: **"When a man's ways please the Lord, He makes even his enemies to be at peace with him"** (Proverbs 16:7), as it was clear to him that Rabbi Ḥiyya had merited divine assistance.

מַאי טַעְמָא עֲבַד מָר הָכִי? אֲמַר לֵיהּ: דִּכְתִיב: "חָכְמוֹת בַּחוּץ תָּרֹנָּה". אֲמַר לֵיהּ: אִם קָרִיתָ – לֹא שָׁנִיתָ, וְאִם שָׁנִיתָ – לֹא שִׁילַּשְׁתָּ, וְאִם שִׁילַּשְׁתָּ, לֹא פֵּירְשׁוּ לָךְ.

§ Concerning the issue with which the entire incident had begun, Rabbi Yehuda HaNasi asked Rabbi Ḥiyya: **What is the reason that** you, **the Master, acted as** you did, ignoring my instructions not to teach Torah in the marketplace? Rabbi Ḥiyya **said to him: As it is written: "Wisdom cries aloud in the streets"** (Proverbs 1:20), which implies that Torah should be publicized in the streets. Rabbi Yehuda HaNasi **said to him: If you read** this verse once, **you** certainly **did not read** it **a second time**[N] in greater depth; **and if you read it a second time, you** certainly **did not read** it **a third time;** and **if you read** it **a third time,** then **it was not** adequately **explained to you,** as it is clear that you do not understand it properly.

"חָכְמוֹת בַּחוּץ תָּרֹנָּה" – כִּדְרָבָא. דְּאָמַר רָבָא: כָּל הָעוֹסֵק בַּתּוֹרָה מִבִּפְנִים – תּוֹרָתוֹ מַכְרֶזֶת עָלָיו מִבַּחוּץ.

The words: **"Wisdom cries aloud in the streets,"** should be understood **in accordance with** the opinion **of Rava. As Rava said:** With regard to **everyone who occupies himself with Torah** study **inside** the privacy of his home, **his Torah** knowledge **will proclaim his** greatness **outside,** as it will be revealed to the masses and they will see his greatness.

וְהָא כְּתִיב: "לֹא מֵרֹאשׁ בַּסֵּתֶר דִּבַּרְתִּי"! הַהוּא בְּיוֹמֵי דְּכַלָּה.

The Gemara asks: **But isn't it written: "From the beginning I have not spoken in secret"** (Isaiah 48:16), implying that the Torah should be taught and proclaimed in public? The Gemara answers: **That** verse is referring to **the days of the *kalla*,**[N] the gathering for Torah study held during Elul and Adar, when many people come to listen to Torah discourses. During this time, it is not only permitted but even recommended to teach Torah to the masses. In this way, the verse can be explained in accordance with the opinion of Rabbi Yehuda HaNasi.

וְרַבִּי חִיָּיא, הַאי "חַמּוּקֵי יְרֵכַיִךְ" מַאי עָבֵיד לַהּ? מוֹקֵי לַהּ בִּצְדָקָה וּבִגְמִילוּת חֲסָדִים.

The Gemara asks: **And what did Rabbi Ḥiyya do with this** verse: **"Your rounded thighs are like jewels"?** How did he understand it? This verse implies that the Torah must be kept hidden in the study hall and not publicized in the marketplace. The Gemara explains: **He interprets it** not as a reference to Torah, but as referring **to** acts of **charity and loving-kindness,** which should certainly be performed in private.

אַלְמָא, נְזִיפָה דִּידְהוּ תְּלָתִין יוֹמִין! נְזִיפַת נָשִׂיא שָׁאנֵי.

This incident demonstrates **that, apparently, admonition of those** who live in Eretz Yisrael lasts for **thirty days** and not for seven days. The Gemara answers that this is not a conclusive proof, since Rabbi Yehuda HaNasi was the *Nasi*. **The admonition of the *Nasi*** of the Sanhedrin **is different** i.e., more severe, than the admonition of anyone else.

וּנְזִיפָה דִּידַן כַּמָּה הָוֵי? חַד יוֹמָא. כִּי הָא דִּשְׁמוּאֵל וּמָר עוּקְבָא, כִּי הָווּ יָתְבִי גָּרְסִי שְׁמַעְתָּא – הֲוָה יָתֵיב מָר עוּקְבָא קַמֵּיהּ דִּשְׁמוּאֵל בְּרִחוּק אַרְבַּע אַמּוֹת, וְכִי הָווּ יָתְבִי בְּדִינָא – הֲוָה יָתֵיב שְׁמוּאֵל קַמֵּיהּ דְּמָר עוּקְבָא בְּרִחוּק אַרְבַּע אַמּוֹת. וְהָווּ חָיְיקִי לֵיהּ דּוּכְתָּא לְמָר עוּקְבָא בְּצִיפְתָּא וְיָתֵיב עִילָּוֵיהּ, כִּי הֵיכִי דְּלִישְׁתַּמְעָן מִילֵּיהּ.

The Gemara asks: **And how long is our admonition**[H] in Babylonia? The Gemara answers: It is only **one day, as in** the case involving **Shmuel and** the Exilarch **Mar Ukva.**[P] **When they would sit and study *halakha*, Mar Ukva would sit before Shmuel at a distance of four cubits** as a sign of respect. Mar Ukva would conduct himself as though Shmuel were his teacher because Shmuel was much greater than him in Torah matters. **And when they would sit** together **in judgment, Shmuel would sit before Mar Ukva at a distance of four cubits** because Mar Ukva was the Exilarch and the chief judge. **But they would lower a place for Mar Ukva in the matting** upon which he sat, **and he would sit on it so that he could hear** Shmuel's **words**[N] of Torah even when they were engaged in judgment.

כָּל יוֹמָא הֲוָה מְלַוֵּי לֵיהּ מָר עוּקְבָא לִשְׁמוּאֵל עַד אוּשְׁפִּיזֵיהּ. יוֹמָא חַד אִיטְּרִיד בְּדִינֵיהּ. הֲוָה אָזֵיל שְׁמוּאֵל בַּתְרֵיהּ. כִּי מְטָא לְבֵיתֵיהּ אֲמַר לֵיהּ: לָא נְגַהּ לָךְ? לִישְׁרֵי לִי מָר בְּתִיגְרֵיהּ! יְדַע דִּנְקַט מִילְּתָא בְּדַעְתֵּיהּ, נְהַג נְזִיפוּתָא בְּנַפְשֵׁיהּ חַד יוֹמָא.

Every day, Mar Ukva would accompany Shmuel to his lodgings, in the manner that a student would show honor toward his teacher. **One day,** Mar Ukva **was** so heavily **preoccupied with a case** that had been brought before him for judgment that he did not realize that **Shmuel was walking behind him** to show him respect due to his position as the Exilarch. **When** Mar Ukva **reached his home,** Shmuel **said to him: Is it not enough for you**[N] that I accompanied you until here? **Release me, Master, from my obligation,** so that I may return home. Mar Ukva **understood that** Shmuel **had taken the matter to heart** and was insulted. Therefore, **he conducted** himself as if he had been **admonished, for one day** as a self-imposed punishment.

הַהִיא אִיתְּתָא דַּהֲוַות יָתְבָה בִּשְׁבִילָא, הֲוַות פָּשְׁטָה כַּרְעָהּ וְקָא מְנִיפָה חוּשְׁלָאֵי, וַהֲוָה חָלֵיף וְאָזֵיל צוּרְבָא מֵרַבָּנָן, וְלָא אִיכַּנְעָה מִקַּמֵּיהּ. אֲמַר: כַּמָּה חֲצִיפָא הַהִיא אִיתְּתָא! אֲתַאי לְקַמֵּיהּ דְּרַב נַחְמָן. אֲמַר לָהּ: מִי שָׁמַעַתְּ שַׁמְתָּא מִפּוּמֵיהּ? אֲמַרָה לֵיהּ: לָא. אֲמַר לָהּ: זִילִי, נְהוֹגִי נְזִיפוּתָא חַד יוֹמָא בְּנַפְשִׁיךְ.

It was related that **a certain woman was sitting alongside a path** with **her leg extended** while **she was sifting barley. A Torah scholar passed** by her on this path, **but she did not yield to him** and move her leg to make room for him. **He said: How rude is that woman!** The woman **came before Rav Naḥman** to ask if this statement should be deemed as excommunication. **He said to her: Did you hear** the word **excommunication** explicitly issue **from his mouth? She said to him: No. He said to her:** If this is the case, then **go and observe an admonition for one day,** as it appears that the Torah scholar sought only to admonish you.

HALAKHA

Our admonition – נְזִיפָה דִּידַן: Admonition lasts for one day (*Shulḥan Arukh, Yoreh De'a* 334:1).

PERSONALITIES

Mar Ukva – מָר עוּקְבָא: Mar Ukva was the Exilarch during the time of Rav and Shmuel. Generally, the title *Mar* was added to the name of the Exilarch and those in his family. He was a direct descendant of the house of David and was appointed by the Persians as Exilarch. For these two reasons, Mar Ukva had authority to rule in monetary cases. In this regard, the great Sages of Babylonia deferred to the Exilarch, and Mar Ukva's court, which had a permanent location near the city of Sura, was considered to be the most respected court.

Mar Ukva was very knowledgeable in Torah, and based upon several sources it seems that he saw himself as the primary student of Shmuel. In fact, many of Shmuel's statements are transmitted through Mar Ukva. There was also a close friendship between them, and Shmuel served as Mar Ukva's doctor. Apparently, Mar Ukva outlived Shmuel.

In addition to his greatness in Torah, Mar Ukva was also very generous. Many stories are told about the charity that he gave, which was not only given in large sums but was also given secretly, so as not to embarrass the recipients. Similarly, due to his modest nature he did not use his position of power to fight those who tried to harm him. Several Sages from the following generation cite statements in his name.

NOTES

So that he could hear Shmuel's words – כִּי הֵיכִי דְּלִישְׁתַּמְעָן מִילֵּיהּ: According to this version of the text, they would give Mar Ukva an elevated seat, on a cushion, so that his words could be heard and so people would humbly accept them (*Talmid Rabbeinu Yeḥiel of Paris*).

Some explain that this statement emphasizes that they would lower Mar Ukva's seat a bit so that his seat would not be much higher than Shmuel's, and that Shmuel was honored by being offered a position from which his words could be heard (manuscript of Rashi). The version of Rashi printed on the page seems to relate to a different version of the talmudic text. According to this version, Mar Ukva lowered his seat so that he would not be far from Shmuel, in order to hear what Shmuel said.

Is it not enough [*nega*] for you – לָא נְגַהּ לָךְ: Some explain that this expression is related to *noga*, light, and Shmuel implied: Have you not yet been enlightened as to how much you are troubling me (Rabbi Shlomo ben HaYatom)? Others claim that the word *nega* means evening, and he implied: Will it become dark while you are still dragging me behind you (manuscript of Rashi)?

זוּטְרָא בַּר טוֹבִיָּה הֲוָה קָפָסֵיק סִידְרָא קַמֵּיהּ דְּרַב יְהוּדָה. כִּי מְטָא לְהַאי פְּסוּקָא: ״וְאֵלֶּה דִּבְרֵי דָוִד הָאַחֲרוֹנִים״, אֲמַר לֵיהּ: אַחֲרוֹנִים – מִכְּלָל דְּאִיכָּא רִאשׁוֹנִים. רִאשׁוֹנִים מַאי נִינְהוּ?

§ **Zutra bar Toviyya** was once **reading the portion**[N] of the Bible **before Rav Yehuda. When he reached the verse: "Now these are the last words of David"** (II Samuel 23:1), Zutra bar Toviyya **said to** Rav Yehuda: If it is written that these are the **last** of David's words, **by inference there are first**[N] words as well. If this is the case, **what are these first** words of David? Prior to this, it mentions only David's song, but not his words.

שָׁתֵיק וְלָא אֲמַר לֵיהּ וְלָא מִידִּי. הֲדַר אֲמַר לֵיהּ: אַחֲרוֹנִים מִכְּלָל דְּאִיכָּא רִאשׁוֹנִים. רִאשׁוֹנִים מַאי הִיא? אֲמַר לֵיהּ: מַאי דַּעְתָּךְ? דְּלָא יָדַע פֵּירוּשָׁא דְּהַאי קְרָא – לָאו גַּבְרָא רַבָּה הוּא? יָדַע דִּנְקַט מִילְּתָא בְּדַעְתֵּיהּ, נְהַג נְזִיפוּתָא בְּנַפְשֵׁיהּ חַד יוֹמָא.

Rav Yehuda **remained silent and said nothing to him.** Zutra bar Toviyya thought that Rav Yehuda did not hear what he had said, so he **then said to him** a second time: If it is written that these are the **last** of David's words, **by inference there are first** words as well. If this is the case, **what are these first** words of David? **He said to him: What do you think?** Do you think that anyone **who does not know the meaning of this verse is not a great man?** Why are you stressing the fact that I do not know the answer to your question? Zutra bar Toviyya **understood that** Rav Yehuda **had taken the matter to heart** and was insulted. Therefore, **he conducted** himself as if had been **admonished for one day** as a self-imposed punishment.

וּדְאָתָן עֲלָהּ, מִיהָא אַחֲרוֹנִים – מִכְּלָל דְּאִיכָּא רִאשׁוֹנִים, רִאשׁוֹנִים מַאי הִיא? ״וַיְדַבֵּר דָּוִד לַה׳ אֶת דִּבְרֵי הַשִּׁירָה הַזֹּאת בְּיוֹם הִצִּיל ה׳ אוֹתוֹ מִכַּף כׇּל אוֹיְבָיו וּמִכַּף שָׁאוּל״.

The Gemara asks: **But** now **that we have come** to discuss this issue, since the verse mentions David's **last** words, **by inference there are** also **first** words. **What** then **are these first** words of David? The Gemara answers: The first words are: **"And David spoke to the Lord the words of this song in the day that the Lord delivered him out of the hand of his enemies, and out of the hand of Saul"** (II Samuel 22:1), as that song is also referred to as words.

אָמַר לוֹ הַקָּדוֹשׁ בָּרוּךְ הוּא לְדָוִד: דָּוִד, שִׁירָה אַתָּה אוֹמֵר עַל מַפַּלְתּוֹ שֶׁל שָׁאוּל? אִלְמָלֵי אַתָּה שָׁאוּל וְהוּא דָּוִד – אִיבַּדְתִּי כַּמָּה דָּוִד מִפָּנָיו.

The Gemara elaborates: **The Holy One, Blessed be He, said to David: David, do you recite a song over the fall of Saul? Had you been Saul**[N] **and he were David,** then **I would have destroyed many Davids before him.** Although I decreed that Saul's kingdom would not continue, as an individual he was far greater and more important than you.

הַיְינוּ דִּכְתִיב: ״שִׁגָּיוֹן לְדָוִד אֲשֶׁר שָׁר לַה׳ עַל דִּבְרֵי כוּשׁ בֶּן יְמִינִי״. וְכִי כּוּשׁ שְׁמוֹ? וַהֲלֹא שָׁאוּל שְׁמוֹ! אֶלָּא: מַה כּוּשִׁי מְשׁוּנֶּה בְּעוֹרוֹ – אַף שָׁאוּל מְשׁוּנֶּה בְּמַעֲשָׂיו.

The response to this admonishment **is** found in the verse, **as it is written: "Shiggaion of David, which he sang to the Lord, concerning the words of Cush the Benjaminite"** (Psalms 7:1). **Is Cush his name? Saul is his name.**[N] **Rather,** this is a designation that indicates: **Just as a Cushite,** a native of the ancient kingdom of Cush in eastern Africa, **is distinguished by his** dark **skin, so too, Saul was distinguished by his actions,**[N] as he was absolutely righteous and performed many good deeds. Therefore, David uses the word *shiggaion* as an allusion to the error [*shegia*] that he had made when he sang a song of praise over Saul's downfall.

כַּיּוֹצֵא בַּדָּבָר אַתָּה אוֹמֵר: ״עַל אוֹדוֹת הָאִשָּׁה הַכּוּשִׁית אֲשֶׁר לָקָח״. וְכִי כּוּשִׁית שְׁמָהּ? וַהֲלֹא צִיפּוֹרָה שְׁמָהּ! אֶלָּא: מַה כּוּשִׁית מְשׁוּנָּה בְּעוֹרָהּ – אַף צִיפּוֹרָה מְשׁוּנָּה בְּמַעֲשֶׂיהָ. כַּיּוֹצֵא בַּדָּבָר אַתָּה אוֹמֵר: ״וַיִּשְׁמַע עֶבֶד מֶלֶךְ הַכּוּשִׁי״. וְכִי כּוּשִׁי שְׁמוֹ? וַהֲלֹא צִדְקִיָּה שְׁמוֹ! אֶלָּא: מַה כּוּשִׁי מְשׁוּנֶּה בְּעוֹרוֹ – אַף צִדְקִיָּה מְשׁוּנֶּה בְּמַעֲשָׂיו.

The Gemara notes: **Similarly, you can explain** the verse: "And Miriam and Aaron spoke against Moses **due to the Cushite woman whom he had married,** for he had taken a Cushite woman" (Numbers 12:1). **But is her name Cushite? Zipporah is her name. Rather, just as a Cushite is distinguished by his** dark skin, **so too, Zipporah was distinguished by her actions.** The Gemara continues: **Similarly, you can explain** the verse: **"Now when Ebed-Melech the Cushite heard"** (Jeremiah 38:7). **Is his name Cushite? Zedekiah is his name. Rather, just as a Cushite is distinguished by his** dark skin, **so too, Zedekiah was distinguished by his** righteous **actions.**[N]

כַּיּוֹצֵא בַּדָּבָר אַתָּה אוֹמֵר: ״הֲלֹא כִבְנֵי כוּשִׁיִּים אַתֶּם לִי בֵּית יִשְׂרָאֵל״. וְכִי כּוּשִׁיִּים שְׁמָן? וַהֲלֹא יִשְׂרָאֵל שְׁמָן! אֶלָּא: מַה כּוּשִׁי מְשׁוּנֶּה בְּעוֹרוֹ – אַף יִשְׂרָאֵל מְשׁוּנִּין בְּמַעֲשֵׂיהֶן מִכׇּל הָאוּמּוֹת.

Similarly, you can explain the verse: **"Are you not as much Mine as the children of the Cushites, O children of Israel?"** (Amos 9:7). **Is their name Cushite? Israel is their name. Rather, just as a Cushite stands out** because of his dark skin, **so too, the Jewish people are distinguished by their actions,** and they are different **from all the** other **nations.**

NOTES

Reading the portion – קָפְסֵיק סִידְרָא: It was customary for the Sages of the Talmud to divide the Bible into portions, so that they would complete all of the Bible in one year. This practice is similar to the current division of the Torah into weekly portions. Perhaps the Sages' division is parallel to the divisions that are used today (see *Talmid Rabbeinu Yeḥiel of Paris*).

Last, by inference there are first – אַחֲרוֹנִים, מִכְּלָל דְּאִיכָּא רִאשׁוֹנִים: According to Rashi, Zutra bar Toviyya asked: How can the verse write "these are the last words of David" (II Samuel 23:1), when "words of David" is a unique expression found only here in the Bible? Where is it possible to find other words of David? Where is similar language used?

Other commentaries understand that Zutra bar Toviyya assumes that the verse in II Samuel, chapter 23, actually refers back to the previous chapter, as the word "these" in "these are the last words of David" can function as a concluding remark on II Samuel, chapter 22, which is a song that David sang after he was saved from Saul. If this is the case, Zutra bar Toviyya asked: Where else did David speak about Saul (Ra'avad; *Tosefot HaRosh*)?

Alternatively, there are those who maintain that "the words of David" indicates prophecy. If so, Zutra bar Toviyya asked: Where is there another case where David relayed words that God had spoken to him, but the text does not explicitly say so (Ritva)?

Had you been Saul – אִלְמָלֵי אַתָּה שָׁאוּל: Many explain that this expression means: Had it not been an issue of destiny, Saul would have prevailed, as he surpassed you, David, in righteousness (Rashi). Some say: If you were Saul, meaning: If you were humble like Saul, then this attribute alone would tip the scale in your favor (see Rabbeinu Gershom *Meor HaGola*). Others say that were it not for the heavenly decree that you, David, would rule, then you would not have been worthy of inheriting the kingship from Saul (Rabbi Shlomo ben HaYatom). Similarly, others explain that were it not stated from the outset that David become king after Saul, then he would not have ruled. It is stated elsewhere in the Talmud that because of his prestigious lineage, Saul's rule did not continue, unlike David, whose lineage was questionable (*Yoma* 22b; Ran; *Tosefot HaRosh*). Others suggest that the tribe of Benjamin, to which Saul belonged, was not chosen to rule forever. Instead, David's tribe, the tribe of Judah, was designated to have lasting monarchy (*Iyyun Ya'akov*).

Cush and Saul – כּוּשׁ וְשָׁאוּל: Some explain that the names Cush and Kish are actually the same name, and the verse in Psalms alludes to Saul, son of Kish (*Talmid Rabbeinu Yeḥiel of Paris*).

Saul was distinguished by his actions – שָׁאוּל מְשׁוּנֶּה בְּמַעֲשָׂיו: Some explain that the term distinguished is referring to Saul's righteousness and humility. Others state that it points to the fact that he was physically outstanding, as he was extremely tall.

Similarly, some say that the term distinguished, in the case of Zipporah, is referring to her good deeds and modesty, while others claim that it points to her unique beauty (manuscript of Rashi; *HaKotev*).

Zedekiah was distinguished by his actions – צִדְקִיָּה מְשׁוּנֶּה בְּמַעֲשָׂיו: According to this explanation, the verse is read as follows: The servant [*eved*] of the king [*melekh*] called Cushite. Zedekiah was called this because he was righteous in a generation of wicked people (*Talmid Rabbeinu Yeḥiel of Paris*).

אָמַר רַבִּי שְׁמוּאֵל בַּר נַחְמָנִי אָמַר רַבִּי יוֹנָתָן: מַאי דִּכְתִיב: ״נְאֻם דָּוִד בֶּן יִשַׁי וּנְאֻם הַגֶּבֶר הוּקַם עָל״? נְאֻם דָּוִד בֶּן יִשַׁי, שֶׁהֵקִים עוּלָּהּ שֶׁל תְּשׁוּבָה.

§ Having mentioned the last words of David, the Gemara continues to explain other expressions in that passage. **Rabbi Shmuel bar Naḥmani said in the name of Rabbi Yonatan: What is** the meaning of that **which is written: "The saying of David, son of Yishai, and the saying of the man who was raised up on high** [*al*]" (II Samuel 23:1)? It means as follows: **The saying of David, son of Yishai, who raised the yoke of** [*ulla*] **repentance,**[N] as through his actions he taught the power of repentance. The word *al*, on high, and the word *ulla* are comprised of the same consonants in Hebrew.

״אָמַר אֱלֹהֵי יִשְׂרָאֵל לִי דִּבֶּר צוּר יִשְׂרָאֵל מוֹשֵׁל בָּאָדָם צַדִּיק מוֹשֵׁל יִרְאַת אֱלֹהִים״. מַאי קָאָמַר? אֲמַר רַבִּי אַבָּהוּ, הָכִי קָאָמַר, אָמַר אֱלֹהֵי יִשְׂרָאֵל: לִי דִּבֶּר צוּר יִשְׂרָאֵל, אֲנִי מוֹשֵׁל בָּאָדָם. מִי מוֹשֵׁל בִּי? צַדִּיק, שֶׁאֲנִי גּוֹזֵר גְּזֵרָה וּמְבַטְּלָהּ.

The passage continues: **"The God of Israel said, the Rock of Israel spoke to me, He that rules over men must be righteous, ruling in the fear of God"** (II Samuel 23:3). The Gemara asks: **What is** this verse **saying?** What does it mean? **Rabbi Abbahu said: This is what** the verse **is saying: The God of Israel said, the Rock of Israel spoke to me:** Although **I rule over man, who rules over Me? It is a righteous person.** How is it possible to say that a righteous person rules over God, as it were? **As I,** God, **issue a decree** and the righteous person **nullifies it.**

״אֵלֶּה שְׁמוֹת הַגִּבּוֹרִים אֲשֶׁר לְדָוִד יוֹשֵׁב בַּשֶּׁבֶת״ וגו׳. מַאי קָאָמַר? אֲמַר רַבִּי אַבָּהוּ, הָכִי קָאָמַר, וְאֵלֶּה שְׁמוֹת גְּבוּרוֹתָיו שֶׁל דָּוִד:

Similarly, the verse states there: **"These are the names of David's warriors; Josheb-Basshebeth** a Tahchemonite, chief of the captains; the same was Adino the Eznite; he raised his spear against eight hundred, whom he slew at one time" (II Samuel 23:8). The Gemara asks: **What is** this verse **saying? Rabbi Abbahu said: This is what** the verse **is saying: These are the names of the mighty actions of David.**[N] These expressions should not be read as names of people but instead as descriptions of David's good deeds.

״יוֹשֵׁב בַּשֶּׁבֶת״ – בְּשָׁעָה שֶׁהָיָה יוֹשֵׁב בִּישִׁיבָה לֹא הָיָה יוֹשֵׁב עַל גַּבֵּי כָּרִים וּכְסָתוֹת, אֶלָּא עַל גַּבֵּי קַרְקַע. דְּכָל כַּמָּה דַּהֲוָה רַבֵּיהּ עִירָא הַיָּאִירִי קַיָּים – הֲוָה מַתְנֵי לְהוּ לְרַבָּנַן עַל גַּבֵּי כָּרִים וּכְסָתוֹת, כִּי נַח נַפְשֵׁיהּ – הֲוָה מַתְנֵי דָּוִד לְרַבָּנַן, וַהֲוָה יָתֵיב עַל גַּבֵּי קַרְקַע. אֲמַרוּ לֵיהּ: לֵיתֵיב מָר אַכָּרִים וּכְסָתוֹת! לָא קַבֵּיל עֲלֵיהּ.

Josheb-Basshebeth [*yoshev bashevet*] indicates that **when** David **would sit** [*yoshev*] **in the study hall, he would not sit upon pillows and cushions,** as an important person ordinarily would. **Rather,** he would sit **on the ground** like one of the students. **For as long as** David's **teacher, Ira the Jairite, was alive,** Ira **would teach the Sages** while sitting **on pillows and cushions. When** Ira **passed away, David would teach the Sages, and he** did this while **sitting on the ground. They said to him: Master,** you **should sit upon pillows and blankets. He did not accept** their suggestions, since in his humility he did not wish to appear as the teacher of the Jewish people.

״תַּחְכְּמוֹנִי״ – אָמַר רַב: אָמַר לוֹ הַקָּדוֹשׁ בָּרוּךְ הוּא, הוֹאִיל וְהִשְׁפַּלְתָּ עַצְמְךָ – תְּהֵא כָּמוֹנִי, שֶׁאֲנִי גּוֹזֵר גְּזֵרָה – וְאַתָּה מְבַטְּלָהּ.

In this verse, David is described as **"a Tahchemonite** [*taḥkemoni*]." **Rav said: The Holy One, Blessed be He, said to him: Since you have humbled yourself, be you** now **like Me** [*tehe kamoni*]. How so? **As I issue a decree, and you,** owing to your righteousness, **may nullify it.**

״רֹאשׁ הַשָּׁלִישִׁים״ – תְּהֵא רֹאשׁ לִשְׁלֹשֶׁת אָבוֹת. ״הוּא עֲדִינוֹ הָעֶצְנִי״ – כְּשֶׁהָיָה יוֹשֵׁב וְעוֹסֵק בַּתּוֹרָה – הָיָה מְעַדֵּן עַצְמוֹ כְּתוֹלַעַת; וּבְשָׁעָה שֶׁיּוֹצֵא לַמִּלְחָמָה – הָיָה מַקְשֶׁה עַצְמוֹ כְּעֵץ.

David is also described here as **"chief of the captains** [*rosh hashalishim*]" because God said to him: **You will be the head** [*rosh*] **of the three** [*sheloshet*] **Patriarchs.**[N] **"The same was Adino the Eznite"**; this alludes to the fact that **when** David **would sit and occupy himself with Torah, he would make himself soft** [*me'aden*] **as a worm,**[N] **and when he would go out to war, he would make himself hard** and strong **as a tree** [*etz*].

״עַל שְׁמוֹנֶה מֵאוֹת חָלָל בְּפַעַם אֶחָת״ – שֶׁהָיָה זוֹרֵק חֵץ וּמַפִּיל שְׁמוֹנֶה מֵאוֹת חָלָל בְּפַעַם אַחַת, וְהָיָה מִתְאַנֵּחַ עַל מָאתַיִם. דִּכְתִיב: ״אֵיכָה יִרְדֹּף אֶחָד אֶלֶף״.

The expression: **"Against eight hundred people, which he slew at one time,"** means **that he would throw an arrow** in the air **and** with it **kill eight hundred people at one time. And** David **would sigh over the two hundred** who were missing from fulfillment of the Torah's promise, **as it is written: "How should one man chase a thousand"** (Deuteronomy 32:30).[N]

יָצְתָה בַּת קוֹל וְאָמְרָה: ״רַק בִּדְבַר אוּרִיָּה הַחִתִּי״.

A Divine Voice issued forth and said by way of explanation as to why the promise was not entirely fulfilled: "Because David did that which was right in the eyes of the Lord, and turned not aside from anything that He commanded him all the days of his life, **save only the matter of Uriah the Hittite"** (I Kings 15:5). Had David not committed this sin, then all of the promises mentioned in the Torah would have been fulfilled in their entirety through him.

NOTES

Who raised the yoke [*ulla*] of repentance – שֶׁהֵקִים עוּלָּהּ שֶׁל תְּשׁוּבָה: Some explain that the word *ulla* is related to the word *ol*, yoke, and repentance rested upon David like a yoke rests upon an ox (*Talmid Rabbeinu Yeḥiel of Paris*). In the manuscript of Rashi, it is understood that, according to this expression, David showed the *to'elet*, great power and value, of repentance.

These are the names of the mighty actions of David – אֵלֶּה שְׁמוֹת גְּבוּרוֹתָיו שֶׁל דָּוִד: It is possible to explain the names listed in the verse as descriptions as David himself because they do not sound like names of people, e.g., Josheb-Basshebeth a Tahchemonite (Ran).

Head of the three Patriarchs – רֹאשׁ לִשְׁלֹשֶׁת אָבוֹת: Rashi and others explain that in the future David will be listed before the three Patriarchs. Rabbi Shlomo ben HaYatom explains this to mean that David will be equivalent to the three Patriarchs. Just as in the *Amida* prayer, the first blessing concludes with: Shield of Abraham, so the Gemara states that the blessing recited after the *haftara*, the portion read from the Prophets, concludes with: Shield of David (*Pesaḥim* 117b). Lastly, there are those who explain that according to this statement, he will be the leader over the descendants of the three Patriarchs (Ran).

He would make himself soft [*me'aden*] as a worm – הָיָה מְעַדֵּן עַצְמוֹ כְּתוֹלַעַת: Some explain that this means that he would bend himself like a worm. David would bend his hands and legs almost like a link in a chain, and this meaning is alluded to in the verse: "Can you bind the chains [*ma'adannot*] of Pleiades" (Job 38:31; manuscript of Rashi). Others explain that this is related to the phrase "polluted garment" [*begged idin*] (Isaiah 64:5), which refers to a decomposing garment that is filled with worms (Ran).

How should one man chase a thousand – אֵיכָה יִרְדֹּף אֶחָד אֶלֶף: Although this verse speaks about the defeat of the Jews at the hands of other nations, God's goodness, when the Jewish people defeat their enemies, will certainly be even greater than this. Therefore, this verse will be fulfilled to an even greater degree when Jews act properly (manuscript of Rashi; see Maharsha).

אָמַר רַבִּי תַּנְחוּם בְּרֵיהּ דְּרַבִּי חִיָּיא אִישׁ כְּפַר עַכּוֹ אָמַר רַבִּי יַעֲקֹב בַּר אַחָא אָמַר רַבִּי שִׂמְלַאי, וְאָמְרִי לַהּ אָמַר רַבִּי תַּנְחוּם אָמַר רַב הוּנָא, וְאָמְרִי לַהּ אָמַר רַב הוּנָא לְחוּדֵיהּ:

The Gemara returns to the *halakhot* of ostracism and mentions that **Rabbi Tanḥum, son of Rabbi Ḥiyya, of the village of Akko, said** that **Rabbi Ya'akov bar Aḥa said** that **Rabbi Simlai said, and** some **say** that this tradition was transmitted in the following manner: **Rabbi Tanḥum said** that **Rav Huna said, and** others **say** that **Rav Huna himself** made this statement without the chain of transmission:

Perek **III**
Daf **17** Amud **a**

תַּלְמִיד שֶׁנִּידָּה לִכְבוֹדוֹ – נִדּוּיוֹ נִידּוּי. דְּתַנְיָא: מְנוּדֶּה לָרַב – מְנוּדֶּה לְתַלְמִיד; מְנוּדֶּה לְתַלְמִיד – אֵינוֹ מְנוּדֶּה לָרַב. לָרַב הוּא דְּאֵינוֹ מְנוּדֶּה, הָא לְכוּלֵּי עָלְמָא – מְנוּדֶּה.

If a **student ostracized** someone else **due to** an insult to **his dignity,** and not because the ostracized person was guilty of some transgression, **his** decree of **ostracism is valid, as it is taught** in a *baraita*: **One who is ostracized by the teacher is** considered **ostracized with regard to the student.** However, **one who is ostracized by the student is not** considered **ostracized with regard to the teacher.** The Gemara attempts to draw an inference from a careful reading of this *baraita*: **He is not** considered **ostracized with regard to the teacher,** which implies **that he is** considered **ostracized with regard to everyone** else.

לְמַאי? אִי בְּמִילֵּי דִּשְׁמַיָּא – "אֵין חָכְמָה וְאֵין תְּבוּנָה וְאֵין עֵצָה לְנֶגֶד ה'"! אֶלָּא לָאו – לִכְבוֹד עַצְמוֹ?

The Gemara clarifies the case: **For what** reason was he ostracized? **If** it was **for a matter relating to Heaven,**[H] i.e., because he sinned, then why, if he was ostracized by the student, should he not be considered ostracized with regard to the teacher? Doesn't the verse state: **"There is no wisdom or understanding or counsel against the Lord"** (Proverbs 21:30)? This means that when a sin is committed and God's name is desecrated, all other considerations are ignored, even the eminence and knowledge of the teacher, and therefore he too must treat the offender as ostracized. **Rather, is it not** that the Gemara is referring to a case where the student ostracized the other person due to an insult **to his** own **dignity?** Therefore, it is apparent that his decree of ostracism is valid and binding upon all, with the exception of his teacher.

אָמַר רַב יוֹסֵף: צוּרְבָא מֵרַבָּנַן עָבֵיד דִּינָא לְנַפְשֵׁיהּ בְּמִילְּתָא דִּפְסִיקָא לֵיהּ.

Rav Yosef said: A Torah scholar may execute judgment for himself[N] **with regard to a matter about which he is certain,**[H] and he is not required to first go to court and have the case decided for him. The same applies when another person behaves in a disrespectful manner toward him; he is permitted to go ahead on his own and ostracize him.

HALAKHA

For a matter relating to Heaven – בְּמִילֵּי דִּשְׁמַיָּא: If one is ostracized over one of the matters that are normally punishable by ostracism, as opposed to acting disrespectfully toward a Torah scholar, then the *Nasi* and all the Jewish people are required to respect the decree of ostracism until it is nullified. This is the *halakha* even if the one who declared the ostracism is the least important person (*Shulḥan Arukh*, *Yoreh De'a* 334:17).

Ruling for himself – עוֹשֶׂה דִּין לְעַצְמוֹ: One may rule for himself when he is certain that the *halakha* is in accordance with his opinion; however, the details of when and how this may be done are very complex (*Shulḥan Arukh*, *Ḥoshen Mishpat* 4).

NOTES

A Torah scholar may execute judgment for himself – צוּרְבָא מֵרַבָּנַן עָבֵיד דִּינָא לְנַפְשֵׁיהּ: Some explain that according to this statement, a Torah scholar may ostracize someone who owes him money, if the loan has not been repaid and it is clear that the *halakha* is in accordance with the opinion of the Torah scholar (Rid; Ran). However, many authorities disagree and say that this behavior could lead to a desecration of God's name. Instead, they explain that the statement in the Gemara is referring to a Torah scholar who ostracizes someone over his honor. If one acts disrespectfully concerning a matter that is explicitly prohibited, then the Torah scholar may ostracize him (Rabbeinu Ḥananel). Others add that in that case, all people must ostracize him (Rosh). Some say that this statement is not referring to ostracism at all; it is actually referring to the more general concept that one is permitted to determine his own ruling with regard to money that has been stolen from him, and he is not required to wait for the court to rule on the issue. If so, the only novel element of this statement is that it teaches that even a Torah scholar is permitted to act in this manner, although it is preferable for a Torah scholar to act generously and to go above and beyond what is strictly permitted by the *halakha* (Ritva; Ran).

ההוא צורבא מרבנן דהוו סנו שומעניה. אמר רב יהודה: היכי ליעביד? לשמתיה – צריכי ליה רבנן. לא לשמתיה – קא מיתחיל שמא דשמיא.

There was a certain Torah scholar who gained a bad reputation[N] due to rumors about his conduct. **Rav Yehuda**[P] **said: What should be done? To excommunicate him** is not an option. **The Sages need him,**[N] as he is a great Torah authority. **Not to excommunicate him** is also not an option, as then **the name of Heaven would be desecrated.**[N]

אמר ליה לרבה בר בר חנה: מידי שמיע לך בהא. אמר ליה: הכי אמר רבי יוחנן, מאי דכתיב: "כי שפתי כהן ישמרו דעת ותורה יבקשו מפיהו כי מלאך ה׳ צבאות הוא"? אם דומה הרב למלאך ה׳ – יבקשו תורה מפיו; ואם לאו – אל יבקשו תורה מפיו.

Rav Yehuda **said to Rabba bar bar Ḥana:** Have **you heard anything with regard to this** issue? **He said to him: Rabbi Yoḥanan said as follows: What is** the meaning of that **which is written: "For the priest's lips should keep knowledge, and they should seek Torah at his mouth; for he is a messenger [*malakh*] of the Lord of hosts"** (Malachi 2:7)? This verse teaches: **If the teacher is similar to an angel [*malakh*] of the Lord,** then **seek Torah from his mouth,** but if he is **not** pure and upright, then **do not seek Torah from his mouth;** even if he is knowledgeable about Torah, do not learn from him.[H]

שמתיה רב יהודה. לסוף איחלש רב יהודה. אתו רבנן לשיולי ביה, ואתא איהו נמי בהדייהו. כד חזייה רב יהודה חייך,

Based on this statement, **Rav Yehuda ostracized** that Torah scholar. **In the end,** after some time had passed, **Rav Yehuda took ill** and was on the verge of death. **The Sages came to inquire about his well-being, and** the ostracized scholar **came** along **with them as well. When Rav Yehuda saw him,** that scholar, **he laughed.**

אמר ליה: לא מסתייך דשמתיה להדהוא גברא אלא אחוכי נמי חייך בי?! אמר ליה: לאו בדידך מחייכנא. אלא דכי אזלינא להדהוא עלמא בדיחא דעתאי, דאפילו לגברא כוותך לא חניפי ליה.

The ostracized scholar **said to him: Was it not enough that you excommunicated that man,** i.e., me, **but** now **you even laugh at me?** Rav Yehuda **said to him: I was not laughing at you; rather, I am happy as I go to that** other **world that I did not flatter even** a great **man like you,** but instead I treated you fairly in accordance with the *halakha*.

נח נפשיה דרב יהודה. אתא לבי מדרשא אמר להו: שרו לי! אמרו ליה רבנן: גברא דחשיב כרב יהודה ליכא הכא דלישרי לך. אלא זיל לגביה דרבי יהודה נשיאה דלישרי לך. אזל לקמיה. אמר ליה לרבי אמי: פוק עיין בדיניה. אי מיבעי למישרא ליה – שרי ליה.

Rav Yehuda died. The ostracized scholar **came to the study hall and said** to the Sages: **Release me** from the decree of ostracism. **The Sages said to him: There is no man here as eminent as Rav Yehuda who can release you** from the ostracism. **Rather, go to Rabbi Yehuda Nesia** in Eretz Yisrael, as only **he can release you.** That scholar **came before** Rabbi Yehuda Nesia. Rabbi Yehuda Nesia **said to Rabbi Ami: Go and examine his case. If it is necessary to release him** from his decree of ostracism, **release him** on my behalf.

עיין רבי אמי בדיניה. סבר למישרא ליה. עמד רבי שמואל בר נחמני על רגליו ואמר: ומה שפחה של בית רבי לא נהגו חכמים קלות ראש בנידויה שלש שנים – יהודה חבירינו על אחת כמה וכמה!

Rabbi Ami examined his case and **thought** at first **to release him** from his ostracism. But **Rabbi Shmuel bar Naḥmani**[P] **rose up on his feet and said: If the maidservant in the house of** Rabbi Yehuda HaNasi once ostracized another person,[N] and **the Sages did not relate frivolously to her** decree of **ostracism** and did not revoke it until **three years** had passed, **all the more so,** with regard to a decree of ostracism placed by **Yehuda our colleague,** we must take it seriously and not release this scholar.

NOTES

Gained a bad reputation – **דהוו סנו שומעניה**: Some say that this Torah scholar engaged in activities that were not appropriate for one of his stature, e.g., frivolous song or studying heretical works (Rabbeinu Ḥananel). Most commentaries explain that he was accused of adultery or some other type of sexual immorality (*Talmid Rabbeinu Yeḥiel of Paris*; Commentary on *Moed Katan*; see *Tosafot*). The Ritva explains that the Torah scholar did not violate any Torah prohibition but instead was lenient or ignored rabbinic prohibitions, such as the *halakhot* pertaining to seclusion with a woman or other similar *halakhot*.

To excommunicate him is not an option, the Sages need him – **לשמתיה צריכי ליה רבנן**: The question is raised: Why would ostracizing him be a problem; it was already stated that one who has been ostracized may study and teach Torah? The Ritva explains that it would not be appropriate for the students to sit four cubits away from him, as was the practice for one who had been ostracized. Some learn from here that there is a distinction between standard ostracism [*niddui*] and a more severe form of ostracism [*shamta*]. Although it is permitted for one who has been ostracized to teach Torah, it is prohibited for one severely ostracized to teach Torah, and that decree does not lapse after thirty days (Rabbeinu Yehonatan of Lunel).

The name of Heaven would be desecrated – **מיתחיל שמא דשמיא**: God's name could be desecrated either because failing to excommunicate could teach others to be lenient with regard to prohibitions, or because others will claim that Torah scholars do not judge fairly and do not render the appropriate punishment for other Sages who have violated transgressions (*Talmid Rabbeinu Yeḥiel of Paris*).

The ostracism of Rabbi Yehuda HaNasi's maidservant – **נדויה של אמתא דרבי**: The early authorities ask: Why was this decree of ostracism, and that of the Torah scholar, nullified only after a period of time had passed? Some say that ostracism cannot be nullified unless the one who has been ostracized abandons the sin for which he was ostracized. In this case, since he did not, his decree of ostracism could not be nullified (Rabbeinu Yehonatan of Lunel). Others say that ostracism cannot be nullified unless those who nullify it are of equal or greater stature than the one who initially declared the ostracism. In this case, Rabbi Yehuda HaNasi's maidservant was wise and sin fearing, and therefore it took a long time to find someone who could nullify the decree of ostracism that she had declared (Rosh, citing Ra'avad).

HALAKHA

A Torah scholar who sins – **תלמיד חכם שסרח**: When a Torah scholar sins, the court does not rush to ostracize him; rather, they distance themselves from him. However, if he is liable to receive lashes for his sin, he may be punished in private. If he has earned a bad reputation by involving himself in prohibited matters, and his fellow scholars are embarrassed due to his behavior, and the name of Heaven is desecrated, then he should be ostracized (*Shulḥan Arukh*, *Yoreh De'a* 334:42).

PERSONALITIES

Rav Yehuda – **רב יהודה**: Rav Yehuda bar Yeḥezkel was one of the great Babylonian Sages of the second generation of *amora'im*. He studied under both Rav and Shmuel. Shmuel's love and respect for Rav Yehuda were such that he often spoke highly of him and even remarked in admiration: This cannot be an ordinary mortal. Following Shmuel's death, Rav Yehuda was appointed head of the Neharde'a academy in his stead. He moved the academy to his hometown of Pumbedita, where it remained for over seven hundred years, producing many prominent Sages.

Rav Yehuda's life was devoted entirely to Torah study, and he lived in poverty until he was instated as head of the academy. Most of scholars of the third generation of *amora'im* were Rav Yehuda's students, including his son, Rav Yitzhak. Even those who studied in the academy in Sura became his students after the death of Rav Huna, head of that academy.

Though Rav Yehuda believed that there are biblical verses prohibiting one from moving to Eretz Yisrael from Babylonia, he was well known for his love of Eretz Yisrael. The majority of his students moved there and became leading *amora'im* of Eretz Yisrael.

Rabbi Shmuel bar Naḥmani – **רבי שמואל בר נחמני**: Rabbi Shmuel bar Naḥmani was an *amora* in Eretz Yisrael during the second to third generation of *amora'im* there. He was probably born in Eretz Yisrael, however he may have also spent some time in Babylonia. He was a main student of the *amora* Rabbi Yoḥanan, but he also studied under Rabbi Yehoshua ben Levi. He was considered to be one of the greatest scholars of *aggada* in the Talmud. He was one of the best known masters of *aggada* of his generation. His statements appear throughout the Jerusalem Talmud and other midrashic literature.

Rabbi Shmuel bar Naḥmani also made halakhic statements, which were transmitted by other Sages. It was primarily the students of Rabbi Yoḥanan who asked him different questions and transmitted Torah statements in his name. Additionally, Rabbi Shmuel bar Naḥmani had a unique status in that he was one of the few Sages who knew the secret of the movement of celestial bodies, necessary for calculating the New Moon. He was called: One of the great men of the generation. He also represented the Jewish people before the Roman Emperor Diocletian.

Rabbi Shmuel bar Naḥmani lived to a very old age, until the time when Rabbi Ami was the head of the study hall, when he no longer was able to go there regularly. However, it appears that he had his own personal study hall, in which the emphasis may have been more on the study of *aggada*.

BACKGROUND

A wasp came and stung him – אֲתָא זִיבּוּרָא וּטְרַקֵיהּ: A wasp sting is very painful, and in a sensitive area this pain is even greater. Approximately one percent of the population is allergic to these stings and the poison injected through the stinger. For such people, even one sting is dangerous and without quick treatment may lead to death.

Wasp stinger with dripping venom about to enter human skin

HALAKHA

One who strikes an adult son – הַמַּכֶּה בְּנוֹ הַגָּדוֹל: A father who strikes his grown child is ostracized for transgressing the prohibition: "You shall not place a stumbling block before the blind." According to some, one's child is an adult child from the age of twenty-two; others say from the age of twenty-four (*Shulḥan Arukh*, *Yoreh De'a* 334:43).

אֲמַר רַבִּי זֵירָא: מַאי דְּקַמָּן דַּאֲתָא הָאִידָּנָא הַאי סָבָא בְּבֵי מִדְרָשָׁא, דְּהָא כַּמָּה שְׁנֵי לָא אֲתָא. שְׁמַע מִינָּהּ לָא מִיבָּעֵי לְמִישְׁרָא לֵיהּ. לָא שְׁרָא לֵיהּ. נְפַק כִּי קָא בָּכֵי וְאָזֵיל.

Rabbi Zeira said: What caused **this Elder,** Rabbi Shmuel bar Naḥmani, **to come before us in the study hall** today **though for many years he did not come,** and now he comes precisely during this discussion. **Learn from this** that **it is not necessary to release him** from his decree of ostracism, as this combination of events is certainly not a coincidence. Rather, it should be viewed as an instructive sign from Heaven. Consequently, Rabbi Ami **did not release him** from the ostracism, and the ostracized scholar **left in tears.**

אֲתָא זִיבּוּרָא וּטְרַקֵיהּ אַאַמְּתֵיהּ, וּשְׁכֵיב. עַיְּילוּהוּ לִמְעָרְתָא דַּחֲסִידֵי – וְלָא קִיבְּלוּהוּ. עַיְּילוּהוּ לִמְעָרְתָא דְּדַיָּינֵי – וְקִיבְּלוּהוּ.

A wasp came and stung the ostracized scholar[B] **on his penis**[N] **and he died.** Because he was a great Torah scholar, **they took him into the caves in which the pious** are interred in order to bury him there, **but** the caves **did not accept him.** A snake stood at the entrance of the caves and did not let them pass. **They** then **took him into the caves of the judges, and they accepted him.**

מַאי טַעְמָא? דַּעֲבַד כְּרַבִּי אִילְעַאי. דְּתַנְיָא, רַבִּי אִילְעַאי אוֹמֵר: אִם רוֹאֶה אָדָם שֶׁיִּצְרוֹ מִתְגַּבֵּר עָלָיו – יֵלֵךְ לְמָקוֹם שֶׁאֵין מַכִּירִין אוֹתוֹ, וְיִלְבַּשׁ שְׁחוֹרִים וְיִתְעַטֵּף שְׁחוֹרִים, וְיַעֲשֶׂה מַה שֶּׁלִּבּוֹ חָפֵץ, וְאַל יְחַלֵּל שֵׁם שָׁמַיִם בְּפַרְהֶסְיָא.

The Gemara asks: **What is the reason** that he was accepted there? The Gemara answers: Even though he sinned, **he** still **acted in accordance with** the opinion of **Rabbi Ilai,**[N] **as it is taught** in a *baraita*: **Rabbi Ilai says: If a person sees that his** evil **inclination is gaining control over him** and he cannot overcome it, then **he should go to a place where he is not known. He should wear black, and he should wrap his** head **in black,** as if he were a mourner. Perhaps these changes will influence him, so that he not sin. Even if these actions do not help, **he should** at least **do as his heart desires** in private **and not desecrate the name of Heaven in public.**[N] Although this person had sinned, he did so in private and in a manner that did not publicly desecrate God's name, and therefore it was fitting that he be given an honorable burial.

שִׁפְחָה שֶׁל בֵּית רַבִּי מַאי הִיא? דְּאַמְתָא דְּבֵי רַבִּי חֲזֵיתֵיהּ לְהַהוּא גַּבְרָא דַּהֲוָה מָחֵי לִבְנוֹ גָּדוֹל. אֲמַרָה: לֶיהֱוֵי הַהוּא גַּבְרָא בְּשַׁמְתָּא, דְּקָעָבַר מִשּׁוּם: "וְלִפְנֵי עִוֵּר לֹא תִתֵּן מִכְשׁוֹל". דְּתַנְיָא: "וְלִפְנֵי עִוֵּר לֹא תִתֵּן מִכְשׁוֹל" – בְּמַכֶּה לִבְנוֹ גָּדוֹל הַכָּתוּב מְדַבֵּר.

The Gemara asks: **What is** the story mentioned by Rabbi Shmuel bar Naḥmani involving **the maidservant in the house of Rabbi** Yehuda HaNasi? It was related **that the maidservant in Rabbi** Yehuda HaNasi's **house saw a certain man who was striking his adult son.**[H] **She said: Let that man be excommunicated, due to** the fact that **he has transgressed** the injunction: **"You shall not place a stumbling block before the blind"** (Leviticus 19:14), **as it is taught** in a *baraita* that the verse states: **"You shall not place a stumbling block before the blind,"** and **the verse speaks** here **of one who strikes his adult son,** as the son is likely to become angry and strike his father back, thereby transgressing the severe prohibition against hitting one's parent.

NOTES

Stung him on his penis [*ametei*] – וּטְרַקֵיהּ אַאַמְּתֵיהּ: Some explain that he was stung on his hand (Ritva), and others have a version of the talmudic text containing the word forehead [*aputei*] (Rabbi Shlomo ben HaYatom).

He acted in accordance with Rabbi Ilai – דַּעֲבַד כְּרַבִּי אִילְעַאי: There are various versions of this text, and consequently there are also many explanations of it. Some say that the question is why the unnamed ostracized scholar was not taken into the cave of the pious. The Gemara answers that this was because he did not act in accordance with Rabbi Ilai, but sinned in his home town. This is based on a version of the text that reads: Because he transgressed the opinion of Rabbi Ilai.

Others understand this Gemara in the opposite way. According to them, the Gemara asks why he was taken into the cave of judges. In response to this question, the Gemara answers that he acted in accordance with Rabbi Ilai. In fact, there are those who say that even if one acts in accordance with Rabbi Ilai but does not overcome his evil inclination, he is not considered to be pious (see *Talmid Rabbeinu Yeḥiel of Paris*; Rabbeinu Yehonatan of Lunel).

One whose evil inclination is gaining control over him – מִי שֶׁיִּצְרוֹ מִתְגַּבֵּר עָלָיו: Rabbeinu Ḥananel explains in the name of the *ge'onim* that this directive does not refer to one who intends to violate actual transgressions. Rather, it applies to someone who plans to enjoy pleasures or spend time in places that the Sages do not approve of. In that case, it is preferable that one who can no longer control himself go to a different place, where he is not known.

Many note, in the name of Rav Hai Gaon, that Rabbi Ilai does not claim that it is permitted for one to sin. Rather, he claims that if one goes to a different place and wears black, which is mourner's clothing, then he will be able to overcome his evil inclination. Similarly, others write that the hassle of traveling will reduce his inclination (Rabbeinu Yehonatan of Lunel). Alternatively, if he goes to a place where he is a stranger and is not respected, he will be humbled (*Talmid Rabbeinu Yeḥiel of Paris*; Rabbeinu Yehonatan of Lunel).

רֵישׁ לָקִישׁ הֲוָה מְנַטֵּר פַּרְדֵּיסָא. אֲתָא הַהוּא גַּבְרָא וְקָאָכֵיל תְּאֵינֵי. רְמָא בֵּיהּ קָלָא, וְלָא אַשְׁגַּח בֵּיהּ. אֲמַר: לֶיהֱוֵי הַהוּא גַּבְרָא בְּשַׁמְתָּא. אֲמַר לֵיהּ: אַדְּרַבָּה, לֶיהֱוֵי הַהוּא גַּבְרָא בְּשַׁמְתָּא! אִם מָמוֹן נִתְחַיַּיבְתִּי לְךָ – נִידּוּי מִי נִתְחַיַּיבְתִּי לְךָ?

Similarly, it was related that **Reish Lakish**[P] **was guarding an orchard** for payment when **a certain man came and ate** some **figs** that were growing there. Reish Lakish **raised his voice** and yelled at him, **but** this man **paid no attention to him** and kept eating. Reish Lakish **said: Let that man be** in a state of **excommunication.** The man eating the figs **said to him: On the contrary, let that man,** i.e., Reish Lakish, **be** in a state of **excommunication,** for even **if I have become liable to you for payment,** as I have eaten of the figs without permission, **have I become liable to you for excommuncation?**[N] With that statement, the man left.

אֲתָא לְבֵי מִדְרְשָׁא. אֲמַר לֵיהּ: שֶׁלּוֹ – נִידּוּי; שֶׁלְּךָ – אֵינוֹ נִידּוּי.

Reish Lakish **went to the study hall** to inquire about the *halakha* with regard to this man. The other Sages **said to him: His** decree of **ostracism is** valid, but **your** decree of **ostracism is not.**[H] In other words, that man was correct and Reish Lakish should not have ostracized him in response to his actions.

וּמַאי תַּקַּנְתֵּיהּ? זִיל לְגַבֵּיהּ דְּלִישְׁרֵי לָךְ. לָא יָדַעְנָא לֵיהּ. אֲמַרוּ לֵיהּ: זִיל לְגַבֵּי נְשִׂיאָה דְּלִישְׁרֵי לָךְ, דְּתַנְיָא: נִידּוּהוּ וְאֵינוֹ יוֹדֵעַ מִי נִידָּהוּ – יֵלֵךְ אֵצֶל נָשִׂיא, וְיַתִּיר לוֹ נִדּוּיוֹ.

Reish Lakish then asked: If so, **what is the remedy** for this decree of ostracism? The Sages answered him: **Go to him so that he may release you** from it. Reish Lakish replied: **I do not know him. They said to him: Go** then **to the** ***Nasi*****, so that he may release you** from the ban, **as it is taught** in a *baraita*: If one **was ostracized, but he does not know who ostracized him,**[H] **he should go to the** ***Nasi*****, and the** *Nasi* **may release** him from **his** decree of **ostracism.**

אָמַר רַב הוּנָא, בְּאוּשָׁא הִתְקִינוּ: אַב בֵּית דִּין שֶׁסָּרַח – אֵין מְנַדִּין אוֹתוֹ, אֶלָּא אוֹמֵר לוֹ: ״הִכָּבֵד וְשֵׁב בְּבֵיתֶךָ״. חָזַר וְסָרַח – מְנַדִּין אוֹתוֹ, מִפְּנֵי חִילּוּל הַשֵּׁם.

The Gemara continues: **Rav Huna said** that **in Usha it was enacted:** If **the president of the court sinned,**[H] **he is not ostracized.** Although this would be the appropriate punishment, he is not ostracized, so as not to cause a desecration of God's name. **Rather,** they **say to him** the words of the verse: **"Keep your honor and stay at home"** (II Kings 14:10).[N] That is to say, to preserve your dignity, it would be best if you were to stay at home, resign your position, and refrain from further public appearances. If **he sins again, he is ostracized, due to the desecration of God's name** that would ensue were people to think that he was spared his rightful punishment due to his high position.

וּפְלִיגָא דְּרֵישׁ לָקִישׁ. דְּאָמַר רֵישׁ לָקִישׁ: תַּלְמִיד חָכָם שֶׁסָּרַח – אֵין מְנַדִּין אוֹתוֹ בְּפַרְהֶסְיָא, שֶׁנֶּאֱמַר: ״וְכָשַׁלְתָּ הַיּוֹם וְכָשַׁל גַּם נָבִיא עִמְּךָ לָיְלָה״ – כַּסֵּהוּ כַּלַּיְלָה.

The Gemara comments: This opinion **disagrees with** that of **Reish Lakish,** for **Reish Lakish said:** If **a Torah scholar sins, he is not ostracized** at all **in public, as it is stated: "Therefore, shall you fall in the day, and the prophet also shall fall with you in the night"** (Hosea 4:5). This is explained to mean: If a prophet or any other important person sins, his offense **should be concealed like the night** and not punished in public.

מָר זוּטְרָא חֲסִידָא, כִּי מִיחַיַּיב צוּרְבָא מֵרַבָּנָן שַׁמְתָּא – בְּרֵישָׁא מְשַׁמֵּית נַפְשֵׁיהּ, וַהֲדַר מְשַׁמֵּית לְדִידֵיהּ. כִּי הֲוָה עָיֵיל בְּאוּשְׁפִּיזֵיהּ – שָׁרֵי לֵיהּ לְנַפְשֵׁיהּ וַהֲדַר שָׁרֵי לֵיהּ לְדִידֵיהּ.

With regard to this issue, it was related that **when a Torah scholar would become liable** to be punished with **excommunication before Mar Zutra the Pious,** Mar Zutra **would first excommunicate himself**[N] as a mark of respect for the Torah scholar, **and afterward he would ostracize** the Torah scholar. This self-imposed excommunication was meant only as a show of honor to the other Torah scholar, and therefore **when** Mar Zutra **would enter his house** of lodging, **he would release his** own excommunication, **and afterward he would release** the other's excommunication.

NOTES

The ostracism that Reish Lakish declared – **נִידּוּיוֹ שֶׁל רֵישׁ לָקִישׁ**: Several questions are asked with regard to this incident. Apparently this person was a thief; why, then, was he not deserving of ostracism? Some say that the common practice in this place was to take fruit and pay afterward (see *Tosafot*). Others explain that Reish Lakish would have been permitted to ostracize the thief before he stole, but not after he had already stolen, when instead Reish Lakish could take him to court and sue for damages (Rosh).

With regard to the ostracism introduced by the phrase: On the contrary, there are those who claim that the ostracism has an impact only when directed toward an important person. Similarly, in the Jerusalem Talmud this story is told somewhat differently. According to that version, those stealing the figs were bandits, and it was Reish Lakish himself who was unsure if it was appropriate to ostracize them. These differences serve as the basis for the dispute between the Babylonian and Jerusalem Talmud with regard to this *halakha*.

Keep your honor and stay at home – **הִכָּבֵד וְשֵׁב בְּבֵיתֶךָ**: Some explain that the president of the court is essentially ostracized, however the court does not make explicit reference to it. Rather, they allude to it by encouraging him to remain at home and not leave (Rabbeinu Yehonatan of Lunel; Ran).

He would first excommunicate himself – **בְּרֵישָׁא מְשַׁמֵּית נַפְשֵׁיהּ**: Some write that this was the common practice when it was necessary to ostracize an important person. The one who would pronounce the ostracism would first ostracize himself, so that he would not cause additional embarrassment to the one being ostracized (Commentary on *Moed Katan*). Some say that the expression: When he would enter his house of lodging, is referring not to Mar Zutra, but to the one who had been ostracized, and his decree of ostracism would be nullified before he returned to his residence (*Talmid Rabbeinu Yeḥiel of Paris*).

HALAKHA

One who incorrectly ostracizes – **הַמְנַדֶּה שֶׁלֹּא כַּדִּין**: If one ostracizes another without a proper basis for doing so, and the second person says to him: On the contrary you are ostracized, then the first is ostracized. This is the *halakha* provided that the second person who declared the ostracism is an important person, even if he is not a Torah scholar (Rema). This is also the case if the first does not know who this second person is, and there is a chance that he is an important person. However, if the second person is not a Torah scholar or a Torah student, then he cannot say: On the contrary, etc. If the first person only stated that the act is punishable by ostracism, and the second person responded: On the contrary, etc., then the first person is not ostracized. The reason for this is because the first person did not explicitly ostracize the second (*Shulḥan Arukh, Yoreh De'a* 334:39, and in the comment of Rema).

If one was ostracized and does not know who ostracized him – **נִידּוּהוּ וְאֵינוֹ יוֹדֵעַ מִי נִידָּהוּ**: If one was ostracized but does not know who ostracized him, then he should go to the *Nasi* to have his decree of ostracism nullified (Rambam *Sefer HaMadda, Hilkhot Talmud Torah* 7:10).

If the president of the court sinned – **אַב בֵּית דִּין שֶׁסָּרַח**: If the head of a court or an eminent Torah scholar sins, he should not be publicly ostracized unless he committed major transgressions and is leading other members of the community astray, like Jeroboam ben Nebat. If he repents but commits other sins, then he should be punished with lashes in private (*Shulḥan Arukh, Yoreh De'a* 334:42).

PERSONALITIES

Reish Lakish – **רֵישׁ לָקִישׁ**: Rabbi Shimon ben Lakish, typically referred to as Reish Lakish, was among the greatest *amora'im* in Eretz Yisrael. He was the friend and brother-in-law of Rabbi Yoḥanan.

Reish Lakish had an amazing life story. He studied Torah from a young age, but, perhaps due to dire financial straits, he sold himself to a Roman circus as a gladiator. There are many stories in the Talmud that attest to his great strength. Sometime later, after meeting Rabbi Yoḥanan, he resumed his Torah study, first as a student of Rabbi Yoḥanan, then as a friend and colleague. He married Rabbi Yoḥanan's sister.

The Talmud records many halakhic disagreements between Reish Lakish and Rabbi Yoḥanan with regard to central issues of *halakha*. Rabbi Yoḥanan treated him with great respect, often saying: My peer disagrees with me. Reish Lakish was known for his strict piety, to the extent that anyone who was seen conversing in public with Reish Lakish was said to be able to borrow money without guarantors, as Reish Lakish only associated with people beyond reproach. When he died, he was survived by his wife and son, who was a child prodigy.

אָמַר רַב גִּידֵּל אָמַר רַב: תַּלְמִיד חָכָם מְנַדֶּה לְעַצְמוֹ, וּמֵיפֵר לְעַצְמוֹ. אָמַר רַב פָּפָּא: תֵּיתֵי לִי דְּלָא שַׁמְּתִי צוּרְבָא מֵרַבָּנַן מֵעוֹלָם. אֶלָּא, כִּי קָא מִיחַיַּיב צוּרְבָא מֵרַבָּנַן שַׁמְתָּא הֵיכִי עָבֵיד? כִּי הָא, דִּבְמַעְרְבָא מִימְנוּ אַנְגִּידָא דְּצוּרְבָא מֵרַבָּנַן וְלָא מִימְנוּ אַשַּׁמְתָּא.

Rav Giddel said that **Rav said: A Torah scholar may ostracize himself,**[N] **and he may** similarly **release himself** from self-imposed ostracism.[H] **Rav Pappa said: I** have good **coming to me,** for I am praiseworthy, **as I have never ostracized a Torah scholar.** The Gemara asks about this: **If so, when a Torah scholar was liable to be ostracized, what would he do?** The Gemara answers: He did **as they do in the West,** Eretz Yisrael, where **they appoint** a court **to give a Torah scholar lashes, but they do not appoint** a court **to ostracize him.** That is to say, lashes were preferred over ostracism.

מַאי שַׁמְתָּא? אָמַר רַב: שָׁם מִיתָה. וּשְׁמוּאֵל אָמַר: שְׁמָמָה יִהְיֶה, וּמְהַנְיָא בֵּיהּ כִּי טִיחְיָא בְּתַנּוּרָא.

The Gemara proceeds with a discussion that explains the severity of the punishment of excommunication: **What** is the meaning of the word **excommunication** [***shamta***]?[L] **Rav said:** This word is a contraction of the expression **there is death** [***sham mita***], alluding to the deathly aspect of excommunication. **And Shmuel said:** *Shamta* means that **he will be a desolation** [***shemama yiheyeh***], **and it is effective upon him like fat** smeared **on an oven.** Just as some of the fat will always remain absorbed in the walls of the oven, so too some aspect of the curse contained in the excommunication will continue to adhere to him even after the excommunication has been nullified.

וּפְלִיגָא דְּרֵישׁ לָקִישׁ. דְּאָמַר רֵישׁ לָקִישׁ: כְּשֵׁם שֶׁנִּכְנֶסֶת בְּמָאתַיִם וְאַרְבָּעִים וּשְׁמוֹנָה אֵיבָרִים, כָּךְ כְּשֶׁהִיא יוֹצְאָה – יוֹצְאָה מִמָּאתַיִם וְאַרְבָּעִים וּשְׁמוֹנָה אֵיבָרִים.

The Gemara comments: **And** this opinion **disagrees with** the opinion of **Reish Lakish, for Reish Lakish said: Just as** ostracism **enters the two hundred and forty-eight organs** of one's body when it is first pronounced, **so too when it leaves, it leaves from** his **two hundred and forty-eight organs.**

כְּשֶׁהִיא נִכְנֶסֶת – דִּכְתִיב: ״וְהָיְתָה הָעִיר חֵרֶם״, ״חֵרֶם״ בְּגִימַטְרִיָּא מָאתַיִם וְאַרְבְּעִים וּשְׁמוֹנָה הָווּ. כְּשֶׁהִיא יוֹצְאָה – דִּכְתִיב: ״בְּרוֹגֶז רַחֵם תִּזְכּוֹר״ ״רַחֵם״ בְּגִימַטְרִיָּא הָכִי הָווּ.

The following allusion is offered in support of the opinion of Reish Lakish: **When it enters,** it enters all the organs, **as it is written: "And the city shall be a curse [*ḥerem*]"** (Joshua 6:17),[N] **and the numerical value [*gimatriyya*]**[L] of the word ***ḥerem***, a concept similar to ostracism, **is two hundred and forty-eight.** Therefore, the verse alludes to the fact that a decree of ostracism penetrates one's two hundred and forty-eight organs. **When it leaves,** it leaves all the organs, **as it is written: "In wrath remember mercy [*raḥem*]"** (Habakkuk 3:2), **and the numerical value** of the word ***raḥem*** **is also** two hundred and forty-eight, thereby teaching that when the decree of ostracism is revoked, it disappears entirely.

אָמַר רַב יוֹסֵף: שְׁדִי שַׁמְתָּא אַגְּנוּבְתָּא דְּכַלְבָּא – וְאִיהִי דִּידַהּ עָבְדָה. דְּהַהוּא כַּלְבָּא דַּהֲוָה אָכֵיל מְסָאנֵי דְּרַבָּנַן, וְלָא הָווּ קָא יָדְעִי מַנּוּ. וְשַׁמְתּוּ לֵיהּ. אִיתְלִי בֵּיהּ נוּרָא בִּגְנוּבְתֵּיהּ, וַאֲכַלְתֵּיהּ.

The Gemara continues discussing the power of a ban. **Rav Yosef said: Cast an excommunication on the tail of a dog and it,** the excommunication, **will do its work** and harm the dog. It was related that there was **a certain dog that would eat the shoes of the Sages, and they did not know who it was** causing this damage. They thought that it was a person, **and** so **they excommunicated** whoever was doing it. Soon thereafter, the dog's **tail caught fire and got burnt.** This shows that excommunication can have a harmful effect even on a dog.

הַהוּא אַלִּמָּא דַּהֲוָה קָא מְצַעֵר לֵיהּ לְהַהוּא צוּרְבָא מֵרַבָּנַן. אֲתָא לְקַמֵּיהּ דְּרַב יוֹסֵף. אֲמַר לֵיהּ: זִיל שַׁמְתֵּיהּ. אָמַר לֵיהּ: מִסְתְּפִינָא מִינֵּיהּ.

It was further related that there was **a violent person who** caused **suffering to a certain Torah scholar.** This Torah scholar **came before Rav Yosef** to ask what he should do. Rav Yosef **said to him: Go and ostracize him.** This Torah scholar **said to him: I am afraid of him,** that he will harass me even more.

אֲמַר לֵיהּ: שְׁקִילִי פְּתִיחָא עֲלֵיהּ. כׇּל שֶׁכֵּן דְּמִסְתְּפִינָא מִינֵּיהּ. אֲמַר לֵיהּ: שְׁקַלֵיהּ אַחֲתֵיהּ בְּכַדָּא,

Rav Yosef **said to him: Take** out, i.e., publish **a written** ostracism **against him.**[B] The Torah scholar said to him: **All the more so I am fearful of him,** for if I publicize the matter he will certainly come after me. Rav Yosef **said to him** to do as follows: **Take** the written ostracism **and place it in a jug,**

NOTES

Ostracizes himself [*le'atzmo*] – מְנַדֶּה לְעַצְמוֹ: The word *le'atzmo* is explained in two ways. Some say it means that he ostracized himself. Others say that it means he may ostracize someone else for his own sake or due to his honor (Rashi manuscript).

And the city shall be a curse [*ḥerem*] – וְהָיְתָה הָעִיר חֵרֶם: The Maharsha comments that the word *ḥerem* is used many times earlier in the Bible, and therefore he asks why the Gemara specifically quotes the verse from the book of Joshua. He explains that the verse's indirect reference to the inhabitants with the word "city" indicates that there is something to be derived from it. He goes on to explain that the Gemara understands the word "city" here as an allusion to the body. Therefore, it is befitting to use this specific verse in a discussion with regard to *ḥerem* and the body. The *Iyyun Ya'akov* explains more simply that this is the first place where the enactment of such a *ḥerem* is found in the Bible.

HALAKHA

A Torah scholar may ostracize himself, and he may release himself – תַּלְמִיד חָכָם מְנַדֶּה לְעַצְמוֹ וּמֵיפֵר לְעַצְמוֹ: A Torah scholar can ostracize himself and release himself from ostracism, even if he was ostracized at the instruction of someone else, or was ostracized because he had sinned. Some say that if he was liable to be ostracized and is deserving of this punishment, he cannot release himself from ostracism (*Shulḥan Arukh, Yoreh De'a* 334:33).

LANGUAGE

Excommunication [*shamta*] – שַׁמְתָּא: This word is Aramaic and means to ostracize or to excommunicate. The explanations offered by the Sages for this word are not meant to teach about its etymology, but rather are meant to allude to the severity of ostracism.

Numerical value [*gimatriyya*] – גִּימַטְרִיָּא: From the Greek γεωμετρία, *geometria*, which means measurement or calculation in general, although it later came to refer to a specific type of calculation. In rabbinic literature, it also refers broadly to mathematical calculations, and specifically for tabulating the numerical value of the letters.

BACKGROUND

Document of ostracism – פְּתִיחָא: The *ge'onim*, who had a tradition with regard to this matter, understood that this is a document written for someone who refuses to appear in court or pay what he owes. It is given this name because it is the first document that the court writes for him. If, after some time, he still does not obey the court's orders, they then write a document of excommunication, which is more severe than the initial document of ostracism (see *Bava Kama* 112b).

וְאַחֲתֵיהּ בֵּי קִבְרֵי, וּקְרִי בֵּיהּ אַלְפָּא שִׁפּוּרֵי בְּאַרְבְּעִין יוֹמִין. אֲזַיל עֲבֵיד הָכִי. פְּקַע כַּדָּא, וּמִית אַלָּמָא. מַאי שִׁפּוּרֵי? שֶׁנִּפְרָעִין מִמֶּנּוּ.

and set it down in a cemetery,[N] where nobody is found, **and sound a thousand,** i.e., many, ***shofar*** **blasts over the course of forty days.**[N] That man **went and did this. The jug burst and the violent man died.** The Gemara asks: **What** is the reason that ***shofarot*** are sounded when a decree of ostracism is pronounced? The *shofarot* allude to the fact **that they extract punishment** [*shenifra'in*] **from** the excommunicated person.

מַאי תַּבְרָא? אָמַר רַב יִצְחָק בְּרֵיהּ דְּרַב יְהוּדָה: תַּבְרֵי בָּתֵּי רָמֵי. דְּתַנְיָא, אָמַר רַבָּן שִׁמְעוֹן בֶּן גַּמְלִיאֵל: כׇּל מָקוֹם שֶׁנָּתְנוּ חֲכָמִים עֵינֵיהֶם – אוֹ מִיתָה אוֹ עוֹנִי.

The Gemara asks further: **What** is the reason that **broken** blasts are sounded on the *shofar* when the excommunication is pronounced? **Rav Yitzḥak, son of Rav Yehuda, said: It breaks tall buildings,**[N] i.e., a decree of ostracism can harm and break even the high and mighty, **as it is taught** in a *baraita*: **Rabban Shimon ben Gamliel said: Wherever** it says that **the Sages set their eyes** in anger upon a particular person, it causes **either death or poverty.**

״וְהַנָּזִיר וְהַמְּצוֹרָע מִטּוּמְאָתוֹ לְטׇהֳרָתוֹ״. בְּעָא מִינֵּיהּ רַבִּי יִרְמְיָה מֵרַבִּי זֵירָא: בְּשֶׁלֹּא הָיָה לָהֶם פְּנַאי, אוֹ דִּלְמָא אַף בְּשֶׁהָיָה לָהֶם פְּנַאי?

§ It is taught in the mishna: **And the nazirite** whose term of naziriteship ended on the intermediate days of a Festival, **and the leper** who needs to purify himself on the intermediate days and must shave his entire body in order to leave **his** state of ritual **impurity** and regain **his** ritual **purity,** these people are permitted to cut their hair on the intermediate days of the Festival because they were not able to do so on the eve of the Festival. **Rabbi Yirmeya raised a question before Rabbi Zeira:** Is this allowance limited to the case **where they did not have the time** to cut their hair before the Festival, as it was prohibited for them to do so beforehand? **Or perhaps** they may cut their hair **even** in a case **where they had the time** to do so beforehand.

אֲמַר לֵיהּ: תָּנֵינָא, כׇּל אֵלּוּ שֶׁאָמְרוּ מוּתָּרִין לְגַלֵּחַ בַּמּוֹעֵד – בְּשֶׁלֹּא הָיָה לָהֶם פְּנַאי, אֲבָל הָיָה לָהֶם פְּנַאי – אֲסוּרִים.

He said to him: We already **learned** this in a *baraita*: With regard to **all those** about whom **the** Sages **said** that they **are permitted to cut their hair on** the intermediate days of **a Festival,** they may do so only **if they did not have time** to cut their hair before the Festival. **But if they had time** before the Festival began, then **they are prohibited** from doing so.

נָזִיר וּמְצוֹרָע, אַף עַל פִּי שֶׁהָיָה לָהֶם פְּנַאי – מוּתָּרִים, שֶׁלֹּא יַשְׁהוּ קׇרְבְּנוֹתֵיהֶן.

However, **a nazirite and a leper, even if they had the time** to do so before the Festival, **they are permitted** to cut their hair. Why are they granted this special allowance? So **that they will not delay** bringing **their offerings.**[N] Both a nazirite and a leper must cut their hair before sacrificing their offerings in completion of their purification process. Therefore, if they are not permitted to cut their hair, they will not be able to sacrifice their offerings at the proper time."[H]

תָּנָא: הַכֹּהֵן וְהָאָבֵל מוּתָּרִין בְּגִילּוּחַ. הַאי אָבֵל הֵיכִי דָּמֵי? אִילֵּימָא שֶׁחָל שְׁמִינִי שֶׁלּוֹ בְּעֶרֶב הָרֶגֶל – אִיבָּעֵי לֵיהּ לְגַלּוֹחֵי בְּעֶרֶב הָרֶגֶל. אֶלָּא שֶׁחָל שְׁמִינִי שֶׁלּוֹ לִהְיוֹת בְּשַׁבָּת עֶרֶב הָרֶגֶל,

In was **taught** in a *baraita*: **A priest and a mourner are permitted to cut their hair** during the intermediate days of a Festival. The Gemara asks: **What are the circumstances** when the **mourner** is permitted to do so? **If we say that the eighth** day **of his** mourning **occurred on the eve of the Festival,** then **he should have cut his hair on the eve of the Festival,** as the more stringent restrictions of his mourning no longer applied. **Rather,** it must be that we are dealing with a case **where the eighth** day **of his** mourning **occurred on a Shabbat**[N] **that was the eve of the Festival,** and so he could not have cut his hair on the Festival eve.

NOTES

Cemetery – **בֵּי קִבְרֵי**: The simple reason for this is because it is a place where people are not present. *Talmid Rabbeinu Yeḥiel of Paris* adds that by doing this, it is as though the dead were his community and they agreed to this decree of ostracism.

A thousand *shofar* blasts over the course of forty days – **אַלְפָּא שִׁפּוּרֵי בְּאַרְבְּעִין יוֹמִין**: Rabbi Shlomo ben HaYatom explains that this does not mean that he should sound the ram's horn exactly one thousand times, but rather that it should be blown numerous times. However, he writes that the number forty alludes to the forty days when a fetus is first formed so that this curse of death parallels the time when this person was first created. See also Maharsha who offers a similar explanation.

It breaks tall buildings [*tavrei batei ramei*] – **תַּבְרֵי בָּתֵּי רָמֵי**: In the manuscript of Rashi, it is noted that an alternative version of the Talmud text reads: That breaks, builds, and casts away [*tavrei, batei, verami*] (see Commentary on *Moed Katan*).

So that they will not delay bringing their offerings – **שֶׁלֹּא יַשְׁהוּ קׇרְבְּנוֹתֵיהֶם**: Rabbi Shlomo ben HaYatom writes that one who is required to bring these offerings transgresses a positive mitzva every day that he delays doing so. *Talmid Rabbeinu Yeḥiel of Paris* explains that in this case the Sages did not prohibit haircutting during the intermediate days, as they did not want their decree to prevent one from bringing his offering in the proper time.

Tosafot ask: The nazirite's haircut is not a prerequisite for sacrificing his offering, so why is he permitted to cut his hair during the intermediate days? They answer that although he is not required to do so, it is a mitzva for him to cut his hair at that time. *Talmid Rabbeinu Yeḥiel of Paris* adds that normally one wants to perform all of the associated mitzvot at the same time, and if he is not permitted to cut his hair then he will similarly delay bringing his offering.

Where the eighth day…occurred on a Shabbat – **שֶׁחָל שְׁמִינִי...בְּשַׁבָּת**: *Tosafot* note that the mourning period begins only once the deceased has been buried. Since burials may not be performed on Shabbat, how is it possible for the eighth day of the mourning period to fall on Shabbat? This question is answered by the Jerusalem Talmud in several different ways: Either the deceased was killed and dragged away by a wild animal on Shabbat, in which case there is no burial and the mourning period begins immediately, or gentiles completed the burial after Shabbat had already begun. The Meiri adds that it is possible that the deceased drowned on a boat on Shabbat.

HALAKHA

Haircutting for a nazirite and leper during the intermediate days – **תִּגְלַחַת נָזִיר וּמְצוֹרָע בַּמּוֹעֵד**: When it is time for a nazirite or a leper to cut his hair, he is permitted to do so, even during the intermediate days of the Festival, so that he does not delay bringing his offerings. Even if his time to cut his hair occurred before the Festival, but he delayed for whatever reason, he may still cut his hair during the intermediate days to avoid further delay in bringing his offerings (Rambam *Sefer Zemanim*, *Hilkhot Yom Tov* 7:19).

HALAKHA

The time that a mourner may cut his hair – זמן גילוח לאבל: If one buried his deceased relative seven days before the Festival and mourned for seven days, the Festival cancels the thirty-day period of mourning known as *sheloshim*. This applies even if the seventh day occurs on the day before the Festival, due to the principle that part of a day has the halakhic status of an entire day, in accordance with the opinion of Abba Shaul. In addition, such mourners are permitted to cut their hair, launder their clothes, and bathe on the day before a Festival, close to nightfall. On the day before Passover, a mourner may perform these activities from midday onward so that he may bring the Paschal offering at the proper time. Others say that it is preferable for him to cut his hair before midday (Rema).

Similarly, if the eighth day of his mourning falls on Shabbat on the day before a Festival, then he may cut his hair, launder his clothes, and bathe on Friday, which is his seventh day of mourning. If he did not cut his hair in these cases, then he is prohibited from doing so during the intermediate days. However, he may do so after the conclusion of the Festival. If his seventh day of mourning falls on Shabbat on the day before a Festival, then he is permitted to cut his hair during the intermediate days, since he was unable to do so before the Festival (*Shulḥan Arukh, Yoreh De'a* 399:3).

A priest serving immediately prior to the Festival – כהן המשמש סמוך לרגל: The members of the priestly watch whose week of Temple service ends during the Festival may cut their hair during the intermediate days. However, if the watch completed its service on the day before a Festival, then the priests should cut their hair at that time, and they are prohibited from cutting their hair during the Festival (Rambam *Sefer Zemanim, Hilkhot Yom Tov* 7:19 and *Sefer Avoda, Hilkhot Biat HaMikdash* 1:13).

Watches during the Festivals – המשמרות ברגלים: During the three pilgrimage Festivals, all of the priestly watches have equal standing; they equally divide the shewbread and all of the offerings that were sacrificed during the Festival. Additionally, on *Shavuot* they share the two loaves (Rambam *Sefer Avoda, Hilkhot Kelei HaMikdash* 4:4–5).

BACKGROUND

The shewbread – לחם הפנים: The Torah describes the offering of the twelve loaves of shewbread that were placed on the sacred table in the Sanctuary each Shabbat (Leviticus 24:5–9). The bread of the previous week was divided among the priests and eaten by them. The shewbread was unleavened and placed on the table in two arrangements of six loaves each. Two bowls of frankincense were placed between them, or, according to other opinions, on top of them.

Priests with shewbread

איבעי ליה לגלוחי ערב שבת, דאמר רב חסדא אמר רבינא בר שילא: הלכה כאבא שאול. ומודים חכמים לאבא שאול בשחל שמיני שלו להיות בשבת ערב הרגל, שמותר לגלח בערב שבת!

But if this is the case, **he should have cut his hair on Friday, for Rav Ḥisda said** that **Ravina bar Sheila said: The *halakha* is in accordance with** the opinion of **Abba Shaul.** If the deceased was buried seven days before the Festival, then not only has the mourner completed the seven-day mourning period, but he is even regarded as having begun the thirty-day mourning period, and so the Festival cancels this thirty-day period of mourning. **And the Rabbis concede** to the opinion of **Abba Shaul when the eighth** day of **his** mourning **occurs on a Shabbat that is the eve of the Festival,** and they maintain **that he is permitted to cut his hair on Friday.** Since he is unavoidably prevented from cutting his hair on the eighth day, the Rabbis allowed him to cut it already on the seventh day.[H]

לא צריכא, שחל שביעי שלו להיות בשבת ערב הרגל.

The Gemara answers: **No,** the ruling of the *baraita* is **necessary** in the case **where the seventh** day of **his** mourning **occurs on a Shabbat that is the eve of the Festival.** In that case, he certainly cannot cut his hair on Friday because it is only the sixth day of his mourning, and so he is permitted to cut his hair on the intermediate days of the Festival.

תנא ברא סבר לה כאבא שאול, דאמר מקצת היום ככולו, ויום שביעי עולה לו לכאן ולכאן. וכיון דשבת הוי – אנוס הוא.

The Gemara comments: **The *tanna* of the *baraita*,** who permits a mourner to cut his hair during the intermediate days of the Festival, **holds in accordance with** the opinion of **Abba Shaul, who said:** The legal status of **part of the day is like** that of **an entire** day, **and** therefore **the seventh** day **counts as both** the final day of the seven-day mourning period and the first day of the thirty-day mourning period. From the perspective of the *halakhot* of mourning, one would be permitted to cut his hair; however **since** this day **is Shabbat, he is unavoidably prevented** from doing so, and therefore he is permitted to cut his hair during the intermediate days of the Festival.

תנא דידן סבר לה כרבנן, דאמרי: לא אמרינן מקצת היום ככולו, ואכתי לא שלים אבילות דשבעה.

The *tanna* of **our** mishna, on the other hand, who does not mention that a mourner is permitted to cut his hair on the intermediate days of a Festival, **holds in accordance with** the opinion of the **Rabbis, who say: We do not say** that the legal status of **part of the day is like** that of **an entire** day for a mourner. Therefore, **he has not yet completed** his **seven**-day period of **mourning,** and consequently he will not be permitted to cut his hair even after the Festival, until the completion of the thirty-day mourning period.

האי כהן היכי דמי? אילימא דשלים משמרתו ערב הרגל – איבעי ליה לגלוחי ערב הרגל!

The Gemara continues and asks: The case of **this priest,** who is permitted to cut his hair during the intermediate days of a Festival, **what are the circumstances? If we say that he completed his watch on the eve of the Festival,** then **he should have cut his hair on the eve of the Festival.**

לא צריכא, דשלים משמרתו ברגל. תנא דידן סבר: כיון דתנן: בשלשה פרקים בשנה היו כל המשמרות שוות באימורי הרגלים ובחילוק לחם הפנים. כמאן דלא שלים משמרתו ברגל דמי. ותנא ברא סבר: אף על גב דשייך בהנך משמרות – משמרתיה מיהא שלימא ליה.

The Gemara answers: **No,** the ruling of the *baraita* is **necessary** in the case **where one completed his watch during the Festival** week itself.[H] **The *tanna*** of **our** mishna **holds** that **since we learned** in a mishna (*Sukka* 55b): **At the year,** i.e., the three pilgrimage Festivals, **all of the priestly watches share equally in the Festival offerings**[N] **and in the division of the shewbread**[B] among the priests on Shabbat that occurs on the Festival,[H] therefore, **he is** considered **like one whose watch was not completed during the Festival,** and he may not cut his hair until after the Festival. **And the *tanna*** of **the *baraita* holds that although** he **belongs** also **to those** other **watches** serving during the Festival, **nevertheless, his own watch was completed** before the Festival, and so he is permitted to cut his hair.[N]

NOTES

The Festival offerings [*imurei*] – אימורי הרגלים: In tractate *Sukka*, it is explained that the term used here for offerings refers specifically to those portions that were burnt on the altar. The priests have no benefit from those portions. Some explain that the word *imurei* here should be understood not as offerings, but as: What is said [*ne'emar*] to be done during the Festivals, or to the other offerings from which the priests would receive a portion (*Talmid Rabbeinu Yeḥiel of Paris*; Ritva).

A priest's haircut – תגלחת הכהן: Rashi asks: Why does he not cut his hair on Thursday, just before the conclusion of his watch? In answer, he explains that the *baraita* refers to a case where the Festival itself occurs on Thursday. The Meiri offers a similar explanation. Rashi in the manuscript writes that initially the priest is permitted only to launder his clothes, but not to cut his hair on Thursday. The Ritva offers a similar explanation.

תָּנוּ רַבָּנַן: כׇּל אֵלּוּ שֶׁאָמְרוּ מוּתָּרִין לְגַלֵּחַ בַּמּוֹעֵד – מוּתָּרִין לְגַלֵּחַ בִּימֵי אֶבְלָן.

§ **The Sages taught** the following *baraita*: **All those about whom it was said** that they **are permitted to cut their hair on** the intermediate days of **a Festival**[H] because they were unable to do so beforehand, **they may** similarly **cut their hair during the period of their mourning** if they had been unable to do so beforehand.

וְהָתַנְיָא אֲסוּרִים! אָמַר רַב חִסְדָּא אָמַר רַב שֵׁילָא: כִּי תַּנְיָא הָכָא מוּתָּרִין – בְּשֶׁתְּכָפוּהוּ אֲבֵלָיו.

The Gemara asks: **But isn't it taught** in another *baraita*: **They are** nevertheless **prohibited** from cutting their hair during the period of their mourning? **Rav Ḥisda said** that **Rav Sheila said: When it is taught** in the *baraita* that **they are permitted** to cut their hair, it is referring to one **for whom** two periods of **mourning applied in succession.** In other words, this person was required to practice one period of mourning immediately following another period of mourning, and he is unable to endure the prescribed restrictions for such an extended period.

אִי בְּשֶׁתְּכָפוּהוּ אֲבֵלָיו מַאי אִירְיָא כׇּל אֵלּוּ שֶׁאָמְרוּ? אֲפִילּוּ כּוּלֵּי עָלְמָא נַמִּי! דְּתַנְיָא: תְּכָפוּהוּ אֲבֵלָיו זֶה אַחַר זֶה, הִכְבִּיד שְׂעָרוֹ – מֵיקֵל בְּתַעַר, וּמְכַבֵּס כְּסוּתוֹ בְּמַיִם!

The Gemara asks: **If** this is referring to a case **where his mourning applied in succession,** then **why specifically** does the *baraita* discuss **all those about whom it was said** that they may cut their hair? The allowance should apply **even to everyone,** not only to those who had been unavoidably prevented from cutting their hair in the preceding period, **as it is taught** in a *baraita*: **If one's mourning** periods **applied in succession, one after the other,** and **his hair** grew long and **became heavy, he may lighten** it by cutting his hair **with a razor,**[N] **and he may wash his garment in water,** so that he does not suffer for such a long time without cutting his hair or washing his clothes.

הָא אִתְּמַר עֲלָהּ, אָמַר רַב חִסְדָּא: בְּתַעַר וְלֹא בְּמִסְפָּרַיִם; בְּמַיִם וְלֹא בְּנֶתֶר וְלֹא בְּאָהָל. אָמַר רַב חִסְדָּא: זֹאת אוֹמֶרֶת: אָבֵל אָסוּר בְּתִכְבּוֹסֶת.

The Gemara answers: **But wasn't it said with regard to that** *baraita*: **Rav Ḥisda said:** When it states that one may cut his hair, it means that he may do so **with a razor, but not with scissors?** Similarly, when it states that one may wash his clothes, it means that he may launder them **with water, but not with** ***neter***[B] **or soap.**[B] Therefore, the *baraita* teaches that if one had been unavoidably prevented from performing these actions beforehand and then had to observe a double mourning period, he may cut his hair in an ordinary manner, without performing these actions in an altered way. **Rav Ḥisda said: That is to say** that, generally speaking, **a mourner is prohibited from laundering** his clothes.[NH]

תָּנוּ רַבָּנַן: כְּשֵׁם שֶׁאָמְרוּ אָסוּר לְגַלֵּחַ בַּמּוֹעֵד – כָּךְ אָסוּר לִיטּוֹל צִפּוֹרְנַיִם בַּמּוֹעֵד, דִּבְרֵי רַבִּי יְהוּדָה. וְרַבִּי יוֹסֵי מַתִּיר.

The Sages taught the following *baraita*: **Just as** the Sages **said** that **it is prohibited to cut one's hair during the** intermediate days of **a Festival, so too it is prohibited to cut one's nails during the** intermediate days of **a Festival;**[N] this is **the statement of Rabbi Yehuda, whereas Rabbi Yosei permits** cutting nails.

BACKGROUND

Neter – נֶתֶר: This is apparently sodium carbonate, Na_2CO_3, which is found in colorless clusters that crystallize from evaporating water. In nature, sodium carbonate is found in desert regions. However, in ancient times it was often produced from the ash of sea algae. Also called washing soda, this compound easily dissolves in water, and its solubility causes a strong basic reaction. Due to hydrolysis, which produces Na_2, it can dissolve many different types of fats, and therefore it was used as a cleaning agent, even during the biblical period. Some say that it refers to natron, a naturally occurring mixture of sodium carbonate decahydrate.

Soap [*ohal*] – אָהָל: Many plants with the name *ohal* are found in Eretz Yisrael. One of them, known as the common ice plant or *Mesembryanthemum crystallinum* L., is an annual plant that grows in the Sharon and Shephela regions of Eretz Yisrael, in rocks and walls that face the sea. The surface of these plants is covered in small translucent sacs that appear like ice crystals, which give it the name ice plant. This plant contains a noticeable amount of raw soda and was used for laundering clothes and bathing.

Common ice plant

HALAKHA

Those who are permitted to cut their hair on the intermediate days of a Festival, etc. – הַמּוּתָּרִים לְהִתְגַּלֵּחַ בַּמּוֹעֵד וכו׳: If one from those categories of people whom the Sages permitted to cut their hair during the intermediate days becomes a mourner, it is prohibited for him to cut his hair during the mourning period. However, if he had two consecutive mourning periods, he may cut his hair in an ordinary manner during the second seven-day period. Anyone else who has two consecutive periods of mourning may cut his hair in an unusual manner, such as with a razor, as opposed to using scissors. This must be done in private (*Shulḥan Arukh*, *Yoreh De'a* 390:3, and in the comment of Rema).

A mourner is prohibited from laundering his clothes – אָבֵל אָסוּר בְּתִכְבּוֹסֶת: A mourner may not launder his clothes for the entire seven-day period of mourning, and he is similarly prohibited from wearing freshly laundered clothes. After these seven days, it is permitted. However, the common practice is to refrain from wearing freshly laundered clothes for the entire thirty-day period. In order to observe this custom, it is common practice to permit the mourner to wear clean clothes after they have first been worn by another person for a short time (Rema).

If a person in one of the categories of people who are permitted to launder their clothes during the intermediate days became a mourner, he is prohibited from laundering his clothes while in mourning. However, if he experiences two consecutive periods of mourning, then he may launder clothes in an ordinary manner in private.

Anyone who experiences two consecutive periods of mourning may launder clothes only in water, without soap or lye. If he must wash his clothes because they are dirty and he is not doing so for pleasure, then he is permitted to launder them properly (*Shulḥan Arukh*, *Yoreh De'a* 389:1; *Pitḥei Teshuva*, citing *Responsa Laḥmei Toda*).

NOTES

Lighten it with a razor – מֵיקֵל בְּתַעַר: According to some, this expression means that one is permitted only to neaten his hair by trimming several of the longer strands, but he may not have a proper haircut (*Talmid Rabbeinu Yeḥiel of Paris*). Others write that this means that he may cut the lower parts of his hair so that the haircut is not apparent to others (Rid). The Ran presents both opinions.

That is to say a mourner is prohibited from laundering his clothes – זֹאת אוֹמֶרֶת אָבֵל אָסוּר בְּתִכְבּוֹסֶת: The early authorities ask: Why did Rav Ḥisda need to make this statement when it was already taught that a mourner may not launder his clothes, based on the instructions given to the Tekoite woman (see *Tosafot*)? *Talmid Rabbeinu Yeḥiel of Paris* writes that the verse cannot serve as a proof but merely as an allusion to the *halakha*, making Rav Ḥisda's statement necessary. Others write that there the *baraita* taught only about laundering clothes in an ordinary manner. However, here Rav Ḥisda teaches that it is prohibited to launder clothes even in cold water (Ran; Ritva; see *Tosefot HaRosh*).

Cutting nails during the intermediate days – נְטִילַת צִפּוֹרְנַיִם בַּמּוֹעֵד: Some explain that according to Rabbi Yosei's opinion nothing is accomplished by cutting one's nails before a Festival because they grow so quickly. Even cutting them immediately before the Festival does not prevent the need to cut them during the intermediate days (Ran). Others suggest that long fingernails are especially repulsive, and the Sages were not strict with such a minor type of work (Ritva).

And just as the Sages **said** that **a mourner is prohibited from cutting his hair during the period of his mourning, so too he is prohibited from cutting his nails during the period of his mourning;** this is **the statement of Rabbi Yehuda, whereas Rabbi Yosei permits** a mourner to cut his nails.[N]

וּכְשֵׁם שֶׁאָמְרוּ: אָבֵל אָסוּר לְגַלֵּחַ בִּימֵי אֶבְלוֹ – כָּךְ אָסוּר לִיטּוֹל צִפּוֹרְנַיִם בִּימֵי אֶבְלוֹ, דִּבְרֵי רַבִּי יְהוּדָה. וְרַבִּי יוֹסֵי מַתִּיר.

Ulla said: The *halakha* is in accordance with the opinion of **Rabbi Yehuda with regard to mourning, but the *halakha* is in accordance with** the opinion of **Rabbi Yosei with regard to the** intermediate days of the **Festival. Shmuel said:**

אָמַר עוּלָּא: הֲלָכָה כְּרַבִּי יְהוּדָה בְּאָבֵל, וַהֲלָכָה כְּרַבִּי יוֹסֵי בְּמוֹעֵד, שְׁמוּאֵל אָמַר:

NOTES

Nail cutting for a mourner – נְטִילַת צִפּוֹרְנַיִם בְּאָבֵל: The Ran writes in the name of Rabbi Aaron HaLevi that it is possible to derive the prohibition against nail cutting during the mourning period from the biblical passage that describes the beautiful captive woman. She must mourn for her family for seven days, and it is written that she must "do her nails" (Deuteronomy 21:12). This is understood as meaning that she must let her nails grow during the period when she mourns her family.

Rabbi Yosei does not learn this derivation, either because the mitzva that the beautiful woman grow her nails is part of the requirement that she make herself unattractive, or because he maintains that "do her nails" does not mean grow her nails, but rather cut her nails (Ran; see Ritva).

Perek **III**
Daf **18** Amud **a**

The *halakha* is in accordance with the opinion of **Rabbi Yosei with regard to** the intermediate days of **the Festival**[H] **and with regard to mourning, as Shmuel said** this general principle: **The *halakha* is in accordance with the statement of the** more **lenient** authority **in** matters relating to **mourning.**[H]

הֲלָכָה כְּרַבִּי יוֹסֵי בְּמוֹעֵד וּבְאָבֵל. דְּאָמַר שְׁמוּאֵל: הֲלָכָה כְּדִבְרֵי הַמֵּיקֵל בְּאָבֵל.

It was related that **something** unpleasant **happened to Pineḥas, brother of Mar Shmuel,** that is to say, one of his close relatives died. **Shmuel entered to ask him the reason,** i.e., to console him. **He saw that** Pineḥas's **nails were long,** and **said to him: Why do you not cut them?** Pineḥas **replied: If it were your** relative who died,[N] and you were in mourning, **would you treat** the matter **so lightly** and cut your nails?

פִּנְחָס אֲחוּהּ דְּמָר שְׁמוּאֵל, אִיתְרַע בֵּיהּ מִילְּתָא. עָל שְׁמוּאֵל לְמִישְׁאַל טַעְמָא מִינֵּיהּ. חַזְנְהוּ לְטוּפְרֵי דַּהֲווּ נְפִישָׁן. אֲמַר לֵיהּ: אַמַּאי לָא שָׁקְלַתְּ לְהוּ? אֲמַר לֵיהּ: אִי בְּדִידֵיהּ הֲוָה, מִי מְזַלְזְלַתְּ בֵּיהּ כּוּלֵּי הַאי?

Pineḥas's words **were: "Like an error that proceeds from a ruler"** (Ecclesiastes 10:5).[N] As soon as he uttered them they came true, even though he did not intend them. Shortly after Pineḥas made his comment, **something** unpleasant **happened to Shmuel,** and one of his close relatives died. **Pineḥas, his brother, entered to ask him the reason,** i.e., to offer words of comfort. Shmuel **took his nails and cast them in** Pineḥas's face.[N] Shmuel then **said to him:** Do **you not** know the principle that **a covenant is made with the lips?** In other words, do you not know that what one says influences future events?

הֲוַאי ״כִּשְׁגָגָה שֶׁיֹּצָא מִלִּפְנֵי הַשַּׁלִּיט״, וְאִיתְרַע בֵּיהּ מִילְּתָא בִּשְׁמוּאֵל. עָל פִּנְחָס אֲחוּהּ לְמִישְׁאַל טַעְמָא מִינֵּיהּ, שַׁקְלִינְהוּ לְטוּפְרֵיהּ חַבְטִינְהוּ לְאַפֵּיהּ. אֲמַר לֵיהּ: לֵית לָךְ בְּרִית כְּרוּתָה לַשְּׂפָתַיִם?

HALAKHA

Cutting nails during the intermediate days of a Festival – נְטִילַת צִפּוֹרְנַיִם בְּמוֹעֵד: It is permitted to cut both one's fingernails and toenails during the intermediate days of a Festival, even using a pair of scissors. This is because the *halakha* is in accordance with the opinion of Rabbi Yosei, as is stated by Shmuel.

The Rema writes that there are those who rule stringently and prohibit the use of scissors. The custom is not to cut one's nails using any implement, with the exception of a woman preparing for mandatory ritual immersion, who may cut her nails in an ordinary manner. However, even according to those who are strict, it is permitted to trim nails with one's teeth or hands. In exceptional circumstances, if one was preoccupied before the Festival, then he may cut his nails with scissors during the Festival, even according to those who are stringent (*Arukh HaShulḥan*). Practically speaking, Ashkenazic communities follow the Rema, and even many Sephardic communities do as well, and one should not act differently in a place where this is the custom (*Kaf HaḤayyim*; *Shulḥan Arukh*, *Oraḥ Ḥayyim* 532:1).

Cutting nails while in mourning – נְטִילַת צִפּוֹרְנַיִם בְּאָבֵל: The *halakha* follows the opinion of Rabbi Yosei, as ruled by Shmuel, that a mourner may cut his nails. However, the *halakha* also follows the opinion of Rav, and the nails should be cut with one's hands or teeth but not with a utensil.

Once the first seven days of mourning have passed, but before the thirty-day period of mourning is over, a woman who is preparing for her ritual immersion should ask a gentile woman to cut her nails for her. Some say that another Jewish woman may also cut them on her behalf (Rema). However, others disagree and say that it is prohibited for another Jewish woman to cut them for her (*Shakh*), but this is not the custom (*Arukh HaShulḥan*; *Shulḥan Arukh*, *Yoreh De'a* 390:7).

NOTES

If it were your relative who died – אִי בְּדִידֵיהּ הֲוָה: This refers to a child, rather than any other relative, which explains why it was a close relative of Pineḥas, but not a close relative of Pineḥas's brother, Shmuel (Rashi manuscript).

Like an error that proceeds from a ruler – כִּשְׁגָגָה שֶׁיֹּצָא מִלִּפְנֵי הַשַּׁלִּיט: In the manuscript of Rashi, it is explained: This is similar to a case where a ruler stated that a person deserves to be sentenced to death. Although the ruler did not actually intend for him to be killed, his servant carried out this order.

Took his nails and cast them in his face – שַׁקְלִינְהוּ לְטוּפְרֵיהּ חַבְטִינְהוּ לְאַפֵּיהּ: Shmuel was not concerned about throwing his fingernail clippings on the ground, although subsequently the Gemara explains that one who does so is wicked. Shmuel was not concerned, either because he collected them afterward (Rashi), or because he was in a place where women were not present (*Talmid Rabbeinu Yeḥiel of Paris*).

דְּאָמַר רַבִּי יוֹחָנָן: מִנַּיִן שֶׁבְּרִית כְּרוּתָה לִשְׂפָתַיִם – שֶׁנֶּאֱמַר: ״וַיֹּאמֶר אַבְרָהָם אֶל נְעָרָיו שְׁבוּ לָכֶם פֹּה עִם הַחֲמוֹר וַאֲנִי וְהַנַּעַר נֵלְכָה עַד כֹּה וְנִשְׁתַּחֲוֶה וְנָשׁוּבָה אֲלֵיכֶם״, וְאִיסְתַּיְּיעָא מִלְּתָא דַּהֲדוּר תַּרְוַיְיהוּ.

This is as **Rabbi Yoḥanan said: From where** is it derived **that a covenant is made with the lips,** and that one's speech has the power to change events? **For it is stated: "And Abraham said to his young men: Stay here with the donkey, and I and the lad will go onward; and we will worship, and we will come back to you"** (Genesis 22:5). Abraham said this even though he thought that he was going to sacrifice his son as an offering and that Isaac would not be returning, **yet this had an influence and they both came back.**

סְבוּר מִינַּהּ: דְּיָד – אִין, דְּרֶגֶל – לָא. אָמַר רַב עָנָן בַּר תַּחְלִיפָא: לְדִידִי מְפָרְשָׁא לִי מִינֵּיהּ דִּשְׁמוּאֵל: לָא שְׁנָא דְּיָד, וְלָא שְׁנָא דְּרֶגֶל.

With regard to this *halakha* pertaining to a mourner cutting his nails: They initially **concluded from this:** With regard to the nails on his **hand, yes,** a mourner may cut them; but as for the nails on his **foot, no,** he may not cut them, because long toenails are less repulsive. **Rav Anan bar Taḥlifa said: It was explained to me by Shmuel** himself: **It is not different** if it is the nails on the **hand and it is not different** if it is the nails on the **foot,** as in both cases cutting the nails is permitted.

אָמַר רַב חִיָּיא בַּר אַשִׁי אָמַר רַב: וּבִגְנוּסְטְרָא אָסוּר. אָמַר רַב שֶׁמֶן בַּר אַבָּא: הֲוָה קָאֵימְנָא קַמֵּיהּ דְּרַבִּי יוֹחָנָן בֵּי מִדְרְשָׁא בְּחוּלּוֹ שֶׁל מוֹעֵד, וְשַׁקְלִינְהוּ לְטוּפְרֵיהּ בְּשִׁינֵּיהּ וְזַרְקִינְהוּ.

Rav Ḥiyya bar Ashi said that **Rav said: But with scissors** [*genustera*][L] specifically for nail cutting **it is prohibited,** i.e., the mourner should cut his nails in an alternate manner. **Rav Shemen bar Abba said:** I once **stood before Rabbi Yoḥanan in the study hall during the intermediate days of a Festival, and he cut his nails with his teeth and threw them** down.

שְׁמַע מִינַּהּ תְּלָת; שְׁמַע מִינַּהּ: מוּתָּר לִיטּוֹל צִפָּרְנַיִם בְּחוּלּוֹ שֶׁל מוֹעֵד. וּשְׁמַע מִינַּהּ: אֵין בָּהֶן מִשּׁוּם מִיאוּס. וּשְׁמַע מִינַּהּ: מוּתָּר לְזוֹרְקָן.

The Gemara comments: **Learn from this** incident of Rabbi Yoḥanan **three** *halakhot*:[N] **Learn from this** that **it is permitted to cut one's nails on the intermediate days of a Festival. And learn from this** that nails **have no** prohibition **due to** the fact that they are **repulsive,** i.e., there is no prohibition against biting them on that basis. Inasmuch as one is prohibited from placing something repulsive in his mouth, this incident teaches that nails do not fall into this category. **And** also **learn from this** that **it is permitted** to throw **nails** away.

אִינִי? וְהָתַנְיָא: שְׁלֹשָׁה דְּבָרִים נֶאֶמְרוּ בְּצִפָּרְנַיִם: הַקּוֹבְרָן – צַדִּיק; שׂוֹרְפָן – חָסִיד; זוֹרְקָן – רָשָׁע. טַעְמָא מַאי? שֶׁמָּא תַּעֲבוֹר עֲלֵיהֶן אִשָּׁה עוּבָּרָה וְתַפִּיל.

The Gemara asks: **Is that so? But isn't it taught** in a *baraita*: **Three things were said about nails: One who buries them** in the ground **is** deemed **righteous. One who burns them** is even better, as he **is** considered **pious.**[N] **One who** merely **throws them** away is regarded as **wicked.**[H] The Gemara explains: **What is the reason** that it is prohibited to throw away nail clippings? This is prohibited **lest a pregnant women pass over them**[N] **and miscarry,** for the Sages had a tradition that it is dangerous for a pregnant woman to walk over fingernails.

אִשָּׁה בֵּי מִדְרְשָׁא לָא שְׁכִיחָא. וְכִי תֵּימָא: זִימְנִין דְּמִיכַּנְּשִׁי לְהוּ וְשָׁדֵי לְהוּ אַבָּרַאי, כֵּיוָן דְּאִשְׁתַּנֵּי – אִשְׁתַּנֵּי.

The Gemara answers: **A woman is not usually** found **in the study hall,** and therefore Rabbi Yoḥanan was not concerned about throwing his nail clippings there. **If you say** that **sometimes** the nails **are gathered** together when the floor is swept **and** then **thrown outside** where a pregnant woman may walk over them, this is not a problem. **Once** their place **has changed**[N] the nails themselves **change** and are no longer harmful.

אָמַר רַב יְהוּדָה אָמַר רַב: זוּג בָּא מֵחַמְתָּן לִפְנֵי רַבִּי, וּמָר זוּטְרָא מַתְנֵי: זוּג בָּא מֵחַמְתָּן לִפְנֵי רַבִּי, וּבִקְּשׁוּ מִמֶּנּוּ צִפָּרְנַיִם – וְהִתִּיר לָהֶם. וְאִם בִּקְּשׁוּ מִמֶּנּוּ שָׂפָה – הִתִּיר לָהֶם. וּשְׁמוּאֵל אָמַר: אַף בִּקְּשׁוּ מִמֶּנּוּ שָׂפָה וְהִתִּיר לָהֶם.

Rav Yehuda said that **Rav said: A pair** of Sages **from Ḥamatan came before Rabbi** Yehuda HaNasi. **And Mar Zutra taught**[N] it without the names of Rav Yehuda and Rav, simply as: **A pair** of Sages **from Ḥamatan came before Rabbi** Yehuda HaNasi. **And they asked him** whether or not a mourner is permitted to cut his **nails, and he permitted** it **to them. And had they asked him** whether or not a mourner may trim his **mustache, he would** also **have permitted** it to them. **And Shmuel said: They also asked him** about trimming **a mustache,**[N] and **he permitted** it **to them.**

LANGUAGE

Scissors [*genustera*] – **גְּנוּסְטְרָא**: The origin of this word is Greek. Some say it originates from the Greek κνηστήρ, *knestèr*, meaning a nail file, which was used for nail cutting. Others say, based on a version of the Talmud text that reads *negusterei*, that this may be from the Greek ὄνυξ, *onux*, meaning nail, and ῥίνη, *rhinè*, meaning clipper or cutter, which also refers to a utensil used for cutting nails.

NOTES

Learn from this incident three ***halakhot*** **– שְׁמַע מִינַּהּ תְּלָת:** Based on the fact that the Gemara specifically mentions three *halakhot* and not four, there are those who understand that Rabbi Yoḥanan's actions do not teach the prohibition against cutting fingernails on the intermediate days with scissors (Rif). Instead, he did not use scissors either because he did not have any available to him at that time or because one may not take metal tools into a study hall (Rabbi Shlomo ben HaYatom; see Ran). Some say that there is no evidence as to whether or not one may use scissors to cut nails on the intermediate days because this list of three only includes leniencies and not stringencies (Rid; see Ran).

One who burns them is pious – שׂוֹרְפָן חָסִיד: There are several reasons why such a person is called pious: Perhaps it is difficult to find an appropriate place to burn fingernails; burning fingernails smell unpleasant; or it may be particularly painful for one to burn something that was once part of his body (*Talmid Rabbeinu Yeḥiel of Paris*).

Lest a pregnant woman pass over them – שֶׁמָּא תַּעֲבוֹר עֲלֵיהֶן אִשָּׁה עוּבָּרָה: Some say that this means that the fingernails are repulsive and may thereby cause her to miscarry (*Talmid Rabbeinu Yeḥiel of Paris*). However, others explain that there is a spiritual reason that fingernails cause women to miscarry. For example, *Eliya Rabba* gives kabbalistic reasons for this.

Once their place has changed – כֵּיוָן דְּאִשְׁתַּנֵּי: Based on this expression, most explain that once nail clippings have been moved they no longer have the power to cause harm. Others suggest that once a certain amount of time has passed their power is negated (see *Talmid Rabbeinu Yeḥiel of Paris*).

Mar Zutra taught – וּמָר זוּטְרָא מַתְנֵי: According to the text of the Babylonian Talmud, there is no difference between the two versions of this statement, aside from the fact that Mar Zutra taught this statement as a *baraita* and not as a statement made by Rav. According to Rabbi Shlomo ben HaYatom, the text should read: A pair came from Ḥamatan before Rabbi Ḥiyya. In the Jerusalem Talmud, it is stated that two pairs of Sages came, each one from a different place, and each asked a different question.

They also asked him about a mustache – אַף בִּקְּשׁוּ מִמֶּנּוּ שָׂפָה: Rabbeinu Gershom *Me'or HaGola* and Rashi explain this question to be: In general, is trimming a mustache prohibited as a form of removing one's beard? However, most commentaries explain that the question is whether or not it is permitted to trim one's mustache during the intermediate days of a Festival (Rid; Rabbeinu Yehonatan of Lunel; *Talmid Rabbeinu Yeḥiel of Paris*). In the Jerusalem Talmud, there is a long dispute as to whether the question applies to the intermediate days of a Festival or to a mourning period. According to the Ra'avad, a mourner may not trim his mustache. In order to support his opinion, he cites Mephibosheth, who did not trim his mustache while he was mourning (II Samuel 19:25).

HALAKHA

What is done with nail clippings – מָה עוֹשִׂים בְּצִפָּרְנַיִם: When one cuts his nails it is preferable that he does not throw away the clippings, but instead he should bury or burn them (*Shulḥan Arukh*, *Oraḥ Ḥayyim* 260:1; *Magen Avraham*).

אָמַר אֲבִיטוּל סָפְרָא מִשְּׁמֵיהּ דְּרַב פָּפָּא: שָׂפָה מִזָּוִית לְזָוִית. אָמַר רַבִּי אַמִי: וּבְשָׂפָה הַמְעַכֶּבֶת. אֲמַר רַב נַחְמָן בַּר יִצְחָק: לְדִידִי כְּשָׂפָה הַמְעַכֶּבֶת דָּמֵי לִי.

Avitul the scribe said in the name of Rav Pappa: A mustache may be trimmed **from** one **corner to** the other **corner**[N] of the mouth. **Rabbi Ami said:** One may trim only the portion of the **mustache that interferes** with normal eating, but one may not trim the mustache for beautification. **Rav Naḥman bar Yitzḥak said: For me,** my entire mustache **is** considered **like a mustache that interferes** with normal eating, as I am particularly sensitive, and so I may trim my entire mustache.[H]

וְאָמַר אֲבִיטוּל סָפְרָא מִשְּׁמֵיהּ דְּרַב פָּפָּא: פַּרְעֹה שֶׁהָיָה בִּימֵי מֹשֶׁה הוּא אַמָּה וּזְקָנוֹ אַמָּה, וּפַרְמַשְׁתָּקוֹ אַמָּה וָזֶרֶת, לְקַיֵּים מַה שֶּׁנֶּאֱמַר: ״וּשְׁפַל אֲנָשִׁים יְקִים עֲלַיהּ״.

§ Having mentioned Avitul the scribe, the Gemara records other statements of his: **And Avitul the scribe said in the name of Rav Pappa:** The **Pharaoh who lived in the days of Moses**[N] **was a cubit** tall, his **beard was a cubit** long, **and his penis** [*parmashtako*][L] was **a cubit and a span,** i.e., a cubit and the distance between the thumb and the little finger, in length, **in order to fulfill what is stated: "And He sets up over it the lowest of men"** (Daniel 4:14), which teaches that Pharaoh was extremely short and lowly.

וְאָמַר אֲבִיטוּל סָפְרָא מִשְּׁמֵיהּ דְּרַב פָּפָּא: פַּרְעֹה שֶׁהָיָה בִּימֵי מֹשֶׁה אַמְגּוּשִׁי הָיָה, שֶׁנֶּאֱמַר: ״הִנֵּה יוֹצֵא הַמַּיְמָה״ וגו׳.

Avitul the scribe also **said in the name of Rav Pappa:** The **Pharaoh who lived in the days of Moses was a sorcerer** [*amgushi*],[L] **as it is stated: "Behold, he goes out to the water"** (Exodus 7:15). Pharaoh would regularly go out to the water in order to engage in witchcraft.

״וְאֵלּוּ מְכַבְּסִין בַּמּוֹעֵד הַבָּא מִמְּדִינַת הַיָּם״. אָמַר רַב אַסִי אָמַר רַבִּי יוֹחָנָן: מִי שֶׁאֵין לוֹ אֶלָּא חָלוּק אֶחָד – מוּתָּר לְכַבְּסוֹ בְּחוּלּוֹ שֶׁל מוֹעֵד.

§ The mishna taught: **And these** people **may launder** their clothes **on** the intermediate days of **a Festival: One who comes from a country overseas. Rav Asi said** that **Rabbi Yoḥanan said: Anyone who has only one shirt is permitted to launder it on the intermediate days of a Festival.**[H]

מְתִיב רַבִּי יִרְמְיָה: אֵלּוּ מְכַבְּסִין בַּמּוֹעֵד, הַבָּא מִמְּדִינַת הַיָּם כו׳. הָנֵי – אִין, מִי שֶׁאֵין לוֹ אֶלָּא חָלוּק אֶחָד – לָא!

Rabbi Yirmeya raised an objection from what was taught in the mishna: **And these** people **may launder** their clothes **on the** intermediate days of a **Festival: One who comes from a country overseas,** and one who is released from a house of captivity, and one who comes out of prison, and one who had been ostracized and the Rabbis released him from his decree of ostracism, **etc.** It may be inferred: **Those** who are mentioned in the mishna, **yes,** they may launder their clothes during the intermediate days of the Festival, but **one who has only one shirt** may **not** launder it.

אֲמַר לֵיהּ רַבִּי יַעֲקֹב לְרַבִּי יִרְמְיָה: אַסְבְּרָהּ לָךְ. מַתְנִיתִין – אַף עַל גַּב דְּאִית לֵיהּ תְּרֵי וּמְטַנְּפִי.

Rabbi Ya'akov said to Rabbi Yirmeya: I will explain it to you. The mishna is referring to those cases where one is permitted to launder his clothes even if **he has two** changes of garments **and** they are **dirty.** Rabbi Yoḥanan speaks about one who has only one garment, and he rules that he may launder it in all circumstances.

שְׁלַח רַב יִצְחָק בַּר יַעֲקֹב בַּר גִּיּוֹרֵי מִשְּׁמֵיהּ דְּרַבִּי יוֹחָנָן: כְּלֵי פִּשְׁתָּן מוּתָּר לְכַבְּסָן בְּחוּלּוֹ שֶׁל מוֹעֵד. מְתִיב רָבָא: מִטְפְּחוֹת הַיָּדַיִם, מִטְפְּחוֹת

Rav Yitzḥak bar Ya'akov bar Giyorei sent a message **in the name of Rabbi Yoḥanan:** With regard to **linen garments,**[N] **it is permitted to launder them during the intermediate days of the Festival** because they are easily soiled.[H] **Rava raised an objection** from what is taught in the mishna: **Hand towels, the towels**

NOTES

A mustache may be trimmed from one corner to the other corner – **שָׂפָה מִזָּוִית לְזָוִית**: Many of the early authorities have a version of the text that includes the expression: But any part of the *hanaha* is prohibited. However, it is not in the standard text because in the manuscript of Rashi it is written that he did not find a way to explain the term *hanaha*. Neither the Rif nor the Rambam had these words in their talmudic text.

Many early authorities understand that *hanaha* refers to the sides of the mouth, and it means that one is permitted to cut only the mustache itself, but hair on the sides of the mouth must be left untrimmed, along with the rest of the beard, unless it interferes with eating (Rabbeinu Ḥananel).

Others explain that the terms mustache here refers to the hair immediately above the mouth, and the word *hanaha* refers to the hair above that (Meiri). Alternatively, there are those who claim the word *hanaha* refers to the hair near the lower lip, which is below [*naha*] the mouth (see Ritva).

Pharaoh who lived in the days of Moses – **פַּרְעֹה שֶׁהָיָה בִּימֵי מֹשֶׁה**: Rabbi Shlomo ben HaYatom has a different version of the Talmud text. It adds that Pharaoh's name was Girsi. The verse: "He sets up over it the lowest of men," is actually referring to Nebuchadnezzar, who was only one cubit tall. However, the Gemara understands that Pharaoh was also this height (*Talmid Rabbeinu Yeḥiel of Paris*).

Linen garments – **כְּלֵי פִּשְׁתָּן**: Some say that the reason for this allowance is that they become dirty quickly and can be laundered without much effort (Rashi manuscript).

LANGUAGE

His penis [*parmashtako*] – **פַּרְמַשְׁתָּקוֹ**: This word appears to be Persian. However, its actual source is unclear. Although there are similar words in Persian and Sanskrit, none of them have the meaning that Rashi and others ascribe to it.

It is possible that the depiction of Pharaoh here is based on other similar ancient Egyptian statues and objects that show dwarflike figures containing all the elements of the description here.

Sorcerer [*amgushi*] – **אַמְגּוּשִׁי**: The origin of the word is magus, a term used for Zoroastrian priests in Iranian languages. It was then adopted by Greek and Aramaic.

HALAKHA

Cutting one's mustache – **נְטִילַת שָׂפָם**: One may trim the mustache hairs above his upper lip during the intermediate days of the Festival, even in public (*Shulḥan Arukh, Oraḥ Ḥayyim* 531:8, and in the comment of Rema).

One who has one shirt – **מִי שֶׁיֵּשׁ לוֹ חָלוּק אֶחָד**: One who has only one garment may launder it in an ordinary manner during the intermediate days of a Festival, and he may even use different types of soap and launder it in public. However, he may launder only one garment at a time. One may wash other items, such as children's clothes or diapers, if they are soiled, in larger quantities (*Shulḥan Arukh, Oraḥ Ḥayyim* 534:1).

Laundering linen garments – **כִּיבּוּס כְּלֵי פִשְׁתָּן**: In accordance with Rabbi Yoḥanan's opinion, one may launder linen garments during the intermediate days of the Festival. However, the common practice is to refrain from doing so. This type of laundering falls into the category of activities that are customarily avoided, although they are technically permitted. Therefore, one may not openly state that such an activity is permitted. Some say that one may give such garments to a gentile to be laundered during the intermediate days (*Ḥayyei Adam*, citing *Eliya Rabba* and *Perisha*; *Shulḥan Arukh, Oraḥ Ḥayyim* 534:2).

הַסַּפָּרִים. הָנֵי – אִין, כְּלֵי פִּשְׁתָּן – לָא!

of barbers that are used to cover a person having a haircut, and body-drying towels may all be laundered on the intermediate days of a Festival. This statement implies that **these** garments, **yes,** they may be laundered, but other types of **linen garments, no,** they may not be laundered.

אֲמַר לֵיהּ אַבַּיֵי: מַתְנִיתִין אֲפִילּוּ דִּשְׁאָר מִינֵי. אֲמַר בַּר הֶדְיָא: לְדִידִי חֲזֵי לִי יַמָּהּ שֶׁל טִבֶּרְיָה, דְּמַפְּקִי לָהּ מְשִׁיכְלֵי דְּמָנֵי כִּיתָּנָא בְּחוּלָּא דְּמוֹעֲדָא.

Abaye said to him: This is not a contradiction: **The mishna** is referring to garments made **even of other types** of materials; linen garments, however, may be laundered even when they serve other purposes. **Bar Hedya said: I myself saw the Sea of Tiberias,**[B] the Sea of Galilee, **to which basins full of linen garments were brought out** to be laundered **during the intermediate days of a Festival.**

מַתְקִיף לָהּ אַבַּיֵי: מַאן לֵימָא לָן דִּבְרְצוֹן חֲכָמִים עָבְדִי? דִּלְמָא שֶׁלֹּא בִּרְצוֹן חֲכָמִים עָבְדִי.

Abaye strongly objects to this: This report cannot be adduced as proof for the *halakha,* for **who says to us** that **they did** this **in accordance with the will of the Sages? Perhaps they did** it **without the will of the Sages.**

מתני׳ וְאֵלּוּ כּוֹתְבִין בַּמּוֹעֵד: קִדּוּשֵׁי נָשִׁים, וְגִיטִּין, וְשׁוֹבְרִין, דְּיַיתֵּיקִי, מַתָּנָה, וּפְרוֹזְבּוֹלִין, אִיגְּרוֹת שׁוּם, וְאִיגְּרוֹת מָזוֹן,

MISHNA **And these** are the documents that **may be written on** the intermediate days of a **Festival:**[NH] Documents of **betrothal of wives,**[N] through which bridegrooms betroth their brides; **bills of divorce;**[N] **receipts** for the repayment of debts; **wills** [***deyateiki***];[L] deeds of **gift;** ***perozbolin,***[L] documents through which lenders authorize the courts to collect their loans on their behalf, thereby preventing the Sabbatical year from canceling their debts; **letters of valuation,** which were drawn up by the court when they valuated property and transferred it to the lender; and **letters of sustenance,**[N] which were drawn up when one accepted upon himself to maintain another, e.g., his step-daughter.

NOTES

These may be written during the intermediate days of a Festival – וְאֵלּוּ כּוֹתְבִין בַּמּוֹעֵד: The early authorities disagree as to why writing these documents during the intermediate days is permitted. Some say that each document is, to some degree, something that would cause a loss, as in each case delaying the writing of the document may cause financial loss or some other type of harm.

Although this reason may not apply in some particular cases, the *halakha* nevertheless applies in every case without distinction. The commentaries explain in detail what the loss is in each case (Rashi manuscript; Rabbeinu Yehonatan of Lunel; *Talmid Rabbeinu Yeḥiel of Paris*; Meiri). Some say that the writing of the prohibited labor is only writing business documents, and none of these documents is directly related to business. For this reason they may be written during the intermediate days of a Festival (Rid; Ran). However, the Rambam explains that most of these documents may be written because the public requires them (see Ra'avad).

Documents of betrothal of wives – קִידּוּשֵׁי נָשִׁים: Although it is explained in the Talmud that this refers to financial documents, the conclusion indicates that it also applies to actual documents of betrothal (Rashi manuscript; Rabbeinu Yehonatan of Lunel).

Bills of divorce – גִּיטִּין: Rashi in the manuscript explains that this is referring to a case where one is setting out on a journey during the intermediate days and does not wish to leave his wife bound in the event that he does not return. Alternatively, it is referring to one who is on his deathbed and wants to prevent his wife from having to marry in a levirate marriage. Rabbi Shlomo ben HaYatom explains that by giving his wife a bill of divorce, a husband ends the fighting within his home, and therefore writing such a document is considered to be for the sake of the joy of the Festival. In the Jerusalem Talmud, it is asked why writing a divorce document is permitted. Since it causes pain, it should not be an appropriate activity for a time of joy. It is explained there that once one has made up his mind to divorce his wife, it is no longer considered to be painful for him to give her the document of divorce.

Letters of sustenance – אִגְּרוֹת מָזוֹן: Some explain that such a document guaranteed that a widow would receive money for her basic needs from the property of her deceased husband (Jerusalem Talmud; Rabbeinu Yehonatan of Lunel).

LANGUAGE

Wills [*deyateiki*] – דְּיַיתֵּיקִי: From the Greek διαθήκη, *diatèkè*, meaning a will. The Sages expound upon it as though it were Aramaic: *Da tehei lemeikam* meaning: This will stand.

Perozbul – פְּרוֹזְבּוּל: Through this document one transfers all outstanding loans owed to him to the court, so that the court will collect them. This was instituted by Hillel to circumvent the cancellation of loans in the Sabbatical Year and to thereby prevent lenders from refusing to grant loans.

The origin of the word is Greek, although it is unclear exactly which word it was taken from. Some say that it was related to the word προβολή, *probolè*, meaning the presentation of a message to the court or to a public gathering. It can also refer to a loan. Some say that it is related to the Greek προσβολή, *prosbolè*, which means application or the conclusion of a sale. However, the issue has not been conclusively resolved and there are also other opinions with regard to the word's origins.

BACKGROUND

Sea of Tiberias – יַמָּהּ שֶׁל טִבֶּרְיָה:

Aerial view of the Sea of Tiberias, also known as the Sea of Galilee

HALAKHA

Writing during the intermediate days of a Festival – כְּתִיבָה בְּחוֹל הַמּוֹעֵד: During the intermediate days of the Festival it is permitted to write documents of betrothal; documents of stipulation; bills of divorce; receipts for repayment of debt; wills; gift documents; *perozbolin*; letters of valuation; letters of sustenance, and some say this includes a document in which a man writes that he will support his step-daughter (Rema); documents of *ḥalitza*; documents of refusal; documents of arbitration; and decrees of the court.

Some say that it is permitted to write a marriage document, and some say that it is prohibited (Rema). Some permit one to write down novel ideas he has about Torah, lest he forget them. Some permit the writing of greeting letters, based on the Jerusalem Talmud, and others prohibit it. In many places it is customary to be stringent (Rema).

Some authorities say that writing is permitted, as long as it is not in the script used for writing Torah scrolls, because ordinary script is not considered to be the work of an expert. Those who write in an ordinary manner during the intermediate days of the Festival do so based on this opinion. Some require that each letter be written in an unusual manner (*Taz*; *Shulḥan Arukh, Oraḥ Ḥayyim* 545:5).

שְׁטָרֵי חֲלִיצָה, וּמֵיאוּנִים, וְשִׁטְרֵי בֵּירוּרִין, גְּזֵרוֹת בֵּית דִּין, וְאִיגְּרוֹת שֶׁל רָשׁוּת.

The list continues: **Documents of the ritual through which the brother-in-law frees the *yevama* of her levirate bonds [*ḥalitza*],** thereby freeing her from the obligation to marry one of her deceased husband's brothers; documents in which the court records the **refusal** of a girl upon reaching majority to remain married to the man to whom her mother or brothers married her as a minor after the death of her father; **documents of arbitration,**[N] in which the court summarizes a conflict that had been resolved through arbitration; **court rulings; and** the official **correspondence of the** ruling **authorities.**[N]

גמ׳ אָמַר שְׁמוּאֵל: מוּתָּר לְאָרֵס אִשָּׁה בְּחוּלּוֹ שֶׁל מוֹעֵד, שֶׁמָּא יְקַדְּמֶנּוּ אַחֵר. לֵימָא מְסַיַּיע לֵיהּ: וְאֵלּוּ כּוֹתְבִין בַּמּוֹעֵד: קִדּוּשֵׁי נָשִׁים.

GEMARA **Shmuel said: It is permitted to betroth** a woman **on the intermediate days of a Festival, lest another** come and betroth her **first.** The Gemara asks: **Let us say that** the mishna **supports** Shmuel, who said: **And these** are the documents that **may be drawn up on the** intermediate days of **a Festival: Documents of betrothal.**

מַאי לָאו שִׁטְרֵי קִדּוּשִׁין מַמָּשׁ? לָא, שִׁטְרֵי פְּסִיקָתָא, וְכִדְרַב גִּידֵּל אָמַר רַב.

What, is the mishna **not** referring to **actual documents of betrothal,** through which one would actually betroth a woman? The Gemara rejects this: **No,** the mishna is referring to **documents of stipulation** recording the amounts that the parents agree to pay as the dowry of their respective son or daughter, **in accordance with** what **Rav Giddel said** that **Rav said.**

דְּאָמַר רַב גִּידֵּל אָמַר רַב: ״כַּמָּה אַתָּה נוֹתֵן לִבְנְךָ״ – כָּךְ וְכָךְ; ״כַּמָּה אַתָּה נוֹתֵן לְבִתְּךָ״ – כָּךְ וְכָךְ. עָמְדוּ וְקִידְּשׁוּ – קָנוּ. הֵן הֵן הַדְּבָרִים הַנִּקְנִין בַּאֲמִירָה.

For **Rav Giddel said** that **Rav said:** When two families negotiate the terms of marriage for their respective children, and one side says to the other: **How much do you give**[H] **to your son** as a dowry? And the second side says: I give **such and such** amount; **how much do you give to your daughter?** And the first side responds: **Such and such** amount, then, once the bride and groom **arose and** pronounced **the betrothal** formula, then all of these obligations are **acquired** and therefore binding. **These are** among **the things that are acquired through words** alone. In other words, there is no need to perform an additional act of acquisition in order to confirm the agreement, and the mishna is referring to a document recording such an agreement. Although such a document may be drawn up even on the intermediate days of a Festival, this does not mean that one may actually betroth a woman during this period.

לֵימָא מְסַיַּיע לֵיהּ: אֵין נוֹשְׂאִין נָשִׁים בַּמּוֹעֵד, לֹא בְּתוּלוֹת וְלֹא אַלְמָנוֹת, וְלֹא מְיַבְּמִין, מִפְּנֵי שֶׁשִּׂמְחָה הִיא לוֹ. הָא לְאָרֵס – שָׁרֵי!

The Gemara asks: **Let us say** that the following mishna **supports** Shmuel: **One may not marry a woman on the** intermediate days of **a Festival, neither a virgin nor a widow; nor may one** then **perform levirate marriage** with his sister-in-law, if his brother died childless, **because that** would be **a joyous** occasion **for him.** This statement implies that it is only marrying that is prohibited, **but betrothing is permitted.**

לָא מִיבַּעְיָא קָאָמַר; לָא מִיבַּעְיָא לְאָרֵס – דְּלָא קָעָבֵיד מִצְוָה, אֶלָּא אֲפִילּוּ לִישָּׂא נַמִי, דְּקָא עָבֵיד מִצְוָה – אָסוּר.

The Gemara rejects this argument: This is not the correct way to understand the mishna, as **it is speaking in the style of: Needless to say.** It is **needless to say** that **betrothal** is not permitted, **because** the groom **does not perform a mitzva**[N] through betrothal. **Rather,** the same is true **even of marriage, through which one performs a mitzva,** as marriage is preparation for fulfilling the mitzva of procreation. It is still **not permitted.**

תָּא שְׁמַע, דְּתָנָא דְּבֵי שְׁמוּאֵל: מְאָרְסִין אֲבָל לֹא כּוֹנְסִין, וְאֵין עוֹשִׂין סְעוּדַּת אֵירוּסִין, וְלֹא מְיַבְּמִין, מִפְּנֵי שֶׁשִּׂמְחָה הִיא לוֹ. שְׁמַע מִינַּהּ.

The Gemara offers another support for Shmuel: **Come** and **hear that which** a Sage of **the school of Shmuel taught** in the following *baraita*: **One may betroth** a woman on the intermediate days of a Festival,[H] **but he may not marry** her, **nor may he make a betrothal feast, nor may he perform levirate marriage, because that** would be **a joyous** occasion **for him,** and one may not mix the joy of a wedding with the joy of the Festival. The Gemara concludes: **Learn from this** a support for Shmuel's opinion.

NOTES

Documents of arbitration – שִׁטְרֵי בֵּירוּרִין: Rashi, the Rid, and Ran explain that this means arbitration to resolve a dispute. In the Jerusalem Talmud it is explained that this document gives power of attorney to investigators to look into a dispute (a similar explanation appears in the Rashi manuscript, and in Rambam's Commentary on the Mishna). Others explain that these documents contained each side's claims before the court (Riaz).

Official correspondence of the authorities [*rashut*] – אִגְּרוֹת שֶׁל רָשׁוּת: The early authorities disagree about the way this word should be vocalized and consequently also about its meaning. According to those who read the word *rashut*, these were official documents sent to the ruling government (Rashi) or they contained calculations that were delivered to the government (Meiri). The *ge'onim* explain that it refers to a document in which the *Nasi* or the Exilarch appoints a judge for a certain community (see Rabbeinu Yehonatan of Lunel). However, others read this word *reshut*, based on the Jerusalem Talmud, where it is stated that this expression refers to letters of greetings. Some explain that it is permitted to write such letters because doing so does not require a great deal of precision, and is therefore considered a layman's activity (Rambam).

Some explain that the *halakha* permitting letters of greeting specifically refers to a case in which one will not find a messenger with whom he can send the letter after the Festival, and therefore he will incur some degree of loss by not mailing such a letter at this time (*Tosefot HaRosh*). Others suggest that this type of correspondence will increase the joy of the Festival (Ritva).

Betrothal, because he does not perform a mitzva – לְאָרֵס, דְּלָא קָעָבֵיד מִצְוָה: The later authorities mention that the Rambam, apparently, disagrees with this Gemara. He maintains that there is a mitzva to betroth a woman. Rabbi Shlomo ben HaYatom explains that there is no apparent contradiction, as this opinion in the Gemara holds that betrothal does not complete the mitzva, as marriage does.

HALAKHA

How much do you give – כַּמָּה אַתָּה נוֹתֵן: When there is an arrangement between a man and a woman that they will marry, the man asks his future wife: How much money will you give to me as a dowry? She answers that it will be a particular amount of money. He makes a similar statement to her. After the betrothal declaration has been made, this money is transferred through their statement, provided that the property belonged to them when they committed to it, and they do not need to perform any other method of transfer. There is no distinction between a first and second marriage (*Shulḥan Arukh, Even HaEzer* 51:1, and in the comment of Rema).

Betrothal during the intermediate days of a Festival – אֵירוּסִין בַּמּוֹעֵד: One may not marry or perform levirate marriage during the intermediate days of a Festival. However, one may betroth a woman, though without a betrothal feast, during the intermediate days (*Shulḥan Arukh, Oraḥ Ḥayyim* 546:1).

ומי אמר שמואל שמא יקדמנו אחר? והאמר רב יהודה אמר שמואל: בכל יום ויום בת קול יוצאת ואומרת: בת פלוני לפלוני, שדה פלוני לפלוני!

The Gemara raises a question about the ruling itself: **And did Shmuel** actually **say** that we are concerned that **perhaps another** man will come and betroth the woman **first? But didn't Rav Yehuda say that Shmuel said: Every day a Divine Voice issues forth and says: The daughter of so-and-so is** destined to be the wife of **so-and-so; the field of so-and-so** will belong **to so-and-so?**[N] If this is the case, why should one be concerned lest another betroth her first? It is predestined that he will marry his designated mate.

אלא: שמא יקדמנו אחר ברחמים.

Rather, Shmuel's statement should be understood as follows: **Perhaps another** man will come and betroth her **first by means of** praying for divine **mercy.** In other words, Shmuel is concerned that the rival may beseech God to cancel the decree of the Divine Voice, and therefore the first man needs to hurry and betroth the woman before the other one has a chance to pray that he should take her from him.

כי הא דרבא שמעיה לההוא גברא דבעי רחמי ואמר: תזדמן לי פלניתא. אמר ליה: לא תיבעי רחמי הכי. אי חזיא לך – לא אזלא מינך; ואי לא – כפרת בה׳. בתר הכי שמעיה דקאמר: או איהו לימות מקמה, או איהי תמות מקמיה. אמר ליה: לאו אמינא לך לא תיבעי עלה דמילתא?

This is **like this** incident, in **which Rava heard a certain man asking for mercy,** i.e., praying, **who said: Grant me so-and-so** as a wife. Rava **said to him: Do not** pray and **ask for mercy** in **this** way. **If** she **is fit for you,** and it has been decreed that she will be your wife, **she will not go away from you. And if** she is **not** destined to be your wife, **you will** come to **deny the Lord**[N] when you see that your prayer is not answered. **After** the man married this woman, Rava **heard him say** in prayer: Please **either let him die before her or let her die before him.** He was speaking about himself and his wife because he had grown to hate her so much. Rava **said to him: Did I not say to you not to pray for this matter?**

הכי אמר רב משום רבי ראובן בן אצטרובילי: מן התורה ומן הנביאים ומן הכתובים מה׳ אשה לאיש. מן התורה – דכתיב: ״ויען לבן ובתואל ויאמרו מה׳ יצא הדבר״. מן הנביאים – דכתיב: ״ואביו ואמו לא ידעו כי מה׳ היא״. מן הכתובים – דכתיב: ״בית והון נחלת אבות ומה׳ אשה משכלת״.

Rav said in the name of Rabbi Reuven ben Itzterobili[P] **as follows: From the Torah, and from the Prophets, and from the Writings;**[N] it implies that the decree that a specific **woman** is destined to be married **to** a specific **man is from God.** From where is this derived? It is **from the Torah, as it is written: "Then Laban and Bethuel answered and said: The thing comes from the Lord,** we cannot speak to you either bad or good" (Genesis 24:50). **From the Prophets, as it is written: "But his father and his mother knew not that it was of the Lord"** (Judges 14:4). **From the Writings, as it is written: "House and riches are the inheritance of fathers; but a prudent woman is from the Lord"** (Proverbs 19:14).

ואמר רב משום רבי ראובן בן אצטרובילי, ואמרי לה במתניתא תנא, אמר רבי ראובן בן אצטרובילי: אין אדם נחשד בדבר אלא אם כן עשאו; ואם לא עשה כולו – עשה מקצתו; ואם לא עשה מקצתו – הרהר בלבו לעשותו; ואם לא הרהר בלבו לעשותו – ראה אחרים שעשו, ושמח.

§ Apropos a teaching of Rabbi Reuven ben Itzterobili, the Gemara states that **Rav said in the name of Rabbi Reuven ben Itzterobili, and some say** that **it was taught in a** ***baraita*** that **Rabbi Reuven ben Itzterobili said: A man is suspected of** having done **something** wrong **only if he has** indeed **done so. And if he did not do it wholly,** then probably **he did it partly. And if he did not do it** even **partly,** then probably **he thought in his heart to do it. And if he did not** even **think to** himself **to do it,** then certainly **he saw others doing it and was happy.** Suspicions do not arbitrarily arise about a person; therefore is certainly some basis for them.

מתיב רבי יעקב: ״ויחפאו בני ישראל דברים אשר לא כן על ה׳ אלהיהם״! התם להכעיס הוא דעבוד.

Rabbi Ya'akov raised an objection: Does the verse not say: **"And the children of Israel fabricated matters that were not right against the Lord their God"** (II Kings 17:9), which indicates that it is possible to make up stories about someone else even though they are entirely baseless. The Gemara answers: **There they did it in order to anger** God, but they did not actually think that what they were saying was true.

NOTES

The field of so-and-so to so-and-so – שדה פלוני לפלוני: According to the Ran, this statement is also connected to marriage, as it refers to property transferred to the groom through the dowry.

You will come to deny the Lord – כפרת בה׳: The commentary here follows Rashi's version of the text, according to which, in this case, unanswered prayers lead one to heresy, while answered prayers do not actually benefit him. The *Arukh* explains the passage in a similar manner. However, others have a version of the text which reads: You will come to deny her, meaning that such a person will renounce this woman in the end. In other words, he will regret having married this woman and he will become disgusted with her (*Talmid Rabbeinu Yeḥiel of Paris*; Ran).

From the Torah and from the Prophets and from the Writings – מן התורה ומן הנביאים ומן הכתובים: Some expound on this statement and note that these three verses refer to three different types of couples. The verse from the Torah describes the marriage of Isaac and Rebecca, which was a marriage between a righteous man and a righteous woman. The verse from the Prophets describes the marriage of Samson and his first wife, which was a marriage between a righteous man and a wicked woman. The verse from Writings speaks in general about a marriage between a wicked man and a righteous woman (Riaf; *Iyyun Ya'akov*).

PERSONALITIES

Rabbi Reuven ben Itzterobili – רבי ראובן בן אצטרובילי: Rabbi Reuven ben Itzterobili was a *tanna* in the generation of Rabbi Akiva. It is told that he was able to intervene with the powerful people in Rome and cancel any decree made against Israel. Several statements are mentioned in his name in the Talmud and midrashic literature. His two sons were also Torah scholars and became students of Rabbi Yehuda HaNasi. The name Itzterobili appears to be from the Greek στρόβιλος, *strobilus*, meaning round, spinning.

תָּא שְׁמַע: ״וַיְקַנְאוּ לְמֹשֶׁה בַּמַּחֲנֶה לְאַהֲרֹן קְדוֹשׁ ה׳״ – רַב שְׁמוּאֵל בַּר יִצְחָק אָמַר: מְלַמֵּד שֶׁכָּל אֶחָד קִינֵּא לְאִשְׁתּוֹ מִמֹּשֶׁה! הָתָם מִשּׁוּם שִׂנְאָה הוּא דַּעֲבוּד.

Come and **hear** a challenge from a different source: The verse states: **"And they were jealous of Moses in the camp, of Aaron the Lord's holy one"** (Psalms 106:16). **Rav Shmuel bar Yitzḥak said:** This verse **teaches that every man warned his wife** against seclusion **with Moses**[N] because he was jealous. This implies that every man thought that his wife had secluded herself with Moses and sinned, although this was certainly not the case. This demonstrates that it is possible to suspect an absolutely innocent person. The Gemara answers: **There they did it out of hatred** for Moses. They did not actually suspect him of wrongdoing. Instead, their goal was to degrade him by leveling these false accusations against him.

תָּא שְׁמַע, אָמַר רַבִּי יוֹסֵי: יְהֵא חֶלְקִי עִם מִי שֶׁחוֹשְׁדִין אוֹתוֹ בְּדָבָר וְאֵין בּוֹ. וְאָמַר רַב פַּפָּא: לְדִידִי חָשְׁדוּן וְלָא הֲוָה בִּי!

The Gemara raises another challenge, based on yet another source: **Come** and **hear that which Rabbi Yosei said: May my portion** in the future world **be with one who is suspected** of a certain wrongdoing **but is innocent,** as the pain that such a person experiences atones for his sins. This statement also appears to imply that it is possible to suspect an absolutely innocent person. **And Rav Pappa said: They suspected me** of a certain wrongdoing **but I was not** guilty.

לָא קַשְׁיָא; הָא – בְּקָלָא דְּפָסֵיק; הָא – בְּקָלָא דְּלָא פָּסֵיק. וְקָלָא דְּלָא פָּסֵיק עַד כַּמָּה? אָמַר אַבַּיֵי: אָמְרָה לִי אֵם: דּוּמֵי דְּמָתָא יוֹמָא וּפַלְגָּא.

The Gemara answers: **It is not difficult. This** is referring **to a rumor that stops,** and therefore it is possible that it is groundless, whereas **that** is referring **to a rumor that does not stop,** and in that case there must be a factual basis for the suspicion. The Gemara asks: To be considered **a rumor that does not stop, for how long** must it persist? **Abaye**[P] **said: My nurse told me: Local gossip lasts for a day and a half,** and then it is deemed to be a rumor that does not stop.

וְהָנֵי מִילֵּי – דְּלָא פְּסַק בֵּינֵי בֵּינֵי; אֲבָל פְּסַק בֵּינֵי בֵּינֵי – לֵית לָן בַּהּ. וְכִי פָּסַק בֵּינֵי בֵּינֵי – לָא אֲמָרַן אֶלָּא דְּלָא פְּסַק מֵחֲמַת יִרְאָה, אֲבָל פְּסַק מֵחֲמַת יִרְאָה – לָא.

The Gemara comments: **This applies only** if the rumor **did not stop in between,** during the day and a half, **but if it stopped in between** then **we have no** problem **with it,** and it is not a persistent rumor. **And if** the rumor **stopped in between, we said** that it is considered baseless **only** if it **stopped** of its own accord and **not out of fear,** i.e., because the suspect is violent and therefore people are afraid to speak badly about him. But if the rumor **stopped out of fear,** then this dispensation does **not** apply, and it is still assumed that there must be some basis to the rumor.

וְלָא אֲמָרַן אֶלָּא דְּלָא הֲדַר נָבַט, אֲבָל הֲדַר נָבַט – לָא. וְלָא אֲמָרַן אֶלָּא דְּלֵית לֵיהּ אוֹיְבִים, אֲבָל אִית לֵיהּ אוֹיְבִים – אוֹיְבִים הוּא דְּאַפְּקוּהָ לְקָלָא.

And we said that a rumor that stopped is assumed to be baseless **only if it did not arise again.**[N] **But if it arose again,** then this does **not** apply. **And we said** that a rumor that does not stop must be taken seriously **only if** the slandered person **has no enemies. But if he has** known **enemies,** then it can be assumed that **it was the enemies who disseminated the rumor.**

מתני׳ אֵין כּוֹתְבִין שְׁטָרֵי חוֹב בַּמּוֹעֵד. וְאִם אֵינוֹ מַאֲמִינוֹ, אוֹ שֶׁאֵין לוֹ מַה יֹּאכַל – הֲרֵי זֶה יִכְתּוֹב.

MISHNA **One may not write bills of debt on** the intermediate days of **a Festival. But if** the lender **does not trust** the borrower, and he is concerned that the borrower will later deny the loan, **or** if the scribe **has nothing to eat,** then **he may write** a bill of debt during the Festival week.

אֵין כּוֹתְבִין סְפָרִים, תְּפִילִּין וּמְזוּזוֹת בַּמּוֹעֵד, וְאֵין מַגִּיהִין אוֹת אַחַת אֲפִילּוּ בְּסֵפֶר עֶזְרָא. רַבִּי יְהוּדָה אוֹמֵר: כּוֹתֵב אָדָם תְּפִילִּין וּמְזוּזוֹת לְעַצְמוֹ,

One may not write Torah **scrolls,**[H] **phylacteries, or *mezuzot* on the** intermediate days of **a Festival, nor may one correct a single letter, even in the** Torah **scroll of Ezra,**[N] which was kept in the Temple and upon which all the Jewish communities relied. **Rabbi Yehuda says: One may write phylacteries and *mezuzot* for himself** on the intermediate days of a Festival if he needs them.

NOTES

Warned his wife against seclusion with Moses – קִינֵּא לְאִשְׁתּוֹ מִמֹּשֶׁה: This statement is based primarily on the similarity between the verse: "And they were jealous of Moses [*vaykanu leMoshe*]" (Psalms 106:16), and the verse that describes what happens when a man becomes suspicious about his wife: "And the spirit of jealousy come upon him, and he be jealous of his wife [*vekineh et ishto*]" (Numbers 5:14).

Many explanations are offered for this somewhat surprising statement. Some say that because Moses had a tent outside the camp, people were suspicious that the women who came there would be alone with him in a prohibited manner (Riaf). The author of the commentary *HaKotev* in the *Ein Ya'akov* explains that the Gemara is referring to the congregation of Korah, who warned their wives that Moses was power hungry.

Did not arise again – דְּלָא הֲדַר נָבַט: Rashi in the manuscript has a different version of the talmudic text. He explains that when people other than the rumor's subject actively deny and try to quiet it, it is considered a rumor that stops.

Even in the Torah scroll of Ezra [*sefer Ezra*] – אֲפִילּוּ בְּסֵפֶר עֶזְרָא: This is Rashi's version of the talmudic text, according to which this statement is referring to the Torah scroll written by Ezra. This scroll was central in that it was the Torah scroll that was used to correct every other Torah scroll (Meiri).

However, most authorities have a version of the Gemara that reads: The Torah scroll of the courtyard [*sefer azara*]. This term refers to the Torah scroll that was kept in the Temple courtyard. It was used by the High Priest when he read on Yom Kippur (Rabbeinu Yehonatan of Lunel; see Rashi manuscript). Others suggest that it was the king who read from this Torah scroll during the time of *hakhel* (Rabbi Shlomo ben HaYatom; Meiri).

PERSONALITIES

Abaye – אַבַּיֵי: Abaye was one of the most famous of the Babylonian *amora'im*. The disagreements between Abaye and his colleague Rava recorded in the Gemara are so essential that the Gemara itself is referred to as the discussions of Abaye and Rava. Among those hundreds of discussions, the ruling follows Abaye in only six cases.

Abaye was orphaned at the time of his birth and raised bsy his paternal uncle, Rabba. The nurse who raised him impressed upon him many life lessons, which he quotes in the Gemara in her name. There are a number of stories in the Gemara that illustrate his intelligence even as a child, including some in which Rabba tests him with questions.

Abaye was chosen to head the academy in Pumbedita. He celebrated the study of Torah and would announce a holiday for the scholars whenever one of them completed a tractate. Growing up in his uncle's home, he was aware of the difficulties of scholars who were without financial means. The Gemara in tractate *Berakhot* (35b) relates that he testified that many were successful following the path of Rabbi Yishmael, who instructed his students to plow, plant, and harvest in the appropriate time. Only very few were successful following the path of Rabbi Shimon bar Yoḥai, who taught that one should devote himself entirely to Torah and ignore worldly concerns.

HALAKHA

Writing a Torah scroll – כְּתִיבָה בְּסֵפֶר: It is prohibited to write or correct even one letter in a Torah scroll during the intermediate days of a Festival. Some say this is prohibited even if it is needed for communal use during the Festival. The accepted custom is to permit writing in ordinary handwriting and to prohibit only the special scribal writing used for Torah scrolls (*Shulḥan Arukh*, *Oraḥ Ḥayyim* 545:1, and in the comment of Rema).

וְטוֹוֶה עַל יְרֵיכוֹ תְּכֵלֶת לְצִיצִיתוֹ.

And one may spin sky-blue wool[B] **for** his **ritual fringes on his thigh,**[HB] but not in the ordinary manner with a spindle, as this procedure must be performed in an altered manner on the intermediate days of a Festival.

גמ׳ תָּנוּ רַבָּנַן: כּוֹתֵב אָדָם תְּפִילִּין וּמְזוּזוֹת לְעַצְמוֹ, וְטוֹוֶה עַל יְרֵיכוֹ תְּכֵלֶת לְצִיצִיתוֹ; וְלַאֲחֵרִים בְּטוֹבָה, דִּבְרֵי רַבִּי מֵאִיר. רַבִּי יְהוּדָה אוֹמֵר מַעֲרִים וּמוֹכֵר אֶת שֶׁלּוֹ, וְחוֹזֵר וְכוֹתֵב לְעַצְמוֹ. רַבִּי יוֹסֵי אוֹמֵר: כּוֹתֵב וּמוֹכֵר כְּדַרְכּוֹ כְּדֵי פַּרְנָסָתוֹ.

GEMARA **The Sages taught** the following *baraita*: **A person may write phylacteries**[N] **and** ***mezuzot*** **for himself**[N] **and spin sky-blue** wool **for his fringes on his thigh. And for others** he may do these things **as a favor,** but not for payment. This is **the statement of Rabbi Meir. Rabbi Yehuda says:** If he initially made them for himself, **he may employ artifice, sell his own and** then **go back and write** new ones **for himself. Rabbi Yosei says: He may write and sell** them **in his** usual **manner,** in the amount that is **enough** to provide **for his livelihood.**[N]

BACKGROUND

Sky-blue wool – תְּכֵלֶת: This was made with a special dye produced from a species of snail. In talmudic times, this dye was already quite rare, and the means of preparing it, including the species of snail used, were eventually forgotten. In recent generations, efforts have been made to identify the snail and to resume use of the dye. A common identification today is the *Murex trunculus*. Others have suggested the common cuttlefish, *Sepia officinalis*, or the raft snail, *Janthina janthina*.

The Torah requires wool that is dyed sky-blue for two purposes: It is used for ritual fringes; some of the four threads of each fringe must be dyed with this special blue dye, and they are wound around the other threads. However, the mitzva to wear fringes is not contingent on one of the threads being dyed, and today all ritual fringes are made without the dyed thread. In addition, in the priestly vestments, wool dyed this color is used in all or part of the sash, the entire cloak, the *ephod*, and the breastplate.

Murex

Common cuttlefish

Raft snail

Methods of spinning – דַּרְכֵי טְוִיָּה: Spinning fibers of linen, cannabis, cotton, or wool in order to form strings was done with special utensils and complex spindles. Instead of a spindle, which is turned in order to wind the strings, it is also possible to use a stone. Without a spindle or stone, it is possible to spin in a simpler way, without the use of any external utensil, by winding strings around one's thigh.

Woman spinning wool with a spindle

HALAKHA

Making phylacteries and ritual fringes during a Festival – עֲשִׂיַּית תְּפִילִּין וְצִיצִית בַּמּוֹעֵד: One may write phylacteries and *mezuzot* for himself and spin strings on his thigh for ritual fringes. If his income is minimal or if he needs to make more money in order to cover the expenses of the Festival then he may write these items and sell enough of them to others so that he can earn a living. If he writes phylacteries in order to wear them during the intermediate days of the Festival then it is permitted for him to write them in any case (Rema), because the *halakha* is in accordance with the opinion of Rabbi Yehuda and Rabbi Yosei (*Shulḥan Arukh, Oraḥ Ḥayyim* 545:3).

NOTES

A person may write phylacteries – כּוֹתֵב אָדָם תְּפִילִּין: Nevertheless, one may not write a Torah scroll. This is because the mitzvot of fringes and phylacteries are completed when work on them is finished. However, the mitzva pertaining to a Torah scroll is not completed when it is written, as Torah scrolls are written in order to fulfill the mitzva of teaching Torah (*Commentary on Rif*).

Write phylacteries…for himself – כּוֹתֵב...תְּפִילִּין...לְעַצְמוֹ: Many of the early authorities discuss a question not mentioned by the Gemara: Should one wear phylacteries during the intermediate days of a Festival? The dispute exists primarily between the early authorities, many of whom say that one may not wear phylacteries during the intermediate days because this period is considered to be like a Festival, during which wearing phylacteries is prohibited (Rif; Rambam; Rashba). The Meiri states that this was the common custom in Spain. Others say that one is required to wear phylacteries during the intermediate days (Rash; Ritva; *Sefer HaMeorot*). The Meiri writes that this is the accepted custom in all of France. Some say that since there is a doubt with regard to this issue, it is preferable to wear phylacteries without reciting a blessing (see Ran; Meiri). This dispute remains unresolved, and the standard Ashkenazic custom is to wear phylacteries and recite the blessings over them (Rema). However, the Sephardic and Hasidic customs, and the custom in Eretz Yisrael, is to not wear phylacteries during this period.

The simple explanation of the statements of the *tanna'im* in the *baraita* is in accordance with those who are of the opinion that phylacteries should be worn during the intermediate days of a Festival, and this also seems to be the opinion stated in the Jerusalem Talmud (see Meiri).

According to those who say that phylacteries should not be worn during the intermediate days of a Festival, this *baraita* is referring to one who is writing phylacteries for himself so that he will have them immediately after the Festival. Similarly, one who is selling phylacteries to others is doing this so that other people will have them when they are needed (Rif).

Some explain that the question of whether or not phylacteries are worn on the intermediate days is the basis of the dispute in the mishna. Rabbi Meir and Rabbi Yehuda claim that one is required to wear phylacteries during the intermediate days of a Festival because they say, in accordance with an opinion that is rejected, that one is required to wear phylacteries on Shabbat and on Festivals as well. However, Rabbi Yosei holds that one may not wear phylacteries during the intermediate days of a Festival (Rabbeinu Yehonatan of Lunel).

Enough to provide for his livelihood – כְּדֵי פַּרְנָסָתוֹ: The *Ba'al Halakhot Gedolot* explains that this expression refers to one who has nothing to eat. Many of the early authorities challenge this opinion, as if this were the case then certainly even Rabbi Meir would agree that it would be permitted. Consequently, they explain that the expression: Enough to provide for his livelihood, includes earning enough to cover expenses beyond one's most basic needs, such as the additional expenses of the Festival. With regard to the reason for this, some explain that once writing phylacteries is permitted, it is possible to expand this leniency and claim that one may write phylacteries in order to sell them (Rid).

אוֹרֵי לֵיהּ רַב לְרַב חֲנַנְאֵל, וְאָמְרִי לָהּ רַבָּה בַּר בַּר חָנָה לְרַב חֲנַנְאֵל: הֲלָכָה, כּוֹתֵב וּמוֹכֵר כְּדַרְכּוֹ כְּדֵי פַּרְנָסָתוֹ.

Rav ruled for Rav Ḥananel, and some say it was **Rabba bar bar Ḥana** who ruled **for Rav Ḥananel: The *halakha* is** that **one may write and sell** them **in his** usual **manner,** in the amount that is **enough** to provide **for his livelihood.**

״וְטוֹוֶה עַל יְרֵיכוֹ תְּכֵלֶת״. תָּנוּ רַבָּנַן: טוֹוֶה אָדָם עַל יְרֵיכוֹ תְּכֵלֶת לְצִיצִיתוֹ, אֲבָל לֹא בְּאֶבֶן, דִּבְרֵי רַבִּי אֱלִיעֶזֶר. וַחֲכָמִים אוֹמְרִים: אַף בְּאֶבֶן. רַבִּי יְהוּדָה אוֹמֵר מִשְּׁמוֹ: בְּאֶבֶן, אֲבָל לֹא בְּפֶלֶךְ. וַחֲכָמִים אוֹמְרִים: בֵּין בְּאֶבֶן בֵּין בְּפֶלֶךְ.

§ The mishna taught: **And one may spin sky-blue** wool **for** his **ritual fringes on his thigh. The Sages taught** a *baraita*: **A person may spin sky-blue** wool **for his ritual fringes on his thigh, but not with a stone,** which can be used to form a small spindle and ease the spinning process; this is **the statement of Rabbi Eliezer. But the Rabbis say:** One may spin the sky-blue wool **even with a stone. Rabbi Yehuda said in** the name of Rabbi Eliezer: It is permitted **with a stone, but not with a spindle. And the Rabbis say:** One may spin this wool **with either a stone or a spindle.**

אָמַר רַב יְהוּדָה אָמַר שְׁמוּאֵל, וְכֵן אָמַר רַבִּי חִיָּיא בַּר אַבָּא אָמַר רַבִּי יוֹחָנָן: הֲלָכָה, בֵּין בְּאֶבֶן בֵּין בְּפֶלֶךְ. וַהֲלָכָה: כּוֹתֵב כְּדַרְכּוֹ וּמוֹכֵר כְּדֵי פַּרְנָסָתוֹ.

Rav Yehuda said that **Shmuel said, and similarly Rabbi Ḥiyya bar Abba said** that **Rabbi Yoḥanan said:** The *halakha* is that one may spin the sky-blue wool for fringes on the intermediate days of a Festival, **both with a stone and with a spindle,** owing to the importance of the mitzva of ritual fringes. **And** similarly **the *halakha* is: One may write** phylacteries and *mezuzot* on the intermediate days of a Festival **in his** usual **manner and sell enough** to provide **for his livelihood.**

מתני׳ הַקּוֹבֵר אֶת מֵתוֹ שְׁלֹשָׁה יָמִים קוֹדֶם לָרֶגֶל – בָּטְלָה הֵימֶנּוּ גְּזֵרַת שִׁבְעָה. שְׁמוֹנָה – בָּטְלוּ הֵימֶנּוּ גְּזֵרַת שְׁלֹשִׁים.

MISHNA One who buries his deceased relative **three days before a pilgrimage Festival**[N] has **the decree of** the **seven**-day period of mourning, i.e., the *halakhot* and prohibitions associated with that period, **nullified for him** by the Festival. He is not required to complete this seven-day mourning period after the Festival. If one buries his deceased relative **eight** days before a pilgrimage Festival, then **the decree of thirty** days **is nullified for him.** The restrictions that ordinarily apply during this thirty-day mourning period no longer apply after the Festival.[N]

מִפְּנֵי שֶׁאָמְרוּ: שַׁבָּת עוֹלָה וְאֵינָהּ מַפְסֶקֶת, רְגָלִים – מַפְסִיקִין וְאֵינָן עוֹלִין.

This is **because** the Sages **said**[N] a principle with regard to this issue: **Shabbat counts** as one of the days of mourning, although one may not mourn on it **and it does not interrupt**[H] the mourning period, which continues after Shabbat. The **pilgrimage Festivals,** on the other hand, **interrupt** the mourning period,[N] so that if one began mourning before such a Festival, then the mourning period is canceled by the Festival. **They do not,** however, **count.**[H] If one did not begin mourning before the Festival, or if his relative died during the Festival, then he is required to complete his mourning period afterward, as the days of the Festival do not count toward the requisite days of mourning.

רַבִּי אֱלִיעֶזֶר אוֹמֵר: מִשֶּׁחָרַב בֵּית הַמִּקְדָּשׁ עֲצֶרֶת כְּשַׁבָּת.

Rabbi Eliezer says: From the time that the Temple was destroyed, *Shavuot* is like Shabbat, because nowadays the days following *Shavuot* are not treated like Festival days. When the Temple stood, many of the Festival's offerings that could not be sacrificed on *Shavuot* itself would be sacrificed during the six days following the Festival. Nowadays, however, when offerings are no longer sacrificed, *Shavuot* lasts for only one day in Eretz Yisrael, and therefore it is treated like Shabbat with regard to mourning: It counts as one of the days of mourning, but does not interrupt the period of mourning.

NOTES

Three days before a pilgrimage Festival – שְׁלֹשָׁה יָמִים קוֹדֶם הָרֶגֶל: The reason for this is because the first three days of mourning are considered to be the most stringent in several ways, as will be explained later. Consequently, they are treated as a separate entity, e.g., with regard to wearing phylacteries according to many authorities (Ritva; see *Sefat Emet*).

The decree of seven…the decree of thirty – גְּזֵרַת שִׁבְעָה...גְּזֵרַת שְׁלֹשִׁים: They are referred to by the term decree because all the *halakhot* of mourning are based on rabbinic decree (Rabbi Shlomo ben HaYatom).

Because they said – מִפְּנֵי שֶׁאָמְרוּ: The Ritva questions this wording, which seems to introduce a new issue, but in fact only restates what is previously mentioned in the mishna. He explains that because all the *halakhot* of mourning are of rabbinic origin, it is the Sages who decide both what the *halakhot* of mourning are and how they are counted. Rabbi Shlomo ben HaYatom explains that the phrase: Because they said, introduces a quotation of a tradition that was transmitted by Moses from Sinai, and this quotation serves as the basis for the *halakha* in the mishna.

Shabbat and Festivals – שַׁבָּת וְיוֹם טוֹב: Several explanations are offered for the difference between Shabbat and Festivals. Some say that the difference between them is that one may not perform a public display of mourning on Shabbat; however, mourning applies in private. For this reason, Shabbat counts as part of the mourning period. It has already been noted that this opinion fits with the opinion that there is no private mourning during a Festival (see Jerusalem Talmud, Rambam's Commentary on the Mishna; Rabbeinu Yehonatan of Lunel).

In the Jerusalem Talmud it is explained that Shabbat does not interrupt the mourning because if it did then there would never be a seven-day period of mourning. Some of the early authorities (*Ba'al Halakhot Gedolot*; *She'iltot*) make the following distinction: One is required to have enjoyment from Shabbat, and therefore one may not engage in public displays of mourning during it. Yet one may still be slightly sad during Shabbat. On the other hand, one is commanded to be joyous during the Festival, and therefore the *halakhot* of mourning are nullified altogether.

HALAKHA

Shabbat counts and it does not interrupt – שַׁבָּת עוֹלָה וְאֵינָהּ מַפְסֶקֶת: Shabbat is counted as one of the days of mourning, although the restrictions of mourning do not apply during it. It does not interrupt the mourning period (*Shulḥan Arukh, Yoreh De'a* 400:1).

Festivals interrupt, they do not count – רְגָלִים מַפְסִיקִין וְאֵינָן עוֹלִין: If one began mourning before a Festival, the Festival interrupts his mourning, and he does not continue mourning upon the conclusion of the Festival. However, if he did not begin observing mourning practices before the Festival, then the days of the Festival are not counted toward his mourning period, and he must observe the mourning in its entirety afterward. In the Diaspora, where two Festival days are observed, the last day of the Festival is counted as one of the seven days of mourning, so only six more days are observed after the Festival ends (*Shulḥan Arukh, Yoreh De'a* 399:2).

רַבָּן גַּמְלִיאֵל אוֹמֵר: רֹאשׁ הַשָּׁנָה וְיוֹם הַכִּפּוּרִים כִּרְגָלִים. וַחֲכָמִים אוֹמְרִים: לֹא כְּדִבְרֵי זֶה וְלֹא כְּדִבְרֵי זֶה, אֶלָּא: עֲצֶרֶת – כִּרְגָלִים, רֹאשׁ הַשָּׁנָה וְיוֹם הַכִּפּוּרִים – כְּשַׁבָּת.

Rabban Gamliel says: Even **Rosh HaShana and Yom Kippur** are considered **like** the **pilgrimage Festivals,** in that they interrupt the mourning period but are not counted toward the days of mourning.[H] **And the Rabbis say:** The *halakha* **is neither in accordance with the statement of** Rabbi Eliezer **nor in accordance with the statement of** Rabban Gamliel. **Rather,** with regard to mourning, ***Shavuot*** is treated **like the** other **pilgrimage Festivals,** whereas **Rosh HaShana and Yom Kippur** are treated **like Shabbat.**[N]

גמ׳ אָמַר רַב: גְּזֵרַת – בָּטְלוּ, יָמִים – לֹא בָּטְלוּ. וְכֵן אָמַר רַבִּי הוּנָא: גְּזֵרַת – בָּטְלוּ, יָמִים – לֹא בָּטְלוּ. וְרַב שֵׁשֶׁת אָמַר: אֲפִילּוּ יָמִים נַמִי בָּטְלוּ.

GEMARA With regard to the mishna's statement that the seven- and thirty-day periods of mourning are nullified, **Rav said:** The **decree,** meaning the main prohibitions of the period, **was nullified,** but **the days** of mourning themselves **were not** entirely **nullified.**[N] Instead, these periods of mourning remain to some degree. **And so said Rav Huna: The decree was nullified,** but **the days** of mourning themselves **were not nullified. And Rav Sheshet said: Even the days** of mourning **were also nullified.**

מַאי טַעְמָא יָמִים לֹא בָּטְלוּ? שֶׁאִם לֹא גִּילַּח עֶרֶב הָרֶגֶל – אָסוּר לְגַלֵּחַ אַחַר הָרֶגֶל.

The Gemara asks: **What is the reason that the days** themselves **were not nullified?** The Gemara explains: It is so **that if** one observed eight days of mourning before the Festival, so that the prohibition against hair cutting was nullified before the Festival, but for whatever reason **he did not cut his hair on the eve of the Festival, he is prohibited from cutting his hair after the Festival** until the end of the thirty-day period of mourning. In other words, the mourning period was not entirely nullified, and since he did not take advantage of the allowance to cut his hair before the Festival, he must observe the prohibitions applying during the thirty-day period of mourning after the Festival as well.

HALAKHA

Rosh HaShana and Yom Kippur with regard to mourning – רֹאשׁ הַשָּׁנָה וְיוֹם כִּפּוּר בַּאֲבֵילוּת: The *halakha* is in accordance with the opinion of Rabban Gamliel that Rosh HaShana and Yom Kippur have the same status as other Festivals with regard to mourning (*Shulḥan Arukh, Yoreh De'a* 399:6).

NOTES

The opinions of the *tanna'im* in the mishna – שִׁיטוֹת הַתַּנָּאִים בַּמִּשְׁנָה: The Ramban explains that, according to Rabbi Eliezer, because Passover and *Sukkot* last for seven days, it interrupts the mourning and ends all of the mourning obligations. However, this does not apply to a Festival that lasts for only one day, and after the Temple was destroyed *Shavuot* was celebrated for only one day. It is therefore treated like Shabbat.

Alternatively, Rabban Gamliel says that the difference between Shabbat and Festivals with regard to mourning is related to the nature of the days and not to their length. Festivals, which are days of joy, cancel mourning entirely, and therefore all Festivals are included in this group, even *Shavuot*. The Rabbis essentially agree with Rabbi Eliezer; however, they say that since the additional six days were added to make up the offerings of *Shavuot*, it therefore falls into the same category as other Festivals, especially since it is listed together with them in the Bible. However, this is not the case with regard to Rosh HaShana and Yom Kippur.

The days were not nullified – יָמִים לֹא בָּטְלוּ: Some explain that, according to Rav, the harsh decrees of mourning are nullified. However, the days of mourning themselves are not nullified. Therefore, after the Festival one is required to make up the days on which he did not mourn by refraining from cutting his hair during that time (Rabbi Shlomo ben HaYatom).

Perek **III**
Daf **19** Amud **b**

וְהָתַנְיָא: הַקּוֹבֵר אֶת מֵתוֹ שְׁלֹשָׁה יָמִים קוֹדֶם לָרֶגֶל – בָּטְלָה הֵימֶנּוּ גְּזֵרַת שִׁבְעָה. שְׁמוֹנָה יָמִים קוֹדֶם לָרֶגֶל – בָּטְלָה הֵימֶנּוּ גְּזֵרַת שְׁלֹשִׁים. וּמְגַלֵּחַ עֶרֶב הָרֶגֶל. אִם לֹא גִּילַּח עֶרֶב הָרֶגֶל – אָסוּר לְגַלֵּחַ אַחַר הָרֶגֶל.

But isn't it taught[N] in a *baraita*: In the case of **one who buries his dead** relative **three days before a pilgrimage Festival, the decree of the seven**-day period of mourning is **nullified for him.** If one buries his dead relative **eight** days before a Festival, **the decree of thirty** days **is nullified for him,** and therefore he may **cut his hair on the eve of the Festival. If,** however, **he did not cut his hair on the eve of the Festival, he is prohibited from cutting his hair after the Festival**[N] until the end of the thirty-day period of mourning.

אַבָּא שָׁאוּל אוֹמֵר: מוּתָּר לְגַלֵּחַ אַחַר הָרֶגֶל. שֶׁכְּשֵׁם שֶׁמִּצְוַת שְׁלֹשָׁה מְבַטֶּלֶת גְּזֵרַת שִׁבְעָה – כָּךְ מִצְוַת שִׁבְעָה מְבַטֶּלֶת גְּזֵרַת שְׁלֹשִׁים.

Abba Shaul says: Even if he failed to cut his hair on the eve of the Festival, **he is permitted to cut his hair after the Festival, for just as** his observance of **the mitzva of three** days of mourning prior to the Festival **cancels the decree of** the **seven**-day period of mourning, and so if the deceased was buried three days before the Festival, the mourner is no longer required to continue this period of mourning after the Festival, **so too,** his observance of **the mitzva of seven** days of mourning before the Festival **cancels the decree** of the **thirty**-day period of mourning.

NOTES

But isn't it taught – וְהָתַנְיָא: Most of the commentaries explain that the expression: But isn't it taught, which normally introduces a challenge, introduces a support in this case. However, there is a dispute about the details of this support. Some say that it serves as proof for Rav Huna's opinion, based on the first *tanna*, who makes an explicit statement in accordance with his opinion (*Tosafot*, see *Yad David*). Some say the expression: But isn't it taught, means here: Like the dispute between *tanna'im*, and note that the dispute between Rav Huna and Rav Sheshet parallels an explicit tannaitic dispute (Rid; *Talmid Rabbeinu Yeḥiel of Paris*; Ritva). However, others claim that it is not possible to say that this dispute is like the dispute between *tanna'im* because the dispute between *amora'im* is about how to explain the mishna. It is not a dispute concerning the *halakha* itself (*Tal Ḥayyim*).

There is another opinion, according to which the expression: But isn't it taught, is meant to introduce a challenge by Rav to Rav Huna's opinion, based on Abba Shaul's statement, which is the accepted *halakha*. According to this explanation, it was not Abaye who said that the *halakha* is in accordance with the opinion of Abba Shaul with regard to the seventh day of mourning, but Rav. This also explains Rav's answer that the *halakha* is not in accordance with Abba Shaul with regard to every issue (Rabbeinu Ḥananel).

He is prohibited from cutting his hair after the Festival – אָסוּר לְגַלֵּחַ אַחַר הָרֶגֶל: Some say that this serves as a sort of punishment. Because this mourner did not mind entering into the Festival while he was disheveled, the Festival no longer cancels the restrictions that apply during his thirty-day period of mourning (*Talmid Rabbeinu Yeḥiel of Paris*).

שִׁבְעָה? וְהָאֲנַן שְׁמוֹנָה תְּנַן! קָסָבַר אַבָּא שָׁאוּל: מִקְצָת הַיּוֹם כְּכוּלּוֹ, וְיוֹם שְׁבִיעִי עוֹלֶה לוֹ לְכָאן וּלְכָאן. אָמַר רַב חִסְדָּא אָמַר רָבִינָא בַּר שֵׁילָא: הֲלָכָה כְּאַבָּא שָׁאוּל.

The Gemara asks: Why does Abba Shaul speak of the observance of **seven** days of mourning? **But didn't we learn** in the mishna that it requires **eight** days? The Gemara explains: **Abba Shaul maintains** that the legal status of **part of the day is like** that of **an entire day,** and therefore **the seventh day counts as both** the final day of the seven-day period of mourning and the first day of the thirty-day period of mourning. **Rav Ḥisda said** that **Ravina bar Sheila said: The *halakha* is in accordance with** the opinion of **Abba Shaul.**[H]

וּמוֹדִים חֲכָמִים לְאַבָּא שָׁאוּל כְּשֶׁחָל שְׁמִינִי שֶׁלּוֹ לִהְיוֹת בְּשַׁבָּת עֶרֶב הָרֶגֶל, שֶׁמּוּתָּר לְגַלֵּחַ בְּעֶרֶב שַׁבָּת.

And furthermore, even **the Rabbis concede to Abba Shaul that when one's eighth** day of mourning **occurs on a Shabbat,** which is also **the eve of a Festival, he is permitted to cut his hair on Friday,** which is the seventh day. Since he is unavoidably prevented from cutting his hair on the eighth day, as it is prohibited for him to cut his hair on Shabbat, he may do so already on Friday, although it is only his seventh day of mourning.

כְּמַאן אָזְלָא הָא דְּאָמַר רַב עַמְרָם אָמַר רַב: אָבֵל, כֵּיוָן שֶׁעָמְדוּ מְנַחֲמִין מֵאֶצְלוֹ – מוּתָּר בִּרְחִיצָה. כְּמַאן? כְּאַבָּא שָׁאוּל.

The Gemara asks: **In accordance with whose** opinion **is that which Rav Amram said** that **Rav said:** With regard to **a mourner, once the comforters have stood up** to leave **his** house on the seventh day of his mourning, **he is immediately permitted to bathe? In accordance with whose** opinion? **In accordance** with the opinion of **Abba Shaul.** He maintains that a part of the seventh day is treated as an entire day with regard to this issue.

אָמַר אַבַּיֵי: הֲלָכָה כְּאַבָּא שָׁאוּל בְּיוֹם שִׁבְעָה, וּמוֹדִים חֲכָמִים לְאַבָּא שָׁאוּל בְּיוֹם שְׁלֹשִׁים, דְּאָמְרִינַן: מִקְצָת הַיּוֹם כְּכוּלּוֹ.

Abaye said: The *halakha* is in accordance with the opinion of **Abba Shaul with regard to the seventh** day of mourning, **and the Rabbis concede to Abba Shaul with regard to the thirtieth day,**[N] for with regard to the thirtieth day **we** certainly **say** that the legal status of **part of the day is like** that of **an entire** day, and so a mourner may already cut his hair on the morning of the thirtieth day.

רָבָא אָמַר: הֲלָכָה כְּאַבָּא שָׁאוּל בְּיוֹם שְׁלֹשִׁים, וְאֵין הֲלָכָה כְּאַבָּא שָׁאוּל בְּיוֹם שִׁבְעָה. וּנְהַרְדְּעֵי אָמְרִי: הֲלָכָה כְּאַבָּא שָׁאוּל בְּזוֹ וּבְזוֹ. דְּאָמַר שְׁמוּאֵל: הֲלָכָה כְּדִבְרֵי הַמֵּיקֵל בְּאֵבֶל.

Rava said: The *halakha* is in accordance with the opinion of **Abba Shaul with regard to the thirtieth day** of mourning, **but the *halakha* is not in accordance with Abba Shaul with regard to the seventh** day. **And** the Sages of **Neharde'a say: The *halakha* is in accordance with** the opinion of **Abba Shaul with regard to both** the seventh day and the thirtieth day, **for Shmuel said: The *halakha* follows the statement of the** more **lenient** authority **in** matters relating to **mourning.**

שְׁלֹשִׁים יוֹם מְנָלַן? יָלֵיף ״פֶּרַע״ ״פֶּרַע״ מִנָּזִיר. כְּתִיב הָכָא: ״רָאשֵׁיכֶם אַל תִּפְרָעוּ״, וּכְתִיב הָתָם: ״גַּדֵּל פֶּרַע שְׂעַר רֹאשׁוֹ״, מַה לְּהַלָּן שְׁלֹשִׁים – אַף כָּאן שְׁלֹשִׁים.

§ The Gemara asks now about the thirty-day mourning period: **From where do we** derive the **thirty-day** period of mourning?[N] The Gemara answers: **It is learned** by way of a verbal analogy **between** one instance of the word ***pera*** and a different instance of the word ***pera*** stated with regard to **a nazirite. Here,** in the instructions given to Aaron not to mourn the deaths of his sons, **it is written: "Let the hair of your heads not grow loose [*tifra'u*]"** (Leviticus 10:6), which indicates that ordinary mourners are required to grow their hair long. **And there,** with regard to a nazirite, **it is written: "He shall let the hair of his head grow long [*pera*]"** (Numbers 6:5). **Just as there,** in the case of the nazirite, he must grow his hair for **thirty** days, **so too, here** a mourner must grow his hair for **thirty** days.

וְהָתָם מְנָלַן? אָמַר רַב מַתָּנָה: סְתָם נְזִירוּת שְׁלֹשִׁים יוֹם. מַאי טַעְמָא? אָמַר קְרָא: ״קָדוֹשׁ יִהְיֶה״. יִהְיֶה בְּגִימַטְרִיָּא תְּלָתִין הָווּ.

The Gemara asks: **And there,** with regard to a nazirite, **from where do we** derive that he must grow his hair for thirty days? Nowhere is this explicitly stated with regard to a nazirite. The Gemara answers: **Rav Mattana said: An unspecified nazariteship,**[H] when one takes a vow of naziriteship without specifying for how long, extends for **thirty days. What is the reason** for this? **The verse states: "He shall be sacred,** and he shall let the hair of his head grow" (Numbers 6:5), and **"He shall be [*yihye*],"** which is written *yod, heh, yod, heh,* **has a numerical value [*gimatriyya*] of thirty,** as *yod* has a numerical value of ten and *heh* has a numerical value of five. This implies that an unspecified naziriteship extends for thirty days, and by way of the verbal analogy, this is applied to mourning as well.

HALAKHA

The *halakha* is in accordance with the opinion of Abba Shaul – הֲלָכָה כְּאַבָּא שָׁאוּל: The *halakha* is in accordance with the opinion of Abba Shaul with regard to the seven- and thirty-day mourning periods, and it is in accordance with the Sages of Neharde'a, based on the principle that the *halakha* follows the lenient opinion with regard to mourning. Therefore, once those who have come to console the mourner stand to leave on the seventh day, the prohibitions of the seven-day mourning period cease to apply. Similarly, the legal status of part of the day is like that of an entire day with regard to the thirty-day period of mourning, and the restrictions of mourning cease at sunrise of the thirtieth day. The Rema writes, based on the Rosh, that in places where the consolers do not come on the seventh day, the restrictions of the seven-day period end one hour after the time of prayer (*Shulḥan Arukh, Yoreh De'a* 395:1).

Unspecified naziriteship – סְתָם נְזִירוּת: If one took an oath to become a nazirite without specifying for how long it would be in effect, he is required to act as a nazirite for thirty days (Rambam *Sefer Hafla'a, Hilkhot Nezirut* 3:1).

NOTES

The Rabbis concede…with regard to the thirtieth day – וּמוֹדִים חֲכָמִים...בְּיוֹם שְׁלֹשִׁים: The reason for this is because the thirty-day period of mourning is considered to be a less serious type of mourning, and therefore the Rabbis are not stringent with regard to this issue. Instead ,they agree that one may rely upon the principle that a portion of the day is considered to be like the entire day (Rabbeinu Yehonatan of Lunel; *Talmid Rabbeinu Yeḥiel of Paris*).

From where do we derive the thirty-day period of mourning – שְׁלֹשִׁים יוֹם מְנָלַן: As is explained in a later passage (20a), the seven-day period of mourning is derived from the Bible (Rashi manuscript). In addition, this derivation from a nazirite serves as the basis for the dispute between the Rabbis and Abba Shaul. In the case of a nazirite, the unique restrictions apply to him for thirty days, and he is permitted to cut his hair on the thirtieth day itself. However, the *tanna'im* disagree as to why the *halakhot* of a nazirite should be compared to the *halakhot* of a mourner (*Tosefot HaRosh*; see *Tosafot*).

אָמַר רַב הוּנָא בְּרֵיהּ דְּרַב יְהוֹשֻׁעַ: הַכֹּל מוֹדִין כְּשֶׁחָל שְׁלִישִׁי שֶׁלּוֹ לִהְיוֹת עֶרֶב הָרֶגֶל שֶׁאָסוּר בִּרְחִיצָה עַד הָעֶרֶב.

Rav Huna, son of Rav Yehoshua, said: Everyone, including Abba Shaul, who says that part of a day is treated like a full day, **agrees** that **when his third** day of mourning **occurs**[N] **on the eve of the Festival,**[H] the mourner **is prohibited from bathing** his body **until the evening.** In this case, the principle that the legal status of part of the day is like that of an entire day does not apply. Rather, one must observe three full days of mourning. He must therefore wait until the evening and wash himself with cold water, or wait until the intermediate days of the Festival and bathe in hot water.

אָמַר רַב נְחֶמְיָה בְּרֵיהּ דְּרַב יְהוֹשֻׁעַ: אַשְׁכַּחְתִּינְהוּ לְרַב פַּפִּי וּלְרַב פָּפָּא דְּיָתְבִי וְקָאָמְרִי: הֲלָכָה כְּרַב הוּנָא בְּרֵיהּ דְּרַב יְהוֹשֻׁעַ. אִיכָּא דְּאָמְרִי, אָמַר רַב נְחֶמְיָה בְּרֵיהּ דְּרַב יוֹסֵף: אַשְׁכַּחְתִּינְהוּ לְרַב פַּפִּי וּלְרַב פָּפָּא וּלְרַב הוּנָא בְּרֵיהּ דְּרַב יְהוֹשֻׁעַ דְּיָתְבִי וְקָאָמְרִי: הַכֹּל מוֹדִים שֶׁאִם חָל שְׁלִישִׁי שֶׁלּוֹ לִהְיוֹת עֶרֶב הָרֶגֶל – שֶׁאָסוּר בִּרְחִיצָה עַד הָעֶרֶב.

Rav Neḥemya, son of Rav Yehoshua, said: I once **found Rav Pappi**[P] **and Rav Pappa sitting** together **and saying: The** ***halakha*** **is in accordance with** the opinion of **Rav Huna, son of Rav Yehoshua. There are** those who **say** a different version of this tradition: **Rav Neḥemya, son of Rav Yosef, said: I** once **found Rav Pappi, Rav Pappa, and Rav Huna, son of Yehoshua, sitting** together **and saying: Everyone concedes** that **when the third** day of mourning **occurs on the eve of a Festival,** the mourner **is prohibited from bathing** his body **until the evening.**[N]

בְּעָא מִינֵּיהּ אַבָּיֵי מֵרָבָא: קְבָרוֹ בָּרֶגֶל, רֶגֶל עוֹלֶה לוֹ לְמִנְיַן שְׁלֹשִׁים, אוֹ אֵין רֶגֶל עוֹלֶה לוֹ לְמִנְיַן שְׁלֹשִׁים? לְמִנְיַן שִׁבְעָה לָא קָמִיבַּעְיָא לִי – דְּלָא נָהֲגָא מִצְוַת שִׁבְעָה בָּרֶגֶל. כִּי קָא מִיבַּעְיָא לִי – לְמִנְיַן שְׁלֹשִׁים, דְּקָא נָהֲגָא מִצְוַת שְׁלֹשִׁים בָּרֶגֶל. מַאי?

Abaye inquired of Rava: If **one buried** his dead relative **on the Festival** itself, **does the Festival count toward his thirty**-day period of mourning, **or does the Festival not count toward his thirty**-day period of mourning? Abaye elaborated on his question: **I do not ask** whether or not the Festival counts toward his **seven**-day period of mourning because **the obligation** to observe **seven** days of mourning **does not apply** at all **during the Festival,** and therefore he must certainly observe the seven-day mourning period, beginning from after the Festival. **What I am asking is** with regard to the **thirty**-day period of mourning, because certain aspects of the **mitzva of** the **thirty**-day mourning period **do** in fact **apply during the Festival,**[N] e.g., the prohibitions to launder clothes and cut hair. **What,** then, is the *halakha*: Do the days of the Festival count toward the thirty days or not?

אָמַר לֵיהּ: אֵינוֹ עוֹלֶה. אֵיתִיבֵיהּ: הַקּוֹבֵר אֶת מֵתוֹ שְׁנֵי יָמִים קוֹדֶם הָרֶגֶל – מוֹנֶה חֲמִשָּׁה יָמִים אַחַר הָרֶגֶל, וּמְלַאכְתּוֹ נַעֲשֵׂית עַל יְדֵי אֲחֵרִים, וַעֲבָדָיו וְשִׁפְחוֹתָיו עוֹשִׂים בְּצִינְעָא בְּתוֹךְ בֵּיתוֹ, וְאֵין רַבִּים מִתְעַסְּקִין עִמּוֹ,

Rava **said to him:** The Festival **does not count** toward the thirty days. Abaye **raised an objection to** Rava's opinion from the following *baraita*: If **one buries his dead** relative **two days before a Festival, he must count five days** of mourning **after the Festival, and** during this period **his work is performed** for him **by others.**[N] **And his menservants and maidservants do** this work **in private inside his house, and the public need not occupy themselves with him** by coming to console him,

HALAKHA

The third day occurs on the eve of the Festival – חָל שְׁלִישִׁי בְּעֶרֶב הָרֶגֶל: If a Festival interrupts one's seven-day mourning period, he may launder his clothes on the day preceding the Festival, though he may not wear laundered clothes until the Festival begins at night. However, he is prohibited from bathing until nightfall. Some permit him to bathe after the afternoon prayer, immediately before it becomes dark. The Rema writes that this is prohibited because the custom not to bathe during the thirty-day period applies, as the Festival does not cancel the thirty-day period of mourning. The same is true with regard to laundering in places where it is customary for a mourner to refrain from laundering his clothes for thirty days. However, it is the common practice to be lenient (*Magen Avraham*; Rema; *Shakh*; *Taz* on *Shulḥan Arukh, Yoreh De'a* 399:5; *Shulḥan Arukh, Oraḥ Ḥayyim* 548:10).

PERSONALITIES

Rav Pappi – רַב פַּפִּי: Rav Pappi was one of the fourth generation of *amora'im* in Babylonia and a primary student of Rava. There are cases of Rav Pappi discussing halakhic issues with his colleagues, mainly with other students of Rava, such as Rav Huna, son of Rabbi Yehoshua, and Rav Pappa. It appears that Rav Pappi was connected to the house of the Exilarch, that there were warm relations between them, and that eventually he joined the Exilarch's court.

Several members of the next generation of Sages and even his younger colleagues transmitted statements in his name, and the *amora* Rav Ashi is listed as one of his students.

NOTES

When his third day of mourning occurs – כְּשֶׁחָל יוֹם שְׁלִישִׁי שֶׁלּוֹ: There are those who explain that this statement specifically refers to the third day (see *Or Zarua* and Ra'avya). However, most of the commentaries explain that the prohibition against bathing on the eve of the Festival before nightfall does not specifically apply to the third day. Rather, this *halakha* applies to any day during the seven-day period of mourning, with the exception of the seventh day. This day is mentioned only because the wording of the mishna is preserved (*Ba'al Halakhot Gedolot*).

He is prohibited from bathing until the evening – אָסוּר בִּרְחִיצָה עַד הָעֶרֶב: The halakhic authorities explain that bathing is specifically prohibited until the evening. However, this is not the case with regard to laundering and cutting hair, which are permitted on account of the principle that the legal status of part of the day is like that of an entire day. The reason for this distinction is because the latter group of activities may not be performed during the Festival itself, whereas bathing may be performed in a certain way during the Festival (Ra'avad; Rosh).

Certain aspects of the mitzva of the thirty-day mourning period do apply during the Festival – דְּקָא נָהֲגָא מִצְוַת שְׁלֹשִׁים בָּרֶגֶל: Some explain that this does not mean that the thirty-day period of mourning actually applies during the Festival. However, since it is prohibited to launder clothes and cut one's hair during the intermediate days of the Festival, it is as though the restrictions of the thirty-day period of mourning extended into the Festival itself (Rashi; Rabbeinu Ḥananel; Rid).

However, there are others who hold that the thirty-day period of mourning actually applies during the Festival, and therefore a mourner may not wear ironed clothes during the Festival. Similarly, he must avoid joyous social gatherings. According to this opinion, because laundering and hair cutting are similarly prohibited during the Festival, observing these restrictions does not appear to be a public display of mourning (Ramban; Ran).

His work is performed by others – מְלַאכְתּוֹ נַעֲשֵׂית עַל יְדֵי אֲחֵרִים: *Tosafot* question the reasoning behind this leniency. The Ramban explains that because one is not permitted to perform work during the Festival, the Sages were not stringent and did not prohibit him from having his work performed by others after the Festival.

שֶׁכְּבָר נִתְעַסְּקוּ בּוֹ בָּרֶגֶל. כְּלָלוֹ שֶׁל דָּבָר: כׇּל שֶׁהוּא מִשּׁוּם אֵבֶל – רֶגֶל מַפְסִיקוֹ; וְכׇל שֶׁהוּא מִשּׁוּם עִסְקֵי רַבִּים – אֵין רֶגֶל מַפְסִיקוֹ.

for they already occupied themselves with him when they came to console him **during the Festival. The** general **principle with regard to the matter** is as follows: **Any** activity **that** is prohibited to the mourner **because it is** an expression of **mourning is interrupted by the Festival**[N] and remains prohibited afterward. **And anything that involves the public's occupation** with the mourner,[N] e.g., coming to the mourner to offer him comfort and condolence, **is not interrupted by the Festival,** for people console the mourner during the Festival as well.

קְבָרוֹ שְׁלֹשָׁה יָמִים בְּסוֹף הָרֶגֶל – מוֹנֶה שִׁבְעָה אַחַר הָרֶגֶל. אַרְבָּעָה יָמִים הָרִאשׁוֹנִים – רַבִּים מִתְעַסְּקִין בּוֹ. שְׁלֹשָׁה יָמִים הָאַחֲרוֹנִים – אֵין רַבִּים מִתְעַסְּקִין בּוֹ, שֶׁכְּבָר נִתְעַסְּקוּ בָּרֶגֶל, וְרֶגֶל עוֹלֶה לוֹ.

If **he** buries his relative **three days** before **the end of the Festival,** the mourner **must count seven** days of mourning **after the Festival** because his mourning never began. On the **first four days** of his mourning, **the public must occupy themselves with him** and come to console him. On **the three last days,** however, **the public need not occupy themselves with him, as they already occupied themselves with him during the Festival.** That is to say, they certainly came to console him during the Festival, although the period of mourning did not actually begin until afterward. **And the Festival counts for him** toward the thirty-day mourning period.

מַאי לָאו אַסֵּיפָא? לָא, אַרֵישָׁא.

With regard to the statement of the *baraita* that the Festival counts toward the thirty-day period of mourning: **What, is it not** referring to **the latter clause**[N] of that *baraita,* which speaks about a case where the burial was performed during the Festival itself? If this is the case, then a refutation of Rava's opinion is stated explicitly, that the Festival counts toward the thirty-day mourning period, even if the deceased was buried on the Festival itself. Rava rejects this argument: **No,** it is referring to **the first clause,** which discusses a case where the burial was performed before the Festival, and since rites of mourning were observed already before the Festival, the Festival is counted toward the thirty-day period of mourning. Therefore, it is not a refutation of Rava's *halakha.*

אֵיתִיבֵיהּ: רֶגֶל עוֹלֶה לוֹ לְמִנְיַן שְׁלֹשִׁים. כֵּיצַד? קְבָרוֹ בִּתְחִילַּת הָרֶגֶל – מוֹנֶה שִׁבְעָה אַחַר הָרֶגֶל, וּמְלַאכְתּוֹ נַעֲשֵׂית עַל יְדֵי אֲחֵרִים, וַעֲבָדָיו וְשִׁפְחוֹתָיו עוֹשִׂין בְּצִנְעָא בְּתוֹךְ בֵּיתוֹ, וְאֵין רַבִּים מִתְעַסְּקִין בּוֹ, שֶׁכְּבָר נִתְעַסְּקוּ בּוֹ בָּרֶגֶל, וְרֶגֶל עוֹלֶה לוֹ! תְּיוּבְתָּא.

Abaye **raised an objection to** Rava's opinion from another *baraita,* in which it was taught: **A pilgrimage Festival counts toward the thirty**-day period of mourning. **How so?** If one **buried** his dead relative **at the beginning of a pilgrimage Festival,**[N] **he must count seven** days of mourning **after the Festival, and** during this period **his work is performed by others. And his menservants and maidservants perform** this work **in private inside his house, and the public need not occupy themselves with him** and come to console him, **for they already occupied themselves with him during the Festival. And the Festival counts for him.** Here it is explicitly stated that the Festival counts toward the thirty-day period of mourning, even when the deceased was buried during the Festival itself. The Gemara concludes: This is indeed **a conclusive refutation** of Rava's opinion.

כִּי אֲתָא רָבִין אָמַר רַבִּי יוֹחָנָן: אֲפִילּוּ קְבָרוֹ בָּרֶגֶל. וְכֵן אוֹרֵי לֵיהּ רַבִּי אֶלְעָזָר לְרַבִּי פְּדָת בְּרֵיהּ: אֲפִילּוּ קְבָרוֹ בָּרֶגֶל.

When Ravin came from Eretz Yisrael to Babylonia, **he said** that **Rabbi Yoḥanan said: Even if one buried** his dead relative **during the Festival,** the Festival counts toward his thirty-day period of mourning. **And, similarly, Rabbi Elazar ruled for Rabbi Pedat, his son: Even if one buried** his dead relative **during the Festival** it counts towards his thirty days.[H]

תָּנוּ רַבָּנַן, קִיֵּים כְּפִיַּית הַמִּטָּה שְׁלֹשָׁה יָמִים קוֹדֶם הָרֶגֶל – אֵינוֹ צָרִיךְ לְכְפוֹתָהּ אַחַר הָרֶגֶל, דִּבְרֵי רַבִּי אֱלִיעֶזֶר. וַחֲכָמִים אוֹמְרִים: אֲפִילּוּ יוֹם אֶחָד, אֲפִילּוּ שָׁעָה אַחַת.

§ **The Sages taught** the following *baraita*: If **one fulfilled the** obligation of **overturning the bed**[N] **for three days before the pilgrimage Festival, he is no** longer **required to overturn it after the Festival;** this is **the statement of Rabbi Eliezer. But the Rabbis say: Even** if one overturned his bed for only **one day,** or **even for** only **one hour,** he is not required to overturn it after the Festival.

NOTES

It…is interrupted by the Festival – רֶגֶל מַפְסִיקוֹ: Some note that the expression: Is interrupted by the Festival, does not mean the same thing here as it does in most other places. Usually the phrase means that the Festival nullifies the rest of the mourning period. However, in this case the term means that the mourning is put on hold and is continued after the conclusion of the Festival (Rashi manuscript).

Public's occupation with the mourner – עִסְקֵי רַבִּים: According to all opinions, this expression refers to people coming to console the mourner. With regard to the meal eaten after the burial, some say that it is eaten even during the intermediate days (Ritva; see *Tosafot*). However, according to the Jerusalem Talmud, this meal may not be eaten during the intermediate days of the Festival, or on Hanukah or Purim.

What, is it not referring to the latter clause – מַאי לָאו אַסֵּיפָא: In other words, does it not refer to all of the *halakhot* stated in this *baraita,* including those mentioned it the latter clause? (Ritva).

He buried his relative at the beginning of a pilgrimage Festival – קְבָרוֹ בִּתְחִילַּת הָרֶגֶל: The Gemara is referring only to the beginning of the Festival in order to present the most extreme case. Although an entire seven-day Festival passed since one relative died, he is still required to observe seven days of mourning (*Talmid Rabbeinu Yeḥiel of Paris*).

He fulfilled the overturning of the bed – קִיֵּים כְּפִיַּית הַמִּטָּה: From the wording of this *baraita,* the Ra'avad learns that the matter is not connected to one's status as a mourner, but rather to his observance of even some of the *halakhot* of mourning, for the Gemara mentions only overturning the bed but not the relative's burial. This is also the opinion of most authorities. However, the Meiri states that the wording used is not conclusive. In his opinion, the Festival nullifies the mourning of one who has buried his relative, even if he had not yet observed the mourning customs.

HALAKHA

Someone whose relative died during the Festival – מִי שֶׁמֵּת לוֹ מֵת בָּרֶגֶל: One whose close relative dies during the intermediate days of a Festival observes the *halakhot* of acute mourning before the burial, and afterward he privately observes the customs of mourning. In such a case, the Festival counts toward the thirty-day mourning period. The public comes to console him during the Festival, and he may perform any work if refraining from it would cause him to incur a loss, as is the case for anyone else during the intermediate days. Any work that does not fall into this category may be performed by his servants and maidservants in private (Rema). Once seven days have passed from the time of the burial, even though he has not completed his seven-day mourning period, his work may be performed by others in their houses. Consolation by others is only for the remainder of the seven days minus the days that he was mourning during the Festival. He practices the seven-day mourning period in an ordinary manner after the Festival. In the Diaspora, he includes the last day of the Festival as one of his seven days, although in practice he does not mourn on it, and therefore he observes only six days of mourning (*Shulḥan Arukh, Yoreh De'a* 399:2).

אָמַר רַבִּי אֶלְעָזָר בְּרַבִּי שִׁמְעוֹן: הֵן הֵן דִּבְרֵי בֵּית שַׁמַּאי, הֵן הֵן דִּבְרֵי בֵּית הִלֵּל. שֶׁבֵּית שַׁמַּאי אוֹמְרִים: שְׁלֹשָׁה יָמִים, וּבֵית הִלֵּל אוֹמְרִים: אֲפִילּוּ יוֹם אֶחָד.

Rabbi Elazar, son of Rabbi Shimon, said: This is the statement of Beit Shammai, and **that is the statement of Beit Hillel.** In other words, Rabbi Eliezer and the Rabbis disagreed about a matter that was the subject of an earlier dispute between Beit Shammai and Beit Hillel, **for Beit Shammai say: Three days, and Beit Hillel say: Even one day.**

אָמַר רַב הוּנָא אָמַר רַבִּי חִיָּיא בַּר אַבָּא אָמַר רַבִּי יוֹחָנָן, וְאָמְרִי לָהּ אָמַר לֵיהּ רַבִּי יוֹחָנָן לְרַבִּי חִיָּיא בַּר אַבָּא וּלְרַב הוּנָא: אֲפִילּוּ יוֹם אֶחָד, אֲפִילּוּ שָׁעָה אַחַת. רָבָא אָמַר: הֲלָכָה כְּתַנָּא דִּידַן, דְּאָמַר שְׁלֹשָׁה.

Rav Huna said that **Rabbi Ḥiyya bar Abba said** that **Rabbi Yoḥanan said, and some say** a different version of this line of transmission: **Rabbi Yoḥanan said to Rabbi Ḥiyya bar Abba and to Rav Huna: Even one day, even one hour.** The Gemara cites **Rava,** who **said: The *halakha* is in accordance with** the opinion of **the *tanna*** of **our** mishna, who **said three** days. Based on this, we rule that the mourning rites are not canceled after the Festival unless they were observed for at least three days before the Festival.[H]

רָבִינָא אִיקְּלַע לְסוּרָא דִּפְרָת. אֲמַר לֵיהּ רַב חֲבִיבָא לְרָבִינָא: הִלְכְתָא מַאי? אֲמַר לֵיהּ אֲפִילּוּ יוֹם אֶחָד, וַאֲפִילּוּ שָׁעָה אַחַת.

Ravina happened to come to the city of **Sura on the** banks of the **Euphrates** River. **Rav Ḥaviva said to Ravina: What is the *halakha*** with regard to this issue? **He said to him: Even one day, and even one hour.**

יְתֵיב רַבִּי חִיָּיא בַּר אַבָּא וְרַבִּי אַמִּי וְרַבִּי יִצְחָק נַפָּחָא אַקִּילְעָא דְּרַבִּי יִצְחָק בֶּן אֶלְעָזָר. נְפַק מִילְּתָא מִבֵּינַיְיהוּ: מִנַּיִן לַאֲבֵילוּת שִׁבְעָה? דִּכְתִיב: ״וְהָפַכְתִּי חַגֵּיכֶם לְאֵבֶל״ מַה חַג שִׁבְעָה – אַף אֲבֵילוּת שִׁבְעָה.

§ It was related that **Rabbi Ḥiyya bar Abba, Rabbi Ami, and Rabbi Yitzḥak Nappaḥa were** once **sitting in the pavilion of Rabbi Yitzḥak ben Elazar** and were conversing. **A matter emerged from among them: From where** is it derived that the rites of **mourning** are observed for **seven** days?[N] **As it is written: "And I will turn your Festivals into mourning"** (Amos 8:10).[N] **Just as a Festival** lasts for **seven** days, **so too mourning** lasts for **seven** days.

וְאֵימָא עֲצֶרֶת, דְּחַד יוֹמָא! הַהוּא מִיבָּעֵי לֵיהּ לְכִדְרֵישׁ לָקִישׁ, דְּאָמַר רֵישׁ לָקִישׁ מִשּׁוּם רַבִּי יְהוּדָה נְשִׂיאָה: מִנַּיִן לִשְׁמוּעָה רְחוֹקָה שֶׁאֵינָהּ נוֹהֶגֶת אֶלָּא יוֹם אֶחָד? דִּכְתִיב: ״וְהָפַכְתִּי חַגֵּיכֶם לְאֵבֶל״, וְאַשְׁכְּחַן עֲצֶרֶת דְּאִיקְּרִי חַד יוֹמָא חַג.

The Gemara asks: **And say** that perhaps mourning is like ***Shavuot*, which is only one day.** The Gemara rejects this argument: **That** derivation, from the one day of *Shavuot*, **is required for** what was stated by **Reish Lakish, as Reish Lakish said in the name of Rabbi Yehuda Nesia: From where** is it derived **that** mourning in the case of **distant tidings,** i.e., when one hears that one of his relatives died a long time ago, **applies for only one day? As it is written: "And I will turn your Festivals into mourning," and we find** with regard to ***Shavuot*** **that one day is** also **called a Festival.**

תָּנוּ רַבָּנַן: שְׁמוּעָה קְרוֹבָה נוֹהֶגֶת שִׁבְעָה וּשְׁלֹשִׁים; שְׁמוּעָה רְחוֹקָה אֵינָהּ נוֹהֶגֶת אֶלָּא יוֹם אֶחָד. אֵיזוֹ הִיא קְרוֹבָה וְאֵיזוֹ הִיא רְחוֹקָה? קְרוֹבָה – בְּתוֹךְ שְׁלֹשִׁים; רְחוֹקָה – לְאַחַר שְׁלֹשִׁים, דִּבְרֵי רַבִּי עֲקִיבָא. וַחֲכָמִים אוֹמְרִים: אַחַת שְׁמוּעָה קְרוֹבָה וְאַחַת שְׁמוּעָה רְחוֹקָה – נוֹהֶגֶת שִׁבְעָה וּשְׁלֹשִׁים.

The Sages taught the following *baraita*: In the case of **recent tidings** of a relative's death, mourning **applies for seven- and thirty-**day periods. In the case of **distant tidings, it applies only for one day. What are** considered **recent tidings and what are** considered **distant tidings? Recent** tidings are news that arrives **within thirty** days of the person's death. **Distant** tidings are news that arrives **after thirty** days; this is **the statement of Rabbi Akiva. And the Rabbis say: Both** in the case of **recent tidings and** in the case of **distant tidings,** mourning **applies for seven- and thirty-**day periods.[H]

HALAKHA

One who buries his dead before a Festival – הַקּוֹבֵר מֵתוֹ לִפְנֵי לְרֶגֶל: When one buries a close relative before a Festival and begins observing mourning practices, even in private, and even for a short period of time, the remainder of his seven days of mourning are nullified by the Festival. In such a case, the days of the Festival also count toward the thirty-day period of mourning.

However, if one did not observe any mourning practices beforehand, whether intentionally or accidentally, the Festival does not nullify the mourning. Therefore, one must observe the mourning customs in private during the Festival, and comforters come to visit and console him in his home. Then he observes the seven-day period of mourning after the Festival. During those days, his work is performed by others, since he refrained from working during the Festival and was consoled. However, the Festival counts toward the thirty-day mourning period, because he observed the customs of this thirty-day period during the intermediate days of the Festival (*Shulḥan Arukh, Yoreh De'a* 399:1).

Recent and distant tidings – שְׁמוּעָה קְרוֹבָה וּשְׁמוּעָה רְחוֹקָה: If one receives news that his relative has passed away within thirty days of the death, then he acts as if the day he heard this news were the day of the burial, even if this news arrives on the thirtieth day. Therefore, the mourner rends his clothes and observes the seven- and thirty-day periods of mourning.

If one heard about the death after the thirtieth day, then he is required to observe mourning only for one hour, whether he heard this news during the day or at night, because of the principle that the legal status of part of a day is like that of a whole day.

For one's father or mother, mourning practices are observed even after the thirtieth day, and one may not cut his hair until others rebuke him for looking disheveled. If one receives news about his father's or mother's death more than twelve months after it occurred, then he practices only one day of mourning (*Shulḥan Arukh, Yoreh De'a* 402:1).

NOTES

From where is it derived that the rites of mourning are observed for seven days – מִנַּיִן לַאֲבֵילוּת שִׁבְעָה: The Jerusalem Talmud offers different sources for the seven-day mourning period, and the clearest of them is based on the verse that states that Joseph "made seven days of mourning for his father" (Genesis 50:10). However, this proof is rejected by the Jerusalem Talmud because *halakha* cannot be derived from events that occurred before the giving of the Torah. Furthermore, *Tosafot* point out that Joseph's mourning occurred before the burial, and therefore is not a valid source for current practice. Another source is from that which is stated before the flood: "And it came to pass after the seven days, that the waters of the flood were upon the earth" (Genesis 7:10). This is understood as a reference to either God's or Methuselah's time of mourning for the world that would be destroyed. Similarly a proof is derived from a verse describing Miriam, who was afflicted with leprosy and confined for seven days. The verse says there: "Let her not, I pray, be as one dead" (Numbers 12:12), and therefore her case is compared to that of the dead. The Jerusalem Talmud there mentions the details of each of these proof texts and the difficulties with learning from each one.

And I will turn your Festivals into mourning – וְהָפַכְתִּי חַגֵּיכֶם לְאֵבֶל: The Ritva writes that Reish Lakish bases his exposition on the word "Festivals," in plural. He maintains that this word must be referring to two Festivals: A seven-day Festival in the case of recent tidings and a one-day Festival in the case of distant tidings. In the Jerusalem Talmud, it is asked: Why can't this verse be used to conclude that there is an eight-day mourning period from the festival of *Sukkot*, which is eight days long? The answer given there is that the Eighth Day of Assembly is a separate Festival, and therefore none of the Festivals are longer than seven days.

אָמַר רַבָּה בַּר בַּר חָנָה אָמַר רַבִּי יוֹחָנָן: כׇּל מָקוֹם שֶׁאַתָּה מוֹצֵא יָחִיד מֵקִיל וְרַבִּים מַחְמִירִין – הֲלָכָה כְּרַבִּים, חוּץ מִזּוֹ, שֶׁאַף עַל פִּי שֶׁרַבִּי עֲקִיבָא מֵקִיל וַחֲכָמִים מַחְמִירִין – הֲלָכָה כְּרַבִּי עֲקִיבָא. דְּאָמַר שְׁמוּאֵל: הֲלָכָה כְּדִבְרֵי הַמֵּקִיל בְּאֵבֶל.

Rabba bar bar Ḥana said that **Rabbi Yoḥanan said: Wherever you find an individual being lenient and the majority being stringent, the *halakha* is in accordance with the majority, except for this** case, **for even though Rabbi Akiva is lenient and the Rabbis are stringent, the *halakha* is in accordance with** the opinion of **Rabbi Akiva.** This is in keeping with the principle **stated by Shmuel: The *halakha* follows the statement of the** more **lenient** authority **in** matters relating to **mourning.**

רַב חֲנִינָא אָתְיָא לֵיהּ שְׁמוּעָה דַּאֲבוּהּ מִבֵּי חוֹזָאִי. אֲתָא לְקַמֵּיהּ דְּרַב חִסְדָּא. אֲמַר לֵיהּ: שְׁמוּעָה רְחוֹקָה אֵינָהּ נוֹהֶגֶת אֶלָּא יוֹם אֶחָד. רַב נָתָן בַּר אַמִי אֲתָא לֵיהּ שְׁמוּעָה דְּאִימֵּיהּ מִבֵּי חוֹזָאִי. אֲתָא לְקַמֵּיהּ דְּרָבָא. אֲמַר לֵיהּ: הֲרֵי אָמְרוּ: שְׁמוּעָה רְחוֹקָה אֵינָהּ נוֹהֶגֶת אֶלָּא יוֹם אֶחָד בִּלְבָד.

It was related that **Rav Ḥanina received** distant **tidings of his father's** death **from Bei Ḥozai.**[B] **He came before Rav Ḥisda** to ask what he should do. Rav Ḥisda **said to him:** In the case of **distant tidings,** mourning **applies for only one day.** It was similarly related that **Rav Natan bar Ami received a report about his mother's** death **from Bei Ḥozai. He came before Rava,** and Rava **said to him: They said** that in the case of **distant tidings,** mourning **applies for only one day.**

אֵיתִיבֵיהּ: בַּמֶּה דְּבָרִים אֲמוּרִים – בַּחֲמִשָּׁה מֵתֵי מִצְוָה, אֲבָל עַל אָבִיו וְעַל אִמּוֹ – שִׁבְעָה וּשְׁלֹשִׁים!

Rav Natan **raised an objection to** Rava's opinion based on what was taught in a *baraita*: **In what** case **is this statement** that mourning applies for only one day **said?** In the case of **the** other **five close relatives,** over whose **death** it is **a mitzva** to mourn, i.e., son, daughter, brother, sister, and spouse. **But for one's father or mother,** one is required to mourn for **seven and thirty** days, even when the report of the parent's death is received some time after the event.

אֲמַר לֵיהּ: יְחִידָאָה הִיא, וְלָא סְבִירָא לַן כְּוָותֵיהּ. דְּתַנְיָא: מַעֲשֶׂה וּמֵת אָבִיו שֶׁל רַבִּי צָדוֹק בְּגִינְזַק, וְהוֹדִיעוּהוּ לְאַחַר שָׁלֹשׁ שָׁנִים, וּבָא וְשָׁאַל אֶת אֱלִישָׁע בֶּן אֲבוּיָה וּזְקֵנִים שֶׁעִמּוֹ, וְאָמְרוּ: נְהוֹג שִׁבְעָה וּשְׁלֹשִׁים. וּכְשֶׁמֵּת בְּנוֹ שֶׁל רַבִּי אֲחִיָּיה בַּגּוֹלָה יָשַׁב עָלָיו שִׁבְעָה וּשְׁלֹשִׁים.

Rava **said to him: This is an individual** opinion,[N] **and we do not hold in accordance with his** opinion, **as it is taught** in a *baraita*: There was **an incident and the father of Rabbi Tzadok died in** the city of **Ginzak,**[B] **and they informed him** of his father's passing only **after three years. He came and asked Elisha ben Avuya and the Elders with him** what he should do. **And** Elisha ben Avuya **said** to him: **Observe** the rites of mourning for **seven and thirty** days. **And when the son of Rabbi Aḥiyya died in the Diaspora,** and Rabbi Aḥiyya was informed about his passing a long time afterward, he **sat** in mourning for **seven and thirty** days. Therefore, it is clear that this opinion was held only by a few individual Sages, but it was not generally accepted.

אִינִי? וְהָא רַב, בַּר אֲחוּהּ דְּרַבִּי חִיָּיא, דְּהוּא בַּר אַחְתֵּיהּ דְּרַבִּי חִיָּיא. כִּי סְלֵיק לְהָתָם, אֲמַר לֵיהּ: אַבָּא קַיָּים?

The Gemara asks: **Is that so,** that this is Rabbi Aḥiyya's opinion? **But Rav was the son of Rabbi Ḥiyya's brother and** also **the son of Rabbi Ḥiyya's sister,** for Rav's father, Aivu, was Rabbi Ḥiyya's paternal half brother, and Rav's mother was Rabbi Ḥiyya's maternal half sister. **When** Rav **went there,** Eretz Yisrael, his uncle Rabbi Ḥiyya **said to him:** Is your **father,** Aivu, still **alive?**

BACKGROUND

Bei Ḥozai – **בֵּי חוֹזָאִי:** This is the Aramaic name for the portion of the Persian kingdom near Shatt al Arab, the river formed by the confluence of the Euphrates and the Tigris. Bei Ḥozai is known today as Khuzestan, which is derived from the original name Ḥozai. This area was distant from the centers of Jewish life in Babylonia, and it took several months to make the trip. However, due to the strong business relations between Bei Ḥozai, Babylonia, and Eretz Yisrael, there was constant contact between these places.

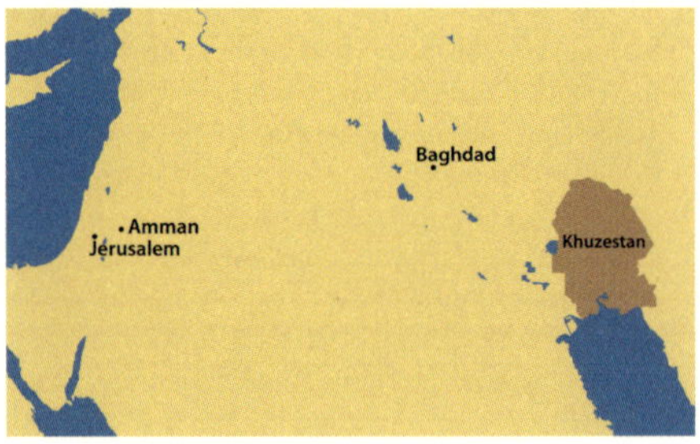

Khuzestan

Ginzak – **גִּינְזַק:** The Sages identify Ginzak as the biblical Gozan (see I Chronicles 5:26). However, the location of the city is unknown. Some explain that this is the ancient city Ganzak, which stood somewhere south of Lake Urmia. Others hold that it is south of the Caspian Sea, while still others maintain that it is in the vicinity of Nahrawan. It seems that this Jewish center was separate from the primary centers of Jewish life in Babylonia, though it was important enough that several Jewish leaders visited there.

NOTES

This is an individual opinion – **יְחִידָאָה הִיא:** In other words, this is the opinion only of Elisha ben Avuya, as will be explained shortly. However, as noted by *Tosafot*, it seems that there are other Sages who also hold that one is required to observe seven- and thirty-day periods of mourning in the case of distant tidings. Therefore, this statement is referring only to the opinion in the *baraita* that accepts the distinction between recent and distant tidings. Elisha ben Avuya essentially agrees with Rabbi Akiva's opinion. However, he also presents a third opinion, according to which Rabbi Akiva's opinion distinguishes between mourning a parent and mourning another relative, and in this respect his is an individual opinion (see Ritva; see *Sefat Emet*, and *Tal Ḥayyim*).

One can ask why this opinion is called individual when it was held by other Sages as well as Elisha ben Avuya. The answer is that, notwithstanding their numbers, they are referred to as an individual in opposition to the majority, which does not accept their opinion (*Tosefot HaRosh*; see Ya'avetz). This supports the Rambam's opinion, according to which even when an individual opinion is mentioned in the Mishna, it does not mean that it was held by only one Sage. Rather, the individual Sage represented the most important member from among the group of minority Sages who agree with him.

אֲמַר לֵיהּ: אִימָּא קַיֶּימֶת? אֲמַר לֵיהּ: אִימָּא קַיֶּימֶת? אֲמַר לֵיהּ: אַבָּא קַיָּים?! אֲמַר לֵיהּ לְשַׁמָּעֵיהּ: חֲלוֹץ לִי מִנְעָלַי, וְהוֹלֵךְ אַחֲרַי כֵּלַי לְבֵית הַמֶּרְחָץ.

Not wishing to deliver unfortunate news, Rav **said to him: Is** my **mother** still **alive?**[N] In other words, why do you not ask me about my mother, who is your sister, whether she is still among the living? Rabbi Ḥiyya **said to him: Is** your **mother** still **alive?** Rav **said to him: Is** my **father** still **alive?** Rabbi Ḥiyya understood from Rav's failure to provide him with straight answers that both his brother and his sister had passed away.[P] Rabbi Ḥiyya immediately **said to his servant: Remove my shoes** as a sign of mourning, and afterward **carry my clothes behind me,** as I am going **to the bathhouse.**

שְׁמַע מִינַּהּ תְּלָת: שְׁמַע מִינָּהּ: אָבֵל אָסוּר בִּנְעִילַת הַסַּנְדָּל; וּשְׁמַע מִינָּהּ: שְׁמוּעָה רְחוֹקָה אֵינָהּ נוֹהֶגֶת אֶלָּא יוֹם אֶחָד; וּשְׁמַע מִינָּהּ: מִקְצָת הַיּוֹם כְּכוּלּוֹ.

The Gemara comments: **Learn three** *halakhot* **from this**[N] incident with Rabbi Ḥiyya. **Learn from this** that **a mourner is prohibited from wearing shoes,**[N] and therefore Rabbi Ḥiyya removed his shoes upon hearing of the deaths of his brother and sister. **And learn from this** that in the case of **distant tidings** of a relative's death, the mourning rites **apply for only one day** and no more. **And learn from this** that the legal status of **part of the day is like** that of **an entire** day, as immediately following the removal of his shoes, Rabbi Ḥiyya went to the bathhouse.

רַבִּי חִיָּיא – לְחוּד, רַבִּי אֲחִיָּיה – לְחוּד.

In any case, Rabbi Ḥiyya observed only one day of mourning after receiving a belated report of his siblings' passing, in contrast to Rabbi Aḥiyya, who observed seven and thirty days. The Gemara's question assumes that Rabbi Ḥiyya and Rabbi Aḥiyya are the same person. The Gemara answers: This is not difficult, for **Rabbi Ḥiyya is a discrete** person **and Rabbi Aḥiyya is a discrete** person; despite the similarity between their names, these are two different people.[L]

אָמַר רַבִּי יוֹסֵי בַּר אָבִין: שָׁמַע שְׁמוּעָה קְרוֹבָה בָּרֶגֶל, וּלְמוֹצָאֵי הָרֶגֶל נַעֲשֵׂית רְחוֹקָה – עוֹלֶה לוֹ, וְאֵינוֹ נוֹהֵג אֶלָּא יוֹם אֶחָד. תָּנֵי רַבִּי אַדָּא דְּמִן קֵסָרִי קַמֵּיהּ דְּרַבִּי יוֹחָנָן: שָׁמַע שְׁמוּעָה קְרוֹבָה בְּשַׁבָּת, וּלְמוֹצָאֵי שַׁבָּת נַעֲשֵׂית רְחוֹקָה – אֵינוֹ נוֹהֵג אֶלָּא יוֹם אֶחָד.

§ **Rabbi Yosei bar Avin said:** If **one received recent tidings** of a relative's death **during a Festival,** when it is prohibited to mourn, **and after the Festival they became distant** tidings, as after the Festival thirty days had already elapsed since the relative's passing, the Festival **counts for him** toward the number of days that make it a belated report. **And,** consequently, after the Festival **he observes only one day** of mourning.[H] Similarly, **Rabbi Adda of Caesarea taught** a *baraita* **before Rabbi Yoḥanan:** If **one received recent tidings** of a relative's passing **on Shabbat, and at the conclusion of Shabbat it became distant tidings, he observes only one day** of mourning.

PERSONALITIES

Rabbi Ḥiyya and Rav – רַבִּי חִיָּיא וְרַב: This diagram shows the relationship between Rabbi Ḥiyya and Rav. Rabbi Abba married his first wife and had a son named Ḥana, the father of Rabba bar Ḥana. He also had three other sons, Sheila, Marta, and Aivu. Aivu was Rav's father. Afterward, Rabbi Abba married his second wife, who brought with her a daughter called Ima, from a previous marriage. Rabbi Abba and the second wife had a son named Ḥiyya. Later, Aivu, Rabbi Ḥiyya's half brother, married his stepsister, the daughter of Rabbi Ḥiyya's mother, and their son was named Rav. Therefore, Rav was the son of Rabbi Ḥiyya's brother as well as the son of his sister.

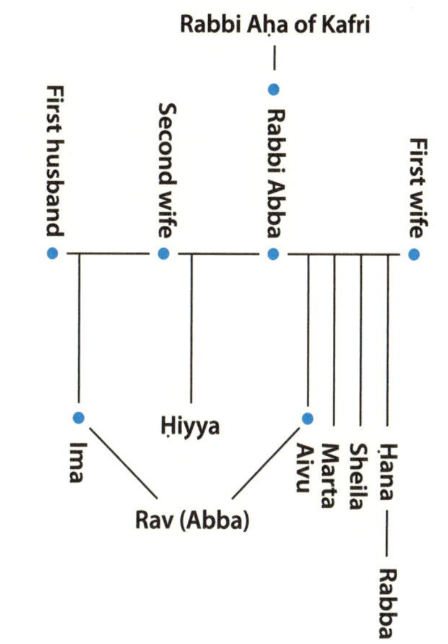

Family tree of Rabbi Ḥiyya and Rav

HALAKHA

Distant tidings on Shabbat and Festivals – שְׁמוּעָה רְחוֹקָה בְּשַׁבָּת וּמוֹעֵד: If one hears on Shabbat or a Festival that a close relative has passed away, and by the end of that day the news will become a distant tiding, then news of the passing is already considered to be a distant tiding when it is received. Consequently, the mourner observes mourning practices in private on Shabbat or the Festival itself. On the following day, he observes only a single day of public mourning (*Shulḥan Arukh*, *Yoreh De'a* 402:5).

LANGUAGE

Ḥiyya, Aḥiyya – חִיָּיא, אֲחִיָּיה: The name Ḥiyya, like the names of many other *tanna'im* and *amora'im*, is Aramaic. However, there were many common Hebrew names that had an Aramaic version or a shortened form, while the person's actual Hebrew name was rarely used. The name Yosei, which is referred to in the Jerusalem Talmud as Yosa either with an *alef* or a *heh* at the end, is a shortened form of the Hebrew name Yosef. In addition, some say that the name Ezra is actually an Aramaic nickname for the Hebrew name Azariya. The same applies for many different names. Consequently, the Gemara thought that the name Ḥiyya was an Aramaic version of the name Aḥiyya, which is both phonetically similar and has a similar meaning to the name Ḥiyya.

NOTES

He said to him, Is mother alive – אֲמַר לֵיהּ, אִימָּא קַיֶּימֶת: There are many different versions of this story, and there are different explanations of each version. Rabbeinu Ḥananel and other early authorities had a version that read: Is Father alive? He said to him: Abba is alive. He said to him: Is Mother alive? He said to him: Imma is alive.

According to this version of the story, Rabbi Ḥiyya asked about the well-being of his own father and mother, i.e., Rabbi Abba bar Aḥa and his wife, who were Rav's grandfather and grandmother. Rav responded that Rav's father, Aivu, and his mother, who were the brother and sister of Rabbi Ḥiyya, were alive, and based on this Rabbi Ḥiyya understood that his own father and mother had died. Rabbeinu Ḥananel derives from here the *halakha* in a case of distant tidings with regard to one's parents.

However, there is another version of the story that is more similar to the one in the Gemara, and most commentaries base their explanations on it. According to this version, Rabbi Ḥiyya asked about Rav's father, Aivu, and his mother. Rav answered with two other questions: Is mother alive, and is father alive? Based on this, Rabbi Ḥiyya understood that his brother and sister had died (Rashi; Rabbeinu Yehonatan of Lunel; Ran).

Some explain, based on this version, that Rav's words constituted a statement rather than a question: My mother is alive, and: My father is alive, and Rabbi Ḥiyya understood, based on the fact that Rav did not answer him directly, that they were no longer alive. Rashi, who offers this explanation, questions it, as it is inconceivable that Rav would tell a lie. Rabbi Shlomo ben HaYatom explains that Rav was speaking through euphemism, as it is stated elsewhere that the righteous are considered alive even after their death. For this reason, he stated that they were alive.

Learn three *halakhot* from this – שְׁמַע מִינָּהּ תְּלָת: There are two other *halakhot* that can be learned from this story: One can fulfill his obligation to mourn over several deceased relatives at one time (Rabbi Yitzḥak ibn Giat), and one may rely on the testimony of an individual relative with regard to mourning (Ramban). The Ritva writes that these *halakhot* are not mentioned in the Talmud because they were considered to be obvious.

A mourner is prohibited from wearing shoes – אָבֵל אָסוּר בִּנְעִילַת הַסַּנְדָּל: This *halakha*, as it applies to a mourner, is certainly not novel, and therefore some explain that this statement indicates that one who is mourning over distant tidings is prohibited from wearing shoes. According to the Ramban, it means that one can fulfill his obligation to mourn with even a small act, e.g., removing his shoes.

HALAKHA

Rending garments over distant tidings – קְרִיעָה עַל שְׁמוּעָה רְחוֹקָה: One is not required to rend his clothes upon hearing distant tidings for other relatives. However, one is always required to rend his clothes upon hearing about the death of a parent or a great person with whom he discussed *halakha* (*Shakh*). This ruling is in accordance with the opinions of Rabbi Mani and Rabbi Zeira (*Shulḥan Arukh*, *Yoreh De'a* 402:4).

One did not have his own garment – מִי שֶׁאֵין לוֹ חָלוּק: One who does not have a garment when he hears that his close relative has died may rend his clothes later if he happens to acquire a garment during the seven-day period of mourning. However, after hearing about the death of one of his parents, he is required to rend his garment at any time afterward, in accordance with the opinion of Rabbi Zeira (*Shulḥan Arukh*, *Yoreh De'a* 340:18).

קוֹרֵעַ אוֹ אֵינוֹ קוֹרֵעַ? רַבִּי מָנִי אָמַר: אֵינוֹ קוֹרֵעַ. רַבִּי חֲנִינָא אָמַר: קוֹרֵעַ. אָמַר לֵיהּ רַבִּי מָנִי לְרַבִּי חֲנִינָא: בִּשְׁלָמָא לְדִידִי, דְּאָמֵינָא אֵינוֹ קוֹרֵעַ, הַיְינוּ דְּלָא אִיכָּא אֲבֵילוּת שִׁבְעָה. אֶלָּא לְדִידָךְ דְּאָמְרַתְּ קוֹרֵעַ, קְרִיעָה בְּלָא שִׁבְעָה מִי אִיכָּא?

§ The Gemara asks: Upon receiving a belated report of a close relative's passing, **does one rend** his garment **or does he not rend** it?[N] **Rabbi Mani said: He does not rend** it, whereas **Rabbi Ḥanina said:** He does **rend** it.[H] **Rabbi Mani said to Rabbi Ḥanina: Granted,** it makes sense **that according to my** position this is consistent, **as I say** that **he does not rend** his garment, and **this is because there is no seven**-day period of **mourning. But according to you, who says** that **he does rend** his garment, **is there rending without a seven**-day period of **mourning** afterward?[N]

וְלָא? וְהָתַנְיָא אִיסִי אֲבוּהּ דְּרַבִּי זֵירָא, וְאָמְרִי לַהּ אֲחוּהּ דְּרַבִּי זֵירָא קַמֵּיהּ דְּרַבִּי זֵירָא: מִי שֶׁאֵין לוֹ חָלוּק לִקְרוֹעַ, וְנִזְדַּמֵּן לוֹ בְּתוֹךְ שִׁבְעָה – קוֹרֵעַ; לְאַחַר שִׁבְעָה – אֵינוֹ קוֹרֵעַ.

The Gemara asks: Is there **not? But isn't it taught** in a *baraita* reported by **Isi, father of Rabbi Zeira, and some say** it was taught by **the brother of Rabbi Zeira before Rabbi Zeira:**[P] If at first **one did not have** his own **garment**[N] **to rend,**[H] **and he acquired** one **during the seven**-day period of mourning, he should **rend** it then. But if he acquired it only **after the seven**-day period of mourning, **he does not rend** it.

עָנֵי רַבִּי זֵירָא בַּתְרֵיהּ: בַּמֶּה דְּבָרִים אֲמוּרִים – בַּחֲמִשָּׁה מֵתֵי מִצְוָה, אֲבָל עַל אָבִיו וְעַל אִמּוֹ – קוֹרֵעַ וְהוֹלֵךְ!

Rabbi Zeira explained the *baraita* **after him,** filling in a missing element: **In what** case **is this statement** that one does not rend his garment after the seven-day period of mourning **said?** In the case of **the** other **five close relatives** over whose **death** it is **a mitzva** to mourn, i.e., son, daughter, brother, sister, and spouse. **But for one's father or mother, one continues** to be obligated **to rend** his garment if he receives the garment after the seven-day mourning period as well. This apparently contradicts Rabbi Mani's statement that there is no rending without seven days of mourning.

כִּי תַּנְיָא הַהִיא – לִכְבוֹד אָבִיו וְאִמּוֹ.

The Gemara answers: **When that** *baraita* **is taught,** it is referring to a symbolic act meant **to honor his father or mother.**[N] It is for one's father or mother that he must rend his garment, even if it becomes available only after the seven-day period of mourning. Essentially, however, the obligation to rend one's garments applies only when it is followed by a seven-day period of mourning.

NOTES

Does one rend it or does he not rend it – קוֹרֵעַ אוֹ אֵינוֹ קוֹרֵעַ: Most authorities explain that the question applies to any type of distant tidings (Rif; Ramban; Rosh; Ritva). However, others explain that this applies only to one who received these tidings on a day when he is prohibited from mourning, and they became distant tidings afterward (*Tosafot*; *Talmid Rabbeinu Yeḥiel of Paris*; see *Tosefot HaRosh*).

Rending without a seven-day period of mourning – קְרִיעָה בְּלָא שִׁבְעָה: There is a *halakha* that one is required to rend his clothes at the death of his teacher or the *Nasi* of the Sanhedrin, despite the fact that this is not followed by seven days of mourning. Still, the question here is referring specifically to mourning over family members (*Tosefot HaRosh*; Ritva).

One did not have his own garment – מִי שֶׁאֵין לוֹ חָלוּק: *Tosafot* explain that this person was wearing a borrowed garment, which he cannot rend (see *Talmid Rabbeinu Yeḥiel of Paris*). Some explain that this refers to a case where one was wearing an outer garment, which is not torn (Rabbeinu Yehonatan of Lunel). The Ramban explain that this refers either to one who was half naked or to one who was wearing a garment that was already torn.

To honor his father or mother – לִכְבוֹד אָבִיו וְאִמּוֹ: Some say that this means that since the mourning over one's father and mother is more serious, one is required to rend his garments even after the seven-day mourning period, as long as it is still within thirty days of the burial (Ra'avad). Others explain that after seven days, rending is no longer obligatory but only a mark of respect. Therefore, it does not apply to the case of distant tidings (Commentary on *Moed Katan*; Ramban; *Sefer HaMeorot*).

PERSONALITIES

Rabbi Zeira – רַבִּי זֵירָא: Born in Babylonia, Rabbi Zeira, known in the Jerusalem Talmud as Rabbi Ze'eira, became one of the great third-generation *amora'im* in Eretz Yisrael. His father was a tax collector for the Persian government and was praised as one of the few who filled that position properly.

When Rabbi Zeira emigrated to Eretz Yisrael, he wanted to immerse himself completely in the Torah of Eretz Yisrael. The Gemara relates that he observed one hundred fasts in order to forget the Torah that he had studied in Babylonia.

Rabbi Zeira was famous for his sharp intellect and was the author of incisive *halakhot*. He was also known as an extremely God-fearing man and the Gemara records several stories related to his distinction in that area. He did not even want to be ordained with the title Rabbi, due to his modesty. He relented only after he was told that with ordination comes atonement for his sins.

The Gemara relates that he observed one hundred additional fasts so that the fire of Gehenna would not harm him, and he would periodically check whether the fasts worked by entering a fiery furnace. On one occasion, his legs were scorched, and from then on he was called: The little man with the scorched legs.

He was a contemporary of Rav Ḥisda, Rav Sheshet, and Rabba in Babylonia and one of the disciples of Rabbi Yoḥanan in Eretz Yisrael, and he engaged in extensive halakhic discourse with them. Apparently, he was a flax merchant in Eretz Yisrael, and it is conceivable that he had occasion in the course of his business to return to Babylonia several times.

The text of the beginning of the eulogy for Rabbi Zeira is preserved in the Talmud: The land of Shinar, Babylonia, conceived and gave birth; the land of splendor, Eretz Yisrael, raised her plaything. Woe unto her, said Reket, Tiberias, for she has lost her beloved vessel.

He had a son, Rabbi Ahava, who was also an *amora*.

תָּנוּ רַבָּנַן: כׇּל הָאָמוּר בְּפָרָשַׁת כֹּהֲנִים, שֶׁכֹּהֵן מִיטַּמֵּא לָהֶן – אָבֵל מִתְאַבֵּל עֲלֵיהֶן. וְאֵלּוּ הֵן: אִשְׁתּוֹ, אָבִיו, וְאִמּוֹ, אָחִיו, וַאֲחוֹתוֹ, בְּנוֹ, וּבִתּוֹ. הוֹסִיפוּ עֲלֵיהֶן אָחִיו וַאֲחוֹתוֹ הַבְּתוּלָה מֵאִמּוֹ, וַאֲחוֹתוֹ נְשׂוּאָה בֵּין מֵאָבִיו בֵּין מֵאִמּוֹ.

§ **The Sages taught:** With regard to **all** of the relatives **mentioned in the** Torah in the **passage** referring to **priests,**[N] **for which a priest becomes impure, a mourner must mourn for them. And they are: His wife, his father, and his mother, his brother and his** unmarried **sister** from the same father, **his son, and his daughter.**[H] The Sages **added** other relatives **to** this list: **His** maternal **brother and his unmarried sister from the same mother, and his married sister, whether from the same father or from the same mother.** One mourns for these relatives, **although** a priest would not become impure for them.

וּכְשֵׁם שֶׁמִּתְאַבֵּל עֲלֵיהֶם – כָּךְ מִתְאַבֵּל עַל שְׁנִיִּים שֶׁלָּהֶם, דִּבְרֵי רַבִּי עֲקִיבָא. רַבִּי שִׁמְעוֹן בֶּן אֶלְעָזָר אוֹמֵר: אֵינוֹ מִתְאַבֵּל אֶלָּא עַל בֶּן בְּנוֹ וְעַל אֲבִי אָבִיו. וַחֲכָמִים אוֹמְרִים: כׇּל שֶׁמִּתְאַבֵּל עָלָיו – מִתְאַבֵּל עִמּוֹ.

Just as one mourns for them, so too he mourns for their relatives' relatives, who are his **second-degree relatives.**[N] That is to say, just as one is required to mourn over his close relatives, so too he is required to mourn over his relatives' close relatives, which are known as second-degree relatives. For example, if his father's father, his son's son, his brother's son, or the like passed away, he must join his relatives in their mourning; this is **the statement of Rabbi Akiva. Rabbi Shimon ben Elazar says: He mourns only over his son's son and his father's father,** but not over the other relatives of his relatives. **And the Rabbis say: Any** relative **over whom one would mourn** if that person died, **one mourns with him** when he is in mourning.[NH]

חֲכָמִים הַיְינוּ תַּנָּא קַמָּא! אִיכָּא בֵּינַיְיהוּ עִמּוֹ בַּבַּיִת. כִּי הָא דַּאֲמַר לֵיהּ רַב לְחִיָּיא בְּרֵיהּ, וְכֵן אֲמַר לֵיהּ רַב הוּנָא לְרַבָּה בְּרֵיהּ: בְּאַפָּהּ – נְהוֹג אֲבֵילוּתָא; בְּלָא אַפָּהּ – לָא תִּינְהוֹג אֲבֵילוּתָא.

The Gemara asks: The statement of **the Rabbis is** identical to the statement of the **first** ***tanna***, Rabbi Akiva. What does their statement add? The Gemara answers: The practical difference **between them** is with regard to whether one mourn **with him** only **in the** same **house.** According to the Rabbis, one is required to mourn with his relative only while he is with him in the same house, whereas according to Rabbi Akiva, he is required to observe mourning even when he is not with him. This is **like what Rav said to his son, Ḥiyya, and** it is **similarly** like what **Rav Huna said to his son Rabba,** when the latter's wife was in mourning: **In her presence practice**[N] **mourning,** but **out of her presence do not practice mourning.**

מָר עוּקְבָא שְׁכִיב לֵיהּ בַּר חֲמוּהּ. סְבַר לְמֵיתַב עֲלֵיהּ שִׁבְעָה וּשְׁלֹשִׁים. עָל רַב הוּנָא לְגַבֵּיהּ, אַשְׁכְּחֵיהּ. אֲמַר לֵיהּ: צוּדָנִיָּיתָא בָּעֵית לְמֵיכַל? לֹא אָמְרוּ לִכְבוֹד אִשְׁתּוֹ אֶלָּא חָמִיו וַחֲמוֹתוֹ.

It is related that **the son of Mar Ukva's father-in-law,** i.e., Mar Ukva's brother-in-law, **died,** and Mar Ukva **thought to sit** in mourning **over him for the seven- and thirty-**day periods of mourning. **Rav Huna went into his** house, **found him** observing the rites of mourning, and **said to him: Do you desire to eat mourners' food** [***tzudaniyyata***]**?**[L] The Sages **said** that one should observe mourning **in honor of his wife only** when she is in mourning over the death **of his father-in-law or his mother-in-law.**

NOTES

All those mentioned in the passage of priests – כׇּל הָאָמוּר בְּפָרָשַׁת כֹּהֲנִים: It is stated in the passage: "Except for his close relatives, for his mother, and for his father, and for his son, and for his daughter, and for his brother; and for his virgin sister, that is near unto him, that has had no husband, for her he may make himself impure" (Leviticus 21:2–3). The Sages understand that the brother mentioned in the verse is referring to the priest's paternal brother, who inherits from him, and not to a maternal brother. With regard to his wife, the Sages derive the requirement to become impure for her from the expression: "Except for his close relatives."

However, many of the early authorities had a version of the Gemara text that did not include his wife in the list of permitted relatives. Some explain that the reason for this is because certain distinctions are made depending on the status of his wife, e.g., whether he was betrothed to her or married and whether she was permitted to marry a priest or not. Similarly, with regard to mourning over her relatives, she is not listed with the others (see Ritva). According to the Rambam, one's wife is considered one of his close family members by rabbinic decree.

Their second-degree relatives – שְׁנִיִּים שֶׁלָּהֶם: Some say that the second-degree relatives mentioned are the generations above and below, such as a father's father or a son's son (*Tosefot HaRosh*). Others hold that this category applies only to relatives with whom one has a blood relationship, but not to those to whom he is related through marriage, whether his marriage or his relatives' marriage. Alternatively, this *halakha* applies only to relatives on his father's side, to whom the *halakhot* of inheritance apply (see Ramban).

One mourns with him – מִתְאַבֵּל עִמּוֹ: The reason for this is due to their relationship and the desire to maintain peace within the home (Rabbeinu Yehonatan of Lunel). Based on this, the early authorities write that if a one's relatives are not concerned whether he mourns with them or not, they may forgo this honor. The common practice nowadays is to assume that everyone forgoes this honor, and no one observes these customs.

In her presence practice – בְּאַפָּהּ נְהוֹג: This does not mean that he is required to observe customs of mourning only when she is looking, for acting in this manner would make the issue seem trivial. Instead, this means that he is required to observe the mourning customs only when he is actually with her (Ramban; Ritva).

LANGUAGE

Mourners' food [*tzudaniyyata*] – צוּדָנִיָּיתָא: Many different versions of this word exist, and many different sources are used in order to offer an explanation for it. The version of the word in the Gemara appears to be related to the word *tzeida*, meaning provisions. In this context, the word means food prepared for a specific purpose, such as *tzeida laderekh*, provisions for a journey.

HALAKHA

Over whom does one mourn – עַל מִי מִתְאַבְּלִים: One is required to mourn over all relatives for which a priest becomes ritually impure, including one's father, mother, son, daughter, paternal brother, unmarried paternal sister, and wife. The Sages added that one should also mourn over his maternal brother and his sister, whether she is married or unmarried and whether they share the same father or mother. Just as a man mourns for his wife, so a woman is required to mourn for her husband (*Shulḥan Arukh, Yoreh De'a* 374:4).

Any relative over whom one would mourn, one mourns with him – כׇּל שֶׁמִּתְאַבֵּל עָלָיו, מִתְאַבֵּל עִמּוֹ: One is required to mourn with any family member over whom he would mourn if they were to die. This applies when they are in his presence. However, outside of their presence one is not required to observe mourning practices, in accordance with the opinion of the Rabbis.

Although a man is required to mourn for his wife, he mourns with her only over the death of her father or mother. Similarly, she is required to mourn with him only when one of his parents dies, but not when he loses another close family member.

The Rema writes that nowadays the custom is to be lenient with regard to this type of mourning, and one does not observe mourning practices for second-degree relatives (see *Tur*, citing Ramban and Rosh). This has become the common practice, and one who is stringent with regard to this issue is considered to be acting in a peculiar manner.

It is generally accepted that one practices certain customs of mourning during the first week after the death of a relative who is not one of those for whom one is required to mourn formally. This includes all those whose family relationship would prohibit giving joint testimony. In such circumstances, one does not bathe or change clothes, and in some places other customs of mourning are observed as well. This applies specifically to recent tidings.

One who wishes may act stringently and mourn formally for a person for whom he is not required to mourn or wear black clothes for him (*Shulḥan Arukh, Yoreh De'a* 374:6).

דְּתַנְיָא: מִי שֶׁמֵּת חָמִיו אוֹ חֲמוֹתוֹ – אֵינוֹ רַשַּׁאי לָכוֹף אֶת אִשְׁתּוֹ לִהְיוֹת כּוֹחֶלֶת וְלִהְיוֹת פּוֹקֶסֶת. אֶלָּא כּוֹפֶה מִטָּתוֹ, וְנוֹהֵג עִמָּהּ אֲבֵילוּת. וְכֵן הִיא שֶׁמֵּת חָמִיהָ אוֹ חֲמוֹתָהּ – אֵינָהּ רַשָּׁאָה לִהְיוֹת כּוֹחֶלֶת וְלִהְיוֹת פּוֹקֶסֶת, אֶלָּא כּוֹפָה מִטָּתָהּ וְנוֹהֶגֶת עִמּוֹ אֲבֵילוּת.

As it is taught in a *baraita*: **One whose father-in-law or mother-in-law died may not force his wife to paint [*koḥelet*]** her eyelids[B] **or put rouge [*pokeset*]**[L] on her face while she is in mourning. **Rather, he should overturn his bed, and observe** the rites of **mourning with her. And similarly, when her father-in-law or mother-in-law dies, she may not paint** her eyelids **or put rouge** on her face. **Rather, she should overturn her bed and practice** the rites of **mourning with him.**

וְתַנְיָא אִידָךְ: אַף עַל פִּי שֶׁאָמְרוּ אֵינוֹ רַשַּׁאי לָכוֹף אֶת אִשְׁתּוֹ לִהְיוֹת כּוֹחֶלֶת וְלִהְיוֹת פּוֹקֶסֶת, בֶּאֱמֶת אָמְרוּ: מוֹזֶגֶת לוֹ אֶת הַכּוֹס, וּמַצַּעַת לוֹ מִטָּה, וּמַרְחֶצֶת לוֹ פָּנָיו יָדָיו וְרַגְלָיו. קַשְׁיָין אַהֲדָדֵי!

And it was taught in another *baraita*: **Even though** the Sages **said that** a husband **may not force his wife to paint** her eyelids **or put rouge** on her face when she is in mourning, i.e., that she may not treat her mourning lightly, **actually, they said** that **she may pour his cup**[N] of wine, **make his bed, and wash his face, hands, and feet,**[H] as these activities are expressions of affection between husband and wife rather than unnecessary adornment or a belittlement of the mourning. These two *baraitot* **contradict each other:** The first *baraita* indicates that the husband must practice the rites of mourning together with his wife, whereas the second one bars him only from forcing her to treat her own mourning lightly.

אֶלָּא לָאו שְׁמַע מִינָּהּ: כָּאן – בְּחָמִיו וַחֲמוֹתוֹ, כָּאן – בִּשְׁאָר קְרוֹבִים? שְׁמַע מִינָּהּ. תַּנְיָא נַמִי הָכִי: לֹא אָמְרוּ לִכְבוֹד אִשְׁתּוֹ – אֶלָּא חָמִיו וַחֲמוֹתוֹ בִּלְבַד.

Rather, must one **not conclude from this** as follows: **Here,** where one is required to observe the *halakhot* of mourning together with his wife, the *baraita* is referring to the death of **his father-in-law or mother-in-law. There,** where one is not required to mourn, the *baraita* is referring to the death of his wife's **other relatives** for whom she is required to mourn. The Gemara summarizes: **Conclude from this** that this is the case. **This is also taught** in a *baraita*: The Sages **said** that one is required to observe the rites of mourning **in honor of his wife only** when she is in mourning over **his father-in-law or his mother-in-law.**

אַמֵימָר שְׁכִיב לֵיהּ בַּר בְּרֵיהּ, קְרַע עִילָּוֵיהּ. אֲתָא בְּרֵיהּ – קְרַע בְּאַפֵּיהּ. אִידְּכַר דִּמְיוֹשָּׁב קְרַע – קָם קְרַע מְעוּמָּד.

It was further related that **the son of Ameimar's son died,** and Ameimar **rent** his garment **over him. His son came** before him, and **he rent** his garments again **in the presence of his** son,[N] as an expression of empathy with the his son's pain and grief. Later, **he remembered** that when he rent his garments in his son's presence **he rent** them while **sitting,** and therefore **he stood up** and **rent** his garment again while **standing.**

אֲמַר לֵיהּ רַב אַשִׁי לְאַמֵימָר: קְרִיעָה דִּמְעוּמָּד מְנָלַן? דִּכְתִיב: ״וַיָּקׇם אִיּוֹב וַיִּקְרַע אֶת מְעִילוֹ״.

With regard to this issue, the Gemara reports that **Rav Ashi said to Ameimar: From where do we** derive that **rending** must be done while **standing?** He responded: **As it is written** about the deaths of Job's sons: **"Then Job arose, and rent his coat"** (Job 1:20).

NOTES

She may pour his cup, etc. – מוֹזֶגֶת לוֹ אֶת הַכּוֹס וכו׳: This list includes tasks that were customarily performed by a wife for her husband. Although all of these actions increase affection between the couple, and therefore a woman may not perform them when she is impure due to menstruation, the Sages did not prohibit them when she is in mourning (*Talmid Rabbeinu Yeḥiel of Paris*, based on tractate *Ketubot*).

There are several explanations as to how the act of the wife pouring wine for her husband shows that he does not observe mourning practices with his wife. Some say that based on the statement that she may make his bed, it is implied that he is not required to overturn it (Rashi). Alternatively, this is derived by the fact that such a requirement is not stated explicitly (Ra'avad). Others suggest that since she may wash his face, with hot water according to some, he is clearly not observing the practices of mourning (see Commentary on *Moed Katan* and *Sefat Emet*).

His son came and he rent his garments in the presence of his son – אֲתָא בְּרֵיהּ, קְרַע בְּאַפֵּיהּ: Some explain that Ameimar forgot and rent his garments while sitting, and his son did not wish to tell him that he had acted incorrectly, out of respect for his father. Instead, he rent his garment while standing, and then Ameimar realized that he had rent his garment incorrectly (*Talmid Rabbeinu Yeḥiel of Paris*; see *Tosefot HaRosh* and *Tosafot*).

HALAKHA

One's wife in mourning – אֵשֶׁת אִישׁ בִּזְמַן אֲבֵלָה: When the close relative of a married woman dies, she is not permitted to wear makeup, and her husband cannot force her to do so. However, she may make his bed and pour him a cup of wine, or any other similar act. A married woman is permitted to wear makeup after the seven-day mourning period, so that she will not appear ugly to her husband (*Shulḥan Arukh*, *Yoreh De'a* 381:6).

BACKGROUND

To paint [*koḥelet*] her eyelids – לִהְיוֹת כּוֹחֶלֶת: The Hebrew term refers to kohl, a dark blue or black color that is extracted from the sulfide mineral stibnite, Sb_2S_3, sometimes referred to as antimonite. In antiquity, the crystals of the mineral were ground up and used by women for painting their eyelashes, eyebrows, and eyelids, thereby accenting their eyes and giving the impression that their eyes were larger than they actually were. Kohl was also used for healing the eyes.

Stibnite crystal

Ancient Egyptian kohl tube

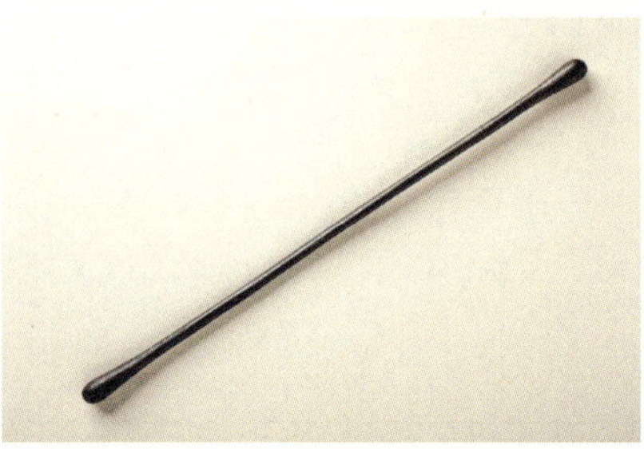

Ancient kohl applicator

LANGUAGE

Rouge [*pokeset*] – פּוֹקֶסֶת: From the Greek φῦκος, *fukos*, meaning the color red. See also LANGUAGE, p. 53.

אֶלָּא מֵעַתָּה – "וְעָמַד וְאָמַר לֹא חָפַצְתִּי לְקַחְתָּהּ" הָכָא נָמֵי? וְהָא תַּנְיָא: בֵּין יוֹשֵׁב בֵּין עוֹמֵד בֵּין מוּטֶּה!

Rav Ashi challenged him: **However, if** that is **so,** one should be required to stand while performing the ritual through which the brother-in-law frees the *yevama* of her levirate bonds [*ḥalitza*], as the verse states: **"And if he stands and he says: I do not wish to take her"** (Deuteronomy 25:8). **Here** must he **also** stand for the ceremony? **But isn't it taught** in a *baraita* that *ḥalitza* may be performed **whether** the man is **sitting,**[H] **or standing,**[N] **or reclining?**

אֲמַר לֵיהּ: הָתָם לָא כְּתִיב "וַיַּעֲמֹד וַיֹּאמַר"; הָכָא כְּתִיב "וַיָּקָם וַיִּקְרַע".

He said to him: There, in the case of *ḥalitza,* **it is not written: And he will stand**[N] **and he will say,** which would imply an obligation to stand; whereas **here,** in the case of rending, **it is written: "Then** Job **arose, and rent** his coat" (Job 1:20).

אָמַר רָמִי בַּר חָמָא: מִנַּיִן לִקְרִיעָה שֶׁהִיא מְעוּמָּד? שֶׁנֶּאֱמַר: "וַיָּקָם אִיּוֹב וַיִּקְרַע". דִּלְמָא מִילְּתָא יְתֵירְתָא הוּא דַּעֲבַד? דְּאִי לָא תֵּימָא הָכִי – "וַיָּגָז אֶת רֹאשׁוֹ" הָכִי נָמֵי?

Rami bar Ḥama said: From where is it derived **that rending must be** performed while **standing?**[H] **As it is stated: "Then Job arose, and tore** his coat" (Job 1:20). The Gemara asks: **Perhaps he did something extra** beyond what is required, and actually there is no obligation to stand; **as, if you do not say** that he did more than what was required of him, then how do you explain the continuation of the verse: **"And he shaved his head"** (Job 1:20)? Is every mourner required to act in **this** manner **also** and shave his head?

אֶלָּא מֵהָכָא: "וַיָּקָם הַמֶּלֶךְ וַיִּקְרַע אֶת בְּגָדָיו". וְדִלְמָא מִילְּתָא יְתֵירְתָא עֲבִיד? דְּאִי לָא תֵּימָא הָכִי – "וַיִּשְׁכַּב אָרְצָה" הָכִי נָמֵי?

The Gemara concludes: **Rather,** this source must be rejected, and instead the *halakha* is derived **from here,** the verse that describes David's mourning over his son: **"Then the king arose, and rent his garments"** (II Samuel 13:31). The Gemara asks: But **perhaps he** too **did something extra** beyond what is required, and he was not actually obligated to stand; **as, if you do not say** that he did more than what was required of him, then how do you explain the continuation of the verse: **"And he lay on the earth"** (II Samuel 13:31)? Is every mourner required to act in **this** manner **also?**

וְהָתַנְיָא: יָשַׁב עַל גַּבֵּי מִטָּה, עַל גַּבֵּי כִּסֵּא, עַל גַּבֵּי אוּדְיָינֵי גְּדוֹלָה, עַל גַּבֵּי קַרְקַע – מִכּוּלָּן לֹא יָצָא יְדֵי חוֹבָתוֹ. וְאָמַר רַבִּי יוֹחָנָן: שֶׁלֹּא קִיֵּים כְּפִיַּית הַמִּטָּה.

But isn't it taught in a *baraita*: If a mourner **sat on a bed, on a chair, on a large mortar** [*udyanei*],[NL] **or on the ground, he does not fulfill his obligation through any of them.**[H] **And Rabbi Yoḥanan said:** This is **because he did not fulfill** his obligation to **overturn his bed,** even if he lay on the ground. This indicates that there is no requirement whatsoever to lie on the ground.

אֲמַר לֵיהּ: כְּעֵין אַרְצָה.

Ameimar **said to** Rav Ashi: The verse does not mean that David actually lay on the ground. Rather, it was **as if** he were **on the ground,** since he overturned his bed and brought it closer to the ground. If this is the case, then Ameimar acted correctly, and a mourner should rend his garments while standing.

NOTES

Whether sitting or standing – בֵּין יוֹשֵׁב בֵּין עוֹמֵד: The question is not with regard to the obligation to rend garments *ab initio*, as it is also clear that it is preferable to perform both rending and *ḥalitza* while standing. Rather, the question concerns Ameimar's decision to rend his garment again, which implies that, even after the fact, if one was not standing the rending is invalid. Consequently, the Gemara asks what the difference is between rending and *ḥalitza*, since the word standing is used in reference to both (Ramban).

It is not written: And he will stand – לָא כְּתִיב וַיַּעֲמֹד: This derivation is based not on the difference in tense but on the structure of the verses. If the word "stand" had been stressed, this would have indicated that there is a specific requirement to stand. However, in the verses of *ḥalitza* all the actions are written in the same form, thereby conveying some degree of continuity, and the word "stand" is not stressed (Ritva).

Alternatively, some explain that the phrase: "And if he stands," does not mean that one is actually required to stand. Instead, it means: Come forward, or: Prepare yourself to perform a certain act (*Tosafot*; *Talmid Rabbeinu Yeḥiel of Paris*).

Large mortar – אוּדְיָינֵי גְּדוֹלָה: Some explain that this refers to a large mortar (Rashi; Rabbeinu Ḥananel), which people could sit on by placing it upside down. However, others say that this refers to a covering for a pit (Rashi, from manuscript; Rashbam). There are also those who claim that this means an overturned kneading bowl or a bathtub (see Ran).

HALAKHA

Ḥalitza while sitting – חֲלִיצָה בִּישִׁיבָה: During all parts of the *ḥalitza* ceremony, the judges sit, while the man and woman performing the ceremony stand. If the man is old or weak he may lean on a cane (*Be'er Heitev*). If he is incapable of standing at all, he may sit (*Shulḥan Arukh, Even HaEzer* 169:12, and in the comment of Rema).

Rending while standing – קְרִיעָה שֶׁהִיא מְעוּמָּד: Rending garments as a sign of mourning must be done while standing. If one performed this while sitting, he is required to rend the garments a second time (*Shulḥan Arukh, Yoreh De'a* 340:1).

The mitzva of overturning the bed – מִצְוַת כְּפִיַּית הַמִּטָּה: It is not enough for one simply to overturn his bed; he must sleep on the overturned bed in order to fulfill his obligation. Therefore, if one slept on a chair, wardrobe, or the ground, then has not fulfilled this obligation (Rambam *Sefer Shofetim, Hilkhot Evel* 5:18). However, nowadays the custom is not to overturn beds at all (*Shulḥan Arukh, Yoreh De'a* 387:2).

LANGUAGE

Mortar [*udyanei*] – אוּדְיָינֵי: Several different versions of this word exist, and therefore there are also many different interpretations of its meaning. Some say that it is related to the Aramaic *udna*, meaning handle or ear, and in this context it refers to a vessel with a handle.

Large mortar

תָּנוּ רַבָּנַן, וְאֵלּוּ דְּבָרִים שֶׁאָבֵל אָסוּר בָּהֶן: אָסוּר בִּמְלָאכָה, וּבִרְחִיצָה, וּבְסִיכָה, וּבְתַשְׁמִישׁ הַמִּטָּה, וּבִנְעִילַת הַסַּנְדָּל, וְאָסוּר לִקְרוֹת בַּתּוֹרָה וּבַנְּבִיאִים וּבַכְּתוּבִים, וְלִשְׁנוֹת בַּמִּשְׁנָה, בַּמִּדְרָשׁ וּבַהֲלָכוֹת וּבַתַּלְמוּד וּבַאֲגָדוֹת. וְאִם הָיוּ רַבִּים צְרִיכִין לוֹ – אֵינוֹ נִמְנָע. וּמַעֲשֶׂה וּמֵת בְּנוֹ שֶׁל רַבִּי יוֹסֵי בְּצִיפּוֹרִי, וְנִכְנַס לְבֵית הַמִּדְרָשׁ וְדָרַשׁ כָּל הַיּוֹם כּוּלּוֹ.

§ **The Sages taught: These are the activities that a mourner is prohibited from** engaging **in:**[N] **He is prohibited from working, and from bathing, and from anointing** himself with oil, **and from engaging in sexual relations, and from wearing shoes. And he is prohibited from reading in the Torah,**[NH] **and in the Prophets, and in the Writings, and from studying in the Mishna, in the midrash, and in the *halakhot*, and in the Talmud, and in the *aggadot*. But if the public needs him** to teach them these things, **he need not refrain** from doing so. **There was an incident that the son of Rabbi Yosei**[P] **died in Tzippori, and** Rabbi Yosei **entered the study hall and expounded** there **for the entire day.**

רַבָּה בַּר בַּר חָנָה אִיתְרְעָא בֵּיהּ מִילְּתָא. סָבַר דְּלָא לְמֵיפַּק לְפִירְקָא. אֲמַר לֵיהּ רַבִּי חֲנִינָא: אִם הָיוּ רַבִּים צְרִיכִין לוֹ – אֵינוֹ נִמְנָע. סָבַר לְאוֹקְמֵי אָמוֹרָא עֲלֵיהּ – אֲמַר לֵיהּ רַב, תַּנְיָא: וּבִלְבַד שֶׁלֹּא יַעֲמִיד תּוּרְגְּמָן.

It was related that **a calamity,** i.e., a death in the family, once **befell Rabba bar bar Ḥana, and he thought not to go out to** deliver **his exposition. Rabbi Ḥanina said to him:** Is it not taught that **if the public needs him** to teach them these things, **one need not refrain** from doing so? **He** then **thought to place an interpreter**[B] **alongside him,** who would sound his words to the public, as was normally done for such an exposition. **Rav said to him: It is taught** in a *baraita* similarly: **Provided that he does not place the disseminator** alongside him.

NOTES

These are the activities that a mourner is prohibited from engaging in – וְאֵלּוּ דְּבָרִים שֶׁאָבֵל אָסוּר בָּהֶן: *Tosafot* note that not all of the activities that are prohibited to a mourner are mentioned here, and they explain why only some of these prohibitions are mentioned (see Ran). All the activities that are prohibited to a mourner are detailed in tractate *Semaḥot*.

He is prohibited from reading in the Torah, etc. – אָסוּר לִקְרוֹת בַּתּוֹרָה וכו׳: The Ramban discusses whether the fact that learning Torah is a mitzva is sufficient to permit a mourner to study Torah in certain situations; or perhaps it is permitted after the first day, similar to donning phylacteries; or perhaps since it gives pleasure it is not permitted for the entire week. In the Jerusalem Talmud, it is explained that one is permitted to study a Torah text that he is unfamiliar with, because this is not as enjoyable as other study. Similarly, it is stated there that one who is intensely passionate about Torah study may learn Torah, since refraining from Torah study would be a form of affliction, and one is not required to afflict himself when in mourning.

HALAKHA

Torah study while in mourning – לִימּוּד תּוֹרָה בְּאֵבֶל: A mourner is prohibited from studying Torah for all seven days of the mourning period, but he may read the book of Lamentations, prophecies about catastrophic events, and the *halakhot* of mourning. If the community requires it, a mourner is permitted to expound in public. However, if he expounds through an interpreter then there must be an intermediary between him and the interpreter, in order to deviate from his ordinary way of speaking. A scholar who is in mourning may give a halakhic ruling to an individual who asks him a question. However, he may not teach a *halakha* to his students. This is the common practice; however, some are lenient with regard to this (*Shulḥan Arukh, Yoreh De'a* 384:1, and in the comment of Rema).

PERSONALITIES

Rabbi Yosei – רַבִּי יוֹסֵי: This is Rabbi Yosei ben Ḥalafta, one of the greatest of the *tanna'im*. He lived in the generation prior to the redaction of the Mishna, and the influence of his teachings is evident throughout tannaitic literature. His father, known as Abba Ḥalafta, was also considered one of the great Sages of his generation. According to one tradition, his family was descended from Jehonadab, son of Rechab (see II Kings 10:15).

In addition to studying with his father, Rabbi Yosei was also an outstanding student of Rabbi Akiva. Rabbi Yosei and his contemporaries, Rabbi Meir, Rabbi Yehuda, Rabbi Shimon bar Yoḥai, and other students of Rabbi Akiva, formed the center of talmudic creativity of that entire generation. In his halakhic approach, as in his way of life, Rabbi Yosei was moderate, and he refrained from taking extreme opinions on halakhic issues. A well-known principle in the *halakha* is that Rabbi Yosei's opinions are based on sound reasoning, and therefore the *halakha* is always in accordance with his opinion.

In addition to being a great master of *halakha*, Rabbi Yosei was also famous for his piety. The Talmud relates many stories about his modesty, humility, and holiness. It is related that Elijah the Prophet would appear to him every day, and several conversations between Elijah and Rabbi Yosei are recorded in the Talmud. Rabbi Yosei was the primary redactor of a series of *baraitot* on the history of the Jewish people known as *Seder Olam*. For many years, he lived in Tzippori in the Galilee and earned his living as a tanner.

Many of the prominent Sages of the following generation, including Rabbi Yehuda HaNasi, the redactor of the Mishna, were his students. But his main students were his five sons, all of whom were Sages in their generation. The most famous of them were Rabbi Eliezer, son of Rabbi Yosei, one of the great masters of *aggada*, and Rabbi Yishmael, son of Rabbi Yosei.

BACKGROUND

Interpreter [*amora*] – אָמוֹרָא: In this context, the word *amora*, literally speaker, has the same meaning as the word *meturgeman*, disseminator, used in the Mishna. This disseminator of the Sages' expositions was often a scholar himself, sometimes even an important Sage, whose job it was to translate the exposition from Hebrew to Aramaic and to project it so that it could be heard by everyone. Sometimes, there was more than one disseminator if the speech needed to be projected to a large group. Often, the disseminator would not only translate but also explain the exposition, as the Sage would say the most basic ideas, and the disseminator would expand and develop them. For this reason, the Sages of the talmudic period describe themselves as *amora'im*, as they saw their job as being similar to that of these interpreters for the Sages of the Mishna.

וְאֶלָּא הֵיכִי עָבֵיד? כִּי הָא דְּתַנְיָא: מַעֲשֶׂה וּמֵת בְּנוֹ שֶׁל רַבִּי יְהוּדָה בַּר אִילְעַאי, וְנִכְנַס לְבֵית הַמִּדְרָשׁ. וְנִכְנַס רַבִּי חֲנַנְיָה בֶּן עֲקַבְיָא וְיָשַׁב בְּצִדּוֹ, וְלָחַשׁ הוּא לְרַבִּי חֲנַנְיָה בֶּן עֲקַבְיָא, וְרַבִּי חֲנַנְיָה בֶּן עֲקַבְיָא לְתוּרְגְּמָן, וְתוּרְגְּמָן הִשְׁמִיעַ לָרַבִּים.

The Gemara asks: **But how,** then, should he **act** so that he can be heard? The Gemara answers: It is **like that which is taught** in a *baraita*: There was **an incident and the son of Rabbi Yehuda bar Ilai died, and** Rabbi Yehuda **entered the study hall. And Rabbi Ḥananya ben Akavya** entered after him and **sat by his side.** Rabbi Yehuda bar Ilai then **whispered** his lecture **to Rabbi Ḥananya ben Akavya, and Rabbi Ḥananya ben Akavya** whispered it **to the disseminator, and the disseminator sounded to the public** what had been told to him. In this way, it became known that Rabbi Yehuda bar Ilai was in mourning.

תָּנוּ רַבָּנַן: אָבֵל, שְׁלֹשָׁה יָמִים הָרִאשׁוֹנִים אָסוּר לְהָנִיחַ תְּפִילִּין. מִשְּׁלִישִׁי וְאֵילָךְ, וּשְׁלִישִׁי בִּכְלָל – מוּתָּר לְהָנִיחַ תְּפִילִּין. וְאִם בָּאוּ פָּנִים חֲדָשׁוֹת – אֵינוֹ חוֹלֵץ, דִּבְרֵי רַבִּי אֱלִיעֶזֶר. רַבִּי יְהוֹשֻׁעַ אוֹמֵר: אָבֵל, שְׁנֵי יָמִים הָרִאשׁוֹנִים – אָסוּר לְהָנִיחַ תְּפִילִּין. מִשֵּׁנִי וְשֵׁנִי בִּכְלָל – מוּתָּר לְהָנִיחַ תְּפִילִּין. וְאִם בָּאוּ פָּנִים חֲדָשׁוֹת – חוֹלֵץ.

§ **The Sages taught** the following *baraita*: For **the first three days, a mourner is prohibited from donning phylacteries.**[H] **From the third** day **and on, and including the third** day, **he is permitted to don phylacteries. And if new faces,**[N] i.e., people who had not yet come to console him, **come, he need not remove** them, although these people may falsely conclude that he had also donned phylacteries during the first two days of his mourning; this is **the statement of Rabbi Eliezer. Rabbi Yehoshua says: For the first two days, a mourner is prohibited from donning** phylacteries. **From the second** day, **and including the second** day, **he is permitted to wear** phylacteries. **But if new faces come in** to console him, **he must remove** his phylacteries.

אָמַר רַב מַתָּנָה: מַאי טַעְמָא דְּרַבִּי אֱלִיעֶזֶר? דִּכְתִיב: ״וַיִּתְּמוּ יְמֵי בְכִי אֵבֶל מֹשֶׁה״. אָמַר רַב עֵינָא: מַאי טַעְמָא דְּרַבִּי יְהוֹשֻׁעַ? דִּכְתִיב: ״וְאַחֲרִיתָהּ כְּיוֹם מָר״.

Rav Mattana said: What is the reason of Rabbi Eliezer?[N] **As it is written: "And the days of weeping and mourning for Moses ended"** (Deuteronomy 34:8). The plural term "days" implies a minimum of two, and it indicates that the main portion of the mourning period is the first two full days. **Rav Eina said: What is the reason of Rabbi Yehoshua? As it is written:** "And I will make it as the mourning for an only son, **and its end as a bitter day"** (Amos 8:10), i.e., a single "day."

וְרַבִּי יְהוֹשֻׁעַ נַמִי, הָא כְּתִיב: ״וַיִּתְּמוּ יְמֵי״ וגו׳! אָמַר לָךְ: שָׁאנֵי מֹשֶׁה, דְּתַקִּיף אֶבְלֵיהּ. וְרַבִּי אֱלִיעֶזֶר נַמִי, הָא כְּתִיב: ״וְאַחֲרִיתָהּ כְּיוֹם מָר״! עִיקַּר מְרִירָא חַד יוֹמָא הוּא.

The Gemara asks: **But also** for **Rabbi Yehoshua, isn't it written** in the Torah: **"And the days** of weeping and mourning for Moses **ended,"** thereby implying that this period lasts for two days? The Gemara answers: He could have **said to you** that **Moses was different, because the mourning for him was more intense,** and the people mourned for him longer than usual. The Gemara asks: **But also** for **Rabbi Eliezer, isn't it written** in the Torah: **"And its end as a bitter day"**? The Gemara answers: He could have said to you that **the main bitterness is** only **one day,** but the severity of the mourning lasts for two days.

אָמַר עוּלָּא: הֲלָכָה כְּרַבִּי אֱלִיעֶזֶר בַּחֲלִיצָה, וַהֲלָכָה כְּרַבִּי יְהוֹשֻׁעַ בַּהֲנָחָה.

Ulla said: The ***halakha*** **is in accordance with** the opinion of **Rabbi Eliezer with regard to the removal** of phylacteries. A mourner need not remove them when new people come in to console him. **And the** ***halakha*** **is in accordance with** the opinion of **Rabbi Yehoshua with regard to the donning** of phylacteries, and so a mourner may already don phylacteries on the second day.

אִיבַּעְיָא לְהוּ: בְּשֵׁנִי לְעוּלָּא, חוֹלֵץ אוֹ אֵינוֹ חוֹלֵץ?

A dilemma was raised before the scholars: **According** to **Ulla,** who rules in accordance with Rabbi Yehoshua that a mourner may don phylacteries **on** his second **day** of mourning, is the mourner required to **remove** them if new people arrive on that day, **or** is he **not** required to **remove** them?

תָּא שְׁמַע, אָמַר עוּלָּא: חוֹלֵץ וּמֵנִיחַ אֲפִילּוּ מֵאָה פְּעָמִים. תַּנְיָא נַמִי הָכִי, יְהוּדָה בֶּן תֵּימָא אוֹמֵר: חוֹלֵץ וּמֵנִיחַ אֲפִילּוּ מֵאָה פְּעָמִים.

The Gemara answers: **Come** and **hear** what **Ulla said** explicitly: **One removes** his phylacteries when new people come to console him, **and he dons** them again when they leave, **even** if he must don and remove them **a hundred times. This is also taught** in a *baraita*: **Yehuda ben Teima says: He removes** his phylacteries **and dons** them again, **even** if he must do so **a hundred times.**

רָבָא אָמַר: כֵּיוָן שֶׁהֵנִיחַ – שׁוּב אֵינוֹ חוֹלֵץ. וְהָא רָבָא הוּא דְּאָמַר: הֲלָכָה כְּתַנָּא דִּידַן, דְּאָמַר: שְׁלֹשָׁה!

Rava said: Once he dons his phylacteries, **he does not remove** them again. The Gemara asks: **But wasn't it Rava** himself **who said: The** ***halakha*** **is in accordance with** the opinion of **the** ***tanna*** **of our** mishna, **who said** that the most serious period of mourning is **three** days? How then does he rule in accordance with the *baraita* that a mourner may don phylacteries during these days?

HALAKHA

A mourner is prohibited from donning phylacteries – **אָבֵל...אָסוּר לְהָנִיחַ תְּפִילִּין**: A mourner is prohibited from wearing phylacteries on his first day of mourning, but he is required to wear them from the second day and onward. This ruling is in accordance with the opinion of Rabbi Yehoshua, as the *halakha* is in accordance with his opinion in disputes with Rabbi Eliezer. It is also in accordance with the opinion of Rava (*Shulḥan Arukh, Yoreh De'a* 388:1).

NOTES

New faces – **פָּנִים חֲדָשׁוֹת**: Most commentaries explain here, similar to the case with the seven-day period following marriage, that the phrase new faces refers to people who have not yet come to visit. Others explain that the term refers to other mourners who are joining this mourning (Rabbeinu Yehonatan of Lunel). There are also those who understand that the term refers to additional relatives who die while the mourner is still in mourning (Rabbi Shlomo ben HaYatom).

Some explain that the reason for removing the phylacteries is lest new people come, see him wearing phylacteries, and think that he is doing so on the first day of mourning and thereby acting disrespectfully toward the laws of mourning (*Talmid Rabbeinu Yeḥiel of Paris*; Ran; Meiri).

Others say that when new people come and begin speaking about the mourner's deceased relative, the mourner's pain will be renewed, and therefore the sadness becomes like that on the first day (Ritva). This is similar to the explanation of the *ge'onim*, mentioned by the Ramban, according to which a mourner may not wear phylacteries because one wearing phylacteries is prohibited from taking his mind off them. When the new guests weep and eulogize the deceased, the mourner may forget that he is wearing phylacteries.

The reasons of Rabbi Eliezer and Rabbi Yehoshua – **טַעֲמָם שֶׁל רַבִּי אֱלִיעֶזֶר וְרַבִּי יְהוֹשֻׁעַ**: It is mentioned in the name of the Ra'avad that Rabbi Eliezer's opinion can be explained as follows: "The days…ended" indicates that they were completed, and if this is the case then there were two full days of mourning. A part of the third day was added according to rabbinic law (see *Talmid Rabbeinu Yeḥiel of Paris*). Although the verse is describing events that happened thirty days after Moses' death, the derivation is based on the expression: "Days of weeping," i.e., the first two days of weeping before the rest of the days of mourning (see Ritva). With regard to the verse: "Its end as a bitter day," the expression "as…a day" also means a little more than a complete day, and therefore includes part of the second day.

מִצְוָה שָׁאנֵי.

The Gemara answers: **A mitzva is different,**[N] and since it is a mitzva to put on phylacteries, the mourner is required to do so, even during the first three days.

תָּנוּ רַבָּנַן: אָבֵל, שְׁלֹשָׁה יָמִים הָרִאשׁוֹנִים – אָסוּר בִּמְלָאכָה, וַאֲפִילּוּ עָנִי הַמִּתְפַּרְנֵס מִן הַצְּדָקָה. מִכָּאן וְאֵילָךְ – עוֹשֶׂה בְּצִינְעָא בְּתוֹךְ בֵּיתוֹ. וְהָאִשָּׁה טוֹוָה בְּפֶלֶךְ בְּתוֹךְ בֵּיתָהּ.

§ **The Sages taught** the following *baraita*: **During the first three days** after his bereavement, **a mourner is prohibited from working,**[NH] **even if he is a poor person who is supported by charity. From this** point **forward, he may do** work **privately in his own home** if he needs to do so. **And** similarly **a woman may spin** thread **on a spindle**[N] **in her** own **home** when she is mourning.

תָּנוּ רַבָּנַן: אָבֵל, שְׁלֹשָׁה יָמִים הָרִאשׁוֹנִים – אֵינוֹ הוֹלֵךְ לְבֵית הָאָבֵל; מִכָּאן וְאֵילָךְ – הוֹלֵךְ, וְאֵינוֹ יוֹשֵׁב בִּמְקוֹם הַמְנַחֲמִין אֶלָּא בִּמְקוֹם הַמִּתְנַחֲמִין.

The Sages taught in another *baraita*: **A mourner during the first three days** after his bereavement **may not go to** another **mourner's house**[N] to console him.[H] **From this** point **forward, he may go, but he may not sit among the consolers, but rather in the place of those being consoled,**[N] i.e., with the mourners in that house.

תָּנוּ רַבָּנַן: אָבֵל, שְׁלֹשָׁה יָמִים הָרִאשׁוֹנִים – אָסוּר בִּשְׁאִילַת שָׁלוֹם; מִשְּׁלֹשָׁה וְעַד שִׁבְעָה – מֵשִׁיב וְאֵינוֹ שׁוֹאֵל; מִכָּאן וְאֵילָךְ – שׁוֹאֵל וּמֵשִׁיב כְּדַרְכּוֹ.

§ **The Sages taught** in yet another *baraita*: **A mourner, during the first three days** after his bereavement, **is prohibited from extending greetings** to others. **From the third** day **to the seventh** day, **he may respond** when other people address him, **but he may not extend greetings**[N] to them. **From this** point **forward, he may extend greetings and respond in his** usual **manner."**[H]

שְׁלֹשָׁה יָמִים הָרִאשׁוֹנִים אָסוּר בִּשְׁאִילַת שָׁלוֹם? וְהָתַנְיָא: מַעֲשֶׂה וּמֵתוּ בָּנָיו שֶׁל רַבִּי עֲקִיבָא, נִכְנְסוּ כׇּל יִשְׂרָאֵל וְהִסְפִּידוּם הֶסְפֵּד גָּדוֹל.

The Gemara asks: Is he really **prohibited** from extending **greetings during the first three** days of mourning? **But isn't it taught** in a *baraita*: There was **an incident and the sons of Rabbi Akiva**[P] **died, and all the Jews entered to eulogize them with a great eulogy.**

NOTES

A mitzva is different – מִצְוָה שָׁאנֵי: Some have a version of the text that reads: The mitzva of phylacteries is different. This means that since the mitzva to wear phylacteries is from the Torah, it takes precedence over mourning, which is rabbinic (Rabbi Shlomo ben HaYatom; see Ritva).

The first three days a mourner is prohibited from working – אָבֵל, שְׁלֹשָׁה יָמִים הָרִאשׁוֹנִים אָסוּר בִּמְלָאכָה: Some write that the prohibition against working, and similarly the permission to work in private after the first three days, applies to everyone, although in practice, one who does not require the money is unlikely to perform work. Still, there is an opinion that one who needs the money is permitted to do so and others are similarly permitted (Rid). This opinion is not accepted by most commentaries and halakhic authorities, who say that only poor people with nothing to eat may work during the seven-day mourning period (see Riaz).

A woman may spin on a spindle – הָאִשָּׁה טוֹוָה בְּפֶלֶךְ: Most commentaries explain that this specifically refers to a poor woman, and the Sages permitted her to perform this type of work in her house because she needs to earn a livelihood. If she is unable to support herself with this work, then she may perform other types of work (see Ramban). There are those who write that any woman may do this work and not just a poor woman (Radbaz).

Go to another mourner's house – הוֹלֵךְ לְבֵית הָאָבֵל: Some say this means that he may go to a mourner's house only when he is related to the deceased, and this is why he sits with the other mourners, but he may not go to visit other mourners (Rabbeinu Yehonatan of Lunel; see Ran). However, most halakhic authorities hold that there is no distinction.

He sits in the place of those being consoled – יוֹשֵׁב בִּמְקוֹם הַמִּתְנַחֲמִים: Based on this, some halakhic authorities rule that a mourner is permitted to go to the synagogue on the Ninth of Av, as at that time the synagogue is a place of mourners, and everyone is considered to be like the consoled (see *Tosafot*). The *halakha* follows this opinion (*Shulḥan Arukh*, *Oraḥ Ḥayyim* 568:6).

He may respond but he may not extend greetings – מֵשִׁיב וְאֵינוֹ שׁוֹאֵל: The reason for this is explained in tractate *Berakhot*, where it is noted that people must be very careful to respond when a person extends greetings toward them, so as not to insult the greeter. The great people of every generation would respond to every person when greeted, regardless of his status. Therefore, the Sages permitted a mourner to respond when greeted, even when it would not be permitted for him to extend greetings to someone else. Even when it is not permitted for him to respond, he is still required to explain that he is not responding because he is mourning.

HALAKHA

A mourner is prohibited from working – אָבֵל...אָסוּר בִּמְלָאכָה: A mourner is prohibited from working during the first three days of mourning, even if he is poor and must take his livelihood from charity. From then onward, if he has nothing to eat he may perform work in the privacy of his own home (*Shulḥan Arukh*, *Yoreh De'a* 380:2).

Going to the house of another mourner – הֲלִיכָה לְבֵית הָאָבֵל: A mourner during the first three days of mourning may not attend a funeral unless there is no one else who can appropriately accompany the deceased or bury him. After the first three days of mourning, one may go to the funeral of someone from his neighborhood who has passed away, and may also visit a house of mourning. However, instead of sitting among the consolers he should sit with the mourners.

The Rema writes that today it is customary for the mourner not to leave his house for all seven days, even if he wishes to go to another house of mourning (*Shulḥan Arukh*, *Yoreh De'a* 393:1).

Greeting during mourning – שְׁאִילַת שָׁלוֹם בְּאֵבֶל: For the first three days, a mourner may not extend greetings to anyone. If people do not know that he is mourning and extend greetings to him, he should not respond to them. Instead, he should inform them that he is mourning.

From the third to the seventh day, he should not initiate extending greetings. However, if someone extends greetings to him then he may respond. From the seventh to the thirtieth days, he may extend greetings to others and respond. However, one should not extend greetings toward him.

After thirty days he is treated as any other person, if he is mourning for relatives other than his parents. One who is mourning for his father or mother may extend greetings to others after seven days, but others should not extend greetings to him until twelve months have passed. In order to show respect to a group he may say: Go in peace. Some permit extending greetings nowadays. However, this does not appear to be an appropriate custom unless he uses different wording and does not use the word: *Shalom* (*Shulḥan Arukh*, *Yoreh De'a* 385:1; Rema; *Shakh*).

PERSONALITIES

Rabbi Akiva – רַבִּי עֲקִיבָא: Akiva ben Yosef was one of the greatest of the *tanna'im*. He lived from just after the destruction of the Second Temple until the bar Kokheva revolt. He was one of the leading Sages at the time of Rabban Gamliel II in Yavne.

According to legend, Rabbi Akiva began his studies at the age of forty, when Rachel, the daughter of the wealthy Kalba Savua, agreed to marry him on condition that he went to study Torah. Rabbi Akiva became the student of Rabbi Eliezer ben Hyrcanus and Rabbi Yehoshua ben Ḥananya. Ultimately, he became a great scholar with twenty-four thousand students.

Among Rabbi Akiva's first students were Shimon ben Azzai and Shimon ben Zoma, with whom he entered the orchard (see *Ḥagiga* 14b), studying esoteric elements of the Torah. Subsequently, Rabbi Meir and Rabbi Shimon bar Yoḥai, among others, became his students.

He was a staunch supporter of bar Kokheva's revolt against Rome, and even declared him the Messiah. During the period of the Roman Emperor Hadrian's decrees, Torah study was prohibited, but Rabbi Akiva continued convening assemblies and teaching Torah. Ultimately, he was apprehended and executed, and he is one of the ten martyrs whose execution is described in liturgy.

Rabbi Akiva collected early rabbinic teachings and worked to organize the Oral Torah. The work done by Rabbi Akiva and his students served as the basis for the Mishna that was edited by Rabbi Yehuda HaNasi and his disciples.

בִּשְׁעַת פְּטִירָתָן עָמַד רַבִּי עֲקִיבָא עַל סַפְסָל גָּדוֹל וְאָמַר: אַחֵינוּ בֵּית יִשְׂרָאֵל שִׁמְעוּ! אֲפִילּוּ שְׁנֵי בָּנִים חֲתָנִים – מְנוּחָם הוּא בִּשְׁבִיל כָּבוֹד שֶׁעֲשִׂיתֶם. וְאִם בִּשְׁבִיל עֲקִיבָא בָּאתֶם – הֲרֵי כַּמָּה עֲקִיבָא בַּשּׁוּק. אֶלָּא כָּךְ אֲמַרְתֶּם: ״תּוֹרַת אֱלֹהָיו בְּלִבּוֹ״ וְכׇל שֶׁכֵּן שֶׁשְּׂכַרְכֶם כָּפוּל. לְכוּ לְבָתֵּיכֶם לְשָׁלוֹם.

When they were about to take leave, Rabbi Akiva stood on a large bench[L] **and said: Our brothers, the house of Israel, listen! Even had my two sons been bridegrooms, I would have been consoled on account of the honor you have shown** them. **If you came** to console **for the sake of Akiva, there are many Akivas in the marketplace** whom the Jews do all not come to console. **Rather,** certainly **this is** what **you said** to yourselves: **"The Torah of his God is in his heart"** (Psalms 37:31), and you wished to show your respect for the Torah. **All the more so is your reward doubled,** for you have consoled mourners and shown respect for the Torah. **Return** now **to your homes in peace.** This indicates that a mourner may greet other people even on the first day of his mourning.

כְּבוֹד רַבִּים שָׁאנֵי.

The Gemara answers: Showing **respect for the public is different.** Rabbi Akiva was permitted to greet them to demonstrate courtesy and respect.

מִשְּׁלֹשָׁה וְעַד שִׁבְעָה – מֵשִׁיב וְאֵינוֹ שׁוֹאֵל; מִכָּאן וְאֵילָךְ – שׁוֹאֵל וּמֵשִׁיב כְּדַרְכּוֹ.

§ It was taught in the aforementioned *baraita*: **From the third** day **to the seventh** day, **he may respond** when other people address him, **but he may not extend greetings** to them. **From this point forward, he may extend greetings and respond in his** usual **manner.**

וּרְמִינְהוּ: הַמּוֹצֵא אֶת חֲבֵירוֹ אָבֵל, בְּתוֹךְ שְׁלֹשִׁים יוֹם – מְדַבֵּר עִמּוֹ תַּנְחוּמִין וְאֵינוֹ שׁוֹאֵל בִּשְׁלוֹמוֹ; לְאַחַר שְׁלֹשִׁים יוֹם – שׁוֹאֵל בִּשְׁלוֹמוֹ וְאֵינוֹ מְדַבֵּר עִמּוֹ תַּנְחוּמִין.

And the Gemara **raises a contradiction** from another *baraita* that states: **One who finds another in mourning during the** first **thirty days** of that person's bereavement **may** still **speak words of consolation to him, but he should not extend greetings toward him.** If he finds him **after thirty days, he may extend greetings toward him, but he should not speak words of consolation to him,** so as not to remind him of his pain.

מֵתָה אִשְׁתּוֹ וְנָשָׂא אִשָּׁה אַחֶרֶת – אֵינוֹ רַשַּׁאי לִיכָּנֵס לְבֵיתוֹ לְדַבֵּר עִמּוֹ תַּנְחוּמִין. מְצָאוֹ בַּשּׁוּק – אוֹמֵר לוֹ בְּשָׂפָה רָפָה וּבְכוֹבֶד רֹאשׁ!

If it was the mourner's **wife** who **died and he married another woman**[N] within thirty days of his first wife's death, **one may not enter his house to speak words of consolation with him,** so as not to offend his new wife. If, however, **he finds him** alone **in the marketplace, he may speak to him with gentle words and in a serious manner.** This indicates that the prohibition against extending greetings lasts for thirty days and not just seven.

אָמַר רַב אִידִי בַּר אָבִין: הוּא שׁוֹאֵל בִּשְׁלוֹם אֲחֵרִים – שֶׁאֲחֵרִים שְׁרוּיִין בְּשָׁלוֹם; אֲחֵרִים אֵין שׁוֹאֲלִין בִּשְׁלוֹמוֹ – שֶׁהוּא אֵינוֹ שָׁרוּי בְּשָׁלוֹם.

Rav Idi bar Avin said: The two *baraitot* refer to different situations: The first *baraita* is referring to the mourner **himself, who may extend greetings** [*shalom*] **to others** after the completion of his seven days of mourning, **as the others are at peace** [*shalom*]. The second *baraita*, which speaks of a prohibition that lasts thirty days, is referring to **other people, who may not extend greetings to him, as he,** the mourner, **is not at peace.**

וְהָא מִדְּקָתָנֵי מֵשִׁיב – מִכְּלָל דְּשָׁיְילִינַן לֵיהּ! דְּלָא יָדְעִי.

The Gemara challenges: **But from** the fact **that it teaches** in a *baraita* that after the third day of his bereavement, the mourner may **respond** when other people address him, **by inference** others **may extend greetings to him.** The Gemara answers: This is referring to a case where people **did not know** that he was in mourning and unknowingly extended greetings to him.

אִי הָכִי, הָתָם נַמִי! הָתָם מוֹדַע לְהוּ, וְלָא מְהַדַּר לְהוּ; הָכָא – לָא צָרִיךְ לְאוֹדוֹעִינְהוּ.

The Gemara asks: **If so,** if the *baraita* speaks of a case where the people who greeted him were unaware that he was in mourning, then **there also,** during the first three days of his bereavement, he should be permitted to respond when other people address him. The Gemara answers: **There,** during the first three days, **he must inform them** that he is in mourning **and not respond** to their greetings. **Here,** after the first three days, **he need not inform them** about his bereavement, but rather he may respond to their greetings.

וּרְמִינְהוּ: הַמּוֹצֵא אֶת חֲבֵרוֹ אָבֵל, בְּתוֹךְ שְׁנֵים עָשָׂר חֹדֶשׁ – מְדַבֵּר עִמּוֹ תַּנְחוּמִין וְאֵינוֹ שׁוֹאֵל בִּשְׁלוֹמוֹ; לְאַחַר שְׁנֵים עָשָׂר חֹדֶשׁ – שׁוֹאֵל בִּשְׁלוֹמוֹ וְאֵינוֹ מְדַבֵּר עִמּוֹ תַּנְחוּמִין, אֲבָל מְדַבֵּר עִמּוֹ מִן הַצַּד.

And the Gemara **raises a contradiction** from another *baraita* that states: **One who finds another in mourning during** his **twelve months** of bereavement **may** still **speak words of consolation to him, but he should not extend greetings toward him.** If he finds him **after twelve months, he may extend greetings toward him, and he should not speak words of consolation to him. He may, however, speak to him indirectly,** i.e., he may say to him: May you be consoled, without mentioning the name of the deceased.

LANGUAGE

Bench [*safsal*] – סַפְסָל: The origin of this word is the Latin *subsellium*, meaning low seat or bench. Often this word was used to refer to the seats of judges or other leaders. Some say that the origin of the word is from the Hebrew word *sefel*, meaning mug, or at least influenced to some degree by the Hebrew, as it was common for people to sit on large overturned mugs.

Ancient figurine of a person sitting on a large overturned mug

NOTES

The mourner's wife died and he married another woman – מֵתָה אִשְׁתּוֹ וְנָשָׂא אִשָּׁה אַחֶרֶת: The commentaries explain that one may marry another woman this soon after the death of his first wife only if he has not yet fulfilled the mitzva of procreation or if he has small children who need a mother to take care of them. It is in these situations that one must be careful not to offend his second wife by mentioning the previous one.

אָמַר רַבִּי מֵאִיר: הַמּוֹצֵא אֶת חֲבֵרוֹ אָבֵל לְאַחַר שְׁנֵים עָשָׂר חֹדֶשׁ, וּמְדַבֵּר עִמּוֹ תַּנְחוּמִין, לְמָה הוּא דּוֹמֶה? לְאָדָם שֶׁנִּשְׁבְּרָה רַגְלוֹ וְחָיְתָה, מְצָאוֹ רוֹפֵא וְאָמַר לוֹ: כַּלֵּךְ אֶצְלִי, שֶׁאֲנִי שׁוֹבְרָהּ וַאֲרַפְּאֶנָּה, כְּדֵי שֶׁתֵּדַע שֶׁסַּמְמָנִין שֶׁלִּי יָפִין!

Rabbi Meir said: One who finds another in mourning after twelve months and speaks to him words of consolation, to what may this situation **be likened? To a person who broke his leg and it healed,** and afterward a physician **found him and said to him: Come to me, for I will break it** a second time **and** then **I will heal it, so that you may know how good my medicines are** and how well they work. One who consoles his friend after so much time has passed acts in a similar fashion, stirring up an old wound and then trying to heal it. In any event, it appears that one must not extend greetings to a mourner during the entire twelve-month mourning period.

לָא קַשְׁיָא: הָא – בְּאָבִיו וְאִמּוֹ; הָא – בִּשְׁאָר קְרוֹבִים.

The Gemara answers: **This is not difficult. This** *baraita*, which says that one must not extend greetings to a mourner for twelve months, is referring to one who lost **his father or mother. That** *baraita*, which teaches that a mourner may be greeted after seven days,[H] is referring to one who is in mourning over **other relatives.**

הָתָם נַמִי יְדַבֵּר עִמּוֹ תַּנְחוּמִין מִן הַצַּד! אִין, הָכִי נַמִי. וּמַאי אֵינוֹ מְדַבֵּר עִמּוֹ תַּנְחוּמִין? כְּדַרְכּוֹ, אֲבָל מְדַבֵּר עִמּוֹ מִן הַצַּד.

The Gemara asks: **There too,** in the case of other relatives after thirty days, **let him speak words of consolation to him indirectly.** Why does the *baraita* say that after thirty days he should not speak words of consolation to him at all? The Gemara answers: **Yes, it is indeed so. And what** is meant by the words: **He should not speak words of consolation to him?** This means that he may not console him **in his** usual **manner, but he may speak to him indirectly.**

תָּנוּ רַבָּנַן: אָבֵל, שְׁלֹשָׁה יָמִים הָרִאשׁוֹנִים בָּא מִמָּקוֹם קָרוֹב – מוֹנֶה עִמָּהֶן; בָּא מִמָּקוֹם רָחוֹק – מוֹנֶה לְעַצְמוֹ. מִכָּאן וְאֵילָךְ, אֲפִילּוּ בָּא מִמָּקוֹם קָרוֹב – מוֹנֶה לְעַצְמוֹ. רַבִּי שִׁמְעוֹן אוֹמֵר: אֲפִילּוּ בָּא בַּיּוֹם הַשְּׁבִיעִי מִמָּקוֹם קָרוֹב – מוֹנֶה עִמָּהֶן.

§ **The Sages taught** the following *baraita*: If **a mourner comes** to the house of mourning **from a nearby place**[N] **during the first three days** of mourning, **he counts** his days of mourning **with** the other mourners from the time of the burial and completes his mourning with them. This is the case even if he may end up observing mourning for only five or six days. But if **he came from a distant place, he counts on his own** seven complete days from the time that he was informed of his relative's death. **From this** point **forward,** i.e., after the first three days of mourning, **even if he came from a nearby place, he counts** seven days **on his own. Rabbi Shimon says: Even** if **he came on the seventh day from a nearby place, he counts** and completes the seven-day period of mourning **with** the other mourners.[H]

אָמַר מָר: שְׁלֹשָׁה יָמִים הָרִאשׁוֹנִים, בָּא מִמָּקוֹם קָרוֹב – מוֹנֶה עִמָּהֶן. אָמַר רַבִּי חִיָּיא בַּר אַבָּא אָמַר רַבִּי יוֹחָנָן: וְהוּא שֶׁיֵּשׁ גְּדוֹל הַבַּיִת בַּבַּיִת.

The Master said, citing the *baraita*: If **a mourner comes** to the house of mourning **from a nearby place during the first three days** of mourning, **he counts** his days of mourning **with** the other mourners and completes his mourning with them. **Rabbi Ḥiyya bar Abba said that Rabbi Yoḥanan said: This is** in a case **where the principal** member **of the household**[N] **is in the house,** and therefore all the other family members follow his mourning. If, however, it is the principal member of the family who comes home, he certainly does not follow the other members, but rather he counts seven days on his own.

אִיבַּעְיָא לְהוּ:

A dilemma was raised before the scholars:

HALAKHA

Consoling mourners after seven days – נִחוּם אֲבֵלִים לְאַחַר שִׁבְעָה: One who meets a mourner within the latter's thirty-day period of mourning should speak words of consolation to him and should not extend greetings. After thirty days, he may extend greetings toward him, but he may not speak words of consolation to him explicitly. However, he may say: You should be consoled, without mentioning the name of the deceased.

If a man's wife passes away and he marries another woman, one should not enter his house to console him. If he finds him on the street then he may say in an undertone: You should be consoled. If he did not marry another wife, then one may console him until three pilgrimage Festivals have passed.

One may speak words of consolation to a mourner whose father or mother has passed away within the last twelve months, and afterward he may console him without mentioning the name of the deceased (*Shulḥan Arukh, Yoreh De'a* 385:2).

How does one join the counting of seven – כֵּיצַד מִצְטָרֵף לְמִנְיַן שִׁבְעָה: In a case where one's close family member died and he did not know until he reached the place of the mourners, if he came from a nearby place, which is less than ten parasangs away, then he joins with the other mourners, even if he arrives on the seventh day. Nowadays, a nearby place is defined as any distance that one can reach in a single day's travel using modern forms of transportation (*Arukh HaShulḥan*). One joins the mourners if he still finds people who came to console the principal member of the household, even if they have stood up to leave. Similarly, such a person also counts the thirty-day period of mourning with this group. If he does not find consolers, there then he observes seven days of mourning on his own. Similarly, one who comes from a distant place counts his own seven- and thirty-day periods of mourning from the day on which he arrived, even if he arrives on the second day of mourning (*Shulḥan Arukh, Yoreh De'a* 375:8).

NOTES

One who comes from a nearby place – בָּא מִמָּקוֹם קָרוֹב: There is a tradition in the name of the *ge'onim* that a distant place refers to one that is more than a day's travel away from the place of the other mourners. The Rif explains that within this distance it is possible for a messenger to reach this relative and for him to arrive within the first three days after the death. As mentioned above, three days is referred to as the main portion of the mourning, and as long as one is close enough to the other mourners to reach them in this time period, he is joined together with the other mourners.

The principal member of the household – גְּדוֹל הַבַּיִת: Some commentaries explain that this term does not refer to a specific person, e.g., the oldest brother. Rather, it refers to the most important member of that family, whom everyone else follows with regard to mourning. This is the case even if he is a son or the youngest of the brothers (Rabbi Yitzḥak ibn Giat).

הָלַךְ גָּדוֹל הַבַּיִת לְבֵית הַקְּבָרוֹת מַהוּ?

If **the principal** member **of the household went**[N] with the remains of the deceased **to the cemetery** and did not return for several days,[H] **what is** the *halakha*? If another mourner came to the house of mourning during his absence, does he follow the principal member of the household and count from the time of the burial, or does he count from the time that the funeral procession departed, like the other members of the household?

תָּא שְׁמַע, דְּאָמַר רַבִּי חִיָּיא בַּר אַבָּא אָמַר רַבִּי יוֹחָנָן: אֲפִילּוּ הָלַךְ גָּדוֹל הַבַּיִת לְבֵית הַקְּבָרוֹת מוֹנֶה עִמָּהֶן. מוֹנֶה עִמָּהֶן? וְהָתַנְיָא מוֹנֶה לְעַצְמוֹ!

The Gemara answers: **Come and hear that which Rabbi Ḥiyya bar Abba said that Rabbi Yoḥanan said: Even** if the **principal** member **of the household went to the cemetery,** the mourner who comes home during his absence **counts with them,** i.e., the other members of the household who did not go to the cemetery. The Gemara asks: Does **he** really **count** and complete his mourning **with them? But isn't it taught** otherwise in a *baraita*, that **he counts** seven days **on his own?**

לָא קַשְׁיָא: הָא – דְּאָתָא בְּגוֹ תְּלָתָא, וְהָא – דְּלָא אָתָא בְּגוֹ תְּלָתָא. כִּי הָא דַּאֲמַר לְהוּ רַב לִבְנֵי הַצְלְפּוֹנִי: דְּאָתוּ בְּגוֹ תְּלָתָא – לִימְנוּ בַּהֲדַיְיכוּ; דְּלָא אָתוּ בְּגוֹ תְּלָתָא – לִימְנוּ לְנַפְשַׁיְהוּ.

The Gemara answers: **This is not difficult. This** statement, that he counts with them, is referring to a case **where** the principal member of the household **came** home **within three** days. **And the other** ruling, that he counts on his own, is referring to a case **where he did not come** home **within three** days. This conclusion is **similar to** what **Rav said to the sons of Hatzleponi**[N] when they were in mourning: **Those who come** home **within three** days **should count with you;** whereas **those who do not come** home **within three** days **should count on their own.**

אֲמַר לְהוּ רָבָא לִבְנֵי מְחוֹזָא: אַתּוּן דְּלָא אָזְלִיתוּ בָּתַר עַרְסָא, מִכִּי מְהַדְרִיתוּ אַפַּיְיכוּ מִבָּבָא דְּאַבּוּלָּא – אַתְחִילוּ מְנוּ.

Rava said to the people of Meḥoza:[B] Those of **you who do not follow the coffin** all the way to the place of interment **should begin counting** your days of mourning **from when you turn your faces**[H] **from the city gates**[N] to return home. Since the dead were commonly transported long distances and buried far away, most of the mourners did not accompany their deceased relatives to the actual site of burial.

״רַבִּי שִׁמְעוֹן אוֹמֵר אֲפִילּוּ בָּא בַּיּוֹם הַשְּׁבִיעִי מִמָּקוֹם קָרוֹב מוֹנֶה עִמָּהֶן״. אָמַר רַבִּי חִיָּיא בַּר גַּמְדָּא אָמַר רַבִּי יוֹסֵי בֶּן שָׁאוּל אָמַר רַבִּי: וְהוּא שֶׁבָּא וּמָצָא מְנַחֲמִין אֶצְלוֹ.

§ The Gemara cites the *baraita* taught above: **Rabbi Shimon says: Even** if one of the mourners **came on the seventh day from a nearby place, he counts with** the other mourners and completes the seven-day period of mourning with them. **Rabbi Ḥiyya bar Gamda said that Rabbi Yosei ben Shaul said that Rabbi** Yehuda HaNasi **said: And this is the** *halakha*, provided that **he came and found consolers** still present **in the house.**

בְּעֵי רַב עָנָן: נִנְעֲרוּ לַעֲמוֹד וְלֹא עָמְדוּ, מַהוּ? תֵּיקוּ.

§ **Rav Anan asks:** If the consolers **had** already **stirred** themselves **to stand up** and leave but **did not** yet actually **stand up** and leave, **what is** the *halakha*? Is it considered as if the consolers have already left or not? This question was not answered, and the dilemma **stands** unresolved.

HALAKHA

The principal member of the household went – הָלַךְ גָּדוֹל הַבַּיִת: Some say that in a case where a person arrives and finds that the principal member of the household has gone to tend to the needs of the dead, then if the principal member returns within three days, it is as though he was home when this person arrived, and this person is considered to be one of the members of the household. Therefore, he counts the days of his mourning period with this group (Rema; *Shulḥan Arukh, Yoreh De'a* 375:8).

When you turn your faces – מִכִּי מְהַדְרִיתוּ אַפַּיְיכוּ: In places where the deceased are carried to another city in order to be buried, those who remain in the city should begin counting the seven-day period of mourning once they turn away from the funeral procession. Those who accompany the deceased and those relatives who live near the place of burial begin to observe their mourning after the burial itself.

If the principal member of the household accompanies the deceased, then even those who stay at home must wait until the deceased has been buried to start counting the seven days of mourning. Everyone follows the principal member of the household, regardless of whether he is the eldest member or if he is young, though some say that he must be at least thirteen years old. When a married woman is the deceased, her husband is considered to be the principal member of the household (*Shakh*, citing Rashba; *Shulḥan Arukh, Yoreh De'a* 375:2).

BACKGROUND

Meḥoza – מְחוֹזָא: A city on the Tigris, located near the Malka River, Meḥoza was a large commercial city and most of its inhabitants were Jews. Unlike most other Jewish communities, the Jews of Meḥoza generally earned their living from commerce. The Jewish community included a large number of converts as well as Jews from many different countries. After Neharde'a was destroyed in 259 CE the Neharde'a yeshiva relocated to Meḥoza. Meḥoza became the Torah center of leading scholars such as Rav Naḥman; Rav Sheshet; Rava, who later became head of the Meḥoza Yeshiva; Ameimar; and Rav Kahana, who was Rav Ashi's teacher. After the death of Abaye in 338 CE, the Pumbedita yeshiva, which was then headed by Rava, also moved for a period to Meḥoza.

NOTES

The principal member of the household went, etc. – הָלַךְ גָּדוֹל הַבַּיִת וכו׳: The early authorities disagree about how to understand this *halakha*, and their dispute is based on, among other issues, whether this statement and those after it are a continuation of what was previously stated or separate from it.

Some explain that the question of the Gemara concerns the principal member of the household himself. If he accompanied the deceased to the cemetery and was not home when the rest of the family began their mourning, then the issue is whether he joins with their mourning or not. The conclusion is that if he returns within three days, then he joins with them; if not, he counts on his own (Rashi, from manuscript; Ra'avad; Rabbeinu Yehonatan of Lunel).

According to this explanation, the Babylonian Talmud contradicts the principle stated in the Jerusalem Talmud, that all mourning is based on the principal member of the family. In the Jerusalem Talmud, it is maintained that if the principal member remains in that place, the other mourners count with him; if he goes to accompany the dead, then they count with him after the burial.

However, others understand this as a continuation of the previous case, where a person comes and joins other mourners. This issue depends on the principal member of the household, and this case concerns the *halakha* when the principal member of the household is not present at that time that this other person came to the house of mourning. For example, if the principal member of the household went to accompany the deceased and returns within three days, it is as though he were there the entire time. Therefore, the newly arrived mourner joins with the rest of the mourners in that household (Rabbeinu Gershom Meor HaGola; *Talmid Rabbeinu Yeḥiel of Paris*; Rabbi Shlomo ben HaYatom).

There is another entirely different explanation, which understands the phrase: The principal member of the household went to the cemetery, to mean that the principal member of the household passed away. According to this explanation, the Gemara asks if the mourners follow the principal person who remains, or if the *halakha* of the principal member of the household no longer applies (Rashi, from manuscript; Commentary on *Moed Katan*).

Hatzleponi – הַצְלְפּוֹנִי: Some explain this to be the name of a place, while others understand it to be a family name (Rashi, from manuscript). There are also those who hold that this was the name of their father who passed away (*Talmid Rabbeinu Yeḥiel of Paris*).

The city gates – בָּבָא דְּאַבּוּלָּא: Rabbeinu Gershom Meor HaGola explains that this refers to the gate in the house of mourning, and some have a version of the text that reflects this explanation.

גְּמִירִי חַבְרֵיהּ דְּרַבִּי אַבָּא בַּר חִיָּיא מֵרַבִּי אַבָּא, וּמַנּוּ – רַבִּי זֵירָא, וְאָמְרִי לַהּ: חַבְרֵיהּ דְּרַבִּי זֵירָא מֵרַבִּי זֵירָא, וּמַנּוּ – רַבִּי אַבָּא בְּרֵיהּ דְּרַבִּי חִיָּיא בַּר אַבָּא, אָמַר רַבִּי יוֹחָנָן: הֲלָכָה כְּרַבָּן שִׁמְעוֹן בֶּן גַּמְלִיאֵל בִּטְרֵיפוֹת, וַהֲלָכָה כְּרַבִּי שִׁמְעוֹן בְּאֵבֶל.

The Gemara relates that **a colleague of Rabbi Abba bar Ḥiyya learned** the following principle as a tradition **from Rabbi Abba.** The Gemara asks: **And who** was this colleague? It was **Rabbi Zeira. And some say** a different version of this tradition: **A colleague of Rabbi Zeira** learned a tradition **from Rabbi Zeira.** The Gemara asks: **And who is** this colleague? It was **Rabbi Abba, son of Rabbi Ḥiyya bar Abba: Rabbi Yoḥanan said: The *halakha* is in accordance with** the opinion of **Rabban Shimon ben Gamliel with regard to** an animals that is unsuitable for human consumption because of severe organic disease or congenital defect, making it a ***tereifa*, and the *halakha* is in accordance with** the opinion of **Rabbi Shimon with regard to** the *halakhot* of **mourning.**

כְּרַבִּי שִׁמְעוֹן בְּאֵבֶל – הָא דַּאֲמַרַן. כְּרַבָּן שִׁמְעוֹן בֶּן גַּמְלִיאֵל בִּטְרֵיפוֹת – דִּתְנַן: בְּנֵי מֵעַיִם שֶׁנִּיקְּבוּ וְלֵיחָה סוֹתַמְתָּן – כְּשֵׁרָה, דִּבְרֵי רַבָּן שִׁמְעוֹן בֶּן גַּמְלִיאֵל.

The Gemara explains: The *halakha* is **in accordance with** the opinion of **Rabbi Shimon with regard to mourning, concerning that which we** just **said** about a mourner who arrives on the seventh day. The *halakha* is **in accordance with** the opinion of **Rabban Shimon ben Gamliel with regard to** defects in animals that render them ***tereifa*** concerning **that which we learned** in a *baraita*: If the animal's **intestines became perforated, but** the hole **was stopped up by mucus,**[H] so that nothing comes out of this hole, the animal is **fit.** Unlike an ordinary hole in the intestines, this hole does not render the animal a *tereifa* and make it unfit for consumption. This is **the statement of Rabban Shimon ben Gamliel.**

מַאי לֵיחָה? אֲמַר רַב כַּהֲנָא: שִׁירְקָא דִּמְעַיָּא דְּנָפֵיק אַגַּב דּוּחְקָא. אָמַר מַאן דְּהוּא: אִיזְכֵּי וְאַסֵּיק וְאֶגְמְרָא לִשְׁמַעְתָּא מִפּוּמֵיהּ דְּמָרֵיהּ.

The Gemara asks: **What** is this **mucus? Rav Kahana said: The fat [*shirka*]**[L] **of the intestines**[BN] **that comes out under pressure. Someone** whose name was not given **said: May I merit to go up** to Eretz Yisrael **and learn this *halakha* from the mouth of its author.**

כִּי סְלֵיק אַשְׁכְּחֵיהּ לְרַבִּי אַבָּא בְּרֵיהּ דְּרַבִּי חִיָּיא בַּר אַבָּא, אֲמַר לֵיהּ: אֲמַר מָר הֲלָכָה כְּרַבָּן שִׁמְעוֹן בֶּן גַּמְלִיאֵל בִּטְרֵיפוֹת? אֲמַר לֵיהּ: אֲנָא ״אֵין הֲלָכָה״ אֲמָרִי.

When he went up from Babylonia to Eretz Yisrael, **he found Rabbi Abba, son of Rabbi Ḥiyya bar Abba,** and **said to him: Did the Master say** that **the *halakha* is in accordance with** the opinion of **Rabban Shimon ben Gamliel with regard to** defects that render the animal a ***tereifa*? He said to him: I said** just the opposite, namely, that **the *halakha* is not** in accordance with Rabban Shimon ben Gamliel, and therefore such a hole in the animal's intestine makes it unfit for eating.

כְּרַבִּי שִׁמְעוֹן בְּאֵבֶל מַאי? אֲמַר לֵיהּ: פְּלוּגְתָּא נִינְהוּ. דְּאִיתְּמַר, רַב חִסְדָּא אָמַר: הֲלָכָה; וְכֵן אָמַר רַבִּי יוֹחָנָן: הֲלָכָה; רַב נַחְמָן אָמַר: אֵין הֲלָכָה.

He asked him again: **What** about the other ruling reported in your name, that the *halakha* **is in accordance with** the opinion of **Rabbi Shimon with regard to mourning?** Is this accurate? **He said to him:** This issue is **subject to dispute, as it was stated: Rav Ḥisda said: The *halakha*** is in accordance with the opinion of Rabbi Shimon, **and similarly Rabbi Yoḥanan said:** It is the ***halakha*.** But **Rav Naḥman said: It is not the *halakha*.**

וְאֵין הֲלָכָה כְּרַבָּן שִׁמְעוֹן בֶּן גַּמְלִיאֵל בִּטְרֵיפוֹת. וַהֲלָכָה כְּרַבִּי שִׁמְעוֹן בְּאֵבֶל. דְּאָמַר שְׁמוּאֵל: הֲלָכָה כְּדִבְרֵי הַמֵּיקֵל בְּאֵבֶל.

The Gemara concludes: **The *halakha* is not in accordance with** the opinion of **Rabban Shimon ben Gamliel with regard to** the aforementioned issue of ***tereifa*, and the *halakha* is in accordance with Rabbi Shimon with regard to mourning, as Shmuel stated** a principle: **The *halakha* follows the opinion of the** more **lenient** authority **in** matters relating to **mourning.**

עַל כָּל הַמֵּתִים כּוּלָּן, מַדְחֶה מִטָּתוֹ – הֲרֵי זֶה מְשׁוּבָּח; עַל אָבִיו וְעַל אִמּוֹ – הֲרֵי זֶה מְגוּנֶּה. הָיָה עֶרֶב שַׁבָּת, אוֹ עֶרֶב יוֹם טוֹב – הֲרֵי זֶה מְשׁוּבָּח, שֶׁאֵינוֹ עוֹשֶׂה אֶלָּא לִכְבוֹד אָבִיו וְאִמּוֹ.

§ It was taught in a *baraita*: **With regard to all** other **deceased** relatives, it **is praiseworthy** for **one** to be **quick** in taking **the bier**[NH] out for burial. But **in the case of one's father or mother,** acting in this manner **is condemnable,** as one should draw out the period of acute mourning for his parent. If, however, **it was Friday**[N] **or the eve of a Festival,** then **one is praiseworthy** for expediting his parent's burial because **he does this only out of respect for his father or mother,** as he does not want them to remain unburied for the duration of Shabbat or the Festival.

עַל כָּל הַמֵּתִים כּוּלָּן, רָצָה מְמַעֵט בְּעִסְקוֹ, רָצָה אֵינוֹ

With regard to all other **dead,** if the mourner **wishes** he may **reduce his business**[NH] due to mourning. If, however, **he wishes** not to do so, he **need not**

HALAKHA

Intestines became perforated, but the hole was stopped up by mucus – נִקְבוּ הַדַּקִּים וְלֵיחָה סוֹתַמְתָּן: A hole in the small intestine qualifies an animal as a *tereifa*; even if liquid sticks to this hole and blocks it the animal may not be eaten. As is stated in the Gemara, the *halakha* is not in accordance with the opinion of Rabban Shimon ben Gamliel (*Shulḥan Arukh, Yoreh De'a* 46:1).

One to be quick in taking the bier – מַדְחֶה מִיטָּתוֹ: For most deceased relatives, it is praiseworthy to complete the burial as quickly as possible. However, in the case of one's father or mother, this is considered to be disrespectful, unless it is Friday, the eve of a Festival, or it is raining and the corpse will get wet. In these situations, it is preferable to conduct the burial quickly, out of respect for one's parents (*Shulḥan Arukh, Yoreh De'a* 357:2).

He may reduce his business – מְמַעֵט בְּעִסְקוֹ: One who is mourning over a close relative may choose whether or not to limit his involvement in business activities. However, one who is mourning over his father or mother is required to lessen his involvement in these activities (*Shulḥan Arukh, Yoreh De'a* 380:24).

LANGUAGE

Fat [*shirka*] – שִׁירְקָא: Apparently from the Middle Iranian širak, referring to secreted fatty liquid.

BACKGROUND

The fat of the intestines – שִׁירְקָא דִּמְעַיָּא: This refers to the mucus membrane that covers the intestines, the *muscosa tunica*, which contains protrusions that enter into the intestines. This soft membrane is not considered to be enough of a protection if the intestine is punctured, as even if it manages to close the intestine for a short period of time the food in the intestines will eventually leave the intestinal tract from this hole.

NOTES

The fat of the intestines – שִׁירְקָא דִּמְעַיָּא: Some say that this is a soft membrane that covers the intestines (Commentary on *Moed Katan*). It is said in the name of Rav Hai Gaon that this refers to the soft layer of fat that covers the walls of the intestines. Others claim that it refers to food that has not been entirely digested (see Commentary on *Moed Katan*).

One to be quick in taking the bier – מַדְחֶה מִטָּתוֹ: Since one does not speak a lengthy eulogy over other relatives, it is preferable not to delay the burial unless it is for their honor (Rabbeinu Yehonatan of Lunel). Some say that one who buries the deceased quickly shows that he has accepted Heaven's decree with love, and that he is not challenging God's judgment (*Talmid Rabbeinu Yeḥiel of Paris*).

Friday, etc. – עֶרֶב שַׁבָּת וכו׳: It is preferable to show respect toward Shabbat or a Festival, which require preparation, rather than spend time eulogizing the dead. Similarly, there is also concern that if the burial is delayed there may not be time to complete the burial, causing the deceased to remain unburied for an additional day, in violation of the *halakha* (*Talmid Rabbeinu Yeḥiel of Paris*).

He may reduce his business – מְמַעֵט בְּעִסְקוֹ: Rav Hai Gaon explains that one who spends all day in his business must work for fewer hours. In the Jerusalem Talmud it explains that one who is mourning over his father or mother may not leave his home for business endeavors, even after thirty days, until such time as his colleagues rebuke him.

מְמַעֵט; עַל אָבִיו וְעַל אִמּוֹ – מְמַעֵט.

reduce it. In the case of **his father or mother,** he must always **reduce** his business.

עַל כָּל הַמֵּתִים כּוּלָּן, רָצָה – חוֹלֵץ, רָצָה – אֵינוֹ חוֹלֵץ. עַל אָבִיו וְעַל אִמּוֹ – חוֹלֵץ.

With regard to all other **deceased** relatives, if the mourner **wishes, he may remove**[N] his garment from one of his shoulders,[BH] and if **he wishes** not to remove it, **he need not remove** it. However, in the case of **his father or mother, he** must always **remove** his garment from one of his shoulders.

וּמַעֲשֶׂה בִּגְדוֹל הַדּוֹר אֶחָד שֶׁמֵּת אָבִיו וּבִיקֵּשׁ לַחֲלוֹץ, וּבִיקֵּשׁ גְּדוֹל הַדּוֹר אַחֵר שֶׁעִמּוֹ לַחֲלוֹץ – וְנִמְנַע וְלֹא חָלַץ.

There was **an incident when the father of a leading authority of** his **generation died, and** the authority **wished to remove** his garment from one shoulder. **Another leading authority of the generation** also **wished to remove** his own garment together **with him,** in order to join him in his mourning, **but** due to this the first person **refrained and did not remove**[N] his garment, so that his colleague would not remove his garment as well.

אָמַר אַבָּיֵי: גְּדוֹל הַדּוֹר – רַבִּי; גְּדוֹל הַדּוֹר שֶׁעִמּוֹ – רַבִּי יַעֲקֹב בַּר אַחָא. וְאִיכָּא דְּאָמְרִי: גְּדוֹל הַדּוֹר – רַבִּי יַעֲקֹב בַּר אַחָא; גְּדוֹל הַדּוֹר שֶׁעִמּוֹ – רַבִּי.

Abaye said: The leading authority of the generation mentioned here is **Rabbi** Yehuda HaNasi, and **the leading authority of the generation** who was **with him** was **Rabbi Ya'akov bar Aḥa. And some say: The leading authority of the generation** was **Rabbi Ya'akov bar Aḥa,** and **the leading authority of the generation** who was **with him** was **Rabbi** Yehuda HaNasi.

בִּשְׁלָמָא לְמַאן דְּאָמַר גְּדוֹל הַדּוֹר שֶׁעִמּוֹ רַבִּי – הַיְינוּ דְּנִמְנַע וְלֹא חָלַץ.

The Gemara examines this issue: **Granted, according to the one who said** that **the leading authority of the generation** who was **with him was Rabbi** Yehuda HaNasi, **this is** the reason that **he refrained and did not remove** his garment from his shoulder. That is to say, Rabbi Ya'akov bar Aḥa refrained from doing so because he did not wish to cause the *Nasi* to remove his own garment.

אֶלָּא לְמַאן דְּאָמַר רַבִּי יַעֲקֹב בַּר אַחָא – אַמַּאי נִמְנַע וְלֹא חָלַץ? רַבָּן שִׁמְעוֹן בֶּן גַּמְלִיאֵל נָשִׂיא הֲוָה, וְכוּלֵּי עָלְמָא מִיחַיְּיבִי לְמִיחְלַץ! קַשְׁיָא.

But according to the one who said that it is **Rabbi Ya'akov bar Aḥa** who was the leader of the generation with him, **why did** Rabbi Yehuda HaNasi **refrain and not remove** his garment from his shoulder? **Rabban Shimon ben Gamliel,**[P] the father of Rabbi Yehuda HaNasi, was also **the *Nasi*, and everyone is required to remove** his garment from his shoulder for him, as was the accepted practice. Therefore, Rabbi Ya'akov bar Aḥa would also have been required to bare his shoulder. Why, then, did Rabbi Yehuda HaNasi prevent him from doing so? The Gemara concludes: Indeed **this is difficult.**

NOTES

He may remove [*ḥoletz*] – חוֹלֵץ: The *ge'onim* explain that this means removing the garment from one's shoulder and exposing the shoulder. There is also support for this explanation from several places in the Talmud (Ramban). However, some explain slightly differently, maintaining that one is required to rend his garment until he exposes his shoulder (Rashi, from manuscript; *Talmid Rabbeinu Yeḥiel of Paris*). Others understand that this means removing one's outer garment, like a person who shows that he is about to engage in an act that requires physical exertion. By doing so, this mourner demonstrates that he is putting effort into showing honor for the deceased (Ramban; Ran citing *Tosefot of Rabbi Shimshon of Saens*).There are also those who understand that the word *ḥoletz* in this context means removing one's shoes, and that a mourner is required to remove his shoes and walk barefoot in order to honor the dead, not as an act of mourning. Therefore, one performs this act before the requirements of mourning take effect, when he is accompanying the body on the way to burial (see Rosh).

He refrained and did not remove – נִמְנַע וְלֹא חָלַץ: Although there is a mitzva to remove one's garment in order to show respect for the deceased, maintaining the honor of a Torah scholar of this stature is a greater mitzva and takes precedence. Perhaps one of the reasons that the custom of exposing the shoulder is no longer practiced is that there is concern that in the Diaspora it will cause the mourners to be treated disrespectfully by their gentile neighbors (Ramban).

BACKGROUND

Removal of the garment from one's shoulder – חֲלִיצַת כָּתֵף: Removing the garment from one's shoulder is similar to a symbolic rending of one's garment, and doing so is considered like removing one's garment in mourning. As is stated in the Gemara, the more one wishes to emphasize the mourning, and the more honor one wishes to show the deceased, the more he removes his garment.

Garment removed from the shoulder

HALAKHA

Removing a garment from the shoulder for a mourner – חֲלִיצַת כָּתֵף לְאָבֵל: One is required to remove his garment while walking with the bier of his father or mother, until the burial has been completed. If the mourner is an important person and it would be seen as dishonorable for him to remove his garment, then he is not required to do so. For all other deceased relatives, he is not required to remove his garment from his shoulder if he does not want to. The Rema writes, based on the *Kolbo*, that nowadays it is customary not to remove one's garment at all (*Shulḥan Arukh, Yoreh De'a* 340:16–17).

PERSONALITIES

Rabban Shimon ben Gamliel – רַבָּן שִׁמְעוֹן בֶּן גַּמְלִיאֵל: Rabban Shimon ben Gamliel II was head of the Sanhedrin following the bar Kokheva revolt. He was a member of the dynasty of Hillel the Elder. His grandfather, Rabban Shimon ben Gamliel the Elder, headed the Sanhedrin at the time of the destruction of the Temple and was one of the Ten Martyrs killed by the Romans.

Rabban Shimon ben Gamliel II was a young man studying in Beitar at the time of the bar Kokheva revolt. He escaped from the city before it was destroyed. When the Sanhedrin was reconstituted in Usha, he was chosen to preside there in place of his late father. The Talmud records that he studied Greek philosophy, and it appears that he was knowledgeable in a wide range of scholarly disciplines, including science and medicine.

He tended to be lenient in his halakhic rulings, often stating his concern that people not be overly inconvenienced. All of his rulings were accepted as *halakha*, with only three exceptions. His teachings included attempts to limit arguments and disputes. One example is his statement that no court can nullify the ruling of another court unless it is greater in wisdom and number. In tractate *Avot* (1:17), the following maxim is cited in his name: On three things the world is sustained: On truth, on judgment, and on peace.

עַל כָּל הַמֵּתִים כּוּלָּן מִסְתַּפֵּר לְאַחַר שְׁלֹשִׁים יוֹם; עַל אָבִיו וְעַל אִמּוֹ – עַד שֶׁיִּגְעֲרוּ בּוֹ חֲבֵרָיו. עַל כָּל הַמֵּתִים כּוּלָּן – נִכְנָס לְבֵית הַשִּׂמְחָה לְאַחַר שְׁלֹשִׁים יוֹם; עַל אָבִיו וְעַל אִמּוֹ – לְאַחַר שְׁנֵים עָשָׂר חֹדֶשׁ.

§ The Gemara returns to the continuation of the *baraita*: **With regard to all deceased** relatives except for parents, **one may cut his hair after thirty days. In the case of one's father or mother,** one may not cut his hair **until his colleagues have rebuked him** for his hair being too long.[H] **With regard to all** other **deceased** relatives, **he may enter a place** where **a joyous** celebration is taking place **after thirty days; in the case of his father or mother,** he may enter such a place only **after twelve months.**

אָמַר רַבָּה בַּר בַּר חָנָה: וּלְשִׂמְחַת מְרֵיעוּת. מֵיתִיבִי: וּלְשִׂמְחָה וְלִמְרֵיעוּת שְׁלֹשִׁים יוֹם! קַשְׁיָא.

Rabba bar bar Ḥana said: The ruling that a mourner may enter a house of joy after thirty days applies specifically **to a joyous social gathering,** that is to say, to the joyous meals that a group of friends would eat together, each taking a turn hosting. But this ruling does not apply to a large joyous occasion, such as a wedding feast. The Gemara **raises an objection** from a *baraita* which adds: **And** also **for joyous social gatherings, thirty days.**[N] This implies that when the *baraita* speaks of joyous celebrations without further specification, it is not referring to joyous social gatherings, but even to weddings and other joyous occasions. The Gemara concludes: Indeed, **it is difficult.**

אַמֵימָר מַתְנֵי הָכִי: אָמַר רַבָּה בַּר בַּר חָנָה, וּלְשִׂמְחַת מְרֵיעוּת – מוּתָּר לִיכָּנֵס לְאַלְתַּר. וְהָא תַּנְיָא: לְשִׂמְחָה שְׁלֹשִׁים, וְלִמְרֵיעוּת שְׁלֹשִׁים!

Ameimar taught the previous discussion **as follows: Rabba bar bar Ḥana said** an alternative version of the discussion: **For a joyous social gathering one is permitted to enter immediately.** The Gemara poses a question: **But isn't it taught** in a *baraita*: **For joyous celebrations and for joyous social gatherings,** one must wait **thirty** days?

לָא קַשְׁיָא; הָא בַּאֲרִיסוּתָא; הָא – בְּפוּרְעָנוּתָא.

The Gemara answers: **This is not difficult. This** ruling, of the *baraita*, is referring **to an initial** gathering,[N] when the mourner is the first in the group of friends to host. The *baraita* teaches that in such a situation the mourner is required to wait thirty days before doing so. **That** ruling, of Rabba bar bar Ḥana, is referring **to a reciprocal** gathering. The mourner's friends have already hosted these gatherings, and now it is his turn to host. Since he is required to host such a gathering for his colleagues, he need not postpone it. Rather, he may host the group immediately.[H]

עַל כָּל הַמֵּתִים כּוּלָּן – קוֹרֵעַ טֶפַח; עַל אָבִיו וְעַל אִמּוֹ – עַד שֶׁיְּגַלֶּה אֶת לִבּוֹ. אָמַר רַבִּי אַבָּהוּ: מַאי קְרָא? "וַיַּחֲזֵק דָּוִד בִּבְגָדָיו וַיִּקְרָעֵם", וְאֵין אֲחִיזָה פָּחוֹת מִטֶּפַח.

The *baraita* continues: **With regard to all** other **deceased** relatives, **one rends** his garment the length **of a handbreadth,** and that suffices. **In the case of his father or mother,** he must rend his garment **until he reveals his heart.**[NH] **Rabbi Abbahu said: What is the verse** that teaches that the rent must be a handbreadth? **"And David took hold of his clothes and rent them"** (II Samuel 1:11), **and taking hold cannot** be done for a garment **less than a handbreadth.**

NOTES

A joyous social gathering and other types of joyous celebrations – שִׂמְחַת מְרֵעוּת וְשִׂמְחָה אַחֶרֶת: The differences between the two versions in the Talmud are based on the issue of which is more likely to be prohibited to a mourner: Should a joyous social gathering be delayed until after thirty days because it is purely social and not a mitzva? Or, perhaps the celebration for a mitzva, such as a wedding, must be postponed. Since the joy is greater, a mourner should not take part until after this time. This issue is the subject of a disagreement between the early authorities.

Initial gathering [*arisuta*] – אֲרִיסוּתָא: According to most early authorities, the correct version of the text is *arishuta* or *rashuta*, which are derived from the Aramaic *rashu*, meaning creditor. These meals are considered like a form of a loan that must be repaid to one's friends by hosting them. Therefore, if the mourner is begins a cycle of social meals, he must postpone hosting because he does not yet owe anyone the invitation. However, when others have already hosted him and it is his turn to repay the debt, he is permitted to host the meal. Some have asked why the mourner cannot host the meal or repay the loan without actually taking part himself. They answer that to do so would be insulting for his friends, since they would be eating in his house without him present.

Until he reveals his heart – עַד שֶׁיְּגַלֶּה אֶת לִבּוֹ: In the Jerusalem Talmud, it is explained that by performing this act the mourner expresses his pain that the mitzva to honor one's father and mother no longer applies to him.

HALAKHA

Haircut for a mourner – תִּסְפּוֹרֶת לְאָבֵל: One who is mourning a deceased relative other than his parents may cut his hair after thirty days. After the death of his mother or father, he mourner must wait to cut his hair until his colleagues rebuke him, and a Festival does not interrupt this aspect of mourning. There is dispute with regard to the amount of rebuke he must receive, and the accepted practice is to wait three months to cut the hair on one's head. However, a man may trim his beard before this (*Pitḥei Teshuva*, citing *Noda Bihuda*). In some places, it is customary for a mourner not to cut his hair for twelve months, if it is not absolutely necessary to do so (*Shulḥan Arukh, Yoreh De'a* 390:4, and in the comment of Rema).

A mourner with regard to a party – אָבֵל לְעִנְיַן מִשְׁתֶּה: One who is mourning for a deceased relative may go to a celebration after thirty days, but one who is mourning over his father or mother is required to wait twelve months before doing so. In a leap year, which has an additional month, the mourner is required to wait for twelve months, not a full year. If one is required to host a social gathering to repay those who have hosted him in the past, he may do so after the seven-day mourning period has ended. However, one mourning for his father or mother may not host such a gathering under any circumstances for twelve months. With regard to a joyous mitzva celebration, if there is a concern that the event will not take place at all if he will not attend, such as when two orphans get married, then he may go, provided it takes place after the thirty-day mourning period.

A mourner may take part in a mitzva feast that is not especially joyful, such as a meal after a circumcision or for the redemption of the first born, even during the seven days of mourning, provided he does not have to leave his house. However, the custom is for a mourner not to take part in any feast outside of his house for twelve months.

If one's son is being circumcised or if the mourner is performing the circumcision, he may wear Shabbat clothes and join the feast, provided that it occurs after the thirty-day period of mourning (Rema). Some permit one mourning his parents to join a feast within twelve months, provided that he helps prepare the wedding or serves those in attendance in some way (*Shulḥan Arukh, Yoreh De'a* 391:2).

Rending – קְרִיעָה: One who is mourning a deceased relatives other than a parent is required to rend only his outer garment one handbreadth; if he tore his inner garment, it is acceptable after the fact (*Pitḥei Teshuva*, citing *Keneset HaGedola*), although others disagree and require him to tear his outer garment (Rabbi Akiva Eiger, citing *Torat Ḥayyim*). At the death of one's father or mother, he is required to tear all of his garments until he exposes his heart. It is also the accepted practice to rend one's garment on the left side over one's father or mother and on the right side for other deceased relatives (*Shakh*, citing Maharshal).

There is a dispute with regard to the term *apikarsuto*: Some say that it refers to an undergarment that is worn directly against the skin, and others say that it refers to an outer garment. The accepted practice is never to rend an outer cloak; however an undergarment should be rent. The Rema writes that the Ashkenazic custom is to tear neither one's outer garment nor one's innermost garment. Instead, one is required to tear his second outermost garment over a deceased relatives; over one's father or mother, he must rend all the middle garments between the outer one and the one closest to his body (*Shulḥan Arukh, Yoreh De'a* 340:9–10).

עַל כָּל הַמֵּתִים כּוּלָּן, אֲפִילּוּ לָבוּשׁ עֲשָׂרָה חֲלוּקִין – אֵינוֹ קוֹרֵעַ אֶלָּא עֶלְיוֹן. עַל אָבִיו וְעַל אִמּוֹ – קוֹרֵעַ אֶת כּוּלָּן, וְאַפִּיקַרְסוּתוֹ אֵינָהּ מְעַכֶּבֶת.

The *baraita* teaches further: **With regard to all** other deceased relatives, **even if he is wearing ten garments,** one on top of the other, **he rends only** his **outer** garment. But **in** the case of **his father or mother, he must rend them all.** Failure to rend **his undergarment,**[NL] however, **does not invalidate** the fulfillment of the mitzva.

אֶחָד הָאִישׁ וְאֶחָד אִשָּׁה. רַבִּי שִׁמְעוֹן בֶּן אֶלְעָזָר אוֹמֵר: הָאִשָּׁה קוֹרַעַת אֶת הַתַּחְתּוֹן, וּמַחֲזִירַתּוֹ לַאֲחוֹרֶיהָ, וְחוֹזֶרֶת וְקוֹרַעַת אֶת הָעֶלְיוֹן.

Both a man and a woman are required to rend their garments. **Rabbi Shimon ben Elazar says: A woman** first **rends** her **inner** garment **and turns** it **around,** so that the tear is **on her back. And** only **afterward** does **she rend** her **outer** garment, so that she does not expose her chest.[H]

עַל כָּל הַמֵּתִים כּוּלָּן רָצָה – מַבְדִּיל קַמֵּי שָׂפָה שֶׁלּוֹ, רָצָה – אֵינוֹ מַבְדִּיל. עַל אָבִיו וְעַל אִמּוֹ – מַבְדִּיל.

With regard to all other **deceased** relatives, if **one wishes he may rip apart** his garment **on the hem,**[NH] rather than merely expanding the neck hole, so that the tear stands out distinctly from the opening of the garment. If he **wishes** not to do this, **he does not rip apart** the hem in this manner. That is to say, one may simply enlarge the neck hole, although rending a garment in this way makes the tear less prominent. **In the case of one's father or mother,** however, **he must** always **rip apart** the hem.

רַבִּי יְהוּדָה אוֹמֵר: כָּל קְרִיעָה שֶׁאֵינוֹ מַבְדִּיל קַמֵּי שָׂפָה שֶׁלּוֹ – אֵינוֹ אֶלָּא קֶרַע שֶׁל תִּיפְלוּת. אָמַר רַבִּי אַבָּהוּ: מַאי טַעְמָא דְּרַבִּי יְהוּדָה? דִּכְתִיב: ״וַיַּחֲזֵק בִּבְגָדָיו וַיִּקְרָעֵם לִשְׁנַיִם קְרָעִים״. מִמַּשְׁמַע שֶׁנֶּאֱמַר ״וַיִּקְרָעֵם״ אֵינִי יוֹדֵעַ שֶׁהֵן לִשְׁנַיִם? אֶלָּא: שֶׁנִּרְאִין קְרוּעִים כִּשְׁנַיִם.

Rabbi Yehuda says: Any rending that does not rip apart his garment **on the hem** of the garment **is nothing other than a frivolous rent** of no significance, as it must be evident that one has rent his garment in mourning and that the rent is not merely an imperfection in the garment. **Rabbi Abbahu said: What is the reason** for **Rabbi Yehuda's** opinion? **As it is written: "And he took hold of his own clothes and he rent them in two pieces"** (II Kings 2:12). **From that which is stated: "And he rent," do I not know that** he rent them **in two? Rather,** these words teach **that** the rent clothes must **appear as if they were torn into two** pieces, i.e., the tear must be obvious and visible.

עַל כָּל הַמֵּתִים כּוּלָּן – שׁוֹלֵל לְאַחַר שִׁבְעָה, וּמְאַחֶה לְאַחַר שְׁלֹשִׁים. עַל אָבִיו וְעַל אִמּוֹ – שׁוֹלֵל לְאַחַר שְׁלֹשִׁים, וְאֵינוֹ מְאַחֶה לְעוֹלָם. וְהָאִשָּׁה שׁוֹלַלְתּוֹ לְאַלְתַּר, מִפְּנֵי כְּבוֹדָהּ.

The *baraita* continues: **With regard to all** other **deceased** relatives, **one may tack** the tear with rough stitches **after seven days, and one may join** the edges more carefully **after thirty** days. But **in** the case of **one's father or mother, he may tack** the tear only **after thirty days, and he may never** again **join** the edges more carefully. **A woman,** however, **may tack** the tear **immediately, due to her honor,** for it would be dishonorable for her to be seen with torn garments.[H]

כִּי אֲתָא רָבִין אָמַר רַבִּי יוֹחָנָן: עַל כָּל הַמֵּתִים, רָצָה – קוֹרֵעַ בַּיָּד, רָצָה – קוֹרֵעַ בִּכְלִי. עַל אָבִיו וְעַל אִמּוֹ – בַּיָּד.

When Ravin came from Eretz Yisrael to Babylonia, **he said that Rabbi Yoḥanan said: With regard to all** other **deceased** relatives, **if one wishes, he may rend** his garment **with his hand;** and if **he wishes, he may rend** it **with a utensil** in a way that will preserve it. But **in the case of his father or mother,** he must rend his garment **with his hand** in a manner that will utterly ruin it.[H]

NOTES

Undergarment – אַפִּיקַרְסוּתוֹ: According to the *ge'onim*, cited by the *Arukh* and the Ramban, this word refers to undergarments worn directly on one's skin, which are not important enough to have the same status as other clothes. Others explain this term as having the opposite meaning, i.e., it refers to an outer garment or a type of cloak that was worn only for honor, and therefore it was not considered to be an ordinary garment (Ra'avad; *Sefer HaMeorot*; Ritva; Meiri). There are also those who hold that this refers to a turban whose ends rests on the neck (Rashi, from manuscript; *Tosefot HaRosh*).

On the hem [*safa*] – קַמֵּי שָׂפָה: Some explain that the *safa* mentioned here is the opening of the garment around the neck, and the phrase: On the hem, means in front of it. In other words, according to this understanding one should not rend his garment from the neck, since he appears to be enlarging this opening. Instead, he should rend his garment near this opening, so that the rending will be more apparent (Rabbeinu Gershom Meor HaGola; Rashi). Others explain that the expression refers to the hem itself, which if not torn will leave the top of the tear closed. In that case, the tear will appear more like a hole and the garment will not look like it has been torn (Rid; *Talmid Rabbeinu Yeḥiel of Paris*; Ran).

LANGUAGE

Undergarment [*apikarsuto*] – אַפִּיקַרְסוּתוֹ: Apparently from the Greek ἐπικάρσιον, *epikarsiyon*, meaning a striped garment. The Sages generally use the word to refer to an undergarment.

HALAKHA

How does a woman rend her garment – כֵּיצַד קוֹרַעַת אִשָּׁה: A woman is required to rend all of her garments, in accordance with the opinion of Rabbi Shimon ben Elazar. However, these tears should not be one directly under the another in a manner that exposes her body. If a woman cannot turn some of her garments around, then she is not required to tear all of them (*Arukh HaShulḥan*; *Shulḥan Arukh, Yoreh De'a* 340:11).

Ripping apart on the hem – מַבְדִּיל קַמֵּי שָׂפָה: Some say that over deceased relatives one is not required to rip on the hem, in accordance with the opinion of the first *tanna*, and therefore one may leave the hem of the garment intact and tear only below it. However, for one's father or mother one is required to tear the edge of the garment. Others say that the *halakha* is in accordance with Rabbi Yehuda, and one must tear the hem of the garment for any relative (*Mordekhai*). This opinion is the basis for the common practice (*Shulḥan Arukh, Yoreh De'a* 340:12 and in the comment of Rema).

Sewing the tear – תְּפִירַת הַקֶּרַע: After the death of a man's mother or father, he may tack the tear rent in his garment only after thirty days, and he may never mend it. A woman may tack the tear immediately, due to her honor. For other deceased relatives, one may tack the tear with loose stitches after seven days, and he may mend it properly after thirty days. In some places, it is customary not to tack the tear within thirty days, even for rents torn for a relative other than a parent. In such a place, the ends of the tear may not be attached even with a safety pin (*Shulḥan Arukh, Yoreh De'a* 340:15, and in the comment of Rema).

Rending by hand or with a utensil – קְרִיעָה בַּיָּד אוֹ בִּכְלִי: Over deceased relatives, one may tear the garment by hand or with a utensil, but over one's father or mother one must tear the garment by hand (*Shulḥan Arukh, Yoreh De'a* 340:14).

וְאָמַר רַבִּי חִיָּיא בַּר אַבָּא אָמַר רַבִּי יוֹחָנָן: עַל כָּל הַמֵּתִים כּוּלָּן – מִבִּפְנִים; עַל אָבִיו וְעַל אִמּוֹ – קוֹרֵעַ מִבַּחוּץ. אָמַר רַב חִסְדָּא: וְכֵן לְנָשִׂיא.

And Rabbi Ḥiyya bar Abba said that Rabbi Yoḥanan said: **With regard to all** other **deceased** relatives, one rends his garment **on the inside,** meaning, he rends his inner garment and not necessarily his outermost garment. **In** the case of **one's father or mother,** however, **he must rend** the garment **on the outside,** i.e., the outermost garment.[NH] **Rav Ḥisda said: And likewise, over a** ***Nasi***, one is required to rend his garment as he does over his father.

מֵיתִיבִי: לֹא הוּשְׁווּ לְאָבִיו וּלְאִמּוֹ אֶלָּא לְאִיחוּי בִּלְבַד.

The Gemara **raises an objection** from a *baraita* in which it was taught: The *halakhot* of rending for the death of other people referred to in the *baraita,* e.g., a *Nasi*, a president of the court, or one's teacher, **were likened to** the *halakhot* of rending for **one's father or mother only with regard to** the issue of carefully **rejoining** the edges of the rent, as in all of these cases it is prohibited to mend one's garment with precise stitches.

מַאי לָאו – אֲפִילּוּ לְנָשִׂיא? לָא, לְבַר מִנָּשִׂיא.

What, is this *baraita* **not** also referring **even** to one who rends his garment **for the** ***Nasi***? The Gemara rejects this: **No,** the *baraita* is referring to the other people, **aside** from one who rends his garment for the *Nasi*, as rending for the *Nasi* is the same as rending for one's father with regard to all aspects of the rending.[H]

נְשִׂיאָה שְׁכֵיב. אֲמַר לֵיהּ רַב חִסְדָּא לְרַב חָנָן בַּר רָבָא: כְּפֵי אָסִיתָא וְקוּם עֲלַהּ, וְאַחְוֵי קְרִיעָה לְעָלְמָא.

It was related that the ***Nasi*** **died,** and **Rav Ḥisda said to Rav Ḥanan bar Rava: Turn the mortar over and stand on it, and show** the **rent to everyone.** Everyone will then rend his garment in this manner, as everyone is required to rend his garment over the death of the *Nasi*.

עַל חָכָם חוֹלֵץ מִיָּמִין; עַל אַב בֵּית דִּין מִשְּׂמֹאל; עַל נָשִׂיא – מִכָּאן וּמִכָּאן.

§ It was further taught: **For** mourning **a Sage, one removes** his garment **from the right** shoulder. **For the president of the court**[B] he removes his garment **from the left** shoulder. **For the** ***Nasi*** he removes his garment **from here and from here,** from both shoulders.[N]

תָּנוּ רַבָּנַן: חָכָם שֶׁמֵּת – בֵּית מִדְרָשׁוֹ בָּטֵל; אַב בֵּית דִּין שֶׁמֵּת – כָּל בָּתֵּי מִדְרָשׁוֹת שֶׁבְּעִירוֹ בְּטֵלִין, וְנִכְנָסִין לְבֵית הַכְּנֶסֶת, וּמְשַׁנִּין אֶת מְקוֹמָן: הַיּוֹשְׁבִין בַּצָּפוֹן – יוֹשְׁבִין בַּדָּרוֹם, הַיּוֹשְׁבִין בַּדָּרוֹם – יוֹשְׁבִין בַּצָּפוֹן. נָשִׂיא שֶׁמֵּת – בָּתֵּי מִדְרָשׁוֹת כּוּלָּן בְּטֵלִין, וּבְנֵי הַכְּנֶסֶת נִכְנָסִין לְבֵית הַכְּנֶסֶת,

The Sages taught the following *baraita*: When **a Sage dies, his study hall ceases** its regular study[N] as a sign of mourning over him. When **the president of the court dies, all of the study halls in his city cease** their regular study, and everyone **enters the synagogue and changes their places** there as a sign of mourning over him. **Those who** ordinarily **sit in the north** should **sit in the south, and those who** ordinarily **sit in the south** should **sit in the north.** When a ***Nasi*** **dies, all study halls cease** their regular study. On Shabbat, **the members of the synagogue enter the synagogue** for public Torah reading, which requires a congregation of ten,[H]

NOTES

On the inside and on the outside – מִבִּפְנִים וּמִבַּחוּץ: Some explain that the term outside in this context means in public, and the term inside means that one may rend his garment even inside his house (Rashi, from manuscript; Commentary on *Moed Katan*). Others explain that the term inside means under his other garments, and in this case one is not required to make the tear noticeable on the outside (Rabbeinu Gershom Meor HaGola; Rabbi Yitzḥak ibn Giat). Rabbeinu Yehonatan of Lunel, the Rambam, and the Meiri give both explanations for these terms.

Removal from the right and the left – חֲלִיצָה מִיָּמִין וּמִשְּׂמֹאל: Removing one's garment from the right shoulder does not appear to be a display of mourning, as sometimes a person will do so when carrying a load or performing another type of work. However, if one removes the left side of his garment, and even more so if he removes both sides, then it is clear that he is doing so as a sign of mourning (Rabbeinu Yehonatan of Lunel; *Talmid Rabbeinu Yeḥiel of Paris*).

His study hall ceases its regular study – בֵּית מִדְרָשׁוֹ בָּטֵל: The early authorities disagree as to whether this is done as a sign of mourning and is therefore practiced only for one day, like other acts of mourning for one's teacher (*Talmid Rabbeinu Yeḥiel of Paris*), or if it is done so that longer eulogies will be given and the public mourning will not be lessened in order to return to their studies. If the reason is the latter, the custom should apply for the entire seven-day mourning period, during which the deceased is spoken about and praised (Ramban; *Tosefot HaRosh*).

HALAKHA

Rending on the inside and on the outside – קְרִיעָה מִבִּפְנִים וּמִבַּחוּץ: Over deceased relatives, one may tear his garments in private. As the tear need not be visible to others, the inside of the garment may be torn. However, over one's father or mother, one must tear the garment in public. The tear should be on the outside of the garment, so that it will be visible to others (*Shulḥan Arukh, Yoreh De'a* 340:13).

Rending over the ***Nasi*** – קְרִיעָה עַל נָשִׂיא: One has the same obligations for one's father and for a *Nasi* with regard to removing one's garment from one's shoulder, having the tear visible to others, and mending the tear (*Shulḥan Arukh, Yoreh De'a* 340:17).

Mourning over the leaders of the generation – אֵבֶל עַל גְּדוֹלֵי הַדּוֹר: When a Sage dies, his study hall ceases its regular study, and he is spoken about and praised for seven days. Even after the eulogy, his students may not gather in the study hall. Instead, they study in pairs at home. However, other study halls are active, even during the time of these eulogies. When the president of the court dies, all the study halls in that city cease their regular study, and the members of these study halls change their seats in the synagogue. If the *Nasi* dies, then all the study halls in which he is eulogized cease their regular study. Even after the eulogies, they do not enter the study hall, but study in pairs at home. The residents of the city pray in the mourner's house; however, they come to the synagogue for Torah reading. Today, when there is no *Nasi* and no Sanhedrin, these mourning customs are not practiced (*Arukh HaShulḥan*; *Shulḥan Arukh, Yoreh De'a* 344:18).

BACKGROUND

A Sage [*Ḥakham*] and the president of the court – חָכָם וְאַב בֵּית דִּין: When used as a specific title, and not just as an ordinary honorific term, the word *ḥakham* can have either of two meanings. In certain cases, it refers to the rabbi of a city or of a specific synagogue. However, in the context of this Gemara, the term seems relate to the basic structure of the court, which replaced the Sanhedrin after the destruction of the Temple, and could therefore be translated as court officer.

The head of the court was the *Nasi*, who was a descendent of Hillel the Elder. In addition to being the head of the court, he was a political leader for the Jews in Eretz Yisrael and represented them to the foreign authorities. The *Nasi* could trace his lineage back to the Davidic line, and the position therefore represented the kingship of the house of David. Similarly, the Exilarch in Babylonia, who also descended from the Judean kings, was a reminder of the Davidic kingship, and the *halakhot* of mourning a *Nasi* applied to him as well. The honor shown to the *Nasi* was not only due to his Torah knowledge and his character traits, but also, to a large extent, because he represented independent Jewish rule.

The president of the court [*av beit din*] was considered to be second to the *Nasi* in terms of honor. His job was to actually head the central court. After the generation of Rabbi Yehuda HaNasi, the president of the court was also the head of the central study hall, and he was therefore the spiritual leader of that generation.

The *Ḥakham* mentioned in the Gemara refers to the third in command in the Sanhedrin. The *Ḥakham* was often one of the brightest scholars, but did not have the official position as the head of the study hall. The Gemara relates that these positions, and the honors associated with each one, were established during the time of Rabban Shimon ben Gamliel II, and, with slight modifications, they continued to exist for many generations.

וְקוֹרִין שִׁבְעָה וְיוֹצְאִין. רַבִּי יְהוֹשֻׁעַ בֶּן קׇרְחָה אוֹמֵר: לֹא שֶׁיֵּלְכוּ וִיטַיְּילוּ בַּשּׁוּק, אֶלָּא יוֹשְׁבִין וְדוֹמְמִין.

and seven people **read**[N] from the Torah. **And** then **they leave** and pray on their own. **Rabbi Yehoshua ben Korḥa says:** It is **not that they stroll** afterward **in the marketplace,** but **rather they sit** at home **in silent** mourning.

וְאֵין אוֹמְרִים שְׁמוּעָה וְאַגָּדָה בְּבֵית הָאֵבֶל. אָמְרוּ עָלָיו עַל רַבִּי חֲנַנְיָה בֶּן גַּמְלִיאֵל שֶׁהָיָה אוֹמֵר שְׁמוּעָה וְאַגָּדָה בְּבֵית הָאֵבֶל.

And furthermore, **one may not speak** about ***halakha***[N] **or *aggada* in a house of mourning,** as this is an activity that brings people joy.[H] **It was said of Rabbi Ḥananya ben Gamliel**[N] **that he would speak about *halakha* and *aggada* in a house of mourning.**

תָּנוּ רַבָּנַן: אָבֵל, שַׁבָּת רִאשׁוֹנָה – אֵינוֹ יוֹצֵא מִפֶּתַח בֵּיתוֹ; שְׁנִיָּה – יוֹצֵא וְאֵינוֹ יוֹשֵׁב בִּמְקוֹמוֹ; שְׁלִישִׁית – יוֹשֵׁב בִּמְקוֹמוֹ וְאֵינוֹ מְדַבֵּר; רְבִיעִית – הֲרֵי הוּא כְּכׇל אָדָם.

§ **The Sages taught** the following *baraita*: During the **first week** after his bereavement, **the mourner may not go out**[N] **of the opening of his house.**[N] During the **second** week, **he may go out, but he may not sit in his** usual **place**[N] in the synagogue. During the **third week, he may sit in his** usual **place but he may not speak.** During the **fourth** week, **he is like any** other **person.**[H]

רַבִּי יְהוּדָה אוֹמֵר: לֹא הוּצְרְכוּ לוֹמַר שַׁבָּת רִאשׁוֹנָה לֹא יֵצֵא מִפֶּתַח בֵּיתוֹ – שֶׁהֲרֵי הַכֹּל נִכְנָסִין לְבֵיתוֹ לְנַחֲמוֹ. אֶלָּא: שְׁנִיָּה – אֵינוֹ יוֹצֵא מִפֶּתַח בֵּיתוֹ; שְׁלִישִׁית – יוֹצֵא וְאֵינוֹ יוֹשֵׁב בִּמְקוֹמוֹ; רְבִיעִית – יוֹשֵׁב בִּמְקוֹמוֹ וְאֵינוֹ מְדַבֵּר; חֲמִישִׁית – הֲרֵי הוּא כְּכׇל אָדָם.

Rabbi Yehuda says: They did not need to say that **during the first week** the mourner **may not go out of the opening of his house.** This teaches us nothing new, **as** at that time **everyone goes into his house to console him. Rather,** during the **second** week, he may **not go out of the opening of his house.** During the **third** week, **he may go out, but he may not sit in his** usual **place** in the synagogue. During the **fourth** week, **he may sit in his** usual **place, but he may not speak.** During the **fifth** week, **he is like any** other **person.**

NOTES

And seven read – וְקוֹרִין שִׁבְעָה: Some write that they would each pray alone at home (Rabbeinu Gershom Meor HaGola, Rashi; *Talmid Rabbeinu Yeḥiel of Paris*; Commentary on *Moed Katan*). Others say that they would pray in the mourner's house, but they would go to read the Torah in the synagogue (Ritva; see *Divrei David*).

One may not speak about *halakha* – אֵין אוֹמְרִים שְׁמוּעָה: This refers to the weekdays during the mourning period. However, many understand that *halakha* should not be discussed even on Shabbat. The Ran explains that the reason is that if people become engaged in Torah study they may forget about their mourning. A similar explanation is offered by the Ramban and Rabbeinu Yehonatan of Lunel. The Ritva mentions an explanation based on tractate *Semaḥot*, according to which this statement is a continuation of what was stated above with regard to the death of a *Nasi*.

Rabbi Ḥananya ben Gamliel, etc. – רַבִּי חֲנַנְיָה בֶּן גַּמְלִיאֵל וכו׳: It appears that this applies specifically to Shabbat, and Rabbi Ḥanina's practice was in accordance with the opinion that mourning does not apply on Shabbat at all (Jerusalem Talmud). This is discussed in 23b as well.

During the first week [*shabbat*] the mourner may not go out, etc. – אָבֵל, שַׁבָּת רִאשׁוֹנָה אֵינוֹ יוֹצֵא וכו׳: Some explain that in this context the word *shabbat* means week (Rashi; *Talmid Rabbeinu Yeḥiel of Paris*). However, others say that the word *shabbat* here refers to Shabbat itself, and during the other days of the week a mourner may leave his house if he needs to do so (Rabbeinu Yehonatan of Lunel; Ra'avad; Ran).

May not go out of the opening of his house – אֵינוֹ יוֹצֵא מִפֶּתַח בֵּיתוֹ: With regard to this issue, there are different customs for the residents of Babylonia and Eretz Yisrael. In Babylonia, it was the practice for the mourners to go to the synagogue every day. However, in Eretz Yisrael the custom was for mourners not to attend synagogue but to host a prayer group in their home. This is the common practice today (see Meiri).

He may not sit in his place – אֵינוֹ יוֹשֵׁב בִּמְקוֹמוֹ: This *halakha* applies in any place with assigned seats, e.g., the synagogue and the study hall (*Talmid Rabbeinu Yeḥiel of Paris*).

HALAKHA

One may not speak about *halakha* – אֵין אוֹמְרִים שְׁמוּעָה וכו׳: One may not speak about *halakha* or *aggada* in the house of a mourner (*Shulḥan Arukh, Yoreh De'a* 378:7).

First and second week, etc. – שָׁבוּעַ רִאשׁוֹן וְשֵׁנִי וכו׳: During the first week of mourning, a mourner may not leave his house, even to attend a wedding or circumcision ceremony. Some are lenient and permit him to go out at night if there is a reasonable need to do so. The prohibition against leaving the house applies only to one who goes to stroll or to engage in business. However, one who goes at the order of the ruler or in other cases of great need is permitted to leave, and this is the common practice (Rema).

During the second week, the mourner may leave his house. However, he may neither sit in his ordinary seat nor may he speak. During the third week he may sit in his regular seat, but may not speak. Alternatively, he may choose not to sit in his regular seat and is then permitted to speak. It is the accepted practice that a mourner does not sit in his ordinary seat for the entirety of the thirty-day period of mourning over a relative; when mourning one's father or mother this practice lasts for twelve months. Although this custom has no basis in the Gemara, it is not proper to deviate from the local custom (Rema). During the fourth week, the mourner is like everyone else.

For the purposes of these *halakhot*, the weeks are not counted from the beginning of the mourning, but rather from the beginning of the week, e.g., the Sunday after the third week ends is counted as the beginning of the fourth week (*Shulḥan Arukh, Yoreh De'a* 393:2).

תָּנוּ רַבָּנַן: כׇּל שְׁלֹשִׁים יוֹם לְנִישּׂוּאִין. מֵתָה אִשְׁתּוֹ – אָסוּר לִישָּׂא אִשָּׁה אַחֶרֶת, עַד שֶׁיַּעַבְרוּ עָלָיו שְׁלֹשָׁה רְגָלִים. רַבִּי יְהוּדָה אוֹמֵר: רֶגֶל רִאשׁוֹן וְשֵׁנִי – אָסוּר, שְׁלִישִׁי – מוּתָּר.

§ **The Sages taught** another *baraita*: During **the entire thirty-day** period of mourning, it is prohibited **to marry.**[H] **If one's wife died, it is prohibited to marry another wife until three Festivals pass**[N] since her death.[H] **Rabbi Yehuda says:** Until the **first and second** Festivals have passed, **he is prohibited** from marrying; before the **third** Festival, however, he is **permitted** to do so.

וְאִם אֵין לוֹ בָּנִים – מוּתָּר לִישָּׂא לְאַלְתַּר, מִשּׁוּם בִּיטּוּל פְּרִיָּה וּרְבִיָּה. הִנִּיחָה לוֹ בָּנִים קְטַנִּים – מוּתָּר לִישָּׂא לְאַלְתַּר, מִפְּנֵי פַּרְנָסָתָן.

And if he does not have children, he is permitted to marry another wife **immediately due to** the need to not **neglect** the mitzva to **be fruitful and multiply.** Since he has not yet fulfilled the mitzva of procreation, he is still required to marry a wife. Any delay might result in a lost opportunity for marriage. Similarly, if his wife died and **left him young children, he is permitted to marry** another wife **immediately, so that** she might **take care of them.**

מַעֲשֶׂה שֶׁמֵּתָה אִשְׁתּוֹ שֶׁל יוֹסֵף הַכֹּהֵן, וְאָמַר לַאֲחוֹתָהּ בְּבֵית הַקְּבָרוֹת: לְכִי וּפַרְנְסִי אֶת בְּנֵי אֲחוֹתֵךְ. וְאַף עַל פִּי כֵן לֹא בָּא עָלֶיהָ אֶלָּא לִזְמַן מְרוּבֶּה. מַאי לִזְמַן מְרוּבֶּה? אָמַר רַב פָּפָּא: לְאַחַר שְׁלֹשִׁים יוֹם.

There was **an incident when the wife of Yosef the Priest died, and he said to her sister at the cemetery** immediately after the funeral: **Go and care for your sister's children.** In other words, he alluded that he wished to marry her immediately. **But even though** he married her immediately, **he did not engage in sexual relations with her for a long time** afterward. The Gemara asks: **What** is the meaning of the term: **A long time? Rav Pappa said: After thirty days.**

תָּנוּ רַבָּנַן: כׇּל שְׁלֹשִׁים יוֹם לְגִיהוּץ, אֶחָד כֵּלִים חֲדָשִׁים וְאֶחָד כֵּלִים יְשָׁנִים יוֹצְאִין מִתּוֹךְ הַמַּכְבֵּשׁ. רַבִּי אוֹמֵר: לֹא אָסְרוּ אֶלָּא כֵּלִים חֲדָשִׁים בִּלְבַד. רַבִּי אֶלְעָזָר בְּרַבִּי שִׁמְעוֹן אוֹמֵר: לֹא אָסְרוּ אֶלָּא כֵּלִים חֲדָשִׁים לְבָנִים בִּלְבַד.

§ **The Sages taught** yet another *baraita*: During **the entire thirty-day** period of mourning, it is prohibited **to wear ironed**[B] garments, **whether they are new garments or old garments taken out of the press,**[HB] as ironed garments appear to be new. **Rabbi** Yehuda HaNasi disagrees and **says:** The Sages **prohibited** wearing **only new garments. Rabbi Elazar, son of Rabbi Shimon, says: They prohibited** wearing **only new white garments.**

NOTES

It is prohibited to marry…until three Festivals pass – אָסוּר לִישָּׂא...עַד שֶׁיַּעַבְרוּ עָלָיו שְׁלֹשָׁה רְגָלִים: Several reasons for this decree are mentioned by *Tosafot*: This decree is either so that the mourner will not forget his first wife or so that when he is with his new wife he will not still be thinking about his previous wife. Rabbeinu Yehonatan of Lunel and the Ramban explain similarly.

It is also suggested that the mourner must wait this amount of time so that he will not constantly tell his new wife about his previous wife's actions. Some explain that since the Sages said that one's wife dies over unfulfilled vows, the mourning period lasts for three Festivals in order to correspond to vows, which remain in effect for the same amount of time (see Ramban).

Others explain that the mourner will forget his previous wife due to the joy of the three Festivals. This is the basis for those who say that these three Festivals do not refer specifically to the pilgrimage Festivals, but to any days that interrupt the mourning.

The early authorities write that this *halakha* applies specifically to a man. When a woman's husband dies, she is not required to wait for three Festivals to pass before she remarries. Several explanations are offered for this difference. Some explain that it is the ordinary way of the world for a man to pursue a woman and not the opposite. Therefore, when a woman finds someone who wishes to marry her, it is preferable not to delay the marriage, since she does not know when her next opportunity will arise (Rabbeinu Yehonatan of Lunel; see *Shakh* on *Yoreh De'a* 392:2).

BACKGROUND

Ironing – גִּיהוּץ: The origin of this word is unclear, and it has been compared to similar words in other languages, yet no exact match has been found. There are different opinions as to exactly which activity this is. It is clear that it involved taking a worn, dirty garment and making it look as though it were new. This includes laundering the garment with specific substances, e.g., soap, laundering soda, or the like, and pressing it flat with a stone or piece of metal.

Press – מַכְבֵּשׁ:

Fresco of a laundry press from Pompeii during the time of the Mishna

HALAKHA

Marriage of a mourner – נִישּׂוּאִין שֶׁל אָבֵל: It is prohibited for a mourner to remarry during the thirty-day mourning period. After thirty days, he may marry and have a wedding feast, even if he is mourning for his father or mother. Some say that one may even betroth a woman on the day of the death itself, as long as he does not prepare a feast. However, others say that a mourner may not betroth a woman within thirty days, and this is the accepted opinion (Rema, citing Rosh and Ramban). It is permitted to arrange a marriage within thirty days (*Shakh*; *Baḥ*; *Shulḥan Arukh*, *Yoreh De'a* 392:1).

Marriage after his wife's death – נִישּׂוּאִין לְאַחַר מוֹת אִשְׁתּוֹ: If a man's wife dies then he is not permitted to remarry until three Festivals have passed; the Eighth Day of Assembly is considered to be its own Festival in this regard (*Dagul Merevava*). Similarly, some say that Rosh HaShana and Yom Kippur are also considered to be Festivals for this purpose (*Taz*), however others disagree (*Arukh HaShulḥan*).

If one has not yet fulfilled the mitzva to procreate, or if he has young children, or if he needs someone to care for him, then he may betroth a woman immediately and marry her after seven days. However, some say that betrothing is also prohibited until the initial seven days of mourning have passed (*Shakh*). In such a case, he should not engage in sexual relations with his second wife until the thirty-day period of mourning has concluded, unless he has not fulfilled the mitzva of procreation.

Some say that even if one is wealthy and can hire many servants, he may marry before the established time if he is lonely without a wife. It is then considered as if he has no one to care for him. This is the basis for the common practice for people to remarry before the established time. However, one who is able to wait should be strict with himself (Rema).

A woman whose husband dies is not required to wait for three Festivals. Instead, with regard to the laws of mourning, she is permitted to marry even within thirty days. However, she is required to wait three months in case she is pregnant, in order to determine the father of the child (*Shakh*, citing the Rif; *Shulḥan Arukh*, *Yoreh De'a* 392:2).

Ironed garment – בֶּגֶד מְגוּהָץ: For thirty days, a mourner is prohibited from wearing or spreading underneath himself a white, new, ironed garment, even if it is made of linen. This ruling is in accordance with the opinion of Rabbi Elazar, son of Rabbi Shimon (*Shulḥan Arukh*, *Yoreh De'a* 389:5).

אַבַּיֵי נָפֵיק בְּגַרְדָּא דִּסַרְבָּלָא, כְּרַבִּי. רָבָא נָפֵיק בְּחִימוּצְתָּא רוֹמִיתָא סוּמָקְתָּא חַדְתִּי, כְּרַבִּי אֶלְעָזָר בְּרַבִּי שִׁמְעוֹן.

The Gemara relates that **Abaye went out** while he was in mourning **in an old white garment, in accordance with** the opinion of **Rabbi** Yehuda HaNasi. **Rava,** on the other hand, **went out in a new, red Roman cloak,**[NL] as he acted **in accordance with** the opinion of **Rabbi Elazar, son of Rabbi Shimon.**

״מִפְּנֵי שֶׁאָמְרוּ שַׁבָּת עוֹלָה וְאֵינָהּ מַפְסֶקֶת״. בְּנֵי יְהוּדָה וּבְנֵי גְּלִילָא – הָנֵי אָמְרִי:

It was taught in the mishna: This is **because** the Sages **said** that **Shabbat counts** as one of the days of mourning, **but it does not interrupt** the mourning period, which continues after Shabbat. It is stated that with regard to mourning on Shabbat, there is a difference in practice between **the residents of Judea and the residents of the Galilee.**[B] **These say:**

NOTES

Cloak – חִימוּצְתָּא: Some explain that this refers to a type of shirt (Rashi; *Talmid Rabbeinu Yeḥiel of Paris*). Others claim that it is a garment made of silk or another similar material (Rabbi Shlomo ben HaYatom).

BACKGROUND

The residents of Judea and the residents of the Galilee – בְּנֵי יְהוּדָה וּבְנֵי גְּלִילָא: In the times when the Jewish community was well established in Eretz Yisrael, it was divided into three parts: Judea, the Galilee, and the East Bank of the Jordan, each of which had its own geography, climate, and traditions.

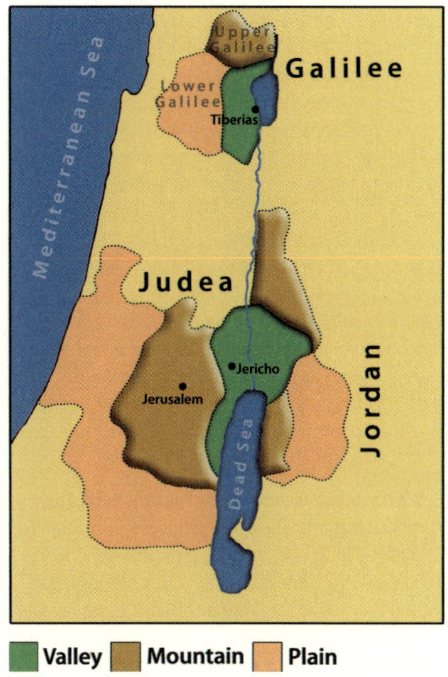

Map of the three regions of Eretz Yisrael

LANGUAGE

Cloak [*ḥimutzeta*] – חִימוּצְתָּא: This word appears to be Semitic and is similar to the Arabic خميصة, *ḫamīṣa*, a type of robe that is decorated around the edges.

Perek **III**
Daf **23** Amud **b**

יֵשׁ אֲבֵילוּת בְּשַׁבָּת, וְהָנֵי אָמְרִי: אֵין אֲבֵילוּת בְּשַׁבָּת.

There is some **mourning on Shabbat,** i.e., with regard to mourning rites that can be observed privately in the mourner's home and will go unnoticed by other people; **whereas those say: There is no mourning on Shabbat**[N] at all.

מַאן דְּאָמַר יֵשׁ אֲבֵילוּת בְּשַׁבָּת – דְּקָתָנֵי: עוֹלָה. מַאן דְּאָמַר אֵין אֲבֵילוּת בְּשַׁבָּת – דְּקָתָנֵי: אֵינָהּ מַפְסֶקֶת.

The Gemara explains: **The ones who said** that **there is** some **mourning on Shabbat** rely on **that** which is **taught,** that Shabbat **counts** as one of the days of mourning, implying that some degree of mourning applies on that day. **The ones who said** that **there is no mourning on Shabbat** at all base this on **that** which is **taught** that Shabbat **does not interrupt** the mourning period.

NOTES

Mourning on Shabbat – אֲבֵילוּת בְּשַׁבָּת: The early authorities disagree about the meaning of the expression: There is mourning on Shabbat. There are those who say that this means that all of the *halakhot* of mourning, in their entirety, apply on Shabbat as they do during weekdays (Ramban). The Ra'avad holds that the customs of mourning do not obligate one to mourn Shabbat. Some hold that mourning is voluntary on Shabbat, while others have a custom that mourning is prohibited.

However, most of the early authorities hold that the disagreement in the Gemara is only whether mourning applies to what is done in private on Shabbat (*Tosafot*; Ritva). With regard to the source of this *halakha*, some early authorities write that on a Festival there is a mitzva to be joyous, but on Shabbat the mitzva is to delight, which is of lesser intensity (see *She'iltot*). Therefore, it is possible for the mourner to mourn in his heart while still delighting in Shabbat. Alternatively, it is stated in the Jerusalem Talmud, with regard to the verse: "The blessing of the Lord makes rich, and toil [*etzev*] adds nothing to it," (Proverbs 10:22) that "the blessing of the Lord" is Shabbat, which God blessed when He created the world. "And toil [*etzev*] adds nothing to it," means that one does not makes one's self sad [*lehitatzev*] on Shabbat at all.

אי סלקא דעתך יש אבילות בשבת – השתא אבילות נהגא, אפסוקי מיבעיא?

The latter argue as follows: **If it should enter your mind** to say that **there is** some **mourning on Shabbat,** there is a difficulty, for **now** that it has been stated that actual **mourning applies** on Shabbat, **is** it **necessary** to teach us that this day does not **interrupt** the mourning period? Rather, the conclusion must be that there is no mourning on Shabbat whatsoever.

ואלא הא קתני עולה! איידי דקבעי למיתנא סיפא אינן עולים, תנא רישא עולה.

The Gemara asks: **But isn't it taught** in the mishna that Shabbat **counts**[N] as one of the days of mourning, implying that it is just like the other days of mourning, and at least some mourning rites are practiced on it? The Gemara answers: **Since** the mishna **wished to teach** in **the latter clause** that the days of a Festival **do not count** toward the requisite days of mourning, **it taught** also **in the first clause** that Shabbat **counts** as one of the days of mourning, although no mourning rites are practiced on it.

ולמאן דאמר יש אבילות בשבת, הא קתני אינה מפסקת! משום דקבעי למיתנא סיפא מפסיקין – תנא רישא אינה מפסקת.

The Gemara asks: **And according to the ones who said** that **there is** some **mourning on Shabbat, isn't it** taught in the mishna that **it does not interrupt** the mourning period, which would have been unnecessary to say if the mourning rites are practiced on it? The Gemara answers: This was not necessary for itself, but **due to** the fact that the since the mishna **wished to teach** in **the latter clause** that the Festivals **interrupt** the mourning, **it taught** also **in the first clause** that Shabbat **does not interrupt** it.

לימא כתנאי: מי שמתו מוטל לפניו – אוכל בבית אחר. אין לו בית אחר – אוכל בבית חברו. אין לו בית חברו – עושה לו מחיצה עשרה טפחים. אין לו דבר לעשות מחיצה – מחזיר פניו ואוכל.

The Gemara asks: **Let us say** that this is **parallel to** a dispute between ***tanna'im*** with regard to whether or not some mourning rites are observed even on Shabbat, for it was taught in a *baraita*: **One whose deceased** relative **is laid out before him**[NH] **eats in another room. If he does not have another room, he eats in the house of a friend. If he does not have a friend's house** available, **he makes a partition ten handbreadths** high between him and the deceased, so that he may eat. If **he does not have material with which to make a partition, he averts his face** from the dead **and eats.**

ואינו מיסב ואוכל, ואינו אוכל בשר, ואינו שותה יין, ואין מברך, ואין מזמן, ואין מברכין עליו, ואין מזמנין עליו, ופטור מקריאת שמע, ומן התפלה, ומן התפילין, ומכל מצות האמורות בתורה.

And in any case, **he does not recline while he eats,** as reclining is characteristic of a festive meal; **and he neither eats meat**[N] **nor drinks wine; and he does not recite a blessing**[N] before eating to exempt others from their obligation; **and he does not** recite the formula to **invite** the participants in the meal to join together in the Grace after Meals, **and they do not recite a blessing over him**[N] **nor do others invite him** to join in the Grace after Meals, as he cannot be a member of the three required to recite the formula. **And he is exempt from the recitation of *Shema*,**[N] **and from** the *Amida* **prayer, and from** donning **phylacteries, and from** performing **all of the mitzvot mentioned in the Torah.**

HALAKHA

One whose deceased relative is laid out before him – מי שמתו מוטל לפניו: If one's relative has died but has not yet been buried, then he is referred to as an acute mourner. During this time he may not eat in the same room as the body. Instead, he must eat in a different room. If he does not have another room, he should eat in the house of a friend. If he does not have a friend with a house, then he should make a partition, even out of a sheet, and then he may eat. If he has nothing with which to make a partition, he should avert his face, and then he may eat.

Until the deceased is buried, an acute mourner may not recline and eat, he may not eat meat, and he may not drink wine. He does not recite the blessing before eating bread. Other people may not recite a blessing on his behalf or invite him to join them in Grace after Meals, and he is exempt from all the mitzvot stated in the Torah. This is the case even if the acute mourner is not required to make preparations for the burial, and even when he is in a different city from the deceased. However, if there is a group of people in that city who are responsible for the burial of the dead and the preparations for burial, known today as the *ḥevra kadisha*, then once he gives over the body to them he immediately becomes obligated in all mitzvot (*Peri Megadim*; *Ḥokhmat Adam*; *Sha'arei Teshuva*; *Derekh HaḤayyim*; *Mishna Berura*).

One who is an acute mourner on Shabbat or a Festival may eat meat or drink wine if he wishes (Rema). Similarly, on Shabbat he recites blessings, is obligated in all the mitzvot, and goes to pray in the synagogue. However, he may not engage in sexual relations. If he sets out on Shabbat to walk to the city limit, so that he can prepare for the burial immediately once Shabbat ends, then the prohibitions pertaining to acute mourning apply to him immediately, even though Shabbat has not yet ended. Similarly, if he wishes to hire gentile workers to perform the burial on the first day of a Festival, and all the more so on the second day of the Festival in the Diaspora, then all the *halakhot* of acute mourning apply to him. Some say that if a rabbi dies and has not yet been buried, his student is prohibited to eat meat or to drink wine on weekdays (*Shulḥan Arukh*, *Yoreh De'a* 341:1, and in the comment of Rema).

NOTES

But isn't it taught that Shabbat counts [*ola*] – ואלא הא קתני עולה: The proofs brought in this discussion, which are based on close readings of the language of the mishna, are not entirely clear. The early authorities attempt to explain them in several different ways (see *Tosafot*) but many of them have difficulty explaining this sentence. The Rid goes so far as to say that the sentence is an error and should be erased from the text. This also appears to be the opinion of the Ra'avad.

However, there are those who explain that the word *ola*, counted, has two different meanings. It either means that Shabbat is counted as one of the days of mourning, and all the *halakhot* of mourning apply on it, or it means that Shabbat is counted in the mourning period, even though mourning is not practiced on it. Based on this distinction, it would have been more correct to state explicitly that it counts toward the number [*ola min haminyan*]. However, since the expression: Do not count [*ainam olim*], is used in the end of the mishna, the *tanna* did not wish to alter the style. This is the opinion of *Talmid Rabbeinu Yeḥiel of Paris*, and a similar statement is made in *Tosefot HaRosh* in the name of Rabbeinu Tam.

One whose deceased relative is laid out before him – מי שמתו מוטל לפניו: There are two types of mourning recognized by *halakha*: One type is known as acute mourning, which applies from the time of death until the burial. It appears that the *halakhot* of acute mourning are meant to enable the mourner to properly prepare for and organize the burial. Since it is a mitzva to arrange the burial, the mourner is exempt from all other mitzvot. Alternatively, the rationale for the acute mourner's exemption from mitzvot is that it is not appropriate for the relatives to continue their lives in an ordinary manner before the deceased has been buried. These two reasons are discussed explicitly in the Jerusalem Talmud. The second type of mourning is the ordinary period of mourning that begins once the deceased has been buried, and it includes all the ways that the mourner expresses pain over his deceased relative.

And he neither eats meat, etc. – ואינו אוכל בשר וכו׳: The Ran writes that the food restrictions are so that he will not get carried away with his eating and delay the burial. Since the *halakhot* of mourning do not yet apply to him, the prohibition against eating meat is not a sign of mourning.

And he does not recite a blessing – ואין מברך: Some say that this statement means that the acute mourner should not recite a blessing before eating his food because he is exempt from performing mitzvot (Rashi, from manuscript; Rashi on tractate *Berakhot*; Ran). Others write that the mourner is required to recite a blessing before eating, as it is not appropriate for him to benefit from the world without doing so (*Kolbo*). Instead, this phrase in the *baraita* means that he may not recite a blessing on behalf of others (Rabbeinu Gershom Meor HaGola; Rashi). Others claim that it refers specifically to the Grace after Meals, which he does not recite (*Talmid Rabbeinu Yeḥiel of Paris*).

And they do not recite a blessing over him – ואין מברכין עליו: *Tosefot HaRosh* explain that no blessing may be recited on his behalf, for not only should he not recite a blessing, but others should not even fulfill his obligation for him.

And he is exempt from the recitation of *Shema* – ופטור מקריאת שמע: In the Jerusalem Talmud, in tractate *Berakhot*, an allusion is offered for this based on the verse: "So that you remember the day you left Egypt all the days of your life" (Deuteronomy 16:3). This means that you are obligated to remember the Exodus and recite *Shema* only on days during which you are involved in life, and not when you are occupied with the dead.

וּבְשַׁבָּת – מֵסֵב וְאוֹכֵל, וְאוֹכֵל בָּשָׂר, וְשׁוֹתֶה יַיִן, וּמְבָרֵךְ, וּמְזַמֵּן, וּמְבָרְכִין וּמְזַמְּנִין עָלָיו, וְחַיָּיב בִּקְרִיאַת שְׁמַע וּבִתְפִילָּה וּבִתְפִילִּין וּבְכָל מִצְוֹת הָאֲמוּרוֹת בַּתּוֹרָה. רַבָּן גַּמְלִיאֵל אוֹמֵר: מִתּוֹךְ שֶׁנִּתְחַיֵּיב בְּאֵלּוּ – נִתְחַיֵּיב בְּכוּלָּן.

But on Shabbat **he reclines** at the meal, as per his custom, **and eats; and he eats meat and drinks wine; and he recites blessings** to exempt others from their obligation; **and** he recites the formula to **invite** the participants in the meal to join together in the Grace after Meals, **and others may recite blessings on his behalf and invite** him to join in the Grace after Meals. **And he is** also **obligated in the recitation of *Shema*, and in** the *Amida* **prayer, and in** the mitzva of **phylacteries,**[N] **and in all the mitzvot mentioned in the Torah. Rabban Gamliel says: Since he is obligated** to fulfill **these** mitzvot associated with Shabbat, **he is obligated** to fulfill **all**[N] of the mitzvot on Shabbat.

וְאָמַר רַבִּי יוֹחָנָן: תַּשְׁמִישׁ הַמִּטָּה אִיכָּא בֵּינַיְיהוּ.

Rabban Gamliel's statement is vague. The following clarifies it: **Rabbi Yoḥanan said:** The practical difference **between them,** the opinion of the anonymous first *tanna* and Rabbi Yoḥanan's opinion, is with regard to **sexual relations.** According to Rabban Gamliel, the acute mourner is obligated in the mitzva to engage in marital intercourse with his wife on Shabbat, just as he is obligated in all the other mitzvot.

מַאי לָאו בְּהָא קָא מִיפַּלְגִי; דְּמָר סָבַר: יֵשׁ אֲבֵילוּת בְּשַׁבָּת, וּמָר סָבַר: אֵין אֲבֵילוּת בְּשַׁבָּת.

The Gemara asks: **What, is it not with regard to this** issue that **they disagree:**[N] Is it not **that** one **Sage,** the anonymous first *tanna,* **holds** that **there is** some **mourning on Shabbat** with regard to private issues, and therefore the mourner does not engage in sexual relations; **and** one **Sage,** Rabban Gamliel, **holds** that **there is no mourning on Shabbat** at all?

מִמַּאי? דִּלְמָא עַד כָּאן לָא קָאָמַר תַּנָּא קַמָּא הָתָם – אֶלָּא מִשּׁוּם דְּמֵתוֹ מוּטָל לְפָנָיו, אֲבָל הָכָא דְּאֵין מֵתוֹ מוּטָל לְפָנָיו – לָא.

The Gemara rejects this argument: **From where** do you reach this conclusion? **Perhaps the first *tanna*** is **saying** that it is prohibited for the grieving relative to engage in sexual relations in the case dealt with **only there, because his deceased** relative **is laid out before him** and has not yet been buried. **But here,** with regard to the period of mourning, when **his dead** has been buried and **is no** longer **laid out before him,** sexual relations are **not** prohibited.

וְעַד כָּאן לָא קָאָמַר רַבָּן גַּמְלִיאֵל הָתָם – דְּאַכַּתִּי לָא חָל אֲבֵילוּת עֲלֵיהּ, אֲבָל הָכָא דְּחָל אֲבֵילוּת עֲלֵיהּ – הָכִי נַמִי.

And alternatively, perhaps **Rabban Gamliel is saying** that the grieving relative is permitted to engage in sexual relations **only there, where** the *halakhot* of **mourning have not** yet **taken effect,** as mourning begins only after the burial. **But here, where** the *halakhot* of **mourning** have already **taken effect,** he may **also** prohibit sexual relations.

Perek **III**
Daf **24** Amud **a**

בְּעָא מִינֵּיהּ רַבִּי יוֹחָנָן מִשְּׁמוּאֵל: יֵשׁ אֲבֵילוּת בְּשַׁבָּת אוֹ אֵין אֲבֵילוּת בְּשַׁבָּת? אֲמַר לֵיהּ: אֵין אֲבֵילוּת בְּשַׁבָּת.

Rabbi Yoḥanan asked of Shmuel: Is there some **mourning** on **Shabbat or is there no mourning on Shabbat** at all?[H] **He said to him: There is no mourning on Shabbat** at all.

NOTES

And he is obligated in phylacteries – וְחַיָּיב בִּתְפִילִּין: The early authorities ask how one can be obligated to wear phylacteries on Shabbat when phylacteries are not worn by anyone on Shabbat. Because of this difficulty, some explain that this expression should be erased (Rashi, from manuscript). Others say that this obligation is mentioned only here because the *baraita* is speaking in general terms. Yet others say that it teaches the *halakha* for the intermediate days of a Festival (*Talmid Rabbeinu Yeḥiel of Paris*; *Magen Avraham*). Alternatively, this statement may be in accordance with the opinion of those *tanna'im* who hold that phylacteries may be worn on Shabbat and Festivals.

He is obligated to fulfill all – נִתְחַיֵּיב בְּכוּלָּן: The early authorities explain that this expression does not describe a true obligation. Instead, this expression in this context means that performing mitzvot on Shabbat is permitted (*Talmid Rabbeinu Yeḥiel of Paris*). However, there are those who say that even the first *tanna* does not believe that any of these actions are prohibited. They explain that, according to the first *tanna*, these activities are permitted, and according to Rabban Gamliel there is an obligation to perform them (Rabbi Zeraḥya HaLevi).

What, is it not with regard to this issue that they disagree – מַאי לָאו בְּהָא קָא מִיפַּלְגִי: This question is based on the assumption that the *halakha* of acute mourning is included within the *halakhot* of ordinary mourning, and everything stated with regard to ordinary mourning applies also to acute mourning. The Gemara rejects this comparison and states that these are two separate concepts. One cannot derive the halakhot of one from other, neither to be lenient nor to be stringent (Ritva).

HALAKHA

Mourning on Shabbat – אֲבֵילוּת בְּשַׁבָּת: On Shabbat, the restrictions of mourning apply in private. This is the opinion of Rabbi Yoḥanan, and the *halakha* is in accordance with him, even when he argues against Rav and Shmuel. This is also the *halakha* according to a similar discussion in tractate *Ketubot*.

Therefore, a mourner is prohibited from engaging in sexual relations or bathe even on Shabbat. However, he may not show any public signs of mourning, and therefore he may not wrap his head in mourning like the Ishmaelites (Rema). He wears shoes, sets his bed upright, and does not wear a torn garment. If he has no other garment, then he should reverse the garment so that the tear is in the back.

Torah study is prohibited, as it is considered a private matter. However, he may read the Torah portion twice and its translation once, as this type of study is considered to be similar to the recitation of the *Shema*. If the mourner is called to the Torah, he should go up to the Torah, for not going is a public display of mourning. Similarly, one who is called to the Torah every week or a priest in a synagogue where there are no other priests may also read from the Torah (*Shulḥan Arukh*, *Yoreh De'a* 400:1, and in the comment of Rema).

יָתְבִי רַבָּנַן קַמֵּיהּ דְּרַב פָּפָּא וְקָאָמְרִי מִשְּׁמֵיהּ דִּשְׁמוּאֵל: אָבֵל שֶׁשִּׁימֵּשׁ מִטָּתוֹ בִּימֵי אֶבְלוֹ – חַיָּיב מִיתָה. אֲמַר לֵיהּ רַב פָּפָּא: אָסוּר אִתְּמַר, וּמִשְּׁמֵיהּ דְּרַבִּי יוֹחָנָן אִתְּמַר.

The Sages sat before Rav Pappa and said in the name of Shmuel: A mourner who engaged in sexual relations during his days of mourning is liable to receive **the death penalty**[N] at the hand of Heaven. **Rav Pappa said to them: It was said** that sexual relations are **prohibited,** but not that the offender is guilty of a capital crime. **And** the ruling **was said in the name of Rabbi Yoḥanan,** and not in the name of Shmuel.

וְאִי שְׁמִיעָא לְכוּ מִשְּׁמֵיהּ דִּשְׁמוּאֵל – הָכִי שְׁמִיעַ לְכוּ: אָמַר רַב תַּחְלִיפָא בַּר אֲבִימִי אָמַר שְׁמוּאֵל: אָבֵל שֶׁלֹּא פָּרַע וְשֶׁלֹּא פֵּירֵם – חַיָּיב מִיתָה, שֶׁנֶּאֱמַר: ״רָאשֵׁיכֶם אַל תִּפְרָעוּ וּבִגְדֵיכֶם לֹא תִפְרוֹמוּ וְלֹא תָמוּתוּ״ וגו׳, הָא אַחֵר שֶׁלֹּא פָּרַע וְשֶׁלֹּא פֵּירֵם – חַיָּיב מִיתָה.

And if you heard a statement on this issue **in the name of Shmuel,** then **you heard as follows: Rav Taḥlifa bar Avimi said** that **Shmuel said: A mourner who did not let** his hair **grow wild and did not rend** his garments[H] **is liable** to receive **the death penalty** at the hand of Heaven, **as it is stated** following the deaths of Nadab and Abihu concerning the surviving sons of Aaron: **"Let not the hair of your heads go loose, neither rend your clothes, that you not die"** (Leviticus 10:6). They were instructed not to mourn, so as not to interfere with the dedication of the Tabernacle. From here it may be deduced **that** any **other** mourner[N] **who did not let** his hair **grow wild or rend** his clothes **is liable** to receive **the death penalty.**

אָמַר רַפְרָם בַּר פָּפָּא, תָּנָא בְּאֵבֶל רַבָּתִי: אָבֵל אָסוּר לְשַׁמֵּשׁ מִטָּתוֹ בִּימֵי אֶבְלוֹ. וּמַעֲשֶׂה בְּאֶחָד שֶׁשִּׁימֵּשׁ מִטָּתוֹ בִּימֵי אֶבְלוֹ, וְשָׁמְטוּ חֲזִירִים אֶת גְּוִיָּיתוֹ.

Rafram bar Pappa said: A Sage **taught in** ***Evel Rabbati*,**[B] a separate tractate devoted to the *halakhot* of mourning: **A mourner is prohibited from engaging in sexual relations during his days of mourning.** There was **an incident with one who engaged in sexual relations during his days of mourning and** he was punished, for after his death **pigs dragged away his corpse.**[N]

אָמַר שְׁמוּאֵל: פח״ז – חוֹבָה; נת״ר – רְשׁוּת.

Shmuel offered a mnemonic device with regard to the observance of mourning rites on Shabbat, and **said:** ***Peh, ḥet, zayin*** **are obligatory.**[N] These letters combine to create a mnemonic standing for: Uncovering the head [*periat rosh*], reversing the torn garment [*ḥazarat kera*], and standing the bed upright [*zekifat hamitta*]. However, ***nun, tav, reish,*** which stand for: Wearing shoes [*ne'ilat hasandal*], marital relations [*tashmish hamitta*], and hand washing [*reḥitzat yadayim*], **are optional.**

פְּרִיעַת הָרֹאשׁ, חֲזָרַת קֶרַע לַאֲחוֹרָיו, זְקִיפַת הַמִּטָּה – חוֹבָה. נְעִילַת הַסַּנְדָּל, תַּשְׁמִישׁ הַמִּטָּה, רְחִיצַת יָדַיִם וְרַגְלַיִם בְּחַמִּין עַרְבִית – רְשׁוּת. וְרַב אָמַר: אַף פְּרִיעַת הָרֹאשׁ רְשׁוּת.

This is explained: **Uncovering the head,** i.e., removing the head covering usually worn by a mourner; **reversing the tear to the back,** so that it will not be visible; and **standing the bed upright** in the usual position, so that it is not overturned, are all **obligatory** for the mourner to uphold in honor of Shabbat. However, **wearing shoes, engaging in sexual relations,** and **washing one's hands and feet in hot water in the evening are optional** activities on Shabbat. If a mourner wishes to refrain from them he may do so. **And Rav said: Uncovering the head is also an optional** activity.

NOTES

Liable to receive the death penalty – חַיָּיב מִיתָה: The early authorities write that this phrase does not mean that such a mourner who engaged in sexual relations would actually be executed at the hand of Heaven, for doing so is not listed in tractate *Sanhedrin* among the sins that are punishable by death. Instead, it is meant to be a harsh expression that emphasizes the seriousness of the sin. This is similar to what is stated elsewhere: Anyone who transgresses the words of the Sages is liable to receive the death penalty (Ramban). All such cases are based on the verse: "One who breaks through a fence, a serpent shall bite him" (Ecclesiastes 10:8), as rabbinic law is considered a fence meant to protect the Torah (*Talmid Rabbeinu Yeḥiel of Paris*).

That you not die…any other mourner, etc. – וְלֹא תָמוּתוּ...הָא אַחֵר וכו׳: The Ramban, in his glosses to *Sefer HaMitzvot* and in his commentary on the Torah, writes that the phrase: "That you not die," can be understood in two different ways. It can be understood either as a simple statement, or as a warning.

As a statement, it means the following: You are not required to practice mourning. Despite the general principle that one who is obligated to mourn and does not do so will receive the death penalty, you will not die because God commanded you not to mourn. Based on this, the Gemara concludes that others who are required to practice mourning and do not do so are liable to receive the death penalty. However, if it is a warning, it means: You are prohibited from practicing mourning, for if you practice mourning you will die.

His corpse – גְּוִיָּיתוֹ: Some explain that this word means his corpse; others say that it refers to his penis (Rashi, from manuscript; Rabbi Shlomo ben HaYatom). According to this second explanation, this man was punished measure for measure; he both sinned and was punished through the same body part (*Talmid Rabbeinu Yeḥiel of Paris*).

Peh, ḥet, zayin **are obligatory – פח״ז חוֹבָה:** On Shabbat, a distinction is made between mourning practices that are public and those that are private. Alternatively, the distinction is between those actions that make it obvious to others that one is mourning and those actions that are not noticeable signs of mourning (Ritva).

HALAKHA

The obligation to rend – חִיּוּב קְרִיעָה: A mourner is obligated to rend his garment over a deceased relative. This *halakha* is alluded to in the Bible but is a rabbinic enactment (Rambam *Sefer Shofetim*, *Hilkhot Evel* 8:1).

BACKGROUND

Evel Rabbati **– אֵבֶל רַבָּתִי:** This is referring to one of the minor tractates not included in the six orders of Mishna. These tractates are primarily collections of *baraitot* organized according to topic. *Evel Rabbati* has fourteen chapters, though the early authorities apparently had a longer version. It deals with people who are near death, the *halakhot* of funerals, rending garments, eulogizing, and mourning. The tractate is called *Evel Rabbati* in order to distinguish it from *Evel Zutarti*, which mostly deals with one who is dangerously ill. The tractate *Evel Rabbati* is found in most versions of the Talmud with the other minor tractates, at the end of the order of *Nezikin*. Most early authorities refer to it euphemistically as the *Tractate of Joys*.

וּשְׁמוּאֵל, מַאי שְׁנָא נְעִילַת הַסַּנְדָּל דִּרְשׁוּת? דְּלָאו כּוּלֵּי עָלְמָא עֲבִידִי דְּסַיְּימִי מְסָאנַיְיהוּ; פְּרִיעַת הָרֹאשׁ נָמֵי לָאו כּוּלֵּי עָלְמָא עֲבִידִי דְּמִגַּלּוּ רֵישַׁיְיהוּ!

The Gemara asks: **According to Shmuel, what is different about wearing shoes** that it is **optional?** His reasoning presumably is that **not everyone wears shoes** at all times, and therefore not wearing shoes will not be perceived by others as a sign of mourning. If so, the same thing may be said about **uncovering the head also,** i.e., **not everyone uncovers his head** at all times, as some people always walk around with their heads wrapped. This, too, should not be seen as a clear display of mourning, and therefore uncovering one's head should also be treated as optional.

שְׁמוּאֵל לְטַעְמֵיהּ, דְּאָמַר שְׁמוּאֵל: כׇּל קֶרַע שֶׁאֵינוֹ בִּשְׁעַת חִימּוּם – אֵינוֹ קֶרַע, וְכׇל עֲטִיפָה שֶׁאֵינָהּ כַּעֲטִיפַת יִשְׁמְעֵאלִים – אֵינָהּ עֲטִיפָה. מַחְוֵי רַב נַחְמָן עַד גּוֹבֵי דְּדִיקְנָא.

The Gemara answers: **Shmuel** conforms **to his** standard line of **reasoning,** for **Shmuel said: Any rending** of garments **that is not** done **at the time of** the **most intense** grief, i.e., the time of death, **is not** considered proper **rending** of garments.[H] **And any wrapping** of the head **that is not** done **in the manner of the wrapping of the Ishmaelites,**[B] who wrap their heads on all sides, **is not** considered proper **wrapping.**[H] Since Shmuel requires that a mourner wrap his head in this special manner, one who acts in this way on Shabbat openly displays his mourning, as people do not ordinarily wrap their heads in this manner. What is this wrapping? **Rav Naḥman demonstrated** the procedure by covering up his face to the **sides of the beard,**[N] leaving only the center of his face exposed.

אָמַר רַבִּי יַעֲקֹב אָמַר רַבִּי יוֹחָנָן: לֹא שָׁנוּ אֶלָּא שֶׁאֵין לוֹ מִנְעָלִים בְּרַגְלָיו, אֲבָל יֵשׁ לוֹ מִנְעָלִים בְּרַגְלָיו – מִנְעָלָיו מוֹכִיחִין עָלָיו.

Rabbi Ya'akov said that **Rabbi Yoḥanan said: They taught** that a mourner is required to remove his head covering on Shabbat **only when he has no shoes on his feet,** so that he not appear too obviously to be in mourning. **But if he has shoes on his feet,** then **his shoes prove** that **he** is not observing the rites of mourning on Shabbat.

BACKGROUND

Wrapping of the Ishmaelites – עֲטִיפַת יִשְׁמְעֵאלִים: Wrapping a shawl so that one side of the shawl rests on the shoulder is called Ishmaelite wrapping because nomadic Arabs would wrap themselves in this manner as protection from the cold or sand.

Ishmaelite wrapping

HALAKHA

Rending garments at the time of most intense grief – קֶרַע בִּשְׁעַת חִימּוּם: The primary mitzva for the mourner to rend his garments applies from the time of death until the burial. If one did not rend his garments during this time he may rend them anytime during the seven-day mourning period, as this entire time falls into the category of the most intense moment of grief. However, if did not rend his garments during the seven days either, he should not do so afterward. Over one's father or mother one is required to rend garments in their honor, even after this time, if he has not already done so (*Shulḥan Arukh, Yoreh De'a* 340; see *Arukh HaShulḥan*).

Wrapping for mourners – עֲטִיפַת אֲבֵלִים: A mourner is required to wrap his head with a scarf or shawl, and one corner should reach across his mouth and his nose. The mourner must keep this wrapping in place for the entire day, except for when others come to console him. At that time, he removes it as a sign of respect toward those who have come to visit him. The Rema writes that this is not the accepted practice in European regions, and one does not deviate from the local custom to act in a more stringent manner. However, it is appropriate to perform an act similar to wrapping, such as lowering one's hat over one's face slightly (*Shakh*; *Taz*; *Shulḥan Arukh, Yoreh De'a* 386:1).

NOTES

Sides of the beard – גּוֹבֵי דְּדִיקְנָא: Rashi and others explain that this refers to the indentations in the jaw slightly below the mouth. Rav Hai Gaon explains that this refers to the hair on the cheeks. The halakhic authorities disagree with regard to how and where this wrapping is performed: If it extends below the mouth or not and whether or not the nose must be covered. Although for many generations it has not been the common practice to perform this wrapping as a sign of mourning, this style of wrapping still has practical ramifications with regard to the manner in which one must wrap one's prayer shawl.

NOTES

He rent twelve garments on account of him – קְרַע עֲלֵיהּ תְּרֵיסַר מָנֵי: A similar story is related in the Jerusalem Talmud, where it is added that Rabbi Yoḥanan took out his Shabbat clothes and tore them over the death of Rabbi Ḥanina. Apparently, many of the commentaries understood that he tore his clothes in this manner for many days. Each time he needed a new garment, he would tear it first (see Rashi, from manuscript; *Haggahot Maimoniyyot*).

Of whom I was in fear – דַּהֲוָה מִסְתְּפֵינָא מִינֵּיהּ: Rashi and others explain that Shmuel was afraid of the challenges that Rav raised against his opinions. Rabbi Shlomo ben HaYatom writes that he was awed and ashamed before him, due to Rav's greatness and wisdom. The Ra'avad explains that as long as Rav was alive, Shmuel felt that he needed to be precise with his speech, as Rav, who was greater than him, would critique everything he said. Now that Rav passed away, Shmuel was afraid that he would err.

The Maharsha describes a different type of fear, and writes that Shmuel said that Rav was the perfect Torah scholar, and the Sages said that one is required to fear Torah scholars, as fear of them is compared to the fear of Heaven.

And if he comes to change clothing – וְאִם בָּא לְהַחֲלִיף: The Ra'avad writes that a mourner may change into another garment only if the first one requires laundering. The Meiri writes that one may change from a lightweight garment to a warmer one if the weather changes. This implies that a mourner may change garments only if there is a reason to do so.

LANGUAGE

Wool [*mileta*] – מִילָתָא: Apparently from the Greek μηλωτή, *mèlotè*, meaning wool. However, there are those who say that this word is related to the city of Miletus, which was a center for wool trading.

Garments [*itztelei*] – אִצְטְלֵי: From the Greek στολά, *stola*, meaning garment or cloak.

HALAKHA

Tears that may not be mended – קְרָעִים שֶׁאֵינָם מִתְאַחִים: A garment that was torn in mourning over one's father or mother may never be mended, even if it was not torn at the time of most intense grief. This is in accordance with the opinion of Rabbi Oshaya and based on a ruling in the Jerusalem Talmud (Rosh; *Shulḥan Arukh*, *Yoreh De'a* 340:14).

כָּל קֶרַע שֶׁאֵינוֹ בִּשְׁעַת חִימּוּם אֵינוֹ קֶרַע. וְהָא אָמְרוּ לֵיהּ לִשְׁמוּאֵל: נָח נַפְשֵׁיהּ דְּרַב. קְרַע עֲלֵיהּ תְּרֵיסַר מָנֵי, אָמַר: אָזַל גַּבְרָא דַּהֲוָה מִסְתְּפֵינָא מִינֵּיהּ. אֲמַר לֵיהּ לְרַבִּי יוֹחָנָן: נָח נַפְשֵׁיהּ דְּרַבִּי חֲנִינָא. קְרַע עֲלֵיהּ תְּלֵיסַר אִצְטְלֵי מִלְתָא, אָמַר: אָזַל גַּבְרָא דַּהֲוָה מִסְתְּפֵינָא מִינֵּיהּ!

The Gemara returns to Shmuel's statement that **any rending** of garments **that is not** done **at the time of most intense** grief and pain **is not** considered proper **rending** of garments. The Gemara poses a question: **But when they said to Shmuel** that **Rav had passed away, he rent twelve garments on account of him,**[N] **and said: The man of whom I was in fear,**[N] owing to his great learning, **has gone** and died. Similarly, when **they told Rabbi Yoḥanan**[P] that **Rabbi Ḥanina**[P] **had passed away, he rent thirteen** expensive **wool** [*mileta*][L] **garments** [*itztelei*][L] **on account of him, and said: The man of whom I was in fear has gone.** When each of these Sages received the news that their distinguished colleague had died, it was no longer the time of the most intense grief, i.e., the time of death, and yet they rent their garments.

שָׁאנֵי רַבָּנַן, דִּכְיוָן דְּכׇל שַׁעְתָּא מִדְּכְרִי שְׁמַעְתַּיְיהוּ – כִּשְׁעַת חִימּוּם דָּמֵי.

The Gemara answers: **The Sages are different. Since their teachings are mentioned all the time,** every time they are mentioned **is like the time of most intense** grief, as the pain over their death is once again renewed.

אֲמַר לֵיהּ רָבִין בַּר אַדָּא לְרָבָא: אָמַר תַּלְמִידָךְ רַב עַמְרָם, תַּנְיָא: אָבֵל, כׇּל שִׁבְעָה – קוֹרְעוֹ לְפָנָיו; וְאִם בָּא לְהַחֲלִיף – מַחֲלִיף, וְקוֹרֵעַ. בַּשַּׁבָּת – קוֹרְעוֹ לַאֲחוֹרָיו; וְאִם בָּא לְהַחֲלִיף – מַחֲלִיף, וְאֵינוֹ קוֹרֵעַ.

Ravin bar Adda said to Rava: Your student, Rav Amram, said that **it is taught** in a *baraita* as follows: For **all seven days** of mourning, **a mourner** must keep **the tear** in his garment **before him** so that it will be seen. **And if he comes to change** clothing,[N] **he changes and rends** the new garment. **On Shabbat,** he turns **the tear to his back, and if he comes to change** clothing, **he changes but does not tear** the second garment. From here it seems that there is an obligation to rend garments during the entire week of mourning, not only at the most intense moment of grief.

כִּי תַּנְיָא הַהִיא – בִּכְבוֹד אָבִיו וְאִמּוֹ.

The Gemara answers: **When that** *baraita* **is taught,** it is referring to the specific case of rending one's garment **in honor of his father or mother.** Owing to the special honor due to one's parents, it is inappropriate for the child to wear a garment that is not torn. Consequently, if he changes clothing, he must tear the new garment, even if it is no longer the most intense time of grief.

אוֹתָן קְרָעִין מִתְאַחִין אוֹ אֵין מִתְאַחִין? פְּלִיגִי בָּהּ אֲבוּהּ דְּרַב אוֹשַׁעְיָא וּבַר קַפָּרָא. חַד אָמַר: אֵין מִתְאַחִין, וְחַד אָמַר: מִתְאַחִין.

The Gemara asks: **Those** additional **tears** that are made in honor of one's father or mother, **may they be** properly **mended** at the end of the son's period of mourning, **or may they not be** properly **mended,** like the tear made for one's father or mother at the most intense moment of grief? The Gemara answers: **They disagree about** this issue, **the father of Rav Oshaya and bar Kappara. One said: They may not be mended, and one said: They may be mended.**[H]

PERSONALITIES

Rabbi Yoḥanan – רַבִּי יוֹחָנָן: Rabbi Yoḥanan bar Nappaḥa was one of the greatest *amora'im*. His teachings are fundamental components of both the Babylonian and the Jerusalem Talmud. He resided in Tiberias and lived to an advanced age. Almost nothing is known of his family background. He was orphaned at a young age and, although his family apparently owned considerable property, he spent virtually all of his resources in his devotion to the study of Torah and eventually became impoverished.

In his youth, he had the privilege of studying under Rabbi Yehuda HaNasi, the redactor of the Mishna, but most of his Torah learning came from Rabbi Yehuda HaNasi's students: Ḥizkiya ben Ḥiyya, Rabbi Oshaya, Rabbi Ḥanina, and Rabbi Yannai, who lavished praise upon him. In time, he became the head of the yeshiva in Tiberias, at which point his fame and influence increased greatly.

For a long time, Rabbi Yoḥanan was the leading rabbinic scholar in the entire Jewish world, not only in Eretz Yisrael, but in Babylonia as well, where he was respected by the Babylonian Sages. Many of them came to Eretz Yisrael and became his outstanding students. He was a master of both *halakha* and *aggada*, and his teachings in both disciplines are found throughout both the Babylonian and the Jerusalem Talmud. In recognition of his intellectual and spiritual stature, the *halakha* is ruled in accordance with his opinion in almost every case, even when Rav or Shmuel, the preeminent *amora'im* of Babylonia, whom he treated deferentially, disagreed with him. Only in disputes with his teachers in Eretz Yisrael, such as Rabbi Yannai and Rabbi Yehoshua ben Levi, is the *halakha* not ruled in accordance with his opinion.

Rabbi Ḥanina – רַבִּי חֲנִינָא: This is Rabbi Ḥanina bar Ḥama, who lived in the transitional generation between the *tanna'im* and *amora'im*. Rabbi Ḥanina was born in Babylonia but emigrated to Eretz Yisrael at a very young age, where he studied Torah from Rabbi Yehuda HaNasi. His teacher was very fond of him, saying that Rabbi Ḥanina was not a human being but an angel. Rabbi Ḥanina also studied under Rabbi Yehuda HaNasi's greatest students, in particular Rabbi Ḥiyya. At the time of his death, Rabbi Yehuda HaNasi appointed Rabbi Ḥanina as head of the yeshiva, but in his humility, Rabbi Ḥanina refused to accept the position during the lifetime of his older colleague, Rabbi Afes.

Rabbi Ḥanina lived in the city of Tzippori, where he dealt in the honey trade, from which he grew wealthy. He used his money to build a large study hall. Rabbi Ḥanina is considered one of the cleverest scholars of his generation and was also renowned for his righteousness and kindness.

Rabbi Ḥanina's halakhic and aggadic statements abound both in the Jerusalem and Babylonian Talmud. He enjoyed a long and healthy life and taught many students over several generations. Rabbi Yehoshua ben Levi was his student and colleague, and he was also privileged to teach Rabbi Yoḥanan for many years. The *amora* Rabbi Ḥama, son of Rabbi Ḥanina, was possibly his son.

תִּסְתַּיֵּים דַּאֲבוּהּ דְּרַב אוֹשַׁעְיָא דְּאָמַר אֵין מִתְאַחִין, דְּאָמַר רַב אוֹשַׁעְיָא, אֵין מִתְאַחִין. מִמַּאן שְׁמִיעַ לֵיהּ? לָאו מֵאֲבוּהּ? לָא, מִבַּר קַפָּרָא רַבֵּיהּ שְׁמִיעַ לֵיהּ.

The Gemara comments: **Conclude that** it was **Rav Oshaya's father who said** that such rents **may not be** properly **mended, for Rav Oshaya said:** Such rents **may not be** properly **mended. From whom did he hear** this *halakha*? Was it **not from his father?** The Gemara rejects this argument: **No,** this cannot be offered as a proof, as perhaps **he heard it from bar Kappara,** who was **his teacher.**

אָמַר רָבָא: אָבֵל מְטַיֵּיל בְּאוּנְקְלִי בְּתוֹךְ בֵּיתוֹ. אַבָּיֵי אַשְׁכְּחֵיהּ לְרַב יוֹסֵף דִּפְרִיס לֵיהּ סוּדָרָא אַרֵישֵׁיהּ, וְאָזֵיל וְאָתֵי בְּבֵיתֵיהּ. אָמַר לֵיהּ: לָאו סָבַר לַהּ מָר אֵין אֲבֵילוּת בְּשַׁבָּת? אָמַר לֵיהּ: הָכִי אָמַר רַבִּי יוֹחָנָן: דְּבָרִים שֶׁבְּצִינְעָא נוֹהֵג.

§ **Rava said: A mourner may walk about his house in** a torn **robe** [*unkali*][NL] on Shabbat, since he is not doing so in public. It was related that **Abaye found Rav Yosef walking back and forth in his house** on Shabbat when he was in mourning **with a scarf spread over his head** in the manner of mourning. **He said to him: Master, do you not maintain** that **there is no mourning on Shabbat? He said to him: This is what Rabbi Yoḥanan said: Matters that are in private apply,** and so when one is in his house he must observe the rites of mourning even on Shabbat.

"רַבִּי אֱלִיעֶזֶר אוֹמֵר מִשֶּׁחָרַב בֵּית הַמִּקְדָּשׁ עֲצֶרֶת כְּשַׁבָּת" וכו׳. אָמַר רַב גִּידֵּל בַּר מְנַשְּׁיָא אָמַר שְׁמוּאֵל: הֲלָכָה כְּרַבָּן גַּמְלִיאֵל.

§ The mishna taught: **Rabbi Eliezer says: Since the Temple was destroyed,** ***Shavuot*** **is like Shabbat** with regard to mourning. Rabban Gamliel says: Even Rosh HaShana and Yom Kippur are considered like Festivals. The Gemara comments that **Rav Giddel bar Menashya said** that **Shmuel said: The** ***halakha*** **is in accordance with** the opinion of **Rabban Gamliel.**

וְאִיכָּא דְּמַתְנֵי לְהָא דְּרַב גִּידֵּל בַּר מְנַשְּׁיָא אַהָא: כָּל שְׁלֹשִׁים יוֹם תִּינוֹק יוֹצֵא בְּחֵיק, וְנִקְבָּר בְּאִשָּׁה אַחַת וּשְׁנֵי אֲנָשִׁים, אֲבָל לֹא בְּאִישׁ אֶחָד וּשְׁתֵּי נָשִׁים.

And some teach this ruling **of Rav Giddel bar Menashya** as referring **to the following** case: It is taught in a *baraita*: Within the first **thirty days** after birth, **an infant** that dies **is taken out** for burial **in** one's **bosom,**[N] that is to say, he is carried to his grave in one's arms, not in a coffin. **And he is buried by one woman and two men,** there being no need for a quorum of ten men. **But** he should **not** be taken out **by one man and two women,**[N] because it is prohibited for one man to seclude himself with two women.

Perek **III**
Daf **24** Amud **b**

אַבָּא שָׁאוּל אוֹמֵר: אַף בְּאִישׁ אֶחָד וּשְׁתֵּי נָשִׁים. וְאֵין עוֹמְדִין עָלָיו בְּשׁוּרָה, וְאֵין אוֹמְרִים עָלָיו בִּרְכַּת אֲבֵלִים וְתַנְחוּמֵי אֲבֵלִים.

Abba Shaul says: The infant may be taken out **even by one man and two women,**[N] for there is no concern with regard to seclusion in a time of mourning. **And** for such an infant, people **do not stand in a line** to offer their condolences to the mourners, as is ordinarily done after a burial; **nor do** others **recite over him the mourners' blessing,**[N] which is recited in the courtyard of the graveyard after the burial; **nor** is the usual formula for the **consolation of mourners** recited during the seven days of mourning.

NOTES

Robe [*unkali*] – אוּנְקְלִי: Many commentaries explain that *unkali* refers to a garment that is worn directly on one's skin. They explain that Rava permits a mourner to wear a torn undergarment within his home on Shabbat, if the mourner does not wish to change his garments (Rabbeinu Gershom Meor HaGola; Rashi). Rabbeinu Ḥananel explains that *unkali* refers to a type of turban that would cover the head of a mourner while he was mourning. This explanation is based on the opinion that holds that a mourner is not required to wrap his head specifically in the manner of the Ishmaelites. Some explain that the word *unkali* means a hook or clasp, and it refers to a torn garment that is held together by a clasp (Ramban; Ran).

Within the first thirty days an infant that dies is taken out for burial in one's bosom – כָּל שְׁלֹשִׁים יוֹם תִּינוֹק יוֹצֵא בְּחֵיק: The reason for this is that until a baby has survived for thirty days, it is not considered viable. As a result, mourning for the death of such an infant is not as intense as for an older child or an adult. The early authorities write that these *halakhot* do not apply to a stillborn child.

One man and two women – אִישׁ אֶחָד וּשְׁתֵּי נָשִׁים: In tractate *Kiddushin*, it is stated that one man may not be alone with two women due to the prohibition of seclusion. According to the first *tanna*, there is no distinction between a time of mourning and any other time, because the case is one in which the child died within thirty days. Therefore, the grief is less intense, and it is possible that the mourners will come to sin (Rashi, from manuscript; Commentary on *Moed Katan*).

LANGUAGE

Robe [*unkali*] – אוּנְקְלִי: From the Greek ἀνάκωλος, *anakolos*, meaning short or cut off. It is used in reference to a lower garment that reached the knees.

NOTES

Even by one man, etc. – אַף בְּאִישׁ אֶחָד וכו׳: *Tosafot* explain: Although there is generally concern about the seclusion of one man with two women, Abba Shaul holds that one's sexual desire are not as strong during mourning. It can also be deduced from this Gemara that although there is no requirement for ten people to take part in a burial, there must be at least three people present (Ran).

Nor do others recite over him the mourners' blessing – וְאֵין אוֹמְרִים עָלָיו בִּרְכַּת אֲבֵלִים: This implies that there is no public mourning for a small child who dies. However, it is not clear whether the relatives are required to mourn for their child. There was a difference in practice between the residents of the Diaspora and the residents of Eretz Yisrael. In the Diaspora, the custom was not to mourn for a baby unless it had survived for at least thirty days; whereas the residents of Eretz Yisrael mourned over any baby, even if it lived for only one day. This custom was based on a mishna (*Nidda* 5:3) concerning mourning that states that a newborn baby is to his father, his mother, and all of his relatives like a fully grown groom.

בֶּן שְׁלֹשִׁים יוֹצֵא בִּדְלוּסְקְמָא. רַבִּי יְהוּדָה אוֹמֵר: לֹא דְּלוּסְקְמָא הַנִּיטֶּלֶת בְּכָתֵף, אֶלָּא הַנִּיטֶּלֶת בַּאֲגַפַּיִם. וְעוֹמְדִין עָלָיו בְּשׁוּרָה, וְאוֹמְרִים עָלָיו בִּרְכַּת אֲבֵלִים וְתַנְחוּמֵי אֲבֵלִים.

A thirty-day-old infant that dies **is taken out** for burial **in a coffin** [*deluskema*].[HL] **Rabbi Yehuda says: Not in** a small **coffin that is carried on** one's **shoulder, but rather** in a coffin that is carried **in the arms** of two people. **And** for such an infant, people **stand in a line** to offer their condolences to the mourners. **And** others **recite the mourners' blessing** at the cemetery. **And** people recite **the consolation of mourners** during the week of mourning.

בֶּן שְׁנֵים עָשָׂר חֹדֶשׁ – יוֹצֵא בְּמִטָּה. רַבִּי עֲקִיבָא אוֹמֵר: הוּא בֶּן שָׁנָה וְאֵבָרָיו כְּבֶן שְׁתַּיִם, הוּא בֶּן שְׁתַּיִם וְאֵבָרָיו כְּבֶן שָׁנָה – יוֹצֵא בְּמִטָּה.

A twelve-month-old infant **is taken out** for burial **on a bier,** just as an adult is. **Rabbi Akiva says:** This *halakha* applies if the infant that dies **is one year old and his limbs are like** those of **a two year old,** so that he looks older, or if **he is two years old and his limbs are like** those of **a one-year-old.** Only then **he is taken out on a bier.**

רַבִּי שִׁמְעוֹן בֶּן אֶלְעָזָר אוֹמֵר: הַיּוֹצֵא בְּמִטָּה – רַבִּים מַצְהִיבִין עָלָיו. אֵינוֹ יוֹצֵא בְּמִטָּה – אֵין רַבִּים מַצְהִיבִין עָלָיו. רַבִּי אֶלְעָזָר בֶּן עֲזַרְיָה אוֹמֵר: נִיכָּר לָרַבִּים – רַבִּים מִתְעַסְּקִים עִמּוֹ; אֵינוֹ נִיכָּר לָרַבִּים – אֵין רַבִּים מִתְעַסְּקִים עִמּוֹ.

Rabbi Shimon ben Elazar says: For one that is taken out on a bier, the public should grieve [*matzhivin*].[L] **For one that is not taken out on a bier, the public need not grieve. Rabbi Elazar ben Azarya says:** The *halakha* is as follows: If the infant was **known to the public,** because he regularly left the house and many people knew him, **the public must occupy themselves with him** and participate in his burial. If **he was not known to the public, the public need not occupy themselves with him.**

וּמַה הֵן בְּהֶסְפֵּד? רַבִּי מֵאִיר בְּשֵׁם רַבִּי יִשְׁמָעֵאל אוֹמֵר: עֲנִיִּים – בְּנֵי שָׁלֹשׁ; עֲשִׁירִים – בְּנֵי חָמֵשׁ. רַבִּי יְהוּדָה אוֹמֵר מִשְּׁמוֹ: עֲנִיִּים – בְּנֵי חָמֵשׁ; עֲשִׁירִים – בְּנֵי שֵׁשׁ. וּבְנֵי זְקֵנִים כִּבְנֵי עֲנִיִּים.

And what is the status of deceased infants **with regard to eulogy?**[N] **Rabbi Meir said in the name of Rabbi Yishmael:** The children of **the poor**[N] are eulogized from **the age of three,** whereas the children of **the wealthy** are eulogized from **the age of five.** This is because a child is the sole source of joy for the poor, and so the pain and grief of the poor over the death of a child is greater than that of the wealthy. **Rabbi Yehuda said in the name of** Rabbi Yishmael: The children of **the poor** are eulogized from **the age of five,** whereas the children of **the wealthy** are eulogized from **the age of six.**[H] **And the children of the elderly**[N] **are** treated **like the children of the poor,** for the death of a child is particularly painful for an older person.[H]

אָמַר רַב גִּידֵּל בַּר מְנַשְּׁיָא אָמַר רַב: הֲלָכָה כְּרַבִּי יְהוּדָה שֶׁאָמַר מִשּׁוּם רַבִּי יִשְׁמָעֵאל.

Rav Giddel bar Menashya said that **Rav said: The** *halakha* **is in accordance with** the opinion of **Rabbi Yehuda, who stated it in the name of Rabbi Yishmael.**

HALAKHA

Less than thirty days old – פָּחוֹת מִבֶּן שְׁלֹשִׁים: A baby who dies within thirty days of birth is carried to burial in one's hands and there is no requirement to bury him in a coffin (*Shakh*, citing *Or Zarua*). The baby should be buried by one woman and two men, but not by one man and two women, due to the prohibition of seclusion, as mentioned by the first *tanna*. There is no requirement for others to stand in a line to comfort the mourners after his death (*Shakh*, citing Rashi). Similarly, the mourners' blessing and the consolation of mourners are not said after the baby's death, even when it is clear that the infant was not a stillbirth but was fully formed baby (*Shulḥan Arukh, Yoreh De'a* 353:3).

The burial of a child – קְבוּרַת יֶלֶד: If a child dies more than thirty days after his birth, he is carried to burial in a coffin that is held by two people. People stand in a line to comfort the mourners over his death, and the mourners' blessing and the consolation of mourners are said after his death. If the child was more than twelve months old then, he is carried for burial on a bier, just as an adult. Anyone who is carried on a bier should be mourned by the public. The public is involved with the funeral of any child that is known to them, and if he is not known to them they are not involved in his funeral, in accordance with the opinions of Rabbi Shimon ben Elazar and Rabbi Elazar ben Azarya (*Shulḥan Arukh, Yoreh De'a* 353:5).

Eulogies over children – הֶסְפֵּד עַל יְלָדִים: The children of the wealthy are eulogized if they are older than six, and the children of the poor or the elderly are eulogized from the age of five. The *Shulḥan Arukh* holds that the blessing: The true Judge and the mourners' prayer are recited from the age of thirty days in all cases. The Rema disagrees and writes that the custom is to recite this only if the child was at least twelve months old (*Shakh*; *Shulḥan Arukh, Yoreh De'a* 344:4).

LANGUAGE

Coffin [*deluskema*] – דְּלוּסְקְמָא: From the Greek γλωσσόκομος, *glossokomos*, meaning case. Originally, it referred specifically to a case in which to keep mouthpieces of wind-instruments. The meaning was expanded so that it referred to any box or crate, including a coffin or ossuary.

Ossuary

Grieve [*matzhivin*] – מַצְהִיבִין: The meaning of this word and its root, *tz-h-v*, are possibly related to the color *tzahov*, which in modern Hebrew means yellow, but in the Gemara can also refer to a more reddish color. The meaning of the word here is to make one's face redden with emotion, either with grief or anger.

NOTES

What is the status with regard to eulogy – מַה הֵן בְּהֶסְפֵּד: It is stated in a *baraita* in tractate *Semaḥot* that if it is possible to praise the child and his deeds, then he should be eulogized in the merit of his deeds. If this is not the case, then he should be eulogized in the merits of his forefathers.

The children of the poor – בְּנֵי עֲנִיִּים: Rashi explains, and before him Rav Hai Gaon explained, that the poor do take pleasure from what they have, and consequently they feel more pain when their one joy, their child, dies. Others say that they are more pained by their children's death because they rely on them for financial support once they grow older (Rashi, from manuscript). Others write that since the poor must eat sparingly in order to provide for their children, they become more attached to them (Ran). There are also those who suggest that this decree was made because the poor are constantly living in pain and suffering, and if they do not eulogize their children there is a concern that people will suspect that they are not showing honor for their child because of their poverty (Rabbi Shlomo ben HaYatom).

The children of the elderly [*zekenim*] – בְּנֵי זְקֵנִים: Most commentaries note that this is because the elderly no longer have hope that they will have other children, and therefore their pain is greater (Rabbi Shlomo ben HaYatom; Ran). Or, it is possible that the reason for this is because they hope that their child will care for them in their old age. Others write that the word *zekenim*, literally Elders, refers to Sages, and more honor should be shown for Torah scholars.

דָּרַשׁ רַבִּי עֲנָנִי בַּר שָׂשׂוֹן אַפִּיתְחָא דְּבֵי נְשִׂיאָה: יוֹם אֶחָד לִפְנֵי עֲצֶרֶת וַעֲצֶרֶת – הֲרֵי כָּאן אַרְבָּעָה עָשָׂר. שְׁמַע רַבִּי אַמִּי וְאִיקְפַּד. אֲמַר: אִטּוּ דִּידֵיהּ הִיא? דְּרַבִּי אֶלְעָזָר אָמַר רַבִּי אוֹשַׁעְיָא הִיא!

Rabbi Anani bar Sason taught at the entrance to the house of the *Nasi*: If one suffered the loss of a close relative shortly before the festival of *Shavuot*, his **one day** of mourning **before *Shavuot*[H] and *Shavuot*** itself together count as **fourteen** days. The day before the Festival counts as seven full days of mourning because the Festival interrupts the seven-day period of mourning, and the Festival itself is counted as a seven-day Festival. Even though it is a one-day Festival, it is counted as seven days because it has the same *halakha* as the other Festivals. After *Shavuot*, then, only sixteen days are left to complete the thirty-day mourning period. **Rabbi Ami heard** this **and became angry** with him. **He said: Is that to say** that it is **his own** opinion?[N] **It is** the opinion **that Rabbi Elazar said** that **Rabbi Oshaya** said.

דָּרַשׁ רַבִּי יִצְחָק נַפָּחָא אַקִּילְעָא דְּרֵישׁ גָּלוּתָא: יוֹם אֶחָד לִפְנֵי עֲצֶרֶת, וַעֲצֶרֶת – הֲרֵי כָּאן אַרְבָּעָה עָשָׂר. שְׁמַע רַב שֵׁשֶׁת אִיקְפַּד, אֲמַר: אִטּוּ דִּידֵיהּ הִיא? דְּרַבִּי אֶלְעָזָר אָמַר רַבִּי אוֹשַׁעְיָא הִיא.

Similarly **Rabbi Yitzḥak Nappaḥa taught in the pavilion [*kila*][L] of the Exilarch:** If one's relative died shortly before the festival of *Shavuot*, his **one day** of mourning **before *Shavuot* and *Shavuot*** itself count as **fourteen** days. **Rav Sheshet heard and became angry.** He **said: Is that to say** that it is **his own** opinion? **It is** the opinion **that Rabbi Elazar said** that **Rabbi Oshaya** said.

דְּאָמַר רַבִּי אֶלְעָזָר אָמַר רַבִּי אוֹשַׁעְיָא: מִנַּיִן לַעֲצֶרֶת שֶׁיֵּשׁ לָהּ תַּשְׁלוּמִין כָּל שִׁבְעָה? שֶׁנֶּאֱמַר: ״בְּחַג הַמַּצּוֹת וּבְחַג הַשָּׁבוּעוֹת״ – מָה חַג הַמַּצּוֹת יֵשׁ לָהּ תַּשְׁלוּמִין כָּל שִׁבְעָה – אַף חַג הַשָּׁבוּעוֹת יֵשׁ לָהּ תַּשְׁלוּמִין כָּל שִׁבְעָה.

In both of these cases, a Sage presented an opinion as their own, without attributing it to the original Sage who stated it, **for Rabbi Elazar said** that **Rabbi Oshaya said: From where** is it derived **that the *Shavuot*** offerings **have redress all seven** subsequent **days?**[H] That is to say, if someone failed to bring the Festival offering on the Festival itself, he has six more days to bring it. **As it is stated:** "Three times a year shall all your males appear before the Lord your God in the place that He shall choose; **on the festival of Passover, and on the festival of *Shavuot*,** and on the festival of *Sukkot*" (Deuteronomy 16:16). **Just as** the offerings of **the festival of Passover have redress all seven** days, as Passover is seven days long, **so too** the offerings of **the festival of *Shavuot* have redress all seven** days, during the week following *Shavuot*. From this we learn that *Shavuot* is treated like a seven-day Festival for all halakhic purposes.

אַדְבָּרֵיהּ רַב פַּפָּא לְרַב אָוְיָא סָבָא, וְדָרַשׁ: יוֹם אֶחָד לִפְנֵי רֹאשׁ הַשָּׁנָה, וְרֹאשׁ הַשָּׁנָה – הֲרֵי כָּאן אַרְבָּעָה עָשָׂר. אָמַר רָבִינָא: הִלְכָּךְ, יוֹם אֶחָד לִפְנֵי הֶחָג, וְחַג, וּשְׁמִינִי שֶׁלּוֹ – הֲרֵי כָּאן עֶשְׂרִים וְאֶחָד יוֹם.

Rav Pappa granted permission[B] **to Rav Avya the Elder** to speak **and he taught** the following in public: If one's relative died shortly before Rosh HaShana, his **one day** of mourning **before Rosh HaShana**[NH] **and Rosh HaShana** itself together count as **fourteen** days, because Rosh HaShana is treated like a seven-day Festival. **Ravina said: Therefore,** if a one's relative died shortly before *Sukkot*, his **one day** of mourning **before the Festival** of *Sukkot*,[H] **and the Festival** of *Sukkot* itself, which is seven days, **and its Eighth** day of Assembly, which is considered to be a separate Festival, count as **twenty-one** days, and he must observe only nine more days of mourning to complete the thirty-day period of mourning.

NOTES

Is that to say that it is his own opinion – אִטּוּ דִּידֵיהּ הִיא: Some say that Rabbi Ami became angry because one must be careful to cite words of Torah in the name of the person who originally said them, as is noted in numerous places in the Gemara. This is important both in terms of determining the *halakha* and also to honor the speaker and his Torah. Numerous stories are told both in the Jerusalem and the Babylonian Talmud about how the Sages were careful to quote statements they heard in the name of those who originally said them (Rabbi Shlomo ben HaYatom).

The Ramban holds that Rabbi Ami became angry because he thought that Rabbi Anani bar Sason based his statement incorrectly on what Rabbi Oshaya said. This is because Rabbi Oshaya's statement applies only when the Temple stood, as he refers to offerings when he discusses their redress. Therefore, this statement cannot be used as a basis for mourning practices after the destruction of the Temple.

One day before Rosh HaShana, etc. – יוֹם אֶחָד לִפְנֵי רֹאשׁ הַשָּׁנָה: The early authorities question the purpose of this *halakha*, as Yom Kippur is also considered to be a Festival (Ra'avad; *Tosafot*). Therefore, if someone begins mourning on the day before Rosh HaShana, the seven days ends with Rosh HaShana, and Yom Kippur itself should end the thirty-day mourning period. For what purpose is it necessary to state that the day before Rosh HaShana together with Rosh HaShana count as fourteen days? The *Ba'al Halakhot Gedolot* explains that since one leniency is applied to this period of mourning with regard to Rosh HaShana, another leniency cannot be applied in the case of Yom Kippur. Therefore, the latter is not also counted as seven days.

Tosafot also state in the name of Rabbeinu Yitzḥak and Rabbeinu Shimshon that after Rosh HaShana, the mourner is considered to already be in his third week of mourning, and therefore he may sit in his place in synagogue.

HALAKHA

One day before *Shavuot* – יוֹם אֶחָד לִפְנֵי עֲצֶרֶת: One who observed mourning practices for at least one day before *Shavuot* is considered as though he observed mourning for seven days, and *Shavuot* itself is counted as another seven days. Therefore, after the Festival he has only sixteen days of mourning left. The second day of the Festival that is observed in the diaspora is included in this number, in accordance with the opinions of Rabbi Anani bar Sason and Rabbi Oshaya (*Shulḥan Arukh, Yoreh De'a* 399:8).

Redress for the offerings of *Shavuot* – תַּשְׁלוּמֵי עֲצֶרֶת: One who did not bring the Festival peace-offerings on *Shavuot* may bring them for an additional six days after the Festival and thereby fulfills his obligation (Rambam *Sefer Korbanot, Hilkhot Ḥagiga* 1:7).

One day before Rosh HaShana – יוֹם אֶחָד לִפְנֵי רֹאשׁ הַשָּׁנָה: If one observed mourning practices for a deceased relative for even an hour before Rosh HaShana, then Rosh HaShana cancels the seven-day period of mourning. The thirty-day period of mourning is canceled by Yom Kippur, and one may cut his hair on the day before Yom Kippur, in accordance with the opinion of Rav Pappa (*Shulḥan Arukh, Yoreh De'a* 399:9).

One day before the Festival of *Sukkot* – יוֹם אֶחָד לִפְנֵי הֶחָג: If one observed mourning for a short time before the Festival of *Sukkot*, it is considered to be seven days of mourning. The Festival itself counts as an additional seven days, and the Eighth Day of Assembly also counts as seven days. Therefore, he needs to complete only nine days of mourning after the Festival, in order to finish his thirty-day period of mourning. In the Diaspora, *Simḥat Torah* counts as one day towards this number (*Shulḥan Arukh, Yoreh De'a* 399:11).

LANGUAGE

Pavilion [*kila*] – קִילְעָא: This word refers to any temporary structure built from screens or panels. Therefore, it means a tent or any other temporary partition.

BACKGROUND

Granted permission – אַדְבָּרֵיהּ: The expression refers to the granting of permission to teach *halakha* in public. Occasionally, this means that the Sage granting the permission also gave his approval to the teaching. There are a number of instances in the Gemara in which a Sage gave permission to different people from the house of the Exilarch to give these types of public lessons.

רָבִינָא אִיקְּלַע לְסוּרָא דִּפְרָת. אֲמַר לֵיהּ רַב חֲבִיבָא מִסּוּרָא דִּפְרָת לְרָבִינָא: אָמַר מָר יוֹם אֶחָד לִפְנֵי רֹאשׁ הַשָּׁנָה וְרֹאשׁ הַשָּׁנָה הֲרֵי כָּאן אַרְבָּעָה עָשָׂר? אֲמַר לֵיהּ: אֲנָא מִסְתַּבְרָא כְּרַבָּן גַּמְלִיאֵל הוּא דְּאָמֵינָא.

It was related that **Ravina happened** to come **to** the city of **Sura on the Euphrates** River. **Rav Ḥaviva from Sura on the Euphrates said to Ravina:** Did the **Master say** that **one day** of mourning **before Rosh HaShana and Rosh HaShana** itself count **as fourteen** days? **He said to him: I said that it stands to reason** that this is so **according to Rabban Gamliel,**[N] who maintains that Rosh HaShana is treated like a pilgrimage Festival. But I did not rule in accordance with this opinion.

מתני׳ אֵין קוֹרְעִין, וְלֹא חוֹלְצִין, וְאֵין מַבְרִין, אֶלָּא קְרוֹבָיו שֶׁל מֵת. וְאֵין מַבְרִין אֶלָּא עַל מִטָּה זְקוּפָה.

MISHNA Mourners **do not rend**[N] their garments during the intermediate days of a Festival[H] **and do not remove** their garments from their shoulders. **And** others **do not provide them with a meal**[N] [*mavrin*][L] after the burial, **except for close relatives of the deceased. And** the consolers **provide the** first **meal** after the burial **only** while the mourner is sitting **on an upright bed,** and not on one that is overturned.

NOTES

It stands to reason according to Rabban Gamliel – מִסְתַּבְרָא כְּרַבָּן גַּמְלִיאֵל: It is explained that Ravina did not rule in this manner explicitly. Instead, he said that since the *halakha* is in accordance with Rabban Gamliel, that Rosh HaShana is considered to interrupt mourning like the Festivals, it is should also be considered to be like a Festival and count as seven days. He did not mean that the *halakha* is in accordance with Rabban Gamliel's opinion; rather, he was just explaining his reasoning.

According to the Rambam, Ravina did not agree with this ruling. Although the *halakha* is in accordance with Rabban Gamliel, that Rosh HaShana interrupts mourning, Ravina did not agree that Rosh HaShana should count as seven days. This is because it is not a pilgrimage Festival at all, and the comparison between *Shavuot* and *Sukkot* cannot be applied to Rosh HaShana. Other halakhic authorities hold that Rosh HaShana is considered to be like a pilgrimage Festival because all Festivals are compared to each other.

Mourners do not rend, etc. – אֵין קוֹרְעִין וכו׳: Most of the early authorities explain that this entire mishna specifically discusses the *halakhot* of mourning during the intermediate days of the Festival. However, this implies that on non-festive days mourners must rend their clothes (*ge'onim*; Ra'avad; Ramban). This also appears to be the conclusion in the Jerusalem Talmud. However, there are some who understand this mishna to be dealing with mourning during weekdays, and according to their explanation it is entirely prohibited to rend their garments (Rashi).

Others do not provide them with a meal, etc. – אֵין מַבְרִין: According to those who understand the mishna to be speaking of the intermediate days of the Festival, a mourner is not required to overturn his bed because mourning does not apply during this time. According to those who understand that this *halakha* was said with regard to regular weekdays, there are those who understand it to mean that the consolers sit on an upright bed, and not with the mourner on an overturned bed (Rashi; Rabbeinu Gershom Meor HaGola; Rabbeinu Yehonatan of Lunel). However, others explain that both out of respect for the consolers and so that they will not have to sit in separate place, the Sages even permitted the mourner to eat the feast after the burial on an upright bed (Ra'avad; Ramban).

HALAKHA

Rending during the Festival – קְרִיעָה בְּמוֹעֵד: One may rend his garment over a death during the intermediate days of the Festival only when rending the garment is required according to *halakha*. Some disagree and say that one may not rend garments at all during the intermediate days of the Festival. It is the Ashkenazic custom for one to rend his garments during the intermediate days of the Festival only when mourning his father or mother. When mourning any other relatives one rends his garments after the Festival (Rema). However, in Poland it was customary to rend one's garments when mourning all relatives (*Magen Avraham*). The Sephardic communities of Jerusalem, Izmir, and Thessaloniki, had a similar custom to the Ashkenazic one; however, every place should act in accordance with the local custom there (*Kaf HaḤayyim*; *Shulḥan Arukh*, *Oraḥ Ḥayyim* 547:6).

LANGUAGE

Provide a meal [*mavrin*] – מַבְרִין: The root *v-r-h* means to eat and is found several times in the Bible (see II Samuel, chapter 13). The custom for mourners to eat their first meal after the burial from other people's food is very ancient and is first mentioned in the book of II Samuel: "And the people came to feed David bread" (3:35). Similarly, the custom is mentioned when Ezekiel the prophet is prohibited from acting like an ordinary mourner: "And people's bread you shall not eat" (Ezekiel 24:17–22). This meal is referred to as the *se'udat havra'a*, meaning the meal at which the mourners are fed.

גמ׳ וַאֲפִילּוּ חָכָם? וְהָתַנְיָא: חָכָם שֶׁמֵּת – הַכֹּל קְרוֹבָיו.

GEMARA The mishna teaches that only the relatives of the deceased rend their clothes. The Gemara asks: **And** is this the case **even** if the deceased was a Torah **Sage? But isn't it taught** otherwise in a *baraita*: When a Torah **scholar dies, everyone is his relative.**[H]

הַכֹּל קְרוֹבָיו סָלְקָא דַעְתָּךְ?! אֶלָּא: הַכֹּל כִּקְרוֹבָיו – הַכֹּל קוֹרְעִין עָלָיו, וְהַכֹּל חוֹלְצִין עָלָיו, וְהַכֹּל מַבְרִין עָלָיו בָּרְחָבָה! לָא צְרִיכָא דְּלָאו חָכָם הוּא.

The Gemara clarifies: **Does it enter your mind** to say that **everyone is his relative? Rather,** this *baraita* should be understood as follows: **Everyone is** considered to be **like his relative** in the sense that **everyone rends his** garment in anguish **over him, and everyone bares**[H] his shoulder **over him** in mourning, **and everyone eats the mourner's meal over him**[H] **in the public square** as mourners do. The death of a Torah scholar is a personal loss for every Jew. So why is the mishna limited to only relatives? The Gemara answers: **No,** it is **necessary** for the mishna to teach this *halakha* in a case **where** the deceased **is not a** Torah **scholar.**

וְאִי אָדָם כָּשֵׁר הוּא – חִיּוּבֵי מִיחַיַּיב לְמִיקְרַע, דְּתַנְיָא: מִפְּנֵי מָה בָּנָיו וּבְנוֹתָיו שֶׁל אָדָם מֵתִים כְּשֶׁהֵן קְטַנִּים – כְּדֵי שֶׁיִּבְכֶּה וְיִתְאַבֵּל עַל אָדָם כָּשֵׁר.

The Gemara asks: **And if** the deceased **was an upright person** who feared Heaven and performed good deeds, then aren't all those present at his death **obligated to rend** their garments over his death?[H] **As it is taught** in a *baraita*: **For what reason do a person's sons and daughters die when they are young?** They die **so that he will cry and mourn** over the death of **an upright person.**

יִבְכֶּה וְיִתְאַבֵּל? עַרְבוֹנָא קָא שָׁקֵיל מִינֵּיהּ?! אֶלָּא: מִפְּנֵי שֶׁלֹּא בָּכָה וְהִתְאַבֵּל עַל אָדָם כָּשֵׁר. שֶׁכָּל הַבּוֹכֶה וּמִתְאַבֵּל עַל אָדָם כָּשֵׁר – מוֹחֲלִין לוֹ עַל כָּל עֲוֹנוֹתָיו בִּשְׁבִיל כָּבוֹד שֶׁעָשָׂה לוֹ! דְּלָאו אָדָם כָּשֵׁר הוּא.

The Gemara questions the formulation: They die so that **he will cry and mourn? Is security,** i.e., his children, **taken from him** in advance to ensure that in the future he will mourn over the death of an upright person? **Rather** the *baraita* means as follows: His children died **because he did not cry or mourn over an upright person**[N] who died. **As** with regard to **anyone who cries and mourns over an upright person** who died, **they forgive him** for **all his transgressions because of the honor he accorded** to the deceased. If this is the case, one also rends his clothes over an upright person. The Gemara answers: Rather, the mishna is referring only to one **who** was **not an upright person.**

NOTES

Because he did not cry…over an upright person – מִפְּנֵי שֶׁלֹּא בָּכָה...עַל אָדָם כָּשֵׁר: In punishment for not crying over an upright person, this person will cry over the death of his children, who were certainly upright because they were not yet old enough to sin. Therefore, the punishment is tailored to the sin (Maharsha).

HALAKHA

Rending garments over a Torah scholar – קְרִיעָה עַל חָכָם: When a Torah scholar dies, everyone rends his garment over him on the day of burial or when they hear of his death, provided it is within thirty days of his passing. Additionally, one rends his garment over him at the time of the eulogy if the eulogy is within thirty days of the death (*Shakh*; *Baḥ* citing Rosh and Ra'avad). If one did not rend his garment on the day when he heard the news or during the eulogy, then he may no longer rend his garment (Rema). In this context anyone who is asked questions about *halakhot* and knows the answers is called a Torah scholar. When rendering garments over one's own rabbi, one tears until he exposes his chest. When rending one's garments over other Torah scholars, even if they are equal in wisdom to the mourner, the tear is one handbreadth in length. Some say that one rends his garments only over his rabbi or over one who taught him Torah. The common practice is to be lenient and not rend a garment over one's rabbi (*Shulḥan Arukh*, *Yoreh De'a* 340:7, and in the comment of Rema).

Everyone bares – הַכֹּל חוֹלְצִין: When one's rabbi dies he should uncover his garment from his shoulder, similar to the practice over the passing of his father or mother. Some say that this act of mourning is no longer performed, and this is the common practice (*Shulḥan Arukh*, *Yoreh De'a* 340:17).

Everyone eats the mourner's meal over him – הַכֹּל מַבְרִין עָלָיו: Everyone eats the mourner's meal over the death of a Torah scholar in the public square, even during the intermediate days of a Festival, because everyone is considered to be like his relative (*Shulḥan Arukh*, *Yoreh De'a* 401:4).

Rending garments over an upright person – קְרִיעָה עַל אָדָם כָּשֵׁר: When an upright person dies, one rends his garment between the time of death and burial as a sign of mourning. An upright person is one who is not suspected of committing grave sins or avoiding performance of any mitzva, even if he is not knowledgeable in Torah. Some say that a person does not fall into this category unless he is well known for his acts of kindness (*Shakh*, *Baḥ* citing Rabbeinu Yona and Ramban). Torah scholars are not required to rend their garments over such a person; however, some Torah scholars are strict and rend their garments nevertheless (*Shakh*, citing Ra'avad and Rosh).

Others say that only one who is present at the time of the departure of the soul is required to rend his garment over an upright person, however one is required to cry and mourn over him in every case. It is the accepted practice to be lenient and not to rend one's garment (*Shulḥan Arukh*, *Yoreh De'a* 340:6 and in the comment of Rema).

אִי דְּקָאֵי הָתָם בִּשְׁעַת יְצִיאַת נְשָׁמָה – חִיּוּבֵי מִיחַיַּיב, דְּתַנְיָא, רַבִּי שִׁמְעוֹן בֶּן אֶלְעָזָר אוֹמֵר: הָעוֹמֵד עַל הַמֵּת בִּשְׁעַת יְצִיאַת נְשָׁמָה – חַיָּיב לִקְרוֹעַ. לְמָה זֶה דּוֹמֶה? לְסֵפֶר תּוֹרָה שֶׁנִּשְׂרָף, שֶׁחַיָּיב לִקְרוֹעַ!

The Gemara challenges: But **if one was standing there at the time of the soul's departure,** i.e., at the time of death, he **is** also **obligated** to rend his clothes. **As it is taught** in a *baraita*: **Rabbi Shimon ben Elazar says: One who stands over the deceased at the time of the soul's departure is obligated to rend** his clothes.[H] **To what may this be likened? To a Torah scroll that is burned,**[N] for which anyone present **is obligated to rend** his clothes.

דְּלָא קָאֵי הָתָם בִּשְׁעַת יְצִיאַת נְשָׁמָה.

The Gemara answers: The mishna must be referring to a person **who was not standing there at the time of the soul's departure** but who heard that someone who is not a close relative died, and the deceased was neither a Torah scholar nor an upright person.

כִּי נָח נַפְשֵׁיהּ דְּרַב סָפְרָא לָא קְרָעוּ רַבָּנַן עֲלֵיהּ. אָמְרִי: לָא גָּמְרִינַן מִינֵּיהּ. אֲמַר לְהוּ אַבַּיֵי: מִי תַּנְיָא הָרַב שֶׁמֵּת? חָכָם שֶׁמֵּת תַּנְיָא. וְעוֹד: כׇּל יוֹמָא שְׁמַעְתָּתֵיהּ בְּפוּמִין בְּבֵי מִדְרְשָׁא.

§ The Gemara relates that **when Rav Safra**[P] **passed away the** other **Sages did not rend** their garments **over him.**[N] **They said: We did not learn from him,** as he did not disseminate his Torah knowledge to the public. **Abaye** berated them and **said to them: Is it taught** in the *baraita*: If one's **teacher died? It is taught:** If a Torah **scholar died,** and Rav Safra was certainly a Torah scholar. **And furthermore, every day his teachings are in our mouths in the study hall,** so that even if we did not learn directly from him, we should still be considered his students.

סְבוּר: מַה דַּהֲוָה – הֲוָה. אֲמַר לְהוּ אַבַּיֵי, תָּנֵינָא: חָכָם, כׇּל זְמַן שֶׁעוֹסְקִין בְּהֶסְפֵּד – חַיָּיבִין לִקְרוֹעַ. סְבוּר לְמִיקְרַע לְאַלְתַּר. אֲמַר לְהוּ אַבַּיֵי, תַּנְיָא: חָכָם כְּבוֹדוֹ בְּהֶסְפֵּידוֹ.

The other Sages **thought that what was** done **was** done, and it was now too late for them to rend their garments. **Abaye said to them: We learned:** With regard to a Torah **scholar, as long as they are engaged in eulogizing** him, then people **are obligated to rend** their garments, even after the time of his death. **They** then **thought to rend** their garments **immediately. Abaye said to them: It is taught** in a *baraita*: **A** Torah **scholar's honor is at** the time of **his eulogy,** and so you should wait until the time of the eulogy before rending your garments.

כִּי נָח נַפְשֵׁיהּ דְּרַב הוּנָא, סְבוּר לְאוֹתוּבֵי סֵפֶר תּוֹרָה אַפּוּרְיֵיהּ. אֲמַר לְהוּ רַב חִסְדָּא: מִילְּתָא דִּבְחַיֵּיהּ לָא סְבִירָא לֵיהּ, הָשְׁתָּא לֵיקוּם לֵיהּ לִיעֲבַד לֵיהּ? דְּאָמַר רַב תַּחְלִיפָא: אֲנָא חֲזִיתֵיהּ לְרַב הוּנָא דְּבָעֵי לְמֵיתַב אַפּוּרְיֵיהּ, וַהֲוָה מַנַּח סֵפֶר תּוֹרָה עֲלֵיהּ, וְכָף כַּדָּא אַאַרְעָא וְאוֹתִיב סֵפֶר תּוֹרָה עִילָּוֵיהּ. אַלְמָא קָסָבַר: אָסוּר לֵישֵׁב עַל גַּבֵּי מִטָּה שֶׁסֵּפֶר תּוֹרָה מוּנָּח עָלֶיהָ.

§ The Gemara relates another incident: **When Rav Huna**[P] **died they thought to place a Torah scroll on his bier,** as was commonly done after the death of a Torah scholar, as if to say that the deceased fulfilled everything written in the scroll. **Rav Ḥisda said to them:** This is **a practice that he did not hold with during his lifetime; now should we stand up and do it for him** when he is dead? **As Rav Taḥlifa said:** I myself **saw Rav Huna, who wished to sit on his bed, and there was a Torah scroll placed on it. And he turned a jug over and placed the Torah scroll on it** so that he could then sit on the bed. **Apparently he holds** that **it is prohibited to sit on a bed upon which a Torah scroll lies.**[H] Therefore, it would be inappropriate to lay a Torah scroll next to his body after he died.[H]

HALAKHA

Rending garments at the time of the soul's departure – קְרִיעָה בִּשְׁעַת יְצִיאַת נְשָׁמָה: One who is in the presence of a Jew whose soul departs is required to rend his garment. This applies whether the deceased is a man or a woman, but does not apply to a minor who has died (*Shakh*, citing Maharshal), unless he has already studied Torah (*Shakh*, citing *Baḥ*). This applies even if he was not an upright person, and it is known that he occasionally sinned due to his desires or was negligent and did not trouble himself to perform a certain mitzva. However, one does not rend his garment over one who habitually sins, and even more so over an apostate (*Shulḥan Arukh, Yoreh De'a* 340:5).

A Torah scroll on the bier of a Torah scholar's – סֵפֶר תּוֹרָה עַל מִיטַּת חָכָם: A Torah scroll is not placed on the bier of a Torah scholar who died, as demonstrated in the incident with Rav Huna (*Shulḥan Arukh, Yoreh De'a* 353:2).

Sitting in a place on which a Torah scroll is resting – יְשִׁיבָה בְּמָקוֹם שֶׁמּוּנָּח סֵפֶר תּוֹרָה: It is prohibited to sit on a chair or bench on which a Torah scroll is resting. It is appropriate to be stringent and to raise the Torah ten handbreadths from where one is sitting, or at least three (*Shakh*, citing *Beit Yosef*), but after the fact, one handbreadth is sufficient (*Shakh*; *Shulḥan Arukh, Yoreh De'a* 282:7).

NOTES

To a Torah scroll that is burned – לְסֵפֶר תּוֹרָה שֶׁנִּשְׂרָף: The early authorities offer several explanations for this comparison. Rashi and Rabbeinu Gershom Meor HaGola explain that as one's soul and a Torah scroll are both likened to a candle of God, the mourning for both should be the same. The text of Rashi printed alongside the Rif, and cited in Rashi's name by the Ran, states that since the deceased could have studied more Torah during his lifetime but did not succeed in doing so, it is comparable to a Torah scroll that was burned.

The Ramban writes that just as one rends his garment for a Torah scroll that is burned, so too one rends them over a person who observes the Torah's mitzvot. He similarly explains that the relationship between the body and the soul is similar to that between the parchment and the letters. Once a scroll is burned the letters leave the page, just like the soul departs from the body. Others write that one rends his garment because of the sanctity of the soul that departs from the body (Commentary on *Moed Katan*). Rashi writes in tractate *Shabbat* that since even the most ignorant Jew is filled with mitzvot, every person is similar to a Torah scroll.

The Sages did not rend their garments over him – לָא קְרָעוּ רַבָּנַן עֲלֵיהּ: The early authorities ask: Even if Rav Safra was not their teacher, he was certainly an upright person, so why did they not rend their clothes over him? Some say that rending garments over an upright person is only done between the death and the burial. Since this discussion occurred after the burial the Sages thought that they did not need to rend their garments (Ra'avad). Others write that Torah scholars do not rend their garments over an upright person unless he is a Torah scholar of their stature (Ramban).

PERSONALITIES

Rav Safra – רַב סָפְרָא: Rav Safra was an *amora* from the third and fourth generation of *amora'im* in Babylonia. The Talmud records that Rav Safra discussed halakhic matters as a disciple-colleague of the greatest Sages of the third generation of *amora'im*, such as Rabba and Rav Yosef, and continued to flourish into the time of their students Abaye and Rava. Apparently Rav Safra was a merchant, and visited Eretz Yisrael, where he interacted with Sages such as Rabbi Abba and Rabbi Abbahu. He was primarily knowledgeable about *halakha*, and devoted less attention to the study of *aggada* or Bible. Rav Safra was also well known for his character traits, particularly with regard to his desire to entirely avoid falsehood. Because Rav Safra traveled from place to place he did not have his own academy and he was often absent from the study hall. Therefore, some Sages thought that he did not qualify as a Sage for whom everyone mourns.

Rav Huna – רַב הוּנָא: One of the greatest second-generation of *amora'im* in Babylonia, Rav Huna succeeded his primary teacher, Rav, as the head of the academy in Sura. After Shmuel passed away Rav Huna was considered by all to be the most learned scholar in Babylonia.

Under his tenure, the yeshiva of Sura experienced significant growth, both in the number of its students and in their quality. Almost all of the Sages of the next generation were considered Rav Huna's students to a certain degree. This included Rav Ami and Rav Asi, who studied from Rav Huna in Babylonia. Even after they moved to Eretz Yisrael and were recognized as the leading Sages there, they considered themselves subordinate to Rav Huna.

According to a tradition recorded by the *ge'onim*, Rav Huna was from the family of the Exilarch. Nonetheless, he was very poor in his youth, but he studied Torah despite his poverty. He became wealthy later in life (see 27b). The Talmud recounts numerous anecdotes about Rav Huna's piety (see *Ta'anit* 20b), and his wisdom was legendary.

Rav Huna lived for over eighty years, and after his death he was brought with great honor to Eretz Yisrael, where he was buried next to the great Sage Rabbi Ḥiyya.

Rav Huna's son, Rabba bar Rav Huna, was among the most prominent *amora'im* of the next generation.

לָא הֲוָה נְפֵיק פּוּרְיָא מִבָּבָא, סְבוּר לְשַׁלְשׁוּלֵי דֶּרֶךְ גַּגִּין. אֲמַר לְהוּ רַב חִסְדָּא: הָא גְּמִירְנָא מִינֵּיהּ: חָכָם כְּבוֹדוֹ דֶּרֶךְ פֶּתַח.

When they tried to remove his corpse from his house for the burial, **the bier would not** fit **through the** narrow **door. They** then **thought to lower** the bier **from the roof. Rav Ḥisda said to them: This I learned from him,** Rav Huna himself: **A scholar's honor** is for him to be taken out **through the** main **opening,** and not in any other manner.

סְבוּר לְאַשְׁנוּיֵי מִפּוּרְיָא לְפוּרְיָא. אֲמַר לְהוּ רַב חִסְדָּא, הָכִי גְּמִירְנָא מִינֵּיהּ: חָכָם, כְּבוֹדוֹ בְּמִטָּה רִאשׁוֹנָה. דַּאֲמַר רַב יְהוּדָה אָמַר רַב: מִנַּיִן לְחָכָם שֶׁכְּבוֹדוֹ בְּמִטָּה רִאשׁוֹנָה? שֶׁנֶּאֱמַר: ״וַיַּרְכִּיבוּ אֶת אֲרוֹן הָאֱלֹהִים אֶל עֲגָלָה חֲדָשָׁה״. פְּרוּס בָּבָא, וְאַפְּקוּהָ.

They then **thought to move him from** his **bier to** a narrower **bier** so that it would fit through the door. But **Rav Ḥisda said to them: I learned from him,** Rav Huna himself, **as follows: A scholar's honor is** for him to be taken out **on the first bier.**[H] **As Rav Yehuda said** that **Rav said: From where** is it derived that **a scholar's honor is** for him to be taken out **on the first bier? As it is stated: "And they set the Ark of God upon a new cart"** (II Samuel 6:3).[N] When taking the Ark to Jerusalem, King David had it placed back on the cart upon which it had been returned by the Philistines, and a Torah scholar is considered to be similar to the Ark of the Covenant. When they saw that there was nothing else that they could do, **they broke the doorway and took him out** through it.

פְּתַח עֲלֵיהּ רַבִּי אַבָּא: רָאוּי הָיָה רַבֵּינוּ שֶׁתִּשְׁרֶה עָלָיו שְׁכִינָה, אֶלָּא שֶׁבָּבֶל גָּרְמָה לֵיהּ.

Rabbi Abba opened his eulogy for **him: Our Rabbi was worthy that the Divine Presence should rest upon him, except** for the fact **that Babylonia caused it** not to rest. In other words, it was only because he lived in Babylonia and not in Eretz Yisrael that the Divine Presence did not rest upon him.

מְתִיב רַב נַחְמָן בַּר חִסְדָּא, וְאָמְרִי לָהּ רַב חָנָן בַּר חִסְדָּא: ״הָיֹה הָיָה דְבַר ה׳ אֶל יְחֶזְקֵאל בֶּן בּוּזִי הַכֹּהֵן בְּאֶרֶץ כַּשְׂדִּים״!

Rav Naḥman bar Ḥisda raised an objection against this, **and some say** that it was **Rav Ḥanan bar Ḥisda:** Is it not stated: **"The word of the Lord came [*hayo haya*] to Ezekiel the priest, son of Buzi, in the land of the Chaldeans"** (Ezekiel 1:3), thereby implying that a prophet can prophesy outside of Eretz Yisrael?

טְפַח לֵיהּ אֲבוּהּ בְּסַנְדָּלֵיהּ. אֲמַר לֵיהּ: לָאו אָמִינָא לָךְ לָא תִּיטְרוֹד עָלְמָא? מַאי ״הָיָה״? שֶׁהָיָה כְּבָר.

His father tapped him with his sandal on his foot, thereby hinting to him that he should be quiet. **He said to him: Have I not told you not to trouble everyone** with questions in the middle of a eulogy? The Gemara answers the question: **What** is the meaning of the doubling of the word **"came [*hayo haya*]"?** It implies **that it had already come** before,[N] i.e., that Ezekiel had already begun to prophesy in Eretz Yisrael, and his prophecy in Babylonia was merely a continuation of that prophecy.

כִּי אַסְקוּהּ לְהָתָם אֲמָרוּ לֵיהּ לְרַבִּי אַמִי וּלְרַבִּי אַסִי: רַב הוּנָא אָתֵי. אֲמָרוּ: כִּי הֲוֵינַן הָתָם לָא הֲוָה לָן לְדַלּוּיֵי רֵישִׁין מִינֵּיהּ, הָשְׁתָּא אָתֵינַן הָכָא אֲתָא בַּתְרִין?

§ The Gemara relates that **when they took** Rav Huna **there,** to Eretz Yisrael, for burial **they said to Rabbi Ami and Rabbi Asi: Rav Huna has come,** and they misunderstood and thought that he was still alive. **They said: When we were there,** in Babylonia, we **did not have strength to lift our heads before him. Now** that **we have come here, has he come after us?**

אֲמָרוּ לֵיהּ: אֲרוֹנוֹ בָּא. רַבִּי אַמִי וְרַבִּי אַסִי נְפוּק, רַבִּי אִילָא וְרַבִּי חֲנִינָא לָא נְפוּק. אִיכָּא דְּאָמְרִי: רַבִּי אִילָא נְפַק, רַבִּי חֲנִינָא לָא נְפַק.

They said to them: His coffin has come. Rabbi Ami and Rabbi Asi went out to meet his funeral procession. **Rabbi Ila and Rabbi Ḥanina did not go out. Some say** that **Rabbi Ila went out,** but **Rabbi Ḥanina did not go out.**

HALAKHA

A scholar's honor is on the first bier – חָכָם, כְּבוֹדוֹ בְּמִטָּה רִאשׁוֹנָה: It accords honor to a deceased Torah scholar to take his body out of his house through the doorway and not by lowering him from the roof. Similarly he should not be moved from one bier to another. Nowadays people are not particular about this (*Arukh HaShulḥan*; *Shulḥan Arukh*, *Yoreh De'a* 353:3).

NOTES

And they set…upon a new cart – וַיַּרְכִּיבוּ...אֶל עֲגָלָה חֲדָשָׁה: Rashi explains that the cart mentioned here is the one on which the Philistines returned the Ark (I Samuel, chapter 6). See also Rabbeinu Gershom Meor HaGola and the Commentary on *Moed Katan*. The early authorities ask with regard to Rashi's explanation: It is stated explicitly (I Samuel 6:14) that this cart was destroyed and its wood was used to burn the cows that dragged the cart, as a burnt offering. There are some who explain that the cart was not entirely destroyed. However, this explanation is implausible. Some explain that the new cart refers to a different cart that was constructed in order to transport the ark (*Tosefot HaRosh*; see *HaKotev* on *Ein Ya'akov*). The Meiri adds to this explanation that the fact that Uzza died as a punishment (II Samuel 6:7) shows that moving the Ark to a new cart, and not transporting it on the original, was itself a transgression.

That it had already come – שֶׁהָיָה כְּבָר: Although there were prophets who prophesied outside of Eretz Yisrael, that happened only before the Jewish people entered their land, and from that point onward prophets prophesied only in Eretz Yisrael (*HaKotev* in *Ein Ya'akov*). The explanation that Ezekiel was a prophet even before he was exiled to Babylonia, which is mentioned in Rashi, is also mentioned in *midrashim* (see Maharsha). The *Kuzari* explains Ezekiel's prophecy differently, and notes that Ezekiel was able to prophesy in the Diaspora because he did so for the sake of Eretz Yisrael.

HALAKHA

A passing coffin – אָרוֹן מֵתִים הָעוֹבֵר: When a coffin is passing from place to place, if the skeleton of the deceased is still intact and there are mourners in that place then they stand in a line to honor the deceased and say the mourners' blessing and the consolation of mourners. If the skeleton is no longer intact then there is no need to do so (*Shulḥan Arukh, Yoreh De'a* 345:8).

NOTES

Who will take him in – מַאן מְעַיֵּיל לֵיהּ: Tractate *Bava Metzia* describes the great respect with which Rabbi Ḥiyya's grave was treated. Only a few unique individuals were able to enter and exit safely. The pillar of fire that accompanied Rabbi Ḥiyya is also mentioned there. Similarly, the sanctity of Rabbi Ḥiyya and his sons is compared to that of the Patriarchs. In the Jerusalem Talmud it is told that the Sages suspected that Rav Ḥagga, who was already old, wished to enter the grave so that he himself would also die in this holy burial place. The qualifications Rav Ḥagga presented are sufficient to explain why he was fit to enter and exit that cave.

One of the straps of his phylacteries turned around – אִתְהַפִּיכָא לֵיהּ רְצוּעָה דִּתְפִילִּין: Some explain that the strap turned over so that the black side, which should face outward, could not be seen (Rabbeinu Gershom Meor HaGola). Others say it was not the straps that turned over, but the letters of God's name, which are formed by the straps of the phylacteries, that were turned over. According to those who explain the passage in this manner, Rav Huna fasted so much because he was concerned that he had not properly fulfilled the mitzva and thought that this might have been a desecration of God's name. There are also those who explain that Rav Huna thought that if this happened to him it must be because he had accidentally sinned in another matter (Commentary on *Moed Katan*).

He stood up Rav Huna's coffin – דִּזְקַפֵּיהּ לַאֲרוֹנֵיהּ דְּרַב הוּנָא: Many of the early authorities had a version of this text that states that because of this action the Exilarch is never fully punished by Heaven for his sins. Rabbeinu Ḥananel explains that through the merit of Rav Huna, who was descended from the family of the Exilarch, and through the symbolic act of standing up the coffin, all of his family were privileged to enjoy greatness, even though they did not always deserve it.

דִּנְפַק מַאי טַעֲמֵיהּ? דְּתַנְיָא: אָרוֹן הָעוֹבֵר מִמָּקוֹם לְמָקוֹם – עוֹמְדִים עָלָיו בְּשׁוּרָה, וְאוֹמְרִים עָלָיו בִּרְכַּת אֲבֵלִים וְתַנְחוּמֵי אֲבֵלִים. דְּלָא נְפַק מַאי טַעֲמָא? דְּתַנְיָא: אָרוֹן הָעוֹבֵר מִמָּקוֹם לְמָקוֹם – אֵין עוֹמְדִין עָלָיו בְּשׁוּרָה, וְאֵין אוֹמְרִים עָלָיו בִּרְכַּת אֲבֵלִים וְתַנְחוּמֵי אֲבֵלִים.

The Gemara asks: Those who **went out, what is the reason** that they went? **As it is taught** in a *baraita*: When **a coffin is passing from place to place,**[H] the people **stand in a line** to show respect **for** the deceased, **and they recite the mourners' blessing and the consolation of the mourners over it.** Those **who did not go out, what is the reason** that they did not? **As it is taught** in another *baraita*: When a **coffin is passing from place to place, they do not stand in a line** to show respect **for** the deceased, **and they do not recite the mourners' blessing** or the **consolation of the mourners for him.**

קַשְׁיָין אַהֲדָדֵי! לָא קַשְׁיָא, כָּאן – שֶׁשִּׁלְדּוֹ קַיֶּימֶת; כָּאן – בְּשֶׁאֵין שִׁלְדּוֹ קַיֶּימֶת. וְרַב הוּנָא שִׁלְדּוֹ קַיֶּימֶת הֲוָה. דְּלָא נְפַק – לָא סַיְּימוּהּ קַמֵּיהּ.

The Gemara asks: If so, **these** two tannaitic statements **contradict each other.** The Gemara answers: **It is not difficult: Here,** the *baraita* is referring to a case **where the skeleton** of the deceased **is still intact,** and the mourning practices must be observed. **And there** the *baraita* is referring to a case **where the skeleton** of the deceased **is no longer intact,** and it is not necessary to observe the customs of mourning. **And Rav Huna's skeleton was** still **intact.** The reason that the **one** Sage **did not go out** was that **they did not confirm for him** that the skeleton was still intact.

אָמְרִי: הֵיכָא נֵינְחֵיהּ? רַב הוּנָא רִיבֵּץ תּוֹרָה בְּיִשְׂרָאֵל וְרַבִּי חִיָּיא רִיבֵּץ תּוֹרָה בְּיִשְׂרָאֵל הֲוָה.

The Sages of Eretz Yisrael **said: Where shall we bury him?** They concluded: **Rav Huna disseminated Torah to** the people **of Israel,** and similarly **Rabbi Ḥiyya disseminated Torah to** the people of **Israel;** therefore, it is appropriate to bury Rav Huna next to Rabbi Ḥiyya.

מַאן מְעַיֵּיל לֵיהּ? אֲמַר לְהוּ רַב חַגָּא: אֲנָא מְעַיֵּילְנָא לֵיהּ, דְּאוֹקַמְתֵּיהּ לְתַלְמוּדַאי כִּי הֲוֵינָא בַּר תְּמָנֵי סְרֵי שְׁנִין וְלָא חֲזֵי לִי קֶרִי, וּמְשַׁמַּשְׁנָא לֵיהּ קַמֵּיהּ וְיָדַעְנָא בְּעוֹבָדֵיהּ. דְּיוֹמָא חַד אִתְהַפִּיכָא לֵיהּ רְצוּעָה דִּתְפִילִּין, וִיתֵיב עֲלָהּ אַרְבָּעִין תַּעֲנִיָּתָא.

They asked: **Who will take him in**[N] to Rabbi Ḥiyya's burial cave, as few are fit to enter it? **Rav Ḥagga**[P] **said to them: I will take him into** the cave, **for I presented my studies** before him **when I was** just **eighteen, never having experiencing a seminal emission. And so too I attended to him and knew his** great **deeds.** For example, **one day one of the straps of his phylacteries turned around,**[N] the unpainted side being turned outward, **and he observed forty fasts for this,** as he had acted negligently, allowing the black side to face inward.

עַיְּילֵיהּ, הֲוָה גָּנֵי יְהוּדָה מִימִינֵיהּ דַּאֲבוּהּ, וְחִזְקִיָּה מִשְּׂמָאלֵיהּ. אֲמַר לֵיהּ יְהוּדָה לְחִזְקִיָּה: קוּם מִדּוּכְתִּיךְ, דְּלָאו אוֹרַח אַרְעָא דְּקָאִים רַב הוּנָא. בַּהֲדֵי דְּקָאִים קָם בַּהֲדֵיהּ עַמּוּדָא דְּנוּרָא, חַזְיֵיהּ רַב חַגָּא, אִיבְעִית, זְקַפֵּיהּ לַאֲרוֹנֵיהּ וּנְפַק, אֲתָא. וְהַאי דְּלָא אִיעֲנַשׁ עֲנַשׁ – מִשּׁוּם דִּזְקַפֵּיהּ לַאֲרוֹנֵיהּ דְּרַב הוּנָא.

Rav Ḥagga **took him in.** The body of Rabbi Ḥiyya's son **Yehuda lay** buried **to the right of his father, and** the body of his other son **Ḥizkiyya** lay **to his left.** The spirit of **Yehuda said to** the spirit of **Ḥizkiyya: Rise from your place,** as it is **not proper conduct** to remain lying when the body of **Rav Huna is standing here. When** Ḥizkiyya's corpse stood **up, a pillar of fire rose with him.** When **Rabbi Ḥagga saw this, he was frightened** by what he saw, and so **he stood up** Rav Huna's **coffin**[N] **and went away.** The Gemara comments: **And he was not punished** or harmed by this pillar of fire **because he set up Rav Huna's coffin** as protection for himself.

כִּי נָח נַפְשֵׁיהּ דְּרַב חִסְדָּא סְבוּר לְאוֹתוּבֵי סֵפֶר תּוֹרָה אַפּוּרְיֵיהּ. אֲמַר לְהוּ רַבִּי יִצְחָק: מִילְּתָא דִּלְרַבֵּיהּ לָא סְבִירָא לֵיהּ, אֲנַן נֵיקוּם נַעֲבֵיד לֵיהּ?

§ The Gemara relates another story about the burial of one of the Sages: **When Rav Ḥisda died they thought to place a Torah scroll on his bier. Rabbi Yitzḥak said to them:** This is **a practice that this Rabbi did not hold with during his lifetime; should we stand up and do it for him** now that he is dead?

PERSONALITIES

Rav Ḥagga – רַב חַגָּא: Rav Ḥagga was a Babylonian *amora* who moved to Eretz Yisrael and was active there. Rav Ḥagga was apparently a disciple-colleague of Rav Huna, as this is consistent with the chronological calculation. In the Jerusalem Talmud, where he is known by the name Rabbi Ḥaggai, it is told that when Rav Ḥagga brought Rav Huna for his burial he was already eighty years old, and it is known that he lived for a time afterward. In Eretz Yisrael he interacted with the students of Rabbi Yoḥanan, although he also transmitted statements from the Sages of previous generations. It appears that he served as a judge in his city and several stories about his activity there are related in the Jerusalem Talmud and in the *midrashim*. The Sages of the following generations received numerous traditions in his name, and he became known as one of the leaders of his generation.

סְבוּר דְּלָא לְמִישְׁלַל קְרָעַיְיהוּ. אֲמַר לְהוּ רַבִּי יִצְחָק בַּר אַמִי: חָכָם, כֵּיוָן שֶׁהֶחְזִירוּ פְּנֵיהֶם מֵאֲחוֹרֵי הַמִּטָּה – שׁוֹלְלִין.

They then **thought not to tack,** i.e., sew up, **the tears** that they had made in their clothes. **Rabbi Yitzḥak bar Ami said to them:** When the deceased is **a Torah Sage, they may tack** the tears **once they turn their faces from the bier.**[H]

כִּי נָח נַפְשֵׁיהּ דְּרַבָּה בַּר הוּנָא וְרַב הַמְנוּנָא אַסְקִינְהוּ לְהָתָם,

The Gemara relates that **when Rabba bar Huna and Rav Hamnuna died, they took them** both **up there,** to Eretz Yisrael.

HALAKHA

Tacking a tear made over the death of a Sage – שְׁלִילַת קֶרַע עַל חָכָם: A tear made in mourning for the death of a Sage may be tacked and mended once one has turned his face from the coffin of the deceased (*Shulḥan Arukh, Yoreh De'a* 340:17).

Perek **III**
Daf **25** Amud **b**

כִּי מְטוֹ אַגִּישְׁרָא קָמוּ גַּמְלֵי. אֲמַר לְהוּ הַהוּא טַיְיעָא: מַאי הַאי? אֲמַרוּ לֵיהּ: רַבָּנַן דְּקָא עָבְדִי יְקָרָא אַהֲדָדֵי. מָר אָמַר: מָר נֵיעוּל בְּרֵישָׁא, וּמָר אָמַר: מָר נֵיעוּל בְּרֵישָׁא. אֲמַר: דִּינָא הוּא דְּרַבָּה בַּר הוּנָא לֵיעוּל בְּרֵישָׁא. חֲלֵיף גַּמְלֵיהּ דְּרַבָּה בַּר הוּנָא, נְתוּר כַּכֵּיהּ וְשִׁנֵּיהּ דְּהַהוּא טַיְיעָא.

When they reached a bridge that could be crossed only in single file, **the camels** carrying the two Sages **stood** in their places and would not cross the bridge. **A certain Arab** [*Tayya'a*][L] who witnessed what was happening **said to them: What is this** phenomenon that the camels have stopped moving? **They said to him:** The deceased **Sages are showing honor to each other.** It is as if one **Sage is saying: The Master should go** and cross the bridge **first,** while at the same time the other **Sage is saying: The Master should go** and cross **first.** The Arab **said: By law**[N] **Rabba bar Huna should go first,** since he is the son of a great man, and **the camel** carrying **Rabba bar Huna** then **passed** first. Shortly thereafter, **the molars and** other **teeth of that Arab fell out** due to the disrespect he showed Rav Hamnuna.

פְּתַח עֲלֵיהּ הַהוּא יָנוּקָא: "גֶּזַע יְשִׁישִׁים עָלָה מִבָּבֶל וְעִמּוֹ סֵפֶר מִלְחָמוֹת. קָאַת וְקִפּוֹד הוּכְפְּלוּ, לִרְאוֹת בְּשׁוֹד וְשֶׁבֶר הַבָּא מִשִּׁנְעָר. קָצַף עַל עוֹלָמוֹ וְחָמַס מִמֶּנּוּ נְפָשׁוֹת, וְשָׂמַח בָּהֶם כְּכַלָּה חֲדָשָׁה. רוֹכֵב עֲרָבוֹת שָׂשׂ וְשָׂמַח בְּבֹא אֵלָיו נֶפֶשׁ נָקִי וְצַדִּיק".

When they reached Tiberias **a certain child opened** his eulogy saying as follows: **The shoot of an ancient line,** i.e., Rabba bar Rav Huna, who was the descendant of great people, **has ascended from Babylonia, and with him is the book of wars,** i.e., Rav Hamnuna, who was great in Torah, which is referred to as the book of the Wars of the Lord (Numbers 21:14). **The** curses of the **pelican and the bittern,** which are symbols of the destruction of the Temple (Isaiah 34:11), **have been doubled,**[N] **to see the ruin and brokenness that has come from Shinar,** i.e., Babylonia. The Lord **became angry with His world and seized souls from it, and He rejoices over them** when they come to Him **like a new bride.** God **who rides upon the clouds is joyous and happy when an innocent and righteous soul comes to Him.**

כִּי נָח נַפְשֵׁיהּ דְּרָבִינָא פְּתַח עֲלֵיהּ הַהוּא סַפְדָּנָא: "תְּמָרִים הָנִיעוּ רֹאשׁ עַל צַדִּיק כַּתָּמָר, נָשִׁים לֵילוֹת כְּיָמִים" – עַל מֵשִׂים לֵילוֹת כְּיָמִים.

§ The Gemara continues recounting other famous eulogies. **When Ravina**[P] **passed away, a certain eulogizer opened** his eulogy **for him** with the following words: **Date-palms, hang** your **heads** in sadness **over the righteous man who may be likened to a date-palm. Women,** make your **nights like days** in weeping, **over** a man who **made** his **nights like days** studying the Torah.

LANGUAGE

Arab [*Tayya'a*] – **טַיָּיעָא**: The origin of this word appears to be the name of a specific Arab tribe called الطائي, *al-ṭā'ī*. The Arab tribes that resided in the desert area between Arabia and Babylonia would come to trade even as far as Babylonia.

PERSONALITIES

Ravina – **רָבִינָא**: Ravina was a sixth generation Babylonian sage, whose major work was assisting Rav Ashi in editing the Babylonian Talmud. In his youth he studied under the direction of Rava. He passed away in the year 422. Ravina and Rav Ashi discuss matters of *halakha* in many places throughout the Talmud.

NOTES

By law [*dina hu*], **etc.** – **דִּינָא הוּא וכו׳**: Most versions of the talmudic text read: In my judgment [*bedina didi*], i.e., in my opinion, the great man who is also the son of a great man should go in front, before Rav Hamnuna who was not the son of a great man. This Arab was punished because it was not appropriate for him to offer his opinion on the issue, especially since there were people far more learned than him present at the time (*Iyyun Ya'akov*).

The curses of the pelican and the bittern have been doubled [*hukhpalu*] – **קָאַת וְקִפּוֹד הוּכְפְּלוּ**: Several explanations are offered for this poetic expression. Rashi explains that the pelican and bittern are mentioned as signs of a curse, and therefore this means that the curse was doubled, as two great people died. Some explain that *hukhpalu* should be related to as an Aramaic word, meaning to strive. According to this, the expression means that even these birds made an effort to attend the funeral of the righteous men (*Arukh*; Rabbeinu Gershom Meor HaGola; Commentary on *Moed Katan*; Ran). Some understand this as a reference to the Arabs who joined them on the funeral procession (Maharsha). The Meiri explains that the pelican and bittern are symbolic and allude to the increase of weeping and eulogies.

אָמַר לֵיהּ רַב אַשִׁי לְבַר קִיפּוֹק: הָהוּא יוֹמָא מַאי אָמְרַתְּ? אָמַר לֵיהּ, אָמֵינָא: אִם בָּאֲרָזִים נָפְלָה שַׁלְהֶבֶת – מָה יַעֲשׂוּ אֵיזוֹבֵי קִיר, לִוְיָתָן בְּחַכָּה הוּעֲלָה – מָה יַעֲשׂוּ דְּגֵי רְקָק, בְּנַחַל שׁוֹטֵף נָפְלָה חַכָּה – מָה יַעֲשׂוּ מֵי גְבִים.

The Gemara relates that prior to Ravina's death, **Rav Ashi**[P] **said to bar Kippok,** who was a famous eulogizer: **On that day** when Ravina will die, **what will you say?**[N] **He said to him: I shall** begin my eulogy and **say** as follows: **If the cedars went up in flame, what shall the hyssop of the wall do? If the leviathan was lifted by a hook, what shall the** tiny **fish of the marsh do? If dryness overtook a flowing river, what can the water of puddles do?**

אָמַר לֵיהּ בַּר אָבִין: חַס וְשָׁלוֹם דְּחַכָּה וְשַׁלְהֶבֶת בְּצַדִּיקֵי אָמֵינָא. וּמַאי אָמְרַתְּ? אָמֵינָא: בְּכוּ לָאֲבֵלִים וְלֹא לָאֲבֵידָה, שֶׁהִיא לִמְנוּחָה וְאָנוּ לַאֲנָחָה.

Bar Avin, who was also a eulogizer, **said to him: God forbid** that the words **hook and flame** should be **said with regard to the righteous,** as these are not expressions of honor. Rav Ashi asked him: **And what will you say?** He said to him: **I shall say: Cry for the mourners and not for that which was lost,** as that which was lost, i.e., the soul of Ravina, has gone **to** its eternal **rest, while we,** the mourners, are left with our **sighs.**

חֲלַשׁ דַּעְתֵּיהּ עֲלַיְיהוּ, וְאִתְהַפּוּךְ כַּרְעַיְיהוּ. הָהוּא יוֹמָא לָא אָתוּ לְאַסְפּוֹדֵיהּ. וְהַיְינוּ דְּאָמַר רַב אַשִׁי: לָא בַּר קִיפּוֹק חָלֵיץ, וְלָא בַּר אָבִין חָלֵיץ.

Rav Ashi **was offended by them,**[N] as their words of praise for Ravina might have been understood as a show of disrespect to Rav Ashi, since they likened Ravina to a cedar and the other Sages, Rav Ashi included, to hyssops of the wall. Due to Rav Ashi's anger, **their feet turned** inward and became crooked. **On that day** when Ravina actually died, **neither** of them **came to eulogize him. This is what Rav Ashi said** using a metaphor to describe this incident: **Neither bar Kippok can perform *ḥalitza*, nor can bar Avin perform *ḥalitza*,** because their feet are crooked and so their shoes cannot be removed from their feet in the proper manner.

רָבָא, כִּי הֲוָה אָתָא לְדִגְלַת אָמַר לֵיהּ לְבַר אָבִין: קוּם אֵימָא מִילְּתָא. קָאֵי וְאָמַר: בָּאוּ רוֹב שְׁלִישִׁית בַּמַּיִם, זְכוֹר וְרַחֵם. תָּעִינוּ מֵאַחֲרֶיךָ כְּאִשָּׁה מִבַּעְלָהּ, אַל תַּזְנִיחֵנוּ כְּאוֹת מֵי מָרָה.

When Rava once **came to the Tigris**[N] River, and he was concerned that he might be swept away by the water, **he said to bar Avin: Rise** and **say** a prayer on our behalf. **He rose and said: Most of the third,** a poetic reference to the Jewish people (Isaiah 19:24), **has come**[N] **in the water,** implying that Rava was equal in importance to the majority of the Jewish people. **Remember** then **and have mercy** on us. Although **we have strayed from you like an** unfaithful **woman** strays **from her husband, do not forsake** and punish **us like the sign of the bitter water,** with which a woman suspected of adultery is tested. That is to say, do not punish us with water.

חָנִין יוֹחָנָן זֵירָא אַבָּא יַעֲקֹב יוֹסֵי שְׁמוּאֵל חִיָּיא מְנַחֵם – סִימָן.

Apropos eulogies for righteous men, the Gemara presents the names: **Ḥanin, Yoḥanan, Zeira, Abba, Ya'akov, Yosei, Shmuel, Ḥiyya,** and **Menaḥem;** this is a **mnemonic device** for the stories that follow.

רַבִּי חָנִין חַתְנֵיהּ דְּבֵי נְשִׂיאָה הֲוָה. לָא קָא הָווּ לֵיהּ בְּנֵי, בְּעָא רַחֲמֵי וַהֲווּ לֵיהּ. הָהוּא יוֹמָא דַּהֲוָה לֵיהּ – נָח נַפְשֵׁיהּ. פְּתַח עֲלֵיהּ הָהוּא סַפְדָּנָא: ״שִׂמְחָה לְתוּגָה נֶהֶפְכָה, שָׂשׂוֹן וְיָגוֹן נִדְבְּקוּ, בְּעֵת שִׂמְחָתוֹ נֶאֱנַח, בְּעֵת חֲנִינָתוֹ אָבַד חֲנִינוֹ״. אַסִּיקוּ לֵיהּ חָנָן עַל שְׁמֵיהּ.

It was related that **Rabbi Ḥanin was a son-in-law in the house of the *Nasi*.** At first **he did not have** any **children,** but **he prayed** that God have **mercy** on him, **and** then **had** a child. **On the** same **day that** a son **was** born **to him,** he himself **passed away. A** certain **eulogizer opened** his eulogy **for him** with the following words: **Happiness has been turned into sorrow; joy and suffering have become joined together.**[N] **At the moment of his happiness he sighed** his dying breath. **At the moment he was graced** with a son, his own **grace was lost. And they named** the child **Ḥanan after** his father.

NOTES

On that day what will you say – הָהוּא יוֹמָא מַאי אָמְרַתְּ: Some explain that Rav Ashi asked: What will the eulogizers say when our older colleague Ravina passes away? (Rabbeinu Ḥananel; Rashi, from manuscript). Others explain that he asked what the eulogizer would say when Rav Ashi himself died (Rashi; Rabbi Shlomo ben HaYatom; Ran).

Rav Ashi was offended by them – חֲלַשׁ דַּעְתֵּיהּ עֲלַיְיהוּ: According to those who understand this to be describing a eulogy for Ravina, the reason that he was offended is because the eulogizer implied that all other Sages, including Rav Ashi himself, were of lesser stature than Ravina.

Those who understand this to be a description of the eulogy for Rav Ashi explain that the wording of the eulogy made it seem as though the death of the righteous person was an accident, and not the result of Divine providence (see Maharsha). Rabbi Shlomo ben HaYatom explains simply that Rav Ashi was insulted because they should have first reassured him that he will live for a very long time, so that it would not appear as though they were already ready to eulogize him.

When Rava once came to the Tigris – רָבָא כִּי הֲוָה אָתָא לְדִגְלַת: Most of the early authorities explain that this prayer was said when the Tigris River began to overflow (Rashi). According to other versions of the text, Rava requested that bar Avin pray that he would not drown in the river (see Commentary on *Moed Katan* in the *Ein Ya'akov* and Rashi there).

Most of the third has come – בָּאוּ רוֹב שְׁלִישִׁית: As the verse says: "And Israel shall be the third [*shelishiyya*]" (Isaiah 19:24), some explain that the term third, *shelishit*, refers to the Jewish people (Rashi; Rashi, from manuscript). Others explain that this term refers to the settled third of the world, and the flood was threatening to overtake a portion of the settled region. Alternatively, it is possible that the Tigris River itself is called the third because it is the third river listed in Genesis, chapter 2. The prayer means that this third river threatens to flood everything with its water (Ran).

Joy and suffering have become joined together – שָׂשׂוֹן וְיָגוֹן נִדְבְּקוּ: The Maharsha writes that the days of celebration over the birth of the child were exactly the same as the days of mourning over the father: The day of Rav Ḥanin's death was the day that the child was born, the day of his circumcision was on the seventh day of mourning, counting from the day of the funeral. The redemption of the firstborn was at the end of the thirty-day mourning period for Rav Ḥanin.

PERSONALITIES

Rav Ashi – רַב אַשִׁי: Rav Ashi was a sixth generation Babylonian sage whose major work was editing the Babylonian Talmud, together with Ravina. He was born in the year 352 and studied with Rav Kahana. Rav Ashi reestablished the academy in Sura, which had not functioned since the days of Rav Ḥisda, and he led that yeshiva for sixty years.

Rav Ashi and Ravina were not the first ones to edit the oral traditions, as there are many discussions in the Talmud whose language and style show that they were prepared long before Rav Ashi. Rav Ashi arranged the material that he received from previous generations, which emanated from different academies and was written in different styles, to produce an organized and uniform Talmud.

Various factors helped Rav Ashi undertake this great project, which ultimately was completed over a period of several hundred years. It is likely that Rav Ashi was assisted by a committee of scholars who gathered in the academy in Sura. It was due to the unique political environment and economic conditions at that time that a mission of this scope could be launched. The Babylonian king Yazdegerd I treated all of his citizens fairly and showed particular interest in the Jewish community, whose Sages he respected. Under his reign, the economic situation of the Jews of Babylonia was excellent, and they enjoyed relative freedom. These conditions allowed the Babylonian Sages to commit themselves to this the vast enterprise of redacting the Gemara.

כִּי נָח נַפְשֵׁיהּ דְּרַבִּי יוֹחָנָן פְּתַח עֲלֵיהּ רַבִּי יִצְחָק בֶּן אֶלְעָזָר: קָשֶׁה הַיּוֹם לְיִשְׂרָאֵל כְּיוֹם בֹּא הַשֶּׁמֶשׁ בַּצָּהֳרַיִם, דִּכְתִיב: "וְהָיָה בַּיּוֹם הַהוּא וְהֵבֵאתִי הַשֶּׁמֶשׁ בַּצָּהֳרָיִם". וְאָמַר רַבִּי יוֹחָנָן: זֶה יוֹמוֹ שֶׁל יֹאשִׁיָּהוּ.

When Rabbi Yoḥanan passed away, Rabbi Yitzḥak ben Elazar opened his eulogy for him as follows: Today is as difficult for the Jewish people as the day that the sun set at noon, as it is written: "And it shall come to pass on that day, says the Lord God, that I will cause the sun to go down at noon, and I will darken the earth in the clear day. And I will turn your feasts into mourning, and all your songs into lamentation; and I will bring up sackcloth upon all loins, and baldness upon every head; and I will make it as the mourning for an only son, and its end like a bitter day" (Amos 8:9–10). And Rabbi Yoḥanan said: This was the day on which King Josiah was killed (see II Chronicles 35:20–24). This demonstrates that the most righteous person of the generation is described as the sun.

כִּי נָח נַפְשֵׁיהּ דְּרַבִּי יוֹחָנָן יְתֵיב רַבִּי אַמִי שִׁבְעָה וּשְׁלֹשִׁים. אָמַר רַבִּי אַבָּא בְּרֵיהּ דְּרַבִּי חִיָּיא בַּר אַבָּא: רַבִּי אַמִי דַּעֲבַד – לְגַרְמֵיהּ הוּא דַּעֲבַד. דְּהָכִי אָמַר רַבִּי חִיָּיא בַּר אַבָּא אָמַר רַבִּי יוֹחָנָן: אֲפִילּוּ רַבּוֹ שֶׁלִּימְּדוֹ חָכְמָה – אֵינוֹ יוֹשֵׁב עָלָיו אֶלָּא יוֹם אֶחָד.

It was further related that when Rabbi Yoḥanan passed away, Rabbi Ami sat in mourning for him for seven days and for thirty days as though he had lost a close relative. Rabbi Abba, son of Rabbi Ḥiyya bar Abba, said: What Rabbi Ami did, he did on his own, but this practice does not reflect the *halakha*. For Rabbi Ḥiyya bar Abba said that Rabbi Yoḥanan said as follows: Even for the death of his teacher who taught him wisdom, one sits in mourning over him for only one day and no more.[H]

כִּי נָח נַפְשֵׁיהּ דְּרַבִּי זֵירָא, פְּתַח עֲלֵיהּ הַהוּא סַפְדָּנָא: "אֶרֶץ שִׁנְעָר הָרָה וְיָלְדָה אֶרֶץ צְבִי גִּידְּלָה שַׁעֲשׁוּעֶיהָ. אוֹי נָא לָהּ אָמְרָה רַקַּת, כִּי אִבְּדָה כְּלִי חֶמְדָּתָהּ".

The Gemara tells of another incident about a eulogy: When Rabbi Zeira died, a certain eulogizer opened his eulogy for him saying: The land of Shinar conceived and gave birth to him, as he was originally Babylonian, but the land of beauty, i.e., Eretz Yisrael, raised the darling of Babylonia, as he later moved to Eretz Yisrael and grew up there. Woe to her, said Rakkath, a poetic name for Tiberias, for her dearest vessel has been lost.

כִּי נָח נַפְשֵׁיהּ דְּרַבִּי אַבָּהוּ אַחִיתוּ עַמּוּדֵי דְּקִסְרִי מַיָּא; דְּרַבִּי יוֹסֵי – שָׁפְעוּ מַרְזְבֵי דְּצִיפּוֹרִי דְּמָא; דְּרַבִּי יַעֲקֹב – אִתְחַמִיאוּ כּוֹכְבֵי בִּימָמָא; דְּרַבִּי אַסִי – אִיעַקְרוּ כָּל אִילָנַיָּא; דְּרַבִּי חִיָּיא – נְחִיתוּ כֵּיפֵי דְנוּרָא מֵרְקִיעָא; דְּרַבִּי מְנַחֵם בְּרַבִּי יוֹסֵי – אִישְׁתָּעוּ צַלְמָנַיָּא וַהֲווּ לְמֶחְלְצַיָּיא;

The Gemara continues to discuss the death of the righteous: When Rabbi Abbahu passed away, the pillars of Caesarea, his city, ran with water[N] as if they were shedding tears over him. When Rabbi Yosei passed away, the gutters of Tzippori, his city, flowed with blood. When Rabbi Ya'akov passed away, the stars were visible during the day. When Rabbi Asi passed away, all the trees were uprooted in a storm. When Rabbi Ḥiyya passed away, fiery stones fell from the sky. When Rabbi Menaḥem, son of Rabbi Yosei, passed away, the faces of the statues became smooth as if they had been smoothed with a plasterer's trowel [*meḥlatzaya*].[L]

דְּרַבִּי תַּנְחוּם בַּר חִיָּיא – אִיתְקַצְּצוּ כָּל אַנְדַּרְטַיָּא; דְּרַבִּי אֶלְיָשִׁיב – אִיחַתְּרוּ שִׁבְעִין מַחְתַּרְתָּא בִּנְהַרְדְּעָא; דְּרַב הַמְנוּנָא – נְחִיתוּ כֵּיפֵי דְבַרְדָּא מֵרְקִיעָא; דְּרַבָּה וְרַב יוֹסֵף – נְשׁוּק כֵּיפֵי דִּפְרָת אַהֲדָדֵי; דְּאַבַּיֵי וְרָבָא – נְשׁוּק כֵּיפֵי דִּדְגַלַת אַהֲדָדֵי; כִּי נָח נַפְשֵׁיהּ דְּרַבִּי מְשַׁרְשְׁיָא טְעוּן דִּיקְלֵי שִׁיצֵי.

When Rabbi Tanḥum bar Ḥiyya passed away, every statue [*andartaya*][L] of the king were mutilated. When Rabbi Elyashiv passed away, seventy tunnels of thieves were dug[N] in Neharde'a, because as long as he was alive there were no thieves in the town due to his merit. When Rav Hamnuna passed away, hail stones fell from the sky. When Rabba and Rav Yosef passed away, the tops of the bridges of the Euphrates collapsed and touched each other. When Abaye and Rava passed away, the tops of the bridges of the Tigris collapsed and touched each other. When Rabbi Mesharshiyya passed away, the palm trees became laden with thorns [*shitzei*].[L]

תָּנוּ רַבָּנַן:

§ The Gemara returns to the subject of tearing garments in mourning: The Sages taught the following *baraita*:

NOTES

The pillars of Caesarea ran with water – אַחִיתוּ עַמּוּדֵי דְּקִסְרִי מַיָּא: Rav Hai Gaon writes that the events described here were miraculous occurrences that happened in those days so that everyone would recognize what was lost when the righteous person passed away. However, the Meiri explains that all of these statements do not refer to actual events and instead are portions of eulogies, with each description being a colorful explanation of mourning for the death (see Ran). In any event, there is a relationship between what is stated here and the personalities of those who passed away. For example, for Rabbi Abbahu, who was the leader of the Jewish people and based in Caesarea, even the pillars of Caesarea shed tears. When the stars were visible during the day it was because the sky became dark in the middle of the day. When the faces of the statues were smoothed it was because Rabbi Menaḥem bar Yosei would not look at any image, even if there was only a slight concern that it was used for idol worship. Similarly, when the bridges collapsed, it was because bridges represent something that holds a community together.

Tunnels of thieves were dug – אִיחַתְּרוּ...מַחְתַּרְתָּא: Some explain that this means that the number of thieves increased greatly, as during his life they were kept in check due to his merit. Others explain that these tunnels were holes that opened by themselves in the ground, alluding to the same idea (Commentary on *Moed Katan*).

LANGUAGE

Plasterer's trowel [*meḥlatzaya*] – מֶחְלְצַיָּא: Some explain that this word means plasterer's trowel, and in this context it means that the statues' faces were so smooth it was as though they had been smoothed over with a trowel. Others explain that the word means reed mats [*maḥatzalot*], and in this case the statues' faces were covered by mats. This also appears to be the meaning in other, parallel, sources.

Statue [*andartaya*] – אַנְדַּרְטַיָּא: Apparently from the Greek ἀνδριάντος, *andriantos*, meaning a statue of a person.

Thorns [*shitzei*]– שִׁיצֵי: This Aramaic word is ordinarily used to describe the hardened branches of a palm tree, which become quite sharp and thorny after several years.

Thorny palm branch

HALAKHA

Mourning over the death of a teacher – אֵבֶל עַל מוֹת הָרַב: One rends all of his garments in mourning when his primary Torah teacher dies. Similarly, a convert rends his garments over the death of the rabbi who accepted him as a convert (*Pitḥei Teshuva*, citing *Sha'arei Efrayim*). Some say that he rends only one handbreadth of his garment, but he may never mend this tear. In addition he should practice all the customs of mourning for a portion of the day on the day of death or the day on which he receives news of the death (*Shulḥan Arukh*, *Yoreh De'a* 242:25).

HALAKHA

Rending garments over one's teacher – קְרִיעָה עַל רַבּוֹ: If one's teacher dies, from whom he had learned the majority of his Torah, whether it be Bible, Mishna, or Gemara, he must rend his garments until his heart is revealed, and some say that he is required to rend only one handbreadth of his garments. These tears may never be sewn, even if they were made upon hearing of the death only some time later. However, if one did not acquire most of his knowledge from this teacher, then he rends his garment over his death as he would over other relatives for whom he is required to mourn. Even if one learned only one thing from his teacher, he should rend his garments over this teacher's death. Some say that even a tear made over a teacher who was not one's primary teacher may not be sewn (Rema). Some say that colleagues who study with each other treat each other as their primary teacher, and some say that they treat each other like other teachers. There are also those who say that rending garments over a colleague or over a teacher from whom one learned a single thing is merely a stringency. Therefore, the common practice is to be lenient (*Shulḥan Arukh, Yoreh De'a* 340:8).

Rending garments over bad tidings – קְרִיעָה עַל שְׁמוּעוֹת רָעוֹת: Upon hearing bad tidings, e.g., a large part of the community went out to war, one makes a tear that may never be mended, even if only a few people died or were taken captive (Rema). In addition, this tear may be tacked only on the day following hearing the news (*Shakh*, citing *Beit Yosef*). This ruling is in accordance with the *baraita* and the Gemara's conclusion (*Shulḥan Arukh, Yoreh De'a* 340:36).

וְאֵלּוּ קְרָעִין שֶׁאֵין מִתְאַחִין: הַקּוֹרֵעַ עַל אָבִיו, וְעַל אִמּוֹ, וְעַל רַבּוֹ שֶׁלִּימְּדוֹ תּוֹרָה, וְעַל נָשִׂיא, וְעַל אַב בֵּית דִּין, וְעַל שְׁמוּעוֹת הָרָעוֹת, וְעַל בִּרְכַּת הַשֵּׁם, וְעַל סֵפֶר תּוֹרָה שֶׁנִּשְׂרַף, וְעַל עָרֵי יְהוּדָה, וְעַל הַמִּקְדָּשׁ, וְעַל יְרוּשָׁלַיִם. וְקוֹרֵעַ עַל מִקְדָּשׁ וּמוֹסִיף עַל יְרוּשָׁלַיִם.

And these are the rents of mourning **that may never be** properly **mended: One who rends** his garments **for the death his father, or for his mother, or for his teacher who taught him Torah, or for the** ***Nasi*****, or for the president of the court; or upon** hearing **evil tidings;** or hearing God's **name being blessed,** which is a euphemism for hearing God's name being cursed; **or when a Torah scroll has been burned; or upon** seeing **the cities of Judea** that were destroyed **or the** destroyed **Temple or Jerusalem** in ruins. This is the way one conducts himself when approaching Jerusalem when it lies in ruin: **He** first **rends** his garments **for the Temple and** then **extends** the rent **for Jerusalem.**

אָבִיו וְאִמּוֹ וְרַבּוֹ שֶׁלִּימְּדוֹ תּוֹרָה מְנָלַן? דִּכְתִיב: "וֶאֱלִישָׁע רֹאֶה וְהוּא מְצַעֵק אָבִי אָבִי רֶכֶב יִשְׂרָאֵל וּפָרָשָׁיו". "אָבִי אָבִי" – זֶה אָבִיו וְאִמּוֹ; "רֶכֶב יִשְׂרָאֵל וּפָרָשָׁיו" – זֶה רַבּוֹ שֶׁלִּימְּדוֹ תּוֹרָה.

The Gemara elaborates upon the *halakhot* mentioned in this *baraita*: **From where do we** derive that one must rend his clothing for **his father, his mother, and his teacher who taught him Torah?**[H] **As it is written** with regard to the prophet Elijah, when he ascended to Heaven in a tempest: **"And Elisha saw it, and he cried, My father, my father, the chariots of Israel and their horsemen"** (II Kings 2:12). The Gemara interprets this verse as follows: **"My father, my father"; this** comes to teach that one must rend his garments for the death of **his father or mother. "The chariots of Israel and their horsemen"; this** comes to include also **one' teacher who taught him Torah.**

מַאי מַשְׁמַע? כִּדְמְתַרְגֵּם רַב יוֹסֵף: רַבִּי רַבִּי, דְּטַב לְהוֹן לְיִשְׂרָאֵל בִּצְלוֹתֵיהּ מֵרְתִיכִין וּפָרָשִׁין.

The Gemara asks: **From where** may it **be inferred** that this is referring to one's teacher? The Gemara explains: **As** the verse **was translated by Rav Yosef:**[N] **My teacher, my teacher, who was better for** the protection of the **Jewish people with his prayers than** an army with **chariots and horsemen.**

וְלָא מִתְאַחִין מְנָלַן? דִּכְתִיב: "וַיַּחֲזֵק בִּבְגָדָיו וַיִּקְרָעֵם לִשְׁנַיִם קְרָעִים". מִמַּשְׁמַע שֶׁנֶּאֱמַר "וַיִּקְרָעֵם" אֵינִי יוֹדֵעַ שֶׁלִּשְׁנַיִם?! אֶלָּא, מְלַמֵּד שֶׁקְּרוּעִים וְעוֹמְדִים לִשְׁנַיִם לְעוֹלָם.

And from where do we derive that these rents **are never** to be properly **mended? As it is written: "And he took hold of his own clothes, and rent them in two pieces"** (II Kings 2:12). **From the fact that** it is **stated: "And he rent them," do I not know that** he rent them **in two** pieces? **Rather,** when the verse adds that they were torn into two pieces, **it teaches that they must remain torn in two** pieces **forever.** Accordingly, this rent must never be properly mended.

אֲמַר לֵיהּ רֵישׁ לָקִישׁ לְרַבִּי יוֹחָנָן: אֵלִיָּהוּ חַי הוּא! אֲמַר לֵיהּ: כֵּיוָן דִּכְתִיב: "וְלֹא רָאָהוּ עוֹד" – לְגַבֵּי דִּידֵיהּ כְּמֵת דָּמֵי.

Reish Lakish said to Rabbi Yoḥanan: But isn't **Elijah** still **alive?** Why, then, did Elisha rend his garments for him? **He said to him: Since it is written: "And he saw him no more"** (II Kings 2:12), Elijah was **considered dead from** Elisha's perspective, and so Elisha rent his clothing for him.

נָשִׂיא וְאַב בֵּית דִּין וּשְׁמוּעוֹת הָרָעוֹת מְנָלַן? דִּכְתִיב: "וַיַּחֲזֵק דָּוִד בִּבְגָדָיו וַיִּקְרָעֵם, וְגַם כָּל הָאֲנָשִׁים אֲשֶׁר אִתּוֹ. וַיִּסְפְּדוּ וַיִּבְכּוּ וַיָּצוּמוּ עַד הָעָרֶב עַל שָׁאוּל וְעַל יְהוֹנָתָן בְּנוֹ וְעַל עַם ה׳ וְעַל בֵּית יִשְׂרָאֵל, כִּי נָפְלוּ בֶּחָרֶב".

§ **From where do we** derive that one must rend his clothing for the death of the ***Nasi*** or the **president of the court and** upon hearing **evil bad tidings?**[H] **As it is written,** when David heard about the defeat of Israel and the death of Saul and his sons: **"Then David took hold of his clothes, and rent them; and likewise all the men that were with him: And they mourned, and wept, and fasted until evening, for Saul and for Jonathan his son, and for the people of the Lord, and for the house of Israel; because they were fallen by the sword"** (II Samuel 1:11–12).

"שָׁאוּל" – זֶה נָשִׂיא; "יְהוֹנָתָן" – זֶה אַב בֵּית דִּין; "עַל עַם ה׳ וְעַל בֵּית יִשְׂרָאֵל" – אֵלּוּ שְׁמוּעוֹת הָרָעוֹת.

The Gemara explains how the aforementioned *halakhot* are derived from the verse: **"Saul"; this is** a reference to the ***Nasi*****,** as Saul was king of Israel. **"Jonathan"; this is** a reference to the **president of the court. "For the people of the Lord, and for the house of the Israel"; these are** a reference to **evil tidings.**

NOTES

As it was translated by Rav Yosef, etc. – כִּדְמְתַרְגֵּם רַב יוֹסֵף וכו׳: This explanation is necessary because without it we would think that Elisha rent his garments over the death of Elijah because Elijah was a prophet. We learn from this translation that Elisha rent his garments over him because Elijah was his teacher (Ritva).

אֲמַר לֵיהּ רַב בַּר שַׁבָּא לְרַב כָּהֲנָא: וְאֵימָא עַד דְּהָווּ כּוּלְּהוּ! אֲמַר לֵיהּ: ״עַל״ ״עַל״ הִפְסִיק הָעִנְיָן.

Rav bar Shaba said to Rav Kahana: But perhaps you can **say** that one need not rend his clothing **until all these** calamities occur together, and that rending clothing is performed only over a tragedy of this magnitude. **He said to him:** The repetition of the word "for": "**For Saul,**" "**for** Jonathan," and "for the people of the Lord" **divides the matter** and teaches that each individual misfortune is sufficient cause to rend one's garments.

וּמִי קָרְעִינַן אַשְּׁמוּעוֹת הָרָעוֹת? וְהָא אֲמָרוּ לֵיהּ לִשְׁמוּאֵל: קְטַל שָׁבוֹר מַלְכָּא תְּרֵיסַר אַלְפֵי יְהוּדָאֵי בִּמְזִיגַת קֵסָרִי, וְלָא קְרַע! לֹא אָמְרוּ אֶלָּא בְּרוֹב צִבּוּר, וּכְמַעֲשֶׂה שֶׁהָיָה.

The Gemara asks: **But do we** actually **rend** our clothing upon hearing **evil tidings? But didn't they say to Shmuel: King Shapur killed twelve thousand Jews in Mezigat**[L] **Caesarea,**[B] **and** Shmuel **did not rend** his clothing? The Gemara answers: **They said** that one must rend his clothing upon hearing evil tidings **only** in a case where the calamity involved **the majority of the community** of Israel **and resembles the incident that occurred** when Saul was killed and the entire nation of Israel suffered defeat.

וּמִי קְטַל שָׁבוֹר מַלְכָּא יְהוּדָאֵי? וְהָא אֲמַר לֵיהּ שָׁבוֹר מַלְכָּא לִשְׁמוּאֵל: תֵּיתֵי לִי, דְּלָא קְטַלִי יְהוּדִי מֵעוֹלָם! הָתָם אִינְהוּ גְּרַמִי לְנַפְשַׁיְיהוּ. דְּאָמַר רַבִּי אַמִי: לְקַל יְתֵירֵי דִּמְזִיגַת קֵסָרִי פְּקַע שׁוּרָא דְּלוּדְקִיָא.

The Gemara tangentially asks: **Did King Shapur** really **kill Jews? But didn't King Shapur say to Shmuel: I have** a blessing **coming to me, for I have never killed a Jew?** The Gemara answers: King Shapur never instigated the killing of Jews; **there,** however, **they brought it upon themselves, as Rabbi Ami said** in an exaggerated manner: **Due to the noise of the** harp **strings** of **Mezigat Caesarea, the walls of Laodicea were breached,** for the residents of the city celebrated when they rebelled against King Shapur. Because they rebelled against him and threatened his rule, he was forced to kill them.

עַל בִּרְכַּת הַשֵּׁם מְנָלַן? דִּכְתִיב: ״וַיָּבֹא אֶלְיָקִים בֶּן חִלְקִיָּה אֲשֶׁר עַל הַבַּיִת וְשֶׁבְנָא הַסּוֹפֵר וְיוֹאָח בֶּן אָסָף הַמַּזְכִּיר אֶל חִזְקִיָּהוּ קְרוּעֵי בְגָדִים״.

§ The Gemara continues its analysis of the *baraita*: **From where do we** derive that one must rend his garments **upon** hearing God's **name being blessed,** i.e., cursed?[NH] **As it is written** with regard to the blasphemous words said by Rab-shakeh: "**Then came Eliakim, son of Hilkiya, who was over the household, and Shebna the scribe, and Joah, son of Asaph, the recorder, to Hezekiah with their clothes rent**" (II Kings 18:37).

תָּנוּ רַבָּנַן: אֶחָד הַשּׁוֹמֵעַ וְאֶחָד הַשּׁוֹמֵעַ מִפִּי הַשּׁוֹמֵעַ חַיָּיב לִקְרוֹעַ, וְהָעֵדִים אֵינָן חַיָּיבִין לִקְרוֹעַ, שֶׁכְּבָר קָרְעוּ בְּשָׁעָה שֶׁשָּׁמְעוּ.

The Sages taught a *baraita* with regard to this issue: Both **one who** actually **hears** the curse **and one who hears from the mouth of** the one **who heard** the curse **are obligated to rend** their garments. **But the witnesses** who testify against the person who uttered the blasphemy **are not obligated to rend** their clothing when they testify as to what they heard **because they already rent** their clothing **when they heard** the curse the first time.

בְּשָׁעָה שֶׁשָּׁמְעוּ מַאי הָוֵי? הָא קָא שָׁמְעִי הַשְׁתָּא! לָא סָלְקָא דַּעְתָּךְ, דִּכְתִיב: ״וַיְהִי כִּשְׁמוֹעַ הַמֶּלֶךְ חִזְקִיָּהוּ וַיִּקְרַע אֶת בְּגָדָיו״ – הַמֶּלֶךְ קָרַע, וְהֵם לֹא קָרְעוּ.

The Gemara asks: **What** difference **does** it make that they rent their garments **when they heard** the curse the first time? **Didn't they hear** it again **now?** The Gemara rejects this argument: **This will not enter your mind, as it is written: "And it came to pass, when King Hezekiah heard it, that he rent his clothes"** (II Kings 19:1). This indicates that **the king rent** his garments, **but** those who reported the blasphemy to him **did not rend** theirs, as they had already rent their garments the first time.

וְלָא מִתְאַחִין מְנָלַן? אָתְיָא קְרִיעָה קְרִיעָה.

And from where do we derive that these rents **may not be** properly **mended?**[N] **This is derived** by way of a verbal analogy between the verb **rending** used here with regard to Hezekiah and the verb **rending** used in the case of Elijah and Elisha.

LANGUAGE

Mezigat – מְזִיגַת: The variation *megizat* appears to be preferable, as it means passage or path and is similar to the Arabic مَجَاز, *majāz*.

BACKGROUND

King Shapur and Mezigat Caesarea – שָׁבוֹר מַלְכָּא וּמְזִיגַת קֵיסָרִי: The King Shapur mentioned here refers to the king of Persia, Shahpuhr the first, who ruled from 241–272 CE. He had especially close ties with the Sage Shmuel. King Shapur was the founder of the great Sassanid Empire, and he expanded its borders while waging numerous wars against the Romans. Through wartime journeys, he reached Anatolia and even Syria. Mezigat Caesarea appears to be the city of Kayseri in modern day Turkey, which was the capital of Cappadocia in that time. The residents of this place, including the Jewish residents, rebelled against the king. During the ensuing battle, the area changed hands many times. Due to the strategic importance of this area, this rebellion had an extremely great influence, and consequently, they said in an exaggerated manner that the walls of Laodicea, which was hundreds of kilometers away, shook due to this rebellion. Because of its strategic importance, the rebellion was strongly crushed by King Shapur, even though he ordinarily had warm relations with the Jews.

Bas-relief sculpture depicting the triumph of Shapur I over the Roman emperor Valerian

NOTES

From where do we upon hearing God's name being blessed, i.e., cursed – עַל בִּרְכַּת הַשֵּׁם מְנָלַן: Although it is not explicitly stated that God's name was cursed, Rab-Shakeh's statement implied disrespect toward God, for he compared the Holy One, Blessed be He, to the gods of others nations, and this is considered to be like a curse (Rashi on II Kings 18:37; see Maharsha).

And from where do we derive that these rents may not be properly mended – וְלָא מִתְאַחִין מְנַיִין: The Rosh disagrees with this derivation by means of verbal analogy. He prefers a textual variation mentioned by the Ra'avad: It is stated: "With torn garments" (II Kings 18:37). It is derived from this statement that the garments must remain torn forever.

HALAKHA

Rending garments over the cursing of God's name – קְרִיעָה עַל בִּרְכַּת הַשֵּׁם: One who hears a Jew curse God's name, even if the blasphemer uses another term to refer to God or speaks in a foreign language (Rema), is required to rend his garments. One who hears the Tetragrammaton being cursed is required to rend his garments, even if it is uttered by a gentile (*Shakh*, citing Ramban). However, one is not required to rend his garments upon hearing a gentile curse God's name more generally. Some say that today an apostate is considered to be like a gentile in this regard (Rema). If a Jew came and said that he heard a certain curse, then one who hears this report is required to rend his garments. Even when one hears from the witnesses in court who testify that so-and-so cursed God's name, he is required to rend his garments. Some say that if the witnesses do not explicitly state the curse, then one is not required to rend their garments (*Pitḥei Teshuva*, citing Rambam and *Semag*). The witnesses themselves, who have already rent their garments, are not required to do so a second time (*Shulḥan Arukh*, *Yoreh De'a* 340:37).

HALAKHA

Rending garments over the burning of the Torah – קְרִיעָה עַל שְׂרֵיפַת הַתּוֹרָה: One is required to rend his garments twice upon seeing a Torah scroll, phylacteries, or even a scroll of Prophets or Writings being burned, erased, or torn by force, in order to destroy it (*Shulḥan Arukh, Yoreh De'a* 340:37).

NOTES

For the Lord has afflicted her [*hoga*] – כִּי ה׳ הוֹגָהּ: Some explain that the word *hoga* can be read as *haga*, uttered, meaning that it was the Lord who said this (Rashi, from manuscript).

By inference they were required to rend their clothing – מִכְּלָל דְּבָעוּ לְמִיקְרַע: The Rosh comments that the derivation mentioned here does not imply that it is prohibited to mend a tear made for a burned Torah scroll. Instead, he holds that it is possible to derive this through an *a fortiori* inference. If one rends his garments and may never mend them over the deaths of those who study the Torah, i.e., one's teachers, shouldn't this be the case all the more for the Torah itself?

Sitting before Rabbi Abba – יָתְבֵי קַמֵּיהּ דְּרַבִּי אַבָּא: Some change the text of the Gemara, removing the phrase: Were sitting before, as how could Rabbi Abba sit before himself? Rav Betzalel Ronsburg explains that there is no need to alter the text, for there were several *amora'im* known as Rabbi Abba.

By force and it resembles the incident that occurred – בְּזוֹרוֹעַ וּכְמַעֲשֶׂה שֶׁהָיָה: Some explain that this term means specifically with violence and not by accident. One rends his garments only when the destruction occurs through human action and in a situation where the person seeing the burning cannot prevent it. However, one is not required to rend his garments if it occurred through an accident (Rashi, from manuscript). Some say that this applies only when the tearing was specifically done in order to anger God. Some of the later authorities suggest that one is required to rend his garments only when the act is performed by a Jew by force, as was the case with Jehoiakim (see *Tal Ḥayyim*).

סֵפֶר תּוֹרָה שֶׁנִּשְׂרַף מְנָלַן? דִּכְתִיב: ״וַיְהִי כִּקְרֹא יְהוּדִי שָׁלֹשׁ דְּלָתוֹת וְאַרְבָּעָה יִקְרָעֶהָ בְּתַעַר הַסֹּפֵר וְהַשְׁלֵךְ אֶל הָאֵשׁ אֲשֶׁר אֶל הָאָח״ וגו׳. מַאי ״שָׁלֹשׁ דְּלָתוֹת וְאַרְבָּעָה״?

§ **From where do we** derive that one must rend his garments when **a Torah scroll has been burned?**[H] **As it is written: "And it came to pass, that when Jehudi had read three or four leaves, he would cut it with a penknife, and cast it into the fire that was in the brazier"** (Jeremiah 36:23). With regard to the verse itself the Gemara asks: **What** is meant by **"three or four leaves,"** and why did he cut the book only at that point?

אֲמָרוּ לֵיהּ לִיהוֹיָקִים: כָּתַב יִרְמְיָה סֵפֶר קִינוֹת. אֲמַר לְהוּ: מַה כְּתִיב בֵּיהּ? ״אֵיכָה יָשְׁבָה בָדָד״. אֲמַר לְהוּ: אֲנָא מַלְכָּא. אֲמַרוּ לֵיהּ ״בָּכֹה תִבְכֶּה בַּלַּיְלָה״. אֲנָא מַלְכָּא. ״גָּלְתָה יְהוּדָה מֵעֹנִי״ – אֲנָא מַלְכָּא. ״דַּרְכֵי צִיּוֹן אֲבֵלוֹת״ – אֲנָא מַלְכָּא.

The Gemara explains: **They said to Jehoiakim: Jeremiah has written a book of Lamentations** over the future downfall and destruction of Jerusalem. **He said to them: What is written in it?** They read him the first verse: **"How does the city sit solitary"** (Lamentations 1:1). **He said to them: I am king,** and this does not apply to me. **They read him** the second verse: **"She weeps sore in the night"** (Lamentations 1:2). He said to them: **I am king,** and this does not apply to me. They read him the third verse: **"Judah is gone into exile due to affliction"** (Lamentations 1:3). He said to them: **I am king.** They read to him: **"The ways of Zion do mourn"** (Lamentations 1:4). He said to them: **I am king.** These are the four leaves, or verses, that he read first.

״הָיוּ צָרֶיהָ לְרֹאשׁ״ – אֲמַר לְהוּ: מַאן אֲמָרָהּ? ״כִּי ה׳ הוֹגָהּ עַל רֹב פְּשָׁעֶיהָ״. מִיָּד קָדַר כָּל אַזְכָּרוֹת שֶׁבָּהּ וּשְׂרָפָן בָּאֵשׁ. וְהַיְינוּ דִּכְתִיב: ״וְלֹא פָחֲדוּ וְלֹא קָרְעוּ אֶת בִּגְדֵיהֶם״, מִכְּלָל דְּבָעוּ לְמִיקְרַע.

They read him an additional verse: **"Her adversaries have become the chief"** (Lamentations 1:5), i.e., the reigning king will be removed from power. Once he heard this, **he said to them: Who said** this? They said to him: This is the continuation of the verse: **"For the Lord has afflicted her**[N] **for the multitude of her transgressions"** (Lamentations 1:5). **Immediately, he cut out all the names** of God **from** the book **and burned them in fire. This is as it is written: "Yet they were not afraid, nor rent their garments,** neither the king, nor any of his servants that heard all these words" (Jeremiah 36:24). **By inference,** this shows **that** they **were required to rend** their clothing[N] when they saw this.

אֲמַר לֵיהּ רַב פַּפָּא לְאַבַּיֵי: אֵימַר מִשּׁוּם שְׁמוּעוֹת הָרָעוֹת! אֲמַר לֵיהּ: שְׁמוּעוֹת רָעוֹת בְּהַהִיא שַׁעְתָּא מִי הָווּ?

Rav Pappa said to Abaye: Perhaps you can **say** that they should have rent their garments **due to the evil tidings** contained in the scroll and not because of the destruction of the book? Abaye **said to him: Were they evil tidings at that time?** This was a prophecy and not an account of current events.

אָמַר רַבִּי חֶלְבּוֹ אָמַר רַב הוּנָא: הָרוֹאֶה סֵפֶר תּוֹרָה שֶׁנִּקְרַע חַיָּיב לִקְרוֹעַ שְׁתֵּי קְרִיעוֹת: אֶחָד עַל הַגְּוִיל וְאֶחָד עַל הַכְּתָב, שֶׁנֶּאֱמַר: ״אַחֲרֵי שְׂרֹף הַמֶּלֶךְ אֶת הַמְּגִלָּה וְאֶת הַדְּבָרִים״.

Rabbi Ḥelbo said that **Rav Huna said: One who sees a Torah scroll that was torn is obligated to make two rents, one for the parchment** that was damaged **and one for the writing, as it is stated:** "Then the word of the Lord came to Jeremiah, **after the king had burned the scroll and the words"** (Jeremiah 36:27). This implies that a separate rent must be made for each of them, both the parchment and the writing.

רַבִּי אַבָּא וְרַב הוּנָא בַּר חִיָּיא הָווּ יָתְבֵי קַמֵּיהּ דְּרַבִּי אַבָּא. בְּעָא לְאִפַּנּוֹיֵי, שְׁקַלֵיהּ לְטוֹטַפְתֵּיהּ אַחְתֵּיהּ אַבֵּי סָדְיָא. אֲתַאי בַּת נַעֲמִיתָא בְּעָא לְמִיבְלְעֵיהּ.

It was related that **Rabbi Abba and Rav Huna bar Ḥiyya were sitting before Rabbi Abba.**[N] Rabbi Abba **needed to relieve himself. He removed his phylacteries** from his head and **placed them on the cushion** on which he was sitting. **An ostrich**[B] **came and wanted to swallow** the phylacteries.

אֲמַר: הַשְׁתָּא אִיחַיְּיבִין לִי שְׁתֵּי קְרִיעוֹת, אֲמַר לֵיהּ: מְנָא לָךְ הָא? וְהָא בְּדִידִי הֲוָה עוּבְדָּא, וַאֲתַאי לְקַמֵּיהּ דְּרַב מַתָּנָה וְלָא הֲוָה בִּידֵיהּ, אֲתַאי לְקַמֵּיהּ דְּרַב יְהוּדָה, וַאֲמַר לִי: הָכִי אֲמַר שְׁמוּאֵל, לֹא אָמְרוּ אֶלָּא בְּזְרוֹעַ, וּכְמַעֲשֶׂה שֶׁהָיָה.

He said: Now, had it succeeded to swallow it, **I would have been obligated to make two rents. He said to him: From where do you** derive **this? There was an incident in which I** was involved **and I came before Rav Mattana** asking what to do, **but he did not have** an answer readily available. I then **came before Rav Yehuda, and he said to me: Shmuel said as follows: They said** that one is obligated to rend his clothing **only** when a Torah scroll or some other sacred book is torn **by force, and it resembles the incident that occurred**[N] with Jehoiakim.

BACKGROUND

Ostrich – בַּת נַעֲמִיתָא: The bird mentioned here is among those ordinarily found in the desert. However, elsewhere ostriches were also raised domestically, apparently for their feathers. These birds are well known for their inclination to swallow almost anything, even objects normally considered to be inedible.

עָרֵי יְהוּדָה מְנָלַן? דִּכְתִיב: ״וַיָּבֹאוּ אֲנָשִׁים מִשְּׁכֶם מִשִּׁילוֹ וּמִשֹּׁמְרוֹן שְׁמֹנִים אִישׁ מְגוּלְּחֵי זָקָן וּקְרוּעֵי בְגָדִים וּמִתְגּוֹדְדִים וּמִנְחָה וּלְבוֹנָה בְּיָדָם לְהָבִיא בֵּית ה׳״ וגו׳.

§ From where do we derive that one must rend his garments upon seeing **the cities of Judea** in ruin?[NH] **As it is written: "There came certain men from Shechem, from Shiloh, and from Samaria, eighty people, their beards shaven, and their clothes rent, and having cut themselves, with offerings and incense in their hand, to bring to the house of the Lord"** (Jeremiah 41:5). This indicates that they rent their garments upon seeing the destruction.

אָמַר רַבִּי חֶלְבּוֹ אָמַר עוּלָּא בִּירָאָה אָמַר רַבִּי אֶלְעָזָר, הָרוֹאֶה עָרֵי יְהוּדָה בְּחוּרְבָּנָן – אוֹמֵר: ״עָרֵי קָדְשְׁךָ הָיוּ מִדְבָּר״, וְקוֹרֵעַ. יְרוּשָׁלַיִם בְּחוּרְבָּנָהּ – אוֹמֵר: ״צִיּוֹן מִדְבָּר הָיָתָה יְרוּשָׁלַיִם שְׁמָמָה״, וְקוֹרֵעַ. בֵּית הַמִּקְדָּשׁ בְּחוּרְבָּנוֹ – אוֹמֵר ״בֵּית קָדְשֵׁנוּ וְתִפְאַרְתֵּנוּ אֲשֶׁר הִלְלוּךָ אֲבוֹתֵינוּ הָיָה לִשְׂרֵיפַת אֵשׁ וְכָל מַחֲמַדֵּינוּ הָיָה לְחָרְבָּה״, וְקוֹרֵעַ.

Rabbi Ḥelbo said that **Ulla Bira'a said** that **Rabbi Elazar said: One who sees the cities of Judea in their desolation says: "Your sacred cities are become a wilderness"** (Isaiah 64:9), and then **rends** his garments. One who sees **Jerusalem in its desolation says: "Zion is a wilderness, Jerusalem a desolation"** (Isaiah 64:9), **and then rends** his garments. One who sees **the Temple in its desolation says: "Our sacred and our beautiful house, where our fathers praised You, is burned with fire; and all our pleasant things are laid waste"** (Isaiah 64:10), **and then rends** his garments.

״קוֹרֵעַ עַל מִקְדָּשׁ וּמוֹסִיף עַל יְרוּשָׁלַיִם״. וּרְמִינְהוּ: אֶחָד הַשּׁוֹמֵעַ וְאֶחָד הָרוֹאֶה, כֵּיוָן שֶׁהִגִּיעַ לַצּוֹפִים – קוֹרֵעַ, וְקוֹרֵעַ עַל מִקְדָּשׁ בִּפְנֵי עַצְמוֹ וְעַל יְרוּשָׁלַיִם בִּפְנֵי עַצְמָהּ!

It was taught in the *baraita*: **He** first **rends** his garments **for the Temple and** then **extends** the rent **for Jerusalem. And they raise a contradiction** from another *baraita* that states: Both **one who hears** that Jerusalem is in ruin **and one who sees** the destruction, **once he reaches** Mount Scopus [*Tzofim*],[B] **rends** his garments. **And he rends** his garments **for the Temple separately and for Jerusalem separately.**

לָא קַשְׁיָא: הָא – דְּפָגַע בַּמִּקְדָּשׁ בְּרֵישָׁא, הָא – דְּפָגַע בִּירוּשָׁלַיִם בְּרֵישָׁא.

The Gemara answers: **This is not difficult. This** *baraita*, which states that instead of making a separate rent for Jerusalem one may extend the first rent that he had made for the Temple, is referring to the case where **one reached the Temple first,** before seeing the rest of Jerusalem, and saw it in ruin. **That** *baraita*, which states that one must make separate rents for Jerusalem and for the Temple, is referring to the case where **one reached Jerusalem first,** and only afterward the Temple.

תָּנוּ רַבָּנַן: וְכוּלָּן רַשָּׁאִין לְשׁוֹלְלָן, וּלְמוֹלְלָן, וּלְלוֹקְטָן וְלַעֲשׂוֹתָן כְּמִין סוּלָּמוֹת, אֲבָל לֹא לְאַחוֹתָן.

§ **The Sages taught** the following *baraita*: **And all of these** rents, **one may tack them** together with loose stitches,[H] **and hem them,**[N] **and gather them, and fix them** with imprecise **ladder-like** stitches.[B] **But one may not mend them** with precise stitches.

אָמַר רַב חִסְדָּא:

Rav Ḥisda said:

BACKGROUND

Tzofim – צוֹפִים: Some people explain that the word *tzofim* refers to a specific place, perhaps what is referred to today as Mount Scopus, from which one could see Jerusalem and the Temple. Others say that *tzofim* more generally refers to any place from which one can see the city of Jerusalem.

View of Jerusalem from Mount Scopus

View of Mount Scopus from Jerusalem

Ladder-like stitches – כְּמִין סוּלָּמוֹת: Connecting a tear with parallel stitches creates a ladder-like form

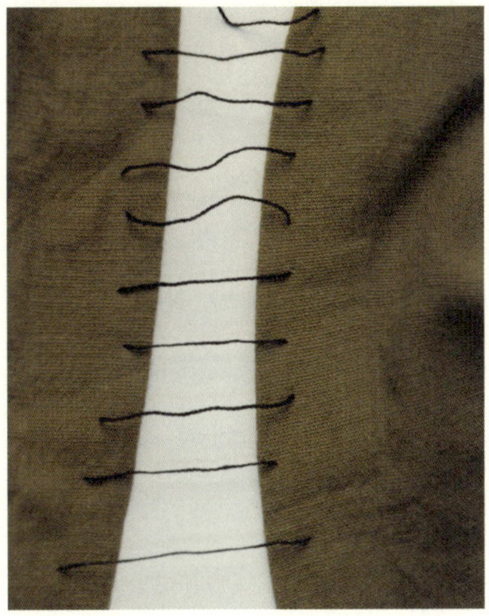

Ladder-like stitching

NOTES

From where do we derive that one must rend his garments upon seeing the cities of Judea in ruin – עָרֵי יְהוּדָה מְנָלַן: The Gemara does not mention the cities of the kingdom of Israel is because in Judah it was known which cities had always been Jewish. However, in the Galilee, which was only partially settled by those who returned from Babylonia, they were unsure which cities were considered to be Jewish cities (Maharsha).

Tack them [*sholelan*] and hem them [*molelan*], etc. – לְשׁוֹלְלָן וּלְמוֹלְלָן: Several explanations are offered with regard to the details of these actions. Rabbeinu Yehonatan of Lunel explains that the words *shelila* and *melila* refer to types of tying without the use of a needle. However, when the Gemara refers to gathering them and fixing them with ladder-like stitches it means using an imprecise type of stitch, which does not fall into the category of sewing. Rashi explains that *sholelan* refers to tacking with wide stitches, *molelan* refers to binding the two edges of a tear together with two stitches, and gathering [*loktan*] refers to sewing a tear from top to bottom with proper stitching (Rashi, from manuscript).

HALAKHA

Rending garments over the cities of Israel and the Temple – קְרִיעָה עַל עָרֵי יִשְׂרָאֵל וְהַמִּקְדָּשׁ: If one sees the cities of Judea in their destroyed state, as he approaches he says: "Your sacred cities have become a wilderness" (Isaiah 64:9), and rends his garments. Even if the cities are inhabited by Jews, they are still considered to be destroyed as long as they are under foreign, gentile rule. As one approaches Jerusalem and reaches Mount Scopus [*Tzofim*], he recites the verse: "Zion has become a wilderness, Jerusalem a desolation" (Isaiah 64:9), and rends his garments. Some say that *tzofim* refers to a specific place, while others understand it to be any place from which Jerusalem is visible (see *Magen Avraham*). Practically speaking, since the area surrounding Jerusalem is built up one does not rend his garments before seeing the walls of the Old City (*Kaf HaḤayyim*). Afterward, when he sees the site where the Temple stood, he says: "Our holy and our beautiful Temple, where our fathers praised You, is burned with fire; and all our pleasant things are laid waste" (Isaiah 64:10), and he rends his garments a second time. These tears should be at least one handbreadth in length. If one arrives from the east and sees the ruins of the Temple first, then he should rend his garments over the Temple and extend this tear over Jerusalem. Anyone who has not seen the destroyed cities or the ruins of the Temple for thirty days must rend his garments again (*Shulḥan Arukh, Oraḥ Ḥayyim* 561:1–2 and Rema).

Tacking the tears – לִשְׁלוֹל הַקְּרָעִים: Tears made over the death of one's father or Torah teacher, bad tidings, the burning of the Torah, the cities of Judea, or the Temple may never be sewn. However, they may be tacked and closed up in a different manner on the following day (*Shulḥan Arukh, Yoreh De'a* 340:39).

וּבְאִיחוּי אֲלֶכְּסַנְדְּרִי.

And the reference here is **to** the **Alexandrian** method of **mending,**[BNH] a type of sewing performed in Alexandria, which is considered to be of exceptional quality and after which the tear is no longer visible.

תָּנוּ רַבָּנַן: הַקּוֹרֵעַ מִתּוֹךְ הַשְּׁלָל, מִתּוֹךְ הַמְּלָל, מִתּוֹךְ הַלֶּקֶט, מִתּוֹךְ הַסּוּלָּמוֹת – לֹא יָצָא. מִתּוֹךְ הָאִיחוּי – יָצָא. אָמַר רַב חִסְדָּא: וּבְאִיחוּי אֲלֶכְּסַנְדְּרִי.

The Sages taught the following *baraita*: **One who rends** his garment in a place **that had been** loosely **tacked** together, or **from the hem of the garment,**[H] or **on the gathering,** or **on the ladder-like stiches has not fulfilled** his obligation to rend it. But if he rends it in a place **that had been** carefully **mended, he has fulfilled** his obligation, because such a garment is regarded as whole. **Rav Ḥisda said: And** here, too, the reference is **to** the **Alexandrian** method of **mending** and not to ordinary sewing.

תָּנוּ רַבָּנַן: רַשַּׁאי לְהוֹפְכוֹ לְמַטָּה וּלְאַחוֹתוֹ. רַבִּי שִׁמְעוֹן בֶּן אֶלְעָזָר אוֹסֵר לְאַחוֹתוֹ. וּכְשֵׁם שֶׁהַמּוֹכֵר אָסוּר לְאַחוֹתוֹ – כָּךְ הַלּוֹקֵחַ אָסוּר לְאַחוֹתוֹ. וּלְפִיכָךְ מוֹכֵר צָרִיךְ לְהוֹדִיעוֹ לַלּוֹקֵחַ.

The Sages taught another *baraita*: One is **permitted to turn** a garment that was rent on the upper edge **upside down and** then **mend** it in a precise fashion. **Rabbi Shimon ben Elazar prohibits** careful **mending** in this case as well. **And** if one wishes to sell a garment that he had previously rent in mourning, **just as the seller,** who had rent the garment, **is prohibited from** carefully **mending** the garment, **so too the buyer,** who purchases it from him, **is prohibited from mending it. The seller must therefore inform the buyer** that the rent was made on account of mourning and may not be mended.[H]

תָּנוּ רַבָּנַן: תְּחִילַּת קְרִיעָה טֶפַח, וְתוֹסֶפֶת שָׁלֹשׁ אֶצְבָּעוֹת, דִּבְרֵי רַבִּי מֵאִיר. רַבִּי יְהוּדָה אוֹמֵר: תְּחִילַּת קְרִיעָה שָׁלֹשׁ אֶצְבָּעוֹת, וְתוֹסֶפֶת כָּל שֶׁהוּ.

The Sages taught a *baraita*: **The initial rending is a handbreadth** in length, **and the extension,** if one is obligated to rend his garment for other deceased relatives and he wishes to use the same rent for this purpose, **is three fingerbreadths;** this is **the statement of Rabbi Meir. Rabbi Yehuda says:** The **initial rending is three fingerbreadths**[N] in length, **and** its **extension is any amount,** with no minimum measure.[H]

אָמַר עוּלָּא: הֲלָכָה כְּרַבִּי מֵאִיר בִּקְרִיעָה, וַהֲלָכָה כְּרַבִּי יְהוּדָה בְּתוֹסֶפֶת. תַּנְיָא נַמִי הָכִי, רַבִּי יוֹסֵי אוֹמֵר: תְּחִילַּת קְרִיעָה טֶפַח וְתוֹסֶפֶת כָּל שֶׁהוּ.

Ulla said: The *halakha* is in accordance with the opinion of **Rabbi Meir that** the initial **rending** is one handbreadth in length, **and the *halakha* is in accordance with** the opinion of **Rabbi Yehuda that an extension** can be any length. The Gemara comments: **That is also taught** in a *baraita*: **Rabbi Yosei says:** The **initial rending** is **one handbreadth, and** the size of the **extension is any** minimal **amount.** By tradition, the *halakha* is in accordance with the opinion of Rabbi Yosei when he disagrees with any one of his colleagues.

BACKGROUND

Alexandrian mending – אִיחוּי אֲלֶכְּסַנְדְּרִי: This refers to the city of Alexandria in Egypt. In ancient times, it was the center of science and technology in the Middle East, and perhaps in the entire world. Items of high quality were named for the city, and consequently the highest quality of sewing is referred to as Alexandrian sewing.

NOTES

Alexandrian mending – אִיחוּי אֲלֶכְּסַנְדְּרִי: Some say that this refers to precise sewing, in which the stitching is straight and smooth on the outer side of the garment, although it protrudes from the inner side of the garment (Ra'avad; Rabbeinu Yehonatan of Lunel). Others say that this refers to a type of mending through which the torn threads are removed and replaced and new threads are woven into the garment (Rabbeinu Ḥananel; Ramban; see Jerusalem Talmud). The Ritva writes that since the definition of Alexandrian sewing disputed, one should act stringently in accordance with both opinions. Therefore, it is prohibited for a mourner to mend a garment from one side. Conversely, only a garment that is properly mended may be rent in mourning. Some write that Alexandrian sewing refers to strong stitching, as opposed to tacking, which is imprecise, temporary stitching (Commentary on *Moed Katan*; Rabbi Shlomo ben HaYatom; Meiri).

The initial rending is three fingerbreadths – תְּחִילַּת קְרִיעָה שָׁלֹשׁ אֶצְבָּעוֹת: *Tosafot* ask how this measure is derived. Earlier (22b) the Gemara cited the verse "and he took hold" (II Kings 2:12) as a source. Some explain that this does not refer to holding with the entire hand, as it would then be a handbreadth; rather, it refers to the way people ordinarily hold a garment, with three fingers (Ritva).

HALAKHA

With Alexandrian mending – בְּאִיחוּי אֲלֶכְּסַנְדְּרִי: If a tear may not be mended, this prohibition includes Alexandrian sewing, in accordance with the opinion of Rav Ḥisda (Rambam *Sefer Shofetim, Hilkhot Evel* 9:3).

One who rends…from the hem, etc. – הַקּוֹרֵעַ...מִתּוֹךְ הַמְּלָל וכו׳: One who rends his garment in mourning from within a hem, or in a similar manner, does not fulfill his obligation to rend his garment. However, if he rends something that was attached with Alexandrian sewing, i.e., stitching that is not noticeable from the outside, then he fulfills his obligation in accordance with the opinion of Rav Ḥisda (*Shulḥan Arukh, Yoreh De'a* 340:20).

Tears that may not be sewn – קְרָעִים שֶׁאֵינָם מִתְאַחִים: All tears in this category may never be sewn, even if one turns the garment upside down so that the torn portion is on the bottom. Similarly, it is prohibited to purchase such a garment in order to sew it; therefore, one who sells a garment that was rent in mourning must inform the buyer (*Shulḥan Arukh, Yoreh De'a* 340:19).

The measure of the tear – שִׁיעוּר קְרִיעָה: One must tear his garment one handbreadth as a sign of mourning. If his garment was already torn and he heard within seven days of the death that another family member died, then he extends this tear one handbreadth. If the second death occurred more than seven days after the first death, then he may add any amount to the first tear. This ruling is in accordance with the opinion of Rabbi Yosei. However, it applies only to mourning over other relatives; for a father and mother, one is required to rend his garment until he reaches the point in the garment that covers his heart (*Shulḥan Arukh, Yoreh De'a* 340:3).

תָּנוּ רַבָּנַן: אָמְרוּ לוֹ מֵת אָבִיו, וְקָרַע, מֵת בְּנוֹ, וְהוֹסִיף, תַּחְתּוֹן מִתְאַחֶה, עֶלְיוֹן אֵינוֹ מִתְאַחֶה.

The Sages taught the following *baraita*: If **they** first **said to** a person that **his father died, and he rent** his garment, and afterward they told him that **his son died, and he added** to the same rent, in such a case the **lower** portion of the rent that had been made for his son **may be mended.** The is because, after completing the period of mourning, one is permitted to mend a rent made for relatives other than one's parents. However, the **upper** portion of the rent **may not be mended,** as a tear made for one's father may never be carefully sewn back together.

מֵת בְּנוֹ וְקָרַע, מֵת אָבִיו וְהוֹסִיף, עֶלְיוֹן מִתְאַחֶה, תַּחְתּוֹן אֵינוֹ מִתְאַחֶה.

If, on the other hand, they said to him first that **his son died, and he rent** his garment, and afterward they told him that **his father died, and he added** to the same rent, then in that case the **upper** portion of the rent, which that had been made for his son, **may be mended,** but **the lower** portion of the rent, which had been made for his father, **may not be mended.**

מֵת אָבִיו, מֵת אִמּוֹ, מֵת אָחִיו, מֵתָה אֲחוֹתוֹ, קוֹרֵעַ קֶרַע אֶחָד לְכוּלָּן. רַבִּי יְהוּדָה בֶּן בְּתֵירָה אוֹמֵר: עַל כּוּלָּן קֶרַע אֶחָד, עַל אָבִיו וְאִמּוֹ קֶרַע אֶחָד, לְפִי שֶׁאֵין מוֹסִיפִין עַל קֶרַע אָבִיו וְאִמּוֹ.

If they said to him all at one time that **his father died, his mother died, his brother died, and his sister died,** then **he may make one rent for all of them. Rabbi Yehuda ben Beteira says: For all** of his other relatives he makes **one rent,** and **for his father and mother** he makes **another rent, as one must not add** to **a rent** made **for his father and mother.**[H]

מַאי טַעְמָא? אָמַר רַב נַחְמָן בַּר יִצְחָק: לְפִי שֶׁאֵינָן בְּתוֹסֶפֶת.

The Gemara asks: **What is the reason** for Rabbi Yehuda ben Beteira's opinion that one may not add to the rent torn for a mother or father? **Rav Naḥman bar Yitzḥak said: Because they cannot be added;**[N] one has only one father and one mother and cannot add others.

אָמַר שְׁמוּאֵל: הֲלָכָה כְּרַבִּי יְהוּדָה בֶּן בְּתֵירָה. וּמִי אָמַר שְׁמוּאֵל הָכִי? וְהָאָמַר שְׁמוּאֵל: הֲלָכָה כְּדִבְרֵי הַמֵּיקֵל בְּאֵבֶל! אֲבֵילוּת לְחוּד, קְרִיעָה לְחוּד.

Shmuel said: The *halakha* is in accordance with the opinion of **Rabbi Yehuda ben Beteira.** The Gemara asks: **And did Shmuel** actually **say this? But didn't Shmuel say** the principle is that **the *halakha* is in accordance with the statement** of the **lenient** Sage with regard to **mourning;** yet here he rules in accordance with the more stringent opinion. The Gemara answers: The *halakhot* of **mourning are discrete** and the *halakhot* **of rending are discrete,**[N] and it is only with regard to the *halakhot* of mourning that Shmuel rules consistently in accordance with the lenient opinion.

עַד הֵיכָן קוֹרֵעַ? עַד טִיבּוּרוֹ, וְיֵשׁ אוֹמְרִים: עַד לִבּוֹ. אַף עַל פִּי שֶׁאֵין רְאָיָה לַדָּבָר – זֵכֶר לַדָּבָר, שֶׁנֶּאֱמַר: "וְקִרְעוּ לְבַבְכֶם וְאַל בִּגְדֵיכֶם".

It was taught in a *baraita*: **Until where** may **he rend** his garment,[H] if he continues to rend the same garment for additional relatives? He may continue rending **until** the point where the garment covers **his navel. Some say: Until** the point where the garment covers **his heart. Although there is no** absolute **proof for the matter** that one may rend the garment until this point, there is **an allusion to this matter, as it is stated: "And rend your hearts, and not your garments"** (Joel 2:13), thereby intimating that one may extend the rent in his garment only until he reaches the point where the garment covers his heart.

HALAKHA

Extending a tear – תּוֹסֶפֶת קְרִיעָה: If one rends his garment in mourning over his mother or father, and after seven days another one of his relatives dies, and he extends this tear, then the upper portion of the tear may never be sewn but the lower portion may be sewn. However, if one rends his garment over one of his other relatives and afterward hears that his father or mother died, then he should make a new tear and not extend the first one. The latter ruling is in accordance with the opinion of Rabbi Yehuda ben Beteira (Ramban; Rabbeinu Yeruḥam; *Shulḥan Arukh, Yoreh De'a* 340:22).

Until where may he rend his garment – עַד הֵיכָן קוֹרֵעַ: One who rent his garment in mourning and then extended this tear for other relatives may continue extending the tear until it reaches the point on the garment that covers his navel. If he becomes obligated to rend his garment again, then he must rend it from the edge of the garment three fingerbreadths away from the first tear. If the garment has tears in the front, then he may turn it around and rend it from the portion of the garment that is now in front of him. If the upper portion is torn, he may turn the garment over and rend what was formerly the bottom. If every portion of the garment is torn, then he is considered like one who has no garment and he does not rend it (*Shulḥan Arukh, Yoreh De'a* 340:21).

NOTES

Because they cannot be added – לְפִי שֶׁאֵינָן בְּתוֹסֶפֶת: Some explain that due to the honor one must show toward his parents, it is not appropriate for him to extend the tear rent over them as mourning for another relative (see Rashi). Others explain that because a mourner must make a longer tear for his father and mother, with no maximum size, any extension will not be noticeable (Ra'avad; Rid; Rosh). Rabbi Yitzḥak ibn Giat explains that one is required to rend his garment for his father and mother until he reaches the point on the garment which covers his navel, and since one may not tear below this, it is impossible to extend the tear (see Ramban and Ritva).

There are also those who understand this not as a halakhic statement but as a moral explanation for this ruling. One will never have another father or mother, and therefore it is not appropriate to add to the tear made as a sign of mourning for one's parents (*Tal Torah*). One may, however, have relatives in other categories in the future, e.g., children or even half siblings from his surviving parent.

***Halakhot* of mourning are discrete and *halakhot* of rending are discrete – אֲבֵילוּת לְחוּד, קְרִיעָה לְחוּד:** Some say that this is because rending garments is a Torah law, as derived from the verses concerning the sons of Aaron, while the *halakhot* of mourning are of rabbinic origin (Ra'avad; see *Tosefot HaRosh*). The Ramban writes that the mitzva of rending is not itself a Torah law. Rather, it is a rabbinic law with supporting verses from the Torah. The *Nimmukei Yosef* writes simply that these two practices do not fall into the same category. Rending is performed before the mourning actually begins, and therefore Shmuel's principle that the *halakha* is ruled in accordance with the opinion of the lenient Sage with regard to mourning does not apply to it.

הִגִּיעַ לְטִיבּוּרוֹ, מַרְחִיק שָׁלֹשׁ אֶצְבָּעוֹת וְקוֹרֵעַ. נִתְמַלֵּא מִלְּפָנָיו – מַחְזִירוֹ לַאֲחוֹרָיו. נִתְמַלֵּא מִלְּמַעְלָה – הוֹפְכוֹ מִלְּמַטָּה. וְהַקּוֹרֵעַ מִלְּמַטָּה וּמִן הַצְּדָדִין לֹא יָצָא. אֶלָּא שֶׁכֹּהֵן גָּדוֹל פּוֹרֵם מִלְּמַטָּה.

If **he** tore his garment until he **reached** the point where it covers **his navel,** he should not continue rending in the same place. Instead, **he should move away** a space of **three fingerbreadths** from the first rent **and make** a new **rent.** If the garment **became full** of rents **in the front, he should turn** the garment **front to back** and make a rent on the other side. If **it became full** of rents **above, he should turn it** top to bottom and make a rent on what used to be **the bottom. But one who rends** his garment **at the bottom or at the sides has not fulfilled** his obligation, as rending may be done only at the top of the garment.[H] **The High Priest, however,** who is prohibited from rending his garments in mourning, **may tear** his garment **at the bottom**[N] to mark his mourning in a symbolic manner.[H]

פְּלִיגוּ בָּהּ רַב מַתָּנָה וּמַר עוּקְבָא, וְתַרְוַיְיהוּ מִשְּׁמֵיהּ דַּאֲבוּהּ דִּשְׁמוּאֵל וְלֵוִי; חַד אָמַר: כָּל שִׁבְעָה קוֹרֵעַ, לְאַחַר שִׁבְעָה מוֹסִיף. וְחַד אָמַר: כָּל שְׁלֹשִׁים קוֹרֵעַ, לְאַחַר שְׁלֹשִׁים מוֹסִיף.

Rav Mattana and Mar Ukva disagreed about the following issue, **and both of them** stated their respective opinions **in the name of Shmuel's father and Levi. One said:** During **all seven** days of mourning, if the mourner hears that another relative of his passed away, **he makes** a new **rent; after seven** days of mourning **he** merely **adds** to the first one. **And one said:** During **all** of the first **thirty days he makes** a new rent; **after thirty** days **he** merely **adds** to the first one.

מַתְקִיף לָהּ רַבִּי זֵירָא: מַאן דְּאָמַר כָּל שִׁבְעָה קוֹרֵעַ, אַמַּאי? דְּלֹא נִיתַּן לְשׁוֹלְלוֹ. אֶלָּא הָא דְּאָמַר מָר: הָאִשָּׁה שׁוֹלַלְתּוֹ לְאַלְתַּר, הָכָא נַמִי?

Rabbi Zeira strongly objects to this: According to **the one who said** that during **all seven** days of mourning **he makes** a new **rent, why** is it not enough to add to the first one? It is because **he may not tack it** until the end of the seven-day period of mourning, and therefore if he adds to the rent it will look like a continuation of the previous tear. **But** then, with regard to **that which the Master said** in the *baraita*: After **a woman** rends her garment, she **may tack** the tear **immediately,** would you say that **here also** she may add to the first rent for a new bereavement during the seven-day period of mourning?

הָתָם מִשּׁוּם כְּבוֹד אִשָּׁה הוּא.

The Gemara answers: **There** the woman is permitted to tack the rent **due to the woman's honor,** as it would be dishonorable for her to be seen wearing torn garments. However, halakhically the rent is considered as if it still exists, and therefore she must make a new rent for a new bereavement and not merely add to the previous one.

מַאן דְּאָמַר כָּל שְׁלֹשִׁים קוֹרֵעַ, אַמַּאי? דְּלֹא נִיתַּן לְאַחוֹתוֹ. אֶלָּא לְאָבִיו וּלְאִמּוֹ, דְּלֹא נִיתַּן לְאַחוֹתוֹ לְעוֹלָם, הָכִי נַמִי?

Rabbi Zeira asked further: According to **the one who said** that **all thirty days** of mourning **one must make** a new **rent** rather than add to the existing tear, **why** does he say this? It is because during the thirty days **one is not given** permission to properly **mend** the garment, and so it still appears to be torn. **But** then, in a case of a rent made **for one's father or mother,** for **which** he **is not given** permission to **ever** properly **mend it,** would you say that he should **so too** be forever barred from adding to the rent for a new bereavement and is instead obligated to make a new rent?

הָתָם מִשּׁוּם כְּבוֹד אָבִיו וְאִמּוֹ הוּא.

The Gemara answers: **There** he may not properly mend the rent **due to the honor due to his father and mother.** Essentially, however, the tear is considered as if it had been sewn up after the thirty-day period, and therefore the son may extend it in the case of a new bereavement.

NOTES

The High Priest may tear his garment at the bottom – כֹּהֵן גָּדוֹל פּוֹרֵם מִלְּמַטָּה: Although a High Priest is prohibited from rending his garment as a sign of grief (Leviticus 21:10), he may perform a symbolic act that does not fall into the category of actual rending (Rashi, from manuscript).

HALAKHA

The place of the rending – מְקוֹם הַקְּרִיעָה: Rending may be performed on any part of the front of a garment, from the neck. One who rends the garment from the bottom or from the sides does not fulfill his obligation. Others hold that one can fulfill his obligation by rending from the sides of the garment. It is customary to rely on this lenient opinion when rending over the dead to whom one is not related, e.g., when one is present at the time when the soul departs (*Shakh*). However, one who rends his garment over relatives for whom he is required to rend it must do so from the neckline (*Shulḥan Arukh*, *Yoreh De'a* 340:2, and in the comment of Rema).

Rending of a High Priest – קְרִיעַת כֹּהֵן גָּדוֹל: A High Priest, who is prohibited from rending his garment, may tear the bottom of his garment near his feet (Rambam *Sefer Avoda*, *Hilkhot Kelei HaMikdash* 5:6).

תָּנוּ רַבָּנַן: הַיּוֹצֵא בְּבֶגֶד קָרוּעַ לִפְנֵי הַמֵּת הֲרֵי זֶה גּוֹזֵל אֶת הַמֵּתִים וְאֶת הַחַיִּים.

The Sages taught the following *baraita*: **One who goes out before the deceased in a rent garment** that he had previously torn[H] over another bereavement, thereby giving the appearance of having rent his garment for him, **steals from the dead,**[N] as he did not rend a garment for him. **And** he similarly steals **from the living,** who see him and think that he made the tear in honor of the deceased, when in reality he is deceiving them.

רַבָּן שִׁמְעוֹן בֶּן גַּמְלִיאֵל אוֹמֵר, הָאוֹמֵר לַחֲבֵירוֹ: ״הַשְׁאִילֵנִי חֲלוּקְךָ וְאֵלֵךְ וְאֲבַקֵּר אֶת אַבָּא שֶׁהוּא חוֹלֶה״, וְהָלַךְ וּמְצָאוֹ שֶׁמֵּת – קוֹרֵעַ, וּמְאַחוֹ. וּכְשֶׁיָּבֹא לְבֵיתוֹ מַחֲזִיר לוֹ חֲלוּקוֹ וְנוֹתֵן לוֹ דְּמֵי קְרָעוֹ. וְאִם לֹא הוֹדִיעוֹ – הֲרֵי זֶה לֹא יִגַּע בּוֹ.

Rabban Shimon ben Gamliel says: In the case of **one who says to his fellow: Lend me your cloak and I will go and visit my father because he is sick, and he goes and finds that** his father **has died, he rends** the cloak **and** may then **mend it** in the proper manner. **And when he returns home, he returns the cloak** to his fellow **and pays him the value of the rent,** i.e., the depreciation in the value of the cloak that resulted from the tear. The assumption is that the lender considered the possibility that the sick father might die, and lent the garment anyway, understanding that he might have to tear it. **But if one did not inform** his fellow that he was going to visit his sick father, **he must not touch it,** as he was not granted permission to tear the garment belonging to someone else.[H]

תָּנוּ רַבָּנַן: חוֹלֶה שֶׁמֵּת לוֹ מֵת – אֵין מוֹדִיעִין אוֹתוֹ שֶׁמֵּת, שֶׁמָּא תִּטָּרֵף דַּעְתּוֹ עָלָיו. וְאֵין מְקָרְעִין בְּפָנָיו, וּמַשְׁתִּיקִין אֶת הַנָּשִׁים מִפָּנָיו.

The Sages taught the following *baraita*: When a relative **of a sick** person **dies,**[H] those around him **do not inform him that** this relative **died, lest he lose control of his mind** due to his emotional state and his grief exacerbate his physical health. **And** other people **may not rend** their garments **in his presence,** so that he will not know that one of his relatives passed away. **And we silence the women** who weep **in his presence,** so that he will not know that his relative is no longer alive.

וּמְקָרְעִין לְקָטָן מִפְּנֵי עָגְמַת נֶפֶשׁ. וְקוֹרְעִין עַל חָמִיו וְעַל חֲמוֹתוֹ מִפְּנֵי כְּבוֹד אִשְׁתּוֹ.

And the relatives **rend** the garment **of a minor child** when there is mourning in his family **in order to arouse grief. Although** a minor is not required to rend his garments, this will add to the grief of those who see that even the garments of children are rent. **And one rends** his garment **for his father-in-law or mother-in-law, although** he is not required to mourn for them, **due to the honor of his wife,** to show her that he joins in her mourning.[H]

וְאָמַר רַב פָּפָּא, תָּנָא בְּאֵבֶל רַבָּתִי: אָבֵל לֹא יָנִיחַ תִּינוֹק בְּתוֹךְ חֵיקוֹ מִפְּנֵי שֶׁמְּבִיאוֹ לִידֵי שְׂחוֹק, וְנִמְצָא מִתְגַּנֶּה עַל הַבְּרִיּוֹת.

And Rav Pappa said: A Sage **taught in** ***Evel Rabbati*****: A mourner should not place** a young **child in his lap because** the child **will bring him to laughter, and he will be disgraced in** the eyes of **other people** because he laughed while in mourning.[H]

״וְאֵין מַבְרִין עַל מִטּוֹת זְקוּפוֹת״. תָּנוּ רַבָּנַן: הַהוֹלֵךְ לְבֵית הָאָבֵל, אִם הָיָה לִבּוֹ גַּס בּוֹ – יַבְרוּהוּ עַל מִטּוֹת כְּפוּיוֹת; וְאִם לָאו – יַבְרוּהוּ עַל מִטּוֹת זְקוּפוֹת.

§ The mishna taught: **And** the consolers **provide the first meal** after the burial **only** while the mourner sits **on an upright bed** and not on one that is overturned. **The Sages taught** in a *baraita*: With regard to **one who goes to the house of the mourner, if he is confident** in his friendship **with him**[N] because they are close friends, **they provide him with the meal of comfort** while both he and the mourner sit **on overturned beds. And if** he is **not** confident in his friendship with him, both **he** and the mourner **should be fed on upright beds.**

רָבָא אִיתְרַע בֵּיהּ מִילְּתָא. עַל לְגַבֵּיהּ אַבָּא בַּר מַרְתָּא, דְּהוּא אַבָּא בַּר מְנִיּוֹמֵי. רָבָא – זְקִיף, אַבָּא בַּר מַרְתָּא – כָּפֵי. אָמַר: כַּמָּה לֵית בֵּיהּ דַּעְתָּא לְהַאי צוּרְבָא מֵרַבָּנַן.

The Gemara relates that **something** unpleasant **happened to Rava,** i.e., one of his close relatives died, and **Abba bar Marta,** who was also known as **Abba bar Minyomi, entered** to visit **him. Rava stood** the bed **upright,** treating him like any other person who came to comfort him. **Abba bar Marta overturned** the bed because he saw himself as being on very familiar terms with Rava. Rava **said: How lacking in sense**[N] **is this Torah scholar.** Rava had shown from the outset that he did not consider Abba bar Marta to be a close friend, yet the latter ignored this message and viewed himself as being exceptionally close to Rava.

תָּנוּ רַבָּנַן: הַהוֹלֵךְ מִמָּקוֹם לְמָקוֹם,

The Sages taught a *baraita*: If **one who was going from place to place**[H] learned of the death of a close relative, so that he must now observe the rites of mourning,

HALAKHA

One who goes out in a rent garment that he had previously torn – הַיּוֹצֵא בְּבֶגֶד קָרוּעַ: One who goes out before the dead in a garment that was previously torn in order to make it appear as though he rent this garment in honor of the deceased is considered as though he has stolen both from the living and from the dead (*Shulḥan Arukh, Yoreh De'a* 340:33).

Rending a borrowed garment – קְרִיעַת בֶּגֶד שָׁאוּל: One who is wearing a borrowed garment when one of his relatives dies may not rend it, and one who does rend such a garment does not fulfill his obligation (*Shakh*). However, if one told the lender that he was going to visit the sick relative, then the borrower may rend the borrowed garment and pay the owner for the damage, in accordance with the opinion of Rabban Shimon ben Gamliel (*Shulḥan Arukh, Yoreh De'a* 340:34).

When a relative of a sick person dies – חוֹלֶה שֶׁמֵּת לוֹ מֵת: When the relative of a sick person's dies, even if it is not a close relative, he should not be informed of the death, lest his grief makes his condition worsen. Similarly, he does not rend his garment, and he is not told to rend it even if he knows about the death. Others should not cry or eulogize the deceased in his presence (*Shulḥan Arukh, Yoreh De'a* 337:1, see *Shakh* and *Baḥ*).

One rends his garment for his father-in-law or mother-in-law – קוֹרְעִין עַל חָמִיו וַחֲמוֹתוֹ: Both men and women should rend their garments over their father- and mother-in-law. However, the custom nowadays is not to rend the garment in such a case (*Shulḥan Arukh, Yoreh De'a* 340:4, and in the comment of Rema).

A mourner is prohibited from being joyous – אָבֵל אָסוּר בְּשִׂמְחָה: A mourner should not place a child on his lap for all seven days of mourning, lest the child take his mind off of his mourning. When a mourner recites *havdala*, he should not recite the verses of joy. Rather, he should begin from the blessings (*Pitḥei Teshuva*; *Shulḥan Arukh, Yoreh De'a* 391:1).

Who was going from place to place – הַהוֹלֵךְ מִמָּקוֹם לְמָקוֹם: With regard to one who was traveling when he heard news of a death, if he can entirely avoid doing business in that place then this is preferable. However, if business transactions are unavoidable because if he does not make a purchase there he will not be able to find food elsewhere, then he should purchase the minimal essentials for the rest of his journey (*Shulḥan Arukh, Yoreh De'a* 380:23).

NOTES

Steals from the dead – גּוֹזֵל אֶת הַמֵּתִים: If one was obligated to rend his garment and did not do so, he stole the honor due to the deceased (see Rabbeinu Yehonatan of Lunel). Rav Hai Gaon writes, based on *Evel Rabbati*, that stealing from the dead is very serious because one cannot ask forgiveness from the deceased, as he can with a living person whom he has dishonored.

If he is confident in his friendship with him – אִם הָיָה לִבּוֹ גַּס בּוֹ: Some explain that this means that the mourner is close to the consoler. Since they are so familiar with each other the mourner does not need to honor the consoler. The mourner is not required to turn the bed upright as a sign of respect for the guest because he knows that the guest will not be offended (Ramban). Others write that the consoler might see sitting on an overturned bed as a bad omen, and if he is not a regular visitor to this place then the mourners must take care not to upset him (Rabbeinu Yehonatan of Lunel; see *Nimmukei Yosef*).

Alternatively, this expression refers to the mourner. If the mourner is so friendly that he becomes happy, then the consolers must also overturn their beds in order to reach his heart and remind him of his mourning (Rashi, from manuscript).

How lacking in sense – כַּמָּה לֵית בֵּיהּ דַּעְתָּא: Some explain this to mean that Rava acted appropriately and stood up both beds, yet his guest overturned his own one. He thereby put Rava in an inappropriate situation where he, a mourner, was sitting on an upright bed while his guest was sitting on an overturned bed (Rabbi Shlomo ben HaYatom).

אִם יָכוֹל לְמַעֵט בְּעִסְקוֹ – יְמַעֵט; וְאִם לָאו – יְגַלְגֵּל עִמָּהֶן.

if he can reduce his business, he should reduce it; **and if not, he may carry on with them,**[N] i.e., his business partners. He may act in partnership with the members of the group with which he is traveling, but he may not engage in business independently.

תָּנוּ רַבָּנַן: מֵאֵימָתַי כּוֹפִין אֶת הַמִּטּוֹת? מִשֶּׁיֵּצֵא מִפֶּתַח בֵּיתוֹ, דִּבְרֵי רַבִּי אֱלִיעֶזֶר. רַבִּי יְהוֹשֻׁעַ אוֹמֵר: מִשֶּׁיִּסָּתֵם הַגּוֹלֵל.

§ **The Sages taught** the following *baraita*: **From when do** the mourners **overturn** their **beds?**[N] **From when** the corpse **is taken out of the opening of his house;** this is **the statement of Rabbi Eliezer. Rabbi Yehoshua says: From when the** tomb **is sealed** with **the grave cover.**[BH]

מַעֲשֶׂה שֶׁמֵּת רַבָּן גַּמְלִיאֵל הַזָּקֵן. כֵּיוָן שֶׁיָּצָא מִפֶּתַח בֵּיתוֹ אָמַר לָהֶם רַבִּי אֱלִיעֶזֶר: כְּפוּ מִטּוֹתֵיכֶם. וְכֵיוָן שֶׁנִּסְתַּם הַגּוֹלֵל, אָמַר לָהֶם רַבִּי יְהוֹשֻׁעַ: כְּפוּ מִטּוֹתֵיכֶם. אָמְרוּ לוֹ: כְּבָר כָּפִינוּ עַל פִּי זָקֵן.

There was **an incident in which** the *Nasi* **Rabban Gamliel the Elder**[P] **died,** and **once** his body **left the opening of his house, Rabbi Eliezer said to** the members of the household: **Overturn your beds. And once the** tomb **was sealed** with **the grave cover, Rabbi Yehoshua said to them: Overturn your beds. They** then **said to him: We already overturned** them **in accordance with the Elder,** i.e., Rabbi Eliezer.

תָּנוּ רַבָּנַן: מֵאֵימָתַי זוֹקְפִין אֶת הַמִּטּוֹת בְּעֶרֶב שַׁבָּת? מִן הַמִּנְחָה וּלְמַעְלָה. אָמַר רַבָּה בַּר הוּנָא: אַף עַל פִּי כֵן, אֵינוֹ יוֹשֵׁב עָלֶיהָ עַד שֶׁתֶּחְשַׁךְ. וּלְמוֹצָאֵי שַׁבָּת, אַף עַל פִּי שֶׁאֵין לוֹ לֵישֵׁב אֶלָּא יוֹם אֶחָד – חוֹזֵר וְכוֹפֶה.

The Sages taught in a *baraita*: **From when do** the mourners **stand** their **beds upright on Friday;**[H] as the rites of mourning are not observed on Shabbat, and the beds must be returned to their ordinary position beforehand? **From** ***minḥa*** time **onward. Rabba bar Huna said: Even so, one may not sit down on** his upright bed immediately. Rather, he must wait **until it becomes dark** to do so. **And at the conclusion of Shabbat, even if he has only one** more **day to sit** in mourning, i.e., his period of mourning concludes on Sunday, **he must** once **again overturn** his bed.

תָּנוּ רַבָּנַן: הַכּוֹפֶה מִטָּתוֹ, לֹא מִטָּתוֹ בִּלְבַד הוּא כּוֹפֶה, אֶלָּא כׇּל מִטּוֹת שֶׁיֵּשׁ לוֹ בְּתוֹךְ בֵּיתוֹ הוּא כּוֹפֶה. וַאֲפִילּוּ יֵשׁ לוֹ עֶשֶׂר מִטּוֹת בַּעֲשָׂרָה מְקוֹמוֹת כּוֹפֶה אֶת כּוּלָּן. וַאֲפִילּוּ חֲמִשָּׁה אַחִין וּמֵת אֶחָד – כּוּלָּן כּוֹפִין.

The Sages taught in a *baraita*: With regard to **one who** is in mourning and must **overturn his bed,**[N] **he overturns not only his own bed, but rather he overturns all the beds he has**[N] **in his house. And even if he has ten beds**[N] **in ten** different **places, he overturns them all. And even** if there are **five brothers and one** of them **died, all of them overturn** their beds wherever they live.[H]

NOTES

He should reduce his business…and he may carry on with them – יְמַעֵט בְּעִסְקוֹ...וִיגַלְגֵּל עִמָּהֶן: Two explanations are offered for this expression. Some say that the phrase: He should reduce, means that he should not engage in business at all, and if he absolutely must do so he may purchase only the minimal amount to eat on the journey home (Rabbeinu Ḥananel; Rosh). Some explain the expression: He may carry on with them, to mean that he should not perform business on his own at all. Instead, he should join in partnership with others or others may engage in business on his behalf (Rashi; Rabbeinu Gershom Meor HaGola; Rabbeinu Yehonatan of Lunel).

From when do they overturn their beds – מֵאֵימָתַי כּוֹפִין אֶת הַמִּטּוֹת: Overturning the bed signifies the beginning of all of the mourning practices. Since the activities of removing shoes or wrapping the head are not applicable to all, the Gemara referred to overturning the bed because it applies equally to all (*Tosefot HaRosh*).

Overturning of the bed – כְּפִיַּית הַמִּיטָּה: The early authorities mention a statement in the Jerusalem Talmud that a guest in an inn does not overturn his bed because the gentiles there are likely to think that he is engaging in witchcraft. Based on this, they explain why it is no longer customary for a mourner to overturn his bed. When the Jewish people are in exile, it is as though they are always residing in temporary accommodations. Additionally, it is explained that modern beds have pieces that protrude upward, and overturning them would not be noticeable or practical; therefore, it became customary not to overturn one's bed at all (see Rosh).

All the beds he has – כׇּל מִיטּוֹת שֶׁיֵּשׁ לוֹ: Some of the early authorities explain that a mourner must overturn all of the beds in his house, whether they belong to him, to the members of his household, or to others. However, guests who are not mourners stand these beds upright when they wish to use them (Ramban). According to the Ra'avad, a mourner is required to overturn only the beds belonging to the members of his household (see Rosh).

And even if he has ten beds, etc. – וַאֲפִילּוּ יֵשׁ לוֹ עֶשֶׂר מִיטּוֹת וכו׳: Rabbeinu Yehonatan of Lunel writes that the principle behind this *halakha* is that the obligation to overturn one's bed does not apply specifically to the house where the person died. Rather, it is the obligation of every mourner. Therefore, if the mourner sleeps in several different places, he is required to overturn his bed in each place. Similarly, brothers who are each mourning in their own homes are required to overturn their beds.

BACKGROUND

Grave cover – גּוֹלֵל: The grave cover was a large stone that was rolled onto the grave to seal it. In burial caves, these stones, which cover the entrance to the cave, are considered like large stone wheels that are not susceptible to ritual impurity and that can be rolled away when people wish to enter the cave.

Stone used to seal a burial cave

HALAKHA

When is the beginning of mourning – מֵאֵימָתַי תְּחִילַּת אֲבֵילוּת: Mourning begins when the deceased is buried and the grave is covered with dirt, in accordance with the opinion of Rabbi Yehoshua. At this point, the mourner is also required to wrap his head. However, he does not remove his shoes until he reaches his house. Nowadays, it is customary to remove one's shoes immediately after the grave has been sealed. If one thought that the grave had been sealed and he began mourning, and it later became known to him that he had made a mistake, then he should count his mourning period from the time of the actual burial (*Shulḥan Arukh, Yoreh De'a* 375:1, and in the comment of Rema).

The time of the standing up of the bed – זְמַן זְקִיפַת הַמִּיטָּה: A mourner stands his bed upright on Friday from the time of the afternoon prayer and onward. However, he should not sit on an upright bed until it becomes dark. At the conclusion of Shabbat, he again overturns the bed, even if he has only one day of mourning left (*Shulḥan Arukh, Yoreh De'a* 400:1).

Which beds are overturned – אֵלּוּ מִטּוֹת כּוֹפִים: A mourner who is required to overturn his bed is required to overturn not only his own bed, but also all the beds in his house. If he has many houses in various places, then he must overturn all of the beds in each house. This obligation applies to all of the mourners. However, the obligation applies only to beds intended for lying on. A bed that has been designated for storing garments or for some other use need not be overturned. Similarly, a bed with large posts need not be overturned. With regard to a *dargash*, one should untie its loops rather than overturning it (Rambam *Sefer Shofetim, Hilkhot Evel* 5:18). Nowadays, the custom is not to overturn beds at all (*Shulḥan Arukh, Yoreh De'a* 387:2).

PERSONALITIES

Rabban Gamliel the Elder – רַבָּן גַּמְלִיאֵל הַזָּקֵן: Rabban Gamliel is referred to as the Elder to distinguish him from his grandson, whose name was also Rabban Gamliel, and who was referred to as Rabban Gamliel of Yavne. He was a grandson of Hillel the Elder and served as the head of the Sanhedrin for many years during the Temple period.

It seems that Rabban Gamliel was the first to receive the honorary title Rabban because he was accepted by all the Sages of the Jewish people. Many of his rulings were cited in subsequent generations. He enacted many important rulings, e.g., that a woman may remarry based on the testimony of a single witness that her previous husband has died. He enacted other rulings as well, in order to improve public welfare. During his time, people would study Torah only while standing, but that practice ceased when he died. Therefore, it is said that when Rabban Gamliel died, honor for the Torah ceased (Sota 49a).

His son was Rabban Shimon ben Gamliel, who led the Jewish people during the era of the Great Revolt and who was later executed by the Romans.

וְאִם הָיְתָה מִטָּה הַמְיוּחֶדֶת לְכֵלִים – אֵין צָרִיךְ לְכַפּוֹתָהּ. דַּרְגָּשׁ – אֵין צָרִיךְ לְכַפּוֹתוֹ, אֶלָּא זוֹקְפוֹ. רַבָּן שִׁמְעוֹן בֶּן גַּמְלִיאֵל אוֹמֵר: דַּרְגָּשׁ, מַתִּיר אֶת קַרְבִּיטָיו וְהוּא נוֹפֵל מֵאֵילָיו.

If, however, it is a bed designated for the storage of **garments** and not for sleeping, **he is not required to overturn it. It is also not necessary to overturn a *dargash*,**[N] **but rather he stands it upright. Rabban Shimon ben Gamliel says:** With regard to a ***dargash*, one loosens its loops** [***karbitav***],[L] which hold up the pillows, **and it falls on its own.**

מַאי דַּרְגָּשׁ? אֲמַר עוּלָּא: עַרְסָא דְּגַדָּא.

The Gemara asks: **What is the meaning of the word *dargash*? Ulla said:** It is a good-**luck** [***gada***] **bed,** as it was common to have ornamental beds for good luck, which were not used for sleeping.

אֲמַר לֵיהּ רַבָּה: אֶלָּא מֵעַתָּה גַּבֵּי מֶלֶךְ, דִּתְנַן: כׇּל הָעָם מְסוּבִּים עַל הָאָרֶץ וְהוּא מֵיסֵב עַל הַדַּרְגָּשׁ, מִי אִיכָּא מִידֵּי דְּעַד הָאִידָּנָא לָא אוֹתְבִינֵיהּ – וְהָשְׁתָּא מוֹתְבִינַן לֵיהּ?

Rabba said to him: However, if that is so, then the following statement **with regard to a king** is difficult, **as we learned** in a mishna (*Sanhedrin* 20a): When the mourner's meal is served to the king and his family, **all the people recline on the ground, and he,** the king, due to his honor, **reclines on a *dargash*.**[H] **Is there anything upon which we would not have seated him until now,** when he was not a mourner, **but now,** specifically during the mourning period, **we seat him on it?**

מַתְקִיף לַהּ רַב אַשִׁי: מַאי קוּשְׁיָא? מִידֵּי דַּהֲוָה אַאֲכִילָה וּשְׁתִיָּה, דְּעַד הָאִידָּנָא – לָא אוֹכְלִינֵיהּ וְלָא אַשְׁקִינֵיהּ, הָשְׁתָּא – אוֹכְלִינֵיהּ וְאַשְׁקִינֵיהּ!

Rav Ashi strongly objects to this: What is the difficulty raised by Rabba? One can answer: The *halakha* is **just as it is in** the case of **eating and drinking,** that **until now,** before one became a mourner, **we did not feed him or give him drink,** but **now** that he is a mourner **we feed him and give him drink** during the first meal after the burial.

אֶלָּא, אִי קַשְׁיָא – הָא קַשְׁיָא: דִּתְנַן: דַּרְגָּשׁ אֵינוֹ צָרִיךְ לְכַפּוֹתוֹ אֶלָּא זוֹקְפוֹ, וְאִי עַרְסָא דְּגַדָּא – אַמַּאי אֵינוֹ צָרִיךְ לְכַפּוֹתוֹ? הָא תְּנַן: הַכּוֹפֶה מִטָּתוֹ – לֹא מִטָּתוֹ בִּלְבַד הוּא כּוֹפֶה, אֶלָּא כׇּל מִטּוֹת שֶׁיֵּשׁ לוֹ בְּתוֹךְ בֵּיתוֹ כּוֹפֶה!

Rather, if it is difficult, this is difficult, as we learned in a *baraita*: **It is not necessary to overturn a *dargash*, but rather he stands it upright. But if it is a good-luck bed, why is it not necessary to overturn it? Didn't we learn: One who** is in mourning and must **overturn his bed overturns not only his own bed, but rather he overturns all the beds in his house,** including this good luck bed?

וּמַאי קַשְׁיָא? מִידֵּי דַּהֲוָה אַמִּטָּה הַמְיוּחֶדֶת לְכֵלִים, דְּתַנְיָא: אִם הָיְתָה מִטָּה הַמְיוּחֶדֶת לְכֵלִים – אֵינוֹ צָרִיךְ לְכַפּוֹתָהּ!

The Gemara rejects this: **And what is difficult** in this? One can answer: The *halakha* is **just as it is in** the case of **a bed designated** for the storage of **garments, as it is taught** in a *baraita*: **If it is a bed designated for** the storage of **garments,** and not for sleeping, **one is not required to overturn it.** So too, one is not required to overturn a *dargash*, as it is a bed that is not used for sleeping.

אֶלָּא, אִי קַשְׁיָא הָא קַשְׁיָא: רַבָּן שִׁמְעוֹן בֶּן גַּמְלִיאֵל אוֹמֵר: דַּרְגָּשׁ, מַתִּיר קַרְבִּיטָיו וְהוּא נוֹפֵל מֵאֵילָיו. וְאִי סָלְקָא דַּעְתָּךְ עַרְסָא דְּגַדָּא – מַאי קַרְבִּיטִין אִית לֵיהּ?

Rather if it is difficult, this is the difficulty: It was taught in a *baraita*: **Rabban Shimon ben Gamliel says:** With regard to a ***dargash*, one loosens the loops** that hold up the pillows, **and it falls on its own. And if it enters your mind** to say that a *dargash* **is a good-luck bed,** it is like other beds, so **what loops does it have?**

כִּי אֲתָא רָבִין אֲמַר לֵיהּ הַהוּא מֵרַבָּנַן, וְרַב תַּחֲלִיפָא בַּר מַעַרְבָא שְׁמֵיהּ, דַּהֲוָה שְׁכִיחַ בְּשׁוּקָא דְּגִילְדָאֵי: מַאי דַּרְגָּשׁ? עַרְסָא דְּצַלָּא.

When Ravin came from Eretz Yisrael to Babylonia, **one of the Sages, whose name was Rav Taḥalifa from the West,** and **who was frequently** found **in the market of leather workers, said to him: What is a *dargash*?** It is **a leather bed.**

אִיתְּמַר נַמִי, אָמַר רַבִּי יִרְמְיָה: דַּרְגָּשׁ – סִירוּגוֹ מִתּוֹכוֹ; מִטָּה – סִירוּגָהּ עַל גַּבָּהּ.

It was also stated that **Rabbi Yirmeya said: A *dargash*** has **its interlacing from the inside,**[B] i.e., attached to loops that go through holes that are made in the bed frame itself; whereas a **bed** has **its interlacing from the outside,**[B] i.e., the strapping itself is looped around the wood of the frame, and therefore it cannot be loosened.

אָמַר רַבִּי יַעֲקֹב בַּר אַחָא אָמַר רַבִּי יְהוֹשֻׁעַ בֶּן לֵוִי: הֲלָכָה כְּרַבָּן שִׁמְעוֹן בֶּן גַּמְלִיאֵל. אִיתְּמַר נַמִי, אָמַר רַבִּי יַעֲקֹב בַּר אַחָא אָמַר רַבִּי אַסִי: מִטָּה שֶׁנַּקְלִיטֶיהָ יוֹצְאִין – זוֹקְפָהּ, וְדַיּוֹ.

Rabbi Ya'akov bar Aḥa said in the name of Rabbi Yehoshua ben Levi: The *halakha* is in accordance with the opinion of **Rabban Shimon ben Gamliel** with regard to a *dargash*. **It was also stated** that **Rabbi Ya'akov bar Aḥa said in the name of Rabbi Asi: A bed whose posts** [***naklitin***][NLB] **extend,** meaning that they are very long so that the bed will remain high off the ground even if it is overturned, **may be stood upright and that is sufficient.** That is to say, one is not required to overturn such a bed.

NOTES

It is not necessary to overturn a *dargash* – דַּרְגָּשׁ, אֵין צָרִיךְ לְכַפּוֹתוֹ: According to the Meiri, this is because it is not readily apparent if the *dargash* is overturned, since it is always low to the ground. The Ritva writes that because a *dargash* is made of expensive leather, there is concern that it will be damaged if it is overturned, and therefore it is sufficient to stand it on its side as a sign of mourning.

Whose posts extend – נַקְלִיטֶיהָ יוֹצְאִין: Rabbeinu Yehonatan of Lunel writes that the posts are two poles that stick out from the middle of the ends of the bed. Therefore, it is impossible to overturn such a bed.

LANGUAGE

Loops [*karbitin*] – קַרְבִּיטִין: From the Greek κράββατος, *krabatos*, meaning mattress, cushion, or interlacing of the bed.

Posts [*naklitin*] – נַקְלִיטִין: Probably from the Greek ἀνάκλιτα, *anaklita*, or ἀνάκλιτος, *anaklitos*, meaning leaning back in a bed or chair.

HALAKHA

The first meal for a king after the burial – סְעוּדַת הַבְרָאָה לַמֶּלֶךְ: When a king eats the first meal after the burial of his relative, everyone else sits on the ground and he sits on a *dargash* (Rambam *Sefer Shofetim*, *Hilkhot Evel* 7:8).

BACKGROUND

Interlacing from the inside – סֵירוּגוֹ מִתּוֹכוֹ:

Interlacing from the outside – סֵירוּגָהּ עַל גַּבָּהּ:

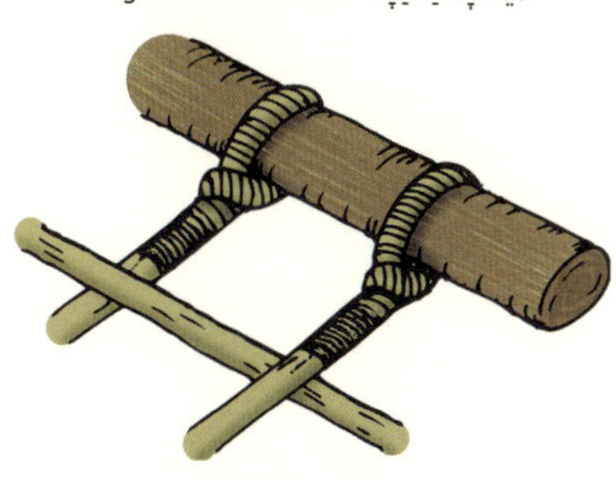

Bed and bedpost – מִטָּה וְנַקְלִיטִין: On the bed depicted in the image, the supports at the head and the foot, which may be the posts referred to by the Gemara, extend from the bed, and therefore it is difficult to overturn it. Furthermore, overturning it would not be immediately noticeable.

Ancient Roman bed from mishnaic period

תָּנוּ רַבָּנַן: יָשֵׁן עַל גַּבֵּי כִּסֵּא, עַל גַּבֵּי אוּדְיָינֵי גְּדוֹלָה, עַל גַּבֵּי קַרְקַע – לֹא יָצָא יְדֵי חוֹבָתוֹ. אָמַר רַבִּי יוֹחָנָן: שֶׁלֹּא קִיֵּים כְּפִיַּית הַמִּטָּה.

The Sages taught the following *baraita*: If the mourner **sleeps on a chair,** or **on a large** overturned **mortar,** or **on the ground, he does not fulfill his obligation,** even though he is uncomfortable while sleeping. **Rabbi Yoḥanan said:** This is **because he did not fulfill** the mitzva of **overturning the bed.**[H]

תָּנוּ רַבָּנַן: מְכַבְּדִין וּמַרְבִּיצִין בְּבֵית הָאֵבֶל, וּמַדִּיחִין קְעָרוֹת וְכוֹסוֹת וּצְלוֹחִיּוֹת וְקִיתוֹנִיּוֹת בְּבֵית הָאֵבֶל, וְאֵין מְבִיאִין אֶת הַמּוּגְמָר וְאֶת הַבְּשָׂמִים לְבֵית הָאֵבֶל.

The Sages taught another *baraita*: **One may sweep and sprinkle** water[H] on a dirt floor **in the house of a mourner, and one may wash bowls, cups, jugs, and pitchers in the house of a mourner. But one may not bring incense or** fragrant **spices into the house of a mourner.**

אִינִי: וְהָא תָּנֵי בַּר קַפָּרָא: אֵין מְבָרְכִין לֹא עַל הַמּוּגְמָר וְלֹא עַל הַבְּשָׂמִים בְּבֵית הָאֵבֶל. בָּרוּכֵי הוּא דְּלָא מְבָרְכִין, הָא אַתּוּיֵי – מַיְיתִינַן!

The Gemara asks: **Is that so? But doesn't bar Kappara teach** the following *baraita*: **One may not recite a blessing either over incense or over fragrant spices in the house of a mourner?** From this one may infer that **one may not recite a blessing** over these incense or spices, **but one may bring them** into the house of the mourner. This appears to contradict the previous *baraita*.

לָא קַשְׁיָא; הָא – בְּבֵית הָאֵבֶל, הָא – בְּבֵית הַמְנַחֲמִין.

The Gemara explains: **It is not difficult. Here,** the *baraita* is referring **to the house of a mourner,** into which spices should not be taken; **there,** the *baraita* that states that one may not recite a blessing over them, is referring **to the house of the consolers,** his relatives, into which spices may be brought.[N]

מתני׳ אֵין מוֹלִיכִין לְבֵית הָאֵבֶל לֹא בְּטַבְלָא וְלֹא בְּאִסְקוּטְלָא וְלֹא בְּקָנוֹן, אֶלָּא בְּסַלִּים. וְאֵין אוֹמְרִים בִּרְכַּת אֲבֵלִים בַּמּוֹעֵד, אֲבָל עוֹמְדִין בְּשׁוּרָה, וּמְנַחֲמִין, וּפוֹטְרִין אֶת הָרַבִּים.

MISHNA One does not bring[N] the first meal after the burial **to the house of mourning on a small tray** [*tavla*],[L] **in a bowl** [*iskutla*],[NL] **or in a narrow-mouthed basket** [*kanon*],[L] **but rather in** ordinary **baskets. And the mourners' blessing is not recited on** the intermediate days of **a Festival, but** the consolers may **stand in a row** when the mourners leave the cemetery **and console** them. **And** the mourners **dismiss the many** consolers,[N] by telling them that they may return home after they have fulfilled the mitzva of consoling the mourners.[H]

אֵין מַנִּיחִין אֶת הַמִּטָּה בָּרְחוֹב שֶׁלֹּא לְהַרְגִּיל אֶת הַהֶסְפֵּד. וְלֹא שֶׁל נָשִׁים לְעוֹלָם, מִפְּנֵי הַכָּבוֹד.

The bier of the deceased **is not set down in the street** during the intermediate days of a Festival[H] **so as not to encourage eulogies.** On an ordinary weekday, people would gather in the street around the bier to eulogize the deceased, but this should be avoided during the intermediate days of the Festival. **And the** biers **of women** are **never** set down, even if it is not the intermediate days of a Festival, **due to their honor.** Blood might drip from their bodies, and it would cause them dishonor if their blood stained the street.

HALAKHA

Sleeping on an overturned bed – שֵׁינָה עַל מִיטָּה כְּפוּיָה: It is not enough for a mourner to overturn his bed; he must sleep on it overturned as well (Rambam *Sefer Shofetim, Hilkhot Evel* 5:18).

Sweep and sprinkle water – מְכַבְּדִין וּמַרְבִּיצִין: It is permitted to sweep and sprinkle water on the dirt floor in a mourners' house. Similarly, one may wash dishes there as well. However, one should not bring any type of fragrant spices there. Spices may be taken into a house in which a dead body is present, but one does not recite a blessing over those spices (*Shulḥan Arukh, Yoreh De'a* 378:7).

Customs of mourning during the intermediate days of the Festival – מִנְהַג אֲבֵילוּת בַּמּוֹעֵד: The mourners' blessing is not recited in open areas during the intermediate days of a Festival. However, the consolers stand in a line and the mourners dismiss the masses (*Tur, Yoreh De'a* 401).

Placing a bier during the intermediate days of the Festival – הֲנָחַת הַמִּיטָּה בַּמּוֹעֵד: The bier is not placed in the street during the intermediate days of a Festival, so as not to encourage eulogizing at that time. On these days, eulogies are given only in honor of a Torah scholar. A bier is not taken for burial during the intermediate days of the Festival until the grave has already been prepared (*Shulḥan Arukh, Yoreh De'a* 401:1).

LANGUAGE

Tray [*tavla*] – טַבְלָא: From the Greek τάβλα, *tabla*, which is borrowed from the Latin tabula. Ordinarily, it refers to a tablet that was used for writing or on which objects were placed. By extension, the word is used here in reference to a flat tray that is similar to a tablet. See also LANGUAGE, p. 54.

Bowl [*iskutla*] – אִסְקוּטְלָא: From the Latin scutella, meaning flat dish.

Narrow-mouthed basket [*kanon*] – קָנוֹן: From the Greek κάνεον, *kaneon*, or κανῶν, *kanon*, meaning breadbasket, or a basket in which items were taken as gifts or to be sacrificed as offerings. According to the description in the Talmud, this basket had a narrow opening.

NOTES

The house of the mourner and the house of the consolers – בֵּית הָאֵבֶל וּבֵית הַמְנַחֲמִין: The authorities disagree with regard to the meaning of the expression: House of the mourner. Some say that the house of the mourner refers to a house where the mourner alone is present, and the house of the consolers refers to the place where people come to comfort him (Ra'avad; Rabbeinu Yehonatan of Lunel).

Others explain that the house of the mourner refers to a house that still contains the body of the deceased, and the more correct name would be the house of the mourning; whereas the house of the consolers is the room that no longer contains the body of the deceased, where others come to console the mourners (Rosh).

Similarly, there is a dispute with regard to the *halakha*, as there are those who say that it is permitted to bring fragrant spices into a house where the body of the deceased is present, to remove any unpleasant odor, however such spices may not be brought to a place where there is no dead body (Rabbi Yitzḥak ibn Giat; Ritva; Meiri). Some say that in a house where only the mourner is present one may not bring fragrant spices because it is not appropriate for the mourner to take pleasure while he is mourning. However, in honor of the consolers one may bring such spices (Rabbeinu Ḥananel).

One does not bring – אֵין מוֹלִיכִין: Some say that this mishna refers to the intermediate days of the Festival. Despite the honor of the intermediate days of the Festival, one may not take food to the mourner's house in elaborately decorated vessels. This is all the more so prohibited on an ordinary weekday (Ritva).

In a bowl – בְּאִסְקוּטְלָא: Some explain that this refers to a type of large bowl (Rashi) or that it was a gold or silver bowl (*Arukh*). Others understand it to be a small table (Rabbeinu Yehonatan of Lunel), or a fine tablecloth (Rabbi Shlomo ben HaYatom).

And dismiss the many consolers – וּפוֹטְרִים אֶת הָרַבִּים: Some explain that the mourners would dismiss the consolers immediately, telling them that they have not fulfilled their obligation since they cannot recite the mourners' blessing (Rabbeinu Yehonatan of Lunel). Those who came to console were also exempt after the Festival from reciting the mourners' blessing (Ra'avad). Some say that in honor of the Festival it is permitted to tell the consolers: Go in peace (Ran).

גמ׳ תָּנוּ רַבָּנַן: בָּרִאשׁוֹנָה הָיוּ מוֹלִיכִין בְּבֵית הָאֵבֶל, עֲשִׁירִים – בְּקָלָתוֹת שֶׁל כֶּסֶף וְשֶׁל זָהָב, וַעֲנִיִּים – בְּסַלֵּי נְצָרִים שֶׁל עֲרָבָה קְלוּפָה. וְהָיוּ עֲנִיִּים מִתְבַּיְּישִׁים, הִתְקִינוּ שֶׁיְּהוּ הַכֹּל מְבִיאִין בְּסַלֵּי נְצָרִים שֶׁל עֲרָבָה קְלוּפָה, מִפְּנֵי כְּבוֹדָן שֶׁל עֲנִיִּים.

GEMARA **The Sages taught** the following *baraita*: **At first,** the meal after the burial **would be brought to the house of the mourner** in various ways. **The wealthy** would bring the meal **in baskets of silver and gold, and the poor** would bring it in **baskets of peeled willow branches. And the poor were embarrassed,**[N] as everyone would see that they were poor. The Sages **instituted that everyone should bring** the meal **in baskets of peeled willow branches,**[H] **due to the honor of the poor.**

תָּנוּ רַבָּנַן: בָּרִאשׁוֹנָה הָיוּ מַשְׁקִין בְּבֵית הָאֵבֶל, עֲשִׁירִים – בִּזְכוּכִית לְבָנָה, וַעֲנִיִּים – בִּזְכוּכִית צְבוּעָה, וְהָיוּ עֲנִיִּים מִתְבַּיְּישִׁין. הִתְקִינוּ שֶׁיְּהוּ הַכֹּל מַשְׁקִין בִּזְכוּכִית צְבוּעָה, מִפְּנֵי כְּבוֹדָן שֶׁל עֲנִיִּים.

The Sages taught a similar *baraita*: **At first, they would serve** wine **in the house of the mourner** during the first meal after the burial; the **wealthy** would do so **in** cups made from **white glass, and the poor** would serve this wine **in** cups of **colored glass.**[B] **And the poor were embarrassed,** as everyone would see that they were poor. The Sages **instituted that all should serve drinks** in the house of the mourner **in colored glass** cups, **due to the honor of the poor.**

בָּרִאשׁוֹנָה הָיוּ מְגַלִּין פְּנֵי עֲשִׁירִים, וּמְכַסִּין פְּנֵי עֲנִיִּים, מִפְּנֵי שֶׁהָיוּ מוּשְׁחָרִין פְּנֵיהֶן מִפְּנֵי בַּצּוֹרֶת, וְהָיוּ עֲנִיִּים מִתְבַּיְּישִׁין. הִתְקִינוּ שֶׁיְּהוּ מְכַסִּין פְּנֵי הַכֹּל, מִפְּנֵי כְּבוֹדָן שֶׁל עֲנִיִּים.

Furthermore, **at first they would uncover the faces of the wealthy**[N] who passed away **and cover the faces of the poor, because their faces were blackened by famine. And the poor were embarrassed** because they were buried in a different manner. The Sages **instituted that everyone's face should be covered, due to the honor of the poor.**[H]

בָּרִאשׁוֹנָה הָיוּ מוֹצִיאִין עֲשִׁירִים בְּדַרְגָּשׁ, וַעֲנִיִּים

Additionally, **at first the wealthy would take** the deceased **out** for burial **on a** ***dargash*****, and the poor** would take the deceased out

HALAKHA

Baskets of peeled willow branches – סַלֵּי נְצָרִים שֶׁל עֲרָבָה קְלוּפָה: Food for the first meal after burial may be transferred only in simple willow baskets (Rambam *Sefer Shofetim*, *Hilkhot Evel* 13:7).

Covering the faces of the dead – כִּיסּוּי פְּנֵי הַמֵּת: The faces of the deceased should be covered, regardless of whether they were wealthy or poor, in accordance with the enactment of the Sages (*Shulḥan Arukh*, *Yoreh De'a* 353:1).

NOTES

Would be brought…and the poor were embarrassed – הָיוּ מוֹלִיכִין...וְהָיוּ עֲנִיִּים מִתְבַּיְּישִׁים: There is a dispute as to whether the concern is for the honor of the mourners or the consolers. According to one opinion, people would use inexpensive vessels to bring food to the mourners who were from poor households, and the Sages were concerned about the honor of the poor. Alternatively, this ordinance was instituted because the poor consolers would bring simple utensils, and the Sages were concerned about the honor of the consolers (Rabbeinu Yehonatan of Lunel; see *Nimmukei Yosef*).

Uncover the faces of the wealthy – מְגַלִּין פְּנֵי עֲשִׁירִים: Uncovering the face was done to increase the eulogies because people would be pained when they saw the face of the deceased. Or perhaps those present, when seeing the deceased, would realize that despite how beautiful he had once been his body will nevertheless soon become dirt and decay. This leads to an understanding of the frailty of life (Rabbeinu Yehonatan of Lunel).

BACKGROUND

Colored glass – זְכוּכִית צְבוּעָה:

Roman glassware in various colors

Perek **III**
Daf **27** Amud **b**

בִּכְלִיכָה, וְהָיוּ עֲנִיִּים מִתְבַּיְּישִׁין. הִתְקִינוּ שֶׁיְּהוּ הַכֹּל מוֹצִיאִין בִּכְלִיכָה, מִפְּנֵי כְּבוֹדָן שֶׁל עֲנִיִּים.

on a plain bier made from poles that were strapped together, **and the poor were embarrassed.** The Sages **instituted that everyone should be taken out** for burial **on a plain bier, due to the honor of the poor.**

בָּרִאשׁוֹנָה הָיוּ מַנִּיחִין אֶת הַמּוּגְמָר תַּחַת חוֹלֵי מֵעַיִם מֵתִים, וְהָיוּ חוֹלֵי מֵעַיִם חַיִּים מִתְבַּיְּישִׁין, הִתְקִינוּ שֶׁיְּהוּ מַנִּיחִין תַּחַת הַכֹּל, מִפְּנֵי כְּבוֹדָן שֶׁל חוֹלֵי מֵעַיִם חַיִּים.

Similarly, **at first they would place incense under** the beds of **those who died with an intestinal disease,** because the body emitted an especially unpleasant odor. **And those who were alive with an intestinal disease were embarrassed** when they understood that they, too, would be treated in this manner after their death, and that everyone would know the cause of their death. The Sages **instituted that incense should be placed under everyone, due to the honor of those with an intestinal disease who were** still **living.**

בָּרִאשׁוֹנָה הָיוּ מַטְבִּילִין אֶת הַכֵּלִים עַל גַּבֵּי נִדּוֹת מֵתוֹת, וְהָיוּ נִדּוֹת חַיּוֹת מִתְבַּיְּישׁוֹת. הִתְקִינוּ שֶׁיְּהוּ מַטְבִּילִין עַל גַּבֵּי כָּל הַנָּשִׁים, מִפְּנֵי כְּבוֹדָן שֶׁל נִדּוֹת חַיּוֹת. בָּרִאשׁוֹנָה מַטְבִּילִין עַל גַּבֵּי זָבִין מֵתִים, וְהָיוּ זָבִין חַיִּים מִתְבַּיְּישִׁין. הִתְקִינוּ שֶׁיְּהוּ מַטְבִּילִין עַל גַּב הַכֹּל, מִפְּנֵי כְּבוֹדָן שֶׁל זָבִין חַיִּים.

Moreover, **at first they would** ritually **immerse** all **the utensils** that had been used **by** women who **died** while **menstruating,** which had thereby contracted ritual impurity. **And** due to this, **the living menstruating women were embarrassed.** The Sages **instituted that** the utensils that had been used **by all** dying **women must be immersed, due to the honor of living menstruating women.** And, **at first they would** ritually **immerse** all **the utensils** that had been used by ***zavin***, men suffering from gonorrhea, **who died,** as the utensils had thereby contracted ritual impurity. **And** due to this **the living** ***zavin*** **felt embarrassed.** The Sages **instituted that** the utensils that had been used **by all** men **must be immersed, due to the honor of the living** ***zavin*****.**

בְּרִאשׁוֹנָה הָיְתָה הוֹצָאַת הַמֵּת קָשָׁה לִקְרוֹבָיו יוֹתֵר מִמִּיתָתוֹ, עַד שֶׁהָיוּ קְרוֹבָיו מַנִּיחִין אוֹתוֹ וּבוֹרְחִין. עַד שֶׁבָּא רַבָּן גַּמְלִיאֵל וְנָהַג קַלּוּת רֹאשׁ בְּעַצְמוֹ וְיָצָא בִּכְלֵי פִשְׁתָּן, וְנָהֲגוּ הָעָם אַחֲרָיו לָצֵאת בִּכְלֵי פִשְׁתָּן. אָמַר רַב פָּפָּא: וְהָאִידָּנָא נְהוּג עָלְמָא אֲפִילּוּ בְּצַרְדָּא בַּר זוּזָא.

Likewise, **at first taking the dead out** for burial **was more difficult for the relatives than the** actual **death,** because it was customary to bury the dead in expensive shrouds, which the poor could not afford. The problem grew **to the point that relatives would** sometimes **abandon** the corpse **and run away.** This lasted **until Rabban Gamliel came and acted**[N] with **frivolity,** meaning that he waived his dignity, by leaving instructions that he be **taken out** for burial **in linen garments. And the people** adopted this **practice after him** and had themselves **taken out** for burial **in linen garments.**[H] **Rav Pappa said: And nowadays, everyone follows the practice** of taking out the dead for burial **even in** plain **hemp garments** [*tzerada*][L] that cost only **a dinar.**[N]

"אֵין מַנִּיחִין אֶת הַמִּטָּה בָּרְחוֹב". אָמַר רַב פָּפָּא: אֵין מוֹעֵד בִּפְנֵי תַלְמִיד חָכָם, וְכׇל שֶׁכֵּן חֲנוּכָּה וּפוּרִים.

It is taught in the mishna: **The bier** of the deceased **is not set down in the street** during the intermediate days of a Festival, **so as not to encourage eulogies. Rav Pappa said:** There are **no** restrictions on eulogizing on the intermediate days of **a Festival in the presence** of a deceased **Torah scholar,**[H] and therefore he may be eulogized in the ordinary manner during the Festival week. **And all the more so** a Torah scholar may be eulogized on the days of **Hanukkah and Purim,** which have less sanctity than the intermediate days of a Festival.

וְהָנֵי מִילֵּי – בְּפָנָיו, אֲבָל שֶׁלֹּא בְּפָנָיו – לָא. אִינִי? וְהָא רַב כָּהֲנָא סַפְדֵיהּ לְרַב זְבִיד מִנְּהַרְדְּעָא בְּפוּם נַהֲרָא! אָמַר רַב פַּפִּי: יוֹם שְׁמוּעָה הֲוָה, וְכִבְפָנָיו דָּמֵי.

The Gemara comments: **But this** allowance to eulogize a Torah scholar during the intermediate days of a Festival **applies only** when the eulogy is **in** the **presence** of the deceased, before the bier. **However,** giving a eulogy that is **not in his presence** is **not** permitted. The Gemara asks: **Is that so? But didn't Rav Kahana eulogize Rav Zevid from Neharde'a in** his city **Pum Nahara** during the intermediate days of a Festival? **Rav Pappa said: It was the day** on which Rav Kahana received the **news** of Rav Zevid's death, **and** a eulogy in such a situation **is considered as** if it is **in his presence.**

אָמַר עוּלָּא: הֶסְפֵּד עַל לֵב, דִּכְתִיב: "עַל שָׁדַיִם סֹפְדִים"; טִיפּוּחַ – בְּיָד; קִילּוּס – בְּרֶגֶל.

The Gemara continues its discussion of the *halakhot* of mourning: **Ulla said:** Although *hesped* usually refers to a eulogy, strictly speaking, ***hesped*** is referring to striking oneself **on the heart, as it is written: "Striking [*sofedim*] the breasts"** (Isaiah 32:12). The term ***tipuaḥ*** is referring to striking **with** one **hand** against the other hand, i.e., clapping. The term ***killus***[L] is referring to stomping **with** one's **foot**[N] on the ground.

תָּנוּ רַבָּנַן: הַמְקַלֵּס – לֹא יְקַלֵּס בְּסַנְדָּל, אֶלָּא בְּמִנְעָל, מִפְּנֵי הַסַּכָּנָה.

The Sages taught a *baraita*: **One who stomps his foot on the ground** as a sign of mourning **should not stomp with a sandal,**[N] **but rather** he should do so wearing **a shoe, due to the danger** of being hurt. Because a sandal is easily torn, it is possible that something sharp on the ground will puncture his foot, or that he will suffer some other injury.

אָמַר רַבִּי יוֹחָנָן: אָבֵל, כֵּיוָן שֶׁנִּיעְנַע רֹאשׁוֹ – שׁוּב אֵין מְנַחֲמִין רַשָּׁאִין לֵישֵׁב אֶצְלוֹ.

Rabbi Yoḥanan said: Once a mourner nods his head[NH] to show that his grief has slightly diminished, **the consolers may no longer sit next to him,** as with his action the mourner shows that he no longer desires their presence.

NOTES

Rabban Gamliel came and acted – בָּא רַבָּן גַּמְלִיאֵל וְנָהַג: He was remembered for this practice throughout the generations, since he did it for the sake of the masses. It was such an important act that when people would drink cups of wine in the house of the mourner, as was the custom then, they would also drink an extra cup in honor of Rabban Gamliel (*Ketubot* 8b).

Hemp garments that cost one dinar – צַרְדָּא בַּר זוּזָא: Some explain that this is a simple thick garment (Rabbi Shlomo ben HaYatom).

***Killus* is referring to stomping with one's foot** – קִילּוּס בְּרֶגֶל: This custom is mentioned in the Bible as a mourning custom, as it is stated: "Stamp your feet and say: Alas!" (Ezekiel 6:11). This custom continued for a long time as a sign of mourning in Eretz Yisrael (Rabbi Shlomo ben HaYatom; *Tosefot HaRosh*).

Should not stomp with a sandal – לֹא יְקַלֵּס בְּסַנְדָּל: One version of the text inverts the statement and says: One should not stomp with a shoe, because it has a soft sole and one may injure himself. On the other hand, a sandal has a hard sole, which was made from wood (Rashi manuscript). There is another version that reads: Not with a shoe and not with a sandal, lest one become distracted and be injured.

Once a mourner nods his head – אָבֵל, כֵּיוָן שֶׁנִּיעְנַע רֹאשׁוֹ: Some explain that when a mourner nods his head he displays that he has already been somewhat consoled, and it is no longer necessary to sit with him and trouble him with conversation (Rabbeinu Gershom Meor HaGola; Rabbeinu Yehonatan of Lunel). Some say that since he is sitting with his face wrapped and he is required to sit quietly, if he wishes to hint that he is tired or that it is difficult for him to be in the company of others, then he should do so only with a nod of his head (Rav Hai Gaon).

LANGUAGE

Hemp garments [*tzerada*] – צַרְדָּא: According to most commentaries this refers to a simple linen or hemp garment. It is apparently related to the Middle Persian čādur, meaning a veil.

Killus – קִילּוּס: Apparently a Greek word, although there is dispute with regard to its precise origin. Some say that it is derived from κλῆσις, *klèsis*, meaning to raise one's voice or to call.

HALAKHA

The people adopted…burial in linen garments – נָהֲגוּ הָעָם...בִּכְלֵי פִשְׁתָּן: It is customary not to bury the dead in expensive shrouds, even if he was a great person (*Shulḥan Arukh*, *Yoreh De'a* 352:1).

There are no restrictions of a Festival in the presence of a deceased Torah scholar – אֵין מוֹעֵד בִּפְנֵי תַלְמִיד חָכָם: When a Torah scholar dies, even during the intermediate days of a Festival, and all the more so on Hanukkah, Purim, or a New Moon, he is eulogized as he would be during a weekday, as a sign of respect. The eulogy must be delivered in the presence of his body, and if the body is not present it is prohibited to eulogize the deceased. One may also eulogize a Torah scholar on the day one hears about his death, even if it is not in the presence of his body. The custom today is to eulogize the deceased during the intermediate days of a Festival or on holidays only if the deceased is a Torah scholar and it is in his presence (*Arukh HaShulḥan*; *Shulḥan Arukh*, *Yoreh De'a* 401:5).

Once a mourner nods his head – אָבֵל, כֵּיוָן שֶׁנִּיעְנַע רֹאשׁוֹ: Once the consolers see that the mourner wants them to leave then they must leave, even if he does not say so explicitly. For example, they should leave even if he simply nods his head or motions in any other way (see *Arukh HaShulḥan*; *Shulḥan Arukh*, *Yoreh De'a* 376:1).

וְאָמַר רַבִּי יוֹחָנָן: הַכֹּל חַיָּיבִין לַעֲמוֹד מִפְּנֵי נָשִׂיא, חוּץ מֵאָבֵל וְחוֹלֶה. וְאָמַר רַבִּי יוֹחָנָן: לְכֹל אוֹמְרִים לָהֶם ״שְׁבוּ״ חוּץ מֵאָבֵל וְחוֹלֶה.

Rabbi Yoḥanan further said: All are obligated to stand in the **presence of the *Nasi*, except for a mourner**[H] **and one who is sick. Rabbi Yoḥanan said: To all** who stand before a great person **one says: Be seated,**[NH] and only then may they sit down, **except for a mourner and one who is sick.** If they stood up they do not need permission to sit down, but rather they may do so if they wish.

אָמַר רַב יְהוּדָה אָמַר רַב: אָבֵל, יוֹם רִאשׁוֹן – אָסוּר לֶאֱכוֹל לֶחֶם מִשֶּׁלּוֹ, מִדְּאָמַר לֵיהּ רַחֲמָנָא לִיחֶזְקֵאל: ״וְלֶחֶם אֲנָשִׁים לֹא תֹאכֵל״. רַבָּה וְרַב יוֹסֵף מְחַלְּפִי סְעוּדָּתַייהוּ לַהֲדָדֵי.

Rav Yehuda said in the name of Rav: A mourner on the **first day** of his mourning **is prohibited from eating of his own bread.**[NH] From where is this derived? **From what the Merciful One says to Ezekiel** when the latter is in mourning: **"Nor eat the bread of men"** (Ezekiel 24:17), which indicates that other mourners must eat bread made by others. It was related that when **Rabba and Rav Yosef** were in mourning they **would exchange their meals**[N] **with each other.**

וְאָמַר רַב יְהוּדָה אָמַר רַב: מֵת בָּעִיר – כׇּל בְּנֵי הָעִיר אֲסוּרִין בַּעֲשִׂיַּית מְלָאכָה.

And Rav Yehuda said in the name of Rav: When a person **dies in a city,**[N] **all of the residents of that city are prohibited from performing work** until he has been buried.[H]

רַב הַמְנוּנָא אִיקְּלַע לְדָרוּמָתָא. שְׁמַע קוֹל שִׁיפּוּרָא דְּשָׁכְבָא. חֲזָא הָנָךְ אִינָשֵׁי דְּקָא עָבְדִי עֲבִידְתָּא, אֲמַר לְהוּ: לֶיהֱווּ הָנָךְ אֱינָשֵׁי בְּשַׁמְתָּא! לָא שְׁכָבָא אִיכָּא בְּמָתָא? אֲמַרוּ לֵיהּ: חֲבוּרָתָא אִיכָּא בְּמָתָא. אֲמַר לְהוּ: אִי הָכִי – שְׁרָיָא לְכוּ.

The Gemara relates that when **Rav Hamnuna** once **happened** to come to a place called **Darumata he heard the sound of a *shofar*** announcing that a person **had died** in the town. When **he saw some people doing work he said to them: Let these people be under an excommunication. Is there not a dead** person **in town? They said to him: There are** separate **groups in the town,** each one responsible for its own dead. Knowing that the deceased was not from our group, we continued our work. **He said to them: If so, it is permitted** to you,[N] and he revoked his excommunication.

וְאָמַר רַב יְהוּדָה אָמַר רַב: כׇּל הַמִּתְקַשֶּׁה עַל מֵתוֹ יוֹתֵר מִדַּאי – עַל מֵת אַחֵר הוּא בּוֹכֶה. הַהִיא אִיתְּתָא דַּהֲוַת בְּשִׁיבָבוּתֵיהּ דְּרַב הוּנָא, הֲווֹ לַהּ שִׁבְעָה בְּנֵי. מֵת חַד מִינַּיְיהוּ, הֲוַת קָא בָכְיָא בֵּיתֵירְתָּא עֲלֵיהּ. שְׁלַח לַהּ רַב הוּנָא: לָא תַּעַבְדִי הָכִי! לָא אַשְׁגַּחָה בֵּיהּ. שְׁלַח לַהּ: אִי צַיְּיתַתְּ – מוּטָב; וְאִי לָא – צְבִית זְווֹדְתָּא לְאִידָּךְ מֵית. וּמִיתוּ כּוּלְּהוּ. לְסוֹף אֲמַר לַהּ: תִּימוֹשׁ זְווֹדְתָּא לְנַפְשִׁיךְ, וּמִיתָא.

And Rav Yehuda said further in the name of Rav: Anyone who grieves excessively over his dead[NH] and does not allow himself to be consoled **will** in the end **weep for another** person.[N] The Gemara relates that **a certain woman** who lived **in the neighborhood of Rav Huna had seven sons. One of them died and she wept for him excessively. Rav Huna sent** a message **to her: Do not do this.** But **she took no heed of him. He** then **sent** another message **to her: If you listen to me, it is well, but if not, prepare shrouds for another death.** But she would not listen **and they all died. In the end,** when she continued with her excessive mourning, **he said to her:** Since you are acting in this way, **prepare shrouds for yourself, and** soon thereafter **she died.**

NOTES

To all who stand one says, Be seated – לְכֹל אוֹמְרִים שְׁבוּ: The early authorities write that saying: Be seated, to a mourner is a bad omen, as if saying to him that he should remain in mourning. *Tosefot HaRosh* writes that in the Bible the word sitting means remaining and continuing. Some say that this custom applies only during the time of the ritual sitting and standing after the burial, when one may not say to the mourners: Be seated (Rabbeinu Yehonatan of Lunel). Others explain that if mourners stand before an important person he should not say to them: Be seated, but should instead use different language that does not contain a bad omen (see Ran).

Is prohibited from eating of his own – אָסוּר לֶאֱכוֹל...מִשֶּׁלּוֹ: The early authorities write that it is implied in the Jerusalem Talmud that if a mourner does not wish to eat or to accept assistance from other people then he may fast for the first day.

Exchange their meals – מְחַלְּפִי סְעוּדָּתַייהוּ: Some explain that this refers to a case in which they were both mourning at the same time (Commentary on *Moed Katan*).

When a person dies in a city – מֵת בָּעִיר וכו׳: Some explain that the *halakha* that all residents of a city must refrain from work in order to involve themselves in the burial applies specifically to a corpse with no one to bury it [*met mitzva*], whom everyone is obligated to bury (*Be'er Halakhot Gedolot*). However, most of the early authorities do not accept this explanation and state that the obligation to refrain from working refers to whenever there is any dead person in the city.

It is permitted to you – שְׁרָיָא לְכוּ: Some explain this expression to mean that you are permitted to act in accordance with your custom, while others say that it means that the excommunication that he had just declared was nullified (Rashi manuscript).

One who grieves excessively [*hamitkashe*] over his dead – הַמִּתְקַשֶּׁה עַל מֵתוֹ יוֹתֵר מִדַּאי: Some, including Rashi in the manuscript, have a version that reads: Passionately eulogizes [*hamakshir*] or [*hamitkashir*], which is understood to mean that he excessively eulogizes his dead, as in the expression: Tied eulogy [*hesped kashur*] (Jerusalem Talmud, *Yevamot* 16:4), which refers to the custom of tying something to the doorway of a house so that passersby would know it was a house of mourning (*Korban HaEda*).

Will in the end weep for another person – עַל מֵת אַחֵר הוּא בּוֹכֶה: The early authorities explain this statement in two different ways. Perhaps he will continue to weep because he shows that he does not accept God's judgment upon himself. If so, his punishment corresponds to his transgression in that he is punished by having to mourn again. Alternatively, it is possible that he is punished for a similar reason to when the Jewish people in the desert were punished for crying without cause upon hearing the report of the spies (see *Iyyun Ya'akov*).

HALAKHA

A mourner is not required to stand – אֵין אָבֵל חַיָּיב לַעֲמוֹד: A mourner, and similarly a sick person, is not required to stand in respect in the presence of the *Nasi* (*Shulḥan Arukh Yoreh De'a* 376:1, and in the comment of Rema).

To all who stand one says, Be seated – לְכֹל אוֹמְרִים שְׁבוּ: One who wishes to honor his fellow should say to him: Be seated. However, one does not say this to a mourner or to a sick person (*Shulḥan Arukh, Yoreh De'a* 376:2).

The first meal after the burial – סְעוּדַּת הַבְרָאָה: During the first meal after the burial it is prohibited for the mourner to eat his own food, and it is a mitzva for his neighbors to bring him food to eat. However, if no one sends him food or he has no neighbors he may eat his own food and is not required to starve himself (*Taz*). It was the common practice in the time of the Gemara to prepare special foods as a sign of mourning, such as eggs or lentils, and in many places it is customary to serve the mourner a cup of wine. Nowadays there are many different customs. One may bring food to another when he is mourning and that person can return the favor and bring food to the first if he is subsequently in mourning, like Rabba and Rav Yosef, provided that this condition to repay the meal is not stated explicitly (*Shulḥan Arukh, Yoreh De'a* 378:1).

Prohibition against working when there is a dead person in the city – אִיסּוּר מְלָאכָה כְּשֶׁמֵּת בָּעִיר: When there is an unburied dead person in a city all of the residents of that city are prohibited from working until he is buried. Anyone who sees a funeral and does not join is deserving of excommunication. If there are assigned groups that care for the dead, then other people in this city may perform work. However, at the time when the deceased is taken out for burial everyone must refrain from working (Shulḥan Arukh, Yoreh De'a 343:1).

One who grieves excessively over his dead – הַמִּתְקַשֶּׁה עַל מֵתוֹ יוֹתֵר מִדַּאי: One should not excessively mourn over his dead. Instead there should be three days of mourning, seven days for eulogizing, and thirty days during which it is prohibited to cut one's hair or iron one's clothes (*Shulḥan Arukh, Yoreh De'a* 394:1).

NOTES

To one who leaves the world without children – לַהוֹלֵךְ בְּלֹא בָּנִים: Some write that since, as the Sages say, one who does not have children is considered to be as though he is dead, it is as though this person died twice, once during his lifetime and once after his death. Therefore, the grief over his demise is much greater (*Iyyun Ya'akov*). This issue is explained in several other ways, based on both its simple meaning and the mystical meaning.

Rav Huna said this is one who committed a transgression – רַב הוּנָא אָמַר זֶה שֶׁעָבַר עֲבֵירָה: Many of the early authorities hold that Rav Huna does not dispute the first explanation of the verse. Rather, he bases his teaching on the second half of the same verse: "He shall return no more, nor see his native land," meaning that the sinner will not find a path of repentance for himself (see Ran; Meiri).

Between his two thighs – בֵּין שְׁתֵּי יְרֵכוֹתָיו: Many have a version of the text that reads: Between his shoulders, meaning that the mourner stands bowed over in the manner of one who stands in fear lest he be stabbed in the back with a sword, and must consequently be fearful and submissive at every moment (Rabbeinu Yehonatan of Lunel). *Tosafot* cite a parallel statement from the Jerusalem Talmud. It is also stated there that if a child is born within that family, it is a good sign that the family has been healed.

"אל תבכו למת ואל תנודו לו" – "אל תבכו למת" – יותר מדאי; "ואל תנודו לו" – יותר מכשיעור. הא כיצד? שלשה ימים – לבכי, ושבעה – להספד, ושלשים – לגיהוץ ולתספורת. מכאן ואילך – אמר הקדוש ברוך הוא: אי אתם רחמנים בו יותר ממני.

The Sages taught in a *baraita* with regard to the verse that states: **"Weep not for the dead, neither bemoan him"** (Jeremiah 22:10): **"Weep not for the dead"** is referring to **excessive** mourning; **"neither bemoan him" more than the** appropriate **measure** of time. **How so?** What is the appropriate measure? **Three days for weeping, and seven for eulogizing, and thirty for** the prohibition against **ironing** clothing **and for** the prohibition against **cutting hair. From this** point **forward the Holy One, Blessed be He, says: Do not be more merciful with** the deceased **than I am.** If the Torah commands one to mourn for a certain period of time, then that suffices.

"בכו בכו להולך", אמר רב יהודה: להולך בלא בנים. רבי יהושע בן לוי לא אזל לבי אבלא אלא למאן דאזיל בלא בני, דכתיב: "בכו בכו להולך כי לא ישוב עוד וראה את ארץ מולדתו". רב הונא אמר: זה שעבר עבירה ושנה בה.

It is stated in the continuation of the verse: **"Weep sore for him that goes away." Rav Yehuda said:** This is referring **to one who leaves** the world **without children**[N] to survive him, since mourning for him is much more intense. It was related that **Rabbi Yehoshua ben Levi** would **go to a house of mourning only for one who passed away without children, as it is written: "Weep sore for him that goes away; for he shall return** [*yashuv*] **no more, nor see his native land"** (Jeremiah 22:10). **Rav Huna** disagreed with the interpretation of the verse and **said:** "Him that goes" **is one who committed a transgression**[N] **and** then **repeated it,** i.e., one who sins constantly and does not repent [*yashav*], and therefore loses his portion in the World-to-Come, his "native land."

רב הונא לטעמיה, דאמר רב הונא: כיון שעבר אדם עבירה ושנה בה – הותרה לו. הותרה לו סלקא דעתך?! אלא אימא: נעשית לו כהיתר.

The Gemara notes that **Rav Huna** conforms **to his** standard line **of reasoning,** as **Rav Huna said: Once a person commits a transgression and repeats it, it becomes permitted to him.** The Gemara questions the wording used here: **Does it enter your mind** that it is actually **permitted?** How could it possibly be permitted for him to sin? **Rather, say** instead: **It becomes as though it were permitted,** for after doing it twice he no longer relates to his action as the violation of a serious prohibition.

אמר רבי לוי: אבל שלשה ימים הראשונים – יראה את עצמו כאילו חרב מונחת לו בין שתי יריכותיו. משלשה עד שבעה – כאילו מונחת לו כנגדו בקרן זוית. מכאן ואילך – כאילו עוברת כנגדו בשוק.

Rabbi Levi said: A mourner during **the first three days** of his mourning **should see himself as though a sword were lying between his two thighs,**[N] meaning that he too may be facing imminent death. During this period he should live in dread. **From the third to the seventh** days he should conduct himself **as if** the sword **were lying opposite him in the corner,** but still threatening him. **From this** point **forward it is as if** the sword **was moving before him in the marketplace,** and the fear is not as great.

"ולא של נשים לעולם מפני הכבוד". אמרי נהרדעי: לא שנו

§ The mishna teaches: **And** the biers **of women** are **never** set down, **due to** their **honor.** The Sages of **Neharde'a say: They only taught** this

Perek **III**
Daf **28** Amud **a**

NOTES

Even other women – אֲפִילּוּ שְׁאָר הַנָּשִׁים: Some say that not placing the bier of women in the street is a Torah law, as it is derived from the Torah's description of Miriam's death. Others say that it was due to the honor of the community (Meiri). Some suggest that it is done on account of the women's honor and that it is not appropriate for a woman to be displayed in burial shrouds before all (Rabbeinu Yehonatan).

אלא חיה, אבל שאר נשים – מניחין.

with regard to **a woman** who died **in childbirth,** and therefore continues to bleed. **But** the biers of **other women may be set down** in the street.

רבי אלעזר אמר: אפילו שאר הנשים, דכתיב: "ותמת שם מרים ותקבר שם" – סמוך למיתה קבורה.

Rabbi Elazar said: Even the biers of **other women**[N] must not be set down in the street,[H] **as it is written: "And Miriam died there and was buried there"** (Numbers 20:1), which teaches that **the** site of her **burial was close to** the place of her **death.** Therefore, it is preferable to bury a woman as close as possible to the place where she died.

HALAKHA

The bier of a woman in the street – מִיטַּת אִשָּׁה בָּרְחוֹב: The bier of a deceased woman is never placed in the street, even if she did not die in childbirth, in accordance with the opinion of Rabbi Elazar (*Shulḥan Arukh, Yoreh De'a* 355:1).

וְאָמַר רַבִּי אֶלְעָזָר: אַף מִרְיָם בִּנְשִׁיקָה מֵתָה. אָתְיָא "שָׁם" "שָׁם" מִמֹּשֶׁה. וּמִפְּנֵי מָה לֹא נֶאֱמַר בָּהּ "עַל פִּי ה'" – מִפְּנֵי שֶׁגְּנַאי הַדָּבָר לְאוֹמְרוֹ.

With regard to that same verse **Rabbi Elazar said** further: **Miriam also died by** the divine **kiss,** just like her brother Moses. What is the source for this? **This is derived** through a verbal analogy between the word **"there"** stated with regard to Miriam and the word **"there"**[N] mentioned **with regard to Moses.** With regard to Moses it says: "So Moses the servant of the Lord died there in the land of Moab by the mouth of the Lord" (Deuteronomy 34:5). **For what** reason **was it not** explicitly **stated with regard to her,** as it is stated with regard to Moses, that she died **"by the mouth of the Lord"?** It is **because it would be unseemly to say such a thing,** that a woman died by way of a divine kiss, and therefore it is not said explicitly.

אָמַר רַבִּי אַמִי: לָמָּה נִסְמְכָה מִיתַת מִרְיָם לְפָרָשַׁת פָּרָה אֲדוּמָּה? לוֹמַר לְךָ: מַה פָּרָה אֲדוּמָּה מְכַפֶּרֶת – אַף מִיתָתָן שֶׁל צַדִּיקִים מְכַפֶּרֶת. אָמַר רַבִּי אֶלְעָזָר: לָמָּה נִסְמְכָה מִיתַת אַהֲרֹן לְבִגְדֵי כְּהוּנָּה? מַה בִּגְדֵי כְּהוּנָּה מְכַפְּרִין – אַף מִיתָתָן שֶׁל צַדִּיקִים מְכַפֶּרֶת.

Rabbi Ami said: Why was the Torah portion that describes the **death of Miriam juxtaposed to the portion** dealing with **the red heifer? To tell you: Just as the red heifer atones** for sin, **so too, the death of the righteous atones** for sin. **Rabbi Elazar said: Why was** the Torah portion that describes the **death of Aaron juxtaposed to** the portion discussing **the priestly garments?** This teaches that **just as the priestly garments atone** for sin, **so too, the death of the righteous atones** for sin.[N]

תָּנוּ רַבָּנַן: מֵת פִּתְאוֹם – זוֹ הִיא מִיתָה חֲטוּפָה. חָלָה יוֹם אֶחָד וּמֵת – זוֹ הִיא מִיתָה דְּחוּפָה. רַבִּי חֲנַנְיָא בֶּן גַּמְלִיאֵל אוֹמֵר: זוֹ הִיא מִיתַת מַגֵּפָה, שֶׁנֶּאֱמַר: "בֶּן אָדָם הִנְנִי לוֹקֵחַ מִמְּךָ אֶת מַחְמַד עֵינֶיךָ בְּמַגֵּפָה" וּכְתִיב: "וָאֲדַבֵּר אֶל הָעָם בַּבֹּקֶר וַתָּמָת אִשְׁתִּי בָּעָרֶב".

§ **The Sages taught** the following *baraita*: If one **dies suddenly** without having been sick, **this is death** through **snatching.** If he **became sick for a day and died, this is an expedited**[N] death. **Rabbi Ḥananya ben Gamliel says: This is death at a stroke, as it is stated: "Son of man, behold, I am about to take away from you the delight of your eyes at a stroke"** (Ezekiel 24:16). **And** when this prophecy is fulfilled **it is written: "So I spoke to the people in the morning and at evening my wife died"** (Ezekiel 24:18).

שְׁנֵי יָמִים וּמֵת – זוֹ הִיא מִיתָה דְּחוּיָה; שְׁלֹשָׁה – גְּעָרָה; אַרְבָּעָה – נְזִיפָה; חֲמִשָּׁה – זוֹ הִיא מִיתַת כָּל אָדָם.

If he was sick for **two days and died, this is a quickened death.** If he was sick for **three** days and died, this is a death of **rebuke.** If he died after being sick for **four** days, this is a death of **reprimand.** If one died after a sickness lasting **five** days, **this is the** ordinary **death of all people.**

אָמַר רַבִּי חָנִין: מַאי קְרָא? "הֵן קָרְבוּ יָמֶיךָ לָמוּת", "הֵן" – חַד; "קָרְבוּ" – תְּרֵי; "יָמֶיךָ" – תְּרֵי; הָא חֲמִשָּׁה. "הֵן" חַד – שֶׁכֵּן בִּלְשׁוֹן יְוָנִי קוֹרִין לְאַחַת "הֵן".

Rabbi Ḥanin said: What is the verse from which this is derived? It is stated: **"Behold, your days approach that you must die"** (Deuteronomy 31:14).[N] This verse is expounded in the following manner: **"Behold [*hen*]"** indicates **one; "approach [*karvu*],"** a plural term, indicates **two; "your days [*yamekha*],"** also a plural term, indicates another **two;** and therefore in total **this is five.** How does the word ***hen*** indicate **one? Because in the Greek language they call** the number **one *hen*.**[L]

מֵת בַּחֲמִשִּׁים שָׁנָה – זוֹ הִיא מִיתַת כָּרֵת; חֲמִשִּׁים וּשְׁתַּיִם שָׁנָה זוֹ הִיא מִיתָתוֹ שֶׁל שְׁמוּאֵל הָרָמָתִי; שִׁשִּׁים – זוֹ הִיא מִיתָה בִּידֵי שָׁמַיִם.

The Gemara discusses the significance of death at different ages: If one **dies when** he is **fifty years** old, **this is death through *karet*,**[N] the divine punishment of excision, meted out for the most serious transgressions. If he dies when he is **fifty-two years** old, **this is the death of Samuel from Ramah.** If he dies at the age of **sixty, this is death at the hand of Heaven.**

אָמַר מָר זוּטְרָא: מַאי קְרָא? דִּכְתִיב: "תָּבֹא בְכֶלַח אֱלֵי קָבֶר". "בְּכֶלַח" בְּגִימַטְרִיָּא שִׁיתִּין הָווּ.

Mar Zutra said: What is the verse from which this is derived? **As it is written: "You shall come to your grave in a ripe age [*bekhelaḥ*]"** (Job 5:26). The word **"ripe age" [*bekhelaḥ*] has the numerical value of sixty,** and it is alluded to there that dying at this age involves a divine punishment.

שִׁבְעִים – שֵׂיבָה, שְׁמוֹנִים – גְּבוּרוֹת, דִּכְתִיב: "יְמֵי שְׁנוֹתֵינוּ בָהֶם שִׁבְעִים שָׁנָה וְאִם בִּגְבוּרוֹת שְׁמוֹנִים שָׁנָה". אָמַר רַבָּה: מֵחֲמִשִּׁים וְעַד שִׁשִּׁים שָׁנָה – זוֹ הִיא מִיתַת כָּרֵת. וְהַאי דְּלָא חָשֵׁיב לְהוּ – מִשּׁוּם כְּבוֹדוֹ שֶׁל שְׁמוּאֵל הָרָמָתִי.

One who dies at the age of **seventy** has reached **old age.** One who dies at the age of **eighty** dies in **strength, as it is written: "The days of our years are seventy, or if by reason of strength, eighty years"** (Psalms 90:10). **Rabba said:** Not only is death at the age of fifty a sign of *karet*, but even death **from fifty to sixty years** of age **is death by *karet*. And** the reason that **all of these years were not counted** in connection with *karet* is **due to the honor of Samuel from Ramah,** who died at the age of fifty-two.

NOTES

This is derived between the word there and there – אָתְיָא שָׁם שָׁם: In this version of the text the derivation is from the verses describing the death of Moses. However, there is a different version of the talmudic text in which the fact that Miriam died by divine kiss is derived through a verbal analogy to the verses describing Aaron's death. Rabbi Eliyahu Mizraḥi explains similarly (*Beit Moed*).

The death of Aaron and the priestly garments – בִּגְדֵי כְּהוּנָּה וּמִיתַת אַהֲרֹן: See Rashi manuscript and *Tosafot*, who explain that the Torah describes Aaron's removal of his priestly garments before his death. This detail is unnecessary for the narrative, and is mentioned by the Torah only to teach that there is a relationship between these garments and Aaron's death. The atonement performed by the priestly garments is described in tractate *Zevaḥim*, and each individual garment atones for a specific sin. The Torah states explicitly that the frontplate of the High Priest atones for sin.

Snatching, expedited – חֲטוּפָה, דְּחוּפָה: The death of the wicked is sudden, as the verse states: "Like the passing of the storm, and there is no wickedness" (Proverbs 10:25), and therefore it is a bad sign when one dies in this manner. Death through snatching is extremely sudden, while expedited death is also quick, but not quite as sudden. Quickened death [*mita deḥuya*], literally, pushed death, is analogous to when one pushes something and it rolls away gradually. Expedited death [*mita deḥufa*] is analogous to pushing something which falls immediately and is lost (Rabbi Shlomo ben HaYatom).

Behold, your days approach that you must die – הֵן קָרְבוּ יָמֶיךָ לָמוּת: The early authorities question this, as the verse refers to Moses, who was not sick at all prior to his death. Some write that this was said to Moses in order to inform him that this is the way that a person ordinarily dies, but that one who is completely righteous like him does not require this (*Tosefot HaRosh*). Some say that the reason ordinary people die in this manner is to give them time to prepare for their death, and therefore God informed Moses that he should prepare himself (Ritva).

The age of fifty and *karet* – חֲמִשִּׁים מִיתַת כָּרֵת: A proof is offered in the Jerusalem Talmud based on the verses stated with regard to the Levites: "You shall not cut the staff of the families of the Kohathites" (Numbers 4:18), meaning that precautions should be taken that they not die while serving in the Temple. Because Levites served in the Temple until the age of fifty, it is deduced that anyone who dies up to this point dies through *karet*. See the Ran, who offers another reason for this statement: Since the lifespan of strength is eighty years, and the first twenty years, during which one is not punished by divine intervention, are removed from the equation, then one who does not live for half of these remaining years fits the description "They shall not live half of their days" (Psalms 55:24).

LANGUAGE

One [*hen*] – הֵן: From the Greek ἕν, *hen*, meaning one.

רַב יוֹסֵף, כִּי הֲוָה בַּר שִׁיתִּין עֲבַד לְהוּ יוֹמָא טָבָא לְרַבָּנָן. אֲמַר: נְפַקִי לִי מִכָּרֵת. אֲמַר לֵיהּ אַבַּיֵי: נְהִי דִּנְפַק לֵיהּ מָר מִכָּרֵת דִּשְׁנֵי, מִכָּרֵת דְּיוֹמֵי מִי נָפֵיק מָר? אֲמַר לֵיהּ: נְקוֹט לָךְ מִיהָא פַּלְגָא בִּידָךְ.

The Gemara relates that **when Rav Yosef turned sixty he made a holiday for the Sages.** Explaining the cause for his celebration, **he said: I have passed** the age of *karet*. **Abaye said to him:** **Master,** even **though you have passed the** *karet* **of years, have you, Master, escaped the** *karet* **of days?** As previously mentioned, sudden death is also considered to be a form of *karet*. **He said to him: Grasp at least half in your hand,** for I have at least escaped one type of *karet*.

רַב הוּנָא נָח נַפְשֵׁיהּ פִּתְאוֹם. הָווּ קָא דָּיְיגִי רַבָּנַן. תָּנָא לְהוּ זוּגָא דְּמֵהַדַּיֵיב: לֹא שָׁנוּ אֶלָּא שֶׁלֹּא הִגִּיעַ לִגְבוּרוֹת, אֲבָל הִגִּיעַ לִגְבוּרוֹת – זוֹ הִיא מִיתַת נְשִׁיקָה.

It was related that **Rav Huna died suddenly,** and **the Sages were concerned** that this was a bad sign. The Sage **Zuga**[N] **from Hadayeiv taught them** the following: **They taught** these principles **only when** the deceased **had not reached** the age of **strength,** i.e., eighty. **But if he had reached** the age of **strength** and then died suddenly, **this is death by way of a** divine **kiss.**

אֲמַר רָבָא: חַיֵּי, בְּנֵי וּמְזוֹנֵי, לָא בִּזְכוּתָא תַּלְיָא מִילְּתָא, אֶלָּא בְּמַזָּלָא תַּלְיָא מִילְּתָא. דְּהָא רַבָּה וְרַב חִסְדָּא תַּרְוַיְיהוּ רַבָּנַן צַדִּיקֵי הָווּ, מָר מְצַלֵּי וְאָתֵי מִיטְרָא, וּמָר מְצַלֵּי וְאָתֵי מִיטְרָא.

Rava said: Length of **life, children, and sustenance do not depend on** one's **merit,**[N] **but rather they depend upon fate. As, Rabba**[P] **and Rav Ḥisda were both pious Sages;** one Sage would **pray** during a drought **and rain would fall, and** the other Sage would **pray and rain would fall.**

רַב חִסְדָּא חָיָה תִּשְׁעִין וְתַרְתֵּין שְׁנִין – רַבָּה חָיָה אַרְבְּעִין. בֵּי רַב חִסְדָּא – שִׁיתִּין הִלּוּלֵי; בֵּי רַבָּה – שִׁיתִּין תִּיכְלֵי.

And nevertheless, their lives were very different. **Rav Ḥisda lived for ninety-two years,** whereas **Rabba lived for** only **forty** years. **The house of Rav Ḥisda** celebrated **sixty wedding feasts,** whereas the **house of Rabba** experienced **sixty calamities.** In other words, many fortuitous events took place in the house of Rav Ḥisda and the opposite occurred in the house of Rabba.

בֵּי רַב חִסְדָּא – סְמִידָא לְכַלְבֵּי וְלָא מִתְבְּעֵי; בֵּי רַבָּה – נַהֲמָא דְּשַׂעֲרֵי לֶאֱינָשֵׁי, וְלָא מִשְׁתַּכַּח.

In the house of Rav Ḥisda there was bread from **the finest flour** [*semida*][L] even **for the dogs, and it was not asked after,** as there was so much food. **In the house of Rabba,** on the other hand, there was coarse **barley bread** even **for people, and it was not found** in sufficient quantities. This shows that the length of life, children, and sustenance all depend not upon one's merit, but upon fate.

וְאָמַר רָבָא: הָנֵי תְּלָת מִילֵּי בְּעַאִי קַמֵּי שְׁמַיָּא, תַּרְתֵּי יְהַבוּ לִי, חֲדָא לָא יְהַבוּ לִי; חוּכְמָתֵיהּ דְּרַב הוּנָא וְעוּתְרֵיהּ דְּרַב חִסְדָּא – וִיהַבוּ לִי; עַנְוְתָנוּתֵיהּ דְּרַבָּה בַּר רַב הוּנָא – לָא יְהַבוּ לִי.

Apropos Rav Ḥisda's great wealth, the Gemara reports that **Rava said: These three things I requested from Heaven, two** of which **were given to me,** and **one was not given to me:** I requested the **wisdom of Rav Huna and the wealth of Rav Ḥisda and they were given to me.** I also requested the **humility of Rabba bar Rav Huna,** but **it was not given to me.**

רַב שְׂעוֹרִים אֲחוּהּ דְּרָבָא הֲוָה יָתֵיב קַמֵּיהּ דְּרָבָא. חַזְיֵיהּ דַּהֲוָה קָא מְנַמְנֵם. אֲמַר לֵיהּ: לֵימָא לֵיהּ מָר דְּלָא לְצַעֲרַן! אֲמַר לֵיהּ: מָר לָאו שׁוֹשְׁבִינֵיהּ הוּא? אֲמַר לֵיהּ: כֵּיוָן דְּאִימְּסַר מַזָּלָא – לָא אַשְׁגַּח בִּי. אֲמַר לֵיהּ: לִיתְחֲזֵי לִי מָר. אִיתְחֲזֵי לֵיהּ. אֲמַר לֵיהּ: הֲוָה לֵיהּ לְמָר צַעֲרָא? אֲמַר לֵיהּ: כִּי רִיבְדָּא דְּכוּסִילְתָּא.

The Gemara continues its discussion of the deaths of the righteous. **Rav Seorim, Rava's brother, sat before Rava,** and **he saw that** Rava **was dozing,** i.e., about to die. Rava **said to** his brother: **Master, tell him,** the Angel of Death, **not to torment me.** Knowing that Rava was not afraid of the Angel of Death, Rav Seorim **said to** him: **Master, are you not a friend of** the Angel of Death?[N] Rava **said to him: Since** my **fate has been handed over** to him, and it has been decreed that I shall die, the Angel of Death **no longer pays heed to me.** Rav Seorim **said to** Rava: **Master, appear to me** in a dream after your death. And Rava **appeared to him.** Rav Seorim **said to** Rava: **Master, did you have pain** in death? **He said to him: Like the prick** of the knife **when letting blood.**

PERSONALITIES

Rabba – רַבָּה: Rav Abba bar Naḥmani HaKohen, popularly referred to as Rabba throughout the Babylonian Talmud, was a third-generation Babylonian *amora*. Rabba was a student of Rav Huna, who himself was a student of Rav. Therefore, Rabba's opinions on *halakha* were in concert with Rav's teachings. Rabba was considered the sharpest among his peers, to the extent that he was referred to as one who uproots mountains, in contrast with his colleague Rav Yosef, whose expertise was in his broad knowledge, and who was consequently referred to as Sinai. In almost every disagreement between them, the ruling follows Rabba's opinion.

Rabba had many students, and virtually all of the Sages of the following generation studied under him. His personal life was one of great tragedy; it appears that his children died during his lifetime. He was poverty stricken his entire life, eking out a living from agricultural work. When his nephew Abaye became orphaned at a young age, Rabba took him in and raised him.

LANGUAGE

Finest flour [*semida*] – סְמִידָא: This word is similar to the Greek σεμίδαλις, *semidalis*, meaning fine wheat flour.

NOTES

Zuga – זוּגָא: In an alternative version of the text his name appears as Zawa. Rashi in the manuscript understands that Zuga is not a name, but refers to a pair [*zug*] of Sages.

Do not depend on merit – לָא בִּזְכוּתָא תַּלְיָא: Some of the early authorities write that this opinion is rejected, as it is said elsewhere that Jews are not under the authority of fate (Meiri). However, others say that one's fortune depends not only upon his actions, but also on his fate, as although one's merit may change his fate, it does not always change it completely (Ran; Ritva; *Tosafot*).

Are you not a friend of the Angel of Death – לָאו שׁוֹשְׁבִינֵיהּ הוּא: Many stories are told in the Talmud about different Sages who engaged in discussions with various angels, including the Angel of Death (see *Berakhot* 51a, *Ḥagiga* 4b, and *Ketubot* 77b) The Angel of Death takes the righteous into account and does not kill them in a disgraceful manner.

רָבָא הֲוָה יָתֵיב קַמֵּיהּ דְּרַב נַחְמָן. חַזְיֵיהּ דְּקָא מְנַמְנֵם. אֲמַר לֵיהּ: לֵימָא לֵיהּ מָר דְּלָא לְצַעֲרַן. אֲמַר לֵיהּ: מָר לָאו אָדָם חָשׁוּב הוּא? אֲמַר לֵיהּ: מַאן חֲשִׁיב, מַאן סְפִין, מַאן רְקִיעַ?

It was similarly related that **Rava sat before Rav Naḥman,** and **he saw that** Rav Naḥman **was dozing,** i.e., slipping into death. Rav Naḥman **said to** Rava: **Master, tell** the Angel of Death **not to torment me.** Rava **said to him: Master, are you not an important person** who is respected in Heaven? Rav Naḥman **said to him:** In the supernal world **who is important? Who is honorable? Who is complete?**[N]

אֲמַר לֵיהּ: לִיתְחֲזֵי לִי מָר. אִתְחֲזֵי לֵיהּ. אֲמַר לֵיהּ: הֲוָה לֵיהּ לְמָר צַעֲרָא? אֲמַר לֵיהּ: כְּמִישְׁחַל בִּנִיתָא מֵחֶלְבָּא. וְאִי אֲמַר לִי הַקָּדוֹשׁ בָּרוּךְ הוּא זִיל בְּהַהוּא עָלְמָא כַּד הֲוֵית – לָא בָּעֵינָא, דְּנָפֵישׁ בִּיעֲתוּתֵיהּ.

Rava **said to** Rav Naḥman: **Master, appear to me** in a dream after your death. And **he appeared to him.** Rava **said to him: Master, did you have pain** in death? Rav Naḥman **said to him: Like the removal of hair from milk,** which is a most gentle process. But nevertheless, **were the Holy One, Blessed be He, to say to me: Go** back **to that world,** the physical world, **as you were, I would not want to go, for the fear of** the Angel of Death **is great.**[N] And I would not want to go through such a terrifying experience a second time.

רַבִּי אֶלְעָזָר הֲוָה קָאָכֵיל תְּרוּמָה, אִיתְחֲזֵי לֵיהּ. אֲמַר לֵיהּ: תְּרוּמָה קָא אָכֵילְנָא, וְלָאו קוֹדֶשׁ אִיקְרֵי? חָלְפָא לֵיהּ שַׁעֲתָא.

The Gemara relates that **Rabbi Elazar was** once **eating *teruma*,** when the Angel of Death **appeared to him. He said to** the Angel of Death: **I am eating *teruma*; is it not called sacred?** It would be inappropriate for me to die now and thereby defile this sacred *teruma*. The Angel of Death accepted his argument and left him. **The moment passed,** and he lived for some time afterward.

רַב שֵׁשֶׁת אִיתְחֲזֵי לֵיהּ בְּשׁוּקָא. אֲמַר לֵיהּ: בְּשׁוּקָא כִּבְהֵמָה? אִיתָא לְגַבֵּי בֵּיתָא.

It was similarly related that the Angel of Death once **appeared to Rav Sheshet in the marketplace.** Rav Sheshet **said to** the Angel of Death: Shall I die **in the market like an animal? Come to** my **house** and kill me there like a human being.

רַב אַשִׁי אִיתְחֲזֵי לֵיהּ בְּשׁוּקָא. אֲמַר לֵיהּ: אִיתְרַח לִי תְּלָתִין יוֹמִין, וַאֲהַדְרִי לְתַלְמוּדַאי. דְּאָמְרִיתוּ: אַשְׁרֵי מִי שֶׁבָּא לְכָאן וְתַלְמוּדוֹ בְּיָדוֹ. בְּיוֹם תְּלָתִין אֲתָא. אֲמַר לֵיהּ: מַאי כּוּלֵּי הַאי? קָא דָּחֲקָא רַגְלֵיהּ דְּבַר נָתָן, וְאֵין מַלְכוּת נוֹגַעַת בַּחֲבֶירְתָּהּ אֲפִילּוּ כִּמְלֹא נִימָא.

So too, the Angel of Death **appeared to Rav Ashi in the marketplace.** Rav Ashi **said to** the Angel of Death: **Give me thirty days so that I may review my studies, for you say** above: **Fortunate is he who comes here** to Heaven **with his learning in his hand. On the thirtieth day** the Angel of Death **came** to take him. Rav Ashi **said to** the Angel of Death: **What is all of this?** Why are you in such a hurry to take me? Why can you not postpone my death? He said to him: **The foot of** Rav Huna **bar Natan**[P] **is pushing** you, as he is ready to succeed you as the leader of the generation, **and one sovereignty does not overlap with its counterpart, even by one hairbreadth.** Therefore, you cannot live any longer.

רַב חִסְדָּא לָא הֲוָה יָכֵיל לֵיהּ, דְּלָא הֲוָה שָׁתֵיק פּוּמֵּיהּ מִגִּירְסָא. סְלֵיק יְתֵיב בְּאַרְזָא דְּבֵי רַב. פְּקַע אַרְזָא וּשְׁתַק וְיָכֵיל לֵיהּ.

The Angel of Death **was unable** to take **Rav Ḥisda because his mouth was never silent from study.** So the Angel of Death **went** and **sat on the cedar** column that supported the roof of **the study hall of the Sages. The cedar cracked and** Rav Ḥisda **was silent** for a moment, as he was startled by the sound. At that point the Angel of Death was **able to** take **him.**

רַבִּי חִיָּיא לָא הֲוָה מָצֵי לְמִיקְרְבָא לֵיהּ. יוֹמָא חַד אִידַּמִּי לֵיהּ כְּעַנְיָא, אֲתָא טָרֵיף אַבָּבָא, אֲמַר לֵיהּ: אַפֵּיק לִי רִיפְתָּא. אַפִּיקוּ לֵיהּ. אֲמַר לֵיהּ: וְלָאו קָא מְרַחֵם מָר אַעַנְיָא? אַהַהוּא גַּבְרָא אַמַּאי לָא קָא מְרַחֵם מָר? גַּלֵּי לֵיהּ, אַחֲוֵי לֵיהּ שׁוֹטָא דְּנוּרָא, אַמְצֵי לֵיהּ נַפְשֵׁיהּ.

The Angel of Death **could not come near Rabbi Ḥiyya,** owing to his righteousness. **One day** the Angel of Death **appeared to him as a poor person. He came and knocked on the door. He said to** Rabbi Ḥiyya: **Bring out bread for me,** and **he took out** bread **for him.** The Angel of Death then **said** to Rabbi Ḥiyya: **Master, do you not have mercy on a poor person? Why, then, do you not have mercy upon that man,** i.e., upon me, and give me what I want? The Angel of Death then **revealed** his identity **to him,** and **showed him a fiery rod** in order to confirm that he was the Angel of Death. At this point Rav Ḥiyya **surrendered** himself **to him.**

PERSONALITIES

Bar Natan – בַּר נָתָן: Apparently bar Natan refers to Rav Huna bar Rav Natan. It was said that with regard to the combination of Torah and greatness in one place, he was second only to Rav Ashi himself (*Gittin* 59a). According to the tradition of Rav Sherira Gaon, Rav Huna bar Natan was the Exilarch in the time of Rav Ashi. However, due to Rav Ashi's greatness he was also submissive before him. It seems that he was Rav Pappa's student, and he studied Torah under the other leaders of that generation as well. Occasionally the Gemara records his discussions with Rav Ashi.

NOTES

Who is honorable [*sefin*], who is complete [*rekia*] – מַאן סְפִין, מַאן רְקִיעַ: Some explain that the word *sefin* means important or respected (Rabbi Shlomo ben HaYatom). Others say that the word *sefin*, similarly to the term afraid [*mistafina*], refers to one who is feared and is therefore respected (Rashi manuscript). Or perhaps the word means high (Rashi on *Ein Ya'akov*). *Tosefot HaRosh* explains that the word *sefin* is similar to what is stated with regard to Moses: "For there a portion of a ruler [*safun*] was reserved" (Deuteronomy 33:21).

The word *rekia* is explained by some to mean complete (*ge'onim*). Others claim that it means simple or smooth, and that this is an honorific adjective for a righteous person (Rabbi Shlomo ben HaYatom). Still others say that the word refers to one who ascends into the sky [*rakia*] like Moses (*Tosefot HaRosh*).

The fear…is great – נָפֵישׁ בִּיעֲתוּתֵיהּ: Most of the commentaries explain that Rav Naḥman was very fearful of the Angel of Death. This is also the version of the text in the *Ein Ya'akov*. Therefore, he did not wish to die a second time. However, others say that he was fearful of this world and its physical and spiritual dangers (Rabbi Shlomo ben HaYatom).

HALAKHA

On the intermediate days of a Festival women may wail – נָשִׁים בַּמּוֹעֵד מְעַנּוֹת: It is permitted to wail during the intermediate days of a Festival when everyone wails a single lament together; however, one may not clap. On New Moons, Hanukkah, and Purim they may wail and clap but not lament, in accordance with the opinion of the first *tanna*. All of this applies only in the presence of the deceased (*Shulḥan Arukh*, *Yoreh De'a* 401:5).

BACKGROUND

Shekhantziv – שְׁכַנְצִיב: It is believed that the city of Shekhantziv was on the banks of the Tigris River. It was an important center of Torah, and several Sages were active there.

The residents of this city were well known for their wit and even warned others to stay away from their sharp speech and scoffing. This Gemara demonstrates that the sayings of the women of Shekhantziv were complex and clever.

מתני׳ נָשִׁים בַּמּוֹעֵד מְעַנּוֹת, אֲבָל לֹא מְטַפְּחוֹת. רַבִּי יִשְׁמָעֵאל אוֹמֵר: הַסְּמוּכוֹת לַמִּטָּה מְטַפְּחוֹת.

MISHNA **On the intermediate days of a Festival women may wail**[H] in grief over the deceased, **but they may not clap** [*metapeḥot*] their hands in mourning. **Rabbi Yishmael says: Those who are close to the bier may clap.**

בְּרָאשֵׁי חֳדָשִׁים, בַּחֲנוּכָּה וּבַפּוּרִים – מְעַנּוֹת וּמְטַפְּחוֹת, בָּזֶה וָזֶה – לֹא מְקוֹנְנוֹת. נִקְבַּר הַמֵּת – לֹא מְעַנּוֹת וְלֹא מְטַפְּחוֹת.

On New Moons, Hanukkah and Purim, which are not Festivals by Torah law, the women **may** both **wail and clap** their hands in mourning. **On both** the intermediate days of a Festival **and on** New Moons, Hanukkah and Purim **they may not lament.** After **the deceased has been buried they may neither wail nor clap.**

אֵיזֶהוּ עִינּוּי – שֶׁכּוּלָּן עוֹנוֹת כְּאַחַת; קִינָה – שֶׁאַחַת מְדַבֶּרֶת וְכוּלָּן עוֹנוֹת אַחֲרֶיהָ, שֶׁנֶּאֱמַר: ״וְלַמֵּדְנָה בְנוֹתֵיכֶם נֶהִי וְאִשָּׁה רְעוּתָהּ קִינָה״.

The mishna explains: **What is considered wailing?** This is **when they all wail together** simultaneously. And what is considered **a lament?** This is **when one speaks and they all answer after her** with a repeated refrain, **as it is stated: "And teach your daughters wailing and everyone her neighbor lamentation"** (Jeremiah 9:19).

אֲבָל לֶעָתִיד לָבֹא הוּא אוֹמֵר: ״בִּלַּע הַמָּוֶת לָנֶצַח וּמָחָה ה׳ אֱלֹהִים דִּמְעָה מֵעַל כָּל פָּנִים״ וגו׳.

In order to conclude on a positive note, the mishna says: **But with regard to the future,**[N] the verse **states: "He will destroy death forever; and the Lord, God, will wipe away tears from off all faces** and the reproach of His people He will take away from off all the earth" (Isaiah 25:8).

גמ׳ מַאי אָמְרָן? אָמַר רַב: וַיי לְאָזְלָא, וַיי לַחֲבִילָא.

GEMARA **What do** the women who wail over the dead **say? Rav said:** They say: **Woe over him who is** now **departing; woe over** him who is now returning **the pledge,** i.e., his soul, which had been deposited in his hands all the years of his life.

אָמַר רָבָא, נְשֵׁי דִּשְׁכַנְצִיב אָמְרָן הָכִי: וַיי לְאָזְלָא, וַיי לַחֲבִילָא. וְאָמַר רָבָא, נְשֵׁי דִּשְׁכַנְצִיב אָמְרָן: גּוּד גַּרְמָא מִכַּכָּא, וְנִמְטֵי מַיָּא לְאַנְטִיכֵי.

Rava said: The women in the city of **Shekhantziv,**[NB] who were known for their wisdom, **would say as follows: Woe over him who is** now **departing; woe over** him who is now returning **the pledge.**[N] **And Rava said: The women of Shekhantziv would say** about an elderly person: **The bone has been removed from the jaw and the water returns to the kettle.**[N]

NOTES

But with regard to the future – אֲבָל לֶעָתִיד לָבֹא: *Tosafot* explain that this statement is made in order to conclude on a positive note, because according to their ordering of the tractates, *Moed Katan* is the final tractate in the order of *Moed*. However, according to the Rambam's order of the tractates, *Ḥagiga* is the final tractate. Even so, it is possible to say that the editors of the mishna also wished to conclude each tractate with more positive material (Rabbi Ovadya MiBartenura). Other tractates have similar endings as well.

The women of Shekhantziv – נְשֵׁי דִּשְׁכַנְצִיב: Rabbi Shlomo ben HaYatom writes that the women of Shekhantziv spoke through deep riddles. He offers explanations from the *ge'onim* but suggests that there may be alternative explanations. Many textual variations exist for these riddles, and different explanations are offered for each variation.

Woe over him who is departing, woe over the pledge [*laḥavila*] – וַיי לְאָזְלָא, וַיי לַחֲבִילָא: Some explain the word *laḥavila* to be a pledge, and they explain allegorically that a person's soul is a deposit or a security that must be returned upon his death (Rabbeinu Ḥananel). Others explain that they would say this when a person died in poverty, as his children and the members of his household would have to give security to repay their debts (*Tosefot HaRosh*; Meiri).

There are also those who say that the word *ḥavila* means destruction or pain, and consequently the expression means: Woe over the suffering one endures in death (*ge'onim*). Some explain that the word means load and the expression means: Woe over the load that one must carry (Rabbi Betzalel Ransburg, citing an earlier commentary). Still others say that the expression means: Woe over the package, and the knot that became undone (Commentary on *Moed Katan*).

The bone has been removed from the jaw and the water returns to the kettle [*antikhei*] – גּוּד גַּרְמָא מִכַּכָּא וְנִמְטֵי מַיָּא לְאַנְטִיכֵי: Some explain that this means that when the bone that one eats is uprooted from his mouth, i.e., he stops eating it, his temperature rises like water in a kettle (Rabbeinu Ḥananel). Others say it means: The teeth fall out of the mouth, and the hot water may be returned to the vessel, as one can no longer drink it (Commentary on *Moed Katan*).

Other commentaries have a version of the text that reads: The water is returned to Antioch [*la'Antokhia*], which was a city very far away. According to this version of the text, the statement means that the water can now go to a very distant place, as there is no longer any need for it. Some see this as an allusion to what happens after death; the women meant that when one dies the soul goes to the place where it was at first (Rabbi Shlomo ben HaYatom).

The *Tosefot HaRosh* understands the text differently, explaining that this refers to a case where one's son died, and the women told the father to remove one of his teeth so as to remember him in the future. Afterward he should heat water and wash the tooth, in order to increase the crying and the eulogizing (see Meiri). Elsewhere (*Berakhot* 5b) the Gemara relates that Rabbi Yoḥanan acted similarly, and kept a bone from his youngest son who had died.

וְאָמַר רָבָא, נְשֵׁי דְשָׁכַנְצִיב אָמְרָן: עַטוּף וּכְסוּ טוּרֵי, דְּבַר רָמֵי וּבַר רַבְרְבֵי הוּא. וְאָמַר רָבָא, נְשֵׁי דְשָׁכַנְצִיב אָמְרָן: שַׁיּוּל אִצְטְלָא דְמַלְתָּא לְבַר חוֹרִין דִּשְׁלִימוּ זְוָודֵיהּ.

And Rava said: The women of Shekhantziv would say at a time of bereavement: **Wrap and cover the mountains**[N] in mourning, as the deceased is **the son of the high and distinguished. Rava said: The women of Shekhantziv would say: Lend out a cloak of fine wool**[N] to serve as a burial shroud **for a free man whose sustenance has been depleted.** In other words, a wealthy person who loses his fortune would rather die than live in poverty.

וְאָמַר רָבָא, נְשֵׁי דְשָׁכַנְצִיב אָמְרָן: רָהֵיט וְנָפֵיל אַמַּעְבְּרָא, וִיזוֹפְתָּא יָזֵיף. וְאָמַר רָבָא, נְשֵׁי דְשָׁכַנְצִיב אָמְרָן: אַחְנָא תַּגָּרֵי אַזְבְּזָגֵי מִיבַּדְקוּ. וְאָמַר רָבָא, נְשֵׁי דְשָׁכַנְצִיב אָמְרָן: מוֹתָא כִּי מוֹתָא, וּמַרְעִין – חִיבּוּלְיָא.

And Rava said: The women of Shekhantziv would say: A person **runs and tumbles at the ford**[N] and still **he borrows. And Rava said: The women of Shekhantziv would say: Our brothers, the merchants, will be examined**[N] **at their places** of business to see if they are honest businessmen. **And Rava said: The women of Shekhantziv would say: Death is like death,** as everyone must die, **and suffering is like interest.**[N]

תַּנְיָא, הָיָה רַבִּי מֵאִיר אוֹמֵר: "טוֹב לָלֶכֶת אֶל בֵּית אֵבֶל" וגו׳ עַד "וְהַחַי יִתֵּן אֶל לִבּוֹ" דְּבָרִים שֶׁל מִיתָה. דְּיִסְפַּד – יִסְפְּדוּנֵיהּ, דְּיִקְבַּר – יִקְבְּרוּנֵיהּ, דְּיִטְעַן – יִטְעֲנוּנֵיהּ. דְּיִדַּל – יִדְלוּנֵיהּ.

It is taught in a *baraita* that **Rabbi Meir would say** with regard to the verse **"It is better to go to the house of mourning** than to go to the house of feasting, for that is the end of all men; **and the living will lay it to his heart"** (Ecclesiastes 7:2): What should the living lay to his heart? **Matters relating to death.** And these matters are as follows: He **that eulogizes will be eulogized** by others. He **that buries** others **will be buried** by others. He **that loads** many words of praise and tribute into the eulogies that he delivers for others **will be** similarly **treated** by others. He **that raises** his voice in weeping over others **will** have others **raise** their voices **over him.**

וְאִיכָּא דְּאָמְרִי: דְּלָא יִדַּל – יִדְלוּנֵיהּ, דִּכְתִיב: "כִּי טוֹב אֲמָר לְךָ עֲלֵה הֵנָּה" וגו׳.

And some say: One **who does not raise himself** with pride, but chooses his place among the lowly, **will be raised**[N] by others, **as it is written:** "Do not exalt yourself in the king's presence, and stand not in the place of great men. **For it is better to be told, step up here,** than to be degraded in the presence of the great" (Proverbs 25:6–7).

NOTES

Wrap [*atuf*] and cover the mountains – עַטוּף וּכְסוּ טוּרֵי: Some explain that this is a poetic call for the mountains to wrap themselves in fine clothes in order to greet a great person. Alternatively, it may mean that many people should gather to accompany the deceased, thereby wrapping and concealing the mountains with their multitudes (Rabbeinu Ḥananel). Others explain similarly, but understand the verb *atuf* to mean darken, i.e., that the mountains should darken themselves (Rashi, Rabbeinu Gershom Meor HaGola).

Some understand this phrase as an allegory that means that the great people, who are referred to as mountains, should come to the funeral (Commentary on *Moed Katan*). Others say that this refers to one who was buried in a mountain cave, so that the mountains become his burial shroud (Ran).

Lend [*shayyul*] a cloak of fine wool, etc. – שַׁיּוּל אִצְטְלָא דְמַלְתָּא וכו׳: Some explain that this means that it is preferable for a formerly wealthy person who has no food to eat to find a burial shroud, as it is preferable for him to die and not be ashamed (Rabbeinu Ḥananel). Alternatively, it means that one should prepare fine clothes in order to join the funeral of a person from a wealthy family who died in poverty (Rabbeinu Ḥananel). Others suggest that it means that one should prepare a fine burial shroud for such a person (Rabbi Shlomo ben HaYatom). Rabbeinu Gershom Meor HaGola explains that the word *shayyul* is similar to the word *She'ol* meaning underworld or death, which is the best state for such a person.

Runs and tumbles at the ford [*amabra*] – רָהֵיט וְנָפֵיל אַמַּעְבְּרָא: Many different textual variations and explanations exist for this statement. Some explain that this was said about one who did not work during his life and now must borrow for the sake of the *mabarot*, the burial shrouds (*ge'onim*; see Ran and Maharsha). Others suggest that this refers to one who ran his entire life earning money but fell in with people who lost all of his money, and in the end he no longer had money at the ford, meaning for his burial (Rabbeinu Ḥananel).

Similarly, the passage is explained in many other ways, based on numerous textual variations that exist. One version reads: Run and go, son of divers, meaning that a diver who makes a living by swimming in deep waters must borrow money to pass over a small river at a ford (*Tosefot HaRosh*; see Meiri).

The merchants [*azavzagei*] will be examined – אַזְבְּזָגֵי מִיבַּדְקוּ: Another version of the text has the word purchases [*azbinei*], so that this means: The merchants will be examined not by their speech but by the way in which they conducted their business (Rabbeinu Ḥananel). Some explain that the merchants will be examined at the end of their lives to see how much they actually profited (Rabbi Betzalel Ransburg). Others have a version that reads *azla bazag*, meaning that the traveling merchants eventually go to the grave (Rabbi Shlomo ben HaYatom).

Suffering is like interest – וּמַרְעִין, חִיבּוּלְיָא: Some explain: The length of one's sickness until he dies is like interest on the capital, i.e., death (Rabbeinu Ḥananel). Others explain that diseases are additional pain and suffering (Ran).

One who does not raise himself will be raised [*dela yiddal yidlunei*] – דְּלָא יִדַּל יִדְלוּנֵיהּ: Rabbeinu Ḥananel has a version that reads *la yiddal de'idlonei*, meaning that one should not raise himself, so that he will not be lifted and taken down from his place. Others explain, in accordance with our version of the text, that one who does not raise himself will either be raised through receiving honor (Commentary on *Moed Katan*), or other people will carry his bier and eulogize him with honor. Consequently, the verse is an allusion to the matter and the essence of the concept (Rabbi Shlomo ben HaYatom).

תָּנוּ רַבָּנַן: כְּשֶׁמֵּתוּ בָּנָיו שֶׁל רַבִּי יִשְׁמָעֵאל נִכְנְסוּ אַרְבָּעָה זְקֵנִים לְנַחֲמוֹ: רַבִּי טַרְפוֹן, וְרַבִּי יוֹסֵי הַגְּלִילִי, וְרַבִּי אֶלְעָזָר בֶּן עֲזַרְיָה, וְרַבִּי עֲקִיבָא. אָמַר לָהֶם רַבִּי טַרְפוֹן: דְּעוּ שֶׁחָכָם גָּדוֹל הוּא, וּבָקִי בָּאַגָּדוֹת, אַל יִכָּנֵס אֶחָד מִכֶּם לְתוֹךְ דִּבְרֵי חֲבֵירוֹ. אָמַר רַבִּי עֲקִיבָא: וַאֲנִי אַחֲרוֹן.

The Sages taught the following *baraita*: **When the sons of Rabbi Yishmael**[P] **died, four Elders entered to console him: Rabbi Tarfon, Rabbi Yosei HaGelili, Rabbi Elazar ben Azarya, and Rabbi Akiva. Rabbi Tarfon said to them: Know that** Rabbi Yishmael **is a great Sage**[N] **and well versed in *aggadot*. Let none of you interrupt the words of another,** but rather each person should say something novel of his own. **Rabbi Akiva said: And I** shall speak **last.**

פָּתַח רַבִּי יִשְׁמָעֵאל וְאָמַר: רַבּוּ עֲוֹנוֹתָיו, תְּכָפוּהוּ אֲבֵלָיו, הִטְרִיחַ רַבּוֹתָיו פַּעַם רִאשׁוֹנָה וּשְׁנִיָּה.

Rabbi Yishmael, the mourner, **opened and said** about himself: **Many are his sins.** Due to this, **his bereavements came in** quick **succession** and **he troubled his teachers once and** then **a second time** to come and console him.

נַעֲנָה רַבִּי טַרְפוֹן וְאָמַר: ״וַאֲחֵיכֶם כָּל בֵּית יִשְׂרָאֵל יִבְכּוּ אֶת הַשְּׂרֵפָה״, וַהֲלֹא דְּבָרִים קַל וָחוֹמֶר: וּמַה נָּדָב וַאֲבִיהוּא שֶׁלֹּא עָשׂוּ אֶלָּא מִצְוָה אַחַת, דִּכְתִיב: ״וַיַּקְרִיבוּ בְּנֵי אַהֲרֹן אֶת הַדָּם אֵלָיו״ – כָּךְ, בָּנָיו שֶׁל רַבִּי יִשְׁמָעֵאל – עַל אַחַת כַּמָּה וְכַמָּה.

Having been granted permission to speak, **Rabbi Tarfon answered and said:** With regard to the death of Aaron's sons it says: **"But let your brethren, the whole house of Israel, bewail the burning that the Lord has kindled"** (Leviticus 10:6). **Are** these **matters not** inferred ***a fortiori*: If, with regard to Nadav and Avihu, who had performed only one mitzva**[N] that is explicitly mentioned in the Bible, **as it is written: "And the sons of Aaron brought the blood to him"** (Leviticus 9:9), **this** was nevertheless stated about them, then with regard to **the sons of Rabbi Yishmael,** who were well known for their performance of many mitzvot, **all the more so** should the entire Jewish people bewail their death.

נַעֲנָה רַבִּי יוֹסֵי הַגְּלִילִי וְאָמַר: ״וְסָפְדוּ לוֹ כָּל יִשְׂרָאֵל וְקָבְרוּ אוֹתוֹ״. וַהֲלֹא דְּבָרִים קַל וָחוֹמֶר: וּמָה אֲבִיָּה בֶּן יָרָבְעָם שֶׁלֹּא עָשָׂה אֶלָּא דָּבָר אֶחָד טוֹב, דִּכְתִיב בֵּיהּ: ״יַעַן נִמְצָא בוֹ דָּבָר טוֹב״ – כָּךְ, בָּנָיו שֶׁל רַבִּי יִשְׁמָעֵאל – עַל אַחַת כַּמָּה וְכַמָּה.

Rabbi Yosei HaGelili answered and said: With regard to Abijah, son of King Jeroboam, the verse states: **"And all Israel shall mourn for him, and bury him"** (I Kings 14:13). **Are** these **matters not** inferred ***a fortiori*: If, with regard to Abijah, son of Jeroboam, who did only one good thing, as it is written: "Because in him there is found some good thing** toward the Lord God of Israel" (I Kings 14:13), i.e., he did only one good thing, and **this** was his reward, then with regard to **the sons of Rabbi Yishmael all the more so** should they be rewarded by having the entire Jewish people mourn for them and bury them.

מַאי דָּבָר טוֹב? רַבִּי זֵירָא וְרַבִּי חִינָּנָא בַּר פַּפָּא; חַד אָמַר: שֶׁבִּיטֵּל מִשְׁמַרְתּוֹ וְעָלָה לָרֶגֶל; וְחַד אָמַר: שֶׁבִּיטֵּל פַּרְדָּסָאוֹת שֶׁהוֹשִׁיב יָרָבְעָם אָבִיו עַל הַדְּרָכִים שֶׁלֹּא יַעֲלוּ יִשְׂרָאֵל לָרֶגֶל.

The Gemara asks: **What** was this **one** good **thing** that Abijah did? **Rabbi Zeira and Rabbi Ḥinnana bar Pappa** disagreed about this issue. **One said: He abandoned his guard post.** His father, Jeroboam, had assigned him to serve as one of the guards whose mission it was to prevent people from going up to Jerusalem on the pilgrimage Festivals. **And he** himself **went up** to Jerusalem **for the pilgrimage Festival. And one said: He removed the guards** [*pardesaot*][L] **that his father, Jeroboam, had placed along the roads so that** the people of **Israel would not go up** to Jerusalem **for the pilgrimage Festivals.**

נַעֲנָה רַבִּי אֶלְעָזָר בֶּן עֲזַרְיָה וְאָמַר: ״בְּשָׁלוֹם תָּמוּת וּבְמִשְׂרְפוֹת אֲבוֹתֶיךָ הַמְּלָכִים הָרִאשׁוֹנִים [אֲשֶׁר הָיוּ לְפָנֶיךָ כֵּן] יִשְׂרְפוּ לָךְ״. וַהֲלֹא דְּבָרִים קַל וָחוֹמֶר: וּמַה צִּדְקִיָּהוּ מֶלֶךְ יְהוּדָה, שֶׁלֹּא עָשָׂה אֶלָּא מִצְוָה אַחַת, שֶׁהֶעֱלָה יִרְמְיָה מִן הַטִּיט – כָּךְ, בָּנָיו שֶׁל רַבִּי יִשְׁמָעֵאל – עַל אַחַת כַּמָּה וְכַמָּה.

The *baraita* continues: **Rabbi Elazar ben Azarya answered and said:** With regard to King Zedekiah, the verse states: **"But you shall die in peace; and with the burnings of your fathers, the former kings that were before you, so shall they make a burning for you"** (Jeremiah 34:5). **Are** these **matters not** inferred ***a fortiori*: If, with regard to Zedekiah, king of Judea, who had performed** only **one mitzva** that is explicitly mentioned in the Bible, **for he had Jeremiah lifted out of the mire** (Jeremiah 38:10), **this** was nevertheless stated about him, then with regard to **the sons of Rabbi Yishmael all the more so** should they be rewarded by dying in peace.

נַעֲנָה רַבִּי עֲקִיבָא וְאָמַר: ״בַּיּוֹם הַהוּא יִגְדַּל הַמִּסְפֵּד בִּירוּשָׁלַםִ כְּמִסְפַּד הֲדַדְרִימּוֹן [בְּבִקְעַת מְגִדּוֹן]״. וְאָמַר רַב יוֹסֵף: אִלְמָלֵא תַּרְגּוּמֵיהּ דְּהַאי קְרָא לָא הֲוָה יָדַעְנָא מַאי קָאָמַר:

Rabbi Akiva answered and said: The verse states: **"On that day shall there be a great mourning in Jerusalem, like the mourning of Hadadrimmon in the valley of Megiddon"** (Zechariah 12:11). The Gemara comments: With regard to this verse, **Rav Yosef said: Had it not been for the** Aramaic **translation of this verse, we would not have known what it is saying,** as nowhere in the Bible do we find this incident involving Hadadrimmon.

PERSONALITIES

Rabbi Yishmael – רַבִּי יִשְׁמָעֵאל: Rabbi Yishmael ben Elisha II was the grandson of Rabbi Yishmael ben Elisha, the High Priest who served in the Temple at the end of the Second Temple period. The grandson is the *tanna* who is usually referred to simply as Rabbi Yishmael throughout the Talmud. As a young man, he was imprisoned by the Romans. He was redeemed by Rabbi Yehoshua and ultimately became his student. Later he became one of the renowned scholars in Yavne, where he was a close friend and intellectual adversary of Rabbi Akiva. Each of them developed a unique system of biblical hermeneutics. The thirteen principles of interpretation formulated by Rabbi Yishmael serve as the foundation for halakhic midrash, which derives Jewish *halakha* from the Torah. We find many of his teachings throughout the Mishna. There are many more in the Talmud, which are taught by his students under the rubric: It was taught in the school of Rabbi Yishmael.

It appears that Rabbi Yishmael passed away prior to the bar Kokheva revolt. The Talmud mentions his sons and daughters; it is likely that the *tanna* Rabbi Eliezer, son of Rabbi Yishmael, was among his children.

NOTES

Know that Rabbi Yishmael is a great Sage, etc. – דְּעוּ שֶׁחָכָם גָּדוֹל וכו׳: Therefore, each one of you should say something novel that Rabbi Yishmael has not yet heard. The phrase: Let none of you interrupt the words of another, means that you should not cite the statement of one of your colleagues and begin to discuss it. Consequently, Rabbi Akiva's choice to volunteer to say something novel after everyone else was the most difficult of the options (Ran). Some explain that the Sages were told not to discuss another's statement lest Rabbi Yishmael forget his mourning. It was best for them to speak in an orderly fashion so that Rabbi Yishmael would listen and not speak (Maharsha).

Who had performed only one mitzva – שֶׁלֹּא עָשׂוּ אֶלָּא מִצְוָה אַחַת: It is explained that this means that they performed only one mitzva, for which they earned merit, and through which they died (Commentary on *Moed Katan*). Others say that this means that they performed a mitzva that is relevant and applicable to all of Israel (Maharsha).

LANGUAGE

Guards [*pardesaot*] – פַּרְדָּסָאוֹת: From the Latin praesidia, meaning guards. In other tractates and other manuscripts this word is written as *peruzdaot*.

בְּעִידָּנָא הַהוּא יִסְגֵּי מִסְפְּדָא בִּירוּשְׁלֵם כְּמִסְפְּדָא דְּאַחְאָב בַּר עָמְרִי דִּקְטַל יָתֵיהּ הֲדַדְרִימּוֹן בַּר טַבְרִימּוֹן, וּכְמִסְפֵּד דְּיֹאשִׁיָּה בַּר אָמוֹן דִּקְטַל יָתֵיהּ פַּרְעֹה חֲגִירָא בְּבִקְעַת מְגִידוֹ.

The Aramaic translation reads as follows: **At that time the mourning in Jerusalem will be as great as the mourning over Ahab, son of Omri, who was slain by Hadadrimmon, son of Tabrimmon, and like the mourning over Josiah, son of Amon, who was slain by Pharaoh the lame in the valley of Megiddon.**

וַהֲלֹא דְּבָרִים קַל וָחוֹמֶר: וּמָה אַחְאָב מֶלֶךְ יִשְׂרָאֵל, שֶׁלֹּא עָשָׂה אֶלָּא דָּבָר אֶחָד טוֹב, דִּכְתִיב: ״וְהַמֶּלֶךְ הָיָה מָעֳמָד בַּמֶּרְכָּבָה נֹכַח אֲרָם״ – כָּךְ, בָּנָיו שֶׁל רַבִּי יִשְׁמָעֵאל – עַל אַחַת כַּמָּה וְכַמָּה.

The *baraita* continues: **Are these matters not** inferred ***a fortiori*: If, with regard to Ahab, king of Israel, who did** only **one good thing** that is explicitly mentioned in the Bible, **as it is written: "And the king was propped up in his chariot facing Aram"** (I Kings 22:35), as he did not want the Jewish people to see that he was mortally wounded and flee, and **this,** that he was greatly mourned, was nevertheless stated about him, then **all the more so** will **the sons of Rabbi Yishmael** be greatly mourned.

אֲמַר לֵיהּ רָבָא לְרַבָּה בַּר מָרִי, כְּתִיב בֵּיהּ בְּצִדְקִיָּהוּ ״בְּשָׁלוֹם תָּמוּת״, וּכְתִיב ״וְאֶת עֵינֵי צִדְקִיָּהוּ עִוֵּר״! אֲמַר לֵיהּ: הָכִי אֲמַר רַבִּי יוֹחָנָן: שֶׁמֵּת נְבוּכַדְנֶאצַּר בְּיָמָיו.

The Gemara discusses issues in the aforementioned verses: **Rava said to Rabba bar Mari: It is written with regard to Zedekiah: "You shall die in peace," but** elsewhere **it is written: "And he put out Zedekiah's eyes"** (Jeremiah 39:7). Rabba bar Mari **said to him: Rabbi Yoḥanan said as follows:** The first verse: "You shall die in peace," means **that Nebuchadnezzar died in** Zedekiah's **lifetime** and consequently the latter died in peace, having seen the death of the wicked.

וַאֲמַר רָבָא לְרַבָּה בַּר מָרִי: כְּתִיב בֵּיהּ בְּיֹאשִׁיָּהוּ: ״לָכֵן הִנְנִי אוֹסִפְךָ עַל אֲבוֹתֶיךָ וְנֶאֱסַפְתָּ אֶל קִבְרוֹתֶיךָ בְּשָׁלוֹם״ וּכְתִיב: ״וַיֹּרוּ הַיֹּרִים לַמֶּלֶךְ יֹאשִׁיָּהוּ״, וְאָמַר רַב יְהוּדָה אָמַר רַב: שֶׁעֲשָׂאוּהוּ כִּכְבָרָה!

And Rava further **said to Rabba bar Mari: It is written with regard to Josiah: "Behold, therefore I will gather you unto your fathers, and you shall be gathered into your grave in peace"** (II Kings 22:20), **and** elsewhere **it is written: "And the archers shot at King Josiah;** and the king said to his servants, Get me away; for I am grievously wounded" (II Chronicles 35:23). **And** with regard to this verse **Rabbi Yehuda said** that **Rav said:** With their many arrows, **they made** his body **like a sieve.**

אֲמַר לֵיהּ, הָכִי אֲמַר רַבִּי יוֹחָנָן: שֶׁלֹּא חָרַב בֵּית הַמִּקְדָּשׁ בְּיָמָיו.

Rabba bar Mari **said to him: Rabbi Yoḥanan said as follows:** The words "in peace" stated with regard to King Josiah refer to the fact **that the Temple was not destroyed in his lifetime,** as the verse itself continues: "And your eyes shall not see all the evil that I will bring upon this place" (II Kings 22:20).

אָמַר רַבִּי יוֹחָנָן: אֵין מְנַחֲמִין רַשָּׁאִין לוֹמַר דָּבָר עַד שֶׁיִּפְתַּח אָבֵל, שֶׁנֶּאֱמַר: ״אַחֲרֵי כֵן פָּתַח אִיּוֹב אֶת פִּיהוּ״ וַהֲדַר ״וַיַּעַן אֱלִיפַז הַתֵּימָנִי״.

The Gemara returns to examining the *halakhot* of consolation. **Rabbi Yoḥanan said: The consolers are not permitted to speak words** of consolation **until the mourner opens** and speaks first.[H] **As it is stated:** "And they sat down with him upon the ground for seven days and seven nights, and none spoke a word to him; for they saw that his suffering was very great. **After this Job opened his mouth"** (Job 2:13–3:1). **And afterward: "And Eliphaz the Temanite answered** and said" (Job 4:1).

אָמַר רַבִּי אַבָּהוּ: מִנַּיִן לְאָבֵל שֶׁמֵּיסֵב בָּרֹאשׁ? שֶׁנֶּאֱמַר: ״אֶבְחַר דַּרְכָּם וְאֵשֵׁב רֹאשׁ וְאֶשְׁכּוֹן כְּמֶלֶךְ בַּגְּדוּד כַּאֲשֶׁר אֲבֵלִים יְנַחֵם״.

Rabbi Abbahu said: From where is it derived that **the mourner reclines at the head** [*rosh*] of the table? **As it is stated: "I chose out their way, and sat as chief** [*rosh*], **and dwelt as a king in the army, as one that comforts** [*yenaḥem*] **the mourners"** (Job 29:25). This indicates that the mourner sits at the head of the table, as the chief.

״יְנַחֵם״ אַחֲרִינֵי מַשְׁמַע! אָמַר רַב נַחְמָן בַּר יִצְחָק: יִנָּחֵם כְּתִיב.

The Gemara raises an objection: But the word ***yenaḥem* means that he comforts others,** thereby implying that one who comforts the mourners sits at the head of the table. **Rav Naḥman bar Yitzḥak said:** The word **is written** as ***yinaḥem***,[N] meaning: Will be comforted, and therefore can be understood as referring to the mourner.

HALAKHA

The custom of the consolers – מִנְהַג מְנַחֲמִים: The consolers may not begin speaking until the mourner speaks first. However, this applies only when one eats in a mourner's house and not when he merely visits (*Arukh HaShulḥan*; *Shulḥan Arukh*, *Yoreh De'a* 376:1).

NOTES

It is written *yinaḥem* – יִנָּחֵם כְּתִיב: The early authorities have a version that reads: It is written *yenuḥam*, he who is consoled. They comment that this statement does not imply that the word is actually written in this manner; rather, it means that the word can be read in this way as well (Ritva).

LANGUAGE

Mirzaḥ – מַרְזֵחַ: The origin of this word is unclear, even in its Aramaic form, *marziḥa*. However, from the verse: "Enter not into the house of mourning [*mirzaḥ*]" (Jeremiah 16:5), it appears to mean a house of mourning. Some explain that the meaning of the root *r-z-ḥ* is to raise one's voice, whether in weeping or in joy.

HALAKHA

A priest at the head – כֹּהֵן בָּרֹאשׁ: When many people sit together to eat, the greatest person there should recite the blessing over the bread and cut it. If a groom is present and it is the day of his wedding, then he should cut the bread, even when there is a greater person there (*Magen Avraham*, citing *Beit Yosef*). If everyone is of equal stature and there is a priest present, then it is a mitzva for him to do so first. However, if the priest is an ignoramus and there is a Torah scholar present, then the Torah scholar cuts the bread first (*Magen Avraham*). If the priest is also a Torah scholar, he should be first, even if there is a greater scholar present, but this is not required (Rema). It is a mitzva to first present a priest who is a Torah scholar with any honor related to a mitzva. However, he may pass the honor to someone else in his place (Rema, citing *Smag*; *Shulḥan Arukh*, *Oraḥ Ḥayyim* 167:14, 201:2).

מָר זוּטְרָא אָמַר מֵהָכָא: ״וְסָר מִרְזַח סְרוּחִים״, מַרְזֵחַ – נַעֲשָׂה שַׂר לִסְרוּחִים.

Mar Zutra said: A proof may be derived **from here:** The verse **"And the revelry [*mirzaḥ*] of those who stretched themselves out shall pass away [*sar*]"** (Amos 6:7) means that ***mirzaḥ*,**[L] he who is bitter [*mar*] and whose mind is overwrought [*zaḥ*] due to grief, **is made a prince [*sar*] over those who** sit beside him **stretched out** below him to comfort him.

אָמַר רַבִּי חָמָא בַּר חֲנִינָא: מִנַּיִן לְחָתָן שֶׁמֵּיסֵב בָּרֹאשׁ? שֶׁנֶּאֱמַר: ״כֶּחָתָן יְכַהֵן פְּאֵר״, מַה כֹּהֵן בָּרֹאשׁ – אַף חָתָן בָּרֹאשׁ.

Rabbi Ḥama bar Ḥanina said: From where is it derived **that a groom reclines at the head** of the table? **As it is stated: "As a bridegroom decks himself [*yekhahen*] with a garland"** (Isaiah 61:10). **Just as a priest [*kohen*] is at the head** of the table, **so too, a bridegroom is at the head** of the table.

וְכֹהֵן גּוּפֵיהּ מְנָלַן? דְּתָנָא דְּבֵי רַבִּי יִשְׁמָעֵאל: ״וְקִדַּשְׁתּוֹ״ – לְכָל דָּבָר שֶׁבִּקְדוּשָּׁה, לִפְתּוֹחַ רִאשׁוֹן, וּלְבָרֵךְ רִאשׁוֹן, וְלִיטּוֹל מָנָה יָפָה רִאשׁוֹן.

The Gemara asks: **From where do we** derive that **the priest himself** sits at the head?[H] The Gemara answers: **As the school of Rabbi Yishmael taught:** With regard to a priest it says: **"You shall sanctify him,** for he offers the bread of your God" (Leviticus 21:8), meaning that you are to sanctify him **with regard to all matters of sanctity: To be first to begin** reading the Torah, **to be first to recite the Grace** after Meals, **and to be first to take a portion** during a meal.

אָמַר רַבִּי חֲנִינָא: קָשָׁה יְצִיאַת נְשָׁמָה מִן הַגּוּף

§ The Gemara returns to its discussion of death: **Rabbi Ḥanina said: The soul's departure from the body is as difficult**

Perek **III**
Daf **29** Amud **a**

LANGUAGE

Halyard [*pitirei*] – פִּטִירֵי: According to those who understand that this word means a kind of ship's rope, it is similar to the expression "knobs and open flowers [*peturei tzitzim*]" (I Kings 6:18), which Rashi explains to mean decorated ropes.

HALAKHA

One who departs from the deceased – הַנִּפְטָר מִן הַמֵּת: Based on the verse "and you shall go to your fathers in peace" (Genesis 15:15), those who have accompanied the deceased say after the burial: Go in peace (Rambam *Sefer Shofetim*, *Hilkhot Evel* 4:4).

כְּצִיפּוֹרִי בְּפִי הַוֶּושֶׁט. רַבִּי יוֹחָנָן אָמַר: כִּפְטִירֵי בְּפִי וֶושֶׁט.

as it is **for a knotted rope [*tzippori*]**[N] **to pass through an eye [*veshet*]** in a ship's rigging. **Rabbi Yoḥanan said:** It is as difficult as it is **for a halyard [*pitirei*]**[L] **to pass through an eye [*veshet*].**[N]

וְאָמַר רַבִּי לֵוִי בַּר חַיְתָא: הַנִּפְטָר מִן הַמֵּת לֹא יֹאמַר לוֹ ״לֵךְ לְשָׁלוֹם״ אֶלָּא ״לֵךְ בְּשָׁלוֹם״. הַנִּפְטָר מִן הַחַי לֹא יֹאמַר לוֹ ״לֵךְ בְּשָׁלוֹם״, אֶלָּא ״לֵךְ לְשָׁלוֹם״.

And Rabbi Levi bar Ḥayyata said: One who departs from the deceased[H] **should not say to him: Go to peace, but rather** he should say: **Go in peace.**[N] **One who departs from the living should not say to him: Go in peace, but rather** he should say: **Go to peace.**

הַנִּפְטָר מִן הַמֵּת לֹא יֹאמַר לוֹ ״לֵךְ לְשָׁלוֹם״ אֶלָּא ״לֵךְ בְּשָׁלוֹם״ – שֶׁנֶּאֱמַר: ״וְאַתָּה תָּבֹא אֶל אֲבוֹתֶיךָ בְּשָׁלוֹם״.

One who departs from the deceased should not say to him: Go to peace, but rather: Go in peace, as it is stated: "And you shall go to your fathers in peace; you shall be buried in a good old age" (Genesis 15:15).

NOTES

Like a knotted rope [*tzippori*] to pass through an eye [*veshet*] in a ship's rigging – כְּצִיפּוֹרִי בְּפִי הַוֶּושֶׁט: Some explain that the word *tzippori* means: Like the knot of a rope (Rashi). Others explain that it refers to a rope made from the fibers of a coconut tree, which was used to tie ships (*Arukh*). Still others say that the word is related to the term "young goat [*tzefir izim*]" (Daniel 8:8) and means that death is as difficult as the birth of a firstborn goat (Rabbi Shlomo ben HaYatom).

There are some with a version of the text that reads: Like a bird [*tzippor*] caught in the esophagus [*veshet*]. They say that the expression refers to the difficulty of swallowing a bird in a single gulp (*ge'onim*). The Ran has a version that reads: Like a fingernail [*tzipporen*] caught in the esophagus, which would cause great pain. Most commentaries explain that the metaphor is meant to compare death to something that has become stuck in the esophagus [*veshet*] and can be swallowed only with difficulty and great pain.

As a halyard [*pitirei*] to pass through an eye – כִּפְטִירֵי בְּפִי וֶושֶׁט: Most commentaries explain that the word *pitirei* is similar in meaning to the word *tzippori*, and it denotes a thick rope used on a ship. The *ge'onim* explain that it means mushroom [*pitria*], so that death is compared to one who swallows a mushroom whole (see Ran).

Go to peace…go in peace – לֵךְ לְשָׁלוֹם...לֵךְ בְּשָׁלוֹם: With regard to the difference between these expressions, some say that: Go in peace, means that this person should be in a place where there is peace, i.e., to the grave. Meanwhile, the phrase: Go to peace, refers to the person's direction. Using this time alludes to a person going towards greatness, symbolized by the letter *lamed*, which is the tallest of all the letters (Rabbi Shlomo ben HaYatom). The Ran explains that: Go in peace, means that one's journey should be in peace; however, it does not refer to his destination. Therefore, it is appropriate to say this only with regard to the dead and not the living.

The Ritva explains that the dead no longer need to be concerned about future calamities, and everything that will happen to them in the future depends on what they did in this world. Therefore, those present bless the dead with the words: Go in peace, meaning that this person's passing will be complete and in peace. However, with regard to the living, they have already left in peace and now need only a blessing that they should go peacefully to their future destination.

הַנִּפְטָר מִן הַחַי לֹא יֹאמַר לוֹ ״לֵךְ בְּשָׁלוֹם״ אֶלָּא ״לֵךְ לְשָׁלוֹם״, שֶׁהֲרֵי דָּוִד שֶׁאָמַר לְאַבְשָׁלוֹם ״לֵךְ בְּשָׁלוֹם״ – הָלַךְ וְנִתְלָה. יִתְרוֹ שֶׁאָמַר לְמֹשֶׁה ״לֵךְ לְשָׁלוֹם״ – הָלַךְ וְהִצְלִיחַ.

One who departs from the living[H] **should not say to him: Go in peace, but rather: Go to peace, as David said to Absalom: "Go in peace"** (II Samuel 15:9), **and he** subsequently **went and was hanged;** whereas **Jethro said to Moses: "Go to peace"** (Exodus 4:18), and **he went and was successful.**

וְאָמַר רַבִּי לֵוִי: כׇּל הַיּוֹצֵא מִבֵּית הַכְּנֶסֶת לְבֵית הַמִּדְרָשׁ, וּמִבֵּית הַמִּדְרָשׁ לְבֵית הַכְּנֶסֶת – זוֹכֶה וּמְקַבֵּל פְּנֵי שְׁכִינָה, שֶׁנֶּאֱמַר: ״יֵלְכוּ מֵחַיִל אֶל חָיִל יֵרָאֶה אֶל אֱלֹהִים בְּצִיּוֹן״.

And Rabbi Levi said: Anyone who leaves from the synagogue and goes **to the study hall**[NH] **or** goes **from the study hall to the synagogue,** i.e., he goes from the mitzva of prayer to the mitzva of Torah study or vice versa, **merits to receive the Divine Presence, as it is stated: "They go from strength to strength, every one of them appears before God in Zion"** (Psalms 84:8).

אָמַר רַב חִיָּיא בַּר אַשִׁי אָמַר רַב: תַּלְמִידֵי חֲכָמִים אֵין לָהֶם מְנוּחָה אֲפִילּוּ לָעוֹלָם הַבָּא, שֶׁנֶּאֱמַר: ״יֵלְכוּ מֵחַיִל אֶל חָיִל יֵרָאֶה אֶל אֱלֹהִים בְּצִיּוֹן״.

With regard to the same verse, **Rav Ḥiyya bar Ashi said** that **Rav said: Torah scholars have no rest,**[N] **even in the World-to-Come,** as even there they remain in constant movement and ascent, **as it is stated: "They go from strength to strength, every one of them appears before God in Zion."** Even when they are in the World-to-Come, they continue to go from strength to strength, until the final redemption will arrive in the end of days and God will appear in Zion.

הדרן עלך ואלו מגלחין
וסליקא לה מסכת מועד קטן

HALAKHA

One who departs from the living – **הַנִּפְטָר מִן הַחַי**: One should not say to his friend: Go in peace, rather he should say: Go to peace (*Magen Avraham*; *Shulḥan Arukh, Oraḥ Ḥayyim* 110).

From the synagogue to the study hall – **מִבֵּית הַכְּנֶסֶת לְבֵית הַמִּדְרָשׁ**: After leaving the synagogue, one should go to the study hall and set aside time to study. He must establish a regular time to study, so that he will not skip it, even if an opportunity arises during that time to make a large profit. Even one who does not know how to study Torah should go to the study hall so that he will receive reward for walking there (Rabbeinu Yona). One should establish a fixed place for himself in the study hall, so that he can study what he is capable of studying and contemplate his actions, so as to develop the fear of Heaven (*Shulḥan Arukh, Oraḥ Ḥayyim* 155:1, and in the comment of Rema).

NOTES

From the synagogue to the study hall – **מִבֵּית הַכְּנֶסֶת לְבֵית הַמִּדְרָשׁ**: By doing so, one shows that engaging in Torah and mitzvot is his primary intent and goal; however, in order to make a living he must also engage in other activities.

Have no rest – **אֵין לָהֶם מְנוּחָה**: This is a continuation of what is stated with regard to one who goes from the synagogue to the study hall. In the World-to-Come, there is no break, and he goes from strength to strength there as well (*Yad David*). The early authorities write that this is based on what is mentioned in many places in the Talmud, that in the supernal world souls engage in Torah study and understanding of the Creator (*Tosefot HaRosh*; Rabbi Shlomo ben HaYatom). The Rambam writes in *Sefer HaMadda* that the reward of the righteous will be that they will know the truth of the Creator, things that they could not know when they were in a body.

Summary of **Perek III**

Many different areas of *halakha* were discussed and ruled on in this chapter. With regard to the intermediate days of a Festival, it was explained that one who was prevented due to duress is permitted to cut his hair and wash his clothing on these days, whether the duress was due to an external factor, such as being locked up in prison, or whether due to his halakhic status, for example if he was a mourner or had been excommunicated. Similarly, even though it is normally prohibited to write on the intermediate days of a Festival, it is permitted to do so in cases of loss, or for the sake of dire financial need.

This chapter also discussed those *halakhot* and restrictions of the intermediate days of a Festival that are shared by a leper, a mourner, and one who is ostracized, e.g., haircutting, laundering, and greeting others. Similarly, they are prohibited from wearing leather shoes, from engaging in marital relations, and from donning phylacteries, and all are required to wrap their heads.

The Gemara explained that there is a difference between the more lenient form of ostracism and the more stringent excommunication, which are applied to those who transgress various prohibitions or who do not listen to the rulings of the court. The most stringent form of excommunication involves a higher degree of isolation from others, and contains an aspect of curse.

This chapter is the main source in the Talmud for the *halakhot* of mourning. It explained most of the *halakhot* of mourning, of rending garments, and of comforting mourners. There is a distinction made between rending at the time of death over any person, particularly an upright person, rending over a relative for whom one is obligated to mourn, and rending over a parent, a teacher, or the *Nasi*. For a relative other than one's parents there is a specific time to rend and a minimum size for the tear. For a mother, father, teacher, or *Nasi* one must make a tear that is more visible, and it may never be fully mended. The Gemara also discusses other times when one must rend one's garments as a sign of mourning.

The *halakhot* of the meal of comfort for the mourners were also explained in this chapter, as well as how one comforts the mourners, both during their mourning period and afterward.

The Gemara discussed the various degrees of mourning, which lessen with the passage of time. Acute mourning begins before the burial of the deceased; mourning is most stringent on the first day; for seven days the mourner must remain in his home, may not work, and must observe all the stringencies of mourning; for thirty days there are public signs of mourning for relatives; and for twelve months there are mourning practices observed after the death of a parent. The *halakhot* of distant tidings, i.e., if one hears of the death only after some time has passed, were also discussed.

The Gemara concluded that on Shabbat and Festivals there is no public mourning, and even during the intermediate days of a Festival one may not eulogize excessively or do other activities that lead to emotional pain. Furthermore, the days of a Festival sometimes cancel the mourning, or at least shorten the length of the mourning period.

Index of **Background**

Index of **Language**

Index of **Personalities**

Image **Credits**

Introduction to Ḥagiga

Tractate *Ḥagiga* deals with the *halakhot* of the mitzva to ascend and appear in the Temple on the three pilgrimage Festivals. The analysis of these *halakhot* can be divided into two main categories: The offerings which the pilgrims must bring, and ritual purity and impurity, especially those aspects which are relevant to the Festivals.

The mitzvot of the Torah to ascend to the Temple and to celebrate and rejoice on the Festivals are expressed in both general and specific terms. The general obligation, "Three times a year all your males shall appear before the Lord God" (Exodus 23:17), is supplemented by a practical means of implementation by the Torah itself: "And none shall appear before Me empty-handed" (Exodus 23:15). As is clear from several places in the Torah (e.g., Deuteronomy 12:11–12), this means that pilgrims must bring with them special offerings for the Festivals. In other words, in addition to the fixed, communal Festival offerings, the details of which are set out mainly in Leviticus 23 and Numbers 28–29, each individual pilgrim must sacrifice special offerings brought for the Festival. Similarly, the other, undefined commandments, i.e., the celebration of and rejoicing in the Festival, are fulfilled in a highly practical manner, through the sacrifice of certain animal offerings.

The Torah itself does not state which offerings must be brought by individuals, as the verses themselves provide mere allusions in this regard. However, by tradition of the Sages there are three types of Festival offerings: The burnt-offering of appearance, the Festival peace-offering, and the peace-offering of rejoicing. Every individual pilgrim who appears before God in the Temple must bring a burnt-offering of appearance. The Festival peace-offering is likewise obligatory, while the peace-offering of rejoicing is a separate offering that has no fixed requirement; it is brought if more meat is necessary for the rejoicing of the Festival.

In addition to these offerings, pilgrims would ascend to Jerusalem for the Festivals with the other offerings and gifts they were obligated to bring to the Temple or to the city. These included the various obligatory offerings, e.g., burnt-offerings, sin-offerings and guilt-offerings for specific sins, offerings brought in fulfillment of a vow, firstborns, animal tithe, and second tithe produce and its redemption money. These were typically brought on the Festival, not only for reasons of convenience so as to avoid several trips to Jerusalem, but also because the connection between one's sacrificial obligations and the rejoicing of the Festivals is established by the Torah itself (see, for example, Deuteronomy 12:6–12).

The numerous offerings brought by pilgrims raises the problem of the relationship between the obligatory Festival offerings and those which are not connected to the festivities of the day. The general principle that one cannot fulfill the duty to bring one offering by the sacrifice of another is applicable here, and therefore one must bring special offerings for the Festival. However, it is necessary to determine the minimum requirement of these offerings, as well as whether this measure applies by Torah law or whether the Torah simply imposes a general obligation and the Sages established a fixed value for these offerings. In the Jerusalem Talmud (*Pe'a* 1:1 and the beginning of *Ḥagiga*) this is treated as a general inquiry with regard to all halakhic measurements that are not mentioned in the Torah itself. Conversely, the Babylonian Talmud apparently considers this a specific problem involving the Festival offerings, which are not detailed at all in the Torah.

In any case, there are certain ways to combine an obligatory offering with animals or money that are designated for a different offering. Furthermore, they can be used for the fulfillment of the peace-offerings of rejoicing, whose obligation is less clearly delineated than that of the other two categories.

The classification of these offerings as Festival offerings raises a series of questions. First, the period of the Festival must be defined: Does it refer only to the Festival itself, or are the intermediate days of the Festival also included? If the obligation applies solely on the Festival day, how should one treat the animals sacrificed thereon?

It is prohibited to perform labor on a Festival, and several of the mitzvot of an animal offering involve the performance of labor, especially the placing of one's hands on an offering, an act that is not indispensible for the sacrificial rite. Although these mitzvot were performed regularly, and therefore one would expect there to have been an established custom in this regard, certain details of the rite were nevertheless subject to ancient disputes that were left unresolved.

Another topic dealt with in this tractate is the *halakhot* of ritual purity and impurity. These *halakhot* are tightly bound to the Temple and to consecrated items. In essence, the use of ritually impure objects is not forbidden in and of itself, but only when one will come into contact with *teruma* or the Temple and its sacred articles.

Nevertheless, many Jews would be careful to remain in a state of ritual purity at all times, even when they dealt with non-sacred objects and foods. These people were called *ḥaverim*. The opposite category of people, i.e., those who were not scrupulous with regard to ritual purity and impurity as well as with regard to several other areas of *halakha*, were known as *amei ha'aretz*. Due to the care that must be taken to preserve ritual purity, and because of the severity of the *halakhot* of ritual impurity, which include numerous rabbinic ordinances, the Sages decreed that *amei ha'aretz* should be considered ritually impure at all times. However, this level of caution and separation could be maintained only in the rest of the country and not in the Temple itself, which is shared by all Jews.

The problem of the ritual purity of sacred articles was resolved in two main ways. On the one hand, the Sages instituted a large number of restrictive decrees with regard to ritual purity and impurity which went far beyond the *halakhot* of the Torah. These ordinances and restrictions were designed to ensure that no ritual impurity that applied by Torah law would be found in the Temple precincts, especially concerning the red heifer and the waters of the purification offering. On the other hand, even *amei ha'aretz*, who were not particular about the observance of every mitzva, treated the Temple with great respect and were careful about its sanctity and ritual purity. Consequently, they too were considered trustworthy when it came to any questions involving the ritual purity of sacred articles. Furthermore, the Sages added a special decree that applied to the Festival period: When all Jews ascend to Jerusalem for the pilgrimage Festivals they are considered "Knit together [*ḥaverim*] as one man" (Judges 20:11) in every regard. In the words of the psalmist, "Jerusalem is built as a city that is compact together," at those times when "the tribes ascended there…to give thanks to the name of the Lord" (Psalms 122:3–4).

Ritual purity and impurity is the most difficult and complex area of *halakha*. An entire order of the Mishna is devoted to the analysis of these *halakhot* (see the introduction of the Rambam to the order of *Teharot* in his Commentary on the Mishna). The discussion in tractate *Ḥagiga* focuses mainly on the differences between the *halakhot* of ritual purity and impurity in general and their particular application to sacred articles, concerning which many stringencies and higher standards are imposed both by Torah law and by rabbinic law. At the same time, the tractate also deals with the trustworthiness of all Jews in this regard, and the leniencies that are invoked during the pilgrimage Festivals.

Incidental to the general discussion concerning the *halakhot* of the Festival offerings, which are only alluded to in the Torah, an entire section of the tractate deals with areas of the Torah that are not detailed and elucidated in the Torah itself. In some cases these topics are *halakhot* mentioned in Torah in the form of allusions, while their main explication is found in the traditions of the Oral Law. Other matters are kept hidden by their very nature, as they are not meant to be studied by all people. These issues, which were not taught in public lectures, were called *Ma'aseh Bereshit*, the Act of Creation, which deals with the secrets of the creation of the world, and *Ma'aseh Merkava*, the Design of the Divine Chariot, which concerns the lofty, upper world and Divine Providence.

Tractate *Ḥagiga* does not clarify these esoteric subjects, but it does explain their permitted and prohibited areas of inquiry as well as why the Sages were reluctant to publicize these ideas. Moreover, they are not matters of *halakha* and are not connected at all to the mitzvot of the pilgrimage Festivals, yet the main analysis in the Talmud of these esoteric issues appears in this tractate. Indeed, there is an intimate connection between esoterica, which involve the heavenly entourage and the Temple of above, and tractate *Ḥagiga*, which deals with the obligations of those pilgrims who ascend to "appear before the Lord God."

Tractate *Ḥagiga* consists of three chapters, which move back and forth from one topic to another.

Chapter One deals with the basic pilgrimage obligation and the Festival offerings, as well as the various areas of the Torah that are merely alluded to in the Torah itself and which are elucidated by the tradition of the Sages.

Chapter Two covers those matters which may not be taught in public, the manner of bringing offerings on a Festival day, and the differences between the *halakhot* of ritual purity and impurity as they apply to non-sacred items, *teruma*, and the sacred articles of the Temple.

Chapter Three discusses the higher standard that is conferred on sacred articles beyond that of *teruma*, and the leniencies that the Sages applied to the ritual purity of consecrated items in Jerusalem, particularly during the Festival period.

Introduction to **Perek I**

Three times you shall keep a feast to Me in the year.

(Exodus 11:11–12)

And you shall keep the feast of weeks to the Lord your God after the measure of the free-will offering of your hand, which you shall give, as the Lord your God blesses you. And you shall rejoice before the Lord your God, you, and your son, and your daughter, and your servant, and your maidservant, and the Levite who is within your gates, and the stranger, and the orphan, and the widow, who are in your midst, in the place that the Lord your God shall choose to cause His name to dwell there.

(Deuteronomy 16:10–11)

Three times a year shall all your males appear before the Lord your God at the place that He shall choose; on the feast of unleavened bread, and on the feast of weeks, and on the feast of tabernacles; and they shall not appear before the Lord empty-handed. Every man shall give as he is able, according to the blessing of the Lord your God that He has given you.

(Deuteronomy 16:16–17)

The mitzvot of the pilgrimage Festivals: To "keep a feast," to "rejoice before the Lord your God," and to "appear before the Lord your God," are not fully clarified in the Torah. Not only are the details of these commandments left unstated, their very meaning is vague. According to the tradition of the Sages, in addition to their broader connotations, these mitzvot are fulfilled by means of defined actions. One who undertakes the pilgrimage to the Temple must bring a burnt-offering of appearance, and two types of peace-offerings: The Festival peace-offering and the peace-offering of rejoicing. The relationship between the general meaning of these mitzvot and their precise manner of fulfillment is the subject of much debate. Furthermore, the details of the performance of these mitzvot in practice require elucidation.

Several practical questions must be addressed. First, who is obligated in the mitzva of the Festival pilgrimage and who is exempt from this obligation? Is there a connection between those who are required to fulfill this mitzva and those who are obligated to bring the Festival offerings? Second, what exactly are these offerings? Must they be of a particular value, or does this depend on the wishes and funds of each individual pilgrim? Furthermore, do these differ from voluntary offerings? May one fulfill these obligations by means of a combination with other obligatory offerings?

Another question concerns the days of the Festival on which one can fulfill this mitzva. Does the mitzva, or at least the main obligation, apply only on the first day or on all the Festival days, or even after the conclusion of the Festival?

The detailed analysis and elucidation of these questions is the topic of this chapter.

מתני׳ הַכֹּל חַיָּיבִין בִּרְאִיָּיה, חוּץ מֵחֵרֵשׁ, שׁוֹטֶה, וְקָטָן; וְטוּמְטוּם, וְאַנְדְּרוֹגִינוֹס, וְנָשִׁים, וַעֲבָדִים שֶׁאֵינָם מְשׁוּחְרָרִים; הַחִיגֵּר, וְהַסּוּמָא, וְהַחוֹלֶה, וְהַזָּקֵן, וּמִי שֶׁאֵינוֹ יָכוֹל לַעֲלוֹת בְּרַגְלָיו.

MISHNA **All are obligated** on the three pilgrimage Festivals **in the** mitzva of **appearance,**[NH] i.e., to appear in the Temple as well as to sacrifice an offering, **except for a deaf-mute,**[N] **an imbecile, and a minor; and a** ***tumtum*****,**[NB] **and a hermaphrodite, and women, and slaves**[N] **who are not emancipated; and the lame, and the blind, and the sick, and the old, and one who is unable to ascend**[N] to Jerusalem **on his own legs.**

אֵיזֶהוּ קָטָן – כֹּל שֶׁאֵינוֹ יָכוֹל לִרְכּוֹב עַל כְּתֵפָיו שֶׁל אָבִיו וְלַעֲלוֹת מִירוּשָׁלַיִם לְהַר הַבַּיִת, דִּבְרֵי בֵּית שַׁמַּאי. וּבֵית הִלֵּל אוֹמְרִים: כֹּל שֶׁאֵינוֹ יָכוֹל לֶאֱחוֹז בְּיָדוֹ שֶׁל אָבִיו וְלַעֲלוֹת מִירוּשָׁלַיִם לְהַר הַבַּיִת, שֶׁנֶּאֱמַר: ״שָׁלֹשׁ רְגָלִים״.

Who has the status of **a minor** with regard to this *halakha*? **Any** child **who is unable to ride on his father's shoulders and ascend from Jerusalem to the Temple Mount;** this is **the statement of Beit Shammai. And Beit Hillel say: Any** child **who is unable to hold his father's hand and ascend** on foot **from Jerusalem to the Temple Mount, as it is stated: "Three times [*regalim*]"** (Exodus 23:14). Since the term for feet is *raglayim*, Beit Hillel infer from here that the obligation to ascend involves the use of one's legs.

בֵּית שַׁמַּאי אוֹמְרִים: הָרְאִיָּיה שְׁתֵּי כֶסֶף, וְהַחֲגִיגָה מָעָה כֶסֶף. וּבֵית הִלֵּל אוֹמְרִים: הָרְאִיָּיה מָעָה כֶסֶף, וְהַחֲגִיגָה שְׁתֵּי כֶסֶף.

Beit Shammai say: The burnt-offering of **appearance** brought on a pilgrimage Festival must be worth at least **two silver** coins, **and the Festival peace**-offering must be worth at least one **silver** ***ma'a***[B] coin. **And Beit Hillel say: The** burnt-offering of **appearance** must be worth at least one **silver** ***ma'a*** **and the Festival peace**-offering at least **two silver** coins.

גמ׳ לְאֵתוֹיֵי מַאי? לְאֵתוֹיֵי מִי שֶׁחֶצְיוֹ עֶבֶד וְחֶצְיוֹ בֶּן חוֹרִין. וּלְרָבִינָא, דְּאָמַר: מִי שֶׁחֶצְיוֹ עֶבֶד וְחֶצְיוֹ בֶּן חוֹרִין פָּטוּר מִן הָרְאִיָּיה, ״הַכֹּל״ לְאֵתוֹיֵי מַאי? לְאֵתוֹיֵי חִיגֵּר בְּיוֹם רִאשׁוֹן וְנִתְפַּשֵּׁט בְּיוֹם שֵׁנִי.

GEMARA The Gemara asks: When the mishna states that all are obligated in the mitzva of appearance in the Temple, the term: All, comes **to add what** in the mishna's ruling? The Gemara answers: It serves **to add one who is half-slave half-freeman.** The Gemara asks: **And according to** the opinion of **Ravina, who said: One who is half-slave half-freeman is exempt from the appearance** in the Temple, the term: **All,** comes **to add what?** The Gemara answers: It comes **to add** one who was **lame on** the **first day** of the Festival and was unable to travel, **and was healed on** the **second day** of the Festival. This man is obligated to appear before the end of the Festival.

הָנִיחָא לְמַאן דְּאָמַר כּוּלָּן תַּשְׁלוּמִין זֶה לָזֶה, אֶלָּא לְמַאן דְּאָמַר כּוּלָּן תַּשְׁלוּמִין דְּרִאשׁוֹן – ״הַכֹּל״ לְאֵתוֹיֵי מַאי? לְאֵתוֹיֵי סוּמָא בְּאַחַת מֵעֵינָיו.

The Gemara asks: **This works out well according to the one who said** that **all** seven days of the Festival **redress one another,** i.e., the obligation to appear applies equally on all days of the Festival. Consequently, one who was unable to travel on the first day may do so on the second day. **However, according to the one who said** that the main obligation is on the first day and **all** the remaining days merely **redress the first**[H] day, and therefore one who was exempt from appearing on the first day of the Festival remains exempt throughout the rest of the Festival, the term: **All,** comes **to add what?** The Gemara answers: It comes **to add** one who is **blind in one of his eyes.**[H]

NOTES

Appearance – רְאִיָּיה: The commentaries analyze the nature of the mitzva of appearance mentioned here. Some explain that this refers to the obligation to visit the Temple on the three pilgrimage Festivals (Rashi; Rambam). Others maintain, as noted in the Jerusalem Talmud, that the mitzva of appearance in the Mishna refers to the mitzva of sacrificing the burnt-offering of appearance on the Festivals (Rav Hai Gaon). In the Jerusalem Talmud it is noted that besides the mitzva for every adult male to bring a burnt-offering of appearance on each Festival, there is an obligation to appear in the Temple that applies equally to the entire Jewish people, including women and children.

Except for a deaf-mute, etc. – חוּץ מֵחֵרֵשׁ וכו׳: Those who are exempt from the mitzva of appearance are divided by the mishna into different categories based on the reason for their exemption. Some are exempt because they are not of sound mind; others because they are not defined as: "All your males" (Exodus 23:17); while yet others are exempt due to the fact that they are unable to ascend to the Temple by foot.

And a ***tumtum*****, etc.** – וְטוּמְטוּם וכו׳: The commentaries note that elsewhere the *tumtum* and hermaphrodite are listed after women, whereas here they are mentioned first. The reason is that in other cases their disqualification is due to their possible status as women (*Turei Aven*). Here, however, they are exempt in their own right, as explained in the Gemara (4a).

Women and slaves – נָשִׁים וַעֲבָדִים: Why are all the exemptions listed in the singular form except for those of women and slaves (*Tosafot*)? Some suggest that this is because there are many women and slaves in society (*Tiferet Yisrael*). Alternatively, the other people mentioned in the mishna are exempt due to a particular characteristic or flaw, whereas women and slaves by definition are not obligated in the first place (*Ḥeshek Shlomo*). Others explain simply that this is the usual expression, as the trio of the deaf-mute, imbecile, and minor are always listed together as a unit, as are women and slaves (*Melekhet Shlomo*; *Petaḥ Einayim*).

One who is unable to ascend – מִי שֶׁאֵינוֹ יָכוֹל לַעֲלוֹת: The case of one who is unable to ascend from Jerusalem to the Temple Mount is an extreme example; this exemption certainly applies to one who is unable to reach Jerusalem in the first place (*Tosafot*, citing Rashi). Others explain that this refers to an unusually delicate individual who never travels by foot (Rambam). Yet others say that the reference is to one who is unable to walk barefoot. Since it is prohibited to enter the Temple wearing shoes, he may not walk in the sacred place (Rashi on 4b; see Meiri).

BACKGROUND

Tumtum – טוּמְטוּם: A *tumtum* is one whose external sexual organs are indeterminate, and it is unclear whether the person is male or female. In certain cases, the gender of the *tumtum* is established at a later stage, which is described in the language of the *halakha* as: A *tumtum* who was torn, revealing his gender. At that point this person is considered a full-fledged member of that gender.

Silver ***ma'a*** – מָעָה כֶּסֶף: A small silver coin, worth thirty-two *peruta*, or one-sixth of a dinar. The *ma'a*, the equivalent of the biblical *gera*, weighed sixteen barleycorns of silver, about 384 mg.

HALAKHA

Those who are obligated in the mitzva of appearance – הַחַיָּיבִין בִּרְאִיָּיה: Women and slaves are exempt from the mitzva of appearance in the Temple. All men are obligated to appear, except for a deaf-mute, a mute, an imbecile, a minor, a blind person, a lame person, one who is ritually impure, and one who is uncircumcised. Other exemptions include the elderly, the sick, and a delicate person, all of whom are physically unable to ascend by foot (Rambam *Sefer Korbanot*, *Hilkhot Ḥagiga* 2:1).

All redress the first – כּוּלָּן תַּשְׁלוּמִין דְּרִאשׁוֹן: All the days of the Festival redress the first day, i.e., the main obligation of appearance in the Temple applies on the first day, while the remaining Festival days merely provide another opportunity for one who failed to arrive at the Temple on the first day to fulfill the mitzva (Rambam *Sefer Korbanot*, *Hilkhot Ḥagiga* 1:4).

Blind in one of his eyes – סוּמָא בְּאַחַת מֵעֵינָיו: One who is blind, even in one eye, is exempt from the mitzva of appearance in the Temple, in accordance with the opinion of Yoḥanan ben Dehavai (Rambam *Sefer Korbanot*, *Hilkhot Ḥagiga* 2:1).

NOTES

As it is stated…will appear [*yera'e*]…will see [*yireh*] – **שֶׁנֶּאֱמַר: "יֵרָאֶה" "יִרְאֶה"**: Since the Gemara is not vocalized, there is some dispute as to which verb appears first in the text. According to Rashi and others, the reading is *yireh*, i.e., will see, followed by *yera'e*, i.e., will appear, meaning that just as God, Who is complete, sees the pilgrim, the pilgrim must likewise be seen before God in a complete and unblemished state, i.e., with two functional eyes.

Here it is in accordance with the initial version of the mishna, etc. – **כָּאן כְּמִשְׁנָה רִאשׁוֹנָה וכו׳**: The Gemara does not explain which source is referred to by the term: Here. There are two interpretations of this entire passage. Some say that the phrase: The initial version of the mishna, refers to Ravina's opinion. In other words, the assumption that a half-slave is exempt from the mitzva of appearance is in accordance with the ruling of the initial mishna, before Beit Hillel retracted. The ruling that a half-slave and half-freeman is obligated in the mitzva of appearance follows the ultimate version of the mishna, i.e., after Beit Hillel's retraction. The reasoning for this interpretation is as follows: Since Beit Hillel concede that the master is obligated to emancipate his slave, it is considered as though he were already freed, which means he is obligated in mitzvot (Rabbeinu Ḥananel; Rashi; Rabbeinu Gershom *Me'or HaGola* on *Arakhin*; Rid).

Alternatively, the ruling of the initial version of the mishna is that a half-slave is obligated to appear at the Temple, as during the period when he is a freeman he is obligated in all the mitzvot. According to this explanation, Ravina's opinion is in accordance with the ultimate version of the mishna. The logic of this claim is that although the man must be freed, until he is fully emancipated he retains the halakhic status of a slave (Rambam; Rabbi Ovadya MiBartenura; see Meiri).

וּדְלָא כִּי הַאי תַּנָּא. דְּתַנְיָא, יוֹחָנָן בֶּן דְּהַבַאי אוֹמֵר מִשּׁוּם רַבִּי יְהוּדָה: סוּמָא בְּאַחַת מֵעֵינָיו פָּטוּר מִן הָרְאִיָּיה, שֶׁנֶּאֱמַר: "יֵרָאֶה" "יִרְאֶה", כְּדֶרֶךְ שֶׁבָּא לִרְאוֹת כָּךְ בָּא לֵירָאוֹת, מָה לִרְאוֹת בִּשְׁתֵּי עֵינָיו – אַף לֵירָאוֹת בִּשְׁתֵּי עֵינָיו.

The Gemara notes: **And** this is **not in accordance with** the opinion of **this** ***tanna*****, as it is taught** in a *baraita* that **Yoḥanan ben Dehavai says in the name of Rabbi Yehuda:** One who is **blind in one of his eyes is exempt from the** mitzva of **appearance, as it is stated:** "Three occasions in the year all your males **will appear** [***yera'e***] before the Lord God" (Exodus 23:17). Since there are no vowels in the text, this can be read as: All your males **will see** [***yireh***][N] the Lord God. This teaches that **in the** same **manner that one comes to see, so he comes to be seen: Just as** the usual way **to see is with both one's eyes, so too** the obligation **to be seen** applies only to one who comes **with** the sight of **both his eyes.** Therefore, one who is blind in one eye is not obligated in the mitzva of appearance in the Temple.

וְאִיבָּעֵית אֵימָא: לְעוֹלָם כִּדְאָמְרִי מֵעִיקָּרָא, וּדְקָא קַשְׁיָא לָךְ הָא דְּרָבִינָא – לָא קַשְׁיָא; כָּאן – כְּמִשְׁנָה רִאשׁוֹנָה, כָּאן – כְּמִשְׁנָה אַחֲרוֹנָה. דִּתְנַן: מִי שֶׁחֶצְיוֹ עֶבֶד וְחֶצְיוֹ בֶּן חוֹרִין – עוֹבֵד אֶת רַבּוֹ יוֹם אֶחָד וְאֶת עַצְמוֹ יוֹם אֶחָד, דִּבְרֵי בֵּית הִלֵּל.

And if you wish, say instead: **Actually,** it is **as we said initially,** that it comes to include one who is half-slave and half-freeman. **And** as for that **which** poses **a difficulty to** the opinion **of Ravina,** it is **not difficult: Here** it is in accordance with **the initial** version of the **mishna,**[N] whereas **there,** Ravina's statement, is **in accordance with the ultimate** version of the **mishna. As we learned** in a mishna (*Pesaḥim* 88a): **One who is half-slave half-freeman serves his master one day** and works for **himself one day.** This is **the statement of Beit Hillel.**

אָמְרוּ לָהֶם בֵּית שַׁמַּאי:

Beit Shammai said to them:

Perek **I**
Daf **2** Amud **b**

HALAKHA

One who is a half-slave – **מִי שֶׁחֶצְיוֹ עֶבֶד**: Since a man who is a half-slave and half-freeman cannot marry, his master is forced to free him, at which point the slave writes the master a promissory note for half his worth. The *halakha* is in accordance with the opinion of Beit Shammai, as Beit Hillel ultimately conceded to their opinion (*Shulḥan Arukh*, *Yoreh De'a* 267:62).

תִּקַּנְתֶּם אֶת רַבּוֹ, וְאֶת עַצְמוֹ לֹא תִּקַּנְתֶּם; לִישָּׂא שִׁפְחָה – אֵינוֹ יָכוֹל, בַּת חוֹרִין – אֵינוֹ יָכוֹל.

You have remedied the situation of **his master,**[N] who benefits fully from all his rights to the slave, **but his own** situation **you have not remedied.** How so? **He is unable to marry a maidservant,**[N] as half of him is already free, and a free Jew may not marry a Canaanite maidservant. **He** is likewise **unable** to marry **a free woman,** as half of him is still a slave.[H]

NOTES

You have remedied the situation of his master – **תִּקַּנְתֶּם אֶת רַבּוֹ**: The term remedied is apparently inaccurate, as this arrangement does not provide a solution for his master (see *Tosafot* for a different version of the text). Some explain that a half-freeman is not required to do any work at all, or he can work whenever he pleases, as his master cannot constrain him to a specific time or activity. Therefore, Beit Hillel instituted that he should work every other day. According to this interpretation, Beit Hillel's ruling does offer a remedy for the master (*Zekher LaḤagiga*).

He is unable to marry a maidservant – **לִישָּׂא שִׁפְחָה אֵינוֹ יָכוֹל**: Since he is a half-freeman it is prohibited for him to marry a female slave, in accordance with the interpretation accepted by the Sages for the verse: "There shall be no male prostitutes among the men of Israel" (Deuteronomy 23:18). Similarly, Onkelos translates this verse as follows: And a man from the nation of Israel shall not marry a female slave. The suggestion that he should marry a child born from an incestuous or adulterous relationship [*mamzer*] is not viable, as the Sages do not institute ordinances that will increase the number of illegitimate children (*Tosafot*; see Meiri). Some say that even according to the ruling of the Rambam that a female slave may marry a *mamzer*, a male slave may not marry a *mamzeret*, a female *mamzer* (Maharsha).

לִיבַּטֵּיל? וַהֲלֹא לֹא נִבְרָא הָעוֹלָם אֶלָּא לִפְרִיָּה וּרְבִיָּה, שֶׁנֶּאֱמַר: "לֹא תֹהוּ בְרָאָהּ לָשֶׁבֶת יְצָרָהּ"! אֶלָּא, מִפְּנֵי תִּיקּוּן הָעוֹלָם כּוֹפִין אֶת רַבּוֹ וְעוֹשֶׂה אוֹתוֹ בֶּן חוֹרִין, וְכוֹתֵב לוֹ שְׁטָר עַל חֲצִי דָמָיו. וְחָזְרוּ בֵּית הִלֵּל לְהוֹרוֹת כְּדִבְרֵי בֵּית שַׁמַּאי.

And if you say **he should be idle** and not marry, **but isn't it** true that **the world was created only for procreation, as it is stated: "He did not create it to be a waste;**[N] **He formed it to be inhabited"** (Isaiah 45:18)? **Rather, for the betterment of the world we force his master to make him a freeman,** and the slave **writes a bill to** his master accepting his responsibility to pay **half his value** to him. **And Beit Hillel** ultimately **retracted** their opinion, **to rule in accordance with the statement of Beit Shammai** that a half-slave must be set free.

"חוּץ מֵחֵרֵשׁ שׁוֹטֶה וְקָטָן" כו׳. קָתָנֵי חֵרֵשׁ דּוּמְיָא דְּשׁוֹטֶה וְקָטָן, מָה שׁוֹטֶה וְקָטָן – דְּלָאו בְּנֵי דֵעָה, אַף חֵרֵשׁ – דְּלָאו בַּר דֵּעָה הוּא. וְקָא מַשְׁמַע לָן כְּדִתְנַן: חֵרֵשׁ שֶׁדִּיבְּרוּ חֲכָמִים בְּכׇל מָקוֹם – שֶׁאֵינוֹ שׁוֹמֵעַ וְאֵינוֹ מְדַבֵּר. הָא מְדַבֵּר וְאֵינוֹ שׁוֹמֵעַ, שׁוֹמֵעַ וְאֵינוֹ מְדַבֵּר – חַיָּיב.

§ The mishna taught: **Except for a deaf-mute, an imbecile, and a minor.** The Gemara notes: By listing these three cases together the mishna **is teaching** that **a deaf-mute is similar to an imbecile and a minor: Just as an imbecile and a minor** are among those **who are not of sound mind, so too the deaf-mute** [*ḥeresh*] mentioned here is one **who is not of sound mind. And** this **teaches us as we learned** in a mishna (*Terumot* 1:2): **The *ḥeresh*, whom the Sages**[N] **discussed everywhere,** is one **who does not hear and does not speak,**[N] and therefore his mind is not lucid. It can be inferred from this that **one who speaks but does not hear** and **one who hears but does not speak are obligated** in mitzvot like any other person.

תָּנֵינָא לְהָא, דְּתָנוּ רַבָּנַן: הַמְדַבֵּר וְאֵינוֹ שׁוֹמֵעַ – זֶהוּ חֵרֵשׁ. שׁוֹמֵעַ וְאֵינוֹ מְדַבֵּר זֶהוּ אִלֵּם. זֶה וָזֶה הֲרֵי הֵן כְּפִקְחִין לְכׇל דִּבְרֵיהֶם.

The Gemara notes: **We** already **learned this, as the Sages taught** in the *Tosefta* (*Terumot* 1:2): **One who speaks but does not hear, this is a deaf** person. One who **hears but does not speak, this is a mute.** Both **this** one **and that** one **are** in the same legal category **as those who can see and hear** with regard **to all matters.**[H] This shows that the *ḥeresh* exempted by the Sages is one who neither hears nor speaks.

וּמִמַּאי דִּמְדַבֵּר וְאֵינוֹ שׁוֹמֵעַ זֶהוּ חֵרֵשׁ, שׁוֹמֵעַ וְאֵינוֹ מְדַבֵּר זֶהוּ אִלֵּם? דִּכְתִיב: "וַאֲנִי כְחֵרֵשׁ לֹא אֶשְׁמָע וּכְאִלֵּם לֹא יִפְתַּח פִּיו". וְאִיבָּעֵית אֵימָא, כִּדְאָמְרִי אֱינָשֵׁי: אִישְׁתַּקֵּיל מִילּוּלֵיהּ.

The Gemara asks: **And from where** is it derived **that one who speaks but does not hear is a deaf** person, and one who **hears but does not speak is a mute? As it is written: "But I am as a deaf man, I hear not; and I am as a dumb man [*illem*] who does not open his mouth"** (Psalms 38:14). **If you wish, say** instead that this is **as people say: His speech has been taken [*Ishtakeil Milulei*]**; the term *illem* is an acronym for this phrase.

"מְדַבֵּר וְאֵינוֹ שׁוֹמֵעַ שׁוֹמֵעַ וְאֵינוֹ מְדַבֵּר חַיָּיב". וְהָתַנְיָא: מְדַבֵּר וְאֵינוֹ שׁוֹמֵעַ, שׁוֹמֵעַ וְאֵינוֹ מְדַבֵּר – פָּטוּר!

The *Tosefta* taught that **one who speaks but does not hear** and **one who hears but does not speak** are **obligated** in mitzvot. The Gemara asks: **Isn't it taught** in a *baraita* that **one who speaks but does not hear** and **one who hears but does not speak** are **exempt?**

אָמַר רָבִינָא וְאִיתֵּימָא רָבָא: חַסּוֹרֵי מִיחַסְּרָא, וְהָכִי קָתָנֵי: הַכֹּל חַיָּיבִין בִּרְאִיָּיה וּבְשִׂמְחָה, חוּץ מֵחֵרֵשׁ הַמְדַבֵּר וְאֵינוֹ שׁוֹמֵעַ, שׁוֹמֵעַ וְאֵינוֹ מְדַבֵּר, שֶׁפָּטוּר מִן הָרְאִיָּיה. וְאַף עַל פִּי שֶׁפָּטוּר מִן הָרְאִיָּיה – חַיָּיב בְּשִׂמְחָה. וְאֶת שֶׁאֵינוֹ לֹא שׁוֹמֵעַ וְלֹא מְדַבֵּר, וְשׁוֹטֶה וְקָטָן – פָּטוּר אַף מִן הַשִּׂמְחָה, הוֹאִיל וּפְטוּרִים מִכׇּל מִצְוֹת הָאֲמוּרוֹת בַּתּוֹרָה.

Ravina said, and some say it was **Rava** who said: The mishna **is incomplete**[N] **and is teaching the following:**[B] **All are obligated in** the mitzvot of **appearance** in the Temple **and rejoicing** during the pilgrimage Festival by eating the sacrificial meat, **except for a deaf** person **who speaks but does not hear** and mute person **who hears but does not speak,**[H] each of whom **is exempt from** the mitzva of **appearance. And even though he is exempt from** the mitzva of **appearance, he is obligated in** the mitzva of **rejoicing. But one who does not hear and does not speak, and an imbecile and a minor,** each of these is **exempt even from rejoicing, since they are exempt from all the mitzvot mentioned in the Torah,** as they are not of sound mind.

תַּנְיָא נָמֵי הָכִי: הַכֹּל חַיָּיבִין בִּרְאִיָּיה וּבְשִׂמְחָה – חוּץ מֵחֵרֵשׁ הַמְדַבֵּר וְאֵינוֹ שׁוֹמֵעַ, שׁוֹמֵעַ וְאֵינוֹ מְדַבֵּר – שֶׁפְּטוּרִין מִן הָרְאִיָּיה. וְאַף עַל פִּי שֶׁפָּטוּר מִן הָרְאִיָּיה

That opinion **is also taught** in a *baraita*: **All are obligated in** the mitzva of **appearance and in rejoicing, except for a deaf** person **who speaks but does not hear** and **one who hears but does not speak, as they are exempt from** the mitzva of **appearance. And even though they are exempt from** the mitzva of **appearance,**

NOTES

He did not create it to be a waste – לֹא תֹהוּ בְרָאָהּ: The Gemara cites this verse instead of the positive mitzva: "Be fruitful and multiply" (Genesis 1:28), as the verse from Isaiah emphasizes more sharply the fundamental role of procreation in the world (*Tosafot*). To fulfill the requirement of the second half of the verse in Isaiah: "He formed it to be inhabited," certain activities are permitted that would not be allowed for the sake of other mitzvot. This is why there is no violation here of the prohibition against emancipating one's slave. Alternatively, the verse from Genesis could not be cited because a slave is not obligated in the mitzva of: "Be fruitful and multiply" (see Maharsha). Therefore, the Gemara cites the phrase: "He formed it to be inhabited," which applies to all people, even those who are exempt from the mitzva of procreation (see *Turei Aven*).

The *ḥeresh* whom the Sages discussed, etc. – חֵרֵשׁ שֶׁדִּבְּרוּ חֲכָמִים וכו׳: The following formula is stated in the Jerusalem Talmud: The principles of Rabbi Yehuda HaNasi are not principles. This means that one should not learn from generalizations stated in the Mishna, like this one, as there are invariably many exceptions to these generalizations. In this case, too, there are times when it is clear that the *ḥeresh*, even when mentioned together with an imbecile and minor, does not refer to a deaf-mute (see Rabbi Ovadya MiBartenura).

One who does not hear and does not speak – שֶׁאֵינוֹ שׁוֹמֵעַ וְאֵינוֹ מְדַבֵּר: Some commentaries explain that a deaf-mute is referred to only as deaf, *ḥeresh*, because this term generally refers to one who was born deaf and consequently never learned how to speak. Therefore, the Sages referred to him by his primary disability (Rambam's Commentary on the Mishna, *Terumot* 1:1).

Incomplete, etc. – חַסּוֹרֵי מִיחַסְּרָא וכו׳: According to the explanation of Ravina that this mishna refers not only to the mitzva of appearance but also to the mitzva of rejoicing, each section of the mishna must be analyzed on its own merits. Certain sections of the mishna refer solely to the mitzva of appearance while others refer both to that mitzva and the mitzva of rejoicing (*Tosefot Rid*).

HALAKHA

As those who can see and hear with regard to all matters – כְּפִקְחִין לְכׇל דִּבְרֵיהֶם: One who can hear but cannot speak, even if he is mute from birth, has the legal status of one who is of sound mind with regard to all matters of *halakha*. This individual can divorce his wife by means of hand motions, and his business dealings are valid. He may likewise confer gifts, although his bestowal must be confirmed either by an outside source or by written confirmation in his handwriting. Similarly, one who is hard of hearing has the same legal status as that of a regular person (*Shulḥan Arukh*, *Even HaEzer* 121:6, *Ḥoshen Mishpat* 235:18).

A deaf person and a mute – חֵרֵשׁ וְאִילֵּם: A deaf person and a mute are exempt from the mitzva of appearance in the Temple. However, they must rejoice on the pilgrimage Festivals, as they are obligated in other mitzvot like all members of the Jewish people. Conversely, a deaf-mute is exempt from all mitzvot, including rejoicing on a Festival (Rambam *Sefer Korbanot*, *Hilkhot Ḥagiga* 2:1–4).

BACKGROUND

The mishna is incomplete and is teaching the following – חַסּוֹרֵי מִיחַסְּרָא וְהָכִי קָתָנֵי: This method of explanation is often found in the Gemara. Generally speaking, it does not suggest an actual emendation of the text of the mishna. Rather, the addition introduced by the Gemara is a necessary elaboration upon what is written in the mishna, which is insufficiently clear in its current form. The addition provides the necessary clarification.

חַיָּיב בְּשִׂמְחָה. וְאֶת שֶׁאֵינוֹ לֹא שׁוֹמֵעַ וְלֹא מְדַבֵּר, וְשׁוֹטֶה וְקָטָן – פְּטוּרִין אַף מִן הַשִּׂמְחָה, הוֹאִיל וּפְטוּרִין מִכׇּל מִצְוֹת הָאֲמוּרוֹת בַּתּוֹרָה. מַאי שְׁנָא לְעִנְיַן רְאִיָּה דִּפְטִירִי, וּמַאי שְׁנָא לְעִנְיַן שִׂמְחָה דְּמִחַיְּיבִי?

they are **obligated in rejoicing. And one who does not hear and does not speak, an imbecile, and a minor are** all **exempt even from rejoicing, since they are exempt from all the mitzvot mentioned in the Torah.** The Gemara asks: **What is different with regard to** the mitzva of **appearance, that** a deaf person and a mute **are exempt** from this mitzva? **And what is different with regard to** the mitzva of **rejoicing, that they are obligated?**

לְעִנְיַן רְאִיָּה גָּמַר "רְאִיָּה" "רְאִיָּה" מֵהַקְהֵל, דִּכְתִיב: "הַקְהֵל אֶת הָעָם הָאֲנָשִׁים וְהַנָּשִׁים וְהַטַּף", וּכְתִיב: "בְּבֹא כׇל יִשְׂרָאֵל לֵרָאוֹת".

The Gemara explains: **With regard to** their exemption from the obligation of **appearance,** the *tanna* **derives** this *halakha* by means of a verbal analogy between the term **appearance** stated with regard to the mitzva of appearance at the Temple on the pilgrimage Festival and the term **appearance** stated with regard to the mitzva **of assembly,**[NB] i.e., the obligation to assemble in the Temple on *Sukkot* in the year following the Sabbatical Year. **As it is written,** with regard to the mitzva of assembly: **"Assemble the people, the men and the women and the little ones"** (Deuteronomy 31:12), **and it is written** in that context: **"When all of Israel come to appear"** (Deuteronomy 31:11). Just as a deaf person and a mute are not obligated to attend the assembly, they are likewise exempt from appearing in the Temple on the Festivals.[H]

וְהָתָם מְנָלַן? דִּכְתִיב: "לְמַעַן יִשְׁמְעוּ וּלְמַעַן יִלְמְדוּ", וְתַנְיָא: "לְמַעַן יִשְׁמְעוּ" – פְּרָט לִמְדַבֵּר וְאֵינוֹ שׁוֹמֵעַ; "וּלְמַעַן יִלְמְדוּ" – פְּרָט לְשׁוֹמֵעַ וְאֵינוֹ מְדַבֵּר.

The Gemara asks: **And there,** with regard to the mitzva of assembly, **from where do we** derive that a deaf person and a mute are exempt? **As it is written** there: **"That they may hear, and that they may learn"** (Deuteronomy 31:12), **and it is taught** in a *baraita* that the phrase **"that they may hear" excludes one who speaks but does not hear;** and the phrase **"and that they may learn" excludes one who hears but does not speak,** as he is unable to learn.

לְמֵימְרָא דְּכִי לָא מִשְׁתָּעֵי לָא גָּמַר? וְהָא הָנְהוּ תְּרֵי אִילְּמֵי דַּהֲווּ בְּשֵׁבָבוּתֵיהּ דְּרַבִּי, בְּנֵי בְּרַתֵּיהּ דְּרַבִּי יוֹחָנָן בֶּן גּוּדְגְּדָא, וְאָמְרִי לַהּ בְּנֵי אַחְתֵּיהּ דְּרַבִּי יוֹחָנָן, דְּכׇל אֵימַת דַּהֲוָה עָיֵיל רַבִּי לְבֵי מִדְרָשָׁא הָווּ עָיְילִי וְיָתְבִי קַמַּיְיהוּ, וּמְנַיְּידִי בְּרֵישַׁיְיהוּ וּמְרַחֲשִׁין שִׂפְוָותַיְיהוּ.

The Gemara asks: **Is that to say that one who** is **not** able to **speak** is **not** able to **learn?** But consider the following incident. There were **two mute people who were in the neighborhood of Rabbi** Yehuda HaNasi.[P] They were the **sons of the daughter of Rabbi Yoḥanan ben Gudgeda, and some say** that they were the **sons of the sister of Rabbi Yoḥanan** ben Gudgeda. **Whenever Rabbi** Yehuda HaNasi **would enter the study hall they would** also **enter and sit before** the Sages, **and they would nod their heads** as if they understood **and move their lips.**

וּבָעֵי רַבִּי רַחֲמֵי עֲלַיְיהוּ וְאִיתַּסּוּ, וְאִשְׁתַּכַּח דַּהֲווּ גְּמִירִי הִלְכְתָא וְסִפְרָא וְסִפְרֵי וְכוּלַּהּ תַּלְמוּדָא!

And Rabbi Yehuda HaNasi **prayed for** God to have **mercy upon them, and they were healed. And it was discovered that they had learned** and were proficient in ***halakha***, i.e., Mishna; ***Sifra***, the halakhic midrash on Leviticus; ***Sifrei***, the halakhic midrash on Numbers and Deuteronomy; **and the entire Talmud.** This shows that those who cannot speak are able to learn.

אָמַר מָר זוּטְרָא: קְרִי בֵּיהּ "לְמַעַן יְלַמְּדוּ". רַב אַשִׁי אֲמַר: וַדַּאי "לְמַעַן יְלַמְּדוּ" הוּא, דְּאִי סָלְקָא דַּעְתָּךְ "לְמַעַן יִלְמְדוּ", וְכֵיוָן דְּלָא מִשְׁתָּעֵי לָא גָּמַר, וְכֵיוָן דְּלָא שָׁמַע לָא גָּמַר –

Mar Zutra said that one should **read into** the verse: **That they may teach** [*yelamdu*],[N] instead of: "That they may learn [*yilmedu*]" (Deuteronomy 31:12). Even if a mute person is able to learn he cannot teach others. **Rav Ashi said** that the verse **is certainly** to be read: **That they may teach. As, if it enters your mind** that one should read: **"That they may learn,"** as it is written, **and** you will explain that **since he is not** able to **speak he** is **not** able to **learn,** and similarly the reason for the exemption of a deaf person is that **since he is not** able to **hear he is not** able to **learn,** you will have erred. According to this interpretation, it is clear from the context that a deaf person is exempted by the phrase: "That they may hear," not merely due to his lack of hearing but because his inability to hear prevents him from learning.

NOTES

With regard to appearance, he derives…with regard to the mitzva of assembly – לְעִנְיַן רְאִיָּה גָּמַר...מֵהַקְהֵל: Why is it necessary for the Gemara to cite the verse: "Assemble the people, the men and the women and the little ones"; it is apparently enough to quote the previous verse, which includes the phrase: Appearance. One explanation is that a person might have thought that the verbal analogy between the mitzva of assembly and the mitzva of appearance is not absolute, as women are exempt from the mitzva of appearance but are obligated in the mitzva of assembly. Therefore, the Gemara cites this verse to indicate that the Torah explicitly included women in this particular obligation, whereas with regard to a deaf person the verbal analogy is indeed absolute (*Siaḥ Yitzḥak*; *Turei Aven*; and the later authorities).

Read into it, That they may teach – קְרִי בֵּיהּ לְמַעַן יְלַמְּדוּ: In the Jerusalem Talmud this derivation is presented in slightly different terms. The commentaries discuss whether the derivation in the Jerusalem Talmud is ultimately the same as that of the Babylonian Talmud, or whether it is based on the additional letter *vav* in the verse, meaning "and": "And that they may learn," which can be interpreted as an indication that they must be able to teach others (*Korban HaEda*). Additionally, the Jerusalem Talmud indicates that one who is unable to teach others is deficient in his own learning.

BACKGROUND

Assembly – הַקְהֵל: The Torah commands that the Jewish people must assemble in the Temple courtyard once every seven years to hear a public reading of the book of Deuteronomy by the king (Deuteronomy 31:10–13). This assembly was held during the festival of *Sukkot* in the year following the Sabbatical Year. The entire nation, including men, women, and children, attended.

HALAKHA

The obligation of appearance and assembly – חִיּוּב בִּרְאִיָּיה וּבְהַקְהֵל: All those who are exempt from the mitzva of appearance in the Temple are likewise exempt from the mitzva of assembly, except for women, children, and the uncircumcised, who are exempt from appearance but are obligated in assembly (Rambam *Sefer Korbanot, Hilkhot Ḥagiga* 3:2).

PERSONALITIES

Rabbi Yehuda HaNasi – רַבִּי יְהוּדָה הַנָּשִׂיא: The period of *tanna'im* concluded with Rabbi Yehuda HaNasi's arrangement of the Mishna. The son of Rabbi Shimon ben Gamliel II, Rabbi Yehuda HaNasi lived from 135–220 CE When he was thirty years old he was appointed *Nasi*, or prince, but due to his great scholarship the Talmud refers to him simply as: Rabbi. Rabbi Yehuda HaNasi spoke Greek, which was the language of the elite in Eretz Yisrael, and he was friendly with the Roman Emperor, Antoninus. His knowledge of Hebrew was legendary, to the extent that the Sages learned the meaning of difficult words from servants who worked in his house. According to the Gemara (*Gittin* 59a), from the time of Moses, there was not found another individual who had the combined qualities of Torah scholarship and prominent leadership to the extent of Rabbi Yehuda HaNasi. Rabbi Yehuda HaNasi's lifework was the collection of oral traditions and opinions that he wove into the Mishna. His Mishna serves as the basis for the Talmud that is studied to this day. Rabbi Yehuda HaNasi's students were the Sages of the first generation of *amora'im*, including Rabbi Yoḥanan, Rabbi Ḥiyya, bar Kappara, and Rav.

הַאי מִ״לְמַעַן יִשְׁמְעוּ״ נָפְקָא! אֶלָּא וַדַּאי ״לְמַעַן יְלַמְּדוּ״ הוּא.

However, this is incorrect, for if so, **this** exemption of a mute could also be **derived from: "That they may hear,"** as the verse has already taught the basic principle that anyone who cannot learn is not obligated in the mitzva of assembly. **Rather,** the verse **is certainly** to be read as: **"That they may teach,"** which indicates that although a mute is able to learn himself, and therefore he is not exempted by the previous verse, he is nevertheless exempt because he is unable to teach others.

אָמַר רַבִּי תַּנְחוּם: חֵרֵשׁ בְּאׇזְנוֹ אַחַת פָּטוּר מִן הָרְאִיָּה, שֶׁנֶּאֱמַר: ״בְּאׇזְנֵיהֶם״.

Rabbi Tanḥum said: One who is deaf in one ear[H] **is exempt from** the mitzva of **appearance** in the Temple, **as it is stated** with regard to the mitzva of assembly: "When all Israel comes to appear before the Lord your God in the place that He shall choose, you shall read this law before all Israel **in their ears**" (Deuteronomy 31:11).[N] This verse indicates that the obligation of assembly applies only to those who can hear with both ears. Since the two mitzvot are connected by verbal analogy, as explained above, this *halakha* applies to the mitzva of appearance as well.

וְהַאי ״בְּאׇזְנֵיהֶם״ מִבְּעֵי לֵיהּ: בְּאׇזְנֵיהֶם דְּכוּלְּהוּ יִשְׂרָאֵל! הַהוּא מִ״נֶּגֶד כׇּל יִשְׂרָאֵל״ נָפְקָא. אִי מִ״נֶּגֶד כׇּל יִשְׂרָאֵל״ הֲוָה אָמֵינָא: אַף עַל גַּב דְּלָא שָׁמְעִי, כְּתַב רַחֲמָנָא ״בְּאׇזְנֵיהֶם״ – וְהוּא דְּשָׁמְעִי!

The Gemara asks: **But this** phrase: **"In their ears," is necessary** to teach that the reading of the Torah at the assembly must enter **the ears of the entire Jewish people.** Consequently, it cannot serve as the source of the *halakha* concerning one who is deaf in one ear. The Gemara answers: **That** *halakha*, that the reading of the Torah must be heard by the entire Jewish people, **is derived from** the phrase: **"Before all Israel"** (Deuteronomy 31:11). The Gemara asks: **If** that *halakha* were derived **from: "Before all Israel," I would say** that the mitzva applies **even though they cannot hear;** therefore, **the Merciful One writes: "In their ears," and that** indicates that **they** must be able to **hear.** If so, this phrase is not available for deriving the *halakha* of someone who is deaf in one ear.

הַהוּא מִ״לְמַעַן יִשְׁמְעוּ״ נָפְקָא.

The Gemara answers: **That** *halakha*, that the people must hear, **is derived from: "That they may hear"** (Deuteronomy 31:12).[N] Therefore, the phrase: "In their ears," is not required for that purpose. Rather, it teaches that only those who can hear with both ears are obligated in the mitzva of assembly, and by extension, in the mitzva of appearance as well.

אָמַר רַבִּי תַּנְחוּם: חִיגֵּר בְּרַגְלוֹ אַחַת – פָּטוּר מִן הָרְאִיָּה, שֶׁנֶּאֱמַר: ״רְגָלִים״.

Rabbi Tanḥum said: One who is lame in one leg[H] **is exempt from** the mitzva of **appearance, as it is stated:** "Three **times** [***regalim***][N] shall you keep a feast for Me in the year" (Exodus 23:14). Since the term for feet is *raglayim*, it can be inferred from here that the obligation to ascend involves the use of both of one's legs.

וְהָא ״רְגָלִים״ מִבְּעֵי לֵיהּ פְּרָט לְבַעֲלֵי קַבַּיִין! הַהוּא מִ״פְּעָמִים״ נָפְקָא. דְּתַנְיָא: ״פְּעָמִים״, אֵין פְּעָמִים אֶלָּא רְגָלִים. וְכֵן הוּא אוֹמֵר: ״תִּרְמְסֶנָּה רָגֶל רַגְלֵי עָנִי פַּעֲמֵי דַלִּים״ וְאוֹמֵר: ״מַה יָּפוּ פְעָמַיִךְ בַּנְּעָלִים בַּת נָדִיב״.

The Gemara asks: **But** the term **"*regalim*" is necessary** to **exclude people with artificial legs.**[N] Although these people are capable of walking, as they do not have two natural legs they are exempt from ascending to the Temple. The Gemara responds: **That** *halakha* is **derived from:** "Three **occasions** [***pe'amim***] in the year all your males will appear before the Lord God" (Exodus 23:17). The term *pe'amim* can also mean legs, **as it is taught** in a *baraita*, with regard to the term **"*pe'amim*": *Pe'amim* means nothing other than legs. And so it says: "The foot shall tread it down, even the feet of the poor and the steps [*pa'amei*] of the needy"** (Isaiah 26:6), **and it says: "How beautiful are your feet [*fe'amayikh*]**[N] **in sandals, daughter of the prince"** (Song of Songs 7:2).

NOTES

As it is stated, In their ears – שֶׁנֶּאֱמַר בְּאׇזְנֵיהֶם: The Gemara here derives the *halakha* from the fact that the Torah uses the plural form: Ears. *Tosafot* cite the Jerusalem Talmud, which also asks whether an individual who is deaf in one ear is obligated in the mitzva of appearance. According to the Jerusalem Talmud the answer depends upon the correct interpretation of the Torah's use of the plural in general. For example, the Torah states: "And for Aaron's sons you shall make tunics" (Exodus 28:40). One opinion is that this means two tunics for each son. Others claim that it can mean even one tunic for each son. The question here is the same: Is it necessary for each person to be able to hear in both ears, or is it enough if he has one good ear?

That is derived from, That they may hear – הַהוּא מִלְּמַעַן יִשְׁמְעוּ נָפְקָא: This version of the text reflects the opinion that the derivation is from the phrase: "That they may hear," i.e., it must be a complete hearing with two ears (Rambam).

As it is stated, times [*regalim*] – שֶׁנֶּאֱמַר רְגָלִים: The commentaries explain that the *halakha* that a lame person is exempt from the mitzva of appearance is derived from the use of the term: "times" [*regalim*], which alludes to legs [*raglayim*]. Since the Torah uses the synonymous term "occasions" [*pe'amim*] elsewhere (e.g., Exodus 34:23), the specific use of *regalim* indicates that one must be able to ascend to the Temple by foot (Rambam).

To exclude people with artificial legs – פְּרָט לְבַעֲלֵי קַבַּיִין: According to this opinion, anyone with a permanent blemish, i.e., one who does not have any legs at all, is exempt from the mitzva of appearance, whereas a lame person is obligated in this mitzva (*Turei Aven*).

And it says, How beautiful are your feet [*fe'amayikh*] – וְאוֹמֵר מַה יָּפוּ פְעָמַיִךְ: It can be derived from this verse that the term *pe'amim*, which is from the same root as *fe'amayikh*, is a synonym for feet. Additionally, through the use of the word "sandals," this verse teaches that the term includes shoes as well. Consequently, anyone who is unable to put on shoes is not obligated in the mitzva of appearance (Rashi; see *Siaḥ Yitzḥak*).

HALAKHA

Deaf in one ear – חֵרֵשׁ בְּאׇזְנוֹ אַחַת: An individual who is deaf in one ear is exempt from the mitzva of appearance, in accordance with the opinion of Rabbi Tanḥum (Rambam *Sefer Korbanot*, *Hilkhot Ḥagiga* 2:1).

Lame in one leg – חִיגֵּר בְּרַגְלוֹ אַחַת: An individual who is lame in one leg is exempt from the mitzva of appearance, in accordance with the opinion of Rabbi Tanḥum (Rambam *Sefer Korbanot*, *Hilkhot Ḥagiga* 2:1).

דָּרַשׁ רָבָא: מַאי דִּכְתִיב "מַה יָּפוּ פְעָמַיִךְ בַּנְּעָלִים בַּת נָדִיב"? כַּמָּה נָאִין רַגְלֵיהֶן שֶׁל יִשְׂרָאֵל בְּשָׁעָה שֶׁעוֹלִין לָרֶגֶל. "בַּת נָדִיב" – בִּתּוֹ שֶׁל אַבְרָהָם אָבִינוּ שֶׁנִּקְרָא נָדִיב, שֶׁנֶּאֱמַר: "נְדִיבֵי עַמִּים נֶאֱסָפוּ עַם אֱלֹהֵי אַבְרָהָם". "אֱלֹהֵי אַבְרָהָם" וְלֹא אֱלֹהֵי יִצְחָק וְיַעֲקֹב? אֶלָּא: אֱלֹהֵי אַבְרָהָם שֶׁהָיָה תְּחִילָּה לַגֵּרִים.

With regard to the aforementioned verse, **Rava taught: What is** the meaning of that **which is written: "How beautiful**[N] **are your feet in sandals, daughter of the prince** [*nadiv*]**"? How pleasant are the feet** [*raglehen*] **of the Jewish people when they ascend** to Jerusalem **on the pilgrimage Festival** [*regel*]. **"Daughter of the prince":**[N] this is referring to **the daughter of Abraham our father who is called a prince, as it is stated: "The princes of the peoples are gathered together, the people of the God of Abraham"** (Psalms 47:10). The Gemara asks: Is God only **"the God of Abraham," and not the God of Isaac and Jacob? Rather,** the verse mentions **"the God of Abraham," as he was the first of the converts.**[N] Abraham was the first prince, as all converts who follow in his path are called "the princes of the peoples."

אָמַר רַב כָּהֲנָא, דָּרַשׁ רַב נָתָן בַּר מַנְיוֹמִי מִשּׁוּם רַבִּי תַּנְחוּם: מַאי דִּכְתִיב "וְהַבּוֹר רֵק אֵין בּוֹ מָיִם". מִמַּשְׁמַע שֶׁנֶּאֱמַר "וְהַבּוֹר רֵק" אֵינִי יוֹדֵעַ שֶׁאֵין בּוֹ מָיִם? אֶלָּא: מַיִם אֵין בּוֹ, אֲבָל נְחָשִׁים וְעַקְרַבִּים – יֵשׁ בּוֹ.

The Gemara cites another statement of Rabbi Tanḥum. **Rav Kahana said** that **Rabbi Natan bar Manyumi taught in the name of Rabbi Tanḥum: What is** the meaning of **that which is written** with regard to Joseph: "And they took him, and cast him into the pit; **and the pit was empty, there was no water in it"** (Genesis 37:24). **By inference from that which is stated: "And the pit was empty," don't I know that there was no water in it? Rather,** this teaches that **there was no water in it, but there were snakes and scorpions**[N] **in it.**

תָּנוּ רַבָּנַן: מַעֲשֶׂה בְּרַבִּי יוֹחָנָן בֶּן בְּרוֹקָה וְרַבִּי אֶלְעָזָר בֶּן חִסְמָא שֶׁהָלְכוּ לְהַקְבִּיל פְּנֵי רַבִּי יְהוֹשֻׁעַ בִּפְקִיעִין. אָמַר לָהֶם: מַה חִידּוּשׁ הָיָה בְּבֵית הַמִּדְרָשׁ הַיּוֹם? אָמְרוּ לוֹ: תַּלְמִידֶיךָ אָנוּ, וּמֵימֶיךָ אָנוּ שׁוֹתִין. אָמַר לָהֶם: אַף עַל פִּי כֵן, אִי אֶפְשָׁר לְבֵית הַמִּדְרָשׁ בְּלֹא חִידּוּשׁ.

§ **The Sages taught:** There was **an incident involving Rabbi Yoḥanan ben Beroka and Rabbi Elazar ben Ḥisma, when they went to greet Rabbi Yehoshua in Peki'in.** Rabbi Yehoshua **said to them: What novel** idea was taught **today in the study hall? They said to him: We are your students**[N] **and we drink** from **your water,** i.e., all of our Torah knowledge comes from you, and therefore how can we tell you something you have not already learned? **He said to them: Even so, there cannot be a study hall without a novelty.**

שַׁבָּת שֶׁל מִי הָיְתָה? שַׁבָּת שֶׁל רַבִּי אֶלְעָזָר בֶּן עֲזַרְיָה הָיְתָה. וּבַמֶּה הָיְתָה הַגָּדָה הַיּוֹם? אָמְרוּ לוֹ: בְּפָרָשַׁת הַקְהֵל. וּמַה דָּרַשׁ בָּהּ?

He asked them: **Whose week was it,** i.e. who was the lecturer this week? They said to him: **It was Rabbi Elazar ben Azarya's**[P] **week.** He inquired: **And on what** subject **was the lecture today? They said to him:** He spoke **about the portion of** the mitzva of **assembly.** Rabbi Yehoshua persisted: **And what** verse **did he interpret homiletically with regard to** this mitzva?

"הַקְהֵל אֶת הָעָם הָאֲנָשִׁים וְהַנָּשִׁים וְהַטַּף" אִם אֲנָשִׁים בָּאִים לִלְמוֹד, נָשִׁים בָּאוֹת לִשְׁמוֹעַ, טַף לָמָּה בָּאִין? כְּדֵי לִיתֵּן שָׂכָר לִמְבִיאֵיהֶן. אָמַר לָהֶם: מַרְגָּלִית טוֹבָה הָיְתָה בְּיֶדְכֶם וּבִקַּשְׁתֶּם לְאַבְּדָהּ מִמֶּנִּי!

They said to him that Rabbi Elazar ben Azarya interpreted the following verse: **"Assemble the people, the men and the women and the little ones"** (Deuteronomy 31:12). This verse is puzzling: **If men come to learn,** and **women,** who might not understand, **come** at least **to hear, why do the little ones come?** They come **in order** for God **to give a reward to those who bring them,**[N] i.e., God credits those who bring their children to the assembly. Rabbi Yehoshua **said to them:** This **good pearl** of wisdom **was in your hands, and you tried to conceal it from me?**

וְעוֹד דָּרַשׁ: "אֶת ה' הֶאֱמַרְתָּ הַיּוֹם וַה' הֶאֱמִירְךָ הַיּוֹם" –

Upon seeing that Rabbi Yehoshua was pleased to hear this idea, Rabbi Yoḥanan ben Beroka and Rabbi Elazar ben Ḥisma said to him: **Additionally,** Rabbi Elazar **interpreted** the following verses **homiletically: "You have affirmed, this day,** that **the Lord** is your God, and that you will walk in His ways and keep His statutes, His mitzvot, and His ordinances, and listen to His voice. **And the Lord has affirmed you, this day,** to be His treasure, as He promised you, and that you should keep all His mitzvot" (Deuteronomy 26:17–18).

אָמַר לָהֶם הַקָּדוֹשׁ בָּרוּךְ הוּא לְיִשְׂרָאֵל: אַתֶּם עֲשִׂיתוּנִי חֲטִיבָה אַחַת בָּעוֹלָם, וַאֲנִי אֶעֱשֶׂה אֶתְכֶם חֲטִיבָה אַחַת בָּעוֹלָם. אַתֶּם עֲשִׂיתוּנִי חֲטִיבָה אַחַת בָּעוֹלָם דִּכְתִיב: "שְׁמַע יִשְׂרָאֵל ה' אֱלֹהֵינוּ ה' אֶחָד", וַאֲנִי אֶעֱשֶׂה אֶתְכֶם חֲטִיבָה אַחַת בָּעוֹלָם, שֶׁנֶּאֱמַר:

Rabbi Elazar explained: **The Holy One, Blessed be He, said to the Jewish people: You have made Me a single entity in the world,** as you singled Me out as separate and unique. **And** therefore **I will make you a single entity**[N] **in the world,** as you will be a treasured nation, chosen by God. **You have made Me a single entity in the world, as it is written: "Hear, O Israel, the Lord our God, the Lord is One"** (Deuteronomy 6:4). **And** therefore **I will make you a single entity in the world, as it is stated:**

NOTES

Rava taught…how beautiful – דָּרַשׁ רָבָא...מַה יָּפוּ: A similar interpretation appears in the Aramaic translation of Song of Songs: How pleasant are the feet of Israel when they ascend to appear before God three times a year. According to some versions of the text, the derivation is based on the term "sandals" [*ne'alim*], which is similar to the term for ascending [*aliya*].

Daughter of the prince [*nadiv*] – בַּת נָדִיב: The connection to Abraham is that just as Abraham gave of himself [*nitnadev*] to ascend to Eretz Yisrael, the pilgrims on a Festival likewise make great efforts to reach Jerusalem (Riaf).

As he was the first of the converts – שֶׁהָיָה תְּחִילָּה לַגֵּרִים: The commentaries explain that Abraham was the first convert, as he recognized the Creator on his own (*Tosafot*; *Petaḥ Einayim*). The Sages also teach that he fulfilled all the mitzvot of the Torah even before it was given on Mount Sinai. Furthermore, Abraham started the unique existence of the Jewish people as a distinct group, which no longer belonged to the children of Noah (*Turei Aven*).

But there were snakes and scorpions, etc. – אֲבָל נְחָשִׁים וְעַקְרַבִּים וכו׳: The phrase: "And the pit was empty," indicates that it was entirely empty, and therefore when the verse adds: "There was no water in it," it teaches that the pit was actually lacking only water but it was not completely empty (see Rabbi Eliyahu Mizraḥi and Maharsha). However, it remains unclear how it is derived from here that the pit contained snakes specifically. One suggestion is that a pit can be described as empty even if snakes and scorpions are present, as these creatures tend to hide in the holes and crevices of a pit. Therefore, when the verse emphasizes that the pit contained no water, this indicates that there were snakes inside (*Petaḥ Einayim*, citing Ari).

We are your students, etc. – תַּלְמִידֶיךָ אָנוּ וכו׳: Rabbi Yoḥanan ben Beroka and Rabbi Elazar ben Ḥisma emphasized both that they received the Torah knowledge they already have from Rabbi Yehoshua, and that they are continually learning more Torah from him (*Petaḥ Einayim*). Some explain their comment as follows: Although what we studied was a novelty for us, we are sure it would not be a novelty for our teacher (*Leḥem Shlomo*).

In order for God to give a reward to those who bring them – כְּדֵי לִיתֵּן שָׂכָר לִמְבִיאֵיהֶן: Some commentaries question the need for this statement, for if the adults are all obligated to come, who will watch the children at home? They explain that although the parents have no choice, nevertheless the act of bringing the children is a meritorious act deserving of its own reward (*Derashot Mahari Mintz*; Riaf).

A single entity, etc. – חֲטִיבָה אַחַת וכו׳: There are different explanations of this expression, each of which emphasizes a particular aspect of the relationship between God and the Jewish people. Some explain the phrase "has affirmed you" (Deuteronomy 26:18) in the sense of praise and glory (Rashi). Others say that "affirm" [*he'emir*] means to exalt and make great, like an *amir*, a treetop. Yet others associate it with the Arabic أمير, *'amīr*, a leader (Rav Se'adya Gaon). Some maintain that the phrase: A single entity, refers to something for which there is no similar model in the world (Rav Hai Gaon). Alternatively, the statement means: You prepared for Me a portion in this world and I will prepare for you a portion in the World-to-Come (*Arukh*; Maharsha).

״וּמִי כְּעַמְּךָ יִשְׂרָאֵל גּוֹי אֶחָד בָּאָרֶץ״.

"And who is like Your people, Israel, one nation in the land?" (I Chronicles 17:21).

וְאַף הוּא פָּתַח וְדָרַשׁ: ״דִּבְרֵי חֲכָמִים כַּדָּרְבֹנוֹת וּכְמַשְׂמְרוֹת נְטוּעִים בַּעֲלֵי אֲסֻפּוֹת נִתְּנוּ מֵרוֹעֶה אֶחָד״. לָמָּה נִמְשְׁלוּ דִּבְרֵי תוֹרָה לְדָרְבָן? לוֹמַר לָךְ: מַה דָּרְבָן זֶה מְכַוֵּין אֶת הַפָּרָה לְתַלְמֶיהָ לְהוֹצִיא חַיִּים לָעוֹלָם, אַף דִּבְרֵי תוֹרָה מְכַוְּונִין אֶת לוֹמְדֵיהֶן מִדַּרְכֵי מִיתָה לְדַרְכֵי חַיִּים. אִי מַה דָּרְבָן זֶה מִטַּלְטֵל אַף דִּבְרֵי תוֹרָה מִטַּלְטְלִין – תַּלְמוּד לוֹמַר: ״מַשְׂמְרוֹת״.

The Gemara adds: **And** Rabbi Elazar ben Azarya **also commenced**[N] his lecture **and taught:** It is written: **"The words of the wise are as goads, and as nails well fastened are those that are composed in collections; they are given from one shepherd"** (Ecclesiastes 12:11). **Why are matters of Torah compared to a goad? To tell you** that **just as this goad directs the cow to her furrow to bring forth** sustenance for **life to the world, so too the words of Torah direct those who study them from the paths of death to the paths of life.** The Gemara asks: **If so,** derive the following from that same analogy: **Just as this goad is movable** and not rigid, **so too matters of Torah are movable** in accordance with circumstance and are not permanent. Therefore, **the verse states: "Nails,"** which are permanent.

אִי מַה מַּסְמֵר זֶה חָסֵר וְלֹא יָתֵר, אַף דִּבְרֵי תוֹרָה חֲסֵירִין וְלֹא יְתֵירִין – תַּלְמוּד לוֹמַר: ״נְטוּעִים״, מַה נְּטִיעָה זוֹ פָּרָה וְרָבָה – אַף דִּבְרֵי תוֹרָה פָּרִין וְרָבִין. ״בַּעֲלֵי אֲסֻפּוֹת״ – אֵלּוּ תַּלְמִידֵי חֲכָמִים שֶׁיּוֹשְׁבִין אֲסוּפּוֹת אֲסוּפּוֹת וְעוֹסְקִין בַּתּוֹרָה, הַלָּלוּ מְטַמְּאִין וְהַלָּלוּ מְטַהֲרִין, הַלָּלוּ אוֹסְרִין וְהַלָּלוּ מַתִּירִין, הַלָּלוּ פּוֹסְלִין וְהַלָּלוּ מַכְשִׁירִין.

The Gemara further asks: **If so,** one can explain as follows: **Just as this nail is diminished**[N] in size **and does not expand,** as it wastes away over time, **so too matters of Torah are** gradually **diminished and do not expand.** Therefore, **the verse states: "Well fastened [*netuim*]." Just as this plant [*neti'a*] flourishes and multiplies, so too matters of Torah flourish and multiply. "Those that are composed in collections [*ba'alei asufot*]": These are Torah scholars who sit in many groups [*asupot*] and engage in Torah** study. There are often debates among these groups, as some of **these** Sages **render** an object or person **ritually impure and these render it pure; these prohibit** an action **and these permit** it; **these deem** an item **invalid and these deem it valid.**

שֶׁמָּא יֹאמַר אָדָם: הֵיאָךְ אֲנִי לָמֵד תּוֹרָה מֵעַתָּה? תַּלְמוּד לוֹמַר: כּוּלָּם ״נִתְּנוּ מֵרוֹעֶה אֶחָד״ – אֵל אֶחָד נְתָנָן, פַּרְנָס אֶחָד אֲמָרָן, מִפִּי אֲדוֹן כָּל הַמַּעֲשִׂים בָּרוּךְ הוּא, דִּכְתִיב: ״וַיְדַבֵּר אֱלֹהִים אֵת כָּל הַדְּבָרִים הָאֵלֶּה״.

Lest a person say: Now, how can I study Torah when it contains so many different opinions? **The verse states** that **they are all "given from one shepherd."**[N] **One God gave them; one leader,** i.e., Moses, **said them from the mouth of the Master of all creation, Blessed be He, as it is written: "And God spoke all these words"** (Exodus 20:1). The plural form "words" indicates that God transmitted all the interpretations of the Ten Commandments. Since the Sages invariably utilize the Torah itself or the statements of the prophets as the sources for their opinions, there is a certain unity to the study of Torah, despite the numerous explanations and applications.

אַף אַתָּה עֲשֵׂה אָזְנֶיךָ כַּאֲפַרְכֶּסֶת, וּקְנֵה לְךָ לֵב מֵבִין לִשְׁמוֹעַ אֶת דִּבְרֵי מְטַמְּאִים וְאֶת דִּבְרֵי מְטַהֲרִים, אֶת דִּבְרֵי אוֹסְרִין וְאֶת דִּבְרֵי מַתִּירִין, אֶת דִּבְרֵי פּוֹסְלִין וְאֶת דִּבְרֵי מַכְשִׁירִין. בַּלָּשׁוֹן הַזֶּה אָמַר לָהֶם: אֵין דּוֹר יָתוֹם שֶׁרַבִּי אֶלְעָזָר בֶּן עֲזַרְיָה שָׁרוּי בְּתוֹכוֹ.

So too you, the student, **make your ears like a funnel**[B] **and acquire for yourself an understanding heart to hear** both **the statements of** those **who render** objects **ritually impure and the statements of** those **who render** them **pure; the statements of** those **who prohibit** actions **and the statements of** those **who permit** them; **the statements of** those **who deem** items **invalid and the statements of** those **who deem** them **valid.** When Rabbi Yehoshua heard these interpretations, **he said to them in these words: No generation** is considered **orphaned,** i.e. without a leader, **if Rabbi Elazar ben Azarya dwells among it.**

וְלֵימְרוּ לֵיהּ בְּהֶדְיָא? מִשּׁוּם מַעֲשֶׂה שֶׁהָיָה. דְּתַנְיָא: מַעֲשֶׂה בְּרַבִּי יוֹסֵי בֶּן דּוּרְמַסְקִית שֶׁהָלַךְ לְהַקְבִּיל פְּנֵי רַבִּי (אֶלְעָזָר) אֱלִיעֶזֶר בְּלוֹד. אָמַר לוֹ: מַה חִידּוּשׁ הָיָה בְּבֵית הַמִּדְרָשׁ הַיּוֹם?

The Gemara asks: **But** Rabbi Yoḥanan ben Beroka and Rabbi Elazar ben Ḥisma **should have told** Rabbi Yehoshua these statements of Rabbi Elazar ben Azarya **directly,** without delay. Why did they hesitate at first? The Gemara answers: They were hesitant **due to an incident that occurred. As it is taught** in a *baraita*: There was **an incident involving Rabbi Yosei ben Durmaskit, who went to greet Rabbi Eliezer in Lod.** Rabbi Elazar **said to him: What novel** idea **was taught today in the study hall?**

NOTES

And he also commenced – וְאַף הוּא פָּתַח: Some explain that this refers to Rabbi Yehoshua, who added a statement of his own (Maharsha). Many commentaries note that the parallel versions of the text indicate otherwise.

Just as this nail is diminished – מַה מַּסְמֵר זֶה חָסֵר: Rashi explains, perhaps based on a variant text, that the nail diminishes objects, i.e., it pierces and removes matter from the place where it is inserted (see Maharsha). Some explain that the size of the nail itself decreases when it is nailed into the wall (*Anaf Yosef*).

They are all given from one shepherd – כּוּלָּם נִתְּנוּ מֵרוֹעֶה אֶחָד: The notion that all opinions in a dispute involving Torah are of value is also taught in the well-known saying: Both these and those are the words of the living God. This idea is dealt with at length and in depth by the early and later authorities (see *Akedat Yitzḥak*). Many explain that the Torah was transmitted with numerous different, yet legitimate, interpretations, each of which possesses an element of truth. Although the Sages must issue practical halakhic decisions, this does not negate the truth of the opinions that are not accepted (see *Otzar HaKavod*; *Be'er HaGola*).

BACKGROUND

Make your ears like a funnel – עֲשֵׂה אָזְנֶיךָ כַּאֲפַרְכֶּסֶת:

Ancient Roman funnel

אָמַר לֵיהּ, נִמְנוּ וְגָמְרוּ: עַמּוֹן וּמוֹאָב מְעַשְּׂרִין מַעְשַׂר עָנִי בַּשְּׁבִיעִית.

Rabbi Yosei ben Durmaskit **said to him:** The Sages assembled, **counted** the votes, **and concluded** that although the lands of **Ammon and Moab**[B] on the eastern side of the Jordan River are not part of Eretz Yisrael, and therefore the *halakhot* of the Sabbatical Year and tithes should not apply to them, as these lands are adjacent to Eretz Yisrael, **one separates the poor man's tithe**[BNH] there **in the Sabbatical Year.**[B] Since the Sages debated which tithes should be separated, they had to take a vote to determine the *halakha* in this regard.

אָמַר לוֹ: יוֹסֵי! פְּשׁוֹט יָדֶיךָ וְקַבֵּל עֵינֶיךָ. פָּשַׁט יָדָיו וְקִבֵּל עֵינָיו. בָּכָה רַבִּי אֱלִיעֶזֶר וְאָמַר: ״סוֹד ה׳ לִירֵאָיו וּבְרִיתוֹ לְהוֹדִיעָם״.

Rabbi Elazar **said to him** in anger: **Yosei, extend your hands and catch your eyes,**[N] which are about to come out of their sockets. **He extended his hands and caught his eyes. Rabbi Elazar wept**[N] **and said** the verse: **"The counsel of the Lord is with them who fear Him; and His covenant, to make them know it"** (Psalms 25:14), i.e., the Sages arrived at the correct conclusion, although they were unaware of the proper rationale behind it.

אָמַר לוֹ: לֵךְ אֱמוֹר לָהֶם: אַל תָּחוּשׁוּ לְמִנְיַינְכֶם. כָּךְ מְקוּבְּלַנִי מֵרַבָּן יוֹחָנָן בֶּן זַכַּאי, שֶׁשָּׁמַע מֵרַבּוֹ, וְרַבּוֹ מֵרַבּוֹ: הִלְכְתָא לְמֹשֶׁה מִסִּינַי, עַמּוֹן וּמוֹאָב מְעַשְּׂרִין מַעְשַׂר עָנִי בַּשְּׁבִיעִית. מַה טַּעַם? הַרְבֵּה כְּרַכִּים כָּבְשׁוּ עוֹלֵי מִצְרַיִם וְלֹא כְּבָשׁוּם עוֹלֵי בָבֶל,

Rabbi Elazar **said to** Rabbi Yosei to **go** and **say to** the Sages in the study hall: **Do not be concerned** with regard **to your counting,** that you might not have ruled properly, as you have not in fact instituted a new ordinance at all. **This is** the tradition that **I received from Rabban Yoḥanan ben Zakkai, who heard from his teacher, and his teacher from his teacher:** It is a ***halakha*** transmitted **to Moses from Sinai**[N] that in **Ammon and Moab one separates the poor man's tithe in the Sabbatical Year. What is the reason? Those who ascended from Egypt conquered many cities,**[N] **and those who ascended from Babylonia did not conquer them** after the destruction of the First Temple.

BACKGROUND

Ammon and Moab – עַמּוֹן וּמוֹאָב:

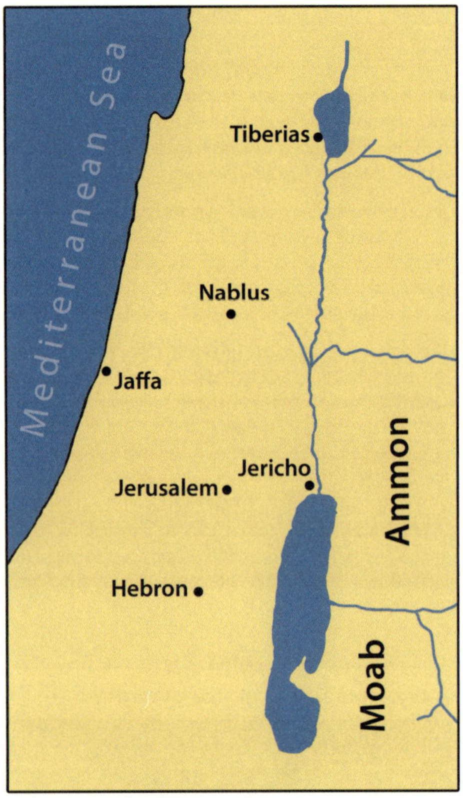

Location of Ammon and Moab

Poor man's tithe – מַעְשַׂר עָנִי: The poor man's tithe is a special tithe set aside from agricultural produce and distributed to the poor. During the third and sixth years of the Sabbatical cycle, after the priests' share of the produce and the first tithe have been set aside, one-tenth of the remaining produce is distributed to the poor. During the other years of the Sabbatical cycle, the second tithe is set aside instead of the poor man's tithe. Although the poor man's tithe is not sanctified, until it has been set aside the produce is deemed *tevel*, untithed produce, and may not be eaten. The poor man's tithe is separated from doubtfully tithed produce but it is not given to the poor, as the principle that the burden of proof rests upon the claimant applies to this case. In other words, a poor person who lays claim to the poor man's tithe has to prove that the tithe had not already been separated from this produce.

The Sabbatical Year – שְׁבִיעִית: The seventh year is the last year of the Sabbatical cycle. The first of these cycles began after the conquest of Canaan by Joshua. It is also known as *shemitta*, literally, abandonment, or release. The *halakhot* of the Sabbatical Year are based on Torah law (Leviticus 25:1–7; Deuteronomy 15:1–6); however, most authorities maintain that the conditions for the applicability of this Torah mitzva have lapsed, and its present-day observance is based on rabbinic decree. During the Sabbatical Year all agricultural land in Eretz Yisrael must be left to lie fallow. It is prohibited to work the land, except for what is necessary to keep existing crops alive. All produce that does grow is ownerless and must be left unguarded in the fields for ready access to any creature, including wild animals and birds. As long as produce can still be found in the fields it may be eaten, although it may not be bought and sold in the normal manner or used for purposes other than food. By rabbinic decree it is prohibited to consume produce that grew from seeds during the Sabbatical Year, even if it grew by itself. According to some authorities, this prohibition applies by Torah law.

HALAKHA

In Ammon and Moab one separates the poor man's tithe – עַמּוֹן וּמוֹאָב מְעַשְּׂרִין מַעְשַׂר עָנִי: It is a *halakha* transmitted to Moses from Sinai that one must separate the poor man's tithe during the Sabbatical Year in the lands of Ammon and Moab (Rambam *Sefer Zera'im*, *Hilkhot Mattenot Aniyyim* 6:5).

NOTES

In Ammon and Moab one separates the poor man's tithe – עַמּוֹן וּמוֹאָב מְעַשְּׂרִין מַעְשַׂר עָנִי: This *halakha* is extensively debated by the early authorities, as it was prohibited for the Jewish people to conquer the lands of Ammon and Moab. How then could it be considered that these lands might possess the sanctity of Eretz Yisrael? The commentaries suggest that this refers to the lands of Sihon, king of the Emorites, and of Og, king of the Bashan, who conquered parts of Ammon and Moab. At that point, as these lands were under the control of another nation, it became permitted for the Jewish people to conquer them (Rabbeinu Tam in *Tosafot*). However, those areas were never sanctified, as although the land of Sihon is in the territory of the Emorites, which is part of the inheritance of the Jewish people, the lands of Ammon and Moab are called: "The Kinite, the Kenizzite, and the Kadmonite" (Genesis 15:19), which will be inherited by the Jewish people only in the future age of the ultimate redemption. See the *Kesef Mishne*, as well as other commentaries on the Rambam, with regard to the Rambam's opinion in this regard.

Extend your hands and catch your eyes – פְּשׁוֹט יָדֶיךָ וְקַבֵּל עֵינֶיךָ: Rashi says that Rabbi Elazar was angered that they attributed this *halakha* to the Sages of Yavne. Others likewise explain that he was annoyed that the Sages assembled a majority and voted, a move he felt was unnecessary seeing that it is a *halakha* transmitted to Moses from Sinai (Rabbeinu Ḥananel). Conversely, others contend that Rabbi Elazar was angry because they did not preface their remarks with the formula: We are your students, etc., which he deemed disrespectful (Rabbeinu Shimshon of Saens; Maharsha). Yet others maintain that the quickness of the response upset him. Rabbi Yoḥanan ben Beroka and Rabbi Elazar ben Ḥisma learned from this incident that one must be extremely careful when addressing one's teacher (*Petaḥ Einayim*).

Rabbi Elazar wept – בָּכָה רַבִּי אֱלִיעֶזֶר: Some explain that Rabbi Elazar cried because he was unable to enter the study hall due to the fact that the Sages had excommunicated him. Had he been present, this issue would not have become the subject of dispute, as he had a clear tradition in this regard (*Petaḥ Einayim*, in the name of Rabbi Betzalel Ashkenazi; see Rambam's Commentary on the Mishna, *Yadayim* 4:3).

A *halakha* transmitted to Moses from Sinai – הִלְכְתָא לְמֹשֶׁה מִסִּינַי: Many commentaries explain that this is actually an ordinance enacted by the Sages, as this expression merely serves to convey the idea that the matter is as clear as a *halakha* transmitted to Moses from Sinai (Rabbeinu Shimshon of Saens; Rosh; and many later authorities). However, the *Tosefta* indicates that this is an actual *halakha* transmitted to Moses from Sinai (Rabbeinu Shimshon; Rambam).

What is the reason…many cities – מַה טַּעַם, הַרְבֵּה כְּרַכִּין: Some commentaries maintain that this statement was not issued by Rabbi Elazar himself; rather, it is an unattributed opinion in the Gemara (Rabbeinu Tam in *Sefer HaYashar*). In practice, the authorities differentiate between the *halakhot* of tithes in those parts of Eretz Yisrael that were conquered only by those who ascended from Egypt and not by those who returned from Babylonia, and the *halakhot* that apply on the eastern side of the Jordan River (see Rambam).

מִפְּנֵי שֶׁקְּדוּשָּׁה רִאשׁוֹנָה קִדְּשָׁה לִשְׁעָתָהּ וְלֹא קִדְּשָׁה לֶעָתִיד לָבֹא, וְהִנִּיחוּם כְּדֵי שֶׁיִּסְמְכוּ עֲלֵיהֶן עֲנִיִּים בִּשְׁבִיעִית.

This difference is important, **because the first consecration**[H] of Eretz Yisrael, by those who ascended from Egypt, caused **it** to be **sanctified** only **for its time and it** was **not sanctified forever,** as that depended on the renewed conquest of the land by the Jewish people. **And** those who ascended from Babylonia **left those** cities aside and did not consider them part of Eretz Yisrael even after Jewish settlement was renewed there. They would plow and harvest in these places in the Sabbatical Year and tithe the poor man's tithe, **so that the poor** of Eretz Yisrael, who did not have sufficient income from the previous years, **could rely upon** that produce **in the Sabbatical Year,** receiving help from this tithe.

תָּנָא: לְאַחַר שֶׁנִּתְיַישְּׁבָה דַּעְתּוֹ, אָמַר: יְהִי רָצוֹן שֶׁיַּחְזְרוּ עֵינֵי יוֹסֵי לִמְקוֹמָן. וְחָזְרוּ.

It was **taught** that **after** Rabbi Elazar's **mind was put at ease, he said: May it be** God's **will that Rabbi Yosei's eyes should return to their place. And** indeed his eyes **returned.** Due to this event, in which Rabbi Elazar responded harshly when his disciple related what he considered a novel idea, the students of Rabbi Yehoshua hesitated to recount what they had heard until their teacher encouraged them to do so.

תָּנוּ רַבָּנַן: אֵיזֶהוּ שׁוֹטֶה? הַיּוֹצֵא יְחִידִי בַּלַּיְלָה, וְהַלָּן בְּבֵית הַקְּבָרוֹת, וְהַמְקָרֵעַ אֶת כְּסוּתוֹ. אִיתְּמַר, רַב הוּנָא אָמַר: עַד שֶׁיְּהוּ כּוּלָּן בְּבַת אַחַת. רַבִּי יוֹחָנָן אָמַר: אֲפִילּוּ בְּאַחַת מֵהֶן.

§ **The Sages taught: Who is** considered **an imbecile?**[HN] **One who goes out alone at night, and one who sleeps in a cemetery, and one who rends his garment. It was stated** that **Rav Huna said:** One does not have the halakhic status of an imbecile **until there are all** of these signs present in him **at the same time. Rabbi Yoḥanan said:** He is considered an imbecile **even** due to the appearance **of one of** these signs.

הֵיכִי דָּמֵי? אִי דְּעָבֵיד לְהוּ דֶּרֶךְ שְׁטוּת – אֲפִילּוּ בַּחֲדָא נַמֵי. אִי דְּלָא עָבֵיד לְהוּ דֶּרֶךְ שְׁטוּת – אֲפִילּוּ כּוּלְּהוּ נַמֵי לָא!

The Gemara asks: **What are the circumstances** of the case under discussion? **If he performs them in a deranged manner,** then **even** the appearance **of one** sign should be enough to classify him as an imbecile. **If** he **does not perform these** actions **in a deranged manner,** but has a reason to act this way, then **even** if he performs **all of them** he should **not** be deemed an imbecile.

לְעוֹלָם דְּקָא עָבֵיד לְהוּ דֶּרֶךְ שְׁטוּת, וְהַלָּן בְּבֵית הַקְּבָרוֹת – אֵימוּר כְּדֵי שֶׁתִּשְׁרֶה עָלָיו רוּחַ טוּמְאָה הוּא דְּקָא עָבֵיד. וְהַיּוֹצֵא יְחִידִי בַּלַּיְלָה – אֵימוּר גַּנְדְּרִיפַּס אַחַדְיֵהּ. וְהַמְקָרֵעַ אֶת כְּסוּתוֹ – אֵימוּר בַּעַל מַחֲשָׁבוֹת הוּא. כֵּיוָן דַּעֲבַדִינְהוּ לְכוּלְּהוּ – הָוֵה לְהוּ

The Gemara answers: **Actually,** the *baraita* is referring to one **who performs these** actions **in a deranged manner, but** each action on its own could be explained rationally. With regard to **one who sleeps in the cemetery,** one could **say that he is doing** so **in order that an impure spirit should settle upon him.** Although it is inappropriate to do this, as there is a reason for this behavior it is not a sign of madness. **And** with regard to **one who goes out alone at night,** one could **say** that perhaps **a fever took hold of him** and he is trying to cool himself down. **And** as for **one who tears his garments,** one could **say** that **he is a man** engaged in **thought,** and out of anxiety he tears his clothing unintentionally. Despite these possible explanations, **since one performed all of these** together **they are** considered

---

HALAKHA

First and second consecrations – קְדוּשָּׁה רִאשׁוֹנָה וּשְׁנִיָּה: All the areas possessed by those who ascended from Egypt were endowed with the sanctity of Eretz Yisrael. When the Jews were exiled from Eretz Yisrael, that sanctity was nullified. Later, when those who ascended from Babylonia arrived and took possession of part of the land, it was endowed with a second, permanent sanctity. However, those places that were conquered only by those who ascended from Egypt were not exempted from tithes and *teruma* in the Sabbatical Year, so that the poor would have something to eat (Rambam *Sefer Zera'im, Hilkhot Mattenot Aniyyim* 6:5, *Hilkhot Terumot* 1:5).

Who is an imbecile – אֵיזֶהוּ שׁוֹטֶה: With regard to one who goes out alone at night, tears his garments, sleeps in the cemetery, or loses whatever he is given (Jerusalem Talmud; *Tosefta*), if he performs any one of these actions in a deranged manner he has the halakhic status of an imbecile, in accordance with the opinion of Rabbi Yoḥanan. However, this applies only if he regularly behaves in this manner. If not, he does not have the halakhic status of an imbecile even if performs the act in a deranged manner (*Shakh*, in the name of *Beit Yosef*). Similarly, one whose mind is consistently impaired in one aspect, even if he is otherwise coherent, is considered an imbecile (*Shulḥan Arukh, Yoreh De'a* 1:5 and *Ḥoshen Mishpat* 35:8).

NOTES

Who is an imbecile – אֵיזֶהוּ שׁוֹטֶה: An imbecile as discussed by the Sages is one who is mentally imbalanced either due to illness or from birth. Everyone agrees that the characteristics listed in the Gemara are not the exclusive signs of an imbecile (see *Or HaYashar*).

Perek **I**
Daf **4** Amud **a**

כְּמִי שֶׁנָּגַח שׁוֹר חֲמוֹר וְגָמָל, וְנַעֲשָׂה מוּעָד לַכֹּל. אָמַר רַב פָּפָּא: אִי שְׁמִיעַ לֵיהּ לְרַב הוּנָא הָא דְּתַנְיָא: אֵי זֶהוּ שׁוֹטֶה – זֶה הַמְאַבֵּד כׇּל מַה שֶּׁנּוֹתְנִים לוֹ, הֲוָה הָדַר בֵּיהּ.

like the actions of a forewarned ox **that gored an ox, a donkey, and a camel.** Since this ox gored three different animals on three separate occasions, it is considered predisposed to gore **and becomes forewarned for every** type of animal. Likewise, if someone performs three different deranged actions, it is assumed that there is no logical reason for his behavior and he is classified as an imbecile. **Rav Pappa said: If Rav Huna had heard that which is taught** in a *baraita*: **Who is an imbecile? This is one who destroys whatever is given to him, he would have retracted** his statement that one is an imbecile only if he performs three deranged actions.

HALAKHA

Mitzvot in which women are obligated – מִצְוֹת שֶׁהַנָּשִׁים חַיָּיבוֹת בָּהֶן: Women are obligated in all the negative mitzvot in the Torah, just like men, with the exception of the prohibitions: "You shall not round the corners of your heads, nor shall you mar the corners of your beard" (Leviticus 19:27) and the prohibition against priests becoming ritually impure by contact with a corpse. Women are exempt from all positive, time-bound mitzvot, except for *kiddush* on Shabbat, eating *matza* on the first night of Passover, slaughtering and eating the Paschal offering, the assembly, and rejoicing on the Festival (Rambam *Sefer HaMadda*, *Hilkhot Avoda Zara* 12:3).

A *tumtum* and a hermaphrodite with regard to the mitzva of appearance – טוּמְטוּם וְאַנְדְּרוֹגִינוֹס בִּרְאִיָּיה: A *tumtum* and an hermaphrodite are exempt from appearing in the Temple on a Festival (Rambam *Sefer Korbanot*, *Hilkhot Ḥagiga* 2:1).

אִיבַּעֲיָא לְהוּ: כִּי הֲוָה הָדַר בֵּיהּ – מִמְּקָרֵעַ כְּסוּתוֹ הוּא דַּהֲוָה הָדַר בֵּיהּ, דְּדָמְיָא לְהָא, אוֹ דִּלְמָא מִכּוּלְּהוּ הֲוָה הָדַר? תֵּיקוּ.

A dilemma was raised before the Sages with regard to Rav Pappa's statement: **When** Rav Pappa claims that Rav Huna **would have retracted** his statement, **would he have retracted** only **from** the case of **one who tears his garments, as** this person **is similar** to one who destroys whatever is given to him? **Or perhaps he would have retracted** his opinion with regard to **all of** the signs of an imbecile? The Gemara states that the dilemma **shall stand** unresolved, as no answer was found.

״וְטוּמְטוּם וְאַנְדְּרוֹגִינוֹס״ כו׳. תָּנוּ רַבָּנַן: ״זָכוּר״, לְהוֹצִיא אֶת הַנָּשִׁים; ״זְכוּרְךָ״, לְהוֹצִיא טוּמְטוּם וְאַנְדְּרוֹגִינוֹס; ״כָּל זְכוּרְךָ״ – לְרַבּוֹת אֶת הַקְּטַנִּים.

§ The mishna taught: **And a *tumtum* and a hermaphrodite** are exempt from the mitzva of appearance in the Temple. **The Sages taught,** with regard to the verse: "Three occasions in the year all your males will appear before the Lord God" (Exodus 23:17), had the verse simply said **"males,"** this would serve **to exclude women**[H] from this mitzva. By specifying **"your males,"**[N] it comes **to exclude a *tumtum* and a hermaphrodite**[H] as well. Furthermore, when the verse adds **"all your males,"** this serves **to include** male **minors.**

אָמַר מָר: ״זָכוּר״ – לְהוֹצִיא אֶת הַנָּשִׁים. הָא – לָמָּה לִי קְרָא? מִכְּדִי מִצְוַת עֲשֵׂה שֶׁהַזְּמַן גְּרָמָא הוּא, וְכָל מִצְוַת עֲשֵׂה שֶׁהַזְּמַן גְּרָמָא נָשִׁים פְּטוּרוֹת!

The Master said in the *baraita*: **"Males"** comes **to exclude women.** The Gemara asks: **Why do I** need **a verse** for **this** *halakha*? **After all,** the obligation of appearance on a Festival **is a positive, time-bound mitzva, and women are exempt from any positive, time-bound mitzva.**

אִצְטְרִיךְ; סָלְקָא דַּעְתָּךְ אָמִינָא: נֵילַף רְאִיָּיה רְאִיָּיה מֵהַקְהֵל; מַה לְּהַלָּן נָשִׁים חַיָּיבוֹת – אַף כָּאן נָשִׁים חַיָּיבוֹת. קָא מַשְׁמַע לָן.

The Gemara answers: This statement **was necessary,** as otherwise **it could enter your mind to say: Let us derive** by means of a verbal analogy between the term: **Appearance,** which appears here, and the term: **Appearance,** stated **with** regard to the mitzva of **assembly** (Deuteronomy 31:11), which is also a positive, time-bound mitzva. **Just as there, women are obligated** in the mitzva of assembly, **so too here, women are obligated** in the mitzva of appearance on the Festival. Therefore, the *baraita* **teaches us** that women are exempt.

אָמַר מָר: ״זְכוּרְךָ״ – לְהוֹצִיא טוּמְטוּם וְאַנְדְּרוֹגִינוֹס. בִּשְׁלָמָא אַנְדְּרוֹגִינוֹס – אִצְטְרִיךְ. סָלְקָא דַּעְתָּךְ אָמִינָא: הוֹאִיל וְאִית לֵיהּ צַד זַכְרוּת – לִיחַיֵּיב. קָא מַשְׁמַע לָן דִּבְרִיָּה בִּפְנֵי עַצְמוֹ הוּא.

The Master said in the *baraita*: **"Your males"** comes **to exclude a *tumtum* and a hermaphrodite.** The Gemara asks: **Granted,** the exclusion of **a hermaphrodite was necessary,** as **it could enter your mind to say** that **since he possesses an aspect of masculinity,** i.e., he has a male sexual organ, **he should be obligated** like a male. Therefore, the *baraita* **teaches us** that a hermaphrodite **is a being unto itself,** which is neither male nor female.

אֶלָּא טוּמְטוּם סְפֵיקָא הוּא, מִי אִצְטְרִיךְ קְרָא לְמַעוּטֵי סְפֵיקָא? אָמַר אַבַּיֵי: כְּשֶׁבֵּיצָיו מִבַּחוּץ.

However, as the status of **a *tumtum*,** who lacks external sexual organs, **is a** halakhic **uncertainty, is a verse necessary to exclude an uncertainty?**[N] **Abaye said:** It is referring to a case **when** the **testicles** of a *tumtum* **are on the outside,** although his penis is not visible. The verse teaches that this *tumtum* is not obligated in the mitzva of appearance, despite the fact that he is certainly male.

NOTES

Males…Your males – זָכוּר...זְכוּרְךָ: The term: "Males," serves to exclude women. The more restrictive phrase: "Your males," refers to those who are undoubtedly male, not those whose masculinity is uncertain. Therefore, the Sages interpreted the verse as excluding the *tumtum* and hermaphrodite (see *Zekher LaḤagiga*).

A verse necessary to exclude an uncertainty – אִצְטְרִיךְ קְרָא לְמַעוּטֵי סְפֵיקָא: This phrase, which appears in several places in the Talmud, is generally explained by Rashi as a question: Would the Torah exclude an uncertainty? Why would one think that a case of an uncertainty is prohibited or that one should rule stringently in this case, so that it would be necessary for the Torah to explicitly exclude it? Alternatively, there is no need to exclude a doubtful case, as an uncertainty results from a lack of knowledge. God clearly does not lack this knowledge, and therefore the Torah does not address cases of uncertainty (Rashi on *Ḥullin* 22b). In this regard the early authorities cite a fundamental halakhic discussion. There is a general principle that one rules stringently with regard to an uncertainty involving a Torah law. The commentaries dispute whether the principle itself is instituted by rabbinic law, whereas by Torah law every uncertainty is treated leniently (Rambam), or whether the *halakha* that an uncertainty involving Torah law is treated stringently is a principle imposed by Torah law (Rashba).

אָמַר מָר: ״כָּל זְכוּרְךָ״ – לְרַבּוֹת אֶת הַקְּטַנִּים. וְהָתְנַן: חוּץ מֵחֵרֵשׁ שׁוֹטֶה וְקָטָן! אָמַר אַבָּיֵי: לָא קַשְׁיָא; כָּאן – בְּקָטָן שֶׁהִגִּיעַ לְחִינּוּךְ, כָּאן – בְּקָטָן שֶׁלֹּא הִגִּיעַ לְחִינּוּךְ. קָטָן שֶׁהִגִּיעַ לְחִינּוּךְ דְּרַבָּנַן הִיא! אִין הָכִי נַמִּי, וּקְרָא אַסְמַכְתָּא בְּעָלְמָא.

The Master said in the *baraita*: **"All your males"** comes **to include minors.**[H] The Gemara asks: **Didn't we learn** in the mishna: All are obligated to appear, **except for a deaf-mute, an imbecile, and a minor? Abaye said:** This is **not difficult. Here,** the *baraita* that obligates minors is referring **to a minor who has reached** the age of **training** in mitzvot. **There,** the mishna is referring **to a minor who has not** yet **reached** the age of **training** in mitzvot, and therefore he is exempt from the mitzva of appearance. The Gemara asks: The obligation of **a minor who has reached** the age of **training is** one that applies **by rabbinic law.** How then can the *baraita* derive this *halakha* from a verse? The Gemara answers: **Yes, it is indeed so, and the verse is a mere support** for this rabbinic obligation.

וְאֶלָּא קְרָא לְמַאי אֲתָא? לְכִדְאַחֵרִים. דִּתְנַן, אֲחֵרִים אוֹמְרִים: הַמְקַמֵּץ, וְהַמְצָרֵף נְחֹשֶׁת, וְהַבּוּרְסִי – פְּטוּרִין מִן הָרְאִיָּיה, מִשּׁוּם שֶׁנֶּאֱמַר: ״כָּל זְכוּרְךָ״, מִי שֶׁיָּכוֹל לַעֲלוֹת עִם כָּל זְכוּרְךָ, יָצְאוּ אֵלּוּ שֶׁאֵינָן רְאוּיִין לַעֲלוֹת עִם כָּל זְכוּרְךָ.

The Gemara asks: **Rather, for what** purpose **does the verse:** "All your males," **come?** It comes to teach **that which *Aḥerim*** taught. **As it is taught** in a *baraita*: ***Aḥerim* say** that **a scrimper,** one who gathers dog feces to give them to tanners for the purpose of tanning hides; **and a melder**[HN] **of copper,** who purifies copper from dross; **and a tanner** of hides, **are** all **exempt from** the mitzva of **appearance,** as their occupation inflicts upon them a particularly unpleasant odor. This is **because it is stated: "All your males,"** which indicates that only **one who is able to ascend with all your males** is obligated, **excluding those who are not suited to ascend with all your males,** as people avoid their company.

״נָשִׁים וַעֲבָדִים שֶׁאֵינָן מְשׁוּחְרָרִים״ וכו׳. בִּשְׁלָמָא נָשִׁים – כְּדַאֲמַרַן; אֶלָּא עֲבָדִים מְנָלַן? אָמַר רַב הוּנָא, אָמַר קְרָא: ״אֶל פְּנֵי הָאָדוֹן ה׳״ – מִי שֶׁאֵין לוֹ אֶלָּא אָדוֹן אֶחָד, יָצָא זֶה שֶׁיֵּשׁ לוֹ אָדוֹן אַחֵר.

§ The mishna taught that **women and slaves who are not emancipated** are exempt from the mitzva of appearance. The Gemara asks: **Granted, women** are exempt, **as we said** earlier that this is derived from the phrase: "Your males." **However,** with regard to **slaves, from where do we** derive[N] that they are exempt? **Rav Huna said** that **the verse states: "Before the Lord God"** (Exodus 23:17). This indicates that **one who has** only **one Master** is obligated, which **excludes this** slave, **who has another master.**

הָא לָמָּה לִי קְרָא? מִכְּדִי, כָּל מִצְוָה שֶׁהָאִשָּׁה חַיֶּיבֶת בָּהּ – עֶבֶד חַיָּיב בָּהּ, כָּל מִצְוָה שֶׁאֵין הָאִשָּׁה חַיֶּיבֶת בָּהּ – אֵין הָעֶבֶד חַיָּיב בָּהּ, דְּגָמַר ״לָהּ״ ״לָהּ״ מֵאִשָּׁה!

The Gemara asks: **Why do I** need **a verse** to teach this *halakha*? **After all,** with regard to **every mitzva in which a woman is obligated, a slave is** also **obligated in that** mitzva; and with regard to **every mitzva in which a woman is not obligated, a slave is not obligated in it** either. The reason for this principle is **that it is derived** by means of a verbal analogy between the phrase: **"To her"** (Leviticus 19:20), written with regard to a designated maidservant, and the phrase: **"To her"** (Deuteronomy 24:3), written with regard **to** a divorced **woman.**[N]

אָמַר רָבִינָא: לֹא נִצְרְכָה אֶלָּא לְמִי שֶׁחֶצְיוֹ עֶבֶד וְחֶצְיוֹ בֶּן חוֹרִין. דַּיְקָא נַמִּי, דְּקָתָנֵי: נָשִׁים וַעֲבָדִים שֶׁאֵינָן מְשׁוּחְרָרִין. מַאי שֶׁאֵינָן מְשׁוּחְרָרִין? אִילֵימָא שֶׁאֵינָן מְשׁוּחְרָרִין כְּלָל – לִיתְנֵי עֲבָדִים סְתָמָא! אֶלָּא לָאו: שֶׁאֵינָן מְשׁוּחְרָרִין לְגַמְרֵי. וּמַאי נִינְהוּ? מִי שֶׁחֶצְיוֹ עֶבֶד וְחֶצְיוֹ בֶּן חוֹרִין. שְׁמַע מִינָּהּ.

Ravina said: This verse **is necessary only** to teach the exemption **of one who is half-slave half-freeman.** The Gemara notes that the language of the mishna **is also precise, as it teaches: Women and slaves who are not emancipated. What is** the purpose of specifying: **Who are not emancipated? If we say** that this means **that they are not emancipated at all, let it** simply **teach: Slaves, without** any further **description. Rather, is it not** the case **that** the mishna is referring to slaves **who are not entirely emancipated? And who are these** slaves? **One who is half-slave half-freeman.** The Gemara concludes: **Learn from this** that this is correct.

״וְהַחִיגֵּר וְהַסּוּמָא וְחוֹלֶה וְהַזָּקֵן״. תָּנוּ רַבָּנַן: ״רְגָלִים״ – פְּרָט לְבַעֲלֵי קַבַּיִן. דָּבָר אַחֵר: ״רְגָלִים״ – פְּרָט לְחִיגֵּר, וּלְחוֹלֶה, וּלְסוּמָא, וּלְזָקֵן, וּלְשֶׁאֵינוֹ יָכוֹל לַעֲלוֹת בְּרַגְלָיו. וְשֶׁאֵינוֹ יָכוֹל לַעֲלוֹת בְּרַגְלָיו לְאֵתוּיֵי מַאי? אָמַר רָבָא: לְאֵתוּיֵי

The mishna further taught: **And the lame, and the blind, and the sick, and the old** are all exempt from the mitzva of appearance. **The Sages taught: "Times [*regalim*]"** (Exodus 23:14) alludes to the use of one's feet [*raglayim*], and therefore it **excludes people with artificial legs.** Although they are able to walk, they are exempt from traveling, as they do not have feet. **Alternatively,** the term ***"regalim"*** comes to **exclude the lame, the sick, the blind, the old, and one who is unable to ascend on his** own **feet.**[H] The Gemara asks: The last category of **one who is unable to ascend on his feet,** comes **to add what?** The *baraita* already taught that the lame and the sick are exempt. **Rava said:** It comes **to add**

HALAKHA

A minor with regard to the mitzva of appearance – קָטָן בִּרְאִיָּיה: If a minor is able to hold his father's hand and ascend from Jerusalem to the Temple Mount, his father is obligated to bring him along to the Temple to train him in the observance of mitzvot (Rambam *Sefer Korbanot*, *Hilkhot Ḥagiga* 2:3).

A scrimper and a melder with regard to the mitzva of appearance – הַמְקַמֵּץ וְהַמְצָרֵף בִּרְאִיָּיה: The Rambam rules that a scrimper and a melder of copper, as well as other craftsmen who have a foul odor, must wash themselves and their clothes and ascend on the Festivals like the rest of the nation (*Sefer Korbanot*, *Hilkhot Ḥagiga* 2:2). There are two explanations as to why the Rambam's ruling does not contradict the *baraita* here, which explicitly states that all of these people are exempt from this obligation. First, the phrase: *Aḥerim* say, indicates that this is the opinion of an individual Sage, which is not accepted by the Rabbis, and the *halakha* is in accordance with the majority opinion (*Kesef Mishne*). Second, the ruling of *Aḥerim* applies only when these people are covered in filth. However, once they clean themselves they are considered like everyone else (*Kesef Mishne*; Rabbi Yosef Kurkus).

One who is unable to ascend on his feet – מִי שֶׁאֵינוֹ יָכוֹל לַעֲלוֹת בְּרַגְלָיו: One who is unable to ascend to the Temple by foot is not obligated in the mitzva of appearance. Consequently, the lame, the sick, the old, and the unusually delicate are all exempt, in accordance with the opinion of Rava (Rambam *Sefer Korbanot*, *Hilkhot Ḥagiga* 2:1).

NOTES

A scrimper and a melder – הַמְקַמֵּץ וְהַמְצָרֵף: The commentaries explain that these malodorous people are exempt from the mitzva of appearance not for the good of the general public but for their own honor. It would be insulting for them were they to ascend to the Temple with everyone keeping their distance from them. Consequently, they are exempt from this obligation (*ge'onim*).

Slaves, from where do we derive – עֲבָדִים מְנָלַן: Many commentaries note that this section of the discussion is apparently self-contradictory. At first the Gemara inquires into the source exempting slaves, which indicates that this source is necessary. Subsequently, the Gemara questions why this source is required, as the exemption can be derived from the case of women. Some explain that the phrase: "All your males," can be explained as referring to male slaves as well, and therefore one might have thought that in this case the *halakha* of slaves cannot be derived from that of women (*Mishḥat Aharon*; see the Jerusalem Talmud). Others explain that the question concerning the possible derivation of the exemption of slaves from the *halakha* of women is the continuation of the statement of Rav Huna. There are passages elsewhere in the Gemara that follow a similar structure (see *Petaḥ Einayim* for examples). Some commentaries cite yet another source for the exemption of slaves: "When all of Israel come" (Deuteronomy 31:11), as slaves are not considered part of the Jewish people (Rambam; Rabbi Ovadya MiBartenura).

It is derived by: To her, to her, with regard to a woman – גָּמַר ״לָהּ״ ״לָהּ״ מֵאִשָּׁה: Although the first "to her" is actually stated with regard to a maidservant, not a male slave, the derivation is still legitimate. This is because the verbal analogy is not required to exempt a maidservant from the mitzvot in which women are not obligated, as there is no reason to think that she should have a higher level of obligation than a Jewish woman. Alternatively, one might think that slaves should not be obligated in mitzvot at all, as they are neither Jews nor converts. Therefore, once it is derived by verbal analogy that maidservants have the same halakhic obligations as Jewish women, the same applies to male slaves as well (see *Turei Aven*).

NOTES

Delicate – מְפַנְּקֵי: Some explain that this refers to delicate people who are not used to walking barefoot. Since it is prohibited for one to enter the Temple while wearing shoes, which is considered trampling the sacred courtyards, he is exempt from ascending for the pilgrimage Festivals (Rashi). Alternatively, the term refers to those who are so frail they are not used to walking at all. Since they walk in a feeble manner, even were they to reach the Temple, their arrival would be deemed trampling on the sacred (Rambam; *Siaḥ Yitzḥak*).

The uncircumcised as the ritually impure – לְעָרֵל כְּטָמֵא: The Gemara indicates that the uncircumcised are exempt from the mitzva of appearance because the Torah equates them with the ritually impure concerning the prohibition against eating sacred meat. Some commentaries are puzzled by this claim, as there are several verses that explicitly state that the uncircumcised are prohibited from eating sacred food, e.g., the Paschal offering. If the explanation of the Gemara is accepted, these verses are superfluous, as this *halakha* can also be derived from that of the ritually impure. One answer is that there is a difference between one who willfully remains uncircumcised and someone uncircumcised for health reasons, who cannot be compared to a ritually impure person (*Tosafot*). Others maintain that the Gemara here is not referring to the prohibition against eating sacred meat at all. Rather, an uncircumcised man is considered repulsive, like the ritually impure, and therefore he too is kept at a distance (Rambam; see *Yevamot* 72b, *Nedarim* 31a).

When he reached this verse, will see, shall appear – כִּי מָטֵי לְהַאי קְרָא ״יִרְאֶה״ ״יֵרָאֶה״: The commentaries are perplexed by the mention of the derivation of: "Will see," "shall appear," in this context, as it is apparently irrelevant to the topic at hand. Indeed, certain versions of the text state only: "Will see." Some maintain that Rav Huna does not accept the idea that this verse comes to exclude one who does not have two eyes. Instead, he explains that just as God wants the Jewish people to ascend to see Him, so too He wants to see them (*Petaḥ Einayim*). Others state similarly that Rav Huna learns from this verse only that the Jewish people are beloved by God to such an extent that He wants to see them and to be seen by them (Maharsha).

HALAKHA

The uncircumcised and the ritually impure with regard to the mitzva of appearance – עָרֵל וְטָמֵא בִּרְאִיָּיה: The uncircumcised and the ritually impure are exempt from the mitzva of appearance, as stated in the *baraita* (Rambam *Sefer Korbanot*, *Hilkhot Ḥagiga* 2:1).

מְפַנְּקֵי, דִּכְתִיב: ״כִּי תָבֹאוּ לֵרָאוֹת פָּנָי מִי בִקֵּשׁ זֹאת מִיֶּדְכֶם רְמֹס חֲצֵרָי״.

a delicate[N] man, who cannot walk without shoes. **As it is written: "When you come to appear before Me, who has required this at your hand, to trample My courts?"** (Isaiah 1:12). Entering the Temple with shoes is described by the prophet as trampling, and therefore one who cannot enter barefoot is exempt from the mitzva of appearance.

תָּנָא: הֶעָרֵל וְהַטָּמֵא פְּטוּרִין מִן הָרְאִיָּיה. בִּשְׁלָמָא טָמֵא – דִּכְתִיב: ״וּבָאתָ שָׁמָּה״ ״וַהֲבֵאתֶם שָׁמָּה״, כֹּל שֶׁיֶּשְׁנוֹ בְּבִיאָה – יֶשְׁנוֹ בַּהֲבָאָה, וְכֹל שֶׁאֵינוֹ בְּבִיאָה – אֵינוֹ בַּהֲבָאָה.

It is **taught: The uncircumcised and the ritually impure are exempt from** the mitzva of **appearance.**[H] The Gemara comments: **Granted, a ritually impure** person is exempt, **as it is written: "And there you shall come"** (Deuteronomy 12:5), followed by: **"And there you shall bring"** (Deuteronomy 12:6). The juxtaposition of these verses teaches: **Anyone included in** the mitzva of **coming,** i.e., anyone who may enter the Temple, **is** also included **in** the obligation of **bringing** offerings; **and anyone not** included **in** the mitzva of **coming is not** included **in** the obligation of **bringing** either. Since it is prohibited for a person who is ritually impure to enter the Temple, he is also exempt from the obligation to bring a burnt-offering of appearance.

אֶלָּא עָרֵל מְנָלַן? הָא מַנִּי? רַבִּי עֲקִיבָא הִיא, דִּמְרַבֵּי לְעָרֵל כְּטָמֵא. דְּתַנְיָא, רַבִּי עֲקִיבָא אוֹמֵר: ״אִישׁ אִישׁ״ – לְרַבּוֹת אֶת הֶעָרֵל.

However, with regard to **the uncircumcised, from where do we** derive that he is exempt? The Gemara answers: In accordance with **whose** opinion **is this** *baraita*? **It is** in accordance with the opinion of **Rabbi Akiva, who amplifies** the *halakha* so **that the uncircumcised** is included in the same category **as the ritually impure.**[N] **As it is taught** in a *baraita*: **Rabbi Akiva says,** with regard to the verse: **"Any man** [*ish ish*] of the seed of Aaron that is a leper or has an issue; he shall not eat of the sacred things" (Leviticus 22:4), the double use of the term: "Ish," comes **to include the uncircumcised.** Like the ritually impure, the uncircumcised may neither eat sacrificial meat nor bring offerings to the Temple.

תָּנוּ רַבָּנַן: טָמֵא פָּטוּר מִן הָרְאִיָּיה, דִּכְתִיב: ״וּבָאתָ שָׁמָּה״ ״וַהֲבֵאתֶם שָׁמָּה״, כֹּל שֶׁיֶּשְׁנוֹ בְּבִיאָה – יֶשְׁנוֹ בַּהֲבָאָה, וְכֹל שֶׁאֵינוֹ בְּבִיאָה – אֵינוֹ בַּהֲבָאָה.

The Sages taught: A ritually impure person **is exempt from** the mitzva of **appearance, as it is written: "And there shall you come," "and there you shall bring." Anyone** included **in coming is** also **included in** the obligation of **bringing** offerings; **and anyone not** included **in coming is not** included **in** the obligation of **bringing** either.

רַבִּי יוֹחָנָן בֶּן דַּהֲבַאי אוֹמֵר מִשּׁוּם רַבִּי יְהוּדָה: סוּמָא בְּאַחַת מֵעֵינָיו פָּטוּר מִן הָרְאִיָּיה, שֶׁנֶּאֱמַר: ״יֵרָאֶה״ ״יִרְאֶה״ – כְּדֶרֶךְ שֶׁבָּא לִרְאוֹת כָּךְ בָּא לֵירָאוֹת, מַה בָּא לִרְאוֹת בִּשְׁתֵּי עֵינָיו – אַף לֵירָאוֹת בִּשְׁתֵּי עֵינָיו.

Rabbi Yoḥanan ben Dehavai says in the name of Rabbi Yehuda: One who is blind in one of his eyes is exempt from the mitzva of **appearance, as it is stated:** "Three times a year all your males **shall appear** [*yera'e*] before the Lord God" (Exodus 23:17). Since there are no vowels in the text, this can be read as: All your males **will see** [*yireh*] the Lord God. This teaches that **in the same manner that one comes to see, so he comes to be seen: Just as one comes to see with both his eyes, so too** the obligation **to be seen** applies only to one who comes **with both his eyes.** Therefore, one who is blind in one eye is exempt from the mitzva of appearance in the Temple.

רַב הוּנָא, כִּי מָטֵי לְהַאי קְרָא ״יִרְאֶה״ ״יֵרָאֶה״ בָּכֵי, אָמַר: עֶבֶד שֶׁרַבּוֹ מְצַפֶּה לוֹ לִרְאוֹתוֹ יִתְרַחֵק מִמֶּנּוּ? דִּכְתִיב: ״כִּי תָבוֹאוּ לִרְאוֹת פָּנָי מִי בִקֵּשׁ זֹאת מִיֶּדְכֶם רְמֹס חֲצֵרָי״.

The Gemara relates that **when Rav Huna reached this verse,** which can be read as: **"Will see"** [*yireh*] and **"shall appear"** [*yera'e*],[N] **he cried. He said:** Can it happen to **a slave whose master expects to see him,** that the master **will** eventually **distance himself from him** and not want him anymore? **As it is written: "When you come to appear before Me, who has required this at your hand, to trample My courts?"** (Isaiah 1:12).

רַב הוּנָא כִּי מָטֵי לְהַאי קְרָא בָּכֵי: ״וְזָבַחְתָּ שְׁלָמִים וְאָכַלְתָּ שָּׁם״, עֶבֶד שֶׁרַבּוֹ מְצַפֶּה לֶאֱכוֹל עַל שֻׁלְחָנוֹ יִתְרַחֵק מִמֶּנּוּ? דִּכְתִיב: ״לָמָּה לִּי רֹב זִבְחֵיכֶם יֹאמַר ה׳״.

Similarly, when Rav Huna reached this verse, he cried: "And you shall sacrifice peace-offerings, and you shall eat there" (Deuteronomy 27:7). Can it happen to **a slave whose master expects** him **to eat at his table,** that his master **will** eventually **distance himself from him? As it is written: "To what purpose is the multitude of your offerings to Me? says the Lord"** (Isaiah 1:11).

רַבִּי אֶלְעָזָר כִּי מָטֵי לְהַאי קְרָא בָּכֵי: ״וְלֹא יָכְלוּ אֶחָיו לַעֲנוֹת אֹתוֹ כִּי נִבְהֲלוּ מִפָּנָיו״. וּמַה תּוֹכֵחָה שֶׁל בָּשָׂר וָדָם – כָּךְ, תּוֹכֵחָה שֶׁל הַקָּדוֹשׁ בָּרוּךְ הוּא – עַל אַחַת כַּמָּה וְכַמָּה! רַבִּי אֶלְעָזָר כִּי מָטֵי לְהַאי קְרָא בָּכֵי: ״וַיֹּאמֶר שְׁמוּאֵל אֶל שָׁאוּל לָמָּה הִרְגַּזְתַּנִי לְהַעֲלוֹת אוֹתִי״. וּמַה שְּׁמוּאֵל הַצַּדִּיק הָיָה מִתְיָירֵא מִן הַדִּין, אָנוּ – עַל אַחַת כַּמָּה וְכַמָּה!

The Gemara similarly relates: **When Rabbi Elazar reached this verse, he cried: "And his brethren could not answer him, for they were affrighted at his presence"** (Genesis 45:3). He said, in explanation of his emotional reaction: **If the rebuke of** a man **of flesh and blood** was **such** that the brothers were unable to respond, when it comes to **the rebuke of the Holy One, Blessed be He, all the more so.**[N] **When Rabbi Elazar reached this verse, he cried: "And Samuel said to Saul: Why have you disquieted me, to bring me up"** (1 Samuel 28:15).[NB] He said: **If Samuel the righteous was afraid of judgment**[N] when he was raised by necromancy, as he thought he was being summoned for a Divine judgment, **all the more so** that **we** should be afraid.

שְׁמוּאֵל מַאי הִיא? דִּכְתִיב: ״וַתֹּאמֶר הָאִשָּׁה אֶל שָׁאוּל אֱלֹהִים רָאִיתִי עוֹלִים״, ״עוֹלִים״ – תְּרֵי מַשְׁמַע, חַד – שְׁמוּאֵל, וְאִידָךְ – דַּאֲזַל שְׁמוּאֵל וְאַתְיֵיהּ לְמֹשֶׁה בַּהֲדֵיהּ. אֲמַר לֵיהּ: דִּלְמָא חַס וְשָׁלוֹם לְדִינָא מִתְבָּעֵינָא, קוּם בַּהֲדַאי דְּלֵיכָּא מִילְּתָא דִּכְתַבְתְּ בְּאוֹרַיְיתָא דְּלָא קַיֵּימְתִּיהָ.

The Gemara asks: In the case of **Samuel, what is it** that he feared? **As it is written: "And the woman said to Saul, I see a godlike being coming up** [*olim*] out of the earth" (1 Samuel 28:13). **"*Olim*,"** in the plural form, **indicates** that there were **two** of them. **One** of them was **Samuel, but the other,** who was he? The Gemara explains **that Samuel went and brought Moses with him.**[N] **He said to** Moses: **Perhaps, Heaven forbid, I was summoned for judgment** by God; **stand with me** and testify on my behalf **that there is nothing that you wrote in the Torah that I did not fulfill.**

רַבִּי אַמִי כִּי מָטֵי לְהַאי קְרָא בָּכֵי: ״יִתֵּן בֶּעָפָר פִּיהוּ אוּלַי יֵשׁ תִּקְוָה״, אֲמַר: כּוּלֵּי הַאי – וְאוּלַי?! רַבִּי אַמִי כִּי מָטֵי לְהַאי קְרָא בָּכֵי: ״בַּקְּשׁוּ צֶדֶק בַּקְּשׁוּ עֲנָוָה אוּלַי תִּסָּתְרוּ בְּיוֹם אַף ה׳״, אֲמַר: כּוּלֵּי הַאי – וְאוּלַי?! רַבִּי אַסִי, כִּי מָטֵי לְהַאי קְרָא בָּכֵי: ״שִׂנְאוּ רָע וְאֶהֱבוּ טוֹב וְהַצִּיגוּ בַשַּׁעַר מִשְׁפָּט אוּלַי יֶחֱנַן ה׳ [אֱלֹהֵי] צְבָאוֹת״, כּוּלֵּי הַאי – וְאוּלַי?!

When Rabbi Ami reached this verse, he cried: "Let him put his mouth in the dust, perhaps there may be hope" (Lamentations 3:29). **He said:** A sinner suffers through **all this** punishment **and** only **perhaps**[N] there may be hope? **When Rabbi Ami reached this verse, he cried: "Seek righteousness, seek humility; perhaps you shall be hidden on the day of the Lord's anger"** (Zephaniah 2:3). **He said: All of this** is expected of each individual, **and** only **perhaps** God's anger may be hidden? Likewise, **when Rabbi Asi reached this verse, he cried: "Hate the evil, and love the good, and establish justice in the gate; perhaps the Lord, the God of hosts, will be gracious"** (Amos 5:15). **He said: All of this, and only perhaps?**

רַב יוֹסֵף כִּי מָטֵי לְהַאי קְרָא בָּכֵי: ״וְיֵשׁ נִסְפֶּה בְּלֹא מִשְׁפָּט״ אֲמַר: מִי אִיכָּא דְּאָזֵיל בְּלָא זִמְנֵיהּ? אִין, כִּי הָא דְּרַב בֵּיבָי בַּר אַבַּיֵּי הֲוָה שְׁכִיחַ גַּבֵּיהּ מַלְאַךְ הַמָּוֶת. אֲמַר לֵיהּ לִשְׁלוּחֵיהּ: זִיל אַיְיתִי לִי מִרְיָם מְגַדְּלָא שֵׂיעַר נְשַׁיָּיא. אֲזַל אַיְיתִי לֵיהּ מִרְיָם מְגַדְּלָא דַּרְדְּקֵי.

When Rav Yosef reached this verse, he cried: "But there are those swept away without justice" (Proverbs 13:23). **He said: Is there one who goes before his time** and dies for no reason? The Gemara answers: **Yes, like this** incident of **Rav Beivai bar Abaye, who would be frequented** by the company of **the Angel of Death**[N] and would see how people died at the hands of this angel. The Angel of Death **said to his agent: Go and bring me,** i.e., kill, **Miriam the raiser,** i.e., braider, **of women's hair. He went,** but instead **brought him Miriam,** the **raiser of babies.**

אֲמַר לֵיהּ: אֲנָא מִרְיָם מְגַדְּלָא שֵׂיעָר נְשַׁיָּיא אֲמָרִי לָךְ! אֲמַר לֵיהּ: אִי הָכִי אַהַדְרַהּ! אֲמַר לֵיהּ: הוֹאִיל וְאַיְיתִיתַהּ – לֶיהֱוֵי לְמִנְיָינָא. אֶלָּא הֵיכִי יָכְלַתְּ לָהּ? הֲוַת נְקִיטָא מְתָארָא בִּידַהּ, וַהֲוַת קָא שָׁגְרָא

The Angel of Death **said to him: I told you** to bring **Miriam,** the **raiser** of **women's hair.** His agent **said to him: If so, return her** to life. **He said to him: Since you** have already **brought her, let her be counted**[N] toward the number of deceased people. Apparently, this woman died unintentionally. Rav Beivai asked the agent: **But** as her time to die had not yet arrived, **how were you able** to kill **her?** The agent responded that he had the opportunity, as **she was holding a shovel in her hand and** with it she **was lighting**

NOTES

If the rebuke of flesh and blood was such, the rebuke of the Holy One…all the more so – וּמַה תּוֹכֵחָה שֶׁל בָּשָׂר וָדָם, כָּךְ תּוֹכֵחָה שֶׁל הַקָּדוֹשׁ בָּרוּךְ הוּא עַל אַחַת כַּמָּה וְכַמָּה: The Maharsha notes that the Torah does not in fact record that Joseph rebuked his brothers. Therefore, he explains this statement as follows: If Joseph's brothers, who merely feared the possibility of rebuke, were unable to respond, all the more so when a man stands before God. However, others write that the midrash indicates that Joseph actually reprimanded his brothers (Riaf; *Iyyun Ya'akov*).

Disquieted me to bring me up – הִרְגַּזְתַּנִי לְהַעֲלוֹת אוֹתִי: In the Jerusalem Talmud the verse is explained in two ways. The phrase "disquieted me" might indicate anger, i.e., Samuel is saying: Is it not enough that you transgressed the Torah, now you are also using me to commit the sin of resurrection by means of necromancy? Alternatively, the term "disquieted" denotes fear, as in several other places (e.g., Deuteronomy 2:25). If so, Samuel is saying that he feared being resurrected.

Was afraid of judgment – הָיָה מִתְיָירֵא מִן הַדִּין: Some write that although Samuel did not believe he was being called to the ultimate Day of Judgment, nevertheless, as this incident occurred within a year of his death, he feared that he was perhaps being called to the court of heaven before arriving at his resting place in the Garden of Eden (*Yeshuot Meshiḥo*).

And he brought Moses with him – וְאַתְיֵיהּ לְמֹשֶׁה בַּהֲדֵיהּ: Some explain that the phrase: "I see a godlike being [*elohim*]," itself alludes to this explanation, as only Moses of all the prophets and righteous people is described by the Torah as "*elohim*" (Exodus 7:1). This term can mean a judge or leader, but is also a name of God.

All this and only perhaps – כּוּלֵּי הַאי וְאוּלַי: The commentaries explain that the Sages cried because these verses describe the highest qualities of modesty and humility as well as other admirable qualities. If even one who possesses these is not guaranteed salvation, what will be the fate of others? (Maharsha).

He would be frequented by the Angel of Death, etc. – הֲוָה שְׁכִיחַ גַּבֵּיהּ מַלְאַךְ הַמָּוֶת וכו׳: The commentaries explain that Rav Beivai was well versed in esoteric matters. They further suggest that this might have been a dream or a vision (*ge'onim*). This story teaches the important idea that some people die not as a result of their sins but simply due to circumstances, or, in the terms of the Gemara, a mistake of the agent. However, God does not deprive anyone of his reward in the World-to-Come, and his suffering and untimely death are taken into account. Some suggest that the agent of the Angel of Death does not always act upon the will of God. Furthermore, sometimes one dies for a specific sin even if it is not one that normally renders him deserving of death by the hands of Heaven (*Zohar*, *Parashat Vayera*).

Let her be counted – לֶיהֱוֵי לְמִנְיָינָא: Let her be counted only among the dead, not among those who were liable to receive the death penalty (*Tosefot Rid*).

BACKGROUND

And Samuel said to Saul, Why have you disquieted me to bring me up – וַיֹּאמֶר שְׁמוּאֵל אֶל שָׁאוּל לָמָּה הִרְגַּזְתַּנִי לְהַעֲלוֹת אוֹתִי: Although some early authorities maintain that magical powers do exist, other commentaries explain Samuel's appearance after death as a miraculous event arranged by God rather than by the necromancy of the medium of En-Dor (Rav Hai Gaon; Rav Sa'adia Gaon). The purpose of this miracle was to convey a specific message to Saul by the only means available. In contrast, some claim that the medium of En-Dor was a woman experienced in deceptive methods who recognized Saul beneath his disguise and decided to provide him with a purported prophecy of destruction that would discourage him, leading to his ultimate defeat and death (*Midrash Shlomo*).

NOTES

I shepherd them – דָּרְעֵינָא לְהוּ אֲנָא: This cryptic idea is based on the verse: "Like sheep they are appointed for the netherworld; death shall be their shepherd; and the upright shall have dominion over them in the morning; and their form shall be for the netherworld to wear away, that there be no habitation for it" (Psalms 49:15). The verse depicts death as a shepherd for the souls until they arrive in the netherworld. Furthermore, the verse also alludes to the idea that Torah scholars who are willing to bear insults are granted extra years, as: "The upright shall have dominion over them" (*Petaḥ Einayim*, citing Rabbi Yitzḥak Luria).

Others incite him and he is incited – מְסִיתִין לוֹ וְנִיסַּת: Some commentaries note that according to the midrashic tradition that Job was one of Pharaoh's advisors, he deserved to be punished, as he should have protested against Pharaoh's evil ways (*Turei Aven*). Even so, it is possible that the incitement mentioned here refers to the unnecessarily harsh manner of his punishment. Others say that this statement in is accordance with the opinion of Rabbi Yoḥanan (*Bava Batra* 16a) that Job lived in a later time period and was not guilty of sin (see *Iyyun Ya'akov*).

וּמְחַרְיָא תַּנּוּרָא. שְׁקַלְתָּא וְאַנַּחְתָּא אַגַּבָּה דְּכַרְעָהּ, קְדַחָא וְאִיתְרַע מַזָּלָהּ, וְאַיְיתִיתָהּ.

and sweeping the oven. She took the fire **and set it on her foot; she was scalded and her luck suffered,** which gave me the opportunity, **and I brought her.**

אֲמַר לֵיהּ רַב בֵּיבָי בַּר אַבָּיֵי: אִית לְכוּ רְשׁוּתָא לְמֶיעְבַּד הָכִי? אֲמַר לֵיהּ: וְלָא כְּתִיב ״וְיֵשׁ נִסְפֶּה בְּלֹא מִשְׁפָּט״? אֲמַר לֵיהּ: וְהָכְתִיב: ״דּוֹר הוֹלֵךְ וְדוֹר בָּא״!

Rav Beivai bar Abaye said to the Angel of Death: Do **you have the right to act in this** manner, to take someone before his time? The Angel of Death **said to him: And is it not written: "But there are those swept away without justice"** (Proverbs 13:23)? Rav Beivai **said to him: And isn't it written: "One generation passes away, and another generation comes"** (Ecclesiastes 1:4), which indicates that there is a predetermined amount of time for the life of every generation.

אֲמַר: דָּרְעֵינָא לְהוּ אֲנָא עַד דִּמְלוּ לְהוּ לְדָרָא, וְהָדַר מַשְׁלִימְנָא לֵיהּ לְדוּמָה. אֲמַר לֵיהּ: סוֹף סוֹף, שְׁנֵיהּ מַאי עָבְדַתְּ? אֲמַר: אִי אִיכָּא צוּרְבָא מֵרַבָּנַן דְּמַעֲבִיר בְּמִילֵּיהּ מוֹסִיפְנָא לְהוּ לֵיהּ, וְהָוְיָא חִלּוּפֵיהּ.

He said to him: **I shepherd them,**[N] not releasing them **until** the years of **the generation are completed, and then I pass them on to** the angel **Duma** who oversees the souls of the dead. Rav Beivai **said to him: Ultimately, what do you do** with **his** extra **years,** those taken away from this individual? The Angel of Death **said** to him: **If there is a Torah scholar who disregards his** personal **matters,** i.e., who overlooks the insults of those who wrong him, **I add those** years **to him and he becomes** the deceased's **replacement** for that time.

רַבִּי יוֹחָנָן כִּי מָטֵי לְהַאי קְרָא בָּכֵי: ״וַתְּסִיתֵנִי בוֹ לְבַלְּעוֹ חִנָּם״ עֶבֶד שֶׁרַבּוֹ מְסִיתִין לוֹ וְנִיסַּת, תַּקָּנָה יֵשׁ לוֹ? רַבִּי יוֹחָנָן כִּי מָטֵי לְהַאי קְרָא בָּכֵי: ״הֵן בִּקְדֹשָׁיו לֹא יַאֲמִין״, אִי בִּקְדוֹשָׁיו לֹא יַאֲמִין – בְּמַאן יַאֲמִין?

§ The Gemara returns to the previous topic. **When Rabbi Yoḥanan reached this verse, he cried,** as God said to the Satan about Job: **"Although you did incite Me against him, to destroy him without cause"** (Job 2:3). Rabbi Yoḥanan said: With regard to **a slave whose master** is one whom others **incite** to act harshly against the slave **and** the master **is incited**[N] to do so, **is there a remedy for** the slave? Additionally, **when Rabbi Yoḥanan reached this verse, he cried: "Behold He puts no trust in His sacred ones"** (Job 15:15), saying: **If He does not place trust in His sacred ones, in whom** does **He place trust?**

יוֹמָא חַד הֲוָה קָא אָזֵיל בְּאוֹרְחָא, חַזְיֵיהּ לְהָהוּא גַּבְרָא דַּהֲוָה מְנַקֵּיט תְּאֵנֵי, שָׁבֵיק הָנָךְ דִּמְטוּ, וְשָׁקֵיל הָנָךְ דְּלָא מְטוּ. אֲמַר לֵיהּ: לָאו הָנֵי מַעֲלָן טְפֵי? אֲמַר לֵיהּ: הָנֵי לְאוֹרְחָא בָּעֵינַן לְהוּ, הָנֵי – נָטְרָן, וְהָנֵי – לָא נָטְרָן. אֲמַר: הַיְינוּ דִּכְתִיב ״הֵן בִּקְדוֹשָׁיו לֹא יַאֲמִין״.

The Gemara relates: **One day** Rabbi Yoḥanan **was walking along the road,** and **he saw a certain man who was picking figs** in an unusual manner: **He left the ones that had reached** the stage of ripeness **and took those that had not** yet **reached** that state. Rabbi Yoḥanan **said to him: Aren't these** ripe ones **much better? He said to him: I need these** dates **for the road; these** that are not yet ripe **will be preserved, and these** that are already ripe **will not be preserved.** Rabbi Yoḥanan **said: This is** the same **as is written: "Behold He puts no trust in His sacred ones";** there are righteous people whom God takes from this world before their time, as He knows that in the future they will stumble.

אִינִי? וְהָא הַהוּא תַּלְמִידָא דַּהֲוָה בְּשִׁיבָבוּתֵיהּ דְּרַבִּי אֲלֶכְּסַנְדְּרִי וְשָׁכֵיב אַדְּזוּטַר, וַאֲמַר: אִי בָּעֵי הַאי מֵרַבָּנַן הֲוָה חָיֵי. וְאִם אִיתָא – דִּלְמָא מֵ״הֵן בִּקְדוֹשָׁיו לֹא יַאֲמִין״ הֲוָה? הַהוּא מְבַעֵט בְּרַבּוֹתָיו הֲוָה.

The Gemara asks: **Is that so? But there was a certain student in the neighborhood of Rabbi Alexandri, and he died while** he was still **young. And** Rabbi Alexandri **said: If this** young **Sage had wanted, he would have lived,** i.e., his actions caused him to die young. **And if it is so,** as Rabbi Yoḥanan suggested, **perhaps** this student was **from** those concerning whom it is written: **"Behold he puts no trust in his sacred ones,"** and it was not his sins that caused his death. The Gemara answers: **That** student **was** one who acted **irreverently toward his teachers,** and Rabbi Alexandri knew of his improper behavior.

רַבִּי יוֹחָנָן כִּי מָטֵי לְהַאי קְרָא בָּכֵי: ״וְקָרַבְתִּי אֲלֵיכֶם לַמִּשְׁפָּט וְהָיִיתִי עֵד מְמַהֵר בַּמְכַשְּׁפִים וּבַמְנָאֲפִים וּבַנִּשְׁבָּעִים לַשָּׁקֶר וּבְעֹשְׁקֵי שְׂכַר שָׂכִיר״, עֶבֶד שֶׁרַבּוֹ מְקָרְבוֹ לְדוּנוֹ, וּמְמַהֵר לְהָעִידוֹ, תַּקָּנָה יֵשׁ לוֹ?

When Rabbi Yoḥanan reached this verse, he cried: "And I will come near to you to judgment; and I will be a swift witness against the sorcerers, and against the adulterers, and against false witnesses, and against those who oppress the hireling in his wages, the widow, and the fatherless, and who turn aside the convert from his right, and do not fear Me, says the Lord" (Malachi 3:5). He said: With regard to **a slave whose master comes near to him to judge him and is swift to testify** against **him, is there a remedy for him?**

אָמַר רַבִּי יוֹחָנָן בֶּן זַכַּאי: אוֹי לָנוּ שֶׁשָּׁקַל עָלֵינוּ הַכָּתוּב קַלּוֹת כַּחֲמוּרוֹת.

With regard to that same verse, **Rabbi Yoḥanan ben Zakkai said: Woe to us, as the verse weighs lenient** mitzvot **for us like** more **stringent** mitzvot, as it lists both those who violate sins punishable by death, e.g., sorcerers and adulterers, with those who violate apparently less severe sins, e.g., those who withhold payment from a hired worker.

אָמַר רֵישׁ לָקִישׁ: כָּל הַמַּטֶּה דִּינוֹ שֶׁל גֵּר – כְּאִילּוּ מַטֶּה דִּינוֹ שֶׁל מַעְלָה, שֶׁנֶּאֱמַר: "וּמַטֵּי גֵר" – וּמַטִּי כְּתִיב. אָמַר רַבִּי חֲנִינָא בַּר פַּפָּא: כָּל הָעוֹשֶׂה דָּבָר וּמִתְחָרֵט בּוֹ – מוֹחֲלִין לוֹ מִיָּד, שֶׁנֶּאֱמַר: "וְלֹא יְרֵאוּנִי", הָא יְרֵאוּנִי – מוֹחֲלִין לָהֶם מִיָּד.

Reish Lakish said: Anyone who distorts the judgment of a convert,[N] **it is considered as if he distorted the judgment of** the One **above, as it is stated: "And who turn aside [*umattei*] the convert"** (Malachi 3:5). This term **is written** as: ***Umatti***,[N] turn Me aside, i.e., one who distorts the judgment of a convert it considered as though he distorts the judgment of God, as it were. **Rabbi Ḥanina bar Pappa said: Anyone who does something** sinful **and regrets it,**[N] **he is forgiven immediately, as it is stated: "And do not fear Me"** (Malachi 3:5), which indicates that if **they** do **fear Me** and are embarrassed to sin before God, **they are forgiven immediately.**

רַבִּי יוֹחָנָן כִּי מָטֵי לְהַאי קְרָא בָּכֵי: "כִּי אֶת כָּל מַעֲשֶׂה הָאֱלֹהִים יָבִיא בְמִשְׁפָּט עַל כָּל נֶעְלָם", עֶבֶד שֶׁרַבּוֹ שׁוֹקֵל לוֹ שְׁגָגוֹת כִּזְדוֹנוֹת תַּקָּנָה יֵשׁ לוֹ?

Additionally, **when Rabbi Yoḥanan reached this verse, he cried: "For God shall bring every work into the judgment concerning every hidden thing"** (Ecclesiastes 12:14). He said: With regard to **a slave whose master weighs his unwitting** sins **like intentional** ones,[N] i.e., God punishes him even for an action that was hidden from him, **is there a remedy for him?**

מַאי "עַל כָּל נֶעְלָם"? אָמַר רַב: זֶה הַהוֹרֵג כִּינָּה בִּפְנֵי חֲבֵרוֹ וְנִמְאָס בָּהּ. וּשְׁמוּאֵל אָמַר: זֶה הָרָק בִּפְנֵי חֲבֵירוֹ וְנִמְאָס.

The Gemara asks: **What** sin is the verse referring to when it states: **"Concerning every hidden thing"? Rav said: This** is referring to **one who kills a louse in the presence of another and** his friend **is disgusted by it.** God judges him for the unintentional discomfort he caused. **And** similarly, **Shmuel said: This** is referring to **one who spits in the presence of another** and his friend **is disgusted** by his action.

מַאי "אִם טוֹב וְאִם רָע"? אָמְרִי דְּבֵי רַבִּי יַנַּאי: זֶה הַנּוֹתֵן צְדָקָה לְעָנִי בְּפַרְהֶסְיָא. כִּי הָא דְּרַבִּי יַנַּאי חַזְיֵיהּ לְהַהוּא גַּבְרָא דְּקָא יָהֵיב זוּזָא לְעָנִי בְּפַרְהֶסְיָא, אֲמַר לֵיהּ: מוּטָב דְּלָא יְהַבַת לֵיהּ מֵהָשְׁתָּא דִּיהַבְתְּ לֵיהּ וְכַסַּפְתֵּיהּ.

The Gemara asks: **What** is the meaning of the end of that verse: **"Whether it be good, or whether it be evil"** (Ecclesiastes 12:14)? This verse indicates that God judges man harshly even for the good deeds he performs. The Sages **from the school of Rabbi Yannai say: This** verse is referring to **one who gives charity to a poor person in public.**[N] Although he performed a good deed, he embarrassed the pauper, **as in this case of Rabbi Yannai,** who **saw a certain man who was giving a dinar to a poor person in public. He said to him:** It would have been **better had you not given** it **to him than** what you did, as **now you gave** it to **him and embarrassed him.**

NOTES

Anyone who distorts the judgment of a convert – כָּל הַמַּטֶּה דִּינוֹ שֶׁל גֵּר: The same applies to one who distorts the judgment of any Jew. However, one who distorts the judgment of a convert receives a harsher punishment. Furthermore, one is punished for distorting the judgment of a Jew only if he himself actually performs the act, whereas in the case of a convert one is punished even if he indirectly causes a distortion in judgment (*Turei Aven*).

It is written, *Umatti* – וּמַטִּי כְּתִיב: Apparently, there is no special exposition here from the manner in which the term is written, as both readings: *Umatti* and *Umattei*, are written the same way. Some explain that the term is read: *Umattei*, whereas it is written: *Umatti* (Rabbeinu Ḥananel; see Maharsha). Others note that the rest of the sinners listed in the verse are preceded by the letter *bet*, which means against. However, this prefix is missing in the case of one who turns aside a convert, which indicates that it is as if he is exploiting God Himself (*Iyyei HaYam*).

Anyone who does something and regrets it – כָּל הָעוֹשֶׂה דָּבָר וּמִתְחָרֵט בּוֹ: A similar statement appears in *Berakhot* (12b): One who commits an act of transgression and is ashamed of it, all of his transgressions are forgiven. Apparently, there is a difference between one who is ashamed by his sins and one who merely regrets his sins; in the former case, all of his transgressions are forgiven, and in the latter case, only that particular transgression is forgiven (*Dikdukei Soferim*).

Weighs his unwitting sins like intentional ones – שׁוֹקֵל לוֹ שְׁגָגוֹת כִּזְדוֹנוֹת: This is puzzling; is it possible that God would judge man's unwitting sins as though they were intentional? One explanation is that Rabbi Yoḥanan does not mean that God equates the two; rather, the point is that God does not discount unwitting transgressions (*Mesillat Yesharim*).

One who gives charity to a poor person in public – הַנּוֹתֵן צְדָקָה לְעָנִי בְּפַרְהֶסְיָא: The commentaries explain that this applies specifically to one who gives a small gift to the poor (Meiri). One version of the text supports this interpretation, as it reads: One who gives a *peruta* to the poor, an insignificant sum. Others explain that this refers to one who gives money to a poor person who did not request it, and therefore this public donation is a source of embarrassment (*Gilyonei Yoel*).

דְּבֵי רַבִּי שֵׁילָא אָמְרִי: זֶה הַנּוֹתֵן צְדָקָה לְאִשָּׁה בְּסֵתֶר, דְּקָא מַיְיתֵי לָהּ לִידֵי חֲשָׁדָא. רָבָא אָמַר: זֶה הַמְשַׁגֵּר לְאִשְׁתּוֹ בָּשָׂר שֶׁאֵינוֹ מְחוּתָּךְ בְּעַרְבֵי שַׁבָּתוֹת.

The Sages from **the school of Rabbi Sheila say: This** verse is referring to **one who gives charity to a woman in private, as he subjects her to suspicion,**[N] for people might think that he is engaging her services as a prostitute. **Rava said: This** is referring to **one who sends his wife meat that is not sliced,** i.e., that has not yet had the prohibited sciatic nerve removed, **on Shabbat eve.** Since she is in a hurry she might not notice and will perhaps cook the prohibited meat.

וְהָא רָבָא מְשַׁגֵּר! שָׁאנֵי בַּת רַב חִסְדָּא דְּקִים לֵיהּ בְּגַוָּהּ דִּבְקִיאָה.

The Gemara asks: **But** yet **Rava** himself would **send** this type of meat to his wife on Shabbat eve. The Gemara answers: **The daughter of Rav Ḥisda,** Rava's wife, **is different, as he was certain about her that she was an expert** in this matter. Rava trusted that his wife would realize the sciatic nerve had not been removed even when she was in a hurry on Shabbat eve.

רַבִּי יוֹחָנָן כִּי מָטֵי לְהַאי קְרָא בָּכֵי: "וְהָיָה כִּי תִמְצֶאןָ אוֹתוֹ רָעוֹת רַבּוֹת וְצָרוֹת" עֶבֶד שֶׁרַבּוֹ מַמְצִיא לוֹ רָעוֹת וְצָרוֹת תַּקָּנָה יֵשׁ לוֹ?

Additionally, **when Rabbi Yoḥanan reached this verse, he cried: "Then it shall come to pass, when many evils and troubles are come upon them"** (Deuteronomy 31:21). He said: With regard to **a slave whose master brings upon him evils and troubles, is there a remedy for him?**

מַאי "רָעוֹת וְצָרוֹת"? אָמַר רַב: רָעוֹת שֶׁנַּעֲשׂוֹת צָרוֹת זוֹ לָזוֹ, כְּגוֹן זִיבּוּרָא וְעַקְרַבָּא.

The Gemara asks: **What is** the verse referring to when it states: **"Evils and troubles"? Rav said: Evils that become troubles for one another,**[N] i.e., the remedy for one problem has a deleterious effect on the other. **For example,** one who is stung by a **hornet and a scorpion.** The sting of a hornet must be treated only with a cold ointment, while that of a scorpion must be treated with a hot ointment. As these medicaments are mutually exclusive, one cannot treat both stings at the same time.

וּשְׁמוּאֵל אָמַר: זֶה הַמַּמְצִיא לוֹ מָעוֹת לְעָנִי בִּשְׁעַת דּוֹחֲקוֹ. אֲמַר רָבָא: הַיְינוּ דְּאָמְרִי אֱינָשֵׁי "זוּזָא לְעַלְלָא לָא שְׁכִיחָא, לִתְלֵיתָא – שְׁכִיחַ".

And Shmuel said: This verse is referring to **one who provides money to a poor person**[N] as a loan **during his exigent** financial **circumstances,** but immediately after the borrower is released from the initial pressure by receiving the loan, the lender begins to demand repayment, subjecting the recipient to further pressure. **Rava said** that **this** explains the folk saying **that people say: A dinar for produce is not found; for hanging** it can be **found.** A poor person cannot find money to buy basic necessities; however, when the lenders hang on and pressure him he must come up with the money somehow.

"וְחָרָה אַפִּי בוֹ בַיּוֹם הַהוּא וַעֲזַבְתִּים וְהִסְתַּרְתִּי פָנַי מֵהֶם", אָמַר רַב בַּרְדְּלָא בַּר טַבְיוּמֵי אָמַר רַב: כֹּל שֶׁאֵינוֹ בְּהֶסְתֵּר פָּנִים – אֵינוֹ מֵהֶם, כֹּל שֶׁאֵינוֹ בִּ"וְהָיָה לֶאֱכוֹל"

On the same topic the Gemara states: **"Then My anger shall be kindled against them in that day, and I will forsake them, and I will hide My face from them,** and they shall be devoured" (Deuteronomy 31:17). **Rav Bardela bar Tavyumei said** that **Rav said: Anyone who is not subject to** His **hiding of the face,** i.e., whose prayers are invariably answered, **is not from** the Jewish people, as the verse states about the Jewish people that God will hide His face from them as a result of their sins. Similarly, **anyone** who **is not subject to: "And they shall be devoured,"** i.e., gentiles do not steal his money,

NOTES

Subjects her to suspicion – מַיְיתֵי לָהּ לִידֵי חֲשָׁדָא: Some commentaries ask why the Gemara is concerned only about suspicions concerning her and not him, as presumably he would be suspected of sinning as well (*Turei Aven*; *Zekher LaHagiga*). One answer is that as he gave the charity secretly, his identity remains unknown. In contrast, if a poor woman suddenly comes into possession of money, people will suspect her of earning it by immoral means (*Iyyei HaYam*).

Evils and troubles – רָעוֹת וְצָרוֹת: This idea, that the verse is referring to evils that become troubles for one another, is derived from the unusual phrasing of the verse, as in Hebrew the term "many" appears between "evils and troubles." This indicates that "troubles" is an adjective of "evils." Rashi explains that "troubles" connotes proximity, i.e., one experiences many hardships without respite (see *Tzlaḥ*).

One who provides money to a poor person – הַמַּמְצִיא לוֹ מָעוֹת לְעָנִי: The commentaries contrast this idea with a statement of the Sages that one who loans money to a poor person in his time of need is praiseworthy (*Tosafot*). One explanation is that sometimes when a poor person borrows money in his time of need he must provide a substantial collateral, which he would not need to do if he were more comfortable (*Tosefot Rid*). Others suggest that this refers to one who gives enough money so that the recipient no longer has the status of a poor person to whom it is required to give charity, while still leaving him in dire financial straits (*Or Zarua*; see Jerusalem Talmud, *Pe'a*, chapter 1).

אֵינוֹ מֵהֶם. אֲמָרוּ לֵיהּ רַבָּנַן לְרָבָא: מָר לָא בְּהֶסְתֵּר פָּנִים אִיתֵיהּ, וְלָא בְּ״וְהָיָה לֶאֱכוֹל״ אִיתֵיהּ! אֲמַר לְהוּ: מִי יָדְעִיתוּ כַּמָּה מְשַׁדַּרְנָא בְּצִנְעָא בֵּי שָׁבוֹר מַלְכָּא? אֲפִילּוּ הָכִי יְהַבוּ בֵּיהּ רַבָּנַן עֵינַיְיהוּ. אַדְּהָכִי שְׁדוּר דְּבֵי שָׁבוֹר מַלְכָּא וּגְרַבוּהוּ. אֲמַר, הַיְינוּ דְּתַנְיָא, אָמַר רַבָּן שִׁמְעוֹן בֶּן גַּמְלִיאֵל: כׇּל מָקוֹם שֶׁנָּתְנוּ חֲכָמִים עֵינֵיהֶם – אוֹ מִיתָה אוֹ עוֹנִי.

is not from among **them.**[N] **The Sages said to Rava: Master, you are not subject to** His **hiding** of the **face,** as your prayers are heard, **and you are not subject to: "And they shall be devoured,"** as the authorities take nothing from you. **He said to them: Do you know how many gifts I send in private to the house of King Shapur?**[P] Although it might seem that the monarchy does not take anything from me, in actuality I am forced to give many bribes. **Even so, the Sages looked upon** Rava with suspicion. **In the meantime,** messengers **from the house of King Shapur sent** for him **and imprisoned him** to extort more money from him. Rava **said: This is as it is taught** in a *baraita* that **Rabban Shimon ben Gamliel said: Wherever the Sages looked upon** someone, it resulted in **either death or poverty.**

״וְאָנֹכִי הַסְתֵּר אַסְתִּיר פָּנַי בַּיּוֹם הַהוּא״, אָמַר רָבָא, אָמַר הַקָּדוֹשׁ בָּרוּךְ הוּא: אַף עַל פִּי שֶׁהִסְתַּרְתִּי פָּנַי מֵהֶם – ״בַּחֲלוֹם אֲדַבֶּר בּוֹ״. רַב יוֹסֵף אָמַר: יָדוֹ נְטוּיָה עָלֵינוּ, שֶׁנֶּאֱמַר: ״וּבְצֵל יָדִי כִּסִּיתִיךָ״.

With regard to the verse: **"And I will hide my face in that day"** (Deuteronomy 31:18), **Rava said** that **the Holy One, Blessed be He, said: Even though I hid my face from them** and My Divine Presence is not revealed, nevertheless: **"I speak with him in a dream"** (Numbers 12:6).[N] **Rav Yosef said: His hand is outstretched,** guarding **over us, as it is stated: "And I have covered you in the shadow of my hand"** (Isaiah 51:16).

רַבִּי יְהוֹשֻׁעַ בֶּן חֲנַנְיָה הֲוָה קָאֵי בֵּי קֵיסָר. אַחֲוֵי לֵיהּ הַהוּא מִינָא: עַמָּא דְּאַהַדְרִינְהוּ מָרֵיהּ לְאַפֵּיהּ מִינֵּיהּ. אַחֲוֵי לֵיהּ: יָדוֹ נְטוּיָה עָלֵינוּ. אֲמַר לֵיהּ קֵיסָר לְרַבִּי יְהוֹשֻׁעַ: מַאי אַחֲוֵי לָךְ? עַמָּא דְּאַהַדְרִינְהוּ מָרֵיהּ לְאַפֵּיהּ מִינֵּיהּ, וַאֲנָא מַחֲוֵינָא לֵיהּ: יָדוֹ נְטוּיָה עָלֵינוּ.

The Gemara relates: **Rabbi Yehoshua ben Ḥananya**[P] **was standing** in the **house of the Caesar. A certain heretic,** who was also present, **gestured to him,** indicating that his was **the nation whose Master,** God, **turned His face** away **from it.** Rabbi Yehoshua **gestured to him** that **His hand is outstretched over us** in protection. **The Caesar said to Rabbi Yehoshua: What did he gesture to you,** and how did you respond? He replied: He indicated that mine is **the nation whose Master turned His face from it, and I gestured to him** that **His hand is outstretched over us.**

אֲמָרוּ לֵיהּ לְהַהוּא מִינָא: מַאי אַחֲוֵיית לֵיהּ? עַמָּא דְּאַהַדְרִינְהוּ מָרֵיהּ מִינֵּיהּ. וּמַאי אַחֲוֵי לָךְ? לָא יָדַעְנָא. אֲמָרוּ: גַּבְרָא דְּלָא יָדַע מַאי מַחֲווּ לֵיהּ, בְּמָחוֹג יַחֲוֵי קַמֵּי מַלְכָּא?! אַפְּקוּהוּ וְקַטְלוּהוּ.

The members of the Caesar's household **said to that heretic: What did you gesture to him?** He said to them: I gestured that his is **the nation whose Master has turned** His face **from it.** They asked: **And what did he gesture to you?** He said to them: **I don't know;** I did not understand. **They said:** How can **a man who does not know what** others **gesture to him** dare to **gesture in the presence of the king? They took him out and killed him.**

NOTES

Is not from them – אֵינוֹ מֵהֶם: These statements teach that one should not question the ways of God, as the current era, since the destruction of the Temple, is one in which God's face is hidden (Meiri). Some commentaries write that God acts in this manner out of love for the Jewish people by exacting punishment for their sins a little at a time, and not leaving it all for the Day of Judgment, after which no further atonement is possible (*Turei Aven*).

I speak with him in a dream – בַּחֲלוֹם אֲדַבֶּר בּוֹ: Some explain that there is a state of revelation in which God approaches man face to face, which starkly contrasts with the current situation in which He hides and does not reveal Himself to the world at all. Rava teaches that even so, a minor form of revelation is possible even nowadays through dreams. Similarly, the Gemara in tractate *Berakhot* (55b) teaches that some dreams are a minor prophecy (*Otzar HaKavod*). Alternatively, Rav Yosef considers God's hiding of His face as part of the punishment of exile, and he adds that nevertheless God still protects the Jewish people (see Maharsha).

PERSONALITIES

King Shapur – שָׁבוֹר מַלְכָּא: King Shapur, or Shavor Malka, was the name of several Persian kings. The Gemara is apparently referring to the second King Shapur, who lived from 303–380 CE, during the period of the third and fourth generations of *amora'im* in Babylonia. He was a zealous supporter of Zoroastrianism, a religion he tried to impose on the minorities under his rule, especially Christians. During his reign, the Jewish community suffered from taxes, levies, and various decrees. When the Persian army was stationed in the city of Meḥoza, the local population, most of which was comprised of Jews, was obliged to maintain it.

Bas-relief sculpture depicting the triumph of King Shapur over the Roman emperor Valerian

Rabbi Yehoshua ben Ḥananya – רַבִּי יְהוֹשֻׁעַ בֶּן חֲנַנְיָה: Rabbi Yehoshua ben Ḥananya the Levite was one of the leading Sages in the generation after the destruction of the Second Temple. Earlier, Rabbi Yehoshua served as one of the Levite singers in the Temple. After its destruction, he was among the students who accompanied their teacher, Rabban Yoḥanan ben Zakkai, to Yavne. Unlike his colleague Rabbi Eliezer, Rabbi Yehoshua entirely adhered to the opinion of his teacher and Beit Hillel.

Rabbi Yehoshua was recognized by Jews and gentiles alike as a leading scholar not only in Torah matters but in general knowledge as well. He was renowned as an expert in science, from astronomy to zoology. Rabbi Yehoshua was unimpressive in appearance, and the Talmud quotes the Caesar's daughter as exclaiming that his brilliant knowledge was contained in an ugly vessel.

Despite living a life of poverty working as a blacksmith, Rabbi Yehoshua was widely recognized as one of the leading religious authorities. Although he disagreed with many of Rabban Gamliel's rulings, he accepted the authority of the *Nasi*. Ultimately, he was appointed leader of the Sages after Rabban Gamliel's death.

כִּי קָא נָיְחָא נַפְשֵׁיהּ דְּרַבִּי יְהוֹשֻׁעַ בֶּן חֲנַנְיָה אֲמָרוּ לֵיהּ רַבָּנַן: מַאי תֶּיהֱוֵי עֲלַן מִמִּינָאֵי? אֲמַר לְהֶם: ״אָבְדָה עֵצָה מִבָּנִים נִסְרְחָה חָכְמָתָם״. כֵּיוָן שֶׁאָבְדָה עֵצָה מִבָּנִים – נִסְרְחָה חָכְמָתָן שֶׁל אוּמּוֹת הָעוֹלָם.

The Gemara relates: **When Rabbi Yehoshua ben Ḥananya was dying, the Sages said to him: What will become of us, from** the threat of **the heretics,** when there is no scholar like you who can refute them? **He said to them** that the verse states: "Is wisdom no more in Teiman? **Has counsel perished from the prudent? Has their wisdom vanished?"** (Jeremiah 49:7). He explained: **Since counsel has perished from the prudent,** from the Jewish people, the **wisdom of the nations of the world has vanished** as well, and there will be no superior scholars among them.

וְאִי בָּעֵית אֵימָא מֵהָכָא: ״וַיֹּאמֶר נִסְעָה וְנֵלֵכָה וְאֵלְכָה לְנֶגְדֶּךָ״.

And if you wish, say instead that the same idea can be derived **from here: "And he said: Let us take our journey, and let us go, and I will go corresponding to you"** (Genesis 33:12). Just as the Jewish people rise and fall, so too, the nations of the world simultaneously rise and fall, and they will never have an advantage.

רַבִּי אִילָא הֲוָה סָלֵיק בְּדַרְגָּא דְּבֵי רַבָּה בַּר שֵׁילָא. שְׁמָעֵיהּ לְיַנּוּקָא דַּהֲוָה קָא קָרֵי: ״כִּי הִנֵּה יוֹצֵר הָרִים וּבוֹרֵא רוּחַ וּמַגִּיד לְאָדָם מַה שֵּׂיחוֹ״. אָמַר: עֶבֶד שֶׁרַבּוֹ מַגִּיד לוֹ מַה שֵּׂיחוֹ, תַּקָּנָה יֵשׁ לוֹ?! מַאי ״מַה שֵּׂיחוֹ״? אָמַר רַב: אֲפִילּוּ שִׂיחָה יְתֵירָה שֶׁבֵּין אִישׁ לְאִשְׁתּוֹ מַגִּידִים לוֹ לְאָדָם בִּשְׁעַת מִיתָה.

The Gemara relates that **Rabbi Ila was ascending the stairs in the house of Rabba bar Sheila,** a children's teacher. **He heard a child**[N] **who was reading** a verse out loud: **"For, lo, He Who forms the mountains, and creates the wind, and declares to man what is his speech"** (Amos 4:13). Rabbi Ila **said:** With regard to **a servant whose master declares to him what is his** proper **speech, is there a remedy for him?** The Gemara asks. **What** is the meaning of the phrase: **"What is his speech"? Rav said: Even frivolous speech**[H] **that is between a man and his wife** before engaging in relations **is declared to a person at the time of death,** and he will have to account for it.

אִינִי? וְהָא רַב כָּהֲנָא הֲוָה גָּנֵי תּוּתֵי פּוּרְיֵיהּ דְּרַב, וּשְׁמָעֵיהּ דְּסָח וְצָחַק וְעָשָׂה צְרָכָיו. אֲמַר: דָּמֵי פּוּמֵיהּ דְּרַב כְּמַאן דְּלָא טְעִים לֵיהּ תַּבְשִׁילָא. אֲמַר לֵיהּ: כָּהֲנָא, פּוּק, לָאו אוֹרַח אַרְעָא!

The Gemara asks: **Is that so?** Is it prohibited for a man to speak in this manner with his wife? **Wasn't Rav Kahana lying beneath Rav's bed, and he heard** Rav **chatting and laughing** with his wife, **and performing his needs,** i.e., having relations with her. Rav Kahana **said** out loud: **The mouth of Rav is like** one who **has never eaten a cooked dish,** i.e., his behavior is lustful. Rav **said to him: Kahana, leave,** as this is **not proper conduct.** This shows that Rav himself engaged in frivolous talk before relations.

לָא קַשְׁיָא; כָּאן – דִּצְרִיךְ לְרַצּוּיַהּ, הָא – דְּלָא צָרִיךְ לְרַצּוּיַהּ.

The Gemara answers: This is **not difficult. Here,** where this type of speech is permitted, it is referring to a situation **where he must appease** his wife before relations, and therefore this speech is appropriate. However, **this** statement, that it is prohibited, is referring to a situation **where he doesn't need to appease her.** In these circumstances, it is prohibited to engage in excessively lighthearted chatter with one's wife.

״וְאִם לֹא תִשְׁמָעוּהָ בְּמִסְתָּרִים תִּבְכֶּה נַפְשִׁי מִפְּנֵי גֵוָה״. אָמַר רַב שְׁמוּאֵל בַּר אִינְיָא מִשְּׁמֵיהּ דְּרַב: מָקוֹם יֵשׁ לוֹ לְהַקָּדוֹשׁ בָּרוּךְ הוּא וּמִסְתָּרִים שְׁמוֹ. מַאי ״מִפְּנֵי גֵוָה״? אָמַר רַב שְׁמוּאֵל בַּר יִצְחָק: מִפְּנֵי גַּאֲוָתָן שֶׁל יִשְׂרָאֵל שֶׁנִּיטְּלָה מֵהֶם וְנִתְּנָה לְגוֹיִם. רַבִּי שְׁמוּאֵל בַּר נַחְמָנִי אָמַר: מִפְּנֵי גַּאֲוָתָהּ שֶׁל מַלְכוּת שָׁמַיִם.

The verse states: **"But if you will not hear it, my soul shall weep in secret [*bemistarim*] for your pride"** (Jeremiah 13:17). **Rav Shmuel bar Inya said in the name of Rav: The Holy One, Blessed be He, has a place** where He cries, **and its name is Mistarim. What** is the meaning of **"for your pride"?**[N] **Rav Shmuel bar Yitzḥak said:** God cries **due to the pride of the Jewish people, which was taken from them and given to** the gentile **nations. Rav Shmuel bar Naḥmani said:** He cries **due to the pride of the kingdom of Heaven,** which was removed from the world.

וּמִי אִיכָּא בְּכִיָּה קַמֵּיהּ הַקָּדוֹשׁ בָּרוּךְ הוּא? וְהָאָמַר רַב פַּפָּא: אֵין עֲצִיבוּת לִפְנֵי הַקָּדוֹשׁ בָּרוּךְ הוּא, שֶׁנֶּאֱמַר: ״הוֹד וְהָדָר לְפָנָיו עֹז וְחֶדְוָה בִּמְקוֹמוֹ״. לָא קַשְׁיָא: הָא – בְּבָתֵּי גַּוָּאֵי, הָא – בְּבָתֵּי בָּרָאֵי.

The Gemara asks: **But is there crying before the Holy One, Blessed be He? Didn't Rav Pappa say: There is no sadness before the Holy One, Blessed be He, as it is stated: "Honor and majesty are before Him; strength and gladness are in His place"** (I Chronicles 16:27)? The Gemara responds: This is **not difficult. This** statement, that God cries, is referring to **the innermost chambers,** where He can cry in secret, whereas **this** statement, that He does not cry, is referring to **the outer chambers.**[N]

NOTES

He heard a child, etc. – שְׁמָעֵיהּ לְיַנּוּקָא וכו׳: But is it possible that Rabbi Ila was unfamiliar with this verse until he heard it from a child? Some suggest that the child read the verse with a slight error, which accentuated this particular interpretation. Specifically, he read *siḥo*, which clearly refers to speech, rather than *"seiḥo,"* which bears other meanings, e.g., actions (see Ibn Ezra on Amos 4:13; see also Riaf and *Iyyun Ya'akov*).

For your pride [*geva*] – מִפְּנֵי גֵוָה: *Geva* is explained as a form of *ga'ava*, pride, i.e., God cries over the degradation of the exalted. The two explanations mentioned in the Gemara are similar to one another, as God Himself is the pride of the Jewish people (see Deuteronomy 33:29; Psalms 89:18), while the fall of the Jewish people is considered the degradation of the glory of the heavens (see *Otzar HaKavod*; Maharsha).

This is referring to the outer chambers – הָא בְּבָתֵּי בָּרָאֵי: Rashi explains that that God cries in the innermost chambers, whereas He does not cry in the outer chambers. Some commentaries suggest the opposite explanation, apparently based on a textual variant (Rabbeinu Ḥananel). According to this interpretation, there is always strength and gladness in God's inner chambers, whereas in the outer chambers He cries. Many commentaries understand similarly, that in the inner presence of God there is no sadness at all, as crying always relates to the external reality of the world.

HALAKHA

Frivolous speech – שִׂיחָה יְתֵירָה: A man should not act frivolously with his wife and should not defile his mouth with idle talk, even in private conversations between the two of them. Furthermore, he should not speak of other matters with her while engaged in marital relations. However, it is permitted to talk with her about issues related to intercourse. If they had quarreled beforehand, he may converse with her so as to appease her, as indicated by both the *baraita* and Rav's behavior (*Shulḥan Arukh*, *Even HaEzer* 25:2).

וּבְבָתֵּי בָּרָאֵי לָא? וְהָא כְּתִיב: ״וַיִּקְרָא אֲדֹנָי ה׳ צְבָאוֹת בַּיּוֹם הַהוּא לִבְכִי וּלְמִסְפֵּד וּלְקָרְחָה וְלַחֲגוֹר שָׂק״! שָׁאנֵי חוּרְבַּן בֵּית הַמִּקְדָּשׁ, דַּאֲפִילּוּ מַלְאֲכֵי שָׁלוֹם בָּכוּ, שֶׁנֶּאֱמַר: ״הֵן אֶרְאֶלָּם צָעֲקוּ חוּצָה מַלְאֲכֵי שָׁלוֹם מַר יִבְכָּיוּן״.

The Gemara asks: **And doesn't** God cry **in the outer chambers? Isn't it written: "And on that day the Lord, the God of hosts, called to weeping, and to mourning, and to baldness, and to girding with sackcloth"** (Isaiah 22:12)? The Gemara responds: **The destruction of the Temple is different, as even the angels of peace cried, as it is stated: "Behold, their valiant ones cry without; the angels of peace weep bitterly"** (Isaiah 33:7).

״וְדָמֹעַ תִּדְמַע וְתֵרַד עֵינִי דִּמְעָה כִּי נִשְׁבָּה עֵדֶר ה׳״ אָמַר רַבִּי אֶלְעָזָר: שָׁלֹשׁ דְּמָעוֹת הַלָּלוּ לָמָּה? אַחַת – עַל מִקְדָּשׁ רִאשׁוֹן; וְאַחַת – עַל מִקְדָּשׁ שֵׁנִי; וְאַחַת – עַל יִשְׂרָאֵל שֶׁגָּלוּ מִמְּקוֹמָן. וְאִיכָּא דְּאָמְרִי: אַחַת עַל בִּיטּוּל תּוֹרָה.

The verse continues: **"And my eye shall weep sore, and run down with tears, because the Lord's flock is carried away captive"** (Jeremiah 13:17). **Rabbi Elazar said: Why these three** references to **tears** in the verse? **One is for the First Temple; one is for the Second Temple; and one is for the Jewish people who were exiled from their place. And there are** those **who say:** The last **one is for** the unavoidable **dereliction** of the study of **Torah** in the wake of the exile.

בִּשְׁלָמָא לְמַאן דְּאָמַר עַל יִשְׂרָאֵל שֶׁגָּלוּ – הַיְינוּ דִּכְתִיב: ״כִּי נִשְׁבָּה עֵדֶר ה׳״. אֶלָּא לְמַאן דְּאָמַר עַל בִּיטּוּל תּוֹרָה, מַאי ״כִּי נִשְׁבָּה עֵדֶר ה׳״? כֵּיוָן שֶׁגָּלוּ יִשְׂרָאֵל מִמְּקוֹמָן – אֵין לְךָ בִּיטּוּל תּוֹרָה גָּדוֹל מִזֶּה.

The Gemara asks: **Granted, according to the one who said** that the last tear is **for the Jewish people who were exiled, this is as it is written: "Because the Lord's flock is carried away captive." However, according to the one who said** that this tear is **for the dereliction** of the study of **Torah, what is** the meaning of: **"Because the Lord's flock is carried away captive"?** The Gemara answers: **Since the Jewish people were exiled from their place, there is no greater** involuntary **dereliction** of the study of **Torah than** that which was caused by **this.**

תָּנוּ רַבָּנַן: שְׁלֹשָׁה הַקָּדוֹשׁ בָּרוּךְ הוּא בּוֹכֶה עֲלֵיהֶן בְּכָל יוֹם: עַל שֶׁאֶפְשָׁר לַעֲסוֹק בַּתּוֹרָה וְאֵינוֹ עוֹסֵק, וְעַל שֶׁאִי אֶפְשָׁר לַעֲסוֹק בַּתּוֹרָה וְעוֹסֵק, וְעַל פַּרְנָס הַמִּתְגָּאֶה עַל הַצִּבּוּר.

The Sages taught that there are **three** types of people **for whom the Holy One, Blessed be He, cries**[N] **every day:** For one **who is able to engage in Torah** study **and does not engage** in it; **and for** one **who is unable to engage in Torah** study and nevertheless he endeavors and **engages** in it;[N] **and for a leader who lords over the community.**

רַבִּי הֲוָה נָקֵיט סֵפֶר קִינוֹת וְקָא קָרֵי בְּגַוֵּיהּ. כִּי מְטָא לְהַאי פְּסוּקָא: ״הִשְׁלִיךְ מִשָּׁמַיִם אֶרֶץ״ – נְפַל מִן יְדֵיהּ. אֲמַר: מֵאִיגְּרָא רָם לְבֵירָא עֲמִיקְתָּא.

The Gemara relates: **Rabbi** Yehuda HaNasi **was holding** the **book of Lamentations and was reading from it. When he reached the verse: "He has cast down from heaven to earth** the beauty of Israel" (Lamentations 2:1), in his distress the book **fell from his hand. He said: From a high roof to a deep pit,** i.e., it is terrible to tumble from the sky to the ground.

רַבִּי וְרַבִּי חִיָּיא הֲווּ שָׁקְלִי וְאָזְלִי בְּאוֹרְחָא. כִּי מְטוֹ לְהָהוּא מָתָא אָמְרִי: אִיכָּא צוּרְבָא מֵרַבָּנַן הָכָא, נֵיזִיל וְנִיקַבֵּיל אַפֵּיהּ. אָמְרִי: אִיכָּא צוּרְבָא מֵרַבָּנַן הָכָא, וּמְאוֹר עֵינַיִם הוּא. אֲמַר לֵיהּ רַבִּי חִיָּיא לְרַבִּי: תִּיב אַתְּ, לָא תְּזַלְזֵל בִּנְשִׂיאוּתָךְ. אֵיזִיל אֲנָא וַאֲקַבֵּיל אַפֵּיהּ.

§ The Gemara relates: **Rabbi** Yehuda HaNasi **and Rabbi Ḥiyya were walking along the road. When they arrived at a certain city, they said: Is there a Torah scholar here whom we can go and greet?** The people of the city **said: There is a Torah scholar here but he is blind. Rabbi Ḥiyya said to Rabbi** Yehuda HaNasi: **You sit here; do not demean your** dignified status as *Nasi* to visit someone beneath your stature. **I will go and greet him.**

NOTES

Three for whom the Holy One, Blessed be He, cries – שְׁלֹשָׁה הַקָּדוֹשׁ בָּרוּךְ הוּא בּוֹכֶה עֲלֵיהֶן: The reason for this crying is unclear. One explanation is that God decrees one's life path from the outset, whether he will be wealthy or poor, of a lowly or high status. Occasionally, it is decreed that a certain individual will be rich and therefore will have ample time to study Torah. However, he fails to utilize this opportunity. Conversely, if one is decreed for financial struggles there is no expectation that he will have time for Torah study, and yet some manage to do so regardless. The same applies to one who was granted a position of greatness that he uses improperly. In all these cases, God cries over the decree (*Mishḥat Aharon*).

For one who is unable to engage in Torah study…and engages in it – עַל שֶׁאִי אֶפְשָׁר לוֹ לַעֲסוֹק בַּתּוֹרָה וְעוֹסֵק: Why does God cry over this individual? He should rejoice over him (see Maharsha). Some explain that God does not cry for him, but for those who had the ability to support him and failed to do so (*Gilyonei Yoel*). Alternatively, this does not refer to one who is unable to study due to financial difficulties but to one who is hampered by intellectual deficiencies. He strives to learn on a level beyond his ability but is unable to understand his studies (*Zekher LaḤagiga*).

תְּקָפֵיהּ וַאֲזַל בַּהֲדֵיהּ. כִּי הָווּ מִיפַּטְרִי מִינֵּיהּ, אֲמַר לְהוּ: אַתֶּם הִקְבַּלְתֶּם פָּנִים הַנִּרְאִים וְאֵינָן רוֹאִין – תִּזְכּוּ לְהַקְבִּיל פָּנִים הָרוֹאִים וְאֵינָן נִרְאִין. אֲמַר לֵיהּ: אִיכּוּ הָשְׁתָּא מְנַעְתַּן מֵהַאי בִּירְכָתָא.

Rabbi Yehuda HaNasi **grabbed him and went with him** anyway, and together they greeted the blind scholar. **When they were leaving him, he said to them: You greeted** one who is **seen and does not see; may you be worthy to greet** the One Who **sees and is not seen.** Rabbi Yehuda HaNasi **said to** Rabbi Ḥiyya: **Now, if** I had listened to you and not gone to greet him, **you would have prevented me from receiving this blessing.**

אֲמַרוּ לֵיהּ: מִמַּאן שְׁמִיעָא לָךְ? מִפִּרְקֵיהּ דְּרַבִּי יַעֲקֹב שְׁמִיעַ לִי. דְּרַבִּי יַעֲקֹב אִישׁ כְּפַר חִיטַּיָּא הֲוָה מַקְבִּיל אַפֵּיהּ דְּרַבֵּיהּ כָּל יוֹמָא. כִּי קָשׁ אֲמַר לֵיהּ: לָא נִצְטַעֵר מָר, דְּלָא יָכֵיל מָר.

They said to the blind scholar: **From whom did you hear**[N] that we are worthy of this blessing? He said to them: **I heard** it **from the instruction of Rabbi Ya'akov, as Rabbi Ya'akov of the village of Ḥitiyya would greet his teacher every day. When** Rabbi Ya'akov **grew elderly,** his teacher **said to him: Do not despair, my Master, that my Master is unable** to make the effort to greet me. It is better that you should not visit me.

אֲמַר לֵיהּ: מִי זוּטָר מַאי דִּכְתִיב בְּהוּ בְּרַבָּנַן: ״וִיחִי עוֹד לָנֶצַח לֹא יִרְאֶה הַשָּׁחַת כִּי יִרְאֶה חֲכָמִים יָמוּתוּ״? וּמָה הָרוֹאֶה חֲכָמִים בְּמִיתָתָן יִחְיֶה, בְּחַיֵּיהֶן – עַל אַחַת כַּמָּה וְכַמָּה!

Rabbi Ya'akov **said to him: Is it** a **minor** matter, **that which is written about the Sages: "That he should still live always, that he should not see the pit. For he sees that wise men die"** (Psalms 49:10–11)? In this regard an *a fortiori* reference applies: **Just as one who sees Sages in their death will live, all the more so** one who sees them **in their lifetime.** From here the blind scholar learned the importance of greeting Torah scholars, which is why he blessed the Sages who came to greet him.

רַב אִידִי אֲבוּהּ דְּרַבִּי יַעֲקֹב בַּר אִידִי הֲוָה רָגִיל דַּהֲוָה אָזֵיל תְּלָתָא יַרְחֵי בְּאוֹרְחָא וְחַד יוֹמָא בְּבֵי רַב. וְהָווּ קָרוּ לֵיהּ רַבָּנַן ״בַּר בֵּי רַב דְּחַד יוֹמָא״. חֲלַשׁ דַּעֲתֵיהּ. קָרֵי אַנַּפְשֵׁיהּ: ״שְׂחוֹק לְרֵעֵהוּ אֶהְיֶה״ וגו׳. אֲמַר לֵיהּ רַבִּי יוֹחָנָן: בְּמָטוּתָא מִינָּךְ לָא תַּעֲנִישׁ לְהוּ רַבָּנַן.

The Gemara relates: **Rav Idi, father of Rabbi Ya'akov bar Idi, would regularly travel three months on the road** to reach the study hall **and** as he would immediately travel back again to arrive home for the festival of *Sukkot*, he spent only **one day in the school of Rav. And the Sages would** disparagingly **call him: A student** of Torah **for one day. He was offended** and **read** the following verse **about himself: "I am as one that is a laughingstock to his neighbor,** a man who calls upon God, and He answers him" (Job 12:4). **Rabbi Yoḥanan said to him: Please do not punish the Sages,** i.e., do not take offense and be harsh with them, as this will cause them to be punished by God.

נְפַק רַבִּי יוֹחָנָן לְבֵי מִדְרָשָׁא וְדָרַשׁ: ״וְאוֹתִי יוֹם יוֹם יִדְרֹשׁוּן וְדַעַת דְּרָכַי יֶחְפָּצוּן״. וְכִי בַּיּוֹם דּוֹרְשִׁין אוֹתוֹ וּבַלַּיְלָה אֵין דּוֹרְשִׁין אוֹתוֹ? אֶלָּא לוֹמַר לְךָ: כָּל הָעוֹסֵק בַּתּוֹרָה אֲפִילּוּ יוֹם אֶחָד בַּשָּׁנָה – מַעֲלֶה עָלָיו הַכָּתוּב כְּאִילּוּ עָסַק כָּל הַשָּׁנָה כּוּלָּהּ.

Rabbi Yoḥanan left Rav Idi and went **to the study hall and taught: "Yet they seek Me daily, and delight to know My ways"** (Isaiah 58:2). **But is** it possible that only **during the day they seek Him and at night they do not seek Him?** What is the meaning of daily? **Rather,** this verse comes **to say to you** that with regard to **anyone who engages in Torah** study **even one day a year, the verse ascribes him** credit **as though he engaged** in Torah study **the entire year.**

וְכֵן בְּמִדַּת פּוּרְעָנוּת, דִּכְתִיב: ״בְּמִסְפַּר הַיָּמִים אֲשֶׁר תַּרְתֶּם אֶת הָאָרֶץ״. וְכִי אַרְבָּעִים שָׁנָה חָטְאוּ? וַהֲלֹא אַרְבָּעִים יוֹם חָטְאוּ! אֶלָּא לוֹמַר לְךָ: כָּל הָעוֹבֵר עֲבֵירָה אֲפִילּוּ יוֹם אֶחָד בַּשָּׁנָה – מַעֲלֶה עָלָיו הַכָּתוּב כְּאִילּוּ עָבַר כָּל הַשָּׁנָה כּוּלָּהּ.

And the same applies **to the attribute of punishment, as it is written: "After the number of the days in which you spied out the land,** even forty days, for every day a year, shall you bear your iniquities" (Numbers 14:34). **But did they sin** for **forty years? Didn't they sin** for only **forty days? Rather,** this comes **to say to you** that **anyone who transgresses a sin even one day a year, the verse ascribes him** liability **as though he transgressed the entire year.**

״אֵי זֶהוּ קָטָן? כָּל שֶׁאֵינוֹ יָכוֹל לִרְכּוֹב עַל כְּתֵפוֹ שֶׁל אָבִיו״. מַתְקִיף לָהּ רַבִּי זֵירָא:

§ The mishna taught: **Who is a minor** who is exempt from the mitzva of appearance in the Temple? **Any** child **who is unable to ride on his father's shoulders** and ascend from Jerusalem to the Temple Mount. **Rabbi Zeira strongly objects to this:**

NOTES

From whom did you hear – מִמַּאן שְׁמִיעָא לָךְ: One version of the text cites this question in the singular form, i.e., Rabbi Ḥiyya asked Rabbi Yehuda HaNasi where he learned the importance of the mitzva to greet a Torah scholar (*Dikdukei Soferim*). The story is much simpler according to this version, which resolves several of the difficulties raised by the commentaries.

עַד הָכָא מַאן אַתְיֵיהּ?

Who brought him to here, all the way to Jerusalem? If the father could bring his child to Jerusalem, why can't he bring him to the Temple Mount?

אֲמַר לֵיהּ אַבָּיֵי: עַד הָכָא, דְּמִיחַיְּיבָא אִימֵּיהּ בְּשִׂמְחָה – אַיְיתִיתֵיהּ אִימֵּיהּ. מִכָּאן וְאֵילָךְ, אִם יָכוֹל לַעֲלוֹת וְלֶאֱחוֹז בְּיָדוֹ שֶׁל אָבִיו מִירוּשָׁלַיִם לְהַר הַבַּיִת – חַיָּיב; וְאִי לָא – פָּטוּר.

Abaye said to him: With regard to the way **to here, as his mother is** also **obligated in rejoicing**[NH] on the Festival, **his mother brought him** when she herself ascended to the capital. **From this point forward, if he is able to ascend and hold his father's hand from Jerusalem to the Temple Mount,**[N] **he is obligated, and if not, he is exempt.**

הֵשִׁיב רַבִּי תַּחַת בֵּית הִלֵּל: לְדִבְרֵי בֵית שַׁמַּאי, "וְחַנָּה לֹא עָלָתָה כִּי אָמְרָה לְאִישָׁהּ עַד יִגָּמֵל הַנַּעַר וַהֲבִיאוֹתִיו", וְהָא שְׁמוּאֵל דְּיָכוֹל לִרְכּוֹב עַל כְּתֵיפוֹ שֶׁל אָבִיו הֲוָה!

It is taught in a *baraita* that **Rabbi** Yehuda HaNasi **responded in place of Beit Hillel,** that **according to the statement of Beit Shammai** that a child who is unable to ride on his father's shoulders is not obligated in the mitzva of appearance, they must explain a verse that deals with Hanna, Samuel's mother: **"But Hanna did not ascend, for she said to her husband: Until the child is weaned, when I will bring him"** (I Samuel 1:22). **But Samuel was able to ride on his father's shoulders.** The age of weaning is twenty-four months, before which Samuel was already old enough to ride on his father's shoulders, and yet he was not ready to ascend to the Tabernacle. This shows that only a child who is able to walk on his own is obligated in the mitzva of appearance.

אֲמַר לֵיהּ אֲבוּהּ: וּלְטַעֲמִיךְ, תִּיקְשֵׁי לָךְ חַנָּה גּוּפַהּ, מִי לָא מִיחַיְּיבָא בְּשִׂמְחָה? אֶלָּא, חַנָּה מִפַּנְקוּתָא יְתֵירְתָּא חָזְיָיא בֵּיהּ בִּשְׁמוּאֵל, וְחָשְׁשָׁא בֵּיהּ בִּשְׁמוּאֵל לְחוּלְשָׁא דְּאוֹרְחָא.

Rabbi Yehuda HaNasi's **father said to him: According to your reasoning, ask about Hanna herself: Wasn't she obligated in rejoicing?** Why didn't she travel to the Tabernacle to fulfill a mitzva in which she herself was obligated? **Rather, Hanna saw in Samuel** the need for **extra pampering, and she was concerned about Samuel** lest he experience **weakness from the journey.** Since she was unable to bring him, she herself did not come.

בָּעֵי רַבִּי שִׁמְעוֹן: קָטָן חִיגֵּר לְדִבְרֵי בֵית שַׁמַּאי וְסוּמָא לְדִבְרֵי שְׁנֵיהֶם, מַהוּ?

Rabbi Shimon raises a dilemma:[N] With regard to **a minor** who is **lame** and yet he is able to ascend on his father's shoulders, **according to the statement of Beit Shammai, and** likewise a minor who is **blind** but is able to hold his father's hand and ascend, **according to the statements of both** Beit Shammai and Beit Hillel, **what is** the *halakha*? Are these children obligated in the mitzva of appearance?

הֵיכִי דָּמֵי? אִילֵּימָא בְּחִיגֵּר שֶׁאֵינוֹ יָכוֹל לְהִתְפַּשֵּׁט, וְסוּמָא שֶׁאֵינוֹ יָכוֹל לְהִתְפַּתֵּחַ, הַשְׁתָּא גָּדוֹל פָּטוּר, קָטָן מִיבַּעְיָא?! לָא צְרִיכָא, בְּחִיגֵּר שֶׁיָּכוֹל לְהִתְפַּשֵּׁט, וְסוּמָא שֶׁיָּכוֹל לְהִתְפַּתֵּחַ, מַאי?

The Gemara inquires: **What are the circumstances** of this case? **If we say** that it is referring **to a lame** minor **who cannot be healed, and a blind** child **who cannot develop** sight, what is the dilemma? **Now,** if **an adult** in this state **is exempt,** is it **necessary** to ask about **a minor?** Since this minor will never be obligated in the mitzva, even when he is an adult, there is no need to train him in its performance. The Gemara explains: **No;** it is **necessary** to ask with regard **to a lame** minor **who can be healed and a blind** minor **who can develop** sight. **What** is the *halakha*? Since the minor might eventually be obligated, is it necessary to train him at this point?

NOTES

As his mother is obligated in rejoicing – דְּמִיחַיְּיבָא אִימֵּיהּ בְּשִׂמְחָה: The obligation of women in the mitzva of rejoicing on the Festival is derived from the verse: "And you shall rejoice, you, and your household" (Deuteronomy 14:26). However, the manner of the fulfillment of this mitzva in practice is unclear. Rashi says that this mitzva is not related to the offerings; rather, husbands must ensure that their wives rejoice on the Festival. Naturally, women should be with their husbands on the Festival so that they can enable them to rejoice. Some commentaries indicate that the mitzva is for women to participate in the Festival peace-offerings (*Tosafot*). However, even *Tosafot* agree that the obligation to bring the offerings does not apply to women themselves. Rather, their husbands must bring these offerings and thereby cause their wives to rejoice. Yet others maintain that women are personally obligated to bring the Festival peace-offering, and they must ascend to the Temple for that reason (see HALAKHA).

To ascend…from Jerusalem to the Temple Mount – לַעֲלוֹת...מִירוּשָׁלַיִם לְהַר הַבַּיִת: In the Jerusalem Talmud a question is raised concerning the distance one must be able to walk for him to be obligated to ascend to the Temple. Is it measured from the city wall or from some other spot? The conclusion of the Gemara there is that the measurement is from the Siloam pool, i.e., one who is able to walk from the Siloam pool to the Temple Mount is obligated in the mitzva of appearance.

Rabbi Shimon raises a dilemma, etc. – בָּעֵי רַבִּי שִׁמְעוֹן וכו׳: A similar problem is cited in the Jerusalem Talmud with regard to a deaf minor, although there the dilemma is attributed to an *amora*. The Gemara there asks how it can even be suggested that a minor might be obligated in a mitzva from which an adult is exempt. The answer given is that the verse from which the obligation of minors is derived: "All your males" (Exodus 23:17), is unrelated to the verse that serves as the source for the *halakha* that certain people are exempt from the obligation to ascend to the Temple. Therefore, it is possible that these exemptions do not apply to minors.

HALAKHA

As his mother is obligated in rejoicing – דְּמִיחַיְּיבָא אִימֵּיהּ בְּשִׂמְחָה: One of the mitzvot of the pilgrimage Festivals is to sacrifice regular peace-offerings, in addition to the Festival peace-offerings. These regular offerings are called the peace-offerings of rejoicing, and women are also obligated in this mitzva. Some maintain that women are not obligated to bring this offering at all; rather, they need only fulfill the mitzva to rejoice, i.e., when a woman ascends with her husband to the Temple, he must enable her to rejoice (Ra'avad). There is a dispute with regard to the opinion of the Rambam, as some (*Leḥem Mishne*) say he rules that women are obligated to bring the offering, whereas others (*Kesef Mishne*) maintain that according to the opinion of the Rambam women fulfill the mitzva by means of their husbands' peace-offerings of rejoicing (Rambam *Sefer Korbanot, Hilkhot Ḥagiga* 1:1).

אָמַר אַבַּיֵי: כָּל הֵיכָא דְּגָדוֹל מִיחַיַּיב מִדְּאוֹרַיְיתָא – קָטָן נַמִי מְחַנְּכִינַן לֵיהּ מִדְּרַבָּנַן; כָּל הֵיכָא דְּגָדוֹל פָּטוּר מִדְּאוֹרַיְיתָא – מִדְּרַבָּנַן קָטָן נַמִי פָּטוּר.

Abaye said: Anywhere that an adult is obligated by Torah law, one must **also train a minor** in that state of health **by rabbinic law. Anywhere that an adult is exempt**[NH] **by Torah law, a minor** in that same state **is also exempt by rabbinic law.** Since in this current condition an adult would be exempt, there is no obligation to train this minor either, despite the fact that he might become obligated in the future.

"בֵּית שַׁמַּאי אוֹמְרִים הָרְאִיָּיה שְׁתֵּי כֶסֶף" כו׳.

§ The mishna taught that **Beit Shammai say:** The burnt-offering of **appearance,** brought by a pilgrim when he appears at the Temple on a Festival, must be worth at least **two silver** coins, and the Festival peace-offering must be worth at least one silver *ma'a* coin. And Beit Hillel say: The burnt-offering of appearance must be worth at least one silver *ma'a* and the Festival peace-offering at least two silver coins.

תָּנוּ רַבָּנַן, בֵּית שַׁמַּאי אוֹמְרִים: הָרְאִיָּיה שְׁתֵּי כֶסֶף, וְהַחֲגִיגָה מָעָה כֶּסֶף. שֶׁהָרְאִיָּיה עוֹלָה כּוּלָּהּ לַגָּבוֹהַּ, מַה שֶּׁאֵין כֵּן בַּחֲגִיגָה. וְעוֹד: מָצִינוּ בַּעֲצֶרֶת, שֶׁרִיבָּה בָּהֶן הַכָּתוּב בְּעוֹלוֹת יוֹתֵר מִבִּשְׁלָמִים.

The Sages taught in a *baraita* that **Beit Shammai say:** The burnt-offering of **appearance** must be worth **two silver** coins, **and the Festival peace**-offering need be worth only one **silver** *ma'a.* The reason the burnt-offering must be worth more is **that** the burnt-offering of **appearance** goes **up entirely to God, which is not so with regard to the Festival peace**-offering, as parts of **a peace**-offering are eaten by its owner while other portions are consumed by the priests. **And furthermore,** another reason for this difference is that **we find with regard to** the festival of **Assembly,**[N] i.e., *Shavuot,* **that the verse includes more burnt**-offerings **than peace**-offerings. The sacrificial requirement consists of one bull, two rams, and seven sheep as burnt-offerings, but only two sheep for peace-offerings.

וּבֵית הִלֵּל אוֹמְרִים: הָרְאִיָּיה מָעָה כֶסֶף וַחֲגִיגָה שְׁתֵּי כֶסֶף. שֶׁחֲגִיגָה יֶשְׁנָהּ לִפְנֵי הַדִּיבּוּר, מַה שֶּׁאֵין כֵּן בָּרְאִיָּיה. וְעוֹד: מָצִינוּ בַּנְּשִׂיאִים שֶׁרִיבָּה בָּהֶן הַכָּתוּב בִּשְׁלָמִים יוֹתֵר מִבְּעוֹלוֹת.

And Beit Hillel say: The burnt-offering of **appearance** must be worth **one silver** *ma'a* **and the Festival peace**-offering must be worth **two silver** coins. The reason for this difference is **that the Festival peace**-offering **existed before the speech**[N] of God, i.e., before the giving of the Torah on Mount Sinai, **which is not so with regard to** the mitzva of **appearance. And furthermore,** another reason is that **we find with regard to** the offerings of the princes during the dedication of the Tabernacle **that the verse includes more peace**-offerings **than burnt**-offerings. Each prince brought one cow, a ram, and a sheep as burnt-offerings, but two cows, two rams, five goats, and five sheep as peace-offerings.

וּבֵית הִלֵּל, מַאי טַעְמָא לָא אָמְרִי כְּבֵית שַׁמַּאי? דְּקָא אָמְרַתְּ רְאִיָּיה עֲדִיפָא, דְּעוֹלָה כּוּלָּהּ לַגָּבוֹהַּ – אַדְּרַבָּה, חֲגִיגָה עֲדִיפָא, דְּאִית בָּהּ שְׁתֵּי אֲכִילוֹת. וּדְקָא אָמְרַתְּ נֵילַף מֵעֲצֶרֶת – דָּנִין קָרְבַּן יָחִיד מִקָּרְבַּן יָחִיד, וְאֵין דָּנִין קָרְבַּן יָחִיד מִקָּרְבַּן צִבּוּר.

The Gemara asks: **And Beit Hillel, what is the reason** that **they do not say in accordance with** the opinion of **Beit Shammai?** Beit Hillel would respond to both claims of Beit Shammai. With regard to **that which you said,** that the burnt-offering of **appearance is superior because it** goes **up entirely to God, on the contrary, the Festival peace**-offering **is superior,**[N] **as it has two consumptions,** by God on the altar and by people. **And** with regard to **that which you said** that **we derive** this *halakha* **from** the festival of **Assembly,** i.e., *Shavuot,* one could argue instead that **one** should **derive** the *halakhot* of **the offering of an individual from** another **offering of an individual,** i.e., the princes; **and one does not derive** the *halakhot* **of the offering of an individual from the communal offering** of *Shavuot.*

וּבֵית שַׁמַּאי, מַאי טַעְמָא לָא אָמְרִי כְּבֵית הִלֵּל? דְּקָאָמְרַתְּ חֲגִיגָה עֲדִיפָא דְּיֶשְׁנָהּ לִפְנֵי הַדִּיבּוּר – רְאִיָּיה נַמִי יֶשְׁנָהּ לִפְנֵי הַדִּיבּוּר.

The Gemara asks the reverse question: **And what is the reason** that **Beit Shammai do not say in accordance with** the opinion of **Beit Hillel?** Beit Shammai would respond to the arguments of Beit Hillel: **With regard to that which you said,** that **the Festival peace**-offering **is superior, as it existed before the speech** of God, the burnt-offering of **appearance also existed before the speech.** According to the opinion of Beit Shammai, the Jewish people sacrificed burnt-offerings at Mount Sinai before the giving of the Torah.

NOTES

Anywhere that an adult is exempt, etc. – כָּל הֵיכָא דְּגָדוֹל פָּטוּר וכו׳: Some commentaries cite this statement as proof of the following broad claim: Due to the fact that the mitzva to train children in the performance of mitzvot applies by rabbinic law, it does not include mitzvot that are themselves obligatory by rabbinic law, as that would be combining two rabbinic laws. Although the practice is to train minors in certain mitzvot that apply by rabbinic law, e.g., Hanukkah and the recitation of blessings, there is a specific reason in each of those cases. Others explain that a special *halakha* applies to this case, as the Sages did not require one to train a child who has a condition that would render even an adult exempt (see *Birkei Yosef* and *Yad David*).

We find with regard to the festival of Assembly, etc. – מָצִינוּ בַּעֲצֶרֶת וכו׳: On other Festivals the additional offerings consist solely of burnt-offerings, while no communal peace-offerings are brought at all. Why, then, didn't the Gemara cite these cases as evidence that the burnt-offering is superior? The commentaries explain that when no peace-offering is sacrificed at all there is no room for comparison. The only way to determine whether the burnt-offering is superior to the peace-offering is by a direct comparison between the two when both types of offerings are brought, and both are sacrificed only on *Shavuot* (*Turei Aven*).

Existed before the speech – יֶשְׁנָהּ לִפְנֵי הַדִּיבּוּר: Rashi and others explain that the phrase: Before the speech, means before the giving of the Torah. Others explain that it means before God spoke to Moses from the Tent of Meeting (*Tosefot Rid*). According to this explanation, the Gemara is far more straightforward.

On the contrary, the Festival peace-offering is superior – אַדְּרַבָּה, חֲגִיגָה עֲדִיפָא: It is generally assumed that the burnt-offering is the most important offering, as it is entirely burnt. If so, it is unclear how it can be suggested that the Festival peace-offering is superior. Some commentaries explain that the Gemara is not asking which offering has a more sacred status, as that is certainly the burnt-offering. Rather, the issue is how much money must be spent on each of these offerings. Since the peace-offering is consumed by the owner as well, it is possible that it is appropriate to spend more on it (*Sefat Emet*).

HALAKHA

Anywhere that an adult is exempt – כָּל הֵיכָא דְּגָדוֹל פָּטוּר: With regard to a minor who is lame, deaf, or blind, even if he could potentially be healed his father is not obligated to bring him to the Temple in order to fulfill the mitzva to train him. The reason is that in any case where an adult is exempt by Torah law, one is exempt by rabbinic law from training a minor who has the same condition. This *halakha* is in accordance with the opinion of Abaye (Rambam *Sefer Korbanot, Hilkhot Ḥagiga* 2:3).

וּדְקָאָמְרַתְּ נֵילַף מִנְּשִׂיאִים – דָּנִין דָּבָר הַנּוֹהֵג לְדוֹרוֹת מִדָּבָר הַנּוֹהֵג לְדוֹרוֹת, וְאֵין דָּנִין דָּבָר הַנּוֹהֵג לְדוֹרוֹת מִדָּבָר שֶׁאֵינוֹ נוֹהֵג לְדוֹרוֹת.

And with regard to that which you said, that **one derives** the *halakhot* of these offerings **from** the offerings of **the princes,** one could argue that **one derives** the *halakhot* **of a matter that is performed in all generations,** i.e., the value of the different Festival offerings, **from** another **matter that is performed in** all **generations,** i.e., the offerings brought on *Shavuot.* However, **one does not derive** the *halakhot* **of a matter that is performed** in all generations **from a matter that is not performed in** all **generations,** as the offerings of the princes was a specific mitzva for the Tabernacle in the wilderness.

וּבֵית הִלֵּל, מַאי שְׁנָא חֲגִיגָה דְּיֶשְׁנָהּ לִפְנֵי הַדִּיבּוּר, דִּכְתִיב: ״וַיִּזְבְּחוּ זְבָחִים שְׁלָמִים״ – רְאִיָּיה נַמִי, הָכְתִיב: ״וַיַּעֲלוּ עוֹלוֹת״!

The Gemara asks: **And** according to the opinion of **Beit Hillel, what is different** about **the Festival peace**-offering, **that it existed before the speech** of God, **as it is written: "And they sacrificed peace-offerings**[N] of bulls to the Lord" (Exodus 24:5)? The burnt-offering of **appearance** is **also** mentioned, as **isn't it written** in the same verse: **"And they sacrificed burnt**-offerings"?

קָסָבְרִי בֵּית הִלֵּל: עוֹלָה שֶׁהִקְרִיבוּ יִשְׂרָאֵל בַּמִּדְבָּר עוֹלַת תָּמִיד הֲוַאי. וּבֵית שַׁמַּאי סָבְרִי: עוֹלָה שֶׁהִקְרִיבוּ יִשְׂרָאֵל בַּמִּדְבָּר עוֹלַת רְאִיָּיה הֲוַאי.

The Gemara responds: **Beit Hillel hold** that **the burnt**-offering **that the Jewish people sacrificed in the desert** at Mount Sinai **was the daily burnt**-offering,[NB] which is a communal offering, as there were no individual burnt-offerings before the giving of the Torah. **And Beit Shammai hold** that **the burnt**-offering **that the Jewish people sacrificed in the desert** at Mount Sinai **was a burnt**-offering **of appearance,** which is an individual offering.

אָמַר אַבַּיֵי: בֵּית שַׁמַּאי, וְרַבִּי אֶלְעָזָר, וְרַבִּי יִשְׁמָעֵאל – כּוּלְּהוּ סְבִירָא לְהוּ: עוֹלָה שֶׁהִקְרִיבוּ יִשְׂרָאֵל בַּמִּדְבָּר עוֹלַת רְאִיָּיה הֲוַאי. וּבֵית הִלֵּל, וְרַבִּי עֲקִיבָא, וְרַבִּי יוֹסֵי הַגְּלִילִי – כּוּלְּהוּ סְבִירָא לְהוּ: עוֹלָה שֶׁהִקְרִיבוּ יִשְׂרָאֵל בַּמִּדְבָּר עוֹלַת תָּמִיד הֲוַאי.

Abaye said: Beit Shammai, Rabbi Elazar, and Rabbi Yishmael all hold that **the burnt**-offering **that the Jewish people sacrificed in the desert** at Mount Sinai **was a burnt**-offering **of appearance. And Beit Hillel, Rabbi Akiva, and Rabbi Yosei HaGelili all hold** that **the burnt**-offering **that the Jewish people sacrificed in the desert** at Mount Sinai **was a daily burnt**-offering, not an individual offering.

בֵּית שַׁמַּאי – הָא דַּאֲמָרַן. רַבִּי יִשְׁמָעֵאל – דְּתַנְיָא, רַבִּי יִשְׁמָעֵאל אוֹמֵר: כְּלָלוֹת נֶאֶמְרוּ בְּסִינַי

The Gemara explains the source for each opinion. **Beit Shammai** is **that which we said. Rabbi Yishmael, as it is taught** in a *baraita* that **Rabbi Yishmael says: General statements were said at Sinai,** i.e., Moses received general mitzvot at Sinai, including the Ten Commandments.

NOTES

And they sacrificed peace-offerings – וַיִּזְבְּחוּ זְבָחִים שְׁלָמִים: The connection between these offerings and the Festival peace-offering is explained in the Jerusalem Talmud: It is with regard to these, i.e., the Festival peace-offerings, that the verse states: "Let My people go, that they may hold a Festival for Me in the wilderness" (Exodus 5:1).

Was the daily burnt-offering – עוֹלַת תָּמִיד הֲוַאי: Although this episode occurred before the giving of the Torah, when the daily burnt-offering was presumably commanded, it is possible that this mitzva was among those given at Mara even before the giving of the Torah (Meiri).

BACKGROUND

Daily burnt-offering – עוֹלַת תָּמִיד: This refers to the daily offering of two lambs, one in the morning and one in the afternoon, sacrificed each day in the Temple (see Numbers 28:1–8).

Perek **I**
Daf **6** Amud **b**

וּפְרָטוֹת בְּאֹהֶל מוֹעֵד, וְרַבִּי עֲקִיבָא אוֹמֵר: כְּלָלוֹת וּפְרָטוֹת נֶאֶמְרוּ בְּסִינַי, וְנִשְׁנוּ בְּאֹהֶל מוֹעֵד, וְנִשְׁתַּלְּשׁוּ בְּעַרְבוֹת מוֹאָב. וְאִי סָלְקָא דַּעְתָּךְ עוֹלָה שֶׁהִקְרִיבוּ יִשְׂרָאֵל בַּמִּדְבָּר עוֹלַת תָּמִיד הֲוַאי,

And the details of the mitzvot, e.g., the particulars of the sacrificial process, were said to Moses at a later time **in the Tent of Meeting. And Rabbi Akiva says:** Both **general statements and the details** of mitzvot **were said at Sinai and** later **repeated in the Tent of Meeting, and** reiterated **a third time** by Moses to the Jewish people **in the plains of Moab,** as recorded in the book of Deuteronomy. **And if it enters your mind** to say that Rabbi Yishmael holds that **the burnt**-offering **that the Jewish people sacrificed in the desert** at Mount Sinai **was the daily burnt**-offering, rather than the burnt-offering of an individual, the following question arises:

מִי אִיכָּא מִידֵי דְּמֵעִיקָּרָא לָא בָּעֵי הֶפְשֵׁט וְנִיתּוּחַ וּלְבַסּוֹף בָּעֵי הֶפְשֵׁט וְנִיתּוּחַ?

Is there any offering **that initially did not require skinning**[N] **and cutting** into pieces, as these details of the daily burnt-offering were transmitted later in the Tent of Meeting, **and ultimately,** when these details were added, the offering **required skinning and cutting?** It is not plausible that the details of a mitzva would change over time. Therefore, it is clear that according to the opinion of Rabbi Yishmael the Jews did not sacrifice the daily burnt-offering before the giving of the Torah, which means that the burnt-offering sacrificed at Mount Sinai must have been a burnt-offering of appearance.

NOTES

That initially did not require skinning – דְּמֵעִיקָּרָא לָא בָּעֵי הֶפְשֵׁט: Burnt-offerings did not require skinning or cutting into pieces before the giving of the Torah, as the details of the burnt-offering are presented as novel *halakhot* in Leviticus. No such requirements pertained to the burnt-offerings brought by the descendants of Noah either before the Torah was given or afterward. Many sources, such as the Jerusalem Talmud (*Megilla* 1:11), cite support for this claim from this verse: "Sacrificed burnt-offerings and sacrificed peace-offerings [*shelamim*]" (Exodus 24:5). They read the last word as: Complete [*sheleimim*], which indicates that these burnt-offerings were neither skinned nor cut into pieces.

רַבִּי אֶלְעָזָר דְּתַנְיָא: ״עוֹלַת תָּמִיד הָעֲשׂוּיָה בְּהַר סִינַי״, רַבִּי אֶלְעָזָר אוֹמֵר: מַעֲשֶׂיהָ נֶאֶמְרוּ בְּסִינַי, וְהִיא עַצְמָהּ לֹא קָרְבָה.

The Gemara cites the source for the opinion of **Rabbi Elazar. As it is taught** in a *baraita*: **"It is a daily burnt**-offering, **which was performed on Mount Sinai"** (Numbers 28:6). **Rabbi Elazar says:** The details of **its performance were said at Sinai, but it itself was not sacrificed** until the Tabernacle was erected. This indicates that the offering brought on Mount Sinai was a burnt-offering of appearance.

רַבִּי עֲקִיבָא אוֹמֵר: קָרְבָה וְשׁוּב לֹא פָּסְקָה. אֶלָּא מָה אֲנִי מְקַיֵּים: ״הַזְּבָחִים וּמִנְחָה הִגַּשְׁתֶּם לִי בַמִּדְבָּר אַרְבָּעִים שָׁנָה בֵּית יִשְׂרָאֵל״?

Rabbi Akiva says: It was sacrificed when they stood at Mount Sinai **and** its sacrifice **never ceased.** The Gemara asks: **But** if so, **how do I uphold,** i.e., how does Rabbi Akiva explain the following verse: **"Did you bring to Me sacrifices and offerings for forty years in the wilderness, house of Israel?"** (Amos 5:25). This verse indicates that they did not sacrifice these offerings.

שִׁבְטוֹ שֶׁל לֵוִי שֶׁלֹּא עָבְדוּ עֲבוֹדָה זָרָה, הֵן הִקְרִיבוּ אוֹתָהּ.

The Gemara answers: **The tribe of Levi,**[N] **which did not commit** the sin of **idol worship, sacrificed it** from their own funds. Since the rest of the Jewish people did not contribute the funds for the daily burnt-offering, it is as though they did not sacrifice this offering. This concludes the list of sources of the opinions of those Sages who hold that the daily burnt-offering was not sacrificed at Mount Sinai, and the offering that was sacrificed there was a burnt-offering of appearance.

בֵּית הִלֵּל – הָא דַּאֲמָרַן. רַבִּי עֲקִיבָא – הָא נַמִי דַּאֲמָרַן. רַבִּי יוֹסֵי הַגְּלִילִי – דְּתַנְיָא, רַבִּי יוֹסֵי הַגְּלִילִי אוֹמֵר: שָׁלֹשׁ מִצְוֹת נִצְטַוּוּ יִשְׂרָאֵל בַּעֲלוֹתָם לָרֶגֶל: רְאִיָּה, וַחֲגִיגָה, וְשִׂמְחָה.

The Gemara cites the sources for the opinions that the daily burnt-offering was sacrificed at Mount Sinai. **Beit Hillel: That which we said. Rabbi Akiva: Also that which we said,** in the aforementioned dispute with Rabbi Elazar. **Rabbi Yosei HaGelili: As it is taught** in a *baraita* that **Rabbi Yosei HaGelili says: The Jewish people were commanded** to perform **three mitzvot when they ascended** to the Temple **for** the pilgrimage **Festivals:**[H] The burnt-offering of **appearance, and the Festival peace**-offering, **and the** peace-offering of **rejoicing.**

יֵשׁ בָּרְאִיָּה שֶׁאֵין בִּשְׁתֵּיהֶן, וְיֵשׁ בַּחֲגִיגָה שֶׁאֵין בִּשְׁתֵּיהֶן, יֵשׁ בַּשִּׂמְחָה שֶׁאֵין בִּשְׁתֵּיהֶן. יֵשׁ בָּרְאִיָּה שֶׁאֵין בִּשְׁתֵּיהֶן – שֶׁהָרְאִיָּה עוֹלָה כּוּלָּהּ לַגָּבוֹהַּ, מַה שֶּׁאֵין כֵּן בִּשְׁתֵּיהֶן.

Rabbi Yosei HaGelili continues. **There is** an element **of the** burnt-offering of **appearance that is not** present **in** the other **two; there is** an element **of the Festival peace**-offering **that is not** present **in** the other **two;** and **there is** an element **of the** peace-offering of **rejoicing**[N] **that is not** present **in** the other **two.** He elaborates: **There is** an element **of the** burnt-offering of **appearance that is not** present **in** the other **two, as the** burnt-offering of **appearance** goes **up entirely to God, which is not so with regard to** the other **two,** as the majority portion of the other two offerings is eaten.

יֵשׁ בַּחֲגִיגָה מַה שֶּׁאֵין בִּשְׁתֵּיהֶן – שֶׁחֲגִיגָה יֶשְׁנָהּ לִפְנֵי הַדִּיבּוּר, מַה שֶּׁאֵין בִּשְׁתֵּיהֶן. יֵשׁ בַּשִּׂמְחָה מַה שֶּׁאֵין בִּשְׁתֵּיהֶן – שֶׁהַשִּׂמְחָה נוֹהֶגֶת בַּאֲנָשִׁים וּבְנָשִׁים, מַה שֶּׁאֵין בִּשְׁתֵּיהֶן.

There is an element **of the Festival peace**-offering **that is not** present **in** the other **two, as the Festival peace**-offering **existed before the speech** of God at Mount Sinai,[N] **which is not so with regard to** the other **two.** Finally, **there is** an element **of the** peace-offering of **rejoicing that is not** present **in** the other **two, as the** peace-offering of **rejoicing is performed by** both **men and by women, which is not so with regard to** the other **two.** This shows that Rabbi Yosei HaGelili holds that the burnt-offering of appearance was not sacrificed at Mount Sinai, which means that the burnt-offering mentioned in that context must have been the daily burnt-offering.

וְרַבִּי יִשְׁמָעֵאל, מַאי טַעְמָא קָא מוֹקְמַתְּ לֵיהּ כְּבֵית שַׁמַּאי? אִי סָלְקָא דַּעְתָּךְ עוֹלָה שֶׁהִקְרִיבוּ יִשְׂרָאֵל בַּמִּדְבָּר עוֹלַת תָּמִיד הֲוַאי – מִי אִיכָּא מִידֵּי דְּמֵעִיקָּרָא לָא בָּעֵי הֶפְשֵׁט וְנִיתּוּחַ וּלְבַסּוֹף בָּעֵי הֶפְשֵׁט וְנִיתּוּחַ?

The Gemara asks a question with regard to Abaye's explanation. **And** with regard to **Rabbi Yishmael, what is the reason** that **you established** his ruling **in accordance with** the opinion of **Beit Shammai** that the burnt-offering sacrificed at Mount Sinai was a burnt-offering of appearance? The explanation for his opinion was: **If it enters your mind** that the **burnt**-offering **the Jewish people sacrificed in the desert was a daily burnt**-offering, **is there any** offering **that initially did not require skinning and cutting** into pieces **and ultimately required skinning and cutting** into pieces?

NOTES

The tribe of Levi, etc. – שִׁבְטוֹ שֶׁל לֵוִי וכו׳: Some commentaries maintain that the Jewish people was partially excommunicated after the sin of the Golden Calf, and only the tribe of Levi, which did not sin, brought offerings in the Tabernacle (Rashi here and on *Yevamot* 72a). Others contend that it was not prohibited for the rest of the Jewish people to bring offerings due to their excommunication; however, as they were chastened before God it was inappropriate for them to do so (*Turei Aven*). Some explain that the Jewish people were barred from sacrificing offerings not because of the sin of the Golden Calf, for which they were forgiven after the building of the Tabernacle, but due to the sin of the spies (*Tosafot* on *Yevamot* 72a). Others say that for practical reasons they were unable to sacrifice offerings in the desert (Ibn Ezra on Amos 5:25).

There is an element of the peace-offering of rejoicing, etc. – יֵשׁ בַּשִּׂמְחָה וכו׳: The commentaries cite another difference mentioned in the *Tosefta*: The peace-offering of rejoicing is brought every day of the seven-day Festival, whereas the other two offerings are brought only once (*Tosafot*). Some say that this difference is not mentioned because it does not apply to *Shavuot*, which lasts only one day (*Sefat Emet*). In the Jerusalem Talmud additional differences between the peace-offering of rejoicing and the other two offerings are discussed. For example, one can fulfill the obligation to bring the peace-offering of rejoicing both with his own money and with the money of another, and one can fulfill this mitzva even with non-sacred meat, according to the opinion of Rabbi Yehoshua ben Levi.

As the Festival peace-offering existed before the speech – שֶׁחֲגִיגָה יֶשְׁנָהּ לִפְנֵי הַדִּיבּוּר: It is noted in the Jerusalem Talmud that the Festival peace-offering is brought when one ascends to the Temple, which was clearly not possible before the giving of the Torah, as the Jewish people had not yet been commanded about the pilgrimage Festivals. Nevertheless, the term Festival [*ḥagiga*] appears even before the giving of the Torah: "That they may hold a Festival [*veyaḥogu*] for Me in the wilderness" (Exodus 5:1).

HALAKHA

Three mitzvot of the pilgrimage Festival – שָׁלֹשׁ מִצְוֹת בָּרֶגֶל: The Jewish people were commanded to perform three mitzvot upon their ascent to the Temple for the pilgrimage Festivals: The burnt-offering of appearance, the Festival peace-offering, and the peace-offering of rejoicing, in accordance with the opinion of Rabbi Yosei HaGelili (Rambam *Sefer Korbanot*, *Hilkhot Ḥagiga* 1:1).

וְהָא רַבִּי יוֹסֵי הַגְּלִילִי דְּאָמַר עוֹלָה שֶׁהִקְרִיבוּ יִשְׂרָאֵל בַּמִּדְבָּר עוֹלַת תָּמִיד הוּאִי, מֵעִיקָּרָא לָא בָּעֵי הֶפְשֵׁט וְנִיתּוּחַ וּלְבַסּוֹף בָּעֵי הֶפְשֵׁט וְנִיתּוּחַ.

But wasn't it Rabbi Yosei HaGelili who said: The burnt-offering **that the Jewish people sacrificed in the desert** at Mount Sinai **was the daily burnt**-offering? Nevertheless, he holds that **initially** it **did not require skinning and cutting** into pieces, **and ultimately** it **required skinning and cutting** into pieces.[N]

דְּתַנְיָא, רַבִּי יוֹסֵי הַגְּלִילִי אוֹמֵר: עוֹלָה שֶׁהִקְרִיבוּ יִשְׂרָאֵל בַּמִּדְבָּר אֵינָהּ טְעוּנָה הֶפְשֵׁט וְנִיתּוּחַ, לְפִי שֶׁאֵין הֶפְשֵׁט וְנִיתּוּחַ אֶלָּא מֵאֹהֶל מוֹעֵד וָאֵילָךְ! סְמִי מִכָּאן רַבִּי יִשְׁמָעֵאל.

As it is taught in a *baraita* that **Rabbi Yosei HaGelili says: The burnt**-offering **that the Jewish people sacrificed in the desert did not require skinning and cutting** into pieces, **because** the requirement of **skinning and cutting** offerings applied **only from** the time God commanded this mitzva in **the Tent of Meeting and onward.** The Gemara concludes: There is no clear evidence as to what Rabbi Yishmael actually maintains in this regard, and therefore one should **delete Rabbi Yishmael from** this list **here,** i.e., the list of those who hold that the burnt-offering sacrificed in the desert was a burnt-offering of appearance.

בָּעֵי רַב חִסְדָּא, הַאי קְרָא הֵיכִי כְּתִיב? ״וַיִּשְׁלַח אֶת נַעֲרֵי בְּנֵי יִשְׂרָאֵל וַיַּעֲלוּ עוֹלוֹת״ – כְּבָשִׂים; ״וַיִּזְבְּחוּ זְבָחִים שְׁלָמִים לַה׳ פָּרִים״? אוֹ דִּלְמָא אִידֵי וְאִידֵי פָּרִים הֲווֹ?

Rav Ḥisda raises a dilemma: This verse, how is it written, i.e., how should it be understood? Should the following verse be read as two separate halves, with the first part consisting of: **"And he sent the young men of the children of Israel, and they sacrificed burnt**-offerings" (Exodus 24:5), which were **sheep;** and the second part consisting of the rest of the verse: **"And they sacrificed peace-offerings of bulls to the Lord,"** i.e., these peace-offerings alone were bulls? **Or perhaps both of these** were **bulls,** as the term: "Bulls," refers both to the burnt-offerings and the peace-offerings.

לְמַאי נָפְקָא מִינַּהּ? מָר זוּטְרָא אָמַר: לְפִיסּוּק טְעָמִים.

The Gemara asks: **What is the practical difference** between the two readings? **Mar Zutra said:** The practical difference is with regard **to the punctuation of** the cantillation **notes,** whether there should be a break in the verse after: "And they sacrificed burnt-offerings," indicating that these offerings consisted of sheep; or whether it should read: "And they sacrificed burnt-offerings and sacrificed peace-offerings of bulls," as one clause.

רַב אַחָא בְּרֵיהּ דְּרָבָא אָמַר: לְאוֹמֵר ״הֲרֵי עָלַי עוֹלָה כָּעוֹלָה שֶׁהִקְרִיבוּ יִשְׂרָאֵל בַּמִּדְבָּר״. מַאי? פָּרִים הֲווֹ אוֹ כְּבָשִׂים הֲווֹ? תֵּיקוּ.

Rav Aḥa, son of Rava, said that the difference between these two readings of the verse is **for one who says** in the form of a vow: It is incumbent **upon me** to bring **a burnt**-offering **like the burnt**-offering **that the Jewish people sacrificed in the desert** at Mount Sinai. **What** is he required to bring? **Were they bulls** or **were they sheep?**[N] The Gemara does not provide an answer and states that the question **shall stand** unresolved.

תְּנַן הָתָם: אֵלּוּ דְּבָרִים שֶׁאֵין לָהֶם שִׁיעוּר:

We learned in a mishna **there** (*Pe'a* 1:1): **These are** the mitzvot **that have no measure:**[N]

NOTES

And ultimately it required skinning and cutting into pieces – וּלְבַסּוֹף בָּעֵי הֶפְשֵׁט וְנִיתּוּחַ: According to the opinion of Rabbi Yosei HaGelili, and perhaps according to the opinion of Rabbi Yishmael as well, the burnt-offering at Mount Sinai was the daily burnt-offering. Although the *halakhot* of this offering were explicated only later in the Tent of Meeting, the initial offering at Mount Sinai was a daily burnt-offering, not a free-will burnt-offering of appearance in honor of the giving of the Torah.

Were they bulls or were they sheep – פָּרִים הֲווֹ אוֹ כְּבָשִׂים הֲווֹ: Some commentaries attempt to prove that the first half of the verse can reasonably be explained as referring to sheep, which would mean that this offering is similar to the daily burnt-offering sacrificed in the Temple (Meiri).

That have no measure – שֶׁאֵין לָהֶם שִׁיעוּר: The following list (next *amud*) is not an exhaustive list of all the mitzvot that have no measure, with regard to neither a maximum nor a minimum measure (see Jerusalem Talmud). One common denominator of the mitzvot on this list is that the more often one performs them the greater the fulfillment of the mitzva. Other mitzvot, for which there is no benefit derived from increasing the number of times they are performed, are excluded from this list.

הַפֵּאָה, וְהַבִּכּוּרִים, וְהָרְאָיוֹן, וּגְמִילוּת חֲסָדִים, וְתַלְמוּד תּוֹרָה.

Produce in the corner of the field that must be left unharvested, **which is given to the poor** [*pe'a*];[H] **and the first fruits,** which are brought to the Temple;[H] **and the appearance** in the Temple on the pilgrimage Festivals;[H] **and acts of loving-kindness;**[H] **and Torah study.**[NH]

אָמַר רַבִּי יוֹחָנָן: כִּסְבוּרִין אָנוּ לוֹמַר הָרְאָיוֹן אֵין לוֹ שִׁיעוּר לְמַעְלָה, אֲבָל יֵשׁ לוֹ שִׁיעוּר לְמַטָּה. עַד שֶׁבָּא רַבִּי אוֹשַׁעְיָא בְּרַבִּי וְלִימֵּד: הָרְאָיוֹן אֵין לוֹ שִׁיעוּר לֹא לְמַעְלָה וְלֹא לְמַטָּה. אֲבָל חֲכָמִים אוֹמְרִים: הָרְאִיָּיה מָעָה כֶּסֶף, וְהַחֲגִיגָה שְׁתֵּי כֶסֶף.

Rabbi Yoḥanan said: We thought to say[N] **that the** mitzva of **appearance** in the Temple **does not have a maximum measure, but it does have a minimum measure; until Rabbi Oshaya the Distinguished** [***beRabbi***],[L] **came and taught: The** mitzva of **appearance has neither a maximum nor a minimum measure. However, the Rabbis say:** The burnt-offering of **appearance** must be worth one **silver** ***ma'a*** **and the Festival peace**-offering **two silver** coins.

מַאי הָרְאָיוֹן? רַבִּי יוֹחָנָן אָמַר: רְאִיַּית פָּנִים בָּעֲזָרָה, וְרֵישׁ לָקִישׁ אָמַר: רְאִיַּית פָּנִים בְּקָרְבָּן.

§ **What is the** mitzva of **appearance** to which this mishna is referring? **Rabbi Yoḥanan said:** It is the mitzva of **the appearance of** one's **face**[H] in the Temple **courtyard.** One may appear in the Temple as often as he likes over the course of a Festival. **And Reish Lakish said:** It is **the appearance of** one's **face** in the Temple **with an offering.** There is no measure in this regard, as every time one appears in the Temple during a Festival he must bring an offering.

בְּעִיקַּר הָרֶגֶל – כּוּלֵּי עָלְמָא לָא פְּלִיגִי דִּרְאִיַּית פָּנִים בְּקָרְבָּן. כִּי פְּלִיגִי – בִּשְׁאָר יְמוֹת הָרֶגֶל. כָּל הֵיכָא דְּאָתָא וְאַיְיתֵי – כּוּלֵּי עָלְמָא לָא פְּלִיגִי דִּמְקַבְּלִינַן מִינֵּיהּ. כִּי פְּלִיגִי – דְּאָתָא וְלָא אַיְיתֵי.

The Gemara explains: **On the main** i.e., on the first, day of **the pilgrimage Festival,**[NH] **everyone agrees that the appearance of** one's **face** must be accompanied **by an offering. When they disagree,** it is with regard **to the rest of the days of the pilgrimage Festival,** i.e., whether or not one who appears must sacrifice an offering. Furthermore, **anywhere,** i.e., in any case **that one comes and brings** an offering, **everyone agrees that we accept it from him. When they disagree,** it is **when he comes and does not bring** an offering. Is this man obligated to bring an offering or not?

NOTES

Acts of loving-kindness and Torah study – **גְּמִילוּת חֲסָדִים וְתַלְמוּד תּוֹרָה**: Some commentaries claim that these two mitzvot are distinct from the others on the list (*Turei Aven*). The other mitzvot are limited by a measure prescribed by the Sages, whereas the mitzvot of learning Torah and acts of loving-kindness, which one fulfills with his body and not with his possessions, have no prescribed measure at all.

We thought to say – **כִּסְבוּרִים אָנוּ לוֹמַר**: The phrasing of the Gemara indicates that Rabbi Yoḥanan changed his mind and holds in accordance with the opinion of Rabbi Oshaya. However, this is less clear in the Jerusalem Talmud, and some dispute this interpretation here as well. It is explained in the Jerusalem Talmud that Rabbi Yoḥanan and Rabbi Oshaya disagree over a fundamental point.

According to the opinion of Rabbi Oshaya, any measure not explicitly written in the Torah applies by rabbinic law, whereas Rabbi Yoḥanan holds that some measures are *halakhot* transmitted to Moses from Sinai. According to this explanation, the opinion of Reish Lakish is in accordance with that of Rabbi Oshaya. See *Tosafot* and Meiri, who discuss this issue at length.

On the main day of the pilgrimage Festival – **בְּעִיקַּר הָרֶגֶל**: The commentaries disagree over the meaning of this term. Some say it refers to the first day of the Festival, as the remaining days are considered merely redress with regard to the burnt-offering of appearance (see Rabbeinu Ḥananel). Others explain that it means the first day one comes to the Temple to sacrifice the burnt-offering of appearance, even if this is one of the intermediate days of the Festival (see Rambam and *Kesef Mishne*).

LANGUAGE

BeRabbi – **בְּרַבִּי**: This appellation, *beRabbi* or *beRibbi*, is an abbreviation for son of Rabbi [*ben Rabbi*]. However, already in the times of the *tanna'im* this term was used as an honorific for a distinguished Torah scholar, indicating that he is the son of great people or Sages. The label was applied whether the Sage in question was actually the son of Torah scholars, e.g., Rabbi Oshaya, son of Rabbi Ḥama ben Rabbi Kisa, or not. Occasionally, a Torah Sage was referred to simply as *BeRabbi*, without mention of his own name at all.

HALAKHA

The measure of produce of the corners – **שִׁיעוּר פֵּאָה**: There is no measurement for produce of the corners by Torah law, as one can fulfill his obligation by leaving even one stalk in his field. However, by rabbinic law one must leave no less than one-sixtieth of the field. It is appropriate to increase this amount in accordance with the size of the field, its current yield, and the requirements of the poor in that area (Rambam *Sefer Zera'im*, *Hilkhot Mattenot Aniyyim* 1:15).

The measure of the first fruits – **שִׁיעוּר בִּיכּוּרִים**: There is no measure for first fruits by Torah law, although by rabbinic law one must bring at least one-sixtieth of the harvest. One may render his entire field first fruits if he so desires (Rambam *Sefer Zera'im*, *Hilkhot Bikkurim* 2:17).

The measure of appearance – **שִׁיעוּר הָרְאָיוֹן**: By Torah law there is no fixed measure for the Festival offerings. However, the Sages declared that one should spend no less than one silver *ma'a* for the burnt-offering of appearance and no less than two silver *ma'a* for a Festival peace-offering. This is in accordance with the opinion of Rabbi Oshaya, Rabbi Yoḥanan's teacher (Rambam *Sefer Korbanot*, *Hilkhot Ḥagiga* 1:2).

Acts of loving-kindness – **גְּמִילוּת חֲסָדִים**: It is a positive mitzva by rabbinic law to visit the sick, comfort mourners, eulogize the deceased and arrange their funeral and burial, raise funds for brides in need, and increase the joy of a bride and groom. These and similar mitzvot are all acts of loving-kindness that have no specified measure. Although the mitzvot listed here apply by rabbinic law, nevertheless, they are included in the verse (Leviticus 19:18): "You shall love your neighbor as yourself" (Rambam *Sefer Shofetim*, *Hilkhot Evel* 14:1).

Torah study – **תַּלְמוּד תּוֹרָה**: There is no measure for the mitzva of Torah study, and one is obligated to learn Torah all the days of his life (*Shulḥan Arukh*, *Yoreh De'a* 246:3).

The appearance of one's face – **רְאִיַּית פָּנִים**: One who comes to the Temple courtyard during the Festival after having already sacrificed the burnt-offering of appearance is not obligated to bring another offering. However, if he does so it is accepted. This is because there is no measure for the number of burnt-offerings of appearance that one may bring (Rambam *Sefer Korbanot*, *Hilkhot Ḥagiga* 2:6).

Appearance on the main day of the pilgrimage Festival – **רְאִיָּיה בְּעִיקַּר הָרֶגֶל**: The mitzva of appearance is fulfilled by coming to the Temple and sacrificing a burnt-offering of appearance on the first day of a pilgrimage Festival. One may fulfill his obligation with either an animal offering or a bird-offering (see the *Kesef Mishne* with regard to the possibility of a burnt-offering of birds). One who comes to the Temple on the first day of the Festival without an offering has violated both a negative and a positive mitzva. The prohibition is: "And none shall appear before Me empty-handed" (Exodus 23:15). However, one is not flogged for this transgression, as it does not involve an action (Rambam *Sefer Korbanot*, *Hilkhot Ḥagiga* 1:1).

דְּרַבִּי יוֹחָנָן סָבַר: רְאִיַּית פָּנִים בָּעֲזָרָה, דְּכָל אֵימַת דְּאָתֵי לָא צָרִיךְ לְאַתּוּיֵי. רֵישׁ לָקִישׁ אָמַר: רְאִיַּית פָּנִים בְּקָרְבָּן, דְּכָל אֵימַת דְּאָתֵי צָרִיךְ לְאַתּוּיֵי.

The Gemara explains **that Rabbi Yoḥanan holds** that the mitzva is merely **the appearance of** one's **face in the** Temple **courtyard.** Therefore, one **doesn't need to bring** an offering **whenever he comes** to the Temple. **Reish Lakish said** that the mitzva is **the appearance of** one's **face with an offering,** which means that **whenever one comes he must bring** an offering with him.

אֵיתִיבֵיהּ רֵישׁ לָקִישׁ לְרַבִּי יוֹחָנָן: ״וְלֹא יֵרָאוּ פָּנַי רֵיקָם״! אֲמַר לֵיהּ: בְּעִיקַּר הָרֶגֶל.

Reish Lakish raised an objection to the opinion of **Rabbi Yoḥanan.** The verse states: "Three times you shall keep a feast for Me in the year… **and none shall appear before Me empty-handed**" (Exodus 23:14–15). This verse indicates that one must bring an offering whenever he appears in the Temple. Rabbi Yoḥanan **said to him:** That obligation applies only **on the main** day of **the pilgrimage Festival,** but not on the rest of the Festival days.

אֵיתִיבֵיהּ: ״וְלֹא יֵרָאוּ פָּנַי רֵיקָם״ – בִּזְבָחִים. אַתָּה אוֹמֵר בִּזְבָחִים, אוֹ אֵינוֹ אֶלָּא בְּעוֹפוֹת וּמְנָחוֹת? וְדִין הוּא: נֶאֶמְרָה חֲגִיגָה לְהֶדְיוֹט וְנֶאֶמְרָה רְאִיָּיה לַגָּבוֹהַּ. מַה חֲגִיגָה הָאֲמוּרָה לְהֶדְיוֹט – זְבָחִים, אַף רְאִיָּיה הָאֲמוּרָה לַגָּבוֹהַּ – זְבָחִים.

Reish Lakish **raised an objection to** the opinion of Rabbi Yoḥanan from a *baraita*: **"And none shall appear**[N] **before Me empty-handed."** This teaches that Festival pilgrims must appear **with animal offerings.** Do **you say** that they must appear **with animal offerings, or** perhaps **it is only with bird-offerings**[N] **or meal-offerings? And it is** possible to determine the answer **by logical derivation: It is stated** that one must bring **a Festival peace-offering for a commoner**[N] to eat, **and it is stated** that one must bring a burnt-offering of **appearance,** which is **for God. Just as the Festival peace-offering that is stated for a commoner** is referring to **animal offerings, so too,** the burnt-offering of **appearance that is stated** to be sacrificed wholly **for God** is referring to **animal offerings.**

וּמַה הֵן זְבָחִים? עוֹלוֹת. אַתָּה אוֹמֵר עוֹלוֹת, אוֹ אֵינוֹ אֶלָּא שְׁלָמִים? וְדִין הוּא: נֶאֶמְרָה חֲגִיגָה לְהֶדְיוֹט, וְנֶאֶמְרָה רְאִיָּיה לַגָּבוֹהַּ, מַה חֲגִיגָה הָאֲמוּרָה לְהֶדְיוֹט – בָּרָאוּי לוֹ, אַף רְאִיָּיה הָאֲמוּרָה לַגָּבוֹהַּ – בָּרָאוּי לוֹ.

And what are these **animal offerings** that the Festival pilgrims sacrifice to God? **Burnt**-offerings. Do **you say** that they are **burnt**-offerings, **or** perhaps **it is only** that they are **peace**-offerings? **And it is** possible to determine the answer **by logical derivation: It is stated** that one must bring a **Festival peace**-offering **for a commoner, and** it **is stated** that one must bring a burnt-offering of **appearance,** which is solely **for God. Just as the Festival peace**-offering **that is stated for a commoner** is referring to an offering that is **fitting for him** to eat, i.e., a peace-offering, **so too,** the burnt-offering of **appearance that is stated** to be **for God** is referring to an offering that is **fitting for Him,** i.e., a burnt-offering, which is entirely consumed on the altar.

וְכֵן בְּדִין, שֶׁלֹּא יְהֵא שׁוּלְחָנְךָ מָלֵא וְשׁוּלְחַן רַבְּךָ רֵיקָם! אֲמַר לֵיהּ: בְּעִיקַּר הָרֶגֶל.

And similarly, one can learn **by logical derivation that your table should not be full** of meat **while your Master's table,** i.e., the altar, **is empty.** This indicates that one must sacrifice a burnt-offering whenever one appears in the Temple, which contradicts the opinion of Rabbi Yoḥanan. Rabbi Yoḥanan again **said to him:** This obligation applies only **on the main** day of **the pilgrimage Festival.**

אֵיתִיבֵיהּ, רַבִּי יוֹסֵי בְּרַבִּי יְהוּדָה אוֹמֵר: שָׁלֹשׁ רְגָלִים בַּשָּׁנָה נִצְטַוּוּ יִשְׂרָאֵל לַעֲלוֹת בָּרֶגֶל: בְּחַג הַמַּצּוֹת וּבְחַג הַשָּׁבוּעוֹת, וּבְחַג הַסּוּכּוֹת. וְאֵין נִרְאִין חֲצָאִין – מִשּׁוּם שֶׁנֶּאֱמַר ״כָּל זְכוּרְךָ״, וְאֵין נִרְאִין רֵיקָנִים – מִשּׁוּם שֶׁנֶּאֱמַר ״וְלֹא יֵרָאוּ פָּנַי רֵיקָם״! אֲמַר לֵיהּ: בְּעִיקַּר הָרֶגֶל.

Reish Lakish **raised** another **objection to** the opinion of Rabbi Yoḥanan. **Rabbi Yosei, son of Rabbi Yehuda, says: Three times a year the Jewish people were commanded to ascend on the pilgrimage Festival: On Passover, on *Shavuot*, and on *Sukkot*. They may not appear partially,** i.e., only some of the people, **because it is stated: "All your males"** (Exodus 23:17). **And they may not appear empty-handed, because it is stated: "And none shall appear before Me empty-handed"** (Exodus 23:15). Rabbi Yoḥanan **said to him:** That too is referring to **the main** day of **the pilgrimage Festival.**

אֵיתִיבֵיהּ רַבִּי יוֹחָנָן לְרֵישׁ לָקִישׁ: ״יִרְאֶה״ ״יֵרָאֶה״ – מָה אֲנִי בְּחִנָּם אַף אַתֶּם בְּחִנָּם!

Rabbi Yoḥanan raised an objection to the opinion of **Reish Lakish** from a *baraita*: The verse states: "All your males shall appear." Although the verse as written can be read: **"Will see [*yireh*],"** it is actually read: **"Shall be seen [*yera'e*]."**[N] The *baraita* derives that **just as I,** God, come to see you **for free,** as He has no obligation to bring an offering when He comes to see us in the Temple, **so too, you** may come to see Me in the Temple **for free,** i.e., there is no requirement to bring an offering. The Gemara accepts this objection and therefore proceeds to explain the dispute between Rabbi Yoḥanan and Reish Lakish in a different manner.

NOTES

Reish Lakish raised an objection to the opinion of Rabbi Yoḥanan, And none shall appear – אֵיתִיבֵיהּ וְלֹא יֵרָאוּ: The commentaries point out that it is unclear what this *baraita* adds to the discussion, as the same objection against Rabbi Yoḥanan could be raised from the previously cited verse and the same answer would apply to this *baraita* as well (Rabbi Akiva Eiger). One answer is that the objection is not from the *halakha* of the *baraita*, but from the logical derivation it states below: That your table should not be full of meat while your Master's table is empty. This reasoning can be applied to all the days of the Festival, not only the first (*Siaḥ Yitzḥak*).

Or it is only with bird-offerings – אוֹ אֵינוֹ אֶלָּא בְּעוֹפוֹת: Many commentaries are puzzled by the Rambam's ruling that one can fulfill his obligation of the burnt-offering of appearance with a bird. Some early authorities claim that the Rambam had a different version of the Gemara here. That reading was likely similar to the version in the *Mekhilta*, which states: Perhaps it is only with money. According to this version, birds were never excluded from the burnt-offering of appearance. Others say that if one may bring only animals, it could turn out that he will sacrifice more burnt-offerings than peace-offerings, as each time he appears at the Temple he is obligated to sacrifice a burnt-offering. This is inappropriate according to the opinion of Beit Hillel. If it is permitted for one to use birds, there will still be more peace-offerings than burnt-offerings, at least in terms of the total amount of meat (*Tzlaḥ*). Another possible answer is that the last logical derivation: So too, the burnt-offering of appearance is for God and must be fitting for Him, includes birds, as they too are entirely burnt on the altar. Only meal-offerings are excluded, as they are eaten in part by the priests (*Porat Yosef*).

It is stated one must bring a Festival peace-offering for a commoner – נֶאֶמְרָה חֲגִיגָה לְהֶדְיוֹט: Some commentaries cite proof from the verse: "You shall keep it a feast" (Exodus 12:14), that the Festival peace-offering is meant to be eaten by the people and not consumed entirely on the altar (*Tosefot Yom Tov*).

Will see [*yireh*], shall be seen [*yera'e*] – יִרְאֶה, יֵרָאֶה: Some commentaries ask why Reish Lakish doesn't refute this proof by stating that a different *halakha* is learned from this verse, e.g., Rabbi Yoḥanan ben Dehavai's derivation that someone blind in one eye is excluded from this obligation (see 2a). They answer that when a term can be written and read in two different ways, and the way it is written and read are both used for *halakhot*, it is considered as though the two terms were juxtaposed. Consequently, there is no limit to the number of *halakhot* that can be derived from this juxtaposition, as whatever applies to one case applies equally to the other (*Siaḥ Yitzḥak*).

אֶלָּא: כׇּל הֵיכָא דַּאֲתָא וְלָא אַיְיתֵי – דְּכוּלֵּי עָלְמָא לָא פְּלִיגִי דְּעָיֵיל, וּמִתְחֲזֵי וְנָפֵיק, כִּי פְּלִיגִי – דַּאֲתָא וְאַיְיתֵי.

Rather, with regard to **anywhere that one comes** to the Temple courtyard after the initial time on the first day of the Festival **and he does not bring** an offering, **everyone agrees that one enters,**[N] **appears, and exits** without having to bring an offering. **When they disagree** it is in a case **where one comes and brings** an offering.

רַבִּי יוֹחָנָן דְּאָמַר רְאִיַּית פָּנִים בָּעֲזָרָה; רְאִיַּית פָּנִים הוּא דְּאֵין לָהּ שִׁיעוּר, הָא לְקׇרְבָּן – יֵשׁ לָהּ שִׁיעוּר. וְרֵישׁ לָקִישׁ אָמַר: רְאִיַּית פָּנִים בְּקׇרְבָּן, דַּאֲפִילּוּ קׇרְבָּן נַמִי אֵין לוֹ שִׁיעוּר.

The Gemara explains: **Rabbi Yoḥanan, who says** that the appearance mentioned in the mishna is referring to **the appearance of** one's **face in the** Temple **courtyard,** maintains that **it is this appearance** itself **that has no** maximum **measure,** i.e., one may appear as often as he wishes without an offering. However, **there is** a maximum **measure,** i.e., a limited number **of offerings,** that one may bring; only one burnt-offering of appearance per Festival. **And Reish Lakish said: The appearance of** one's **face** means **with an offering, as even offerings have no** maximum **measure.** One may bring as many offerings during the Festival as he wishes.

אֵיתִיבֵיהּ: ״הֹקַר רַגְלְךָ מִבֵּית רֵעֶךָ״! הָתָם בְּחַטָּאוֹת וַאֲשָׁמוֹת,

Rabbi Yoḥanan **raised an objection to** the opinion of Reish Lakish: **"Let your foot be seldom**[N] **in your neighbor's house,**[N] lest he be sated with you, and hate you" (Proverbs 25:17). It can be inferred from this verse that one should not bring extra gifts, i.e., offerings, to God. The Gemara responds: **There,** the verse is referring **to sin**-offerings **and guilt**-offerings, i.e., it is better not to sin in the first place.

כִּדְרַבִּי לֵוִי, דְּרַבִּי לֵוִי רָמֵי: כְּתִיב ״הֹקַר רַגְלְךָ מִבֵּית רֵעֶךָ״ וּכְתִיב ״אָבֹא בֵיתְךָ בְעוֹלוֹת״! לָא קַשְׁיָא; כָּאן – בְּחַטָּאוֹת וַאֲשָׁמוֹת, כָּאן – בְּעוֹלוֹת וּשְׁלָמִים.

This explanation is **in accordance with** the opinion of **Rabbi Levi, as Rabbi Levi raised a contradiction** between two verses. **It is written: "Let your foot be seldom in your neighbor's house," and it is written: "I will come into Your house with burnt**-offerings, I will perform for You my vows" (Psalms 66:13). Rabbi Levi explained: This is **not difficult; here,** the verse is referring **to sin**-offerings **and guilt**-offerings, **and there,** it is referring **to burnt**-offerings **and peace**-offerings, concerning which one may bring as many as he likes.

תַּנְיָא נַמִי הָכִי: ״הֹקַר רַגְלְךָ מִבֵּית רֵעֶךָ״ – בְּחַטָּאוֹת וַאֲשָׁמוֹת הַכָּתוּב מְדַבֵּר. אַתָּה אוֹמֵר בְּחַטָּאוֹת וַאֲשָׁמוֹת, אוֹ אֵינוֹ אֶלָּא בְּעוֹלוֹת וּשְׁלָמִים? כְּשֶׁהוּא אוֹמֵר ״אָבוֹא בֵיתְךָ בְעוֹלוֹת אֲשַׁלֵּם לְךָ נְדָרָי״ – הֲרֵי עוֹלוֹת וּשְׁלָמִים אָמוּר. הָא מָה אֲנִי מְקַיֵּים ״הֹקַר רַגְלְךָ מִבֵּית רֵעֶךָ״ – בְּחַטָּאוֹת וַאֲשָׁמוֹת הַכָּתוּב מְדַבֵּר.

That opinion **is also taught** in a *baraita*: **"Let your foot be seldom in your neighbor's house." The verse is speaking of sin**-offerings **and guilt**-offerings. Do **you say** it is referring **to sin-offerings and guilt**-offerings, **or** perhaps **it is only** referring **to burnt**-offerings **and peace**-offerings? **When it says: "I will come into Your house with burnt**-offerings, **I will perform for You my vows," burnt**-offerings **and peace-offerings are mentioned,** as these are more pleasant to sacrifice to God. **How** then **do I uphold** the meaning of the verse: **"Let your foot be seldom in your neighbor's house"? The verse is speaking of sin**-offerings **and guilt**-offerings.

״וְאֵין נִרְאִין חֲצָאִין״ כו׳. סָבַר רַב יוֹסֵף לְמֵימַר: מַאן דְּאִית לֵיהּ עֲשָׂרָה בָּנִים לָא לִיסְקוּ הָאִידָּנָא חֲמִשָּׁה וּלְמָחָר חֲמִשָּׁה.

§ Earlier the *baraita* taught: The people **may not appear partially,** as the verse states: "All your males" (Exodus 23:17). **Rav Yosef thought to say: One who has ten sons**[N] should **not let five ascend now and** the other **five tomorrow.** Rather, they must all ascend to the Temple together.

NOTES

Everyone agrees that one enters, etc. – **דְּכוּלֵּי עָלְמָא לָא פְּלִיגִי דְּעָיֵיל וכו׳:** This statement is problematic, as the previous discussion between the two *amora'im* indicates that they do dispute the case of one who appears in the Temple without bringing an offering. Some commentaries have a different version of the text, according to which anyone who comes to the Temple on the Festival is certainly obligated to bring an offering (Rabbeinu Ḥananel). The dispute according to this version is whether or not one who comes multiple times on the first day is obligated to bring another offering each time he comes. Conversely, others simply delete this line (*Benei Shmuel*).

Some explain that this is the style of the Gemara: occasionally it will attribute questions and answers to particular Sages, in this case Rabbi Yoḥanan and Reish Lakish, when really it is the Gemara itself discussing their opinions (*Siaḥ Yitzḥak*, citing *Yavin Shemua*).

Rabbi Yoḥanan an objection to the opinion of Reish Lakish, Let your foot be seldom – **אֵיתִיבֵיהּ: הֹקַר רַגְלְךָ:** It is unclear which Sage is raising this objection (see *Zekher LaḤagiga*, who discusses this at length). Some maintain that this question is asked of Reish Lakish, as according to his opinion one may come to the Temple as often as he wishes (*Petaḥ Einayim*).

Let your foot [*raglekha*] be seldom in your neighbor's [*re'ekha*] house – **הֹקַר רַגְלְךָ מִבֵּית רֵעֶךָ:** Although this verse from Proverbs has nothing to do with offerings per se, it is well-known that the book of Proverbs contains numerous parables, and therefore an apparently homiletic interpretation of a verse might well be its plain meaning. Additionally, the phrase: "Your foot [*raglekha*]," is similar to the word *regalim*, Festivals (Maharsha). Rabbi Levi maintains that the term *raglekha* is related to *hergel*, meaning customary practice (Meiri).

Rashi cites this verse as evidence that God considers the Jewish people His brethren and companions [*re'im*] (see Psalms 122:8). Others mention verses from Song of Songs in this connection, in which God refers to the Jewish people as: My lover, and: My friend [*re'i*], e.g., Song of Songs 5:16. Elsewhere Rashi quotes in this regard the verse "Your own friend [*re'ekha*], and your father's friend, forsake not" (Proverbs 27:10). In any case, the term neighbor [*re'a*] in this context means a shepherd and a provider, as is explained by the Sages in many instances (see *Otzar HaKavod*).

Who has ten sons – **דְּאִית לֵיהּ עֲשָׂרָה בָּנִים:** Some commentaries explain that according to the opinion of Rav Yosef, young children are also obligated in the mitzva of appearance, and therefore the father is obligated to bring all of his children with him. This explanation resolves Abaye's subsequent questions (*Zekher LaḤagiga*).

אֲמַר לֵיהּ אַבַּיֵי: פְּשִׁיטָא, הֵי מִינַּיְיהוּ מְשַׁוֵּית לְהוּ פּוֹשְׁעִים וְהֵי מִינַּיְיהוּ מְשַׁוֵּית לְהוּ זְרִיזִין!

Abaye said to him: This **is obvious; which of** his sons would **he render sinners,** who are too lazy to ascend, **and which of them** would **he render vigilant,** eager to perform the mitzva at the first opportunity?

אֶלָּא קְרָא לְמַאי אֲתָא? לְכִדְאַחֵרִים. דְּתַנְיָא, אֲחֵרִים אוֹמְרִים: הַמְקַמֵּץ, וְהַמְצָרֵף נְחֹשֶׁת, וְהַבּוּרְסִי – פְּטוּרִין מִן הָרְאִיָּיה, שֶׁנֶּאֱמַר: "כָּל זְכוּרְךָ" – מִי שֶׁיָּכוֹל לַעֲלוֹת עִם כָּל זְכוּרְךָ, יָצְאוּ אֵלּוּ שֶׁאֵין יְכוֹלִין לַעֲלוֹת עִם כָּל זְכוּרְךָ.

Rather, for what purpose **does the verse:** "All your males," **come?** It comes to teach **that which *Aḥerim*** taught. **As it is taught** in a *baraita*: ***Aḥerim* say** that **a scrimper,** one who gathers dog feces to give them to tanners for the purpose of tanning hides; **a melder of copper,** who purifies copper from dross; **and a tanner** of hides are all **exempt from** the mitzva of **appearance,** as their occupation inflicts upon them an unpleasant odor. **As it is stated: "All your males,"**[N] which indicates that only **one who is able to ascend with all your males** is obligated, **excluding these.** As people avoid their company, **they cannot ascend with all your males.**

מתני׳ עוֹלוֹת בַּמּוֹעֵד בָּאוֹת מִן הַחוּלִּין, וְהַשְּׁלָמִים מִן הַמַּעֲשֵׂר. יוֹם טוֹב הָרִאשׁוֹן שֶׁל פֶּסַח, בֵּית שַׁמַּאי אוֹמְרִים: מִן הַחוּלִּין, וּבֵית הִלֵּל אוֹמְרִים: מִן הַמַּעֲשֵׂר.

MISHNA **Burnt**-offerings that one sacrifices **on** the intermediate days of **the Festival** must **come from non-sacred** property, not from sacred property such as second-tithe money. **But the peace**-offerings may be brought **from the** second **tithe,**[NB] i.e., from money with which one redeemed second tithe, which is subsequently used to purchase food in Jerusalem. With regard to the Festival peace-offering sacrificed on **the first day of the festival of Passover, Beit Shammai say:** It must come **from non-sacred** property, **and Beit Hillel say:** It may be brought even **from the** second **tithe.**

יִשְׂרָאֵל יוֹצְאִין יְדֵי חוֹבָתָן בִּנְדָרִים וּנְדָבוֹת וּבְמַעְשַׂר בְּהֵמָה, וְהַכֹּהֲנִים בְּחַטָּאוֹת וַאֲשָׁמוֹת וּבַבְּכוֹר וּבֶחָזֶה וָשׁוֹק, אֲבָל לֹא בָּעוֹפוֹת וְלֹא בַּמְּנָחוֹת.

In general, **Israelites fulfill their obligation**[N] to eat peace-offerings of rejoicing **with** their voluntary **vows and gift** offerings donated during the year and sacrificed on the Festival; **and** likewise **with animal tithes.**[B] **And the priests** fulfill their obligation of rejoicing **with** the meat of **sin-offerings and guilt**-offerings **and with firstborn** offerings, as the priests receive a portion of these, **and with the breast and thigh** of peace-offerings, to which they are also entitled. **However,** they do **not** fulfill their obligation **with birds,** e.g., a bird sacrificed as a sin-offering, **nor with meal**-offerings, as only the eating of meat constitutes rejoicing.[H]

NOTES

As it is stated, All your males – **שֶׁנֶּאֱמַר, כָּל זְכוּרְךָ:** In the Jerusalem Talmud the exemption of men who are engaged in these occupations is derived from a different verse: "When all of Israel come to appear before the Lord" (Deuteronomy 31:11). This indicates that anyone who cannot come together with the rest of the Jewish people is exempt from ascending to Jerusalem on the pilgrimage Festivals. The Gemara there adds that in addition to people who have an offensive odor, those afflicted with contagious diseases are also exempt.

Peace-offerings from the second tithe – **שְׁלָמִים מִן הַמַּעֲשֵׂר:** The term peace-offerings can be interpreted in several ways in this context. It might be referring solely to Festival peace-offerings. If so, the mishna first mentions items concerning which there is no dispute, as burnt-offerings must come from non-sacred property and peace-offerings of rejoicing may come from second tithe. Subsequently, it discusses Festival peace-offerings, about which there is a dispute. It is also possible that the term peace-offerings serves as a general heading, after which the mishna distinguishes between different types of peace-offerings (*Siaḥ Yitzḥak*).

Israelites fulfill their obligation, etc. – **יִשְׂרָאֵל יוֹצְאִין יְדֵי חוֹבָתָן וכו׳:** Rashi notes that the term Israelites is unusual in this context, as this obligation applies equally to priests. He explains that it was necessary to state Israelites, as only priests can fulfill their obligation of peace-offerings of rejoicing with the offerings mentioned subsequently. However, some commentaries explain that the ruling of the mishna is in accordance with the opinion that priests are not obligated in animal tithes. If so, the term Israelites is precise (see *Yad David*).

BACKGROUND

The tithe – **הַמַּעֲשֵׂר:** In this context the term: Tithe, refers to the second tithe that is set aside after *teruma* has been given to the priests and the first tithe to the Levites. Second tithe was given during the first, second, fourth, and fifth years of the Sabbatical cycle. After second tithe was set aside, it was brought to Jerusalem to be eaten there by its owner. If the journey to Jerusalem was so long that it would be difficult to transport all the second-tithe produce, or if the produce became ritually impure, it could be redeemed for an equivalent sum of money. If the owner redeemed his own produce, he had to add one-fifth of its value. This redemption money was brought to Jerusalem, where it was spent on food. Second tithe could be redeemed only with minted coins bearing an imprint; unstamped coins and promissory notes could not be used. Today, second tithe is still redeemed, but only for a nominal sum, as in the absence of the Temple it is no longer brought to Jerusalem. The *halakhot* of second tithe are discussed in tractate *Ma'aser Sheni*.

Animal tithes – **מַעְשַׂר בְּהֵמָה:** On three occasions each year, the owner of a herd of kosher animals was required to gather all the animals born during the preceding period into an enclosure and let them out one by one. These animals were passed "under the shepherd's rod" (Leviticus 27:32), and every tenth animal was marked with red paint to indicate that it was sacred. The sacred animals were called animal tithes. If it was fit to be sacrificed, the animal tithe was brought to the Temple and sacrificed in a manner similar to that of a peace-offering. Its blood was sprinkled on the altar, and its meat was eaten by its owner. The details of the *halakhot* of animal tithes are elucidated in tractate *Bekhorot*.

HALAKHA

Peace-offerings of rejoicing – **שַׁלְמֵי שִׂמְחָה:** One fulfills his obligation of eating peace-offerings of rejoicing not only with peace-offerings themselves, but with any offering that may be eaten. Consequently, Israelites fulfill their obligation with vow offerings, gift offerings, and animal tithes. Priests may fulfill their obligation even with sin-offerings, guilt-offerings, firstborn offerings, and the breast and thigh they receive from other offerings. However, they do not fulfill their obligation by eating bird-offerings or meal-offerings (Rambam *Sefer Korbanot*, *Hilkhot Ḥagiga* 2:10).

גמ׳ אֶלָּא עוֹלוֹת, בַּמּוֹעֵד הוּא דְּבָאוֹת מִן הַחוּלִּין. הָא בְּיוֹם טוֹב – מִן הַמַּעֲשֵׂר. אַמַּאי? דָּבָר שֶׁבְּחוֹבָה הִיא, וְכׇל דָּבָר שֶׁבְּחוֹבָה אֵינוֹ בָּא אֶלָּא מִן הַחוּלִּין!

GEMARA When the mishna states that **burnt**-offerings sacrificed **during the** intermediate days of **the Festival may come from non-sacred** property, this leads to the surprising conclusion that **on the Festival** they may even come **from the second tithe.**[N] The Gemara asks: **Why** should this be the case? The burnt-offering **is an obligatory matter, and** there is a principle that **any obligatory matter** with regard to offerings **may come only from non-sacred** property that was consecrated expressly for this purpose alone, not from property that was previously consecrated for another purpose.

וְכִי תֵּימָא: הָא קָא מַשְׁמַע לָן דְּעוֹלוֹת, בַּמּוֹעֵד – בָּאוֹת, בְּיוֹם טוֹב – אֵינָן בָּאוֹת, כְּמַאן? כְּבֵית שַׁמַּאי?!

And if you would say that **this teaches us that burnt**-offerings **may come,** i.e., be sacrificed, **on** the intermediate days of **the Festival,** whereas **on the Festival they may not come** at all, **in accordance with whose** opinion is this mishna? It is **in accordance with** the opinion of **Beit Shammai.**

דִּתְנַן: בֵּית שַׁמַּאי אוֹמְרִים: מְבִיאִין שְׁלָמִים וְאֵין סוֹמְכִין עֲלֵיהֶן, אֲבָל לֹא עוֹלוֹת. וּבֵית הִלֵּל אוֹמְרִים: מְבִיאִין שְׁלָמִים וְעוֹלוֹת, וְסוֹמְכִין עֲלֵיהֶן!

As we learned in a mishna (*Beitza* 19a) that **Beit Shammai say: One brings peace**-offerings on a Festival, **but one does not place** his hands **on them,**[N] as placing one's hands on an animal on a Festival is prohibited by rabbinic law. **However,** one may **not** sacrifice **burnt**-offerings at all, as they are not eaten, and slaughtering is permitted on a Festival only for human needs. **And Beit Hillel say: One brings** both **peace**-offerings **and burnt**-offerings, **and one does place** his hands **on them.** It is unlikely that an anonymous mishna would follow the opinion of Beit Shammai, whose rulings are not accepted as *halakha*.

חַסּוּרֵי מִיחַסְּרָא וְהָכִי קָתָנֵי: עוֹלוֹת נְדָרִים וּנְדָבוֹת, בַּמּוֹעֵד – בָּאוֹת, בְּיוֹם טוֹב – אֵינָן בָּאוֹת, וְעוֹלַת רְאִיָּה – בָּאָה אֲפִילּוּ בְּיוֹם טוֹב. וּכְשֶׁהִיא בָּאָה – אֵינָהּ בָּאָה אֶלָּא מִן הַחוּלִּין. וְשַׁלְמֵי שִׂמְחָה בָּאִין אַף מִן הַמַּעֲשֵׂר. וַחֲגִיגַת יוֹם טוֹב הָרִאשׁוֹן שֶׁל פֶּסַח, בֵּית שַׁמַּאי אוֹמְרִים: מִן הַחוּלִּין. וּבֵית הִלֵּל אוֹמְרִים: מִן הַמַּעֲשֵׂר.

The Gemara answers: This mishna **is incomplete, and this** is what **it is teaching: Burnt**-offerings brought as a fulfillment of one's **vow or as gift** offerings **may come on** the intermediate days of **the Festival.** However, **on the Festival** itself **they may not come. And the burnt**-offering **of appearance comes even on the Festival, but when it comes, it may come only from non-sacred** property,[H] as it is obligatory. **And peace**-offerings **of rejoicing may come even from the** second **tithe.**[H] **And** with regard to **the Festival peace**-offering brought on **the first day of Passover, Beit Shammai say:** It may come only **from non-sacred** property, **and Beit Hillel say:** It may come even **from the** second **tithe.**

תַּנְיָא נַמִּי הָכִי: עוֹלוֹת נְדָרִים וּנְדָבוֹת, בַּמּוֹעֵד – בָּאוֹת, בְּיוֹם טוֹב – אֵינָן בָּאוֹת. וְעוֹלַת רְאִיָּה – בָּאָה אֲפִילּוּ בְּיוֹם טוֹב. וּכְשֶׁהִיא בָּאָה – אֵינָהּ בָּאָה אֶלָּא מִן הַחוּלִּין. וְשַׁלְמֵי שִׂמְחָה בָּאִין אַף מִן הַמַּעֲשֵׂר. וַחֲגִיגַת יוֹם טוֹב הָרִאשׁוֹן שֶׁל פֶּסַח, בֵּית שַׁמַּאי אוֹמְרִים: מִן הַחוּלִּין, וּבֵית הִלֵּל אוֹמְרִים: מִן הַמַּעֲשֵׂר.

That opinion **is also taught** in a *baraita*: **Burnt**-offerings brought as a fulfillment of one's **vow or** as **gift** offerings **may come on** the intermediate days of **the Festival.**[H] However, **on** the Festival **itself they may not come. And the burnt**-offering **of appearance comes even on the Festival, but when it comes it may come only from non-sacred** property. **And peace-offerings of rejoicing may come even from the** second **tithe. And** with regard to **the Festival peace**-offering brought on **the first day of the festival of Passover, Beit Shammai say:** It may come only **from non-sacred** property, **and Beit Hillel say:** It may come even **from the** second **tithe.**

NOTES

On the Festival they may come from the second tithe – **הָא בְּיוֹם טוֹב מִן הַמַּעֲשֵׂר:** Some commentaries contend that this inference, i.e., that one may not bring a burnt-offering from second-tithe money on the Festival itself, is imprecise. In fact, one may never bring a burnt-offering from second-tithe funds, as that money must be used for food, and one may not eat from a burnt-offering. Rather, the Gemara means that it is prohibited to use funds that were previously designated for any other purpose, e.g., for a gift offering.

But one does not place his hands on them – **וְאֵין סוֹמְכִין עֲלֵיהֶן:** This issue of placing one's hands on offerings on a Festival is one of the most ancient disputes (see 17a). Some suggest, based on the Gemara in tractate *Beitza* (20a), that this dispute is connected to Beit Shammai's opinion that there is no requirement to place one's hands on peace-offerings at all (*Turei Aven*). Furthermore, Beit Shammai hold that the placing of one's hands does not have to be performed immediately before slaughtering an offering, which means that it can be performed on the eve of the Festival.

HALAKHA

Burnt-offering of appearance from non-sacred property – **עוֹלַת רְאִיָּה מִן הַחוּלִּין:** The burnt-offering of appearance may come only from non-sacred property, like all other obligatory offerings (Rambam *Sefer Korbanot*, *Hilkhot Ḥagiga* 2:8).

Festival offerings on the pilgrimage Festival day – **קׇרְבְּנוֹת הָרֶגֶל בְּיוֹם טוֹב:** Since burnt-offerings of appearance, Festival peace-offerings, and peace-offerings of rejoicing are all obligations of the Festival day, one may bring them on the first day of the Festival. When doing so, one places his hands on them in the manner of a weekday. This is in accordance with the opinion of Beit Hillel (Rambam *Sefer Korbanot*, *Hilkhot Ḥagiga* 1:8–9).

Vow or gift offerings on the intermediate days of the Festival – **נְדָרִים וּנְדָבוֹת בַּמּוֹעֵד:** It is permitted to sacrifice voluntary vow offerings and gift offerings on the intermediate days of a Festival. Furthermore, it is permitted on these days to bring obligatory offerings that have no set time (Rambam *Sefer Korbanot*, *Hilkhot Ḥagiga* 1:10).

מַאי שְׁנָא חֲגִיגַת יוֹם טוֹב הָרִאשׁוֹן שֶׁל פֶּסַח? אָמַר רַב אַשִׁי: הָא קָא מַשְׁמַע לָן, חֲגִיגַת חֲמִשָּׁה עָשָׂר – אִין, חֲגִיגַת אַרְבָּעָה עָשָׂר – לָא.

The Gemara asks: **What is different** about **the Festival peace-**offering brought on **the first day of the festival of Passover? Rav Ashi said: This** emphasis on the specific date **teaches us** that for **the Festival peace-**offering **of the fifteenth,** i.e., the pilgrimage Festival offerings brought on the first day of Passover, **yes,** this restriction applies; however, for **the Festival peace-**offering **of the fourteenth, no,** this limitation is not in force. If the Paschal lamb was too small for a group, they would bring an additional peace-offering so that the Paschal lamb could be eaten when one was full. This offering was called the Festival peace-offering of the fourteenth of Nisan. Since this offering is not obligatory, everyone agrees that it may be purchased with second-tithe money.

Perek **I**
Daf **8** Amud **a**

אַלְמָא קָסָבַר: חֲגִיגַת אַרְבָּעָה עָשָׂר לָאו דְּאוֹרַיְיתָא.

Apparently, he holds that **the Festival peace-**offering **of the fourteenth**[NH] does **not** apply **by Torah law,** and therefore one may bring it even from second-tithe funds.

אָמַר מָר: בֵּית הִלֵּל אוֹמְרִים: מִן הַמַּעֲשֵׂר. אַמַּאי? דָּבָר שֶׁבְּחוֹבָה הוּא, וְכָל דָּבָר שֶׁבְּחוֹבָה אֵינוֹ בָּא אֶלָּא מִן הַחוּלִּין! אָמַר עוּלָּא: בְּטוֹפֵל.

§ **The Master said** in the *baraita* that **Beit Hillel say:** Festival peace-offerings may be brought even **from the** second **tithe.** The Gemara asks: **Why? It is an obligatory matter, and any obligatory matter may come only from non-sacred** property. **Ulla said:** This is referring to a case **where one combines,**[H] i.e., the offering is purchased with a combination of second-tithe funds and non-sacred money. The Gemara adds that *amora'im* dispute the details of this *halakha*.

חִזְקִיָּה אָמַר: טוֹפְלִין בְּהֵמָה לִבְהֵמָה וְאֵין טוֹפְלִין מָעוֹת לְמָעוֹת. וְרַבִּי יוֹחָנָן אָמַר: טוֹפְלִין מָעוֹת לְמָעוֹת וְאֵין טוֹפְלִין בְּהֵמָה לִבְהֵמָה.

Ḥizkiya said: One may combine one **animal with** another **animal.** If one has a large household for which one animal will not suffice, he brings one animal for the Festival offering from non-sacred money and he may combine funds of second tithe to purchase a second animal. Since he has fulfilled his obligation of the Festival offering by bringing one animal from non-sacred money, he may bring the others from second tithe or animal tithes. **But one may not combine money with** other **money,** i.e., one may not combine second-tithe funds with non-sacred money toward the purchase of one animal for the Festival offering. **And Rabbi Yoḥanan said:** **One** may **combine money with** other **money, but one may not combine** one **animal with** another **animal.**

תַּנְיָא כְּוָותֵיהּ דְּחִזְקִיָּה, תַּנְיָא כְּוָותֵיהּ דְּרַבִּי יוֹחָנָן. תַּנְיָא כְּוָותֵיהּ דְּרַבִּי יוֹחָנָן: "מִסַּת" – מְלַמֵּד שֶׁאָדָם מֵבִיא חוֹבָתוֹ מִן הַחוּלִּין. וּמִנַּיִן שֶׁאִם רָצָה לְעָרֵב מְעָרֵב? תַּלְמוּד לוֹמַר: "כַּאֲשֶׁר יְבָרֶכְךָ ה׳ אֱלֹהֶיךָ".

The Gemara comments: **It is taught** in a *baraita* **in accordance with** the opinion of **Ḥizkiya, and it is taught** in another *baraita* **in accordance with** the opinion of **Rabbi Yoḥanan.** The Gemara elaborates: **It is taught** in a *baraita* **in accordance with** the opinion of **Rabbi Yoḥanan: "After the measure** of the gift offering of your hand" (Deuteronomy 16:10). This **teaches that a person brings his obligatory** offering **from non-sacred** property. **And from where** is it derived **that if one wishes to mix**[N] he may **mix? The verse states: "As the Lord your God blesses you"** (Deuteronomy 16:10), i.e., one may use any money with which God has blessed him, even second tithe. The term: Mix, means combining money from different sources.

תַּנְיָא כְּוָותֵיהּ דְּחִזְקִיָּה: "מִסַּת" – מְלַמֵּד שֶׁאָדָם מֵבִיא חוֹבָתוֹ מִן הַחוּלִּין. בֵּית שַׁמַּאי אוֹמְרִים: יוֹם רִאשׁוֹן מִן הַחוּלִּין, מִכָּאן וְאֵילָךְ מִן הַמַּעֲשֵׂר. וּבֵית הִלֵּל אוֹמְרִים: אֲכִילָה רִאשׁוֹנָה מִן הַחוּלִּין, מִכָּאן וְאֵילָךְ מִן הַמַּעֲשֵׂר.

It is taught in a *baraita* **in accordance with** the opinion of **Ḥizkiya: "After the measure"** (Deuteronomy 16:10). This **teaches that a person brings his obligatory** offering **from non-sacred** property. Beit Shammai and Beit Hillel disagree with regard to this issue, as **Beit Shammai say:** On **the first day** one may bring only **from non-sacred** property. **From this** point **forward** one may buy the animal **from the** second-**tithe** money. **And Beit Hillel say: The first eating** must be **from non-sacred** property. **From this** point **forward** one may bring **from the** second-**tithe** money. The phrase: The first eating, means the first animal that one eats, which is in accordance with Ḥizkiya's opinion.

NOTES

The Festival peace-offering of the fourteenth – חֲגִיגַת אַרְבָּעָה עָשָׂר: The Sages dispute the nature of this unique offering. According to the mishna (*Pesaḥim* 69b), the Festival peace-offering of the fourteenth of Nisan is merely an optional addition to the Paschal offering, brought only so that each individual will eat the Paschal lamb on a full stomach if one lamb or ewe is not enough for all the members of the group. This additional offering may also be brought from cattle. The commentaries note that with regard to this offering the Sages were stringent and stipulated that it may be eaten only for one day and one night, to prevent people from confusing the meat of the Paschal lamb with that of the Festival peace-offering (Meiri, citing the Jerusalem Talmud). Since this offering is optional, it is not brought at all when Passover eve occurs on Shabbat. However, some Sages maintain that the Festival peace-offering of the fourteenth applies by Torah law, and therefore it overrides Shabbat (see *Pesaḥim* 70b). Support is derived for this opinion from the verse "And you shall sacrifice the Paschal offering to the Lord your God, of the sheep and the cattle" (Deuteronomy 16:2). Since the Paschal offering may be brought only from sheep, the term "cattle" must be referring to the additional Festival offering that is brought on the fourteenth.

That if one wishes to mix – שֶׁאִם רָצָה לְעָרֵב: The commentaries explain that the term mix applies only to money, i.e., it is permitted to buy one animal with a combination of money from different funds. However, this term is not applicable to animals (*ge'onim*; Rashi). Accordingly, the phrase: First eating from non-sacred property, refers to an animal purchased exclusively with non-sacred property, as in that case there is a recognizable difference between the first eating and the second.

HALAKHA

The Festival peace-offering of the fourteenth – חֲגִיגַת אַרְבָּעָה עָשָׂר: The Festival peace-offering of the fourteenth of Nisan is optional, and therefore one does not fulfill his obligation of the Festival peace-offering with it. However, he does fulfill his obligation of the peace-offering of rejoicing with it (Rambam *Sefer Korbanot, Hilkhot Ḥagiga* 2:10).

From which funds may one bring Festival peace-offerings – מִמַּה מְבִיאִים שַׁלְמֵי חֲגִיגָה: It is permitted to bring Festival peace-offerings from second-tithe funds combined with non-sacred money, provided that there is enough non-sacred money to purchase a proper measure of meat for the first eating. The *halakha* is in accordance with the opinions of Beit Hillel, Rabbi Yoḥanan, and Ulla (Rambam *Sefer Korbanot, Hilkhot Ḥagiga* 2:8).

וּשְׁאָר כָּל יְמוֹת הַפֶּסַח – אָדָם יוֹצֵא יְדֵי חוֹבָתוֹ בְּמַעְשַׂר בְּהֵמָה. בְּיוֹם טוֹב מַאי טַעְמָא לָא?

The *baraita* concludes: All this applies on the first day of the Festival. **But** with regard to **all the other days of Passover,**[N] on which one is obligated to bring peace-offerings of rejoicing, **a person fulfills his obligation** even **with animal tithes,**[N] and certainly with funds of second tithe.[H] The Gemara asks: **What is the reason that one does not** fulfill his obligation with animal tithes **on the Festival?**

אָמַר רַב אַשִׁי: דִּלְמָא אָתֵי לְעַשּׂוּרֵי בְּיוֹם טוֹב, וְאִי אֶפְשָׁר לְעַשֵּׂר בְּיוֹם טוֹב מִשּׁוּם סִקְרָתָא.

Rav Ashi said: There is a concern that if one requires additional animals, **perhaps he may come to separate tithes on the Festival** itself, **and one may not separate tithes on the Festival due to the red dye** [*sikrata*].[BL] Every tenth animal is marked with red dye, and as it is prohibited to dye on a Festival due to the labor of writing, one may not separate tithes on a Festival.

מַאי מַשְׁמַע דְּהַאי "מִסַּת" לִישָּׁנָא דְּחוּלִּין הוּא? דִּכְתִיב: "וַיָּשֶׂם הַמֶּלֶךְ אֲחַשְׁוֵרוֹשׁ מַס עַל הָאָרֶץ".

The Gemara asks: **From where may it be inferred that this: "After the measure** [*missat*],"[N] mentioned in the verse, **is a term for non-sacred** property? The Gemara answers: **As it is written: "And the king Ahasuerus laid a tribute** [*mas*] **upon the land"** (Esther 10:1), which is clearly referring to a tribute of non-sacred property.

"יִשְׂרָאֵל יוֹצְאִין יְדֵי חוֹבָתָן בִּנְדָרִים וּנְדָבוֹת". תָּנוּ רַבָּנַן: "וְשָׂמַחְתָּ בְּחַגֶּךָ" – לְרַבּוֹת כָּל מִינֵי שְׂמָחוֹת לְשִׂמְחָה. מִכָּאן אָמְרוּ חֲכָמִים: יִשְׂרָאֵל יוֹצְאִין יְדֵי חוֹבָתָן בִּנְדָרִים וּנְדָבוֹת וּבְמַעְשַׂר בְּהֵמָה,

§ The mishna stated that **Israelites fulfill their obligation** to eat peace-offerings of rejoicing **with** their **vow** offerings **and gift** offerings. **The Sages taught** that the verse: **"And you shall rejoice in your feast"** (Deuteronomy 16:14) comes **to include all types of rejoicing as** constituting a fulfillment of the mitzva of **rejoicing. From here the Sages stated: Israelites fulfill their obligation** to eat peace-offerings of rejoicing **with** their **vow** offerings **and gift** offerings **and** likewise **with animal tithes.**

וְהַכֹּהֲנִים בְּחַטָּאת וְאָשָׁם וּבִבְכוֹר וּבְחָזֶה וָשׁוֹק. יָכוֹל אַף בְּעוֹפוֹת וּבִמְנָחוֹת – תַּלְמוּד לוֹמַר: "וְשָׂמַחְתָּ בְּחַגֶּךָ",

And the priests fulfill their obligation of rejoicing **with** the meat of **sin**-offerings **and guilt**-offerings, **and with firstborn** offerings, **and with the breast and thigh**[B] of peace-offerings. One **might** have thought that they can fulfill their obligation **even by** eating **bird**-offerings **and meal**-offerings. Therefore, **the verse states: "And you shall rejoice in your feast."**

HALAKHA

Festival peace-offerings from the second tithe – שַׁלְמֵי חֲגִיגָה מִן הַמַּעֲשֵׂר: Although one can fulfill his obligation to bring a Festival peace-offering with funds from animal tithes, one may not bring this offering on the Festival itself. Instead, he should wait until the intermediate days of the Festival, lest one separate the tithe on the Festival. This opinion is in accordance with that of Rav Ashi (Rambam *Sefer Korbanot, Hilkhot Ḥagiga* 2:9).

LANGUAGE

Red dye [*sikrata*] – סִקְרָתָא: Similar to the Hebrew *serak*, meaning rouge. Apparently, this dye was created from minerals, possibly lead oxide.

BACKGROUND

Due to the red dye – מִשּׁוּם דְּסִקְרָתָא: The proper method of tithing animals is described in several places. The owner would allow to pass through a narrow opening all the young sheep and cattle that were born in the course of one year and count them. Every tenth animal passing by would be marked with dye, in fulfillment of the verse: "Whatsoever passes under the shepherd's rod" (Leviticus 27:32).

Breast and thigh – חָזֶה וָשׁוֹק: The breast and thigh refer to sections of the peace-offering that are given to the priests as one of the twenty-four priestly gifts (see Leviticus 7:29–34). In contrast to some of the other priestly gifts, which may be eaten only by male priests inside the precincts of the Temple, the breast and thigh may be eaten by male or female members of the priestly family throughout the city of Jerusalem. This difference stems from the fact that the breast and thigh come from the portion that belongs to the one who brought the offering, whereas the priest's portion of a sin-offering, for example, comes from the part that is set aside for God.

NOTES

But all the other days of Passover – וּשְׁאָר כָּל יְמוֹת הַפֶּסַח: Although this *halakha* is not limited to Passover, as the same applies on *Sukkot*, this *baraita* specifies Passover because the mishna dealt with this Festival. The mishna chose the example of Passover so as to distinguish this offering from the Festival peace-offering of the fourteenth of Nisan (*Zekher LaḤagiga*).

With animal tithes – בְּמַעְשַׂר בְּהֵמָה: The halakhic authorities ask why it is permitted to bring an animal tithe for the purpose of the Festival peace-offering *ab initio*. The commentaries on the Rambam write that although according to some opinions second-tithe money is consecrated property and therefore should not be used for personal consumption, the animal tithe actually belongs to its owners (*Leḥem Mishne*).

From where may it be inferred that this…measure [*missat*] – מַאי מַשְׁמַע דְּהַאי מִסַּת: In the Jerusalem Talmud a different *halakha* is derived from the term measure, i.e., that it is permitted to bring the Festival peace-offering from second-tithe money. This is based on a verbal analogy between the term *missat* stated with regard to the Festival peace-offering and the phrase: "Carry it [*se'eto*]" (Deuteronomy 14:24), which appears in connection with second tithe. A similar verbal analogy is based on the term rejoicing, which features in both of these contexts. Furthermore, the Gemara there cites in this context the verse: "Benjamin's tribute [*masat Binyamin*]" (Genesis 43:34), as there too the term means an addition beyond the basic amount.

מִי שֶׁחֲגִיגָה בָּאָה מֵהֶם, יָצְאוּ אֵלּוּ שֶׁאֵין חֲגִיגָה בָּאָה מֵהֶם.

This teaches that eating **those** animals **from which the Festival** peace-offering **may come,**[N] i.e., sheep and cattle, is a fulfillment of the mitzva of rejoicing. This **excludes these,** i.e., bird-offerings and meal-offerings, **from which the Festival peace**-offering **may not come.**[NH]

רַב אַשִׁי אָמַר: מִ״וְשָׂמַחְתָּ״ נָפְקָא, יָצְאוּ אֵלּוּ שֶׁאֵין בָּהֶן שִׂמְחָה.

Rav Ashi said: There is no need to derive this *halakha* from "And you shall rejoice in your feast" by explaining that the word feast is referring to the Festival peace-offering. Rather, this *halakha* **is derived** simply **from** the phrase **"And you shall rejoice."** This **excludes those** bird-offerings and meal-offerings **that do not have** an element of **rejoicing,** as the joy of eating is provided only by animal meat.

וְרַב אַשִׁי, הַאי ״בְּחַגֶּךָ״ מַאי עָבֵיד לֵיהּ? הַהוּא לְכִדְרַב דָּנִיֵּאל בַּר קְטִינָא. דְּאָמַר רַב דָּנִיֵּאל בַּר קְטִינָא אָמַר רַב: מִנַּיִין שֶׁאֵין נוֹשְׂאִין נָשִׁים בַּמּוֹעֵד – שֶׁנֶּאֱמַר: ״וְשָׂמַחְתָּ בְּחַגֶּךָ״ – וְלֹא בְּאִשְׁתְּךָ.

The Gemara asks: **And what does Rav Ashi do with** the phrase: **"In your feast"?** The Gemara answers: **That** phrase comes to teach **in accordance with** the statement **of Rav Daniel bar Ketina. As Rav Daniel bar Ketina said** that **Rav said: From where** is it derived **that one may not marry a woman on** the **intermediate days of the Festival? As it is stated: "And you shall rejoice in your feast,"** indicating that one should rejoice only in your feast **and not with your wife.**[NH]

מתני׳ מִי שֶׁיֵּשׁ לוֹ אוֹכְלִים מְרוּבִּים וּנְכָסִים מוּעָטִים – מֵבִיא שְׁלָמִים מְרוּבִּים וְעוֹלוֹת מוּעָטוֹת. נְכָסִים מְרוּבִּים וְאוֹכְלִין מוּעָטִין – מֵבִיא עוֹלוֹת מְרוּבּוֹת וּשְׁלָמִים מוּעָטִין.

MISHNA **One who has many eaters,** i.e., members of his household, **and a small** amount of **property, may bring many peace-offerings and few burnt**-offerings, so he can feed the members of his household with the peace-offerings. If one has **much property and few eaters, he** should **bring many burnt**-offerings **and few peace**-offerings.

זֶה וָזֶה מוּעָט – עַל זֶה נֶאֱמַר: ״מָעָה כֶּסֶף״ ״שְׁתֵּי כֶסֶף״. זֶה וָזֶה מְרוּבִּים – עַל זֶה נֶאֱמַר: ״אִישׁ כְּמַתְּנַת יָדוֹ כְּבִרְכַּת ה׳ אֱלֹהֶיךָ אֲשֶׁר נָתַן לָךְ״.

If both **these and those,** his property and the members of his household, **are few, with regard to this** individual **it is stated** in the mishna (2a) that the Sages established the smallest amount of one **silver** *ma'a* for the burnt-offering of appearance in the Temple and **two silver** coins for the Festival peace-offerings. **If both** his eaters and his property **are many, with regard to this** individual **it is stated: "Every man shall give as he is able,**[N] **according to the blessing of the Lord your God, which He has given you"** (Deuteronomy 16:17).[H]

גמ׳ שְׁלָמִים מְרוּבִּים מֵהֵיכָא מַיְיתִי? הָא לֵית לֵיהּ! אָמַר רַב חִסְדָּא: טוֹפֵל וּמֵבִיא פַּר גָּדוֹל. אָמַר לֵיהּ רַב שֵׁשֶׁת: הֲרֵי אָמְרוּ טוֹפְלִין בְּהֵמָה לִבְהֵמָה!

GEMARA With regard to the mishna's statement that one who has many eaters and a small amount of property may bring many peace-offerings, the Gemara asks: **From where can he bring many peace**-offerings? **He does not have** much property. **Rav Ḥisda said: He combines** his property with the second-tithe money **and brings a large bull.** In this way he will have a lot of meat from the peace-offering. **Rav Sheshet said to him:** The Sages **said** that **one may combine an animal with** another **animal.**

מַאי קָאָמַר לֵיהּ? אִילֵימָא הָכִי קָאָמַר לֵיהּ: הֲרֵי אָמְרוּ טוֹפְלִין בְּהֵמָה לִבְהֵמָה אֲבָל לֹא מָעוֹת לְמָעוֹת – וְלֵימָא לֵיהּ: אֵין טוֹפְלִין מָעוֹת לְמָעוֹת! אֶלָּא הָכִי אָמַר לֵיהּ: הֲרֵי אָמְרוּ אַף טוֹפְלִין בְּהֵמָה לִבְהֵמָה!

Since Rav Sheshet's objection is unclear, the Gemara asks: **What is he saying to** Rav Ḥisda? **If we say** that **he was saying to him as follows: They said** that **one may** only **combine an animal with** another **animal, but one** may **not** combine **money with** other **money** to purchase one large bull, then **let him** simply **say: One may not combine money with** other **money. Rather, this is what he said to him:** The Sages **said** that **one may even combine an animal with** another **animal.** Why did you, Rav Ḥisda, limit him to the purchase of one large animal? Why not also suggest that this individual may bring other animals from second-tithe money?

NOTES

Those from which the Festival peace-offering may come – **מִי שֶׁחֲגִיגָה בָּאָה מֵהֶם:** This does not mean that all the details of the *halakhot* of peace-offerings of rejoicing are precisely the same as those of Festival peace-offerings. Rather, it simply means that the animals that can be used for Festival peace-offerings are also those suitable for peace-offerings of rejoicing (*Zekher LaHagiga*).

From which the Festival peace-offering may not come – **שֶׁאֵין חֲגִיגָה בָּאָה מֵהֶם:** In the Jerusalem Talmud this *halakha* is derived from the chapter that deals with the ceremony on Mount Gerizim and Mount Ebal. Indeed, several *halakhot* pertaining to the Festival peace-offering are derived from these verses. It is stated there: "And you shall sacrifice [*vezavaḥta*] peace-offerings" (Deuteronomy 27:7), and sacrificing [*zeviḥa*] refers only to animal offerings, not bird-offerings or meal-offerings.

In your feast and not with your wife – **בְּחַגֶּךָ וְלֹא בְּאִשְׁתְּךָ:** Why does the term "your feast" specifically exclude a wife? Some commentaries explain that this is because the phrase "you and your household," i.e., husband and wife together, is mentioned in connection with the mitzva of rejoicing on the Festival. Therefore, it is necessary to state that the rejoicing of the Festival must be focused on the Festival itself, not on one's new wife (*Zekher LaHagiga*).

Every man shall give as he is able, etc. – **אִישׁ כְּמַתְּנַת יָדוֹ וגו׳:** Rashi explains that the phrase "every man shall give as he is able" refers to multiple burnt-offerings, while "according to the blessing of the Lord" means peace-offerings. Others interpret in the opposite manner: "Every man shall give as he is able" refers specifically to peace-offerings, as one not only brings these as offerings, but he also gives them to the members of his household to eat (Maharsha).

HALAKHA

From which the Festival peace-offering may not come – **שֶׁאֵין חֲגִיגָה בָּאָה מֵהֶם:** The Festival peace-offering must be an animal (Rambam *Sefer Korbanot*, *Hilkhot Ḥagiga* 1:1).

One may not marry…on the intermediate days of the Festival – **אֵין נוֹשְׂאִים בַּמּוֹעֵד:** One may not marry on the intermediate days of a Festival, even if he does not celebrate the marriage with a feast (*Magen Avraham*), nor may one perform levirate marriage during the intermediate days of a Festival. However, it is permitted to betroth a woman on these days, provided that he does not celebrate by holding a betrothal feast at the home of his betrothed, although he may do so in another place. Furthermore, it is permitted to remarry one's divorced wife on the intermediate days of the Festival (*Shulḥan Arukh*, *Oraḥ Ḥayyim* 546:1–2 and *Even HaEzer* 64:6).

Peace-offerings and burnt-offerings on the pilgrimage Festival – **שְׁלָמִים וְעוֹלוֹת בָּרֶגֶל:** One who has a large household and few possessions brings many Festival peace-offerings and few burnt-offerings of appearance in the Temple. If his household is small but he has many possessions, he brings many burnt-offerings of appearance and few Festival peace-offerings. If he has a small household and few possessions, he offers the minimum value of each offering: One silver *ma'a* for a burnt-offering of appearance and two silver coins for a Festival peace-offering. If he has a large household and is wealthy, with regard to him the verse states: "According to the blessing of the Lord your God, which He has given you" (Rambam *Sefer Korbanot*, *Hilkhot Ḥagiga* 1:11).

NOTES

The *baraitot* do not disagree – מַתְנְיָיתָא לָא פְּלִיגִי: Rashi explains that the *baraitot* disagree only with regard to combining animals, not combining money. Others maintain that the *baraitot* do not disagree at all, as each is dealing with a particular circumstance that does not negate the other (*Tosefot Rid*). According to this opinion, from the fact that one *baraita* is apparently referring to money in particular, the Gemara infers that the other *baraita* refers specifically to animals (see *Turei Aven*).

He may return and sacrifice – חוֹזֵר וּמַקְרִיב: There are three main explanations of the dispute between Reish Lakish and Rabbi Yoḥanan. Some say that they are arguing over one's obligation, i.e., is one obligated to sacrifice the animals that he did not bring on the first day, or perhaps this is merely optional (Meiri). Others maintain that the question is whether he is permitted to return and sacrifice more after he stopped, or whether any further sacrifice of these offerings violates the prohibition: Do not add to the mitzvot (Rashi; Rambam). According to these two opinions, the term: The second day of the Festival, is actually referring to all the remaining days of the Festival, including the intermediate days. The third opinion is that the issue being debated is whether the remaining animals are considered part of the obligatory Festival peace-offering, and therefore it would be permitted to sacrifice them on the last day of the Festival, or whether they are gift offerings, which means that one may not sacrifice them on a Festival day (Rabbeinu Ḥananel). See *Tosafot* and Meiri, who maintain that the Jerusalem Talmud supports this last interpretation.

כְּמַאן? דְּלָא כְּחִזְקִיָּה וּדְלָא כְּרַבִּי יוֹחָנָן!

The Gemara asks: **In accordance with whose** opinion did Rav Sheshet say this? It is **not in accordance with** the opinion of **Ḥizkiya,** who said that one may combine only one animal with another animal, **and not in accordance with** the opinion of **Rabbi Yoḥanan,** who said that one may combine only money with other money.

וְכִי תֵּימָא אָמוֹרָאֵי הוּא דִּפְלִיגִי, מַתְנְיָיתָא לָא פְּלִיגִי – וְהָא קָתָנֵי: אֲכִילָה רִאשׁוֹנָה מִן הַחוּלִּין!

And if you would say: It is the *amora'im* who disagree, whereas **the *baraitot*** that were cited in support of their opinions **do not disagree**[N] **and** therefore Rav Sheshet may present his own opinion on the matter, this cannot be the case, as the *baraita* **teaches: The first eating** must come **from non-sacred** property. In other words, the first animal one eats must come entirely from non-sacred property, and combining is permitted only for the second animal. This indicates that although one may combine an additional animal with that first one, one may not combine money with other money to purchase even one animal.

מַאי אֲכִילָה רִאשׁוֹנָה? שִׁיעוּר דְּמֵי אֲכִילָה רִאשׁוֹנָה מִן הַחוּלִּין.

The Gemara explains. **What is** the meaning of: **The first eating?** This means that when one combines non-sacred money with second-tithe money, **the monetary** value **of** the required **measure** of the **first eating** from the offering must come **from non-sacred** funds. However, the remaining value of that animal may come from second-tithe funds. Therefore, according to the opinion of Rav Sheshet, one may combine an animal with another animal, i.e., by purchasing two separate animals, one from non-sacred funds and one from second-tithe money. Another option is to purchase one animal with combined funds, provided that the first eating is from non-sacred funds.

אָמַר עוּלָּא אָמַר רֵישׁ לָקִישׁ: הִפְרִישׁ עֶשֶׂר בְּהֵמוֹת לַחֲגִיגָתוֹ, הִקְרִיב חָמֵשׁ בְּיוֹם טוֹב רִאשׁוֹן – חוֹזֵר וּמַקְרִיב חָמֵשׁ בְּיוֹם טוֹב שֵׁנִי. רַבִּי יוֹחָנָן אָמַר: כֵּיוָן שֶׁפָּסַק – שׁוּב אֵינוֹ מַקְרִיב.

§ **Ulla said** that **Reish Lakish said:** If one **separated ten animals for** the purpose of **his Festival peace**-offering, and **he sacrificed five** of them **on the first** day of **the Festival, he may return and sacrifice**[N] the remaining **five on the second day of the Festival,** or on any of the other days. There is no concern for the prohibition of: "You shall not add" (Deuteronomy 13:1), as though he were celebrating the first day twice, because the remaining offerings merely complete the first day's offerings. **Rabbi Yoḥanan said: Since he stopped** after the first five offerings on the day on which he first brought the Festival peace-offerings, **he may no longer sacrifice** the remaining animals on the other days, as that would be considered celebrating an extra day.

אָמַר רַבִּי אַבָּא: וְלָא פְּלִיגִי: כָּאן – בִּסְתָם, כָּאן – בִּמְפָרֵשׁ.

Rabbi Abba said: And these *amora'im* **do not disagree,** as they are referring to different circumstances. **Here,** Rabbi Yoḥanan is speaking of a case **where one did not specify** when he intended to sacrifice these offerings, and therefore it is assumed that he meant to sacrifice them all on the first day. **There,** Reish Lakish is referring to a case **where one explicitly** said at the outset that he intended to bring them on all the days of the Festival (Rabbeinu Ḥananel).

הַאי סְתָם הֵיכִי דָמֵי? אִילֵימָא דְּלֵיכָּא שְׁהוּת בַּיּוֹם לְקָרֵב, הַאי דְּלָא אַקְרְבִינְהוּ – דְּלֵיכָּא שְׁהוּת בַּיּוֹם.

The Gemara asks: With regard to **this** case where he **did not specify, what are the circumstances? If we say that there was no time** left **in the day to sacrifice,** i.e., he brought all his animals on the first day and realized that there was not enough time to sacrifice all of them, one can assume that the reason **that he did not bring them is that there was no time** left **in the day.** If so, his offering on another day is certainly considered merely the completion of the obligations of the first day. In this case his bringing of the additional offerings is not prohibited.

וְאֶלָּא דְּלֵית לֵיהּ אוֹכְלִין, הַאי דְּלָא אַקְרְבִינְהוּ – דְּלֵית לֵיהּ אוֹכְלִין!

But rather, you must say that this is referring to a case **where he does not have** enough **eaters** in his household, and as one may not have leftovers, he did not sacrifice the remaining offerings. Here too, the fact **that he did not sacrifice them is because he does not have** enough **eaters.** Again, this cannot be the case in which it is prohibited to sacrifice the extra offerings.

לָא צְרִיכָא, דְּאִיכָּא שְׁהוּת בַּיּוֹם וְאִית לֵיהּ אוֹכְלִין. מִדְּבְקַמָּא לָא אַקְרְבִינְהוּ – שְׁמַע מִינָּהּ שַׁיּוּרֵי שַׁיְּירִינְהוּ.

The Gemara answers: **No,** it is **necessary** to teach this ruling **only** in a case **where there is time** left **in the day and he has eaters** in his household. **From** the fact **that he did not sacrifice them on the first** day of the Festival, one can **conclude from** it that **he left them** intentionally. Therefore, he is no longer permitted to sacrifice them on the other days of the Festival.[NH]

וְהָכִי נַמִי מִסְתַּבְּרָא, דְּכִי אֲתָא רָבִין אָמַר רַבִּי יוֹחָנָן: הִפְרִישׁ עֶשֶׂר בְּהֵמוֹת לַחֲגִיגָתוֹ, הִקְרִיב חָמֵשׁ בְּיוֹם טוֹב רִאשׁוֹן – חוֹזֵר וּמַקְרִיב חָמֵשׁ בְּיוֹם טוֹב שֵׁנִי. קַשְׁיָין אַהֲדָדֵי!

The Gemara comments: **So too, it is reasonable** that Rabbi Yoḥanan agrees that if one specifies his intentions he may sacrifice the offerings on the remaining days, **as when Ravin came** from Eretz Yisrael to Babylonia he said that **Rabbi Yoḥanan said:** If **one separated ten animals for his Festival peace-**offering, and **he sacrificed five on the first day** of **the Festival, he may return and sacrifice** the other **five on the second** day of the **Festival.** These two statements of Rabbi Yoḥanan, cited by Ulla and Ravin respectively, apparently **contradict each other.**

אֶלָּא לָאו שְׁמַע מִינָּהּ: כָּאן – בִּסְתָם, כָּאן – בִּמְפָרֵשׁ? שְׁמַע מִינָּהּ.

Rather, isn't it correct to **conclude from** this contradiction that this statement **here** is dealing with a case **where** one **did not specify,** whereas **there** it is referring to a situation **where** one stated his intentions **explicitly?** The Gemara concludes: **Indeed, conclude from** here that it is so.

אִיתְּמַר נַמִי, אָמַר רַב שֶׁמֶן בַּר אַבָּא אָמַר רַבִּי יוֹחָנָן:

It **was also stated** that **Rav Shemen bar Abba said** that **Rabbi Yoḥanan said:**

NOTES

May he sacrifice the rest or not – מַקְרִיב אוֹ אֵינוֹ מַקְרִיב הַשְּׁאָר: In the Jerusalem Talmud this dispute between Rabbi Yoḥanan and Reish Lakish is compared to the dispute between Ḥizkiya and Rabbi Yoḥanan with regard to combining. Since Rabbi Yoḥanan holds that one may combine money from one source with money from a different source, he evidently maintains that the sacrifice of each animal partially fulfills the obligation of the Festival peace-offering. Consequently, one may sacrifice these animals on the second Festival day, i.e., the first intermediate Festival day. However, according to the opinion that one may combine only one animal with another, as the remaining animals are no longer considered full-fledged Festival peace-offerings, their sacrifice does not override the Festival day.

HALAKHA

One who did not sacrifice all the offerings he separated – מִי שֶׁלֹּא הִקְרִיב כָּל הַקָּרְבָּנוֹת שֶׁהִפְרִישׁ: If one separated many animals for his Festival peace-offering but sacrificed only some of them on the first Festival day, he may not go back and sacrifice the rest, as he left them over by choice. However, if he could not sacrifice them that same day due to time constraints, he may sacrifice them the following day. This is in accordance with the opinion of Rabbi Yoḥanan, as the *halakha* follows his opinion when he disagrees with Reish Lakish (Rambam *Sefer Korbanot*, *Hilkhot Ḥagiga* 2:7).

Perek **I**
Daf **9** Amud **a**

לֹא שָׁנוּ אֶלָּא שֶׁלֹּא גָּמַר, אֲבָל גָּמַר – חוֹזֵר וּמַקְרִיב.

They taught that one may sacrifice the Festival peace-offering on the first Festival day but not on all seven days, as recorded in the *baraita* on this *amud* below, **only** in a case **where he did not finish. However, if he finished, he may go back and sacrifice.**

מַאי גָּמַר? אִילֵימָא גָּמַר קָרְבְּנוֹתָיו – מַאי מַקְרִיב? אֶלָּא שֶׁלֹּא גָּמַר הַיּוֹם, אֲבָל גָּמַר הַיּוֹם – חוֹזֵר וּמַקְרִיב.

The Gemara asks: **What is** the meaning of the term: **Finish,** in this context? **If we say** it means that he **finished** sacrificing all of **his offerings, what** is **he** going back to **sacrifice? Rather,** it means **that** if **the day did not end** and he still has offerings left over, he may not return to sacrifice those on other Festival days. **However, if the day ended** and he had not finished sacrificing his offerings, **he may go back and sacrifice** them. This shows that Rabbi Yoḥanan concedes that in these circumstances it is permitted to sacrifice Festival peace-offerings during the remaining days of the Festival.

מתני׳ מִי שֶׁלֹּא חַג בְּיוֹם טוֹב הָרִאשׁוֹן שֶׁל חָג – חוֹגֵג אֶת כָּל הָרֶגֶל, וְיוֹם טוֹב הָאַחֲרוֹן שֶׁל חָג.

MISHNA With regard to **one who did not celebrate** by bringing **the Festival** peace-offering **on the first day of the festival** of *Sukkot*, he **may celebrate** and bring it during **the entire** remaining days of **the pilgrimage Festival,**[N] **and** even **on the final day of the Festival,** i.e., on the Eighth Day of Assembly.[H]

HALAKHA

One who did not celebrate on the first day – מִי שֶׁלֹּא חַג בָּרִאשׁוֹן: One who did not bring his obligatory burnt-offering of appearance and Festival peace-offering on the first day of a Festival may sacrifice them on the remaining days of the Festival (Rambam *Sefer Korbanot*, *Hilkhot Ḥagiga* 1:4).

NOTES

May celebrate during the entire pilgrimage Festival, etc. – חוֹגֵג אֶת כָּל הָרֶגֶל וכו׳: Some commentaries point out an apparent contradiction: The first use in the mishna of the term festival refers solely to the festival of *Sukkot*, not including the Eighth Day of Assembly. However, when it states a few lines later: If the Festival passed and he did not celebrate by bringing the Festival peace-offering, the term apparently includes even the Eighth Day of Assembly (*Turei Aven*).

The *Turei Aven* explains that in each instance the term Festival refers only to the first seven days, as the status of the eighth day is different from the rest: One who was not fit to sacrifice an offering during the first seven days may not do so on the eighth day, which serves merely as redress for the missed offerings of one who was qualified to offer at that time. This is true even according to the opinion that each day is available for redress for the others. Others claim that the Eighth Day of Assembly is a separate Festival, and therefore one is obligated to bring a separate Festival peace-offering for this day even if he was exempt during the entire festival of *Sukkot* (Ritva; see *Zekher LaḤagiga* at length).

עָבַר הָרֶגֶל וְלֹא חָג – אֵינוֹ חַיָּיב בְּאַחֲרָיוּתוֹ. עַל זֶה נֶאֱמַר: "מְעֻוָּת לֹא יוּכַל לִתְקֹן וְחֶסְרוֹן לֹא יוּכַל לְהִמָּנוֹת".

If **the pilgrimage Festival passed and one did not celebrate**[H] by bringing **the Festival** peace-offering, **he is not obligated** to pay **restitution** for it. Even if he consecrated an animal for this purpose and it was lost, once the Festival is over he has no obligation to replace it, as he has missed the opportunity for performing this mitzva. And **about this it is stated: "That which is crooked cannot be made straight; and that which is wanting cannot be numbered"** (Ecclesiastes 1:15).[N]

רַבִּי שִׁמְעוֹן בֶּן מְנַסְיָא אוֹמֵר: אֵיזֶהוּ מְעֻוָּת שֶׁאֵינוֹ יָכוֹל לְהִתָּקֵן? זֶה הַבָּא עַל הָעֶרְוָה וְהוֹלִיד מִמֶּנָּה מַמְזֵר. אִם תֹּאמַר בְּגוֹנֵב וְגוֹזֵל – יָכוֹל הוּא לְהַחֲזִירוֹ וְיִתָּקֵן.

Rabbi Shimon ben Menasya says: Who is the **crooked that cannot be made straight? This** verse is referring to **one who engaged in intercourse with a woman forbidden to him and fathered a *mamzer***[B] **with her.** This individual is unable to rectify his sin, because the status of the illegitimate child is permanent. And **if you say** that it is referring **to one who steals or robs,**[N] although he is crooked **he can return** what he stole **and** in this manner his sin **will be rectified.**

רַבִּי שִׁמְעוֹן בֶּן יוֹחַי אוֹמֵר: אֵין קוֹרִין מְעֻוָּת אֶלָּא לְמִי שֶׁהָיָה מְתוּקָּן בַּתְּחִילָּה וְנִתְעַוֵּות, וְאֵי זֶה? זֶה תַּלְמִיד חָכָם הַפּוֹרֵשׁ מִן הַתּוֹרָה.

Rabbi Shimon ben Yoḥai says: One calls crooked only someone who was initially straight and subsequently **became crooked. And who is this? This is a Torah scholar who leaves** his **Torah** study. Here is an example of something straight that became crooked.

גמ׳ מְנָהָנֵי מִילֵּי? אָמַר רַבִּי יוֹחָנָן מִשּׁוּם רַבִּי יִשְׁמָעֵאל: נֶאֱמַר "עֲצֶרֶת" בִּשְׁבִיעִי שֶׁל פֶּסַח, וְנֶאֱמַר "עֲצֶרֶת" בִּשְׁמִינִי שֶׁל חָג. מָה לְהַלָּן לְתַשְׁלוּמִין – אַף כָּאן לְתַשְׁלוּמִין.

GEMARA The mishna taught that if one did not bring his Festival peace-offering on the first day of the festival of *Sukkot*, he may bring it even on the Eighth Day of Assembly, despite the fact that it is a separate Festival. The Gemara asks: **From where are these matters** derived?[N] **Rabbi Yoḥanan said in the name of Rabbi Yishmael** that this *halakha* is derived by means of a verbal analogy. **It is stated: "Assembly"** (Deuteronomy 16:8), with regard **to the seventh day of Passover, and it is stated: "Assembly"** (Leviticus 23:36), with regard **to the eighth day of the festival** of *Sukkot*. **Just as there,** with regard to Passover, the day of assembly, i.e., the seventh day of Passover, is available **for redress,** as it is certainly part of the Festival, **so too here,** in the case of *Sukkot*, the Eighth Day of Assembly is available **for redress.**

מוּפְנֶה, דְּאִי לָאו מוּפְנֶה – אִיכָּא לְמִיפְרַךְ: מָה לִשְׁבִיעִי שֶׁל פֶּסַח – שֶׁכֵּן אֵינוֹ חָלוּק מִשֶּׁלְּפָנָיו, תֹּאמַר בִּשְׁמִינִי שֶׁל חָג שֶׁחָלוּק מִשֶּׁלְּפָנָיו.

The Gemara adds that the term assembly in each of these contexts is **free** for this verbal analogy, i.e., it is superfluous in both contexts. **As, if it is not free**[N] the verbal analogy **can be refuted,** because each context in which the term appears contains features that do not apply to the other one. **What** can one say **about the seventh** day **of Passover? That it is not distinct from** the days **preceding it** with regard to the Festival offerings and the prohibition against eating leavened bread. Can **you say** the same **with regard to the eighth** day **of the festival** of *Sukkot*, **which is distinct from** the days **preceding it,** i.e., that the Eighth Day of Assembly does not involve the same mitzvot as the festival of *Sukkot*?

לָאֵיי, אַפְנוּיֵי מוּפְנֶה. מִכְּדִי, מַאי עֲצֶרֶת – עָצוּר בַּעֲשִׂיַּית מְלָאכָה. הָכְתִיב: "לֹא תַעֲשֶׂה מְלָאכָה"! "עֲצֶרֶת" דִּכְתַב רַחֲמָנָא לָמָּה לִי? אֶלָּא שְׁמַע מִינָּהּ לְאַפְנוּיֵי.

However, this is **not so** [*la'ei*],[L] as the term assembly is certainly **free. Now, what is** the meaning of: **"assembly** [*atzeret*]**"?** It means that one is **stopped** [*atzur*], i.e., prohibited, **from performing labor. But isn't it** already **written: "You shall not perform labor"** (Deuteronomy 16:8)? **Why** then **do I** need this term ***atzeret*** **that the Merciful One writes? Rather, learn from here** that it is **free** for the verbal analogy.

וְתַנָּא מַיְיתֵי לַהּ מֵהָכָא, דְּתַנְיָא: "וְחַגּוֹתֶם אוֹתוֹ חַג לַה׳ שִׁבְעַת יָמִים", יָכוֹל יְהֵא חוֹגֵג וְהוֹלֵךְ כָּל שִׁבְעָה – תַּלְמוּד לוֹמַר: "אוֹתוֹ", אוֹתוֹ, אַתָּה חוֹגֵג, וְאִי אַתָּה חוֹגֵג כָּל שִׁבְעָה. אִם כֵּן לָמָּה נֶאֱמַר "שִׁבְעָה" – לְתַשְׁלוּמִין.

The Gemara comments: **And a *tanna* cites** proof **from here, as it is taught** in a *baraita* with regard to a verse that deals with the festival of *Sukkot*: **"And you shall keep it a feast to the Lord seven days"** (Leviticus 23:41). One **might** have thought that one **may continue to celebrate** by bringing the Festival peace-offering **all seven** days of the Festival. Therefore, **the verse states: "It,"** which teaches: **It,** i.e., the first day of the Festival, **you shall celebrate** with these offerings, **and you may not celebrate all seven** days. **If so, why is "seven" stated? For redress,** i.e., if one failed to bring an offering on the first day he may do so all seven days.

HALAKHA

If the pilgrimage Festival passed and one did not celebrate – עָבַר הָרֶגֶל וְלֹא חָג: If one did not sacrifice the Festival offerings and the Festival passed, he is not obligated to make restitution for them. With regard to this situation the verse states: "That which is crooked cannot be made straight" (Rambam *Sefer Korbanot*, *Hilkhot Ḥagiga* 1:6).

NOTES

About this it is stated, that which is crooked, etc. – עַל זֶה נֶאֱמַר, מְעֻוָּת וכו׳: Since the neglect of any positive mitzva that has a limited time for its performance cannot be rectified, why is the verse interpreted with regard to this case in particular (*Turei Aven*)? The *Turei Aven* answers that this animal consecrated for the Festival peace-offering retains consecrated status and must be sacrificed as a gift offering. Consequently, the mishna stresses that even so, the obligation of the individual is no longer in effect, and therefore if the animal is lost or dies he has no obligation to bring another Festival peace-offering in its place.

One who steals or robs – גּוֹנֵב וְגוֹזֵל: Several commentaries provide suggestions as to why one might think that these individuals' sins cannot be rectified. One reason is that if they stole from the public they cannot make full restitution, even if there are various ways for the robber or thief to return the stolen property (Maharsha; see *Yad David*).

From where are these matters derived – מְנָהָנֵי מִילֵּי: This question refers only to the Eighth Day of Assembly; the Gemara does not explain from where this principle is derived with regard to the first seven days. Some explain that it is derived from the verse that deals with *Sukkot*: "And you shall keep it a Festival to the Lord seven days" (Leviticus 23:41). By juxtaposition, the same applies to the other two pilgrimage Festivals (Rabbeinu Ḥananel).

Free, as, if it is not free – מוּפְנֶה, דְּאִי לָא מוּפְנֶה: The terms used in a verbal analogy must be superfluous in their respective contexts, and therefore free for the analogy. If only one of the terms is extraneous, the Sages dispute the validity of the analogy. Rabbi Yishmael holds that it is entirely valid, whereas others invoke the principle: One can derive from a verbal analogy of this kind and one can refute it logically. In other words, one may reject it on the basis of a suitable challenge. Everyone agrees that this principle applies to a verbal analogy in which both words are necessary in their own contexts. In this specific case, some claim that the term assembly that appears in Deuteronomy is necessary for another *halakha* and therefore this verbal analogy is not completely free. Others explain that this verbal analogy is derived in accordance with the opinion of Rabbi Yishmael (see Rashash; Rabbi Shlomo Cohen).

BACKGROUND

***Mamzer* – מַמְזֵר:** A *mamzer* is a child born from relations between a married woman and a man other than her husband, or between relatives who are forbidden to marry by Torah law, where the participants in such a relationship are subject to the punishment of *karet*. An exception to this principle is a menstruating woman, with whom sexual relations are forbidden under penalty of *karet*, but whose offspring is not a *mamzer*. The offspring of an unmarried couple is not a *mamzer*. A *mamzer* inherits his natural father and is halakhically considered his father's son in all respects. A *mamzer* may marry only a female *mamzer* or a convert. Likewise, a female *mamzer* may marry only a *mamzer* or a convert.

LANGUAGE

Not so [*la'ei*] – לָאֵיי: From the context, this term means: Therefore, or: Certainly this is so. However, its source is unknown. Some maintain that it is an amalgamation of the Aramaic term for no [*la*] and the Greek for son, υἱέ, *huye* (*Arukh*). If so, it means: No, my son.

וּמִנַּיִן שֶׁאִם לֹא חַג יוֹם טוֹב הָרִאשׁוֹן שֶׁל חָג שֶׁחוֹגֵג וְהוֹלֵךְ אֶת כָּל הָרֶגֶל וְיוֹם טוֹב הָאַחֲרוֹן? תַּלְמוּד לוֹמַר: ״בַּחֹדֶשׁ הַשְּׁבִיעִי תָּחֹגּוּ אוֹתוֹ״. אִי ״בַּחֹדֶשׁ הַשְּׁבִיעִי״ – יָכוֹל יְהֵא חוֹגֵג וְהוֹלֵךְ הַחֹדֶשׁ כּוּלּוֹ? תַּלְמוּד לוֹמַר: ״אוֹתוֹ״ – אוֹתוֹ אַתָּה חוֹגֵג, וְאִי אַתָּה חוֹגֵג חוּצָה לוֹ.

And from where is it derived **that if one did not celebrate** by bringing the Festival peace-offering **on the first day of the festival** of *Sukkot* **that he may continue to celebrate throughout the pilgrimage Festival and** even on **the last festival day** of *Sukkot*, which is the Eighth Day of Assembly? **The verse states: "You shall keep it in the seventh month"** (Leviticus 23:41), which indicates that one may bring the Festival offerings even after the seven days of the Festival. **If** the verse said only: **"In the seventh month,"** one **might** have thought that **one** may **continue to celebrate** by bringing the offering at any time during the rest of **the entire month.** Therefore, **the verse states: "It,"** indicating that **you celebrate it**, i.e., any of the Festival days, **and you may not celebrate outside of** these days.

וּמַאי תַּשְׁלוּמִין? רַבִּי יוֹחָנָן אָמַר: תַּשְׁלוּמִין לְרִאשׁוֹן. וְרַבִּי אוֹשַׁעְיָא אָמַר: תַּשְׁלוּמִין זֶה לָזֶה.

§ The Gemara asks: **What is** the meaning of the concept of **redress** mentioned in the *baraita*? The Gemara answers that **Rabbi Yoḥanan said:** The other days are **redress for the first** day. If one did not bring the Festival offering on the first day, he may still do so on the remaining days of the Festival. **And Rabbi Oshaya said:** The days are **redress for one another.** Each day can be considered the main day of obligation, i.e., if one did not bring the offering on the first available day he may do so on the remaining days.[H]

מַאי בֵּינַיְיהוּ? אָמַר רַבִּי זֵירָא: חִיגֵּר בְּיוֹם רִאשׁוֹן וְנִתְפַּשֵּׁט בְּיוֹם שֵׁנִי אִיכָּא בֵּינַיְיהוּ. רַבִּי יוֹחָנָן אָמַר: תַּשְׁלוּמִין לְרִאשׁוֹן, כֵּיוָן דְּלָא חֲזִי בְּרִאשׁוֹן – לָא חֲזִי בְּשֵׁנִי. וְרַבִּי אוֹשַׁעְיָא אָמַר: תַּשְׁלוּמִין זֶה לָזֶה. אַף עַל גַּב דְּלָא חֲזִי בְּרִאשׁוֹן – חֲזִי בְּשֵׁנִי.

The Gemara asks: **What is** the practical difference **between** these two explanations? **Rabbi Zeira said:** The practical difference **between them** is in a case of one who was **lame on the first day**[HN] of the Festival **and was healed on the second day. Rabbi Yoḥanan said** that the other days are **redress for the first** day; **since he was not fit**, i.e., was not qualified to sacrifice his offerings **on the first** day, **he is not fit** to do so even **on the second,** as the second day is redress for the first. The second day is not for those who were completely exempt on the first, but for those who were obligated to sacrifice but neglected to do so. **And Rabbi Oshaya said** that the days are **redress for one another.** Consequently, **even though he was not fit** to bring the offering **on the first** day, he **is fit** to do so **on the second.** Since a separate obligation applies on each day, even if one was unfit to bring the offering on the first day he must do so when he becomes fit.

וּמִי אָמַר רַבִּי יוֹחָנָן הָכִי?

The Gemara asks: **And did Rabbi Yoḥanan** actually **say this?** Rabbi Yoḥanan was involved in a dispute with regard to a nazirite. A nazirite who becomes ritually impure as a result of contact with a corpse must undergo a seven-day process of ritual purification, after which he must bring a set of offerings and restart counting the days of his nazirite period. Usually, a nazirite may bring one set of offerings even for many occurrences of ritual impurity. However, if he came into contact with a corpse for a second time on the eighth day after he first became ritually impure he must bring two sets of offerings, as the second impurity occurred at a time when he could have begun counting the days of his nazirite vow again. The *amora'im* dispute the details of this *halakha*.

וְהָאָמַר חִזְקִיָּה: נִטְמָא בַּיּוֹם – מֵבִיא, בַּלַּיְלָה – אֵינוֹ מֵבִיא.

The Gemara continues. **Didn't Ḥizkiya say** that if a nazirite **became ritually impure on** the eighth **day**[N] itself, **he brings** a second set of offerings? However, if he became ritually impure **on the** previous **night**[H] **he does not bring** an additional set of offerings, because he could not have brought the offering at night. Although seven complete days have passed, as he did not yet have the opportunity to bring the offering, it is as though his seven days were not yet complete. Consequently, he may still bring one set of offerings for the two instances of ritual impurity.

HALAKHA

The nature of the days of redress – מַהוּת יְמֵי הַתַּשְׁלוּמִין: Any offerings sacrificed after the first day of the Festival are considered redress for the first day (Rambam *Sefer Korbanot, Hilkhot Ḥagiga* 1:6). This ruling is in accordance with the opinion of Rabbi Yoḥanan, despite the fact that Rabbi Oshaya was his teacher, as the Gemara discusses Rabbi Yoḥanan's opinion in a manner that indicates that this is the *halakha* (*Kesef Mishne*). Some explain that the Rabbi Oshaya mentioned here is a different *amora*, who was not Rabbi Yoḥanan's teacher (*Leḥem Mishne*).

One who was lame on the first day – חִיגֵּר בְּיוֹם רִאשׁוֹן: One who was lame or blind on the first Festival day is exempt from the mitzva of appearance in the Temple. Even if he was healed after the first day he is still not obligated, as the remaining days of the Festival are merely redress for the first day. The *halakha* is in accordance with the opinion of Rabbi Yoḥanan (Rambam *Sefer Korbanot, Hilkhot Ḥagiga* 2:5).

He became ritually impure in the day or at night – נִטְמָא בַּיּוֹם וּבַלַּיְלָה: One who became ritually impure on the first night of the Festival is exempt from appearing in the Temple even if he was purified the following day. However, if he became ritually impure on the first day of the Festival he is obligated to bring his burnt-offering of appearance as well as his Festival peace-offering sometime during the Festival, when he is purified. The *halakha* is in accordance with the opinion of Ḥizkiya, who was Rabbi Yoḥanan's teacher. Furthermore, the conclusion of the Gemara indicates that Rabbi Yoḥanan conceded to Ḥizkiya's opinion (Rambam *Sefer Korbanot, Hilkhot Ḥagiga* 2:5).

NOTES

One who was lame on the first day – חִיגֵּר בְּיוֹם רִאשׁוֹן: The commentaries discuss whether this dispute also applies to one who was a minor on the first day and became an adult during the Festival. Was he never obligated in this mitzva, or was his obligation merely delayed until later in the Festival? (see *Petaḥ Einayim*).

A nazirite became ritually impure on the eighth day – נִטְמָא בַּיּוֹם: Many commentaries maintain that this dispute refers to a nazirite (Rashi; *Tosafot*; Rabbeinu Ḥananel; Rabbeinu Gershom Meor HaGola on *Keritot* 8a). Others contend that this dispute also concerns the Festival peace-offering itself: If one became ritually impure on the first night he has no further obligation, despite the fact that he could not have sacrificed the offering at that time (Rambam; Meiri). This explains why the Rambam rules in accordance with the opinion of Rabbi Yoḥanan as opposed to that of Rabbi Oshaya, as Ḥizkiya agrees with Rabbi Yoḥanan's ruling, which means that Rabbi Yoḥanan's ruling is the majority opinion (see *Sefat Emet*).

וְרַבִּי יוֹחָנָן אָמַר: אַף בַּלַּיְלָה נַמִי מֵבִיא!

And Rabbi Yoḥanan said: Even if the nazirite became ritually impure **on the night** on which the eighth day begins, **he also brings** a second set of offerings. Rabbi Yoḥanan maintains that this nazirite is effectively ready to begin counting the days of his vow again, as only the technicality that one may not bring offerings at night prevents him from doing so. This shows that according to the opinion of Rabbi Yoḥanan, even when one is incapable of sacrificing his offerings, his obligation remains intact. So too, in the case of a lame person, his obligation to bring the Festival offering applies in theory even on the first day, which means that he should be able to bring the offerings at a later date during the Festival.

אָמַר רַבִּי יִרְמְיָה: שָׁאנֵי טוּמְאָה דְּיֵשׁ לָהּ תַּשְׁלוּמִין בְּפֶסַח שֵׁנִי.

Rabbi Yirmeya said: The case of one who cannot bring an offering due to **ritual impurity is different.** He is not completely disqualified, **as there is redress for** ritual purity. This can be demonstrated from the *halakha* **of the second *Pesaḥ*.** Just as one who is ritually impure and may not sacrifice the Paschal offering has the opportunity to redress the situation by means of the second *Pesaḥ*, so too, anyone who cannot bring an offering due to impurity may redress this at a later date.

מַתְקִיף לָהּ רַב פָּפָּא: הָנִיחָא לְמַאן דְּאָמַר: פֶּסַח

Rav Pappa strongly objects to this reasoning: **This works out well according to the one who said** that **the second *Pesaḥ***

Perek **I**
Daf **9** Amud **b**

שֵׁנִי תַּשְׁלוּמִין דְּרִאשׁוֹן הוּא. אֶלָּא לְמַאן דְּאָמַר שֵׁנִי רֶגֶל בִּפְנֵי עַצְמוֹ הוּא – מַאי אִיכָּא לְמֵימַר?

is redress for the first Paschal offering. According to this opinion, it is clear that ritual impurity does not nullify one's obligation. **However, according to the one who said** that **the second *Pesaḥ*[HN] is a separate pilgrimage Festival,** established for those who were unable to sacrifice the Paschal offering at the proper time, **what is there to say?** In that case, Rav Yirmeya's answer does not apply, and therefore it remains unclear that Rabbi Yoḥanan holds that one who is not obligated in the Festival offerings on the first day is exempt during the remaining days.

אֶלָּא אָמַר רַב פָּפָּא: קָסָבַר רַבִּי יוֹחָנָן לַיְלָה אֵינוֹ מְחוּסַּר זְמַן. וּמִי אָמַר רַבִּי יוֹחָנָן הָכִי?

Rather, Rav Pappa said: Rabbi Yoḥanan holds that **night** is **not** considered part of a date **whose time has not yet** arrived. Although one may not sacrifice offerings at night, the date itself has arrived and his period of impurity is complete, which is why any further impurity requires a second set of offerings. Consequently, Rabbi Yoḥanan's opinion with regard to a lame person does not contradict his ruling concerning a nazirite. The Gemara asks: **And did Rabbi Yoḥanan** actually **say this,** that night is not considered part of a date whose time has not yet arrived?

HALAKHA

The second *Pesaḥ* – פֶּסַח שֵׁנִי: The second *Pesaḥ* is a separate Festival, not merely redress for the first *Pesaḥ*. Furthermore, the second *Pesaḥ* offering overrides Shabbat. One who neglects to bring this offering when he is obligated to do so is liable to receive *karet* (Rambam *Sefer Korbanot*, *Hilkhot Korban Pesaḥ* 5:1).

NOTES

The second *Pesaḥ* – פֶּסַח שֵׁנִי: The *halakha* of the second *Pesaḥ* is stated explicitly in the Torah (Numbers 9:9–14). One who was ritually impure or far from Jerusalem at the time for the sacrificing of the Paschal offering must sacrifice that offering one month later, on the fourteenth of Iyyar. The *tanna'im* dispute whether the second *Pesaḥ* is merely redress for the Paschal offering's omission, or whether it is a separate Festival that is incumbent only upon one who did not sacrifice the Paschal offering (*Pesaḥim* 93a). The practical differences between these opinions concern two main areas: What is the *halakha* if someone intentionally refrained from bringing the Paschal offering. Does he have an opportunity for rectification on the second *Pesaḥ*? If the second *Pesaḥ* is redress for the first, an intentional sinner does not have recourse to this option. Furthermore, what happens if one who is obligated to observe the second *Pesaḥ* intentionally neglects this offering? If it is considered a Festival in its own right he is liable to receive *karet* for this willful sin. Likewise, there is a difference with respect to one who was not obligated to bring a Paschal offering on the fourteenth of Nisan but who is obligated to perform mitzvot at the time of the second *Pesaḥ*, e.g., a convert or a minor. If the second *Pesaḥ* is redress for the first, he does not bring this offering.

וְהָאָמַר רַבִּי יוֹחָנָן: רָאָה אַחַת בַּלַּיְלָה וּשְׁתַּיִם בַּיּוֹם – מֵבִיא;

But didn't Rabbi Yoḥanan say: A *zav* at the end of his seven-day purification process who **saw**[N] that he experienced **one** emission **at night**[H] **and** then **two in the day brings** additional offerings for the second impurity? Had he experienced the emissions before he became ritually pure, he would have been required to bring only one set of offerings. However, once his purification is complete he must bring a separate set. In this case, the first emission occurred before he was able to sacrifice the offerings for his initial period of impurity. Nevertheless, as the two subsequent sightings occurred during the day, and they alone would suffice to confer upon him the status of a *zav*, they combine with the one from the previous night and he is required to bring new offerings.

שְׁתַּיִם בַּלַּיְלָה וְאַחַת בַּיּוֹם – אֵינוֹ מֵבִיא. וְאִי סָלְקָא דַּעְתָּךְ קָסָבַר רַבִּי יוֹחָנָן לַיְלָה אֵינוֹ מְחוּסַּר זְמַן, אֲפִילּוּ שְׁתַּיִם בַּלַּיְלָה וְאַחַת בַּיּוֹם מֵבִיא!

However, if he saw **two** emissions **at night and one in the day, he does not bring** additional offerings, because at night he could not yet sacrifice the offerings owed due to his current status, and without those two new sightings he would not become a *zav* again. **And if it enters your mind that Rabbi Yoḥanan holds that night** is **not** considered a date **whose time has not yet** arrived, then **even** in the case where he saw **two** emissions **at night and one in the day he** should have to **bring** another set of offerings. He already reached the date of sacrificing the previous offerings before these new emissions occurred. This indicates that Rabbi Yoḥanan holds that night is considered part of a date whose time has not yet arrived.

כִּי קָאָמַר רַבִּי יוֹחָנָן – לְדִבְרֵי הָאוֹמֵר לַיְלָה מְחוּסַּר זְמַן. לְדִבְרֵי הָאוֹמֵר? פְּשִׁיטָא! שְׁתַּיִם בַּיּוֹם וְאַחַת בַּלַּיְלָה אִצְטְרִיכָא לֵיהּ.

The Gemara answers: **When Rabbi Yoḥanan said** this statement, he spoke **according to the one who says** that **night**[H] is considered part of a date **whose time has not yet** arrived.[N] However, he himself maintains that even if a *zav* saw all three emissions at night he must bring another offering. The Gemara asks: If he spoke only **according to the one who says** that opinion, it **is obvious** that no new offerings are required; what novel idea did Rabbi Yoḥanan intend to express? The Gemara answers: Nevertheless, **it was necessary for him** to teach the case of a *zav* who saw **two in the day and one at night.**

סָלְקָא דַּעְתָּךְ אָמִינָא כְּאַתְקַפְתָּא דְּרַב שֵׁישָׁא בְּרֵיהּ דְּרַב אִידִי. קָא מַשְׁמַע לָן כְּדְרַב יוֹסֵף.

The Gemara elaborates: It was necessary for Rabbi Yoḥanan to say this, lest it **enter your mind to say** in the manner **of the strong objection of Rav Sheisha, son of Rav Idi** (see *Keritot* 8a), who holds that there is no reason to distinguish between a *zav* seeing one or two emissions at night. Therefore, Rabbi Yoḥanan **teaches us** that the *halakha* is **in accordance with** the opinion **of Rav Yosef**, that the first sighting confers merely the status of ritual impurity of one who has a seminal emission, and he is not yet classified as a *zav*. Consequently, there is a difference between one who experienced one emission at night and one who experienced two.

״עָבַר הָרֶגֶל וְלֹא חַג אֵינוֹ חַיָּיב בְּאַחֲרָיוּתוֹ. וְעַל זֶה נֶאֱמַר: ׳מְעֻוָּת לֹא יוּכַל לִתְקֹן וְחֶסְרוֹן לֹא יוּכַל לְהִמָּנוֹת׳״.

§ The mishna taught that if **the pilgrimage Festival passed and one did not celebrate** it by sacrificing **a Festival** peace-offering, **he is not obligated** to pay **restitution for it. And about this it is stated: "That which is crooked cannot be made straight; and that which is wanting cannot be numbered"** (Ecclesiastes 1:15).

אֲמַר לֵיהּ בַּר הֵי הֵי לְהִלֵּל: הַאי ״לְהִמָּנוֹת״? לְהִמָּלְאוֹת מִיבָּעֵי לֵיהּ! אֶלָּא זֶה שֶׁמָּנוּהוּ חֲבֵירָיו לִדְבַר מִצְוָה וְהוּא לֹא נִמְנָה עִמָּהֶן.

The Sage **bar Hei Hei**[P] **said to Hillel** that if this is the correct interpretation of the verse, **this** term: **"Be numbered [*lehimanot*]"**[N] is apparently inappropriate. **It should have said: Be filled. Rather, this** verse is referring to one **whose friends reached a consensus [*manuhu*]** with regard **to a matter of a mitzva and he was not part of their consensus,** and therefore he missed his opportunity to join them in the performance of the mitzva.

NOTES

Saw – רָאָה: This refers to a *zav*, a man suffering from gonorrhea. The *halakhot* of the severe ritual impurity caused by this condition are detailed in the Torah (Leviticus 15:1–15) and in tractate *Zavim*. The *zav* becomes ritually impure as a result of the secretion of a white, pus-like discharge from his penis. A man who sees, i.e., experiences, a discharge of that kind on one occasion becomes ritually impure for one day, like a man who discharges semen. If he experiences a second discharge on the same day or the following day, or a prolonged initial discharge, he contracts the more severe ritual impurity of a *zav*, which lasts seven days. If he experiences a third discharge within the next twenty-four hours, he is obligated to bring a pair of doves as part of his purification process, one for a sin-offering and the other for a burnt-offering.

Night is part of a date whose time has not yet arrived – לַיְלָה מְחוּסַּר זְמַן: It is clear that one may not sacrifice offerings at night. However, some Sages maintain that this is merely a technical issue, which does not negate the fact that the same status applies to the night as it does to the following day. Conversely, others maintain that since one may sacrifice offerings only from the following morning, no obligations concerning that offering exist at night. Nazirites are included among those ritually impure people who have completed their purification process but have not yet brought their offerings and therefore lack atonement, as their purity is determined not only by a particular date but also by an offering. With regard to these individuals, there are practical ramifications to this apparently theoretical issue: Are events that occur at night related to the following day or not?

Be numbered – לְהִימָּנוֹת: Some explain that the mishna is referring to one who failed to arrive and be counted as part of a communal prayer, which is something wanting that cannot be numbered (Maharsha).

HALAKHA

Who saw one emission at night, etc. – רָאָה אַחַת בַּלַּיְלָה וכו׳: If a *zav* whose secretions ceased and who counted seven clean days subsequently experienced an emission on the eighth night and two more on the eighth day, these sightings combine and he is obligated to bring a second set of offerings. If he experienced two sightings of a *zav* on the eighth night and one on the eighth day, these sightings do not combine and he is not obligated to bring a second set. The *halakha* is in accordance with the opinion of Rabbi Yoḥanan (Rambam *Sefer Korbanot*, *Hilkhot Meḥusrei Kappara* 3:5).

Night – לַיְלָה: Night is considered part of a date whose time has not yet arrived, as one cannot sacrifice an offering at night (Rambam *Sefer Korbanot*, *Hilkhot Meḥusrei Kappara* 3:4).

PERSONALITIES

Bar Hei Hei – בַּר הֵי הֵי: The tradition is that this Sage and his colleague ben Bag Bag were converts. Some say they were converted by Hillel the Elder, against the advice of Shammai, as related in *Shabbat* 30b. The name bar Hei Hei alludes to his status as a convert, as the letter *hei* was added to the name of Abraham, considered the first convert (see 3a). It is also likely that he was called by this name to hide his identity from the government. Bar Hei Hei is cited at the end of *Avot* (chapter 5) as the author of the saying: According to the exertion is the reward, which fits in well with the story cited here.

תַּנְיָא נַמִּי הָכִי: ״מְעֻוָּת לֹא יוּכַל לִתְקוֹן״ – זֶה שֶׁבִּיטֵּל קְרִיאַת שְׁמַע שֶׁל שַׁחֲרִית, אוֹ קְרִיאַת שְׁמַע שֶׁל עַרְבִית, אוֹ שֶׁבִּיטֵּל תְּפִלָּה שֶׁל שַׁחֲרִית, אוֹ תְּפִלָּה שֶׁל עַרְבִית, ״וְחֶסְרוֹן לֹא יוּכַל לְהִימָּנוֹת״ – זֶה שֶׁנִּמְנוּ חֲבֵירָיו לִדְבַר מִצְוָה וְהוּא לֹא נִמְנָה עִמָּהֶן.

This explanation **is also taught** in a *baraita*. The meaning of the verse "That which is crooked cannot be made straight; and that which is wanting cannot be numbered" is as follows: **"That which is crooked cannot be made straight"** is referring to **one who omitted the recitation of the morning *Shema* or the recitation of the evening *Shema*, or who omitted the morning prayer or the evening prayer.**[H] **"And that which is wanting cannot be numbered"** is referring to **one whose friends reached a consensus** with regard **to a matter of a mitzva and he was not part of their consensus.**

אֲמַר לֵיהּ בַּר הֵי הֵי לְהִלֵּל: מַאי דִּכְתִיב: ״וְשַׁבְתֶּם וּרְאִיתֶם בֵּין צַדִּיק לְרָשָׁע בֵּין עוֹבֵד אֱלֹהִים לַאֲשֶׁר לֹא עֲבָדוֹ״? הַיְינוּ ״צַדִּיק״ הַיְינוּ ״עוֹבֵד אֱלֹהִים״, הַיְינוּ ״רָשָׁע״ הַיְינוּ ״אֲשֶׁר לֹא עֲבָדוֹ״! אֲמַר לֵיהּ: ״עֲבָדוֹ״ וְ״לֹא עֲבָדוֹ״ – תַּרְוַיְיהוּ צַדִּיקֵי גְּמוּרֵי נִינְהוּ. וְאֵינוֹ דּוֹמֶה שׁוֹנֶה פִּרְקוֹ מֵאָה פְּעָמִים לְשׁוֹנֶה פִּרְקוֹ מֵאָה וְאֶחָד.

The Gemara records another discussion between bar Hei Hei and Hillel. **Bar Hei Hei said to Hillel: What is** the meaning of that **which is written: "Then you shall again discern between the righteous and the wicked, between he who serves God and he who does not serve Him"** (Malachi 3:18). There are two redundancies here: **"The righteous"** is the same as **"he who serves God,"** and **"the wicked"** is the same as **"he who does not serve Him."** Hillel **said to him:** The one **"who serves Him"** and the one **"who does not serve Him" are both** referring to **completely righteous people. But** the verse is hinting at a distinction between them, as **one who reviews his studies one hundred times is not comparable to one who reviews his studies one hundred and one** times.[N]

אֲמַר לֵיהּ: וּמִשּׁוּם חַד זִימְנָא קָרֵי לֵיהּ ״לֹא עֲבָדוֹ״? אֲמַר לֵיהּ: אִין. צֵא וּלְמַד מִשּׁוּק שֶׁל חַמָּרִין: עֲשָׂרָה פַּרְסֵי – בְּזוּזָא, חַד עֲשַׂר פַּרְסֵי – בִּתְרֵי זוּזֵי.

Bar Hei Hei **said to him: And due to one** extra **time** that he did not review, **the verse calls him** a person **"who does not serve Him"? He said to him: Yes. Go and learn from the market of donkey drivers.** One can hire a driver to travel up to **ten parasangs for one dinar.** However, he will travel **eleven parasangs** only **for two dinars.** This shows that any departure beyond the norm is considered a significant difference.

אֲמַר לֵיהּ אֵלִיָּהוּ לְבַר הֵי הֵי וְאָמְרִי לַהּ לְרַבִּי אֶלְעָזָר: מַאי דִּכְתִיב: ״הִנֵּה צְרַפְתִּיךָ וְלֹא בְכָסֶף בְּחַרְתִּיךָ בְּכוּר עוֹנִי״? מְלַמֵּד שֶׁחָזַר הַקָּדוֹשׁ בָּרוּךְ הוּא עַל כָּל מִדּוֹת טוֹבוֹת לִיתֵּן לְיִשְׂרָאֵל, וְלֹא מָצָא אֶלָּא עֲנִיּוּת. אֲמַר שְׁמוּאֵל וְאִיתֵימָא רַב יוֹסֵף, הַיְינוּ דְּאָמְרִי אֱינָשֵׁי: יָאָה עֲנִיּוּתָא לִיהוּדָאֵי כִּי בַּרְזָא סוּמָּקָא לְסוּסְיָא חִיוָּרָא.

The Gemara relates that **Elijah** the prophet **said to bar Hei Hei, and some say** that he said this **to Rabbi Elazar: What is** the meaning of that **which is written: "Behold, I have refined you, but not as silver;[N] I have tried you in the furnace of affliction [oni]"** (Isaiah 48:10)? This **teaches that the Holy One, Blessed be He, sought after all good character traits to impart** them **to the Jewish people, and He found only poverty** [*aniyut*] capable of preventing them from sin. **Shmuel said, and some say** it was **Rav Yosef: This** explains the folk saying **that people say: Poverty is good for the Jewish people like a red bridle [*barza*][NL] for a white horse.** Just as a red bridle accentuates the white color of the horse, so the challenge of poverty draws out the purity of the Jewish people.

״רַבִּי שִׁמְעוֹן בֶּן מְנַסְיָא אוֹמֵר: אֵי זֶה הוּא ״מְעֻוָּת לֹא יוּכַל לִתְקוֹן״ – זֶה הַבָּא עַל הָעֶרְוָה וְהוֹלִיד מִמֶּנָּה מַמְזֵר״, וכו׳. הוֹלִיד – אִין, לֹא הוֹלִיד – לָא?

§ The mishna taught that **Rabbi Shimon ben Menasya says: Who is the crooked that cannot be made straight? This** verse is referring to **one who engaged in intercourse with a woman forbidden to him and fathered a *mamzer* with her.** The Gemara infers from the mishna: If **he fathers a child, yes,** this verse applies, as he cannot remedy the situation; if **he does not father a child, no,** the verse does not apply, as he can make amends.

וְהָא תַּנְיָא, רַבִּי שִׁמְעוֹן בֶּן מְנַסְיָא אוֹמֵר: גּוֹנֵב אָדָם – אֶפְשָׁר שֶׁיַּחֲזִיר גְּנֵבוֹ וִיתַקֵּן, גּוֹזֵל אָדָם – אֶפְשָׁר שֶׁיַּחֲזִיר גְּזֵלוֹ וִיתַקֵּן, אֲבָל הַבָּא עַל אֵשֶׁת אִישׁ וַאֲסָרָהּ לְבַעְלָהּ – נִטְרַד מִן הָעוֹלָם וְהָלַךְ לוֹ.

The Gemara asks: **Isn't it taught** in a *baraita* that **Rabbi Shimon ben Menasya says:** If **a person steals it is possible that he** might **return his stolen property and be made straight;** if **a person robs from another it is possible that he** might **return his robbed property and be made straight. However, one who has sexual relations with a married woman** with her consent **and** thereby **renders her forbidden to her husband is banished from the world and passes away.** There is no way for him to rectify the situation and achieve atonement, because a married woman who willingly has sexual relations with another man is permanently forbidden to her husband.

HALAKHA

One who omitted a prayer – מִי שֶׁבִּטֵּל תְּפִלָּה: One who intentionally failed to pray cannot redress this omission. If he wishes, he may recite a voluntary prayer without adding a novel element to his prayer, despite the fact that generally one may recite a voluntary prayer only if he adds a novel aspect to his prayers, i.e. something reflecting his personal needs (see *Berakhot* 29b). This is the case provided that he prays shortly after the missed prayer. Some say he is not permitted to pray voluntarily without adding a new element to his prayer (*Baḥ*). Others distinguish between one who intentionally missed the afternoon prayer, who may pray the evening prayer twice, and one who omitted the evening and morning prayers, in which case he must add a novel element if he adds a voluntary prayer (*Ateret Zahav*). According to the *Kaf HaḤayyim*, nowadays one should not recite a voluntary prayer at all (*Shulḥan Arukh, Oraḥ Ḥayyim* 108:7).

NOTES

One hundred, and one hundred and one – מֵאָה וּמֵאָה וְאַחַת: One who regularly reviews his studies one hundred times and no more is called "he who does not serve Him." This is because true service of God involves performing actions beyond one's regular routine. Many commentaries suggest that there are special meanings to this extra review. Some interpret the term: One, as a reference to the lofty soul of a human being, the divine spark within him, beyond the regular service of God (see Maharsha). Others interpret this statement based on the numerical value of Hebrew letters: The number one hundred has the same numerical value as one of the names of Satan, *Sam*, whereas one hundred and one represents Michael, the protecting angel of Israel (Maharsha; Riaf).

I have refined you but not as silver – צְרַפְתִּיךָ וְלֹא בְכֶסֶף: Rashi apparently interprets this phrase as: And not as silver is refined. Others explain: I have chosen for you the proper remedy and it is not with silver. Rather, the remedy is through a lack of silver, i.e., money (Maharsha). According to this interpretation, the two halves of the verse bear parallel meanings.

Like a red bridle – כִּי בַּרְזָא סוּמָּקָא: Some explain that this bridle is not pretty in its own right, but becomes a beautiful decoration when placed upon a white horse. Similarly, although poverty is not inherently appealing, it serves to elevate the Jewish people.

LANGUAGE

Bridle [*barza*] – בַּרְזָא: Apparently derived from the Aramaic, meaning strap or halter. Others say it is from the Greek βυρσίνη, *bursinè*, meaning a leather mat placed on a horse (see *Arukh*).

רַבִּי שִׁמְעוֹן בֶּן יוֹחַי אוֹמֵר: אֵין אוֹמֵר "בִּקְרוּ גָּמָל", "בִּקְרוּ חֲזִיר". אֶלָּא: "בִּקְרוּ טָלֶה". וְאֵי זֶה? זֶה תַּלְמִיד חָכָם שֶׁפֵּירַשׁ מִן הַתּוֹרָה.

Rabbi Shimon ben Yoḥai says: Someone who wants to examine an animal for blemishes to bring it as an offering **does not say: Inspect the camel, or: Inspect the pig,** as these are inherently disqualified for the altar. **Rather,** he says: **Inspect the lamb.** Similarly, the term: "Crooked," applies only to one who was previously straight. **And who is this? This is a Torah scholar who leaves** his **Torah** study.

רַבִּי יְהוּדָה בֶּן לָקִישׁ אָמַר: כָּל תַּלְמִיד חָכָם שֶׁפֵּירַשׁ מִן הַתּוֹרָה עָלָיו הַכָּתוּב אוֹמֵר: "כְּצִפּוֹר נוֹדֶדֶת מִן קִנָּהּ כֵּן אִישׁ נוֹדֵד מִמְּקוֹמוֹ", וְאוֹמֵר: "מַה מָּצְאוּ אֲבוֹתֵיכֶם בִּי עָוֶל כִּי רָחֲקוּ מֵעָלָי"?!

Rabbi Yehuda ben Lakish said: Any Torah scholar who leaves the Torah, about him the verse says: "As a bird that wanders[N] **from her nest, so is a man who wanders from his place"** (Proverbs 27:8). **And it says: "What unrighteousness have your fathers found in Me, that they are gone far from Me?"** (Jeremiah 2:5). This indicates that the punishment is greater for one who was close to God and became distant from Him. In any case, there is a contradiction here, as in the mishna Rabbi Shimon ben Menasya says that the act of one who fathers an illegitimate child is crooked and cannot be straightened, whereas in the *baraita* he says the same applies to anyone who has forbidden sexual relations, regardless of whether or not he fathers a child.

לָא קַשְׁיָא; כָּאן – בַּאֲחוֹתוֹ פְּנוּיָה, כָּאן – בְּאֵשֶׁת אִישׁ. וְאִי בָּעֵית אֵימָא: הָא וְהָא בְּאֵשֶׁת אִישׁ, וְלָא קַשְׁיָא; כָּאן

The Gemara answers: This is **not difficult. Here,** the mishna is dealing with a case where he had forbidden sexual relations **with his unmarried sister.** Although the intercourse itself is a severe sin, if he does not sire a child it can be rectified through repentance. **There,** in the *baraita,* it is referring to a case where he sinned **with a married woman,** causing irreparable damage to her marriage. **And if you wish, say** instead: **This and that** are both referring **to a married woman. And** it is **not difficult. Here,** the mishna is dealing

NOTES

As a bird that wanders, etc. – **כְּצִפּוֹר נוֹדֶדֶת וכו׳**: A Sage is constantly reciting Torah, just as a bird is always chirping and singing. One who abandons the study hall may continue to speak, but no longer talks of Torah; this is like a bird that has wandered from its place (Maharsha).

בְּאוֹנֶס, כָּאן – בְּרָצוֹן. וְאִיבָּעֵית אֵימָא: הָא וְהָא בְּאוֹנֶס, וְלָא קַשְׁיָא: כָּאן – בְּאֵשֶׁת כֹּהֵן, כָּאן – בְּאֵשֶׁת יִשְׂרָאֵל.

with a rape, in which case it is not prohibited for the woman to return to her husband. **There,** it is referring to a woman who had relations **willfully,** and therefore she is forbidden to her husband. **And if you wish, say** that **this and that** are both dealing **with a rape, and** it is still **not difficult. Here,** where the transgression cannot be rectified, it is referring **to** one who raped **the wife of a priest,** as it is forbidden for a priest to have relations with his wife once she has intercourse with any other man, even unwillingly. **There,** it is referring **to** one who raped **the wife of an Israelite,** in which case there is no prohibition against her returning to her husband.

"וְלַיּוֹצֵא וְלַבָּא אֵין שָׁלוֹם", אָמַר רַב: כֵּיוָן שֶׁיּוֹצֵא אָדָם מִדְּבַר הֲלָכָה לִדְבַר מִקְרָא – שׁוּב אֵין לוֹ שָׁלוֹם.

Since the Gemara mentioned a Torah scholar who abandons the study of Torah, it cites a relevant verse: **"Neither was there any peace to him that went out or came in** due to the adversary" (Zechariah 8:10). **Rav said: Once a person leaves** the study **of *halakha*,** i.e., Mishna and Gemara, even **for** the study **of the Torah** itself, **he will no longer have peace.**[N] The verses of the Torah are often obscure and it is difficult to learn *halakha* directly from them without the aid of the interpretations of the Talmud.

וּשְׁמוּאֵל אָמַר: זֶה הַפּוֹרֵשׁ מִתַּלְמוּד לְמִשְׁנָה, וְרַבִּי יוֹחָנָן אָמַר: אֲפִילּוּ מִתַּלְמוּד לְתַלְמוּד.

And Shmuel said: This is referring to **one who leaves** the study **of Talmud to** learn **Mishna.** Whereas the reasoning of the Talmud is relatively clear, the Mishna cites legal rulings without explaining their reasoning. **And Rabbi Yoḥanan said:** The verse applies **even** to one who leaves the study **of** one **Talmud for** the other **Talmud,**[N] i.e., who leaves off his study of the Jerusalem Talmud to begin the Babylonian Talmud, as he will encounter difficulties with the new style of learning.

NOTES

Once a person leaves the study of *halakha* for the study of the Torah he will no longer have peace – **כֵּיוָן שֶׁיּוֹצֵא אָדָם מִדְּבַר הֲלָכָה לִדְבַר מִקְרָא שׁוּב אֵין לוֹ שָׁלוֹם**: If one who is familiar with the Sages' explanations of Torah verses studies the simple meaning of the verses, he will find it difficult to reconcile many of the rabbinic interpretations with the text itself. On occasion there are even rabbinic explanations of certain verses that uproot the plain meaning of the text, to the extent that the ruling of the Sages stands in direct opposition to the apparent meaning of the verse. One example of this is the interpretation of "An eye for an eye" (Exodus 21:24) as requiring monetary payment. Rav is suggesting that these experiences can be disturbing to a student of *halakha*, who must come to accept that rabbinic traditions often differ from the plain meaning of the verse, despite the saying of the Sages that a verse always maintains its plain meaning (*Midrash Shlomo*).

Talmud for Talmud – **מִתַּלְמוּד לְתַלְמוּד**: Rashi explains that this is referring to a change from the Jerusalem Talmud to the Babylonian Talmud, which has more complex reasoning and is more confusing. Others maintain the opposite, that this refers to a change from the Babylonian Talmud to the Jerusalem Talmud, whose methodologies of learning are not identical (Rabbeinu Ḥananel). Others likewise explain that this refers to a change from the detailed Babylonian Talmud, with its well-defined, conceptual analysis, to the shorter and more obscure discussions of the Jerusalem Talmud (*Tosefot Rid*).

מתני׳ הֶיתֵּר נְדָרִים פּוֹרְחִין בָּאֲוִיר וְאֵין לָהֶם עַל מַה שֶּׁיִּסְמֹכוּ.

MISHNA Incidental to the Festival peace-offering, the mishna describes the nature of various areas of Torah study. The *halakhot* of the **dissolution of vows,** when one requests from a Sage to dissolve them, **fly in the air**[N] **and have nothing to support them,** as these *halakhot* are not mentioned explicitly in the Torah. There is only a slight allusion to the dissolution of vows in the Torah, which is taught by the Sages as part of the oral tradition.

הִלְכוֹת שַׁבָּת חֲגִיגוֹת וְהַמְּעִילוֹת – הֲרֵי הֵם כַּהֲרָרִים הַתְּלוּיִן בְּשַׂעֲרָה, שֶׁהֵן מִקְרָא מוּעָט וַהֲלָכוֹת מְרוּבּוֹת. הַדִּינִין וְהָעֲבוֹדוֹת, הַטְּהָרוֹת וְהַטְּמָאוֹת, וַעֲרָיוֹת – יֵשׁ לָהֶן עַל מַה שֶּׁיִּסְמֹכוּ, וְהֵן הֵן גּוּפֵי תוֹרָה.

The ***halakhot*** **of Shabbat, Festival peace**-offerings, **and misuse** of consecrated property **are like mountains suspended by a hair,**[N] **as they** have **little** written about them in **the Torah, and** yet the details of their ***halakhot*** **are numerous.** The details of **monetary law,** sacrificial **rites, ritual purity and impurity, and** the *halakhot* of **those with whom relations are forbidden** all **have something to support them,** i.e., there is ample basis in the Torah for these *halakhot*, **and these are the essential parts of Torah.**

גמ׳ תַּנְיָא, רַבִּי אֱלִיעֶזֶר אוֹמֵר: יֵשׁ לָהֶם עַל מַה שֶּׁיִּסְמֹכוּ, שֶׁנֶּאֱמַר: ״כִּי יַפְלִיא״ ״כִּי יַפְלִיא״ שְׁתֵּי פְעָמִים, אַחַת הַפְלָאָה לְאִיסּוּר וְאַחַת הַפְלָאָה לְהֶיתֵּר.

GEMARA **It is taught** in a *baraita* that **Rabbi Eliezer said:** The *halakhot* of the dissolution of vows[N] **have something to support them,**[N] **as it is stated: "When** a man shall **clearly utter** a vow" (Leviticus 27:2), and: **"When** either man or woman shall **clearly utter** a vow" (Numbers 6:2), i.e., the words "clearly utter" appear **twice. One clear utterance is for prohibition,**[N] i.e., when one states his intention to accept the vow, **and one clear utterance is for dissolution,** when he provides the Sage with a reason why the vow should no longer apply. This is an allusion in the Torah to the annulment of vows.

רַבִּי יְהוֹשֻׁעַ אוֹמֵר: יֵשׁ לָהֶם עַל מַה שֶּׁיִּסְמֹכוּ, שֶׁנֶּאֱמַר: ״אֲשֶׁר נִשְׁבַּעְתִּי בְאַפִּי״ – בְּאַפִּי נִשְׁבַּעְתִּי, וְחָזַרְתִּי בִּי.

Rabbi Yehoshua likewise **says:** These *halakhot* **have something to support them, as it is stated: "Wherefore I swore in My wrath"** (Psalms 95:11), meaning: **In my wrath I swore, and I retracted.**[N] This is the basis for the dissolution of vows, in which the one who uttered the vow tells the Sage that he regrets it, as he did so in a moment of anger.

רַבִּי יִצְחָק אוֹמֵר: יֵשׁ לָהֶם עַל מַה שֶּׁיִּסְמֹכוּ, שֶׁנֶּאֱמַר: ״כֹּל נְדִיב לִבּוֹ״. חֲנַנְיָה בֶּן אֲחִי רַבִּי יְהוֹשֻׁעַ אוֹמֵר: יֵשׁ לָהֶם עַל מַה שֶּׁיִּסְמֹכוּ, שֶׁנֶּאֱמַר: ״נִשְׁבַּעְתִּי וָאֲקַיֵּימָה לִשְׁמוֹר מִשְׁפְּטֵי צִדְקֶךָ״.

Rabbi Yitzḥak says: These *halakhot* **have something to support them, as it is stated: "Whoever is of a willing heart,** let him bring it" (Exodus 35:5). This verse indicates that as long as one retains the same desire to fulfill the vow, he must continue to fulfill it, but if he regrets taking the vow he may arrange for it to be dissolved. **Ḥananya, son of Rabbi Yehoshua's brother,** also **says: They have something to support them, as it is stated: "I have sworn, and have fulfilled it, to observe your righteous ordinances"** (Psalms 119:106). This verse indicates that certain oaths need not be fulfilled, i.e., those that have been dissolved.

אָמַר רַב יְהוּדָה אָמַר שְׁמוּאֵל: אִי הֲוַאי הָתָם אֲמָרִי לְהוּ: דִּידִי עֲדִיפָא מִדִּידְכוּ, שֶׁנֶּאֱמַר: ״לֹא יַחֵל דְּבָרוֹ״, הוּא אֵינוֹ מוֹחֵל, אֲבָל אֲחֵרִים מוֹחֲלִין לוֹ. אָמַר רָבָא: לְכוּלְּהוּ אִית לְהוּ פִּירְכָא, לְבַר מִדִּשְׁמוּאֵל דְּלֵית לֵיהּ פִּירְכָא.

Rav Yehuda said that **Shmuel said: If I had been there,**[N] sitting with those Sages, I would have **said to them:** My source **is better than yours, as it is stated: "He shall not nullify his word"** (Numbers 30:3), from which it may be inferred: **He** himself **cannot nullify his word; however, others,** i.e., a Sage, **may nullify** it **for him** by dissolving his vow. **Rava said: For all of** the suggested sources for the dissolution of vows **there is** a possible **refutation, except for that of Shmuel, for which there is no refutation.**

דְּאִי מִדְּרַבִּי אֱלִיעֶזֶר – דִּלְמָא כִּדְרַבִּי יְהוּדָה שֶׁאָמַר מִשּׁוּם רַבִּי טַרְפוֹן. דְּתַנְיָא, רַבִּי יְהוּדָה אוֹמֵר מִשּׁוּם רַבִּי טַרְפוֹן: לְעוֹלָם אֵין אֶחָד מֵהֶם נָזִיר, שֶׁלֹּא נִיתְּנָה נְזִירוּת אֶלָּא לְהַפְלָאָה.

Rava elaborates. **As,** if it is derived **from** the statement **of Rabbi Eliezer, perhaps** the phrase: "Clearly utter" should be understood **in accordance with** the opinion of **Rabbi Yehuda, who said** an alternative interpretation **in the name of Rabbi Tarfon. As it is taught** in a *baraita* with regard to two people who are arguing whether or not someone who passed before them is a nazirite, each of them declaring that if he is correct he himself will become a nazirite, **Rabbi Yehuda says in the name of Rabbi Tarfon: Actually, neither of them is a nazirite, as naziriteship is effected only by** means of a **clear utterance** and neither party is certain they will be a nazirite at the time of their utterance. He derives this *halakha* from this phrase: "Clearly utter."

NOTES

Fly in the air – פּוֹרְחִין בָּאֲוִיר: The difference between *halakhot* described as flying in the air and those defined as mountains suspended by a hair is that the former are not based on any explicit Torah source, as they are all derived from subtle allusions. By contrast, those *halakhot* described as mountains suspended by a hair do have an explicit source in the Torah, but the source does not include the many details of the *halakhot* (see *Turei Aven*).

Mountains suspended by a hair – הֲרָרִים הַתְּלוּיִן בְּשַׂעֲרָה: Some commentaries explain that this refers to two mountains hanging by one thread, which do not fall or crash into each other (Maharsha).

The dissolution of vows – הֶיתֵּר נְדָרִים: The Torah does delineate the *halakhot* of the annulment of vows (Numbers, chapter 26): A father can annul his daughter's vows and a husband has the power to annul his wife's vows. However, the Torah does not say that one who regrets his vow may request that a Sage dissolve it. Although the Sages dispute the parameters of this *halakha*, they all agree in principle that dissolution can be performed, notwithstanding the fact that at the time of his vow this individual intended to accept it upon himself and he was of sound mind and free to make informed decisions.

The ***halakhot*** **have something to support them** – יֵשׁ לָהֶם עַל מַה שֶּׁיִּסְמֹכוּ: This does not mean that these *halakhot* are mentioned explicitly in the Torah. Rather, the idea is that they can be derived directly from the verses (Meiri). Some commentaries maintain that these *halakhot* are supported by a verbal analogy, which is a traditionally acceptable mode of derivation (*Turei Aven*).

Clear utterance is for prohibition – הַפְלָאָה לְאִיסּוּר: Some commentaries maintain that this concept of a clear utterance for prohibition concerns a different issue, i.e., that the vows of a minor one year before he or she reaches majority are of substance (*Tosefot Rid*).

In my wrath I swore and I retracted – בְּאַפִּי נִשְׁבַּעְתִּי וְחָזַרְתִּי בִּי: The commentaries raise a difficulty: This verse is apparently referring to God's oath, in the wake of the sin of the spies, that He would not bring that generation of Jews into Eretz Yisrael. If so, the statement of Rabbi Yehoshua is puzzling, as God did not retract this vow (*Tosafot*). Rashi explains that Rabbi Yehoshua maintains that the mention of God's anger indicates that He could have retracted the vow because it was uttered in anger, although He chose not to do so. *Tosafot* answer that the verse is referring to the World-to-Come, as indicated by its continuation: "Into My rest." If so, it is reasonable to suggest that God did retract His vow and that generation merited the World-to-Come.

If I had been there – אִי הֲוַאי הָתָם: In the Jerusalem Talmud a reference to the dissolution of vows is derived from the fact that the topic of vows was taught "to the heads of the tribes" (Numbers 30:2). It can be inferred from this verse that vows may be dissolved by those heads of tribes. Some explain that although the Babylonian Talmud accepts that this *halakha* is derived from the verse in this manner, it is nevertheless correct to say that these *halakhot* fly in the air, as this entire issue is not explicitly mentioned in the Torah (*Siaḥ Yitzḥak*).

אִי מִדְּרַבִּי יְהוֹשֻׁעַ – דִּלְמָא הָכִי קָאָמַר: בְּאַפִּי נִשְׁבַּעְתִּי וְלָא הֲדַרְנָא בִּי. אִי מִדְּרַבִּי יִצְחָק – דִּלְמָא לְאַפּוֹקֵי מִדִּשְׁמוּאֵל. דְּאָמַר שְׁמוּאֵל: גָּמַר בְּלִבּוֹ – צָרִיךְ שֶׁיּוֹצִיא בִּשְׂפָתָיו, וְהָא קָא מַשְׁמַע לַן: דְּאַף עַל גַּב דְּלָא הוֹצִיא בִּשְׂפָתָיו.

Similarly, **if** it is derived **from** the statement **of Rabbi Yehoshua, perhaps this is what** the verse **is saying: In my wrath I swore and I do not take it back,** despite the fact that it was stated in a moment of anger. **If** it is derived **from** the statement **of Rabbi Yitzḥak, perhaps** the phrase "a willing heart" comes **to exclude** the statement **of Shmuel, as Shmuel said: If one decided in his heart** but did not verbalize a vow, it is insufficient, as **he must verbally express** it. **And** therefore **this** phrase **teaches us that even though he did not verbally express** the vow he is still obligated to fulfill it.[H]

אִי מִדַּחֲנַנְיָה בֶּן אֲחִי רַבִּי יְהוֹשֻׁעַ – דִּלְמָא כְּרַב גִּידֵּל אָמַר רַב. דְּאָמַר רַב גִּידֵּל אָמַר רַב: מִנַּיִן שֶׁנִּשְׁבָּעִין לְקַיֵּים אֶת הַמִּצְוָה? שֶׁנֶּאֱמַר: ״נִשְׁבַּעְתִּי וָאֲקַיֵּימָה לִשְׁמוֹר מִשְׁפְּטֵי צִדְקֶךָ״.

Finally, **if** it is derived **from** the statement **of Rabbi Ḥananya, son of Rabbi Yehoshua's brother, perhaps** the phrase "and fulfilled it" should be explained **in accordance with** the opinion of **Rav Giddel,** who said that **Rav said** a different interpretation of this verse. **As Rav Giddel said** that **Rav said: From where** is it derived **that** although one is already obligated to fulfill all mitzvot **one may take an oath to fulfill a mitzva,**[HN] and this is not considered an oath taken in vain? **As it is stated: "I have sworn, and have fulfilled it, to observe Your righteous ordinances"** (Psalms 119:106).

אֶלָּא דִּשְׁמוּאֵל לֵית לֵיהּ פִּירְכָא. אֲמַר רָבָא וְאִיתֵימָא רַב נַחְמָן בַּר יִצְחָק: הַיְינוּ דְּאָמְרִי אֱינָשֵׁי: טָבָא חֲדָא פִּלְפַּלְתָּא חֲרִיפְתָּא מִמְּלֵי צַנָּא דִּקְרֵי.

Rav concludes. **However,** for **Shmuel's** source **there is no refutation. Rava said,** and **some say** it was **Rav Naḥman bar Yitzḥak** who said: **This** explains the folk saying **that people say: One spicy pepper is better than a basketful of squash,** as the single pepper has more flavor than all the squash combined.

״הִלְכוֹת שַׁבָּת״ מִיכְתַּב כְּתִיבָן! לָא צְרִיכָא, לְכִדְרַבִּי אַבָּא. דְּאָמַר רַבִּי אַבָּא: הַחוֹפֵר גּוּמָּא בְּשַׁבָּת וְאֵין צָרִיךְ אֶלָּא לַעֲפָרָהּ – פָּטוּר עָלֶיהָ.

§ The mishna stated that **the** ***halakhot*** **of Shabbat** are like mountains suspended by a hair. The Gemara asks: But the *halakhot* of Shabbat **are written,** i.e., the prohibition against performing labor is explicit in the Torah. The Gemara answers: **No,** it is **necessary** to say this **in accordance with** the opinion of **Rabbi Abba. As Rabbi Abba said: One who digs a hole**[N] **on Shabbat**[H] **only** because he **needs its dirt** and not for the hole itself **is exempt from** liability for that act, as this is not the labor of digging prohibited on Shabbat by Torah law.

כְּמַאן? כְּרַבִּי שִׁמְעוֹן, דְּאָמַר: מְלָאכָה שֶׁאֵינָהּ צְרִיכָה לְגוּפָהּ פָּטוּר עָלֶיהָ.

The Gemara asks: **In accordance with whose** opinion did Rabbi Abba issue this ruling? It is **in accordance with** the opinion of **Rabbi Shimon, who said:** One who performs on Shabbat a **labor** that is **not necessary for its own sake,** i.e., he performs the labor for a purpose other than the direct result of the action, is **exempt from** liability **for it.**

אֲפִילּוּ תֵּימָא לְרַבִּי יְהוּדָה, הָתָם – מְתַקֵּן, הָכָא – מְקַלְקֵל הוּא.

The Gemara offers an alternative possibility. This ruling can be explained **even if you say** that Rabbi Abba holds **in accordance with** the opinion of **Rabbi Yehuda,** that one is liable for a labor that is not necessary for its own sake. **There,** in other cases, Rabbi Yehuda deems one liable because his purpose is **creative. Here,** where one is digging the hole for the dirt, the purpose **is destructive,** as the action damages the ground. Therefore, Rabbi Yehuda concedes that in this case he is exempt.

מַאי כַּהֲרָרִין הַתְּלוּיִין בְּשַׂעֲרָה?

The Gemara returns to the mishna. **What** then does the mishna mean by the phrase: **Like mountains suspended by a hair?**

NOTES

One may take an oath to fulfill a mitzva – נִשְׁבָּעִין לְקַיֵּים אֶת הַמִּצְוָה: Some commentaries explain that one may take an oath to fulfill a mitzva, even by mentioning God's name, and this is not considered taking God's name in vain (Rashi; *Tosafot*). According to the opinion of Rashi, it is even a mitzva to undertake this type of oath. Some further maintain that this oath is effective to the extent that if one does not fulfill the mitzva concerning which he took the oath, he is flogged like one who violates a regular oath (Ran, *Nedarim* 7b; see *Turei Aven*).

One who digs a hole – הַחוֹפֵר גּוּמָּא: The commentaries note that the particulars of this *halakha* are not essential for this discussion (*Siaḥ Yitzḥak*). The main point is that the Torah does not explicitly state that one is not liable for a destructive act on Shabbat, even when it is a complete act of labor. Everyone agrees with this *halakha* in principle, even Rabbi Yehuda, and even those who maintain that one is liable for digging a hole in this manner (see Meiri).

HALAKHA

He decided in his heart and did not verbally express it – גָּמַר בְּלִבּוֹ וְלֹא הוֹצִיא בִּשְׂפָתָיו: A vow or oath takes effect only if one decides upon the oath in his heart and gives it verbal expression (*Shulḥan Arukh, Yoreh De'a* 210:1, 239:1).

Taking an oath to perform mitzvot – נִשְׁבָּעִין עַל הַמִּצְוֹת: One is permitted to take an oath that he will perform a mitzva, despite the fact that he is obligated by oath to do so from the time of the acceptance of the Torah on Mount Sinai (Rambam *Sefer Hafla'a, Hilkhot Shevuot* 11:3).

One who digs a hole on Shabbat – הַחוֹפֵר גּוּמָּא בְּשַׁבָּת: One who digs a hole on Shabbat but requires only its dirt has performed a destructive act for which he is not liable. This is in accordance with the opinion of Rabbi Abba (Rambam *Sefer Zemanim, Hilkhot Shabbat* 1:17).

NOTES

Planned, creative labor – מְלֶאכֶת מַחֲשֶׁבֶת: A large proportion of the *halakhot* of Shabbat are derived by juxtaposition with the instructions of the building of the Tabernacle (see Exodus, chapter 35). This juxtaposition teaches that forms of labor that are prohibited on Shabbat are derived from the various forms of labor performed in the Tabernacle. With regard to the labor of the Tabernacle it is stated: "Creative labor [*melekhet maḥshevet*]" (Exodus 35:33), from which it is derived that the labors prohibited on Shabbat must be purposeful and creative. Many fundamental *halakhot* of Shabbat observance involve this principle, e.g., an act of labor is prohibited only when it is performed with forethought. Even the *tanna'im* who disagree over several cases related to this topic merely debate the scope of this definition, not the principle itself.

Celebrate a Festival – חוֹגוּ חַגָּא: Rashi explains that the term Festival might simply mean a time of celebration and rejoicing. Others suggest that the phrase: Celebrate a Festival [*ḥogu ḥagga*], might be associated with dance [*ḥog*], i.e., they should perform joyous dances in honor of the occasion (*Tosafot*; *Tosefot Yom Tov*).

However, if that is so, those that are brought during a Festival, etc. – אֶלָּא מֵעַתָּה, הַבָּא בִּזְמַן חַג וכו׳: The commentaries ask: Even if this verse is not referring to the Festival as a particular date in time, but is speaking of the Festival offering as per its plain meaning, the same problem still remains: The verse indicates that the prohibition against leaving over until the morning applies only to this offering, which is not the case. The answer is that if the verse is referring to the Festival offering, one can say that it is dealing with the *halakhot* of a peace-offering, and is simply adding to what is stated elsewhere with regard to a burnt-offering. In contrast, if the term Festival is a designation of time, then the verse apparently limits the prohibition against leaving over any offering to the time of the Festival (*Tosafot*, as explained by *Sefat Emet*).

HALAKHA

Planned, creative labor – מְלֶאכֶת מַחֲשֶׁבֶת: The Torah prohibits on Shabbat only creative, purposeful, and productive labor (Rambam *Sefer Zemanim*, *Hilkhot Shabbat* 1:9).

מְלֶאכֶת מַחֲשֶׁבֶת אָסְרָה תּוֹרָה, וּמְלֶאכֶת מַחֲשֶׁבֶת לָא כְּתִיבָא.

The Gemara answers: **The Torah prohibited** only planned, **creative labor**[NH] on Shabbat. An act of labor that is not intended, or whose result is unintended, or whose consequence is destructive, is not included in this category. Therefore, one who performs labor in this manner is exempt. **And** limitation of the prohibition against **creative labor is not written** anywhere in the Torah with regard to the laws of Shabbat. Admittedly, this principle is written in connection with the Tabernacle, and there is an established exegetical link between the building of the Tabernacle and Shabbat. Nevertheless, as this fundamental principle concerning the *halakhot* of Shabbat does not appear explicitly, it is compared to mountains suspended by a hair.

"חֲגִיגוֹת": מִיכְתַּב כְּתִיבָן! לָא צְרִיכָא, לְכִדְאָמַר לֵיהּ רַב פָּפָּא לְאַבָּיֵי: מִמַּאי דְּהַאי "וְחַגּוֹתֶם אוֹתוֹ חַג לַה׳" זְבִיחָה? דִּלְמָא חוֹגוּ חַגָּא קָאָמַר רַחֲמָנָא!

§ The mishna taught that the *halakhot* of **Festival peace**-offerings are like mountains suspended by a hair. The Gemara asks: But **they are written** in the Torah. The Gemara answers: **No,** it is **necessary** to say this **in accordance with that which Rav Pappa said to Abaye: From where** is it derived **that this** verse: **"And you shall celebrate it as a Festival** [*veḥagotem*] **to the Lord"** (Leviticus 23:41), is referring to **an animal offering? Perhaps the Merciful One is** simply **saying: Celebrate a Festival.**[N]

אֶלָּא מֵעַתָּה, דִּכְתִיב: "וְיָחוֹגּוּ לִי בַּמִּדְבָּר" הָכִי נַמִי דְּחוֹגוּ חַגָּא הוּא? וְכִי תֵּימָא הָכִי נַמִי – וְהָכְתִיב: "וַיֹּאמֶר מֹשֶׁה גַּם אַתָּה תִּתֵּן בְּיָדֵינוּ זְבָחִים וְעוֹלוֹת"!

Abaye responded: **However, if that is so,** consider **that it is written:** "Let My people go, **that they may hold a feast** [*veyaḥogu*] **to Me in the wilderness"** (Exodus 5:1). **So too,** the meaning of this verse **is that** they will merely **celebrate a Festival,** and not bring an offering. **And if you would say that is** indeed **so,** that this means that they should celebrate a Festival, **but isn't it written: "And Moses said: You must also give into our hand sacrifices and burnt-**offerings, that we may sacrifice to the Lord our God" (Exodus 10:25)? This shows that the command is referring to offerings.

דִּלְמָא הָכִי קָאָמַר רַחֲמָנָא: אִכְלוּ וּשְׁתוּ וְחוֹגוּ חַגָּא קַמַּאי. לָא סָלְקָא דַּעְתָּךְ, דִּכְתִיב: "וְלֹא יָלִין חֵלֶב חַגִּי עַד בֹּקֶר", וְאִי סָלְקָא דַּעְתָּךְ דְּחוֹגָא הוּא – תַּרְבָּא לְחַגָּא אִית לֵיהּ?!

The Gemara raises a difficulty. But **perhaps this is what the Merciful One said:** Slaughter animals so that you can **eat, drink, and celebrate a Festival before Me,** but no offerings are necessary. The Gemara answers: This **cannot enter your mind, as it is written: "The fat of My Festival feast** [*ḥagi*] **shall not remain all night until the morning"** (Exodus 23:18). **And if it enters your mind** to say **that it is** referring to a regular **Festival feast** and not an offering, **does a Festival feast have** forbidden **fats?**

וְדִלְמָא הָכִי קָאָמַר רַחֲמָנָא: חֵלֶב הַבָּא בִּזְמַן חַג – לֹא יָלִין?

The Gemara asks: **But perhaps this is what the Merciful One states** in the Torah: The **fats** of gift offerings **that are brought during a Festival may not remain all night.** If so, the phrase "My Festival feast" is not referring to a type of offering at all, but to a particular time.

אֶלָּא מֵעַתָּה: הַבָּא בִּזְמַן חַג – הוּא דְּלֹא יָלִין, הָא דְּכָל הַשָּׁנָה כּוּלָּהּ יָלִין? "כׇּל הַלַּיְלָה עַד הַבֹּקֶר" כְּתִיב!

The Gemara answers: **However, if that is so,** this verse indicates that it is only those fats **that are brought during a Festival**[N] **that may not remain overnight.** It may be inferred from here **that** fats which are brought **throughout the year may remain all night.** But **it is written** about burnt-offerings: "On its firewood upon the altar **all night into the morning"** (Leviticus 6:2). This shows that burnt-offerings must burn upon the altar all night.

דִּלְמָא, אִי מֵהַהוּא הֲוָה אָמֵינָא: הַהוּא לַעֲשֵׂה. כְּתַב רַחֲמָנָא הַאי לְלָאו!

The Gemara further asks: **Perhaps if** this *halakha* was derived **from that** verse, **I would say that** verse serves as the source **of a positive mitzva.** Therefore, **the Merciful One writes this** verse: "Shall not remain all night," **as a prohibition** as well.

לְלָאו כְּתַב קְרָא אַחֲרִינָא: "וְלֹא יָלִין מִן הַבָּשָׂר אֲשֶׁר תִּזְבַּח בָּעֶרֶב בַּיּוֹם הָרִאשׁוֹן לַבֹּקֶר". וְדִלְמָא לַעֲבוֹר עָלָיו בִּשְׁנֵי לָאוִין וַעֲשֵׂה!

The Gemara responds. With regard **to the prohibition** against leaving over an offering on a Festival, **another verse was written: "Neither shall any of the flesh, which you sacrifice the first day at evening, remain all night until the morning"** (Deuteronomy 16:4). The Gemara asks: **But perhaps** the verse: "Shall not remain all night" comes to teach that one who does so **violates two prohibitions and a positive mitzva.**

אֶלָּא: אָתְיָא "מִדְבָּר" "מִדְבָּר". כְּתִיב הָכָא: "וְיָחוֹגּוּ לִי בַּמִּדְבָּר", וּכְתִיב הָתָם: "הַזְּבָחִים וּמִנְחָה הִגַּשְׁתֶּם לִי בַּמִּדְבָּר", מַה לְּהַלָּן זְבָחִים – אַף כָּאן זְבָחִים.

Rather, the Gemara rejects this explanation in favor of the claim that the source for a Festival peace-offering **comes** from a verbal analogy between the term **"wilderness"** stated here and the term: **"wilderness"** stated elsewhere. **It is written here: "They shall make an offering to Me in the wilderness"** (Exodus 5:1), **and it is written there: "Did you bring to Me sacrifices and offerings** forty years **in the wilderness,** house of Israel?" (Amos 5:25). **Just as there** it is referring to actual **animal offerings, so too here,** it is referring to **animal offerings,** not merely the celebration of a Festival.

וּמַאי כַּהֲרָרִין הַתְּלוּיִין בְּשַׂעֲרָה? דִּבְרֵי תוֹרָה מִדִּבְרֵי קַבָּלָה לָא יָלְפִינַן.

The Gemara asks: **And** in light of this verbal analogy, in **what** way is this *halakha* **like mountains suspended by a hair?** The Gemara answers: The textual evidence is not that strong, as generally **one does not derive Torah matters from texts of the tradition,**[N] i.e., Prophets and Writings. Since the prophets were not permitted to introduce new *halakhot,* as the Torah is the only authoritative source in that regard, this verbal analogy does not carry the same weight as a *halakha* derived from the Torah itself.

"מְעִילוֹת": מִיכְתַּב כְּתִיבָן! אֲמַר רָמִי בַּר חָמָא: לָא נִצְרְכָא אֶלָּא לְכִדְתְנַן: הַשָּׁלִיחַ שֶׁעָשָׂה שְׁלִיחוּתוֹ – בַּעַל הַבַּיִת מָעַל. לֹא עָשָׂה שְׁלִיחוּתוֹ – שָׁלִיחַ מָעַל.

§ The mishna taught that the details of the *halakhot* of **misuse** of consecrated property[N] are like mountains suspended by a hair. The Gemara asks: But **they are written** in the Torah (Leviticus 5:14–16). **Rami bar Ḥama said:** This statement **is necessary only for that which we learned** in a mishna (*Me'ila* 20a): With regard to **an agent who performs his agency,**[H] e.g., when a homeowner sends someone to buy an object with consecrated money and the agent does as he was instructed, **the homeowner has misused** consecrated property and must bring an offering for the actions of the agent performed on his behalf. However, if the agent **did not perform his agency,** but in some way acted on his own account, **the agent has misused** consecrated property, and he is the one obligated to bring the offering.

וְכִי עָשָׂה שְׁלִיחוּתוֹ אַמַּאי מָעַל? וְכִי זֶה חוֹטֵא וְזֶה מִתְחַיֵּיב?! הַיְינוּ כַּהֲרָרִין הַתְּלוּיִין בְּשַׂעֲרָה.

The Gemara explains: **And when he performed his agency, why** is the owner considered to have **misused** consecrated property? **And is it** possible **that this one sins and that one is rendered liable?** Since this *halakha* is counterintuitive, it is not apparent from the verses. **This is** what the mishna was referring to when it said that these *halakhot* are **like mountains suspended by a hair.**

אֲמַר רָבָא: וּמַאי קוּשְׁיָא? דִּלְמָא שָׁאנֵי מְעִילָה, דְּיָלְפָא "חֵטְא" "חֵטְא" מִתְּרוּמָה, מַה הָתָם שְׁלוּחוֹ שֶׁל אָדָם כְּמוֹתוֹ – אַף כָּאן שְׁלוּחוֹ שֶׁל אָדָם כְּמוֹתוֹ?

Rava said: And what is the logical **difficulty** with this *halakha?* **Perhaps** the transgression of **misuse** of consecrated property **is different, as it is derived** through a verbal analogy from the parallel term **"sin"** (Leviticus 5:6) and **"sin"** (Numbers 18:9), **from** the case of *teruma:* **Just as there,** with regard to *teruma,* the legal status of **a person's agent is like** that of **himself,**[H] and therefore the agent may separate *teruma* on behalf of the owner of the produce, **so too here,** with regard to misuse of consecrated property, the legal status of **a person's agent is like** that of **himself,** which means that when the agent properly performs his agency the owner is liable.

HALAKHA

An agent with regard to misuse of consecrated property – שָׁלִיחַ בִּמְעִילָה: With regard to one who unwittingly takes a consecrated object and gives it to an agent for a mundane purpose, if the agent performs his agency properly, the homeowner is liable for misuse of consecrated property and he must bring a guilt offering. If the agent deviates from his agency and acts on his own accord, he is liable (Rambam *Sefer Avoda, Hilkhot Me'ila* 7:1).

A person's agent is like that of himself – שְׁלוּחוֹ שֶׁל אָדָם כְּמוֹתוֹ: One may appoint an agent to separate *terumot* and tithes on his behalf (*Shulḥan Arukh, Yoreh De'a* 331:29).

NOTES

Torah matters from texts of the tradition [*divrei kabbala*] **– דִּבְרֵי תוֹרָה מִדִּבְרֵי קַבָּלָה:** The books of the Prophets and the books of the Writings are sometimes referred to as texts of the tradition, which literally means: Received matters. Some explain that this is because all the prophets received their prophetic status from Moses, the father of all prophets (*Shita Mekubbetzet*). Alternatively, the prophets passed down the tradition from the time of Joshua (*Maḥzor Vitri*). Others say that this appellation refers to the fact that every prophet receives the prophecy his generation requires (Rashi). Some read the phrase as: *Divrei kevala,* matters of complaint, as the prophets mainly complain and protest over the sins of the Jewish people (*Shita Mekubbetzet,* citing Rabbeinu Peretz). Although many halakhic concepts are derived from the statements of the prophets, verbal analogies derived from the Prophets do not have the same status as do those derived from the Torah itself. Therefore, this is not a full-fledged verbal analogy.

Misuse of consecrated property – מְעִילָה: The *halakhot* of misuse of consecrated property are detailed extensively in tractate *Me'ila.* The essential point is that it is prohibited to use a consecrated object for one's own purpose. However, one is liable to bring an offering for this misuse only when the action is performed unwittingly, as offerings generally atone for unwitting sins. This obligation applies not only when one forgets that a certain item was consecrated, but also when he was not aware of its consecrated status at all. Furthermore, this *halakha* is one of the few instances in which one is liable for a transgression performed by his agent, despite the principle that there is no agent for transgression. The Sages explain this principle in the following terms: If one is confronted with a command of his teacher and an opposing command of a student, whose command should he follow? In other words, one must never follow the instructions of another when they conflict with the will of God. However, with regard to misuse of consecrated property, this reasoning does not apply, as one is liable to bring an offering only when the act is performed unwittingly. See *Turei Aven* and *Siaḥ Yitzḥak,* who debate at length the various opinions in this regard.

אֶלָּא אֲמַר רָבָא: לָא נִצְרְכָא אֶלָּא לְכִדְתַנְיָא: נִזְכַּר בַּעַל הַבַּיִת וְלֹא נִזְכַּר שָׁלִיחַ – שָׁלִיחַ מָעַל. שָׁלִיחַ עַנְיָא מַאי קָא עָבֵיד? הַיְינוּ כַּהֲרָרִין הַתְּלוּיִין בְּשַׂעֲרָה.

Rather, Rava said: The mishna's statement with regard to mountains **is necessary only for that which is taught** in a *baraita*: If, after he sent an agent to use a consecrated object, **the homeowner remembered**[H] that it was a consecrated item **and the agent did not remember, the agent has misused** consecrated property despite the fact that he was merely performing his agency. This is because one is liable for the misuse of consecrated property only if he acted unwittingly. In this instance, **what did the poor agent do?**[N] He simply performed his agency on behalf of the owner, and yet because the owner remembered about the consecrated object, the agent is liable. **This is** what the mishna is referring to when it says that these *halakhot* are **like mountains suspended by a hair.**

אֲמַר רַב אַשִׁי: מַאי קוּשְׁיָא? דִּלְמָא מִידֵּי דַּהֲוָה אַמּוֹצִיא מְעוֹת הֶקְדֵּשׁ לְחוּלִּין?

Rav Ashi said: And **what is** the logical **difficulty** with this *halakha*? **Perhaps** this **is just as it is** with regard to **one who spends consecrated money for non-sacred** purposes. Although this individual did not know that the money was consecrated, he is nevertheless obligated to bring an offering. Here too, once the owner canceled the agency upon realizing the money was consecrated, the agent unwittingly misused consecrated property, and therefore he is liable.

אֶלָּא אֲמַר רַב אַשִׁי: לָא נִצְרְכָא אֶלָּא לְכִדְתְנַן: נָטַל אֶבֶן אוֹ קוֹרָה שֶׁל הֶקְדֵּשׁ – הֲרֵי זֶה לֹא מָעַל, נְתָנָהּ לַחֲבֵירוֹ – הוּא מָעַל, וַחֲבֵירוֹ לֹא מָעַל. מִכְּדִי מִישְׁקַל שְׁקַלָהּ, מַה לִּי הוּא וּמַה לִּי חֲבֵירוֹ? הַיְינוּ כַּהֲרָרִין הַתְּלוּיִין בְּשַׂעֲרָה.

Rather, Rav Ashi said: The mishna **is necessary only for that which we learned** in a mishna (*Me'ila* 19b): If one **picked up a consecrated stone or beam,**[H] **he has not misused** consecrated property merely by this action. However, if he **gave it to another, he has misused** consecrated property **and the other** person **has not misused** consecrated property. The Gemara analyzes this case: **Since he picked it up, what** difference **is** there **to me** if **he** keeps it, **and what** difference **is** there **to me** if he gives it to **another?** What is the basis for the distinction between the two cases? Rather, **this is** the case the mishna is referring to when it says that these *halakhot* are **like mountains suspended by a hair.**

וּמַאי קוּשְׁיָא? דִּלְמָא כִּדִשְׁמוּאֵל, דְּאָמַר שְׁמוּאֵל: הָכָא

The Gemara raises a difficulty. **What is** the logical **difficulty** with this *halakha*? **Perhaps** it should be explained **in accordance with** the opinion **of Shmuel, as Shmuel said: Here,** this mishna is not referring to an ordinary person who picked up a consecrated stone for himself.

HALAKHA

The homeowner remembered – נִזְכַּר בַּעַל הַבַּיִת: If one unwittingly sends consecrated money with an agent to buy an object for him, and subsequently remembers that this money is consecrated property, the agent is liable, as he acted unintentionally. The homeowner is considered to have acted intentionally and therefore is not liable for misuse of consecrated property (Rambam *Sefer Avoda*, *Hilkhot Me'ila* 7:5).

One picked up a consecrated stone or beam – נָטַל אֶבֶן אוֹ קוֹרָה שֶׁל הֶקְדֵּשׁ: With regard to one who picks up a consecrated stone or beam, if they are in his domain, i.e., in a case where he was the one who consecrated them (Ra'avad), or if they are in in the Temple treasury, he is not liable for misuse of consecrated property until he uses the stone or beam. If he removes the stone or beam from his domain or that of the treasury, or from the domain of the one who consecrated them, he is considered to have misused consecrated property at that point (Rambam *Sefer Avoda*, *Hilkhot Me'ila* 6:7–8).

NOTES

The poor agent, etc. – שָׁלִיחַ עַנְיָא וכו׳: The agent is liable in this instance, as the *halakha* of misuse of consecrated property applies only to an act performed unwittingly. Since the owner became aware that the object was consecrated, the agent alone is considered to have performed the unwitting act. Likewise, if the agent was reminded, the one who received the money he took from the homeowner would be liable when he uses it. With regard to other *halakhot*, one might consider this case as involving circumstances beyond the agent's control. However, in this area of *halakha* one is liable even if he had no knowledge that the object was consecrated.

Perek **I**
Daf **11** Amud **a**

בְּגִזְבָּר הַמְּסוּרוֹת לוֹ אַבְנֵי בִנְיָן עָסְקִינַן, דְּכָל הֵיכָא דְּמַנְחָה – בִּרְשׁוּתָא דִּידֵיהּ מַנְחָה.

Rather, **we are dealing with the treasurer** of the Temple, **to whom the** consecrated **building stones were transferred** for safekeeping. The reason for the exemption is **that anywhere that** the stone **is resting, it is** considered to be **resting within his domain.** Consequently, he is not liable for picking up the stone or beam, as he is permitted to carry it. However, he does not have permission to give it to someone else, and therefore when he hands it over to someone else he has misused consecrated property. If so, this *halakha* is also perfectly logical and should not be considered like mountains suspended by a hair.

אֶלָּא מִסֵּיפָא: בְּנָאָהּ בְּתוֹךְ בֵּיתוֹ – הֲרֵי זֶה לֹא מָעַל, עַד שֶׁיָּדוּר תַּחְתֶּיהָ בְּשָׁוֶה פְּרוּטָה. מִכְּדִי, שַׁנּוּיֵי שַׁנְּיָיהּ, מַה לִּי דָּר וּמַה לִּי לֹא דָּר? הַיְינוּ כַּהֲרָרִין הַתְּלוּיִין בְּשַׂעֲרָה.

Rather, the comparison of these *halakhot* to mountains suspended by a hair is based **on the latter clause** of that same mishna: **If he built** the stone **into his house,**[H] **he has not misused** consecrated property **until he dwells under it** an amount of time **that is worth a** ***peruta*****.**[N] **Since he has changed** the stone by incorporating it into his house, **what** difference **is** there **to me** if **he dwelt** there, **and what** difference **is** there **to me** if he did **not dwell** there? Apparently, **this is** the *halakha* considered **like mountains suspended by a hair.**

HALAKHA

He built the stone into his house – בְּנָאָהּ בְּתוֹךְ בֵּיתוֹ: One who inserted a consecrated stone or beam into his house has misused consecrated property. If he placed it on top of his window and did not attach it, he misuses the stone or beam only if he derives benefit worth a *peruta* by dwelling under it. The *halakha* is in accordance with the opinion of Rav (Rambam *Sefer Avoda*, *Hilkhot Me'ila* 6:8).

NOTES

Worth a ***peruta*** **– בְּשָׁוֶה פְּרוּטָה:** Some commentaries maintain that as soon as one derives a *peruta* of benefit he is liable for misuse of consecrated property, but the stone or the beam retains its sanctified status (*Tosafot*). Others hold that once he violates the prohibition the stone or beam loses its sanctified status, as one cannot violate the prohibition against misuse twice with the same object.

ומאי קושיא? דלמא לכדרב, דאמר רב: כגון שהניחה על פי ארובה. אי דר ביה – אין. לא דר ביה – לא.

The Gemara rejects this claim. **And what is** the logical **difficulty** with this *halakha*? **Perhaps** it is stated **in accordance with** the opinion **of Rav. As Rav said:** This mishna is referring to a case **where he placed** the stone **over a window,** but he did not make any adjustment to the stone itself. **If he dwelt in** the house, **yes,** he has misused consecrated property, as he derived benefit from it. If **he did not dwell in it, no,** he has not misused consecrated property, as he gained no benefit from the stone.

אלא לעולם כדרבא. ודקא קשיא לך מידי דהוה אמוציא מעות הקדש לחולין – התם מידע ידע דאיכא זוזי דהקדש, איבעיא ליה לעיוני. הכא – מי ידע? היינו כהררין התלויין בשערה.

Rather, the reason is **actually in accordance with** the aforementioned opinion **of Rava,** who holds that the innovative element of this *halakha* involves a case where the homeowner remembered, which caused the agent to misuse consecrated property. **And** with regard to that **which** posed **a difficulty for you,** i.e., that the *halakha* here should be **just as it is with** regard to **one who spends consecrated money for non-sacred** purposes, the two cases are not identical. **There,** in the case that Rava mentioned, the agent **knew that he** also **had consecrated coins** and therefore **he should have examined** carefully whether this money was consecrated. **Here, did** the agent **know** that there was a possibility that the money was consecrated? **This is** why this *halakha* is **like mountains suspended by a hair.**

"מקרא מועט והלכות מרובות". תנא: נגעים ואהלות – מקרא מועט והלכות מרובות. נגעים מקרא מועט? נגעים מקרא מרובה הוא! אמר רב פפא, הכי קאמר: נגעים – מקרא מרובה והלכות מועטות. אהלות – מקרא מועט והלכות מרובות.

§ The mishna explained that those matters that are like mountains suspended by a hair have **little** written about them in **the Torah, and** yet the details of their ***halakhot* are numerous.** A Sage **taught** in the *Tosefta*: The *halakhot* of **leprosy and** the *halakhot* of ritual impurity imparted by **tents**[N] in which a corpse lies have **little in the Torah and** their ***halakhot* are numerous.** The Gemara asks: With regard to **leprosy,** is there **little** about their *halakhot* in **the Torah? Leprosy is** something about which there are **numerous** details stated in **the Torah** (see Leviticus, chapters 13–14). **Rav Pappa said** that **this is what** the mishna **is saying: Leprosy has numerous** details in **the Torah but** relatively **few *halakhot*.** In contrast, the case of ritual impurity imparted by **tents** has **little** in **the Torah but numerous *halakhot*.**

ומאי נפקא מינה? אי מספקא לך מילתא בנגעים – עיין בקראי. ואי מספקא לך מילתא באהלות – עיין במתניתין.

The Gemara asks: **And what is the practical difference** whether there are numerous or few references to a particular *halakha* in the Torah? The Gemara answers: **If you are uncertain** about **a matter with** regard to the *halakhot* of **leprosy, delve into the verses,** as it is treated extensively there. **And if you are uncertain** about **a matter with** regard to the *halakhot* of the ritual impurity imparted by **tents, delve into the Mishna,** as these *halakhot* are not sufficiently explicated in the Torah.

"דינין" מיכתב כתיבן! לא נצרכא אלא לכדרבי.

§ The mishna taught that **monetary law** is one of those matters that have something to support them in the Torah. The Gemara asks: Monetary laws **are written** in the Torah; why does the mishna merely say it has something to support it? The Gemara answers: This **is necessary only** according to the opinion **of Rabbi** Yehuda HaNasi.

דתניא, רבי אומר: "נפש תחת נפש" – ממון. אתה אומר ממון, או אינו אלא נפש ממש? נאמרה נתינה למטה ונאמרה נתינה למעלה. מה להלן ממון – אף כאן ממון.

The Gemara elaborates. **As it is taught** in a *baraita* that **Rabbi** Yehuda HaNasi **says:** "But if any harm follow, then you shall give **life for life**"[N] (Exodus 21:23). This verse is referring to a payment of **money. Do you say money, or** perhaps **it is solely an actual life** that is demanded? The term **giving is stated below:** "You shall give life for life," **and giving is stated above,** in the previous verse: "And he shall give as the judges determine" (Exodus 21:22). **Just as there,** the giving is in the form of **money, so too here,** it is referring to a payment of **money.** Although this *halakha* is not explicit in the Torah, the verses lend support to it.

NOTES

Leprosy and tents – **נגעים ואהלות:** These two topics are not mentioned in the mishna because their basic *halakhot* appear in the Torah. The main difference between them is that the *halakhot* of leprosy are described extensively in the Torah (Leviticus, chapters 13–14), whereas many details of the *halakhot* of impurity imparted by tents are left unexplained (Numbers 19:14–15). These *halakhot* are clarified mainly in the Mishna, not in the Torah.

Life for life – **נפש תחת נפש:** Rabbi Yehuda HaNasi cites this *halakha* in particular, rather than mentioning the derivation that "an eye for an eye" (Exodus 21:24) means money. This is because the concept of "an eye for an eye" as referring to monetary compensation is unanimously accepted, as it is clear from the continuation of the discussion in the Torah and from elsewhere that in that case one must make monetary restitution. However, with regard to an act of killing that is not completely intentional, the *tanna'im* disagree whether or not the punishment is in accordance with the plain meaning of the verse. Therefore, it is necessary to derive the *halakha* by means of a verbal analogy.

״עֲבוֹדוֹת״ מִיכְתַּב כְּתִיבָן! לָא נִצְרְכָא אֶלָּא לְהוֹלָכַת הַדָּם. דְּתַנְיָא: ״וְהִקְרִיבוּ״ – זוֹ קַבָּלַת הַדָּם.

§ The mishna stated that the *halakhot* of sacrificial **rites** have something to support them. The Gemara asks: Sacrificial rites **are written** explicitly in the Torah. The Gemara answers: It **is necessary** to state that sacrificial rites have merely something to support them **only with regard to** the rite of **carrying the blood** to the altar. **As it is taught** in a *baraita*: "And Aaron's sons, the priests, **shall offer** the blood" (Leviticus 1:5); **this is** referring to **collecting the blood,** which is the stage before carrying the blood to the altar.

וְאַפְּקָהּ רַחֲמָנָא בִּלְשׁוֹן הוֹלָכָה, דִּכְתִיב: ״וְהִקְרִיב הַכֹּהֵן אֶת הַכֹּל וְהִקְטִיר הַמִּזְבֵּחָה״ וְאָמַר מָר: זוֹ הוֹלָכַת אֵבָרִים לַכֶּבֶשׁ,

And the Merciful One expressed collecting the blood **in the language of carrying,** i.e., by means of the term offer. **As it is written: "And the priest shall offer the whole, and make it smoke upon the altar"** (Leviticus 1:13). **And the Master said** that this term, "offer," is not referring to sacrificing on the altar, as that is expressed by the phrase: "Make it smoke upon the altar." Rather, **this is** referring to **carrying the limbs to the ramp** next to the altar, from where it is placed on the altar itself.

לְמֵימְרָא דְּהוֹלָכָה לָא תַּפְקָהּ מִכְּלַל קַבָּלָה.

Evidently, the Torah is referring to collecting the blood with the same terminology it used when referring to carrying. **That is to say that carrying should not be excluded from the category of collecting.**[N] In other words, all the *halakhot* that pertain to collecting the blood of offerings, e.g., that it must be performed by a priest with his right hand, apply equally to carrying the blood.

״טְהָרוֹת״. מִיכְתַּב כְּתִיבָן! לָא נִצְרְכָא אֶלָּא לְשִׁיעוּר מִקְוֶה, דְּלָא כְּתִיבָא. דְּתַנְיָא: ״וְרָחַץ אֶת בְּשָׂרוֹ בַּמַּיִם״ – בְּמֵי מִקְוֶה. ״אֶת כָּל בְּשָׂרוֹ״ – מַיִם שֶׁכָּל גּוּפוֹ עוֹלֶה בָּהֶן. וְכַמָּה הֵן? אַמָּה עַל אַמָּה בְּרוּם שָׁלֹשׁ אַמּוֹת. וְשִׁיעֲרוּ חֲכָמִים: מֵי מִקְוֶה אַרְבָּעִים סְאָה.

§ The mishna further taught that the *halakhot* of **ritual purity** have something to support them. The Gemara again asks: But ritual purity **is written** explicitly in the Torah. The Gemara answers: The observation that the *halakhot* of ritual purity merely have something to support them **is necessary only for** the minimum **measure of a ritual bath,**[N] **which is not written** explicitly in the Torah. **As it is taught** in a *baraita*: **"And he shall bathe his flesh in water"** (Leviticus 14:9). This means **in the water of a ritual bath.**[NH] And it is stated: "And he shall wash **all his flesh** in water" (Leviticus 15:16), which indicates that it must contain **water in which his whole body can enter. And how much** water **is this? One cubit by one cubit with a height of three cubits. And the Sages estimated** that the measure for **ritual bath water** is **forty *se'a*.**[B]

״טְמֵאוֹת״ מִיכְתַּב כְּתִיבָן! לָא נִצְרְכָא אֶלָּא לְכַעֲדָשָׁה מִן הַשֶּׁרֶץ, דְּלָא כְּתִיבָא. דְּתַנְיָא: ״בָּהֶם״.

§ The mishna stated that the *halakhot* of **ritual impurity** also have something to support them. Once again the Gemara asks: Ritual impurity **is written** explicitly in the Torah. The Gemara answers: This **is necessary only with regard to the** size **of a lentil-bulk from a creeping animal,**[H] **which is not written. As it is taught** in a *baraita* with regard to a verse that deals with creeping animals: "Whoever touches **them** when they are dead shall be impure" (Leviticus 11:31).

יָכוֹל בְּכוּלָּן – תַּלְמוּד לוֹמַר ״מֵהֶם״. יָכוֹל בְּמִקְצָתָן – תַּלְמוּד לוֹמַר ״בָּהֶם״.

One **might** have thought that only someone who touches **an entire,** whole creeping animal becomes ritually impure. **The verse states:** "And upon whatever any **of them** falls, when they are dead, it shall be impure" (Leviticus 11:32). "Of them" indicates that this *halakha* applies even if one comes into contact with a part of them. One **might** have thought that even **some of them** suffices to impart impurity. **The verse states: "Them,"** i.e., all of them. This conclusion apparently contradicts the first ruling.

הָא כֵּיצַד? עַד שֶׁיִּגַּע בְּמִקְצָתוֹ שֶׁהוּא כְּכוּלּוֹ. שִׁיעֲרוּ חֲכָמִים בְּכַעֲדָשָׁה, שֶׁכֵּן חוֹמֶט תְּחִלָּתוֹ בְּכַעֲדָשָׁה. רַבִּי יוֹסֵי בְּרַבִּי יְהוּדָה אוֹמֵר: כִּזְנַב הַלְּטָאָה.

How can this apparent contradiction be resolved? One does not become impure **until he touches some of it that is like the whole,** i.e., a significant amount. And **the Sages estimated** this measure as the size **of a lentil-bulk.** The reason is **that** in **its early** stages, **the *ḥomet*,**[B] the smallest of these creeping animals, is the size **of a lentil-bulk. Rabbi Yosei, son of Rabbi Yehuda, says:** The size of a lentil-bulk is that **of a lizard's tail,** which is considered a part that is like the whole. The tail of a lizard can be cut off easily, and as it continues to twitch even after it has been cut off, it has the appearance of life. Consequently, it is fitting to label it as a part that is like the whole.

NOTES

Collecting and carrying – קַבָּלָה וְהוֹלָכָה: There are four regular sacrificial rites pertaining to offerings: Slaughtering the animal, collecting its blood in a vessel, carrying the blood to the altar, and sprinkling the blood on the altar. Although collecting the blood is not mentioned explicitly as a unique rite, it is a necessary stage in the process of the Temple service described in the Torah. Conversely, the carrying of the blood is not an essential rite in practical terms; if the offering was slaughtered close to the altar it is possible to sprinkle the blood immediately without carrying it. In fact, Rabbi Shimon maintains that carrying is not an essential rite at all, and the *halakhot* pertaining to other sacrificial rites do not apply to it. Consequently, it is possible that the claim of the Gemara is not unanimous (see *Turei Aven*). Some say that even Rabbi Shimon concedes that as carrying is necessary on Yom Kippur, this action has the same status as the other rites, and therefore the Gemara here is in accordance with the opinions of all the *tanna'im* (*Siaḥ Yitzḥak*).

The measure of a ritual bath – שִׁיעוּר מִקְוֶה: Apparently, the measure of a ritual bath is derived from the Torah itself, as it says that one must immerse his whole body in water and he cannot be ritually purified any other way. If so, the measure is clearly the amount required to fit one's body. Nevertheless, there is a novelty to the established measure of the Sages: Even someone of short stature who can immerse his entire body in a volume of less than forty *se'a* does not fulfill his obligation in this manner, as the measure of a ritual bath is a *halakha* transmitted to Moses from Sinai.

In water, in the water of a ritual bath – בַּמַּיִם בְּמֵי מִקְוֶה: Rashi writes here that this comes to exclude water that does not gather on its own but was drawn. Others explain that it serves to emphasize that the water must be gathered in one place (*Tosafot*). In *Eiruvin* 4b Rashi explains that the phrase: Water of a ritual bath, comes to exclude spring water, i.e., for most ritual impurity there is no need for spring water in particular, as the water of any ritual bath is sufficient (see *Turei Aven*).

HALAKHA

Water of a ritual bath – מֵי מִקְוֶה: A menstruating woman and anyone else ritually impure with a stringent level of impurity, i.e., who were rendered impure by contact with the dead, purify themselves by immersing their entire body at one time in a spring or ritual bath containing at least forty *se'a* of water (*Shulḥan Arukh, Yoreh De'a* 201:1).

Ritual impurity imparted by a creeping animal – טוּמְאַת הַשֶּׁרֶץ: The remains of a creeping animal impart ritual impurity only if it is the size of a lentil-bulk. If one touches many creeping animals at the same time, which together are the size of a lentil-bulk, he is rendered ritually impure (Rambam *Sefer Tahara, Hilkhot She'ar Avot HaTumot* 4:2).

BACKGROUND

Forty *se'a* – אַרְבָּעִים סְאָה: This is the minimum volume of water necessary for a ritual bath; it is the equivalent of 80 *hin* or 5,760 egg-bulks. The forty-*se'a* measure is the basis of all modern halakhic calculations of the various measures of volume. According to the Na'e scale, a ritual bath must contain 332 ℓ of water. According to the opinion of the Ḥazon Ish, the required volume is 573 ℓ.

***Ḥomet* – חוֹמֶט:** The *ḥomet* is mentioned in the Torah's list of ritually impure creeping animals (Leviticus 11:30); however, its identification is uncertain. According to the translation of the Septuagint the *ḥomet* is a type of lizard, whereas some commentaries maintain that it is a chameleon (Rav Se'adya Gaon). According to this interpretation, the Gemara here is apparently referring to the size of this reptile's eggs. Rashi explains that the *ḥomet* is a snail.

״עֲרָיוֹת״: מִיכְתַּב כְּתִיבָן! לָא נִצְרְכָא

§ The mishna further taught that the *halakhot* of those with whom relations are forbidden have something to support them. The Gemara asks: The *halakhot* of **those with whom relations are forbidden are written** explicitly in the Torah. The Gemara answers: This **is necessary only**

לְבִתּוֹ מֵאֲנוּסָתוֹ דְּלָא כְּתִיבָא.

with regard **to his daughter** born **from the woman he raped,**[N] **which is not written** explicitly in the Torah. It is forbidden for this man to have sexual relations with this daughter, despite the fact that she is not the daughter of his wife, as he did not marry her mother.

דְּאָמַר רָבָא, אֲמַר לִי רַבִּי יִצְחָק בַּר אַבְדִּימִי: אָתְיָא ״הֵנָּה״ ״הֵנָּה״,

As Rava said: Rabbi Yitzḥak bar Avdimi said to me that this *halakha* is **derived** by means of a verbal analogy between the term **they** [***hena***], an unusual form of this word, written in one context, and the same term, **they,** written elsewhere. As it is written: "The nakedness of a woman and her daughter…you shall not take…they [*hena*] are near kinswomen; it is lewdness" (Leviticus 18:17). And it is written: "The nakedness of your son's daughter, or of your daughter's daughter, even their nakedness you shall not uncover; for they [*hena*] are your own nakedness" (Leviticus 18:10). This indicates that every daughter, even from the rape of a woman who is not one's wife, is forbidden, just like one's daughter from his wife.

אָתְיָא ״זִימָּה״ ״זִימָּה״.

Furthermore, the punishment for this transgression is **derived** from a verbal analogy between: "It is **lewdness** [*zima*]" (Leviticus 18:17), which is written with regard to a woman and her daughter, and the same term **"lewdness"** that appears elsewhere, as it is stated: "And if a man take with his wife also her mother, it is lewdness [*zima*]: They shall be burnt with fire, both he and they" (Leviticus 20:14).

״הֵן הֵן גּוּפֵי תוֹרָה״: הָנֵי אִין, הָנָךְ לָא?! אֶלָּא, אֵימָא: הֵן וְהֵן גּוּפֵי תוֹרָה.

§ The mishna taught: **These** [***hen hen***] **are the essential parts of the Torah.**[N] The Gemara asks: **These,** the topics mentioned in the mishna, which are not written explicitly but for which there is ample basis in the Torah, **yes,** they are the essential parts of Torah, whereas **those** other categories listed in the mishna that are written explicitly, **no,** they are not essential? **Rather,** one must **say** that both **these and those** [***hen vehen***] **are the essential parts of the Torah.** Every part of the Torah is essential, whether or not it is written explicitly.

הדרן עלך הכל חייבין

NOTES

His daughter from the woman he raped – בִּתּוֹ מֵאֲנוּסָתוֹ: As stated in the Gemara, the prohibition against marrying a woman and her daughter, even if she is not his daughter, is explicit in the Torah. Similarly, the prohibition against marrying one's granddaughter is written in the Torah as well, and the verses do not distinguish whether or not she is his granddaughter from a woman he married. However, the Torah does not explicitly state that it is forbidden for one to have sexual relations with one's daughter, although, as Rashi explains, this is clearly understood to be the case. With regard to the possible distinction between the daughter of one's wife and the daughter of a woman he raped, there are certain sexual relationships that are forbidden only due to a familial relationship through marriage. Therefore, one might have thought that this distinction is valid.

These [*hen hen*] are the essential parts of the Torah – הֵן הֵן גּוּפֵי תוֹרָה: Some commentaries explain that the repetitious phrase *hen hen* is not a figure of speech but an inclusive expression that means: All the cases listed in the mishna, both those that have an explicit source and those that are based on mere textual allusion, are essential parts of the Torah (Rambam's Commentary on the Mishna).

Summary of **Perek I**

With regard to the question of who is obligated to ascend to the Temple on the pilgrimage Festivals, the Gemara established several general principles. First of all, as this is a positive, time-bound mitzva, only men are obligated to ascend to the Temple, in accordance with the verse: "All your males" (Exodus 23:17), which includes emancipated slaves. Children who have reached the age of training in mitzvot are obligated by rabbinic law. Excluded from this obligation are women and slaves, even if they are half-free. Second, one who is unable to ascend by foot, due to either illness or weakness, is likewise exempt from the mitzva. Furthermore, a man is who unable to arrive together with the rest of the Jewish people because everyone shuns his company is also exempt.

The Festival offerings must be worth a minimum amount. The burnt-offering of appearance must be at least one silver *ma'a* in value, while the Festival peace-offering must be worth no less than two *ma'a*. However, there is no set value for the other peace-offering brought on a Festival, the peace-offering of rejoicing. The obligatory offerings for which there is a fixed sum must be brought from non-sacred funds, although one can add money designated for other offerings to increase the size of the peace-offering.

The general obligation to rejoice on the pilgrimage Festivals applies to women as well as men. However, in the case of men this obligation is fulfilled in a defined manner, by eating the peace-offerings of rejoicing. This mitzva is performed through the consumption of any animal offering that may be eaten.

The main mitzva of Festival offerings applies on the first Festival day. However, one who neglected to sacrifice his offerings on the first day can redress this deficiency on the rest of the days of the Festival. In the case of *Shavuot*, redress can be performed even after the Festival, as will be explained in the next chapter.

Incidental to these *halakhot*, this chapter discussed two broader issues: Which transgressions of positive mitzvot and prohibitions can be remedied by means of repentance, and which cannot be fully atoned for through repentance alone. It also analyzed the relationship between those *halakhot* that are explained in great depth by the Sages and their sources in the Torah itself, especially those whose source verse is brief and obscure, occasionally no more than a mere allusion.

Introduction to **Perek II**

And he shall lay his hand upon the head of his offering, and slaughter it before the tent of meeting; and Aaron's sons shall sprinkle its blood against the altar round about.

(Leviticus 3:8)

Three times a year shall all your males appear before the Lord your God at the place that He shall choose; on the feast of unleavened bread, and on the feast of weeks, and on the feast of tabernacles; and they shall not appear before the Lord empty-handed.

(Deuteronomy 16:16)

Continuing the discussion in the previous chapter concerning matters that the Bible does not mention explicitly but only alludes to or conceals, and which are explained and expanded in the Oral Law, this chapter relates to additional matters that are to be kept concealed. This is due to the complexity of these topics, which may lead unworthy students to err. It is necessary to explain which topics may not be taught publicly and openly like all other sections of the Torah, and to provide the reasons for this prohibition.

Later, the chapter returns to the main concern of the tractate: The Festival offering brought on the Festival. The most ancient rabbinic dispute in a halakhic matter known to us is discussed in this chapter. It concerns whether or not one may place his hands on the head of the Festival offering. Another related dispute concerns the types of offerings one is allowed to bring on the actual day of the Festival: Whether only peace-offerings, most of which are consumed by the owner and the priests, are permitted, or whether one may also bring burnt-offerings, although people do not consume them.

The pilgrimage to the Temple is a time when the entire people of Israel ascends to Jerusalem as one: Wise sages and ignorant simpletons alike, those who are stringent regarding mitzva observance along with those who are less stringent. The pilgrims were accustomed to bringing their *teruma* and tithes along with them, in accordance with rabbinic ordinances and decrees. It was therefore necessary to review the laws of ritual purity and impurity regarding these items and others. According to both Torah law and rabbinic law, with regard to the laws of ritual impurity and the process of purification, there are differences between non-sacred food, *teruma*, and sacred offerings. Different levels of stringency apply to each, according to their level of sanctity and importance. The main concern of this chapter is the clarification of these issues and other related topics.

מתני׳ אֵין דּוֹרְשִׁין בַּעֲרָיוֹת בִּשְׁלֹשָׁה, וְלֹא בְּמַעֲשֵׂה בְרֵאשִׁית בִּשְׁנַיִם, וְלֹא בַּמֶּרְכָּבָה בְּיָחִיד, אֶלָּא אִם כֵּן הָיָה חָכָם וּמֵבִין מִדַּעְתּוֹ.

MISHNA One may not expound[N] the topic of **forbidden sexual relations before three** or more individuals; **nor** may one expound the **act of Creation** and the secrets of the beginning of the world **before two** or more individuals;[N] **nor** may one expound **by oneself the** Design of the Divine **Chariot,**[NH] a mystical teaching with regard to the ways God conducts the world, **unless** he is **wise and understands** most matters **on his own.**

כָּל הַמִּסְתַּכֵּל בְּאַרְבָּעָה דְּבָרִים רָתוּי לוֹ כְּאִילּוּ לֹא בָּא לָעוֹלָם: מַה לְּמַעְלָה, מַה לְּמַטָּה, מַה לְּפָנִים, וּמַה לְּאָחוֹר. וְכׇל שֶׁלֹּא חָס עַל כְּבוֹד קוֹנוֹ – רָתוּי לוֹ שֶׁלֹּא בָּא לָעוֹלָם.

The mishna continues in the same vein: **Whoever looks at four matters, it would have been better for him had he never entered the world:** Anyone who reflects upon **what is above**[N] the firmament and **what is below** the earth, **what was before** Creation, **and what** will be **after** the end of the world. **And anyone who has no concern for the honor of his Maker,**[N] who inquires into and deals with matters not permitted to him, **deserves to have never come to the world.**

גמ׳ אָמְרַתְּ בְּרֵישָׁא ״וְלֹא בַּמֶּרְכָּבָה בְּיָחִיד״, וַהֲדַר אָמְרַתְּ: אֶלָּא אִם כֵּן הָיָה חָכָם וּמֵבִין מִדַּעְתּוֹ!

GEMARA The Gemara poses a question: **You said in the first clause** of the mishna: **Nor** may one expound **the** Design of the Divine **Chariot by oneself,** which indicates that the topic may not be learned at all, **and yet you subsequently said: Unless** he is **wise and understands** most things **on his own,** which indicates that an individual is permitted to study the Design of the Divine Chariot.

הָכִי קָאָמַר: אֵין דּוֹרְשִׁין בַּעֲרָיוֹת לִשְׁלֹשָׁה, וְלֹא בְּמַעֲשֵׂה בְרֵאשִׁית לִשְׁנַיִם, וְלֹא בַּמֶּרְכָּבָה לְיָחִיד, אֶלָּא אִם כֵּן הָיָה חָכָם וּמֵבִין מִדַּעְתּוֹ.

The Gemara explains: **This is what the mishna is saying: One may not expound the** topic of **forbidden sexual relations before three** students, **nor the act of Creation before two, nor** may one teach **the** Divine **Chariot to one, unless** that student **was wise and understands on his own.**

״אֵין דּוֹרְשִׁין בַּעֲרָיוֹת בִּשְׁלֹשָׁה״. מַאי טַעְמָא? אִילֵימָא מִשּׁוּם דִּכְתִיב: ״אִישׁ אִישׁ אֶל כׇּל שְׁאֵר בְּשָׂרוֹ״, ״אִישׁ אִישׁ״ – תְּרֵי; ״שְׁאֵר בְּשָׂרוֹ״ – חַד; וְאָמַר רַחֲמָנָא ״לֹא תִקְרְבוּ לְגַלּוֹת עֶרְוָה״.

§ The Gemara continues to clarify the mishna, which reads: **One may not expound** the topic of **forbidden sexual relations before three** individuals. **What is the reason** for this? **If we say** it is **because it is written: "None of you [*ish, ish*] shall approach any near of kin** to uncover their nakedness" (Leviticus 18:6). *Ish, ish,* literally means: Man, man. It is understood as an allusion to the number of students permitted to study the topic. This is as it is explained immediately: **"Man, man"** equals **two; "any near of kin** to him" is **one; and the Merciful One states: "You shall not approach to uncover their nakedness,"** which indicates that one may not expound the *halakhot* of forbidden sexual relations in the presence of three individuals.

אֶלָּא מֵעַתָּה, דִּכְתִיב: ״אִישׁ אִישׁ כִּי יְקַלֵּל אֱלֹהָיו״, ״אִישׁ אִישׁ אֲשֶׁר יִתֵּן מִזַּרְעוֹ לַמּוֹלֶךְ״, הָכִי נַמִי?

They ask: **If that is so,** then what of **this verse: "Any man [*ish, ish*] who curses his God"** (Leviticus 24:15), or **"Any man [*ish, ish*] who gives of his seed to the *Molekh*"** (Leviticus 20:2), which is a form of idol worship? In both cases the double expression implies the number two. **So too** there, will you say that it is prohibited to teach these *halakhot* before two individuals?

NOTES

One may not expound – **אֵין דּוֹרְשִׁין**: The *Zekher LaḤagiga* explains the connection between the content of this first mishna and the rest of tractate *Ḥagiga*: The subject of this chapter is the mitzva to approach God in His Temple, a complex, profound topic that must not be taken at face value. This mishna was needed in order to explain how very profound the matter of approaching God is. It was also necessary to emphasize how careful one must be when explaining such matters to the general public.

The act of Creation before two – **בְּמַעֲשֵׂה בְרֵאשִׁית בִּשְׁנַיִם**: This prohibition is explained in *Otzar HaKavod* in a manner similar to the Gemara's reasoning in the case of forbidden relations: If a teacher instructs two students, they may become involved in a discussion that will lead them to erroneous conclusions.

The act of Creation and the Design of the Divine Chariot – **מַעֲשֵׂה בְרֵאשִׁית וּמַעֲשֵׂה מֶרְכָּבָה**: The Rambam and others explain that the act of Creation refers to the understanding of nature in general, while the Design of the Divine Chariot refers to the knowledge of metaphysical matters. Many commentaries note that the details of the Gemara's discussion do not accord with this approach. See *Tosafot* and Rabbi Ovadya MiBartenura, who explain that the act of Creation and the Design of the Divine Chariot refer to delving into the secrets of Creation and divine providence by means of studying the sacred names of God. The *Tosefot Yom Tov* explains that the mishna does not relate to merely theoretical analysis, but to the performance of supernatural deeds through the use of the secrets of the Torah as well. In general terms, Rabbi Ḥayyim Vital explains, citing the Ari, that the act of Creation means the secrets of Creation, referred to as chaos and rectification, whereas the Design of the Divine Chariot refers to the study and knowledge of the secret details of the way God conducts the world.

What is above, etc. – **מַה לְּמַעְלָה וכו׳**: *Tosafot* claim that these terms can be understood spatially, i.e., referring to anything outside the boundaries of the world, as well as temporally or qualitatively. The Recanati states, citing Rav Hai Gaon, that it is impossible to study matters that lie completely outside the boundaries of our world, as our conceptual understanding is limited to those matters directly or indirectly within our grasp. The *Pardes Rimmonim* maintains that the term: Above, refers to the nature of God, while the word: Below, means divine providence, both of which, as the Rambam explains in *Sefer HaMadda*, are part of God's sovereign essence and knowledge, which are beyond the comprehension of man. The Meiri explains the phrase: What is before, in a similar manner: One should not seek proof for Creation, but should rely on faith with regard to such a complex issue.

Who has no concern for the honor of his Maker – **שֶׁלֹּא חָס עַל כְּבוֹד קוֹנוֹ**: It is explained in Rambam's Commentary on the Mishna that the phrase: The honor of his Maker refers to human intelligence, the honor bestowed upon man by God, which one must be careful not to spoil by harboring futile thoughts.

HALAKHA

The act of Creation and the Design of the Divine Chariot – **מַעֲשֵׂה בְרֵאשִׁית וּמַעֲשֵׂה מֶרְכָּבָה**: One may teach the act of Creation to one student to the extent that he is able to grasp the topic, but the Design of the Divine Chariot may be taught only in the form of outlines, and only to a wise person capable of understanding of his own accord, as these matters cannot be fully comprehended by everyone (Rambam *Sefer HaMadda*, *Hilkhot Yesodei HaTorah* 4:10–11).

אֶלָּא, הָנְהוּ מִיבָּעֵי לֵיהּ לְרַבּוֹת אֶת הַגּוֹיִם, שֶׁמּוּזְהָרִין עַל בִּרְכַּת הַשֵּׁם וְעַל עֲבוֹדָה זָרָה כְּיִשְׂרָאֵל,

The Gemara answers: **Rather, those** instances of the double expression: Man, man, **are required for him,** the *tanna*, in order **to include gentiles,**[N] **who are commanded with regard to blessing,** a euphemism for cursing, **God, and with regard to idol worship just as Jews** are commanded.[H]

הַאי נַמִי מִיבָּעֵי לֵיהּ לְרַבּוֹת אֶת הַגּוֹיִם, שֶׁמּוּזְהָרִין עַל הָעֲרָיוֹת כְּיִשְׂרָאֵל!

But if so, **this** mention of "man, man" in the case of forbidden relations is **also required for him to include gentiles, who are commanded with regard to forbidden sexual relations, as Jews** are.[H]

אֶלָּא: מִדִּכְתִיב "וּשְׁמַרְתֶּם אֶת מִשְׁמַרְתִּי", "וּשְׁמַרְתֶּם" – תְּרֵי; "מִשְׁמַרְתִּי" – חַד; וְאָמַר רַחֲמָנָא "לְבִלְתִּי עֲשׂוֹת מֵחֻקּוֹת הַתּוֹעֵבוֹת".

Rather, the Gemara rejects the previous explanation, and suggests that the prohibition against teaching three is derived **from the** following **verse** stated with regard to forbidden sexual relations: **"And you shall observe My charge"** (Leviticus 18:30), which is explained as follows: **"And you shall observe** [*ushmartem*]," in the plural, indicates at least **two; "My charge"** is **one; and the Merciful One states** at the conclusion of this verse: "That you **do not perform any of these abominable customs"** (Leviticus 18:30), indicating that this topic may not be taught to three.

אֶלָּא מֵעַתָּה, דִּכְתִיב: "וּשְׁמַרְתֶּם אֶת הַשַּׁבָּת", "וּשְׁמַרְתֶּם אֶת הַמַּצּוֹת", "וּשְׁמַרְתֶּם אֶת מִשְׁמֶרֶת הַקֹּדֶשׁ", הָכִי נַמִי?!

The Gemara asks: **However, if that is so,** then what of **that which is written: "And you shall observe the Shabbat"** (Exodus 31:14), and **"And you shall observe the festival of *matzot*"** (Exodus 12:17), and **"And you shall observe the charge of the sacred things"** (Numbers 18:5); **so too,** will you say that none of these subjects may be taught to three?

אֶלָּא אָמַר רַב אַשִׁי: מַאי אֵין דּוֹרְשִׁין בָּעֲרָיוֹת בִּשְׁלֹשָׁה? אֵין דּוֹרְשִׁין בְּסִתְרֵי עֲרָיוֹת בִּשְׁלֹשָׁה.

Rather, Rav Ashi said: These scriptural allusions are all unacceptable. **What is the meaning of: One may not expound the** topic of **forbidden sexual relations before three?** It means: **One may not expound the concealed** laws of **forbidden sexual relations**[N] **before three.**[H] The prohibition against teaching before three applies to *halakhot* of forbidden sexual relations that are not explicitly stated in the Torah but are derived by expounding the verses or through analogy.

מַאי טַעְמָא? סְבָרָא הוּא: בֵּי תְּרֵי כִּי יָתְבִי קַמֵּי רַבַּיְיהוּ, חַד שָׁקֵיל וְטָרֵי בַּהֲדֵי רַבֵּיהּ, וְאִידָּךְ מַצְלֵי אוּדְנֵיהּ לִגְמָרָא. תְּלָתָא, חַד שָׁקֵיל וְטָרֵי בַּהֲדֵי רַבֵּיהּ, וְהָנָךְ תְּרֵי – שָׁקְלוּ וְטָרוּ בַּהֲדֵי הֲדָדֵי, וְלָא יָדְעִי מַאי קָאָמַר רַבַּיְיהוּ, וְאָתוּ לְמִישְׁרֵי אִיסּוּרָא בַּעֲרָיוֹת.

What is the reason? It is due not to a biblical allusion, but rather **it is** based on **logical reasoning: When two** students **sit before their teacher, one** of them **is** typically **involved in a discussion** of *halakha* **with his teacher, while the other lends his ear** to listen **to the teaching.** However, if there are **three** students, **one** of them **is involved in a discussion with his teacher while the** other **two are engaged in a discussion with one another, and they do not know what their teacher is saying, and may come to** render **permitted a forbidden relation** by following their own reasoning rather than the explanation provided by their teacher.

אִי הָכִי כָּל הַתּוֹרָה נַמִי!

The Gemara raises a difficulty: **If so, the entire Torah** should **likewise** be taught only to two individuals, to prevent similar errors.

עֲרָיוֹת שָׁאנֵי, דְּאָמַר מָר: גֶּזֶל וַעֲרָיוֹת נַפְשׁוֹ מְחַמַּדְתָּן, וּמִתְאַוָּה לָהֶם.

The Gemara answers: The *halakha* of **forbidden sexual relations is different, for the Master said: Robbery and forbidden sexual relations** are sins that one's **soul covets and lusts after.** Therefore, we are concerned that one who has not properly studied these matters with his teacher will rule leniently for himself.

אִי הָכִי גֶּזֶל נַמִי! עֲרָיוֹת, בֵּין בְּפָנָיו בֵּין שֶׁלֹּא בְּפָנָיו נָפֵישׁ יִצְרֵיהּ. גֶּזֶל, בְּפָנָיו נָפֵישׁ יִצְרֵיהּ, שֶׁלֹּא בְּפָנָיו – לָא נָפֵישׁ יִצְרֵיהּ.

The Gemara asks: **If so, robbery** should **also** not be taught to more than two, for this very reason. The Gemara responds: There is a difference between the lust for forbidden sexual relations and the lust for robbery. In the case of **those with whom relations are forbidden, his** evil **inclination is strong whether or not** the objects of desire **are before him.**[N] With regard to **robbery,** however, if the object presents a direct temptation **before him his inclination is strong,** but when it is **not before him his inclination is not strong,** and we are therefore less concerned.

NOTES

To include gentiles – לְרַבּוֹת אֶת הַגּוֹיִם: The *Turei Aven* points out that the Gemara in tractate *Sanhedrin*, which discusses the Noahide commandments in great detail, states that the obligation of Noahides to fulfill these commandments is derived from a different source. The teaching cited here does not refer to the obligation of Noahides to refrain from idolatry, cursing God, and incestuous relations, but to certain additional details of these *halakhot* derived not from Genesis but from the mitzvot given exclusively to Israel.

The concealed laws of forbidden sexual relations – סִתְרֵי עֲרָיוֹת: Rashi explains that the concealed laws of forbidden sexual relations refers to those *halakhot* of prohibited relationships that are not explicitly stated in the Torah, but are derived from allusions and expositions. The Rid questions why the discussion of such matters, which are merely stringencies, should be prohibited. He explains that the phrase: Concealed laws of forbidden relations, denotes the leniencies in this area of *halakha*, which may not be discussed in public. Rabbeinu Ḥananel maintains that the phrase refers to the precise definitions of this category of prohibitions, including those cases that do not incur the death penalty. See the later authorities, who attempt to combine these opinions with the approach of the Jerusalem Talmud. However, the Jerusalem Talmud itself is unclear in this regard; the *Penei Moshe* and *Korban HaEda* dispute the meaning of the phrase. The *Otzar HaKavod* explains that this expression refers to the reasoning for the prohibitions against forbidden sexual relations and why some of them were permitted in earlier generations. The Maharsha explicates this phrase in a similar vein.

His inclination is strong whether or not the objects of desire are before him – שֶׁלֹּא בְּפָנָיו נָפֵישׁ יִצְרֵיהּ: Even though the Gemara in tractate *Sota* states that the evil inclination for forbidden relations has power over an individual only with regard to a woman he sees, once a man has seen a woman, his inclination will continue to tempt him even when she is no longer visible to him (*Mishḥat Aharon*).

HALAKHA

Idolatry and cursing God by Noahides – עֲבוֹדָה זָרָה וּבִרְכַּת הַשֵּׁם בִּבְנֵי נֹחַ: If a Noahide engages in idolatry in its customary manner, he is liable to receive the death penalty. A Noahide is executed for any form of idol worship for which one is liable to be put to death at the hands of a Jewish court. It is also prohibited for him to engage in other forms of idolatry, although he is not put to death for them. A Noahide who curses God is liable to be put to death, whether he uses the Tetragrammaton or any other appellation, and in any language (Rambam *Sefer Shofetim*, *Hilkhot Melakhim* 9:2–3).

Forbidden relations for Noahides – אִיסּוּרֵי עֲרָיוֹת לִבְנֵי נֹחַ: Six forbidden sexual relations apply to Noahides: One's mother, the wife of one's father, a married woman, one's maternal half sister, males, and animals (Rambam *Sefer Shofetim*, *Hilkhot Melakhim* 9:5).

Expounding the concealed laws of forbidden sexual relations – דְּרָשָׁה בְּסִתְרֵי עֲרָיוֹת: One may not expound the concealed laws of forbidden sexual relations before three students, in case two of them become involved in a discussion of the *halakha* and fail to hear their teacher, leading them to issue erroneously lenient rulings (Rambam *Sefer Kedusha*, *Hilkhot Issurei Bia* 22:17).

״וְלֹא בְּמַעֲשֵׂה בְרֵאשִׁית בִּשְׁנַיִם״. מְנָא הָנֵי מִילֵּי? דְּתָנוּ רַבָּנַן: ״כִּי שְׁאַל נָא לְיָמִים רִאשֹׁנִים״ – יָחִיד שׁוֹאֵל, וְאֵין שְׁנַיִם שׁוֹאֲלִין.

§ It is taught in the mishna: **"Nor the act of Creation before two."** The Gemara poses a question: **From where are these matters** derived? The Gemara explains: **As the Sages taught** that the verse states: **"For ask now of the days past,** which were before you" (Deuteronomy 4:32); since this verse is stated in the singular, it teaches that **an individual may ask** questions with regard to Creation, i.e., "the days past," **but two may not ask,** which indicates that one may teach such matters to only one student.

יָכוֹל יִשְׁאַל אָדָם קוֹדֶם שֶׁנִּבְרָא הָעוֹלָם – תַּלְמוּד לוֹמַר: ״לְמִן הַיּוֹם אֲשֶׁר בָּרָא אֱלֹהִים אָדָם עַל הָאָרֶץ״.

One **might** have thought that **a person may ask** questions with regard to matters **preceding the creation of the world.** Therefore, **the** continuation of the **verse states: "Since the day that God created man upon the earth,"** but not earlier.

יָכוֹל לֹא יִשְׁאַל אָדָם מִשֵּׁשֶׁת יְמֵי בְרֵאשִׁית – תַּלְמוּד לוֹמַר: ״לְיָמִים רִאשֹׁנִים אֲשֶׁר הָיוּ לְפָנֶיךָ״.

One **might** have thought that **a person may not ask** questions with regard to matters that occurred **during the six days of Creation** before the creation of man. Therefore, **the verse states:** "For ask now **of the days past, which were before you,"** indicating that one may inquire about the days preceding the creation of man.

יָכוֹל יִשְׁאַל אָדָם מַה לְּמַעְלָה וּמַה לְּמַטָּה, מַה לְּפָנִים וּמַה לְּאָחוֹר – תַּלְמוּד לוֹמַר: ״וּלְמִקְצֵה הַשָּׁמַיִם וְעַד קְצֵה הַשָּׁמָיִם״ – מִ״לְּמִקְצֵה הַשָּׁמַיִם וְעַד קְצֵה הַשָּׁמָיִם״ אַתָּה שׁוֹאֵל, וְאֵין אַתָּה שׁוֹאֵל מַה לְּמַעְלָה מַה לְּמַטָּה, מַה לְּפָנִים מַה לְּאָחוֹר.

One **might** have thought that **a person may ask** questions with regard to **what is above, what is below, what was before,** and **what is after** the world. Therefore, **the** same **verse states: "From one end of the heavens to the other"** (Deuteronomy 4:32), which is explained as follows: **With regard to that** which is **from one end of the heavens to the other,** within the boundaries of the world, **you may ask, but you may not ask what is above, what is below, what was before,** or **what is after.**

Perek **II**
Daf **12** Amud **a**

הָשְׁתָּא דְּנָפְקָא לֵיהּ מִ״לְּמִקְצֵה הַשָּׁמַיִם וְעַד קְצֵה הַשָּׁמָיִם״, ״לְמִן הַיּוֹם אֲשֶׁר בָּרָא אֱלֹהִים אָדָם עַל הָאָרֶץ״ לָמָּה לִי?

The Gemara poses a question: **Now that it is derived from** the phrase **"from one end of the heavens to the other," why do I need** the phrase **"since the day**[N] **that God created man upon the earth"?**

כִּדְרַבִּי אֶלְעָזָר. דְּאָמַר רַבִּי אֶלְעָזָר: אָדָם הָרִאשׁוֹן מִן הָאָרֶץ עַד לָרָקִיעַ, שֶׁנֶּאֱמַר: ״לְמִן הַיּוֹם אֲשֶׁר בָּרָא אֱלֹהִים אָדָם עַל הָאָרֶץ״. וְכֵיוָן שֶׁסָּרַח – הִנִּיחַ הַקָּדוֹשׁ בָּרוּךְ הוּא יָדָיו עָלָיו וּמִיעֲטוֹ, שֶׁנֶּאֱמַר: ״אָחוֹר וָקֶדֶם צַרְתָּנִי וַתָּשֶׁת עָלַי כַּפֶּכָה״.

The Gemara answers that this phrase teaches us something else, **according to Rabbi Elazar. As Rabbi Elazar said:** The height of **Adam the first man**[N] reached **from the ground to the skies, as it is stated: "Since the day that God created man upon the earth,** and from one end of the heavens" (Deuteronomy 4:32). **When he sinned, the Holy One, Blessed be He, placed His hand upon him and diminished him, as it is stated: "You fashioned me behind and before, and laid Your hand upon me"** (Psalms 139:5).

אָמַר רַב יְהוּדָה אָמַר רַב: אָדָם הָרִאשׁוֹן – מִסּוֹף הָעוֹלָם וְעַד סוֹפוֹ הָיָה, שֶׁנֶּאֱמַר: ״לְמִן הַיּוֹם אֲשֶׁר בָּרָא אֱלֹהִים אָדָם עַל הָאָרֶץ וּלְמִקְצֵה הַשָּׁמַיִם וְעַד קְצֵה הַשָּׁמָיִם״. כֵּיוָן שֶׁסָּרַח – הִנִּיחַ הַקָּדוֹשׁ בָּרוּךְ הוּא יָדוֹ עָלָיו וּמִיעֲטוֹ, שֶׁנֶּאֱמַר: ״וַתָּשֶׁת עָלַי כַּפֶּכָה״.

Rav Yehuda said that Rav said: The size of Adam the first man was from one end of the world to the other, as it is stated: "Since the day that God created man upon the earth, and from one end of the heavens to the other," which indicates that he spanned the entire length of the world. **Once he sinned, the Holy One, Blessed be He, placed His hand upon him and diminished him, as it states: "And laid Your hand upon me."**

אִי הָכִי קָשׁוּ קְרָאֵי אַהֲדָדֵי! אִידִי וְאִידִי חַד שִׁיעוּרָא הוּא.

The Gemara asks: **If so, the** two parts of the **verse contradict each other,** since one indicates that his height reached the heavens while the other says it reached the end of the earth. The Gemara answers: Both **this and that are one,** the same, **measure.**

NOTES

Why do I need the phrase "since the day" – לְמִן הַיּוֹם...לָמָּה לִי: In the Jerusalem Talmud a different explanation is given with regard to the necessity of both phrases. The phrase "since the day God created man upon the earth" teaches that one may inquire about Creation only from the day of the creation of man onward, while the phrase "for ask now of the days past" approves of inquiring back to infinity. Since the second part of the verse amplifies the first and is also restricted by it, we learn that one may inquire about the six days of Creation and no earlier.

The height of Adam the first man – קוֹמָתוֹ שֶׁל אָדָם הָרִאשׁוֹן: This teaching and the ensuing discussion in the Gemara are related to the act of Creation and are therefore written in cryptic style (see Meiri). The explanations provided by the Sages on these issues should be taken as allusions to a deeper meaning. For example, with regard to Adam's height, the *Nefesh HaḤayyim* states that his essence and personality extended from one end of the world to the other, from the uppermost level of Creation to its lowest rung. It is for this reason that his height was diminished after his sin.

וְאָמַר רַב יְהוּדָה אָמַר רַב: עֲשָׂרָה דְּבָרִים נִבְרְאוּ בְּיוֹם רִאשׁוֹן, וְאֵלּוּ הֵן: שָׁמַיִם וָאָרֶץ, תֹּהוּ וָבֹהוּ, אוֹר וָחֹשֶׁךְ, רוּחַ וּמַיִם, מִדַּת יוֹם וּמִדַּת לַיְלָה.

§ The Gemara continues to discuss Creation: **Rav Yehuda said** that **Rav said: Ten things were created on the first day** of Creation, **and they are** as follows: **Heaven and earth;** ***tohu*** **and** ***vohu***, i.e., unformed and void; **light and darkness; wind and water; the length of day and the length of night.**

שָׁמַיִם וָאָרֶץ – דִּכְתִיב: ״בְּרֵאשִׁית בָּרָא אֱלֹהִים אֵת הַשָּׁמַיִם וְאֵת הָאָרֶץ״. תֹּהוּ וָבֹהוּ – דִּכְתִיב: ״וְהָאָרֶץ הָיְתָה תֹהוּ וָבֹהוּ״. אוֹר וָחֹשֶׁךְ – חֹשֶׁךְ דִּכְתִיב: ״וְחֹשֶׁךְ עַל פְּנֵי תְהוֹם״. אוֹר דִּכְתִיב: ״וַיֹּאמֶר אֱלֹהִים יְהִי אוֹר״. רוּחַ וּמַיִם – דִּכְתִיב: ״וְרוּחַ אֱלֹהִים מְרַחֶפֶת עַל פְּנֵי הַמָּיִם״. מִדַּת יוֹם וּמִדַּת לַיְלָה – דִּכְתִיב: ״וַיְהִי עֶרֶב וַיְהִי בֹקֶר יוֹם אֶחָד״.

All of these are derived from the Torah: **Heaven and earth, as it is written: "In the beginning God created the heaven and the earth"** (Genesis 1:1). ***Tohu*** **and** ***vohu***, **as it is written: "And the earth was unformed and void [*tohu vavohu*]"** (Genesis 1:2). **Light and darkness; darkness, as it is written: "And darkness was upon the face of the deep"** (Genesis 1:2); **light, as it is written: "And God said: Let there be light"** (Genesis 1:3). **Wind and water, as it is written: "And the wind of God hovered over the face of the waters"** (Genesis 1:2). **The length of day and the length of night, as it is written: "And there was evening, and there was morning, one day"** (Genesis 1:5).

תָּנָא: תֹּהוּ – קַו יָרוֹק שֶׁמַּקִּיף אֶת כׇּל הָעוֹלָם כּוּלּוֹ, שֶׁמִּמֶּנּוּ יָצָא חֹשֶׁךְ, שֶׁנֶּאֱמַר: ״יָשֶׁת חֹשֶׁךְ סִתְרוֹ סְבִיבוֹתָיו״. בֹּהוּ – אֵלּוּ אֲבָנִים הַמְפוּלָּמוֹת הַמְשׁוּקָּעוֹת בַּתְּהוֹם, שֶׁמֵּהֶן יוֹצְאִין מַיִם, שֶׁנֶּאֱמַר: ״וְנָטָה עָלֶיהָ קַו תֹהוּ וְאַבְנֵי בֹהוּ״.

It was taught in the *Tosefta*: ***Tohu*** **is a green line that encompasses the entire world, and from which darkness emerges, as it is stated: "He made darkness His hiding place round about Him"** (Psalms 18:12), indicating that a line of darkness surrounds the world. ***Vohu***; **these are damp**[L] **stones submerged in the depths, from which water emerges, as it is stated: "And He shall stretch over it the line of** ***tohu*** **and stones of** ***vohu***" (Isaiah 34:11), which demonstrates that *tohu* is a line and that *vohu* is referring to stones.[N]

וְאוֹר בְּיוֹם רִאשׁוֹן אִיבְּרִי? וְהָכְתִיב: ״וַיִּתֵּן אוֹתָם אֱלֹהִים בִּרְקִיעַ הַשָּׁמָיִם״, וּכְתִיב: ״וַיְהִי עֶרֶב וַיְהִי בֹקֶר יוֹם רְבִיעִי״!

The Gemara poses a question: **And was light created on the first day? But isn't it written: "And God set them in the firmament of the heaven"** (Genesis 1:17), **and it is also written: "And there was evening, and there was morning, a fourth day"** (Genesis 1:19), indicating that light was created on the fourth day.

כִּדְרַבִּי אֶלְעָזָר, דְּאָמַר רַבִּי אֶלְעָזָר: אוֹר שֶׁבָּרָא הַקָּדוֹשׁ בָּרוּךְ הוּא בְּיוֹם רִאשׁוֹן – אָדָם צוֹפֶה בּוֹ מִסּוֹף הָעוֹלָם וְעַד סוֹפוֹ. כֵּיוָן שֶׁנִּסְתַּכֵּל הַקָּדוֹשׁ בָּרוּךְ הוּא בְּדוֹר הַמַּבּוּל וּבְדוֹר הַפְּלַגָּה וְרָאָה שֶׁמַּעֲשֵׂיהֶם מְקוּלְקָלִים – עָמַד וּגְנָזוֹ מֵהֶן, שֶׁנֶּאֱמַר: ״וְיִמָּנַע מֵרְשָׁעִים אוֹרָם״.

The Gemara answers: This should be understood **in accordance with Rabbi Elazar, as Rabbi Elazar said:** The **light that the Holy One, Blessed be He, created on the first day** was not that of the sun but a different kind of light, **through which man could observe from one end of the world to the other. But when the Holy One, Blessed be He, looked upon the generation of the Flood and the generation of the Dispersion and saw that their ways were corrupt** and that they might misuse this light for evil, **He arose and concealed it from them, as it is stated: "And from the wicked their light is withheld"** (Job 38:15).

וּלְמִי גְּנָזוֹ? לַצַּדִּיקִים לֶעָתִיד לָבֹא, שֶׁנֶּאֱמַר: ״וַיַּרְא אֱלֹהִים אֶת הָאוֹר כִּי טוֹב״, וְאֵין טוֹב אֶלָּא צַדִּיק, שֶׁנֶּאֱמַר: ״אִמְרוּ צַדִּיק כִּי טוֹב״.

And for whom did He conceal it? For the righteous people in the future, as it is stated: "And God saw the light, that it was good" (Genesis 1:4), **and "good" is referring to none** other than the **righteous, as it is stated: "Say of the righteous that it shall be good** for them, for they shall eat the fruit of their actions" (Isaiah 3:10).

כֵּיוָן שֶׁרָאָה אוֹר שֶׁגְּנָזוֹ לַצַּדִּיקִים שָׂמַח, שֶׁנֶּאֱמַר: ״אוֹר צַדִּיקִים יִשְׂמָח״.

When the light saw that it had been concealed for the righteous, it rejoiced, as it is stated: "The light for the righteous shall rejoice" (Proverbs 13:9).[N]

כְּתַנָּאֵי: אוֹר שֶׁבָּרָא הַקָּדוֹשׁ בָּרוּךְ הוּא בְּיוֹם רִאשׁוֹן אָדָם צוֹפֶה וּמַבִּיט בּוֹ מִסּוֹף הָעוֹלָם וְעַד סוֹפוֹ, דִּבְרֵי רַבִּי יַעֲקֹב. וַחֲכָמִים אוֹמְרִים: הֵן הֵן מְאוֹרוֹת שֶׁנִּבְרְאוּ בְּיוֹם רִאשׁוֹן וְלֹא נִתְלוּ עַד יוֹם רְבִיעִי.

The Gemara comments: This is **like** a dispute between ***tanna'im***: The **light that the Holy One, Blessed be He, created on** the first day was so profound that **man could observe through it from one end of the world to the other;** this is **the statement of Rabbi Ya'akov. And the Rabbis say:** This light **is the very same as the lights created on the first day, but they were not suspended** in their designated places in the firmament **until the fourth day.**

אָמַר רַב זוּטְרָא בַּר טוֹבִיָּא אָמַר רַב: בַּעֲשָׂרָה דְּבָרִים נִבְרָא הָעוֹלָם: בְּחׇכְמָה, וּבִתְבוּנָה, וּבְדַעַת, וּבְכֹחַ, וּבִגְעָרָה, וּבִגְבוּרָה, בְּצֶדֶק, וּבְמִשְׁפָּט, בְּחֶסֶד, וּבְרַחֲמִים.

§ **Rav Zutra bar Tuvya said** that **Rav said: The world was created through ten attributes:**[N] **Through wisdom, through understanding, through knowledge, through strength, through rebuke, through might, through righteousness, through justice, through kindness, and through mercy.**

LANGUAGE

Damp [*mefulamot*] – מְפוּלָּמוֹת: This word derives from the Greek πήλωμα, *pèloma*, meaning mud or moisture. Therefore, in this context, it refers to moist, muddy stones.

NOTES

A green line, stones – קַו יָרוֹק, אֲבָנִים: Explained in a mystical vein, the green line refers to God's essence, from which all the other basic elements of the world are formed, while the stones are the building blocks of primeval matter (*Otzar HaKavod*; see Maharsha). The commentaries point out that the darkness mentioned here is not to be understood as the opposite of light or the lack thereof, but as an obscure entity that is called darkness because it is undefined and indistinct. The philosophical term for this substance is "the foundation of the first fire" (see *Guide of the Perplexed*, part 2, chapter 30).

The light for the righteous shall rejoice – אוֹר צַדִּיקִים יִשְׂמָח: According to this version of the Gemara, it is the light itself that rejoices over having been preserved for the righteous alone, as this light is depicted as a spiritual entity containing a kind of lofty inspiration that allows insight into concealed matters. Other readings of the text imply that it is the Holy One, Blessed be He, Who rejoiced over hiding the light, and several later authorities explain likewise.

The world was created through ten attributes – בַּעֲשָׂרָה דְּבָרִים נִבְרָא הָעוֹלָם: The commentaries write that these ten attributes allude to the ten utterances of Creation mentioned in Genesis, which begin with the words "and God said," as well as the ten kabbalistic emanations of God [*sefirot*] that correspond to them (*Otzar HaKavod*; Maharsha).

בְּחָכְמָה וּבִתְבוּנָה - דִּכְתִיב: ״ה׳ בְּחָכְמָה יָסַד אָרֶץ כּוֹנֵן שָׁמַיִם בִּתְבוּנָה״. בְּדַעַת - דִּכְתִיב: ״בְּדַעְתּוֹ תְּהוֹמוֹת נִבְקָעוּ״. בְּכֹחַ וּגְבוּרָה - דִּכְתִיב: ״מֵכִין הָרִים בְּכֹחוֹ נֶאְזָר בִּגְבוּרָה״. בִּגְעָרָה - דִּכְתִיב: ״עַמּוּדֵי שָׁמַיִם יְרוֹפָפוּ וְיִתְמְהוּ מִגַּעֲרָתוֹ״. בְּצֶדֶק וּמִשְׁפָּט - דִּכְתִיב: ״צֶדֶק וּמִשְׁפָּט מְכוֹן כִּסְאֶךָ״. בְּחֶסֶד וְרַחֲמִים - דִּכְתִיב: ״זְכֹר רַחֲמֶיךָ ה׳ וַחֲסָדֶיךָ כִּי מֵעוֹלָם הֵמָּה״.

Scriptural proof is provided for this statement as follows: It was created **through wisdom and through understanding, as it is written: "The Lord founded earth with wisdom, and established the heavens with understanding"** (Proverbs 3:19); **through knowledge, as it is written: "With His knowledge the depths were broken up"** (Proverbs 3:20); **through strength and through might, as it is written: "Who by Your strength sets fast the mountains, who is girded about with might"** (Psalms 65:7); **through rebuke, as it is written: "The pillars of heaven tremble and are astonished at His rebuke"** (Job 26:11); **through righteousness and justice, as it is written: "Righteousness and justice are the foundation of Your throne"** (Psalms 89:15); **through kindness and mercy, as it is written: "Remember Your mercies, O Lord, and Your kindnesses, for they are from times of old"** (Psalms 25:6).

וְאָמַר רַב יְהוּדָה אָמַר רַב: בְּשָׁעָה שֶׁבָּרָא הַקָּדוֹשׁ בָּרוּךְ הוּא אֶת הָעוֹלָם הָיָה מַרְחִיב וְהוֹלֵךְ כִּשְׁתֵּי פְקָעִיּוֹת שֶׁל שְׁתִי, עַד שֶׁגָּעַר בּוֹ הַקָּדוֹשׁ בָּרוּךְ הוּא וְהֶעֱמִידוֹ, שֶׁנֶּאֱמַר: ״עַמּוּדֵי שָׁמַיִם יְרוֹפָפוּ וְיִתְמְהוּ מִגַּעֲרָתוֹ״. וְהַיְינוּ דְּאָמַר רֵישׁ לָקִישׁ, מַאי דִּכְתִיב: ״אֲנִי אֵל שַׁדַּי״? אֲנִי הוּא שֶׁאָמַרְתִּי לָעוֹלָם דַּי. אָמַר רֵישׁ לָקִישׁ: בְּשָׁעָה שֶׁבָּרָא הַקָּדוֹשׁ בָּרוּךְ הוּא אֶת הַיָּם הָיָה מַרְחִיב וְהוֹלֵךְ, עַד שֶׁגָּעַר בּוֹ הַקָּדוֹשׁ בָּרוּךְ הוּא וְיִבְּשׁוֹ, שֶׁנֶּאֱמַר: ״גּוֹעֵר בַּיָּם וַיַּבְּשֵׁהוּ וְכָל הַנְּהָרוֹת הֶחֱרִיב״.

And Rav Yehuda said that Rav said, with regard to the same matter: **When the Holy One, Blessed be He, created the world, it continued to expand like two balls of a warp,**[NB] whose cord lengthens as they unravel, **until the Holy One, Blessed be He, rebuked it and made it stand still, as it is stated: "The pillars of heaven tremble and are astonished at His rebuke"** (Job 26:11). **And this is** the same as that which **Reish Lakish said: What is** the meaning of that **which is written: "I am the Almighty God [*El Shaddai*]"** (Genesis 17:1)? It means: **I am He Who said to the world "enough [dai],"** instructing it to stop expanding. Similarly, **Reish Lakish said: When the Holy One, Blessed be He, created the sea, it continued to expand until the Holy One, Blessed be He, rebuked it and made it dry, as it is stated: "He rebukes the sea and makes it dry, and desiccates all the rivers"** (Nahum 1:4).

תָּנוּ רַבָּנַן: בֵּית שַׁמַּאי אוֹמְרִים: שָׁמַיִם נִבְרְאוּ תְּחִלָּה וְאַחַר כָּךְ נִבְרֵאת הָאָרֶץ, שֶׁנֶּאֱמַר: ״בְּרֵאשִׁית בָּרָא אֱלֹהִים אֵת הַשָּׁמַיִם וְאֵת הָאָרֶץ״. וּבֵית הִלֵּל אוֹמְרִים: אֶרֶץ נִבְרֵאת תְּחִלָּה וְאַחַר כָּךְ שָׁמַיִם, שֶׁנֶּאֱמַר: ״בְּיוֹם עֲשׂוֹת ה׳ אֱלֹהִים אֶרֶץ וְשָׁמָיִם״.

§ Beit Shammai and Beit Hillel dispute the order of Creation, as **the Sages taught: Beit Shammai say: The heavens were created first and afterward the earth was created, as it is stated: "In the beginning God created the heaven and the earth"** (Genesis 1:1), which indicates that heaven came first. **And Beit Hillel say:** The **earth was created first, and heaven after it, as it is stated: "On the day that the Lord God made earth and heaven"** (Genesis 2:4).

אָמַר לָהֶם בֵּית הִלֵּל לְבֵית שַׁמַּאי: לְדִבְרֵיכֶם, אָדָם בּוֹנֶה עֲלִיָּיה וְאַחַר כָּךְ בּוֹנֶה בַּיִת?! שֶׁנֶּאֱמַר: ״הַבּוֹנֶה בַשָּׁמַיִם מַעֲלוֹתָיו וַאֲגֻדָּתוֹ עַל אֶרֶץ יְסָדָהּ״. אָמְרוּ לָהֶם בֵּית שַׁמַּאי לְבֵית הִלֵּל: לְדִבְרֵיכֶם אָדָם עוֹשֶׂה שְׁרַפְרַף וְאַחַר כָּךְ עוֹשֶׂה כִּסֵּא?! שֶׁנֶּאֱמַר: ״כֹּה אָמַר ה׳ הַשָּׁמַיִם כִּסְאִי וְהָאָרֶץ הֲדוֹם רַגְלָי״. וַחֲכָמִים אוֹמְרִים: זֶה וָזֶה כְּאַחַת נִבְרְאוּ, שֶׁנֶּאֱמַר: ״אַף יָדִי יָסְדָה אֶרֶץ וִימִינִי טִפְּחָה שָׁמָיִם קוֹרֵא אֲנִי אֲלֵיהֶם יַעַמְדוּ יַחְדָּו״.

Beit Hillel said to Beit Shammai: According to your words, does **a person build a second floor and build** the first floor of **the house afterward? As it is stated: "It is He Who builds His upper chambers in the heaven, and has founded His vault upon the earth"** (Amos 9:6), indicating that the upper floor, heaven, was built above the earth. **Beit Shammai said to Beit Hillel: According to your words,** does **a person make a stool** for his feet, **and make a seat afterward? As it is stated: "So said the Lord: The heavens are My seat, and the earth My footstool"** (Isaiah 66:1). **But the Rabbis say:** Both **this and that were created as one, for it is stated: "Indeed, My hand has laid the foundation of the earth, and My right hand has spread out the heavens; when I call to them, they stand up together"** (Isaiah 48:13), implying that they were created as one.

וְאִידָךְ - מַאי ״יַחְדָּו״? דְּלָא מִשְׁתַּלְּפִי מֵהֲדָדֵי. קָשׁוּ קְרָאֵי אַהֲדָדֵי! אָמַר רֵישׁ לָקִישׁ: כְּשֶׁנִּבְרְאוּ - בָּרָא שָׁמַיִם וְאַחַר כָּךְ בָּרָא הָאָרֶץ. וּכְשֶׁנָּטָה - נָטָה הָאָרֶץ וְאַחַר כָּךְ נָטָה שָׁמַיִם.

The Gemara asks: **And the others,** Beit Shammai and Beit Hillel, **what,** in their opinion, **is** the meaning of **"together"?** The Gemara responds: It means **that they do not separate from each other.** In other words, the term "together" is referring not to the moment of their creation but to the manner of their positioning. The Gemara comments: In any case, **the verses contradict each other,** as heaven is sometimes mentioned first, while on other occasions earth is listed beforehand. **Reish Lakish said: When they were created,** He first **created** the **heavens and afterward created the earth, but when He spread** them out and fixed them in their places, **He spread out the earth and afterward He spread** out **the heavens.**

NOTES

Continued to expand like two balls of a warp – הָיָה מַרְחִיב וְהוֹלֵךְ כִּשְׁתֵּי פְקָעִיּוֹת שֶׁל שְׁתִי: The commentaries note that these teachings relate to the potentially limitless character of Creation, on the one hand, and to the limitation of the divine, which establishes the boundaries of being, on the other. This explains the combination of kindness and mercy alongside the rebuke in the process of Creation (see Maharsha). Potentially, the created world should be limitless in all its aspects, but a different divine force restrains it and holds it back. The dispute with regard to heaven and earth is also connected with this issue.

BACKGROUND

Balls of a warp – פְּקָעִיּוֹת שֶׁל שְׁתִי: Before being placed in the loom, the threads of the warp are wrapped around balls, called clews. When a ball of this kind falls, the thread unravels from it. The threads of the warp are generally thinner than those of the woof, and therefore such a ball is more likely to come loose.

NOTES

Esh umayim, fire and water – **אֵשׁ וּמַיִם**: The *Panim Yafot* explains that according to this answer, *shamayim* is read as *sha-mayim*, with the first syllable reversed, leaving *esh-mayim*, fire-water.

Shamayim **is the name of the Holy One, Blessed be He – שָׁמַיִם שְׁמוֹ שֶׁל הַקָּדוֹשׁ בָּרוּךְ הוּא**: In other words, one should not entertain the thought that heaven and earth might possess divine qualities, as they constitute primordial matter used by God to create His world. Rather, they are created objects no different from anything else He created (Maharsha).

מַאי שָׁמַיִם? אָמַר רַבִּי יוֹסֵי בַּר חֲנִינָא: שֶׁשָּׁם מַיִם. בְּמַתְנִיתָא תָּנָא: אֵשׁ וּמַיִם. מְלַמֵּד שֶׁהֱבִיאָן הַקָּדוֹשׁ בָּרוּךְ הוּא וּטְרָפָן זֶה בָּזֶה, וְעָשָׂה מֵהֶן רָקִיעַ.

Incidental to the above, the Gemara asks: **What is** the meaning and source of the word **"heaven"** [*shamayim*]**? Rabbi Yosei bar Ḥanina said:** It is an acronym, ***shesham mayim***, meaning: That water is there. **It was taught in a *baraita*:** *Shamayim* means ***esh umayim***, fire and water,[N] which **teaches that the Holy One, Blessed be He, brought them** both **and combined them together, and made** the **firmament from them.**

שָׁאַל רַבִּי יִשְׁמָעֵאל אֶת רַבִּי עֲקִיבָא כְּשֶׁהָיוּ מְהַלְּכִין בַּדֶּרֶךְ, אָמַר לֵיהּ: אַתָּה שֶׁשִּׁימַּשְׁתָּ אֶת נַחוּם אִישׁ גַּם זוֹ עֶשְׂרִים וּשְׁתַּיִם שָׁנָה שֶׁהָיָה דּוֹרֵשׁ כׇּל אֶתִין שֶׁבַּתּוֹרָה, ״אֵת הַשָּׁמַיִם וְאֵת הָאָרֶץ״ מָה הָיָה דּוֹרֵשׁ בָּהֶן? אָמַר לֵיהּ: אִילּוּ נֶאֱמַר שָׁמַיִם וָאָרֶץ הָיִיתִי אוֹמֵר: שָׁמַיִם – שְׁמוֹ שֶׁל הַקָּדוֹשׁ בָּרוּךְ הוּא. עַכְשָׁיו שֶׁנֶּאֱמַר: ״אֵת הַשָּׁמַיִם וְאֵת הָאָרֶץ״. שָׁמַיִם – שָׁמַיִם מַמָּשׁ, אֶרֶץ – אֶרֶץ מַמָּשׁ.

§ The Gemara relates: **Rabbi Yishmael**[P] **asked Rabbi Akiva**[P] a question **when they were walking along the way. He said to him: You who served Naḥum of Gam Zu for twenty-two years, who would expound** and learn that **every** appearance of the word ***et* in the Torah** is meant to teach something, **what would he expound from** the phrase: **"The heaven and the earth"** [*et hashamayim ve'et ha'aretz*] (Genesis 1:1)? **He said to him:** These words should be expounded as follows: **Had it stated:** In the beginning God created *hashamayim veha'aretz*, i.e., the heaven and the earth, without the word *et*, **I would have said: *Shamayim* is the name of the Holy One, Blessed be He,**[N] and the same goes for *aretz*, and the verse would sound as if it meant that God, whose name is *Shamayim* and *Aretz*, created the world. **Since it states *"et hashamayim ve'et ha'aretz,"*** it is clear that these are created objects and that ***shamayim*** means the **actual heaven** and ***aretz*** is the **actual earth.** It is for this reason that the word *et* is necessary.

PERSONALITIES

Rabbi Yishmael – רַבִּי יִשְׁמָעֵאל: Rabbi Yishmael ben Elisha II was the grandson of Rabbi Yishmael ben Elisha the High Priest, who served in the Second Temple during the period preceding its destruction. The grandson is the *tanna* who is usually referred to simply as Rabbi Yishmael throughout the Talmud. As a young man, he was imprisoned by the Romans and was ransomed by Rabbi Yehoshua, whose student he ultimately became. After a while, he developed into one of the most renowned scholars in Yavne, where he was the close friend and intellectual adversary of Rabbi Akiva.

Both Rabbi Yishmael and Rabbi Akiva developed a unique system of biblical hermeneutics. The thirteen principles of interpretation formulated by Rabbi Yishmael serve as the foundation for the halakhic midrash, which derives Jewish law from the Torah. Many of his teachings appear throughout the Mishna, and many more in the Talmud were taught by his students under the rubric of: It was taught in the school of Rabbi Yishmael.

It appears that Rabbi Yishmael passed away prior to the bar Kokheva revolt. The Talmud mentions his sons and daughters; it is likely that the *tanna* Rabbi Eliezer, son of Rabbi Yishmael, was one of his children.

Rabbi Akiva – רַבִּי עֲקִיבָא: Akiva ben Yosef was one of the greatest of the generation of *tanna'im* who were active from just after the destruction of the Second Temple until the bar Kokheva revolt. He was one of the leading Sages during the lifetime of Rabban Gamliel II in Yavne.

According to legend, Rabbi Akiva began his studies at the age of forty, when Rachel, the daughter of the wealthy Kalba Savua, agreed to marry him on condition that he went to study Torah. Rabbi Akiva became the student of Rabbi Eliezer ben Hyrcanus and Rabbi Yehoshua ben Ḥananiah. Ultimately, he became a great scholar with twenty-four thousand students.

Among Rabbi Akiva's first students were Shimon ben Azzai and Shimon ben Zoma, with whom he entered what is known as the orchard, studying esoteric elements of the Torah. Later on, he taught Rabbi Meir and Rabbi Shimon bar Yoḥai, among others. He supported bar Kokheva's revolt against the Roman authorities, declaring him to be the Messiah. Due to Hadrian's decrees Torah study was prohibited, but Rabbi Akiva continued gathering Jews and teaching them Torah. Ultimately, he was captured and executed as one of the ten martyrs.

Rabbi Akiva collected early rabbinic teachings and worked to organize the Oral Torah. The work done by Rabbi Akiva and his students served as the basis for the Mishna that was edited by Rabbi Yehuda HaNasi and his disciples.

״אֵת הָאָרֶץ״ לָמָּה לִי – לְהַקְדִּים שָׁמַיִם לָאָרֶץ. ״וְהָאָרֶץ הָיְתָה תֹהוּ וָבֹהוּ״ מִכְּדִי בְּשָׁמַיִם אַתְחֵיל בְּרֵישָׁא, מַאי שְׁנָא דְּקָא חָשֵׁיב מַעֲשֵׂה אֶרֶץ? תָּנָא דְּבֵי ר׳ יִשְׁמָעֵאל: מָשָׁל לְמֶלֶךְ בָּשָׂר וָדָם שֶׁאָמַר לַעֲבָדָיו: הַשְׁכִּימוּ לְפִתְחִי. הִשְׁכִּים וּמָצָא נָשִׁים וַאֲנָשִׁים, לְמִי מְשַׁבֵּחַ – לְמִי שֶׁאֵין דַּרְכּוֹ לְהַשְׁכִּים וְהִשְׁכִּים.

Why do I need "and the earth" [*et ha'aretz*]? To teach that **heaven preceded earth**[N] in the order of Creation. The next verse states: **"And the earth was unformed and void"** (Genesis 1:2). The Gemara asks: **After all,** the Bible **began with heaven first; what is different** about the second verse? Why does the Bible **recount the creation of earth** first in the second verse? **The Sage of the school of Rabbi Yishmael taught:** This can be explained by **a parable of a flesh-and-blood king who said to his servants: Rise early** and come **to my entrance. He arose and found women and men** waiting for him. **Whom does he praise? Those who are unaccustomed to rising early but** yet **rose early,** the women. The same applies to the earth: Since it is a lowly, physical sphere, we would not have expected it to be created together with heaven. Therefore, it is fitting to discuss it at greater length.

תַּנְיָא, רַבִּי יוֹסֵי אוֹמֵר: אוֹי לָהֶם לַבְּרִיּוֹת שֶׁרוֹאוֹת וְאֵינָן יוֹדְעוֹת מָה רוֹאוֹת, עוֹמְדוֹת – וְאֵין יוֹדְעוֹת עַל מָה הֵן עוֹמְדוֹת. הָאָרֶץ עַל מָה עוֹמֶדֶת? עַל הָעַמּוּדִים, שֶׁנֶּאֱמַר: ״הַמַּרְגִּיז אֶרֶץ מִמְּקוֹמָהּ וְעַמּוּדֶיהָ יִתְפַּלָּצוּן״. עַמּוּדִים – עַל הַמַּיִם, שֶׁנֶּאֱמַר: ״לְרוֹקַע הָאָרֶץ עַל הַמָּיִם״. מַיִם – עַל הֶהָרִים, שֶׁנֶּאֱמַר: ״עַל הָרִים יַעַמְדוּ מָיִם״. הָרִים – בְּרוּחַ, שֶׁנֶּאֱמַר: ״כִּי הִנֵּה יוֹצֵר הָרִים וּבוֹרֵא רוּחַ״. רוּחַ – בִּסְעָרָה, שֶׁנֶּאֱמַר: ״רוּחַ סְעָרָה עוֹשָׂה דְבָרוֹ״. סְעָרָה תְּלוּיָה בִּזְרוֹעוֹ שֶׁל הַקָּדוֹשׁ בָּרוּךְ הוּא, שֶׁנֶּאֱמַר: ״וּמִתַּחַת זְרוֹעוֹת עוֹלָם״.

§ **It is taught** in a *baraita*: **Rabbi Yosei says: Woe to them, the creations,**[N] **who see and know not what they see; who stand and know not upon what they stand.** He clarifies: **Upon what does the earth stand? Upon pillars, as it is stated: "Who shakes the earth out of its place, and its pillars tremble"** (Job 9:6). These **pillars** are positioned **upon water, as it is stated: "To Him Who spread forth the earth over the waters"** (Psalms 136:6). These **waters** stand **upon mountains, as it is stated: "The waters stood above the mountains"** (Psalms 104:6). The **mountains** are upon the **wind, as it is stated: "For behold He forms the mountains and creates the wind"** (Amos 4:13). The **wind** is **upon a storm, as it is stated: "Stormy wind, fulfilling His word"** (Psalms 148:8). The **storm hangs upon the arm of the Holy One, Blessed be He,**[N] **as it is stated: "And underneath are the everlasting arms"** (Deuteronomy 33:27), which demonstrates that the entire world rests upon the arms of the Holy One, Blessed be He.

וַחֲכָמִים אוֹמְרִים: עַל שְׁנֵים עָשָׂר עַמּוּדִים עוֹמֶדֶת, שֶׁנֶּאֱמַר: ״יַצֵּב גְּבוּלוֹת עַמִּים לְמִסְפַּר בְּנֵי יִשְׂרָאֵל״. וְיֵשׁ אוֹמְרִים: שִׁבְעָה עַמּוּדִים, שֶׁנֶּאֱמַר: ״חָצְבָה עַמּוּדֶיהָ שִׁבְעָה״. רַבִּי אֶלְעָזָר בֶּן שַׁמּוּעַ אוֹמֵר: עַל עַמּוּד אֶחָד, וְצַדִּיק שְׁמוֹ, שֶׁנֶּאֱמַר: ״וְצַדִּיק יְסוֹד עוֹלָם״.

And the Rabbis say: The earth **stands on twelve pillars, as it is stated: "He set the borders of the nations according to the number of the children of Israel"** (Deuteronomy 32:8). Just as the children of Israel, i.e., the sons of Jacob, are twelve in number, so does the world rest on twelve pillars. **And some say:** There are **seven pillars, as it is stated: "She has hewn out her seven pillars"** (Proverbs 9:1). **Rabbi Elazar ben Shammua says:** The earth rests **on one pillar and a righteous person is its name, as it is stated: "But a righteous person is the foundation of the world"** (Proverbs 10:25).

אָמַר רַב יְהוּדָה: שְׁנֵי רְקִיעִים הֵן, שֶׁנֶּאֱמַר: ״הֵן לַה׳ אֱלֹהֶיךָ הַשָּׁמַיִם וּשְׁמֵי הַשָּׁמָיִם״.

§ **Rabbi Yehuda said: There are two firmaments, as it is stated: "Behold, to the Lord your God belongs the heaven and the heaven of heavens"** (Deuteronomy 10:14), indicating that there is a heaven above our heaven.

רֵישׁ לָקִישׁ אָמַר: שִׁבְעָה. וְאֵלּוּ הֵן: וִילוֹן, רָקִיעַ, שְׁחָקִים, זְבוּל, מָעוֹן, מָכוֹן, עֲרָבוֹת. וִילוֹן – אֵינוֹ מְשַׁמֵּשׁ כְּלוּם, אֶלָּא נִכְנָס שַׁחֲרִית וְיוֹצֵא עַרְבִית, וּמְחַדֵּשׁ בְּכָל יוֹם מַעֲשֵׂה בְרֵאשִׁית, שֶׁנֶּאֱמַר: ״הַנּוֹטֶה כַדּוֹק שָׁמַיִם וַיִּמְתָּחֵם כָּאֹהֶל לָשָׁבֶת״. רָקִיעַ – שֶׁבּוֹ חַמָּה וּלְבָנָה כּוֹכָבִים וּמַזָּלוֹת קְבוּעִין, שֶׁנֶּאֱמַר: ״וַיִּתֵּן אוֹתָם אֱלֹהִים בִּרְקִיעַ הַשָּׁמַיִם״. שְׁחָקִים – שֶׁבּוֹ רֵחַיִם עוֹמְדוֹת וְטוֹחֲנוֹת מָן לַצַּדִּיקִים – שֶׁנֶּאֱמַר: ״וַיְצַו שְׁחָקִים מִמָּעַל וְדַלְתֵי שָׁמַיִם פָּתָח וַיַּמְטֵר עֲלֵיהֶם מָן לֶאֱכוֹל״ וגו׳.

Reish Lakish said: There are **seven** firmaments,[N] **and they are as follows:** ***Vilon,***[NL] ***Rakia, Sheḥakim, Zevul, Ma'on, Makhon,*** and ***Aravot.***[N] The Gemara proceeds to explain the role of each firmament: ***Vilon,*** curtain, is the firmament that **does not contain anything, but enters at morning and departs** in the **evening,** and **renews the act of Creation daily, as it is stated: "Who stretches out the heavens as a curtain** [*Vilon*], **and spreads them out as a tent to dwell in"** (Isaiah 40:22). ***Rakia,*** firmament, is the one **in which the sun, moon, stars, and zodiac signs are fixed, as it is stated: "And God set them in the firmament** [*Rakia*] **of the heaven"** (Genesis 1:17). ***Sheḥakim,*** heights, is the one **in which mills stand and grind manna for the righteous, as it is stated: "And He commanded the heights** [*Shehakim*] **above, and opened the doors of heaven; and He caused manna to rain upon them for food,** and gave them of the corn of heaven" (Psalms 78:23–24).

NOTES

That heaven preceded earth – לְהַקְדִּים שָׁמַיִם לָאָרֶץ: *Bereshit Rabba* and other midrashic sources cite the continuation of this discussion between Rabbi Akiva and Rabbi Yishmael. Rabbi Yishmael has a different approach than that of Rabbi Akiva, as he learns from the two occurrences of the word *et* that the hosts of the heavens and the hosts of the earth were included in Creation as well. The basic difference between the two opinions is whether the verse is meant to negate erroneous beliefs or merely to describe reality (see *Otzar HaKavod*). It appears that according to Rabbi Akiva, the word *et* before the word *ha'aretz* is not to be understood in the usual manner as an expression of inclusion. Rather, it serves to separate earth from heaven, thereby emphasizing that they were not created together (see Rabbeinu Ḥananel).

Woe to them, the creations, etc. – אוֹי לָהֶם לַבְּרִיּוֹת וכו׳: The Maharsha explains why it is considered negative for one not to understand the matters of Creation. The phrase: Woe to them, refers not to the physical aspects of Creation but to issues involving the service of God and the power of choice to change the world. When people do not realize that they possess that power, it is detrimental for the world.

Upon the arm of the Holy One, Blessed be He – בִּזְרוֹעוֹ שֶׁל הַקָּדוֹשׁ בָּרוּךְ הוּא: The *Arukh*, citing Rabbeinu Ḥananel, writes that the arm refers to God's might, upon which the world rests (see *Ḥiddushei Aggadot LaRashba*).

Seven firmaments – שִׁבְעָה רְקִיעִים: Rav Hai Gaon attempts to connect the list of seven firmaments to the number of zodiac signs of the seven planets, but he admits that they do not correspond precisely. The *Tzlaḥ* writes that the details provided by the Gemara make it clear that these firmaments are not physical entities, not even ones extremely vague in form, but spiritual ones.

***Vilon* – וִילוֹן:** *Tosafot* suggest that *Vilon* enters in the morning and conceals the splendor of the firmament before departing in the evening, thereby revealing the stars. The *Sefat Emet* points out that according to this explanation, *Vilon* comes to conceal the splendor of the sun slightly; this is the meaning of the talmudic phrase sheath of the sun. However, the straightforward meaning of the Gemara indicates that not only does *Vilon* not contain anything, but it is of no substance and merely serves to renew the world each day.

The number of firmaments – מִסְפַּר הָרְקִיעִים: The early authorities explain that the opinions of Rav Yehuda and Reish Lakish complement each other. Rav Yehuda speaks in general terms of a heaven above the heavens, whereas Reish Lakish lists the various heavens in detail (see *Otzar HaKavod* and Maharsha).

LANGUAGE

***Vilon* – וִילוֹן:** From the Latin velum, perhaps by way of the Greek βῆλον, whose meanings include a screen; possibly from the Greek form βηλός/βηλόν, *bēlos/bēlon*, meaning curtain or threshold.

זְבוּל – שֶׁבּוֹ יְרוּשָׁלַיִם וּבֵית הַמִּקְדָּשׁ, וּמִזְבֵּחַ בָּנוּי, וּמִיכָאֵל הַשַּׂר הַגָּדוֹל עוֹמֵד וּמַקְרִיב עָלָיו קׇרְבָּן, שֶׁנֶּאֱמַר: ״בָּנֹה בָנִיתִי בֵּית זְבֻל לָךְ מָכוֹן לְשִׁבְתְּךָ עוֹלָמִים״. וּמְנָלַן דְּאִיקְּרִי שָׁמַיִם? דִּכְתִיב: ״הַבֵּט מִשָּׁמַיִם וּרְאֵה מִזְּבֻל קׇדְשְׁךָ וְתִפְאַרְתֶּךָ״.

Zevul, abode, **is the location of** the heavenly **Jerusalem**[N] **and** the heavenly **Temple, and** there the heavenly **altar is built, and** the angel **Michael, the great minister, stands and sacrifices an offering upon it, as it is stated: "I have surely built a house of** ***Zevul*** **for You, a place for You to dwell forever"** (I Kings 8:13). **And from where do we derive that** ***Zevul*** **is called heaven? As it is written: "Look down from heaven and see, from Your holy and glorious abode [*Zevul*]"** (Isaiah 63:15).

מָעוֹן – שֶׁבּוֹ כִּיתּוֹת שֶׁל מַלְאֲכֵי הַשָּׁרֵת, שֶׁאוֹמְרוֹת שִׁירָה בַּלַּיְלָה וְחָשׁוֹת בַּיּוֹם, מִפְּנֵי כְּבוֹדָן שֶׁל יִשְׂרָאֵל, שֶׁנֶּאֱמַר: ״יוֹמָם יְצַוֶּה ה׳ חַסְדּוֹ וּבַלַּיְלָה שִׁירֹה עִמִּי״.

Ma'on, habitation, **is where** there are **groups of ministering angels who recite song at night and are silent during the day out of respect for Israel,** in order not to compete with their songs, **as it is stated: "By day the Lord will command His kindness, and in the night His song is with me"** (Psalms 42:9), indicating that the song of the angels is with God only at night.

אָמַר רֵישׁ לָקִישׁ: כׇּל הָעוֹסֵק בַּתּוֹרָה בַּלַּיְלָה – הַקָּדוֹשׁ בָּרוּךְ הוּא מוֹשֵׁךְ עָלָיו חוּט שֶׁל חֶסֶד בַּיּוֹם, שֶׁנֶּאֱמַר: ״יוֹמָם יְצַוֶּה ה׳ חַסְדּוֹ״. וּמָה טַּעַם ״יוֹמָם יְצַוֶּה ה׳ חַסְדּוֹ״? מִשּׁוּם ״וּבַלַּיְלָה שִׁירֹה עִמִּי״. וְאִיכָּא דְּאָמְרִי, אָמַר רֵישׁ לָקִישׁ: כׇּל הָעוֹסֵק בַּתּוֹרָה בָּעוֹלָם הַזֶּה, שֶׁהוּא דּוֹמֶה לְלַיְלָה – הַקָּדוֹשׁ בָּרוּךְ הוּא מוֹשֵׁךְ עָלָיו חוּט שֶׁל חֶסֶד לָעוֹלָם הַבָּא, שֶׁהוּא דּוֹמֶה לְיוֹם, שֶׁנֶּאֱמַר: ״יוֹמָם יְצַוֶּה ה׳ חַסְדּוֹ וּבַלַּיְלָה שִׁירֹה עִמִּי״.

With regard to the aforementioned verse, **Reish Lakish said: Whoever occupies** himself **with Torah at night,**[H] **the Holy One, Blessed be He, extends a thread of kindness over him by day, as it is stated: "By day, the Lord will command His kindness,"** and **what is the reason** that **"by day, the Lord will command His kindness"? Because "and in the night His song,"** i.e., the song of Torah, **"is with me." And some say** that **Reish Lakish said: Whoever occupies himself with Torah in this world, which is comparable to night, the Holy One, Blessed be He, extends a thread of kindness over him in the World-to-Come, which is comparable to day, as it is stated: "By day, the Lord will command His kindness, and in the night His song is with me."**

אָמַר רַבִּי לֵוִי: כׇּל הַפּוֹסֵק מִדִּבְרֵי תוֹרָה וְעוֹסֵק בְּדִבְרֵי שִׂיחָה – מַאֲכִילִין אוֹתוֹ גַּחֲלֵי רְתָמִים, שֶׁנֶּאֱמַר: ״הַקּוֹטְפִים מַלּוּחַ עֲלֵי שִׂיחַ וְשֹׁרֶשׁ רְתָמִים לַחְמָם״. וּמְנָלַן דְּאִיקְּרִי שָׁמַיִם – שֶׁנֶּאֱמַר: ״הַשְׁקִיפָה מִמְּעוֹן קׇדְשְׁךָ מִן הַשָּׁמַיִם״.

With regard to the same matter, **Rabbi Levi said: Anyone who pauses from words of Torah to occupy himself with mundane conversation will be fed with the coals of the broom tree, as it is stated: "They pluck saltwort [*maluah*] with wormwood [*alei siah*], and the roots of the broom tree [*retamim*]**[B] **are their food"** (Job 30:4). The exposition is as follows: Those who pluck, i.e., pause, from learning Torah, which was given upon two tablets, *luhot*, which sounds similar to *maluah*, for the purpose of *siah*, idle chatter, are punished by having to eat coals made from "the roots of the broom tree." **And from where do we** derive **that** *Ma'on* **is called heaven? As it is stated: "Look forth from Your holy** ***Ma'on*****, from heaven"** (Deuteronomy 26:15).

מָכוֹן – שֶׁבּוֹ אוֹצְרוֹת שֶׁלֶג וְאוֹצְרוֹת בָּרָד, וַעֲלִיַּית טְלָלִים רָעִים, וַעֲלִיַּית אֲגָלִים, וְחַדְרָהּ שֶׁל סוּפָה [וּסְעָרָה], וּמְעָרָה שֶׁל קִיטוֹר, וְדַלְתוֹתֵיהֶן אֵשׁ, שֶׁנֶּאֱמַר: ״יִפְתַּח ה׳ לְךָ אֶת אוֹצָרוֹ הַטּוֹב״.

Makhon, dwelling place, **is where there are storehouses of snow and storehouses of hail, and the upper chamber of harmful dews, and the upper chamber of drops, and the room of tempests and storms, and the cave of mist. And the doors** of all these are made of **fire.** How do we know that there are storehouses for evil things? **For it is stated: "The Lord will open for you His good storehouse,**[N] the heavens" (Deuteronomy 28:12), which indicates the existence of a storehouse that contains the opposite of good.

הָנֵי בִּרְקִיעָא אִיתְנְהוּ? הָנֵי בְּאַרְעָא אִיתְנְהוּ! דִּכְתִיב: ״הַלְלוּ אֶת ה׳ מִן הָאָרֶץ תַּנִּינִים וְכׇל תְּהֹמוֹת אֵשׁ וּבָרָד שֶׁלֶג וְקִיטוֹר רוּחַ סְעָרָה עֹשָׂה דְבָרוֹ״! אָמַר רַב יְהוּדָה אָמַר רַב: דָּוִד בִּיקֵּשׁ עֲלֵיהֶם רַחֲמִים, וְהוֹרִידָן לָאָרֶץ. אָמַר לְפָנָיו: רִבּוֹנוֹ שֶׁל עוֹלָם, ״לֹא אֵל חָפֵץ רֶשַׁע אָתָּה לֹא יְגֻרְךָ רָע״. צַדִּיק אַתָּה ה׳ – לֹא יָגוּר בִּמְגוּרְךָ רָע. וּמְנָלַן דְּאִיקְּרִי שָׁמַיִם? דִּכְתִיב: ״וְאַתָּה תִּשְׁמַע הַשָּׁמַיִם מְכוֹן שִׁבְתֶּךָ״.

The Gemara asks a question: With regard to **these** things listed above, are they **located in heaven?** It is obvious that **they** are **located on the earth. As it is written:** "Praise the Lord from the earth, sea monsters and all depths, fire and hail, snow and mist, stormy wind, fulfilling His word" (Psalms 148:7–8). The verse seems to indicate that all these things are found on the earth. **Rav Yehuda said** that **Rav said: David requested mercy with regard to them,** that they should not remain in heaven, **and He brought them down to earth. He said before Him: Master of the Universe, "You are not a God that has pleasure in wickedness, evil shall not sojourn with You"** (Psalms 5:5). In other words, **You are righteous, O Lord.** Nothing **evil should sojourn in Your vicinity.** Rather, it is better that they remain close to us. **And from where do we** derive **that** this place **is called** "**heaven**"? **As it is written: "And You shall hear in heaven, the** ***Makhon*** **of Your dwelling"** (I Kings 8:39).

NOTES

Is the location of Jerusalem, etc. – **שֶׁבּוֹ יְרוּשָׁלַיִם וכו׳:** The Sages learn from the verse "a place for You to dwell forever" that the heavenly Jerusalem will never be destroyed. It contains an everlasting altar for God, with the sacred service administered by means of spiritual offerings. The *Tur* explains the prayer: And accept in love and favor the offerings of Israel, recited in the *Amida* as a reference to the spiritual offerings sacrificed on High even today, when the earthly Temple is no longer standing.

Will open for you His good storehouse – **יִפְתַּח...לְךָ אֶת אוֹצָרוֹ הַטּוֹב:** This verse implies the existence of an additional storehouse that is not good. Other versions of the text cite a different verse that states explicitly that there is a storehouse above containing instruments of retribution: "The Lord has opened His armory, and has brought forth the weapons of His indignation" (Jeremiah 50:25).

HALAKHA

Whoever occupies himself with Torah at night – **כׇּל הָעוֹסֵק בַּתּוֹרָה בַּלַּיְלָה:** Although the Sages dispute the ideal time for Torah study, they nevertheless agree that with regard to one who occupies himself with Torah at night, a thread of kindness is extended over him by day (Rambam *Sefer HaMadda, Hilkhot Talmud Torah* 3:13).

BACKGROUND

Broom tree [*rotem*] – **רֹתֶם:** The *rotem* is probably the plant known as the white broom, *Retama raetam*, a shrub from the Fabaceae family. This plant grows to a height of 1–2 m and has small green leaves that it sheds in the summer, while only its green branches continue to grow. With its extremely fragrant white flowers, the shrub can be found in all areas of Israel. Coals made from the roots of the broom tree are of excellent quality, and preserve their heat for an extended period of time.

Blossoming white broom tree

עֲרָבוֹת – שֶׁבּוֹ צֶדֶק, מִשְׁפָּט וּצְדָקָה, גִּנְזֵי חַיִּים וְגִנְזֵי שָׁלוֹם וְגִנְזֵי בְּרָכָה, וְנִשְׁמָתָן שֶׁל צַדִּיקִים, וְרוּחוֹת וּנְשָׁמוֹת שֶׁעָתִיד לְהִיבָּרְאוֹת, וְטַל שֶׁעָתִיד הַקָּדוֹשׁ בָּרוּךְ הוּא לְהַחֲיוֹת בּוֹ מֵתִים. צֶדֶק וּמִשְׁפָּט – דִּכְתִיב: "צֶדֶק וּמִשְׁפָּט מְכוֹן כִּסְאֶךָ". צְדָקָה – דִּכְתִיב: "וַיִּלְבַּשׁ צְדָקָה כַּשִּׁרְיָן". גִּנְזֵי חַיִּים – דִּכְתִיב: "כִּי עִמְּךָ מְקוֹר חַיִּים". וְגִנְזֵי שָׁלוֹם – דִּכְתִיב: "וַיִּקְרָא לוֹ ה' שָׁלוֹם". וְגִנְזֵי בְּרָכָה – דִּכְתִיב: "יִשָּׂא בְרָכָה מֵאֵת ה'".

Aravot, skies, is the firmament **that contains righteousness; justice; righteousness,** i.e., charity; **the treasuries of life; the treasuries of peace; the treasuries of blessing; the souls of the righteous; the spirits and souls that are to be created; and the dew that the Holy One, Blessed be He, will use to revive the dead.** The Gemara proves this statement: **Righteousness and justice** are found in heaven, **as it is written: "Righteousness and justice are the foundation of Your throne"** (Psalms 89:15); **righteousness, as it is written: "And He donned righteousness as armor"** (Isaiah 59:17); **the treasuries of life, as it is written: "For with You is the source of life"** (Psalms 36:10). **And the treasuries of peace** are found in heaven, **as it is written: "And he called Him the Lord of peace"** (Judges 6:24), implying that peace is God's name and is therefore found close to Him. **And the treasuries of blessing, as it is written: "He shall receive a blessing from the Lord"** (Psalms 24:5).

נִשְׁמָתָן שֶׁל צַדִּיקִים – דִּכְתִיב: "וְהָיְתָה נֶפֶשׁ אֲדֹנִי צְרוּרָה בִּצְרוֹר הַחַיִּים אֵת ה' אֱלֹהֶיךָ". רוּחוֹת וּנְשָׁמוֹת שֶׁעָתִיד לְהִיבָּרְאוֹת – דִּכְתִיב: "כִּי רוּחַ מִלְּפָנַי יַעֲטוֹף וּנְשָׁמוֹת אֲנִי עָשִׂיתִי". וְטַל שֶׁעָתִיד הַקָּדוֹשׁ בָּרוּךְ הוּא לְהַחֲיוֹת בּוֹ מֵתִים – דִּכְתִיב: "גֶּשֶׁם נְדָבוֹת תָּנִיף אֱלֹהִים נַחֲלָתְךָ וְנִלְאָה אַתָּה כוֹנַנְתָּהּ".

The souls of the righteous are found in heaven, **as it is written: "And the soul of my master shall be bound in the bundle of life with the Lord, your God"** (I Samuel 25:29). **Spirits and souls that are to be created** are found there, **as it is written: "For the spirit that enwraps itself is from Me, and the souls that I have made"** (Isaiah 57:16), which indicates that the spirit to be released into the world, wrapped around a body, is located close to God. **The dew that the Holy One, Blessed be He, will use to revive the dead** is found in heaven, **as it is written: "A bountiful rain You will pour down, God; when Your inheritance was weary, You confirmed it"** (Psalms 68:10).

שָׁם אוֹפַנִּים וּשְׂרָפִים וְחַיּוֹת הַקֹּדֶשׁ, וּמַלְאֲכֵי הַשָּׁרֵת, וְכִסֵּא הַכָּבוֹד, מֶלֶךְ אֵל חַי רָם וְנִשָּׂא שׁוֹכֵן עֲלֵיהֶם בַּעֲרָבוֹת, שֶׁנֶּאֱמַר: "סֹלּוּ לָרוֹכֵב בָּעֲרָבוֹת בְּיָהּ שְׁמוֹ". וּמְנָלַן דְּאִיקְרִי שָׁמַיִם? אָתְיָא "רְכִיבָה" "רְכִיבָה"; כְּתִיב הָכָא: "סֹלּוּ לָרוֹכֵב בָּעֲרָבוֹת", וּכְתִיב הָתָם: "רוֹכֵב שָׁמַיִם בְּעֶזְרֶךָ".

There, in the firmaments, are the ***ofanim***, the **seraphim,** the **holy divine creatures, and the ministering angels, and the Throne of Glory. The King, God,** the **living, lofty, exalted One dwells above them in *Aravot*, as it is stated: "Extol Him Who rides upon the skies [*Aravot*], Whose name is God"** (Psalms 68:5). **And from where do** we derive **that *Aravot* is called "heaven"?** This is **learned** by using a verbal analogy between two instances of **"rides" and "rides": Here, it is written: "Extol Him Who rides upon the skies [*Aravot*]," and there, it is written: "Who rides upon the heaven as your help"** (Deuteronomy 33:26).

וְחֹשֶׁךְ וְעָנָן וַעֲרָפֶל מַקִּיפִין אוֹתוֹ, שֶׁנֶּאֱמַר: "יָשֶׁת חֹשֶׁךְ סִתְרוֹ סְבִיבוֹתָיו סֻכָּתוֹ חֶשְׁכַת מַיִם עָבֵי שְׁחָקִים". וּמִי אִיכָּא חֲשׁוֹכָא קַמֵּי שְׁמַיָּא? וְהָכְתִיב: "הוּא גָּלֵא עַמִּיקָתָא וּמְסַתְּרָתָא יָדַע מָה בַחֲשׁוֹכָא וּנְהוֹרָא עִמֵּהּ שְׁרֵא"! לָא קַשְׁיָא: הָא

And darkness and clouds and fog surround Him, as it is stated: "He made darkness His hiding place, His pavilion round about Him; darkness of waters, thick clouds of the skies" (Psalms 18:12). The Gemara asks: **And is there darkness before Heaven,** i.e., before God? **But isn't it written: "He reveals deep and secret things, He knows what is in the darkness, and the light dwells with Him"** (Daniel 2:22), demonstrating that only light, not darkness, is found with God? The Gemara answers: This is **not difficult. This** verse, which states that only light dwells with Him, is referring

Perek **II**
Daf **13** Amud **a**

בְּבָתֵּי גַוָּאֵי, הָא – בְּבָתֵּי בָרָאֵי. וְאָמַר רַב אַחָא בַּר יַעֲקֹב: עוֹד רָקִיעַ אֶחָד יֵשׁ לְמַעְלָה מֵרָאשֵׁי הַחַיּוֹת, דִּכְתִיב: "וּדְמוּת עַל רָאשֵׁי הַחַיָּה רָקִיעַ כְּעֵין הַקֶּרַח הַנּוֹרָא".

to the **inner houses,** where there is only light; **that** source, according to which He is surrounded by darkness, is referring **to the outer houses. And Rav Aḥa bar Ya'akov said: There is one more firmament**[N] above these, which is **above the heads of the divine creatures, as it is written: "And over the heads of the divine creatures there was the likeness of a firmament, like the color of the terrible ice"** (Ezekiel 1:22).

NOTES

One more firmament – עוֹד רָקִיעַ אֶחָד: The commentaries write that this firmament is not included in the list of seven firmaments because it is prohibited to discuss it due to its lofty status. In other contexts as well, with regard to certain acts that are performed to correspond to the number of firmaments, the number seven is always used.

עַד כָּאן יֵשׁ לְךָ רְשׁוּת לְדַבֵּר; מִכָּאן וְאֵילָךְ – אֵין לְךָ רְשׁוּת לְדַבֵּר, שֶׁכֵּן כָּתוּב בְּסֵפֶר בֶּן סִירָא: בַּמּוּפְלָא מִמְּךָ אַל תִּדְרוֹשׁ, וּבַמְכוּסֶּה מִמְּךָ אַל תַּחְקוֹר, בַּמֶּה שֶׁהוּרְשֵׁיתָ הִתְבּוֹנֵן, אֵין לְךָ עֵסֶק בַּנִּסְתָּרוֹת. תַּנְיָא, אָמַר רַבָּן יוֹחָנָן בֶּן זַכַּאי: מַה תְּשׁוּבָה הֱשִׁיבַתּוּ בַּת קוֹל לְאוֹתוֹ רָשָׁע, בְּשָׁעָה שֶׁאָמַר: ״אֶעֱלֶה עַל בָּמֳתֵי עָב אֶדַּמֶּה לְעֶלְיוֹן״? יָצְתָה בַּת קוֹל וְאָמְרָה לוֹ: רָשָׁע בֶּן רָשָׁע, בֶּן בְּנוֹ שֶׁל נִמְרוֹד הָרָשָׁע, שֶׁהִמְרִיד כָּל הָעוֹלָם כּוּלּוֹ עָלָיו בְּמַלְכוּתוֹ!

The Gemara comments: **Until here, you have permission to speak; from this** point **forward you do not have permission to speak, as it is written in the book of Ben Sira:**[NB] **Seek not things concealed from you, nor search those hidden from you. Reflect on that which is permitted to you; you have no business with secret matters. It is taught** in a *baraita*: **Rabban Yoḥanan ben Zakkai said: What response did the Divine Voice provide to that wicked man,** Nebuchadnezzar, **when he said: "I will ascend above the heights of the clouds; I will be like the Most High"** (Isaiah 14:14), thereby intending to rise to heaven? **A Divine Voice came and said to him: Wicked man, son of a wicked man, descendant,** i.e., follower of the ways, **of Nimrod**[N] **the wicked, who caused the entire world to rebel against Him during** the time of **his reign.**

כַּמָּה שְׁנוֹתָיו שֶׁל אָדָם? שִׁבְעִים שָׁנָה, שֶׁנֶּאֱמַר: ״יְמֵי שְׁנוֹתֵינוּ בָהֶם שִׁבְעִים שָׁנָה וְאִם בִּגְבוּרוֹת שְׁמוֹנִים שָׁנָה״. וַהֲלֹא מִן הָאָרֶץ עַד לָרָקִיעַ מַהֲלַךְ חֲמֵשׁ מֵאוֹת שָׁנָה, וְעוֹבְיוֹ שֶׁל רָקִיעַ מַהֲלַךְ חֲמֵשׁ מֵאוֹת שָׁנָה, וְכֵן בֵּין כָּל רָקִיעַ וְרָקִיעַ.

How many are the years of man? Seventy years, as it is stated: "The span of our life is seventy years, or if we are strong, eighty years" (Psalms 90:10). **Now is there not from the earth to the firmament a walking** distance **of five hundred years, and the thickness of the firmament** itself is **a walking** distance **of five hundred years, and a** similar distance exists **between each and every one of the firmaments?**

לְמַעְלָה מֵהֶן חַיּוֹת הַקֹּדֶשׁ; רַגְלֵי הַחַיּוֹת כְּנֶגֶד כּוּלָּם. קַרְסוּלֵּי הַחַיּוֹת כְּנֶגֶד כּוּלָּן, שׁוֹקֵי הַחַיּוֹת כְּנֶגֶד כּוּלָּן, רְכוּבֵּי הַחַיּוֹת כְּנֶגֶד כּוּלָּן, יַרְכֵי הַחַיּוֹת כְּנֶגֶד כּוּלָּן, גּוּפֵי הַחַיּוֹת כְּנֶגֶד כּוּלָּן, צַוְּארֵי הַחַיּוֹת כְּנֶגֶד כּוּלָּן, רָאשֵׁי הַחַיּוֹת כְּנֶגֶד כּוּלָּן, קַרְנֵי הַחַיּוֹת כְּנֶגֶד כּוּלָּן, לְמַעְלָה מֵהֶן כִּסֵּא כָּבוֹד; רַגְלֵי כִּסֵּא הַכָּבוֹד כְּנֶגֶד כּוּלָּן, כִּסֵּא הַכָּבוֹד כְּנֶגֶד כּוּלָּן, מֶלֶךְ אֵל חַי וְקַיָּם רָם וְנִשָּׂא שׁוֹכֵן עֲלֵיהֶם. וְאַתָּה אָמַרְתָּ: ״אֶעֱלֶה עַל בָּמֳתֵי עָב אֶדַּמֶּה לְעֶלְיוֹן״ – ״אַךְ אֶל שְׁאוֹל תּוּרָד אֶל יַרְכְּתֵי בוֹר״!

And **above them,** above all the firmaments, **are the divine creatures. The feet of the divine creatures**[N] correspond in distance **to all** the firmaments; **the ankles of the animals correspond to all of them, the shins of the animals correspond to all of them, the knees of the animals correspond to all of them, the thighs of the animals correspond to all of them, the bodies of the animals correspond to all of them, the necks of the animals correspond to all of them, the heads of the animals correspond to all of them,** and **the horns of the animals correspond to all of them. Above them** is the **Throne of Glory: The feet of the Throne of Glory correspond to all of them, the Throne of Glory corresponds to all of them,** and **the living, almighty, lofty, exalted King dwells above them. And you,** Nebuchadnezzar, **say: "I will ascend above the heights of the clouds; I will be like the Most High"** (Isaiah 14:15), but the next verse states: **"Yet you shall be brought down to the netherworld, to the uttermost parts of the pit"** (Isaiah 14:15).

״וְלֹא בַּמֶּרְכָּבָה בְּיָחִיד״. תָּנֵי רַבִּי חִיָּיא: אֲבָל מוֹסְרִין לוֹ רָאשֵׁי פְרָקִים. אָמַר רַבִּי זֵירָא: אֵין מוֹסְרִין רָאשֵׁי פְרָקִים אֶלָּא לְאַב בֵּית דִּין, וּלְכָל מִי שֶׁלִּבּוֹ דּוֹאֵג בְּקִרְבּוֹ. אִיכָּא דְּאָמְרִי: וְהוּא שֶׁלִּבּוֹ דּוֹאֵג בְּקִרְבּוֹ.

§ It is taught in the mishna, according to the Gemara's explanation: **Nor** may one expound **the** Design of the Divine **Chariot to an individual. Rabbi Ḥiyya taught: But one may transmit to him,** an individual, **the outlines**[N] of this topic, leaving him to comprehend the rest on his own.[H] **Rabbi Zeira said: One may transmit the outlines** of the Design of the Divine Chariot **only to the president of the court,** who needs to know them due to his wisdom and meritorious deeds, **and to anyone whose heart inside him is concerned,** i.e., one who is concerned about his sins and desires to achieve full repentance. **There are** those **who say** that this does not refer to two separate individuals, but to the president of the court, **whose heart inside him is concerned.**

NOTES

As it is written in the book of Ben Sira – שֶׁכֵּן כָּתוּב בְּסֵפֶר בֶּן סִירָא: In the book of Ben Sira itself (3:21–22), this passage appears slightly differently. In the Jerusalem Talmud and other sources it is also cited with a slightly different reading: "What can you know of that which is concealed from you? What can you investigate of that which is deeper than the netherworld? Reflect on that which you have been permitted; you have no business with hidden matters." Some explain that Ben Sira's proverb alludes to all matters whose public exposition was prohibited by the Sages: The act of Creation, the Design of the Divine Chariot, the *halakhot* of forbidden sexual relations, and the secrets of the Torah. In *Ḥiddushei Aggadot LaRashba*, the upper firmament and the concealed matters are associated with the kabbalistic *sefira* known as *Keter Elyon*, Loftiest Crown.

Descendant of Nimrod – בֶּן בְּנוֹ שֶׁל נִמְרוֹד: *Tosafot* point out that Nebuchadnezzar could not have been an actual descendant of Nimrod, as Nimrod was descended from Ḥam, while Nebuchadnezzar was descended from Shem. Rather, he is considered his descendant due to their similarly evil deeds (see *Turei Aven* and Maharsha). The Rashash notes that an individual is at times referred to as son on account of his actions, for example, in the expression: Son of a worthless man [*ben beliya'al*].

The feet of the divine creatures, etc. – רַגְלֵי הַחַיּוֹת וכו׳: This list implies that each level includes the one beneath it, forming a hierarchy. It should certainly not be taken as a literal description of the form of the divine creatures.

One may transmit to him the outlines – מוֹסְרִין לוֹ רָאשֵׁי פְּרָקִים: In conclusion, it appears that it is prohibited to teach the Design of the Divine Chariot in a comprehensive manner. With regard to the outlines, certain matters may be taught in outline form to one who is worthy of studying them due to his knowledge and positive character traits, whereas matters that are beyond the level of the electrum may be transmitted only to one who is wise and understands on his own accord.

The Rambam's Commentary on the Mishna explains the reasoning for this: Since one can grasp such lofty, abstract ideas only by means of parables and metaphors, anyone teaching the topic to another must necessarily make use of his own personal perception of the images. Since different teachers are likely to use different metaphors, it is impossible to convey the meaning of the biblical verses to others without becoming entangled in error. Consequently, only the outlines may be taught, and the student must fill in the gaps by means of his own intellect.

As the Gemara will explain later, the student may provide an account to his teacher of his understanding of these matters, so that the latter can examine whether he has understood them properly (see the Jerusalem Talmud).

HALAKHA

Studying the Design of the Divine Chariot – לִימּוּד מַעֲשֵׂה מֶרְכָּבָה: The Sages render prohibited expounding on the Design of the Divine Chariot. However, it is permitted to transmit its outlines to a scholar such as Rav Ḥiyya, who is capable of understanding the details on his own. It is certainly prohibited to lecture in public on such profound and obscure matters. Whoever understands these matters should keep the knowledge to himself (Rambam *Sefer HaMadda, Hilkhot Yesodei HaTorah* 2:12).

BACKGROUND

The book of Ben Sira – סֵפֶר בֶּן סִירָא: The book of Ben Sira was one of the first books composed after the canonization of the Bible. It was written by Shimon ben Yehoshua ben Sira, a resident of Jerusalem and a younger contemporary of Shimon HaTzaddik, before the Hasmonean period. The book was held in high regard. Its translation into Greek by the author's grandson in Alexandria in 132 BCE facilitated its circulation among those who were unfamiliar with Hebrew. The Septuagint includes the book of Ben Sira among the books of the Bible, leading many other translations to do the same. Although the Sages decided that this book was apocryphal, they did not refrain from quoting it in a most respectful manner. Occasionally they even considered it as if it were part of the Bible. It is possible that they rendered its study prohibited because the original volume was frequently confused with a different book, Alpha Beta of Ben Sira, a popular work filled with many dubious statements.

אָמַר רַבִּי אַמִי: אֵין מוֹסְרִין סִתְרֵי תוֹרָה אֶלָּא לְמִי שֶׁיֵּשׁ בּוֹ חֲמִשָּׁה דְּבָרִים: ״שַׂר חֲמִשִּׁים וּנְשׂוּא פָנִים וְיוֹעֵץ וַחֲכַם חֲרָשִׁים וּנְבוֹן לָחַשׁ״. וְאָמַר רַבִּי אַמִי: אֵין מוֹסְרִין דִּבְרֵי תוֹרָה לְגוֹי, שֶׁנֶּאֱמַר: ״לֹא עָשָׂה כֵן לְכָל גּוֹי וּמִשְׁפָּטִים בַּל יְדָעוּם״.

Rabbi Ami said: The secrets of the Torah may be transmitted only to one who possesses the following **five characteristics: "The captain of fifty,**[N] **and the man of favor, and the counselor, and the cunning charmer, and the skillful enchanter"** (Isaiah 3:3). **And Rabbi Ami said** further: **The words of Torah may not be transmitted to a gentile,**[N] **as it is stated: "He has not dealt so with any nation, and as for His ordinances, they have not known them"** (Psalms 147:20).

אָמַר לֵיהּ רַבִּי יוֹחָנָן לְרַבִּי אֶלְעָזָר: תָּא אַגְמְרָךְ בְּמַעֲשֵׂה הַמֶּרְכָּבָה! אָמַר לֵיהּ: לָא קְשַׁאי. כִּי קַשׁ – נָח נַפְשֵׁיהּ דְּרַבִּי יוֹחָנָן. אָמַר לֵיהּ רַבִּי אַסִי: תָּא וְאַגְמְרָךְ בְּמַעֲשֵׂה מֶרְכָּבָה! אָמַר לֵיהּ: אִי זְכַאי – גְּמִירְתָּא מֵרַבִּי יוֹחָנָן רַבָּךְ.

§ The Gemara relates: **Rabbi Yoḥanan**[P] **said to Rabbi Elazar:**[P] **Come and I will teach you the Design of the** Divine **Chariot.** Rabbi Elazar **said to him:** I have **not** yet **aged** sufficiently, as one must be very settled in one's mind for these studies. **When he grew old, Rabbi Yoḥanan had** already **passed away. Rabbi Asi said to him: Come and I will teach you the Design of the** Divine **Chariot. He said to him: Had I merited, I would have learned** it **from Rabbi Yoḥanan, your teacher.** It therefore appears that I am unworthy of studying it.

רַב יוֹסֵף הֲוָה גְּמִיר מַעֲשֵׂה הַמֶּרְכָּבָה. סָבֵי דְּפוּמְבְּדִיתָא הָווּ תָּנוּ בְּמַעֲשֵׂה בְּרֵאשִׁית. אָמְרוּ לֵיהּ: לִיגְמוֹר לָן מָר מַעֲשֵׂה מֶרְכָּבָה! אָמַר לְהוּ: אַגְמְרוּן לִי מַעֲשֵׂה בְרֵאשִׁית! בָּתַר דְּאַגְמְרוּן, אָמְרוּ לֵיהּ: לִיגְמְרוּן מָר בְּמַעֲשֵׂה מֶרְכָּבָה! אָמַר לְהוּ: תָּנֵינָא בְּהוּ: ״דְּבַשׁ וְחָלָב תַּחַת לְשׁוֹנֵךְ״ – דְּבָרִים הַמְתוּקִין מִדְּבַשׁ וְחָלָב יְהוּ תַּחַת לְשׁוֹנֵךְ.

The Gemara relates: **Rav Yosef would study the Design of the** Divine **Chariot** and was familiar with the subject, whereas **the Elders of Pumbedita would study the act of Creation. They said to** Rav Yosef: **Let the Master teach us the Design of the** Divine **Chariot. He said to them:** You **teach me**[N] **the act of Creation. After they taught him** that subject, **they said to him: Let the Master teach us the Design of the** Divine **Chariot. He said to them: We learned with regard to them** the secrets of the Torah: **"Honey and milk are under your tongue"** (Song of Songs 4:11), meaning that **matters that are sweeter than honey and milk should remain under your tongue.** In other words, one should not speak of such matters, and anyone who is familiar with them may not reveal them to others.

רַבִּי אַבָּהוּ אָמַר מֵהָכָא: ״כְּבָשִׂים לִלְבוּשֶׁךָ״ – דְּבָרִים שֶׁהֵן כִּבְשׁוֹנוֹ שֶׁל עוֹלָם יִהְיוּ תַּחַת לְבוּשְׁךָ. אָמְרוּ לֵיהּ: תָּנֵינַן בְּהוּ עַד ״וַיֹּאמֶר אֵלַי בֶּן אָדָם״. אָמַר לְהוּ: הֵן הֵן מַעֲשֵׂה הַמֶּרְכָּבָה.

Rabbi Abbahu said: It is derived from **here,** from the following verse: **"The lambs** [*kevasim*] **will be for your clothing"** (Proverbs 27:26), which he expounds as though it were written with the letter *shin, kevashim,* meaning concealed matters: **Things that constitute the concealed matters of the world should be under your clothing;** you should not reveal them. When the Elders of Pumbedita saw that Rav Yosef was not going to teach them, **they said to him: We have learned them,** the verses concerning the Design of the Divine Chariot written in the book of Ezekiel, **up to** the verse **"And He said to me, son of man"** (Ezekiel 2:1). **He said to them:** If so, **these** verses **are** the very essence of the **Design of the** Divine **Chariot,**[N] as they provide the main details of the topic.

NOTES

The captain of fifty – שַׂר חֲמִשִּׁים: The Gemara addresses each of these terms later. The *Turei Aven* explains that the student must be at least fifty years old in order to study these lofty matters, which is why the Gemara continues with the story of Rabbi Elazar.

The words of Torah may not be transmitted to a gentile – אֵין מוֹסְרִין דִּבְרֵי תוֹרָה לְגוֹי: Several commentaries are puzzled by the fact that the *halakha* with regard to transmitting words of Torah to a gentile is not cited by the halakhic decisors. The *Sefat Emet* writes that once the Torah was translated into Greek, it was no longer possible to issue a blanket prohibition in this regard. Others claim that the statement with regard to transmitting the words of Torah to a gentile does not refer to the words of the Torah themselves, but only to the secrets of the Torah (Responsa *Be'er Sheva*; see Maharsha). The Meiri follows his consistent approach and maintains that this prohibition applies only to gentiles who actually worship idols, but not to those who believe in one God.

He said to them teach me, etc. – אָמַר לְהוּ אַגְמְרוּן לִי וכו׳: This appears to be a form of deception, as they agreed to teach him only because they anticipated that he would teach them the Design of the Divine Chariot in return. The commentaries point out that the *Mekhilta* and other sources explicitly permit one to steal, so to speak, words of Torah in such a manner, and say that there was no moral wrongdoing involved in his conduct. Furthermore, since they were unworthy of learning the Design of the Divine Chariot, it was prohibited for him to teach it to them in any case (Rabbi Yehuda of Barcelona, citing Rav Hai Gaon).

These verses are the very essence of the Design of the Divine Chariot – הֵן הֵן מַעֲשֵׂה הַמֶּרְכָּבָה: Rashi understands that Rav Yosef is confirming that the students had in fact studied the topic previously, so that it was unnecessary for him to teach it to them. However, the Rid explains that Rav Yosef meant to say that these verses may not be taught to others at all.

PERSONALITIES

Rabbi Yoḥanan – רַבִּי יוֹחָנָן: This is Rabbi Yoḥanan bar Nappaḥa, one of the greatest *amora'im*, whose teachings are fundamental components of both the Babylonian and the Jerusalem Talmuds. He resided in Tiberias and lived to an advanced age. Almost nothing is known of his family origins. He was orphaned at a young age, and although his family apparently owned considerable property, in his devotion to the study of Torah, he spent virtually all of his resources and eventually became impoverished. In his youth, he had the privilege of studying under Rabbi Yehuda HaNasi, the redactor of the Mishna, but most of his Torah learning was accomplished under the students of Rabbi Yehuda HaNasi: Ḥizkiya ben Ḥiyya, Rabbi Oshaya, Rabbi Ḥanina, and Rabbi Yannai, who lavished praise upon him. In time, he became the head of the yeshiva in Tiberias, at which point his fame and influence increased greatly.

For a long time, Rabbi Yoḥanan was the leading rabbinic scholar in the entire Jewish world, not only in Eretz Yisrael, but in Babylonia as well, where he was respected by the Babylonian Sages. Many of them ascended to Eretz Yisrael and became his outstanding students.

He was a master of both *halakha* and *aggada*; his teachings in both disciplines are found throughout both Talmuds. In recognition of his intellectual and spiritual stature, the *halakha* is ruled in accordance with his opinion in almost every case, even when Rav or Shmuel, the preeminent *amora'im* of Babylonia, whom he treated deferentially, disagree with him. Only in disputes with his teachers in Eretz Yisrael, such as Rabbi Yannai and Rabbi Yehoshua ben Levi, is the *halakha* not ruled in accordance with his opinion.

Rabbi Yoḥanan had many students. In fact, all of the *amora'im* of Eretz Yisrael in succeeding generations were his students and benefited from his teachings, to the extent that he is considered the author of the Jerusalem Talmud. His greatest students were his brother-in-law Reish Lakish, Rabbi Elazar, Rabbi Ḥiyya bar Abba, Rabbi Abbahu, Rabbi Yosei bar Ḥanina, Rabbi Ami, and Rabbi Asi.

Rabbi Elazar – רַבִּי אֶלְעָזָר: In the Gemara, citations of Rabbi Elazar, with no patronymic, refer to Rabbi Elazar ben Pedat, a second-generation *amora* in Eretz Yisrael. He was born in Babylonia, where he was a student of both Rav and Shmuel. In his youth, he immigrated to Eretz Yisrael, where he married. In Eretz Yisrael, he became the primary student of Rabbi Yoḥanan. The connection between them was so close that when the Gemara raises a contradiction between their statements it also expresses or implies surprise that they would hold different opinions.

NOTES

Indeed, that man is remembered, etc. – בְּרַם זָכוּר וכו׳: This statement, which is not connected to the Design of the Divine Chariot, is cited here only as a preamble to the subsequent incident, recounting that the Sages also wished to suppress the book of Ezekiel due to the Torah secrets it contains (*Turei Aven*).

That its words contradicted, etc. – שֶׁהָיוּ דְּבָרָיו סוֹתְרִין וכו׳: Rashi explains that the description of the sacrificial services in the book of Ezekiel contradicts Torah law in some instances. In tractate *Shabbat* he explains that this statement is referring to the contradiction with regard to the prohibition against eating an unslaughtered animal [*neveila*], which, according to the book of Ezekiel, seems to apply only to priests.

PERSONALITIES

Ḥananya ben Ḥizkiya – חֲנַנְיָה בֶּן חִזְקִיָּה: Ḥananya ben Ḥizkiya ben Garon, or Guryon, was one of the most prominent Sages of the generation following Shammai and Hillel. His upper chamber served as a meeting place for the scholars of the generation, and many important decisions were made there. One of his important projects was the composition of *Megillat Ta'anit*, the first written book of Oral Law, which lists and details festive days established in commemoration of various historical events. As explained here and elsewhere, Ḥananya also went to great lengths to ensure that the book of Ezekiel would not be suppressed despite the numerous difficulties it presents.

מֵיתִיבִי: עַד הֵיכָן מַעֲשֵׂה הַמֶּרְכָּבָה? רַבִּי אוֹמֵר: עַד ״וָאֵרֶא״ בַּתְרָא. רַבִּי יִצְחָק אוֹמֵר, עַד ״הַחַשְׁמַל״. עַד ״וָאֵרֶא״ – מְגַמְרִינַן; מִכָּאן וְאֵילָךְ – מָסְרִינַן רָאשֵׁי פְּרָקִים. אִיכָּא דְּאָמְרִי: עַד ״וָאֵרֶא״ – מָסְרִינַן רָאשֵׁי פְּרָקִים; מִכָּאן וְאֵילָךְ, אִם הוּא חָכָם מֵבִין מִדַּעְתּוֹ – אִין; אִי לָא – לָא.

The Gemara **raises an objection** to this from a *baraita*: **Until where is the Design of the** Divine **Chariot** related? **Rabbi** Yehuda HaNasi **says: Until the latter "And I saw"** (Ezekiel 1:27), not including the last verse. **Rabbi Yitzḥak says: Until** the word **"the electrum"** (Ezekiel 1:27). Neither of these opinions accord with Rav Yosef's opinion that the Design of the Divine Chariot continues until the end of the chapter. The Gemara answers: **Until "And I saw," we teach** those worthy of it; **from this** point **forward,** we **transmit** only the **outlines. There are** those **who say: Until "And I saw," we transmit the outlines; from this** point **forward, if he is wise** and **can understand of his own accord, yes,** we teach him. **If not,** we do **not** teach him even the outlines.

וּמִי דָּרְשִׁינַן בְּחַשְׁמַל? וְהָא הַהוּא יָנוֹקָא דְּדָרַשׁ בְּחַשְׁמַל וּנְפַקָא נוּרָא וַאֲכַלְתֵּיהּ! שָׁאנֵי יָנוֹקָא דְּלָאו מָטֵי זִימְנֵיהּ.

The Gemara poses a question: **And may one teach about the electrum** of the Design of the Divine Chariot at all? **But wasn't there a certain youth** who **expounded the electrum, and fire came out and consumed him,** showing that such study is highly dangerous? The Gemara answers: That **youth was different, for his time** to study such matters **had not** yet **arrived.** Therefore, he was punished.

אָמַר רַב יְהוּדָה: בְּרַם, זָכוּר אוֹתוֹ הָאִישׁ לְטוֹב, וַחֲנַנְיָה בֶּן חִזְקִיָּה שְׁמוֹ, אִלְמָלֵא הוּא נִגְנַז סֵפֶר יְחֶזְקֵאל, שֶׁהָיוּ דְּבָרָיו סוֹתְרִין דִּבְרֵי תוֹרָה. מֶה עָשָׂה? הֶעֱלוּ לוֹ שְׁלֹשׁ מֵאוֹת גַּרְבֵּי שֶׁמֶן, וְיָשַׁב בַּעֲלִיָּיה וּדְרָשׁוֹ.

Rav Yehuda said: Indeed, that man is remembered[N] **for good, and Ḥananya ben Ḥizkiya**[P] **was his name,** because **were it not for him, the book of Ezekiel would have been suppressed.** Why did they wish to suppress it? Because they found **that its words contradicted**[N] **the words of Torah,** as its later chapters contain many *halakhot* that appear not to accord with those of the Torah. **What did he do? They brought up to him three hundred barrels of oil,** for light and sustenance, **and he sat in an upper chamber and expounded it,** to reconcile its teachings with those of the Torah.

תָּנוּ רַבָּנַן: מַעֲשֶׂה בְּתִינוֹק אֶחָד שֶׁהָיָה קוֹרֵא בְּבֵית רַבּוֹ בְּסֵפֶר יְחֶזְקֵאל, וְהָיָה מֵבִין בְּחַשְׁמַל, וְיָצְאָה אֵשׁ מֵחַשְׁמַל וּשְׂרָפַתּוּ. וּבִיקְּשׁוּ לִגְנוֹז סֵפֶר יְחֶזְקֵאל. אָמַר לָהֶם חֲנַנְיָה בֶּן חִזְקִיָּה: אִם זֶה חָכָם – הַכֹּל חֲכָמִים הֵן?!

The Sages taught: An incident occurred **involving a youth who was reading the book of Ezekiel in the house of his teacher, and** he was able to **comprehend the electrum, and fire came out of the electrum and burned him. And they sought to suppress the book of Ezekiel** due to the danger it posed. **Ḥananya ben Ḥizkiya said to them: If this** youth happened to be **wise,** are **all** people **wise** enough to understand this book?

מַאי חַשְׁמַל? אָמַר רַב יְהוּדָה:

The Gemara asks: **What is the electrum? Rav Yehuda said:**

Perek **II**
Daf **13** Amud **b**

NOTES

Are silent and speak – חָשׁוֹת וּמְמַלְּלוֹת: When God reveals Himself to the prophets, He first delivers His divine speech to the angels and the divine creatures, who remain silent throughout. Afterward, the creatures speak in order to inform the relevant prophet of the prophecy at hand (Rabbi Betzalel Ashkenazi, citing *Petaḥ Einayim*).

LANGUAGE

Lightning [*bazak*] – בָּזָק: The meaning of this word in the Bible is not at all clear. In the context of the Gemara here, the Sages associate it with the Aramaic *bazaka*, earthenware shards.

חַיּוֹת אֵשׁ מְמַלְּלוֹת. בְּמַתְנִיתָא תָּנָא: עִתִּים חָשׁוֹת עִתִּים מְמַלְּלוֹת. בְּשָׁעָה שֶׁהַדִּיבּוּר יוֹצֵא מִפִּי הַקָּדוֹשׁ בָּרוּךְ הוּא – חָשׁוֹת; וּבְשָׁעָה שֶׁאֵין הַדִּיבּוּר יוֹצֵא מִפִּי הַקָּדוֹשׁ בָּרוּךְ הוּא – מְמַלְּלוֹת.

It refers to **speaking animals of fire.** Electrum [*ḥashmal*] is an acrostic of this phrase [*ḥayyot esh memallelot*]. **It was taught in a *baraita*: At times they are silent; at times they speak.**[N] **When the divine speech emerges from the mouth of the Holy One, Blessed be He, they are silent; and when the divine speech does not emerge from the mouth of the Holy One, Blessed be He, they speak.**

״וְהַחַיּוֹת רָצוֹא וָשׁוֹב כְּמַרְאֵה הַבָּזָק״. מַאי רָצוֹא וָשׁוֹב? אָמַר רַב יְהוּדָה: כְּאוּר הַיּוֹצֵא מִפִּי הַכִּבְשָׁן. מַאי ״כְּמַרְאֵה הַבָּזָק״? אָמַר רַבִּי יוֹסֵי בַּר חֲנִינָא: כְּאוּר הַיּוֹצֵא מִבֵּין הַחֲרָסִים.

§ The verse states: **"And the divine creatures ran and returned like the appearance of a flash of lightning [*bazak*]"** (Ezekiel 1:14). **What is the meaning of "ran and returned"? Rav Yehuda said: Like fire that is emitted from a furnace,** whose flame is continuously bursting out and withdrawing. **What is** the meaning of **"like the appearance of a flash of lightning"? Rabbi Yosei bar Ḥanina said: Like the fire that is emitted** from **between** pieces of **earthenware** used for refining gold, as an additional meaning ascribed to the word *bazak*[L] is shards of earthenware.

״וָאֵרֶא וְהִנֵּה רוּחַ סְעָרָה בָּאָה מִן הַצָּפוֹן עָנָן גָּדוֹל וְאֵשׁ מִתְלַקַּחַת וְנוֹגַהּ לוֹ סָבִיב וּמִתּוֹכָהּ כְּעֵין הַחַשְׁמַל מִתּוֹךְ הָאֵשׁ״. לְהֵיכָן אֲזַל? אָמַר רַב יְהוּדָה אָמַר רַב: שֶׁהָלַךְ לִכְבּוֹשׁ אֶת כָּל הָעוֹלָם כּוּלּוֹ תַּחַת נְבוּכַדְנֶצַּר הָרָשָׁע. וְכָל כָּךְ לָמָּה? שֶׁלֹּא יֹאמְרוּ אוּמּוֹת הָעוֹלָם: בְּיַד אוּמָּה שְׁפֵלָה מָסַר הַקָּדוֹשׁ בָּרוּךְ הוּא אֶת בָּנָיו. אָמַר הַקָּדוֹשׁ בָּרוּךְ הוּא: מִי גָּרַם לִי שֶׁאֶהְיֶה שַׁמָּשׁ לְעוֹבְדֵי פְּסִילִים? עֲוֹנוֹתֵיהֶן שֶׁל יִשְׂרָאֵל הֵן גָּרְמוּ לִי.

The verse states: **"And I looked and, behold, a stormy wind came out of the north, a great cloud, with a fire flashing up, so that a brightness was round about it; and out of its midst was like the color of electrum, out of the midst of the fire"** (Ezekiel 1:4). The Gemara poses a question: **Where did** that wind **go? Rav Yehuda said** that **Rav said: It went to conquer the entire world under the wicked Nebuchadnezzar. And why was all of this necessary?** Why was it necessary that the entire world be subjected to his dominion? **So that the nations of the world would not say: The Holy One, Blessed be He, delivered His children into the hands of a lowly nation.** Since it was already decreed that the kingdom of Israel would fall into the hands of Nebuchadnezzar, God made him into a great conqueror, so that Israel would not be ashamed of being defeated by him. **The Holy One, Blessed be He, said** with regard to this: **Who caused Me to be an attendant to worshippers of molten images,** forcing Me to wage their wars? **It was the sins of Israel that led Me** to do so.

״וָאֵרֶא הַחַיּוֹת וְהִנֵּה אוֹפַן אֶחָד בָּאָרֶץ אֵצֶל הַחַיּוֹת״, אָמַר רַבִּי אֶלְעָזָר: מַלְאָךְ אֶחָד שֶׁהוּא עוֹמֵד בָּאָרֶץ, וְרֹאשׁוֹ מַגִּיעַ אֵצֶל הַחַיּוֹת. בְּמַתְנִיתָא תָּנָא: סַנְדַּלְפוֹן שְׁמוֹ, הַגָּבוֹהַּ מֵחֲבֵרוֹ מַהֲלַךְ חֲמֵשׁ מֵאוֹת שָׁנָה, וְעוֹמֵד אֲחוֹרֵי הַמֶּרְכָּבָה, וְקוֹשֵׁר כְּתָרִים לְקוֹנוֹ. אִינִי? וְהָכְתִיב: ״בָּרוּךְ כְּבוֹד ה׳ מִמְּקוֹמוֹ״, מִכְּלָל דִּמְקוֹמוֹ לֵיכָּא דְּיָדַע לֵיהּ! דְּאָמַר שֵׁם אַתָּגָא, וְאָזַל וְיָתֵיב בְּרֵישֵׁיהּ.

Another verse in the same chapter states: **"Now as I beheld the divine creatures, behold, one wheel [*ofan*] was upon the earth near the divine creatures"** (Ezekiel 1:15). **Rabbi Elazar said:** This wheel is **a certain angel who stands on the earth and its head reaches the divine creatures. It was taught in a *baraita*:** This angel **is named Sandalfon,**[L] **who is taller than his colleague by a distance of five hundred years, and he stands behind the** Divine **Chariot and weaves crowns for his Maker.**[N] The Gemara asks: **Is that so?** Can crowns be woven for God? **But isn't it written: "Blessed be the Lord's glory from His place"** (Ezekiel 3:12), which proves **by inference that no one knows His place?** Therefore, how can crowns be woven for Him? Rather, it can be done **by saying a name for the crown, and** then the crown **goes and sits on** God's **head** of its own accord.

אָמַר רָבָא: כָּל שֶׁרָאָה יְחֶזְקֵאל רָאָה יְשַׁעְיָה. לְמָה יְחֶזְקֵאל דּוֹמֶה? לְבֶן כְּפָר שֶׁרָאָה אֶת הַמֶּלֶךְ. וּלְמָה יְשַׁעְיָה דּוֹמֶה? לְבֶן כְּרַךְ שֶׁרָאָה אֶת הַמֶּלֶךְ. אָמַר רֵישׁ לָקִישׁ: מַאי דִּכְתִיב: ״אָשִׁירָה לַה׳ כִּי גָאֹה גָּאָה״? שִׁירָה לְמִי שֶׁמִּתְגָּאֶה עַל הַגֵּאִים. דְּאָמַר מָר: מֶלֶךְ שֶׁבַּחַיּוֹת – אֲרִי; מֶלֶךְ שֶׁבַּבְּהֵמוֹת – שׁוֹר; מֶלֶךְ שֶׁבָּעוֹפוֹת – נֶשֶׁר; וְאָדָם מִתְגָּאֶה עֲלֵיהֶן, וְהַקָּדוֹשׁ בָּרוּךְ הוּא מִתְגָּאֶה עַל כּוּלָּן וְעַל כָּל הָעוֹלָם כּוּלּוֹ.

§ **Rava said: All that Ezekiel saw,** the prophet **Isaiah saw** as well, but the latter did not find it necessary to describe his vision in such detail. **To what may Ezekiel be compared? To a villager who saw the king** and is excited by all the extravagances of the king's palace and everything it contains, as he is unaccustomed to them. **And to what may Isaiah be compared? To a city dweller**[N] **who saw the king.** Such an individual focuses on the encounter with the king, and is oblivious to all the distractions. **Reish Lakish said: What is** the meaning of that **which is written: "I will sing to the Lord, for He is highly exalted"** (Exodus 15:1)? It is fitting to **sing to He Who is exalted above the exalted. As the Master said: The king of the beasts** is **the lion, the king of the domestic animals** is **the ox, the king of the birds** is **the eagle, and man is exalted** and lords **over them, but the Holy One, Blessed be He, is exalted above all of them and above the entire world,** as the creatures that appear in the Divine Chariot are the ox, the lion, the eagle, and man.

כָּתוּב אֶחָד אוֹמֵר: ״וּדְמוּת פְּנֵיהֶם פְּנֵי אָדָם וּפְנֵי אַרְיֵה אֶל הַיָּמִין לְאַרְבַּעְתָּם וּפְנֵי שׁוֹר מֵהַשְּׂמֹאל לְאַרְבַּעְתָּן וגו׳״, וּכְתִיב: ״וְאַרְבָּעָה פָּנִים לְאֶחָד פְּנֵי הָאֶחָד פְּנֵי הַכְּרוּב וּפְנֵי הַשֵּׁנִי פְּנֵי אָדָם וְהַשְּׁלִישִׁי פְּנֵי אַרְיֵה וְהָרְבִיעִי פְּנֵי נָשֶׁר״, וְאִילּוּ שׁוֹר לָא קָא חָשֵׁיב! אֲמַר רֵישׁ לָקִישׁ: יְחֶזְקֵאל בִּיקֵּשׁ עָלָיו רַחֲמִים וַהֲפָכוֹ לִכְרוּב. אָמַר לְפָנָיו: רִבּוֹנוֹ שֶׁל עוֹלָם! קַטֵּיגוֹר יֵעָשֶׂה סַנֵּיגוֹר?!

The Gemara poses a question with regard to the animals of the Divine Chariot: **One verse states: "As for the likeness of their faces, they had the face of a man; and the four had the face of a lion on the right side; and the four had the face of an ox on the left side"** (Ezekiel 1:10). **And it is** also **written: "And each one had four faces: The first face was the face of the cherub, and the second face was the face of a man, and the third the face of a lion, and the fourth the face of an eagle"** (Ezekiel 10:14), **but it does not include** the face of **an ox** in this second list. **Reish Lakish said: Ezekiel requested mercy** with regard **to it,**[N] i.e., the face of the ox, **and had it turned into a cherub. He said before Him** as follows: **Master of the Universe.** Shall **an accuser [*kateigor*]**[L] **become a defender [*saneigor*]?**[L] As the face of an ox recalls Israel's sin of the Golden Calf, it would be preferable for there to be a different face on the Divine Chariot.

LANGUAGE

Sandalfon – סַנְדַּלְפוֹן: If this name carries any meaning, it is similar to the Greek Συνάδελφος, *sunadelphos*, which means one who has brothers or sisters or one who belongs to a group or a sect.

Accuser [*kateigor*] – קַטֵּיגוֹר: From the Greek κατήγορος, *kategoros*, the prosecutor in a court of law.

Defender [*saneigor*] – סַנֵּיגוֹר: From the Greek συνήγορος, *sunègoros*, the representative of the defendant who pleads his case in court.

NOTES

Weaves crowns for his Maker – קוֹשֵׁר כְּתָרִים לְקוֹנוֹ: According to several *midrashim*, these crowns are understood to refer to words of prayer. Indeed, human beings recite praises with regard to God's crown in the additional prayer. The angels are portrayed as creating crowns from these prayers for God.

A villager and a city dweller – בֶּן כְּפָר וּבֶן כְּרַךְ: Rashi and Rabbeinu Ḥananel explain that city dwellers are not as impressed by superficial adornments as villagers are. However, *Tosafot* explain that the key factor is not the character of the prophet but the location where the vision is experienced. The revelation of the Divine Presence in Babylonia is an unusual phenomenon, requiring it to be presented in greater detail.

The Maharsha explains, similarly to Rashi, that a city dweller is accustomed to seeing kings and palaces, whereas Ezekiel, the villager, was unaccustomed to royal ways. The *Shita Mekubbetzet* explains that the difference does not lie in the particular prophet but in the inhabitants of his locale, as villagers require detailed descriptions, unlike city dwellers.

The *Zohar* states that since the Jewish people were at the lowest point of their exile and had lost all hope, Ezekiel provided an elaborate depiction of the greatness of the Divine Chariot in order to raise their spirits.

Ezekiel requested mercy with regard to it – יְחֶזְקֵאל בִּיקֵּשׁ עָלָיו רַחֲמִים: According to one opinion, this face was originally that of a baby who resembled Joseph, but Moses transformed it and gave it the features of an ox, as the verse with regard to Joseph's tribe in Deuteronomy 33:17 reads: "His firstborn ox, majesty is his." Later, Ezekiel requested that this feature be omitted, as it calls attention to Israel's transgression in the incident of the Golden Calf (*Otzar HaKavod*).

מַאי כְּרוּב? אָמַר רַבִּי אַבָּהוּ: כְּרַבְיָא, שֶׁכֵּן בְּבָבֶל קוֹרִין לְיַנּוּקָא רַבְיָא. אֲמַר לֵיהּ רַב פַּפָּא לְאַבַּיֵי: אֶלָּא מֵעַתָּה, דִּכְתִיב: "פְּנֵי הָאֶחָד פְּנֵי הַכְּרוּב וּפְנֵי הַשֵּׁנִי פְּנֵי אָדָם וְהַשְּׁלִישִׁי פְּנֵי אַרְיֵה וְהָרְבִיעִי פְּנֵי נֶשֶׁר" – הַיְינוּ פְּנֵי כְרוּב הַיְינוּ פְּנֵי אָדָם! אַפֵּי רַבְרְבֵי וְאַפֵּי זוּטְרֵי.

The Gemara asks: **What is** the meaning of "**cherub**"? **Rabbi Abbahu said: Like a baby** [*keravya*], **for in Babylonia they call a baby** *ravya*. **Rav Pappa said to Abaye: However, if that is so, what is** the meaning of **that which is written: "The first face was the face of the cherub, and the second face was the face of a man, and the third the face of a lion, and the fourth the face of an eagle"? The face of a cherub is** the same as **the face of a man**; what is the difference between them? He replied: The difference is that the face of a man is referring to **a large face,** whereas the face of a cherub means the **small face** of a baby.

כָּתוּב אֶחָד אוֹמֵר: "שֵׁשׁ כְּנָפַיִם שֵׁשׁ כְּנָפַיִם לְאֶחָד", וְכָתוּב אֶחָד אוֹמֵר: "וְאַרְבָּעָה פָנִים לְאַחַת וְאַרְבַּע כְּנָפַיִם לְאַחַת לָהֶם"! לָא קַשְׁיָא: כָּאן – בִּזְמַן שֶׁבֵּית הַמִּקְדָּשׁ קַיָּים; כָּאן – בִּזְמַן שֶׁאֵין בֵּית הַמִּקְדָּשׁ קַיָּים. כִּבְיָכוֹל שֶׁנִּתְמַעֲטוּ כַּנְפֵי הַחַיּוֹת.

The Gemara asks another question: **One verse states: "Each one had six wings;** with two it covered its face and with two it covered its feet, and with two it flew" (Isaiah 6:2), **and another verse states: "And every one had four faces, and every one of them had four wings"** (Ezekiel 1:6). The Gemara answers: This is **not difficult,** as **here,** when the verse states they each had six wings, it is referring **to the time when the Temple is standing,** while **there,** where four wings are described, it is referring **to the time when the Temple is not standing,** for **it is as if** the number of **the wings of the animals were diminished** so that they now have only four.

הֵי מִינַּיְיהוּ אִימְעוּט? אָמַר רַב חֲנַנְאֵל אָמַר רַב: אוֹתָן שֶׁאוֹמְרוֹת שִׁירָה בָּהֶן. כְּתִיב הָכָא: "וּבִשְׁתַּיִם יְעוֹפֵף וְקָרָא זֶה אֶל זֶה וְאָמַר", וּכְתִיב: "הֲתָעִיף עֵינֶיךָ בּוֹ וְאֵינֶנּוּ".

The Gemara asks: **Which of** the wings **were diminished? Rav Ḥananel said** that **Rav said: Those with which they recite song.** The proof is that **it is written here: "And with two it flew** [*yeofef*]. **And one called to the other and said"** (Isaiah 6:2–3), **and it is written: "Will you set** [*hata'if*] **your eyes upon it? It is gone"** (Proverbs 23:5), implying that the flight of these wings had ceased.

וְרַבָּנַן אָמְרִי: אוֹתָן שֶׁמְּכַסּוֹת בָּהֶן רַגְלֵיהֶם, שֶׁנֶּאֱמַר: "וְרַגְלֵיהֶם רֶגֶל יְשָׁרָה" וְאִי לָאו דְּאִימְעוּט – מְנָא הֲוָה יָדַע? דִּלְמָא דְּאִיגְּלַאי וַחֲזָא לֵיהּ. דְּאִי לָא תֵּימָא הָכִי – "וּדְמוּת פְּנֵיהֶם פְּנֵי אָדָם" הָכִי נַמִי דְּאִימְעוּט? אֶלָּא – דְּאִיגְּלַאי וַחֲזָא לֵיהּ; הָכָא נַמִי – דְּאִיגְּלַאי וַחֲזָא לֵיהּ.

And the Rabbis say that the wings they lost are **those with which they cover their feet, for it is stated: "And their feet were straight feet"** (Ezekiel 1:7). **Now if** these wings **had not been diminished, how would he know** what their feet looked like? Clearly their feet were no longer covered. The Gemara rejects this: This is no proof, for **perhaps they were** momentarily **revealed,** allowing him to **see them. Because if you do not say so,** that he saw them for a moment, then with regard to the verse: **"And the likeness of their faces, they had the face of a man"** (Ezekiel 1:10), **so too** will you say **that these** the wings covering their faces **were diminished** as well? **Rather,** it must be **that they were revealed and he saw them. Here too, they were revealed and he saw them.**

הָכִי הָשְׁתָּא! בִּשְׁלָמָא אַפֵּיהּ – אוֹרַח אַרְעָא לְגַלּוּיֵי קַמֵּיהּ רַבֵּיהּ; כַּרְעֵיהּ – לָאו אוֹרַח אַרְעָא לְגַלּוּיֵי קַמֵּיהּ רַבֵּיהּ.

The Gemara refutes this: **How can** these cases **be compared? Granted,** it is logical that **his face** was revealed, as **it is proper conduct** for an angel **to reveal** his face **before his Master,** and therefore it is possible that they would have revealed their faces at certain times; but with regard to **his feet,** it is **not proper conduct to reveal** them **before his Master.** Therefore, they must have lacked wings to cover their feet.

כָּתוּב אֶחָד אוֹמֵר: "אֶלֶף אַלְפִין יְשַׁמְּשׁוּנֵּיהּ וְרִבּוֹ רִבְבָן קֳדָמוֹהִי יְקוּמוּן", וְכָתוּב אֶחָד אוֹמֵר: "הֲיֵשׁ מִסְפָּר לִגְדוּדָיו"! לָא קַשְׁיָא: כָּאן – בִּזְמַן שֶׁבֵּית הַמִּקְדָּשׁ קַיָּים; כָּאן – בִּזְמַן שֶׁאֵין בֵּית הַמִּקְדָּשׁ קַיָּים. כִּבְיָכוֹל שֶׁנִּתְמַעֲטָה פָּמַלְיָא שֶׁל מַעְלָה.

§ The Gemara continues to address apparent contradictions between verses concerning similar matters: **One verse states: "A thousand thousands ministered to Him, and ten thousand times ten thousand stood before him"** (Daniel 7:10), **and another verse states: "Is there a number to His troops?"** (Job 25:3), implying that they are even more numerous than "ten thousand times ten thousand." The Gemara answers: This is **not difficult,** for **here,** when they are without number, the verse is referring **to the time when the Temple is standing; there,** the other verse is referring **to the time when the Temple is not standing, for it is as though the heavenly entourage** [*pamalya*][L] **were diminished.**

LANGUAGE

Entourage [*pamalya*] – **פָּמַלְיָא:** From the Latin familia, which means household, i.e., the attendants and all those tied to a family estate. The heavenly *pamalya* therefore refers to all those who minister to God.

תַּנְיָא, רַבִּי אוֹמֵר מִשּׁוּם אַבָּא יוֹסֵי בֶּן דּוֹסַאי: ״אֶלֶף אַלְפִין יְשַׁמְּשׁוּנֵּיהּ״ – מִסְפַּר גְּדוּד אֶחָד, ״וְלִגְדוּדָיו אֵין מִסְפָּר״. וְרַבִּי יִרְמְיָה בַּר אַבָּא אָמַר: ״אֶלֶף אַלְפִין יְשַׁמְּשׁוּנֵּיהּ״ – לִנְהַר דִּינוּר, שֶׁנֶּאֱמַר: ״נְהַר דִּינוּר נָגֵד וְנָפֵק מִן קֳדָמוֹהִי אֶלֶף אַלְפִין יְשַׁמְּשׁוּנֵּיהּ וְרִבּוֹ רִבְבָן קֳדָמוֹהִי יְקוּמוּן״.

It is taught in a *baraita*: **Rabbi** Yehuda HaNasi **says in the name of Abba Yosei ben Dosai: "A thousand thousands ministered to Him"** is referring to the **number** of angels in **a single troop**, but with regard to the number of his troops, it can be said: **"And to his troops, there is no number." And Rabbi Yirmeya bar Abba said:** There is no contradiction, since with regard to the phrase **"a thousand thousands ministered to Him,"** the pronoun "Him" can be literally translated as: It, referring not to those who serve God Himself, but to those who administer **to the River Dinur, as it is stated: "A fiery [dinur] river issued and came forth from before him; a thousand thousands ministered to it, and a myriad myriads stand before it"** (Daniel 7:10). The ministers of God, however, are indeed too numerous to count.

מֵהֵיכָן נָפֵיק? מִזֵּיעָתָן שֶׁל חַיּוֹת. וּלְהֵיכָן שָׁפֵיךְ? אָמַר רַב זוּטְרָא בַּר טוֹבִיָּה אָמַר רַב: עַל רֹאשׁ רְשָׁעִים בְּגֵיהִנָּם, שֶׁנֶּאֱמַר: ״הִנֵּה סַעֲרַת ה׳ חֵמָה יָצְאָה וְסַעַר מִתְחוֹלֵל עַל רֹאשׁ רְשָׁעִים יָחוּל״. וְרַב אַחָא בַּר יַעֲקֹב אָמַר: עַל אֲשֶׁר קוּמְּטוּ, שֶׁנֶּאֱמַר: ״אֲשֶׁר קוּמְּטוּ וְלֹא עֵת נָהָר יוּצַק יְסוֹדָם״. תַּנְיָא, אָמַר רַבִּי שִׁמְעוֹן הֶחָסִיד: אֵלּוּ תְּשַׁע מֵאוֹת וְשִׁבְעִים וְאַרְבַּע דּוֹרוֹת שֶׁקּוּמְּטוּ לְהִיבָּרְאוֹת

The Gemara asks: **From where does** this river **flow?** The Gemara answers: **From the perspiration of the divine creatures.**[N] **And where does** it **flow to? Rav Zutra bar Toviya said that Rav said: Upon the heads of the wicked in Gehenna, as it is stated: "Behold, a storm of the Lord has gone forth in fury, a whirling storm; it shall whirl upon the head of the wicked"** (Jeremiah 23:19). **And Rav Aḥa bar Ya'akov said:** The river flows **over those who were snatched away,** i.e., the generations that were never created, **as it is stated: "Who were snatched away before their time, whose foundation was poured out as a stream"** (Job 22:16), implying that the River Dinur flows over them. **It is taught** in a *baraita*: **Rabbi Shimon HeḤasid said** in explanation of this verse: **These** people "who were snatched away" are **those nine hundred and seventy-four generations that were snatched away;** they were to have **been created**

NOTES

From the perspiration of the divine creatures – מִזֵּיעָתָן שֶׁל חַיּוֹת: The River Dinur represents the lower, more limited flow of the creatures' power. This is alluded to in the verse "His throne was fiery flames [*dinur*]" (Daniel 7:9), implying that the River Dinur, mentioned in the subsequent verse, flows from the fiery sparks emitted from the creatures carrying the Divine Chariot (Maharsha).

Perek **II**
Daf **14** Amud **a**

קוֹדֶם שֶׁנִּבְרָא הָעוֹלָם וְלֹא נִבְרְאוּ. עָמַד הַקָּדוֹשׁ בָּרוּךְ הוּא וּשְׁתָלָן בְּכׇל דּוֹר וָדוֹר, וְהֵן הֵן עַזֵּי פָּנִים שֶׁבַּדּוֹר.

before the creation of the world, but they were not created. The Torah was supposed to have been given a thousand generations after the world was created, as it is written: "He commanded His word for a thousand generations" (Psalms 105:8), but God gave it earlier, after only twenty-six generations, so that nine-hundred and seventy-four generations should have been created but were not. **The Holy One, Blessed be He, acted by planting** a few of **them**[N] **in each and every generation, and they are the insolent ones of the generation,** as they belonged to generations that should not have been created at all.

וְרַב נַחְמָן בַּר יִצְחָק אָמַר: ״אֲשֶׁר קוּמְּטוּ״ – לִבְרָכָה הוּא דִּכְתִיב, אֵלּוּ תַּלְמִידֵי חֲכָמִים שֶׁמְּקַמְּטִין עַצְמָן עַל דִּבְרֵי תוֹרָה בָּעוֹלָם הַזֶּה, הַקָּדוֹשׁ בָּרוּךְ הוּא מְגַלֶּה לָהֶם סוֹד לָעוֹלָם הַבָּא, שֶׁנֶּאֱמַר: ״נָהָר יוּצַק יְסוֹדָם״.

And Rav Naḥman bar Yitzḥak said that the verse: **"Who were snatched [*kumtu*]"** (Job 22:16), **is written for a blessing,**[N] as the verse is not referring to lowly, cursed people, but to the blessed. **These are Torah scholars, who shrivel [*mekamtin*],** i.e., humble, **themselves over the words of Torah in this world. The Holy One, Blessed be He, reveals a secret to them in the World-to-Come, as it is stated: "Whose foundation [*yesodam*] was poured out as a stream"** (Job 22:16), implying that He will provide them with an abundant knowledge of secret matters [*sod*].

אֲמַר לֵיהּ שְׁמוּאֵל לְחִיָּיא בַּר רַב: בַּר אַרְיָא! תָּא, אֵימָא לָךְ מִילְּתָא מֵהָנֵי מִילֵּי מַעַלְיוּתָא דַּהֲוָה אָמַר אֲבוּךְ: כׇּל יוֹמָא וְיוֹמָא נִבְרָאִין מַלְאֲכֵי הַשָּׁרֵת מִנְּהַר דִּינוּר, וְאָמְרִי שִׁירָה וּבָטְלִי, שֶׁנֶּאֱמַר: ״חֲדָשִׁים לַבְּקָרִים רַבָּה אֱמוּנָתֶךָ״. וּפְלִיגָא דְּרַבִּי שְׁמוּאֵל בַּר נַחְמָנִי, דְּאָמַר רַבִּי שְׁמוּאֵל בַּר נַחְמָנִי אָמַר רַבִּי יוֹנָתָן: כׇּל דִּיבּוּר וְדִיבּוּר שֶׁיּוֹצֵא מִפִּי הַקָּדוֹשׁ בָּרוּךְ הוּא נִבְרָא מִמֶּנּוּ מַלְאָךְ אֶחָד, שֶׁנֶּאֱמַר: ״בִּדְבַר ה׳ שָׁמַיִם נַעֲשׂוּ וּבְרוּחַ פִּיו כׇּל צְבָאָם״.

Shmuel said to Ḥiyya bar Rav: Son of great ones, come and I will tell you something of the great things that your father would say: Each and every day, ministering angels are created from the River Dinur, and they recite song to God **and** then immediately **cease** to exist, **as it is stated: "They are new every morning; great is Your faithfulness"** (Lamentations 3:23), indicating that new angels praise God each morning. The Gemara comments: **And** this opinion **disagrees with** that **of Rabbi Shmuel bar Naḥmani, as Rabbi Shmuel bar Naḥmani said** that **Rabbi Yonatan said:** With **each and every word that emerges from the mouth of the Holy One, Blessed be He, an angel is created, as it is stated: "By the word of the Lord the heavens were made, and by the breath of His mouth all their hosts"** (Psalms 33:6). The hosts of heaven are the angels, who, he claims, are created from the mouth of God, rather than from the River Dinur.

NOTES

The Holy One, Blessed be He, acted by planting a few of them – עָמַד הַקָּדוֹשׁ בָּרוּךְ הוּא וּשְׁתָלָן: *Tosafot* write that God foresaw the wickedness of the members of that generation and therefore removed them from the world, or, at the very least, dispersed them among those of other generations (see Maharsha).

Snatched is written for a blessing – קוּמְּטוּ לִבְרָכָה הוּא דִּכְתִיב: The Maharsha explains that the phrase: "Before their time" (Job 22:16), refers to reward in the World-to-Come. Alternatively, it is a reference to those scholars who continue studying Torah beyond the regular hours of study (*Melo HaRo'im*).

כָּתוּב אֶחָד אוֹמֵר: ״לְבוּשֵׁיהּ כִּתְלַג חִיוָּר וּשְׂעַר רֵישֵׁיהּ כַּעֲמַר נְקֵא״, וּכְתִיב: ״קְוֻצּוֹתָיו תַּלְתַּלִּים שְׁחוֹרוֹת כָּעוֹרֵב״! לָא קַשְׁיָא: כָּאן בִּישִׁיבָה, כָּאן – בְּמִלְחָמָה. דְּאָמַר מָר: אֵין לְךָ נָאֶה בִּישִׁיבָה אֶלָּא זָקֵן, וְאֵין לְךָ נָאֶה בְּמִלְחָמָה אֶלָּא בָּחוּר.

§ The Gemara continues to reconcile verses that seem to contradict each other: **One verse states: "His raiment was as white snow, and the hair of his head**[N] **like pure** white **wool"** (Daniel 7:9), **and it is written: "His locks are curled, black as a raven"** (Song of Songs 5:11). The Gemara answers: This is **not difficult. Here** the verse in Daniel is referring to when He is **in the** heavenly **academy,** while **there** the verse in Song of Songs speaks of when He is **at war, for the Master said: There is no finer** individual to study Torah **in an academy than an old man, and there is no finer** individual to wage war **than a youth.** A different metaphor is therefore used to describe God on each occasion.

כָּתוּב אֶחָד אוֹמֵר: ״כָּרְסְיֵהּ שְׁבִיבִין דִּינוּר״, וְכָתוּב אֶחָד אוֹמֵר: ״עַד דִּי כָרְסָוָן רְמִיו וְעַתִּיק יוֹמִין יְתִיב״! לָא קַשְׁיָא: אֶחָד לוֹ וְאֶחָד לְדָוִד. כִּדְתַנְיָא: אֶחָד לוֹ וְאֶחָד לְדָוִד, דִּבְרֵי רַבִּי עֲקִיבָא. אָמַר לוֹ רַבִּי יוֹסֵי הַגְּלִילִי: עֲקִיבָא! עַד מָתַי אַתָּה עוֹשֶׂה שְׁכִינָה חוֹל! אֶלָּא: אֶחָד לְדִין וְאֶחָד לִצְדָקָה.

The Gemara poses another question: **One verse states: "His throne was fiery flames"** (Daniel 7:9), **and** another phrase in the same **verse states: "Till thrones were placed, and one who was ancient of days sat,"** implying the existence of two thrones. The Gemara answers: This is **not difficult. One** throne is **for Him and one is for David,**[N] **as it is taught** in a *baraita* with regard to this issue: **One** throne **for Him and one for David;** this is **the statement of Rabbi Akiva. Rabbi Yosei HaGelili said to him: Akiva, how long shall you make the Divine Presence profane,** by presenting it as though one could sit next to Him? **Rather,** the two thrones are designated for different purposes: **One for judgment and one for righteousness.**

קִיבְּלָהּ מִינֵּיהּ אוֹ לָא קִיבְּלָהּ מִינֵּיהּ? תָּא שְׁמַע: אֶחָד לְדִין וְאֶחָד לִצְדָקָה, דִּבְרֵי רַבִּי עֲקִיבָא. אָמַר לוֹ רַבִּי אֶלְעָזָר בֶּן עֲזַרְיָה: עֲקִיבָא! מַה לְּךָ אֵצֶל הַגָּדָה? כְּלָךְ מִדַּבְּרוֹתֶיךָ אֵצֶל נְגָעִים וְאֳהָלוֹת. אֶלָּא: אֶחָד לְכִסֵּא וְאֶחָד לְשַׁרְפְרַף. כִּסֵּא – לֵישֵׁב עָלָיו, שַׁרְפְרַף – לַהֲדוֹם רַגְלָיו, שֶׁנֶּאֱמַר: ״הַשָּׁמַיִם כִּסְאִי וְהָאָרֶץ הֲדוֹם רַגְלָי״.

The Gemara asks: Did Rabbi Akiva **accept** this rebuff **from him, or did he not accept** it **from him?** The Gemara offers a proof: **Come** and **hear** the following teaching of a different *baraita*: **One** throne is **for judgment and one** is **for righteousness;** this is **the statement of Rabbi Akiva. Rabbi Elazar ben Azarya**[P] **said to him: Akiva, what are you doing** occupying yourself **with** the study of ***aggada***? This is not your field of expertise. **Take** [*kelakh*][L] **your words to** the topics of **plagues and tents.** Meaning, it is preferable that you teach the *halakhot* of the impurity of leprosy and the impurity of the dead, which are within your field of expertise. **Rather,** with regard to the two thrones: **One** throne is **for a seat and one** is **for a small seat.** The **seat** is **to sit on,** and the **small seat** is **for His footstool, as it is stated: "The heavens are My seat, and the earth My footstool"** (Isaiah 66:1).

כִּי אֲתָא רַב דִּימִי אֲמַר: שְׁמוֹנֶה עֶשְׂרֵה קְלָלוֹת קִילֵּל יְשַׁעְיָה אֶת יִשְׂרָאֵל, וְלֹא נִתְקָרְרָה דַּעְתּוֹ עַד שֶׁאָמַר לָהֶם הַמִּקְרָא הַזֶּה: ״יִרְהֲבוּ הַנַּעַר בַּזָּקֵן וְהַנִּקְלֶה בַּנִּכְבָּד״.

§ The Gemara stated earlier that one who studies the secrets of Torah must be "a captain of fifty and a man of favor" (Isaiah 3:3), but it did not explain the meaning of these requirements. It now returns to analyze that verse in detail. **When Rav Dimi came** from Israel to Babylonia, **he said: Isaiah cursed Israel with eighteen curses, and his mind was not calmed,** i.e., he was not satisfied, **until he said to them the** great curse of the **following verse: "The child shall behave insolently against the aged, and the base against the honorable"** (Isaiah 3:5).

שְׁמוֹנֶה עֶשְׂרֵה קְלָלוֹת מַאי נִינְהוּ? דִּכְתִיב: ״כִּי הִנֵּה הָאָדוֹן ה׳ צְבָאוֹת מֵסִיר מִירוּשָׁלַםִ וּמִיהוּדָה מַשְׁעֵן וּמַשְׁעֵנָה כֹּל מִשְׁעַן לֶחֶם וְכֹל מִשְׁעַן מָיִם. גִּבּוֹר וְאִישׁ מִלְחָמָה שׁוֹפֵט וְנָבִיא וְקוֹסֵם וְזָקֵן. שַׂר חֲמִשִּׁים וּנְשׂוּא פָנִים וְיוֹעֵץ וַחֲכַם חֲרָשִׁים וּנְבוֹן לָחַשׁ. וְנָתַתִּי נְעָרִים שָׂרֵיהֶם וְתַעֲלוּלִים יִמְשְׁלוּ בָם״ וגו׳.

The Gemara asks: **What are these eighteen curses?** The Gemara answers: **As it is written: "For behold, the Master, the Lord of hosts, shall take away from Jerusalem and from Judah support and staff, every support of bread, and every support of water; the mighty man, and the man of war; the judge, and the prophet, and the diviner, and the elder; the captain of fifty, and the man of favor, and the counselor, and the cunning charmer, and the skillful enchanter. And I will make children their princes, and babes shall rule over them"** (Isaiah 3:1–4). The eighteen items listed in these verses shall be removed from Israel.

״מַשְׁעֵן״ – אֵלּוּ בַּעֲלֵי מִקְרָא, ״מַשְׁעֵנָה״ – אֵלּוּ בַּעֲלֵי מִשְׁנָה, כְּגוֹן רַבִּי יְהוּדָה בֶּן תֵּימָא וַחֲבֵירָיו. פְּלִיגוּ בָּהּ רַב פַּפָּא וְרַבָּנַן. חַד אֲמַר: שֵׁשׁ מֵאוֹת סִדְרֵי מִשְׁנָה, וְחַד אֲמַר: שְׁבַע מֵאוֹת סִדְרֵי מִשְׁנָה.

The Gemara proceeds to clarify the homiletical meaning of these terms: **"Support"; these are masters of the Bible. "Staff"; these are masters of Mishna, such as Rabbi Yehuda ben Teima and his colleagues.** The Gemara interjects: **Rav Pappa and the Rabbis disagreed with regard to this. One** of them **said:** They were proficient in **six hundred orders of Mishna,**[N] **and the other one said:** In **seven hundred orders of Mishna,** only six of which remain today.

NOTES

And the hair of his head, etc. – **וּשְׂעַר רֵישֵׁיהּ וכו׳**: The image of God presented here is not really an image of God Himself but a certain image shown to those who are able to see it, as revelation is specific to each viewer and to the topic of the message being relayed to him (Rabbeinu Ḥananel; *Otzar HaKavod*).

The teaching of this Gemara is rendered into poetic form in the Song of Glory recited at the conclusion of Sabbath and Festival prayer services: They represented you in many visions; through them all, You are One without divisions. They saw in You old age and youth, and the hair of Your head hoary and black; elderly on the day of judgment, and young on the day of battle.

Alternatively, Rabbeinu Ḥananel suggests that the changing image in prophetic visions is not that of God, but rather that of the angel who appears to the prophets (see Rav Sa'adia Gaon, *Emunot VeDe'ot*, II, 6).

One for Him and one for David – **אֶחָד לוֹ וְאֶחָד לְדָוִד**: The commentaries explain that Rabbi Akiva did not mean that David's throne should be placed alongside that of the Divine Presence. Rather, he was referring to a level of the Divine Presence entitled David, known in kabbalistic terminology as *malkhut*, majesty. Rabbi Yosei the Galilean and Rabbi Elazar ben Azarya are therefore referring to the same phenomenon. The former took issue with Rabbi Akiva only because he felt that his image and choice of words would invite a mundane interpretation (*Otzar HaKavod*; see *Turei Aven*). According to this understanding, Rabbi Akiva was told that despite his knowledge of the Design of the Divine Chariot, it would be inappropriate for him to expound on this matter, as his listeners might misunderstand him.

Six hundred orders of Mishna – **שֵׁשׁ מֵאוֹת סִדְרֵי מִשְׁנָה**: These orders comprise the entirety of the Oral Law from the days of Moses until the days of the *tanna'im*. However, when the knowledge of Torah decreased in the times of Hillel and Shammai, due to persecutions and troubles, the Sages decided that it was not possible to remember all of them, so they consolidated the six hundred volumes of Mishna into the current form of six orders. The *ge'onim* are quoted as saying that this abridgement of orders occurred in the days of Hillel (see the *Petaḥ Einayim*).

PERSONALITIES

Rabbi Elazar ben Azarya – **רַבִּי אֶלְעָזָר בֶּן עֲזַרְיָה**: One of the most significant *tanna'im* in the generation following the destruction of the Temple, Rabbi Elazar ben Azarya descended from a family of great wisdom, distinguished lineage, and wealth.

His father, Azarya, was also a Torah scholar and an extremely wealthy man. Azarya supported his brother Shimon, one of the Sages. For this reason, he is referred to as Shimon, brother of Azarya.

Rabbi Elazar ben Azarya's family was a family of priests descended from Ezra the Scribe, and there are traditions that tell of similarities between them. The Gemara describes how his knowledge, wealth, and family lineage made him the Sages' choice to replace Rabban Gamliel as *Nasi*, when he was removed from his position of leadership after embarrassing Rabbi Yehoshua (*Berakhot* 27b).

LANGUAGE

Take [*kelakh*] – **כְּלָךְ**: This appears to be a shortened expression. Based on parallel texts, it is an abbreviated form of *lekha lakh*, meaning: Go, take yourself. Others hold that it is short for *keleh velekh*, meaning: Finish and go.

״כֹּל מִשְׁעַן לֶחֶם״ – אֵלּוּ בַּעֲלֵי תַּלְמוּד, שֶׁנֶּאֱמַר: ״לְכוּ לַחֲמוּ בְלַחְמִי וּשְׁתוּ בְּיַיִן מָסָכְתִּי״. ״וְכֹל מִשְׁעַן מָיִם״ – אֵלּוּ בַּעֲלֵי אַגָּדָה, שֶׁמּוֹשְׁכִין לִבּוֹ שֶׁל אָדָם כַּמַּיִם בְּאַגָּדָה. ״גִּבּוֹר״ – זֶה בַּעַל שְׁמוּעוֹת. ״וְאִישׁ מִלְחָמָה״ – זֶה שֶׁיּוֹדֵעַ לִישָּׂא וְלִיתֵּן בְּמִלְחַמְתָּהּ שֶׁל תּוֹרָה. ״שׁוֹפֵט״ – זֶה דַּיָּין שֶׁדָּן דִּין אֱמֶת לַאֲמִיתּוֹ. ״נָבִיא״ – כְּמַשְׁמָעוֹ. ״קוֹסֵם״ – זֶה מֶלֶךְ, שֶׁנֶּאֱמַר: ״קֶסֶם עַל שִׂפְתֵי מֶלֶךְ״. ״זָקֵן״ – זֶה שֶׁרָאוּי לִישִׁיבָה.

"Every support of bread"; these are masters of Talmud, as it is stated: "Come, eat of my bread, and drink of the wine that I have mingled" (Proverbs 9:5). "And every support of water"; these are the masters of *aggada*, who draw people's hearts like water by means of *aggada*. "The mighty man"; this is the master of halakhic tradition,[N] one who masters the *halakhot* transmitted to him from his rabbis. "And the man of war"; this is one who knows how to engage in the discourse of Torah, generating novel teachings in the war of Torah. "A judge"; this is a judge who judges a true judgment truthfully. "A prophet"; as it literally indicates. "A diviner"; this is a king.[N] Why is he called a diviner? For it is stated: "A divine sentence is on the lips of the king" (Proverbs 16:10). "An elder"; this is one fit for the position of head of an academy.

״שַׂר חֲמִשִּׁים״ – אַל תִּקְרֵי ״שַׂר חֲמִשִּׁים״ אֶלָּא שַׂר חוּמְשִׁין, זֶה שֶׁיּוֹדֵעַ לִישָּׂא וְלִיתֵּן בַּחֲמִשָּׁה חוּמְשֵׁי תוֹרָה. דָּבָר אַחֵר: ״שַׂר חֲמִשִּׁים״ – כִּדְרַבִּי אַבָּהוּ. דְּאָמַר רַבִּי אַבָּהוּ: מִכָּאן שֶׁאֵין מַעֲמִידִין מְתוּרְגְּמָן עַל הַצִּבּוּר פָּחוֹת מֵחֲמִשִּׁים שָׁנָה. ״וּנְשׂוּא פָנִים״ – זֶה שֶׁנּוֹשְׂאִין פָּנִים לְדוֹרוֹ בַּעֲבוּרוֹ. לְמַעְלָה – כְּגוֹן רַבִּי חֲנִינָא בֶּן דּוֹסָא. לְמַטָּה – כְּגוֹן רַבִּי אַבָּהוּ בֵּי קֵיסָר.

"A captain of fifty," do not read it as "*sar ḥamishim*," rather read it as "*sar ḥumashin*"; this is one who knows how to engage in discourse with regard to the five books of [*ḥamisha ḥumshei*] the Torah. Alternatively, "a captain of fifty" should be understood in accordance with Rabbi Abbahu, for Rabbi Abbahu said: From here we learn that one may not appoint a disseminator over the public[N] to transmit words of Torah or teachings of the Sages if he is less than fifty years of age. "And the man of favor"; this is one for whose sake favor is shown to his generation. The Gemara provides different examples of this: Some garner favor above, such as Rabbi Ḥanina ben Dosa,[P] whose prayers for his generation would invariably be answered. Others gain favor below, for example: Rabbi Abbahu, who would plead Israel's case in the house of the emperor.

״יוֹעֵץ״ – שֶׁיּוֹדֵעַ לְעַבֵּר שָׁנִים וְלִקְבּוֹעַ חֳדָשִׁים, ״וַחֲכַם״ – זֶה תַּלְמִיד הַמַּחְכִּים אֶת רַבּוֹתָיו. ״חֲרָשִׁים״ – בְּשָׁעָה שֶׁפּוֹתֵחַ בְּדִבְרֵי תוֹרָה הַכֹּל נַעֲשִׂין כְּחֵרְשִׁין. ״וּנְבוֹן״ – זֶה הַמֵּבִין דָּבָר מִתּוֹךְ דָּבָר. ״לָחַשׁ״ – זֶה שֶׁרָאוּי לִמְסוֹר לוֹ דִּבְרֵי תוֹרָה שֶׁנִּיתְּנָה בְּלַחַשׁ.

"The counselor"; this is referring to one who knows how to intercalate years and determine months, due to his expertise in the phases of the moon and the calculation of the yearly cycle. "The cunning"; this is a student[N] who makes his rabbis wise through his questions. "Charmer [*ḥarashim*]"; this is referring to one so wise that when he begins speaking matters of Torah, all those listening are as though deaf [*ḥershin*], as they are unable to comprehend the profundity of his comments. "The skillful"; this is one who understands something new from something else he has learned. "Enchanter [*laḥash*]"; this is referring to one who is worthy of having words of the Torah that were given in whispers [*laḥash*], i.e., the secrets of the Torah, transmitted to him.

״וְנָתַתִּי נְעָרִים שָׂרֵיהֶם״. מַאי ״וְנָתַתִּי נְעָרִים שָׂרֵיהֶם״? אָמַר רַבִּי אֶלְעָזָר: אֵלּוּ בְּנֵי אָדָם שֶׁמְּנוֹעָרִין מִן הַמִּצְוֹת.

The Gemara continues to interpret this verse: "And I will make children their princes" (Isaiah 3:4). The Gemara asks: What is the meaning of "And I will make children [*ne'arim*] their princes"? Rabbi Elazar said: These are people who are devoid [*menu'arin*] of mitzvot; such people will become the leaders of the nation.

PERSONALITIES

Rabbi Ḥanina ben Dosa – רַבִּי חֲנִינָא בֶּן דּוֹסָא: A *tanna* who lived at the end of the Second Temple period, Rabbi Ḥanina ben Dosa was a disciple of Rabban Yoḥanan ben Zakkai. However, he is best known as the performer of miraculous acts, a righteous man whose prayers were always heard on high. The Talmud is replete with stories of miracles that took place for him and for those close to him. He was indigent and earned a very meager living. He is the Talmud's paradigm of a full-fledged righteous man who received no reward in this world. In tractate *Avot*, several of his ethical teachings are cited. They underscore the primacy of the fear of Heaven and the need for mutual affection in interpersonal relationships.

NOTES

The mighty man, this is the master of halakhic tradition – גִּבּוֹר זֶה בַּעַל שְׁמוּעוֹת: Because this man has learned many *halakhot* from his rabbis, he can safely rely on them and is therefore considered mighty in Torah learning (Maharsha).

A diviner, this is a king – קוֹסֵם זֶה מֶלֶךְ: The term diviner cannot be understood literally, as divination is prohibited by the Torah, and the abolishment of diviners would not be viewed as a curse. Therefore, it is interpreted as referring to a king (Maharsha).

A disseminator over the public, etc. – מְתוּרְגְּמָן עַל הַצִּבּוּר וכו׳: Rashi indicates that one who is less than fifty years of age is not yet worthy of delivering public lectures with the aid of a disseminator. A variant version of the text reads as follows: We do not appoint a disseminator for a small gathering but only for a group of at least fifty individuals.

Cunning [*ḥakham*], this is a student, etc. – חָכָם זֶה תַּלְמִיד וכו׳: The Gemara did not explain *ḥakham* literally, as wise man, because the word is used as part of an expression, "cunning charmer." According to the explanation offered here, the *ḥakham* is the student of a charmer (Maharsha).

״וְתַעֲלוּלִים יִמְשְׁלוּ בָם״ – אָמַר רַב פַּפָּא בַּר יַעֲקֹב: תַּעֲלֵי בְּנֵי תַּעֲלֵי. וְלֹא נִתְקָרְרָה דַּעְתּוֹ עַד שֶׁאָמַר לָהֶם ״יִרְהֲבוּ הַנַּעַר בַּזָּקֵן וְהַנִּקְלֶה בַּנִּכְבָּד״ – אֵלּוּ בְּנֵי אָדָם שֶׁמְּנוֹעָרִין מִן הַמִּצְוֹת, יִרְהֲבוּ בְּמִי שֶׁמְּמוּלָּא בְּמִצְוֹת כָּרִמּוֹן. ״וְהַנִּקְלֶה בַּנִּכְבָּד״ – יָבֹא מִי שֶׁחֲמוּרוֹת דּוֹמוֹת עָלָיו כְּקַלּוֹת וְיִרְהֲבוּ בְּמִי שֶׁקַּלּוֹת דּוֹמוֹת עָלָיו כַּחֲמוּרוֹת.

"And babes [*ta'alulim*] shall rule over them"; Rav Pappa bar Ya'akov said: *Ta'alulim* means foxes [*ta'alei*], sons of foxes. In other words, inferior people both in terms of deeds and in terms of lineage. And the prophet Isaiah's **mind was not calmed**[N] **until he said to them: "The child shall behave insolently against the aged, and the base against the honorable"** (Isaiah 3:5). "The child" [*na'ar*]; **these are people who are devoid of mitzvot,** who **will behave insolently toward one who is as filled with mitzvot as a pomegranate. "And the base** [*nikleh*] **against the honorable** [*nikhbad*]"; this means that **one for whom major** [*kaved*] transgressions **are like minor ones** [*kalot*] **in his mind will come and behave insolently with one for whom** even **minor** transgressions **are like major ones in his mind.**

אָמַר רַב קְטִינָא: אֲפִילּוּ בִּשְׁעַת כִּשְׁלוֹנָהּ שֶׁל יְרוּשָׁלַיִם לֹא פָּסְקוּ מֵהֶם בַּעֲלֵי אֲמָנָה, שֶׁנֶּאֱמַר: ״כִּי יִתְפֹּשׂ אִישׁ בְּאָחִיו בֵּית אָבִיו שִׂמְלָה לְךָ קָצִין תִּהְיֶה לָּנוּ״ – דְּבָרִים שֶׁבְּנֵי אָדָם מִתְכַּסִּין כְּשִׂמְלָה יֶשְׁנָן תַּחַת יָדֶךָ.

§ The Gemara continues its explanation of the chapter in Isaiah. **Rav Ketina said: Even at the time of Jerusalem's downfall, trustworthy men did not cease to exist** among its people, **as it is stated: "For a man shall take hold of his brother of the house of his father,** and say: **You have a cloak, be our ruler"** (Isaiah 3:6). The Gemara explains that they would approach someone and say to him: **Things that people** are careful to keep **covered as with a cloak,** i.e., words of Torah that are covered and concealed, **are under your hand,** as you are an expert with regard to them.

״וְהַמַּכְשֵׁלָה הַזֹּאת״. מַאי ״וְהַמַּכְשֵׁלָה הַזֹּאת״? דְּבָרִים שֶׁאֵין בְּנֵי אָדָם עוֹמְדִין עֲלֵיהֶן אֶלָּא אִם כֵּן נִכְשַׁל בָּהֶן, יֶשְׁנָן תַּחַת יָדֶךָ. ״יִשָּׂא בַיּוֹם הַהוּא לֵאמֹר לֹא אֶהְיֶה חוֹבֵשׁ וּבְבֵיתִי אֵין לֶחֶם וְאֵין שִׂמְלָה לֹא תְשִׂימוּנִי קְצִין עָם״. ״יִשָּׂא״ – אֵין יִשָּׂא אֶלָּא לְשׁוֹן שְׁבוּעָה, שֶׁנֶּאֱמַר: ״לֹא תִשָּׂא אֶת שֵׁם ה׳ אֱלֹהֶיךָ״. ״לֹא אֶהְיֶה חוֹבֵשׁ״ – לֹא הָיִיתִי מֵחוֹבְשֵׁי בֵּית הַמִּדְרָשׁ. ״וּבְבֵיתִי אֵין לֶחֶם וְאֵין שִׂמְלָה״ – שֶׁאֵין בְּיָדִי לֹא מִקְרָא וְלֹא מִשְׁנָה וְלֹא גְּמָרָא.

What is the meaning of the end of that verse: **"And this stumbling block"** (Isaiah 3:6)? **Things that people cannot grasp unless they have stumbled over them,** as they can be understood only with much effort, **are under your hand. Although** they will approach an individual with these statements, he **"shall swear that day, saying: I will not be a healer, for in my house there is neither bread nor a cloak; you shall not make me ruler of a people"** (Isaiah 3:7). When the verse states: **"Shall swear** [*yissa*]," *yissa* **is none** other **than an expression of an oath, as it is stated: "You shall not take** [*tissa*] **the name of the Lord your God** in vain" (Exodus 20:6). Therefore, the inhabitant of Jerusalem swears: **"I will not be a healer** [*ḥovesh*]" (Isaiah 3:7), which means: **I was never** one **of those who sit** [*meḥovshei*] **in the study hall; "for in my house there is neither bread nor a cloak,"** as **I possess** knowledge of **neither the Bible, nor Mishna, nor Gemara.** This shows that even at Jerusalem's lowest spiritual ebb, its inhabitants would admit the truth and own up to their complete ignorance.

וְדִלְמָא שָׁאנֵי הָתָם, דְּאִי אֲמַר לְהוּ גָּמֵירְנָא – אָמְרִי לֵיהּ: אֵימָא לָן! הֲוָה לֵיהּ לְמֵימַר גָּמַר וְשָׁכַח. מַאי ״לֹא אֶהְיֶה חוֹבֵשׁ״? לֹא אֶהְיֶה חוֹבֵשׁ כְּלָל.

The Gemara raises a difficulty: **But perhaps it is different there, for if he had said: I have learned, they would have said to him: Tell us,** and people do not lie about things that can be easily verified. The Gemara rejects this claim: If he were a liar, **he would have said** that **he learned and forgot,** thereby avoiding shame. **What is** the meaning of **"I will not be a healer,"** which seems to imply that he had learned in the past? It means: **I will not be a healer**[N] **at all,** as I have never learned. Consequently, there were trustworthy men in Jerusalem after all.

אִינִי?! וְהָאָמַר רָבָא: לֹא חָרְבָה יְרוּשָׁלַיִם עַד שֶׁפָּסְקוּ מִמֶּנָּה בַּעֲלֵי אֲמָנָה, שֶׁנֶּאֱמַר: ״שׁוֹטְטוּ בְּחוּצוֹת יְרוּשָׁלַםִ וּרְאוּ נָא וּדְעוּ וּבַקְשׁוּ בִרְחוֹבוֹתֶיהָ אִם תִּמְצְאוּ אִישׁ אִם יֵשׁ עֹשֶׂה מִשְׁפָּט מְבַקֵּשׁ אֱמוּנָה וְאֶסְלַח לָהּ״! לָא קַשְׁיָא:

The Gemara raises another difficulty: **Is that so? But didn't Rava say: Jerusalem was not destroyed until trustworthy men ceased to exist in it, as it is stated: "Run to and fro through the streets of Jerusalem, and see now and know, and seek in its broad places, if you can find a man, if there is any that acts justly, that seeks truth, and I will pardon her"** (Jeremiah 5:1), implying there were no trustworthy people at that time? The Gemara answers: This is **not difficult:**

NOTES

And his mind was not calmed – וְלֹא נִתְקָרְרָה דַּעְתּוֹ: How is it possible that the prophet was not appeased until he had cursed Israel with such a terrible curse? One answer is that the prophet was in fact upset about having to relate all these curses and objected to doing so, until he was informed that in that generation "the child shall behave insolently against the aged, etc." This calmed him, for he now understood the justification for all these severe punishments (*Petaḥ Einayim*).

I will not be a healer – לֹא אֶהְיֶה חוֹבֵשׁ: Rashi explains that the future tense in this context, as is often the case, should be understood as the present continuous, so that: I will not be, should be understood as: I am not used to being, or: I do not deal with such matters.

הָא – בְּדִבְרֵי תוֹרָה, הָא – בְּמַשָּׂא וּמַתָּן. בְּדִבְרֵי תוֹרָה – הָווּ, בְּמַשָּׂא וּמַתָּן – לָא הָווּ.

This case is referring **to words of Torah,** while **that** case is referring **to commerce. With regard to words of Torah, they were** trustworthy; **with regard to commerce, they were not.**

תָּנוּ רַבָּנַן: מַעֲשֶׂה בְּרַבָּן יוֹחָנָן בֶּן זַכַּאי שֶׁהָיָה רוֹכֵב עַל הַחֲמוֹר, וְהָיָה מְהַלֵּךְ בַּדֶּרֶךְ, וְרַבִּי אֶלְעָזָר בֶּן עֲרָךְ מְחַמֵּר אַחֲרָיו. אָמַר לוֹ: רַבִּי! שְׁנֵה לִי פֶּרֶק אֶחָד בְּמַעֲשֵׂה מֶרְכָּבָה! אָמַר לוֹ: לֹא כָּךְ שָׁנִיתִי לָכֶם: וְלֹא בַּמֶּרְכָּבָה בְּיָחִיד אֶלָּא אִם כֵּן הָיָה חָכָם מֵבִין מִדַּעְתּוֹ? אָמַר לוֹ: רַבִּי, תַּרְשֵׁינִי לוֹמַר לְפָנֶיךָ דָּבָר אֶחָד שֶׁלִּמַּדְתַּנִי. אָמַר לוֹ: אֱמוֹר.

§ The Gemara returns to the topic of the Design of the Divine Chariot. **The Sages taught: An incident** occurred **involving Rabban Yoḥanan ben Zakkai,**[P] **who was riding on a donkey and was traveling along the way, and** his student, **Rabbi Elazar ben Arakh,**[P] **was riding a donkey behind him.** Rabbi Elazar **said to him: My teacher, teach me one chapter in the Design of the** Divine **Chariot. He said to him:** Have **I not taught you: And one may not** expound the Design of the Divine Chariot **to an individual, unless he is a Sage who understands on his own accord?** Rabbi Elazar **said to him: My teacher, allow me to say before you one thing that you taught me.** In other words, he humbly requested to recite before him his own understanding of this issue. **He said to him: Speak.**

מִיָּד יָרַד רַבָּן יוֹחָנָן בֶּן זַכַּאי מֵעַל הַחֲמוֹר, וְנִתְעַטֵּף וְיָשַׁב עַל הָאֶבֶן תַּחַת הַזַּיִת. אָמַר לוֹ: רַבִּי, מִפְּנֵי מָה יָרַדְתָּ מֵעַל הַחֲמוֹר? אָמַר: אֶפְשָׁר אַתָּה דּוֹרֵשׁ בְּמַעֲשֵׂה מֶרְכָּבָה, וּשְׁכִינָה עִמָּנוּ, וּמַלְאֲכֵי הַשָּׁרֵת מְלַוִּין אוֹתָנוּ, וַאֲנִי אֶרְכַּב עַל הַחֲמוֹר?! מִיָּד פָּתַח רַבִּי אֶלְעָזָר בֶּן עֲרָךְ בְּמַעֲשֵׂה הַמֶּרְכָּבָה וְדָרַשׁ, וְיָרְדָה אֵשׁ מִן הַשָּׁמַיִם וְסִיבְּבָה כָּל הָאִילָנוֹת שֶׁבַּשָּׂדֶה, פָּתְחוּ כּוּלָּן וְאָמְרוּ שִׁירָה.

Immediately, Rabban Yoḥanan ben Zakkai alighted from the donkey, and wrapped his head in his cloak in a manner of reverence, **and sat on a stone under an olive tree.** Rabbi Elazar **said to him: My teacher, for what reason did you alight from the donkey? He said:** Is it **possible that** while **you are expounding the Design of the** Divine **Chariot, and the Divine Presence is with us, and the ministering angels are accompanying us, that I should ride on a donkey? Immediately, Rabbi Elazar ben Arakh began** to discuss **the Design of the** Divine **Chariot and expounded, and fire descended from heaven and encircled all the trees in the field, and all** the trees **began reciting song.**

מַה שִּׁירָה אָמְרוּ? ״הַלְלוּ אֶת ה׳ מִן הָאָרֶץ תַּנִּינִים וְכָל תְּהוֹמוֹת...עֵץ פְּרִי וְכָל אֲרָזִים... הַלְלוּיָהּ״. נַעֲנָה מַלְאָךְ מִן הָאֵשׁ וְאָמַר: הֵן הֵן מַעֲשֵׂה הַמֶּרְכָּבָה. עָמַד רַבָּן יוֹחָנָן בֶּן זַכַּאי, וּנְשָׁקוֹ עַל רֹאשׁוֹ, וְאָמַר: בָּרוּךְ ה׳ אֱלֹהֵי יִשְׂרָאֵל שֶׁנָּתַן בֵּן לְאַבְרָהָם אָבִינוּ שֶׁיּוֹדֵעַ לְהָבִין וְלַחְקוֹר וְלִדְרוֹשׁ בְּמַעֲשֵׂה מֶרְכָּבָה. יֵשׁ נָאֶה דּוֹרֵשׁ וְאֵין נָאֶה מְקַיֵּים, נָאֶה מְקַיֵּים וְאֵין נָאֶה דּוֹרֵשׁ, אַתָּה נָאֶה דּוֹרֵשׁ וְנָאֶה מְקַיֵּים. אַשְׁרֶיךָ אַבְרָהָם אָבִינוּ שֶׁאֶלְעָזָר בֶּן עֲרָךְ יָצָא מֵחֲלָצֶיךָ.

What song did they recite? "Praise the Lord from the earth, sea monsters and all depths... fruit trees and all cedars... praise the Lord" (Psalms 148:7–14). **An angel responded from the fire, saying: This is the very Design of the** Divine **Chariot,** just as you expounded. **Rabban Yoḥanan ben Zakkai stood and kissed** Rabbi Elazar ben Arakh **on his head, and said: Blessed be God, Lord of Israel, who gave our father Abraham a son** like you, **who knows** how to **understand, investigate, and expound the Design of the** Divine **Chariot.** There **are some who expound** the Torah's verses **well but do not fulfill** its imperatives **well,** and there are some **who fulfill** its imperatives **well but do not expound** its verses **well,** whereas **you expound** its verses **well and fulfill** its imperatives **well. Happy are you, our father Abraham, that Elazar ben Arakh came from your loins.**

PERSONALITIES

Rabban Yoḥanan ben Zakkai – רַבָּן יוֹחָנָן בֶּן זַכַּאי: Rabban Yoḥanan ben Zakkai headed the Sanhedrin after the destruction of the Second Temple. He was one of the greatest leaders of the Jewish people in all of its history.

Rabban Yoḥanan ben Zakkai was the youngest of Hillel the Elder's students. He lived to an advanced age and acted as the leader of the Jewish people for many years. It was said of him that there was not a single area of Torah that he neglected. His greatness notwithstanding, he was a modest individual who greeted every person he met, even gentiles in the marketplace.

Already when the Temple stood, he was acknowledged as a leading scholar, and most of the third generation of *amora'im* in Eretz Yisrael were his students. When the Great Revolt broke out, Rabban Yoḥanan took a strong stance against it, attempting to bring it to a peaceful close. As a leading resident of the besieged Jerusalem, he realized that the city would soon fall, and he succeeded in escaping with a number of his students. Appearing before Vespasian, he was warmly received, and when his prophecy that Vespasian would be appointed emperor was fulfilled, Vespasian rewarded him by allowing him to establish a new center of Jewish Torah study and leadership in Yavne. Rabban Yoḥanan ben Zakkai took this opportunity to save the life of Rabban Gamliel as well.

In Yavne, Rabban Yoḥanan succeeded in instituting a wide range of regulations that served to memorialize the Temple and promised the possibility of its ultimate rebuilding, which offered hope for Jewish continuity in the absence of the Temple. His success in this endeavor is felt to this day in religious practice.

His students taught Torah throughout the Eretz Yisrael following the destruction of the Temple. Rabban Yoḥanan served as a mentor for Rabban Gamliel of Yavne, who followed him in the capacity of *Nasi*.

Rabbi Elazar ben Arakh – רַבִּי אֶלְעָזָר בֶּן עֲרָךְ: Rabbi Elazar ben Arakh was one of the greatest students of Rabban Yoḥanan ben Zakkai, who called him an ever-increasing wellspring because of his creative powers. According to one tradition, his rabbi even compared his greatness to that of all the rest of Israel combined, preferring his opinion to that of his colleagues with regard to several issues. The Talmud relates that Rabbi Elazar ben Arakh relocated to Emmaus, a place without scholars, hoping that the Sages of the generation would follow him there to learn from him. However, the scholars stayed in Yavne, and Rabbi Elazar ben Arakh, who remained alone, neglected his studies until he forgot all that he had learned. One tradition maintains that the Sages prayed for his learning to be restored to him. From then on, he became known as Rabbi Nehorai, meaning, the one who enlightens. In any case, only a few statements of *halakha* and *aggada* are attributed to him in talmudic literature.

LANGUAGE

Halls [*teraklin*] – טְרַקְלִין: From the Greek τρικλίνιον, *triklinyon*, a chamber in which couches were laid out and guests dined on them.

וּכְשֶׁנֶּאֶמְרוּ הַדְּבָרִים לִפְנֵי רַבִּי יְהוֹשֻׁעַ הָיָה הוּא וְרַבִּי יוֹסֵי הַכֹּהֵן מְהַלְּכִים בַּדֶּרֶךְ. אָמְרוּ: אַף אָנוּ נִדְרוֹשׁ בְּמַעֲשֵׂה מֶרְכָּבָה. פָּתַח רַבִּי יְהוֹשֻׁעַ וְדָרַשׁ. וְאוֹתוֹ הַיּוֹם תְּקוּפַת תַּמּוּז הָיָה, נִתְקַשְּׁרוּ שָׁמַיִם בְּעָבִים וְנִרְאָה כְּמִין קֶשֶׁת בֶּעָנָן, וְהָיוּ מַלְאֲכֵי הַשָּׁרֵת מִתְקַבְּצִין וּבָאִין לִשְׁמוֹעַ, כִּבְנֵי אָדָם שֶׁמִּתְקַבְּצִין וּבָאִין לִרְאוֹת בְּמַזְמוּטֵי חָתָן וְכַלָּה.

The Gemara relates: **And when** these **matters,** this story involving his colleague Rabbi Elazar ben Arakh, **were recounted before Rabbi Yehoshua, he was walking along the way with Rabbi Yosei the Priest. They said: We too shall expound the Design of the** Divine **Chariot. Rabbi Yehoshua began expounding. And that was the day of the summer solstice,** when there are no clouds in the sky. Yet the **heavens became filled with clouds, and there was the appearance of a kind of rainbow in a cloud. And ministering angels gathered and came to listen, like people gathering and coming to see the rejoicing of a bridegroom and bride.**

הָלַךְ רַבִּי יוֹסֵי הַכֹּהֵן וְסִיפֵּר דְּבָרִים לִפְנֵי רַבָּן יוֹחָנָן בֶּן זַכַּאי, וְאָמַר: אַשְׁרֵיכֶם וְאַשְׁרֵי יוֹלַדְתְּכֶם, אַשְׁרֵי עֵינַי שֶׁכָּךְ רָאוּ. וְאַף אֲנִי וְאַתֶּם בַּחֲלוֹמִי מְסוּבִּין הָיִינוּ עַל הַר סִינַי, וְנִתְּנָה עָלֵינוּ בַּת קוֹל מִן הַשָּׁמַיִם: עֲלוּ לְכָאן, עֲלוּ לְכָאן! טְרַקְלִין גְּדוֹלִים וּמַצָּעוֹת נָאוֹת מוּצָּעוֹת לָכֶם. אַתֶּם וְתַלְמִידֵיכֶם וְתַלְמִידֵי תַלְמִידֵיכֶם מְזוּמָּנִין לַכַּת שְׁלִישִׁית.

Rabbi Yosei the Priest went and recited these **matters before Rabban Yoḥanan ben Zakkai,** who **said** to him: **Happy are** all **of you, and happy are** the mothers **who gave birth to you;**[N] **happy are my eyes that saw this,** students such as these. **As for you and I,** I saw **in my dream** that **we were seated at Mount Sinai,**[N] **and a Divine Voice came to us from heaven: Ascend here, ascend here,** for **large halls** [*teraklin*][L] **and pleasant couches are made up for you. You, your students, and the students of your students are invited to the third group,**[N] those who will merit to welcome the Divine Presence.

אִינִי? וְהָתַנְיָא, רַבִּי יוֹסֵי בְּרַבִּי יְהוּדָה אוֹמֵר: שְׁלֹשָׁה הַרְצָאוֹת הֵן: רַבִּי יְהוֹשֻׁעַ הִרְצָה דְּבָרִים לִפְנֵי רַבָּן יוֹחָנָן בֶּן זַכַּאי, רַבִּי עֲקִיבָא הִרְצָה לִפְנֵי רַבִּי יְהוֹשֻׁעַ, חֲנַנְיָא בֶּן חֲכִינַאי הִרְצָה לִפְנֵי רַבִּי עֲקִיבָא. וְאִילּוּ רַבִּי אֶלְעָזָר בֶּן עֲרָךְ לָא קָא חָשֵׁיב? דְּאַרְצִי וְאַרְצוּ קַמֵּיהּ – קָחָשֵׁיב; דְּאַרְצִי וְלָא אַרְצוּ קַמֵּיהּ – לָא קָא חָשֵׁיב. וְהָא חֲנַנְיָא בֶּן חֲכִינַאי דְּלָא אַרְצוּ קַמֵּיהּ וְקָא חָשֵׁיב! דְּאַרְצִי מִיהָא קַמֵּיהּ מַאן דְּאַרְצִי.

The Gemara poses a question: **Is that so? But isn't it taught** in a *baraita*: **Rabbi Yosei, son of Rabbi Yehuda, says: There are three lectures.**[N] In other words, there are three Sages with regard to whom it states that they delivered lectures on the mystical tradition: **Rabbi Yehoshua lectured** on these **matters before Rabban Yoḥanan ben Zakkai; Rabbi Akiva lectured before Rabbi Yehoshua;** and **Ḥananya ben Ḥakhinai lectured before Rabbi Akiva. However, Rabbi Elazar ben Arakh was not included** in the list, despite the testimony that he lectured before Rabban Yoḥanan. The Gemara explains: Those **who lectured and were** also **lectured to were included;** but those **who lectured and were not lectured to were not included.** The Gemara asks: **But wasn't there Ḥananya ben Ḥakhinai, who was not lectured to, and yet he is included?** The Gemara answers: Ḥananya ben Ḥakhinai **actually lectured**[N] **before one who lectured** in front of his own rabbi, so he was also included in this list.

NOTES

Happy are all of you and happy are the mothers who gave birth to you – אַשְׁרֵיכֶם וְאַשְׁרֵי יוֹלַדְתְּכֶם: It has been noted that this expression resembles the words of praise uttered by Rabban Yoḥanan ben Zakkai with regard to his student Rabbi Yehoshua: Happy is she who gave birth to him (*Avot* 2:8).

We were seated at Mount Sinai – מְסוּבִּין הָיִינוּ עַל הַר סִינַי: This alludes to the idea that any innovation that will one day be uttered by a learned student has already been taught to Moses at Sinai. Rabban Yoḥanan's vision of his students dining there therefore attests to the fact that their words of Torah are true and that they originated at Sinai (Maharsha).

Third group – כַּת שְׁלִישִׁית: The Maharsha writes that this statement is perhaps connected to the three groups mentioned in the expression: You, and your students, and the students of your students. However, in the Jerusalem Talmud it is explicitly stated that this expression is related to the tradition that seven groups will merit welcoming the Divine Presence. *Midrash Rabba* explains that there is a celestial body that corresponds to each of these groups. The third group corresponds to the firmament, in accordance with the verse (Daniel 12:3): "And they that are wise shall shine [*yazhiru*] as the brightness of the firmament." The Introduction to the *Zohar* states that the name *Zohar* is derived from this verse.

There are three lectures – שְׁלֹשָׁה הַרְצָאוֹת: It is stated in the Jerusalem Talmud that from that day forward, the minds of these three scholars were no longer clear, and that they no longer merited the opportunity expound the Design of the Divine Chariot.

Actually lectured – דְּאַרְצִי מִיהָא: It appears that these three lectures are presented as a kind of tradition transmitted from one generation to another, and therefore Rabbi Elazar ben Arakh is excluded, as no one lectured before him (see *Tosafot*).

תָּנוּ רַבָּנַן: אַרְבָּעָה נִכְנְסוּ בַּפַּרְדֵּס, וְאֵלּוּ הֵן: בֶּן עַזַּאי, וּבֶן זוֹמָא, אַחֵר, וְרַבִּי עֲקִיבָא. אָמַר לָהֶם רַבִּי עֲקִיבָא: כְּשֶׁאַתֶּם מַגִּיעִין אֵצֶל אַבְנֵי שַׁיִשׁ טָהוֹר אַל תֹּאמְרוּ ״מַיִם מַיִם״! מִשּׁוּם שֶׁנֶּאֱמַר: ״דּוֹבֵר שְׁקָרִים לֹא יִכּוֹן לְנֶגֶד עֵינָי״.

§ **The Sages taught: Four entered the orchard**[N] [*pardes*],[L] i.e., dealt with the loftiest secrets of Torah, **and they are as follows: Ben Azzai; and ben Zoma;**[P] ***Aḥer*,**[L] the other, a name for Elisha ben Avuya;[P] **and Rabbi Akiva. Rabbi Akiva,** the senior among them, **said to them: When,** upon your arrival in the upper worlds, **you reach pure marble stones, do not say: Water, water,** although they appear to be water, **because it is stated: "He who speaks falsehood shall not be established before My eyes"** (Psalms 101:7).

בֶּן עַזַּאי הֵצִיץ וָמֵת, עָלָיו הַכָּתוּב אוֹמֵר: ״יָקָר בְּעֵינֵי ה׳ הַמָּוְתָה לַחֲסִידָיו״. בֶּן זוֹמָא הֵצִיץ וְנִפְגַּע, וְעָלָיו הַכָּתוּב אוֹמֵר: ״דְּבַשׁ מָצָאתָ אֱכוֹל דַּיֶּךָּ פֶּן תִּשְׂבָּעֶנּוּ וַהֲקֵאתוֹ״. אַחֵר קִיצֵּץ בִּנְטִיעוֹת. רַבִּי עֲקִיבָא יָצָא בְּשָׁלוֹם.

The Gemara proceeds to relate what happened to each of them: **Ben Azzai glimpsed** at the Divine Presence **and died. And with regard to him the verse states: "Precious in the eyes of the Lord is the death of His pious ones"** (Psalms 116:15). **Ben Zoma glimpsed** at the Divine Presence **and was harmed,** i.e., he lost his mind. **And with regard to him the verse states: "Have you found honey? Eat as much as is sufficient for you, lest you become full from it and vomit it"** (Proverbs 25:16). ***Aḥer* chopped down the shoots** of saplings. In other words, he became a heretic. **Rabbi Akiva came out safely.**

שָׁאֲלוּ אֶת בֶּן זוֹמָא: מַהוּ לְסָרוּסֵי כַּלְבָּא? אָמַר לָהֶם: ״וּבְאַרְצְכֶם לֹא תַעֲשׂוּ״ – כֹּל שֶׁבְּאַרְצְכֶם לֹא תַעֲשׂוּ. שָׁאֲלוּ אֶת בֶּן זוֹמָא: בְּתוּלָה שֶׁעִיבְּרָה מַהוּ לְכֹהֵן גָּדוֹל? מִי חָיְישִׁינַן לְדִשְׁמוּאֵל, דְּאָמַר שְׁמוּאֵל:

The Gemara recounts the greatness of ben Zoma, who was an expert interpreter of the Torah and could find obscure proofs: **They asked ben Zoma: What is** the *halakha* with regard to **castrating a dog?**[N] The prohibition against castration appears alongside the sacrificial blemishes, which may imply that it is permitted to castrate an animal that cannot be sacrificed as an offering. **He said to them:** The verse states "That which has its testicles bruised, or crushed, or torn, or cut, you shall not offer to God, nor **shall you do so in your land"** (Leviticus 22:24), from which we learn: With regard to **any** animal **that is in your land, you shall not do** such a thing.[H] **They** also **asked ben Zoma:** A woman considered **to be a virgin who became pregnant,**[N] **what** is the *halakha*? **A High Priest** may marry only a virgin; is he permitted to marry her? The answer depends on the following: **Are we concerned for** the opinion of **Shmuel? Shmuel says:**

PERSONALITIES

Ben Zoma – בֶּן זוֹמָא: Shimon ben Zoma, one of the greatest scholars of the generation of the destruction of the Temple, was a student of Rabbi Yehoshua. Despite being considered one of the foremost Sages of his time, Shimon ben Zoma was not ordained, perhaps due to his youth, and therefore he was not called Rabbi. He was sometimes known only by his father's name. A considerable number of legal and aggadic sayings are cited in his name, and he was especially renowned for his expositions of the Bible, so much so that it was said: After ben Zoma died, the expositors ceased.

Elisha, *Aḥer* – אֱלִישָׁע, אַחֵר: Elisha ben Avuya was born in Jerusalem toward the end of the Second Temple period. His family was one of the most prominent and wealthy in the city, but, as related by the Jerusalem Talmud, it was under the sway of foreign cultures and did not maintain deep ties with Judaism. Unique circumstances lead to Elisha receiving an extensive Jewish education, and his great talents earned him a place among the chief scholars of the day. Nevertheless, even when he was a member of the academy, Elisha continued to maintain ties with Greek culture in its various manifestations and took an interest in and read heretical works.

In addition to the story reported here, the Talmud offers other accounts of how severe emotional traumas, perhaps connected to the Hadrianic persecutions, caused Elisha to leave Judaism entirely. Certain sources suggest that not only did he transgress the mitzvot, but that he even collaborated with the Romans against his Jewish brethren. Many acts of cruelty are ascribed to him.

This explains the enmity directed at him as early as during the time of Rabbi Yehuda HaNasi. In his own generation, Rabbi Meir was apparently the only person to maintain personal ties with the renegade. He even continued to study Torah from Elisha, which was controversial at the time.

In talmudic sources, the feeling of regret and pain that such a great scholar turned into a heretic appears to have been more lasting than the immediate feelings of antagonism toward him. It is also implied that *Aḥer* remained miserable even during his rebellion but could not find the courage to repent after having acted so wickedly. It is due to this remorse that his teachings are preserved. A proverb of his can be found in *Pirkei Avot* (4:20), while *Avot DeRabbi Natan* features an entire chapter of his Torah teachings. According to the version of the Gemara here, the *tanna* Rabbi Ya'akov was the son of the daughter of *Aḥer*, who is discussed later (15b).

NOTES

Four entered the orchard – אַרְבָּעָה נִכְנְסוּ בַּפַּרְדֵּס: Entering the orchard, i.e., delving into the deepest secrets of Torah knowledge, does not leave anyone unaffected. Ben Azzai's death and ben Zoma's insanity are not presented as punishments but as the natural consequences of their investigation. Ben Azzai, whose soul yearned for the purity of Torah knowledge, subjugated his physical self to the extent that his spirit cleaved to the Almighty, destroying his physical being. Ben Zoma, who desired to investigate areas of wisdom that were beyond his comprehension, suffered a loss of intellectual function. *Aḥer* was overwhelmed by his experience and lost the ability to distinguish between the Creator and His creations, meaning that he confused Mitatron, who was God's angel, with the Creator Himself. This heresy is described by the Gemara as separating the root from the sapling. Only Rabbi Akiva, who was able to understand the depths of the Torah, survived unscathed (*Midrash Shlomo*).

Castrating a dog – לְסָרוּסֵי כַּלְבָּא: Rashi and *Tosafot* ask why this question was asked specifically concerning a dog, rather than any animal unfit for an offering. They answer that because the law of castration is mentioned in the context of animals that are disqualified as offerings, one may have thought that the law does not apply to dogs, which are completely distanced from offerings by the prohibition against using the price paid for a dog to purchase an offering (Deuteronomy 23:19). The *Zohar* says that ben Zoma answered that despite the Torah's view of dogs as despised animals, even these animals have a right to exist in the world. Consequently, it is prohibited to interfere with their procreation.

Virgin who became pregnant – בְּתוּלָה שֶׁעִיבְּרָה: High Priests are permitted to marry only virgins (Leviticus 21:13). The question being discussed here is whether the woman's pregnancy proves that she is not a virgin. The early and later authorities discuss whether the Gemara is referring to a woman who only claims to be a virgin or to a female who was examined and found to be one (see *Turei Aven* and *Sefat Emet*).

LANGUAGE

Orchard [*pardes*] – פַּרְדֵּס: This word appears in the Bible as well (e.g., Song of Songs 4:13). It probably comes from an ancient Persian word meaning a fenced-off place or garden. Different forms of this word are featured in many other languages. In the Septuagint, παραδεισον, *pardisyon*, is used as the translation of Garden of Eden. Here, in the context of the four who entered the *pardes*, the word also alludes to a celestial garden.

***Aḥer* – אַחֵר:** *Aḥer* can be understood literally as: A different person, one who was unknown beforehand. However, the word apparently included a negative connotation as well, similar to the use of the term *Aḥerim*, literally, others, in rabbinic literature as a reference to gentiles. It is also possible that it is related to the verb *aḥar*, which means: In heat, enslaved to his lusts.

HALAKHA

The prohibition against castration – אִיסּוּר סֵירוּס: It is prohibited to destroy the sexual organs of humans and animals, including beast and fowl. *Pitḥei Teshuva* includes fish as well. The prohibition applies to both ritually pure and impure animals in both Eretz Yisrael and the Diaspora. One who castrates any of these species is liable to receive lashes. It is also prohibited to castrate female species, but if one does so he is exempt from lashes (*Shulḥan Arukh*, *Even HaEzer* 5:11).

BACKGROUND

Conceived in a bath – בְּאַמְבַּטִי עִיבְּרָה: Even in regular pregnancies, isolated spermatozoa rarely reach the womb and fertilize the female. Semen from sexual relations is ejaculated with force and lands closer to the womb, thereby increasing the chances of pregnancy. The spermatozoa of healthy semen can travel a considerable distance in the womb when ejaculated with force. The odds that a woman will become impregnated as a result of the chance infiltration of a sperm cell into her womb are of course extremely slight, but it is nevertheless possible.

LANGUAGE

Bath [*ambati*] – אַמְבַּטִי: From the Greek ἐμβατή, *embatè*, meaning a tub or other washing vessel.

יָכוֹל אֲנִי לִבְעוֹל כַּמָּה בְּעִילוֹת בְּלֹא דָּם, אוֹ דִּלְמָא דִּשְׁמוּאֵל לָא שְׁכִיחָא? אֲמַר לְהוּ: דִּשְׁמוּאֵל לָא שְׁכִיחַ, וְחָיְישִׁינַן שֶׁמָּא בְּאַמְבַּטִי עִיבְּרָה.

I can engage in intercourse several times without blood. In other words, I can have relations with a woman while leaving her hymen intact. If this is so, it is possible that the assumed virgin had intercourse in this manner and is forbidden to the High Priest. **Or, perhaps** a person who can act like **Shmuel is not common** and the *halakha* is not concerned with this case. **He said to them:** One like **Shmuel is not common, and we are concerned that she may have conceived in a bath.**[NBL] Perhaps she washed in a bath that contained a man's semen, from which she became impregnated while remaining a virgin.

וְהָאָמַר שְׁמוּאֵל: כׇּל שִׁכְבַת זֶרַע שֶׁאֵינוֹ יוֹרֶה כַּחֵץ אֵינוֹ מַזְרַעַת! מֵעִיקָּרָא נָמֵי יוֹרֶה כַּחֵץ הֲוָה.

The Gemara asks: How could she possibly become pregnant in such a manner? **Didn't Shmuel say: Any semen that is not shot like an arrow cannot fertilize?** The Gemara answers: This does not mean that it must be shot like an arrow at the moment of fertilization. Even if **initially,** when released from the male, **it was shot as an arrow,** it can **also** fertilize a woman at a later moment.

תָּנוּ רַבָּנַן: מַעֲשֶׂה בְּרַבִּי יְהוֹשֻׁעַ בֶּן חֲנַנְיָה שֶׁהָיָה עוֹמֵד עַל גַּב מַעֲלָה בְּהַר הַבַּיִת, וְרָאָהוּ בֶּן זוֹמָא וְלֹא עָמַד מִלְּפָנָיו. אָמַר לוֹ: מֵאַיִן וּלְאַיִן בֶּן זוֹמָא? אָמַר לוֹ: צוֹפֶה הָיִיתִי בֵּין מַיִם הָעֶלְיוֹנִים לַמַּיִם הַתַּחְתּוֹנִים, וְאֵין בֵּין זֶה לָזֶה אֶלָּא שָׁלֹשׁ אֶצְבָּעוֹת בִּלְבַד, שֶׁנֶּאֱמַר: ״וְרוּחַ אֱלֹהִים מְרַחֶפֶת עַל פְּנֵי הַמָּיִם״ – כְּיוֹנָה שֶׁמְּרַחֶפֶת עַל בָּנֶיהָ וְאֵינָהּ נוֹגַעַת. אָמַר לָהֶן רַבִּי יְהוֹשֻׁעַ לְתַלְמִידָיו: עֲדַיִין בֶּן זוֹמָא מִבַּחוּץ.

With regard to the fate of ben Zoma, **the Sages taught: There was once an incident with regard to Rabbi Yehoshua ben Ḥananya, who was standing on a step on the Temple Mount, and ben Zoma saw him and did not stand before him** to honor him, as he was deep in thought. Rabbi Yehoshua **said to him: From where** do you come **and where are you going, ben Zoma,** i.e., what is on your mind? **He said to him:** In my thoughts **I was looking upon** the act of Creation, at the gap **between the upper waters and the lower waters,**[N] **as there is only** the breadth of **a mere three fingers**[N] **between them, as it is stated: "And the spirit of God hovered over the face of the waters"** (Genesis 1:2), **like a dove hovering over its young without touching** them. **Rabbi Yehoshua said to his students** who had overheard this exchange: **Ben Zoma is still outside;**[N] he has not yet achieved full understanding of these matters.

מִכְּדִי ״וְרוּחַ אֱלֹהִים מְרַחֶפֶת עַל פְּנֵי הַמָּיִם״ אֵימַת הֲוַי? בְּיוֹם רִאשׁוֹן, הַבְדָּלָה – בְּיוֹם שֵׁנִי הוּא דַּהֲוַאי, דִּכְתִיב: ״וִיהִי מַבְדִּיל בֵּין מַיִם לָמָיִם״. וְכַמָּה? אָמַר רַב אַחָא בַּר יַעֲקֹב: כִּמְלֹא נִימָא. וְרַבָּנַן אָמְרִי: כִּי גּוּדָא דִּגְמַלָּא. מָר זוּטְרָא וְאִיתֵּימָא רַב אַסִּי אָמַר: כִּתְרֵי גְּלִימֵי דִּפְרִיסִי אַהֲדָדֵי, וְאָמְרִי לַהּ: כִּתְרֵי כָּסֵי דִּסְחִיפִי אַהֲדָדֵי.

The Gemara explains: **Now, this verse: "And the spirit of God hovered over the face of the waters," when was** it stated? **On the first day,** whereas **the division** of the waters **occurred on the second day, as it is written: "And let it divide the waters from the waters"** (Genesis 1:6). How, then, could ben Zoma derive a proof from the former verse? The Gemara asks: **And how much,** in fact, is the gap between them? **Rav Aḥa bar Ya'akov said: Like the thickness of a thread; and the Rabbis said: Like** the gap between **the boards of a bridge. Mar Zutra, and some say** it was **Rav Asi, said: Like two robes spread one over the other,** with a slight gap in between. **And some said: Like two cups placed one upon the other.**

NOTES

She may have conceived in a bath – שֶׁמָּא בְּאַמְבַּטִי עִיבְּרָה: The Gemara's statement here is a key source for the contemporary legal debate with regard to human artificial insemination and the legal status of a child born from such a procedure. Several early authorities discuss this issue in theory (see *Tosafot* and Rosh on *Gittin* 19a), and it is likewise addressed by several later authorities (see *Turei Aven*). Nowadays, the question has resurfaced as a practical concern. Various arguments have been put forward, with some scholars permitting artificial insemination in all cases and others issuing blanket prohibitions, as well as a range of opinions between the two extremes.

The upper waters and lower waters – מַיִם הָעֶלְיוֹנִים לַמַּיִם הַתַּחְתּוֹנִים: Much has been written with regard to this statement. Rashi explains that it refers to the difference between the dome of the firmament and the earth, while the Rambam maintains that it means the distance between the firmaments and the various spheres. The *Otzar HaKavod* writes that the upper and lower waters are spiritual terms that correspond to the source of ethereal and earthly entities. According to this explanation, Rabbi Yehoshua's claim is that on the first day, there was no difference between these entities; they all constituted a single creation. Others explain that according to ben Zoma, the description in Genesis follows the order of Creation, whereas Rabbi Yehoshua is of the opinion that certain things mentioned in Genesis as having been created on the first day did not come into being until a later stage.

Three fingers – שָׁלֹשׁ אֶצְבָּעוֹת: The *Turei Aven* writes that this breadth is equivalent to the distance of a dove from its young when it hovers above them. They add that there is no special scriptural source for this particular measurement.

Ben Zoma is still outside – עֲדַיִין בֶּן זוֹמָא מִבַּחוּץ: This means that ben Zoma had yet to achieve a full understanding of secret matters. An alternate version of the text reads: Ben Zoma is already outside, reflecting Rabbi Yehoshua's recognition that his mind was occupied with matters that would lead to his impending demise.

אַחֵר קִיצֵּץ בִּנְטִיעוֹת. עָלָיו הַכָּתוּב אוֹמֵר: "אַל תִּתֵּן אֶת פִּיךָ לַחֲטִיא אֶת בְּשָׂרֶךָ". מַאי הִיא? חֲזָא מִיטַטְרוֹן דְּאִתְיְהֲבָא לֵיהּ רְשׁוּתָא לְמֵיתַב לְמִיכְתַּב זַכְוָותָא דְּיִשְׂרָאֵל. אֲמַר: גְּמִירָא דִּלְמַעְלָה לָא הָוֵי לֹא יְשִׁיבָה וְלֹא תַּחֲרוּת וְלֹא עוֹרֶף וְלֹא עִיפּוּי. שֶׁמָּא חַס וְשָׁלוֹם שְׁתֵּי רָשׁוּיוֹת הֵן.

§ The Gemara stated earlier that *Aḥer* **chopped down the saplings,** becoming a heretic. **With regard to him, the verse states: "Do not let your mouth bring your flesh into guilt"** (Ecclesiastes 5:5). The Gemara poses a question: **What was** it that led him to heresy? **He saw** the angel **Mitatron,**[NL] **who was granted permission to sit and write the merits of Israel. He said:** There is a **tradition** that in the world **above there is no sitting; no competition; no** turning one's **back before Him,** i.e., all face the Divine Presence; **and no lethargy.** Seeing that someone other than God was seated above, **he said: Perhaps,** the Gemara here interjects, **Heaven forbid, there are two authorities,** and there is another source of power in control of the world in addition to God. Such thoughts led *Aḥer* to heresy.

אַפְּקוּהוּ לְמִיטַטְרוֹן וּמַחְיוּהוּ שִׁיתִּין פּוּלְסֵי דְּנוּרָא. אָמְרוּ לֵיהּ: מַאי טַעְמָא כִּי חֲזִיתֵיהּ לָא קַמְתְּ מִקַּמֵּיהּ? אִיתְיְהִיבָא לֵיהּ רְשׁוּתָא לְמִימְחַק זַכְוָותָא דְּאַחֵר. יָצְתָה בַּת קוֹל וְאָמְרָה: "שׁוּבוּ בָּנִים שׁוֹבָבִים" חוּץ מֵאַחֵר.

The Gemara relates: **They removed Mitatron** from his place in heaven **and smote him**[N] **with sixty rods** [*pulsei*][L] **of fire,** so that others would not make mistake that *Aḥer* made. **They said** to the angel: **What is the reason** that **when you saw** Elisha ben Avuya **you did not stand before him?** Despite this conduct, since Mitatron was personally involved, he **was granted permission to erase the merits of** *Aḥer* and cause him to stumble in any manner. **A Divine Voice went forth saying: "Return, rebellious children"** (Jeremiah 3:22), **apart from** *Aḥer*.[N]

אֲמַר: הוֹאִיל וְאִיטְרִיד הַהוּא גַּבְרָא מֵהַהוּא עָלְמָא לֵיפּוּק לִיתְהַנֵּי בְּהַאי עָלְמָא. נְפַק אַחֵר לְתַרְבּוּת רָעָה. נְפַק אֶשְׁכַּח זוֹנָה, תְּבָעָהּ. אֲמַרָה לֵיהּ: וְלָאו אֱלִישָׁע בֶּן אֲבוּיָה אַתְּ? עָקַר פּוּגְלָא מִמֵּישְׁרָא בְּשַׁבָּת וִיהַב לָהּ. אָמְרָה: אַחֵר הוּא.

Upon hearing this, Elisha ben Avuya **said: Since that man,** meaning himself, **has been banished from that world, let him go out and enjoy this world.** *Aḥer* **went astray. He went** and **found a prostitute** and **solicited her** for intercourse. **She said to him: And** are **you not Elisha ben Avuya?** Shall a person of your stature perform such an act? **He uprooted a radish from a patch** of radishes **on Shabbat and gave it to her,** to demonstrate that he no longer observed the Torah. The prostitute **said: He is other** than he was. He is not the same Elisha ben Avuya, he is *Aḥer*, other.

שָׁאַל אַחֵר אֶת רַבִּי מֵאִיר לְאַחַר שֶׁיָּצָא לְתַרְבּוּת רָעָה, אֲמַר לֵיהּ: מַאי דִּכְתִיב: "גַּם אֶת זֶה לְעוּמַּת זֶה עָשָׂה הָאֱלֹהִים"? אָמַר לוֹ: כׇּל מַה שֶּׁבָּרָא הַקָּדוֹשׁ בָּרוּךְ הוּא – בָּרָא כְּנֶגְדּוֹ. בָּרָא הָרִים – בָּרָא גְּבָעוֹת; בָּרָא יַמִּים – בָּרָא נְהָרוֹת.

The Gemara relates: *Aḥer* **asked Rabbi Meir**[NP] a question, **after he had gone astray. He said to him: What is** the meaning of that **which is written: "God has made even the one as well as the other"** (Ecclesiastes 7:14)? Rabbi Meir **said to him: Everything that the Holy One, Blessed be He, created, He created** a similar creation **corresponding to it. He created mountains, He created hills; He created seas, He created rivers.**

NOTES

He saw Mitatron, etc. – חֲזָא מִיטַטְרוֹן וכו׳: The kabbalistic Sages discuss this passage at length. Various midrashic sources imply that Mitatron is the minister of the world, i.e., the angel appointed over the entire world. Seeing Mitatron in this capacity led *Aḥer* to entertain the erroneous notion of the existence of two different thrones, that of God above the entire world and a separate domain of the minister of the world. This view is similar to that of certain Gnostic sects.

They removed Mitatron and smote him – אַפְּקוּהוּ לְמִיטַטְרוֹן וּמַחְיוּהוּ: Some explain that *Aḥer* was shown Mitatron being beaten, so that he would recognize that his status was that of a mere messenger, just like other angels (Rabbeinu Ḥananel; *ge'onim*; see *Otzar HaKavod*).

Apart from *Aḥer* – חוּץ מֵאַחֵר: This is because God knew that *Aḥer* would never fully repent (Rabbeinu Ḥananel). The different versions of the text provide a reason for this: Since as a great scholar he possessed knowledge of the glory of God, he was a willful sinner, and he had therefore forfeited the assistance usually granted to one who wishes to achieve repentance.

***Aḥer* asked Rabbi Meir – שָׁאַל אַחֵר אֶת רַבִּי מֵאִיר:** The Maharsha writes that *Aḥer* was alluding to himself in these questions, as implied by the other questions he posed. Some write that Rabbi Meir deliberately provided answers that would lead *Aḥer* to state the explanations that were applicable to himself, so that Rabbi Meir could reply by imploring that he repent.

LANGUAGE

Mitatron – מִיטַטְרוֹן: The linguistic origin of this word is unclear. Some claim it derives from the Latin metator, meaning a guide or a planner. Others maintain it comes from the Greek μετά θρόνος, *meta thronos*, meaning behind the throne. According to the latter explanation, it refers to the angel standing behind the Throne of Glory, as it were, the highest minister of the World Above.

Rods [*pulsei*] – פּוּלְסֵי: Some claim that this word is derived from the Latin pulsus, meaning a blow or a strike.

PERSONALITIES

Rabbi Meir – רַבִּי מֵאִיר: Rabbi Meir was one of the greatest *tanna'im* of the generation that preceded the redaction of the Mishna. There is no clear information available concerning Rabbi Meir's parents, though it is told that he descended from a family of converts from the house of the Roman emperors.

His exceptional brilliance in Torah study was evident from a very early age, and he was a student of the two greatest scholars of the generation, Rabbi Yishmael and Rabbi Akiva. He was also the only Sage who continued to study with Elisha ben Avuya, despite the latter's estrangement from Judaism. His primary teacher was Rabbi Akiva, who ordained him at a very young age, which is the reason that he was ordained a second time by Rabbi Yehuda ben Bava. In recognition of his outstanding scholarship, Rabbi Meir was officially appointed *Hakham*, literally, wise man, the third level below *Nasi*, head of the Sanhedrin. The halakhic discussions between him and his colleagues, Rabbi Yehuda, Rabbi Yosei, Rabbi Shimon, and Rabbi Elazar, form an important foundation of the Mishna.

Rabbi Meir's greatest undertaking appears to have been a structured, oral redaction of the Oral Law, including establishing specific formats for the *halakhot*. Apparently, Rabbi Yehuda HaNasi followed in Rabbi Meir's footsteps and incorporated his work into the Mishna. Consequently, it is a well-known principle that the author of an unattributed statement in the Mishna is Rabbi Meir, as the assumption is that it was one of the *mishnayot* he formulated.

Due to his involvement in the attempt to depose Rabban Shimon ben Gamliel, the *Nasi* of the Sanhedrin, he was punished by the latter, and for a long period his teachings were not cited in his name but were introduced with the words: Others say.

His private life was replete with suffering. His two sons died during his lifetime, and his extraordinary wife Berurya also died under painful circumstances. Nevertheless, it is known that a daughter of his survived. He was eventually forced into exile to Asia Minor, where he died, with the order that his coffin be transferred to Eretz Yisrael and that he be temporarily interred on the shore of the sea whose waves reach the Holy Land.

Rabbi Meir was famous in his lifetime, not only for his sharp intellect, which exceeded that of all his peers, but also for his personal attributes, his efforts as a peacemaker and his willingness to relinquish personal honor for the good of others. He was known as a magnificent public speaker. It is said that following his death, those who composed parables ceased. Several of his parables relating to animals were repeated for many generations. He was also renowned as a miracle worker. For many years a charity fund named after him, Rabbi Meir the Miracle Worker [*Ba'al HaNes*], served as the main source of funding for the Jews in Eretz Yisrael.

LANGUAGE

Curtain [*pargod*] – פרגוד: It appears that this word is of Persian origin, a transposition of pargad, meaning a screen. It refers to the screen that divides the king from his palace retinue.

אמר לו: רבי עקיבא רבך לא אמר כך, אלא: ברא צדיקים – ברא רשעים, ברא גן עדן – ברא גיהנם. כל אחד ואחד יש לו שני חלקים, אחד בגן עדן ואחד בגיהנם. זכה צדיק – נטל חלקו וחלק חברו בגן עדן. נתחייב רשע – נטל חלקו וחלק חברו בגיהנם.

Aḥer **said to him: Rabbi Akiva, your teacher, did not say so, but** explained the verse as follows: Everything has its opposite: **He created the righteous, He created the wicked; He created the Garden of Eden, He created Gehenna. Each and every** person **has two portions, one in the Garden of Eden and one in Gehenna.** If he **merits** it, by becoming **righteous, he takes his portion and the portion of his** wicked **colleague**[N] **in the Garden of Eden;** if he is found **culpable** by becoming **wicked, he takes his portion and the portion of his colleague in Gehenna.**

אמר רב משרשיא: מאי קראה? גבי צדיקים כתיב: "לכן בארצם משנה יירשו". גבי רשעים כתיב: "ומשנה שברון שברם".

Rav Mesharshiyya said: What is the verse from which it is derived? **With regard to the righteous, it is stated: "Therefore in their land they shall possess double"** (Isaiah 61:7); whereas **with regard to the wicked, it is stated: "And destroy them with double destruction"** (Jeremiah 17:18); therefore, each receives a double portion.

שאל אחר את רבי מאיר לאחר שיצא לתרבות רעה: מאי דכתיב: "לא יערכנה זהב וזכוכית ותמורתה כלי פז"? אמר לו: אלו דברי תורה, שקשין לקנותן ככלי זהב וכלי פז, ונוחין לאבדן ככלי זכוכית. אמר לו: רבי עקיבא רבך לא אמר כך, אלא: מה כלי זהב וכלי זכוכית, אף על פי שנשברו יש להם תקנה – אף תלמיד חכם, אף על פי שסרח יש לו תקנה. אמר לו: אף אתה חזור בך! אמר לו: כבר שמעתי מאחורי הפרגוד: שובו בנים שובבים – חוץ מאחר.

Aḥer **asked Rabbi Meir** another question, again **after he had gone astray. What is** the meaning of that **which is written: "Gold and glass cannot equal it; neither shall its exchange be vessels of fine gold"** (Job 28:17)? If it is referring to the praise and honor of the Torah, it should have compared it only to gold, not to glass. **He said to him:** This is referring to **words of Torah, which are as difficult to acquire as gilded vessels and vessels of fine gold but are as easy to lose as glass vessels.** *Aḥer* **said to him: Rabbi Akiva, your teacher, did not say so, but** taught as follows: **Just as golden vessels and glass vessels have a remedy even when they have broken,** as they can be melted down and made into new vessels, **so too a Torah scholar, although he has transgressed, has a remedy.** Rabbi Meir **said to him:** If so, **you too, return** from your ways. **He said to him: I have already heard** the following declaration **behind the** dividing **curtain,**[L] which conceals God from the world: **"Return, rebellious children,"** (Jeremiah 3:22) **apart from** ***Aḥer.***

תנו רבנן: מעשה באחר שהיה רוכב על הסוס בשבת, והיה רבי מאיר מהלך אחריו ללמוד תורה מפיו. אמר לו: מאיר, חזור לאחריך, שכבר שיערתי בעקבי סוסי עד כאן תחום שבת. אמר ליה: אף אתה חזור בך. אמר ליה: ולא כבר אמרתי לך: כבר שמעתי מאחורי הפרגוד "שובו בנים שובבים" – חוץ מאחר.

The Gemara cites a related story: **The Sages taught: There was once an incident involving** ***Aḥer,*** **who was riding on a horse on Shabbat, and Rabbi Meir was walking behind him to learn Torah from him.** After a while, *Aḥer* **said to him: Meir, turn back, for I have already estimated** and measured **according to the steps of my horse**[N] that **the Shabbat boundary ends here,** and you may therefore venture no further. Rabbi Meir **said to him: You, too, return** to the correct path. **He said to him: But have I not already told you** that **I have already heard behind the** dividing **curtain: "Return, rebellious children," apart from** ***Aḥer?***

תקפיה, עייליה לבי מדרשא. אמר ליה לינוקא: פסוק לי פסוקך! אמר לו: "אין שלום אמר ה' לרשעים". עייליה לבי כנישתא אחריתי, אמר ליה לינוקא: פסוק לי פסוקך! אמר לו: "כי אם תכבסי בנתר ותרבי לך בורית נכתם עונך לפני". עייליה לבי כנישתא אחריתי, אמר ליה

Nevertheless, Rabbi Meir **took hold of him** and **brought him to the study hall.** *Aḥer* **said to a child,** by way of divination: **Recite your verse** that you studied today **to me.**[N] **He recited** the following verse **to him: "There is no peace, said the Lord, concerning the wicked"** (Isaiah 48:22). **He brought him to another study hall.** *Aḥer* **said to a child: Recite your verse to me. He recited to him: "For though you wash with niter, and take for you much soap, yet your iniquity is marked before Me"** (Jeremiah 2:22). **He brought him to another study hall.** *Aḥer* **said to**

NOTES

He takes his portion and the portion of his colleague – נטל חלקו וחלק חברו: This is because one who causes many others to sin is punished for their sins as well. Similarly, a righteous person brings merit to many others (Rabbeinu Ḥananel).

For I have already estimated according to the steps of my horse – שכבר שיערתי בעקבי סוסי: The Maharsha explains that the intention of *Aḥer* was to mock Rabbi Meir, as it is easier to measure distances by the pace of a person than by a horse's gait. However, in the Jerusalem Talmud it is indicated that this serves to emphasize the wisdom of *Aḥer*. Even while talking of other matters and while riding, he was able to estimate the distance he had traveled.

Recite your verse to me – פסוק לי פסוקך: It was the custom for each child learning in a synagogue to memorize a verse each day. The Gemara elsewhere states that Sages would ask children to recite their verse as a way of divining the future (see *Ḥullin* 95b).

לינוקא: פסוק לי פסוקך! אמר ליה: ״ואת שדוד מה תעשי כי תלבשי שני כי תעדי עדי זהב כי תקרעי בפוך עיניך לשוא תתיפי״ וגו׳.

a child: Recite your verse to me. He recited to him: "And you, spoiled one, what are you doing, that you clothe yourself with scarlet, that you deck yourself with ornaments of gold, that you enlarge your eyes with paint? In vain you make yourself fair" (Jeremiah 4:30).

עייליה לבי כנישתא אחריתי, עד דעייליה לתליסר בי כנישתא. כולהו פסקו ליה כי האי גוונא. לבתרא אמר ליה: פסוק לי פסוקך! אמר ליה: ״ולרשע אמר אלהים מה לך לספר חקי״ וגו׳. ההוא ינוקא הוה מגמגם בלישניה, אשתמע כמה דאמר ליה ״ולאלישע אמר אלהים״. איכא דאמרי: סכינא הוה בהדיה וקרעיה, ושדריה לתליסר בי כנישתי. ואיכא דאמרי, אמר: אי הואי בידי סכינא – הוה קרענא ליה.

He brought him to another synagogue, until he had brought him into thirteen synagogues, where **all** the children **recited to him similar** verses that speak of the hopeless situation of the wicked. **At the last one, he said to him: Recite your verse to me. He recited to him: "And to the wicked [*velerasha*] God says, what is it for you to declare My statutes"** (Psalms 50:16). The Gemara relates: **That child had a stutter,** so it **sounded as though he were saying to him: *Vele'elisha*,** i.e., and to Elisha, **God says.** This made Elisha think the child was deliberately insulting him. **Some say *Aḥer* had a knife, and he tore** the child **apart and sent him** to the **thirteen synagogues. And others say** that *Aḥer* merely **said: Had I a knife, I would have torn him apart.**

כי נח נפשיה דאחר אמרי: לא מידן לידייניה, ולא לעלמא דאתי ליתי. לא מידן לידייניה – משום דעסק באורייתא, ולא לעלמא דאתי ליתי – משום דחטא. אמר רבי מאיר: מוטב דלידייניה וליתי לעלמא דאתי. מתי אמות ואעלה עשן מקברו. כי נח נפשיה דרבי מאיר סליק קוטרא מקבריה דאחר.

The Gemara relates: **When *Aḥer* passed away,** the Heavenly Court **declared** that **he should not be judged, nor brought into the World-to-Come. He should not be judged** in a manner befitting his deeds, **because he occupied** himself **with Torah,** whose merit protects him. **And he should not be brought into the World-to-Come because he sinned. Rabbi Meir said: It is better that he be judged** properly **and be brought into the World-to-Come. When I die** I will request this of Heaven, **and I will cause smoke to rise up from his grave,**[N] as a sign that he is being sentenced in Gehenna. The Gemara relates: **When Rabbi Meir passed away, smoke rose up from** the **grave of *Aḥer*,** implying that Rabbi Meir's wish was granted.

אמר רבי יוחנן: גבורתא למיקלא רביה?! חד הוה בינגא ולא מצינן לאצוליה. אי נקטיה ביד – מאן מרמי ליה. מאן?! אמר: מתי אמות ואכבה עשן מקברו! כי נח נפשיה דרבי יוחנן – פסק קוטרא מקבריה דאחר. פתח עליה ההוא ספדנא: אפילו שומר הפתח לא עמד לפניך, רבינו.

Rabbi Yoḥanan said: Was this **a mighty** deed on Rabbi Meir's part, **to burn his teacher?** Was this the only remedy available? Can it be that there **was one** Sage **among us** who left the path **and we cannot save him? If we hold him by the hand, who will remove him** from our protection; **who?** Rabbi Yoḥanan continued and **said: When I die I will have** the **smoke extinguished from his grave,** as a sign that he has been released from the sentence of Gehenna and brought to the World-to-Come. Indeed, **when Rabbi Yoḥanan passed away,** the **smoke ceased** to rise up **from the grave of *Aḥer*. A certain eulogizer** began his eulogy of Rabbi Yoḥanan with the following: **Even the guard at the entrance could not stand before you, our rabbi.** The guard at the entrance to Gehenna could not prevent Rabbi Yoḥanan from arranging the release of *Aḥer*.

בתו של אחר אתיא לקמיה דרבי, אמרה ליה: רבי, פרנסני. אמר לה: בת מי את? אמרה לו: בתו של אחר אני. אמר לה: עדיין יש מזרעו בעולם? והא כתיב: ״לא נין לו ולא נכד בעמו ואין שריד במגוריו״! אמרה לו: זכור לתורתו ואל תזכור מעשיו. מיד ירדה אש וסכסכה ספסלו של רבי. בכה ואמר רבי: ומה למתגנין בה – כך, למשתבחין בה – על אחת כמה וכמה!

The Gemara relates: **The daughter of *Aḥer* came before Rabbi** Yehuda HaNasi and **said to him: Rabbi, provide me with sustenance,** as she was in need of food. **He said to her: Whose daughter are you? She said to him: I am the daughter of *Aḥer*. He said to her,** angrily: **Is there still of his seed** remaining **in the world? But isn't it stated: "He shall have neither son**[N] **nor grandson among his people or any remaining in his dwellings"** (Job 18:19)? **She said to him: Remember his Torah, and do not remember his deeds. Immediately, fire descended and licked Rabbi** Yehuda HaNasi's **bench. Rabbi** Yehuda HaNasi **wept and said:** If God protects the honor of **those who treat** the Torah **with contempt** in **such** a manner, as *Aḥer* despised the Torah and relinquished its teachings, **how much more so** would He do **for those who treat it with honor.**

NOTES

I will cause smoke to rise up from his grave – אעלה עשן מקברו: Obviously, not all those who are sentenced to Gehenna have smoke rising from their graves. Rabbi Meir, however, requested that God provide a sign so that all would know that *Aḥer* had been judged and would eventually be rehabilitated (Maharsha).

But isn't it stated, he shall have neither son, etc. – והא כתיב, לא נין וכו׳: According to the Jerusalem Talmud, Rabbi Yehuda HaNasi cited a different verse: "Let there be none to extend kindness to him; nor let there be any to be gracious to his fatherless children" (Psalms 109:12), which means that one should not give charity even to the children of one such as *Aḥer*, who sinned so greatly and desecrated God's Name. He subsequently retracted his statement when he realized that *Aḥer* had merited God-fearing daughters (see *Dikdukei Soferim*).

וְרַבִּי מֵאִיר הֵיכִי גָּמַר תּוֹרָה מִפּוּמֵיהּ דְּאַחֵר? וְהָאָמַר רַבָּה בַּר בַּר חָנָה אָמַר רַבִּי יוֹחָנָן: מַאי דִּכְתִיב: ״כִּי שִׂפְתֵי כֹהֵן יִשְׁמְרוּ דַעַת וְתוֹרָה יְבַקְשׁוּ מִפִּיהוּ כִּי מַלְאַךְ ה׳ צְבָאוֹת הוּא״? אִם דּוֹמֶה הָרַב לְמַלְאַךְ ה׳ צְבָאוֹת – יְבַקְשׁוּ תוֹרָה מִפִּיהוּ. וְאִם לָאו – אַל יְבַקְשׁוּ תוֹרָה מִפִּיהוּ!

The Gemara poses a question: **And Rabbi Meir, how could he learn Torah from the mouth of *Aḥer*? But didn't Rabba bar bar Ḥana say that Rabbi Yoḥanan said: What is the** meaning of that **which is written: "For the priest's lips should keep knowledge, and they should seek Torah from his mouth; for he is an angel of the Lord of hosts"** (Malachi 2:7)? The verse teaches: **If the rabbi is similar to an angel of the Lord of hosts,** perfect in his ways, **they should seek Torah from his mouth; but if not, they should not seek Torah from his mouth.**[H]

אָמַר רֵישׁ לָקִישׁ: רַבִּי מֵאִיר קְרָא אַשְׁכַּח וְדָרַשׁ: ״הַט אָזְנְךָ וּשְׁמַע דִּבְרֵי חֲכָמִים וְלִבְּךָ תָּשִׁית לְדַעְתִּי״. לְדַעְתָּם לֹא נֶאֱמַר, אֶלָּא לְדַעְתִּי.

Reish Lakish said: Rabbi Meir found a verse and interpreted it homiletically: "Incline your ear, and hear the words of the wise, and apply your heart to My knowledge" (Proverbs 22:17). **It does not state "to their knowledge," but "to My knowledge."** In other words, one must listen to the words of **the Sages,** despite their flaws, provided that their opinion concurs with that of God.

רַב חֲנִינָא אָמַר מֵהָכָא: ״שִׁמְעִי בַת וּרְאִי וְהַטִּי אָזְנֵךְ וְשִׁכְחִי עַמֵּךְ וּבֵית אָבִיךְ״ וגו׳.

Rav Ḥanina said that one can find support for this idea **from here: "Listen, daughter and consider, and incline your ear; forget also your own people and your father's house"** (Psalms 45:11), which likewise indicates that one must listen to the words of a Sage while forgetting, i.e., ignoring, the faulty aspects of his teachings.

קָשׁוּ קְרָאֵי אַהֲדָדֵי! לָא קַשְׁיָא, הָא – בְּגָדוֹל, הָא – בְּקָטָן.

The Gemara asks: If so, **the verses contradict each other,** for one source states that one may learn only from a scholar who is perfect in his ways, while the other indicates that it is permitted even to learn from one whose character is flawed. The Gemara answers: This is **not difficult. This** case, in which it is permitted to a flawed scholar, is referring **to an adult;** whereas **that** case, which prohibits doing so, is referring **to a minor,**[N] who should learn only from a righteous person, so that his ways are not corrupted by a teacher with flawed character.

כִּי אֲתָא רַב דִּימִי אֲמַר, אָמְרִי בְּמַעֲרָבָא: רַבִּי מֵאִיר אֲכַל תַּחְלָא וּשְׁדָא שִׁיחֲלָא לְבָרָא. דָּרַשׁ רָבָא: מַאי דִּכְתִיב: ״אֶל גִּנַּת אֱגוֹז יָרַדְתִּי לִרְאוֹת בְּאִבֵּי הַנָּחַל״ וגו׳? לָמָּה נִמְשְׁלוּ תַּלְמִידֵי חֲכָמִים לֶאֱגוֹז? לוֹמַר לְךָ: מָה אֱגוֹז זֶה, אַף עַל פִּי שֶׁמְּלוּכְלָךְ בְּטִיט וּבְצוֹאָה – אֵין מַה שֶּׁבְּתוֹכוֹ נִמְאָס, אַף תַּלְמִיד חָכָם, אַף עַל פִּי שֶׁסָּרַח – אֵין תּוֹרָתוֹ נִמְאֶסֶת.

When Rav Dimi came from Eretz Yisrael to Babylonia, **he said: In the West,** Eretz Yisrael, they **say: Rabbi Meir ate a half-ripe date**[N] **and threw the peel away.** In other words, he was able to extract the important content from the inedible shell. **Rava taught: What is** the meaning of that **which is written: "I went down into the garden of nuts, to look at the green plants of the valley"** (Song of Songs 6:11)? **Why are Torah scholars compared to nuts? To tell you: Just as this nut, despite being soiled with mud and excrement, its content is not made repulsive,** as only its shell is soiled; **so too a Torah scholar, although he has sinned, his Torah is not made repulsive.**

אַשְׁכְּחֵיהּ רַבָּה בַּר שֵׁילָא לְאֵלִיָּהוּ, אֲמַר לֵיהּ: מַאי קָא עָבֵיד הַקָּדוֹשׁ בָּרוּךְ הוּא? אֲמַר לֵיהּ: קָאָמַר שְׁמַעְתָּא מִפּוּמַיְיהוּ דְּכוּלְּהוּ רַבָּנַן, וּמִפּוּמֵיהּ דְּרַבִּי מֵאִיר לָא קָאָמַר. אֲמַר לֵיהּ: אַמַּאי? מִשּׁוּם דְּקָא גָּמַר שְׁמַעְתָּא מִפּוּמֵיהּ דְּאַחֵר. אֲמַר לֵיהּ: אַמַּאי? רַבִּי מֵאִיר רִמּוֹן מָצָא, תּוֹכוֹ אָכַל, קְלִיפָּתוֹ זָרַק! אֲמַר לֵיהּ: הָשְׁתָּא קָאָמַר: מֵאִיר בְּנִי אוֹמֵר: בִּזְמַן שֶׁאָדָם מִצְטַעֵר שְׁכִינָה מַה לָּשׁוֹן אוֹמֶרֶת? קַלַּנִי מֵרֹאשִׁי, קַלַּנִי מִזְּרוֹעִי. אִם כָּךְ הַקָּדוֹשׁ בָּרוּךְ הוּא מִצְטַעֵר עַל דָּמָן שֶׁל רְשָׁעִים – קַל וָחוֹמֶר עַל דָּמָן שֶׁל צַדִּיקִים שֶׁנִּשְׁפַּךְ.

The Gemara relates: **Rabba bar Sheila found Elijah** the prophet, who had appeared to him. He **said to** Elijah: **What is the Holy One, Blessed be He, doing?** Elijah **said to him: He is stating *halakhot* transmitted by all of the Sages, but in the name of Rabbi Meir He will not speak. He said to him: Why?** He replied: **Because he learned *halakhot* from the mouth of *Aḥer*. He said to him: Why** should he be judged unfavorably for that? **Rabbi Meir found a pomegranate** and **ate its contents** while **throwing away its peel. He said to him:** Indeed, your defense has been heard above. **Now God is saying:**[N] **My son, Meir, says: When a person suffers,** e.g., by receiving lashes or the death penalty at the hands of the court, **how does the Divine Presence express itself? Woe is Me from My head,**[N] **woe is Me from My arm,** as God empathizes with the sufferer. **If the Holy One, Blessed be He, suffers** to **such** an extent **over the blood of the wicked, how much more so** does He suffer **over the blood of the righteous that is spilled.**

HALAKHA

From whom is it proper to learn – מִמִּי רָאוּי לִלְמוֹד: One may not learn from a teacher who behaves improperly, even if he is a great Torah scholar, until the scholar mends his ways. The Sages say that if a teacher is not similar to an angel of God, one should not seek Torah from his mouth (*Shulḥan Arukh, Yoreh De'a*, 246:8).

NOTES

This is referring to an adult [*gadol*], that is referring to a minor [*katan*] – הָא בְּגָדוֹל, הָא בְּקָטָן: The commentaries ask why the Rambam and the *Shulḥan Arukh* do not cite this distinction in their codes of law. They answer that nowadays, there are no scholars of such caliber who can learn Torah from a teacher without being influenced by his ways (*Leḥem Mishne*; *Shakh*). The *Yad David* writes that the word *gadol*, literally, great one, refers to an individual who is unique in his generation. Only such a person is permitted to learn from a teacher who behaves inappropriately, while an ordinary adult is prohibited to do so. The *Zekher LaHagiga* suggests an alternative explanation: The words great and small do not refer to the student but to the teacher himself: If the teacher who sinned is such a great individual that the court does not place him under a ban, it is permitted to study from him.

Ate a half-ripe date [*taḥla*] – אֲכַל תַּחְלָא: Rashi explains that *taḥla* in this context is a type of date whose peel is inedible. The Maharsha notes that this metaphor alludes to the double nature of the corruption of *Aḥer*, which was both internal, in terms of his heretical views, as well as external, in terms of his conduct. Rabbi Meir consequently threw away both the bad peel as well as the inedible pit within, keeping only the words of Torah themselves.

Now God is saying, etc. – הָשְׁתָּא קָאָמַר וכו׳: Many commentaries are puzzled by this passage. Why were words of Torah not cited in Rabbi Meir's name, and how did Rabba bar Sheila's argument cause this to change? One explanation is that God was, of course, aware of the purity of Rabbi Meir's intentions and of the fact that he had not been affected by his teacher's opinions. However, those observing Rabbi Meir may have viewed such learning in a negative light. Since one must also be innocent in the eyes of others, learning from *Aher* was considered a flaw. Once it became evident that there are those in the world below such as Rabba bar Sheila, who understood the positive nature of Rabbi Meir's behavior, the latter was demonstrated as worthy of having teachings ascribed to him.

Woe is Me [*kalani*] from My head, etc. – קַלַּנִי מֵרֹאשִׁי וכו׳: The meaning of this expression, which concerns God's identification with the pain of the Jewish people, is debated by *amora'im* (*Sanhedrin* 47a). The *ge'onim* explain *kalani* as two words: *Kal ani*, I am light, as one who is unwell feels so weak that even a light gust of wind could knock him over. Mystical significance has been ascribed to the terms My head and My arm in this context (*Otzar HaKavod*). The *Zekher LaHagiga* explains that these expressions allude to the midrashic teaching that God wears phylacteries on His head and arm, upon which the name of Israel is inscribed. When a Jew suffers, it is as though these phylacteries were damaged and fell; therefore, it is as if His head and arm become lighter.

אַשְׁכְּחֵיהּ שְׁמוּאֵל לְרַב יְהוּדָה דְּתָלֵי בְּעִיבְרָא דְּדַשָּׁא וְקָא בָּכֵי. אֲמַר לֵיהּ: שִׁינְנָא, מַאי קָא בָּכֵית? אֲמַר לֵיהּ מִי זוּטְרָא מַאי דִּכְתִיב בְּהוּ בְּרַבָּנַן: ״אַיֵּה סוֹפֵר אַיֵּה שׁוֹקֵל אַיֵּה סוֹפֵר אֶת הַמִּגְדָּלִים״? ״אַיֵּה סוֹפֵר״ – שֶׁהָיוּ סוֹפְרִים כָּל אוֹתִיּוֹת שֶׁבַּתּוֹרָה. אַיֵּה שׁוֹקֵל – שֶׁהָיוּ שׁוֹקְלִים קַלִּין וַחֲמוּרִין שֶׁבַּתּוֹרָה. ״אַיֵּה סוֹפֵר אֶת הַמִּגְדָּלִים״ – שֶׁהָיוּ שׁוֹנִין שְׁלֹשׁ מֵאוֹת הֲלָכוֹת בְּמִגְדָּל הַפּוֹרֵחַ בָּאֲוִיר.

The Gemara relates: **Shmuel found Rav Yehuda leaning on the bar of the door, crying. He said to him: Long-toothed one** [*shinnana*],[L] **what are you crying for? He said to him: Is it a small** matter, **that which is written with regard to Sages** who have sinned: **"Where is he who counted, where is he who weighed? Where is he who counted the towers?"** (Isaiah 33:18). He proceeded to explain: **"Where is he who counted"; for they would count all the letters of the Torah. "Where is he who weighed"; for they would weigh** and compare the **minor and major** transgressions **of the Torah. "Where is he who counted the towers"; for they would teach three hundred *halakhot*** concerning the details of tent impurity **involving** a wooden **closet floating in the air.**[N] If they studied a subject so removed from reality in such depths, how much more so did they analyze other issues.

וַאֲמַר רַבִּי אַמִי: תְּלַת מְאָה בְּעָיֵי בָּעוּ דּוֹאֵג וַאֲחִיתוֹפֶל בְּמִגְדָּל הַפּוֹרֵחַ בָּאֲוִיר. וּתְנַן: שְׁלֹשָׁה מְלָכִים וְאַרְבָּעָה הֶדְיוֹטוֹת אֵין לָהֶם חֵלֶק לָעוֹלָם הַבָּא. אֲנַן מַה תֶּהֱוֵי עֲלַן?! אֲמַר לֵיהּ: שִׁינְנָא, טִינָא הָיְתָה בְּלִבָּם.

And Rabbi Ami said: Doeg asked Ahithophel three hundred questions with regard to a closet floating in the air, as they were both great Torah scholars. **And we learned** in a mishna (*Sanhedrin* 90a): **Three kings and four commoners have no portion in the World-to-Come,** a list that includes Doeg and Ahithophel. If such great Sages could sin and forfeit their share in the World-to-Come, **we,** who are less knowledgeable than they, **what will be of us? He said to him: Long-toothed one, there was mud** [*tina*][L] **in their hearts,** i.e., they had certain flaws that prevented their Torah learning from protecting them.

אַחֵר מַאי? זֶמֶר יְוָונִי לָא פְּסַק מִפּוּמֵּיהּ. אָמְרוּ עָלָיו עַל אַחֵר, בְּשָׁעָה שֶׁהָיָה עוֹמֵד מִבֵּית הַמִּדְרָשׁ הַרְבֵּה סִפְרֵי מִינִין נוֹשְׁרִין מֵחֵיקוֹ.

The Gemara explains: ***Aḥer*, what** was his failing? **Greek tunes never ceased from his mouth.** He would constantly hum Greek songs, even when he was among the Sages. This shows that from the outset he was drawn to gentile culture and beliefs. Similarly, **they said about *Aḥer*: When he would stand** after learning **in the study hall, many heretical books,** which he had been reading, would **fall from his lap.** Therefore, he was somewhat unsound even when among the Sages.

שָׁאַל נִימוֹס הַגַּרְדִּי אֶת רַבִּי מֵאִיר: כָּל עֲמַר דְּנָחִית לְיוֹרָה סְלֵיק? אֲמַר לֵיהּ: כָּל מַאן דַּהֲוָה נָקִי אַגַּב אִימֵּיהּ – סְלֵיק; כָּל דְּלָא הֲוָה נָקִי אַגַּב אִימֵּיהּ – לָא סְלֵיק.

The gentile philosopher, **Nimos HaGardi,**[P] **asked Rabbi Meir:** Does **all wool that enters the cauldron** to be dyed **emerge colored?** In other words, do all those who learn Torah emerge as decent and worthy? **He said to him: Whoever was clean when** he was **with his mother,** from the outset, will **emerge** decent and worthy, but **all** those who were **not clean when** they were **with their mother** will **not emerge** worthy. One who approaches Torah study having been flawed from the outset will not be properly influenced by it.

רַבִּי עֲקִיבָא עָלָה בְּשָׁלוֹם וְיָרַד בְּשָׁלוֹם, וְעָלָיו הַכָּתוּב אוֹמֵר: ״מָשְׁכֵנִי אַחֲרֶיךָ נָרוּצָה״. וְאַף רַבִּי עֲקִיבָא בִּקְּשׁוּ מַלְאֲכֵי הַשָּׁרֵת לְדוֹחֲפוֹ. אָמַר לָהֶם הַקָּדוֹשׁ בָּרוּךְ הוּא: הַנִּיחוּ לְזָקֵן זֶה, שֶׁרָאוּי לְהִשְׁתַּמֵּשׁ בִּכְבוֹדִי.

§ The Gemara returns to the four who entered the orchard. It is stated above that **Rabbi Akiva ascended in safety and descended safely. With regard to him, the verse states: "Draw me, we will run after you;** the king has brought me into his chambers" (Song of Songs 1:4). The Gemara relates: **And even Rabbi Akiva, the ministering angels sought to push** him out of the orchard. **The Holy One, Blessed be He, said to them: Leave this Elder, for he is fit to serve My glory.**[N]

LANGUAGE

Long-toothed one [*shinnana*] – **שִׁינְנָא:** According to many commentaries, Rashi among them, *shinnana* means sharp. It is an honorific that Shmuel conferred upon his most prominent student. However, the *ge'onim* explain, based on old Aramaic vernacular, that *shinnana* means the one with the large teeth, and that this was Rav Yehuda's nickname.

Mud [*tina*] – **טִינָא:** Probably similar in meaning to the word's form in Arabic, طين, *ṭīn*, meaning mud or dirt, or, according to some scholars, rust. It subsequently came to refer to anything unclean in the spiritual sense, i.e., something resulting from envy, hatred, lust, and related traits.

NOTES

Closet [*migdal*] **floating in the air – מִגְדָּל הַפּוֹרֵחַ בָּאֲוִיר:** Rashi provides three explanations of this expression. According to Rashi's own opinion, it refers to the *halakhot* of a tent over a corpse. The specific case here is that of a wooden closet suspended in the air in the space between various areas of a house (see Mishna *Oholot* 4:1). Many *halakhot* depend on whether the impurity is considered to be in the house or the closet. Rabbeinu Ḥananel explains this expression similarly.

Rashi provides two additional explanations of this phrase, both of which are metaphorical. First, the word *migdal* includes the letter *lamed*, which is shaped like a closet in the air, as it is the only letter to continue above a line when written. It alludes to the Sages being so thorough in their interpretation of the Torah, that they found meaning even in part of one letter. Second, the word *migdal* alludes to the Tower of Babel, which was built high in the air with the end of defeating God. This story is one of the sections of the Torah that the Sages expounded upon. The *Otzar HaKavod* attempts to reconcile Rashi's explanations while elucidating some of the secret teachings involved, relating to the Divine Presence in the world.

However, some *ge'onim* maintain that it is possible, by various means, for a closet to actually fly in the air. The legal ramifications of such a case are connected to the *halakhot* of a portable tent. Others maintain that this case is cited as an example in order to show that despite the fact that such a flying object could not have existed in those days, the Sages did not refrain from discussing the detailed *halakhot* of something that was of mere theoretical importance.

For he is fit to serve My glory – שֶׁרָאוּי לְהִשְׁתַּמֵּשׁ בִּכְבוֹדִי: Rabbi Akiva was careful not to proceed beyond the boundaries of human comprehension in his studies. This protected him from an error that would cost him his sanity or his life (*Otzar HaKavod*).

PERSONALITIES

Nimos HaGardi – נִימוֹס הַגַּרְדִּי: This is probably the man referred to elsewhere as Avnimos HaGardi, from the Greek name **Οἰνόμαος**, *Oinomaos*. Some maintain that it refers to a Greek philosopher from the town of Gader, which explains the surname. He was a fierce opponent of paganism. Various sources relate discussions that he conducted with the Sages of Israel. It appears that he and Rabbi Meir held each other in mutual respect. The Sages greatly praised his wisdom, to the extent that they said that there were no philosophers in the nations as great as Balaam and Nimos HaGardi.

LANGUAGE

Exemplary [*dugma*] – דּוּגְמָא: From the Greek δεῖγμα, *deigma*, meaning an example or pattern.

NOTES

Six statements were said with regard to demons – שִׁשָּׁה דְּבָרִים נֶאֶמְרוּ בַּשֵּׁדִים: Additional aspects of similarity between demons and humans are mentioned elsewhere in the Gemara. Those additional aspects, however, are considered by the Gemara to relate to a broader definition of demons, so they are not mentioned here. According to the Gemara, demons are harmful creatures that are comprised of matter and spirit, like humans, although their material nature is not identical to that of humans (see Ramban on Leviticus, chapter 17).

Speak in the holy tongue – מְסַפְּרִים בִּלְשׁוֹן הַקּוֹדֶשׁ: This does not refer exclusively to the holy tongue, but rather to the ability to speak in general, which is common to both angels and humans. Since the Gemara is comparing humans to angels, who converse exclusively in the holy tongue, it describes people in similar terms (Maharsha).

מַאי דָּרַשׁ? אָמַר רַבָּה בַּר בַּר חָנָה אָמַר רַבִּי יוֹחָנָן: ״וְאָתָא מֵרִבְבֹת קֹדֶשׁ״ – אוֹת הוּא בְּרִבָּבָה שֶׁלּוֹ.

The Gemara asks: **What** verse did Rabbi Akiva **expound** that prevented him from making the same mistake as *Aḥer*? **Rabba bar bar Ḥana said** that **Rabbi Yoḥanan said:** It was the following: **"And He came [*ve'ata*] from the holy myriads"** (Deuteronomy 33:2), which he explained in this manner: **He,** God, **is unique [*ot*] among His myriads** of angels. Therefore, he knew that he had merely seen an angel.

וְרַבִּי אַבָּהוּ אָמַר: ״דָּגוּל מֵרְבָבָה״ – דּוּגְמָא הוּא בְּרִבָּבָה שֶׁלּוֹ.

And Rabbi Abbahu said: Rabbi Akiva expounded the verse: **"Preeminent above a myriad"** (Song of Songs 5:10) to indicate that **He is exemplary**[L] **among His myriad.**

וְרֵישׁ לָקִישׁ אָמַר: ״ה׳ צְבָאוֹת שְׁמוֹ״ – אָדוֹן הוּא בַּצָּבָא שֶׁלּוֹ.

And Reish Lakish said: He expounded the verse: **"The Lord of hosts is His name"** (Isaiah 48:2); **He is the Master in His host.**

וְרַבִּי חִיָּיא בַּר אַבָּא אָמַר רַבִּי יוֹחָנָן: ״לֹא בָרוּחַ ה׳ וְאַחַר הָרוּחַ רַעַשׁ לֹא בָרַעַשׁ ה׳ וְאַחַר הָרַעַשׁ אֵשׁ לֹא בָאֵשׁ ה׳ וְאַחַר הָאֵשׁ קוֹל דְּמָמָה דַקָּה״, ״וְהִנֵּה ה׳ עוֹבֵר״.

And Rav Ḥiyya bar Abba said that **Rabbi Yoḥanan said:** He expounded the verses: **"But the Lord was not in the wind. And after the wind, an earthquake; the Lord was not in the earthquake. And after the earthquake, fire;** but **the Lord was not in the fire. And after the fire, a still, small voice,"** and it states in that verse: **"And behold, the Lord passed by"** (I Kings 19:11–12). Rabbi Akiva used this verse in order to recognize the place of His presence and refrain from trespassing there.

תָּנוּ רַבָּנַן: שִׁשָּׁה דְּבָרִים נֶאֶמְרוּ בַּשֵּׁדִים, שְׁלֹשָׁה כְּמַלְאֲכֵי הַשָּׁרֵת וּשְׁלֹשָׁה כִּבְנֵי אָדָם. שְׁלֹשָׁה כְּמַלְאֲכֵי הַשָּׁרֵת: יֵשׁ לָהֶם כְּנָפַיִם כְּמַלְאֲכֵי הַשָּׁרֵת, וְטָסִין מִסּוֹף הָעוֹלָם וְעַד סוֹפוֹ כְּמַלְאֲכֵי הַשָּׁרֵת, וְיוֹדְעִין מַה שֶּׁעָתִיד לִהְיוֹת כְּמַלְאֲכֵי הַשָּׁרֵת.

§ The Gemara returns to discussing the heavenly beings. **The Sages taught: Six** statements **were said with regard to demons:**[N] In **three** ways they are **like ministering angels, and** in **three** ways they are **like humans.** The *baraita* specifies: In **three** ways they are **like ministering angels: They have wings like ministering angels; and they fly from one end of the world to the other like ministering angels; and they know what will be in the future like ministering angels.**

יוֹדְעִין סָלְקָא דַעְתָּךְ?! אֶלָּא: שׁוֹמְעִין מֵאֲחוֹרֵי הַפַּרְגּוֹד כְּמַלְאֲכֵי הַשָּׁרֵת.

The Gemara is puzzled by this last statement: **Should it enter your mind that they know** this? Not even the angels are privy to the future. **Rather, they hear from behind the curtain** when God reveals something of the future, **like ministering angels.**

וּשְׁלֹשָׁה כִּבְנֵי אָדָם: אוֹכְלִין וְשׁוֹתִין כִּבְנֵי אָדָם, פָּרִין וְרָבִין כִּבְנֵי אָדָם, וּמֵתִים כִּבְנֵי אָדָם.

And in **three** ways they are similar **to humans: They eat and drink like humans; they multiply like humans; and they die like humans.**

שִׁשָּׁה דְּבָרִים נֶאֶמְרוּ בִּבְנֵי אָדָם, שְׁלֹשָׁה כְּמַלְאֲכֵי הַשָּׁרֵת, שְׁלֹשָׁה כִּבְהֵמָה. שְׁלֹשָׁה כְּמַלְאֲכֵי הַשָּׁרֵת: יֵשׁ לָהֶם דַּעַת כְּמַלְאֲכֵי הַשָּׁרֵת, וּמְהַלְּכִין בְּקוֹמָה זְקוּפָה כְּמַלְאֲכֵי הַשָּׁרֵת, וּמְסַפְּרִים בִּלְשׁוֹן הַקֹּדֶשׁ כְּמַלְאֲכֵי הַשָּׁרֵת. שְׁלֹשָׁה כִּבְהֵמָה: אוֹכְלִין וְשׁוֹתִין כִּבְהֵמָה, וּפָרִין וְרָבִין כִּבְהֵמָה, וּמוֹצִיאִין רְעִי כִּבְהֵמָה.

Six statements **were said with regard to humans:** In **three** ways, they are **like ministering angels,** and in **three** ways they are **like animals.** The *baraita* explains: In **three** ways they are **like ministering angels: They have intelligence like ministering angels; and they walk upright like ministering angels; and they speak in the holy tongue**[N] **like ministering angels.** In **three** ways humans are **like animals: They eat and drink like animals; and they multiply like animals; and they emit excrement like animals.**

״כׇּל הַמִּסְתַּכֵּל בְּאַרְבָּעָה דְּבָרִים רָתוּי לוֹ שֶׁלֹּא בָּא לָעוֹלָם״ כו׳. בִּשְׁלָמָא מָה לְמַעְלָה מָה לְמַטָּה מָה לְאָחוֹר – לְחַיֵּי; אֶלָּא לְפָנִים – מָה דַּהֲוָה הֲוָה!

§ The mishna taught: **Whoever looks at four things, it would have been better for him had he never entered the world:** Anyone who reflects upon that which is above the firmament; that which is below the earth; what was before the creation of the world; and what will be after the end of the world. The Gemara asks: **Granted,** it is prohibited to reflect on **what is above, what is below,** and **what is after.** This is fine, since one is examining things that are not part of the world but lie beyond it. **But before** the creation of the world, **what has happened has happened.** Why is it prohibited to reflect upon this?

רַבִּי יוֹחָנָן וְרַבִּי אֶלְעָזָר דְּאָמְרִי תַּרְוַיְיהוּ: מָשָׁל לְמֶלֶךְ בָּשָׂר וָדָם שֶׁאָמַר לַעֲבָדָיו: בְּנוּ לִי פַּלְטֵירִין גְּדוֹלִין עַל הָאַשְׁפָּה. הָלְכוּ וּבָנוּ לוֹ, אֵין רְצוֹנוֹ שֶׁל מֶלֶךְ לְהַזְכִּיר שֵׁם אַשְׁפָּה.

The Gemara explains: **Rabbi Yoḥanan and Rabbi Elazar both say:** This can be demonstrated through **a parable** with regard to **a flesh-and-blood king who said to his servants: Build for me large palaces**[L] **on a garbage dump.**[N] **They went and built** them **for him.** Clearly, in that case, **the king does not desire** that they **mention the garbage dump.** Here too, God does not want people to concern themselves with the chaos that preceded the world.

״כׇּל שֶׁלֹּא חָס עַל כְּבוֹד קוֹנוֹ רָתוּי לוֹ שֶׁלֹּא בָּא לָעוֹלָם״. מַאי הִיא? רַבִּי אַבָּא אָמַר: זֶה הַמִּסְתַּכֵּל בַּקֶּשֶׁת. רַב יוֹסֵף אָמַר: זֶה הָעוֹבֵר עֲבֵירָה בְּסֵתֶר. מִסְתַּכֵּל בַּקֶּשֶׁת – דִּכְתִיב: ״כְּמַרְאֵה הַקֶּשֶׁת אֲשֶׁר יִהְיֶה בֶעָנָן בְּיוֹם הַגֶּשֶׁם כֵּן מַרְאֵה הַנֹּגַהּ סָבִיב הוּא מַרְאֵה דְּמוּת כְּבוֹד ה׳״.

It is taught in the mishna: **Whoever has no concern for the honor of his Maker deserves to have never come to the world.** The Gemara asks: **What is** lack of concern for the honor of one's Maker? **Rabbi Abba said: This is one who looks at a rainbow.**[NB] **Rav Yosef said: This is one who commits a transgression in private.** They proceed to clarify their opinions: **Looking at a rainbow** constitutes an act of disrespect toward the Divine Presence, **as it is written: "As the appearance of the bow that is in the cloud in the day of rain so was the appearance of the brightness round about. This was the appearance of the likeness of the glory of the Lord"** (Ezekiel 1:28), and it is a dishonor to God to stare at His likeness.

רַב יוֹסֵף אָמַר: זֶה הָעוֹבֵר עֲבֵירָה בְּסֵתֶר, כִּדְרַבִּי יִצְחָק. דְּאָמַר רַבִּי יִצְחָק: כׇּל הָעוֹבֵר עֲבֵירָה בְּסֵתֶר כְּאִילּוּ דּוֹחֵק רַגְלֵי שְׁכִינָה, שֶׁנֶּאֱמַר: ״כֹּה אָמַר ה׳ הַשָּׁמַיִם כִּסְאִי וְהָאָרֶץ הֲדוֹם רַגְלָי״.

Rav Yosef said: This is one **who commits a transgression in private, in accordance with Rabbi Yitzḥak, as Rabbi Yitzḥak said: Whoever commits a transgression in private, it is as though he pushed** away **the feet of the Divine Presence, as it is stated: "Thus said the Lord: The heavens are My seat, and the earth My footstool"** (Isaiah 66:1). If one believes that no one can see what he is doing in private, it is as though he said that God is absent from that place. He is therefore compared to one who attempts to remove God from His footstool.

אִינִי? וְהָאָמַר רַבִּי אֶלְעָא הַזָּקֵן: אִם רוֹאֶה אָדָם שֶׁיִּצְרוֹ מִתְגַּבֵּר עָלָיו – יֵלֵךְ לְמָקוֹם שֶׁאֵין מַכִּירִין אוֹתוֹ, וְיִלְבַּשׁ שְׁחוֹרִין וְיִתְעַטֵּף שְׁחוֹרִין, וְיַעֲשֶׂה מַה שֶּׁלִּבּוֹ חָפֵץ, וְאַל יְחַלֵּל שֵׁם שָׁמַיִם בְּפַרְהֶסְיָא! לָא קַשְׁיָא: הָא – דְּמָצֵי כָּיֵיף לֵיהּ לְיִצְרֵיהּ, הָא דְּלָא מָצֵי כָּיֵיף לְיִצְרֵיהּ.

The Gemara raises a difficulty: And **is that so? But didn't Rabbi Ela the Elder say: If a person sees that his inclination is overcoming him, he should go to a place where he is unknown, and wear black,**[N] **and wrap himself in black,** in the manner of mourners, because he should be ashamed of his weakness, **and do there what his heart desires, but let him not desecrate the Name of Heaven in public.** This shows that sinning in private is sometimes preferable to the public performance of a transgression. The Gemara answers: This is **not difficult. This** case, where one who commits a transgression in public has no concern for the honor of his Maker, occurs **when one is capable of overcoming his inclination** and fails to do so. **That** case, where it is preferable to sin in private, occurs **when one is incapable of overcoming his inclination.** He is therefore advised to, at the very least, refrain from desecrating God's name in public.

LANGUAGE

Palaces [*palterin*] – פַּלְטֵירִין: From the Greek παλάτιον, *palatiyon*, meaning a palace.

BACKGROUND

Rainbow – קֶשֶׁת: A rainbow is an optical and meteorological phenomenon that causes a spectrum of light to appear in the sky when the sun shines on droplets of moisture in the Earth's atmosphere. It takes the form of a multicolored arc.

NOTES

Palaces on a garbage dump – פַּלְטֵירִין...עַל הָאַשְׁפָּה: The early and later authorities discuss the significance and nature of this dump. In the Jerusalem Talmud, it is indicated that it refers to the chaos that preceded Creation, when the world was entirely filled with water. The Rid explains that it refers to the nothingness that preceded Creation. This parable corresponds to the kabbalistic doctrine of the breaking of the vessels and the assertion that flawed worlds existed before ours was created (see *Bereshit Rabba*).

One who looks at a rainbow – הַמִּסְתַּכֵּל בַּקֶּשֶׁת: This does not mean that the rainbow resembles the actual likeness of God. Rather, the obscure nature of the rainbow, as those who observe it see different hues depending on their position of observation, is comparable to the glory of the Divine Presence (Rid).

In our physical reality, it is the natural world that testifies most clearly to the work of the Creator. At the same time, God cannot be perceived in a physical sense, and the world that He created does not fully reflect His greatness. The rainbow is a metaphor for this state of affairs, since the rainbow has no physical essence; it is merely the product of light shining on droplets of moisture in the atmosphere. Just as the individual who looks at the rainbow and believes that he is looking at a tangible material is making a serious error, so too, the individual who gazes upon God's creations and believes that he can fully understand His reality is dishonoring God (*Midrash Shlomo*).

Wear black, etc. – יִלְבַּשׁ שְׁחוֹרִין וכו׳: Rabbeinu Ḥananel explains that acting in this manner will cause the sinful inclination to leave him, as the hardships of the journey and the humiliation he suffers from wandering and wearing unseemly clothes will inevitably have an effect. However, *Tosafot* explain this passage in a straightforward manner: One who intends to sin should, at the very least, avoid desecrating God's name publicly.

דָּרַשׁ רַבִּי יְהוּדָה בְּרַבִּי נַחְמָנִי, מְתוּרְגְּמָנֵיהּ דְּרֵישׁ לָקִישׁ: כָּל הַמִּסְתַּכֵּל בִּשְׁלֹשָׁה דְּבָרִים עֵינָיו כֵּהוֹת: בַּקֶּשֶׁת, וּבַנָּשִׂיא, וּבַכֹּהֲנִים. בַּקֶּשֶׁת – דִּכְתִיב: ״כְּמַרְאֵה הַקֶּשֶׁת אֲשֶׁר יִהְיֶה בֶעָנָן בְּיוֹם הַגֶּשֶׁם הוּא מַרְאֵה דְּמוּת כְּבוֹד ה׳״. בַּנָּשִׂיא – דִּכְתִיב: ״וְנָתַתָּה מֵהוֹדְךָ עָלָיו״. הַמִּסְתַּכֵּל בַּכֹּהֲנִים בִּזְמַן שֶׁבֵּית הַמִּקְדָּשׁ קַיָּים, שֶׁהָיוּ עוֹמְדִין עַל דּוּכָנָן וּמְבָרְכִין אֶת יִשְׂרָאֵל בַּשֵּׁם הַמְפוֹרָשׁ.

Rabbi Yehuda, son of Rabbi Naḥmani, the disseminator of **Reish Lakish, interpreted** a verse **homiletically: Whoever looks at** the following **three things,**[N] **his eyes will grow dim:** One who looks **at a rainbow,**[H] **at a *Nasi*, and at the priests.**[H] He explains: **At a rainbow, as it is written: "As the appearance of the bow that is in the cloud on the day of rain,** so was the appearance of the brightness round about, **this was the appearance of the likeness of the glory of the Lord"** (Ezekiel 1:28). **At a *Nasi*, as it is written: "And you shall put of your splendor upon him"** (Numbers 27:20), which indicates that the splendor of the Divine Presence rested upon Moses, who was the *Nasi* of Israel. The third item, looking at priests, is referring to one **who looks at the priests when the Temple is standing, as they would stand on their platform and bless Israel with the ineffable name,** at which point the Divine Presence would rest above the joints of their fingers.

דָּרַשׁ רַבִּי יְהוּדָה בְּרַבִּי נַחֲמָנִי מְתוּרְגְּמָנֵיהּ דְּרֵישׁ לָקִישׁ: מַאי דִּכְתִיב: ״אַל תַּאֲמִינוּ בְרֵעַ אַל תִּבְטְחוּ בְּאַלּוּף״? אִם יֹאמַר לְךָ יֵצֶר הָרַע חֲטוֹא וְהַקָּדוֹשׁ בָּרוּךְ הוּא מוֹחֵל – אַל תַּאֲמִן, שֶׁנֶּאֱמַר: ״אַל תַּאֲמִינוּ בְרֵעַ״, וְאֵין רַע אֶלָּא יֵצֶר הָרָע, שֶׁנֶּאֱמַר: ״כִּי יֵצֶר לֵב הָאָדָם רַע״,

Apropos this Sage, the Gemara cites another statement of his: **Rabbi Yehuda, son of Rabbi Naḥmani, the disseminator** of **Reish Lakish, interpreted** a verse **homiletically: What is** the meaning of that **which is written: "Trust not in a companion, do not put your confidence in an intimate friend"** (Micah 7:5)? **If the evil inclination says to you: Sin,**[N] **and the Holy One, Blessed be He, will forgive, do not trust** it, **since it is stated: "Trust not in a companion** [*rei'a*]." **And** *rei'a* **is referring to none other** than **the evil** [*ra*] **inclination, as it is stated: "For the inclination of the heart of man is evil** [*ra*]" (Genesis 8:21).

וְאֵין אַלּוּף אֶלָּא הַקָּדוֹשׁ בָּרוּךְ הוּא, שֶׁנֶּאֱמַר: ״אַלּוּף נְעוּרַי אָתָּה״. שֶׁמָּא תֹּאמַר: מִי מֵעִיד בִּי? אַבְנֵי בֵיתוֹ וְקוֹרוֹת בֵּיתוֹ שֶׁל אָדָם, הֵם מְעִידִין בּוֹ, שֶׁנֶּאֱמַר: ״כִּי אֶבֶן מִקִּיר תִּזְעָק וְכָפִיס מֵעֵץ יַעֲנֶנָּה״.

And "intimate friend" is referring to none other than **the Holy One, Blessed be He, as it is stated: "You are the intimate friend of my youth"** (Jeremiah 3:4). **Lest you say:** Since I am acting in private, **who will testify against me? The stones of the house and the beams of the house of** each **person testify against him, as it is stated:** "For the stone shall cry out of the wall, and the beam out of the timber shall answer it" (Habakkuk 2:11).

וַחֲכָמִים אוֹמְרִים: נִשְׁמָתוֹ שֶׁל אָדָם מְעִידָה בּוֹ, שֶׁנֶּאֱמַר: ״מִשֹּׁכֶבֶת חֵיקֶךָ שְׁמוֹר פִּתְחֵי פִיךָ״. אֵי זוֹ הִיא דָּבָר שֶׁשּׁוֹכֶבֶת בְּחֵיקוֹ שֶׁל אָדָם? הֱוֵי אוֹמֵר זוֹ נְשָׁמָה. רַבִּי זְרִיקָא אָמַר: שְׁנֵי מַלְאֲכֵי הַשָּׁרֵת הַמְלַוִּין אוֹתוֹ הֵן מְעִידִין בּוֹ, שֶׁנֶּאֱמַר: ״כִּי מַלְאָכָיו יְצַוֶּה לָּךְ לִשְׁמָרְךָ בְּכָל דְּרָכֶיךָ״. וַחֲכָמִים אוֹמְרִים: אֵבָרָיו שֶׁל אָדָם מְעִידִין בּוֹ, שֶׁנֶּאֱמַר: ״וְאַתֶּם עֵדַי נְאֻם ה׳ וַאֲנִי אֵל״.

And the Sages say: A person's soul shall itself **testify against him, as it is stated: "Guard the doors of your mouth from she who lies in your bosom"** (Micah 7:5). **What thing lies in a person's bosom? You must say it is** his **soul. Rabbi Zerika said:** The **two ministering angels who accompany him,** i.e., each individual, **they testify against him, as it is stated: "For He will command his angels over you, to guard you in all your ways"** (Psalms 91:11). **And the Sages say: A person's limbs testify against him, as it is stated: "Therefore you are My witnesses, says the Lord, and I am God"** (Isaiah 43:12), which indicates that each individual becomes his own witness and testifies against himself on the Day of Judgment.

NOTES

Whoever looks at the following three things – כָּל הַמִּסְתַּכֵּל בִּשְׁלֹשָׁה דְּבָרִים: Since each of these represents an aspect of the glory of the Divine Presence, it is improper to gaze upon them (Rabbeinu Ḥananel).

There are several phenomena whose spiritual grandeur should cause the one gazing upon them to recognize God's greatness. Among them are natural phenomena such as a rainbow; intellectual phenomena, such as the *Nasi*, who is, according to the Rambam, the creative and intellectual giant whose mental capacity is considered a level of prophecy; and religious phenomena, such as the Temple priests who offer the Godly, threefold Priestly Benediction with love. Someone who witnesses one of these and is unable to recognize God's presence in them has missed an opportunity for communion with God, and his eyes grow dim in a metaphorical sense (Rabbi Joseph B. Soloveitchik, *Al HaTeshuva*).

If the evil inclination says to you, sin – אִם יֹאמַר לְךָ יֵצֶר הָרַע חֲטוֹא: Some commentaries take this to mean that the evil inclination says: Sin, and God will pardon you even without repentance. Alternatively, the evil inclination is inciting one to sin and repent later, despite the principle that one who says he will sin and repent is not provided with the opportunity to do so (Maharsha). The *Tzlaḥ* explains that the evil inclination is assuring the individual that it will leave him alone after he has succumbed to sin, whereas the truth is that sinning makes one more likely to transgress again.

HALAKHA

One who looks at a rainbow – הַמִּסְתַּכֵּל בַּקֶּשֶׁת: It is prohibited to stare at a rainbow or to prostrate oneself upon seeing one because one appears as though he were bowing down to it. One should, however, recite a blessing over seeing a rainbow, and the same should be done each time he sees an additional rainbow, even if they appear within thirty days of each other (*Shulḥan Arukh, Oraḥ Ḥayyim* 229:1).

And at the priests – וּבַכֹּהֲנִים: It is prohibited to look at the priests while they are blessing the congregation. However, the reason that the Gemara provides for this prohibition, the pronouncing of the ineffable name, applies only in the Temple. Today, one may not look at the priests when they are blessing the people so as to avoid distracting them (*Magen Avraham*; *Taz*, citing *Beit Yosef*) and due to the glory of the Divine Presence that rests upon their hands even now (*Kaf HaḤayyim*, citing the *Zohar*). According to the letter of the law, it is permitted to glance at the priests briefly, but the custom is to refrain from looking at them entirely (*Mishna Berura*; *Shulḥan Arukh*, *Oraḥ Ḥayyim* 128:23).

מתני׳ יוֹסֵי בֶּן יוֹעֶזֶר אוֹמֵר שֶׁלֹּא לִסְמוֹךְ, יוֹסֵף בֶּן יוֹחָנָן אוֹמֵר לִסְמוֹךְ. יְהוֹשֻׁעַ בֶּן פְּרַחְיָה אוֹמֵר שֶׁלֹּא לִסְמוֹךְ, נִיתַּאי הָאַרְבֵּלִי אוֹמֵר לִסְמוֹךְ. יְהוּדָה בֶּן טַבַּאי אוֹמֵר שֶׁלֹּא לִסְמוֹךְ. שִׁמְעוֹן בֶּן שָׁטַח אוֹמֵר לִסְמוֹךְ. שְׁמַעְיָה אוֹמֵר לִסְמוֹךְ, אַבְטַלְיוֹן אוֹמֵר שֶׁלֹּא לִסְמוֹךְ. הִלֵּל וּמְנַחֵם לֹא נֶחְלְקוּ. יָצָא מְנַחֵם נִכְנַס שַׁמַּאי. שַׁמַּאי אוֹמֵר שֶׁלֹּא לִסְמוֹךְ, הִלֵּל אוֹמֵר לִסְמוֹךְ.

MISHNA **Yosei ben Yo'ezer says not to place** one's hands on offerings before slaughtering them on a Festival because this is considered performing labor with an animal on a Festival. His colleague, **Yosef ben Yoḥanan, says to place** them;[H] **Yehoshua ben Peraḥya says not to place** them; **Nitai HaArbeli says to place** them; **Yehuda ben Tabbai says not to place** them; **Shimon ben Shataḥ says to place** them; **Shemaya says to place** them; **Avtalyon says not to place** them. **Hillel and Menaḥem did not disagree**[N] with regard to this issue. **Menaḥem departed** from his post, and **Shammai entered** in his stead. **Shammai says not to place** them; **Hillel says to place** them.

HALAKHA

Placing hands on an offering on a Festival – סְמִיכָה בְּיוֹם טוֹב: The *halakha* is in accordance with the opinion that one places his hands on all offerings brought on Festivals (Rambam *Sefer Korbanot*, *Hilkhot Ḥagiga* 1:9).

NOTES

Hillel and Menaḥem did not disagree – הִלֵּל וּמְנַחֵם לֹא נֶחְלְקוּ: The Rambam maintains that they did not dispute concerning this matter because they did not serve simultaneously for a long period. Therefore, Menaḥem's opinion was never fully established. However, others maintain that Menaḥem in fact agreed with Hillel (*Peri Ḥadash*; Rashash; see Meiri).

Perek **II**
Daf **16** Amud **b**

הָרִאשׁוֹנִים הָיוּ נְשִׂיאִים, וּשְׁנִיִּים לָהֶם אֲבוֹת בֵּית דִּין.

The first members of each pair **served as *Nasi*, and their counterparts** served as **deputy *Nasi*.**

גמ׳ תָּנוּ רַבָּנַן שְׁלֹשָׁה מִזּוּגוֹת הָרִאשׁוֹנִים שֶׁאָמְרוּ שֶׁלֹּא לִסְמוֹךְ, וּשְׁנַיִם מִזּוּגוֹת הָאַחֲרוֹנִים שֶׁאָמְרוּ לִסְמוֹךְ, (הָרִאשׁוֹנִים) הָיוּ נְשִׂיאִים, וּשְׁנִיִּים לָהֶם אֲבוֹת בֵּית דִּין, דִּבְרֵי רַבִּי מֵאִיר. וַחֲכָמִים אוֹמְרִים: יְהוּדָה בֶּן טַבַּאי – אַב בֵּית דִּין, וְשִׁמְעוֹן בֶּן שָׁטַח – נָשִׂיא.

GEMARA **The Sages taught: Three of the first pairs who say not to place hands and two of the last pairs who say to place hands served as *Nasi*, and their counterparts** served as **deputy *Nasi***; this is **the statement of Rabbi Meir. And the Rabbis say** the opposite: **Yehuda ben Tabbai** was **deputy *Nasi* and Shimon ben Shataḥ** was the ***Nasi*.**

מַאן תְּנָא לְהָא דְּתָנוּ רַבָּנַן: אָמַר רַבִּי יְהוּדָה בֶּן טַבַּאי: אֶרְאֶה בַּנֶּחָמָה אִם לֹא הָרַגְתִּי עֵד זוֹמֵם, לְהוֹצִיא מִלִּבָּן שֶׁל צְדוֹקִין, שֶׁהָיוּ אוֹמְרִים: אֵין עֵדִים זוֹמְמִין נֶהֱרָגִין עַד שֶׁיֵּהָרֵג הַנִּידּוֹן.

The Gemara asks: **Who is the *tanna*** who taught **that which the Sages taught** in a *baraita*: **Rabbi Yehuda ben Tabbai said:** I swear that **I will not see the consolation** of Israel **if I did not kill a conspiring witness.**[N] This means that Rabbi Yehuda ben Tabbai sentenced a conspiring witness to death, in order **to counter the views of the Sadducees, who would say: Conspiring witnesses are not executed unless the sentenced one has been executed.** Their views opposed the traditional view, which maintains that conspiring witnesses are executed only if the one sentenced by their testimony has not yet been executed.[N]

אָמַר לוֹ שִׁמְעוֹן בֶּן שָׁטַח: אֶרְאֶה בַּנֶּחָמָה אִם לֹא שָׁפַכְתָּ דָּם נָקִי, שֶׁהֲרֵי אָמְרוּ חֲכָמִים: אֵין עֵדִים זוֹמְמִין נֶהֱרָגִין – עַד שֶׁיּוּזַמּוּ שְׁנֵיהֶם, וְאֵין לוֹקִין – עַד שֶׁיּוּזַמּוּ שְׁנֵיהֶם, וְאֵין מְשַׁלְּמִין מָמוֹן – עַד שֶׁיּוּזַמּוּ שְׁנֵיהֶם.

Shimon ben Shataḥ said to him: I swear that **I will** not **see the consolation** of Israel **if you did not shed innocent blood, as the Sages said: Conspiring witnesses are not executed unless they are both found to be conspirators;**[N] if only one is found to be a conspirator, he is not executed. **And they are not flogged** if they are liable to such a penalty, **unless they are both found to be conspirators. And** if they testified falsely that someone owed money, **they do not pay money unless they are both found to be conspirators.**[H]

HALAKHA

When are conspiring witnesses punished – מָתַי נֶעֱנָשִׁים עֵדִים זוֹמְמִים: A pair of witnesses found to be conspiring are executed only if both of them conspired to have someone executed. Similarly, a pair of witnesses can be sentenced to receive lashes or pay a fine only if both of them were found to be conspiring. The same *halakha* applies to a group of three or more witnesses (Rambam *Sefer Shofetim*, *Hilkhot Edut* 20:1).

NOTES

If I did not kill a conspiring witness – אִם לֹא הָרַגְתִּי עֵד זוֹמֵם: The Rid claims that in this particular case, only one witness, not two, testified and was found to have conspired against the defendant. Rabbi Yehuda ben Tabbai thought, in accordance with the opinion of the Sages, that since false, conspiring witnesses are punished for the conspiracy itself, a single witness should also be punished, despite the fact that his testimony is not accepted. According to this approach, Rabbi Yehuda ben Tabbai chose this particular case to act as he did in order to stress that the *halakha* follows the Sages, not the Sadducees.

Conspiring witnesses – עֵדִים זוֹמְמִים: The law with regard to conspiring witnesses appears in the Torah: "If an unrighteous witness rises up against any man to bear perverted witness against him…And the judges shall inquire diligently; and, behold, if the witness is a false witness…then you shall do to him as he conspired to do to his brother" (Deuteronomy 19:16–19). The specifics of this law are analyzed in great detail in tractate *Makkot*.

The *halakha* is such that not all witnesses whose testimony has been rejected, including proven liars, are considered conspiring witnesses. A witness has the status of a conspiring witness only if there is proof that he could not possibly have been at the place of his testimony at the particular time that he claimed to have been there. The Sadducees understood the Bible as saying that a conspiring witness is punished for causing bodily or monetary harm to another, whereas the tradition of the Sages, based on a careful reading of the phrase "as he conspired to do," is that such a witness is punished only if he conspired to bring about a sentence that was not actually carried out.

This tradition is considered a Torah edict not requiring a logical reason. However, logical reasons for this *halakha* can be suggested. First, the conspiring witnesses brought about the death of an innocent person, their sin cannot be atoned by their execution. Second, were the conspiring witnesses to be executed, it would become publicly known that the court erred in its judgment, and this would harm the authority of the court (Meiri).

Unless they are both found to be conspirators – עַד שֶׁיּוּזַמּוּ שְׁנֵיהֶם: It appears that Rabbi Yehuda ben Tabbai's error was based on the wording of the verse "and behold, if the witness is a false witness" (Deuteronomy 19:18), which seems to indicate that even one witness is held culpable. However, the tradition of the Sages is that the word "witness" should not be understood as referring to a single individual, but rather as a general term referring to an entire group of witnesses that offers testimony, as is evident from the law stated earlier in the chapter (Deuteronomy 19:15).

מִיָּד קִבֵּל עָלָיו יְהוּדָה בֶּן טַבַּאי שֶׁאֵינוֹ מוֹרֶה הֲלָכָה אֶלָּא בִּפְנֵי שִׁמְעוֹן בֶּן שָׁטַח.

Hearing this, **Yehuda ben Tabbai immediately accepted upon himself not to rule** on any matter of **law unless he was in the presence of Shimon ben Shataḥ**, as he realized he could not rely on his own judgment.

כָּל יָמָיו שֶׁל יְהוּדָה בֶּן טַבַּאי הָיָה מִשְׁתַּטֵּחַ עַל קִבְרוֹ שֶׁל אוֹתוֹ הָרוּג, וְהָיָה קוֹלוֹ נִשְׁמָע. כִּסְבוּרִין הָעָם לוֹמַר שֶׁקּוֹלוֹ שֶׁל הָרוּג הוּא. אָמַר לָהֶם: קוֹלִי הוּא, תֵּדְעוּ שֶׁלְּמָחָר הוּא מֵת וְאֵין קוֹלוֹ נִשְׁמָע.

The *baraita* further relates: **All of Yehuda ben Tabbai's days, he would prostrate himself on the grave of that executed** individual, to request forgiveness, **and his voice was heard** weeping. **The people thought that it was the voice of that executed** person, rising from his grave. Yehuda ben Tabbai **said to them: It is my voice,** and **you** shall **know** that it is so, **for tomorrow,** i.e., sometime in the future, **he will die, and his voice will no** longer **be heard.** Yehuda ben Tabbai was referring to himself, but he did not want to mention something negative about himself in direct terms.

אֲמַר לֵיהּ רַב אַחָא בְּרֵיהּ דְּרָבָא לְרַב אָשֵׁי: וְדִלְמָא פִּיּוּסֵי פַּיְיסֵיהּ, אוֹ בְּדִינָא תַּבְעֵיהּ?

Rav Aḥa, son of Rava, said to Rav Ashi: This provides no conclusive proof that the voice was not that of the executed man, as **perhaps** ben Tabbai **appeased** the executed individual in the World-to-Come. **Or,** alternatively, the latter may have **prosecuted him by the law** of Heaven, and that is why his voice can no longer be heard.

מַנִּי הָא? אִי אָמְרַתְּ בִּשְׁלָמָא רַבִּי מֵאִיר, דְּאָמַר: שִׁמְעוֹן בֶּן שָׁטַח אַב בֵּית דִּין, רַבִּי יְהוּדָה בֶּן טַבַּאי נָשִׂיא – הַיְינוּ דְּקָא מוֹרֵי הֲלָכָה בִּפְנֵי שִׁמְעוֹן בֶּן שָׁטַח. אֶלָּא אִי אָמְרַתְּ רַבָּנַן, דְּאָמְרִי: יְהוּדָה בֶּן טַבַּאי אַב בֵּית דִּין, שִׁמְעוֹן בֶּן שָׁטַח נָשִׂיא – אַב בֵּית דִּין בִּפְנֵי נָשִׂיא מִי מוֹרֶה הֲלָכָה?

The Gemara returns to its original question: **Whose** opinion does **this** *baraita* follow? **Granted, if you say** it is in accordance **with** that of **Rabbi Meir,** who **said** that **Shimon ben Shataḥ was deputy *Nasi*** while **Rabbi Yehuda ben Tabbai was *Nasi*, that** explains why **he** had previously **issued a halakhic ruling in the presence of Shimon ben Shataḥ** to execute the conspiring witness, and only after that unfortunate incident did he undertake to issue rulings only in the presence of his colleague. **But if you say** that the *baraita* is in accordance with **the Sages, who said: Yehuda ben Tabbai** was **deputy *Nasi*** and **Shimon ben Shataḥ** the ***Nasi***, why did he need to make such a commitment? **May** the **deputy *Nasi* issue a halakhic ruling in the presence of** the ***Nasi*?**

לָא. מַאי קִבֵּל עָלָיו דְּקָאָמַר? לְאִצְטְרוֹפֵי, דַּאֲפִילּוּ אִצְטְרוֹפֵי נָמֵי לָא מִצְטְרֵיפְנָא.

The Gemara refutes this: **No; what** did he mean by **accepting upon himself** not to rule on his own? **He spoke** with regard **to joining** the ruling of others: **Even** with regard to **joining** the ruling of others, **I will also not join** until I have first heard the view of Shimon ben Shataḥ.

״יָצָא מְנַחֵם וְנִכְנַס שַׁמַּאי״ כו׳. לְהֵיכָן יָצָא? אַבַּיֵי אָמַר: יָצָא לְתַרְבּוּת רָעָה. רָבָא אָמַר: יָצָא לַעֲבוֹדַת הַמֶּלֶךְ. תַּנְיָא נָמֵי הָכִי: יָצָא מְנַחֵם לַעֲבוֹדַת הַמֶּלֶךְ, וְיָצְאוּ עִמּוֹ שְׁמוֹנִים זוּגוֹת תַּלְמִידִים לְבוּשִׁין סִירִיקוֹן.

§ It is taught in the mishna: **Menaḥem**[P] **departed and Shammai entered.** The Gemara asks: **To where did** Menaḥem **depart? Abaye said: He departed and went astray.** Therefore, the mishna did not wish to delve into the details of his case. **Rava said: He departed for the king's service.** He received a post from the king and had to leave the court. **This is also taught** in a *baraita*: **Menaḥem departed for the king's service, and eighty pairs of students dressed in silk robes**[L] **left with him** to work for the king, and that they no longer studied Torah.

אָמַר רַב שֶׁמֶן בַּר אַבָּא אָמַר רַבִּי יוֹחָנָן: לְעוֹלָם אַל תְּהֵא שְׁבוּת קַלָּה בְּעֵינֶיךָ, שֶׁהֲרֵי סְמִיכָה אֵינָהּ אֶלָּא מִשּׁוּם שְׁבוּת, וְנֶחְלְקוּ בָּהּ גְּדוֹלֵי הַדּוֹר.

§ **Rav Shemen bar Abba said** that **Rabbi Yoḥanan said: A rabbinic decree [*shevut*]**[N] **should never be taken lightly in your eyes, since placing hands** on the head of an offering on a Festival **is prohibited only as a rabbinic decree** because it is considered making use of an animal, which is not considered a prohibited labor but merely resembles one, and yet **the greatest** scholars **of each generation disputed it.**

פְּשִׁיטָא! שְׁבוּת מִצְוָה אִצְטְרִיכָא לֵיהּ.

The Gemara is puzzled by this statement: This **is obvious.** Since it is an accepted rabbinic decree, why should people take it lightly? The Gemara answers: It was **necessary for him** to state it because it is **a rabbinic decree related to a mitzva.** In other words, although this rabbinic decree of placing the hands on an animal is not performed for one's own sake but for the purpose of a mitzva, it was nevertheless a serious matter in the eyes of the Sages.

הָא נָמֵי פְּשִׁיטָא! לְאַפּוֹקֵי מִמַּאן דְּאָמַר בִּסְמִיכָה גּוּפָהּ פְּלִיגִי. קָא מַשְׁמַע לָן בִּשְׁבוּת הוּא דִּפְלִיגִי.

The Gemara remains puzzled: **This too is obvious.** In that case as well, the act is prohibited by the Sages. The Gemara responds: Rabbi Yoḥanan's statement comes **to exclude** the opinion **of the one who said** that **they disagree with regard to the actual** obligation of **placing hands,** i.e., whether or not obligatory peace-offerings require placing the hands. **He** therefore **teaches us** that **it is a rabbinic decree** that is the subject **of their dispute,**[N] not the requirement itself.

PERSONALITIES

Menaḥem – מְנַחֵם: The identity of the Menaḥem mentioned here and the nature of his departure remain unknown. He is perhaps the Sage mentioned in the books of Josephus as prophesying to Herod that the latter would achieve greatness, and he may have actively supported him later on. Therefore, the Gemara says: Departed for the king's service. Since Herod was considered by the Sages to be an evil usurper, they did not want to elaborate on Menaḥem's actions.

LANGUAGE

Silk [*sirikon*] – סִירִיקוֹן: From the Greek σηρικόν, *sèrikon*, meaning silk or made from silk.

NOTES

Rabbinic decree [*shevut*] – שְׁבוּת: This type of rabbinic decree is a unique category of prohibition that applies to Shabbat and Festivals. Various forms of activity that are not considered prohibited labor by Torah law were nevertheless prohibited by the Sages because their performance would likely to lead to a labor prohibited by Torah law. Certain prohibitions in this category are already mentioned by the prophets, such as engaging in commercial activity on Shabbat, which is alluded to in the book of Amos and mentioned explicitly in Nehemiah. The Gemara in tractate *Beitza* (36b) differentiates between two types of rabbinic decrees: Those that involve entirely optional acts and those that are prohibited despite the fact that they are related to a mitzva.

It is a rabbinic decree that is the subject of their dispute – בִּשְׁבוּת הוּא דִּפְלִיגִי: The *Turei Aven* asks: Since the Sages hold that rabbinic decrees do not apply in the Temple, why did they prohibit the act of placing? He answers as follows: Beit Shammai maintain that there is no requirement that the act of placing hands be performed immediately before slaughtering; it can be performed even on the preceding day. Therefore, the location of placing hands is similarly optional, and it may be performed outside the Temple. Since, according to this approach, the act of placing hands is not necessarily related to the Temple, it is not permitted on the Festival.

אֲמַר רָמִי בַּר חָמָא: שְׁמַע מִינַּהּ סְמִיכָה בְּכׇל כֹּחוֹ בָּעֵינַן. דְּאִי סָלְקָא דַּעְתָּךְ לָא בָּעֵינַן בְּכׇל כֹּחוֹ – מַאי קָא עָבֵיד? לִיסְמוֹךְ!

Rami bar Ḥama said: You can **learn from here,** from this dispute, that the mitzva of **placing hands** requires not only placing one's hands on the animal's head, but **we also require** that one places his hands **with all his strength.**[H] **For if it enters your mind that we do not require all his strength, what** prohibition **does one violate** by placing his hands? **Let him place** them on a Festival as well, as this does not resemble a prohibited action at all.

מֵיתִיבִי: "דַּבֵּר אֶל בְּנֵי יִשְׂרָאֵל וְסָמַךְ", בְּנֵי יִשְׂרָאֵל סוֹמְכִין וְאֵין בְּנוֹת יִשְׂרָאֵל סוֹמְכוֹת. רַבִּי יוֹסֵי וְרַבִּי יִשְׁמָעֵאל אוֹמְרִים: בְּנוֹת יִשְׂרָאֵל סוֹמְכוֹת רְשׁוּת.

The Gemara raises an objection to this from a *baraita*: **"Speak to the children of** [*benei*] **Israel"** (Leviticus 1:2). The word *benei* literally means: Sons of. And it states nearby: **"And he shall place** his hand on the head of the burnt-offering" (Leviticus 1:4), from which we learn that **the sons of Israel place** their hands, **but the daughters of Israel do not place** them.[HN] **Rabbi Yosei and Rabbi Yishmael say: It is optional for the daughters of Israel to place** their hands. They may place their hands if they so choose, although they are not obligated to do so.

אָמַר רַבִּי יוֹסֵי: סָח לִי אַבָּא אֶלְעָזָר: פַּעַם אַחַת הָיָה לָנוּ עֵגֶל שֶׁל זִבְחֵי שְׁלָמִים, וֶהֱבֵיאנוּהוּ לְעֶזְרַת נָשִׁים, וְסָמְכוּ עָלָיו נָשִׁים. לֹא מִפְּנֵי שֶׁסְּמִיכָה בְּנָשִׁים – אֶלָּא כְּדֵי לַעֲשׂוֹת נַחַת רוּחַ לַנָּשִׁים. וְאִי סָלְקָא דַּעְתָּךְ סְמִיכָה בְּכׇל כֹּחוֹ בָּעֵינַן – מִשּׁוּם נַחַת רוּחַ דְּנָשִׁים עָבְדִינַן עֲבוֹדָה בְּקָדָשִׁים? אֶלָּא לָאו שְׁמַע מִינַּהּ: לָא בָּעֵינַן בְּכׇל כֹּחוֹ.

Rabbi Yosei said: The Sage **Abba Elazar related to me** the following incident: **On one occasion, we had a calf for a peace-offering, and we brought it to the Women's Courtyard, and women placed** their hands **on it.** We did this **not because there** is an obligation of **placing hands in** the case of **women, but in order to please the women,** by allowing them to sacrifice an offering, in all of its particulars, as men do. Now, **if it enters your mind** that **we require** placing hands **with all one's strength,** would **we perform work with consecrated** offerings **in order to please** the **women?** Placing one's hands forcefully on an animal is considered performing work with it, and if one does it without being obligated to do so, he has thereby performed work with an offering. **Rather, isn't it** correct to **conclude from this** that **we do not require** placing hands **with all one's strength?**

לְעוֹלָם אֵימָא לָךְ בָּעֵינַן בְּכׇל כֹּחוֹ. דְּאָמַר לְהוּ: אַקְפּוּ יְדַיְיכוּ. אִי הָכִי "לֹא מִפְּנֵי שֶׁסְּמִיכָה בְּנָשִׁים"? תֵּיפוֹק לֵיהּ דְּאֵינָהּ לִסְמִיכָה כְּלָל!

The Gemara rejects this: **Actually, I** could **say to you** that **we do require** placing hands **with all one's strength,** but here they allowed women to place their hands **by saying to them: Ease your hands** and do not press forcefully, so that their hand placing should not constitute work. The Gemara retorts: **If so,** then the reason formulated as: **Not because there** is an obligation to **place hands in** the case of **women,** is irrelevant to this law. **Let him derive** the permission for women to do so from the reason that **it is not** considered **placing hands at all.** If placing hands must be performed with all one's strength, this action the women are performing does not constitute placing hands.

אָמַר רַבִּי אַמִי: חֲדָא וְעוֹד קָאָמַר; חֲדָא – דְּלֵיתָא לִסְמִיכָה כְּלָל! וְעוֹד: כְּדֵי לַעֲשׂוֹת נַחַת רוּחַ לַנָּשִׁים.

Rabbi Ami said: He stated one reason **and another. One** reason is **that it is not** considered **placing hands at all,** as it is not performed with all of one's strength; **and another** reason is that they allowed it **in order to please the women.**

אָמַר רַב פַּפָּא: שְׁמַע מִינַּהּ צְדָדִין אֲסוּרִין. דְּאִי סָלְקָא דַּעְתָּךְ צְדָדִין מוּתָּרִין – לִסְמוֹךְ לִצְדָדִין. אֶלָּא לָאו שְׁמַע מִינַּהּ: צְדָדִין אֲסוּרִין?

Rav Pappa said: Learn from this that anything upon which one may not place objects or upon which one may not sit on Shabbat, its **sides are** likewise **prohibited, for if it enters your mind** to say that the **sides are permitted,** they could have told the women **to place** their hands **on the sides,** i.e., on the head of the animal rather than on its back, as the head of the animal is considered as if it were one of its sides. **Rather,** must one **not conclude from this** that the **sides are prohibited?**

Perek **II**
Daf **17** Amud **a**

רַב אַשִׁי אָמַר: אֲפִילּוּ תֵּימָא צְדָדִין מוּתָּרִין. כׇּל דִּבְהָדֵי גַּבָּהּ – כְּגַבָּהּ דָּמֵי.

Rav Ashi said: Even if **you say that sides are permitted** in general, there is no proof from here, since **anything that is near** the animal's **back** is **considered as its back.** Therefore, placing the hands on the head of the animal is the same as placing them on the animal itself, as opposed to its sides.

HALAKHA

Places his hands with all his strength – סְמִיכָה בְּכׇל כֹּחוֹ: One who is placing his hands on an animal must do so by placing his hands on the animal's head and leaning into them with all of his strength, in accordance with Rami bar Ḥama and Rav Pappa (Rambam *Sefer Avoda, Hilkhot Ma'aseh HaKorbanot* 3:11).

Placing hands by women – סְמִיכַת נָשִׁים: Women do not perform the act of placing on offerings, in accordance with the opinion of the Sages (Rambam *Sefer Avoda, Hilkhot Ma'aseh HaKorbanot* 3:5).

NOTES

The daughters of Israel do not place them – אֵין בְּנוֹת יִשְׂרָאֵל סוֹמְכוֹת: It appears from the discussion here and in other places in the Gemara that the first *tanna* not only maintains that women are not obligated to place their hands, but it is in fact prohibited for them to do so.

This prohibition is understandable according to Rashi (e.g., on *Rosh HaShana* 33a), as he claims that women who perform mitzvot without being obligated to do so transgress the prohibition against adding to the mitzvot. However, most authorities reject this view. Instead, they state that a prohibition exists in this case due to the concern that it may appear as if the women were performing work with sacred offerings (see *Tosafot* on *Rosh HaShana*). This explanation also clarifies the dispute between the *tanna'im*: The lenient view maintains that there is no reason to be stringent with regard to this *halakha*, as the act is prohibited only due to the appearance of prohibition.

מתני׳ בֵּית שַׁמַּאי אוֹמְרִים: מְבִיאִין שְׁלָמִים וְאֵין סוֹמְכִין עֲלֵיהֶם, אֲבָל לֹא עוֹלוֹת. וּבֵית הִלֵּל אוֹמְרִים: מְבִיאִין שְׁלָמִים וְעוֹלוֹת וְסוֹמְכִין עֲלֵיהֶם.

MISHNA **Beit Shammai say:**[N] **One may bring peace-offerings** on a Festival because both the owners and the priests partake of them, **but one may not place** his hands **on them,**[N] on the peace-offerings before sacrificing them. **However,** one may **not** bring **burnt-offerings** at all because they are not eaten, and labor is permitted on Festivals only for the sake of preparing food for humans. **And Beit Hillel say: One may bring peace-offerings and** also **burnt-offerings, and one places** his **hands on** both of **them.**[H]

עֲצֶרֶת שֶׁחָל לִהְיוֹת בְּעֶרֶב שַׁבָּת, בֵּית שַׁמַּאי אוֹמְרִים: יוֹם טְבוֹחַ אַחַר הַשַּׁבָּת. וּבֵית הִלֵּל אוֹמְרִים: אֵין יוֹם טְבוֹחַ אַחַר הַשַּׁבָּת. וּמוֹדִים שֶׁאִם חָלָה לִהְיוֹת בַּשַּׁבָּת, שֶׁיּוֹם טְבוֹחַ אַחַר הַשַּׁבָּת.

If **the festival of *Shavuot* occurs on the eve of Shabbat, Beit Shammai say: The day of slaughter** is **after Shabbat,**[N] on Sunday. This is the day on which the animals brought in honor of the pilgrimage Festival are slaughtered, since they maintain that the Festival burnt-offering is not sacrificed on the Festival day itself but on the following day, and all burnt-offerings vowed by individuals are postponed to the following day. **And Beit Hillel say: The day of slaughter is not after Shabbat.** Since the slaughter may be performed on the Festival day itself, it is unnecessary to postpone it. **But** they **concede that if *Shavuot* occurs on Shabbat, the day of slaughter** is **after Shabbat.**

אֵין כֹּהֵן גָּדוֹל מִתְלַבֵּשׁ בְּכֵלָיו, וּמוּתָּרִין בְּהֶסְפֵּד וּבְתַעֲנִית, שֶׁלֹּא לְקַיֵּים דִּבְרֵי הָאוֹמְרִין: עֲצֶרֶת אַחַר הַשַּׁבָּת.

The mishna relates that when the day of slaughter was on a Sunday, **the High Priest would not dress in his** festive **garments**[N] but would wear his regular clothing. **And all were permitted to eulogize**[N] **and fast** on this day. This was done in order **not to uphold** and reinforce **the opinion of** the Sadducees, **who would say: *Shavuot*** must always occur **after Shabbat.**[B] As the day of slaughter was on Sunday, it was necessary to demonstrate that we do not accept the view of the Sadducees, and that the day is not a Festival.

גמ׳ אָמַר רַבִּי אֶלְעָזָר אָמַר רַבִּי אוֹשַׁעְיָא: מִנַּיִין לַעֲצֶרֶת שֶׁיֵּשׁ לָהּ תַּשְׁלוּמִין כָּל שִׁבְעָה? שֶׁנֶּאֱמַר: ״בְּחַג הַמַּצּוֹת וּבְחַג הַשָּׁבוּעוֹת וּבְחַג הַסּוּכּוֹת״, מַקִּישׁ חַג הַשָּׁבוּעוֹת לְחַג הַמַּצּוֹת: מַה חַג הַמַּצּוֹת יֵשׁ לָהּ תַּשְׁלוּמִין כָּל שִׁבְעָה, אַף חַג הַשָּׁבוּעוֹת יֵשׁ לָהּ תַּשְׁלוּמִין כָּל שִׁבְעָה.

GEMARA **Rabbi Elazar said** that **Rabbi Oshaya said: From where** is it derived **that** the ***Shavuot*** offerings **can be redressed,**[N] i.e., that the obligatory Festival offerings can be sacrificed **all seven** days following the Festival?[H] **As it is stated:** "Three times a year all your males shall appear… **on the festival of Passover, and on the festival of *Shavuot,* and on the festival of *Sukkot*"** (Deuteronomy 16:16). The verse compares **the festival of *Shavuot* to the festival of Passover by analogy: Just as one can redress the failure to bring the offering on the festival of Passover on all seven** days of the Festival, **so too, on the festival of *Shavuot,* one can redress the failure to bring the offering for all seven,** i.e., *Shavuot* and the six days following it.

HALAKHA

Festival offerings and placing hands on them – קָרְבְּנוֹת הֶחָג וּסְמִיכָה עֲלֵיהֶם: Festival offerings that are obligatory for that day are sacrificed on the Festival. This applies both to peace-offerings and burnt-offerings. Hands are placed on these offerings, in accordance with the opinion of Beit Hillel (Rambam *Sefer Korbanot, Hilkhot Ḥagiga* 1:8–9).

Redress for *Shavuot* offerings – תַּשְׁלוּמֵי עֲצֶרֶת: Even though *Shavuot* lasts only one day, Sages maintained the tradition that one may bring the obligatory Festival offerings throughout the six days following the Festival (Rambam *Sefer Korbanot, Hilkhot Ḥagiga* 1:7).

BACKGROUND

Who would say, *Shavuot* must always occur after Shabbat – הָאוֹמְרִין עֲצֶרֶת אַחַר הַשַּׁבָּת: According to tractate *Rosh HaShana* (22a) it was the Boethusians, a cult that broke away from the traditions of the Sages, who maintained this view. They explained the verse: "And you shall count for yourselves from the morrow of Shabbat" (Leviticus 23:15), as referring to the Shabbat that occurs during Passover. Accordingly, the festival of *Shavuot* in their calendar always occurs on a Sunday.

The members of this sect, who were allies of the Sadducees, constituted a minority of the Jewish people at the time, but it appears that they were powerful and wealthy, and they were even prepared to deploy various types of manipulation and deceit to ensure that all would follow their practices. For this reason, the Sages found it necessary to institute several decrees to counter their views, in order to emphasize and publicly demonstrate that the Boethusian approach is to be entirely rejected.

NOTES

Beit Shammai, etc. – בֵּית שַׁמַּאי וכו׳: *Tosafot* note that the first section of the mishna, which appears in tractate *Beitza*, is cited here only incidentally. Therefore, the mishna does not discuss it at length. Others, however, claim that this is not necessarily the case. The dispute can be understood as referring to the Festival peace-offering, which would render it relevant to the topic of this tractate (see *Zekher LaḤagiga*).

But one may not place his hands on them – וְאֵין סוֹמְכִים עֲלֵיהֶם: The Gemara in tractate *Beitza* cites several opinions with regard to the nature of this dispute. One view is that the dispute with regard to placing the hands applies only to obligatory Festival peace-offerings, as the mitzva of placing the hands on peace-offerings is stated in the Torah only with regard to voluntary peace-offerings and not with regard to obligatory ones (Leviticus, chapter 3). An alternative explanation maintains that the dispute pertains to whether placing the hands must be performed immediately before slaughtering, or whether it can perhaps be done prior to the Festival.

Day of slaughter after Shabbat – יוֹם טְבוֹחַ אַחַר הַשַּׁבָּת: The novelty of this opinion is as follows: Although the Sages instituted several decrees to publicize their opposition to the Sadducean view that *Shavuot* must always occur on a Sunday, Beit Shammai nevertheless maintains that Sunday is the day of slaughter even when it does not immediately follow the Festival. This also explains why the dispute is mentioned with regard to *Shavuot*, despite the fact that Beit Shammai claim that a similar day of slaughter follows the other Festivals as well (*Siaḥ Yitzḥak*; see *Zekher LaḤagiga*).

The High Priest would not dress in his garments – אֵין כֹּהֵן גָּדוֹל מִתְלַבֵּשׁ בְּכֵלָיו: According to the explanation of *Tosafot*, the High Priest would not wear priestly garments at all on this day. The day was marked by his avoidance of any service, as opposed to Festivals, when the High Priest would sacrifice offerings (see Meiri).

And all were permitted to eulogize – וּמוּתָּרִין בְּהֶסְפֵּד: This indicates that if not for the need to mark this day, eulogies would have been prohibited on it. With regard to those who sacrifice their offerings on that day, the question has been raised as to whether they are prohibited from eulogizing, as anyone who sacrifices an offering observes that day as a Festival (see *Mishne LaMelekh* and *Yad David*). The *Levush* writes that since nowadays we are no longer concerned about the Sadducean views, it is indeed prohibited to eulogize on the days that were once intended for the redress of the *Shavuot* offerings, and we do not recite the supplication prayer [*taḥanun*] on these days. This is, in fact, the custom of most communities.

Redress for *Shavuot* offerings – תַּשְׁלוּמֵי עֲצֶרֶת: The Jerusalem Talmud presents the following difficulty: One verse: "You shall do no kind of laborious work" (Leviticus 23:21), indicates that labor is prohibited on *Shavuot*, whereas another verse states: "And the Festival of harvest, the first fruits of your labor" (Exodus 23:16), implying that labor is performed on this day. The explanation there is that no labor may be performed on the Festival itself, but it is permitted on the days during which its offerings are redressed.

וְאֵימָא: מַקִּישׁ לְחַג הַסּוּכּוֹת, מָה חַג הַסּוּכּוֹת יֵשׁ לָהּ תַּשְׁלוּמִין כׇּל שְׁמוֹנָה – אַף חַג הַשָּׁבוּעוֹת יֵשׁ לָהּ תַּשְׁלוּמִין כׇּל שְׁמוֹנָה! שְׁמִינִי רֶגֶל בִּפְנֵי עַצְמוֹ הוּא.

The Gemara raises a difficulty: **But perhaps** you should **say** instead that the verse compares *Shavuot* **to the festival of *Sukkot* by analogy: Just as the Festival** day **of *Sukkot* can be redressed for all eight** days, as the Eighth Day of Assembly is part of the Festival, **so too can the festival of *Shavuot* be redressed for all eight** days. The Gemara answers: The **Eighth** Day of Assembly **is an independent pilgrimage Festival** and is not considered part of *Sukkot*.

אֵימוּר דְּאָמְרִי שְׁמִינִי רֶגֶל בִּפְנֵי עַצְמוֹ הוּא, הָנֵי מִילֵּי לְעִנְיַן פז״ר קש״ב, אֲבָל לְעִנְיַן תַּשְׁלוּמִין – תַּשְׁלוּמִין דְּרִאשׁוֹן הוּא? דִּתְנַן: מִי שֶׁלֹּא חָג בְּיוֹם טוֹב הָרִאשׁוֹן שֶׁל חַג – חוֹגֵג אֶת כׇּל הָרֶגֶל וְיוֹם טוֹב הָאַחֲרוֹן!

The Gemara continues to ask: You can **say that** when **they said that** The **Eighth** Day of Assembly **is an independent pilgrimage Festival, this applies only to the issue of** ***peh, zayin, reish, kuf, shin, beit,***[NH] an acronym for the six *halakhot* that differentiate The **Eighth** Day of Assembly from the festival of *Sukkot*. **But with regard to the redress** of the Festival offerings, **it** is considered a day of **redress for the first** Festival day, **as we learned** in a mishna (9a): **One who did not celebrate** by sacrificing the Festival offerings **on the first day of the** *Sukkot* **Festival can celebrate** by sacrificing them **throughout the pilgrimage Festival** of *Sukkot* **and** on **the last day** of that Festival. If so, the question remains: Why do we not compare *Shavuot* to *Sukkot* and allow its offerings to be completed on all eight days?

תָּפַשְׂתָּ מְרוּבֶּה – לֹא תָּפַשְׂתָּ, תָּפַשְׂתָּ מוּעָט – תָּפַשְׂתָּ.

The Gemara answers by implementing the following principle: **If you grasped many, you did not grasp anything; if you grasped few, you grasped something.** In other words, when one must choose between a smaller number and a larger one, there is more certainty in choosing the smaller one. Even if that choice turns out to be erroneous, it is preferable to the larger one, as it is included in it. In this case, seven is included in eight. Therefore, it is preferable to compare *Shavuot* to the seven days of Passover than to the eight days of *Sukkot*.

אֶלָּא לְמַאי הִלְכְתָא כְּתַבֵיהּ רַחֲמָנָא לְחַג הַסּוּכּוֹת? לְאַקּוֹשֵׁי לְחַג הַמַּצּוֹת, מָה חַג הַמַּצּוֹת טָעוּן לִינָה – אַף חַג הַסּוּכּוֹת טָעוּן לִינָה.

The Gemara asks: **But** if we do not compare *Shavuot* to *Sukkot*, **for** the sake of **what *halakha* did the Merciful One write**[N] **the festival of *Sukkot*** in this context? The laws of all the Festivals were already listed, so the Torah must have mentioned their names again in order to compare them for a particular reason. The Gemara answers: The festival of *Sukkot* was mentioned in order **to compare** it by **analogy to the festival of Passover,** in the following manner: **Just as the festival of Passover requires lodging** overnight in Jerusalem after the conclusion of the Festival, as one may not depart that night, **so too the festival of *Sukkot* requires lodging** in Jerusalem after *Sukkot* has ended.

וְהָתָם מְנָלַן?

The Gemara asks: **And there,** with regard to Passover itself, **from where do we** derive that it requires lodging?

Perek **II**
Daf **17** Amud **b**

דִּכְתִיב: ״וּפָנִיתָ בַבֹּקֶר וְהָלַכְתָּ לְאֹהָלֶיךָ״.

The Gemara answers: One may leave Jerusalem only in the morning, after staying there for the night following the Festival, **as it is written** following the laws of the Paschal offering: **"And you shall turn**[N] **in the morning and go to your tents"** (Deuteronomy 16:7).

NOTES

Peh, zayin, reish, kuf, shin, beit – **פז״ר קש״ב:** This acronym stands for the six unique aspects of the Eighth Day of Assembly: First, a new lottery [*payis*] is performed to determine which priests will sacrifice the day's offerings, and the arrangement established on *Sukkot* is not continued. Second, the blessing for time [*zeman*] is recited: Who has given us life, sustained us, and brought us to this time, just as it is recited at the outset of each Festival. Third, it is considered a pilgrimage Festival [*regel*] in and of itself, in that it is referred to as the Eighth Day of Assembly rather than *Sukkot*. Fourth, the additional offerings [*korban*] are unique to this day and do not follow the model of the additional offerings of *Sukkot*. Fifth, the song [*shir*] of the day sung by the Levites is unique to this day rather than being a continuation of the Psalms sung on *Sukkot*. Lastly, the day has its own blessing [*berakha*] inserted in Grace after Meals and in prayer (see *Tosafot*), which is different than that recited on *Sukkot*.

For what *halakha* did the Merciful One write – **לְמַאי הִלְכְתָא כְּתַבֵיהּ רַחֲמָנָא:** The *Bayit Ḥadash* asks: If so, perhaps this verse was stated only with regard to lodging, and there is no proof that *Shavuot* has days of redress. He answers that according to the principle: There is no analogy by half-measures, the fact that the Festivals are compared to one another with regard to one aspect implies that they are comparable with regard to other aspects, including the observance of days of redress.

HALAKHA

Peh, zayin, reish, kuf, shin, beit – **פז״ר קש״ב:** On the first day of *Sukkot*, a lottery is conducted between the priestly watches to determine which of them will sacrifice the bulls of the additional Festival offering and in what order. On the Eighth Day of Assembly, a new lottery is performed, as it is for any other Festival. The additional offering of the Eighth Day of Assembly does not follow the order of the *Sukkot* offerings but consists of a bull, a ram, seven lambs as burnt-offerings, and one goat as a sin-offering (Rambam *Sefer Avoda, Hilkhot Temidin UMusafin* 10:5).

Sukkot is not mentioned in the prayers and blessings of the Eighth Day of Assembly. Rather, the day has a name of its own: The Eighth Day; this festival of Assembly (*Shulḥan Arukh*); or the Eighth day of Assembly, this Festival (*Magen Avraham*, citing Maharshal; *Taz*). The blessing for time is recited on the Eighth Day of Assembly as part of *kiddush* (*Shulḥan Arukh, Oraḥ Ḥayyim* 668:1).

NOTES

As it is written, And you shall turn, etc. – **דִּכְתִיב: וּפָנִיתָ וגו׳:** According to Rashi, the verse, "And you shall turn in the morning," must refer to the morning of the first intermediate day of the Festival, rather than the Festival itself, because one may not venture beyond the Shabbat boundaries on a Festival. Other commentaries raise various difficulties with regard to this reasoning. According to the Rid, the verse is referring to the morning following the final day of the Festival, as all seven days of the Festival are considered a single unit (see *Tosafot*). The Meiri addresses a different aspect of the mitzva of lodging. He claims that the mitzva of lodging is unrelated to the prohibition against venturing beyond the boundary, and one who has brought an offering may not leave Jerusalem that night even if he remains within the boundary. Rather, he must stay overnight as a sign of respect to the Temple, thereby demonstrating that he is not in a hurry to leave immediately upon the fulfillment of his duty.

NOTES

What, is it not that it does not have a day of slaughter at all – מַאי לָאו, אֵין לָהּ יוֹם טְבוֹחַ כְּלָל: Many commentaries are puzzled by this statement: How can the Gemara suggest that there is no day of slaughter at all according to Beit Hillel, when the mishna states that they concede that there is a day of slaughter when *Shavuot* occurs on a Shabbat? Some commentaries distinguish between a general day of slaughter and the particular circumstance of redressing offerings that could not be sacrificed on Shabbat. Beit Hillel concede only that there is a day for redressing the Shabbat offerings, since they are postponed by the Torah itself (see Maharsha and *Siaḥ Yitzḥak*). The *Turei Aven*, based on the reasoning above and on additional reasons, explains that throughout this entire discussion, all concur that there is at least one day of slaughter for redressing the offerings. However, when the Gemara refers to a day of slaughter, it does not mean that it is held on the day after the Festival but later in that week.

So too *Shavuot* is sanctified for the unit of time by which it is counted – אַף עֲצֶרֶת לְמִנּוּיֶיהָ: The difficulty posed by the Gemara, that perhaps *Shavuot* should have only one day of redress, is also addressed by the Jerusalem Talmud. The answer offered there is that there is indeed a difference between the first day of redress and the six additional days: The first day of slaughter is considered the main day of redress, whereas the role of the others is merely to supplement it.

So too *Shavuot* is one day – אַף עֲצֶרֶת יוֹם אֶחָד: The *Turei Aven* raises the following difficulty: The Torah states explicitly that *Shavuot* is celebrated for one day; why then is it necessary to learn this through an analogy to the New Moon? He answers, in accordance with his general approach, that this statement is referring to the additional day of slaughter. Without the analogy, one may have mistakenly thought that the period of redress for *Shavuot* lasts only one day.

תְּנַן: עֲצֶרֶת שֶׁחָל לִהְיוֹת עֶרֶב שַׁבָּת, בֵּית שַׁמַּאי אוֹמְרִים: יוֹם טְבוֹחַ אַחַר הַשַּׁבָּת, וּבֵית הִלֵּל אוֹמְרִים: אֵין לָהּ יוֹם טְבוֹחַ. מַאי לָאו – אֵין לָהּ יוֹם טְבוֹחַ כְּלָל? לֹא, שֶׁאֵינָהּ צְרִיכָה יוֹם טְבוֹחַ.

§ **We learned** in the mishna: If **the festival of *Shavuot* occurs on the eve of Shabbat, Beit Shammai say: The day of slaughter is after Shabbat; and Beit Hillel say: It does not have a day of slaughter. What, is it not that it does not have a day of slaughter at all;**[N] i.e., there are no days of redress for an offering that was meant to be sacrificed on the festival of *Shavuot* itself? The Gemara rejects this: **No,** Beit Hillel means that **it does not require a day of slaughter.**

וּמַאי קָא מַשְׁמַע לַן? דְּמַקְרְבִינַן בְּיוֹמֵיהּ. הָא אִיפְלִיגוּ בָּהּ חֲדָא זִימְנָא. דִּתְנַן: בֵּית שַׁמַּאי אוֹמְרִים: מְבִיאִין שְׁלָמִים וְאֵין סוֹמְכִין עֲלֵיהֶם, אֲבָל לֹא עוֹלוֹת. וּבֵית הִלֵּל אוֹמְרִים: מְבִיאִין שְׁלָמִים וְעוֹלוֹת וְסוֹמְכִין עֲלֵיהֶם!

The Gemara asks: **And what does this teach us; that** all offerings **are sacrificed on their day? But they have** already **disputed this once, as we learned** in a mishna: **Beit Shammai say: One may bring peace-offerings** on a Festival **but one may not place** his **hands on them. However,** one may **not** bring **burnt-offerings** at all; **and Beit Hillel say: One may bring peace-offerings and** also **burnt-offerings, and one places** his **hands on** both of **them.** Why is it necessary to restate this argument in different terms?

צְרִיכָא. דְּאִי אַשְׁמְעִינַן בְּהָא – בְּהָא קָא אָמְרִי בֵּית שַׁמַּאי, מִשּׁוּם דְּאֶפְשָׁר לְמָחָר, אֲבָל הָכָא, אֵימָא מוֹדוּ לְהוּ לְבֵית הִלֵּל.

The Gemara answers: It is **necessary, for had** the mishna **taught us** only **this** case, that Beit Shammai prohibits bringing burnt-offerings on a Festival, we might have said: It is **with regard to this** case, a regular Festival followed by a weekday, **that Beit Shammai state** their opinion, **because** it is **possible** to sacrifice these burnt-offerings **on the following day,** on the day of slaughter after the Festival; **but there,** with regard to a *Shavuot* that occurs on a Friday, when one cannot sacrifice offerings on the following day, **you** might perhaps **say** that **they agree with Beit Hillel** that the burnt-offerings should be sacrificed on the Festival itself. It was therefore necessary to state that Beit Shammai's view is the same in both cases.

וְאִי אַשְׁמְעִינַן בְּהָא – בְּהָא קָאָמְרִי בֵּית הִלֵּל, מִשּׁוּם דְּלָא אֶפְשָׁר לְמָחָר, אֲבָל בְּהָא – אֵימָא מוֹדוּ לְבֵית שַׁמַּאי. צְרִיכָא.

The reverse also applies: **And had it taught us** only **that** case, that there is no day of slaughter after Shabbat, we might have said: It is **with regard to that** case **that Beit Hillel state** their view, that the offerings should be sacrificed on the Festival itself, **because** it is **not possible** to sacrifice them **on the following day,** which is Shabbat; **but here,** on a regular Festival followed by a weekday, **you** might **say** that perhaps **they agree with Beit Shammai.** It is therefore **necessary** for the mishna to specify both cases. The question of whether there days of redress for *Shavuot* according to Beit Hillel therefore remains unresolved.

תָּא שְׁמַע: מִי שֶׁלֹּא חָג שִׁבְעַת יְמֵי הַפֶּסַח, וּשְׁמוֹנַת יְמֵי הֶחָג, וְיוֹם טוֹב הָרִאשׁוֹן שֶׁל עֲצֶרֶת – שׁוּב אֵינוֹ חוֹגֵג. מַאי לָאו – יוֹם טוֹב שֶׁל עֲצֶרֶת? לֹא, יוֹם טְבוֹחַ. אִי הָכִי נִיפְשׁוֹט מִינַּהּ דְּחַד יוֹם טְבוֹחַ! אֵימָא: יְמֵי טְבוֹחַ.

The Gemara suggests: **Come** and **hear** a proof from a different source: **One who did not celebrate** by sacrificing the peace-offerings of the Festival on **the seven days of Passover, or** on **the eight days of the festival** of *Sukkot*, **or** on **the first day of *Shavuot* may no longer celebrate** and sacrifice those offerings. The Gemara infers: **Does** this **not** mean that if one did not sacrifice on **the Festival day of *Shavuot*** itself, this lapse cannot be remedied, thereby demonstrating that there are no days of redress for *Shavuot*? The Gemara refutes this: **No,** the term Festival day is referring to the **day of slaughter,** rather than the Festival itself. The Gemara immediately counters: **If so, let us** at least **resolve from here,** i.e., the mishna **that** there is only **one day of slaughter** and not seven days. The Gemara rejects this: **Say** that the wording of the mishna should be corrected, so that instead of: A day of slaughter, it reads: **Days of slaughter.**

תָּא שְׁמַע, דְּתָנֵי רַבָּה בַּר שְׁמוּאֵל: אָמְרָה תּוֹרָה מְנֵה יָמִים וְקַדֵּשׁ חֹדֶשׁ, מְנֵה יָמִים וְקַדֵּשׁ עֲצֶרֶת. מָה חֹדֶשׁ לְמִנּוּיָיו – אַף עֲצֶרֶת לְמִנּוּיֶיהָ. מַאי לָאו גָּמַר מֵחֹדֶשׁ, מָה חֹדֶשׁ יוֹם אֶחָד – אַף עֲצֶרֶת יוֹם אֶחָד!

The Gemara suggests further: **Come** and **hear** a proof from another source, **as Rabba bar Shmuel taught** the following *baraita*: The **Torah said** to **count** thirty **days, as it is stated:** "A month of days" (Numbers 11:20), **and** then **sanctify** the **month** with offerings. And the Torah also said to **count days** from Passover **and** then **sanctify the festival of *Shavuot*** with offerings, **as it is stated: "You shall count fifty days"** (Leviticus 23:16). From this comparison, we learn the following *halakha*: **Just as** the new **month is** sanctified **for** the unit of time **by which it is counted,** i.e., for one day, **so too, *Shavuot*** is sanctified for the unit of time by which it is counted,[N] i.e., for one full week, as it is stated: "Seven complete weeks shall there be" (Leviticus 23:15). The Gemara infers from this: **Does** this **not** mean that **we learn from** the **month?** If so, we can also learn that **just as** the festival of **a month,** the New Moon, is **one day, so too *Shavuot*** is only **one day,**[N] without days of redress.

אָמַר רָבָא: וְתִסְבְּרָא? אַטּוּ עֲצֶרֶת, יוֹמֵי מָנֵינַן שָׁבוּעֵי לָא מָנֵינַן? וְהָאָמַר אַבַּיֵי: מִצְוָה לְמִימְנֵי יוֹמֵי – דִּכְתִיב: ״תִּסְפְּרוּ חֲמִשִּׁים יוֹם״, וּמִצְוָה לְמִימְנֵי שָׁבוּעֵי – דִּכְתִיב: ״שִׁבְעָה שָׁבוּעוֹת תִּסְפָּר לָךְ״. וְעוֹד: ״חַג שָׁבוּעוֹת״ כְּתִיב.

Rava said: And how can you understand it that way? **Is that to say that for *Shavuot* we count days but we do not count weeks?**[N] **Didn't Abaye say:** It is **a mitzva to count days,** in the counting of the *omer*, **as it is written:** "Until the morrow of the seventh week, **you shall count fifty days**" (Leviticus 23:16); **and** it is also **a mitzva to count weeks,**[N] **as it is written: "Seven weeks you shall count for yourself,** from when the sickle is first put to the standing corn" (Deuteronomy 16:9); **and further, it is written: "The festival of weeks [*shavuot*]"** (Deuteronomy 16:10), which indicates that it is a Festival that is established through a count of weeks? Consequently, the days of redress for *Shavuot* should last a week, in accordance with its components.[H]

דְּבֵי רַבִּי אֱלִיעֶזֶר בֶּן יַעֲקֹב תָּנָא: אָמַר קְרָא: ״וּקְרָאתֶם״ ״וּבְקֻצְרְכֶם״ – אֵיזֶהוּ חַג שֶׁאַתָּה קוֹרֵא וְקוֹצֵר בּוֹ – הֱוֵי אוֹמֵר זֶה חַג עֲצֶרֶת.

§ In **the school of Rabbi Eliezer ben Ya'akov,** a Sage **taught** the following: **The verse states** with regard to *Shavuot*: **"And you shall make a proclamation** on this very day, it shall be a holy convocation, you shall do no kind of laborious work" (Leviticus 23:21), and it states in the same chapter: **"And when you reap** the harvest of your land" (Leviticus 23:22). **Which is the Festival on which you make a proclamation and** also **reap,** i.e., which Festival occurs in the harvest season? **You must say it is the festival of *Shavuot*.**

אֵימַת? אִילֵימָא בְּיוֹם טוֹב – קְצִירָה בְּיוֹם טוֹב מִי שָׁרֵי? אֶלָּא לָאו – לְתַשְׁלוּמִין.

The Gemara proceeds to analyze the teaching: **When** exactly does this refer to? **If we say** it is referring **to the Festival day** itself, is it **permitted to reap on a Festival?**[N] Obviously, ordinary work is prohibited on Festivals. **Rather,** is it **not** referring **to** the issue of **redress?** In other words, it speaks of those days on which redress can be made for the offerings of the Festival, i.e., the days of slaughter, on which one may indeed reap because they are regular weekdays, and they nevertheless have a festive quality.

וְאַף עַל גַּב דְּאִיתְּמַר דְּרַבִּי אֶלְעָזָר אָמַר רַבִּי אוֹשַׁעְיָא, אִצְטְרִיךְ דְּרַבִּי אֱלִיעֶזֶר בֶּן יַעֲקֹב. דְּאִי מִדְּרַבִּי אֶלְעָזָר אָמַר רַבִּי אוֹשַׁעְיָא – הֲוָה אָמִינָא: מַה תַּשְׁלוּמִין שֶׁל חַג הַמַּצּוֹת אָסוּר בַּעֲשִׂיַּית מְלָאכָה – אַף תַּשְׁלוּמֵי עֲצֶרֶת נַמִי אָסוּר בַּעֲשִׂיַּית מְלָאכָה. קָמַשְׁמַע לָן דְּרַבִּי אֱלִיעֶזֶר בֶּן יַעֲקֹב. וְאִי מִדְּרַבִּי אֱלִיעֶזֶר בֶּן יַעֲקֹב

The Gemara comments: **And even though** the teaching **that Rabbi Elazar** said that **Rabbi Oshaya said,** that the *halakha* of the redress for *Shavuot* is derived from the comparison to Passover, **was stated,** it was nevertheless **necessary** to state the teaching of **Rabbi Eliezer ben Ya'akov** as well, **for if** we had learned only the proof **that Rabbi Elazar** said that **Rabbi Oshaya said, I would say** the following: **Just as on the** days of **redress for the festival of Passover it is prohibited to perform** any **work** that will not cause irretrievable loss, as they are part of the Festival, **so too** on **the** days of **redress for *Shavuot* it is also prohibited to perform work.**[N] We are therefore **taught** the statement of **Rabbi Eliezer ben Ya'akov** as well, that on these festive days one may reap, as they are weekdays. Conversely, **if** we had learned the *halakha* only **from** the words of **Rabbi Eliezer ben Ya'akov,**

HALAKHA

The mitzva of the counting of the *omer* – מִצְוַות סְפִירַת הָעוֹמֶר: One must count both the days and weeks to fulfill the obligation of counting the *omer*, as stated by Abaye. For example, one recites: Today is eight days, which are one week and one day of the *omer* [*la'omer*] (*Roke'aḥ*; Rashba; *Beit Yosef*; *Shela*; a similar view is attributed to the Ari). This is the custom according to *Nusaḥ Sefarad*, one version of Ashkenazic liturgy. Others say: In the *omer* [*ba'omer*] (Rema; *Taz*); this is the custom according to *Nusaḥ Ashkenaz*, another version of Ashkenazic liturgy. However, the Sephardic custom is to adjust the order slightly and say: Today is eight days of the *omer*, which are one week and one day. If one counts the days without the weeks or only the weeks without the days, some say that he fulfills his obligation (Rema; *Ḥavvot Ya'ir*), while others disagree (*Peri Ḥadash*). One should therefore count again in the proper manner but without a blessing (*Beur Halakha*; *Shulḥan Arukh*, *Oraḥ Ḥayyim* 489:1).

NOTES

Is that to say that for *Shavuot*…we do not count weeks – אַטּוּ עֲצֶרֶת...שָׁבוּעֵי לָא מָנֵינַן: Why isn't the principle: If you grasped few, you grasped something, applied to this case as well, resulting in the conclusion that there should be only one day of redress rather than an entire week? It is possible that the Gemara adds the reason relating to the festival of weeks in order to counter this possibility. The verse indicates that the counting leading up to *Shavuot* is fundamentally linked to weeks and does not merely consist of a number of individual days; therefore, an entire week should be devoted to the redress of the *Shavuot* offerings (*Siaḥ Yitzḥak*, citing the Rashba on tractate *Rosh HaShana*).

And it is a mitzva to count weeks – וּמִצְוָה לְמִימְנֵי שָׁבוּעֵי: Most authorities understand Abaye to mean that on each day of the *omer* we count the weeks as well as the days. However, some early authorities maintain that Abaye means that the number of weeks need only be mentioned at the conclusion of each week (Razah; *Sefer HaḤinnukh*).

Is it permitted to reap on a Festival – קְצִירָה בְּיוֹם טוֹב מִי שָׁרֵי: Later authorities point out that this statement assumes that reaping on Festivals is prohibited by Torah law. This presents a difficulty for several authorities, who claim that any labor prohibited on Shabbat that involves the preparation of food, including reaping, is permitted on a Festival by Torah law, and the prohibition against reaping on a Festival is by rabbinic law. According to this approach, standard reaping is prohibited, as it is not performed for the preparation of food for the day of the Festival itself. Therefore, a Festival day cannot be described as a day on which one reaps (see *Turei Aven* and *Zekher LaHagiga*).

So too on the days of the redress of *Shavuot* it is also prohibited to perform work – אַף תַּשְׁלוּמֵי עֲצֶרֶת נַמִי אָסוּר בַּעֲשִׂיַּית מְלָאכָה: The Jerusalem Talmud indicates that it is indeed prohibited to perform regular work on the day of slaughter, which is treated similarly to the intermediate Festival days. The Rambam also cites this law, although he adds that this prohibition is not an accepted law, but a custom (see Meiri).

לָא יָדְעִנָא כַּמָּה, קָא מַשְׁמַע לָן דְּרַבִּי אֶלְעָזָר אָמַר רַבִּי אוֹשַׁעְיָא.

I would not know how many days of redress there are. The Gemara therefore **teaches us,** from the statement **that Rabbi Elazar** said that **Rabbi Oshaya said,** that there are seven days of redress.

וְרֵישׁ לָקִישׁ אָמַר: ״וְחַג הַקָּצִיר״. אֵיזֶהוּ חַג שֶׁאַתָּה חוֹגֵג וְקוֹצֵר בּוֹ? הֱוֵי אוֹמֵר זֶה עֲצֶרֶת. אֵימַת? אִילֵימָא בְּיוֹם טוֹב – קְצִירָה בְּיוֹם טוֹב מִי שָׁרֵי? אֶלָּא לָאו – לְתַשְׁלוּמִין.

And Reish Lakish said, providing a different proof: From the very name of the day: **"And the Festival of harvest"** (Exodus 23:16), we can learn the following: **On which Festival do you celebrate and harvest? You must say it is** ***Shavuot.*** **When** exactly does this apply? **If we say** that it is **on the Festival day** itself, **is harvesting permitted on a Festival? Rather, is it not** referring to the day of **redress?**

אָמַר רַבִּי יוֹחָנָן, אֶלָּא מֵעַתָּה: ״חַג הָאָסִיף״, אֵי זֶהוּ חַג שֶׁיֵּשׁ בּוֹ אֲסִיפָה? הֱוֵי אוֹמֵר זֶה חַג הַסּוּכּוֹת. אֵימַת? אִילֵימָא בְּיוֹם טוֹב – מְלָאכָה בְּיוֹם טוֹב מִי שָׁרֵי? אֶלָּא בְּחוּלּוֹ שֶׁל מוֹעֵד. חוּלּוֹ שֶׁל מוֹעֵד מִי שָׁרֵי? אֶלָּא: חַג הַבָּא בִּזְמַן אֲסִיפָה; הָכָא נַמִי: חַג הַבָּא בִּזְמַן קְצִירָה.

Rabbi Yoḥanan said to Reish Lakish: **However, if that is so,** you should likewise say with regard to **"the Festival of gathering"** (Exodus 23:16): On **which Festival is there gathering? You must say it is the festival of** ***Sukkot.*** **When** exactly? **If we say** it is **on the Festival** day itself, **is labor permitted on a Festival? Rather,** it is referring **to the intermediate Festival days.** But on **the intermediate Festival days,** too, **is it permitted?** One may perform only work that, if neglected, would result in irretrievable loss. **Rather,** you must explain that "the Festival of gathering" is referring to the season of the year, i.e., the **Festival that occurs during the time of gathering.**[N] **Here too:** "The Festival of harvest" means **a Festival that occurs during the time of** harvest.

מִכְּלָל דְּתַרְוַיְיהוּ סְבִירָא לְהוּ דְּחוּלּוֹ שֶׁל מוֹעֵד אָסוּר בַּעֲשִׂיַּית מְלָאכָה.

§ The Gemara comments: Since Reish Lakish does not dispute the accuracy of Rabbi Yoḥanan's statement, **it may be inferred** from their statements **that both** of them **hold** that **the performance of labor** during **the intermediate Festival days is prohibited**[N] by the Torah.[H]

מְנָהָנֵי מִילֵּי? דְּתָנוּ רַבָּנַן: ״אֶת חַג הַמַּצּוֹת תִּשְׁמוֹר שִׁבְעַת יָמִים״ – לִימֵּד עַל חוּלּוֹ שֶׁל מוֹעֵד שֶׁאָסוּר בַּעֲשִׂיַּית מְלָאכָה, דִּבְרֵי רַבִּי יֹאשִׁיָּה. רַבִּי יוֹנָתָן אוֹמֵר: אֵינוֹ צָרִיךְ, קַל וָחוֹמֶר: וּמַה רִאשׁוֹן וּשְׁבִיעִי שֶׁאֵין קְדוּשָּׁה לִפְנֵיהֶן וּלְאַחֲרֵיהֶן – אָסוּר בַּעֲשִׂיַּית מְלָאכָה, חוּלּוֹ שֶׁל מוֹעֵד שֶׁיֵּשׁ קְדוּשָּׁה לִפְנֵיהֶן וּלְאַחֲרֵיהֶן – אֵינוֹ דִּין שֶׁיְּהֵא אָסוּר בַּעֲשִׂיַּית מְלָאכָה?!

The Gemara proceeds to ask: **From where are these matters** derived; what is the biblical source for this prohibition? **As the Sages taught: "You shall observe the festival of Passover seven days"** (Exodus 23:15).[N] This **teaches that the performance of labor is prohibited during the intermediate Festival days,** as "observe" denotes a negative commandment; this is **the statement of Rabbi Yoshiyya. Rabbi Yonatan says:** This proof **is not necessary,**[N] as it does not accord with the straightforward meaning of the verse. Rather, it is learned from **an** ***a fortiori*** inference, as follows: **If the performance of labor** on the **first and seventh** days of Passover, **which are not preceded and followed by sanctity** as the days before the first day and after the seventh day are weekdays, is nevertheless **prohibited, is it not right that** on the days of **the intermediate Festival days, which are preceded and followed by sanctity,**[N] i.e., the first and last days of the Festival, **the performance of labor should be prohibited?**

שֵׁשֶׁת יְמֵי בְרֵאשִׁית יוֹכִיחוּ, שֶׁיֵּשׁ קְדוּשָּׁה לִפְנֵיהֶן וּלְאַחֲרֵיהֶן וּמוּתָּרִין בַּעֲשִׂיַּית מְלָאכָה! מַה לְּשֵׁשֶׁת יְמֵי בְרֵאשִׁית – שֶׁאֵין בָּהֶן קׇרְבַּן מוּסָף, תֹּאמַר בְּחוּלּוֹ שֶׁל מוֹעֵד – שֶׁיֵּשׁ בּוֹ קׇרְבַּן מוּסָף. רֹאשׁ חֹדֶשׁ יוֹכִיחַ, שֶׁיֵּשׁ בּוֹ קׇרְבַּן מוּסָף – וּמוּתָּר בַּעֲשִׂיַּית מְלָאכָה! מַה לְּרֹאשׁ חֹדֶשׁ שֶׁאֵין קָרוּי ״מִקְרָא קֹדֶשׁ״, תֹּאמַר בְּחוּלּוֹ שֶׁל מוֹעֵד שֶׁקָּרוּי ״מִקְרָא קֹדֶשׁ״, הוֹאִיל וְקָרוּי מִקְרָא קֹדֶשׁ – דִּין הוּא שֶׁאָסוּר בַּעֲשִׂיַּית מְלָאכָה.

The Gemara questions this conclusion: The **six days of Creation,** i.e., the days of the week, **shall prove** this, **since** they **are preceded and followed by the sanctity** of Shabbat, **and yet the performance of labor on them is permitted.** The Gemara rejects this difficulty: **What** of the fact that the **six days of Creation** are regular weekdays **on which there is no additional offering;** can **you say** the same **with regard to the intermediate Festival days, on which there is an additional offering,** bestowing these days with a measure of sanctity? The Gemara counters this: **The New Moon shall prove this, since it has an additional offering, and the performance of labor is** nevertheless **permitted on it.** The Gemara refutes this argument: **What** of the fact that **the New Moon is not called "a holy convocation";** can **you say** the same **with regard to the intermediate Festival days, which** are **called "a holy convocation"?**[N] **Since** they are **called "a holy convocation" it is logical that the performance of labor should be prohibited on them.**

NOTES

A Festival that occurs during the time of gathering – חַג הַבָּא בִּזְמַן אֲסִיפָה: This statement teaches that the year must be intercalated when necessary in order to ensure that *Sukkot* occurs during the period of gathering, i.e., the harvest.

The performance of labor during the intermediate Festival days is prohibited – חוּלּוֹ שֶׁל מוֹעֵד אָסוּר בַּעֲשִׂיַּית מְלָאכָה: The Gemara indicates that this is the view of both Rabbi Yoḥanan and Reish Lakish, as well as that of certain *tanna'im*. However, as explained in *Tosafot*, most Sages maintain that the prohibition against working during the intermediate Festival days is rabbinic and the verses cited as proof merely serve to support the *halakhot* instituted by the Sages.

You shall observe…seven days – תִּשְׁמוֹר שִׁבְעַת יָמִים: The verse states: "You shall observe the festival of Passover; seven days you shall eat *matzot* as I commanded you, at the appointed time in the month of Aviv" (Exodus 23:15). According to a straightforward reading of the verse, the words "seven days" refer to the obligation to eat *matza*. However, since the verse is phrased so that the words "seven days" appear in the middle, they may be expounded as referring both to the preceding clause as well as to the one that follows it. Here, the preceding clause relates to refraining from work (*Turei Aven*).

Is not necessary – אֵינוֹ צָרִיךְ: This expression is common in halakhic midrash. It indicates the rejection of the exposition of one Sage by another, who proceeds to suggest an alternative. Generally, it should be understood as though the Sage were saying: The previous exposition with its attending difficulties is not needed, as I have a preferable exposition, which is either more straightforward or less flawed than the previous one. The attending difficulties are usually left unexplained.

Which are preceded and followed by sanctity – שֶׁיֵּשׁ קְדוּשָּׁה לִפְנֵיהֶן וּלְאַחֲרֵיהֶן: The *Turei Aven* notes that there is one major difficulty with regard to this *a fortiori* inference: It views the intermediate Festival days as a single unit. He claims that the inference must be understood in reference to each day on its own. Once it is used for the first day, the result can be used as the basis of a further *a fortiori* inference for the second day, and so on for all the Festival days. This type of inference is known as an *a fortiori* inference that is a consequence of an *a fortiori* inference.

The intermediate Festival days which are called a holy convocation – בְּחוּלּוֹ שֶׁל הַמּוֹעֵד שֶׁקְּרוּיִ מִקְרָא קֹדֶשׁ: The *Zekher LaHagiga* points out that, in fact, no source explicitly refers to the intermediate Festival days as holy convocations. Therefore, it can be assumed that the *baraita* here is relying on a verse that appears toward the conclusion of the main Torah passage relating to the Festivals: "These are the appointed seasons of the Lord, which you shall proclaim to be holy convocations, to bring an offering made by fire to the Lord, a burnt-offering, and a meal-offering, a sacrifice, and libations, each on its own day" (Leviticus 23:37), which appears to include the intermediate Festival days as well.

HALAKHA

The intermediate days of the Festivals – חוֹל הַמּוֹעֵד: Certain forms of work are prohibited on the intermediate Festival days while others are permitted, in accordance with the approach of the Sages with regard to each particular issue (Rema). One must honor the intermediate days of the Festivals by eating special foods and drinks and by wearing festive clothing, as on the Festival days themselves (*Magen Avraham*, citing *Tanya*; *Shulḥan Arukh*, *Oraḥ Ḥayyim* 530:1).

תַּנְיָא אִידָךְ: ״כׇּל מְלֶאכֶת עֲבוֹדָה לֹא תַעֲשׂוּ״ – לִימֵּד עַל חוּלּוֹ שֶׁל מוֹעֵד שֶׁאָסוּר בַּעֲשִׂיַּית מְלָאכָה, דִּבְרֵי רַבִּי יוֹסֵי הַגְּלִילִי. רַבִּי עֲקִיבָא אוֹמֵר: אֵינוֹ צָרִיךְ. הֲרֵי הוּא אוֹמֵר: ״אֵלֶּה מוֹעֲדֵי ה׳״ וגו׳; בַּמֶּה הַכָּתוּב מְדַבֵּר? אִם בָּרִאשׁוֹן – הֲרֵי כְּבָר נֶאֱמַר שַׁבָּתוֹן, אִם בַּשְּׁבִיעִי – הֲרֵי כְּבָר נֶאֱמַר שַׁבָּתוֹן. הָא אֵין הַכָּתוּב מְדַבֵּר אֶלָּא בְּחוּלּוֹ שֶׁל מוֹעֵד, לְלַמֶּדְךָ שֶׁאָסוּר בַּעֲשִׂיַּית מְלָאכָה.

It is taught in **another** *baraita* concerning the same topic: With regard to the first day of Passover and *Sukkot*, the verse states: **"You shall do no kind of laborious work"** (Leviticus 23:35), followed by "seven days, you shall bring an offering made by fire to the Lord," which **teaches that the performance of labor is prohibited during the intermediate Festival days;** this is **the statement of Rabbi Yosei the Galilean. Rabbi Akiva says:** This **is not necessary, since it is stated** earlier in that chapter: **"These are the appointed Festivals of the Lord,** holy convocations, which you shall proclaim in their appointed season" (Leviticus 23:4). **With regard to what is the verse speaking? If** it is referring **to the first** day of the Festival, **it has already** explicitly **stated "a solemn rest"** (Leviticus 23:39) with regard to that day; **if** it is referring **to the seventh, it has already stated "a solemn rest"** (Leviticus 23:39) with regard to that day as well. **Therefore, the verse can be speaking only of the intermediate Festival days, teaching you that the performance of labor is prohibited on them.**

תַּנְיָא אִידָךְ: ״שֵׁשֶׁת יָמִים תֹּאכַל מַצּוֹת וּבַיּוֹם הַשְּׁבִיעִי עֲצֶרֶת לַה׳״, מָה שְׁבִיעִי עָצוּר – אַף שֵׁשֶׁת יָמִים עֲצוּרִין. אִי מָה שְׁבִיעִי עָצוּר בְּכׇל מְלָאכָה – אַף שֵׁשֶׁת יָמִים עֲצוּרִין בְּכׇל מְלָאכָה?

It is taught in **another** *baraita*: The verse states: **"Six days you shall eat unleavened bread, and on the seventh day**[N] there **shall be a solemn assembly for the Lord** your God; on it, you shall do no work" (Deuteronomy 16:8). **If so, just as the seventh** day of the Festival **is precluded** from the performance of labor, **so are the six** intermediate Festival **days precluded,** since the word "and" in the phrase "and on the seventh day" connects it to the previous days. **If so,** perhaps: **Just as the seventh day is precluded from the performance of all labor, so too the six** intermediate **days are precluded from the performance of all labor,** even those whose performance prevents irretrievable loss.

תַּלְמוּד לוֹמַר: ״וּבַיּוֹם הַשְּׁבִיעִי עֲצֶרֶת״ – הַשְּׁבִיעִי עָצוּר בְּכׇל מְלָאכָה, וְאֵין שִׁשָּׁה יָמִים עֲצוּרִין בְּכׇל מְלָאכָה. הָא לֹא מְסָרָן הַכָּתוּב אֶלָּא לַחֲכָמִים. לוֹמַר לְךָ אֵי זֶה יוֹם אָסוּר וְאֵי זֶה יוֹם מוּתָּר, אֵי זוֹ מְלָאכָה אֲסוּרָה וְאֵי זוֹ מְלָאכָה מוּתֶּרֶת.

The verse therefore **states: "And on the seventh day there shall be a solemn assembly,"** literally, pause. This indicates that **the seventh** day alone **is precluded from the performance of all labor, but** the other **six days are not precluded from the performance of all labor** but only from certain forms of work. Since the Bible does not specify which types of work are prohibited, **the verse has therefore entrusted the** matter **to the Sages exclusively, to tell you** on **which day** work **is prohibited and** on **which day** it **is permitted,** and similarly **which labor is prohibited and which labor is permitted.**

״וּמוּתָּרִין בְּהֶסְפֵּד וְתַעֲנִית שֶׁלֹּא לְקַיֵּים אֶת דִּבְרֵי הָאוֹמְרִין עֲצֶרֶת אַחַר הַשַּׁבָּת״. וְהָאִיתְּמַר: מַעֲשֶׂה וּמֵת אֲלֶכְּסָא בְּלוֹד, וְנִכְנְסוּ כׇּל יִשְׂרָאֵל לְסׇפְדוֹ, וְלֹא הִנִּיחָם רַבִּי טַרְפוֹן, מִפְּנֵי שֶׁיּוֹם טוֹב שֶׁל עֲצֶרֶת הָיָה.

§ The mishna taught: **All were permitted to eulogize and fast** on the days of slaughter, in order **not to uphold the opinion of** the Sadducees, **who would say:** ***Shavuot*** must always occur **after Shabbat.** The Gemara raises a difficulty: **But wasn't it stated: An incident** occurred when **Alexa**[L] **died in Lod,**[B] **and all of Israel gathered to eulogize him, but Rabbi Tarfon would not allow them** do so **because it was the Festival day of** ***Shavuot*****?**

יוֹם טוֹב סָלְקָא דַּעְתָּךְ?! אִי בְּיוֹם טוֹב, מִי קָאָתוּ? אֶלָּא אֵימָא: מִפְּנֵי שֶׁיּוֹם טְבוֹחַ הָיָה! לָא קַשְׁיָא: כָּאן – בְּיוֹם טוֹב שֶׁחָל לִהְיוֹת אַחַר הַשַּׁבָּת; כָּאן – בְּיוֹם טוֹב שֶׁחָל לִהְיוֹת בַּשַּׁבָּת.

The Gemara analyzes this passage: **Can it enter your mind** to say that it was **a Festival day? If it had been a Festival day, would they have come?** Certainly they would not have assembled to eulogize someone on the Festival itself. **Rather, say** that they were prohibited to eulogize **because it was the Festival day of slaughter.**[N] The Gemara answers: This is **not difficult,** since **here,** the incident in Lod, is referring **to a Festival that occurs after Shabbat,** whose day of slaughter does not fall on a Sunday. The day of slaughter retains a measure of the sanctity of *Shavuot* through the offering of Festival offerings and should therefore be treated as a Festival. **There,** however, the mishna is referring **to a Festival that occurs on Shabbat.** Since in that case the day of slaughter occurs on a Sunday, it cannot be observed as a Festival, in order to counter the view of the Sadducees.

NOTES

And on the seventh day – וּבַיּוֹם הַשְּׁבִיעִי: This exposition is apparently based on two well-known principles of halakhic midrash: The word "and" links the seventh day to the days preceding it. This teaches that the law that is applicable to the sixth day of the Festival applies to the seventh as well. However, the word "the" in "the seventh day" indicates that they cannot be compared: It refers to the seventh day specifically, and no other. Since there are two expositions that appear to contradict one another, a middle ground must be found. In other words, the intermediate Festival days should be somewhat similar, but not entirely identical, to the actual Festival days. Since the nature of this difference is not specified by the Torah, the Sages of each generation have the power to determine the precise laws pertaining to days that are neither Festival days nor proper weekdays (see *Turei Aven*).

It was the Festival day of slaughter – שֶׁיּוֹם טְבוֹחַ הָיָה: This appears to imply that Rabbi Tarfon rules in accordance with Beit Shammai, since Beit Hillel maintain that a day of slaughter is held only when *Shavuot* occurs on a Shabbat. The Rid explains that even according to Beit Hillel, a day of slaughter would be held after *Shavuot* no matter the day of the week, as it was not physically possible for all the Festival offerings to be sacrificed on a single day. The only exception would be when *Shavuot* occurs on a Friday. Others claim that this law does not refer exclusively to the festival of *Shavuot*, but rather, as explained in the Jerusalem Talmud, it refers to a general *halakha* that the day after a Festival, called *Isru Ḥag*, must be observed in a festive manner, without eulogies or fasting (see *Siaḥ Yitzḥak*).

LANGUAGE

Alexa – אֲלֶכְּסָא: From the Greek name Ἀλεξῶ', *Alekso*, probably short for Alexander.

BACKGROUND

Lod – לוֹד: Lod was one of the oldest towns in Judea. It grew significantly toward the end of the Second Temple period and served as an important cultural center for many generations after the destruction of the Temple. Some of the greatest *tanna'im* lived there; among them were Rabbi Eliezer ben Hyrcanus, also known as Rabbi Eliezer the Great, Rabbi Tarfon, and others. Several important ordinances were instituted in the upper chamber of the house of Nit'za in Lod. After the bar Kokheva revolt, the town remained an important Torah center, especially for the scholars of southern Israel. Among the great *amora'im* who lived there were Rabbi Yehoshua ben Levi, Rabbi Simlai, Rabbi Yitzḥak bar Naḥmani, Rabbi Shimon ben Pazi, his son Rabbi Yehuda, and Rabbi Aḥa.

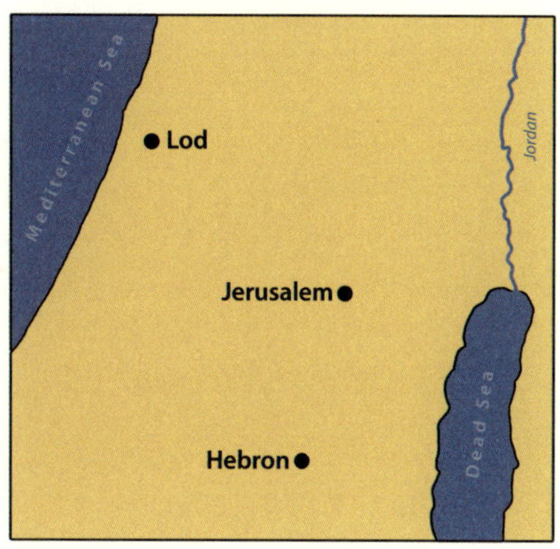

Location of Lod

After discussing many issues unrelated to the main topic of the tractate, the Gemara now begins to discuss the topic of ritual purity and will do so for the remainder of the tractate. These *halakhot* are relevant to the pilgrimage Festivals, as all are obligated to purify themselves in order to enter the Temple and sacrifice offerings.

מתני׳ נוֹטְלִין לַיָּדַיִם לַחוּלִּין וְלַמַּעֲשֵׂר וְלַתְּרוּמָה. וְלַקּוֹדֶשׁ – מַטְבִּילִין, וְלַחַטָּאת, אִם נִטְמְאוּ יָדָיו – נִטְמָא גּוּפוֹ.

MISHNA **One must wash his hands**[N] by pouring a quarter-*log* of water over them before eating **non-sacred** food,[NH] **and for tithes and for *teruma*;**[HB] **but for** eating **sacrificial** food **one must immerse** one's hands in **purification** waters, such as those of a ritual bath.[H] **And with** regard to one who wishes to touch the **purification** waters of the red heifer used for sprinkling, concerning which the Sages ordained further measures of sanctity, **if one's hands were rendered impure** even by rabbinical ritual impurity, which usually only renders the hands impure, **his** entire **body is rendered impure,** and he must immerse himself in a ritual bath.[H]

NOTES

One must wash his hands, etc. – **נוֹטְלִין לַיָּדַיִם וכו׳**: The early and later authorities disagree about the exact case discussed in this mishna. Some say that this mishna is referring to the regular washing of hands performed by one who is uncertain that his hands are impure. He is required to wash them due to the assumption that: Hands tend to be busy, i.e., they are liable to have been rendered impure unless particular care was taken. Alternatively, the mishna might be dealing with hands that have definitely been rendered impure by something that contaminates them with rabbinic, second-degree ritual impurity.

Washing hands for non-sacred food – **נְטִילַת יָדַיִם לַחוּלִּין**: The requirement to wash one's hands before eating non-sacred produce is a special ordinance that is essentially unrelated to the ritual purity of the food in question. According to Torah law, there is no obligation to be pure when partaking of non-sacred food, and one may eat such foods while his body is impure. Nevertheless, one is required to wash his hands before eating bread, even if he is certainly impure. The ordinance of washing hands for non-sacred produce was established due to the ancillary to *teruma*: The Sages decreed that the hands must be washed before eating bread so that people would remember to maintain themselves in a state of ritual purity when touching *teruma* and certainly when eating it.

HALAKHA

Washing hands for non-sacred food – **נְטִילַת יָדַיִם לַחוּלִּין**: One who wishes to eat bread, whose blessing is: Who brings forth [*hamotzi*] bread from the earth, must first wash his hands and recite the blessing: Who has commanded us about washing the hands, even if to his knowledge, his hands have not touched any sort of ritual impurity (*Shulḥan Arukh*, *Oraḥ Ḥayyim* 158:1).

Washing hands for *teruma* – **נְטִילַת יָדַיִם לִתְרוּמָה**: Anyone who eats *teruma*, including fruit, must wash his hands, even if they are ritually pure (Rambam *Sefer Zera'im*, *Hilkhot Terumot* 11:7).

Immersing hands for sacrificial food – **נְטִילַת יָדַיִם לְקוֹדֶשׁ**: If even a single hand of an individual is impure with the type of ritual impurity that affects only the hands, it renders the other hand impure upon contact, so that they both require immersion for sacrificial food (Rambam *Sefer Tahara*, *Hilkhot Avot HaTumot* 8:7).

Purification for the purification waters – **טָהֳרָה לַחַטָּאת**: One whose hands are rendered impure with a ritual impurity that affects only the hands must undergo a full immersion before touching the purification waters. Although the rest of his body is ritually pure with regard to sacrificial food and he is required only to immerse his hands for them, for the purposes of the red heifer, his entire body is considered impure (Rambam *Sefer Tahara*, *Hilkhot Para Aduma* 13:4).

BACKGROUND

Teruma – **תְּרוּמָה**: The Torah commands that the first fruit of one's grain, wine, and oil be given to a priest (Deuteronomy 18:4; Numbers 18:12). The Sages extended the scope of this mitzva to include all produce. This mitzva applies only in Eretz Yisrael. After one sets aside the first fruits, a certain portion of the produce must be set aside for priests. The Torah does not specify the amount of *teruma* that must be set aside; theoretically, one may fulfill his obligation by giving even a single kernel of grain from an entire crop. The Sages established a measure: One-fortieth for a generous gift, one-fiftieth for an average gift, and one-sixtieth for a miserly gift. One should not set aside the other tithes until he has set aside *teruma*. Whenever the term *teruma* appears without qualification, it refers to this offering, *teruma gedola*, also called the great *teruma*.

Teruma is considered sacred and may be eaten only by a priest and his household while they are in a state of ritual purity (see Leviticus 22:9–15). To highlight that state of ritual purity, the Sages obligated the priests to wash their hands before partaking of it. This is the source for the practice of washing the hands before partaking of bread today.

A ritually impure priest or a non-priest who eats *teruma* is subject to the penalty of death at the hand of Heaven. If *teruma* contracts ritual impurity, it may no longer be eaten and must be burned. Nevertheless, it remains the property of the priest, and he may benefit from its burning. Nowadays, *teruma* is not given to the priests because they have no definite proof of their priestly lineage. Nevertheless, the obligation to separate *teruma* still remains, but only a small portion of the produce is separated.

טָבַל לְחוּלִּין – הוּחְזַק לְחוּלִּין, אָסוּר לְמַעֲשֵׂר. טָבַל לְמַעֲשֵׂר – הוּחְזַק לְמַעֲשֵׂר, אָסוּר לִתְרוּמָה. טָבַל לִתְרוּמָה – הוּחְזַק לִתְרוּמָה, אָסוּר לְקוֹדֶשׁ. טָבַל לְקוֹדֶשׁ – הוּחְזַק לְקוֹדֶשׁ, אָסוּר לְחַטָּאת. טָבַל לְחָמוּר – מוּתָּר לְקַל. טָבַל וְלֹא הוּחְזַק – כְּאִילּוּ לֹא טָבַל.

The mishna continues to list additional differences between various levels of ritual purity: If **one immersed for** the purpose of eating **non-sacred** food, he **assumes a presumptive status** of ritual purity **for non-sacred** food,[N] and **it is prohibited for him** to eat **tithes,** as he did not purify himself with the intention of eating tithes. If one **immersed to** eat **tithes, he assumes a presumptive status for tithes,** but he is **prohibited from** eating ***teruma*.** If one **immersed for *teruma*, he assumes a presumptive status for *teruma*,** but he is **prohibited from** eating **sacrificial** food. If he **immersed for sacrificial** food, **he assumes a presumptive status for sacrificial** food, but he is **prohibited from** coming in contact with the **purification** waters. The principle is as follows: One who **immersed to** eat a food in **a stringent** category **is permitted to** eat a food in **a lenient** one. Another principle: One who **immersed without** the intention to **assume a presumptive status** of ritual purity, i.e., one who immersed but did not intend to purify himself, it is **as though he has not immersed** at all.[H]

בִּגְדֵי עַם הָאָרֶץ מִדְרָס לִפְרוּשִׁין; בִּגְדֵי פְרוּשִׁין מִדְרָס לְאוֹכְלֵי תְרוּמָה; בִּגְדֵי אוֹכְלֵי תְרוּמָה מִדְרָס לְקוֹדֶשׁ; בִּגְדֵי קוֹדֶשׁ מִדְרָס לְחַטָּאת.

The mishna continues: **The garments of an *am ha'aretz*,**[H] one who is not careful with regard to the laws of ritual purity, **are** considered impure with the ritual impurity imparted by the **treading** of a *zav*. That is considered a primary level of impurity **for individuals who are scrupulous with regard to impurity [*perushin*]. The garments of *perushin*** are considered impure by the **treading** of a *zav* **for** priests **who eat *teruma*; the garments of** those **who eat *teruma***[H] are considered impure by the **treading** of a *zav* **for** those who eat **sacrificial** food; and likewise **the garments of** those who eat **sacrificial** food[H] are considered impure by the **treading** of a *zav* **for** those dealing with the preparation of the **purification** waters.

יוֹסֵף בֶּן יוֹעֶזֶר הָיָה חָסִיד שֶׁבַּכְּהוּנָּה, וְהָיְתָה מִטְפַּחְתּוֹ מִדְרָס לְקוֹדֶשׁ. יוֹחָנָן בֶּן גּוּדְגְּדָא הָיָה אוֹכֵל עַל טׇהֳרַת הַקּוֹדֶשׁ כׇּל יָמָיו וְהָיְתָה מִטְפַּחְתּוֹ מִדְרָס לְחַטָּאת.

The mishna relates: **Yosef ben Yo'ezer**[P] **was the most pious** member **of the priesthood** and was extremely careful to eat *teruma* in a state of ritual purity, **and** yet **his cloth was** considered impure by the **treading** of a *zav* **for** those who ate **sacrificial** food. **Yoḥanan ben Gudgeda would eat** non-sacred food while following the laws of **ritual purity for sacrificial** food **all his days, and** nevertheless **his cloth was** considered impure by the **treading** of a *zav* **for** those preparing the **purification** waters.

NOTES

Immersion for non-sacred food – טְבִילָה לַחוּלִּין וכו׳: The nature of this immersion is also the subject of dispute. Some authorities maintain that it is the full immersion of one's entire body, while others claim that this statement continues the earlier statement pertaining to washing the hands. Immersing the hands would consequently be similar to washing them, except that immersing is performed with the waters of a ritual bath (see *Turei Aven*).

HALAKHA

Levels of immersion – מַעֲלוֹת בִּטְבִילָה: The Sages instituted levels of immersion: Anyone who immersed without intention is pure only with regard to non-sacred food, but he may not partake of the second tithe until he immerses with that particular level of purification in mind. If he immersed for the second tithe, it is still prohibited for him to eat *teruma*. Similarly, one who immerses for *teruma* remains impure for sacrificial food; even if he immerses for the latter, he is not presumed to be ritually pure for the waters of the red heifer.

However, one who immerses for the purification waters of the red heifer is considered ritually pure with regard to everything, as immersing for the sake of something stringent establishes one's status for a more lenient matter, but not vice versa. Likewise, one who purifies his hands must intend to do so only for the sake of tithes and all higher levels of ritual purity. All these levels are rabbinic, since according to Torah law any immersion renders one pure for all purposes (Rambam *Sefer Tahara*, *Hilkhot Avot HaTumot* 13:2).

The garments of an *am ha'aretz* – בִּגְדֵי עַם הָאָרֶץ: An *am ha'aretz*, even one who observes Torah and mitzvot, is considered impure. Furthermore, his clothes render items impure like the treading of a *zav* (Rambam *Sefer Tahara*, *Hilkhot Metamei Mishkav UMoshav* 10:1).

The garments of those who eat *teruma* – בִּגְדֵי אוֹכְלֵי תְרוּמָה: Although individuals who eat *teruma* are pure and are careful not to become impure, with regard to sacrificial food their clothes are nevertheless considered ritually impure by the treading of a *zav* (Rambam *Sefer Tahara*, *Hilkhot Avot HaTumot* 12:4).

The garments of those who eat sacrificial food – בִּגְדֵי קוֹדֶשׁ: Any vessel or object that is susceptible to ritual impurity imparted by one who reclines or sits upon it, although it is ritually pure with regard to sacrificial food, it is nevertheless considered as if it had been tread upon by a *zav* with regard to the waters of the red heifer. It is purified for this purpose only when immersed with the latter in mind (Rambam *Sefer Tahara*, *Hilkhot Para Aduma* 13:2).

PERSONALITIES

Yosei ben Yo'ezer – יוֹסֵי בֶּן יוֹעֶזֶר: Yosei ben Yo'ezer of Tzereida, referred to as Yosef in the Gemara here, was the first of the pairs of teachers who formed the spiritual leadership of the Jewish people at the outset of the period of the *tanna'im*. He was a student of Antigonus of Sokho. During that period, Sages were not granted honorary titles but were known by first name alone. Based on the accounts of the Talmud, Yosei ben Yo'ezer lived in an era when Hellenists controlled Jerusalem. He was executed, probably by his sister's son, the wicked priest Alkimos, and died a martyr's death. Together with his colleague Yosei ben Yoḥanan, Yosei ben Yo'ezer decreed that lands outside Israel and glass vessels be considered impure. Conversely, testimony is provided in tractate *Eduyyot* with regard to his lenient rulings with regard to several *halakhot*, to such an extent that he was called Yosei the Lenient. The Sages of the Mishna discussed his teachings at length (see *Pesaḥim*, chapter 1), and said that his death brought an end to the *eshkolot*, clusters, the scholars with expertise in all areas of the Torah.

גמ׳ חוּלִּין וּמַעֲשֵׂר מִי בָּעוּ נְטִילַת יָדַיִם?

GEMARA Before discussing the details of the *halakhot* listed in the mishna, the Gemara poses a basic question: **Do non-sacred** foods **and tithes** indeed **require washing the hands?**

וּרְמִינְהִי: הַתְּרוּמָה וְהַבִּיכּוּרִים – חַיָּיבִין עֲלֵיהֶן מִיתָה, וְחוֹמֶשׁ, וְאָסוּר לְזָרִים, וְהֵן נִכְסֵי כֹהֵן, וְעוֹלִין בְּאֶחָד וּמֵאָה, וּטְעוּנִין נְטִילַת יָדַיִם, וְהֶעֱרֵב שֶׁמֶשׁ, הֲרֵי אֵלּוּ בִּתְרוּמָה וּבִיכּוּרִים – מַה שֶּׁאֵין כֵּן בְּמַעֲשֵׂר, וְכׇל שֶׁכֵּן בְּחוּלִּין.

The Gemara **raises a contradiction** to the mishna, from the following mishna in tractate *Bikkurim* (2:1): With regard to ***teruma***[H] **and first fruits,**[HB] **one is liable to** the **death** penalty **for them,** e.g., if a non-priest ate them intentionally; if he did so unintentionally, he must restore the amount he ate with the addition of **a fifth; and they are prohibited to non-priests;**[N] **and they are the property of the priest.**[H] Consequently, a priest can purchase anything he wishes with them, or betroth a woman with them. **And** if they fell into non-sacred produce and became mixed with it, **they are nullified** only **in** a mixture that contains **one hundred and one**[H] times their amount; **and they require washing of the hands and the setting of the sun**[H] before they can be eaten, i.e., an impure priest who has immersed at the proper time must still wait for the sun to set before he is fit to eat them. **These** laws apply **to *teruma* and first fruits, but not to tithes.**[HN] The mishna adds: **And all the more so** do they not apply **to non-sacred** food.

HALAKHA

Teruma **for non-priests** – **תְּרוּמָה לְזָרִים**: One who is not a priest may not eat *teruma*, even if he resides with a priest or is employed by one. If a non-priest ate *teruma* intentionally, he receives lashes. If he was not punished by the court, he is liable to death at the hand of Heaven. If he ate *teruma* unintentionally he must pay its value plus one-fifth (Rambam *Sefer Zera'im*, *Hilkhot Terumot* 6:5–6).

First fruits for non-priests – **בִּיכּוּרִים לְזָרִים**: Non-priests may not eat first fruits. One who did so after the first fruits entered the walls of Jerusalem is liable to death at the hand of Heaven (Rambam *Sefer Zera'im*, *Hilkhot Bikkurim* 4:15; 3:1).

The property of a priest – **נִכְסֵי כֹהֵן**: First fruits and *teruma* are the property of the priest. He may sell them to priests or use them in any manner that does not debase or waste them (Rambam *Sefer Zera'im*, *Hilkhot Bikkurim* 4:14).

They are nullified only in a mixture that contains one hundred and one – **וְעוֹלִין בְּאֶחָד וּמֵאָה**: *Teruma* that fell into non-sacred produce is nullified if the non-sacred produce is at least one-hundred times its quantity (Rambam *Sefer Zera'im*, *Hilkhot Terumot* 13:1).

Like *teruma*, first fruits are also nullified if the non-sacred produce is at least one-hundred times its quantity. However, if first fruits are mixed with non-sacred produce of the same type in Jerusalem, the mixture cannot be nullified at all because it falls under the category of an object whose prohibition is temporary (Rambam *Sefer Zera'im*, *Hilkhot Bikkurim* 4:15).

The setting of the sun – **הֶעֱרֵב שֶׁמֶשׁ**: Ritually impure individuals may not partake of *teruma* until they have immersed and the sun has set on the day of their purification. This is because a *tevul yom*, an individual who has immersed and is waiting for the sun to set before he is fully purified, is prohibited from *teruma* and first fruits (Rambam *Sefer Zera'im Hilkhot Terumot* 7:2).

Tithes – **מַעֲשֵׂר**: Non-priests may eat the second tithe, as long as they are not in a state of ritual impurity. One who eats second tithe in a state of impurity receives lashes, in accordance with the opinion of the Sages. However, a *tevul yom,* who has immersed and is waiting for the sun to set before he is fully purified, may partake of the second tithe (Rambam *Sefer Zera'im Hilkhot Ma'aser Sheni* 3:1, 4).

BACKGROUND

First fruits – **בִּיכּוּרִים**: The first fruits of the new harvest were given to the priests (see Deuteronomy, chapter 26). When the Temple stood, a farmer would select the first fruits of the seven types of fruit with which Eretz Yisrael is especially favored (Deuteronomy 8:8). According to rabbinic decree, one is required to give at least one-sixtieth of his harvest for this purpose. He would bring the fruits to the Temple in a basket, place them before the altar, and recite prayers of thanks to God. Afterward, the fruits were given to the priests and eaten under the same provisions that govern *teruma*. The first fruits were brought to the Temple between the festivals of *Shavuot* and *Sukkot*. If they were not brought within this period, an extension was granted until Hanukkah. An entire tractate of the Mishna, *Bikkurim*, is devoted to the laws and practices governing this mitzva.

NOTES

Prohibited to non-priests – **וְאָסוּר לְזָרִים**: The Rid is puzzled by this statement, as the mishna has already stated that one who eats *teruma* is liable to the death penalty. Why, then, is it necessary to say that *teruma* is prohibited to non-priests? He explains that the phrase: Liable to the death penalty, adds that even a priest who partakes of *teruma* in a state of ritual impurity is liable to the death penalty. This differs from the *halakha* with regard to tithes, where one who eats them is not liable to the death penalty, even according to the view that they must be eaten in a state of ritual purity. Others explain the phrase: Prohibited to non-priests, as follows: Not only is it prohibited for one to consume *teruma*, but no benefit may be derived from it in the process of destroying it (Rabbeinu Tam; Meiri; Rabbi Shimshon of Saens). Alternatively: Prohibited to non-priests, indicates that it is prohibited to eat even less than the amount for which one is obligated to bring a sin-offering (*Arukh*; *Tosafot* on *Yevamot* 73a; see Meiri).

Second tithe – **מַעֲשֵׂר שֵׁנִי**: There are several disputes between *tanna'im* with regard to the status and sanctity of the second tithe. The biblical verses merely describe the obligation to separate this tithe and eat it in Jerusalem (Deuteronomy 12:17–20). Some *tanna'im* are of the opinion that the second tithe is considered property of the Most High, which means that its owner is granted permission to eat it, in a similar manner to offerings, but it is not considered his property in any other regard. Some authorities maintain that it is sacred and must therefore be consumed in a state of ritual purity, unlike non-sacred produce.

קַשְׁיָא מַעֲשֵׂר אַמַּעֲשֵׂר, קַשְׁיָא חוּלִּין אַחוּלִּין!

This is **difficult:** The *halakha* of **tithes** stated in *Bikkurim* seems to contradict the *halakha* of **tithes** taught in the mishna here, which states that the hands must be washed before tithes are eaten. Additionally, it is **difficult** with regard to the *halakha* of **non-sacred** food, as it contradicts the *halakha* applicable to **non-sacred** food stated in the mishna here.

בִּשְׁלָמָא מַעֲשֵׂר אַמַּעֲשֵׂר לָא קַשְׁיָא: הָא – רַבִּי מֵאִיר, וְהָא – רַבָּנַן.

The Gemara comments: **Granted,** one of the laws with regard to **tithes,** as opposed to the other law with regard to **tithes, is not difficult,** since the contradiction can be resolved as follows: **This** case, the mishna in *Bikkurim*, is in accordance **with Rabbi Meir, while that** case, the mishna here, follows **the Rabbis.**

דִּתְנַן: כׇּל הַטָּעוּן בִּיאַת מַיִם מִדִּבְרֵי סוֹפְרִים מְטַמֵּא אֶת הַקּוֹדֶשׁ, וּפוֹסֵל אֶת הַתְּרוּמָה, וּמוּתָּר לַחוּלִּין וְלַמַּעֲשֵׂר, דִּבְרֵי רַבִּי מֵאִיר. וַחֲכָמִים אוֹסְרִים בַּמַּעֲשֵׂר. אֶלָּא חוּלִּין אַחוּלִּין קַשְׁיָא!

As we learned in a mishna (*Para* 11:5): **Anything that requires immersion in water**[H] **by rabbinic law renders sacrificial food impure.** If it touches a consecrated item, the latter is itself rendered impure with a second-degree ritual impurity. It also renders impure any other consecrated object that comes into contact with it with a third-degree ritual impurity **and invalidates** ***teruma,*** meaning that it renders the *teruma* itself impure, but not to the extent that the *teruma* can render other *teruma* impure. **And** anything that requires immersion in water by rabbinic law **is permitted for non-sacred** produce **and for tithes,** meaning that it does not render these items impure, as something impure to such a low degree does not invalidate even non-sacred food. This is **the statement of Rabbi Meir. But the Rabbis prohibit** this **in** the case of **tithes,** meaning that they are invalidated. This source demonstrates that according to the Rabbis, the *halakha* that applies to tithes differs from that of non-sacred produce, which explains why one must wash his hands for tithes. **However,** the law with regard to **non-sacred** food as opposed to the other law of **non-sacred** food is still **difficult.**

לָא קַשְׁיָא; כָּאן – בַּאֲכִילָה, כָּאן – בִּנְגִיעָה.

The Gemara responds: It is **not difficult. Here** the mishna is referring **to eating,** before which one must wash his hands. **There** the mishna in *Bikkurim* deals **with touching** alone, for which prior washing of the hands is not necessary.

מַתְקִיף לַהּ רַב שִׁימִי בַּר אַשִׁי: עַד כָּאן לָא פְּלִיגִי רַבָּנַן עֲלֵיהּ דְּרַבִּי מֵאִיר אֶלָּא בַּאֲכִילָה דְּמַעֲשֵׂר, אֲבָל בִּנְגִיעָה דְּמַעֲשֵׂר וּבַאֲכִילָה דְּחוּלִּין – לָא פְּלִיגִי! אֶלָּא: אִידִי וְאִידִי בַּאֲכִילָה, וְלָא קַשְׁיָא: כָּאן – בַּאֲכִילָה דְּנַהֲמָא, כָּאן – בַּאֲכִילָה דְּפֵירֵי. דְּאָמַר רַב נַחְמָן: כׇּל הַנּוֹטֵל יָדָיו לְפֵירוֹת – הֲרֵי זֶה מִגַּסֵּי הָרוּחַ.

Rav Shimi bar Ashi strongly objects to this: The Rabbis disagree with Rabbi Meir only with regard to eating tithes, but with regard to touching tithes and eating non-sacred food **they do not disagree** with him. Therefore, the Gemara's resolution of the difficulty with regard to non-sacred food is not acceptable. **Rather,** the previous explanation is to be rejected in favor of the following: Both **this** mishna **and that** mishna are referring **to eating, and** it is **not difficult: Here** the mishna is dealing **with eating bread,** which requires washing one's hands, whereas **there,** in *Bikkurim*, the mishna is referring **to eating non-sacred fruit,** for which one need not wash his hands, **for Rav Naḥman said: Anyone who washes his hands for fruit is of the haughty of spirit** because he shows himself to be more particular than required by the Sages.[H]

תָּנוּ רַבָּנַן: הַנּוֹטֵל יָדָיו, נִתְכַּוֵּון – יָדָיו טְהוֹרוֹת; לֹא נִתְכַּוֵּון – יָדָיו טְמֵאוֹת. וְכֵן הַמַּטְבִּיל יָדָיו, נִתְכַּוֵּון – יָדָיו טְהוֹרוֹת; לֹא נִתְכַּוֵּון – יָדָיו טְמֵאוֹת. וְהָתַנְיָא: בֵּין נִתְכַּוֵּון בֵּין לֹא נִתְכַּוֵּון – יָדָיו טְהוֹרוֹת! אָמַר רַב נַחְמָן: לָא קַשְׁיָא; כָּאן – לַחוּלִּין,

§ **The Sages taught: One who washes his hands,** if **he intended** to purify them, **his hands are pure; if he did not intend**[N] to do so, **his hands are impure.**[H] **Similarly,** in the case of **one who immerses his hands** in forty *se'a* of water, if **he intended** to purify them, **his hands are pure; if he did not** so **intend, his hands are impure.** The Gemara raises a difficulty: **But isn't it taught** in a *baraita* that **his hands are pure whether he did or did not intend** to purify them? **Rav Naḥman said:** This is **not difficult,** as **there,** the second *baraita* is referring **to non-sacred** food, for which one need not have the intention to purify his hands;

HALAKHA

Things that require immersion in water – הַטָּעוּן בִּיאַת מַיִם: Certain objects require immersion by rabbinic decree, including hands, which are generally considered to have second-degree ritual impurity. Since second-degree of impurity does not render non-sacred produce impure to the third degree, such an individual may touch non-sacred foods. However, he invalidates *teruma* and renders sacrificial food impure with contact (Rambam *Sefer Tahara, Hilkhot Tumat Okhalin* 16:8).

Washing hands for fruit – נְטִילַת יָדַיִם לְפֵירוֹת: One who washes his hands for fruit that is not wet is considered haughty of spirit, as stated by Rav Naḥman (*Shulḥan Arukh HaRav*). This applies only if he does so in order to fulfill a mitzva, but he may wash them for purposes of cleanliness (Rema). Some say that roasted meat with gravy is similar to fruit in this regard, as well as cooked grains that are dry when eaten (*Shulḥan Arukh, Oraḥ Ḥayyim* 158:5).

Intention with regard to washing hands – כַּוָּונָה לִנְטִילַת יָדַיִם: At the outset, one who washes his hands must intend to make them fit for eating. The relevant intention is that of the one who pours the water over the hands, not one whose hands are being washed by another (Rema). If the pourer did not have intention at all, it appears that washing must be repeated. According to the Rashba, his hands are pure with regard to touching non-sacred food but not for the purpose of eating it (*Magen Avraham*; *Shulḥan Arukh, Oraḥ Ḥayyim* 159:13).

NOTES

Intention when washing the hands – כַּוָּונָה בִּנְטִילַת יָדַיִם: The Rashba's view is that intention is indeed required when washing one's hands before eating bread, and that washing without intention is not considered washing at all. However, according to this opinion, it is unclear why Rav Naḥman did not differentiate between touching and eating. The *Siaḥ Yitzḥak* answers that Rav Naḥman preferred to provide a simple and straightforward response.

HALAKHA

A wave…became detached – גַּל שֶׁנִּתְלַשׁ: If a wave containing forty *se'a* became detached from the sea and fell on an individual or on vessels, they are ritually pure for the purpose of non-sacred produce, as one who immerses himself for non-sacred produce is not required to have intention. If one was sitting and watching for a wave to fall, the immersion is effective for whatever purpose he intended (Rambam *Sefer Tahara, Hilkhot Mikvaot* 9:17).

LANGUAGE

Flow [*ḥardalit*] – חַרְדָּלִית: The *ge'onim* have a version in which this is *hardalit*, spelled with a *heh*, not a *ḥet*, and they explain that this word is a compound of *har dala*, meaning something that flows down a mountain. Others claim that the word is related to one of the meanings of *ḥared*, meaning quick, and consequently refers to a quick flow. Yet others maintain that it is derived from the Greek χαράδρα, *kharadra*, meaning a flow of water descending from a mountain.

BACKGROUND

Edges and arcs of a wave – רָאשִׁין וְכֵיפִין:

Structure of a wave

כָּאן – לְמַעֲשֵׂר. וּמְנָא תֵּימְרָא דְּחוּלִּין לָא בָּעוּ כַּוָּונָה, דִּתְנַן: גַּל שֶׁנִּתְלַשׁ וּבוֹ אַרְבָּעִים סְאָה, וְנָפַל עַל הָאָדָם וְעַל הַכֵּלִים – טְהוֹרִין. קָתָנֵי אָדָם דּוּמְיָא דְּכֵלִים, מַה כֵּלִים דְּלָא מְכַוְּונִי – אַף אָדָם דְּלָא מְכַוֵּין.

whereas **here,** the first *baraita* is referring **to tithes,** for which intention to purify oneself is required. **And from where do you say** this, **that non-sacred food**[N] **does not require** the **intention**[N] that one is purifying himself for the sake of eating it? **As we learned** in a mishna (*Mikvaot* 5:6): **If a wave containing forty *se'a*** of water **became detached**[NH] from the sea **and fell on a person or on vessels, they are ritually pure.** The mishna **teaches that a person is similar to vessels: Just as vessels do not intend** to be purified, as they obviously harbor no intentions, **so too,** the case of **a person** is referring to a situation **in which he does not intend** to purify himself, thereby implying that people can be ritually purified even without intention.

וּמִמַּאי? דִּלְמָא בְּיוֹשֵׁב וּמְצַפֶּה אֵימָתַי יִתָּלֵשׁ הַגַּל עָסְקִינַן, וְכֵלִים דּוּמְיָא דְּאָדָם, מַה אָדָם דְּבַר כַּוָּונָה – אַף כֵּלִים דִּמְכַוֵּין לְהוּ?

The Gemara rejects this proof: **And from where** is it clear that this is the meaning of the mishna? **Perhaps we are dealing with** one who **is sitting and awaiting** for **when a wave will detach** and fall on the vessels, and the implication is the opposite: **Vessels are similar** to **a person: Just as a person** is **capable of intention** to ritually purify himself, **so too** the case of the **vessels** mentioned in the mishna is referring to a situation **where one intends on their behalf** that they be purified.

וְכִי תֵּימָא: בְּיוֹשֵׁב וּמְצַפֶּה מַאי לְמֵימְרָא?

And if you would say that the mishna is indeed is referring **to** one who **is sitting and awaiting, what** is the purpose **of stating** this?[N] Such a *halakha* would not appear to offer a novelty; why would it be necessary to state it?

סָלְקָא דַּעְתָּךְ אָמִינָא: לִיגְזוֹר דִּלְמָא אָתֵי לְמִיטְבַּל בְּחַרְדָּלִית שֶׁל גְּשָׁמִים, אִי נַמִי נִגְזוֹר רָאשִׁין אַטּוּ כֵּיפִין. קָא מַשְׁמַע לָן דְּלָא גָּזְרִינַן.

The Gemara responds: It nevertheless provides a novel teaching, as **it might enter your mind to say that it should be decreed** that a detached wave does not affect purification, **lest one come to immerse in a flow**[L] **of rainwater** whose volume is forty *se'a*. In other words, one might think that immersion in a flood of rainwater effects purification, whereas the *halakha* is that rainwater purifies only if it is gathered in one location. **Alternatively,** you might think that **it should be decreed** that purification by means of **the edges** of the waves that comes in contact with the ground should be ineffective **due to** the upper **arcs** of the waves.[B] The mishna therefore **teaches us that we do not** so **decree.**

NOTES

And from where do you say that non-sacred food – וּמְנָא תֵּימְרָא דְּחוּלִּין וכו׳: This question is difficult, since the *baraita* explicitly states that one fulfills the duty of washing his hands whether or not he had the proper intention. One explanation is that since washing hands is a mitzva by rabbinic law, it is possible that in certain cases one can ritually purify himself without intention. The question in this case is referring to immersion of the entire body, or to purification whose obligation is by Torah law (*Turei Aven*; see *Tosafot* on *Ḥullin*).

Non-sacred food does not require intention – חוּלִּין לָא בָּעוּ כַּוָּונָה: The early authorities point out that the issue of intention during immersion is unrelated to the broader question of whether or not mitzvot require intention (Ran, citing Ramban). Here, intention does not relate to the fulfillment of the mitzva of immersing but to one's desire to ritually purify himself through this immersion. It is similar to the basic level of intention to fulfill a mitzva, which consists merely of awareness of the act being performed, e.g., one who hears a *shofar* must know it is a *shofar*.

A wave…became detached – גַּל שֶׁנִּתְלַשׁ: The Meiri explains that although the wave is connected to the sea, and connection to the sea renders water as eligible to serve as a ritual bath, it is necessary for the wave to consist of at least forty *se'a* of water because the water one immerses in must suffice to cover one's entire body. Even if the individual who is immersing is short, the waters of the wave will not cover his entire body if they measure less than this amount, as they spread out.

Others imply that the Gemara is referring to a wave that has become entirely removed from its place, so that it is no longer attached to the sea at all (*Tosafot*; *Siaḥ Yitzḥak*).

To one who is sitting and awaiting, what is the purpose of stating this – בְּיוֹשֵׁב וּמְצַפֶּה מַאי לְמֵימְרָא: Early and later authorities ask the following question: This seems to be a highly novel teaching, since there is a dispute in a mishna as to whether sea waters purify like the waters of a spring, and are therefore valid even when flowing, or whether they have the status of a ritual bath and have the power to purify only when gathered together in one spot, like a pond. If this mishna teaches that one may ritually purify himself in a moving wave, this would prove that sea water is like a spring. Some authorities say that this source indicates that the wave is not considered similar to flowing water but to a pond, because at the moment the wave falls on a person it is gathered in one spot (see Ra'avad and *Yad David*). The Meiri offers an alternative reason, explaining why waves are not considered flowing water: Since sea water is always moving, the movement of a wave is not considered to be a flow, and it is equivalent to a ritual bath.

וּמְנָא תֵּימְרָא דְּלָא מַטְבִּילִין בְּכֵיפִין? דְּתַנְיָא: מַטְבִּילִין בְּרָאשִׁין וְאֵין מַטְבִּילִין בְּכֵיפִין, לְפִי שֶׁאֵין מַטְבִּילִין בָּאֲוִיר.

And from where do you say that one may not immerse in the arcs? As it is taught in a *baraita*: **One may immerse in the edges**[H] of waves, **but one may not immerse in** their **arcs, because one may not immerse in air.** The area under the arc of a wave is considered mere air, despite the fact that the individual is surrounded by water on all sides.

אֶלָּא מֵהָא, דִּתְנַן: פֵּירוֹת שֶׁנָּפְלוּ לְתוֹךְ אַמַּת הַמַּיִם, וּפָשַׁט מִי שֶׁיָּדָיו טְמֵאוֹת וּנְטָלָן – יָדָיו טְהוֹרוֹת, וּפֵירוֹת אֵינָן בְּ״כִי יוּתַּן״.

Rather, the proof that the purification with regard to non-sacred produce does not require intention is **from that which we learned** in a mishna (*Makhshirin* 4:7): In the verse that is referring to the preconditions required for fruit and seeds to be susceptible to ritual impurity, it is stated: "If water be put on seeds, and any of their carcasses fall there, it shall be impure to you" (Leviticus 11:38). **If fruit fell into a water channel, and one whose hands were ritually impure extended his hands and lifted them up** with the goal of removing them from the water channel, **his hands are ritually pure,** as he has purified them by inserting them into the water channel, **and** these **fruits are not** included **in** the category of **"if water be put** on seeds."[B] The verse is referring only to fruit that has intentionally been brought into contact with water. Since the fruit in this case was not intentionally made wet, it cannot as yet contract impurity.

וְאִם בִּשְׁבִיל שֶׁיּוּדְחוּ יָדָיו – יָדָיו טְהוֹרוֹת, וְהַפֵּירוֹת הֲרֵי הֵן בְּ״כִי יוּתַּן״.

And if he put his hands into the water channel **in order to wash his hands, his hands are ritually pure, and the fruit is** included **in** the category of **"if water be put** on seeds."[H] Since he intended to wet his hands, the contact of the fruit with this water renders them susceptible to ritual impurity. In any case, the mishna teaches that his hands are ritually pure in either situation, indicating that no special intention is required for purification.

אֵיתִיבֵיהּ רַבָּה לְרַב נַחְמָן: הַטּוֹבֵל לְחוּלִּין וְהוּחְזַק לְחוּלִּין – אָסוּר לְמַעֲשֵׂר. הוּחְזַק – אִין, לֹא הוּחְזַק – לָא!

Rabba raised an objection to Rav Naḥman from the mishna here: **One who immersed for** the purpose of eating **non-sacred** food **and assumes a presumptive status** of ritual purity **for non-sacred** food **is** still **prohibited** from eating **tithes. The Gemara infers: If one** immersed with the intention of **assuming a presumptive status** of ritual purity for non-sacred food, **yes,** he assumes that status; **if he did not** immerse with the intention of **assuming that presumptive status, no, he does not** assume that status. This proves that even for the sake of non-sacred produce, one must intend to assume the appropriate status of ritual purity.

הָכִי קָאָמַר: אַף עַל פִּי שֶׁהוּחְזַק לְחוּלִּין – אָסוּר לְמַעֲשֵׂר.

Rav Naḥman refutes this proof: **This is what** the mishna **is saying: Even though he assumes a presumptive status** of ritual purity **for non-sacred** produce, **he is prohibited from** eating **tithes.** In other words, the mishna does not teach that intention is required for eating non-sacred food in a state of ritual purity. Rather, it teaches that even if one intended to purify himself for non-sacred food, he is not purified with regard to tithes.

אֵיתִיבֵיהּ: טָבַל וְלֹא הוּחְזַק – כְּאִילּוּ לֹא טָבַל. מַאי לָאו – כְּאִילּוּ לֹא טָבַל כְּלָל!

He, Rabba, **raised an objection to him** from another teaching of our mishna: With regard to one who **immersed without** intending to **assume a presumptive status of ritual purity,** it is **as if he has not immersed. What, is it not** teaching that it is **as if he had not immersed at all?**

לָא, כְּאִילּוּ לֹא טָבַל לְמַעֲשֵׂר, אֲבָל טָבַל לְחוּלִּין. הוּא סָבַר דָּחֵי קָא מַדְחֵי לֵיהּ. נְפַק, דָּק וְאַשְׁכַּח, דְּתַנְיָא: טָבַל וְלֹא הוּחְזַק – אָסוּר לְמַעֲשֵׂר וּמוּתָּר לְחוּלִּין.

Rav Naḥman rejected this proof as well: **No,** it means that it is **as if he has not immersed for tithes, but he is** considered to have **immersed for non-sacred** produce, for which no intention is necessary. The Gemara comments: **He,** i.e., Rabba, **thought** that Rav Naḥman **was** merely **refuting his** proof by saying that the wording of the mishna does not conclusively prove his case, but he did not actually think that the mishna should be understood differently. However, he subsequently **went** and **examined** the sources **and found that** a *baraita* **was** explicitly **taught** in accordance with the opinion of Rav Naḥman: One who **immersed and** did not intend to **assume a presumptive status**[H] of ritual purity **is prohibited from** eating **tithes, but is permitted to** eat **non-sacred** produce, even if he eats non-sacred produce only when ritually pure.

HALAKHA

One may immerse in the edges, etc. – מַטְבִּילִין בְּרָאשִׁין וכו׳: If the two edges of a wave are touching the ground, one may immerse in it, but one may not immerse in the arc of a wave, as its legal status is that of air (Rambam *Sefer Tahara, Hilkhot Mikvaot* 9:18).

Fruit that fell – פֵּירוֹת שֶׁנָּפְלוּ: If fruit fell into water, and one inserted his hands and removed the fruit, the fruit is not susceptible to contracting ritual impurity. But if one also intended to wash his hands, the water on his hands renders the fruit susceptible to impurity (Rambam *Sefer Tahara, Hilkhot Tumat Okhalin* 12:10).

One who immersed and did not intend to assume a presumptive status – טָבַל וְלֹא הוּחְזַק: One who immersed without intending to assume a presumptive status of ritual purity is considered ritually pure only with regard to non-sacred food. With regard to other items, it is as if he had never immersed (Rambam *Sefer Tahara, Hilkhot Mikvaot* 1:8; see 11:12).

BACKGROUND

In the category of "if water be put on seeds" – ״בְּ״כִי יוּתַּן״: In order for agricultural produce to become susceptible to contracting ritual impurity, it must be detached from the earth and then come into contact with water or certain other liquids. The particular formulation employed in the verse implies that the owner of the produce must approve of the fact that the produce became wet. If the owner is not pleased, the produce is not susceptible to ritual impurity. The Talmud contains numerous discussions about specific instances in which there is uncertainty whether or not the conditions that create susceptibility to ritual impurity have been fulfilled.

אמר רבי אלעזר: טבל ועלה – מחזיק עצמו לכל מה שירצה.

§ With regard to assuming a presumptive status of ritual purity, **Rabbi Elazar said:** If one **immersed** without any particular intention **and ascended** from his immersion, **he may assume a presumptive status**[N] of ritual purity after his immersion **for whatever he wishes.** In his opinion, there is no need to have a definite intention in mind at the actual moment of immersion.

מיתיבי: עודהו רגלו אחת במים, הוחזק לדבר קל – מחזיק עצמו לדבר חמור. עלה – שוב אינו מחזיק.

The Gemara **raises an objection** to this from the following *baraita*: In a case where one has immersed and is ascending, **and one of his feet is still in the water, if he** had originally intended to **assume presumptive status** of ritual purity **for a minor matter, he may** still intend to **assume presumptive status for a major matter.** But if he has fully **ascended, he may no longer** intend to **assume a presumptive status** for any other matter.

מאי לאו – אינו מחזיק כלל?

The Gemara infers from this *baraita*: **What, is it not** teaching that if one has ascended **he may not** intend to **assume a presumptive status** of ritual purity **at all,** which proves that one may do so only if he is still at least partially in the water?

לא, עודהו – אף על פי שהוחזק – מחזיק. עלה – אם לא הוחזק – מחזיק. ואם הוחזק – אינו מחזיק.

The Gemara rejects this inference: **No,** it should be understood as follows: If **he is still** in the water, then although **he** previously intended to **assume a presumptive status** of ritual purity for a minor matter, **he may** now intend to **assume a presumptive status** of ritual purity for whatever purpose he wishes, since one can adjust his intention during his immersion. Once he has already **ascended, if he did not** intend to **assume a presumptive status** of ritual purity at all, but immersed without any intention, **he may** intend to **assume a presumptive status** of ritual purity for whatever he wishes even after ascending from the ritual bath; **but if he did** intend to **assume a presumptive status** of ritual purity for a minor matter, **he may not** intend to **assume a presumptive status** of ritual purity for a major matter, as his intention was fixed when he ascended from the ritual bath.

מאן תנא עודהו רגלו אחת במים? אמר רבי פדת: רבי יהודה היא. דתנן: מקוה שנמדד ויש בו ארבעים סאה מכוונות, וירדו שנים וטבלו זה אחר זה – הראשון טהור והשני טמא. אמר רבי יהודה: אם היו רגליו של ראשון נוגעות במים – אף השני טהור.

In relation to the above, the Gemara explains: **Who** is the *tanna* who **taught** that one **whose foot is still in the water** is considered to be still immersing himself? **Rabbi Pedat said: It is** the opinion of **Rabbi Yehuda, as we learned** in a mishna (*Mikvaot* 7:6): In the case of **a ritual bath that was measured**[B] **and** found to **contain exactly forty** ***se'a*** of water, **and** then **two** individuals **descended and immersed one after the other, the first one is ritually pure,** since he immersed in a valid ritual bath, **but the second is ritually impure.** Because a small amount of water clings to the first individual, the ritual bath subsequently holds less than the requisite amount. Therefore, it does not purify the second individual.[H] **Rabbi Yehuda said: If the feet of the first one were** still **touching the water,** so that he had not yet exited the ritual bath entirely while the second one immersed, **the second is also ritually pure.** This teaches that Rabbi Yehuda is of the opinion that one who still has a foot in the water is considered to be inside the ritual bath.

אמר רב נחמן אמר רבה בר אבוה: מחלוקת במעלות דרבנן, אבל מטומאה לטהרה – דברי הכל אף השני טמא. והיינו דרבי פדת.

Rav Naḥman said that **Rabba bar Avuh said:** This **dispute** between the Rabbis and Rabbi Yehuda pertains **to higher standards of ritual purity** established **by the Sages,**[N] where the obligation to immerse is due to a rabbinical ordinance. **However,** when the purpose of the immersion is to transition **from** full-fledged **ritual impurity to purity, everyone agrees** that **the second** individual **is impure. And this is** in accordance with the statement **of Rabbi Pedat** on this topic, who asserts that only Rabbi Yehuda maintains that one may assume a presumptive ritually pure status if one of his feet is still in the ritual bath.

NOTES

If one immersed and ascended, he may assume a presumptive status – **טבל ועלה מחזיק עצמו**: The commentaries discuss the reasoning behind this *halakha*: How can one intend to assume a presumptive status of ritual purity for whatever he wishes? *Tosafot* claim that one can intend to assume a presumptive status of purity only while he is still wet; as long as one is not yet dry, it is as if his immersion were ongoing.

The Meiri, however, claims that one can intend to assume a presumptive status of purity even after his body is dry. It appears that his opinion is similar to that of the *Turei Aven*, who maintains that this *halakha* follows the principle of retroactive designation [*bereira*], meaning that intention can be established retroactively. Later authorities point out that Rabbi Eliezer's statement is in accordance with the opinion in the *Kesef Mishne*, whereby the purification of a ritual bath does not occur while one is still in the water but only upon his ascent (see *Zekher LaḤagiga* and *Shalmei Ḥagiga*).

This dispute pertains to higher standards of ritual purity established by the Sages – **מחלוקת במעלות דרבנן**: In the Jerusalem Talmud, a similar opinion is attributed to Reish Lakish, whereby only one whose immersion is for impurity by rabbinic law can establish his status for whatever he wishes. This opinion is rejected there entirely.

BACKGROUND

A ritual bath that was measured – **מקוה שנמדד**: At times, people would build ritual baths that were very small, which contained only the minimum measure of water. Once one individual immersed, the ritual bath may not have contained the requisite quantity of water.

Small ritual bath excavated at Masada in the Judean Desert

HALAKHA

Immersion in a ritual bath of minimum measure – **טבילה במקוה מצומצם**: In a case where two individuals immersed one after the other in a ritual bath that contains exactly forty *se'a*, the immersion of the second individual is ineffective, even if the feet of the first one were still in contact with the water when the second immersed. This ruling is in accordance with the opinion of first *tanna* (*Shulḥan Arukh*, *Yoreh De'a* 201:62). The *Arukh HaShulḥan* claims that the same *halakha* applies even if the entire body of the first individual, apart from his head, was still in the water.

אִיכָּא דְּאָמְרִי, אָמַר רַב נַחְמָן אָמַר רַבָּה בַּר אֲבוּהּ: מַחְלוֹקֶת מִטּוּמְאָה לְטָהֳרָה, אֲבָל בְּמַעֲלוֹת דְּרַבָּנַן – דִּבְרֵי הַכֹּל אַף הַשֵּׁנִי טָהוֹר. וּפְלִיגָא דְּרַבִּי פְּדָת.

There are those who say a different version of this statement: **Rav Naḥman said** that **Rabba bar Avuh said:** This **dispute** is referring only to one who is obligated to immerse in order to transition **from ritual impurity to purity, but with regard to higher standards of ritual purity** established **by the Sages, everyone agrees** that **even the second** individual **is ritually pure** if the foot of the first is still in contact with the water. **And** consequently, this opinion **disagrees** with the statement **of Rabbi Pedat**, since, according to this version, all agree that with regard to higher standards of ritual purity, the immersion continues as long as a single foot remains in the water.

אֲמַר עוּלָּא, בְּעֵי מִינֵּיהּ מֵרַבִּי יוֹחָנָן: לְרַבִּי יְהוּדָה, מַהוּ לְהַטְבִּיל מְחָטִין וְצִינּוֹרִיּוֹת בְּרֹאשׁוֹ שֶׁל רִאשׁוֹן?

With regard to the discussion above, **Ulla said: I asked Rabbi Yoḥanan: According to Rabbi Yehuda, what is** the *halakha* with regard to **immersing** small vessels, such as **needles and knitting needles, on the head of the first** individual immersing himself? Since Rabbi Yehuda maintains that one whose foot is still in the water is considered as immersed in the ritual bath, does this mean that his body and even his wet hair can serve as part of the ritual bath?

גּוּד אַחֵית – אִית לֵיהּ לְרַבִּי יְהוּדָה, גּוּד אַסֵּיק – לֵית לֵיהּ? אוֹ דִּלְמָא: גּוּד אַסֵּיק נַמִי אִית לֵיהּ?

The Gemara clarifies the dilemma raised by this question: Does **Rabbi Yehuda accept** only the principle of **lowering the partition,** meaning that an item positioned above another item is considered as if it continued downward, and therefore the water on the body of the one immersing is viewed as descending into the ritual bath, so that the bath retains its requisite size; but **he does not accept** the concept of **raising the partition,**[N] so that the water in the ritual bath is not considered to rise up to one's head, making him part of the ritual bath as well? **Or, perhaps he also accepts** the principle of **raising the partition,** which means that one is indeed considered part of the ritual bath?

אֲמַר לֵיהּ תְּנֵיתוּהָ: שָׁלֹשׁ גְּמָמִיּוֹת בְּנַחַל: הָעֶלְיוֹנָה, הַתַּחְתּוֹנָה וְהָאֶמְצָעִית. הָעֶלְיוֹנָה וְהַתַּחְתּוֹנָה שֶׁל עֶשְׂרִים עֶשְׂרִים סְאָה, וְהָאֶמְצָעִית שֶׁל אַרְבָּעִים סְאָה, וְחַרְדָּלִית שֶׁל גְּשָׁמִים עוֹבֶרֶת בֵּינֵיהֶן. רַבִּי יְהוּדָה אוֹמֵר, מֵאִיר הָיָה אוֹמֵר: מַטְבִּיל בָּעֶלְיוֹנָה.

Rabbi Yoḥanan **said to him: You** already **learned** it in the *Tosefta* (*Mikvaot* 3:3): If there are **three depressions**[H] **in** the bed of **a stream that** are not completely dry, **an upper one, a lower one, and a middle one;** and **the upper and lower ones** hold **twenty** *se'a* **each, while the middle one** contains **forty** *se'a*, **and a flow of rain runs between them,** thereby linking the depressions one to another, **Rabbi Yehuda says:** My colleague, Rabbi **Meir, would say:** One may **immerse in the upper one.** This indicates that Rabbi Meir holds that the waters of the middle depression, which contains the requisite amount of water for a ritual bath, are considered to have ascended by means of the rainwater into the higher depression. Since Rabbi Yehuda cites his colleague's statement without comment, he evidently accepts the principle of raising the partition.

וְהָתַנְיָא, רַבִּי יְהוּדָה אוֹמֵר,

Ulla raised a difficulty: **But isn't it taught** in a *baraita*: **Rabbi Yehuda says:**

Perek **II**
Daf **19** Amud **b**

מֵאִיר הָיָה אוֹמֵר: מַטְבִּיל בָּעֶלְיוֹנָה, וַאֲנִי אוֹמֵר: בַּתַּחְתּוֹנָה וְלֹא בָּעֶלְיוֹנָה! אֲמַר לֵיהּ: אִי תַּנְיָא – תַּנְיָא.

Rabbi **Meir would say:** One may **immerse in the upper one, and I say: In the lower one but not in the upper one.** This demonstrates that Rabbi Yehuda does not accept the principle of raising the partition. Rabbi Yoḥanan **said to him: If this** *baraita* **is taught, it is taught,** and I cannot take issue with it. Therefore, it is clear that the matter is held in dispute between *tanna'im* and that Rabbi Yehuda does not accept the principle of raising the partition.

״הַטּוֹבֵל לְחוּלִּין וְהוּחְזַק לְחוּלִּין״ כו׳. מַנִּי מַתְנִיתִין? רַבָּנַן הִיא, דְּשָׁנֵי לְהוּ בֵּין חוּלִּין לְמַעֲשֵׂר.

§ It is taught in the mishna: **One who immersed for** the purpose of eating **non-sacred** food with the intention of **assuming a presumptive status** of ritual purity **for non-sacred** food **it is prohibited for him** to eat **tithes.** The Gemara comments: **Whose** opinion is expressed in **the mishna? It is** that of **the Rabbis, who differentiate between non-sacred** produce **and tithes,**[N] since they maintain the following: If one who is required by rabbinic law to immerse touches non-sacred food, it remains pure, but if he comes into contact with tithes they are rendered ritually impure.

NOTES

Lowering the partition and raising the partition – גּוּד אַחֵית וְגוּד אַסֵּיק: These principles are applied in various areas of *halakha*. They are based on the idea that two items that are not necessarily attached but are positioned opposite each other can be viewed as if they extended toward each other and came into contact. The word partition is derived from cases of building a *sukka*, the classic context where it is applied, where a partial wall is viewed as forming a full partition. Since gravity makes objects descend naturally, the logic of lowering the partition is generally easier to accept than that of raising the partition.

HALAKHA

Three depressions – שָׁלֹשׁ גְּמָמִיּוֹת: If a stream has three depressions, the middle of which contains forty *se'a* while the upper and lower ones hold less, only the middle one is fit for immersion because it is the only one that contains the requisite quantity of water. This is the case even if flowing rainwater passes between them. However, if a rush of rainwater passes between them, one may immerse in any of the depressions (*Shulḥan Arukh*, *Yoreh De'a* 201:60; *Shakh*).

NOTES

Who differentiate between non-sacred produce and tithes – דְּשָׁנֵי לְהוּ בֵּין חוּלִּין לְמַעֲשֵׂר: The *Turei Aven* asks why the Rabbis saw fit to add an extra level of purity for those who eat tithes, as the previous discussion of the Gemara concluded that one need not wash his hands to touch tithes. He answers that since the Rabbis differentiated between the eating of non-sacred food and tithes, they also had to create a level for those who partake of tithes, in order to emphasize that tithes are considered an intermediate level between non-sacred produce and *teruma*.

HALAKHA

The levels of ritual purity for garments – **מַעֲלוֹת הַטָּהֳרָה בִּבְגָדִים**: The Sages ordained five levels of ritual purity with regard to clothing: (1) The garments of an *am ha'aretz* are considered ritually impure by treading for those who eat non-sacred produce in a state of purity, and *amei ha'aretz* themselves are likewise considered as *zavim* in this regard. (2) The garments of those who eat non-sacred produce in a state of ritual purity are impure by treading for those who partake of second-tithe produce, but the individuals themselves are pure even with regard to *teruma*. (3) The garments of those who eat second-tithe produce are ritually impure by treading for those who eat *teruma*, while (4) the garments of those who eat *teruma* are ritually impure by treading for those who partake of sacrificial food; however, they themselves are ritually pure with regard to sacrificial food. (5) The garments but not the bodies of those who eat sacrificial food are ritually impure by treading for the waters of the red heifer (Rambam *Sefer Tahara, Hilkhot Avot HaTuma* 13:1).

אֵימָא סֵיפָא: בִּגְדֵי עַם הָאָרֶץ מִדְרָס לְפְרוּשִׁין. בִּגְדֵי פְּרוּשִׁין מִדְרָס לְאוֹכְלֵי תְרוּמָה.

However, in that case, **say the latter clause** of the mishna, which states that **the garments of an *am ha'aretz*,** who is not careful with regard to the *halakhot* of ritual purity, **are** considered to be rendered ritually impure by the impurity imparted by the **treading**[N] of a *zav*, which is considered a primary source of ritual impurity, **for *perushin*,** individuals who are careful to eat even non-sacred food in a state of purity. **The garments of *perushin*,** although they are careful to remain ritually pure, are nevertheless considered to be rendered impure by the **treading**[N] of a *zav* **for** priests who partake of ***teruma***. Consequently, the latter clause differs from the opinion of the Rabbis in the earlier clause.[H]

אֲתָאן לְרַבִּי מֵאִיר, דְּאָמַר: חוּלִּין וּמַעֲשֵׂר כַּהֲדָדֵי נִינְהוּ. רֵישָׁא רַבָּנַן וְסֵיפָא רַבִּי מֵאִיר? אִין, רֵישָׁא רַבָּנַן וְסֵיפָא רַבִּי מֵאִיר.

Therefore, **we have arrived at** the opinion of **Rabbi Meir, who said: Non-sacred** produce **and tithes are similar to one another,** as this clause of the mishna does not distinguish between those eating non-sacred food and those eating tithes. Is **the earlier clause** the opinion of **the Rabbis and the latter clause** the opinion of **Rabbi Meir?**[N] The Gemara answers: **Yes;** although it is unusual, in this instance we must explain that **the earlier clause** was said by **the Rabbis and the latter clause** by **Rabbi Meir.**

רַב אַחָא בַּר אַדָּא מַתְנֵי לַהּ בְּסֵיפָא חָמֵשׁ מַעֲלוֹת, וּמוֹקֵי לַהּ כּוּלַּהּ כְּרַבָּנַן.

However, **Rav Aḥa bar Adda would teach** that **five levels** of ritual purity are listed **in the latter clause** of the mishna, by counting the clause that states that the clothes of those who eat non-sacred produce in a state of purity are ritually impure for tithes, **and** in this way **he establishes** the **entire** mishna **in accordance with** the opinion of **the Rabbis.**

אָמַר רַב מָרִי: שְׁמַע מִינַּהּ, חוּלִּין שֶׁנַּעֲשׂוּ עַל טׇהֳרַת הַקּוֹדֶשׁ כְּקוֹדֶשׁ דָּמוּ. מִמַּאי?

§ **Rav Mari said:** They **learn from** the mishna that **non-sacred** produce **that was prepared according to** the level of **ritual purity** required **for sacrificial** food,[N] i.e., with the same stringencies as required for sacrificial food, is **like sacrificial** food. **From where** is this deduced?

NOTES

The garments of an *am ha'aretz* are considered to be rendered ritually impure by the impurity imparted by treading – **בִּגְדֵי עַם הָאָרֶץ מִדְרָס**: The problem with regard to ritual impurity imparted by treading is as follows: Did the Sages decree that individuals who are less strict with regard to ritual purity should be considered as if they themselves were *zavim* with regard items with high-level sanctity, or did their decree apply exclusively to their garments? This question is addressed in the Jerusalem Talmud. The answer there is that the basic decree applies exclusively to garments.

However, the Rambam writes that the Sages were of the opinion that the case of an *am ha'aretz* is an exception, and they themselves are considered to be impure. The Rabbis decreed that they should have the status of *zavim*. It is important to note that this ruling is not at all unequivocal (see *Tosafot*).

The Meiri points out that the various statements of the Talmud are not always consistent with regard to this issue, as it sometimes appears that the decree was applied across the board by dint of one being an *am ha'aretz*, whereas on other occasions it seems that the Sages decreed this only due to a specific concern that they may have become impure. For example, both the Babylonian Talmud and the Jerusalem Talmud state the concern that the menstruating wife of an *am ha'aretz* may have sat on his garments, thereby rendering them impure upon contact, and since an *am ha'aretz* is not careful with regard to ritual impurity he might consequently be wearing impure garments.

The garments of *perushin* are considered to be rendered impure by treading, etc. – **בִּגְדֵי פְּרוּשִׁין מִדְרָס וכו׳**: Since all agree that there is no concern about possible bodily impurity of those who eat *teruma* and the like, the Meiri explains that the Sages enacted this decree because of the assumption that one who immerses does so only in order to establish his status, and all the more so his garments and any other vessels he immerses, for the level of ritual purity he requires. Therefore, those who partake of *teruma* purify their garments for the purpose of *teruma* alone, and as we learn in the mishna, this does not suffice for them to be considered ritually pure with regard to sacrificial food. The garments of those who eat *teruma* are therefore viewed as impure in relation to higher levels of purity.

Is the earlier clause the opinion of the Rabbis and the latter clause the opinion of Rabbi Meir – **רֵישָׁא רַבָּנַן וְסֵיפָא רַבִּי מֵאִיר**: Even though Rabbi Yehuda HaNasi, who redacted the Mishna, gathered together collections of *mishnayot* from various houses of study, it is nevertheless assumed that any unattributed mishna and the *mishnayot* adjacent to it reflect the opinion of a single *tanna*. Certain Sages, such as Rabbi Yoḥanan, would invest great effort to establish the mishna in accordance with the opinion of a single *tanna* rather than two, even if this required him to use a far-fetched explanation.

Non-sacred produce…according to the level of ritual purity required for sacrificial food – **חוּלִּין...עַל טׇהֳרַת הַקּוֹדֶשׁ**: Rashi explains that in order to avoid error, certain individuals who often partake of consecrated offerings, primarily priests, would always prepare their food according to the purity required for sacrificial food. However, those who had the custom of eating non-sacred produce in a state of ritual purity did so as an extra measure of sanctity they accepted upon themselves, but not as a safeguard against error.

מִדְּלָא קָתָנֵי בְּהוּ מַעֲלָה.

It is deduced **from** the fact **that it is not taught in their regard** that those who eat non-sacred produce according to the level of ritual purity required for sacrificial food must treat the produce with **a higher standard** with regard to their degree of purity, like those who actually partake of sacrificial food.

וְדִלְמָא הַאי דְּלָא קָתָנֵי בְּהוּ מַעֲלָה, דְּאִי דָּמוּ לִתְרוּמָה – הָא תָּנֵי תְּרוּמָה, וְאִי דָּמוּ לְחוּלִּין – הָא תָּנֵי לְחוּלִּין. דִּתְנַן: חוּלִּין שֶׁנַּעֲשׂוּ עַל טׇהֳרַת הַקּוֹדֶשׁ הֲרֵי הֵן כְּחוּלִּין, רַבִּי אֶלְעָזָר בְּרַבִּי צָדוֹק אוֹמֵר: הֲרֵי הֵן כִּתְרוּמָה?

The Gemara asks: **But perhaps** the reason for **this** fact, **that a higher standard is not taught with regard to those** who actually partake of sacrificial food, is that these foods are not on a distinct level of ritual purity, **as, if they are similar to** the level of ***teruma, teruma* has** already been **taught; and if they are similar to non-sacred** produce, **non-sacred produce has** also already been **taught. As we learned** in a *baraita* that they are not considered to be on a level of their own: **Non-sacred** foods **prepared according to the** level of ritual **purity** required **for sacrificial** food[H] **are like non-sacred** food; **Rabbi Elazar, son of Rabbi Tzadok, says: They are like *teruma*,** but not like sacrificial food. Therefore, the fact that this level is not explicitly mentioned affords no proof.

אֶלָּא מִסֵּיפָא: יוֹסֵי בֶּן יוֹעֶזֶר הָיָה חָסִיד שֶׁבַּכְּהוּנָּה, וְהָיְתָה מִטְפַּחְתּוֹ מִדְרָס לַקּוֹדֶשׁ. יוֹחָנָן בֶּן גּוּדְגְּדָא הָיָה אוֹכֵל עַל טׇהֳרַת הַקּוֹדֶשׁ כׇּל יָמָיו, וְהָיְתָה מִטְפַּחְתּוֹ מִדְרָס לַחַטָּאת.

Rather, the proof is derived from **the last clause** in the mishna: **Yosei ben Yo'ezer was the most pious** member **of the priesthood, and** yet **his cloth was** considered impure by the **treading** of a *zav* **for** those who ate **sacrificial** food. **Yoḥanan ben Gudgeda would eat** non-sacred foods prepared **according to the** level of ritual **purity** required **for sacrificial** food **all his days, and** nevertheless **his cloth was** considered rendered impure by the **treading** of a *zav* **for** those preparing the **purification** waters.

לַחַטָּאת – אִין, לַקּוֹדֶשׁ – לָא. אַלְמָא קָסָבַר: חוּלִּין שֶׁנַּעֲשׂוּ עַל טׇהֳרַת קוֹדֶשׁ – כְּקוֹדֶשׁ דָּמוּ.

The Gemara infers from this: **For the purifying** waters, **yes,** his cloth was considered to have ritual impurity imparted by treading, but **for sacrificial** food, **no,** it was not considered to have ritual impurity imparted by treading. **Apparently, he maintains** that **non-sacred** produce **prepared according to** the level of ritual **purity** required **for sacrificial** food **is like sacrificial** food, as one who is particular to preserve the ritual purity required for sacrificial food even with regard to non-sacred produce is considered pure even with regard to sacrificial food themselves.

אָמַר רַבִּי יוֹנָתָן בֶּן אֶלְעָזָר: נָפְלָה מַעֲפַרְתּוֹ הֵימֶנּוּ, אָמַר לַחֲבֵירוֹ "תְּנָה לִי", וּנְתָנָהּ לוֹ – טְמֵאָה. אָמַר רַבִּי יוֹנָתָן בֶּן עַמְרָם: נִתְחַלְּפוּ לוֹ כֵּלִים שֶׁל שַׁבָּת בְּכֵלִים שֶׁל חוֹל וּלְבָשָׁן – נִטְמְאוּ.

§ With regard to the particular care that must be taken to prevent any suspicion that one's clothes have contracted impurity, **Rabbi Yonatan ben Elazar said: If the shawl of** one who was stringent with regard to ritual purity **fell**[H] **off of him, and he said to another** person: **Give it to me, and he gave it to him,** the shawl is **impure.** Even if the other individual is himself pure, since his attention was diverted at that moment from being cautious with regard to impurity, it is as though the shawl were rendered impure. Similarly, **Rabbi Yonatan ben Amram says: If one's Shabbat clothes were switched**[H] **for his weekday clothes and he wore them, they are impure.** His assumption that they were different clothes than the clothes he had intended to wear is enough of a distraction to spoil his caution against impurity.

אָמַר רַבִּי אֶלְעָזָר בַּר צָדוֹק: מַעֲשֶׂה בִּשְׁתֵּי נָשִׁים חֲבֵירוֹת שֶׁנִּתְחַלְּפוּ לָהֶן כְּלֵיהֶן בְּבֵית הַמֶּרְחָץ, וּבָא מַעֲשֶׂה לִפְנֵי רַבִּי עֲקִיבָא וְטִימְּאָן.

Rabbi Elazar bar Tzadok said: There was **an incident involving two women who were wives of *ḥaverim*,** who are meticulous in observance of *halakha* especially with regard to matters of impurity, **whose clothes were switched in the bathhouse; and the incident came before Rabbi Akiva and he declared** the clothes **impure.**[H] This demonstrates that an unintentional act is considered a lapse of attention, which renders the items impure, even if there was no other reason to consider them impure.

מַתְקִיף לַהּ רַבִּי אוֹשַׁעְיָא: אֶלָּא מֵעַתָּה, הוֹשִׁיט יָדוֹ לַסַּל לִיטּוֹל פַּת חִטִּין וְעָלְתָה בְּיָדוֹ פַּת שְׂעוֹרִים – הָכִי נַמִי דְּנִטְמֵאת?

Rabbi Oshaya strongly objects to this: However, if that is so, one who **inserted his hand into a basket to take a loaf of wheat** bread, **and a loaf of barley bread came up in his hand** instead; **in that case, too,** will you say that the loaf **is rendered impure?**

HALAKHA

Non-sacred produce prepared according to the level of ritual purity required for sacrificial food – חוּלִּין שֶׁנַּעֲשׂוּ עַל טׇהֳרַת הַקֹּדֶשׁ: Non-sacred produce that was prepared according to the level of ritual purity required for sacrificial food is considered non-sacred food with regard to ritual impurity. Its second degree of impurity is invalid, not impure, so that if it comes into contact with a third object, it does not render it ritually impure. This is the Rambam's ruling, in accordance with the opinion of the first *tanna*. The Ra'avad, however, maintains that non-sacred food prepared according to the level of ritual purity required for sacrificial food has the status of sacrificial food, in accordance with the opinion of Rabbi Elazar, son of Rabbi Tzadok, following the discussion in tractate *Ḥullin* (Rambam *Sefer Tahara, Hilkhot Avot HaTumot* 11:15; 12:16).

If the shawl of one fell – נָפְלָה מַעֲפַרְתּוֹ: If one's shawl fell, and he asked another to give it to him, and the latter did so, it is ritually impure, as stated by Rabbi Yonatan ben Elazar (Rambam *Sefer Tahara, Hilkhot Metamei Mishkav UMoshav* 13:6).

One's…clothes were switched – נִתְחַלְּפוּ לוֹ כֵּלִים: In a case when one wore Shabbat clothes because he mistook them for his weekday garments, the Shabbat clothes are rendered impure, as his assumption that they are weekday clothes causes him to guard them less scrupulously than usual, as stated by Rabbi Yonatan ben Amram (Rambam *Sefer Tahara, Hilkhot Metamei Mishkav UMoshav* 13:6).

Women whose garments were switched – נָשִׁים שֶׁנִּתְחַלְּפוּ בִּגְדֵיהֶן: There was an incident involving two women who were wives of *ḥaverim* whose garments became switched in a bathhouse, and the Sages declared all the clothes ritually impure (Rambam *Sefer Tahara, Hilkhot Metamei Mishkav UMoshav* 13:6).

וְכִי תֵּימָא הָכִי נַמִי – וְהָתַנְיָא: הַמְשַׁמֵּר אֶת הֶחָבִית בְּחֶזְקַת שֶׁל יַיִן וְנִמְצֵאת שֶׁל שֶׁמֶן – טְהוֹרָה מִלְּטַמֵּא! וּלְטַעֲמִיךְ, אֵימָא סֵיפָא: וַאֲסוּרָה מִלֶּאֱכוֹל. אַמַּאי?

And if you would say, indeed, this is correct, **but isn't it taught** in a *baraita*: **One who is minding a barrel** to ensure its ritual purity **on the assumption** that it is a barrel **of wine and** it **is found** to be **of oil, it is ritually pure** in the sense that it does not **transmit impurity?** This indicates that one's lack of knowledge with regard to the identity of the item he is minding does not itself cause impurity. The Gemara rejects this: **But according to your** line of **reasoning, say the latter clause** of that same *baraita*: **And it is prohibited to be eaten,** which indicates that the supervision is insufficient in this case. The Gemara asks: **Why** is it that the barrel's status is pure and yet there is a prohibition against eating its contents? If the supervisor's error does not harm the food's ritually pure status, one should likewise be permitted to eat it.

אָמַר רַבִּי יִרְמְיָה: בְּאוֹמֵר: שְׁמַרְתִּיהָ מִדָּבָר הַמְטַמְּאָהּ וְלֹא מִדָּבָר הַפּוֹסְלָהּ.

Rabbi Yirmeya said: The *baraita* is referring **to one who says: I guarded it from things that render it impure but not from things that invalidate it.**[N] In other words, he was careful to guard it only from being rendered impure with a severe degree of impurity, which causes anything it renders impure to render others impure in turn, but not from a lesser degree of impurity that merely invalidates it for use but does not enable it to render other items ritually impure. Since he guarded it from impurity, it is considered pure with regard to rendering other items impure, but it still may not be eaten, in case it was invalidated by an impure object.

וּמִי אִיכָּא נְטִירוּתָא לְפַלְגָא? אִין. וְהָתַנְיָא: הוֹשִׁיט יָדוֹ בַּסַּל, וְהַסַּל עַל כְּתֵיפוֹ, וְהַמַּגְרֵיפָה בְּתוֹךְ הַסַּל, וְהָיָה בְּלִבּוֹ עַל הַסַּל וְלֹא הָיָה בְּלִבּוֹ עַל הַמַּגְרֵיפָה – הַסַּל טָהוֹר וְהַמַּגְרֵיפָה טְמֵאָה.

The Gemara asks: **And is there guarding by half** measures; can it be said that one was careful with regard to only a particular type of impurity? The Gemara responds: **Yes, as it is** indeed **taught** in a *baraita*: **If one inserted his hand into a basket** filled with figs, **and the basket** was placed **on his shoulder, and a shovel**[B] was **in the basket, and his mind was on the basket** to guard it from impurity, **but his mind was not on the shovel, the basket is pure and the shovel is impure.**

הַסַּל טָהוֹר? תְּטַמֵּא הַמַּגְרֵיפָה לַסַּל! אֵין כְּלִי מְטַמֵּא כְּלִי. וְלִיטַמֵּא מַה שֶּׁבַּסַּל! אָמַר רָבִינָא, בְּאוֹמֵר: שְׁמַרְתִּיו מִדָּבָר שֶׁמְּטַמְּאוֹ, וְלֹא מִדָּבָר הַפּוֹסְלוֹ.

The Gemara asks: Why is **the basket pure? Let the shovel render the basket ritually impure,** if the former is in fact impure. The Gemara answers: The *halakha* is that **a vessel cannot render** a different **vessel impure.** Therefore, the basket remains pure. The Gemara asks another question: **And let it render impure** any food **that is inside the basket,** as food is not a vessel and can therefore be rendered impure by a vessel. **Ravina said:** The *baraita* is referring **to one who says: I guarded** the shovel **from things that render it ritually impure,**[N] which is why it cannot render other objects impure, **but** I did **not** guard it **from things that invalidate it,** so it is impure.[H] Consequently, there is no proof from here that the contents of the barrel in the earlier case may not be eaten.

מִכָּל מָקוֹם קַשְׁיָא.

Returning to the prior discussion, the Gemara states that **in any case** it is **difficult.** Why should an object be impure just because the one guarding it was mistaken with regard to the identity of its contents; how would this accord with the *baraita* that explicitly taught that if one minds a barrel under the assumption that it is wine and it turns out to contain oil, the oil is pure and cannot render others impure?

וְעוֹד, מוֹתִיב רַבָּה בַּר אֲבוּהּ: מַעֲשֶׂה בְּאִשָּׁה אַחַת שֶׁבָּאת לִפְנֵי רַבִּי יִשְׁמָעֵאל, וְאָמְרָה לוֹ: רַבִּי! בֶּגֶד זֶה אֲרַגְתִּיו בְּטָהֳרָה, וְלֹא הָיָה בְּלִבִּי לְשׁוֹמְרוֹ בְּטָהֳרָה. וּמִתּוֹךְ בְּדִיקוֹת שֶׁהָיָה רַבִּי יִשְׁמָעֵאל בּוֹדְקָהּ, אָמְרָה לוֹ: רַבִּי, נִדָּה מָשְׁכָה עִמִּי בַּחֶבֶל. אָמַר רַבִּי יִשְׁמָעֵאל: כַּמָּה גְּדוֹלִים דִּבְרֵי חֲכָמִים שֶׁהָיוּ אוֹמְרִים: בְּלִבּוֹ לְשׁוֹמְרוֹ – טָהוֹר, אֵין בְּלִבּוֹ לְשׁוֹמְרוֹ – טָמֵא.

And Rabba bar Avuh raised a further objection:[N] There was an **incident involving a certain woman who came before Rabbi Yishmael and said to him: Rabbi, I wove this garment in a ritually pure state, but my mind was not on it to guard its** state of **purity.** In other words, although I did not intend to guard it in this manner, I am certain that no impurity came into contact with it. **And during the interrogations that Rabbi Yishmael conducted with her,** to see if it had remained in a state of purity, **she** happened to **say to him: Rabbi, a menstruating woman pulled the rope with me** as I was weaving, and the garment was therefore rendered fully impure by a menstruating woman moving it. **Rabbi Yishmael said: How great are the words of the Sages when they said:** If **one's mind** is focused **on guarding it, it is pure; if one's mind is not** focused **on guarding it, it is impure.** Since she was not focused on preserving the garment's pure state, it contracted impurity without her noticing.

NOTES

From things that render it ritually impure but not from things that invalidate it – מִדָּבָר הַמְטַמְּאָהּ וְלֹא מִדָּבָר הַפּוֹסְלָהּ: The Rid explains that this statement is not referring to the ritual impurity of the barrel itself, but to the liquids it contains, which are rendered ritually impure by coming into contact with impure objects. Although liquids can generally be rendered impure by all types of ritual impurity, there are exceptions to this rule, such as the contact of a *tevul yom*, an individual who has immersed and is waiting for the sun to set before he is fully purified, which only invalidates and does not render impure.

I guarded it from things that render it impure, etc. – שְׁמַרְתִּיו מִדָּבָר שֶׁמְּטַמְּאוֹ וכו׳: The Rid and *Tosafot* explain that by Torah law, liquids have the power to render only food impure, but by rabbinic law, they can render vessels impure as well. In this case, it may be that the liquid did not render the non-sacred food in the basket impure, and yet the shovel would nevertheless be considered to be impure with regard to both *teruma* and sacrificial food.

Rabba bar Avuh raised a further objection – מוֹתִיב רַבָּה בַּר אֲבוּהּ: Rabbi Akiva Eiger comments that there seems to be no difficulty here: There appears to be no direct correlation between the various incidents with regard to the women and the topic at hand. Rabbi Ya'akov Yalish writes that the proof of the principle that mere lack of awareness does not suffice to render the item impure is from the fact that Rabbi Yishmael cross-examined the woman to see if there had been an actual cause of impurity, demonstrating that distraction alone would not have been enough to cause ritual impurity.

BACKGROUND

Shovel – מַגְרֵיפָה: There are a number of utensils referred to by the Gemara as shovels, but in the context of a basket and shovel combination, the usual reference is to an implement used for raking clay. This type of tool typically had a long handle and a wide head, and it was made of either wood or metal. A common secondary use for such a shovel was to separate dried figs.

HALAKHA

A basket and a shovel – סַל וּמַגְרֵיפָה: If a *ḥaver* was carrying a basket that contained a shovel on his shoulder, and he had in mind to guard the basket's ritual purity while intending to guard the shovel only from something that renders it impure but not from things that invalidate it, the shovel is impure and renders *teruma* ritually impure upon contact (Rambam *Sefer Tahara, Hilkhot Metamei Mishkav UMoshav* 13:6).

שׁוּב מַעֲשֶׂה בְּאִשָּׁה אַחַת שֶׁבָּאת לִפְנֵי רַבִּי יִשְׁמָעֵאל, אָמְרָה לוֹ: רַבִּי, מַפָּה זוֹ אֲרַגְתִּיהָ בְּטָהֳרָה וְלֹא הָיָה בְּלִבִּי לְשׁוֹמְרָהּ. וּמִתּוֹךְ בְּדִיקוֹת שֶׁהָיָה רַבִּי יִשְׁמָעֵאל בּוֹדְקָהּ, אָמְרָה לוֹ: רַבִּי, נִימָא נִפְסְקָה לִי וְקָשַׁרְתִּיהָ בְּפֶה.

There was **another incident involving a certain woman who came before Rabbi Yishmael** and **said to him: Rabbi, I wove this cloth in** a state of ritual **purity, but my mind was not on it to guard it** from impurity. **And during the interrogations that Rabbi Yishmael conducted with her, she said to him: Rabbi, a thread** of **mine** that was woven into the cloth **snapped and I tied it with my mouth.** It can be assumed that the thread became moist from her spittle, which means that if that thread was touched by a source of impurity, the cloth would be rendered ritually impure by contact with impure liquids. This is because the Sages decreed that any impurity that touches liquid renders the liquid ritually impure to the first degree, so any vessel that comes into contact with the liquid would be impure to the second degree.

אָמַר רַבִּי יִשְׁמָעֵאל: כַּמָּה גְּדוֹלִים דִּבְרֵי חֲכָמִים, שֶׁהָיוּ אוֹמְרִים: בְּלִבּוֹ לְשׁוֹמְרוֹ – טָהוֹר, אֵין בְּלִבּוֹ לְשׁוֹמְרוֹ – טָמֵא.

Rabbi Yishmael said: How great are the words of the Sages when they said: If **one's mind is** focused **on guarding it, it is pure; if one's mind is not** focused **on guarding it, it is impure.** In any case, if one intends to keep something in a state of ritual purity, a mistake on his part with regard to its identity is not considered enough of a distraction to render the item impure, unlike the *baraita* that explicitly taught that if one minds a barrel under the assumption that it is wine and it turns out to contain oil, the oil is pure and cannot render others impure.

בִּשְׁלָמָא לְרַבִּי אֶלְעָזָר בַּר צָדוֹק – כָּל אַחַת וְאַחַת אוֹמֶרֶת חֲבֶרְתִּי אֵשֶׁת עַם הָאָרֶץ, וּמַסְּחָה דַּעְתָּהּ מִינֵּהּ.

The Gemara clarifies: **Granted, according to Rabbi Elazar bar Tzadok** there is no difficulty, as in the case of the two wives of *ḥaverim* whose garments were switched it can be said that **each of them says** to herself: **My colleague is the wife of an *am ha'aretz*,** and not a *ḥaver*. **And she diverts her mind from** her garments, as she is certain that they have already been rendered impure, and a distraction of this kind makes it likely that the garment contracted impurity. It is therefore considered impure.

לְרַבִּי יוֹנָתָן בֶּן עַמְרָם נַמִּי, כֵּיוָן דִּכְלֵים דְּשַׁבָּת עָבֵיד לְהוּ שִׁימּוּר טְפֵי – מַסַּח דַּעֲתֵיהּ מִינַּיְיהוּ. אֶלָּא לְרַבִּי יוֹנָתָן בֶּן אֶלְעָזָר – נַעֲבֵיד לְהוּ שִׁימּוּר בִּידֵיהּ דְּחַבְרֵיהּ!

Likewise, **according to Rabbi Yonatan ben Amram** there is no difficulty either, as with regard to the case of one who switched his Shabbat clothes with his weekday clothes, it can **also** be said that **since he is more protective of Shabbat clothes, he will divert his mind from** that higher level of protection if he thinks that they are weekday garments. A distraction of this kind makes it likely that the garment contracted impurity, so it is considered impure. **But according to Rabbi Yonatan ben Elazar,** who deals with the case where one's shawl fell and another person lifts it up, why should this be considered a distraction? **Let him guard** his garments from ritual impurity while they are **in the other person's hands;** why should they be considered impure?

אָמַר רַבִּי יוֹחָנָן: חֲזָקָה, אֵין אָדָם מְשַׁמֵּר מַה שֶּׁבְּיַד חֲבֵרוֹ. וְלֹא?!

Rabbi Yoḥanan said: It is **a presumption** that **a person does not guard that which is in another's hand.**[NH] Since the object is in the hands of another, he will inevitably be distracted from guarding it. The Gemara asks: **And** can one indeed **not** guard an item in the hand of another?

NOTES

A person does not guard that which is in another's hand – אֵין אָדָם מְשַׁמֵּר מַה שֶּׁבְּיַד חֲבֵרוֹ: Several commentaries are puzzled with regard to the reason and source of the principle stated by Rabbi Yoḥanan. Some explain along the lines of Rashi, that once an object is transferred for safekeeping to one who does not know whether or not it is ritually pure, the one who transferred it will no longer guard it. Some later authorities discuss whether this principle should be applied to other mitzvot as well, such as ensuring that *matza* has not become leavened (see *Zekher LaHagiga*; see the Meiri).

HALAKHA

Does not guard that which is in another's hand – אֵין...מְשַׁמֵּר מַה שֶּׁבְּיַד חֲבֵרוֹ: It is a presumption that one does not guard the ritual purity of vessels that do not belong to him in the same manner that he safeguards his own vessels, unless he is informed that the owner is relying on him to guard them from impurity (Rambam *Sefer Tahara, Hilkhot Metamei Mishkav UMoshav* 13:1, 6).

וְהָתַנְיָא: הֲרֵי שֶׁהָיוּ חַמָּרָיו וּפוֹעֲלָיו טְעוּנִין טְהָרוֹת, אַף עַל פִּי שֶׁהִפְלִיג מֵהֶן יוֹתֵר מִמִּיל – טְהָרוֹתָיו טְהוֹרוֹת. וְאִם אָמַר לָהֶם: לְכוּ וַאֲנִי אָבוֹא אַחֲרֵיכֶם – כֵּיוָן שֶׁנִּתְעַלְּמוּ עֵינָיו מֵהֶן טְהָרוֹתָיו טְמֵאוֹת.

But isn't it taught in a *baraita*: With regard to **one whose donkey drivers and workers,** who were *amei ha'aretz,* **were bearing pure** food,[H] without touching the pure food itself but only the earthenware vessels containing them, even if **he distanced himself from them** as they walked by **more than a *mil*,**[L] **his pure** foods **are pure.** Since the workers are unaware of his departure, he is still considered to be guarding the food in their possession and need not be concerned that they may have touched the pure foods. **But if he said to them: Go, and I will follow behind you,** then **once they are no longer within his eyesight, his pure** foods **are impure.**

מַאי שְׁנָא רֵישָׁא וּמַאי שְׁנָא סֵיפָא? אָמַר רַבִּי יִצְחָק נַפָּחָא: רֵישָׁא בִּמְטַהֵר חַמָּרָיו וּפוֹעֲלָיו לְכָךְ.

The Gemara asks: **What is different** in **the first clause** of the *baraita*, where the food remains pure, **and what is different** in **the latter clause,**[N] where the food is impure? **Rabbi Yitzḥak Nappaḥa said: The first clause** is referring **to one who purifies his donkey drivers and workers for this** purpose,[N] meaning that he ensured that they immersed and purified themselves beforehand, so that concern for impurity was removed.

אִי הָכִי, סֵיפָא נַמִי! אֵין עַם הָאָרֶץ מַקְפִּיד עַל מַגַּע חֲבֵירוֹ.

The Gemara questions this: **If so,** in **the latter clause** they should **also** be pure. The Gemara responds: **An *am ha'aretz* is not particular about the contact of his colleague,** and therefore there is concern that they might have encountered another *am ha'aretz* on the way, who touched the produce and thereby rendered it impure.

אִי הָכִי רֵישָׁא נַמִי! בְּבָא לָהֶם דֶּרֶךְ עֲקַלָּתוֹן.

The Gemara counters: **If so,** in **the first** clause of the *baraita* there should **also** be concern that they might have met an *am ha'aretz,* and despite the employer's warning to his workers to stay ritually pure, they are not careful with regard to the impurity of another *am ha'aretz.* The Gemara answers: The first clause is referring to a situation **when he comes across them** via **a circuitous path.**[N] Since he is not walking directly behind them but can appear from the sides, they cannot always see him. Consequently, they are concerned that he may return at any moment. Therefore, they are careful not to render themselves ritually impure, and they are also wary of the contact of other *amei ha'aretz,* although they are not usually particular about the contact of their colleagues.

אִי הָכִי סֵיפָא נַמִי! כֵּיוָן דְּאָמַר לְהוּ ״לְכוּ וַאֲנִי אָבוֹא אַחֲרֵיכֶם״ – מִיסְמַךְ סָמְכָא דַּעְתַּיְיהוּ.

The Gemara raises a difficulty: **If so,** in **the latter clause, too,** since he can arrive from around a corner at any given moment, they should certainly be cautious. The Gemara responds: **Since he said to them: Go and I will follow behind you, they rely** on this, and they do not consider themselves to be under observation. Consequently, they are not particular about the contact of another *am ha'aretz.*

הדרן עלך אין דורשין

HALAKHA

One whose donkey drivers and workers were bearing pure food – חַמָּרָיו וּפוֹעֲלָיו טְעוּנִין טְהָרוֹת: If donkey drivers and workers who are *amei ha'aretz* are bearing pure food and went far ahead of their employer, a *ḥaver*, and he can encounter them via a circuitous path, all the produce remains pure because they are afraid to touch it, as their employer may arrive at any moment. This ruling is in accordance with the opinion of Rabbi Yitzḥak Nappaḥa (*Kesef Mishne*). However, if the employer said to them: Go, and I will follow behind you, then as soon as they are no longer within eyeshot, all the food is impure (Rambam *Sefer Tahara, Hilkhot Metamei Mishkav UMoshav* 13:5).

LANGUAGE

Mil – מִיל: From the Latin mille, meaning a measure of length equal to one thousand double steps. It is the equivalent of two thousand cubits, or 960–1200 m, according to the various opinions concerning measurements.

NOTES

What is different in the first clause of the *baraita* and what is different in the latter clause – מַאי שְׁנָא רֵישָׁא וּמַאי שְׁנָא סֵיפָא: Rashi maintains that this sentence is not a part of the original Gemara text. According to those who have this version of the text, this phrase should be understood is a type of preliminary question leading into a discussion of the *baraita* itself. The Gemara often begins its discussion of a quoted *baraita* by clarifying the wording or any other internal problems in it. The Gemara then proceeds to address the question for which it was cited.

One who purifies his donkey drivers and workers for this purpose – מְטַהֵר חַמָּרָיו וּפוֹעֲלָיו לְכָךְ: This suggestion not only answers the question of why the donkey drivers are relied upon not to touch the food, but it also resolves the difficulty as to how the owner can be relied upon to guard the food when it is in the possession of his workers. The reasoning behind the principle that one does not guard pure items in the possession of another is either because one believes that his guarding would serve no purpose, as he cannot control the actions of the one possessing the items, or because he is not particular when guarding the possession of another. In this case, however, since the owner has purified his donkey drivers and workers in order to keep the food pure, he has demonstrated that he expects them to guard the produce. Therefore, he will continue to guard it as well. Consequently, this source does not contradict Rabbi Yoḥanan's statement.

When he comes across them by a circuitous path – בְּבָא לָהֶם דֶּרֶךְ עֲקַלָּתוֹן: According to *Tosafot*, this answer completes the previous one: It is insufficient that he has purified the workers for this purpose; they must also be concerned about his unexpected arrival. The Rambam indicates that the second answer renders the first answer redundant, as the reason an individual cannot guard something that is in another's hand is because one is not careful with regard to the property of someone else (see *Kesef Mishne*). In this case, however, since the workers are subservient to the owner and are intimidated by him, their guarding is sufficient (see *Zekher LaḤagiga*).

Summary of **Perek II**

Three major Torah issues may be taught in public, but only in very small groups: The laws of forbidden sexual relations, the Act of Creation, and the Design of the Divine Chariot. This chapter focused on the two latter issues, which are related to divine secrets. The Gemara discussed which topics are included in the Act of Creation and the Design of the Divine Chariot, emphasizing how critical it is to take care not to study these topics, which are directly related to God's honor, unless one is thoroughly prepared. Even then, one who studies them may be in great danger, as the chapter described in detail.

The dispute with regard to placing the hands on Festival offerings, which continued throughout the generation of the pairs until Hillel and Shammai and their students, ended in favor of Beit Hillel, who ruled that one may bring both peace-offerings and burnt-offerings on the Festival and that one may place the hands on them.

With regard to the topic of purity and impurity, several levels of purity were discussed: Non-sacred food, i.e., tithes; *teruma*; sacred offerings; and the purifying waters of the red heifer. An additional difference between levels of purity pertains to washing one's hands from the impurity. The Rabbis ordained that with regard to the hands, in order to eat non-sacred food and teruma washing one's hands is sufficient, but in order to consume sacred offerings or for the sprinkling of the purifying waters a full immersion is required.

The major principle with regard to levels of purity was also explained in this chapter. Anything that is on a lower level of sanctity is considered as if it were impure with regard to things on a higher level of sanctity. An additional principle is that with regard to whether an item is completely ritually pure or not, one must have full intention and awareness that it has indeed maintained its pure status. In the absence of such awareness its status may no longer be relied upon, especially with regard to items that are of a higher level of sanctity.

Introduction to **Perek III**

They shall keep My charge, lest they bear sin for it, and die thereby, if they profane it: I am the Lord Who sanctifies them.

(Leviticus 22:9)

Our feet were standing within your gates, O Jerusalem. Jerusalem, that is built as a city that is compact together.

(Psalms 122:2–3)

The Torah stresses several times its insistence on maintaining *teruma* and sacrificial items in a state of ritual purity, as well as the severe penalties for eating *teruma* or sacrificial food in a state of ritual impurity. In light of the Torah's directives to make safeguards for its commandments in general and for the maintenance of ritual purity for holy foods in particular, the Sages instituted various stringencies and decrees in order to, in their words: Make safeguards for the safeguards.

These rabbinic safeguards and decrees for the maintenance of ritual purity are stricter or more lenient in accordance with the level of sanctity of the item for which they were intended. Thus, they were more stringent regarding sacrificial food than regarding *teruma*, and stricter still for the purification ashes of the red heifer.

The concept of instituting stricter standards for sacrificial food is found in the Torah itself. To this the Sages added various decrees to the effect that the slightest possibility of defilement or lack of care in the handling of sacrificial food should render it unfit or impure. The difference between unfit and impure is that the former would invalidate the item for use but would not defile other foods that came into contact with it, while the latter indicates something whose impurity can be passed on to other sacred foods.

Despite this general trend, there are certain situations in which the Sages were stricter with *teruma* than with sacrificial food. This is because *teruma* is set aside by everyone and is eaten by any priest in his own house, without the rabbinic supervision that prevailed in the Temple's sacrificial service, and not all priests were well versed in the laws or sufficiently meticulous about them.

In general, there were many people who lived during the Second Temple period who were not meticulous about observing the laws of ritual purity. These people are referred to as *amei ha'aretz*, common folk, while those who did maintain the strictures of ritual purity at all times were called *ḥaverim*, literally, colleagues. Since *teruma* perforce often involved contact with *amei ha'aretz*, the Sages on occasion saw fit to apply stricter standards to *teruma* than to sacred foods, for which even *amei ha'aretz* could be relied upon to adhere to the highest standard.

The elaboration of the Sages' enactments and decrees in these matters, both the strictures they imposed for sacrificial food and the leeway they occasionally granted for an item, in Jerusalem and specifically in the Temple, and especially during the Festival periods, are the major focus of this chapter.

מתני׳ חוֹמֶר בַּקֹּדֶשׁ מִבַּתְּרוּמָה: שֶׁמַּטְבִּילִין כֵּלִים בְּתוֹךְ כֵּלִים לִתְרוּמָה – אֲבָל לֹא לַקֹּדֶשׁ; אֲחוֹרַיִים וְתוֹךְ וּבֵית הַצְּבִיטָה בִּתְרוּמָה – אֲבָל לֹא בַּקֹּדֶשׁ;

MISHNA Concerning several matters there is greater **stringency with regard to sacrificial** food[NH] **than with regard to** ***teruma*****,** a portion of the produce designated for the priest. This expresses itself in many ways, the first being **that one may immerse vessels inside** other **vessels** to purify them **for** ***teruma*****; but not for sacrificial** food, for which one must immerse each vessel separately. Another difference is that the *halakhot* of **the back** of a vessel **and** its **inside and** its **place for gripping** apply **to** vessels used for ***teruma*****,** meaning that each part of the vessel has its own use and is considered a separate vessel in that it does not convey impurity to the other parts of the vessel when it contracts impurity; **but not to sacrificial** food, for which an impure section of the vessel does convey impurity to all the other sections.

הַנּוֹשֵׂא אֶת הַמִּדְרָס נוֹשֵׂא אֶת הַתְּרוּמָה – אֲבָל לֹא אֶת הַקֹּדֶשׁ; בִּגְדֵי אוֹכְלֵי תְרוּמָה מִדְרָס לְקֹדֶשׁ.

Likewise, **one who carries an object trodden** on by a *zav*, a man suffering from gonorrhea, **may carry** ***teruma*** at the same time, if he is careful that neither he nor the impure object should come into contact with the *teruma*, **but** this may **not** be done with **sacrificial** food. **The garments of those who eat** ***teruma*** are like an object trodden on by a *zav* **with regard to sacrificial** food.

לֹא כְּמִדַּת הַקֹּדֶשׁ מִדַּת הַתְּרוּמָה: שֶׁבַּקֹּדֶשׁ מַתִּיר וּמְנַגֵּב וּמַטְבִּיל וְאַחַר כָּךְ קוֹשֵׁר, וּבִתְרוּמָה קוֹשֵׁר וְאַחַר כָּךְ מַטְבִּיל;

The mishna lists other stringencies that apply to sacrificial foods but not to *teruma*: **The characteristics of** ***teruma*** **are not like the characteristics of sacrificial** food,[N] **as in** the case of vessels that are used with **sacrificial** food, if one has a garment or vessel that is tied up **he must untie** it **and dry** it[N] if there was any moisture on it, as both a knot and absorbed moisture are considered interpositions that prevent the water of the ritual bath from reaching the entire garment. **And he may** then **immerse** them, **and afterward he may tie** them up again if he wishes. **But with regard to** ***teruma*** **he may,** if he so desires, **tie** up the garment **and then immerse** it[N] without any concern that the knot might be considered an interposition.

כֵּלִים הַנִּגְמָרִים בְּטׇהֳרָה צְרִיכִין טְבִילָה לַקֹּדֶשׁ, אֲבָל לֹא לִתְרוּמָה; הַכְּלִי מְצָרֵף מַה שֶּׁבְּתוֹכוֹ לַקֹּדֶשׁ – אֲבָל לֹא לִתְרוּמָה;

Vessels that were fashioned and **completed in purity** nevertheless **require immersion** to be considered pure **for sacrificial foods, but not for** ***teruma*****. A vessel combines** all the food **that is in it** with regard **to sacrificial** food, meaning that if one piece of food becomes impure all the other pieces become impure as well; **but not** with regard **to** ***teruma*****,** concerning which each piece is treated independently.

הָרְבִיעִי בַּקֹּדֶשׁ פָּסוּל, וְהַשְּׁלִישִׁי בִּתְרוּמָה. וּבִתְרוּמָה, אִם נִטְמֵאת אַחַת מִיָּדָיו – חֲבֶירְתָּהּ טְהוֹרָה, וּבַקֹּדֶשׁ מַטְבִּיל שְׁתֵּיהֶן, שֶׁהַיָּד מְטַמָּא אֶת חֲבֶירְתָּהּ בַּקֹּדֶשׁ אֲבָל לֹא בִּתְרוּמָה. אוֹכְלִין אוֹכָלִים נְגוּבִין בְּיָדַיִם מְסוֹאָבוֹת בִּתְרוּמָה, אֲבָל לֹא בַּקֹּדֶשׁ.

The mishna continues the list of differences between sacrificial food and *teruma*. **Sacrificial** food **that is impure with fourth-degree** impurity **is disqualified,** meaning that the sacrificial food is rendered impure but it does not impart impurity to other items. ***Teruma*** **is disqualified when it is impure with third-degree** impurity; it is not susceptible to fourth-degree impurity at all. **And with regard to** ***teruma*****, if one of one's hands became impure** by rabbinic law that renders only the hands impure, **its counterpart,** i.e., the other hand, remains **pure. But with regard to sacrificial** food, if one hand becomes impure **he must immerse them both, as one hand renders its counterpart impure with regard to sacrificial** food **but not with regard to** ***teruma*****. One may eat dry foods,** i.e., foods that have never come into contact with liquid and are therefore not susceptible to impurity, **with impure hands when** it is ***teruma*****, but not** when it is **sacrificial** food.

NOTES

There is greater stringency with regard to sacrificial food – חוֹמֶר בַּקּוֹדֶשׁ: The plain meaning of this mishna appears to be that these stringencies result from the extra care and rigor that must be observed concerning sacrificial foods, as the Torah is more particular about preserving them in a full state of purity. We see this, for instance, in the fourth degree of impurity, which applies only to sacrificial foods. An alternative opinion suggested by the Jerusalem Talmud is that those who eat *teruma* are meticulous, as *teruma* may be eaten only by priests, who are generally careful with regard to purity. By contrast, sacrificial foods are eaten by regular Israelites as well, not all of whom are so scrupulous with regard to purity. Therefore, the Sages were more stringent in the latter case.

The characteristics of ***teruma*** **are not like the characteristics of sacrificial food – לֹא כְּמִדַּת הַקֹּדֶשׁ מִדַּת הַתְּרוּמָה:** *Tosafot* comment on the insertion of this general phrase in the middle of the mishna's list of differences between *teruma* and sacrificial food. They explain that since the list is so lengthy the mishna divides it up with this clause.

Turei Aven notes a peculiarity in the listing. In the first section the *tanna* first states the leniency of *teruma* and then contrasts it with the stringency of sacrificial food, whereas in the second section, for the most part, he reverses the order and refers to the stringency of the sacrificial foods first. He explains that in the earlier section of the mishna one might have thought that the stringency applies to *teruma* as well, and therefore it begins each clause by stating that it does not. In the second section, however, one would not have thought this stringency should apply in any case, so the mishna begins by stating that it does apply to sacrificial food, going on to elaborate that it does not apply to *teruma* (see *Zekher LaHagiga*).

He must untie it and dry it – מַתִּיר וּמְנַגֵּב: The Rambam, in his Commentary on the Mishna, explains that the term drying, here, is referring to wiping off any fat from the vessel that might be considered an interposition between the water and the vessel. In *Porat Yosef* it is demonstrated that the term drying can sometimes refer to a thorough cleaning.

He may tie it up and then immerse it – קוֹשֵׁר וְאַחַר כָּךְ מַטְבִּיל: The Rambam explains that the mishna is not referring to a garment knotted together but to one who ties together a vessel made of separate parts. In the case of *teruma* one may immerse the entire vessel, but for sacrificial food one must immerse each part of the vessel separately (see Meiri).

HALAKHA

There is greater stringency with regard to sacrificial food – חוֹמֶר בַּקּוֹדֶשׁ: The Sages enacted many stringencies for the purity of sacrificial foods, both with regard to the requirement to keep them from any kind of impurity and with regard to the manner of immersion of impure vessels to be used for them (Rambam *Sefer Tahara, Hilkhot She'ar Avot HaTumot* 12:1–7, 11–16).

הָאוֹנֵן וּמְחוּסַּר כִּפּוּרִים צְרִיכִין טְבִילָה לַקֹּדֶשׁ, אֲבָל לֹא לַתְּרוּמָה.

An acute mourner [***onen***],[N] i.e., someone who has experienced the loss of a close relative on that day, who had not come into contact with the deceased; **and one who is lacking atonement,** i.e., someone who still needs to bring an offering to complete his purification procedure, such as a *zav* or a woman after childbirth, both **require immersion** in order **to** eat **sacrificial** food.[N] The *onen* would immerse after the day has passed and the one lacking atonement would immerse after the requisite offering is brought. **However,** immersion in these cases is **not** necessary **for** eating ***teruma*****.**

גמ׳ בַּקֹּדֶשׁ מַאי טַעְמָא לָא? אָמַר רַבִּי אִילָא: מִפְּנֵי שֶׁכְּבֵידוֹ שֶׁל כְּלִי חוֹצֵץ.

GEMARA It is taught in the mishna that one may not immerse one vessel inside another if they will be used for sacrificial food, though this may be done for *teruma*. The Gemara asks: **With regard to sacrificial** food, **what is the reason** that one may **not** immerse vessels in this manner? **Rabbi Ila said: Because the weight of the** inner **vessel causes an interposition**[N] between the water and the vessels. That is, the innermost vessel weighs down on the bottom one, not allowing the water to reach the two vessels' point of contact.

וְהָא מִדְּסֵיפָא מִשּׁוּם חֲצִיצָה, רֵישָׁא לָאו מִשּׁוּם חֲצִיצָה, דְּקָתָנֵי סֵיפָא: וְלֹא כְּמִדַּת הַקֹּדֶשׁ מִדַּת הַתְּרוּמָה, שֶׁבַּקֹּדֶשׁ מַתִּיר וּמְנַגֵּב וּמַטְבִּיל וְאַחַר כָּךְ קוֹשֵׁר, וּבַתְּרוּמָה קוֹשֵׁר וְאַחַר כָּךְ מַטְבִּיל!

The Gemara poses a question on this explanation: **But is it not so that since the latter clause** of the mishna mentions that sacrificial foods and *teruma* differ **with regard to** matters of **interposition,**[N] **the first clause** of the mishna must **not** be **with regard to** matters of **interposition,** but is referring to a different consideration? **As it teaches in the latter part** of the mishna: **The characteristics of *teruma* are not like the characteristics of sacrificial** food, **as in** the case of **sacrificial** food, if one has a garment or vessel that is tied up **he must untie** it **and dry** it, **and he may** then **immerse** them, **and afterward he may tie** them up again if he wishes; **but with regard to *teruma* he may tie** up the garment **and then immerse** it. This latter clause shows that there the Sages were concerned for any possibility of interposition with regard to sacrificial food, so most likely the earlier clause of the mishna is due to a different reason.

רֵישָׁא וְסֵיפָא מִשּׁוּם חֲצִיצָה. וּצְרִיכָא. דְּאִי אַשְׁמְעִינַן רֵישָׁא, הֲוָה אָמִינָא: הַיְינוּ טַעְמָא דִּלְקֹדֶשׁ לָא, מִשּׁוּם כְּבֵידוֹ שֶׁל כְּלִי דְּאִיכָּא, אֲבָל סֵיפָא, דְּלֵיכָּא כְּבֵידוֹ שֶׁל כְּלִי – אֵימָא לַקֹּדֶשׁ נַמִי לָא הָוֵי חֲצִיצָה. וְאִי אַשְׁמְעִינַן סֵיפָא, הֲוָה אָמִינָא: הַיְינוּ טַעְמָא דִּלְקֹדֶשׁ לָא, מִשּׁוּם

The Gemara answers: No, this is not necessarily so. In both **the first clause and the latter clause** of the mishna the concern is **due to interposition, and** it is nevertheless **necessary** to teach us both cases. **For had** the mishna **taught us** only **the first clause,** i.e., that one may not immerse one vessel within another, **I would have said** that **this is the reason** one may **not** do so **for sacrificial** food: **Because there is the weight of** the interior **vessel**[N] that must be taken into account. **But** in **the latter clause, where there is no weight of a vessel** to be considered, **I will say** that **it is not** considered an interposition **for sacrificial** food **either. And had it taught** us only **the latter clause** dealing with the knotted garments, **I would have said** that **this is the reason one may not** do so **for sacrificial** food: **Because** it is possible

NOTES

An acute mourner [*onen*] – אוֹנֵן: The *Turei Aven* addresses the duration of the acute mourner status. Rashi in tractate *Pesaḥim*, citing *Zevaḥim* 100b, states that it lasts only until the deceased is buried. However, this is difficult, as all opinions in the Gemara passage there agree that the status of acute mourner continues throughout the day of death, even after burial. The later commentaries discuss this problem. *Sefat Emet* asserts that Rashi is not referring to the day of death, but rather to a situation in which the burial does not take place on the day of death. He is stating that the mourner remains an acute mourner until the burial on the subsequent day.

Immersion in order to eat sacrificial food – טְבִילָה לַקֹּדֶשׁ: See *Turei Aven* for a discussion of the question of whether this immersion is required only for eating sacrificial foods, or whether such people may not even touch them.

Because the weight of the inner vessel causes an interposition – מִפְּנֵי שֶׁכְּבֵידוֹ שֶׁל כְּלִי חוֹצֵץ: This principle is quantified in the Jerusalem Talmud as follows: A vessel that weighs a *litra*, a pound, or more is considered heavy enough to cause an interposition between another vessel and the water.

Since the latter clause is with regard to matters of interposition – מִדְּסֵיפָא מִשּׁוּם חֲצִיצָה: Some note (see *Siaḥ Yitzḥak*) that the Gemara seemingly could have proven that if the two *halakhot* had the same reason, as Rabbi Ila asserts, they should have been juxtaposed in the mishna. However, even according to Rava's explanation of the mishna, presented later in the Gemara, the arrangement of the items in the mishna's list seems to be random rather than grouped by topics. Therefore, the Gemara did not use this point against Rabbi Ila, assuming simply that the items are not arranged in any logical order, but were enumerated by the *tanna* in the order in which he heard them from his teacher.

Because there is the weight of the interior vessel – מִשּׁוּם כְּבֵידוֹ שֶׁל כְּלִי דְּאִיכָּא: Some say that Rabbi Ila accepts Rava's opinion, presented by the Gemara later, that interposition is not the only reason for the mishna's principle (see *Turei Aven* and *Zekher LaḤagiga*).

דְּקִיטְרָא בְּמַיָּא אַהֲדוּקֵי מִיהְדַק. אֲבָל רֵישָׁא, דְּמַיָּא אַקְפּוּיֵי מַקְפּוּ לֵיהּ לְמָנָא – לָא הָוְיָא חֲצִיצָה. צְרִיכָא.

that it is the nature of **knots** to **tighten** even more **in water,**[N] creating an interposition that bars the water from entering all the way, **but** in the case of **the first clause** of the mishna, which deals with one vessel inside another and **where water** by nature **causes the** top **vessel to** lighten and **float** away from the lower vessel rather than weigh down on it, I would have said that **it is not** considered an **interposition.** It is therefore **necessary** for the *halakha* to be stated in both cases.[H]

רַבִּי אִילָא לְטַעְמֵיהּ, דְּאָמַר רַבִּי אִילָא אָמַר רַבִּי חֲנִינָא בַּר פָּפָּא: עֶשֶׂר מַעֲלוֹת שָׁנוּ כָּאן, חָמֵשׁ רִאשׁוֹנוֹת – בֵּין לַקֹּדֶשׁ בֵּין לַחוּלִּין שֶׁנַּעֲשׂוּ עַל טׇהֳרַת הַקֹּדֶשׁ; אַחֲרוֹנוֹת – לַקֹּדֶשׁ אֲבָל לֹא לַחוּלִּין שֶׁנַּעֲשׂוּ עַל טׇהֳרַת הַקֹּדֶשׁ.

The Gemara comments: **Rabbi Ila** here conforms **to his** standard line of **reasoning** in considering these two issues as one, **as Rabbi Ila said** that **Rabbi Ḥanina bar Pappa said: They taught ten stringencies**[N] of sacrificial food **here** in this mishna, rather than the apparent eleven. The **first five** stringencies apply **both to the sacrificial** foods themselves and **to non-sacred** food **that was prepared according to** the standards of **purity of sacrificial** food, whereas the **last** five apply only **to** actual **sacrificial** food **but not to non-sacred** food **that was prepared according to** the standards of **purity of sacrificial** food. The fact that Rabbi Ila counts only ten cases in the mishna shows that he considered the two cases discussed above to be of the same category, and therefore they are counted together as one stringency.

מַאי טַעְמָא? חָמֵשׁ קַמַּיְיתָא דְּאִית לְהוּ דְּרָרָא דְּטוּמְאָה מִדְּאוֹרַיְיתָא – גְּזַרוּ בְּהוּ רַבָּנַן בֵּין לַקֹּדֶשׁ בֵּין לַחוּלִּין שֶׁנַּעֲשׂוּ עַל טׇהֳרַת הַקֹּדֶשׁ, בָּתְרַיְיתָא דְּלֵית לְהוּ דְּרָרָא דְּטוּמְאָה מִדְּאוֹרַיְיתָא – גְּזַרוּ בְּהוּ רַבָּנַן לַקֹּדֶשׁ, לַחוּלִּין שֶׁנַּעֲשׂוּ עַל טׇהֳרַת הַקֹּדֶשׁ – לֹא גְּזַרוּ בְּהוּ רַבָּנַן.

The Gemara explains Rabbi Ila's statement. **What is the reason** for this distinction? With regard to the **first five** stringencies, **which have a connection to impurity** as defined **by Torah law** because ignoring them can lead to a case of impurity by Torah law as opposed to merely rabbinic law, **the Sages decreed these** stringencies **both for** actual **sacrificial** food **and for non-sacred** food **prepared according to** the standards of **purity of sacrificial** food. However, with regard to the **last** five, **which do not have a connection to impurity by Torah law,**[N] as their entire impurity is based on a rabbinic decree, **the Sages decreed these** stringencies only **for** actual **sacrificial** food. But **with regard to non-sacred** food **made according to** the standards of **purity of sacrificial** food, **the Sages did not decree** these stringencies **for** such foods.

HALAKHA

Immersing one vessel inside another for sacrificial food – טְבִילַת כְּלִי בְּתוֹךְ כְּלִי לְקוֹדֶשׁ: It is permitted to immerse one vessel inside another when the vessels are used for *teruma* but not if they are used for sacrificial food. This was decreed lest one do so when the mouth of the outer vessel is narrower than the tube of a wineskin, in which case the water in the vessel is not considered attached to the water of the ritual bath. This applies only if the outer vessel was pure and not in need of immersion itself. If the outer vessel was impure, since the immersion is effective for the outer vessel, it is effective for the inner one as well, even for sacrificial food, as stated by Rava (Rambam *Sefer Tahara, Hilkhot She'ar Avot HaTumot* 12:1).

NOTES

That it is the nature of knots to tighten even more in water – דְּקִיטְרָא בְּמַיָּא אַהֲדוּקֵי מִיהְדַק: *Tosafot* question why the Gemara ignores the additional requirement to dry the vessels, which appears to be due to interposition as well. The *Turei Aven* explains that the mishna's word, *umenagev*, should be translated as, or dry, rather than, and dry, meaning that the interposition must be removed one way or another.

Ten stringencies – עֶשֶׂר מַעֲלוֹת: The Gemara (22a) cites Rabba bar Avuh's opposing opinion that there are eleven stringencies in the mishna, and states that Rava's interpretation of the mishna, cited shortly, accords with that opinion as well. It is stated in the Jerusalem Talmud, however, that there is a dispute between *tanna'im* with regard to whether there are twelve or thirteen stringencies that regulate sacrificial food but not *teruma*, including some that are not listed in this mishna. *Tosafot* and other commentaries also point out that there are additional stringencies not listed in the mishna, some of which are mentioned in the previous chapter. Furthermore, it is possible to count more than eleven stringencies in our mishna, for instance, by separating the untying and the drying of garments into two distinct stringencies.

Which do not have a connection to impurity by Torah law – דְּלֵית לְהוּ דְּרָרָא דְּטוּמְאָה מִדְּאוֹרַיְיתָא: Rashi details at length how each of the first five stringencies has a connection with impurity by Torah law, either due to a concern regarding the purification of the vessel, e.g., due to interposition, or because the Sages' decree is based on a similarity to a Torah law case of impurity. However, with regard to the last five cases, or six, depending on the two explanations of the mishna, two of them also appear to have a connection with impurity by Torah law, i.e., the application of a fourth degree of impurity for sacrificial food, and the *halakha* that a vessel combines the food within it. *Tosafot* cite Rabbeinu Yitzḥak's answer that these two cases are also included in the category of things that do not have a connection to impurity by Torah law, because these *halakhot* are not prescribed by Torah law in general, but are unique to the case of sacrificial food.

BACKGROUND

The tube of a wineskin – שְׁפוֹפֶרֶת הַנּוֹד: Wineskins were made out of whole hides stripped from various animals. Such flasks served many uses, mainly as containers for objects and various foods. When these wineskins were used for holding liquids, such as water, wine, or oil, they would make sure to remove the hide without perforating it or removing the skin of the legs. A tube, usually made out of a reed, would subsequently be inserted into one of the legs, from which the liquid would be poured out of the wineskin.

Wineskin

רָבָא אָמַר: מִדְּסֵיפָא הָוֵי מִשּׁוּם חֲצִיצָה – רֵישָׁא לָאו מִשּׁוּם חֲצִיצָה. וְרֵישָׁא הַיְינוּ טַעְמָא: גְּזֵירָה שֶׁלֹּא יַטְבִּיל מְחָטִין וְצִינּוֹרוֹת בִּכְלִי שֶׁאֵין בְּפִיו כִּשְׁפוֹפֶרֶת הַנּוֹד. כִּדְתְנַן: עֵירוּב מִקְוָואוֹת כִּשְׁפוֹפֶרֶת הַנּוֹד, כְּעוּבְיָהּ

Rava disagreed with Rabbi Ila. He **said** that **since** the reason for the stringency in **the latter clause is due to** concern for interposition, this implies that the reason for the stringency in **the first clause is not due to interposition,** but to a different reason. **And** with regard to the stringency in **the first clause** that one may not immerse one vessel within another, **this is the reasoning:** It is a rabbinic **decree** to ensure **that one not immerse** small vessels, such as **needles and hooks, inside a vessel whose mouth** is less than the width of **the tube of a wineskin.**[B] In such a case the water in the bottle would not be considered attached to the rest of the ritual bath, **as we learned** in a mishna (*Mikvaot* 6:7): **The joining of** different bodies of water in cases of **ritual baths**[H] takes place if the opening between the two bodies is at least as wide **as** the width of **the tube of a wineskin,** counting both the **thickness** of the wall of the tube

HALAKHA

The joining of different bodies of water in cases of ritual baths – עֵירוּב מִקְוָואוֹת: If one wishes to join an invalid or incomplete ritual bath to a valid one, the hole between them must be at least the size of the tube of a wineskin, with the flow of the water filling the width of the hole. Once the two bodies of water have been joined together, they both remain valid even if the opening was made smaller or closed up. If there are many small holes between the two bodies of water, if they add up together to the required width of the tube of a wineskin, the two bodies of water are considered joined. However, if both bodies contain less than the requisite amount of forty *se'a* of water and one wishes to join them so that the requisite amount is reached, a single hole the size of the tube of a wineskin is required. Similarly, if a ritual bath was divided into two sections by means of a sackcloth or a basket that is full of tiny holes, if neither section of the ritual bath has forty *se'a* in it, it is invalid (Rema). Based on these principles, it is permitted to dig a ditch alongside a river to use as a ritual bath, even if the ditch does not contain forty *se'a* (Rema), for the river's water seeps in through the porous ground (*Shulḥan Arukh*, *Yoreh De'a* 201:52).

Perek **III**
Daf **22** Amud **a**

HALAKHA

Stringencies of sacrificial food – מַעֲלוֹת הַקּוֹדֶשׁ: The Sages instituted eleven stringencies, as stated by Rabba bar Avuh, that apply to sacrificial food as opposed to *teruma*. The first six apply also to non-sacred food prepared according to the standards of purity of sacrificial food, whereas the last five refer only to sacrificial food itself (Rambam *Sefer Tahara*, *Hilkhot She'ar Avot HaTumot* 12:1, 16).

Counting both the thickness of the wall of the tube and its space – כְּעוּבְיָהּ וְכַחֲלָלָהּ: The measurement of the tube of a wineskin is equivalent to the width of two fingers, i.e., the forefinger and middle finger, which can be inserted into this space and moved around easily. It makes no difference whether the hole is round or square, as long as it is of this size (*Shulḥan Arukh*, *Yoreh De'a* 201:40).

וְכַחֲלָלָהּ בִּשְׁתֵּי אֶצְבָּעוֹת חוֹזְרוֹת לִמְקוֹמָן.

and its space,[H] **which is equivalent to** the width of **two fingers going around in their place,** i.e., a space large enough to insert two fingers and twist them around inside. If one body of water contains the requisite forty *se'a*, while another, adjacent body is lacking this amount, then if the opening between the two bodies of water is wider than this measurement, the two bodies are considered as one, and the smaller body is also considered an acceptable ritual bath. Since any opening smaller than this is not considered to connect two bodies of water, the water inside a bottle with a narrow mouth would be considered disconnected from the water of the ritual bath, and smaller vessels inside such a narrow-necked vessel would not be considered as having come into contact with the water of the ritual bath. The Sages therefore enacted a decree rendering prohibited the immersion of any vessel inside another vessel.

סָבַר לַהּ כְּהָא דְּאָמַר רַב נַחְמָן אָמַר רַבָּה בַּר אֲבוּהּ: אַחַת עֶשְׂרֵה מַעֲלוֹת שָׁנוּ כָּאן; שֵׁשׁ רִאשׁוֹנוֹת בֵּין לַקּוֹדֶשׁ בֵּין לַחוּלִּין שֶׁנַּעֲשׂוּ עַל טׇהֳרַת הַקּוֹדֶשׁ, אַחֲרוֹנוֹת – לַקּוֹדֶשׁ אֲבָל לֹא לַחוּלִּין שֶׁנַּעֲשׂוּ עַל טׇהֳרַת הַקּוֹדֶשׁ.

The Gemara notes: Rava **holds in accordance with this** statement **that Rav Naḥman said** that **Rabba bar Avuh said: They taught eleven stringencies** of sacrificial food **here** in this mishna, rather than Rabbi Ila's ten. The **first six** stringencies apply **both to sacrificial** food itself and **to non-sacred** food **that was prepared according to** the standards of **purity of sacrificial** food, whereas the **last** five apply only **to** actual **sacrificial** food **but not to non-sacred** food **that was prepared according to** the standards of **purity of sacrificial** food.[H]

מַאי אִיכָּא בֵּין דְּרָבָא לְדְרַבִּי אִילָא?

The Gemara asks: **What** practical difference **is there between** the opinion **of Rava,** i.e., that the Sages rendered it prohibited to immerse one vessel inside of another because they were concerned lest one immerse needles in a vessel whose mouth is narrower than the tube of a wineskin, **and** the opinion **of Rabbi Ila,**[N] who holds that their concern was about interposition?

אִיכָּא בֵּינַיְיהוּ סַל וְגַרְגּוּתְנִי שֶׁמִּילְּאָן כֵּלִים וְהִטְבִּילָן. לְמַאן דְּאָמַר מִשּׁוּם חֲצִיצָה – אִיכָּא. לְמַאן דְּאָמַר מִשּׁוּם גְּזֵירָה שֶׁמָּא יַטְבִּיל מְחָטִין וְצִינּוֹרִיּוֹת בִּכְלִי שֶׁאֵין בְּפִיו כִּשְׁפוֹפֶרֶת הַנּוֹד – סַל וְגַרְגּוּתְנִי שֶׁאֵין בְּפִיהֶן כִּשְׁפוֹפֶרֶת הַנּוֹד לֵיכָּא.

The Gemara answers: **The** practical difference **between them** is in the case of **a basket or** a wicker **bin [*gargutni*]**[NL] **that one has filled** with smaller **vessels and** has **immersed them** all together. **According to** Rabbi Ila, **the one who said** it is prohibited to immerse one vessel inside another **due to** the concern of **interposition,** in this case as well **there is** such a concern, as the inner vessels might weigh down against the basket and prevent the water from touching the contact points.[H] But **according to** Rava, **the one who said** it is prohibited **due to** a rabbinic **decree lest one immerse needles and hooks inside a vessel whose mouth does not have** the width of **the tube of a wineskin, there are no** such things as **baskets and** wicker **bins whose mouth does not have** the width of **the tube of a wineskin,** and therefore the decree would not apply to them.

רָבָא לְטַעֲמֵיהּ, דְּאָמַר רָבָא: סַל וְגַרְגּוּתְנִי שֶׁמִּילְּאָן כֵּלִים וְהִטְבִּילָן – טְהוֹרִין.

The Gemara notes: **And Rava follows his** line of **reasoning, as Rava said: A basket or** wicker **bin that one has filled** with smaller **vessels and** has **immersed them** all together, **they are pure** in all regards, even for sacrificial food.

וּמִקְוֶה שֶׁחִלְּקוֹ בְּסַל וְגַרְגּוּתְנִי – הַטּוֹבֵל שָׁם לֹא עָלְתָה לוֹ טְבִילָה, דְּהָא אַרְעָא כּוּלָּהּ חַלְחוּלֵי מְחַלְחְלָא, וּבָעֵינַן דְּאִיכָּא אַרְבָּעִים סְאָה בְּמָקוֹם אֶחָד.

Rava stated a second teaching with regard to baskets and bins as well: **And** in the case of **a ritual bath that one divided** into two sections **by** inserting **a basket**[N] **or** wicker **bin,** so that each section is left with less than the required forty *se'a*, if **one immerses there, his immersion is ineffective for him.** Despite the certainty that water seeps through the basket or bin, this is not enough to join the two incomplete sections of the ritual bath to be counted as one. We know that this is so, **for the earth is entirely porous, and** nevertheless **we** do not rely on this to allow several adjacent, small ditches full of water to add up to forty *se'a*, but rather **require that there be forty *se'a*** together **in one place.**

וְהָנֵי מִילֵּי – בִּכְלִי טָהוֹר. אֲבָל בִּכְלִי טָמֵא – מִיגּוֹ דְּסָלְקָא טְבִילָה לְכוּלֵּיהּ גּוּפֵיהּ דְּמָנָא – סָלְקָא לְהוּ נַמִי לְכֵלִים דְּאִית בֵּיהּ.

The Gemara comments: **And this** *halakha*, that small vessels such as needles cannot be immersed inside a vessel with a narrow opening,[N] **applies** only if he immersed them **in a pure vessel,** which does not require purification on its own. **But** if he did so **in an impure vessel,** which requires purification in its own right, **since the immersion is effective for the whole of the** outer **vessel,** including its inside, **it is also effective for** the **vessels that are inside of it.** Since the water that enters the outer vessel is considered attached to the rest of the ritual bath for purposes of purification of the outer vessel, so is it considered attached with regard to the purification of the inner vessels.[H]

דִּתְנַן: כֵּלִים שֶׁמִּילְּאָן כֵּלִים וְהִטְבִּילָן – הֲרֵי אֵלּוּ טְהוֹרִין. וְאִם לֹא טָבַל, מַיִם הַמְעוֹרָבִים – עַד שֶׁיִּהְיוּ מְעוֹרָבִין כִּשְׁפוֹפֶרֶת הַנּוֹד. מַאי קָאָמַר: ״וְאִם לֹא טָבַל״? הָכִי קָאָמַר: וְאִם אֵינוֹ צָרִיךְ לְהַטְבִּילוֹ, וּמַיִם הַמְעוֹרָבִין – עַד שֶׁיְּהוּ מְעוֹרָבִין כִּשְׁפוֹפֶרֶת הַנּוֹד.

We know this, **as we learned** in a mishna (*Mikvaot* 6:2): With regard to **vessels that one filled with** other **vessels and immersed them** all together, **they are pure,** regardless of the width of the opening of the outer vessel. **And if he did not immerse, the joining of waters** is not effective **until they are joined like the** width of the **tube of a wineskin.** This second sentence of the mishna is unclear, and the Gemara seeks to clarify it. **What is the** mishna **saying** here when it says: **And if he did not immerse?** The Gemara explains. **This is what** the mishna **is saying: And if he has no need to immerse** the outer vessel, as it was already pure, **and** similarly in a case of two bodies of **water** that are **joined** together by means of a hole, it is not valid **until** the water **is joined** through a space as wide **as the tube of a wineskin.**

NOTES

What practical difference is there between the opinion of Rava and of Rabbi Ila, etc. – מַאי אִיכָּא בֵּין דְּרָבָא לְדְרַבִּי אִילָא וכו׳: *Tosafot* point out that there are other, more obvious differences between them as well. The later commentaries offer various reasons as to why the Gemara ignores these other differences. The *Sefat Emet* says that although there are in fact several differences between them, the Gemara mentions the case of the basket or bin because it is a situation with regard to which there is much to discuss.

Basket or bin – סַל וְגַרְגּוּתְנִי: The Rid writes that the difference between these vessels and others is that the mouths of these are always equal in width to their bases, whereas other vessels come in various shapes, with wider or narrower mouths. Therefore, the Sages decreed, without differentiation between various shapes, not to allow immersion of vessels within those other vessels. Others point out that in addition to the width of their mouths there is another difference that distinguishes baskets and bins from other vessels, which is that their woven design allows water to penetrate through their sides as well (see *Zekher LaHagiga*).

A ritual bath that one divided into two sections by inserting a basket, etc. – מִקְוֶה שֶׁחִלְּקוֹ בְּסַל וכו׳: Although it is obvious that water will pass through the holes of the basket, and one may immerse vessels inside a burlap sack for this reason (see Mishna, *Mikvaot* 6:5), since he has placed it as a kind of partition within the ritual bath, it no longer has the appearance of a vessel being immersed, but rather of a ritual bath split into two (Rid).

And this applies only if he immersed them in a pure vessel – וְהָנֵי מִילֵּי בִּכְלִי טָהוֹר: According to Rabbeinu Hananel, this paragraph is not dealing with the immersion of one vessel inside another for use with sacrificial food, for that would be prohibited even if the outer vessel were impure. Rather, it is dealing with the case of partitioning a ritual bath by placing a basket in the middle of it. See the Meiri on the mishna, who discusses this issue at length.

LANGUAGE

Bin [*gargutni*] – גַּרְגּוּתְנִי: From the Greek γύργαθος, *gurgathos*, meaning a wicker basket.

HALAKHA

Immersing vessels inside a basket – טְבִילַת כֵּלִים בְּסַל: One may not immerse vessels used for sacrificial food inside other vessels, including wide baskets or bins, but for *teruma* one may use them (Rambam *Sefer Tahara*, *Hilkhot Mikvaot* 3:26).

Immersing utensils inside an impure vessel – טְבִילָה בְּתוֹךְ כְּלִי טָמֵא: If one immersed utensils by inserting them inside an impure vessel the immersion is effective, even if the mouth of the outer vessel is very narrow. But if he tilted the outer vessel onto its side, the immersion is effective only if its mouth is as wide as the tube of a wineskin. In the case of sacrificial food, one may not immerse vessels inside other vessels at all (Rambam *Sefer Tahara*, *Hilkhot Mikvaot* 3:26).

וְהָא דְּרָבָא וּדְרַבִּי אִילָא תַּנָּאֵי הִיא. דְּתַנְיָא: סַל וְגַרְגּוּתְנִי שֶׁמִּילְאָן כֵּלִים וְהִטְבִּילָן, בֵּין לַקּוֹדֶשׁ בֵּין לַתְּרוּמָה – טְהוֹרִין, אַבָּא שָׁאוּל אוֹמֵר: לַתְּרוּמָה אֲבָל לֹא לַקּוֹדֶשׁ.

§ The Gemara notes: **And this** dispute between **Rava and Rabbi Ila is** also a dispute between ***tanna'im*. As it is taught** in a *baraita*: With regard to **a basket or a** wicker **bin that one filled** with **vessels and** then **immersed them, whether for** purposes of **sacrificial** food **or for** purposes of ***teruma*, they are pure.** This is identical to Rava's opinion. **Abba Shaul says:** They are pure **for** purposes of ***teruma* but not for** purposes of **sacrificial** food.[N] This is identical to Rabbi Ila's opinion.

אִי הָכִי תְּרוּמָה נַמִי! לְמַאן קָאָמְרִינַן? חֲבֵרִים; חֲבֵרִים מֵידַע יָדְעִי!

The Gemara asks: **If so,** in light of these two reasons we have given for concern with regard to immersing vessels inside other vessels, this should **not** be permitted for ***teruma* either.**[N] The Gemara responds: **For whom do we say** the principle that one vessel may not be immersed inside another? For ***ḥaverim*,** individuals devoted to the meticulous observance of mitzvot, especially *halakhot* of ritual purity. Others do not carefully follow these *halakhot* in any event. And ***ḥaverim* know** such things **well,** that water is considered detached from the ritual bath if it is separated by a narrow opening, and that if one vessel is weighing down on another, preventing the water from reaching that spot, the top vessel must be lifted to allow the water to touch all parts of the vessel. Therefore, there is no need to apply these concerns and stringencies to the case of *teruma*.

אִי הָכִי קוֹדֶשׁ נַמִי! חָזֵי לֵיהּ עַם הָאָרֶץ וְאָזֵיל מַטְבִּיל.

The Gemara counters with another question. **If so,** we should say the same thing in the case of **sacrificial** food **too,** i.e., that all these *halakhot* are for *ḥaverim*, who meticulously follow ritual purity for sacrificial food and inquire about such *halakhot*. Why, then, did the Sages apply these concerns and stringencies to the case of sacrificial food? The Gemara responds: With regard to sacrificial food they were concerned that a **common person** [***am ha'aretz***], who is not meticulous about ritual purity, may **see** the *ḥaver* immersing small vessels inside of large vessels, **and** will then **go and immerse** vessels of his own in this manner. But he will not take the same precautions as the *ḥaver* would, ensuring that the outer vessel has a wide opening and that the vessels on top do not weigh down on the lower ones.

תְּרוּמָה נַמִי חָזֵי לֵיהּ עַם הָאָרֶץ וְאָזֵיל מַטְבִּיל! לָא מְקַבְּלִינַן מִינַּיְיהוּ.

The Gemara objects: But the same concern could be raised with regard to ***teruma* as well.** It is possible that **an *am ha'aretz*** may **see** the *ḥaver* immerse vessels for *teruma* in this manner, **and** he will then **go and immerse** his vessels this way, without taking the precautions that the *ḥaver* would take. The Gemara answers: **We do not accept** *teruma* **from** *amei ha'aretz*, as they are not trustworthy with regard to the *halakhot* of ritual purity, and therefore it does not matter if the vessels he uses for *teruma* are not immersed properly. Therefore, the Sages were not concerned that the *am ha'aretz* may come to a misunderstanding when observing a *ḥaver* immersing vessels within vessels.

קוֹדֶשׁ נַמִי לָא נְקַבֵּיל מִינַּיְיהוּ! הָוְיָא לֵיהּ אֵיבָה.

The Gemara continues its line of questioning. If so, **we should likewise not accept sacrificial** food **from** *amei ha'aretz*, since they are not sufficiently meticulous with ritual purity, and we should therefore not care if they immerse their vessels improperly. The Gemara responds: The *am ha'aretz* **will have** feelings of **antagonism** if sacrificial food is not accepted from him, and this would lead to internal discord and conflict within Israel.

NOTES

A basket or a bin with regard to sacrificial food – סַל וְגַרְגּוּתְנִי לַקּוֹדֶשׁ: See HALAKHA, previous page, for the Rambam's ruling, which is in accordance with Abba Shaul's opinion that one may not immerse other vessels inside such utensils. Although this appears to contradict the Rambam's basic approach, which follows Rabba bar Avuh, whom the Gemara identifies with Rava, whereas Abba Shaul's opinion is identified with that of Rabbi Ila, it is possible that the Rambam relied on a specific ruling of the Jerusalem Talmud in this instance. Additionally, the explanation that an *am ha'aretz* might see the *ḥaver* and copy his actions perhaps convinced Rava to retract his opinion and agree that a basket should be prohibited, as an *am ha'aretz* might not distinguish between baskets and other vessels (*Siaḥ Yitzḥak*).

If so, this should not be permitted for *teruma* either – אִי הָכִי תְּרוּמָה נַמִי: The Gemara mentions this case rather than any of the other differences between *teruma* and sacrificial food listed in the mishna because the concern here is that the inner vessels might not become purified at all, whereas the other differences stem from special stringencies that were added for sacrificial food (*Turei Aven*). Alternatively, the Gemara's question is directed only at the opinion of Rava, who bases the prohibition on the concern that people might perform immersion in a truly ineffectual manner. This leads to the question of why we are not concerned that they might do the same with regard to *teruma* as well (see *Siaḥ Yitzḥak*).

תְּרוּמָה נַמִּי הָוְיָא לֵיהּ אֵיבָה! לָא אִיכְפַּת לֵיהּ, דְּאָזֵיל יָהֵיב לֵיהּ לְכֹהֵן עַם הָאָרֶץ חַבְרֵיהּ.

The Gemara asks: If so, in the case of ***teruma* he will also have** feelings of **antagonism** if *teruma* is not accepted from him. Why were the Sages concerned about this factor only with regard to sacrificial food and not *teruma*? The Gemara replies: An *am ha'aretz* **does not care** if his *teruma* is not accepted by *ḥaverim*, **as** he can always **go** and **give** his *teruma* **to an *am ha'aretz* priest** who is **his friend** and who will accept it from him. In the case of sacrificial food, however, there is only one Temple, and care must be taken not to make the *amei ha'aretz* feel they are being rejected.

וּמַאן תַּנָּא דְּחָיֵישׁ לְאֵיבָה? רַבִּי יוֹסֵי הִיא, דְּתַנְיָא, אָמַר רַבִּי יוֹסֵי: מִפְּנֵי מָה הַכֹּל נֶאֱמָנִין עַל טָהֳרַת יַיִן וְשֶׁמֶן כָּל יְמוֹת הַשָּׁנָה? כְּדֵי שֶׁלֹּא יְהֵא כָּל אֶחָד וְאֶחָד הוֹלֵךְ וּבוֹנֶה בָּמָה לְעַצְמוֹ, וְשׂוֹרֵף פָּרָה אֲדוּמָּה לְעַצְמוֹ.

The Gemara notes that this sensitivity of not causing offense to the *am ha'aretz* is expressed elsewhere as well: **And who is the *tanna* that is concerned for** such **antagonism** of *amei ha'aretz*? **It is Rabbi Yosei,**[N] **as it is taught** in a *baraita*: **Rabbi Yosei said: For what** reason are **all** people, i.e., even *amei ha'aretz*, **trusted with regard to the purity of** their **wine and oil**[H] that they bring to the Temple for sacrificial purposes **throughout the year?** Why is the status of these items not investigated to determine that they were prepared with the necessary regard for ritual purity? In order to avoid schisms among the people, **so that each and every individual should not go off and build** a private **altar for himself and burn a red heifer for himself.**[N] Were the Sages to reject sacrificial wine and oil from *amei ha'aretz*, they would become alienated and go off and create schisms, going so far as to build their own separate temples and bring their own private offerings.

אֲמַר רַב פַּפָּא: כְּמַאן מְקַבְּלִינַן הָאִידָּנָא סַהֲדוּתָא מֵעַם הָאָרֶץ? כְּמַאן? כְּרַבִּי יוֹסֵי.

Rav Pappa said: In accordance with whose opinion **do we accept testimony nowadays from an *am ha'aretz*,** despite the concern of some Sages that their carelessness with regard to observance of *halakha* might also lead to personal untrustworthiness? **In accordance with whom** is this done? **In accordance with** the opinion of **Rabbi Yosei.**[H]

וְנֵיחוּשׁ לִשְׁאֵלָה?

§ We have established that the reason for leniency with regard to immersing one vessel inside another for *teruma* is based on the fact that we do not care if the vessels *amei ha'aretz* use for *teruma* are improperly purified, since we do not accept *teruma* from them in any event. The Gemara asks: **But let us be concerned about borrowing** vessels from them. Although *ḥaverim* do not accept *teruma* from an *am ha'aretz*, they do sometimes borrow their vessels and use them for *teruma*. It should therefore be a matter of concern for us if those vessels are not properly purified.

דִּתְנַן: כְּלִי חֶרֶס מַצִּיל עַל הַכֹּל, דִּבְרֵי בֵית הִלֵּל. בֵּית שַׁמַּאי אוֹמְרִים: אֵינוֹ מַצִּיל אֶלָּא עַל אוֹכָלִים וְעַל הַמַּשְׁקִים וְעַל כְּלֵי חֶרֶס.

The Gemara proves that it is acceptable to borrow vessels from an *am ha'aretz*: **As we learned** in a mishna (*Eduyyot* 1:14): **An earthenware vessel** of an *am ha'aretz* **shields** all kinds of items from the ritual impurity imparted by a corpse. There are two applications of this fact: If there are objects or foods inside a tightly sealed earthenware vessel located inside a room containing a corpse, the vessel prevents the impurity from reaching the items inside it. Also, if there is a corpse in the first floor of a house and food or vessels are located in a second story of the same building, with an opening such as a skylight in the floor between the two stories, an earthenware vessel plugging up the opening will prevent the ritual impurity from spreading to the second story. This is **the statement of Beit Hillel. Beit Shammai say: It shields only food, drink,**[N] **and earthenware vessels,** but not utensils of metal, wood, cloth, etc.[H]

אָמְרוּ לָהֶם בֵּית הִלֵּל לְבֵית שַׁמַּאי: מִפְּנֵי מָה? אָמְרוּ בֵּית שַׁמַּאי: מִפְּנֵי שֶׁהוּא טָמֵא עַל גַּבֵּי עַם הָאָרֶץ, וְאֵין כְּלִי טָמֵא חוֹצֵץ. אָמְרוּ לָהֶם בֵּית הִלֵּל: וַהֲלֹא טִיהַרְתֶּם אוֹכָלִין וּמַשְׁקִין שֶׁבְּתוֹכוֹ! אָמְרוּ לָהֶם בֵּית שַׁמַּאי: כְּשֶׁטִּיהַרְנוּ אוֹכָלִין וּמַשְׁקִין שֶׁבְּתוֹכוֹ

The mishna continues: **Beit Hillel said to Beit Shammai: For what** reason do you make this distinction? It is clear that a closed, pure earthenware vessel serves as a barrier, blocking the spread of impurity in a room with a corpse (see Numbers 19:15). **Beit Shammai said** to them: **Because** the earthenware vessel itself **is impure on account of** its contact with **an *am ha'aretz*.** The Sages decreed that anything touched by an *am ha'aretz* is impure, since such people are not meticulous or sufficiently knowledgeable about the *halakhot* of purity; therefore his vessels are considered impure. **And** the principle is that **an impure vessel does not serve as a barrier** from impurity. **Beit Hillel said to them: But didn't you declare the food and drink inside** the earthenware vessel to be **pure?** If the vessel of an *am ha'aretz* cannot serve as a barrier, why do you say that some items inside it are pure? **Beit Shammai said to them: When we declared the food and drink inside it to be pure,**

NOTES

Who is the *tanna* that is concerned for antagonism of *amei ha'aretz*? It is Rabbi Yosei – מַאן תַּנָּא דְּחָיֵישׁ לְאֵיבָה, רַבִּי יוֹסֵי הִיא: The implication is that the other Sages were not concerned about the possibility of antagonizing *amei ha'aretz*, and did not permit them to give testimony. There are different opinions among the early commentaries as to whether there is a real dispute here, because some maintain that the various *halakhot* with regard to *amei ha'aretz* depend on the character of the *am ha'aretz* involved: Rabbi Yosei was lenient only with regard to an *am ha'aretz* who observes mitzvot and has a sense of basic decency, while the other Rabbis were stringent only in the case of *amei ha'aretz* who had not read Torah or studied the Oral Law at all, and who did not possess a measure of basic decency.

And burn a red heifer for himself – וְשׂוֹרֵף פָּרָה אֲדוּמָּה לְעַצְמוֹ: This detail is not relevant to the trustworthiness of *amei ha'aretz* with regard to sacrificial food, but to another established *halakha*: *Amei ha'aretz* are trusted with regard to the water of purification of the red heifer, as this water was also prepared on behalf of all Israel, and it therefore might lead to enmity if the *amei ha'aretz* were not trusted with it (*Turei Aven*).

It shields only food, drink, etc. – אֵינוֹ מַצִּיל אֶלָּא עַל אוֹכָלִים וְעַל הַמַּשְׁקִים וכו׳: The Rambam maintains that Beit Shammai applies this decree universally, both to earthenware vessels belonging to *amei ha'aretz* and to those of *ḥaverim*, whereas Rabbeinu Shimshon states that the discussion here speaks only of earthenware vessels owned by *amei ha'aretz*.

HALAKHA

All people are trusted with regard to the purity of wine and oil – הַכֹּל נֶאֱמָנִין עַל טָהֳרַת יַיִן וְשֶׁמֶן: Everyone, including *amei ha'aretz*, is trusted with regard to the purity of wine and oil for libations. Therefore, if they say it is pure, it is accepted as such (Rambam *Sefer Tahara, Hilkhot Metamei Mishkav UMoshav* 11:1).

Accepting testimony from an *am ha'aretz* – קַבָּלַת עֵדוּת מֵעַמֵּי הָאָרֶץ: Even though the *halakha* follows Rav Pappa's ruling that testimony from *amei ha'aretz* is accepted, this applies only to one who observes mitzvot, performs acts of kindness, and behaves in a generally decent manner, despite the fact that he is not versed in either the written Torah or the Oral Law. If the above conditions do not apply, the *am ha'aretz* is assumed to be untrustworthy (*Shulḥan Arukh, Ḥoshen Mishpat* 34:17).

Shielding from impurity by means of a tightly closed vessel – הַצָּלָה בִּכְלִי הַסָּגוּר בְּצָמִיד פָּתִיל: By Torah law, all earthenware vessels shield their contents from impurity in a room with a corpse if they are tightly closed. However, the Sages decreed that such a vessel shields only food, drink, and other earthenware vessels, while clothes and vessels that can be purified in a ritual bath are considered impure. In this case the *halakha* follows Beit Shammai, in accordance with the reason mentioned to Rabbi Yehoshua, as described subsequently in the Gemara, and was accepted as *halakha* in practice (Rambam *Sefer Tahara, Hilkhot Tumat Met* 23:1).

HALAKHA

An impure bowl and pure dough – עֲרֵיבָה טְמֵאָה וְעִיסָּה טְהוֹרָה: The Sages decreed that if an earthenware vessel is blocking a hole between the stories of a building, with a corpse on the first floor, the vessel shields only food and drink in the second story from the impurity of the corpse, but not people or metal vessels. If such a vessel contains food and drink, the vessel is impure with the impurity of seven days, but the food and drink it contains remain pure (Rambam *Sefer Tahara, Hilkhot Tumat Met* 23:4).

LANGUAGE

Pitcher [*login*] – לוֹגִין: From the Latin lagena, or, alternatively, derived from the Greek λάγυνον, *lagunos*, a drinking jug.

לְעַצְמוֹ טִהַרְנוּ.

we declared them **pure for** the *am ha'aretz* **himself,** not for *ḥaverim*, since *ḥaverim* in any event do not consider anything touched by an *am ha'aretz* to be pure. A *ḥaver* would therefore never relate to the food of an *am ha'aretz* as pure, and he would not use the earthenware vessels of an *am ha'aretz* for preparation of pure food, since an earthenware vessel cannot be purified through immersion. However, he might borrow a metal vessel, for instance, and purify it through immersion before using it for pure food.

אֲבָל נְטַהֵר אֶת הַכְּלִי שֶׁטׇּהֳרָתוֹ לְךָ וְלוֹ?

But how **can we purify a vessel** of metal and other materials, **whose purity** would be relevant both **for you and for him?** A *ḥaver* may one day borrow a metal vessel from the *am ha'aretz*, and not realize that it was once inside an earthenware vessel in the same room as a corpse and as a result requires extensive purification from corpse contamination through the ashes of the red heifer, rather than mere immersion. Therefore, the *am ha'aretz* is informed that his vessels of metal and other materials have contracted impurity from the corpse, and must undergo the extensive purification process, and after this is done these vessels will now be fit for use of the *ḥaver* after mere immersion.

תַּנְיָא, אָמַר רַבִּי יְהוֹשֻׁעַ: בּוֹשְׁנִי מִדִּבְרֵיכֶם, בֵּית שַׁמַּאי! אֶפְשָׁר, אִשָּׁה לָשָׁה בַּעֲרֵיבָה – אִשָּׁה וַעֲרֵיבָה טְמֵאִין שִׁבְעָה וּבָצֵק טָהוֹר?! לוֹגִין מָלֵא מַשְׁקִין, – לוֹגִין טָמֵא טוּמְאַת שִׁבְעָה וּמַשְׁקִין טְהוֹרִין?!

It is taught in a *baraita* with regard to this debate between Beit Shammai and Beit Hillel: **Rabbi Yehoshua said: I am ashamed of your words, Beit Shammai,** for they are illogical. Is it **possible** that there should be a corpse on the first floor, with an earthenware vessel blocking the opening to the second story, and **a woman** is standing upstairs **kneading** dough **in a** metal **bowl,** and the **woman and the bowl are impure** for **seven** days owing to the impurity of the corpse, **while** the **dough** inside the trough **is pure?**[H] For that would be the result according to Beit Shammai, who distinguishes between food and earthenware vessels on the one hand and metal vessels on the other. Similarly: Is it possible that there is **a** metal **pitcher** [***login***][L] **full of liquid** in the second story, and the **pitcher** should be **impure with impurity of seven** days, **while the liquids** remain **pure?**

נִטְפַּל לוֹ תַּלְמִיד אֶחָד מִתַּלְמִידֵי בֵית שַׁמַּאי, אָמַר לוֹ: אוֹמַר לְךָ טַעְמָן שֶׁל בֵּית שַׁמַּאי. אָמַר לוֹ: אֱמוֹר. אָמַר לוֹ: כְּלִי טָמֵא חוֹצֵץ אוֹ אֵינוֹ חוֹצֵץ? אָמַר לֵיהּ: אֵינוֹ חוֹצֵץ. כְּלִי שֶׁל עַם הָאָרֶץ טָמֵא אוֹ טָהוֹר? אָמַר לוֹ: טָמֵא. וְאִם אַתָּה אוֹמֵר לוֹ "טָמֵא", כְּלוּם מַשְׁגִּיחַ עָלֶיךָ? וְלֹא עוֹד, אֶלָּא שֶׁאִם אַתָּה אוֹמֵר לוֹ "טָמֵא", אוֹמֵר לָךְ "שֶׁלִּי טָהוֹר וְשֶׁלָּךְ טָמֵא".

After Rabbi Yehoshua posed this question, **one student from among the students of Beit Shammai approached him** and **said to him: I will tell you Beit Shammai's reasoning. He said to him: Speak. He said to him: Does an impure vessel serve as a barrier** to corpse contamination **or does it not serve as a barrier?** Rabbi Yehoshua **said to him: It does not serve as a barrier.** The student asked further: And **is a vessel of an** ***am ha'aretz*** **pure or impure? He said to him: Impure.** The student responded: **And if you tell him** that his vessel **is impure, will he pay attention to you at all?** Clearly he will not. **What is more, if you say to him** that it is **impure, he will say to you:** On the contrary, **my** vessel **is pure and yours is impure.**

וְזֶהוּ טַעְמָן שֶׁל בֵּית שַׁמַּאי.

And that is Beit Shammai's reasoning: Food, drink, and earthenware vessels inside a sealed earthenware vessel remain pure, as, since they belong to an *am ha'aretz*, a *ḥaver* will not eat the food or borrow the earthenware vessel. Vessels of metal or similar materials may one day be borrowed by a *ḥaver*, however, and therefore Beit Shammai declared these to be impure.

מִיָּד הָלַךְ רַבִּי יְהוֹשֻׁעַ וְנִשְׁתַּטַּח עַל קִבְרֵי בֵּית שַׁמַּאי, אָמַר: נַעֲנֵיתִי לָכֶם עַצְמוֹת בֵּית שַׁמַּאי, וּמָה סְתוּמוֹת שֶׁלָּכֶם כָּךְ – מְפוֹרָשׁוֹת עַל אַחַת כַּמָּה וְכַמָּה. אָמְרוּ: כׇּל יָמָיו הוּשְׁחֲרוּ שִׁינָּיו מִפְּנֵי תַּעֲנִיּוֹתָיו.

Once he heard the logic behind Beit Shammai's opinion, **Rabbi Yehoshua immediately went and prostrated himself on the graves of Beit Shammai,** i.e., the students and proponents of Shammai, and **said: I humble myself before you, bones of Beit Shammai. If such** clarity and wisdom is **found in your** rulings that you stated and left **unexplained, all the more so** must this be the case **in your** rulings when they were stated and **explained.** People **said** of Rabbi Yehoshua: **Throughout his days his teeth darkened because of all his fasts** that he undertook to atone for having spoken inappropriately of Beit Shammai.

קָתָנֵי מִיהַת: לְךָ וְלוֹ. אַלְמָא: שָׁאֲלִינַן מִינַּיְיהוּ! כִּי שָׁיְילִינַן מִינַּיְיהוּ – מַטְבְּלִינַן לְהוּ.

The Gemara returns to its main point. **In any event,** this mishna **teaches** that the status of the vessels of an *am ha'aretz* is relevant both **for you and for him. Apparently,** then, **we** *ḥaverim* **may borrow** vessels **from** *amei ha'aretz*. The question therefore arises: Why are the Sages not concerned that *amei ha'aretz* may immerse vessels inside of other vessels in an inappropriate way, so that they will remain unpurified when borrowed by a *ḥaver*? The Gemara answers: **For when we** *ḥaverim* **borrow** vessels **from them we immerse them** before using them.[H] It is therefore inconsequential to us if their vessels were not immersed properly beforehand.

אִי הָכִי נִיהַדְרוּ לְהוּ בֵּית הִלֵּל לְבֵית שַׁמַּאי: כִּי שָׁאֲלִינַן מִינַּיְיהוּ מַטְבְּלִינַן לְהוּ! טְמֵא מֵת בָּעֵי הַזָּאָה שְׁלִישִׁי וּשְׁבִיעִי, וּמָנָא לְשִׁבְעָה יוֹמֵי לָא מוֹשְׁלֵי אֱינָשֵׁי.

The Gemara asks: **If so, let Beit Hillel respond to Beit Shammai.** They can respond as follows: **When we borrow** vessels **from them we immerse them,** and that is why we rule that vessels of metal or similar materials are pure. The Gemara explains: That dispute is referring to the impurity of a corpse. **And that which becomes impure by** proximity to **a corpse requires sprinkling** of the red heifer's ashes on the **third and seventh** days of its purification,[H] **and people do not** generally **lend vessels for seven days.**[N] The solution the *ḥaver* implements of immersing vessels that he borrows from an *am ha'aretz* is effective only for other impurities, but not for the impurity imparted by a corpse.

וְאַטְבִּילָה לָא מְהֵימְנִי? וְהָתַנְיָא: נֶאֱמָנִין עַמֵּי הָאָרֶץ עַל טָהֳרַת טְבִילַת טְמֵא מֵת!

The Gemara poses a question with regard to the *halakha* that a *ḥaver* must immerse vessels that he borrows from an *am ha'aretz*: **But** is it so that *amei ha'aretz* **are not trusted with regard to immersion? Isn't it taught** in a *baraita*: ***Amei ha'aretz* are trusted with regard to the purification** process **of immersion of that which has become impure by** contact with **a corpse?** In addition to being sprinkled with purification water on the third and seventh days, a person or article that has been in contact with a corpse must also undergo immersion on the seventh day. An *am ha'aretz* is believed when he says that he has performed this immersion.

אָמַר אַבַּיֵי: לָא קַשְׁיָא: הָא – בְּגוּפוֹ, הָא – בְּכֵלָיו. רָבָא אָמַר: אִידִי וְאִידִי בְּכֵלָיו, וְלָא קַשְׁיָא; הָא – דְּאָמַר מֵעוֹלָם לֹא הִטְבַּלְתִּי כְּלִי בְּתוֹךְ כְּלִי, וְהָא דְּאָמַר ״הִטְבַּלְתִּי אֲבָל לֹא הִטְבַּלְתִּי בִּכְלִי שֶׁאֵין בְּפִיו כִּשְׁפוֹפֶרֶת הַנּוֹד״.

The Gemara presents two answers for this question. **Abaye said** one answer: This is **not difficult. This** *baraita,* which teaches that an *am ha'aretz* is trusted, is referring **to** the immersion of **his body,**[NH] whereas **this** teaching of the Gemara that *amei ha'aretz* are not trusted concerning immersion deals **with his vessels. Rava said** a different answer: Both **this and that,** both the *baraita* and the Gemara's teaching, refer **to the vessels** of an *am ha'aretz,* **and it is** nevertheless **not difficult. This** *baraita,* which teaches that an *am ha'aretz* is trusted, is referring to an *am ha'aretz* **who said: I never immersed one vessel inside another,** which is a statement that we accept. **And this** teaching of the Gemara that *amei ha'aretz* are not trusted deals with one **who said: I have immersed** vessels inside of other vessels, **but I did not immerse with a vessel whose mouth does not have** the width of **the tube of a wineskin.**[N] It is with regard to such details that an *am ha'aretz* cannot be trusted.

HALAKHA

When we borrow vessels from them we immerse them – כִּי שָׁיְילִינַן מִינַּיְיהוּ מַטְבְּלִינַן לְהוּ: When a *ḥaver* borrows vessels from an *am ha'aretz*, he immerses them and they become pure when evening arrives (Rambam *Sefer Tahara, Hilkhot Tumat Met* 23:1).

Requires sprinkling on the third and seventh days – בָּעֵי הַזָּאָה שְׁלִישִׁי וּשְׁבִיעִי: In order for one to purify himself from the impurity of a corpse, he must be sprinkled with the purification waters on the third and seventh days after separating from the impurity (Rambam *Sefer Tahara, Hilkhot Para Aduma* 11:1).

The trustworthiness of an *am ha'aretz* concerning the impurity of the dead – נֶאֱמָנוּת עַם הָאָרֶץ בְּטוּמְאַת הַמֵּת: If an *am ha'aretz* states that he, or a vessel in his possession, is pure from the impurity of the dead, he is believed. His vessel then requires immersion only from the impurity of the *am ha'aretz*, and becomes pure after sunset (Rambam *Sefer Tahara, Hilkhot Metamei Mishkav UMoshav* 11:12).

NOTES

Vessels for seven days – מָנָא לְשִׁבְעָה יוֹמֵי: *Zekher LaHagiga* explains that people do not borrow vessels in order to use them seven days later. If one borrows a vessel it must therefore be because he requires it at that point in time.

This is referring to his body – הָא בְּגוּפוֹ: Abaye's reasoning is that the purity of his body is important to an *am ha'aretz*, as it is relevant to the purity of the Temple, but he is not particular about the purity of his vessels and therefore does not immerse them properly (*Siaḥ Yitzḥak*).

And this deals with one who said, I have immersed, but I did not immerse…the tube of a wineskin – וְהָא דְּאָמַר הִטְבַּלְתִּי אֲבָל לֹא הִטְבַּלְתִּי...כִּשְׁפוֹפֶרֶת הַנּוֹד: The reason the statement of the *am ha'aretz* is not accepted is not that he is not trusted, because according to legal principles he should be believed, since he himself offered the information that he immersed vessels inside of vessels. However, due to the lack of knowledge of an *am ha'aretz*, we assume that he did not check the vessel carefully at the time, and therefore his claim regarding the width of the vessel's mouth is deemed unreliable (*Turei Aven*).

NOTES

The back of a vessel – אֲחוֹרַיִם: In his commentary on the mishna, Rashi explains that the back of a vessel refers to a part of the vessel's outside that is concave, such as the bottom of a vessel with a hollow stem, which can be used to contain something. See the Rid, who rejects this explanation.

BACKGROUND

Rim and handle – אוֹגֶן וְאוֹזֶן:

Rim and handle of ancient vessel

וְהָתַנְיָא: נֶאֱמָן עַם הָאָרֶץ לוֹמַר ״פֵּירוֹת לֹא הוּכְשְׁרוּ״, אֲבָל אֵינוֹ נֶאֱמָן לוֹמַר ״פֵּירוֹת הוּכְשְׁרוּ אֲבָל לֹא נִטְמְאוּ״.

And so it was taught in a *baraita* to this effect: **An** ***am ha'aretz*** **is trusted to say** that **produce has not been made susceptible** to impurity, i.e., that it has never come into contact with water,[H] **but he is not trusted to say** that the **produce has been made susceptible** to impurity **but has not** actually **become impure.** This *baraita* shows that *amei ha'aretz* are trusted concerning basic facts, but not concerning matters that require detailed knowledge and scrupulous care.

וְאַגּוּפוֹ מִי מְהֵימַן? וְהָתַנְיָא: חָבֵר שֶׁבָּא לְהַזּוֹת – מַזִּין עָלָיו מִיָּד. עַם הָאָרֶץ שֶׁבָּא לְהַזּוֹת – אֵין מַזִּין עָלָיו עַד שֶׁיַּעֲשֶׂה בְּפָנֵינוּ שְׁלִישִׁי וּשְׁבִיעִי!

The Gemara poses a question with regard to Abaye's opinion: **And is an** *am ha'aretz* really **trusted** concerning **his body,** when he claims to have immersed? **Isn't it taught** in a *baraita*: Concerning **a** ***ḥaver*** **who comes** before those in charge of sprinkling water of purification **to be sprinkled** with that water, and claims that the requisite three days have passed since his contamination by a corpse, **they may sprinkle upon him immediately. But** concerning **an** ***am ha'aretz*** **who comes** before them and claims that three days have passed, **they may not sprinkle upon him until he performs** and counts **in our presence** the **third** day **and** the **seventh** day? This shows that an *am ha'aretz* is not trusted concerning the purity of his own body.[H]

אֶלָּא אָמַר אַבַּיֵי: מִתּוֹךְ חוֹמֶר שֶׁהֶחְמַרְתָּ עָלָיו בִּתְחִילָּתוֹ – הֵיקַלְתָּ עָלָיו בְּסוֹפוֹ.

Rather, Abaye said, modifying his previous explanation: **Because of the stringency that you applied to** the *am ha'aretz* **in his beginning,** i.e., at the beginning of the purification process, by not allowing him to purify himself without first ensuring that he has not been in contact with a corpse for three days, **you** may **be lenient with him in his end,** in that he is trusted regarding having immersed at the end of the seven days, removing the impurity contracted through contact with a corpse.

״אֲחוֹרַיִם וְתוֹךְ״. מַאי אֲחוֹרַיִם וְתוֹךְ?

§ The mishna teaches: The *halakhot* of **the back** of a vessel[N] **and** its **inside**[H] apply to vessels used for *teruma*, but not for sacrificial food. The Gemara asks: **What is** the meaning of: **The back and** its **inside?**

כְּדִתְנַן: כְּלִי שֶׁנִּטְמָא אֲחוֹרָיו בְּמַשְׁקִין – אֲחוֹרָיו טְמֵאִין, תּוֹכוֹ אוֹגְנוֹ אָזְנוֹ וְיָדָיו – טְהוֹרִין. נִטְמָא תּוֹכוֹ – כּוּלּוֹ טָמֵא.

The Gemara explains. **As we learned** in a mishna (*Keilim* 25:6): **A vessel whose back** part, as opposed to its inside, **was defiled by** contact with impure **liquid. Its back is impure,** while its other parts, such as **its inside, its rim, its ear-shaped handles,**[B] **and its** straight **handles are pure.** By Torah law, foods and liquids cannot impart ritual impurity to a vessel at all, but by rabbinic law liquids can. In order to clarify that it is only a rabbinic decree, they instituted that the impurity thereby imparted, if the liquid touched the outside of the vessel, should affect only the part touched by the liquid, but not its inside or the other parts of its outside. However, if **its inside was defiled,** even by impurity only according to rabbinic law, **it is all impure.** This *halakha* applies only to *teruma*, but regarding offerings, the defilement of any part of the vessel renders it all impure.

HALAKHA

The trustworthiness of an ***am ha'aretz*** **concerning food – נֶאֱמָנוּת עַם הָאָרֶץ עַל אוֹכָלִין:** An *am ha'aretz* is believed when he says that foods have not been made susceptible to impurity (Rambam *Sefer Tahara*, *Hilkhot Tumat Okhalin* 16:2).

An ***am ha'aretz*** **and a** ***ḥaver*** **concerning sprinkling – עַם הָאָרֶץ וְחָבֵר בְּהַזָּאָה:** If a *ḥaver* comes before us to purify himself from the impurity of the dead and says that he has already counted three days or more, we immediately sprinkle the purification waters upon him and his vessels. In the case of an *am ha'aretz*, however, he must begin a new count in our presence, and we sprinkle on him on the third and seventh days of this counting (Rambam *Sefer Tahara*, *Hilkhot Para Aduma* 11:2).

The back and inside of vessels – אֲחוֹרַיִם וְתוֹךְ: If the back of a vessel came into contact with impure liquids, only its back is defiled but not its inside and its handles. This *halakha* applies to non-sacred vessels, and even to vessels used for *teruma*. In the case of sacrificial foods, however, the whole of a vessel whose back was defiled by impure liquid becomes impure to the second degree (Rambam *Sefer Tahara*, *Hilkhot She'ar Avot HaTumot* 7:3, 12:2).

"וּבֵית הַצְּבִיטָה" וכו׳. מַאי בֵּית הַצְּבִיטָה? אָמַר רַב יְהוּדָה אָמַר שְׁמוּאֵל: מָקוֹם שֶׁצּוֹבְטוֹ. וְכֵן הוּא אוֹמֵר: "וַיִּצְבָּט לָהּ קָלִי". רַבִּי אַסִּי אָמַר רַבִּי יוֹחָנָן: מָקוֹם שֶׁנְּקִיֵּי הַדַּעַת צוֹבְעִין.

§ The mishna teaches: **And its place for gripping.** The Gemara asks: **What is** the meaning of: **Place for gripping [*beit hatzevita*]?**[NB] **Rav Yehuda said** that **Shmuel said:** It is the **place** where **he** grips the vessel in order to **pass [*tzovet*]** it, a kind of indentation used for grasping the vessel. **And similarly it states: "And he pinched [*vayitzbat*] some parched corn for her"** (Ruth 2:14), which means that he gave her a little of the corn. Therefore, the term is referring to a place on the vessel used to grasp it. **Rabbi Asi** said that **Rabbi Yoḥanan said:** It is the **place that fastidious people** use for **dipping.** A small receptacle for spices and the like would be attached to the sides of vessels for dipping one's food.

תָּנֵי רַב בֵּיבָי קַמֵּיהּ דְּרַב נַחְמָן: כָּל הַכֵּלִים אֵין לָהֶם אֲחוֹרַיִם וְתוֹךְ, אֶחָד קָדְשֵׁי הַמִּקְדָּשׁ וְאֶחָד קָדְשֵׁי הַגְּבוּל. אֲמַר לֵיהּ: קָדְשֵׁי הַגְּבוּל מַאי נִינְהוּ? תְּרוּמָה. וְהָתְנַן: אֲחוֹרַיִם וְתוֹךְ וּבֵית הַצְּבִיטָה לַתְּרוּמָה!

Rav Beivai taught the following *baraita* **before Rav Naḥman: No vessels have** this difference between **the back and inside, whether** they are vessels used for **consecrated** foods **of the Temple or** those used for **consecrated** foods **of outlying areas,** i.e., outside the Temple. In these cases, if one of the parts of the vessel was defiled with impure liquids the entire vessel becomes impure. Rav Naḥman **said to him: What are these consecrated** foods **of outlying areas** mentioned in the *baraita*? This term is usually applied to **teruma,** but if so the *baraita* contradicts the mishna. For **didn't we learn** in the mishna: The *halakhot* of **the back** of a vessel **and its inside and its place for gripping** apply **to** vessels used for ***teruma*?**

דִּלְמָא לַחוּלִּין שֶׁנַּעֲשׂוּ עַל טׇהֳרַת הַקּוֹדֶשׁ קָאָמְרַתְּ.

Rav Naḥman continued: **Perhaps** when you said the consecrated foods of outlying areas you were not referring to *teruma*, but rather **you are speaking of non-sacred** food **prepared according to the** standards of **purity of sacrificial** food, and you called them consecrated foods of outlying areas because this level of purity can be observed outside the Temple as well.

אַדְכַּרְתָּן מִילְּתָא דְּאָמַר רַבָּה בַּר אֲבוּהּ: אַחַת עֶשְׂרֵה מַעֲלוֹת שָׁנוּ כָּאן; שֵׁשׁ רִאשׁוֹנוֹת – בֵּין לַקּוֹדֶשׁ בֵּין לַחוּלִּין שֶׁנַּעֲשׂוּ עַל טׇהֳרַת הַקּוֹדֶשׁ; אַחֲרוֹנוֹת – לַקּוֹדֶשׁ, אֲבָל לֹא לַחוּלִּין שֶׁנַּעֲשׂוּ עַל טׇהֳרַת הַקּוֹדֶשׁ.

In the course of this discussion Rav Naḥman said to Rav Beivai: **You have** now **reminded me** of something that **Rabba bar Avuh said** concerning this issue: **They taught eleven stringencies** of sacrificial food **here** in the mishna. The **first six** apply **both to sacrificial** food **and to non-sacred** food **prepared according to the** standards of **purity of sacrificial** food, whereas **the last** five **apply** only **to sacrificial** foods **but not to non-sacred** food **prepared according to the** standards of **purity of sacrificial** food. Rabba bar Avuh's statement therefore corroborates the interpretation of the *baraita* as dealing with non-sacred food prepared according to the standards of purity of sacrificial foods.

"הַנּוֹשֵׂא אֶת הַמִּדְרָס נוֹשֵׂא אֶת הַתְּרוּמָה אֲבָל לֹא אֶת הַקּוֹדֶשׁ". קוֹדֶשׁ מַאי טַעְמָא לָא? מִשּׁוּם מַעֲשֶׂה שֶׁהָיָה. דְּאָמַר רַב יְהוּדָה אָמַר שְׁמוּאֵל: מַעֲשֶׂה בְּאֶחָד שֶׁהָיָה מַעֲבִיר חָבִית שֶׁל יַיִן קוֹדֶשׁ מִמָּקוֹם לְמָקוֹם

§ The mishna teaches: **One who carries an object trodden** by a *zav* may **carry *teruma*** at the same time, if he is careful that neither he nor the impure object come into contact with the *teruma*, **but** this may **not** be done with **sacrificial** food. The Gemara asks: Concerning **sacrificial** food, **what is the reason** that he may **not** carry it? As long as contact with the food is prevented, why should he not carry sacrificial food as well? The Gemara answers: This enactment was made **due to an incident that occurred.**[H] **As Rav Yehuda said** that **Shmuel said:** There was once **an incident involving someone who was transferring a barrel of sacrificial wine from one place to another,**

NOTES

Place for gripping [*beit hatzevita*] – **בֵּית הַצְּבִיטָה:** It appears that even before the time of the earliest commentaries there were two readings of this item, *beit hatzevia* and *beit hatzevita*. The Gemara's interpretations of the term can fit either reading. The Rambam and Meiri state that *beit hatzevita* refers to a depression on the vessel where one placed his finger [*etzba*] to grasp it. The Rid explains that it was a hollowed-out area on the bottom of the vessel, such as the hollow stem of a cup, by which it could be held. Fastidious people would hold the cup upside down and dip their food in this reverse side rather than in the vessel itself. According to Rashi, a *beit hatzevita* is a small receptacle carved into the inside base of the vessel, and was used for containing dips.

BACKGROUND

Place for gripping [*beit hatzevita*] – **בֵּית הַצְּבִיטָה:** Below is a depiction of an ancient vessel that has a small area near its rim used to hold small vessels or spices. This is one interpretation of the term: Place for gripping, since this part of the vessel was also used to pick the entire vessel up.

Vessel with a place for gripping

HALAKHA

One who carries both an object trodden by a *zav* and something pure – הַנּוֹשֵׂא מִדְרָס וְדָבָר טָהוֹר: A person carrying an object trodden by a *zav* may hold something pure at the same time, including *teruma*, as long as the two do not come into contact with each other. However, he may not carry sacrificial food together with an object trodden by a *zav*, as the Sages made a decree against this due to an incident that occurred (Rambam *Sefer Tahara, Hilkhot She'ar Avot HaTumot* 12:3).

וְנִפְסְקָה רְצוּעָה שֶׁל סַנְדָּלוֹ. וּנְטָלָהּ וְהִנִּיחָהּ עַל פִּי חָבִית, וְנָפְלָה לַאֲוִיר הֶחָבִית, וְנִטְמֵאת. בְּאוֹתָהּ שָׁעָה אָמְרוּ: הַנּוֹשֵׂא אֶת הַמִּדְרָס נוֹשֵׂא אֶת הַתְּרוּמָה, אֲבָל לֹא אֶת הַקֹּדֶשׁ.

and the strap of his sandal, which had been rendered ritually impure by being trodden by a *zav*, **broke off, and he picked up** the strap **and placed it**[N] on top **of the mouth of** the **barrel,**[N] **and** it **fell into the airspace of the barrel,** thereby **rendering** the entire barrel **impure. At that time** the Sages **said** and issued a permanent decree that **one who carries an object that is impure by having been trodden** by a *zav* **may carry** ***teruma*** at the same time, **but not sacrificial** food.

אִי הָכִי תְּרוּמָה נַמִּי! הָא מַנִּי? רַבִּי חֲנַנְיָה בֶּן עֲקַבְיָא הִיא, דְּאָמַר: לֹא אָסְרוּ אֶלָּא בְּיַרְדֵּן וּבִסְפִינָה, וּכְמַעֲשֶׂה שֶׁהָיָה.

The Gemara asks: **If so,** if they prohibited doing so due to that incident, they should have made the same decree with regard to ***teruma*** **also,** because if the same incident would occur with *teruma* it would defile the *teruma* as well. The Gemara answers: In accordance with **whose** opinion **is this** stated? **It is** that of **Rabbi Ḥananya ben Akavya,**[N] **who said** concerning a similar issue: **They prohibited** it **only in the Jordan** River, **and** only **in a boat,** in a situation **similar to the incident that occurred,** which triggered the enactment. In his opinion, whenever the Sages enacted a decree prohibiting something due to a particular incident, they did not extend the prohibition to related cases, but only to the same set of circumstances that pertained to that specific incident.

מַאי הִיא? דְּתַנְיָא: לֹא יִשָּׂא אָדָם מֵי חַטָּאת וְאֵפֶר חַטָּאת וְיַעֲבִירֵם בְּיַרְדֵּן וּבִסְפִינָה, וְלֹא יַעֲמוֹד בְּצַד זֶה וְיִזְרְקֵם לְצַד אַחֵר, וְלֹא יְשִׁיטֵם עַל פְּנֵי הַמַּיִם, וְלֹא יִרְכַּב עַל גַּבֵּי בְהֵמָה, וְלֹא עַל גַּבֵּי חֲבֵירוֹ, אֶלָּא אִם כֵּן הָיוּ רַגְלָיו נוֹגְעוֹת בַּקַּרְקַע. אֲבָל מַעֲבִירָן עַל גַּבֵּי הַגֶּשֶׁר וְאֵינוֹ חוֹשֵׁשׁ. אֶחָד הַיַּרְדֵּן וְאֶחָד שְׁאָר הַנְּהָרוֹת. רַבִּי חֲנַנְיָה בֶּן עֲקַבְיָא אוֹמֵר: לֹא אָסְרוּ אֶלָּא בְּיַרְדֵּן, וּבִסְפִינָה, וּכְמַעֲשֶׂה שֶׁהָיָה.

The Gemara presents the background to Rabbi Ḥananya ben Akavya's statement: **What is that** enactment that Rabbi Ḥananya ben Akavya was referring to? **As it is taught** in a *baraita*: **A person may not carry the water of purification and the ashes of purification and transport them across the Jordan** River, **and** this is if he is **on a boat. Nor may he stand on one side** of the river **and throw them to the other side. Nor may he float them** across the river. **Nor may he** ford the river **riding on an animal or on his friend** and carrying the water or ashes of purification, **unless his feet are touching the ground** as he fords the river. **But he may transfer them** across the river **over a bridge without concern** about transferring them improperly. This decree applies **both** to **the Jordan and to other rivers. Rabbi Ḥananya ben Akavya says:** The Sages **prohibited** these acts **only in the Jordan** River, **and** only if he transports them **in a boat, and** in circumstances exactly **like** those of **the incident that occurred.**[H]

מַאי מַעֲשֶׂה שֶׁהָיָה? דְּאָמַר רַב יְהוּדָה אָמַר רַב: מַעֲשֶׂה בְּאָדָם אֶחָד שֶׁהָיָה מַעֲבִיר מֵי חַטָּאת וְאֵפֶר חַטָּאת בְּיַרְדֵּן וּבִסְפִינָה, וְנִמְצָא כַּזַּיִת מֵת תָּחוּב בְּקַרְקָעִיתָהּ שֶׁל סְפִינָה. בְּאוֹתָהּ שָׁעָה אָמְרוּ: לֹא יִשָּׂא אָדָם מֵי חַטָּאת וְאֵפֶר חַטָּאת וְיַעֲבִירֵם בְּיַרְדֵּן בִּסְפִינָה.

The Gemara inquires: **What was the incident that occurred? Rav Yehuda said** that **Rav said:** There was once **an incident involving a person who was transferring water of purification and ashes of purification in the Jordan, and** he was **on a boat, and an olive-bulk** from **a corpse was discovered stuck**[N] **in the floor of the boat,** over which the water of purification had passed, thereby rendering them impure and invalid. **At that time the Sages said: A person may not carry water of purification and ashes of purification and transport them across the Jordan,** and this is if he is **on a boat.** Just as in that case, Rabbi Ḥananya ben Akavya stated that the decree was limited to the specific circumstances of the original incident, here too, he would say that since the original incident involved sacrificial food and not *teruma* the Sages did not apply the decree to *teruma*.

NOTES

And he picked it up and placed it, etc. – **וּנְטָלָהּ וְהִנִּיחָהּ וכו׳**: The early commentaries ask the following question: The detached sandal strap should be considered a broken part of a vessel, which is not subject to ritual impurity at all. *Tosefot Rid* explains that for this reason an alternative reading with masculine endings should be adopted, indicating that it was the broken sandal which could no longer be worn, which was picked up and placed over the barrel (see Meiri).

On the mouth of the barrel – **עַל פִּי חָבִית**: There is a slightly different version of this incident related in the Jerusalem Talmud: The barrel he was carrying developed a hole and he plugged it up with his sandal. The early commentaries point out that this version of the story resolves several problems presented by the incident as it is recounted here.

In accordance with whose opinion is this…Rabbi Ḥananya ben Akavya, etc. – **הָא מַנִּי, רַבִּי חֲנַנְיָה בֶּן עֲקַבְיָא וכו׳**: The *Kesef Mishne* addresses the apparent contradiction in the conclusions of the Rambam. One the one hand, he rules in accordance with the mishna regarding one who carries sacrificial food, which, the Gemara states, is in accordance with Rabbi Ḥananya's limitations of decrees to situations resembling the original incident. At the same time, however, he rules in accordance with the Sages regarding the water of purification. *Siaḥ Yitzḥak* states that the Gemara does not mean to say that the *halakha* of the mishna does not follow the opinion of the Rabbis, but merely that here the decree was not extended to other circumstances beyond a certain limit, similar to Rabbi Ḥananya's position, but not necessarily in accordance with his opinion. Others say it is understandable why the decree against carrying an impure sandal with sacrificial food was not broadened to *teruma* as well, in light of the Jerusalem Talmud's opinion that the Sages did not apply such decrees to those who eat *teruma*, as they were generally meticulous (*Yad David*). It is also possible to explain that the decree concerning the water of purification was not extended to other situations because the entire susceptibility of the ashes of purification to ritual impurity is only a rabbinic stringency (see *Turei Aven*).

An olive-bulk from a corpse was discovered stuck, etc. – **נִמְצָא כַּזַּיִת מֵת תָּחוּב וכו׳**: The early commentaries address the fundamental question of why the ashes of the red heifer, which are neither a vessel nor food, should be susceptible to impurity at all. The answer appears to be that the great importance of the purification ashes bestows upon them the ability to contract impurity (see *Turei Aven*; Responsa of the Rashba).

HALAKHA

The manner of transporting water of purification – **כֵּיצַד נוֹשְׂאִים מֵי חַטָּאת**: Due to an incident that once occurred, the Sages decreed that one may not transfer either the water of purification or the ashes of purification over a river on a boat, nor should they be floated over the water, nor should they be thrown to the other side of the river. But it is permitted to traverse the water on foot or over a bridge, in accordance with the opinion of the Rabbis (Rambam *Sefer Tahara*, *Hilkhot Para Aduma* 10:2).

אִיבַּעְיָא לְהוּ: סַנְדָּל טָמֵא. סַנְדָּל טָהוֹר מַהוּ? חָבִית פְּתוּחָה. חָבִית סְתוּמָה מַהוּ? עָבַר וְנָשָׂא מַהוּ?

Several **dilemmas were raised before** the scholars: It is clear that this *halakha*, like the incident itself, applies to an object that has actually contracted impurity by being trodden by a *zav*, such as an **impure sandal.** But if it is **a pure sandal, what is** the *halakha*?[N] Is the decree so far-reaching as to include a prohibition against carrying even a pure sandal together with sacrificial food? Similarly, the *halakha* certainly applies to **an open barrel,** where there is a danger that the sandal may enter the airspace of the barrel, as in the original incident, but if it was **a closed barrel,** where there is no such danger, **what is** the *halakha*? Does the decree apply in this case as well? Another question: If someone **transgressed** this decree **and carried** an impure sandal together with sacrificial food, **what is** the *halakha*?[N] Did the Sages decree that the sacrificial food would become defiled because their decree was transgressed or not?

רַבִּי אִילָא אָמַר: אִם עָבַר וְנָשָׂא – טָמֵא. רַבִּי זֵירָא אָמַר: עָבַר וְנָשָׂא – טָהוֹר.

The Gemara presents a conclusion for the last dilemma. **Rabbi Ila said: If one transgressed and carried** sacrificial food together with an impure sandal, **it is** indeed rendered **impure. Rabbi Zeira said:** If **he transgressed and carried** sacrificial food in this manner, **it is** still **pure.**

״כֵּלִים הַנִּגְמָרִים בְּטׇהֳרָה״ כו׳. דִּגְמָרִינְהוּ מַאן? אִילֵימָא דִּגְמָרִינְהוּ חָבֵר – לָמָּה לְהוּ טְבִילָה?

§ The mishna states: **Vessels that were** fashioned and **completed in purity** require immersion for sacrificial food but not for *teruma*. The Gemara asks: **Who completed** the work of these vessels? **If we say that** it was a ***ḥaver***, an individual who is meticulous about the *halakhot* of ritual purity, who **completed them, why** should **they** require **immersion,** given that he is meticulous about the *halakhot* of purity?

אֶלָּא דִּגְמָרִינְהוּ עַם הָאָרֶץ – נִגְמָרִין בְּטׇהֳרָה קָרֵי לְהוּ?! אָמַר רַבָּה בַּר שֵׁילָא אָמַר רַב מַתָּנָה אָמַר שְׁמוּאֵל: לְעוֹלָם דִּגְמָרִינְהוּ חָבֵר, וּמִשּׁוּם צִינּוֹרָא דְּעַם הָאָרֶץ.

Rather, it must mean **that an *am ha'aretz* completed them.** But can one **call these** vessels **completed in purity?** The very touch of an *am ha'aretz* renders them impure. **Rabba bar Sheila said** that **Rav Mattana said** that **Shmuel said: Actually,** the mishna is dealing with vessels **that a *ḥaver* completed,** and the Sages declared them impure for sacrificial food **due to** a concern that the **spittle**[N] **of an *am ha'aretz*** might have fallen on them, which would render them impure if he were a *zav*.[H]

דְּנָפֵל אֵימַת? אִילֵימָא מִקַּמֵּי דְּלִיגְמְרֵיהּ – הָא לָאו מָנָא הוּא. אֶלָּא בָּתַר דִּגְמָרֵיהּ – מִיזְהָר זְהִיר בְּהוּ! לְעוֹלָם מִקַּמֵּיהּ דִּגְמָרֵיהּ, וְדִלְמָא בְּעִידָּנָא דִּגְמָרֵיהּ עֲדַיִין לַחָה הִיא.

The Gemara asks: **When did** this hypothetical spittle **fall** on the vessel? **If we say** it was **before he completed** the vessel, in **that** case **it is not** yet **a vessel,** and therefore cannot contract impurity at that stage at all. **Rather,** it must have sprayed onto the vessel **after he completed it.** But at that point, since he is a *ḥaver*, **he is careful about it.** He would ensure that no spittle would fall on it, so there is no danger that it might have become defiled. The Gemara responds: **Actually,** we must explain that the spittle fell **before he completed it,** when the *ḥaver* was not yet guarding it against impurity, **and** the Sages were concerned that **perhaps at the moment when he completed** the vessel the spittle **was still moist,** and thus still capable of defiling the finished vessel, for the continued presence of the spittle on the vessel might have escaped the attention of the *ḥaver* craftsman.

טְבִילָה – אִין, הֶעֱרֵב שֶׁמֶשׁ – לָא.

The Gemara comments: The mishna states that the vessel requires immersion, implying: **Immersion, yes,**[N] but **the setting of the sun** after immersion, **not,**[N] i.e., it is considered pure immediately after immersion, even though generally the purification engendered by immersion does not take effect until sunset.

NOTES

A pure sandal, what is the *halakha* – סַנְדָּל טָהוֹר מַהוּ: The question is that since the original incident involved a sandal it is reasonable to assert that the decree included all sandals (see *Siaḥ Yitzḥak* and Rashash).

If someone transgressed and carried, what is the *halakha* – עָבַר וְנָשָׂא מַהוּ: In *Siaḥ Yitzḥak* it is explained that the Gemara asks this question only concerning this particular case, not the previous stringencies listed in the mishna, as it was clear to the Sages of the Talmud that in those other cases the item in question is impure even after the fact. The question arises only in this case because here the decree was instituted as a result of a specific incident. In *Zekher LaḤagiga*, however, the exact opposite approach is taken, i.e., that the Gemara assumes that the other cases are not considered impure if the relevant stringency was not followed. This is because the other cases do not involve a concern for actual impurity but involve merely a far-fetched safeguard, whereas here it is possible that the food in the barrel may actually become impure.

Spittle – צִינּוֹרָא: This Aramaic word has various meanings. It often refers to a pipe or spout for flowing water. Here it is used in a similar sense, to refer to a spray of spittle.

Immersion, yes – טְבִילָה אִין: *Tosafot* ask how it is inferred from the mishna that the setting of the sun is not necessary. *Turei Aven* answers that the mishna could have stated simply that these vessels are impure, and it would be obvious that they require immersion. Since the mishna says instead that they "require immersion," it must be emphasizing that it requires immersion alone and nothing else.

The setting of the sun, not – הֶעֱרֵב שֶׁמֶשׁ לָא: In light of the Gemara's conclusion that the impurity of this vessel is due to the fact that the spittle of a *zav* might have defiled it, this line in the Gemara seems difficult, because such defilement by a *zav* does indeed require the setting of the sun. The *Turei Aven* answers that the possibility of spittle on the vessel not drying until the vessel is completed is actually a far-fetched concern, and therefore the required immersion is merely a stringency, to maintain extra purity. Therefore, the principles of the spittle of a *zav* were not applied to the fullest extreme.

HALAKHA

Immersing vessels that were completed in purity – טְבִילַת כֵּלִים הַנִּגְמָרִים בְּטׇהֳרָה: For sacrificial food, vessels that were completed in purity require immersion, but not the setting of the sun, even if they were made by a learned person. For *teruma*, however, the vessels may be used without immersion (Rambam *Sefer Tahara*, *Hilkhot She'ar Avot HaTumot* 12:6).

מתניתין דלא כרבי אליעזר. דתנן: שפופרת שחתכה לחטאת, רבי אליעזר אומר: יטבול מיד. רבי יהושע אומר: יטמא ואחר כך יטבול. והוינן בה: דחתכה מאן? אילימא דחתכה חבר – למה לי טבילה? ואלא דחתכה עם הארץ – בהא לימא רבי יהושע יטמא ויטבול? הא טמא וקאי!

The Gemara asks: If so, **the mishna is not in accordance with** the opinion of **Rabbi Eliezer. As we learned** in a mishna (*Para* 5:4): Regarding **a tube** of reed, **which one cut for** storing ashes of **purification,**[H] **Rabbi Eliezer says: He should immerse** it **immediately; Rabbi Yehoshua says: He should** first **render** it **impure** by touching it to an actual source of impurity **and** only **after that immerse** it. **And we discussed** the mishna's case, asking: **Who cut** this tube? **If we say a *ḥaver* cut it, why do I** need **immersion?** The *ḥaver* prepared it with the strictest adherence to the *halakhot* of purity. **Rather,** it must be that an *am ha'aretz* **cut it.** But **in that case, would Rabbi Yehoshua say** that **he should** first **render** it **impure and** only then **immerse** it? **Isn't it already impure,** due to the handling of the *am ha'aretz*?

ואמר רבה בר שילא אמר רב מתנה אמר שמואל: לעולם דחתכה חבר, ומשום צינורא דעם הארץ. דנפל. אימת? אילימא מקמי דליחתכה – הא לאו מנא הוא. ואלא בתר דחתכה – מיזהר זהיר בה! לעולם מקמי דליחתכה, דלמא בעידנא דחתכה עדיין לחה היא.

And in response to this question, **Rabba bar Sheila said** that **Rav Mattana said** that **Shmuel said: Actually,** the case is **that a *ḥaver* cut it, and** the reason it requires immersion is **because** the Sages were concerned that the **spittle of an *am ha'aretz*** might have touched it. The Gemara asks: **When did** this hypothetical spittle **fall** on the tube? **If we say** it was **before he cut** the tube, in **that** case **it is not** yet **a vessel** and therefore cannot contract impurity at that stage. **Rather,** it must have sprayed onto the vessel **after he completed it.** But at that point, since he is a *ḥaver*, **he is careful about it** and would ensure that no spittle would fall on it, so there is no danger that it might have become impure. The Gemara responds: **Actually** we must explain that the spittle fell **before he cut it, and** the Sages were concerned that **perhaps at the moment when he cut** the tube the spittle **was still moist,** and thus still capable of rendering the finished tube impure.

בשלמא לרבי יהושע – היינו דאיכא היכירא לצדוקין.

The Gemara continues: **Granted, according to Rabbi Yehoshua it** is found **that there is** an act of **recognition** performed in opposition **to the Sadducees,** in order to demonstrate that the Sages do not take their opinions into account.

דתנן: מטמאין היו את הכהן השורף את הפרה, להוציא מלבן של צדוקין, שהיו אומרים: במעורבי שמש היתה נעשית.

As we learned in a mishna (*Para* 3:7): **They would render impure the priest who burns the** red **heifer,**[H] **in order to counter the opinion of** the **Sadducees,**[N] **who used to say:** The ritual of the red heifer **was** to be **performed by those who had experienced sunset** after their immersion. The Sadducee opinion was that all those involved in the preparation of the red heifer must be completely pure, having undergone immersion as well as having waited until after sunset, when the purification takes full effect. The Sages, however, maintain that the red heifer may be prepared by people immediately after immersion, without waiting for sunset. In order to clearly demonstrate their rejection of the Sadducee opinion they would deliberately defile the people involved with preparing the red heifer and then immerse them. It is for this reason as well that Rabbi Yehoshua ruled that the tube must be rendered impure before it is immersed.

אלא לרבי אליעזר, אי אמרת בשלמא בעלמא בעינן הערב שמש – היינו דאיכא היכירא לצדוקין. אלא אי אמרת בעלמא לא בעינן הערב שמש, מאי היכירא לצדוקין איכא!

But according to Rabbi Eliezer, granted, if you say that **generally, the setting of the sun is required** after a vessel is completed, **it is** found **that there is** some act of **recognition** in opposition **to** the **Sadducees,** as according to him, the tube used for the red heifer ashes, which should normally have required the setting of the sun, is used without waiting for sunset. **But if you say** that **generally the setting of the sun is not required** to remove the impurity caused by the touch of an *am ha'aretz*, and immersion alone is sufficient, **what** act of **recognition** in opposition **to** the **Sadducees is there** here? It must be, therefore, that Rabbi Eliezer requires the setting of the sun for purification from the impurity imparted by an *am ha'aretz*. Therefore, the mishna, which implies that immersion alone is sufficient, does not accord with Rabbi Eliezer's opinion.

אמר רב:

Rav said: Indeed, Rabbi Eliezer does not require the setting of the sun for vessels that have been completed in purity, but there is nevertheless a demonstrative sign that the opinion of the Sadducees is rejected,

HALAKHA

A tube cut for the water of purification – שפופרת שחתכה לחטאת: One who cuts a reed tube for the water of purification should first defile it and subsequently immerse and use it, in accordance with Rabbi Yehoshua, as the *halakha* follows his opinion in opposition to Rabbi Eliezer (Rambam *Sefer Tahara, Hilkhot Para Aduma* 1:15).

They would render impure the priest who burns the red heifer – מטמאין היו את הכהן השורף את הפרה: Because the Sadducees claimed that actions performed on the red heifer are valid only if carried out by those for whom the sun has set after their immersion, the members of the court during the time of the Second Temple would defile the priest designated for burning the heifer by touching him with a dead creeping animal or something similar. He would then immerse and go on to burn the heifer. This was done as a public demonstration that the Sadducee opinion was not accepted as *halakha* (Rambam *Sefer Tahara, Hilkhot Para Aduma* 1:14).

NOTES

To counter the opinion of the Sadducees – להוציא מלבן של צדוקין: The Sadducees claimed that those who are involved with the preparation of the red heifer must be entirely pure. The Sages, however, expounded that the words "the clean person" (Numbers 19:18–19) mean that he must be pure to a certain degree, even if he is not completely pure. In order to emphasize and publicize their opinion, the Sages would intentionally defile those who would handle the red heifer and subsequently immerse them, despite the fact that a wholly pure person was, of course, also fit for the task. Since this act constituted a certain detraction from the strict purity of the water of purification, the Sages added many decrees to the purity of the red heifer, to ensure that the rite would be carried out with the utmost regard to the *halakhot* of purity.

עֲשָׂאוּהָ כִּטְמֵא שֶׁרֶץ.

as **they treated** the tube with severity **as** though it had been **rendered impure** by contact with a dead **creeping animal.** Therefore, in not requiring the setting of the sun they made it noticeable that they were opposed to the Sadducees.

אֶלָּא מֵעַתָּה לֹא תְּטַמֵּא אָדָם! אַלְמָּה תַּנְיָא: חוֹתְכָהּ וּמַטְבִּילָהּ – טָעוּן טְבִילָה! וְאֶלָּא, עֲשָׂאוּהָ כִּטְמֵא מֵת. אִי הָכִי, תִּיבְעֵי הַזָּאַת שְׁלִישִׁי וּשְׁבִיעִי!

The Gemara raises a difficulty. **However, if** that is **so,** that the tube is treated as if defiled by a creeping animal, **it should not render a person impure,**[N] as something defiled by a creeping animal is impure to the first degree of ritual impurity, which cannot impart ritual impurity to people. **Why,** then, **is it taught** in a *baraita*: The one who **cuts and immerses** the tube for the red heifer ashes **requires immersion** himself, which shows that the tube does defile people? **But rather,** say that **they treated it as** something **made impure by** contact with **a corpse,** for such objects do defile people as well. The Gemara asks: **If that is so,** the tube **should** also **require the sprinkling** of the water of purification on the **third and seventh** days of its purification, like all things defiled by a corpse.

אַלְמָּה תַּנְיָא: חוֹתְכָהּ וּמַטְבִּילָהּ – טָעוּן טְבִילָה. טְבִילָה – אִין, הַזָּאַת שְׁלִישִׁי וּשְׁבִיעִי – לָא! אֶלָּא: עֲשָׂאוּהָ כִּטְמֵא מֵת בִּשְׁבִיעִי שֶׁלּוֹ.

Why, then, **is it taught** in a *baraita*: The one who **cuts and immerses it**[H] **requires immersion,** which indicates that **immersion** for the tube, **yes,** this is required, but **sprinkling of the third and the seventh** day, **no. Rather,** you must say that **they treated it as** something **made impure by** contact with **a corpse** that is already **in its seventh** day, after its sprinklings, when it is still impure and imparts impurity to those who touch it, but requires only immersion and no further sprinkling.

וְהָתַנְיָא: מֵעוֹלָם לֹא חִידְּשׁוּ דָּבָר בְּפָרָה!

The Gemara asks: **But isn't it taught** in a *baraita*: The Sages **never made any innovations** in the *halakhot* of impurity **with regard to the** red **heifer** procedure.[N] In other words, although the Sages added stringencies to the red heifer procedure, they never created new *halakhot* for it that do not exist elsewhere in other areas of *halakha*. We have said that the tube is treated as if it had had contact with a corpse even though it did not; this is an innovation that is not found anywhere else.

אָמַר אַבָּיֵי: שֶׁלֹּא אָמְרוּ קוֹרְדוֹם מְטַמֵּא מוֹשָׁב. כִּדְתַנְיָא: "וְהַיּוֹשֵׁב עַל הַכְּלִי", יָכוֹל כָּפָה סְאָה וְיָשַׁב עָלֶיהָ, תַּרְקַב וְיָשַׁב עָלֶיהָ, יְהֵא טָמֵא?

The Gemara answers: **Abaye said:** When they said that the Sages did not make innovations, they were not referring to something of this nature, but meant that **they did not say** that **a spade** upon which a *zav* sits **can become impure as a seat.** They thereby preserved the basic *halakhot* of impurity, **as it is taught** in a *baraita*: It states with regard to a *zav*: **"And he who sits on any object** whereon the *zav* sits shall wash his clothes and bathe himself in water, and be unclean until the evening" (Leviticus 15:6). One **might** have thought that if a *zav* **turned over** a vessel used to measure **a *se'a***[H] **and sat on it,** or if he turned over a vessel used to measure **a *tarkav*,**[L] i.e., a half-*se'a*, **and sat on it,** that the vessel **should be** rendered **impure** as a seat upon which a *zav* sat.

תַּלְמוּד לוֹמַר: "וְהַיּוֹשֵׁב עַל הַכְּלִי אֲשֶׁר יֵשֵׁב עָלָיו...יִטְמָא" – מִי שֶׁמְּיוּחָד לִישִׁיבָה, יָצָא זֶה, שֶׁאוֹמְרִים לוֹ עֲמוֹד וְנַעֲשֶׂה מְלַאכְתֵּנוּ.

The *baraita* concludes: Therefore, **the verse states: "And he who sits on any object whereon** the *zav* **sits…and be unclean** until the evening" (Leviticus 15:6). The wording of the verse indicates that it is speaking of an object **that is designated for sitting,** i.e., upon which people generally sit, **excluding such** a vessel for **which we would say to** someone sitting on it: **Stand up, so we can do our work.** A spade and a measuring bowl, then, are not subject to the impurity of the seat of a *zav*, even if a *zav* sat on them. Rather, they are considered to be on the lower level of impurity transmitted through simple contact with a *zav*. The same *halakha* was applied to the vessels used in preparation of the red heifer; the Sages did not add stringency and decree that a vessel not generally used for sitting should be considered as the seat of a *zav*.

NOTES

It should not render a person impure – לֹא תְּטַמֵּא אָדָם: The *Turei Aven* asks: The principle is that the Sages did not apply the ordinary decreasing levels of impurity regarding the red heifer (see Mishna, *Para* 12:7–8), so that there is no difference between the first and second degrees of ritual impurity. Rather, an impure object can defile another object, which can in turn defile another, even up to the hundredth object. In light of this, why does the Gemara find difficulty with the tube defiling a person? *Zekher LaHagiga* answers that the above applies only to definite impurity, whereas here the impurity of the tube is only a decree made in order to demonstrate the rejection of the Sadducee opinion.

The Sages never made any innovations with regard to the red heifer procedure – לֹא חִידְּשׁוּ דָּבָר בְּפָרָה: Although the Sages instituted numerous decrees and stringencies concerning the purity of the red heifer beyond the ordinary *halakhot* of offerings, the method of these decrees was to apply to the water of purification stringencies found elsewhere, even in situations where they would not normally be applied, without innovating any new type of impurity. Abaye's response is that this principle means that whenever they applied a particular *halakha* they followed the principles of that *halakha* in its original context. This does not, however, contradict the fact that the Sages also instituted decrees for the heifer that cannot be found elsewhere.

HALAKHA

The one who cuts and immerses it, etc. – חוֹתְכָהּ וּמַטְבִּילָהּ וכו׳: The one who cuts and immerses a tube made for ashes of the red heifer becomes ritually impure thereby. He requires immersion, but not sprinkling on the third and seventh days, as the Sages treated the tube as a vessel defiled by a corpse on its seventh day (Rambam *Sefer Tahara, Hilkhot Para Aduma* 1:15).

If a *zav* turned over a vessel used to measure a *se'a*, etc. – כָּפָה סְאָה וכו׳: If a *zav* trod upon a vessel that is not designated for lying, sitting, or riding, even if the vessel is fit for such a use, it remains pure, as it is designated for other uses. Therefore, if a *zav* turned over a vessel used to measure a *se'a* and sat on it, it is not defiled by the ritual impurity imparted by treading (Rambam *Sefer Tahara, Hilkhot Metamei Mishkav UMoshav* 7:8).

LANGUAGE

***Tarkav* – תַּרְקַב:** A *tarkav* is a vessel used to measure a half-*se'a*. The early commentaries explained it as being derived from the words two [*trei*] and *kav*, i.e., two *kav* plus another *kav*, three *kav* in all; for a *se'a* consists of six *kav*. It is likely, however, that it is derived from the Greek τρίκαβος, *trikabos*, meaning three *kabos*.

"הַכְּלִי מְצָרֵף מַה שֶּׁבְּתוֹכוֹ לַקֹּדֶשׁ אֲבָל לֹא לַתְּרוּמָה". מְנָא הָנֵי מִילֵּי? אָמַר רַבִּי חָנִין, דְּאָמַר קְרָא: "כַּף אַחַת עֲשָׂרָה זָהָב מְלֵאָה קְטֹרֶת" – הַכָּתוּב עֲשָׂאוֹ לְכָל מַה שֶּׁבַּכַּף אַחַת.

§ The mishna states: **A vessel combines**[HN] all the food that is in it with regard **to sacrificial** food **but not** with regard **to *teruma*.** The Gemara asks: **From where are these matters** derived? What is the source for this stringency? **Rabbi Ḥanin said: The verse states** with regard to the sacrificial donations of the tribal princes: **"One golden pan of ten shekels, full of incense"** (Numbers 7:14), which teaches us that **the verse treats everything inside the pan** as **one** unit, even if the items are not attached to each other.

מְתִיב רַב כָּהֲנָא: הוֹסִיף רַבִּי עֲקִיבָא: הַסֹּלֶת וְהַקְּטֹרֶת וְהַלְּבוֹנָה וְהַגֶּחָלִים, שֶׁאִם נָגַע טְבוּל יוֹם בְּמִקְצָתוֹ – פָּסַל אֶת כּוּלּוֹ.

Rav Kahana raised an objection against this based on the mishna that teaches (*Eduyyot* 8:1): **Rabbi Akiva added** to the list of items that are considered combined when in the same vessel **fine flour,**[N] **incense, frankincense, and coals,** saying **that if one who immersed himself that day** but has not waited until sunset **touched** a **part** of the contents of a vessel containing these substances, **all of** the vessel's contents **are disqualified,** as the vessel combines them.

וְהָא דְּרַבָּנַן הִיא! מִמַּאי? מִדְּקָתָנֵי רֵישָׁא: הֵעִיד רַבִּי שִׁמְעוֹן בֶּן בְּתֵירָא עַל אֵפֶר חַטָּאת שֶׁנָּגַע הַטָּמֵא בְּמִקְצָתוֹ, שֶׁטִּימֵּא אֶת כּוּלּוֹ. וְקָתָנֵי: הוֹסִיף רַבִּי עֲקִיבָא!

Isn't this *halakha* that these substances are considered combined **by rabbinic law? From where** do we know that this is so? **From** the fact **that it teaches in the first clause** of that mishna: **Rabbi Shimon ben Beteira testified with regard to ashes of purification** in a vessel **that** if **an impure** person or object **touched part of it, it renders all of it impure.**[H] The purification ashes of the red heifer are neither food nor a sacrificial item, so Rabbi Ḥanin's verse does not apply to the ashes, and the vessel certainly does not combine the ashes together by Torah law, but by rabbinic law. **And it is taught** immediately following this: **Rabbi Akiva added,** which shows that Rabbi Akiva's *halakha*, like the previous *halakha*, deals with an additional level of impurity instituted by the Sages rather than a Torah law.

אָמַר רֵישׁ לָקִישׁ מִשּׁוּם בַּר קַפָּרָא:

Reish Lakish said in the name of Bar Kappara:

HALAKHA

A vessel combines – הַכְּלִי מְצָרֵף: If a vessel was filled with separate items, such as produce, and something impure touches one of them, all its contents are defiled in the case of sacrificial food, but not in the case of *teruma*. This stringency is from a decree of the Sages (Rambam *Sefer Tahara, Hilkhot She'ar Avot HaTumot* 12:7). This is in accordance with Rabbi Yoḥanan (see 24a) rather than Rabbi Ḥanin here, as the former was greater than him in Torah (*Kesef Mishne*).

Combining with regard to the ashes of the red heifer – צֵירוּף בְּאֵפֶר הַפָּרָה: If something impure touches part of the ashes of the red heifer, it disqualifies all of the ashes (Rambam *Sefer Tahara, Hilkhot Para Aduma* 13:5).

NOTES

A vessel combines – הַכְּלִי מְצָרֵף: In other words, the vessel turns all of its contents into a single unit, even if they are not physically connected to one another. The later commentaries discuss whether this principle applies only if the items in the vessel are of the same type, or also if the items therein are different types of objects. The later commentaries likewise address the issue of whether the vessel combines only those items that were inside it when the impurity touched one of them, or whether something added later also contracts impurity as though it had been present when the initial items became impure (see *Turei Aven* and *Zekher LaHagiga*).

Rabbi Akiva added…flour, etc. – הוֹסִיף רַבִּי עֲקִיבָא, הַסֹּלֶת וכו׳: See *Tosafot*, who cite several sources which state that the *halakha* that frankincense and coals can contract ritual impurity, despite being neither vessels nor food, is derived from a particular verse in the Torah. Rabbi Akiva adds that not only are they susceptible to impurity, but the *halakha* of combining in a vessel applies to them as well. The Gemara states that this is impurity by rabbinic law. They infer this from the comparison to the ashes of the red heifer, which certainly are not combined by being in a single vessel according to Torah law, either because they are not included in the verse "One golden pan, full of incense" (see *Turei Aven*), or because their entire impurity is undoubtedly rabbinic in nature (see Rid).

Perek **III**
Daf **24** Amud **a**

לָא נִצְרְכָא אֶלָּא לִשְׁיָרֵי מִנְחָה. דְּאוֹרָיְיתָא, צָרִיךְ לַכְּלִי הַכְּלִי מְצָרְפוֹ, שֶׁאֵין צָרִיךְ לַכְּלִי – אֵין כְּלִי מְצָרְפוֹ,

Rabbi Akiva's testimony is not needed to teach the basic *halakha* that a vessel combines its ingredients, which is Torah law; **it is necessary only for the remainders of the meal-offering,**[N] the part of a meal-offering left over after a fistful of it and its frankincense have been sacrificed on the altar, which is eaten by a priest. In such a case the *halakha* of combining applies only by rabbinic law, for **by Torah law** only when an item **requires a vessel** in order for it to be sanctified does **the vessel combine it** with regard to impurity, even if its parts are not touching each other. But in the case of something **that does not require a vessel,**[H] the **vessel does not combine it.** The remainder of a meal-offering no longer requires a vessel, since it is given to a priest after the fistful is sacrificed, so the flour in a vessel would not be considered combined according to Torah law.

NOTES

It is necessary only for the remainders of the meal-offering – לָא נִצְרְכָא אֶלָּא לִשְׁיָרֵי מִנְחָה: It is stated in the Jerusalem Talmud that this applies only to the remainders of the meal-offering, because even though they do not need a vessel presently, they did at a previous time, i.e., before the scooping of the fistful. Items that never required a vessel, however, cannot be subject to combining in a vessel even by rabbinic law. It is specified there that the coals combined in a vessel refers only to the coals used on Yom Kippur, which require a special pan, but not to other coals.

HALAKHA

Requires a vessel…that does not require a vessel – צָרִיךְ לַכְּלִי...שֶׁאֵין צָרִיךְ לַכְּלִי: If there are two separate items in a vessel, with a third item between them, and one of them was defiled, if the object between them is one that requires a vessel, the vessel combines them and everything is defiled. But if that object does not require a vessel, only the part that came into contact with the impurity is defiled; the impurity is not transferred throughout the vessel (Rambam *Sefer Tahara, Hilkhot She'ar Avot HaTumot* 12:8). The Ra'avad disagrees with this understanding of the *halakha*, and states that a third item does not constitute a separation between the other two, even if that item does not require a vessel. Rather, things that require a vessel are always combined by a vessel containing them. Only the object that does not need the vessel remains pure, although it is situated in the middle.

וְאָתוּ רַבָּנַן וְגָזְרוּ דְּאַף עַל גַּב דְּאֵינוֹ צָרִיךְ לִכְלִי – כְּלִי מְצָרְפוֹ.

And the Sages came and decreed that even if something **does not require a vessel,** such as the leftover flour of the meal-offering, the **vessel** nevertheless **combines it.**

תֵּינַח סֹלֶת. קְטוֹרֶת וּלְבוֹנָה מַאי אִיכָּא לְמֵימַר? אָמַר רַב נַחְמָן אָמַר רַבָּה בַּר אֲבוּהּ: כְּגוֹן שֶׁצְּבָרָן עַל גַּבֵּי קַרְטַבְלָא. דְּאוֹרָיְיתָא, יֵשׁ לוֹ תּוֹךְ מְצָרֵף, אֵין לוֹ תּוֹךְ – אֵינוֹ מְצָרֵף, וְאָתוּ רַבָּנַן וְתִיקְּנוּ דְּאַף עַל גַּב דְּאֵין לוֹ תּוֹךְ – מְצָרֵף.

The Gemara raises a difficulty: It **works out well** in the case of **flour,** which can be said to refer to the flour left over from meal-offerings, but with regard to **incense and frankincense, what is there to say?** In these cases a vessel is certainly required, but if the *halakha* of combining applies to them from the Torah, why did Rabbi Akiva include them in his list? **Rav Naḥman said** that **Rabba bar Avuh said: For example, if he piled them up on a leather board [*kartavla*],**[L] rather than in a containing vessel. **By Torah law** a vessel that **has an inside combines** its ingredients, but **one that** is flat and **does not have an inside does not combine.**[N] **And the Sages came and decreed that even if it does not have an inside it** nevertheless **combines** what is placed on it.

וּפְלִיגָא דְּרַבִּי חָנִין אַדְּרַבִּי חִיָּיא בַּר אַבָּא. דְּאָמַר רַבִּי חִיָּיא בַּר אַבָּא אָמַר רַבִּי יוֹחָנָן: מֵעֵדוּתוֹ שֶׁל רַבִּי עֲקִיבָא נִשְׁנֵית מִשְׁנָה זוֹ.

The Gemara comments: **And** this opinion **of Rabbi Ḥanin's,** that impurity by combining is derived from the Torah, **disagrees with** the opinion **of Rabbi Ḥiyya bar Abba. For Rabbi Ḥiyya bar Abba said** that **Rabbi Yoḥanan said** in reference to our mishna: **This mishna was taught based on Rabbi Akiva's testimony.** In other words, the mishna's teaching that a vessel combines its contents follows the statement of Rabbi Akiva, indicating that it is by rabbinic law, unlike Rabbi Ḥanin, who said that it is based on a source from the Torah.

״הָרְבִיעִי בְּקֹדֶשׁ פָּסוּל״. תַּנְיָא, אָמַר רַבִּי יוֹסֵי: מִנַּיִן לָרְבִיעִי בְּקֹדֶשׁ שֶׁהוּא פָּסוּל? וְדִין הוּא: וּמָה מְחוּסַּר כִּפּוּרִים שֶׁמּוּתָּר בִּתְרוּמָה – פָּסוּל בְּקֹדֶשׁ, שְׁלִישִׁי שֶׁפָּסוּל בִּתְרוּמָה – אֵינוֹ דִּין שֶׁיַּעֲשֶׂה רְבִיעִי לְקֹדֶשׁ? וְלָמַדְנוּ שְׁלִישִׁי לְקֹדֶשׁ מִן הַתּוֹרָה, וּרְבִיעִי בְּקַל וָחוֹמֶר.

§ It was taught in the mishna: **The fourth degree** of impurity, **with regard to sacrificial** food, is **disqualified.**[H] **It is taught** in a *baraita*: **Rabbi Yosei said: From where** is it derived with regard **to the fourth degree** of ritual impurity, that **with regard to sacrificial** food it **is disqualified? It is a logical derivation,** by *a fortiori*: **If one who is lacking atonement,** an impure person who is obligated to bring an offering to complete his purification process, **who is permitted to** eat ***teruma,*** is nevertheless **disqualified with regard to** the consumption of **sacrificial** food, as specified in the Torah, then concerning something that is impure to the **third** degree of ritual impurity, **which is disqualified** if it is ***teruma,* is it not right that it should engender a fourth** degree of ritual impurity when it touches **sacrificial** food? Therefore, **we have learned** that there is a **third** degree of impurity with regard **to sacrificial food from the Torah, and** that there is a **fourth** degree of impurity **from *a fortiori*** reasoning.

שְׁלִישִׁי לְקֹדֶשׁ מִן הַתּוֹרָה מִנַּיִן? דִּכְתִיב: ״וְהַבָּשָׂר אֲשֶׁר יִגַּע בְּכָל טָמֵא לֹא יֵאָכֵל״, מִי לָא עָסְקִינַן דְּנָגַע בְּשֵׁנִי – וְקָאָמַר רַחֲמָנָא: ״לֹא יֵאָכֵל״. רְבִיעִי מִקַּל וָחוֹמֶר – הָא דַּאֲמַרַן.

The above *baraita* taught that there is a **third** degree of impurity **for sacrificial** food **from the Torah.** The Gemara asks: **From where** is this derived? **As it is written: "And the meat that touches any impure thing shall not be eaten"** (Leviticus 7:19). **Is it not** so that **we are not dealing** in that verse with meat that touches any "impure thing" at all, even **if it touched** something that is of the **second** degree of ritual impurity, which is also called an "impure thing"? **And** yet **the Merciful One states** with regard to that meat, which having touched a second-degree impurity is now impure to the third degree: **"It shall not be eaten,"** meaning that it has been rendered unfit due to impurity. And as for the *baraita's* statement that the **fourth** level of impurity is derived **by an *a fortiori* inference** – it is **as we said** just above, the *a fortiori* inference put forth by Rabbi Yosei.

״וּבִתְרוּמָה אִם נִטְמֵאת״ כו׳. אָמַר רַב שֵׁיזְבִי: בְּחִיבּוּרִין שָׁנוּ, אֲבָל שֶׁלֹּא בְּחִיבּוּרִין – לֹא.

§ It was taught in the mishna: **And with regard to *teruma,* if** one of one's hands **became impure** with impurity by rabbinic law that renders only the hands impure, its counterpart, the other hand, remains pure. But with regard to sacrificial food, if one hand becomes impure he must immerse them both. **Rav Sheizevi said:** When they said that with regard to sacrificial food a hand that is rendered impure renders the other hand impure as well, **they taught** this only for a situation **when** the pure hand is **in contact**[N] with the sacrificial food when the impure hand touches it. **But** if the pure hand is **not in contact** with the sacrificial food, **no,** the pure hand is not rendered impure by touching the impure hand. According to Rav Sheizevi, the Sages enacted the decree that one hand renders the other impure because they were concerned that the impure hand may have touched the sacrificial food directly without being noticed. Therefore, the decree applies only when the pure hand is touching the sacrificial food.

LANGUAGE

Leather board [*kartavla*] – קַרְטַבְלָא: Probably derived from the Greek καταβολή, *katbolè*, meaning the laying of a foundation.

NOTES

One that is flat and does not have an inside does not combine – אֵין לוֹ תּוֹךְ, אֵינוֹ מְצָרֵף: According to the Gemara's conclusion that the entire principle of combining in a vessel is by rabbinic law, Rabbi Akiva adds that vessels combine their contents even with regard to impurity imparted by one who has immersed himself during the day, before the sun sets (*Siaḥ Yitzḥak*, based on Rabbi Ovadya MiBartenura; see *Zekher LaHagiga* for an alternative explanation of this whole discussion).

They taught this only when the pure hand is in contact – בְּחִיבּוּרִין שָׁנוּ: There are different explanations of the term: In contact, in this context. Rashi maintains that it means that the pure hand is in contact with sacrificial foods when the impure hand touches the pure hand. The Meiri, however, explains that it means that the pure hand is touching the impure hand when the latter is still in contact with the item that is making it impure. This is also how the Ramban appears to understand the Ra'avad's opinion. Rabbeinu Ḥananel, the *Ba'al HaMaor*, and the Ramban give yet another interpretation: In contact, means that the impure hand defiles the pure one only if it actually comes into contact with it, as opposed to the pure hand becoming impure automatically by virtue of the other hand's impurity. See the Ramban, who cites proofs for this opinion. This also appears to be the explanation of the *ge'onim* for this passage. The Gemara's citation of the dispute between Rabbi Yoḥanan and Reish Lakish immediately after this discussion fits in well with this opinion.

HALAKHA

The fourth degree of ritual impurity – רְבִיעִי לְטוּמְאָה: The fourth degree of ritual impurity is unfit with regard to sacrificial food, although it does not convey impurity to others items, but it is pure with regard to *teruma* (Rambam *Sefer Tahara, Hilkhot She'ar Avot HaTumot* 12:11).

NOTES

A dry hand – **יָד נְגוּבָה**: The *Ba'al HaMaor* explains the term dry hand here to mean a single hand that has not been immersed and is therefore still impure, as opposed to a hand that has been immersed, removing its impurity. See the Meiri, who notes that the Rambam's ruling seems to combine several different interpretations of this passage.

They taught that one hand renders the other impure only if it is his own hand, etc. – לֹא שָׁנוּ אֶלָּא יָדוֹ וכו׳: Many early commentaries interpret these words, or they may even have a textual reading that states explicitly, that one hand defiles the other only if they are in contact, referring to Rabbeinu Ḥananel's explanation of that expression cited earlier. Based on this interpretation, they infer that the *halakha* follows Rav Sheizevi, as it emerges that both Reish Lakish and Rabbi Yoḥanan agree with his opinion (Rabbeinu Ḥananel; *ge'onim*; see Ramban). However, according to those explanations that understand: In contact, differently, as cited above, it is clear that the dispute of Rabbi Yoḥanan and Reish Lakish is not related to Rav Sheizevi's statement.

HALAKHA

A dry hand – **יָד שֶׁאֵינָהּ נְגוּבָה**: The Rambam (*Sefer Tahara, Hilkhot She'ar Avot HaTumot* 12:12) states that if one of one's hands is impure and wet, the other hand becomes impure as well, even if the two hands did not touch at all, and they must both be purified before touching sacrificial food. The Ra'avad, however, holds that the wet hand must touch the other one in order to render it impure.

אֵיתִיבֵיהּ אַבָּיֵי: יָד נְגוּבָה – מְטַמְּאָה חֲבֵירְתָּהּ, לְטַמֵּא לַקֹּדֶשׁ, אֲבָל לֹא לִתְרוּמָה, דִּבְרֵי רַבִּי. רַבִּי יוֹסֵי בְּרַבִּי יְהוּדָה אוֹמֵר: לִפְסוֹל, אֲבָל לֹא לְטַמֵּא.

Abaye raised an objection to Rav Sheizevi from the following teaching: Even **a dry hand**[N] that is impure **renders its counterpart,** i.e., the other hand, **impure, to** the extent that the second hand will now **render impure** any food that it touches.[H] This is true with regard **to sacrificial** food **but not** with regard **to *teruma*.** This is **the statement of Rabbi** Yehuda HaNasi. **Rabbi Yosei, son of Rabbi Yehuda, says:** The second hand is not rendered impure to such a severe extent. It can merely **disqualify** sacrificial food that it touches, by rendering it impure to the fourth degree, **but not render** it **impure** with third-degree impurity.

אִי אָמְרַתְּ בִּשְׁלָמָא שֶׁלֹּא בְּחִיבּוּרִין – הַיְינוּ רְבוּתֵיהּ דִּנְגוּבָה. אֶלָּא אִי אָמְרַתְּ בְּחִיבּוּרִין אִין, שֶׁלֹּא בְּחִיבּוּרִין לָא – מַאי רְבוּתָא דִּנְגוּבָה?

Granted, if you say that the second hand becomes impure even **when it is not in contact** with the sacrificial food, **this** would explain **the noteworthiness of a dry** hand rendering its counterpart impure. It teaches that even though normally a dry hand would not render another hand impure, the Sages nevertheless declared it impure with regard to sacrificial food. **But if you say** that when the second hand is **in contact** with sacrificial food, **yes,** the decree that the second hand becomes impure applies, lest the impure hand touch the sacrificial food directly, but **when it is not in contact, no,** the decree does not apply, then **what is the noteworthiness** of stating that it applies in the case of a **dry** hand?

אִיתְּמַר נָמֵי, אָמַר רֵישׁ לָקִישׁ: לֹא שָׁנוּ אֶלָּא יָדוֹ,

It was also stated that *amora'im* disputed a similar issue: **Reish Lakish said: They taught** that one hand renders the other impure **only** if the second hand is **his** own **hand,**[N]

Perek **III**
Daf **24** Amud **b**

HALAKHA

One hand renders its counterpart impure – **יָד מְטַמְּאָה חֲבֵירְתָּהּ**: If one whose hand was impure by rabbinic law touches his other hand or that of another person, it confers third-degree impurity on that other hand. He should therefore not touch sacrificial food with that second hand, in accordance with Rabbi Yoḥanan and Reish Lakish (Rambam *Sefer Tahara, Hilkhot She'ar Avot HaTumot* 12:12).

אֲבָל יַד חֲבֵירוֹ לֹא. וְרַבִּי יוֹחָנָן אָמַר: אֶחָד יָדוֹ וְאֶחָד יַד חֲבֵירוֹ, בְּאוֹתָהּ הַיָּד, לִפְסוֹל אֲבָל לֹא לְטַמֵּא.

but an impure hand does **not** render impure **the hand of another. And Rabbi Yoḥanan said:** An impure hand renders another hand impure **whether it is his** own **hand or the hand of another,** provided the second hand is touched **by the same hand** that came into contact with the impurity. Moreover, the impure hand affects the food it touches only **to disqualify** it, **but not to render** it **impure.**

מִמַּאי? מִדְּקָתָנֵי סֵיפָא: שֶׁהַיָּד מְטַמְּאָה חֲבֵירְתָּהּ לַקֹּדֶשׁ, אֲבָל לֹא לִתְרוּמָה. הָא תּוּ לָמָּה לִי? הָא תָּנָא לֵיהּ רֵישָׁא! אֶלָּא לָאו שְׁמַע מִינַּהּ: לְאֵתוֹיֵי יַד חֲבֵירוֹ.

The Gemara elaborates on Rabbi Yoḥanan's opinion. **From where** did he learn this? **From the fact that it teaches in a latter clause** in the mishna: **For one renders its counterpart,** i.e., the other hand, **impure**[H] with regard **to sacrificial** food **but not** with regard **to *teruma*. Why do I need this** phrase **as well? It was** already **taught in the first clause** that one hand renders the other hand impure with regard to sacrificial food. **Rather,** must one **not conclude from** this added phrase that it comes **to include** the rendering impure of **the hand of another** as well as his own other hand?

וְאַף רֵישׁ לָקִישׁ הֲדַר בֵּיהּ, דְּאָמַר רַבִּי יוֹנָה אָמַר רַבִּי אַמֵּי אָמַר רֵישׁ לָקִישׁ: אֶחָד יָדוֹ וְאֶחָד יַד חֲבֵירוֹ, בְּאוֹתָהּ הַיָּד – לִפְסוֹל אֲבָל לֹא לְטַמֵּא.

The Gemara observes: **And Reish Lakish, too, retracted** his own opinion in favor of Rabbi Yoḥanan's opinion. For **Rabbi Yona said** that **Rabbi Ami said** that **Reish Lakish said:** The decree that one hand renders another impure applies **whether it is his** own **hand or the hand of another,** provided the second hand is touched **by the same hand** that came into contact with the impurity. Moreover, the impure hand affects the food it touches only **to disqualify render** it, **but not to render** it **impure.**

וְלִפְסוֹל אֲבָל לֹא לְטַמֵּא תַּנָּאֵי הִיא. דִּתְנַן: כָּל הַפּוֹסֵל בִּתְרוּמָה – מְטַמֵּא יָדַיִם לִהְיוֹת שְׁנִיּוֹת, וְיַד מְטַמֵּא חֲבֶירְתָּהּ, דִּבְרֵי רַבִּי יְהוֹשֻׁעַ. וַחֲכָמִים אוֹמְרִים: יָדַיִם שְׁנִיּוֹת הֵן, וְאֵין שֵׁנִי עוֹשֶׂה שֵׁנִי בְּחוּלִּין.

The Gemara comments: **And** this opinion, that an impure hand affects the sacrificial food only **to disqualify** it **but not to render** it **impure, is** a dispute between ***tanna'im*****. As we learned** in a mishna (*Yadayim* 3:2): **Anything that disqualifies *teruma*** by contact with it, i.e., anything that is impure at least to the second degree, **renders the hands impure** to the **second** degree. **And** furthermore, **a hand** that is impure to the second degree **renders its counterpart,** the other hand, **impure;** this is **the statement of Rabbi Yehoshua. But the Rabbis say: Hands** themselves **are** impure to the **second** degree,[H] **and** that which is impure to the **second** degree **cannot impart** second-degree impurity to something else **with regard to non-sacred** food.

מַאי לָאו – שֵׁנִי הוּא דְּלָא עָבֵיד, הָא שְׁלִישִׁי – עָבֵיד!

From the Rabbis' response to Rabbi Yehoshua it is clear that the latter's opinion is that the second hand is indeed rendered impure to the second degree, imparting third-degree impurity to sacrificial food that it touches. Moreover: **What, is it not** correct to infer from the Rabbis' words that **it is** impurity to the **second** degree **that** the first hand **does not impart** to for the second hand by touching it, **but** impurity to the **third** degree it **does impart** to the second hand? The second hand would thus only disqualify the sacrificial food that it touches by imparting to it a fourth-degree impurity. Therefore, the Rabbis and Rabbi Yehoshua are arguing about this very point: Does the second hand only disqualify sacrificial food by imparting to it fourth-degree impurity, or does it render the food impure with third-degree impurity?

דִּלְמָא לָא שֵׁנִי עָבֵיד, וְלֹא שְׁלִישִׁי.

The Gemara rejects this proof: **Perhaps** the Rabbis meant that the first hand does **not impart** impurity to the second hand to **either the second or the third** degree, for in their opinion one impure hand does not defile the other hand at all, in contradiction to the mishna, whereas the opinion expressed in the mishna would be following Rabbi Yehoshua.

אֶלָּא כִּי הָנֵי תַּנָּאֵי, דְּתַנְיָא: יָד נְגוּבָה מְטַמָּא אֶת חֲבֶירְתָּהּ לְטַמֵּא בַּקֹּדֶשׁ, אֲבָל לֹא לִתְרוּמָה, דִּבְרֵי רַבִּי. רַבִּי יוֹסֵי בְּרַבִּי יְהוּדָה אוֹמֵר: אוֹתָהּ יָד לִפְסוֹל, אֲבָל לֹא לְטַמֵּא.

Rather, the issue of which degree of impurity is imparted to the second hand is **like** the following dispute between ***tanna'im*****, as it is taught** in the *baraita* cited earlier: Even **a dry hand** that is impure **renders its counterpart,** i.e., the other hand, **impure to** the extent that the second hand will now **render impure** food that it touches. This is true with regard **to sacrificial** food **but not** with regard **to *teruma*.** This is **the statement of Rabbi** Yehuda HaNasi. **Rabbi Yosei, son of Rabbi Yehuda, says: The** second **hand** is not rendered impure to such a severe extent. It can merely **disqualify** sacrificial food that it touches, by making it impure to the fourth degree, **but not render** it **impure** to the third degree.

"אוֹכְלִין אוֹכָלִים נְגוּבִין בְּיָדַיִם מְסוֹאָבוֹת" כו׳. תַּנְיָא, אָמַר רַבִּי חֲנִינָא בֶּן אַנְטִיגְנוֹס: וְכִי יֵשׁ נְגוּבָה לַקֹּדֶשׁ? וַהֲלֹא חִיבַּת הַקֹּדֶשׁ מַכְשַׁרְתָּן!

§ It was taught in the mishna: **One may eat dry** foods, i.e., foods that have never been wetted and are thus not susceptible to impurity, **with impure hands** in the case of *teruma*, but not in the case of sacrificial food. **It is taught** in a *baraita* that there is a difficulty with this statement of the mishna: **Rabbi Ḥanina ben Antigonus said: Now, is there** such a possibility as **dry** food, i.e., food that is not susceptible to impurity, with regard **to sacrificial** food? **Is it not so that the reverence** accorded **to sacrificial** food itself **renders it fit** to contract impurity[N] even if it has never been in contact with liquid at all? All sacrificial food is thus automatically susceptible to impurity, and whether it is dry, i.e., it has never been wetted, or not is irrelevant.

לָא צְרִיכָא כְּגוֹן שֶׁתָּחַב לוֹ חֲבֵירוֹ לְתוֹךְ פִּיו, אוֹ שֶׁתָּחַב הוּא לְעַצְמוֹ בְּכוּשׁ וּבְכַרְכַּר, וּבִיקֵּשׁ לֶאֱכוֹל צְנוֹן וּבָצָל שֶׁל חוּלִּין עִמָּהֶן.

The Gemara answers: **No,** it is **necessary** for the mishna to state this. And the case is not one of dry sacrificial food, as was first assumed. Rather, the mishna is dealing with a case in **which, for example, his friend inserted** sacrificial food or *teruma* **into his mouth, or,** alternatively, a case in **which he inserted** it **into his own** mouth **by** means of **a spindle or whorl,**[NB] which are wooden vessels without receptacles that cannot contract impurity. In either event the food arrives in his mouth without being rendered impure by his impure hands. **And** then, while the sacrificial food or *teruma* is still in his mouth, he **wishes to** put into his mouth and **eat a non-sacred radish or onion along with them.**

HALAKHA

Hands are impure to the second degree – **יָדַיִם שְׁנִיּוֹת הֵן**: The Sages decreed that when hands become impure it is always to the second degree (Rambam *Sefer Tahara, Hilkhot She'ar Avot HaTumot* 8:2).

NOTES

Is it not so that the reverence accorded to sacrificial food renders it fit to contract impurity – **וַהֲלֹא חִיבַּת הַקֹּדֶשׁ מַכְשַׁרְתָּן**: The question is asked: Perhaps the mishna means to tell us just this, that sacrificial food, unlike *teruma*, requires no wetting to make it susceptible to impurity. What, then, is the problem that Rabbi Ḥanina ben Antigonus is raising here? Some commentaries explain that he means to say that the *halakhot* of purity that stem from the reverence accorded to sacrificial food do not belong to the list of stringencies stated in the mishna, as that list consists of rabbinic stringencies, whereas Rabbi Ḥanina maintains that the reverence accorded to sacrificial food renders it fit to contract impurity by Torah law (*Rishon LeTziyyon*). *Yad David* explains that Rabbi Ḥanina means that if the basic reason for the *halakha* of the mishna were due to the reverence accorded sacrificial food, this should have been stated more clearly by the mishna. Rather, Rabbi Ḥanina deduced, the mishna must be referring to a stringency that is over and beyond the concept of reverence sacrificial food is accorded.

He inserted it…by means of a spindle or whorl – **תָּחַב...בְּכוּשׁ וּבְכַרְכַּר**: Although, as the Gemara teaches in tractate *Ḥullin* (107a), it is generally prohibited to allow someone to put food in one's mouth if the person eating has not washed his hands, lest the eater touch it inadvertently, placing food in another's mouth by means of a whorl or spindle is an unusual manner of eating, and would serve as a reminder to the eater that he must not touch the food with impure hands. A problem would arise only if he decided to add a non-sacred onion or radish afterward, in which case there is a concern that while doing so he might touch the sacrificial food in his mouth (*Turei Aven*).

BACKGROUND

Spindle or whorl – **כּוּשׁ וְכַרְכַּר**: A whorl is a circular weight used to balance a spindle while spinning wool. Below is an image of an ancient spindle with two whorls.

Ancient spindle and whorls

לַקֹּדֶשׁ – גָּזְרוּ בְּהוּ רַבָּנַן, לַתְּרוּמָה – לֹא גָּזְרוּ בְּהוּ רַבָּנַן.

Non-sacred food is not rendered impure by being touched with impure hands, so it should not be problematic to put a radish or onion into one's mouth with his hands. However, **regarding sacrificial food the Sages enacted a decree against** doing so, lest the person inadvertently touch the sacrificial food in his mouth with his impure hand. This decree, the mishna teaches, applies only to sacrificial food, **but in** a case in which he had ***teruma*** in his mouth **the Sages did not enact a decree against it.**[H]

"הָאוֹנֵן וּמְחוּסַּר כִּפּוּרִים" כו׳. מַאי טַעְמָא? כֵּיוָן דְּעַד הָאִידָּנָא הֲווּ אֲסִירִי – אַצְרְכִינְהוּ רַבָּנַן טְבִילָה.

§ It was taught in the mishna: **An acute mourner and one who is lacking atonement**[N] require immersion[H] in order to eat sacrificial food, but this is not necessary for *teruma*. The Gemara explains: **What is the reason** for this decree? **Since until now it was prohibited** for **them** to partake of sacrificial food and they therefore might not have guarded themselves properly from impurity, **the Sages required them** to undergo **immersion** before eating sacrificial food.

מתני׳ חוֹמֶר בַּתְּרוּמָה, שֶׁבִּיהוּדָה נֶאֱמָנִין עַל טׇהֳרַת יַיִן וָשֶׁמֶן כׇּל יְמוֹת הַשָּׁנָה, וּבִשְׁעַת הַגִּיתּוֹת וְהַבַּדִּים – אַף עַל הַתְּרוּמָה.

MISHNA The previous mishna listed stringencies that apply to sacrificial food but not to *teruma*. However, there are also **stringencies** that apply **to *teruma*** over sacrificial food: **In Judea** all people, even people who are not generally meticulous in their observance of the *halakhot* of ritual purity [*amei ha'aretz*], **are trusted with regard to the purity of** consecrated **wine and oil**[N] throughout **all the days of the year. And during the period of the winepress and olive press,** when grapes and olives are pressed and made into wine and oil, respectively, they are trusted **even with regard to** the purity of ***teruma***, as all people, including *amei ha'aretz*, purify their vessels for this season.[H]

עָבְרוּ הַגִּיתּוֹת וְהַבַּדִּים וְהֵבִיאוּ לוֹ חָבִית שֶׁל יַיִן שֶׁל תְּרוּמָה – לֹא יְקַבְּלֶנָּה מִמֶּנּוּ, אֲבָל מַנִּיחָהּ לַגַּת הַבָּאָה. וְאִם אָמַר לוֹ: הִפְרַשְׁתִּי לְתוֹכָהּ רְבִיעִית קֹדֶשׁ – נֶאֱמָן.

But once **the** periods of the **winepress and olive press have passed,** if *amei ha'aretz* **brought to him,** i.e., to a priest who is meticulous concerning the *halakhot* of ritual purity [*ḥaver*], a **barrel of *teruma* wine, he may not accept it from them,** as *amei ha'aretz* are not trusted with regard to matters of ritual purity during the rest of the year. **But** the giver **may leave it** over **for the following winepress** season, in the following year, at which point the *ḥaver* priest may accept it from him, although it was prohibited for him to accept the same barrel beforehand. **And if** the giver **said to** the priest: **I separated** and placed **into** this barrel of *teruma* **a quarter-*log* of sacrificial** wine or oil, **he is trusted** with regard to the entire contents of the barrel. Since an *am ha'aretz* is trusted with regard to the purity of sacrificial food, he is also believed with regard to *teruma* that is mingled with the sacrificial food.[H]

כַּדֵּי יַיִן וְכַדֵּי שֶׁמֶן

With regard to **jugs of wine and jugs of oil**

HALAKHA

Eating food that has not been rendered susceptible to impurity – אֲכִילַת אוֹכָלִים שֶׁלֹּא הוּכְשְׁרוּ לְטוּמְאָה: It is permitted to eat with impure hands *teruma* that has never been made susceptible to impurity, but one may not do so with sacrificial food, as the reverence accorded to sacrificial food renders it susceptible to impurity automatically. Even if he does not touch the sacrificial food with his hands at all but merely eats it with a utensil, it is nevertheless prohibited (Rambam *Sefer Tahara, Hilkhot She'ar Avot HaTumot* 12:13).

An acute mourner and one who is lacking atonement require immersion – אוֹנֵן וּמְחוּסַּר כִּפּוּרִים צְרִיכִים טְבִילָה: An acute mourner after his period of acute mourning has ended and one who had been lacking atonement after he has brought his offering are both permitted to eat *teruma* immediately, but before they partake of sacrificial foods they must immerse (Rambam *Sefer Tahara, Hilkhot She'ar Avot HaTumot* 12:15).

Trustworthiness of *amei ha'aretz* regarding sacrificial food – נֶאֱמָנוּת עַמֵּי הָאָרֶץ בְּקָדָשִׁים: *Amei ha'aretz* are trusted with regard to the purity of wine and oil prepared for sacrificial purposes, and it is permissible to rely upon them if they say they are pure. They are likewise trusted with regard to purity of *teruma* during the seasons of the winepress and the olive press (Rambam *Sefer Tahara, Hilkhot Metamei Mishkav UMoshav* 11:1).

If they brought him a barrel of *teruma* – הֵבִיאוּ לוֹ חָבִית תְּרוּמָה: If an *am ha'aretz* brought a barrel of *teruma* wine or oil to a *ḥaver* priest, the latter may not accept it from him, as it is assumed to be impure. However, if he said that he added into the barrel a quarter-*log* of sacrificial wine or oil, he is believed regarding its purity, and one may take it from him (Rambam *Sefer Tahara, Hilkhot Metamei Mishkav UMoshav* 11:2, 4).

NOTES

An acute mourner and one who is lacking atonement, etc. – הָאוֹנֵן וּמְחוּסַּר כִּפּוּרִים וכו׳: The reference is to an acute mourner after his period of acute mourning has ended, and to one who had been lacking atonement after he has brought his offering, as the Torah explicitly states that they may not eat offerings before this stage. They are required to immerse in case they have not properly preserved themselves in a state of purity. The question of why they are not considered impure even with regard to *teruma*, seeing as the reason is due to insufficient attention to impurity, is addressed in the Jerusalem Talmud. See Rashi, who notes that *teruma* may be eaten by an acute mourner and one who is lacking atonement. Accordingly, it could be argued that with regard to eating *teruma* there was no time in which one could drop his guard against impurity for *teruma*.

All people are trusted with regard to the purity of consecrated wine and oil – נֶאֱמָנִין עַל טׇהֳרַת יַיִן וָשֶׁמֶן: The Rambam explains that even *amei ha'aretz* were careful to maintain strict standards of purity for sacrificial food. Therefore, anyone who prepares wine or oil for sacrificial purposes is believed when he claims to have maintained the requisite level of purity. During the periods of the winepress and the olive press, people would also purify themselves properly, but this care would not extend beyond those periods. However, the Meiri and others imply that the reason for this lenient ruling is similar to that of the general leniency with regard to *amei ha'aretz* and offerings mentioned earlier (22a), i.e., that since everyone comes to a single Temple, the Sages were concerned lest the *am ha'aretz* feel offended that his offering is rejected, leading to ill will and schisms within Israel.

הַמְדוּמָּעוֹת – נֶאֱמָנִין עֲלֵיהֶם בִּשְׁעַת הַגִּיתּוֹת וְהַבַּדִּים, וְקוֹדֶם לַגִּיתּוֹת שִׁבְעִים יוֹם.

that are mingled, *amei ha'aretz* **are trusted with regard to them during the period of the winepress and the olive press, and** also up to **seventy days before the winepress,** for that is when people begin to purify their vessels in preparation for the wine-pressing season.

גמ׳ בִּיהוּדָה – אִין, וּבַגָּלִיל – לָא. מַאי טַעְמָא?

GEMARA The mishna teaches that *amei ha'aretz* are trusted with regard to the purity of sacrificial wine and oil in Judea. The Gemara infers: **In Judea, yes, but in the Galilee, no. What is the reason** for this distinction between the two places?

אָמַר רֵישׁ לָקִישׁ: מִפְּנֵי שֶׁרְצוּעָה שֶׁל כּוּתִים מַפְסֶקֶת בֵּינֵיהֶן.

Reish Lakish said: It is **because a strip** of land inhabited **by Samaritans** [*Kutim*][B] **separates**[N] **between** Judea and the Galilee, and it is impossible to travel from one land to the other without traversing this strip. The Sages decreed that lands inhabited by non-Jewish nations[N] are considered ritually impure, so that it would be impossible to transport food from the Galilee to Judea, where the Temple is located, without the food becoming impure. Therefore, even oil and wine prepared by *ḥaverim* who lived in the Galilee were not accepted for sacrificial use.

וְנֵיתֵיב בִּשִׁידָּה תֵּיבָה וּמִגְדָּל! הָא מַנִּי? רַבִּי הִיא, דְּאָמַר: אֹהֶל זָרוּק לָאו שְׁמֵיהּ אֹהֶל. דְּתַנְיָא: הַנִּכְנָס לְאֶרֶץ הָעַמִּים בְּשִׁידָּה תֵּיבָה וּמִגְדָּל, רַבִּי מְטַמֵּא, וְרַבִּי יוֹסֵי בְּרַבִּי יְהוּדָה מְטַהֵר.

The Gemara raises a difficulty: **And let** the residents of the Galilee **place** the wine and oil and transport it to Judea **in a** closed **box, a chest, or a closet,** whose contents cannot contract impurity, as they have the status of separate tents. The Gemara answers: In accordance with **whose** opinion **is this** mishna? **It is** in accordance with the opinion of **Rabbi** Yehuda HaNasi, **who said: A thrown tent,** i.e., a moving tent, **is not called** a proper **tent,**[N] and therefore its contents are subject to impurity. In our case, then, the contents would contract the impurity decreed upon the lands of non-Jewish nations. **As it is taught** in a *baraita*: Concerning **one who enters a land of non-Jewish nations** sitting **in a box,**[H] **a chest, or a closet, Rabbi** Yehuda HaNasi **declares** him to be **impure, and Rabbi Yosei, son of Rabbi Yehuda, declares** him to be **pure.**

וְלַיְיתוּהּ בִּכְלִי חֶרֶס הַמּוּקָּף צָמִיד פָּתִיל! אָמַר רַבִּי אֱלִיעֶזֶר: שׁוֹנִין, אֵין הַקֹּדֶשׁ נִיצּוֹל בְּצָמִיד פָּתִיל.

The Gemara raises a further difficulty: **And let them bring** oil and wine to the Temple **in an earthenware vessel sealed** with **a tightly bound cover,** which cannot contract impurity even if it is in the same tent as a corpse, as it states: "And every open vessel, which has no covering tightly bound upon it, is unclean" (Numbers 19:15). **Rabbi Eliezer said:** The Sages **taught** in a *baraita*: **Sacrificial** food, unlike other items, **is not spared** from impurity **by** being in a container with **a tightly bound cover.**[NH]

NOTES

A strip of land inhabited by Samaritans separates – רְצוּעָה שֶׁל כּוּתִים מַפְסֶקֶת: The question is raised: If so, how did the inhabitants of the Galilee ever make the Festival pilgrimage to Jerusalem? One answer is that they would arrive seven days before the Festival and purify themselves from the impurity of the dead before the onset of the Festival (*Sha'ar Efrayim*; *Turei Aven*). Others maintain that during the time of the Temple the Samaritan strip did not completely separate the two areas, so that it was possible to travel from one land to the other in purity (see *Siaḥ Yitzḥak*; *Zekher LaḤagiga*).

Lands inhabited by non-Jewish nations – אֶרֶץ הָעַמִּים: The basic idea behind the principle that the lands of the non-Jewish nations, which include every place outside Eretz Yisrael, are impure is found in various forms in the Bible itself (see Amos 7:17). The Sages, however, took this concept a step further and decreed that the impurity of lands of non-Jewish nations can also include parts of Eretz Yisrael, and that they should be considered on the level of impurity imparted by a corpse. The main reason for this is that they were concerned that a body might be buried in any place, even outside of a cemetery. It remains a matter of dispute elsewhere in the Gemara whether it is only the earth of non-Jewish lands that defiles or its airspace as well.

A thrown tent is not called a proper tent – אֹהֶל זָרוּק לָאו שְׁמֵיהּ אֹהֶל: The Rid writes that whether or not a moving tent can protect the one inside it from impurity depends in part on the dispute mentioned in the previous note concerning the airspace of non-Jewish lands, as according to the opinion that even the airspace of these lands causes defilement, this would certainly apply even to a moving tent. However, according to the opinion that it is only the earth of these lands that causes impurity, it can be debated, as it is in the Gemara, whether or not a portable tent can be considered a tent in order to spare what is inside it from contracting impurity.

Sacrificial food is not spared from impurity by a tightly bound cover – אֵין הַקֹּדֶשׁ נִיצּוֹל בְּצָמִיד פָּתִיל: The *Turei Aven* notes that the discussion here indicates that not only foods that have already been consecrated, but even regular produce contained inside such a vessel are not spared from impurity by a tightly bound cover.

BACKGROUND

A strip of land inhabited by Samaritans – רְצוּעָה שֶׁל כּוּתִים: The Kutim, or Samaritans, a group of people of questionable Jewishness, lived in Samaria, in the area adjacent to Shechem. This area was not fully defined politically, and the area of territory containing a heavy Samaritan population changed over time. During the Hasmonean period this strip of land dwindled significantly, while at other times the Samaritans broadened their settlements to a great extent. This strip effectively reached the coastal plains during certain eras, thus forming a Samaritan buffer between the two main Jewish settlements, Judea and the Galilee. When the Sages decreed that Samaritans should be considered gentiles, this meant that there was a strip of land belonging to a non-Jewish nation running right through the middle of Eretz Yisrael, thereby preventing the transfer of objects in purity from the Galilee to Judea.

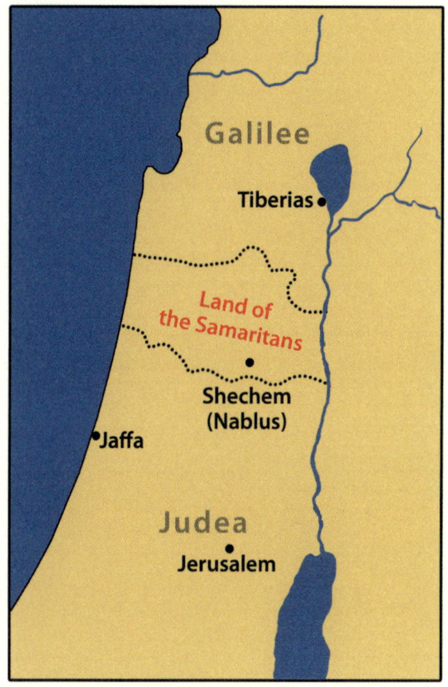

Strip of land inhabited by Samaritans

HALAKHA

One who enters a land of non-Jewish nations in a box, etc. – הַנִּכְנָס לְאֶרֶץ הָעַמִּים בְּשִׁידָּה וכו׳: One who enters the land of non-Jewish nations in a box, a chest, or a closet that does not touch the ground is nevertheless impure, for a moving tent is not considered a tent, as the *halakha* follows Rabbi Yehuda HaNasi rather than any one of his colleagues (Rambam *Sefer Tahara*, *Hilkhot Tumat Met* 11:5).

Sacrificial food is not spared from impurity by a tightly bound cover – אֵין הַקֹּדֶשׁ נִיצּוֹל בְּצָמִיד פָּתִיל: Sacrificial food and drink are not spared from impurity when placed inside a tightly bound vessel. However, water or an empty vessel that has been prepared for holding the ashes of the red heifer is spared from impurity, as stated by Rabbi Eliezer (Rambam *Sefer Tahara*, *Hilkhot Para Aduma* 14:4).

HALAKHA

Water of purification is not spared from impurity by a tightly bound cover – אֵין חַטָּאת נִיצֶּלֶת בְּצָמִיד פָּתִיל: If a vessel containing ashes of purification or water of purification is tightly bound and located inside a tent containing a corpse, the ashes and water are impure (Rambam *Sefer Tahara, Hilkhot Para Aduma* 14:3).

וְהָתַנְיָא: אֵין חַטָּאת נִיצֶּלֶת בְּצָמִיד פָּתִיל. מַאי לָאו, הָא קֹדֶשׁ נִיצּוֹל! לֹא, הָא מַיִם שֶׁאֵינָן מְקוּדָּשִׁים נִיצּוֹלִין בְּצָמִיד פָּתִיל.

The Gemara asks: **But isn't it taught** in a *baraita*: Water of **purification** containing ashes from the red heifer **is not spared** from impurity **by** being in a vessel with **a tightly bound cover?**[HN] **What, is it not** implied in the *baraita* **this** inference: That **sacrificial** food **is spared** from impurity in such a situation? The *baraita* seems to imply that this is a special stringency for water of purification, which does not apply to anything else, including sacrificial food. The Gemara rejects this: **No,** the *baraita's* inference should be understood differently, as **this: Water that has not** yet **been consecrated** by being mixed with ashes of the red heifer **is spared** from impurity **by** being in a vessel with **a tightly bound cover,** even if they are designated for such a use at a later stage.

וְהָאָמַר עוּלָּא: חַבְרַיָּיא מְדַכַּן בְּגָלִילָא! מַנִּיחִין, וְלִכְשֶׁיָּבֹא אֵלִיָּהוּ וִיטַהֲרֶנָּה.

The Gemara raises another difficulty: **But didn't Ulla say:** *Ḥaverim* **purify** their wine and oil, i.e., they produce their wine and oil by the standards of purity used for sacrificial food **in the Galilee,**[N] to be used for sacrificial purposes? This indicates that there must have been some way of transporting them from the Galilee to the Temple, for otherwise why would they have prepared such items? The Gemara answers: Indeed, they could not transfer these items to the Temple. Rather, they would **leave** them in their place, **and** their thought was that **when Elijah comes** in messianic times and **purifies** the road from Galilee to Judea, these items will become eligible for use.

״וּבִשְׁעַת הַגִּיתּוֹת נֶאֱמָנִין אַף עַל הַתְּרוּמָה״. וּרְמִינְהִי: הַגּוֹמֵר זֵיתָיו – יְשַׁיֵּיר קוּפָּה אַחַת, וְיִתְּנֶנָּה לַעֲנִי כֹּהֵן!

§ It was taught in the mishna: **And during the period of the winepress** and olive press, *amei ha'aretz* **are trusted even with regard to** the purity of *teruma.* **And** the Gemara **raises a contradiction** from the following teaching: An *am ha'aretz* **who finishes** pressing **his olives should leave over one sack** of unpressed olives, **and give it to a poor priest**[N] as *teruma,* so that the priest himself can make ritually pure oil from it. This shows that even during the period of the olive press the *am ha'aretz* is not trusted to make pure olive oil himself.

אָמַר רַב נַחְמָן: לָא קַשְׁיָא: הָא – בְּחָרְפֵי, הָא – בְּאַפְלֵי. אֲמַר לֵיהּ רַב אַדָּא בַּר אַהֲבָה: כְּגוֹן מַאי? כְּאוֹתָן שֶׁל בֵּית אָבִיךָ.

Rav Naḥman said: This is **not difficult. This** case of the mishna, where *amei ha'aretz* are trusted to produce pure olive oil themselves, is referring **to** people who press their olives **early,** during the regular season of the olive press, while **that** case is referring **to** those who press their olives **later,** after the period when most people press their olives has passed. **Rav Adda bar Ahava said to him:** Such as **what** case, **for example?** Such **as those** olives **of your father's house.** Rav Naḥman's father had many olives, and he often pressed them after the regular pressing season.

NOTES

Water of purification is not spared from impurity by a tightly bound cover – אֵין חַטָּאת נִיצֶּלֶת בְּצָמִיד פָּתִיל: The *Sifrei* derives this from the verse that states the ashes of the red heifer must be "in a pure place" (Numbers 19:9), which is not applicable to a tent containing a corpse. The Rambam cites this source as well.

***Ḥaverim* purify their wine and oil in the Galilee** – חַבְרַיָּיא מְדַכַּן בְּגָלִילָא: *Tosefot Rid* explains that there was a supply of red heifer ashes in the Galilee, which had been brought there before the Samaritan settlements made transporting them in purity impossible.

And he should give it to a poor priest – וְיִתְּנֶנָּה לַעֲנִי כֹּהֵן: The early commentaries had two versions of this text, one stating that he should give it to a poor [*le'ani*] priest, the other stating that he should give it before the eyes [*le'einei*] of a priest. Most prefer the second reading, which means that the *am ha'aretz* should separate a certain amount of his olives before pressing, when the priest can see for himself that they have not become susceptible to impurity, and give it to the priest as *teruma*; the priest himself would then press the olives into oil with the required standards of purity (see *Tosefot Rid*).

Rabbi Ovadya MiBartenura (*Teharot* 9:4) explains that the reading that states: To a poor priest, means that since it is only a small amount it would more likely to be given to a poor priest. The Meiri explains that since the priest prepares the wine or oil himself, if he is wealthy it will appear that he is pressing the olives as a service for the giver of the *teruma*, and it is prohibited for a priest to work in the threshing floor in order to receive his *teruma*. However, if he is poor, people will not think that he is taking the olives as *teruma*, but they will assume that he is working for the olive grower for a salary.

רַב יוֹסֵף אָמַר: בְּגָלִילָא שָׁנוּ. אֵיתִיבֵיהּ אַבַּיֵי: עֵבֶר הַיַּרְדֵּן וְהַגָּלִיל – הֲרֵי הֵן כִּיהוּדָה, נֶאֱמָנִין עַל הַיַּיִן בִּשְׁעַת הַיַּיִן, וְעַל הַשֶּׁמֶן בִּשְׁעַת הַשֶּׁמֶן. אֲבָל לֹא עַל הַיַּיִן בִּשְׁעַת הַשֶּׁמֶן, וְלֹא עַל הַשֶּׁמֶן בִּשְׁעַת הַיַּיִן!

Rav Yosef said a different resolution of the above contradiction. The source that states that *amei ha'aretz* are not trusted **was taught** with **regard to the Galilee,**[N] and as the mishna taught earlier concerning sacrificial wine and oil, *amei ha'aretz* are trusted only in Judea and not in the Galilee. **Abaye raised an objection to him** from a *baraita*: **Transjordan and the Galilee are like Judea,** in that **they are trusted with regard to wine** of *teruma* **during the period of wine** production, **and with regard to oil** of *teruma* **during the period of oil** production. **However,** they are **not** trusted **with regard to wine during the period of oil** production, **nor** are they trusted **with regard to oil during the period of wine** production. This *baraita* shows that with regard to *teruma* there is no difference between the trustworthiness of *amei ha'aretz* who live in the Galilee and that of those who live in Judea.

אֶלָּא מְחַוַּורְתָּא כִּדְשָׁנִין מֵעִיקָּרָא.

Rather, Rav Yosef's answer must be rejected, and **it is clear** that the correct answer is **as we answered initially,** that it is speaking of the period following the conclusion of the winepress.

"עָבְרוּ הַגִּיתּוֹת וְהַבַּדִּים וְהֵבִיאוּ לוֹ חָבִית שֶׁל יַיִן לֹא יְקַבְּלֶנָּה הֵימֶנּוּ, אֲבָל מַנִּיחָהּ לְגַת הַבָּאָה". בָּעוּ מִינֵּיהּ מֵרַב שֵׁשֶׁת: עָבַר וְקִיבְּלָהּ, מַהוּ שֶׁיַּנִּיחֶנָּה לַגַּת הַבָּאָה? אֲמַר לְהוּ: תְּנִיתוּהָ,

§ It was taught in the mishna: Once **the** periods of the **winepress and olive press have passed,** if *amei ha'aretz* **brought to** a *ḥaver* priest a **barrel of** *teruma* **wine, he may not accept it from them. But** the giver **may leave it** over **for the following winepress** season, in the following year. **They raised a dilemma before Rav Sheshet:** If the priest **violated** the *halakha* **and did accept** the wine from an *am ha'aretz*, **what is** the *halakha*? Is it permissible **that he should leave it** over for himself **for the following winepress** season? Since it is permissible to accept the wine and oil of an *am ha'aretz* intentionally left until that time, perhaps it is also permissible if the priest himself intentionally leaves it over until that time. **He said to him: You learned it** in a mishna (*Demai* 6:9):

NOTES

The source that states that *amei ha'aretz* are not trusted was taught with regard to the Galilee – בְּגָלִילָא שָׁנוּ: *Tosafot* indicate that this answer was stated in explanation and as a continuation of Rav Naḥman's statement. Rashi, however, views it as an independent response.

Perek **III**
Daf **25** Amud **b**

חָבֵר וְעַם הָאָרֶץ שֶׁיָּרְשׁוּ אֶת אֲבִיהֶם עַם הָאָרֶץ, יָכוֹל לוֹמַר לוֹ: טוֹל אַתָּה חִטִּין שֶׁבְּמָקוֹם פְּלוֹנִי, וַאֲנִי חִטִּין שֶׁבְּמָקוֹם פְּלוֹנִי.

In the case of a **ḥaver** and an *am ha'aretz*,[N] who are brothers and **inherited** property from **their father,** who was also **an** *am ha'aretz*, the *ḥaver* **can say to** his *am ha'aretz* brother: **You take** the **wheat that is in such and such a place and I** will take the **wheat that is in such and such a place.** The *ḥaver* knows that the former batch of wheat had been made susceptible to impurity, and he would therefore have no use for it, while the latter batch had not been made susceptible to impurity.

טוֹל אַתָּה יַיִן שֶׁבְּמָקוֹם פְּלוֹנִי, וַאֲנִי יַיִן שֶׁבְּמָקוֹם פְּלוֹנִי.

The mishna continues: Similarly, the *ḥaver* brother may say to the *am ha'aretz* brother: **You take** the **wine that is in such and such a place and I** will take the **wine that is in such and such a place.** The *ḥaver* knows that the latter batch of wine has not been rendered impure, and he wants to take that batch as his share. When brothers inherit a quantity of a certain item they will each end up receiving an equal share of that item. Therefore, the principle of retroactive designation applies, meaning that it is considered that whatever portion any particular brother receives in the end is the one that had been designated for him as his inheritance from the beginning. It is not considered to be a trade or a business transaction with the other brothers in exchange for their portions.

NOTES

A *ḥaver* and an *am ha'aretz*, etc. – חָבֵר וְעַם הָאָרֶץ וכו׳: The context of this Gemara indicates that the case here is that some of the inherited produce is susceptible to impurity and some is not, and the *ḥaver* wants to receive only the produce not susceptible to impurity. However, since this mishna is found in tractate *Demai*, the Rambam and other commentaries on the Mishna explain that it involves a completely different issue, the prohibition against selling doubtfully tithed produce to an *am ha'aretz*. Since the deceased was an *am ha'aretz*, the produce that was in his possession is considered doubtfully tithed, and it would be prohibited for the *ḥaver* brother to trade any produce with his brother, for that would be tantamount to selling doubtfully tithed produce to an *am ha'aretz*.

NOTES

You take the wet and I will take the dry produce – טוֹל אַתָּה לַח וַאֲנִי יָבֵשׁ: The Meiri explains that wet and dry produce differ in price, and therefore they are considered like two separate commodities, similar to wheat and barley.

That *ḥaver* must burn the wet produce – אוֹתוֹ חָבֵר שׂוֹרֵף הַלַּח: The reference is to *teruma* or to non-sacred produce that is being kept pure according to the standard of *teruma*. Since the *teruma* of an *am ha'aretz* is considered impure, all the produce that is susceptible to impurity must be burnt (Meiri).

HALAKHA

Dividing an inheritance with an *am ha'aretz* – חֲלֻקַּת יְרוּשַּׁת עַם הָאָרֶץ: If a *ḥaver* and an *am ha'aretz* who are brothers inherit property from their *am ha'aretz* father, the *ḥaver* can say: You take the wheat from that place, or: You take the wine from there, leaving the *ḥaver* to take a different portion that he knows is pure. They may not, however, divide it up so that he takes dry produce instead of wet, and the like (Rambam *Sefer Zera'im*, *Hilkhot Ma'aser* 11:6).

A person may blow at the ground of a *beit haperas*, etc. – מְנַפֵּחַ אָדָם בֵּית הַפְּרָס כו׳: If one has to pass through a *beit haperas* on his way to performing the paschal offering he may blow at the ground in front of him as he walks, and after passing in this manner he may partake of the paschal offering. Likewise, a *beit haperas* that has been trodden by others is considered pure for those performing the paschal offering, in accordance with the statements of Shmuel and Ulla (Rambam *Sefer Korbanot*, *Hilkhot Korban Pesaḥ* 6:8).

אֲבָל לֹא יֹאמַר לוֹ: טוֹל אַתָּה לַח וַאֲנִי יָבֵשׁ, טוֹל אַתָּה חִטִּין וַאֲנִי שְׂעוֹרִים.

The mishna continues: **But** the *ḥaver* brother **may not say to** the *am ha'aretz* brother: **You take** the **wet** produce **and I** will take the **dry** produce.[N] Nor may he say: **You take** the **wheat, and I** will take the **barley.**[H] The principle of retroactive designation does not apply to objects of different types. If one brother would take wheat and the other barley it would be considered a trade. And it is prohibited for a *ḥaver* to sell or transfer impure produce or produce that is susceptible to impurity to an *am ha'aretz*, who does not strictly follow the principles of purity, as this would involve the prohibition of "You shall not place a stumbling-block before the blind" (Leviticus 19:14).

וְתָנֵי עֲלַהּ: אוֹתוֹ חָבֵר שׂוֹרֵף הַלַּח וּמַנִּיחַ אֶת הַיָּבֵשׁ.

And it is taught in a *baraita* **with regard to** this mishna: If the *ḥaver* receives a share that consists of some items that are wet and some that are dry, **that *ḥaver* must burn the wet** produce[N] if it was *teruma*, as it has certainly been defiled and impure *teruma* is burned, **but he may leave the dry** produce and use it, as it can be assumed that it has not been defiled.

אַמַּאי? יַנִּיחֶנָּה לַגַּת הַבָּאָה! בְּדָבָר שֶׁאֵין לוֹ גַּת. וְיַנִּיחֶנּוּ לָרֶגֶל! בְּדָבָר שֶׁאֵינוֹ מִשְׁתַּמֵּר לָרֶגֶל.

The Gemara draws a conclusion based on this *baraita*: **Why** must he burn the wet *teruma*? **Let him leave it over until the following winepress** season, during which time *teruma* from an *am ha'aretz* is considered pure. The fact that this option is not taken into account indicates that one may not intentionally leave over *teruma* received from an *am ha'aretz* until the next winepress season, which would resolve the dilemma presented to Rav Sheshet. The Gemara rejects this proof: Here it is referring **to something that does not have a winepress,** i.e., to liquids that are never used in the Temple service, as *amei ha'aretz* are careful only with regard to liquids that may be used in the Temple service. The Gemara asks: Even so, there is another option: **And let him leave it for the** next **pilgrimage Festival,** for the mishna later teaches (26a) that *amei ha'aretz* are assumed to observe all laws of ritual purity on Festivals. The Gemara answers: It is referring **to something that would not last until the** next **pilgrimage Festival,** but which would spoil beforehand. The dilemma presented to Rav Sheshet therefore remains unresolved.

״וְאִם אָמַר הִפְרַשְׁתִּי לְתוֹכָהּ רְבִיעִית קֹדֶשׁ נֶאֱמָן״. תְּנַן הָתָם: מוֹדִין בֵּית שַׁמַּאי וּבֵית הִלֵּל שֶׁבּוֹדְקִין לְעוֹשֵׂי פֶסַח, וְאֵין בּוֹדְקִין לְאוֹכְלֵי תְרוּמָה.

§ It was taught in the mishna: **And if** the giver **says** to the priest: **I separated** and placed **into** this barrel of *teruma* **a quarter-*log* of sacrificial** wine or oil, **he is deemed credible.** The Gemara proceeds to cite a mishna in tractate *Oholot*, the discussion of which ultimately relates to this mishna here: **We learned** in a mishna **elsewhere** (*Oholot* 18:4): **Beit Shammai and Beit Hillel agree that one may examine** the ground **for those performing the paschal** offering, **but one may not examine** the ground **for those who eat *teruma*.**

מַאי בּוֹדְקִין? אָמַר רַב יְהוּדָה אָמַר שְׁמוּאֵל: מְנַפֵּחַ אָדָם בֵּית הַפְּרָס וְהוֹלֵךְ.

The Gemara asks: **What is** the meaning of: **One may examine? Rav Yehuda said** that **Shmuel said: A person may blow** at the ground of **a *beit haperas***[HL] **and walk** through it as he does so. A *beit haperas* is a patch of ground with a grave in it that was subsequently plowed over. The Sages were concerned that there might be small pieces of human bone scattered in the field, which would impart impurity to anyone moving them with his foot. Therefore, they decreed that whoever traverses such a field becomes impure. However, the Sages allowed one to pass through the field while maintaining his purity if he blows on the ground as he goes, the assumption being that any small pieces of bone would thereby be blown out of his path. This is the examination to which this mishna refers. The mishna teaches that this examination is sufficient to allow one to retain his purity as he goes to perform the paschal offering, but not to allow one to retain his purity with regard to the eating of *teruma*.

LANGUAGE

Beit haperas – בֵּית הַפְּרָס: There are different opinions with regard to the source of this term. Rashi and *Tosafot* explain that it derives from the root *p-r-s*, meaning to break up, as its impurity comes from bones broken by a plow. The Rambam indicates that it is derived from a different meaning of this root, to spread, for the impurity is spread about throughout the area. Others claim that the word is derived from the Greek πάρος, *paros*, meaning before. It also means a courtyard, in this case the yard around a grave. Yet others relate it to the Greek ἄπορος, *aporos*, a place without passage.

וְרַבִּי חִיָּיא בַּר אַבָּא מִשְּׁמֵיהּ דְּעוּלָּא אָמַר: בֵּית הַפְּרָס שֶׁנִּדַּשׁ טָהוֹר לְעוֹשֵׂי פֶּסַח, לֹא הֶעֱמִידוּ דִּבְרֵיהֶן בִּמְקוֹם כָּרֵת.

And Rabbi Ḥiyya bar Abba said in the name of Ulla: A ***beit haperas*** **that has been trodden** by passersby who have beaten a path through it **is** considered **pure for those who** are on their way to **perform the paschal** offering, as the assumption is that no more bone fragments remain on the surface of the ground. The examination referred to in the mishna, then, is referring to ascertaining whether a particular *beit haperas* has been trodden or not. The reason for this leniency is that the impure status of a *beit haperas* is only a rabbinical decree, and the Sages **did not uphold their words** decreeing the field to be impure **in a place** where this affects one's ability to perform a mitzva involving ***karet***; and failure to bring a paschal offering is punishable by *karet*.

לְאוֹכְלֵי תְרוּמָה – הֶעֱמִידוּ דִּבְרֵיהֶן בִּמְקוֹם מִיתָה.

However, with regard **to those who** wish to **eat** ***teruma*** after traversing a *beit haperas*, the Sages **did uphold their words** decreeing the field to be impure **in a place** of a sin involving the punishment of **death**[N] by God's hand. The sin of eating *teruma* in a state of impurity is punishable by death by God's hand, and the Sages were therefore strict in insisting that one not eat it after traversing a *beit haperas*.

אִיבַּעְיָא לְהוּ: בָּדַק לְפִסְחוֹ, מַהוּ שֶׁיֹּאכַל בִּתְרוּמָתוֹ? עוּלָּא אָמַר: בָּדַק לְפִסְחוֹ מוּתָּר לֶאֱכוֹל בִּתְרוּמָתוֹ. רַבָּה בַּר עוּלָּא אָמַר: בָּדַק לְפִסְחוֹ – אָסוּר לֶאֱכוֹל בִּתְרוּמָתוֹ.

A dilemma was raised before the scholars: If **one examined** a *beit haperas* **for** the purpose of bringing **his paschal** offering, **what is** the *halakha* with regard to *teruma* after he has traversed the field? Is it permissible **that he** can rely on this examination to **eat his** ***teruma*** as well, since his passage through the field has been established as not having defiled him? **Ulla said:** If he **examined** the ground **for** purposes of bringing **his paschal** offering, **he is permitted** afterward **to eat his** ***teruma***, for once he is declared pure with regard to the offerings it would be inconsistent to declare him at the same time impure with regard to *teruma*. But **Rabba bar Ulla said:** If one **examined** the ground **for** purposes of bringing **his paschal** offering, it **is prohibited** for him **to eat his** ***teruma***.

אֲמַר לֵיהּ הַהוּא סָבָא: לָא תִּפְלוֹג עֲלֵיהּ דְּעוּלָּא, דִּתְנַן כְּוָותֵיהּ: וְאִם אָמַר: הִפְרַשְׁתִּי לְתוֹכָהּ רְבִיעִית קֹדֶשׁ – נֶאֱמָן. אַלְמָא: מִדִּמְהֵימַן אַקֹּדֶשׁ – מְהֵימַן נַמִי אַתְּרוּמָה; הָכָא נַמִי: מִדִּמְהֵימַן אַפֶּסַח – מְהֵימַן נַמִי אַתְּרוּמָה.

A certain older man said to Rabba bar Ulla: **Do not argue with Ulla, as we learned** in the mishna **in accordance with his** opinion, for the mishna states: **And if** the *am ha'aretz* **says** to the priest: **I separated** and placed **into** this barrel of *teruma* **a quarter-*log*** of **sacrificial** wine or oil, **he is deemed credible. Apparently, then, once** the *am ha'aretz* **is deemed credible** with regard to the **sacrificial** items in the barrel **he is also deemed credible** with regard to the ***teruma*** in it. **Here too,** the same principle should be applied, so **once he is deemed credible** and is considered pure with regard to the **paschal** offering, **he is also deemed credible with regard to** ***teruma***.

״כַּדֵּי יַיִן וְכַדֵּי שֶׁמֶן״ כו׳. תָּנָא: אֵין נֶאֱמָנִין לֹא עַל הַקַּנְקַנִּים וְלֹא עַל הַתְּרוּמָה. קַנְקַנִּים דְּמַאי? אִי קַנְקַנִּים דְּקֹדֶשׁ – מִיגּוֹ דִּמְהֵימַן אַקֹּדֶשׁ, מְהֵימַן נַמִי אַקַּנְקַנִּים! אֶלָּא קַנְקַנִּים דִּתְרוּמָה? פְּשִׁיטָא! הָשְׁתָּא אַתְּרוּמָה לָא מְהֵימַן – אַקַּנְקַנִּים מְהֵימַן?!

§ It was taught in the mishna: Concerning **jugs of wine and jugs of oil** that are mingled, *amei ha'aretz* are deemed credible during the period of the winepress and the olive press. A Sage **taught** in a *baraita*: *Amei ha'aretz* **are not deemed credible, neither with regard to flasks**[H] **nor with regard to** ***teruma***. The Gemara asks: **Flasks of what? If** it is referring to **flasks of sacrificial** food, **since** an *am ha'aretz* **is deemed credible** concerning the **sacrificial** items it contains, he must necessarily be **deemed credible** concerning the **flasks as well. Rather,** it is referring to **flasks of** ***teruma***. But this **is obvious: Now,** if he **is not deemed credible** concerning the ***teruma*** itself, is it possible that he would be **deemed credible** concerning the **flasks** containing it?

אֶלָּא בְּרֵיקָנִים דְּקֹדֶשׁ וּבִשְׁאָר יְמוֹת הַשָּׁנָה, וּבִמְלֵאִין דִּתְרוּמָה וּבִשְׁעַת הַגִּיתּוֹת.

The Gemara answers: **Rather,** it is referring **to empty** flasks that had contained **sacrificial** food **during the rest of the days of the year,** i.e., during all the days of the year, for an *am ha'aretz* is deemed credible with regard to sacrificial food throughout the year, yet he is not deemed credible with regard to its flask once the food has been removed, **and** it is referring as well **to** flasks **full of** ***teruma*** wine **during the period of the winepress,** when they are deemed credible with regard to the *teruma* itself, but not the vessels.

NOTES

They did uphold their words in a place of death – הֶעֱמִידוּ דִּבְרֵיהֶם בִּמְקוֹם מִיתָה: The early commentaries quote a variant text of the Gemara that reads: They did uphold their words in a place where there is a positive mitzva. This would mean that since eating *teruma* is merely a positive mitzva, the Sages upheld their words decreeing that a *beit haperas* conveys impurity and preferred that the person neglect this mitzva rather than impinge on the rabbinical decree of impurity.

HALAKHA

Amei ha'aretz **are not deemed credible neither with regard to flasks – אֵין נֶאֱמָנִין לֹא עַל הַקַּנְקַנִּים:** Even during the period of the wine and olive presses, when *amei ha'aretz* are deemed credible with regard to the purity of *teruma*, they are not deemed credible to declare an empty vessel pure for *teruma*. Similarly, they are never deemed credible to say an empty vessel is pure for sacrificial food (Rambam *Sefer Tahara, Hilkhot Metamei Mishkav UMoshav* 11:4).

תְּנַן: כַּדֵּי יַיִן וְכַדֵּי שֶׁמֶן הַמְדוּמָּעוֹת. מַאי לָאו מְדוּמָּעוֹת דִּתְרוּמָה? אָמְרִי דְּבֵי רַבִּי חִיָּיא: מְדוּמָּעוֹת דְּקֹדֶשׁ.

The Gemara asks a question: **We learned** in the mishna: With regard to **jugs of wine and jugs of oil that are mingled** [*meduma*], *amei ha'aretz* are deemed credible during the period of the winepress and the olive press, and seventy days before the winepress. The Gemara asks: **What, is it not so that mingled** means that there is a mixture **of *teruma*** oil or wine in the jug, and yet the mishna states that *amei ha'aretz* are deemed credible with regard to the jugs? This would appear to contradict the ruling of the *baraita* that they are not deemed credible with regard to flasks containing *teruma*. The Gemara answers: **In the school of Rabbi Ḥiyya they say** that the mishna in fact is referring to ordinary oil or wine **mingled with sacrificial** wine or oil, so that it contains a certain amount of sacrificial liquid.

וּמִי אִיכָּא דִּימּוּעַ לַקֹּדֶשׁ? אָמְרִי דְּבֵי רַבִּי אֶלְעַאי: בִּמְטַהֵר אֶת טִבְלוֹ לִיטּוֹל מִמֶּנּוּ נְסָכִים.

The Gemara asks: **And does** the concept of *meduma* **apply to sacrificial** foods[N] at all? This term *meduma* applies only to *teruma*, not to sacrificial items. In **the school of Rabbi Elai they say** that the *halakha* of the mishna is stated **with regard to one who is keeping his** wine ***tevel***, i.e., produce from which the requisite *teruma* and tithes have not yet been separated, **in purity,** because he intends **to take** wine for **libations from it.**[H] It is therefore in a sense a mixture of sacrificial food, *teruma* and non-sacred food all in one, and accordingly the term *meduma* is applicable. The mishna is teaching that since the *am ha'aretz* is deemed credible with regard to the sacrificial food in this mixture, he is also deemed credible with regard to the *teruma* and the jugs.[N]

"קוֹדֶם לַגִּיתּוֹת שִׁבְעִים יוֹם". אָמַר אַבַּיֵי, שְׁמַע מִינָּהּ: דִּינָא הוּא דְּעִילָוֵיהּ אָרִיסָא לְמִיטְרַח אַגּוּלְפֵי שִׁבְעִים יוֹמִין מִקַּמֵּי מַעֲצַרְתָּא.

§ It is taught in the mishna that apart from the period of the winepress itself, *amei ha'aretz* are also deemed credible **seventy days before** the period of **the winepress. Abaye said:** You can **learn from here,** incidental to the laws of purity, that **the law is that a tenant** farmer in a vineyard **must make the effort** of acquiring **flasks** for the wine **seventy days before** the time of **the winepress,** for the mishna considers this amount of time the period of preparation for the pressing of grapes.

מתני׳ מִן הַמּוֹדִיעִים וְלִפְנִים – נֶאֱמָנִין עַל כְּלֵי חֶרֶס. מִן הַמּוֹדִיעִים וְלַחוּץ – אֵין נֶאֱמָנִין. כֵּיצַד? הַקַּדָּר שֶׁהוּא מוֹכֵר הַקְּדֵרוֹת נִכְנַס לִפְנִים מִן הַמּוֹדִיעִים, הוּא הַקַּדָּר וְהֵן הַקְּדֵרוֹת וְהֵן הַלּוֹקְחִין – נֶאֱמָן. יָצָא – אֵינוֹ נֶאֱמָן.

MISHNA **From Modi'im and inward** toward Jerusalem,[NB] i.e., in the area surrounding Jerusalem, up to the distance of the town of Modi'im, which is fifteen *mil* from Jerusalem, all potters, including *amei ha'aretz*, **are deemed credible with regard to** the purity of **earthenware vessels** that they have produced. Because these places supplied earthenware vessels for the people in Jerusalem, the Sages did not decree impurity for them. **From Modi'im and outward,** however, **they are not deemed credible.** The details of this ruling are specified: **How so? A potter who sells pots,** if he **entered within Modi'im** from outside it, although **the potter, and the pots,**[H] **and the customers** were all previously located outside Modi'im, where he is not deemed credible with regard to purity, **he is** now **deemed credible.** And the opposite is true of the opposite case: If the same person who was deemed credible inside **left** the boundaries of Modi'im, **he is no** longer **deemed credible.**

NOTES

And does the concept of *meduma* apply to sacrificial foods – וּמִי אִיכָּא דִּימּוּעַ לַקֹּדֶשׁ: The term *dimua* or *meduma*, mingling, is derived from a verse that is referring to *teruma*: "The fullness of your harvest, and the outflow [*dimakha*] of your presses" (Exodus 22:28), and therefore it is not a correct term for a mixture of sacrificial foods. See the Rambam's comments in his Commentary to the Mishna on the difference between the Babylonian Talmud and the Jerusalem Talmud with regard to the meaning of this statement and its implications for *halakha*.

Trustworthiness with regard to earthenware vessels – נֶאֱמָנוּת עַל כְּלֵי חֶרֶס: According to the conclusion of the Gemara that this trustworthiness refers only to vessels used for sacrificial food, the mishna should be seen as a continuation of the list of things by which *teruma* is more stringent than sacrificial food, as *amei ha'aretz* are not deemed credible with regard to such vessels for *teruma* (Meiri).

From Modi'im and inward toward Jerusalem – מִן הַמּוֹדִיעִים וְלִפְנִים: Various commentaries point out that it does not state here, as in similar cases, that this refers not only to Modi'im but to the equivalent distance in all directions, even though it seems that it would be true in this case as well (Rid). *Tosefot Yom Tov* suggests that the mishna does not mention other places for the practical reason that there was an earthenware industry in Modi'im.

BACKGROUND

From Modi'im and inward toward Jerusalem – מִן הַמּוֹדִיעִים וְלִפְנִים: The town of Modi'im in the vicinity of Lod, also referred to as Modi'in and Modi'it, is significant in several regards. A company of priests lived here, including the Hasmonean family. Modi'im served as the residence of the *tanna* Elazar the Modi'ite. Additionally, the distance between Modi'im and Jerusalem serves as the standard measurement for the concept of the "distant path" with regard to the exemption from bringing the paschal offering (Numbers 9:10). It likewise appears that the categorization of Modi'im as a "distant path" has ramifications for the issue in this Gemara, in that the area between Modi'im and Jerusalem is considered near the Temple and served the requirements of the Sanctuary in various ways.

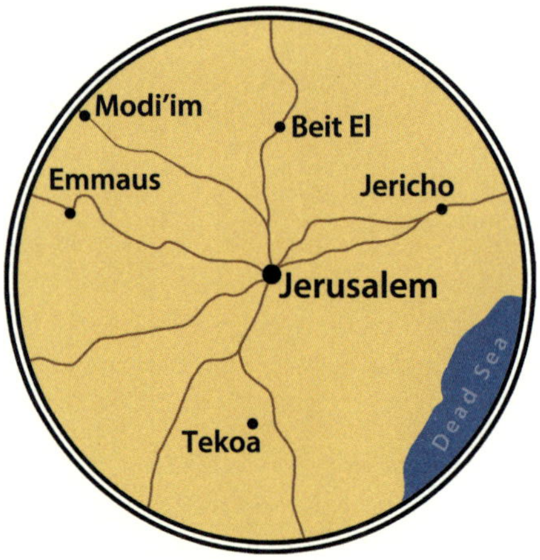

Relative locations of Jerusalem and Modi'im

HALAKHA

With regard to one who is keeping his *tevel* in purity – בִּמְטַהֵר אֶת טִבְלוֹ: If a vessel containing wine or oil was preserved in purity by an *am ha'aretz* in order to use it for libations, he is deemed credible with regard to its purity during the period of the wine and olive presses and seventy days beforehand, but not during the rest of the year (Rambam *Sefer Tahara, Hilkhot Metamei Mishkav UMoshav* 11:5).

Although the potter, and the pots, etc. – הוּא הַקַּדָּר וְהֵן הַקְּדֵרוֹת וכו׳: Although the Sages deemed credible *amei ha'aretz* with regard to the purity of earthenware vessels from Modi'im inward, they are not deemed credible outside that area, even with regard to the identical potter, the same pots, and the same customers (Rambam *Sefer Tahara, Hilkhot Metamei Mishkav UMoshav* 11:7).

גמ׳ תָּנָא: מוֹדִיעִים, פְּעָמִים כְּלִפְנִים, פְּעָמִים כְּלַחוּץ. כֵּיצַד? קַדָּר יוֹצֵא וְחָבֵר נִכְנָס – כְּלִפְנִים. שְׁנֵיהֶן נִכְנָסִין

GEMARA A *tanna* **taught** in a *baraita*: With regard to **Modi'im** itself, **there are times** that it is considered **like inside** the perimeter surrounding Jerusalem, and **there are times** that it is considered **like outside** that perimeter. **How so?** If **a potter is leaving** the perimeter **and a *ḥaver* is entering** it, and they meet in Modi'im, it is considered **like inside,** and the *ḥaver* may purchase the jugs.[H] However, if **both are entering** the perimeter

HALAKHA

The trustworthiness of a potter with regard to earthenware vessels – נֶאֱמָנוּת קַדָּר עַל כְּלֵי חֶרֶס: From Modi'im and inward a potter is deemed credible with regard to the purity of earthenware vessels, but from Modi'im outward he is not deemed credible. As for Modi'im itself, it is sometimes considered outside of the defined area and sometimes it is considered as inside the defined area: If the seller and buyer are both entering or leaving, it is considered outside; if the *ḥaver* is entering and the *am ha'aretz* is leaving with the earthenware vessel in hand, it is considered inside. The Ra'avad maintains that according to the conclusion of the Gemara, the trustworthiness of the potter applies only to small earthenware vessels used for offerings (Rambam *Sefer Tahara, Hilkhot Metamei Mishkav UMoshav* 11:6).

Perek **III**
Daf **26** Amud **a**

אוֹ שְׁנֵיהֶן יוֹצְאִין – כְּלַחוּץ.

or both are leaving it, it is considered **like outside** the perimeter and the *ḥaver* may not acquire vessels from him. The reason is that if they are both entering the perimeter they can easily wait until they are inside and then conduct the transaction, and if they are both leaving they should have completed the deal beforehand, and the *ḥaver* may not make up for this lapse by doing so now.

אָמַר אַבָּיֵי, אַף אֲנַן נָמֵי תְּנֵינָא: הַקַּדָּר שֶׁמָּכַר אֶת הַקְּדֵירוֹת וְנִכְנַס לִפְנִים מִן הַמּוֹדִיעִים. טַעְמָא – דִּלְפְנִים מִן הַמּוֹדִיעִים, הָא מוֹדִיעִים גּוּפָהּ – לָא מְהֵימַן. אֵימָא סֵיפָא: יָצָא – אֵינוֹ נֶאֱמָן, הָא מוֹדִיעִים גּוּפָהּ – נֶאֱמָן! אֶלָּא לָאו שְׁמַע מִינַּהּ: כָּאן – בְּקַדָּר יוֹצֵא וְחָבֵר נִכְנָס, כָּאן – בִּשֶׁשְּׁנֵיהֶן יוֹצְאִין אוֹ שְׁנֵיהֶן נִכְנָסִין? שְׁמַע מִינַּהּ.

Abaye said: We, too, learn this in the mishna. For it is taught there: **A potter who was selling pots and entered within the Modi'im** area is deemed credible, which indicates that **the** only **reason** he is deemed credible is **that** he is **inside** the **Modi'im** area, **thus** implying that in **Modi'im itself he is not deemed credible.** But now **say the latter clause** of the mishna: If he **left he is not deemed credible, thus** implying that in **Modi'im itself he is deemed credible,** which contradicts the previous inference. **Rather,** must one **not conclude from** the mishna the following distinction: **Here,** in the latter clause, it is referring **to a potter** who is **leaving and a *ḥaver*** who is **entering,** in which case he is deemed credible; and **there,** in the first clause, it is referring **to** a situation **where they are both leaving or both entering,** in which case he is not deemed credible. Consequently, both inferences from the mishna are upheld. The Gemara concludes: Indeed, **learn from here** that this is the case.

תָּנָא: נֶאֱמָנִין בִּכְלֵי חֶרֶס הַדַּקִּין לַקּוֹדֶשׁ. אָמַר רֵישׁ לָקִישׁ: וְהוּא שֶׁנִּיטָּלִין בְּיָדוֹ אַחַת. וְרַבִּי יוֹחָנָן אָמַר: אֲפִילּוּ שֶׁאֵין נִיטָּלִין בְּיָדוֹ אַחַת.

§ A *tanna* **taught** in the *Tosefta* (3:33): All people, including *amei ha'aretz*, **are deemed credible** with regard to purity from Modi'im and inward only **with regard to small earthenware vessels,** and they may be used **for sacrificial** food. Since these small vessels were needed by all, the Sages deemed the *amei ha'aretz* credible concerning them. The *amora'im* discussed the meaning of the term small vessels. **Reish Lakish said: It is** speaking of those vessels **that can be picked up in one hand,** but no larger. **And Rabbi Yoḥanan said: Even if they cannot be picked up in one hand,** they can still be called small vessels.

אָמַר רֵישׁ לָקִישׁ: לֹא שָׁנוּ אֶלָּא רֵיקָנִין, אֲבָל מְלֵאִין – לֹא. וְרַבִּי יוֹחָנָן אָמַר: אֲפִילּוּ מְלֵאִים, וַאֲפִילּוּ אַפִּיקַרְסוּתוֹ לְתוֹכוֹ. וְאָמַר רָבָא: וּמוֹדֶה רַבִּי יוֹחָנָן בְּמַשְׁקִין עַצְמָן שֶׁהֵן טְמֵאִין. וְאַל תִּתְמַהּ, שֶׁהֲרֵי לָגִין מָלֵא מַשְׁקִין, לָגִין טָמֵא טוּמְאַת שִׁבְעָה וּמַשְׁקִין טְהוֹרִין.

Reish Lakish said further: **They taught** in the *baraita* **only** that *amei ha'aretz* are deemed credible with regard to **empty** vessels, **but** if they are **full** of liquid they are **not** deemed credible.[N] **And Rabbi Yoḥanan said: Even** if the jugs are **full, and even** if **his garment** [***apikarsuto***][L] **is inside** the vessel, the Sages were not concerned about impurity, as they did not apply their decree to such vessels at all. **And Rava said: And Rabbi Yoḥanan concedes with regard to the liquids themselves** in the vessel **that they are impure,** for although the Sages declared the vessels to be pure they did not waive the decree that liquids touched by *amei ha'aretz* are impure.[H] **And do not be perplexed**[N] by this apparent contradiction, **for** there is a similar *halakha* in a case of an earthenware **pitcher full of liquid** in a room with a corpse and the pitcher is tightly sealed with another earthenware vessel of an *am ha'aretz*, where the *halakha* is that the **pitcher is impure** with a **seven**-day **impurity, while the liquids** remain **pure.**

NOTES

But if they are full, they are not deemed credible – אֲבָל מְלֵאִים לֹא: It appears that Rabbeinu Ḥananel had a different version of the text, according to which Reish Lakish states that even though he is not deemed credible with regard to the purity of the full vessels themselves, he is deemed credible concerning the liquids in them.

And do not be perplexed by this apparent contradiction – וְאַל תִּתְמַהּ: In the Jerusalem Talmud, Rabbi Yoḥanan cites a long list of similar laws in which the Sages limited their decrees in a manner that seems to be self-contradictory.

LANGUAGE

Garment [*apikarsuto*] – אַפִּיקַרְסוּתוֹ: From the Greek, ἐπικάρσιον, *epikarsiyon*, a type of striped garment.

HALAKHA

Credibility regarding earthenware vessels in Jerusalem – נֶאֱמָנוּת עַל כְּלֵי חֶרֶס בִּירוּשָׁלַיִם: All people are deemed credible in Jerusalem at all times to say that an earthenware vessel is pure for sacrificial use, whether it was large or small, full or empty. Although the liquids it contains are considered impure, every person is nevertheless deemed credible with regard to the vessel itself. Even if one's garment, which is considered impure with regard to sacrificial food, is inside the vessel, the vessel remains pure for sacred foods, in accordance with the statement of Rabbi Yoḥanan (Rambam *Sefer Tahara, Hilkhot Metamei Mishkav UMoshav* 11:5).

מתני׳ הגבאין שנכנסו לתוך הבית, וכן הגנבים שהחזירו את הכלים, נאמנין לומר ״לא נגענו״, ובירושלים נאמנין על הקודש, ובשעת הרגל אף על התרומה.

MISHNA In the case of *amei ha'aretz* tax **collectors who entered a house** to collect items for a tax, **and similarly thieves who returned the vessels** they had stolen, **they are deemed credible when they say: We did not touch** the rest of the objects in the house, and those items remain pure. **And in Jerusalem** all people, even *amei ha'aretz,* **are deemed credible with regard to sacrificial** food[N] throughout the year, **and during a pilgrimage Festival** they are deemed credible **even with regard to *teruma*.**

גמ׳ ורמינהי: הגבאין שנכנסו לתוך הבית, הבית כולו טמא! לא קשיא: הא – דאיכא גוי בהדייהו, הא – דליכא גוי בהדייהו. דתנן: אם יש גוי עמהן – נאמנין לומר ״לא נכנסנו״, אבל אין נאמנים לומר ״נכנסנו אבל לא נגענו״.

GEMARA And the Gemara **raises a contradiction** from a different mishna (*Teharot* 7:6): If *amei ha'aretz* tax **collectors entered a house,**[H] **the entire house is impure.** The Gemara answers: It is **not difficult,** as **that** mishna is referring to a situation **where there is a gentile with them,**[N] in which case they conduct a thorough search in the whole house, and certainly will have touched everything; whereas **this** mishna deals with a case **when there is no gentile with them,** and their claim not to have touched anything is therefore accepted. **As we learned** in a mishna (*Teharot* 7:6): **If there is a gentile with** the tax collectors, **they are deemed credible** if they were **to say: We did not enter** the house at all; **but they are not deemed credible** if they were **to say: We entered** the house **but did not touch** its vessels.

וכי איכא גוי בהדייהו מאי הוי? רבי יוחנן ורבי אלעזר, חד אמר: אימת גוי עליהן. וחד אמר: אימת מלכות עליהן. מאי בינייהו? איכא בינייהו גוי שאינו חשוב.

The Gemara raises a question: **And when there is a gentile with them, what of it?** Why does this affect the *halakha*? **Rabbi Yoḥanan and Rabbi Elazar** disputed this issue. **One said: The fear of the gentile,** who is their senior, **is upon them,** for they are afraid he might punish them. **And one said: The fear of the kingdom,** i.e., the government, **is upon them,** as the gentile might report them to the authorities if they do not carry out a thorough search. The Gemara asks: **What is** the practical difference **between them?** The Gemara responds: **The** practical difference **between them** is the case of **a gentile who is not important,** i.e., he does not have senior authority. In that case they are not afraid of him personally, but there is still concern that he might report them to the government authorities.

״וכן הגנבים שהחזירו את הכלים״. ורמינהי: הגנבים שנכנסו לתוך הבית – אינו טמא אלא מקום דריסת רגלי הגנבים! אמר רב פנחס משמיה דרב: כשעשו תשובה. דיקא נמי, דקתני: ״שהחזירו את הכלים״. שמע מינה.

§ It is taught in the mishna: **And similarly thieves who returned vessels** are deemed credible. **And** the Gemara **raises a contradiction** from the following mishna (*Teharot* 7:6): Concerning **the thieves who entered**[N] a house, **only the place where the feet of the thieves had trodden is impure.** The implication is that all the vessels of the section of the house where they had entered are impure, and they are not deemed credible if they say that they did not touch a particular item. **Rav Pinḥas said in the name of Rav:** The mishna here is referring to a case **where** the thieves **repented,** which is why they are deemed credible, whereas the mishna in *Teharot* is referring to a case in which the thieves did not repent.[H] The Gemara comments: The language of the mishna **is also precise, as it teaches:** Thieves **who returned vessels,** which indicates that they repented and made restoration willingly. The Gemara concludes: Indeed, **learn from here** that this is the case.

״ובירושלים נאמנין על הקודש״. תנא: נאמנין על כלי חרס גסין לקודש. וכל כך למה? שאין עושין כבשונות בירושלים.

§ The mishna teaches: **And in Jerusalem** all people **are deemed credible with regard to sacrificial** food.[H] A *tanna* **taught** in a *baraita*: **They are deemed credible** even **with regard to large earthenware vessels**[N] **for sacrificial** food, and not only small ones. **And why** did the Sages exhibit **so much** leniency, waiving their regular decrees of impurity within Jerusalem for large vessels and all the way to Modi'im for small vessels? Because there is a principle that potters' **kilns may not be made in Jerusalem,** in order to preserve the quality of the air in the city. It is therefore necessary to bring in earthenware vessels from outside the city, and consequently the Sages were lenient concerning such utensils.

NOTES

And in Jerusalem all are deemed credible with regard to sacrificial food – ובירושלים נאמנין על הקודש: Most commentaries view this as a continuation of the previous statement with regard to the trustworthiness of an *am ha'aretz* concerning the purity of earthenware vessels used for sacrificial food. However, the Rid and others claim that this clause in the mishna is not dealing with vessels but with sacrificial food itself. Although the mishna above (24b) taught that *amei ha'aretz* are deemed credible with regard to sacrificial food anywhere in Judea, that mishna was dealing with sacrificial food made by the *amei ha'aretz* themselves. However, if they touch the sacrificial food of others, it would be considered impure. The mishna here comes to add that in Jerusalem *amei ha'aretz* are deemed credible completely, even concerning the sacrificial food of others.

When there is a gentile with them – הא דאיכא גוי בהדייהו: Several early commentaries had a different version of this text, which implies the opposite: If the tax collectors are accompanied by a gentile they are wary of touching everything, but if they are by themselves it can be assumed they have touched all the vessels in the house (Rabbeinu Ḥananel; Rid). The Rambam rules in accordance with this reading as well. This also answers the questions posed by the Ra'avad and Meiri, who did not have this reading.

And the Gemara raises a contradiction concerning the thieves who entered, etc. – ורמינהי הגנבים שנכנסו וכו׳: It is not immediately clear why the Gemara considers this mishna to be a contradiction to our mishna. Already in the time of the *ge'onim* difficulty was found with the Gemara's question. One explanation is that the statement that the place where they trod is impure implies that they are considered definitely impure, without any possibility of claiming that they did not touch certain items. This is in opposition to our mishna.

They are deemed credible with regard to large earthenware vessels – נאמנין על כלי חרס גסין: With regard to small earthenware vessels *amei ha'aretz* are deemed credible even in the surroundings of Jerusalem, as everyone needed vessels for cooking their sacred food, and therefore such vessels were in high demand. Large vessels, however, were in less demand, as they were required only for storage (see Rashi; Rid).

HALAKHA

Tax collectors who entered a house – הגבאין שנכנסו לתוך הבית: If government tax collectors entered a house in order to confiscate vessels as pledges, all the contents of the house are considered impure. If they were accompanied by a gentile, they are deemed credible if they say they did not touch a certain object, because they are afraid of the gentile. This applies only if witnesses saw them enter or if the pledge was in their possession, but if it was otherwise unknown that they had entered the house they are deemed credible if they say: We entered the house but did not touch the vessels (Rambam *Sefer Tahara, Hilkhot Metamei Mishkav UMoshav* 12:12).

They repented – עשו תשובה: Thieves or government tax collectors who repented and restored the property they took of their own accord, without any coercion, are deemed credible if they say they did not touch the vessels of the house, even concerning those parts of the house they had entered (Rambam *Sefer Tahara, Hilkhot Metamei Mishkav UMoshav* 12:14).

The purity of the Jewish people on a pilgrimage Festival – טהרת ישראל ברגל: During pilgrimage Festivals all members of the Jewish people are considered pure, including their vessels, drinks, and food. They are likewise deemed credible with regard to all purity, whether that of sacrificial food or *teruma*. Once the Festival has ended, they return to their impure state (Rambam *Sefer Tahara, Hilkhot Metamei Mishkav UMoshav* 11:9).

"וּבִשְׁעַת הָרֶגֶל אַף עַל הַתְּרוּמָה". מְנָהָנֵי מִילֵּי? אָמַר רַבִּי יְהוֹשֻׁעַ בֶּן לֵוִי: דְּאָמַר קְרָא: "וַיֵּאָסֵף כָּל אִישׁ יִשְׂרָאֵל אֶל הָעִיר כְּאִישׁ אֶחָד חֲבֵרִים" – הַכָּתוּב עֲשָׂאָן כּוּלָּן חֲבֵרִים.

§ It was taught in the mishna: **And during a pilgrimage Festival** they are deemed credible **even with regard to *teruma*.** The Gemara poses a question: **From where are these matters** derived, i.e., that there is a difference between Festival days and other periods? **Rabbi Yehoshua ben Levi said: The verse states** concerning the incident of the concubine in Gibeah: **"And all the men of Israel gathered to the city, like one man, united [*ḥaverim*]"** (Judges 20:11).[N] This verse is interpreted to teach that whenever the entire people of Israel gathers together in a single place, **the Torah makes,** i.e., considers, **all of them *ḥaverim*.** The final word of the phrase, *ḥaverim*, is a reference to the members of a group dedicated to scrupulous observance of mitzvot, as the term is used by the Sages.

מתני׳ הַפּוֹתֵחַ אֶת חָבִיתוֹ, וְהַמַּתְחִיל בְּעִיסָּתוֹ עַל גַּב הָרֶגֶל, רַבִּי יְהוּדָה אוֹמֵר: יִגְמוֹר, וַחֲכָמִים אוֹמְרִים: לֹא יִגְמוֹר.

MISHNA In the case of **one who opens his barrel** of wine for public sale, **and** similarly **one who starts** selling **his dough during the time of the pilgrimage Festival,** and these items perforce come into contact with *amei ha'aretz*, **Rabbi Yehuda says:** Since the food was pure, despite its contact with *amei ha'aretz*, when he began selling it, **he may finish** selling it in a state of purity even after the Festival, and there is no concern about the contact that has been made by *amei ha'aretz* during the Festival. **But the Rabbis say: He may not finish** selling it.[H]

גמ׳ יָתִיב רַבִּי אַמִּי וְרַבִּי יִצְחָק נַפָּחָא אַקִּילְעָא דְּרַבִּי יִצְחָק נַפָּחָא. פְּתַח חַד וְאָמַר: מַהוּ שֶׁיַּנִּיחֶנָּה לָרֶגֶל אַחֵר?

GEMARA **Rabbi Ami and Rabbi Yitzḥak Nappaḥa were** once **sitting in the courtyard of Rabbi Yitzḥak Nappaḥa. One of them opened** the discussion **and said: What is** the *halakha* **with regard to** the possibility of **him leaving** his wine **for another,** subsequent **pilgrimage Festival** and continuing to sell it at that point? Although according to the Rabbis one may not continue selling it once the Festival has concluded, may he leave the barrel aside until the next Festival, at which point it would once again be able to be sold in purity?

אֲמַר לֵיהּ אִידָּךְ: יַד הַכֹּל מְמַשְׁמְשִׁין בָּהּ, וְאַתְּ אָמְרַתְּ יַנִּיחֶנָּה לָרֶגֶל אַחֵר?! אֲמַר לֵיהּ: אַטּוּ עַד הָאִידָּנָא לָאו יַד הַכֹּל מְמַשְׁמְשִׁין בָּהּ? אֲמַר לֵיהּ: הָכִי הַשְׁתָּא! בִּשְׁלָמָא עַד הָאִידָּנָא – טוּמְאַת עַם הָאָרֶץ בָּרֶגֶל רַחֲמָנָא טַהֲרָהּ. אֶלָּא הַשְׁתָּא – טְמֵאָה הִיא.

The other Sage **said to him: Everyone's hand has touched it, and** yet **you are saying that** perhaps **he may leave it for another pilgrimage Festival** and then sell it in purity? How could such a possibility even be considered? **He said** back **to him: Is that to say** that **until now,** throughout the Festival, **everyone's hand was not touching it?** It was permitted during the Festival despite the fact that everyone was touching it; apparently, their touching did not render it impure at all. **He said to him: How can** these cases **be compared? Granted, until now, the Merciful One declares pure the impurity of the *am ha'aretz* during the Festival,** and consequently his impurity is disregarded, **but now** that the Festival has passed, the touch of an *am ha'aretz* **is** once again considered **impure.**

נֵימָא כְּתַנָּאֵי; דְּתָנֵי חֲדָא: יַנִּיחֶנָּה לָרֶגֶל אַחֵר. וְתַנְיָא אִידָּךְ: לֹא יַנִּיחֶנָּה לָרֶגֶל אַחֵר. מַאי לָאו תַּנָּאֵי הִיא!

The Gemara suggests: **Let us say** this dispute between *amora'im* is **parallel to** a dispute between ***tanna'im*. For it is taught** in **one** *baraita*: **He may leave it for another pilgrimage Festival** and then continue to sell it. **And it was taught in a different** *baraita*: **He may not leave it for another Festival. What, is it not** so that this very issue **is** a dispute between these two ***tanna'im*,** the authors of these two *baraitot*?

NOTES

Like one man, united – **כְּאִישׁ אֶחָד חֲבֵרִים**: The Jerusalem Talmud cites a different source verse: "Jerusalem, that is built as a city that is compact [*ḥubra*] together" (Psalms 122:3), which is interpreted to mean that Jerusalem makes all who are inside it into *ḥaverim*. And when is this so? As the following verse goes on to state: "When the tribes went up there, the tribes of the Lord" (Psalms 122:4). The Rambam provides a rationale for this principle: That it can be assumed that everyone purifies themselves properly in order to bring the Festival offerings, and therefore one may rely upon all the people. He adds this reason because the verses adduced by the Talmud are intended merely as nominal allusions, which makes it necessary to provide a more concrete justification for this law (*Tosefot Yom Tov*).

HALAKHA

One who opens his barrel on a pilgrimage Festival, etc. – **הַפּוֹתֵחַ חָבִיתוֹ בָּרֶגֶל וכו׳**: If one opened his barrel to sell wine or began selling his dough on a pilgrimage Festival, the remainder of the barrel or dough is considered impure after the Festival has ended. It is assumed to have been touched on the Festival by *amei ha'aretz*, who are pure only during the Festival itself, in accordance with the Rabbis. Likewise, the remainder of wine or dough may not be left for the following Festival, although the conclusion of the Gemara seems to indicate otherwise, for the answer provided in the Gemara was not a substantial refutation (Rambam *Sefer Tahara, Hilkhot Metamei Mishkav UMoshav* 11:10 and *Kesef Mishne* there).

NOTES

They pass all the vessels of the Temple courtyard through a process of purification – מַעֲבִירִין עַל טָהֳרַת הָעֲזָרָה: Rashi explains that the mishna uses this expression because they would pass the Temple vessels from their usual places in order to purify them. The Rid understands the term pass in a similar manner to its use in the verse: "And they passed a proclamation throughout the camp" (Exodus 36:6), so that it means that they proclaimed the need to purify the vessels. The Meiri explains that pass means they would hurry to complete the task as soon as possible.

And they say to the *am ha'aretz* priests – וְאוֹמְרִים לָהֶם: Some maintain that this was said to the priests during the Festival, for although the impurity of *amei ha'aretz* is suspended during the Festival, the status of impurity would return immediately following the Festival (Rashi; Rambam). Others explain that they said this to the priests after the Festival, when they were busy purifying the vessels, in order to prevent them from touching the table of the shewbread at that point (Meiri).

HALAKHA

Immersing the Temple vessels – מַטְבִּילִין כְּלֵי הַמִּקְדָּשׁ: On the night of the conclusion of a pilgrimage Festival they would immerse all the Temple vessels, since they were touched by *am ha'aretz* priests during the Festival. They would therefore warn *am ha'aretz* priests not to touch the table of the shewbread so that it should not require immersion followed by the setting of the sun, as this would lead to the suspension of the mitzva of (Exodus 25:30): "Shewbread before Me always" (Rambam *Sefer Tahara*, *Hilkhot Metamei Mishkav UMoshav* 11:11).

לָא. הָא דְּקָתָנֵי יַנִּיחֶנָּה – רַבִּי יְהוּדָה. וְהָא דְּקָתָנֵי לֹא יַנִּיחֶנָּה – רַבָּנַן. וְתִסְבְּרָא?! הָא רַבִּי יְהוּדָה ״יִגְמוֹר״ קָאָמַר! אֶלָּא: הָא דְּקָתָנֵי לֹא יַנִּיחֶנָּה – רַבִּי יְהוּדָה, וְהָא דְּקָתָנֵי יַנִּיחֶנָּה – רַבָּנַן. וּמַאי לֹא יַנִּיחֶנָּה? שֶׁאֵין צָרִיךְ לְהַנִּיחָהּ.

The Gemara rejects this suggestion: **No,** it is possible that **this** *baraita*, **which teaches** that **he may leave it,** follows the opinion, cited in the mishna, of **Rabbi Yehuda,** who allows the wine seller to finish selling his wine after the Festival, **whereas that** *baraita*, **which teaches** that **he may not leave it,** is in accordance with the opinion of **the Rabbis,** who prohibit him to finish it. The Gemara questions this conclusion: **And** how can **you understand** it that way? **Didn't Rabbi Yehuda say he may finish** it after the Festival? Consequently, there would be no need for him to leave it for another Festival. **Rather,** say as follows: **This** *baraita*, **which teaches** that **he may not leave it,** is in accordance with the opinion of **Rabbi Yehuda, whereas that** *baraita*, **which teaches** that **he may leave it,** is in accordance with the opinion of **the Rabbis. And what is** the meaning of the statement: **He may not leave it** for another Festival? It means **that he has no need to leave it** for another Festival, as Rabbi Yehuda maintains he can finish selling it in purity immediately.

מתני׳ מִשֶּׁעָבַר הָרֶגֶל מַעֲבִירִין עַל טָהֳרַת הָעֲזָרָה. עָבַר הָרֶגֶל לְיוֹם שִׁשִּׁי – לֹא הָיוּ מַעֲבִירִין, מִפְּנֵי כְּבוֹד הַשַּׁבָּת. רַבִּי יְהוּדָה אוֹמֵר: אַף לֹא בְּיוֹם חֲמִישִׁי, שֶׁאֵין הַכֹּהֲנִים פְּנוּיִין.

MISHNA **Once the pilgrimage Festival has passed by,** the priests **pass** all the vessels of **the Temple courtyard** through a process of **purification,**[N] since they were touched by *am ha'aretz* priests during the Festival.[H] If **the Festival passed by into a Friday,** i.e., if the Festival ended on Thursday night, **they would not pass** the vessels through the purification process on that day, **due to the honor of Shabbat,** in order to give the priests time to prepare the requirements of Shabbat. **Rabbi Yehuda says:** They do **not even** purify them **on Thursday,** in the event that the Festival ended on Wednesday night, because **the priests are not free** to do so.

גמ׳ תָּנָא: שֶׁאֵין הַכֹּהֲנִים פְּנוּיִין מִלְּהוֹצִיא בַּדֶּשֶׁן.

GEMARA A *tanna* **taught** in a *baraita*, in explanation of Rabbi Yehuda's words: The priests do not purify the vessels of the Temple courtyard on Thursday, **as the priests are not free from removing the ashes.** During the Festival days a large quantity of ash would accumulate on the altar, due to the large number of offerings brought at that time. Because they would not remove the ashes on the Festival itself, they would have to remove a very large amount afterward. Consequently, all the priests were kept busy with this task upon the conclusion of the Festival, which did not leave them with enough time to deal with other matters.

מתני׳ כֵּיצַד מַעֲבִירִין עַל טָהֳרַת עֲזָרָה? מַטְבִּילִין אֶת הַכֵּלִים שֶׁהָיוּ בַּמִּקְדָּשׁ, וְאוֹמְרִין לָהֶם: הִזָּהֲרוּ

MISHNA **How do they pass** all the vessels of the Temple **courtyard** through a process of **purification? They immerse the vessels that were in the Temple. And they say to** the *am ha'aretz* priests[N] who served in the Temple during the Festival: **Be careful**

Perek **III**
Daf **26** Amud **b**

NOTES

That you not touch the table – שֶׁלֹּא תִּגְּעוּ בַּשּׁוּלְחָן: *Tosafot* explain that this refers to priests entering the Sanctuary to prostrate themselves, which leads the later commentaries to ask how this could be, as it is prohibited to enter the Sanctuary except for the purpose of the Temple service. The Rambam maintains that it speaks of the priests who would lift up the table to display it before the pilgrims.

HALAKHA

All the vessels…had second, etc. – כָּל הַכֵּלִים...יֵשׁ לָהֶם שְׁנִיִּים וכו׳: All the Temple vessels had two or three replacements, which were used if the originals contracted impurity (Rambam *Sefer Avoda*, *Hilkhot Kelei HaMikdash* 7:19).

שֶׁלֹּא תִּגְּעוּ בַּשֻּׁלְחָן.

that you not touch the table[N] of the shewbread. If you defile it by touching it, it would need to be removed for immersion, and this would lead to the temporary suspension of the mitzva of the shewbread, which had to be on the table at all times.

כָּל הַכֵּלִים שֶׁהָיוּ בַּמִּקְדָּשׁ יֵשׁ לָהֶם שְׁנִיִּים וּשְׁלִישִׁים, שֶׁאִם נִטְמְאוּ הָרִאשׁוֹנִים – יָבִיאוּ שְׁנִיִּים תַּחְתֵּיהֶן. כָּל הַכֵּלִים שֶׁהָיוּ בַּמִּקְדָּשׁ טְעוּנִין טְבִילָה, חוּץ מִמִּזְבַּח הַזָּהָב, וּמִזְבַּח הַנְּחֹשֶׁת, מִפְּנֵי שֶׁהֵן כְּקַרְקַע, דִּבְרֵי רַבִּי אֱלִיעֶזֶר. וַחֲכָמִים אוֹמְרִים: מִפְּנֵי שֶׁהֵן מְצוּפִּין.

The mishna continues: **All the vessels that were in the Temple had second**[H] **and third** substitute vessels, **so that if the first ones became impure they could bring the second ones in their place. All the vessels that were in the Temple required immersion** after the Festival, **apart from the golden altar and the bronze altar, because they are** considered **like the ground** and therefore, like land itself, not susceptible to impurity. This is **the statement of Rabbi Eliezer. And the Rabbis say:** It is **because they are coated.**

גמ׳ תָּנָא: הִזָּהֲרוּ שֶׁמָּא תִּגְּעוּ בַּשּׁוּלְחָן, וּבַמְּנוֹרָה. וְתַנָּא דִּידַן, מַאי טַעְמָא לָא תָּנֵי מְנוֹרָה? שֻׁלְחָן – כְּתִיב בֵּיהּ ״תָּמִיד״; מְנוֹרָה לָא כְּתִיב בָּהּ ״תָּמִיד״.

GEMARA A *tanna* **taught** in a *baraita* that they would say to the *am ha'aretz* priests: **Be careful lest you touch the table,** as explained above, **or the candelabrum,** as the Gemara will explain. The Gemara asks: **And** regarding **the *tanna* of our** mishna, **what is the reason he did not teach** that they were instructed not to touch the **candelabrum** as well? The Gemara answers: **With regard to the table it is written:** "Shewbread before Me **always**" (Exodus 25:30), indicating that the table holding the shewbread must always be in its place, whereas **with regard to the candelabrum it is not written "always,"**[N] and therefore it can be removed for immersing.

וְאִידָךְ: כֵּיוָן דִּכְתִיב: ״וְאֶת הַמְּנֹרָה נֹכַח הַשֻּׁלְחָן״ כְּמַאן דִּכְתִיב בָּהּ תָּמִיד דָּמֵי. וְאִידָךְ: הַהוּא לִקְבּוֹעַ לָהּ מָקוֹם הוּא דַּאֲתָא.

The Gemara asks: **And** regarding **the other** *tanna*, in the *baraita*, why does he include the candelabrum? The Gemara answers: **Since it is written: "And** you shall set the table without the veil **and the candelabrum opposite the table"** (Exodus 26:35), indicating that the candelabrum must always be placed opposite the table; **it is as though it is written "always" with regard to** the candelabrum as well. **And the other** *tanna*, in the mishna, who does not object to removing the candelabrum for immersion, would reply: **That** verse **comes** only **to establish a place for** the candelabrum, to describe where it must be positioned, but it does not mean to say that it must be opposite the table at all times.

וְתִיפּוֹק לִי דִּכְלִי עֵץ הֶעָשׂוּי לְנַחַת הוּא, וְכָל כְּלִי עֵץ הֶעָשׂוּי לְנַחַת לָא מְטַמֵּא. מַאי טַעְמָא? דּוּמְיָא דְּשַׂק בָּעֵינַן, מָה שַּׂק מִיטַּלְטֵל מָלֵא וְרֵיקָם – אַף כָּל מִיטַּלְטֵל מָלֵא וְרֵיקָם?

The Gemara poses a question concerning the requirement to keep *amei ha'aretz* away from the table: **And let us derive it,** i.e., let it be established, that it is not necessary to take care against contact with the table, as it is incapable of contracting ritual impurity. This is **because it is a wooden vessel designated to rest**[H] in a fixed place, **and** the *halakha* is that **any** large, **wooden vessel designated to rest** in a fixed place **cannot become impure. What is the reason** for this *halakha*? Since wooden vessels and sacks are juxtaposed in the verse describing their impurity (Leviticus 11:32), **we require** a wooden vessel **to be similar to a sack** in order to be capable of contracting impurity, in the following manner: **Just as a sack is carried** when it is both **full and empty, so too any** wooden vessel that is **carried full and empty** can contract impurity, as opposed to vessels, such as the table, that are designated to rest in a fixed place. The table should therefore not be susceptible to impurity at all.

הַאי נָמֵי מִיטַּלְטֵל מָלֵא וְרֵיקָם הוּא, כִּדְרֵישׁ לָקִישׁ. דְּאָמַר רֵישׁ לָקִישׁ: מַאי דִּכְתִיב: ״עַל הַשֻּׁלְחָן הַטָּהוֹר״? מִכְּלָל שֶׁהוּא טָמֵא.

The Gemara answers: The table **too is** in fact **carried full and empty, in accordance with** the words **of Reish Lakish. For Reish Lakish said: What is** the meaning of that **which is written:** "And you shall set them in two rows, six in a row, **upon the pure table"** (Leviticus 24:6)? The words "pure table" teach **by inference that it is** capable of becoming **impure,** and therefore the Torah warns us to make sure it is pure when the twelve loaves of bread are placed there.

וְאַמַּאי? כְּלִי עֵץ הֶעָשׂוּי לְנַחַת הוּא, וְאֵינוֹ מְקַבֵּל טוּמְאָה! אֶלָּא מְלַמֵּד שֶׁמַּגְבִּיהִין אוֹתוֹ, וּמַרְאִין בּוֹ לְעוֹלֵי רְגָלִים לֶחֶם הַפָּנִים, וְאוֹמְרִים לָהֶם: רְאוּ חִיבַּתְכֶם לִפְנֵי הַמָּקוֹם, סִילּוּקוֹ כְּסִידּוּרוֹ. דְּאָמַר רַבִּי יְהוֹשֻׁעַ בֶּן לֵוִי: נֵס גָּדוֹל נַעֲשָׂה בְּלֶחֶם הַפָּנִים – כְּסִידּוּרוֹ כָּךְ סִילּוּקוֹ, שֶׁנֶּאֱמַר: ״לָשׂוּם לֶחֶם חוֹם בְּיוֹם הִלָּקְחוֹ״.

And why indeed is the table susceptible to ritual impurity, being that **it is a wooden vessel designated to rest** in a fixed place **and** should therefore **not** be **susceptible to impurity? Rather,** this verse **teaches that they** would **lift** the table with the shewbread on it **to display the shewbread to the pilgrims** standing in the Temple courtyard, as it was prohibited for Israelites to enter the Sanctuary, where the table stood, **and they would say to them: Behold your affection before God,** Who performs a perpetual miracle with the bread, for when **it is removed** from the table on Shabbat it is just as fresh **as when it was arranged** on the previous Shabbat. **As Rabbi Yehoshua ben Levi said: A great miracle was performed with the shewbread: As its** condition during its **arrangement, so was its** condition during its **removal, as it is stated: "To place hot bread on the day when it was taken away"** (I Samuel 21:7), indicating that it was as hot on the day of its removal as it was on the day when it was placed.

NOTES

With regard to the candelabrum it is not written "always" – **מְנוֹרָה לָא כְּתִיב בָּהּ תָּמִיד:** Rashi raises the obvious question that the Torah does indeed explicitly state "always" with regard to the candelabrum as well, as in Exodus 27:20: "To cause a lamp to burn always." He answers that although the term "always" is used for the candelabrum, it was nevertheless not necessary for the lamp to burn at all times without interruption (see *Tosafot*). The Meiri explains that the verse states "always" with regard to the placement of the table and its bread in a fixed place, whereas it does not say "always" with regard to the placement of the candelabrum, but only concerning the continuous, i.e., daily, obligation to light it. The rest of the discussion of the Gemara fits in well with this opinion.

HALAKHA

A wooden vessel designated to rest – **כְּלִי עֵץ הֶעָשׂוּי לְנַחַת:** A wooden vessel designated to rest in one place is not capable of contracting impurity at all, neither by Torah law nor by Rabbinic law, even if it has only a small capacity. For if it can hold forty *se'a*, it is considered as though it was designated to be fixed in one place permanently (Rambam *Sefer Tahara*, *Hilkhot Kelim* 3:1).

LANGUAGE

Dulpaki – דּוּלְפְּקִי: Probably from the Greek Δέλφιξ, *delfix*, with the genitive δελφικός, *delfikos*, meaning a tripod, a table made of three legs in the style of the city of Delphi.

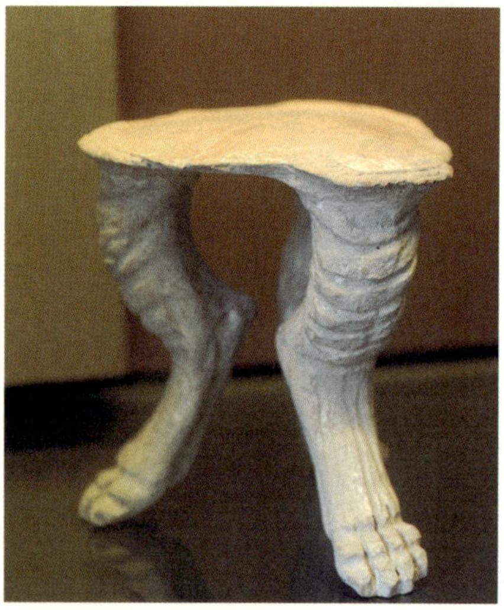

Ancient tripod table

Akhselag – אַכְסְלַג: There are many different versions of this word, whose meaning remains unclear. It seems to be derived from the Greek ἀξιόλογος, *axiologos*, meaning important, noteworthy. If so, it does not refer to a particular type of tree, but rather serves as a generic term for valuable wood.

Masmi – מַסְמִי: The source of this word and its meaning are unclear. The *ge'onim* explain that it refers to the ebony tree, a tough, very heavy tree, usually black in color, which is imported from the tropics. Even nowadays this wood is considered elegant and valuable.

Rim – לִבְזְבְּזִין: From the Greek λαβίς, *labis*, a handle. The Talmud uses the word in reference to the part of a vessel added to be decorative.

BACKGROUND

A place for placing cups – מְקוֹם הֲנָחַת כּוֹסוֹת: A vacant space, without a tablecloth or covering vessel, was sometimes left in the middle of a table upon which they would place the vessels used in the meal, which were often too hot or charred to place on the table proper. The finished, decorative part of the table's surface was for use by the diners as they ate.

HALAKHA

A coated table and a *dulpaki* – הַשּׁוּלְחָן וְהַדּוּלְפְּקִי הַמְחוּפִּים: A table or *dulpaki* that was coated with marble is susceptible to impurity if a spot large enough for placing cups was left uncovered. If it was entirely coated it is pure, and it makes no difference if it was a fixed or removable coating, or if its rims were coated, or if it was made from expensive or cheap wood, in accordance with the statements of first *tanna* and Rabbi Yoḥanan (Rambam *Sefer Tahara*, *Hilkhot Kelim* 6:15).

וְתֵיפּוּק לִי מִשּׁוּם צִיפּוּי, דִּתְנַן: הַשֻּׁלְחָן וְהַדּוּלְפְּקִי שֶׁנִּפְחֲתוּ אוֹ שֶׁחִיפָּן בְּשַׁיִישׁ, וְשִׁיֵּיר בָּהֶם מְקוֹם הֲנָחַת כּוֹסוֹת – טָמֵא. רַבִּי יְהוּדָה אוֹמֵר: מְקוֹם הֲנָחַת הַחֲתִיכוֹת.

The Gemara asks another question: **Let us derive** this fact, i.e., that the table can contract ritual impurity, not because it is portable but **due to** its golden **coating.**[N] **For didn't we learn** in a mishna (*Kelim* 22:1): Concerning **a table and a *dulpaki*[NL] that** some of its surface **became broken off, or that one coated with marble,** i.e., stone not being susceptible to impurity: If **he left on them a place** on the surface that remained unbroken or uncoated, big enough **for placing cups,**[B] **it** remains **susceptible to impurity** as a wooden vessel. **Rabbi Yehuda says:** It must have an unbroken and uncoated **place** big enough **for placing pieces** of meat and bread as well in order to maintain susceptibility to impurity as a wooden vessel.[H] It is clear from this mishna that if a table is completely coated with stone it is not susceptible to impurity, showing that the status of a vessel follows its external coating, not its main material. The Temple table, which was coated with gold, should have the status of a metal vessel.

וְכִי תֵּימָא שָׁאנֵי עֲצֵי שִׁטִּים דַּחֲשִׁיבִי וְלָא בָּטְלִי – הָנִיחָא לְרֵישׁ לָקִישׁ, דְּאָמַר: לֹא שָׁנוּ אֶלָּא בִּכְלֵי אַכְסְלַגִּים הַבָּאִין מִמְּדִינַת הַיָּם, אֲבָל בִּכְלֵי מַסְמִים – לָא בָּטְלִי, שַׁפִּיר. אֶלָּא לְרַבִּי יוֹחָנָן, דְּאָמַר: אֲפִילּוּ בִּכְלֵי מַסְמִים נַמִי בָּטְלִי, מַאי אִיכָּא לְמֵימַר?

The Gemara proposes a possible answer: **And if you would say** that **acacia wood,** from which the Temple table was made, **is different,** as it is an **important,** valuable kind of wood **and is** therefore **not nullified** by a coating, **this works out well according to Reish Lakish, who said: They taught** that a wooden vessel is nullified by its coating **only with regard to vessels** made of cheap *akhselag*[L] wood **which comes from overseas, but** vessels made of expensive *masmi*[L] wood **are not nullified** by a coating. According to this opinion it is **fine,** for we can say that the acacia wood of the table is also not nullified by its golden coating. **But according to Rabbi Yoḥanan, who said: Even** expensive ***masmi* vessels are also nullified** by a coating, **what is there to say?**

וְכִי תֵּימָא: כָּאן – בְּצִיפּוּי עוֹמֵד, כָּאן – בְּצִיפּוּי שֶׁאֵינוֹ עוֹמֵד, הָא בְּעָא מִינֵּיהּ רֵישׁ לָקִישׁ מֵרַבִּי יוֹחָנָן: בְּצִיפּוּי עוֹמֵד אוֹ בְּצִיפּוּי שֶׁאֵינוֹ עוֹמֵד, בְּחוֹפֶה אֶת לִבְזְבְּזָיו אוֹ בְּשֶׁאֵינוֹ חוֹפֶה אֶת לִבְזְבְּזָיו?

The Gemara proposes another possible answer: **And if you would say** that the mishna is not applicable because **here** in the mishna the wood is nullified by its coating because it is speaking **of a fixed coating,**[N] whereas **there** in the case of the Temple table the golden **coating** is **not fixed** onto the wood, this is impossible. For **didn't Reish Lakish inquire of Rabbi Yoḥanan:** Does this law that vessels follow their coating deal only **with a fixed coating or** even **with a coating that is not fixed?** And he asked him further: Does it deal only **with** a coating **that covers the** table's **rim**[L] as well as the table itself, **or** even **with one that does not cover its rim?**

וְאָמַר לֵיהּ: לָא שְׁנָא בְּצִיפּוּי עוֹמֵד, וְלָא שְׁנָא בְּצִיפּוּי שֶׁאֵינוֹ עוֹמֵד, לָא שְׁנָא בְּחוֹפֶה אֶת לִבְזְבְּזָיו וְלֹא שְׁנָא בְּשֶׁאֵינוֹ חוֹפֶה אֶת לִבְזְבְּזָיו! אֶלָּא: שָׁאנֵי שֻׁלְחָן

And Rabbi Yoḥanan **said to him** in response: **It is not different** if it **is a fixed coating and it is not different** if it is **a coating that is not fixed;** and **it is not different** if the coating **covers** the table's **rim and it is not different** if **it does not cover its rim.** Therefore, since the coating always determines the status of the vessel, the Temple table, with its gold coating, should be susceptible to impurity. **Rather,** we must say a different explanation as to why the coating does not make the table susceptible to impurity: The **table is different**

NOTES

Let us derive it due to its coating – וְתֵיפּוּק לִי מִשּׁוּם צִיפּוּי: It appears that the Rambam had a different version of this discussion, for he rules that wooden vessels coated with marble do not contract impurity, not because they are nullified by their marble coating, marble being a material that is not susceptible to impurity, but due to a special principle that coated vessels do not contract impurity at all. According to this opinion the mishna's statement about the altars: "Because they are coated," can be explained in a straightforward manner, in that the Rabbis are saying that altars cannot be defiled because they are coated, and wooden vessels that have a coating are not capable of contracting impurity (*Kesef Mishne*, citing Rav Yosef Corcos).

However, it has already been pointed out by the *Kesef Mishne* that the discussion below (27a) cannot be explained in this manner, which means we would have to accept the rather forced explanation that the discussion there follows a different opinion, similar to that of Rashi and the Ra'avad.

Dulpaki – דּוּלְפְּקִי: Rashi explains that this term refers to a kind of folding chair with a leather seat. In tractate *Menaḥot* 96b he explains that it is a leather-topped table. The *ge'onim* in *Seder Teharot* imply that it means a sort of shelf upon which cups are placed.

A fixed coating – צִיפּוּי עוֹמֵד: Rashi explains that this refers to coating fixed tightly to the vessel. The *ge'onim*, however, maintain that this term, literally: A standing coating, means a coating that can stand on its own, without the support of the vessel for which it provides the coating. This is likewise indicated in the Jerusalem Talmud (see *Tosafot*).

דְּרַחֲמָנָא קַרְיֵיהּ עֵץ, דִּכְתִיב: ״הַמִּזְבֵּחַ עֵץ שָׁלֹשׁ אַמּוֹת גָּבֹהַּ וְאָרְכּוֹ שְׁתַּיִם אַמּוֹת וּמִקְצְעוֹתָיו לוֹ וְאָרְכּוֹ וְקִירוֹתָיו עֵץ וַיְדַבֵּר אֵלַי זֶה הַשֻּׁלְחָן אֲשֶׁר לִפְנֵי ה׳״.

because the Merciful One called it: "Wood," as it is **written** with regard to the table of the shewbread: **"The altar, three cubits high,**[N] **and its length two cubits, was of wood, and so its corners, its length, and its walls were also of wood, and he said to me: This is the table that is before the Lord"** (Ezekiel 41:22). This verse indicates that even though the table was coated, its identity as a wooden vessel was preserved, which means that, like all wooden vessels, it would not be susceptible to impurity were it not for the fact that they took it out to show to the pilgrims.

פָּתַח בְּמִזְבֵּחַ וְסִיֵּים בְּשֻׁלְחָן. רַבִּי יוֹחָנָן וְרֵישׁ לָקִישׁ דְּאָמְרִי תַּרְוַייהוּ: בִּזְמַן שֶׁבֵּית הַמִּקְדָּשׁ קַיָּים מִזְבֵּחַ מְכַפֵּר עַל אָדָם; עַכְשָׁיו – שֻׁלְחָנוֹ שֶׁל אָדָם מְכַפֵּר עָלָיו.

As the Gemara has cited the above verse, it clarifies a puzzling aspect of it: The verse **began with the** word **"altar" and ended with the** word **"table,"** both words describing the same item. **Rabbi Yoḥanan and Reish Lakish both say** the following exposition: **When the Temple is standing the altar atones for a person; now** that the Temple has been destroyed, it is **a person's table** that **atones for him,**[N] for his feeding of needy guests atones for his sins.

״כׇּל הַכֵּלִים שֶׁבַּמִּקְדָּשׁ יֵשׁ לָהֶם שְׁנִיִּים״ כּו׳. מִזְבַּח הַנְּחוֹשֶׁת – דִּכְתִיב: ״מִזְבַּח אֲדָמָה תַּעֲשֶׂה לִּי״. מִזְבַּח הַזָּהָב – דִּכְתִיב: ״הַמְּנוֹרָה וְהַמִּזְבְּחוֹת״ – אִיתְקוּשׁ מִזְבְּחוֹת זֶה לָזֶה.

§ The mishna taught: **All the vessels that were in the Temple had second** and third substitute vessels, **etc.** All the vessels that were in the Temple required immersion, apart from the golden altar and the bronze altar, because they are considered like the ground. The Gemara cites the relevant sources: **The bronze altar** is considered like the ground, **as it written** concerning this altar: **"An altar of earth you shall make for Me"** (Exodus 20:21). **The golden altar** is considered like the ground, **as it is written: "The candelabrum and the altars"** (Numbers 3:31). The plural word "altars" indicates that **the** two **altars** of the Temple, the bronze one and the golden one, **are compared to each other,** teaching that just as the bronze altar is like the ground in that it cannot contract impurity, the same applies to the golden altar.

״וַחֲכָמִים אוֹמְרִים מִפְּנֵי שֶׁהֵן מְצוּפִּין״. אַדְּרַבָּה, כֵּיוָן דִּמְצוּפִּין נִינְהוּ מִיטַּמְּאוּ! אֵימָא: וַחֲכָמִים מְטַמְּאִין מִפְּנֵי שֶׁהֵן מְצוּפִּין.

§ According to the mishna, Rabbi Eliezer maintains that the altars are pure because they are like the ground, **and the Rabbis say:** It is **because they are coated.** The mishna seems to be saying that the Rabbis are offering a different reason for the altars not being susceptible to impurity, namely, that they are coated. The Gemara is puzzled by this: **On the contrary, since they are coated** with gold or bronze that is a reason that they should **contract impurity,** as the metal coating makes the entire altar considered as a metal vessel, as stated above, and metal is susceptible to impurity. The Gemara answers: **Say** and emend the mishna text as follows: **And the Rabbis** disagree with Rabbi Eliezer altogether, and **declare** the altars **to be susceptible to impurity, because they are coated.**

וְאִיבָּעֵית אֵימָא: רַבָּנַן לְרַבִּי אֱלִיעֶזֶר קָאָמְרִי: מַאי דַּעְתִּיךְ? מִשּׁוּם דִּמְצוּפִּין?

And if you wish, say that that our text of the mishna is correct, and we should understand that **the Rabbis were saying** their statement in response **to Rabbi Eliezer: What is your reasoning** for stating that the altars are not susceptible to impurity because they are like the ground? Why didn't you say simply that they are wooden vessels fixed in one place? For that is sufficient reason for them not to be susceptible to impurity. Is it **because** they **are coated** with metal, and therefore they would be considered metal vessels rather than wooden ones, and susceptible to impurity, were it not for the fact that they are considered like the ground?

מִיבְטַל בְּטִיל צִפּוּיָין גַּבַּיְיהוּ.

This is a mistake, for the coating is not important, and **their coating is nullified** and considered subordinate **to them,** so that they are indeed considered wooden vessels in a fixed place and therefore not susceptible to impurity.[H] Although generally the status of a vessel does follow its coating, the Temple table and its altars are exceptions, as derived from the verse in Ezekiel cited above (41:22). There is therefore no need to mention that they are compared to the ground. Since these altars are made of wood they do not contract impurity, irrespective of whether or not they are attached to the ground.

NOTES

The altar, three cubits high – הַמִּזְבֵּחַ עֵץ שָׁלֹשׁ אַמּוֹת גָּבֹהַּ: This verse is speaking of the Temple table, and not its altar in the literal sense (Rashi on Ezekiel 41:22; *Tosafot* on *Menaḥot* 97a, based on *Targum Yonatan*).

A person's table atones – שֻׁלְחָנוֹ שֶׁל אָדָם מְכַפֵּר: Rashi explains that nowadays atonement is achieved through hospitality, by feeding people at one's table. The Maharsha maintains that one receives atonement by limiting his consumption of food for the sake of Heaven, i.e., in memory of the Temple, or for ascetic reasons. Others explain that one's table becomes like the altar if he says words of Torah at it (see tractate *Avot*, chapter 3).

HALAKHA

Immersing the Temple vessels – טְבִילַת כְּלֵי הַמִּקְדָּשׁ: All the Temple vessels require immersion and the setting of the sun after the Festival, apart from the bronze and golden altars, because their coating was considered nullified and subordinate to the wooden altars themselves (Rambam *Sefer Tahara*, *Hilkhot Metamei Mishkav UMoshav* 11:11). This is stated by the Rabbis and is in accordance with the last answer of the Gemara, for the *halakha* generally follows the last answer (*Kesef Mishne*).

אָמַר רַבִּי אַבָּהוּ אָמַר רַבִּי אֶלְעָזָר: תַּלְמִידֵי חֲכָמִים אֵין אוּר שֶׁל גֵּיהִנָּם שׁוֹלֶטֶת בָּהֶן, קַל וָחוֹמֶר מִסָּלָמַנְדְּרָא; וּמַה סָּלָמַנְדְּרָא שֶׁתּוֹלֶדֶת אֵשׁ הִיא – הַסָּךְ מִדָּמָהּ אֵין אוּר שׁוֹלֶטֶת בּוֹ, תַּלְמִידֵי חֲכָמִים שֶׁכָּל גּוּפָן אֵשׁ, דִּכְתִיב: "הֲלוֹא כֹה דְבָרִי כָּאֵשׁ נְאֻם ה'" – עַל אַחַת כַּמָּה וְכַמָּה.

§ Apropos the coating of the altar, the Gemara cites an Aggadic teaching: **Rabbi Abbahu said** that **Rabbi Elazar said: The fire of Gehenna has no power over Torah scholars.** This can be derived by an ***a fortiori*** inference **from the salamander** [***salamandra***],[LB] a creature created out of fire and immune to its effects, and whose blood is fireproof: **If a salamander, which is** merely **a product of fire,** and nevertheless when **one anoints** his body **with its blood, fire has no power over him, all the more so** should fire not have any power over **Torah scholars, whose entire bodies are fire, as it is written: "Surely My words are as fire, says the Lord"** (Jeremiah 23:29), and the words of Torah become part of the Torah scholars' very bodies.

אָמַר רֵישׁ לָקִישׁ: אֵין אוּר שֶׁל גֵּיהִנָּם שׁוֹלֶטֶת בְּפוֹשְׁעֵי יִשְׂרָאֵל, קַל וָחוֹמֶר מִמִּזְבַּח הַזָּהָב; מַה מִּזְבַּח הַזָּהָב שֶׁאֵין עָלָיו אֶלָּא כְּעוֹבִי דִּינַר זָהָב, כַּמָּה שָׁנִים אֵין הָאוּר שׁוֹלֶטֶת בּוֹ, פּוֹשְׁעֵי יִשְׂרָאֵל שֶׁמְּלֵאִין מִצְוֹת כָּרִמּוֹן, דִּכְתִיב: "כְּפֶלַח הָרִמּוֹן רַקָּתֵךְ", אַל תִּקְרִי "רַקָּתֵךְ" אֶלָּא רֵיקָנִין שֶׁבָּךְ – עַל אַחַת כַּמָּה וְכַמָּה.

Reish Lakish said: The **fire of Gehenna has no power over the sinners of Israel** either. This can be derived by **an *a fortiori*** inference **from the golden altar: If the golden altar, which** has **on it** a coating that is **no more than the thickness of a gold dinar,**[N] and which has incense burning on it **for many years** and yet **fire has no power over it,** as the gold miraculously remained undamaged, **all the more so** should immunity from fire be granted to **the sinners of Israel, who are filled with good deeds as a pomegranate** is full of seeds,[N] **as it is written: "Your temples** [***rakatekh***] **are like a pomegranate split open"** (Song of Songs 4:3), which is to be expounded as follows: **Do not read** this word as ***rakatekh***, **rather** read it as ***reikanin shebakh***, meaning the empty, worthless people among you; even these people are as full of good deeds as a pomegranate is full of seeds.

הדרן עלך חומר בקודש
וסליקא לה מסכת חגיגה

LANGUAGE

Salamander [*salamandra*] – סָלָמַנְדְּרָא: From the Greek σαλαμάνδρα, *salamandra*, a tailed amphibian.

BACKGROUND

Salamander – סָלָמַנְדְּרָא: Salamander is the name, of Greek origin, for a group of tailed animals that includes hundreds of species. The common salamander, *Salamandra salamandra*, also known as fire salamander, lives near swamps and streams in Israel, as in many places in the world. It looks like a fat lizard, about 30 cm in length, with slimy skin. The salamander feeds on bugs and small animals found in the water.

The word *salamandra* is also used to refer to a creature formed by fire. *Midrashim* include various descriptions of the salamander's creation from fire, and the ability of its blood and skin to grant immunity from fire. Rabbi Binyamin Mussafia claims that these depictions refer to the same creature, whose resistance to fire he believes to be on account of the moistness of its skin. However, the descriptions in the *midrashim* and other places do not accord with this explanation.

Fire salamander

NOTES

No more than the thickness of a gold dinar – כְּעוֹבִי דִּינַר זָהָב: Rashi explains that the gold coating of the altar remained undamaged despite its thinness and the repeated burning of incense on it. *Tosafot* explain that the Gemara is referring to the wood of the golden altar that was under the coating, which was not burned over the course of the years (see Maharsha). It is stated in the Jerusalem Talmud that it was a heavenly, supernatural fire that descended upon the golden altar, and yet the altar itself was unharmed. The lesson from this is that just as even a divinely created fire did not affect the altar, similarly the divinely created fire of Gehenna will not affect the Torah scholars.

The sinners of Israel, who are filled with good deeds as a pomegranate is full of seeds – פּוֹשְׁעֵי יִשְׂרָאֵל שֶׁמְּלֵאִין מִצְוֹת כָּרִמּוֹן: The meaning of this *aggada* is that the words of the Torah, which are called "More pleasant than gold and much fine gold" (Psalms 19:11), serve to protect Israel. The *Sefat Emet* connects this teaching to the earlier discussion about the purity of all Israel on Festivals, which similarly emphasizes the importance and value of even common, uneducated people in the eyes of God.

Summary of **Perek III**

The Sages enumerated ten stringencies that apply to sacrificial food and the vessels used in its preparation and storage which do not apply to *teruma* and its vessels, owing to the greater level of sanctity inherent in the former. Some of these stringencies have a basis in the Torah or are hinted at in verses, but they were expanded in scope and breadth by the Sages. Others are rabbinic decrees designed to avoid outright contamination of the sacred food. On the other hand, in view of the fact that everyone, including *amei ha'aretz,* adhered to the strictest standards in the preparation of sacrificial items, the Sages relied on *amei ha'aretz* for certain matters pertaining to sacrificial food, though ordinarily such people were not considered trustworthy regarding issues of ritual impurity.

In actuality the trustworthiness afforded by the Sages in matters pertaining to sacrificial food was expanded beyond the sacrifices themselves, and was applied as well to other items that have a relationship to sacrifices. Consequently, the people of Judea, which is in close proximity to the Temple, were considered more trustworthy than others regarding the observance of ritual purity. The Sages showed leniency regarding certain other matters pertaining to the honor and sanctity of Jerusalem.

Perhaps most sweeping of all was the leniency shown by the Sages during the time of the pilgrimage Festivals. These occasions, when all of Israel assembled before God at the Temple, were considered times in which it was possible to rely completely on *amei ha'aretz* in all matters regarding ritual purity. This was based on the necessity to maintain harmony among all the various factions and individuals in Israel at this time of unity, when, in the words of the biblical verse, "All the men of Israel gathered… knit together [*ḥaverim*] as one man" (Judges 20:11).

Index of Background

Index of **Language**

Index of **Personalities**

Image **Credits**

Common **Acronyms**

Since the publication of the first volume of the *Koren Talmud Bavli* we have employed some transliterated acronyms, such as Rambam, to give the translation a more authentic flavor. These acronyms are used throughout this volume where they are well known and where the acronym helps readers easily identify the author in question. The following chart provides the full name of each author or work alongside its common acronym.

Acronym	Full Name
HaAri	Rabbi Yitzḥak Luria
Ba'al HaMaor	Rabbi Zeraḥya HaLevi
Baḥ	*Bayit Ḥadash*
Beur HaGra	Commentary of Rabbi Eliyahu of Vilna on the *Shulḥan Arukh*
Derashot Mahari Mintz	Homilies of Rabbi Yehuda Mintz
Derashot Ra'anaḥ	Homilies of Rabbi Eliyahu ben Ḥayyim
Geranat	Rabbi Naftali Trop
Gilyon Maharsha	Marginalia of Rabbi Shlomo Eiger
Gra	Rabbi Eliyahu of Vilna, the Vilna Gaon
Graḥ	Rabbi Ḥayyim Soloveitchik
Grib	Rabbi Yehuda Bakhrakh
Griz	Rabbi Yitzḥak Ze'ev Soloveitchik
Haggahot HaGra	Comments of Rabbi Eliyahu of Vilna on the Talmud
Haggahot Maharsha	Comments of Rabbi Shmuel Eliezer Eidels
Hassagot HaRa'avad	Comments of Rabbi Avraham ben David on the Rambam's *Mishne Torah*
Ḥida	Rabbi Ḥayyim David Azulai
Ḥiddushei Aggadot LaMaharal	*Ḥiddushei Aggadot* by Rabbi Yehuda Loew of Prague
Ḥiddushei Aggadot LaRashba	*Ḥiddushei Aggadot* by Rabbi Shlomo ben Adderet
Ḥiddushei HaGeranat	*Ḥiddushei* Rabbi Naftali Trop
Ḥiddushei HaGriz	*Ḥiddushei* Rabbi Yitzḥak Ze'ev Soloveitchik
Ḥiddushei HaRim	*Ḥiddushei* Rabbi Yitzḥak Meir of Gur
Ḥiddushei Ri Ḥaver	*Ḥiddushei* Rabbi Yitzḥak Isaac Ḥaver
Kitzur Piskei HaRosh	Abridged Halakhic Rulings of Rabbeinu Asher ben Rabbi Yeḥiel
Mabit	Rabbi Moshe ben Yosef di Trani
Maharal	Rabbi Yehuda Loew of Prague
Maharam Alashkar	Rabbi Moshe Alashkar
Maharam Brisk	Rabbi Mordekhai Brisk
Maharam Ḥalawa	Rabbi Moshe Ḥalawa
Maharam Lublin	Rabbi Meir of Lublin

Acronym	Full Name
Maharam Mintz	Rabbi Moshe Mintz
Maharam of Rothenburg	Rabbi Meir of Rothenburg
Maharam Padua	Rabbi Meir of Padua
Maharam Schick	Rabbi Moshe Schick
Maharam Schiff	Rabbi Meir Schiff
Maharatz Ḥayyut	Rabbi Tzvi Hirsch Chajes
Mahari Abuhav	Rabbi Yitzḥak Abuhav
Mahari Bassan	Rabbi Yeḥiel Bassan
Mahari Beirav	Rabbi Ya'akov Beirav
Mahari ben Lev	Rabbi Yosef ben Lev
Mahari ben Malkitzedek	Rabbi Yitzḥak ben Malkitzedek
Mahari Berona	Rabbi Yisrael Berona
Mahari Kurkus	Rabbi Yosef Kurkus
Mahari Mintz	Rabbi Yehuda Mintz
Mahari Weil	Rabbi Ya'akov Weil
Mahariḥ	Rabbi Yeḥezkia ben Ya'akov of Magdeburg
Maharik	Rabbi Yosef Colon
Maharikash	Rabbi Ya'akov Castro
Maharil	Rabbi Ya'akov HaLevi Molin
Maharit	Rabbi Yosef di Trani
Maharit Algazi	Rabbi Yom Tov Algazi
Maharsha	Rabbi Shmuel Eliezer Eidels
Maharshal	Rabbi Shlomo Luria
Malbim	Rabbi Meir Leibush ben Yeḥiel Michel Wisser
Netziv	Rabbi Naftali Tzvi Yehuda Berlin
Nimmukei HaGrib	Comments of Rabbi Yehuda Bakhrakh on the Maharsha
Piskei HaRid	Halakhic Rulings of Rabbi Yeshaya di Trani the Elder
Piskei Riaz	Halakhic Rulings of Rabbi Yeshaya di Trani the Younger
Ra'ah	Rabbi Aharon HaLevi
Ra'anaḥ	Rabbi Eliyahu ben Ḥayyim
Ra'avad	Rabbi Avraham ben David
Ra'avan	Rabbi Eliezer ben Natan
Ra'avya	Rabbi Eliezer ben Yoel HaLevi
Rabbi Avraham ben HaRambam	Rabbi Avraham, son of the Rambam
Rabbi Shlomo ben Rashbatz	Rabbi Shlomo, son of Rabbi Shimon ben Tzemaḥ Duran
Radak	Rabbi David Kimḥi
Radbaz	Rabbi David ben Zimra
Ralbag	Rabbi Levi ben Gershon
Ramah	Rabbi Meir HaLevi
Rambam	Rabbi Moshe ben Maimon
Ramban	Rabbi Moshe ben Naḥman

Acronym	Full Name
Ran	Rabbeinu Nissim ben Reuven of Gerona
Rashash	Rabbi Shmuel Strashun
Rashba	Rabbi Shlomo ben Adderet
Rashbam	Rabbi Shmuel ben Meir
Rashbatz	Rabbi Shimon ben Tzemaḥ Duran
Rashi	Rabbi Shlomo Yitzḥaki
Re'em Horowitz	Rabbi Elazar Moshe Horowitz
Rema	Rabbi Moshe Isserles
Ri HaLavan	Rabbeinu Yitzḥak ben Ya'akov of Prague
Ri Ḥaver	Rabbi Yitzḥak Isaac Ḥaver
Ri Migash	Rabbi Yosef Migash
Riaf	Rabbi Yoshiya Pinto
Riaz	Rabbi Yeshaya di Trani the Younger
Rid	Rabbi Yeshaya di Trani the Elder
Ridvaz	Rabbi Ya'akov David ben Ze'ev Wilovsky
Rif	Rabbi Yitzḥak Alfasi
Rim	Rabbi Yitzḥak Meir of Gur
Ritva	Rabbi Yom Tov ben Avraham Asevilli (of Seville)
Riva	Rabbeinu Yitzḥak ben Asher
Rivam	Rabbi Yitzḥak ben Meir
Rivan	Rabbi Yehuda bar Natan
Rivash	Rabbi Yitzḥak ben Sheshet
Rosh	Rabbeinu Asher ben Rabbi Yeḥiel
Shakh	*Siftei Kohen* by Rabbi Shabtai Cohen Rappaport
Shas	The Six Orders of the Mishna
She'elat Ya'avetz	Responsa of Rabbi Ya'akov Emden
Shela	*Shenei Luḥot HaBerit* by Rabbi Yeshaya HaLevi Horowitz
Siddur Rashi	Siddur compiled by Rashi's students
Sma	*Sefer Meirat Einayim* by Rabbi Yehoshua Falk
Smag	*Sefer Mitzvot Gadol* by Rabbi Moshe of Coucy
Smak	*Sefer Mitzvot Katan* by Rabbi Yitzḥak ben Yosef of Corbeil
Talmid HaRa'ah	A student of Rabbi Aharon HaLevi
Talmid HaRashba	A student of Rabbi Shlomo ben Adderet
Tashbetz	Responsa of Rabbi Shimon ben Tzemaḥ Duran
Taz	*Turei Zahav* by Rabbi David HaLevi
Tosefot HaRosh	*Tosefot* of Rabbeinu Asher ben Rabbi Yeḥiel
Tosefot Ri HaLavan	*Tosefot* of Rabbeinu Yitzḥak ben Ya'akov of Prague
Tosefot Rid	*Tosefot* of Rabbi Yeshaya di Trani the Elder
Tur	*Sefer HaTurim* by Rabbi Ya'akov ben Asher
Tzlaḥ	*Tziyyun LeNefesh Ḥayya* by Rabbi Yeḥezkel Landau
Ya'avetz	Rabbi Ya'akov Emden

תלמוד בבלי

— מהדורת נאה —

מועד קטן · חגיגה

Steinsaltz Center

KOREN

תלמוד בבלי

הוצאת קוֹרֵן ירושלים

מהדורת נאה

מועד קטן · חגיגה

COMMENTARY BY

Rabbi Adin Even-Israel Steinsaltz

EDITOR-IN-CHIEF

Rabbi Dr Tzvi Hersh Weinreb

EXECUTIVE EDITOR

Rabbi Joshua Schreier

•

STEINSALTZ CENTER
KOREN PUBLISHERS JERUSALEM

משקין

אבית השלחין במועד •ובשביעית, בין ממעיין שיצא בתחילה, בין ממעיין שלא יצא בתחילה. באבל אין משקין לא ממי הגשמים, ולא ממי הקילון. גואין עושין *עוגיות לגפנים. רבי אלעזר בן עזריה אומר: אין עושין את האמה בתחילה במועד ובשביעית, וחכמים אומרים: דעושין את האמה בתחילה בשביעית, הומתקנין את המקולקלות במועד. (א) ומתקנין את קלקולי המים שברשות הרבים, וחוטטין אותן, זומתקנין את הדרכים ואת הרחובות ואת (ב) מקוות המים, ועושין כל צורכי הרבים, ומציינין את הקברות, חויוצאין אף על הכלאים.§ גמ' השתא יש לומר ממעיין שיצא בתחילה, דאתי לאינפולי – משקין, ממעיין שלא יצא בתחילה, דלא אתי לאינפולי, מיבעיא? אמרי: אצטריך; אי תנא מעיין שיצא בתחילה – הוה אמינא: הכא הוא דבית השלחין – אין, בית הבעל – לא, משום דאתי לאינפולי. אבל מעיין שלא יצא בתחילה, דלא אתי לאינפולי, אימא אפילו בית הבעל נמי, קא משמע לן: לא שנא מעיין שיצא בתחילה, ולא שנא מעיין שלא יצא בתחילה, בית השלחין – אין, בית הבעל – לא. ומאי משמע דהאי בית השלחין לישנא דצחותא היא – דכתיב *°"ואתה עיף ויגע" (דברים כה) ומתרגמינן: ואת משלהי ולאי. ומאי משמע דהאי בית הבעל לישנא דמייתבותא היא – דכתיב: °"כי יבעל בחור בתולה" (ישעיה סב), ומתרגמינן: ארי כמה דמיתותב עולם עם בתולתא יתייתבון בגויך בניך. מאן תנא טדפסידא – אין, הרווחה – לא, יואפילו במקום פסידא מיטרח נמי לא טרחינן? אמר רב הונא: ר' אליעזר בן יעקב היא. דתנן, *רבי אליעזר בן יעקב אומר: מושכין את המים מאילן לאילן, ובלבד שלא ישקה את השדה כולה. אימור דשמעת ליה לרבי אליעזר הרווחה דלא, טירחא במקום פסידא מי שמעת ליה? אלא אמר רב פפא: הא מני – רבי יהודה היא, דתניא: *מעיין היוצא בתחילה משקין ממנו אפילו שדה בית הבעל, דברי רבי מאיר. רבי יהודה אומר: כאין משקין אלא שדה בית השלחין שחרבה. רבי אלעזר בן עזריה אומר: לא כך ולא כך. יתר על כן אמר רבי יהודה: לא יפנה אדם אמת המים וישקה לגינתו ולחורבתו בחולו של מועד. מאי חרבה? אילימא חרבה ממש – למה לי דמשקי לה?(ג) אמר אביי: שחרבה ממעיין זה, ויצא לה מעיין אחר. רבי אלעזר בן עזריה אומר לא כך ולא כך. לא שנא חרב מעיינה ולא שנא לא חרב מעיינה, מעיין שיצא בתחילה – לא. וממאי? דלמא עד כאן לא קאמר רבי יהודה בית השלחין אין, בית הבעל לא – אלא מעיין שיצא בתחילה, דלמא

רש"י

משקין בית השלחין במועד. שדה שהיא עומדת בצר, וצריך להשקותה תמיד – משקין אותה, אפילו בחולו של מועד. לפי שהוא לו הפסד גדול אם אינו משקה אותה. ודבר של הפסד התירו חכמים לטרוח בו בחולו של מועד, כמו שאנו אומרין במסכת חגיגה (דף יח.), דכתיב (דברים טז): "ששת ימים תאכל מצות וביום השביעי עצרת לה' אלהיך" מה שביעי עצור בעשיית מלאכה – אף ששה עצורים בעשיית מלאכה. אי מה שביעי עצור בכל מלאכה – אף ששה עצורין בכל מלאכה? תלמוד לומר: "השביעי" שביעי – עצור בכל מלאכה, ואין ששה עצורין בכל מלאכה. הא לא מסרן הכתוב אלא לחכמים, לומר לך איזו מלאכה אסורה בחוה"מ ואי זו מותרת. ומלאכה שיש בה הפסד אם אינו עושה אותה, כגון להשקות בית השלחין – התירו חכמים: ובשביעית. מפרש בגמרא: ממעיין שיצא בתחילה. דעכשיו מתחיל לנבוע, שעדיין לא החזיקה דרכה: בין ממעיין שלא יצא בתחילה. אלא מעיין נובע מזמן מרובה: אבל לא ממי גשמים. משום דאית ביה טירחא יתירא, כדמפרש בגמרא: גמ' דאתי לאינפולי. הקרקע שסביבה, דעדיין לא החזיקה דרכה: משקין. בחולו של מועד, ולא חיישינן דלמא נפיל, ואזיל וטרח טירחא יתירא: מעיין שלא יצא בתחילה. שכבר החזיק דרכו: מיבעיא. דמשקה ממנו בחולו של מועד: בית הבעל. שדה הוא בעמק, ואינו צריך להשקותה, ואין בה הפסד אם אין משקה אותה: קא משמע לן. מתניתין, דתני: בין ממעיין שלא יצא בתחילה: בית השלחין אין בית הבעל. אפילו ממעיין שלא יצא בתחילה – לא: (*מישלהי). וה"א מתחלף בחי"ת: מאן תנא. דמתני', דפסידא שרי למיטרח בה בחוה"מ, כגון בית השלחין: הרווחה לא. כגון דבית הבעל, דאסור להשקותה מאחר שאין בה הפסד, שאין צריך להשקותה אלא להרווחה דמילתא, לשוויה אפלי חרפי: אפילו במקום פסידא מיטרח לא טרחינן. דקתני מתניתין: אבל לא ממי גשמים כו' – משום דאית ביה טירחא: מושכין המים מאילן לאילן. בחולו של מועד, אם יש מים תחת אילן אחד – עושין דרך קטן מאילן לאילן, כדי שימשכו המים מאילן זה לאילן אחר: (ד)לא ישקה את השדה כולה. כבית הבעל קמייתי, דהרווחה היא, אלמא: דהרווחה דמילתא אסר ר' אליעזר: אילימא חרבה ממש. שנעשה בור, למה לי למשקה להיאך? דהא אין לה תקנה לעולם: שחרבה ממעיין זה ויצא לה מעיין אחר. שחרב מעיינה שרגילה לשתות ממנו, דכיון שרגילה לשתות, אי לא משקה לה עכשיו – אית ליה פסידא יתירא. אפילו הכי לא שרי ר' יהודה אלא ממעיין שיצא לה, דלאו טירחא הוא – אבל מי גשמים ומי קילון, דטירחא הוא – לא שרי אפילו לבית השלחין. ועוד: חזינן דקאמר רבי יהודה לא יפנה(ה) מים כו' אלמא: דלא שרי ר' יהודה, טירחא יתירא. אלמא מתני' ר' יהודה היא, דהא ראב"ע ל"ש חרב מעיינה ממעיינה שיצא לה בתחילה, ול"ש לא חרב – תרוייהו אסר: דלמא

תוספות

משקין בית השלחין. שדה שאינה מסתפקת במי גשמים וצריך להשקותה תמיד, ואם אין משקין אותה תדיר – נפסדת, והלכך משקין אותה בחוה"מ, ומשום פסידא שרו ליה רבנן. כדאמרינן בפ' "אין דורשין" (חגיגה דף יח. ושם), תניא אידך: "ששת ימים תאכל מצות וביום השביעי עצרת לה' אלהיך" מה שביעי עצור – אף ששה עצורים, אי מה שביעי עצור מכל מלאכה – אף כל ששה עצורים מכל מלאכה? תלמוד לומר: השביעי, ה"א יתירא, השביעי עצור מכל מלאכה ואין הששה עצורים מכל מלאכה. הא לא מסרן הכתוב אלא לחכמים, ללמדך איזה יום אסור ואיזה יום מותר, איזו מלאכה אסורה ואיזו מלאכה מותרת:

וחוטטין אותה. שאם נתמלא הבור – מותר לחטוט להעמיקו, שהעפר תיחוח, אבל לחופרה בתחילה, שהקרקע קשה – לא, משום דאיכא טירחא יתירא:

ומציינין דליכא טירחא:

ויוצאין על הכלאים. מצוה הוא לצאת, כדאמרינן בגמ'. ולא דמי להני אחריני דקתני ומתקנין, דהאי חובה הוא, כדמוכח בגמרא:

עיף ויגע. צמא, למים כדכתיב *"הרויתי נפש עיפה" (ירמיה לא):

מאן תנא פסידא אין. משום דאשכחן לקמן דרבי מאיר פליג עלה דמתני', והאי סתם מתניתין לא אתיא אליביה כשאר סתמי, משום הכי קבעי התלמוד: מאן תנא?

מושכין אמת המים כו'. שאם יש שם מים תחת אילן זה – יכול למושכם במועד תחת אילן אחר, משום דאילן כבית השלחין דמי, וצריכין למים טפי, והא דתנא מושכין ולא תנא משקין – אורחא דמילתא קתני, דבענין זה רגילין להשקות אילנות: יתר על כן אמר רבי יהודה. עוד היה מחמיר יותר, אפילו בבית השלחין קא אסר להפנות משום דהוי טירחא יתירא:

לגינתו ולחורבתו. של בית השלחין. גינה – מקום זרעים, חורבה – מקום שחרבו אילנותיו, וחרשו וזרעו ונטעו. ושמא הוא צריך למים יותר, ולא זו אף זו קתני. אי נמי: חרב ביתו ועשאו גינה, וצריכה מים תדיר יותר משאר בית השלחין, ומשום דאיכא טירחא יתירא – לא:

אם

רבינו חננאל

משקין בית השלחין במועד ובשביעי' בין ממעין שיצא בתחלה ובין ממעין כו' ומקשינן השתא יש לומר ממעין שיצא בתחלה דחיישינן דלמא אתי לאינפולי ובני ליה אמרת משקין ממעין שכבר יצא וניתקן ועמד מיבעיא. ופרקינן איצטריך לאשמועינן דאפי' ממעין ישן דליכא חששא דלמא נפיל ובני ליה אין משקין אלא בית השלחין שהן נטועין וצמאין למים מלשון שלהי כדמתרגמי' והוא עיף ומשלהי. אבל בית הבעל שכבר גדל והשריש שרשים בקרקע כמו בעל באשתו כדכתיב והולידה והצמיחה. בין ממעין שיצא בתחלה ובין ממעין שלא יצא בתחלה אין משקין שדה בית הבעל. ואמרינן מאן תנא דחייש לפסידא דבית השלחין כדי שלא יפסידו וייבשו והתיר להשקותם ואפי' הכי לא התיר אלא דבר שאין בו טורח. אבל להשקות ממי גשמים וכיוצא בהן שיש טורח בהן לא התיר. אמר רב הונא ר' אליעזר בן יעקב היא דתנא ר' אליעזר בן יעקב אומר מושכין מים מאילן לאילן אבל לא ישקה את כל השדה ודחינן אימור דשמעת לר' אליעזר דלא שרי הרווחה מדקתני לא ישקה את כל השדה אבל שלא להטריח במקום שיש פסידא מי שמעת ליה. ובא רב פפא ואוקמה לר' יהודה דתני אין משקין ממעין היוצא בתחלה אלא שדה בית השלחין שחרבה. ומקשינן אי חרבה למה לי השקאה אמר אביי מאי חרבה דקתני חרב מעיינה ויצא לה מעין אחר בתחלה וסבר ר' יהודה ל"ש מעין שיצא בתחלה ולא שנא מעין שלא יצא בתחלה אין משקין אלא בית השלחין. והא דקתני מעין שיצא בתחלה איידי דאמר ר' מאיר מעין שיצא בתחלה משקין ממנו אפי' שדה

עין משפט נר מצוה

א א מיי' פ"ז מהלכות יו"ט הלכה ב ופ"א מהלכות שמטה הלכה ח סמג לאוין עה ועשין דרבנן ב טוש"ע א"ח סי' תקלז סעיף א:

ב ב מיי' פ"ז מהלכות יו"ט שם טוש"ע שם סעיף ב:

ג ג מיי' פ"ח מהלכות י"ט הלכה ג טוש"ע שם סעיף ה:

ד ד מיי' פ"א מהלכות שמטה הלכה ט:

ה ה מיי' פ"ח מהלכות יו"ט הלכה ג טוש"ע שם סעיף ו:

ו ו מיי' שם פ"ז הלכה י טוש"ע שם סי' תקמד סעיף ב:

ז ז מיי' שם טוש"ע שם סעיף א:

ח ח מיי' פ"ז מהלכות י"ט הלכה יא:

ט ט י מיי' שם הלכה ב טוש"ע שם סי' תקלז סעיף א ב:

י כ מיי' שם טוש"ע שם סעיף א:

[הגוסחא הישנה ונפש עיפה למים לא נמצא בתנ"ך עיין תוי"ט]

מסורת הש"ס

[עי' פרש"י לקמן ד: ד"ה עוגיות]

[נ"ל משלהי]

[גי' הערוך בערך שלה ה דכתיב והוא עיף (בראשית כה) תרגומו והוא משלהי]

לקמן ו:

[ע"ש תוספתא]

גליון הש"ס

מתני' ובשביעית בין ממעיין. עיין לקמן דף ו ע"ב תוס' ד"ה מרבילין:

הגהות הב"ח

(א) מתני' ומתקנין את קלקולי המים. נ"ב עי' פרש"י בדף ה ע"א: (ב) שם ואת מקוואות המים ועושין: (ג) גמ' למשקי לה ואמר אביי שחרבה כו' לא חרב מעיינה ממעיין שיצא בתחלה: (ד) רש"י ד"ה שלא ישקה: (ה) ד"ה שחרבה כו' דקאר"י לא יפנה אדם אמת המים כו' אלמא וכו' ל"ש חרב מעיינה ול"ש לא חרב תרווייהו אסר ממעיין שיצא לה בתחילה כצ"ל והס"ד:

יא א מיי' פ"ח מהלכות שבת הלכה ב:
יב ב מיי' שם הלכה ד:
יג ג מיי' פ"א מהלכות כלאים הלכה ב סמג לאוין רעט טוש"ע י"ד סי' רצז סעיף א:
יד ד מיי' פ"ט מהלכות שמטה הלכה ב סמג לאוין ער וסמג עשין קמט:

דִּלְמָא אָתֵי לְאִינְפּוּלֵי. אֲבָל מַעְיָן שֶׁלֹּא יָצָא בַּתְּחִילָּה, דְּלָא אָתֵי לְאִינְפּוּלֵי — אֲפִילּוּ בֵּית הַבַּעַל נַמִּי. אִם כֵּן מַתְנִיתִין אַמַּאן תַּרְמְיָהּ? אֶלָּא: לְרַבִּי יְהוּדָה לָא שְׁנָא מַעְיָן שֶׁיָּצָא בַּתְּחִילָּה וְלָא שְׁנָא מַעְיָן שֶׁלֹּא יָצָא בַּתְּחִילָּה, בֵּית הַשְּׁלָחִין — אִין, בֵּית הַבַּעַל — לָא. וְהַאי דְּקָתָנֵי מַעְיָן שֶׁיָּצָא בַּתְּחִילָּה — לְהוֹדִיעֲךָ כֹּחוֹ דְּר' מֵאִיר, דַּאֲפִילּוּ מַעְיָן הַיּוֹצֵא בַּתְּחִילָּה מַשְׁקִין מִמֶּנּוּ אֲפִילּוּ שְׂדֵה הַבַּעַל. אִתְּמַר, הַמְנַכֵּשׁ וְהַמַּשְׁקֶה מַיִם לִזְרָעִים בְּשַׁבָּת, מִשּׁוּם מַאי מַתְרִינַן בֵּיהּ? רַבָּה אָמַר: מִשּׁוּם חוֹרֵשׁ, רַב יוֹסֵף אָמַר: [א]מִשּׁוּם זוֹרֵעַ. אָמַר רַבָּה: כְּוָותִי דִּידִי מִסְתַּבְּרָא, מַה דַּרְכּוֹ שֶׁל חוֹרֵשׁ — לְרַפּוּיֵי אַרְעָא, הַאי נַמִּי מְרַפּוּיֵי אַרְעָא. אָמַר רַב יוֹסֵף: כְּוָותִי דִּידִי מִסְתַּבְּרָא, מַה דַּרְכּוֹ שֶׁל זוֹרֵעַ — לְצַמּוּחֵי פֵּירָא, הָכָא נַמִּי מְצַמַּח פֵּירָא. אֲמַר לֵיהּ אַבַּיֵי לְרַבָּה: לְדִידָךְ קַשְׁיָא, וּלְרַב יוֹסֵף קַשְׁיָא. לְדִידָךְ קַשְׁיָא: מִשּׁוּם חוֹרֵשׁ אִין, מִשּׁוּם זוֹרֵעַ לָא? לְרַב יוֹסֵף קַשְׁיָא: מִשּׁוּם זוֹרֵעַ אִין, מִשּׁוּם חוֹרֵשׁ לָא? וְכִי תֵּימָא כָּל הֵיכָא דְּאִיכָּא תַּרְתֵּי לָא מִיחַיַּיב אֶלָּא חֲדָא, וְהָאָמַר רַב כַּהֲנָא: *[ב]זוֹמֵר וְצָרִיךְ לָעֵצִים — חַיָּיב שְׁתַּיִם, אַחַת מִשּׁוּם נוֹטֵעַ וְאַחַת מִשּׁוּם קוֹצֵר. קַשְׁיָא. אֵיתִיבֵיהּ רַב יוֹסֵף לְרַבָּה: *[ג]הַמְנַכֵּשׁ וְהַמְחַפֶּה לְכִלְאַיִם — לוֹקֶה, רַבִּי עֲקִיבָא אוֹמֵר: אַף *הַמְקַיֵּים. בִּשְׁלָמָא לְדִידִי דְּאָמִינָא מִשּׁוּם זוֹרֵעַ — הַיְינוּ דַּאֲסִירָא זְרִיעָה בְּכִלְאַיִם, אֶלָּא לְדִידָךְ דְּאָמְרַתְּ מִשּׁוּם חוֹרֵשׁ — חֲרִישָׁה בְּכִלְאַיִם מִי אֲסִירָא? אֲמַר לֵיהּ: מִשּׁוּם מְקַיֵּים. וְהָא מִדְּקָתָנֵי סֵיפָא: ר"ע אוֹמֵר אַף הַמְקַיֵּים, מִכְּלָל דְּתַנָּא קַמָּא לָאו מִשּׁוּם מְקַיֵּים הוּא! כּוּלָּהּ ר' עֲקִיבָא הִיא, וּמַאי טַעַם קָאָמַר; מַאי טַעַם הַמְנַכֵּשׁ וְהַמְחַפֶּה בְּכִלְאַיִם לוֹקֶה — מִשּׁוּם מְקַיֵּים, שֶׁר"ע אוֹמֵר אַף הַמְקַיֵּים. מַאי טַעְמָא דְּר' עֲקִיבָא — דְּתַנְיָא: °"שָׂדְךָ לֹא תִזְרַע כִּלְאָיִם" אֵין לִי אֶלָּא זוֹרֵעַ, מְקַיֵּים מִנַּיִין? תַּלְמוּד לוֹמַר "כִּלְאַיִם שָׂדְךָ לֹא". תְּנַן: מַשְׁקִין בֵּית הַשְּׁלָחִין בַּמּוֹעֵד וּבַשְּׁבִיעִית. בִּשְׁלָמָא מוֹעֵד מִשּׁוּם טִירְחָא הוּא, וּבִמְקוֹם פְּסֵידָא שָׁרוּ רַבָּנַן. אֶלָּא שְׁבִיעִית, בֵּין לְמַאן דְּאָמַר מִשּׁוּם זוֹרֵעַ, וּבֵין לְמַאן דְּאָמַר מִשּׁוּם חוֹרֵשׁ — זְרִיעָה וַחֲרִישָׁה בַּשְּׁבִיעִית מִי שָׁרֵי?! אָמַר אַבַּיֵי: בַּשְּׁבִיעִית בַּזְּמַן הַזֶּה, וְרַבִּי הִיא. דְּתַנְיָא, *רַבִּי אוֹמֵר: °"וְזֶה דְּבַר הַשְּׁמִטָּה שָׁמוֹט" — [ד]בִּשְׁתֵּי שְׁמִיטּוֹת הַכָּתוּב מְדַבֵּר, אַחַת שְׁמִיטַּת קַרְקַע וְאַחַת שְׁמִיטַּת כְּסָפִים. בִּזְמַן שֶׁאַתָּה מְשַׁמֵּט קַרְקַע — אַתָּה מְשַׁמֵּט כְּסָפִים, וּבִזְמַן שֶׁאִי אַתָּה מְשַׁמֵּט קַרְקַע — אִי אַתָּה מְשַׁמֵּט כְּסָפִים. רָבָא אָמַר: אֲפִילּוּ תֵּימָא רַבָּנַן, אָבוֹת אָסַר רַחֲמָנָא,

תּוֹלָדוֹת

ויקרא יט | דברים טו

רש"י

דִּלְמָא אָתֵי לְאִינְפּוּלֵי. אֲבָל מִמַּעְיָן שֶׁלֹּא יָצָא בַּתְּחִילָּה אֲפִילּוּ בֵּית הַבַּעַל נַמִּי שָׁרֵי רַבִּי יְהוּדָה, וּמַתְנִיתִין דְּקָתָנֵי נַמִּי מִמַּעְיָן שֶׁלֹּא יָצָא בַּתְּחִילָּה בֵּית הַשְּׁלָחִין אִין בֵּית הַבַּעַל לָא, לָאו רַבִּי יְהוּדָה הִיא: אִם כֵּן מַתְנִיתִין אַמַּאן תַּרְמְיָיהּ. לָא ר"א בֶּן יַעֲקֹב כִּדְאָמְרַן, וְלָא כְּר"מ דְּשָׁרֵי אֲפִילּוּ בֵּית הַבַּעַל, וְלָא כְּר' אֶלְעָזָר בֶּן עֲזַרְיָה דַּאֲפִילּוּ בֵּית הַשְּׁלָחִין לָא שָׁרֵי מִמַּעְיָן שֶׁיָּצָא בַּתְּחִילָּה: אֶלָּא לְרַבִּי יְהוּדָה וְלָא שְׁנָא כו'. וּמַתְנִיתִין ר' יְהוּדָה הִיא: לְהוֹדִיעֲךָ כֹּחוֹ דְּרַבִּי מֵאִיר. דַּאֲפִילּוּ מִמַּעְיָן שֶׁיָּצָא בַּתְּחִילָּה שָׁרֵי אֲפִילּוּ לְבֵית הַבַּעַל: מְנַכֵּשׁ. תּוֹלֵשׁ עֲשָׂבִים רָעִים מִתּוֹךְ הַטּוֹבִים, וְכִי עָקְרֵי לְהוּ נָמְחֵי הָנֵי טְפֵי: מַשְׁקֶה מַיִם בִּזְרָעִים. שֶׁזּוֹרֵק מַיִם בְּעִיקְרֵי הָעֲשָׂבִים: מִשּׁוּם מַאי מַתְרִינַן בֵּיהּ. דְּמַאי מְלָאכָה קָא חָשְׁבִינַן לֵיהּ דְּוַדַּאי קוֹצֵר לָא חָשְׁבִינַן, שֶׁאֵינוֹ מִתְכַּוֵּין לִיטּוֹל הָעֲשָׂבִים אֶלָּא לְתַקֵּן עֲשָׂבִים הַטּוֹבִים שֶׁבַּשָּׂדֶה: חוֹרֵשׁ וְזוֹרֵעַ וְקוֹצֵר אֲבוֹת מְלָאכוֹת הֵן בְּפֶרֶק "כְּלָל גָּדוֹל" (שבת דף עג.): לְרַפּוּיֵי. לְרַכֵּךְ: מִשּׁוּם חוֹרֵשׁ אִין מִשּׁוּם זוֹרֵעַ לָא. אַמַּאי לָא מִיחַיַּיב בְּתַרְוַויְיהוּ? הָא עָבֵיד תַּרְוַויְיהוּ, וְאַשְׁכְּחִינַן בִּמְלָאכָה דְּמִיחַיַּיב תַּרְתֵּי: זוֹמֵר. בְּשַׁבָּת: וְצָרִיךְ לָעֵצִים חַיָּיב. מִשּׁוּם קוֹצֵר שֶׁהֲרֵי צָרִיךְ לָעֵצִים, וְחַיָּיב מִשּׁוּם נוֹטֵעַ דְּמִשּׁוּם הַזִּימּוּר גָּדְלֵי טְפֵי: הַמְחַפֶּה. שֶׁמְּכַסֶּה אֶת הַזְּרָעִים בֶּעָפָר: לוֹקֶה. מִשּׁוּם: "לֹא תִזְרַע כִּלְאָיִם" (ויקרא יט): אַף הַמְקַיֵּים. שֶׁרוֹאֶה כִּלְאַיִם זָרוּעַ וְאֵינוֹ מְבַטְּלוֹ: בִּשְׁלָמָא לְדִידִי דְּאָמִינָא. דִּמְנַכֵּשׁ הָוֵי מִשּׁוּם זוֹרֵעַ, מִשּׁוּם הָכִי מְנַכֵּשׁ בְּכִלְאַיִם לוֹקֶה דְּהָא אֲסִירָא זְרִיעָה בְּכִלְאַיִם דִּכְתִיב: "לֹא תִזְרַע": חֲרִישָׁה. לְצוֹרֶךְ זְרִיעַת כִּלְאַיִם מִי אֲסִירָא? דִּבְשַׁעַת חֲרִישָׁה לֵיכָּא כִּלְאַיִם כְּלָל: אָמַר לֵיהּ. מְנַכֵּשׁ אֵינוֹ לוֹקֶה אֶלָּא מִשּׁוּם מְקַיֵּים: תַּלְמוּד לוֹמַר כִּלְאַיִם שָׂדְךָ לֹא. וְאַע"ג דִּכְתִיב לֹא תִזְרַע כִּלְאָיִם *גּוֹרְעִין וְדוֹרְשִׁין: לֹא כִּלְאַיִם — לֹא יְהֵא כִּלְאַיִם מִכָּל מָקוֹם, שֶׁחַיָּיב אַתָּה לְבַטְּלוֹ: בִּשְׁלָמָא מוֹעֵד. מִשּׁוּם הָכִי שָׁרֵי, דְּלָא אֲסִיר מִשּׁוּם מְלָאכָה, אֶלָּא מִשּׁוּם טִירְחָא: וְכָל מְקוֹם פְּסֵידָא שָׁרוּ רַבָּנַן. לְמִיטְרַח בְּחוּלּוֹ שֶׁל מוֹעֵד בִּמְקוֹם פְּסֵידָא, כִּדְפָרְשִׁינַן לְעֵיל: בֵּין לְמַאן דְּאָמַר מִשּׁוּם חוֹרֵשׁ. דִּפְלִיגֵי רַבָּה וְרַב יוֹסֵף לְעֵיל בְּמַשְׁקֶה מַיִם לִזְרָעִים, דְּחַד אָמַר מִשּׁוּם חוֹרֵשׁ, וְחַד אָמַר מִשּׁוּם זוֹרֵעַ: חֲרִישָׁה בַּשְּׁבִיעִית מִי שָׁרֵי. הָא נָפְקָא מִ"בֶּחָרִישׁ וּבַקָּצִיר תִּשְׁבּוֹת" דְּאָמְרִינַן: אִם אֵינוֹ עִנְיָן לְשַׁבָּת שֶׁאֵינוֹ צָרִיךְ, שֶׁהֲרֵי כְּבָר נֶאֱמַר "כָּל מְלָאכָה" — תְּנֵהוּ עִנְיָן לַשְּׁבִיעִית: בַּשְּׁבִיעִית בַּזְּמַן הַזֶּה. דְּרַבָּנָן: וְרַבִּי הִיא. דְּאָמַר דְּהוּא מִדְּרַבָּנָן, וּמִילְּתָא דִּפְסִידָא — שָׁרוּ רַבָּנַן: וְזֶה דְּבַר הַשְּׁמִטָּה שָׁמוֹט. כְּתִיב בְּהַשְׁמָטַת כְּסָפִים — אַמַּאי כְּתִיב תְּרֵי זִימְנֵי "שְׁמִטָּה" "שָׁמוֹט": בִּזְמַן שֶׁאִי אַתָּה מְשַׁמֵּט קַרְקַע כו'. מִכְּלָל דְּאִיכָּא זְמַן דְּלָא מְשַׁמֵּט קַרְקַע, וְאֵיזֶה זֶה — בַּזְּמַן הַזֶּה: אֲפִילּוּ תֵּימָא רַבָּנַן. דִּפְלִיגֵי עֲלֵיהּ דְּרַבִּי, וְאָמְרֵי דִּשְׁבִיעִית בַּזְּמַן הַזֶּה דְּאוֹרַיְיתָא: אָבוֹת מְלָאכוֹת. אָסַר רַחֲמָנָא בַּשְּׁבִיעִית:

תּוֹלָדוֹת

תוספות

אם כן אמאן תרמייה. ואם נפשך לומר: ממאי דרמינן אליבא דר' יהודה יותר מר"א? כמו דאקשינן לעיל לר"א – הכי נמי פרכינן אליבא דרבי יהודה, ומאי אלימא להש"ס מילתא דרבי יהודה דמוכח מיניה דמתניתין אתיא אליביה, יותר מדרבי אליעזר? איכא למימר: משום דבתרתי מילי אשכחן בהדיא במילתיה דר"י כמו במתניתין, דפסידא – אין, הרווחה – לא, ובמקום פסידא נמי מיטרח לא טרח. אבל לר"א ליכא לאוכוחי ממילתיה אלא חד מילתא כדלעיל, דהרווחה אסיר. הלכך ניחא ליה לאוקמי כר' יהודה, ולא כרבי אליעזר: **כחו** דר' מאיר דמיקל. ואם תאמר: וליתני שלא יצאו בתחילה – להודיען כחו דר' יהודה דמחמיר! (א)כח דהתירא עדיף:

משום מאי מתרינן. דאין אדם לוקה ולא נהרג אלא בהתראה, שמתרינן בו: לא תעשה הך איסורא, כדמפקינן בסנהדרין (דף מא.) מקרא, דצריך לפרש שם האיסור בהדיא: **קא** מרפויי ארעא. דבתר עיקר המלאכה אזלינן, ודומה לחורש. ורב יוסף, אע"ג דעיקר מלאכה דומה לחורש – מחשבת הנפש לאו לרפויי ארעא. ובהכי פליגי: דרבה סבר לבתר המעשה מדמינן לה, ולא אחר המחשבה. ורב יוסף סבר: בתר מחשבה אזלינן, דהויא עיקר, ולא אזלינן בתר הדמיון:

וצריך לעצים. אבל אם אין צריך לעצים – לא נאמר בו דחייב משום קצירה, דלא דמיא לקצירה דקוצרין למאכל, או מידי שצריכין לאיזה דבר, כגון רפואה וכיוצא בהן. ואי לאו שקוצרין לצורך גופו – פטור, דלא מיחייב אפילו משום תולדה. דתולדה צריך שתהא דמי לאב מלאכה: **חייב** שתים. קשיא לרבה דאזיל בתר הדמיון, דהכא זומר לא דמי כלל לנוטע – ואעפ"כ חייב משום נוטע. וקשיא לרב יוסף, דאפילו אינו מתכוין לנמוח הגפן, כיון דודאי מלמחה מחמת הזימור – חייב משום נוטע. דהא סתם קאמר רב כהנא, אפילו לא חישב ליטע. ואי קשיא: הא דאמרינן בדוכתא אחריתי (כתובות דף לז.): משום רשעה אחת אתה מחייבו, ואי אתה מחייבו משום שתי רשעיות! תריץ הכי: כגון דאיכא מיתה ומלקות. אבל תרתי מילי דאסירן, דדמיין להדדי בשתי מלקיות – תרווייהו חד רשעה הוא, ולא ממעטי מ"רשעתו" דכל שם מלקות – חד רשעה הוא. והכי נמי אמר במס' פסחים בפ' "כל שעה" (דף כד. ושם) אמר אביי: אכל פוטיתא – לוקה ארבע. ואע"ג דרב כהנא אמורא הוא – מקשי מיניה לרבה ורב יוסף משום דגברא רבה הוה, כדאשכחן (ב"ק דף קיז.) במעשה דר' יוחנן דהוה חריף טובא. ◐וקשיא, ל"ג, כיון דלאו תנא הוא לא חשיב לה כל כך, ופליגי עליה:

אף

רבינו חננאל

שדה הבעל תנא איהו נמי מעין שיצא בתחלה. אתמר המנכש פי' החופר בית הזרעים והממשיך מים לזרעי' בשבת משום מאי מתרינן ביה. רבה אמר משום חורש מה דרך החורש לרפויי ארעא הכא נמי מרפי ארעא נינהו. ורב יוסף אמר משום זורע. מה דרך הזורע לאצמוחי פירא הכא נמי קא מצמחי פירא. ומקשי אביי לתרווייהו ואמאי לא מתרינן ביה משום חורש ומשום זורע דהא דמיא להא ודמיא נמי להא. וכי תימא כל היכא דאיכא מלאכה מעין שתים לא מחייבינן אלא חדא. והאמר רב כהנא הזומר וצריך לעצים חייב שתים אחת משום זורע ואחת משום קוצר ולאפירקו לנפשייהו איתיביה רב יוסף לרבה המנכש פי' חופר אצל הכלאים ולוקח העפר ומחפה בו את הכלאים כדי שיצמח והמחפה בכלאים לוקה. ר' עקיבא אומר אף המקיים. בשלמא לרב יוסף דא' מנכש משום זורע חייב היינו דאסירא זריעה בכלאים. אלא לרבה דאמר משום חורש חרישה בכלאים מי אסירא. ופריק רבה מאי לוקה דקתני משום מקיים בכלאים וכולה ר' עקיבא היא. ומה טעם קאמר והכי קתני המנכש והמחפה בכלאים לוקה. מ"ט משום מקיים שר' עקיבא אומר אף המקיים בכלאים לוקה. פי' מקיים בכלאים שמצא שדה זרועה כלאים ועבדה הוא וצמחה ונתקיים הכלאים בעבודתו שגורם לו הצמחה והפרחת פירי. מ"ט אמר קרא לא תזרע כרמך כלאים. אין לי אלא זורע תבואה בכרם מקיים מנין תלמוד לומר לא כלאים. כלומר האי לא דכתב רחמנא דרוש אותו בזורע דהוה ליה למכתב לא תזרע כרמך ולישתוק. ואנא ידענא דאין זריעה אלא בתבואה פי' וממילא שמעינן שאסר זריעת התבואה בכלאים. *) למה עוד אמר כלאים כדכתיב וזרעתם את השנה ההיא וגו' אבל באילנות נטיעה היא כדכתיב ונטעתם כל עץ מאכל. כלאים דכתב רחמנא למה לי לרבות המקיים בכלאים בלאו. ומקשינן לרבה ורב יוסף ממתניתין דתנן משקין בית השלחין במועד ובשביעית. בשלמא מועד משום טירחא הוא דאסורה וכל מקום פסידא שרו רבנן. אלא בשביעית בין למ"ד משקה מים לזרעים חייב משום זורע. ובין למ"ד חייב משום חורש תרווייהו חרישה וזריעה בשביעית אסירי היכי שרו ופירק אביי בשביעית בזמן הזה. ורבי היא דתניא רבי אומר וזה דבר השמטה שמוט כתיב שמיטה וכתיב שמוט בב' שמיטות הכתוב מדבר אחת שמיטת קרקע ואחת שמיטת כספים. בזמן שאתה משמט קרקע כו' והאידנא דאין שמיטה בקרקע שא"י בידי עובדי כוכבים היא. שביעית בזמן הזה דרבנן ובמקום פסידא שרו רבנן. רבא אמר לא תימא מתני' רבי היא ולא רבנן. אלא אפי' תימא רבנן הניכוש והחיפוי בכלאים תולדות נינהו

ובשביעית

*) לכאורה נראה שצ"ל שאסר זריעת התבואה בכלאים כדכתיב וזרעתם את וכו' ונטעתם כל עץ מאכל למה עוד אמר כלאים לרבות המקיים כו'.

[שעשה להן סייג וגדר רש"י ע"ז סד. וע"ש בתוס']

[שבת עג:]

[תוספ' כלאים פ"א] מכות כא: ע"ז סד.

[ועי' פי' ריב"ן למכות ובכל מקום פי' בסגנון אחר]

גיטין לו. קדושין לח.

הגהות הב"ח

(א) תוס' ד"ה כחו כו' דר' יהודה דמחמיר וי"ל כח דהתירא:

גליון הש"ס

תוס' ד"ה חייב שתים וכו' וקשיא ל"ג. עיין ב"ב דף כב ע"ב:

תולדות לא אסר רחמנא, דכתיב: "ובשנה השביעית שבת שבתון יהיה לארץ שדך לא תזרע" וגו'. מכדי, זמירה בכלל זריעה, ובצירה בכלל קצירה, למאי הלכתא כתבינהו רחמנא? למימרא: דאהני תולדות — מיחייב, אאחרנייתא — לא מיחייב. ולא? והתניא: "שדך לא תזרע וכרמך לא תזמור", אין לי אלא זירוע וזימור, מנין לניכוש ולעידור ולכיסוח? ת"ל: "שדך לא" "כרמך לא". לא כל מלאכה שבשדך, ולא כל מלאכה שבכרמך. מנין שאין מקרסמין, ואין מזרדין, ואין מפסגין באילן — ת"ל: "שדך לא" "כרמך לא", לא כל מלאכה שבשדך ולא כל מלאכה שבכרמך. מנין שאין מזבלין, ואין מפרקין, ואין *מאבקין, ואין מעשנין באילן — ת"ל: "שדך לא" "כרמך לא", כל מלאכה שבשדך לא, וכל מלאכה שבכרמך לא. יכול לא יקשקש תחת הזיתים, ולא יעדר תחת הגפנים, ולא ימלא נקעים מים, ולא יעשה עוגיות לגפנים — ת"ל: "שדך לא תזרע" זריעה בכלל היתה, ולמה יצתה — להקיש אליה, לומר לך: מה זריעה מיוחדת, עבודה שבשדה ושבכרם — אף כל שהיא עבודה שבשדה ושבכרם! מדרבנן, וקרא — אסמכתא בעלמא. *וקשקוש בשביעית מי שרי? והא כתיב: "והשביעית תשמטנה ונטשתה". "תשמטנה" — מלקשקש, "ונטשתה" — מלסקל! אמר רב עוקבא בר חמא: *תרי קשקושי הוו; חד — אברויי אילני, וחד — סתומי פילי. אברויי אילן — אסור, סתומי פילי — שרי. איתמר, החורש בשביעית, ר' יוחנן ור' אלעזר. חד אמר: לוקה, וחד אמר: אינו לוקה. לימא בדר' אבין אמר רבי אילעא קמיפלגי, דאמר *רבי אבין אמר ר' אילעא: כל מקום שנאמר כלל בעשה, ופרט בלא תעשה — אין דנין אותו בכלל ופרט וכלל. מאן דאמר לוקה — לית ליה דרבי אבין אמר רבי אילעא, ומאן דאמר אינו לוקה — אית ליה דר' אבין! לא, דכולי עלמא לית ליה דרבי אבין אמר ר' אילעא. מאן דאמר לוקה — שפיר. ומאן דאמר אינו לוקה — אמר לך: מכדי, זמירה בכלל זריעה, ובצירה בכלל קצירה, למאי הלכתא כתבינהו רחמנא? למימר דאהני תולדות הוא דמיחייב, אתולדה אחרינא — לא מיחייב. ולא? והתניא: "שדך לא תזרע וכרמך לא תזמור" אין לי אלא זירוע וזימור, מנין לעידור ולקישקוש ולכיסוח — ת"ל: "שדך לא" "כרמך לא", לא כל מלאכה שבשדך, ולא כל מלאכה שבכרמך. ומנין שאין מקרסמין ואין מזרדין ואין מפסגין באילן — ת"ל: "שדך לא", "כרמך לא", כל מלאכה שבשדך לא, כל מלאכה שבכרמך לא. מנין שאין מזבלין ואין מפרקין ואין מעשנין באילן — ת"ל: "שדך לא" "כרמך לא", כל מלאכה שבשדך לא, וכל מלאכה שבכרמך לא. יכול לא יקשקש תחת הזיתים, ולא יעדר תחת הגפנים, ולא ימלא נקעים מים, ולא יעשה עוגיות לגפנים — תלמוד לומר: "שדך לא תזרע", זריעה בכלל היתה, ולמה יצתה — להקיש אליה, לומר לך: מה זריעה מיוחדת — עבודה שבשדה ושבכרם, אף כל שהיא עבודה שבשדה ושבכרם! מדרבנן, וקרא אסמכתא בעלמא.

כי

רש"י

תולדות. כגון משקה זרעים שלא היה במשכן — לא אסר רחמנא: זמירה בכלל זריעה. שדרכו של זומר לצמוחי פירי כזורע: בצירה. בענבים כקצירה בתבואה — וקצירה אב מלאכה היא, בפ' כלל גדול (שבת דף עג.) בצירה בכלל קצירה, דשניהן חותכין: זימור. מחתך ענפים יבשין של גפן: עידור. שחופר תחת הגפנים, לרפויי ארעא: כיסוח. בעשבים, שחותך הרעים מן הטובים. ולא היינו ניכוש, דמעקר העיקרים מן הקרקע. דהוה אין עוקרין, אלא חותכין למעלה: תלמוד לומר שדך לא כרמך לא. מדלא כתיב: "לא תזרע שדך לא תזמור כרמך" אלא "שדך לא תזרע כרמך לא תזמור" משמע: שדך לא, כרמך לא: מקרסמין. היינו, זימור, אלא שקירסום שייך באילנות: מזרדין. מחתך ענפים יבשים ולחים, לפי שיש לאילן ענפים יותר מדאי: מפסגין. סומכים האילן שהוא רענן יותר מדאי: מזבלין. מניחים זבל בעיקרי האילן: מפרקין. אבנים שעל עיקרי האילן: מאבקים. שששרשיו נראין, ומכסין אותו באבק: מעשנין. עושין עשן תחת האילן, כדי שיגשרו התולעים שעליו: יקשקש. היינו עידור, אלא שעידור בגפנים וקשקוש בזיתים: עוגיות. חופר גומא תחת הגפן ליתן בו מים: זריעה בכלל היתה. "ובשנה השביעית שבת שבתון" וגו': אף כל עבודה שהיא בשדה ובכרם. כגון כל הני (א) פרטי, יצא קשקוש ועידור ומים בנקעים ועוגיות שאינן בשניהן כו': לא יקשקש תחת הזיתים ולא יעדר כו'. ואם תקשי: הא אסר עידור לעיל! קא תריץ לקמן בעוגיות, הא — בחדתי, והא — בעתיקי. והוא הדין לעידור: (ב) כל הני מדרבנן. אבל מדאורייתא לא הוי אלא זמירה ובצירה, כדאמרינן לעיל: הני — אין, מידי אחרינא — לא: מלסקל. להוציא אבנים מן הכרם: (ג) סתומי פילי. שמסתם בקעים של אילן: שרי. דאית ביה משום פסידא: אברויי אילני אסור. דהוי משום רווחא, והאי דשרי קשקוש — היינו סתומי פילי, והאי דאסיר — היינו אברויי אילני: כל מקום שנאמר כלל בעשה ופרט בלא תעשה. כגון הכא, דכתיב (ויקרא כה): "ובשנה השביעית שבת שבתון יהיה לארץ" — כלל היינו עשה, "שדך לא תזרע וכרמך לא תזמור" — פרט, היינו לא תעשה: אין דנין אותו בכלל ופרט וכלל. ואף על גב דכתיב כלל בתריה, כגון הכא דכתיב בתריה: "(*שבת) שבתון" כלומר: אין לו דין דשאר כלל ופרט וכלל שכתובין כולו בעשה או בלאו, דאמר: כלל ופרט וכלל אי אתה דן אלא כעין הפרט, דמרבי כל מידי דדמי לפרט. אלא דיינינן ליה בכלל ופרט, הואיל דנשתנה משאר כלל ופרט וכלל, אמרינן: אין בכלל אלא מה שבפרט, הני — אין, מידי אחרינא — לא: דכולי עלמא לית להו דרבין כו' מאן דאמר לוקה שפיר. כדאמר, דדרשינן בכלל ופרט וכלל: אחרינא לא. להכי חורש אינו לוקה:

תוספות

אף כל שבשדה ושבכרם. וכל הני עבודות דלעיל — נוהגות בין בשדה ובין בכרם. ואפילו שיש מהן שאין עתה נוהגין כן — י"ל שבמקומן היו עושין כך, ורגילין לעשותן בשדה ובכרם: אין דנין אותו בכלל ופרט וכלל. הכי הוה שמיע ליה לר' אילעא, דכיון דהפרט בלא תעשה — הכלל האחרון אינו מוציא הפרט ממשמעותיה, ואינו כלל ופרט וכלל, דדיינינן ליה בכלל ופרט. ולא נהירא לי: דמנלן דרבי אילעא ס"ל הכי? אימא דהפרט שהוא בלא תעשה — בטל, אבל הכלל עומד במקומו, לפי דבריו! ועוד: לפי לשון זה קשה לי אמאי תירץ דכולי עלמא לית להו דר' אבין? והא הוה מצי לתרוצי דכולי עלמא אית להו! דבכל מקום סוגיית התלמוד היא, דכיון דמצי למימר דכולי עלמא אית להו סברת האמורא — לא מתרצינן לית להו. ולימא הכי: דכולי עלמא אית להו דרבי אבין, מאן דאמר אינו לוקה — שפיר, ומאן דאמר לוקה — סבירא ליה כי הך ברייתא דמפקא ליה לתולדות מקרא, וקסבר: לאו אסמכתא הוא, אלא דרשה גמורה היא. ולי נראה: דהא לימא בדר' אבין אמר ר' אילעא וכו' — קאזיל בכה"ג דליכא הכא אלא כלל ופרט, דכלל בתרא לא חשיב. כיון דהאי כלל בקרא אחרינא וחשיב בכלל המרוחק זה מזה, כיון דלא הוו בחד קרא. דהכי מוכח בפ"ק דפסחים (דף ו: ושם), דאיכא למאן דאמר כיון דהוו בתרי קראי — לא מילטרפי למיהוי כלל ופרט וכלל. והכא נמי לא הוי אלא כלל ופרט, והכי איכא (ד) הגירסא [בירושלמי דכלאים] בפ"ח: חד אמר לוקה, סבר לה כרבי אילעא. דאינו נדון בכלל ופרט, כיון דהפרט בלא תעשה — הפרט בטל, והכלל במקומו עומד. ולפיכך אמר: כל החורש בשביעית — לוקה. וחד אמר: החורש בשביעית אינו לוקה, לא סבר להא דר' אילעא, אלא דנין אותו בכלל ופרט; הני — אין, מידי אחרינא — לא. ודחי לה: דכולהו אית להו דרבי אילעא, מאן דאמר לוקה — שפיר, ומאן דאמר אינו לוקה — מכדי זמירה בכלל זריעה ובצירה כו'. ואם נפשך לומר: למאן דאמר לוקה אמאי כתב רחמנא זמירה ובצירה? שמא קסבר ללאו יתירא אתי, אי נמי קסבר: כרם משדה לא הוה יליף, הלכך הוצרך למיכתב בין בשדה בין בכרם:

רבינו חננאל

ובשביעית אבות אסר רחמנא תולדות לא אסר רחמנא שמעינן לה מדכתיב שדך לא תזרע וכרמך לא תזמור. מכדי (זריעה) [זמירה] מכלל (זמירה) [זריעה] היא דכיון שזומר ועוזק צומח ובצירה בכלל קצירה למאי הלכתא דכ' רחמנא ללמדך דאהני תולדות מיחייב בשביעית אתולדות אחרנייתא לא מיחייב. איני והתניא שדך לא תזרע וכרמך לא וגו' אין לי שחייב בשביעית אלא זורע וזומר בלבד מנין למנכש ולעודר ולמכסח ת"ל שדך לא וגו' פי' הוה ליה למכתב לא תזרע ואנא ידענא דאין זריעה אלא בשדה. שדך דכתב רחמנא למה לי לרבות כל מלאכות שבשדה. מנין שאין מזבלין ואין מפרקין ואין מאבקין ואין מעשנין ת"ל כרמך לא לרבות כל מלאכות שבכרם שאסורות. קתני מיהא דמנכש אסור בשביעית ופרקינן האי איסורא מדרבנן היא וקרא אסמכתא כו'. יכול לא יקשקש תחת הזיתים ולא יעדר תחת הגפנים ולא ימלא נקעים מים ולא יעשה עוגיאיות לגפנים בין אילן לחברו ת"ל שדך לא תזרע. זריעה וזמירה בכלל שבת שבתון יהיה (לכם) [לארץ] היו ולמה יצאת להקיש אליה לומר לך מה זריע' מיוחד' עבודת שדות וכרמים אף כל עבודת שדות וכרמים למעוטי קשקוש ועידור וביקוע ועישון דעבודת אילנות הן ולא עבודת שדות וזרעים. והלכך שרי קשקוש בשביעית פי' *) תרי קישקושי הוו חד לאברויי אילני כלומ' להברות האילן כגון גיזום שאמרו במס' ע"ז ואסור וחד לסתומי פילי לסתום הסדקין ושרי. איתמר החורש בשביעית ר' יוחנן ור' אלעזר חד אמר לוקה. סבר לה כר' אלעא דא' מקום שאתה מוצא כלל בעשה כגון ובשנה השביעית שבת וגו' שבת לה' הרי כלל כל מלאכות שביעית. ועוד פרט בלא עשה שנאמר שדך לא תזרע וכרמך לא תזמור. ואת ענבי נזירך לא תבצור שנת שבתון יהיה לארץ. ומרבה כל מלאכה ואפילו החורש בשביעית לוקה. וחד אמר החורש בשביעית אינו לוקה לא סבר לה דר' אלעא (דאמר) [אלא ס"ל] דנין אותו בכלל ובפרט. הני אין כלומר אלו בלבד המפורשין הם במלקות מידי אחרינא לא ודחינא לא דכ"ע אית להו דר' אלעא מ"ד לוקה שפיר. ומ"ד אינו לוקה מכדי זמירה בכלל זריעה ובצירה כו': ירושלמי בשביעית פ"ב (ה"ג) מיבלין מעבירין היבלת מפרקין בעלין מאבקין עושין להן אבק מעשנין מתנינן לה מזהמין מתליעין בשביעית מה בין זוהם לעושה בית המזוהם אינו אלא כמושיב שומר. עושה בית מציל עליה והיא גדילה מחמתו. מה בין מחפה באבנים ובתבן ובקש שהוא מותר למחפה בעפר שאסור המחפה בקש ובתבן ובאבנים אינו אלא כמושיב שומר. המחפה בעפר עושה לו טינא והיא גדילה מחמתו: כי אתא רב

*) נראה לחסר בדברי רבינו וצ"ל איני והא כתיב והשביעית תשמטנה וכו' מלקשקש ומשנינן תרי קשקושי. **) גירסת רבינו הובא בתוס' ד"ה אין דנין בשם רבינו לפי מה שהגיה הב"ח והדין עמו דאלו בירושלמי שם אדרבה הגירסא כמו גירסת הש"ס כאן ע"ש.

עין משפט נר מצוה

טו א מיי' פ"א מהלכות שמטה הלכה ב ג:
טז ב ג ד ה מיי' שם הלכה ד ה:
יז ה מיי' שם הלכה ז:
יח ו ז מיי' שם הל' ט:
יט ח מיי' שם הלכה ג:
כ ט מיי' שם הל' ז:
כא כ מיי' שם הל' ז:

מסורת הש"ס

[פי' מסירין האבק מעליהן. ערוך]

[סוכה מד:]

[ע"ז נ:]

[סנהדר' קיג.]

הגהות הב"ח

(א) רש"י ד"ה אף כל כו' כל הני פרטי דפרט יצא קשקוש כו': (ב) ד"ה לא יקשקש וכו' וה"א לעידור הס"ד ואח"כ מה"ד מדרבנן כל הני מדרבנן אבל מדאורייתא' כו': (ג) ד"ה סתומי פילי כו' נ"ב ע' פרק פ"ד דסוכה דף מד ע"ב: (ד) תוס' ד"ה אין כו'. והכי איתא הגירסא בפר"ח חד אמר:

גליון הש"ס

גמ' מנין לעידור ולקשקוש ולכיסוח כצ"ל לענ"ד:

כי אתא רב דימי אמר: יכול ילקה על התוספת – ונסיב לה תלמודא לפטורא, ולא ידענא מאי תלמודא ומאי תוספת. ר' אלעזר אמר: חרישה, והכי קאמר: יכול ילקה על חרישה, דאתיא מכלל ופרט וכלל, ונסיב ליה תלמודא לפטורא, דאם כן, כל הני פרטי למה לי? ור' יוחנן אמר: ימים שהוסיפו חכמים לפני ראש השנה, והכי קאמר: יכול ילקה על תוספת ראש השנה, דאתיא °מ"בחריש ובקציר תשבות", ונסיב לה תלמודא לפטורא, כדבעינן למימר לקמן. מאי ימים שלפני ראש השנה? כדתנן: *עד מתי חורשין בשדה אילן ערב שביעית? בית שמאי אומרים: כל זמן שיפה לפרי, וב"ה אומרים:[א] אעד העצרת. וקרובין דברי אלו להיות כדברי אלו. *ועד מתי חורשין שדה הלבן ערב שביעית – משתכלה הלחה, וכל זמן שבני אדם חורשים ליטע מקשאות ומדלעות. ר' שמעון אומר: א"כ – נתנה תורה שיעור לכל אחד ואחד בידו! באלא: בשדה הלבן – עד הפסח, ובשדה האילן – עד העצרת. (*וב"ה אומרים: עד הפסח) ואמר ר' שמעון בן פזי אמר רבי יהושע בן לוי משום בר קפרא: רבן גמליאל ובית דינו גנמנו על שני פרקים הללו ובטלום. אמר ליה רבי זירא לר' אבהו, ואמרי לה ריש לקיש לר' יוחנן: רבן גמליאל ובית דינו היכי מצו מבטלי תקנתא דב"ש וב"ה והא תנן: *דאין ב"ד יכול לבטל דברי בית דין חבירו אלא אם כן גדול ממנו בחכמה ובמנין! *°"אשתומם כשעה חדא", אמר ליה: אימור כך התנו ביניהן: כל הרוצה לבטל – יבוא ויבטל. דידהו היא? הלכה למשה מסיני היא! דאמר ר' אסי אמר ר' יוחנן משום ר' נחוניא איש בקעת בית חורתן: *העשר נטיעות, ועֲרבה, זוניסוך המים – הלכה למשה מסיני. אמר רבי יצחק: כי גמירי הלכתא – שלשים יום לפני ראש השנה, ואתו הני תקון מפסח ומעצרת. ואתנו בדידהו: כל הרוצה לבטל – יבוא ויבטל. והני הלכתא נינהו? קראי נינהו. (*דתנן:) °"בחריש ובקציר תשבות", ר' עקיבא אומר: אין צריך לומר חריש וקציר של שביעית – שהרי כבר נאמר: °"שדך לא תזרע וכרמך לא תזמור", אלא חריש של ערב שביעית שנכנס

תורה אור: שמות לד | דניאל ד | ויקרא כה

רש"י

כי אתא רב דימי. מארץ ישראל לבבל: אמר. שמעית דאמרי בא"י: יכול ילקה על תוספת: ושמעית דנסיב עליה תלמודא לפטורא. ולא ידענא מאי תוספת ולא פטור: רבי אלעזר אמר חרישה. בשביעית. להכי קרי ליה תוספת, דלא נפיק עיקרו מן התורה אלא מכלל ופרט וכלל, כדאמרי' לעיל: ונסיב תלמודא לפטורא. כדאמרינן: הני – אין: דאם כן. דהוי לקי: כל הני פרטי. דפריט בהדיא דאסור בשביעית זריעה וזימור, קצירה ובצירה: למה לי. דכתב רחמנא? אלא למימרא דאהנך הוא דלוקה וכו'. שמע מינה: אחרישה לא לקי: ימים שלפני ראש השנה. של שביעית, שהוא תוספת על השביעית: דאתיא מבחריש ובקציר. כדאמר לקמן: אם אינו ענין לשביעית, שהרי כתיב "שדך לא תזרע וכרמך לא תזמור" – תנהו לענין ששית שנכנס לשביעית, דבשביעית נמי אסור: כדבעינן למימר לקמן. גמר שבת שבתון משבת בראשית: כל זמן שיפה לפרי. כלומר: כל זמן שחרישה יפה לפירות שגדלו בששית, דהיינו נמי קרוב לעצרת. אבל מכאן ואילך – לא, דהוי כמתקן פירות שביעית: שדה לבן. של תבואה: שתכלה הלחה. שכלין הגשמים של שנה ששית. דעד ההיא שעתא מהני חרישה לזריעה דשנה זו, אבל משתכלה הלחה – אינו יכול לחרוש, דמחזי כחורש לצורך שביעית, דהיינו כל זמן שבני אדם חורשין ליטע מקשאות: נתנה תורה שיעור לכל אחד ואחד בידו. כלומר, נתת דבריך לשיעורין, שפעמים זה חורש קודם חבירו ליטע מקשאות: על שני פרקים. דפסח ועצרת: ובטלום. דחורשין עד ראש השנה: תקנתא דשמאי והלל. דרבי שמעון דאמר עד פסח ועד עצרת – והיינו אליבא דב"ש וב"ה: כך התנו. שמאי והלל בשעת תקנתם: דידהו היא. תקנתם היא? חורתן. מקום: י' נטיעות. המפוזרות בתוך בית סאה, שהוא נ' על נ' – חורשין כל השדה שלה בשבילן בערב שביעית עד ר"ה. ואמרי: הני, הואיל וילדות הן – איכא פסידא יתירא, לכך חורשין עד ראש השנה. אבל זקינה – אין חורשין עד ראש השנה. אלמא: דהלכה למשה מסיני הן: וערבה. להקיף המזבח: כי גמירי הלכתא. דאין חורשין לזקינה עד ראש השנה, אבל חורשין עד שלשים יום לפני ראש השנה: (א)ואתו. בתקנה דידהו, דהרחיקו עד הפסח ועד העצרת: וכל הרוצה לבטל יבוא ויבטל. ורבן גמליאל דבטל לא בטל אלא מפסח ומעצרת, עד שלשים יום לפני ראש השנה: שנכנס

תוספות

רבי אלעזר אומר חרישה. מהא ליכא למימר(ב) תסתייס דר' אלעזר לעיל דאמר אינו לוקה. דאיכא למימר דרבי אלעזר לא שמיע ליה הא דאמר לקמן דהתירו תוספת שביעית, הלכך הוה אמר הכי. דליכא לפרש מילתא דרב דימי אלא בחרישה, אבל לדידיה – אסור ולוקה, דלא ס"ל. אי נמי: דכיון דאיתא בהדיא כי הך דלעיל במילי דחרישה – אינו צריך לומר תסתייס, דאין דרך התלמוד לומר תסתייס בדבר המפורש בהדיא כל כך:

יכול ילקה על תוספת של ראש השנה. ואם תאמר: מלקות מנלן? והלא לא כתיב בתוספת לאו, אלא עשה גרידא: "בחריש ובקציר תשבות"! איכא למימר: דמבחריש ובקציר מפקינן דצריך תוספת. כלומר, שהשביעית מתחלת משנה הששית, וכל דין שביעית יהיה לששית. דהכי קאמר רחמנא: דשביעית מתחלת קודם שנת שביעית, וא"כ הוא כשביעית:

עד עצרת. דהיינו יותר. דבכל מקום בית שמאי לחומרא ובית הלל לקולא, לבד מאותן דברים דקחשיב בעדיות (פ"ה):

וקרובים דברי אלו. קא משמע לן דאין ב"ש מחמירין אלא מעט על ב"ה ולאשמועינן מילתייהו דבית שמאי פירש הכי:

כל הרוצה לבטל יבא ויבטל. שמא יתקלקלו הקרקעות, ואינן מגדלין תבואה בלא חרישה לאחר זמן. זה התנו שיהא כח להתיר לצריכים, שחשו להפסד רבים, שלא גרמו רעה לעולם:

הלכה למשה מסיני. מהכא איכא לדקדק: מדשרא רחמנא ילדה – מכלל דזקינה אסורה. הרי על ידי הלכה למשה מסיני נאסרה תוספת שביעית. אבל להתירא לחוד לילדה – לא אצטריך, דמהיכא תיתי לאסור?

נטיעות. תנן במסכת שביעית פרק קמא: עד אימתי נקראו נטיעות? ר' אלעזר בן עזריה אומר: עד שיחולו, רבי יהושע אומר: בת שבע שנים, רבי עקיבא אומר: נטיעה כשמה. אילן שנגמם, פירוש: שנחתך והוציא חליפין, מטפח ולמטה – כנטיעה, מטפח ולמעלה – כאילן, דברי רבי שמעון:

ניסוך המים. והא דאמרינן בעלמא (שבת דף קג:) מ"ם יו"ד מ"ם – לרבות ניסוך המים מן התורה! אינו אלא אסמכתא בעלמא, כפר"ת:

שהרי כבר נאמר שדך לא תזרע וגו'. ואם כן כתיב: "את ספיח קצירך לא תקצור" אלמא: קצירה לא אצטריך. ואפילו אם תימצי לומר חרישה צריכה, דאזהרת חרישה לא אשכחן אלא הכא, מיהא קצירה לא אצטריך. ולהכי דרשא דאתיא קצירה – אתיא חרישה, כיון דכתבינהו גבי הדדי. אי נמי ס"ל לר"ע כי ההיא דאמרן לעיל, דלוקה על חרישה, וכדאמרינן טעמא לעיל: סבר ר' עקיבא, ותרוייהו מיותרין. ואליבא דר' עקיבא קפריש ואזיל, דר' עקיבא סבר: אם אינו ענין לשבת – תנהו גבי שביעית.(ג) ובמשמעות שבא להחמיר ולא להקל. ולא בעי לאוקמי בשבת כר' ישמעאל להקל, דהכי עדיפא ליה. ור' ישמעאל עדיפא ליה לאוקמי בשבת, דפשטיה דקרא מיירי ביה ואפילו להקל, מלאוקמי בשביעית דלא מיירי ביה ולהחמיר: אלא

עין משפט נר מצוה

כב א ב ג מיי' פ"ג מהלכות שמיטה הלכה א סמג לאוין רסו:
כג ד מיי' פ"ב מהלכות ממרים הלכה ב:
כד ה מיי' פ"ג מהל' שמיטה הלכה ה:
כה ו מיי' פ"ז מהלכות לולב הלכה כ:
כו ז מיי' פ"ו מהלכות תמידין הלכה ו:

מסורת הש"ס

שביעית פ"א מ"א | שם פ"ב מ"א ע"ש | [ליתא במשנה דשביעית] | מגילה ב. גיטין לו: עדיות פ"א מ"ה ע"ז לו. | סוכה לד. מד. תענית ג. זבחים קי: | שביעית פ"א מ"ד ר"ה ט. מכות ח: | [שבת מז. סוכה מד. קידושין לט. חולין כח.]

[נ"ל דהתניא משום דבמשנ' דשביעית לא נזכר ר' עקיבא אלא סתמא דת"ק וגם הא דאתמר הכא שהרי כבר נאמר כו' לא נזכר במשנה דהתם וכ"מ בהר"ש שם בפירושו בשביעית דהך דמייתי הכא וכן בר"ה ט. ברייתא היא לכך שפי' גרסי' דתניא]

הגהות הגר"א

[א] גמ' וב"ה כו'. נ"ב בירושלמי [שביעית פ"א] ולמה לא תניתוה מקולי ב"ש ומחומרי ב"ה פעמים שאין הגשמים מצויין ואין הליחה מצויה [דלא כתוס' ד"ה עד עצרת]:

הגהות הב"ח

(א) רש"י ד"ה ואתו ב"ש וב"ה וגזרו מפסח ומעצרת ואתו בתקנתא דידהו וכו' ועד העצרת דכל הרוצה לבטל כו' לא בטל אלא הפסח והעצרת עד ל' כו' כצ"ל והד"א: (ב) תום' ד"ה ר"א כו' מהא ליכא למימר לעיל תסתייס דר"א דאמר וכו' לא שמיע ליה. נ"ב כלומר לא סבירא ליה הא דאמר דהתירו תוספת שביעית ולכך הוה אמר הכי משום דליכא לפרש כצ"ל: (ג) ד"ה שהרי וכו' תנהו גבי שביעית ובמשמעותיה דקרא שבא להחמיר:

רבינו חננאל

רב דימי אמר יכול ילקה על התוספת ונסיב לה תלמודא לפטורא. מאי תוספת. ר' אלעזר אמר חרישה שהיא תוספת על הזריעה ועל הקצירה דאתיא מכלל ופרט *) א"כ כל הני פרטי למה לי והדין הוא תלמודא דנסיב לפטורא פרטיהן הזורע והזומר וקוצר ובוצר למה לי אלא ללמדך דאהני תולדות דזומר ובוצר הוא דמיחייב אתולדות אחרנייתא לא מיחייב. ור' יוחנן אמר ימים שהוסיפו חכמים לפני ר"ה להיות חורשין באילן ערב שביעית עד העצרת אע"פ שנהנה האילן בחרישה זו בשנה השביעית ובשדה הלבן עד הפסח. וכך אמרו יכול ילקה על תוספת ר"ה וכר"ע דמרבה להו מבחריש ובקציר תשבות ואמר אין צ"ל חריש וקציר של שביעית שהרי כתיב שדך לא תזרע אלא חריש של ערב שביעית שנכנס בשביעית כו' ונסיב לה קרא לפטורא כדאמרן. ירושלמי בשביעית [פ"ק ה"א] באיסור ב' פרקים הללו התירו ובאו אחרי כן בשעה שאסרו והתירו למקרא סמכו בחריש (ובחריש) [ובקציר] איזהו חריש אסור בחריש שקצירו אסור. ואיזהו חריש של ערב שביעית שיצא למוצאי שביעית וכשהתירו אחריהן למקרא סמכו (והא) כתיב הכא בשביעית שבת. וכתיב בשבת בראשית שבת מה ערב שבת בראשית אתה מותר לעשות עד שתשקע החמה אף ערב שבת שביעית אתה מותר לעשות עד שתשקע החמה. א"כ למה נאמר עד העצרת שעד כאן יפה לפרי. ומיכן ואילך מנבל פירותיו. ומקשינן היכי מבטל ר"ג תקנת הלל ושמאי והתנן אין ב"ד יכול לבטל דברי ב"ד חבירו אא"כ גדול ממנו בחכמה ובמנין. ופרקינן תיקנו שמאי והלל תקנה זו והתנו שכל הרוצה לבטל יבוא ויבטל. ומקשינן וכי דבית הלל ושמאי הן והא הל"מ הן דא"ר יוחנן עשר נטיעות והן אלו ששנינו במס' [שביעית] פרק ראשון עשר נטיעות מפוזרות בתוך בית סאה חורשין כל בית סאה בשבילן עד ר"ה. פירוש מהכא שמעינן שהנטיעות הן שמותר לו לחרוש להן בששית עד ראש השנה. אבל האילנות שכבר עשו פירי וזיקנו אין חורשין להן בששית עד ר"ה ובתחלת פרק ראשון ממס' שביעית עד מתי חורשין שדה האילן ערב שביעית בש"א כל זמן שהוא יפה לפרי שהחרישה תועיל לפירות שבאילן שהן הפירות השנה הששית אבל אם נכנס הקיץ וגמרו הפירות ואין החרישה מועלת לאותן הפירות כלום נאסר בחרישה שהחרישה אותו העת אינה מועלת לשנה הששית כלום ונעשה כאילו הוא חורש בשביעית ושיערו ב"ה אותו העת עצרת וקרובים דברי אלו להיות כדברי אלו. ומנא תימרא דשני לן בין נטיעה לאילן כדתנן במס' שביעית פ"א עד אימתי נקראו נטיעות ר' אלעזר בן עזריה אומר עד שיחולו ר' יהושע אומר בת ז' שנים ר"ע אומר נטיעה כשמה. אילן שנגמם פי' שנחתך והוציא חילופין מטפח ולמטה כנטיעה מטפח ולמעלה כאילן. דברי ר' שמעון (מכיון) [אלמא] דשני לן בין נטיעה לאילן. ש"מ מדהתיר לחרוש לנטיעות.
עד

*) נראה דצ"ל ונסיב לה תלמודא לפטורא דא"כ כל הני. **) נראה דצ"ל ר"ג ובית דינו התירו באיסור ב' פרקים הראשונים ר' אחא בשם ר"י בשעה שאסרו למקרא סמכו ובשעה שהתירו למקרא סמכו בחריש ובקציר איזהו חריש שקצירו אסור זהו חריש של ערב שביעית שנכנס לשביעית וקציר של שביעית שיוצא למוצאי שביעית וכו'.

שנכנס לשביעית, וקציר של שביעית שיצא למוצאי שביעית. ר' ישמעאל אומר: מה חריש רשות — אף קציר רשות, [א]יצא קציר העומר שהיא מצוה. אלא אמר רב נחמן בר יצחק: כי גמירי הלכתא — למישרי ילדה, קראי — למיסר זקינה. וכיון דהלכתא למשרי ילדה לאו ממילא זקינה אסירה? אלא: הלכתא לרבי ישמעאל, קראי לר' עקיבא. ור' יוחנן אמר: רבן גמליאל ובית דינו מדאורייתא בטיל להו. מאי טעמא? גמר "שבת" "שבת" משבת בראשית, מה להלן היא אסורה, לפניה ולאחריה — מותרין, אף כאן, היא אסורה, לפניה ולאחריה — מותרין. מתקיף לה רב אשי: מאן דאמר הלכתא — אתיא גזרה שוה עקרה הלכתא? ומאן דאמר קרא — אתיא גזרה שוה עקרה קרא?! אלא אמר רב אשי: רבן גמליאל ובית דינו סברי לה כרבי ישמעאל דאמר הלכתא גמירי לה, וכי גמירי הלכתא — בזמן שבית המקדש קיים, דומיא דניסוך המים. אבל בזמן שאין בית המקדש קיים — לא.§ "אבל לא ממי הגשמים וממי הקילון".§ (א) בשלמא מי קילון — איכא טירחא יתירא, אלא מי גשמים מאי טירחא איכא? אמר ר' אילעא א"ר יוחנן: גזירה מי גשמים אטו מי קילון. רב אשי אמר: מי גשמים גופייהו לידי מי קילון אתו. וקמיפלגי בדר' זירא. דאמר ר' זירא אמר רבה בר ירמיה אמר שמואל: [ב]נהרות המושכין מים מן האגמים — מותר להשקות מהן בחולו של מועד. מר אית ליה דרבי זירא, ומר לית ליה דרבי זירא. גופא, אמר ר' זירא אמר רבה בר ירמיה אמר שמואל: נהרות המושכין מים מן האגמים — מותר להשקות מהן בחולו של מועד. איתיביה רבי ירמיה לרבי זירא: אבל לא ממי גשמים ולא ממי קילון! אמר ליה: ירמיה ברי, [ג]הני אגמים דבבל — כמיא דלא פסקי דמו. תנו רבנן: [ד]הפסיקות והבריכות שנתמלאו מים מעיו"ט — אסור להשקות מהן בחולו של מועד, ואם היתה אמת המים עוברת ביניהן — מותר. אמר רב פפא: והוא שרובה של אותה שדה שותה מאותה אמת המים. רב אשי אמר: [ה]אע"פ שאין רובה של אותה שדה שותה, כיון דקא משכא ואתיא — מימר אמר: אי לא שתיא לחד יומא — תשתי לתרי ותלתא יומי. ת"ר: [ו]בריכה שנוטפת מים משדה בית השלחין זו — מותר להשקות ממנה שדה בית השלחין אחרת. והא עבידא דפסקא! אמר ר' ירמיה: [ז]ועדיין היא מטפטפת. אמר אביי: [ח]והוא שלא פסק מעיין ראשון. תניא, ר' שמעון בן מנסיא אומר: שתי ערוגות זו למעלה מזו — לא ידלה מן התחתונה וישקה את העליונה. יותר על כן אמר *רבי אלעזר בר שמעון: [ט]אפילו ערוגה אחת, חציה נמוך וחציה גבוה — לא ידלה ממקום נמוך וישקה למקום גבוה. תנו רבנן: [י]מדלין לירקות כדי לאוכלן, ואם בשביל לייפותן — אסור. רבינא ורבה תוספאה הוו קא אזלי באורחא, חזו לההוא גברא דהוה דלי דוולא בחולא דמועדא. אמר ליה רבה תוספאה לרבינא: ליתי מר לשמתיה! א"ל: והתניא: מדלין לירקות כדי לאוכלן! א"ל: מי סברת מאי מדלין — מדלין מיא? מאי מדלין

רש"י

שנכנס לשביעית. כל שיש לו ליכנס לשביעית, שאסור לחרוש לפני ר"ה: מה חריש רשות. בכל מקום: קציר העומר. מותר לקצור בשבת: שהיא של מצוה. אע"פ שמצא קצור — קוצר, דבעינן קצירה לשמה. אבל אם מצא חרוש — אינו חורש: הלכתא למישרא ילדה. עשר נטיעות עד ר"ה: קראי למיסר זקינה. שלשים יום קודם ראש השנה. ואתו בית שמאי והלל וגזרו מפסח ועד עצרת: ממילא שמעת מינה. דזקינה אסור לחרוש: אלא הלכתא לרבי ישמעאל. דלא נפיק ליה מקראי, דדריש לקרא לדרשה אחרינא: להוציא קציר העומר: מדאורייתא בטלו. כלומר, אסמכוה סמך מן התורה, להכי בטלו הלכתא: מאן דאמר הלכתא. דלפני ר"ה אסור: אתא גזירה שוה עקרה להלכתא. כלומר, משום גזרה שוה דאינהו גמירו מנפשייהו משבת — בטלו הלכתא? הא אין אדם דן ג"ש מעצמו! כי גמירו הלכתא בזמן שבית המקדש קיים. וכי שרו רבן גמליאל ובית דינו — בזמן שאין בית המקדש קיים: גזירה מי גשמים. דלמא אתי למעבד מי קילון: מי גשמים נמי אתי לידי מי קילון. כלומר, כי מדלו מינה(ב) דלא הויא מליאה — נעשית ממילא מי קילון, שאינו מלא, וטריחא מלתא: נהרות המושכין מן האגמים. השתא משמע ליה מי אגמים, עבידא דפסקי:(ג) מותר להשקות מהן בחולו של מועד. ולא גזרי דלמא פסיקא מי אגמים, ואזיל וטרח ואייתי מן נהר אחר: ר' אילעא אמר ר' יוחנן. דאמר גזרינן מי גשמים אפילו היכא דלא פסקי אטו מי קילון מדקאמר רב אשי מי גשמים לידי(ד) קילון אתי מכלל דר' יוחנן אסר אפילו דלא אתיא לידי מי קילון לית ליה דר' זירא דלא גזר: מיתיבי אבל לא מי קילון. דלמא מפסקי, וטרח להוציא מן העמוק. הכא נמי: אמאי לא ניחוש דלמא מפסקי מי אגמים? א"ל כמיא דלא פסקי דמו. וליכא למיחש: פסיקות ובריכות. חדא מילתא היא: אם אמת המים עוברת ביניהן. בין הבריכות הללו — מותר להשקות ממי גשמים, דאי פסקי מי גשמים — משקה מאמת המים: והוא שרובה של אותה שדה שותה מאותה אמת המים כו'. שיכול להשקות רוב השדה בפעם אחת מאותה אמת המים. אבל אם אינו יכול להשקות בפעם אחת מאותה אמת המים רוב של שדה — אינו משקה מפסיקות ובריכות, דלמא מפסיק ואזיל: תישתי לתרי או תלתא יומי. מהאי אמת המים, ולא טרח ומייתי מאמת המים אחרינא: בריכה שנטפה משדה בית השלחין זו מותר להשקות ממנה בית השלחין אחר. בית השלחין שהיה גבוה, והיה מעיין נובע מתוכו, ובצד אחד היה בית השלחין נמוך. ובין אלו בית השלחין היה בצד השלחין הנמוך בריכה קטנה, וכשמשקים בית השלחין הגבוה מן המעיין נוטף טיפין מן בית השלחין הגבוה לבריכה הנמוכה — מותר להשקות אותו בית השלחין הנמוך מאותה בריכה, אע"ג דבריכה עבידא דפסקא. הואיל ומטפטף בו מבית השלחין הגבוה מים שבאו לו מחמת המעיין: והא עבידא דפסקא. בריכה, ואזיל ומייתי(ה): עדיין היא מטפטפת. מבית השלחין גבוה לתוך הבריכה, דודאי לא פסקא: אמר אביי והוא שלא פסק מעיין. המטפטף מבית השלחין גבוה לבריכה — מותר להשקות מבריכה לבית השלחין נמוך. אבל אי פסיק מעיין, אע"ג דעדיין מטפטף מבית השלחין גבוה לתוך הבריכה — אין משקין מן הבריכה לבית השלחין נמוך, דלמא פסיק, ואזיל וטרח ומייתי ממעיין אחר: לא ידלה מן התחתון וישקה לעליון. דאיכא טירחא יתירא: מדלין לירקות. משמע שהוא דולה מים ומשקה לירקות, כדי לאוכלן בחולו של מועד: ואם בשביל לייפותן. שיגדלו הירקות — אסור, דהרווחה היא: דהוה דלי דוולא. דולה דליות מים לירקות. וחכמים לא התירו כי אם לבית השלחין בלבד: שלופי

[תוספתא פ"א]

תוספות

אלא אמר רב נחמן בר יצחק. האי "אלא" קאי אהאי דרבי יצחק (ו) לעיל: כי גמירי הלכתא לשלשים יום לפני ראש השנה, דהיינו באילנות זקנים. לא תימא דלהכי אתיא הלכתא, אלא סבר רב נחמן דאיסור שלשים לפי אומד חכמים, ואף החמירו בהם בדבריהם. ויש דמשבשי ליה להאי 'אלא' דרב נחמן, ואין להאריך בדבריהם:

מה להלן היא אסורה לפניה ולאחריה מותרין. ואי קשיא: והא מפקינן מקרא במס' יומא פרק בתרא (דף פא:) דצריך לעשות תוספת גבי שבת, בין בכניסתה בין ביציאתה, להוסיפה מחול על הקודש! איכא למימר: ההוא פורתא לא קא חשיב, כיון דלא הוי אלא כל שהוא. וכי ההוא שיעורא נמי יהא מודה רבן גמליאל דצריך להוסיף:

אלא אמר רב אשי רבן גמליאל כו'. כלומר, ודאי מדאורייתא בטיל. ולאו היינו טעמא כדקאמר, אלא סבירא ליה כרבי ישמעאל. וקא דייק רבן גמליאל מה שייכא תוספת שביעית גבי ניסוך, שניתנו למשה גבי הדדי, (ז) דבכל מקום שונה הני שלשה ביחד, דכך ניתנו. אלא ודאי — למילף סמכינהו רחמנא:

בשלמא מי קילון כו' אלא מי גשמים. מיירי בכי האי גוונא דקים לן דלא פסקי, ולית בהו איסור אלא מהאי טעמא דמפרש. אבל אי פסקי — אית להו איסורא, כדלקמן. דבכל מידי דפסיק — איכא איסורא משום דאזיל ומייתי ממקום רחוק כיון שהתחיל להשקות, שלא יפסיד שדהו. הלכך, איכא לאוקמי הכא דלא פסקי:

מדלין

עין משפט נר מצוה

כז א מיי' פ"ז מהלכות תמידין הלכה ו סמג עשין קנט:

כח ב ג ד ה ו ז ח מיי' פ"ח מהלכות יו"ט הלכה א טוש"ע א"ח סי' תקלז סעיף ג:

כט ט מיי' שם הלכה ב טוש"ע שם סעיף ב:

ל י מיי' שם טוש"ע שם סעיף ז:

רבינו חננאל

עד ר"ה מכלל שאין חורשין לאילן עד ר"ה. ומן ההלכה שמענו. ולא מדב"ש וב"ה וערבה וניסוך המים הל"מ הן. ופריק ר' יצחק כי אתאי הלכתא א) פי' כדתנן בשביעית בפ' שני אין נוטעין ואין מבריכין ואין מרכיבין ערב שביעית פחות משלשים יום קודם ר"ה ואתו ב"ש ובית הלל התקינו מפסח לשדה לבן ומעצרת לשדה האילן ושקלו וטרו כי אתאי הלכתא למישרא ילדה. פי' כגון עשר נטיעות המפוזרות בבית סאה שהל"מ לחרוש להן כל בית סאה עד ר"ה למישרי ילדה להתיר החרישה לנטיעה שהיא ילדה. קראי למיסר זקינה פי' בחריש ובקציר שלמדנו ממנו איסור חרישה קודם ר"ה האיסור הזה לאילן שכבר עשה פרי וכבר זקן ואקשינן וכיון שהלכה להתיר החרישה לנטיעה הלא מתוך זאת אתה למד שהחרישה לאילן אסורה. (והשבנו שר' ישמעאל הוא שלמד איסור החרישה מן ההלכה דר' ישמעאל מוציא בחריש ובקציר לטעם אחר להתיר קצירת העומר בשבת ולפיכך הוא נצרך להלכה ללמד איסורי החרישה). ואסיקנא לה ר' ישמעאל סבר הל"מ הוא פי' כי הוא מוציא בחריש ובקציר לטעם אחר להתיר קצירת העומר [בשבת] ור"ע פליג עליה ואמר לאו הל"מ נינהו אלא קרא פי' מן בחריש ובקציר נינהו. ור' יוחנן אמר ר"ג מדאוריי' שרא להו גמר שבת שבת בראשית בג"ש מה ערב שבת בראשית מותר לעשות מלאכה עד שתחשך כלומר לפניה ולאחריה מותר אף ערב שביעית מותר עד ר"ה פירוש לפניה ולאחריה מותר. ודחי רב ששת מ"ד הלכה אתאי גזרה שוה ועקרתה להלכתא כו' אלא אמר רב אשי ר"ג ובית דינו סברי לה כר' ישמעאל דאמר הלכתא גמירי לה וכי גמירי הלכתא בזמן שבהמ"ק קיים דומיא דניסוך המים. אבל בזמן שאין בית המקדש קיים לא ולפיכך התיר. אבל אין משקין את השלחין לא ממי הגשמים ולא ממי הקילון ומקשינן בשלמא מי הקילון שהן כמו בור מושך מים וצריך לדלות ולהשקות דאיכא טירחא לא. אלא מי גשמים דפתיחה סגי ליה מאי טירחא איכא. א"ר יוחנן גזירה כו'. רב אשי אמר גשמים שבפשטם המטר אתי לידי מי קילון. כלומר צריך למלאות מהן בדלי במקום שנתקבצו ופליגא דאמר נהרות המושכין מן האגם מותר להשקות מהן בחולו של מועד. ר' יוחנן אית ליה דר' זירא. ואסיקנא דהני נהרות המושכין מן האגמים מותר משום דאגמי בבל כמיא דלא פסקי דמו. ת"ר הבריכות והפסיקות שנתמלאו מים ב) בחולו של מועד דחיישינן שמא יפסקו ויבואו למלאות בדלי ואם היתה אמת המים עוברת עליהן מותר. אמר רב אשי ואע"פ שאין רוב אותה שדה שותה מאותה אמת המים שרינן. מ"ט כיון דמשכה אותה אמת המים ואתיא לה לא חייש לפסידא מימר אמר אי לא שתי לחד יומא שתי לתרי יומא ותלת יומא: תנו רבנן בריכה שנטפה מים. כלומר נתמצו ונתקבצו בתוכה התמצית שלחין אחדא. תנינן המים המתמצין משדה בית השלחין משקה בית השלחין אחר כ"ז שמטפטפת ולא פסק מעין ראשון. ותניא ר"ש בן מנסיא אומר ב' ערוגות זו למעלה מזו לא ידלה מן התחתונה וישקה לעליונה ואפי' ערוגה אחת חציה נמוך וחציה גבוה לא ידלה מן הנמוך וישקה את הגבוה. ת"ר מדלין מים כו'. ואסיקנא

א) נ"ל כי אתאי הלכתא ל' יום לפני ר"ה פי' כדתנן וכו'. ב) נ"ל שנתמלאו מים מעיו"ט אסור להשקות מהן בחולו של מועד.

הגהות הב"ח

(א) גמ' בשלמא מי קילון. נ"ב ל' הרמב"ם קילון כלומר בור עמוק וכן מי גשמים שמתקבצי' מהם אגמים וכשהגשמים פוסקים יתמו המים הבאים לאגמים ויצטרך להשקות מהם בדלי: (ב) רש"י ד"ה מי גשמים כו' כי מדלו מינה עד דלא הוי מליאה: (ג) ד"ה מותר כו' וד"ה רבי אילעא כו' הס"ד: (ד) ד"ה אילעא כו' לידי מי קילון: (ה) ד"ה והא עבידא כו' ואזיל ומייתי ממעיין אחר הס"ד: (ו) תום' ד"ה אלא כו' אהאי דר' יצחק לעיל דקאמר כי גמירי כו' לפי אומד חכמים הוא ואף: (ז) ד"ה אלא אר"א כו' דבכל מ"ש שונה הני שלשה ביחד. נ"ב אבל רש"י ז"ל פי' במס' סוכה דף לד דאלו שלשה נשאלו בבית המדרש ושמע השומע וגרסם כסדר ששמעם:

מַדְלִין — שַׁלּוּפֵי. כִּדְתְנַן: *הַמֵּידֵל בַּגְּפָנִים, כְּשֵׁם שֶׁהוּא מֵידֵל בְּשֶׁלּוֹ — כָּךְ הוּא מֵידֵל בְּשֶׁל עֲנִיִּים, דִּבְרֵי ר׳ יְהוּדָה. רַבִּי מֵאִיר אוֹמֵר: בְּשֶׁלּוֹ — רַשַּׁאי, וְאֵינוֹ רַשַּׁאי בְּשֶׁל עֲנִיִּים. אֲמַר לֵיהּ: וְהָתַנְיָא: מַדְלִין מַיִם לַיְּרָקוֹת כְּדֵי לְאוֹכְלָן! אֲמַר לֵיהּ: *אִי תַּנְיָא — תַּנְיָא. § "וְאֵין עוֹשִׂין עוּגִיּוֹת לַגְּפָנִים". § מַאי עוּגִיּוֹת? אָמַר רַב יְהוּדָה: בִּנְכֵי. *תַּנְיָא נַמִּי הָכִי: אֵלּוּ הֵן עוּגִיּוֹת — בְּדִידִין שֶׁבְּעִיקְּרֵי זֵיתִים וְשֶׁבְּעִיקְּרֵי גְּפָנִים. אִינִי? וְהָא רַב יְהוּדָה שְׁרָא לִבְנֵי בַּר צִיתַאי לְמֶעֱבַד בִּנְכֵי לְכַרְמֵיהוֹן! לָא קַשְׁיָא, [א]הָא — בַּחֲדַתֵי, הָא — בְּעַתִּיקֵי. § "ר׳ אֶלְעָזָר בֶּן עֲזַרְיָה אוֹמֵר אֵין עוֹשִׂין אֶת הָאַמָּה". § בִּשְׁלָמָא מוֹעֵד — מִשּׁוּם דְּקָא טָרַח, אֶלָּא שְׁבִיעִית — מַאי טַעְמָא? פְּלִיגוּ בָּהּ רַבִּי זֵירָא וְרַבִּי אַבָּא בַּר מֶמֶל. חַד אָמַר: מִפְּנֵי שֶׁנִּרְאֶה כְּעוֹדֵר, וְחַד אָמַר: מִפְּנֵי שֶׁמַּכְשִׁיר אֲגַפֶּיהָ לִזְרִיעָה. מַאי בֵּינַיְיהוּ? אִיכָּא בֵּינַיְיהוּ דְּקָא אָתוּ מַיָּא בַּתְרֵיהּ. מַאן דְּאָמַר מִפְּנֵי שֶׁמַּכְשִׁיר אֲגַפֶּיהָ לִזְרִיעָה — אִיכָּא, ומ"ד מִפְּנֵי שֶׁנִּרְאֶה כְּעוֹדֵר — לֵיכָּא. וּלְמַאן דְּאָמַר מִפְּנֵי שֶׁנִּרְאֶה כְּעוֹדֵר — לֵיחוּשׁ מִפְּנֵי שֶׁמַּכְשִׁיר אֲגַפֶּיהָ לִזְרִיעָה! אֶלָּא: אִיכָּא בֵּינַיְיהוּ דְּקָא שָׁקֵיל מִינֵּיהּ וְשָׁדֵי לְבָרַאי. לְמַאן דְּאָמַר מִפְּנֵי שֶׁמַּכְשִׁיר אֲגַפֶּיהָ לִזְרִיעָה — לֵיכָּא, לְמ"ד מִפְּנֵי שֶׁנִּרְאֶה כְּעוֹדֵר — אִיכָּא. וּלְמ"ד מִפְּנֵי שֶׁמַּכְשִׁיר אֲגַפֶּיהָ לִזְרִיעָה, לֵיחוּשׁ מִפְּנֵי שֶׁנִּרְאֶה כְּעוֹדֵר? עוֹדֵר נַמִּי, כִּי קָא שָׁקֵיל — בְּדוּכְתֵּיהּ מַנַּח לֵיהּ. אַמֵּימַר מַתְנֵי לָהּ מִפְּנֵי שֶׁנִּרְאֶה כְּעוֹדֵר, וְקַשְׁיָא לֵיהּ דְּרַבִּי אֶלְעָזָר בֶּן עֲזַרְיָה אַדְּר׳ אֶלְעָזָר בֶּן עֲזַרְיָה: וּמִי אָמַר ר׳ אֶלְעָזָר בֶּן עֲזַרְיָה כָּל שֶׁנִּרְאֶה כְּעוֹדֵר אָסוּר? וּרְמִינְהִי: *[ב]עוֹשֶׂה אָדָם אֶת זִבְלוֹ אוֹצָר. ר׳ מֵאִיר אוֹסֵר עַד שֶׁיַּעֲמִיק שְׁלֹשָׁה טְפָחִים, אוֹ עַד שֶׁיַּגְבִּיהַּ ג׳ טְפָחִים. הָיָה לוֹ דָּבָר מוּעָט — מוֹסִיף עָלָיו וְהוֹלֵךְ. רַבִּי אֶלְעָזָר בֶּן עֲזַרְיָה אוֹסֵר עַד שֶׁיַּעֲמִיק שְׁלֹשָׁה, אוֹ עַד שֶׁיַּגְבִּיהַּ שְׁלֹשָׁה, אוֹ עַד שֶׁיִּתֵּן עַל הַסֶּלַע. ר׳ זֵירָא וְר׳ אַבָּא בַּר מֶמֶל, חַד אָמַר: כְּגוֹן שֶׁהֶעֱמִיק, וְחַד אָמַר: זִיבְלוֹ מוֹכִיחַ עָלָיו. § "וּמְתַקְּנִין אֶת הַמְקוּלְקֶלֶת בַּמּוֹעֵד". § מַאי מְקוּלְקֶלֶת? אָמַר רַבִּי אַבָּא: [ג]שֶׁאִם הָיְתָה עֲמוּקָּה טֶפַח — מַעֲמִידָהּ עַל שִׁשָּׁה טְפָחִים. פְּשִׁיטָא, חֲצִי טֶפַח עַל שְׁלֹשָׁה טְפָחִים, כֵּיוָן דְּלָא עָבַר מַיָּא — לָאו כְּלוּם הוּא. טְפָחַיִים עַל שְׁנֵים עָשָׂר, דְּקָא טָרַח טִירְחָא יְתֵירָא — לָא. טְפָחַיִים עַל שִׁבְעָה מַהוּ? [ד]הָכָא חֲמִשָּׁה קָא מַעֲמִיק וְהָכָא חֲמִשָּׁה קָא מַעֲמִיק, אוֹ דִּלְמָא, כֵּיוָן דְּאִיכָּא טֶפַח יְתֵירָא — אִיכָּא טִירְחָא טְפֵי? תֵּיקוּ. אַבַּיֵי [ה]שְׁרָא לִבְנֵי בַּר הַמְדָּךְ לְשַׁחוּפֵי נַהֲרָא. רַבִּי יִרְמְיָה [ו]שְׁרָא לְהוּ לִבְנֵי סְכוּתָא לְמִכְרָא נַהֲרָא טְמִימָא. רַב אַשִׁי שְׁרָא לְהוּ לִבְנֵי מָתָא מְחַסְיָא לְאַקְדּוּחֵי נְהַר בּוֹרְנִיץ. אֲמַר: כֵּיוָן דְּשָׁתוּ מִינֵּיהּ רַבִּים — כְּרַבִּים דָּמֵי, וּתְנַן: עוֹשִׂין כָּל צוֹרְכֵי רַבִּים. § "וּמְתַקְּנִין אֶת קִילְקוּלֵי

שַׁלּוּפֵי. כְּשֶׁהַיְּרָקוֹת רְצוּפִין נוֹטֵל מֵהֶן מִבֵּינְתַיִים לְאוֹכְלָן – מוּתָּר, לְיַפּוֹתָן – אָסוּר, בִּשְׁבִיל לְיַפּוֹתָן אוֹתָם שֶׁנִּשְׁאָרִים: הַמֵּידֵל. תּוֹלֵשׁ בַּגְּפָנִים שֶׁיֶּשְׁנָן בְּיַחַד יוֹתֵר מִדַּאי: בְּשֶׁל עֲנִיִּים. בְּפֵאָה. א"נ, עוֹלֵלוֹת – שֶׁאֵין לוֹ לֹא כָּתֵף וְלֹא נָטֵף: בִּנְכֵי. כּוֹרוֹת תַּחַת הַגְּפָנִים וְזֵיתִים וְנוֹתֵן בָּהֶם מַיִם: עוּגִיּוֹת. עִגּוּל סָבִיב, כְּמוֹ "עָג עוּגָה וְעָמַד בְּתוֹכָהּ" (תענית דף יט.) וּבְדִידִין נַמִּי הֵן גּוּמוֹת: צִיתַאי. מָקוֹם: לְמֶעֱבַד בִּנְכֵי. עוּגִיּוֹת. וְהֵיכִי שָׁרֵי? וְהָא תְּנַן: אֵין עוֹשִׂין עוּגִיּוֹת! הָא בַּחֲדַתֵי. שֶׁמֵּעוֹלָם לֹא הָיוּ שָׁם עוּגִיּוֹת – אָסוּר לַעֲשׂוֹת בְּחוּלּוֹ שֶׁל מוֹעֵד, דְּאִיכָּא טִירְחָא יְתֵירָא. אֲבָל עַתִּיקֵי, שֶׁכְּבָר הָיוּ לוֹ שָׁם עוּגִיּוֹת וְנִסְתְּמוּ – מוּתָּר לַחֲזוֹר וּלְחוֹפְרָן בְּחוּלּוֹ שֶׁל מוֹעֵד: מִפְּנֵי שֶׁנִּרְאֶה כְּעוֹדֵר. לְצוֹרֶךְ שְׁבִיעִית, שֶׁהֲרֵי חוֹפֵר כְּעוֹדֵר: שֶׁמַּכְשִׁיר אֲגַפֶּיהָ לִזְרִיעָה. כְּשֶׁחוֹפֵר הָאַמָּה וּמַנִּיחַ הֶעָפָר שֶׁבָּאַמָּה עַל שְׂפַת הָאַמָּה – מְתַקֵּן אֲגַפֶּיהָ לִזְרִיעָה, דְּעָבֵיד לַהּ אַרְעָא רַכִּיכָא: דְּקָא אָתוּ מַיָּא בַּתְרֵיהּ. דְּכִי חָפַר בָּאַמָּה אָתוּ לְאַלְתַּר מַיִם בַּהֲדֵי חֲפִירָה: מ"ד מִפְּנֵי שֶׁמַּכְשִׁיר אֲגַפֶּיהָ לִזְרִיעָה אִיכָּא. אע"ג דְּאָתֵי מַיָּא בַּתְרֵיהּ, דְּהָא שְׁדָא אַרְעָא רַכִּיכָא אֲגַפֵּי הָאַמָּה: וּמ"ד מִפְּנֵי שֶׁנִּרְאֶה כְּעוֹדֵר לֵיכָּא. דְּהָא אָתֵי מַיָּא, וּבְעוֹדֵר לֵיכָּא מַיִם, וּלְכָךְ לָא דָּמֵי לְעוֹדֵר: אֶלָּא. לְעוֹלָם דְּלָא אָתוּ מַיָּא בַּתְרֵיהּ. וְאִיכָּא בֵּינַיְיהוּ דְּשָׁקֵיל וְשָׁדֵי לְבָרַאי. דְּחָפֵיר בָּאַמָּה וְשָׁדֵי עָפָר לְבָרַאי, רָחוֹק מֵאֲגַפֵּי אַמָּה, דְּלָא מַכְשִׁיר אֲגַפֶּיהָ לִזְרִיעָה: מַאן דְּאָמַר מִפְּנֵי שֶׁנִּרְאֶה כְּעוֹדֵר אִיכָּא. דְּהָא חָפֵיר וְלָא אָתוּ מַיָּא בַּתְרֵיהּ: בְּדוּכְתֵּיהּ מַנַּח לֵיהּ. דְּלָא שָׁדֵי אַרְעָא לְבָרַאי, דְּלָא עָבֵיד אֶלָּא מְרַכֵּךְ אַרְעָא. אֲבָל הָכָא – שָׁדֵי לְבָרַאי, לְכָךְ לָא דָּמֵי לְעוֹדֵר: אַמֵּימַר מַתְנֵי. בְּהֶדְיָא, הָא דְּאָמַר ר׳ אֶלְעָזָר אֵין עוֹשִׂין אֶת הָאַמָּה בַּשְּׁבִיעִית מִפְּנֵי שֶׁנִּרְאֶה כְּעוֹדֵר: עוֹשֶׂה אָדָם זִבְלוֹ אוֹצָר. שֶׁמַּכְנִיס כָּל זִבְלוֹ בַּשְּׁבִיעִית בַּשָּׂדֶה, וְלָא אָמְרִינַן דְּנִרְאֶה כִּמְזַבֵּל שָׂדֵהוּ בַּשְּׁבִיעִית: עַד שֶׁיַּעֲמִיק שְׁלֹשָׁה טְפָחִים. וּמַכְנִיס הַזֶּבֶל לְשָׁם, דְּמוֹכְחָא מִלְּתָא דְּלָא עָבֵיד כְּדֵי לְזַבֵּל שָׂדֵהוּ בַּשְּׁבִיעִית: הָיָה לוֹ מְעַט זֶבֶל. בְּאוֹתָהּ שָׂדֶה קוֹדֶם שְׁבִיעִית, מוֹסִיף עָלָיו זֶבֶל וְהוֹלֵךְ בַּשְּׁבִיעִית, וְאֵין צָרִיךְ לְהַעֲמִיק: רַבִּי אֶלְעָזָר אוֹסֵר. אֲפִילּוּ אִם הָיָה שָׁם מְעַט זֶבֶל קוֹדֶם שְׁבִיעִית, לְהוֹסִיף עָלָיו בַּשְּׁבִיעִית: עַד שֶׁיַּעֲמִיק שְׁלֹשָׁה. אוֹ שֶׁיִּתֵּן הַזֶּבֶל עַל הַסֶּלַע שֶׁבַּשָּׂדֶה, דְּלָא נִרְאֶה כִּמְזַבֵּל וְהֵיכִי שָׁרֵי רַבִּי אֶלְעָזָר לַחְפּוֹר וּלְהַעֲמִיק בַּשְּׁבִיעִית וְלָא חָיֵישׁ לְנִרְאֶה כְּעוֹדֵר? כְּגוֹן שֶׁהֶעֱמִיק. קוֹדֶם לָכֵן. כְּלוֹמַר, הָא דְּאָמַר רַבִּי אֶלְעָזָר עַד שֶׁיַּעֲמִיק – לָא אָמַר עַד שֶׁיַּעֲמִיק בַּשְּׁבִיעִית, אֶלָּא שֶׁהָיָה עָמוֹק קוֹדֶם שְׁבִיעִית: זִבְלוֹ מוֹכִיחַ עָלָיו. כְּלוֹמַר, אע"ג דְּמַעֲמִיק בַּשְּׁבִיעִית הוּא נִרְאֶה כְּעוֹדֵר וְאָסוּר – הָכָא מוּתָּר, שֶׁהֲרֵי זִבְלוֹ שֶׁמַּנִּיחַ לְשָׁם מוֹכִיחַ עָלָיו דְּלָא עָבֵיד מִשּׁוּם עוֹדֵר: שֶׁאִם הָיְתָה עֲמוּקָּה טֶפַח. כְּלוֹמַר, שֶׁלְּכַתְּחִילָּה הָיָה שָׁם אַמַּת הַמַּיִם בַּת שִׁשָּׁה טְפָחִים, וְנִסְתְּמָה עַד טֶפַח[א] – מַעֲמִידָהּ עַל שִׁשָּׁה טְפָחִים, כְּלוֹמַר: חוֹזֵר וּמַעֲמִיק אוֹתָן חֲמִשָּׁה טְפָחִים שֶׁנִּסְתְּמָה: חֲצִי טֶפַח עַל שְׁלֹשָׁה. אִם הָיְתָה בִּתְחִלָּה בַּת שְׁלֹשָׁה טְפָחִים, וְנִסְתְּמָה עַד חֲצִי טֶפַח, דְּוַדַּאי אֵינוֹ חוֹזֵר וְחוֹפֵר אוֹתָן שְׁנֵי טְפָחִים וּמֶחֱצָה. אע"ג דְּהָוֵי דּוּמְיָא דְּהָיְתָה עֲמוּקָּה טֶפַח וּמַעֲמִידָהּ עַל ו׳ טְפָחִים: כֵּיוָן דְּמֵעִיקָּרָא לָא עָבְרִי בָּהּ מַיָּא. כְּלוֹמַר, וַדַּאי בְּאַמָּה בַּת שְׁלֹשָׁה טְפָחִים לָא עָבְרִי בָּהּ מַיָּא שַׁפִּיר, לֹא קוֹדֶם לָכֵן וְלֹא עַכְשָׁיו – הָוֵי טִירְחָא דְּלָא צָרִיךְ: טְפָחַיִים עַל שְׁנֵים עָשָׂר. דִּלְכַתְּחִילָּה הָיְתָה שֶׁל שְׁנֵים עָשָׂר, וְנִסְתְּמָה עַד שְׁנֵי טְפָחִים – אָסוּר לְהַעֲמִיק עוֹד עַד י׳ טְפָחִים עַל אוֹתָן שְׁנַיִם הָרִאשׁוֹנִים, מִשּׁוּם דְּהָוֵי טִירְחָא יְתֵירָא, דְּקָא מַעֲמִיק כָּל כָּךְ וּלְהַגְבִּיהַּ קַרְקָעִית הַגּוּמָא לְמַעְלָה מִשִּׁשָּׁה טְפָחִים: טְפָחַיִים עַל שִׁבְעָה טְפָחִים. וְנִסְתְּמָה עַד שְׁנֵי טְפָחִים: מַהוּ. לְהַעֲמִיק אוֹתָן חֲמִשָּׁה שֶׁנִּשְׁתַּיְּירוּ: הָכָא חֲמִשָּׁה קָא מַעֲמִיק. דְּהָיְתָה עֲמוּקָּה טֶפַח וּמַעֲמִידָהּ עַל שִׁשָּׁה וְלָא הָוֵי טִירְחָא יְתֵירָא לְהַעֲמִיק כָּל כָּךְ בַּקַּרְקַע: וְהָכָא. נַמִּי לֹא מַעֲמִיק בַּמּוֹעֵד אֶלָּא חֲמִשָּׁה טְפָחִים: כֵּיוָן דְּאִיכָּא טֶפַח יְתֵירָא. דְּלָא צָרִיךְ כָּל הַטֶּפַח [דְּסַגֵּי בְּד׳]: אִיכָּא טִירְחָא טְפֵי. שֶׁשּׁוֹחֶה עַצְמוֹ בִּשְׁבִיל אוֹתוֹ טֶפַח יוֹתֵר מִדַּאי: לְשַׁחוּפֵי נַהֲרָא. לַעֲקוֹר עַנְפֵי אִילָנוֹת הַגְּדֵלִים בַּנָּהָר: לְמִכְרָא נַהֲרָא טְמִימָא. לְפַנּוֹת מְקוֹר הַמַּעְיָין שֶׁנִּסְתַּם: לְאַקְדּוּחֵי נַהֲרָא. לְפַנּוֹת שִׁירְטוֹן שֶׁבְּאֶמְצַע הַנָּהָר: בּוֹרְנִיץ. שֵׁם הַנָּהָר: קִילְקוּלֵי

---

*מדלין לירקות. ממקום עמוק קרי דילוי, ואע"ג דאיכא טירחא יתירא, בשביל לאכול – התירו. אבל לייפות, אפילו ליכא טירחא – לא התירו: כך מידל בשל עניים. דכי אסר רחמנא ליקח עוללות – ה"מ בשעת בצירה, כדכתיב (דברים כד): "כי תבצור כרמך לא תעולל" – איסור עוללות עלייהו:

מפני שמכשיר אגפיה לזריעה. ונראית חרישה ממש, שסבורין הרואין שלכך מתכוין. אי נמי: חשיב ליה עבודת קרקע ממש. ואע"ג שאינו מתכוין לכך – מיהו מלאכה היא. ואע"ג דאמר ר' שמעון דבר שאין מתכוין מותר – הא אמרינן: *מודה ר' שמעון בפסיק רישיה ולא ימות. ורבנן סברי: כיון דע"י שינוי עביד ליה – לאו מלאכה היא, ומותר, דלא שמיה חרישה:

זבלו מוכיח עליו. דליכא למיחש להא, דמאן דחזי החפירה (*לא) חזי ליה[ב] לזבל שבחפירה:

*) [נ"ל הא וכן איתא בתוי"ט לאתויי דשביעית פ"ג מ"ג]

רבינו חננאל

ואסיקנא מדלין מים לירקות כדי לאוכלן ואם בשביל לייפותן אסור. ולית האי מדלין מלשון שלופי כדתנן המדל בגפנים כו' [ואין עושין עוגיות] פי' עוגה והן בדידין שבעיקרי אילנות כדתנן במס' כלים פ' כ"ט יד הבדיד ד' והנ"מ בחדתא אבל בעתיקא למיעבד בנכי שרי: (מתני') [פיסקא] ר' אלעזר בן עזריה אומר אין עושין את האמה בתחלה בין [במועד ובין] בשביעית. ומקשינן בשלמא במועד משום טירחא אלא שביעית אמאי לא. ופרקינן כיון שחופר נראה כעושה מלאכה בשביעית בשדה. וי"א מפני שמכשיר אגפיה לזריעה כלומר כיון שחופר נמצא כחורש באמצע ומכשיר הצדדין לזריעה כו'. אמימר מתני לה מפני שנראה כעודר. וקשיא ליה ומי א"ר אלעזר הכי שכל החופר ומעמיק נראה כעודר. והא איהו דאמר שחופר עד ג' ולא גזר משום עודר דתנן במס' שביעית פ"ג עושה אדם זבלו אוצר ר"מ אוסר עד שיעמיק ג' טפחים או עד שיגביה ג' או שיתן על הסלע ופרקינן ר' זירא ור' אבא בר ממל חד אמר כגון שהעמיק קודם לכן וחד אמר זבלו מוכיח עליו שאינו עודר: **פיסקא.** וחכ"א עושה אדם אמת המים בתחלה בשביעית ומתקנין את המתקלקלות במועד. מאי מקולקלות. א"ר אבהו שאם היתה עמוקה טפח חופרה ומעמידה עד ששה טפחים נמצא מוסיף ה' טפחים. ומיבעיא לן אמה שיש בה טפחיים מהן לחפור ה' האחרות ולהעמידה על ז' טפחים דחמשה נמי הוא דקא מוסיף ועלתה בתיקו: ומתקנין קילקולי המים שברה"ר. אביי שרא לבני בר הרמך לסחופי נהרא. ור' ירמיה שרא לבני סכותא למכרא נהרא סתום ולפותחו ור' אסי שרא לאקדוחי נהר ביצין אמר כיון דשתו מיניה רבים כרבים דמי ותנן עושין כל צורכי רבים:

פיסקא

עין משפט נר מצוה

שייך מעב"ל

לא א מיי' פ"ח מהלכות י"ט הלכה ג טוש"ע א"ח סי' תקלז סעיף ה:

לב ב מיי' פ"ב מהלכות שמיטה הלכה ב:

לג ג ד מיי' פ"ח מהל' י"ט הלכה ג סמג לאוין עה טוש"ע א"ח סי' תקלז סעיף ו:

לד ה ו מיי' שם הלכה ד סמג שם טוש"ע א"ח סי' תקמד ס"ב:

שבת עה.

מסורת הש"ס

פאה פ"ז מ"ה

[שבת קטו: וש"נ]

[תוספתא פ"א ע"ש תוספתא דשביעית פ"א]

[שביעית פ"ג מ"ג]

הגהות הב"ח

(א) רש"י ד"ה שאם היתה כו' ונסתמה עד טפח וחוזר ומעמידה עד ששה:

(ב) תוס' ד"ה זבלו כו' חזי ליה נמי לזבל:

קִילְקוּלֵי הַמַּיִם שֶׁבִּרְה"ר" וכו'.§ חֲטִיטָה — אִין, חֲפִירָה — לָא. אָמַר ר' יַעֲקֹב אָמַר ר' יוֹחָנָן: לֹא שָׁנוּ אֶלָּא שֶׁאֵין רַבִּים צְרִיכִין לָהֶם, אֲבָל רַבִּים צְרִיכִין לָהֶם — אֲפִילּוּ חֲפִירָה מוּתָּר. וְכִי רַבִּים צְרִיכִין לָהֶם מִי שָׁרֵי? וְהָתַנְיָא: חוֹטְטִין בּוֹרוֹת שִׁיחִין וּמְעָרוֹת שֶׁל יָחִיד, וְאֵין צָרִיךְ לוֹמַר שֶׁל רַבִּים, וְאֵין חוֹפְרִין בּוֹרוֹת שִׁיחִין וּמְעָרוֹת שֶׁל רַבִּים, וְאֵין צָרִיךְ לוֹמַר שֶׁל יָחִיד. מַאי לָאו — בְּשֶׁרַבִּים צְרִיכִין לָהֶם! לֹא, בְּשֶׁאֵין רַבִּים צְרִיכִין לָהֶם. דִּכְוָותָהּ גַּבֵּי יָחִיד — שֶׁאֵין יָחִיד צָרִיךְ לָהֶם, חֲטִיטָה מִי שָׁרֵי? וְהָתַנְיָא: בּוֹרוֹת שִׁיחִין וּמְעָרוֹת שֶׁל יָחִיד — כּוֹנְסִין מַיִם לְתוֹכָן, אֲבָל לֹא חוֹטְטִין,(א) וְלֹא שָׁפִין אֶת סִדְקֵיהֶן. וְשֶׁל רַבִּים — חוֹטְטִין אוֹתָן וְשָׁפִין אֶת סִדְקֵיהֶן. וְאֶלָּא מַאי — בְּשֶׁיָּחִיד צָרִיךְ לָהֶם, דִּכְוָותָהּ גַּבֵּי רַבִּים — בְּשֶׁרַבִּים צְרִיכִין לָהֶם, חֲפִירָה מִי אֲסִיר? וְהָתַנְיָא: בּוֹרוֹת שִׁיחִין וּמְעָרוֹת שֶׁל יָחִיד כּוֹנְסִין מַיִם לְתוֹכָן, וְחוֹטְטִין אוֹתָן, אֲבָל לֹא שָׁפִין אֶת סִדְקֵיהֶן, וְלֹא חוֹטְטִין לְתוֹכָן, וְלֹא סָדִין אוֹתָן בְּסִיד. וְשֶׁל רַבִּים — חוֹפְרִין אוֹתָן, וְסָדִין אוֹתָן בְּסִיד. אֶלָּא קַשְׁיָא הַךְ קַמַּיְיתָא! תְּרֵיץ הָכִי: חוֹטְטִין בּוֹרוֹת שֶׁל יָחִיד — [א]בְּשֶׁיָּחִיד צָרִיךְ לָהֶם, וְאֵין צָרִיךְ לוֹמַר בְּשֶׁל רַבִּים כְּשֶׁרַבִּים צְרִיכִין לָהֶם, [ב]דַּאֲפִילּוּ חֲפִירָה מוּתָּר, וְאֵין חוֹפְרִין בּוֹרוֹת שִׁיחִין וּמְעָרוֹת שֶׁל רַבִּים [ג]בְּשֶׁאֵין רַבִּים צְרִיכִין לָהֶם, וְאֵין צָרִיךְ לוֹמַר שֶׁל יָחִיד, דְּכִי אֵין יָחִיד צָרִיךְ לָהֶם — [ד]אֲפִילּוּ חֲטִיטָה נַמִּי אָסוּר. אָמַר רַב אַשִׁי: מַתְנִיתִין נַמִּי דַּיְקָא, דְּקָתָנֵי: עוֹשִׂין כָּל צוֹרְכֵי רַבִּים. "כָּל" לְאַתּוּיֵי מַאי — לָאו לְאַתּוּיֵי חֲפִירָה? לָא, לְאַתּוּיֵי הָא דְּתַנְיָא: [ה]יוֹצְאִין לְקַוֵּץ אֶת הַדְּרָכִים, וּלְתַקֵּן אֶת הָרְחוֹבוֹת וְאֶת *הָאִסְטְרָטָאוֹת, וְלָמוֹד אֶת הַמִּקְוָאוֹת. וְכָל מִקְוֶה שֶׁאֵין בּוֹ אַרְבָּעִים סְאָה מַרְגִּילִין לְתוֹכוֹ אַרְבָּעִים סְאָה. וּמִנַּיִן שֶׁאִם לֹא יָצְאוּ וְעָשׂוּ כָּל אֵלּוּ, שֶׁכָּל דָּמִים שֶׁנִּשְׁפְּכוּ שָׁם מַעֲלֶה עֲלֵיהֶם הַכָּתוּב כְּאִילּוּ הֵם שְׁפָכוּם? ת"ל °"וְהָיָה עָלֶיךָ דָּמִים". הָא — בְּהֶדְיָא קָתָנֵי לָהּ: וּמְתַקְּנִין אֶת הַדְּרָכִים, וְאֶת הָרְחוֹבוֹת, וְאֶת הַמִּקְוָאוֹת, וְעוֹשִׂין כָּל צוֹרְכֵי רַבִּים. לְאַתּוּיֵי מַאי, לָאו לְאַתּוּיֵי חֲפִירָה? שְׁמַע מִינָּהּ.§ [ו]"מְצַיְּינִין אֶת הַקְּבָרוֹת".§ אָמַר ר"ש בֶּן פָּזִי: רֶמֶז לְצִיּוּן קְבָרוֹת *מִן הַתּוֹרָה מִנַּיִן — תַּלְמוּד לוֹמַר: °"וְרָאָה עֶצֶם אָדָם וּבָנָה אֶצְלוֹ צִיּוּן". א"ל רָבִינָא לְרַב אַשִׁי: הָא מִקַּמֵּי דַּאֲתָא יְחֶזְקֵאל מַאן אֲמַר? וְלִיטַעְמִיךְ, הָא *דְּאָמַר רַב חִסְדָּא: דָּבָר זֶה מִתּוֹרַת מֹשֶׁה רַבֵּינוּ לֹא לָמַדְנוּ, מִדִּבְרֵי יְחֶזְקֵאל בֶּן בּוּזִי לָמַדְנוּ: °"כָּל בֶּן נֵכָר עֶרֶל לֵב וְעֶרֶל בָּשָׂר לֹא יָבֹא אֶל מִקְדָּשִׁי (*לְשָׁרְתֵנִי"), מִקַּמֵּי דַּאֲתָא יְחֶזְקֵאל מַאן אֲמַר? אֶלָּא: גְּמָרָא גְּמִירִי לָהּ, וַאֲתָא יְחֶזְקֵאל וְאַסְמְכָהּ אַקְּרָא. הָכָא נַמִּי: גְּמָרָא גְּמִירִי לָהּ וַאֲתָא יְחֶזְקֵאל וְאַסְמְכָהּ אַקְּרָא. רַבִּי אַבָּהוּ אָמַר מֵהָכָא: °"וְטָמֵא טָמֵא יִקְרָא" — טוּמְאָה קוֹרְאָה לוֹ, וְאוֹמֶרֶת לוֹ: פְּרוֹשׁ. וְכֵן אָמַר רַבִּי עוּזִּיאֵל בַּר בְּרֵיהּ דְּרַבִּי עוּזִּיאֵל רַבָּה: טוּמְאָה קוֹרְאָה לוֹ וְאוֹמֶרֶת לוֹ: פְּרוֹשׁ. וְהַאי לְהָכִי הוּא דַּאֲתָא? הַהוּא מִיבְּעֵי לֵיהּ לְכִדְתַנְיָא: "וְטָמֵא טָמֵא יִקְרָא" — *[ז]צָרִיךְ לְהוֹדִיעַ צַעֲרוֹ לָרַבִּים, וְרַבִּים מְבַקְּשִׁין עָלָיו רַחֲמִים! א"כ לִיכְתּוֹב "וְטָמֵא יִקְרָא" מַאי "וְטָמֵא טָמֵא" — שָׁמְעַתְּ מִינָּהּ תַּרְתֵּי. אַבָּיֵי אָמַר מֵהָכָא: °"וְלִפְנֵי עִוֵּר לֹא תִתֵּן מִכְשׁוֹל". רַב פַּפָּא אָמַר: (ב)°"וְאָמַר סֹלּוּ סֹלּוּ פַּנּוּ דָרֶךְ". רַב חִינְּנָא אָמַר: "הָרִימוּ מִכְשׁוֹל מִדֶּרֶךְ עַמִּי". ר' יְהוֹשֻׁעַ בְּרֵיהּ דְּרַב אִידִי אָמַר: °"וְהוֹדַעְתָּ לָהֶם אֶת הַדֶּרֶךְ (אֲשֶׁר) יֵלְכוּ בָהּ". מָר זוּטְרָא אָמַר: °"וְהִזַּרְתֶּם אֶת בְּנֵי יִשְׂרָאֵל מִטֻּמְאָתָם". רַב אַשִׁי אָמַר: *°"וּשְׁמַרְתֶּם אֶת מִשְׁמַרְתִּי" — עֲשׂוּ מִשְׁמֶרֶת לְמִשְׁמַרְתִּי. רָבִינָא אָמַר: °"וְשָׂם דֶּרֶךְ אַרְאֶנּוּ בְּיֵשַׁע אֱלֹהִים". אָמַר ריב"ל: *כָּל הַשָּׂם אוֹרְחוֹתָיו — זוֹכֶה וְרוֹאֶה בִּישׁוּעָתוֹ שֶׁל הַקָּדוֹשׁ בָּרוּךְ הוּא, שֶׁנֶּאֱמַר "וְשָׂם דֶּרֶךְ", אַל תִּקְרֵי "וְשָׂם" אֶלָּא "וְשָׁם דֶּרֶךְ" — אַרְאֶנּוּ בְּיֵשַׁע אֱלֹהִים. רַבִּי יַנַּאי הֲוָה לֵיהּ הַהוּא תַּלְמִידָא דְּכָל יוֹמָא הֲוָה מַקְשֵׁי לֵיהּ, בְּשַׁבְּתָא דְּרִיגְלָא לָא הֲוָה מַקְשֵׁי לֵיהּ. קָרֵי

תורה אור: דברים יט | יחזקאל לט | שם מד | ויקרא יג | ויקרא יט | ישעיה נז | שמות יח | ויקרא טו | שם יח | תהלים נ

רש"י

קִילְקוּלֵי הַמַּיִם. כְּגוֹן אֲבָנִים שֶׁנָּפְלוּ מֵחֲמַת הַבּוֹר: חוֹטְטִין. נָפְלוּ צְרוֹרוֹת בְּקַרְקָעִית הַבּוֹר מַעֲלֶה אוֹתָן בַּמּוֹעֵד: אֲבָל לֹא חוֹטְטִין אוֹתָן. אִי אֲמַרְתְּ בִּשְׁלָמָא הָא דְּקָתָנֵי הַהִיא בָּרַיְיתָא שֶׁלְּמַעְלָה(ג) שֶׁל יָחִיד — הַיְינוּ בְּשֶׁיָּחִיד צָרִיךְ לוֹ, אִיכָּא לְאוֹקְמֵי הַאי דְּקָתָנֵי הַאי בָּרַיְיתָא אֲבָל לֹא חוֹטְטִין — בְּשֶׁאֵין יָחִיד צָרִיךְ לוֹ. אֶלָּא אִי אוֹקְמַת לַהּ הָא דְּחוֹטְטִין בְּשֶׁאֵין יָחִיד צָרִיךְ לוֹ, א"כ הַאי דְּקָתָנֵי אֲבָל לֹא חוֹטְטִין בְּמַאי מוֹקְמַת לַהּ? אֶלָּא מַאי בְּשֶׁיָּחִיד צָרִיךְ לוֹ כו'. כְּלוֹמַר, בְּמַאי מוֹקְמַת הַאי דְּקָתָנֵי חוֹטְטִין — בְּשֶׁרַבִּים צְרִיכִים לָהֶן, וְהָתַנְיָא כו' שֶׁל רַבִּים חוֹפְרִין אוֹתָן: אֶלָּא קַשְׁיָא קַמַּיְיתָא. דְּקָתָנֵי: אֵין חוֹפְרִין בּוֹרוֹת שֶׁל רַבִּים — בְּשֶׁרַבִּים צְרִיכִין לוֹ, קַשְׁיָא לְהָא בָּרַיְיתָא דְּקָתָנֵי הָכָא: שֶׁל רַבִּים — חוֹפְרִין אוֹתָן: אֶלָּא תְּרֵיץ הָכִי. וְאֵין צָרִיךְ לוֹמַר בְּשֶׁל רַבִּים, דַּאֲפִילּוּ חֲפִירָה מוּתָּר. וְלָא קַשְׁיָא לְרַבִּי יוֹחָנָן דַּאֲמַר לֹא שָׁנוּ כו': מַתְנִיתִין נַמִּי דַּיְקָא. דִּבְשֶׁרַבִּים צְרִיכִין לוֹ, דַּחֲפִירָה נַמִּי מוּתָּר: לְקַוֵּץ אֶת הַדְּרָכִים. לְפַנּוֹת קוֹצִים שֶׁבַּדְּרָכִים: מַרְגִּילִין לִהְיוֹת בְּתוֹכוֹ אַרְבָּעִים סְאָה. שֶׁמַּרְגִּילִין שֶׁיְּהֵא (ד)נוֹגֵעַ בַּמִּקְוֶה אַמַּת הַמַּיִם, כְּדֵי שֶׁיְּהֵא בּוֹ אַרְבָּעִים סְאָה: כָּל דָּמִים שֶׁנִּשְׁפְּכוּ שָׁם. כְּגוֹן בְּקוֹצִים שֶׁבַּדְּרָכִים: הָא. דְּקָאָמְרַתְּ דִּלְאַתּוּיֵי הָנֵי נַמִּי בְּהֶדְיָא קָתָנֵי בְּמַתְנִי' מְתַקְּנִין כו'. אֶלָּא וַדַּאי הָא דְּקָתָנֵי וְעוֹשִׂין כָּל צוֹרְכֵי רַבִּים — לְאַתּוּיֵי חֲפִירָה קָא אָתוּ: *מְצַיְּינִין אֶת הַקְּבָרוֹת. שֶׁעוֹשִׂין סִימָנִים עַל הַקְּבָרוֹת בְּסִיד. כִּדְאָמַר בְּ"מְרוּבֶּה" (ב"ק דף סט.): שֶׁל קְבָרוֹת בְּסִיד, דְּחִוָּור כַּעֲצָמוֹת, כְּדֵי שֶׁלֹּא יֵלְכוּ אוֹכְלֵי תְּרוּמָה לְשָׁם: דִּכְתִיב וְרָאָה עֶצֶם וכו'. יְחֶזְקֵאל מִתְנַבֵּא עַל הֶעָתִיד לָבֹא, שֶׁיַּעֲשׂוּ יִשְׂרָאֵל צִיּוּנִים עַל עַצְמוֹת הַפְּגָרִים הַמּוּשְׁלָכִין.(ה) וְרֶמֶז הוּא, שֶׁלֹּא בָּא הַכָּתוּב *אֶלָּא לְהַזְהִיר וּלְלַמֵּד שֶׁיְּהֵא אָדָם עוֹשֶׂה צִיּוּן: כָּל בֶּן נֵכָר(ו) וְעֶרֶל בָּשָׂר. שֶׁמֵּתוּ אֶחָיו מֵחֲמַת מִילָה וְלֹא רָצוּ לְמוּלוֹ, שֶׁיִּרְאוּ פֶּן יָמוּת גַּם הוּא כְּאֶחָיו — לֹא יָבֹא אֶל מִקְדָּשִׁי לְשָׁרְתֵנִי, שֶׁאֲסוּרִין בָּעֲבוֹדָה: גְּמִירִי. מִסִּינַי: טוּמְאָה קוֹרְאָה לוֹ פְּרוֹשׁ. כְּלוֹמַר, עוֹשִׂים סִימָנִים עַל הַטּוּמְאָה, כְּדֵי שֶׁיְּהֵא מַרְגִּישׁ וּפוֹרֵשׁ: (ז)לִפְנֵי עִוֵּר לֹא תִתֵּן מִכְשׁוֹל. כְּלוֹמַר, עֲשׂוּ דָּבָר עַל הַטּוּמְאָה שֶׁלֹּא יְהוּ נִכְשָׁלִים בָּהּ נוֹשְׂאֵי תְּרוּמָה וּטְהָרוֹת: וְהִזַּרְתֶּם. וּמְתַרְגְּמִינַן: וְתַפְרְשׁוּן: עֲשׂוּ מִשְׁמֶרֶת לְמִשְׁמַרְתִּי. עֲשׂוּ מִשְׁמֶרֶת לְאוֹכְלֵי תְּרוּמָה, דִּכְתִיב בָּהּ 'מִשְׁמֶרֶת' דִּכְתִיב (במדבר יח): "וַאֲנִי נָתַתִּי לְךָ אֶת מִשְׁמֶרֶת תְּרוּמוֹתָי" שֶׁלֹּא יְהוּ מִטַּמְּאִים: וְשָׁם דֶּרֶךְ. שֶׁעוֹשִׂין סִימָן בְּאֵיזֶה דֶּרֶךְ יֵלְכוּ: אַרְאֶנּוּ בְּיֵשַׁע אֱלֹהִים. זֶה הַשָּׁם אוֹרְחוֹתָיו, הַמְחַשֵּׁב הֶפְסֵד מִצְוָה כְּנֶגֶד שְׂכָרָהּ וּשְׂכַר עֲבֵירָה כְּנֶגֶד הֶפְסֵדָהּ. וְשָׁם — כְּמוֹ שָׁמִין: בְּשַׁבְּתָא דְּרִיגְלָא לָא הֲוָה מַקְשֵׁי לֵיהּ. מִשּׁוּם דַּאֲתוּ כּוּלֵּי עָלְמָא לְפִירְקָא, וְאִי מַקְשֵׁי לֵיהּ וְלָא הֲוֵה מָצֵי לְפָרוֹקֵי — הֲוֵה מַכְסִיף:

תוספות

לאתויי הך דתניא. קא סלקא דעתיה: דהאי דקפריך הכא דבכלל מתקנין הדרכים לא הוי קוון דרכים — דתיקון משמע שמתקן הגבשושיות והגומות, הלכך פריך הכי. ומתרץ: כל אלו בהדיא קתני להו דהוו בכלל מתקנין כו'. א"נ: האי דמקשה הך קושיא — לא היתה מתניתא שגורה בפיו, ולא הוי ידע *דגרס בה "ומתקנין את הדרכים":

והיה עליך דמים. פי' רבינו חננאל: נקיט ליה להאי קרא מפרשת* מעקה דדמי להאי דהוי מכשול. ממתני' עם הגמרא יש ללמד שאסור להשקות קרקעות אלא אותן דהוו דבר האבד, שיתקלקלו התבואה והאילנות הנטועים בה. והוא הדין לשאר עבודת קרקע — אסור בחולו של מועד. והא דאמרינן דמותר להשקות — הני מילי כגון מאמת המים העוברת בשדה עצמו, דליכא טירחא יתירא. ומותר לתקן בורות שיחין ומערות של יחיד, ושל רבים מותר לחפור לכתחילה, כיון דצריכי למים. דהכי תניא לעיל כדפרישית:

רמז לציון. דהאי קרא לא כתיב אלא לעתיד, אבל לא בזמן הזה. ומיהו, משני דאיכא למילף מהתם:

הא מקמי דליתי יחזקאל. כלומר: לדידך דאמרת דבזמן הזה הויא[א] *מדאורייתא, אם כן מקמי דליתי יחזקאל הוה ליה להקדוש ברוך הוא לאשמועינן דצריך ציון! ומתרץ: הרבה דברים דקים לן דאסורין מן התורה, דלא כתיב בקרא אלא בהלכה, עד דאתא יחזקאל. והאי הכי נמי:

רב פפא אמר סלו סלו. כל חד וחד נקיט מאי דהוה מסיק אדעתיה, ולא פליגי, אלא אורחיה דמלתא דכל חד מסיק אדעתיה מאי דלא מסיק חבריה אדעתיה:

בשבתא דריגלא. שבת של יום הרגל, שהיו דורשין, והיו מתקבצין כל בני העיר לשמוע הלכות של רגל:

אין

רבינו חננאל

פיסקא וחוטטין אותו חטיטה אין חפירה לא ותריצנא הכי חוטטין בורות שיחין ומערות יחיד בשיחיד צריך להן ואצ"ל של רבים וכי רבים צריכין להם אפי' חפירה נמי שרי ואין חופרין של יחיד דכי אין יחיד צריך להן אפי' חטיטה נמי אסור אמר רב אשי מתניתין נמי דיקא דקתני עושין כל צרכי רבים לאתויי מאי לאו לאתויי חפירה. ודחינן לא לאתויי הא דתניא יוצאין לקוץ את הדרכי' ולתקן את הרחובות והאסטרטאות ולמוד המקואות וכל מקוה שאין בו מ' סאה מרגילין לתוכו מ' סאה. ומניין שאם לא יצאו ותיקנו כל אלו כל דמים שנשפכו שם מעלה אני עליהם כאילו הם שפכום שנאמר ועשית מעקה לגגך וגו' וכתיב והיה עליך דמים. ופריק הא בהדיא קתני לה. מתקנין את הדרכים כו' כל צרכי רבים לאתויי מאי לאתויי חפירה של רבים שהיא מותרת ש"מ. תניא בורות שיחין ומערות של יחיד כונסין לתוכן מים במועד אבל לא חוטטין אותן ולא שפין את סדקיהן ושל רבים חופרין אותן וסדין אותן בסיד. ומציינין את הקברות רמז לציון מנא לן מדכתיב וראה עצם אדם ובנה אצלו ציון ועד דלא אתא יחזקאל מאן אמרה אלא גמרה גמירי לה ויחזקאל אסמכה אקרא. רבי אבהו אמר מהכא וטמא טמא יקרא. טומאה קוראה לו ואומרת פרוש פרוש וש"מ נמי כל מי שאירע בו דבר כגון המצורע וכיוצא בו צריך להודיע לרבים ורבים מבקשין עליו רחמים שנא' וטמא טמא יקרא ורבנן אחריני נמי אמרי מהני קראי. ולפני עור לא תתן מכשול. וכתיב הרימו מכשול מדרך עמי והודעת להם את הדרך ילכו בה. רב אשי אמר ושמרתם את משמרתי עשו משמרת למשמרתי. רבינא אמר ושם דרך אראנו בישע אלהים. וכל השם אורחותיו זוכה ויושב ורואה בישועתו של הקב"ה שנאמר ושם דרך אראנו בישע אלהים קרי ביה ושם דרך. ר' ינאי הוה ליה ההוא תלמידא כל שתא הוה מקשי ובשבתא

עין משפט נר מצוה

לה א מיי' פ"ח מהל' י"ט הלכה ד סמג לאוין עה טוש"ע א"ח סי' תקמד סעיף ב:

לו ב ג מיי' פ"ז שם הלכה י סמג לאוין שם טוש"ע שם:

לז ד מיי' שם פ"ח הלכה ד סמג וטוש"ע שם:

לח ה מיי' שם פ"ז הלכה י סמג שם טוש"ע שם סעיף ב:

לט ו מיי' פ"ח מהלכות טומאת מת הלכה ט סמג עשין רלג:

מ ז מיי' פ"ו מהלכות טומאת צרעת הלכה ו סמג עשין רלה:

[עי' תוס' פסחים נז. ד"ה אלא וכו']

[ומשם לא מוכח מידי ושם כתיב קרא אחרינא ונראה דצ"ל מפ' מקלט העתק מחילופי גרסאות]

[ועי' תוס' ב"ב קמז. ד"ה מנין]

מסורת הש"ס

[שייך למשנה דלעיל ב.]

[פי' דרכים המפולשין]

[בר"ש בעין יעקב ליתא תיבת אלא]

[עי' תוס' ב"ב קמז. ד"ה מנין]

תענית יז: יומא עא: סנהדרין כב: פג: זבחים יח: [כב:]

[סוטה לב: נדה סו. שבת סז. חולין עח.]

[יבמות כח.]

[סוטה ה:]

הגהות מהר"ב רנשבורג

א] תוס' ד"ה הא מקמי וכו' מדאורייתא. נ"ב עיין נדה דף נז ע"א דמדרבנן הוא וכו'. ועיין בב"ב קמז ע"א תוס' ד"ה מנין כו' ודו"ק שוב נדפס ספר יד דוד ולהרב שהרגיש בזה:

גליון הש"ס

גמ' ת"ל וראה עצם אדם. עי' נדה דף נז ע"א תוס' ד"ה ובנה.

הגהות הב"ח

(א) גמ' אבל לא חוטטין אותן ולא שפין: (ב) שם רב פפא אמר מהכא ואמר סלו כו' רב חיננא אמר מהכא הרימו כו' ר"י בריה דר"א אמר מהכא והודעת כו' מר זוטרא אמר מהכא והזרתם כו' רב אשי אמר מהכא ושמרתם כו' רבינא אמר מהכא ושם דרך כו': (ג) רש"י ד"ה אבל כו' ברייתא שלמעלה חוטטין של יחיד היינו: (ד) ד"ה מרגילין כו' שיהא נובע במקום כו' ונ"ב נראה דפי' זה הוא של רבינו הלוי דס"ל דזכה טעונה מים חיים אבל לדעת רש"י דס"ל דלא בעי' מים חיים צ"ל מרגילין לתוכו מ' סאה היינו מי גשמים עי' בפ' במה אשה שבת דף סה ע"ב ובבכורות דף כה ע"ב: (ה) ד"ה דכתיב כו' הפגרים המושלכין בארצם ורמז הוא (שלא בא הכתוב וכו' עושה ציון) תא"מ ונ"ב ס"א שלא בא הכתוב להזהיר ואמר שיהא אדם עושה ציון דמש"ה א"צ ציון דכיון שאין מטמא באהל מכסהו בקרקע ואין צריך לציין: (ו) ד"ה כל בן נכר ערל לב שנתנכרו מעשיו לאביו שבשמים שנעשה ערל לב ועע"ז כדמפרש בפ"ב דמנחות וערל בשר שמתו כו': (ז) ד"ה לפני כו' וטהרות הס"ד ואח"כ מה"ד פנו דרך. עשו דרך פנוי ללכת בו הס"ד:

מא א ב ג ד ה מיי' פ"ח מהל' טומאת מת הלכה ט סמג עשין רלח:
מב ו מיי' שם פ"י הל"א סמג עשין רלח:
מג ז ח מיי' פ"ו מהל' ק"פ הלכה ח:
מד ט מיי' פ"ח מהל' טומאת מת הלכה א סמג עשין לא:
מה י מיי' שם פ"י הלכה א סמג שם:
מו כ מיי' שם פ"ח הלכה ד:
מז ל מיי' שם הלכה י ופ"י הלכה י:
מח מ מיי' שם פ"י הל"י:

קָרֵי עֲלֵיהּ: °"וְשָׂם דֶּרֶךְ אַרְאֶנּוּ בְּיֵשַׁע אֱלֹהִים". תהלים נ

תָּנוּ רַבָּנַן: *אאֵין מְצַיְּינִין לֹא עַל כַּזַּיִת מִן הַמֵּת, וְלֹא עַל עֶצֶם כִּשְׂעוֹרָה, וְלֹא עַל דָּבָר שֶׁאֵינוֹ מְטַמֵּא בְּאֹהֶל. אֲבָל מְצַיְּינִין עַל הַשִּׁדְרָה, וְעַל הַגּוּלְגּוֹלֶת, עַל רוֹב בִּנְיָן וְעַל רוֹב מִנְיַן הַמֵּת. בוְאֵין מְצַיְּינִין עַל הַוַּודָּאוֹת, אֲבָל מְצַיְּינִין עַל הַסְּפֵיקוֹת. וְאֵלּוּ הֵן הַסְּפֵיקוֹת: סְכָכוֹת, וּפְרָעוֹת, וּבֵית הַפְּרָס. *גוְאֵין מַעֲמִידִין צִיּוּן בִּמְקוֹם טוּמְאָה — שֶׁלֹּא לְהַפְסִיד אֶת הַטְּהָרוֹת, *דוְאֵין מַרְחִיקִין צִיּוּן מִמְּקוֹם טוּמְאָה — שֶׁלֹּא לְהַפְסִיד אֶת אֶרֶץ יִשְׂרָאֵל. וְכַזַּיִת מִן הַמֵּת אֵינוֹ מְטַמֵּא בְּאֹהֶל? וְהָא (*תַּנְיָא:) *אֵלּוּ שֶׁמְּטַמְּאִין בְּאֹהֶל — כַּזַּיִת מִן הַמֵּת! אָמַר רַב פַּפָּא: הָכָא בְּכַזַּיִת המְצוּמְצָם עָסְקִינַן, דְּסוֹף סוֹף מִיחְסַר חָסַר, מוּטָב יִשָּׂרְפוּ עָלָיו תְּרוּמָה וְקָדָשִׁים לְפִי שָׁעָה, וְאַל יִשָּׂרְפוּ עָלָיו לְעוֹלָם. וְאֵלּוּ הֵן הַסְּפֵיקוֹת: סְכָכוֹת וּפְרָעוֹת; *סְכָכוֹת — אִילָן הַמֵּיסֵךְ עַל הָאָרֶץ, פְּרָעוֹת[א] — *אֲבָנִים פְּרוּעוֹת הַיּוֹצְאוֹת מִן הַגָּדֵר. בֵּית הַפְּרָס — כִּדְתְנַן: *והַחוֹרֵשׁ אֶת הַקֶּבֶר הֲרֵי הוּא עוֹשֶׂה בֵּית הַפְּרָס, וְכַמָּה הוּא עוֹשֶׂה — מְלֹא מַעֲנֶה מֵאָה אַמָּה. וּבֵית הַפְּרָס מִי מְטַמֵּא בְּאֹהֶל? *וְהָאָמַר רַב יְהוּדָה אָמַר שְׁמוּאֵל: זמְנַפֵּחַ אָדָם בֵּית הַפְּרָס וְהוֹלֵךְ. וְרַב יְהוּדָה בַּר *אַמֵּי מִשְּׁמֵיהּ דְּעוּלָּא אָמַר: חבֵּית הַפְּרָס שֶׁנִּידַּשׁ טָהוֹר! אָמַר רַב פַּפָּא: לָא קַשְׁיָא; כָּאן — בְּשָׂדֶה שֶׁאָבַד בָּהּ קֶבֶר, כָּאן — בְּשָׂדֶה שֶׁנֶּחֱרַשׁ בָּהּ קֶבֶר. וְשָׂדֶה[ב] שֶׁנֶּחֱרַשׁ בָּהּ קֶבֶר "בֵּית הַפְּרָס" קָרֵי לֵיהּ? אִין, וְהָתְנַן: *שְׁלֹשָׁה בֵּית הַפְּרָס הֵן: טשָׂדֶה שֶׁנֶּאֱבַד בָּהּ קֶבֶר, יוְשָׂדֶה שֶׁנֶּחֱרַשׁ בָּהּ קֶבֶר, כוּשְׂדֵה[ג] בּוֹכִין. מַאי שְׂדֵה בּוֹכִין? רַב יְהוֹשֻׁעַ בַּר אַבָּא מִשְּׁמֵיהּ דְּעוּלָּא אָמַר: שָׂדֶה שֶׁמַּפְטִירִין בָּהּ מֵתִים. וְטַעֲמָא מַאי? אָמַר אֲבִימִי: מִשּׁוּם יֵאוּשׁ בְּעָלִים נָגְעוּ בָּהּ. וְשָׂדֶה שֶׁנֶּחֱרַשׁ בָּהּ קֶבֶר לָא בָּעֵי צִיּוּן? וְהָא תַּנְיָא: *למָצָא שָׂדֶה מְצוּיֶּינֶת, וְאֵין יָדוּעַ מַה טִּיבָהּ. יֵשׁ בָּהּ אִילָנוֹת — *בְּיָדוּעַ שֶׁנֶּחֱרַשׁ בָּהּ קֶבֶר, אֵין בָּהּ אִילָנוֹת בְּיָדוּעַ שֶׁאָבַד בָּהּ קֶבֶר. מר' יְהוּדָה אוֹמֵר: עַד שֶׁיְּהֵא שָׁם זָקֵן אוֹ תַּלְמִיד, לְפִי שֶׁאֵין הַכֹּל בְּקִיאִין בַּדָּבָר. אָמַר רַב פַּפָּא: כִּי תַּנְיָא הַהִיא — בְּשָׂדֶה שֶׁאָבַד בָּהּ קֶבֶר, דְּצִיְּינוּהָ. יֵשׁ בָּהּ אִילָנוֹת — בְּיָדוּעַ שֶׁנֶּחֱרַשׁ בָּהּ קֶבֶר. אֵין בָּהּ אִילָנוֹת — בְּיָדוּעַ שֶׁאָבַד בָּהּ קֶבֶר. וְלֵיחוּשׁ דִּלְמָא אִילָנוֹת מִגַּוַּאי וְקֶבֶר מִבָּרַאי! כִּדְאָמַר עוּלָּא: בְּעוֹמְדִין עַל הַגְּבוּלִין, הָכָא נַמִּי: בְּעוֹמְדִין עַל הַגְּבוּלִין. וְדִלְמָא

אין מציינין. אין לריך ליון. ואי גבי יום טוב איירי הברייתא — איכא לפרש: אסור ללוין (ג) ואסור לטרוח ביום טוב:
עצם כשעורה. והוא הדין יותר מכשעורה כדמוכח בסמוך, אינו מטמא באהל. והאי דנקט כשעורה — משום דבהאי שיעורא מטמא במגע, דהכי הלכה למשה מסיני כדאמרינן בשחיטת חולין (חולין דף קכו:): **שאינו** מטמא באהל. א] כגון תרווד רקב, כדאיתא ב"העור והרוטב" (חולין דף קכו: ושם), ושדה שנחרש בה קבר כדלקמן בשמעתין. ואפילו איכא ספק טומאה, שמטמא בהיסט בלא נגיעה — לא הלריכוה ליון, דהיסט לאו מילתא דשכיחא היא שידרוס על קנה שטומאה עליו, ולכך לא החמירו חכמים לליין משום היסט:
אילן המיסך על הארץ. סמוך לבית הקברות. דמספקא לן אי איכא טומאה תחתיו אי לא, מסתמא אמרינן דמת תחתיו, כיון דדרך מקום לנוע הוא, ולכך בעי ליון. ע"א: דידעינן ודאי דאיכא טומאה תחת נוף אחד של אילן, ויש הפרש בין נוף לחבירו, ואין ידוע באיזה מקום ישנה. והכי נמי איכא לפרש גבי אבנים: שיש אבנים זו אצל זו הבולטות מן הגדר:
מנפח אדם בין הפרס והולך. דמסתמא ליכא למימר שהגיעה המחרישה עד המת, וליכא לאחזוקי מקום טהור בטמא מספק. אלא חכמים החמירו משום חומרא דטהרות. ומשום הכי הקילו, (ד) דליכא ספיקא דאורייתא, הם אמרו והם אמרו. ולא היו רגילים לקבור מתים בעומק כי השתא בזמן הזה, הילכך לא חיישינן שמא המת בעומק תחת המחרישה. ומן הדין אפילו נפוח לא לריך, כי אם חומרא בטהרות שהחמירו חכמים בדבר. ואמאי לא חייש שיהא מת בקרקע, ואין נוגע בו ומטמא באהל? אי נמי: בלא המאהילים מן הצדדים הוו מטמאין לאדם באהל. אלא שמע מינה דלא מטמא באהל:
יש בה אילנות בידוע שנחרש בה קבר אין בה אילנות בידוע שאבד בה קבר. דתניא התם (תוספתא דאהלות פי"ז): שדה שאבד בה קבר — אינה ניטעת כל נטע. וכגון שראויה לאילנות, ויש לנו לומר דמסתמא אם לא שאבד בה קבר היו נוטעים בתוכה. ⊕אי נמי: בידוע לאו דוקא, ואגב דנקט רישא בידוע — נקט סיפא בידוע. וכן נ"ל לפי' הקונטרס: אם

קָרֵי עֲלֵיהּ וְשָׂם דֶּרֶךְ. שֶׁמְּחַשֵּׁב בַּשָּׁעוֹת, אֵי זֶה מֵהֶן לְהַקְשׁוֹת אֵי זֶה מֵהֶן שֶׁלֹּא לְהַקְשׁוֹת: אֲבָל מְצַיְּינִין עַל הַשִּׁדְרָה. שֶׁאע"פ שֶׁאֵינָהּ אֶלָּא עֶצֶם אֶחָד — מְטַמֵּא טוּמְאָה בְּאֹהֶל: רוֹב בִּנְיָנוֹ. כְּגוֹן עֲצָמוֹת גְּדוֹלוֹת, כְּגוֹן קוּלְיוֹת, אע"פ שֶׁאֵין בּוֹ רוֹב מִנְיָנוֹ: רוֹב מִנְיָנוֹ. רוֹב הָעֲצָמוֹת, וְאע"פ שֶׁאֵין בּוֹ רוֹב בִּנְיָנוֹ: אֵין מְצַיְּינִין עַל הַוַּודָּאוֹת. הוֹאִיל דְּבָרוּר לְכוּלֵּי עָלְמָא דְּאִית בֵּיהּ טוּמְאָה וַדָּאִית — לָא מְטַלְטְלֵי בְּאוֹתוֹ מָקוֹם טְהָרוֹת: אֲבָל מְצַיְּינִין עַל הַסְּפֵיקוֹת. שֶׁיֵּשׁ עֲלֵיהֶן אֹהֶל, כְּגוֹן סְכָכוֹת וּפְרָעוֹת (א) הַסְּמוּכוֹת לרה"ר הַסָּמוּךְ לְבֵית הַקְּבָרוֹת, דִּמְסַפְּקָא לָן בְּהוּ טוּמְאָה. דְּכֵיוָן דְּיֵשׁ עֲלֵיהֶן אֹהֶל — רְגִילִים לִקְבּוֹר שָׁם בְּמָקוֹם צָנוּעַ: סְכָכוֹת וּפְרָעוֹת וּבֵית הַפְּרָס. מְפָרֵשׁ לְקַמָּן: אֵין מַעֲמִידִין הַצִּיּוּן עַל הַטּוּמְאָה שֶׁלֹּא לְהַפְסִיד טְהָרוֹת. שֶׁאִם הַטּוּמְאָה מַמָּשׁ תַּחַת הַצִּיּוּן — אֵינוֹ מַרְגִּישׁ עַד שֶׁבָּא עַל הַצִּיּוּן פִּתְאוֹם, וְיִטַּמְּאוּ הַטְּהָרוֹת, שֶׁהֲרֵי הַטּוּמְאָה תַּחַת הַצִּיּוּן. אֶלָּא עוֹשִׂין הַצִּיּוּן סָמוּךְ לַטּוּמְאָה בְּרִחוּק כָּל שֶׁהוּא, וּכְשֶׁבָּא עַל הַצִּיּוּן — מַרְגִּישׁ מִן הַטּוּמְאָה, וְאֵינוֹ הוֹלֵךְ עָלֶיהָ: אֵין מַרְחִיקִין אֶת הַצִּיּוּן מִמְּקוֹם טוּמְאָה. יוֹתֵר מִכָּל שֶׁהוּא: שֶׁלֹּא לְהַפְסִיד אֶרֶץ יִשְׂרָאֵל. שֶׁכְּשֶׁרוֹאֶה הַסִּימָן מִיָּד פּוֹרֵשׁ, וְנִמְצָא אֶרֶץ יִשְׂרָאֵל בְּטוּמְאָה שֶׁלֹּא לְצוֹרֶךְ: וְכַזַּיִת מִן הַמֵּת אֵינוֹ מְטַמֵּא בְּאֹהֶל. דְּקָתָנֵי: אֵין מְצַיְּינִין עַל כַּזַּיִת מִן הַמֵּת, וְלֹא עַל כָּל דָּבָר שֶׁאֵינוֹ מְטַמֵּא בְּאֹהֶל: אָמַר רַב פַּפָּא. לְעוֹלָם כַּזַּיִת מְטַמֵּא בְּאֹהֶל, וְהָא דְּקָתָנֵי אֵין מְצַיְּינִין — בְּכַזַּיִת מְצוּמְצָם עָסְקִינַן, דְּמִחְסַר חָסַר בַּקַּרְקַע, וּלְהָכִי אֵין מְצַיְּינִין: יִשָּׂרְפוּ עָלָיו [תְּרוּמוֹת] וּטְהָרוֹת שָׁעָה אַחַת. דְּכָל הָעוֹבֵר עַל אוֹתוֹ כַּזַּיִת כְּשֶׁנִּקְבַּר מֵחָדָשׁ — שׂוֹרְפִין טְהָרוֹתָיו, דַּעֲדַיִין לֹא חָסַר: וְאַל יִשָּׂרְפוּ עָלָיו לְעוֹלָם. שֶׁאִם מְצַיְּינִין אוֹתוֹ — שׂוֹרְפִין עָלָיו (עַל) כָּל תְּרוּמָה שֶׁעוֹבְרִין עַל אוֹתוֹ צִיּוּן לְעוֹלָם, שֶׁלֹּא לְצוֹרֶךְ, שֶׁהֲרֵי חָסַר. וְזִימְנִין דְּלָא חֲזֵי לֵיהּ, כְּגוֹן בַּלַּיְלָה, וְכִי הָדַר חֲזֵי לֵיהּ וְאָמַר: נִטְמֵאת תְּרוּמָתִי, וְשָׂרַף לָהּ, וְהִיא לֹא נִטְמֵאת — דְּהַהִיא כַּזַּיִת כְּבָר חָסַר. וּכְשֶׁאֵין מְצַיְּינִין אוֹתוֹ אֵין שׂוֹרְפִין עָלָיו אֶלָּא מֵחָדָשׁ, שֶׁלֹּא חָסַר: אִילָן הַמֵּיסֵךְ עַל הָאָרֶץ. וְטוּמְאָה תַּחַת נוֹף אֶחָד, וְאֵינוֹ יוֹדֵעַ תַּחַת אֵיזֶה נוֹף — עוֹשֶׂה לִיּוּן: בֵּית הַפְּרָס. *חֲלִי מַעֲנָה = תֶּלֶם אֶחָד שֶׁל מֵאָה אַמָּה: מְנַפֵּחַ אָדָם. הַהוֹלֵךְ לִשְׁחוֹט פִּסְחוֹ. דְּאִם יֵשׁ עֶצֶם כִּשְׂעוֹרָה הַמְטַמֵּא בְּהֶיסֵּט — מִתְפַּזֵּר בָּרוּחַ, וְעוֹשֶׂה פֶּסַח בְּבֵית הַפְּרָס אָזִיל לוֹ. וְאִי מְטַמֵּא בְּאֹהֶל — הֵיכִי אָזִיל עָלֶיהָ? בְּשָׂדֶה שֶׁאָבַד בָּהּ קֶבֶר. קָתָנֵי דִּמְלַיְּינִין, דִּמְטַמֵּא בְּאֹהֶל. אֲבָל בְּשָׂדֶה שֶׁנֶּחֱרַשׁ בָּהּ קֶבֶר — אֵין צָרִיךְ לְלַיֵּין, וְלֹא מְטַמֵּא בְּאֹהֶל, דְּנִימָא מַחְרֵישָׁה סִלְּקֵיהּ לַטּוּמְאָה: שְׁלֹשָׁה בֵּית הַפְּרָס הֵן. שֶׁאֵין הוֹלְכִין בּוֹ אוֹכְלֵי תְרוּמָה: שֶׁמַּפְטִירִין בָּהּ אֶת הַמֵּתִים. שֶׁכְּשֶׁמְּבִיאִין מֵתִים מִמָּקוֹם לְמָקוֹם לִקְבּוֹר, כְּשֶׁבָּאִין בְּשָׂדֶה סָמוּךְ לָעִיר נִפְטָרִין אֵלּוּ שֶׁהֱבִיאוּם מִמְּקוֹמָן וְהוֹלְכִין לָהֶם, וּבָאִין אַנְשֵׁי הַמָּקוֹם (ב) וּמְקַבְּלִין אוֹתָן וְרוֹחֲצִין אוֹתָן שָׁם, וְקוֹבְרִין אוֹתָן: וְטַעְמָא מַאי. חוֹשְׁשִׁין בֵּיהּ מִשּׁוּם טוּמְאָה: מִשּׁוּם יֵאוּשׁ בְּעָלִים. לְפִי שֶׁהֱבִיאוּם מִמָּקוֹם רָחוֹק נִדַּלְדֵּל אֵבֶר וְנָפַל שָׁם, וְנִתְיָיאֲשׁוּ אֵלּוּ וְהֵיכִּיחוּהוּ שָׁם: וְשָׂדֶה שֶׁנֶּחֱרַשׁ בָּהּ קֶבֶר לָא בָּעֵי צִיּוּן. דְּקָא מַתְרֶצֶת הָא דְּקָתָנֵי מְנַפֵּחַ אָדָם בֵּית הַפְּרָס כְּשֶׁנֶּחְרַשׁ: וְאֵינוֹ יוֹדֵעַ מַה טִּיבָהּ. אִם הוּא שָׂדֶה שֶׁנֶּחֱרַשׁ בָּהּ קֶבֶר וְיָכוֹל לֵילֵךְ בְּנִיפּוּחַ, וְאִם מִפְּנֵי שֶׁנֶּאֱבַד בָּהּ קֶבֶר וְאֵינוֹ יָכוֹל לְהִכָּנֵס בָּהּ בִּנְפִיחָה, דִּמְטַמֵּא בְּאֹהֶל: יֵשׁ בָּהּ אִילָנוֹת בְּיָדוּעַ שֶׁנֶּחֱרַשׁ. הַשָּׂדֶה לְצוֹרֶךְ הָאִילָנוֹת, וְיָכוֹל לְהַלֵּךְ, שֶׁאֵינוֹ מְטַמֵּא בְּאֹהֶל. אַלְמָא: מִדְּקָתָנֵי בָּהּ מָצָא שָׂדֶה מְצוּיֶּינֶת — דִּמְלַיְּינִין בֵּית הַפְּרָס שֶׁנֶּחֱרַשׁ: אֵין בָּהּ אִילָנוֹת בְּיָדוּעַ שֶׁאָבַד בָּהּ קֶבֶר. וְלֹא נֶחְרַשׁ, וּמְטַמֵּא בְּאֹהֶל: רַבִּי יְהוּדָה אוֹמֵר. לְעוֹלָם לֹא הָוֵי בְּחֶזְקַת שֶׁנֶּחְרַשׁ, עַד שֶׁיְּהֵא שָׁם זָקֵן אוֹ ת"ח שֶׁיְּהֵא יוֹדֵעַ שֶׁנֶּחֱרַשׁ: אָמַר רַב פַּפָּא. לְעוֹלָם בֵּית הַפְּרָס שֶׁנֶּחֱרַשׁ לָא בָּעֵי לִיּוּן. וְהַאי דְּקָתָנֵי בְּיָדוּעַ שֶׁנֶּחֱרַשׁ בָּהּ קֶבֶר — בְּשָׂדֶה שֶׁאָבַד בָּהּ קֶבֶר, וְלַיְּינָהּ לְאַלְתַּר: יֵשׁ בָּהּ אִילָנוֹת בְּיָדוּעַ שֶׁנֶּחֱרַשׁ. לְאַחַר שֶׁלַּיְּינוּהָ. וּלְעוֹלָם בֵּית הַפְּרָס שֶׁנֶּחֱרַשׁ לֹא בָּעֵי לִיּוּן: אֵין בָּהּ אִילָנוֹת בְּיָדוּעַ שֶׁאָבַד בָּהּ קֶבֶר. וְלֹא נֶחְרַשׁ: וְלֵיחוּשׁ דִּלְמָא אִילָנוֹת מִגַּוַּאי וְטוּמְאָה מֵאַבָּרַאי. וְלֹא נֶחְרַשׁ בִּמְקוֹם טוּמְאָה מִבַּחוּץ לָאִילָנוֹת, אֶלָּא בֵּין הָאִילָנוֹת, וְהָוֵי שָׂדֶה שֶׁאָבַד בָּהּ קֶבֶר וְלֹא נֶחְרַשׁ. וְאַמַּאי קָאָמַר בְּיָדוּעַ שֶׁנֶּחֱרַשׁ בָּהּ קֶבֶר: בְּעוֹמְדִין הָאִילָנוֹת עַל הַגְּבוּלִין. שֶׁל רְשׁוּת הָרַבִּים, דְּוַדַּאי לֵיכָּא טוּמְאָה מִבָּרַאי, דְּלָא קָבְרֵי אִינָשֵׁי בִּרְשׁוּת הָרַבִּים. אֶלָּא בֵּין הָאִילָנוֹת הָוְיָא טוּמְאָה וְנֶחְרַשׁ בִּשְׁבִיל הָאִילָנוֹת: וְדִלְמָא

רבינו חננאל

ובשבתא דריגלא לא הוה מקשי והוה קרי עליה ושם דרך אראנו בישע אלהים: ת"ר אין מציינין על כזית מצומצמת מן [המת] דסופו מיחסר חסר. ותנן באהלות פרק שני אלו אם חסרו טהורין כזית מן המת כזית נצל כו' ולא על הבשר שסופו מתאכל והולך ולא על עצם כשעורה ולא על כל דבר שאינו מטמא באהל אבל מציינין על השדרה ועל הגלגולת ועל רוב בנינו של מת ועל מנינו. ואין מציינין על הוודאות אלא על הספיקות. ואלו הן הספיקות סככות ופרעות פי' דתנן באהלות פ' ח' הזיזין *) והגודריות כו' עד והסככות והפרעות (אינן) [שהן] יכולין לקבל מעזיבה כו' ואלו הן הסככות אילן המיסך על הארץ והפרעות אבנים היוצאות מן הגדר ומציינין על בית הפרס בשדה שאבד בה קבר ואין מעמידין ציון במקום טומאה עצמה שלא להפסיד את הטהרות אלא מרחיקין מעט. ואין מרחיקין ציון ממקום הטומאה שלא להפסיד את א"י. ואין מציינין על השדה שנחרש בה קבר וכ"ש שנידש. תניא ג' בית הפרס הן. שדה שנחרש בה קבר ושנאבד בה קבר ושדה בוכים. פי' דתנן באהלות פרק י"ח ג' בית הפרס הן החורש את הקבר נוטעת כל נטע כו'. עד ומטמאין במגע ובמשא ואינן מטמאין באהל. שדה שנאבד בה קבר בתוכה כו' עד ומטמא במגע ובמשא ובאהל. מאי שדה בוכים שדה שמפטירין בתוכה מתים. פי' דתנן באהלות פרק י"ח שדה בוכים לא ניטעת ולא ניזרעת ועפרה טהור כו' מ"ט יאוש בעלים נגעו בה ומקשינן שדה שנחרש בה קבר לא בעיא ציון והתניא מצא שדה מצויינת ואין ידוע מה טיבה. יש בה אילנות בידוע שנחרש בה קבר. אין בה אילנות בידוע שאבד בה קבר. ופריק רב פפא כי תניא ההיא בשדה שאבד בה קבר וציינוה אם יש בה אילנות בידוע שאחרי שציינוה שנחרש אותו הקבר. וניחוש דלמא אילנות גואי. פי' לא חרשו מקום הטומאה וטומאה מבראי קאי. ואמרינן בשאילנות עומדין

*) שם במשנה איתא והגיזוזטראות.

[תוספ' שקלים פ"א]
[לקמן ו.]
[אהלות רפ"ב]
[אהלות פי"ח מ"ב נזיר נה:]
אהלות פי"ז מ"א [תמורה יג. ע"ש]
ברכות יט: פסחים צב: חגיגה כה: כתובות כח: נדה נז: בכורות כט.
אהלות פי"ח מ"ג מ"ד
תוספתא דאהלות פי"ז
[עיין תוס' כתובות כח: ד"ה בית הפרס]
נ"ל שבל מלה
[עי' גירסת התוס' לקמן ו. ד"ה לאמר]
[נ"ל תנן]
[תוספתא דאהלות פ"ט]
[ועי' מש"כ עה"ג ברכות יט:]

הגהות הגר"א

[א] גמ' פרעות פרעות היוצאין מן הגדר כצ"ל (כ"ה במתני' דאהלות פ"ח מ"ב ובנזיר נד ב ועי' תוי"ט באהלות שם): [ב] שנחרש. נ"ל שאבד: [ג] בוכין. נ"ב ובתוספתא (פי"ז דאהלות) גרסינן בוכין (וכן פי' בערוך לחד פי'):

הגהות מהר"ב רנשבורג

א] תוס' ד"ה שאינו וכו' כגון תרווד רקב וכו'. נ"ב דבריהם תמוהים דבחולין שם מפורש דלמטמא באהל וכן הוא משנה מפורשת פ"ב דאהלות ועיין באהלות בספר שושנים לדוד עמד על דבריהם ועי' גם בספר יד דוד:

גליון הש"ס

תוס' ד"ה יש בה אילנות וכו' אי נמי בידוע לאו דוקא. עיין נדה דף סד ע"ב תוס' ד"ה ע"ג כולם:

הגהות הב"ח

(א) רש"י ד"ה אבל מציינין כו' כגון סככות ופרעות הסמוכות לרשות הרבים. נ"ב עי' פרש"י במס' נדה דף נז ע"א וז"ל אילן המיסך על הארץ והוא סמוך לדרך בית הקברות וזימנין דמתרמי בין השמשות וקברי התם כו': (ב) ד"ה שמפטירין כו' ובאין אנשי המקום כו'. נ"ב לשון הערוך בערך בך ונקרא בוכים שכן דרך כשמתועדין יחד אלו עם אלו כולם בוכים ועי' בתוס' ס"פ דם הנדה: (ג) תוס' ד"ה אין כו' אסור ללוין לאסור לטרוח: (ד) ד"ה מנפח כו' ומשום הכי הקילו דכיון דליכא ספיקא:

ודלמא טומאה מגואי ואילנות מבראי! במסובכין. ואיבעית אימא: הא אמרן *אין מרחיקין ציון ממקום טומאה, שלא להפסיד את א"י. ר' יהודה אומר: עד שיהא שם זקן או תלמיד, לפי שאין הכל בקיאין בדבר. אמר אביי: שמע מינה: צורבא מרבנן דאיכא במתא — כל מילי דמתא עליה רמיא. אמר רב יהודה: [א]מצא אבן מצויינת — תחתיה טמא. שתים, אם יש סיד ביניהן — טמא, ואם אין סיד ביניהן — ביניהן טהור. ואע"ג דליכא חורש? והתניא: *מצא אבן אחת מצויינת — תחתיה טמא. שתים, אם יש חורש ביניהן — ביניהן טהור, ואם לאו — ביניהן טמא! אמר רב פפא: [ב]הכא כשהסיד שפוך על ראשיהן ומרודה לכאן ולכאן. אי איכא חורש ביניהן — ביניהן טהור, דאימור מחמת חורש הוא(א) דאיקפל. ואי לא — סיד דביני ביני הוא, וטמא. א"ר אסי: [ג]מצר אחד מצוין — הוא טמא, וכל השדה כולה טהורה. שנים — הם טמאין, וכל השדה כולה טהורה. שלשה — הם טמאין, וכל השדה כולה טהורה. ארבעה — הן טהורין, וכל השדה כולה טמאה. דאמר מר: *אין מרחיקין ציון ממקום טומאה, שלא להפסיד את א"י.§ "ויוצאין אף על הכלאים".§ ואכלאים בחולו של מועד נפקינן? ורמינהו: *[ד]באחד באדר משמיעין על השקלים [ה]ועל הכלאים, [ו]בחמשה עשר בו קורין את המגילה בכרכים, ויוצאין לקווץ את הדרכים, ולתקן הרחובות, ולמוד המקואות, ועושין כל צורכי רבים, ומציינין את הקברות, ויוצאין על הכלאים! רבי אלעזר ורבי יוסי בר חנינא; חד אמר: [ז]כאן — בבכיר, כאן — באפיל. וחד אמר: כאן — בזרעים, כאן — בירקות. א"ר אסי א"ר יוחנן: [ח]לא שנו אלא שאין ניצן ניכר, אבל ניצן ניכר — יוצאין עליהן. מאי שנא בחולו של מועד דנפקינן? אמר רבי יעקב אמר רבי יוחנן: משום שכר פעולה, דמוזלי גבן. אמר רב זביד ואיתימא רב משרשיא: שמע מינה כי יהבינן להו שכר — מתרומת הלשכה יהבינן להו. דאי סלקא דעתך מדידהו יהבינן להו — מאי נפקא לן מינייהו, כל כמה דבעו ליתן להו! ועד כמה? אמר רב שמואל בר יצחק: [ט]כאותה ששנינו: *כל סאה שיש בה רובע

רש"י

ודלמא טומאה מגואי. ולא בין האילנות, ולא נחרש במקום טומאה: (ב) מסובכין. שאינן עומדין בשורה אחת סביב הגבולין, אלא מעורבין בכל השדה, דודאי נחרש כל השדה בשביל האילנות: הא אמרן אין מרחיקין ציון ממקום טומאה. וכיון שסמוך לאילנות הציון — ודאי טומאה בין האילנות היא, ונחרש בשביל האילנות: כל מילי דמתא עליה רמיא. דתלמיד בקי הוא: מצא אבן אחת מצויינת. בסיד, תחתיה טמא. ומפי מורי הזקן: אבן אחת מצויינת — שיש סיד על גבה, דאינו צריך להרחיק הציון מן האבן, לפי שהאבן גבוה על גבי קרקע ורואה את הציון מיד קודם שיהא נוגע בו. אבל בשדה — מרחיקין ליה ציון בסמוך, דזמנין לא חזי ציון עד דאתי ונגע ומאהיל: שתים. מצויינות תחתיהן טמא. אבל ביניהן, אם יש סיד ביניהם על הארץ — טמא, דמשום ציון הוא: אע"ג דליכא חורש. שלא חרש ביניהם מעולם — טהור כי ליכא סיד: אם אין חורש ביניהן טמא. ואע"ג דליכא סיד. לפי שציין את האבנים שמכאן ומכאן — לא חשש לציין בינתים: הכא. דקתני כי ליכא חורש טמא — כגון סיד שפוך על ראשי אבנים ומרודה לכאן ולכאן ביניהן. דאי איכא חורש — מחמת חורש הוא (ג) דאיקלף, שנקלף מן האבנים ונפלו שם ביניהם, וטהור. ואי לא — סיד דביני ביני הוא, ומחמת ציון נעשה שם, להודיע שיש גם ביניהם טומאה: אין מרחיקין ציון ממקום טומאה. ולהכי לציין כל ארבעה מצדדיו, דתהא כל השדה נטמאה. ובציון דמצר אחד לא סגי לכולה, דאין מרחיקין ציון ממקום טומאה: ואכלאים בחולו של מועד נפקינן ורמינהו באחד באדר משמיעין על השקלים. שיהו ישראל מביאין תרומת שקלים בניסן, דכתיב: "בחדשו לחדשי השנה" — חדש והבא לי קרבן מתרומה חדשה: בכרכים. המוקפין חומה מימות יהושע בן נון: ואת מקואות המים. מקואות המים של מ' סאה, שחוטטין אותן מן הזבל שנכנס לתוכן כל ימות הגשמים. והאי דלא פריך נמי בגמרא אשאר מתני', דתני ומתקנים הדרכים והרחובות בחולו ש"מ, והכא תנא בט"ו באדר — משום דלאו פירכא הוא, דדין הוא דמתקנין להו תרי זימני. דכי מתקן בט"ו באדר — אתו גשמים ומקלקלי להו, והדרי ומתקני להו, בחולו של מועד. אבל אכלאים, כיון דעקרו להו לגמרי בחמשה עשר באדר למה לי — למיפק בו בחולו של מועד? ולהכי קא מיבעיא: כאן בבכיר כאן באפיל. על הבכירות יוצאים בט"ו באדר, על האפילות בחולו של מועד דפסח: בזרעים. על התבואה יוצאין בט"ו באדר, שקודמין לירקות: לא שנו. דאין יוצאין עליהן קודם אדר וקודם חולו של מועד: משום שכר פעולה דמוזלי גבן. כלומר, שיכול לשכור פועלין בזול, לפי שאינן עוסקין במלאכה בחולו של מועד: שמע מינה. מדעסקינן לשכור פועלים בזול: כי יהבינן להו. שכירות לפועלים דבטלי כלאים: דאי סלקא דעתך מדידהו. דבעל הבית (ד) יהיב להו, אמאי יוצאין להכי בחולו של מועד משום שכר פעולה? לבטלו בכל זמן, אף על גב דליכא שכר פעולה בזול, וכל מה דבעי — ליתב להו. אלא מתרומת הלשכה יהבינן להו, וכל כמה דמלינן לאלמס מעות דהקדש — עבדינן: ועד כמה. הוי כלאים דחייב לבטלו: רובע

תוספות

אם יש סיד ביניהם. הציון הוא מסיד, כדתנן פרק ה' דמעשר שני (מ"א), ומייתי לה פרק "מרובה" (ב"ק סט. ושם). אם יש סיד ביניהם — לא ידענא כמה: אע"ג דליכא חרס. גרסינן. ומצאתי מפרש: חרס — דומה הוא לחרסית, ואין לבן כמו סיד. ונ"ל פירושו: אם יש חרסית ביניהם (ה) — דומה שמציינין להודיע שהוא טהור, שעד שם אין בית הקברות שאינה לבן בינתים:

אמר רב פפא כשהסיד שפוך. פירוש: ודאי כי ליכא סיד וחרסית — טהורין, אבל כשהוא מרובה ושפוך על ראשו — אז צריך חרסית. שאם יש חרסית — יש לתלות שנתן לצידי האבן חרסית, והסיד נתחבר בו ונרפו הסיד שעל ראשו עמה, ואם אין חרסית — א"כ סיד הוא של ציון בינתים. ולפירוש הקונטרס גרסינן: אף על גב דליכא חורש. (ו) ומפרש: ביניהם טהור — דאינתקא לה טומאה, דהוי לה קבר שנחרש, ותימה לי: נהי דטהור מטומאת אהל — טהור לא הוי! דהוי כמו שדה שנחרש בה קבר! ושמא טהור מאהל קאמר. א"נ: לגמרי, ע"י דישה וניפוח. א"נ: ביניהם איכא טובא ספיקות, ושרי. ספק אי איכא ציון (ז) הטומאה שביניהם אי לא, ואפילו איכא ציון — הרי נחרש. ומצאתי מפרש: דהשתא סלקא דעתיה דה"פ: אם יש ביניהם חורש טהור, דודאי לא היה שם טומאה, דאם היה ביניהם — לא היה חורשו אדם. תימה לי: אמאי לא פריך דקתני בקמייתא: אם יש סיד ביניהם — בינתים טמא, אע"ג דאיכא חורש. והכא קתני: אם יש חורש ביניהם — טהור, ואע"ג דאיכא סיד! ונ"ל: דסלקא דעתיה דהך בתרייתא איירי בדליכא סיד, דכי איכא סיד — לא היה טהור לעולם, דהא אין מציינין אם לאו על הטומאה. (ח) וכי חורשו — לא יהא טהור. ולהכי לא מקשה כי אם מסיפא דברייתא קמייתא, דאיירי בדליכא סיד:

דאמר מר אין מרחיקים. כך פירש בתוספתא, ובקונט'. ובספרים מצאתי: דאמר מר אין מעמידין ציון כו'. ולפי זה אינו נותן טעם למה כל השדה טמא, אלא נותן טעם למה תחתיהן טהורין — דאין מעמידין ציון במקום הטומאה. ונהי דברות אחד או שנים או שלשה יש לנו לומר דכל תחתיה טמא כי אין הטומאה בפחות מן הציון, אבל בארבעה — יש לתלות הטומאה בכל השדה, לפיכך תחתיהן טהורים:

ואכלאים בחולו של מועד נפקינן. במשנה פי' מאי טעמא לא מקשה על אינך. ובירושל' מקשה: מציינין על הקברות ולא כבר ציינו? ומתרץ: כגון שירד שטף מים של גשמים ושטפו:

בט"ו קורין את המגילה. הוי מצי למתני בי"ד בו *)(בכפרים), אלא משום דט"ו זמן לדברים אחרים הוא, כגון ומתקנין את הדרכים וכו':

דמוזלי גבן. למ"ד לקמן (דף יג.) שכר פעולה שאין לו מה יאכל שרי — ניחא שיכולין ליטול שכרן. אלא למאן דאמר אסור, לא ידעינן היכן ישכרו פועלים במועד? ושמא יש לומר: דהני דמצות התירו:

מתרומת הלשכה. אין להקשות: הא אית בהן מעילה! דלב ב"ד מתנה עלייהו. ובפרק בתרא דכתובות (דף קו. ושם) איכא מילי טובא שנוטלין שכרן מתרומת הלשכה:

שיש בה רובע. פירוש: כשרוצה לזרוע. דהא קתני סיפא, ר' יוסי אומר: יבור. והא לא שייך בנזרע כבר. ובפרק "המוכר פירות" (ב"ב דף לז. ושם) מייתי לה. מיהו, בשמעתין דאיירי בנזרע כבר — יש לומר דלא פליגי: ואין

*) [נ"ל בשאר עיירות]

רבינו חננאל

עומדין על הגבולין וניחוש דלמא טומאה גואי ואילנות על הגבולין בראי. ופרקינן במסובכין. איבעית אימא כדאמר אין מרחיקין ציון ממקום הטומאה שלא להפסיד את א"י. ר' יהודה אומר עד שיהא שם זקן או תלמיד שתיקן זה הציון לפי שאין הכל בקיאין בדבר. ש"מ צורבא מדרבנן דאיתיה במתא כל מילי דמתא עליה רמיא. אמר רב יהודה מצא אבן אחת מצויינת תחתיה טמא שתים אם יש סיד ביניהן טמא ואם לאו טהור ואם היה הסיד שפוך על ראשיהן ומרודה לכאן ולכאן אי*) איכא חרש ביניהן טמא דאמרי' מחמת חרש הוא דאיקפל ואם לאו סיד דביני ביני הוא וטהור. א"ר אסי מצא ציון מצד אחד הוא הצד טמא וכל השדה טהורה וכן ג' הן טמאין וכל השדה טהורה ד' השדה כולה טמאה והציונין שהציון בהן טהורין. דאמר מר אין מרחיקין ציון ממקום טומאה שלא להפסיד את א"י כו': ויוצאין אף על הכלאים. ומקשינן איני דבחולו של מועד יוצאין על הכלאים והתנן בט"ו באדר יוצאין על הכלאים. ופרקינן בבכיר יוצאין בט"ו באדר. באפיל יוצאין בחולו של מועד וי"א כאן בזרעים וכאן בירקות וא"ר יוחנן לא שנו בחולו של מועד אלא שאין ניצן ניכר פי' ציץ שלהן ניכר. אבל אם הציץ שלהן ניכר שהוא כלאים יוצאין לאלתר ואין שוהין אותן עד חולו של מועד. ומ"ש בחולו של מועד יוצאין על הכלאים א"ר יוחנן משום שכר פעולה עת שהפועלים בטלין ונשכרין בזול לעקור הזרעים ולהשליכן ובעינן למיתן להו אגרייהו מתרומת הלשכה. והני מילי במשנה שתתקנו להיות עוקרין הכלאים בלבד מתוך התבואה ומשליכין. אבל מה שהתקינו להיות מפקירין כל השדה כולה יוצאין אפי' בשאר הימים. ועושין כל צרכי רבים.

עין משפט נר מצוה

מט א ב ג מיי' פ"ח מהלכות טומאת מת הלכה יא:
נ ד מיי' פ"א מהלכות שקלים הלכה ט סמג עשין מה:
נא ה מיי' פ"ב מהל' כלאים הלכה טו:
נב ו מיי' פ"א מהל' מגילה הל' ד סמג עשין דרבנן ד טוש"ע א"ח סי' תרפח סעיף א:
נג ז ח מיי' פ"ב מהל' כלאים הלכה טו והלכה יז:
נד ט מיי' שם הלכה טז:

מסורת הש"ס

[לעיל ה:]
[תוספתא שקלים פ"א]
[לעיל ה:]
מגילה יג: כט. שקלים פ"א מ"א
כלאים פ"ב מ"א ב"ב לז.

ירושלמי אלו הן צרכי רבים דנין דיני נפשות ודיני ממונות ודיני מכות ופדיון שבוים ודיני ערכין והחרמין והקדשות וההשקאות ועריפת עגלה וטהרת מצורע ורציעת עבד עברי. וכן מפרקין מנעל מעל האמום אבל אין מחזירין. ומציינין על הקברות. והלא ציין באדר כגון שרבו המים ושטפום. ויוצאין אף על הכלאים והלא כבר יצאו מאדר תיפתר שהיתה השנה אפילה ולא היו הצמחים ניכרים באדר: מתני'

*) אולי צ"ל לא איכא חרש ביניהם טהור כו' דביני ביני הוא וטמא ואולי דרבינו היה לו גרסא אחרת.

הגהות הב"ח

(א) גמ' דאימור מחמת חורש הוא דאיקלף ואי לא סיד: (ב) רש"י ד"ה מסובכין נ"ל במסובכין: (ג) שם ד"ה הכא כו' מחמת חורש הוא הס"ד ואח"כ מה"ד דאיקלף כו' ועוד הס"ד ומה"ד ואי לא כו': (ד) ד"ה דאי ס"ד מדידהו דבעל הבית דביכן להו אמאי: (ה) תוס' ד"ה אע"ג כו' אם יש חרסית ביניהם שאינה לבן בינתים דומה שמציינין וכו' אין בית הקברות הס"ד: (ו) ד"ה אמר כו' אע"ג דליכא חורש ביניהם טהור ומפרש דאינתקא כו': (ז) בא"ד אי איכא ציון על הטומאה שביניהן: (ח) בא"ד אם לאו על הטומאה ואפילו חורשו לא:

תורה אור

רובע זֶרַע מִמִּין אַחֵר – ^אימַעֵט. וְהָתַנְיָא: הִתְקִינוּ שֶׁיְּהוּ מַפְקִירִין כָּל הַשָּׂדֶה כּוּלָּהּ! לָא קַשְׁיָא: כָּאן – קוֹדֶם תַּקָּנָה, כָּאן – לְאַחַר תַּקָּנָה. דְּתַנְיָא: *^בבָּרִאשׁוֹנָה הָיוּ עוֹקְרִין וּמַשְׁלִיכִין לִפְנֵי בְהֶמְתָּן, וְהָיוּ בַּעֲלֵי בָתִּים שְׂמֵחִין שְׁתֵּי שְׂמָחוֹת: אַחַת – שֶׁמְּנַכְּשִׁין לָהֶם שְׂדוֹתֵיהֶן, וְאַחַת – שֶׁמַּשְׁלִיכִין לִפְנֵי בְהֶמְתָּם, הִתְקִינוּ שֶׁיְּהוּ עוֹקְרִין וּמַשְׁלִיכִין עַל הַדְּרָכִים. וַעֲדַיִין הָיוּ שְׂמֵחִין שִׂמְחָה גְּדוֹלָה שֶׁמְּנַכְּשִׁין שְׂדוֹתֵיהֶן, הִתְקִינוּ שֶׁיְּהוּ מַפְקִירִין כָּל הַשָּׂדֶה כּוּלָּהּ.§ **מתני'** *ר"א בֶּן יַעֲקֹב אוֹמֵר: ^גמוֹשְׁכִין אֶת הַמַּיִם מֵאִילָן לְאִילָן, וּבִלְבַד שֶׁלֹּא יַשְׁקֶה אֶת כָּל הַשָּׂדֶה. ^דזְרָעִים שֶׁלֹּא שָׁתוּ לִפְנֵי הַמּוֹעֵד – לֹא יַשְׁקֵם בַּמּוֹעֵד. וַחֲכָמִים מַתִּירִין בָּזֶה וּבָזֶה.§ **גמ'** אָמַר רַב *יְהוּדָה: ^האִם הָיְתָה שָׂדֶה מְטוּנֶּנֶת – מוּתָּר. תַּנְיָא נַמִּי הָכִי: *כְּשֶׁאָמְרוּ אָסוּר לְהַשְׁקוֹתָן בַּמּוֹעֵד – לֹא אָמְרוּ אֶלָּא בִּזְרָעִים שֶׁלֹּא שָׁתוּ מִלִּפְנֵי הַמּוֹעֵד, אֲבָל זְרָעִים שֶׁשָּׁתוּ לִפְנֵי הַמּוֹעֵד – מוּתָּר לְהַשְׁקוֹתָן בַּמּוֹעֵד. וְאִם הָיְתָה שָׂדֶה מְטוּנֶּנֶת – מוּתָּר. וְאֵין[א] מַשְׁקִין שְׂדֵה גָּרִיד בַּמּוֹעֵד, וַחֲכָמִים מַתִּירִין בָּזֶה וּבָזֶה. אֲמַר *רָבִינָא: שְׁמַע מִינָּהּ, הַאי תַּרְבִּיצָא שָׁרֵי לְתַרְבּוּצֵי בְּחוּלָּא דְמוֹעֲדָא. שְׂדֵה גָּרִיד מַאי טַעְמָא – דְּאַפְלָא מְשַׁוֵּי לָהּ חַרְפָּא, ה"נ – אַפְלָא מְשַׁוֵּי לָהּ חַרְפָּא. ת"ר:[ב] מַרְבִּיצִין שְׂדֵה לָבָן בַּשְּׁבִיעִית, אֲבָל לֹא בַּמּוֹעֵד. וְהָא תַּנְיָא: ^ומַרְבִּיצִין בֵּין בַּמּוֹעֵד בֵּין בַּשְּׁבִיעִית! אָמַר רַב הוּנָא: לָא קַשְׁיָא: הָא – ר"א בֶּן יַעֲקֹב, הָא – רַבָּנַן. תַּנְיָא אִידָךְ: מַרְבִּיצִין שְׂדֵה לָבָן עֶרֶב שְׁבִיעִית כְּדֵי שֶׁיֵּצְאוּ יְרָקוֹת בַּשְּׁבִיעִית, וְלֹא עוֹד אֶלָּא שֶׁמַּרְבִּיצִין שְׂדֵה לָבָן בַּשְּׁבִיעִית כְּדֵי שֶׁיֵּצְאוּ יְרָקוֹת לְמוֹצָאֵי שְׁבִיעִית.§ **מתני'** צָדִין אֶת הָאִישׁוּת וְאֶת הָעַכְבָּרִים מִשְּׂדֵה הָאִילָן וּמִשְּׂדֵה הַלָּבָן כְּדַרְכּוֹ, בַּמּוֹעֵד וּבַשְּׁבִיעִית. *^זוְחכ"א: מִשְּׂדֵה הָאִילָן – כְּדַרְכּוֹ, וּמִשְּׂדֵה הַלָּבָן – שֶׁלֹּא כְּדַרְכּוֹ. ^חוּמְקָרִין אֶת הַפִּירְצָה בַּמּוֹעֵד, ^טוּבַשְּׁבִיעִית בּוֹנֶה כְּדַרְכּוֹ.§ **גמ'** מַאי אִישׁוּת? אָמַר רַב יְהוּדָה: בִּרְיָה שֶׁאֵין לָהּ עֵינַיִם. אָמַר רָבָא בַּר יִשְׁמָעֵאל, וְאִיתֵּימָא רַב יֵימַר בַּר שֶׁלֶמְיָא: מַאי קְרָא? °"כְּמוֹ שַׁבְּלוּל תֶּמֶס יַהֲלֹךְ נֵפֶל אֵשֶׁת בַּל חָזוּ שָׁמֶשׁ". (תהלים נח) ת"ר: צָדִין אֶת הָאִישׁוּת וְאֶת הָעַכְבָּרִים מִשְּׂדֵה הַלָּבָן וּמִשְּׂדֵה הָאִילָן כְּדַרְכּוֹ, *וּמַחְרִיבִין חוֹרֵי נְמָלִים, כֵּיצַד מַחֲרִיבִין? רשב"ג אוֹמֵר: מֵבִיא עָפָר מֵחוֹר זֶה וְנוֹתֵן לְתוֹךְ חוֹר זֶה, וְהֵן חוֹנְקִין זֶה אֶת זֶה. אָמַר רַב יֵימַר בַּר שֶׁלֶמְיָא מִשְּׁמֵיהּ דְּאַבַּיֵי: וְהוּא דְּקָאֵי בִּתְרֵי עֶבְרֵי נַהֲרָא, וְהוּא דְּלֵיכָּא גִּשְׁרָא, וְהוּא דְּלֵיכָּא גַּמְלָא, וְהוּא דְּלֵיכָּא מִצְרָא.

עַד

רש"י

רוֹבַע. הַקַּב, אֶחָד מכ"ד בִּסְאָה: הָכִי גָּרֵס יְמַעֵט. שֶׁאִם זָרַע רוֹבַע הַקַּב – יְמַעֲטֶנּוּ וְיַעַקְרֶנּוּ: וְהָתַנְיָא כָּל הַשָּׂדֶה כּוּלָּהּ. וְאַתְּ אָמַרְתְּ: יְמַעֵט: שֶׁמְּנַכְּשִׁין שְׂדוֹתֵיהֶן. שְׁלוּחֵי ב"ד מִשֶּׁלָּהֶן, דִּכְשֶׁמּוּטָלִין הַכִּלְאַיִם – מֵאֵלָיו מִתְנַכֵּשׁ: **מתני'** מוֹשְׁכִין הַמַּיִם מֵאִילָן לְאִילָן. דְּהָוֵי כִּשְׂדֵה בֵּית הַשְּׁלָחִין, דִּפְסֵידָא יְתֵירָא אִיכָּא. אֲבָל לֹא יַשְׁקֶה אֶת הַשָּׂדֶה כּוּלָּהּ, שְׂדֵה בֵּית הַבַּעַל: זְרָעִים שֶׁלֹּא שָׁתוּ לִפְנֵי הַמּוֹעֵד. שֶׁלֹּא הָיוּ מְלוּמָּדִין לִשְׁתּוֹת תָּמִיד לִפְנֵי הַמּוֹעֵד: לֹא יַשְׁקֵם בַּמּוֹעֵד. דְּהוֹאִיל וְלֹא מַשְׁקֶה לְהוּ תָּדִיר לִפְנֵי הַמּוֹעֵד – לָא הָוֵי לֵיהּ פְּסֵידָא אִי לֹא מַשְׁקֶה לְהוּ בַּמּוֹעֵד: וַחֲכָמִים מַתִּירִים בָּזֶה וּבָזֶה. לְהַשְׁקוֹת אֶת כָּל הַשָּׂדֶה כּוּלָּהּ, וּלְהַשְׁקוֹת בַּמּוֹעֵד זְרָעִים שֶׁלֹּא שָׁתוּ לִפְנֵי הַמּוֹעֵד. וְהַאי חֲכָמִים – הַיְינוּ ר"מ, דְּאָמַר לְעֵיל (דף ב.): מַשְׁקִין מִמֶּנּוּ אֲפִי' שְׂדֵה בֵּית הַבַּעַל: **גמ'** אָמַר רַב יְהוּדָה. הָא דְּאָמַר ר"א אֲבָל לֹא יַשְׁקֶה [ג] אֶת הַשָּׂדֶה כּוּלָּהּ, אֲבָל אִם הָיְתָה שָׂדֶה מְטוּנֶּנֶת – לַחָה וִיבֵשָׁה – מוּתָּר לְהַשְׁקוֹתָהּ אע"ג דַּהֲוָה שְׂדֵה בֵּית הַבַּעַל. דְּכֵיוָן דַּהֲוָיָא לַחָה עַד הַשְׁתָּא, אִי לֹא מַשְׁקֶה לָהּ – הָוֵי פְּסֵידָא יְתֵירָא: שְׂדֵה גָּרִיד. יְבֵשָׁה מֵעוֹלָם, שֶׁאֵין צָרִיךְ לְהַשְׁקוֹתָהּ: בָּזֶה וּבָזֶה. בִּשְׂדֵה גָּרִיד, וּבִזְרָעִים שֶׁלֹּא שָׁתוּ לִפְנֵי הַמּוֹעֵד: תַּרְבִּיצָא. גִּינָּה: שָׁרֵי לְתַרְבּוּצֵי. לִזַלֵּף עָלֶיהָ מַיִם, אע"ג דְּלֵיכָּא פְּסֵידָא לְתַרְבּוּצֵי. לְהַשְׁקוֹת, לְשׁוֹן "אֵין מְכַבְּדִין וְאֵין מַרְבִּיצִין" – הַיְינוּ הַשְׁקָאָה פּוּרְתָּא, כְּדֵי שֶׁיִּגְדְּלוּ הַיְּרָקוֹת, וּכְדִמְפָרֵשׁ בְּאִידָךְ בָּרַיְיתָא לְקַמֵּיהּ. וּמַשְׁקִין – הַיְינוּ הַשְׁקָאָה גְּמוּרָה שֶׁל בֵּית הַשְּׁלָחִין: אַפְלָא לְשַׁוּוּיֵי חַרְפָּא. דְּלֵיכָּא פְּסֵידָא, וְאפ"ה שָׁרֵי לְהַשְׁקוֹתָהּ כָּךְ וּלְהַשְׁבִּיחָהּ – ה"נ בְּגִינָּה מַרְבִּילִין: שְׂדֵה לָבָן. בֵּית הַבַּעַל: הָא. דְּקָתָנֵי אֲבָל לֹא יַשְׁקֵם בַּמּוֹעֵד – הַיְינוּ ר"א בֶּן יַעֲקֹב, דְּאָמַר: אֲבָל לֹא יַשְׁקֶה אֶת כָּל הַשָּׂדֶה כּוּלָּהּ. וְהָא דְּתָנֵי בֵּין בַּמּוֹעֵד בֵּין בַּשְּׁבִיעִית – הַיְינוּ חֲכָמִים, דְּמַתִּירִין לְהַשְׁקוֹת אֲפִי' כָּל הַשָּׂדֶה: כְּדֵי שֶׁיֵּצְאוּ בַּשְּׁבִיעִית. אֲבָל לֹא יַשְׁקֶה בַּשְּׁבִיעִית כְּדֵי שֶׁיִּגְדְּלוּ בַּשְּׁבִיעִית: **מתני'** צָדִין הָאִישׁוּת. בִּשְׂדֵה הָאִילָן בַּמּוֹעֵד, מִפְּנֵי שֶׁמַּפְסִידִין בּוֹ: כְּדַרְכּוֹ. שֶׁאֵין צָרִיךְ לְשַׁנּוֹת בִּצֵידָה: וּבַשְּׁבִיעִית. אע"ג דְּמְתַקֵּן הַשָּׂדֶה: בִּשְׂדֵה הָאִילָן. צָד כְּדַרְכּוֹ, מִפְּנֵי שֶׁהֶפְסֵד מְרוּבֶּה הוּא: וּבִשְׂדֵה לָבָן שֶׁלֹּא כְּדַרְכּוֹ. וְאֵינוֹ יָכוֹל לָצוּד כְּדַרְכּוֹ בִּשְׂדֵה לָבָן, מִשּׁוּם דְּלֹא מַפְסִיד כּוּלֵּי הַאי בִּשְׂדֵה לָבָן: וּמְקָרִין אֶת הַפִּירְצָה. שֶׁאִם נָפְלָה מְקַלַּקְתָּהּ – חוֹזֵר וּמְתַקְּנָהּ בַּמּוֹעֵד: וּבַשְּׁבִיעִית בּוֹנֶה כְּדַרְכּוֹ. מִתְּחִילָּה, אע"ג דְּמִיחְזֵי דְּעָבֵיד נְטִירוּתָא לַפֵּירֵי: **גמ'** בִּרְיָה שֶׁאֵין לָהּ עֵינַיִם. וְחוֹפֵר בְּקַרְקַע: מַאי קְרָא. דְּאִישׁוּת בִּרְיָה שֶׁאֵין לָהּ עֵינַיִם: דִּכְתִיב כְּמוֹ שַׁבְּלוּל תֶּמֶס יַהֲלֹךְ. שַׁבְּלוּל שֶׁקּוֹרִין לִימְלוּ"ץ, תֶּמֶס יַהֲלֹךְ – כְּלוֹמַר כְּשֶׁיּוֹצֵא חוּץ מִנַּרְתִּיקוֹ (א) רִירוֹת נוֹפְלוֹת מִמֶּנּוּ, עַד שֶׁהוּא נִימּוֹחַ וּמֵת. תֶּמֶס – כְּמוֹ "וְנָמֵס": נֵפֶל אֵשֶׁת בַּל חָזוּ שָׁמֶשׁ. כְּלוֹמַר: כָּךְ אִישׁוּת נוֹפְלוֹת פִּתְאוֹם לָאָרֶץ וּמֵתִים, דְּלָא חָזוּ: וְחוֹנְקִין זוֹ אֶת זוֹ. מִפְּנֵי שֶׁמְּרִיחִין אֶת הֶעָפָר, וְאֵין מַכִּירִין בְּאוֹתוֹ עָפָר: וְהוּא דְּקָאֵי בִּתְרֵי עֶבְרֵי נַהֲרָא. דְּכֵיוָן דְּאִיכָּא הֶפְסֵק מַיִם בֵּין הָנֵי תַּרְתֵּי חוֹרֵי נְמָלִים – אֵין מַכִּירִים הָנֵי בֶּעָפָר דְּהָנֵי: גִּישְׁרָא. גֶּשֶׁר: גַּמְלָא. שֶׁאֵין לוֹ גֶּשֶׁר אֶלָּא מִנֶּסֶר אֶחָד: וּמִצְרָא. עֲדַיִין קָטָן מִגַּמְלָא, אֵין יָכוֹל לְהַלֵּךְ עָלָיו אֶלָּא כְּשֶׁקּוֹשְׁרִים חֶבֶל אֶחָד מִשְּׁנֵי עֶבְרֵי הַנָּהָר בִּשְׁתֵּי יְתֵידוֹת, וְאוֹחֲזִין בּוֹ, וְהוֹלְכִין עַל אוֹתוֹ גֶּשֶׁר צַר. אֲבָל אִי אִיכָּא חַד מֵהֶן – מַכִּירִין הָנֵי בְּחוֹרֵי דְּהָנֵי:

עַד

תוספות

ואין משקין שדה גריד. פי': בית הבעל, לפי שהוא רגיל להיות יבש. וגריד בדל"ת, וכן פירש בערוך. [ובתוס'] הרב – ברי"ש, כמו "חמרא מיגרר גריר" (פסחים דף קז:):

וחכמים מתירין בזה ובזה. והני תרי פלוגתא דבהך ברייתא, היינו כעין פלוגתא במתניתין, ות"ק דהכא הוא ר"א בן יעקב: **שרי** לתרבוצי. וקשה: הא קיימא לן משנת ר"א (ב) קב ונקי! ועוד הקשה בתוספות: דרבינא גופיה, דאמר לעיל (דף ד.): מדלין ירקות כדי לאוכלן, אבל לייפותן – אסור. אלמא: הרוחא אסור! ותירץ: דתרבילא אינה כ"א השקאה פורתא. ולפ"ז נראה דה"פ: דהאי תרבילא שרי לתרבולי אפילו לראב"י, דכי היכי דשרו רבנן אפלא לשוויי חרפא – גם לראב"י, יתיר ג"כ השקאה פורתא. או שמא סבר כר"א בהשקאה, ופליג בהרבלה. וי"מ: דפלוגתא דשדה גריד לאו היינו פלוגתא דמתני' דמיירי בה ראב"י וחכמים. ופליגי באפלא לשווי חרפא, ת"ק חשיב ליה הרווחא ואסור, ורבנן סברי דלאו היינו הרווחא, דיש אוהב יותר אפלא ויהיו נגמרים יותר ומבושלים בטוב. ור"ח פי': אמר רבינא שמע מינה האי תרבילא, פי': שדה שאין זרוע עדיין, שכבר השקוהו קודם – מותר להשקותו במועד לזורעו אחר המועד. דסבר לה כראב"י, דאמר: זרעים ששתו לפני המועד, (ג) וקסבר: תרבילא הוי כמו זרעים ששתו לפני המועד. דהיינו שם תרבילא – שהרבילוהו קודם המועד. (ד) ומקשינן עלה: שדה גריד אסור משום דאי משקי ליה האידנא יבכיר קודם, אבל לא פסיד, תרבילא נמי אי משקה האידנא – קדים ובכיר ולא פסיד. וזה השיטה הולכת דסבירא לן כראב"י – כך פירש ר"ח: **מרביצין** שדה לבן בשביעית. לגבי שביעית פי' הקונטרס השקאה פורתא. ונראה שחזר בו ממה שפירש במשנה משקין בית השלחין במועד, ולגבי שביעית שרי אפילו בית הבעל. ואני פירשתי במשנה דשביעית נמי לא שרי אלא בבית השלחין, כדפי' בקונטרס כאן. אבל ק"ל: שמא הכא איירי בהשקאה גמורה, דפליגי לגבי מועד ראב"י ורבנן, ופלוגתייהו הוי בהשקאה מרובה. ואדרבה, נראה לי דמיירי בהשקאה גמורה. אלא, לגבי שלחין שצריך השקאה נקט משקין, וגבי בית הבעל קרוי הרבצה. לכן נראה יותר פי' הקונטרס שבמשנה. ולפי' דהכא נ"ל דהשקאה גמורה אסורה בבית הבעל, והרבצה מועטת שרי בשביעית. ובמועד אסור אפילו הרבצה מועטת לר"א בן יעקב, ולרבנן שרי אפי' השקאה גמורה:

צדין את האישות במועד ובשביעי'. תימה: מאי קמ"ל בשביעית? והלא אין זו עבודת קרקע, ורבי יהודה מאי טעמא לאסר כדרכו? וי"ל: דודאי צריך למיסקל אבנים מתוך שדהו כשמפנה האישות. ותנן פ"ג דשביעית: המסקל שדהו – נוטל העליונות ומניח התחתונות הנוגעות בארץ, וכן גרגיר של צרורות וכו'. אישות, מפורש בירושלמי: חולדה:

עד

רבינו חננאל

מתני' ר' אליעזר בן יעקב אומר מושכין המים כו' אמר רב הונא אם היתה השדה מטוננת פי' לחה כגון שרבו המים מקודם ועדיין ליחלוחיתה קיימת מותר. תניא כוותיה כשאמרו אסור להשקות במועד לא אמרו אלא זרעים שלא שתו מלפני המועד אבל זרעים ששתו מלפני המועד מותר להשקותן. ואם היתה שדה מטוננת מותר ואין משקין שדה גריד במועד פי' כדתנן בנזיקין בפ' איזהו נשך כל ימי גריד אחד כל ימי רביעה אחד. וחכמים מתירין בזה ובזה. אמר רב כהנא ש"מ האי תרביצא פי' שדה זרועה *) עדיין שכבר השקוה מקודם מותר להשקותה גם במועד לזורעה אחר המועד. ומקשינן עלה גריד אמאי אסור משום דאי משקת ליה האידנא מקדים ליה ובכיר תרביצא נמי אי משקת ליה האידנא קדים ומציץ בכיר. ולא איפריק והא דתניא מרביצין בשביעית אבל לא במועד ר' אליעזר בן יעקב היא והא דתניא מרביצין בין במועד בין בשביעית רבנן היא. תניא מרביצין שדה לבן בערב שביעית כדי שיצמחו ירקות בשביעית ולא עוד אלא שמרביצין שדה לבן בשביעית כדי שיצמחו ירקות במוצאי שביעית. אישות פי' בריה שאין לה עינים כדכתיב נפל אשת בל חזו שמש: **ירושלמי** אישות זה חולדה: ת"ר צדין את האישות ואת העכברים משדה אילן ומשדה הלבן. ומחריבין חורי נמלים. כיצד עושה מביא עפר תיחוח עם הנמלים מחור זה ונותן לתוך חור זה והן חונקין זה את זה. והוא דקיימי אילן החורין בתרי עברי נהרא וליכא התם לא גשר ולא גמלא ולא מיצרא ולא תיתורא שיכולין לחזור בחור שלהן וכמה יהא בין חור לחור פרסה.

רבי

*) נ"ל שדה שאינה זרועה עדיין וכו' תרבילא נמי וכו' קדים ובכיר כל"ל וכ"ה בתוס' כאן בשם רבינו.

עין משפט נר מצוה

נה א מיי' פ"ב מהל' כלאים הלכה א טוש"ע י"ד סי' רלז סעיף ה:
נו ב מיי' שם הל' טז:
נז ג מיי' פ"ח מהל' יו"ט הלכה ג סמג לאוין עה טוש"ע א"ח סי' תקלז סעיף ז:
נח ד מיי' שם הל' ד:
נט ה מיי' שם הל' ג טוש"ע שם:
ס ו מיי' פ"א מהלכות שמיטה הלכה ט ופ"ח מהלכות יו"ט הלכה ג:
סא ז מיי' פ"ח מהלכות יו"ט הלכה ה טוש"ע א"ח סי' תקלז סעיף יג:
סב ח מיי' שם הלכה ו טוש"ע שם סי' תקמ סעיף א:
סג ט מיי' פ"ב מהל' שמיטה הלכה יד:

[בשאלתות פרשת הברכה סי' קט איתא ר"א בן יעקב אומר כשאמרו כו']

מסורת הש"ס

[שקלים ג. עוד שם פרק א מ"ב]

לעיל ב.

[בשאלתות פ' הברכה אי' רב הונא]

[שם אי' רבא]

[עיין ר"ש פ"ב דשביעית מ"י]

ס"א ר' יהודה וכן גירסת התוספות (וכן ברי"ף והרא"ש וכן בשאלתות פרשת הברכה סי' קט וכן בפיסקי' לקמן ז. ר' יהודה אומר וכו')

[תוספת' פ"א]

הגהות הגר"א

[א] גמ' משקין נ"ל מרבילין (וע' ג"י): [ב] שם ת"ר אין מרבילין שדה לבן בשביעית ולא במועד כל"ל: [ג] רש"י ד"ה אמר רב יהודה כו' ר"א אבל לא ישקה כו'. נ"ב אבל הטור פי' דקאי אזרעים שלא שתו וכן פי' הר"ן:

הגהות הב"ח (א) רש"י ד"ה הולא הולי דקל הס"ד ומה"ד דפנא ענפי עץ שקורין לו"ר ופרי שלו קורין בי"ש וקעבד גלר: (ב) תוס' ד"ה אמר רבי כו' ואי בעי שתיק ורבי יוסי קסבר לעולם כו' ולדברי ר' יוסי לא תמלא: (ג) ד"ה בהסבר כו' תחילת הסבר ראשון שיכול לשתוק דהא:

עַד כַּמָּה — עַד פַּרְסָה.§ "רַבִּי יְהוּדָה אוֹמֵר מְשַׁדֵּה הָאִילָן כְּדַרְכּוֹ וּמְשַׁדֵּה הַלָּבָן שֶׁלֹּא כְּדַרְכּוֹ".§ תָּנוּ רַבָּנַן: אכֵּיצַד כְּדַרְכּוֹ — חוֹפֵר גּוּמָא, וְתוֹלֶה בָּהּ מְצוּדָה. כֵּיצַד שֶׁלֹּא כְּדַרְכּוֹ — נוֹעֵץ שַׁפּוּד, וּמַכֶּה בְּקוּרְדּוֹם, *וּמְרַדֶּה הָאֲדָמָה מִתַּחְתֶּיהָ. תַּנְיָא, (*ר"ש בֶּן אֶלְעָזָר) אוֹמֵר: בכְּשֶׁאָמְרוּ "מְשַׁדֵּה לָבָן שֶׁלֹּא כְּדַרְכּוֹ" — לֹא אָמְרוּ אֶלָּא בִּשְׂדֵה לָבָן הַסְּמוּכָה לָעִיר, אֲבָל בִּשְׂדֵה לָבָן הַסְּמוּכָה לִשְׂדֵה הָאִילָן — אֲפִילּוּ כְּדַרְכּוֹ, שֶׁמָּא יֵצְאוּ מִשְּׂדֵה הַלָּבָן וְיַחֲרִיבוּ אֶת הָאִילָנוֹת.§ "וּמְקָרִין אֶת הַפִּירְצָה בַּמּוֹעֵד".§ כֵּיצַד מְקָרִין? רַב יוֹסֵף אָמַר: *גבְּהוּצָא וְדַפְנָא. בְּמַתְנִיתָא תָּנָא: דצָר בִּצְרוֹר וְאֵינוֹ טָח בְּטִיט. אָמַר רַב חִסְדָּא: לֹא שָׁנוּ אֶלָּא כּוֹתֶל הַגִּינָּה, אֲבָל הכּוֹתֶל הֶחָצֵר — בּוֹנֶה כְּדַרְכּוֹ. לֵימָא מְסַיֵּיעַ לֵיהּ: *וכּוֹתֶל *הַגּוֹחֶה לִרְשׁוּת הָרַבִּים — סוֹתֵר וּבוֹנֶה כְּדַרְכּוֹ מִפְּנֵי הַסַּכָּנָה. הָתָם כִּדְקָתָנֵי טַעְמָא: מִפְּנֵי הַסַּכָּנָה. וְאִיכָּא דְּאָמְרִי, תָּא שְׁמַע: כּוֹתֶל הַגּוֹחֶה לרה"ר — סוֹתֵר וּבוֹנֶה כְּדַרְכּוֹ מִפְּנֵי הַסַּכָּנָה. מִפְּנֵי הַסַּכָּנָה — אִין, שֶׁלֹּא מִפְּנֵי הַסַּכָּנָה — לֹא. לֵימָא תֶּיהֱוֵי תְּיוּבְתֵּיהּ דְּרַב חִסְדָּא! אָמַר לָךְ רַב חִסְדָּא: הָתָם — סוֹתֵר וּבוֹנֶה, הָכָא — בּוֹנֶה וְלֹא סוֹתֵר. הָתָם נַמִּי לִיסְתּוֹר וְלָא לִיבְנֵי! א"כ מִימְנַע וְלֹא סוֹתֵר. אָמַר רַב אַשִׁי: מַתְנִיתִין נַמִּי דַּיְקָא, דְּקָתָנֵי: וּבַשְּׁבִיעִית בּוֹנֶה כְּדַרְכּוֹ. דְּהֵיכָא? אִילֵימָא דְּחָצֵר — צְרִיכָא לְמֵימַר? אֶלָּא לָאו — דְּגִינָּה, וְאע"ג דְּמֶיחֱזֵי כְּמַאן דְּעָבֵיד נְטִירוּתָא לְפֵירֵי — שְׁמַע מִינַּהּ.§

מתני' ר' מֵאִיר אוֹמֵר: רוֹאִין אֶת הַנְּגָעִים (*בַּתְּחִילָּה) לְהָקֵל, אֲבָל לֹא לְהַחְמִיר. זוַחֲכָמִים אוֹמְרִים: לֹא לְהָקֵל וְלֹא לְהַחְמִיר.§

גמ' תַּנְיָא, רַבִּי מֵאִיר אוֹמֵר: *רוֹאִין אֶת הַנְּגָעִים לְהָקֵל, אֲבָל לֹא לְהַחְמִיר. רַבִּי יוֹסֵי אוֹמֵר: לֹא לְהָקֵל וְלֹא לְהַחְמִיר. שֶׁאִם אַתָּה נִזְקָק לוֹ לְהָקֵל — נִזְקָק לוֹ אַף לְהַחְמִיר. אָמַר רַבִּי: נִרְאִין דִּבְרֵי רַבִּי מֵאִיר בְּמוּסְגָּר, וְדִבְרֵי רַבִּי יוֹסֵי בְּמוּחְלָט. אָמַר רָבָא: בְּטָהוֹר — כ"ע לָא פְּלִיגִי דְּלָא חָזוּ לֵיהּ, [א]בְּהֶסְגֵּר רִאשׁוֹן — דכ"ע לָא פְּלִיגִי דְּחָזֵי לֵיהּ, כִּי פְּלִיגִי — בְּהֶסְגֵּר

רש"י

עַד כַּמָּה. מְרוּחָקִין הָנֵי תְּרֵי חוֹרֵי נְמָלִים, דְּכִי אִיכָּא נַהֲרָא בֵּינַיְיהוּ וְלֵיכָּא גִּישְׁרָא דְּאֵין מַכִּירִין הָנֵי בְּחוֹרֵי דְּהָנֵי: עַד פַּרְסָה. אִי לֵיכָּא פַּרְסָה בֵּינַיְיהוּ, אע"ג דְּאִיכָּא נַהֲרָא וְלֵיכָּא מַעֲבָר — מַכִּירִין הָנֵי בְּחוֹרֵי דְּהָנֵי: נוֹעֵץ שַׁפּוּד. בְּמָקוֹם שֶׁהֵן מְלוּיִן, וּמְרַדֶּה הָאֲדָמָה, וּמְמַעֵךְ אוֹתָן: הוּצָא. (א) עַנְפֵי דֶּקֶל דִּתְמָרִים: דַּפְנָא. דָּיֵיר, וְקָעָבֵד גָּדֵר מִדַּפְנָא, וּמְגַדֵּל אוֹתָהּ מֵהוּלֵי הַדֶּקֶל: צָר בִּצְרוֹר. מַנִּיחַ אֲבָנִים זֶה עַל גַּב זֶה: אָמַר רַב חִסְדָּא לֹא שָׁנוּ. דְּאָמַר: מַתְנִי' מְקָרִין, אֲבָל אֵינוֹ בּוֹנֶה כְּדַרְכּוֹ: בְּכוֹתֶל גִּינָּה. דְּלֵיכָּא פְּסֵידָא יְתֵירָא אִי עָיְילֵי בָּהּ אֱינָשֵׁי: אֲבָל בְּכוֹתֶל חָצֵר בּוֹנֶה כְּדַרְכּוֹ. דְּאִיכָּא פְּסֵידָא יְתֵירָא אִי עָיְילֵי בָּהּ גַּנָּבֵי וְגָנְבֵי מָמוֹנֵיהּ: גּוֹחֶה. שׁוֹחֶה וְנָטוּי: סוֹתֵר וּבוֹנֶה כְּדַרְכּוֹ. דְּהַיְינוּ כּוֹתֶל חָצֵר, מְסַיֵּיעַ לֵיהּ לְרַב חִסְדָּא: מִפְּנֵי הַסַּכָּנָה. שֶׁלֹּא תִּפּוֹל עַל הוֹלְכֵי בִּרְשׁוּת הָרַבִּים: שֶׁלֹּא מִפְּנֵי הַסַּכָּנָה לֹא. קַשְׁיָא לְרַב חִסְדָּא, דְּאָמַר בְּכוֹתֶל חָצֵר בּוֹנֶה כְּדַרְכּוֹ, אע"פ דְּלֵיכָּא סַכָּנָה: תְּרֵיץ. לֹא קַשְׁיָא לְרַב חִסְדָּא, דְּהָא דְּקָתָנֵי בִּמְקוֹם סַכָּנָה — הַיְינוּ דְּסָתַר לָהּ כְּשֶׁגּוֹחֶה, וּבוֹנֶה לָהּ שַׁפִּיר: הָכָא. דְּקָאָמַר רַב חִסְדָּא שֶׁלֹּא בִּמְקוֹם סַכָּנָה בּוֹנֶה כְּדַרְכָּהּ — כְּשֶׁהָיְתָה סְתוּרָה קוֹדֶם לָכֵן, אֲבָל לֹא סָתַר לָהּ בַּמּוֹעֵד: הָתָם. בִּמְקוֹם סַכָּנָה, לִסְתּוֹר מִשּׁוּם דְּאִיכָּא סַכָּנָה, וְלֹא לִיבְנֵי — דְּבִבְנְיָן לֵיכָּא סַכָּנָה: א"כ. דְּלָא בָּנֵי: מִמְנְעִי וְלָא סָתְרִי. וְהָוֵי סַכָּנָה: מַתְנִיתִין נַמִּי דַּיְקָא. כְּרַב חִסְדָּא, דְּגִינָּה אֵינוֹ בּוֹנֶה בַּמּוֹעֵד כְּדַרְכּוֹ: אֶלָּא לָאו בְּגִינָּה. וּבַשְּׁבִיעִית בּוֹנֶה כְּדַרְכּוֹ, אֲבָל בַּמּוֹעֵד אֵינוֹ בּוֹנֶה כְּדַרְכּוֹ: **מתני'** רוֹאִין אֶת הַנְּגָעִים לְהָקֵל. כְּלוֹמַר, רוֹאֶה הַכֹּהֵן נֶגַע צָרַעַת בַּמּוֹעֵד לְטַהֵר: לֹא לְהַחְמִיר. שֶׁאִם רוֹאֶה הַכֹּהֵן שֶׁהוּא טָמֵא — אֵינוֹ אוֹמֵר כְּלוּם. שֶׁאִם מְטַמְּאוֹ — נִמְצָא מְצַעֲרוֹ בַּמּוֹעֵד, וְרַחֲמָנָא אָמַר (דברים טז): "וְשָׂמַחְתָּ בְּחַגֶּךָ": **גמ'** שֶׁאִם אַתָּה נִזְקָק לוֹ לְהָקֵל אַתָּה נִזְקָק לוֹ לְהַחְמִיר. כְּלוֹמַר: מֵאַחַר שֶׁרוֹאֵהוּ הַכֹּהֵן — אוֹמֵר, בֵּין הוּא טָמֵא בֵּין הוּא טָהוֹר: א"ר נִרְאִין לִי דִּבְרֵי ר' מֵאִיר בְּמוּסְגָּר. שֶׁרוֹאִין, וְדִבְרֵי רַבִּי יוֹסֵי בְּמוּחְלָט: בְּהֶסְגֵּר רִאשׁוֹן. שֶׁאִם מְטַהֵר לֵיהּ מְשַׂמַּח לֵיהּ, אִי לָא מְטַהֵר לֵיהּ — לָא מְטַמֵּא לֵיהּ יוֹתֵר מִדְּמֵעִיקָּרָא, אֶלָּא מְסַגֵּר לֵיהּ פַּעַם שְׁנִיָּה: בְּהֶסְגֵּר

תוספות

עד כמה עד פרסה. דאין מכירין זה את זה ביותר מפרסה, אפי' בלא נהר. א"נ, ה"פ: כשיש נהר, מתי קרויין מכירין – עד פרסה, אבל ביותר – מיקרי אין מכירין, ודוקא דאיכא נהר: **תניא** ר"ש בן אלעזר אומר. לא ידענא מה הוא, אם הוא תנא שלישי, או שמא מילתיה דת"ק מפרש, או שמא י"ל דרבי יהודה מודה בשדה לבן הסמוכה לשדה האילן, וחכמים מיירי בשדה הסמוכה לבית השלחין לא בשדה הסמוכה לבית האילן. ונראה לי דגרסינן הכי: באיזה שדה לבן מתירין חכמים. ויש ספרים שכתוב בהן: כשאמרו בשדה לבן שלא כדרכו לא אמרו אלא בשדה לבן הסמוכה לעיר, וקאי על דברי רבי יהודה כו':

אמר רב אשי מתניתין נמי דיקא. פסק בתוס' דהר"ר פרץ דהלכתא הכי, דכותל חצר מותר לבנותו. ופירש: דהיינו דוקא במקום סמוך לרה"ר, שיש לו לחוש לגנבים. אבל בין חצר לחצר, ומשום בני חצר – אסור לבנותו כדרכו:

אמר רבי נראין דברי ר"מ במוסגר. מה שפירש בקונטרס דמוסגר אסור בתשמיש המטה – לא נדע מנין לו. דהא תנן בפרק קמא דמגילה (ד' ח:) אין בין מוסגר למוחלט אלא פריעה ופרימה, משמע דלענין תשמיש המטה – שוין, דלמאן דאמר מוחלט מותר – כל שכן דמוסגר מותר. ולמ"ד דמוחלט אסור – ה"ה מוסגר אסור. דהא מוחלט מאי טעמא דאסור – משום דאיכא ק"ו לימי חלוטו, כדאמרינן בשמעתין. והכי נמי ק"ו לימי הסגירו, וגמרינן ימי הסגר מימי ספרו. ואי משום דאין טעון פריעה ופרימה – בימי ספרו נמי אין טעון פריעה ופרימה. והא דקאמר התם בגמרא הא לענין שילוח טומאה זה וזה שוין – ה"ה לענין תשמיש המטה הן שוין, אלא לא פסיק ליה לאיסור או להיתר. וגם מה שפירש בקונט' דמוסגר אינו משתלח חוץ לג' מחנות – מזה חזר בו, דהא בפרק קמא דמגילה (ד' ח:) קאמר: הא לענין שילוח – זה וזה שוין. ולפי זה קשה: מאי שייך לוותא דאשתו ולוותא דעלמא במוסגר ובמוחלט? בשלמא לוותא דעלמא – יש ליישב שהוא צריך פריעה ופרימה כשהוא מוחלט, וטמא טמא יקרא, ופורש מבני אדם בימי חלוטו יותר מבימי הסגירו. אבל לתשמיש שניהן שוין. ע"כ נראה דהא דקאמר: מר סבר: לוותא דעלמא ניחא ליה, ומר סבר: לוותא דאשתו עדיף – אמוחלט קאי. וה"פ: נראין דברי ר' מאיר במוחלט, דרואין. דאי מטמא ליה – תחילה נמי טמא הוה. ואי מטהר ליה – מאי אפסדיה? דלוותא דאשתו אינו חושש, דלוותא דעלמא עדיפא ליה. ונראין דברי ר' יוסי במוסגר, דמטמא ליה ופסיד לוותא דעלמא, שיהיה טעון פריעה ופרימה וטמא טמא יקרא וצריך לפרוש מבני אדם. וגם יפסיד, שילטער שעד עתה היה מצפה להיות טהור ואין מצפה עתה ליטהר. ותנא אחרינא סבר: לוותא דאשתו ניחא ליה. והכי פירושו: נראין דברי ר' מאיר דרואין במוסגר, דאי מטמא ליה – לא יפסיד, דשניהן, מוסגר ומוחלט, דינם שוה חוץ מפריעה ופרימה, ובהן הפסד אינו חושש, אפי' קרינא ליה הפסד לוותא דעלמא כדפי' אינו חושש אלא אלוותא דאשתו. אבל מוחלט אין רואין, דאי מטהר ליה – יפסיד לוותא דאשתו, דקסבר: לוותא דאשתו עדיפא ליה מלוותא דעלמא. וקצת ק"ל: מהו נראין דברי ר"מ? הא לית ליה לרבי מאיר כלל דהכהן מחויב לומר, ואי בעי שתיק. ור' (ב) קסבר דלעולם כהן אינו רשאי לשתוק כלל. ולדברי ר' לא תמצא בשום אחד רואין להקל ולא להחמיר, דאינו רשאי לשתוק כלל. והכי הוה ליה למימר: נראין דברי ר' יוסי כו' ואין נראין דברי יוסי כו'. והכי איתא בשמעתין דטיפת חלב (חולין ד' קט.): **בהסגר** ראשון כולי עלמא לא פליגי. מה שפירש בקונטרס בסוף הסגר ראשון, ומשום הכי רואין, אי טהור – שפיר, ואי עומד בעיניו – תחילה נמי בבית הכלא היה עומד, וקשה: דלמא פשה הנגע ויהיה טמא מוחלט? והכי משמע בנגעים פ"א: דארבע מראות הללו מצטרפין זה עם זה לפטור את העומד סוף שבוע שני, להחליט את שנולד בו מחיה או שער לבן בתחילה בסוף שבוע ראשון או בסוף שני לאחר הפטור, להחליט את שנולד בו פיסיון בסוף שבוע ראשון או בסוף שבוע שני! ויש לפרש: בהסגר ראשון כ"ע לא פליגי דחזי ליה, הוי הטעם משום ד"לטהרו או לטמאו" לא שייך למדרש עד שעה שצריך לטמאותו, דהיינו בסוף הסגר שני. אבל בסוף הסגר ראשון – ראוי הוא להסגיר עוד, ולא יטמאנו. וכל זה דוחק. לכך נראה דברי רבינו יצחק: בהסגר ראשון – היינו תחילת הסגר ראשון, שיכול (ג) לשמח בהן דהא לא שייך לטהרו או לטמאו. בהסגר שני והוא בתחילת הסגר שני – שמא אינו יכול לשתוק, והוא הדין בסוף הסגר שני: לטהרו

מסורת הש"ס

[נ"ל ומרדד כך אי' בתוספ' פ"א וכ"א בשאלתות]

[לקמן יח.]

[תוספתא פ"א לקמן יג.]

[עי' בתוי"ט]

[תוספתא פ"א]

עין משפט נר מצוה

סד א מיי' פ"ח מהל' י"ט הל' ה טוש"ע א"ח סי' תקלז סעיף יג:

סה ב מיי' שם טוש"ע שם:

סו ג ד ה ו מיי' פ"ח מהל' י"ט הלכה ו סמג לאוין עה טוש"ע א"ח סי' תקמ סעיף א:

סז ז מיי' פ"ז מהל' י"ט הלכה טז:

[בשאלתות אי' ר"א ב"י]

[בערוך אי' הגוהה וכ"א בשאלתות וכ"ה בתוספתא ולקמן יג.]

רבינו חננאל

ר' יהודה אומר צדין משדה האילן כדרכו ומשדה הלבן שלא כדרכו: ת"ר כיצד כדרכו חופר גומא ותולה בה מצודה. כיצד שלא כדרכו נועץ שפוד ומכה בקורדום ומרדה בעפר תחתיה: ומקרין הפירצה במועד. רב יוסף אמר בהוצא ודפנא במתניתא תנא צר בצרור כלומר עולה באבנים זו על גב זו ואינו טח בטיט. אמר רב חסדא לא שנו שמקרין את הפירצה אלא כותל גינה [אבל כותל חצר] שנפל בונה כדרכו אמר רב אשי מתני' נמי דיקא דעל כותל גינה אמר' המשנה ומקרין את הפירצה במועד דקתני ובשביעית בונה כדרכו דהיכא אי נימא דחצר צריכא למימר דבונה בשביעית וכי בנין בשביעית מי אסיר אלא לאו דגינה *) (ובונה כדרכו מפני הסכנה שלא יפול על בני אדם) ואע"ג דמיחזי כמאן דעביד נטירותא לפירי. תניא כותל הגוחה לרה"ר סותר ובונה כדרכו מפני הסכנה שלא יפול על בני אדם: **מתני'** רמ"א רואין את הנגעים וכו' תניא ר' מאיר אומר רואין את הנגעים להקל כדי לטהרו אבל לא להחמיר שאם אתה נוקק לו להקל אתה נוקק לו להחמיר שנא' לטהרו או לטמאו. א"ר נראין דברי רבי מאיר במוסגר כי רואין להקל לטהר אבל לא להחמיר שאם יראה כי הוא טמא ישתוק ואוקמה רבה בהסגר שני. ור' מאיר סבר בכהן תליא מילתא

*) אלו תיבות המוקפים נראה שמיותרים הם.

גליון הש"ס

תום' ד"ה אמר רבי נראין וכו' צריך פריעה ופרימה כשהוא מוחלט וטמא טמא יקרא. עיין תוי"ט פ"א מ"ז דמגילה:

הגהות הב"ח

(א) רש"י ד"ה הוצא הוצי דקל הס"ד ומה"ד דפנא ענפי עץ שקורין לו"ר ופרי שלו קורין ביי"ש וקעבד גדר: (ב) תוס' ד"ה אמר רבי כו' ואי בעי שתיק ורבי יוסי קסבר דלעולם כו' ולדברי ר' יוסי לא תמצא: (ג) ד"ה בהסגר כו' תחילת הסגר ראשון שיכול לשתוק דהא:

הגהות הגר"א

[א] גמ' בהסגר שני כ"ע ל"פ דחזי ליה כי פליגי בהסגר ראשון כצ"ל:

עין משפט נר מצוה

סח א מיי' פ"י מהל' טומאת צרעת הל' ו סמג עשין רלה:
סט ב מיי' פ"ט שם הלכה ח:

בְּהֶסְגֵּר שֵׁנִי. מָר סָבַר: בְּכֹהֵן תַּלְיָא מִילְּתָא, אִי טָהוֹר — אָמַר לֵיהּ טָהוֹר, וְאִי טָמֵא — שָׁתֵיק. וּמָר סָבַר: "לְטַהֲרוֹ אוֹ לְטַמְּאוֹ" כְּתִיב. (ויקרא יג) אָמַר מָר, אָמַר רַבִּי: נִרְאִין דִּבְרֵי רַבִּי יוֹסֵי בְּמוּחְלָט וְדִבְרֵי ר' מֵאִיר בְּמוּסְגָּר. וְהָתַנְיָא אִיפְּכָא! תַּנָּאֵי הִיא אַלִּיבָּא דְּרַבִּי, מָר סָבַר צַוְותָא דְּעָלְמָא עָדִיף לֵיהּ, וּמָר סָבַר צַוְותָא דְּאִשְׁתּוֹ עֲדִיפָא לֵיהּ. לְמֵימְרָא דְּמוּחְלָט מוּתָּר בְּתַשְׁמִישׁ הַמִּטָּה? [א]אִין, וְהָתַנְיָא: *°"וְיָשַׁב מִחוּץ לְאָהֳלוֹ שִׁבְעַת יָמִים" (שם יד) — שֶׁיְּהֵא אָסוּר בְּתַשְׁמִישׁ הַמִּטָּה, וְאֵין אָהֳלוֹ אֶלָּא אִשְׁתּוֹ, שֶׁנֶּאֱמַר: °"לֵךְ אֱמוֹר לָהֶם שׁוּבוּ לָכֶם לְאָהֳלֵיכֶם" (דברים ה). א] רַבִּי יְהוּדָה אוֹמ' °"שִׁבְעַת יָמִים יִסְפְּרוּ לוֹ" (יחזקאל מד) — *יְמֵי סְפִירוֹ, וְלֹא יְמֵי חִלּוּטוֹ. ר' יוֹסֵי בְּר' יְהוּדָה אוֹמֵר: ז' יְמֵי סְפִירוֹ, ק"ו לִימֵי חִלּוּטוֹ. וְא"ר חִיָּיא: דַּנְתִּי לִפְנֵי רַבִּי: לִימַּדְתָּנוּ רַבֵּינוּ, יוֹתָם לֹא הָיָה לוֹ לְעוּזִּיָּהוּ אֶלָּא בִּימֵי חִלּוּטוֹ, אָמַר לוֹ: אַף אֲנִי כָּךְ אָמַרְתִּי. בְּמַאי קָמִיפַּלְגִי? ר' יוֹסֵי בְּר' יְהוּדָה סָבַר: גַּלֵּי רַחֲמָנָא בִּימֵי סְפִירוֹ, וְכ"ש בִּימֵי חִלּוּטוֹ. וּמָר סָבַר: *מַאי דְּגַלֵּי — גַּלֵּי, וּמַאי דְּלָא גַּלֵּי — לָא גַּלֵּי. לְמֵימְרָא דִּבְכֹהֵן תַּלְיָא מִילְּתָא? אִין, וְהָתַנְיָא: °"וּבְיוֹם הֵרָאוֹת בּוֹ" (ויקרא יג) — יֵשׁ יוֹם שֶׁאַתָּה רוֹאֶה בּוֹ, וְיֵשׁ יוֹם שֶׁאִי אַתָּה רוֹאֶה בּוֹ. מִכָּאן אָמְרוּ: *חָתָן שֶׁנּוֹלַד בּוֹ נֶגַע — נוֹתְנִין לוֹ ז' יְמֵי הַמִּשְׁתֶּה, לוֹ וּלְבֵיתוֹ וְלִכְסוּתוֹ. וְכֵן בָּרֶגֶל, נוֹתְנִין לוֹ שִׁבְעַת יְמֵי הָרֶגֶל, דִּבְרֵי רַבִּי יְהוּדָה. א] ר' אוֹמֵר: אֵינוֹ צָרִיךְ, ב]הֲרֵי הוּא אוֹמֵר: °"וְצִוָּה הַכֹּהֵן וּפִנּוּ אֶת הַבַּיִת" (שם יד), אִם מַמְתִּינִים לוֹ לִדְבַר הָרְשׁוּת — כׇּל שֶׁכֵּן לִדְבַר מִצְוָה. מַאי בֵּינַיְיהוּ? אָמַר אַבַּיֵי: מַשְׁמָעוּת דּוֹרְשִׁין אִיכָּא בֵּינַיְיהוּ. וְרָבָא אָמַר: דְּבַר הָרְשׁוּת אִיכָּא בֵּינַיְיהוּ. וְרַבִּי יְהוּדָה: מֵהָתָם לָא גָּמְרִינַן, דְּחִידּוּשׁ הוּא דְּהָא

רש"י

בְּהֶסְגֵּר שֵׁנִי. דְּאִי מְטַמֵּא לֵיהּ מַחְלִיט לֵיהּ בְּטוּמְאָה חֲמוּרָה, וּמְצַעֵר לֵיהּ: מָר. ר"מ, דְּאָמַר רוֹאֶה לְהָקֵל, לְטַהֵר אֲבָל לֹא לְטַמֵּא: סָבַר בְּכֹהֵן תָּלָא רַחֲמָנָא. דְּאִי מְטַמֵּא לֵיהּ הָוֵי טָמֵא, וְאִי לָא בָּעֵי מְטַמֵּא לֵיהּ — לָא הָוֵי טָמֵא וּלְהָכִי חָזֵי לֵיהּ לְהָקֵל אֲבָל לֹא לְהַחְמִיר. דְּאִי חָזֵי לֵיהּ דְּהָוֵי טָמֵא — לָא לֵימָא לֵיהּ כְּלוּם, וְלֹא הָוֵי טָמֵא: וּמָר. ר' יוֹסֵי, דְּאָמַר לֹא לְהָקֵל: סָבַר לְטַהֲרוֹ וּלְטַמְּאוֹ כְּתִיב. דְּכִי חָזֵי לֵיהּ כֹּהֵן דְּטָמֵא — לָא מָצֵי לְמִשְׁתַּק, וּדְלָמָא הָוֵי טָמֵא, וְנִמְצָא מְצַעֲרוֹ שֶׁמְּטַמְּאוֹ בַּמּוֹעֵד: וְהָא תַּנְיָא אִיפְּכָא. דִּבְרֵי ר"מ בְּמוּחְלָט, דִּבְרֵי רַבִּי יוֹסֵי בְּמוּסְגָּר: מָר סָבַר צַוְותָא דְּאִשְׁתּוֹ עָדִיף לֵיהּ. וּלְהָכִי חָזֵי לֵיהּ בַּמּוֹעֵד בְּהֶסְגֵּר שֵׁנִי. דְּאִי מְטַהֲרוֹ — מְשַׂמְּחוֹ, וַאֲפִי' מְטַמֵּא לֵיהּ וּמַחְלִיט לֵיהּ וּמְשַׁדֵּר לֵיהּ חוּץ מִג' מַחֲנוֹת, וְלֵית לֵיהּ לְווֹתָא דַּאֲיָנָשֵׁי דְּעָלְמָא — אפ"ה לֵית לֵיהּ צַעֲרָא, דְּהָא אִית לֵיהּ לְווֹתָא דְּאִשְׁתּוֹ וּמוּתָּר הוּא בְּאִשְׁתּוֹ לְהִתְיַחֵד עִמָּהּ בִּימֵי חִלּוּטוֹ. וְדִבְרֵי ר' יוֹסֵי בְּמוּחְלָט, דַּאֲפִי' מְטַהֵר לֵיהּ, דְּאע"ג דְּשָׁרֵי לֵיהּ לְמַחֲנֵה יִשְׂרָאֵל — אִית לֵיהּ צַעֲרָא, דְּלֵית לֵיהּ לְווֹתָא דְּאִשְׁתּוֹ, דְּאָסוּר הוּא. דְּכֵיוָן דִּמְטַהֵר לֵיהּ מֵחִלּוּטוֹ — מִיבָּעֵי לֵיהּ לְמִימְנֵי שֶׁבַע יְמֵי סְפִירוֹ, וּבִימֵי סְפִירוֹ אָסוּר בְּתַשְׁמִישׁ הַמִּטָּה, דִּכְתִיב: "וְיָשַׁב מִחוּץ לְאָהֳלוֹ שִׁבְעַת יָמִים" וְאָהֳלוֹ זוֹ אִשְׁתּוֹ, דִּכְתִיב: "שׁוּבוּ לָכֶם לְאָהֳלֵיכֶם": וּמָר סָבַר צַוְותָא דְּעָלְמָא עָדִיף לֵיהּ. הַאי תַּנָּא דְּאָמַר א"ר נִרְאִין דִּבְרֵי ר"מ בְּמוּחְלָט וְדִבְרֵי ר' יוֹסֵי בְּמוּסְגָּר, סָבַר: לְווֹתָא דְּעָלְמָא עָדִיף לֵיהּ, וּלְהָכִי חָזֵי בִּימֵי חִלּוּטוֹ. דְּאִי מְטַמְּאוֹ — לֹא מְטַמֵּא יוֹתֵר מִדְּמֵעִיקָּרָא, וְאִי מְטַהֲרוֹ — מְשַׂמְּחוֹ, דְּאִית לֵיהּ לְווֹתָא דְּעָלְמָא. אַף עַל גַּב דְּאָסוּר בְּתַשְׁמִישׁ הַמִּטָּה — לְווֹתָא דְּעָלְמָא עָדִיף לֵיהּ. וְדִבְרֵי רַבִּי יוֹסֵי בְּמוּסְגָּר דְּלָא חָזֵי לֵיהּ — דִּלְמָא מְטַמֵּא לֵיהּ חוּץ לְג' מַחֲנוֹת, וְלֵית לֵיהּ לְווֹתָא דְּעָלְמָא, וּמְצַעֵר לֵיהּ: יְמֵי סְפִירוֹ. אָסוּר בְּתַשְׁמִישׁ הַמִּטָּה, וְלֹא יְמֵי חִלּוּטוֹ: יוֹתָם לֹא הָיָה לְעוּזִּיָּהוּ אֶלָּא בִּימֵי חִלּוּטוֹ. כְּלוֹמַר, לֹא נִתְעַבְּרָה אִמּוֹ דְּיוֹתָם אֶלָּא בִּימֵי חִלּוּטוֹ דְּעוּזִּיָּהוּ. דְּעוּזִּיָּהוּ הָיָה מְצוֹרָע, וְלֹא נִזְקַק לְאִשְׁתּוֹ בִּימֵי סְפִירוֹ אֶלָּא בִּימֵי חִלּוּטוֹ: אַף אֲנִי כָּךְ אָמַרְתִּי. דִּמְצוֹרָע מוּתָּר בְּתַשְׁמִישׁ הַמִּטָּה, דְּ"וְיָשַׁב מִחוּץ לְאָהֳלוֹ" — בִּימֵי סְפִירוֹ כְּתִיב: וְרַבִּי סָבַר מַאי דְּגַלֵּי גַּלֵּי. לְהָכִי אָמְרִי': יְמֵי סְפִירוֹ וְלֹא יְמֵי חִלּוּטוֹ: לְמֵימְרָא דִּבְכֹהֵן תַּלְיָא מִילְּתָא. פָּרֵיךְ בֵּין לְר"מ בֵּין לְרַבִּי יוֹסֵי. דְּר"מ אוֹמֵר בְּהֶדְיָא: אִי טָמֵא — שָׁתֵיק, וְרַבִּי יוֹסֵי קָאָמַר אֵין רוֹאִין — כְּלָל מִכְּלָל דְּרַבִּי יוֹסֵי סָבַר: אִי לָא בָּעֵי — לָא חָזֵי לֵיהּ, וְלָא הָוֵי טָמֵא: נוֹתְנִין לוֹ ז' יְמֵי הַמִּשְׁתֶּה. דְּלָא חָזֵי לֵיהּ, דִּלְמָא מְטַמֵּא לֵיהּ: וְלִכְסוּתוֹ. אִם נִרְאֶה הַנֶּגַע בִּכְסוּתוֹ: אִם מַמְתִּינִין לִדְבַר הָרְשׁוּת. הֲרֵי מַמְתִּינִין לוֹ, שֶׁאֵין מְטַמְּאִין עַד שֶׁמְּפַנֶּה כׇּל הַכֵּלִים שֶׁבַּבַּיִת. וְיָלְפִי' מִינֵּהּ דְּבְטוּמְאָה דְּבְגוּפֵיהּ נַמִּי מַמְתִּין לִדְבַר הָרְשׁוּת, דּוּמְיָא דְּהָכָא. כֵּיוָן דְּאַשְׁכְּחַן דְּבְטוּמְאָה דְּגוּפֵיהּ מַמְתִּינִין לוֹ לִדְבַר הָרְשׁוּת — כ"ש דְּמַמְתִּינִין לוֹ לִדְבַר מִצְוָה, כְּגוֹן חָתָן וָרֶגֶל: מַשְׁמָעוּת דּוֹרְשִׁין. דְּמָר דָּרֵישׁ מֵהַאי קְרָא, וּמָר דָּרֵישׁ מֵהַאי קְרָא: דְּבַר הָרְשׁוּת אִיכָּא בֵּינַיְיהוּ. רַבִּי יְהוּדָה דְּמַפִּיק מִ"בְּיוֹם הֵרָאוֹת בּוֹ" וּמִכָּאן אָמְרוּ: חָתָן וְרֶגֶל, דְּהַיְינוּ מִצְוָה — מַמְתִּינִין לוֹ. אֲבָל לִדְבַר הָרְשׁוּת — אֵין מַמְתִּינִין לוֹ בְּטוּמְאָה דְּגוּפֵיהּ. וְרַבִּי סָבַר: דְּלִדְבַר רְשׁוּת נַמִּי מַמְתִּינִין לוֹ, כִּדְאָמְרִינַן לְעֵיל: דְּרַבִּי יָלֵיף טוּמְאָה דְּגוּפֵיהּ לְהַמְתִּין לוֹ מִטּוּמְאָה דְּבֵיתוֹ: לֹא גָּמְרִינַן. דְּהָוֵי חִידּוּשׁ, וּמֵחִידּוּשׁ לֹא יָלְפִינַן. דְּכׇל הֵיכָא דְּאִיכָּא חִידּוּשׁ — אֵין לְךָ דָּבָר בּוֹ אֶלָּא חִידּוּשׁוֹ: דְּהָא

תוספות

לטהרו או לטמאו כתיב. בפ' בתרא דנזיר (דף סה: ושם) דריש מיניה: פתח הכתוב בטהרה תחילה גבי ספק שער לבן קודם לבהרת, והתם דריש מדכתיב "לטהרו" ברישא, והכא דריש מגופיה דקרא: **ה"ג** בתורת כהנים: שבעת ימים ימי ספירו וכו'. ואגב שנכתב (א) בפסוק בתר "ואחרי טהרתו" וגו' כתבוהו כאן:

יותם לא היה לו לעוזיהו אלא בימי חלוטו. פירש הר"ר קלונימוס: דכתיב (ישעיה ז) "ובעוד ששים וחמש שנה יחת אפרים מעם" — והיינו מנבואת עמוס, אע"פ שישעיה אמרה. וישעיה נתנבא בשעה שנתנגע עוזיהו, כדמוכח קראי שהיה רעש ע"י שרעשו עליונים לשורפו ותחתונים לבלעו, הוא מונה לנבואת עמוס שנתנבא שנתים לפני הרעש, "וישראל גלה יגלה מעל אדמתו" (עמוס ז) שאז נגזרה גזירה. וכמה יש עד גלות הושע בן אלה, שהיה בשנת שש לחזקיהו — חשבונו ס"ה שנים. ב' שנים קודם נִגְעוֹ. וכ"ה דְּנִגְעוֹ, דעוזיהו נתנגע כ"ה שנים לפני מותו, וי"ו דיותם, ושש עשרה דאחז, ושש לחזקיה היה הגלות — הרי ס"ה שנים. ויותם בן כ"ה שנים כשמלך, וא"כ היה עיבורו בימי חלוטו. מכל מקום אין ר' יוסי בר' יהודה מוקשה, די"ל: דנתנגע בסוף השנה, ועיבורו היתה בתחילת השנה. ובפי' נביאים פרש"י חשבון זה, וכן מוכיח בסדר עולם. ומאחר שזה אמת — נמצא שצריך ליישב: והלא עוזיהו וירבעם מלכו כאחת! דהא ירבעם מלך מ"א שנה, וא"כ כשמת היה מ"א למלכות עוזיהו, והכתוב אומר בשנת שלשים ושמנה לעזריה מלך יהודה מלך זכריה בן ירבעם וא"כ חסר ג' שנים! וי"ל: דמָלַךְ ג' שנים בחיי אביו, וכן הגיה במקלת פירושים דהכי הוה מעשה, דזכריה מלך בחיי ירבעם אביו ג' שנים:

מאי דלא גלי לא גלי. יש מקשין: למה אין רבי דורש ק"ו! הא אדם דן ק"ו מעצמו! *) ושמא יש שם פירכא, או שמא מצורע חידוש הוא. א"נ: ז' ימים משמע מיעוט, לאפוקי ימי חלוטו, ואידך דמצטריך לגופיה. מיהו (ב) מדכתיב ביה "לו" שמע מינה למעוטי: ב]**ויש** יום שאי אתה רואה בו. תימה: לר"מ למה אינו רואה להקל? ועוד: לְמַאי דפי' רבינו יצחק דלכולי עלמא בתחילת הסגר רואין להקל — לעולם יכול לראות! ועוד: "ופינו את הבית" עד שיראו — למה טורח לפנות? שמא ימצא טהור:

משמעות דורשין איכא בינייהו. ר' דורש מ"ופינו", "וביום" אצטריך למידרש ביום ולא בלילה כדלקמן. וי"ו לא משמע ליה. ור' יהודה דורש מ"וביום", אבל "ופינו את הבית" — שמא אצטריך לרבי יהודה, אפי' חבילי קש וחבילי עצים, כדתנן בנגעים (פ' י"ב מ"ה) לרבי יהודה:

דבר הרשות איכא בינייהו. דרבי יהודה סבר: חידוש הוא, ואין ללמוד הימנה שאר המתנות. ומ"ביום הראות בו" לא משמע אלא המתנה דמצוה, דמשמע דתלוי הדבר בקביעת היום, כגון רגל, והוא הדין לחתן. ורבי סבר: לרבות נמי המתנה שאינה מצוה, וגמרינן שפיר להמתנה מ"ופינו". כל דבר הרשות בבית לא פליגי — דהא בהדיא כתיב "ופינו את הבית", אלא דבר הרשות דגופיה איכא בינייהו. ואין נראה לפרש שאר דברי רשות, כגון חבילי קש, ופליגי בבתים, ג]דלרבי יהודה דאמר חידוש הוא — לא ילפינן: דהא

*) [כדאיתא נדה יט:]

רבינו חננאל

אי טהור א"ל טהור אי טמא שתיק דבמילתא דכהן תליא מילתא ועד שאמר טמא בחזקה קאי ואמר ר' נראין דברי ר' יוסי שאמר אין רואין כלל במוחלט והתניא איפכא נראין דברי ר' מאיר במוחלט ודברי ר' יוסי במוסגר ופרקינן תרי תנאי ואליבא דרבי. האי תנא דתני אמר רבי נראין דברי רבי מאיר במוחלט שרואין סבר דלמא אחזי ליה לטהרו וצוותא דעלמא עדיפא ליה מצוותא דאשתו והאי תנא דתני אמר ר' נראין דברי ר' יוסי במוחלט סבר אי חזי ליה טהרה מצריכו לספירת שבעה ואוסרו באשתו שהיה מותר בה בכל ימי חלוטו וצוותא דאשתו עדיפא ליה מצוותא דעלמא לפיכך קתני נראין דברי ר' יוסי דאמר אין רואין במוחלט כו' ואמרינן למימרא דר' סבר מוחלט מותר באשתו. ואמר הין. והתניא דרבי סבר המוחלט מותר באשתו דתניא וישב מחוץ לאהלו שבעת ימים שיהא כמנודה וכאבל שאסור בתשמיש המטה ואין אהלו אלא אשתו כדכתיב שובו לכם לאהליכם בז' ימי ספרו ולא בז' ימי חלוטו דברי רבי ורבי יוסי אומר *) דנתי לפני ר' לימדתנו רבינו יותם לא היה לעוזיהו אלא בימי חלוטו א"ל אף אני אומר כן כי בימי חלוטו מותר הוא ואינו אסור בתשמיש המטה אלא בימי ספרו ולא אמרינן ק"ו אלא בימי ספרו דגלי רחמנא ביה איסורא אסיר אבל חלוט דלא גלי ביה רחמנא איסורא שרי. למימרא דבדיבורא דכהן תליא מילתא דכתיב וביום הראות בו בשר חי יטמא ומה ת"ל וביום לימא ובהראות בו יטמא וביום למה לי אלא יש יום שאתה רואה ויש יום שאי אתה רואה מכאן אמרו חתן שנולד בו נגע נותנין לו ז' ימי המשתה ולאיצטליתו ולכסותו וכן ברגל נותנין לו כל ימי הרגל דברי רבי ר' יוסי אומר אינו צריך הרי הוא אומר וצוה הכהן ופנו את הבית אם ממתינין לו לפנות את כליו שהוא דבר הרשות ק"ו שממתינין לו בימי חתונתו ובימי הרגל שמצוה לשמוח בהן. ור' יהודה מצוה **) בכהן לא גמרי' דחדוש הוא דהא עצים ואבנים בעלמא לא מיטמו והכא מיטמו בנגעים הלכך חדוש הוא ומחדושא לא גמרינן ופשוטה היא.

*) גי' רבינו צ"ע לכאורה ואולי דטס"ה וצ"ל דברי ר' ר' יוסי בר"י אומר בימי ספירו ק"ו לימי חלוטו וא"ר חייא דנתי וכו'. **) אולי צ"ל מצוה מכלים לא גמרינן.

מסורת הש"ס

לקמן טו:
[תוספתא נגעים פ"ח]
[זבחים ז: יל: מנחות נב:]
נגעים פ"ג מ"ב [בכורות לד:]

הגהות הב"ח

(א) תום' ד"ה ה"ג כו' ואגב שנכתב בפרק בתרא ואחרי טהרתו. נ"ב פירוש דהאי קרא דיחזקאל שבעת ימים יספרו לו מיירי אם נטרע כדמוכח בפרק בתרא דף ע"ו מפרש"י והתוס' בהדיא לשם מ"מ לא היה צריך להאי דמוישב מחוץ לאהלו גרידא דריש ימי ספירו ולא ימי חלוטו אלא אגב דמייתי להאי קרא בפ' בתרא כתבוהו כאן: (ב) ד"ה מאי כו' מדכתיב ביה לו. נ"ב עיין בספרי דדרשינן לו משמע ימי ספירו ולא ימי חלוטו:

הגהות מהר"י לנדא

א] גמ' רבי יהודה אומר שבעת ימים יספרו לו. רבי אומר וכן הוא בתורת כהנים ועיין במס' חולין דף קמא ע"א ודו"ק:

הגהות מהר"ב רנשבורג

א] גמ' רבי אומר אינו צריך כו'. נ"ב ותימה דבסמוך קאמרינן אליבא דרבא ורבי אומר איצטריך וכו' וא"כ מאי אינו צריך דקאמר הכא ולע"ג וי"ל דכוונת הברייתא דא"צ לקרא לדבר מצוה וה"ל רק לכתוב לדבר הרשות דגופיה וכ"ש לדבר מצוה דגופיה והוי כמילתא דאתיא בק"ו טרח וכתב לה קרא וכמ"ש תוס' בדף הסמוך בד"ה נפקא ליה וכו' יעוש"ה ועפ"ז מיושב מה שתמה מהרש"א שם על דבריהם כנלע"ד ודוק היטב: ב] תוס' ד"ה יש יום שאי אתה רואה בו. עי' על דבריהם במשנה למלך פ"ז מהלכות יו"ט הלכה ט"ז: ג] ד"ה דבר הרשות איכא בינייהו כו' דלר' יהודה דאמר חידוש הוא לא ילפינן. עיין קרבן אהרן פ' תזריע דף קל"ח:

דְּהָא עֵצִים וַאֲבָנִים בְּעָלְמָא לָא מְטַמְּאוּ, וְהָכָא מְטַמְּאוּ. וְרַבִּי אָמַר: אִצְטְרִיךְ, דְּאִי כְּתַב רַחֲמָנָא "וּבְיוֹם הֵרָאוֹת בּוֹ" — הֲוָה אָמֵינָא: לִדְבַר מִצְוָה — אִין, לִדְבַר הָרְשׁוּת — לָא. כְּתַב רַחֲמָנָא "וְצִוָּה הַכֹּהֵן". וְאִי כְּתַב רַחֲמָנָא "וְצִוָּה הַכֹּהֵן" — הֲוָה אָמֵינָא: הָנֵי — אִין, דְּלָאו טוּמְאָה דְּגוּפֵיהּ. אֲבָל טוּמְאָה דְּגוּפֵיהּ — אֵימָא מֶיחֱזָא חָזֵיא לֵיהּ, צְרִיכָא. אָמַר מָר: יֵשׁ יוֹם שֶׁאַתָּה רוֹאֶה בּוֹ וְיֵשׁ יוֹם שֶׁאִי אַתָּה רוֹאֶה בּוֹ. מַאי מַשְׁמַע? אָמַר אַבַּיֵי: א"כ לִיכְתּוֹב רַחֲמָנָא "בְּיוֹם", מַאי "וּבְיוֹם" — שְׁמַע מִינָּהּ: יֵשׁ יוֹם שֶׁאַתָּה רוֹאֶה בּוֹ וְיֵשׁ יוֹם שֶׁאִי אַתָּה רוֹאֶה בּוֹ. רָבָא אָמַר: כּוּלֵּהּ קְרָא יְתֵירָא הוּא. דְּא"כ לִכְתּוֹב רַחֲמָנָא "וּבְהֵרָאוֹת" מַאי "וּבְיוֹם" — שְׁמַע מִינָּהּ: יֵשׁ יוֹם שֶׁאַתָּה רוֹאֶה בּוֹ, וְיֵשׁ יוֹם שֶׁאִי אַתָּה רוֹאֶה בּוֹ. וְאַבַּיֵי: הַהוּא מִיבְּעֵי לֵיהּ: [א]בַּיּוֹם וְלֹא בַּלַּיְלָה. וְרָבָא, בַּיּוֹם וְלֹא בַּלַּיְלָה מְנָא לֵיהּ? נָפְקָא לֵיהּ °מִ"לְּכָל מַרְאֵה עֵינֵי הַכֹּהֵן". וְאַבַּיֵי: הַהוּא מִיבְּעֵי לֵיהּ [ב]לְמַעוּטֵי סוּמָא בְּאַחַת מֵעֵינָיו. וְרָבָא נַמִּי מִיבְּעֵי לֵיהּ לְהָכִי! אִין, הָכִי נַמִּי. וְאֶלָּא בַּיּוֹם וְלֹא בַּלַּיְלָה מְנָא לֵיהּ? נָפְקָא לֵיהּ °מִ"כְּנֶגַע נִרְאָה לִי בַּבָּיִת", לִי — וְלֹא לְאוֹרִי, וְאַבַּיֵי: אִי מֵהָתָם הֲוָה אָמֵינָא: הָנֵי מִילֵּי — טוּמְאָה דְּלָאו דְּגוּפֵיהּ, אֲבָל טוּמְאָה דְּגוּפֵיהּ — אֲפִילּוּ לְאוֹרוֹ נַמִּי, קָא מַשְׁמַע לָן.§

מתני' וְעוֹד אָמַר ר' מֵאִיר: מְלַקֵּט אָדָם עַצְמוֹת אָבִיו וְאִמּוֹ, מִפְּנֵי שֶׁשִּׂמְחָה הִיא לוֹ. ר' יוֹסֵי אוֹמֵר: [ג]אֵבֶל הוּא לוֹ. [ד]לֹא יְעוֹרֵר אָדָם עַל מֵתוֹ וְלֹא יַסְפִּידֶנּוּ קוֹדֶם לָרֶגֶל שְׁלֹשִׁים יוֹם.§

גמ' וּרְמִינְהוּ: *[ה]הַמְלַקֵּט עַצְמוֹת אָבִיו וְאִמּוֹ — הֲרֵי זֶה מִתְאַבֵּל עֲלֵיהֶם כָּל הַיּוֹם, וְלָעֶרֶב אֵין מִתְאַבֵּל עֲלֵיהֶן. וְאָמַר רַב חִסְדָּא: [ו]אֲפִילּוּ צְרוּרִין לוֹ בִּסְדִינוֹ. אָמַר אַבַּיֵי: אֵימָא, מִפְּנֵי שֶׁשִּׂמְחַת הָרֶגֶל עָלָיו.§ "וְלֹא יְעַרְעֵר עַל מֵתוֹ".§ מַאי לֹא יְעַרְעֵר עַל מֵתוֹ? אָמַר רַב: כַּד הָדַר סַפְדָּנָא בְּמַעַרְבָא אָמְרִי: יִבְכּוּן עִמֵּיהּ כָּל מְרִירֵי לִיבָּא.§ "קוֹדֶם הָרֶגֶל שְׁלֹשִׁים יוֹם".§ מַאי שְׁנָא שְׁלֹשִׁים יוֹם? אָמַר רַב כַּהֲנָא *אָמַר רַב יְהוּדָה אָמַר רַב: מַעֲשֶׂה בְּאָדָם אֶחָד שֶׁכִּינֵּס מָעוֹת לַעֲלוֹת לָרֶגֶל, וּבָא סַפְדָּן וְעָמַד עַל פֶּתַח בֵּיתוֹ, וּנְטָלָתַן אִשְׁתּוֹ וּנְתָנָתַן לוֹ, וְנִמְנַע וְלֹא עָלָה. בְּאוֹתָהּ שָׁעָה אָמְרוּ: לֹא יְעוֹרֵר עַל מֵתוֹ, וְלֹא יַסְפִּידֶנּוּ קוֹדֶם לָרֶגֶל שְׁלֹשִׁים יוֹם. וּשְׁמוּאֵל אָמַר: לְפִי

ויקרא יג — "לכל מראה עיני הכהן"; שם יד — "כנגע נראה לי בבית"

רש"י

דְּהָא עֵצִים. פְּשׁוּטֵי כְּלֵי עֵץ לָא מְקַבְּלֵי טוּמְאָה: וְרַבִּי אָמַר אִצְטְרִיךְ. כְּלוֹמַר אע"ג דְּיָלֵיף טוּמְאָה דְּגוּפֵיהּ מִטּוּמְאָה דְּלָאו גּוּפֵיהּ לִדְבַר הָרְשׁוּת, מִ"וְצִוָּה הַכֹּהֵן", אִיצְטְרִיךְ "בְּיוֹם הֵרָאוֹת בּוֹ": אֲבָל טוּמְאָה דְּגוּפֵיהּ אֵימָא לָא. דְּלָא יָלֵיף טוּמְאָה דְּגוּפֵיהּ מִטּוּמְאָה דְּלָאו גּוּפֵיהּ לִדְבַר הָרְשׁוּת מִ"וְצִוָּה הַכֹּהֵן". דַּהֲוָה אָמֵינָא חִידּוּשׁ הוּא, קמ"ל "וּבְיוֹם הֵרָאוֹת" דְּהַיְינוּ טוּמְאָה דְּגוּפֵיהּ, דְּמַמְתִּינִין לוֹ לִדְבַר מִצְוָה. וְהוֹאִיל וְאַשְׁכְּחַן דְּמַמְתִּינִין לוֹ לְטוּמְאָה דְּגוּפֵיהּ מִיהָא לִדְבַר מִצְוָה — אִית לֵיהּ נַמִּי כֹּחַ לְמֵילַף מִ"וְצִוָּה הַכֹּהֵן" דְּמַמְתִּינִין לְטוּמְאָה דְּגוּפֵיהּ לִדְבַר הָרְשׁוּת נַמִּי, אַף עַל גַּב דְּחִידּוּשׁ הוּא: כּוּלֵּהּ קְרָא יְתֵירָא. כְּלוֹמַר, כּוּלָּהּ תֵּיבָה דְ"בְּיוֹם הֵרָאוֹת" קְרָא יְתֵירָא: מַרְאֵה עֵינֵי הַכֹּהֵן. מַשְׁמַע: בַּיּוֹם שֶׁיָּכוֹל לִרְאוֹת: לִי וְלֹא לְאוֹרִי. שֶׁאֵין צָרִיךְ לְאוֹר הַנֵּר, דְּהַיְינוּ בַּיּוֹם וּבְהַהוּא שַׁעְתָּא נַמִּי "וּבָא הַכֹּהֵן" — אַלְמָא: דְּאֵין רוֹאִין אֶלָּא בַּיּוֹם: קמ"ל. "וּבְיוֹם הֵרָאוֹת בּוֹ" דְּ"בּוֹ" הַיְינוּ טוּמְאָה דְּגוּפֵיהּ:

מתני' מְלַקֵּט אָדָם עַצְמוֹת אָבִיו וְאִמּוֹ. וּמוֹלִיכָן לְמָקוֹם אַחֵר לְקוֹבְרָן בְּקִבְרוֹת אֲבוֹתָם: מִפְּנֵי שֶׁשִּׂמְחָה הִיא לוֹ. שֶׁקּוֹבְרָן בְּקִבְרֵי אֲבוֹתָיו, וְלָא מִצְטַעֵר בַּמּוֹעֵד: רַבִּי יוֹסֵי אוֹמֵר. לָא יְלַקֵּט, מִפְּנֵי שֶׁאֵבֶל הוּא לוֹ: לֹא יְעַרְעֵר עַל מֵתוֹ. אִם מֵת לוֹ מֵת אֹדֶשׁ אוֹ חֳדָשִׁים קוֹדֶם הַמּוֹעֵד — לָא יְעַרְעֵר. מְפָרֵשׁ בַּגְּמָ': כַּד הָדַר סַפְדָּנָא בְּמַעַרְבָא. כְּלוֹמַר, שֶׁלֹּא יִשְׂכּוֹר סַפְדָּן לַחֲזוֹר עַל קְרוֹבָיו לוֹמַר: בְּכוּ עִמִּי כָּל מָרֵי נֶפֶשׁ: לֹא יַסְפִּידֶנּוּ. שֶׁאִם מֵת לוֹ מֵת בְּתוֹךְ שְׁלֹשִׁים יוֹם לִפְנֵי הָרֶגֶל — לֹא יִשְׂכּוֹר סַפְדָּן לְהַסְפִּידוֹ. וּשְׁלֹשִׁים יוֹם אַתַּרְוַיְיהוּ קָאֵי וְטַעְמָא דִּשְׁלֹשִׁים יוֹם מְפָרֵשׁ בַּגְּמָ': **גמ'** הֲרֵי הוּא מִתְאַבֵּל עֲלֵיהֶן. וְקַשְׁיָא לְרַבִּי מֵאִיר, דְּאָמַר: מִפְּנֵי שֶׁשִּׂמְחָה הִיא לוֹ: אֲפִילּוּ צְרוּרִין בִּסְדִינוֹ. שֶׁאֵינוֹ מְלַקְּטָן, וְאֵינוֹ רוֹאֶה אוֹתָן — הֲרֵי זֶה מִתְאַבֵּל כָּל זְמַן שֶׁלֹּא נִקְבְּרוּ: מִפְּנֵי שֶׁשִּׂמְחַת הָרֶגֶל עָלָיו. כְּלוֹמַר, הַרְבֵּה הוּא עוֹסֵק בְּשִׂמְחַת הָרֶגֶל וְאֵינוֹ מִצְטַעֵר בִּמְלַקֵּט עַצְמוֹת אָבִיו וְאִמּוֹ: יִבְכּוּן עִמֵּיהּ. (אֲפִילּוּ) הָכִי אָסוּר לְמֵימַר בַּמּוֹעֵד, הַיְינוּ לָא יְעוֹרֵר עַל מֵתוֹ: אָמַר רַב (נַחְמָן) מַעֲשֶׂה כו'. כְּלוֹמַר, שֶׁהָיוּ לוֹ מָעוֹת מְזוּמָּנִין לְצוֹרֶךְ לַעֲלוֹת לָרֶגֶל, וּנְתָנָתַן אִשְׁתּוֹ לְהַסְפְּדָנִים, וְנִמְנַע מִלַּעֲלוֹת לָרֶגֶל: לְפִי

תוספות

דהא עצים ואבנים לא מטמאו. ואפ"ה מטמאו כאן. עלים ואבנים לאו דוקא, דהא תנן במסכת נגעים (פי"ב מ"ה): לרבי יהודה אפילו חבילי קש וחבילי תבן. וא"כ צריך לומר א] דרבי נמי מודה לר' יהודה. וכן משמע, מדלא מסיק דרבי סבר לה כר' שמעון דפליג התם:

מאי וביום יש יום שאתה רואה. משמע לאביי דר' יהודה דריש וי"ו. וכן פ"ק דסנהדרין (דף יד. ושם) גבי "ושופטיך" ופ' "אלו מציאות" (ב"מ דף כז.) גבי "ומצאת". וקשה: איהו גופיה לא דריש וי"ו ד"ואם המר ימיר" בפ"ק דתמורה (דף ג:), ובסוף פרק "טרף בקלפי" (יומא ד' מה.) גבי "והאש"! ושמא דריש ליה לדרשה אחרינא. מיהו הכא קשה טפי: כיון דר' יהודה דריש וי"ו — מאי טעמא לא אמר רבא דהכא נמי דריש וי"ו? למה חולק על אביי, היה לו להזכירה! ושמא רבא קאמר: אפילו לא דריש ר' יהודה וי"ו הכא להאי דרשה — יש לייתבה*:

נפקא ליה מכנגע נראה לי ולא לאורי. תימה: דהא לעיל אמר רבא לר' יהודה חידוש הוא, ולא גמרינן מיניה. ב] ולפירוש שפירש דרבי יהודה לטעמיה, דמצריך ופינו בעלים ובאבנים — ניחא, דלענין פינו דוקא חידוש. ועי"ל: כיון דלאורו (א) אינו יכול לראות בלא נר — א"כ פוסל מטעם ראיה, יש לנו ללמוד הימנו, כיון דחזינן דבעלמא נמי אשכחנא קפידא בראיה טפי מעולי רגלים, *דבעינן שתי עינים, ובעינן נמי שלא יהא יום המעונן. ותימה: דהכא משמע דרבא ממעט לילה מהאי קרא, ובפ' "אחד דיני ממונות" (סנהדרין ד' לד: ושם) מייתי קרא "וביום הראות בו" והיינו כאביי! (ב) וי"ל: דאורחיה דהתלמוד א) לאתויי דרשות הפשוטים יותר. ושמא אי לא כתב "כנגע נראה לי" הוה מוקמינן "וביום הראות" — למעוטי לילה, וכן בפ"ב דמגילה (דף כ.) ולא מוהלין אלא ביום, דריש התם מ"ביום השמיני" — ביום ולא בלילה. ובפ' "ר' אליעזר דמילה" (שבת קלב. ושם), דריש מיניה "ביום" — אפילו בשבת, ומ"בן שמונת ימים" דרשינן ימים ולא לילות, ובפ'ב "החובל" (ב"ק דף פז.) מייתי שבח נעורים לאביה מ"בנעוריה בית אביה" ובריש פ"ק דקדושין (דף ג:) מוקי לה בהפרת נדרים דוקא, ושבח נעורים נפקי מ"וכי ימכור" וגו'. וכן בפ' קמא דקדושין (ג: יד.) מייתי: ספר כורתה ואין דבר אחר כורתה מ"ספר כריתות", ובפרק ["המביא גט"] (גיטין דף כא:) מפקי לה רבנן מ"וכתב לה", ו"ספר כריתות" אצטריך לדרשה אחרינא. ומיהו, תימה: היאך נוכל ליישב הסוגיא דפרק "אחד דיני ממונות" (סנהדרין דף לד:) אליבא דרבא, דמייתי לה התם למיגמר דין ביום מנגעים? ובשלמא אי מייתי מ"וביום הראות בו" — מצינו לאוקמי בגמר דין. אלא "כנגע (ג)נראה לי" — היינו תחלת דין. (ג) ואביי דאמר אי מהתם הני מילי דטומאה לאו דגופיה *וקיימא פירכא דלעיל, דמגופיה דאית ליה לאביי משמעות דורשין איכא בינייהו, דמשמע דרבי יהודה לא דריש מ"ופינו" הוה דריש ליה נמי שפיר, ואצטריך "וביום הראות". ע"כ נראה לי דה"פ לעיל: משמעות דורשין איכא בינייהו, רבי סבר: ד"ביום הראות" אצטריך לדרשה אחרינא, דביום ולא בלילה, כדפרישית נמי לעיל. ורבי יהודה סבר: דתרוייהו דרשינן, ואיצטריך לתרי קראי. כי היכי דאית ליה לרבי דמ"ופינו" ה"א טומאה דלאו גופיה — קמ"ל "וביום", ו"מביום" לא שמעינן אלא לדבר מצוה, קמ"ל "ופינו". ולפי זה לכ"ע ממתינין לדבר הרשות, דהא תרווייהו דרשי ופינו, כדפרישית. ד]ומלתא דאתיא מק"ו — טרח וכתב לה קרא, דהיינו דבר מצוה. וקשה קצת אליבא דרבי יהודה: שמה שיש בחומרא חידוש אין ללמוד הימנו קולא, דקאמר משום דחידוש הוא דהא עלים ואבנים לא מטמאו — אין ללמוד ממנה, אלא דכוותיה אמרינן פרק "כל הבשר" (חולין ד' קח. ושם): בשר בחלב חידוש הוא, ופירש רבינו יעקב: דאי תרי ליה כולי יומא בחלבא — שרי, וכי מבשל ליה — אסור. והחידוש אינו מן האיסור, דבהדי הדדי אסור והאי לחודיה והאי לחודיה שרי. דהא כלאים נמי, כל חדא שרי ובהצטרפות אסירי, כדמסיק בפ' "אלו עוברין" (פסחים דף מד:) א] משמע כשהאיסור חידוש — אין ללמוד ממנו קולא. מהאי טעמא היה מיישב רבינו יצחק בר אברהם ההיא דעדים זוממין, דחידוש הוא*:

ורמינהו המלקט כו'. במס' שמחות (פרק יב ע"ש). והוה מצי לשנויי: הא מני — ר' יוסי היא, דאמר במשנה: אבל הוא לו: **ולערב** אינו מתאבל ואמר רב חסדא. בלא דרב חסדא קשה היטב, אלא כך רגילות התלמוד אגב גררא להביא פירוש הברייתא, דאפילו צרורין לו בסדינו אינו מתאבל לערב. ויש מפרשים דארישא קאי: אפילו צרורין לו בסדינו כמה ימים צריך להתאבל כל זמן שרואה אותן. ופי' קמא ניחא טפי, אבל לא שייך הכא כל כך לפירוש ראשון, דהא מסיפא אינו מתאבל לערב לא מצי להקשות על המשנה כי אם מרישא! וצריך לומר: דמייתי סיפא אגב גררא, והא דרב חסדא אגב גררא לגררא:

דקא

א) [וכ"כ תוספות מגילה כ. ובסנהדרין לד: בד"ה דכתי' ובזבחים קיז. ד"ה והתורה] ב) [בגמ' שם לא מייתי שום קרא ערש"י שם ותוספות]

[וע"ע תוספות מנחות נה: ד"ה וי"ו ותוספות סנהדרין יד. ד"ה ור"ש]

[כדאיתא ריש חגיגה]

רבינו חננאל

ועוד אמר ר"מ מלקט אדם עצמות אביו ואמו במועד: *) אוקמא מפני ששמחת הרגל עליו ואינו מתאבל עליהן אבל בשאר הימים זולתי המועד המלקט עצמו' אביו ואמו מתאבל עליהן כל היום ולערב אינו מתאבל עליהן אמר רב חסדא ואפילו צרורין בסדינין: **ירושלמי** תני המעביר ארון ממקום למקום אין בו משום ליקוט עצמות ר' יוסי אומר לעולם אין בהן משום ליקוט אלא אם (חסר בכ"י) **) כר אחא דאמר יש ליקוט עצמות בארון של עץ והורה לו שלא להטמאות כר' יוסי דאמר אין ליקוט עצמות בארון ואפי' של עץ תני ליקוט עצמות אין אומרים עליהן קינין ונהי. ואין אומרין עליהן ברכת אבלים ולא תנחומי אבלים ואלו הן ברכת אבלים שאומרים בבהכ"נ. ותנחומי אבלים שאומרים בשורה. תני' אבל אומרים עליהן דברי' רבנן דקיסרי אמרי (רבנן) קילוסין. ולא יעורר על מתו. איזהו עירעור מזכירו בין המתים. הספד מספידו בפני עצמו. תני אשה לא תעורר על לווייתה

*) נ"ל אמר אביי אימא מפני וכו'.

**) לפנינו בירושלמי הגי' אלא המעביר באפיקרסין ממקום למקום וכו' ר' מנא הורי לר' הלל לקרוע ולהתאבל כר' אחא דאמר כו'.

עין משפט נר מצוה

ע א מיי' פ"ט מהלכות טומאת צרעת הלכה ו סמג עשין רלד:

עא ב מיי' שם הל' ה:

עב ג מיי' פי"א מהל' אבל הלכה ג סמג לאוין עה ועשין דרבנן ב טוש"ע י"ד סי' תג סעיף ד:

עג ד מיי' שם הלכה ו ופ"ו מהלכות י"ט הלכה כד סמג לאוין עה טוש"ע א"ח סי' תקמז סעיף ג וטוש"ע י"ד סי' שמז סעיף א:

עד ה ו מיי' פי"ב מהל' אבל הלכה ח טור ש"ע י"ד סי' תג סעיף א:

הגהות מהר"י לנדא

א] תוס' ד"ה נפקא לי' וכו' משמע כשהאיסור חידוש אין ללמוד ממנו קולא. נ"ל כשהיתר חידוש אין ללמוד ממנו איסור ועי' בתוס' סנהדרין כז ע"א בד"ה ואין לך וכו'. ועי' בנודע ביהודה תנינא בהשמטות לספר י"ז בחלק י"ד:

גליון הש"ס

תוס' ד"ה נפקא ליה וכו' וספר כריתות אצטריך לדרשה אחרינא. וע"ע תוס' זבחים דף קיז ע"ב ד"ה והתורה ובכריתות דף טו ע"א תוס' ד"ה עירות:

שמחות פי"ב

[בכה"ש ובכי"י איתא ואמרי לה כו']

[וקיימא פירכא דלעיל דמגופי' ולאצטריך ובקיום הראות והא אית ליה לאביי ומופינו הוי דריש ליה נמי שפיר ע"כ עד על כן נראה לי כל"ל וכ"ה בחילופי גרסאות]

[וע"ע תוס' סנהדרין כז. ד"ה אין לך]

הגהות הב"ח

(א) תוס' ד"ה נפקא כו' ועוד י"ל כיון דלאורו לא אינו אלא משום דאינו יכול לראות בלא נר כו' קפידא בראייה כגון עולי רגלים: (ב) בא"ד וי"ל דאורחיה דהש"ס כו'. נ"ב וכה"ג כתבו התוס' במסכת סוכה בדף כד ובדף ל ע"ש: (ג) בא"ד היינו תחלת דין הס"ד ואח"כ מה"ד ואביי אי מהתם ה"א הני מילי טומאה דלאו דגופי' וקשה דלעיל משמע דלא ס"ל פירכא דמגופיה דאית ליה לאביי כו' דמשמע דר' יהודה דלא דריש מופינו הוה דריש ליה נמי שפיר אלא דאיצטריך לחבילי קש וחבילי עלים לכך דריש וביום הראות כו' דמופינו ה"א ה"מ טומאה דלאו כו' הימנו קולא דקאמר הכא חידוש הוא כו' ממנה אלא דכוותיה דהכי אמרינן פ' כל הבשר כו' ופירש רבינו יעקב דזהו חידושו דאי תרו ליה. נ"ב שם בדף קח קאמר בסתם דבשר בחלב חידוש הוא ופירש בקונטרס לחידושו דכניסת מין היתר זה לבדו וזה לבדו וכשנתערבו נאסרין ובתוס' הקשו עליו דטעם זה לא יתכן דבפרק אלו עוברין דף מד ובפ' ג' מינים דף לח קאמר בהדיא דאין זה חידושו דהא כלאים נמי הכי הוה אלא זהו חידושו דאי תרו כו':

הגהות מהר"ב רנשבורג

א] תוס' ד"ה דהא וכו' דרבי נמי מודה לר' יהודה. נ"ב עי' במ"ל פי"ד מהלכות טומאת צרעת הלכה ד ודוק: ב] ד"ה נפקא לי' וכו' ולפי' שפי' דר"י לטעמיה דמצריך ופינו בעלים ובאבנים ניחא נ"ב עיין במ"ל הנ"ל: ג] בא"ד נ"ל היינו תחלת דין. נ"ב כאן הס"ד ואח"כ מתחיל הדיבור ואביי וכו'. וכ"כ בס' שמע שלמה פ' תזריע ועי' בקרבן אהרן דף קלח ריש ע"ב: ד] בא"ד ומלתא דאתיא מק"ו טרח וכתב לה קרא. נ"ב כוונת דבריהם כמ"ש לעיל עה"ג דלא היה צריך קרא דוביום הראות וגו' לכתוב משמעותו לדבר מצוה רק הו"ל לפרש להדי' דבר הרשות דגופי' ולק"מ קו' מהרש"א בזה על התוס' ודו"ק כי משמעות קרא דביום משמע להדי' לדבר מצוה וכמ"ש תוס' לעיל ד"ה דבר הרשות כו':

אלפי *שאין המת משתכח מן הלב שלשים יום. מאי בינייהו? איכא בינייהו דקעביד בחנם.§ **מתני'** באין חופרין כוכין וקברות במועד, גאבל מחנכין את הכוכין במועד. דועושין נברכת במועד, וארון עם המת בחצר. רבי יהודה אוסר, אלא אם כן יש עמו נסרים.§ **גמ'** מאי כוכין ומאי קברות? אמר רב יהודה: כוכין – בחפירה, וקברות – בבנין. תניא נמי הכי: אלו הן כוכין ואלו הן קברות, כוכין – בחפירה, וקברות – בבנין.§ "אבל מחנכין את הכוכין".§ כיצד מחנכין? אמר רב יהודה: השאם היה ארוך – מקצרו. במתניתא תנא: *מאריך בו ומרחיב בו.§ "ועושין נברכת" כו'.§ מאי נברכת? אמר רב יהודה: זו בקיע. והתניא: הנברכת והבקיע! אמר אביי ואיתימא רב כהנא: גיהא ובר גיהא.§ "וארון עם המת בחצר".§ תנינא להא דתנו רבנן: ועושין כל צורכי המת: גוזזין לו שערו, ומכבסין לו כסותו, ועושין לו ארון מנסרין המנוסרין מערב יו"ט. רבן שמעון בן גמליאל אומר: אף מביאין עצים, ומנסרן בצינעא בתוך ביתו.§ **מתני'** *זאין נושאין נשים במועד, לא בתולות ולא אלמנות, ולא מייבמין, מפני ששמחה היא לו, אבל מחזיר הוא את גרושתו. חועושה אשה תכשיטיה במועד, רבי יהודה אומר: לא תסוד, מפני שניוול הוא לה. *טההדיוט תופר כדרכו, יוהאומן מכליב. כומסרגין את המטות, רבי יוסי אומר: ממתחין.§ **גמ'** וכי שמחה היא לו מאי הוי? אמר רב יהודה אמר שמואל, וכן אמר רבי אלעזר אמר רבי אושעיא, ואמרי לה אמר ר' אלעזר אמר ר' חנינא: ללפי שאין מערבין שמחה בשמחה. רבה בר [רב] הונא אמר: מפני שמניח שמחת הרגל ועוסק בשמחת אשתו. אמר ליה אביי לרב יוסף: הא דרבה בר [רב] הונא – דרב הוא, דאמר רב דניאל בר קטינא אמר רב: *מנין שאין נושאין נשים במועד – שנאמר: °"ושמחת בחגך", בחגך – ולא באשתך. עולא אמר: מפני הטורח. רבי יצחק נפחא אמר: מפני ביטול פריה ורביה. מיתיבי: כל אלו שאמרו אסורין לישא במועד מותרין

תורה אור: דברים טז

רש"י

לפי שאין המת משתכח מן הלב שלשים יום. כלומר, כיון דמת אין משתכח מן הלב שלשים יום, אם מספידו פחות משלשים יום לפני הרגל – אתי למספד ברגל, דעדיין לא שכחו: דעביד בחנם. מ"ד משום מעות שזימן לרגל, כיון דספדן עביד בחנם – שפיר דמי, ומ"ד לפי שאין המת משתכח מן הלב שלשים יום – בחנם נמי אסור: **מתני'** אין חופרין כוכין וקברות. לצורך מתים. שדרכן לחפור כוכין וקברות לזמנן לצורך מתים שימותו, דטירחא יתירא הוא: מחנכין. מפרש בגמ': נברכת. בריכה של כובסין, ולית ביה טירחא כולי האי: וארון עם המת בחצר. שהמת שם, מותר לעשות ארון ולנסר הנסרים מתחילה לצורך הארון ולעשותו כולו. אבל לא בחצר אחרת, שלא יאמרו מלאכה אחרת היא: ר' יהודה אוסר. להביא עצים ולעשותן נסרים לצורך הארון, אא"כ היו מנוסרים בתחילה קודם י"ט: **גמ'** גיהא ובר גיהא. (א)בריכה גדולה שעושין בחצר שיכנסו בו כל השופכים. בקיע – בר גיהא, בריכה קטנה שעושין סמוך לגדולה כדי שיכנסו המים היוצאין מן הגדולה לקטנה, שהיא מליאה ונכנסין לקטנה: וארון עם המת בחצר. כלומר: כשמת בחצר (שפיר דמי), דמוכחא מילתא דלצורך המת עבידא – מאי למיעבד ארון, ובאותה חצר: מנסרין המנוסרין. יש עמו נסרין מתוקנין מערב המועד, דטורח גדול לעשותן במועד: **מתני'** מפני ששמחה היא לו. מפרש בגמ': מחזיר גרושתו. דאינה שמחה כל כך: ועושה אשה תכשיטיה. הני תכשיטין דקא מפרש בגמ': לא תסוד. בסיד, מפני שניוול הוא אלא עכשיו במועד שהיא תסוד בסיד, ומצטערת: ומסרגין את המטות. בגמ' מפרש: **גמ'** מאי הוי. וכי שמחה אסורה ביו"ט: דאין מערבין שמחה בשמחה. כלומר: בעינן דלישמח בשמחת מועד לחודיה: מפני הטורח. ליטרח לצורך נישואין, וטירחא במועד אסור: משום ביטול פריה ורביה. דאי שרי נשואין ביו"ט – אין אדם נושא אשה כל השנה כולה, אלא ממתין עד המועד, שיהא עושה סעודה אחת למועד ולנשואין: מותרין

תוספות

דקא עביד בחנם. ונראה דהלכה כרב באיסורי.* ואפילו לשמואל י"ל דלא אסירי אלא ע"י ספדנא, אבל הוא עצמו – שרי, יותר מתפקק מצערו על ידי צעקה וישמח לאחר זמן: **אין** חופרין כוכין וקברות במועד. פי' בקונטרס: לצורך מתים הוא עושה, אפילו כשאין צריך עתה. כדתנן ב"המוכר פירות" (ב"ב דף ק:): המוכר מקום לחבירו לעשות לו קבר – עושה רחבה של מערה. אבל לצורך המת שמת כבר – מותר אפילו ביו"ט שני למיגז ליה גלימא ולמיגז ליה אסא, כדאמר בפ"ק דביצה (דף ו. ושם), כ"ש – חול המועד. ואע"פ שיש לחלק, דחול המועד דאורייתא ויו"ט שני דרבנן, כמו יו"ט שני דעצרת ויו"ט שני דשביעי של פסח ושמיני עצרת – אין נראה, דבכל יום שני קאמר בביצה. ועוד: כל ענין מלאכה חמיר טפי י"ט שני מחול המועד. וכמו שפירש בקונטרס דאיירי בחופר מחיים כך פר"ח, אבל לאחר מיתה – שרי. והא דתנינן כוכין וקברות – אפילו בלא מת, וארון – דוקא עם המת? שמא כשחופר הוא רגיל לחפור בבית, והוי הכירא דצריך למת. נראה לי. והא דלא שרי הכא לר' יהודה אלא נסרים המנוסרים מערב יו"ט, והתם שרי למיגז ליה גלימא ואסא – שמא נסרים יכולים למצוא מנוסרים הרבה, אבל גלימא ואסא לא ימצא עשויים. או, שמא, בנסירת נסרים יש קול ופירסום גדול. וי"מ: דאין חופרין – מיירי אפילו לאחר מיתה, דומיא דמחנכין, דמשמע לאחר מיתה. דמפרש בגמ': שאם היה ארוך – מקצרו. ומחיים אין רגילות לשנותו, כי אינו יודע מי ישים בו. ויש לפרש: שעושה לצורכו או לצורך אחר, וכמו שפירש שהיו עושין. והא דשרינן בפ"ק דביצה (דף ו. ושם) למיגז ליה גלימא ואסא – היינו דוקא כדפרישית, שלא ימצא גלימא ואסא עשוי מערב יו"ט. אבל כוכין וקברות – ימצא הרבה, שהיו רגילים לחפור מחיים. ומהאי טעמא יכול להיות מותר בזמן הזה, לפי שאין עושין כוכין וקברות מחיים: **ועושין** נברכת במועד. תימה: ואמאי צריך במועד? והלא אין מכבסין במועד! וי"ל: לצורך כל אותם שהתירו חכמים לכבס, לקמן בפרק בתרא (דף יג:) וי"מ: לרחוץ את המת ותכריכין: **וארון** עם המת בחצר. אמרינן בירושלמי, אמר רבי מנא: הדא דאמר – במת שאינו מפורסם, אבל במת שמפורסם – עושין לו ארון אפילו בשוק – כהדא דרבי חנינא חברייהו דרבנן דמך בחול המועד, עבדי ליה ארון בשוקא. ונראה, דלדידן שיש קהלות מועטין – חשבינן להו מפורסם לכולהו מתים: **גיהא** ובר גיהא. פי' ר"ח: מחמכן ונדיין דפרק "לא יחפור" (ב"ב דף יט.). וליתא, דהתם: מרחיקין את הנברכת שלשה טפחים, וקאמרינן בגמ': לא שנו אלא מן החמכן אבל מן הנדיין ארבע אמות. ובתוספתא* תני: מרחיקין את הנברכת ואת הבקיעה שלשה טפחים: **ומנסרן** בצנעא. ואסור בפרהסיא. ויש ליתן טעם דלא דמי להההיא (שבת דף קמו:) דכל שאסרו חכמים משום מראית העין כו'. ודמי טפי להההיא דפ' "אע"פ" (כתובות ס. ושם): ליגור שעלו בו קשקשים כו': **אבל** מחזיר גרושתו. בירושלמי: הדא דתימא מהנישואין, פירוש: גרשה אחר נישואין והחזיר, אבל לא מן האירוסין: **לפי** שאין מערבין שמחה בשמחה. גזירת הכתוב, כדדריש לקמן מקרא דשלמה. ובירושלמי דריש מדכתיב: "מלא שבוע זאת". וטעם נראה קצת דכמו שאין עושין מצות חבילות* דבעינן שיהא לבו פנוי למצוה אחת ולא יפנה עצמו הימנה, וכן שמחה בשמחה – יהיה לבו פנוי בשמחה: **בחגך** ולא באשתך. °עיקר דרשה הוא, ולא אסמכתא. כדאמרינן פ"ק דחגיגה (ד' ח: ושם): ורב אשי – האי "בחגך" מאי דריש ביה? מפני הטורח. ומתניתין הכי פי': מפני ששמחה היא לו – וטורח בה יותר מדאי: **מפני** ביטול פריה ורביה. ומתני' ה"פ: מפני ששמחה היא לו. ומשהה אותה ברצון עד הרגל שיהא שמח, או שיהיה פנוי. והא דקתני אבל מחזיר גרושתו – שאין שמחה לו, ולא שייך עירוב(ב) בשמחה. ולא מניח שמחת הרגל, וגם אין טורח בה, וגם ביטול פריה ורביה אין כאן, שהיה לו אשה כבר, וסתמא דמילתא יש לו בנים. וגם אין רגיל לשהות דבר זה עד הרגל. וסעודת ברית מילה מותר לעשות בחול המועד – דליכא שמחה, כדאמרינן פ' קמא דכתובות (ד' ח.) דלא מברכין "שהשמחה במעונו" משום דאית ליה צערא לינוקא. אי נמי, כיון שזמנו קבוע – אין לבטל זה מפני זה. אבל סעודת פדיון הבן – צריך עיון אם מותר לעשות במועד, ואין לומר הא זמנה קבוע! תינח – בזמנה, שלא בזמנה – היאך יהא מותר? ונראה לי: דקיימא לן כרב אשי דדריש בחגיגה בפ"ק (ד' ח: ושם) "בחגך" ולא באשתך, ואינו אסור לערב שמחה בשמחה. ועי"ל: דלא חשיבי שמחה בשמחה כי אם סעודת נישואין לבד:

איבעי

עין משפט נר מצוה

[כלאיחא בכורות מט:]

עה א מיי' פ"ג מהלכות אבל הלכה ז:

עו ב ג מיי' פ"ז מהל' י"ט הלכה יב סמג לאוין עה טוש"ע א"ח סי' תקמז סעיף יא:

עז ד מיי' שם הלכה ד:

עח ה מיי' שם הלכה ח טוש"ע שם:

עט ו מיי' פ"ז מהלכות י"ט הלכה טו סמג לאוין עה טוש"ע שם סעיף ו:

פ ז מיי' פ"ז מהלכות י"ט הלכה טז ופ"י מהלכות אישות הלכה יד סמג לאוין שם טוש"ע א"ח סי' תקמו סעיף א ב וטוש"ע אה"ע סי' סד סעיף ב:

פא ח מיי' פ"ז מהלכות י"ט הלכה כ טוש"ע שם א"ח שם סעיף ה:

פב ט י מיי' פ"ז מהל' י"ט שם סי' תקמא סעיף ה:

פג כ מיי' שם פ"ה הלכה יג טוש"ע שם שם סעיף ב:

פד ל מיי' שם פ"ז הלכה טז ופ"י מהל' אישות הלכה יד טוש"ע אה"ע סי' סב סעיף ב:

רבינו חננאל

במועד שנאמר העתידין עורר לויתן: קודם לרגל שלשים יום. דאמר רב מעשה באחד שקבץ מעות לרגל בא ספדן ועמד על פתח ביתו נטלן ונתנן לו ונמנע לעלות לרגל התקינו שלא יעורר כו': [מתני'] אין חופרין כוכין וקברות במועד. פי' להקבר בהן לאחר הרגל תניא הן כוכין הן קברות אלא שהכוכין בחפירה והקברו' בבנין. ומחנכין אותן. כיצד מחנכין אותן. אמר רב יהודה אם היה ארוך מקצרו ובמתניתא תנא מאריך ומרחיב בו. ועושין נברכת במועד. מאי נברכת. גוהא בר ירושלמי פי' ירושלמי נברכת זה בקיע. ועושין ארון עם המת בחצר. פי' שאם יעשו את הארון בחוץ יאמרו כל העם מותר לעשות במועד שאינן יודעין שמת לו מת. כדתניא עושין כל צרכי המת גוזזין שערו ומכבסין את כסותו ועושין לו ארון מנסרין את המנוסרין מעיו"ט. ר"ש בן גמליאל אף מביא עצים ומנסרן בצינעא לתוך ביתו. ירושלמי ל"ש אלא באדם שאינו מפורסם כלומר אינו אדם חשוב אבל אם הוא אדם חשוב עושין לו ארון אפילו בשוק כד דמך ר' חנינא חברין דרבנן עבדו ליה ארון בשוק. והכל מודים שלא יקוץ ארזים ודכוותה לא יחצוב לו אבנים ואם היו חצובות פלוגתא דר' יהודה ורבנן: מתני' אין נושאין נשים במועד כו'. מ"ט א"ר חנינא מפני שמערבין שמחה בשמחה אשתו הרגל בשמחת רב אמר מפני שנאמר ושמחת בחגך ולא באשתך. עולא אמר מפני הטורח רבי יצחק נפחא אומר משום ביטול פריה ורביה שאם אתה מתירו להכניסה במועד אף מעבירה הוא בכל השנה כולה שלא יבטל ממלאכתו ומכניסה ברגל ונמצא מבטל כל אותה שנה. ומותבינן כל אלו שאמרו כגון בתולות אלמנות כו' אסורות לישא במועד ומותרין בערב הרגל קשיא

מסורת הש"ס

[ברכות נח: ע"ש]
[תוספתא פ"א]
[לקמן יח:]
[לקמן יג. פסחים נה:]
חגיגה ח:
[דב"ב פ"א]
[ברכות מט.]

הגהות הב"ח

(א) רש"י ד"ה גיהא ובר גיהא בריכה גדולה שעושין כו' היוצאין מן הגדולה כשהיא מלאה כו' כנ"ל ותיבת לקטנה נמחק: (ב) תום' ד"ה מפני ביטול כו' ולא שייך עירוב שמחה ולא:

גליון הש"ס

תום' ד"ה בחגך כו' עיקר דרשה כו'. ועי' כתובות דף מז ע"א תוס' ד"ה דמסר:

מותרין לישא ערב הרגל. כלומר, מותר לכתחלה. ואע"ג דשבעת ימים של סעודה יהיו ברגל: עיקר שמחה. דנישואין חד יומא. ובשאר יומי לא חשיב מערב שמחה בשמחה: עיקר טירחא. דנישואין ביום ראשון דנישואין: לחד יומא לא משהו אינשי. כלומר, כיון שאינו יכול להתחיל אלא בערב הרגל – אין ממתינין עד הרגל. דדלמא מתרמי מילתא דלא מצי מתחיל בערב הרגל, ולא מתחיל כל הרגל: ועביד ז'. יומי שמחה להכא ולהכא, לחנוכת הבית ולרגל: ודלמא מינטר לא נטרינן. נישואין עד הרגל, כי היכי דלא נטר שלמה, אבל אי מתרמי ליה – עביד: אי הכי. דהיכא דאי איקרי ליה עביד – איבעי ליה לשיורי בבנין עד הרגל, כי היכי דליתרמי ליה חנוכת הבית ברגל: אמה כליא עורב. הגג כלה ומקלר למעלה עד כאמה, ומחפין אותו שם בברזל ובמסמרים כדי שלא ישבו העורבים עליו, זהו לא חשיב כבנין: ודלמא אמה כליא עורב נמי צורך בנין הוא. להכי לא שייריה, אלא כל היכא דאיתרמי ליה לנישואין ברגל – לא ידעינן מנלן דלא עבדינן: שמע מינה הני לחוד. דלא מצי למיעבד ליה ביחד, אפילו מתרמי: לא עשו ישראל יום כפורים. לפי ששבעה ימים שלפני סוכות כל יום עשו שמחה ומשתה, דכתיב: "ויעש שלמה בעת ההיא את החג שבעת ימים ושבעת ימים ארבעה עשר יום": וקרבן יחיד. של נשיאים: דאיסור סקילה. דחמור מכרת: וקרבן צבור. דמה שהיו מקריבין בימי חנוכת הבית – קרבן צבור הוא: התם. במשכן דגבוה – הוו קרבנות: הכא. בחנוכת הבית דהדיוט – משתה: הכא נמי לעבדו. קרבנות, מיכל לא ליכלו: ביום השביעי. ומשמע לן: יום ז' היינו שבת: דלמא שביעי לקרבנות. שאם הקריב נשיא שני בערב שבת – מקריב נשיא שביעי באחד בשבת, ומאי שביעי – שביעי לקרבן נשיא: ביום עשתי עשר יום. האי יום יתירא משמע: מה יום רצוף, שאין בו הפסק – אף כולהו י"א יום רצוף, דליכא הפסק בינתיים, אפילו בשבת: דלמא ימים הראויין. למשתה, עביד משתה, לאפוקי יום הכפורים: גמר יום יום מהתם. מנשיאים דמשכן, דגמרינן מתרי קראי דהוו רצופים אפילו בשבת. אף משתה דחנוכת הבית – הוו י"ד רצופים, ואפילו [ביוה"כ]: כ"ד רננות. כתיבי בפרשה, בין רנה ותחנה ותפלה ובקשה: פרשת נדרים. מסכת נדרים: ביום השמיני. של חג, היינו בעשרים ושתים: וכתיב וביום עשרים ושלשה. אלמא דבעשרים ושתים, ובעשרים ושלשה איפטרו מיניה: של צורה. כלומר: חכמים: פלס מעגל רגלך. כלומר: שקול מצות ועיין בהן. איזו מצוה גדולה, ועשה הגדולה: וכתיב ארח חיים פן תפלס. דמשמע: כל מצוה שתבא לידך – עשה אותה, בין גדולה בין קטנה, ואל תניח קטנה מפני הגדולה: מצוה שאפשר לעשותה ע"י אחרים. תפלס. פלס מעגל רגלך, שתעשה אתה הגדולה, וחבריך יעשו קטנה: ובמצוה

תורה אור

מותרין לישא ערב הרגל. קשיא לכולהו! לא קשיא; למאן דאמר משום שמחה – עיקר שמחה חד יומא הוא. למ"ד משום טירחא – עיקר טירחא חד יומא הוא. למ"ד משום ביטול פריה ורביה – לחד יומא לא משהי איניש נפשיה. ודאין מערבין שמחה בשמחה מנלן? דכתיב: °"ויעש שלמה בעת ההיא את החג וכל ישראל עמו קהל גדול מלבוא חמת עד נחל מצרים [לפני ה' אלהינו] שבעת ימים ושבעת ימים ארבעה עשר יום". ואם איתא דמערבין שמחה בשמחה – איבעי ליה למינטר עד החג, ומיעבד שבעה להכא ולהכא. ודלמא: מינטר – לא נטרינן, והיכא דאתרמי – עבדינן! איבעי ליה לשיורי פורתא. שיורי בנין בהמ"ק לא משיירינן! איבעי ליה לשיורי *באמה (א) כליא עורב. אמה כליא עורב צורך בנין הבית הוא! אלא, מדמייתר קרא; מכדי כתיב: "ארבעה עשר יום", "שבעת ימים ושבעת ימים" למה לי? שמע מינה: הני לחוד, והני לחוד. א"ר פרנך א"ר יוחנן: אותה שנה לא עשו ישראל את יום הכפורים, והיו דואגים ואומרים: שמא נתחייבו שונאיהן של ישראל כלייה, יצתה בת קול ואמרה להם: כולכם מזומנין לחיי העולם הבא. מאי דרוש? אמרו: קל וחומר; ומה משכן שאין קדושתו קדושת עולם, וקרבן יחיד – דוחה שבת, דאיסור סקילה, מקדש, •דקדושתו קדושת עולם, וקרבן צבור, ויום הכפורים דענוש כרת – לא כ"ש? אלא אמאי היו דואגים? התם – צורך גבוה, הכא – צורך הדיוט. הכא נמי, מיעבד – ליעבדו, מיכל לא ניכלו ולא לישתו! אין שמחה בלא אכילה ושתיה. ומשכן דדחי שבת מנלן? אילימא מדכתיב: °"ביום הראשון... וביום השביעי" – דלמא שביעי לקרבנות! אמר רב נחמן בר יצחק: אמר קרא: °"ביום עשתי עשר יום", מה יום כולו רצוף – אף עשתי עשר כולן רצופין. ודלמא ימים הראויין! כתיב קרא אחרינא: °"ביום שנים עשר יום", מה יום כולו רצוף – אף שנים עשר יום כולן רצופין. ודלמא הכא נמי: ימים הראויין! אם כן, תרי קראי למה לי? ומקדש דדוחה יום הכפורים מנלן? אילימא מדכתיב: "ארבעה עשר יום" – ודלמא ימים הראויין? גמר "יום" "יום" מהתם. יצתה בת קול ואמרה להם: כולכם מזומנין לחיי העולם הבא. ומנלן דאחיל להו – דתני תחליפא: *°"ביום השמיני שלח את העם ויברכו את המלך וילכו לאהליהם שמחים וטובי לב על כל הטובה אשר עשה ה' לדוד עבדו ולישראל עמו". "לאהליהם" – שהלכו ומצאו נשיהם בטהרה, "שמחים" – שנהנו מזיו השכינה, "וטובי לב" – שכל אחד ואחד נתעברה אשתו בבן זכר, "על כל הטובה" – שיצתה בת קול ואמרה להם: כולכם מזומנין לחיי העולם הבא. "לדוד עבדו ולישראל עמו" בשלמא לישראל עמו – דאחיל להו עון יום הכפורים, אלא לדוד עבדו מאי היא? אמר רב יהודה אמר רב: *בשעה שביקש שלמה להכניס ארון למקדש דבקו שערים זה לזה, אמר שלמה עשרים וארבע רננות ולא נענה. פתח ואמר: °"שאו שערים ראשיכם" וגו' ולא נענה. כיון שאמר: °"ה' אלהים אל תשב פני משיחך זכרה לחסדי דוד עבדך" – מיד נענה. באותה שעה נהפכו פני שונאי דוד כשולי קדירה וידעו הכל שמחל לו הקב"ה על אותו עון. ר' יונתן בן עסמיי *ורבי יהודה בן גרים תנו פרשת נדרים בי ר' שמעון בן יוחי, איפטור מיניה באורתא. לצפרא הדור וקא מפטרי מיניה, אמר להו: ולאו איפטריתו מיני באורתא? אמרו ליה: למדתנו רבינו, *תלמיד שנפטר מרבו ולן באותה העיר – צריך ליפטר ממנו פעם אחרת, שנאמר: "ביום השמיני שלח את העם ויברכו את המלך" וכתיב: °"וביום עשרים ושלשה לחדש השביעי שלח את העם"! אלא מכאן לתלמיד הנפטר מרבו ולן באותה העיר – צריך ליפטר ממנו פעם אחרת. א"ל לבריה: בני אדם הללו אנשים של צורה הם, זיל גביהון דליברכוך. אזל, אשכחינהו דקא רמו קראי אהדדי; כתיב: °"פלס מעגל רגלך וכל דרכיך יכונו" וכתיב: °"אורח חיים פן תפלס"! לא קשיא: כאן – במצוה שאפשר לעשותה ע"י אחרים, כאן

איבעי ליה למינטר עד החג. כדי שלא יתבטלו ישראל ממלאכתן כל כך: איבעי ליה לשיורי באמה כליא עורב. שלא היה צורך הבנין כ"כ, ואע"פ שהוא מהבנין, כדי שלא יבאו הטומאה – אין זה צורך כל כך. וגם בשעת הבנין, בזמן שלא היה השכינה שורה בו – לא היה צורך*:

רבינו חננאל

קשיא לכולהו. ופרקינן מאן דאמר משום שמחה חד יומא הוה והוא יום הכנסת הכלה בערב יום טוב. וכן נמי מי שאמר משום טרחא *) כר' אבא דאמר עלת כלתא נפקת טרחותא מאן דאמר משום פריה ורביה לחד יומא לא משהי נפשיה. ומנ"ל דאין מערבין שמחה בשמחה דכתיב ויעש שלמה את החג וכל ישראל עמו קהל גדול מלבוא חמת עד נחל מצרים לפני ה' אלהינו שבעת ימים ושבעת ימים ארבעה עשר יום ואסיקנא מדמייתר קרא מכדי כתיב ארבעה עשר יום שבעת ימים ושבעת ימים למה לי אלא ש"מ שמחת חינוך לבד ושמחת החג לבד. אמר רבי פרנך א"ר יוחנן אותה שנה לא צמו ביוה"כ דכתיב שמחה ואי שמחה בלא אכילה מאי דרוש ק"ו ומה משכן שאין קדושתו קדושת עולם דהא יש אחריו קדושה וקרבן הנשיאים קרבן יחיד הוא ולא קרבן צבור ודחי שבת שהוא איסור סקילה. והקריבו בשבת כדכתיב ביום עשתי עשר יום. ביום ביום דכתב קרא למה לי אלא ללמד מה יום כולו רצוף אף שנים עשר כולן רצופין הקריבו בהן והשבת בכללן. מקדש קדושתו קדושת עולם דאין אחריו היתר וקרבן צבור ויוה"כ דאיסור כרת הוא לא כ"ש דנידחי ליה והיו דואגין שמא נתחייבו כלייה דאמרי התם במשכן לא דחו שבת אלא בהקרבת קרבנות דצורך גבוה נינהו אבל יום הכפורים דאסור באכילה ושתיה שהוא צורך הדיוט. יצאת ב"ק ואמרה להן כולכם מזומנים לחיי העולם הבא שלא נתכוונתם אלא למצוה. ומניין שמחל להם שנא' וביום השמיני שלח את העם ויברכו את המלך וילכו לאהליהם שהלכו ומצאו נשיהן טהורות שמחים שנהנו מזיו השכינה וטובי לב שכל אחד ואחד נתעברה אשתו זכר על כל הטובה אשר עשה ה' לדוד עבדו שהודיע לכל שמחל לו עון בת שבע ומיתת אוריה שלא נענה שלמה בנו בעת שדבקו שערים זה בזה ולא נפתחו שיכנס הארון אלא כשאמר ה' אלהים אל תשב פני משיחך זכרה לחסדי דוד עבדך מיד נודע לכל שמחל הקב"ה לדוד עבדו אותו עון ולישראל עמו שיצאת ב"ק ואמרה כולכם מזומנים לחיי העולם הבא. ר' יונתן בן עבראי ור' יהודה בן גרים תנו נדרים בי רשב"י איפטור מיניה באורתא בצפרא נמי אתו וקא מיפטרי אמר להו ולאו כבר איפטריתו אמרו לו לימדתנו רבינו תלמיד הנפטר מרבו ולן וכו' שדר לגבייהו בריה ליברכיה אזל אשכחינהו דמפרשי פלס מעגל רגלך במצוה (שאי אפשר) [שאפשר] לעשותה ע"י אחרים

*) דברי ר' אבא נמצא בירושלמי כאן הלכה ז' א"ר בא עלת כלתא נפקת טרחותא.

פה א טוש"ע י"ד סי' רמב סעיף טז בהגה"ה:

מ"א ח

[שבת ל. ערכין ו. ע"ש מנחות קז.] מגלה פ"ד מ"ו

[עי' תוספות שבת ל. ד"ה מכלאת ותוס' מנחות קז. ד"ה כליא ובערכין ו. ד"ה כגון]

במדבר ז

שם

שם

[שבת ל. ע"ש]

מ"א ח

שבת ל. סנהדרין קז:

תהלים כד

דה"ב ו

שבת לג:

דה"ב ז

משלי ד

שם ה

גליון הש"ס

גמ' דקדושתו קדושת עולם. עיין שבועות דף טז ע"ב תוס' ד"ה קדושתו:

הגהות הב"ח

(א) גמ' באמה כליא עורב נ"ב לשון כלוי ומניעת העורבי' מלישב וכן פי' הערוך אלא שכתב דבמקדש ראשון לא היה צריך כליא עורב ע"ש והתוס' בפרק ר' עקיבא כתבו דמוכח כאן שהיה במקדש ראשון כליא עורב:

עין משפט נר מצוה

מסורת הש"ס

כאן – במצוה שא"א לעשותה על ידי אחרים. הדר יתבי וקא מבעי להו: כתיב: °"יקרה היא מפנינים וכל חפציך לא ישוו בה", הא חפצי שמים – ישוו בה, וכתיב: °"כל חפצים לא ישוו בה" – דאפילו חפצי שמים לא ישוו בה! כאן – במצוה שאפשר לעשותה ע"י אחרים, כאן – במצוה שאי אפשר לעשותה ע"י אחרים. אמרו ליה: מאי בעית הכא? אמר להו: דאמר לי אבא: זיל גבייהו דליברכוך. אמרו ליה: יהא רעוא דתזרע ולא תחצד, תעייל ולא תיפוק, תיפוק ולא תעייל, ליחרוב ביתך וליתוב אושפיזך, לבלבל פתורך, ולא תחזי שתא חדתא. כי אתא לגבי אבוה, א"ל: לא מבעיא דברוכי לא בירכן – אבל צעורי צעורן. א"ל: מאי אמרו לך? הכי והכי אמרו לי. א"ל: הנך כולהו ברכתא נינהו; תזרע ולא תחצד – תוליד בנים ולא ימותו. תעייל ולא תיפוק – תעייל כלתא ולא לימותו בנך דליפקון. תיפוק ולא תעייל – תוליד בנתא ולא ימותו גוברייהו וליהדרו לותיך. ליחרוב ביתך וליתוב אושפיזך – דהאי עלמא אושפיזך והאי עלמא ביתא, דכתיב: °"קרבם בתימו לעולם" אל תקרי "קרבם" אלא "קברם". לבלבל פתורך – בבני ובנתא, ולא תיחזי שתא חדתא – דלא תמות אנתתך ולא תנסב איתתא אחריתי. ר' שמעון בן חלפתא אפטר מיניה דרב, א"ל (*אבוה:) זיל לגביה דליברכך. א"ל: יהא רעוא דלא תבייש ולא תתבייש. *אתא גבי אבוה. א"ל: מאי אמר לך? א"ל: מילין בעלמא הוא דאמר לי. א"ל: בירכך ברכתא דברכן קודשא בריך הוא לישראל ותנא בה, דכתיב: °"ואכלתם אכול ושבוע והללתם וגו' ולא יבושו עמי לעולם וידעתם כי בקרב ישראל אני וגו' ולא יבושו עמי לעולם". § "ועושה אשה תכשיטיה". ת"ר: אאלו הן תכשיטי נשים: כוחלת, ופוקסת, ומעבירה (*סרק) על פניה, ואיכא דאמרי: מעברת[א] סרק על פניה של מטה. דביתהו דרב חסדא מקשטא באנפי כלתה. יתיב רב הונא בר חיננא קמיה דרב חסדא, ויתיב וקאמר: לא שנו אלא ילדה, אבל זקנה – לא. א"ל: האלהים! אפילו אמך, ואפילו אימא דאימך, ואפילו עומדת על קברה. דאמרי אינשי: בת שיתין כבת שית, לקל טבלא רהטא. § "ר' יהודה אומר לא תסוד". § תניא, רבי יהודה אומר: *אשה לא תסוד, (א) מפני שניוול הוא לה. ומודה ר' יהודה בבסיד שיכולה לקפלו במועד שטופלתו במועד, שאע"פ שמצירה היא עכשיו – שמחה היא לאחר זמן. ומי אית ליה לרבי יהודה האי סברא? והתנן, *רבי יהודה אומר: נפרעין מהן מפני שמצר. גאמרו לו: אע"פ שמצר עכשיו – שמח הוא לאחר זמן! אמר רב נחמן בר יצחק: הנח להלכות מועד, דכולהו מצר עכשיו ושמח לאחר זמן נינהו. רבינא אמר: גוי לענין פרעון לעולם מצר. *אמר רב יהודה: בנות ישראל שהגיעו לפירקן ולא הגיעו לשנים, עניות – טופלות אותן בסיד, עשירות – טופלות אותן בסולת, בנות מלכים – בשמן המור, שנאמר: °"ששה חדשים בשמן המור". *מאי שמן המור? רב הונא בר חייא אמר: סטכת. *)רב ירמיה בר אמי אמר: שמן זית שלא הביא שליש. תניא, רבי יהודה אומר: אנפיקנון – שמן זית שלא הביא שליש. ולמה סכין אותו – שמשיר את השער ומעדן את הבשר. *רב ביבי הוה ליה ברתא, טפלה אבר אבר, שקל בה ד' מאה זוזי. הוה ההוא גוי בשבבותיה דה"ל ברתא, טפלה בחד זמנא – ומתה. אמר: קטלא ביבי לברתי. אמר רב נחמן: רב ביבי דשתי שיכרא – בעיין בנתיה טפלא, אנן דלא שתינן שיכרא. לא בעיין בנתין טפלא. §

משלי ג | שם ח | תהלים מט | יואל ב | אסתר ב | [בבא מציעא פ: פ"ב]

ההדיוט

וּבמצוה שא"א לעשותה ע"י אחרים. אל תפלס. אלא מצוה שבאה לידך, בין גדולה בין קטנה – עשה: וכל חפציך לא ישוו בה. שתבטל כל חפציך בשביל שתעסוק בתורה: חפצי שמים ישוו בה. כלומר, שאם יש לך לעסוק במצוה – תבטל תלמוד תורה, ועסוק במצוה: דאפילו חפצי שמים לא. דמבטל מצוה ועוסק בתלמוד תורה: תעייל ולא תיפוק תיפוק ולא תעייל. משמע ליה בסחורה; תעייל ולא תיפוק – שתביא סחורה ולא תמכרנה, תיפוק ולא תעייל – שתוליא בסחורה במקום אחר ולא תביאנה: תעייל כלתא. שדרך כלתא הולכת אצל הבעל: ולא תיפוק. דלא לימות בנך, דהדרי נפקי מינך והדרי לבי נשייהו: שתא חדתא. זו שנה ראשונה של נישואין, דכתיב: "כי יקח איש אשה חדשה לא יצא" וגו' (דברים כד): ליחרב ביתך. בית קברתך. דלא תמות, אלא תחיה לאורך ימים: לא תבוש ולא תתבייש. לא תיבוש אחרים, כדי שלא תתבייש, שלא תבא לידי כך פן תתבייש: ותנא בה. ושנה בה: "לא יבושו עמי לעולם" והיינו: לא תבייש ולא תתבייש: כוחלת. נותנת כחול בין עיניה, כדי שדומות נאים: פוקסת. מחלקת שערה לכאן ולכאן*: ומעברת סרק על פניה. סם אחד, כדי שתראה אדומה: סכין על פניה של מטה. כדי להעביר שער של מטה: היתה מיקשטא. כי הני קשוטין, כדאמר הכא: באנפי כלתה. שהיתה כל כך זקינה שהיתה לה כלה, שהיא אשת בנה: לא שנו. הא דאמר עושה אשה תכשיטיה: אלא ילדה. בחורה, שדרכה בכך, ולהכי הוי לה שמחה במועד: אבל זקינה לא. והיכי עבדא אשתך הכי, דמיקשטא? הא הויא זקינה! ואפילו עומדת על פתח קברה. שריא להתקשט: לקל טבלא רהטא. פירוש: קשקוש הזוג. ר"ל: מיני זמר בהילולא. וכי היכי דרהטא ילדה בת שית לקל הילולא – הכי עבדא (ב) בת שיתין, והכי נמי מיקשטא: שניוול הוא לה. שגנאי הוא לה וניוול בסיד, ומלטטרת בסיד: שיכולה לקפלו במועד. אע"פ שהיא מנוולת בסיד: שמחה היא לאחר זמן. במועד. לסוף המועד, לאחר שקפלתו את הסיד שטפלה. לפי שמשיר את השער ומעדן את הבשר. והואיל דהאי סיד משמחתה לאחר זמן – להכי שרי לה לטופלו במועד, אע"פ שהיא מלירה עכשיו: ומי אית ליה לרבי יהודה האי סברא. אע"ג שהיא מלירה עכשיו שמחה וכו': נפרעים מהם. מהגוים ביום חגם, מפני שהוא מלער. דכל אדם שפורע מילר. אבל לא משלמים להם ממון ביום חגם – לפי שמשמח ביום חגם, ומודה לע"ז, כדפי' במס' ע"ז: שמח הוא לאחר זמן. שפרע לו. ואמאי נפרע מהן? אבל לרבי יהודה לא אית ליה האי סברא דמשום שמילר עכשיו שרי, והיכי אית ליה האי סברא גבי טפול, אע"ג שהיא מלירה עכשיו שמחה היא לאחר זמן? הנח להלכות מועד. להכי א"ר יהודה הכא דשרי אע"פ שהיא מלירה כו': דכולהו הלכות מועד. דשרי, משום האי טעמא נמי שרו כגון אפייה ובישול, דמלער השפחה כשהוא אופה ומבשל. ולהכי שרי, דשמח הוא כשהוא אוכל אפייתו ובישולו בי"ט: גוי לעולם מיצר. שפורע. ולהכי לא אית ליה לר' יהודה התם אף על פי שמילר שמח וכו'. אבל לעיל, גבי טפול – אית ליה לר' יהודה אע"פ שמלירה עכשיו שמחה לאחר זמן: שהגיעו לפירקן. לשיער: ולא הגיעו לשנים. שאינן בנות י"ב שנה ויום אחד, שעדיין אינו דין שיהא להן שער ובושות על כך: עניות טופלות. השיער בסיד ומשירות אותן: אנפיקנון. היינו אנפיקינון דקתני התם במנחות (דף פה:): אנפיקינון לא יביא, היינו אותו שמן שעושין מזיתים: שלא הביאו שליש. שלא בישלו שליש: ולמה סכין אותו. אלא הני קא מהדר, דקאמר טופלין כו': ושקל בה ארבע מאה זוזי. שנתייפת, ונטל מבעלה כך: טפלה כולה בחד זימנא. דסבר למיעבד כרב ביבי, ומתה: בעיין בנתין טפלא. דשכר מגדל השער ומעבה את הבשר:

תופר

כאן במצוה שאי אפשר לעשותה ע"י אחרים. עשיית מלוה עדיף, שהרי מפסיקין אפילו לר"ש בן יוחי לעושה סוכה ולולב, כדאי' בירושלמי.* אבל בהפסקה דתפלה ⊕וק"ש אין מפסיקין לר"ש בן יוחי. (ג) א] ובירושלמי: זה שנינו וזה שנינו, ואין מפסיקין שנינו מפני שנינו:

פוקסת. פי' בקונטרס: מתקנת שער שלא יתפזר. וקשה: דבפרק "המלניע" (שבת דף לד: ושם) אמר (ד) דמתחייב בשבת משום טוה. ועוד, דסורקת ה"ל למיתני, כמו גבי נזיר (נזיר מב.). ובפ' קמא דכתובות (דף ד: ושם) *פירש בקונטרס: קליעת שער. וקשיא: דבפרק "המלניע" שונה גודלת ופוקסת. ואין לפרש מעברת סרק על פניה – דהכא תני תרוייהו, וגם בפ' *קמא דכתובות. ויש לפרש: דמתקנת שערה בידיה חוץ לצעיף. וריב"א מפרש: שנותנת חוטין של בצק (ה) [דקין] על פניה להאדיס הבשר, והיינו טוייה. והאי דקורא ליה בירושלמי לובע – שהוא מאדים הבשר. ובנין נמי שייך בתיקון האשה, לאמר דמפורש סוף "המלניע" (שבת דף לה.) משום בונה, ומייתי קרא ד"ויבן את הצלע": סטכת. בפרק "כל הקרבנות" (מנחות דף פו.) מפרש דשמן המור הוא סטכת. ובפ' קמא דמגילה (דף יג.): מאי שמן המור? רב הונא אמר רבי חייא: סטכת:

רבינו חננאל

אבל מצוה שאי אפשר לעשותה ע"י אחרים אורח חיים פן תפלס. תוב כתיב יקרה היא מפנינים וכל חפציך לא ישוו בה הא חפצי שמים ישוו בה במצוה (שאפשר) [שאי אפשר] לעשותה ע"י אחרים. כל חפצים לא ישוו בה במצוה (שאי אפשר) [שאפשר] לעשות' ע"י אחרים אמר להו אבא שדרני לגביכו דתתברכון יתי אמרו ליה תהא רעוא דתזרע ולא תחצד פי' דתוליד בנים ולא תקברם תעייל ולא תיפוק תעייל כלתך לביתך ולא תוציאם תיפוק ולא תעייל תוציא בנות לבית בעליהן ולא ימותו בעליהן וישובו אליך ליחרב ביתך וליתוב אושפיזך. פי' יהיה ביתך חרבה והוא מקום קברך שאתה עתיד להקבר בו כי הוא מקום של אדם. כלומר תאריך ימים בעולם הזה הנקרא אושפיזא. וישאר מקום קברך חרב הנקרא ביתך שנאמר קרבם בתימו לעולם. ליבלבל פתורך. כלומר יהיו לך בנים הרבה ויבלבלו שלחנך ולא תיחזי שתא חדתא דלא תימות אתתך ותיתב אחריתי א"ל ר' לבריה זיל לגביה ר"ש בן חלפתא דליברכך אזל לגביה א"ל תהא רעוא דלא תיבוש ולא תתבייש. א"ל אבוה ברי ברכך ברכתא דברכינהו הקדוש ב"ה לישראל ותנא ביה שנא' ואכלתם אכול ושבוע וגו': ועושה תכשיטיה במועד: ת"ר אלו הן תכשיטי נשים גודלת כוחלת פוקסת *) נוטלת שערה וציפרניה ומעברת שרק על פניה איכא דאמרי מעברת סכין על פניה של מטה. דביתהו דרב חסדא הוה מתקשטא באנפי כלותיה כו'. ואפי' עומדת על פתח קברה דאמרי אינשי בת שיתין כבת שית לקל טבלא רהטא. ר"י אומר לא תסוד כו'. תניא ר' יהודה אומר אשה לא תסוד במועד מפני שניול הוא לה אם היא תשאר בסיד. ומודה בסיד שיכולה לקפלו במועד שטופלתו במועד ואע"פ שמצירה עכשיו שמחה היא לאחר זמן. ומי אית ליה לר' יהודה האי סברא והתנן במס' ע"ז ר' יהודה אומר נפרעין מהן מפני שהוא מיצר כו'. ופירק רב נחמן בר יצחק הנח להלכות מועד דכולהו אע"פ שמצירות עכשיו שמחות לאחר זמן. אמר רב יהודה אמר רב בנות ישראל שהגיעו לפירקן ולא הגיעו לשנים עניות טופלות אותן בסיד עשירות בסולת בנות מלכים בשמן המור והוא סטכת איכא דאמרי שמן זית שלא הביא שליש. תניא אפיקנון שמן זית שלא הביא שליש סכין אותו שמשיר

*) כ"ה נוסחת הברייתא בירושלמי כאן הלכה ז':

[פ"ק דשבת סוף הלכה ב]

פו א ב מיי' פ"ג מהל' יום טוב הלכה כ סמג לאוין עה טוש"ע א"ח סי' תקמו סעיף ה:

פז ג מיי' פ"ט מהלכות ע"ז הלכה א סמג לאוין מה טוש"ע י"ד סי' קמח סעיף ח:

נ"ל מפרש בגמ' דפוקסת היינו פירכוס וסס יז. פי' בקונט' דפירכוס היינו קליעת שער ע"ש תוס' ז: ד"ה פוקסת

[נ"ל שני]

רש"א

הגהות הגר"א

[א] גמ' וא"ד מעברת סכין ע"פ של מטה כנ"ל. (וכ"ה ברש"י ורי"ף ורא"ש ומרדכי):

הגהות מהר"ב רנשבורג

א] תוס' ד"ה כאן במצוה שאי אפשר וכו' ובירושלמי זה שנינו וכו'. הוא מלשון ושננתם כמ"ש מהרש"א. וכן הוא בלשון הירושלמי הנ"ל זה שינון וזה שינון:

גליון הש"ס

תוס' ד"ה כאן במצוה וכו' וק"ש אין מפסיקין. להדיא איתא בשבת דף יא ע"א דלק"ש מפסיקין וצ"ע:

כן פי' הערוך ערך פקס ועיין פי' רש"י שבת סד: ד"ה ולא תפקוס ושני הפירושים שהביא שם לז: ד"ה וכן הפוקסת

[נ"ל לבריה כ"ה בע"י]

[כי]

[נ"ל שרק עי' רש"י וכן גי' הערוך]

ע"ז ו:

שם ב.

שבת פ: ע"ש פסחי' מג. ע"ש

מגילה יג. מנחות פו. ע"ש

*) [עי' רש"י מנחות פו. ד"ה סטכתא]

הגהות הב"ח

(א) גמ' אשה לא תסוד במועד מפני שניוול כו' מפני שמילר הוא אמרו לו אע"פ שמילר הוא עכשיו שמח: (ב) רש"י ד"ה לקל טבלא כו' הכי עבדא לרהוט בת שיתין: (ג) תוס' ד"ה כאן כו' בן יוחי כדאמרינן בירושלמי זה שננו: (ד) ד"ה פוקסת כו' דבפרק המלניע אמר דפוקסת מתחייבת בשבת: (ה) בא"ד חוטין של בצק והוא תקון על פניה:

"הַהֶדְיוֹט תּוֹפֵר כְּדַרְכּוֹ".§ הֵיכִי דָּמֵי הֶדְיוֹט? אָמְרִי דְּבֵי רַבִּי יַנַּאי: כָּל שֶׁאֵינוֹ יָכוֹל לְהוֹצִיא מְלֹא מַחַט בְּבַת אַחַת. רַבִּי יוֹסֵי בַּר חֲנִינָא אָמַר: כָּל שֶׁאֵינוֹ יָכוֹל לְכַוֵּין אִימְרָא בְּחֵפֶת חֲלוּקוֹ.§ "וְהָאוּמָּן מַכְלִיב".§ מַאי מַכְלִיב? רַבִּי יוֹחָנָן אָמַר: מַפְסִיעַ, רַבָּה בַּר שְׁמוּאֵל אָמַר: שִׁינֵּי כַּלְבְּתָא.§ "מְסָרְגִין אֶת הַמִּטּוֹת".§ מַאי מְסָרְגִין וּמַאי מְמַתְּחִין? כִּי אֲתָא רַב דִּימִי אֲמַר: פְּלִיגִי בָּהּ ר' חִיָּיא בַּר אַבָּא וְר' אַסִּי, וְתַרְוַיְיהוּ מִשְּׁמֵיהּ דְּחִזְקִיָּה וְר' יוֹחָנָן; חַד אָמַר: מְסָרְגִין – שְׁתִי וָעֵרֶב, וּמְמַתְּחִין – שְׁתִי בְּלֹא עֵרֶב. וְחַד אָמַר: מְסָרְגִין שְׁתִי בְּלֹא עֵרֶב, וּמְמַתְּחִין – שֶׁאִם הָיָה רָפוּי מְמַתְּחוֹ. אִינִי? וְהָא תָּנֵי רַב תַּחְלִיפָא בַּר שָׁאוּל: וְשָׁוִין שֶׁאֵין מַפְשִׁילִין חֲבָלִים לְכַתְּחִלָּה. בִּשְׁלָמָא לְמַאן דְּאָמַר מְסָרְגִין שְׁתִי וָעֵרֶב, וּמְמַתְּחִין שְׁתִי בְּלֹא עֵרֶב – הַיְינוּ דְּקָתָנֵי רַב תַּחְלִיפָא בַּר שָׁאוּל: אוְשָׁוִין שֶׁאֵין מַפְשִׁילִין חֲבָלִים לְכַתְּחִלָּה. אֶלָּא לְמַאן דְּאָמַר: מְסָרְגִין – שְׁתִי בְּלֹא עֵרֶב, מְמַתְּחִין – שֶׁאִם הָיָה רָפוּי הָיָה מְמַתְּחוֹ. הַשְׁתָּא שְׁתִי וָעֵרֶב אָמְרַתְּ לָא, חֲבָלִים לְכַתְּחִלָּה מִיבַּעְיָא! קַשְׁיָא. א"ל רַב נַחְמָן בַּר יִצְחָק לְרַבִּי חִיָּיא בַּר אָבִין: מִי אִיכָּא לְמַאן דְּאָמַר מְסָרְגִין שְׁתִי בְּלֹא עֵרֶב? וְהָתְנַן, *רַבִּי מֵאִיר אוֹמֵר: הַמִּטָּה – מִשֶּׁיִּסְרוֹג בָּהּ שְׁלֹשָׁה בָּתִּים! אֶלָּא, כִּי אֲתָא רָבִין אֲמַר: בִּמְסָרְגִין – כּוּלֵּי עָלְמָא לָא פְּלִיגִי דִּשְׁתִי וָעֵרֶב. אֶלָּא כִּי פְּלִיגִי – בִּמְמַתְּחִין, מָר סָבַר: מְמַתְּחִין שְׁתִי בְּלֹא עֵרֶב, וּמָר סָבַר: שֶׁאִם הָיָה רָפוּי – מְמַתְּחוֹ. מֵיתִיבִי: מְסָרְגִין אֶת הַמִּטָּה וְאֵין צָרִיךְ לוֹמַר שֶׁמְּמַתְּחִין, דִּבְרֵי ר' מֵאִיר. ר' יוֹסֵי אוֹמֵר: מְמַתְּחִין, אֲבָל לֹא מְסָרְגִין. וְי"א: אֵין מְמַתְּחִין כָּל עִיקָּר. בִּשְׁלָמָא לְמַאן דְּאָמַר מְמַתְּחִין שְׁתִי בְּלֹא עֵרֶב – הַיְינוּ דְּאָתוּ יֵשׁ אוֹמְרִים לְאִיפְּלוּגֵי. אֶלָּא לְמַאן דְּאָמַר שֶׁאִם הָיָה רָפוּי מְמַתְּחוֹ, לְיֵשׁ אוֹמְרִים מְמַתְּחוֹ נַמִי לָא? אִין, כֵּיוָן דְּאֶפְשָׁר לְמַמְלְיֵיהּ בְּמָאנֵי – לָא טָרְחִינַן.§

מתני' • במַעֲמִידִין תַּנּוּר וְכִירַיִם גוְרֵיחַיִם בַּמּוֹעֵד. ר' יְהוּדָה אוֹמֵר: אֵין מְכַבְּשִׁין אֶת הָרֵיחַיִם בַּתְּחִילָּה.§

גמ' מַאי מְכַבְּשִׁין? רַב יְהוּדָה אָמַר: מְנַקֵּר רֵיחַיָא, רַב יְחִיאֵל אָמַר: בַּת עֵינָא. מֵיתִיבִי: מַעֲמִידִין תַּנּוּר וְכִירַיִם בַּמּוֹעֵד, וּבִלְבַד שֶׁלֹּא יִגְמוֹר מְלַאכְתָּן, דִּבְרֵי רַבִּי אֱלִיעֶזֶר. וַחֲכָמִים אוֹמְרִים: אַף יִגְמוֹר. רַבִּי יְהוּדָה אוֹמֵר מִשְּׁמוֹ: מַעֲמִידִין אֶת הַחֲדָשָׁה, וּמְכַבְּשִׁין אֶת הַיְשָׁנָה. וְיֵשׁ אוֹמְרִים: אֵין מְכַבְּשִׁין כָּל עִיקָּר. בִּשְׁלָמָא לְמַאן דְּאָמַר מְכַבְּשִׁין מְנַקֵּר רֵיחַיָא – הַיְינוּ דְּמַשְׁכַּחַתְּ לָהּ בִּישָׁנָה. אֶלָּא לְמַאן דְּאָמַר בַּת עֵינָא – יְשָׁנָה, בַּת עֵינָא לָמָּה לָהּ? כְּגוֹן דְּקָא בָּעֵי לְאַרְווֹחֵי טְפֵי פּוּרְתָּא. רַב הוּנָא שְׁמָעֵיהּ לְהַהוּא גַּבְרָא דְּקָא מְנַקֵּר רֵיחַיָא בְּחוּלָּא דְּמוֹעֲדָא, אֲמַר: מַאן הַאי? *אִיתְחִיל גּוּפֵיהּ דְּקָא מְחִיל חוּלָּא דְּמוֹעֲדָא. סָבַר לָהּ כְּיֵשׁ אוֹמְרִים. דָּרַשׁ רַב חָמָא: דנוֹקְרִין רֵיחַיִם בַּמּוֹעֵד. מִשּׁוּם (א) רַבִּי מֵאִיר אָמַר: אֲפִילּוּ סוּס שֶׁרוֹכֵב עָלָיו וַחֲמוֹר שֶׁרוֹכֵב עָלָיו ה(*וּמוּתָּר) לִיטּוֹל צִפָּרְנַיִם בְּחוּלּוֹ שֶׁל מוֹעֵד

אֲבָל

רש"י

תּוֹפֵר כְּדַרְכּוֹ. בְּחוּלּוֹ שֶׁל מוֹעֵד: הֵיכִי דָּמֵי הֶדְיוֹט. שֶׁאֵינוֹ אוּמָּן, שֶׁתּוֹפֵר כְּדַרְכּוֹ: מְלֹא מַחַט בְּבַת אַחַת. שֶׁאֵינוֹ יָכוֹל לִלְקוֹט נִימֵי הַתְּפִירָה שֶׁל חָלוּק כְּדֵי לִתְפּוֹר. כְּשֶׁהוּא תּוֹפֵר תּוֹחֵב תְּחִיבוֹת הַרְבֵּה כִּמְלֹא אוֹרֶךְ הַמַּחַט, וְאַחַ"כ מוֹשְׁכָהּ מִן הַבֶּגֶד, וְנִמְלְאוּ תְּפִירוֹת הַרְבֵּה בִּמְשִׁיכָה אַחַת. וְהַיּוֹדֵעַ לַעֲשׂוֹת כֵּן – אוּמָּן הוּא: שֶׁאֵינוֹ יָכוֹל לְכַוֵּין אִימְרָא בְּחֵפֶת חֲלוּקוֹ. שֶׁאֵינוֹ יוֹדֵעַ לִתְחוֹב אוֹתוֹ בֶּגֶד עַד שֶׁעוֹשִׂין מִמֶּנּוּ אִימְרָא בְּחֵפֶת חֲלוּקוֹ, אֶלָּא שֶׁבְּמָקוֹם אֶחָד מְקַצְּרוֹ וּבְמָקוֹם אֶחָד מַרְחִיבוֹ: הָאוּמָּן. הַחַיָּיט מַכְלִיב: מַפְסִיעַ. שֶׁאֵינוֹ תּוֹפֵר בְּיוֹשֶׁר, אֶלָּא מְפַזֵּר הַתְּפִירָה. וּלְהָכִי קָרֵי מַכְלִיב – שֶׁדּוֹמִין תְּחוּבֵי הַמַּחַט לְשִׁינֵּי הַכֶּלֶב, רְחוֹקוֹת זוֹ מִזּוֹ כְּשִׁינֵּי הַכֶּלֶב: כַּלְבְּתָא. שֶׁאֵינוֹ תּוֹפֵר כְּדַרְכּוֹ, (ב)תּוֹחֵב זֶה בְּסָמוּךְ זֶה, אֶלָּא שֶׁתּוֹחֵב הַמַּחַט פַּעַם אַחַת לְמַעְלָה וּפַעַם אַחַת לְמַטָּה. וּלְהָכִי קָרֵי לֵיהּ כַּלְבְּתָא, דְּהָכִי קָיְימִי שִׁינֵּי הַכֶּלֶב – שֵׁן אֶחָד גָּבוֹהַּ מֵחֲבֵירוֹ: מְסָרְגִין שְׁתִי וָעֵרֶב. שֶׁאוֹרְגִין מִטָּה שֶׁל חֲבָלִים בִּשְׁתִי וָעֵרֶב: שְׁתִי בְּלֹא עֵרֶב. שֶׁמּוֹתֵחַ הַשְּׁתִי, וְאֵינוֹ אוֹרֵג בָּהּ הָעֵרֶב: שֶׁאִם הָיָה רָפוּי. זֶה שֶׁנֶּאֱרַג יָמִים רַבִּים, וְהָיוּ הַחֲבָלִים רְפוּיִין וּתְלוּיִין לְמַטָּה, שֶׁאֵינָן מְתוּחִין – מְמַתְּחָן: וְשָׁוִין. רַבִּי מֵאִיר וְר' יוֹסֵי: שֶׁאֵין מַפְשִׁילִין חֲבָלִים לְכַתְּחִלָּה. שֶׁאֵין גּוֹדְלִים חֲבָלִים לְכַתְּחִלָּה: הַמִּטָּה. לְעוֹלָם אֵינָהּ מְקַבֶּלֶת טוּמְאָה עַד שֶׁיִּסָּרֵג בָּהּ ג' בָּתֵּי נִירִין. שֶׁהַשְּׁתִי כְּבָר מָתוּחַ, וְאוֹרֵג בָּהּ שְׁלֹשָׁה בָּתֵּי נִירִין דְּעֵרֶב. אַלְמָא, דִּמְסָרְגִין קָרֵי שְׁתִי וָעֵרֶב: הַיְינוּ דְּאָתוּ יֵשׁ אוֹמְרִים לְאִפְּלוּגֵי. דַּאֲפִילּוּ שְׁתִי בְּלֹא עֵרֶב לָא מָצֵי: מְמַתֵּחַ נַמִּי לָא. בִּתְמִיהָ: אָתוּ יֵשׁ אוֹמְרִים לְמֵיסַר נַמִּי מַתּוּחֵי? וְאַמַּאי הָא לָא קָעָבֵיד מְלָאכָה! וְאִי לָא עָבֵיד הָכִי – לָא מָצֵי לְמִיזְגָא עֲלַהּ: אִין. וַדַּאי אָתוּ יֵשׁ אוֹמְרִים לְמֵיסַר נַמִּי מַתּוּחֵי, מִשּׁוּם דְּהוֹאִיל וְאֶפְשָׁר לְמַלְיֵיהּ לְמַטָּה בְּמָאנֵי עַד לְעֵיל, וְהָדַר מָצֵי לְמִירְמָא עֲלַיְיהוּ כָּרִים וּכְסָתוֹת לְמִיזְגָא עֲלַיְיהוּ: לָא טָרְחִינַן. דְּהָוֵי טוֹרַח דְּלָא צָרִיךְ: **מתני'** מַעֲמִידִין תַּנּוּר וְכִירַיִם. שֶׁעוֹשִׂין אוֹתָם לְכַתְּחִלָּה, כִּדְאָמְרִינַן לְקַמָּן. תַּנּוּר – תּוֹכוֹ חָלוּל, מְקוֹם שְׁפִיתַת (ג)שְׁתֵּי קְדֵירוֹת. כִּירָה – מְקוֹם שְׁפִיתַת קְדֵירָה אַחַת: מְכַבְּשִׁין. אבַּגְּמָ' מְפָרֵשׁ: **גמ'** מְנַקֵּר רֵיחַיָא. שֶׁכְּשֶׁהִיא יְשָׁנָה וַחֲלָקָה וְאֵין הַחִטִּין יְכוֹלִין לִפְרוֹךְ – מְנַקְּרִין אוֹתָהּ, חוֹתְכִין אוֹתָהּ כְּדֵי שֶׁלֹּא יְהֵא שָׁוֶה, כְּדֵי שֶׁיִּפָּרְכוּ הַחִטִּין תַּחְתֶּיהָ: בַּת עֵינָא. נֶקֶב שֶׁעוֹשִׂין בְּאֶמְצַע הָרֵיחַיִם, שֶׁהַתְּבוּאָה נוֹפֶלֶת לְתוֹכָהּ: הַיְינוּ דְּמַשְׁכַּחַתְּ לָהּ בִּישָׁנָה. לְפִי שֶׁהַיְשָׁנָה צְרִיכָה לְכָךְ, שֶׁכְּבָר הִיא חֲלָקָה, לְפִי שֶׁתָּדִיר הִיא טוֹחֶנֶת: אֶלָּא לְמַאן דְּאָמַר. דִּמְכַבְּשִׁין הַיְינוּ בַּת עֵינָא, יְשָׁנָה בַּת עֵינָא לָמָּה? וַהֲלֹא כְּבָר אִית לָהּ בַּת עֵינָא, שֶׁכְּבָר הִיא יְשָׁנָה מִלִּטְחוֹן, וְאִי לָא הֲוֵי לָהּ בַּת עֵינָא – לָא מָצֵי לְמִיטְחַן: כְּגוֹן דְּבָעֵי לְאַרְווֹחֵי. הַאי בַּת עֵינָא טְפֵי, וְכִי הַאי גַּוְונָא מַשְׁכַּחַתְּ לָהּ בִּישָׁנָה: מְנַקֵּר רֵיחַיָא. בִּישָׁנָה: אִיתְחִיל גּוּפֵיהּ. יִתְחַלֵּל גּוּפוֹ: מוּתָּר לִיטּוֹל. לָהֶן לְפָרְנַיִם כְּדֶרֶךְ הָעוֹשִׂין עַכְשָׁיו לַסּוּסִים שֶׁלָּנוּ, דְּאִי לָא עָבֵיד לֵיהּ הָכִי – הָוֵה לֵיהּ צַעֲרָא, וְלָא מָצֵי אָזֵיל:

אֲבָל

תוספות

ההדיוט תופר כדרכו. נראה, דוקא לצורך המועד, אבל בחנם – למה יתירו אפילו על ידי שינוי? מיהו, לא איירי בדבר האבד. דהיכא דאיכא דבר האבד – קיימא לן כר' יוסי, דאין מצריך שינוי בדבר האבד. והיכא דבגדיו או מנעליו מקורעין, ואם יניח אותן עד לאחר מועד יתקלקלו – ראיתי רבותי שאין מקילין כלל להתיר, אפילו על ידי נכרי, כדאמרינן לקמן (דף יב.): כל שאינו עושה – אינו אומר לנכרי ועושה. ושמא לא היו חושבים אותו דבר האבד, או שמא אין כל דבר האבד מותר בלא שינוי, דבפ' "מקום שנהגו" (פסחים דף נה:) משמע: דוקא עולי רגלים מתקנין מנעלים במועד*:

במסרגין כולי עלמא לא פליגי דשתי וערב. תימה: היאך מותר לעשות מלאכה כי האי בלא שינוי? **ממתוחי** נמי לא. בלאו הכי נמי נראה דמצי לאקשויי: היכי קאמר ר' יוסי שאם היה רפוי ממתחו, אבל לא מסרגין שתי וערב? הא אפילו בשתי בלא ערב אסור!

כיון דאפשר למלויי במאני. משמע דאין מותר אלא לצורך המועד:

ה"ג: **רבי** יהודה אומר אין מכבשין את הריחים בתחילה. ובחדשה קאמר. דהא בגמרא מתיר ישנה. ואין נראה לומר דבגמ' דמתיר ישנה משום ר' אליעזר קאמר, והא משמיה דידיה. כי למה נדחוק לעשות מחלוקת חנם? ועוד: דלכתחילה משמע חדשה. ואם תאמר: כבוש מאן דכר שמיה? י"ל: תנא קמא אמר מעמידין, ובחדשה קאמר, ומשמע אפילו כבוש. ור' יהודה אוסר בכבוש. ואית דגרים: ר' יהודה אומר מכבשין את הריחים, ולא גרס לכתחילה, והיא היא, אבל עתה קשיא יותר כבוש מאן דכר שמיה. תנא קמא נמי שרי! יש לומר: דת"ק שרי העמדה בעלמא, שאין זה בנין גמור, (ד)וה"ה דאסר כבוש בין בחדשה בין בישנה. ור' יהודה שרי כבוש בישנה. וגירסא ראשונה נראה לרבי. ומעמידין – נראה דוקא העמדה דתנור אין זה בנין בתחילה, אלא הוא עשוי כבר, אבל אינו מחובר בקרקע וצריך לחברו ולטפלו בארץ, כדמפרש בפרק "כל הכלים" (שבת דף קכה.). אי נמי: כי ההוא דפ' "המביא כדי יין" (ביצה לד.) גבי תנור, דבי"ט אין סכין אותו ואין טשין אותו במטלית וכו' – הכא במועד שרי. ולקמן בשמעתין נמי קאמר: ושוין שאין גודלים תנור בתחילה, ובירושלמי תני ר' חלפתא: ובלבד שלא יגלחנו בתחילה. ופירש בתוספ' דלא ידע מאי גילות. ול"נ: דגרסינן שלא יגדלנו: **סום** שרוכב עליו. פי' בתוספתא: לצורך המועד. משמע שאסור לרכוב בחנם: למישקל

רבינו חננאל

שמשיר את השיער ומעדן את הבשר: ההדיוט תופר כדרכו בתלמו"ד א"י מפור"ש לפיכ"ך כתבנ"ו והנחנ"ו ז"ה. דבי ר' ינאי אמרי כדרכו ממלא את המחט. מכליב אחת אחת ר' יוחנן א' כדרכו (אפי') אחת אחת. מכליב. מפסיע. כלומר מדלג. מתני' מסייע לר' יוחנן הרצענין מכלבין במועד אין תימר חדא חדא היינו אורחייהו כך היא אומנותן *) של מפסע. ר' יוסי ב"ר חנינא אומר המזווג את האמריות **) זהו אומן וכל מי שאינו מזווג אינו אומן א"ר סימון הדיוט תופר כיסין כיסין. מסרגין את המטות. ר' יוסי אומר ממתחין. ר' חייא בר אבא ור' אמי פליגי תרוייהו משום דחזקיה ור' יוחנן (אמרו) חד אמר מסרגין כגון אריגה שתי וערב ממתחין שתי בלא ערב. וחד אמר מסרגין שתי בלא ערב. ממתחין שאם היה רפוי ממתחו. איני והתני ר' חלפתא בן שאול ושוין פי' ת"ק ור' יוסי שאין מפשילין חבלים לכתחלה. ומתמה רב נחמן בר יצחק מי איכא מ"ד מסרגין שתי בלא ערב. והתנן ר"מ אומר המטה משיסרוג בה שלשה בתים מי אפשר לעשות בית בלא שתי וערב אלא כ"ע מסרגין שתי וערב כי פליגי בממתחין. ולא איפשיט לן בהדיא האי מיתוח מה הוא אי שתי בלא ערב. או אם היה רפוי ממתחו. אפשר למימליא במני. אפשר למלאות רפיון חבלי המטה בכסתות הרבה: [מתני'] מעמידין תנור וכירים במועד ר"י אומר אין מכבשין את הריחים במועד בתחלה. מאי מכבשין. רב יהודה אמר מנקר ריחיא פי' כיון שיעמדו הריחים מלטחון מנקרין בהן נקרין קטנים כמין חידודין כדי לטחון במהרה רב יחיאל אמר בת עינא. ומקשינן עליה דרב יחיאל ומפרק כגון דנקרה ובעי לארווחי בי טפי רב הונא שמע להוא גברא דהוה מנקר ריחיא בחולו של מועד אמר מאן האי דמחיל י"ט ליתחיל גופיה. ורב הונא סבר לה כי"א דאמרו אין מכבשין כל עיקר. דרש רב חמא נוקרין ריחים בחולו של מועד משום רבינו אמרו אפי' סוס שרוכב עליו וחמור

עין משפט נר מצוה

פח א טוש"ע א"ח סי' תקמה סעיף ב:

פט ב מיי' פ"ח מהלכות י"ט הלכה יג טוש"ע שם סי' תקמ סעיף ז:

צ ג ד מיי' שם טור ש"ע שם סעיף ח:

צא ה מיי' שם הלכה טו טוש"ע שם סי' תקלו סעיף א:

[וע"ש בפסחים תוס' ד"ה עולי רגלים]

מסורת הש"ם

כלים פט"ז מ"א

[עירובין קד.]

[נ"ל מותר]

הגהות הב"ח

(א) גמ' נוקרין ריחים במועד משום רבינו אמרו (אפילו) תז"מ ונ"ב בס"א ל"ג ליה. עוד נ"ב ונראה דרבינו הוא רב ועי' במ"ק פ' לולב הגזול דף לג ע"א אפרש"י רבינו רבי שם הארכתי על זה: (ב) רש"י ד"ה כלבתא כו' כדרכו לתחוב זה: (ג) ד"ה מעמידין כו' מקום שפיתת קדירה אחת כירה מקום שפיתת שתי קדירות. נ"ב כ"ה בריש פ' כירה: (ד) תום' ד"ה ה"ג ר"י כו' שאין זה בנין גמור אבל בנין בתחילה אסור וה"ה לאסור כבוש:

גליון הש"ם

מתני' מעמידין תנור וכירים וריחים כצ"ל:

הגהות מהר"ב רנשבורג

א] רש"י ד"ה מכבשין בגמ' מפרש. נ"ב עי' נדה כו ע"ב בתוס' ד"ה בפלוגתא וכו' ועיין ודו"ק:

---

*) בירושלמי שם הגי' אלא כי אנן קיימין במפסיע. **) לפנינו בירושלמי איתא כל שהוא מזווג את האמריות זהו הדיוט ופשוט דטס"ה וצ"ל כגי' רבינו ז"ל.

אבל חמרא דריחיא – לא. רב יהודה שרי למישקל טופריה לחמרא דריחיא, ולאוקומי ריחיא, ולמיבני ריחיא, ולמיבני אמת ריחיא, ולמיבני אוריא. (*רבא) שרא לסרוקי סוסיא, ולמיבני אקרפיטא, ולמיבני איצטבא. רבא שרא למישקל דמא לבהמה בחולא דמועדא. א"ל אביי: תניא דמסייע לך: מקיזין דם לבהמה, ואין מונעין רפואה לבהמה בחולו של מועד. רבא שרא לכסכוסי קירמי. מ"ט – מעשה הדיוט הוא. אמר רב יצחק בר אמי אמר רב חסדא: *קיטורי *בירי [ו] – אסיר, מ"ט – מעשה אומן הוא. אמר רבא: *מאן דמתקיל (א) ארעא, אדעתא דבי דרי – שרי, אדעתא דארעא – אסיר. היכי דמי? מוליא *במוליא ונצא בנצא (ב) – אדעתא דבי דרי, שקל מוליא ושדא בנצא – אדעתא דארעא. ואמר רבא: האי מאן דזכי זיכי אדעתא דציבי – שרי, אדעתא דארעא – אסיר. *היכי דמי? שקיל רברבי ושביק זוטרי – אדעתא דציבי, שקל רברבי וזוטרי – אדעתא דארעא. ואמר רבא: האי מאן דפתח מיא לארעיה, אדעתא דכוורי – שרי, אדעתא דארעא – אסיר. היכי דמי? *פתח תרי בבי, חד מעילאי וחד מתתאי – אדעתא דכוורי, פתח חד בבא – אדעתא דארעא. ואמר רבא: האי מאן דפשח דיקלא אדעתא דחיותא – שרי, אדעתא דדיקלא – אסיר. היכי דמי? *שקיל כוליה מחד גיסא – אדעתא דחיותא, מהאי גיסא ומהאי גיסא – אדעתא דדיקלא, ואסיר. ואמר רבא: הני תמרי תוחלני, מיגזרינהו – שרי, מייצינהו – אסיר. רב פפא אמר: כיון דמתלעי – *כפרקמטיא האבד דמי, ושרי. ואמר רבא: פרקמטיא כל שהוא אסור. א"ר יוסי בר אבין: ובדבר האבד – מותר. רבינא הוה ליה ההוא עיסקא דהוה מזדבן בשיתא אלפי, שהייה לזבוניה בתר חולא דמועדא וזבניה בתריסר אלפי. רבינא הוה מסיק זוזי בבני *אקרא דשנואתא, אתא לקמיה דרב אשי, א"ל: מהו למיזל האידנא עלייהו? א"ל: כיון דהאידנא הוא דמשכחת להו, ביומי אחריני לא משכחת להו – כפרקמטיא האבד דמי, ושרי. תניא נמי גבי ע"ז כי האי גוונא: הולכין ליריד

רש"י

אבל חמרא דריחיא. שכך עושין, שהיו טוחנים אגב חמורים – לא מלי למישקל להוא חמרא לפרניו. דלא מלי למטחן במועד אלא לצורך מועד, כדמפרש לקמן פרק "מי שהפך" (דף יב:). הלכך טחינה מועטת יכול לטחון בחמור ולא מרעי ליה גידול לפרניו: **לאוקומי ריחיא.** להעמיד, להשים הריחים זו על גב זו: **אמת ריחיא.** העץ שהריחים בנוי עליו: **ולמיבני אוריא.** רפת בקר: **לסרוקי סוסיא.** להסריק סוסים במסרק של ברזל: **למיבני אקורפיטא.** מה שמשימין התבואה לתוכו לפני הסוסים, שקורין מנייטור"ה בלע"ז: **איצטבא.** בנין אבנים: **למישקל דמא.** להקיז: **לכסכוסי.** גיהוץ, שקורין קודילו"ר: **קרמין.** *בגדים: **מעשה הדיוט.** דמותר לעשותו בחולו של מועד, דלאו מעשה אומן הוא: **קיטורי בירי אסיר.** למיעבד במועד. שכך היו עושין, שהיו נוטלין כלים חלוקין והיו מחליקין עליהן בית יד של חלוקיהם – מעשה אומן הוא ואסור. ל"א: לכוין קמטין שאדם עושה בבית יד, שממלאים אותה בקנה של שבלים חלקים ומקמטין, פרוונלי"א בלע"ז: **דמתקיל תיקלא.** שחופר משם האדמה לצורך הגורן לחבוט שם חטין לצורך המועד. היינו אדעתא דבי דרי, ושרי: **אדעתא דארעא.** שחופר שדהו לצורך זריעה – אסור, משום דדמי כחורש בי"ט: **מוליא במוליא.** שנוטל הקרקע ממקום גבוה, ומניחו שם על גבי מקום גבוה – היינו מליא במוליא: **או נצא בנצא.** שחופר במקום נמוך ומניחו במקום נמוך, דהיינו אדעתא דארעא – ואסור. דזה דרכו של חורש שדהו (ג) שאינו משגיח באיזה מקום שירד המחרישה בקרקע, אפילו במקום נמוך – חורש, והיינו דומיא דחרישה ואסור: **אבל שקל מוליא.** שנוטל הקרקע ממקום גבוה: **ושדא בנצא.** במקום נמוך, היינו אדעתא דבי דרי, אדעתא דגורן. שכך דרכו של גורן, שמשוה הגרנות – וזה מותר: **דזכי זיכיא.** שמכבד את הקרקע מעלים קטנים שעליה, שנוטלם: **אדעתא דציבי.** אם ליקטן אדעתא דעלים להסיקן, דנקט רברבי ושבק זוטרי: **אדעתא דארעא.** דלהכי ליקטן, שרוצה לזרוע הקרקע, שלוקט גדולים וקטנים – אסור (ד): **אדעתא דכוורי.** שעושין המים שיוצאין מן הגומא של ביבר לחוץ, אם לצורך שיצאו המים וישתיירו הדגים – מותר: כגון דפתח תרי בבי. חד שבו נכנסין המים לגומא ונכנסין אף הדגים לגומא, וחד שהמים יוצאין חוץ לגומא, והדגים משתיירים בתוכה ולוקחים אותם – שרי, דהיינו אדעתא דכוורי: **דארעא.** דפתח חד בבא שבו נכנסים המים לגומא, ואידך פתח שבו יוצאין המים לחוץ לא פתח: **אדעתא דארעא.** שכשהגומא מליאה מים יוצאין המים למעלה ומשקין כל השדה, וכי האי גוונא אסור: **דפשח דיקלא.** שזומר הדקל מן הענפים שבו: **אדעתא דחיותא.** דראויין למאכל בהמה, דנקט מן הענפים דמחד גיסא בין לחין בין יבשין, לצורך מאכל בהמה, היינו דחיותא – ושרי: דנקיט מהאי גיסא. **דדיקלא.** ומהאי גיסא ענפים יבשין שבו, היינו אדעתא דדיקלא – ואסור: **הני תמרי תוחלני.** תמרים שלא נתבשלו כל צרכן: **מיגזרינהו.** לחותכן לשנים ולאוכלן הכי בי"ט – שרי, דלצורך יום טוב קעביד: **מייצינהו אסור.** לכותשן במשוי, ומוציא ליחה שבהן לחוץ – היינו אסור. שעכשיו אינן נתלעים, אלא לעשות מהן לימוקים לאכלן בחול הוא מכוין – ואסור לתקן ביום טוב מאכל דחול: **כיון דמתלעי.** אי לאו דמיילינהו: **כדבר האבד.** כלומר: כסחורה שאדם יכול לעשותה במועד כדי שלא יפסיד בה אם לא עשאה, הכי נמי מלי למיילינהו. דאי לא עביד הכי – מיתלעי, ושרי: **פרקמטיא כל שהוא.** לעשות סחורה בחולו של מועד: **ובדבר האבד מותר.** שאם יש לו הפסד אם לא יעשנה לאותה סחורה – מותר לעשותה, אבל בחנם שלא להרויח – אסור: **הוה מסיק זוזי.** שהיו חייבין לו מעות באותו מקום:

יריד

תוספות

למישקל טופרי. פירש (ה) בתוספתא: דה"ה לדידן, שמותר לתקן ברזלים, דקרקע קשה ומתקלקל. ומשום שאין ברזלים בימי חכמים, שאין צריך רק למשקל טופריה, שהיה הקרקע מטוננת כמו ברוסי"א – היה אסור: **איצטבא** ואקרופיטא. עניני ספסל, וקלא הם חלוקים. כדאמרינן בריש פרק "עשרה יוחסין" (קדושין דף ע.) ליתיב מר אקרופיטא. אמר ליה: מי סני ספסל כדאמרי רבנן, או איצטבא כדאמרי אינשי:

ואין מונעין רפואה מבהמה. (ו) דברפואה דבהמה שיש בה מלאכה איירי. אבל רפואה שאין בה איסור מלאכה, רק גזירה משום שחיקת סממנין – אפילו בשבת איכא מאן דשרי. והלכה כמאן דשרי, כדאי' בפ' "במה בהמה" (שבת דף נג:): דרש רבא: הלכה כרבי יאשיה, דלית ליה גזירה משום שחיקת סממנין ברפואה דבהמה. פי' לסרוקי סוסיא, שפירש בקונטרס אושטלי"ר בלעז – אין נראה לי. דהא קי"ל דבין קירוד ובין קירצוף שרי, (ז) כדאי' סוף פרק שני דביצה (דף כג.), לר' שמעון דאמר דבר שאין מתכוין מותר, וקיימא לן כוותיה. אלא ענין אחר הוא:

כסכוסי. פי' בקונטרס: אנפשיי"ר בלע"ז. ויש מפרשים: ליקיי"ר. ולשון כסכוס משמע כן, כדאי' פ' "תולין" (שבת דף קמא. ושם): מכסכסו מבפנים ואין מכסכסו מבחוץ, גבי טיט: **קיטורי** בירי. גרסינן ברי"ש ולא בידי בדלי"ת. (ח) והוי מענין בירית טהורה בפ' "במה אשה יוצאה" (שם דף סג.) (ובפרק "חזקת הבתים") (ב"ב דף נד):

מוליא במוליא ונצא בנצא אדעתא (ט) דבי דרי שקל מוליא ושדי בנצא אדעתא דארעא. [א] וכן גרס רבינו גרשון. ורב אלפס גרס בהפך: מוליא במוליא ונצא בנצא – אדעתא דארעא, מוליא בנצא – אדעתא דבי דרי. משמע שיותר קרקע שוה צריך לחרוש מלידוש. ואיפכא מסתברא טפי, דלדידן צריך קרקע שוה לידוש יותר מלחרוש. ושמא לפי שהיו דשין במוריגין אין צריך קרקע שוה. ויש מפרשים כדי לעשות דיר של בהמה*):

פרקמטיא כל שהוא. פי' רבינו יצחק בתשובתו: כי רבינו יעקב לא היה חושב הלואת רבית פרקמטיא. והא דאמר: רבינא הוה מסיק זוזי בבני אקרא דשנואתא משמע דחשיב פרקמטיא, ולא שרי אלא משום דבר האבד! היה אומר רבינו יעקב דסחורת יין היתה, כדאמרינן ב"איזהו נשך" (ב"מ עג:): רבינא הוה יהיב זוזי לבני אקרא דשנואתא, ושפכי ליה טפי כופייתא. אבל הלואה דשולחנות בקביעות וחילוף – נראה (י) דחשיב פרקמטיא:

ובדבר האבד מותר. פירוש: בדבר שאם לא ימכרנה עתה – שמא לא ימכרנה יפה פעם אחרת, ויפסיד מן הקרן. אבל אם לא יפסיד מן הקרן, אלא שלא ירויח כל כך – אין זה חשוב דבר האבד. וכל שכן לקנות סחורה שמא תהיה יותר ביוקר אחר המועד, אבל לקנות יין כשר בתוך המועד – מותר. והר"ר יוסף פירש: דיש לאסור, דאף על פי שלא ימצא ביוקר, ואין זה דבר האבד: הרי ימצא בזול –

כוורא

*) [ועי' תוס' ב"ב נד. ד"ה מוליא].

רבינו חננאל

וחמור שרוכב עליו מותר ליטול צפרניו. אבל חמור הטוחן בריחים לא ר' יהודה שרא ליטול צפרנים של חמור הטוחן בריחים ולאוקמי ריחיא ולמבני ריחיא ולמיבני אמת הריחים ולמיבני אוריא פי' אורוות סוסים רבא שרא לסרוקי סוסיא ולמיבני אקרפיטא ואיצטבא. רבא שרא למשקל דמא תניא נמי הכי מקיזין דם לבהמה. ואין מונעין רפואה לבהמה בחולו של מועד. רבא שרא לכסכוסי קירמי. ופירשו הגאונים *) תרטיב ר' אמתענה ותליינא אמר רב חסדא קיטורא בידא אסור מעשה אומן הוא במס' יו"ט פ"ב (דף כג) אמר רבא מאן דתקיל תיקלא **) פי' אולח וגה אל ארץ ונעל הא מועתר אל אי שקיל ויהיב מוליא במוליא ונצא בנצא העפר הרך נותן ברך והקשה בקשה אדעתא דבי דרי עביד ושרי פי' מוליא בנצא הרך בקשה אדעתא דארעא ואסיר. וכן מאן דזכי זביא. פי' מסקל ומנקה הקרקע שקיל רברבי פי' העצים הגדולים נוטל ומניח הקיסמין קטנים אדעתא דציבי ושרי שקיל רברבי וזוטרי אדעתא דארעא עביד ואסיר. וכן מאן דפתח מיא בארעיה דעיילי מהאי גיסא ודנפקי מהאי גיסא אדעתא למיצד כוורי הוא ושרי מחד גיסא אסיר. וכן מאן דפשח דיקלא מחד גיסא אדעתא דחיותא שרי מהאי גיסא ומהאי גיסא אדעתא דדיקלא ואסיר והני תוחלני שרי למגזרינהו מייצינהו אסור. בחגיגה בפרק אין דורשין אומר שם משל אי משכחת תוחלא אכול כו' והם התמרים הרכים הנקראים בטיית שודאך רטב והדקל אשר בו אלו התמרים עליו דיבר בכאן והתיר לחותכם מן הדקל ולא התיר לדורכן בנרתק שלהן לעשותן כמו אלו הנקראים בטיית אל לוג. ורב פפא התיר את זאת מפני שמתליעין. רב פפא אמר כיון דמתלען כפרקמטיא האבד דמי ושרי. ואמר רבא פרקמטיא כל שהוא אסור. א"ר אסי בר אבין ובדבר האבד מותר. רבינא הוה ליה עיסקא דהוה מזדבנא בשיתא אלפי שהייה לבתר מועדא וזבניה בי"ב אלפי. רבינא הוה מסיק זוזי בבני אקרא דשנואתא אתא לקמיה דרב אשי א"ל כיון דהאידנא משכחת להו וביומי אחריני לא משכחת להו

*) לפי הנראה הוראת הדברים בלה"ק שרא לרטוב נרכי הבית כדי לנקותם. **) הוראת הדברים בלה"ק ענינו דקירה. ופי' דקר את פני הארץ כי יעשה עפר.

עין משפט נר מצוה

צב א מיי' פ"ח מהל' י"ט הלכה טו סמג לאוין עה טוש"ע א"ח סי' תקמ סעיף ח:
צג ב מיי' שם טוש"ע א"ח סי' תקלו ס"ב:
צד ג טוש"ע א"ח סי' תקמ סעיף ה:
צה ד מיי' שם הלכה ז טוש"ע שם סעיף ו:
צו ה מיי' שם הלכה טו טוש"ע א"ח סי' תקלו סעיף ג:
צז ו מיי' שם הלכה יד טוש"ע א"ח סי' תקמא סעיף ג:
[ו מיי' שם טוש"ע שם]:
צח ז מיי' פ"ח הלכה יב שם ופ"ב מהל' זכיה ומתנה מהל' ד עד הלכה ט טוש"ע א"ח סי' תקלז סעיף ט וטור ש"ע ח"מ סי' רעה סעיף יז יח יט כ:
צט ח טוש"ע א"ח שם סעיף י:
ק ט טוש"ע שם ס"ח:
קא י טוש"ע שם סעיף יא:
קב כ טוש"ע שם סי' תקלג סעיף ג:
קג ל מ נ מיי' פ"ז שם הלכה כב טוש"ע שם סי' תקלט סעיף א:

מסורת הש"ס

[צ"ל רב וכ"א בר"ח ובערוך ערך אקרפיטא] [בב"י סי' תקמ העתיקו נוסח הגמ' קטורי בי ידי ע"ש] ב"ב נד. [שם] [שם] [שם] [לקמן יח.] [עי' ב"מ עג.]

גליון הש"ס

תוס' ד"ה ואין מונעין וכו' אין נ"ל דהא קיי"ל. עיין ברא"ש דהגירסא הכא רב. ולפ"ז לק"מ דרב לשיטתיה דס"ל דבר שאין מתכוין אסור. ואסור קרלוף בי"ט:

הגהות הגר"א

[א] תוס' ד"ה מוליא במוליא כו' וכן גרס ר"ג ורב אלפס משמע שיותר קרקע שוה צריך לחרוש כו' ושמא לפי שהיו דשין כו' וי"מ כדי לעשות דיר כו' ורש"י גריס בהיפך מוליא במוליא ונצא בנצא אדעתא דארעא מוליא בנצא אדעתא דבי דרי כצ"ל:

הגהות הב"ח

(א) אמר רבא מאן דמתקיל תיקלא אדעתא. נ"ב כן היא גירסת רש"י ונימוקי יוסף ופירוש מסקל השדה: (ב) שם ונצא בנצא אדעתא דארעא שקל מוליא ושדא בנצא אדעתא דבי דרי כו' כצ"ל: (ג) רש"י ד"ה או נצא כו' שאינו משגיח באיזה מקום. נ"ב פירוש דרכו של חורש אינו אלא לרפויי ארעא עי' לעיל דף ב ע"ב: (ד) ד"ה אדעתא דארעא דלהכי כו' אסור מה"ד דפתח מיא כו' והמים יוצאין מן הגומא: (ה) תוס' ד"ה למישקל כו' פי' בתוספות כו' לתקן ברזלים לכיון דהקרקע קשה ומתקלקל: (ו) ד"ה ואין מונעין רפואה מבהמה נראה דברפואה דבהמה: (ז) בא"ד וכן קרלוף שרי אפילו בי"ט כדאיתא: (ח) ד"ה קיטורי כו' נ"ב פירוש דיש גורסין בידי בדלי"ת ופי' לעשות קשרי בית ידים אסור מפני שעושה מעשה אומן וכך היא גירסת הרמב"ם: (ט) ד"ה מוליא כו' אדעתא דארעא שקל מוליא ושדי בנצא אדעתא דבי דרי וכן גרס ר"ג ור"א גרס בהיפך כו' בנצא אדעתא דבי דרי מוליא בנצא אדעתא דארעא משמע שיותר כו' כצ"ל: (י) ד"ה פרקמטיא כו' בקביעות וחילוף נראה דלא חשיב פרקמטיא:

גמרא

*לְיָרִיד שֶׁל גּוֹיִם, [א]וְלוֹקְחִים בְּהֵמָה עֲבָדִים וּשְׁפָחוֹת בָּתִּים שָׂדוֹת וּכְרָמִים, וְכוֹתֵב וּמַעֲלֶה בְּעַרְכָּאוֹת שֶׁלָּהֶן, מִפְּנֵי שֶׁהוּא כְּמַצִּיל מִיָּדָן. רַב [ב]שְׁרָא לְחִיָּיא בַּר אַשִׁי לְמִיגְדַּל אוֹהֲרֵי בְּחוּלָּא דְמוֹעֲדָא. מַאי טַעְמָא — מַעֲשֵׂה הֶדְיוֹט הוּא, אֲבָל [ג]אִיזְלֵי — אָסוּר, מַאי טַעְמָא — מַעֲשֵׂה אוּמָּן הוּא. רַב יְהוּדָה [ד]שְׁרָא לְאַמֵּי תַּנּוּרָא לְמִיגְדַּל תַּנּוּרֵי, וּלְרַב' בַּר עַשָּׂבֵי לְמִיגְדַּל מְהוּלָתָא. אִינִי? וְהָא תָּנֵי רַבָּה בַּר שְׁמוּאֵל: וְשָׁוִין שֶׁאֵין גּוֹדְלִין תַּנּוּר לְכַתְּחִילָּה! לָא קַשְׁיָא: [ה]כָּאן — בִּימוֹת הַחַמָּה, כָּאן — בִּימוֹת הַגְּשָׁמִים.§ **מתני'** [ו]עוֹשִׂין מַעֲקֶה לַגַּג וְלַמִּרְפֶּסֶת מַעֲשֵׂה הֶדְיוֹט, אֲבָל לֹא מַעֲשֵׂה אוּמָּן. [ז]שָׁפִין אֶת הַסְּדָקִין וּמַעְגִּילִין אוֹתָן בְּמַעְגִּילָה בַּיָּד וּבָרֶגֶל, אֲבָל לֹא בְּמַחֲלָצַיִם. [ח]הַצִּיר וְהַצִּינּוֹר וְהַקּוֹרָה וְהַמַּנְעוּל וְהַמַּפְתֵּחַ שֶׁנִּשְׁבְּרוּ — מְתַקְּנָן בַּמּוֹעֵד, [ט]וּבִלְבַד שֶׁלֹּא יִתְכַּוֵּין לַעֲשׂוֹת מְלַאכְתּוֹ בַּמּוֹעֵד. [י]וְכָל כְּבָשִׁין שֶׁהוּא יָכוֹל לֶאֱכוֹל מֵהֶן בַּמּוֹעֵד — כּוֹבְשָׁן.§ **גמ'** הֵיכִי דָּמֵי מַעֲשֵׂה הֶדְיוֹט? רַב יוֹסֵף אָמַר: *בְּהוּצָא וְדַפְנָא. בְּמַתְנִיתָא תָּנָא: צָר בִּצְרוֹר וְאֵינוֹ טָח בְּטִיט.§ "שָׁפִין אֶת הַסְּדָקִין וּמַעְגִּילִין אוֹתָן בְּמַעְגִּילָה".§ הַשְׁתָּא בְּמַעְגִּילָה אָמְרַתְּ שָׁרֵי, בַּיָּד וּבָרֶגֶל מִיבַּעְיָא?! הָכִי קָאָמַר: שָׁפִין אֶת הַסְּדָקִין וּמַעְגִּילִין אוֹתָן כְּעֵין מַעְגִּילָה בַּיָּד וּבָרֶגֶל, אֲבָל לֹא בְּמַחֲלָצַיִם.§ "הַצִּיר וְהַצִּינּוֹר וְהַקּוֹרָה וְהַמַּנְעוּל וְהַמַּפְתֵּחַ שֶׁנִּשְׁבְּרוּ מְתַקְּנָן בַּמּוֹעֵד".§ וּרְמִינְהִי: *עַד יָמָיו הָיָה פַּטִּישׁ מַכֶּה בִּירוּשָׁלַיִם כו'. עַד יָמָיו — אִין, מִכָּאן וְאֵילָךְ — לָא! לָא קַשְׁיָא; כָּאן — בִּדְנַפָּחֵי. כָּאן — בִּדְנַגָּרֵי. מַתְקִיף לָהּ רַב חִסְדָּא: [כ]אָמְרוּ קָלָא רַבָּה — אָסִיר, קָלָא זוּטָר — שָׁרֵי! אֶלָּא אָמַר: רַב חִסְדָּא: לָא קַשְׁיָא; הָא — בְּמַגְלֵי, הָא — בַּחֲצִינֵי. רַב פַּפָּא אָמַר: כָּאן — קוֹדֶם גְּזֵירָה, כָּאן — לְאַחַר גְּזֵירָה. רַב אַשִׁי אָמַר: הָא — ר' יְהוּדָה, הָא — ר' יוֹסֵי. דְּאָמַר ר' יִצְחָק בַּר אַבְדִּימִי: *מַאן תְּנָא שִׁינּוּי בַּמּוֹעֵד בְּדָבָר הָאָבֵד — דְּלָא כְּר' יוֹסֵי. אָמַר רָבִינָא: כְּמַאן מַדְלֵינַן הָאִידָּנָא קַבְיוּתָא דְּדַשָּׁא בְּחוּלָּא דְמוֹעֲדָא, כְּמַאן — כְּר' יוֹסֵי.§ "כְּבָשִׁין שֶׁהוּא יָכוֹל לֶאֱכוֹל בַּמּוֹעֵד — כּוֹבְשָׁן".§ (א) בְּדִיתָא לְבָאֵי כַּוְורֵי. אֲזַל כּוּלֵּי עָלְמָא צוּד, אַיְיתוּ כַּוְורָא. שְׁרָא לְהוּ רָבָא לְמִימְלַח מִינַּיְיהוּ. אֲמַר לֵיהּ אַבַּיֵי: וְהָא תְּנַן: כְּבָשִׁין שֶׁהוּא יָכוֹל לֶאֱכוֹל מֵהֶן בַּמּוֹעֵד — כּוֹבְשָׁן! אֲמַר לֵיהּ: כֵּיוָן דְּמֵעִיקָּרָא אַדַּעְתָּא דַּאֲכִילָה אַיְיתִינְהוּ, וְאִי שָׁבֵיק לְהוּ פָּסְדִי — *כִּפְרַקְמַטְיָא הָאָבֵד דָּמֵי, וְשָׁרֵי. וְאִיכָּא דְּאָמְרִי: [כ]שָׁרֵי לְהוּ רָבָא מֵיצַד, מֵיזַל, אַיְיתוּיֵי, וּמִימְלַח. אֲמַר לֵיהּ אַבַּיֵי: וְהָא אֲנַן "כְּבָשִׁין שֶׁהוּא יָכוֹל לֶאֱכוֹל מֵהֶן (ב) כּוֹבְשָׁן" תְּנַן! אֲמַר לֵיהּ: הָנֵי נַמִי מִיתְאַכְלֵי אַגַּב אִיצְצָא. כִּי הָא דִּשְׁמוּאֵל עֲבַדוּ לֵיהּ שִׁיתִּין אִיצְצֵי, וַאֲכַל. רָבָא אִיקְלַע לְבֵי רֵישׁ גָּלוּתָא, עָבְדִי לֵיהּ שִׁיתִּין אִיצְצֵי וַאֲכַל. רַב אִיקְלַע לְבֵי רַב שַׁפִּיר, אַיְיתוּ לְקַמֵּיהּ הַהוּא כַּוְורָא, תִּילְתָּא בִּישׁוּלָא, תִּילְתָּא מִילְחָא, וְתִילְתָּא טַוְויָא. אֲמַר רַב, אֲמַר לִי אַדָּא צַיָּידָא: כַּוְורָא, סָמוּךְ לְמִיסְרְחֵיהּ מַעֲלֵי. וַאֲמַר רַב, אֲמַר לִי אַדָּא צַיָּידָא: כַּוְורָא, טַוְויָא בַּאֲחוּהּ, אַסּוּקֵיהּ בַּאֲבוּהּ, מֵיכְלֵי בִּבְרֵיהּ, אִשְׁתֵּי עֲלֵיהּ אֲבוּהּ. וַאֲמַר רַב, אֲמַר לִי אַדָּא צַיָּידָא: כַּוְורָא תַּחְלֵי וְחַלְבָּא לִיטְעוֹן גּוּפָא וְלָא לִיטְעוֹן פּוּרְיָא. וַאֲמַר רַב, אֲמַר לִי אַדָּא צַיָּידָא: כַּוְורָא, תַּחְלֵי, וְחַלְבָּא — מַיָּא וְלָא שִׁיכְרָא, שִׁיכְרָא וְלָא חַמְרָא.§

הדרן עלך משקין בית השלחין

רש"י

יָרִיד שֶׁל גּוֹיִם. יוֹמָא דְשׁוּקָא: וּמַעֲלֶה בְּעַרְכָּאוֹת. לְקַיְּימָן בַּחֲתִימָתָן. דְּכֵיוָן דְּהַשְׁתָּא הוּא דְמַשְׁכַּח לְהוּ, וּלְיוֹמָא אַחֲרִינָא לָא — שָׁרֵי: אוֹהֲרֵי. שֶׁצָּדִין בּוֹ דָּגִים, שֶׁקּוֹרִין רוש"א: אִיזְלֵי. רְשָׁתוֹת שֶׁצָּדִין בּוֹ עוֹפוֹת: לְמִגְדַּל תַּנּוּרָא. לַעֲשׂוֹת הַתַּנּוּר מֵחָדָשׁ: מְהוּלָתָא. נָפָה: בִּימוֹת הַחַמָּה. כְּלוֹמַר, כְּשֶׁיֵּשׁ יְמוֹת הַחַמָּה, כְּגוֹן בְּפֶסַח דְּחָבוּל עָלְמָא שֶׁאֵין יוֹרְדִין בּוֹ גְּשָׁמִים — מוּתָּר לַעֲשׂוֹת בּוֹ תַּנּוּר, לְפִי שֶׁנִּתְחַמֵּר יָבֵשׁ וִיכוֹלִין לֶאֱפוֹת בּוֹ פַּת בָּרֶגֶל לְצוֹרֶךְ הָרֶגֶל: כָּאן בִּימוֹת הַגְּשָׁמִים. כְּלוֹמַר, כְּשֶׁיּוֹרְדִין הַגְּשָׁמִים בָּרֶגֶל, כְּגוֹן בְּסוּכּוֹת — אֵין עוֹשִׂין תַּנּוּר, לְפִי שֶׁאֵינוֹ יָבֵשׁ לְהִתְחַמֵּר עַד לְאַחַר הָרֶגֶל, וְעָבֵיד טִירְחָא שֶׁלֹּא לְצוֹרֶךְ הָרֶגֶל:

מתני' מַעֲקֶה לְמִרְפֶּסֶת. כּוֹתֶל קְטַנָּה הָעוֹשִׂין עַל הָאִיצְטַבּוֹת שֶׁלִּפְנֵי הָעֲלִיּוֹת גְּדוֹלוֹת, כְּעֵין שֶׁיֵּשׁ עַל שְׂפַת נְהַר רַיְינִיס: שָׁפִין אֶת הַסְּדָקִים. שֶׁבַּתַּנּוּר: וּמַעְגִּילִין אוֹתָן בְּמַעְגִּילָה. שֶׁגּוֹלְלִין עַל קַרְקְעוֹת הַתַּנּוּר עֵץ גָּדוֹל עָגוֹל, כְּדֵי לִסְתּוֹם הַסְּדָקִין: בַּיָּד וּבָרֶגֶל. (ג)שֶׁלּוֹקֵחַ בְּיָדוֹ עֵץ וּבוֹעֲטִין בַּיָּד עַל הַתַּנּוּר לִסְתּוֹם הַסְּדָקִים, אוֹ בּוֹעֵט בְּרַגְלוֹ עַל קַרְקְעוֹת הַתַּנּוּר: מַחֲלָצַיִם. עֵץ כְּעֵין רֶגֶל, שֶׁדּוֹחֲקוֹ בְּמַעֲזִיבָה לִסְתּוֹם הַסְּדָקִין. וְיֵשׁ בּוֹ מַעֲשֵׂה אוּמָּן יוֹתֵר מִמַּעְגִּילָה: צִיר. רֶגֶל הַדֶּלֶת, כְּמוֹ "הַדֶּלֶת תִּסּוֹב עַל צִירָהּ" (משלי כו): צִינּוֹר. הוּא הַחוֹר שֶׁבָּאַסְקוּפָּה הַתַּחְתּוֹנָה, כְּמוֹ *צִינּוֹרָא דְּדָשָׁא: הַקּוֹרָה. מָה שֶׁעַל הַפֶּתַח שֶׁתַּחֲזוֹר בּוֹ הַדֶּלֶת, וְקוֹרִין אוברטו"ר: מַנְעוּל. בלנדור"א: וּבִלְבַד שֶׁלֹּא יִתְכַּוֵּין לַעֲשׂוֹת מְלַאכְתּוֹ בַּמּוֹעֵד. כְּשֶׁיֵּשׁ לוֹ לְתַקֵּן כָּל אֵילּוּ בִּשְׁאָר יְמוֹת הַשָּׁנָה, וּמַנִּיחוֹ עַד הַמּוֹעֵד: וּכְבָשִׁין. שֶׁל צִיר. כְּלוֹמַר, דָּגִים וּשְׁאָר דְּבָרִים שֶׁכּוֹבְשִׁים בְּמֶלַח, שֶׁיָּכוֹל לְאוֹכְלָן בַּמּוֹעֵד שֶׁלֹּא יְהֵא צָרִיךְ לְהַמְתִּין בַּאֲכִילָתָן עַד לְאַחַר הַמּוֹעֵד, שֶׁיְּהוּ נִכְבָּשִׁין מַהֵר וּרְאוּיִין לֶאֱכוֹל מִיָּד: **גמ'** הוּצָא. הוּלֵי דֶּקֶל: (ד)דּוּפְנָא. עָבְדִי לְחַיֵּיס שֶׁל גָּדֵר: וְאֵינוֹ טָח בְּטִיט. זֶה הוּא מַעֲשֵׂה הֶדְיוֹט: מַעְגִּילָה. דֶּרֶךְ אוּמָּנוּת יוֹתֵר: בַּיָּד וּבָרֶגֶל. דְּלָאו מַעֲשֵׂה אוּמָּן הוּא, לֹא כָּל שֶׁכֵּן: כְּעֵין מַעְגִּילָה. וְלֹא מַעְגִּילָה מַמָּשׁ, אֶלָּא כְּעֵין מַעְגִּילָה בַּיָּד וּבָרֶגֶל: עַד יָמָיו. שֶׁל יוֹחָנָן כ"ג הָיָה פַּטִּישׁ מַכֶּה בִּירוּשָׁלַיִם בְּחוּלּוֹ שֶׁל מוֹעֵד. וְהוּא גָּזַר עָלָיו וּבִטְּלוֹ. אַלְמָא אָסוּר. וּמַתְנִי' קָתָנֵי וּמְתַקְּנִין מַנְעוּל וּמַפְתֵּחַ: מַתְנִיתִין דְּמִתַּקְּנִין אֵלּוּ בְּחוש"מ בִּדְנַגָּרֵי. בְּמַנְעוּל שֶׁל עֵץ — שָׁרֵי, דְּלָא הָוֵי קָלָא רַבָּה: בִּדְנַפָּחֵי. דְּפַטִּישׁ הַיְינוּ קוּרְנָס — אָסוּר, דְּהָוֵי קָלָא רַבָּה, וְאוֹלוּדֵי קָלָא אָסוּר: מַגְלֵי. מַסָּר הַגָּדוֹל שָׁרֵי, דְּלָא מוֹלִיד קָלָא כְּלוּם: בַּחֲצִינֵי. ברר"א. אָסִיר, דְּהָוֵי אוֹלוּדֵי קָלָא טְפֵי: לְאַחַר שֶׁגָּזַר. יוֹחָנָן כ"ג: הָא ר' יְהוּדָה הָא ר' יוֹסֵי. בְּפִירְקָא דִּלְקַמָּן (דף יב.), דְּרַבִּי יוֹסֵי לָא בָּעֵי לְשַׁנּוּיֵי לְדָבָר הָאָבֵד. וּמַתְנִי' דְּשָׁרֵי הָכָא כָּל הָנֵי בְּלָא שִׁינּוּי — ר' יוֹסֵי הִיא:

כְּמַאן מַדְלֵינַן הָאִידָּנָא קַבְיוּתָא דְּדַשָּׁא. כְּשֶׁיּוֹלְאִין מַסְמְרִים שֶׁל עֵץ מִן הַקּוֹרָה שֶׁעַל הַפֶּתַח, דְּשָׁרֵי לְמֵיעְבַד בְּלָא שִׁינּוּי: בְּדִיתָא. שֵׁם נָהָר: לְבָאֵי. שֵׁם מָקוֹם: כַּוְורֵי. הָכִי עָשׂוּ דֶּרֶךְ לַנָּהָר שֶׁיָּצְאוּ מֵימָיו, וְנִשְׁתַּיְּירוּ שָׁם דָּגִים הַרְבֵּה: לְמִימְלַח.(ה) הַרְבֵּה, אע"פ שֶׁאֵין יְכוֹלִים לְאוֹכְלָן בַּמּוֹעֵד, שֶׁהֲרֵי הָיוּ מְלוּחִין הַרְבֵּה: כְּבָשִׁין. בְּחוֹמֶץ וּבְמֶלַח, שֶׁקּוֹרִין קונפוסט"א. וְהָכָא נַמִי, כֵּיוָן שֶׁמְּלָחָן הַרְבֵּה כְּדֵי לְהַצְנִיעָן — תּוּ לָא חֲזוּ בַּמּוֹעֵד: אֲמַר לֵיהּ הָנֵי נַמִי.(ו) דְּמַלְחִינְהוּ: מִתְאַכְלֵי. בַּמּוֹעֵד: אַגַּב אִיצְצָא. שֶׁמּוֹשֵׁךְ הַמֶּלַח מֵהֶן:(ז) שִׁיתִּין אִיצְצֵי. כְּלוֹמַר: רוֹחֲצִין אוֹתוֹ הַרְבֵּה פְּעָמִים, מְנַלֵּי לֵיהּ שִׁשִּׁים זִימְנֵי: רַב אִיקְלַע. בַּמּוֹעֵד: תִּילְתָּא מִילְחָא. אַגַּב אִיגְּלָא: סָמוּךְ לְמִיסְרְחֵיהּ מַעֲלֵי. כְּלוֹמַר: יָפֶה הוּא לְאַחַר זְמַן שֶׁנִּיצּוֹד יוֹתֵר מֵהַסְרָחָה שֶׁעָתָה דְּנִיצּוֹד: טַוְויָא בַּאֲחוּהּ. בְּמֶלַח, שֶׁהַמֶּלַח נִבְרָא מִן הַמַּיִם כַּדָּגִים: אַסְּקֵיהּ בַּאֲבוּהּ. לְאַחַר שֶׁצְּלָאוֹ נוֹתְנוֹ בַּמַּיִם לוֹנָן: אַכְלֵיהּ בִּבְרֵיהּ. מַטִּילִין אוֹתוֹ בְּצִיר הַיּוֹצֵא מִן הַדָּגִים, וְאוֹכְלִין אוֹתוֹ: מִשְׁתְּיָא עֲלֵיהּ אֲבוּהּ. שֶׁשּׁוֹתִין עָלָיו מַיִם, שֶׁדָּגִים נִבְרְאוּ מִן הַמַּיִם: לִטְעוֹן גּוּפָא. כְּלוֹמַר: לְאַחַר אֲכִילָתוֹ מְהַלֵּךְ הַרְבֵּה קוֹדֶם שֶׁיִּישַׁן: וְלָא לִטְעוֹן פּוּרְיָא. לֹא יִשַׁן לְהִתְחַמֵּר אַחֲרֵיהֶם: תַּחְלֵי. שַׁחֲלַיִם: מַיָּא וְלָא שִׁכְרָא. מוּטָב לִשְׁתּוֹת אַחֲרֵיהֶן מַיִם, וְלֹא שֵׁכָר: הדרן עלך משקין בית השלחין

תוספות

כוורא סמוך למסרחיה מעלי. ובזמן הזה תופסים סכנה למיכל סמוך לסירחון. וגם משתי עלה אבוה, דאמר בסמוך דמעלי, ושמא נשתנו, כמו הרפואות שבתלמוד שאינן טובות בזמן הזה. או שמא נהרות דבבל מעלו לו טפי. ויש מפרשים: דכוורא לא בכלל דגים מיירי, ושם דג ששמו כוורא, ומשונה בדברים האלו משאר דגים. כדאמרינן פ' "כל הבשר" (חולין דף קט:): אסר לן גירותא, שרא לן לישנא דכוורא. ואין נראה שיהא בכל הלשונות של דגים טעם אחד:

הדרן עלך משקין בית השלחין

עין משפט נר מצוה

קד א מיי' פ"ט מהלכות ע"ז הלכה יד טוש"ע י"ד סי' קמט סעיף ג:

קה ב ג טוש"ע א"ח סי' תקמא סעיף א:

קו ד ה מיי' פ"ח מהל' י"ט הלכה יג טוש"ע א"ח סי' תקמ סעיף ז:

קז ו מיי' שם הלכה ו טוש"ע שם סעיף א:

קח ז מיי' שם פ"ז הלכה ה טוש"ע שם סעיף ג:

קט ח מיי' שם פ"ח הלכה ז טוש"ע שם סעיף ד:

קי ט מיי' שם פ"ז הלכה ד טוש"ע שם סי' תקלח סעיף ו:

קיא י מיי' שם הלכה ז טוא"ח סי' תקלג:

קיב כ מיי' שם טוש"ע שם סעיף ד:

מסורת הש"ס

עירובין מז. ע"ז יג.

[ברכות יח:]

לעיל ז.

מע"ש פ"ה מט"ו סוטה מז:

[לקמן יב: ע"ש]

[לעיל י:]

רבינו חננאל

להו כפרקמטיא האבוד דמי ושרי. רב שרא לר' חייא בר אשי למיגדל אהורי. פי' במס' גיטין בסוף פרק הניזקין (דף ס' ע"ב) ומפרשי רבנן אוזלי שבאו מעולא תרגום ויביאו מטוה כד עזיל ומפרשי אוהורי אלפכוך. מ"ט מעשה הדיוט אבל איזלי אסיר מ"ט מעשה אומן הוא. רב יהודה שרא לאביי תנוראה למגדל תנורא בחולי דמועדא. ולרבא בר עישבי שרא למגדל מחולתא בחולי דמועדא. ועושין מעקה לגג ולמרפסת מעשה הדיוט אבל לא מעשה אומן. היכי דמי מעשה הדיוט בהוצא ודפנא. במתניתא תנא צר בצרור ואינו טח בטיט ושפין את הסדקין ומעגילין אותן במעגילה ביד וברגל אבל לא במחלצים: **מתני'** הציר והצינור והקורה והמנעול והמפתח שנשברו מתקנן במועד ובלבד שלא יכוין מלאכתו במועד. איני והא תנן בסוף מס' סוטה עד כל ימיו פטיש היה מכה בירושלים עד ימיו של יוחנן כהן גדול אין מיכן ואילך לא. ופריק רב הונא האי פטיש דאסיר מיכן ואילך בדנפחי. והא דתנן הצינור כו' בדנגרי הוא ושרי. מתקיף ליה רב חסדא ונדחה ופריק בחציני אסיר ומתניתין דהכא במגלא ושרי *) קודם גזירה פירש קודם גזירת יוחנן כ"ג ורב אשי אמר מתני' דהתם ר' יהודא היא ומתני' דהכא ר' יוסי דאמר רב יצחק בר אבא מאן תנא דבעי שינוי במועד בדבר האבד דלא כר' יוסי דאי ר' יוסי הא אמר זולף וגומר וגף כדרכו. אמר רבינא כמאן מדלינן האידנא כו'. וכבשין שיכול לאכול מהן במועד מכבשן. רבא שרא לבני בדיתא לבאי למיצד ולמימלח א"ל אביי והתנן כבשין שיכול לאכול מהן מכבשן. שיכול אין לא יכול לא. א"ל הני נמי מתאכלי אגב איצצא כשיכבשום דחוקים כי הא דשמואל עבדו ליה ששים איצצי ואכל. פי' מיני תבשיל. אמר רב אמר לי אדא ציידא כוורא סמוך למיסרחי מעלי. ותוב אמר דג טוויא באחווה פירוש המלח מן הים והדג מן הים נמצא שניהן אביהן הים והן כמו אחים. וא"ל מלח הדג במלח שהוא אחיו וצלה אותו במלח. אסוקיה באבוה. פי' כשתעלהו מן האש שוטפהו במים מלוחין שהן אביו אוכליה בבריה פירוש אכול אותו בבנו והוא ציר של דגים שהוא יוצא מן השמנונית של דג כי הוא חשוב לדג כבנו. וכשתאכלהו שתה אחריו המים כי באותה העת ובאותו מקום היו אומרים להם הרופאים כשתאכל דגים שתה אחריו המים ולא יין **) או יין ולא שכר. כוורא תחלי וחלבא ליטעון גופא ולא ליטעון פוריא. פי' כשיאכל אותם עד שיתעכלו במעיו לא ישן כי השינה מיד מזיקתו: **הדרן עלך משקין בית השלחין.**

*) נראה דצ"ל רב פפא אמר כאן קודם גזרה כו'. **) לפנינו בגמ' הגרסא להיפך. ואולי דרבינו היה לו גי' אחרת.

הגהות הב"ח

(א) גמ' בדיתא לבאי כוורא. נ"ב כך הוא גירסת האלפס בפומבדיתא לבאי כוורא ופי' הר"ן פוס שם המקום היושב על נהר בדיתא לבאי כוורא לדו והביאו דגים רבים שנתייבש הנהר ומתו הדגים עכ"ל: (ב) שם והא אנן כבשין שהוא יכול לאכול מהן במועד כובשן תנן: (ג) רש"י ד"ה ביד וברגל (שלוקח בידו עץ) תא"מ ונ"ב נ"ל טעות: (ד) ד"ה דופנא כו'. נ"ב עי' לעיל בפירושו בדף ז' ע"א: (ה) ד"ה למימלח למולחן הרבה אע"פ: (ו) ד"ה א"ל הני נמי אע"ג דמלחינהו: (ז) ד"ה אגב כו' המלח מהן הס"ד ואח"כ מה"ד עבדו ליה שיתין איצצי כלומר רוחצין אותו הרבה פעמים הס"ד ואח"כ מה"ד שיתין אוללי ששים פעמים הס"ד:

עין משפט נר מצוה

א א מיי' מהל' י"ט הלכה ג טוש"ע א"ח סי' תקלח סעיף א:

ס"א ושמא

[עי' תוס' דחגיגה יח. ד"ה חולו ותוס' ע"ז כב. ד"ה תיפוק ליה]

ב ב מיי' פ"ה מהלכות אבל הלכה י טוש"ע י"ד סי' שפ סעיף י:

ג ג מיי' שם:

ד ד ה טור יו"ד סי' שפ:

ה ו מיי' שם הלכה יא טוש"ע שם סעיף יב:

ו ז ח מיי' שם טוש"ע שם סעיף יד:

ז ט מיי' שם הלכה יב טוש"ע שם סעיף יג:

ח י מיי' שם הלכה יג טוש"ע שם סעיף יז:

ט כ מיי' שם טוש"ע שם סעיף יח:

י ל מ טוש"ע שם סעיף כא:

משנה

מי שֶׁהָפַךְ אֶת זֵיתָיו, וְאֵירְעוֹ אֵבֶל אוֹ אוֹנֶס, אוֹ שֶׁהִטְעוּהוּ פּוֹעֲלִים — טוֹעֵן קוֹרָה רִאשׁוֹנָה, וּמַנִּיחָהּ לְאַחַר הַמּוֹעֵד, דִּבְרֵי ר' יְהוּדָה. רַבִּי יוֹסֵי אוֹמֵר: [א]זוֹלֵף וְגוֹמֵר וְגָף כְּדַרְכּוֹ.

גמרא

§ **גמ'** פָּתַח בְּאֵבֶל וְסַיֵּים בְּמוֹעֵד! אָמַר רַב שֵׁישָׁא בְּרֵיהּ דְּרַב אִידִי: [ב]זֹאת אוֹמֶרֶת דְּבָרִים הַמּוּתָּרִין בַּמּוֹעֵד — אֲסוּרִים בִּימֵי אֶבְלוֹ. רַב אַשִׁי אָמַר: לָא מִיבַּעְיָא קָאָמַר: לָא מִיבַּעְיָא בִּימֵי אֶבְלוֹ דְּמִדְּרַבָּנָן הוּא, וְשָׁרֵי, אֶלָּא אֲפִילּוּ בַּמּוֹעֵד, דְּאִיסּוּר מְלָאכָה מִדְּאוֹרַיְיתָא, בִּמְקוֹם פְּסֵידָא — שָׁרוּ רַבָּנַן. תַּנְיָא כְּוָותֵיהּ דְּרַב שֵׁישָׁא בְּרֵיהּ דְּרַב אִידִי: [ג]אֵלּוּ דְּבָרִים הָעוֹשִׂין לָאָבֵל בִּימֵי אֶבְלוֹ: *זֵיתָיו הֲפוּכִין — טוֹעֲנִין לוֹ, וְכַדּוֹ לָגוּף, וּפִשְׁתָּנוֹ לְהַעֲלוֹת מִן הַמִּשְׁרָה, וְצַמְרוֹ לְהַעֲלוֹת מִן הַיּוֹרָה, וּמַרְבִּיצִים שָׂדֵהוּ מִשֶּׁתַּגִּיעַ עוֹנַת הַמַּיִם שֶׁלּוֹ. ר' יְהוּדָה אוֹמֵר: אַף זוֹרְעִין לוֹ שְׂדֵה נִיר, וְשָׂדֶה הָעוֹמֶדֶת לְפִשְׁתָּן. אָמְרוּ לוֹ: אִם לֹא תִּזָּרַע בִּבְכִיר — תִּזָּרַע בְּאָפֵל, אִם לֹא תִּזָּרַע פִּשְׁתָּן — תִּזָּרַע מִמִּין אַחֵר. [ד]רַבָּן שִׁמְעוֹן בֶּן גַּמְלִיאֵל אוֹמֵר: זֵיתָיו הֲפוּכִין וְאֵין שָׁם אוּמָּן אֶלָּא הוּא, כַּדּוֹ לָגוּף וְאֵין שָׁם אוּמָּן אֶלָּא הוּא, פִּשְׁתָּנוֹ לְהַעֲלוֹת מִן הַמִּשְׁרָה, וְצַמְרוֹ לְהַעֲלוֹת מִן הַיּוֹרָה וְאֵין שָׁם אוּמָּן אֶלָּא הוּא — הֲרֵי זֶה יַעֲשֶׂה בְּצִינְעָא. [ה]יָתֵר עַל כֵּן אָמַר רַבָּן שִׁמְעוֹן בֶּן גַּמְלִיאֵל: אִם הָיָה אוּמָּן לָרַבִּים, וְסַפָּר וּבַלָּן לָרַבִּים, וְהִגִּיעַ עֵת הָרֶגֶל וְאֵין שָׁם אוּמָּן אֶלָּא הוּא — הֲרֵי זֶה יַעֲשֶׂה. [ו]הָאֲרִיסִין וְהַחֲכִירִין וְהַקַּבְּלָנִין — הֲרֵי אֵלּוּ יַעֲשׂוּ אֲחֵרִים בִּשְׁבִילָן. [ז]הַחַמָּרִין הַגַּמָּלִין וְהַסַּפָּנִין — הֲרֵי אֵלּוּ לֹא יַעֲשׂוּ. [ח]וְאִם הָיוּ מוּחְכָּרִין אוֹ מוּשְׂכָּרִין אֵצֶל אֲחֵרִים — הֲרֵי אֵלּוּ יַעֲשׂוּ. [ט]שְׂכִיר יוֹם, אֲפִילּוּ בְּעִיר אַחֶרֶת — לֹא יַעֲשֶׂה. הָיְתָה מְלֶאכֶת אֲחֵרִים בְּיָדוֹ, אע"פ שֶׁבְּקִיבּוֹלֶת לֹא יַעֲשֶׂה. אַף עַל פִּי שֶׁבְּקִיבּוֹלֶת וְלָא מִיבַּעְיָא שֶׁאֵינָהּ קִיבּוֹלֶת?! אַדְּרַבָּה, קִיבּוֹלֶת כְּדִידֵיהּ דָּמֵי! אֶלָּא, אֵימָא: [י]בֵּין קִיבּוֹלֶת בֵּין שֶׁאֵינָהּ קִיבּוֹלֶת לֹא יַעֲשֶׂה. [כ]הָיְתָה מְלַאכְתּוֹ בְּיַד אֲחֵרִים, בְּבֵיתוֹ — לֹא יַעֲשׂוּ, בְּבֵית אַחֵר — יַעֲשׂוּ. מָרְיוֹן בְּרֵיהּ דְּרָבִין וּמָר בְּרֵיהּ דְּרַב אַחָא בְּרֵיהּ דְּרָבָא [ל]הֲוָה לְהוּ הַהוּא גַּמְלָא דְּתוֹרָא בַּהֲדֵי הֲדָדֵי, אִיתְרְעָא בֵּיהּ מִילְּתָא בְּמָר בְּרֵיהּ דְּרַב אַחָא בְּרֵיהּ דְּרָבָא, וּפַסְקֵיהּ לְגַמְלֵיהּ. אָמַר רַב אַשִׁי: גַּבְרָא רַבָּה כְּמָר בְּרֵיהּ דְּרַב אַחָא עָבֵיד הָכִי?! נְהִי דִּלְפְסֵידָא דִּידֵיהּ לָא חָיֵישׁ, אַדַּאֲחֵרִים לָא חָיֵישׁ? וְהָא תַּנְיָא: אִם הָיוּ מוּשְׂכָּרִין אוֹ מוּחְכָּרִין אֵצֶל אֲחֵרִים — הֲרֵי אֵלּוּ יַעֲשׂוּ! וְהוּא סָבַר: *[מ]אָדָם חָשׁוּב שָׁאנֵי.

אָמַר

רש"י

מי שֶׁהָפַךְ אֶת זֵיתָיו. שֶׁהִזְמִינָן לִיתֵּן עַל גַּבֵּי הַבַּד לְהוֹצִיא מֵהֶן שֶׁמֶן: וְאֵירְעוֹ אֵבֶל. בִּשְׁאָר יְמוֹת הַשָּׁנָה, שֶׁלֹּא סָמוּךְ לָרֶגֶל, וְאֵינוֹ יָכוֹל לִיתְּנָם עַל גַּבֵּי הַבַּד, לְפִי שֶׁאָבֵל אָסוּר בַּעֲשִׂיַּית מְלָאכָה: אוֹ אוֹנֶס. הַיְינוּ מִילְּתָא אַחֲרִיתֵי. כְּלוֹמַר, מִי שֶׁהָפַךְ אֶת זֵיתָיו לִפְנֵי הָרֶגֶל וְאֵירְעוֹ אוֹנֶס, וְלֹא הָיָה יָכוֹל לִיתְּנָם עַל גַּבֵּי בֵּית הַבַּד, וּבָא הָרֶגֶל: אוֹ שֶׁהִטְעוּהוּ פּוֹעֲלִים. שֶׁהִשְׂכִּיר לִיתְּנָם עַל גַּבֵּי בֵּית הַבַּד קוֹדֶם הָרֶגֶל, וְלֹא בָּאוּ: טוֹעֵן קוֹרָה רִאשׁוֹנָה. כְּלוֹמַר: נוֹתְנָן עַל גַּבֵּי בֵּית הַבַּד בָּרֶגֶל וְסוֹחֵט עֲלֵיהֶן הַקּוֹרָה פַּעַם אַחַת, דְּאִי לָא עָבֵיד הָכִי — אִיכָּא פְּסֵידָא יְתֵירָא: וּמַנִּיחָהּ. בּוֹ, שֶׁלֹּא יִסְחוֹט יוֹתֵר עַד לְאַחַר הַמּוֹעֵד: זוֹלֵף וְגוֹמֵר כְּדַרְכּוֹ. כְּלוֹמַר, נוֹתְנוֹ עַל גַּבֵּי בֵּית הַבַּד וְסוֹחֵט הַכֹּל. כָּל מִידֵי דְּשָׁפוּךְ קָרֵי זִילּוּף:

גמ' פָּתַח בְּאֵבֶל וְסַיֵּים בַּמּוֹעֵד. דְּקָתָנֵי: מִי שֶׁהָפַךְ אֶת זֵיתָיו וְאֵירְעוֹ אֵבֶל וְלֹא פֵּירֵשׁ אִם יָכוֹל לִטְעוֹן קוֹרָה בַּאֲבֵילוּת אִם לָאו, אֶלָּא מִילֵּי דְּמוֹעֵד קָא פָּרֵישׁ, דְּכִי אֵירַע לוֹ קוֹדֶם הַמּוֹעֵד אוֹנֶס — טוֹעֵן קוֹרָה רִאשׁוֹנָה בַּמּוֹעֵד: אָסוּר בִּימֵי אֶבְלוֹ. כְּלוֹמַר: לְהָכִי לָא פָּרֵישׁ, דְּאָסוּר לוֹ לִטְעוֹן אֲפִילּוּ קוֹרָה רִאשׁוֹנָה בִּימֵי אֶבְלוֹ: לָא מִבַּעְיָא בִּימֵי אֶבְלוֹ. דְּאֵין אָסוּר בִּמְלָאכָה אֶלָּא מִדְּרַבָּנָן, דְּשָׁרֵי לִטְעוֹן קוֹרָה רִאשׁוֹנָה: אֶלָּא אֲפִילּוּ. חוּלּוֹ שֶׁל מוֹעֵד דַּאֲסִירָא בֵּיהּ מְלָאכָה מִדְּאוֹרַיְיתָא, דִּכְתִיב (שמות כג): "אֶת חַג הַמַּצּוֹת תִּשְׁמוֹר שִׁבְעַת יָמִים" — לִימֵּד עַל כָּל הֶחָג שֶׁהוּא אָסוּר: בִּמְקוֹם פְּסֵידָא שָׁרוּ רַבָּנַן. לִטְעוֹן קוֹרָה רִאשׁוֹנָה: הָעוֹשִׂין לָאָבֵל. אֲחֵרִים, אֲבָל הוּא עַצְמוֹ אֵינוֹ רַשַּׁאי: כַּדּוֹ לָגוּף. מְגוּפַת הֶחָבִית: וְזֵיתָיו הֲפוּכִין. נוֹתְנִין אוֹתָן עַל בֵּית הַבַּד, וְטוֹעֲנִין לוֹ קוֹרָה רִאשׁוֹנָה. אֲבָל הוּא עַצְמוֹ אֵינוֹ עוֹשֶׂה, הַיְינוּ כְּרַב שֵׁישָׁא, דְּאָמַר: דְּבָרִים הַמּוּתָּרִין בְּחוש"מ אֲסוּרִין בִּימֵי אֶבְלוֹ: וּפִשְׁתָּנוֹ לְהַעֲלוֹת מִן הַמִּשְׁרָה. כָּל הָנֵי אִית בְּהוּ פְּסֵידָא אִי לָא עָבֵיד לְהוּ: מִשֶּׁתַּגִּיעַ עוֹנַת הַמַּיִם שֶׁלּוֹ. כְּשֶׁהִגִּיעַ זְמַנּוֹ לְהַשְׁקוֹת הַשָּׂדֶה, שֶׁכָּךְ הָיוּ נוֹהֲגִין: כָּל אֶחָד וְאֶחָד מַשְׁקֶה כָּל הַשָּׂדוֹת שֶׁבַּבִּקְעָה, אִישׁ יוֹמוֹ אוֹ שָׁבוּעַ אֶחָד: שְׂדֵה נִיר. שָׂדֶה חֲרוּשָׁה: שָׂדֶה הָעוֹמֶדֶת לְפִשְׁתָּן. שֶׁאִם לֹא תִּזָּרַע עַכְשָׁו, מִכָּאן וְאֵילָךְ — אֵינוֹ רָאוּי לְפִשְׁתָּן: אָמְרוּ לוֹ. לֹא תִּזָּרַע שְׂדֵה נִיר וּשְׂדֵה פִּשְׁתָּן. שֶׁאִם לֹא תִּזָּרַע בִּבְכִיר בִּשְׂדֵה נִיר — תִּזָּרַע בְּאָפֵל, וְלָא הָוֵי פְּסֵידָא יְתֵירָא: בַּלָּן. שׁוֹמֵר בֵּית הַמֶּרְחָץ, וּמְשַׁמֵּשׁ בְּבֵית הַמֶּרְחָץ, וְנוֹטֵל מִכָּל אֶחָד שְׂכָרוֹ: וְהִגִּיעַ עֵת הָרֶגֶל. שֶׁהַכֹּל צְרִיכִין לוֹ — הֲרֵי זֶה יַעֲשֶׂה, כֵּיוָן דְּאִית לֵיהּ פְּסֵידָא, וְאִיכָּא נַמִּי צוֹרֶךְ רַבִּים. וְל"ג הָכָא בְּצִינְעָא — דְּהָא רַבִּים הוּא: הָאֲרִיסִין. מְקַבְּלֵי הַשָּׂדוֹת לְשְׁנַיִם לִשְׁלִישׁ וְלִרְבִיעַ: הַחֲכִירִים. שֶׁקִּיבֵּל לִשְׁמִירָה וּלְעוֹבְדָהּ לִסְכוּם, כָּךְ וְכָךְ כּוֹרִין אֲנִי נוֹתֵן לְךָ מִמֶּנָּה: וְהַקַּבְּלָנִים. שֶׁקִּיבְּלוּ לְשׁוֹמְרָהּ לִזְמַן פְּלוֹנִי בִּסְכוּם כָּךְ וְכָךְ, בֵּין יִהְיֶה הַרְבֵּה אוֹ מְעַט — הֲרֵי אֵלּוּ יַעֲשׂוּ אֲחֵרִים בִּשְׁבִילָם: הַגַּמָּלִים וְהַסַּפָּנִים הֲרֵי אֵלּוּ לֹא יַעֲשׂוּ. לֹא יַשְׂכִּירוּ לְכַתְּחִילָּה, לְפִי שֶׁהַמְּלָאכָה שֶׁלָּהֶם הוּא: וְאִם הָיוּ מוּחְכָּרִין אוֹ מוּשְׂכָּרִין. הֵם אוֹ בְּהֶמְתָּם אֵצֶל אֲחֵרִים לְמֵהַלֵּךְ חֹדֶשׁ אוֹ חֳדָשִׁים — הֲרֵי אֵלּוּ יַעֲשׂוּ הֵם לְעַצְמָן, וְלֹא יַפְסִידוּ כָּל שְׂכָרָן, וּבְעָלִים נַמִּי לֹא יַפְסִידוּ. וְהָכָא לֹא קָתָנֵי עַל יְדֵי אֲחֵרִים — שֶׁהֲרֵי הֵן בְּעַצְמָן מוּשְׂכָּרִין. אֲבָל אֲרִיסִים — אֶפְשָׁר לָהֶם עַל יְדֵי אֲחֵרִים בַּעֲבוֹדַת קַרְקַע: שְׂכִיר יוֹם. אֶחָד, וַאֲפִילּוּ בְּעִיר אַחֶרֶת וְאֵין יוֹדְעִין שָׁם שֶׁהוּא אָבֵל, וְלֵיכָּא מִשּׁוּם מַרְאִית הָעַיִן: לֹא יַעֲשֶׂה. הוֹאִיל וּבְיָדוֹ לַחֲזוֹר כִּדְאָמְרִינַן (ב"ק דף קטז:) פּוֹעֵל חוֹזֵר, וַאֲפִילּוּ בַּחֲצִי הַיּוֹם, וְלֵיכָּא פְּסֵידָא כּוּלֵּי הַאי: אִם הָיְתָה מְלֶאכֶת אֲחֵרִים בְּיָדוֹ. כְּגוֹן בֶּגֶד לֶאֱרוֹג. הוֹאִיל וּבִרְשׁוּתֵיהּ לְגוֹמְרוֹ לְאַחַר זְמַן — הֲרֵי (א)אֵלּוּ לֹא יַעֲשׂוּ: וְאע"פ שֶׁבְּקִיבּוֹלֶת. אֲחֵרִים הִיא, שֶׁקִּיבֵּל עָלָיו לְמִיתוּת אוֹתוֹ בֶּגֶד לְאוֹרְגוֹ בְּכָךְ וְכָךְ: קִיבּוֹלֶת. לַעֲשׂוֹת בְּכָךְ וְכָךְ (שָׁרֵי): כְּדִידֵיהּ דָּמְיָא. וְאָסוּר. אֲבָל שֶׁאֵינָהּ קִיבּוֹלֶת, דְּלָא הָוֵה כְּדִידֵיהּ — שָׁרֵי: בְּבֵיתוֹ. שֶׁל אָבֵל לֹא יַעֲשׂוּ אוֹתוֹ,(ב) מִשּׁוּם חֲשָׁד, שֶׁיֹּאמְרוּ: הוּא בְּעַצְמוֹ מְסַיֵּיעַ בַּמְּלָאכָה. אִי נַמִּי: שֶׁלֹּא יֹאמְרוּ בִּימֵי אֶבְלוֹ הִשְׂכִּירוּ לָזֶה הַפּוֹעֵל: גַּמְלָא. צֶמֶד בָּקָר בֵּין שְׁנֵיהֶם, שׁוֹר אֶחָד לָזֶה וְשׁוֹר אֶחָד לָזֶה: אִיתְרַע בֵּיהּ מִילְּתָא. אֲבֵילוּת: פַּסְקֵיהּ לְגַמְלֵיהּ. הִפְסִיק שׁוֹרוֹ מִן הַצֶּמֶד, וְלֹא שְׁלָחוֹ לַחֲרוֹשׁ בַּשָּׂדֶה. לְפִי שֶׁהָיָה אָבֵל וּמְצוּוֶּה עַל שְׁבִיתַת בְּהֶמְתּוֹ מִדְּרַבָּנָן: לְהֶפְסֵד דִּידֵיהּ לָא חָיֵישׁ. דְּלָא קָא מְעַבֵּד אַרְעָא מִגַּמְלֵיהּ, מִשּׁוּם דְּאָבֵל הוּא: לִפְסֵידָא דַּאֲחֵרִינֵי. כְּגוֹן מָרְיוֹן — לָא חָיֵישׁ?! דְּלָא קָא מְשַׁדֵּר לְגַמְלֵיהּ הָוֵי לֵיהּ פְּסֵידָא, דְּלָא הֲוָה לֵיהּ בְּהֵמָה לַחֲרוֹשׁ. וְכֵיוָן דְּשָׁרֵי כִּדְתַנְיָא: אִם הָיוּ מוּחְכָּרִין וכו' — הֲוָה לֵיהּ לְמֵיחַשׁ אַפְּסֵידָא דְּחַבְרֵיהּ: הוּא סָבַר. מָר בְּרֵיהּ דְּרַב אַחָא: אָדָם חָשׁוּב שָׁאנֵי. דְּהָא וְהָא אָסוּר לְדִידֵיהּ לְמֵיעֲבַד:

מְקַבְּלֵי

תוספות

רבי יוסי אומר זולף וגומר וגף כדרכו. פי' בקונטרס, לישנא אחרינא: וגף — משום (ג)דאיכא פסידא שמוליכן בלא מגופה. וי"ל: דצריך לכסותו מפני השרצים. ומיהו, מגופה לא היה צריך, דדיו בכיסוי מועט *ושמן חדש מתקלקל: **אפילו** חול המועד דאסורא במלאכה מדאורייתא *פרק קמא (דף ב. בד"ה משקין) פירשתי: **רבי** יהודה אומר אף זורעים כו'. במתניתין מחמיר רבי יהודה, וכאן מיקל: **בורו** לגוף. ספרים אחרים: כדו: **רבן** שמעון בן גמליאל אומר כו'. ואף על גב דרבן שמעון בן גמליאל נמי מודה לדרב שישא בריה דרב אידי, דאסורין בימי אבלו — מודה היכא דאין שם אומן אלא הוא, דשרי, ובצינעא (ד) יעשו ע"י אחרים, משום פסידא דמשכיר שרינן, וגבי אבלו דשרינן הוא עצמו באין שם שיעשה כמותו, ואומן לרבים וספר וכו' — משום דצורך דרבים ורגילא שריא לעיל. ויש מפרשים: דהא דשרינן לאבל עצמו (ה) — כשלא ימצא אחרים, כדמשמע הלשון: ואין שם אומן אלא הוא. אבל לכתחילה — צריך לעשות על ידי אחרים. מיהו, לפי הטעם הזה לא ידענא בחמרין וספרין כשמושכרין אצל אחרים למה אין מצריך בסמוך על ידי אחרים? ולפי טעם קמא ניחא, דאין מי שיעשה דבר זה באותו שיש (ו) אומנות דחמר וגמל וספן:

אמר

רבינו חננאל

מי שהפך את זיתיו לטחנן ואירעו אבל או אונס או שהטעוהו הפועלים ונכנס המועד טוען קורה ראשונה ומניחם לאחר המועד דברי ר"י ר' יוסי אומר זולף וגומר *) כדרכו ומקשינן מתניתין באבל ולא פירש אם מותר לעשות מלאכתו במקום פסידא אם לא. וקפץ ומורה לנו בחולו של מועד שמותר במקום פסידא. ופירק רב שישא בריה דרב אידי זאת אומרת דברים המותרין בחוש"מ אסורין לעשותן בימי אבלו. תניא כותיה אלו דברים שעושין לאבל בימי אבלו. פירוש התירו משום פסידא לעשות לו אחרים ולא הוא אבל ע"י אחרים התירו לו להפוך זיתיו ולגוף בדיו ולהעלות פשתנו מן המשרה וצמרו מן היורה ומרביצין שדהו משתגיע עונת המים שלו. ר' יהודה אומר אף זורעין כו' ר' שמעון בן גמליאל אומר זיתיו הפוכין פשתנו במשרה צמרו ביורה ואין שם אומן אלא הוא הרי זה עושה בצנעא בתוך ביתו וכן היה אומר אם היה ספר או בלן לרבים והגיע הרגל ואין שם אלא הוא הרי זה יעשה. האריסין והחכירין והקבלנין בשדותיו הרי אלו יעשו אבל החמרין והגמלין והספינה שלו לא יעשה בהן מלאכה בימי אבלו ואם היו מקודם מושכרין ביד אחרים עושין. שכיר יום שלו אפילו בעיר אחרת לא יעשה היתה מלאכת אחרים בידו בין בקיבולת בין שאינה בקיבולת לא יעשה היתה מלאכתו ביד אחרים בביתו לא יעשה בבית אחר יעשה. מריון ומר בריה דרב אחא הוו שותפי אירע ביה במר בריה דרב אחא אבל. שדר ופסקיה לגמליה. אמר רב אשי והתניא אם היו מושכרין אצל אחרים שרו ודחינן הני מילי באיניש דעלמא אבל אדם חשוב אפי' מושכרין לא:

אמר

*) רבינו לא גרס וגף גבי זיתים וכ"כ ברש"י בא"לפס ובנ"י שם דלא גרסינן וגף.

הגהות הב"ח

(א) רש"י ד"ה אם היתה כו' לאחר זמן הרי לא יעשה אף על פי שבקיבולת כו' כן צריך להיות והד"א ותיבת אלו נמחק: (ב) ד"ה בביתו של אבל לא יעשו אותו אחרים משום חשד: (ג) תוס' ד"ה רבי יוסי כו' דאיכא פסידא כשמוליכן. נ"ב לשון הר"ן וגף לא גרסי גבי זיתים משום דאין דרך לעשות לזיתים מגופה דאפי' הניחו מגולה לא פסדי וכן נמצא בפרש"י באלפס ובנימוקי יוסף ע"ש אבל בלשון אחר פירש דגרסי' ליה אע"ג דליכא פסידא לזיתים בלא מגופה מ"מ ודאי כשמוליכין אותן איכא פסידא שניתז השמן בלא מגופה: (ד) ד"ה רשב"ג כו' ובצינעא והאריסין יעשו: (ה) בא"ד דשרינן לאבל עצמו היינו דוקא כשלא ימצא: (ו) בא"ד באותו שיש לו אומנות:

גליון הש"ס

גמ' לא מיבעיא בימי אבלו דמדרבנן. עיין לקמן דף יד ע"ב תוס' ד"ה עשה דיחיד:

שמחות פ"ה

[לקמן יב. שבת נא. וש"נ]

ס"א אינו

אָמַר שְׁמוּאֵל: מְקַבְּלֵי קִיבּוֹלֶת, בְּתוֹךְ הַתְּחוּם אָסוּר, חוּץ לַתְּחוּם — מוּתָּר. אָמַר רַב פָּפָּא: וַאֲפִי' חוּץ לַתְּחוּם לָא אֲמַרַן אֶלָּא דְּלֵיכָּא מָתָא דְּמִקַּרְבָא לְהָתָם, אֲבָל אִיכָּא מָתָא דְּמִקַּרְבָא לְהָתָם — אָסוּר. אָמַר רַב מְשַׁרְשְׁיָא: וְכִי לֵיכָּא מָתָא דְּמִקַּרְבָא לְהָתָם נַמִּי, לָא אֲמַרַן אֶלָּא בְּשַׁבָּתוֹת וּבְיָמִים טוֹבִים, דְּלָא שְׁכִיחִי אֱנָשֵׁי דְּאָזְלִי לְהָתָם. אֲבָל בְּחוש"מ דִּשְׁכִיחִי אֱנָשֵׁי דְּאָזְלִי וְאָתוּ לְהָתָם — אָסוּר. מָר זוּטְרָא בְּרֵיהּ דְּרַב נַחְמָן בָּנוּ לֵיהּ אַפַּדְנָא מְקַבְּלֵי קִיבּוֹלֶת חוּץ לַתְּחוּם. אִיקְלַע רַב סָפְרָא וְרַב הוּנָא בַּר חִינָּנָא, וְלָא עָלוּ לְגַבֵּיהּ. וְאִיכָּא דְּאָמְרִי: הוּא נַמִּי לָא עָל בְּגַוֵּויהּ. וְהָאָמַר שְׁמוּאֵל: מְקַבְּלֵי קִיבּוֹלֶת, בְּתוֹךְ הַתְּחוּם — אָסוּר, חוּץ לַתְּחוּם — מוּתָּר! *אָדָם חָשׁוּב שָׁאנֵי. וְאִיכָּא דְּאָמְרֵי: סַיּוּעֵי סַיֵּיע בְּתִיבְנָא בַּהֲדַיְיהוּ, רַב חָמָא שְׁרָא לְהוּ (א) לְאַבּוּנַגְרֵי דְּבֵי רֵישׁ גָּלוּתָא לְמֶיעֱבַד לְהוּ עֲבִידְתָּא בְּחוּלָּא דְּמוֹעֲדָא. אֲמַר: כֵּיוָן דַּאֲגַר לָא קָא שָׁקְלִי — שַׁרְשׁוּיֵי הוּא דְּקָא מְשַׁרְשׁוּ לֵיהּ. וְלֵית לַן בָּהּ. תָּנוּ רַבָּנַן: מְקַבְּלִין קִיבּוֹלֶת בַּמּוֹעֵד לַעֲשׂוֹתָהּ לְאַחַר הַמּוֹעֵד, וּבַמּוֹעֵד — אָסוּר. כְּלָלוֹ שֶׁל דָּבָר: כׇּל שֶׁהוּא עוֹשֶׂה — אוֹמֵר לְגוֹי וְעוֹשֶׂה, וְכׇל שֶׁאֵינוֹ עוֹשֶׂה — אֵינוֹ אוֹמֵר לְגוֹי וְעוֹשֶׂה. תַּנְיָא אִידַּךְ: *מְקַבְּלִין קִיבּוֹלֶת בַּמּוֹעֵד לַעֲשׂוֹתָהּ לְאַחַר הַמּוֹעֵד, וּבִלְבַד שֶׁלֹּא יִמְדּוֹד וְשֶׁלֹּא יִשְׁקוֹל וְשֶׁלֹּא יִמְנֶה כְּדֶרֶךְ שֶׁהוּא עוֹשֶׂה בַּחוֹל. ת"ר: *אֵין מַרְבִּיעִין בְּהֵמָה בְּחוּלּוֹ שֶׁל מוֹעֵד, כַּיּוֹצֵא בּוֹ אֵין מַרְבִּיעִין בִּבְכוֹר, וְלֹא בִּפְסוּלֵי הַמּוּקְדָּשִׁין. תַּנְיָא אִידַּךְ: אֵין מַרְבִּיעִין בְּהֵמָה בְּחוּלּוֹ שֶׁל מוֹעֵד, ר' יְהוּדָה אוֹמֵר: *חֲמוֹרָה שֶׁתָּבְעָה — מַרְבִּיעִין עָלֶיהָ זָכָר בִּשְׁבִיל שֶׁלֹּא תִּצְטַנֵּן, וּשְׁאָר כׇּל הַבְּהֵמוֹת מַכְנִיסִין אוֹתָן לַבְּקָרוֹת. ת"ר: *אֵין מְדַיְּירִין לֹא בְּשַׁבָּתוֹת, וְלֹא בְּיָמִים טוֹבִים. וְלֹא בְּחוּלּוֹ שֶׁל מוֹעֵד. וְאִם בָּאוּ מֵאֲלֵיהֶן — מוּתָּר. וְאֵין מְסַיְּיעִין אוֹתָן, וְאֵין מוֹסְרִין לָהֶם שׁוֹמֵר לְנַעֵר אֶת צֹאנָם. הָיָה שְׂכִיר שַׁבָּת, שְׂכִיר חֹדֶשׁ, שְׂכִיר שָׁנָה, שְׂכִיר שָׁבוּעַ — מְסַיְּיעִין אוֹתָן,[א] *וּמוֹסְרִין לָהֶם שׁוֹמֵר לְנַעֵר אֶת צֹאנָם. [ב]ר' אוֹמֵר: בְּשַׁבָּת — בְּטוֹבָה, בְּיו"ט — בִּמְזוֹנוֹת, בַּמּוֹעֵד — בְּשָׂכָר. אָמַר רַב יוֹסֵף: הִלְכְתָא כְּרַבִּי.§ **מתני'** וְכֵן מִי שֶׁהָיָה יֵינוֹ בְּתוֹךְ הַבּוֹר וְאֵירְעוֹ אֵבֶל אוֹ אוֹנֶס, אוֹ שֶׁהִטְעוּהוּ — *זוֹלֵף וְגוֹמֵר וְגָף כְּדַרְכּוֹ, דִּבְרֵי ר' יוֹסֵי. ר' יְהוּדָה אוֹמֵר: עוֹשֶׂה לוֹ לִימּוּדִים בִּשְׁבִיל שֶׁלֹּא יַחְמִיץ.§ **גמ'** וּצְרִיכָא, דְּאִי אַשְׁמְעִינַן קַמַּיְיתָא — בְּהַהִיא קָאָמַר ר' יוֹסֵי, מִשּׁוּם דְּמִישְׁחָא נְפִישׁ פְּסֵידֵיהּ. אֲבָל חַמְרָא דְּלָא נְפִישׁ פְּסֵידֵיהּ — אֵימָא מוֹדֵי לֵיהּ לְרַבִּי יְהוּדָה. וְאִי אַשְׁמְעִינַן בְּתַרְיְיתָא — בְּהַהִיא קָאָמַר רַבִּי יְהוּדָה, אֲבָל בְּהַךְ אֵימָא — מוֹדֶה לְר' יוֹסֵי, צְרִיכָא. אָמַר רַב יִצְחָק בַּר אַבָּא: *מַאן תְּנָא שִׁינּוּי בַּמּוֹעֵד בְּדָבָר הָאָבֵד — דְּלָא כְּר' יוֹסֵי. אָמַר רַב יוֹסֵף: הֲלָכָה כְּר' יוֹסֵי. בָּעוּ מִינֵּיהּ מֵרַב נַחְמָן בַּר יִצְחָק: מַהוּ לְמֵישַׁע חָבִיתָא דְּשִׁיכְרָא בְּחוּלָּא דְּמוֹעֲדָא? אֲמַר לְהוּ: *סִינַי אֲמַר: הֲלָכָה כְּר' יוֹסֵי. אֵימוּר דַּאֲמַר רַבִּי יוֹסֵי בְּחַמְרָא, בְּשִׁיכְרָא מִי אֲמַר? חַמְרָא טַעְמָא מַאי — מִשּׁוּם דִּנְפִישׁ פְּסֵידֵיהּ, שִׁיכְרָא נַמִּי אִית בָּהּ פְּסֵידָא. דַּאֲמַר אַבָּיֵי, *אָמְרָה לִי אֵם: בַּר שִׁית סָאוֵי וְשָׁיֵיעַ — מִבַּר תְּמָנֵי וְלָא שָׁיֵיעַ. אָמַר רַב חָמָא בַּר גּוּרְיָא אָמַר רַב: הִלְכוֹת מוֹעֵד כְּהִלְכוֹת כּוּתִים *) בַּהֲלָכָה. לְמַאי הִלְכְתָא? אָמַר רַב דָּנִיאֵל *בַּר קְטִינָא **) (אָמַר רַב:) לוֹמַר שֶׁהֵן עֲקוּרוֹת, וְאֵין לְמֵידוֹת זוֹ מִזּוֹ. דְּאָמַר שְׁמוּאֵל: זוֹפְתִין כּוּזְתָא, וְאֵין זוֹפְתִין חָבִיתָא. רַב דִּימִי מִנְּהַרְדְּעָא אָמַר: זוֹפְתִין חָבִיתָא וְאֵין זוֹפְתִין כּוּזְתָא. מָר חָיֵישׁ לִפְסֵידָא, וּמָר חָיֵישׁ לְטִירְחָא. אָמַר אַבָּיֵי: *נָקְטִינַן, הִלְכוֹת מוֹעֵד כְּהִלְכוֹת שַׁבָּת; יֵשׁ

*) [תיבת בהלכה ליתא בהרי"ף ובהרא"ש]. **) [ליתא בהרא"ש].

רש"י

מקבלי קיבולת בתוך התחום אסור. ליתן מלאכה לגוי בקיבולת כי עבדי ליה בשבתא, דידעי כולי עלמא ואמרי: היום בשבת יהב ליה. והא דשרי בית הלל בפ"ק דשבת (ד' יז:) ליתן כלים לכובס בע"ש עם חשיכה, ואפי' בתוך התחום, משום דכביסה בגוי מידי דלא מינכר, וליכא חשדא. אבל מידי דמינכר — בתוך התחום אסור, משום חשדא: אבל אי איכא מתא דמקרבא להתם. אותן פועלים גוים אסורים, דאינהו ידעי דהני גוים עבדי ליה מלאכה ואמרי: בשבתא יהב להו: אסור. דאמרי: היום יהבו ליה: סיועי הוה מסייע בתיבנא. שהיה נותן להם תבן למלאכה. דהואיל והוא מסייע בהדייהו — אסור: אבונגרי. מסדרי שולחנות: למיעבד עבידתייהו. אם נשבר השלחן — שרי לתקנו: שרשויי. ריוח בעלמא, כדי סעודתם דקא אכלי בהדייהו, ולא קא חשיב מלאכה: מקבלין קיבולת. נותנה לגוי לעשותה אחר המועד: אין מרביעין בהמה. משום דעביד מלאכה בחולו של מועד: אין מרביעין. אין אוחזין הבהמה ומביאין עליה זכר: בבכור. דקעביד ביה מלאכה, וכתיב: (דברים טו) "לא תעבוד בבכור שורך": לבקרות. מקום שיש שם בהמות, והיא רובעת מעצמה: מדיירין. מכניסין בהמה לשדה, כדי שיוטילו זבל, ומזבלין השדה: אין מסייעין אותן. לבהמה לבא בשדה, או אם גוים הם — אין מסייעין להם להסיען ממקום למקום כדי שתזבל כל השדה, אפילו בבאין מעצמם: לנער. לשמור, כגון אם גוים הם: שכיר שבת. שמשכרו כל השבוע לדייר שדהו: שבוע. שמיטה: מסייעין. כאילו של גוים הוא: ה"ג: ועושה גוי בשבת וי"ט ומסייעין במועד. דלא טרח מלאכה. כלומר, יכולין לסייע לאותו שכיר לדייר: ומוסרין לו רועה אחד לנער צאנו. שמדיירין אותה, הואיל ואינו שכיר לשבת ממש: רבי אומר בשבת בטובה. אם רוצה שום אדם לסייע לאותו שכיר בטובתו — עושה, כלומר: בחנם ולא בשכר: **מתני'** בתוך הבור. שלפני הגת אותו כלי שהיין נופל בו מן הגת קרוי בור: זולף וגומר כדרכו. כלומר: מריק אותו בחבית, וגף החבית במגופה גמורה: עושה לו למודים. אינו יכול לגוף כדרכו אלא שיחפם,(ב) היינו לימודין, בשביל שלא יחמיץ. שאם אינו סותמו — מחמיץ: **גמ'** וצריכא. למימר בתרוייהו, בשני בבי דמתני', דמשחא ודחמרא, ר' יוסי אומר זולף כו': בההיא. רישא דמתניתין: קאמר רבי יוסי. זולף כדרכו: דמשחא. יקיר, ואיכא פסידא יתירא: מודה ליה לר' יהודה. דאינו זולף וגף ממש, אלא עושה לימודים עראי: דלא כר' יוסי. דאמר: גומר כדרכו ואינו צריך שינוי: למישע. לגוף החבית: סיני. *)רב יוסף: הלכה כר' יוסי. דגף כדרכו: בר שית סאוי ושייע מבר תמני ולא שייע. כלומר: יפה שכר מוגף שמחזיק ששה סאין, משכר שהוא בכלי גדול שמחזיק שמונה סאין: כהלכות כותים. דאמרינן (חולין דף ד.): היכא דאחזיק — אחזיק, היכא דלא אחזיק — לא אחזיק: עקורות. כאשה עקרה, שאין לאדם ממנה פרי, אלא גופה: ואין למידין זו מזו. דאימא: כשם שזו מותרת, כך זו מותרת. כמו בכותים ולא אמרינן: כי היכי דמחזיק בהאי, מחזיק בהאי אלא לא ילפי הני מהני: מר. דאמר זופתין חביתא חייש לפסידא, ובחביתא איכא פסידא יתירא אי לא זפתי לה, משום דנפיש יינא. ובכוזתא ליכא פסידא יתירא. כוזא — כלי קטן: מר. דאמר זופתין לכוזא, דחייש לטירחא יתירא, ובכוזא ליכא טירחא יתירא, ובחביתא איכא טירחא יתירא:

*) ברכות סד. הוריות יד.

תוספות

אמר שמואל מקבלי קיבולת בתוך התחום. הא דשרינן כלים לכובס גוי, פירש בקונט' דלא מינכר שהוא של ישראל. ור' יעקב לא היה מחלק. ואומר דשרי במועד וגם בשבת, דהא ריחים של מים איכא השמעת קול, ושרינן בפ"ק דשבת (דף יח. ושם). ובפ"ק דע"ז (דף כא: ושם) שרינן להשכיר שדה לגוי, משום דאריסותיה קעביד, וכ"ש קבלנות, שאין הבית מתעלה בכך אלא ממהר לעשות. ואע"ג דר' שמעון בן אלעזר פליג — מסתמא הלכה כר' שמעון בן גמליאל דקא אסר התם מרחץ במשנה, משמע: הא שדה — שרי, כדדייק התם. ותניא בפ"ק דשבת (דף יט.) גבי ספינה: פוסק עמו על מנת לשבות, ואינו שובת. אלמא אין הגוי מניח לעשות קבלנותו בשביל ישראל. ואיכא מאן דאמר: אפי' לפסוק אין צריך. ובשמעתין דאסר שמואל — מפרש רבינו יעקב כאותו פירוש שמעמידין כולהו שמעתתא באבל, וכדרב שישא דאמר (לעיל יא:): דברים המותרי' בחש"מ אסורין בימי אבלו, דהוי דאורייתא או כעין דאורייתא. אבל במועד — הקילו, וכ"ש שיש להן להקל בשבת, דלא חיישינן כל כך דלא ליזלזל ביה. וא"ת: כיון דבאבילות איירי שמואל, היכי קאמר וכי ליכא מתא דמיקרבא להתם,(ג) לא אמרן אלא בשבתות וימים טובים דלא שכיחי דאזלי מדוכתא, אבל בחולו של מועד — אסור וצריך עיון: **דברי** רבי יוסי. בשמן. (ד) תניא מילתא דר' יהודה ברישא, וכיון דאתחיל מילתא דרבי יוסי — מסיים לה. וגף ביין לא ידענא אי אבור אי אחבית קאי. מיהו, לכאורה אחבית קאי, דשייך בה מגופה, ומדקתני בה זולף וגומר — משמע דאבור קאי, דאחבית לא שייך, משמע דגף אחרי כן, וגם עושין לו לימודין משמע דקאי אבור. ולית ליה זולף וגומר, דאחבית לא שייך לימודין, דסגי בכיסוי קטן:

מכניס

עין משפט נר מצוה

יא א מיי' פ"ו מהל' שבת הל' יד טוש"ע א"ח סי' רמד סעיף א:
יב ב מיי' פ"ז מהל' יו"ט הלכה כה טוש"ע שם סי' תקמג סעיף ב:
יג ג טוש"ע שם סי' תקמב סעיף א:
יד ד מיי' שם טוש"ע שם סי' תקמג סעיף ג:
טו ה מיי' שם הל' כד טוש"ע שם סעיף א:
טז ו מיי' שם הלכה כה טוש"ע שם סעיף ג:
יז ז מיי' שם פ"ח הלכה טו טוש"ע שם סי' תקלו סעיף ג:
יח ח מיי' פ"א מהל' מעילה הלכה ט:
יט ט י מיי' פ"ח מהל' יו"ט הל' יא טוש"ע שם סי' תקלז סעיף יד:
כ כ מיי' פ"ז מהלכות יו"ט הלכה ג (ופי"ג מהל' אבל הל' ו) טוש"ע א"ח סי' תקלח סעיף א:
כא ל מיי' פ"ז מהל' יו"ט הל' ג ופ"ח הלכה ז טוש"ע שם סי' תקלז סעיף א:
כב מ מיי' שם פ"ח הלכה יד:
כג נ ס מיי' שם טוש"ע שם סי' תקלח סעיף א:

רבינו חננאל

אמר שמואל מקבלי קיבולת. פי' אם קיבלו קיבולת בתוך התחום אסור. חוץ לתחום מותר. ואסיקנא הני מילי בשבתות ובי"ט דלא שכיחי אינשי דנפקי חוץ לתחום אבל בחולו של מועד דאיכא דנפקי חוץ לתחום אסור מר זוטרא בנו ליה גוים בקיבולת אפדנא חוץ לתחום ולא עיילי רבנן בההוא אפדנא איכא דאמרי הוא נמי לא על בההוא אפדנא. ואע"ג דאמר שמואל כי האי גוונא שרי אדם חשוב שאני איכא דאמרי עבדיה סייע בהדייהו בתיבנא רב חמא שרא לאבונגרי דבי ריש גלותא למיעבד להון עבידתא בחולי דמועדא מ"ט דכיון דלא אגרא שקלי שרשויי הוא דמשרשי להו כגון דורון הוא ושרי: ת"ר מקבלין קיבולת במועד לעשותה לאחר המועד ובלבד שלא ישקול ושלא ימדוד ושלא ימנה כדרך שהוא עושה בחול וכן אינו נותן בקיבולת לגוי במועד. כללו של דבר כל דבר שמותר לו לעשותו אומר לגוי ועושה וכל שאינו מותר לעשותו אינו אומר לגוי ועושה: ת"ר אין מרביעין בהמה בחולו של מועד. כיוצא בו אין מרביעין בבכור ולא בפסולי המוקדשין. ר' יהודה אומר חמורה שתבעה מרביעין עליה בשביל שלא תצטנן ושאר כל הבהמות מכניסין אותן לבקרות: **ת"ר** אין מדיירין בחולו של מועד פי' מכניסין הבהמות לדיר כדי שיטול זבלן לזבל השדות והאילנות ואם באו מאליהן מותר אבל אין מסייעין הרועים

גליון הש"ס

גמ' וכל שאינו עושה אינו אומר. עיין בכ"מ דף צ ע"א תוס' ד"ה אבל הכא:

מסורת הש"ס

[שבת נא. וש"נ]
[תוספתא פ"ב]
[שם]
[שם]
[עי' בתוספתא ספ"ב דשביעי']
ס"א ועושה נכרי בשבת ויו"ט ומסייעין במועד
שמחות פ"ה
[לעיל יא. ע"ש]
[ברכות סד.]
[קידושין לא. וש"נ]
גי' הרי"ף והרא"ש בר רב קטינא
[עי' פרש"י בעירובין ה. ד"ה והאמר ר"נ]

הגהות הב"ח

(א) גמ' רב חמא שרא להו לאבונגרי. נ"ב עי' סוף דף יח בפרש"י ד"ה לעלמו: (ב) רש"י ד"ה עושה כו' אלא שיחפם בנסרים היינו לימודין: (ג) תוס' ד"ה אמר כו' מתא דמיקרבא להתם נמי לא אמרן: (ד) ד"ה דברי ר' יוסי בשמן תנן מילתא דר' יהודה ברישא וביין תנן מילתא דר' יוסי ברישא דכיון דאתחיל במילתא דר' יוסי וכו' אי אבור קאי אי אחבית וכו' משמע דאבור קאי. נ"ב כלומר דפי' זולף היינו שסוחט וממלא וכשהוא בבור שייך לומר דממלא כל היין לתוך הבור וגומר כדרכו כולו ולהורידו לבור אבל אחבית לא שייך זולף וגומר כל עיקר אלא אבור קאי וקאמר וגף כדרכו דאח"כ כשסחט וממלא הכל מניח מגופה על הבור שהיין בתוכו ומכסהו כדרכו וזה עולה כגירסת הספרים בורו לגוף:

הגהות הגר"א

[א] גמ' שכיר שבוע מסייעין אותן נ"ב במועד. ומה שנדפס בלדו ס"א ועושה כו' נמחק: [ב] שם ר' אומר בשבת בטובה. נ"ב פי' דקאי ארישא באינו שכיר שבת ובאו מאליהן מותר במועד אפי' נותן לו שכר אח"כ ובסיפא שכיר שבת מסייעין כו' דוקא במועד לבד ומוסרין לו שומר לנער אף בשכר [עי' מ"א] (עמש"ש) [שו"ע] אבל הרמב"ם מפרש אסיפא (וכ"כ המ"מ) לכן השמיט שבת ויו"ט דס"ל דבהם בכל ענין אסור ובמועד כו' אף לשכור מותר (ועמ"ש רבינו בא"ח סי' תקל"ז):

יש מהן פטור אבל אסור, ויש מהן מותר לכתחלה. רב הונא חצדו ליה חצדא במועדא. איתיביה רבה בר רב הונא לרב הונא: טוחנין קמח במועד לצורך המועד, ושלא לצורך המועד – אסור. *[א]דבר שאבוד במועד – מותר לעשותו במועד, דבר שאינו אבוד במועד – אסור. במה דברים אמורים – בתלושין מן הקרקע, אבל מחובר לקרקע – אפי' כולו אבוד אסור. [ב]ואם אין לו מה יאכל – קוצר, ומעמר, ודש, וזורה, ובורר, וטוחן, [ג]ובלבד שלא ידוש בפרות. אמר ליה: יחידאה היא, ולא סבירא לן כוותיה. דתניא, כלל אמר רבן שמעון בן גמליאל משום ר' יוסי: דבר התלוש מן הקרקע, אפילו מקצתו אבוד – מותר. והמחובר לקרקע – אפי' כולו אבוד אסור. ואי ר' יוסי – ידוש נמי בפרות, הא אמר רב יצחק בר אבא: *מאן תנא שינוי במועד – בדבר האבד דלא כר' יוסי! אמר לך: ה"נ כיון דכל יומא לאו בפרות דיישי – האידנא נמי לאו שינוי הוא.

ת"ר: [ד]טוחנין במועד לצורך המועד, ושלא לצורך המועד – אסור. ואם טחן והותיר – הרי זה מותר. קוצצין עצים במועד, לצורך המועד ושלא לצורך המועד – אסור, ואם קצץ והותיר – הרי זה מותר. *[ה]מטילין שכר במועד לצורך המועד, ושלא לצורך המועד – אסור, ואם הטיל והותיר – הרי זה מותר. ובלבד שלא יערים. ורמינהו: מטילין שכר במועד לצורך המועד, ושלא לצורך המועד – אסור. אחד שכר תמרים, ואחד שכר שעורים. ואע"פ שיש לו ישן – [ו]מערים ושותה מן החדש! תנאי היא; דתניא: אין מערימין בכך, ר' יוסי בר יהודה אומר: מערימין. רב חצדו ליה חצדא בחולא דמועדא, שמע שמואל איקפד. לימא שמואל כיחידאה סבירא ליה? לא, חצדא דחיטי הוה, דלא הוה פסיד. ורב מאי טעמא עביד הכי? "אין לו מה יאכל" הוה. ושמואל – לא סיימוה קמיה. אי נמי: *אדם חשוב שאני. ר' יהודה נשיאה נפק (א) בחומרתא דמדושא, ואשתי מיא דאחים קפילא ארמאה. שמע ר' אמי *איקפד. אמר רב יוסף: מאי טעמא איקפד? (א) אי משום חומרתא דמדושא – הא תניא: *השירין הנזמים והטבעות – הרי הן ככל הכלים הניטלין בחצר. אי משום דאישתי מיא דאחים קפילא ארמאה – הא אמר (ב) שמואל בר יצחק אמר רב: *[ז]כל שנאכל כמות שהוא חי – אין בו משום בישולי גוים! אדם חשוב שאני. אמר רב חננאל אמר רב: קוצץ אדם דקל במועד, אע"פ שאינו צריך אלא לנסורת שלו. *לייט עלה אביי. רב אשי הוה ליה אבא בשלניא, אזל למיקצייה בחולא דמועדא. אמר ליה רב שילא משלנייא לרב אשי: מאי דעתיך – דקאמר רב חננאל אמר רב: קוצץ אדם דקל במועד אע"פ שאינו צריך אלא לנסורת שלו, הא לייט עלה אביי! אמר ליה: *לא שמיע לי, כלומר: לא סבירא לי. אישתמיט נרגא, בעי למיפסקיה לשקיה. שבקיה, והדר אתא. רב יהודה [ח]שרא למיעקר כיתנא, ולמיקטל כשותא, ולמיעקר שומשמי. אמר ליה אביי לרב יוסף: בשלמא כיתנא – חזי לחפיפה, כשותא – חזי לשיכרא, אלא שומשמי למאי חזי? חזי לנזיי דאית בהו. רבי ינאי הוה ליה ההוא פרדיסא דמטא זמניה בחולא דמועדא, קטפיה. לשנה שהיוה כולי עלמא לפרדיסייהו לחולא דמועדא. אפקריה רבי ינאי לפרדיסיה ההוא שתא.§

מתני' [ט]מכנים אדם פירותיו מפני הגנבים, [י]ושולה פשתנו מן המשרה בשביל שלא תאבד, [כ]ובלבד שלא יכוין את מלאכתו במועד. [ל]וכולן, אם כוונו מלאכתן במועד – יאבדו.§

גמ' תנא: [מ]ובלבד שיכניסם בצנעא לתוך ביתו. רב יוסף הוה ליה *כשורי, עיילינהו ביממא. אמר ליה אביי, והתניא: ובלבד שיכניסם בצנעא בתוך ביתו! אמר ליה: צנעא דהני – יממא הוא, [נ]כיון דבליליא בעו גברא יתירי, ובעו *מדוכרי דנורא – אוושא מילתא. "ושולה פשתנו מן המשרה" כו'.§ (ג) בעי מיניה רבי ירמיה מרבי זירא: ג) כוון מלאכתו במועד ומת, מהו שיקנסו בניו אחריו? אם תימצי לומר. צרם

א) [עי' מה שפירשו תוס' שבת מו: ד"ה ואמר עולא ותוס' עירובין סט. ד"ה כיון].
ב) [עי' תוס' בכורות לז: ד"ה בעא]. ג) גיטין מד. וע"ש בכורות לז:

יש מהן פטור אבל אסור. והא דקתני אין זופתין – אסור למיעבד לכתחילה, אבל בדיעבד – לא הוי חייב. והא דקתני זופתין – הוי מותר לכתחילה: למיחצד. לקצור. ורב הונא יש לו מה יאכל הוה, ואמאי שרי ליה? אמר ליה. האי דקתני מחובר אפי' כולו אבוד נמי אסור – ר' יוסי היא, ויחידאה היא ולא סבירא לן כוותיה: כיון דכל יומא לאו בפרות דיישי האידנא לאו שינוי הוא. כי דיישי בלא פרות. ולעולם ר' יוסי היא, והא דאסר בפרות – משום דאוושא מילתא היא: ואם טחן. במועד לצורך המועד, והותיר עד לאחר המועד: מותר. לאכלו אחר המועד: ובלבד שלא יערים. שלא יעשה הרבה, ויאמר: לצורך המועד אני עושה, ומתכוין כדי שתשתייר לאחר המועד: מערים ושותה מן החדש. שיכול לומר: לצורך המועד הטילו: לימא שמואל. דאקפיד, כיחידאה סבירא ליה, כההיא מתניתא (ג) במחובר אפי' כולו אבוד נמי אסור, ואוקימנא כר' יוסי יחידאה: חצדא דחיטי דלא הוה פסידא. להכי איקפד. אבל בחצדא דשערי – לא סבר לה כר' יוסי דאסיר: אין לו מה יאכל הוה. להכי עביד הכי: לא סיימוה קמיה. לא אמרו לו דלא הוה ליה מה יאכל, להכי איקפד: אדם חשוב שאני. רב לא הוה ליה למיעבד הכי אפי' אין לו מה יאכל: נפק. בחצר בשבת: בחומרתא דמדושא. טבעת, היא של מתכת וחותמה של אלמוג: שירין. נושקי"א בלעז: כל שהוא נאכל כמות שהוא חי. ומיא שתו אינשי כמות שהן: אדם חשוב שאני. יש לו להחמיר על עצמו יותר, ולא הוה ליה למיפק בחומרתא דמדושא, ולא למישתי מיא דאחים קפילא גוי: לנסורת. עלים דקים שנופלין מן החתיכה: אבא. יער: בשלניא. פירוש: שם העיר. כלומר, היה לו יער באותו מקום: אישתמיט נרגא בעי למיפסקיה לשקיה. דרב אשי, משום דעבר אדאביי: שבקיה. לאבא, דלא קצייה במועד, שהרגיש משום דעבר אדאביי נפל ליה נרגא: למיעקר כיתנא. בחולא דמועדא: למיקטל. לחתוך: כשותא. הומלו"ן: לחפיפה. לכסות בו מאכל, כגון תאנים ותמרים לצורך המועד: לנזיי. כמו נזייתא דשיכרא (ב"ק דף לה.). לנזיי – גרעינין דאית בהו בשומשמין, דחזו למיעבד בהו משחא: אפקריה רבי ינאי לפרדיסיה. משום דעל ידו היה תקלה לעלמא, דשהו עד לחולא דמועדא וקטפי:

מתני' שולה. מעלה: שלא יכוין מלאכתו במועד. שיש לו פנאי בשאר ימות השנה, והוא משהה למועד: יאבדו. שאסור ליהנות מהן:

גמ' צינעא דידהו יממא הוא. אפי' בלילה כיממא דמי, ולא סגי ליה שלא להכניסן. להכי מכניסן נמי ביום: מדוכרי דנורא. אבוקות: מהו שיקנסו בניו אחריו. לבניו נמי יהא אסור אותה מלאכה. דכיון דכוון מלאכתו במועד – דין הוא שיהו אסורין ליהנות ממנה, כשם שהיה אביהם קיים: נרס

[תוספתא פ"ב] [לעיל יא. ע"ש] [שבת קלט:] [לעיל יא: שבת נא. וש"נ] [שבת נא.] [שם מו:] [שבת נא. יבמות מו. ע"ש לח. נט.] [קדושין לג: וש"נ] [עירובין קב: וש"נ]

פי' נ"י קורות כבידים וגדולים

[גי' הערוך בע' מדכר מדכורי דטרא פי' אבוקות]

מכנים אדם פירותיו מפני הגנבים. פירש בתוספות הרב: דאסיפת פירות איכא מלאכה, כדאמרינן פרק "אין דורשין" (חגיגה דף יח.) גבי חג האסיף: אסיפה במועד מי שרי? ואיני יודע מה מלאכה. (ד) וצריך עיון אי טרח בלא מלאכה אסיר, כי היכי דאסירי בפרקמטיא. ולקמן בשמעתין (דף יג.) אמר: מועד משום טירחא ולא טירחא הוא. ושמא היינו דוקא בדבר שהוא מלאכה:

אם תימצי לומר צרם אזן הבכור ומת קנסו בנו אחריו. משום דאיסורא עשה. אבל כוון מלאכתו – לא עשה איסורא עדיין. ולא צריך להגיה דאוריי'. אבל בפ' "השולח" (גיטין מד. ושם) דגבי מכר ומת (ה)בעי אי קנסו בנו אחריו – התם גרסינן ודאי איסורא דאורייתא, משום דמכר ומת נמי עבד איסור', אלא דלא הוי דאוריי': נטייה

כד א מיי' פ"ז מהלכות יו"ט הל' ב טוש"ע א"ח סי' תקלז סעיף א:
כה ב ג מיי' שם הלכה ו טוש"ע שם סעיף טו:
כו ד מיי' שם טוש"ע שם סי' תקלג סעיף א:
כז ה ו מיי' פ"ז שם הלכה ח טוש"ע שם:
כח ז מיי' פי"ז מהל' מאכלות אסורות הלכה יד סמג לאוין קמב טוש"ע י"ד סי' קיג סעיף א:
כט ח מיי' פ"ח מהל' יו"ט הלכה יוד טוש"ע א"ח סי' תקלג סעיף ב:
ל ט מיי' שם פ"ז הל' ג טוש"ע שם סי' תקלח סעיף ב:
לא י כ מיי' שם והל' ד טוש"ע שם סעיף ג:
לב ל מיי' שם הל' ד טוש"ע שם סעיף א:
לג מ נ מיי' שם הל' ג טוש"ע שם סעיף ב:

רבינו חננאל

ואין מוסרין להם שומר לנער את צאנן ואם היה שכיר שנה שכיר חדש שכיר שבת מסייעין הרועין ומוסרין להם שומר לנער צאנן ר' אומר אם באו בשבת במובה בלא כלום הנאה או ביום טוב במזונות בלבד כלומר שכירותכם היא סעודתכם במועד אפי' בשכר אמר רב יוסף הלכתא כרבי: **מתני'** וכן מי שהיה יינו בבור ואירעו אבל או אונס או שהטעוהו פועלים ר' יוסי אומר זולף וגומר כדרכו. ר' יהודה אומר עושה לו לימודים כו' פירוש לימודים מכסהו וצריכא דאי אשמועינן משחא משום דנפיש פסידיה משום הכי שרי ר' יוסי אבל חמרא כו' אמר ר' יצחק בר אבא מאן תנא שינוי במועד בדבר האבד דלא כר' יוסי דהא ר' יוסי שרי כדרכו בלא שינוי אמר רב יוסף הלכתא כר' יוסי: בעא מיניה מרב נחמן בר יצחק מהו למישעיה לחביתא דשיכרא בחולו של מועד אמר להו רב יוסף דהוא סיני כדגרסינן בסוף הוריות רבה עוקר הרים רב יוסף סיני הוא דאמר הלכה כר' יוסי דאמר זולף וגומר וגף כדרכו אמרו ליה אימור דאמר ר' יוסי גף כדרכו בחמרא דאי שבקת ליה מגולה מפסיד שיכרא מי אמר אמר להו שיכרא נמי אית ביה פסידא טובא דאמר אביי אמרה לי אם חביתא דאית בה שית סאוי תמרי או כיוצא בהן ושייעא כה אותו השכר חזק א) כמו חבית שיש בה שמונת סאין ולא שיעא כלומר אם תשאר מגולה יש בשכר הפסד: **אמר** רב הלכות מועד כהלכות כותים למאי הלכתא לומר שעקרות הן ואין למידות זו מזו. דאמר שמואל זופתין כותתא ואין זופתין חבית והלא זו וזו זיפות הוא אלא אין למידין זו מזו ב) זיפות הכותתא אם תשאר בלא זיפות. פי' חייש לטירחא ומר חייש לפסידא מפורש בירושלמי. שמואל אמר זפתין גרבא ולא זפתין כותתא ג) דזיפתא גלידא. רב הונא חצדו ליה בחולא דמועדא איתיביה רבה בר רב הונא והתניא דבר האבד מותר לעשותו במועד ושאינו אבד אסור לעשותו בד"א בתלוש אבל במחובר אפילו כולו אבד אסור ואם אין לו מה יאכל קוצר ומעמר ודש כו'. ובלבד שלא ידוש בפרות. אמר ליה רב הונא הא מתניתא יחידאה היא דהא רשב"ג תני לה משום ר' יוסי ולא סמכינן עליה אי הכי דר' יוסי היא ידוש בפרות דהא ר' יוסי לא בעי שינוי ופרקינן כיון דכל יומא איכא דדיש בלא פרות לאו שינוי: **תנו** רבנן טוחנין קמח במועד לצורך המועד שלא לצורך המועד אסור ואם טחן לצורך המועד והותיר מותר כיוצא בו קוצצין קוצין במועד לצורך המועד ושלא לצורך המועד אסור וכו' וכן מטילין שכר לצורך המועד כו' ובלבד שלא יערים. איני והתניא אע"פ שיש לו שכר ישן מערים ושותה מן החדש. ופרקינן תנאי היא דתניא אין מערימין בכך משום ר' יוסי בר' יהודה אמרו מערימין ואע"ג דלמיחצד למי שאין לו מה יאכל שרי איקפד שמואל עליה דרב ואמר אפילו הכי אדם חשוב שאני. ר' יהודה נשיאה נפק בחומרתא דמדושא ואשתי מיא דאחים קפילא ארמאה. ואיקפד ר' אמי עליה. ואמר רב יוסף תרוייהו שרו להו רבנן חומרתא דמדושא דתניא השירים והצמידים והטבעות הרי הן ככל הכלים הניטלין בחצר ואי מיא דאחים קפילא גוי האמר שמואל בר רב יצחק כל הנאכל כמות שהוא חי אין בו משום בשולי גוים ואמרינן אפילו הכי אדם חשוב שאני לא הוה ליה למיעבד הכי. אמר רב חננאל אמר רב קוצץ אדם דקל במועד אע"פ שאין צריך לו אלא לנסורת שלו לייט עלה אביי אזל רב אשי למקצץ ההיא אבא ואישתמיט נרגא ובעא למיפסקיה לשקיה ושבקיה והדר רב יהודה שרא למיעקר כיתנא ולמיקטל כשותא ולמיעקר שומשמי אמר אביי בשלמא כיתנא חזי לחפיפה כשותא חזי לשיכרא אלא שומשמי למאי חזו ואמרינן לנזיי דאית בהו. רבי ינאי קטף פרדיסאה בחולי דמועדא וחשש לפסידא לשנה אחרת שהו כ"ע לפרדיסייהו וקטפוה בחולי דמועדא אפקר ר' ינאי לפרדיסיה ההיא שתא: **ירושלמי** אמר ילפין מקלקלתא ולא ילפי מתקנייא. ר' יעקב בר אחא בשם ר' אבין פרקמטיא אבידה שריא מטלטלתא במועדא. שיירתא שרי מיזבון מינה במועדא: **מתני'** מכנים אדם פירותיו מפני הגנבים כו'. תניא ובלבד שיכנים בצינעא לתוך ביתו ואי הוו כעין כשורי דרב יוסף דבליליא בעו גברי יתירי ובעי אבוקות של אש ואוושא מילתא טפי עדיף לעיילינהו ביממא. שולה פשתנו מן המשרה שלא תאבד

א) נראה מזה דרבינו היה גורס ככר תמניא. ב) אולי צ"ל אם תשאר בלא זיפות תפסיד רב דימי וכו' אמר זופתין חביתא ואין זופתין כותתא פי' מר חייש. ג) אולי צ"ל זפתין גרבא דזיפתא דקקירלא ולא זפתין כותתא דזיפתא גלידא.

הגהות הב"ח (א) גמ' אי משום חומרתא דמדושא הא תניא השירין נ"ב עי' מ"ש פ' הכל דף סט בתוס': (ב) שם הא אמר רב שמואל: (ג) רש"י ד"ה לימא וכו' דמחובר אפי': (ד) תום' ד"ה מכנים כו' ואיני יודע מה מלאכה איכא באסיפה וצריך עיון: (ה) ד"ה אם כו' דגבי מכר ומת דבעי אי קנסו בנו אחריו התם ודאי גרסינן איסורא דאורייתא:

צָרַם אֹזֶן בְּכוֹר קָנְסוּ בְּנוֹ אַחֲרָיו — מִשּׁוּם דְּאִיסּוּרָא דְּאוֹרַיְיתָא. וְאִם תִּמְצֵי לוֹמַר: מָכַר עַבְדּוֹ לְגוֹי וּמֵת קָנְסוּ בְּנוֹ אַחֲרָיו — מִשּׁוּם דְּכׇל יוֹמָא מַפְקַע לֵיהּ מִמִּצְוֹת, הָכָא מַאי? גַּבְרָא קָנֵיס רַבָּנַן — וְהָא לֵיתֵיהּ, אוֹ דִּלְמָא: מָמוֹנָא קָנֵיס רַבָּנַן, וְהָא אִיתֵיהּ! א"ל: תְּנֵיתוּהָ, *שָׂדֶה [א]שֶׁנִּתְקַוְּוצָה בַּשְּׁבִיעִית — תִּזָּרַע לְמוֹצָאֵי שְׁבִיעִי' [ב]נִטַּיְּיבָה אוֹ נִדַּיְּירָה — לֹא תִּזָּרַע לְמוֹצָאֵי שְׁבִיעִית. וְאָמַר ר' יוֹסֵי בַּר חֲנִינָא: [ג]*נְקָטִינַן, הֵטִיבָהּ וּמֵת — בְּנוֹ זוֹרְעָהּ. אַלְמָא: לְדִידֵיהּ — קָנְסוּ רַבָּנַן, לִבְרֵיהּ — לָא קָנְסוּ רַבָּנַן. ה"נ לְדִידֵיהּ — קָנְסוּ רַבָּנַן, לִבְרֵיהּ — לָא קָנְסוּ רַבָּנַן. אָמַר אַבַּיֵי: *[ד]נְקָטִינַן, טִימֵּא טׇהֳרוֹתָיו וּמֵת — לֹא קָנְסוּ בְּנוֹ אַחֲרָיו. מַאי טַעְמָא — *[ה]הֶיזֵּק שֶׁאֵינוֹ נִיכָּר לָא שְׁמֵיהּ הֶיזֵּק. לְדִידֵיהּ — קָנְסוּ רַבָּנַן, לִבְרֵיהּ — לָא קָנְסוּ רַבָּנַן.§ **מתני'** [ו]אֵין לוֹקְחִין בָּתִּים, עֲבָדִים וּבְהֵמָה אֶלָּא לְצוֹרֶךְ הַמּוֹעֵד, אוֹ לְצוֹרֶךְ הַמּוֹכֵר שֶׁאֵין לוֹ מַה יֹּאכַל.§ **גמ'** בְּעָא מִינֵּיהּ רָבָא מֵרַב נַחְמָן: שְׂכַר פְּעוּלָּה שֶׁאֵין לוֹ מַה יֹּאכַל מַהוּ? א"ל: תְּנֵינָא, אוֹ לְצוֹרֶךְ הַמּוֹכֵר שֶׁאֵין לוֹ מַה יֹּאכַל. לְאַתּוֹיֵי מַאי — לָאו לְאַתּוֹיֵי שְׂכַר פְּעוּלָּה? א"ל: לָא, פָּרוֹשֵׁי קָא מְפָרֵשׁ. אֵיתִיבֵיהּ אַבַּיֵי: *[ז]אֵין כּוֹתְבִין שְׁטָרֵי חוֹב בַּמּוֹעֵד, וְאִם אֵינוֹ מַאֲמִינוֹ (א) אוֹ שֶׁאֵין לוֹ מַה יֹּאכַל — ה"ז יִכְתּוֹב. שֶׁאֵין לוֹ מַה יֹּאכַל לְאַתּוֹיֵי מַאי — לָאו [ח]לְאַתּוֹיֵי שְׂכַר פְּעוּלָּה? שְׁמַע מִינַּהּ. מוֹתִיב רַב שֵׁשֶׁת: *וְחכ"א: [ט]שָׁלֹשׁ אוּמָּנִיּוֹת עוֹשִׂין מְלָאכָה בְּעַרְבֵי פְּסָחִים עַד חֲצוֹת: הַחַיָּיטִין, וְהַסַּפָּרִין, וְהַכּוֹבְסִין. *הַחַיָּיטִין — שֶׁכֵּן *הֶדְיוֹט תּוֹפֵר כְּדַרְכּוֹ בְּחוּלּוֹ שֶׁל מוֹעֵד, הַסַּפָּרִין וְהַכּוֹבְסִין — שֶׁכֵּן הַבָּאִין מִמְּדִינַת הַיָּם וְהַיּוֹצֵא מִבֵּית הָאֲסוּרִין מוּתָּרִין לְסַפֵּר וּלְכַבֵּס בְּחוּלּוֹ שֶׁל מוֹעֵד. וְאִי ס"ד שְׂכַר פְּעוּלָּה שֶׁאֵין לוֹ מַה יֹּאכַל שָׁרֵי — כׇּל מְלָאכוֹת נָמֵי לִישְׁתְּרוּ, דְּהָא אִיכָּא שְׂכַר פְּעוּלָּה שֶׁאֵין לוֹ מַה יֹּאכַל! מַתְקִיף לַהּ רַב פָּפָּא: אֶלָּא מֵעַתָּה, בִּנְיָן לִישְׁתְּרֵי, שֶׁכֵּן *כּוֹתֶל הַגּוֹהֶה לִרה"ר — סוֹתֵר וּבוֹנֶה כְּדַרְכּוֹ מִפְּנֵי הַסַּכָּנָה! מַתְקִיף לַהּ רָבִינָא: אֶלָּא מֵעַתָּה, לַבְלָר לִישְׁתְּרֵי, שֶׁכֵּן כּוֹתְבִין *קִידּוּשֵׁי נָשִׁים גִּיטִּין וְשׁוֹבָרִין! אֶלָּא אָמַר רַב אָשֵׁי: מוֹעֵד אַאַרְבָּעָה עָשָׂר קָא רָמֵית?! מוֹעֵד — מִשּׁוּם טִירְחָא הוּא, וּבִמְקוֹם פְּסֵידָא — שָׁרוּ רַבָּנַן. אַרְבָּעָה עָשָׂר — מִשּׁוּם צוֹרֶךְ יוֹם טוֹב הוּא, מִידֵּי דְּצוֹרֶךְ יו"ט — שָׁרוּ רַבָּנַן, מִידֵּי דְּלָאו צוֹרֶךְ יוֹם טוֹב — לָא שָׁרוּ רַבָּנַן.§ **מתני'** [י]אֵין מְפַנִּין מִבַּיִת לְבַיִת, אֲבָל מְפַנֶּה הוּא לַחֲצֵרוֹ. אֵין מְבִיאִין כֵּלִים מִבֵּית הָאוּמָּן, אִם חוֹשֵׁשׁ לָהֶם — מְפַנָּן לְחָצֵר אַחֶרֶת.§ **גמ'** וְהָאָמְרַתְּ רֵישָׁא אֵין מְפַנִּין כְּלָל! אָמַר אַבַּיֵי: [כ]סֵיפָא אֲתָאן לְבַיִת שֶׁבֶּחָצֵר.§ "וְאֵין מְבִיאִין כֵּלִים מִבֵּית הָאוּמָּן".§ *אָמַר רַב פָּפָּא: בְּדִיק לַן רָבָא: תְּנַן, אֵין מְבִיאִין כֵּלִים מִבֵּית הָאוּמָּן. וּרְמִינְהוּ: מוֹלִיכִין וּמְבִיאִין כֵּלִים מִבֵּית הָאוּמָּן וְאַע"פ שֶׁאֵינָן לְצוֹרֶךְ הַמּוֹעֵד! וְשַׁנֵּינַן לֵיהּ: [ל]כָּאן — בְּאַרְבָּעָה עָשָׂר, כָּאן — בְּחוּלּוֹ שֶׁל מוֹעֵד. אִיבָּעֵית אֵימָא: הָא וְהָא בְּחוּלּוֹ שֶׁל מוֹעֵד; כָּאן — בְּמַאֲמִינוֹ, כָּאן — בְּשֶׁאֵינוֹ מַאֲמִינוֹ. וְהָתַנְיָא

צָרַם אֹזֶן בְּכוֹר. חָתַךְ מֵאׇזְנוֹ מְעַט, כְּדֵי שֶׁיְּהֵא בַּעַל מוּם וִיהֵא מוּתָּר לוֹ. וְאָסוּר לַעֲשׂוֹת כֵּן מִשּׁוּם "מוּם לֹא יִהְיֶה בּוֹ" (ויקרא כב) כְּלוֹמַר, לֹא תַּטִּיל בּוֹ מוּם. וְאִם הִטִּיל בּוֹ מוּם — קָנְסוּהוּ רַבָּנַן דְּלֹא יֵהָנֶה מִמֶּנּוּ, וְאִם מֵת — אֵין בָּנָיו נֶהֱנִין מִמֶּנּוּ: מִשּׁוּם דְּאִיסּוּרָא דְּאוֹרַיְיתָא הוּא. אֲבָל הַאי דְּכִוֵּון מְלַאכְתּוֹ בַּמּוֹעֵד, דְּלָאו אִיסּוּרָא דְּאוֹרַיְיתָא הוּא, דְּהָא בְּלֹא מִתְכַּוֵּין מוּתָּר לְגַמְרֵי: מָכַר עַבְדּוֹ לְגוֹי. קָנְסוּהוּ רַבָּנַן, וְיָצָא לְחֵירוּת, דְּאִי בָּרַח מִן הַגּוֹי — אֵין יִשְׂרָאֵל יָכוֹל לְכוֹפוֹ לַעֲבוֹדָתוֹ, וְאִם מֵת — אֵין בָּנָיו יְכוֹלִין לְכוֹפוֹ: דְּכׇל יוֹמָא מַפְקַע לֵיהּ מִמִּצְוֹת. דְּכׇל זְמַן שֶׁהוּא בִּרְשׁוּת הַגּוֹי אֵינוֹ עוֹסֵק בְּמִצְוֹת: גַּבְרָא. דְּנִתְכַּוֵּין לַעֲשׂוֹת מְלָאכָה, קָנְסוּ רַבָּנַן שֶׁלֹּא לֵיהָנוֹת מִמֶּנָּה: מָמוֹנָא קַנְסוּהָ רַבָּנַן. וַאֲפִילּוּ בָּנָיו אֵין יְכוֹלִין לֵיהָנוֹת מִמֶּנָּה: שֶׁנִּתְקַוְּוצָה. נִיטְּלוּ מִמֶּנָּה קוֹצִים שֶׁבָּהּ: נִטַּיְּיבָה. נִזְדַּבְּלָה, שֶׁהוֹלִיךְ הַזֶּבֶל בַּעֲגָלוֹת וּמַשָּׂאוֹת: נִדַּיְּירָה. עַל יְדֵי דִּיר בְּהֵמָה. (ב) לְזַבְּלָהּ עֲבוֹדַת קַרְקַע הִיא (נִזְדַּבְּלָה). כׇּל הָנֵי מִדְּרַבָּנָן נִינְהוּ, וְאעפ"כ קָנְסוּ, דְּלֹא תִּזָּרַע לְמוֹצָאֵי שְׁבִיעִית: טִימֵּא טׇהֳרוֹתָיו. שֶׁל חֲבֵירוֹ, קָנְסוּ דְּחַיָּיב לְפׇרְעוֹ: הֶיזֵּק שֶׁאֵינוֹ נִיכָּר הוּא. דְּהָא בְּעֵינֵיהּ הוּא: שְׂכַר פְּעוּלָּה שֶׁאֵין לוֹ מַה יֹּאכַל. שֶׁאֵין לוֹ לַפּוֹעֵל מַה יֹּאכַל: מַהוּ. שֶׁיִּתֵּן לוֹ מְלָאכָה, וְלִשְׂכְּרוֹ כְּדֵי שֶׁיְּהֵא לוֹ מַה לֶּאֱכוֹל: לְאַתּוֹיֵי מַאי. אִי לַמּוֹכֵר — הָא תָּנֵי לֵיהּ לְצוֹרֶךְ (ג) הַמּוֹעֵד. אֶלָּא לְאַתּוֹיֵי שְׂכַר פְּעוּלָּה, שֶׁאֵין לוֹ מַה יֹּאכַל, דְּמוּתָּר: פָּרוֹשֵׁי קָא מְפָרֵשׁ. לְצוֹרֶךְ (ד) הַמּוֹעֵד כֵּיצַד? כְּגוֹן שֶׁאֵין לוֹ לַמּוֹכֵר מַה יֹּאכַל. וּלְעוֹלָם לָא תִּיפְשׁוֹט מִינָּהּ לִשְׂכַר פְּעוּלָּה: וְאִם אֵינוֹ מַאֲמִינוֹ. מַלְוֶה לַלֹּוֶה: שֶׁאֵין לוֹ מַה יֹּאכַל לְאַתּוֹיֵי מַאי. אִם מִשּׁוּם לֹוֶה — הָא קָאָמַר אִם אֵינוֹ מַאֲמִינוֹ מוּתָּר. וְהָכָא לָא מָצֵי לְתָרוֹצֵי פָּרוֹשֵׁי קָא מְפָרֵשׁ, דְּהָכִי מִיתְרְמֵי מִילְּתָא דְּאִם אֵינוֹ מַאֲמִינוֹ שֶׁאֵין לוֹ מַה יֹּאכַל — לָאו מִילְּתָא הִיא, דְּהָא מוּתָּר בְּלָאו הָכִי: לָאו לְאַתּוֹיֵי שְׂכַר פְּעוּלָּה. שֶׁאֵין לוֹ לַסּוֹפֵר מַה יֹּאכַל — שָׁרֵי בְּחוּלּוֹ שֶׁל מוֹעֵד: כׇּל מְלָאכָה נָמֵי תִּשְׁתְּרֵי. בְּעֶרֶב הַפֶּסַח, דְּהָא אִישְׁתְּרֵי שְׂכַר פְּעוּלָּה בְּחוּלּוֹ שֶׁל מוֹעֵד. אֶלָּא תִּיפְשׁוֹט מִינֵּיהּ דִּשְׂכַר פְּעוּלָּה שֶׁאֵין לוֹ מַה יֹּאכַל — אָסוּר בְּחוּלּוֹ שֶׁל מוֹעֵד: מַתְקִיף לָהּ רַב פָּפָּא. אַדְּרַב שֵׁשֶׁת פָּרֵיךְ. מִדְּפָרֵיךְ מֵהַאי דִּתְנַן שָׁלֹשׁ אוּמָּנִיּוֹת עוֹשִׂין מְלָאכָה בְּעַרְבֵי פְּסָחִים כו' — אַלְמָא סָבַר: כׇּל מְלָאכָה שֶׁרַשַּׁאי אַתָּה לַעֲשׂוֹת בְּחוּלּוֹ שֶׁל מוֹעֵד עוֹשִׂין אוֹתָהּ בְּעֶרֶב הַפֶּסַח: א"כ בִּנְיָן לִישְׁתְּרֵי. בְּעֶרֶב הַפֶּסַח, דְּהָא כּוֹתֶל הַגּוֹהֶה לרה"ר מוּתָּר לִבְנוֹתוֹ בְּחוּלּוֹ שֶׁל מוֹעֵד: מַתְקִיף לָהּ רָבִינָא. סָבַר נָמֵי כְּרַב פָּפָּא: ה"ג: אֶלָּא אָמַר רַב אָשֵׁי: מִשּׁוּם צוֹרֶךְ י"ט. שָׁרֵי, כְּגוֹן ג' אוּמָּנִיּוֹת וְתוּ לָא. וְהוּא הַדִּין אִם אֵין לוֹ מַה יֹּאכַל, דְּאֵין צוֹרֶךְ י"ט גָּדוֹל מִזֶּה: **מתני'** אֲבָל מְפַנֶּה הוּא לַחֲצֵרוֹ. וְהָא מַשְׁמַע לֵיהּ עַכְשָׁיו שֶׁמֵּבִיא מִבַּיִת שֶׁבְּחָצֵר אַחֶרֶת לַחֲצֵרוֹ: אִם חוֹשֵׁשׁ. שֶׁמָּא יִגְנְבוּ: **גמ'** וְהָא אָמְרַתְּ רֵישָׁא אֵין מְפַנִּין. מִבַּיִת לְבַיִת: סֵיפָא אֲתָאן לְבַיִת שֶׁבֶּחָצֵר. וְהָכִי קָתָנֵי: מְפַנֶּה הוּא מִבַּיִת שֶׁבַּחֲצֵרוֹ לַחֲצֵרוֹ: בָּדִיק לָן. אִי יָדְעִינַן לְתָרוֹצֵי: בי"ד. מוֹלִיכִין וּמְבִיאִין כֵּלִים: בְּחוּלּוֹ שֶׁל מוֹעֵד. אֵין מְבִיאִין: כָּאן בְּמַאֲמִינוֹ. לָאוּמָּן — אֵין מְבִיאִין, דְּשֶׁלֹּא לְצוֹרֶךְ הוּא: אֵין מַאֲמִינוֹ. מְבִיאִין: וְהָתַנְיָא

נטייבה או נדיירה. פי' בקונטרס: היינו מלאכה שבקרקע מדרבנן. אבל נטלו קוליס — אין זו עבודת קרקע. ובגיטין (ד' מד: ושם) פירש בקונטרס: דבקוולה מלאכה דרבנן! וצ"ל דאיירי בקוליס תלושים, דמחוברים כל דהו — הוי דאורייתא, דאמרינן בשבת (ד' קג.): התולש עולשין והמזרד זרדין, אם ליפות את הקרקע — כל שהוא. ואע"פ שאין מכוין ליפות, דקאמר התם דפטור גבי שבת, כגון בארעא דחבריה — אבל גבי שביעית לא בעינן מלאכת מחשבת:

נטייבה. פי' בקונטרס: זבל בהמות. ובפי' ר"ת: חורש בה חרישה יתירא. ובירושלמי מפרש כן. ומ"מ אין נראה שתהא מן התורה — וקשה: היכי מוכח מיניה בבכורות (ד' לד:) בעיא דצרם אוזן בבכור דהוי דאורייתא? ומוכר עבדו נמי, בפ' "השולח" (גיטין מד:)? הא גבי עבד דכ"ע (ה)דפקע ממצות חמיר טפי! ואומר ר"ת: דבשביעית נחמיר, כדאמר בקדושין פ"ק (ד' כ.): כמה קשה אבקה של שביעית, משום הכי יש לפשוט כל הני. א"נ: ראוי להחמיר טפי(ו) מבשום מקום — משום דהיו מזלזלין בה, כדאמר (*בסוף) הניזקין (דף נד.) שהיו חשודין על השביעית, לכך מייתי שפיר מינה:

אין לוקחין בתים עבדים כו' אלא לצורך המועד. פי' הר"ר יוסף: הוא הדין בשאר דברים צריך לצורך המועד, דהא אסור למכור פירות אלא לצורך המועד, אלא רבותא קמ"ל, דאפי' הני דהוין בפרהסיא — שרי לצורך המועד. וצריך עיון אי צריך (ז) הני לינעל כמו בההיא דפירות כסות וכלים (לקמן ע"ב), וההיא דלעיל (דף יב:) מכניס פירות — מצריך בגמ' לינעל, אע"פ שאינו במשנה:

אין מפנין מבית לבית. בירושלמי מתיר מבית אחר לביתו, שערב לאדם לדור בשלו:

רבינו חננאל

ובלבד שלא יכוין מלאכתו במועד וכולן שכוונו מלאכתן במועד יאבדו. בעי ר' ירמיה הרי הצורם אוזן בבכור קנסו בנו אחריו משום דההוא איסורא דאוריי' הוא וכן המוכר עבדו לגוי משום דכל יומא מפקע ליה ממצות מכוין מלאכתו במועד קנסו בנו אחריו או לא. ופשטנא א"ר יוסי ב"ר חנינא נקטינן הטיבה ומת זורעה בנו אחריו אלמא לדידיה קנסו. לבריה לא קנסו רבנן: (פיסקא) [מתני'] אין לוקחין בתים ועבדים*) ואבנים אלא לצורך [המועד] או לצורך המוכר שאין לו מה יאכל בעי רבא שכר פעולה מאי פירוש שאין לו לפועל מה יאכל במועד כגון הסופר שאין לו אלא שכר שטר המקנה. וכן כיוצא בו הפועלים מהו שיתירו לו למכור ולקנות כדי שיקחו אלו שכרם. ופשטנא דאפילו לשכר פעולה שרי. ומותיב רב ששת ג' אומניות עושין מלאכתן בערבי פסחים עד חצות החייטין כו'. ואי ס"ד דכל מי שאין לו מה יאכל שרינן לשכר פעולה כל אומניות לישתרי דהא מי שאין לו מה יאכל וצריך שכר פעולה שרי ורב פפא מתקיף הכי כל בנין לישתרי דהא כותל הגוהה לרה"ר סותרו ובונהו כדרכו מפני הסכנה. ורבינא מתקיף כל לבלר לישתרי דהא כותבין גיטי נשים כו'. ופריק רב אשי י"ד אדמועד קרמית מועד משום טירחא ולא טירחא הוא במקום פסידא שרו רבנן. י"ד משום י"ט הוא מידי דהוי צורך יו"ט שרי ליה רבנן דלא צורך י"ט לא שרו ליה רבנן: **ירושלמי** א"ר יוסי א"ר אבין קרנא ואגרא קרן **) או ידע דמזבן ופחת מן קרנא יזבין ואי לא לא יזבון ר' חנניא חברין דרבנן אמר פרקמטיא ניגבת מנכסי יתומים קטנים הוין בעי למימר בשיש עדים יודעין הא אין עדים יודעין נעשית כפקדון כך אנו אומרים פקדון לא ניתנה לגבות מנכסי יתומין קטנים מה בינה למלוה מלוה להוצאה ניתנה. וזו לא ניתנה להוצאה. א"ר אבא בר ממל אילו היה מי שימנה עמי הייתי מתיר המלאכה. כלום אסרו המלאכה בחולו של מועד אלא שיהו אוכלין ושותין ויגיעם בתורה. והאידנא אוכלין ושותין ופוחזין. ריב"ל שאל לרשב"ל. מהו ליקח בתים מן הגוי בשבת א"ל תני בשבת מותר כיצד עושה מראה לו כיסין של דינרים והגוי חותם ומעלה בערכאין וכן מצינו שנכבשה יריחו בשבת שנא' כה תעשה ששת ימים וכתיב וביום השביעי תסובו את העיר ז' פעמים וכתיב עד רדתה אפי' בשבת: (פיסקא) [מתני'] אין מפנין לבית אבל מפנה הוא בבית שבחצירו: **ירושלמי** אין מפנין לא מדירה נאה לדירה נאה ולא מדירה נאה לדירה כעורה ובתוך שלו אפילו מדירה נאה של חבירו לדירה כעורה שלו מפנין מפני ששמחה היא לו להיות דר בתוך שלו אין מפנין מת ולא עצמות מקבר לקבר ממכובד למכובד ולא מבזוי לבזוי. ואצ"ל ממכובד לבזוי ובתוך שלו אפילו ממכובד לבזוי ערב לאדם בשעה שהוא נינח אצל אבותיו: (פיסקא) [מתני'] אין מביאין כלים מבית האומן אם חשש להן מפנן לחצר אחרת ומקשינן והתנינן מוליכין ומביאין מבית האומן ופרקי' הא בי"ד מתני' דהכא בחולו של מועד.

*) רבינו היה גורס במשנה ואבנים וכ"ה הגי' במשנה שבירושלמי וכ"ה גי' הרי"ף והרא"ש ז"ל ועי' בירושלמי דמפרש איזה צורך המועד שייך באבנים ע"ש. **) לפנינו הגי' בירושלמי אין ידע דלא מזבן והוא פחת מן קרנא וכו' וע"ש במפרש.

שביעית פ"ד מ"ב גיטין מד: בכורות לד:
[עי' פרש"י עירובין ה. בד"ה והאמר ר"נ]
גיטין מד: בכורות לד:
[גיטין נג. וש"נ]
לקמן יח:
פסחים נה. [תוספתא שם פ"ג]
[פסחים נה:]
[לעיל ז. ע"ש]
[לקמן יח:]
[פסחים נה:]
[לעיל ח:]

לד א מיי' פ"א מהל' שמיטה ויובל הל' יד סמג לאוין רסז:
לה ב ג מיי' שם הל' יג:
לו ד ה מיי' פ"ז מהל' חובל ומזיק הל' א ב ג סמג עשין ע טוש"ע ח"מ סי' שפה סעיף א:
לז ו מיי' פ"ז מהלכות י"ט הלכה כב טוש"ע א"ח סי' תקלט סעיף יב:
לח ז מיי' שם הל' יב טוש"ע שם סי' תקמה סעיף ו:
לט ח מיי' שם טוש"ע שם סי' תקמב סעיף ב:
מ ט מיי' שם פ"ח הלכה יט טוש"ע שם סי' תמח סעיף ה:
מא י כ מיי' שם הל' טז טוש"ע שם סי' תקלה סעיף א:
מב ל מיי' שם הל' כא טוש"ע שם סי' תסח סעיף י:

הגהות הב"ח

(א) גמ' ואם אינו מאמינו או תיבת או מוקף וכ"כ מפרש"י משמע דלא גרס או: (ב) רש"י ד"ה נידיירה ע"י דיר בהמה ניזדבלה עבודת קרקע: (ג) ד"ה לאתויי כו' הא תנא ליה לצורך המוכר אלא לאתויי: (ד) ד"ה פרושי קא מפרש לצורך המוכר כילד כגון: (ה) תוספות ד"ה נטייבה פי' כו' גבי עבד דכולי עלמא דמפקע ליה ממצות חמיר טפי: (ו) בא"ד ראוי להחמיר טפי בשביעית מבשום מקום: (ז) ד"ה אין לוקחין כו' וצ"ע אי צריך בהכי לינעל כו' והיא דלעיל גבי מכניס:

וְהָתַנְיָא: *[א]מְבִיאִין כֵּלִים מִבֵּית הָאוּמָּן כְּגוֹן כַּד מִבֵּית הַכַּדָּר, וְכוֹס מִבֵּית הַזַּגָּג, אֲבָל לֹא צֶמֶר מִבֵּית הַצַּבָּע, וְלֹא כֵּלִים מִבֵּית הָאוּמָּן. וְאִם אֵין לוֹ מַה יֹּאכַל — נוֹתֵן לוֹ שְׂכָרוֹ, וּמַנִּיחוֹ אֶצְלוֹ. וְאִם אֵינוֹ מַאֲמִינוֹ — מַנִּיחוֹ בַּבַּיִת הַסָּמוּךְ לוֹ, וְאִם חוֹשֵׁשׁ לָהֶם שֶׁמָּא יִגָּנְבוּ — [א]א (*מְפַנָּן לְחָצֵר אַחֶרֶת, וְאִם אֵינוֹ מַאֲמִינוֹ) — מְבִיאָן בְּצִנְעָה בְּתוֹךְ בֵּיתוֹ. תֵּרַצְתָּ מְבִיאִין, מוֹלִיכִין — קַשְׁיָא! דְּקָתָנֵי: אֵין מְבִיאִין, וְכׇל שֶׁכֵּן שֶׁאֵין מוֹלִיכִין! אֶלָּא: מְחַוַּוְרְתָּא כְּדְשַׁנִּיִּין מֵעִיקָּרָא.§

מתני' [ב]מְחַפִּין אֶת הַקְּצִיעוֹת בְּקַשׁ, רַבִּי יְהוּדָה אוֹמֵר: [ג]אַף מְעַבִּין. [ד]מוֹכְרֵי פֵּירוֹת, כְּסוּת וְכֵלִים — מוֹכְרִים בְּצִנְעָה לְצוֹרֶךְ הַמּוֹעֵד. [ה]הַצַּיָּידִין וְהַדָּשׁוֹשׁוֹת וְהַגָּרוֹסוֹת — עוֹשִׂין בְּצִנְעָה לְצוֹרֶךְ הַמּוֹעֵד. רַבִּי יוֹסֵי אוֹמֵר: הֵם הֶחְמִירוּ עַל עַצְמָן.§ **גמ'** פְּלִיגִי בָּהּ רַבִּי חִיָּיא בַּר אַבָּא וְרַבִּי אַסִּי, וְתַרְוַיְיהוּ מִשְּׁמֵיהּ דְּחִזְקִיָּה וְרַבִּי יוֹחָנָן. חַד אָמַר: מְחַפִּין — אַקְלוּשֵׁי, מְעַבִּין — אַסְמוּכֵי. וְחַד אָמַר: מְחַפִּין — בֵּין אַקְלוּשֵׁי בֵּין אַסְמוּכֵי, מְעַבִּין — עוֹשֶׂה אוֹתוֹ כְּמִין כְּרִי. תַּנְיָא נַמִי הָכִי: מְעַבִּין — עוֹשֶׂה אוֹתוֹ כְּמִין כְּרִי, דִּבְרֵי ר' יְהוּדָה.§ "מוֹכְרֵי פֵּירוֹת כְּסוּת וְכֵלִים מוֹכְרִין בְּצִנְעָה" וכו'.§ אִיבַּעְיָא לְהוּ: הֵן הֶחְמִירוּ עַל עַצְמָן — דְּלָא הָווּ עָבְדִי כְּלָל, אוֹ דִּלְמָא: דְּהָווּ עָבְדִי בְּצִנְעָה? ת"ש: מוֹכְרֵי פֵּירוֹת כְּסוּת וְכֵלִים מוֹכְרִין בְּצִנְעָה לְצוֹרֶךְ הַמּוֹעֵד, ר' יוֹסֵי אוֹמֵר: תַּגָּרֵי טְבֶרְיָא הֵן הֶחְמִירוּ עַל עַצְמָן שֶׁלֹּא יְהוּ מוֹכְרִין כׇּל עִיקָּר. [ו]צַיָּדֵי חַיּוֹת וְעוֹפוֹת וְדָגִים צָדִין בְּצִנְעָה לְצוֹרֶךְ הַמּוֹעֵד, ר' יוֹסֵי אוֹמֵר: צַיָּדֵי עַכּוֹ הֵן הֶחְמִירוּ עַל עַצְמָן שֶׁלֹּא יְהוּ צָדִין כׇּל עִיקָּר. דָּשׁוֹשֵׁי חִילְקָא טַרְגִּים וְטִיסָּנֵי דּוֹשְׁשִׁין בְּצִנְעָה לְצוֹרֶךְ הַמּוֹעֵד. ר' יוֹסֵי אוֹמֵר: דָּשׁוֹשֵׁי צִיפּוֹרִי הֵן הֶחְמִירוּ עַל עַצְמָן שֶׁלֹּא יְהוּ דּוֹשְׁשִׁין כׇּל עִיקָּר. אָמַר אַבַּיֵּי: חִילְקָא — חֲדָא לְתַרְתֵּי, טַרְגִּים — חֲדָא לִתְלָת, טִיסָּנֵי — חֲדָא לְאַרְבְּעָה. כִּי אֲתָא רַב דִּימִי אֲמַר: כּוּנְתָּא. מֵיתִיבִי: *[ז]חִילְקָא טַרְגִּים וְטִיסָּנֵי — טְמֵאִין בְּכׇל מָקוֹם. בִּשְׁלָמָא לְמ"ד חֲדָא לְתַרְתֵּי לִתְלָת וּלְאַרְבְּעָה — מִשּׁוּם הָכִי טְמֵאִין בְּכׇל מָקוֹם, דְּאִתְכַּשּׁוּר, אֶלָּא לְמ"ד כּוּנְתָּא — אַמַּאי טְמֵאִין בְּכׇל מָקוֹם? הָא לָא אִיתְכַּשּׁוּר! כְּגוֹן דְּמִיקַּלְפָן, דְּאִי לָאו דְּשָׁרָא לְהוּ בְּמַיָּא — לָא הֲוָה מִיקַּלְפָא. וְאַמַּאי קָרֵי לֵיהּ חִילְקָא — דְּשָׁקֵיל חֶלְקַיְהוּ. מֵיתִיבִי: *הַנּוֹדֵר מִן הַדָּגָן אָסוּר אַף בַּפּוֹל הַמִּצְרִי יָבֵשׁ, וּמוּתָּר בַּלַּח, וּמוּתָּר בָּאוֹרֶז, בְּחִילְקָא וְטַרְגִּים וְטִיסָּנֵי. בִּשְׁלָמָא לְמ"ד חֲדָא לְתַרְתֵּי חֲדָא לִתְלָת וַחֲדָא לְאַרְבְּעָה — שַׁפִּיר, דְּנָפְקוּ לְהוּ מִתּוֹרַת דָּגָן. אֶלָּא לְמ"ד כּוּנְתָּא — דָּגָן מְעַלְּיָא הוּא! קַשְׁיָא. רַב הוּנָא [ח]שְׁרָא לְהוּ לְהַנְהוּ כְּרוּפַיְיתָא לְמֵיזַל לְזַבּוּנֵי כִּי אוֹרְחַיְיהוּ בְּשׁוּקָא. אֵיתִיבֵיהּ רַב כַּהֲנָא: *[ט]חֲנוּת פְּתוּחָה לְסְטָיו — פּוֹתֵחַ וְנוֹעֵל כְּדַרְכּוֹ, פְּתוּחָה לִרה"ר — פּוֹתֵחַ אַחַת וְנוֹעֵל אַחַת, [י]וְעֶרֶב יוֹם טוֹב הָאַחֲרוֹן שֶׁל חַג — מוֹצִיא, וּמְעַטֵּר אֶת שׁוּקֵי הָעִיר בְּפֵירוֹת בִּשְׁבִיל כְּבוֹד י"ט הָאַחֲרוֹן. מִפְּנֵי כְּבוֹד י"ט הָאַחֲרוֹן — אִין, שֶׁלֹּא מִפְּנֵי כְּבוֹד י"ט — לָא! לָא קַשְׁיָא: [כ]הָא — בְּפֵירֵי, הָא — בְּתַבְלִין.§

הדרן עלך מי שהפך

וְאֵלּוּ [ל]מְגַלְּחִין בַּמּוֹעֵד: הַבָּא מִמְּדִינַת הַיָּם, וּמִבֵּית הַשִּׁבְיָה, וְהַיּוֹצֵא מִבֵּית הָאֲסוּרִין, וְהַמְנוּדֶּה שֶׁהִתִּירוּ לוֹ חֲכָמִים, וְכֵן מִי שֶׁנִּשְׁאַל לְחָכָם וְהוּתַּר, *וְהַנָּזִיר וְהַמְּצוֹרָע (א) מִטּוּמְאָתוֹ לְטׇהֳרָתוֹ. [מ]וְאֵלּוּ מְכַבְּסִין בַּמּוֹעֵד: הַבָּא מִמְּדִינַת הַיָּם וּמִבֵּית הַשִּׁבְיָה, וְהַיּוֹצֵא מִבֵּית הָאֲסוּרִין, וּמְנוּדֶּה

רש"י

וְהָתַנְיָא. סֵיפָא: כַּד וְכוֹס לְצוֹרֶךְ הַמּוֹעֵד הֵן, אֲבָל צֶמֶר וְכֵלִים – אֵין צוֹרֶךְ הַמּוֹעֵד: וְאִם אֵין לוֹ. לָאוּמָּן מַה יֹּאכַל – נוֹתֵן לוֹ שְׂכָרוֹ: מְפַנָּן לְחָצֵר אַחֶרֶת וְאִם אֵינוֹ מַאֲמִינוֹ. בְּחָצֵר אַחֶרֶת: מְבִיאָן לְתוֹךְ בֵּיתוֹ. אַלְמָא: כְּשֶׁאֵינוֹ מַאֲמִינוֹ מְבִיאָן: מוֹלִיכִין קַשְׁיָא. דְּקָתָנֵי מַתְנִי' *דִּפְעָמִים מוֹלִיכִין, וּמַתְנִי' דְּהָכָא קָתָנֵי אֵין מְבִיאִין, כׇּל שֶׁכֵּן דְּאֵין מוֹלִיכִין. וְלֵיכָּא לְתָרֵץ בְּאֵין מַאֲמִינוֹ – דְּמוֹלִיכִין מַאי מַאֲמִינוֹ שַׁיָּיךְ! כְּדְשַׁנִּיִּין מֵעִיקָּרָא. כָּאן בְּאַרְבָּעָה עָשָׂר, כָּאן בְּחוּלּוֹ שֶׁל מוֹעֵד: **מתני'** מְחַפִּין. מְכַסִּין: הַדָּשׁוֹשׁוֹת. שֶׁדָּשִׁין וְכוֹתְשִׁין חִיטִּין לְדַיְיסָא: וְהַגָּרוֹסוֹת. שֶׁטּוֹחֲנִין פּוֹלִין לִגְרִיסִין: בְּצִנְעָה. שֶׁמָּא יֹאמְרוּ: זֶה לוֹקֵחַ שֶׁלֹּא לְצוֹרֶךְ הַמּוֹעֵד: **גמ'** אַקְלוּשֵׁי. שֶׁמְּכַסֵּהוּ בַּעֲנָפִים מְרוּחָקִין זֶה מִזֶּה, דְּלָא הָוֵי כִּסּוּי גָּמוּר: אַסְמוּכֵי. הָעֲנָפִים סוֹמֵךְ זֶה לָזֶה, דְּהָוֵי כִּסּוּי גָּמוּר: כְּמִין כְּרִי. מְכַנְּסִין אוֹתָן בְּיַחַד, כְּדֵי שֶׁיְּהוּ נוֹחִין לְכַסּוֹת: הֶחְמִירוּ עַל עַצְמָם דְּלָא עָבְדִי כְּלָל. וּלְחוּמְרָא: אוֹ דִּלְמָא. הֶחְמִירוּ עַל עַצְמָן לַעֲשׂוֹת בְּצִנְעָה מִדַּעְתָּן, וְאִם רוֹצִין לַעֲשׂוֹת בְּפַרְהֶסְיָא – עוֹשִׂין, וּלְקוּלָּא: דָּשׁוֹשֵׁי. דָּשֵׁי תְּבוּאָה. אִיכָּא דְּאָמְרֵי: דָּשׁוֹשֵׁי – הַמְשַׁבְּרִין תְּבוּאָה חֲדָא לִשְׁנַיִם וְשׁוֹרִין בְּמַיִם כו': כּוּנְתָּא. כּוּסֶּמֶת שֶׁכּוֹתְתִין אוֹתָן, הַיְינוּ חִילְקָא: טְמֵאִים בְּכׇל מָקוֹם. מְקַבְּלִין טוּמְאָה בֵּין בַּכְּפָרִים בֵּין בַּכְּרַכִּים. דְּקַיְימָא לָן (פסחים דף מ.): סוֹלֶת שֶׁל בְּנֵי כְּרַכִּים מְקַבֶּלֶת טוּמְאָה, שֶׁהוּכְשְׁרָה בְּמַיִם. וּבְנֵי כְּפָרִים אֵין מַקְפִּידִין אַסּוֹלֶת נְקִיָּה לִלְתּוֹת בְּמַיִם, וְסוֹלֶת שֶׁלָּהֶן טָהוֹר, שֶׁלֹּא הוּכְשַׁר מֵעוֹלָם. אֲבָל חִילְקָא – טְמֵאִין בְּכׇל מָקוֹם, אֲפִילּוּ בַּכְּפָרִים. דְּאִי אֶפְשָׁר לָהֶם בְּלֹא לְתִיתָה, מִשּׁוּם הָכִי טְמֵאִין, דְּהָא מִיתְכַּשַּׁר, דְּשָׁרֵי לְהוּ בְּמַיָּא: לְעוֹלָם הָוֵי כּוּנְתָּא וּמִיקַּלְּפָן דְּשָׁרֵי לְהוּ בְּמַיָּא דְּשָׁרֵי קְלִיפָּה: דְּשָׁקֵיל חֶלְקַיְיהוּ. כְּלוֹמַר, כְּשֶׁנּוֹטֵל הַקְּלִיפָּה וְהָוֵי חֵלֶק: כְּרוּפַיְיתָא. מוֹכְרֵי בְּשָׂמִים: חֲנוּת פָּתוּחַ לִסְטָיו פּוֹתֵחַ וְנוֹעֵל כְּדַרְכּוֹ. הוֹאִיל וְאֵינוֹ פָּתוּחַ לִרה"ר כִּשְׁאָר חֲנוּיוֹת: פּוֹתֵחַ דֶּלֶת אַחַד וְנוֹעֵל דֶּלֶת אֶחָד. אֲבָל כְּדַרְכּוֹ – לֹא, אֵינוֹ מוֹכֵר כְּדַרְכּוֹ: הָא בְּפֵירֵי. שֶׁיֵּשׁ לַחְשׁוֹד שֶׁקּוֹנֶה לְצוֹרֶךְ (ב) יְמוֹת הַשָּׁנָה: בְּתַבְלִין. מוֹכֵר כְּדַרְכּוֹ, כְּגוֹן כְּרוּב וְכַרְשִׁינִין – הַכֹּל יוֹדְעִין דִּלְצוֹרֶךְ הַמּוֹעֵד הֵן, וְלֵיכָּא חֲשָׁדָא, שֶׁאֵין רְאוּיִן לְהִתְקַיֵּים. הִלְכָּךְ – אֲפִי' בְּפַרְהֶסְיָא מוּתָּר:

הדרן עלך מי שהפך

וְאֵלּוּ מְגַלְּחִין בַּמּוֹעֵד הַבָּא מִמְּדִינַת הַיָּם כו'. בַּמּוֹעֵד, לְפִי שֶׁהָיָה אָנוּס, שֶׁלֹּא הָיָה יָכוֹל לְגַלֵּחַ קוֹדֶם: וּמִי שֶׁנִּשְׁאַל לְחָכָם. שֶׁנָּדַר שֶׁלֹּא לְגַלֵּחַ, וְשָׁאַל לְחָכָם בַּמּוֹעֵד: מִטּוּמְאָתוֹ לְטׇהֳרָתוֹ. נָזִיר טָמֵא כְּשֶׁעָלָה מִטּוּמְאָתוֹ, וְשׁוּב אֵינוֹ מְשַׁמֵּר נִזְרוֹ, וּמְגַלֵּחַ. וְכֵן מְצוֹרָע שֶׁעָלָה מִטּוּמְאָתוֹ – מְגַלֵּחַ בָּרֶגֶל, לְפִי שֶׁלֹּא הָיָה לָהֶם פְּנַאי לְגַלֵּחַ קוֹדֶם הָרֶגֶל:

גמ'

תוספות

בשביל כבוד יום טוב האחרון. אבל מרישא (ג) דחנות פתוחה לרשות הרבים פותח אחת ונועל אחת, ורב הונא מתיר באורחייהו בשוקא – לא פריך. דיש לאוקמיה בי"ט, ולא בחול המועד. ולהכי פריך מסיפא, דמיירי בחול המועד. דהא ערב י"ט האחרון חול המועד: **בתבלין**. פי' בקונט': כרוב וכרשינין. והקשה בתוס' רבי פרץ: דכרוב וקפלוט אינן חשובין תבלין, דהא אמרינן (חולין דף ו.): דתבלין לטעמא עבידי, ואפילו באלף לא בטיל. ולפת וקפלוט – אינו צריך לשער כי אם בששים, כדאיתא פרק "גיד הנשה" (שם דף צז:). (ד) ותבלין כך נידוכין כדרכן, בפ"ק דביצה (דף יד.). א"כ אינו כרוב. ובערוך פירש: מיני בשמים:

הדרן עלך מי שהפך

ואלו מגלחין במועד. משום דתנא באידך פירקין דברים שעושין לצורך המועד, כמו מוכרי פירות דנעשים כדין – קתני נמי ואלו נעשים שלא כדין, לצורך המועד: **והיוצא** מבית האסורים. שאינו יכול לגלח קודם המועד, שאין מניחין לו לגלח. ואפילו מניחין לו – אינו ערב לאדם לגלח בבית האסורין: [כ"ה בירושלמי] ומנודה

עין משפט נר מצוה

מג א מיי' פ"ח מהל' י"ט הל' טז טוש"ע א"ח סי' תקלד סעיף ג:
מד ב ג מיי' פ"ח שם הלכה יד טוש"ע שם סי' תקלח סעיף ד:
מה ד מיי' שם פ"ז הלכה כג טוש"ע שם סימן תקלט סעיף יא:
מו ה ו מיי' שם הלכה ט טוש"ע שם סי' תקלג סעיף ה:
מז ז מיי' פט"ז מהל' טומאת אוכלין הל' א:
מח ח מיי' פ"ז מהל' י"ט הל' כג טוש"ע א"ח סי' תקלט סעיף י:
מט ט י כ מיי' שם טוש"ע שם סעיף יא:
א ל מיי' שם הלכה יז יח טוש"ע שם סי' תקלא סעיף ד:
ב מ מיי' שם סמג לאוין עה טוש"ע שם סי' תקלד סעיף א:

רבינו חננאל

[מתני'] מחפין את הקציעות בקש. ר' יהודה אומר אף מעבין. סוגיא דשמעתא מחפין בעצים של קש דקים בין בעצים של קש עבים. פירוש קלושי דקים. סומכי עבים מעבין עושין אותן כמין כרי כלומר כמו גדיש: **ירושלמי** ר' יהודה אומר יאבד דבר מועט ואל יאבד דבר מרובה. ר' יוסי אומר אל יאבד דבר כל עיקר. כהנא אמר אית מילין דקשין הן (החמירו) מנגעים ואהלות: מוכרי פירות כסות וכלים מוכרין בצינעא לצורך המועד. ר' יוסי אומר הן החמירו על עצמן אוקימנא הן החמירו על עצמן שלא יעשו כל עיקר דתניא מוכרי כסות וכלים מוכרין בצינעא לצורך המועד ר' יוסי [אומר] תגרי טבריא הן החמירו על עצמן שלא יהו עושין כל עיקר. וכן צדי עכו החמירו על עצמן שלא יהו צדין כל עיקר. חילקא חטה אחת נחלקת לשתים טרגין חדא לתלת טיסני חדא לארבע כי אתא רב דימי אמר האי חילקא כתנא הוא איני והתניא חילקא טרגין וטיסני טמאים אי אמרת חטה דשושה לשתים שלש וארבע וכמו הסולת היינו דאיתמר דאיתכשר ומקבלי טומאה אלא כותנא אמאי טמאה והא לא הוכשרה. ופרקינן כגון דמגלפו ההיא כותנא. פי' כוסמת. דאי לאו דשדא בהו מיא לא הוה משלם כלומר מתקפלת הקליפה שלהן. ת"ש הנודר מן הדגן אסור אף בפול המצרי יבש ומותר בלח. ומותר באורז חלקא טרגים וטיסני בשלמא למ"ד דשישי היינו דנפקי להו מתורת דגן אלא למ"ד כותנא דגן גמור הוא כדכתיב והחטה והכוסמת ועלתה בתיובתא לרב דימי. רב יהודה שרא להנהו כרופייתא למיזל ולמיזבני בשוקא כי אורחייהו אוקימנא בתבלי והא דתניא חנות הפתוחה לסטיו פותח ונועל כדרכו כו' אוקימנא בפירות: **ירושלמי** צדי חיה ועופות ודגים צדין בחכה ובמכמורת ולא ממעטין בשמחת הרגל ר' אמי מקיל לון שממעטין בשמחת הרגל: הדרן עלך פרק מי שהפך

מסורת הש"ס

נ"ל דפסחים

[פסחים נה:] ע"ש עה"ג

[כ"ז ליתא בפסחים עי' בב"י סי' תקלד דבספרים שלנו הנוסחא ואם חושש להם שמא יגנבו מביאן בצנעה בתוך ביתו]

מכשירין פ"ו מ"ב

[נדרים נה: תוספתא שם פ"ד]

[תוספ' פ"ב]

[לקמן יז:]

הגהות הב"ח

(א) מתני' והמצורע העולה מטומאתו: (ב) רש"י ד"ה הא בפירי שקונה לצורך שאר ימות השנה: (ג) תוס' ד"ה בשביל כו' אבל מרישא דתני לחנות פתוחה כו' ערב י"ט האחרון חוה"מ הוא: (ד) ד"ה בתבלין כו' כדאיתא פ' גיד הנשה ותנן נמי דתבלין נידוכין כדרכן בפ"ק:

הגהות הגר"א

[א] גמ' (מפנן לחצר אחרת ואם אינו מאמינו) תא"מ (וכן ליתא בדפו"י):

הגהות מהר"ב רנשבורג

א] גמ' מפנן לחצר אחרת ואם אינו מאמינו. זה נמחק ונ"ב בפסחים נה ע"ב כל זה איננו ויעו"ש בתוס' ד"ה ואם מתיירא וכו' ובמהרש"א שם:

ומנודה שֶׁהִתִּירוּ לוֹ חֲכָמִים, וְכֵן מִי שֶׁנִּשְׁאַל לְחָכָם וְהוּתַּר. אמִטְפְּחוֹת *הַיָּדַיִם, וּמִטְפְּחוֹת הַסְּפָרִים, וּמִטְפְּחוֹת הַסְּפָג, בהַזָּבִין וְהַזָּבוֹת וְהַנִּדּוֹת וְהַיּוֹלְדוֹת, וְכָל הָעוֹלִין מִטּוּמְאָה לְטָהֳרָה — הֲרֵי אֵלּוּ מוּתָּרִין. וּשְׁאָר כָּל אָדָם אֲסוּרִין.§ **גמ'** וּשְׁאָר כָּל אָדָם מַאי טַעְמָא אֲסוּרִין? כִּדְתְנַן: *גאַנְשֵׁי מִשְׁמָר וְאַנְשֵׁי מַעֲמָד אֲסוּרִין לְסַפֵּר וּלְכַבֵּס, וּבַחֲמִישִׁי מוּתָּרִין, מִפְּנֵי כְּבוֹד הַשַּׁבָּת. וְאָמַר *רַבָּה בַּר בַּר חָנָה אָמַר ר' אֶלְעָזָר: מ"ט — דכְּדֵי שֶׁלֹּא יִכָּנְסוּ לְמִשְׁמַרְתָּן כְּשֶׁהֵן מְנוּוָּלִין. הָכָא נַמִי: כְּדֵי שֶׁלֹּא יִכָּנְסוּ לָרֶגֶל כְּשֶׁהֵן מְנוּוָּלִין. בָּעֵי ר' זֵירָא: אָבְדָה לוֹ אֲבֵידָה עֶרֶב הָרֶגֶל, כֵּיוָן דַּאֲנִיס — מוּתָּר, אוֹ דִלְמָא: כֵּיוָן דְּלָא מוֹכְחָא מִילְּתָא — לָא? אָמַר אַבַּיֵי, *"יֹאמְרוּ: כָּל הַסְּרִיקִין אֲסוּרִין סְרִיקֵי בַּיְתוֹס מוּתָּרִין"?! וּלְטַעְמִיךְ, הָא דְּאָמַר רַבִּי אַסִי אָמַר רַבִּי יוֹחָנָן: *כָּל מִי שֶׁאֵין לוֹ אֶלָּא חָלוּק אֶחָד — מוּתָּר לְכַבְּסוֹ בְּחוּלּוֹ שֶׁל מוֹעֵד, הָתָם נַמִי: יֹאמְרוּ כָּל הַסְּרִיקִין אֲסוּרִין סְרִיקֵי בַּיְתוֹס מוּתָּרִין! הָא אִתְּמַר עֲלָהּ, אָמַר מָר בַּר רַב אַשִׁי: אֵיזוֹרוֹ מוֹכִיחַ עָלָיו. רַב אַשִׁי מַתְנֵי: בָּעֵי ר' זֵירָא אוּמָּן שֶׁאָבְדָה לוֹ אֲבֵידָה עֶרֶב הָרֶגֶל מַהוּ? כֵּיוָן דְּאוּמָּן הוּא — מוֹכְחָא מִילְּתָא, אוֹ דִלְמָא: כֵּיוָן דְּלָא מוֹכְחָא מִילְּתָא כִּי הָנָךְ — לָא? תֵּיקוּ.§ "מִמְּדִינַת הַיָּם".§ מַתְנִיתִין דְּלָא כְּר' יְהוּדָה, דְּתַנְיָא, *ר' יְהוּדָה אוֹמֵר: הַבָּא מִמְּדִינַת הַיָּם — לֹא יְגַלֵּחַ, מִפְּנֵי שֶׁיָּצָא שֶׁלֹּא בִּרְשׁוּת. אָמַר רָבָא: לָשׁוּט — דִּבְרֵי הַכֹּל אָסוּר, לִמְזוֹנוֹת — דִּבְרֵי הַכֹּל מוּתָּר, לֹא נֶחְלְקוּ אֶלָּא לְהַרְוִיחָא. מָר מְדַמֵּי לֵיהּ כְּלָשׁוּט, הוּמָר מְדַמֵּי לֵיהּ כִּלְמְזוֹנוֹת. מֵיתִיבִי, אָמַר ר' *נִרְאִין דִּבְרֵי ר' יְהוּדָה כְּשֶׁיָּצָא שֶׁלֹּא בִּרְשׁוּת, וְדִבְרֵי חֲכָמִים כְּשֶׁיָּצָא בִּרְשׁוּת. מַאי שֶׁלֹּא בִּרְשׁוּת? אִילֵימָא לָשׁוּט — וְהָאָמַרְתְּ דִּבְרֵי הַכֹּל אָסוּר. וְאֶלָּא לִמְזוֹנוֹת — וְהָאָמַרְתְּ דִּבְרֵי הַכֹּל מוּתָּר! אֶלָּא פְּשִׁיטָא — לְהַרְוִיחָא, אֵימָא סֵיפָא: נִרְאִין דִּבְרֵי חֲכָמִים כְּשֶׁיָּצָא בִּרְשׁוּת. מַאי בִּרְשׁוּת? אִילֵימָא לִמְזוֹנוֹת — הָא אָמַרְתְּ דִּבְרֵי הַכֹּל מוּתָּר, וְאֶלָּא לְהַרְוִיחָא — וְהָא אָמַרְתְּ נִרְאִין דִּבְרֵי רַבִּי יְהוּדָה בְּהָא! הָכִי קָאָמַר: נִרְאִין דִּבְרֵי ר' יְהוּדָה לְרַבָּנַן כְּשֶׁיָּצָא שֶׁלֹּא בִּרְשׁוּת, וּמַאי נִיהוּ — לָשׁוּט, שֶׁאֲפִילּוּ חֲכָמִים לֹא נֶחְלְקוּ עָלָיו אֶלָּא לְהַרְוִיחָא, אֲבָל לָשׁוּט — מוֹדוּ לֵיהּ. וְנִרְאִין דִּבְרֵי רַבָּנַן לְר' יְהוּדָה כְּשֶׁיָּצָא בִּרְשׁוּת, וּמַאי נִיהוּ — לִמְזוֹנוֹת, שֶׁאֲפִילּוּ רַבִּי יְהוּדָה לֹא נֶחֱלַק עֲלֵיהֶם אֶלָּא לְהַרְוִיחָא, אֲבָל לִמְזוֹנוֹת — מוֹדֶה לְהוּ. אָמַר שְׁמוּאֵל: קָטָן הַנּוֹלָד בַּמּוֹעֵד — מוּתָּר לְגַלֵּחַ בַּמּוֹעֵד, שֶׁאֵין לְךָ בֵּית הָאֲסוּרִין גָּדוֹל מִזֶּה. בַּמּוֹעֵד — אִין, מֵעִיקָּרָא — לָא, מְתִיב ר' פִּנְחָס: *כָּל אֵלּוּ שֶׁאָמְרוּ מוּתָּר לְגַלֵּחַ בַּמּוֹעֵד — מוּתָּר לְגַלֵּחַ בִּימֵי אֶבְלוֹ. הָא אָסוּר לְגַלֵּחַ בַּמּוֹעֵד — אָסוּר לְגַלֵּחַ בִּימֵי אֶבְלוֹ.

וְאִי

רש"י

גמ' הָכִי גָּרְסִינַן: **וּשְׁאָר כָּל אָדָם מַאי טַעְמָא אֲסוּרִין? כִּדְתְנַן אַנְשֵׁי מִשְׁמָר כו' וְאָמַר רַבָּה בַּר בַּר חָנָה כו'** עַד כְּשֶׁהֵן מְנוּוָּלִים. וּמַאן דְּמִתְרַשֵּׁל וְלָא גִּילַּח מִקַּמֵּי רֶגֶל, וּמָטֵי זְמַן עֲלַיְיהוּ לְגַלֵּחַ בָּרֶגֶל – הֶחְמִירוּ רַבָּנַן, הוֹאִיל וְלָא מְזָרְזֵי נַפְשַׁיְיהוּ לְסַפֵּר מִקַּמֵּי רֶגֶל, דְּלָא לֶהֱוֵי בָּרֶגֶל מְנוּוָּלִין – אִם הָיוּ מְגַלְּחִין בַּמּוֹעֵד לֹא הָיוּ מְגַלְּחִים לִפְנֵי הַמּוֹעֵד, וְנִכְנָסִין לָרֶגֶל כְּשֶׁהֵן מְנוּוָּלִין: **אָבְדָה לוֹ אֲבֵידָה.** שֶׁלֹּא הָיָה לוֹ פְּנַאי לְגַלֵּחַ קוֹדֶם הָרֶגֶל: **דְּלָא מוֹכְחָא מִילְּתָא.** דְּלָא יָדְעֵי כּוּלֵּי עָלְמָא דְּאָנוּס הָיָה, אֶלָּא יֹאמְרוּ: הוּא מְכַוֵּין לְהַשְׁהוֹת עַד הַמּוֹעֵד: **יֹאמְרוּ כָּל הַסְּרִיקִין אֲסוּרִין וכו'.** כְּלוֹמַר: דְּבַיְיתוֹס הָיָה יָכוֹל לִסְרוֹק חַלּוֹתָיו בְּלִי שָׁהוּת, לְפִי שֶׁהָיָה לוֹ דְּפוּס. וְאעפ"כ אָסְרוּ, מִשּׁוּם דְּאָמְרִי: כָּל הַסְּרִיקִים כו'. הָכָא נַמִי, כֵּיוָן דְּלָא מִיגַּלְיָא לְכוּלֵּי עָלְמָא אוֹנְסֵיהּ – יֹאמְרוּ: כּוּלֵּי עָלְמָא אֲסוּרִין לְגַלֵּחַ, וְזֶה מוּתָּר: **מִי שֶׁאֵין לוֹ אֶלָּא חָלוּק אֶחָד.** נַמִי לָאו מוֹכְחָא מִילְּתָא לְכוּלֵּי עָלְמָא: **אֵיזוֹרוֹ מוֹכִיחַ עָלָיו.** דְּמִי שֶׁאֵין לוֹ אֶלָּא חָלוּק אֶחָד פּוֹשְׁטוֹ וּמִתְעַטֵּף בְּמִקְטְרִינוֹ וְחוֹגְרוֹ בְּאֵיזוֹרוֹ וְעוֹמֵד וּמְכַבֵּס הֶחָלוּק וּמוֹדִיעַ לַכֹּל שֶׁאֵין לוֹ אֶלָּא חָלוּק אֶחָד: **אוּמָּן.** כְּגוֹן סַפָּר, שֶׁהַכֹּל בָּאִים אֶצְלוֹ עֶרֶב הָרֶגֶל וְרוֹאִים שֶׁאָבְדָה לוֹ אֲבֵידָה, וְאָנוּס הוּא, וְאֵינוֹ יָכוֹל לְסַפֵּר עַצְמוֹ: **כִּי הָנָךְ.** דְּמַתְנִיתִין דְּקָתָנֵי מְגַלְּחִין, דְּמֵידַע לַכֹּל: **מִפְּנֵי שֶׁיָּצָא שֶׁלֹּא בִּרְשׁוּת.** כְּלוֹמַר: הוֹאִיל וְלֹא יָצָא בִּרְשׁוּת אֲחֵרִים, אֶלָּא בִּרְצוֹן עַצְמוֹ – לָאו אָנוּס הוּא: **לָשׁוּט.** אִם יָצָא שֶׁלֹּא לְצוֹרֶךְ, וְלֹא יָצָא אֶלָּא כְּדֵי לָשׁוּט בָּעוֹלָם וְלִרְאוֹתוֹ, וְחָזַר בַּמּוֹעֵד: **דִּבְרֵי הַכֹּל אָסוּר.** לְגַלֵּחַ בַּמּוֹעֵד: **לִמְזוֹנוֹת.** שֶׁיָּצָא לַחֲזֵר אַחַר מְזוֹנוֹת, שֶׁאֵין לוֹ מְזוֹנוֹת וְחִזֵּר בַּמּוֹעֵד אַחֲרֵיהֶן – דִּבְרֵי הַכֹּל מוּתָּר לְגַלֵּחַ בַּמּוֹעֵד, לְפִי שֶׁיָּצָא בְּאוֹנֶס: **לְהַרְוִיחָא.** שֶׁיֵּשׁ לוֹ נְכָסִים הַרְבֵּה, וְיוֹצֵא כְּדֵי לְהַרְוִיחַ יוֹתֵר: **נִרְאִין לִי דִּבְרֵי רַבִּי יְהוּדָה.** דְּאָסַר בְּגִילּוּחַ לָבֹא מִמְּדִינַת הַיָּם, כְּשֶׁיָּצָא שֶׁלֹּא בִּרְשׁוּת: **וְדִבְרֵי חֲכָמִים.** הַמַּתִּירִין – כְּשֶׁיָּצָא בִּרְשׁוּת: **אִילֵימָא לָשׁוּט.** דְּקָאָמַר רַבִּי נִרְאִין דִּבְרֵי ר"י בְּיָצָא לָשׁוּט, דְּהַיְינוּ שֶׁלֹּא בִּרְשׁוּת – הָא אָמַרְתְּ וכו', וּמַאי נִרְאִין דִּבְרֵי רַבִּי יְהוּדָה? הֲלֹא שְׁנֵיהֶם מוֹדִים בָּהּ, אֶלָּא פְּשִׁיטָא – לְהַרְוָוחָא, וְאַשְׁמְעִינַן דְּנִרְאִין לוֹ דִּבְרֵי ר' יְהוּדָה שֶׁאוֹסֵר בְּגִילּוּחַ: **וְהָא נִרְאִין דִּבְרֵי רַבִּי יְהוּדָה בְּהָא.** וְקַשְׁיָא דְּרַבִּי אַדְּרַבִּי; דִּבְרֵישָׁא נִרְאֶה לוֹ דִּבְרֵי ר"י דְּאָסַר בְּהַרְוָוחָא, וּבְסֵיפָא נִרְאֶה לוֹ דִּבְרֵי חֲכָמִים דְּמַתִּירִין הַרְוָוחָא. אֶלָּא וַדַּאי אִיכָּא לְמִשְׁמַע מֵהָכָא דְּלָאו הָכִי הוּא כִּדְקָאָמְרַתְּ, דִּבְלָשׁוּט וּבִמְזוֹנוֹת פְּלִיגִי: **ה"ק.** לָאו הֶיתֵּר דִּידֵיהּ אַשְׁמְעִינַן. וְלֹא רוֹאֶה אֲנִי קָאָמַר, אֶלָּא פְּלוּגְתַּיְיהוּ קמ"ל, בְּמַאי פְּלִיגִי, נִרְאִין דִּבְרֵי ר"י הָאוֹסֵר לַחֲכָמִים וכו': **קָטָן הַנּוֹלָד בַּמּוֹעֵד.** וְלוֹ שְׂעָרוֹת גְּדוֹלִים, מוּתָּר לְגַלֵּחַ בַּמּוֹעֵד שְׂעַר רֹאשׁוֹ הַמְלַגְעֲרוֹ: **שֶׁאֵין לְךָ בֵּית הָאֲסוּרִין גָּדוֹל מִזֶּה.** מִמְּעֵי אִמּוֹ שֶׁהָיָה שָׁם, וְאָנוּס הוּא: **מֵעִיקָּרָא לָא.** דְּאִם נוֹלַד קוֹדֶם הָרֶגֶל – אֵינוֹ מְגַלֵּחַ בָּרֶגֶל, הוֹאִיל וְהָיָה יָכוֹל לְגַלֵּחַ קוֹדֶם הָרֶגֶל:

וְאִי

תוספות

ומנודה וכו' ושנשאל. בירושל' מקשה: (א) הני למה התירו? והלא פשע, שלא בא לפני המועד לפני חכמים להתיר לו! ומשני: שכלו לו שלשים יום של נדוי במועד. דאין נדוי פחות משלשים יום. וכן מי שנשאל לנכס מוקי לה כשבא בחול המועד. אי נמי: לפני המועד לא מצאו (ב) בו פתח. וגילוח הראש נמי אסור במועד, דהא אמר בגמ': שלא יכנסו לרגל מנוולין, ואין לך ניוול גדול מזה. ושמא לא קאי טעמא בגמרא אלא אשארא, אבל גילוח של ראשו – אסור משום מלאכה אפילו במקום אונס. ושאר גילוח דבעי בגמרא מאי טעמא אסורין – והיינו גילוח של יפוי, דהוה לן למישרי לצורך המועד, אע"פ שהיא מלאכה. אבל גילוח כל הראש – אסור משום מלאכה. והני (ג) כגון נזיר ומצורע הוא דשרי, משום מצוה. ולפי זה אסור לגלח ראשו במועד. ועוד יש לפרש: שנראה שמותר לגלח ראשו במועד, וא"ת: מאי קא משמע לן נזיר ומצורע? יש לומר: דס"ד דאסור, שלא ישהו קרבנותיהן – קא משמע לן דשרי. ואי מיירי הכא בשלא היה להן פנאי דוקא, והוא כדבעי למימר בגמרא – יש לומר דהכי קאמר: דנזיר ומצורע העולין מטומאה לטהרה – דוקא שעולין עתה, אבל עולין מטומאה לטהרה מקודם רגל – אסורין:

ושאר כל אדם מאי טעמא אסורין. אע"פ שהוא מלאכה – היה לנו להתירה לצורך המועד. (ד) א"נ: [אף] שיש מלאכות אסורות במועד שאין בהן טורח, כגון פרקמטיא, מכל מקום זה שהוא ליפוי ראוי להתיר לכבוד מועד. ויש מפרשים: דקאי על גילוח הראש, דאסרינן משום טירחא. מכל מקום מקשה: דהיה לו להתיר לצורך המועד. ואין זה (ה) נוטה לפי מה שפירש' המשנה דגילוח כל הראש מלאכה גמורה, ואסור!

שאין לו אלא חלוק אחד מותר לכבסו במועד. ואם תאמר: היאך יכבסנו במועד? אם כן ישאר במועד בלא חלוק בשעת כיבוס. כמו כן היה יכול לכבס קודם המועד, ויהיה בלא חלוק בשעת כיבוס! וכי תימא: כשכבסו קודם מועד, ומשום הכי מותר לכבסו במועד – א"כ, תרתי נמי אם יתלכלכו – למה נאסור לו והלא לא פשע! י"ל: דדי לו בשתי חלוקין, אחד ליו"ט ראשון ואחד לי"ט אחרון. בירושלמי אמרו: בגדי קטנים – מותר לכבסן במועד, דניכרים שהם קטנים ומלוכלכין, כמי שאין לו אלא חלוק אחד (ו):

אומן שאבדה לו אבידה ערב הרגל. פירש בקונטרס: דבאומן מבעי' ליה. אבל בני העיר, אע"פ שאין להם (ז) אומן אחר – לא מיבעיא ליה, דפשיטא דאסורים. יש להסתפק אם חלה ונתרפא, אם מותר לגלח, אם מוכחא מילתא כי הני:

מתני' דלא כר"י. תימה: לוקמא אפילו כר"י, ולמזונות אפי' רבי יהודה מודה! ושמא, כיון דקתני ר"י אומר הבא וכו' – משמע שבא לחלוק על המשנה:

אלא להרווחא והא אמרת נראין דברי ר"י בהא. נראה דל"ג ועוד, מכלל דפליגי רבנן אפילו למזונות. ובההיא פ"ק דשחיטת חולין (דף יב.): (ח) נראין דברי רבי יהודה שמלאה באשפה, ל"ג "ועוד":

עשה

מסורת הש"ס

[פרש"י ע"ז לקמן יח. ותוס' שם ע"ב]

תענית טו:

[שם יז. ע"ש]

פסחים לז. חולין קז:

חולין שם [לקמן יח.] תענית כט:

[תוספ' פ"ב]

[תוספתא שם]

[לקמן יז: תוספתא פ"ב]

עין משפט נר מצוה

ג א מיי' פ"ז מהלכות י"ט הלכה כא טוש"ע א"ח סי' תקלד סעיף א:

ד ב מיי' שם:

ה ג ד מיי' פ"ז מהל' כלי המקדש הלכה יא ופ"ז מהל' י"ט הל' יט ופ"א מהל' ביאת מקדש הלכה יב:

ו ה מיי' פ"ז מהלכות י"ט הל' יח טוש"ע א"ח סי' תקלא סעיף ד:

רבינו חננאל

ואלו מגלחין במועד הבא ממדינת הים ומבית השביה והיוצא מבית האסורין כו'. מ"ט כדתנן אנשי משמר ואנשי מעמד אסורין לספר ולכבס ואמרינן מה טעם שלא יכנסו למשמרתן מנוולין דכיון דיודעין דאסורין לכבס אף הן מספרין ומכבסין מקודם ונכנסין מתוקנין ומגוהצין. הכא נמי כדי שלא יכנסו לרגל מנוולין. בעי ר' ירמיה אבדה לו אבידה ערב הרגל כיון דטרוד הוא באבידתו אנוס הוא ומותר לספר ולכבס במועד או דלמא כיון דלא מוכחא מלתא כמו השביה ובית האסורים לא. ועלתה בתיקו. פירוש יאמרו כל הסריקין אסורין כו' הא לגבי מצה בפסח איתמר דאסרו רבנן לעשות מצות סרוקות מפני שהאשה שוהה עליהן ומחמצתן ואמרו בייתוס עושה בדפוס שאין שם שהייה אלא בפעם אחת קובעה בדפוס ונמצאת המצה מצויירת. ומתמהינן התם יאמרו כל הסריקין אסורין סריקי בייתוס מותרין מי יודע כי בדפוס נעשו הכא נמי יאמרו הכל אסורין לספר ולכבס וזה האיש מותר אבל מי שאין לו אלא חלוק אחד מותר לכבסו בחולו של מועד. כי איזורו מוכיח עליו כלומר כשרואין אדם ערום חגור איזור ורוחץ חלוקו כל רואיו יודעין שאין לו אלא חלוק אחד: הבא ממדינת הים. מתניתין דלא כר' יהודה דתניא ר' יהודה אומר הבא ממדינת הים לא יגלח מפני שיצא שלא ברשות אמר רבה לשוט פי' לשוט כמטייל וכמשתעשע כלומר שלא לצורך דברי הכל אסור למזונות כלומר יצא למדינת הים ודחוק לבקש מחיה דברי הכל מותר. כי פליגי ר"י וחכמים כשיצא להרויחא פירוש להתעשר כלומר לסחור ולהרויח. ר"י מדמי ליה לשוט דהא בכאן מחייתו מצויה ואסיר ורבנן מדמו לה ליוצא בבקשת מזון ומותבינן עליה. אמר ר' נראין דברי ר' יהודה שיצא שלא ברשות ונראין דברי חכמים שיצא ברשות ואי אמרינן לא פליגי אלא בהרויחא קשיא א) דר"י ואמר נראין דברי ר' יהודה בהרויחא מכלל דפליגי רבנן עליה ועוד נראין דברי חכמים אלא פליגי אפי' לשוט. והאמרת לשוט דברי הכל אסור. ופרקינן הכי קאמר נראין דברי ר' יהודה לחכמים. ומודה להו כשיצא שלא ברשות ומאי ניהו למזונות שאף ר' יהודה לא חלק אלא בהרויחא וקי"ל כסתמא דמתני' דשרי אפי' מאן דנפיק להרויחא וכן אמר הגאון זצ"ל. אמר שמואל קטן הנולד ברגל מגלחין אותו במועד אין לך בית אסורין גדול ממעי אמו. איני שאם נולד קודם המועד

א) נראה דל"ל קשיא דרבי אדרבי דברישא אמר נראין כו' ובסיפא אמר נראין דברי חכמים וכו'.

הגהות הב"ח

(א) תוס' ד"ה ומנודה כו' בירושלמי מקשה וא"ת הני למה התירו: (ב) בא"ד א"נ לפני המועד לא מצאו לו פתח וגילוח כל הראש נמי גילוח של כל הראש אסור משום: (ג) בא"ד והני דוקא כגון נזיר ומצורע כו' אסור לגלח כל ראשו במועד כו' מותר לגלח כל ראשו: (ד) ד"ה ושאר כו' א"נ אע"פ שיש דברים אסורות במועד שאין בהן מלאכה אלא טורח כגון פרקמטיא: (ה) בא"ד ואין זה נראה לפי מה שפי': (ו) ד"ה שאין כו' כמי שאין לו אלא חלוק אחד דמי הס"ד: (ז) ד"ה אומן כו' אע"פ שאין להם אלא אומן אחד לא מיבעיא ליה: (ח) ד"ה אלא כו' פ"ק דשחיטת חולין דקאמר נראין דברי ר' יהודה שמלאה באשפה נמי ל"ג ועוד:

ז א מיי' פ"ח מהל' אבל הלכה ד טוש"ע י"ד סי' שמ סעיף כז:
ח ב מיי' פ"ז מהלכות י"ט הלכה יט טוש"ע א"ח סי' תקלא סעיף ו:
ט ג מיי' פ"י מהלכות אבל הלכה ג ח טוש"ע א"ח סי' תקמח סעיף א:
י ד טוש"ע י"ד סי' שלד סעיף א:
יא ה ו מיי' פ"ז מהל' י"ט הלכה יב טוש"ע א"ח סי' תקמה סעיף י:
יב ז מיי' פי"ג מהל' סנהדרין הלכה ד סמג לאוין רל:
יג ח מיי' שם הלכה ה:
יד ט מיי' פ"י מהל' טומאת צרעת הל' ו סמג עשין רלה:
טו י מיי' פ"ב מהלכות ביאת המקדש הל' ו:
טז כ מיי' שם הל' ח:
יז ל מיי' פ"י מהלכות טומאת צרעת הל' ו:
יח מ מיי' פ"ה מהל' אבל הל' א ב סמג עשין דרבנן ג טוש"ע י"ד סי' שפ סעיף א וסי' שצ סעיף א:

עשה דיחיד. משמע דאבילות איכא עשה דאורייתא, מדלא קאמר ודחי עשה דרבנן. והאי דקאמר לעיל (דף יא:) לא מבעיא ימי אבלו דרבנן – היינו עשיית מלאכה, דנפקא לן (לקמן טו:) באסמכתא מ"והפכתי חגיכם לאבל". אבל גוף האבילות – דאורייתא. מיהו, נראה לי דשמחת הרגל נמי דרבנן, "ושמחת" – היינו בשלמי שמחה, כדאיתא בחגיגה (ח.): **מהו** שינהוג נידויו ברגל. א]והקשה הרב: הא ליכא אלא עשה,(ג) ואין עשה דוחה עשה! ואפילו עשה ליכא, אלא עזרא גזר, כדלקמן (דף טז.)! והא לאו קושיא היא, דהא נידוי דחי לאו דמקלל חברו, דאיכא לאו. ושמא מסוטה ילפינן. ועוד: כיון שעבר על דברי הדיינין – הרי יש כאן עשה דרבים: **ואי** לא ציית דינא משמתינן ליה. תימה: לימא דאי לא ציית דינא – נחתינן לנכסיה!ב] מיהו, פריך שפיר: **ממנעי** משמחת י"ט. הקשה בתוס' הר"א: היכי קשה ליה, דהא ממנעי משמחת י"ט מאכילה ושתיה, וגוף ההריגה דהוא מלאכה לא חיישינן! ונראה לי מדאסר רחמנא הבערת בת כהן בשבת – מכלל דבמועד שרי. אי נמי: כיון שהיא מצוה – לצורך י"ט קרינא ביה: **נמצאת** אתה מענה את דינו. קשיא לן: דבפ' "אחד דיני ממונות" (סנהדרין דף לה.) בשמעתין דלפיכך אין דנין (*בשבת) מוכח דעינוי הדין לא שייך עד שילינוהו אחר שיגמור הדין. וכי תימא דלעיוני דהכא היינו גמר דין, ולא יהרגוהו עדיין עד אחר הרגל – א"כ אמאי פריך? לימא לעיוני בעלמא: בלא גמר דין, ולא יעשוהו גמר דין עד אחר המועד! וי"ל: דמשתכחי, אף על גב דאיכא סופרי דיינין הכותבים דברי כל אחד – מ"מ הסברא אשר בלב משתכח. ומהאי טעמא אמרינן (שם) דאין דנין בערב שבת, דליכא דאינשי אינשי: **אמר** אביי ת"ש מנודה שהתירו כו'. אביי לטעמיה דדחי ודלמא לעיוני, ואין חושב ראייה להוכחה דלעיל. ואע"ג דדחי דאי לא תימא דקאמ', לא חש באותו דיחויג] ואפי' נראה דיחוי ה"נ מסתברא – מ"מ נוכל לומר לעיוני בלאו הכי נמי מסתברא: **והא** כ"ג דכל השנה כולה ברגל כו'. משמע דאם אין מנודה נוהג נידוי ברגל – הוא הדין כ"ג אינו נוהג נידוי כלל. וקשה: דהא *כ"ג דן ודנין אותו, ואי לא ציית דינא – (לא) משמתינן ליה, ולמאי דפרישית לעיל[ד] דנוכל לומר למיתה לנכסיה – ניחא:

תורה אור

וְאִי אָמְרַתְּ קָטָן אִית בֵּיהּ פְּלוּגְתָּא — נִמְצֵאת אֲבֵילוּת נוֹהֶגֶת בְּקָטָן. וְהַתַנְיָא: *[א]מְקָרְעִין לְקָטָן מִפְּנֵי *עָגְמַת נֶפֶשׁ! אָמַר רַב אַשִׁי, מִי קָתָנֵי: הָא אֲסוּרִין?! דִּלְמָא: יֵשׁ מֵהֶן אָסוּר, וְיֵשׁ מֵהֶן מוּתָּר. אַמֵימָר, וְאִי תֵּימָא רַב שִׁישָׁא בְּרֵיהּ דְּרַב אִידִי, מַתְנֵי הָכִי: אָמַר שְׁמוּאֵל: [ב]קָטָן מוּתָּר לְגַלְּחוֹ בַּמּוֹעֵד, לָא שְׁנָא נוֹלַד בַּמּוֹעֵד וְלָא שְׁנָא נוֹלַד מֵעִיקָּרָא. אָמַר רַב פִּנְחָס, אַף אֲנַן נַמִּי תָּנֵינָא: כׇּל אֵלּוּ שֶׁאָמְרוּ מוּתָּר לְגַלֵּחַ בַּמּוֹעֵד — מוּתָּר לְגַלֵּחַ בִּימֵי אֶבְלוֹ, הָא אֲסוּרִין לְגַלֵּחַ בַּמּוֹעֵד — אֲסוּרִין לְגַלֵּחַ בִּימֵי אֶבְלוֹ. אִי אָמְרַתְּ קָטָן אָסוּר — נִמְצֵאת אֲבֵילוּת נוֹהֶגֶת בְּקָטָן. וְתַנְיָא: מְקָרְעִין לְקָטָן מִפְּנֵי עָגְמַת נֶפֶשׁ. אָמַר רַב אַשִׁי, מִי קָתָנֵי: הָא אֲסוּרִין? דִּלְמָא: יֵשׁ מֵהֶן אָסוּר וְיֵשׁ מֵהֶן מוּתָּר. [ג]אָבֵל אֵינוֹ נוֹהֵג אֲבֵילוּתוֹ בָּרֶגֶל, שֶׁנֶּאֱמַר: "וְשָׂמַחְתָּ בְּחַגֶּךָ" (דברים טז). אִי אֲבֵילוּת דְּמֵעִיקָּרָא הוּא — אָתֵי עֲשֵׂה דְּרַבִּים, וְדָחֵי עֲשֵׂה דְּיָחִיד. וְאִי אֲבֵילוּת דְּהַשְׁתָּא הוּא — לָא אָתֵי עֲשֵׂה דְּיָחִיד וְדָחֵי עֲשֵׂה דְּרַבִּים. [ד]מְנוּדֶּה, מַהוּ שֶׁיִּנְהוֹג נִידּוּיוֹ בָּרֶגֶל? אָמַר רַב יוֹסֵף, [ה]תָּא שְׁמַע: *דָּנִין דִּינֵי נְפָשׁוֹת, וְדִינֵי מַכּוֹת, וְדִינֵי מָמוֹנוֹת. וְאִי לָא צָיֵית דִּינָא — [ו]מְשַׁמְּתִינַן לֵיהּ. וְאִי סָלְקָא דַּעְתָּךְ אֵינוֹ נוֹהֵג נִידּוּיוֹ בָּרֶגֶל — מְשׁוּמַּת וְאָתֵי מֵעִיקָּרָא — אָתֵי רֶגֶל דָּחֵי לֵיהּ, הַשְׁתָּא מְשַׁמְּתִינַן לֵיהּ אֲנַן?! א"ל אַבַּיֵי: וְדִלְמָא לְעַיּוּנֵי בְּדִינֵיהּ, דְּאִי לָא תֵּימָא הָכִי — דִּינֵי נְפָשׁוֹת דְּקָתָנֵי, ה"נ דְּקָטְלִין לֵיהּ? וְהָא קָא מִימַּנְעִי מִשִּׂמְחַת יוֹם טוֹב. דְּתַנְיָא, ר"ע אוֹמֵר: *מִנַּיִן [ז]לְסַנְהֶדְרִין (שֶׁרָאוּ בְּא') שֶׁהָרְגוּ אֶת הַנֶּפֶשׁ שֶׁאֵין טוֹעֲמִין כׇּל אוֹתוֹ הַיּוֹם — ת"ל "לֹא תֹאכְלוּ עַל הַדָּם" (ויקרא יט). אֶלָּא — לְעַיּוּנֵי בְּדִינֵיהּ, ה"נ — לְעַיּוּנֵי בְּדִינֵיהּ. א"ל: אִם כֵּן נִמְצֵאתָ מְעַנֶּה אֶת דִּינוֹ! *[ח]אָתוּ מִצַּפְרָא וּמְעַיְּינִי בְּדִינֵיהּ, וְעָיְילִי וְאָכְלִי וְשָׁתוּ כּוּלֵּי יוֹמָא, וַהֲדַר אָתוּ בִּשְׁקִיעַת הַחַמָּה *וְגָמְרִינַן לְדִינֵיהּ, וְקָטְלוּ לֵיהּ. אָמַר אַבַּיֵי, ת"ש: וּמְנוּדֶּה שֶׁהִתִּירוּ לוֹ חֲכָמִים. אָמַר רָבָא: מִי קָתָנֵי שֶׁהִתִּירוּהוּ חֲכָמִים? שֶׁהִתִּירוּ לוֹ חֲכָמִים קָתָנֵי, דַּאֲזַל וּפַיְּיסֵיהּ לְבַעַל דִּינֵיהּ, וְאָתֵי קַמֵּי דְּרַבָּנַן, וְשָׁרוּ לֵיהּ. מְצוֹרָע מַהוּ שֶׁיִּנְהִיג צָרַעְתּוֹ בָּרֶגֶל? אָמַר אַבַּיֵי, תָּא שְׁמַע: *וְהַנָּזִיר וְהַמְּצוֹרָע (א) מִטּוּמְאָתוֹ לְטׇהֳרָתוֹ. הָא בִּימֵי טוּמְאָתוֹ — נָהֵיג. [ט]לָא מִיבַּעְיָא קָאָמַר; לָא מִיבַּעְיָא בִּימֵי טוּמְאָתוֹ דְּלָא נָהֵיג, אֲבָל לְטׇהֳרָתוֹ — נִיגְזוֹר שֶׁמָּא יַשְׁהֶה קׇרְבְּנוֹתָיו, קמ"ל. אָמַר רָבָא, ת"ש: "וְהַצָּרוּעַ" — *[ט]לְרַבּוֹת כֹּהֵן גָּדוֹל. וְהָא כה"ג דְּכׇל הַשָּׁנָה כְּרֶגֶל (שם יג) לְכוּלֵּי עָלְמָא דָּמֵי, דְּתְנַן: *כֹּהֵן גָּדוֹל [י]מַקְרִיב אוֹנֵן [כ]וְאֵינוֹ אוֹכֵל. שְׁמַע מִינַּהּ: [ל]נוֹהֵג צָרַעְתּוֹ בָּרֶגֶל, שְׁמַע מִינַּהּ. [מ]אָבֵל אָסוּר בְּתִסְפּוֹרֶת, מִדְּקָאָמַר לְהוּ רַחֲמָנָא לִבְנֵי אַהֲרֹן "רָאשֵׁיכֶם אַל תִּפְרָעוּ" (שם י) — מִכְּלָל דְּכוּלֵּי עָלְמָא אָסוּר.

מְנוּדִּין

וְאִי אָמְרַתְּ בְּקָטָן אִית לֵיהּ פְּלוּגְתָּא. חִילּוּק, דְּנוֹלַד קוֹדֶם הָרֶגֶל — אֵינוֹ מְגַלֵּחַ בָּרֶגֶל. וְאִית לָן לְמֵימַר: הוֹאִיל וְאָסוּר לְגַלֵּחַ בָּרֶגֶל — אָסוּר לְגַלֵּחַ נַמִּי בִּימֵי אֶבְלוֹ. א"כ נִמְצֵאתָ אַתָּה אוֹמֵר אֲבֵילוּת אֲפִילּוּ בְּקָטָן: מְקָרְעִין לְקָטָן. אֶת בְּגָדָיו: מִפְּנֵי עָגְמַת נֶפֶשׁ. שֶׁיִּבְכּוּ הָרוֹאִין, וְיַרְבּוּ בִּכְבוֹד הַמֵּת, וְלֹא מִפְּנֵי שֶׁהוּא אָבֵל: מִי קָתָנֵי הָא אֲסוּרִין. דְּמַשְׁמַע: הָאֲסוּרִין לְגַלֵּחַ בַּמּוֹעֵד אֲסוּרִין לְגַלֵּחַ בְּאֵבֶל: יֵשׁ מֵהֶן אֲסוּרִין. בִּשְׁאָר כׇּל אָדָם שֶׁאֲסוּרִין לְגַלֵּחַ בַּמּוֹעֵד (ב) — אֲסוּרִין לְגַלֵּחַ בִּימֵי אֶבְלָן: וְיֵשׁ מֵהֶן מוּתָּרִין. כְּגוֹן קָטָן זֶה, שֶׁנּוֹלַד קוֹדֶם הָרֶגֶל שֶׁאָסוּר לְגַלֵּחַ בָּרֶגֶל — מוּתָּר לְגַלֵּחַ בִּימֵי אֶבְלוֹ: אָתֵי עֲשֵׂה דְּרַבִּים. "וְשָׂמַחְתָּ": וְדָחֵי עֲשֵׂה דְּיָחִיד. אֵבֶל, דִּכְתִיב (ירמיה ו): "אֵבֶל יָחִיד עֲשִׂי לָךְ": דְּהַשְׁתָּא. שֶׁאֵירְעוּ בַּמּוֹעֵד: דָּנִין דִּינֵי נְפָשׁוֹת. בַּמּוֹעֵד, אֲבָל לֹא בְּיוֹם טוֹב, שֶׁאָסוּר מִשּׁוּם שְׁבוּת. וְדָיְיקִינַן מִינַּהּ: מִדְּדָנִין בַּמּוֹעֵד — מִכְּלָל דְּאִי לָא צָיֵית — נַמִּי מְשַׁמְּתִינַן לֵיהּ בַּמּוֹעֵד: אָתֵי רֶגֶל וְדָחֵי לֵיהּ. שֶׁאֵינוֹ נוֹהֵג נִדּוּי בָּרֶגֶל: דִּלְמָא לְעַיּוּנֵי. הָא דְּתָנֵי דָּנִין — לָא אָמְרִי' דְּלֵימָא: "אִישׁ פְּלוֹנִי חַיָּיב אִישׁ פְּלוֹנִי זַכַּאי". וְאִיכָּא לְמֵידַק מִינַּהּ, דְּאִי לָא צָיֵית — מְשַׁמְּתִינַן לֵיהּ. אֶלָּא מְעַיְּינִי בַּדִּין, וְלָא אָמְרִי לֵיהּ כְּלוּם: מְעַנֶּה אֶת דִּינוֹ. דְּכִי לָא אָמְרוּ לֵיהּ דִּינוֹ לְאַלְתַּר, דְּעָיְינִי בֵּיהּ — הֲוָה לֵיהּ עִינּוּי הַדִּין: אֶלָּא. לְעוֹלָם דָּנִין דִּינוֹ וְגוֹמְרִין מַמָּשׁ בַּמּוֹעֵד. וְאִיכָּא לְמֵידַק מִינַּהּ: אִי לָא צָיֵית — מְשַׁמְּתִינַן לֵיהּ. וְאִיכָּא לְמִשְׁמַע מִינַּהּ דְּנוֹהֵג נַמִּי בָּרֶגֶל, וּדְאָמְרַתְּ א"כ מִימְנַע מִשִּׂמְחַת י"ט — הָכָא בְּמַאי עָסְקִינַן דַּאֲתוֹ מִצַּפְרָא כו': ת"ש מְנוּדֶּה שֶׁהִתִּירוּ לוֹ חֲכָמִים. קָא סָלְקָא דַּעְתָּךְ: הִתִּירוּ לְכׇל מְנוּדֶּה נִידּוּיוֹ בָּרֶגֶל, דְּאֵין נִידּוּי נוֹהֵג בָּרֶגֶל: דַּאֲזַיל וּפַיְּיסֵיהּ לְבַעַל דִּינֵיהּ. בָּרֶגֶל, וְהִתִּירוּ לוֹ חֲכָמִים, ב"ד שֶׁבְּאוֹתוֹ דוֹר: שֶׁיַּנְהִיג צָרַעְתּוֹ. שֶׁלֹּא יָבֹא אֶל תּוֹךְ הַמַּחֲנֶה, וְלֹא יְגַלֵּחַ: הָא בִּימֵי טוּמְאָתוֹ נוֹהֵג. צָרַעְתּוֹ בָּרֶגֶל: נִיגְזוֹר. שֶׁלֹּא יְהֵא מְגַלֵּחַ בַּמּוֹעֵד, דְּכֵיוָן דְּגִילַּח צָרִיךְ לְהָבִיא קׇרְבָּן, וְשֶׁמָּא מַשְׁהֶה קׇרְבְּנוֹתָיו עַד לְיוֹם טוֹב הָאַחֲרוֹן וּמַקְרִיבָן. וְאָסוּר לְהַקְרִיב קׇרְבְּנוֹת יָחִיד בְּי"ט: לְרַבּוֹת כ"ג. שֶׁנּוֹהֵג בּוֹ צָרַעַת: הָא כֹּהֵן גָּדוֹל כׇּל הַשָּׁנָה לְדִידֵיהּ כְּרֶגֶל לְכוּלֵּי עָלְמָא דָּמֵי. דִּתְנַן: כ"ג מַקְרִיב אוֹנֵן. מִדְּאָמַר לוֹ אַהֲרֹן לְמֹשֶׁה: "וְאָכַלְתִּי חַטָּאת הַיּוֹם" (ויקרא י) וְלֹא אָמַר לְמֹשֶׁה "וְהִקְרַבְתִּי" — מִכְּלָל דְּהַקְרָבָה בַּאֲנִינוּת. וְלָמַדְנוּ דְּכ"ג מַקְרִיב אוֹנֵן. אֲבָל כּוּלֵּי עָלְמָא בִּשְׁאָר יְמוֹת הַשָּׁנָה — אוֹנֵן אֵינוֹ מְשַׁלֵּחַ קׇרְבְּנוֹתָיו, כִּדְאָמְרִינַן לְקַמָּן (דף טו:): שְׁלָמִים — בִּזְמַן שֶׁהוּא שָׁלֵם וְלֹא בִּזְמַן שֶׁהוּא אוֹנֵן. וּבָרֶגֶל מְשַׁלֵּחַ. וְכֹהֵן גָּדוֹל אוֹנֵן מַקְרִיב כׇּל הַשָּׁנָה, אַלְמָא: כׇּל הַשָּׁנָה לְדִידֵיהּ כְּרֶגֶל דָּמֵי, וְקָתָנֵי דְּנוֹהֵג בּוֹ צָרַעַת. תִּיפְשׁוֹט דְּכׇל מְצוֹרָע נוֹהֵג צָרַעְתּוֹ בָּרֶגֶל: אַל תִּפְרָעוּ. גִּידּוּל שֵׂעָר. וְהַאי קְרָא גַּבֵּי מִיתַת נָדָב וַאֲבִיהוּא כְּתִיב, וּמִדְּאִצְטְרִיךְ קְרָא לְמִישְׁרֵי לְהוּ — מִכְּלָל דַּאֲחֲרִינֵי אֲסוּרִין: מְצוֹרָעִין. אע"ג דִּכְתִיב: "וְרֹאשׁוֹ יִהְיֶה פָרוּעַ" — הָא דָּרֵישׁ לֵיהּ לְקַמָּן לְהַאי פָּרוּעַ לְמִילְּתָא אַחֲרִיתִי:

מְנוּדִּין

[לקמן כו:]
[גי' הערוך אגמת ע"ש]
[תוספתא פ"ב ע"ש]
סנהדרין סג. ע"ש
[אלא כל"ל וכ"ג רש"י]
[נ"ל וגמרי יעב"ץ]
[לעיל יג:]
[לקמן טו.]
יומא יג: הוריות יב: [ב"ק קי. זבחים טז.]

גליון הש"ס

גמ' נמצאת אבלות נוהגת בקטן. ק"ל הא אדרבה כיון דבקטן לא שייך אבלות אין זה יוצא מן הכלל וכל שאסור במועד אסור בימי אבלו דימי אבלו היינו במי שהוא אבל משא"כ קטן דאינו אבל ובמועד אינו איסור על הקטן רק על המגלח אבל באבל דהמגלח אינו אבל ועל קטן ליכא איסור ולצ"ג: **שם** מי קתני. הא אסורין כעין זה זבחים קב ע"א: **שם** לא מיבעיא קאמר. עם עיין לקמן דף יח ע"ב תוס' ד"ה העולים: **שם** מכלל דכולי עלמא אסור. עיין לקמן דף כ"ג ע"ב תוס' ד"ה ואינו אוכל:

הגהות הב"ח (א) גמ' ת"ש והנזיר והמצורע העולה מטומאתו: (ב) רש"י ד"ה יש מהן וכו' לגלח במועד יש מהן אסורין לגלח: (ג) תום' ד"ה מהו כו' הא ליכא אלא עשה דיחיד ואין עשה דיחיד דוחה עשה דרבים ואפילו עשה ליכא:

הגהות מהר"ב רנשבורג

א] תום' ד"ה מהו שינהיג וכו' והקשה הרב כו' אלא עזרא גזר כלדקמן. עיין ריטב"א דבור המתחיל מנודה: ב] ד"ה ואי לא ציית כו' מיהו פריך שפיר. עיין יד דוד: ג] ד"ה אמר אביי כו' אביי לטעמיה כו' ואפילו נראה דיחוי ה"נ מסתברא כו'. בספריהם היה הגירסא א"ל אביי ודלמא לעיוני ה"נ מסתברא דאי לא תימא הכי כו' וק"ל: ד] ד"ה והא כ"ג כו' ולמאי דפרישית לעיל בד"ה ואי לא ציית:

מְנוּדִּין וּמְצוֹרָעִין מַה הֵן בְּתִסְפּוֹרֶת? ת"ש: מְנוּדִּין וּמְצוֹרָעִין אֲסוּרִין לְסַפֵּר וּלְכַבֵּס. מְנוּדֶּה שֶׁמֵּת — ב"ד סוֹקְלִין אֶת אֲרוֹנוֹ, ר' יְהוּדָה אוֹמֵר: לֹא שֶׁיַּעֲמִידוּ עָלָיו גַּל אֲבָנִים כְּגַלּוֹ שֶׁל עָכָן, אֶלָּא: ב"ד שׁוֹלְחִין וּמַנִּיחִין אֶבֶן גְּדוֹלָה עַל אֲרוֹנוֹ. *לְלַמֶּדְךָ שֶׁכָּל הַמִּתְנַדֶּה וּמֵת בְּנִידּוּיוֹ ב"ד סוֹקְלִין אֶת אֲרוֹנוֹ. אָבֵל חַיָּיב בַּעֲטִיפַת הָרֹאשׁ, מִדְּקָאָמַר לֵיהּ רַחֲמָנָא לִיחֶזְקֵאל "וְלֹא תַעְטֶה עַל שָׂפָם" — מִכְּלָל דְּכוּלֵּי עָלְמָא מִיחַיְּיבִי. מְנוּדֶּה מַהוּ בַּעֲטִיפַת הָרֹאשׁ? אָמַר רַב יוֹסֵף, ת"ש: *וְהֵן מִתְעַטְּפִין וְיוֹשְׁבִין כִּמְנוּדִּין וְכַאֲבֵלִים עַד שֶׁיְּרַחֲמוּ עֲלֵיהֶם מִן הַשָּׁמַיִם. א"ל אַבַּיֵי: דִּלְמָא מְנוּדֶּה לַשָּׁמַיִם שָׁאנֵי דַּחֲמִיר. מְצוֹרָע מַהוּ בַּעֲטִיפַת הָרֹאשׁ? ת"ש: "וְעַל שָׂפָם יַעְטֶה" — מִכְּלָל שֶׁחַיָּיב בַּעֲטִיפַת הָרֹאשׁ, ש"מ. *אֲבָל אָסוּר לְהָנִיחַ תְּפִילִּין, מִדְּקָאָמַר לֵיהּ רַחֲמָנָא לִיחֶזְקֵאל: "פְּאֵרְךָ חֲבוּשׁ עָלֶיךָ" — מִכְּלָל דְּכ"ע אָסוּר. א) מְנוּדֶּה מַהוּ בִּתְפִילִּין? תֵּיקוּ. מְצוֹרָע מַהוּ בִּתְפִילִּין? ת"ש: *"וְהַצָּרוּעַ" — לְרַבּוֹת כ"ג, "בְּגָדָיו יִהְיוּ פְרוּמִים" — שֶׁיְּהוּ מְקוֹרָעִים, "וְרֹאשׁוֹ יִהְיֶה פָרוּעַ" — אֵין פְּרִיעָה אֶלָּא גִּידּוּל שֵׂעָר, דִּבְרֵי ר"א. ר"ע אוֹמֵר: נֶאֶמְרָה הֲוָיָה בָּרֹאשׁ וְנֶאֶמְרָה הֲוָיָה בַּבֶּגֶד, מַה הֲוָיָה הָאֲמוּרָה בַּבֶּגֶד — דָּבָר שֶׁחוּץ מִגּוּפוֹ, אַף הֲוָיָה בָּרֹאשׁ — דָּבָר שֶׁחוּץ מִגּוּפוֹ. מַאי לָאו — אַתְּפִילִּין? אָמַר רַב פַּפָּא: לָא, ג) אַכּוּמְתָא וְסוּדָרָא. אָבֵל אָסוּר בִּשְׁאִילַת שָׁלוֹם, דְּקָאָמַר לֵיהּ רַחֲמָנָא לִיחֶזְקֵאל: "הֵאָנֵק דֹּם", מְנוּדֶּה מַהוּ בִּשְׁאִילַת שָׁלוֹם? אָמַר רַב יוֹסֵף: ת"ש: *וּבִשְׁאִילַת שָׁלוֹם שֶׁבֵּין אָדָם לַחֲבֵרוֹ, כִּבְנֵי אָדָם הַנְּזוּפִין לַמָּקוֹם. א"ל אַבַּיֵי: דִּלְמָא מְנוּדֶּה לַשָּׁמַיִם שָׁאנֵי, דַּחֲמִיר. מְצוֹרָע מַהוּ בִּשְׁאִילַת שָׁלוֹם? ת"ש: "וְעַל שָׂפָם יַעְטֶה" — שֶׁיְּהוּ שְׂפָתוֹתָיו מְדוּבָּקוֹת זוֹ בָּזוֹ, שֶׁיְּהֵא כִּמְנוּדֶּה וְכָאָבֵל, וְאָסוּר בִּשְׁאִילַת שָׁלוֹם, ש"מ. וְנִיפְשׁוֹט מִינַּהּ לִמְנוּדֶּה! אָמַר רַב אַחָא בַּר פִּנְחָס מִשְּׁמֵיהּ דְּרַב יוֹסֵף: מִי קָתָנֵי שֶׁאָסוּר? שֶׁיְּהֵא כִּמְנוּדֶּה וְכָאָבֵל [קָתָנֵי] — בְּמִילֵּי אַחֲרָנְיָיתָא, וְאָסוּר נַמִּי בִּשְׁאִילַת שָׁלוֹם. אָבֵל אָסוּר בְּדִבְרֵי תוֹרָה, מִדְּקָאָמַר רַחֲמָנָא לִיחֶזְקֵאל "דֹּם", מְנוּדֶּה מַהוּ בְּדִבְרֵי תוֹרָה? אָמַר רַב יוֹסֵף, ת"ש: מְנוּדֶּה — שׁוֹנֶה וְשׁוֹנִין לוֹ, נִשְׂכָּר וְנִשְׂכָּרִין לוֹ. מוּחְרָם — לֹא שׁוֹנֶה וְלֹא שׁוֹנִין לוֹ, לֹא נִשְׂכָּר וְלֹא נִשְׂכָּרִין לוֹ, אֲבָל שׁוֹנֶה הוּא לְעַצְמוֹ שֶׁלֹּא יַפְסִיק אֶת לִמּוּדוֹ. וְעוֹשֶׂה לוֹ חֲנוּת קְטַנָּה בִּשְׁבִיל פַּרְנָסָתוֹ. וְאָמַר רַב: זַבּוֹנֵי מַיָּא בְּפַקְתָּא דַּעֲרָבוֹת. שְׁמַע מִינַּהּ. מְצוֹרָע מַהוּ בְּדִבְרֵי תוֹרָה? *ת"ש: "וְהוֹדַעְתָּם לְבָנֶיךָ וְלִבְנֵי בָנֶיךָ יוֹם אֲשֶׁר עָמַדְתָּ לִפְנֵי ה' אֱלֹהֶיךָ בְּחֹרֵב", מַה לְּהַלָּן בְּאֵימָה וּבְיִרְאָה וּבִרְתֵת וּבְזִיעָה — מִכָּאן אָמְרוּ: *הַזָּבִין וְהַמְּצוֹרָעִין וּבוֹעֲלֵי נִדּוֹת מוּתָּרִין לִקְרוֹת בַּתּוֹרָה וּבַנְּבִיאִים וּבַכְּתוּבִים, וְלִשְׁנוֹת בַּמִּדְרָשׁ וּבש"ס בַּהֲלָכוֹת וּבָאַגָּדוֹת, וּבַעֲלֵי קְרָיִין אֲסוּרִין, ש"מ. אָבֵל אָסוּר *בְּתִכְבּוֹסֶת, דִּכְתִיב: "וַיִּשְׁלַח יוֹאָב תְּקוֹעָה וַיִּקַּח מִשָּׁם אִשָּׁה חֲכָמָה וַיֹּאמֶר אֵלֶיהָ הִתְאַבְּלִי נָא וְלִבְשִׁי נָא בִגְדֵי אֵבֶל וְאַל תָּסוּכִי שֶׁמֶן וְהָיִית כְּאִשָּׁה זֶה יָמִים רַבִּים מִתְאַבֶּלֶת עַל מֵת". מְנוּדִּין וּמְצוֹרָעִין מַה הֵן בְּתִכְבּוֹסֶת? ת"ש: מְנוּדִּין וּמְצוֹרָעִין אֲסוּרִין לְסַפֵּר וּלְכַבֵּס. ש"מ. אָבֵל חַיָּיב בִּקְרִיעָה דְּקָאָמַר לְהוּ רַחֲמָנָא לִבְנֵי אַהֲרֹן: "לֹא תִפְרוֹמוּ" — מִכְּלָל דְּכ"ע מִיחַיְּיבִי. מְנוּדֶּה מַהוּ בִּקְרִיעָה? תֵּיקוּ. מְצוֹרָע מַהוּ בִּקְרִיעָה? ת"ש: "בְּגָדָיו יִהְיוּ פְרוּמִים" — שֶׁיְּהוּ מְקוֹרָעִין, שְׁמַע מִינַּהּ. אָבֵל חַיָּיב בִּכְפִיַּית הַמִּטָּה, דְּתָנֵי בַּר קַפָּרָא: דְּמוּת

א) [עי' תוס' יבמות נדה ז: ד"ה הקשה ה"ר לאביי"ה וכו']
ב) [פי' כומתא מגבעה רכה שהיא כמלא הראש ואין עולה למעלה מן הראש. ערוך]

רש"י

מְנוּדִּין וּמְצוֹרָעִין מַהוּ. לְהָכִי קָאָמַר לְהוּ בַּהֲדָדֵי — מִשּׁוּם דְּפָשֵׁיט לְהוּ בַּהֲדָדֵי: מְנוּדֶּה שֶׁמֵּת וכו'. סֵיפָא דְּבָרַיְיתָא הִיא: כְּגַלּוֹ שֶׁל עָכָן. דִּכְתִיב (יהושע ז): "וַיָּקִימוּ עָלָיו גַּל אֲבָנִים גָּדוֹל": וְהֵן מִתְעַטְּפִין. מְפוֹרָשׁ בְּמַסֶּכֶת תַּעֲנִית, לְאַחַר שֶׁהִתְעַנּוּ שָׁלֹשׁ עֶשְׂרֵה ת"צ: מְנוּדֶּה לַשָּׁמַיִם. כִּי הָנֵי שָׁאנֵי, דַּחֲמִירֵי, וּלְהָכִי צְרִיכֵי עֲטִיפַת הָרֹאשׁ. אֲבָל אֲחֵרִים — אֵינָן צְרִיכִין עֲטִיפַת הָרֹאשׁ: יַעְטֶה. מַשְׁמַע עֲטִיפַת הָרֹאשׁ: פְּאֵרְךָ. זֶה תְּפִילִּין: דָּבָר שֶׁהוּא חוּץ מִגּוּפוֹ אַף הֲוָיָה. הָאֲמוּרָה בָּרֹאשׁ "רֹאשׁוֹ יִהְיֶה פָרוּעַ" מַשְׁמַע מְגוּלֶּה, כְּעִנְיָן דִּכְתִיב: "וּפָרַע אֶת רֹאשׁ הָאִשָּׁה" (במדבר ה) — דָּבָר שֶׁהוּא חוּץ מִגּוּפוֹ. וְלָא אָמְרִינַן מִשֵּׂעָר, שֶׁהוּא מִגּוּפוֹ: מַאי לָאו. שֶׁיְּהֵא רֹאשׁוֹ מְגוּלֶּה מִתְּפִילִּין: אַכּוּמְתָא וְסוּדָרָא. כְּלוֹמַר שֶׁיְּהֵא רֹאשׁוֹ מְגוּלֶּה מִכּוּמְתָא וְסוּדָרָא, אֲבָל תְּפִילִּין מֵנִיחַ: דְּהָא א"ל רַחֲמָנָא לִיחֶזְקֵאל הֵאָנֵק דֹּם. כְּלוֹמַר, בְּדָבָר זֶה תִּנְהוֹג אֲבֵילוּת: שֶׁתִּדּוֹם וְלֹא תִּשְׁאַל לְשָׁלוֹם: ת"ש. דְּתָנֵי גַּבֵּי תַּעֲנִיּוֹת: הֵן יוֹשְׁבִין כִּמְנוּדִּין וַאֲבֵלִים כו': שָׂפָם. מַשְׁמַע: שְׂפָתוֹתָיו מְדוּבָּקוֹת: מִי קָתָנֵי בִּמְנוּדֶּה. שֶׁאָסוּר בִּשְׁאִילַת שָׁלוֹם: מוּחְרָם. שֶׁמַּחְרִימִין בְּחֵרֶם לְאַחַר ל' יוֹם לְאַחַר הַנִּדּוּי א]: בְּפַקְתָּא דַּעֲרָבוֹת. בַּשּׁוּק שֶׁל אוֹתוֹ מָקוֹם: בַּעֲלֵי קְרָיִין אֲסוּרִין. לְפִי שֶׁבָּא לָהֶם מֵחֲמַת שִׂמְחָה וְקַלּוּת רֹאשׁ, וְלֵיכָּא אֵימָה: דְּמוּת

תוספות

מנודין ומצורעין מה הן בתספורת. ומ"ראשו יהיה פרוע" לא בעי לאוכוחי, דלית ליה דר"א, דמוקי לה לקמן בתספורת. תדע, דלקמן בעי לאוכוחי מינה הנחת תפילין כר"ע: (*מנודה) מהו בעטיפת הראש אמר רב יוסף תא שמע. ולא נראה לו דברי רב פפא דמוקי "ראשו יהיה פרוע" אכומתא וסודרא:

וראשו יהיה פרוע. צריך עיון אי פליגי הכי ב"ראשיכם אל תפרעו ובגדיכם לא תפרומו" דלעיל מייתי (א) עליה תספורת לאבל, ולא מייתי מיניה למצורע, דמשמע דסבר כר"ע, ופליג אדר' אליעזר, כדפרישית לעיל? ושמא ר"ע לא פליג אדרבי אליעזר, דפריעת הראש היינו גידול שער בין במצורע בין באבל, ותרוייהו דורש ר"ע. ולעיל דלא מייתי מיניה למצורע — משום דמשכח ברייתא בהדיא מייתי לה, ואע"ג דברישא דסוגיא מייתי אבל אינו נוהג אבילותו ברגל, ומניח המשנה דלקמן ומייתי קרא ד"ושמחת" — לפי שצריך לפרש מנלן מתני' דאבל אינו נוהג אבילותו ברגל. אבל ראשו יהיה פרוע, דמיירי בגידול שער, דומה לו דבר פשוט וניחא ליה לאתויי ברייתא: אסור בשאילת שלום דקאמר ליה רחמנא ליחזקאל האנק דום. דמשמע שתיקה משאילת שלום. ומתלמוד תורה נמי משמע בסמוך מ"האנק דום". והא דהיה יחזקאל נוהג אבילות ב"האנק דום" ובכל שאר דברים לא היה עושה — שהיה צריך להראות בקצת דברים שהוא אבל, ולא היה נוהג דיני אבל אלא למשל: שיהו שפתותיו מדובקות. לעיל דרשינן מיניה עטיפת הראש. ושמא תרוייהו משמע. א"נ: מדכתיב שפם ולא כתיב שפה:

ובועלי נדות מותרין. אחר שטבל לקרי, אבל לקריו — צריך טבילה. ולרבי יהודה משמע התם דלא צריך טבילה לדברי תורה לבעל קרי, היכא דלא נטהר ע"י טבילה זו. בפרק "מי שמתו" (ברכות דף כו.) במשמשת וראתה דם, ובעל קרי שראה זיבה — צריכין טבילה, ור' יהודה פוטר. והא דהכא בלא טבילה כרבי יהודה — צריך לישב דאיירי רבי יהודה בסיפא דהך ברייתא בפ' "מי שמתו" (שם דף כב.), וקאמר רבי יהודה: שונה הוא בהלכות דרך ארץ. וליכא למימר דלרבי יהודה נמי בועלי נדות חייבין טבילה כמו בעל קרי בעלמא, דהשתא ומה בעל קרי שראה זיבה אחר כך, שהיה חייב כבר — פוטר רבי יהודה, בועל נדה לא כל שכן. מיהו, לכאורה נ"ל דלא פליגי רבי יהודה ורבנן אלא בהני טומאות דדומיא דקרי הוי, דהיינו דטומאה יוצאה עליו מגופו. אבל בטומאת שרצים — מודה רבי יהודה דבהדי קרי צריך טבילה. א"כ ה"נ בועל נדה מודה, דלא חשיב טומאה יוצאה מגופו. ואפילו מאן דבעי למימר בפרק "אלו דברים" בפסחים (דף סח.) ובפ"ק דיומא (דף ו.) דמשתלח חוץ לשתי מחנות כמו בעל קרי — מ"מ לא חשיב טומאה יוצאה מגופו. ורבי יהודה נמי הצריך טבילה לדברי תורה. בתוספ' פי': דכיון דטומאת בועל נדה מכח קרי — רבי יהודה מודה דצריך טבילה:

ה"ג מנודין ומצורעין מה הן בתכבוסת? ת"ש: מנודין ומצורעין אסורין לספר ולכבס. ובספר הרב לא היה כתוב כל זה. והיה קשה לרב: למה לא בעי ליה? ותירץ: דכבר אייתי לעיל הך ברייתא דגבי תספורת. והאי הקשה לקמן גבי עשיית מלאכה קמיבעי, ומביא ברייתא דמתנייא לעיל ונשכרין! ותירץ: דאגב דמצורע קאי בתיקו, קא בעי מנודה, ומייתי לברייתא דלעיל:

ורחילה

רבינו חננאל

מנודה וכן מצורע דתניא מנודין ומצורעין אסורין לספר ולכבס. מנודה שמת ב"ד סוקלין את ארונו. ר' יהודה אומר לא שיעמידו עליו גל אבנים כגל עכן. אלא ב"ד שולחין ומניחין אבן על ארונו כו'. אבל חייב בעטיפת הראש מדאמר ליה רחמנא ליחזקאל לא תעטה על שפם מכלל דכ"ע אסירי וכן מנודה דתנן והן מתעטפין ויושבין כמנודין ואבלין עד שירחמו עליהן מן השמים ודחי אביי ודלמא מנודה לשמים דחמיר חייב בעטיפת הראש אבל מנודה לבני אדם לא. ולקולא עבדינן. ולא מחייבינן למנודה בעטיפת הראש דהא איבעיא ולא איפשיטא. מצורע אסיקנא דחייב בעטיפת הראש. אבל אסור בתפלין מדכתיב ביחזקאל פארך חבוש עליך מכלל דכ"ע אסירי מנודה מהו בתפלין תיקו. מצורע מהו בתפלין ולא איפשיטא בהדיא אבל אסור בשאילת שלום מדכתיב ביחזקאל האנק דום אלא דבר מכלל דכ"ע אסירי. מנודה מאי ת"ש מנודה שונה ושונין לו נשכר ונשכרין לו מוחרם לא שונה ולא שונין לו [לא נשכר] ולא נשכרין לו אבל שונה לעצמו שלא יפסיד תלמודו ועושה לו חנות קטנה בפקתא דערבות שהיא ארץ ציה רחוקה מן הישוב לזבוני מיא כדי פרנסתו וכן מצורע מותר בדברי תורה אבל אסור בתכבוסת ובסיכה שנאמר וישלח יואב תקועה ויקח משם אשה חכמה ויאמר אליה התאבלי נא ולבשי נא בגדי אבל ואל תסוכי שמן והיית כאשה זו ימים רבים מתאבלת על מת. אבל אסור ברחיצה דרחיצה בכלל סיכה היא מנודה ומצורע ברחיצה לא איפשיטא בהדיא. אבל חייב בקריעת בגדיו מדכתיב בבני אהרן ובגדיכם לא תפרומו מכלל דכולי עלמא חייבי וכן מצורע מנודה מאי תיקו אבל חייב בכפיית המטה. מנודים ומצורעים מהו תיקו

גליון הש"ס

תוס' ד"ה ובועלי נדות וכו' ובתוספ' פי' דכיון דטומאת בועל נדה. עיין משנה למלך פ"ג ה"ג מהל' ביאת מקדש:

תורה אור

דמות דיוקני נתתי בהן, ובעונותיהם הפכתיה — כפו מטותיהן עליה. מנודה אומצורע מה הן בכפיית המטה? תיקו. באבל אסור בעשיית מלאכה, דכתיב: °"והפכתי חגיכם לאבל" מה חג אסור במלאכה — אף אבל אסור במלאכה. מנודה מהו בעשיית מלאכה? אמר רב יוסף, ת"ש: *גכשאמרו אסור בעשיית מלאכה — לא אמרו אלא ביום, אבל בלילה מותר. וכן אתה מוצא במנודה ובאבל. מאי לאו — אכולהו? לא, אשארא. ת"ש: מנודה שונה ושונין לו, נשכר ונשכרין לו. שמע מינה. מצורע מהו בעשיית מלאכה? תיקו. דאבל אסור ברחיצה, דכתיב: °"ואל תסוכי שמן", ורחיצה בכלל סיכה. מנודה מהו ברחיצה? אמר רב יוסף, ת"ש: *כשאמרו אסור ברחיצה — הלא אמרו אלא כל גופו, אבל פניו ידיו ורגליו — מותר. וכן אתה מוצא במנודה ובאבל. מאי לאו אכולהו? לא, אשארא. ומצורע מהו ברחיצה? תיקו. *זאבל אסור בנעילת הסנדל, מדקאמר ליה רחמנא ליחזקאל: °"ונעליך תשים ברגליך" — מכלל דכולי עלמא אסור. חמנודה מהו בנעילת הסנדל? אמר רב יוסף, תא שמע: *כשאמרו אסור בנעילת הסנדל — טלא אמרו אלא בעיר, אבל בדרך — מותר. הא כיצד? יצא לדרך — נועל, נכנס לעיר — חולץ, וכן אתה מוצא במנודה ובאבל. מאי לאו אכולהו? לא, אשארא. ימצורע מהו בנעילת הסנדל? תיקו. *כאבל אסור בתשמיש המטה, דכתיב: °"וינחם דוד את בת שבע אשתו ויבא אליה" — מכלל דמעיקרא אסור. מנודה מהו בתשמיש המטה? אמר רב יוסף, ת"ש: כל אותן שנים שהיו ישראל במדבר מנודין היו, ושימשו מטותיהן. א"ל אביי: ודלמא מנודה לשמים שאני, דקיל? קיל?! והא אמרת חמיר! ספוקי מספקא ליה, זיל הכא — קמדחי ליה, וזיל הכא — קמדחי ליה. למצורע מהו בתשמיש המטה? ת"ש, דתניא: °"וישב מחוץ לאהלו" — שיהא כמנודה [א] וכאבל, *ואסור בתשמיש המטה. ואין אהלו אלא אשתו, שנא' °"לך אמור להם שובו לכם לאהליכם" — שמע מינה. וניפשוט נמי למנודה! אמר רב הונא בריה דרב פנחס משמיה דרב יוסף: מי קתני "שאסור"? שיהא כמנודה וכאבל — במילי אחרנייתא, ואסור נמי בתשמיש המטה. מאבל אינו משלח קרבנותיו, דתניא, *ר"ש אומר: "שלמים" — בזמן שהוא שלם, ולא בזמן שהוא אונן. נמנודה מהו שישלח קרבנותיו? אמר רב יוסף, ת"ש: כל אותן שנים שהיו ישראל במדבר מנודין היו, ושלחו קרבנותיהן. א"ל אביי: ודלמא מנודה לשמים שאני, דקיל? קיל?! והאמרת חמיר! ספוקי מספקא ליה, ומדחי ליה. מצורע מהו שישלח קרבנותיו? סת"ש, דתניא: °"ואחרי טהרתו" — אחר פרישתו מן המת, "שבעת ימים יספרו לו" — אלו ז' ימי ספירו, °"וביום באו אל הקודש אל החצר הפנימית לשרת בקודש יקריב חטאתו"

זו

רש"י

דמות דיוקני. "בצלם אלהים עשה את האדם" (בראשית ט): [כשאמרו. חכמים גבי "עברו אלו ולא נענו" (תענית דף יג.) אסור במלאכה וכו' וכן אתה מוצא במנודה]: מאי לאו אכולהו. קאמר, דמנודה אסור: לא אשארא. דקתני (א) אעטיפת הראש, דאמרי' התם (דף יד:): בתענית צבור מתעטפין ויושבין כמנודין: ורחיצה בכלל סיכה. דכתיב: "ותבא כמים בקרבו וכשמן בעצמותיו" (תהלים קט): כשאמרו אסור ברחיצה. בתענית צבור: אכולהו. ארחילה נמי, דמנודה אסור: לא אשארא. קאמר, דמנודה אית ליה דין דהני דתעניות צבור: כשאמרו אסור בנעילת הסנדל. בתענית צבור: ויבא אליה. לאחר אבילות: מנודין היו. למקום: ספיקא הוא. אי קיל אי חמיר: זיל הכא ומדחי. דלקולא *אזלי בהדייהו: לפיכך נקראים שלמים בזמן שהוא שלם. בדעתו, שדעתו מיושבת עליו: יספרו לו. לעיל מיניה כתיב: "ואל מת אדם לא יבא לטמאה" ובכהן משתעי, ואחרי טהרתו — דהיינו מפרישתו מן המת, משפירש מן המת מונין שבעת ימי הזאתו שבעת ימים אחרים יספרו לו. מדאפקיה רחמנא בלשון ספירה ולא נקט הזאה — שמעינן: שבעת ימי ספירו אם נצטרע: וביום באו *ביום טהרתו. כתיב בכהן גדול:

תוספות

ורחיצה בכלל סיכה. תימה: אדבעי מהו ברחילה, אמאי לא בעי מהו בסיכה? לא אשארא. דמיירי התם בסוף פ"ק דתענית (דף יג.) בנעילת הסנדל ועשיית מלאכה. ואעשיית מלאכה לא קאי, דהא מנודה שרי במלאכה, אלא אנעילת סנדל. סוף פ"ק דתענית (שם) מסיק, הלכתא: אבל אסור בין בחמין בין בצונן, אבל לרחוץ פניו ידיו ורגליו בחמין — אסור, בצונן — מותר. ולסוך — אפילו כל שהוא אסור. ובתוס' הרב פי': קשיא ליה מאי שנא בט' באב ויוה"כ אסור לרחוץ אפילו אצבעו, כדמשמע בפרק בתרא דיומא (דף עח.): ומביאין לו מטפחת כו'. והא תרוייהו מסיכה נפקי, אבילות מ"ואל תסוכי שמן", יום הכפורים מ"וסוך לא סכתי" (דניאל י)! ובשם רשב"ם: דלפי המסקנא דמסיק בפ"ק דתענית דאבל מותר לרחוץ פניו ידיו ורגליו בצונן — הוא הדין ט' באב ויוה"כ. ותימה: אמאי לא מייתי בסוגיין דתענית ההיא דמטפחת כו'? ובשם רבינו תם שמעתי שהיה אוסר לרחוץ כלל בט' באב ויוה"כ חוץ מידיו שחרית, דחשיב להו כמו מלוכלכות בטיט ובואה. הואיל ואינו יכול ליגע בפיו ועיניו ומשום בת מלך: לא אשארא. פי': לא קאי אנעילת סנדל אלא ארחילה. וזיל הכא קמדחי ליה, וזיל הכא קמדחי ליה. דאעשיית מלאכה לא קאי, כדפרישית לעיל. וא"ת: ואמאי לא פשיט מר"א דסוף פרק "הזהב" (ב"מ דף נט:*): קרע את בגדיו וחלץ מנעליו! וי"ל: דשמא היה מחמיר על עלמו. אי נמי: מספקא ליה, כי היכי דמספקא לן:

ושמשו מטותיהן. בכל הני דלעיל לא מייתי מבני המדבר, דלא ידעי היאך היו נוהגין. אלא הא פשיטא לן שהיו משמשים מטותיהן — שהרי הם היו פרים ורבים. וכן גבי שלחו קרבנות דבסמוך — שמא יש להוכיח הכי מן הפסוקים:

וישב מחוץ לאהלו. פי': בימי ספרו. ובימי חלוטו פליגי בה לעיל (דף ז:). כי האי גוונא אמרינן אבל אסור להניח תפילין. ולא בכל ימי אבלו קאמרינן, אלא יום ראשון בלבד ושני, כדלקמן (דף כא.):

ואחרי טהרתו. פי' בקונטרס: דבטומאת מת איירי. ז' ימים ימי הזאתו, "יספרו לו" — איירי בימי ספירו. וכמו מילתא אחריתי קמ"ל. וביום באו לעבודה יביא כהן הדיוט עשירית האיפה, "וחטאתו" — כמו חטוי, וקדושתו לעבודה — מילי מילי קאמר. וקשה: אמאי לא מפרש ליה בכהן גדול? ויש לומר: משום דבכהן הדיוט איירי, דכתיב: "כי אם לאב ולאם", ואילו כ"ג לא יטמא לאביו ולאמו. ולא ניחא ליה למימר כדאמרינן בקדושין (דף עח:): רישא בכהן גדול וסיפא בכהן הדיוט. ועוד: דלא הוה קמ"ל מידי. אבל כהן הדיוט ביום חינוכו — אינו כתיב בקרא בפירוש. מיהו, קשה לן: כיון דמילי מילי כתיב, אמאי ר"ש אומר בבאו מקריב — בזמן שראוי לביאה, (ג)וקשה: דבפרק "תמיד נשחט" (פסחים דף סב. ושם), דקאמרינן: כל הזבחים ערל וטמא משלחין קרבנותיהן! ועוד: דהכא נמי לא משמע דאיירי אלא במצורע, דהא דבעי מצורע מהו שישלח קרבנותיו מייתי ליה! ונראה לי, דר"ש לאפוקי מצורע אתי, דרבי יהודה דריש "ביום באו" — ביום שמתחנך לעבודה, ור"ש מוקי ל"ביום באו" — דקאי אדלעיל, דאיירי במצורע, ולא איירי מידי בעשירית האיפה. אלא בא לומר דבמצורע דאיירי בקרא, כשיטהר ויכנס לעזרה, דהיינו לאחר ימי ספרו — אז יקריב חטאתו או שאר קרבנותיו. ובתוספות פי': דערל וטמא משלחין קרבנותיהן(ג) בטומאת שרץ, ולא בטומאה מגופו. והקשה על זה מהא דאמרינן במגילה פ"ק (דף ח.): מזובו ולא מנגעו. משמע, דאם יטהר מזובו — יביא קרבן, אע"פ שהוא מנורע! וכמו כן קשה למאי דפרישית! ותירץ: דלא איירי התם לענין קרבן אלא שיהא טהור מדין משכב ומושב, דחמירא הוה טפי ממצורע. וצ"ע: בפרק "כל הזבחים שנתערבו" (זבחים עד: ושם), ובפרק "כל הגט" (גיטין דף כח: ושם), *מפורש קצת דיני סמיכה שצריך בעלים, ואם כן אין טמא מביא קרבנותיו! [ועי' תוס' יבמות קד: ד"ה דאמר]:

מתרין

רבינו חננאל

אבל אסור בעשיית מלאכה שנאמר והפכתי חגיכם לאבל מה חג אסור בעשיית מלאכה אף אבל אסור. מצורע תיקו אבל מנודה מותר במלאכה. אבל אסור בנעילת הסנדל מדכתיב ביחזקאל ונעליך תשים ברגליך. מכלל דכ"ע אסירי. כשאמרו אסור בנעילת הסנדל לא אמרו אלא בעיר אבל בדרך מותר. יצא לדרך נועל. נכנס לעיר חולץ. וכן המנודה. מצורע תיקו. אבל אסור בתשמיש המטה שנאמר וינחם דוד את בת שבע אשתו ויבא אליה. מכלל דמעיקרא אסיר. מנודה מהו ת"ש כל השנים שהיו ישראל במדבר היו כמנודים והיו משמשין מטותיהן. ודלמא שאני מנודה לשמים דקיל והא אמרת מנודה לשמים חמור הוא ספוקי מספקא ליה אזיל הכא מדחי ליה אזיל הכא מדחי ליה. מצורע מהו בתשמיש המטה ולא איפשיטא בהדיא. אבל אינו משלח קרבנותיו שנאמר שלמים בזמן שהוא שלם ולא בזמן שהוא אונן מנודה מהו ולא איפשיטא מצורע מהו ת"ש

עין משפט נר מצוה

לז א מיי' פ"י מהלכות טומאת צרעת הל' ו סמג עשין רלה:
לח ב מיי' פ"ה מהל' אבל הל' א ג סמג עשין דרבנן ג טוש"ע י"ד סי' שפ סעיף א:
לט ג מיי' פ"ג מהלכות תענית הל' ד טוש"ע א"ח סי' תקנד סעיף ג:
מ ד מיי' פ"ה מהלכות אבל הלכה א ג סמג עשין דרבנן ג טוש"ע י"ד סי' שפ סעיף א:
מא ה מיי' פ"ג מהלכות תענית הל' ז טוש"ע א"ח סי' תקנד סעיף ג:
מב ו מיי' פ"י מהל' טומאת צרעת הל' ו:
מג ז מיי' פ"ה מהל' אבל הל' א ו טוש"ע י"ד סי' שפ סעיף א:
מד ח טוש"ע א"ח סי' שלד סעיף ב:
מה ט מיי' פ"ג מהל' תענית הלכה ז טוש"ע א"ח סי' תקנד סעיף ג:
מו י מיי' פ"י מהלכות טומאת צרעת הל' ו:
מז כ מיי' פ"ה מהל' אבל הלכה א ה סמג עשין דרבנן ג טוש"ע י"ד סי' שפ סעיף א:
מח ל מיי' פ"י מהלכות טומאת צרעת הל' ו:
מט מ נ ס מיי' פ"ב מהלכות ביאת מקדש הלכה יא סמג לאוין שג:

מסורת הש"ס

עמוס ח. שמואל ב יד. תענית יג. [עי' ברא"ש ס"ס נא]. שם [פסחים נג:]. [לקמן כ:]. יחזקאל כד. ביום חיטוטו כתיב בכהן הדיוט כל"ל כפי הסוגיא ופי' התוספות. תוספתא דתענית פ"א. [וע"ש תוספות ד"ה וקרע ובת"י נדה ז: ד"ה הקשה ה"ר דאבי"ה]. [לקמן כא.] שמואל ב יב. ויקרא יד. דברים ה. [לעיל ז:]. [זבחים נט:]. יחזקאל מד. שם. [ובחגיגה טז:]

הגהות הגר"א

[א] גמ' כמנודה מביתו וכאבל כו' כל"ל:

גליון הש"ס

גמ' הא כיצד יצא לדרך. עי' לקמן דף כז ע"א תוס' ד"ה אם יכול: תוס' ד"ה לא אשארא דמיירי כו' משום בת מלך. ע' שבת דף קטו ע"א: ד"ה לא אשארא פי' לא קאי כו' וזיל הכא קמדחי. וכן כתבו כל הפוסקים ותמיה לי לפי ההלכה בתענית דף יג ע"א דבתענית צבור מותר ברחילה כל גופו בצונן אם כן על כרחך הך בריתא מיירי ברחילת חמין וממילא וכן אתה מולא במנודה ובכלל זו לא קאי על רחילה דהא באבל אפילו אצבע אסור בחמין ובכמבואר שם דלהיות דקאי אנעילת סנדל ולא"כ מוכח דקאי אשארא ...

הגהות הב"ח

(א) רש"י ד"ה לא אשארא דקתני התם אעטיפת הראש: (ב) תוס' ד"ה ואחרי כו' בזמן שראוי לביאה דבפ' תמיד נשחט כו' כל"ל ותיבת וקשה נמחק: (ג) בא"ד ובתוס' פי' כו' משלחין קרבנותיהן איירי בטומאת שרץ:

זו עשירית האיפה שלו, דברי רבי יהודה. ר"ש אומר: "בבאו יקריב" — בזמן שראוי לביאה ראוי להקרבה, בזמן שאינו ראוי לביאה — אינו ראוי להקרבה. אמר רבא: (א) מנלן דמשדרין שליחא דבי דינא, ומזמנינן ליה לדינא — דכתיב: "וישלח משה לקרא לדתן ולאבירם בני אליאב". ומנלן דמזמנינן לדינא — דכתיב: "ויאמר משה אל קרח אתה וכל עדתך". לקמי גברא רבה — דכתיב: "לפני ה'", את ופלניא — דכתיב: "אתה והם ואהרן", דקבעינן זימנא — דכתיב: "מחר". זימנא בתר זימנא — דכתיב: "קראו שם פרעה מלך מצרים שאון העביר המועד". ומנלן דאי מתפקר בשליחא דבי דינא, ואתי ואמר, לא מיתחזי כלישנא בישא — דכתיב: "העיני האנשים ההם תנקר". ומנלן דמשמתינן — דכתיב: "אורו מרוז", דהכי סברא דגברא רבה, דכתיב: "אמר מלאך ה'". ומנלן דמחרמינן — דכתיב: "אורו ארור", דאכיל ושתי בהדיה וקאי בארבע אמות דידיה — דכתיב: "יושביה". ומנלן דפרטינן חטאיה בציבורא — דכתיב: "כי לא באו לעזרת ה'". ואמר עולא: בד' מאה שיפורי שמתיה ברק למרוז. איכא דאמרי: גברא רבה הוה, ואיכא דאמרי: כוכבא הוה, שנאמר: "מן שמים נלחמו הכוכבים". ומנלן דמפקרינן נכסיה — דכתיב: "וכל אשר לא יבא לשלשת הימים בעצת השרים והזקנים יחרם כל רכושו והוא יבדל מקהל הגולה". ומנלן דנצינן ולייטינן ומחינן ותלשינן שיער ומשבעינן — דכתיב: "ואריב עמם ואקללם ואכה מהם אנשים ואמרטם ואשביעם". ומנלן דכפתינן ואסרינן ועבדינן הרדפה — דכתיב: "הן למות הן לשרושי הן לענש נכסין ולאסורין". מאי לשרושי? אמר אדא מרי אמר נחמיה בר ברוך אמר רב חייא בר אבין אמר רב יהודה: הרדפה. מאי הרדפה? אמר רב יהודה בריה דרב שמואל בר שילת משמיה דרב: מנדין לאלתר, ושונין לאחר ל' ומחרימין לאחר ששים. א"ל רב הונא בר חיננא, הכי אמר רב חסדא: מתרין ביה שני וחמישי ושני. ה"מ — לממונא. אבל לאפקירותא — לאלתר. ההוא טבחא דאיתפקר ברב טובי בר מתנה, אימנו עליה אביי ורבא ושמתוהו. לסוף אזל פייסיה לבעל דיניה. אמר אביי: היכי ליעביד? לישרי ליה — לא חל שמתא עליה תלתין יומין, לא לישרי ליה — קא בעו רבנן [א]למיעל! א"ל לרב אידי בר אבין: מידי שמיע לך בהא? א"ל: הכי אמר רב תחליפא בר אבימי אמר שמואל: *טוט אסר, וטוט שרי. אמר ליה: ה"מ — לממונא, אבל לאפקירותא — עד דחיילא שמתא עליה תלתין יומין. אלמא קסבר אביי: הני בי תלתא דשמיתו — לא אתו תלתא אחריני ושרו ליה. דאיבעיא להו: הני בי תלתא דשמיתו, מהו למיתי תלתא אחריני ושרו ליה? ת"ש: *מנודה לרב — מנודה לתלמיד, מנודה *לתלמיד — אינו מנודה לרב. מנודה לעירו — מנודה לעיר אחרת, מנודה לעיר אחרת — אינו מנודה לעירו. מנודה לנשיא — מנודה לכל ישראל, מנודה לכל ישראל — אינו מנודה לנשיא. רשב"ג אומר: אחד מן התלמידים שנידה ומת — חלקו אינו מופר. ש"מ תלת: שמע מינה: תלמיד שנידה לכבודו נידויו נידוי, וש"מ: כל אחד ואחד מיפר חלקו, וש"מ: הני בי תלתא דשמיתו — לא אתו תלתא אחריני ושרו ליה. אמר אמימר: הלכתא, הני בי תלתא דשמיתו — אתו בי תלתא אחריני ושרו ליה. א"ל רב אשי לאמימר: והא תניא רשב"ג אומר: אחד מן התלמידים שנידה ומת — חלקו אינו מופר. מאי לאו — אינו מופר כלל? לא, עד דאתו בי תלתא אחריני ושרו ליה. ת"ר: אין נידוי פחות מל' יום, ואין נזיפה פחות מז' ימים. ואף על פי שאין ראיה לדבר — זכר לדבר: שנאמר: "ואביה ירק ירק בפניה הלא תכלם שבעת ימים". אמר רב חסדא: נידוי שלנו כנזיפה שלהן. ונזיפה דידהו שבעה, ותו לא? והא ר"ש בר רבי ובר קפרא הוו יתבי וקא גרסי, קשיא להו שמעתא. א"ל ר"ש לבר קפרא: דבר זה צריך רבי. א"ל בר קפרא לר"ש: ומה רבי אומר בדבר זה? אזל א"ל לאבוה. איקפד. אתא בר קפרא לאיתחזויי ליה, אמר ליה: בר קפרא, איני מכירך מעולם. ידע דנקט מילתא בדעתיה, נהג נזיפותא בנפשיה תלתין יומין. שוב, פעם אחד גזר רבי שלא ישנו לתלמידים בשוק. מאי דרש — *"חמוקי ירכיך *)כמו חלאים", מה ירך בסתר — אף

*) [כמו חלאים אין חלאים אלא רבנן כדגרסינן בנדרים מט. והן שמתעסקין בתורה שהיא מעשה ידי אומן. ערוך בערך חמק]

רש"י

זו עשירית האיפה שלו. שמביא כהן הדיוט כשמחנכין אותו לעבוד תחילה, דכתיב (ויקרא ו): "זה קרבן אהרן ובניו אשר יקריבו לה' ביום המשח אותו עשירית האיפה", ואמרינן (מנחות דף נא:): לרבות עשירית האיפה של כהן הדיוט לחינוך. ולאו אקראי דלעיל קאי, אלא מלות כהנים בעלמא הוא דקאמר יחזקאל. אלמא: שלא היה יכול להקריב קרבנו עשירית האיפה עד שנטהר מטומאת מת, והוא הדין מצרעתו: אמר רבא וכו'. איידי דאיירי במנודה מפרש להו: ומזמינין ליה לדינא. לבעל דין: זימנא בתר זימנא. דאי לא אתי ההוא זימנא — קבעינן ליה זימנא אחריתי: קראו שם. שמתא. כלומר: שמתא לפרעה שהעביר המועד. כלומר שהעביר אותו מועד ששמו אחר מועד ראשון: דאי מתפקר בשליחא דרבנן. כלומר, שחירף שליח ב"ד, ושליח אמר: "חירפני": העיני האנשים ההם תנקר. אי לאו דשליח דא"ל למשה — משה לא הוה ידע: הכי סברא דגברא פלניא. דעת פלוני, שבא לנדות את פלוני, דצריך לנדותו משמו של אותו חכם: אמר מלאך ה'. ברק אמר לשמתו, שהוא שלוחו של מקום: ומחרימין. בחרור: ופרטינן חטאיה. דאמרי לאנשי עירו: משום הכי והכי משמתינן ליה: כוכבא הוה. מזליה דסיסרא: דמפקרינן לנכסיה. דמאן דלא ציית להו לרבנן: יחרם (ב) הוא וכל רכושו. דהפקר ב"ד הפקר — מהכא נפקא לן בכל דוכתי*: ואריב עמם ואקללם. לאותם שהושיבו נשים גויות: דכפתינן. ידיו ורגליו: ואסרינן ליה. שקושרין אותו על העמוד ללקותו: הרדפה. קא מפרש רב יהודה בריה דרב שמואל לרודפו מיד, דכיון דלא ציית דינא — מנדין אותו: ושונין. ומנדין אותו פעם אחרת: לממונא. שחייב ממון לחבירו, ולא רצה לשלם ע"פ ב"ד: לאפקירותא. מבזה תלמידי חכמים: לא חל עליה שמתא ל' יום. ואין שמתא פחותה מל' יום: קא בעו רבנן למיעל. שצריכין לו: טוט אסר טוט שרי. כלומר: מהו למישרי ליה, אע"ג דלא חל עליה ל' יום. דאותו שופר שנדוהו יכול להתיר לו, ומישרי ליה בתוך ל' יום: לא אתו אחריני ושרו ליה. מדמהדר איהו נפשיה למישרי: שנידה לכבודו. ולא לשם שמים, אלא שהתריז נגדו ודאי, כיון דתני אין מנודה לרב — ודאי לא נידה אלא בשביל כבודו, דאי במילי דאיסורא — הוי כמי שמנודה לרב "דאין חכמה ואין עצה וגו'" (משלי כא). וקתני: אין מנודה לרב, אבל לכולי עלמא — מנודה: כל אחד מיפר חלקו. מדקתני: חלקו אינו מופר: לא אתו אחריני ושרו. מדקתני חלקו אינו מופר לעולם, אפי' שרו ליה אחריני: נזיפה. גערה, כדלקמן: נדוי שלנו. בני בבל: כנזיפה שלהן. ארץ ישראל: צריך רבי. רבי, אבוה דר"ש הוה: מה רבי אומר בדבר זה. אין רבי בעולם היודע דבר זה: א"ל לאבוה. לפי תומו, ולאו משום לישנא בישא: לאיתחזויי ליה. לבקר את רבי, שהיה חולה, שקיבל עליו יסורין: אמר ליה בר קפרא איני מכירך. רמז לו שאינו רוצה לראותו: חמוקי ירכיך. כמו "חמק עבר" (שיר ה):

תוספות

מתרין בו שני וחמישי ושני. פירש בקונטרס: שני מתרין בו תחילה, ומנדין אותו, וכן בחמישי, ובשני אחר מחרימין. וא"ל שלשים יום. ויש מפרשים קודם שינדוהו כלל יתרו בו, וכן משמע בפרק "הגוזל בתרא" (ב"ק דף קיג.): וטרקיה

מסורת הש"ס

[נ"ל וביום בואו] [יבמות פט:] [עי' תוספות מנחות לד: ד"ה טט] [לקמן יז.] [עי' תוספות סנהדרין ח. ד"ה מפיקנא] [סוכה מט: ע"ש] ס"א פלניא שופטים ה [שבועות לו.]

הגהות הב"ח

(א) גמ' אמר רבא מנלן דקבעינן דוכתא ומשדרינן שליחא דבי דינא דכתיב וישלח כו' כצ"ל ותיבות ומזמינן ליה לדינא נמחק: (ב) רש"י ד"ה יחרם כל רכושו כו' ותיבת הוא נמחק:

הגהות הגר"א

[א] גמ' למיעל. נ"ב נ"א למיזל [ועיין ר"ן ופרש"י שבריו"ף]:

עין משפט נר מצוה

נ א ב ג מיי' פכ"ה מהלכות סנהדרין הל' ח טוש"ע ח"מ סימן יא סעיף א:
נא ד מיי' שם הלכה ו סמג לאוין רח טוש"ע שם וסימן א סעיף ה בהג"ה:
נב ה מיי' שם הלכה א ופ"ו מהלכות ת"ת הלכה יד ופכ"ד מהלכות סנהדרין הלכה ז טוש"ע ח"מ סימן ב וטוש"ע י"ד סימן שלד סעיף מג:
נג ו מיי' פ"ז מהלכות ת"ת הלכה יג טוש"ע י"ד סי' שלד סעיף ט:
נד ז מיי' פכ"ד מהל' סנהדרין הלכה ז:
נה ח מיי' שם הלכה ו טוש"ע ח"מ סימן ב בהג"ה:
נו ט י מיי' שם הלכה ח והלכה ט:
נז כ מיי' פ"ז מהלכות ת"ת הלכה ד טוש"ע י"ד סימן שלד סעיף א:
נח ל מיי' פכ"ה מהל' סנהדרין הלכה ח טוש"ע י"ד סימן שלד סעיף א בהג"ה וטוש"ע ח"מ סימן ק סעיף ג:
נט מ מיי' פ"ז מהלכות ת"ת הל' יג טוש"ע י"ד סימן שלד סעיף א:
ס נ מיי' שם הלי"ב טוש"ע י"ד סי' שלד סעי' יג:
סא ס מיי' פ"ו שם הל' יג טוש"ע שם סעיף טו:
סב ע מיי' שם טוש"ע שם סעיף כ:
סג פ מיי' שם טוש"ע שם סעיף כא:
סד צ מיי' שם טוש"ע שם סעיף מה:
סה ק טוש"ע שם סעיף כו:
סו ר מיי' פ"ז שם הל' ט טוש"ע שם סעיף כה:
סז ש ת טוש"ע שם סעיף א:

רבינו חננאל

ר"ש אומר כתיב כאן בבאו יקריב עצמו בזמן שראוי לבא בקדש יקריב בזמן שאינו ראוי לביאה אינו ראוי להקרבה. אמר רבא מנ"ל דמשדרינן שליחא מבי דינא ומזמנינן ליה לדינא לקמיה גברא רבה שנאמר ויאמר משה אל קרח אתה וכל עדתך היו לפני ה' ופלניא בעל דינך שנא' אתה והם ואהרן ומנ"ל דקבעינן להו זימנא שנאמר מחר. ומנ"ל דקבעינן זימנא בתר זימנא שנאמר קראו שם פרעה מלך מצרים שאון העביר המועד. העביר המועד שקבעו לו מועד ולא נענש עד אחר כן. מנ"ל דאי מתפקר בשליחא דבי דינא ואתי שליחא ומחוי ליתיה לישנא בישא שנאמר העיני האנשים ההם תנקר לא נעלה ומנ"ל דמשמתינן בהרמנא דגברא רבה שנאמר אורו מרוז אמר וגו' ומנ"ל דמחרמינן ליה נמי דכתיב אורו ארור ומנ"ל דמחרמינן על כל מאן דאכיל ושתי בהדיה וקאי בד' אמות דיליה שנאמר אורו ארור יושביה. ומנ"ל דפרטינן חטאיה שנאמר כי לא באו לעזרת ה' פי' לעזרת עם ה'. איכא דאמרי מרוז אדם גדול הוה ואיכא דאמרי כוכבא הוה והאי דכתיב יושביה כענין עייש על בניה תנחם. ומנ"ל דמאן דמתפקר אבי דינא מפקרינן נכסיה שנאמר וכל אשר לא יבא לשלשת הימים בעצת השרים והזקנים יחרם כל רכושו והוא יבדל מקהל הגולה. ומנ"ל דנצינן ולטינן ומחינן ומתלשינן שיער ומשבעינן דכתיב ואריב עמם ואקללם ואכה מהם אנשים ואמרטם ואשביעם וגו' ומנ"ל דכפתינן ואסרינן ועבדינן הרדפה שנאמר הן למות הן לשרושי הן לענוש נכסין ולאסורין. מאי לשרושי הרדפה. אמר רב יהודה משמיה דרב מנדין לאלתר דמתפקר ושונין לאחר שלשים ומחרימין לאחר ששים. אמרו משמיה דרב חסדא מתרינן ביה שני וחמישי ושני ואח"כ מנדין אותו. והני מילי לממונא אבל לאפקירותא מנדין לאלתר בלא התראה. ההוא טבחא דאתפקר ברב טובי אימנו אביי ורבא ושמתי' אזל פייסיה לרב טובי אמר אביי היכי נעביד נישרי ליה לא חל שמתא עליה שלשים יום נשבקיה בשמתיה קא בעו רבנן לאפטורי. א"ל רב אידי בר אבין הכי אמר שמואל טוט אסר וטוט שרי. כלומר תקיעת השופר היא השמתא הקול שמכריז בתקיעת שופר הוא האוסר הוא המתיר כלומר אינו צריך ימים לחול עליה שמתא א"ל ה"מ לממונא אבל לאפקירותא עד דחייל עליה שמתא שלשים יום. דייקינן מדקאמר אביי בעי רבנן לאפטורי קסבר תלתא דשמיתו לא אתו תלתא אחרינא ושרו מאי ת"ש מנודה לרב מנודה לתלמיד מנודה לתלמיד אינו מנודה לרב מנודה לעירו מנודה לעיר אחרת. מנודה לעיר אחרת אינו מנודה לעירו. מנודה לנשיא מנודה לכל ישראל מנודה לכל ישראל אינו מנודה לנשיא. רשב"ג אומר אחד מן התלמידים שנידה ומת חלקו אינו מופר ש"מ תלת ש"מ מדקתני אחד מן התלמידים שנידה ומת וקתני נמי מנודה לתלמיד אינו מנודה לרב דייקינן מינה דרב אינו מנודה הא לכ"ע מנודה ש"מ תלמיד שנידה לכבודו נידויו נידוי ומדקתני ומת חלקו אינו מופר ש"מ דכל אחד מיפר חלקו. ש"מ נמי דלא אתו אחריני ושרו חלקו א' דמשמתי מופר עד דאתו תלתא אחריני ושרו ליה. *) אמימר הלכתא ת"ר אין נדוי פחות משלשים יום ואין נזיפה פחות משבעה ואע"פ שאין ראיה לדבר זכר לדבר שנאמר ויאמר ה' אל משה ואביה ירק ירק בפניה הלא תכלם שבעת ימים. אמר רב חסדא נידוי שלנו כנזיפה שלהן ונזיפה דידהו שבעה איני והא בר קפרא בעידנא דאמר ליה ר' בר קפרא איני מכירך מעולם וכן כדאמר ליה ר' לר' חייא ראה מה קורא לך בחוץ ידעו דנקיט מילתא עליהו נהגו נזיפתא בנפשייהו תלתין יומין. ואסיקנא נזיפותא דנשיא תלתין יומין. סוגיא דשמעתא כך גזר ר'

*) נ"ל בי תלתא דשמיתו אתו בי תלתא אחרינא ושרו ליה א"ל רב אשי לאמימר והא תניא וכו' חלקו אינו מופר לא אינו מופר עד דאתו וכו'.

*אַף דִּבְרֵי תוֹרָה בְּסֵתֶר. יָצָא רַבִּי חִיָּיא וְשָׁנָה לִשְׁנֵי בְּנֵי אָחִיו בַּשּׁוּק, *לְרַב וּלְרַבָּה בַּר בַּר חָנָה. שְׁמַע רַ' — אִיקְפַּד. אֲתָא ר' חִיָּיא לְאִיתַחֲזוּיֵי לֵיהּ, א"ל: *עִיָּיא, מִי קוֹרֵא לְךָ בַּחוּץ? יָדַע דִּנְקַט מִילְּתָא בְּדַעְתֵּיהּ, נְהַג נְזִיפוּתָא בְּנַפְשֵׁיהּ תְּלָתִין יוֹמִין. בְּיוֹם תְּלָתִין שְׁלַח לֵיהּ: תָּא, הֲדַר שְׁלַח לֵיהּ דְּלָא לֵיתֵי. מֵעִיקָּרָא מַאי סָבַר וּלְבַסּוֹף מַאי סָבַר? מֵעִיקָּרָא סָבַר: *מִקְצָת הַיּוֹם כְּכוּלּוֹ, וּלְבַסּוֹף סָבַר: לָא אָמְרִינַן מִקְצָת הַיּוֹם כְּכוּלּוֹ. לְסוֹף אֲתָא, א"ל: אַמַּאי אָתֵית? א"ל: דִּשְׁלַח לִי מָר דְּלֵיתֵי. וְהָא שְׁלַחִי לָךְ דְּלָא תֵּיתֵי? א"ל: זֶה רָאִיתִי, וְזֶה — לֹא רָאִיתִי. קְרֵי עֲלֵיהּ: °"בִּרְצוֹת ה' דַּרְכֵי אִישׁ גַּם אוֹיְבָיו יַשְׁלִים אִתּוֹ". מ"ט עֲבַד מָר הָכִי? א"ל: דִּכְתִיב: °"חָכְמוֹת בַּחוּץ תָּרֹנָּה". א"ל: *אִם קָרִיתָ — לֹא שָׁנִיתָ, וְאִם שָׁנִיתָ — לֹא שִׁילַּשְׁתָּ, וְאִם שִׁילַּשְׁתָּ, לֹא פֵּירְשׁוּ לְךָ. "חָכְמוֹת בַּחוּץ תָּרֹנָּה" — כִּדְרָבָא. דְּאָמַר רָבָא: כָּל הָעוֹסֵק בַּתּוֹרָה מִבִּפְנִים — תּוֹרָתוֹ מַכְרֶזֶת עָלָיו מִבַּחוּץ. וְהָא כְּתִיב: °"לֹא מֵרֹאשׁ בַּסֵּתֶר דִּבַּרְתִּי"! הַהוּא בְּיוֹמֵי דְּכַלָּה. וְר' חִיָּיא, הַאי "חַמּוּקֵי יְרֵכַיִךְ" מַאי עָבֵיד לָהּ? מוֹקֵי לָהּ בִּצְדָקָה וּבִגְמִילוּת חֲסָדִים. אַלְמָא, נְזִיפָה דִּידְהוּ תְּלָתִין יוֹמִין! נְזִיפַת נָשִׂיא שָׁאנֵי. [א]וּנְזִיפָה דִּידַן כַּמָּה הָוֵי? חַד יוֹמָא. כִּי הָא דִּשְׁמוּאֵל וּמָר עוּקְבָא, כִּי הָווּ יָתְבִי גָּרְסִי שְׁמַעְתָּא — הֲוָה יָתֵיב מָר עוּקְבָא קַמֵּיהּ דִּשְׁמוּאֵל בְּרָחוֹק ד' אַמּוֹת, וְכִי הָווּ יָתְבִי בְּדִינָא — הֲוָה יָתֵיב שְׁמוּאֵל קַמֵּיהּ דְּמָר עוּקְבָא בְּרָחוֹק ד' אַמּוֹת. וְהָווּ חָיְיקִי לֵיהּ דּוּכְתָּא לְמָר עוּקְבָא *בְּצִיפְתָּא וְיָתֵיב עִילָּוֵיהּ, כִּי הֵיכִי דְּלִישְׁתַּמְעָן מִילֵּיהּ. כָּל יוֹמָא הֲוָה מְלַוֵּי לֵיהּ מָר עוּקְבָא לִשְׁמוּאֵל עַד אוּשְׁפִּיזֵיהּ, יוֹמָא חַד אִיטְרִיד בְּדִינֵיהּ. הֲוָה אָזֵיל שְׁמוּאֵל בָּתְרֵיהּ, כִּי מְטָא לְבֵיתֵיהּ א"ל: לָא נְגַהּ לָךְ? לִישְׁרֵי לִי מָר בְּתִיגְרֵיהּ! יָדַע דִּנְקַט מִילְּתָא בְּדַעְתֵּיהּ, נְהַג נְזִיפוּתָא בְּנַפְשֵׁיהּ חַד יוֹמָא. הַהִיא אִיתְּתָא דַּהֲוַות יָתְבָה בִּשְׁבִילָא, הֲוַות פָּשְׁטָה כַּרְעָהּ וְקָא מְנַפְּיָא *חוּשְׁלָאֵי, וַהֲוָה חָלֵיף וְאָזֵיל צוּרְבָּא מֵרַבָּנַן, וְלָא אִיכַּנְעָה מִקַּמֵּיהּ. אָמַר: כַּמָּה חֲצִיפָא הַהִיא אִיתְּתָא! אֲתַאי לְקַמֵּיהּ דְּר"נ, אֲמַר לָהּ: מִי שְׁמַעַתְּ שַׁמְתָּא מִפּוּמֵיהּ? אָמְרָה לֵיהּ: לָא. אֲמַר לָהּ: זִילִי, נְהוֹגִי נְזִיפוּתָא חַד יוֹמָא בְּנַפְשִׁיךְ. זוּטְרָא בַּר טוֹבִיָּה הֲוָה קָפְסֵיק סִידְרָא קַמֵּיהּ דְּרַב יְהוּדָה, כִּי מְטָא לְהַאי פְּסוּקָא: °"וְאֵלֶּה דִּבְרֵי דָוִד הָאַחֲרוֹנִים: א"ל: אַחֲרוֹנִים — מִכְּלָל דְּאִיכָּא רִאשׁוֹנִים, רִאשׁוֹנִים מַאי נִינְהוּ? שָׁתֵיק וְלָא אֲמַר לֵיהּ וְלָא מִידֵי. הֲדַר א"ל: אַחֲרוֹנִים מִכְּלָל דְּאִיכָּא רִאשׁוֹנִים, רִאשׁוֹנִים מַאי הִיא? א"ל: מַאי דַּעְתָּךְ, דְּלָא יָדַע פֵּירוּשָׁא דְּהַאי קְרָא — לָאו גַּבְרָא רַבָּה הוּא? יָדַע דִּנְקַט מִילְּתָא בְּדַעְתֵּיהּ, נְהַג נְזִיפוּתָא בְּנַפְשֵׁיהּ חַד יוֹמָא. וּדְאָתָן עֲלָהּ, מִיהָא אַחֲרוֹנִים — מִכְּלָל דְּאִיכָּא רִאשׁוֹנִים, רִאשׁוֹנִים מַאי הִיא? °"וַיְדַבֵּר דָּוִד לַה' אֶת דִּבְרֵי הַשִּׁירָה הַזֹּאת בְּיוֹם הִצִּיל ה' אוֹתוֹ מִכַּף כָּל אוֹיְבָיו וּמִכַּף שָׁאוּל". אָמַר לוֹ הקב"ה לְדָוִד: •דָּוִד, שִׁירָה אַתָּה אוֹמֵר עַל מַפַּלְתּוֹ שֶׁל שָׁאוּל? *אִלְמָלֵי אַתָּה שָׁאוּל וְהוּא דָּוִד — אִיבַּדְתִּי כַּמָּה דָּוִד מִפָּנָיו. הַיְינוּ דִּכְתִיב: °"שִׁגָּיוֹן לְדָוִד אֲשֶׁר שָׁר לַה' עַל דִּבְרֵי כוּשׁ בֶּן יְמִינִי". וְכִי כּוּשׁ שְׁמוֹ? וַהֲלֹא שָׁאוּל שְׁמוֹ! אֶלָּא: מַה כּוּשִׁי מְשׁוּנֶּה בְּעוֹרוֹ — אַף שָׁאוּל מְשׁוּנֶּה בְּמַעֲשָׂיו. כַּיּוֹצֵא בַּדָּבָר אַתָּה אוֹמֵר: °"עַל אוֹדוֹת הָאִשָּׁה הַכּוּשִׁית אֲשֶׁר לָקָח", וְכִי כּוּשִׁית שְׁמָהּ? וַהֲלֹא צִיפּוֹרָה שְׁמָהּ! אֶלָּא: מַה כּוּשִׁית מְשׁוּנָּה בְּעוֹרָהּ — אַף צִיפּוֹרָה מְשׁוּנָּה בְּמַעֲשֶׂיהָ. כַּיּוֹצֵא בַּדָּבָר אַתָּה אוֹמֵר: °"וַיִּשְׁמַע עֶבֶד מֶלֶךְ הַכּוּשִׁי", וְכִי כּוּשִׁי שְׁמוֹ? וַהֲלֹא צִדְקִיָּה שְׁמוֹ! אֶלָּא: מַה כּוּשִׁי מְשׁוּנֶּה בְּעוֹרוֹ — אַף צִדְקִיָּה מְשׁוּנֶּה בְּמַעֲשָׂיו. כַּיּוֹצֵא בַּדָּבָר אַתָּה אוֹמֵר: °"הֲלֹא כִבְנֵי כֻשִׁיִּים אַתֶּם לִי (*בֵּית) יִשְׂרָאֵל", וְכִי כּוּשִׁיִּים שְׁמָן? וַהֲלֹא יִשְׂרָאֵל שְׁמָן! אֶלָּא: מַה כּוּשִׁי מְשׁוּנֶּה בְּעוֹרוֹ — אַף יִשְׂרָאֵל מְשׁוּנִּין בְּמַעֲשֵׂיהֶן מִכָּל הָאוּמּוֹת. *א"ר שְׁמוּאֵל בַּר נַחְמָנִי א"ר יוֹנָתָן: מַאי דִּכְתִיב: °"נְאֻם דָּוִד בֶּן יִשַׁי וּנְאֻם הַגֶּבֶר הֻקַם עָל" — נְאֻם דָּוִד בֶּן יִשַׁי, שֶׁהֵקִים עוּלָּהּ שֶׁל תְּשׁוּבָה. °"אָמַר אֱלֹהֵי יִשְׂרָאֵל לִי דִבֶּר צוּר יִשְׂרָאֵל מוֹשֵׁל בָּאָדָם צַדִּיק מוֹשֵׁל יִרְאַת אֱלֹהִים", מַאי קָאָמַר? א"ר אֲבָהוּ, ה"ק, אָמַר אֱלֹהֵי יִשְׂרָאֵל: לִי דִּבֵּר צוּר יִשְׂרָאֵל, אֲנִי מוֹשֵׁל בָּאָדָם, מִי מוֹשֵׁל בִּי — צַדִּיק. שֶׁאֲנִי *גּוֹזֵר גְּזֵרָה וּמְבַטְּלָהּ. °"אֵלֶּה שְׁמוֹת הַגִּבֹּרִים אֲשֶׁר לְדָוִד יֹשֵׁב בַּשֶּׁבֶת" וגו' מַאי קָאָמַר? א"ר אֲבָהוּ, ה"ק, וְאֵלֶּה שְׁמוֹת גְּבוּרוֹתָיו שֶׁל דָּוִד: "יוֹשֵׁב בַּשֶּׁבֶת" — בְּשָׁעָה שֶׁהָיָה יוֹשֵׁב בִּישִׁיבָה לֹא הָיָה יוֹשֵׁב עַל גַּבֵּי כָּרִים וּכְסָתוֹת, אֶלָּא עַל גַּבֵּי קַרְקַע. דְּכָל כַּמָּה דַּהֲוָה רַבֵּיהּ עִירָא הַיָּאִירִי קַיָּים — הֲוָה מַתְנֵי לְהוּ לְרַבָּנַן עַל גַּבֵּי כָּרִים וּכְסָתוֹת, כִּי נָח נַפְשֵׁיהּ — הֲוָה מַתְנֵי דָּוִד לְרַבָּנַן, וַהֲוָה יָתֵיב עַל גַּבֵּי קַרְקַע. אָמְרוּ לֵיהּ: לֵיתִיב מָר אַכָּרִים וּכְסָתוֹת! לָא קַבֵּיל עֲלֵיהּ. "תַּחְכְּמֹנִי" — אָמַר רַב: אָמַר לוֹ הקב"ה, הוֹאִיל וְהִשְׁפַּלְתָּ עַצְמְךָ — תְּהֵא כָּמוֹנִי, שֶׁאֲנִי גּוֹזֵר גְּזֵרָה — וְאַתָּה מְבַטְּלָהּ. "רֹאשׁ הַשָּׁלִישִׁים" — תְּהֵא רֹאשׁ לִשְׁלֹשֶׁת אָבוֹת. •"הוּא עֲדִינוֹ הָעֶצְנִי" — כְּשֶׁהָיָה יוֹשֵׁב וְעוֹסֵק בַּתּוֹרָה — הָיָה מְעַדֵּן עַצְמוֹ כְּתוֹלַעַת, וּבְשָׁעָה שֶׁיּוֹצֵא לַמִּלְחָמָה — הָיָה מַקְשֶׁה עַצְמוֹ כָּעֵץ. "עַל שְׁמוֹנֶה מֵאוֹת חָלָל בְּפַעַם אֶחָת" — שֶׁהָיָה זוֹרֵק חֵץ וּמַפִּיל שְׁמוֹנֶה מֵאוֹת חָלָל בְּפַעַם אַחַת, וְהָיָה מִתְאַנֵּחַ עַל מָאתַיִם. דִּכְתִיב: °"אֵיכָה יִרְדֹּף אֶחָד אֶלֶף". יָצְתָה בַּת קוֹל וְאָמְרָה: °"רַק בִּדְבַר אוּרִיָּה הַחִתִּי". אָמַר רַבִּי תַּנְחוּם בְּרֵיהּ דְּרַבִּי חִיָּיא אִישׁ כְּפַר עַכּוֹ אָמַר רַבִּי יַעֲקֹב בַּר אַחָא אָמַר ר' שִׂמְלַאי, וְאָמְרִי לָהּ אָמַר ר' תַּנְחוּם אָמַר רַב הוּנָא, וְאָמְרִי לָהּ אָמַר רַב הוּנָא לְחוֹדֵיהּ:

תַּלְמִיד

רש"י

אַף דִּבְרֵי תוֹרָה בַּסֵּתֶר. דִּכְתִיב בְּסֵיפֵיהּ דִּקְרָא: "מַעֲשֵׂה יְדֵי אָמָּן" — הַתּוֹרָה מַעֲשֵׂה אוּמָנוּתוֹ שֶׁל הַקָּדוֹשׁ בָּרוּךְ הוּא: (א) רַב בַּר אֲחוּהּ דְּרַבִּי חִיָּיא דְּהוּא בַּר אַחְתֵּיהּ, וְרַבָּה בַּר בַּר חָנָה בַּר אֲחוּהּ דְּרַבִּי חִיָּיא [דְּלָאו] בַּר אַחְתֵּיהּ, כִּדְאָמְרִינַן בְּסַנְהֶדְרִין*: עִיָּיא. כָּךְ כִּינּוּי שְׁמוֹ שֶׁל ר' חִיָּיא, לְשׁוֹן גְּנַאי: רְאֵה מִי קוֹרֵא לְךָ. כְּלוֹמַר: לֹא מִכָּאן: תָּא. בּוֹא אֵלַי וְהָדַר שָׁלַח לֵיהּ: לָא תֵּיתֵי: וְזֶה. שָׁלִיחַ שֵׁנִי, לֹא רָאִיתִי: בִּרְצוֹת ה' דַּרְכֵי אִישׁ גַּם אוֹיְבָיו יַשְׁלִים אִתּוֹ. כִּי הוּא עַל כָּרְחוֹ בָּא: מַאי טַעְמָא עֲבַדְתְּ הָכִי. דְּשָׁנִיתָ בַּשּׁוּק: בְּיוֹמָא דְּכַלָּה. דְּרָשָׁה שֶׁהַכֹּל מִתְקַבְּצִין שָׁם: מוֹקִים לֵיהּ בִּצְדָקָה. דְּמִיבָּעֵי לְמֵיעֲבַד בַּסֵּתֶר: מָר עוּקְבָא. כְּתַלְמִיד לִשְׁמוּאֵל, דִּשְׁמוּאֵל גָּדוֹל בַּתּוֹרָה יוֹתֵר מִמָּר עוּקְבָא: כִּי יָתְבָן בְּדִינָא כו'. מִשּׁוּם דְּמָר עוּקְבָא הָיָה נָשִׂיא: חָיְיקִי לֵיהּ דּוּכְתֵּיהּ. מְנַמְּכִין לוֹ מָקוֹם כְּשֶׁיּוֹשֵׁב בַּדִּין: כִּי הֵיכִי דְּמִשְׁתַּמַּע לֵיהּ מִילֵּיהּ. דִּשְׁמוּאֵל רַבֵּיהּ בַּתּוֹרָה: אִיטְרִיד. מָר עוּקְבָא בְּדִינָא, שֶׁהָיָה מְחַשֵּׁב בַּדִּין, וְלָא אִידְּכַר לֵיהּ לְמֵיזַל בָּתַר שְׁמוּאֵל: לֹא נְגַהּ לָךְ. כְּלוֹמַר: לָא סַגִּי לָךְ דַּאֲזֵילְנָא בָּתְרָךְ? לִישְׁרֵי לִי מָר בְּתִיגְרֵיהּ. הַב לִי רְשׁוּתָא לְמֵיהְדַּר: יָדַע. מָר עוּקְבָא: דִּנְקַט. שְׁמוּאֵל בְּדַעְתֵּיהּ, מִשּׁוּם דַּאֲזַל בַּתְרֵיהּ: מִי שְׁמַעַתְּ שַׁמְתָּא מִפּוּמֵיהּ. אִי שָׁמְעַתְּ לָךְ: פָּסֵיק סִידְרָא. לִימֵּד פָּרָשִׁיּוֹת: מִכְּלָל דְּאִיכָּא רִאשׁוֹנִים. וַהֲלֹא לֹא מָצִינוּ שֶׁאָמַר דָּוִד 'דִּבְרֵי' אֶלָּא בַּמִּקְרָא זֶה, דְּ'דִבְרֵי' לְשׁוֹן נְבוּאָה: אַתָּה שָׁאוּל. שֶׁנּוֹלַדְתָּ בְּמַזָּלוֹ: וְהוּא דָּוִד. שֶׁנּוֹלַד בְּמַזָּל שֶׁלְּךָ: אִבַּדְתִּי כַּמָּה דָּוִד. שֶׁהוּא צַדִּיק מִמְּךָ: שִׁגָּיוֹן. שְׁגָגָה הָיְתָה לוֹ: מְשׁוּנֶּה בְּמַעֲשָׂיו. צַדִּיק גָּמוּר: שֶׁהֵקִים עוּלָּהּ שֶׁל תְּשׁוּבָה. שֶׁהוּא שָׁב תְּחִלָּה, וְנָתַן דֶּרֶךְ לַשָּׁבִים. כִּדְאָמְרִינַן בְּפ"ק דְּע"ז (דף ד:): לֹא דָּוִד רָאוּי לְאוֹתוֹ מַעֲשֶׂה, אֶלָּא שֶׁאִם חָטָא יָחִיד — אוֹמְרִים לוֹ: כַּלֵּךְ אֵצֶל דָּוִד, שֶׁמָּחַל לוֹ הקב"ה אוֹתוֹ עָוֹן, אַף אַתָּה — חֲזוֹר בִּתְשׁוּבָה: צוּר יִשְׂרָאֵל. מוֹשֵׁל בָּאָדָם אֲנִי, מִי מוֹשֵׁל בִּי? צַדִּיק מוֹשֵׁל בִּי, וּמְבַטְּלָהּ: עִירָא הַיָּאִירִי. הֲוָה מַתְנֵי לְדָוִד *אַגַּב כָּרִים וּכְסָתוֹת, וְדָוִד הֲוָה מַתְנֵי לְרַבָּנַן עַל גַּבֵּי קַרְקַע: רֹאשׁ לְג' אָבוֹת. שֶׁהוּא הוֹלֵךְ לִפְנֵיהֶם לְעוה"ב: מְעַדֵּן עַצְמוֹ. כּוֹפֵף עַצְמוֹ יָדָיו וְרַגְלָיו בְּיַחַד וְיוֹשֵׁב לָאָרֶץ: בִּדְבַר אוּרִיָּה הַחִתִּי. נָטְלוּ לוֹ מָאתַיִם:

תַּלְמִיד

עין משפט נר מצוה

סח א טוש"ע י"ד סימן רלד סעיף א:

מסורת הש"ס / שולי הגליון

[דף ה.] | סוכה מט: | פסחים ז. | [כריתות ח.] | [פסחים ז. וש"נ] | נ"ל אגבי | משלי טז | שם א | [ברכות יח.] | ישעיה מח | מתנלת עיין רש"י שבת קמ: ד"ה אליפתא חדתא ובערוך ערך לפא ועיין מהרש"א בח"ה ובח"א | שטורין קלופין רש"י סנהדרין כז. ד"ה חושלא והיא היתה מניפה קליפתן מתוכן עיין מהרש"א | שמואל ב כג | שמואל ב כב | [עיין תוספות מגילה כא. ד"ה אלמלא] | תהלים ז | במדבר יב | ירמיה לח | עמוס ט | [נ"ל בני] | ע"ז ה. | שמואל ב כג | שם | [שבת סג. ב"מ פה.] | שם | דברים לב | מלכים א טו

הגהות הב"ח

(א) רש"י ד"ה רב בר אחוה. נ"ב עיין לקמן בדף כ' ע"א:

גליון הש"ס

גמ' דוד שירה אתה אומר. עיין יומא דף כב ע"ב תוספות ד"ה והאמר: **שם** הוא עדינו העצני. עיין רש"י תענית דף כח ע"א ד"ה בני עדין הן הן:

רבינו חננאל

ר' שלא ישנו לתלמידים בשוק שנאמר חמוקי ירכיך כמו חלאים ואין חלאים אלא רבנן כדגרסינן בנדרים (מט.) מאן חולים רבנן והן שמתעסקים בתורה שהיא מעשה ידי אמן ואמר רבי מה ירך זה בסתר אף דברי תורה בסתר והני מילי בשאר ימות השנה. אבל ביומי דכלה לא שנאמר חכמות בחוץ תרונה ברחובות תתן קולה. ונזיפה דידן כמה הוי חד יומא כמר עוקבא כד ידע דנקיט שמואל מלתא בדעתיה נהג נזיפותא בנפשיה חד יומא וכרב נחמן דאמר לההיא דשמעה מפומיה דצורבא מרבנן כמה חציפא הא [אתתא זילי] נהוג בנפשיך חד יומא. מר זוטרא בר טוביה הוה פסיק סידריה קמיה דרב יהודה מטו להאי קרא ואלה דברי דוד האחרונים מכלל דאיכא ראשונים שאליה ולא הגיד ליה. א"ל אטו מאן דלא ידע פירושא דהאי פסוקא לאו גברא רבה הוא ידע דנקיט מילתא בדעתיה נהג נזיפותא בנפשיה חד יומא. פשוטה דראשונים הן דברי השיר אשר שר דוד ביום הציל ה' אותו מכף כל אויביו ומיד שאול. א"ל הקב"ה שירה אתה אומר על מפלתו של שאול כו'. כיון דידע דחטא חזר והודה כי שגג כדכתיב שגיון לדוד אשר שר לה' על דברי כוש בן ימיני ופי' כי כוש הוא שאול. ולפיכך אמר אלה דברי דוד האחרונים נאם דוד בן ישי נאם הגבר הוקם על שהקים עולה של תשובה. רוח ה' דבר בי ומלתו על לשוני. אמר אלהי ישראל לי דבר צור ישראל אמר לי הוא המושל באדם וצדיק הוא המושל ביראת אלהים הוא מושל בדברו כי מבטל בתחינתו גזירות של הקב"ה הרעות מלבוא על עמו ישראל. יושב בשבת תחכמוני כו' עדינו העצני

רש"י

תלמיד חכם שנידה לכבודו. כבר פירשתי למעלה: **עביד** (איניש) **דינא לנפשיה.** דאמר ליה: את מחייבת לי הכי והכי: **דפסיקא ליה.** שודאי הוא לו, ולא ספק: **סנו שומעניה.** שיוצאין עליו שמועות רעות: **צריכי ליה רבנן.** דאתריה, דהוה רבהון: **ואם לאו אל יבקשו תורה.** הואיל וסנו שומעניה, הא דצריכי ליה רבנן לאו כלום הוא, דמוטב דלא ילפי מיניה: **אתא איהו.** האי מנודה נמי בהדייהו: **מאי דקמן.** כלומר, היכי מתרמי דעל האי סבא, ר' שמואל בר נחמני, האידנא לבית המדרש: **שמע מינה.** דלהכי איתרמי דאתא האידנא לבי מדרשא, דלאו מזליה הוא דלישרי ליה: **וטרקיה אאמתיה.** נשכו למנודה באמתו: **ולא קבלוהו.** דהדרא עכנא למערתא, ולא פתחה פיה: **דייני.** ראשי ב"ד. וחסידים עדיפי מינייהו: **מאי טעמא.** קבלוהו: **דעבד כרבי אילעאי וכו'.** בהני שמועות רעות: **מה שלבו חפץ.** עבירה. והואיל ואין מכירין אותו שם ליכא חלול השם. (א) ואמר לן רבי משום רב האי גאון: ויעשה מה שלבו חפץ – רוצה לומר: דודאי כיון שלבוש שחורים וכו' – אני ערב בדבר שאינו חפץ מכאן ואילך בעבירה: **דקא עבר** משום ולפני עור **לא** תתן מכשול. דכיון דגדול הוא, שמא מבעט באביו, והוה ליה איהו מכשילו: **שלך אינו** נידוי. דלאו בדינא שמתיה: **הכבד.** בלשון הזה אומרים לו: עשה עצמך כאדם שכבד עליו ראשו, ושב בביתך. בלשון כבוד אומר לו. (ב) לישנא אחרינא: הכבד = התכבד, כבודך שתשב בביתך: **כסהו.** אל תבזה אותו בפרהסיא: **בלילה.** שחשיכה, ואין אדם רואה: **משמית נפשיה.** משום יקרא דההוא צורבא מדרבנן: **מימנו אנגידא.** מלקות, ומלקות יפה להם יותר משמתא, והוו מלקי להו: **ומהניא כי טיחיא בתנורא.** כשומן שטוחין את התנור ונבלע בתוכו, שאין יוצא לעולם. כלומר: מכה לכל מאן דמשמתינן ליה, דלא נפקא מיניה לעולם: **ופליגא דר"ש** ב"ל. דאמר: יוצאה: **גנובתיה.** זנב: **דידה עבדא.** ומלקי ליה: **מסתפינא מיניה.** דגברא אלמא הוא: **שקיל פתיחא עליה.** כתוב עליו שמתא: **שקליה.** לכתב שמתא: ואחתיה

גמרא

תלמיד שנידה לכבודו – נידויו נידוי. דתניא: – *מנודה לרב – מנודה לתלמיד, מנודה לתלמיד – אינו מנודה לרב. לרב הוא דאינו מנודה, הא לכולי עלמא – מנודה. למאי? אי [א] במילי דשמיא – °"אין חכמה ואין תבונה ואין עצה לנגד ה'"! (משלי כא) אלא לאו – לכבוד עצמו. אמר רב יוסף: צורבא מרבנן [א]עביד דינא לנפשיה במילתא דפסיקא ליה. [ב]ההוא צורבא מרבנן דהוו סנו שומעניה. א"ר יהודה: היכי ליעביד? לשמתיה – צריכי ליה רבנן, לא לשמתיה – קא מיתחיל שמא דשמיא. א"ל לרבב"ח: מידי שמיע לך בהא, א"ל: הכי א"ר יוחנן, *מאי דכתיב: °"כי שפתי כהן ישמרו דעת ותורה יבקשו מפיהו כי מלאך ה' צבאות הוא" (מלאכי ב; חגיגה טו: פ"ה) אם דומה הרב למלאך ה' – יבקשו תורה מפיו, ואם לאו – אל יבקשו תורה מפיו. שמתיה רב יהודה. לסוף איחלש רב יהודה, אתו רבנן לשיולי ביה, ואתא איהו נמי בהדייהו. כד חזייה רב יהודה חייך. אמר ליה: לא מסתייך דשמתיה לההוא גברא אלא אחוכי נמי חייך בי?! א"ל: לאו בדידך מחייכנא אלא דכי אזלינא לההוא עלמא בדיחא דעתאי דאפילו לגברא כוותך לא חניפי ליה. נח נפשיה דרב יהודה, אתא לבי מדרשא אמר להו: שרו לי! אמרו ליה רבנן: גברא דחשיב כרב יהודה ליכא הכא דלישרי לך, אלא זיל לגביה דר' יהודה נשיאה דלישרי לך, אזל לקמיה, א"ל לר' אמי: פוק עיין בדיניה, אי מיבעי למישרא ליה – שרי ליה. עיין ר' אמי בדיניה, סבר למישרא ליה. עמד ר' שמואל בר נחמני על רגליו ואמר: ומה שפחה של בית רבי לא נהגו חכמים קלות ראש בנידויה שלש שנים – יהודה חבירינו על אחת כמה וכמה! א"ר זירא: מאי דקמן דאתא האידנא האי סבא בבי מדרשא, דהא כמה שני לא אתא. ש"מ לא מיבעי למישרא ליה. לא שרא ליה. נפק כי קא בכי ואזיל, אתא זיבורא וטרקיה אאמתיה, ושכיב. עיילוהו למערתא דחסידי – ולא קיבלוהו, עיילוהו למערתא דדייני – וקיבלוהו. מ"ט? דעבד כר' אילעאי. דתניא, *ר' אילעאי אומר: אם רואה אדם שיצרו מתגבר עליו – ילך למקום שאין מכירין אותו, וילבש שחורים ויתעטף שחורים, ויעשה מה שלבו חפץ, ואל יחלל שם שמים בפרהסיא. שפחה של בית רבי מאי היא? דאמתא דבי רבי חזיתיה לההוא גברא דהוה מחי לבנו גדול, [ג]אמרה: ליהוי ההוא גברא בשמתא, דקעבר משום: °"ולפני עור לא תתן מכשול" (ויקרא יט). דתניא: "ולפני עור לא תתן מכשול" – במכה לבנו גדול הכתוב מדבר. ריש לקיש הוה מנטר פרדיסא, אתא ההוא גברא וקאכיל תאיני. רמא ביה קלא, ולא אשגח ביה. אמר: ליהוי ההוא גברא בשמתא. א"ל: אדרבה, ליהוי ההוא גברא בשמתא! אם ממון נתחייבתי לך – נידוי מי נתחייבתי לך? אתא לבי מדרשא. [ד]א"ל: שלו – נידוי, שלך – אינו נידוי. ומאי תקנתיה? זיל לגביה דלישרי לך. לא ידענא ליה. אמרו ליה: זיל לגבי נשיאה דלישרי לך, דתניא: [ה]נידוהו ואינו יודע מי נידהו – ילך אצל נשיא, ויתיר לו נדויו. אמר רב הונא, באושא התקינו: אב בית דין שסרח – אין מנדין אותו, אלא אומר לו: °"הכבד ושב בביתך" (מלכים ב יד). חזר וסרח – מנדין אותו, מפני חילול השם. ופליגא דריש לקיש. *דאמר ריש לקיש: [ו]תלמיד חכם שסרח – אין מנדין אותו בפרהסיא, שנאמר: °"וכשלת היום וכשל גם נביא עמך לילה" (הושע ד) – כסהו כלילה. *מר זוטרא חסידא, כי מיחייב צורבא מרבנן שמתא – ברישא משמית נפשיה, והדר משמית לדידיה. כי הוה עייל באושפיזיה – שרי ליה לנפשיה והדר שרי ליה לדידיה. *אמר רב גידל אמר רב: [ז]ת"ח מנדה לעצמו, ומיפר לעצמו. אמר רב פפא: תיתי לי דלא שמיתי צורבא מרבנן מעולם. אלא, כי קא מיחייב צורבא מרבנן שמתא היכי עביד? כי הא, *דבמערבא [ח]מימנו אנגידא דצורבא מרבנן ולא מימנו אשמתא. מאי שמתא? אמר רב: שם מיתה, ושמואל אמר: שממה יהיה, ומהניא ביה כי טיחיא בתנורא. ופליגא דריש לקיש. דאמר ריש לקיש: כשם שנכנסת במאתים וארבעים ושמונה איברים כך כשהיא יוצאה – יוצאה ממאתים וארבעים ושמונה איברים. כשהיא נכנסת – דכתיב: °"והיתה העיר חרם" (יהושע ו), "חרם" בגימטריא מאתים וארבעים ושמונה הוו. כשהיא יוצאה – דכתיב: °"ברוגז רחם תזכור" (חבקוק ג) "רחם" בגימטריא הכי הוו. אמר: רב יוסף: שדי שמתא אגנובתא דכלבא – ואיהי דידה עבדה. דההוא כלבא דהוה אכיל מסאני דרבנן, ולא הוו קא ידעי מנו. ושמתו ליה. איתלי ביה נורא בגנובתיה, ואכלתיה. ההוא אלמא דהוה קא מצער ליה לההוא צורבא מרבנן, אתא לקמיה דרב יוסף. א"ל: זיל שמתיה. א"ל: מסתפינא מיניה. אמר ליה: שקילי פתיחא עליה. א"ל: כל שכן דמסתפינא מיניה. א"ל: שקליה אחתיה בכדא, ואחתיה

תוספות

וטרקיה. נשכו אאמתו. ויש מפרשים: מדה כנגד מדה, משום דנחשד בזונות: **ולא** קיבלוהו. דהדרא ליה עכנא: **דעבר** אדרבי אילעאי. ולכך לא קיבלוהו, אע"פ שהיה תלמיד חכם. וי"ג: דעבד כר' אילעאי, ומשום הכי קיבלוהו דייני:

אם רואה אדם שיצרו מתגבר עליו. וכתב ר"ח: חס ושלום, לא הותר לו לעשות עבירה, אלא ע"י כך יכנע לבו. בפ"ק דקדושין (דף מ. ושם) פירשתי:*

נידוי מי נתחייבתי לך. אע"פ שמשמתין בעבור ממון, כדאמרינן לעיל (דף טז.): הני מילי לממונא – י"ל: שהיה לו לקרותו לב"ד תחילה, שמא יפרע. ועוד: דבב"ד נמי צריך שני וחמישי ושני, כדפירשתי לעיל, וכדמשמע בפרק "הגוזל בתרא" (ב"ק דף קיג.). ולא דמי לאיסורא (*דמכין) לאלתר, כדאמר *בההוא גברא דקאכל תמרי שנשרו בשבת, וכן [ריש] פרק "הדר" (עירובין דף סג.). ובשם רבינו תם שמעתי שהיו רגילין באותו מקום שאוכלין באילנות ונותן דמים, והשתא לא היו עוברים על הגזל:

משמית נפשיה. משום צער, שצריך לנדות ת"ח. א"נ: כדי שיהא זכור להתיר. והא דלא התיר לחבירו מתחילה – כדאמרינן בשבועות פרק קמא (דף יד.): יבא זכאי ויכפר על החייב, לכך טוב כשיתיר לחבירו – שיהא הוא מותר קודם: שלא

רבינו חננאל

העצני כו' עד רק בדבר אוריה החתי כולן פשוטין הן. עדינו שהיה מעדן עצמו להיות מיושב דעת בדברי תורה וכשיוצא למלחמה קשה כעץ. אמר רב הונא ת"ח שנידה לכבודו נידויו נידוי דדייק מדתניא מנודה לתלמיד אינו מנודה לרב לבדו הא לכ"ע מנודה והני מילי לכבוד עצמו אבל במילי דשמיא אין חכמה ואין תבונה לנגד ה'. אמר רב יוסף צורבא מרבנן עביד דינא לנפשיה. במלתא דפסיקא ליה. כגון הקורא לחבירו עבד יהא בנידוי וכיוצא בו. ההוא צורבא מרבנן דהוה סני שומעניה שהיה שם שמים מתחלל על ידו. כגון הא דגרסינן בסוף יוה"כ מי שיש בידו חילול השם. יצחק דבי ר' אמי אמר כל שחביריו מתביישין משמועתו היכי דמי דאמרי שרי ליה מריה לפלוני. אבל הא דאמר רב כגון אנא דשקילנא בישרא כו'. ודאמר ר' יוחנן כגון אנא דאי מסגינא ד' אמות בלא תורה ובלא תפילין על עצמן בלבד אמרו ולא על זולתם שהיו מחמירין הרבה על עצמם. הלא תראה שכל אחד כך אמר כגון אנא אבל כ"ע כדאמרן וכגון אלישע אחר שהיה מתעסק בספרי מינין ושותה במיני זמר דגרסינן זמר יוני לא פסק מביתו. אמרו עליו על אחר שהיה עומד מבית המדרש הרבה ספרי מינים היו נושרין לו מחיקו וגרסינן נמי השותה במיני זמר כו' וכל צורבא מרבנן דהכי עובדיה מתקריה סנו שומעניה. ואמר רב יהודה בההוא צורבא מרבנן דהוו סני שומעניה כדאמרן היכי נעביד ביה נשמתיה צריכי ליה רבנן לא נשמתיה קא מתחלל שם שמים. א"ל רבה בר בר חנה הכי אמר ר' יוחנן מ"ד כי שפתי כהן ישמרו דעת ותורה יבקשו מפיהו כי מלאך ה' צבאות הוא. אם דומה הרב למלאך ה' צבאות יבקשו תורה מפיהו ואם לאו אל יבקשו תורה מפיהו. שמתיה רב יהודה ולא שרייא לשמתיה לא הוא ולא ר' יהודה נשיאה ואמר רב יהודה בעידנא דשכיב בריתנא דאפילו לגברא רבא כי האי לא חניפי ליה ולא אשכח חד דשרי ליה עד דטרקיה זיבורא אאמתיה ושכיב עיילוה למערתא דחסידי ולא קיבלוה עיילוה למערתא דדייני וקיבלוה. מאי סני שומעניה דעבד כר' אילעאי דתניא ר' אילעאי הזקן אומר אם רואה אדם שיצרו מתגבר עליו פירוש מבקש לשתות במיני זמר ולשמוח בשמחה המרגילה לידי עבירה כגון זה אמר ילך למקום שאין מכירין אותו וילבש שחורין ויכסה שחורין ויעשה מה שלבו חפץ כגון אכילה ושתייה במיני זמר וכיוצא בהן אבל דבר עבירה שיש בה דין אדם או דין שמים ואפילו חייבי לאוין או חייבי עשה וכ"ש למעלה שאיסורן איסור עולם ח"ו שהתיר ר' אילעאי ואפילו בסתר אלא דבר שפירשנו למעלה הוא שאמר לעשות. ואפילו דברים הללו לא התירן לו אלא אמר כמשיא עצה לעשות כך כדי להבריח את יצרו להשלים תאותו וכיון שיראה עצמו לבוש שחורין ועטוף שחורין משתבר יצרו ונמנע ואינו עושה וזה צורבא מרבנן עשה כר' אילעאי ולבש שחורין ונתעטף ואחר זה כולן חזר לשתות במיני זמר כגון שהיה עושה [אלישע] ולפיכך שמתיה רב יהודה תנא דבי ר' ישמעאל ולפני עור לא תתן מכשול זה המכה בנו הגדול שכיון שהוא גדול חוזר גם הוא ומכה אביו זה ונמצא כי אביו גורם לו והכשילו: ריש לקיש הוה מנטר פרדיסא אתא ההוא גברא אכיל תאיני רמא ביה קלא ולא אשגח ביה אמר ליהוי ההוא גברא בשמתא. א"ל אדרבה ליהוי ההוא גברא בשמתא. אם ממון נתחייבתי לך נידוי מי נתחייבתי לך אתא שאיל לבי מדרשא [א"ל] שלו נידוי שלך אינו נידוי זיל לגבי נשיאה דלישרי לך. דתנא נידוהו ואינו יודע מי נדהו ילך אצל נשיא ויפר לו. **ירושלמי** הדא אמרה המנדה למי שאינו צריך וחזר הוא ונידהו נידוי השני נידוי. אמר רב הונא באושא התקינו אב בית דין שסרח אין מנדין אותו אלא אומר לו הכבד ושב בביתך חזר וסרח מנדין אותו מפני חילול השם ריש לקיש אמר תלמיד חכם שסרח אין מבזין אותו בפרהסיא שנאמר וכשלת היום וכשל גם נביא עמך

עין משפט נר מצוה

[סט] [א] מיי' פ"ו מהל' ת"ת הלכה יד טוש"ע י"ד סימן שלד סעיף יז:
סט א מיי' פ"ב מהל' סנהדרין הלכה יב טוש"ע ח"מ סימן ז:
ע ב מיי' פ"ו מהל' ת"ת הל' יד ופ"ז הלכה א טוש"ע י"ד סימן שלד סעיף מב וסעיף מג: [ועי' תוס' חגיגה טז. ד"ה ויעשה וכו']
עא ג מיי' פ"ו מהלכות ת"ת שם ופ"ו מהל' ממרים הלכה ט טוש"ע י"ד סי' שלד סעיף מג:
עב ד מיי' פ"ו מהלכות ת"ת הל' ח טוש"ע שם סעיף לט וסעיף מג:
[נ"ל דמנדין]
[לא נמצא בשום מקום]
עג ה מיי' שם פ"ז הל' א:
עד ו מיי' שם הל' א טוש"ע שם סעי' מב:
עה ז מיי' שם הלכה יא טוש"ע שם סעי' לג:
עו ח מיי' שם הלכה א טוש"ע שם סעי' מב:

מסורת הש"ס

[לעיל טז.]
חגיגה טז. קדושין מ.
[נדרים ז.]
[נדרים ז: וע"ש דפריך פסיעות ומשני]
פסחים נב.

הגהות הב"ח

(א) רש"י ד"ה מה שלבו כו' ואמר לן רבי. נ"ב ולפ"ז ה"ק מ"ט קבלוהו וכ"ה במקצת פרקא: (ב) ד"ה הכבד כו' לישנא אחרינא. נ"ב וכן משמע פי' הקרא במלכים ב יד:

גליון הש"ס

גמ' אי במילי דשמיא. עיין תוס' סנהדרין דף ה ע"א ד"ה מפיקנא: שם למערתא דדייני וקיבלוהו. עי' שבת דף ז ע"א ד"ה הא לבי: שם אמר רב הונא באושא התקינו. בכ"מ פ"ו ה"ח מהל' ת"ת הגירסא אמר רב הונא:

ואחתיה בי קברי, וקרי ביה אלפא שפורי בארבעין יומין. אזיל עביד הכי. פקע כדא, ומית אלמא. מאי שפורי? שנפרעין ממנו. מאי תברא? אמר רב יצחק בריה דרב יהודה: תברי בתי רמי. דתניא, *אמר רבן שמעון בן גמליאל: כל מקום שנתנו חכמים עיניהם – או מיתה או עוני.§ "והנזיר והמצורע מטומאתו לטהרתו".§ בעא מיניה רבי ירמיה מרבי זירא: בשלא היה להם פנאי, או דלמא אף בשהיה להם פנאי? אמר ליה: תנינא, אכל אלו שאמרו מותרין לגלח במועד – בשלא היה להם פנאי, אבל היה להם פנאי – אסורים. בנזיר ומצורע, אע"פ שהיה להם פנאי – מותרים, שלא ישהו קרבנותיהן. תנא: הכהן והאבל מותרין בגילוח. האי אבל היכי דמי? אילימא שחל שמיני שלו בערב הרגל – גאיבעי ליה לגלוחי בערב הרגל, אלא שחל שמיני שלו להיות בשבת ערב הרגל – דאיבעי ליה לגלוחי ערב שבת, דאמר רב חסדא אמר רבינא בר שילא: *ההלכה כאבא שאול, ומודים חכמים לאבא שאול בשחל שמיני שלו להיות בשבת ערב הרגל, שמותר לגלח בערב שבת! לא צריכא, ושחל שביעי שלו להיות בשבת ערב הרגל. תנא ברא סבר לה כאבא שאול, דאמר *זמקצת היום ככולו, ויום שביעי עולה לו לכאן ולכאן. וכיון דשבת הוי – אנוס הוא. תנא דידן סבר לה כרבנן, דאמרי: לא אמרינן מקצת היום ככולו, ואכתי לא שלים אבילות דשבעה. האי כהן היכי דמי? אילימא דשלים משמרתו ערב הרגל – איבעי ליה לגלוחי ערב הרגל! לא צריכא, חדשלים משמרתו ברגל. תנא דידן סבר: כיון *דתנן: טבשלשה פרקים בשנה היו כל המשמרות שוות באימורי הרגלים ובחילוק לחם הפנים. כמאן דלא שלים משמרתו ברגל דמי. ותנא ברא סבר: אע"ג דשייך בהנך משמרות – משמרתיה מיהא שלימא ליה. תנו רבנן: *כל אלו שאמרו מותרין לגלח במועד – מותרין לגלח בימי אבלן. והתניא אסורים! אמר רב חסדא אמר רב שילא: יכי תניא הכא מותרין – בשתכפוהו אבליו, אי בשתכפוהו אבליו מאי איריא כל אלו שאמרו? אפי' כולי עלמא נמי! דתניא: *כתכפוהו אבליו זה אחר זה, הכביד שערו – מיקל בתער, לומכבס כסותו במים. הא אתמר עלה, אמר רב חסדא: מבתער ולא במספרים. נבמים ולא בנתר ולא באהל. אמר רב חסדא: זאת אומרת: *אבל אסור בתכבוסת. ת"ר: *כשם שאמרו אסור לגלח במועד – כך אסור ליטול צפורנים במועד, דברי ר' יהודה. סורבי יוסי מתיר. וכשם שאמרו: אבל אסור לגלח בימי אבלו – כך אסור ליטול צפורנים בימי אבלו, דברי רבי יהודה. ורבי יוסי מתיר. אמר עולא: הלכה כרבי יהודה באבל, והלכה כרבי יוסי במועד, שמואל אמר: הלכה

רש"י

ואחתיה בכדא. תקע בתוך הכד ולא ישמעו: בי קברי. דלא שכיחי תמן אינשי: וקרי ביה. כלומר: תקע ביה אלפין שיפורי: מאי תברי. למה תוקעין תקיעה ושברים? תברי בתי רמי. כלומר: שמחה משבר בתים גבוהים: בשלא היה להן פנאי. דדוקא נקט שעלו מטומאתם ברגל – לפיכך מגלחין, שלא היה להן פנאי לגלח, דעדיין לא עלו מטומאתן: או דלמא אע"פ שהיה להם פנאי. ולא גילחו קודם המועד, מותרים לגלח במועד: שלא ישהו קרבנותיהן. במגלחתן עד לאחר הרגל, דנזיר ומצורע אין מביאין קרבנותיהן עד לאחר גילוח, כדכתיב בהו קראי. הלכך לא קנסינן להו בדלא עבדי מקמי רגל, דזימנין דלא עביד קמי רגל. (א)ומיאסרי להו במועד – נמצא שמשהין הקרבנות ואינן קריבין ביום השמיני בזמנן. לפיכך אמרו מגלח במועד, דמוטב לקרב זמן הקרבה ולא לאחר: איבעי ליה לגלוחי ערב הרגל. דתנן מתניתין (לקמן דף יט.): הקובר מתו שמונה ימים קודם הרגל – בטלו ממנו גזרת ל' יום, ומותר בגילוח. הואיל וכבר התחיל יום אחד מן השלשים. וזה, הואיל ולא גילח ערב הרגל – לא יגלח ברגל: בשבת ערב הרגל. והוי אנוס, דלא מצי לגלח בשמיני ערב הרגל – להכי מגלח ברגל: איבעי ליה לגלוחי ערב שבת. שהוא שביעי: הלכה כאבא שאול. דאפילו לא קבר אלא שבעה ימים קודם הרגל – בטלה ממנו גזרת שלשים: ומודים חכמים לאבא שאול. אע"ג דבעו שמונה: בשחל שמיני להיות בשבת ערב הרגל. דהוי אנוס: שמותר לגלח בערב שבת. שהוא שביעי: האי תנא דברייתא. דתני: אבל מגלח במועד: סבר כאבא שאול. דיום שביעי עולה לכאן ולכאן, לשבעה ולשלשים. וכיון דכבר התחילו שלשים – איבעי ליה לגלוחי קודם הרגל. אלא דשבת הוי, ואנוס הוא, להכי מגלח במועד: ותנא דידן. דתני: אלו מגלחין ברגל, ולא אבל: סבר כרבנן דאמרי לא אמרינן מקצת היום ככולו. אלא שבעה שלימין בעינן, ואכתי לא שלים אבילות דשבעה קודם הרגל, ולא הוי אנוס. דאפי' לא הוי שבת – לא מצי לגלח, להכי אינו מגלח במועד: דשלים משמרתו ערב הרגל. בשבת, דלעולם לא שלמה משמרה אלא בשבת: איבעי ליה לגלוחי ערב הרגל. כלומר, בערב שבת שהוא ערב הרגל. דהא אמרינן (לעיל דף יד.): אנשי משמר אסורין בגילוח, ובחמישי מותרין מפני כבוד השבת: דשלים משמרה ברגל. כגון דהוי יום חמישי יום ראשון של רגל – דלא מצי לגלח דהוי י"ט. ושלים משמרתו בשבת, שהוא יום שלישי לרגל: תנא דידן. דקאמר: אינו מגלח במועד: סבר כיון דתנן בשלשה פרקים. בשלשה רגלים כל המשמרות שוים, אכתי, כמאן דלא שלים משמרתו דמי, ועדיין יש לו חלק באימורי רגלים, ולא שלים משמרתו בכל הרגל, להכי אינו מגלח ברגל. כדתנן: אנשי משמר אסורין לגלח: ותנא ברא. דאמר: מותרין לגלח: אע"ג דשייך בהנך משמרות. [שלים] עיקר משמרתו דידיה, להכי מותר בגילוח: הא אתמר עלה. הא דתני תכפוהו אבליו מיקל בתער ולא במספרים, וקתני ברייתא דכל הני שמותרין לגלח במועד – מותרין לגלח בימי אבלו, כשתכפוהו אבליו, ומגלח במספרים: זאת אומרת. מדתני תכפוהו אבליו מכבס כסותו – מכלל דשאר אבל אסור בתכבוסת:

הלכה

תוספות

שלא ישהו קרבנותיהן. אע"ג דתגלחת דנזיר לא מעכבא – *מכל מקום רגיל הוא לגלח, דמצוה הוא לגלח ולשלוח שערו תחת הדוד: **כשחל** שמיני בשבת. כגון שמע שמועה בשבת, דקבורתו לא היה בשבת, ובירושלמי מוקי לה כשגררתו חיה ונתייאשו לבקש, דמונין לו משעה שנתייאשו:

ותנא דידן סבר לה כרבנן. ואין להקשות: מ"מ יגלח ע"ש, כמו חל שבעה שלו בערב שבת ערב הרגל, דשרו רבנן לגלח, ואע"ג דלית להו מקצת היום ככולו באבילות? דהתם נשלם האבילות קודם יו"ט, אע"ג דמגלח קודם שנשלם, דהא לית להו מקצת היום ככולו באבילות, והכא מיהא אית להו, משום כבוד יו"ט, דאשכחן (יומא דף ו:) בזב וזבה דהויא מקצת היום ככולו, אבל כשיש עדיין ימי אבילות – לא. אבל תימה: (ב)דהיכי אסרינן מהאי דלא תני מתניתין האבל והכהן מותרים לגלח משום דלית ליה פנאי והא מיבעיא לעיל (דף יד.) באבדה לו אבידה, ולא פשיט מדלא תני לה, דאיכא למימר תנא ושייר כמו כן הני – תני ושייר! ויש לומר: כיון דאשכחנא פלוגתא דאבא שאול ורבנן באבל – אית לן למימר דתנא דמתני' וברייתא בהכי פליגי, וכיון דבאבל פליגי – בכהן נמי פליגי:

זאת אומרת אבל אסור בתכבוסת. וא"ת: פשיטא, דהא אפי' שאר מלאכות אסור? וי"ל: משום דקתני לקמן (דף כא.): אלו דברים שאבל אסור בהן ולא קתני תכבוסת. אי נמי: תכבוסת (*חייב) קאמר:

ה"ג: **ושמואל** אמר הלכה כר' יוסי בזו ובזו, דאמר שמואל הלכה כדברי המיקל באבל. וא"ת: בעירובין (דף מו. ושם), דאמר *שמואל: הלכה כדברי המיקל בעירוב, ואמר נמי: הלכה כרבי יוחנן בן נורי. ומקשה התם: תרתי למה לי (ג)כו'! וי"ל: איצטריך הכא לאפוקי מדעולא. וא"ת: וכיון דאית ליה לשמואל רבי יהודה ור' יוסי הלכה כרבי יוסי, כדאמרינן פרק "מי שהוציאוהו" (שם:) למה ליה למימר הכא הלכה כרבי יוסי? וי"ל: לאפוקי מדעולא. ואעולא לא קשיא מידי מהתם, דהיכא דאתמר – אתמר, כדאמר התם:

רבינו חננאל

עמך לילה כסהו כלילה אמר רב תלמיד חכם מנדה לעצמו ומיפר לעצמו רב זוטרא חסידא כי הוה מתחייב ת"ח נידוי הוה משמית נפשיה ברישא והדר משמית ליה. וכד הוה עייל לביתיה הוה א) שרי ליה ברישא והדר שרי לנפשיה. אמר רב פפא תיתי לי דלא שמיתנא צורבא מרבנן מעולם כי הא דבני מערבא מימנו אנגידא דצורבא מרבנן ולא מימנו אשמותיה אלא מכסין אותו. מאי שמתא. רב אמר שם מיתה כלומר מיתה בה ושמואל אמר שם תהא כלומר שם תיתי כדכתיב ובאה אל בית הגנב וגו'. אמר אבוה דשמואל ומהניא כי טחיה בתנורא כלומר אינה יוצאה משם לעולם. ופליגא דר"ל דאמר כשם שנכנס ברמ"ח איברים כדכתיב והיית חרם. חר"ם בגימטריא רמ"ח הוי כך יוצאה ברמ"ח איברים שנאמר ברוגז רחם תזכור.

רח"ם בגימטריא רמ"ח הוי. אמר רב יוסף שדי שמתא אגנובתא דכלבתא והיא דידה עבדה ההוא כלבא דהוה אכיל מסאני דרבנן ולא הוה ידעי מאן דעבד הא מלתא ושמתו ליה ואתלי נורא בגנובתה ואכלתיה ההוא אלמא דהוה מצער ההוא צורבא מרבנן כו'. והאידנא נמי מאן דבעי הכי כרב יוסף רשאי. מאי שיפורא אמר רבא שנפרעין ממנו מאי תברי תברי בתי. תניא אמר ר' שמעון בן גמליאל כל מקום שנתנו חכמים עיניהם בו או מיתה או עוני: **ירושלמי** ריב"ל זמין ליה לחד בר נש ג' זימני ולא אשגח ביה אמר אילולי דלא חרמית ב"נ מן יומא הוינא מחרים ליה. שעל כ"ד דברים מנדין על כבוד הרב וזה אחד מהן שנא' וכל אשר לא יבא לשלשת הימים וכתיב ביה יבדל מקהל הגולה. א"ר יצחק אית סגי מינהון מבדרן במתני'. בתעניות (דף יט) שלח לו שמעון בן שטח צריך אתה נידוי ב) לא נגזרה גזרה בשני אליהו כו'. בר"ה (דף כא) שלח לו ר"ג כל המעכב את הרבים מעשות מצוה ג) צריך נידוי בפסחים (דף נג) אילמלי תודוס אתה גוזרני עליך נידוי. תנא את מי נידו את אלעזר בן חנוך שפקפק בטהרת ידים. הדא אמרה המפקפק אפי' בדבר מדברי סופרים צריך נידוי. בעדיות דכמה השקוה מהו דכמה. דכוותה. פי' גרים שכמותה השקוה. כלומר גינה שמעיה ואבטליון ונידוהו ומת בנדויו וסקלו את ארונו הדא אמרה המבזה זקן אפילו לאחר מיתה צריך נידוי א"ר יוסי נמנו וגמרו לכשיחזור מקרבין אותו. אמתא חזא לחד ספר מהי ינוקא יותר מן צרכיה אמרה יהא ההוא גברא מוחרם. שאלו לר' אחא ואמר צריך למיחש על גרמיה הדא אמרה העושה דבר שלא כשורה צריך נידוי. ר' יעקב בן אביי בשם רב ששת נמנו באושא שלא לנדות זקן [ואתייא כי הא דאמר שמואל בשם ר'] (בר) אבהו דאמר זקן שאירע בו דבר אין מורידין אותו מגדולתו אלא אומרים לו הכבד ושב בביתך. וזקן ששכח תלמודו מחמת אונסו נוהגין בו קדושת הארון ששימש הלוחות. ר' חייא בש"ר יוחנן זקן שנידה לעצמו אפי' כהלכה אין נידויו נידוי. בימי ר' ירמיה אתת עקא על טבראי שלח בעי מנרתא דכספא גבי ר' יעקב ב"ר אבון שלח ליה עדיין לא שב ר' ירמיה מרעתו ובקש לנדותו. וא"ל ר' חייא בר יצחק עטושיא שמעתי שאין מנדין זקן אא"כ עשה כירבעם בן נבט וחביריו שהעמידו עגלים. אמר ליה מי שאמר דכמה השקוה ונידוהו כירבעם בן נבט עשה. ונדון אילין לאילין. וחששו אילין לאילין. וצרכין למשתריא אילין מן אילין:

א) לפנינו הגי' להיפך דשרי ליה לנפשיה בתחלה ואמנם גירסת רבינו נכונה יותר ועי' בתוס' ד"ה משמית ודו"ק. ב) בירושלמי איתא שאילו נגזרה גזרה כשם שנגזרה בימי אליהו וכו'. ג) במשנה שלפנינו ליתא זה אכן בירושלמי משמע דגריס כן.

פיסקא

עין משפט נר מצוה

[מיר מו.]

עז א מיי' פ"ו מהלכות יו"ט הלכה יט סמג לאוין עה טוש"ע א"ח סי' תקלא סעיף ד:

עח ב מיי' שם:

עט ג ד ה מיי' פ"ו מהלכות אבל הל' ז טוש"ע י"ד סימן שצט סעיף ג:

פ ו ז מיי' פ"ז מהלכות יו"ט הלכה יח טוש"ע א"ח סימן תקלא סעיף ה וטוש"ע י"ד סימן שצט סעיף ג:

פא ח מיי' פ"ו מהלכות יו"ט הלכה יט ופ"ו מהלכות ביאת מקדש הלכה יג:

פב ט מיי' פ"ו מהל' כלי המקדש הלכה ד ה:

פג י כ מיי' פ"ו מהל' אבל הל' יג טוש"ע י"ד סימן שצ סעיף ג:

פד ל מיי' שם טוש"ע י"ד סימן שפט סעיף א:

פה מ מיי' שם טוש"ע י"ד סי' שצ סעי' ג:

פו נ מיי' שם טוש"ע י"ד סימן שפט סעיף א:

פז ס מיי' פ"ז מהלכות יו"ט הלכה כ טוש"ע א"ח סי' תקלב סעיף א:

גי' רש"א מיס

[ע"ש לאי' ריב"ל]

מסורת הש"ס

חגיגה ה: נדרים ז: ע"ש סוטה מו:

לקמן יט:

[לעיל טז. פסחים ז. וש"נ]

סוכה נה:

[לעיל יז. תוספתא פ"ב]

תענית יג.

לעיל טו.

[תוספתא פ"ב]

רש"א

הגהות הב"ח

(א) רש"י ד"ה שלא וכו' כו' דלא עביד קמי רגל ולא אסרינן להו במועד: (ב) תוס' ד"ה ותנא כו' אבל תימה דהיכי פשיטא ליה לתנא דידן דהיינו ממאי דלא תני במתני' כו' באבדה לו אבדה ולא פשיטא ליה דאינו מגלח מלתא תני לה: (ג) ד"ה ושמואל כו' ומקשה התם תרתי למה לי הכ"ל קשיא תרתי למה לי וי"ל דאיצטריך הכא:

גליון הש"ס

תוס' ד"ה ותנא דידן וכו' דאיכא למימר תנא ושייר. עיין שבת קה ע"ב תוספות ד"ה חסר וכתובות דף ק"ג תוספות ד"ה ועל הכותל:

הֲלָכָה כְּרַבִּי יוֹסֵי בְּמוֹעֵד. דְּמַתִּיר: אִיתְרַע בֵּיהּ מִילְּתָא. בְּפִנְחָס אֲחוּהּ, *דְּפִנְחָס הֲוָה אָבֵל: עָיֵיל שְׁמוּאֵל לִישְׁאַל בֵּיהּ טַעְמָא. לְדַבֵּר עַל לִבּוֹ דְּפִנְחָס: אִילּוּ בְּדִידֵיהּ הֲוָה. כְּלוֹמַר: אִילּוּ הָיִיתָ אָבֵל: מִי מְזַלְזַלְתְּ בֵּיהּ כּוּלֵּי הַאי. בַּאֲבֵילוּת, דְּשָׁקְלַתְּ לְטוּפְרָךְ: וְאִיתְרַע בֵּיהּ מִילְּתָא. אֲבֵילוּת: שַׁקְלִינְהוּ לְטוּפְרֵיהּ חַבְטִינְהוּ לְאַפֵּיהּ. זַרְקִינְהוּ מֵרוֹב כַּעַס. וַהֲדַר מְכַנֵּס לְהוּ, דְּזוֹרְקָן רָשָׁע: בְּרִית כְּרוּתָה לַשְּׂפָתַיִם. דִּכְתִיב: "וְנִשְׁתַּחֲוֶה וְנָשׁוּבָה אֲלֵיכֶם" וְכֵן הֲוָה, דְּחָזְרוּ תַּרְוַיְיהוּ: סְבוּר מִינֵּיהּ דְּיָד. מוּתָּר בִּימֵי אֶבְלוֹ מִשּׁוּם דְּמָאִיס, דְּרֶגֶל – לֹא: גִּינוּסְטְרֵי. מִסְפָּרַיִם: אֵין בָּהֶם מִשּׁוּם מִיאוּס. מִדְּשָׁקַל לֵיהּ בְּשִׁינֵּיהּ: וּשְׁדִי לֵיהּ לְאַבְרָאֵי. וְעָבְרָה עֲלַיְיהוּ אִיתְּתָא אַבְרָאֵי: כֵּיוָן דְּאִישְׁתַּנֵּי. מֵהֵהוּא דּוּכְתָּא דַּהֲווּ מֵעִיקָּרָא – אִישְׁתַּנֵּי, וְלָא מַזִּיקֵי: וּמָר זוּטְרָא מַתְנֵי. בַּבָּרַיְיתָא, דְּבִקְּשׁוּ מִמֶּנּוּ לְפָרְנַיִם בִּימֵי אֶבְלוֹ, וְלָאו מִשְּׁמֵיהּ דְּרַב יְהוּדָה: וְאִם בִּקְּשׁוּ מִמֶּנּוּ שָׂפָה הָיָה מַתִּיר לָהֶם. כְּלוֹמַר: אֲנָא חֲזֵינָא לְדַעְתֵּיהּ אִי שָׁאֲלוּ לְגַלֵּחַ הַשָּׂפָה – הָיָה מַתִּיר לָהֶם, דְּאֵין בָּהֶם מִשּׁוּם: "בַּל תַּשְׁחִית פְּאַת זְקָנֶךָ" (ויקרא יט): מְזָוִית לְזָוִית. מִסּוֹף הַפֶּה לְסוֹף הָאַחֵר מוּתָּר לְגַלֵּחַ, שֶׁהֲרֵי מְעַכֶּבֶת אֲכִילָה וּשְׁתִיָּה, וּמְאִיס: וּלְדִידִי. דַּאֲנָא דַּעְתִּי – כָּל הַשָּׂפָה כְּשָׂפָה הַמְעַכֶּבֶת דָּמֵי, דַּאֲנָא לִי דַּעְתִּי: פַּרְמַשְׁתָּקוֹ. אַמָּתוֹ: אַמְגּוּשֵׁי הֲוָה דִּכְתִיב הִנֵּה יוֹצֵא הַמַּיְמָה. מַחֲלוֹקֶת בְּמַסֶּכֶת שַׁבָּת (דף עה.), חַד אָמַר: חָרָשֵׁי, לְהָכִי יוֹצֵא לַיְאוֹר בִּשְׁבִיל מְכַשְּׁפוּת. וְאִידָךְ אָמַר: גִּידּוּפֵי, לְהָכִי יוֹצֵא, שֶׁאוֹמֵר: לִי יְאוֹרִי וַאֲנִי עֲשִׂיתִנִי: *מִטְפְּחוֹת יָדַיִם. שֶׁמְּנַגְּבִין בָּהֶן יָדַיִם, מִשּׁוּם דְּמָאִיס: *מִטְפְּחוֹת הַסְּפוֹג. שֶׁמְּנַגְּבִין בָּהֶן עַצְמָן כְּשֶׁיּוֹצְאִין מִבֵּית הַמֶּרְחָץ: וְשֶׁעָלוּ מִטּוּמְאָתָן. בַּמּוֹעֵד: מַתְנִי'. דְּקָתָנֵי "אֵלּוּ מְכַבְּסִין" – אַע"ג דְּאִית לֵיהּ תְּרֵי וּמִטַּנְּפֵי. אֲבָל מִי שֶׁאֵין לוֹ אֶלָּא חָלוּק אֶחָד – דְּכוּלֵּי עָלְמָא שָׁרֵי: כְּלֵי

תורה אור

אהֲלָכָה כְּרַבִּי יוֹסֵי בַּמּוֹעֵד וּבְאֵבֶל. *דְּאָמַר שְׁמוּאֵל: הֲלָכָה כְּדִבְרֵי הַמֵּיקֵל בְּאֵבֶל. פִּנְחָס אֲחוּהּ דְּמָר שְׁמוּאֵל, אִיתְרַע (א) בֵּיהּ מִילְּתָא, עָל שְׁמוּאֵל לְמִישְׁאַל טַעְמָא מִינֵּיהּ. חֲזָנְהוּ לְטוּפְרֵי דַּהֲווּ נְפִישָׁן, אֲמַר לֵיהּ: אַמַּאי לָא שָׁקְלַתְּ לְהוּ? אֲמַר לֵיהּ: אִי בְּדִידֵיהּ הֲוָה, מִי מְזַלְזַלְתְּ בֵּיהּ כּוּלֵּי הַאי? *הֲוַאי °"כִּשְׁגָגָה שֶׁיּוֹצָא מִלִּפְנֵי הַשַּׁלִּיט", וְאִיתְרַע בֵּיהּ מִילְּתָא בִּשְׁמוּאֵל. עָל פִּנְחָס אֲחוּהּ לְמִישְׁאַל טַעְמָא מִינֵּיהּ, שַׁקְלִינְהוּ לְטוּפְרֵיהּ חַבְטִינְהוּ לְאַפֵּיהּ, אֲמַר לֵיהּ: לֵית לָךְ *בְּרִית כְּרוּתָה לַשְּׂפָתַיִם? דְּאָמַר ר' יוֹחָנָן: מִנַּיִן שֶׁבְּרִית כְּרוּתָה לַשְּׂפָתַיִם – שֶׁנֶּאֱמַר: °"וַיֹּאמֶר אַבְרָהָם אֶל נְעָרָיו שְׁבוּ לָכֶם פֹּה עִם הַחֲמוֹר וַאֲנִי וְהַנַּעַר נֵלְכָה עַד כֹּה וְנִשְׁתַּחֲוֶה וְנָשׁוּבָה אֲלֵיכֶם" וְאִיסְתַּיְּיעָא מִלְּתָא דַּהֲדוּר תַּרְוַיְיהוּ. סְבוּר מִינֵּיהּ: דְּיָד – אִין, דְּרֶגֶל – לָא. אָמַר רַב עָנָן בַּר תַּחְלִיפָא: לְדִידִי מְפָרְשָׁא לִי מִינֵּיהּ דִּשְׁמוּאֵל: לָא שְׁנָא דְּיָד, וְלָא שְׁנָא דְּרֶגֶל. אָמַר רַב חִיָּיא בַּר אַשִׁי אָמַר רַב: בוּבְגִנּוּסְטְרָא אָסוּר. אָמַר רַב שֶׁמֶן בַּר אַבָּא: הֲוָה קָאֵימְנָא קַמֵּיהּ דְּר' יוֹחָנָן בֵּי מִדְרָשָׁא בְּחוּלּוֹ שֶׁל מוֹעֵד, וְשַׁקְלִינְהוּ לְטוּפְרֵיהּ בְּשִׁינֵּיהּ וְזַרְקִינְהוּ. שְׁמַע מִינָּהּ תְּלָת; שְׁמַע מִינָּהּ: מוּתָּר לִיטּוֹל צִפָּרְנַיִם בְּחוּלּוֹ שֶׁל מוֹעֵד, וּשְׁמַע מִינָּהּ: אֵין בָּהֶן מִשּׁוּם מִיאוּס, וּשְׁמַע מִינָּהּ: מוּתָּר לְזוֹרְקָן. אִינִי? וְהַתַּנְיָא: *שְׁלֹשָׁה דְּבָרִים נֶאֶמְרוּ בְּצִפָּרְנַיִם: הַקּוֹבְרָן – צַדִּיק, שׂוֹרְפָן – *חָסִיד, זוֹרְקָן – רָשָׁע. טַעְמָא מַאי, שֶׁמָּא תַּעֲבוֹר עֲלֵיהֶן אִשָּׁה עוּבָּרָה וְתַפִּיל – אִשָּׁה בֵּי מִדְרְשָׁא לָא שְׁכִיחָא. וְכִי תֵּימָא: זִימְנִין דְּמִיכַּנְשִׁי לְהוּ וּשְׁדֵי לְהוּ אַבְרָאֵי, כֵּיוָן דְּאִשְׁתַּנֵּי – אִשְׁתַּנֵּי. אָמַר רַב יְהוּדָה אָמַר רַב: זוּג בָּא מֵחַמְתָּן לִפְנֵי רַבִּי, וּמָר זוּטְרָא מַתְנֵי: זוּג בָּא מֵחַמְתָּן לִפְנֵי רַבִּי, וּבִקְּשׁוּ מִמֶּנּוּ צִפָּרְנַיִם – וְהִתִּיר לָהֶם, וְאִם בִּקְּשׁוּ מִמֶּנּוּ שָׂפָה – הִתִּיר לָהֶם. וּשְׁמוּאֵל אָמַר: אַף בִּקְּשׁוּ מִמֶּנּוּ שָׂפָה גוְהִתִּיר לָהֶם אָמַר אֲבִיטוּל סָפְרָא מִשְּׁמֵיהּ דְּרַב (*פַּפָּא:) שָׂפָה מִזָּוִית [א]לְזָוִית. אָמַר רַבִּי אַמִי: וּבְשָׂפָה הַמְעַכֶּבֶת. א"ר נַחְמָן בַּר יִצְחָק: לְדִידִי כְּשָׂפָה הַמְעַכֶּבֶת דָּמֵי לִי. וְאָמַר אֲבִיטוּל סָפְרָא מִשְּׁמֵיהּ דְּרַב (*פַּפָּא:) פַּרְעֹה שֶׁהָיָה בִּימֵי מֹשֶׁה הוּא אַמָּה וּזְקָנוֹ אַמָּה, וּפַרְמַשְׁתָּקוֹ אַמָּה וְזֶרֶת, לְקַיֵּים מַה שֶּׁנֶּאֱמַר: °"וּשְׁפַל אֲנָשִׁים יָקִים עָלֶיהָ". וְאָמַר אֲבִיטוּל סָפְרָא מִשְּׁמֵיהּ דְּרַב (*פַּפָּא:) פַּרְעֹה שֶׁהָיָה בִּימֵי מֹשֶׁה אַמְגּוּשֵׁי הָיָה, שֶׁנֶּאֱמַר: °"הִנֵּה יוֹצֵא הַמַּיְמָה". § "וְאֵלּוּ מְכַבְּסִין בַּמּוֹעֵד הַבָּא מִמְּדִינַת הַיָּם" וגו'. § אָמַר רַב אַסִי א"ר יוֹחָנָן: *) דמִי שֶׁאֵין לוֹ אֶלָּא חָלוּק אֶחָד – מוּתָּר לְכַבְּסוֹ בְּחוּלּוֹ שֶׁל מוֹעֵד. מְתִיב ר' יִרְמְיָה: אֵלּוּ מְכַבְּסִין בַּמּוֹעֵד, הַבָּא מִמְּדִינַת הַיָּם כו'. הָנֵי – אִין, מִי שֶׁאֵין לוֹ אֶלָּא חָלוּק אֶחָד – לָא! אֲמַר לֵיהּ ר' יַעֲקֹב לְר' יִרְמְיָה: אַסְבְּרָהּ לָךְ, מַתְנִי' – אע"ג דְּאִית לֵיהּ תְּרֵי וּמִטַּנְּפֵי. שְׁלַח רַב יִצְחָק בַּר יַעֲקֹב בַּר גִּיּוֹרֵי מִשְּׁמֵיהּ דְּר' יוֹחָנָן: הכְּלֵי פִשְׁתָּן מוּתָּר לְכַבְּסָן בְּחוּלּוֹ שֶׁל מוֹעֵד. מְתִיב רָבָא: *מִטְפְּחוֹת הַיָּדַיִם, מִטְפְּחוֹת הַסְּפָרִים

*) תענית כט: לעיל יז. חולין קז:

ואיסתייעא מילתא דההדור. תימה: דלמא מדה טובה מרובה? והוה ליה לאתויי הא דאמר עולא בעלמא (ברכות דף יט. ע"ש): לעולם אל יפתח אדם פיו לשטן, שנאמר "שמעו דבר ה' קציני סדום" כו' (ישעיה א)! **ובגנוסטרי אסור.** פי' בערוך: * שהוא כלי המתוקן ליטול לפרנים וכך שמו. ומלשון דגנוסטרא אסור – משמע שהיה מתיר בין בתער בין במספרים, ולאו דוקא בשינים. מיהו, קאמר בגמרא רבי יוחנן דשקלינהו בשיניו – משמע דוקא בשיניו שרי. ותימה: דלעיל אמרינן הלכה כר' יוסי במועד לדברי הכל! ושמא רבי יוחנן סבר הלכה כר' יהודה, ומפרש טעמא דמחמרינן במועד טפי מבאבל, ולא כרב שישא בריה דרב אידי דאמר: דברים המותרין בחולו של מועד – אסורין בימי אבלו. ורבינו תם פירש: דכשם שמותר בשיניו – כך מותר ליטול לפרניו [בזו] מחבירתה, דכל זה חשוב שינוי לענין שבת בפ' "המלניע" (שבת דף לד:). ושמעתי בשם רבי שמשון בר אברהם שבחול המועד מותר ליטול לפרנים לנשים, דקתני בירושלמי גבי ועושה אשה תכשיטיה במועד, וחשיב נוטלת שערה ולפרניה, ול"ע: בהלכות גדולות נמי אמרינן: והאשה מותרת בנטילת שער לאחר שבעה! ונראה דבאשה נשואה דוקא קאמר, ומיירי במעברת סרק על פניה וטופלה בסיד, שהוא משום תכשיט שלא תנוול על בעלה, אבל בתספורת ממש – אסורה. וגם בשם רבינו חיים שמעתי שהיה מתיר נטילת לפרנים במועד. ובהלכות גדולות פוסק:(ב) שבעה – אסור בגנוסטרי, בשיניו – מותר, לאחר שבעה – מותר אף בגנוסטרי. ולא ידענא מנא ליה דברייתא איירי תוך שבעה? אי משום דקתני בימי אבלו – ה"נ קתני ימי אבלו גבי גילוח, והיינו כל שלשים. וקאמר: כשם שאסור לגלח בימי אבלו כך אסור ליטול לפרניו בימי אבלו – משמע: כל שלשים. ואי סברי כר' יוסי – יתירו לגמרי! וי"ל: דסברי כר' יוסי, ומסתבר להו דאפילו רבי יוסי היה אוסר בגנוסטרי תוך שבעה, דומיא דמועד או שמא(ג) מעשה דשמואל משמע קלת דשקלינהו לטופריה חבטינהו באפיה – דמיירי תוך שבעה דוקא, דבתוך שבעה היה, ובשיניו היה – מדקא אמרינן בתר הכי ובגנוסטרי אסור. משמע דשמואל לא היה בגנוסטרי, ולא אשכחנא דאסר רק תוך שבעה כשהלך רב פנחס לנחמו: **בקשו** ממנו שפה. יש לפרש: על ידי שינוי, דומיא דלפרנים. ונראה דהכא פירוש דוקא לאחר שבעה: **אע"ג** דאית ליה תרי ומטנפי. מדלא משני הכא במאי עסקינן בשלא כיבסו לפני הרגל, דלא שרינן מי שאין לו אלא חלוק אחד אלא היכא דכבסו לפני הרגל, אבל לא כבסו דפשע – לא שרי. משמע דמי שאין לו אלא חלוק אחד – שרי לכבסו במועד אפילו פשע ולא כבסו לפני המועד, כך נראה לי. ובתוספות מסופק בזה. ונראה לי דהכי משמע, מדלא מפליג. ונראה דגבי אבל לא שרינן כשאין לו אלא חלוק אחד, דהא אפילו אם היו לו מכובסין אסור ללבוש, מה שאין כן ברגל. ל"ע בכהן ששלמה משמרתו ברגל אם מותר לכבס לתנא דלעיל, (דף יז:) דתנא: כהן ואבל. אפילו לתנא דידן, אם חל שלישי להיות בעי"ט, שאסור ברחילה עד הערב. ופירש בקונטרס: עד הלילה בלונן, או עד חול המועד בחמין, ואינו מותר לרחוץ מבעי"ט. מיהו, כשחל שביעי שלו בערב הרגל דאסור לכבס ולרחוץ כל היום – מותר לכבס ברגל. ול"ע: אם אמת הוא שמותר – מאי טעמא לא תני?

עין משפט נר מצוה

פח א ב מיי' פ"ה מהל' אבל הלכה ב סמג עשין דרבנן ג טוש"ע י"ד סי' שצ סעיף ז:

[בערך נגסטר וגרסתו אמר רב ובגנוסטרי אסור וע"ש שהאריך]

פט ג מיי' פ"ז מהלכות יו"ט הלכה כ טור ש"ע א"ח סי' תקלא סעיף ח:

צ ד מיי' שם הלכה כא סמג לאוין סה טור ש"ע א"ח סי' תקלד סעיף א:

צא ה מיי' וסמג שם טוש"ע שם סעיף ב:

[עי' פי' שכתבו תוס' נדה יז. ד"ה שורפן וכו' בשם הערוך]

רבינו חננאל

א)פיסקא דנזיר והמצורע מטומאתו לטהרתו. אוקימנא כדתניא כל אלו שאמרו מותרים לגלח במועד. בשלא היה להן פנאי. אבל היה להן פנאי לגלח ולא גילחו אסורין והנזיר והמצורע אע"פ שהיה להן פנאי לגלח ולא גילחו מותרין שלא ישהו קרבנותיהם. תנא האבל והכהן מותרין לגלח במועד. אוקימנא באבל שחל שביעי שלו להיות בשבת ערב הרגל. תנא ברא סבר לה כאבא שאול דאמר מקצת היום ככולו. ויום שביעי עולה לו לכאן ולכאן. וכיון דשבת הואי אנוס הוא לפיכך מגלח במועד. ותנא דידן סבר לה כרבנן כו'. כהן נמי כגון דשלים ליה משמרתו ברגל כו'. ופשוטה היא: ת"ר תכפוהו אבליו זה אחר זה. פי' קודם שישלים ימי אבל זה מת לו מת אחר וכן עוד בתוך ימי אבל זה מת לו מת אחר הכביד שערו מיקל בתער ומכבס כסותו במים. ואמר רב חסדא נוטל שערו בתער ולא במספריים. מכבס במים לבדם ולא בנתר ולא בחול. זאת אומרת אבל אסור בתכבוסת: ת"ר כשם שאסור לגלח במועד כך אסור ליטול צפרנים. ור' יוסי מתיר ליטול צפרנים במועד ובאבל. ואסיקנא כשמואל דאמר הלכתא כדברי המיקל באבל. דאמר שמואל הלכתא כר' יוסי במועד ובאבל ל"ש צפרנים דיד ל"ש צפרנים דרגל. אמר רב ובגנוסטרא אסור. אמר רב שמן הוה קאימנא קמיה דר' יוחנן בבי מדרשא וחזיתיה דשקלינהו לטופריה בשיניה וזרקינהו. ש"מ תלת. ש"מ מותר ליטול צפרנים במועד וש"מ מדשקלינהו בשיניה אין בהם משום מיאוס. וש"מ מדזרקינהו מותר לזורקן. והתניא ג' דברים נאמרו בצפרנים קוברן צדיק שורפן חסיד זורקן רשע. מ"ט שמא תעבור אשה עוברה עליהן ותפיל. ופרקינן אשה בי מדרשא לא שכיחא. וכי תימא זמנין דמכנשו ושדי להו לבראי כיון דאשתני אישתני. אמר רב יהודה אמר רב זוג בא לפני רבי ובקשו ממנו מהו ליטול צפרנים והתיר להם. ושמואל אמר גם עשיית שפה בקשו ממנו והתיר להם. ואסיקנא עשיית שפה מזוית לזוית. כלומר אם צריכה כולה תקון שרי. אבל מקצתה לא. ב) הנחה כל שהיא מעכבת. פי' אם עשה שפמו והניח מקצתו שאינו עשוי מותר ליטלו כי מעכבתו באכילתו. ג) ובכיוצא בה אמר רב נחמן לדידי שפה כי הנחה מעכבת דמי לי. ואלו כולם שאמרו בתוך שלשים יום. אבל בשבעת ימי האבל אסור בכולן. שמואל נכנס לבקר פנחס אחיו בימי אבלו וראה צפרניו גדולים. אמר ליה אמאי [לא שקלית] להו. א"ל אילו בך היה מי הוית מזלזל כולי האי. הואי כשגגה שיוצא מלפני השליט. ואירע אבל לשמואל נכנס פנחס אחיו לבקרו שקלינהו לטופריה חבטינהו באפיה. א"ל לית לך ברית כרותה לשפתים שנאמר ואני והנער נלכה עד כה ונשתחוה ונשובה אליכם. ואסתייעא מלתא והדרי תרווייהו ואתו. פרעה שהיה בימי משה הוא אמה וזקנו אמה ופרמשתקו אמה וזרת לקיים הכתוב ושפל אנשים יקים עליה: **מתני'** ואלו מכבסין במועד הבא ממדינת הים כו'. א"ר אסי א"ר יוחנן מי שאין לו אלא חלוק אחד מותר לכבסו בחולו של מועד. איני והתנינן אלו מכבסין במועד הבא ממדינת הים כו' וחשיב להו כל מי שהתירו לו חכמים לכבס במועד. ולא תני מי שאין לו אלא חלוק אחד בהדייהו. ופרקינן [מתני' אע"ג דאית לי' תרי ומטנפי] שרי לכבסינהו לכלהו. משמיה דר' יוחנן אמרו כלי פשתן מותר לכבסן במועד. והני מטפחות דתנינן במתני' דלאו

א) מכאן עד ואסיקנא כשמואל דאמר הלכתא כדברי המיקל שייך לעיל יז ע"ב. ב) עי' הגי' בבה"ג ואולם גי' רבינו יותר נכונה. ג) נ"ל דחסר בדברי רבינו ר' אמי אמר שפה נמי כל שמעכבת וכיוצא בה וכו'.

מסורת הש"ס: נ"א דשמואל | עירובין מו. לקמן יט: כב. כו: כתובות מג. חולין נ. | כתובות כג. סנ: ב"מ סח. | סנהדרין קכ. ע"ש | [שייך למתני' דלעיל יז.] | [ג"ז שייך שם] | [בהרא"ש ליתא] | [בילקוט ובע"י ליתא] | [בע"י וגם בתוס' שבת עה. ד"ה אמגושי כו' מוכח דהיא משמי' דרב] | לעיל יד.

הגהות הב"ח

(א) גמ' אחוה דמר שמואל איתרע ליה מילתא: (ב) תוס' ד"ה ובגנוסטרי כו' ובה"ג פוסק תוך שבעה אסור: (ג) בא"ד או שמא ממעשה דשמואל משמע קלת מדשקלינהו לטופריה כו' אסור משמע דמעשה דשמואל לא היה:

הגהות הגר"א

[א] גמ' לזוית. נ"ב הנחה כל שמעכבת ר' אמי ובשפה המעכבת. כ"ה גירסת בה"ג ועי' רא"ש מש"ש. (ועמ"ש רבינו בא"ח סי' תקל"א):

גליון הש"ס

גמ' אשה עוברה ותפיל. עי' סנהדרין דף נט ע"א תד"ה ליכא: תוס' ד"ה ובגנוסטרי וכו' ולא כרב שישא בריה דרב אידי. לעיל דף יא ע"ב:

עין משפט
נר מצוה

[שייך לעיל יד. במשנה]
עיין מהרש"א
[ע"ש הלכה ב]

צב א מיי' פ"ז מהלכות י"ט הלכה יב סמג לאוין עה טוש"ע א"ח סי' תקמה סעיף ה:

שייך לדף יד. במתני'

צג ב מיי' פ"ז מהלכות י"ט הלכה טז סמג לאוין עה טוש"ע א"ח סי' תקמו סעיף א:

צד ג מיי' פכ"ג מהל' אישות הלכה יג ופ"ו מהל' זכייה ומתנה הלכה יז סמג עשין מח טוש"ע אה"ע סי' נא:

צה ד מיי' פ"ז מהלכות י"ט הלכה טז טור ש"ע א"ח סי' תקמו סעיף א:

צו ה מיי' פ"ז מהלכות י"ט הלכה יב סמג לאוין עה טוש"ע א"ח סי' תקמה סעיף ו:

צז ו ז מיי' שם הלכה יג טוש"ע שם סעיף א ג:

תוספות

*הספרים. פירוש להסתפר, ובמסתפר לכל אותם שהתירו חכמים. וי"ג: הספרים, ומטפחת *הספגנין, ובירושלמי קאמר עלה: מטפחת הספרים [אין] מכבסין אותן במי רגלים *מפני הכבוד. ואין נראה לי להביא ראיה דאיירי בכתבי הקדש, דאפילו דאיירי באומן המספר – שייך כבוד המסתפרים, שנותנין אותן בפניהם, וכשמסתפרין אין כבוד להם במטונפין:

*העולים מטומאה לטהרה. במלורע איירי, דהא מלורע אסור לכבס, כדאמר לעיל (דף טו.). ומסופק אם נאמר כן בעולה מטומאת מת ונבילה שלריך לכבס בגדיו, או אמרינן דוקא מלורע, הואיל ואסור לכבס כל בגדיו שלו. מיהו, מה שפירש דבמלורע איירי – קשיא לן: אי אמרינן דמלורע אינו נוהג לרעתו ברגל – א"כ מאי איריא עולים מטומאה לטהרה? אפילו בימי לרעתו נמי מותר לכבס ברגל! דלא מלי למימר לא מיבעיא קאמר, כדלעיל (דף יד:) – דאם כן לא שייך שמא ישהו קרבנותיהן. דבשלמא גילוח הוא בשעת קרבן, אבל כיבוס לא שייך לקרבן! ויש לומר: דכיבוס נמי שייך לקרבן:

מתקיף לה אביי מאן לימא לן. ואע"ג דאביי גופיה שני לעיל מתני' אליבא דרבי יוחנן – אינו סובר כן: ואלו כותבין במועד. נראה דכל הני הוו דבר האבד, פן ימות הנותן או העדים או ב"ד, או ילכו למדינת הים:

ואיגרות רשות. בירושלמי מפרש: פריסת שלום. ויש מפרשים: ליווי השלטון, כמו: אל תתודע לרשות (אבות פ"א מ"י):

אין כותבין שטרי חוב. פירשו בתוספות: הוא הדין שטר מכירה, דהא בהדי אלו כותבין במועד לא חשיב שטר מכירה. ולי נראה: דהא דלא קתני – משום דאין כותבין שטר מכירה אלא על הקרקע, ואמרינן לעיל (דף יג.): אין *מוכרין בתים אלא לצורך המועד. ולצורך המועד פשיטא דשרי. והוא הדין אם מכר קודם המועד ועתה רוצה לכתוב – דשרי במועד, דהא נמי דבר האבד. רק אם היה לו אונס ולא יכול לכתוב קודם המועד:(א) הן הן דברים הנקנין באמירה. בפ' "הנושא" (כתובות דף קב:) מפורש: *ומי אמר שמואל שמא יקדמנו אחר. תימה לי: אמאי לא משני: הא – בזוג שני, הא בזוג ראשון, כדמשני פרק שני דסנהדרין (דף כב.) ובפרק קמא דסוטה (דף ב. ושם):

ל"ל מוקמין

ג"ז שייך לעיל

ועווה

גמרא

הספרים. הני — אין, כלי פשתן — לא! אמר ליה אביי: מתני' אפילו דשאר מיני. אמר בר הדיא: לדידי חזי לי ימה של טבריה, דמפקי לה משיכלי דמני כיתנא בחולא דמועדא. מתקיף לה אביי: *מאן לימא לן דברצון חכמים עבדי? דלמא שלא ברצון חכמים עבדי.§ מתני' [א]ואלו כותבין במועד: קדושי נשים, וגיטין, ושוברין, דייתיקי, מתנה, ופרוזבולין, איגרות שום, ואיגרות מזון, שטרי חליצה, ומיאונים, ושטרי בירורין, גזרות בית דין, ואיגרות של רשות.§ גמ' אמר שמואל: [ב]מותר לארס אשה בחולו של מועד, שמא יקדמנו אחר. לימא מסייע ליה: ואלו כותבין במועד: קדושי נשים. מאי לאו שטרי קדושין ממש? *לא, שטרי פסיקתא, וכדרב גידל אמר רב. *דאמר רב גידל אמר רב: [ג]"כמה אתה נותן לבנך" — כך וכך, "כמה אתה נותן לבתך" — כך וכך. עמדו וקדשו — קנו. הן הן הדברים הנקנין באמירה. לימא מסייע ליה: *אין נושאין נשים במועד, לא בתולות ולא אלמנות, ולא מיבמין, מפני ששמחה היא לו. הא לארס — שרי! לא מיבעיא קאמר; לא מיבעיא לארס — דלא קעביד מצוה, אלא אפילו לישא נמי, דקא עביד מצוה — אסור. תא שמע, דתנא דבי שמואל: מארסין אבל לא כונסין, [ד]ואין עושין סעודת אירוסין, ולא מיבמין, מפני ששמחה היא לו. ש"מ. ומי אמר שמואל שמא יקדמנו אחר? והאמר רב יהודה אמר שמואל: *בכל יום ויום בת קול יוצאת ואומרת: בת פלוני לפלוני, שדה פלוני לפלוני! אלא: שמא יקדמנו אחר ברחמים. כי הא דרבא שמעיה לההוא גברא דבעי רחמי ואמר: תיזדמן לי פלניתא. א"ל: לא תיבעי רחמי הכי. אי חזיא לך — לא אזלא מינך, ואי לא — כפרת בה'. בתר הכי שמעיה דקאמר: או איהו לימות מקמה או איהי תמות מקמיה. א"ל: לאו אמינא לך לא תיבעי עלה דמילתא? הכי אמר רב משום רבי ראובן בן אצטרובילי: מן התורה ומן הנביאים ומן הכתובים מה' אשה לאיש. מן התורה — דכתיב: °"ויען לבן ובתואל ויאמרו מה' יצא הדבר", מן הנביאים — דכתיב: °"ואביו ואמו לא ידעו כי מה' היא". מן הכתובים — דכתיב: °"בית והון נחלת אבות ומה' אשה משכלת". ואמר רב משום רבי ראובן בן אצטרובילי, ואמרי לה במתניתא תנא, א"ר ראובן בן אצטרובילי: אין אדם נחשד בדבר אלא א"כ עשאו, ואם לא עשה כולו — עשה מקצתו, ואם לא עשה מקצתו — הרהר בלבו לעשותו, ואם לא הרהר בלבו לעשותו — ראה אחרים שעשו, ושמח. מתיב רבי יעקב: °"ויחפאו בני ישראל דברים אשר לא כן על ה' אלהיהם" — התם להכעיס הוא דעבוד. *תא שמע: °"ויקנאו למשה במחנה לאהרן קדוש ה'", רב שמואל בר יצחק אמר: מלמד שכל אחד קינא לאשתו ממשה! התם משום שנאה הוא דעבוד. ת"ש: אמר רבי יוסי: *יהא חלקי עם מי שחושדין אותו בדבר ואין בו. ואמר רב פפא: לדידי חשדון ולא הוה בי! לא קשיא; הא — בקלא דפסיק, הא — בקלא דלא פסיק. וקלא דלא פסיק עד כמה? *אמר אביי: אמרה לי אם: *דומי דמתא יומא ופלגא. והני מילי — דלא פסק ביני ביני, אבל פסק ביני ביני — לית לן בה. וכי פסק ביני ביני — לא אמרן אלא דלא פסק מחמת יראה, אבל פסק מחמת יראה — לא. [א]ולא אמרן אלא דלא הדר נבט, אבל הדר נבט — לא. ולא אמרן אלא דלית ליה אויבים, אבל אית ליה אויבים — אויבים הוא דאפקוה לקלא.§ מתני' *[ה]אין כותבין שטרי חוב במועד. ואם אינו מאמינו, או שאין לו מה יאכל — הרי זה יכתוב. [ו]אין כותבין ספרים תפילין ומזוזות במועד, ואין מגיהין אות אחת אפילו בספר עזרא. רבי יהודה אומר: [ז]כותב אדם תפילין ומזוזות לעצמו,

ועווה

(א) שייך לעיל קודם ד"ה אין כותבין.

רש"י

*כלי פשתן. דלא נפיש טירחא: מטפחות הספרים. של פשתן: הני אין. אבל שאר כלי פשתן לא: אפילו דשאר מיני. כלומר, מטפחות דשאר מינין, כגון דצמר, אע"ג דנפיש טירחא – שרי לכבס, אבל שאר כלים דשאר מינין – לא. אבל כלי פשתן שרי לכבס: משיכלי. ספלים:

מתני' קדושי נשים. שכתב בשטר: הרי את מקודשת לי. דאשה נקנית בשטר: דייתיקי. שטר צוואה: פרוזבולין. שכותב מלוה בשטר שאינו משמט, ולא משמיט ליה שמיטה: איגרות שום. בכך שמו בית דין שדה זו, ונתנו לאחים כך וכך נגדו: איגרות מזון. פלוני קבל לזון בת אשתו: שטרי בירורים. בירכו ב"ד חלק זה לזה וחלק זה לזה: גזרות ב"ד. פסקי דינין: ואיגרות של רשות. לווי וקיום של שלטון:

גמ' כדרב גידל. שכותב תנאי זה בשטר: ניקנין באמירה. בלא קנין: דקא עביד מצוה. דעוסק בפריה ורביה: כפרת בה'. באמנה, דקאמר דלא מסייע נלותא כלום, הואיל ולא מזמנא(א) ליה. כלומר, השתא גלינא עלה ולא אסתייעא מילתא: אמר. אי לא מנסבא – או איהי תמות מקמאי, דלא איחזי כד מנסבא לאחר ואיצער בה: או איהו. עצמו ימות מקמי דתינסבא איהי לאידך. ולהכי מארס במועד, שלא יקדמנו אחר ברחמים שתמות היא: נחשד בדבר. עבירה: להכעיס עבוד. וידעי דלא היה: בקלא דפסיק. לא היה בה: קלא דלא פסיק. היה בה: דומי. חשד. כמו: לא ישא בת דומה (סוטה דף כז.): אבל הדר נבט. דבתר דפסיק התחיל קלא. נבט = נשמע. דמיון כמו במסכת תענית (דף ז.): האי לורבא מרבנן דמי לפרלידא דתותי קלא, כיון דנבט נבט. ופי' זה וזה – לשון למח: מתני' ואם אינו מאמינו. המלוה ללוה: או שאין לו מה יאכל. לסופר: אפילו בספר עזרא. ס"ת של עזרא. ואני שמעתי עזרה גרס, ופי': ספר מוגה היה בעזרה, שממנו היו מגיהים כל ספרי גולה: לעצמו. לקיים זה המצוה. אבל לגבור, למכור, דדרך שכירות הוה – חשיב מלאכה, כדאמרינן לעיל (דף יב.): *אונכרא, דכיון דלאו אגרא קשקיל – פרשויי בעלמא הוא, ושרי:

תורה אור

[גיטין מה.]
כתובות קב.
ג"ז שם קדושין ט:
לעיל ח:
סנהדרין כב. ע"ש סוטה ב. ע"ש
[אבוגרי כל"ל]
בראשית כד
שופטים יד
משלי יט
מלכים ב יז
סנהדרין קי. תהלים קו
שבת קיח:
[קידושין לא: וש"נ]
יבמות כה.
[לעיל יג.]

הגהות הב"ח

(א) רש"י ד"ה כפרת כו' הואיל ולא מזמנה לך כלומר:

גליון הש"ס

גמ' מאן לימא לן דברצון חכמים. עיין תשובת מהרי"ט ח"א סי' פג:

רבינו חננאל

כלי פשתן אלא צמר ושל שאר מינין זולתי. אמר בר הדיא אנא חזיתי ים טבריא דמפקי לה משיכלי ומכבסי בהו מאני דכיתנא בחולי דמועדא. א"ל אביי ומאן לימא לן דברצון חכמים עבוד דלמא שלא ברצון חכמים עביד: ירושלמי תני מטפחות ספרים אין מכבסין אותן במי רגלים מפני הכבוד אלא מכבסין אותן בנתר ובורית: מתני' אלו כותבין [במועד] קדושי נשים גיטין ושוברין דיתיקאות מתנות פרוזבולין איגרות שום איגרות מזון שטרי חליצה ומיאונין שטרי ברורין גזירות ב"ד איגרות רשות: ירושל' (שטרי חוב) [ושוברין] אומי לוגיאום. ואיגרות של רשות. איגרות שאילת שלום. איגרות שום. שום היתומים. איגרות מזון מזונות אלמנה של (רשות כו') עד גזירות ב"ד. אלו גזרי דינין (ואיגרות של רשות זו שאילת שלום) קידושי נשים. אוקימנא שטרי פסיקתא. כמה אתה נותן לבנך. כמה אתה נותן לבתך כך וכך ועמדו וקדשו הן הן הדברים הנקנין באמירה: ירושלמי איגרות של רשות זו שאילת שלום. אמר שמואל מותר ליארס בחולו של מועד שמא יקדמנו אחר. איני והא איהו דאמר מ' יום קודם יצירת הולד בכל יום ב"ק יוצאת ומכרזת בת פלוני לפלוני כו'. ופרקינן שמא יקדמנו אחר בתפלה. תנא דבי מנשה מארסין במועד ואין כונסין ואין עושין סעודת אירוסין ולא מייבמין מפני ששמחה היא לו. אבל מחזיר גרושתו. אמר רב מן התורה ומן הנביאים ומן הכתובים מה' אשה לאיש. מן התורה שנאמר מה' יצא הדבר. מן הנביאים שנאמר ואביו [ואמו] לא ידעו כי מה' היה הדבר. מן הכתובים דכתיב בית והון נחלת אבות ומה' אשה משכלת. ואמר רב אין אדם נחשד בדבר אלא אם כן עשאו או כולו או מקצתו או הרהר בלבו לעשותו או ראה אחרים שעשאוהו וייטב בעיניו. איני והכתיב ויחפאו בני ישראל דברים אשר לא כן על ה' אלהיהם. ופרקינן התם להכעיס הוא דעבוד. והכתיב וישמע משה ויפול על פניו. ואמר ר' יוחנן שחשדוהו באשת איש. וכתיב ויקנאו למשה במחנה מלמד שכל אחד ואחד קינא על אשתו. ופרקינן התם משום שנאה עשו כך. ת"ש דא"ר יוסי יהא חלקי עם מי שחושדין אותו בדבר ואין בו. ואמר רב פפא לדידי חשדו לי ולא הוה בי ואסיקנא בקלא דלא פסיק ובאתרא דלית ליה אויבים. אבל היכא דאית ליה אויבים מעיקרא לאו מלתא היא דאויבים הוא דאפקוה לקלא: מתני' אין כותבין שטרי חוב במועד אם אינו מאמינו או שאין לו *) הרי זה יכתוב. אין כותבין סתו"מ. ואין מגיהין אות אחת ואפילו בספר העזרה כו'.

*) אולי צ"ל שאין לו מעות לקנות. ת"ר

הגהות מהר"ב רנשבורג

א] גמ' ולא אמרן אלא דלא הדר נבט. כלומר דלא יצא עכ"ל הערוך בערך נבט ועי' בפרש"י דמפרש מלשון למח. ואיך שיהיה הפי' דלא הדר שוב ונשמע כדפרש"י מעיקרא נבט נשמע וכו' ולפענ"ד דברי הש"ס אלו קא מהדרי אדלעיל דקא משנינן ל"ק הא בקלא דפסיק וכו' וקא מפרש הש"ס בתחילה עד כמה הוי קלא דלא פסיק וכל דיני וחלוקי קלא דלא פסיק והשתא קא מהדר נו לפרושי דקלא דפסיק לא אמרן אלא דלא הדר נבט כו' ודוק היטב. דלפ"ז הוי ג' חלוקים בדבר דבקלא דלא פסיק יומא ופלגא איכ בי' וגלאי משקא. וקלא דפסיק לגמרי דלא הדר נביט לית בי' שום ממש. וקלא דפסיק דהדר נבט אף דלא הוי מיומא ופלגא נהי דלא הדר שוב גמור הוא דאית בי' ממש עכ"פ איכא לספוקי ביה ולא נפיק מתורת חשדא. אולי אית בי'. כנלענ"ד ברור ודוק היטב. ולאיי' גמורה מלאתי לפירושי הזה. דביבמות דף כ"ה ע"א ליתא להך ולא אמרן בתרא יעוש"ה ולדברינו מיושב משום דלענין להוציא אשה מבעלה מיירי ואספיקא לא מפקינן והדר נבט רק ספיקא הוי ודו"ק היטב כי נכון הוא:

אוְטוֹוֶה עַל יְרֵיכוֹ תְּכֵלֶת לְצִיצִיתוֹ.§ **גמ'** ת"ר: כּוֹתֵב אָדָם תְּפִילִּין וּמְזוּזוֹת לְעַצְמוֹ, וְטוֹוֶה עַל יְרֵיכוֹ תְּכֵלֶת לְצִיצִיתוֹ, וְלַאֲחֵרִים בְּטוֹבָה, דִּבְרֵי רַבִּי מֵאִיר. ר' יְהוּדָה אוֹמֵר מַעֲרִים וּמוֹכֵר אֶת שֶׁלּוֹ, וְחוֹזֵר וְכוֹתֵב לְעַצְמוֹ. ר' יוֹסֵי אוֹמֵר: כּוֹתֵב וּמוֹכֵר כְּדַרְכּוֹ כְּדֵי פַּרְנָסָתוֹ. אוֹרֵי לֵיהּ רַב לְרַב חֲנַנְאֵל, וְאָמְרִי לָהּ רַבָּה בַּר בַּר חָנָה לְרַב חֲנַנְאֵל: הֲלָכָה, בכּוֹתֵב וּמוֹכֵר כְּדַרְכּוֹ כְּדֵי פַּרְנָסָתוֹ.§ "וְטוֹוֶה עַל יְרֵיכוֹ תְּכֵלֶת".§ ת"ר: טוֹוֶה אָדָם עַל יְרֵיכוֹ תְּכֵלֶת לְצִיצִיתוֹ, אֲבָל לֹא בְּאֶבֶן, דִּבְרֵי ר' אֱלִיעֶזֶר. וַחֲכָמִים אוֹמְרִים: אַף בְּאֶבֶן. ר' יְהוּדָה אוֹמֵר מִשְּׁמוֹ: בְּאֶבֶן, אֲבָל לֹא בְּפֶלֶךְ. וַחֲכָמִים אוֹמְרִים: בֵּין בְּאֶבֶן בֵּין בְּפֶלֶךְ. אָמַר רַב יְהוּדָה אָמַר שְׁמוּאֵל, וְכֵן א"ר חִיָּיא בַּר אַבָּא א"ר יוֹחָנָן: הֲלָכָה, בֵּין בְּאֶבֶן בֵּין בְּפֶלֶךְ. וַהֲלָכָה: כּוֹתֵב כְּדַרְכּוֹ וּמוֹכֵר כְּדֵי פַּרְנָסָתוֹ.§ **מתני'** *הַקּוֹבֵר אֶת מֵתוֹ שְׁלֹשָׁה יָמִים קוֹדֶם לָרֶגֶל — בָּטְלָה הֵימֶנּוּ גְּזֵרַת שִׁבְעָה, שְׁמוֹנָה — בָּטְלוּ הֵימֶנּוּ גְּזֵרַת שְׁלֹשִׁים. מִפְּנֵי שֶׁאָמְרוּ: גשַׁבָּת עוֹלָה וְאֵינָהּ מַפְסֶקֶת, דרְגָלִים — מַפְסִיקִין וְאֵינָן עוֹלִין, ר' אֱלִיעֶזֶר אוֹמֵר: מִשֶּׁחָרַב בֵּית הַמִּקְדָּשׁ *עֲצֶרֶת כְּשַׁבָּת. רַבָּן גַּמְלִיאֵל אוֹמֵר: הרֹאשׁ הַשָּׁנָה וְיוֹם הַכִּפּוּרִים כִּרְגָלִים. וַחֲכָמִים אוֹמְרִים: *לֹא כְּדִבְרֵי זֶה וְלֹא כְּדִבְרֵי זֶה, אֶלָּא: ועֲצֶרֶת — כִּרְגָלִים, רֹאשׁ הַשָּׁנָה וְיוה"כ — כְּשַׁבָּת.§ **גמ'** אָמַר רַב: גְּזֵרַת — בָּטְלוּ, יָמִים — לֹא בָּטְלוּ. וְכֵן א"ר הוּנָא: גְּזֵרַת — בָּטְלוּ, יָמִים — לֹא בָּטְלוּ. וְרַב שֵׁשֶׁת אָמַר: אֲפִילּוּ יָמִים נַמִּי בָּטְלוּ. מ"ט יָמִים לֹא בָּטְלוּ? שֶׁאִם לֹא גִּילַּח עֶרֶב הָרֶגֶל — אָסוּר לְגַלֵּחַ אַחַר הָרֶגֶל. וְהָתַנְיָא

רש"י

וְטוֹוֶה עַל יְרֵיכוֹ. הַחוּטִין, אֲבָל לֹא בְּיָדוֹ בֵּין אֶצְבְּעוֹתָיו, וּבְפֶלֶךְ, כְּדֶרֶךְ חוֹל: **גמ'** לַאֲחֵרִים בְּטוֹבָה. וְלֹא בְּשָׂכָר: מַעֲרִים וּמוֹכֵר שֶׁלּוֹ. כֵּן עוֹשֶׂה כָּל יְמוֹת הֶחָג: כְּדֵי פַּרְנָסָתוֹ. בְּהַרְוָוחָה. וְלָא מַיְירֵי בְּמִי שֶׁאֵין לוֹ מַה יֹּאכַל: אֲבָל לֹא בְּאֶבֶן. שֶׁתּוֹלֶה בְּחוּט, כְּדֵי שֶׁיּוּכַל לְשׁוֹזְרוֹ יָפֶה:

מתני' הַקּוֹבֵר מֵתוֹ שְׁלֹשָׁה יָמִים קוֹדֶם הָרֶגֶל. הוֹאִיל וְעִיקַּר אֲבֵילוּת אֵינוֹ אֶלָּא שְׁלֹשָׁה יָמִים: בָּטְלָה מִמֶּנּוּ גְּזֵרַת שִׁבְעָה. דִּלְאַחַר הָרֶגֶל אֵינוֹ צָרִיךְ לִמְנוֹת יוֹתֵר: שְׁמוֹנָה יָמִים. קוֹדֶם הָרֶגֶל — בָּטְלָה מִמֶּנּוּ גְּזֵרַת שְׁלֹשִׁים. דְּהוֹאִיל וְהִתְחִיל יוֹם אֶחָד מִן הַשְּׁלֹשִׁים — אֵינוֹ צָרִיךְ לִשְׁמוֹר כְּלוּם לְאַחַר הָרֶגֶל דִּין שְׁלֹשִׁים, אֶלָּא מוּתָּר לְאַלְתַּר בְּתִכְבּוֹסֶת, בְּגִיהוּץ וְתִסְפּוֹרֶת: שַׁבָּת עוֹלָה. אֵירַע שַׁבָּת בִּימֵי אֶבְלוֹ — עוֹלָה לְמִנְיַן שִׁבְעָה: וְאֵינָהּ מַפְסֶקֶת. דִּלְאַחַר שַׁבָּת צָרִיךְ לְהַשְׁלִים שִׁבְעָה יְמֵי אֲבֵלוּת, עִם הַשַּׁבָּת: וְהָרְגָלִים מַפְסִיקִין. דְּכִי קָבַר מֵתוֹ שְׁלֹשָׁה יָמִים קוֹדֶם הָרֶגֶל — מַפְסִיק הָאֲבֵילוּת לְגַמְרֵי, וּלְאַחַר הָרֶגֶל אֵין מַשְׁלִים כְּלוּם: וְאֵין עוֹלִין. דְּכִי קָבַר מֵתוֹ בְּתוֹךְ הָרֶגֶל, דְּלֹא בָּטְלָה מִמֶּנּוּ גְּזֵרַת ז' — אֵין יְמֵי הָרֶגֶל עוֹלִין לְמִנְיַן ז' יְמֵי אֲבֵילוּת, אֶלָּא לְאַחַר הָרֶגֶל צָרִיךְ לֵישֵׁב ז' יְמֵי אֲבֵילוּת — זוֹ הִיא סְבָרָתִי. אֲבָל בְּהֶעְתֵּק מָצָאתִי: וְאֵין עוֹלִין — דְּכִי קָבַר אֶת מֵתוֹ שְׁנֵי יָמִים לִפְנֵי הָרֶגֶל דְּלֹא בָּטְלָה מִמֶּנּוּ גְּזֵרַת שִׁבְעָה — אֵין יְמֵי הָרֶגֶל עוֹלִין לְמִנְיַן שִׁבְעַת יְמֵי אֶבְלוֹ, אֶלָּא לְאַחַר הָרֶגֶל צָרִיךְ לֵישֵׁב ה' יְמֵי אֲבֵלוּת לְהַשְׁלִים לִשְׁנֵי יָמִים שֶׁנָּהַג לִפְנֵי הָרֶגֶל. (א)וַאֲנִי אוֹמֵר כִּי טָעוּת סוֹפֵר הוּא, דְּמָה שֶׁנִּזְכַּר שְׁלֹשָׁה יָמִים לִפְנֵי הָרֶגֶל — לָאו דַּוְקָא, וַאֲפִילּוּ שָׁעָה אַחַת לִפְנֵי הָרֶגֶל — בָּטְלָה מִמֶּנּוּ גְּזֵרַת שִׁבְעָה, דְּהָרֶגֶל מַפְסִיק: מִשֶּׁחָרַב בֵּית הַמִּקְדָּשׁ. שֶׁאֵין לַעֲצֶרֶת תַּשְׁלוּמִין כָּל ז', וְאֵינוֹ אֶלָּא יוֹם אֶחָד: כְּשַׁבָּת. וְדִינוֹ כַּשַּׁבָּת, דְּעוֹלָה וְאֵינָהּ מַפְסֶקֶת: רֹאשׁ הַשָּׁנָה כְּשַׁבָּת. הוֹאִיל וְאֵינוֹ אֶלָּא יוֹם אֶחָד: **גמ'** גְּזֵרַת. שְׁלֹשִׁים בָּטְלוּ, אֲבָל יָמִים לֹא בָּטְלוּ. שְׁלֹשִׁים יוֹם לֹא בָּטְלוּ, דַּעֲדַיִין תְּלוּיִין וְעוֹמְדִים: מַאי טַעְמָא יָמִים לֹא בָּטְלוּ. כְּלוֹמַר: בְּאֵיזֶה עִנְיָן לֹא בָּטְלוּ יָמִים? שֶׁאִם לֹא גִּילַּח עֶרֶב הָרֶגֶל. דְּכִי בָּטְלוּ גְּזֵרַת שְׁלֹשִׁים, וְאִיבָּעֵי לֵיהּ לְגַלּוּחֵי עֶרֶב הָרֶגֶל וְלֹא גִּילַּח: אָסוּר לְגַלֵּחַ אַחַר הָרֶגֶל. כָּל שְׁלֹשִׁים יוֹם: וְהָתַנְיָא

תוספות

וטווה על יריכו תכלת לציציתו. פירוש: ע"י שינוי. אבל בתפילין אי אפשר בשינוי, שצריך כתיבה תמה. ובעשיית תפילין וצילית לא איירי במתני'. ושמא אין איסור כי אם בכתיבה וטוייה. ומה שנהגו לכתוב בעוגל – לא מלינו היתר. (ב) וכן פירש בתוספות הרב בשם רבו. ואפילו על ידי הדחק, על יהודי אחד שתפוס היה – התירו בדוחק. גם על ידי היפוך, שהוא נקרא מלד אחר, לא היו מתירין. וגם אי לא אסור משום מלאכה – הא אסרינן ●אפילו טירחא דלאו מלאכה בפרק קמא (דף ד.). מיהו נהגו לומר דמתני' לא איירי על ידי היפוך. ויש כותבין על ידי חילוק האות, וכן היה עושה רבי זקני. והיו"ד שאי אפשר – היה כותב בכתב הפוך: **רבי** יהודה אומר מערים. לכאורה מחמיר יותר מרבי מאיר שהתיר לאחרים. ובתוספות פירשו דרבי מאיר אינו מתיר אלא בהערמה, ולא הבנתי: **רבי** יוסי אומר כותב ומוכר כדי פרנסתו. דשרי לגמרי לאחרים בשכר, ודוקא כדי פרנסתו. ולכאורה מיקל מכולהו, וכן פ' הר"א. עוד פי': דכולהו הוי שרי כדי פרנסתו דאין לו מה יאכל. ולא איירי אלא כשיש לו מה יאכל, ומחמיר רבי יוסי יותר מכולהו. ולישנא לא משמע הכי, דהוה ליה למימר: אינו כותב אלא כדי פרנסתו. מיהו, במילתא דרבי יהודה קשה נמי קלת: דהוה ליה למימר אינו כותב אלא כדי פרנסתו על ידי אחרים, או על ידי הערמה. והשתא מתני' אתיא כרבי מאיר. ויש מפרשים: דכדי פרנסתו נמי לא משמע דאין לו מה יאכל *שרי, דהואיל דצורך מלוה – מותר להשתכר בה, דבחנם לא ירלה לעשות כן. ומתניתין פירש בתוספות הרב דפליגא אכולהו, ותנא אחר הוא. וה"ר יונה פירש: דאתיא כתנא קמא, והכי פירושו: אין כותבין ספרים תפילין ומזוזות כדי למוכרם או כדי להניחם. ועוד פי': דאתיא כרבי יוסי, לפי מה שפירש שרבי יוסי מחמיר. ואין ראיה מכאן שמותר להניח תפילין, דדלמא רבי מאיר ורבי יהודה לטעמייהו, דסבירא להו פרק "המוצא תפילין" (עירובין דף צו: ושם) שבת זמן תפילין. [ורבנן ורבה בר בר חנה נמי הכי מלי סברי. ואע"ג דכולהו אמוראי דפרק "הקומץ רבה" (מנחות דף לו: ושם) משמע דאית להו שבת לאו זמן תפילין הוא. אבל ר' ילחק בן אברהם היה מביא מן הירושלמי להתיר להניח, דאמר בירושלמי: חד בר נש אובד תפילוי בחולא דמועדא, אתא לקמיה דרב חננאל. פי': שיכתוב לו, לפי שהיה סופר, כדאיתא במגילה (דף יח:). שלחיה לקמיה דרבה בר בר חנה, אמר ליה: זיל הב ליה תפילך, ואת כתב לך. דתנן: כותב אדם תפילין לעצמו. אתא לקמיה דרב, אמר ליה: כתוב ליה. פירוש: בלא הערמה. מתני' פליגא על רב: כותב אדם תפילין ומזוזה לעצמו, הא לאחר – לא. רב פתר לה בכותב להניח. פירוש: רב מעמיד המשנה להניחם אחר המועד, אבל להניחם במועד – שרי. ובהלכות גדולות פסק דאסור להניח תפילין בחולו של מועד. ולטעם שממעט שבתות וימים טובים מ"ימים ימימה" – מסתבר שפיר דממעט חולו של מועד. ולמאן דדריש (מנחות דף לו:) מ"לך לאות" ילאו שבתות וימים טובים שהן בעלמן אות – יש לומר לפי שאין עושין מלאכה כי אם בדבר האבד. אבל קשיא למאי דפרישית לעיל (דף ב. ד"ה משקין) דמלאכה דחול המועד מדרבנן, היכי ממעט להו? יש לומר: הואיל ואוכל מלה ויושב בסוכה – אין לריך אות. ואם הוא אמת דבחול המועד חייב בתפילין – יש לומר: הואיל ועושין מלאכה בו – אין אות, ו"מימים ימימה" נמי לא ממעט אלא יום טוב, דחלוק משאר ימים: **הקובר** את מתו. להכי נקט קובר, דאבילות מתחלת משעת סתימת הגולל, כדאמרינן לקמן (דף כז.): **שלשה** ימים. כך הוא עיקר אבילות לכמה מילי. ואמרינן לקמן (שם:): שלשה ימים לבכי: **מאי** טעמא לא בטלו. הכא הוה ניחא טפי לגרוס ימים לענין מאי לא בטלו, ואין לריך להגיה, דהיא היא: **שאם** לא גילח ערב הרגל כו'. ונראה לי דה"ה לא כיבס ולא רחץ ערב הרגל, אם מותר לרחוץ ולכבס מבערב יו"ט, ולא כיבס ולא רחץ – לא יכבס ברגל. והשתא ניחא הא דקתני: גזרת שבעה בטלו, הא ימים לא בטלו. ומיהו, קשיא לן: דקאמר בסמוך שכשם שמלות שלשה מבטלת גזרת שבעה, אפילו לתנא קמא – דמבטלת אפילו ימים, שמביא אבא שאול ראיה למלות שלשים שבטלו לגמרי, אפילו ימים. והרי"ן פי': דדוקא לא גילח, אבל לא כיבס – לא, דמותר לכבס אפילו לא כיבס, שהוא לורך גדול יותר. ואין נראה לי טעמו, דאם הוא לורך גדול – כ"ש שיש לנו לקנסו בשלא עשה קודם הרגל ונכנס ברגל. ולפירוש הקונטרס, דמפרש לקמן שאם חל שליש להיות ערב הרגל שאסור ברחילה עד הערב – זהו עד שחשכה. אם כן לא שייך לקנסו במה שלא רחץ ולא כבס. וא"כ, ימים לענין מאי לא בטלו גבי שבעה? מיהו, יש לומר: דאם לא רחץ ברגל – אסור לרחוץ אחר הרגל. ועוד יש לומר: אגב דנקט סיפא גזרת נקט ברישא גזרת. ועוד נראה לי: דרישא ה"פ: שלשה ימים בטלה גזרת שבעה, הא שני ימים – לא בטלה גזרת. מ"מ, פי' אמת, מדקאמר בסמוך: שכשם שגזרת שלשה מבטלת גזרת ז' כו', משמע שזה פשוט אפילו לת"ק. והשתא תימה לי: דכי משני שאם לא גילח בו, תינח סיפא אבל ברישא, דקאמר בטלה הימנו גזרת ז' – אמאי נקט גזרת ולענין מאי קאמר ימים לא בטלו? וי"ל: דאגב דנקט סיפא גזרת – תנא נמי רישא גזירת. ועוד נראה לי, דרישא ה"פ: שלשה ימים בטלה גזרת ז', הא שני ימים – בטלו גזרת, הא ימים – לא בטלו, לענין דנוהג דברים שבלינעא:

והתניא

מסורת הש"ס

נזיר טו.

[ע' תוס' לקמן כ. ד"ה עלרת]

תוספ' ע"ז לקמן כ.

עין משפט נר מצוה

צח א ב מיי' פ"ז מהלכות י"ט הלכה יג טוש"ע א"ח סי' תקמה סעיף ג:

צט ג מיי' פ"י מהל' אבל הלכה א סמג עשין ב טוש"ע י"ד סי' ת סעיף א:

ק ד מיי' שם הלכה ג טוש"ע שם סי' שלט סעיף ב:

קא ה מיי' שם טור ש"ע שם סעיף ו:

קב ו מיי' שם טוש"ע שם סעיף ח:

אלא כדי פרנסתו היינו בהרווחה שרי וכו' כן הוא גירסת מהרש"א

רבינו חננאל

ת"ר כותבין תפילין ומזוזות לעצמן ולאחרים בטובה דברי ר' מאיר ר' יהודה אומר מערים ומוכר וחוזר וכותב לעצמו ר' יוסי אומר כותב ומוכר כדרכו כדי פרנסתו. אירי ליה רב לרב חננאל הלכה כותב ומוכר כדרכו כדי פרנסתו: וטווה אדם על יריכו תכלת לציציתו אסיקנא אמר רב יהודה אמר שמואל וכן א"ר חייא בר אבא א"ר יוחנן טווה אדם בין באבן בין בפלך. והלכה כותב ומוכר כדי פרנסתו: **מתני'** הקובר את מתו ג' ימים קודם לרגל בטלה הימנו גזירת שבעה. קברו קודם לרגל שמונה ימים בטלה הימנו גזירת שלשים מפני שאמרו שבת עולה ואינה מפסקת. רגלים מפסיקין ואינן עולין כו'. אמר רב גזרת בטלו. ימים לא בטלו. פי' גזרת בטלו נדחו גזירת האבילות גבי הרגל שיש לו לגלח וזולתי זה מגזירת האבילות. ואם לא גילח ערב הרגל אסור לו לגלח אחר הרגל. כי ימים לא בטלו

הגהות הב"ח

(א) רש"י ד"ה ואין עולין כו' (ואני אומר כי טעות סופר הוא וכו' דהרגל מפסיק) תא"מ ונ"ב הדבר פשוט שאיזה תלמיד טועה כתבו בגליון דהא מוכח לקמן דף כ דלתנא דידן [דוקא שלשה ימים]: (ב) תום' ד"ה וטווה כו' לא מלינו היתר בזה וכן פירש כו' ואפילו ע"י הדחק אסור ועל יהודי אחד:

גליון הש"ס

רש"י ד"ה שמונה ימים וכו' מותר לאלתר בתכבוסת. עי' יבמות דף מג ע"א ברש"י ד"ה מקום שמותר ועיין לקמן דף כג ע"א תום' ד"ה כל שלשים: **ד"ה** ואין עולין וכו' ג"י לאו דוקא. קשה לי הא בהדיא מבואר לקמן דף כ ע"א דלתנא דמתני' דהכא ג"י דוקא כדאמרי' שם הלכה כתנא דידן דאמר שלשה וצ"ע: **תום'** ד"ה וטווה וכו' אפי' טירחא דלאו מלאכה. עי' לעיל דף יב ע"ב תוס' ד"ה מכנים:

קג א ב ג מיי' פ"י מהלכות אבל הלכה ה ו ז טוש"ע י"ד סי' שצט סעיף ג:
קד ד מיי' שם ה"ז סמג עשין דרבנן ב טור ש"ע שם סי' שנה סעיף א:
קה ה מיי' פ"ג מהל' נזירות הלכה א סמג לאוין רב:
קו ו מיי' פ"י מהלכות אבל הלכה ו טוש"ע א"ח סי' תקמח סעיף י וטוש"ע י"ד סי' שצט סעיף ה:

שהרי כשחל שמיני שלו בשבת ערב הרגל מגלח בע"ש ואילו חל שלשים כו' כצ"ל וכ"ה בירושלמי ור"ל אפי' אבא שאול ס"ל כן וא"כ מוכח דהטעם הוא משום כבוד הרגל. העתק מחילופי גרסאות

והתניא: *הקובר את מתו שלשה ימים קודם לרגל – בטלה הימנו גזרת שבעה, שמונה ימים קודם לרגל – בטלה הימנו גזרת שלשים. ומגלח ערב הרגל, אם לא גילח ערב הרגל – אסור לגלח אחר הרגל. אבא שאול אומר: [א]מותר לגלח אחר הרגל. שכשם שמצות שלשה מבטלת גזרת שבעה – כך מצות שבעה מבטלת גזרת שלשים. שבעה? והאנן שמונה תנן! *קסבר אבא שאול: מקצת היום ככולו, ויום שביעי עולה לו לכאן ולכאן. *אמר רב חסדא אמר רבינא בר שילא: [ב]הלכה כאבא שאול. ומודים חכמים לאבא שאול [ג]כשחל שמיני שלו להיות בשבת ערב הרגל, שמותר לגלח בערב שבת. כמאן אזלא הא דאמר רב עמרם אמר רב: אבל, כיון שעמדו מנחמין מאצלו – מותר ברחיצה. כמאן – כאבא שאול. אמר אביי: הלכה כאבא שאול ביום שבעה, ומודים חכמים לאבא שאול ביום שלשים, דאמרינן: מקצת היום ככולו. רבא אמר: הלכה כאבא שאול ביום שלשים, ואין הלכה כאבא שאול ביום שבעה. ונהרדעי אמרי: [ד]הלכה כאבא שאול בזו ובזו. *דאמר שמואל: הלכה כדברי המיקל באבל. שלשים יום מנלן? יליף "פרע" "פרע" מנזיר: כתיב הכא: °"ראשיכם אל תפרעו" וכתיב התם: °"גדל פרע שער ראשו", מה להלן שלשים – אף כאן שלשים. והתם מנלן? *אמר רב מתנה: [ה]סתם נזירות שלשים יום. מאי טעמא – אמר קרא: °"קדוש יהיה". יהיה בגימטריא תלתין הוו. אמר רב הונא בריה דרב יהושע: הכל מודין [ו]כשחל שלישי שלו להיות ערב הרגל – שאסור ברחיצה עד הערב. אמר רב נחמיה בריה דרב יהושע: אשכחתינהו לרב פפי ולרב פפא דיתבי וקאמרי: הלכה כרב הונא בריה דרב יהושע. איכא דאמרי, אמר רב נחמיה בריה דרב יוסף: אשכחתינהו לרב פפי ולרב פפא ולרב הונא בריה דרב יהושע דיתבי וקאמרי: הכל מודים שאם חל שלישי שלו להיות ערב הרגל שאסור ברחיצה עד הערב. בעא מיניה אביי (*מרבא:) קברו ברגל, רגל עולה לו למנין שלשים או אין רגל עולה לו למנין שלשים? •למנין שבעה לא קמיבעיא לי – דלא נהגא מצות שבעה ברגל. כי קא מיבעיא לי – למנין שלשים, דקא נהגא מצות שלשים ברגל. מאי? א"ל: אינו עולה. איתיביה: *הקובר את מתו שני ימים קודם הרגל – מונה חמשה ימים אחר הרגל, ומלאכתו נעשית ע"י אחרים, ועבדיו ושפחותיו עושים בצינעא בתוך ביתו, ואין רבים מתעסקין עמו, שכבר

במדבר ו
שם

והתניא. סייעתא: שכשם (א)שגזרת שלשה מבטלת שבעה. דכי קבר מתו שלשה ימים לפני הרגל אינו יושב לאחר הרגל כלום: כך (ב)גזרת שבעה מבטלת גזרת שלשים. דכי קבר מתו שבעה ימים קודם הרגל – בטלה ממנו גזרת שלשים, דאפילו לא גילח ערב הרגל – מגלח אחר הרגל: ויום(ג) שבעה עולה לכאן ולכאן. דקסבר נמי שמיני: כיון שעמדו מנחמים מאצלו. היינו ביום ז': כמאן כאבא שאול. דאמר: עולה לכאן ולכאן, דקסבר נמי שמיני דמבטל ממנו גזרת שלשים: ומודים הן לאבא שאול. ביום שלשים לקבורת מתו דמותר לגלח, דלא בעינן שלשים שלימין, דאמרינן: מקצת היום ככולו: מנלן. דשלשים יום אסור בגילוח: ראשיכם אל תפרעו. הא שאר אבלים – חייבים משמע: הכל מודים. אפילו אבא שאול, דאמר: מקצת היום ככולו: שאסור ברחיצה עד הערב. דודאי שלש שלימין בעינן עד הערב, ולערב רוחץ בצונן, או ימתין עד חולו של מועד וירחץ בחמין: למנין שבעה לא קמבעיא לי. דודאי אינו עולה, דודאי לא נהגא מצות שבעה ברגל, דהא אינו אסור בנעילת הסנדל, ואינו נוהג בכפיית המטה: דהא נהגא מצות שלשים ברגל. דהא ברגל נמי אסור בגיהוץ ובתספורת כשלשים: ואין רבים מתעסקין עמו. כלומר: אין צריכין לנחמו אחר הרגל, שכבר נחמוהו שבעה ימים ברגל: כל

תורה אור

והתניא. בניחותא הקובר את מתו כו'. הקשה בתוספות הרב: אמאי לא קאמר כתנאי, ורב ששת כאבא שאול, ורב הונא כתנא קמא? א]ושמא משום דברייתא מזכיר לשון בטלו, וקאמר לדידיה ימים לא בטלו – א"כ לא סבירא הברייתא כרב ששת, דרב ששת קאמר ימים נמי בטלו, משום דלשון בטלו משמע בכולו, כן נראה לי: הלכה כאבא שאול. נראה דהלכה כמותו בכל מאי דפליג אתנא קמא, בין במקצת היום ככולו, בין לענין אם לא גילח. מדלא מפליג בהלכה כאבא שאול במקצת היום ככולו ולא בגילוח, הרי"ן. בירושלמי מקשה לרבנן דאבא שאול: מה בין יום שלשים ליום שמיני. דקאמר מקצת היום ככולו ומגלח ערב הרגל, ויום שלשים לא אמר מקצת היום ככולו שיהא מגלח בו? ומשני, משום כבוד הרגל התירו. תדע, *שהרי חל שמיני שלו בערב הרגל, מגלח ערב הרגל ואילו חל שלשים בשבת – אינו מגלח בערב שבת: אתיא פרע פרע מנזיר. יש שאומרים שאסור לאבל להיות סורק ראשו לאחר שבעה, משום דאמרינן (נזיר דף מב.): נזיר חופף ומפספס, אבל לא סורק, ואנן ילפינן מנזיר. ואין נראה כלל, דהא בנזיר אסור ודאי, שאפילו תלש שערו אסור. אבל לענין אבילות, שהוא משום יפוי – לא. ובשעת מעשה שאלתי ממורי ריב"א והתיר לי. והר"ר יום טוב פירש: כיון דקיימא לן מקצת יום שבעה ככולו ועולה לכאן ולכאן – מקצת היום ככולו, ויכול לגלח ביום עשרים ותשעה.ב] ובתוספות הרב לא פירש כן, דלא אמרינן שיהא יום שבעה לשני ימים לענין שלשים יום: תלתין הוו. ולבר פלא דאמר בנזיר בפ"ק (דף ה.) "נזיר להזיר" כ"ט אסור, שלשים שרי. ונזירות הוא עשרים ותשעה יום לדידיה – א"כ סבר על כרחך כדפירש אבא שאול. מיהו, יש לומר: לכתחילה אינו מגלח בנזיר עד שלשים יום מדרבנן, כדמשמע הכא. ובירושלמי מקשה מן המשנה (שם דף טז.) דאמר: גלח ביום שלשים – יצא! ומשני: תמן – לשעבר, הכא – מתחילה, והיינו כדפרישית: שאסור ברחיצה עד הערב. פי' בקונטרס: ולערב יכול לרחוץ גופו בצונן. אי נמי: פניו, ידיו ורגליו, אבל כל גופו בחמין – לא, דאסור לרחוץ בי"ט. א"נ יש לפרש: בחמי טבריא. א"נ: לשטוף מותר, כדאי' פרק "כירה" (שבת דף לט: ושם). אי נמי: בחמין שהוחמו בקרקע. ואמר בפרק "כירה": מחלוקת בחמין שהוחמו בכלי. וא"ת: מאי שנא דלא אמרינן מקצת היום ככולו בשלישי ובשביעי לרבנן, •ובשביעי לאבא שאול שרינן על ידי מקצת היום ככולו? וכי תימא משום דאפשר לרחוץ ביו"ט, ולא יהא ניוול – תינח רחילה, אלא כיבוס מאי איכא למימר? ואין נראה לר"י דכיבוס שרי בשלישי! וי"ל: דבאבילות שבעה חמיר טפי. בה"ג מפרש: הוא הדין רביעי וחמישי אסור, עד הערב, ע"כ פי' בתוספות. •והרי"ט פירש: עד הערב – היינו *מבערב י"ט, ולאפוקי דלא שרי מן הבקר, ונראה דהוא הדין בכיבוס – מותר לערב מעי"ט. ולפירושו נראה דשבעה קודם הרגל איכא דרבנן – מותר מבערב י"ט. *ומדקאמר הכל מודים – פירוש: אפילו אבא שאול דשרי בשביעי מן הבקר – הכא מודה לרבנן דלא שרי מן הבקר, אלא יש לו דין שביעי לרבנן: קברו ברגל רגל עולה לו מן המנין שלשים או אינו עולה. פירש בתוספות: דהוא הדין דמיבעיא לן בקברו שני ימים קודם הרגל. וקשיא לן: דהא בסמוך משמע דפשיטא בקברו שני ימים קודם הרגל, דקאמרינן: מאי לאו אסיפא – לא, ארישא. משמע, דברישא ניחא ליה! ושמא היה הרב רוצה לומר דתרוייהו מיבעי ליה, וכי פשיט – בעי למיפשט הכל. ומשני דלא תיפשוט הכל: דלא נוהגין מצות שבעה ברגל. ומיהו, דברים שבצינעא נוהגין, כדמשמע פ"ק דכתובות (דף ד. ושם) דקאמרינן: כל אותן הימים הוא ישן בין האנשים והיא ישינה בין הנשים, מסייע ליה לרבי יוחנן. וכן פירש הרב בשם רבו. ממתני' מאי למיפשט דאינו עולה למנין שבעה, דקתני: מפסיקין ואין עולין. ולכל הפחות איירי לענין שבעה. ומיהו, יש לומר: דנותן טעם מנין לו פשוט דמתניתין איירי שאינו עולה למנין שבעה, אימא לענין שלשים: ומלאכתו נעשית ע"י אחרים. אפילו בביתו. •אע"ג דאמר לעיל בפ"ב (דף יא:) היתה מלאכתו ביד אחרים, בתוך ביתו – אסור לעשות, בבתיהם – מותר! וי"ל: דהכא איירי בדבר האבד:

שכבר

רבינו חננאל

ומקשינן עליה והתניא הקובר את מתו קודם לרגל ג' ימים בטלה הימנו גזירת שבעה. ח' ימים קודם לרגל בטלה הימנו גזירת שלשים ומגלח ערב הרגל א) אסור לגלח אחר הרגל. אבא שאול אומר אף מגלח אחר הרגל. שכשם שמצות שלשה מבטלת גזירת שבעה. כלומר כיון שקיים מצות אבלות דיי לו. כן מצות ז' מבטלת גזרת שלשים. ומקשינן כך מצות שבעה והאנן שמונה תנן. ופרקינן אבא שאול סבר מקצת היום ככולו ב) ויום השביעי עולה לו למנין שבעה. ושאר יום השביעי כולו עולה לו למנין שלשים. וכיון שקיים מצות שלשים במקצת היום דיי לו. ומגלח ערב הרגל ואם לא גילח ערב הרגל מגלח לאחר הרגל. ואמרו הלכתא כאבא שאול. קשיא לרב דאמר ימים לא בטלו. ג) ופריק רב כי קאמרינן הלכתא כאבא שאול בשבעה ואין צריך שמונה כרבנן דפליגי עליה. ומודים חכמים לאבא שאול ביום ל' שמקצת היום ככולו ואסיקנא הלכתא כאבא שאול בין ביום שביעי בין ביום שלשים דמקצת היום ככולו. והני מילי בתשלום שבעה ובתשלום שלשים. אבל בזמן שהרגל מפסיק האבלות לא כרב הונא בריה דרב יהושע דאמר הכל מודים שאם חל שלישי שלו להיות ערב הרגל שאסור ברחיצה עד הערב. ואמרינן הלכתא כרב הונא בריה דרב יהושע. ד) בעא מיניה אביי מרבה קברו ברגל עולה לו הרגל למנין שלשים או לא. ודאי למנין שבעה אינו עולה דהא לא נהג ביה מצות אבלות דהא פח"ז נת"ר רשות כי תיבעי לך שלשים דהא קיים בה מצות גילוח שהיא מצות שלשים א"ל אין עולה לו אפילו למנין שלשים. ושקלינן וטרינן ודברים פשוטים הן. ומסקנא דשמעתא הלכת למעשה הנקבר אפילו שעה אחת קודם לרגל בטלה הימנו גזרת אבלות. אבל הנקבר ברגל לא חיילא עליה אבלות אלא אחר הרגל ונקיט שבעת ימי אבלות מי"ט האחרון שהוא י"ט שני ואע"ג דלא נהיג ביה אבל עולה למנין שבעה ועצרת ור"ה ויוה"כ מפסיקין אבלות כרגלים כדפסיק רבינא. והלכתא

[נזיר טו.] מס' שמחות פ"ז ע"ש
[לעיל יז: פסחים ז. וש"נ]
לעיל יז.
לעיל יח. וש"נ עירובין מו.
ויקרא י
נזיר ה. לט. תענית יז. [סנהדרין כב:]
[נ"ל מרבה]
[תוספתא פ"ב]
מבערב בערב י"ט כצ"ל
נ"ל ודקאמר

הגהות הב"ח

(א) רש"י ד"ה שכשם שמצות שלשה מבטלת גזירת שבעה דכי קבר מתו: (ב) ד"ה כך מצות שבעה מבטלת: (ג) ד"ה ויום שביעי עולה:

א) נראה דצ"ל ואם לא גילח ערב הרגל אסור לגלח וכו'. ב) אולי צ"ל ומקצת יום השביעי וכו'. ג) נראה מזה שהיה לו גירסא אחרת בסוגיין ולפי גרסא זו משמע דהלכה כרב בזה דימים לא בטלו ועי' ברמב"ן בתוה"א שהאריך להוכיח דהלכה כאב"ש בכולהו ע"ש. ד) והדין דאמרינן בגמרא דמודים חכמים לאב"ש כשחל שמיני שלו וכו' שמותר לגלח בע"ש כתבו רבינו להלן דף כג ע"ב ומש"כ שם בד' רבינו שמותר לגלח ביום שני טס"ה וצ"ל בע"ש.

גליון הש"ס

גמ' למנין שבעה לא קמיבעיא לי דלא נהגא מצות שבעה ברגל. עי' לקמן דף כג ע"ב תוס' ד"ה יש אבילות בשבת: תוס' ד"ה שאסור ברחיצה וכו' ובשביעי לאבא שאול. נ"ל ובשמיני: בא"ד והרי"ט פירש וכו'. עי' לקמן דף כג ע"א תוס' ד"ה ואמר לאחותה: ד"ה ומלאכתו וכו' אע"ג דאמר לעיל. תמוה לי הא הכא מקילי' רק אחר שכלמו ז' ימים מתחילת אבילות ולע"ג:

הגהות מהר"ב רנשבורג

א] תוס' ד"ה והתניא כו' ושמא משום דברייתא מזכיר לשון בטלו וקאמר לדידיה ימים לא בטלו כו'. כוונתם דמש"ה לא קאמר הש"ס כתנאי דניחא ליה למימר בלשון והתניא משום דמייתי סייעתא לר"ה ולאפוקי מר"ש דהא ר"ש פי' לשון בטלו דמתני' דמשמע בכולו ות"ק דברייתא נמי נקט לשון בטלו ואפ"ה קאמר דלא בטלו ימים וזה דלא כר"ש אלא כר"ה. ולזה נתכוון רש"י בד"ה והתניא סייעתא כנלע"ד ודו"ק. ובשו"ת מקום שמואל (סי' מא) הבין דברי התוס' על דרך רחוק ולפיכך כתבתי פה הנלע"ד. אחרי שנים רבות שכתבתי זה נדפס ספר יד דוד וראיתי שכוונתי לדעתו בזה והנאני: ב] בד"ה אתיא פרע פרע מנזיר וכו' ובתוספות הרב לא פירש כן. נ"ב וכן מורין לדברי התוס' בדיבור הקודם בשם הירושלמי לאסור לגלח בע"ש שהוא כ"ט לאבילות שאסור לגלח ודלא כשו"ת האחרונים ז"ל שנשאו ראש להקל בזה. כי מי יקל ראשו נגד ירושלמי המפורש באתרא דלא פליג עליה תלמודא דידן ועיין שו"ת כרם שלמה סי' כח ובד"מ בי"ד סי' ש"ץ אות ד:

כל שהוא משום אבל רגל מפסיקו. שצריך להשלימו אחר הרגל. כיון דכי ישב שני ימים לפני הרגל – צריך להשלים ולישב חמשה ימים אחר הרגל: כל שהוא משום עסקי רבים. כלומר, תנחומי רבים – אין רגל מפסיקו [כדי] שיהא צריך להשלים ולעסוק בו אחר הרגל, אלא מתעסקין בו ברגל: ארבעה ימים הראשונים. של אחר הרגל רבים מתעסקים בו, ומשלימין לשלשה שנתעסקו ברגל, שכבר נתעסקו בו ברגל שלשה ימים: ורגל עולה. למנין שלשים: מאי לאו אסיפא. הא דתני דרגל עולה למנין שלשים – היינו אסיפא, אקברו ברגל. ותיפשוט מינה דכי קברו ברגל – עולה למנין שלשים, וקשיא לרבא, דאמר: אינו עולה: לא, ארישא. קא מהדר, אקברו שני ימים קודם הרגל – רגל עולה לו למנין שלשים. דהתם ודאי עולה לו, הואיל וכבר התחיל באבילות. אבל קברו ברגל – לא ידענא: בתחילת הרגל. ביום ראשון של רגל, וקשיא לרבא: שכבר נתעסקו ברגל. כל שבעה: אפילו קברו ברגל. רגל עולה למנין שלשים, ולא מיבעיא קברו קודם הרגל: תנא דידן. היינו תנא א] (*דברייתא): במה דברים אמורים. שאינה נוהגת אלא יום אחד: אלא חמשה. מהני שבעה מתי מצוה דכתיב בקרא (ויקרא כא): בנו ובתו אחיו ואחותו ואשתו: יחידאה היא. ולא ר' עקיבא. דלר"ע לא שנא אביו ואמו, לא שנא שאר קרוביו: בגינזק. מקום: רב בר אחוה דר' חייא דהוא בר אחתיה דר' חייא. דרבי אחא מכפרי נשא לאה, והוליד ממנה אייבו, מתה ונשא רחל ולה בת מאיש אחר, וממנה נולד רבי חייא. ונשא אייבו הבת, ונולד להן רב. ונמצא: רב בר אייבו בר אחוה דרבי חייא מאבוה, ובר אחתיה מאמיה: כי סליק. רב מעירו דבבל לא"י, שהיה רבי חייא שם: א"ל. רבי חייא לרב: אבא קיים. ר"ל: אייבו אביך, קיים הוא? א"ל

שכבר נתעסקו בו ברגל. כללו של דבר: כל שהוא משום אבל – רגל מפסיקו, וכל שהוא משום עסקי רבים – אין רגל מפסיקו. קברו שלשה ימים בסוף הרגל – מונה שבעה אחר הרגל. ארבעה ימים הראשונים – רבים מתעסקין בו, שלשה ימים האחרונים – אין רבים מתעסקין בו, שכבר נתעסקו ברגל, ורגל עולה לו. מאי לאו אסיפא? לא, ארישא. איתיביה: רגל עולה לו למנין שלשים, כיצד? קברו בתחילת הרגל – מונה שבעה אחר הרגל, [א]ומלאכתו נעשית על ידי אחרים, ועבדיו ושפחותיו עושין בצנעא בתוך ביתו, ואין רבים מתעסקין בו, שכבר נתעסקו בו ברגל, ורגל עולה לו! תיובתא. כי אתא רבין אמר רבי יוחנן: [ב]אפילו קברו ברגל. וכן אורי ליה ר' אלעזר לרבי פדת בריה: אפילו קברו ברגל. ת"ר: *קיים כפיית המטה שלשה ימים קודם הרגל – אינו צריך לכפותה אחר הרגל, דברי רבי אליעזר. וחכמים אומרים: אפי' יום אחד, ואפי' שעה אחת. א"ר אלעזר בר' שמעון: הן הן דברי ב"ש, הן הן דברי בית הלל. שבית שמאי אומרים: שלשה ימים, וב"ה אומרים: אפי' יום אחד. אמר רב הונא אמר ר' חייא בר אבא אמר ר' יוחנן, ואמרי לה אמר(א) (*ליה) ר' יוחנן לר' חייא בר אבא ולרב הונא: אפי' יום אחד, אפי' שעה אחת. רבא אמר: *הלכה כתנא דידן, דאמר שלשה. רבינא איקלע לסורא דפרת, א"ל רב חביבא לרבינא: הלכתא מאי? אמר ליה אפי' יום אחד, [ג]ואפילו שעה אחת. יתיב רבי חייא בר אבא ורבי אמי ור' יצחק נפחא אקילעא דרבי יצחק בן אלעזר, נפק מילתא מביניהו: מנין לאבילות שבעה? דכתיב: °"והפכתי חגיכם לאבל" (עמוס ח) מה חג שבעה – אף אבילות שבעה. ואימא עצרת, דחד יומא! ההוא מיבעי ליה לכדריש לקיש, דאמר ר"ל משום ר' יהודה נשיאה: מנין לשמועה רחוקה שאינה נוהגת אלא יום אחד – דכתיב: "והפכתי חגיכם לאבל" ואשכחן עצרת דאיקרי חד יומא חג. *ת"ר: שמועה קרובה נוהגת שבעה ושלשים, שמועה רחוקה אינה נוהגת אלא יום אחד. [ד]איזו היא קרובה ואיזו היא רחוקה? קרובה – בתוך שלשים, רחוקה – לאחר שלשים, דברי ר"ע. וחכמים אומרים: אחת שמועה קרובה ואחת שמועה רחוקה – נוהגת שבעה ושלשים. אמר רבה בר בר חנה א"ר יוחנן: *כל מקום שאתה מוצא יחיד מקיל ורבים מחמירין – הלכה כרבים, חוץ מזו, שאע"פ שרבי עקיבא מקיל וחכמים מחמירין – [ה]הלכה כרבי עקיבא. *דאמר שמואל: הלכה כדברי המקיל באבל. רב חנינא אתיא ליה שמועה דאבוה מבי חוזאי, אתא לקמיה דרב חסדא. אמר ליה: שמועה רחוקה אינה נוהגת אלא יום אחד. רב נתן בר אמי אתא ליה שמועה דאימיה מבי חוזאי, אתא לקמיה דרבא. אמר ליה: הרי אמרו: שמועה רחוקה אינה נוהגת אלא יום אחד בלבד. איתיביה: במה דברים אמורים – בחמשה מתי מצוה, אבל על אביו ועל אמו – שבעה ושלשים! אמר ליה: יחידאה היא, ולא סבירא לן כוותיה. דתניא: מעשה ומת אביו של רבי צדוק בגינזק, והודיעוהו לאחר שלש שנים, ובא ושאל את אלישע בן אבויה וזקנים שעמו, ואמרו: נהוג שבעה ושלשים. וכשמת בנו של רבי אחיה בגולה ישב עליו שבעה ושלשים. איני? והא *רב, בר אחוה דרבי חייא, דהוא בר אחתיה דר' חייא. כי סליק להתם, אמר ליה: אבא קיים? אמר

שכבר נתעסקו בו ברגל. תנחומין וברכה בשורה. והרי"ט דפירש לענין הבראה חולק על מחזור מויטר"י, שפירש בשם רש"י, שהיה אומר שאין עושים הבראה ברגל, הואיל וליכא אבילות. ולאחר הרגל – נמי לא יעשוה, הואיל ובטלה סעודה ראשונה. פי': דמספקא ליה לרש"י אי הבראה במועד אי לאחר המועד, דשמא הבראה אינו עסקי רבים הואיל ויחיד יכול לעשות. ועל הבראה פירש לקמן, כל יום ראשון אסור לאכול משלו, אפי' אוכל שתי פעמים ביום. דהא לא קאמר גמרא סעודה ראשונה, אלא יום ראשון:

שלשה ימים אחרונים אין רבים מתעסקין בו. פירש בתוספות: דהוא הדין דמלאכתו נעשית ע"י אחרים: **אמר** רבי יוחנן אפילו יום אחד אפי' שעה אחת. קשיא לי: דהא אית ליה לר' יוחנן* הלכה כסתם משנה!

מה חג שבעה. ובירושלמי דייק: אימא שמונה כשמונה דחג? ומשני: שמיני – רגל בפני עצמו הוא, ומ"ויעש לאביו אבל שבעת ימים" (בראשית נ) לא מצי לאתויי, דהתם קודם קבורה היה. ובירושלמי משני דאין למידין מקודם מתן תורה, והתם בירושלמי מייתי קראי טובא:

כל מקום שאתה מוצא יחיד מקיל ורבים מחמירין. והוא הדין יחיד מחמיר ורבים מקילין – הלכה כרבים, ומשום דהכא איירי ביחיד מקיל נקיט הכי. וכל מקום לאו דוקא, דבהרבה מקומות פוסק כדברי היחיד, והיכא דלאתמר אתמר. ועוד: דבעירוב אומר הלכה כדברי המיקל אפי' לגבי רבים. מיהו, התם היינו ריב"ל ולא רבי יוחנן, פר' "מי שהוציאוהו" (עירובין מו.):

יחידאה היא. ואף על גב דלעיל נקיט "וחכ"א":

*__אייבו__ קיים. עדיין לא השיבותיך על אייבו. כך פי' בקונטרס. וקשה: שהיה לר' חייא לומר אמך קיימת, ולא "אימא" דמשמע אמו של ר' חייא? ועוד: דרב היה לו להשיב אבא, ולא היה לו לקרות אביו בשם אייבו? ונראה שר"ח גורס: א"ל: אבא קיים? א"ל: אבא קיים. אימא קיימת? א"ל: אימא קיימת. פירש: ר' חייא היה שואל על אביו ואמו, ורב היה משיב לו על אביו ואם שלו. ואין לנו להקשות: מה לנו לומר דרב בר אחוה דרבי חייא ובר אחתיה? בשלמא לפירוש ראשון – הביאו לומר מה היה חושש ר' חייא על אביו ועל אמו של רב. כי לפירוש זה נמי י"ל דהוצרך יפה, שלא תאמר מה היה לו לרב להשיב על אביו ואמו שלו – כמו כן היה לו להשיב שאר בני אדם קיימין. אבל השתא קמ"ל שהיה משיב לו, לפי שהיה אחיו של ר' חייא ונוח לו להשמיעו חדשות טובות, דלא לימא נא ובשר לקרובים. כדאמרינן בריש פסחים (דף ג: ושם): נא ובשר לסוסים ולחמורים. וי"ג: אמר ליה אבא קיים, אמר ליה אימא קיימת. א"ל: אימא קיימת, אמר ליה: אבא קיים. וכפר"ח. וכענין שפירש ר"ח לגירסת ר"ח. (ב)ורבי חייא היה שואל על אביו ואמו שלו, והוא משיב על אביו ואמו של עצמו. ומה שלא משיב לו כמו גירסת ר"ח – שאם היה משיב לו אבא קיים כשהיה שואל על אביו שלו – משום דהוה משמע שהיה משיב לו על אביו של רבי חייא, שהיה רגיל לקרות אבי אביו אבא:

עולה

רבינו חננאל

והלכתא אפילו יום אחד או שעה אחת נמצאת אומר מי שמת לו מת תוך הרגל נקיט שבעה מיו"ט שני של יו"ט האחרון ואף על פי שיו"ט שני אין נוהג בו אבילות ונקיט ל' מההוא יומא דמית ביה ומאן דשכיב ליה שכבא ביו"ט שני של יו"ט האחרון או ביו"ט שני דעצרת *) נהיג אבל בו ביום דהוא יום קבורה והוא מדאורייתא דכתיב ואכלתי חטאת היום וכתיב נמי ואחריתה כיום מר והוא יום המיתה הלכך יום מיתה מדאורייתא ויו"ט שני מדרבנן אתי דאורייתא ומבטל דרבנן ונהיג ביה אבלות כשאר יומי. מניין לאבלות שהיא שבעה שנאמר והפכתי חגיכם לאבל. מה חג שבעה אף אבלות שבעה. ומניין לשמועה רחוקה שאינה נוהגת אלא יום אחד כבר הקיש הכתוב האבל לחג ומצאנו עצרת שהוא חג והוא יום אחד: ת"ר שמועה קרובה נוהגת שבעה ושלשים שמועה רחוקה אינה נוהגת אלא יום אחד איזו היא קרובה ואיזו היא רחוקה קרובה בתוך ששים לקבורתו רחוקה לאחר שלשים דברי ר' עקיבא וחכמים אומרים אחת זו ואחת זו נוהגת שבעה ושלשים. אמר רבה בר בר חנה אמר רבי יוחנן כל מקום שאתה מוצא יחיד מקיל ורבים מחמירין הלכה כמחמירין חוץ מזו. שאע"פ שר' עקיבא מקיל וחכמים מחמירין הלכה כר' עקיבא דאמר שמואל הלכה כדברי המקיל באבל. והא דתניא בד"א כי שמועה רחוקה אינה נוהגת אלא יום אחד בה' מתי מצוה פי' בחמשה שמצוה להתאבל עליהן. והן בנו ובתו ואחיו ואחותו ואשתו. אבל על אביו ועל אמו אפי' שמועה רחוקה נוהגת שבעה ושלשים לית הלכתא כוותיה דהא יחידאה היא כלומר אלישע בן אבויה וח' זקנים שהיו עמו והורו בשמועה רחוקה לנהוג שבעה ושלשים יחידים הן ולא סבירא לן כוותייהו דהא רב חסדא ורבה הורו על אביו ועל אמו בשמועה רחוקה שלא לנהוג אלא יום

*) כל דברי רבינו אלו הובא בא"ז בח"ב סימן תל"ב בשמו וכן דעת בה"ג ורב אלפס ז"ל וע"ש בא"ז וברא"ש מש"כ על זה.

קז א טוש"ע י"ד סימן שצט סעיף ב:

קח ב מיי' פ"י מהלכות אבל הלכה ח טוש"ע שם:

קט ג מיי' שם הלכה ג סמג עשין דרבנן ב ובלאוין עה טוש"ע שם סעיף א:

קי ד ה מיי' שם פ"ז הלכה א סמג שם טוש"ע י"ד סימן תב סעיף א:

הגהות הב"ח

(א) גמ' ואמרי לה אמר ליה ר' יוחנן לר' חייא בר אבא ור' חייא בר אבא לרב הונא אפילו יום אחד: (ב) תוס' ד"ה אייבו כו' לגירסת ר"ח לר' חייא היה שואל כו' כשהיה שואל על אביו שלו הוה משמע כו' כצ"ל ותיבת משום נמחק:

גליון הש"ס

גמ' אורי ליה רבי אלעזר לרבי פדת בריה. עיין נדה דף ח ע"ב תוס' ד"ה ואמר ר' פדת: שם הן הן כנים זה כתובות דף ס ע"ב: תוס' ד"ה שכבר כו' שאין עושין הבראה ברגל. עי' לקמן דף כד ע"ב תוס' ד"ה אלא:

[תוספ' פ"ב] [נ"ל דמשנה] [נ"ל להון] [לקמן כא.] עירובין מו. [שם] לעיל יח. יבמ' לקמן כב. כו. עירובין מו. [בכורות מט. חולין נ.] נזיר מד. שמחות פי"ב פסחים ז. [סנהדרין ה.]

הגהות מהר"ב רנשבורג

א] רש"י ד"ה תנא דידן היינו תנא דברייתא. נ"ב תנא דמתני' נמי קאמר שלשה ימים קודם הרגל וצ"ע ונלע"ד דרש"י אתי שפיר לשיטתו שפי' במתניתין דלהמשנה לאו דוקא שלשה ימים אלא אפילו שעה אחת והיינו מדקתני במשנה דרגלים מפסיקין מש"כ הכא בברייתא שלשה ימים דוקא דהא לא קתני פסיקין ועוד דפליגי נמי חכמים עלה ולרש"י מיושב קושית התוס' בד"ה אמר ר' יוחנן והתוספות לשיטתם מקשים דפירשו לעיל במשנה כהיש מפרשים דשלשה ימים דוקא וקצת מזה כוונתי לבעל יד דוד וכ"כ בעל שושנים לדוד:

אֲמַר לֵיהּ: אִימָּא קַיֶּימֶת? אֲמַר לֵיהּ: אִימָּא קַיֶּימֶת? א"ל: אַבָּא קַיָּים?! אֲמַר לֵיהּ לְשַׁמָּעֵיהּ: חֲלוֹץ לִי מִנְעָלַי, וְהוֹלֵךְ אַחֲרַי כֵּלַי לְבֵית הַמֶּרְחָץ. שְׁמַע מִינַּהּ תְּלָת: שְׁמַע מִינַּהּ: *אָבֵל אָסוּר בִּנְעִילַת הַסַּנְדָּל, וּשְׁמַע מִינַּהּ: שְׁמוּעָה רְחוֹקָה אֵינָהּ נוֹהֶגֶת אֶלָּא יוֹם אֶחָד, וּשְׁמַע מִינַּהּ: *[א]מִקְצָת הַיּוֹם כְּכוּלּוֹ?! רַבִּי חִיָּיא — לְחוּד, רַבִּי אַחִיָּיה — לְחוּד. אָמַר רַבִּי יוֹסֵי בַּר אָבִין: [ב]שָׁמַע שְׁמוּעָה קְרוֹבָה בָּרֶגֶל, וּלְמוֹצָאֵי הָרֶגֶל נַעֲשֵׂית רְחוֹקָה — עוֹלֶה לוֹ, וְאֵינוֹ נוֹהֵג אֶלָּא יוֹם אֶחָד. תָּנֵי רַבִּי אַדָּא דְּמִן קֵסָרִי קַמֵּיהּ דְּר' יוֹחָנָן: [ג]שָׁמַע שְׁמוּעָה קְרוֹבָה בְּשַׁבָּת, וּלְמוֹצָאֵי שַׁבָּת נַעֲשֵׂית רְחוֹקָה — אֵינוֹ נוֹהֵג אֶלָּא יוֹם אֶחָד. קוֹרֵעַ אוֹ אֵינוֹ קוֹרֵעַ? רַבִּי מָנִי אָמַר: [ד]אֵינוֹ קוֹרֵעַ. רַבִּי חֲנִינָא אָמַר: קוֹרֵעַ. אָמַר לֵיהּ רַבִּי מָנִי לְר' חֲנִינָא: בִּשְׁלָמָא לְדִידִי, דְּאָמִינָא אֵינוֹ קוֹרֵעַ, הַיְינוּ דְּלָא אִיכָּא אֲבֵילוּת שִׁבְעָה. אֶלָּא לְדִידָךְ דְּאָמְרַתְּ קוֹרֵעַ, קְרִיעָה בְּלֹא שִׁבְעָה מִי אִיכָּא? וְלָא? וְהָתַנְיָא אִיסִי אֲבוּהּ דְּרַבִּי זֵירָא, וְאָמְרִי לַהּ אֲחוּהּ דְּרַבִּי זֵירָא קַמֵּיהּ דְּר' זֵירָא: [ה]מִי שֶׁאֵין לוֹ חָלוּק לִקְרוֹעַ, וְנִזְדַּמֵּן לוֹ בְּתוֹךְ שִׁבְעָה — קוֹרֵעַ, לְאַחַר שִׁבְעָה — אֵינוֹ קוֹרֵעַ. עָנֵי ר' זֵירָא בַּתְרֵיהּ: בַּמֶּה דְּבָרִים אֲמוּרִים — בַּחֲמִשָּׁה מֵתֵי מִצְוָה, [ו]אֲבָל עַל אָבִיו וְעַל אִמּוֹ — קוֹרֵעַ וְהוֹלֵךְ! כִּי תַּנְיָא הַהִיא — לִכְבוֹד אָבִיו וְאִמּוֹ. ת"ר: [ז]כָּל הָאָמוּר בְּפָרָשַׁת כֹּהֲנִים, שֶׁכֹּהֵן מִיטַּמֵּא לָהֶן — אָבֵל מִתְאַבֵּל עֲלֵיהֶן, וְאֵלּוּ הֵן: אִשְׁתּוֹ, אָבִיו, וְאִמּוֹ, אָחִיו, וַאֲחוֹתוֹ, בְּנוֹ, וּבִתּוֹ. [א]הוֹסִיפוּ עֲלֵיהֶן אָחִיו וַאֲחוֹתוֹ הַבְּתוּלָה מֵאִמּוֹ, וַאֲחוֹתוֹ נְשׂוּאָה בֵּין מֵאָבִיו בֵּין מֵאִמּוֹ. *וּכְשֵׁם שֶׁמִּתְאַבֵּל עֲלֵיהֶם — כָּךְ מִתְאַבֵּל עַל שְׁנִיִּים שֶׁלָּהֶם, דִּבְרֵי ר"ע. רַבִּי שִׁמְעוֹן בֶּן אֶלְעָזָר אוֹמֵר: אֵינוֹ מִתְאַבֵּל אֶלָּא עַל בֶּן בְּנוֹ וְעַל אֲבִי אָבִיו. וְחכ"א: [ח]כָּל שֶׁמִּתְאַבֵּל עָלָיו — מִתְאַבֵּל עִמּוֹ. חֲכָמִים הַיְינוּ תַּנָּא קַמָּא! אִיכָּא בֵּינַיְיהוּ עִמּוֹ [ט]בַּבַּיִת. *כִּי הָא דַּאֲמַר לֵיהּ רַב לְחִיָּיא בְּרֵיהּ, וְכֵן א"ל רַב הוּנָא לְרַבָּה בְּרֵיהּ: בְּאַפֵּהּ — נְהוֹג אֲבֵילוּתָא, בְּלָא אַפֵּהּ — לָא תִּינְהוֹג אֲבֵילוּתָא. מָר עוּקְבָא שְׁכִיב לֵיהּ בַּר חֲמוּהּ, סָבַר לְמֵיתַב עֲלֵיהּ שִׁבְעָה וּשְׁלֹשִׁים. עָל רַב הוּנָא לְגַבֵּיהּ, אַשְׁכְּחֵיהּ. אֲמַר לֵיהּ: צוּדָנִיָּיתָא בָּעֵית לְמֵיכַל? לֹא אָמְרוּ לִכְבוֹד אִשְׁתּוֹ [י]אֶלָּא חָמִיו וַחֲמוֹתוֹ. דְּתַנְיָא: מִי שֶׁמֵּת חָמִיו אוֹ חֲמוֹתוֹ — [כ]אֵינוֹ רַשַּׁאי לָכוֹף אֶת אִשְׁתּוֹ לִהְיוֹת כּוֹחֶלֶת וְלִהְיוֹת פּוֹקֶסֶת. אֶלָּא כּוֹפֶה מִטָּתוֹ, וְנוֹהֵג עִמָּהּ אֲבֵילוּת. וְכֵן הִיא שֶׁמֵּת חָמִיהָ אוֹ חֲמוֹתָהּ — אֵינָהּ רַשָּׁאָה לִהְיוֹת כּוֹחֶלֶת וְלִהְיוֹת פּוֹקֶסֶת, אֶלָּא כּוֹפָה מִטָּתָהּ וְנוֹהֶגֶת עִמּוֹ אֲבֵילוּת. וְתַנְיָא אִידָךְ: *אַף עַל פִּי שֶׁאָמְרוּ אֵינוֹ רַשַּׁאי לָכוֹף אֶת אִשְׁתּוֹ לִהְיוֹת כּוֹחֶלֶת וְלִהְיוֹת פּוֹקֶסֶת, בֶּאֱמֶת אָמְרוּ: מוֹזֶגֶת לוֹ אֶת הַכּוֹס, וּמַצַּעַת לוֹ מִטָּה, וּמַרְחֶצֶת לוֹ פָּנָיו יָדָיו וְרַגְלָיו. קַשְׁיָין אַהֲדָדֵי! אֶלָּא לָאו שְׁמַע מִינַּהּ: כָּאן — בְּחָמִיו וַחֲמוֹתוֹ, כָּאן — בִּשְׁאָר קְרוֹבִים, שְׁמַע מִינַּהּ. תַּנְיָא נַמִּי הָכִי: לֹא אָמְרוּ לִכְבוֹד אִשְׁתּוֹ — אֶלָּא חָמִיו וַחֲמוֹתוֹ בִּלְבַד. אַמֵּימָר שְׁכֵיב לֵיהּ בַּר בְּרֵיהּ, קָרַע עִילָּוֵיהּ. אֲתָא בְּרֵיהּ — קָרַע בְּאַפֵּיהּ, אִידְּכַר דִּמְיוּשָּׁב קָרַע — קָם קָרַע מְעוּמָּד. אֲמַר לֵיהּ רַב אָשֵׁי לְאַמֵּימָר: קְרִיעָה [ל]דִּמְעוּמָּד *) מְנָלַן? דִּכְתִיב: °"וַיָּקָם אִיּוֹב וַיִּקְרַע אֶת מְעִילוֹ". אֶלָּא

*) [עי' תוספות סנהדרין ס. ד"ה אתיא וכו' מה שהניחו סוגי' דהכא בתימה]

רש"י

א"ל **אימא קיימת**. בלשון שאלה הוא. כלומר,(א) שאתה שואל על אבי — שאל על אמי, שאף היא אחותך: **א"ל**. ר' חייא: ואמך אחותי קיימת היא? **א"ל**. רב: אבא קיים, עדיין לא השכתיך עליו, וממילא הבין. ויש אומרים: בניחותא היה רב משיבו על מי שאינו שואל, כדי שיבין מן הכלל. וקשה בעיני לומר שרב יוציא דבר שקר מפיו: **חלוץ מנעלי**. להתאבל על אחי ואחותי: **והולך** כלי אחרי לבית המרחץ. ללמד הלכה(ב) נתכוין, שאין שמועה רחוקה לאחר שלשים נוהגת אלא יום אחד, ומקצת היום ככולו: **למוצאי הרגל** נעשית רחוקה. דהוי שלשים יום: **אינה נוהגת אלא יום אחד**. אע"פ דכי שמע עדיין היתה קרובה — עולה הרגל להשלים שלשים, דהוי שמועה רחוקה: **אינו קורע**. עכשיו, דנוהג יום אחד לשמועה רחוקה: **היינו דליכא אבילות שבעה**. כלומר, משום דליכא שבעה אינו קורע: **קורע והולך**. אחר שבעה, אע"ג דליכא שבעה: **אבל מתאבל עליהן**. על אותן קרובים: **אחיו מאמו**. שלא מאביו, דקרא משמע מאביו שלא מאמו: **אחותו נשואה בין מאביו בין מאמו**. דבקרא לא אשכחן אלא בבתולה: **על שניים שלהן**. אבי אביו, ועל בן בנו, ועל בן בתו, ועל בן אחותו: **כל שמתאבל עליו מתאבל עמו**. כלומר, מתאבל עם אביו כשהוא מתאבל על אב שלו — נמצא זה מתאבל על אבי אביו. וכן כל שמתאבל עליו, כגון שמתאבל על בנו — מתאבל עמו, כלומר מתאבל עם בנו כשהוא מתאבל (ג)פי' על בן שלו, ונמצא זה מתאבל על בן בנו: **היינו תנא קמא**. של רבי שמעון: **עמו בבית**. דתנא קמא לא בעי שיהא אביו או (בן) בנו עמו בבית ויושב עמו, וחכמים בעו עמו בבית: **כי האי**. ענין דא"ל רב לר' חייא וכו': **באפה**. דאיתתך, כשהיא אבילה. דהאי נמי כל שמתאבל עליו, כגון אשתו — מתאבל עמו בפניו: **צידונייתא**. סעודות דאבל: **קשיין אהדדי**. דהכא קתני: מצעת לו מטתו, והכא קתני: כופה מטתו: **בשאר קרובי אשתו**. מצעת לו מטתו: **אתא בריה**. הדר אמימר קרע באפיה דבריה: **קם קרע**. פעם שלישית: אודייני

תוספות

עולה לו. פירוש הרגל עולה לו למנין שאינו נוהג אלא יום אחד: **קורע** או אינו קורע. דוקא כענין זה מיבעי ליה, לפי שהיה חייב לקרוע בשעת שמועה. אבל שמע שמועה רחוקה בחול — אינו קורע כלל, ואפי' על אביו ואמו. וכן קאמר נמי בסמוך: כי תניא ההיא — בכבוד אביו ואמו. והכי משמע לעיל דלא מצינו לר' חייא שקרע, אע"פ שהיה אביו ואמו לגירסת ר"ת. וא"ת: אי מהא משמע דאינו קורע על אביו ואמו, אמאי לא קאמר ש"מ דאינו קורע? יש לומר: דאינו מביא ש"מ כי אם ממה שראינו שעשה, אבל ממה שלא ראינו — אינו מביא ראיה. מכל מקום, מדלא קבעי התלמוד כלל אם רבי חייא קרע — משמע א"צ לקרוע. ובתשובת רבינו זקיני פי': דאינו קורע על שמועה רחוקה אפי' על אביו ואמו. והרי"ן וגם בתוס' הרב מסופק. והא דאמר בסמוך מי שאין לו חלוק וכו' — מיירי כגון שהיה שאול מחבירו, או נתמלא קרעים. ונראה לי שיש לסמוך יותר על ה"ג מרב למח גאון דאין קורעים לאחר ל' יום אלא על אביו ואמו בלבד. וברכת אבלים נחלקו בה"ג אם שמע בשבת, אם חייב לברך ברכת אבלים. דיש מפרשים דנקרא דברים שבצינעא, וי"א: כיון דמברכין בג' או בעשרה — לאו דברים שבצינעא הוא:

ואחותו נשואה בין מאביו בין מאמו. לא מיבעי מאביו, אלא אפי' מאמו נמי:

על שניים שלהם. פי': הנולדים מהן. אבל באחיהם ובנשותיהם — היה מסופק בתוספות הרב בשם רבו. ולא ידענא מאי שנא:

על אבי אביו ועל בן בנו. פירוש בתוספות הרב בשם רבו: דהוא הדין אבי אמו ובת בתו:

באפה נהוג אבילות. פירוש בתוספות: בכל דיני אבלות, נעילת הסנדל ורחיצה וסיכה וכולן, כל זמן שהוא בפניה. ובפ"ק דכתובות (דף ד:) קאמר: עמו בבית. ושמא באפה דוקא, או שמא בכל הבית:

ומרחצת לו פניו ידיו ורגליו. בחמין קאמר, דאילו בצונן — היא נמי מותרת: **אלא** בחמיו וחמותו. והוא הדין היא נוהגת עמו בחמיה וחמותה. והא דקתני לעיל כל שמתאבל עליו מתאבל עמו — בכל שאר קרובים קאמר. אבל אשתו, יש חילוק בין חמיו וחמותו לשאר קרובים:

אתא בריה קרע באפיה. להיות נוהג עמו אבילות. ותימה: כיון דקרע כבר, וכי צריך לקרוע כלל לפני הקרובים? ושמא לאשמועינן דבאפיה נוהג אבילות. והר"א פירש: אתא בריה קרע באפיה, לפי שאמימר קרע מיושב, ואתא בנו להזכירו שהוא טעה לקרוע מיושב, והקריעה זו עשה בנו של אמימר, ועל ידי כך נזכר אמימר, וקרע פעם שניה מעומד: אלא

רבינו חננאל

אחד. ועוד ר' חייא נהג על אביו ועל אמו בשמועה רחוקה יום אחד ולמדנו ממנו ג' דברים. למדנו כי האבל אסור בנעילת הסנדל. וכי שמועה רחוקה אינה נוהגת אלא יום אחד. וכי מקצת היום ככולו תני ר' אדא קמיה דר' יוחנן שמע שמועה קרובה בשבת ולמו"ש נעשה רחוקה עולה לו ואינה נוהגת אלא יום אחד. וכן א"ר יוסי בר אבין שמע שמועה קרובה ברגל ולמוצאי הרגל נעשית רחוקה אינה נוהגת אלא יום אחד כללו של דבר כל יום שמועה שאינו נוהג בו אבלות כאילו עדיין לא שמע. השומע שמועה רחוקה ברגל קורע או אינו קורע ר' מני אמר אינו קורע ר' חנינא אמר קורע ר' מני אמר אינו קורע דכל היכא דליכא עליה אבלות שבעה אינו קורע איני והא תני איסי אבוה דר' זירא מי שאין לו (אלא חלוק אחד) [חלוק לקרוע] ונזדמן לו חלוק בתוך שבעה קורע לאחר שבעה אינו קורע. הנה קורע בתוך שבעה ואע"פ שאינו נוהג אחר הקריעה שבעה. וכי תימא משום דהיא בתוך שבעה ועוד הא תני ר' זירא בתריה בד"א בה' מתי מצוה פי' חמשה מכלל השבעה שהוא מצוה להתאבל עליהם. אבל על אביו ועל אמו קורע והולך. הנה שאין שם אבלות קורע ופרקינן כי תניא היא דר' זירא לכבוד אביו ואמו: ת"ר כל האמור בפרשת כהנים כהן מיטמא להם אבל מתאבל עליהם. ואלו הן אביו ואמו בנו ובתו אחיו ואחותו ואשתו הוסיפו עליהן אחיו ואחותו בתולה מאמו ואחותו נשואה מאביו וכשם שמתאבל עליהן כך מתאבל על שניים שלהם דברי ר"ע ר"ש בן אלעזר אומר אינו מתאבל אלא על [אבי] אביו ועל בן בנו. וחכמים אומרים כל שמתאבל עליו מתאבל עליהן. וקיי"ל כחכמים. ואוקימנא עמו בבית כגון ראובן שמת לו בן נוהג יעקב אביו עמו בבית בלבד. וכי הא דאמר ליה רב לחייא בריה. ורב הונא אמר לרבה בריה חמיך וחמותך שמתו ואשתך מתאבלת עליהן באפה כלומר בבית עמה נהוג אבלות שלא בפניה לא תנהוג כלל מפני כבוד אשתו א"ל רב הונא למר עוקבא לא אמרו לכבוד אשתו אלא חמיו וחמותו בלבד ותניא כוותיה וכדתניא מי שמת חמיו או חמותו כופה מטתו ונוהג אבלות עמה וכן אם מת חמיה או חמותה אינה רשאה להיות כוחלת ופוקסת אלא כופה מטתה

עין משפט נר מצוה

קיא א מיי' פ"ז מהל' אבל הלכה א סמג עשין דרבנן ב טוש"ע י"ד סימן תב סעיף א:
קיב ב ג מיי' שם הלכה ג וסמג שם טוש"ע י"ד שם סעיף ה:
קיג ד מיי' שם הל' א טוש"ע שם סעי' ד:
קיד ה ו מיי' פ"ח שם הלכה ו טוש"ע י"ד סימן שמ סעיף יח:
קטו ז מיי' שם פ"ב הלכה א סמג שם טוש"ע י"ד סימן שעד סעיף ד:
קטז ח ט י מיי' שם הלכה ד ה טוש"ע שם סעיף ו:
קיז כ מיי' שם הל' ה טוש"ע שם וסימן שפא סעיף ו:
קיח ל מיי' שם פ"ח הלכה א סמג שם טוש"ע י"ד סימן שמ סעיף א:

מסורת הש"ס

[לעיל טו:]
[לעיל טז: פסחים ז. וש"נ]
[שמחות פ"ד]
כתובות ד.
ג"ז שם
ג"ז שם
איוב א

הגהות הב"ח

(א) רש"י ד"ה א"ל אימא כו' כלומר עד שאתה שואל (ב) ד"ה והולך כו' ללמד הלכה לתלמידים נתכוין (ג) ד"ה כל שמתאבל וכו' כשהוא מתאבל על בן של ותיבת פי' נמחק:

גליון הש"ס

גמ' והולך אחרי כלי. עיי לקמן דף כד ע"ב תוספות ד"ה אלא קרוביו: **שם** מי שאין לו חלוק עיין לקמן דף כד ע"ב תוספות ד"ה וכל קרע ובתוספות ד"ה כי תניא:

הגהות מהר"ב רנשבורג

א] גמ' הוספו עליהן אחיו ואחותו הבתולה מאמו ואחותו נשואה כו'. כ"ה עיין ריטב"א:

אֶלָּא מֵעַתָּה — "וְעָמַד וְאָמַר לֹא חָפַצְתִּי לְקַחְתָּהּ" ה"נ? וְהָא תַּנְיָא: בֵּין יוֹשֵׁב בֵּין עוֹמֵד בֵּין מוּטֶּה! א"ל: הָתָם לָא כְּתִיב "וַיַּעֲמֹד וַיֹּאמֶר" הָכָא כְּתִיב "וַיָּקָם וַיִּקְרַע". אָמַר רָמִי בַּר חָמָא: מִנַּיִן לִקְרִיעָה שֶׁהִיא מְעוּמָּד — שֶׁנֶּאֱמַר: "וַיָּקָם אִיּוֹב וַיִּקְרַע". דִּלְמָא מִילְּתָא יְתֵירְתָּא הוּא דַּעֲבַד? דְּאִי לָא תֵּימָא הָכִי — "וַיָּגָז אֶת רֹאשׁוֹ" ה"נ? אֶלָּא מֵהָכָא: "וַיָּקָם הַמֶּלֶךְ וַיִּקְרַע אֶת בְּגָדָיו". וְדִלְמָא מִילְּתָא יְתֵירְתָּא עָבֵיד? דְּאִי לָא תֵּימָא הָכִי — "וַיִּשְׁכַּב אָרְצָה" ה"נ? וְהַתַנְיָא: יָשַׁב עַל גַּבֵּי מִטָּה, עַל גַּבֵּי כִּסֵּא, עַל גַּבֵּי *אוּדְיָינֵי (*גְּדוֹלָה, ע"ג קַרְקַע — מְכוּלָּן) לֹא יָצָא יְדֵי חוֹבָתוֹ, וְא"ר יוֹחָנָן: שֶׁלֹּא קִיֵּים כְּפִיַּית הַמִּטָּה. א"ל: כְּעֵין אַרְצָה. ת"ר, (*וְאֵלּוּ) דְּבָרִים שֶׁאָבֵל אָסוּר בָּהֶן: *אָסוּר בִּמְלָאכָה, *וּבִרְחִיצָה, וּבְסִיכָה, וּבְתַשְׁמִישׁ הַמִּטָּה, וּבִנְעִילַת הַסַּנְדָּל, וְאָסוּר לִקְרוֹת בַּתּוֹרָה וּבַנְּבִיאִים וּבַכְּתוּבִים, וְלִשְׁנוֹת בַּמִּשְׁנָה, בַּמִּדְרָשׁ וּבַהֲלָכוֹת וּבַתַּלְמוּד וּבָאַגָּדוֹת. וְאִם הָיוּ רַבִּים צְרִיכִין לוֹ — אֵינוֹ נִמְנָע. וּמַעֲשֶׂה וּמֵת בְּנוֹ שֶׁל ר' יוֹסֵי בְּצִיפּוֹרִי, וְנִכְנַס לְבֵית הַמִּדְרָשׁ וְדָרַשׁ כָּל הַיּוֹם כּוּלּוֹ. רַבָּה בַּר בַּר חָנָה אִיתְרְעָא בֵּיהּ מִילְּתָא, סָבַר דְּלָא לְמִיפַּק לְפִירְקָא. א"ל ר' חֲנִינָא: אִם הָיוּ רַבִּים צְרִיכִין לוֹ — אֵינוֹ נִמְנָע. סָבַר לְאוֹקְמֵי אָמוֹרָא עֲלֵיהּ — א"ל רַב, תַּנְיָא: וּבִלְבַד שֶׁלֹּא יַעֲמִיד תּוּרְגְּמָן. וְאֶלָּא הֵיכִי עָבֵיד? כִּי הָא דְּתַנְיָא: מַעֲשֶׂה וּמֵת בְּנוֹ שֶׁל ר' יְהוּדָה בַּר אִילְעַאי, וְנִכְנַס לְבֵית הַמִּדְרָשׁ. וְנִכְנַס ר' חֲנַנְיָה בֶּן עֲקַבְיָא וְיָשַׁב בְּצִדּוֹ, וְלָחַשׁ הוּא לְר' חֲנַנְיָה בֶּן עֲקַבְיָא, וְר' חֲנַנְיָה בֶּן עֲקַבְיָא לְתוּרְגְּמָן, וְתוּרְגְּמָן הִשְׁמִיעַ לָרַבִּים. ת"ר: אָבֵל, ג' יָמִים הָרִאשׁוֹנִים אָסוּר לְהָנִיחַ תְּפִילִּין. *מִשְּׁלִישִׁי וְאֵילָךְ, וּשְׁלִישִׁי בִּכְלָל — מוּתָּר לְהָנִיחַ תְּפִילִּין. וְאִם בָּאוּ פָּנִים חֲדָשׁוֹת — אֵינוֹ חוֹלֵץ, דִּבְרֵי ר"א. ר' יְהוֹשֻׁעַ אוֹמֵר: אָבֵל, ב' יָמִים הָרִאשׁוֹנִים — אָסוּר לְהָנִיחַ תְּפִילִּין, *מִשֵּׁנִי וְשֵׁנִי בִּכְלָל — מוּתָּר לְהָנִיחַ תְּפִילִּין, וְאִם בָּאוּ פָּנִים חֲדָשׁוֹת — חוֹלֵץ. אָמַר רַב מַתָּנָה: מַאי טַעְמָא דר"א — דִּכְתִיב: "וַיִּתְּמוּ יְמֵי בְכִי אֵבֶל מֹשֶׁה". אָמַר רַב עֵינָא: מ"ט דְּר' יְהוֹשֻׁעַ — דִּכְתִיב: "וְאַחֲרִיתָהּ כְּיוֹם מָר". וְרַבִּי יְהוֹשֻׁעַ נַמִּי, הָא כְּתִיב: "וַיִּתְּמוּ יְמֵי" וגו'! אָמַר לָךְ: שָׁאנֵי מֹשֶׁה, דְּתַקִּיף אֶבְלֵיהּ. וְר"א נַמִּי, הָא כְּתִיב: "וְאַחֲרִיתָהּ כְּיוֹם מָר"! עִיקַּר מְרִירָא חַד יוֹמָא הוּא. אָמַר עוּלָּא: הֲלָכָה כְּר"א בַּחֲלִיצָה, וַהֲלָכָה כְּר' יְהוֹשֻׁעַ בַּהֲנָחָה. אִיבַּעְיָא לְהוּ: בְּשֵׁנִי לְעוּלָּא, חוֹלֵץ אוֹ אֵינוֹ חוֹלֵץ? ת"ש, אָמַר עוּלָּא: חוֹלֵץ וּמֵנִיחַ אפי' מֵאָה פְּעָמִים. תַּנְיָא נַמִּי הָכִי, יְהוּדָה בֶּן תֵּימָא אוֹמֵר: חוֹלֵץ וּמֵנִיחַ אפי' מֵאָה פְּעָמִים. רָבָא אָמַר: כֵּיוָן שֶׁהֵנִיחַ — שׁוּב אֵינוֹ חוֹלֵץ. וְהָא רָבָא הוּא דְּאָמַר: *הֲלָכָה כְּתַנָּא דִּידַן, דְּאָמַר: שְׁלֹשָׁה — מִצְוָה

רש"י

אוּדְיָינֵי. מַכְתֶּשֶׁת גְּדוֹלָה: מִכּוּלָּם. אָמְרוּ אֲפִי' יָשֵׁן ע"ג קַרְקַע לֹא יָצָא — עַד שֶׁיִּכְפֶּה מִטָּתוֹ וְיֵשֵׁב עָלֶיהָ: כְּעֵין אַרְצָה. כְּלוֹמַר, שֶׁכָּפָה מִטָּתוֹ וְיָשַׁב עָלֶיהָ. וּלְעוֹלָם קְרִיעָה מְעוּמָּד: וְאָסוּר לִקְרוֹת. כִּדְאָמְרִינַן לְעֵיל (דף טו.): מִדְּאָמַר רַחֲמָנָא לִיחֶזְקֵאל: הֵאָנֵק דּוֹם. וְהָא דְּאָמַר (סוכה דף כה.): אָבֵל חַיָּיב בְּכָל הַמִּצְוֹת הָאֲמוּרוֹת בַּתּוֹרָה חוּץ מִן הַתְּפִילִּין — הָתָם שְׁאָר מִצְוֹת בְּעָלְמָא, אֲבָל הָנֵי — אִית בְּהוּ שִׂמְחָה: רַבִּים צְרִיכִים לֵיהּ. לִדְרָשָׁה: סָבַר לְאוֹקְמֵי אֲמוֹרָא עֲלֵיהּ. תּוּרְגְּמָן: וּשְׁלִישִׁי בִּכְלָל. מוּתָּר לְהָנִיחַ תְּפִילִּין. דְּעִיקַּר אֲבֵילוּת אֵינוֹ אֶלָּא ב' יָמִים: וְאִם בָּאוּ פָּנִים חֲדָשׁוֹת. בְּיוֹם ג', אפ"ה אֵינוֹ חוֹלֵץ תְּפִילִּין. אע"ג דְּאִיכָּא לְמֵיחַשׁ דִּלְמָא אָמְרִי [בִּשְׁנֵי] יָמִים הָרִאשׁוֹנִים נַמִּי הֵנִיחַ תְּפִילִּין: רַבִּי יְהוֹשֻׁעַ אוֹמֵר וכו'. דְּעִיקַּר אֲבֵילוּת אֵינוֹ אֶלָּא יוֹם אֶחָד: וְאִם בָּאוּ פָּנִים חֲדָשׁוֹת. בְּיוֹם שֵׁנִי — חוֹלֵץ תְּפִילִּין: מ"ט דר"א. דְּסָבַר עִיקַּר אֲבֵילוּת שְׁנֵי יָמִים: דִּכְתִיב וַיִּתְּמוּ יְמֵי. דְּמַשְׁמַע ב' יָמִים: עִיקַּר מְרִירָא יוֹם אֶחָד. אֲבָל אֲבֵילוּת ב' יָמִים: הֲלָכָה כְּר"א בַּחֲלִיצָה. שֶׁאִם בָּאוּ פָּנִים חֲדָשׁוֹת בְּג' — אֵינוֹ חוֹלֵץ, וַהֲלָכָה כְּרַבִּי יְהוֹשֻׁעַ בַּהֲנָחָה — דְּבַשֵּׁנִי מוּתָּר לְהָנִיחַ תְּפִילִּין: בְּשֵׁנִי לְעוּלָּא חוֹלֵץ. בִּשְׁלִישִׁי קָאָמַר הֲלָכָה כְּר"א דְּאָמַר אֵינוֹ חוֹלֵץ, אֲבָל בַּשֵּׁנִי — לָא יָדַעְנָא אִי חוֹלֵץ אִי לָא: חוֹלֵץ וּמֵנִיחַ. בַּשֵּׁנִי. אֲפִי' מֵאָה פְּעָמִים בַּיּוֹם. וְכִי בָּאוּ פָּנִים חֲדָשׁוֹת — חוֹלֵץ, וְכִי לֵיכָּא פָּנִים חֲדָשׁוֹת — מֵנִיחַ: רָבָא אָמַר כֵּיוָן שֶׁמֵּנִיחַ. בַּשֵּׁנִי, שׁוּב אֵינוֹ חוֹלֵץ לְפָנִים חֲדָשׁוֹת: וְהָאָמַר רָבָא. לְעֵיל (דף כ.) בִּכְפִיַּית הַמִּטָּה, הֲלָכָה כְּתַנָּא דִּידַן דְּאָמַר ג' יָמִים עִיקַּר אֲבֵילוּת. ה"נ — נִבְעֵי ג' יָמִים (א) לְהָנִיחַ תְּפִילִּין:

תוספות

אלא מעתה ועמד ואמר ה"נ. משמע: ועמד ואמר – היינו אפי' מיושב. והא דאמרינן פרק "מצות חליצה" (יבמות דף קו.) בתי עמודי – לכתחילה שמא צריך עמידה מדרבנן. מיהו קשה: ד"ועמדו שני האנשים" (דברים יט) דבעינן עומד! וי"ל: ד"ועמד ואמר" ודאי משמע אפי' מיושב, כמו "ועמדו וקדשו" (לעיל דף יח:) אבל "ועמד" לחוד לא משמע הכי*:

דאי לא תימא הכי וישכב ארצה וכו'. אע"ג ד"ושכב ארצה" כתיב נמי אבל הילד דבת שבע, אע"ג דלא גבי מת כתיב אלא על בנו? ושמא: הואיל והנביא אמר לו "מות ימות" – הרי הוא כמת, ואע"פ שהתפלל עליו שיחיה. וכענין זה אמר בירושלמי: הקב"ה שהיה יודע שעתיד להיות מבול – היה מתאבל על עולמו קודם המבול. ובתוס' הרב הקשה, כי הסוגיא משונה: בתחילה אומר מלתא יתירתא עבד, דאי לא תימא הכי, והדר מקשה דלא יצא ידי חובתו! וי"ל דהכי פי': מלתא יתירתא, וה"נ כפה מטתו ושכב ע"ג קרקע, וא"כ עבד מלתא יתירתא. דליכא למימר ושכב – היינו כפיית המטה – דהא לא יצא ידי חובתו מכפיית המטה. א"ל: כעין, וליכא שום יתור. וניחא ליה לשנויי הכי מלומר שהיה מלתא יתירתא, ולהוכיח קריעה מכפיית המטה:

אלו דברים שאבל אסור בהן. הכא לא חשיב דברים שמצווה עליהן כגון כפיית המטה ועטיפת הראש, דלא חשיב אלא מילי דאסור בהן. תפילין ושאילת שלום לא חשיב, דאין זה כל ימי האבל, כדאמר לקמן. תכבוסת לא חשיב – דהויא בכלל רחילה. אע"ג דלעיל (דף טו.) מייתי תרי קראי לרחילה ולתכבוסת. אבל הני דלא נוהגים כל השבוע – לא. לאפוקי מפי' הר"א שפירש שרבינו שמואל היה מתיר לאבל לעשות מלאכה אחר ג' ימים. ומה שאין נוהגין עתה לעשות עטיפת הראש וכפיית המטה – סמכינן אהא דאמרינן בירושלמי: אכסנאי אינו חייב בכפיית המטה, דלא לימרון חרש הוא. פי': מכשף. וכמו כן, אנו בין הנכרים, ויש בינינו עבדים ושפחות. ועוד יש ליתן טעם בכפיית המטה: לפי שמטות שלנו אין יכולין לשכב בנחת מלד זה כמו מלד זה, ואין ניכרת הכפייה, דיש להן ד' קונדיסים מלמעלה כעין רגלים. וכדאמרינן לקמן: דרגש אין צריך לכפותו. ועוד יש ליתן טעם בעטיפת הראש – שלא היה מביא כי אם לידי שחוק •ענין עטיפת ישמעאלים:

ואסור לקרות בתורה. בתשובת רבינו יצחק זקני כתב כי רבינו יעקב היה אוסר בימי אבלו באיוב ובקינות ובדברים הרעים שבירמיה, מדלא תני ליה בשמעתין, כמו ט' באב שילהי תענית (דף ל.). ובימי זקנותו חזר והתיר. ובירושלמי אמר: אבל שונה במקום שאינו רגיל. משמע ששונה כמו בט' באב, שאומר בפרק בתרא דתענית (שם): אבל קורא במקום שאינו רגיל. וה"ק התם: כל מצות הנוהגות באבל – נוהגות בט' באב, ואסור לקרות בתורה כו' אבל קורא במקום שאינו רגיל, וקורא באיוב וקינות וכו'. משמע לכאורה דאבל וט' באב שוין, כדקאמר בירושלמי. ומיהו, אבל שונה במקום שאינו רגיל, משמע דהא דוקא שרי, ולא באיוב ובקינות ובירמיה. ומה שהביא רבי יצחק ראיה לאסור מדקאמר לעיל (ד' טו.) אסור בדברי תורה, שנאמר "האנק דום" ומשמע הכל – אין נ"ל ראייה, דלא קאמר אלא מדבר המשמחו. כדאמר בתענית (ד' ל.) משום שנאמר "פקודי ה' ישרים משמחי לב". תדע דכולהו לאו דוקא, דהא קאמר אסור בתפילין, שנאמר "פארך חבוש עליך" ואינו אסור כל ימי אבלו:

משלישי ואילך. ושלישי חשבינן [מקצתו] ככולו. ומדרבנן, דהא לא מייתי קרא אלא לשני ימים, דכתיב "ויתמו ימי בכי אבל משה" הר"א. והאי "ויתמו" – בתפילין. וכן "ואחריתה כיום מר" – טפי מכל שאר מילי, דכל שעה שהוא מר נפש מתעולל בעפר ואין זה פאר, כדפירש בקונטרס בכתובות (ד' ו:) ריב"א. ובט' באב היה אומר ר' יצחק זקני דשרי, כמו בשלישי דשרי:

חולץ ומניח אפילו מאה פעמים. פי': חולץ בפנים חדשות, ומניח כשילכו. וכן כל שעה שילכו, מאה פעמים ביום. וטעמיה משום בין לר"א בין לרבי יהושע בפנים חדשות – אסור, לר"א – להניח אסור, ולרבי יהושע – אפי' חולץ:

מכאן

עין משפט נר מצוה

קיט א מיי' פ"ד מהל' יבום וחליצה הל' ו סמג עשין נג טוש"ע אה"ע סי' קסט סעי' סד:

קכ ב מיי' פ"ה שם הלכה יח:

[וע"ע תוס' יבמות קג. ד"ה בין ותוס' שבועות ל. ד"ה מצוה ותוספות זבחים טז. ד"ה מיושב]

קכא ג מיי' שם הל' א סמג עשין דרבנן ג טוש"ע י"ד סימן שפ סעיף א:

קכב ד ה ו ז מיי' שם הלכה טז סמג שם טוש"ע שם וסימן שפד סעיף א:

[גירסת הרי"ף (דף רלה:) גדולה מכולן אמרו אפילו על גבי קרקע לא יצא כו']

קכג ח מיי' שם פ"ד הלכה ט טוש"ע שם סימן שפח סעיף א:

רבינו חננאל

מטתה ונוהגת עמו אבלות. אמימר שכיב ליה בר ברא קרע עליה *) א"ל קרעתי מעומד קם קרע מעומד א"ל רב אשי ומנ"ל דבעינן קריעה מעומד א"ל דכתיב ויקם איוב ויקרע אי הכי בענין חליצה דכתיב ועמד ואמר לא חפצתי הכי נמי דמעומד. והתניא בין עומד בין יושב בין מוטה חליצתה כשרה אלא מהכא ויקם המלך ויקרע את בגדיו ודלמא קריעה מעומד מלתא יתירתא הוא דעבד כמה דעבד בשכיבתו ארצה דלא הוה צריך דתניא ישן על גבי מטה על גבי כסא ע"ג אודייני גדולה מכולן אפילו על גבי קרקע לא יצא וא"ר יוחנן שלא (יצא) קיים כפיית המטה א"ל מאי וישכב ארצה לאו ארצה ממש הוא אלא כעין ארצה כדמפרש בירוש' ר' יוחנן אמר וישבו אתו לארץ אינו כתוב על הארץ אלא לארץ בדבר הסמוך לארץ מיכן שהיו ישינין על מטות כפויות וכיון שישן על מטה כפויה ניעור בלילה ונזכר שהוא אבל: אלו דברים שאבל אסור בהן במלאכה ברחיצה וסיכה ובנעילת הסנדל ובתשמיש המטה ואסור לקרות בתורה בנביאים ובכתובים ולשנות במשנה ובמדרש ובתלמוד בהלכות ובאגדות ואם היו רבים צריכין לו אינו נמנע. ומעשה ומת בנו של ר' יוסי בצפורי ובתו של ר' בבית שערים ויצאו ודרשו כל היום ואסיקנא ובלבד שלא יעמיד המתורגמן אלא יושב לו אחר בצידו של אבל ולוחש לו והוא משמיע לתורגמן והתורגמן משמיע לרבים. גרסינן בפרק יש בכור לנחלה מת הבן ביום שלשים כיום שלפניו פי' כיום ל"א וחייב לתת ה' סלעים לכהן. ר' עקיבא אומר אם נתן לא יטול ואם לא נתן לא יתן. אמר רב אשי הכל מודים לענין אבלות דיום שלשים כיום שלפניו דמי וחשוב כיום שלפניו ובשלשים ואחד שמע והנה **) היא שמועה רחוקה ואינו נוהג אלא יום אחד בלבד כשמואל דאמר הלכה כדברי המיקל באבל: ת"ר אבל שלשה ימים הראשונים אסור להניח תפילין משלישי ושלישי בכלל מניח ואם באו פנים חדשות אינו חולץ דברי רבי אליעזר ורבי יהושע אומר משני ושני בכלל מניח ואם באו פנים חדשות חולץ. אמר עולא הלכתא כרבי אליעזר בחליצה שאם באו פנים חדשות משלישי ואילך אינו חולץ ***) והלכתא כרבא דאמר כיון שהניח אינו חולץ כר' יהושע בהנחה שמיום שני מניח מ"ט דר' אלעזר דכתיב ויתמו

*) אולי צ"ל אמר לא קרעתי מעומד קם וכו'. **) דברי רבינו בכאן הובא ברי"ף כאן בשם איכא מ"ד ועי' היטב מש"כ על דברי רבינו בזה. ***) נראה דצ"ל משלישי ואילך אינו חולץ וכר"י בהנחה שמיום שני מניח והלכתא כרבא דאמר כיון שהניח שוב אינו חולץ.

מסורת הש"ס

יבמות קג.

לקמן כז. ע"ש

[עי' תוס' ב"ב קמב. ד"ה אודייני]

[צ"ל אלו]

[מס' שמחות פ"ו]

[עי' בהר"ן דסוכה (דף רמב.) ד"ה אבל חייב וכו' ותבין למה נקט בהך לישנא]

לעיל כ.

תורה אור

דברים כה; איוב א; שם; שמואל ב יג; שם; דברים לד; עמוס ח

הגהות הב"ח

(א) רש"י ד"ה והאמר רבא כו' נבעי ג' ימים שלא להניח תפילין:

גליון הש"ס

גמ' ודלמא מילתא יתירתא. עיין לקמן דף כו ע"א תד"ה משכם: תום' ד"ה אלו דברים וכו' ענין עטיפת ישמעאלים. עי' לקמן דף כד ע"א תוס' ד"ה ושמואל לטעמיה:

קכד א מיי' פ"ה מהל' אבל הלכה ח סמג עשין דרבנן ב טוש"ע י"ד סימן שפ סעיף ב:
קכה ב מיי' שם פ"ז הלכה ה טוש"ע שם סימן שלג סעיף א:
קכו ג מיי' שם פ"ה הלכה כ טוש"ע שם סימן שפה סעיף א:
קכז ד טוש"ע שם בהג"ה:
קכח ה ו טוש"ע שם סעיף ב:
קכט ז ח ט י מיי' שם הלכה כ וטוש"ע שם סעיף א:
קל כ מיי' שם טוש"ע שם סעיף ב:
קלא ל טוש"ע שם:
קלב מ נ מיי' שם פ"ז הלכה ד סמג עשין דרבנן ב טוש"ע שם סימן שעה סעיף א:

רבינו חננאל

ויתמו ימי בכי אבל משה מיעוט ימי אבל שנים ור' יהושע אמר ואחריתה כיום מר יומא קמא בלבד: ת"ר אבל שלשה ימים הראשונים אסור בעשיית מלאכה ואפילו עני המתפרנס מן הצדקה מיכן ואילך עושה בצנעא בתוך ביתו ואשה טווה בפלך בתוך ביתה: ירושלמי תבא מאירה לשכיניו שהצריכוהו לאבל לעשות ולאכול: ת"ר ג' ימים הראשונים אסור לילך לבית האבל מיכן ואילך הולך כדרכו ואינו יושב במקום המנחמין אלא במקום המתנחמין. ג' ימים הראשונים אסור בשאילת שלום. והא כשמתו בני ר"ע באו כל ישראל והספידום הספד גדול ובשעת פטירתן עמד ר' עקיבא על ספסל גדול ואמר אחינו בית ישראל שמעו אפילו בנים חתנים קבר מנוחם הוא בשביל כבוד שעשיתם וכמה עקיבא בשוק אלא כך אמרתם תורת אלהיו בקרבו לא תמעד אשוריו וכ"ש ששכרכם כפול לכו לבתיכם לשלום. ופרקינן כבוד רבים שאני. ומקשינן מיכן ואילך שואל ומשיב כדרכו והתניא המוצא חבירו אבל בתוך שלשים יום מדבר עמו תנחומין ואינו שואל בשלומו לאחר שלשים יום שואל בשלומו ואינו מדבר עמו תנחומין מתה אשתו ונשא אשה אחרת כו' הנה אין שואלין אפילו לאחר ז' בשלומו ופריק רב אידי בר אבין אחרים אין שואלין בשלומו שהוא אינו שרוי בשלום אבל

תוספות

מכאן ואילך עושה בצינעא בתוך ביתו. פי' בתוספת הרב: במתפרנס מן הצדקה קאי והכי משמע לעיל. דקאמר לעיל (ד' יט:): הקובר מתו ג' ימים קודם הרגל מונה ה' ימים אחר הרגל ומלאכתו נעשית ע"י אחרים. משמע דהאבל אסור כל ז' והתם נמי לא שרינן לעצמו שיהא עושה מלאכה. וה"נ תניא במסכת שמחות (פ"ה): אבל כל ז' ימים, אסור בעשיית מלאכה הוא ובניו ובנותיו ועבדיו ושפחותיו ובהמתו, כשם שהוא אסור לעשות לו – כך אחרים אסורים לעשות לו. פי': חוץ מזיתיו הפוכים ומלאכת האבד. מיום ג' ואילך עושה מלאכה, דוקא במי שמתפרנס מן הצדקה ובצינעא, אבל אמרו חכמים תבא מארה לשכיניו כו'. בר קפרא אומר: אף בשלישי לא יעשה כך. הביא בתוס' הרב. ולכאורה נראה דכיון דילפינן (לעיל דף כ.) מ"והפכתי חגיכם לאבל" מה חג ז', לענין מלאכה איירי. וגם הר"א מסופק דלמא אעני דוקא קאי. אבל בשם רבינו שמואל אמר: בכל אבלים קאי, מדלא קתני מכאן ואילך עושה עני בצינעא ולא כדפרישית:

מכאן ואילך הולך. פי' בתוספת הרב: ועל זה סומכים שבאים בבהכ"נ בט' באב, ואיני יודע אם הוא מנהג טוב. ומדבריו מצינו למדין שחושב ט' באב כמו לאחר שלשה, ונפקא מינה לענין תפילין, כדפי' לעיל:

מדבר עמו תנחומין ואינו שואל. וקשיא למ"ד מכאן ואילך שואל ומשיב:

מתה אשתו ונשא אשה אחרת. משמע בתוך ל' יום דאי לאחר ל' יום היכי קאמר אינו רשאי ליכנס לביתו לדבר עמו תנחומין הא בשאר מתים נמי אמרו אינו מדבר עמו תנחומין וצריך לאוקמי באין לו בנים לפי' ר"ת שמתיר לישא אשה אחר שבעה א"נ בהניחה לו בנים קטנים שמותר לישא מיד ולבעול אחר ל' יום לפירוש רבינו יצחק והאריך בתוספות פרק קמא דכתובות (דף ד. ושם בד"ה אבל איפכא) ובליקוטין כתוב בתשובה:

מקום קרוב. פירשו בהלכות גדולות דהיינו י' פרסאות:

אפילו בא ביום שביעי ממקום קרוב. וא"ת: והא מקצת היום ככולו! וי"ל: א] כגון שלא עמדו עדיין מנחמין מאצלן. ויש נמי בפ"ק דכתובות (דף ח:): ברכת אבלים בעשרה כל ז', ומסתמא היינו ביום. א"נ י"ל: מקצת היום ככולו לא הוי בלילה לענין שום דבר, כדאמרינן במגילה בפ"ב (דף כ.) דשימור לילה לאו שימור הוא, לענין שבעה נקיים:

הלך

גמרא

מִצְוָה שָׁאנֵי. ת"ר: אאָבֵל, ג' יָמִים הָרִאשׁוֹנִים – אָסוּר בִּמְלָאכָה. וַאֲפִילּוּ עָנִי הַמִּתְפַּרְנֵס מִן הַצְּדָקָה. מִכָּאן וְאֵילָךְ – עוֹשֶׂה בְּצִינְעָא בְּתוֹךְ בֵּיתוֹ, וְהָאִשָּׁה טוֹוָה בְּפֶלֶךְ בְּתוֹךְ בֵּיתָהּ. בת"ר: אָבֵל, ג' יָמִים הָרִאשׁוֹנִים – אֵינוֹ הוֹלֵךְ לְבֵית הָאָבֵל, מִכָּאן וְאֵילָךְ – הוֹלֵךְ, וְאֵינוֹ יוֹשֵׁב בִּמְקוֹם הַמְנַחֲמִין אֶלָּא בִּמְקוֹם הַמִּתְנַחֲמִין. גתָּנוּ רַבָּנַן: אָבֵל, ג' יָמִים הָרִאשׁוֹנִים – אָסוּר בִּשְׁאִילַת שָׁלוֹם, מִשְּׁלֹשָׁה וְעַד שִׁבְעָה – מֵשִׁיב וְאֵינוֹ שׁוֹאֵל, מִכָּאן וְאֵילָךְ – שׁוֹאֵל וּמֵשִׁיב כְּדַרְכּוֹ. שְׁלֹשָׁה יָמִים הָרִאשׁוֹנִים אָסוּר בִּשְׁאִילַת שָׁלוֹם? וְהָתַנְיָא: *מַעֲשֶׂה וּמֵתוּ בָּנָיו שֶׁל ר"ע, נִכְנְסוּ כָּל יִשְׂרָאֵל וְהִסְפִּידוּם הֶסְפֵּד גָּדוֹל. בִּשְׁעַת פְּטִירָתָן עָמַד ר"ע עַל סַפְסָל גָּדוֹל וְאָמַר: אַחֵינוּ בֵּית יִשְׂרָאֵל שִׁמְעוּ! אֲפִי' שְׁנֵי בָּנִים חֲתָנִים – מְנוּחָם הוּא בִּשְׁבִיל כָּבוֹד שֶׁעֲשִׂיתֶם. וְאִם בִּשְׁבִיל עֲקִיבָא בָּאתֶם – הֲרֵי כַּמָּה עֲקִיבָא בַּשּׁוּק. אֶלָּא כָּךְ אֲמַרְתֶּם: °"תּוֹרַת אֱלֹהָיו בְּלִבּוֹ" וְכ"ש שֶׁשְּׂכַרְכֶם כָּפוּל, לְכוּ לְבָתֵּיכֶם לְשָׁלוֹם. כְּבוֹד רַבִּים שָׁאנֵי. מג' וְעַד ז' – מֵשִׁיב וְאֵינוֹ שׁוֹאֵל, מִכָּאן וְאֵילָךְ – שׁוֹאֵל וּמֵשִׁיב כְּדַרְכּוֹ. וּרְמִינְהוּ: *הַמּוֹצֵא אֶת חֲבֵירוֹ אָבֵל, בְּתוֹךְ ל' יוֹם – מְדַבֵּר עִמּוֹ תַּנְחוּמִין וְאֵינוֹ שׁוֹאֵל בִּשְׁלוֹמוֹ, לְאַחַר ל' יוֹם – שׁוֹאֵל בִּשְׁלוֹמוֹ וְאֵינוֹ מְדַבֵּר עִמּוֹ תַּנְחוּמִין. מֵתָה אִשְׁתּוֹ וְנָשָׂא אִשָּׁה אַחֶרֶת – אֵינוֹ רַשַּׁאי לִיכָּנֵס לְבֵיתוֹ לְדַבֵּר עִמּוֹ תַּנְחוּמִין. מְצָאוֹ בַּשּׁוּק – אוֹמֵר לוֹ בְּשָׂפָה רָפָה וּבְכוֹבֶד רֹאשׁ! אָמַר רַב אִידִי בַּר אָבִין: הוּא שׁוֹאֵל בִּשְׁלוֹם אֲחֵרִים – שֶׁאֲחֵרִים שְׁרוּיִין בְּשָׁלוֹם, אֲחֵרִים אֵין שׁוֹאֲלִין בִּשְׁלוֹמוֹ – שֶׁהוּא אֵינוֹ שָׁרוּי בְּשָׁלוֹם. וְהָא מִדְּקָתָנֵי מֵשִׁיב – מִכְּלָל דְּשָׁיְילִינַן לֵיהּ! דְּלָא יָדְעִי. אִי הָכִי, הָתָם נַמִּי! הָתָם מוֹדַע לְהוּ, וְלָא מְהַדַּר לְהוּ. הָכָא – לָא צָרִיךְ לְאוֹדוֹעִינְהוּ. וּרְמִינְהוּ: *הַמּוֹצֵא אֶת חֲבֵירוֹ אָבֵל, בְּתוֹךְ י"ב חֹדֶשׁ – מְדַבֵּר עִמּוֹ תַּנְחוּמִין וְאֵינוֹ שׁוֹאֵל בִּשְׁלוֹמוֹ, לְאַחַר י"ב חֹדֶשׁ – שׁוֹאֵל בִּשְׁלוֹמוֹ וְאֵינוֹ מְדַבֵּר עִמּוֹ תַּנְחוּמִין, אֲבָל מְדַבֵּר עִמּוֹ מִן הַצַּד. א"ר מֵאִיר: הַמּוֹצֵא אֶת חֲבֵירוֹ אָבֵל לְאַחַר י"ב חֹדֶשׁ, וּמְדַבֵּר עִמּוֹ תַּנְחוּמִין, לְמָה הוּא דּוֹמֶה – לְאָדָם שֶׁנִּשְׁבְּרָה רַגְלוֹ וְחָיְתָה, מְצָאוֹ רוֹפֵא וְאָמַר לוֹ: כַּלֵּךְ אֶצְלִי, שֶׁאֲנִי שׁוֹבְרָהּ וְאֶרְפָּאֶנָּה, כְּדֵי שֶׁתֵּדַע שֶׁסַּמְמָנִין שֶׁלִּי יָפִין. לָא קַשְׁיָא: הָא – בְּאָבִיו וְאִמּוֹ, הָא – בִּשְׁאָר קְרוֹבִים. הָתָם נַמִּי יְדַבֵּר עִמּוֹ תַּנְחוּמִין מִן הַצַּד! אִין, ה"נ. וּמַאי אֵינוֹ מְדַבֵּר עִמּוֹ תַּנְחוּמִין – כְּדַרְכּוֹ, אֲבָל מְדַבֵּר עִמּוֹ מִן הַצַּד. *ת"ר: אָבֵל, ג' יָמִים הָרִאשׁוֹנִים בָּא מִמָּקוֹם קָרוֹב – מוֹנֶה עִמָּהֶן, בָּא מִמָּקוֹם רָחוֹק – מוֹנֶה לְעַצְמוֹ. מִכָּאן וְאֵילָךְ, אֲפִי' בָּא מִמָּקוֹם קָרוֹב – מוֹנֶה לְעַצְמוֹ. ר"ש אוֹמֵר: אֲפִי' בָּא בַּיּוֹם הַשְּׁבִיעִי מִמָּקוֹם קָרוֹב – מוֹנֶה עִמָּהֶן. אָמַר מָר: ג' יָמִים הָרִאשׁוֹנִים, בָּא מִמָּקוֹם קָרוֹב – מוֹנֶה עִמָּהֶן. א"ר חִיָּיא בַּר אַבָּא א"ר יוֹחָנָן: וְהוּא שֶׁיֵּשׁ גְּדוֹל הַבַּיִת בַּבַּיִת. אִיבַּעְיָא לְהוּ:

הָלַךְ

תורה אור

תהלים לז

עיין שמחות פ"ח

[שמחות פי"ד]

רש"י

מִצְוָה שָׁאנֵי. כְּלוֹמַר: הוֹאִיל וּמִצְוָה לְהָנִיחַ תְּפִילִּין – מָצֵי לְהָנִיחַ לְאַלְתַּר בְּשֵׁנִי: אִשָּׁה. אֲבֵילָה, טוֹוָה בְּפֶלֶךְ: אֶלָּא בִּמְקוֹם הַמִּתְנַחֲמִין. סָמוּךְ לָאֲבֵלִים: אֲפִי' ב' בָּנִים חֲתָנִים. קָבַרְתִּי, מְנוּחָם אֲנִי מֵרוֹב כָּבוֹד שֶׁעֲשִׂיתֶם לִי: וְאִם בִּשְׁבִיל עֲקִיבָא בָּאתֶם הֲרֵי כַּמָּה עֲקִיבָא בַּשּׁוּק. שֶׁלֹּא הֲלַכְתֶּם לְנַחֲמָן: כ"ש שֶׁשְּׂכַרְכֶם כָּפוּל. שֶׁלִּכְבוֹד הַתּוֹרָה בָּאתֶם: לְכוּ לְבָתֵּיכֶם לְשָׁלוֹם. הֲרֵי שָׁאַל בִּשְׁלוֹמָן: וּרְמִינְהוּ. דִּבְתוֹךְ ל' יוֹם אֵינוֹ שׁוֹאֵל: וְנָשָׂא אִשָּׁה. בְּתוֹךְ שְׁלֹשִׁים יוֹם, כְּגוֹן שֶׁאֵין לוֹ בָּנִים, כִּדְלְקַמָּן: אֵינוֹ רַשַּׁאי לִיכָּנֵס לְבֵיתוֹ. לְנַחֲמוֹ, מִשּׁוּם חֲלִישַׁת דַּעַת דְּאִשָּׁה אַחֲרוֹנָה. קָתָנֵי מִיהַת: בְּתוֹךְ ל' יוֹם אֵינוֹ שׁוֹאֵל בִּשְׁלוֹמוֹ. כ"ש שֶׁהָאָבֵל עַצְמוֹ אֵינוֹ שׁוֹאֵל בִּשְׁלוֹמוֹ שֶׁל זֶה. וּלְעֵיל קָתָנֵי: מִשִּׁבְעָה וְאֵילָךְ מֵשִׁיב וְשׁוֹאֵל כְּדַרְכּוֹ: אָמַר רַב אִידִי הוּא שׁוֹאֵל בִּשְׁלוֹם אֲחֵרִים. כְּלוֹמַר: תָּרִיץ הָא דְּתָנֵי מִכָּאן וְאֵילָךְ שׁוֹאֵל כְּדַרְכּוֹ – בְּתוֹךְ שְׁלֹשִׁים יוֹם דְּהוּא שׁוֹאֵל בִּשְׁלוֹם אֲחֵרִים, שֶׁהֵן שְׁרוּיִין בְּשָׁלוֹם וְהָא דְּקָתָנֵי בְּתוֹךְ ל' יוֹם אֵינוֹ שׁוֹאֵל בִּשְׁלוֹמוֹ – אֵין אֲחֵרִים שׁוֹאֲלִין בִּשְׁלוֹמוֹ: מִכְּלָל דְּשָׁיְילֵי. בְּתוֹךְ ל' יוֹם, וְקַשְׁיָא לְמַאן דְּתָנֵי בְּתוֹךְ ל' יוֹם אֵינוֹ שׁוֹאֵל: דְּלָא יָדְעִי. כְּלוֹמַר, הָא דְּתָנֵי דְּמֵשִׁיב – לְהָנֵי דְּשָׁאֲלֵי לֵיהּ וְלָא יָדְעִי דְּאָבֵל הוּא, אֲבָל מַאן דְּיָדַע דְּאָבֵל הוּא – לָא שָׁאֵיל לֵיהּ בְּתוֹךְ ל' יוֹם: אִי הָכִי. דְּאוֹקְמַתְּ לָהּ בְּלָא יָדְעִי, אֲפִי' ג' יָמִים נַמִּי מֵשִׁיב (לְמַאן דְּשָׁאֵיל לֵיהּ (א) וְאָמַר דְּאָבֵל הוּא) לְמַאן דְּלָא יָדַע וְשָׁאֵיל לֵיהּ בְּתוֹךְ ג' יָמִים: הָתָם מוֹדַע לְהוּ. הָא דְּקָתָנֵי כָּל ג' יָמִים אָסוּר בִּשְׁאִילַת שָׁלוֹם – אֲבָל מוֹדַע לְהוּ דְּאָבֵל הוּא, וְלָא מַהְדַּר לְהוּ: הָכָא. לְאַחַר ג' לָא צָרִיךְ לְאוֹדוֹעִינְהוּ לְמַאן דְּלָא יָדְעִי דְּאָבֵל הוּא, אֶלָּא מֵשִׁיב: וּרְמִינְהוּ בְּתוֹךְ י"ב חֹדֶשׁ אֵינוֹ שׁוֹאֵל בִּשְׁלוֹמוֹ. וְקָשֶׁה לְהָךְ דְּתָנֵי לְאַחַר שְׁלֹשִׁים יוֹם שׁוֹאֵל בִּשְׁלוֹמוֹ: מִן הַצַּד. שֶׁאוֹמֵר לוֹ "תִּתְנַחֵם", וְאֵינוֹ מַזְכִּיר שֵׁם הַמֵּת: הָא בְּאָבֵל עַל אָבִיו וְעַל אִמּוֹ. אֵינוֹ שׁוֹאֵל בִּשְׁלוֹמוֹ עַד י"ב חֹדֶשׁ: הָא בִּשְׁאָר קְרוֹבִים. שׁוֹאֵל בִּשְׁלוֹמוֹ לְאַחַר ל' יוֹם: הָתָם נַמִּי. שְׁלֹשִׁים, דְּמוֹקְמַתְּ לֵיהּ בִּשְׁאָר קְרוֹבִים: יְדַבֵּר עִמּוֹ תַּנְחוּמִין מִן הַצַּד. לְאַחַר ל', כִּי הֵיכִי דִּבְאָבִיו וְאִמּוֹ מְדַבֵּר עִמּוֹ תַּנְחוּמִין מִן הַצַּד לְאַחַר י"ב חֹדֶשׁ. וְאַמַּאי קָתָנֵי לְאַחַר ל' אֵינוֹ מְדַבֵּר עִמּוֹ תַּנְחוּמִים כְּלָל? ה"נ. וּמַאי לְאַחַר ל' אֵינוֹ מְדַבֵּר עִמּוֹ תַּנְחוּמִים – כְּדַרְכּוֹ: מוֹנֶה עִמָּהֶן. עִם הָאֲבֵלִים שֶׁבְּאוֹתוֹ מָקוֹם. הוֹאִיל דִּבְמָקוֹם קָרוֹב הֲוָה, וְיָכוֹל לָבֹא בִּתְחִלַּת הָאֲבֵילוּת – חָשְׁבִינַן לֵיהּ כְּמוֹ דְּאַתָּא, דְּאֵינוֹ מוֹנֶה אֶלָּא ה' יָמִים עִם שְׁאָר אֲבֵלִים: מוֹנֶה לְעַצְמוֹ. שִׁבְעָה שְׁלֵימִין: שֶׁיֵּשׁ גְּדוֹל הַבַּיִת בַּבַּיִת. שֶׁבָּא וּמָצָא גְּדוֹל הַבַּיִת בַּבַּיִת – מוֹנֶה עִמָּהֶן עִם אֲבֵילֵי הַבַּיִת. וְזֶה שֶׁבָּא הוּא הַצָּעִיר מִמֶּנּוּ. אֲבָל אִם הָיָה גָּדוֹל בַּדֶּרֶךְ, וּבָא בְּתוֹךְ שְׁלֹשָׁה יָמִים, אֲפִי' מִמָּקוֹם קָרוֹב – מוֹנֶה לְעַצְמוֹ, דְּלָא חָשִׁיב אֲבֵילוּת דְּצָעִיר לְאִצְטְרוּפֵי גָּדוֹל בַּהֲדֵיהּ:

הָלַךְ

הגהות הב"ח

(א) רש"י ד"ה הכי כו' נמי משיב למאן דשאיל ליה הס"ד ואח"כ מה"ד התם מודע להו. הא דקתני כל שלשה אסור בשאלת שלום ולמאן דלא ידע ושאיל ליה בתוך שלשה ימים מודע להו דאבל הוא ולא מהדר להו כצ"ל:

הגהות מהר"ב רנשבורג

א] תוס' ד"ה אפי' וכו וי"ל כגון וכו'. נמחק תיבה כגון וכ"ב כיון כצ"ל לענ"ד ור"ל כיון דלקמן דף כג ע"א מוקמינן לדר"ש והוא שבא ומצא מנחמין אצלו א"כ לא הוי מקצת היום ככולו כל זמן שהמנחמין אצלו ודוק:

הלך גדול הבית לבית הקברות מהו? תא שמע, דאמר רבי חייא בר אבא אמר רבי יוחנן: אפילו הלך גדול הבית לבית הקברות [א]מונה עמהן. מונה עמהן? והתניא מונה לעצמו! לא קשיא: הא — [ב]דאתא בגו תלתא, והא — דלא אתא בגו תלתא. כי הא דאמר להו רב לבני הצלפוני: דאתו בגו תלתא — לימנו בהדייכו, דלא אתו בגו תלתא — לימנו לנפשיהו. אמר להו רבא לבני מחוזא: אתון דלא אזליתו בתר ערסא, [ג]מכי מהדריתו אפייכו מבבא דאבולא — אתחילו מנו. § "ר"ש אומר אפילו בא ביום השביעי ממקום קרוב מונה עמהן". § א"ר חייא בר גמדא א"ר יוסי בן שאול אמר רבי: [ד]והוא שבא ומצא מנחמין אצלו. [ה]בעי רב ענן: נגערו לעמוד ולא עמדו, מהו? תיקו. *גמירי חבריה דר' אבא בר חייא מר' אבא, ומנו — ר' זירא, ואמרי לה: חבריה דר' זירא מרבי זירא, ומנו — ר' אבא בריה דר' חייא בר אבא, א"ר יוחנן: *הלכה כרבי שמעון בן גמליאל בטריפות, והלכה כרבי שמעון באבל. כרבי שמעון באבל — הא דאמרן. כרשב"ג בטריפות — דתנן: בני מעים שניקבו וליחה סותמתן — כשרה, דברי רשב"ג. מאי ליחה? אמר רב כהנא: שירקא דמעיא דנפיק אגב דוחקא. *אמר מאן דהוא: *איזכי ואסיק ואגמרא לשמעתא מפומיה דמריה. כי סליק אשכחיה לר' אבא בריה דרבי חייא בר אבא, א"ל: אמר מר הלכה כרשב"ג בטריפות? א"ל: אנא "אין הלכה" אמרי. כר"ש באבל מאי? א"ל: פלוגתא נינהו. דאיתמר, רב חסדא אמר: הלכה, וכן א"ר יוחנן: הלכה, ר"נ אמר: אין הלכה, [ו]ואין הלכה כרשב"ג בטריפות. והלכה כר"ש באבל. *דאמר שמואל: הלכה כדברי המיקל באבל. *)על כל המתים כולן, [ז]מדחה מטתו — הרי זה משובח, על אביו ועל אמו — הרי זה מגונה. היה ערב שבת, או ערב יום טוב (א) — הרי זה משובח, שאינו עושה אלא לכבוד אביו ואמו. [ח]על כל המתים כולן, ◦רצה ממעט בעסקו, רצה אינו ממעט

*) שמחות פ"ט

רש"י

הלך גדול הבית לבית הקברות. אחר מטתו לקוברו, ושהה שם ג' ימים: מהו. מי חשבינן ליה כמאן דהוי בביתיה, הואיל ולצורך המת הלך אתו: מונה עמהן. דאבילות שלהם התחילה משחזרו פניהם מן המת ואבילות של גדול (ב) עד שיסתום הגולל: לבני הצלפוני. מקום: דלא אזליתו בתר ערסא. דמאן דאזיל בתר ערסא לא חיילא עליה אבילות עד שנסתם הגולל. כשמוליכין המטה מבבל לא"י לקבור, ואין כל הקרובים כולם יכולין לעלות עד א"י, ומלוין המת פרסה או מיל וחוזרים: מכי אהדריתו אפייכו מבבא דאבולא. משער החיצון של העיר ומגרשיה, דאתיתו לביתא: אתחילו מנו. ימי אבילות, אע"ג דלא נקבר המת עד ימים רבים. ואע"ג דאבילות אינו חל עד שיסתום הגולל — לדידכו, דלא מחזי — חזרתכם כנסתם הגולל: ה"ג: והוא שלא עמדו מנחמין מאצלו. שבא בשביעי שחרית, עד שלא עמדו מנחמין אצל זה שבבית: נגערו לעמוד. מנענעים ורוצים לעמוד: אמר מאן דהוא. אדם אחד, מאן דהוה: מפומיה דמריה. מר' אבא בריה דרבי חייא או רבי זירא: אין הלכה אמרי. כלומר: אין הלכה כרבי שמעון: מדחה מטתו. ממהר להוציאו: ממעט בעסקו. כגון סחורה: רצה

תוספות

הלך גדול הבית לבית הקברות מהו. פי': מי מונה לעצמו או לא? דשמא כיון שהוא טרוד בעניני מת, וכששמעו הם שמע גם הוא — ימנה עמהן. או שמא מונה לעצמו. ולא ידענא מאי הוי דינא בגדול הבית שבא ממקום קרוב, אי מונה עמהן הואיל והוא עיקר. ויש ליתן טעם לומר שהוא מונה לבדו, הואיל ואינו יודע האבילות. או טעם להיפך, דהואיל משום המת הלך — ימנה עמהם:

דאתא בגו תלתא יומין. כשאתא גדול הבית בתוך ג' ימים — מונה הוא עמהן. וכדאמרינן לעיל: ג' ימים הראשונים מונה עמהם. וקשיא לי: דהא קיי"ל כר"ש, דאפי' ביום ז' מונה עמהן, כדאמרינן לקמן, וא"כ, מה לי תוך ג' מה לי לאחר ג'? ונראה מתוך ה"ג דאפי' לר"ש (בר יוסי) הוי חילוק, דתוך ג' ואחר ג' מקום רחוק. שפי' הא דאתא בגו תלתא יומי מונה עמהן — אפי' בא ממקום רחוק. אתא לבתר תלתא יומי ממקום קרוב — אפי' תוך ז' מונה עמהן, ובסמוך פירש: אפי' לר"ש אתיא הך מילתא. ועוד יש לפרש, דה"פ: הלך גדול הבית לבית הקברות מהו? דמיבעיא ליה אם אותו שבא מונה עם הנשארים. וכך פי' ר' יצחק ז"ל. והוא כשיש גדול הבית בבית — אז מונה עמהן הבא אצלם ממקום קרוב ומצאם אבלים, שאע"פ שאבלותם חל מקודם לשלו, ומצאם יום או יומים — יסיים עמהן *לרבנן כשבא גדול הבית תוך ג' ימים, שפירש גדול הבית ג' ימים, ולר"ש אפי' ביום השביעי. ודוקא כשיש גדול הבית בבית, כי אז בטל אצלם. והכי פי': איבעיא להו הלך גדול הבית לבית הקברות, פי': הלך ללות מת עד עיר אחרת, וקברו שם, מהו שיהא מונה עמהן אותו שבא אצל אבלים שבעיר, שמת בה מונה עמהן, אע"פ שאין גדול הבית עמהן שם. [או לא?] דהא דבעינן גדול הבית בבית — למעוטי האי נמי קאתי, אע"ג דידע בהאי אבילות ושייך בה. או דלמא לא אתא למעוטי אלא היכא דליתא גדול הבית בדוכתא אחריתי, דלא ידע בהאי אבילות כלל. אבל הלך לבית הקברות, כיון דידע בהאי אבילות — חשיב אבילות דידהו עיקר, ובטל האורח גבייהו. א"ל: מונה עמהן. והתניא מונה לעצמו! לא קשיא: הא — דאתא גדול הבית בגו תלתא יומי מבית הקברות, דאז הוא מונה עמהן, וגם האורח מונה עמהן, אם בא בתוך שלשה לרבנן או בתוך שבעה לרבי שמעון. הא דלא אתא גדול הבית בגו תלתא יומי — דלא חשיב אבילות דידהו עיקר, דלימני הא דאתא מעלמא בהדייהו, מאחר שאין גדול הבית מונה עמהן. ולא מיבעיא לרבנן שאין גדול הבית מונה עמהן כי לא אתא בגו תלתא, אלא אפי' לר"ש דאמר אפי' ביום ז' מונה עמהן — ה"מ אחר דלא הוה ידע ביה בתחילה, ובטל לגבייהו, כיון דגדול הבית נמי מני בהדייהו, והם תחילת האבילות ועיקרו יותר ממנו, שלא ידע בתחילת האבילות. אבל החוזר מבית הקברות, שהיה בתחילת האבילות — אינו מונה עמהן היכא דלא אתא בגו תלתא יומי, בין אם יש גדול הבית בין אם אין גדול הבית. כי הא דא"ל רב לבני הצלפוני דאתי בגו תלתא, החוזר מבית הקברות בגו תלתא — לימנו בהדייכו, דלא אתו בגו תלתא יומי — מימני לנפשיה, עכ"ל. ז"ל הירושלמי: הרי שבא ומצא אבל בתוך ביתו, בשני ובשלישי — משלים עמהן, ברביעי — מונה לעצמו. ר"ש אומר: אפי' בז' משלים עמהם. ריב"ל אומר: הלכה כר"ש כשיש גדול המשפחה בבית, אבל כשאין גדול המשפחה — מונה לעצמו. ולפי הירושלמי היה נ"ל דאינו פוסק כר"ש אלא כשיש גדול המשפחה בבית, אבל אם אין גדול המשפחה — הלכה כרבנן, דבתוך ג' ימים — מונה עמהם, לאחר ג' — מונה לעצמו. ולפ"ז אתי שפיר אפי' אליבא דהלכתא דאתי בגו תלתא — לימנו *בהדייכו בגדול הבית בבית, דכמו שאין גדול הבית הלכתא כרבנן — כמו כן בגדול הבית עצמו, והוי דינא כרבנן:

מהדריתו אפייכו אתחילו מנו. אבל אותם ההולכים עם המת, משיסתם הגולל בין גדול הבית בבית בין הולך לבית הקברות, וכן המנהג. ובירושלמי אינו כן, דהכי תנן מת שהוליכו אותו ממקום למקום, כגון אלו דקברין במקום אחר, אית תניא תני: אלו שכאן מונין משילא המת, ואלו ששם מונין משנסתם הגולל. ואית תני: הני והני משנסתם הגולל. ורב סימון בשם ריב"ל: הכל הולך אחר גדול המשפחה. ר' יעקב בשם ר' יוסי: לחומרין. מהו לחומרין? שאם היה גדול המשפחה כאן — *אלו שכאן מונין משילא המת, ואלו ששם מונין משנסתם הגולל. וגדול המשפחה שם — אלו ואלו מונין משיסתם הגולל. וקשיא: מהו לחומרא? הא זימנין אזלינן לקולא בתר גדול הבית, כגון שגדול המשפחה כאן — שכולם מונין משילא המת מן הבית, דהוה קולא! לכן נראה לפרש: שאם גדול המשפחה כאן — מונין מיד, ומתחילין להתאבל עמו לכבודו מיד כשישמעו, אפי' שלא בפניו. אבל עיקר אבילות יתחילו למנות משיסתום הגולל. וכן איתא בהדיא: ר"ג זוגה, דמכת *אחתיה, סליק אחיה עמה. אמר ליה רבי מנא: כיון שיש גדול הבית — מסלקת גבי אחוך, שלוף סנדלא. ובתוספות הרב פירש שהש"ס אינו מחלק כך:

רבינו חננאל

הוא שואל בשלום אחיו שהן שרויין בשלום: ת"ר אבל ג' ימים הראשונים בא ממקום קרוב מונה עמהן. ואמר ר' חייא בר אבא אמר ר' יוחנן והוא שיש גדול הבית ואפילו הלך גדול הבית לבית הקברות ובא בתוך ג' מונה עמהן. בא לאחר ג' ומצא שהלך גדול הבית לפני הקברות מונה לעצמו כדאמר להו רב לבני הצלבוני דאתו בגו תלתא לימנן בהדייכו דאתו לבתר תלתא לימני לנפשיה. בא ממקום רחוק בתוך ג' מונה לעצמו מיכן ואילך אפילו בא ממקום קרוב מונה לעצמו ר' שמעון אומר אפילו בא ביום ז' ממקום קרוב מונה עמהם ואוקמה ר' יוסי בן שאול והוא שבא ומצא מנחמין אצל אבלים כלומר עדיין לא נסתלקו מן האבלות כדאמרינן מקצת היום ככולו. ואיבעיא להו נגערו האבלים לעמוד ובא ממקום קרוב ומצאן שעדיין לא עמדו מהו ועמדה בתיקו. אמר משמיה דר' יוחנן הלכה כר' שמעון באבל הא דאמרן דאמר שמואל הלכה כדברי המיקל. הא דאמרינן בגררה בהדין אתרא הלכתא כרשב"ג בטריפות כבר פירשנוה בשחיטת חולין ופשוטה היא. אמר להו רבא לבני מחוזא אתון דלא אזליתו בתר ערסא מכי הדריתו אפייכו מבבא דאבולא אתחילו למימני: **ירושלמי** הרי שבא ומצא בתוך ביתו בשני ובשלישי מונה עמהן ברביעי מונה לעצמו ר"ש אומר אפילו *) בששי משלים עמהן אריב"ל הלכה כר' שמעון בשאין גדול משפחה אבל אם הוא גדול משפחה מונה לעצמו. כר' מנא שהורה לר' יעקב ארמניא מכיון שאתה גדול מנה לעצמך: על כל המתים המדחה מטתו משובח על אביו ועל אמו מגונה. אלא אם היה ע"ש או עיו"ט או שהיו גשמים מזלפין על מטתו ועושה לכבוד אביו הרי גם זה משובח על כל המתים אם רצה שלא למעט בעסקו אלא אם רצה לישא וליתן בסחורתו כל היום הרשות בידו. אבל על אביו ועל אמו חייב למעט פי' בשאר מתים אינו ממעט

עין משפט נר מצוה

קלג א ב טוש"ע י"ד סימן שעה סעיף ח בהג"ה:

קלד ג מיי' פ"א מהל' אבל הל' ה טוש"ע שם סעיף ב:

קלה ד ה מיי' שם פ"ז הלכה ד טוש"ע שם סעיף ח:

קלו ו מיי' פ"ו מהל' שחיטה הלכה יד סמג עשין סג טוש"ע י"ד סימן מו סעיף א:

קלז ז מיי' פ"ד מהל' אבל הלכה ז סמג עשין דרבנן ג טוש"ע שם סימן שנז סעיף ב:

קלח ח מיי' שם פ"ו הלכה ט טוש"ע שם סימן שפ סעיף כד:

בחילופי גרסאות מוחק מן תיבת לרבנן עד ביום השביעי. וגורס לעיל מינה עם הנשארים לרבנן כשבא גדול הבית תוך ג' ימים ולר"ש אפילו ביום ז' וכן פי' ר"י וכו'

מסורת הש"ס

חולין נ. ע"ש

[שם]

[ביצה כז.]

חולין נ. [נדה מח.]

[לעיל יח. וש"נ] עירובין מו. לקמן כו:

הגהות הב"ח

(א) גמ' היה ע"ש או עיו"ט או שהיו גשמים מזלפין על מטתו ה"ז משובח: (ב) רש"י ד"ה מונה כו' ואבילות של גדול לא התחיל עד שיסתום הגולל:

גליון הש"ס

גמ' רצה ממעט בעסקו. עיין לקמן דף כז ע"א תוספות ד"ה אם יכול:

בהדייכו כמו בגדול הבית בבית דכשאין גדול הבית כו' עצמו הוי דינא כרבנן כצ"ל

[עי' נוסחת הירושלמי שהביא הרא"ש בסימן לט]

[פי' מתה אחותו]

מעשה

ממעט. על אביו ועל אמו — ממעט. [א]על כל המתים כולן, רצה — חולץ, רצה — אינו חולץ. על אביו ועל אמו חולץ. ומעשה בגדול הדור אחד שמת אביו וביקש לחלוץ, וביקש גדול הדור אחר שעמו לחלוץ — ונמנע ולא חלץ. אמר אביי: גדול הדור — רבי, גדול הדור שעמו — ר' יעקב בר אחא. ואיכא דאמרי: גדול הדור — ר' יעקב בר אחא, גדול הדור שעמו — רבי, בשלמא למ"ד גדול הדור שעמו רבי — היינו דנמנע ולא חלץ. אלא למ"ד רבי יעקב בר אחא — אמאי נמנע ולא חלץ? רשב"ג נשיא הוה, [ב]וכולי עלמא מיחייבי למיחלץ! קשיא. *[ג]על כל המתים כולן מסתפר לאחר ל' יום, על אביו ועל אמו — עד שיגערו בו חבריו. [ד]על כל המתים כולן — נכנס לבית השמחה לאחר ל' יום, על אביו ועל אמו — לאחר י"ב חדש. אמר רבה בר בר חנה: ולשמחת מריעות. מיתיבי: ולשמחה ולמריעות ל' יום! קשיא. אמימר מתני הכי: אמר רבה בר בר חנה, [ה]ולשמחת מריעות — מותר ליכנס לאלתר. והא תניא: לשמחה שלשים, ולמריעות שלשים! ל"ק; [ו]הא — באריסותא, הא — בפורענותא. [ז]על כל המתים כולן — קורע טפח, על אביו ועל אמו — עד שיגלה את לבו. א"ר אבהו: מאי קרא — (שמואל ב א) "ויחזק דוד בבגדיו ויקרעם" ואין אחיזה פחות מטפח. [ח]על כל המתים כולן, אפילו לבוש עשרה חלוקין — אינו קורע אלא עליון. על אביו ועל אמו — קורע את כולן, [ט]ואפיקרסותו אינה מעכבת, אחד האיש ואחד אשה. ר"ש בן אלעזר אומר: [י]האשה קורעת את התחתון, ומחזירתו לאחוריה, וחוזרת וקורעת את העליון. *[כ]על כל המתים כולן רצה — מבדיל קמי שפה שלו, רצה — אינו מבדיל. על אביו ועל אמו — מבדיל. רבי יהודה אומר: [ל]כל קריעה שאינו מבדיל קמי שפה שלו — אינו אלא קרע של תיפלות. אמר רבי אבהו: מ"ט דר' יהודה — דכתיב: (מלכים ב ב) "ויחזק בבגדיו ויקרעם לשנים קרעים", *ממשמע שנאמר "ויקרעם" איני יודע שהן לשנים? אלא: שנראין קרועים כשנים. [מ]על כל המתים כולן — שולל לאחר שבעה, ומאחה לאחר שלשים. על אביו ועל אמו — שולל לאחר ל' ואינו מאחה לעולם. *[נ]והאשה שוללתו לאלתר, מפני כבודה. כי אתא רבין א"ר יוחנן: [ס]על כל המתים, רצה — קורע ביד, רצה — קורע בכלי. על אביו ועל אמו — ביד. וא"ר חייא בר אבא א"ר יוחנן: [ע]על כל המתים כולן — מבפנים, על אביו ועל אמו — קורע מבחוץ. אמר רב חסדא: [פ]וכן לנשיא. מיתיבי: לא הושוו לאביו ולאמו אלא לאיחוי בלבד. מאי לאו — אפילו לנשיא? לא, לבר מנשיא. נשיאה שכיב. א"ל רב חסדא (*לרב חנן בר רבא:) כפי אסיתא וקום עלה, ואחוי קריעה לעלמא. [צ]על חכם חולץ מימין, על אב ב"ד משמאל, על נשיא — מכאן ומכאן. ת"ר: חכם שמת — בית מדרשו בטל, [ק]אב ב"ד שמת — כל בתי מדרשות שבעירו בטלין, ונכנסין לביהכ"נ, ומשנין את מקומן; היושבין בצפון — יושבין בדרום, היושבין בדרום — יושבין בצפון. [ש]נשיא שמת — בתי מדרשות כולן בטילין, ובני הכנסת נכנסין לבית הכנסת, וקורין

(שמואל ב א) (מלכים ב ב) [גי' הערוך בערך אסיתא לרב נחמן בר אמי]

רש"י

רצה חולץ. כתיפו: ונמנע. האבל ולא חלץ, משום כבוד גדול הדור שעמו, שבקש לחלוץ גם הוא: אלא למ"ד גדול הדור שעמו ר' יעקב. ורבי הוה אבל: עד שיגערו בו חבריו. שכבר גידל פרע יותר מדאי: אמר רבה. הא דתניא: נכנס לבית המשתה לאחר ל' יום: לשמחת מריעות. סעודה שעושין ריעים ואוהבים זה עם זה, ולא הוי שמחה כל כך. אבל סעודה דשמחה, כגון דנישואין — לא: הא באריסותא הא בפורענותא. אריסא היינו שמתחיל אחד מהן לעשות סעודה, ומלוה לכולם כדי שיעשו גם הם נמי כך — לאותה סעודה אינו נכנס עד לאחר שלשים יום. אבל בפורענותא, שמשלם להם סעודות שנעשו לו — יכנס לאלתר, שאי אפשר לו שלא לשלם: ואפיקרסותו. שעל ראשו, אינה מעכבת. כלומר, אינו צריך לקורעה: אחד איש ואחד אשה. חייבין לקרוע: האשה. שמת אביה או אמה — קורעת חלוק התחתון משום צניעות: ומחזרת. הקרע לאחוריה: וחוזרת וקורעת העליון. והתחתון מכסה לבה: רצה מבדיל קמי שפה. שאינו בשפה שלפני הצואר, אלא קמי שפה — שלפני השפה, שלפני הצואר, שאינה קרועה, וקורע תחתיה כדי שיהיה נראה הקרע: רצה אינו מבדיל. אלא קורע של בית הצואר, אע"ג דאינו נראה הקרע, דהכל בית הצואר הוא: על אביו ועל אמו מבדיל. קמי שפה, כדי שיהא נראה הקרע: קרע של תיפלה. כלומר: לא יצא ידי קריעה, לפי דנראה דבית צואר הוא הכל: ויקרעם לשנים. אין קורעין, אלא שנראה כשנים, מבדיל קמי שפה, ונראה בית הצואר קרע אחר: שולל. באשטיר"י: מאחה. קוסט"ר, תופר כדרכו: קורע בכלי. סכין, כדי שלא יפסיד הבגד: קורע מבפנים. תחת המקטורן שלו, שאינו קורע מחוץ לעיני הכל: וכן לנשיא. קורע מבחוץ: לא הושוו. רבו ואב ב"ד ונשיא, וכל הנך דתני במתניתא לאביו ולאמו: אלא לאיחוי. שאין מתאחים לעולם. אבל לא הושוו לאביו ולאמו לקרוע מבחוץ. להאי לא הושוו, דעל אביו קורע מבחוץ, ועל כולן אינו קורע מבחוץ: כפי אסיתא. הפוך המכתשת, ועמוד עליה וקרע, כדי שיראוך כל העם כשתקרע: חכם. ממונה על העיר, שמבקשים ממנו הוראה: חולץ. כתף מימין: בית מדרשו בטלין. אותן שרגילין ללמוד תורה מפיו:
וקורין

תורה אור | שמחות פ"ט | הוריות יב. | [לקמן כו. ע"ש סנהדרין ס. ע"ש וע"ש] | [לקמן כו:]

תוספות

מעשה בגדול הדור. אין זה מעשה לסתור דהא דנמנע ולא חלץ — זהו מפני גדול *הדור שעמו. ובמס' שמחות (פ"ט) קתני עלה: ואין ראוי לחלק כבוד לו. והאחרים הראויין לחלוץ, אף על אביו ועל אמו. ואם אינן ראויין — אינו חולץ, כדי שלא יחלצו אחרים ומעשה בר' יעקב כו':

עד שיגערו בו חביריו. נראה דרגל אינו מבטל דבר זה, מדאמרינן בירושלמי: רבי שמואל בר אבדימי דמנה תלתין יומין קמי מועדא, שאיל לרבי מנא. א"ל: כל דבר שהוא תלוי בז' ול' — הרגל מפסיק, ברם הכא — עד שישלח פרע ויגערו בו חביריו, ויאמרו לו לך מעמנו. ובשמחה נמי אשכחנא הכא י"ב חדש, ואין רגל מבטל. ויש ספרים שכתוב בהן: או יגערו בו חביריו, בירושלמי. ונראה שהוא טעות סופרים, כי אם כמו שכתבתי: עד שישלח פרע ויגערו בו:

ולשמחת מריעות. פירש בקונטרס: סעודות שעושים ריעים ואהובים זה לזה. וכ"נ, דדוקא לשמחת מריעות מותר לאחר ל' יום, אבל שמחת חתן — אסור אפילו לאחר ל' יום. והא תניא לשמחה ל' ולמריעות ל'! וה"נ פריך בריש פ"ק דבבא מציעא (דף ג.): והא זה וזה קתני! וכן בפ"ק דסנהדרין (דף ח.) גבי זימון בג', וברכת המזון בג', וטובא איכא. ויש מקומות שאינו שואל, כגון בפ"ק דנדרים (דף ד:) *גבי אסור אסור, ובפרק "גיד הנשה" (חולין דף לא. ושם) גבי אסורות אסורות, ובפרק "בית כור" (ב"ב דף קד.) גבי "בית כור" אני מוכר לך כבית כור. וי"מ: ולשמחת מריעות מותר ליכנס לאלתר. ואנן בסעודת חתן איירינן. הא דאמרינן בירושלמי ובמסכת שמחות (פ"ט): אם היה סעודה של מצוה — מותר, לא ידענא מהו קורא סעודת מצוה להתיר באבל. אם דוקא סעודת קידוש ר"ח. פירש הר"א בשם רבינו שמשון: דלסעודת ברית מילה מותר ליכנס, דלא חשיבא שמחה, כדאמרינן בפ"ק דכתובות (דף ח.) דלא מברכינן בה "שהשמחה במעונו" משום דטרידי, וליכא שמחה. ולהר"א לא היה פשוט דגרע משמחת מריעות. וגם פירש דאסור לאכול אפי' עם המשמשין ואין לחלק בין סעודת המשמשין לסעודה עצמה. ופסק דכניסה בלא אכילה — שרי, דאין שמחה בלא אכילה ושתיה. ובתוספות הרב פוסק כלישנא דאמימר דמיקל טפי:

אחד האיש ואחד האשה. ובתוס' הרב פוסק כר"ש בן אלעזר, דהלכה כדברי המיקל. ולא ידענא מאי קאמר, דלקמן (דף כו:) אמרינן: אבילות לחוד וקריעה לחוד:
רבי

עין משפט נר מצוה

עי' מהרש"א ולפי הנראה יש כאן ערבובי דברים וכצ"ל הדור שעמו ואין ראוי לחלק כבוד לו כדי שלא יחלצו אחרים ובמס' שמחות קתני עלה ואם אין ראוי לחלוץ אף על אביו ואמו לא יחלוץ ומעשה כו' כצ"ל והבוחר יבחר. העתק מחילופי גרסאות

קלט א מיי' פ"ח מהל' אבל הלכה ג סמג עשין דרבנן ב טוש"ע י"ד סימן שמ סעיף טז:

קמ ב מיי' שם פ"ט הלכה טו סמג שם טוש"ע שם סעיף יז:

קמא ג מיי' שם פ"ו הלכה ג סמג שם טוש"ע שם סימן שצ סעיף יז:

קמב ד ה ו מיי' שם הלכה ו ז סמג שם טוש"ע שם סימן שצא סעיף ב:

קמג ז ח ט מיי' שם פ"ח הלכה ב ג סמג שם טוש"ע שם סי' שמ סעיף ט י:

קמד י טוש"ע שם סעיף יא:

קמה כ מיי' שם טוש"ע שם סעיף יב:

קמו ל טוש"ע שם בהג"ה:

קמז מ נ מיי' פ"ט שם הלכה א טוש"ע שם סעיף טו:

[שם בנדרים פריך הש"ס אסור אסור ל"ל וכ"כ תוספות בכורות לא: ד"ה א"כ וכו' דבנדרים פריך כן ולכך צריכים אנו לומר דהכא בדברי תוס' נפל טעות ומ"ש כגון בפ"ק דנדרים גבי אסור אסור שייך לעיל קודם וטובא איכא וכו' ודע עוד דגם במ"ש תוספות הכא ובפ' בית כור וכו' צריך תיקון בזה כי בב"ב קד. שואל הש"ס ע"ש וכך איתא בתוספות בכורות הנ"ל וע"ש]

קמח ס מיי' שם פ"ח הלכה ב ג טוש"ע שם סעיף יד:

קמט ע מיי' שם טוש"ע שם סעיף יג:

קנ פ צ מיי' שם פ"ט הלכה ב יד טו טוש"ע שם סעיף יז:

קנא ק ר ש מיי' שם טוש"ע שם סי' שמ סעיף יח:

רבינו חננאל

ממעט על אביו ועל אמו ממעט בעסקו. ואפילו שהוא על ידי אחרים: ירושל' מרבה בעסקי אביו ואמו משמע בתכריכין והספדו. על כל המתים רצה חולץ פי' חליצת כתף. מוציא ידו מתחת הקרע ונמצאת כתיפו חלוצה מן החלוק. רצה אינו חולץ. על אביו ועל אמו חולץ. ומעשה בגדול הדור שמת אביו ובא לחלוץ. ובקש גדול הדור (עצמו) [שעמו] לחלוץ ולא חלץ. ואסיקנא גדול הדור (שמת) הוא ר' יעקב בר אחא ובקש רבינו הקדוש הוא גדול הדור שעמו לחלוץ עמו מפני כבודו. ונמנע ר' יעקב ולא חלץ. אבל במיתת רשב"ג אבי רבינו הקדוש כ"ע חייבין לחלוץ דנשיא הוא. קיי"ל היכא דחל יום שמיני של אביו ושל אמו להיות בשבת ערב הרגל מגלח ואפילו ביום ששי בע"ש. דלענין כבוד יו"ט ל"ש אב ואם ול"ש שאר קרובים. הלכה כאבא שאול בזה ובזה. על כל המתים מותר להסתפר לאחר שלשים. על אביו ועל אמו מגדל שער עד שיגערו בו חביריו. על כל המתים נכנס לבית המשתה לאחר שלשים יום. ואוקמה אמימר במשתה שמחת מריעות בפורענותא נכנס לאלתר. אבל באריסותא. כלומר הוא אינו פורע אלא הוא מתחיל אחר שלשים יום. אבל על אביו ועל אמו אינו נכנס עד י"ב חדש על כל המתים קורע טפח שנאמר ויחזק בבגדיו ויקרעם לשנים. ואין אחיזה פחותה מטפח. אבל על אביו ועל אמו קורע עד שמגלה את לבו. ואפילו לבוש מאה חלוקים קורע את כולן ומבדיל קמי שפה דבעינן קרע הנראה לשנים קרעים כדכתיב ויקרעם לשנים קרעים ואפיקרסותו אינה מעכבת והאשה על אביה ועל אמה קורעת חלוקה התחתון ומחזרת הקרע לאחוריה וחוזרת וקורעת את העליון. ואינו קורע על אביו ועל אמו בכלי כגון סכין וכיוצא בו אלא בידו קורע ואינו קורע אלא מבחוץ ואינו מאחה הקרע לעולם: ירושלמי זהו איחוי העשוי כאריג אבל על שאר מתים אינו קורע אלא העליון. ואם אינו רוצה להבדיל קמי שפה אינו מבדיל ושולל לאחר שבעה ומאחה לאחר שלשים. והאשה קורעת ושוללתו לאלתר מפני כבודה. ואם רוצה לקרוע בכלי קורע. על אביו ועל אמו קורע מבחוץ. אמר רב חסדא וכן לנשיא. נשיאה שכיב א"ל רב חסדא לרב חנן כפי אסיתא וקום עליה ואחוי קריעה לעלמא. על חכם חולץ מימין על אב ב"ד משמאל. על נשיא מיכן ומיכן. פירוש חליצת כתף. ת"ר חכם שמת מדרשו בטל. אב ב"ד שמת כל מדרשות שבעירו בטילין. ובני הכנסת נכנסין ומשנין את מקומן. היושבין בצפון יושבין בדרום. בדרום יושבין בצפון. נשיא שמת כל בתי מדרשות בטילין ונכנסין לכנסת
וקורין

רבי יהודה אומר לא הוצרכו. בירושלמי פוסק הלכה כדברי המוסיף בימים (שבעה). וראיתי כשהייתי קטן רבינו יצחק זקני שלא היה יושב במקומו עד שבוע רביעי. ולא ידעתי טעמו, שאם היה סובר כר' יהודה – א"כ יסבור כמותו בשניה, שאינו יוצא מפתח ביתו. מיהו, י"ל בהא אשכחנא טובא לעיל דאבילות שבעה, וקי"ל הכי. ושמא טעמו כרבנן, ומשום דצריך לישב במקומו ואינו מדבר – וטוב יותר שישב חוץ למקומו, דשמא אין אסור לדבר כי אם במקומו: **עד** שיעברו שלשה רגלים. עד שיהיה שלשה רגלים בלא שמחה, ולא ישכח אהבת אשתו. אי נמי: כדי שישא אשה אחרת ולא יהא זכור מן הראשונה, [שלא] יהא ב' דעות במטה. ועוד: פן יזכירנה אהבת אשתו, לקנטרה. ודומיא דהכא אמרי' לעיל (ד' כא:): מתה אשתו ונשא אשה אחרת – אינו רשאי ליכנס לביתו כו'. פירש ה"ר יונה: דאין שייך לפסוק כרבי יהודה דאמר שני רגלים משום דקי"ל לעיל (ד' כב.) כדברי המיקל באבל – דהא מילתא דפליגי בה הכא אין זו באבל, דימי אבלו כָּלוּ להן:

ואמר לאחותה בבית הקברות. לאו דוקא, שהאבל כל שבעה אסור. וריב"א מפרש: דזו היא האשה שאומר בזבחים פ' "טבול יום" (ד' ק.) שמתה בערב הפסח, ואמרי' לעיל: אפי' יום אחד אפילו שעה אחת – בטלה ממנו גזרת שבעה. ומיהו, משמע שסובר כאותו הפירוש שפי' למעלה בשם ה"ר יונה: שאסור ברחילה עד הערב – זהו מבעוד יום. ודין הניחה לו בנים קטנים מיד ◦מותר לישא ולבעול, וכן אין לו בנים – פירשתי בתוספות יבמות (ד' מג: ושם*), וכן בכתובות פ"ק (ד' ד.*), ובתשובות. ומה שאמר במס' שמחות (פ"ז) בהאי מילתא דנסיב לאלתר ולא בא עליה עד זמן מרובה. והאי דאמרינן אין לו מי שישמשנו מותר, ואין צריך להמתין שלשה רגלים – כתבתי במקום אחר:

וְקוֹרִין שִׁבְעָה. בְּסֵפֶר תּוֹרָה. דְּאֵין מִתְפַּלְּלִין יַחַד בְּבֵית הַכְּנֶסֶת, אֶלָּא כָּל אֶחָד וְאֶחָד מִתְפַּלֵּל בְּבֵיתוֹ: לֹא הוּצְרְכוּ לוֹמַר שַׁבָּת רִאשׁוֹנָה. שֶׁוַּדַּאי לֹא יֵצֵא מִפֶּתַח בֵּיתוֹ: כָּל שְׁלֹשִׁים יוֹם לְנִישּׂוּאִין. עַד שְׁלֹשִׁים יוֹם לְאַחַר אֶבְלוֹ אֵינוֹ יָכוֹל לִישָּׂא אִשָּׁה: וְאֶחָד כֵּלִים יְשָׁנִים יוֹצְאִין מִתּוֹךְ הַמַּכְבֵּשׁ. פֵּירוּשׁ: שֶׁהֵן כַּחֲדָשִׁים: בְּגַרְדָּא דְּסַרְבְּלָא. מַלְבּוּשׁ לָבָן מְגוֹהָץ יָשָׁן: כְּרַבִּי. דְּאָמַר: לֹא אָסְרוּ לָבָן אֶלָּא חָדָשׁ: בְּחִימוּצְתָּא. חָלוּק: רוֹמִיתָא. שֶׁבָּא מֵרוֹמִי: כְּרַבִּי אֶלְעָזָר. דְּאָמַר: לֹא אָסְרוּ אֶלָּא לְבָנִים, וְזוֹ אֲדוּמָּה הָיְתָה: אַפְסוּקֵי

וְקוֹרִין שִׁבְעָה וְיוֹצְאִין. רַבִּי יְהוֹשֻׁעַ בֶּן קָרְחָה אוֹמֵר: לֹא שֶׁיֵּלְכוּ וִיטַיְּילוּ בַּשּׁוּק, אֶלָּא יוֹשְׁבִין וְדוֹמְמִין. [א]וְאֵין אוֹמְרִים שְׁמוּעָה וְאַגָּדָה בְּבֵית הָאָבֵל. אָמְרוּ עָלָיו עַל ר' חֲנַנְיָה בֶּן גַּמְלִיאֵל שֶׁהָיָה אוֹמֵר שְׁמוּעָה וְאַגָּדָה בְּבֵית הָאָבֵל. *ת"ר: ◦[ב]אָבֵל, שַׁבָּת רִאשׁוֹנָה – אֵינוֹ יוֹצֵא מִפֶּתַח בֵּיתוֹ, שְׁנִיָּה – יוֹצֵא וְאֵינוֹ יוֹשֵׁב בִּמְקוֹמוֹ, (א) שְׁלִישִׁית – יוֹשֵׁב בִּמְקוֹמוֹ וְאֵינוֹ מְדַבֵּר, רְבִיעִית – הֲרֵי הוּא כְּכָל אָדָם. רַבִּי יְהוּדָה אוֹמֵר: לֹא הוּצְרְכוּ לוֹמַר שַׁבָּת רִאשׁוֹנָה לֹא יֵצֵא מִפֶּתַח בֵּיתוֹ – שֶׁהֲרֵי הַכֹּל נִכְנָסִין לְבֵיתוֹ לְנַחֲמוֹ. אֶלָּא: שְׁנִיָּה – אֵינוֹ יוֹצֵא מִפֶּתַח בֵּיתוֹ, שְׁלִישִׁית – יוֹצֵא וְאֵינוֹ יוֹשֵׁב בִּמְקוֹמוֹ, (ב) רְבִיעִית – יוֹשֵׁב בִּמְקוֹמוֹ וְאֵינוֹ מְדַבֵּר, חֲמִישִׁית – הֲרֵי הוּא כְּכָל אָדָם. *ת"ר: [ג]כָּל שְׁלֹשִׁים יוֹם לְנִישּׂוּאִין, מֵתָה אִשְׁתּוֹ – אָסוּר לִישָּׂא אִשָּׁה אַחֶרֶת, עַד שֶׁיַּעַבְרוּ עָלָיו שְׁלֹשָׁה רְגָלִים. רַבִּי יְהוּדָה אוֹמֵר: רֶגֶל רִאשׁוֹן וְשֵׁנִי – אָסוּר, שְׁלִישִׁי – מוּתָּר. [ד]וְאִם אֵין לוֹ בָּנִים – מוּתָּר לִישָּׂא לְאַלְתַּר, מִשּׁוּם בִּיטּוּל פְּרִיָּה וּרְבִיָּה. [ה]הִנִּיחָה לוֹ בָּנִים קְטַנִּים – מוּתָּר לִישָּׂא לְאַלְתַּר, מִפְּנֵי פַּרְנָסָתָן. *מַעֲשֶׂה שֶׁמֵּתָה אִשְׁתּוֹ שֶׁל יוֹסֵף הַכֹּהֵן, וְאָמַר לַאֲחוֹתָהּ בְּבֵית הַקְּבָרוֹת: לְכִי וּפַרְנְסִי אֶת בְּנֵי אֲחוֹתֵךְ. וְאעפ"כ לֹא בָּא עָלֶיהָ אֶלָּא לִזְמַן מְרוּבֶּה. מַאי לִזְמַן מְרוּבֶּה? אָמַר רַב פָּפָּא: [ו]לְאַחַר שְׁלֹשִׁים יוֹם. *ת"ר: כָּל שְׁלֹשִׁים יוֹם לְגִיהוּץ, אֶחָד כֵּלִים חֲדָשִׁים וְאֶחָד כֵּלִים יְשָׁנִים יוֹצְאִין (ג) מִתּוֹךְ הַמַּכְבֵּשׁ. רַבִּי אוֹמֵר: לֹא אָסְרוּ אֶלָּא כֵּלִים חֲדָשִׁים בִּלְבַד. רַבִּי אֶלְעָזָר בר' שִׁמְעוֹן אוֹמֵר: [ז]לֹא אָסְרוּ אֶלָּא כֵּלִים חֲדָשִׁים לְבָנִים בִּלְבַד. אַבַּיֵּי נָפֵיק ◦בְּגַרְדָּא דְּסַרְבְּלָא, כְּרַבִּי. רָבָא נָפֵיק בְּחִימוּצְתָּא רוֹמִיתָא סוּמָקְתָא חַדְתִּי, כְּרַבִּי אֶלְעָזָר בר' שִׁמְעוֹן.§ "מִפְּנֵי שֶׁאָמְרוּ שַׁבָּת עוֹלָה וְאֵינָהּ מַפְסֶקֶת".§ בְּנֵי יְהוּדָה וּבְנֵי גְּלִילָא, הָנֵי אָמְרִי: יֵשׁ

[שמחות פ"י ע"ש] [שמחות פ"ז] [שם וע"ש] [שם וע"ש]

כל שלשים יום לגיהוץ. דוקא גיהוץ אסור, אבל בלא גיהוץ, כגון כיבוס – מותר. דאמרינן לקמן (ד' כז:) "אל תבכו למת" הא כילד? שלשים יום לגיהוץ ולתספורת. ובמסכת שמחות (פ"ז): שלשים יום לגיהוץ כילד כו'. ובירושלמי: גזרת שלשים – גיהוץ ותספורת. אבל כיבוס משמע דשרי, מדאמרינן פ' "החולץ" (יבמות מג:) גבי אלמנה מפני האיבול, וקאמר: באיבול שלה שלשים יום. ופריך: קל וחומר, מה במקום שאסור לכבס – מותר לארס, במקום שמותר לכבס – אינו דין שמותר לארס. והדתניא במסכת שמחות (פ"ז) שמונה ימים קודם הרגל, אם רצה לכבס ולספר – הרשות בידו, לא ספר לא כיבס ערב הרגל – אסור לספר ולכבס עד שישלימו שלשים יום. משמע דכיבוס נמי אסור! נראה ההוא כיבוס היינו גיהוץ, ומאחר דכיבוס שרי – גיהוץ נמי שרי לדידן, כדאמרי' פ"ק דכתובות (ד' י:) ופ"ד דתענית (ד' כט:): דגיהוץ שלנו ככיבוס שלהן. והקשה ה"ר שמואל מוורדו"ס: דהא בשמעתין באביי נפיק כו', והא בבבל הוו קיימי, דגיהוץ דלדידהו אינו אלא כיבוס ומ"מ אסרי! ותירץ רבינו יצחק: דפעמים שהיו מביאים מא"י כלים מגוהצין, או שמא פעמים שמביאין אומנין יודעין לגהץ כבארץ ישראל. והא דתניא בתוספתא (פ"ב): כל אלו שאמרו מותר לספר במועד – מותר לספר בתוך שלשים יום, אבל כל אלו שאמרו מותר לכבס במועד – אסור בתוך שלשים יום של אבל! צריך לומר דכיבוס נמי היינו גיהוץ. ומורי ריב"א זצ"ל היה אוסר לכבס בתוך שלשים יום, ואין נראה לו לדחות כל אלו. והא דקאמר בפרק "החולץ" (יבמות ד' מג. ושם) מקום שמותר לכבס – היינו בהני דהתירו לגלח ולכבס, בריש פירקין (ד' יג:): בא ממדינת הים, ויוצא מבית האסורין. ומה שאסור שם בתשעה באב לכבס – היינו דוקא טעמא שיכול להמתין אחר תשעה באב, הואיל ואיסורו אינו מושך כל כך. וגרסינן שפיר במקום שמותר לספר, כדפרישית. וא"נ לייבשו באשה, או בגילוח כל הראש, כדברי המפרשים שרוצים ליישב גירסת הספרים. והארכתי בתוספות יבמות (ג"ז שם). וגרסינן לקמן (ד' כז:): אל תבכו כו', הא כילד? שלשים יום לתכבוסת ולתספורת. והא דאמר לעיל (ד' טו.) אבל אסור בתכבוסת, משמע לאחר שבעה – שרי! התם במים איירי ולא בנתר וחול, וזה יוכל להיות מותר לאחר שבעה. בתוספות הרב כך פירש לאסור, ובשם רבו פירש היתר. ולפי מה שפירש דכיבוס אסור כמו גיהוץ – ניחא קושיית ה"ר שמואל מוורדו"ס. מיהו, מורי לא היה מפרש ממש לאסור כל כיבוס, אלא היה מפרש: דהאי ברייתא דאסרה כיבוס – היינו בא"י, דכיבוס שלהן כגיהוץ שלנו. והיא דקתני גיהוץ ולא כיבוס – היינו בבבל. מיהו, לפי זה לא היה אסור לדידן כי אם גיהוץ. אכן היה ר"י מפרש בלא ראייה כמו שפירש רבינו יצחק הזקן, דבבבל היו פעמים אומנים מא"י יודעין לגהץ, וכלי פשתן אין בהן משום גיהוץ. וחולק על התלמוד ירושלמי, דקתני התם: כל שלשים יום לגיהוץ אסור ללבוש כלי צמר מגוהצין חדשים, וכלי פשתן מגוהצים לבנים. פירש בתוספות הרב, דהא דאסרי גיהוץ – דוקא ללבוש, אבל לגהץ – מותר. והא דקתני כל שלשים יום לגיהוץ – היינו אסור ללבוש כלים מגוהצין כו'. עד מותר להוליך כלים לגיהוץ בתוך שלשים. ואיני יודע אם היה אומר הרב היתר בכיבוס תוך שבעה, ומחלק נמי בין לכבס או ללבוש. מיהו, רבינו יצחק זקני מפרש בתשובתו דאפי' לכבס ולהניח אסור, מדאסרינן בפרק בתרא דתענית (ד' כט.) לכבס ולהניח. ועוד פירש בתשובתו דכיבוס שלנו מותר בט' באב, כדאמרינן דגיהוץ שלנו ככיבוס שלהן, משמע דכיבוס שלנו אינו ככיבוס שלהם. והכי איתא בהדיא בפ"ק דכתובות (ד' י:). מיהו, לענין ימי אבילות – אסור בכיבוס שלנו. אפי' בתשעה באב מחמירין העולם בכיבוס שלנו מתוך המנהג, כמו שהחמירו לענין אבילות דבשר מליח, דשרי כהלכה ורגילין לנהוג בו איסור. ומיהו, איני מבין מנין לו להקל בתשעה באב יותר מימי אבלו? דאדרבה, בפרק בתרא דתענית (שם) נראה לי שמחמיר יותר לענין גיהוץ כלי פשתן בימי אבלו מבמועד. ובמטפחות ידים השיב רבינו שאף על פי שהתירו במועד – אסורין בימי אבלו, כדאמרינן לעיל (דף יז:): כל שאמרו מותר לגלח במועד כו' והתניא אסורים – ומוקי לה בתכפוהו אבליו: **רבא** נפיק כו'. ופי' בתוספות: דאביי ורבא הלכה כרבא. וא"כ מותר ללבוש כלים מגוהצין לבועין אפילו חדשים, או ישנים אפילו לבנים, וכן פסק ר"ח:

יש

עין משפט נר מצוה

קנב א מיי' פי"ג מהל' אבל הל' ט טוש"ע י"ד סי' שעח סעיף ז:

קנג ב מיי' שם פ"ז הלכה ה סמג עשין ב טוש"ע שם סי' שלג סעיף ב:

קנד ג ד ה ו מיי' שם פ"ו הל' ה טוש"ע שם סי' שלב סעיף א ב:

קנה ז מיי' שם פ"ה הל' ג ופ"ו שם הלכה ד סמג עשין דרבנן ב טוש"ע שם סי' שפט סעיף ה:

רבינו חננאל

וקורין שבעה ויוצאין ודוין א) ולא יטיילו בשוק ואין אומרים שמועה והגדה בבית האבל. אמרו על ר' חנינא בן גמליאל שהיה אומר שמועה והגדה בבית האבל: ת"ר אבל שבת ראשונה אינו יוצא מפתח ביתו. שניה יוצא ואינו יושב במקומו. שלישית יושב ואינו מדבר. רביעית שוה לכל אדם. ר' יהודה אומר לא הצריכו לומר שבת ראשונה שהכל נכנסין אצלו לנחמו אלא שניה אינו יוצא מביתו. שלישית יוצא ואינו יושב במקומו. רביעית יושב ואינו מדבר. חמישית שוה לכל אדם. ב) והיכן דרגילין אבלים לצלויי כנסת קדמי ואתו ויתבי במקום אבלים מצלו. ואיכא נמי בבבל דעבדי הכי: ת"ר כל שלשים אסור לישא. מתה אשתו אסור לישא אחרת עד שיעברו עליו שלש רגלים. ר' יהודה אומר רגל ראשון ושני אסור שלישי מותר ואם אין לו בנים מותר לישא לאלתר משום ביטול פריה ורביה. הניחה לו בנים קטנים מותר לישא אשה לאלתר מפני פרנסתן. ומעשה שמתה אשתו של יוסף הכהן ואמר לאחותה ועדיין הן בבית הקברות לכי ופרנסי בני אחותך ואעפ"כ לא בא עליה אלא לאחר שלשים וכן עשה ר' טרפון ומפורש בתלמוד א"י: ת"ר כל שלשים יום לגיהוץ אחד כלים חדשים ואחד כלים ישנים יוצאין מתחת מכבש רבי אומר לא אמרו אלא כלים חדשים בלבד אביי נפק בגרדא דסרבלא כו'. רבא נפק ג) בהמיצתא רומניתא סומקתא חדתי כר' [אלעזר בר'] שמעון וקיי"ל כרבא ואליבא דר' אלעזר בר' שמעון: **ירושלמי** ב' אחין. ב' שותפין. ב' טבחין ב' חנונין שאירע לאחד מהן דבר הרי אלו נועלין חנותן ופועלים עושין בצינעא במקום אחד: **מתני'** מפני שאמרו שבת עולה ואינה מפסקת בני יהודה ובני גלילא דהני אמרי יש אבלות

א) כ"ה גרסת הרי"ף ויושבין ודוין כו'. ב) וכן הביא הרמב"ן ז"ל בס' תה"א בשער האבלות בשם רב האי גאון ז"ל ועי' ברא"ש כאן. ג) כ"ה גי' הערוך בערך המילתא וע"ע בערך חמלתא והרי"ף ז"ל גרס בהימייטותא רומייתא.

הגהות הב"ח

(א) גמ' שניה יוצא ואינו יושב במקומו ואינו מדבר שלישית יושב במקומו: (ב) שם ואינו יושב במקומו ואינו מדבר רביעית יושב כו': (ג) שם ואחד כלים ישנים יוצאין מתחת המכבש רבי אומר:

גליון הש"ס

גמ' שבת ראשונה אינו יוצא. עיין לקמן דף כז ע"א תוס' ד"ה אם יכול: **שם** בגרדא דסרבלא כרבי. עיין לקמן דף כד ע"ב תוס' ד"ה ברכת אבלים: **תוס'** ד"ה ואמר לאחותה וכו' מותר לישא ולבעול. נ"ל שתיבת ולבעול ט"ס הוא:

קנו א מיי' פ"ד מהל' אבל הל"ז סמג עשין מד"ס ב טוש"ע י"ד סי' שמא סעיף א וטוש"ע א"ח סי' קלט סעיף ה:
קנז ב מיי' פ"י שם הלכה א סמג עשין ב טוש"ע י"ד סי' ת סעיף א:

רבינו חננאל

אבלות בשבת מדקתני במתני' ושבת עולה: והני אמרי אין אבלות בשבת מדקתני אינה מפסקת דאי ס"ד יש אבלות בשבת [השתא אבלות] נהיג אפסוקי דלא מפסקא מיבעיא כו'. לימא כתנאי מי שמתו מוטל לפניו אוכל בבית אחר וכו'. עד ובשבת מיסב ואוכל בשר ושותה יין ומברך ומזמן ומברכין עליו ומזמנין עליו וחייב בתפלה ובק"ש ובתפילין ובכל מצות האמורות בתורה. ר"ג אומר מתוך שנתחייב באלו כך נתחייב בכולן א"ר יוחנן תשמיש המטה איכא בינייהו. מאי לאו בהא קא מיפלגי ת"ק סבר יש אבלות בשבת ור"ג סבר אין אבלות בשבת אפילו תשמיש המטה שרי ודחינן ממאי דלמא עד כאן לא קאמר ת"ק הכא דאסור בתשמיש המטה אלא משום דמתו מוטל לפניו כו':

יֵשׁ אֲבֵילוּת בְּשַׁבָּת, וְהָנֵי אָמְרִי: אֵין אֲבֵילוּת בְּשַׁבָּת. מַאן דְּאָמַר יֵשׁ אֲבֵילוּת בְּשַׁבָּת — דְּקָתָנֵי: עוֹלָה. מַאן דְּאָמַר אֵין אֲבֵילוּת בְּשַׁבָּת — דְּקָתָנֵי: אֵינָהּ מַפְסֶקֶת. אִי סָלְקָא דַעְתָּךְ יֵשׁ אֲבֵילוּת בְּשַׁבָּת — הָשְׁתָּא אֲבֵילוּת נָהֲגָא, אִפְּסוּקֵי מִיבַּעְיָא? וְאֶלָּא הָא קָתָנֵי עוֹלָה! אַיְּידֵי דְּקָבָעֵי לְמִיתְנָא סֵיפָא אֵינָן עוֹלִים, תָּנָא רֵישָׁא עוֹלָה. וּלְמַאן דְּאָמַר יֵשׁ אֲבֵילוּת בְּשַׁבָּת, הָא קָתָנֵי אֵינָהּ מַפְסֶקֶת! מִשּׁוּם דְּקָבָעֵי לְמִיתְנָא סֵיפָא מַפְסִיקִין — תָּנָא רֵישָׁא אֵינָהּ מַפְסֶקֶת. לֵימָא כְּתַנָּאֵי: *אמִי שֶׁמֵּתוֹ מוּטָּל לְפָנָיו — אוֹכֵל בְּבַיִת אַחֵר, אֵין לוֹ בַּיִת אַחֵר — אוֹכֵל בְּבֵית חֲבֵרוֹ, אֵין לוֹ בֵּית חֲבֵרוֹ — עוֹשֶׂה לוֹ מְחִיצָּה עֲשָׂרָה טְפָחִים, אֵין לוֹ דָּבָר לַעֲשׂוֹת מְחִיצָּה — מַחֲזִיר פָּנָיו וְאוֹכֵל. וְאֵינוֹ מֵיסֵב וְאוֹכֵל, וְאֵינוֹ אוֹכֵל בָּשָׂר, וְאֵינוֹ שׁוֹתֶה יַיִן וְאֵין מְבָרֵךְ, וְאֵין מְזַמֵּן, וְאֵין מְבָרְכִין עָלָיו, וְאֵין מְזַמְּנִין עָלָיו, וּפָטוּר מִקְּרִיאַת שְׁמַע, וּמִן הַתְּפִלָּה, וּמִן הַתְּפִילִּין, וּמִכָּל מִצְוֹת הָאֲמוּרוֹת בַּתּוֹרָה. וּבְשַׁבָּת — מֵיסֵב וְאוֹכֵל, וְאוֹכֵל בָּשָׂר, וְשׁוֹתֶה יַיִן, וּמְבָרֵךְ, וּמְזַמֵּן, וּמְבָרְכִין וּמְזַמְּנִין עָלָיו, °וְחַיָּיב בִּקְרִיאַת שְׁמַע וּבִתְפִלָּה וּבִתְפִילִּין וּבְכָל מִצְוֹת הָאֲמוּרוֹת בַּתּוֹרָה. *רַבָּן גַּמְלִיאֵל אוֹמֵר: מִתּוֹךְ שֶׁנִּתְחַיֵּיב בְּאֵלּוּ — נִתְחַיֵּיב בְּכוּלָּן. וְאָמַר ר' יוֹחָנָן: בתַּשְׁמִישׁ הַמִּטָּה אִיכָּא בֵּינַיְיהוּ. מַאי לָאו בְּהָא קָא מִיפַּלְגִי; דְּמָר סָבַר: יֵשׁ אֲבֵילוּת בְּשַׁבָּת, וּמָר סָבַר: אֵין אֲבֵילוּת בְּשַׁבָּת. מִמַּאי? דִּלְמָא עַד כָּאן לָא קָאָמַר תַּנָּא קַמָּא הָתָם — אֶלָּא מִשּׁוּם דְּמֵתוֹ מוּטָּל לְפָנָיו, אֲבָל הָכָא דְּאֵין מֵתוֹ מוּטָּל לְפָנָיו — לֹא. וְעַ"כ לָא קָאָמַר ר"ג הָתָם — דַּאֲכַתִּי לָא חָל אֲבֵילוּת עֲלֵיהּ, אֲבָל הָכָא דְּחָל אֲבֵילוּת עֲלֵיהּ — הָכִי נַמִּי.
בְּעָא

ברכות יז: שמחות פ"י
[במס' שמחות אי' כדהכא אבל בברכו' יח. איתא ר"ש בן גמליאל]

אִפְּסוּקֵי מִבָּעֲיָא. כְּלוֹמַר: מִי צְרִיכָא לְמֵימַר דְּאֵינָהּ מַפְסֶקֶת: **אֵין מְבָרֵךְ.** לְהוֹצִיא אֲחֵרִים יְדֵי חוֹבָתָן: **מִתּוֹךְ שֶׁנִּתְחַיֵּיב בְּאֵלּוּ.** קְרִיאַת שְׁמַע כו' נִתְחַיֵּיב בְּכוּלָּן: **תַּשְׁמִישׁ הַמִּטָּה אִיכָּא בֵּינַיְיהוּ.** הָא דְּאָמַר נִתְחַיֵּיב בְּכוּלָּן — סָבַר: מוּתָּר בְּתַשְׁמִישׁ הַמִּטָּה, וְתַנָּא קַמָּא סָבַר: אָסוּר בְּתַשְׁמִישׁ הַמִּטָּה: **מָר.** דְּאָסַר בְּתַשְׁמִישׁ, סָבַר: יֵשׁ אֲבֵילוּת בְּשַׁבָּת: **וּמָר.** דְּשָׁרֵי, סָבַר כִּשְׁמוּאֵל דְּאָמַר: אֵין אֲבֵילוּת בְּשַׁבָּת: **עֲדַיִין לֹא חָלָה אֲבֵילוּת עֲלֵיהּ.** דְּלֹא נִקְבַּר:
אֲבָל

יש אבילות בשבת. בדברים שבצנעא איירי, כדפירש בקונט'. ובסמוך נמי: לימא כתנאי, מייתי פלוגתא דרשב"ג ורבנן — דהוי דברים שבצנעא. והכי משמע קצת בירושל' דלעיל אמתניתין דהשבת עולה, פליגי רבי יוחנן וריב"ל אם אסור בשבת בתשמיש המטה — משמע דפליגי כעין פלוגתא דהכא, ואליבא דרבי יוחנן יש שאומרים שם מותר, ואותו חולק על התלמוד שלנו, דא"ר יוחנן בפ"ק דכתובות (דף ד. ושם): אע"פ שאמרו אין אבילות בשבת — אבל דברים שבצנעא נוהג. וקצת קשה לי תימה בשמעתין: אביי אשכחיה לרב יוסף דפריס סודרא ארישיה, אמר ליה לא סבר לה מר אין אבילות בשבת? אמר ליה: הכי אמר ר' יוחנן: דברים שבצנעא נוהג! שמא היה סבור דפריס סודרא ארישיה הוה דברים שבפרהסיא, וכמאן דאמר פריעת הראש חובה, ולא היה מחלק בין בביתו בין חוץ לביתו. והוא השיב לו: בביתו חשיב צנעא: **מאן** דאמר יש אבילות בשבת מדקתני עולה. פירש הר"א ז"ל: מדקתני ולא פירש "ואין בה אבילות" — אלמא: אבילות נוהג בה, דאם לא כן — היה לו לפרש הכי בהדיא, אע"ג דעולה לא נהג בה אבילות. דכיון דעולה — משמע דנוהג בה אבילות. ומשני: איידי דקתני סיפא אין עולין סתם, תנא ברישא עולה סתם. ולא נהירא. ופירש ר' שמעון זצ"ל מרבו: מאן דאמר יש אבילות דקתני עולה — משמע דעולה לכל מנין שבעה, ולאבילות — שינהג בשבת מה שנהג אתמול. ומתוך כך תעלה שבת לחשבונו, כשם שע"ש עולה לחשבונו. מ"ד אין אבילות בשבת, דקתני אינה מפסקת, אע"ג דחשיבא כולי האי לבטל אבילות בגוה — מ"מ אינו מפסיק. דאל"כ פשיטא. וקפריך: ואלא הא דקתני עולה, דמשמע דנוהג אבילות כשאר ימים! ומשני: איידי דקתני גבי י"ט אין עולין לגמרי, לא למנין ולא לאבילות, משום שמחה דכתיב בהן כדפרישית, תנא רישא נמי עולה, באותו לשון עצמו דתנא בי"ט תנא בשבת, דלא להפליג בלשון המשנה. ומיהו, עולה דשבת *אינו למנין דלאבילות לא סלקא, אלא אי נהגא אבילות בגויה. וא"כ, לפי פירוש זה ואלא הא דקתני עולה, ומשני לעולם לא נהגא, ואיידי דתנא כו'. וא"כ המשנה — אין שטת התלמוד לומר "איידי דתנא הא תנא נמי הא" — אלא במילתא דאמת, אלא דלא צריכי. אבל דברים נראים שקר — אין לו לשנות! ועוד יש להקשות: לפי מה שמפרש אי הכי ליתני שבת אינו עולה, והוי דומיא דסיפא יותר. עד כאן לשון הר"א. ובתו' הרב מקשה: דמשמע אפילו למאן דאמר דלא נהגא עולה למנין שבעה, וא"כ ברגל נמי, אע"ג דלא נהגא — יהא עולה. ולעיל אמרי' לענין שבעה לא קמבעיא ליה דלא נהגא מצות שבעה ברגל! ומתרץ: אע"ג דשבת עולה — רגל אינו עולה, הואיל ואין אבילות כלל, משום דכתיב בהן שמחה. שבת מיהא לא כתיב שמחה, אפילו אינה נוהגת — עולה. בירושלמי מפרש טעמא דשבת דאין אבילות נוהג בו — משום דכתיב (משלי י) "ברכת ה' היא תעשיר ולא יוסיף עצב עמה" ושבת כתיב ביה ברכה*: **ואינו** אוכל בשר ואינו שותה יין. נראה דכי היכי דשרי בפרק בתרא דתענית (דף ל.) גבי ערב תשעה באב בשר כל זמן שאינו כשלמים, ויין מגתו — הכי נמי שרי באונן. מיהו, אין רגילין לנהוג בהן היתר לא בכאן ולא בתשעה באב. תימה: משמע דאונן חמור מאבל, דלא מצינו אבל שיהא בו איסור בבשר וביין. ולענין קדשים אשכחן דאבל אוכל בקדשים, ואונן אסור. ובשאר דברים החמירו באבילות: בכפיית המטה, ונעילת הסנדל, ועטיפת הראש, וטובא איכא, ובאונן שרי! וי"ל: דדברים שהן משום אבל — מותר גבי אונן, ובאבילות אסורין. אבל דברים שאינם אסורין משום אבילות, אלא משום שיש לו להיות טרוד בקבורת מתו, ולא ימשך אחר דברים אחרים — כגון אכילת בשר ושתיית יין — אסירי באונן דוקא. ותשמיש המטה, דמשמע בסמוך דאסור באונן — בהא נמי שמא ימשך, או שמא שמחה יתירתא וחופה, כך מצאתי, ובתגלחת ובתכבוסת לא ידעינן אי שרי באונן. ואין ללמוד איסור לגלח, מדתני' במס' שמחות*: היה מגלח ואמרו לו מת אחד מקרוביו — הרי זה יגמור. משמע: הא לא התחיל — אסור. דלמא בשמועה איירי, ולאחר שנקבר. ובשם ריב"א כתבתי: דתגלחת אסור, דנפקא לן מ"ראשיכם אל תפרעו" (ויקרא י) הא כולי עלמא — אסירי. ואינהו אוננים הוו. ובתשמיש המטה דאסרינן בסמוך, ורצו להתיר באנינות כדאמרינן פ"ק דכתובות (דף ד. ושם), ובאבילות אסרו. דקאמרינן התם: מכניסין את המת לחדר ובועל בעילת מצוה ופורש. והא דקאמרינן התם אבילות דהכא קילא ואתי לזלזולי בה, ומקשה: מאי קולא? אילימא דקתני בועל בעילת מצוה, משום דלא חיילא אבילות עליה. אינו רוצה לומר שאין קולא בדבר, אלא הכי קאמר: אין קולא באבילות, כי אם באנינות ולא אתי לזלזולי באבילות: **ואין** מברכין עליו. פירש בקונטרס בברכות פרק "מי שמתו" (דף יח. ושם): ברכת המוציא, ואין מזמנין — ברכת המזון. ותימה: גבי המוציא מה שייך לומר אין מברכין עליו? בשלמא גבי ברכת המזון — שייך זירוף, אלא גבי המוציא מאי שייך זירוף? ויש לפרש: דבגמרא קאמרינן דאין מברכין עליו, אלא מצוה לחלק, דהוו כשנים שאכלו שמצוה ליחלק, ואין זה האונן מצטרף עמהן, ואין מזמנין עליהן = עמהן, לומר: נברך שאכלנו משלו. ואי לא הוה תני אלא חדא הוה אמינא: לענין נברך שאכלנו משלו דאין מצטרף אבל מצטרף, להיות להם דין שלשה, לברך אחד מהן בעבור חברו, להכי תני תרתי. וריב"א מפרש: דאין מברכין ומזמנין, חדא לומר "נברך שאכלנו משלו", וחדא לברך בשם, כמו שמזכירין שם בעשרה. פירש בקונטרס בפרק "מי שמתו" (ג"ז שם): ואינו מברך — אין צריך לברך ברכת המזון. משמע מפירושו דאין אסור לברך. ובשמעתין נמי פירש כענין זה. ומיהו, מדקאמר בריש פרק "מי שמתו" התם למאן דאמר [תוך] ארבע אמות הוא דאסור — פירש רבינו יצחק בברכות: דאיכא איסור לברך. וגם בתוספות הרב פירש דאסור לברך. ותימה לרבי יצחק: דהשתא נהגו לברך ולזמן! והיה אומר דלא איירי הכא רק כשהוא עוסק בצרכי המת, שאין לו להתבטל מן המצוה. אבל בשעה שאינו עוסק — שרי. אי נמי: בשעה שאחרים עוסקים, והוא אינו עושה כלום. ומיהו, בירושל' אינו משמע כן, והכי איתא התם*: אינו אוכל כל צורכו, ואינו שותה כל צורכו כו', ואינו מברך. ואם בירך — אין עונין אחריו אמן. ואם ברכו אחרים — אינו עונה אחריהם אמן. ואם משום ביטול מצות עסק במתו — מה ביטול יש בעניית אמן? מיהו, נראה לי משום שמיעת הברכה, שלא תהיה אמן יתומה. ועוד: דאמרינן לקמן הן עומדין ומתפללין והוא יושב ומצדיק עליו את הדין, ומשמע שאינו עוסק בו כלל, אלא יושב ודומם. ונראה דאסור לברך. ושוב מצאתי בירושל' דריש פרק "מי שמתו" תני: אם רצה להחמיר על עצמו — אין שומעין לו, למה — מפני כבודו של מת או משום שאין לו מי שישא משאוי. ופריך: והא תניא פטור מנטילת לולב? וקא סלקא דעתיה דמיירי ביום טוב, ובו אינו טרוד לישא במשאוי! ומשני: תפתר בחול. פירוש: בחולו של מועד. ופריך: והתניא פטור מתקיעת שופר, אית לך למימר בחול ולא ביום טוב? אמר ר' חנינא: מכיון שהיו זקוקים להביא לו ארון ותכריכין, דתנינן תמן: מחשיכין על התחום לפקח על עסקי כלה ועל עסקי המת, להביא ארון ותכריכין — נמי כמו שהוא נושא משאוי דמי.

*משמע דפליגי בשבת וביום טוב דאינו מברך במאי דאמרינן. מיהו, הא קשיא לן: דאמרינן בסיפא: בשבת מברך ומזמן, וצריך עיון:
בעא

אינו אלא למנין דאבילות ולא נהגא אבילות כצ"ל
[ויברך אלהים את יום השביעי כ"ה במ"ר ויחי פ"ק]
פ"ה ה"ח
רש"א
שמחות פ"י
משמע דפליג בשבת כצ"ל

גליון הש"ס

גמ' וחייב בק"ש ובתפלה ובתפילין ובכל מצות. בברכות בברייתא זו איתא וחייב בכל מצות האמורות בתורה ובר"ף שם חייב בק"ש ותפלה ובכל מצות האמורות בתורה.

עין משפט נר מצוה

קנח א מיי' פ"ח מהל' אבל הל' א סמג עשין מד"ס ב:

קנט ב ג מיי' פ"י שם הל' א סמג שם טוש"ע י"ד סי' ת סעי' א:

קס ד מיי' פ"ח שם הל' ג סמג שם טור י"ד סי' שמ:

קסא ה ו מיי' פ"ה שם הל' יט טוש"ע י"ד סי' שפו:

קסב ז מיי' פ"י שם הל' א טוש"ע י"ד סי' ת סעי' א:

קסג ח מיי' שם פ"ט הל' א טוש"ע י"ד סי' שמ סעי' יד:

קסד ט מיי' שם פי"ב הל' י סמג שם טוש"ע י"ד סי' שנג סעי' ז:

גמרא

בעא מיניה ר' יוחנן משמואל: יש אבילות בשבת או אין אבילות בשבת? אמר ליה: אין אבילות בשבת. יתבי רבנן קמיה דרב פפא וקאמרי משמיה דשמואל: אבל ששימש מטתו בימי אבלו – חייב מיתה. א"ל רב פפא: אסור אתמר, ומשמיה דר' יוחנן אתמר. ואי שמיעא לכו משמיה דשמואל – הכי שמיע לכו: אמר רב תחליפא בר אבימי אמר שמואל: אבל שלא פרע ושלא פירם – חייב מיתה, שנאמר: (ויקרא י) "ראשיכם אל תפרעו ובגדיכם לא תפרומו ולא תמותו" וגו', הא אחר שלא פרע ושלא פירם – חייב מיתה. אמר רפרם בר פפא, תנא באבל רבתי: אבל אסור לשמש מטתו בימי אבלו. ומעשה באחד ששימש מטתו בימי אבלו, ושמטו חזירים את גוייתו. אמר שמואל: פח"ז – חובה, נת"ר – רשות. פריעת הראש, חזרת קרע לאחוריו, זקיפת המטה – חובה. נעילת הסנדל, תשמיש המטה, רחיצת ידים ורגלים בחמין ערבית – רשות. ורב אמר: אף פריעת הראש רשות. ושמואל, מאי שנא נעילת הסנדל דרשות – דלאו כולי עלמא עבידי דסיימי מסאנייהו, פריעת הראש נמי לאו כולי עלמא עבידי דמגלו רישייהו! שמואל לטעמיה, דאמר שמואל: כל קרע שאינו בשעת חימום – אינו קרע, וכל עטיפה שאינה כעטיפת ישמעאלים – אינה עטיפה. מחוי ר"נ עד גובי דדיקנא. א"ר יעקב א"ר יוחנן: לא שנו אלא שאין לו מנעלים ברגליו, אבל יש לו מנעלים ברגליו – מנעליו מוכיחין עליו. כל קרע שאינו בשעת חימום אינו קרע? והא אמרו ליה לשמואל: נח נפשיה דרב. קרע עליה תריסר מני, אמר: אזל גברא דהוה מסתפינא מיניה. א"ל לרבי יוחנן: נח נפשיה דר' חנינא. *קרע עליה תליסר אצטלי מלתא, אמר: אזל גברא דהוה מסתפינא מיניה. שאני רבנן, דכיון דכל שעתא מדכרי שמעתייהו – כשעת חימום דמי. א"ל רבין בר אדא לרבא: אמר תלמידך רב עמרם, תניא: אבל, כל שבעה – קורעו לפניו, ואם בא להחליף – מחליף, וקורע. בשבת – קורעו לאחוריו, ואם בא להחליף – מחליף, ואינו קורע! כי תניא ההיא – בכבוד אביו ואמו. אותן קרעין מתאחין או אין מתאחין? פליגי בה אבוה דרב אושעיא ובר קפרא. חד אמר: אין מתאחין, וחד אמר: מתאחין. תסתיים דאבוה דרב אושעיא דאמר אין מתאחין, דאמר רב אושעיא, אין מתאחין. ממאן שמיע ליה – לאו מאבוה? לא, מבר קפרא רביה שמיע ליה. אמר רבא: אבל מטייל באונקלי בתוך ביתו. אביי אשכחיה לרב יוסף דפרים ליה סודרא ארישיה, ואזיל ואתי בביתיה. א"ל: לאו סבר לה מר אין אבילות בשבת? א"ל: הכי א"ר יוחנן: *דברים שבצינעא נוהג. § "ר"א אומר משחרב בית המקדש עצרת כשבת" וכו'. § אמר רב גידל בר מנשיא אמר שמואל: הלכה כר"ג. ואיכא דמתני להא דרב גידל בר מנשיא אהא: כל ל' יום *תינוק יוצא בחיק, ונקבר באשה אחת ושני אנשים, אבל לא באיש אחד ושתי נשים.

אבא

רש"י

אבל רבתי. מסכת שמחות: גוייתו. כל גופו, והיכא דאמרי: חבר שלו: פריעת הראש. שמגלה האבל ראשו בשבת, ואינו מתעטף. וחזרת קרע לאחוריו, וזקיפת המטה – חובה בשבת: נעילת הסנדל. דלאו כולי עלמא סיימי מסאנייהו בשבת, ולא מוכח דאבל הוא: לא כולי עלמא מגלי רישייהו. בשבת, ואע"פ שמתעטף – לא מיחזי כאבל: בשעת חימום. בשעת התחלת הצער, בשעת מיתה: וכל עטיפה שאינה כעטיפת ישמעאלים. הלכך, כיון דכל ימי שבוע שהוא אבל מתעטף כישמעאל, אם אינו נוטלה בשבת – נראה כנוהג אבילות, דכ"ע לא נהיגי בעטיפה זו, אלא אבלים בלבד: מחוי ר"נ. עטיפת ישמעאלים: גובי דיקנא. גומות שבלחי, למטה מפיו: לא שנו. פריעת הראש בשבת, דצריך לגלות חוטמו ושפמו וזקנו שהיה מכוסה בימי אבלו, להודיע כי אין אבילות בשבת: אלא שאין מנעלים ברגליו אבל יש מנעלים ברגליו מנעליו מוכיחים עליו. דאינו אבל. אבל לגלות ראשו – אינו צריך. ואם בא להתעטף בצינעא, אפי' כעטיפת הישמעאלים – אין בכך כלום: דמסתפינא מיניה. בקושיות: מחליף וקורע. אע"פ שאינו שעת חימום: בכבוד אביו. שנו. אבל לכולי עלמא – אין קורע אלא בשעת חימום: ממאן שמיעא. לרב אושעיא הא דאמר אין מתאחין – שמע מינה האי דאמר אין מתאחין – אבוה דרב אושעיא: אונקלי. סייפינ"ש, חלוק שקורעו: בתוך ביתו. שבצינעא מותר לנהוג אבילות בשבת: דפרים סודריה ארישיה. בשבת, משום עטיפה, דנהיג אבילות: כל ל' יום יוצא בחיק. בן ל' יום מוציאו בחיק לבית הקברות, ולא בארון: אבל לא באיש אחד. שאין מתייחדין עם האשה:

דלוסקמא

תוספות

בעא מיניה ר' יוחנן משמואל. מיהו ר' יוחנן לא קיבל משמואל, דאיהו סבירא ליה: דברים שבצינעא נוהג, כדפרישית לעיל:

הא אחר שלא פרע כו'. אע"ג דפשטי' דקרא הא אחר פורע ופורס, ואם הם יעשו ימותו – נראה דאסמכתא בעלמא הוא, דהא לא מייתי להו סוף פרק "הנשרפין" (סנהדרין דף פג.) גבי אלו שבמיתה:

ושמואל לטעמיה. פי' בתוספ' הרב: דרב סבר דעטיפת הראש שאינה כעטיפת ישמעאלים הויא עטיפה, ומסתמא רב ושמואל הלכה כרב. יש מפרשין דרחיצת ידים דקאמר הכא רשות – היינו כמ"ד פרק "במה מדליקין" (שבת דף כה:) דבלא אבילות הוא רשות. אבל לר"נ בר יצחק דאמר התם: ואני אומר מצוה – באבל נמי הוי מצוה, ולא רשות. ונראה דלא צריך למימר הכי, אלא הכי פירושו: הכא דמשום אבילות – אינו חובה להראות אבילות בשבת:

לא שנו שאין לו מנעלים ברגליו. תימה: דכי היכי דמנעליו מוכיחין עליו, אמאי לא אמרי' אחד מהני מוכיחין? ונמצא דאינו חובה כי אם האחד! ושמא במנעלים יש הוכחה יותר:

וכל קרע שאינו בשעת חימום אינו קרע. נראה דהא דאמר לעיל (דף כ:) מי שנזדמן לו חלוק בתוך ז', אע"פ שאינו שעת חימום – שמא דוקא כגון שקרע כבר. והכא איירי בשלא קרע עדיין. א"נ: כגון שאין לו חלוק בשעה ראשונה – חייב לקרוע כשיהיה לו, אפי' שלא בשעת חימום. ולי נראה, דבכל שעה שיוכל להתחמם על מתו, אפי' לזמן מרובה אחר מיתתו – קרוי שפיר בשעת חימום, כמו שאמרו ברבנן: משום דמדכרי שמעתייהו, הוא הדין נמי בכל מת שיוכל להתחמם עליו. והא דפריך בסמוך ולא משני הכי – משום דבלאו הכי משני שפיר:

כי תניא ההיא בכבוד אביו ואמו. ומכאן קשה לי על מה שפי' למעלה (דף כ:) *)דגרסי': רבי חנינא מי שאין לו אלא חלוק אחד, דמיירי בכה"ג דמחליף וקורע. דהא גבי אביו ואמו אמר הכא: מחליף וקורע כל שבעה, ולעיל (שם) אמרי': על אביו ואמו קורע לעולם! וצ"ע:

הכי א"ר יוחנן דברים שבצינעא נוהג. פסק בהלכות גדולות כר' יוחנן, לאפוקי מרב ושמואל דאמרי לעיל: תשמיש המטה רשות, ודברים שבצינעא הוא. ובפ"ק דכתובות (דף ד.) נמי קאמר עלה: מסייע ליה לר' יוחנן, דאביי ורבא סברי כוותיה. ואע"ג דקיימא לן (לעיל דף יח. כב.) הלכה כדברי המיקל – ה"מ במחלוקת של תנאים, אבל במילתא דאמוראי – לא אמרן. מספקא לי, כי היכי דשרי בתוך ביתו הני דברים דקריעה, אי הוה אסור נעילת הסנדל בצנעא, וכל שאר דברים:

*עצרת כשבת. וכ"ש ר"ה ויוה"כ, ר"ג אומר ר"ה ויוה"כ כרגלים וכ"ש עצרת לאחר חורבן. ולישנא לא אתי שפיר, דהוה ליה למתני: ר"ג אומר אף ר"ה ויוה"כ כו':

וחכמים אומרים לא כדברי זה כו'. ולא שייך למימר: היינו תנא קמא! דנימא כולהו אתו לפרש מילתא דתנא קמא, כי ההיא דלא ירדה לו נשים בפרק ב' דסנהדרין (דף כא.), וההיא (דהמקדש):

הלכה כר"ג. תימה: כיון דאמר שמואל (לעיל דף יח. כב.) הלכה כדברי המיקל באבל, אמאי איצטריך למיפסק הלכה כר"ג? וי"ל: דחומרא נמי היא, דאם קברו סמוך לחשיכה ולא היה לו שעה אחת לנהוג בו אבילות, או קברוהו נכרים ביום טוב, או שמע שמועה קרובה ביום טוב, אם הם כרגלים – אינם עולים למנין שבעה, ואם הם כשבת – עולים:

אבא

*) אבל הגי' שם מי שאין לו חלוק לקרוע כו' ואולי גיר' אחרת היתה לפניהם ועיין במהרש"א

רבינו חננאל

בעא מיניה ר' יוחנן משמואל יש אבילות בשבת אי לא. א"ל אין אבילות בשבת. אמרי רבנן משמיה דשמואל אבל ששימש מטתו חייב מיתה. א"ל רב פפא אסור אתמר ומשמיה דר' יוחנן אתמר אמר רב תחליפא אמר שמואל אבל שלא פרע ראשו ולא פירם בגדיו חייב מיתה שנאמר ראשיכם אל תפרעו ובגדיכם לא תפרומו ולא תמותו מכלל שאחר שלא פירע ושלא פירם חייב מיתה. אמר רפרם תנא באבל רבתי אבל אסור לשמש מטתו ומעשה באחד ששימש מטתו בימי אבלו ושמטו חזירים את גויתו. אמרו משמיה דשמואל פח"ז חובה. פריעת הראש. חזרת קרע לאחוריו. זקיפת המטה לעשותן בשבת [חובה] להודיע שאינו נוהג אבל בשבת. אבל נ'ת'ר'. נעילת סנדל. תשמיש המטה. רחיצת ידים ורגלים בחמין רשות. ורב אמר אף פריעת הראש בשבת רשות. מקשינן לשמואל מ"ש נעילת הסנדל דאמר רשות דלאו כ"ע מסגי במסני. פריעת הראש נמי לאו כ"ע עבידי דמגלי רישיהו. ופרקינן שמואל לטעמיה דאמר כל קרע שאינו בשעת חימום אינו קרע. וכל עטיפה שאינה כעטיפת ישמעאלים אינה עטיפה. פי' עטיפת ישמעאלים דאמר שמואל מכסה שפמו וזקנו וחוטמו במצנפתו או בטליתו. והוא אלמתה בלשון ערב. ובשבת צריך לגלות חוטמו ושפמו וזקנו שהיה מכסה בימי אבלו כי אין אבל בשבת אבל לגלות ראשו אין צריך. ועוד כמה מכסי מחוי רב נחמן עד גובי דדיקנא. א"ר יוחנן לא שנו אלא שאין מנעלין ברגליו אבל יש מנעלין ברגליו מנעליו מוכיחין עליו. וקיי"ל כרב דאמר פריעת הראש נמי בשבת רשות. ואם בא להתעטף בצנעא כעטיפת ישמעאלים אין בכך כלום *) ולא בעי עטיפה כולי האי. דהא רב יוסף דהוא בתרא עבד כרב. אמר רבא אבל מטייל באונקלי בתוך ביתו. ואונקלי היא מצנפת כגון מצנפת של כה"ג כדגרסינן בסוף מנחות. מעשה בחוני ושמעי בני שמעון הצדיק הלבישו באונקלי וחגרו בצלצול. אביי אשכחיה [לרב יוסף] דפרים סודרא ארישיה כעטיפת ישמעאלים וקאזיל ואתי בביתיה. א"ל לא סבר לה מר אין אבילות בשבת א"ל דברים שבצנעא נוהג. ומקשינן תוב לשמואל וכל קרע שאינו בשעת חימום אינו קרע. והא אמרו ליה לשמואל נח נפשיה דרב וקרע עליה תליסר כברי מאניה. ור' יוחנן קרע על ר' חנינא י"ג אצטלי דמלתא. א"ל אזל ליה גברא דהוה מסתפינא. הנה קרעו בשעת שמועה שלא בשעת חימום. ופרקינן שאני רבנן דכיון דכל שעתא מדכרי שמועתיה שעת שמועה כשעת חימום דמי. רבא אמר מהכא דתניא אבל כל שבעה קורעו לפניו ואם בא להחליף חלוקו מחליף וקורע החלוק שלובש הנה קריעתה שלא בשעת חימום. ופרקינן כי תניא ההיא שקורע כל חלוק שלובש אפילו כל שבעה בכבוד אביו ואמו: (ירושלמי הרי שהיה מחליף בגדיו) תשלום הברייתא ובשבת קורעו לאחוריו כדאמרן חזרת [קרע לאחוריו בשבת חובה] ואם בא בשבת להחליף חלוקו מחליף ואינו קורע. הרי שהיה מחליף בגדיו [כל] שבעה חייב לקרוע כולן. אותן קרעין מתאחין או אינן מתאחין. אסיקנא חלוקת אבוה דר' אושעיא ובר קפרא: ירושלמי אבל שבא מן הדרך והיה רגליו קיהות מותר לרחוץ שאין רחיצת צונן רחיצה. תני אבל ומנודה שהיו מהלכין בדרך מותרין בנעילת הסנדל. ולכשיבואו לעיר יחלוצו וכן בט' באב. וכן בתענית צבור. תני מקום שנהגו לשאול בשלום אבלים בשבת שואלין. ר' אושעיא חמא אבלין בשבת ואמר להו שלום עליכם כמנהג מקומנו. ר' יוסי בן חלפתא הוה משתבח בר"מ קומי ציפוראי. אדם גדול קדוש צנוע הוא. חד (יומא) זמן חמון ליה שאיל בשלום אבילא בשבת. ותו אמרו ליה ר' אהן הוא דאת משני שבחיה אמר להן [מה עביד] א"ל שאיל בשלום אבילייא בשבתא. אמר לון בעון מידע חייליה. אתא להודעאן דאין אבלות בשבת דכתיב ברכת ה' היא תעשיר. זו ברכת שבת. ולא יוסיף עצב עמה. זו אבלות כמו דאמר נעצב המלך אל בנו. תני ארוסתו לא מתאבל ולא אונן עליה. תני כל שמתאבלין עליו מתאבלין עמו. רב מתה אחותו פקיד לחייא בריה כד תיסליק לגביי של נעליך מעל רגליך. ר' יונה סליק לגביה ר' גוריון בשבת בגו ז' ימי אבלו. נפיק לגביה לביש סנדלי. א"ל אנת הכא דר' דילפון עובדא מינך דבשבת [מותר] בנעילת הסנדל לא ילפון עובדא מבר נש זעיר. אפילו דבר תורה א"ר יוחנן שלא היו יודעין במה לפתוח אם ביסורין שבגופו אם בחסרון ממונו אם בנפש בניו ובנותיו: מתני' משחרב בית המקדש ר' אלעזר אומר עצרת כשבת. ר"ג אומר ר"ה ויוה"כ כרגלים דייקינן מינה וכ"ש עצרת שהיא כרגלים. אמר גידל בן מנשי אמר שמואל הלכה כר"ג

*) נראה דר"ל דלרב גם בחול א"ל להתעטף כעטיפת ישמעאלים ועי' בתוס' ד"ה ושמואל.

מסורת הש"ס / גליון הש"ס

[עי' תוס' כ"ק לח: ד"ה עוכר]

גליון הש"ס: גמ' אסור אתמר ומשמיה דר"י אתמר. לא ידעתי מה חילק בזה הא לאותה בברייתא גמ' לעיל דף כא ע"א אסור בכס וכו' ובתשמיש:

[כתובות ז.]

קידושין פ: שמחות פ"ג

[שייך במשנה דלעיל יט.]

[ג"ז שייך למשנ' דלעיל יט.] [נ"ל דהמזבח מקדש (ל' פג.) וע"ע תוספות פסחים פג. ד"ה ר' שמעון אומר וקף קטו: ותוס' עירובין מח. ד"ה ר' יהודה]

אַבָּא שָׁאוּל אוֹמֵר: אַף בְּאִישׁ אֶחָד וּשְׁתֵּי נָשִׁים. וְאֵין עוֹמְדִין עָלָיו בְּשׁוּרָה, וְאֵין אוֹמְרִים עָלָיו בִּרְכַּת אֲבֵלִים וְתַנְחוּמֵי אֲבֵלִים. בֶּן שְׁלֹשִׁים יוֹצֵא בִּדְלוּסְקְמָא. רַבִּי יְהוּדָה אוֹמֵר: [א]לֹא דְלוּסְקְמָא הַנִּיטֶּלֶת בְּכָתֵף, אֶלָּא הַנִּיטֶּלֶת בַּאֲגַפַּיִם. וְעוֹמְדִין עָלָיו בְּשׁוּרָה, וְאוֹמְרִים עָלָיו בִּרְכַּת אֲבֵלִים וְתַנְחוּמֵי אֲבֵלִים. *[ב]בֶּן י"ב חֹדֶשׁ – יוֹצֵא בְּמִטָּה, ר"ע אוֹמֵר: הוּא בֶּן שָׁנָה וְאֵבָרָיו כְּבֶן שְׁתַּיִם, הוּא בֶּן שְׁתַּיִם וְאֵבָרָיו כְּבֶן שָׁנָה – יוֹצֵא בְּמִטָּה. ר' שִׁמְעוֹן בֶּן אֶלְעָזָר אוֹמֵר: [ג]הַיּוֹצֵא בְּמִטָּה – רַבִּים מַצְהִיבִין עָלָיו, אֵינוֹ יוֹצֵא בְּמִטָּה – אֵין רַבִּים מַצְהִיבִין עָלָיו. ר"א בֶּן עֲזַרְיָה אוֹמֵר: [ד]נִיכָּר לָרַבִּים – רַבִּים מִתְעַסְּקִים עִמּוֹ, אֵינוֹ נִיכָּר לָרַבִּים – אֵין רַבִּים מִתְעַסְּקִים עִמּוֹ. וּמַה הֵן בְּהֶסְפֵּד? רַבִּי מֵאִיר בְּשֵׁם רַבִּי יִשְׁמָעֵאל אוֹמֵר: עֲנִיִּים – בְּנֵי שָׁלֹשׁ, עֲשִׁירִים – בְּנֵי חָמֵשׁ. רַבִּי יְהוּדָה אוֹמֵר מִשְּׁמוֹ: [ה]עֲנִיִּים – בְּנֵי חָמֵשׁ, עֲשִׁירִים – בְּנֵי שֵׁשׁ. וּבְנֵי זְקֵנִים כִּבְנֵי עֲנִיִּים. אָמַר רַב גִּידֵּל בַּר מְנַשְּׁיָא אָמַר רַב: הֲלָכָה כְּרַבִּי יְהוּדָה שֶׁאָמַר מִשּׁוּם רַבִּי יִשְׁמָעֵאל. דָּרַשׁ ר' עֲנָנִי בַּר שָׂשׂוֹן אַפִּיתְחָא דְּבֵי נְשִׂיאָה: [ו]יוֹם אֶחָד לִפְנֵי עֲצֶרֶת וַעֲצֶרֶת – הֲרֵי כָּאן אַרְבָּעָה עָשָׂר. שְׁמַע רַבִּי אַמִּי וְאִיקְפַּד. אֲמַר: אַטּוּ דִּידֵיהּ הִיא? דְּרַבִּי אֶלְעָזָר א"ר אוֹשַׁעְיָא הִיא! דָּרַשׁ רַבִּי יִצְחָק נַפָּחָא אַקִּילְעָא דְּרֵישׁ גָּלוּתָא: יוֹם אֶחָד לִפְנֵי עֲצֶרֶת, וַעֲצֶרֶת – הֲרֵי כָּאן אַרְבָּעָה עָשָׂר. שְׁמַע רַב שֵׁשֶׁת אִיקְפַּד, אֲמַר: אַטּוּ דִּידֵיהּ הִיא? דר"א אָמַר ר' אוֹשַׁעְיָא הִיא. דְּא"ר אֶלְעָזָר א"ר אוֹשַׁעְיָא: [ז]מִנַּיִן *לַעֲצֶרֶת שֶׁיֵּשׁ לָהּ תַּשְׁלוּמִין כָּל שִׁבְעָה – שֶׁנֶּאֱמַר: °"בְּחַג הַמַּצּוֹת וּבְחַג הַשָּׁבֻעוֹת" (א) מַה חַג הַמַּצּוֹת יֵשׁ לָהּ תַּשְׁלוּמִין כָּל שִׁבְעָה – אַף חַג הַשָּׁבוּעוֹת יֵשׁ לָהּ תַּשְׁלוּמִין כָּל שִׁבְעָה. *אַדְבְּרֵיהּ רַב פַּפָּא לְרַב אָוְיָא סָבָא, וְדָרַשׁ: [ח]יוֹם אֶחָד לִפְנֵי רֹאשׁ הַשָּׁנָה, וְרֹאשׁ הַשָּׁנָה – הֲרֵי כָּאן אַרְבָּעָה עָשָׂר. אָמַר רָבִינָא: הִלְכָּךְ, [ט]יוֹם אֶחָד לִפְנֵי הֶחָג, וְחַג, וּשְׁמִינִי שֶׁלּוֹ – הֲרֵי כָּאן עֶשְׂרִים וְאֶחָד יוֹם. רָבִינָא אִיקְלַע לְסוּרָא דִּפְרָת, א"ל *רַב חֲבִיבָא מִסּוּרָא דִּפְרָת לְרָבִינָא: אָמַר מָר יוֹם אֶחָד לִפְנֵי רֹאשׁ הַשָּׁנָה וְרֹאשׁ הַשָּׁנָה הֲרֵי כָּאן אַרְבָּעָה עָשָׂר? אֲמַר לֵיהּ: אֲנָא מִסְתַּבְּרָא כְּרַבָּן גַּמְלִיאֵל הוּא דְּאָמִינָא.§ **מתני'** [י]אֵין קוֹרְעִין, [כ]וְלֹא חוֹלְצִין, [ל]וְאֵין מַבְרִין, אֶלָּא קְרוֹבָיו שֶׁל מֵת. [מ]וְאֵין מַבְרִין אֶלָּא עַל מִטָּה זְקוּפָה.§

גמ'

רש"י

דְּלוּסְקְמָא. אָרוֹן: וְאֵין עוֹמְדִין עָלָיו בְּשׁוּרָה. אֵין צָרִיךְ לַעֲמוֹד עָלָיו בְּשׁוּרָה. כְּשֶׁחוֹזְרִין מִבֵּית הַקְּבָרוֹת עוֹבְרִין לִפְנֵי הָאָבֵל בְּשׁוּרָה, וְכָל אֶחָד אוֹמֵר לוֹ: "תִּתְנַחֵם": בִּרְכַּת אֲבֵלִים. בְּרָכָה שֶׁאוֹמֵר בָּרְחָבָה, כִּדְאָמַר בִּכְתוּבּוֹת (ד' ח:): תַּנְחוּמֵי אֲבֵלִים. כָּל שִׁבְעָה הוֹלְכִין לְנַחֲמוֹ בְּבֵיתוֹ: הַנִּיטֶּלֶת בְּכָתֵף. בְּאָדָם אֶחָד: בַּאֲגַפַּיִם. בִּשְׁנֵי בְּנֵי אָדָם, דֶּרֶךְ כָּבוֹד: וְאֵבָרָיו כְּבֶן שְׁתַּיִם. שֶׁאֵבָרָיו גְּדוֹלִים: מַצְהִיבִין. מַרְגִּישִׁין וּמִצְטַעֲרִין: נִיכָּר לָרַבִּים. שֶׁהָיוּ מַכִּירִין כְּבָר, שֶׁהָיָה רָגִיל לָצֵאת מִן הַבַּיִת: מַה הֵן בְּהֶסְפֵּד. כַּמָּה יְהֵא גָּדוֹל שֶׁמִּצְוָה לְהַסְפִּידוֹ: עֲנִיִּים בְּנֵי שָׁלֹשׁ. לְפִי שֶׁהֶעָנִי מִצְטַעֵר עַל בָּנָיו יוֹתֵר מִן הֶעָשִׁיר, לְפִי שֶׁאֵין לוֹ שִׂמְחָה אַחֶרֶת: יוֹם אֶחָד לִפְנֵי עֲצֶרֶת. הָיָה אָבֵל: הֲרֵי כָּאן אַרְבָּעָה עָשָׂר. דַּעֲצֶרֶת חָשׁוּב כְּשִׁבְעָה, וְזֶהוּ יוֹם שֶׁלִּפְנֵי עֲצֶרֶת – חָשׁוּב ז', דְּסָבַר כִּי הַאי תַּנָּא דִּלְעֵיל (ד' כ.), דְּאָמַר: אֲפִילּוּ יוֹם אֶחָד, אֲפִילּוּ שָׁעָה אַחַת. וּכְמַאן דְּאָמַר עֲצֶרֶת כִּרְגָלִים: **מתני'** עַל מִטָּה זְקוּפָה. יוֹשְׁבִין הַמְנַחֲמִין: חוֹלְצִין. כְּתֵפֵיהֶן:

גמ'

תוספות

אבא שאול אומר אף באיש אחד ושתי נשים. מפורש במסכת קדושין (דף פ: ושם): אע"ג דאין איש אחד מתייחד עם שתי נשים, בשעת אבילות דטרידא – שרי:

ואין אומרים עליו ברכת אבלים. פירש בקונטרס: דמיירי בלא כלו לו חדשיו. ומיהו, אפי' מיירי בכלו לו חדשיו, נהי דמתאבלים עליו, כדאיתא בפרק "ר"א" (שבת ד' קלו. ושם) ובפרק "יש בכור לנחלה" (בכורות דף מט.) – מ"מ אין מחמירין עליו כל כך לצערו. כדאשכחן בהני דסמוך, דלפי מה שהוא גדול מחמירין לכבודו:

ברכת אבלים ותנחומי אבלים. שמנחמים אותו בדברים: לעיל (ע"א) פירש בקונטרס דאם בא להחליף בגדים שכבסו קודם הרגל, ללבוש בגדים שהן מכובסין כי חלוק הוא מַלְבּוּשׁ. ומכאן *משמע שר' שמעון היה מתיר בגדים שכבסו קודם הרגל. ובתוס' פי': אם בא להחליף ללבוש בגדים שאינם מכובסים, כי חלוק הוא מלבוש, ורגילים ללובשו ולהחליף בלא כיבוס. ור' יצחק זקיני סובר כך. ועל פירש"י הקשה: דאי שרי בגדים שכבסו קודם אבלו, ומסתמא הכי נמי שרי בגדים המגוהצים קודם אבילות, וא"כ מנין לו למעלה דאביי כרבי *מנא ב"ר אלעזר בן שמעון? שמא מקודם אבלו היו מגוהצין! וי"ל: דמדשרו הני דוקא ולא חדשים לבנים – ש"מ דסבירא להו הכי. ומיהו, זהו המנהג עתה שמלבישין אותו לאדם אחר יום או חצי יום, ואין זה קרוי בגד מכובס לדידיה: **רבי** עקיבא אומר בן שנה כו'. ולא סגי בי"ב חדשים. ובמסכת שמחות *נראה לי ר"ע כו'. פירוש: דלא בעי ג' שנים, ואם מת ביום שלשים – פוסק בפ' "יש בכור" (בכורות ד' מט.) שלשים יום באדם אינו נפל, ויום שלשים לענין אבילות כיום שלפניו, ואינו מתאבל. וה"ה מסתמא לענין בכור:

דרבי אלעזר א"ר אושעיא היא. והא דלא מייתי ברייתא דר"א בן יעקב, דמפיק תשלומין מ"וקראתם ובקרכס" איזהו חג שאתה קורא וקוצר – הוי אומר זה חג השבועות. וריש לקיש אמר: חג הקציר, איזהו חג שאתה חוגג וקוצר בו – הוי אומר זה עצרת? ויש לומר: דלא ידעינן כמה ימים, אי לאו מדרבי אושעיא. כדאיתא פרק "אין דורשין" (חגיגה דף יז: ושם). אלא קשיא: מנא ליה דעצרת כרגלים בזמן הזה הא ליכא תשלומין! ונהי דמתני' הכי משמע, מדקאמרי עצרת כרגלים – משמע לגמרי, מיהו היא גופא מנא ליה? י"ל: כיון דעצרת חד יומא, ונחשב כמו פסח וסוכות בזמן שבית המקדש קיים לענין תשלומין – חשיב נמי לדידן כרגל דפסח וסוכות. מיהו, בר"ה ויום הכפורים משמע דלא סבירא להו הכי דליהוו חשיבי כשבעה ימים, מדלא נקט אלא עצרת. ולית ליה דרבן גמליאל ורב פפא דבסמוך, דאמרי: אפילו ר"ה ויוה"כ ישנן כרגלים, דלעולם הוא במקום פסח וסוכות. הקשה בתוספות הרב: מה אנו צריכים שיהא ראש השנה כשבעה ימים? בלאו הכי נמי מותר לגלח ערב יום כפורים, דהוי קובר את מתו שמונה ימים קודם יום כפורים – דבטלה הימנו גזרת שלשים! ותירץ: דנפקא מינה אם לא גילח ערב יום כפורים, דאינו מגלח אחר יום כפורים. אבל עתה, דחשבינן ראש השנה כשבעה ויום הכפורים כשבעה, וערב ראש השנה כשבעה ימים קודם, ובין ראש השנה ליום כפורים שבעה, ונקיט ליה בתר יום כפורים שני ימים, ומגלח. ואין נראה לי תירוץ זה, דהא קיימא לן כאבא שאול, דאמר לעיל (ד' יט:): מגלח אחר הרגל. אלא יש לפרש: דנפקא לן מינה לענין שמועה רחוקה, דחשבינן לה שמועה רחוקה בהני שני ימים אחר יום כפורים. וזהו דוחק גדול, כי זה אינו מפורש בשום מקום שתחשב שמועה רחוקה פחות משלשים יום. ויותר היה יכול לומר לענין דחשבינן אחר ראש השנה שבת שלישית, דאמר לעיל: יושב במקומו. מיהו, אין זה נראה שום קושיא כלל, דהא דאמר שמונה ימים קודם הרגל בטלה ממנו גזרת שלשים יום – היינו דוקא היכא דנהג אבילות שבעה ימים, אבל זה שלא נהג אבילות כי אם יום אחד – לא אמרינן יום כפורים תבטל שלשים. ותמהתי למה לא פירש הרב כך, כי דבר זה פשוט! ובסמוך פירש כענין זה הרב, יום אחד לפני החג וחג ושמיני שלו – הרי כאן כ"א יום, דדוקא בהני אומרים דשמיני עצרת הרי כ"א יום. אבל מת ברגל, שלא נהג אבילות קודם הרגל – לא הוי שמיני עצרת כי אם יום אחד למנין שלשים. כך נראה לי, ואיני יודע הבירור. כך פירש הרב. ופירש בהלכות גדולות: דהשתא דאית לן תרי יומי, אי שכיב ליה שיכבא ביום טוב ראשון – לא ינהוג אבילות עד מוצאי יום טוב שני (ימים), ואותו יום טוב שני עולה למנין שבעה. ואי שכיב ביום שני – ההוא יומא נוהג אבילות, דכיון דיום טוב שני דרבנן – אתי אבילות דאורייתא דיום ראשון, דהוי מן התורה, כדאמרינן בזבחים (ד' ק:), ומבטל יום שני דרבנן. ואין נראה לר"י, וגם אין נוהגין כלל. ובמקום אחר פירשתי*:

אלא קרוביו. ירושלמי: ובלבד קרובים הראוין להתאבל. כהדא דרבי אבין דמך במועדא, לא גמל ר' מנא חסדא. אמר: בתר מועדא ניעבדא ליה יקרא, ואסיק: חכם שמת הכל כקרוביו: מברין עליו אלו ואלו. נראה לי: מכאן משמע שיש הבראה בלא אבילות, *כגון ברגל. ולקמן (ד' כה:) אמר: אפי' רבו שלמדו חכמה אינו יושב עליו אלא יום אחד. ותמיהני, אם כן נצטרך הבראה לשמועה רחוקה, ולא מצינו ברבי חייא שעשו לו הבראה, אלא קאמר לעיל (דף כ:): והולך כלי אחרי לבית המרחץ! ושמא לענין הבראה החמירו משום כבוד החכם:

וכך

עין משפט נר מצוה

קסה א ב ג ד מיי' פי"ב הל' אבל הל' י והל' יא טוש"ע יו"ד סי' שנג סעי' ה:

קסו ה מיי' שם הל' ט סמג עשין מד"ס ב טוש"ע י"ד סי' שמד סעיף ד:

קסז ו מיי' פ"י שם הל' ג סמג שם טוש"ע י"ד סי' שלט סעי' ח:

קסח ז מיי' פ"א מהל' חגיגה הלכה ז:

קסט ח מיי' פ"י מהל' אבל הל' ג סמג שם טוש"ע י"ד סי' שלט סעי' ט:

קע ט מיי' שם הל' ד טוש"ע שם סעי' יא:

משמע שרש"י היה מתיר בגדים שכבסו קודם האבל ובתוס' פי' כנ"ל

קעא י מיי' פ"ז מהל' י"ט הל' כג ופי"א מהל' אבל הל' ב סמג שם ולאוין עה טוש"ע א"ח סי' תקמז סעי' ו וטוש"ע י"ד סי' תא סעי' ב:

לאביי כרבי ורבא כראב"ש עי' רש"ש

קעב כ מיי' שם טוש"ע א"ח שם סעי' ז וי"ד שם סעי' ד:

קעג ל מ מיי' שם הל' ג טוש"ע א"ח שם סעי' ח וי"ד שם:

חגיגה יז. ר"ה ד:

פ"ג גרסי' בן ג' שנים יוצא במטה ר' עקיבא כו' פי' דלא בעי ג' כו' כנ"ל

מסורת הש"ס

תורה אור

[שמחות פ"ג ע"ש]

דברים טז

[ע' פרש"י ביצה כט.]

בב"מ סא: הגי' רב חנינא

[עיין תוס' ברכות מז: ד"ה מלוה לרבים שאני]

הגהות הב"ח

(א) גמ' בחג המצות ובחג השבועות ובחג הסוכות: מה חג המצות.

גליון הש"ס

תום' ד"ה אלא כו' כגון ברגל. עיין לעיל דף כ ע"א תד"ה שכבר:

רבינו חננאל

כר"ג. איכא דאמרי להא דרב גידל אהא דתניא תינוק כל ל' יום יוצא בחיק ונקבר באשה אחת ובשני אנשים אבל לא באיש אחד ושתי נשים. אבא שאול אומר אף באיש אחד ובשתי נשים. ואין עומדין עליו בשורה ואין אומרין עליו ברכת אבלים ותנחומי אבלים. בן ל' יום יוצא בדלוסקמא. ר' יהודה אומר לא דלוסקמא הניטלת על הכתף אלא הניטלת על אגפיים. ועומדין עליו בשורה ואומרין עליו ברכת אבלים ותנחומי אבלי'. בן י"ב חודש יוצא במטה. ר' עקיבא אומר בן שנה ואבריו כבן שנתיים בן שנתיים ואבריו כבן שנה יוצא במטה. רבי שמעון בן אלעזר אומר היוצא במטה רבים מצהיבין עליו. ר' אלעזר בן עזריה אומר ניכר לרבים רבים מתעסקין בו. אין ניכר לרבים אין רבים מתעסקין בו מה הן בהספד. ר' מאיר אומר משום ר' ישמעאל עניים בני שלש. עשירים בני חמש. ר' יהודה אומר משום ר' ישמעאל עניים בני חמש. עשירים בני שש. ובני זקנים כבני עניים. אמר גידל בר מנשיא אמר שמואל הלכה כר' יהודה שאמר משום ר' ישמעאל: **ירושלמי** תני אין מראין פנים לא בר"ה ולא ביוה"כ. ר' חזקיה הוה ליה עובדא. סלקין רבנן למחמי ליה אפין בצומא רבא א) אמר לון כלום אמרו אין מראין פנים לא בר"ה ולא ביוה"כ לא מפני התפלה שנייה הוא יוה"כ שחל להיות בשבת. ב) דריש ר' ענני מי שקבר את מתו יום אחד לפני עצרת חשוב כשבעת ימי האבל ופסקו ז' ימי אבלו ועצרת חשוב כשבעת ימי הרגל. דאמר ר' אלעזר מניין לעצרת שיש לה תשלומין שבעה שנאמר בחג המצות ובחג השבועות ובחג הסוכות. מה חג המצות יש לה תשלומין כל שבעה. שאם לא הקריב ביום הראשון יש לו להקריב כל ימי החג. כך עצרת יש לה תשלומין שבעה כחג המצות. הרי ז' לפני עצרת ועצרת ז' הרי י"ד משלים ט"ז יום והרי גמרו לו ל' ומותר בתספורת. אדבריה רב פפא לרב אויא סבא ודרש יום אחד לפני ר"ה ור"ה הרי י"ד אמר רבינא הלכך הקובר את מתו יום אחד לפני החג שבעה והחג שבעה. ושמיני שלו שהוא רגל בפ"ע הרי כאן כ"א יום וזהו שאמר רגל בפ"ע לענין פז"ר קש"ב. פירוש ג) רגל בפ"ע זהו כדי לחשב יום שמיני של חג הסוכות ז' ימים לאבל למנין שלשים: **מתני'** אין קורעין ואין חולצין כתף ולא מברין אלא קרובין של מת

א) פי' ויוה"כ חל אז בשבת. ב) בירושלמי שם איתא שנייה הוא יוה"כ שחל להיות בחול ופי' דאין חילוק דבין שחל בשבת ובין שחל בחול לעולם אין מראין פנים. ג) דברי רבינו אלו הובאו בתוס' ר"ה דף ד' ע"ב ד"ה פז"ר קש"ב בשמו של רבינו ז"ל.

גמ' ואפי' חָכָם? וְהָתַנְיָא: *[א]חָכָם שֶׁמֵּת – הַכֹּל קְרוֹבָיו. הַכֹּל קְרוֹבָיו סָלְקָא דַּעְתָּךְ?! אֶלָּא: הַכֹּל כִּקְרוֹבָיו; [ב]הַכֹּל קוֹרְעִין עָלָיו, [ג]וְהַכֹּל חוֹלְצִין עָלָיו, [ד]וְהַכֹּל מַבְרִין עָלָיו בָּרְחָבָה! לָא צְרִיכָא דְּלָאו חָכָם הוּא. וְאִי אָדָם כָּשֵׁר הוּא – [ה]חִיּוּבֵי מִיחַיַּיב לְמִיקְרַע, דְּתַנְיָא: מִפְּנֵי מָה בָּנָיו וּבְנוֹתָיו שֶׁל אָדָם מֵתִים כְּשֶׁהֵן קְטַנִּים – כְּדֵי שֶׁיִּבְכֶּה וְיִתְאַבֵּל עַל אָדָם כָּשֵׁר. יִבְכֶּה וְיִתְאַבֵּל? עֶרְבוֹנָא קָא שָׁקֵיל מִינֵּיהּ?! אֶלָּא: מִפְּנֵי שֶׁלֹּא בָּכָה וְהִתְאַבֵּל עַל אָדָם כָּשֵׁר. [ו]שֶׁכָּל הַבּוֹכֶה וּמִתְאַבֵּל עַל אָדָם כָּשֵׁר – מוֹחֲלִין לוֹ עַל כָּל עֲוֹנוֹתָיו בִּשְׁבִיל כָּבוֹד שֶׁעָשָׂה לוֹ! דְּלָאו אָדָם כָּשֵׁר הוּא. אִי דְּקָאֵי הָתָם בִּשְׁעַת יְצִיאַת נְשָׁמָה – חִיּוּבֵי מִיחַיַּיב, דְּתַנְיָא, רַבִּי שִׁמְעוֹן בֶּן אֶלְעָזָר אוֹמֵר: *[ז]הָעוֹמֵד עַל הַמֵּת בִּשְׁעַת יְצִיאַת נְשָׁמָה – חַיָּיב לִקְרוֹעַ. לְמָה זֶה דּוֹמֶה – לְסֵפֶר תּוֹרָה שֶׁנִּשְׂרַף, [ח]שֶׁחַיָּיב לִקְרוֹעַ! דְּלָא קָאֵי הָתָם בִּשְׁעַת יְצִיאַת נְשָׁמָה. כִּי נָח נַפְשֵׁיהּ דְּרַב סַפְרָא לָא קָרְעוּ רַבָּנַן עֲלֵיהּ. אָמְרִי: לָא גָּמְרִינַן מִינֵּיהּ. אֲמַר לְהוּ אַבַּיֵי: מִי תַּנְיָא הָרַב שֶׁמֵּת? חָכָם שֶׁמֵּת תַּנְיָא. וְעוֹד: כָּל יוֹמָא שְׁמַעְתָּתֵיהּ בְּפוּמִין בְּבֵי מִדְרְשָׁא. סְבוּר: מַה דַּהֲוָה – הֲוָה. אֲמַר לְהוּ אַבַּיֵי, תְּנֵינָא: חָכָם, כָּל זְמַן שֶׁעוֹסְקִין בְּהֶסְפֵּד – חַיָּיבִין לִקְרוֹעַ. סְבוּר לְמִיקְרַע לְאַלְתַּר. אֲמַר לְהוּ אַבַּיֵי, תַּנְיָא: [ט]חָכָם כְּבוֹדוֹ בְּהֶסְפֵּידוֹ. כִּי נָח נַפְשֵׁיהּ דְּרַב הוּנָא, סְבוּר לְאוֹתוֹבֵי סֵפֶר תּוֹרָה אַפּוּרְיֵיהּ. אֲמַר לְהוּ רַב חִסְדָּא: [י]מִילְּתָא דִּבְחַיֵּיהּ לָא סְבִירָא לֵיהּ, הַשְׁתָּא לֵיקוּם (לֵיהּ) לִיעֲבַד לֵיהּ? דְּאָמַר רַב תַּחְלִיפָא: *אֲנָא חֲזִיתֵיהּ לְרַב הוּנָא דְּבָעֵי לְמֵיתַב אפוריי', וַהֲוָה מַנַּח סֵפֶר תּוֹרָה עֲלֵיהּ, וְכָף כַּדָּא אַאַרְעָא וְאוֹתִיב סֵפֶר תּוֹרָה עִילָּוֵיהּ. אַלְמָא קָסָבַר: [כ]אָסוּר לֵישֵׁב עַל גַּבֵּי מִטָּה שֶׁסֵּפֶר תּוֹרָה מוּנָּח עָלֶיהָ. לָא הֲוָה נָפֵיק פּוּרְיָא מִבָּבָא, סְבוּר לְשַׁלְשׁוּלֵי דֶּרֶךְ גַּגִּין, אֲמַר לְהוּ רַב חִסְדָּא: הָא גְּמִירְנָא מִינֵּיהּ: [ל]חָכָם כְּבוֹדוֹ דֶּרֶךְ פֶּתַח. סְבוּר לְאַשְׁנוּיֵי מִפּוּרְיָא לְפוּרְיָא. אֲמַר לְהוּ רַב חִסְדָּא, הָכִי גְּמִירְנָא מִינֵּיהּ: [מ]חָכָם, כְּבוֹדוֹ בְּמִטָּה רִאשׁוֹנָה. דַּאֲמַר רַב יְהוּדָה אָמַר רַב: מִנַּיִן לְחָכָם שֶׁכְּבוֹדוֹ בְּמִטָּה רִאשׁוֹנָה – שֶׁנֶּאֱמַר: "וַיַּרְכִּיבוּ אֶת אֲרוֹן הָאֱלֹהִים אֶל עֲגָלָה חֲדָשָׁה". פְּרוּם בָּבָא, וְאַפְּקוּהָ. פְּתַח עֲלֵיהּ רַבִּי אַבָּא: רָאוּי הָיָה רַבֵּינוּ שֶׁתִּשְׁרֶה עָלָיו שְׁכִינָה, אֶלָּא שֶׁבָּבֶל גָּרְמָה לֵיהּ. מְתִיב רַב נַחְמָן בַּר *חִסְדָּא, וְאָמְרִי לָהּ רַב חָנָן בַּר חִסְדָּא: "הָיֹה הָיָה דְבַר ה' אֶל יְחֶזְקֵאל בֶּן בּוּזִי הַכֹּהֵן בְּאֶרֶץ כַּשְׂדִּים"! *טְפַח לֵיהּ אֲבוּהּ בְּסַנְדְּלֵיהּ. א"ל: לָאו אֲמִינָא לָךְ לָא תִּיטְרוֹד עָלְמָא? מַאי "הָיָה" – שֶׁהָיָה כְּבָר. כִּי אַסְקוּהּ לְהָתָם אֲמָרוּ לֵיהּ לְר' אַמִי וּלְר' אַסִי: רַב הוּנָא אָתֵי. אָמְרוּ: כִּי הֲוֵינַן הָתָם לָא הֲוָה לָן לְדַלּוּיֵי רֵישִׁין מִינֵּיהּ, הַשְׁתָּא אָתֵינַן הָכָא אָתָא בַּתְרִין? אָמְרוּ (*לֵיהּ:) אֲרוֹנוֹ בָּא. ר' אַמִי וְר' אַסִי נְפוּק, ר' אִילָא וְר' חֲנִינָא לָא נְפוּק. אִיכָּא דְּאָמְרִי: רַבִּי אִילָא נְפַק, ר' חֲנִינָא לָא נְפַק. דִּנְפַק מַאי טַעְמֵיהּ – דְּתַנְיָא: אֲרוֹן הָעוֹבֵר מִמָּקוֹם לְמָקוֹם – עוֹמְדִים עָלָיו בְּשׁוּרָה, וְאוֹמְרִים עָלָיו בִּרְכַּת אֲבֵלִים וְתַנְחוּמֵי אֲבֵלִים. דְּלָא נְפַק מַאי טַעְמָא – דְּתַנְיָא: אֲרוֹן הָעוֹבֵר מִמָּקוֹם לְמָקוֹם – אֵין עוֹמְדִין עָלָיו בְּשׁוּרָה, וְאֵין אוֹמְרִים עָלָיו בִּרְכַּת אֲבֵלִים וְתַנְחוּמֵי אֲבֵלִים. קַשְׁיָין אַהֲדָדֵי! לָא קַשְׁיָא, כָּאן – [נ]שֶׁשִּׁלְדּוֹ קַיֶּימֶת, כָּאן – בְּשֶׁאֵין שִׁלְדּוֹ קַיֶּימֶת, וְרַב הוּנָא שִׁלְדּוֹ קַיֶּימֶת הֲוָה. דְּלָא נְפַק – לָא סַיְּימוּהָ קַמֵּיהּ. אָמְרִי: הֵיכָא נֵינְחֵיהּ? רַב הוּנָא רִיבֵּץ תּוֹרָה בְּיִשְׂרָאֵל וְר' חִיָּיא רִיבֵּץ תּוֹרָה בְּיִשְׂרָאֵל הֲוָה. מַאן מְעַיֵּיל לֵיהּ? אֲמַר לְהוּ רַב חַגָּא: אֲנָא מְעַיֵּילְנָא לֵיהּ, דְּאוֹקַמְתֵּיהּ לְתַלְמוּדַאי כִּי הֲוֵינָא בַּר תְּמָנֵי סְרֵי שְׁנִין וְלָא חֲזֵי לִי קֶרִי, (א) וּמְשַׁמַּע לֵיהּ קַמֵּיהּ וְיָדְעֵי בְּעוֹבָדֵיהּ. דְּיוֹמָא חַד אִתְהַפִּיכָא לֵיהּ רְצוּעָה דִּתְפִילִּין, וִיתֵיב עֲלָהּ אַרְבְּעִין תַּעֲנִיתָא. עַיְילֵיהּ, הֲוָה גָּנֵי יְהוּדָה מִימִינֵיהּ דַּאֲבוּהּ, וְחִזְקִיָּה מִשְּׂמָאלֵיהּ. אֲמַר לֵיהּ יְהוּדָה לְחִזְקִיָּה: קוּם מִדּוּכְתִּיךְ, דְּלָאו אוֹרַח אַרְעָא דְּקָאֵים רַב הוּנָא. בַּהֲדֵי דְּקָאֵים – קָם בַּהֲדֵיהּ עַמּוּדָא דְנוּרָא, חַזְיֵיהּ רַב חַגָּא, אִיבְעִית, זַקְפֵיהּ לַאֲרוֹנֵיהּ וּנְפַק, אֲתָא. וְהַאי דְּלָא אִיעֲנַשׁ עֲנַשׁ – מִשּׁוּם דְּזַקְפֵיהּ לַאֲרוֹנֵיהּ דְּרַב הוּנָא. כִּי נָח נַפְשֵׁיהּ דְּרַב חִסְדָּא סְבוּר לְאוֹתוֹבֵי סֵפֶר תּוֹרָה אַפּוּרְיֵיהּ, אֲמַר לְהוּ ר' יִצְחָק: [ס]מִילְּתָא דְּלְרַבֵּיהּ לָא סְבִירָא לֵיהּ, אֲנַן נֵיקוּם נַעֲבֵיד לֵיהּ? סְבוּר דְּלָא לְמִישְׁלַל קְרָעַיְיהוּ. אֲמַר לְהוּ ר' יִצְחָק בַּר אַמִי: [ע]חָכָם, כֵּיוָן שֶׁהֶחְזִירוּ פְּנֵיהֶם מֵאֲחוֹרֵי הַמִּטָּה – שׁוֹלְלִין. כִּי נָח נַפְשֵׁי' דְּרַבָּה בַּר הוּנָא וְרַב הַמְנוּנָא אַסְקִינְהוּ לְהָתָם, כִּי

רש"י

גמ' לְסֵפֶר תּוֹרָה. דְּתוֹרָה קְרוּיָה נֵר, שֶׁנֶּאֱמַר (משלי ו): "כִּי נֵר מִצְוָה וְתוֹרָה אוֹר", וּנְשָׁמָה נִקְרֵאת נֵר דִּכְתִיב (שם כ): "נֵר *(אֱלֹהִים) נִשְׁמַת אָדָם": שְׁמַעְתָּתֵיהּ בְּפוּמִין. וַהֲוֵי כְּמַאן דִּגְמַרִינַן מִינֵּיהּ: מַאי דַּהֲוָה הֲוָה. הוֹאִיל דְּלֹא קָרְעוּ בִּשְׁעַת מִיתָה – תּוּ לָא קָרְעֵי: לְמִקְרַע לְאַלְתַּר. בְּלֹא הֶסְפֵּד: לְאוֹתוֹבֵי ס"ת אַפּוּרְיֵיהּ. תורה אור

וְלוֹמַר: קַיֵּים זֶה מַה שֶּׁכָּתוּב בָּזֶה: לָא הֲוָה נָפֵיק פּוּרְיָא מִבָּבָא. דְּזוּטָר הֲוֵי בָּבָא: מִפּוּרְיָא לְפוּרְיָא. לְתִתּוֹ בְּמִטָּה אַחֶרֶיתָא, קְטַנָּה, שֶׁתֵּצֵא דֶּרֶךְ הַפֶּתַח: אֶל עֲגָלָה חֲדָשָׁה. אוֹתָהּ עֲגָלָה שֶׁשִּׁגְּרוּהוּ פְּלִשְׁתִּים בָּהּ, וּבְאוֹתָהּ עֲגָלָה הֱבִיאוֹ דָּוִד מִבֵּית אֲבִינָדָב לְעִיר דָּוִד: פְּרוּם בָּבָא. שָׁבְרוּ הַפֶּתַח וְהִרְחִיבוּהוּ: בָּבֶל גָּרְמָה לוֹ. שֶׁאֵין שְׁכִינָה שׁוֹרָה בְּחוּץ לָאָרֶץ: טְפַח לֵיהּ אֲבוּהּ. רַב חִסְדָּא בְּסַנְדָּלָא, שֶׁטָּפַח לוֹ לְרַב נַחְמָן עַל סַנְדָּלוֹ, כְּאָדָם שֶׁנּוֹגֵעַ עַל רֶגֶל חֲבֵירוֹ בַּחֲשַׁאי כְּדֵי שֶׁלֹּא יִשְׁמְעוּ הָעוֹמְדִים סָבִיב מִטָּתוֹ דְּרַב הוּנָא. ע"א: הִכָּהוּ בְּסַנְדָּלוֹ: לָא תִּטְרוֹד עָלְמָא. לֹא תַּטְרַח בְּקוּשְׁיוֹת: שֶׁהָיָה כְּבָר. כְּלוֹמַר: הַהִיא שַׁעְתָּא הֲוָה, וְלֹא יוֹתֵר. וְיֵשׁ אוֹמְרִים: שֶׁהָיָה כְּבָר – בְּאֶרֶץ יִשְׂרָאֵל, שֶׁשָּׁרְתָה עָלָיו רוּחַ הַקּוֹדֶשׁ: כִּי אַסְקוּהּ לְהָתָם. לְאֶרֶץ יִשְׂרָאֵל לְקוֹבְרוֹ, שֶׁכָּל הַנִּקְבָּר שָׁם נִקְבָּר בְּלֹא חֵטְא, *שֶׁנֶּאֱמַר: "הָעָם הַיּוֹשֵׁב בָּהּ נְשׂוּא עָוֹן", כִּדְאִיתָא בִּכְתוּבּוֹת (דף קיא*): לְדַלּוּיֵי רֵישִׁין. דְּאָדָם חָשׁוּב הָיָה, וַהֲוָה לָן בּוֹשֶׁת לְדַלּוּיֵי רֵישִׁין: וְאָתֵי לְהָכָא. דִּסְבוּרִין שֶׁהוּא חַי: שִׁלְדּוֹ. גּוּפוֹ קַיֶּימֶת – יוֹלְאִין: לָא סַיְּימוּהָ קַמֵּיהּ. דְּשִׁלְדּוֹ הֲוָה קַיֶּימֶת: רַב הוּנָא רִיבֵּץ תּוֹרָה. כִּדְאָמְרִי' פֶּרֶק "שְׁנֵי דַּיָּינֵי גְּזֵירוֹת" (כתובות דף קו.): כִּי קָיְימִי רַבָּנַן מִקַּמֵּיהּ וּמְנַפְּצִי גְּלִימַיְיהוּ – מְכַסֵּי לֵיהּ לְיוֹמָא בְּאַבְקָא: רַבִּי חִיָּיא רִיבֵּץ תּוֹרָה. כִּדְאָמְרִינַן בְּבָבָא מְצִיעָא (דף פה:): אֲנָא עָבְדִי לֵיהּ לַתּוֹרָה דְּלָא תִּשְׁתַּכַּח מִיִּשְׂרָאֵל: מַאן מְעַיֵּיל לֵיהּ. מִי יֵלֵךְ לְהַכְנִיסוֹ לִקְבוּרָה אֵצֶל רַבִּי חִיָּיא: אִתְהַפִּיכָא לֵיהּ רְצוּעָה דִּתְפִילִּין. הַשָּׁחוֹר בִּפְנִים. דִּרְצוּעָה שְׁחוֹרָה נִרְאֵית בַּחוּץ הֲלָכָה לְמֹשֶׁה מִסִּינַי: אִיבְעִית. נִבְעַת וְנִפְחַד: זַקְפֵיהּ לַאֲרוֹנָא. דְּרַב הוּנָא לְקַמֵּיהּ עַמּוּדָא דְּנוּרָא, דְּלָא לִיזַּקֵּיהּ: כִּי

תוספות

וכף כדא ארעא ואנח עליה ספר תורה. ונראה דאפילו הספר תורה מונח נגבוה ממנו לא שרי, מדלא אותבוה לספר תורה נגבוה ממנו. וכן פירשתי במנחות בפרק "הקומץ רבה" (דף לג:) *ושם הארכתי:

ורבי חייא ריבץ תורה וכו'. והקשה בתוספות הרב: דמשמע בירושלמי *שרב הונא מת קודם רבי חייא. דאמר ליה לרבי חייא: ארונו בא. והכא משמע שרבי חייא מת קודם רב הונא! ונראה לי: דרב הונא אחר היה, ואותו שבימי רבי חייא – אין זה רב הונא תלמידו דרב, ע"כ. ומיהו, קשה: בירושלמי קאמר בעובדא דהכא רב הונא ריש גלותא, ולפי הענין של הירושלמי היה משמע דזקפיה ר' חגא לארוניה דרב הונא כדי שלא יהא יושב אצל הצדיקים. והכי איתא בפי' רבינו חננאל דרב הונא ריש גלותא:

חכם כיון שהחזיר פניו. פירוש: חכם שמת, כיון שהחזיר פניו אותו שקרע. וגרסינן: אפילו חכם שקרע על החכם, כיון שהחזיר פניו – שולל לאלתר. דמשום כבודו של חכם הקורע התירו, דגנאי הוא לצאת בבגד קרוע. ולא נהיר': ספעו

רבינו חננאל

מת וא"ר ירמיה ובלבד הראויין להתאבל. אוקימנא למתני' באדם שאינו חכם ולא כשר ולא היה עומד שם בשעת יציאת נשמה. אבל בחכם ובכשר חייב לעולם אע"פ שלא היה שם. דתניא חכם שמת הכל חייבין עליו כקרוביו הכל קורעין הכל חולצין והכל מברין והכל עומדין ברחבה. ואי אדם כשר הוא אע"פ שאינו חכם חייב. דתניא מפני מה בניו ובנותיו של בני אדם מתים כשהן קטנים מפני שלא בכה והתאבל על אדם כשר. שכל הבוכה ומתאבל על אדם כשר מוחלין לו על כל עונותיו. ואי עומד על המת בשעת יציאת נשמה חייב. דתניא ר' שמעון בן אלעזר אומר העומד על אדם בשעת יציאת נשמה חייב לקרוע למה זה דומה לס"ת שנשרף שחייב לקרוע. כי נח נפשיה דרב ספרא לא קרעו רבנן עליה. אמרו לא גמרינן מיניה. אמר להו אביי מי תניא הרב שמת חכם שמת תניא. ועוד שמעתתיה בפומין כל יומא בבי מדרשא. סבור מאי דהוה הוה. אמר להו אביי תניא חכם כבודו בהספדו. כי נח נפשיה דרב הונא סבור לאחותי ס"ת אפורייה אמר להו מלתא דבחייה לא סבירא ליה כו'. לא הוה נפיק פורייה לבבא סבור לשלשולי כו'. ואסיקנא חכם כבודו להוציאו דרך פתחים ולא דרך גגות. וכבודו במטה ראשונה ולא ממטה למטה שנאמר וירכיבו את ארון האלהים אל עגלה חדשה. סתרו להו לבבי ואפקוה. פתח עליה ההוא ספדנא ראוי היה רבינו שתשרה עליו שכינה אלא שבבל גרמה לו. וההיא דכתיב היה היה דבר ה' אל יחזקאל בן בוזי הכהן בארץ כשדים על נהר כבר מאי היה היה שכבר הוה. תניא ארון העובר ממקום למקום עומדין עליו בשורה ואומרין עליו ברכת אבלים ותנחומי אבלים. אוקימנא בששלדו קיימת. אבל אין שלדו קיימת לא: **ירושל'** בתחלת משקין (הלכה ה) תני ליקוטי עצמות אין אומרים עליהן קינים ונהי ולא ברכת אבלים ולא תנחומי אבלים. ואלו הן ברכת אבלים *) (מה שאומרים בשורה. אבל אומרים עליהן דברי קילוסין. אמרו מנחייה גבמה בבית הכנסת. אלו הן תנחומי אבלים מה שאומרים בשורה. אבל אומרין עליהן דברי קילוסין): אמרי מנחייה גבי ר' חייא שריבץ תורה כמותו. אמרי מאן ניעייליה. א"ר חנא אנא מעיילנא דאוקימתיה לתלמודא כד הוינא בר תמני סרי ולא חזי לי קרי ומשמע לי קמיה וידענא עובדיה. יומא חד אתהפיכא ליה רצועא דתפלי ויתיב בתעניתא עייליה הוי גני יהודה בריה מימיניה וחזקיה משמאליה. א"ל יהודה לחזקיה קום מדוכתיך דלאו אורח ארעא דקאי רב הונא אבראי. בהדיה דקם. קם בהדיה עמודא דנורא חזייה רב חנא איבעית זקף לארוניה דרב הונא ונפק. והא דלאו מיענשו דבי ריש גלותא משום

*) דברי רבינו כאן בשבוש וכצ"ל ברכת אבלים מה שאומרים בבהכנ"ס אלו הן תנחומי אבלים מה שאומרים בשורה אבל אומרים עליהן דברי קילוסין [וכ"ה בירושלמי פסחים פ"ח ה"ח ובירושלמי דמכילתין נדפס בשבוש וגם חסר שם פירוש דתנחומי אבלים].

הגהות הב"ח

(א) גמ' ומשמע ליה קמיה. נ"ב פירוש הייתי משמש לפניו:

גליון הש"ס

גמ' מילתא דלרביה לא ס"ל אנן ניקום נעביד. עיין בבא קמא דף יז ע"א תד"ה אלא שהניחו:

עין משפט נר מצוה

קעד א ב מיי' פ"ט מהל' אבל הל' יא סמג עשין ב טוש"ע י"ד סי' שמ סעי' ז:

[עיין שם בתוס' ד"ה אסור לישב]

[סוף כלאים ובכתובות פי"ב]

קעה ג מיי' שם טוש"ע שם סעיף יז:

קעו ד מיי' פי"א שם הלכה ב טוש"ע י"ד סי' תא סעיף ד:

קעז ה ו מיי' שם פ"ט הל' יא ופי"ב הל' ב טוש"ע י"ד סי' שמ סעיף ו:

קעח ז מיי' שם פ"ט הלכה יא טוש"ע שם סעי' ה:

קעט ח מיי' שם הלכ' ב טוש"ע שם סעי' לז:

קפ ט מיי' שם הל' יג טוש"ע שם סעי' ז:

קפא י מיי' פי"ב שם הלכה ג טוש"ע שם סי' שנג סעי' ב:

קפב כ מיי' פ"י מהל' תפילין הלכה ו טוש"ע שם סי' רפב סעיף ז:

קפג ל מ מיי' פי"ב מהל' אבל הל' ג טוש"ע שם סי' שנג סעי' ג:

קפד נ מיי' שם הלכה ז סמג עשין מד"ס ב טוש"ע שם סי' שמה סעיף ח:

[בע"י ליתא]

[מנחות לג: ע"ש]

קפה ס מיי' שם פ"ט הלכה יב טוש"ע שם סי' שמ סעיף יז:

מסורת הש"ס

[נ"ל ה']

שבת קה: [תוספתא פ"ב]

[משמע ליה להש"ס דמיירי אפי' באינו כשר כ"כ תוס' בשבת שם ד"ה דתניא]

דכל הדר בא"י שרוי בלא עון

ומנין אף המתים ח"ל וכפר אדמתו עמו עיין בילקוט חלק ב סוף רמז תתלג. ובע"י בפרש"י לא גרס כדאיתא בכתובות והוסיף ואין ישיבה בארץ אלא לקבורה ע"ש

[נ"ל רב חסדא]

[ב"ק לב: ב"ב כב.]

[נ"ל להו]

שמואל ב ו

יחזקאל א

תורה אור

כִּי מָטוּ אַגִּישְׁרָא קָמוּ גְּמָלֵי. אֲמַר לְהוּ הַהוּא טַיָּעָא: מַאי הַאי? אָמְרוּ לֵיהּ: רַבָּנַן דְּקָא עָבְדִי יְקָרָא אַהֲדָדֵי. מָר אֲמַר: מָר נֵיעוּל בְּרֵישָׁא, וּמָר אֲמַר: מָר נֵיעוּל בְּרֵישָׁא. אֲמַר: דִּינָא הוּא דְּרַבָּה בַּר הוּנָא לֵיעוּל בְּרֵישָׁא. חֲלִיף גְּמָלֵיהּ דְּרַבָּה בַּר הוּנָא, נְתוּר כָּבֵיהּ וְשִׁנֵּיהּ דְּהַהוּא טַיָּעָא. פְּתַח עֲלֵיהּ הַהוּא יָנוּקָא: "גֶּזַע יְשִׁישִׁים עָלָה מִבָּבֶל וְעִמּוֹ סֵפֶר מִלְחָמוֹת. *קָאַת וְקִפּוֹד הוּכְפָּלוּ, לִרְאוֹת בְּשׁוֹד וְשֶׁבֶר הַבָּא מִשִּׁנְעָר. קָצַף עַל עוֹלָמוֹ וְחָמַס מִמֶּנּוּ נְפָשׁוֹת, וְשָׂמַח בָּהֶם כְּכַלָּה חֲדָשָׁה. רוֹכֵב עֲרָבוֹת שָׂשׂ וְשָׂמַח בְּבֹא אֵלָיו נֶפֶשׁ נָקִי וְצַדִּיק". כִּי נָח נַפְשֵׁיהּ דְּרָבִינָא פְּתַח עֲלֵיהּ הַהוּא סַפְדָּנָא: "תְּמָרִים הָנִיעוּ רֹאשׁ עַל צַדִּיק כַּתָּמָר נָשִׁים לֵילוֹת כְּיָמִים [עַל מְשִׁים ס"א לֵילוֹת כְּיָמִים".] א"ל רַב אַשִׁי לְבַר קִיפּוֹק: הַהוּא יוֹמָא מַאי אֲמַרְתְּ? אֲמַר לֵיהּ, אָמִינָא: אִם בָּאֲרָזִים נָפְלָה שַׁלְהֶבֶת — מַה יַּעֲשׂוּ אֵיזוֹבֵי קִיר, לִוְיָתָן בְּחַכָּה הוּעֲלָה — מַה יַּעֲשׂוּ דְּגֵי רְקָק, בְּנַחַל שׁוֹטֵף נָפְלָה חַכָּה — מַה יַּעֲשׂוּ מֵי גְּבִים. א"ל בַּר אָבִין: ח"ו דְּחַכָּה וְשַׁלְהֶבֶת בְּצַדִּיקֵי אָמִינָא. וּמַאי אָמַרְתְּ? אָמִינָא: בְּכוּ לָאֲבֵלִים וְלֹא לָאֲבֵידָה, שֶׁהִיא לִמְנוּחָה וְאָנוּ לַאֲנָחָה. חֲלַשׁ דַּעְתֵּיהּ עֲלַיְיהוּ, וְאִתְהַפּוּךְ כַּרְעַיְיהוּ. הַהוּא יוֹמָא לָא אָתוּ לְאַסְפּוֹדֵיהּ. וְהַיְינוּ דְּאָמַר רַב אַשִׁי: *לָא בַּר קִיפּוֹק חָלֵיץ, וְלָא בַּר אָבִין חָלֵיץ. רָבָא, כִּי הֲוָה אֲתָא לְדִגְלַת א"ל לְבַר אָבִין: קוּם אֵימָא מִילְּתָא. קָאֵי וְאָמַר: בָּאוּ רוֹב שְׁלִישִׁית בְּמַיִם, זְכוֹר וְרַחֵם. תָּעִינוּ מֵאַחֲרֶיךָ כְּאִשָּׁה מִבַּעְלָהּ, אַל תַּזְנִיחֵנוּ כְּאוֹת מֵי מָרָה. (חָנִין יוֹחָנָן זֵירָא אַבָּא יַעֲקֹב יוֹסֵי שְׁמוּאֵל חִיָּיא מְנַחֵם — סִימָן.) רַבִּי חָנִין חַתְנֵיהּ דְּבֵי נְשִׂיאָה הֲוָה, לָא קָא הָווּ לֵיהּ בָּנֵי, בְּעָא רַחֲמֵי וְהָווּ לֵיהּ. הַהוּא יוֹמָא דַּהֲוָה לֵיהּ — נָח נַפְשֵׁיהּ. פְּתַח עֲלֵיהּ הַהוּא סַפְדָּנָא: "שִׂמְחָה לְתוּגָה נֶהְפְּכָה, שָׂשׂוֹן וְיָגוֹן נִדְבְּקוּ, בְּעֵת שִׂמְחָתוֹ נֶאֱנַח, בְּעֵת חֲנִינָתוֹ אָבַד חֲנִינוֹ". אַסִּיקוּ לֵיהּ חָנָן עַל שְׁמֵיהּ. כִּי נָח נַפְשֵׁיהּ דְּר' יוֹחָנָן פְּתַח עֲלֵיהּ ר' יִצְחָק בֶּן אֶלְעָזָר: קָשֶׁה הַיּוֹם לְיִשְׂרָאֵל כְּיוֹם בֹּא הַשֶּׁמֶשׁ בַּצָּהֳרַיִם, דִּכְתִיב: °"וְהָיָה בַּיּוֹם הַהוּא (עמוס ח) וְהֵבֵאתִי הַשֶּׁמֶשׁ בַּצָּהֳרָיִם". וְאָמַר ר' יוֹחָנָן: זֶה יוֹמוֹ שֶׁל יֹאשִׁיָּהוּ. כִּי נָח נַפְשֵׁיהּ דְּר' יוֹחָנָן יְתֵיב רַבִּי אַמִּי שִׁבְעָה וּשְׁלֹשִׁים. אָמַר רַבִּי אַבָּא בְּרֵיהּ דְּרַבִּי חִיָּיא בַּר אַבָּא: רַבִּי אַמִּי *דַּעֲבַד — לְגַרְמֵיהּ הוּא דַּעֲבַד. דְּהָכִי אָמַר ר' חִיָּיא בַּר אַבָּא אָמַר ר' יוֹחָנָן: [א]אֲפִילּוּ רַבּוֹ שֶׁלִּימְּדוֹ חָכְמָה — אֵינוֹ יוֹשֵׁב עָלָיו אֶלָּא יוֹם אֶחָד. *כִּי נָח נַפְשֵׁיהּ דְּרַבִּי זֵירָא, פְּתַח עֲלֵיהּ הַהוּא סַפְדָּנָא: "אֶרֶץ שִׁנְעָר הָרָה וְיָלְדָה אֶרֶץ צְבִי גִּידְּלָה שַׁעֲשׁוּעֶיהָ. אוֹי נָא לָהּ אָמְרָה רַקַּת, כִּי אִבְּדָה כְּלִי חֶמְדָּתָהּ". כִּי נָח נַפְשֵׁיהּ דְּרַבִּי אַבָּהוּ אַחִיתוּ עַמּוּדֵי דְקִסְרִי מַיָּא. דְּרַבִּי יוֹסֵי — *שָׁפְעוּ מַרְזְבֵי דְצִיפּוֹרִי דָּמָא, דְּרַבִּי יַעֲקֹב — אִתְחַמִּיאוּ כּוֹכָבֵי בִּימָמָא. דְּר' אַסִּי — אִיעַקְרוּ כָּל אִילָנַיָּא, דְּר' חִיָּיא — נְחִיתוּ כֵּיפֵי דְנוּרָא מֵרְקִיעָא, דְּר' מְנַחֵם *(בְּר' יוֹסֵי) — אִישְׁתָּעוּ צַלְמָנַיָּא וַהֲווֹ לְמֶחְלָצַיָּא, דְּר' תַּנְחוּם בַּר חִיָּיא — אִיתְקַצְּצוּ כָּל אַנְדַּרְטַיָּא, דְּר' אֶלְיָשִׁיב — אִיחַתְרוּ שִׁבְעִין מַחְתַּרְתָּא בִּנְהַרְדְּעָא, דְּרַב הַמְנוּנָא — נְחִיתוּ כֵּיפֵי דְּבַרְדָּא מֵרְקִיעָא, דְּרַבָּה וְרַב יוֹסֵף — נְשׁוּק כֵּיפֵי דִּפְרָת אַהֲדָדֵי, דְּאַבַּיֵי וְרָבָא — נְשׁוּק כֵּיפֵי דְּדִגְלַת אַהֲדָדֵי, כִּי נָח נַפְשֵׁיהּ דְּר' מְשַׁרְשְׁיָא טְעוּן דִּיקְלֵי שִׁיצֵי. ת"ר:
וְאֵלּוּ

רש"י

כי מטו אגישרא. כשהגיעו לעבור בדף של גשר קצר, שעכשיו לא היו יכולין לעבור זה בצד זה, אלא זה אחר זה: קמו גמלי. עמדו הגמלים נושאי המטות במקומן: טייעא. סוחר ישמעאלים: רבנן. דשכיבי, רבה בר רב הונא ורב המנונא: עבדי יקרא. דהא לא בעי האי למיעל מקמי האי: נתור כבי. לחייו, משום דבזי לרב המנונא: ספר מלחמות. ספר תורה. לישנא אחרינא: שנלחם רבה ורב המנונא, ונתור ככי דההוא טייעא. לישנא אחרינא: גזע ישישים — זה רבה בר רב הונא, דהוא בן גדולים, בן רב הונא דהוא ראש גולה, ועדיף מנשיא דארץ ישראל. ועמו ספר מלחמות — עמו רב המנונא: קאת וקיפוד הוכפלו. קללה, כמו: "וירשוה קאת וקיפוד" (ישעיה לד) כלומר: קללה באה והוכפלה בעולם: לראות שוד ושבר. זה שקיצץ הקב"ה על עולמו: נשים לילות כימים. בהספד, על שהם לילות כימים בתורה: בר קיפוק ובר אבין. הוו ספדני: (ההוא יומא. דנח נפשיה): חלש דעתיה. דהאי מדמי ליה לשלהבת, והאי לאבידה: וההוא יומא. דנח נפשיה לא ספדוהו, משום דאירע להו תקלה על ידו: לא בר קיפוק ולא בר אבין חליץ. משום דאיתהפכו כרעייהו. ותניא (יבמות דף קג.): האי מאן דמסגי אלוחתא דריגלא — לא חליץ, דהתורה אמרה "וחלצה נעלו מעל רגלו" ולא מתחת לרגלו: אתי לדגלת. חדקל: רוב שלישית. ישראל נקראו שלישית. ורבא שקול כרוב ישראל, ואמר ליה: קום ואמור מילתא, כלומר: בקש רחמים: כאות במי מרה. שאשה סוטה נבדקת בהן: בעת חנינתו. דולד: אבד חנינו. אביו המתחננו: והבאתי השמש בצהרים. אשקיע השמש בצהרים: יומו של יאשיה. שנהרג יאשיה, קרי יומו שמש: לגרמיה. לדעתיה: רבי זירא היה מבבל, ובה נולד, וגדל בארץ ישראל, והיינו דקאמר: ארץ שנער הרה וילדה ארץ צבי גדלה שעשועיה. ואהכי קרי ליה רבי זירא ורב זירא*: אוי נא לה אמרה רקת. יכולה לומר כן, רקת היא טבריא: אחיתו. הורידו דמעות: איתחמיאו כוכבי. נראו הכוכבים, שנשתנה העולם מרוב צער: כיפי דנורא. אבנים של אור: אשתעו צלמנייא. נימוחו פרצוף שלהן: והוו למחלצייא. כלומר, נחלקה ונתמעכה כל צורת פרצוף של צלמים וצור' המטבעות, מפני צורת הספיד שנשתנית: דרבי מנחם. בנן של קדושים, שלא נסתכל אף בצורה של זוזא, כדאמרינן ב"ערבי פסחים" (דף קד.): והוו למחלצייא. כמו שהולכה במעגל ובמחלצים, שבה מטחין טיט הכותל: אנדרטא. צורת הצלמים שעושין על שם המלך שמת: שבעין מחתרין. דגנבים. דזכותיה לא הוו אתו גנבים: כיפי. נשוק כיפי. כיפות של גשרים נשתברו, ונשקו זו את זו: שיצי. קולים:
ואלו

תוספות

שפעו מרזבי דציפורי דמא. מפרש בירושלמי: דיהב נפשיה על גזרתם. פירוש: נשפך דמו על יחוד השם. תוספתא פ"א: שנתן נפשו על המילה:

__ועל__ רבו שלמדו חכמה. בפרק "אלו מציאות" (ב"מ דף לג. ושם) פליגי רבי יהודה ורבי יוסי, שרבי יהודה אומר: כל שרוב חכמתו הימנו, ורבי יוסי אומר: אפילו לא האיר עיניו אלא במשנה אחת — זהו רבו, ומסיק שם, עולא אמר: תלמידי חכמים שבבבל קורעין זה על זה, כרבי יוסי ס"ל. ופוסק רב ששת כרבי יוסי. ופי' רבינו חננאל דהכי הלכתא. ובשאלתות דרב אחאי) פוסק כרבי יהודה, דאמר: כל שרוב חכמתו הימנו. ומפרש בפר' "אלו מציאות" בתוספתא דהיו קורעין קריעה [דאין] מתאחה. וכן פירש רבי יצחק בר יהודה, ויותר היה נראה לי דמעשה רב, דשמואל עבד כרבי יוסי כדאי' התם. ורבא נמי מפרש מילתא דרבי יוסי, ורבי אלעזר בירושלמי נמי עבד כוותיה. ושמא היו מחמירין על עצמן:

*) [פרשת קרח סי' קלא]

ברכת

עין משפט נר מצוה

קפו א מיי' פ"ט מהל' אבל הלכה יב טוש"ע י"ד סי' רמב סעיף כה:

[שייך לדף כו.]

רבינו חננאל

משום דזקיף ארוניה דרב הונא. כלומר זכותו מגינה עליהם דהוא מדבי ריש גלותא. א"ל רב אשי לרב קיפוק בהא יומא דנח נפשיה דרבינא מאי אמרת עליה. פירוש בר קיפוק הוה ספדנא וכן בר אבין ושאלינהו מהו ההספד שתספדו עליו. וכיון שאמר לו בר קיפוד בארזים נפלה שלהבת מה יעשו אזובי קיר. כלומר כ"ע לגביה כאזוב גבי ארז נינהו כולהו. ובר אבין אמר בכו לאובדין ולא לאבידה כו' חלש דעתיה דרב אשי אמר שויתון לגביה כאזוב של קיר והוא כארז מכלל שהוא גדול ממני. נעשה להן חולי ונהפכו רגליהן שאינן יכולין להלך ולא יצאו בהספד. וזהו שאמר רב אשי כיון שרגליהן של אלו הפוכות אינן ראוין לחליצה. כי נח נפשיה דר' יוחנן יתיב עליה ר' אמי שבעה ושלשים. ואסיקנא אפילו רבו שלמדו תורה אינו יושב עליו אלא יום אחד. וא"ר יצחק בר אמי *)תניא חכם כיון שהחזיר פניו מאחורי המטה שולל. פתח עליה ההוא ספדנא. ארץ שנער הרה וילדה. פי' שנער בבל. ארץ צבי א"י. רקת זו טבריא שמת בה.

[פי' אפי' עופות רעות באות לראות כשמתו ערוך]

יבמות קג. [ע"ש]

[ברכות מח. וש"נ]

מגילה ו.

[וע"ע רש"י כתובות מג: ד"ה אמר ר"ז ועי' תוס' מנחות מ: ד"ה ר"ז אמר]

[סנהדרין קט.]

[נ"ל ברבי סימאי ועי' תוס' שבת קמט. ד"ה ודיוקני ותוס' פסחים קד. ד"ה צלא ותוס' ע"ז נ. ד"ה ה"ג]

ואלו קרעין כו'. באבל רבתי במסכת שמחות (פ"ט): **ברוב ציבור.** רוב ישראל: **וכמעשה שהיה.** בשאול ויהונתן: **גרמו לנפשייהו.** דמרדו ביה. והא דקאמר לא קטלי יהודי – רוצה לומר: בחנם: **לקול יתירי.** לקול כנורות, שמרדו: **באתיא קרע קרע** (*מדוד): **שלש דלתות וארבעה.** כלומר: ארבעה פסוקים: **אנא מלכא.** ואמלכא לא כתיב כלום: **היו צריה לראש.** שהנכרי ראש ולא אתה: **משום שמועות רעות.** על הגלות, איבעי למיקרע: **את המגילה.** זה הגויל: **ואת הדברים.** זה הכתב: **השתא.** אי שקיל להו נעמיתא – איבעי לי למיקרע על הגויל ועל הכתב, דהוי כנשרף: **בזרוע.** שאין יכול להצילו: **וכמעשה שהיה.** דיהויקים. אבל דנעמיתא דמלי להציל – לא מיקרע: **הא דפגע במקדש ברישא.** כגון שנכנס לירושלים בשידה תיבה ומגדל, דלא ראה ירושלים עד שראה בית המקדש – קורע על המקדש, ומוסיף על ירושלים. אבל בשלא נכנס בתיבה ופגע בירושלים ברישא – קורע על ירושלים בפני עצמה ועל המקדש בפני עצמו: **כל הקרעים רשאין למוללן.** לקפל בגד בתפירה: **כעין סולמות.** שאין מלקטין זה סמוך לזה, אבל זה רחוק מזה, שמלקט ברוחב כעין מעלות סולמות:

מתוך

[צ"ל מאלישע]
שמחות פ"ט
[לעיל כה: ע"ש סנהדרין ס.]

תורה אור

*ואלו קרעין שאין מתאחין: הקורע על אביו, ועל אמו, ועל רבו שלימדו תורה, ועל נשיא, ועל אב ב"ד, ועל שמועות הרעות, ועל ברכת השם, ועל ספר תורה שנשרף, ועל ערי יהודה, ועל המקדש, ועל ירושלים. וקורע על מקדש ומוסיף על ירושלים. אביו ואמו ורבו שלימדו תורה מנלן? דכתיב: "ואלישע ראה והוא מצעק אבי אבי רכב ישראל ופרשיו". "אבי אבי" – זה אביו ואמו, "רכב ישראל ופרשיו" – זה רבו שלימדו תורה. מאי משמע? כדמתרגם רב יוסף: רבי רבי, דטב להון לישראל בצלותיה מרתיכין ופרשין. ולא מתאחין מנלן? דכתיב: "ויחזק בבגדיו ויקרעם לשנים קרעים", ממשמע שנאמר *"ויקרעם" איני יודע שלשנים?! אלא, מלמד שקרועים ועומדים לשנים לעולם. אמר ליה ריש לקיש לרבי יוחנן: אליהו חי הוא! אמר ליה: כיון דכתיב: "ולא ראהו עוד" – לגבי דידיה כמת דמי. נשיא ואב בית דין ושמועות הרעות מנלן? דכתיב: "ויחזק דוד בבגדיו ויקרעם וגם כל האנשים אשר אתו ויספדו ויבכו ויצומו עד הערב על שאול ועל יהונתן בנו ועל עם ה' ועל בית ישראל כי נפלו בחרב". "שאול" – זה נשיא, "יהונתן" – זה אב ב"ד, "על עם ה' ועל בית ישראל" – אלו שמועות הרעות. א"ל רב בר שבא לרב כהנא: ואימא עד דהוו כולהו! א"ל: 'על' 'על' הפסיק הענין. ומי קרעינן אשמועות הרעות? והא אמרו ליה לשמואל: קטל שבור מלכא תריסר אלפי יהודאי במזיגת קסרי, ולא קרע. לא אמרו אלא ברוב צבור, וכמעשה שהיה. ומי קטל שבור מלכא יהודאי? והא א"ל שבור מלכא לשמואל: תיתי לי, דלא קטלי יהודי מעולם! התם אינהו גרמי לנפשייהו. דא"ר אמי: לקל יתירי דמזיגת קסרי פקע שורא דלודקיא. על ברכת השם מנלן – דכתיב: "ויבא אליקים בן חלקיה אשר על הבית ושבנא הסופר ויואח בן אסף המזכיר אל חזקיהו קרועי בגדים". *ת"ר: אחד השומע ואחד השומע מפי השומע חייב לקרוע והעדים אינן חייבין לקרוע, שכבר קרעו בשעה ששמעו. בשעה ששמעו מאי הוי, הא קא שמעי השתא! לא ס"ד דכתיב: "ויהי כשמוע המלך חזקיהו ויקרע את בגדיו" – המלך קרע, והם לא קרעו. ולא מתאחין מנלן? *אתיא קריעה קריעה. ספר תורה שנשרף מנלן? דכתיב: "ויהי כקרא יהודי שלש דלתות וארבעה (א) ויקרעה בתער הסופר והשלך אל האש אשר אל האח" וגו'. מאי "שלש דלתות וארבעה"? אמרו ליה ליהויקים: כתב ירמיה ספר קינות. אמר להו: מה כתיב ביה? "איכה ישבה בדד". אמר להו: אנא מלכא. א"ל: "בכה תבכה בלילה". אנא מלכא. "גלתה יהודה מעוני" – אנא מלכא. "דרכי ציון אבלות" – אנא מלכא. "היו צריה לראש" – אמר להו: מאן אמרה? "כי ה' הוגה על רוב פשעיה", מיד קדר כל אזכרות שבה ושרפן באש. והיינו דכתיב: "ולא פחדו ולא קרעו את בגדיהם", מכלל דבעו למיקרע. אמר ליה רב פפא לאביי: אימר משום שמועות הרעות! א"ל: שמועות רעות בההיא שעתא מי הוו? א"ר חלבו אמר רב הונא: הרואה ספר תורה שנקרע חייב לקרוע שתי קריעות: אחד על הגויל ואחד על הכתב. שנאמר: "אחרי שרוף המלך את המגלה ואת הדברים". רבי אבא ורב הונא בר חייא הוו יתבי* [א]קמיה דרבי אבא, בעא לאפנויי, שקליה לטוטפתיה אחתיה אבי סדיא. אתאי בת נעמיתא בעא למיבלעיה, אמר: השתא איחייבין לי שתי קריעות, א"ל: מנא לך הא? והא בדידי הוה עובדא, ואתאי לקמיה דרב מתנה ולא הוה בידיה, אתאי לקמיה דרב יהודה, ואמר לי: הכי אמר שמואל, לא אמרו אלא בזרוע, וכמעשה שהיה. ערי יהודה מנלן? דכתיב: "ויבאו אנשים משכם משילו ומשמרון שמונים איש מגולחי זקן וקרועי בגדים ומתגודדים ומנחה ולבונה בידם להביא בית ה'" וגו'. א"ר (א) חלבו אמר עולא ביראה אמר ר' אלעזר, הרואה ערי יהודה בחורבנן – אומר: "ערי קדשך היו מדבר", וקורע. ירושלים בחורבנה – אומר: "ציון מדבר היתה ירושלים שממה", וקורע. בית המקדש בחורבנו – אומר "בית קדשנו ותפארתנו אשר הללוך אבותינו היה לשריפת אש וכל מחמדינו היה לחרבה", וקורע. "קורע על מקדש ומוסיף על ירושלים". ורמינהו: אחד השומע ואחד הרואה, כיון שהגיע לצופים – קורע, וקורע על מקדש בפני עצמו ועל ירושלים בפני עצמה! לא קשיא: הא – דפגע במקדש ברישא, הא – דפגע בירושלים ברישא. תנו רבנן: וכולן רשאין לשוללן, ולמוללן, וללוקטן ולעשותן כמין סולמות, אבל לא לאחותן. אמר רב חסדא:

ובאיחוי

(א) [בשאלתות איתא אמר ר' יהודה הרואה כו']

מלכים ב ב | שם | שם | שמואל ב א | מלכים ב יח | [סנהדרין ס.] | מלכים ב יט | [סנהדרין שם] | ירמיה לו | איכה א | שם שם שם שם | שם | ירמיה לו | שם | [נ"ל קם רבי אבא] | ירמיה מא | ישעיה סד | שם שם

ברכת השם מנלן. ועל ברכת השם דנכרים פליגי הכא בירושלמי, אית דאמרי: רבשקה ישראל מומר הוה, אבל דנכרי – לא, ואית דאמרי: נכרי הוה. ובפרק "ארבע מיתות" (סנהדרין דף ס.) נמי פליגי בה בש"ס שלנו, ובירושלמי: הוה ריש לקיש קורע על ברכת השם:

ואחד השומע מפי השומעים. פירש בתוס': כגון מן העדים שאומרים זה, ואם הוא אומר יכה יוסי את יוסי – אין קורעין על זה, וכן משמע בפ"ד מיתות (שם דף נו.):

אתיא קריעה. תימה: אם כן, נילף כל קריעות שלא יתאחו מ"קריעה" "קריעה"! ושמא לא מיסתבר ליה:

קדר כל האזכרות. תימה: והא (ב)דקרעה בתער הסופר – משמע כל המגילה! ובירושלמי לא גרסינן האזכרות:

לא אמרו אלא בזרוע. ובירושלמי גרס: ששרפה מלך ישראל בזרוע:

משכם משילו. לא שייך הכא למיפרך: ואימא עד דאיכא תלתא. אבל קצת קשה: דאימר מילתא יתירתא הוא, דמגלחי זקן(ג) ומתגודדים כתיב בהאי קרא! ויש לומר: דלא שייך למימר דלא נילף כלל אלא קריעה, ולעיל (ד' כא.) הכי קאמר נמי: נהי דגמרת שפיר קריעה – מ"מ לא תילף מינה מעומד:

ובאיחוי

קפז א מיי' פ"ט מהל' אבל הלכה ב ג סמג עשין ב טוש"ע י"ד סי' שמ סעיף טו:
קפח ב מיי' שם הלכה ה טוש"ע שם סעיף יז:
קפט ג מיי' שם הלכה ו טוש"ע שם סעיף לו:
קצ ד מיי' שם הלכה י ופ"ה מהלכות תענית הלכה טו יז טוש"ע שם סעיף לח טוש"ע א"ח סי' תקסא סעיף א:
קצא ה מיי' פ"ה מהל' תענית הלכה טז טוש"ע א"ח סעיף ב:
קצב ו מיי' פ"ח מהל' אבל הלכה ג ופ"ט הלכה ב טור ש"ע י"ד סי' שמ סעיף א:
קצג ז מיי' שם פ"ט הלכה ה ופ"ה מהלכות ת"ת הלכה ט סמג עשין ב טוש"ע שם סעיף ח וסי' רמב סעיף כה:
קצד ח מיי' פ"ט מהל' אבל הלכה ב ו טוש"ע י"ד סי' שמ סעיף יז:
קצה ט י מיי' שם טור ש"ע שם סעיף לו:
קצו כ ל מ נ ס מיי' שם הלכה ב ט טוש"ע שם סעיף לז:
קצז ע פ צ מיי' פ"ה מהלכות תענית הלכה טז טוש"ע א"ח סי' תקסא סעיף א ב:
קצח ק מיי' שם הלכה יז ופ"ט מהלכות אבל הלכה ג טוש"ע א"ח שם סעיף ד וטוש"ע י"ד סי' שמ סעיף לט:

הגהות הב"ח

(א) גמ' שלש דלתות וארבעה יקרעה בתער הסופר: (ב) תום' ד"ה קדר כו' והא דיקרעה בתער: (ג) ד"ה משכם כו' דמגלחי זקן וקרועי בגדים ומתגודדים כו' דלא נילף כלל אפילו קריעה:

רבינו חננאל

ת"ר אלו קרעין שאסורין באיחוי פי' עשרה קרעים הללו הקורע על אביו ועל אמו ועל רבו שלמדו חכמה. ועל נשיא ועל אב ב"ד. ועל שמועות הרעות. ועל ברכת השם. ועל ס"ת שנשרף ועל חורבן ערי יהודה ועל חורבן המקדש [ועל ירושלים] וקורע על חורבן בהמ"ק ומוסיף על חורבן ירושלים: אביו ואמו ורבו שלמדו חכמה מהכא ואלישע ראה והוא מצעק אבי אבי רכב ישראל ופרשיו. אבי אבי זה אביו ואמו. רכב ישראל ופרשיו זה רבו שלמדו חכמה. כדמתרגם רבי רבי דטב להון לישראל בצלותך מן רתיכין ופרשין. ואע"ג דאליהו חי הוא כיון דכתיב ביה ולא ראהו עוד כמת הוא לגביה: **ירושלמי** כשם שקורעין על החכמים כך קורעין על תלמידיהן איזהו ת"ח חזקיה אמר כל השונה הלכות *)ועד תורה. א"ר יוסי הדא דאת אמרו בראשונה אבל עכשיו אפילו הלכות. ר' אבהו בשם ר' יוחנן כל שמבטל עסקיו מפני משנתו. תני כל ששואלין אותו ומשיב. א"ר אושעיא כגון אנא דרבבינן משגיחין עלינו וכן מתיבין ליה. א"ר אבא בר ממל כל שיודע לבאר משנתו ואנן אפילו רבבינן לא יכלי לבאר משנתנו איזהו רבו כל שפתח לו תחלה דברי ר' מאיר. ר' יהודה אומר כל שרוב תלמודו ממנו. שמואל חלץ בההוא שהאיר במשנתו. פי' ביאר לו משנתו זו ששנינו בתמיד. ושתי מפתחות היו לו אחד יורד לאמת השחי ואחד פותח כיון. פי' היה מכנים ידו ומורדה עד שיחין שהוא אמה ואח"כ היה מגיע למנעול ופותחו. והאחד היה נכון לפניו מכנים ידו כנגדו ופותח: ולא מתאחין שנאמר ויקרעם לשנים קרעים. ממשמע שנאמר ויקרעם איני יודע שהקריעה לשנים היא אלא מה ת"ל לשנים מלמד שקרועין לעולם לשנים. נשיא ואב ב"ד ושמועת הרעות שנאמר ויחזק דוד בבגדיו ויקרעם וגם כל האנשים אשר אתו ויספדו ויבכו על שאול ועל יהונתן ועל עם ה' ועל בית ישראל כי נפלו בחרב. שאול זה נשיא יהונתן זה אב ב"ד. על עם ה' על בית ישראל אלו שמועות רעות. ומקשינן ואימא לא קרעינן עד דאיכא כולהו. ופרקינן על על הפסיק הענין למימרא דקרעינן על כל אחד ואחד בפ"ע. ואסיקנא לא אמרו דקרעינן על שמועות הרעות אלא ברוב צבור. וכמעשה דשאול דהא שמואל שמע דקטל שבור מלכא י"ב אלפי יהודאי ולא קרע. ועל ברכת השם אחד השומע. ואחד השומע מפי השומע חייבין לקרוע. והעדים אין חייבין לקרוע שכבר קרעו בעת ששמעו. שנאמר ויהי כשמוע המלך את דבריהם ויקרע את בגדיו המלך קרע והם לא קרעו עכשיו שכבר קרעו שנאמר ויבא אליקים בן חלקיהו אשר על הבית ושבנא הסופר ויואח בן אסף המזכיר אל חזקיהו קרועי בגדים ויגידו את דברי רבשקה. ולא מתאחין מנ"ל אתיא קריעה קריעה מהתם: **ירושלמי** מהו לקרוע בזמן הזה משום ר' יוחנן אמרו משרבו הגדפנין בטל מלקרוע. מהו לקרוע על הכנויים נשמעיניה מהדא. ר"ל הוה מהלך בדרך נזדמן לו כותי הוה מגדף והוא קורע נחת מן חמרא ויהב ליה מרתיקא גו ליביה [באבן או באגרוף תרגם מרתוק. פי' הכהו באגרוף על לבו] אמר ליה רשע אית מאנין לאמך מספקא לי אילין שקרעתי הדא אמרת שקורעין על כנויין בזמן הזה: על שריפת התורה. שנאמר ויהי כקרא יהודי שלש דלתות וארבעה יקרעה בתער הסופר והשלך על האש. מהו שלש דלתות וארבע. תלת וארבע פסוקין. ובכולהו אמר אנא מלכא כיון דשמע לפסוקי חמישי היו צריה לראש אמר להו מי אמר אמרו ליה כי ה' הוגה על רוב פשעיה מיד קרעה בתער הסופר. קדר כל האזכרות שבו ושרפן באש. וכתיב ולא פחדו ולא קרעו בגדיהם מכלל דהוה להו למקרע: **ירושלמי** א"ר יוסי בשם רב אין קורעין אלא על ס"ת ששרפו מלך בזרוע. כגון יהויקים בן יאשיהו וחביריו. הרואה ת"ח שמת כרואה ס"ת שנשרף א"ר אבהו יבא עלי אם טעמתי כלום כל אותו היום. ר' יונה הוה בצור שמע [דדמך] בריה דר' אבהו. ואע"ג דאכל גובנא ושתה מיא אסקוה צום כל ההוא יומא. א"ר חלבו אמר רב הונא הרואה ס"ת שנשרף חייב לקרוע שתים. אחת על המגלה ואחת על הדברים. שנאמר ויהי דבר ה' אל ירמיהו אחרי שרוף המלך את המגלה ואת הדברים באש ואסיקנא אמר שמואל אין חייבין לקרוע אלא בשרפת התורה בזרוע כמעשה שהיה. אבל אי בלעה נעמיתה תפילי כדאמר רב הונא בר חייא לא. ערי יהודה שנאמר ויבא אנשים משכם משילו ומשומרון שמונים איש מגולחי זקן וקרועי בגדים. א"ר אלעזר הרואה ערי יהודה בחורבנן אומר ערי קדשך היו מדבר וקורע. הרואה ירושלים בחורבנה אומר ציון מדבר היתה וקורע. בהמ"ק חרב אומר בית קדשנו ותפארתנו אשר הללוך אבותינו היה לשרפת אש וכל מחמדנו היה לחרבה וקורע. ואחד השומע ואחד הרואה כיון שהגיע לצופים קורע. ואי פגע בירושלים תחלה קורע על ירושלים בפ"ע ועל מקדש בפ"ע. ואי פגע במקדש תחלה קורע על המקדש ומוסיף

*) בירושלמי הגי' ועוד תורה וע"ש בפ"מ וכק"ע.

הגהות מהר"ב רנשבורג א] גמ' רבי אבא ורב הונא בר חייא הוו יתבי קמיה דרבי אבא. נמחק תיבות קמיה דר' אבא ונ"ב קם ר' אבא. כך שמעתי וראיתי יש מגיהים ולענ"ד אין צורך לזה דכבר בירר בס' באר שבע בהוריות דף ב' ע"א דתלתא סתם ר' אבא הוו יעוש"ה: ב] רש"י ד"ה אתיא קרע קרע מדוד עכ"ל. עיין שו"ת שער אפרים סי' נו דטעות הדפוס הוא ועיין עוד ספר יד דוד:

ובאיחוי אלכסנדרי. ת"ר: הקורע מתוך השלל, מתוך המלל, מתוך הלקט, מתוך הסולמות – לא יצא. מתוך האיחוי – יצא. אמר רב חסדא: ובאיחוי אלכסנדרי. ת"ר: רשאי להופכו למטה ולאחותו. ר' שמעון בן אלעזר אוסר לאחותו. וכשם שהמוכר אסור לאחותו – כך הלוקח אסור לאחותו. ולפיכך מוכר צריך להודיעו ללוקח. ת"ר: תחילת קריעה טפח, ותוספת שלש אצבעות, דברי רבי מאיר. רבי יהודה אומר: תחילת קריעה שלש אצבעות, ותוספת כל שהו. אמר עולא: הלכה כרבי מאיר בקריעה, והלכה כרבי יהודה בתוספת. תניא נמי הכי, רבי יוסי אומר: תחילת קריעה טפח ותוספת כל שהו. ת"ר: אמרו לו מת אביו, וקרע, מת בנו, והוסיף, תחתון מתאחה, עליון אינו מתאחה. מת בנו וקרע, מת אביו והוסיף, עליון מתאחה, תחתון אינו מתאחה. מת אביו, מת אמו, מת אחיו, מתה אחותו, קורע קרע אחד לכולן. רבי יהודה בן בתירה אומר: על כולן קרע אחד, על אביו ואמו קרע אחד, לפי שאין מוסיפין על קרע אביו ואמו. מאי טעמא? אמר רב נחמן בר יצחק: לפי שאינן בתוספת. אמר שמואל: הלכה כרבי יהודה בן בתירה. ומי אמר שמואל הכי? והאמר שמואל: *הלכה כדברי המיקל באבל! אבילות לחוד, קריעה לחוד. עד היכן קורע? עד טיבורו, ויש אומרים: עד לבו. אע"פ שאין ראיה לדבר – זכר לדבר, שנאמר: "וקרעו לבבכם ואל בגדיכם". הגיע לטיבורו, מרחיק שלש אצבעות וקורע. נתמלא מלפניו – מחזירו לאחוריו. נתמלא מלמעלה – הופכו מלמטה. והקורע מלמטה ומן הצדדין לא יצא. אלא שכהן גדול פורם מלמטה. פליגו בה רב מתנה ומר עוקבא, ותרוייהו משמיה דאבוה דשמואל ולוי; חד אמר: כל שבעה קורע, לאחר שבעה מוסיף. וחד אמר: כל שלשים קורע, לאחר שלשים מוסיף. מתקיף לה רבי זירא: מאן דאמר כל שבעה קורע, אמאי, דלא ניתן לשוללו, אלא הא דאמר מר: *האשה שוללתו לאלתר, ה"נ התם משום כבוד אשה הוא. מאן דאמר כל שלשים קורע, אמאי, דלא ניתן לאחותו. אלא לאביו ולאמו, דלא ניתן לאחותו לעולם, ה"נ התם משום כבוד אביו ואמו הוא. ת"ר: *היוצא בבגד קרוע לפני המת הרי זה גוזל את המתים ואת החיים. *רשב"ג אומר, האומר לחבירו: "השאילני חלוקך ואלך ואבקר את אבא שהוא חולה", והלך ומצאו שמת – קורע, ומאחו. וכשיבא לביתו מחזיר לו חלוקו ונותן לו דמי קרעו. ואם לא הודיעו – הרי זה לא יגע בו. ת"ר: חולה שמת לו מת – אין מודיעין אותו שמת, שמא תטרף דעתו עליו. ואין מקרעין בפניו, ומשתקין את הנשים מפניו. *ומקרעין לקטן מפני עגמת נפש. וקורעין על חמיו ועל חמותו מפני כבוד אשתו. ואמר רב פפא, תנא באבל רבתי: אבל לא יניח תינוק בתוך חיקו מפני שמביאו לידי שחוק, ונמצא מתגנה על הבריות.§ "ואין מברין *על מטות זקופות".§ ת"ר: ההולך לבית האבל, אם היה לבו גס בו – יברוהו על מטות כפויות, ואם לאו – יברוהו על מטות זקופות. רבא איתרע ביה מילתא. על לגביה אבא בר מרתא, דהוא אבא בר מניומי. רבא – זקיף, אבא בר מרתא – כפי. אמר: כמה לית ביה דעתא להאי צורבא מרבנן. תנו רבנן: ההולך ממקום למקום, אם

תורה אור

לעיל יח. וש"נ עירובין מו.

יואל ב

לעיל כב:

שמחות פ"ט

שם [תוספתא ב"מ פ"ח]

לעיל יז:

אלא

רש"י

מתוך השלל. שלא קרע אלא בשלל: מתוך האיחוי. מקרע האיחוי: ובאיחוי אלכסנדרי. דהוה כשלם: רשאי להפכו למטה. שהופך הקרע למטה, והופך שלמטה למעלה, ומאחהו, ועושה בית הצואר ולובשו: ותוספת שלש. כגון שמוסיף קרע אחר על אותו קרע, כגון שאירעו אבל אחר: עליון אין מתאחה. שקרעו על אביו ועל אמו: שאינן בתוספת. כלומר, אין בדין שמוסיף עליהן: הגיע לטיבורו. ומת לו מת אחר: מרחיק שלש אצבעות. בצד אותו קרע, וקורע: נתמלא. קרעים מלפניו, מחזירו לאחוריו וחוזר וקורע לפניו: כל שבעה. אם מת לו מת – קורע קריעה אחרת: לאחר שבעה מוסיף. על קרע ראשון: דלא ניתן לשוללו. תוך שבעה כלל. ואי מוסיף ביה – מיחזי כקרע אחד. אבל לאחר שבעה, דכבר שללו – קורע כל השלילות ומוסיף כל שהו, דמינכר דעל מת אחר קרע: אשה שוללתו לאלתר. אפילו תוך שבעה: הכי נמי. דמוסיף דקורע השלילה, ומוסיף בה פורתא דקא מינכר. וקא פסיק: כל שבעה קורע, ואפילו אשה: משום כבוד האשה הוא. ולא מן הדין: משום כבוד אביו. ולא מן הדין והוי כאיחוי, לפיכך מוסיף בו לאחר שלשים: בבגד קרוע. קודם לכן, גוזל הכל. שמרמה הכל, שמראה להן שקרע על המת: ואם לא הודיעו. שהולך לבקר את אביו: יברוהו. לאותו שבא על מטות כפויות: אבל – ההולך ממקום למקום: יגלגל

תוספות

ובאיחוי אלכסנדרי. בירושלמי: איזהו איחוי – כל שאין מקומו ניכר. ובמסכת שמחות (פ"ט) מפרש: כל שאחוהו כל צורכו: **כך** הלוקח אסור לאחותו. לא שמעתי אם מותר למוכרו לנכרי. נהי דלוקח אסור לאחותו – אם הוא נכרי מותר. ואע"פ דמוכר צריך להודיע ללוקח – היינו כדי שלא יעשה לוקח איסור, אבל אין אנו חוששין אם יתפרנו הנכרי, ולכאורה היה מותר.* ועוד צ"ע. והאי וכשם שהמוכר כו' – הוי פי' לתנא קמא בלא הפיכה, ולר"ש בן אלעזר אפילו על ידי הפיכה. ובמאי דפליגי נראה דהלכה כתנא קמא, וכן פירש הר"א: **תחילת** קריעה שלש אצבעות. לא ידענא *מנא מפיק טעמא, דלעיל (ד' כב:) מפקינן טפח מ"ויחזק": אין אחיזה פחות מטפח: **תניא** נמי הכי. רבי יוסי סובר כן, ורבי יוסי הלכה כמותו גבי דרבי מאיר ורבי יהודה, בפרק "מי שהוציאוהו" (עירובין ד' מו:). ועוד, דה"ל מכריע: **קורע** קרע אחד על כולן. במסכת שמחות (פ"ט): א"ל מת אביו וקרע, והוא אינו אלא אמו – יצא. מתה אמו, והוא אינו אלא אביו – יצא. מת אביו, מתה אמו, וקרע, והוא אינו אלא אחד מן הקרובין – יצא, אחד מן הקרובין וקרע, והוא אינו אלא אביו או אמו – לא יצא. ובירושלמי: אמרו לו מת ראובן וקרע, ואמרו שמעון היה – יצא. אמרו לו מת ראובן וקרע, ואח"כ אמרו לו קיים היה ומת, אית תנא: לא יצא. וכן קרע על אביו ונמצא בנו. אם מת על אתר – אין צריך לקרוע. כמה הוא על אתר – כדי דבור. ובסוף פרק בתרא דנדרים (דף פז.) כמו כן היא שנויה: **אמר** רב נחמן בר יצחק לפי שאינן בתוספת. תימה: מאי מוסיף לפרש הטעם מן הברייתא? ופירש הר"א בשם רבינו שמואל: דלא גרסינן "לפי שאין מוסיפין" בברייתא. והר"י הקשה בתוספות: מאי שייך בתוספת? נראה לי דמצי למימר דסבירא כמאן דאמר עד טיבורו. אי נמי: עד שיגלה את לבו – אין זה כל כך כמו עד לבו. מיהו, יותר נראה לי: דקאמר רב נחמן בר יצחק לפי שאינן בתוספת – שצריך לקרוע עד לבו, ואם אירע כך שלא קרע עד לבו – מ"מ, כיון דלא עשה כמו שהיה צריך – אומר אין שייך תוספת. מיהו, לפירושו קסבר רב נחמן בר יצחק כיש אומרים עד לבו. ואפילו למאן דאמר בסמוך עד טיבורו – יש ליישב כמו שפי', שאין צריך לקרוע על אביו ועל אמו רק עד שיגלה את לבו, מכל מקום אם קרע טפי – שפיר, משום כבוד אביו, ואין כאן "בל תשחית": **פורם** מלמטה. בפ' בתרא דהוריות (ד' יב:) מפרש מה קורע למטה, אם בצואר: **לפי** שאין מוסיפין על אביו ואמו. פי' בקונטרס: דאכולהו קאי, דבין אם קרע על אביו קודם, בין קרע על אחד מקרוביו קודם. ולא ידענא מנא ליה, דלישנא משמע דוקא על קרע אביו ואמו שהיה קודם:
אם

וכמס' שמחות ספ"ט איתא לאסור

[עי' כליס פכ"ד מ"ב ומ"י] אולי צ"ל פכ"ז

עין משפט נר מצוה

קצט א מיי' פ"ט מהל' אבל הלכה ג:

ר ב ג מיי' שם סמג עשין ב טוש"ע י"ד סי' שמ סעיף כ:

רא ד ה מיי' שם והלכה ד סמג שם טוש"ע שם סעיף יט:

רב ו מיי' שם פ"ח הלכה ב י סמג שם טוש"ע שם סעיף ג:

רג ז ח מיי' שם הלכה ט טוש"ע שם סעיף כב:

רד ט מיי' שם הלכה י טוש"ע שם סעיף כא:

רה י מיי' שם הלכה א טוש"ע שם סעיף ב:

רו כ מיי' שם ופ"ז הלכה ו סמג שם וסמג לאוין שא ומיי' פ"ה מהל' כלי המקדש הלכה ו:

רז ל מיי' פ"ח מהלכות אבל הלכה י סמג עשין ב טוש"ע י"ד סי' שמ סעיף כא:

רח מ מיי' שם הלכה ו סמג שם טוש"ע שם סעיף לג:

רט נ מיי' שם הלכה ז טוש"ע שם סעיף לד:

רי ס מיי' שם הלכה ד טוש"ע שם סי' שלז:

ריא ע מיי' שם הלכה ה טוש"ע שם סי' שמ סעיף ד:

ריב פ מיי' שם פ"ה הלכה כ טוש"ע שם וסי' שלא סעיף א:

רבינו חננאל

על ירושלים: ת"ר רשאי להופכו למטה ולעשות לו איחוי. פי' להפך החלוק לחתכו ולתת בית הצואר שלו שולים והשולים יעשה בית שפה. ר' שמעון בן אלעזר אומר באיחוי בין מלמעלן בין מלמטה. וכשם שהבעלים אסורין לאחותו כן הלוקח אסור לאחותו. לפיכך צריך המוכר להודיע ללוקח שזה קרע אסור באיחוי הוא. ת"ר וכולן אלו הקרעין רשאין לשוללן למוללן ללוקטן ולעשותן בתפירה אחת כעין סולמות שיהא ניכר הקרע. אבל אין רשאין לאחותן באיחוי אלכסנדרית שהוא כמין אריגה. ת"ר הקורע מתוך השלל או מתוך המלל או מתוך הליקוט או מתוך הסולמות לא יצא. אבל אם היה איחוי אלכסנדרית שהוא כאריגה יצא ידי קריעה: **ירושלמי** כד דמך ר' יוחנן אורי ר' חייא בר אבא לשלול הקרע בו ביום ולנעול הסנדל בו ביום. א"ל ר' תנחום ב"ר חייא לר' חיננא בר פפא ר' צלי עלן. א"ל יסוג תודעתך שכל אותה שנה הדין מתוח כנגד המשפחה דא"ר יוחנן כל שבעה החרב שלופה עד שלשים יום. ומשלשים היא רופפת ואינה חוזרת לתערה עד י"ב חודש. למה"ד לכיפת אבנים שנתרועעה אחת מהן נתרועעה כולן. א"ר אלעזר אם נולד להן בן באותה משפחה נתרפאת כל המשפחה כולה: **ת"ר** תחלת הקריעה טפח ואם קרע על המת ועוד מת לו מת אחר ובא לקרוע ולהוסיף על הקרע מוסיף ג' אצבעות דברי ר' מאיר *) ותחלת הקריעה ג' אצבעות ותוספת כל שהו. אמר עולא הלכה כר' מאיר בקריעה שתחלת קריעה טפח. והלכתא כר' יהודה בתוספת דדי לו אפילו כל שהו. תניא נמי הכי ר' יוסי אומר תחלת הקריעה טפח ותוספת כל שהו: **ת"ר** מת אביו וקרע. מת בנו והוסיף תחתיו מתאחה. עליון אין מתאחה. מת בנו וקרע מת אביו והוסיף כו'. ר' יהודה בן בתירה אומר על כולן כגון בנו ובתו אחיו ואחותו ואשתו קורעין להן קרע אחד על אביו ועל אמו קורע קרע אחר. לפי שאין מוסיפין על קרע אביו ואמו פי' לפי שאינו בתוספת מפני שקריעתו על אביו ועל אמו מבדיל קמי שפה שלו וקורע והולך עד שמגיע הקרע אל לבו ומגלה. ובשאר מתים קורע טפח ומוסיף כל שהו עד שמגיע אל לבו. ואע"פ שאין ראיה ברורה אשכחן זכר לדבר דכתיב וקרעו לבבכם ואל בגדיכם. אמר שמואל הלכה כר' יהודה בן בתירה. איני והאמר שמואל הלכה כדברי המיקל באבל. ור' יהודה לגבי ת"ק מחמיר הוא. ופרקינן כי קאמר שמואל בענין אבלות ענין קריעה הוא. הלכך הלכתא כר' יהודה בן בתירה. עד היכן קורע עד טיבורו הגיע לטיבורו מרחיק ג' אצבעות וקורע. נתמלא מלפניו מחזירו מלאחוריו נתמלא מלמעלה הופכו למטה (כנגד) מהפך ועושה שולי חלוקו בית הצואר וקורע למעלה. והקורע מלמטה מן השוליים ומן הצדדין לא יצא. אלא שכ"ג פורם מלמטה. פליגי **) עליה משמיה דאבוה דשמואל ולוי. חד אמר כל שבעה לאחר שבעה אם מת לו מת אחר מוסיף על הקרע הראשון כל שהו. וחד אמר כל שלשים יום אם ימות לו מת אחר קורע [קרע] אחר לאחר ל' יום מוסיף. מתקיף ליה ר' זירא מאן דאמר כל שבעה אמאי אינו מוסיף דלא ניתן לשוללו בתוך ז'. אלא קרע של אשה ששוללתו לאלתר הכי נמי שמוספת לאלתר. ופרקינן התם משום כבוד אשה. מ"ד כל ל' יום אם קורע אמאי כו': ת"ר היוצא בבגד לפני המת הרי זה גוזל את החיים ואת המתים רשב"א האומר לחבירו השאילני חלוקך כדי שאלך ואבקר את אבי שהוא חולה. ומצאו שמת קורעו. וכשיבא לביתו מאחו. ומחזירו לבעליו ונותן לו דמי קרעו. ואם לא הודיעו כי הולך לבקר את אביו לא יגע בו. ת"ר חולה שמת לו מת אין מודיעין אותו שמא תטרף דעתו של חולה ואין מקרעין לו ומשתקין הנשים מפניו ומקרעין. לקטן אביו שמת או על אמו. וכיוצא בהן מפני עגמת נפש. וקורע על חמיו ועל חמותו מפני כבוד אשתו: תנא באבל רבתי אבל לא יניח תינוק בחיקו מפני הרבים מפני שמביאו לידי שחוק ונמצא מתגנה על הבריות. ואין מברין אלא על מטות זקופות. ת"ר ההולך לבית האבל אם היה לבו גס בו יברוהו על מטות כפויות. ואם לאו יברוהו על מטות זקופות. רבא איתרע ליה מלתא דאבלות על לגביה רבה וזקף המטה להברותו. על אבא בר מרתא וכפה. אמר לית ביה דעתא [להאי צורבא] מרבנן דכפה דהא אין לבי גס בו. ת"ר אבל ההולך ממקום למקום אם יכול למעט בעסקו כלומר שלא יקנה ולא ימכור [ימעט]. ואם לאו יגלגל עמהן
יקנה

*) חסר כאן וצ"ל ר"י אומר תחלת קריעה ג' אצבעות וכו'. **) צ"ל פליגו בה רב מתנה וכו' משמיה דאבוה דשמואל וכו'.

רש"י

יְגַלְגֵּל עִמָּהֶן. וְאֵינוֹ עוֹשֶׂה סְחוֹרָה בִּפְנֵי עַצְמוֹ, אֶלָּא עִם חֲבוּרָה: אַף עַל גַּב שֶׁאֵין לוֹ. לְאָבֵל אַחַר הַשַּׁבָּת אֶלָּא יוֹם אֶחָד: קַרְבִּיטָיו. רְצוּעוֹתָיו, שֶׁהוּא כְּעֵין תרניפני"א: עַרְסָא דְּגַדָּא. מִטָּה שֶׁמְּיַיחֲדִים אוֹתָהּ לְמַזָּל טוֹב, וְאֵין מִשְׁתַּמְּשִׁין בָּהּ כְּלוּם, אֶלָּא מְיַיחֲדִין אוֹתָהּ לְשָׁרוֹת מַזָּל טוֹב עָלֶיהָ: דְּצַלָּא. עוֹר: סֵירוּגוֹ מִתּוֹכוֹ. מַכְנִיס רְצוּעוֹת מִן חוֹרֵי עֲצֵי הַמִּטָּה: עַל גַּבָּהּ. וְהָעוֹר כָּפוּל עַל הָעֵץ: נַקְלִיטֵי. עֵצִים יוֹצְאִין מְתוּקָּנִין לִמְרַאֲשׁוֹתָיו וּלְמַרְגְּלוֹתָיו, וְנוֹתְנִין עֵץ אָרוֹךְ עֲלֵיהֶן, וְנוֹתֵן הַסְּדִינִין עֲלֵיהֶם לִשְׁמוֹר מֵהַזְּבוּבִים: אֵין מְבָרְכִין. עַל רֵיחַ בְּבֵית הָאָבֵל: הַמְנַחֲמִין. קְרוֹבָיו, מְבִיאִין עֲנָיִים שֶׁל אוֹכָלִין: מתני' אִסְקוּטְלָא. תַּמְחוּי: פּוֹטְרִין אֶת הָרַבִּים. שֶׁאוֹמְרִים לַמְנַחֲמִין: לְכוּ לְבָתֵּיכֶם: אֵין מַנִּיחִין מִטָּה בַּמּוֹעֵד בָּרְחוֹב. לְהַסְפִּידוֹ: וְלֹא שֶׁל נָשִׁים לְעוֹלָם. שֶׁשּׁוֹפְעוֹת זִיבָה: גמ' בְּלִיכָה

גמרא

[א]אִם יָכוֹל לְמַעֵט בְּעִסְקוֹ — יְמַעֵט, וְאִם לָאו — יְגַלְגֵּל עִמָּהֶן. תָּנוּ רַבָּנַן: *מֵאֵימָתַי כּוֹפִין אֶת הַמִּטּוֹת? מִשֶּׁיֵּצֵא מִפֶּתַח בֵּיתוֹ, דִּבְרֵי ר' אֱלִיעֶזֶר. רַבִּי יְהוֹשֻׁעַ אוֹמֵר: *[ב]מִשֶּׁיִּסָּתֵם הַגּוֹלֵל. מַעֲשֶׂה שֶׁמֵּת רַבָּן גַּמְלִיאֵל הַזָּקֵן, כֵּיוָן שֶׁיָּצָא מִפֶּתַח בֵּיתוֹ אָמַר לָהֶם רַבִּי אֱלִיעֶזֶר: כְּפוּ מִטּוֹתֵיכֶם. וְכֵיוָן שֶׁנִּסְתַּם הַגּוֹלֵל, [אָמַר לָהֶם רַבִּי יְהוֹשֻׁעַ: כְּפוּ מִטּוֹתֵיכֶם.] אָמְרוּ לוֹ: כְּבָר כָּפִינוּ עַל פִּי זָקֵן. ת"ר: [ג]מֵאֵימָתַי זוֹקְפִין אֶת הַמִּטּוֹת בְּעֶרֶב שַׁבָּת — מִן הַמִּנְחָה וּלְמַעְלָה. אָמַר רַבָּה בַּר הוּנָא: [ד]אַף עַל פִּי כֵן, אֵינוֹ יוֹשֵׁב עָלֶיהָ עַד שֶׁתֶּחְשַׁךְ. [ה]וּלְמוֹצָאֵי שַׁבָּת, אע"פ שֶׁאֵין לוֹ לֵישֵׁב אֶלָּא יוֹם אֶחָד — חוֹזֵר וְכוֹפֶה. תָּנוּ רַבָּנַן: [ו]הַכּוֹפֶה מִטָּתוֹ, לֹא מִטָּתוֹ בִּלְבַד הוּא כּוֹפֶה, אֶלָּא כָּל מִטּוֹת שֶׁיֵּשׁ לוֹ בְּתוֹךְ בֵּיתוֹ הוּא כּוֹפֶה. וַאֲפִילּוּ יֵשׁ לוֹ עֶשֶׂר מִטּוֹת בַּעֲשָׂרָה מְקוֹמוֹת כּוֹפֶה אֶת כּוּלָּן, וַאֲפִילּוּ חֲמִשָּׁה אַחִין וּמֵת אֶחָד — כּוּלָּן כּוֹפִין. [ז]וְאִם הָיְתָה מִטָּה הַמְיוּחֶדֶת לְכֵלִים — אֵין צָרִיךְ לִכְפּוֹתָהּ. דַּרְגָּשׁ — אֵין צָרִיךְ לִכְפּוֹתוֹ, אֶלָּא זוֹקְפוֹ. רַבָּן שִׁמְעוֹן בֶּן גַּמְלִיאֵל אוֹמֵר: [ח]דַּרְגָּשׁ, מַתִּיר אֶת קַרְבִּיטָיו וְהוּא נוֹפֵל מֵאֵלָיו. *מַאי דַּרְגָּשׁ? אֲמַר עוּלָּא: עַרְסָא דְגַדָּא. אֲמַר לֵיהּ רַבָּה: אֶלָּא מֵעַתָּה גַּבֵּי מֶלֶךְ, *דִּתְנַן: [ט]כָּל הָעָם מְסוּבִּים עַל הָאָרֶץ וְהוּא מֵיסֵב עַל הַדַּרְגָּשׁ, מִי אִיכָּא מִידֵּי דְּעַד הָאִידָּנָא לָא אוֹתְבִינֵיהּ — וְהַשְׁתָּא מוֹתְבִינַן לֵיהּ? מַתְקִיף לַהּ רַב אָשֵׁי: מַאי קוּשְׁיָא? מִידֵּי דַּהֲוָה אַאֲכִילָה וּשְׁתִיָּה, דְּעַד הָאִידָּנָא — לָא אוֹכְלִינֵיהּ וְלָא אַשְׁקִינֵיהּ, הַשְׁתָּא — אוֹכְלִינֵיהּ וְאַשְׁקִינֵיהּ! אֶלָּא, אִי קַשְׁיָא — הָא קַשְׁיָא: (*דִּתְנַן,) דַּרְגָּשׁ אֵינוֹ צָרִיךְ לִכְפּוֹתוֹ אֶלָּא זוֹקְפוֹ, וְאִי עַרְסָא דְגַדָּא — אַמַּאי אֵינוֹ צָרִיךְ לִכְפּוֹתוֹ? הָא (*תְּנַן:) *)הַכּוֹפֶה מִטָּתוֹ — לֹא מִטָּתוֹ בִּלְבַד הוּא כּוֹפֶה, אֶלָּא כָּל מִטּוֹת שֶׁיֵּשׁ לוֹ בְּתוֹךְ בֵּיתוֹ כּוֹפֶה! וּמַאי קַשְׁיָא? מִידֵּי דַּהֲוָה אַמִּטָּה הַמְיוּחֶדֶת לְכֵלִים, דְּתַנְיָא: אִם הָיְתָה מִטָּה הַמְיוּחֶדֶת לְכֵלִים — אֵינוֹ צָרִיךְ לִכְפּוֹתָהּ! אֶלָּא, אִי קַשְׁיָא הָא קַשְׁיָא: רַבָּן שִׁמְעוֹן בֶּן גַּמְלִיאֵל אוֹמֵר: דַּרְגָּשׁ, מַתִּיר קַרְבִּיטָיו וְהוּא נוֹפֵל מֵאֵלָיו. וְאִי סָלְקָא דַּעְתָּךְ עַרְסָא דְגַדָּא — מַאי קַרְבִּיטִין אִית לֵיהּ? *כִּי אֲתָא רָבִין אֲמַר לֵיהּ הַהוּא מֵרַבָּנָן, וְרַב תַּחְלִיפָא בַּר מַעַרְבָא שְׁמֵיהּ, דַּהֲוָה שְׁכִיחַ בְּשׁוּקָא דְגִילְדָאֵי: מַאי דַּרְגָּשׁ — עַרְסָא דְצַלָּא. [א]אִיתְּמַר נַמִּי, אָמַר ר' יִרְמְיָה: דַּרְגָּשׁ — סֵירוּגוֹ מִתּוֹכוֹ, מִטָּה — סֵירוּגָהּ עַל גַּבָּהּ. אָמַר רַבִּי יַעֲקֹב בַּר אַחָא אָמַר רַבִּי יְהוֹשֻׁעַ בֶּן לֵוִי: *הֲלָכָה כְּרַבָּן שִׁמְעוֹן בֶּן גַּמְלִיאֵל. (*אִיתְּמַר נַמִּי,) אָמַר רַבִּי יַעֲקֹב בַּר אַחָא אָמַר רַבִּי אַסִּי: [י]מִטָּה שֶׁנַּקְלִיטֶיהָ יוֹצְאִין — זוֹקְפָהּ, וְדַיּוֹ. *תָּנוּ רַבָּנַן: יָשֵׁן עַל גַּבֵּי כִּסֵּא, עַל גַּבֵּי *אוֹדְיָינֵי גְּדוֹלָה,[ב] עַל גַּבֵּי קַרְקַע — לֹא יָצָא יְדֵי חוֹבָתוֹ. אָמַר רַבִּי יוֹחָנָן: שֶׁלֹּא קִיֵּים כְּפִיַּית הַמִּטָּה. תָּנוּ רַבָּנַן: [כ]מְכַבְּדִין וּמַרְבִּיצִין בְּבֵית הָאָבֵל, וּמַדִּיחִין קְעָרוֹת וְכוֹסוֹת וּצְלוֹחִיּוֹת וְקִיתוֹנִיּוֹת בְּבֵית הָאָבֵל, [ל]וְאֵין מְבִיאִין אֶת הַמּוּגְמָר וְאֶת הַבְּשָׂמִים לְבֵית הָאָבֵל. אִינִי: וְהָא תָּנֵי בַּר קַפָּרָא: אֵין מְבָרְכִין לֹא עַל הַמּוּגְמָר וְלֹא עַל הַבְּשָׂמִים בְּבֵית הָאָבֵל. בָּרוּכֵי הוּא דְּלָא מְבָרְכִין, הָא אַתּוּיֵי — מַיְיתִי! לָא קַשְׁיָא; הָא — בְּבֵית הָאָבֵל, [מ]הָא — בְּבֵית הַמְנַחֲמִין.§

מתני' [נ]אֵין מוֹלִיכִין לְבֵית הָאָבֵל לֹא בְּטַבְלָא וְלֹא בְּאִסְקוּטְלָא וְלֹא בְּקָנוֹן, אֶלָּא בְּסַלִּים. [ס]וְאֵין אוֹמְרִים בִּרְכַּת אֲבֵלִים בַּמּוֹעֵד, אֲבָל עוֹמְדִין בְּשׁוּרָה, וּמְנַחֲמִין, וּפוֹטְרִין אֶת הָרַבִּים. [ע]אֵין מַנִּיחִין אֶת הַמִּטָּה בָּרְחוֹב שֶׁלֹּא לְהַרְגִּיל אֶת הַהֶסְפֵּד. [פ]וְלֹא שֶׁל נָשִׁים לְעוֹלָם, מִפְּנֵי הַכָּבוֹד.§

גמ' תָּנוּ רַבָּנַן: בָּרִאשׁוֹנָה הָיוּ מוֹלִיכִין בְּבֵית הָאָבֵל, עֲשִׁירִים — בְּקַלָּתוֹת שֶׁל כֶּסֶף וְשֶׁל זָהָב, וַעֲנִיִּים — בְּסַלֵּי נְצָרִים שֶׁל עֲרָבָה קְלוּפָה. וְהָיוּ עֲנִיִּים מִתְבַּיְּישִׁים, [צ]הִתְקִינוּ שֶׁיְּהוּ הַכֹּל מְבִיאִין בְּסַלֵּי נְצָרִים שֶׁל עֲרָבָה קְלוּפָה, מִפְּנֵי כְּבוֹדָן שֶׁל עֲנִיִּים. תָּנוּ רַבָּנַן: [ק]בָּרִאשׁוֹנָה הָיוּ מַשְׁקִין בְּבֵית הָאָבֵל, עֲשִׁירִים — בִּזְכוֹכִית לְבָנָה, וַעֲנִיִּים — בִּזְכוֹכִית צְבוּעָה, וְהָיוּ עֲנִיִּים מִתְבַּיְּישִׁין. הִתְקִינוּ שֶׁיְּהוּ הַכֹּל מַשְׁקִין בִּזְכוֹכִית צְבוּעָה, מִפְּנֵי כְּבוֹדָן שֶׁל עֲנִיִּים. [ר]בָּרִאשׁוֹנָה הָיוּ מְגַלִּין פְּנֵי עֲשִׁירִים וּמְכַסִּין פְּנֵי עֲנִיִּים, מִפְּנֵי שֶׁהָיוּ מוּשְׁחָרִין פְּנֵיהֶן מִפְּנֵי בַּצּוֹרֶת, וְהָיוּ עֲנִיִּים מִתְבַּיְּישִׁין. הִתְקִינוּ שֶׁיְּהוּ מְכַסִּין פְּנֵי הַכֹּל, מִפְּנֵי כְּבוֹדָן שֶׁל עֲנִיִּים. *בָּרִאשׁוֹנָה הָיוּ מוֹצִיאִין עֲשִׁירִים בְּדַרְגָּשׁ, וַעֲנִיִּים בִּכְלִיכָה

תוספות

אם יכול למעט בעסקו ימעט. פירש בקונטרס: בסחורתו. ונראה דבדבר האבד קאמר, וכן פי' לעיל (ד' כב.) גבי "על כל המתים כולן רצה ממעט בעסקו רצה אינו ממעט". וגם הרב פירש לעיל בדבר האבד עושה בצנעא בתוך ביתו. נראה לפירושו דהכא איירי באביו ואמו, ומשום דהולך בדרך — התירו לו שיגלגל עמהם אם אינו יכול למעט. דבשאר מתים אינו ממעט כלל אם אינו רוצה. ואי איירי הכא בשאר מתים — צריך לומר להפך: הולך בדרך ואינו נוהג אבילות כל כך, ומתנחם יותר — אסור להרבות בעסקו יותר מאותו שיושב בביתו ואינו מתנחם. וה"ר יוסף פירש: דהכא ימעט בעסקו — לקנות צורכי סעודה, ולפי שהולך בדרך רגיל לקנות צורכי סעודה יותר מבביתו, שיש לו קונים עבורו, וגם מוצא בביתו הרבה. משום הכי נקט הולך בדרך. ומה שפירש בקונטרס דאיירי כשאמרו לו על מיתת קרוביו כשהיה בדרך — לא ידענא אי בעי למימר דאיירי במוליך סחורתו ממקום למקום כדפי' בקונטרס, ור"ל דשמא שרי ליה לדידיה למכור סחורתו, דכיון דהוליך אותה כבר וטרח בה ולא פשע בהליכתו, שלא היה יודע לישב בביתו שיכול לשומרה, או שמא הקונטרס ר"ל משום דאמרינן לעיל (דף כג.) שבת ראשונה אינו יוצא מפתח ביתו. וזה אינו קושיא, דאע"פ שאינו יוצא מפתח ביתו בעיר — הא אמרינן (לעיל דף טו:): יצא לדרך (*הולך ונכנס לעיר). אלמא: מותר לצאת (בו). ושמא דוקא בדבר האבד מותר לצאת לדרך: **מן** המנחה ולמעלה. פי' בתוספות הרב: דמספקא ליה אי מנחה גדולה אי מנחה, קטנה דמקודש לכן אינו יושב עליה. נראה לי, דמכאן סמכו שלא לישב ע"ג כסא וספסל, אע"פ שאין ראיה גמורה, דשאני מטה הואיל וצריך כפייה, ולא מצינו כפייה בכסא וספסל:

ואין מוליכין לבית האבל. זאת המשנה כל כרחין נסדרה בהיפך, ושמא כל זה מן הברייתא דלמעלה, כמו שפירש בתוספות בההיא דלעיל. ותמיהני: מדוע לא פירשו גם כאן כמו שפירש למעלה! ושמא בספר הרב היתה כתובה מגוף הברייתא, ולא הוצרך לפרשו. או לא היה כתוב בספרו כלל: ואין מוליכין כו'. וכן מוכיח מתוך פירוש התוספות שפי': לא ידענא אי קאי האי בראשונה היו מוליכים אמוגמר ובשמים, דאמר אין מברכין. הא אתויי — מייתינן. אי אמתניתין קאי, דקתני: מברין, ואותה הבראה היא בראשונה מוליכין כו' דאמתניתין קאי. ועוד: כיון שפירש התקינו שיהו הכל מוליכין כו', ומתניתין לאחר תקנה:

עין משפט נר מצוה

ריג א מיי' פ"ו מהלכות אבל הלכה י טוש"ע י"ד סי' שפ סעיף כג:
ריד ב מיי' פ"א שם הלכה ב סמג עשין דרבנן ב טוש"ע שם סי' שעה סעיף א:
רטו ג ד ה מיי' שם פ"י הלכה ב טור י"ד סי' ת:
רטז ו ז ח מיי' שם פ"ה הלכה יח טור י"ד סי' שפז:
ריז ט מיי' שם פ"ז הלכה ח ופ"ב מהלכות מלכים הלכה ד:
ריח י מיי' פ"ה מהל' אבל הלכה יח טור י"ד שם:
ריט כ ל מיי' פי"ג שם הלכה ו סמג עשין שם טוש"ע שם סי' שעח סעיף ז:
רכ מ טוש"ע שם:
רכא נ מיי' שם הלכה ז טי"ד סי' תא:
רכב ס מיי' שם פי"א הלכה ג טי"ד שם:
רכג ע מיי' שם ופ"ו מהלכות י"ט הלכה כג טוש"ע י"ד סי' תא סעיף א וטוש"ע א"ח סי' תקמז סעיף א:
רכד פ מיי' שם פי"ב הלכה ה טוש"ע שם סי' שנה:
רכה צ ק מיי' שם פי"ג הלכה ז טי"ד סי' שעח סעיף ה:
רכו ר מיי' שם פ"ד הלכה א טוש"ע שם סי' שנג סעיף א:

[נ"ל טעל נכנס לעיר חולך]

רש"א מ"ז וגורס ואמר

רבינו חננאל

יקנה צרכי הדרך ודברי' שיש בהן חיי נפש: ת"ר מאימתי כופין המטות משיוציאו המת מן הבית. דברי ר' אליעזר ר' יהושע אומר משיסתם הגולל. וקיי"ל כר' יהושע דאין אבילות נוהגת אלא משיקבר המת ויסתום הגולל: ת"ר הכופה מטתו לא מטתו בלבד הוא כופה אלא כל מטות שיש בבית. ואפילו יש לו עשר מטות בעשר מקומות כופה את כולן. ואפילו ה' אחין ומת אחד מהן כולן כופין. ואם היתה מיוחדת לכלים ואינה עשויה לישן אין צריך לכפותה. דרגש א"צ לכפותו אלא זוקפו ודיו ואמר עולא האי דרגש ערסא דגדא הוא פירוש מטה העשויה לכבוד מזל הבית ואין אדם ישן עליה. ונדחו דבריו. ואסיקנא דרגש הוא ערסא דצלא. פירוש מטה של עור. כי פי' צלא עור הוא עור נטוי וקשור בחבלים על המלבנות ומסורגות מלבנות המטה בחבלים הללו והעור בתוכן. וכיון שמעמידין אותה ישנין ע"ג העור. ואמר רשב"ג דרגש מתיר קרביטין והוא נופל. אתמר נמי א"ר ירמיה דרגש סירוגו מתוכו. מטה שנקליטיה יוצאין זוקפה ודיו. כלומר אינו צריך לכפותה: ת"ר מאימתי זוקפין את המטות בע"ש מן המנחה ולמעלה. ואעפ"כ אסור לו לישן עליה עד שתחשך. ובמו"ש אע"פ שלא נשאר לו משבעת ימי אבלו אלא יום אחד בלבד חוזר וכופה מטותיו: ת"ר ישן ע"ג מטה. וע"ג אודיני. וע"ג ספסל ע"ג קרקע לא יצא י"ח. וא"ר יוחנן מפני שלא קיים כפיית המטה: ת"ר מכבדין ומרביצין ומדיחין את הקערות כוסות וקיתוניות וצלוחיות בבית האבל. ואין מביאין מוגמר בבית האבל. ואוקימנא הא דתני בר קפרא אין מברכין על המוגמר ועל הבשמים של בית האבל בהני דמייתי בבית המנחמין: **מתני'** אין אומרים ברכת אבלים במועד. אבל עומדין בשורה ומנחמין ופוטרין את הרבים: ת"ר בראשונה היו מוליכין בבית האבל עשירים בקלתות של כסף ושל זהב ועניים בסלי נצרים כו' וכן היו משקין בבית האבל את העשירים בזכוכית לבנה. ואת העניים בזכוכית צבועה וכו'. וכן היו מגלין את מתין העשירים. והיו מכסין את פני העניים שהיו שחורין מן הרעב וכו' וכן היו מוציאין מתי עשירים בדרגש ועניים בבליכה כו'. ובכל אלו היו העניים מתביישין. התקינו חכמים לעשות לעשירים כדרך שהן עושין לעניים שלא יהא

מסורת הש"ס

שמחות פי"א

כתובות ד: סנהדרין מז: שבת קנב:

רש"א

סנהדרין כ. ע"ש

נדרים נו. ע"ש סנהדרין שם

[נ"ל דתניא]

[נ"ל תניא]

*) ג"ז שם תענית ל: נדרים שם

נדרים נו. סנהדרין כ. ע"ש

נדרים נו: סנהדרין כ: ע"ש

[עי' תוס' ב"ב קמז. ד"ה אודייני]

(לעיל כא. פ"ע)

[תוספתא נדה פ"ט]

הגהות הגר"א

[א] גמ' ערסא דצלא אמר כו' כצ"ל. ומלות אתמר נמי ליתא בסנהד' ועי' הגירסא בנדרים: [ב] שם גדולה מזו ע"ג כו' כצ"ל:

בְּכְלִיכָה, וְהָיוּ עֲנִיִּים מִתְבַּיְּישִׁין, הִתְקִינוּ שֶׁיְּהוּ הַכֹּל מוֹצִיאִין בִּכְלִיכָה, מִפְּנֵי כְּבוֹדָן שֶׁל עֲנִיִּים. בָּרִאשׁוֹנָה הָיוּ מַנִּיחִין אֶת הַמּוּגְמָר תַּחַת חוֹלֵי מֵעַיִם מֵתִים, וְהָיוּ חוֹלֵי מֵעַיִם חַיִּים מִתְבַּיְּישִׁין, הִתְקִינוּ שֶׁיְּהוּ מַנִּיחִין תַּחַת הַכֹּל, מִפְּנֵי כְּבוֹדָן שֶׁל חוֹלֵי מֵעַיִם חַיִּים. *בָּרִאשׁוֹנָה הָיוּ מַטְבִּילִין אֶת הַכֵּלִים עַל גַּבֵּי נִדּוֹת מֵתוֹת, וְהָיוּ נִדּוֹת חַיּוֹת מִתְבַּיְּישׁוֹת, הִתְקִינוּ שֶׁיְּהוּ מַטְבִּילִין עַל גַּבֵּי כָּל הַנָּשִׁים, מִפְּנֵי כְּבוֹדָן שֶׁל נִדּוֹת חַיּוֹת. בָּרִאשׁוֹנָה מַטְבִּילִין עַל גַּבֵּי זָבִין מֵתִים, וְהָיוּ זָבִין חַיִּים מִתְבַּיְּישִׁין. הִתְקִינוּ שֶׁיְּהוּ מַטְבִּילִין עַל גַּב הַכֹּל, מִפְּנֵי כְּבוֹדָן שֶׁל זָבִין חַיִּים. *בָּרִאשׁוֹנָה הָיְתָה הוֹצָאַת הַמֵּת קָשָׁה לִקְרוֹבָיו יוֹתֵר מִמִּיתָתוֹ, עַד שֶׁהָיוּ קְרוֹבָיו מַנִּיחִין אוֹתוֹ וּבוֹרְחִין. עַד שֶׁבָּא רַבָּן גַּמְלִיאֵל וְנָהַג קַלּוּת רֹאשׁ בְּעַצְמוֹ וְיָצָא בִּכְלֵי פִשְׁתָּן, [א]וְנָהֲגוּ הָעָם אַחֲרָיו לָצֵאת בִּכְלֵי פִשְׁתָּן. אָמַר רַב פָּפָּא: וְהָאִידָּנָא נְהוּג עָלְמָא אֲפִילּוּ *בִּצְרָדָא בַּר זוּזָא. § "אֵין מַנִּיחִין אֶת הַמִּטָּה בָּרְחוֹב". § אָמַר רַב פָּפָּא: *[ב]אֵין מוֹעֵד בִּפְנֵי תַּלְמִיד חָכָם, וְכָל שֶׁכֵּן חֲנוּכָּה וּפוּרִים. [ג]וְהָנֵי מִילֵּי — בְּפָנָיו, אֲבָל שֶׁלֹּא בְּפָנָיו — לֹא. אִינִי? וְהָא רַב כַּהֲנָא סַפְדֵיהּ לְרַב זְבִיד מִנְּהַרְדְּעָא בְּפוּם נַהֲרָא! אָמַר רַב פַּפִּי: [ד]יוֹם שְׁמוּעָה הֲוָה, וְכִבְפָנָיו דָּמֵי. אָמַר עוּלָּא: *הֶסְפֵּד עַל לֵב, דִּכְתִיב: °"עַל שָׁדַיִם סוֹפְדִים", טִיפּוּחַ — בַּיָּד, קִילּוּס — בָּרֶגֶל. תָּנוּ רַבָּנַן: הַמְקַלֵּס — לֹא יְקַלֵּס בְּסַנְדָּל, אֶלָּא בְּמִנְעָל, מִפְּנֵי הַסַּכָּנָה. אָמַר רַבִּי יוֹחָנָן: [ה]אָבֵל, כֵּיוָן שֶׁנִּיעְנַע רֹאשׁוֹ — שׁוּב אֵין מְנַחֲמִין רַשָּׁאִין לֵישֵׁב אֶצְלוֹ. וְאָמַר רַבִּי יוֹחָנָן: [ו]הַכֹּל חַיָּיבִין לַעֲמוֹד מִפְּנֵי נָשִׂיא, חוּץ מֵאָבֵל וְחוֹלֶה. וְאָמַר ר' יוֹחָנָן: [ז]לַכֹּל אוֹמְרִים לָהֶם "שְׁבוּ" חוּץ מֵאָבֵל וְחוֹלֶה. אָמַר רַב יְהוּדָה אָמַר רַב: [ח]אָבֵל, יוֹם רִאשׁוֹן — אָסוּר לֶאֱכוֹל לֶחֶם מִשֶּׁלּוֹ, מִדְּאָמַר לֵיהּ רַחֲמָנָא לִיחֶזְקֵאל: °"וְלֶחֶם אֲנָשִׁים לֹא תֹאכֵל". רַבָּה וְרַב יוֹסֵף [ט]מְחַלְּפֵי סְעוּדָתַיְיהוּ לַהֲדָדֵי. וְאָמַר רַב יְהוּדָה אָמַר רַב: [י]מֵת בָּעִיר — כָּל בְּנֵי הָעִיר אֲסוּרִין בַּעֲשִׂיַּית מְלָאכָה. רַב הַמְנוּנָא אִיקְלַע לְדָרוּמָתָא, שְׁמַע קוֹל שִׁיפּוּרָא דְשָׁכְבָא. חֲזָא הָנָךְ אֱנָשֵׁי דְּקָא עָבְדִי עֲבִידְתָּא, אָמַר לְהוּ: לֶיהֱווּ הָנָךְ אִינָשֵׁי בְּשַׁמְתָּא! לָא שָׁכְבָא אִיכָּא בְּמָתָא? אֲמַרוּ לֵיהּ: חֲבוּרְתָּא אִיכָּא בְּמָתָא. אֲמַר לְהוּ: [כ]אִי הָכִי — שַׁרְיָא (א)לְכוּ. וְאָמַר רַב יְהוּדָה אָמַר רַב: [ל]כָּל *הַמִּתְקַשֶּׁה עַל מֵתוֹ יוֹתֵר מִדַּאי — עַל מֵת אַחֵר הוּא בּוֹכֶה. הַהִיא אִיתְּתָא דַּהֲוַת בְּשִׁיבָבוּתֵיהּ דְּרַב הוּנָא, הֲווּ לָהּ שִׁבְעָה בְּנֵי. מֵת חַד מִינַּיְיהוּ, הֲוַת קָא בָּכְיָא בְּיָתֵירְתָּא עֲלֵיהּ. שְׁלַח לָהּ רַב הוּנָא: לָא תַּעַבְדִי הָכִי! לָא אַשְׁגְּחָה בֵּיהּ. שְׁלַח לָהּ: אִי צַיְיתַתְּ — מוּטָב, וְאִי לָא — צְבִית *זְוָודְתָא לְאִידָךְ מִית. וּמִיתוּ כּוּלְּהוּ. לַסּוֹף אֲמַר לָהּ: תִּימוּשׁ זְוָודְתָא לְנַפְשִׁיךְ, וּמִיתָא. °"אַל תִּבְכּוּ לְמֵת וְאַל תָּנוּדוּ לוֹ", "אַל תִּבְכּוּ לְמֵת" — יוֹתֵר מִדַּאי, "וְאַל תָּנוּדוּ לוֹ" — יוֹתֵר מִכְּשִׁיעוּר. הָא כֵּיצַד? [מ]שְׁלֹשָׁה יָמִים — לִבְכִי, וְשִׁבְעָה — לְהֶסְפֵּד, וּשְׁלֹשִׁים — לְגִיהוּץ וּלְתִסְפּוֹרֶת. מִכָּאן וְאֵילָךְ — אָמַר הַקָּדוֹשׁ בָּרוּךְ הוּא: אִי אַתֶּם רַחֲמָנִים בּוֹ יוֹתֵר מִמֶּנִּי. °"בְּכוּ בָכוֹ לַהוֹלֵךְ", *אָמַר רַב יְהוּדָה: בְּלֹא בָּנִים. רַבִּי יְהוֹשֻׁעַ בֶּן לֵוִי לָא אֲזַל לְבֵי *אָבְלָא אֶלָּא לְמַאן דְּאָזֵיל בְּלָא בְּנֵי, דִּכְתִיב: "בְּכוּ בָכוֹ לַהוֹלֵךְ כִּי לֹא יָשׁוּב עוֹד וְרָאָה אֶת אֶרֶץ מוֹלַדְתּוֹ". רַב הוּנָא אָמַר: זֶה שֶׁעָבַר עֲבֵירָה וְשָׁנָה בָּהּ. רַב הוּנָא לְטַעְמֵיהּ, *דְּאָמַר רַב הוּנָא: כֵּיוָן שֶׁעָבַר אָדָם עֲבֵירָה וְשָׁנָה בָּהּ — הוּתְּרָה לוֹ. הוּתְּרָה לוֹ סָלְקָא דַעְתָּךְ?! אֶלָּא אֵימָא: נַעֲשֵׂית לוֹ כְּהֶיתֵּר. אָמַר רַבִּי לֵוִי: [נ]אָבֵל שְׁלֹשָׁה יָמִים הָרִאשׁוֹנִים — יִרְאֶה אֶת עַצְמוֹ כְּאִילּוּ חֶרֶב מוּנַּחַת לוֹ בֵּין שְׁתֵּי (*יַרְיכוֹתָיו,) מִשְּׁלֹשָׁה עַד שִׁבְעָה — לוֹ כְּנֶגְדּוֹ בְּקֶרֶן זָוִית, מִכָּאן וְאֵילָךְ — כְּאִילּוּ עוֹבֶרֶת כְּנֶגְדּוֹ בַּשּׁוּק. § "וְלֹא שֶׁל נָשִׁים לְעוֹלָם מִפְּנֵי הַכָּבוֹד". § אָמְרִי נְהַרְדְּעֵי: לֹא שָׁנוּ אֶלָּא

רש"י

בְּלִיכָה. מִטָּה שֶׁל מֵתִים: עַל גַּבֵּי נִדּוֹת מֵתוֹת. הַכֵּלִים שֶׁנִּשְׁתַּמְּשׁוּ בָּהֶן בְּעוֹדָן בַּחַיִּים, שֶׁנִּטְמְאוּ בִּנְגִיעָתָן. שֶׁהַנִּדָּה מְטַמְּאָה בִּנְגִיעָתָהּ אָדָם וְכֵלִים: וְהָיוּ נִדּוֹת חַיּוֹת מִתְבַּיְּישׁוֹת. שֶׁעוֹשִׂין בָּהֶן מַה שֶּׁאֵין עוֹשִׂין לִשְׁאָר מֵתוֹת: קָשָׁה לִקְרוֹבָיו. בְּתַכְרִיכִין טוֹבִים: צַרְדָא. קַנְבּוֹס: בַּר זוּזָא. הַנִּקְנֶה בְּזוּז: אֵין מוֹעֵד לִפְנֵי חֲכָמִים. שֶׁיְּכוֹלִין לְהַסְפִּידוֹ: עַל לֵב. מְטַפֵּחַ כְּנֶגֶד הַלֵּב: בַּיָּד. קוֹפֵץ יָד זוֹ לְזוֹ: בָּרֶגֶל. מַכֶּה רַגְלוֹ בַּקַּרְקַע: מִפְּנֵי הַסַּכָּנָה. שֶׁהוֹפֵךְ הַסַּנְדָּל וְשׁוֹבֵר רַגְלוֹ: נִיעְנַע רֹאשׁוֹ. שֶׁנִּרְאֶה שֶׁנִּיחַם מֵעַצְמוֹ: לַכֹּל אוֹמְרִים שְׁבוּ. כְּשֶׁעוֹמְדִין לִפְנֵי הַנָּשִׂיא: חֲבוּרְתָא אִיכָּא. חֲבוּרוֹת הֵן, שֶׁאֵלּוּ קוֹבְרִין מֵתִים שֶׁלָּהֶם לְבַדָּם וְאֵלּוּ קוֹבְרִין מֵתִים שֶׁלָּהֶם לְבַדָּם: וְלֹא יָשׁוּב עוֹד וגו'. מַשְׁמַע: מִכָּאן וְאֵילָךְ לֹא יַעֲשֶׂה לְעוֹלָם תְּשׁוּבָה: אֶלָּא

תורה אור

תוספות

בבליכה. גרס בערוך, בשני כפי"ן, ואית דגרסי כליכה בבי"ת השניה, כמו: הללו חוזרין לכלובן (ביצה דף כד.), וכמו "ככלוב מלא עוף" (ירמיה ה), אי נמי כמו "מכליב" (לעיל דף י.). ופירש הקונטרס: כעין סולם, והיינו כעין תפירות רחוקות זו מזו, ומביא הא דאמרינן במדרש: נטלו את הכרובים ונתנום בכליכה. ואם כן צריך לגרוס בפיוט של חרבן בית המקדש בתשעה באב: עמון ומואב הוציאו את הכרובים, וכליכה היו בם מסובבים. וגרס בב' כפי"ן לגירסת הערוך. וכל זה – שלא לבייש מי שאין לו. וכן איתא במסכת בכורים (פ"ג מ"ז): בראשונה מי שהיה יודע לקרו' כו'. ומאותה ההלכ' ⊕מביאין ראיה להא דאמר: שמנה פסוקים שבתורה יחיד קורא אותם, דלא בעי למימר שלא יקרא שליח צבור עמו. כי בימיהם לא היה קורא שליח צבור עם הקורא. ומה שרגילים עתה לקרות – זהו מפני כבודו של קורא, שלא לבייש מי שאינו יודע. וכדאמר גבי בכורים: בראשונה מי שהיה יודע לקרות – קורא, ומי שאינו יודע לקרות (אינו קורא) – מקרין אותו. נמנעו מלהביא בכורים, התקינו שיהו מקרין את הכל (בכורים פ"ג מ"ז): **ונהג** קלות ראש בעצמו. שלוה כן בשעת פטירתו. וי"מ: לאחד מבני ביתו בחייו. ולשון "בעצמו" משמע כפירוש ראשון:

***אבל** לא מטפחות. פירוש: סופק כפיו זו בזו. וא"ת: הא תנן פרק "משילין" (ביצה דף לו:) אין מטפחין ביו"ט, ופי' בקונטרס בפרק "המביא כדי יין" (שם דף ל. בד"ה מרקדין): משום שיר או משום אבל. ומאי איריא בי"ט ומשום שמא יתקן כלי שיר – אפילו בחולו של מועד אסור, משום צער? וצ"ל: דמשום שיר קתני, ולא משום אבל: **טפוח** ביד. כדפרישית: סופק כפיו זו על זו. והכי משמע בהוריות בירושלמי: כשתפס רבי יהודה את ריש לקיש שרי רבי יוחנן טפח בחדא ידיה. [א"ל]: ובחדא ידיה טפחין? כו'. ומספקין, פירש בקונטרס בבילה (דף לו:): כף על ירך. ואם כן "ויספק את כפיו" (במדבר כד) על ירך הן, שתי כפים על שתי ירכים. וצ"ע:

ה"ג ר"ח **לא** יקלס במנעל ולא בסנדל מפני הסכנה. פירוש: דיחף שרי טפי, דנזהר היטב פן ינזק:

ה"ג ר"ח **לכל** אומרים להן שבו חוץ מאבל וחולה. פירוש: תלמידי חכמים שעומדין – צריך לומר שבו. אבל וחולה, אפילו עמדו – אין צריך לומר "שבו". דלא די שעמדו, שאין צריכין לעמוד, ואם כן – פשיטא שישבו בלא רשות: **יום** ראשון אסור לאכול משלו. פירשתי למעלה: אפילו אוכל כמה פעמים באותו יום, דלא קתני סעודה ראשונה: **אסורין** בעשיית מלאכה. משמע דבתלמוד תורה שרי, ולא אסור אלא חכם שמת, דבית מדרשו בטל. *מיהו, בשעת הוצאת מת – אז מבטלין ת"ת, כדאמרינן פ' שני דכתובות (דף יז: ושם) ובפ"ק דמגילה (דף ג:): מבטלין ת"ת להוצאת המת ולהכנסת כלה. ומיהו, היכא דאיכא חבורתא – מספקא ליה. ועוד האריך רבי יצחק בתשובה, והביא ראיה מן הירושלמי: **לגיהוץ** ולתספורת. למעלה* פי' ריב"א היה אומר [שגרסינן] לכבוס ולתספורת, ופירש למעלה *) דאשה מותרת בנטילת שער לאחר ז'. ובתוספות פירש דלא ידע מנא ליה: **מכאן** ואילך כאילו עוברת כנגדו בשוק. עד י"ב חדש. והכי איתא בירושלמי: כל שבעה – החרב היא שלופה, עד שלשים – היא רופפת, לאחר י"ב חודש – היא חוזרת לתערה. ולמה הדבר דומה – לכפה של אבנים, כיון שנזדעזעה אחת מהן – נזדעזעו כולם. ובתלמוד דידן נמי אמרינן (שבת דף קה:): אחד מן האחין שמת – ידאגו כל האחין כו':

מה

רבינו חננאל

יהא הפרש בין עשירים לעניים: ת"ר בראשונה היו מניחין מוגמר תחת מתים בחולי מעיים כו' וכך היו מטבילין את הכלים ע"ג הנשים שהיו מתות נדות וכו' וכך היו מטבילין הכלים ע"ג המתים כשהן זבין והיו בכל אלו החיים מתביישין התקינו שיהו עושין כן לכל. בראשונה היתה הוצאת המת קשה לקרוביו שהיו מוציאין בתכריכין ממון רב והיתה קשה עליהן הוצאתם יותר ממיתתם עד שהיו מניחין ובורחין עד שבא ר"ג וניהג קלות בעצמו וצוה להוציאו בכלי פשתן ונהגו כל העם לצאת בכלי פשתן כמותו. והאידנא נהוג עלמא אפילו בצררא בר זוזא. פי' בחלוק בר זווא: **מתני'** אין מניחין במועד את המטה ברחוב שלא להרגיל ההספד. אמר רבה בר רב הונא אין מועד בפני ת"ח וכ"ש חנוכה ופורים אלא מספידין בהן. וה"מ בפניו אבל שלא בפניו לא. ויום שמועה כבפניו דמי ומותר אפילו במועד. אמר עולא הספד על לב. שנאמר על שדים סופדים *) טיפוח ביד. קילוס ברגל שנאמר (יחזקאל ו) הכה בכפך ורקע ברגלך: ת"ר [המקלס] לא יקלס לא במנעל ולא בסנדל מפני הסכנה. א"ר יוחנן אבל כיון שנענע בראשו שוב אין המנחמין רשאין לישב אצלו. ואמר ר"י הכל חייבין לעמוד לפני נשיא חוץ מאבל וחולה. ואמר ר' יוחנן לכל אומר' להן שבו חוץ מאבל וחולה. אמר רב יהודה אמר רב אבל אסור לאכול ביום ראשון משלו שנאמר ולחם אנשים לא תאכל. רבה ורב יוסף בימי אבלם היו מחלפין סעודתן בהדדי. אמר רב יהודה אמר רב מת בעיר כל בני העיר אסורין בעשיית מלאכה עד שינתן לקבורתו. וכל המתקשה על מתו יותר מדאי על מת אחר הוא בוכה. דההוא אתתא דהוו לה ז' בני ומת חד מינייהו והוות מתקשת יותר מדאי. ושלח לה רב הונא ולא אשגחה ביה ומיתו לה כולהו ומתה היא נמי: ת"ר אל תבכו למת יותר מדאי. ואל תנודו לו יותר מכשיעור. הא כיצד ג' לבכי וז' להספד. ל' לגיהוץ ולתספורת מיכן ואילך הרי הוא קישוי. בכו בכה להולך. אמר רב להולך בלא בנים. ר' יהושע בן לוי לא הוה אזיל לבי אבילא אלא אמאן דשכיב בלא בני. כי לא ישוב עוד וראה את ארץ מולדתו. זה שעבר עבירה ושנה בה. מיכן ואילך שאינו מהרהר בתשובה מפני שנעשית לו כהותר: א"ר לוי אבל ג' ימים הראשונים יראה עצמו כאילו חרב מונחת לו בין כתיפיו. מג' ועד ז' כאילו חרב מונחת בקרן זוית. מיכן ואילך כאילו חרב כנגדו בשוק. ואין מניחין מטה של נשים ברחוב לעולם מפני

*) עי' בערוך ערך טפח ד'.

עין משפט נר מצוה

רכז א מיי' פ"ד מהל' אבל הלכה א טור ש"ע י"ד סי' שנב סעיף א ב:

רכח ב ג ד מיי' פי"א שם הלכה ה ופ"ו מהלכות י"ט הלכה כב סמג עשין ב ולאוין עה טוש"ע שם סי' תא סעיף ה:

רכט ה מיי' פי"ג מהל' אבל הלכה ג סמג עשין ב טוש"ע י"ד סי' שעו סעיף א:

רל ו ז מיי' שם הלכה ה סמג שם טוש"ע שם סעיף א בהג"ה וסעיף ב:

רלא ח ט מיי' שם פ"ד הלכה ט סמג שם טוש"ע שם סי' שעח סעיף א:

רלב י כ מיי' שם פ"ד הלכה י סמג שם טוש"ע שם סי' שמג סעי' א וסי' שסא סעיף ב:

[מגילה ג: ע"ש]

[תוספתא פ"ב]

שייך למתני' דף כח ע"ב

רלג ל מ מיי' שם פי"ג הלכה יא סמג שם טוש"ע שם סי' שלז סעיף א:

רלד נ מיי' שם הלכה יב טוש"ע שם סעי' ז:

מסורת הש"ס

נדה עא. [תוספ' נדה פ"ט עי' תוס' שם ד"ה אלא טעמי']

כתובות ח: [תוספתא שם]

[גי' הערוך צדרא ועי' ב"מ נא. דאיתא התם צדרייתא פרש"י בגדי קנבוס]

ישעיה לב

יחזקאל כד

ירמיה כב

שם

ב"ב קטז. ע"ש

[שם]

יומא פו: פז. ע"ש קדושין כ. מ. סוטה כב. ערכין ל:

[בשאלתות אי' כתיפיו]

[לעיל כב:]

[דף כג. ד"ה כל]

*) [דף יח. בד"ה ובגנוסטרי וע' ברא"ש סי' ק]

הגהות הב"ח

(א) גמ' אי הכי שריא (לכו). תז"מ ונ"ב ס"א להו:

[נ"ל המקשיר הכי איתא בע"י ופרש"י לשון וקשרו מספד]

[פי' תכריכין עי' רש"י עירובין מח: ובע"ז יז. ד"ה בזוודתא]

גליון הש"ס

תוס' ד"ה בכליכה וכו' מביאין ראיה להא דאמר ב"ב ד' טו ע"א:

אֶלָּא חַיָּה, אֲבָל שְׁאָר נָשִׁים – מַנִּיחִין. ר' אֶלְעָזָר אָמַר: אאֲפִילּוּ שְׁאָר הַנָּשִׁים, דִּכְתִיב: °"וַתָּמָת שָׁם מִרְיָם וַתִּקָּבֵר שָׁם" – סָמוּךְ לְמִיתָה קְבוּרָה. וְאָמַר ר' אֶלְעָזָר: *אַף מִרְיָם בִּנְשִׁיקָה מֵתָה, אָתְיָא "שָׁם" "שָׁם" מִמֹּשֶׁה. וּמִפְּנֵי מָה לֹא נֶאֱמַר בָּהּ "עַל פִּי ה'" – מִפְּנֵי שֶׁגְּנַאי הַדָּבָר לְאוֹמְרוֹ. א"ר אַמִי: לָמָּה נִסְמְכָה מִיתַת מִרְיָם לְפָרָשַׁת פָּרָה אֲדוּמָּה – לוֹמַר לְךָ: מַה פָּרָה אֲדוּמָּה מְכַפֶּרֶת – אַף מִיתָתָן שֶׁל צַדִּיקִים מְכַפֶּרֶת. א"ר אֶלְעָזָר: לָמָּה נִסְמְכָה מִיתַת אַהֲרֹן לְבִגְדֵי כְהוּנָּה – מַה בִּגְדֵי כְהוּנָּה מְכַפְּרִין – אַף מִיתָתָן שֶׁל צַדִּיקִים מְכַפֶּרֶת. ת"ר: *מֵת פִּתְאוֹם – זוֹ הִיא מִיתָה חֲטוּפָה, חָלָה יוֹם אֶחָד וּמֵת – זוֹ הִיא מִיתָה דְּחוּפָה. ר' חֲנַנְיָא בֶּן גַּמְלִיאֵל אוֹמֵר: זוֹ הִיא מִיתַת מַגֵּפָה, שֶׁנֶּאֱמַר: °"בֶּן אָדָם הִנְנִי לוֹקֵחַ מִמְּךָ אֶת מַחְמַד עֵינֶיךָ בְּמַגֵּפָה" וּכְתִיב: °"וָאֲדַבֵּר אֶל הָעָם בַּבֹּקֶר וַתָּמָת אִשְׁתִּי בָּעָרֶב". שְׁנֵי יָמִים וּמֵת – זוֹ הִיא מִיתָה דְּחוּיָה, ג' – גְּעָרָה, אַרְבָּעָה – נְזִיפָה, חֲמִשָּׁה – זוֹ הִיא מִיתַת כָּל אָדָם. א"ר חָנִין: מַאי קְרָא? °"הֵן קָרְבוּ יָמֶיךָ לָמוּת", "הֵן" – חַד, "קָרְבוּ" – תְּרֵי, "יָמֶיךָ" – תְּרֵי, הָא חֲמִשָּׁה. "הֵן" חַד – *שֶׁכֵּן בִּלְשׁוֹן יְוָנִי קוֹרִין לְאַחַת "הֵן". מֵת בַּחֲמִשִּׁים שָׁנָה – זוֹ הִיא מִיתַת כָּרֵת *חֲמִשִּׁים וּשְׁתַּיִם שָׁנָה זוֹ הִיא מִיתָתוֹ שֶׁל שְׁמוּאֵל הָרָמָתִי, שִׁשִּׁים – זוֹ הִיא מִיתָה בִּידֵי שָׁמַיִם. אָמַר מָר זוּטְרָא: מַאי קְרָא – דִּכְתִיב: °"תָּבוֹא בְכֶלַח אֱלֵי קָבֶר", "בְּכֶלַח" בְּגִימַטְרִיָּא שִׁיתִּין הָווּ. שִׁבְעִים – שֵׂיבָה, שְׁמוֹנִים – גְּבוּרוֹת, דִּכְתִיב: °"יְמֵי שְׁנוֹתֵינוּ בָהֶם שִׁבְעִים שָׁנָה וְאִם בִּגְבוּרֹת שְׁמוֹנִים שָׁנָה". אָמַר רַבָּה: מֵחֲמִשִּׁים וְעַד שִׁשִּׁים שָׁנָה – זוֹ הִיא מִיתַת כָּרֵת. וְהַאי דְּלָא חָשֵׁיב לְהוּ – מִשּׁוּם כְּבוֹדוֹ שֶׁל שְׁמוּאֵל הָרָמָתִי. רַב יוֹסֵף, כִּי הֲוָה בַּר שִׁיתִּין עֲבַד לְהוּ יוֹמָא טָבָא לְרַבָּנָן. אֲמַר: נְפַקִי לִי מִכָּרֵת. א"ל אַבַּיֵי: נְהִי דִּנְפַק לֵיהּ מָר מִכָּרֵת דִּשְׁנֵי, מִכָּרֵת דְּיוֹמֵי מִי נָפֵיק מָר? א"ל: *נְקוֹט לָךְ מִיהָא פַּלְגָא בִּידָךְ. רַב הוּנָא נָח נַפְשֵׁיהּ פִּתְאוֹם, הָווּ קָא דָּיְיגִי רַבָּנַן. תָּנָא לְהוּ *זוּגָא דְּמֵהַדְיַיב: לֹא שָׁנוּ אֶלָּא שֶׁלֹּא הִגִּיעַ לִגְבוּרוֹת, אֲבָל הִגִּיעַ לִגְבוּרוֹת – זוֹ הִיא מִיתַת נְשִׁיקָה. אָמַר רָבָא: חַיֵּי, בְּנֵי וּמְזוֹנֵי, לָא בִּזְכוּתָא תַּלְיָא מִילְּתָא, אֶלָּא בְּמַזָּלָא תַּלְיָא מִילְּתָא. דְּהָא *רַבָּה וְרַב חִסְדָּא תַּרְוַיְיהוּ רַבָּנַן צַדִּיקֵי הָווּ, מָר מְצַלֵּי וְאָתֵי מִיטְרָא, וּמָר מְצַלֵּי וְאָתֵי מִיטְרָא. רַב חִסְדָּא חָיָה תִּשְׁעִין וְתַרְתֵּין שְׁנִין – רַבָּה חָיָה אַרְבָּעִין, בֵּי רַב חִסְדָּא – שִׁיתִּין הִלּוּלֵי, בֵּי רַבָּה – שִׁיתִּין תִּיכְלֵי. בֵּי רַב חִסְדָּא – סְמִידָא לְכַלְבֵּי וְלָא מִתְבָּעֵי, בֵּי רַבָּה – נַהֲמָא דְּשַׂעֲרֵי לְאֱינָשֵׁי, וְלָא מִשְׁתַּכַּח. וְאָמַר רָבָא: הָנֵי תְּלָת מִילֵּי בְּעַאי קַמֵּי שְׁמַיָּא, תַּרְתֵּי יְהַבוּ לִי, חֲדָא לָא יְהַבוּ לִי; חוּכְמְתֵיהּ דְּרַב הוּנָא וְעוּתְרֵיהּ דְּרַב חִסְדָּא – וִיהַבוּ לִי, עַנְוְתָנוּתֵיהּ דְּרַבָּה בַּר רַב הוּנָא – לָא יְהַבוּ לִי. רַב *שְׂעוֹרִים אֲחוּהּ דְּרָבָא הֲוָה יָתֵיב קַמֵּיהּ דְּרָבָא, חַזְיֵיהּ דַּהֲוָה קָא מְנַמְנֵם. א"ל: לֵימָא לֵיהּ מָר דְּלָא לְצַעֲרַן! א"ל: מָר לָאו שׁוֹשְׁבִינֵיהּ הוּא? א"ל: כֵּיוָן דְּאִימְּסַר מַזָּלָא – לָא אַשְׁגַּח בִּי. א"ל: לִיתְחֲזֵי לִי מָר. אִיתְחֲזֵי לֵיהּ. א"ל: הֲוָה לֵיהּ לְמָר צַעֲרָא? א"ל: *כִּי רִיבְדָּא דְּכוּסִילְתָּא. רָבָא הֲוָה יָתֵיב קַמֵּיהּ דְּר"נ, חַזְיֵיהּ דְּקָא מְנַמְנֵם. א"ל: לֵימָא לֵיהּ מָר דְּלָא לְצַעֲרַן. א"ל: מָר לָאו אָדָם חָשׁוּב הוּא? [א]א"ל: מַאן חָשִׁיב, מַאן סְפִין, מַאן *רְקִיעַ? א"ל: לִיתְחֲזֵי לִי מָר. אִתְחֲזֵי לֵיהּ. א"ל: הֲוָה לֵיהּ לְמָר צַעֲרָא? א"ל: כְּמִישְׁחַל בִּנִיתָא מֵחֶלְבָּא. וְאִי אָמַר לִי הקב"ה זִיל בְּהַהוּא עָלְמָא כַּד הֲוֵית – לָא בָּעֵינָא, דִּנְפִישׁ בִּיעֲתוּתֵיהּ. רַבִּי אֶלְעָזָר הֲוָה קָאָכֵיל תְּרוּמָה, אִיתְחֲזֵי לֵיהּ. [ב] א"ל: תְּרוּמָה קָא אָכֵילְנָא, וְלָאו קוֹדֶשׁ אִיקְרֵי? חָלְפָא לֵיהּ שַׁעְתָּא. רַב שֵׁשֶׁת אִיתְחֲזֵי לֵיהּ בְּשׁוּקָא, אֲמַר לֵיהּ: בְּשׁוּקָא כִּבְהֵמָה? אִיתָא לְגַבֵּי בֵּיתָא. רַב אַשִׁי אִיתְחֲזֵי לֵיהּ בְּשׁוּקָא, א"ל: [א]אִיתְרַח לִי תְּלָתִין יוֹמִין, וְאַהַדְרִי לְתַלְמוּדַאי. דְּאָמְרִיתוּ: *) אַשְׁרֵי מִי שֶׁבָּא לְכָאן וְתַלְמוּדוֹ בְּיָדוֹ. בְּיוֹם תְּלָתִין אֲתָא, אֲמַר לֵיהּ: מַאי כּוּלֵּי הַאי? קָא דָּחֲקָא רִגְלֵיהּ דְּבַר נָתָן, [ג] וְאֵין מַלְכוּת נוֹגַעַת בַּחֲבֶירְתָּהּ אֲפִילּוּ כִּמְלֹא נִימָא. רַב חִסְדָּא לָא הֲוָה יָכֵיל לֵיהּ, דְּלָא הֲוָה שָׁתֵיק פּוּמֵיהּ מִגִּירְסָא. סְלֵיק יָתֵיב בְּאַרְזָא דְּבֵי רַב, פְּקַע אַרְזָא וּשְׁתַק וְיָכֵיל לֵיהּ. ר' חִיָּיא לָא הֲוָה מָצֵי לְמִיקְרְבָא לֵיהּ. יוֹמָא חַד אִידַּמִּי לֵיהּ כְּעַנְיָא, אֲתָא טָרֵיף אַבָּבָא, א"ל: אַפֵּיק לִי רִיפְתָּא. אַפִּיקוּ לֵיהּ. א"ל: וְלָאו קָא מְרַחֵם מָר אַעַנְיָא? אַהַהוּא גַּבְרָא אַמַּאי לָא קָא מְרַחֵם מָר? גַּלֵּי לֵיהּ, אַחֲוֵי לֵיהּ שׁוּטָא דְּנוּרָא, אַמְצֵי לֵיהּ נַפְשֵׁיהּ.§

מתני'

א) [גירסת הערוך איתרה.] ב) [ברכות מח: וש"נ]

*) [פסחים נ. ב"ב י: כתובות עז:]

רש"י

אלא חיה. שמתה מחמת ולד, שהיא שופעת: מת פתאום. שלא חלה: מחמשים שנה. ולמעלה: והאי דלא חשיב ליה. בהדי כרת: כרת דיומי. שמא ימות מיתה חטופה: פלגא. דמכרת דשני מיהא פלטי לי: מנמנם. גוסס: א"ל. רבא לרב שעורים: לימא מר. למלאך המות דלא לצעורי: שושביניה. דמלאך המות: דאימסר מזליה. איתרע מזליה: ליתחזי לי מר. בתר מיתה: מר לאו אדם חשוב. לימא ליה מר: ספין רקיע. מתוקן למיבעי מיניה: ביעתותיה. דמלאך המות: רגליה דבר נתן. למיהוי נשיא: אמאי לא מרחם. דמתפקדנא למייתי ליה למר בההוא עלמא: אחוי ליה שוטא דנורא. וידע דהוא מלאך המות: מתני'

תוספות

מה פרה אדומה מכפרת. פירוש: על מעשה העגל. וכדאמרינן במדרש: משל לבן השפחה שטינף פלטירין של מלך, אומר המלך: תבא אמו וכו': מיתת אהרן לבגדי כהונה. דכתיב (במדבר כ) "והפשט את אהרן את בגדיו ואהרן יאסף ומת שם", וכן פי' בקונטרס. ואין לפרש מיתת בני אהרן ל"בגדי קדש ילבש" – לפי שאינו סמוך כ"כ: מה בגדי כהונה מכפרין. בזבחים כו' (דף פח:):

חטופה ודחופה. לא ידענא מאי שנא הוא, ומנא ליה: ואדבר אל העם בבקר. פי': ואלתה ומתה: הן קרבו וכו'. לאו דוקא, דלא אשכחנא למשה היה חולה. וביום מותו כתב הרבה (סוטה יג:), ופסק כמה פסיעות בבת אחת, כדפירש בפירוש חומש: מת בחמשים זו היא מיתת כרת. בירושלמי (פ"ג דביכורים) דייק מ"אל תכריתו שבט הקהתי" (במדבר ד), ועבודתם עד חמשים דכתיב (שם ח) "מבן חמשים שנה ישוב מצבא העבודה". ועוד: מימי שנותיו ע' שנה, דל עשרין דלא איענש עליהן – נשתיירו חמשים (כדאי' שבת פט:). ותימה לפי', דהא משמע בשמעתין דבחמשים משנולד קאמר. ועוד: יהא חמשים לאחר שנתחייב כרת, והוא מיתת כל אדם: ומיתה בידי שמים בששים. בירושלמי מפיק ממתי מדבר, דאמרינן*: לא מת אחד מהן פחות מבן ששים. וממיתה דהכא משמע זו היא מיתה בידי שמים, וכרת – בחמשים עד ששים, ולא ששים בכלל, וזהו שזרעו נכרת. וי"מ: דחמשים היא מיתה שבידי שמים, וכי איתא בהדי זרעו – הוי כרת, וששים מיתת כל אדם. ובשבת פרק שני (כה. בד"ה כרת) וריש יבמות (ב. בד"ה אשת אחיו) הארכתי: אלא במזלא תליא מילתא. והקשו בתוספות, הא דאמרן בסוף שבת (דף קנו. ושם): אין מזל לישראל! וי"ל: דלפעמים משתנה ע"י מזל, כי הנהו דהתם, ופעמים שאין משתנה, כדאמרינן בתענית (דף כה.) גבי רבי אלעזר בן פדת, דא"ל: ניחא לך דאחריב עלמא דאולי אברי' בעידנא דמזוני: שתין הלולי. יש מפרשים: לאו דוקא: ספין. חשוב, למחר (הוא ו) היא מתה. ואין כל בריה *ספונה (כתובות עב.) פירוש*): חשובה. ובמדרש ילמדנו: אין העובדי כוכבים ספונים כלום, שנא' (ישעיה מ) "כל הגוים כאין נגדו" וכן פירש בערוך*, והביא עדיין ראיות אחרות: מאן רקיע. פי': מתוקן ותפור. "ונעלות בלות ומטולאות" (יהושע ט) תרגום: בלן ומרוקעים. "למתפרות כסתות" (יחזקאל יג) תרגומו: דמתטטים רקיעי. חסוך, והוא לשון ישמעאל, חתיכת בגד תפורה על הקרע, בערוך. ועוד הביא, דאמרינן בפ' "לא יחפור" (ב"ב דף כ.): חזי למרקע לבוש. מיהו, יש ספרים כתוב שם "לקרעא":

*) [ועי' בערוך ערך ספן ב]

בלע

עין משפט נר מצוה

רלה א מיי' פי"ב מהל' אבל הלכה ה סמג עשין ב טוש"ע י"ד סי' שנה:

מסורת הש"ס

[ב"ב יז.] · במדבר כ · שמחות פ"ג · יחזקאל כד · שם · דברים לא · [שבת לא: סנהדרין עו: ע"ש] · שמחות פ"ג תענית ה. · איוב ה · תהלים צ · [סנהדרין ג.] · [בערוך ערך זווא ב' פי' שם האדם ועי' תוס' נדה כו: ד"ה זווא] · [עתוי ר"ה יח. ד"ה רבה ותוס' יבמות קה. ד"ה רבה] · [בכ"מ ענ: אי' רב שעורים אחוה דרבא בסמ"ך] · [ע' פרש"י שבת קכט. וכסנהד' נג:] · [בערוך רקע ז"ל הערוך במ"ך מאן חשיב מאן ספון מאן רקוע כלומר מי יכול להפסעו ולהתגבר באותו שעה עכ"ל נע"ק למעיין בערוך ערך רקע הפני]

רבינו חננאל

מפני הכבוד. אמרי נהרדעי לא שנו אלא חיה דשכיח טינוף אבל של שאר נשים מניחין ר' אלעזר אומר אפילו של שאר נשים אין מניחין שנאמר ותמת שם מרים ותקבר שם תיכף למיתה קבורה א"ר אלעזר אף מרים בנשיקה מתה. אתיא שם שם כתיב הכא ותמת שם מרים וכתיב וימת שם משה עבד ה' מה משה בנשיקה אף מרים בנשיקה. ומפני מה לא נאמר במיתת מרים על פי ה' מפני שגנאי הדבר לאומרו באשה. א"ר אמי למה נסמכה מיתת מרים לפרשת פרה אדומה מה פרה זו מטהרת חטאים ונקראת חטאת וכל חטאת מכפרת עון כך מיתתן של נשים צדקניות מטהרת ומכפרת עונותיהן של ישראל. וכ"ש מיתתן של צדיקים שמכפרת: ירושלמי בתחלת יוה"כ א"ר יודן בר שלום למה נסמכה מיתת אהרן לשבירת הלוחות ללמדך שמיתתן של צדיקים קשה לפני הקב"ה כשבירת הלוחו' כתיב ובני ישראל נסעו מבארת בני יעקן מוסרה שם מת אהרן. וכי אהרן במוסרה מת והלא בהור ההר מת. אלא כיון שמת אהרן נסתלקו ענני הכבוד וכו' ובקשו ישראל לחזור למצרים וחזרו ח' מסעות ורץ שבט לוי והרג מהן ח' משפחות וגם הם הרגו מן הלוים ד' משפחות לעמרמי ליצהרי לחברוני לעוזיאלי כו'. אמרו על מה אירע לנו זה על שלא נתעסקנו בהספדו של צדיק כראוי. מיד ישבו במוסרה והספידו וגמלו לו חסד בהספד כראוי והעלה להן הכתוב כאילו במוסרה מת כו'. א"ר אלעזר למה נסמכה מיתת אהרן לבגדי כהונה לומר לך מה בגדי כהונה מכפרין כדגרסינן (מבחים דף פ"ח:) אף מיתת אהרן מכפרת: ת"ר מת פתאום זו מיתה חטופה. חלה יום אחד ומת זו מיתה דחופה. ר' חנינא בן גמליאל אומר זו מיתת מגפה שנאמר בן אדם הנני לוקח את מחמד עיניך במגפה וכתיב ואדבר אל העם בבקר ותמת אשתי בערב. חלה יומים ומת זו מיתה דחויה חלה ג' ומת זו מיתת גערה. חלה ד' ומת זו היא מיתת נזיפה. חלה ה' ימים ומת זו היא מיתת כל אדם. שמעינן לה מהאי קרא ויאמר ה' אל משה הן קרבו ימיך למות. קרבו תרי. ימיך תרי הן חד הרי ה' ימים. ואח"כ כתיב למות. מי שמת בן חמשים זו היא מיתת כרת. בן נ"ב זו היא מיתתו של שמואל הרמתי. בן ששים זו היא מיתת כל אדם. א"ר זירא מהאי קרא תבא בכלח אלי קבר. בכל"ח בגימטריא שיתין הוו. בן שבעים שיבה. בן שמונים בגבורות שנא' ימי שנותינו בהם שבעים שנה ואם בגבורות שמונים שנה. אמר רבא מי שמת מחמשים ועד ששים מיתת כרת היא. והא דלא חשיב לה משום כבודו של שמואל הרמתי. רב יוסף כי הוה בר שיתין אמר כבר נפקית מכרת דשני. רב הונא נח נפשיה פתאום. הוו רבנן דייגי טובא. תנא להו זווא דמהדייב פי' שם חכם. לא שנו דמיתת פתאום היא מיתה חטופה אלא במי שלא הגיע לגבורות אבל מי שהגיע לגבורות זו היא מיתת נשיקה. אמר רבא חיי בני ומזוני לאו בזכותא תליא מלתא אלא במזלא. דהא רבה ורב חסדא תרוייהו צדיקי גמורי נינהו מר מצלי ואתי מיטרא ומר מצלי ואתי מיטרא. רב חסדא חי' צ"ב שנה. ורבה חיה מ' שנה. בי רב חסדא שיתין הילולי. בי רב חסדא נהמא דסמידא לכלבי. בי רבה [נהמא] דשערי לאינשי לא משתכח אמר רבא תלתא בעאי מקמי שמיא. תרי הבו לי וחד לא הבו לי חכמתיה דרב הונא ועותריה דרב חסדא הבו לי ענוותנותיה דרבה בר רב הונא לא הבו לי. רבה חוה יתיב קמיה דרב נחמן והוה רב נחמן גוסס בעי למינח נפשיה. א"ל בעי רחמי דלא ליצערן מלאכא דמיתותא. א"ל ואנת לאו גברא חשיבא גבי שמיא אנת בעי רחמי עלך א"ל מאן חשוב מן ספון מן רקיע פי' כלומר כיון שנמסר אדם ביד מלאך המות אין שם חשיבותו. א"ל אחרי מיתתו אולי תתראה לי בחלום. ביקש מן הקב"ה כדי שיתראה לו בחלום ונתראה לו. אמר לו היה לך צער בשעת מיתה. א"ל לאו ומשל לו משל כהרמת נימא של שיער מתוך החלב. א"ל אילו היה הקב"ה אומר לי לך חזור וחיי כאשר היית בחייך ואח"כ תמות לא הייתי רוצה שאע"פ שלא היה [לי] צער. אימתו של מה"מ גדולה היא מאד. רבא אתחזי ליה בחלמיה לרב שעורים אחוה. וא"ל הוה לך צערא ואמר לי כי ריבדא דכוסילתא. פי' כמו שריטה ששורטין האומנין בצואר למצוץ דמו. כגון אותו הצער היה לי בעת יציאת הנשמה מן הגוף. רב ששת אתחזי ליה מלאך המות בשוק. א"ל כבהמה איתא לגבי ביתא. רב אסי אתחזי ליה מלאך המות. א"ל אתרח לי ל' יומין דאהדריה לתלמודי. דאמריתו אשרי מי שבא לכאן ותלמודו בידו. ביום שלשים אתא. א"ל מאי כולי האי. א"ל דקא דחקא רגליה דבר נתן:

מתני'

הגהות מהר"ב רנשבורג

א] גמ' א"ל מאן חשיב מאן ספון מאן רקיע. פי' מי הוא חשוב בעיניו ומאן ספון מי הוא אדם ראוי לליסתפו מיניה וחייש לדיבוריה ומאן רקיע מי מתוקן אצלו. מפי' ע"י קטן: ב] שם א"ל תרומה קא אכילנא ולאו קדש איקרי. פי' לאו תרומה אכילנא לאיקרי קודש ואי קטלית לי קא מטמיא וכתיב את משמרת תרומתי שצריך לשומרה בטהרה חלפא ליה שעתא ולא מת באותו פרק. מפי' הנ"ל:

מתני' *[א]נָשִׁים בַּמּוֹעֵד מְעַנּוֹת, אֲבָל לֹא מְטַפְּחוֹת. ר' יִשְׁמָעֵאל אוֹמֵר: הַסְּמוּכוֹת לַמִּטָּה מְטַפְּחוֹת. בְּרָאשֵׁי חֳדָשִׁים, בַּחֲנוּכָּה וּבַפּוּרִים — מְעַנּוֹת וּמְטַפְּחוֹת, בְּזֶה וְזֶה — לֹא מְקוֹנְנוֹת. נִקְבַּר הַמֵּת — לֹא מְעַנּוֹת וְלֹא מְטַפְּחוֹת. אֵיזֶהוּ עִינּוּי — שֶׁכּוּלָּן עוֹנוֹת כְּאַחַת, קִינָה — שֶׁאַחַת מְדַבֶּרֶת וְכוּלָּן עוֹנוֹת אַחֲרֶיהָ, שנא' °"וְלַמֵּדְנָה בְנוֹתֵיכֶם נֶהִי וְאִשָּׁה רְעוּתָהּ קִינָה". אֲבָל לֶעָתִיד לָבֹא הוּא אוֹמֵר: °"בִּלַּע הַמָּוֶת לָנֶצַח וּמָחָה ה' אֱלֹהִים דִּמְעָה מֵעַל כָּל פָּנִים" וגו'. § גמ' מַאי אָמְרָן?

[א]אָמַר רַב: וַיי לְאָזְלָא, וַיי לַחֲבִילָא. אָמַר רָבָא, נְשֵׁי דְשַׁכַנְצִיב אָמְרָן הָכִי: וַיי לְאָזְלָא, וַיי לַחֲבִילָא. וַאֲמַר רָבָא, נְשֵׁי דְשַׁכַנְצִיב אָמְרָן: *גּוּד גַּרְמָא מִכָּבָא, וְנִמְטֵי מַיָּא לְאַנְטִיכֵי. וְאָמַר רָבָא, נְשֵׁי דְשַׁכַנְצִיב אָמְרָן: [ב]*עֲטוּף וּכְסוּ טוּרֵי, דְּבַר רָמֵי וּבַר רַבְרְבֵי הוּא. וַאֲמַר רָבָא, נְשֵׁי דְשַׁכַנְצִיב אָמְרָן: שַׁיְּיוּל אִצְטְלָא דְמֵלְתָא לְבַר חוֹרִין דִּשְׁלִימוּ זְוָודֵיהּ. וַאֲמַר רָבָא, נְשֵׁי דְשַׁכַנְצִיב אָמְרָן: [ג]רָהֵיט וְנָפֵיל אַמַּעְבְּרָא, וִיזוּפְתָּא יָזֵיף. וַאֲמַר רָבָא, נְשֵׁי דְשַׁכַנְצִיב אָמְרָן: [ד]אַחֲנָא תַּגָּרֵי אַזִּבְזַגֵּי מִיבַּדְקוּ. וַאֲמַר רָבָא, נְשֵׁי דְשַׁכַנְצִיב אָמְרָן: [ה]מוֹתָא כִּי מוֹתָא, וּמַרְעִין — חִיבּוּלַיָּא. *תַּנְיָא, הָיָה ר"מ אוֹמֵר: °"טוֹב לָלֶכֶת אֶל בֵּית אֵבֶל" וגו' "עַד וְהַחַי יִתֵּן אֶל לִבּוֹ" דְּבָרִים שֶׁל מִיתָה, דְּיִסְפַּד — יִסְפְּדוּנֵיהּ, דְּיִקְבַּר — יִקְבְּרוּנֵיהּ, דְּיִטְעַן — יִטְעֲנוּנֵיהּ. דְּיִדַּל — יִדְלוּנֵיהּ. וְאִיכָּא דְּאָמְרִי: דְּלָא יִדַּל — יִדְלוּנֵיהּ, דִּכְתִיב: °"כִּי טוֹב אֲמָר לְךָ עֲלֵה הֵנָּה" וגו'. ת"ר: כְּשֶׁמֵּתוּ בָּנָיו שֶׁל רַבִּי יִשְׁמָעֵאל נִכְנְסוּ ד' זְקֵנִים לְנַחֲמוֹ: ר' טַרְפוֹן, וְר' יוֹסֵי הַגְּלִילִי, וְר' אֶלְעָזָר בֶּן עֲזַרְיָה, וְר"ע אָמַר לָהֶם ר' טַרְפוֹן: דְּעוּ שֶׁחָכָם גָּדוֹל הוּא, וּבָקִי בְּאַגָּדוֹת, אַל יִכָּנֵס אֶחָד מִכֶּם לְתוֹךְ דִּבְרֵי חֲבֵירוֹ. אָמַר ר"ע וַאֲנִי אַחֲרוֹן. פָּתַח רַבִּי יִשְׁמָעֵאל וְאָמַר: רַבּוּ עֲוֹנוֹתָיו, תְּכָפוּהוּ אֲבֵלָיו, הִטְרִיחַ רַבּוֹתָיו פַּעַם רִאשׁוֹנָה וּשְׁנִיָּה. נַעֲנָה ר"ט וְאָמַר: °"וַאֲחֵיכֶם כָּל בֵּית יִשְׂרָאֵל יִבְכּוּ אֶת הַשְּׂרֵפָה", וַהֲלֹא דְּבָרִים ק"ו: וּמָה נָדָב וַאֲבִיהוּא שֶׁלֹּא עָשׂוּ אֶלָּא מִצְוָה אַחַת, דִּכְתִיב: °"וַיַּקְרִיבוּ בְּנֵי אַהֲרֹן אֶת הַדָּם אֵלָיו" — כָּךְ, בָּנָיו שֶׁל ר' יִשְׁמָעֵאל — עַל אַחַת כַּמָּה וְכַמָּה. נַעֲנָה ר' יוֹסֵי הַגְּלִילִי וְאָמַר: °"וְסָפְדוּ לוֹ כָל יִשְׂרָאֵל וְקָבְרוּ אוֹתוֹ", וַהֲלֹא דְּבָרִים ק"ו: וּמָה אֲבִיָּה בֶּן יָרָבְעָם שֶׁלֹּא עָשָׂה אֶלָּא דָּבָר אֶחָד טוֹב, דִּכְתִיב בֵּיהּ: °"יַעַן נִמְצָא בוֹ דָּבָר טוֹב" — כָּךְ, בָּנָיו שֶׁל ר' יִשְׁמָעֵאל — עַל אַחַת כַּמָּה וְכַמָּה. מַאי דָּבָר טוֹב? ר' זֵירָא וְר' חִינָּנָא בַּר פָּפָּא; חַד אָמַר: שֶׁבִּיטֵּל *מִשְׁמַרְתּוֹ וְעָלָה לָרֶגֶל, וְחַד אָמַר: שֶׁבִּיטֵּל פַּרְדְּסָאוֹת שֶׁהוֹשִׁיב יָרָבְעָם אָבִיו עַל הַדְּרָכִים שֶׁלֹּא יַעֲלוּ יִשְׂרָאֵל לָרֶגֶל. נַעֲנָה ר' אֶלְעָזָר בֶּן עֲזַרְיָה וְאָמַר: °"בְּשָׁלוֹם תָּמוּת וּבְמִשְׂרְפוֹת אֲבוֹתֶיךָ הָרִאשֹׁנִים [אֲשֶׁר הָיוּ לְפָנֶיךָ כֵּן] יִשְׂרְפוּ לָךְ", וַהֲלֹא דְּבָרִים ק"ו: וּמָה צִדְקִיָּהוּ מֶלֶךְ יְהוּדָה, שֶׁלֹּא עָשָׂה אֶלָּא מִצְוָה אַחַת, שֶׁהֶעֱלָה יִרְמְיָה מִן הַטִּיט — כָּךְ, בָּנָיו שֶׁל רַבִּי יִשְׁמָעֵאל — עַל אַחַת כַּמָּה וְכַמָּה. נַעֲנָה ר"ע וְאָמַר: °"בַּיּוֹם הַהוּא יִגְדַּל הַמִּסְפֵּד בִּירוּשָׁלַםִ כְּמִסְפַּד הֲדַדְרִמּוֹן [בְּבִקְעַת מְגִדּוֹן".] *וְאָמַר רַב יוֹסֵף: אִלְמָלֵא *תַּרְגּוּמֵיהּ דְּהַאי קְרָא לָא הֲוָה יָדַעְנָא מַאי קָאָמַר: בְּעִידָּנָא הַהוּא יִסְגֵּי מִסְפְּדָא בִּירוּשְׁלֵם כְּמִסְפְּדָא דְּאַחְאָב בַּר עָמְרִי דִּקְטַל יָתֵיהּ הֲדַדְרִימּוֹן בַּר טַבְרִימּוֹן, וּכְמִסְפַּד דְּיֹאשִׁיָּה בַּר אָמוֹן דִּקְטַל יָתֵיהּ פַּרְעֹה חֲגִירָא בְּבִקְעַת מְגִדּוֹ. וַהֲלֹא דְּבָרִים ק"ו: וּמָה אַחְאָב מֶלֶךְ יִשְׂרָאֵל, שֶׁלֹּא עָשָׂה אֶלָּא דָּבָר אֶחָד טוֹב, דִּכְתִיב: °"וְהַמֶּלֶךְ הָיָה מָעֳמָד בַּמֶּרְכָּבָה נֹכַח אֲרָם" — כָּךְ, בָּנָיו שֶׁל ר' יִשְׁמָעֵאל — עַל אַחַת כַּמָּה וְכַמָּה. א"ל רָבָא לְרַבָּה בַּר מָרִי, כְּתִיב בֵּיהּ בְּצִדְקִיָּהוּ "בְּשָׁלוֹם תָּמוּת" וּכְתִיב °"וְאֶת עֵינֵי צִדְקִיָּהוּ עִוֵּר"! א"ל: הָכִי א"ר יוֹחָנָן: שֶׁמֵּת נְבוּכַדְנֶאצַּר בְּיָמָיו. וַאֲמַר רָבָא לְרַבָּה בַּר מָרִי: כְּתִיב בֵּיהּ בְּיֹאשִׁיָּהוּ: °"לָכֵן הִנְנִי אוֹסִפְךָ עַל אֲבוֹתֶיךָ וְנֶאֱסַפְתָּ אֶל קִבְרֹתֶיךָ בְּשָׁלוֹם" וּכְתִיב: °"וַיֹּרוּ הַיּוֹרִים לַמֶּלֶךְ יֹאשִׁיָּהוּ"! *וְאָמַר רַב יְהוּדָה אָמַר רַב: שֶׁעֲשָׂאוּהוּ כִּכְבָרָה! א"ל, הָכִי א"ר יוֹחָנָן: שֶׁלֹּא חָרַב בֵּית הַמִּקְדָּשׁ בְּיָמָיו. א"ר יוֹחָנָן: [ב]אֵין מְנַחֲמִין רַשָּׁאִין לוֹמַר דָּבָר עַד שֶׁיִּפְתַּח אָבֵל, שֶׁנֶּאֱמַר: *°"אַחֲרֵי כֵן פָּתַח אִיּוֹב אֶת פִּיהוּ" וַהֲדַר "וַיַּעַן אֱלִיפַז הַתֵּימָנִי". *א"ר אַבָּהוּ: [ג]מִנַּיִן לְאָבֵל שֶׁמֵּיסֵב בָּרֹאשׁ — שֶׁנֶּאֱמַר: °"אֶבְחַר דַּרְכָּם וְאֵשֵׁב רֹאשׁ וְאֶשְׁכּוֹן כְּמֶלֶךְ בַּגְּדוּד כַּאֲשֶׁר אֲבֵלִים יְנַחֵם". "יְנַחֵם" אַחֲרִינֵי מַשְׁמַע! אָמַר רַב נַחְמָן בַּר יִצְחָק: יִנָּחֵם כְּתִיב. מָר זוּטְרָא אָמַר מֵהָכָא: °"וְסָר מִרְזַח סְרוּחִים", מִרְזַח — נַעֲשָׂה שַׂר לִסְרוּחִים. אָמַר ר' חָמָא בַּר חֲנִינָא: מִנַּיִן לְחָתָן שֶׁמֵּיסֵב בָּרֹאשׁ — שֶׁנֶּאֱמַר: °"כֶּחָתָן יְכַהֵן פְּאֵר", מַה כֹּהֵן בָּרֹאשׁ — אַף חָתָן בָּרֹאשׁ. וְכֹהֵן גּוּפֵיהּ מְנָלַן? *דְּתָנָא דְּבֵי ר' יִשְׁמָעֵאל: °"וְקִדַּשְׁתּוֹ" — [ד]לְכָל דָּבָר שֶׁבִּקְדוּשָּׁה, *לִפְתּוֹחַ רִאשׁוֹן, וּלְבָרֵךְ רִאשׁוֹן, וְלִיטּוֹל מָנָה יָפָה רִאשׁוֹן. א"ר חֲנִינָא: קָשָׁה יְצִיאַת נְשָׁמָה מִן הַגּוּף כְּצִיפּוֹרֵי

רש"י

מתני' *בְּלֹא פֵּירוּשׁ: גמ' לַחֲבִילָא. חֲבָלָה: גּוּד גַּרְמָא מִכָּבָא. נָפְלוּ הַלְּחָיַיִם: נִמְטוּ מַיָּא לְאַמְטִיכֵי. כְּלוֹמַר: הָדְרֵי מַיָּא לְמַפְרֵעַ כְּלַפֵּי לְמַעְלָה: שַׁיְּיוּל אִיצְטְלָא דְמַלְתָא. כְּלוֹמַר: יָפָה מִיתָה כְּמַלְבּוּשׁ שֶׁל מֵילָת: דִּשְׁלִימוּ זְוָודֵיהּ. שֶׁכָּלוּ לוֹ מְזוֹנוֹתָיו, שֶׁהוּא עָנִי: עֲטוּף. חוֹשֶׁךְ: אַזִּבְזַגֵּי. קִינֵיהּ: מוֹתָא. כָּל אָדָם מֵת: (מֵרְעָא חֲבִילָא). מַרְעִין חִיבּוּלַיָּא. הָאִיסּוּרִין הֵן כַּבַּיִת: דְּיִדַּל יִדְלוּנֵיהּ. כְּלוֹמַר: מַגְבִּיהִין בְּהֶסְפֵּד לְמִי שֶׁמַּגְבִּיהַּ קוֹלוֹ לְהֶסְפֵּד אֲחֵרִים: הִטְרִיחַ רַבּוֹתָיו. שֶׁבָּאִין לְנַחֲמוֹ: מִשְׁמַרְתּוֹ. שֶׁהוֹשִׁיב יָרָבְעָם שֶׁלֹּא לַעֲלוֹת לָרֶגֶל: מָעֳמָד בַּמֶּרְכָּבָה. שֶׁלֹּא יִכָּשְׁלוּ: יְנַחֵם אֲחֵרִים מַשְׁמַע. שֶׁמְּנַחֲמִין יוֹשְׁבִין בָּרֹאשׁ: סְרוּחִים. לְשׁוֹן רַבִּים: לִפְתּוֹחַ בָּרֹאשׁ. לִקְרוֹת בַּס"ת: וּלְבָרֵךְ. בִּרְכַּת הַמָּזוֹן: כְּלִיפּוֹרֵי

תוספות

בלע המות. כדי לסיים בדבר הטוב. משום דמועד קטן הוא סוף סדר מועד. ומה"ט מתרץ הרב רבי יעקב מאורליינ"ש הא דאתחיל סדר נשים בט"ו נשים, אע"ג דאתחיל בפורענותא לא מתחיל, כדאמרינן ב"ש נוחלין" (ב"ב דף קח.)! ותירץ, דסומכין פורענות דמועד קטן אלא פרענות דיבמות, דסמכינן פורענותא לפורענותא ונחמתא לנחמתא*:

צדקיהו מלך יהודה. לדיק גמור היה. *אבל במקרא לא מלינו יותר כי אם שלוה להעלות ירמיהו מן הטיט:

ינחם כתיב. בכתובות (דף סט:*) פירשנו בענין אחר, שלא כפירוש הקונטרס דהכא:

וליטול מנה יפה ראשון. פי': יש לישראל ליתן לו. אבל הוא אין לו ליטול, כדאמרינן פ' "מקום שנהגו" (פסחים דף נ:): הנותן עיניו בחלק יפה כו'. מיהו, נראה לי דכהן, כיון שזהו דינו — יכול לראות סימן ברכה. ואע"פ שאומרים בפ' "הזרוע" (חולין קלג.): "ונתן". ולא שיטול מעצמו, אין זה לוקח מתנות. כי אם רואה שפיר מה שהוא רוצה ואומר ליתן לו:

[ועי' תוס' גיטין נט: בד"ה וליטול מנה]:

[בכ"מ קמיי' עמ': עירובין ה:]

הדרן עלך ואלו מגלחין
וסליקא לה מסכת מועד קטן

עין משפט נר מצוה

רלו א מיי' פ"ו מהלכות י"ט הלכה כג ופי"א מהל' אבל הלכה ד סמג עשין ב טוש"ע א"ח סי' תקמז סעיף ב וטוש"ע י"ד סי' תא סעיף ה:

[כדאיתא ב"ב יד:]

רלז ב ג מיי' פי"ג מהלכות אבל הלכה ג סמג עשין ב טוש"ע י"ד סי' שעו סעיף א:

[בד"ה אמר ר"נ]

רלח ד מיי' פ"ד מהל' כלי המקדש הלכה ב טוש"ע א"ח סי' קסז סעיף יד בהג"ה וסי' רא סעיף ב:

[כאדם האומר להרים התעטפו והתכסו במלבושים נאים כי זה האיש הבא להקבר אצלכם בן גדולים הוא. ערוך]

[שהושיבו אביו שומר שלא יעלה איש לרגל ובטל משמרתו ועלה. ז"ל רש"י במלכים]

[ואין דובר אליו דבר וכתיב אחרי כן פתח איוב את פיהו וענו חביריו כך מצאתי הגי' בתורת האדם להרמב"ן ז"ל]

מסורת הש"ס

פרש"י על כל עמוד זה תמצא בעין יעקב ע"ש

מגילה ג:

[בערוך ערך גד שני נמצא פירוש ע"ז]

נדרים פג: כתובות עב.

קהלת ז

משלי כה

ויקרא י

שם ט

מלכים א יד

שם

ירמיה לד

זכריה יב

מגילה ג.

[ועי' תוס' ב"ק ג: ד"ה כלדמתרגם]

מלכים א כב

ירמיה לט

מלכים ב כב

דה"ב לה

תענית כב: [סנהדרין מח:]

איוב ג

כתובות סט. איוב כט

עמוס ו

ויקרא כא

ישעיה סא

הוריות יב: נדרים סב. גיטין נט:

[עי' תוס' חולין פז. ד"ה וחייבו]

תורה אור: ירמיה ט; ישעיה כה

רבינו חננאל

מתני' נשים במועד מענות אבל לא מטפחות מאי אמרן. אמר רבא ויי לאזלא ויי לחבלא. פירוש נשי דשכנציב היו חכמות והיו מענות ואומרות אוי להולך כדכתיב כי הולך האדם אל בית עולמו וסבבו וגו' ואוי למי שהוא ממושכן ונתבע לשלם הפקדון שאצלו. כלומר האדם מתמשכן להשלים רוחו שהוא אצלו פקדון לבעליה. פי' חבלא משכון. פירוש גוד גרמא מכבא ונמטי מיא לאנטוכיא חתוך המאכל מן השיניים ויגיע חמות המים באנטיכי. כלומר כיון שנחתך המאכל מפי החולה בוערת בו חמות ומחממת מי רגליו כחמות אנטיכי. דתנן אנטיכי אע"פ שגרופה אין שותין הימנה מפני שמחממת הרבה. פי' שייול אצטלא דמלתא לבר חורי דשלימו זוודיה. כלומר דומה כאצטלא של מילת לבנה לבן טובים שירד מנכסיו. ושלמה הצידה שלו הקבורה טובה לו מחיים. ויש שאומרים מי שאין לו בגדים ללבוש ישאל וילך ללות בן טובים של מת ושלמו ימי חייו. עטוף וכסוי טורי דבר רברבי ובר רמי הוה. פי' כמו אדם האומר להרים התעטפו והתכסו במלבושיכם הנאים כי זה האיש הבא להקבר אצלכם בן גדולים הוא. וי"א לבני אדם אומרים התעטפו והתכסו במלבושיכן ועמדו על ההרים וכסו אותן בשעת קבורתו כי בן גדולים ורמים הוא. אחאנא תגרי דעל זבוגי מיבדקי. פי' אחינו התגרים שעל קניינם מיבדקי. כלומר במקום סחורתן נבדקין הנאמנים הם אם לאו. כמו שאומרים (בעירובין סה) בג' דברים אדם ניכר בכוסו בכיסו ובכעסו. רהיט ונפיל *) בר אודי ואמבדי יוזפתא יזיף. פי' רץ בכל כחו ונופל בין האובדים ועל המעברות מלוה לוה. פי' כמו משל הוא. כלומר אע"פ שאדם רץ בכל כחו כל ימיו כשנופל בין האובדים בין אובדי הדרכים. או כשיגיע לעבור בנהר מתחנן למי שמעבירו ואם אין לו נוטל בהלואה ואינו מוצא. מותא כי מותא. ומרעא חבוליא. פי' המות של זה כמיתת כל אדם. ואריכות חוליו תוספת כמו הרבית על המלוה. שיש מי שפורע חובו היא המלוה שנתנה לו ודיו. ויש מי שפורע **) המלוה היא נשמתו ותוספת על נשמתו צער חליו. תניא היה ר"מ אומר מ"ד טוב ללכת את בית אבל וגו' והחי יתן אל לבו דברים של מיתה. דיספד יספדוניה דיקבר יקברוניה דטעון יטעוניה דידל ידלוניה. איכא דאמרי לא ידל דאדלוניה כדכתיב כי טוב אמר לך עלה הנה מהשפילך לפני נדיב אשר ראו עיניך. כשמתו בניו של ר' ישמעאל נכנסו ד' זקנים לנחמו. ר' יוסי הגלילי. ור' אלעזר בן עזריה ור' עקיבא ור' טרפון. אמר להן ר' טרפון ראו כי חכם גדול ובקי בהגדות הוא אל יכנס אחד לתוך דברי חבירו אמר להן ר' עקיבא ואני אחרון. פתח ר' ישמעאל ואמר רבו עונותיו תכפוהו אבליו הטריח רבותיו פעמים רבות. נענה ר"ט ואמר ואחיכם כל בית ישראל יבכו את השרפה וגו' ומה בני אהרן שלא עשו אלא מצוה אחת שנאמר ויקריבו בני אהרן את הדם אליו. בניו של רבי [ישמעאל] עאכו"כ שחייבין כל ישראל לבכותם. ראב"ע אומר שחייבין כל ישראל לבכות מהכא שנאמר בשלום תמות ובמשרפות אבותיך המלכים הראשונים אשר היו לפניך כן ישרפו לך הוי אדון יספדו לך וגו' והלא דברים ק"ו ומה צדקיה שלא עשה אלא מצוה אחת שהעלה ירמיה מן הטיט זכה לכך. בניו של ר' עאכו"כ. ריה"ג אומר מהכא וספדו לו כל ישראל וקברו אותו כי זה לבדו יבא לירבעם אל קבר יען נמצא בו דבר טוב. והלא דברים ק"ו ומה אביה בן ירבעם שלא עשה אלא דבר אחד שביטל משמרתו ועלה לרגל. וי"א שביטל פרדסאות שהושיב ירבעם שלא יעלו ישראל לרגל כך. בניו של ר' שעשו כמה מצות עאכו"כ. ר"ע אומר מהכא ביום ההוא יגדל המספד בירושלם כמספד הדרימון בבקעת מגידו. ואמר רב יוסף אלמלא תרגומא דהאי קרא לא הוינן ידעי מאי קאמר בעידנא ההיא יסגא מספדא בירושלים כמספד אחאב דקטל יתיה הדרימון בן טברימון. וכמספד יאשיהו בן אמון דקטל יתיה פרעה חגירא בבקעת מגידו. ומה זה שלא עשה אלא דבר אחד דכתיב והמלך היה מעמד במרכבה נוכח ארם עד הערב החזיק בעצמו שלא יאמרו גוסס הוא ויברחו ישראל ותחלת נפילה ניסה בניו של ר' עאכו"כ שכל ישראל חייב לספוד ולבכות עליהם. א"ל רבא לרבה בר מרי כתיב ביה בצדקיהו בשלום

הגהות מהר"ב רנשבורג

א] גמ' אמר רב ויי לאזלא ויי לחבילא. פי' אוי לה להליכה כזו שאינה חוזרת ואוי לה למשאוי כזה שנושאים את המת. פ"א אוי להולך לממושכנים עליו: ב] שם עטוף וכסו טורא. פי' התעטפו והתכסו ההרים בחשך שבן גדולים ובן גבוהים היה המת הזה: ג] שם רהיט ונפיל אמעברא ויזופתא יזיף. פי' רהיט תגר וטורחן היה כל ימיו ועכשיו נפל ריקם בלי ממון אמעברא כשביקש לעבור מן העולם וצריך ללות ממון לתכריכין: ד] שם אחנא תגרי אזבזגי מיבדקו. פי' אחינו הסוחרים לאזבוגי מיבדקו באחריתם נראה עשרם כגון זה שאין לו עכשיו במה לקבור ועל מת עני אומרים אותו כדי שירחמו עליו. מע"י קטן: ה] שם מותא כי מותא ומרעין חיבולא. פי' דמיתתו היה כמיתת כל אדם שהכל מתים. אמנם מרעין חיבולא שיסורים קשים הו"ל יותר מאשר ב"א ג"ז מצאתי בע"י קטן. ונלע"ד לפ"ז דברש"י בד"ה מרעא חבילא וכו' נ"ל היסורין הן בבית עכ"ל וכצ"ל ופי' דבריו דהיסורים הם בפנים ואינן ניכרין אף דמיתתו היתה שלימה כמיתת אחרים ודו"ק:

תורה אור

בְּצִיפּוֹרֵי בְּפִי הַוּוֹשֶׁט. כְּחֶבֶל שֶׁיֵּשׁ בּוֹ קֶשֶׁר, וְיוֹצֵא בְּקוֹשִׁי מִן הַתּוֹרֶן: [נ"ל אמר] פִּיטוּרֵי. שֶׁקּוֹשְׁרִין שְׁתֵּי סְפִינוֹת בְּיַחַד: יֵלְכוּ מֵחַיִל אֶל חָיִל. שֶׁיֵּלְכוּ מִבֵּית הַמִּדְרָשׁ לְבֵית הַכְּנֶסֶת, וּמִבֵּית הַכְּנֶסֶת לְבֵית הַמִּדְרָשׁ – אַחַר יֵרָאֶה אֶל אֱלֹהִים בְּצִיּוֹן, יִזְכּוּ אֵל עֶלְיוֹן:

הדרן עלך ואלו מגלחין
וסליקא לה מסכת מועד קטן

כְּצִיפּוֹרֵי בְּפִי הַוּוֹשֶׁט. רַבִּי יוֹחָנָן אָמַר: כְּפִטְּירֵי בְּפִי וֵושֶׁט. *וְאָמַר *רַבִּי לֵוִי בַּר חַיְּתָא: הַנִּפְטָר מִן הַמֵּת לֹא יֹאמַר לוֹ "לֵךְ לְשָׁלוֹם" אֶלָּא "לֵךְ [א] בְּשָׁלוֹם" הַנִּפְטָר מִן הַחַי לֹא יֹאמַר לוֹ "לֵךְ בְּשָׁלוֹם", אֶלָּא "לֵךְ [ב] לְשָׁלוֹם", הַנִּפְטָר מִן הַמֵּת לֹא יֹאמַר לוֹ "לֵךְ לְשָׁלוֹם" אֶלָּא "לֵךְ בְּשָׁלוֹם" – שֶׁנֶּאֱמַר: °"וְאַתָּה תָּבֹא אֶל אֲבוֹתֶיךָ בְּשָׁלוֹם". (בראשית טו) הַנִּפְטָר מִן הַחַי לֹא יֹאמַר לוֹ "לֵךְ בְּשָׁלוֹם" אֶלָּא "לֵךְ לְשָׁלוֹם", שֶׁהֲרֵי דָּוִד שֶׁאָמַר לְאַבְשָׁלוֹם °"לֵךְ בְּשָׁלוֹם" (ש"ב טו) – הָלַךְ וְנִתְלָה, יִתְרוֹ שֶׁאָמַר לְמֹשֶׁה °"לֵךְ לְשָׁלוֹם" (שמות ד) – הָלַךְ וְהִצְלִיחַ. *וְאָמַר רַבִּי לֵוִי: כָּל הַיּוֹצֵא מִבֵּית הַכְּנֶסֶת [ברכות סד. ע"ש] לְבֵית הַמִּדְרָשׁ, וּמִבֵּית הַמִּדְרָשׁ לְבֵית הַכְּנֶסֶת – זוֹכֶה וּמְקַבֵּל פְּנֵי שְׁכִינָה, שֶׁנֶּאֱמַר: °"יֵלְכוּ מֵחַיִל אֶל חָיִל (תהלים פד) יֵרָאֶה אֶל אֱלֹהִים בְּצִיּוֹן". אָמַר רַב חִיָּיא בַּר אַשִׁי אָמַר רַב: *תַּלְמִידֵי חֲכָמִים אֵין לָהֶם מְנוּחָה אֲפִילּוּ (ברכות סס) לָעוֹלָם הַבָּא, שֶׁנֶּאֱמַר: "יֵלְכוּ מֵחַיִל אֶל חָיִל יֵרָאֶה אֶל אֱלֹהִים בְּצִיּוֹן".§

הדרן עלך ואלו מגלחין וסליקא לה מסכת מועד קטן

ברכות סד. [ע"ש]

[א] [רמב"ם פ"ד מהל' אבל ה"ד]: [ב] [מג"א סי' קי סק"ט]:

רבינו חננאל

בשלום תמות. וכתיב ואת עיני צדקיהו עור. א"ל הכי א"ר יוחנן שמת נבוכדנצר בחייו. א"ל ביאשיהו כתיב לכן הנני אוסיפך (אל) [על] אבותיך [וגו'] בשלום וכתיב ויורו המורים למלך יאשיהו. ואמר רב יהודה א"ר שעשאוהו ככברה. א"ל הכי א"ר יוחנן שלא חרב ביהמ"ק בימיו. אמר רב יהודה אמר רב א) המנחמין רשאין לומר לישב אלא על הקרקע שנאמר וישבו אתו לארץ וכתיב אחרי כן פתח איוב את פיהו וגו'. ואחרי כן ויען אליפז התימני. א"ר אבהו מניין לאבל שיושב בראש שנאמר אבחר דרכם ואשב ראש ב). מר זוטרא אמר מהכא וסר מרזח סרוחים. מרזח נעשה סר לסרוחים. המרזח הוא האבל כלומר הניזח במרירות ומפורש בכתובות (לף סט). הנפטר מן המת לא יאמר לו לך לשלום אלא לך בשלום שנא' ואתה תבא אל אבותיך בשלום והנפטר מן החי לא יאמר לו לך בשלום אלא לך לשלום. שהרי דוד אמר לאבשלום לך בשלום הלך ונתלה באילן ונהרג. יתרו שאמר למשה לך לשלום הלך והצליח. א"ר חמא בר חנינא מניין לחתן שיושב בראש שנאמר כחתן יכהן פאר וגו'. מה כהן בראש דתני דבי ר' ישמעאל וקדשתו לכל דבר שבקדושה לפתוח ראשון ולברך ראשון וכו' כך חתן בראש. א"ר לוי כל היוצא מן הכנסת למדרש ומבית המדרש לבית הכנסת זוכה ומקבל פני שכינה שנאמר ילכו מחיל אל חיל יראה אל אלהים בציון:

א) ע"ס נפל בכאן בדברי רבינו וכצ"ל אין המנחמין רשאין לישב אלא ע"ג קרקע שנאמר וישבו אתו לארץ ואמר רב יהודה אמר רב אין המנחמין רשאין לומר דבר עד שיפתח האבל שנאמר ואין דובר אליו דבר וכתיב אחרי כן פתח איוב וכו' וכ"ה גי' הרי"ף והרא"ש בכאן ובגי' הש"ס שלפנינו חסר מימרא קמייתא דרב יהודה א"ר. ב) נ"ל ואשב ראש וגו' כאשר אבלים ינחם מר זוטרא אמר מהכא.

הדרן עלך ואלו מגלחין במועד. וסליקא לה מסכת מועד קטן בס"ד

The following paragraph is recited three times:

הַדְרָן עֲלָךְ מַסֶּכֶת מוֹעֵד קָטָן וְהַדְרָךְ עֲלָן, דַּעְתָּן עֲלָךְ מַסֶּכֶת מוֹעֵד קָטָן וְדַעְתָּךְ עֲלָן, לָא נִתְנְשֵׁי מִנָּךְ מַסֶּכֶת מוֹעֵד קָטָן וְלָא תִתְנְשֵׁי מִנַּן, לָא בְּעָלְמָא הָדֵין וְלָא בְּעָלְמָא דְאָתֵי.

יְהִי רָצוֹן מִלְּפָנֶיךָ יהוה אֱלֹהֵינוּ וֵאלֹהֵי אֲבוֹתֵינוּ, שֶׁתְּהֵא תוֹרָתְךָ אֻמָּנוּתֵנוּ בָּעוֹלָם הַזֶּה, וּתְהֵא עִמָּנוּ לָעוֹלָם הַבָּא. חֲנִינָא בַּר פָּפָּא, רָמֵי בַּר פָּפָּא, נַחְמָן בַּר פָּפָּא, אַחַאי בַּר פָּפָּא, אַבָּא מָרִי בַּר פָּפָּא, רַפְרָם בַּר פָּפָּא, רָכִישׁ בַּר פָּפָּא, סוּרְחָב בַּר פָּפָּא, אַדָּא בַּר פָּפָּא, דָּרוּ בַּר פָּפָּא.

הַעֲרֶב נָא יהוה אֱלֹהֵינוּ אֶת דִּבְרֵי תוֹרָתְךָ בְּפִינוּ וּבְפִי עַמְּךָ בֵּית יִשְׂרָאֵל, וְנִהְיֶה אֲנַחְנוּ וְצֶאֱצָאֵינוּ (וְצֶאֱצָאֵי צֶאֱצָאֵינוּ) וְצֶאֱצָאֵי עַמְּךָ בֵּית יִשְׂרָאֵל, כֻּלָּנוּ יוֹדְעֵי שְׁמֶךָ וְלוֹמְדֵי תוֹרָתְךָ לִשְׁמָהּ. מֵאֹיְבַי תְּחַכְּמֵנִי מִצְוֺתֶךָ תהלים קיט
כִּי לְעוֹלָם הִיא־לִי: יְהִי־לִבִּי תָמִים בְּחֻקֶּיךָ לְמַעַן לֹא אֵבוֹשׁ: לְעוֹלָם לֹא־אֶשְׁכַּח פִּקּוּדֶיךָ כִּי־בָם חִיִּיתָנִי: בָּרוּךְ אַתָּה יהוה לַמְּדֵנִי חֻקֶּיךָ: אָמֵן אָמֵן אָמֵן סֶלָה וָעֶד.

מוֹדִים אֲנַחְנוּ לְפָנֶיךָ יהוה אֱלֹהֵינוּ וֵאלֹהֵי אֲבוֹתֵינוּ שֶׁשַּׂמְתָּ חֶלְקֵנוּ מִיּוֹשְׁבֵי בֵּית הַמִּדְרָשׁ, וְלֹא שַׂמְתָּ חֶלְקֵנוּ מִיּוֹשְׁבֵי קְרָנוֹת. שֶׁאָנוּ מַשְׁכִּימִים וְהֵם מַשְׁכִּימִים, אָנוּ מַשְׁכִּימִים לְדִבְרֵי תוֹרָה, וְהֵם מַשְׁכִּימִים לִדְבָרִים בְּטֵלִים. אָנוּ עֲמֵלִים וְהֵם עֲמֵלִים, אָנוּ עֲמֵלִים וּמְקַבְּלִים שָׂכָר, וְהֵם עֲמֵלִים וְאֵינָם מְקַבְּלִים שָׂכָר. אָנוּ רָצִים וְהֵם רָצִים, אָנוּ רָצִים לְחַיֵּי הָעוֹלָם הַבָּא, וְהֵם רָצִים לִבְאֵר שַׁחַת, שֶׁנֶּאֱמַר: וְאַתָּה אֱלֹהִים תּוֹרִדֵם לִבְאֵר שַׁחַת תהלים נה
אַנְשֵׁי דָמִים וּמִרְמָה לֹא־יֶחֱצוּ יְמֵיהֶם וַאֲנִי אֶבְטַח־בָּךְ:

יְהִי רָצוֹן מִלְּפָנֶיךָ יהוה אֱלֹהַי, כְּשֵׁם שֶׁעֲזַרְתַּנִי לְסַיֵּם מַסֶּכֶת מוֹעֵד קָטָן כֵּן תְּעַזְּרֵנִי לְהַתְחִיל מַסֶּכְתּוֹת וּסְפָרִים אֲחֵרִים וּלְסַיְּמָם, לִלְמֹד וּלְלַמֵּד לִשְׁמֹר וְלַעֲשׂוֹת וּלְקַיֵּם אֶת כָּל דִּבְרֵי תַלְמוּד תּוֹרָתְךָ בְּאַהֲבָה, וּזְכוּת כָּל הַתַּנָּאִים וְאָמוֹרָאִים וְתַלְמִידֵי חֲכָמִים יַעֲמֹד לִי וּלְזַרְעִי שֶׁלֹּא תָמוּשׁ הַתּוֹרָה מִפִּי וּמִפִּי זַרְעִי וְזֶרַע זַרְעִי
עַד עוֹלָם, וְיִתְקַיֵּם בִּי: בְּהִתְהַלֶּכְךָ תַּנְחֶה אֹתָךְ בְּשָׁכְבְּךָ משלי ו
תִּשְׁמֹר עָלֶיךָ וַהֲקִיצוֹתָ הִיא תְשִׂיחֶךָ: כִּי־בִי יִרְבּוּ יָמֶיךָ משלי ט
וְיוֹסִיפוּ לְּךָ שְׁנוֹת חַיִּים: אֹרֶךְ יָמִים בִּימִינָהּ בִּשְׂמֹאולָהּ משלי ג
עֹשֶׁר וְכָבוֹד: יהוה עֹז לְעַמּוֹ יִתֵּן יהוה יְבָרֵךְ אֶת־עַמּוֹ תהלים כט
בַשָּׁלוֹם:

The following paragraph is recited three times:

הַדְרָן We shall return to you, tractate *Moed Katan,* and your glory is upon us. Our thoughts are upon you, tractate *Moed Katan,* and your thoughts are upon us. We will not be forgotten from you, tractate *Moed Katan,* and you will not be forgotten from us; neither in this world nor in the World-to-Come.

יְהִי רָצוֹן May it be Your will, Lord our God and God of our ancestors, that Your Torah will be our avocation in this world and will accompany us to the World-to-Come. Ḥanina bar Pappa, Ramei bar Pappa, Naḥman bar Pappa, Aḥai bar Pappa, Abba Mari bar Pappa, Rafram bar Pappa, Rakhish bar Pappa, Surḥav bar Pappa, Adda bar Pappa, Daru bar Pappa.

הַעֲרֶב נָא Please, Lord our God, make the words of Your Torah sweet in our mouths and in the mouths of Your people, the house of Israel, so that we, our descendants (and their descendants), and the descendants of Your people, the house of Israel, may all know Your name and
study Your Torah for its own sake. Your commandments *Psalms 119*
make me wiser than my enemies, for they are ever with me. Let my heart be undivided in Your statutes, in order that I may not be put to shame. I will never forget Your precepts, for with them You have quickened me. Blessed are You, O Lord; teach me Your statutes. Amen, Amen, Amen, Selah, Forever.

מוֹדִים We give thanks before You, Lord Our God and God of our ancestors, that You have placed our lot among those who sit in the study hall and that you have not given us our portion among those who sit idly on street corners. We rise early and they rise early. We rise early to pursue matters of Torah and they rise early to pursue frivolous matters. We toil and they toil. We toil and receive a reward and they toil and do not receive a reward. We run and they run. We run to the life of the World-to-Come and they run to the pit of destruction,
as it is stated: But You, God, will bring them down into *Psalms 55*
the pit of destruction; men of blood and deceit shall not live out half their days; but as for me, I will trust in You.

יְהִי רָצוֹן May it be Your will, Lord my God, just as you have assisted me in completing tractate *Moed Katan* so assist me to begin other tractates and books and conclude them to learn and to teach, to observe and to perform, and to fulfill all the teachings of Your Torah with love. And may the merit of all the *tanna'im* and *amora'im* and Torah scholars stand for me and my descendants so that the Torah will not move from my mouth and from the mouths of my descendants and the descendants of my
descendants forever. And may the verse: When you *Proverbs 6*
walk, it shall lead you, when you lie down, it shall watch over you; and when you awaken, it shall talk with you
be fulfilled in me. For in the Torah your days shall be *Proverbs 9*
multiplied, and the years of your life shall be increased.
Length of days is in her right hand; in her left hand are *Proverbs 3*
riches and honor. May the Lord give strength to His *Psalms 29*
people; the Lord will bless His people with peace.

The following קדיש *requires the presence of a* מנין.

יִתְגַּדַּל וְיִתְקַדַּשׁ שְׁמֵהּ רַבָּא
בְּעָלְמָא דְּהוּא עָתִיד לְאִתְחַדָּתָא
וּלְאַחֲיָאָה מֵתַיָּא, וּלְאַסָּקָא יָתְהוֹן לְחַיֵּי עָלְמָא
וּלְמִבְנֵא קַרְתָּא דִירוּשְׁלֵם, וּלְשַׁכְלָלָא הֵיכְלֵהּ בְּגַוַּהּ
וּלְמֶעְקַר פָּלְחָנָא נֻכְרָאָה מֵאַרְעָא
וְלַאֲתָבָא פָּלְחָנָא דִשְׁמַיָּא לְאַתְרֵהּ
וְיַמְלִיךְ קֻדְשָׁא בְּרִיךְ הוּא בְּמַלְכוּתֵהּ וִיקָרֵהּ
(נוסח ספרד: וְיַצְמַח פּוּרְקָנֵהּ וִיקָרֵב מְשִׁיחֵהּ)
בְּחַיֵּיכוֹן וּבְיוֹמֵיכוֹן וּבְחַיֵּי דְכָל בֵּית יִשְׂרָאֵל
בַּעֲגָלָא וּבִזְמַן קָרִיב, וְאִמְרוּ אָמֵן.

יְהֵא שְׁמֵהּ רַבָּא מְבָרַךְ לְעָלַם וּלְעָלְמֵי עָלְמַיָּא.

יִתְבָּרַךְ וְיִשְׁתַּבַּח וְיִתְפָּאַר וְיִתְרוֹמַם וְיִתְנַשֵּׂא
וְיִתְהַדָּר וְיִתְעַלֶּה וְיִתְהַלָּל
שְׁמֵהּ דְּקֻדְשָׁא בְּרִיךְ הוּא
לְעֵלָּא מִן כָּל בִּרְכָתָא
/בעשרת ימי תשובה: לְעֵלָּא לְעֵלָּא מִכָּל בִּרְכָתָא/
וְשִׁירָתָא, תֻּשְׁבְּחָתָא וְנֶחֱמָתָא, דַּאֲמִירָן בְּעָלְמָא
וְאִמְרוּ אָמֵן. (קהל: אָמֵן)

עַל יִשְׂרָאֵל וְעַל רַבָּנָן
וְעַל תַּלְמִידֵיהוֹן וְעַל כָּל תַּלְמִידֵי תַלְמִידֵיהוֹן
וְעַל כָּל מָאן דְּעָסְקִין בְּאוֹרַיְתָא
דִּי בְּאַתְרָא (בארץ ישראל: קַדִּישָׁא) הָדֵין, וְדִי בְּכָל אֲתַר וַאֲתַר
יְהֵא לְהוֹן וּלְכוֹן שְׁלָמָא רַבָּא
חִנָּא וְחִסְדָּא, וְרַחֲמֵי, וְחַיֵּי אֲרִיכֵי, וּמְזוֹנֵי רְוִיחֵי
וּפֻרְקָנָא מִן קֳדָם אֲבוּהוֹן דִּי בִשְׁמַיָּא
וְאִמְרוּ אָמֵן.

יְהֵא שְׁלָמָא רַבָּא מִן שְׁמַיָּא
וְחַיִּים (טוֹבִים) עָלֵינוּ וְעַל כָּל יִשְׂרָאֵל
וְאִמְרוּ אָמֵן.

Bow, take three steps back, as if taking leave of the Divine Presence, then bow, first left, then right, then center, while saying:

עֹשֶׂה שָׁלוֹם/בעשרת ימי תשובה: הַשָּׁלוֹם/ בִּמְרוֹמָיו
הוּא יַעֲשֶׂה בְרַחֲמָיו שָׁלוֹם, עָלֵינוּ וְעַל כָּל יִשְׂרָאֵל
וְאִמְרוּ אָמֵן.

The following Kaddish requires the presence of a minyan.

Magnified and sanctified may His great name be,
in the world that will in future be renewed,
reviving the dead and raising them up to eternal life.
He will rebuild the city of Jerusalem
and in it re-establish His Temple.
He will remove alien worship from the earth
and restore to its place the worship of Heaven.
Then the Holy One, blessed be He,
will reign in His sovereignty and splendor.
May it be in your lifetime and in your days,
(*Nusaḥ Sepharad:* make His salvation flourish,
and hasten His messiah,)
and in the lifetime of all the House of Israel,
swiftly and soon – and say: Amen.

May His great name be blessed for ever and all time.

Blessed and praised,
glorified and exalted,
raised and honored,
uplifted and lauded
be the name of the Holy One,
blessed be He,
beyond any blessing,
song, praise and consolation uttered in the world –
and say: Amen.

To Israel, to the teachers,
their disciples and their disciples' disciples,
and to all who engage in the study of Torah,
in this (*in Israel add:* holy) place or elsewhere,
may there come to them and you great peace,
grace, kindness and compassion,
long life, ample sustenance and deliverance,
from their Father in Heaven –
and say: Amen.

May there be great peace from heaven,
and (good) life for us and all Israel –
and say: Amen.

Bow, take three steps back, as if taking leave of the Divine Presence, then bow, first left, then right, then center, while saying:

May He who makes peace in His high places,
in His compassion make peace for us and all Israel –
and say: Amen.

הַכֹּל

*אחַיָּיבִין בִּרְאִיָּה, חוּץ מֵחֵרֵשׁ, שׁוֹטֶה, וְקָטָן, וְטוּמְטוּם, וְאַנְדְּרוֹגִינוֹס, וְנָשִׁים, וַעֲבָדִים שֶׁאֵינָם מְשׁוּחְרָרִים, הַחִיגֵּר, וְהַסּוּמָא, וְהַחוֹלֶה, וְהַזָּקֵן, וּמִי שֶׁאֵינוֹ יָכוֹל לַעֲלוֹת בְּרַגְלָיו. אֵיזֶהוּ קָטָן — כָּל שֶׁאֵינוֹ יָכוֹל לִרְכּוֹב עַל כְּתֵפָיו שֶׁל אָבִיו וְלַעֲלוֹת מִירוּשָׁלַיִם לְהַר הַבַּיִת, דִּבְרֵי בֵּית שַׁמַּאי. וּבֵית הִלֵּל אוֹמְרִים: בכָּל שֶׁאֵינוֹ יָכוֹל לֶאֱחוֹז בְּיָדוֹ שֶׁל אָבִיו וְלַעֲלוֹת מִירוּשָׁלַיִם לְהַר הַבַּיִת, שֶׁנֶּאֱמַר: °"שָׁלֹשׁ רְגָלִים" (שמות כג). בֵּית שַׁמַּאי אוֹמְרִים: הָרְאִיָּיה שְׁתֵּי כֶסֶף, וְהַחֲגִיגָה מָעָה כֶסֶף. וּבֵית הִלֵּל אוֹמְרִים: גהָרְאִיָּיה מָעָה כֶסֶף, וְהַחֲגִיגָה שְׁתֵּי כֶסֶף.§ **גמ'** *"הַכֹּל" לְאַתּוּיֵי מַאי? לְאַתּוּיֵי *מִי שֶׁחֶצְיוֹ עֶבֶד וְחֶצְיוֹ בֶּן חוֹרִין. וּלְרָבִינָא, דְּאָמַר: מִי שֶׁחֶצְיוֹ עֶבֶד וְחֶצְיוֹ בֶּן חוֹרִין דפָּטוּר מִן הָרְאִיָּיה, "הַכֹּל" לְאַתּוּיֵי מַאי? לְאַתּוּיֵי חִיגֵּר בְּיוֹם רִאשׁוֹן וְנִתְפַּשֵּׁט בְּיוֹם שֵׁנִי. הָנִיחָא לְמַאן דְּאָמַר *כּוּלָּן תַּשְׁלוּמִין זֶה לָזֶה, אֶלָּא לְמַאן דְּאָמַר הכּוּלָּן תַּשְׁלוּמִין דְּרִאשׁוֹן — "הַכֹּל" לְאַתּוּיֵי מַאי? לְאַתּוּיֵי סוּמָא בְּאַחַת מֵעֵינָיו. וּדְלָא כִּי הַאי תַּנָּא. דְּתַנְיָא, *יוֹחָנָן בֶּן דַּהֲבַאי אוֹמֵר מִשּׁוּם ר' יְהוּדָה*: וסוּמָא בְּאַחַת מֵעֵינָיו פָּטוּר מִן הָרְאִיָּיה, שֶׁנֶּאֱמַר: °"יִרְאֶה" (שם) "יֵרָאֶה" — כְּדֶרֶךְ שֶׁבָּא לִרְאוֹת כָּךְ בָּא לֵירָאוֹת, מַה לִּרְאוֹת בִּשְׁתֵּי עֵינָיו — אַף לֵירָאוֹת בִּשְׁתֵּי עֵינָיו, וְאִיבָּעֵית אֵימָא: לְעוֹלָם כִּדְאָמְרִי מֵעִיקָּרָא, וּדְקָא קַשְׁיָא לָךְ הָא דְּרָבִינָא — לָא קַשְׁיָא; כָּאן — כְּמִשְׁנָה רִאשׁוֹנָה, כָּאן — כְּמִשְׁנָה אַחֲרוֹנָה. דִּתְנַן: *מִי שֶׁחֶצְיוֹ עֶבֶד וְחֶצְיוֹ בֶּן חוֹרִין — עוֹבֵד אֶת רַבּוֹ יוֹם אֶחָד וְאֶת עַצְמוֹ יוֹם אֶחָד, דִּבְרֵי בֵּית הִלֵּל. אָמְרוּ לָהֶם בֵּית שַׁמַּאי: תִּקַּנְתֶּם

רש"י

הַכֹּל חַיָּיבִין בִּרְאִיָּה. בְּמִצְוַת רְאִיַּית "כָּל זְכוּרְךָ" (שמות כג), שֶׁצְּרִיכִים לְהִתְרָאוֹת בָּעֲזָרָה בָּרֶגֶל: **חוּץ מֵחֵרֵשׁ שׁוֹטֶה וְקָטָן.** דְּלָאו בְּנֵי דֵּעָה נִינְהוּ, וּפְטוּרִין מִמִּצְוֹת: **הַחִיגֵּר וְהַסּוּמָא.** כּוּלָּהּ יָלֵיף מִקְּרָאֵי בַּגְּמָרָא: **וּמִי שֶׁאֵינוֹ יָכוֹל לַעֲלוֹת בְּרַגְלָיו.** מִירוּשָׁלַיִם לָעֲזָרָה. וּבַגְּמָרָא מְפָרֵשׁ לְהוּ: **אֵי זֶהוּ קָטָן כו'.** אֲבָל מִכָּאן וְאֵילָךְ, אַף עַל פִּי שֶׁאֵינוֹ חַיָּיב מִן הַתּוֹרָה — הֶטִּילוּ חֲכָמִים עַל אָבִיו וְעַל אִמּוֹ לְחַנְּכוֹ בְּמִצְוֹת: **שָׁלֹשׁ רְגָלִים.** הָרָאוּי לַעֲלוֹת בְּרַגְלָיו חַיָּיב הַכָּתוּב. וְכֵיוָן דְּגָדוֹל פָּטוּר מִן הַתּוֹרָה — קָטָן לָאו בַּר חִינּוּךְ הוּא: **בֵּית שַׁמַּאי אוֹמְרִים הָרְאִיָּה שְׁתֵּי כֶסֶף.** גָּדוֹל הַבָּא לְהֵירָאוֹת צָרִיךְ לְהָבִיא עוֹלָה, וְאֵינָהּ פְּחוּתָה מִשְּׁתֵּי כֶסֶף, שְׁתֵּי מָעוֹת כֶּסֶף שֶׁהֵן שְׁלִישׁ דִּינָר, שֶׁנֶּאֱמַר: "וְלֹא יֵרָאוּ פָנַי רֵיקָם" (שם), וְיָלֵיף בַּגְּמָרָא שֶׁצָּרִיךְ לְהָבִיא עוֹלָה, אַף עַל פִּי שֶׁלֹּא נָתְנָה בּוֹ תּוֹרָה שִׁיעוּר — חֲכָמִים נָתְנוּ שִׁיעוּר: **וְהַחֲגִיגָה.** שַׁלְמֵי חֲגִיגָה חַיָּיבִין הַיְּחִידִים לְהָבִיא בָּרֶגֶל, דִּילְפִינַן לָהּ בִּשְׁלְהֵי פִּירְקִין (דף ט.) מִ"וְחַגּוֹתֶם אוֹתוֹ חַג לַה'": **גמ' וּלְרָבִינָא דְּאָמַר כו'.** לְקַמָּן אָמְרִינַן בְּפִירְקִין (דף ד.): **הָנִיחָא לְמַאן דְּאָמַר כו'.** לְקַמָּן אָמְרִינַן בְּפִירְקִין (דף ט.) שֶׁיֵּשׁ לְקָרְבְּנוֹת הֶחָג תַּשְׁלוּמִין כָּל ז'. וְאִיפְּלִיגוּ בָּהּ אָמוֹרָאֵי, אִיכָּא לְמַאן דְּאָמַר תַּשְׁלוּמִין זֶה לָזֶה וְאִיכָּא לְמַאן דְּאָמַר (א) תַּשְׁלוּמִין דְּרִאשׁוֹן הֵן, וְאָמְרִינַן: מַאי בֵּינַיְיהוּ — חִיגֵּר בְּיוֹם רִאשׁוֹן וְנִתְפַּשֵּׁט בְּיוֹם שֵׁנִי אִיכָּא בֵּינַיְיהוּ. מַאן דְּאָמַר כּוּלָּן תַּשְׁלוּמִין לָרִאשׁוֹן, מִי שֶׁמְּחוּיָּיב בָּרִאשׁוֹן וְלֹא הֵבִיא — יָבִיא בְּאֶחָד מִשְּׁאָר הַיָּמִים, וּמִי שֶׁאֵינוֹ מְחוּיָּיב — אֵינוֹ צָרִיךְ תַּשְׁלוּמִין. וּמַאן דְּאָמַר תַּשְׁלוּמִין זֶה לָזֶה, קָסָבַר: הַחוֹבָה מוּטֶּלֶת עַל כָּל אֶחָד מִן שְׁאָר הַיָּמִים, וְלֹא עַל הָרִאשׁוֹן לְבַדּוֹ. הִלְכָּךְ, אַף מִי שֶׁפָּטוּר בָּרִאשׁוֹן וְנִרְאֶה בַּשֵּׁנִי — חַיָּיב לְהָבִיא, וְאִם לֹא יָבִיא בּוֹ בַּיּוֹם — יָבִיא לְמָחָר: (ב) **יִרְאֶה יֵרָאֶה.** [יִרְאֶה] כְּתִיב, וְקָרֵינַן יֵרָאֶה, "יִרְאֶה כָּל זְכוּרְךָ אֶת פְּנֵי הָאָדוֹן" דְּמַשְׁמַע שֶׁהָאָדָם רוֹאֶה אֶת הַשְּׁכִינָה, "יֵרָאֶה כָּל זְכוּרְךָ אֶת פְּנֵי הָאָדוֹן" מַשְׁמַע שֶׁהָאָדוֹן בָּא לִרְאוֹתְךָ. הִקִּישׁ הַכָּתוּב רְאִיָּיתְךָ לִרְאִיָּיתוֹ: **כְּדֶרֶךְ שֶׁבָּא** (ג) **לִרְאוֹתְךָ.** כָּךְ הוּא בָּא לֵירָאוֹת מִמְּךָ: **מַה לִּרְאוֹתְךָ.** בִּשְׁתֵּי עֵינָיו: **אַף.** כָּאן לֵירָאוֹת מִן הָאָדָם — בִּשְׁתֵּי עֵינָיו שֶׁל אָדָם: **מִשְׁנָה רִאשׁוֹנָה.** קוֹדֶם שֶׁחָזְרוּ ב"ה לְהוֹרוֹת כְּדִבְרֵי ב"ש. סֵיפָא דְּמַתְנִי' דְּקָתָנֵי חוּץ מִן הָעֲבָדִים שֶׁאֵינָן מְשׁוּחְרָרִים דְּאוֹקְמָה רָבִינָא בְּמִי שֶׁחֶצְיוֹ עֶבֶד וְחֶצְיוֹ בֶּן חוֹרִין דְּפָטוּר — נִשְׁנֵית קוֹדֶם שֶׁחָזְרוּ ב"ה, אֲבָל לְאַחַר שֶׁהוֹדוּ לב"ש שֶׁיֵּשׁ עַל ב"ד לָכוֹף אֶת אֲדוֹנוֹ לְשַׁחְרְרוֹ, וַהֲוָה לֵיהּ כְּאִלּוּ מְשׁוּחְרָר כְּבָר, וְחַיָּיב. וּמִשְׁנָה שֶׁנִּשְׁנֵית לֹא זָזָה מִמְּקוֹמָהּ:

תוספות

הכל חייבין בראייה. פירש רש"י: במצות "יראה כל זכורך". והקשה הר"ר אלחנן: דהא תני בסמוך, ב"ש אומרים: הראייה שתי כסף, משמע דבקרבן מיירי. ותו, תניא בגמרא*: הערל וטמא פטורין מן הראייה. בשלמא טמא — דכתיב (דברים יב): "ובאת שמה" (ד) כל שישנו בביאה ישנו בהבאה. ועוד אמרינן בירושלמי ריש מכילתין: בד"א — בראיית קרבן, אבל בראיית פנים בעזרה — הכל חייבין כמו בהקהל, האנשים והנשים והטף. ותו: תניא בגמרא*, רבי יוסי אומר: שלש מצות נצטוו ישראל בעלייתן לרגל: ראייה ושמחה וחגיגה. יש בראייה שאין בשתיהן — שהראייה כולה כליל. משמע דסתם ראייה בקרבן מיירי! ע"כ נראה לר"ת דמתני' מיירי בקרבן ובעזרה. ורש"י דנקט בראיית פנים בעזרה — נקט חדא דמשמע תרי, ולפטורא דכולהו אתא, דאף בראיית פנים בעזרה פטירי, וכל שכן בראיית פנים בקרבן. וגם יש ליישב, דמתני' משמע ליה דבראיית פנים (ה) נמי איירי, דקתני בסמוך: איזהו קטן — כל שאין יכול לילך כו'(ו), משמע דבקטן דאיירי ביה קאמר, אלמא: בראיית פנים בעזרה איירי, שאינו יכול לילך לשם. ומיהו, שיטת הירושלמי לא יתכן לפי שיטת שמעתתא שלנו מפני דברים הרבה. דהתם יליף מהקהל לחיוב ואנן לא ילפינן מיניה רק לפטור דחרש. ואע"ג דאמרינן לקמן*: ס"ד אמינא ניליף ראיה ראיה מהקהל — מה להלן נשים חייבות כו', מ"מ מהתם שמעינן דלפי האמת דלא ילפינן מהקהל לחיוב. ועוד: היכי מחייבינן נשים בראיית פנים בעזרה מראייה דהקהל? דהא "ולא יראו" הוא דמוקמינן לקמן בראיית פנים לקרבן, וממעטינן נשים מ"זכורך". ועוד קשיא ליה: דאמרינן לקמן (דף ו.) (ז) מאן אייתי' — אמו דמחייב' בשמחה אייתיה, ולא קאמר דמחייבא בראיית עזרה. משמע דפטורה! ועוד: בגמרא דקאמר שפטורה מראייה וחייבת בשמחה, לפי שיטת הירושלמי הוה מצי למימר שחייבת בראיית עזרה. אלא ודאי כולי שמעתין מוכח דפטירי בכולי ראייה, כדפרישית: **חוץ** מחרש שוטה וקטן. אין למדין מן הכללות אפילו במקום שנאמר בו חוץ, כדאמרינן בריש "בכל מערבין" (עירובין דף כז.) דהא תנא ושייר מקמץ(ח) ובורסי ומי שאין לו קרקע*. ומיהו, אי משום הני — לאו שיורא הוה; דפסול דגופא קחשיב, לאפוקי הני דפסולן מחמת דבר אחר הוא, משום אומנותו. וכי תימא: הא איכא חרש באזנו אחת וחיגר ברגלו אחת, ובעלי קבין! כל הני מכללא אתיין. וטמא פשיטא ליה לפי שאינו בביאה — אינו בהבאה. וערל מרבינן בגמרא* כי טמא, ואליבא דרבי עקיבא, אבל כל הני דמתני' — רבותא אשמעינן, דבעינן מעוטא מקרא: **איזהו** קטן כל שאינו יכול לרכוב. מאם והלאה הוה ליה הגיע לחינוך, ומדרבנן הוא דמחויב, וצריך להביא קרבנותיו נדבה. ולמ"ד (ביצה יט.) אין קריבין ביו"ט — אין קריבין עד למחר בחול המועד. אך קשה למורי: למ"ד תשלומין דראשון נינהו, כיון דלא מצי קריב בראשון — לא קרבי תו, כדאמרינן לקמן (דף ט.) גבי חיגר שנתפשט בשני! וי"ל: דהתם גברא לא חזי, הלכך כיון דלא חזי (ט) בראשונה — לא חזי בשני. אבל הכא — כל חיוב שיש בשני ישנו בראשונה, אלא משום שאינו היום ראוי עכשיו. ודומה לו מצינו בפסחים בפרק "אלו דברים" (דף ע: ושם) גבי חגיגה פעמים ו' פעמים ז', חל יו"ט הראשון להיות בשבת — קרב בששה. אלמא, אע"ג דלא קרב בראשון קרב בשני, כיון דמחמת יום הוא דאתי, כדפרישית. וליכא למימר דלמ"ד דנדרים ונדבות אינן קריבין ביו"ט דרבנן הוא והכא דרבנן תקינו לה שיוכל להביא אף ביו"ט, דהא בפ"ק דביצה (דף יב. ושם) משמע דמדאורייתא הוא, דהא שתי הלחם (*ולחם הפנים) לא דחו יו"ט! וכי תימא: מ"מ, כי מייתי להם נדבה היכי סמיך עלה? דקטן אינו סומך, כדאיתא במנחות בפרק "שתי מדות" (דף צג.)! וי"ל: אע"ג דלא סמיך עליה — מ"מ דמיא לחינוך בנו. ורש"י פירש דאיזהו קטן לא קאי (י) לראייה בראיית קרבן, רק לראיית פנים בעזרה:

הכל לאתויי מאי לאתויי מי שחציו עבד וכו'. ואליבא דמשנה אחרונה. אע"ג (כ) דמתניתין קאמר איפכא, כדדייק בגמרא (דף ד.) מלשון שאינן משוחררים דתלי עבד פטור, מ"מ מתרץ רישא לחיוב לפי מה דסבירא ליה השתא. ואדיוקא לא חש אלישנא דעבדים שאינן משוחררים:

תשלומין דראשון. ואע"ג דגבי חגיגה הוא דכתיב תשלומין — מ"מ ילפינן ראייה מיניה: כולן תשלומין דראשון. והכא גברא לא חזי הוא וכיון דלא חזי בראשון לא חזי בשני. ולא הוה מצי למימר חיגר בשעה ראשונה ונתפשט בשניה! דהא — פשיטא הוא:

יראה יראה כדרך שבא לראות. פרש"י: כלדרך שבא הקב"ה לראותך, דהיינו בשתי עיניו — אף אתה בא (ל) לראותו בשתי עיניך. ולא יתכן לר"ת, דהא לא שייך ביאה גבי שכינה, שבכל מקום הוא! ועוד: דדריש מסורת קודם, אדרבה היו לנו לדרוש המקרא קודם! ע"כ גריס ר"ת: יראה יראה, מה לראות בשתי עיניו, שאדם בא להתראות לפני המקום בשתי עיניו של מקום, אף האדם בא לראות המקום בשתי עיניו. ולא דמי לעוּבָּד ועָבַד (פסחים דף כו:) דדרשינהו תרווייהו, מקרא ומסורת, דהכא כי הדדי נינהו, אבל התם כל חדא חלוק מחבריה:

תקנתם

עין משפט נר מצוה

א א מיי' פ"ב מהלכות חגיגה הלכה א סמג עשין רכז רכח רכט:
ב ב מיי' שם הל' ג:
ג ג מיי' פ"א שם הל' ב סמג שם:
ד ד מיי' שם פ"ב הלכה א סמג שם:
ה ה מיי' שם פ"א הלכה ז סמג שם:
ו ו מיי' שם פ"ב הלכה א סמג שם:

מסורת הש"ס

ערכין ג: | [שם] | [כגון שהיו שני אחין או שני שותפין ששחרר אחד את חלקו רש"י גיטין מא.] | כסנהדרין ד: א"ר בן תימא | פסחים פח. גיטין מא. ב"ב יג. ערכין ב: עדיות פ"א מי"ג | [לקמן ד.] | [לקמן ו.] | [לקמן ד.] | [דף ד.] | [לקמן ט.] | לקמן ד: סנהדרין ד: ערכין ב: [תוספתא פ"א ע"ש] | [פסחים ח:] | [לקמן דף ד:] | [ליתא בביצה כ: ולא א] | [במנחות קו:]

רבינו חננאל

הכל חייבין בראייה חוץ מחרש שוטה וקטן כו'. אתינן לאוקומה למתני' הכל חייבין הכל לאתויי מאי מי שחציו עבד וחציו בן חורין שחייב בראיה. ודחינן ולרבינא דפוטר בהאי מאי ומוקים לה הכל לאתויי מי שהיה חיגר ביום ראשון ולא היה יכול לעלות בהר הבית שפטור ואם נתפשט כלומר נתרפא ביום שני חייב. ואמרינן הניחא לר' אושעי' דאמר כולן תשלומין זה לזה וכיון שהוא יכול לעלות ביום ב' של חג [חייב] בשאר הימים אלא לר' יוחנן דאמר כולן תשלומין דראשון הן כדבעינן למימר לקמן האי הכל דקתני במתניתין לאתויי מאי

הגהות מהר"ב רנשבורג

א] תוס' ד"ה איזהו קטן וכו'. דהא בפ"ק דביצה דף יב ושם. נמחק תיבות בפ"ק דביצה וצ"ב בפ"ב דביצה דף כ ע"ב כצ"ל וכן הגיה בשער המלך פ"א מהלכות חגיגה הלכה ח דף ס"ג ע"א יעו"ש:

הגהות הב"ח

(א) רש"י ד"ה הניחא וכו' ואיכא למאן דאמר כולם תשלומין דראשון הן ואמרינן: (ב) ד"ה יראה יֵרָאֶה כתיב וקרינן יֵרָאֶה יֵרָאֶה כל זכורך וכו' השכינה יֵרָאֶה כל: (ג) ד"ה כדרך שבא לִרְאוֹתְךָ כך הוא בא לֵרָאוֹת מִמְּךָ מה לִרְאוֹתְךָ בשתי עיניו אף בא לֵרָאוֹת מן האדם: (ד) תוס' ד"ה הכל חייבין וכו' ובאת שמה והבאתם שמה כל שישנו וכו' רבי יוסי הגלילי אומר: (ה) בא"ד וגם יש ליישב דמתניתין משמע ליה דבראיית פנים בעזרה איירי כצ"ל ותיבת נמי נמחק: (ו) בא"ד כל שאין יכול לילך כו' אלמא משמע דבקטן דאיירי ביה בראיית פנים בעזרה איירי מדקאמר שאינו יכול לילך כצ"ל ותיבות קאמר אלמא נמחק: (ז) בא"ד דאמרינן לקמן עד הכא מאן אייתיה אמו וכו' דמחייבא בראיית פנים בעזרה וכו' ולפי שיטת הירוש' וכו' שחייבת בראיית פנים בעזרה אלא: (ח) ד"ה חוץ וכו' ושייר מקמץ ומצרף נחשת ובורסי: (ט) ד"ה איזהו וכו' כיון דלא חזי בראשון לא חזי וכו' ישנו בראשון אלא משום שאין היום ראוי: (י) בא"ד לא קאי לראייה בקרבן רק לראיית פנים בעזרה: (כ) ד"ה הכל לאתויי וכו' אע"ג דסיפא דמתניתין קאמר: (ל) ד"ה יראה וכו' אף אתה בא לראות לו מה הוא רואה אותך אף אתה רואה אותו בשתי עיניך ולא יתכן וכו' ע"כ גריס ר"ת יֵרָאֶה יֵרָאֶה מה לִרְאוֹת:

תַּקַּנְתֶּם אֶת רַבּוֹ, וְאֶת עַצְמוֹ לֹא תִקַּנְתֶּם; לִישָּׂא שִׁפְחָה — אֵינוֹ יָכוֹל, בַּת חוֹרִין — אֵינוֹ יָכוֹל, לִיבָּטֵיל? וַהֲלֹא לֹא נִבְרָא הָעוֹלָם אֶלָּא לִפְרִיָּה וּרְבִיָּה, שֶׁנֶּאֱמַר: °"לֹא תֹהוּ בְרָאָהּ לָשֶׁבֶת יְצָרָהּ"! (ישעיה מה) [א]אֶלָּא, מִפְּנֵי תִּיקּוּן הָעוֹלָם כּוֹפִין אֶת רַבּוֹ וְעוֹשֶׂה אוֹתוֹ בֶּן חוֹרִין, וְכוֹתֵב לוֹ שְׁטָר עַל חֲצִי דָמָיו. וְחָזְרוּ בֵּית הִלֵּל לְהוֹרוֹת כְּדִבְרֵי בֵּית שַׁמַּאי.§ "חוּץ מֵחֵרֵשׁ שׁוֹטֶה וְקָטָן" כו'.§ קָתָנֵי חֵרֵשׁ דּוּמְיָא דְשׁוֹטֶה וְקָטָן, מַה שׁוֹטֶה וְקָטָן — *דְּלָאו בְּנֵי דֵעָה, אַף חֵרֵשׁ — דְּלָאו בַּר דֵּעָה הוּא. וְקָא מַשְׁמַע לָן כְּדִתְנַן: *חֵרֵשׁ שֶׁדִּיבְּרוּ חֲכָמִים בְּכָל מָקוֹם — שֶׁאֵינוֹ שׁוֹמֵעַ וְאֵינוֹ מְדַבֵּר. הָא מְדַבֵּר וְאֵינוֹ שׁוֹמֵעַ, שׁוֹמֵעַ וְאֵינוֹ מְדַבֵּר — חַיָּיב. תְּנֵינָא לְהָא, דְּתָנוּ רַבָּנַן: *הַמְדַבֵּר וְאֵינוֹ שׁוֹמֵעַ — זֶהוּ חֵרֵשׁ, שׁוֹמֵעַ וְאֵינוֹ מְדַבֵּר זֶהוּ אִלֵּם, [ב]זֶה וָזֶה הֲרֵי הֵן כְּפִקְחִין לְכָל דִּבְרֵיהֶם. וּמִמַּאי דִּמְדַבֵּר וְאֵינוֹ שׁוֹמֵעַ זֶהוּ חֵרֵשׁ, שׁוֹמֵעַ וְאֵינוֹ מְדַבֵּר זֶהוּ אִלֵּם — דִּכְתִיב: °"וַאֲנִי כְחֵרֵשׁ לֹא אֶשְׁמָע וּכְאִלֵּם לֹא יִפְתַּח פִּיו". (תהלים לח) וְאִיבָּעֵית אֵימָא, כִּדְאָמְרִי אֱנָשֵׁי: אִישְׁתְּקִיל מִילּוּלֵיהּ.§ "מְדַבֵּר וְאֵינוֹ שׁוֹמֵעַ שׁוֹמֵעַ וְאֵינוֹ מְדַבֵּר חַיָּיב".§ וְהָתַנְיָא: [ג]מְדַבֵּר וְאֵינוֹ שׁוֹמֵעַ, שׁוֹמֵעַ וְאֵינוֹ מְדַבֵּר — פָּטוּר! אָמַר רָבִינָא וְאִיתֵּימָא רָבָא: חַסּוּרֵי מִיחַסְּרָא, וְהָכִי קָתָנֵי: הַכֹּל חַיָּיבִין בָּרְאִיָּיה וּבְשִׂמְחָה, חוּץ מֵחֵרֵשׁ הַמְדַבֵּר וְאֵינוֹ שׁוֹמֵעַ, שׁוֹמֵעַ וְאֵינוֹ מְדַבֵּר, שֶׁפָּטוּר מִן הָרְאִיָּיה. וְאַע"פ שֶׁפָּטוּר מִן הָרְאִיָּיה — חַיָּיב בְּשִׂמְחָה. [ד]וְאֶת שֶׁאֵינוֹ לֹא שׁוֹמֵעַ וְלֹא מְדַבֵּר, וְשׁוֹטֶה וְקָטָן — פָּטוּר אַף מִן הַשִּׂמְחָה, הוֹאִיל וּפְטוּרִים מִכָּל מִצְוֹת הָאֲמוּרוֹת בַּתּוֹרָה. תַּנְיָא נַמִי הָכִי: הַכֹּל חַיָּיבִין בָּרְאִיָּיה וּבְשִׂמְחָה — חוּץ מֵחֵרֵשׁ הַמְדַבֵּר וְאֵינוֹ שׁוֹמֵעַ, שׁוֹמֵעַ וְאֵינוֹ מְדַבֵּר — שֶׁפְּטוּרִין מִן הָרְאִיָּיה. וְאַף עַל פִּי שֶׁפָּטוּר מִן הָרְאִיָּיה —

חַיָּיב

רש"י

תִּקַּנְתֶּם אֶת רַבּוֹ וְאֶת עַצְמוֹ לֹא תִקַּנְתֶּם. כָּל תַּקָּנַת רַבּוֹ כָּאן הִיא, אֲבָל תַּקָּנַת הָעֶבֶד אֵין כָּאן. אִם נִתְקַן בְּמִשְׁפַּט הַמָּמוֹן — לֹא נִתְקַן בִּפְרִיָּה וּרְבִיָּה: לִישָּׂא שִׁפְחָה אֵינוֹ יָכוֹל. מִפְּנֵי צַד הַחֵרוּת שֶׁבּוֹ, וּכְתִיב: "לֹא יִהְיֶה קָדֵשׁ" וגו' (דברים כג): בַּת חוֹרִין אֵינוֹ יָכוֹל. מִפְּנֵי צַד עַבְדוּת שֶׁבּוֹ: לֹא תֹהוּ בְרָאָהּ. לֹא בָּרָא הקב"ה אֶת הָאָרֶץ לִהְיוֹת בְּלֹא יִשּׁוּב, אֶלָּא "לָשֶׁבֶת יְצָרָהּ": כִּדְתְנַן. בְּרֵישׁ מַסֶּכֶת תְּרוּמוֹת (מ"ב): חֵרֵשׁ שֶׁדִּבְּרוּ בּוֹ חֲכָמִים בְּכָל מָקוֹם. שֶׁהִשְׁווּ אוֹתוֹ לְשׁוֹטֶה לְפוֹטְרוֹ, לֹא דִּבְּרוּ אֶלָּא בְּמִי שֶׁאֵינוֹ שׁוֹמֵעַ וְאֵינוֹ מְדַבֵּר. הָכִי קִים לְהוּ לְרַבָּנַן, דְּמִי שֶׁאֵינוֹ שׁוֹמֵעַ וְאֵינוֹ מְדַבֵּר — דְּלָאו בְּנֵי דֵעָה נִינְהוּ: מְדַבֵּר וְאֵינוֹ שׁוֹמֵעַ. תְּחִילָּתוֹ הָיָה פִּקֵּחַ עַד שֶׁלָּמַד לְדַבֵּר, וְאַחַ"כ נִתְחָרֵשׁ: תְּנֵינָא. בְּמַתְנִיתִין: לְהָא דְּתָנוּ רַבָּנַן. בַּבָּרַיְיתָא, וְלָמַדְנוּ שֶׁהַבָּרַיְיתָא הַזֹּאת עִיקָּר, וְסוֹמְכִין עָלֶיהָ: זֶה וָזֶה כְּפִקְחִים. הַיְינוּ כְּמַתְנִיתִין, דְּלֹא פָּטַר אֶלָּא חֵרֵשׁ הַדּוֹמֶה לְשׁוֹטֶה: וְאִי בָּעֵית אֵימָא. אִלֵּם כְּמַשְׁמָעוֹ, נוֹטְרִיקוֹן: אִישְׁתַּקִּיל מִלּוּלֵיהּ = נִיטַּל דִּבּוּרוֹ: פָּטוּר. מִן הָרְאִיָּיה. קַשְׁיָין אַהֲדָדֵי מַתְנִיתִין וּבָרַיְיתָא: אָמַר רָבָא. מַתְנִיתִין דְּתָנֵי אֵצֶל רְאִיָּיה חֵרֵשׁ דּוּמְיָא דְשׁוֹטֶה: חַסּוּרֵי מִיחַסְּרָא וְהָכִי קָתָנֵי.(א) דְּאַע"פ דְּלֹא דּוֹמֶה לְשׁוֹטֶה — פָּטוּר. וְכִי תַּנְיָא מַתְנִיתִין דּוּמְיָא דְשׁוֹטֶה — גַּבֵּי שִׂמְחָה הוּא דְּתָנֵי. וּתְרֵי מִינֵי חֵרֵשׁ תָּנָא מַתְנִיתִין, וְחַסּוּרֵי מִיחַסְּרָא מַתְנִיתִין וְהָכִי קָתָנֵי: הַכֹּל חַיָּיבִין בִּרְאִיָּיה חוּץ מֵחֵרֵשׁ כָּל דְּהוּ; אוֹ שׁוֹמֵעַ וְאֵינוֹ מְדַבֵּר אוֹ מְדַבֵּר וְאֵינוֹ שׁוֹמֵעַ: וְאַף עַל פִּי שֶׁהוּא פָּטוּר. בְּעוֹלַת רְאִיָּיה לֵירָאוֹת:

חַיָּיב

תוספות

תקנתם את רבו. במה שהיה לו מעיקרא יש לו עכשיו, שזהו העבדות. ואת עצמו לא תקנתם — שאינו יכול לישא אשה. ואי משום עבדות הא לא איכפת ליה כלל, כיון דמעיקרא היה כולו לרב ועכשיו ביומו לעצמו. והר"ר משולם גרים: תקנתם את עצמו ואת רבו לא תקנתם כלל, שגם הרב מפסיד הוולדות:

לישא שפחה אינו יכול. ולמכור עצמו לא מצי כדי לישא שפחה, דהא גר אינו נמכר בעבד עברי, דבעינן "ושב אל משפחתו" (ויקרא כה) וליכא, כדאיתא ב"איזהו נשך" (ב"מ דף עא.). ועוד: מאחר דלא קיים פריה ורביה ביהדות — לא נסבינן ליה כנענית לצד חירות שבו. ודכוותיה מצינו בפ"ק דקדושין (דף כ.): אין לו אשה ובנים — אין רבו מוסר לו שפחה כנענית. וא"ת: ישא בת מינו — ליתי צד חירות ולישתמיש בצד חירות, וצד עבדות בצד עבדות, דומיא דפרידה שתבעה אין מרביעין עליה לא סוס ולא חמור אלא מינה, בפרק "אותו ואת בנו" (חולין דף עט.)! וי"ל: דהתם לא קפיד קרא אלא בכלאים דתרי מינים, והא ליכא. אבל הכא, אמאן קפיד קרא — אצד חירות, דלא לישתמיש צד חירות בעבדות, והא איתא. ומטעם דשרי הרבעה — שרי גם לרכוב על הפרידה. ובתוספתא דמסכת כלאים (פ"ה ובירושלמי פ"ח) תניא: אמר רבי איסי בן יהודה: אסור לרכוב על הפרידה מק"ו: ומה במקום שמותר ללבוש שתי חלוקין — אסור בתערובתו. מקום שאסור לנהוג שני מינים — אינו דין שאסור בתערובתו! אמרו ליה: והא כתיב(ב) "והרכבתם את שלמה בני על הפרדה" (מלכים א א)! אמר להם: אין למדים תורה מן *התקועה. א"ל: והא כתיבא "ויעש הישר בעיני ה'"(ג):

לישא שפחה אינו יכול. וממזרת לא ישא אע"ג דעבד מותר בממזרת לפי שקדש ועומד, כדתנן פרק "האומר" (קדושין דף סט.): יכולין ממזרים ליטהר, כיצד? ממזר נושא שפחה. ולצד חירות שרי בה, כדתנן פרק "עשרה יוחסין" (שם) שחרורי וממזרי שרו לבא זה בזה. דהא י"ל: דאין לנו לתקן כדי להרבות ממזרים בעולם. ועוד: כיון דתפסי בה קדושין — אתי לצד עבדות ומשתמש באשת איש. ונתינה נמי לא ישא, דאע"ג דממזרת ונתינה ושחרורי מותרין לבא זה בזה, דהא הוה התפסת קדושין — ואתי לצד עבדות ומשתמש באשת איש. אי נמי: נתינה אסור בצד עבדות, דלאו קדש ועומד הוא. אע"ג דמותר בממזרת, משום דלא מקרי קהל — מוזהר בלאו ד"לא יהיה קדש" (דברים כג) וא"ת: וליתי עשה [ד"לשבת יצרה"] ולידחי לאו ד"לא יהיה קדש"! וי"ל: דהכא אפשר לקיים שיכנס על ידי כפייה. אי נמי: דלא אתי עשה ודחי לא תעשה אלא כגון מילה בצרעת, דבעידנא דמעקר לאו מקיים עשה. אבל הכא, משעת הערארה עובר ליה בלאו — ועשה ליכא עד גמר ביאה:

לא תהו בראה. האי עשה אלים טפי מפרו ורבו, כדאמר במגילה בפרק בתרא (דף כז.): מוכר אדם ס"ת לישא אשה וללמוד תורה, ומייתי "לא תהו בראה". אבל י"מ: משום דעבד לא מיפקיד אפריה ורביה, דאמר: *היו לו בנים בעבדותו ונשתחרר — לא קיים פריה ורביה. ולאו מילתא היא, דאמר בירושלמי דמו"ק (פ"א): עבד מהו שישא אשה במועד? אמר להון: נשמעינן מן הָדֵין מתניתין יבטל — והלא לא נברא העולם אלא בשביל פריה ורביה. ואמר שמעון בר אבא משום רבי יוחנן: כל שהוא מצוּוֶּה על פריה ורביה — לא ישא אשה במועד. *ועוד: לישנא דנקט הכא "והלא לא נברא העולם אלא בשביל פריה ורביה" משמע דאתרוייהו קאי. והא דאמרינן לא קיים פריה ורביה — היינו מטעם דבעינן זרעו מיוחס אחריו, ואפילו ישראל שיש לו בן מן השפחה אינו קרוי (ג) "אחריו". ועוד: פרו ורבו אכולהו בני נח כתיב, אף לכנען:

כופין את רבו. אפילו לשמואל, דאמר (גיטין דף לח.): המפקיר עבדו יוצא לחירות וא"צ גט שחרור, הכא דטבא ליה עבדו ליה לעשות שחרור גמור. ואע"ג דאמרינן (ברכות דף מז:): המשחרר עבדו עובר בעשה — ניחא לן דליעבד הרב איסורא זוטא ולא ליעבד העבד איסורא רבה, כדאמר בעירובין בפ' "בכל מערבין" (דף לב: ושם). ולא דמי להההיא דריש שבת (דף ד. ושם): וכי אמרינן לו לאדם עמוד וחטא בשביל שיזכה חבירך? דהתם פושע בדבר הוי, שלא היה לו לאפות הפת. תדע, דשרינן ריש "תמיד נשחט" (פסחים דף נט. ושם) להקריב לכהן אַחַר תמיד של בין הערבים כפרת חבירו, כדי שיאכל קרבן פסח לערב, אע"ג דאיכא עשה דהשלמה*:

***נשים** ועבדים. לא שייך לאקשויי: אמאי תני נשים לשון רבים, ותנא קטן(ד) חרש לשון יחיד! כדדייק בפרק קמא דנדה (דף ח.) גבי קטנות, והכא תנא אשה! דהכא תרי ענייני, ולא דמי חד לאידך. דחרש ושוטה פטור מכל המצות כדאמר לקמן. וקטן לא ידעינן דפטור מקרא רק מק"ו, דנשים פטורות דכתיב "זכורך" טפלים לא כל שכן, דהכי דייקינן בפרק קמא דקדושין (דף לד: ושם), טפלים חייבין נשים לא כל שכן:

***ומי** שאינו יכול לעלות ברגליו. פרש"י: מירושלים לעזרה. ורבותא נקט, דלא מיבעיא מעירו דלא מצי סליק לעזרה. וה"ה נמי אם הוא אינו יכול לעלות מעירו לירושלים דפטור, כדמשמע בגמרא: עד הכא מאן אייתי: **חרש** דומיא דשוטה וקטן. במגילה פ"ב (דף יט:): "הכל כשרין לקרות את המגילה חוץ מחרש שוטה וקטן" כו' לא דייק הכי, דהתם ע"כ במדבר קיימינן, מדקרא את המגילה. וברמיזה לא הוה מפיק אחרים. וכן בחולין (דף ב.): "חוץ מחרש שוטה וקטן שמא יקלקלו את שחיטתן" לא דייק הכי, דהתם הטעם תלוי בכיון, שיוכל לאמן את ידו לשחוט: **המדבר** ואינו שומע זהו חרש. בב"ר מפיק ליה אינו מדבר ואינו שומע דכתיב "מי שם פה לאדם או מי ישום אלם או חרש" (שמות ד), "מי [שם] פה" קאי לתרווייהו:

שומע ואינו מדבר פטור מן הראייה וחייב בשמחה. והא דלא קתני נשים דמחייבי בשמחה בתר הכי — לא חש להכי, למיתני סורסא. וכיוצא בזה מצינו בכמה מקומות. וההיא דלקמן (דף ו:) דאמר: יש בשמחה שאין בשתיהן שנוהגת באנשים ובנשים, מה שאין כן בשתיהן, ולא קחשיב חרש מדבר ואינו שומע — דהתם בחגיגה נמי מיחייב, ולא בעי למיתני יש בשתיהן שאין באחת — כגון חרש מדבר ואינו שומע, דלא נחית למיתני הך כללא רק מה שבאחת שאין בשתים. והכא, כי קאמר דמיחייב בשמחה — הוא הדין בחגיגה, כדפירשתי. אלא שמחה נקט, דנשים חייבות וחרש שוטה וקטן פטירי. וכי תנינן לעיל זה וזה כפיקחין לכל דבריהן — להתחייב בשמחה ובחגיגה קאמר:

גמר

עין משפט נר מצוה

ז א מיי' פ"ז מהלכות עבדים הלכה ז סמג עשין פז טוש"ע י"ד סימן רסז סעיף סב:

ח ב מיי' פ"ב מהלכות אישות הלכה כו ופ"ב מהלכות גירושין הלכה טז ופכ"ט מהלכות מכירה הלכה ב ג טוש"ע א"ה סימן קכא סעיף ו ובח"מ סימן רלה סעיף יח:

ט ג מיי' פ"ב מהלכות חגיגה הלכה א סמג עשין רכו:

י ד מיי' שם הלכה ד סמג שם:

מסורת הש"ס

[יבמות לט: גטין כג. מנחות נג. ערכין ה:]

[נדה יג: תרומות פ"א מ"ב]

גטין עא. [תוספתא תרומות פ"א]

פי' תוקע עלמו לדבר הלכה

א) [נ"ל אשר עשה דוד את הישר וכו' מלכים א טו ה] ב) [ומשני (בירושלמי שם) בכי' מששת ימי בראשית היתה] ובתוספתא לא משני כלום ע"ז

[יבמות סב. וע"ש בתו' ד"ה הכל מודין בעבד שאין לו חיים]

[עיין תוספות גטין מא: ד"ה לא תהו]

[ועי' תוספות פסחים פח: ד"ה כופין]

[שייך לעיל במשנה ועיין תוי"ט]

[שייך למתני']

הגהות הב"ח

(א) רש"י ד"ה חסורי מחסרא והכי קתני דגבי ראייה אע"פ דלא: (ב) תוס' ד"ה לישא שפחה אינו יכול ולמכור וכו' אמר ליה והא כתיב אשר עשה דוד את הישר בעיני ה' ולא סר מכל אשר צוהו כל ימי חייו רק בדבר אוריה החתי הס"ד ונ"ב עיין בר"ש פ' ח' דכלאים פי' תקוע תוקע עלמו לדבר הלכה ולי נראה שדוד [עשה זאת על פי] רבו עירא היאירי שהיה מעיר תקוע: (ג) ד"ה לא תוהו וכו' בן מן השפחה אינו קרוי מיוחס אחריו: (ד) ד"ה נשים וכו' ותנא קטן שוטה חרש לשון יחיד:

רבינו חננאל

ואמרינן (לאתויי מאי) לאתויי סומא באחת מעיניו שחייב בראייה ודלא כיוחנן בן דהבאי שהיה פוטרו ואסיקנא לעולם לאתויי חציו עבד וחציו בן חורין שחייב ומתני' כמשנה אחרונה דתנן כופין את רבו ועושהו בן חורין וחזרו ב"ה להודות לדברי בית שמאי דכיון דודאי לשחרור קאי אע"פ שעדיין לא נשתחרר חייב בראייה: **ירושלמי** מתניתין בראיית קרבן אבל בראיית פנים אפילו קטן אביו חייב להעלותו שנאמר הקהל את העם האנשים והנשים והטף. וסיפא דקתני עבדים שאינן משוחררין לגמרי פטורין כמשנה ראשונה היא שנויה. דרש ר' אלעזר בן עזריה אנשים באין ללמד ונשים באות לשמוע וטף ליתן שכר למביאיהן. חוץ מחרש אתינן לאוקומא בחרש שאינו לא שומע ולא מדבר הא החרש המדבר ואינו שומע או שומע ואינו מדבר חייב. וא' תנינא להא דתנו רבנן חרש מדבר ואינו שומע זהו חרש שומע ואינו מדבר זהו אלם זה וזה הרי הן כפקחין לכל דבריהם. ואקשינן איני והתניא מדבר ואינו שומע שומע ואינו מדבר פטור מן הראייה ואתא רבינא ותרצה ואמר חסורי מחסרא והכי קתני הכל חייבין בראייה ובשמחה חוץ מחרש

גמ׳ חַיָּיב בְּשִׂמְחָה. וְאֶת שֶׁאֵינוֹ לֹא שׁוֹמֵעַ וְלֹא מְדַבֵּר, וְשׁוֹטֶה וְקָטָן — פְּטוּרִין אַף מִן הַשִּׂמְחָה, הוֹאִיל וּפְטוּרִין מִכָּל מִצְוֹת הָאֲמוּרוֹת בַּתּוֹרָה. מַאי שְׁנָא לְעִנְיַן רְאִיָּה דִּפְטִירִי, וּמַאי שְׁנָא לְעִנְיַן שִׂמְחָה דִּמְחַיְּיבִי? לְעִנְיַן רְאִיָּה גָּמַר "רְאִיָּה" "רְאִיָּה" [א]מֵהַקְהֵל, דִּכְתִיב: °"הַקְהֵל אֶת הָעָם הָאֲנָשִׁים וְהַנָּשִׁים וְהַטַּף" וּכְתִיב: °"בְּבֹא כָל יִשְׂרָאֵל לֵרָאוֹת". וְהָתָם מְנָלַן? דִּכְתִיב: °"לְמַעַן יִשְׁמְעוּ וּלְמַעַן יִלְמְדוּ", וְתַנְיָא: "לְמַעַן יִשְׁמְעוּ" — פְּרָט לִמְדַבֵּר וְאֵינוֹ שׁוֹמֵעַ, "וּלְמַעַן יִלְמְדוּ" — פְּרָט לְשׁוֹמֵעַ וְאֵינוֹ מְדַבֵּר. לְמֵימְרָא דְּכִי לָא מִשְׁתָּעֵי לָא גָּמַר? וְהָא הָנְהוּ תְּרֵי אִילְּמֵי דַּהֲווּ בְּשִׁיבָבוּתֵיהּ דְּרַבִּי, בְּנֵי בְּרַתֵּיהּ דְּרַבִּי יוֹחָנָן בֶּן גּוּדְגְּדָא, וְאָמְרִי לַהּ בְּנֵי אֲחָתֵיהּ דְּרַבִּי יוֹחָנָן, דְּכָל אֵימַת דַּהֲוָה עָיֵיל רַבִּי לְבֵי מִדְרְשָׁא הֲווּ עָיְילִי וְיָתְבִי *קַמַּיְיהוּ, וּמְנַיְידִי בְּרֵישַׁיְיהוּ *וּמְרַחֲשִׁין שִׂפְוָותַיְיהוּ. וּבָעֵי רַבִּי רַחֲמֵי עֲלַיְיהוּ וְאִיתַּסּוּ, וְאִשְׁתַּכַּח דַּהֲווּ גְּמִירִי הִלְכְתָא וְסִפְרָא וְסִפְרֵי וְכוּלֵּיהּ תַּלְמוּדָא! אָמַר מָר זוּטְרָא: קְרִי בֵּיהּ "לְמַעַן (א) יְלַמְּדוּ". רַב אַשִׁי אָמַר: וַדַּאי "לְמַעַן יִלְמְדוּ" הוּא, דְּאִי סָלְקָא דַּעְתָּךְ "לְמַעַן יִלְמְדוּ" וְכֵיוָן דְּלָא מִשְׁתָּעֵי לָא גָּמַר, וְכֵיוָן דְּלָא שָׁמַע לָא גָּמַר — הַאי מִ"לְּמַעַן יִשְׁמְעוּ" נָפְקָא! אֶלָּא וַדַּאי "לְמַעַן יְלַמְּדוּ" הוּא. אָמַר ר' תַּנְחוּם: [ב]חֵרֵשׁ בְּאׇזְנוֹ אַחַת פָּטוּר מִן הָרְאִיָּה, שֶׁנֶּאֱמַר: °"בְּאׇזְנֵיהֶם". וְהַאי "בְּאׇזְנֵיהֶם" מִבְּעֵי לֵיהּ: בְּאׇזְנֵיהֶם דְּכוּלְּהוּ יִשְׂרָאֵל! הַהוּא מִ"נֶּגֶד כׇּל יִשְׂרָאֵל" נָפְקָא. אִי מִ"נֶּגֶד כׇּל יִשְׂרָאֵל" הֲוָה אָמִינָא: אַף עַל גַּב דְּלָא שָׁמְעִי, כְּתַב רַחֲמָנָא "בְּאׇזְנֵיהֶם" — וְהוּא דְּשָׁמְעִי! הַהוּא מִ"לְּמַעַן יִשְׁמְעוּ" נָפְקָא. אָמַר רַבִּי תַּנְחוּם: [ג]חִיגֵּר בְּרַגְלוֹ אַחַת — פָּטוּר מִן הָרְאִיָּה, שֶׁנֶּאֱמַר: "רְגָלִים". וְהָא "רְגָלִים" מִבְּעֵי לֵיהּ *פְּרָט לְבַעֲלֵי קַבִּין! הַהוּא מִ"פְּעָמִים" נָפְקָא. דְּתַנְיָא: "פְּעָמִים", אֵין פְּעָמִים אֶלָּא רַגְלַיִם, וְכֵן הוּא אוֹמֵר: °"תִּרְמְסֶנָּה רָגֶל רַגְלֵי עָנִי פַּעֲמֵי דַלִּים" וְאוֹמֵר: °"מַה יָּפוּ פְעָמַיִךְ בַּנְּעָלִים בַּת נָדִיב". *דָּרַשׁ רָבָא: מַאי דִּכְתִיב "מַה יָּפוּ פְעָמַיִךְ בַּנְּעָלִים בַּת נָדִיב" — כַּמָּה נָאִין רַגְלֵיהֶן שֶׁל יִשְׂרָאֵל בְּשָׁעָה שֶׁעוֹלִין לָרֶגֶל, "בַּת נָדִיב" — בִּתּוֹ שֶׁל אַבְרָהָם אָבִינוּ שֶׁנִּקְרָא נָדִיב, שֶׁנֶּאֱמַר: °"נְדִיבֵי עַמִּים נֶאֱסָפוּ עַם אֱלֹהֵי אַבְרָהָם". אֱלֹהֵי אַבְרָהָם וְלֹא אֱלֹהֵי יִצְחָק וְיַעֲקֹב? אֶלָּא: אֱלֹהֵי אַבְרָהָם שֶׁהָיָה תְּחִילָּה לַגֵּרִים. אָמַר רַב כָּהֲנָא, דָּרַשׁ *רַב נָתָן בַּר מַנְיוּמִי מִשּׁוּם ר' תַּנְחוּם: מַאי דִּכְתִיב °"וְהַבּוֹר רֵק אֵין בּוֹ מָיִם" מִמַּשְׁמַע שֶׁנֶּאֱמַר "וְהַבּוֹר רֵק" אֵינִי יוֹדֵעַ שֶׁאֵין בּוֹ מָיִם? אֶלָּא: מַיִם אֵין בּוֹ, אֲבָל נְחָשִׁים וְעַקְרַבִּים — יֵשׁ בּוֹ. ת"ר: *מַעֲשֶׂה בְּרַבִּי יוֹחָנָן בֶּן בְּרוֹקָה וְרַבִּי אֶלְעָזָר (*בֶּן) חִסְמָא שֶׁהָלְכוּ לְהַקְבִּיל פְּנֵי ר' יְהוֹשֻׁעַ בִּפְקִיעִין, אָמַר לָהֶם: מַה חִידּוּשׁ הָיָה בְּבֵית הַמִּדְרָשׁ הַיּוֹם? אָמְרוּ לוֹ: תַּלְמִידֶיךָ אָנוּ, וּמֵימֶיךָ אָנוּ שׁוֹתִין. אָמַר לָהֶם: אַף עַל פִּי כֵן, אִי אֶפְשָׁר לְבֵית הַמִּדְרָשׁ בְּלֹא חִידּוּשׁ, *שַׁבָּת שֶׁל מִי הָיְתָה? שַׁבַּת שֶׁל ר' אֶלְעָזָר בֶּן עֲזַרְיָה הָיְתָה. וּבַמֶּה הָיְתָה הַגָּדָה הַיּוֹם? אָמְרוּ לוֹ: בְּפָרָשַׁת הַקְהֵל. וּמָה דָּרַשׁ בָּהּ? °"הַקְהֵל אֶת הָעָם הָאֲנָשִׁים וְהַנָּשִׁים וְהַטַּף" אִם אֲנָשִׁים בָּאִים לִלְמוֹד, נָשִׁים בָּאוֹת לִשְׁמוֹעַ, טַף לָמָּה בָּאִין? כְּדֵי לִיתֵּן שָׂכָר לִמְבִיאֵיהֶן. אָמַר לָהֶם: מַרְגָּלִית טוֹבָה הָיְתָה בְּיֶדְכֶם וּבִקַּשְׁתֶּם לְאַבְּדָהּ מִמֶּנִּי! וְעוֹד דָּרַשׁ: °"אֶת ה' הֶאֱמַרְתָּ הַיּוֹם וַה' הֶאֱמִירְךָ הַיּוֹם" *אָמַר לָהֶם הַקָּדוֹשׁ בָּרוּךְ הוּא לְיִשְׂרָאֵל: אַתֶּם עֲשִׂיתוּנִי חֲטִיבָה *)אַחַת בָּעוֹלָם, וַאֲנִי אֶעֱשֶׂה אֶתְכֶם חֲטִיבָה אַחַת בָּעוֹלָם — אַתֶּם עֲשִׂיתוּנִי חֲטִיבָה אַחַת בָּעוֹלָם דִּכְתִיב: °"שְׁמַע יִשְׂרָאֵל ה' אֱלֹהֵינוּ ה' אֶחָד", וַאֲנִי אֶעֱשֶׂה אֶתְכֶם חֲטִיבָה אַחַת בָּעוֹלָם שֶׁנֶּאֱמַר: וּמִי

*) [פי' ציור אחד בעולם כלומר דבר הניכר שאין כמותו. ערוך בשם רב האי בערך אמר]

תורה אור: דברים לא | שם | שם | שם | ישעיה כו | שיר ז | תהלים מז | בראשית לז | דברים כו | דברים ו

מסורת הש"ס: [כע"י הגי' קמיה] | [מנחות סג.] | [לקמן ד. יבמות קג. ערכין יט:] | סוכה מט: | שבת כב. | מכילתא פ' בא פר' יז ולהד"ע פרק יח [תוספתא סוטה פ"ז] | ברכות כח. | דברים לא | שם טו | ברכות ו. | דברים ו

רש"י

חַיָּיב בְּשִׂמְחָה. לִשְׂמוֹחַ בֶּחָג, דִּכְתִיב "וְשָׂמַחְתָּ בְּחַגֶּךָ" (דברים טז) וְאָמְרִינַן לְקַמָּן (דף ח.) דְּשִׂמְחָה בִּשְׁלָמִים לֶאֱכוֹל אֶת הַבָּשָׂר, וְיָלְפִינַן לָהּ (פסחים דף קט.) מִ"וְזָבַחְתָּ שְׁלָמִים וְאָכַלְתָּ שָּׁם וְשָׂמַחְתָּ". וּלְקַמָּן פָּרֵיךְ: מ"ש לְעִנְיַן רְאִיָּיה דְּפָטוּר, וּלְעִנְיַן שִׂמְחָה דִּמְחַיֵּיב: וְשֶׁאֵינוֹ לֹא שׁוֹמֵעַ וְלֹא מְדַבֵּר. הַיְינוּ חֵרֵשׁ דְּמַתְנִיתִין, שֶׁסְּמָכוֹ לְשׁוֹטֶה וְקָטָן: רְאִיָּיה מֵהַקְהֵל. דִּכְתִיב בְּפָרָשַׁת הַקְהֵל: "בְּבוֹא כׇל יִשְׂרָאֵל לֵרָאוֹת" וגו', וּפָרָשַׁת הַקְהֵל הַמֶּלֶךְ הָיָה קוֹרֵא מִשְׁנֵה תוֹרָה בָּעֲזָרָה בְּכׇל מוֹצָאֵי שְׁמִטָּה, דִּכְתִיב "מִקֵּץ שֶׁבַע שָׁנִים בְּמוֹעֵד שְׁנַת הַשְּׁמִטָּה" וגו' (דברים לא): פְּרָט לְשׁוֹמֵעַ וְאֵינוֹ מְדַבֵּר. הָשְׁתָּא מַשְׁמַע שֶׁאֵין זֶה רָאוּי לִלְמוֹד: הִלְכְתָא. מִשְׁנָיוֹת: לְמַעַן יְלַמְּדוּ. וְאֵין זֶה רָאוּי לְלַמֵּד אֲחֵרִים: רַב אַשִׁי אָמַר וַדַּאי לְמַעַן יְלַמְּדוּ. כְּלוֹמַר, בְּלָאו קוּשְׁיָא דְּהָנָךְ תְּרֵי אִילְּמֵי לֵיכָּא לְאוֹקְמֵי לִדְרָשָׁה דְּתַנְיָא דְּמָעֵיט מֵהָכָא שׁוֹמֵעַ וְאֵינוֹ מְדַבֵּר, אֶלָּא מִ"לְּמַעַן יְלַמְּדוּ": דְּאִי סָלְקָא דַּעְתָּךְ מִלְּמַעַן יִלְמְדוּ. הוּא דְּמַשְׁמַע לֵיהּ, אַלְמָא סְבִירָא לֵיהּ לְתַנָּא דְּכֵיוָן דְּלָא מִשְׁתָּעֵי — לָא גָּמִיר לְנַפְשֵׁיהּ: וְכֵיוָן דְּלָא שָׁמַע. אֲנַן סָהֲדֵי דְּלָא גָּמִיר, וְכֵיוָן דִּתְנַן "לְמַעַן יִשְׁמְעוּ" פְּרָט לִמְדַבֵּר וְאֵינוֹ שׁוֹמֵעַ, וַאֲנַן סָהֲדֵי דְּטַעְמָא מִשּׁוּם דְּלָא גָּמִיר הוּא, שֶׁלֹּא יָבִין כׇּל מַה שֶּׁאוֹמְרִים לְפָנָיו — לָמָּה לִי לְמֶהְדַּר תּוּ "לְמַעַן יִלְמְדוּ" פְּרָט לְשׁוֹמֵעַ וְאֵינוֹ מְדַבֵּר? כֵּיוָן דִּסְבִירָא לֵיהּ דְּמַאן דְּלָא מִשְׁתָּעֵי נַמִי לָא גָּמִיר, מִ"לְּמַעַן יִשְׁמְעוּ" מְמַעֵט לֵיהּ! אֶלָּא וַדַּאי סְבִירָא לֵיהּ דְּמַאן דְּלָא מִשְׁתָּעֵי נַמִי גָּמִיר, וְלָא מִ"לְּמַעַן יִשְׁמְעוּ" מְמַעֵט, הִלְכָּךְ הֲדַר וּמַעֲטֵיהּ מִ"לְּמַעַן יִלְמְדוּ", הִלְכָּךְ וַדַּאי "לְמַעַן יְלַמְּדוּ" הוּא דְּדָרֵישׁ: פְּרָט לְבַעֲלֵי קַבִּין. כְּשֶׁחָתְכוּ רַגְלֵיהֶם נָתְנוּ קַב קָטָן בְּסוֹף שׁוֹקוֹ, וְנוֹתְנִים בּוֹ מוֹכִין, וְסוֹמֵךְ סוֹף שׁוֹקוֹ עָלָיו: אֶלָּא רַגְלַיִם. אָדָם שֶׁיֵּשׁ לוֹ רַגְלַיִם: פְּעָמַיִךְ בַּנְּעָלִים. אַלְמָא: בְּבַעֲלֵי מִנְעָלִים שַׁיְּיכִי פְּעָמִים. וּבִרְאִיָּיה כְּתִיב "שָׁלֹשׁ פְּעָמִים בַּשָּׁנָה יֵרָאֶה כׇּל זְכוּרְךָ" וגו': שֶׁנִּקְרָא נָדִיב. עַל שֵׁם שֶׁנִּדְּבוֹ לִבּוֹ לְהַכִּיר בּוֹרְאוֹ: נְדִיבֵי עַמִּים. הֵם הַגֵּרִים, הַמִּתְנַדְּבִין מִבֵּין הָעַמִּים לְקַבֵּל עֲלֵיהֶן עוֹל מִצְוֹת: וְהַבּוֹר רֵק. מִשּׁוּם דְּרַבִּי תַּנְחוּם אֲמָרָהּ נָקֵט לָהּ הָכָא גַּבֵּי שְׁמַעְתָּא דְּרַבִּי תַּנְחוּם: אֲבָל נְחָשִׁים וְעַקְרַבִּים יֵשׁ בּוֹ. לֹא הָיָה רֵק אֶלָּא מִמַּיִם: לְהַקְבִּיל פָּנָיו. יוֹם טוֹב הָיָה, שֶׁחַיָּיב אָדָם לְכַבֵּד אֶת רַבּוֹ בְּהַקְבָּלַת פָּנִים, כִּדְאָמְרִינַן בְּמַסֶּכֶת רֹאשׁ הַשָּׁנָה (דף טז:): "מַדּוּעַ אַתְּ הוֹלֶכֶת אֵלָיו הַיּוֹם, לֹא חֹדֶשׁ וְלֹא שַׁבָּת" (מלכים ב ד): תַּלְמִידֶיךָ אָנוּ. וְאֵין לָנוּ לְדַבֵּר בְּפָנֶיךָ: הֶאֱמַרְתָּ. שִׁבַּחְתָּ, כְּמוֹ "יִתְאַמְּרוּ כׇּל פּוֹעֲלֵי אָוֶן" (תהלים צד) — יִשְׁתַּבְּחוּ שֶׁדַּרְכָּן לְכָךְ: חֲטִיבָה אַחַת. שֶׁבַח אֶחָד, שֶׁבַח מְיוּחָד, לוֹמַר: אֵין כָּמוֹךָ, לְכָךְ בַּחַרְנוּךְ לֶאֱלוֹהַּ: וּמַה

תוספות

גמר ראיה ראיה מהקהל. ונשים ליכא לחיובי, דקא ממעטו ליה לקמן מ"זכורך" וכן אמרינן לקמן: הא למה לי קרא? תיפוק לי דמצות עשה שהזמן גרמא, מהו דתימא נילף ראיה מהקהל, מה להלן נשים חייבות. וטפלים לא מחייבינן כמו ב"הקהל" וליתן שכר למביאיהם, כי התם, דמקל וחומר פטרינן ליה, כדפרישית לעיל דנשים פטורות — טפלים לא כל שכן, (ב) ולקמן דמרבינן קטן שהגיע לחינוך מדכתיב "כל" ולא גמרינן מהקהל — התם אסמכתא בעלמא הוא, כדמסיק. ומהאי ק"ו נמי פטור. וכי פריך דרבנן הוא — מצי לאקשויי: למה לי קרא ליגמר מהקהל, אלא עדיפא מינה פריך:

מלמען ישמעו נפקא. דפשטיה דקרא משמע האזינה והבין, שיבין מה שילמדהו. הלכך מה לנו שישמע, כיון דלא גמיר — ממעטינן ליה שפיר:

אלא קרי ביה למען ילמדו. ואף על גב דלא משתעי — גמיר, ולהכי לא נפקא להו מ"למען ישמעו". וכן מדבר ואינו שומע, אפילו שמע עד השתא, דמצי גמיר לאחריני, כיון דלא מצי גמיר בהאי הליכה — מה לו ללכת? וכיון דלא שמע — לא גמיר מכאן ולהבא, אע"ג דגמיר לאחריני עד האידנא, לא יזיל השתא כיון דלא יועיל לו הליכה זו. דהא לא קאמר קרא הקהל אלא שישמעו בקריאת המלך ויבינו מהשתא, ויבאו לידי יראת הבור, דכתיב בסיפיה דקרא "ויראו את ה'" והתלמוד לא חש להביאו, דפשיטא ליה דמשתעי בהני. אבל מ"למען ילמדו" לא מצי מפיק (ג) ב"לא ישמעו" דלא הוינא מפיק מדבר ואינו שומע כיון דשמע מקמי הכי, ושפיר גמיר אף לאחריני וגם יבין למה נקהלו עכשיו וגם (ד) יצטרך ישמעו כדאמרינן לקמן:

חרש באזנו אחת. בירושלמי אמר: ר' יוחנן בעי, חרש באזנו אחת מהו? א"ר יוסי בר בון: פלוגתא דרבי יוסי ורבנן. דתני רבי יוסי: "ולבני אהרן תעשה כתנות" (שמות כח) רבנן אמרי: שתי כתונות לכל אחד, רבי יוסי אמר: אפילו כתונת (ה) לכל אחד ואחד. הכי נמי, רבנן אמרי "באזניהם" — שתי אזנים לכל אחד, ורבי יוסי אמר °אזן לכל אחד ואחד:

אף על גב דלא שמעי. מחמת שהן רחוקים, אבל אם היו חרשין — ממעטינן מבאזניהם:

מפעמים נפקא. וכי אמרינן לקמן: רגלים פרט לבעלי קבין — אסמכתא בעלמא הוא, °דמ"פעמים" נפקא. וכי פריך ב"מצות חליצה" (יבמות דף קג. ושם) ובערכין פרק "האומר משקלי" (דף יט: ושם) ורמינהי: רגלים פרט לבעלי קבין — ההיא (ו) מדסמכיה רגלים קאמר, ולא משום שהוא עיקר דרשה*:

תחילה לגרים. שנצטווה על המילה טפי מכל אותם שלפניו:

נשים לשמוע. אמר בירושלמי: דלא כבן עזאי, *דאמר: חייב אדם ללמד לבתו תורה:

כדי ליתן שכר למביאיהן. ועל זה סמכו *להביא קטנים בבית הכנסת:

ומי

עין משפט נר מצוה: יא א מיי' פ"ג מהלכות חגיגה הלכה ב: | יב ב ג מיי' שם פ"ב הלכה א סמג עשין רכו: | [ועי' תוי"ט סוף פ"ג דאבות] | [וע"ע תוספות בכורות ו. ד"ה רוטב] | [סוטה כ.] | [כ"ה במסכת סופרים פי"ח הלכה ו]

רבינו חננאל

מחרש המדבר ואינו שומע או שומע ואינו מדבר שפטור ואף על פי שפטור מן הראיה חייב בשמחה וחרש שאינו שומע ולא מדבר ושוטה וקטן פטורין אף מן השמחה הואיל ופטורין מכל מצות האמורות בתורה. ומנא לן דהני פטורין מן הראיה דגמר ראיה ראיה מהקהל וכתיב ביה בהקהל למען ישמעו ולמען ילמדו ותניא למען ישמעו פרט למדבר ואינו שומע שפטור למען ילמדו פרט לשומע ואינו מדבר. ומקשינן איני דכל מאן דלא ממלל לא גמר והא הנהו תרי אילמי דבעא רבי רחמי עלייהו ואתפתחו ואשתכחו דהוו גמירי הלכתא וסיפרי וסיפרא ותוספתא וכולה תלמודא ופריק מר זוטרא קרי ביה למען יְלַמְּדוּ הן לאחרים ורב אשי קאי כוותיה דודאי ילמדו פשטיה וכיון דאילמא הוא אע"ג דגמירי לא מצי לאגמורי הוא לאחריני. הא דא"ר תנחום חיגר ברגלו אחת וחרש באזנו אחת פטורין מן הראיה פשוטות הן. בת נדיב בת אברהם שנקרא נדיב כו'. והבור רק אין בו מים מים אין בו אבל נחשים ועקרבים יש בו: ת"ר מעשה בר' יוחנן בן ברוקה ור' אלעזר חסמא שהלכו להקביל פני ר' יהושע בפקיען ואמרו כי ר' אלעזר בן עזריה דרש הקהל את העם האנשים והנשים והטף הא תינח אנשים ונשים וטף למה לי כו'. ועוד דרש את ה' האמרת היום וכו'. אתם עשיתוני חטיבה אחת

הגהות הב"ח

(א) גמ' אמר מר זוטרא קרי ביה למען יְלַמְּדוּ וכו' למען יְלַמְּדוּ הוא דלאי ס"ד למען יִלְמְדוּ: (ב) תוס' ד"ה גמר ראיה וכו' ולקמן דמרבינן. נ"ב וק"ק דהא אצטריך כל דלא תימא נשים פטורין טפלים לכ"ש וי"ל דה"פ הא אי לאו [ק"ו מהקהל שפיר משמע אף קטן שלא] הגיע לחינוך כדקאמר ליתן שכר למביאיהם וכיון דאית לן ריבויא דכל איתרע ק"ו ושפיר נילף מהקהל אף בלא הגיע לחינוך וזה שכתבו התוספות ולקמן דמרבינן קטן שהגיע לחינוך מדכתיב כל ולא גמרינן מהקהל אף בלא הגיע לחינוך כיון דאיתרע ליה ק"ו והא תירצו התם אסמכתא בעלמא הוא כדמסיק ומהאי ק"ו נמי פטור בלא הגיע לחינוך ומסיים התוס' וכי פריך לקמן דף ד' קודם דידע מהירוץ אסמכתא דרבנן הוא הוה מצי לאקשויי ליגמר מהקהל אף בלא הגיע לחינוך: (ג) ד"ה אלא וכו' לא מצי מפיק בלאו למען ישמעו דלא: (ד) בא"ד וגם אצטריך למען ישמעו כדאמרינן לקמן: (ה) ד"ה חרש וכו' ואפי' כתונת אחד לכל אחד וכו' ור' יוסי אומר אפי' אזן אחת לכל אחד: (ו) ד"ה מפעמים וכו' ההיא מדאסמכיה רגלים:

גליון הש"ס

תוספות ד"ה חרש וכו' אזן לכל אחד ואחד. עיין יומא דף לז ע"א וביבמות דף קא ע"ב תוספות ד"ה ש"מ: **ד"ה** מפעמים נפקא וכו' דמפעמים נפקא. עיין תוס' ר"ה דף ה ע"א ד"ה שלמי פסח:

יג א מיי' פ"ו מהלכות מתנות עניים הלכה ה סמג עשין קמב:
יד ב ג מיי' פ"א מהל' תרומות הלכה ה ופ"ו מהלכות בית הבחירה הלכה טז:

בע"י הגרסא כולי האי

טו ד ה מיי' פ"ט מהל' עדות הלכה ט טוש"ע י"ד סימן א סעיף ה וטוש"ע ח"מ סימן לה סעיף ח:

תורה אור

°"ומי כעמך ישראל גוי אחד בארץ". ואף הוא [דה"א יז] פתח ודרש: *°"דברי חכמים כדרבונות [קהלת יב] וכמסמרות נטועים בעלי אסופות נתנו מרועה אחד". למה נמשלו דברי תורה לדרבן? לומר לך: מה דרבן זה מכוין את הפרה לתלמיה להוציא חיים לעולם, אף דברי תורה מכוונין את לומדיהן מדרכי מיתה לדרכי חיים. א]אי מה דרבן זה מטלטל אף דברי תורה מטלטלין — ת"ל: "מסמרות". ב]אי מה מסמר זה חסר ולא יתר אף דברי תורה חסירין ולא יתירין — ת"ל: "נטועים", מה נטיעה זו פרה ורבה — אף דברי תורה פרין ורבין. "בעלי אסופות" — אלו תלמידי חכמים שיושבין אסופות אסופות ועוסקין בתורה, הללו מטמאין והללו מטהרין, הללו אוסרין והללו מתירין, הללו פוסלין והללו מכשירין. שמא יאמר אדם: היאך אני למד תורה מעתה? תלמוד לומר(א): כולם "נתנו מרועה אחד" — אל אחד נתנן, פרנס אחד אמרן, מפי אדון כל המעשים ברוך הוא, דכתיב: °"וידבר אלהים [שמות כ] את כל הדברים האלה". אף אתה עשה אזניך *כאפרכסת, וקנה לך *לב מבין לשמוע את דברי מטמאים ואת דברי מטהרים, את דברי אוסרין ואת דברי מתירין, את דברי פוסלין ואת דברי מכשירין. בלשון הזה אמר להם: *אין דור יתום שר' אלעזר בן עזריה שרוי בתוכו. ולימרו ליה בהדיא? משום מעשה שהיה. דתניא: *מעשה בר' יוסי בן דורמסקית שהלך להקביל פני ר' אלעזר בלוד, אמר לו: מה חידוש היה בבהמ"ד היום? אמר ליה, נמנו וגמרו: *עמון ומואב מעשרין מעשר עני בשביעית. אמר לו: יוסי! פשוט ידיך וקבל עיניך. פשט ידיו וקבל עיניו. בכה ר' אלעזר ואמר: °"סוד ה' ליראיו [תהלים כה] ובריתו להודיעם". אמר לו: לך אמור להם: אל תחושו למנייכם, כך מקובלני מרבן יוחנן בן זכאי, ששמע מרבו, ורבו מרבו: *אהלכתא למשה מסיני, עמון ומואב מעשרין מעשר עני בשביעית. מה טעם? *בהרבה כרכים כבשו [חולין ז.] עולי מצרים ולא כבשום עולי בבל, מפני *שקדושה ראשונה קדשה לשעתה גולא קדשה לעתיד לבא, והניחום כדי שיסמכו עליהן עניים בשביעית. תנא: לאחר שנתיישבה דעתו, אמר: יהי רצון שיחזרו עיני יוסי למקומן. וחזרו. ת"ר: *דאיזהו שוטה? היוצא יחידי בלילה, והלן בבית הקברות, והמקרע את כסותו. איתמר, רב הונא אמר: עד שיהו כולן בבת אחת. ר' יוחנן אמר: האפי' באחת מהן. היכי דמי? אי דעביד להו דרך שטות — אפי' בחדא נמי. אי דלא עביד להו דרך שטות — אפילו כולהו נמי לא! לעולם דקא עביד להו דרך שטות, והלן בבית הקברות — אימור כדי שתשרה עליו רוח טומאה הוא דקא עביד, והיוצא יחידי בלילה — אימור גנדריפס אחדיה, והמקרע את כסותו — אימור בעל מחשבות הוא, כיון דעבדינהו לכולהו — הוה להו כמי

ואף הוא. ג]רבי אלעזר בן עזריה: לתלמיה. שורות המענה: פוסלין ומכשירין. שייך לומר לענין פסול עדות ופסול כהונה: (ב) כולן אל אחד אמרן. אין לך מבני המחלוקת מביא ראיה מתורת אלוה אחר, אלא מתורת אלהינו: פרנס אחד אמרן. אין לך מביא ראייה מדברי נביא הבא לחלוק על משה רבינו: עשה אזניך כאפרכסת. מאחר שכולן לבן לשמים — עשה אזנך שומעת ולמוד, ודע דברי כולן, וכשתדע להבחין אי זה יכשר — קבע הלכה כמותו. אפרכסת = טירמויי"א שעל הריחים: מה מסמר זה. כשנועצין אותו בכותל הוא מחסרו, יכול אף זה כן — תלמוד לומר: "נטועים", כנטיעה שדרכה לפרות ולרבות: ולימרו ליה בהדיא. מיד, למה הוזקקו לומר "תלמידיך אנו": נמנו וגמרו. והתקינו שיהו ישראל הדרין בעבר הירדן, במה שכבשו מסיחון ועוג, ארץ עמון ומואב: מעשרין. עכשיו מעשר עני בשביעית. שהן היו זורעין בשביעית, כדאמרינן לקמן שלא קידשוה עולי גולה כקדושת הארץ: פשוט ידיך וקבל עיניך. הוקשה בעיניו שנתן עטרה לאותו דורש, והלא מימות אנשי כנסת הגדולה היתה תקנה זו: אל תחושו למנייכם. אל יהי לכם שום חשש וגמגום במה שמניתם ותיקנתם, שהרי הסכמתם להלכה: כך מקובלני. שקדושה ראשונה שקידשה יהושע לשעתה לא קידשה לעתיד לבא, אבל קדושה שניה — נתקדשה לעולם, כדתניא ביבמות (דף פב:): קדושה ראשונה ושניה יש להן, שלישית — אין להן. לפיכך בשאר ארץ ישראל אין זריעה בשביעית, אבל עמון ומואב הניחו מלקדשן כדי שיסמכו עליהן עניים בשביעית בלקט שכחה ופאה ובמעשר עני, לכך תקנו להן שיהו מעשרין מעשר עני. ובדרשות החכמים היה להטיל עליהן איזה מעשר שירצו, לפי שאינן חייבין מן התורה: איזהו שוטה. האמור בכל מקום, שפטור מן המצות ומן העונש, ואין קנינו קנין, ואין ממכרו ממכר: והלן בבית הקברות. בלילה: לעולם דקא עביד להו דרך שטות. ואפילו הכי לא מחזקינן ליה בחדא. דהיוצא יחידי בלילה אימור גנדריפס אחדיה — אחזו שמעתי: חולי האוחז מתוך דאגה. ולי נראה: שנתחמם גופו ויוצא למקום האויר: שתשרה עליו רוח טומאה. רוח שדים, שיסייעוהו להיות מכשף: כמו

ומי כעמך ישראל גוי אחד בארץ. אמרינן במדרש: שלשה מעידין זה על זה: ישראל, ושבת, והקדוש ב"ה. ישראל והקדוש ברוך הוא מעידים על השבת שהוא יום מנוחה, ישראל ושבת — על הקדוש ב"ה שהוא אחד, הקב"ה ושבת — על ישראל שהם יחידים באומות. ועל זה סמכינן לומר "אתה אחד" במנחה בשבת, אע"פ שאינו מדבר מעניינא דיומא דשבת *כמו תפלת ערבית ושחרית:

עמון ומואב מעשרין מעשר עני בשביעית. לפי סדר השנים היה להם להפריש מעשר שני, שהוא שנה ראשונה, ומעשר עני נוהג בששית, ולא מלינו מעשר עני שתי שנים רצופים. אלא תקנה תקנו בה, כדי שיסמכו עליהם עניים בשביעית. ובדין הוא דאפי' תרומה גדולה לא ניתקן אלא יהא הכל מעשר עני. אלא שלא רצו לחלק כל כך משאר שנים. פרש"י: דהיינו ארץ סיחון ועוג, כדאמרינן בחולין (דף ס:): עמון ומואב טהרו בסיחון. כלומר, על ידי כבוש סיחון ועוג הותר לישראל ליכבש. והקשה ר"ת: דאמרינן בפרק "מקום שנהגו" (פסחים דף נב: ושם): שלש ארצות לביעור: יהודה, ועבר הירדן, והגליל. ועבר הירדן היינו ארץ סיחון ועוג. (ג)וכ"ת דקדושה ראשונה לא קידשה לעתיד לבא — אם כן תיפשוט מיניה דלרבי אליעזר לא קידשה, אלמה מיבעי' לן בפ"ק דמגילה (דף י. ושם) ובשבועות (דף טז. ושם): מאי סבירא ליה, אי קידשה אי לא קידשה? (ד)ותירץ ר"ת: דיש לחלק, דהכא בעמון ומואב דלא כבשו סיחון ועוג, ולא נתקדשו כלל בקדושת הארץ. ועוד מתרץ: דלא קידשה עבר הירדן רק לארץ סיחון ממש, אבל מה שכבש מעמון — לא נתקדשה:

דרך שטות אפילו בחד נמי. וכי תימא: דלא היה מועד לשטות, רק לאותו דבר, ובעינן תלתא כדי להחזיקו כשוטה לכל מילי, כמו נגח שור וחמור וגמל נעשה מועד לכל. (ה)דהכא לא דמי, דהכא כיון שהוא שוטה באחת — ודאי יש להחזיקו בחזקת שוטה לכל דבר. בירושלמי בפ"ק דתרומות אומר: סימני שוטה היוצא בלילה, והלן בבית הקברות, והמקרע כסותו, (ו)והוא מאבד מה שנותנים לו. א"ר הונא: והוא שיהו כולן בו, דלא כן אומר אני היוצא בלילה יחידי — אימור גנדריפס אחדיה, והלן בבית הקברות — *)לשדים, והמקרע כסותו — אימר בעל מחשבות. מאבד מה שנותנים לו — *קוניקוס. רבי יוחנן אמר: אפילו אחת מהן. אמר ר' אבין: מסתברא כר' יוחנן, בלבד ממאבד מה שנותנין לו, דאפילו שוטה שבשוטים אינו מאבד מה שנותנין לו. קוניקוס — אין בו אחת מכל אלו:

כיון דעבדינהו לכולהו נעשה כמי שנגח כו'. ומחד בשלשה זימנא לא איתחזק, דתלינן בהן דקאמר התלמוד: אימא בעל מחשבות, או אינך: או

*) [מקטיר לשדים כצ"ל]

[הוא נמי חולי של מחשבה מפרש שם]

הגהות מהר"ב רנשבורג

א] אי מה דרבן זה מטלטל. נ"ב ר"ל שאינו מתקיים במקומו מהרש"א ח"א: ב] שם אי מה מסמר זה חסר. נ"ב ר"ל מחסר ומנקב בכותל מהרש"א שם וכן הוא בלשון רש"י ד"ה מה מסמר וכו': ג] רש"י ד"ה ואף הוא ר' אלעזר בן עזריה. נ"ב ומהרש"א בח"א פי' שר' יהושע פתח ודרש ויעו"ש:

הערוך גרס כארפכסת

רבינו חננאל

כו': אף ר' יהושע פתח ודרש דברי חכמים כדרבונות וכמסמרות נטועים בעלי אסופות. אלו ת"ח שיושבין אסופות אסופות ועוסקין בתורה הללו מטהרין והללו מטמאין הללו אוסרין והללו מתירין כו'. וא"ת הואיל וכן היאך אני למד תורה מעתה ת"ל נתנו מרועה אחד כולן מפי אל אחד אמורין שנאמר וידבר אלהים את כל הדברים האלה אלא עשה אזנך כארפכסת וקנה לב לשמוע אלו ואלו שכולן מתבררין לך באיזה מהן הלכה ברורה שאע"פ שנראין כמו חולקין חוזרין ונמנין וגומרין ומסכימין בסוף כדכתיב את והב בסופה כלשון הזה אמר אין דור יתום שר' אלעזר בן עזריה שרוי בתוכו. ומעשה בר' יוסי בן דורמסקית שהלך להקביל פני ר' אלעזר וא"ל בבהמ"ד נמנו וגמרו עמון ומואב מעשרין מעשר שני בשביעית. א"ל ר' אלעזר יוסי פשוט ידיך וקבל עיניך פשט ידיו וקבל עיניו. כעס ר' אלעזר בשביל שא"ל נמנו וגמרו כלומר למה נמנו והלא הלכה למשה מסיני הוא ובכה ואמר סוד ה' ליראיו ובריתו להודיעם ואין בריתו אלא תורה. תנא אחר שנתיישבה דעתו בקש רחמים ואמר יהי רצון שיחזרו עיני יוסי למקומן וחזרו. אמר צא ואמור אל תחושו למניינכם כך מקובלני מריב"ז שקיבל מרבו ורבו מרבו הלכה למשה מסיני עמון ומואב מעשרין מעשר שני בשביעית. מה טעם הרבה כרכים כבשום עולי מצרים ולא כבשו עולי בבל מפני שקדושה ראשונה קדשה לשעתה ולא קדשה לעתיד לבוא

[אבות דר"נ פי"ח תוספתא סוטה פ"ז]

[ברכות כח.]

מכילתא פ' בא פי"ז

[תוספ' ידים פ"ב ע"ש ידים פ"ד מ"ג]

מכילתא פ' בא פי"ז יבמות טז.

כלומר דבר ברור כהלכה למשה מסיני עי' רא"ש בהל' מקואות (סוף נדה) סימן א

מגילה י. [מכות יט. שבועות טז. זבחים ס: קז: חולין ז. תמורה כא. ערכין לב:]

[תוספתא תרומות פ"א]

הגהות הב"ח

(א) גמרא תלמוד לומר נתנו מרועה אחד כולם אל אחד: (ב) רש"י ד"ה פוסלין וכו' כהונה הס"ד ואח"כ מה"ד מה מסמר וכו' ולכבות הס"ד ואח"כ מה"ד כולן אל אחד וכו' שעל הריחים הס"ד ואחר כך מה"ד ולימרו: (ג) תוס' ד"ה עמון וכו' ארץ סיחון ועוג וכן תימה דקאמר הכא לקדושה ראשונה: (ד) בא"ד ותירץ ר"ת. נ"ב ועל קושיא שהקשו אם כן תפשוט אין התירוץ מפורש אבל בפרק קמא דמגילה מפורש בתוס' ע"ש דף י: (ה) ד"ה דרך וכו' נעשה מועד לכל דלא דמי כצ"ל ותיבת דהכא נמחק: (ו) בא"ד והמקרע כסותו והמאבד:

כְּמִי שֶׁנָּגַח שׁוֹר חֲמוֹר וְגָמָל, וְנַעֲשָׂה מוּעָד לַכֹּל. אָמַר רַב פַּפָּא: אִי שְׁמִיעַ לֵיהּ לְרַב הוּנָא הָא דְּתַנְיָא: *אֵי זֶהוּ שׁוֹטֶה – זֶה הַמְאַבֵּד כָּל מַה שֶׁנּוֹתְנִים לוֹ, הֲוָה הָדַר בֵּיהּ. אִיבַּעְיָא לְהוּ: כִּי הֲוָה הָדַר בֵּיהּ – מִמְּקָרֵעַ כְּסוּתוֹ הוּא דַּהֲוָה הָדַר בֵּיהּ, דְּדָמְיָא לְהָא, אוֹ דִּלְמָא מִכּוּלְּהוּ הֲוָה הָדַר? תֵּיקוּ. § "וְטוּמְטוּם וְאַנְדְּרוֹגִינוֹס כו'". תָּנוּ רַבָּנַן: *"זָכוּר", לְהוֹצִיא אֶת הַנָּשִׁים, "זְכוּרְךָ", לְהוֹצִיא טוּמְטוּם וְאַנְדְּרוֹגִינוֹס, "כָּל זְכוּרְךָ" – לְרַבּוֹת אֶת הַקְּטַנִּים. אָמַר מָר: "זָכוּר" – לְהוֹצִיא אֶת הַנָּשִׁים. ◦הָא – לָמָּה לִי קְרָא? מִכְּדִי מִצְוַת עֲשֵׂה שֶׁהַזְּמַן גְּרָמָא הוּא, *[א]וְכָל מִצְוַת עֲשֵׂה שֶׁהַזְּמַן גְּרָמָא נָשִׁים פְּטוּרוֹת! אִצְטְרִיךְ; סָלְקָא דַּעְתָּךְ אָמִינָא: נֵילַף רְאִיָּיה רְאִיָּיה מֵהַקְהֵל; [ב]מָה לְהַלָּן נָשִׁים חַיָּיבוֹת – אַף כָּאן נָשִׁים חַיָּיבוֹת, קָא מַשְׁמַע לָן. אָמַר מָר: "זְכוּרְךָ" – לְהוֹצִיא טוּמְטוּם וְאַנְדְּרוֹגִינוֹס. בִּשְׁלָמָא אַנְדְּרוֹגִינוֹס – אִצְטְרִיךְ, סָלְקָא דַּעְתָּךְ אָמִינָא: הוֹאִיל וְאִית לֵיהּ צַד זַכְרוּת – לִיחַיַּיב, קָא מַשְׁמַע לָן דִּבְרִיָּה בִּפְנֵי עַצְמוֹ הוּא, אֶלָּא טוּמְטוּם סְפֵיקָא הוּא, מִי אִצְטְרִיךְ *קְרָא לְמַעוּטֵי סְפֵיקָא? אָמַר אַבַּיֵי: כְּשֶׁבֵּיצָיו מִבַּחוּץ. אָמַר מָר: "כָּל זְכוּרְךָ" – לְרַבּוֹת אֶת הַקְּטַנִּים. וְהָתְנַן: חוּץ מֵחֵרֵשׁ שׁוֹטֶה וְקָטָן! אָמַר אַבַּיֵי: לָא קַשְׁיָא; [ג]כָּאן – בְּקָטָן שֶׁהִגִּיעַ לְחִינּוּךְ, כָּאן – בְּקָטָן שֶׁלֹּא הִגִּיעַ לְחִינּוּךְ. קָטָן שֶׁהִגִּיעַ לְחִינּוּךְ *דְּרַבָּנַן הִיא! אִין ה"נ, וּקְרָא אַסְמַכְתָּא בְּעָלְמָא. וְאֶלָּא קְרָא לְמַאי אֲתָא? לְכִדְאַחֵרִים. (*דִּתְנַן), *אֲחֵרִים אוֹמְרִים: [ד]הַמְקַמֵּץ, וְהַמְצָרֵף נְחֹשֶׁת, וְהַבּוּרְסִי – פְּטוּרִין מִן הָרְאִיָּיה, מִשּׁוּם שֶׁנֶּאֱמַר: ◦"כָּל זְכוּרְךָ" מִי שֶׁיָּכוֹל לַעֲלוֹת עִם כָּל זְכוּרְךָ, יָצְאוּ אֵלּוּ שֶׁאֵינָן רְאוּיִין לַעֲלוֹת עִם כָּל זְכוּרְךָ. § "נָשִׁים וַעֲבָדִים שֶׁאֵינָן מְשׁוּחְרָרִים וכו'". בִּשְׁלָמָא נָשִׁים – כְּדַאֲמַרַן, אֶלָּא עֲבָדִים מְנָלַן? אָמַר רַב הוּנָא, אָמַר קְרָא: ◦"אֶל פְּנֵי הָאָדוֹן ה'" – מִי שֶׁאֵין לוֹ אֶלָּא אָדוֹן אֶחָד יָצָא זֶה שֶׁיֵּשׁ לוֹ אָדוֹן אַחֵר. הָא לָמָּה לִי קְרָא? מִכְּדִי, [ה]כָּל *מִצְוָה שֶׁהָאִשָּׁה חַיֶּיבֶת בָּהּ – עֶבֶד חַיָּיב בָּהּ, כָּל מִצְוָה שֶׁאֵין הָאִשָּׁה חַיֶּיבֶת בָּהּ – אֵין הָעֶבֶד חַיָּיב בָּהּ, *דְּגָמַר 'לָהּ' 'לָהּ' מֵאִשָּׁה! אָמַר רָבִינָא: *לֹא נִצְרְכָה אֶלָּא [ו]לְמִי שֶׁחֶצְיוֹ עֶבֶד וְחֶצְיוֹ בֶּן חוֹרִין. דַּיְקָא נַמִי, דְּקָתָנֵי: נָשִׁים וַעֲבָדִים שֶׁאֵינָן מְשׁוּחְרָרִין, מַאי שֶׁאֵינָן מְשׁוּחְרָרִין? אִילֵימָא שֶׁאֵינָן מְשׁוּחְרָרִין כְּלָל – לִיתְנֵי עֲבָדִים סְתָמָא! אֶלָּא לָאו: שֶׁאֵינָן מְשׁוּחְרָרִין לְגַמְרֵי, וּמַאי נִינְהוּ – מִי שֶׁחֶצְיוֹ עֶבֶד וְחֶצְיוֹ בֶּן חוֹרִין, שְׁמַע מִינַּהּ. § "וְהַחִיגֵּר וְהַסּוּמָא וְחוֹלֶה וְהַזָּקֵן". תָּנוּ רַבָּנַן: ◦"רְגָלִים" – *פְּרָט לְבַעֲלֵי קַבִּין. דָּבָר אַחֵר: "רְגָלִים" – [ז]פְּרָט לְחִיגֵּר, וּלְחוֹלֶה, וּלְסוּמָא, וּלְזָקֵן, וּלְשֶׁאֵינוֹ יָכוֹל לַעֲלוֹת בְּרַגְלָיו. וְשֶׁאֵינוֹ יָכוֹל לַעֲלוֹת בְּרַגְלָיו לְאַתּוּיֵי מַאי? אָמַר רָבָא: לְאַתּוּיֵי

מְפַנְּקֵי

[לעיל ב. ערכין ג:]

רש"י

כְּמוֹ שֶׁנָּגַח שׁוֹר חֲמוֹר וְגָמָל. דְּבָבָא קַמָּא (דף לז.), דְּנַעֲשָׂה מוּעָד לַכֹּל. וְלֹא אָמְרִינַן עַד שֶׁיְּהֵא מוּעָד בִּשְׁלֹשָׁה בְּכָל מִין וָמִין, דְּהוֹאִיל וְהוּעַד שְׁלֹשָׁה נְגִיחוֹתָיו בִּשְׁלֹשָׁה מִינִין – אֵין זֶה מַקְפִּיד עַל מִין אַחֵר. אַף כָּאן, לֹא בָּאוּ שְׁלֹשָׁה דְּבָרִים לְיָדוֹ בְּבַת אַחַת, אֶלָּא כּוּלָּן מִשּׁוּם שְׁטוּת: אִי שְׁמִיעָא לֵיהּ. הָא דְּתַנְיָא, דְּמַשְׁמַע בְּדָבָר אֶחָד מַחְזִיקִין אוֹתוֹ בְּשׁוֹטֶה – הֲוָה הָדַר בֵּיהּ: זָכוּר. אִם נֶאֱמַר "זָכוּר", אֵין לְךָ לְהוֹצִיא אֶלָּא אֶת הַנָּשִׁים. עַכְשָׁיו שֶׁנֶּאֱמַר "זְכוּרְךָ" – בָּא לְהוֹצִיא אַף טוּמְטוּם וְאַנְדְּרוֹגִינוֹס עִם הַנָּשִׁים: נָשִׁים פְּטוּרוֹת. בְּפ"ק דְּקִדּוּשִׁין (דף לד:) יָלְפִינַן לָהּ: מֵהַקְהֵל. דַּהֲוֵי נַמִי מִצְוַת עֲשֵׂה שֶׁהַזְּמָן גְּרָמָהּ, וְנָשִׁים חַיָּיבוֹת: אָתָא קְרָא לְמַעוּטֵי סְפֵיקָא. בִּתְמִיָּה: לָמָּה לִי קְרָא, מֵהֵיכָא תֵּיתֵי לָן לְחַיּוּבֵיהּ? כְּשֶׁבֵּיצָיו מִבַּחוּץ. אֶלָּא שֶׁהַגִּיד טָמוּן, דְּהָא וַדַּאי זָכָר הוּא, הִלְכָּךְ אִילְטְרִיךְ קְרָא לְמַעוּטֵי: הַמְקַמֵּץ. מְפָרֵשׁ בְּמַסֶּכֶת כְּתוּבּוֹת (דף עז.): הַמְקַמֵּץ בְּיָדוֹ צוֹאַת כְּלָבִים. וְאוֹמֵר אֲנִי: כִּי לְתַקֵּן בָּהֵן עוֹרוֹת, שֶׁקּוֹרִין קורדוו"ן, שֶׁמְּעַבְּדִין אוֹתָן בְּצוֹאַת כְּלָבִים*: וְהַמְצָרֵף נְחֹשֶׁת. שֶׁמְּצָרְפוֹ בַּמָּקוֹם שֶׁחוֹפְרִין אוֹתוֹ מִן הַקַּרְקַע, כִּדְמְפָרֵשׁ בְּמַסֶּכֶת כְּתוּבּוֹת (שם). וְכָל אֵלּוּ רֵיחָן רַע, וְאֵין יְכוֹלִין לַעֲלוֹת עִם חֲבֵירֵיהֶם: כְּדַאֲמַרַן. "זָכוּר" – לְהוֹצִיא אֶת הַנָּשִׁים: לָהּ לָהּ מֵאִשָּׁה. כְּתִיב הָכָא "וְכָתַב לָהּ" (דברים כד), וּכְתִיב הָתָם "אוֹ חֻפְשָׁה לֹא נִתַּן לָהּ" (ויקרא יט): לֹא נִצְרְכָה כו'. מִיהוּ, לְמִשְׁנָה אַחֲרוֹנָה, הוֹאִיל וּבְיָדֵינוּ לָכוֹף אֶת רַבּוֹ – חַיָּיב, דְּאֵין לוֹ אֶלָּא אָדוֹן אֶחָד: דָּבָר אַחֵר כו'. פְּרָט לְבַעֲלֵי קַבִּין מִ"פְּעָמִים" נַפְקָא, כִּדְאָמְרִינַן לְעֵיל. הִלְכָּךְ: "רְגָלִים" לְמַעוּטֵי מִי שֶׁצָּרִיךְ מִשְׁעֶנֶת אַחֶרֶת לְבַד מֵרַגְלָיו:

תוספות

אן דלמא מכולהו. מי אמרינן דכיון (א) דמקרע דדמי להאי הדר ביה – גם לאינך דחשיב בהדי מקרע הדר ביה, או דלמא מהאי לחודיה:

זכורך להוציא טומטום ואנדרוגינוס. בירושלמי בעי: מה אמר רבי יהודה באנדרוגינוס, דשמעינן ליה *דמתיר דמחללין עליו שבת? נשמענה מן הדא, רבי יוחנן בן דהבאי בשם רבי יהודה אומר: אף הסומא*. ולית בר נש אמר אף אלא דהוה מודה על קדמייתא כו'. ומוקי טעמא דהתם גבי שבת* דריש "זכר", מה תלמוד לומר "ערל" – אפילו מקצת ערל, והכא "כל זכורך" – פרט לטומטום ואנדרוגינוס:

אלא טומטום ספיקא הוא. ואע"ג דאנדרוגינוס נמי ספיקא הוא – [אפ"ה מחייבי] מטעם "מקצת זכורך" כדאמר התלמוד. *אלא טומטום, הואיל ונשים פטורות. והאי אימא אשה הוה – ממילא הוה פטרינן ליה, כי היכי דלא לייתי חולין לעזרה. וא"ת: בנדה פרק "המפלת" (דף כח: ושם) מפקינן "מזכר [עד נקבה תשלחו]" (במדבר ה) [זכר] ודאי, נקבה ודאית, ולא טומטום ואנדרוגינוס. ולא פריך מידי! אומר הר"י: דהתם איכא תרי קראי, ומפיק ליה מייתורא דקרא, אבל הכא ליכא אלא חד קרא, הלכך יש לאוקומא באנדרוגינוס, מטעם דקאמר. ולהכי פריך ליה בבכורות בפ' "על אלו מומין" (דף מב: ושם) בגמרא (ב)דרבי ישמעאל אין לך מום גדול מזה, אנדרגינוס – ספיקא הוא, אילטריך קרא למעוטי ספיקא? וכן בפרק "דם שחיטה" (כריתות כא.) גבי כוי. ובריש פרק בתרא דיומא (דף עד.). דבכל הני ליכא רק מחדא קרא, ובהכי יתכן ההיא דשילהי "הערל" (יבמות דף פא.) קאמר רבי שמעון: אנדרוגינוס זכר מאכיל בתרומה. ואלו בפרק "על אלו מומין" (בכורות דף מב.) אמר רבי שמעון בן יהודה בשם רבי שמעון: הרי הוא אומר "הזכר" – להוציא טומטום ואנדרוגינוס. אלא ודאי התם קרא יתירא "הזכר".(ג) ובפרק קמא דב"מ (דף ז.): "העשירי" ודאי אמר רחמנא, ולא ספק. ולא פריך: אלטריך קרא למעוטי ספק, דכולא קרא יתירא להכי. ובשילהי פ"ק דחולין (דף כב: ושם) גבי תחילת הציהוב שבזה ושבזה שפסול, פריך ליה: אלטריך קרא למעוטי ספיקא מתורים ובני יונה? ממה נפשך, או קטן או גדול הוי וכשר לחדא מינייהו, וקמי שמיא גליא היא, ולא למעוטי רק אחד, וליתכשר גבי אידך, בשם רבי יצחק בן ברוך *נ"ע. ויש להקשות: לייתי על תנאי, ואם הוא אשה – ליהוי נדבה. ואפילו למ"ד נדרים ונדבות אין קריבין ביו"ט – ליקרבו למחר, דשפיר (ד)עדיף אפילו למאן דאמר תשלומין דראשון, כדפי' לעיל (דף ג.)! וי"ל: דמבטל ליה מסמיכה. ואע"ג דסמיכה לא מיעכבא, כדאיתא ביומא (דף ה.) – מכל מקום לכתחילה אין לנו לתקן קרבן כדי לבטלו מסמיכה, דהכי קאמר התלמוד פרק "האשה" בפסחים (דף פט.) גבי ה' שנתערבו פסחיהן ונמצא יבלת באחד מהן, ולא דמי לערל וטמא משלחין קרבנותיהן. וגם לקמן ממעטינן ליה, משום דכל שישנו בביאה ישנו בהבאה ולא משום סמיכה – דהתם גברא בר חיובא, ואריא הוא דרביעא עליה שאינו יכול לסמוך. אבל האי – לאו בר חיובא הוי, דאימא איתתא הוא. אבל הא ק"ל: דתיפשוט מהכא דסמיכה בכל כחו בעינן, דאי באקפויי ידיו – לייתי וליתני, ולסמוך. דהכי פריך לקמן פרק שני (דף טז:)! ואיכא למימר: דבכל ענין ממעט ליה קרא:

לא נצרכה אלא לחציו עבד וחציו בן חורין. ולא תימא דקאי עליה ג"ש ד"לה" "לה" מאשה. וקשה: דעליה כתיב "או חופשה לא ניתן לה" (ה)ומוקי לה רבי עקיבא ב"השולח" (גיטין דף מג:* ושם) ובכריתות (דף יא.) בחציה שפחה וחציה בת חורין! וי"ל: מכל מקום אלד עבדות כתיב כדמוכח קרא "או חופשה לא ניתן לה". אך קשה: הכא משמע בחציו עבד לפי משנה אחרונה חייב דלפי משנה ראשונה קיימא הכא כדאיתא לעיל ריש מכילתין, ואלו בגיטין ריש "השולח" (דף מג:*) מיבעי ליה מי שחציו עבד אם יש לו קנס או לא, "שלשים שקלים יתן לאדניו" אמר רחמנא והאי אדון הוא, ולפי משנה אחרונה קאי, דקאמר התם: מאי לאו לפי משנה אחרונה, ואילו הכא פשיטא לן דאין לו אלא אדון אחד, ויש לדחות: דעד כאן לא מחייבי ליה הכא אלא משום דעומד לכוף את רבו כמאן דשיחרר דמי, אבל התם כיון דמית אגליא מילתא דלא הוה עומד לשחרור. והתם בכריתות (דף יא.) מתרץ הר"י בענין אחר:

כי

עין משפט נר מצוה

טז א מיי' פי"ב מהל' ע"ז הלכה ג:

[שבת קלד:]

[פטור מן הראיה]

[שבת קלו:]

יז ב מיי' שם ופ"ג מהל' חגיגה הל' ב:

יח ג מיי' פ"ב מהלכות חגיגה הלכה ג:

יט ד מיי' שם הל' ב:

כ ה ו ז מיי' שם הלכה א:

[א"נ כצ"ל מהרש"א]

רבינו חננאל

לבוא והניחם כדי לסמוך עניים בשביעית. שוטה פטור מן הראייה: ת"ר איזהו שוטה זה היוצא יחידי בלילה והלן בבית הקברות והמקרע את כסותו רב הונא אמר עד דעבדינהו כולהו ר' יוחנן אמר ואפילו אחד מהן והוא דעבדינהו דרך שטות וקיי"ל כר' יוחנן דתניא איזהו שוטה זה המאבד כל מה שנותנין לו. טומטום ואנדרוגינוס פטורין: ת"ר זכור להוציא הנשים שהן פטורות. זכורך להוציא הנשים שהן פטורות. זכורך להוציא טומטום ואנדרוגינוס כל לרבות הקטנים אתינן לאוקומה בקטן שהגיע לחינוך ונדחה דקטנים שהגיעו לחינוך מדרבנן נינהו וקרא לא אתא [אלא] לכדתניא דתניא אחרים אומרים המקמץ והמצרף נחושת והבורסקי פטורין מן הראייה שנא' כל זכורך כל מי שיכול לעלות עם כל זכורך יצאו אלו שאינן יכולין לעלות עם כל זכורך. נשים ועבדים אוקימנה מי שחציו עבד וחציו בן חורין פטורין במשנה ראשונה היא שנויה סיפא במשנה ראשונה ורישא דקתני לאיתויי מי שחציו עבד וחציו בן חורין חייב [כמשנה אחרונה] ומשנה לא זזה ממקומה כל מצוה שהאשה חייבת עבד חייב בה דגמר לה לה כתיב בשפחה או חופשה לא ניתן לה וכתיב באשה וכתב לה ספר כריתות ונתן. ושאינו יכול לעלות

הגהות הב"ח

(א) תוס' ד"ה או דלמא וכו' דכיון דממקרע: (ב) ד"ה אלא וכו' בגמרא אדרבי ישמעאל דאמר אין לך וכו' הני ליכא רק חדא קרא וכו' דקאמר רבי שמעון: (ג) בא"ד קרא יתירא הזכר קדריש ובפרק קמא דב"מ וכו' שבזה ושבזה שפסול פריך ליה שפיר אילטריך קרא למעוטי ספיקא שאם הביא מתורים ובני יונה נפיק ממה נפשך וכו' גליא היא ולא אתא למעוטי: (ד) בא"ד ליקרבו למחר דשפיר עביד אפילו: (ה) ד"ה לא נצרכה וכו' דמוקי לה רבי עקיבא וכו' אלא משום דכיון דעומד לכוף:

מסורת הש"ס

[תוספ' תרומו' פ"א]

[קדושין לד:]

[ברכות כ: ערובין כז. קדושין כט.]

[ועי' ברכות כה. וברש"י שם ד"ה בזמן וברש"י כתובות עז. ד"ה המקמץ כו' ול"ע]

[בכורות מא: חולין כב:]

[סוכה כח:]

[נ"ל דתניא]

לקמן ז:

שמות כג

שם

[נזיר סא. כריתות ז:]

[קדושין כג. גיטין לט: מא:]

שמות כג

לעיל ג. יבמות קג. ערכין יט:

[נ"ל נ"ע]

[ע"ש דלא נזכר ר' עקיבא]

[ע"ש דמיבעי ליה במעוכב גט שחרור ופשיט הש"ס מחצי עבד ועע דתוס' ערכין ב: ד"ה במשנה ראשונה וכו' העתיקו על נכון]

גליון הש"ס

גמרא הא למה לי קרא. עיין שיטה מקובלת רפ"ב דב"מ ד"ה מלא פירות בשם הרמב"ן:

כא א ב מיי' פ"ב מהלכות חגיגה הלכה א סמג עשין רכו:
כב ג מיי' פ"ז מהל' תרומות הלכה י:

אמְפַנְּקֵי, דִּכְתִיב °"כִּי תָבֹאוּ לֵרָאוֹת פָּנָי מִי בִקֵּשׁ זֹאת מִיֶּדְכֶם רְמֹס חֲצֵרָי". תָּנָא: *בהֶעָרֵל וְהַטָּמֵא פְּטוּרִין מִן הָרְאִיָּה. בִּשְׁלָמָא טָמֵא — דִּכְתִיב: °"וּבָאתָ שָׁמָּה" "וַהֲבֵאתֶם שָׁמָּה", כָּל שֶׁיֶּשְׁנוֹ בְּבִיאָה — יֶשְׁנוֹ בַּהֲבָאָה, וְכָל שֶׁאֵינוֹ בְּבִיאָה — אֵינוֹ בַּהֲבָאָה. אֶלָּא עָרֵל מְנָלַן? הָא מַנִּי — רַבִּי עֲקִיבָא הִיא, דִּמְרַבֵּי (א) לְעָרֵל כְּטָמֵא. *דְּתַנְיָא, ר' עֲקִיבָא אוֹמֵר: °"אִישׁ אִישׁ" — גלְרַבּוֹת אֶת הֶעָרֵל. ת"ר: *טָמֵא פָּטוּר מִן הָרְאִיָּה, דִּכְתִיב: "וּבָאתָ שָׁמָּה" "וַהֲבֵאתֶם שָׁמָּה" כָּל שֶׁיֶּשְׁנוֹ בְּבִיאָה — יֶשְׁנוֹ בַּהֲבָאָה, וְכָל שֶׁאֵינוֹ בְּבִיאָה — אֵינוֹ בַּהֲבָאָה. *רַבִּי יוֹחָנָן בֶּן דַּהֲבַאי אוֹמֵר מִשּׁוּם ר' יְהוּדָה: סוּמָא בְּאַחַת מֵעֵינָיו פָּטוּר מִן הָרְאִיָּה, שֶׁנֶּאֱמַר: "יִרְאֶה" "יֵרָאֶה" — כְּדֶרֶךְ שֶׁבָּא (ב) לִרְאוֹת כָּךְ בָּא לֵירָאוֹת, מַה בָּא לִרְאוֹת בִּשְׁתֵּי עֵינָיו — אַף לֵירָאוֹת בִּשְׁתֵּי עֵינָיו.§ רַב הוּנָא, כִּי מָטֵי לְהַאי קְרָא "יִרְאֶה" "יֵרָאֶה" בָּכֵי, אָמַר: עֶבֶד שֶׁרַבּוֹ מְצַפֶּה לוֹ לִרְאוֹתוֹ יִתְרַחֵק מִמֶּנּוּ? דִּכְתִיב: "כִּי תָבֹאוּ לֵרָאוֹת פָּנָי מִי בִקֵּשׁ זֹאת מִיֶּדְכֶם רְמֹס חֲצֵרָי". רַב הוּנָא כִּי מָטֵי לְהַאי קְרָא בָּכֵי: °"וְזָבַחְתָּ שְׁלָמִים וְאָכַלְתָּ שָּׁם", עֶבֶד שֶׁרַבּוֹ מְצַפֶּה לֶאֱכוֹל עַל שֻׁלְחָנוֹ יִתְרַחֵק מִמֶּנּוּ? דִּכְתִיב: °"לָמָּה לִּי רֹב זִבְחֵיכֶם יֹאמַר ה'". ר' אֶלְעָזָר כִּי מָטֵי לְהַאי קְרָא בָּכֵי: °"וְלֹא יָכְלוּ אֶחָיו לַעֲנוֹת אֹתוֹ כִּי נִבְהֲלוּ מִפָּנָיו". וּמַה תּוֹכָחָה שֶׁל בָּשָׂר וָדָם — כָּךְ, תּוֹכָחָה שֶׁל הַקָּדוֹשׁ בָּרוּךְ הוּא — עַל אַחַת כַּמָּה וְכַמָּה! רַבִּי אֶלְעָזָר כִּי מָטֵי לְהַאי קְרָא בָּכֵי: °"וַיֹּאמֶר שְׁמוּאֵל אֶל שָׁאוּל לָמָּה הִרְגַּזְתַּנִי לְהַעֲלוֹת אוֹתִי". וּמַה שְּׁמוּאֵל הַצַּדִּיק הָיָה מִתְיָירֵא מִן הַדִּין, אָנוּ — עַל אַחַת כַּמָּה וְכַמָּה! שְׁמוּאֵל מַאי הִיא? דִּכְתִיב: °"וַתֹּאמֶר הָאִשָּׁה אֶל שָׁאוּל אֱלֹהִים רָאִיתִי עוֹלִים", "עוֹלִים" — תְּרֵי מַשְׁמַע, חַד — שְׁמוּאֵל, וְאִידָךְ — דַּאֲזַל שְׁמוּאֵל וְאַתְיֵיהּ לְמֹשֶׁה בַּהֲדֵיהּ. אֲמַר לֵיהּ: דִּלְמָא חַס וְשָׁלוֹם לְדִינָא מִתְבָּעֵינָא, קוּם בַּהֲדַאי דְּלֵיכָּא מִילְּתָא דִּכְתַבְתְּ בְּאוֹרַיְיתָא דְּלָא קַיֵּימְתִּיהּ. רַבִּי אַמֵּי כִּי מָטֵי לְהַאי קְרָא בָּכֵי: °"יִתֵּן בֶּעָפָר פִּיהוּ אוּלַי יֵשׁ תִּקְוָה", אֲמַר: כּוּלֵּי הַאי — וְאוּלַי?! רַבִּי אַמֵּי כִּי מָטֵי לְהַאי קְרָא בָּכֵי: °"בַּקְּשׁוּ צֶדֶק בַּקְּשׁוּ עֲנָוָה אוּלַי תִּסָּתְרוּ בְּיוֹם אַף ה'", אֲמַר: כּוּלֵּי הַאי — וְאוּלַי?! רַבִּי אַסִי, כִּי מָטֵי לְהַאי קְרָא בָּכֵי: °"שִׂנְאוּ רָע וְאֶהֱבוּ טוֹב וְהַצִּיגוּ בַשַּׁעַר מִשְׁפָּט אוּלַי יֶחֱנַן ה' [אֱלֹהֵי] צְבָאוֹת", כּוּלֵּי הַאי — וְאוּלַי?! רַב יוֹסֵף כִּי מָטֵי לְהַאי קְרָא בָּכֵי: °"וְיֵשׁ נִסְפֶּה בְּלֹא מִשְׁפָּט" (ג) אֲמַר: מִי אִיכָּא דְּאָזֵיל בְּלָא זִמְנֵיהּ? אִין, כִּי הָא דְּרַב בֵּיבַי בַּר אַבַּיֵי הֲוָה שְׁכִיחַ גַּבֵּיהּ מַלְאַךְ הַמָּוֶת. אֲמַר לֵיהּ לִשְׁלוּחֵיהּ: זִיל אַיְיתִי לִי מִרְיָם מְגַדְּלָא שֵׂיעָר נְשַׁיָּיא. אֲזַל אַיְיתִי לֵיהּ מִרְיָם מְגַדְּלָא דַּרְדְּקֵי. אֲמַר לֵיהּ: אֲנָא מִרְיָם מְגַדְּלָא שֵׂיעָר נְשַׁיָּיא אֲמַרִי לָךְ! אֲמַר לֵיהּ: אִי הָכִי אַהַדְרַהּ! אֲמַר לֵיהּ: הוֹאִיל וְאַיְיתִיתַהּ — לֶיהֱוֵי לְמִנְיָינָא. אֶלָּא הֵיכִי יָכְלַתְּ לָהּ? הֲוַת נְקִיטָא *מְתַאֲרָא בִּידַהּ, וַהֲוַת קָא שָׁגְרָא וּמְחַרְיָא

ישעיה א | דברים טז | ויקרא כב | דברים כז | ישעיה א | בראשית מה | שמואל א כח | שם | איכה ג | צפניה ב | עמוס ה | משלי יג

רש"י

מְפַנְּקֵי. שֶׁאֵין הוֹלְכִין בְּלֹא מִנְעָל, דְּאֵין אָדָם נִכְנָס לְהַר הַבַּיִת בְּמִנְעָלוֹ, דִּכְתִיב: "מִי בִקֵּשׁ זֹאת מִיֶּדְכֶם רְמֹס חֲצֵרָי": פְּטוּרִים מִן הָרְאִיָּה. אֵין חַיָּיבִין לִשְׁלוֹחַ עוֹלוֹת רְאִיּוֹתֵיהֶן עַל יְדֵי שָׁלִיחַ: טָמֵא אֵינוֹ (חַיָּיב) בְּבִיאָה, שֶׁאֵינוֹ יָכוֹל לִיכָּנֵס לַמִּקְדָּשׁ, דִּכְתִיב "(*כִּי מִקְדַּשׁ) ה' טִמֵּא וְנִכְרְתָה" (במדבר יט): עָרֵל. יִשְׂרָאֵל שֶׁמֵּתוּ אֶחָיו מֵחֲמַת מִילָה: הָכִי גָּרְסִינַן: דִּמְרַבֵּי לֵיהּ עָרֵל כְּטָמֵא: "אִישׁ אִישׁ. מִזֶּרַע אַהֲרֹן וְהוּא צָרוּעַ אוֹ זָב": לְרַבּוֹת אֶת הֶעָרֵל. שֶׁהוּא כְּטָמֵא, שֶׁלֹּא יֹאכַל תְּרוּמָה אִם כֹּהֵן הוּא: עֶבֶד. שֶׁהוּא חָבִיב לְרַבּוֹ עַד שֶׁרַבּוֹ מְצַפֶּה וְשׁוֹאֵף מָתַי יִרְאֵהוּ, יִתְרַחֵק מֵעָלָיו?! יִתְרַחֵק מֵעָלָיו. אֵיךְ הִגִּיעַ יוֹם שֶׁנֶּהְפַּךְ לוֹ לְשׂוֹנֵא וְרִחֲקוֹ וְצִוָּהוּ שֶׁלֹּא יִרְאֵהוּ שֶׁנֶּאֱמַר: "כִּי תָבֹאוּ" וגו': תּוֹכָחָה. שֶׁמּוֹכִיחַ פִּשְׁעוֹ בְּפָנָיו: מַאי הִיא. מְנָא לָן דְּמִתְיָירָא: כּוּלֵּי הַאי וְאוּלַי. כָּל הַיִּסּוּרִין הַלָּלוּ יְקַבֵּל, וְעוֹדֶנּוּ בְּסָפֵק אִם תִּהְיֶה לוֹ תִּקְוָה: וְיֵשׁ נִסְפֶּה בְּלֹא מִשְׁפָּט. יֵשׁ כָּלֶה וְאֵין עָוֹן בְּיָדוֹ, וְלֹא הָיָה מִשְׁפָּט לִסְפּוֹת: וּמִי אִיכָּא דְּאָזֵיל כו'. הַתַּלְמוּד קָא בָּעֵי לָהּ: אָמַר לֵיהּ. מַלְאָךְ לִשְׁלוּחוֹ: אַיְיתִי לִי מִרְיָם מְגַדְּלָא נְשַׁיָּיא. הֲרוֹג אֶת מִרְיָם הַמְקַלַּעַת שֵׂיעָר הַנָּשִׁים: הֵיכִי יָכְלַתְּ לָהּ. מֵאַחַר שֶׁלֹּא הִגִּיעַ זְמַנָּהּ: הֲוַת נְקִיטָא מְתַאֲרָא בְּיָדָהּ. הָיְתָה אוֹחֶזֶת בְּיָדָהּ הָאוּד שֶׁל תַּנּוּר, שֶׁקּוֹרִין פרגו"ן: וְקָא

[את משכן] | [יבמות עב:] | שם ע. | [תוספתא פ"א] | לעיל ב. סנהדרין ז: ע"ש ערכין כ: [תוספתא שם ע"ש] | [ועיין תוספות בכורות כז. ד"ה בריש] | [פסחים נו.] | [יבמות ע.]

תוספות

כי תבואו לראות פני. פירש רש"י דנפקא ליה מדכתיב "רמוס חצרי" דמשמע דהולך במנעליו. ותימה הוא: דבפרק "הרואה" (ברכות דף סב:) מפיק ליה מדכתיב "של נעלך"! ויש לומר: דהתם עיקר. אבל הכא ניחא ליה לאתויי ראייה כדכתיב "כי תבאו לראות" וכו':

דכתיב ובאת שמה והבאתם שמה. והא דאמרינן (פסחים דף סב.): ערל וטמא משלחין קרבנותיהן, (ד)דאע"ג דליתנהו בביאה — התם איירי בנדרים ונדבות שאין קבועין זמן בהבאת רגלים, והאי קרא לא משתעי אלא בעולת ראייה, דבעינן ביאה. אך קשה, לרבי שמעון דאמר פרק בתרא דמו"ק (דף טו. ושם): "ויבוא בלא יקריב" (יחזקאל מד) בזמן שהוא ראוי לביאה — יקריב, בזמן שאינו ראוי לביאה — לא יקריב. ופשיט מהתם דמצורע לא ישלח קרבנותיו. וכי לית ליה ההוא דלעיל דערל (ה) וטמא? דמשמע דליכא מאן דפליג! ולא מסתבר לחלק דהתם במצורע לחוד והיא בשאר טמאים — דהאי קרא בסתמא כתיב, משמע דאכל טמאים קאי. וכי תימא: משום דכתיב לעיל מינה "שבעת ימים יספרו לו" (שם) דמשמע בימי סיפורו, דקאי דוקא אמצורע — הא אפסקיה למילתיה "ויבוא בלא אל הקודש אל החצר הפנימית" דדרשינן מיניה: זו עשירית האיפה. ועוד: (ו) התם הוה ליה לאתויי להוא ערל וטמא למיפשט מינה דמשלח שפיר! ונראה בעיני דהתם בקרבנות מצורע מצרעתו איירי, ובשמיני לרפואה כי בעי לאתויי קרבנותיו חזר ונצטרע, הלכך האי קרבן דמחויב — לא מצי מייתי, כיון דלאו בר ביאה הוא. אבל בנדרים ונדבות — מביא שפיר אף מצורע כמו שאר טמאים. והתם הארכתי בדבר לפרש מההיא דערל וטמא משלחין קרבנותיהן, ולא בעינן סמיכה, כמו בההיא דהשולח חטאתו ממדינת הים ד"כל הגט" (גיטין דף כח: ושם) דפריך לה: והא בעי סמיכה! ומוקי לה בקרבן נשים, או בחטאת העוף, דהתם בערל שמתו אחיו מחמת מילה, וטמא כמו מצורע או זב דאין טהרתו תלויה רק ברפואה, ואפשר שלא יתרפא לעולם, והוה ליה מחויב קרבן — הלכך טוב לנו שיביא בלא סמיכה. אבל התם בגיטין — יש לנו להמתין עד שיביא. עוד הארכתי התם בפרק ג' דגיטין (שם):

דמרבה ערל כי טמא. אמר הרב ר' אלחנן, דהא דאיצטריך קרא דלעיל למעוטי ליה טומטום ואנדרוגינוס, ולא למעוטי מספק ערל — התם אליבא דרבנן הוא, דלרבי עקיבא לא צריך. ומיהו אך קשה, אמאי איצטריך מיעוט לערל גבי פסח? תיפוק ליה מטמא! וי"ל: (ז) דהתם ממעטינן ערל שמתו אחיו מחמת מילה דלאו כטמא. ומיהו, זהו דוקא לפרש"י דמפרש התם* *ערל, שמתו אחיו מחמת מילה, יש להעמיד הכי, אבל לפר"ת *דמפרש שדואג מחמת הצער, אבל מתו אחיו מחמת מילה הוי אנוס, יש להקשות לרבי עקיבא דמרבה ערל כי טמא: אמאי איצטריך קרא לערל דפסח? תיפוק ליה מטמא! ויש לומר: דמהתם ידעינן ליה בעלמא כיון דמדמה ערל לטמא בפסח — דרשינן נמי מ"איש איש" לרבות ערל כטמא. אבל ליכא למימר דאי ליכא קרא אלא דערל כטמא הייתי אומר דפסח בא בערלות, דאי הוה רובן ערלים כמו בטומאה, דהא מנא ידעינן לרבות ערל כי טמא — מ"איש איש כי יהיה צרוע או זב", והתם לא כתיב רק טומאת צרעת וזיבות, ואנן אמרינן בריש "אלו דברים" (פסחים דף סו.) דלא דחי רק טומאת מת בלבד. והשתא סוגיא דהכא פליגא ארבא דריש "הערל" (יבמות דף עב:) דקאמר: דלא לישתמיט תנא דמרבה ערל כי טמא, ונוקמא כרבי עקיבא. ופריך ליה מהכא דערל וטמא פטורין מן הראייה, ומשני: שאני התם משום דמאיס. ומשמע דאפילו רבנן מודו. כלומר, לאו משום דמרבה ליה כי טמא, אלא משום דמאיס! ומיהו, י"ל דה"פ: שאני התם משום דמאיס, להכי מרבה ערל כי טמא אליבא דרבי עקיבא, אבל לא שיהא ערל מטמא בנגיעה כטמא, להכי לא תנינהו גבי הדדי:

של הקדוש ברוך הוא על אחת כמה וכמה. שלא יוכל להשיב תשובה מעלייתא להיפטר לגמרי. דמכמה דברים מצי לפטור עצמו קצת, כדאיתא בפרק "הדר" (עירובין דף סה.): יכולני לפטור כל העולם מדין של תפלה:

דליכא מילתא דכתיב באורייתא דלא קיימתיה. לא בעי למימר שיעיד לו שקיים הכל דמנא ידע, והא לא היה בדורו! אלא היה אומר: כך וכך דרשתי ועשיתי מעשה, בוא והעידני שכן למדת גם אתה:

אמר מי איכא איניש דאזיל בלא זימניה. ל"ג אמר. שהרי רב יוסף לא היה שואל כך, שעל זה לא מתרץ לו התלמוד כלום, אלא התלמוד קא פריך ליה:

הוה שכיח גביה מלאך המות. דמספר מה שאירע לו כבר. דהאי עובדא דמרים מגדלא נשייא בבית שני היה, דהיתה אמו של פלוני, כדאיתא בשבת (דף קד: ושם):

מוסיפנא

[עיין תוספות זבחים כב: ושייך למשנה דף טו: ערל]

רבינו חננאל

ברגליו לאתויי מפנקי שנאמר כי תבאו לראות פני. תנא הערל והטמא פטורין מן הראיה אוקימנא לרבי עקיבא דמרבי ליה לערל מן הטמא שנאמר איש איש מזרע אהרן והוא צרוע ודחי ליה לערל מן התרומה כטמא ומפורש ביבמות פרק הערל בתחלתו. טמא פטור [מן הראיה] שנאמר ובאת שמה והבאתם שמה כל שישנו בביאה ישנו בהבאה כו' ר' אלעזר כי מטי להאי קרא בכי לכו נא ונוכחה אמר ומה אחי יוסף לא יכלו לענות אותו בתוכחה כי נבהלו מפניו תוכחה של הקב"ה על אחת כמה וכמה. ועוד היה בוכה ואומר ומה שמואל הצדיק היה מתיירא מן הדין שנאמר ויאמר שמואל אל שאול למה הרגזתני להעלות אותי ולא עוד אלא שביקש מרבינו משה לבא עמו שנאמר ותאמר האשה אל שמואל אלהים ראיתי עולים מן הארץ. עולים תרי משמע וכו'. אנו על אחת כמה וכמה. ר' אמי הוה בכי אמר כתיב יתן בעפר פיהו אולי יש תקוה וכתיב בקשו צדק בקשו ענוה אולי תסתרו ביום אף ה' וכתיב שנאו רע ואהבו טוב והציגו בשער משפט אולי יחנן וגו' כולי האי ואולי

הגהות הב"ח

(א) גמ' ר' עקיבא היא דמרבי ליה לערל: (ב) שם כדרך שבא לראות כך בא לראות מה בא לראות בשתי עיניו אף לראות: (ג) שם בלא משפט ומי איכא כצ"ל ותיבת אמר נמחק: (ד) תום' ד"ה דכתיב וכו' ואע"ג וכו' קבועים להם זמן: (ה) בא"ד דלעיל דערל וטמא משלחין קרבנותיהן דמשמע דליכא: (ו) בא"ד ועוד דהתם הוה ליה לאתויי ההוא דערל וטמא וכו' דמשלחין קרבנותיהן שפיר ונראה: (ז) ד"ה דמרבה וכו' וי"ל דמהתם ידעינן ליה בעלמא דכיון דמדמה ערל לטמא דרשינן נמי מאיש איש לרבות ערל כטמא אבל ליכא למימר דאי ליכא קרא דערל גבי פסח הייתי אומר דפסח בא בערלות אי הוה:

וְקָא מַחַרְיָא תַנּוּרָא. מְכַבֶּדֶת אֶת הַתַּנּוּר: אוֹתִיבְתֵּיהּ אַגַּבָּהּ דְּכַרְעָהּ. הוֹשִׁיבַתּוּ עַל גַּב רַגְלָהּ, וְנִכְוֵית וְהוּרַע מַזָּלָהּ: דָּרְעֵינָא לְהוּ אֲנָא. אֵינִי מוֹסְרָן לְשׁוֹמֵר הַמֵּתִים שֶׁשְּׁמוֹ דּוּמָה, אֶלָּא מִתְגַּלְגְּלִין עִמִּי וְשָׁטִין בָּעוֹלָם עַד שֶׁיִּתְמַלְּאוּ שְׁנוֹתָיו, וְהוּא קָרוּי דּוֹר: דְּמַעֲבִיר בְּמִילֵּיהּ. מַעֲבִיר עַל מִדּוֹתָיו: דְּמָטוּ. נִתְבַּשְּׁלוּ: הָנֵי מִינַּטְרַן. אוֹתָן שֶׁלֹּא בִּישְּׁלוּ כָּל צָרְכָּן אֵין מְמַהֲרוֹת לֵירָקֵב: הַיְינוּ דִּכְתִיב כו'.(א) הַטּוֹבוֹת יְרֵאָה פֶּן יֵרָקְבוּ, אַף הַבַּחוּרִים הַצַּדִּיקִים נֶאֱחָזִין לְמִיתָה, פֶּן יֶחֶטְאוּ: אַדְזוּטָר. בְּעוֹדוֹ בָּחוּר: אִי בָּעֵי הַאי מֵרַבָּנַן. לִהְיוֹת הוֹלֵךְ בְּדֶרֶךְ טוֹבִים הֲוֵי חַיֵּי: מְבַעֵט בְּרַבּוֹתָיו הֲוָה. רַבִּי אֲלֶכְּסַנְדְּרִי הָיָה מַכִּיר בּוֹ שֶׁלֹּא הָיָה מִן הַקְּדוֹשִׁים, וּכְתִיב: "וְטוֹב לֹא יִהְיֶה לָרָשָׁע, וְלֹא יַאֲרִיךְ יָמִים כַּצֵּל, אֲשֶׁר אֵינֶנּוּ יָרֵא מִלִּפְנֵי הָאֱלֹהִים" (קהלת ח), וְתַנְיָא בְּמַסֶּכֶת קִדּוּשִׁין (דף לג:): מוֹרָא זוֹ אֵינִי יוֹדֵעַ מַהוּ, כְּשֶׁהוּא אוֹמֵר "וְהָדַרְתָּ פְּנֵי זָקֵן וְיָרֵאתָ מֵאֱלֹהֶיךָ" (ויקרא יט) הֱוֵי אוֹמֵר: מוֹרָא זוֹ כְּבוֹד חֲכָמִים: קַלּוֹת כַּחֲמוּרוֹת. עוֹשְׁקֵי שְׂכַר שָׂכִיר כִּמְנָאֲפִים וּמְכַשְּׁפִים: וּמַטֵּי גֵר. בְּהַאי קְרָא כְּתִיב: וְלֹא יְרֵאוּנִי. וּבְהָא קְרָא כְּתִיב: כִּי אֶת כָּל מַעֲשֶׂה הָאֱלֹהִים יָבִיא בְמִשְׁפָּט עַל כָּל נֶעְלָם. וְאַף עַל הַנֶּעֱלָמוֹת מִמֶּנּוּ, שֶׁעָשָׂה שׁוֹגֵג, הוּא מְבִיאוֹ בְּמִשְׁפָּט: עַל כֹּל. אֲפִי' דָּבָר מוּעָט בְּמַשְׁמַע: וְנִמְאָס. קָצָה דַּעַת חֲבֵירוֹ בַּדָּבָר: מַאי אִם טוֹב. דְּמַשְׁמַע: אַף עַל הַטּוֹבָה מְבִיאוֹ בְּמִשְׁפָּט: שֶׁאֵינוֹ מְחוּתָּךְ. שֶׁאֵינוֹ מְנוּקָּר מִן הַחֵלֶב וּמִן הַגִּידִין הָאֲסוּרִים: בְּעַרְבֵי שַׁבָּתוֹת. שֶׁמִּתּוֹךְ שֶׁמְּמַהֲרִין לַעֲשׂוֹת צָרְכֵי שַׁבָּת אֵינָן נוֹתְנִין לֵב אִם מְנוּקָּר הוּא: צָרוֹת. סְמוּכוֹת זוֹ לָזוֹ, לְשׁוֹן "וְכִעֲסַתָּה צָרָתָהּ" (שמואל א א), שְׁתֵּי נָשִׁים יַחַד: זִיבּוּרָא וְעַקְרַבָּא. *נָקֵיט הָכִי, מִשּׁוּם דְּאָמְרִינַן בְּמַסֶּכֶת ע"ז בְּפֶרֶק "אֵין מַעֲמִידִין" (דף כח:): חֲמִימֵי לְעַקְרַבָּא וּקְרִירֵי לְזִיבּוּרָא, וְחִילּוּפָא סַכַּנְתָּא. הִלְכָּךְ, הֵיכָא דְּנַכְתֵּיהּ זִיבּוּרָא וְעַקְרַבָּא – נַעֲשׂוֹת צָרוֹת זוֹ לָזוֹ, דְּלֵית לֵיהּ תַּקַּנְתָּא לֹא בִּקְרִירֵי – דְּקָשֶׁה לְעַקְרָב, וְלֹא בַּחֲמִימֵי – דְּקָשֶׁה לְזִיבּוּרָא: זֶה הַמַּמְצִיא מָעוֹת לֶעָנִי בִּשְׁעַת דּוֹחֲקוֹ. אַלְּעֵיל קָאֵי "אִם טוֹב וְאִם רָע", הָרָגִיל לְהַמְצִיא לְדָקָתוֹ לֶעָנִי בִּשְׁעַת דּוֹחֲקוֹ וְלֹא קוֹדֶם שְׁעַת הַדְּחָק, שֶׁיָּכוֹל לְבַקֵּשׁ מְזוֹנוֹתָיו וְלִקְנוֹתָן בִּשְׁעַת הַזּוֹל: לְעַלְלָא. לִקְנוֹת הַתְּבוּאָה*, דְּמִתַּרְגֵּם "וְעַלֶּלֶת אַרְעָא" (ויקרא כה): לְתִלֵיתָא. לְהֶפְסֵד וּלְאִיבּוּד, כָּךְ שָׁמַעְתִּי. וְלִי נִרְאֶה: לִקְנוֹת בִּשְׁעַת הַדְּחָק מָזוֹן שֶׁהוּא תּוֹלֶה בְּסַלּוֹ, כִּדְאָמַר מָר (פסחים דף קיא:): תְּלָא סִילְתָא – תְּלָא מְזוֹנֵי, תַּלְאֵי בְּבֵיתָא קָשֶׁה לַעֲנִיּוּתָא:

תורה אור

וּמְחַרְיָא תַנּוּרָא. שְׁקַלְתָּא וְאַנְחָתָא אַגַּבָּהּ דְּכַרְעָהּ, *קָדְחָא וְאִיתְרַע מַזָּלָהּ, וְאַיְיתִיתָהּ. אֲמַר לֵיהּ רַב בֵּיבָי בַּר אַבַּיֵי: אִית לְכוּ רְשׁוּתָא לְמֶיעֱבַד הָכִי? אֲמַר לֵיהּ: וְלָא כְּתִיב "וְיֵשׁ נִסְפֶּה בְּלֹא מִשְׁפָּט"? אֲמַר לֵיהּ: וְהָכְתִיב "דּוֹר הוֹלֵךְ וְדוֹר בָּא"! אֲמַר: דְּרָעֵינָא לְהוּ אֲנָא עַד דְּמָלוּ לְהוּ לְדָרָא, וַהֲדַר מַשְׁלִימְנָא לֵיהּ לְדוּמָה. אֲמַר לֵיהּ: סוֹף סוֹף, שְׁנֵיהּ מַאי עָבְדַתְּ? אֲמַר: אִי אִיכָּא צוּרְבָא מֵרַבָּנַן דְּמַעֲבִיר בְּמִילֵּיהּ מוֹסִיפְנָא לְהוּ לֵיהּ, וְהָוְיָא חִלּוּפֵיהּ. רַבִּי יוֹחָנָן כִּי מָטֵי לְהַאי קְרָא בָּכֵי: "וַתְּסִיתֵנִי בוֹ לְבַלְּעוֹ חִנָּם" עֶבֶד שֶׁרַבּוֹ מְסִיתִין לוֹ וְנִיסַּת, תַּקָּנָה יֵשׁ לוֹ? רַבִּי יוֹחָנָן כִּי מָטֵי לְהַאי קְרָא בָּכֵי: "הֵן בִּקְדֹשָׁיו לֹא יַאֲמִין", אִי בִּקְדוֹשָׁיו לֹא יַאֲמִין – בְּמַאן יַאֲמִין? יוֹמָא חַד הֲוָה קָא אָזֵיל בְּאוֹרְחָא, חַזְיֵיהּ לְהַהוּא גַּבְרָא דַּהֲוָה מְנַקֵּיט תְּאֵינֵי, שָׁבֵיק הָנָךְ דְּמָטוּ, וְשָׁקֵיל הָנָךְ דְּלָא מָטוּ. אֲמַר לֵיהּ: לָאו הָנֵי מַעַלְיָן טְפֵי? אֲמַר לֵיהּ: הָנֵי לְאוֹרְחָא בָּעֵינַן לְהוּ, הָנֵי – נַטְרָן, וְהָנֵי – לָא נַטְרָן. אֲמַר: הַיְינוּ דִּכְתִיב "הֵן בִּקְדוֹשָׁיו לֹא יַאֲמִין". אִינִי? וְהָא הַהוּא תַּלְמִידָא דַּהֲוָה בְּשִׁיבָבוּתֵיהּ דְּרַבִּי אֲלֶכְּסַנְדְּרִי וְשָׁכֵיב אַדְּזוּטָר, וַאֲמַר: *אִי בָּעֵי הַאי מֵרַבָּנַן הֲוָה חַיֵּי. וְאִם אִיתָא – דִּלְמָא מֵ"הֵן בִּקְדוֹשָׁיו לֹא יַאֲמִין" הֲוָה? הַהוּא מְבַעֵט בְּרַבּוֹתָיו הֲוָה. רַבִּי יוֹחָנָן כִּי מָטֵי לְהַאי קְרָא בָּכֵי: "וְקָרַבְתִּי אֲלֵיכֶם לַמִּשְׁפָּט וְהָיִיתִי עֵד מְמַהֵר בַּמְכַשְּׁפִים וּבַמְנָאֲפִים וּבַנִּשְׁבָּעִים לַשָּׁקֶר וּבְעוֹשְׁקֵי שְׂכַר שָׂכִיר", עֶבֶד שֶׁרַבּוֹ מְקָרְבוֹ לְדוּנוֹ, וּמְמַהֵר לְהָעִידוֹ, תַּקָּנָה יֵשׁ לוֹ? אָמַר רַבִּי יוֹחָנָן בֶּן זַכַּאי: אוֹי לָנוּ שֶׁשָּׁקַל עָלֵינוּ הַכָּתוּב קַלּוֹת כַּחֲמוּרוֹת. אָמַר רֵישׁ לָקִישׁ: כָּל הַמַּטֶּה דִּינוֹ שֶׁל גֵּר – כְּאִילּוּ מַטֶּה דִּינוֹ שֶׁל מַעְלָה, שֶׁנֶּאֱמַר: "וּמַטֵּי גֵר" – וּמַטִּי כְּתִיב. א"ר חֲנִינָא בַּר פַּפָּא: כָּל הָעוֹשֶׂה דָּבָר וּמִתְחָרֵט בּוֹ – מוֹחֲלִין לוֹ מִיָּד, שֶׁנֶּאֱמַר: "וְלֹא יְרֵאוּנִי", הָא יְרֵאוּנִי – מוֹחֲלִין *לָהֶם מִיָּד. רַבִּי יוֹחָנָן כִּי מָטֵי לְהַאי קְרָא בָּכֵי: "כִּי אֶת כָּל מַעֲשֶׂה הָאֱלֹהִים יָבִיא בְמִשְׁפָּט עַל כָּל נֶעְלָם", עֶבֶד שֶׁרַבּוֹ שׁוֹקֵל לוֹ שְׁגָגוֹת כִּזְדוֹנוֹת תַּקָּנָה יֵשׁ לוֹ? מַאי "עַל כָּל נֶעְלָם"? אָמַר רַב: זֶה הַהוֹרֵג כִּינָּה בִּפְנֵי חֲבֵרוֹ וְנִמְאָס בָּהּ. וּשְׁמוּאֵל אָמַר: זֶה הָרָק *בִּפְנֵי חֲבֵירוֹ וְנִמְאָס. מַאי "אִם טוֹב וְאִם רָע"? אָמְרִי דְּבֵי ר' יַנַּאי: זֶה הַנּוֹתֵן צְדָקָה לֶעָנִי בְּפַרְהֶסְיָא. כִּי הָא דְּרַבִּי יַנַּאי חַזְיֵיהּ לְהַהוּא גַּבְרָא דְּקָא יָהֵיב זוּזָא לְעָנִי בְּפַרְהֶסְיָא, אֲמַר לֵיהּ: מוּטָב דְּלָא יְהַבְתְּ לֵיהּ מֵהַשְׁתָּא דִּיהַבְתְּ לֵיהּ וְכַסִּפְתֵּיהּ. דְּבֵי ר' שֵׁילָא אָמְרֵי: זֶה הַנּוֹתֵן צְדָקָה לְאִשָּׁה בְּסֵתֶר, דְּקָא מַיְיתֵי לָהּ לִידֵי חֲשָׁדָא. רָבָא אָמַר: זֶה הַמְשַׁגֵּר לְאִשְׁתּוֹ בָּשָׂר שֶׁאֵינוֹ מְחוּתָּךְ בְּעַרְבֵי שַׁבָּתוֹת. *וְהָא רָבָא *מְשַׁגֵּר! שָׁאנֵי בַּת רַב חִסְדָּא דְּקִים לֵיהּ בְּגַוָּוהּ דִּבְקִיאָה. רַבִּי יוֹחָנָן כִּי מָטֵי לְהַאי קְרָא בָּכֵי: "וְהָיָה כִּי תִמְצֶאןָ אוֹתוֹ רָעוֹת רַבּוֹת וְצָרוֹת" עֶבֶד שֶׁרַבּוֹ מַמְצִיא לוֹ רָעוֹת וְצָרוֹת תַּקָּנָה יֵשׁ לוֹ? מַאי "רָעוֹת וְצָרוֹת"? אָמַר רַב: רָעוֹת שֶׁנַּעֲשׂוֹת צָרוֹת זוֹ לָזוֹ, כְּגוֹן זִיבּוּרָא וְעַקְרַבָּא. וּשְׁמוּאֵל אָמַר: זֶה הַמַּמְצִיא לוֹ מָעוֹת לֶעָנִי בִּשְׁעַת דּוֹחֲקוֹ. אָמַר רָבָא: הַיְינוּ דְּאָמְרִי אֱינָשֵׁי: "זוּזָא לְעַלְלָא לָא שְׁכִיחָא, לְתִלֵיתָא – שְׁכִיחַ". "וְחָרָה אַפִּי בוֹ בַיּוֹם הַהוּא וַעֲזַבְתִּים וְהִסְתַּרְתִּי פָנַי מֵהֶם", אָמַר רַב בַּרְדְּלָא בַּר טַבְיוּמֵי אָמַר רַב: כָּל שֶׁאֵינוֹ בְּהֶסְתֵּר פָּנִים – אֵינוֹ מֵהֶם, כָּל שֶׁאֵינוֹ בְּ"וְהָיָה לֶאֱכוֹל" אֵינוֹ

מוסיפנא לו והוה חלופיה. יש להקשות: לרבי עקיבא דאית ליה בשילהי "החולץ" (יבמות דף נ. ושם): משלו הוסיפו לו לחזקיהו, ולית ליה זכה מוסיפין לו, הא משמע הכא דמוסיפין לו! צ"ע:

מבעט ברבותיו הוה. וכן איכא למימר בההיא דפ"ק דשבת, (דף יג.) באחד שמת והיתה אשתו מולכת תפיליו בבית המדרש. אמרה: כתיב "כי היא חייך ואורך ימיך", בעלי שקרא הרבה ושנה הרבה היכי מת בחצי ימיו! ולא השיבו לה דבר, ולא היו אומרים מהני הוה ד"בקדושיו לא יאמין". *אי נמי: לא היה תשובה נלחת:

הא יראוני מוחלין. גבי עושק שכר שכיר כתיב, דהוה ליה לא תעשה. ופליגא[א] דרבי ישמעאל בפרק בתרא דיומא (דף פו.), דאמר: תשובה תולה ויוה"כ מכפר. ואיכא ברייתא אחרת דאמר: על עשה ולא תעשה תשובה מכפרת. (ב)ועוד יש לחלק בין עניני תשובה: יש שב ומוחלין לו מיד, ויש שב דמוחלין לו אבל לא מחילה גמורה ועדיין יש עונש, ואותו עונש תולין. והא דאמרינן בשבועות (דף יב: ושם): העובר על מצות עשה ונתחרט לא זז משם עד שמוחלין לו – היינו מחילה גמורה, ואם שב בכל לבו ע"י יסורין – יתכפרו לו עונותיו:

שנעשות צרות זו לזו כגון זיבורא ועקרבא. פר"ת: רפואה לנשיכה זו קשה לנשיכה זו. וכן אמרינן ריש פרק ב' דע"ז (דף כח: ושם): חמימי לעקרבא קרירי לזיבורא:

זה הממציא מעות לעני בשעת דוחקו. פרש"י דקאי אדלעיל, אם טוב ואם רע, שממתין לו עד שעת היוקר ונמלא קונה ביוקר. לתליתא – לקנות פת לפי שעה, כמו שקונהו בסלו, כדאמרינן תלא לסילתי תלא למזוניה. וקשיא לר"ת: חדא, למה *נקט כולי האי ואפסקיה באידך קרא "והיה כי תמצאן אותו רעות רבות וצרות"! ועוד: דאמרינן המלוה לעני בשעת דוחקו – עליו נאמר "אז תקרא וה' יענה" (ישעיה נח) בפרק "הבא על יבמתו" (יבמות דף סג. ושם)! מיהו, התם מחלק הריב"ן בין מלוה לממציא. ועוד: דנקט התלמוד מילתא דלא שכיח לתלות הלחם, דאמר ב"ערבי פסחים" (דף קיא: ושם) תלאי בביתא – קשי לעניותא! ומפרש ר"ת: צרות רבות ורעות – זהו הממציא מעות לעני בשעת דוחקו, כגון שתפסו המושל ובא זה ואמר לו שילוה לו מעות על קרקעותיו. ואם לא היה זה בא – המושל היה מיקל בפדיונו, לפי שהוא דחוק ועני. זוזי לעללתא לא שכיח, אם היה רוצה לקנות תבואה להאכילו לביתו – אין (ג) מוציאין לו מעות, לתליתא. כמו תלא וזבין (ב"ב דף מז:), כשדוחקין אותו למכור משלו, לתלותו כדי שיפדה עצמו. [וע"ע תוס' סנהדרין דף עו: ד"ה "והמלוה"]:

רבינו חננאל

יש נספה בלא משפט מעשה דמרים מגדלא נשיא ומרים [מגדלא] דרדקי דאתחלף ליה לשליחא ואייתי מרים מגדלא שער נשיא ויש מי שאומר כענין חלום ראה דברים הללו. ולא עוד אלא רב ביבי בן אביי היה מתעסק בראיית השדים לפיכך יש לומר כדרך הזה ראה ואין סומכין עליו ופתרון יש נספה בלא וגו' כגון אדם שהרג חבירו. ותסיתני בו. אתה מעלה בדעתך כיון שאתה בא בדבריך הללו בעקיפין אתה מדמה להסית ואינך יכול להסית אלא (ברבוי מור) מיכן שהשטן של איוב אדם היה. הן בקדושיו לא יאמין כלומר אינו מאמין להם לחיות הרבה שמא בזקנותם יטו מן הדרך הטובה [וקשיא לי דהא אמרינן ביומא כיון שאדם עבר שלשים וששה שנה ולא חטא שוב אינו חוטא] וההוא תלמיד דהוה בשיבבותיה דר' יוחנן ושכיב זוטר. ואמר ר' יוחנן אי בעי להוטובי ארחתיה דלא לבעוט ברבותיו היה חיי. ר' יוחנן הוה בכי אמר כתיב וקרבתי אתכם למשפט והייתי עד ממהר וגו' עבד שרבו מקרבו לדין וממהר להעידו כלום יש בו תקנה. אריב"ז אוי לנו ששקל הקלות עושק שכר שכיר וכיוצא בו הקישו למנאף ולמכשף ר"ל אמר ומטה גר ומטי גר כתיב כלומר כאלו מטה דין של מעלה וכל העושה דבר ומתחרט בו מוחלין לו שנאמר ולא יראוני הא יראוני אני מוחל להם. כי את כל מעשה האלהים יביא במשפט על כל נעלם. היה ר' יוחנן אומר עבד שרבו שוקל שגגות כזדונות תקנה יש לו. על כל נעלם זה שהורג כינה לפני חבירו ונמאס אם טוב ואם רע כלומר אפילו רצה לעשות טוב ועלה בידו רע כגון שנתן צדקה לעני בפרהסיא שנמצא מביישו ר' שילא אמר הנותן צדקה לאשה בסתר ומייתי לה חשדא שמשיאה שם רע רבא אמר זה המשגר לאשתו בשר בע"ש שאינו מחותך אלא אי קים ליה בגווא ובהימנותא *) כרבא בר רב חסדא: והיה כי תמצאן אותו רעות רבות וצרות. אמר רב רעות שנעשות צרות זו לזו כגון זיבורא ועקרבא כגון שעקצו זיבורא ועקרב ביחד לאדם מי שעקצו עקרב [אינו] רוצה דברים קרים נמצא המועיל לאחד מזיק לאחר. שמואל אמר זה הממציא מעות לעני בשעה שהנוגשים עליו ומלוה אותו והנוגשים באין ולוקחין אותו הממון שהלוהו וכי מסתלקי והוא בא ונושה בו בכל יום היינו דאמרי אינשי זוזא לעללא לא שכיח לתוליתא שכיח. פי' זוזא לקנות בו תבואה אינו מצוי ולמי שתולין אותו הנוגשים מצוי. כתיב והסתרתי פני מהם והיה לאכול. אמר רב כל שאין בו והסתרתי פני מהם כלומר שהתפלל **) ואין נענה אין בו והיה לאכול כלומר שמענישין אותו העובדי

*) נראה דל"ל כמו בת רב חסדא אשתו של רבא. **) נראה של"ל ואינו נענה אינו מישראל כל שאין בו והיה לאכול וכו'.

[פי' נשרפה רגלה. ערוך]

הגהות מהר"ב רנשבורג

א] תוס' ד"ה הא ירלאוני כו' ופליגא דר' ישמעאל. נ"ב עי' בסוף ספר מים חיים להפר"ח דף מ"ד ע"ב ד"ה נתקשיתי וכו' וד"ה אמר וכו':

[כתובות קיא.]

[כל זה הדיבור אינו מפרש"י ושייך לתוספות וכ"ה בע"י]

[נ"ל לו וכ"א בילקוט ובע"י]

[ד"ה רבה פ"י]

נ"ל תבואה הארץ ת"א עללת לארעא (ויקרא כג)

[אינו]

דברים לא

הגהות הב"ח

(א) רש"י ד"ה היינו דכתיב כו' כי היכי דבתאנים הטובות ירא: (ב) תוס' ד"ה הא ירלאוני וכו' ועוד יש לחלק. נ"ב כלומר דהשתא לא קאמר הכא הא ירלאוני מוחלין מחילה גמורה אלא כשנתחרט ועדיין לא שב בכל לבו תולין והיינו דקאמר תשובה תולה והא דקאמר בשבועות דף י"ב דבעובר ונתחרט לא זז משם עד שמוחלין לו ומשמע [מחילה גמורה] היינו דוקא במצות עשה והכא ברייתא דאמר על עשה ול"ת תשובה מכפרת מיירי בשב בכל לבו ע"י יסורין שעשה בגופו אז יתכפרו לו לגמרי [והשאר חסר]: (ג) ד"ה זה הממציא וכו' לביתו אין ממציאין לו וכו' כמו תלא וזבין וכו' כדי שיפדה עצמו ממציאין לו מעות הס"ד:

גליון הש"ס

תוס' ד"ה הא ירלאוני וכו' דהוה ליה ל"ת. עיין תשובת פנים מאירות ח"א סימן כ"ו ובספר מים חיים להפר"ח בתשובה האחרונה:

כג א מיי' פ"ה מהל' דעות הלכה ד סמג לאוין פא טוש"ע א"ח סימן רמ סעיף ט [ובאה"ע סימן כה סעיף ב]:

אינו מהם. אמרו ליה רבנן לרבא: מר לא בהסתר פנים איתיה, ולא ב"והיה לאכול" איתיה! אמר להו: מי ידעיתו כמה משדרנא בצנעא בי שבור מלכא? אפי' הכי יהבו ביה רבנן עינייהו. אדהכי שדור דבי שבור מלכא וגרבוהו. אמר, היינו דתניא, אמר רבן שמעון בן גמליאל: *כל מקום שנתנו חכמים עיניהם — או מיתה או עוני. °"ואנכי הסתר אסתיר פני ביום ההוא", אמר *רבא, אמר הקדוש ברוך הוא: אף על פי שהסתרתי פני מהם — בחלום אדבר בו. רב יוסף אמר: ידו נטויה עלינו, שנאמר: °"ובצל ידי כסיתיך". ר' יהושע בן חנניה הוה קאי בי קיסר, אחוי ליה ההוא מינא: עמא דאהדרינהו מריה לאפיה מיניה. אחוי ליה: ידו נטויה עלינו. אמר ליה קיסר לר' יהושע: מאי אחוי לך? עמא דאהדרינהו מריה לאפיה מיניה, ואנא מחוינא ליה: ידו נטויה עלינו. אמרו ליה להוא מינא: מאי אחויית ליה? עמא דאהדרינהו מריה(א) מיניה. ומאי אחוי לך? לא ידענא. אמרו: גברא דלא ידע מאי *מחוו ליה, במחוג יחוי קמי מלכא?! אפקוהו וקטלוהו. כי קא ניחא נפשיה דרבי יהושע בן חנניה אמרו ליה רבנן: מאי תיהוי עלן ממנאי? אמר להם: °"אבדה עצה מבנים נסרחה חכמתם". כיון שאבדה עצה מבנים — נסרחה חכמתן של אומות העולם. ואי בעית אימא מהכא: °"ויאמר נסעה ונלכה ואלכה לנגדך". רבי אילא הוה סליק בדרגא דבי רבה בר שילא, שמעיה לינוקא דהוה קא קרי: °"כי הנה יוצר הרים ובורא רוח ומגיד לאדם מה שיחו". אמר: עבד שרבו מגיד לו מה שיחו, תקנה יש לו?! מאי "מה שיחו"? אמר רב: אפילו *שיחה יתירה שבין איש לאשתו מגידים לו לאדם בשעת מיתה. איני? והא *רב כהנא הוה גני תותי פורייה דרב, ושמעיה דסח וצחק ועשה צרכיו, אמר: דמי פומיה דרב כמאן דלא טעים ליה תבשילא, אמר ליה: כהנא, פוק, לאו אורח ארעא! לא קשיא; כאן — דצריך לרצויה, הא — דלא צריך לרצויה. °"ואם לא תשמעוה במסתרים תבכה נפשי מפני גוה" אמר רב שמואל בר איניא משמיה דרב: מקום יש לו להקב"ה ומסתרים שמו. מאי "מפני גוה"? אמר רב שמואל בר יצחק: מפני גאוותן של ישראל שניטלה מהם ונתנה לגוים. ר' שמואל בר נחמני אמר: מפני גאוותה של מלכות שמים (ב). ומי איכא בכיה קמיה הקדוש ברוך הוא? והאמר רב פפא: אין עציבות לפני הקדוש ברוך הוא, שנאמר: °"הוד והדר לפניו עוז וחדוה במקומו"! לא קשיא: א) הא — בבתי גואי, הא — בבתי בראי. ובבתי בראי לא? והא כתיב: °"ויקרא אדני ה' צבאות ביום ההוא לבכי ולמספד ולקרחה ולחגור שק"! — שאני חרבן בית המקדש, דאפילו מלאכי שלום בכו, שנאמר: °"הן אראלם צעקו חוצה מלאכי שלום מר יבכיון". § °"ודמע תדמע ותרד עיני דמעה כי נשבה עדר ה'" אמר ר' אלעזר: שלש דמעות הללו למה? אחת — על מקדש ראשון, ואחת — על מקדש שני, ואחת — על ישראל שגלו ממקומן. ואיכא דאמרי: אחת על ביטול תורה. בשלמא למאן דאמר על ישראל שגלו — היינו דכתיב: "כי נשבה עדר ה'". אלא למאן דאמר על ביטול תורה, מאי "כי נשבה עדר ה'"! כיון שגלו ישראל ממקומן — אין לך ביטול תורה גדול מזה. תנו רבנן: שלשה הקדוש ברוך הוא בוכה עליהן בכל יום: על שאפשר לעסוק בתורה ואינו עוסק, ועל שאי אפשר לעסוק בתורה ועוסק, ועל פרנס המתגאה על הצבור. רבי הוה נקיט ספר קינות וקא קרי בגויה. כי מטא להאי פסוקא: °"השליך משמים ארץ" — נפל מן ידיה, אמר: מאיגרא רם לבירא עמיקתא. רבי ורבי חייא הוו שקלי ואזלי באורחא, כי מטו להוא מתא אמרי: איכא צורבא מרבנן הכא, נזיל וניקביל אפיה. אמרי: איכא צורבא מרבנן הכא, ומאור עינים הוא. אמר ליה ר' חייא לרבי: תיב את, לא תזלזל בנשיאותך, איזיל אנא ואקביל אפיה. תקפיה ואזל בהדיה. כי הוו מיפטרי מיניה. אמר להו: אתם הקבלתם פנים הנראים ואינן רואין — תזכו להקביל פנים הרואים ואינן נראין, אמר ליה: איכו השתא מנעתן מהאי בירכתא. אמרו ליה: ממאן שמיעא לך? מפרקיה דרבי יעקב שמיע לי. דרבי יעקב איש כפר חיטייא הוה מקביל אפיה דרביה כל יומא, כי קש אמר ליה: לא נצטער מר, דלא יכיל מר. אמר ליה: מי זוטר מאי דכתיב בהו ברבנן °"ויחי עוד לנצח לא יראה השחת כי יראה חכמים ימותו". ומה הרואה חכמים במיתתן יחיה, בחייהן — על אחת כמה וכמה! רב אידי אבוה דרבי יעקב(ג) בר אידי הוה רגיל דהוה אזיל תלתא ירחי באורחא וחד יומא בבי רב. והוו קרו ליה רבנן "בר בי רב דחד יומא". חלש דעתיה. קרי אנפשיה °"שחוק לרעהו אהיה וגו'" אמר ליה ר' יוחנן: במטותא מינך לא תעניש להו רבנן. נפק ר' יוחנן לבי מדרשא ודרש: °"ואותי יום יום ידרשון ודעת דרכי יחפצון", וכי ביום דורשין אותו ובלילה אין דורשין אותו? אלא לומר לך: כל העוסק בתורה אפי' יום אחד בשנה — מעלה עליו הכתוב ג) כאילו עסק כל השנה כולה. וכן במדת פורענות, דכתיב: °"במספר הימים אשר תרתם את הארץ" וכי ארבעים שנה חטאו? והלא ארבעים יום חטאו! אלא לומר לך: כל העובר עבירה אפי' יום אחד בשנה — מעלה עליו הכתוב כאילו עבר כל השנה כולה. § "אי זהו קטן, כל שאינו יכול לרכוב על כתפו של אביו". § מתקיף לה רבי זירא:

עד

(מראי מקומות בגליון: דברים לא; ישעיה נא; ירמיה מט; בראשית לג; עמוס ד; [ברכות סב.]; ירמיה יג; דה"א טז; ישעיה כב; שם לג; ירמיה יג; איכה ב; תהלים מט; איוב יב; ישעיה נח; במדבר יד; [ברכות מו:]; מו"ק יז: סוטה מו: נדרים ז: ע"ש; [יתכן להיות רבה])

הטעיקר חסר מן הספר ובע"י מפני קא דייק וכ"ה שם אע"פ שהסתרתי פני מהם כדכתיב ודבר ה' אל משה פנים וגו' אותן הפנים אסתיר אבל בחלום אדבר בו ע"כ מחילופי גרס'

רש"י

אינו מהן. מזרע ישראל, דכתיב: "והסתרתי פני מהם" (דברים לא), שצועק מצרות הבאות עליו, ואינו נענה שלא יצוהו: והיה לאכול. שהגוים שוללין ממונו: וגרבוהו. שללוהו: בחלום אדבר בו. *"ביום ההוא" קא דייק: ביום ולא בלילה, שמראין לו חלום כדי שיתפלל על הדבר: ידו נטויה. להגן עליו: אפיקורסים. שאינם מאמינים לדברי רז"ל, כגון צדוקים: אחוי ליה. על ידי סימן, רמז לו: החזיר פניו: במחוג. ברמז: נסרחה חכמתם. באדום כתיב: "האין עוד חכמה בתימן, אבדה עצה מבנים" — מישראל: לנגדך. בשוה: שיחה יתירה. דברי שחוק שלפני תשמיש: כדלא טעים תבשילא. שרעב לאכול. כלומר, מתאוה לתשמיש: בבתי גואי. היכא, דכתיב: "במסתרים": הכי גרסינן: ובבתי בראי ליכא? והכתיב ויקרא. וכל קריאה השמעת קול היא: מאיגרא רם לבירא עמיקתא. כמה גדולה נפילה זו! אין לך גבוה ובור עמוק כמשמים לארץ: תקפיה. רבי לר' חייא, ואזיל רבי בהדיה: כי הוו מיפטרי מקמיה. שנטלו ממנו רשות: איכו השתא. אם לא באתי עמך, והאמנתי לך — מנעתני מברכה זו: מנא לך. שכל כך גדולה הקבלת פנים: כדקש. כשהזקין(ג) רבי יעקב: היה רגיל כו'. מהלך שלשה חדשים היה מביתו לבית המדרש, ונוסע מביתו אחר הפסח ולומד יום אחד, וחוזר לביתו לשמח את אשתו בחג הסוכות:

תוספות

שדור בי שבור מלכא וגרבוהו. אומר הר"י דהיינו ההוא דבפרק בתרא דברכות (דף נו.), גבי פשריה דבר הדיא שפתר לו שתמות אשתו ויאבד כל אשר לו מאת המלך:

הן אראלם צעקו חוצה. פשטיה דקרא בישעיה כתיב על המזבח, וכתיב "הוי אריאל" (ישעיה כט):

ויחי עוד לנצח לא יראה השחת. פשטיה דקרא בתמיה הוא: וכי הרשע לא ימות כמו שהחכמים ימותו? דמתייבא

רבינו חננאל

הגוים ואוכלין ממונו אינו מישראל אמרו ליה לרבא והא מר ליתא בוהיה לאכול ומתפלל ונענה. אמר להן לא ידעיתהו כמה משדרנא בצנעא לבי שבור מלכא ואפ"ה לא איפרק דאמור רבנן כ"מ שנתנו חכמים עיניהם או מיתה או עוני. שדרוה ליה שבור מלכא וגרבוה לרבא אמר רבה אע"ג דכתיב והסתרתי פני מהם אמר רחמנא בחלום אדבר בו. רב יוסף אמר ידו נטויה עלינו ובצל ידו אנו סכוכים כו' ענינא כי נח נפשיה דר' יהושע בן חנניא אמרו ליה מה תהא עלן ממינאי כלומר אין אדם בינינו שיש בו כח להשיבם כמותו אמר להם אבדה עצה מבנים נסרחה חכמת האומות: כי הנה יוצר הרים ובורא רוח ומגיד לאדם מה שיחו. אמר רב אפילו שיחה קלה שבין איש לאשתו מגידין לאדם בשעת מיתתו כלומר אין לאדם להרבות שיחה אפילו עם אשתו אלא אם צריך לארצויה כגון שהיא כעוסה ובא לרצותה: ואם לא תשמעוה במסתרים תבכה נפשי מקום שיש למעלה ומסתרים שמו שבוכים שם המלאכים כדכתיב מלאכי שלום מר יבכיון ואע"פ שיש מפורש מלאכי שלום. השלוחים ששלח המלך לעשות שלום לא קבלו מהם וחזרו בוכים במר נפש: מפני גוה מפני גאותן של ישראל שניטלה מהן ונתנה לגוים. ומקשה ומי איכא בכיה קמיה דקב"ה והא כתיב עוז וחדוה במקומו ופרקינן כי ליכא בכיה בבתי גואי ומקום הנקרא מסתרים בבתי בראי הוא. איני ויקרא ה' אלהים צבאות ביום ההוא לבכי ולמספד וגו' הנה הקב"ה קראו לבכי. ופרקינן שאני חורבן ביהמ"ק שאפילו מלאכי שלום בכו שנאמר הן אראלם צעקו חוצה מלאכי שלום מר יבכיון פי' ויקרא ה' אלהים צבאות וגו' קרא אותו היום כלומר קבעו יום בכיה ומספד לדורות. כתיב ודמע תדמע ותרד עיני דמעה. ג' דמעות הללו אחת למקדש ראשון ואחת למקדש שני ואחת כי נשבה עדר ה' דכיון שגלו אין לך ביטול תורה מזה: תנו רבנן שלשה הקב"ה בוכה עליהן בכל יום. פי' אומר הקב"ה ראוי לבכות על אלו בכל יום על מי שאפשר לו לעסוק בתורה [ואינו עוסק ועל שאי אפשר לעסוק בתורה ועוסק] ועל פרנס המתגאה על הצבור בחנם. ר' ור' חייא אקבילו אפיה חד סגי נהורא. אמר להו אתם הקבלתם פנים הנראים ואינם רואים תזכו להקביל פני שכינה שרואין ואינן נראין. הרואה חכמים במיתתם כתיב ויחי עוד לנצח לא יראה השחת כי יראה חכמים ימותו השתא ומה הרואה חכמים במיתתן יחיה בחייהם על אחת כמה וכמה. דרש ר' יוחנן כתיב ואותי יום יום ידרשון וכי ביום דורשין ובלילה אין דורשין אלא לומר לך כל העוסק בתורה אפילו יום אחד בשנה לשמה מעלה עליו הכתוב כאילו עסק כל השנה וכן במדת פורענות כתיב במספר הימים אשר תרתם את הארץ ארבעים יום יום לשנה וכי שנה חטאו והלא לא חטאו אלא ארבעים יום אלא לומר לך כל העובר עבירה אפילו יום אחד בשנה מעלה עליו כאילו עבר כל השנה כולה. איזהו (חייב) [קטן] שאינו חייב בראיה

בה"א

א) [לקמן יג.] ב) [עיין מ"ש בס"ד פסחים מג: על גליון בשם רש"ק בכריתות כה:] ג) [עי' תוספות סוטה יא. ד"ה מריס]

הגהות הב"ח (א) גמרא מריה לאפיה מיניה ומאי אחוי לך: (ב) שם של מלכות שמים שנטלה ומי איכא: (ג) רש"י ד"ה כדקש כשהזקין הס"ד ואח"כ מה"ד רב אידי אבוה דרבי יעקב היה רגיל:

תורה אור

עַד הָכָא מַאן אַתְיֵיהּ? אֲמַר לֵיהּ אַבַּיֵי: עַד הָכָא, (א) [א]דְּמִיחַיְּיבָא אִימֵּיהּ בְּשִׂמְחָה — אַיְיתְיֵיהּ אִימֵּיהּ. מִכָּאן וְאֵילָךְ, אִם יָכוֹל לַעֲלוֹת וְלֶאֱחוֹז בְּיָדוֹ שֶׁל אָבִיו מִירוּשָׁלַיִם לְהַר הַבַּיִת — חַיָּיב, וְאִי לָא — פָּטוּר. הֵשִׁיב רַבִּי תַּחַת בֵּית הִלֵּל: לְדִבְרֵי בֵּית שַׁמַּאי °"וְחַנָּה לֹא עָלָתָה כִּי אָמְרָה לְאִישָׁהּ עַד יִגָּמֵל הַנַּעַר וַהֲבִיאוֹתִיו", וְהָא שְׁמוּאֵל דְּיָכוֹל לִרְכּוֹב עַל כְּתֵיפוֹ שֶׁל אָבִיו הֲוָה! אֲמַר לֵיהּ *אֲבוּהּ: וּלְטַעֲמִיךְ, תִּיקְשֵׁי לָךְ חַנָּה גּוּפַהּ, מִי לָא מִיחַיְּיבָא בְּשִׂמְחָה? אֶלָּא, חַנָּה מִפַּנְקוּתָא יְתֵירְתָא חַזְיָיא בֵּיהּ בִּשְׁמוּאֵל, וְחָשְׁשָׁא בֵּיהּ בִּשְׁמוּאֵל לְחוּלְשָׁא דְּאוֹרְחָא. בָּעֵי רַבִּי שִׁמְעוֹן*: קָטָן חִיגֵּר לְדִבְרֵי בֵּית שַׁמַּאי וְסוּמָא לְדִבְרֵי שְׁנֵיהֶם, מַהוּ? הֵיכִי דָּמֵי! אִילֵּימָא בְּחִיגֵּר שֶׁאֵינוֹ יָכוֹל לְהִתְפַּשֵּׁט, וְסוּמָא שֶׁאֵינוֹ יָכוֹל לְהִתְפַּתֵּחַ, הַשְׁתָּא גָּדוֹל פָּטוּר, קָטָן מִיבַּעְיָא?! לָא צְרִיכָא, בְּחִיגֵּר שֶׁיָּכוֹל לְהִתְפַּשֵּׁט, וְסוּמָא שֶׁיָּכוֹל לְהִתְפַּתֵּחַ, מַאי? אָמַר אַבַּיֵי: [ב]כָּל הֵיכָא דְּגָדוֹל מִיחַיַּיב מִדְּאוֹרַיְיתָא — קָטָן נַמִי מְחַנְּכִינַן לֵיהּ מִדְּרַבָּנַן, כָּל הֵיכָא דְּגָדוֹל פָּטוּר מִדְּאוֹרַיְיתָא — מִדְּרַבָּנַן (ב) קָטָן נַמִי פָּטוּר. § "בֵּית שַׁמַּאי אוֹמְרִים הָרְאִיָּה שְׁתֵּי כֶסֶף כו'". § ת"ר, בֵּית שַׁמַּאי אוֹמְרִים: הָרְאִיָּה שְׁתֵּי כֶסֶף, וְהַחֲגִיגָה מָעָה כֶּסֶף. שֶׁהָרְאִיָּה עוֹלָה כּוּלָּהּ לַגָּבוֹהַּ, מַה שֶּׁאֵין כֵּן בַּחֲגִיגָה. וְעוֹד: מָצִינוּ בָּעֲצֶרֶת, שֶׁרִיבָּה בָּהֶן הַכָּתוּב בְּעוֹלוֹת יוֹתֵר מִבִּשְׁלָמִים. וּבֵית הִלֵּל אוֹמְרִים: הָרְאִיָּה מָעָה כֶסֶף וַחֲגִיגָה שְׁתֵּי כֶסֶף. שֶׁחֲגִיגָה יֶשְׁנָהּ לִפְנֵי הַדִּיבּוּר, מַה שֶּׁאֵין כֵּן בָּרְאִיָּה. וְעוֹד: מָצִינוּ בַּנְּשִׂיאִים שֶׁרִיבָּה בָּהֶן הַכָּתוּב בִּשְׁלָמִים יוֹתֵר מִבְּעוֹלוֹת. וּבֵית הִלֵּל, מַאי טַעְמָא לָא אָמְרִי כְּבֵית שַׁמַּאי? דְּקָא אָמְרַתְּ רְאִיָּה עֲדִיפָא, דְּעוֹלָה כּוּלָּהּ לַגָּבוֹהַּ — אַדְּרַבָּה, חֲגִיגָה עֲדִיפָא, דְּאִית בָּהּ שְׁתֵּי אֲכִילוֹת. וּדְקָא אָמְרַתְּ נֵילַף מֵעֲצֶרֶת — דָּנִין קָרְבַּן יָחִיד מִקָּרְבַּן יָחִיד וְאֵין דָּנִין קָרְבַּן יָחִיד מִקָּרְבַּן צִבּוּר. וּבֵית שַׁמַּאי, מ"ט לָא אָמְרִי כְּבֵית הִלֵּל? דְּקָאָמְרַתְּ חֲגִיגָה עֲדִיפָא דְּיֶשְׁנָהּ לִפְנֵי הַדִּיבּוּר — רְאִיָּה נַמִי יֶשְׁנָהּ לִפְנֵי הַדִּיבּוּר. וּדְקָאָמְרַתְּ נֵילַף מִנְּשִׂיאִים — דָּנִין דָּבָר הַנּוֹהֵג לְדוֹרוֹת מִדָּבָר הַנּוֹהֵג לְדוֹרוֹת, וְאֵין דָּנִין דָּבָר הַנּוֹהֵג לְדוֹרוֹת מִדָּבָר שֶׁאֵינוֹ נוֹהֵג לְדוֹרוֹת. וּבֵית הִלֵּל, מַאי שְׁנָא חֲגִיגָה דְּיֶשְׁנָהּ לִפְנֵי הַדִּיבּוּר, דִּכְתִיב: °"וַיִּזְבְּחוּ זְבָחִים שְׁלָמִים" — רְאִיָּה נַמִי, הָכְתִיב: °"וַיַּעֲלוּ עוֹלוֹת"! קָסָבְרִי בֵּית הִלֵּל: *עוֹלָה שֶׁהִקְרִיבוּ יִשְׂרָאֵל בַּמִּדְבָּר עוֹלַת תָּמִיד הֲוַאי. וּבֵית שַׁמַּאי סָבְרִי: עוֹלָה שֶׁהִקְרִיבוּ יִשְׂרָאֵל בַּמִּדְבָּר עוֹלַת רְאִיָּה הֲוַאי. אָמַר אַבַּיֵי: בֵּית שַׁמַּאי, (ג) וְרַבִּי אֶלְעָזָר, וְר' יִשְׁמָעֵאל — כּוּלְּהוּ סְבִירָא לְהוּ: עוֹלָה שֶׁהִקְרִיבוּ יִשְׂרָאֵל בַּמִּדְבָּר עוֹלַת רְאִיָּה הֲוַאי. וּבֵית הִלֵּל, וְרַבִּי עֲקִיבָא, וְר' יוֹסֵי הַגְּלִילִי — כּוּלְּהוּ סְבִירָא לְהוּ: עוֹלָה שֶׁהִקְרִיבוּ יִשְׂרָאֵל בַּמִּדְבָּר עוֹלַת תָּמִיד הֲוַאי. בֵּית שַׁמַּאי — הָא דַּאֲמַרַן, ר' יִשְׁמָעֵאל — *דְּתַנְיָא, ר' יִשְׁמָעֵאל אוֹמֵר: כְּלָלוֹת נֶאֶמְרוּ בְּסִינַי וּפְרָטוֹת

שמואל א א | שמות כד | שם

רש"י

עַד הָכָא מַאן אַתְיֵיהּ. עַד יְרוּשָׁלַיִם מִי הֱבִיאוֹ (ד)? וַהֲלֹא מִשֶּׁהוּא יָכוֹל לִהְיוֹת חוּץ מֵאִמּוֹ יָכוֹל לֶאֱחוֹז בְּיַד אָבִיו, דִּכְדֵי עֲלִיָּיה מִירוּשָׁלַיִם לְהַר הַבַּיִת אַתָּה אוֹמֵר שֶׁיְּחַנְּכוּהוּ, וְעַד יְרוּשָׁלַיִם מִי הֱבִיאוֹ? מִחַיְּיבָא בְּשִׂמְחָה. לַעֲלוֹת לָרֶגֶל וְלִשְׂמוֹחַ בֶּחָג עִם בַּעְלָהּ, דְּעַל הַשִּׂמְחָה נִצְטַוּוּ נָשִׁים, דִּכְתִיב: "וְשָׂמַחְתָּ אַתָּה וּבֵיתֶךָ" (דברים יד): מִכָּאן וְאֵילָךְ. דְּאִימֵּיהּ לָא מְחַיְּיבָא לְהִתְרָאוֹת בְּהַר הַבַּיִת: עַד יִגָּמֵל. לְסוֹף כ"ד חֹדֶשׁ, שֶׁכֵּן תִּינוֹק יוֹנֵק. וּמִשָּׁנָה רִאשׁוֹנָה הוּא יָכוֹל לִרְכּוֹב עַל כְּתֵיפוֹ שֶׁל אָבִיו כְּדֵי לַעֲלוֹת מִירוּשָׁלַיִם לְהַר הַבַּיִת, וְכָל שֶׁכֵּן מִשִּׁילֹה לַמִּשְׁכָּן: הָכִי גָּרַס: קָטָן חִיגֵּר לְדִבְרֵי בֵּית שַׁמַּאי וְסוּמָא לְדִבְרֵי שְׁנֵיהֶן. דְּאִילּוּ חִיגֵּר לְדִבְרֵי בֵּית הִלֵּל לָא מִיבַּעְיָא לַן דְּלָא מְחַנְּכִינַן לֵיהּ, דְּהָא אָמְרִינַן אֵין מְחַנְּכִין אֶלָּא לְקָטָן שֶׁיָּכוֹל לֶאֱחוֹז וְלַעֲלוֹת בְּרַגְלָיו בִּירוּשָׁלַיִם, וְזֶה אֵינוֹ יָכוֹל. אֲבָל לְבֵית שַׁמַּאי דִּמְחַיְּיבֵי לְחַנְּכוֹ מִשֶּׁיָּכוֹל לִרְכּוֹב — קָטָן חִיגֵּר יָכוֹל לִרְכּוֹב עַל כְּתֵיפוֹ שֶׁל אָבִיו, וְהַסּוּמָא יָכוֹל לֶאֱחוֹז, לְב"ה מַהוּ, צָרִיךְ חִינּוּךְ אוֹ לָא? שֶׁאֵינוֹ יָכוֹל לְהִתְפַּשֵּׁט. שֶׁאֵין סוֹפוֹ לְהִתְפַּשֵּׁט עוֹלָמִית: קָטָן מִבַּעְיָא. הֲלֹא אֵין חִינּוּךְ קָטָן אֶלָּא כְּדֵי לְהַנְהִיגוֹ שֶׁיְּהֵא סָרוּךְ אַחַר מִנְהָגוֹ לִכְשֶׁיַּגְדִּיל — וְכֵיוָן שֶׁזֶּה פָּטוּר לִכְשֶׁיַּגְדִּיל לָמָּה לִי חִינּוּךְ? שֶׁיָּכוֹל לְהִתְפַּתֵּחַ. קוֹדֶם שֶׁיַּגְדִּיל: מָצִינוּ בָּעֲצֶרֶת. בְּפָ' "שׁוֹר אוֹ כֶשֶׂב": "וְהִקְרַבְתֶּם עַל הַלֶּחֶם שִׁבְעַת כְּבָשִׂים תְּמִימִים וּפַר בֶּן בָּקָר אֶחָד וְאֵילִים שְׁנַיִם יִהְיוּ עוֹלָה לַה'", וּכְתִיב: "וּשְׁנֵי כְבָשִׂים בְּנֵי שָׁנָה לְזֶבַח שְׁלָמִים" (ויקרא כג): יֶשְׁנָהּ לִפְנֵי הַדִּיבּוּר. קוֹדֶם מַתַּן תּוֹרָה הִקְרִיבוּ שְׁלָמִים בְּסִינַי, דִּכְתִיב: "וַיִּשְׁלַח אֶת נַעֲרֵי בְּנֵי יִשְׂרָאֵל" (שמות כד). וְאַע"ג דְּהַאי קְרָא כְּתִיב בְּ"וְאֵלֶּה הַמִּשְׁפָּטִים" לְאַחַר עֲשֶׂרֶת הַדִּבְּרוֹת — קוֹדֶם עֲשֶׂרֶת הַדִּבְּרוֹת הֲוָה, וְאֵין מוּקְדָּם וּמְאוּחָר בַּתּוֹרָה. וְהָכִי תַּנְיָא בְּמַסֶּכֶת שַׁבָּת בְּפֶרֶק "ר' עֲקִיבָא": (דף פח.) רַבִּי יוֹסֵי אוֹמֵר, בַּשֵּׁנִי עָלָה וְיָרַד, בַּשְּׁלִישִׁי עָלָה וְיָרַד, בָּרְבִיעִי יָרַד וְשׁוּב לֹא עָלָה, בַּחֲמִישִׁי בָּנָה מִזְבֵּחַ וְהִקְרִיב עָלָיו קָרְבָּן, בַּשִּׁשִּׁי* נִיתְּנָה תוֹרָה. וְאֵין אַתָּה מוֹצֵא בְּנְתִינַת הַתּוֹרָה בִּנְיַן מִזְבֵּחַ אֶלָּא בְּאוֹתוֹ שֶׁנֶּאֱמַר: "וַיִּשְׁלַח אֶת נַעֲרֵי בְּנֵי יִשְׂרָאֵל" וגו'. וּלְקַמָּן פָּרֵיךְ: הָתָם נַמִי עוֹלָה הֲוַאי: נְשִׂיאִים. בַּחֲנוּכַּת הַמִּזְבֵּחַ הִקְרִיבוּ שְׁלָמִים יוֹתֵר מֵעוֹלוֹת, דִּכְתִיב: "כָּל הַבָּקָר לָעוֹלָה" וגו' "וְכָל בְּקַר זֶבַח הַשְּׁלָמִים" וגו' (במדבר ז): שְׁתֵּי אֲכִילוֹת. מִזְבֵּחַ וְאָדָם. נְשִׂיאִים קָרְבַּן יָחִיד, וּרְאִיָּה וַחֲגִיגָה קָרְבַּן יָחִיד, אֲבָל כִּבְשֵׂי עֲצֶרֶת — קָרְבַּן צִבּוּר, וּמִתְּרוּמַת הַלִּשְׁכָּה: רְאִיָּה נַמִי יֶשְׁנָהּ לִפְנֵי הַדִּיבּוּר. דְּעוֹלָה נַמִי הֲוָה הָתָם: מִדָּבָר הַנּוֹהֵג לְדוֹרוֹת. כִּבְשֵׂי עֲצֶרֶת: עוֹלַת תָּמִיד הֲוַאי. חוֹבַת כָּל יוֹם וָיוֹם, וְלָא גָּמְרִינַן מִינָּהּ: עוֹלַת רְאִיָּה הֲוַאי. עַל שֵׁם "וַיֶּחֱזוּ אֶת הָאֱלֹהִים": כְּלָלוֹת נֶאֶמְרוּ בְּסִינַי. הַרְבֵּה דְּבָרִים נֶאֶמְרוּ סְתוּמִים בְּסִינַי שֶׁלֹּא נִתְפָּרְשׁוּ כָּל צָרְכָּן, וּפֵירְשׁוּ לוֹ לְאַחַר שֶׁהוּקַם הַמִּשְׁכָּן בְּאֹהֶל מוֹעֵד. שֶׁהֲרֵי לֹא נִתְפָּרְשׁוּ שָׁם הִלְכוֹת עֲבוֹדָה כְּכָל הַצָּרִיךְ, אֶלָּא "מִזְבַּח אֲדָמָה תַּעֲשֶׂה לִּי וְזָבַחְתָּ עָלָיו אֶת עוֹלוֹתֶיךָ וְאֶת שְׁלָמֶיךָ" (שמות כ) וְלֹא פֵּי' מַתַּן דְּמֵיהֶן, הֶפְשֵׁיטָן וְנִיתּוּחָן שֶׁל עוֹלוֹת, וְהַקְרָבַת אֵימוּרִין שֶׁל שְׁלָמִים:

תוספות

(ה) **דמחייבא** אימיה בשמחה. פירש רש"י בפרק קמא דקדושין (דף לד: ושם) גבי אשה בעלה משמחה, בבגדי צבעונין, בא"י — בבגדי פשתן. והכא משמע דבשלמי שמחה מיירי! והתם (בד"ה אשה) פי', וכן בפ"ק דר"ה (דף ו: ושם):

דיכול לרכוב על כתיפו של אביו. שהיה גדול קצת, אבל לא מצי לאחוז בידו ולעלות ברגליו:

בחיגר שיכול להתפשט. מקמי גדולו, מאי? מי אמרינן: דכיון דגדול המיחייב מדאורייתא — גבי קטן נמי מיחייב בחינוך, דמידי הוא טעמא בקטן — אלא משום לחנכו, דידע כשהוא גדול. או דלמא: כיון דגדול בהכי לא מיחייב — גם קטן לא:

הראייה שתי כסף. ומדרבנן הוא, דמדאורייתא אין לו שיעור לקרבן רק לאשם מעילות (שבועת העדות) דכתיב ביה: "כסף שקלים" (ויקרא ה), ותנן בכריתות (דף כו:): המפריש שתי סלעים לאשם. והא דאמרינן בזבחים (דף מח.): [לא יהא ספיקו חמור מודאו, מה ודאו חטאת בת דנקא — אף ספיקו אשם בר דנקא]. ובמנחות (דף קז:): יביא *אשם הוא ונסכיו בסלע — לאו דוקא קחשיב, דאמרינן בפרק ב' דכריתות (דף י:): יביא *אשם בסלע. וכן הא דאמרינן בפ' "הוציאו לו" ביומא (דף נה:) ניסקול ארבעה זוזי ונשדי בנהרא — לאו דוקא, דלא בעי כולי האי ובפ"ב דמנחות (דף קז: ושם בד"ה כבש) פירשתי*:

ישנה לפני הדבור. וס"ל עולת (ו) ראייה הואי, כדקאמר בסמוך:

***קרבן** יחיד. כגון חגיגה. ובפ"ה דיומא (דף נא. ושם) דקרי ליה קרבן צבור — היינו גבי פסח שני, כדקאמר התם: חגיגה מ"ט מקריא קרבן צבור — דאתיא בכנופיא, פסח נמי אתיא בכנופיא, איכא פסח שני דלא אתיא בכנופיא:

דנין דבר הנוהג לדורות. ולא בעי למימר דנין יו"ט מיו"ט, לאפוקי נשיאים דחול הוי. דלא מלינו ליה האי חילוקא בשום מקום (ז). אע"ג דלקמן, פרק "חומר בקודש" (דף כג: ושם) ילפינן לירוף "כף אחת" הכתוב עשה כל מה שבכף אחת; ולא פרכינן משעה לא ילפינן — דהתם, כיון דליכא למילפי מדורות — ילפינן ליה שפיר משעה. אי נמי: שאני התם דתני ביה קרא תריסר זימני, כדאמרינן בפ"ק דמנחות (דף ח:), ובפרק "הקומץ רבה" (שם דף יט:) גבי כלי הלא מקדש הלא. ויליף שמואל דורות משעה, דתני ביה קרא תריסר זימני:

ורבי ישמעאל ורבי אלעזר וכו'. ואין להקשות: ושבקי ב"ה ועבדי כב"ש? הלא ב"ש במקום בית הלל אינו משנה! וי"ל: דסבירא להו לא נחלקו בית שמאי וב"ה בדבר זה:

בית שמאי הא דאמרן. וליכא לאקשויי: מנא ליה דאית להו עולת ראייה הואי? דלמא לעולם סבירא להו עולת תמיד, וטעמא דידהו עדיף להו, דהכי משמע מדבעי מאי טעמא לא אמר בית הלל כוותייהו? האי לאו מילתא היא, דמיבעיא ליה אמאי לא קאמרי בית הלל עולת ראייה כבית שמאי: מי

עין משפט נר מצוה

כד א מיי' פ"א מהל' חגיגה הלכה א סמג עשין רכו:

כה ב מיי' שם פ"ב הלכה ג:

[בן לקיש וכן איתא בפסחים קיט.]

נ"ל כבש

נ"ל כבש

[וע"ע תוספות ב"ב קסו: ד"ה רבעתים]

[דיבור זה שייך קודם ד"ה ישנה]

הגהות הב"ח

(א) גמרא עד הכא מאן אייתיה אמר ליה אביי עד הכא אימיה דמחייבא בשמחה אייתיתיה מכאן ואילך כנ"ל: (ב) שם דגדול פטור מדאורייתא קטן נמי [פטור] מדרבנן ב"ש אומר: (ג) שם בית שמאי ור' ישמעאל ור' אליעזר כולהו: (ד) רש"י ד"ה עד הכא מאן אייתיה עד ירושלים מי הביאו דכדי עלייה מירושלים וכו' מי הביאו והלא משהוא יכול וכו' לאחוז ביד אביו הס"ד ואח"כ מה"ד דמחייבא: (ה) תום' ד"ה אימיה דמחייבא בשמחה: (ו) ד"ה ישנה וכו' עולת תמיד הואי: (ז) ד"ה דנין וכו' ואף על גב וכו' מכף אחת וכו' משעה משום דתני:

ס"א אביי

[לא היה לו פנאי ואח"כ בשבת כנ"ל להגי' וע"ש]

גליון הש"ס

גמרא עולה שהקריבו ישראל במדבר עולת תמיד הואי. עיין יומא דף לד ע"א תוספות ד"ה שעולה: **תד"ה** הראייה כו' ומדרבנן היא. עי' קדושין

[יבמות ה:]

סוטה לז: זבחים קטו:

רבינו חננאל

בה"א כל שאינו יכול לאחוז בידו של אביו ולעלות מירושלים להר הבית שנאמר שלש רגלים. ממקום מושבותיהם מי הביא הקטנים ופרקינן ממקומם שהיתה אמן חייבת לעלות ולשמוח הביאתו אמו מיכן ואילך שאינה חייבת בראייה משלימתו לאביו ומקשה לב"ש דאמרינן אם יכול לרכוב על כתיפיו של אביו ולעלות חייב. והא שמואל דיכול לרכוב הוה וכתיב וחנה לא עלתה כי אמרה לאישה עד יגמל הנער והביאותיו ונראה את פני ה' וישב שם עד עולם. ודחי ב"ש ולטעמיך חנה גופה אמאי לא עלתה מי לא מיחייבא בשמחה אלא חנה מפנקותא יתירתא חזת בשמואל (והשתא) [וחששה] משום חולשא דאורחא משום הכי חנה נמי פטורה דאמר *) חולין ומשמשיהן פטורין מן הראיה. בעי ר"ש בר אבא קטן חגר שיכול להתפשט לדברי (ב"ה) [ב"ש] וקטן סומא שיכול להתפתח לדברי שניהם מאי ופשטה אביי כל היכא דגדול חייב מן התורה קטן נמי מדרבנן פטור: **מתני'** ב"ש אומרים הראייה שתי כסף כו'. ת"ר הראייה שתי כסף שהיא כולה לגבוה מה שאין כן בחגיגה שהחגיגה החלב והדם לגבוה והבשר לבעלים ועוד מצינו בעצרת שהזהיר הקב"ה לישראל בעולות ושלמים וריבה בעולות. ובה"א החגיגה גדולה מן הראייה שהחגיגה ישנה לפני מתן תורה שנאמר ויזבחו זבחים שלמים לה' פרים וכי תימא והא התם נמי כתיב ויעלו עולות והנה הקריבו נמי קודם מתן תורה עולת ראיה ההיא עולה שהקריבו ישראל קודם מתן תורה עולת תמיד הוא. ועוד מצינו בנשיאים שהקריבו פר ואיל וכבש לעולה והקריבו לזבח שלמים פרים שנים וגו'. ודחינן ב"ה עצרת קרבן צבור ואין דנין קרבן יחיד מקרבן צבור. ודחינן ב"ש עולה שהקריבו ישראל במדבר עולת ראיה הוא. קרבן נשיאים אינו נוהג לדורות. אמר אביי ב"ש ור' ישמעאל ור' אליעזר כולהו סבירא להו עולה שהקריבו ישראל

*) בגמ' לא מלינו זה רק גבי סוכה בסוכה ד' כ"ה ואולי לנ"ל לאמרה ור"ל דחנה סברה כן בדעתה דחולין ומשמשיהן פטורין מן הראיה.

תורה אור

וּפְרָטוֹת בְּאֹהֶל מוֹעֵד, וְר' עֲקִיבָא אוֹמֵר: כְּלָלוֹת וּפְרָטוֹת נֶאֶמְרוּ בְּסִינַי, וְנִשְׁנוּ בְּאֹהֶל מוֹעֵד, וְנִשְׁתַּלְּשׁוּ בְּעַרְבוֹת מוֹאָב. וְאִי סָלְקָא דַּעְתָּךְ עוֹלָה שֶׁהִקְרִיבוּ יִשְׂרָאֵל בַּמִּדְבָּר עוֹלַת תָּמִיד הֲוַאי, מִי אִיכָּא מִידִי דְּמֵעִיקָּרָא לָא בָּעֵי הֶפְשֵׁט וְנִיתּוּחַ וּלְבַסּוֹף בָּעֵי הֶפְשֵׁט וְנִיתּוּחַ? ר' אֱלִיעֶזֶר דְּתַנְיָא: °"עֹלַת תָּמִיד הָעֲשׂוּיָה בְּהַר סִינַי", (במדבר כח) ר' אֱלִיעֶזֶר אוֹמֵר: מַעֲשֶׂיהָ נֶאֶמְרוּ בְּסִינַי, וְהִיא עַצְמָהּ לֹא קָרְבָה, רַבִּי עֲקִיבָא אוֹמֵר: קָרְבָה וְשׁוּב לֹא פָּסְקָה. אֶלָּא מָה אֲנִי מְקַיֵּים: °"הַזְּבָחִים (עמוס ה) וּמִנְחָה הִגַּשְׁתֶּם לִי בַמִּדְבָּר אַרְבָּעִים שָׁנָה בֵּית יִשְׂרָאֵל" — שִׁבְטוֹ שֶׁל לֵוִי שֶׁלֹּא עָבְדוּ ע"ז, הֵן הִקְרִיבוּ אוֹתָהּ. בֵּית הִלֵּל — הָא דַּאֲמָרַן. ר' עֲקִיבָא — הָא נַמִּי דַּאֲמָרַן, ר' יוֹסֵי הַגְּלִילִי — דְּתַנְיָא, ר' יוֹסֵי הַגְּלִילִי אוֹמֵר: *אשָׁלֹשׁ מִצְוֹת נִצְטַוּוּ יִשְׂרָאֵל בַּעֲלוֹתָם לָרֶגֶל: רְאִיָּה, וַחֲגִיגָה, וְשִׂמְחָה. יֵשׁ בָּרְאִיָּה שֶׁאֵין בִּשְׁתֵּיהֶן, וְיֵשׁ בַּחֲגִיגָה שֶׁאֵין בִּשְׁתֵּיהֶן, יֵשׁ בַּשִּׂמְחָה שֶׁאֵין בִּשְׁתֵּיהֶן. יֵשׁ בָּרְאִיָּה שֶׁאֵין בִּשְׁתֵּיהֶן — שֶׁהָרְאִיָּה עוֹלָה כּוּלָּהּ לַגָּבוֹהַּ, מַה שֶּׁאֵין כֵּן בִּשְׁתֵּיהֶן. יֵשׁ בַּחֲגִיגָה מַה שֶּׁאֵין בִּשְׁתֵּיהֶן — שֶׁחֲגִיגָה יֶשְׁנָהּ לִפְנֵי הַדִּיבּוּר, מַה שֶּׁאֵין בִּשְׁתֵּיהֶן. יֵשׁ בַּשִּׂמְחָה מַה שֶּׁאֵין בִּשְׁתֵּיהֶן — שֶׁהַשִּׂמְחָה נוֹהֶגֶת בַּאֲנָשִׁים וּבְנָשִׁים, מַה שֶּׁאֵין בִּשְׁתֵּיהֶן. וְר' יִשְׁמָעֵאל, מַאי טַעְמָא קָא מוֹקְמַתְּ לֵיהּ כְּבֵית שַׁמַּאי? אִי סָלְקָא דַּעֲתָךְ עוֹלָה שֶׁהִקְרִיבוּ יִשְׂרָאֵל בַּמִּדְבָּר עוֹלַת תָּמִיד הֲוַאי — מִי אִיכָּא מִידִי דְּמֵעִיקָּרָא לָא בָּעֵי הֶפְשֵׁט וְנִיתּוּחַ וּלְבַסּוֹף בָּעֵי הֶפְשֵׁט וְנִיתּוּחַ? וְהָא רַבִּי יוֹסֵי הַגְּלִילִי דְּאָמַר עוֹלָה שֶׁהִקְרִיבוּ יִשְׂרָאֵל בַּמִּדְבָּר עוֹלַת תָּמִיד הֲוַאי, מֵעִיקָּרָא לָא בָּעֵי הֶפְשֵׁט וְנִיתּוּחַ וּלְבַסּוֹף בָּעֵי הֶפְשֵׁט וְנִיתּוּחַ. *דְּתַנְיָא, רַבִּי יוֹסֵי הַגְּלִילִי אוֹמֵר: עוֹלָה שֶׁהִקְרִיבוּ יִשְׂרָאֵל בַּמִּדְבָּר אֵינָהּ טְעוּנָה הֶפְשֵׁט וְנִיתּוּחַ, לְפִי שֶׁאֵין הֶפְשֵׁט וְנִיתּוּחַ אֶלָּא מֵאֹהֶל מוֹעֵד וְאֵילָךְ! סְמֵי מִכָּאן ר' יִשְׁמָעֵאל. *בָּעֵי רַב חִסְדָּא, הַאי קְרָא הֵיכִי כְּתִיב: °"וַיִּשְׁלַח (שמות כד) אֶת נַעֲרֵי בְּנֵי יִשְׂרָאֵל וַיַּעֲלוּ עֹלֹת" — כְּבָשִׂים, "וַיִּזְבְּחוּ זְבָחִים שְׁלָמִים לַה' פָּרִים", אוֹ דִּלְמָא אִידִי וְאִידִי פָּרִים הָווּ? לְמַאי נָפְקָא מִינַּהּ? מָר זוּטְרָא אָמַר: לְפִיסּוּק טְעָמִים. רַב אַחָא בְּרֵיהּ דְּרָבָא אָמַר: לְאוֹמֵר "הֲרֵי עָלַי עוֹלָה כְּעוֹלָה שֶׁהִקְרִיבוּ יִשְׂרָאֵל בַּמִּדְבָּר" מַאי, פָּרִים הָווּ אוֹ כְּבָשִׂים הָווּ? תֵּיקוּ. *תְּנַן הָתָם: אֵלּוּ דְּבָרִים שֶׁאֵין לָהֶם שִׁיעוּר: הַפֵּאָה

רש"י

וּפְרָטוֹת בְּאֹהֶל מוֹעֵד. מִשֶּׁהוּקַם הַמִּשְׁכָּן וְדִיבֵּר עִמּוֹ מֵעַל (א) הַפָּרוֹכֶת, שָׁם פֵּירֵשׁ לוֹ הַכָּתוּב, כִּדְכְתִיב: "וַיִּקְרָא אֶל מֹשֶׁה וַיְדַבֵּר ה' אֵלָיו מֵאֹהֶל מוֹעֵד לֵאמֹר". וּבְסֵפֶר תּוֹרַת כֹּהֲנִים, דְּהַיְינוּ וַיִּקְרָא, נִתְפָּרְשׁוּ כָּל הִלְכוֹת קָרְבָּן, וְכֵן דְּבָרִים הַרְבֵּה: וְנִשְׁנוּ. פַּעַם שֵׁנִית, וְכָל מַה שֶּׁנֶּאֱמַר כָּאן נֶאֱמַר כָּאן, וְאַעַ"פ שֶׁלֹּא נִכְתַּב: וְנִשְׁתַּלְּשׁוּ בְּעַרְבוֹת מוֹאָב. מִפִּי מֹשֶׁה לְיִשְׂרָאֵל, שֶׁנֶּאֱמַר: "בְּעֵבֶר הַיַּרְדֵּן בְּאֶרֶץ מוֹאָב הוֹאִיל מֹשֶׁה בֵּאֵר אֶת הַתּוֹרָה" וגו' (דברים א): וְאִי סָלְקָא דַּעְתָּךְ עוֹלַת סִינַי עוֹלַת תָּמִיד הֲוַאי. וְחוֹבַת הַדּוֹרוֹת מִפִּי הַגְּבוּרָה: מִי אִיכָּא מִידֵי כו'. אֶלָּא וַדַּאי עוֹלַת רְאִיָּיה הֲוַאי, וּמֵאֵילֵיהֶם הִקְרִיבוּהָ: וְהִיא עַצְמָהּ לֹא קָרְבָה. וְהָעוֹלָה שֶׁהִקְרִיבוּ הַבְּכוֹרוֹת — עוֹלַת רְאִיָּיה הֲוָה: וּמָה אֲנִי מְקַיֵּים הַזְּבָחִים וּמִנְחָה הִגַּשְׁתֶּם לִי בַּמִּדְבָּר. לְשׁוֹן תְּמִיהָ, וּמַשְׁמַע שֶׁלֹּא הִקְרִיבוּ, לְפִי שֶׁנְּזוּפִין הָיוּ: שִׁבְטוֹ שֶׁל לֵוִי. הִקְרִיבוּהָ מִשֶּׁלָּהֶם: שִׂמְחָה. אַף הֵם שַׁלְמֵי שִׂמְחָה. אִם אֵין לוֹ בְּשַׂר שְׁלָמִים שֶׁל נֶדֶר וּנְדָבָה שֶׁהִתְנַדֵּב כָּל הַשָּׁנָה, שֶׁמְּבִיאִין בָּרֶגֶל, וְלֹא מַעֲשַׂר בְּהֵמָה — מֵבִיא שְׁלָמִים מִשֶּׁלּוֹ, אוֹ מִמְּעוֹת מַעֲשֵׂר שֵׁנִי שֶׁלּוֹ, לִהְיוֹת לוֹ בָּשָׂר לָשׂוֹבַע. שֶׁאֵין שִׂמְחַת הֶחָג אֶלָּא בְּבָשָׂר: שֶׁחֲגִיגָה יֶשְׁנָהּ לִפְנֵי הַדִּיבּוּר. אוֹתָן שְׁלָמִים שֶׁהִקְרִיבוּ הַבְּכוֹרוֹת, אַף עַל פִּי שֶׁלֹּא בָּרֶגֶל הִקְרִיבוּם — חֲגִיגָה נִקְרְאוּ, שֶׁבָּהֶן נִתְקַיֵּים "וְיָחוֹגּוּ לִי בַּמִּדְבָּר" (שמות ה) שֶׁנֶּאֱמַר לָהֶם בְּמִצְרַיִם: הַשִּׂמְחָה נוֹהֶגֶת בְּנָשִׁים. דִּכְתִיב: "וְשָׂמַחְתָּ אַתָּה וּבֵיתֶךָ" (דברים יד): מַה שֶּׁאֵין כֵּן בִּשְׁתֵּיהֶן. דְּמִצְוַת עֲשֵׂה שֶׁהַזְּמָן גְּרָמָא הֵן, וְהַכָּתוּב לֹא רִיבָּה אוֹתָן: הָכִי גָּרְסִינַן: וְרַבִּי יִשְׁמָעֵאל מַאי טַעְמָא קָא מוֹקְמַתְּ לֵיהּ כְּבֵית שַׁמַּאי אִי סָלְקָא דַּעְתָּךְ וכו'. וְלָא גָּרְסִינַן: אָמַר לָךְ. וְהָכִי פֵּירוּשָׁא: לְאַבַּיֵּי פָּרֵיךְ, דְּאָמַר לְעֵיל בֵּית שַׁמַּאי וְרַבִּי יִשְׁמָעֵאל כו', מַאי טַעְמָא מוֹקְמַתְּ לָהּ לְרַבִּי יִשְׁמָעֵאל דְּלָא כְּהִלְכְתָא? דְּבֵית שַׁמַּאי בִּמְקוֹם בֵּית הִלֵּל אֵינוֹ מִשְׁנָה — מִשּׁוּם דְּשָׁמְעַתְּ לֵיהּ דְּאָמַר פְּרָטוֹת לֹא נֶאֶמְרוּ בְּסִינַי, וְקַשְׁיָא לָךְ: אִי סָלְקָא דַּעְתָּךְ עוֹלַת תָּמִיד הֲוַאי — וּמִי אִיכָּא מִידֵי כו' מִשּׁוּם הָכִי לָא הֲוָה לָךְ לְאוֹקְמַהּ כְּבֵית שַׁמַּאי (ב): הָא רַבִּי יוֹסֵי הַגְּלִילִי. דְּשָׁמְעַתְּ לֵיהּ בְּהֶדְיָא דְּאָמַר לְעֵיל עוֹלַת תָּמִיד הֲוַאי וַאֲפִילּוּ הָכִי שָׁמְעִינַן בְּעוֹלַת תָּמִיד דְּלֵית בֵּיהּ הֶפְשֵׁט וְנִיתּוּחַ: לְפִסּוּקֵי טְעָמִים. בִּנְגִינוֹת. אִם תֹּאמַר שְׁנֵי מִינִין — צָרִיךְ אַתָּה לְפִסּוּק הַטַּעַם שֶׁל "וַיַּעֲלוּ עוֹלוֹת" בְּאֶתְנַחְתָּא, כְּמוֹ שֶׁאָנוּ קוֹרִין אוֹתוֹ, אוֹ בִּזְקֵף קָטֹן, טַעַם שֶׁמַּפְסִיק הַדִּבּוּר מִמַּה שֶּׁלְּאַחֲרָיו; וְאִם מִין אֶחָד הָיָה — צָרִיךְ אַתָּה לְקָרוֹתוֹ בְּאַחַד מִשְּׁאָר טְעָמִים שֶׁאֵין מַפְסִיקִין, כְּגוֹן פַּשְׁטָא אוֹ רְבִיעַ: לְאוֹמֵר הֲרֵי עָלַי עוֹלָה כו' גָּרְ', וְלָא גָּרְסִי': כְּאוֹמֵר: נָפְקָא מִינַּהּ לְאוֹמֵר הֲרֵי עָלַי עוֹלָה כְּאוֹתָהּ עוֹלָה. מַה יָּבִיא, פָּרִים אוֹ כְּבָשִׂים? תֵּיקוּ: תְּנַן הָתָם. בְּמַסֶּכֶת פֵּאָה: הַפֵּאָה

תוספות

מי איכא מידי דמעיקרא לא בעי הפשט. דוקא(ג) קא מבעיא ליה, משום דעיקר הפשט כתיב בגופיה. אבל מעולת ראייה, אע"ג דאמת הוא דטעונה הפשט — לא קשה ליה מידי, כיון דלאו בגופיה כתיב: רבי עקיבא וכו'. אע"ג דבחמישי בנה מזבח, ולא ניתנה תורה עד סיני — דריש מאותה שעה דנאמר מעשיה בסיני, כדכתיב "עולת תמיד העשויה בהר סיני". ומאן דלא דריש הכי — מוקי לה דעולה טעונה כלי, וכן פירש רש"י בנימוקי חומש העשויה בהר סיני. ובסיפרי דריש לה: שנעשית בהר סיני קודם לתורה, והיינו בחמישי שבנה מזבח:

יש בשמחה שאין בשתיהן. ובתוספ' גרסינן: שהשמחה יש לה תשלומין כל שבעה, ואלא בשתיהן, ושמעתתא שלנו דלא גריס ליה — סבירא ליה דגם באינך יש להן תשלומין. ולא קאמר יש בשתיהן שצריכין שיעור, מה שאין כן בשמחה — דאימא אף שמחה יש לה שיעור. ומיהו, בלאו הכי ניחא, דלא נחית למיתני הא כללא כדפריש' לעיל (דף ג:*), רק חומרא באחת שאין בשתים. ולהכי לא חשיב שתיהן אינן באין מכל דבר, מה שאין כן בשמחה שבאה מכל דבר, דהא חומרי דשתים לא קא חשיב:

אידי ואידי פרים הוו. אליבא דמ"ד עולת ראייה הואי. ואפי' למ"ד עולת תמיד קודם מתן תורה — היתה של פרים, והדר אישתנו, כמו שנשתנה מן הֶפְשֵׁט וניתוח לרבי יוסי הגלילי:

מאי נפקא מינה. כלומר: מאי דהוה הוה. וכן פריך בפ"ק דיומא (דף ה: ושם) גבי כילד הלבישן, ובפסחים (נו.) גבי אימורי פסחים(ד), ובסנהדרין (דף טו: ושם*) גבי שור סיני בכמה לא בעי, משום דסבירא לאלופי דורות משעה. ובע"ז פרק שני (דף לד.), ובתענית (דף יא:) גבי במה שמש משה כל ימי המלואים דלא פריך ליה — התם נמי למיסבר קראי. לפי שלא מצינו בגדי כהונה רק לאהרן ובניו. ועוד: דאכתי לא נתחנכו הבגדים. דבעינן עלייהו הזאה, ונפקא מינה לעבוד במלואים בלא הזאת בגדים:

לפסוקי טעמא. ולא דמי לה' מקראות שאין להן הכרע (יומא דף נב.), ולא אזלינן בתר פסוקי טעמא? התם לא מצי קאי רק לחד מינייהו, דאין משמעות שתיהן שוה, אבל הכא מצי קאי לתרווייהו:

שאין להן שיעור הפאה. דכתיב: "לא תכלה פאת שדך" (ויקרא יט) ומדאורייתא היא, דאילו מדרבנן (ה) אמר בפרק "ראשית הגז" (חולין דף קלז: ושם): אין פותחין (*לעני בגורן פחות) מששים, ופליגי אמוראי בירושלמי, חד אמר: אין להם שיעור למעלה ולא למטה, כלומר: יוכל לפחות עד חטה, ולמעלה כל שדהו. וחד אמר: למעלה אין לה שיעור, הא למטה — יש לה. ובעי: מאי בינייהו? כלומר, ודאי לכולי עלמא איכא! ומשני: אם פיחת מששים, למאן דאמר אין לו שיעור כלל, מה שנתן — נתן, ופטור מפאה, ואם הוסיף — חייב במעשר. ולמאן דאמר יש לו שיעור למטה, מה שנתן — נתן, ואינו פטור מפאה, וזכה העני, ומחויב במעשר עד שישלם שיעור ששים בבת אחת. דלא הוי פאה אם לא שילם לו בבת אחת כו'. ופריך: אמאי לא חשיב תרומה? ומשני: תפתר מפני המחלוקת. לשון פלוגתא, דומיא דמחלוקת בששיהן אדוקין בתורף (ב"מ דף ז:), כלומר: שיש בה חילוק, דאמר רבי יוחנן: עושה אדם כל שדהו בכורים, ולא אמר עושה כל שדהו תרומה — דהא בעינן ראשית ששיריה ניכרים בפרק "בכל מערבין". התיבון: הרי פאה, דאין אדם עושה כל שדהו פאה! ומשני: עד שלא קצר שבולת לא נתחייב שדהו פאה. כלומר: דכתיב "פאת שדך בקוצרך", תלה רחמנא פאה בקציר. והכי קאמר: דמשנתחייב בפאה אין לה שיעור. וכי תימא בכורים נמי — הכתיב "ראשית" וליבעי שיריס ניכרים כמו בתרומה, דמרבינן ליה התם "ראשית כל בכורי כל". ואני הייתי מפרש: מפני המחלוקת — עין יפה עין רעה ובינונית, לאפוקי הך דעניינם שוה. ועוד, דפליגי במסכת תרומה (פרק ד מ"ה): המרבה בתרומה, רבי אליעזר אומר: אחד מעשרה, יתר מכאן — יעשה תרומת מעשר למקום אחר. רבי ישמעאל אומר: מחצה חולין ומחצה תרומה. ר' עקיבא אומר: עד שישייר שם חולין. ומפרש בירושלמי טעמא דרבי ישמעאל: ד"ראשית דגנך" — דיו לראשית שיהו כדגן:

והבכורים

עין משפט נר מצוה

כו א מיי' פ"א מהל' חגיגה הלכה א:

רבינו חננאל

ישראל במדבר עולת ראיה הואי וב"ה ורבי עקיבא ור' יוסי הגלילי סברי עולת תמיד הואי ב"ש הא דאמרן ר' ישמעאל דתניא כללות נאמרו בסיני ופרטות באהל מועד וליכא מידי דבסיני לא בעי הפשט ונתוח דהא אמרת כללות נאמרו בסיני ובסוף בעי הפשט ונתוח שנאמר והפשיט את העולה ונתח אותה לנתחיה. אלא לאו ש"מ לאו עולת תמיד הואי. אלא עולת ראיה הואי. ר' אליעזר נמי דתניא עולת תמיד העשויה בהר סיני ר' אליעזר אומר מעשיה נאמרו בסיני והיא עצמה לא קרבה ר' עקיבא אומר היא עצמה קרבה בסיני ושוב לא פסקה. וכי תימא איני והכתיב הזבחים ומנחה הגשתם לי במדבר ארבעים שנה בית ישראל *) שעבדו ע"ז הקריבו עולת תמיד בכל ארבעים שנה שהיו ישראל במדבר ותוב א"ר עקיבא כללות ופרטות נאמרו בסיני ונשנו באהל מועד ונשתלשו בערבות מואב ב"ה ור"ע הני דאמרן ר' יוסי הגלילי דתניא ר' יוסי הגלילי אומר ג' מצות נצטוו ישראל בעלייתן לרגל ראיה חגיגה ושמחה יש בראיה משא"כ בשתיהן שהראיה כולה לגבוה משא"כ בשתיהן. ויש בחגיגה משא"כ בשתיהן שהחגיגה ישנה לפני הדבור מה שאין כן בשתיהן ויש בשמחה שהשמחה נוהגת בנשים כבאנשים מה שאין כן בשתיהן. קתני מיהא שהחגיגה ישנה לפני הדבור מה שאין כן בעולת ראיה ובשמחה ש"מ דסבר ר' יוסי הגלילי עולה שהקריבו בני ישראל במדבר עולת תמיד הואי. ואמרינן אמאי מוקמת ליה לר' ישמעאל כב"ש משום דליכא מידי דמעיקרא לא בעי הפשט ונתוח ובסוף בעי הא ר' יוסי הגלילי דאוקימתא כב"ה תני בהדיא רבי יוסי הגלילי אומר עולה שהקריבו בני ישראל במדבר לא בעי הפשט ונתוח אלא מאהל מועד ואילך. ואסיקנא סמי ר' ישמעאל מב"ש **): בעי רב חסדא האי קרא היכי פירושיה וישלח את נערי בני ישראל ויעלו עולות כבשים ויזבחו זבחים שלמים לה' פרים או דלמא אידי ואידי כלומר העולות והשלמים כולן פרים היו ואמרינן מאי נפקא לן מינה [מאי] דהוה הוה. ואמר מר זוטרא לפיסוק טעמי' כלומר אם אלו כבשים ואלו פרים קרא צריך לאפסוקינהו ואי לא [לא] צריך רב אחא אמר לנודר. באומר הרי עלי עולה כעולה שהקריבו ישראל במדבר מאי פר מחייבת ליה או כבש תיקו. תנן התם אלו

*) נראה דל"ל שבטו של לוי שלא עבדו ע"ז וכו'. **) לכאורה נ"ל דלא סבר לה כב"ש או דל"ל דסמי ר' ישמעאל מדברי אביי.

מסורת הש"ס

(תוספתא פ"א)

זבחים קטו: ע"ש וקף קכ. (תוספתא) דפרה פ"ג

יומא נב:

פאה פ"א מ"א חולין קלז:

[ועי' תוס' ד"ה שור סיני]

הגהות הב"ח

(א) רש"י ד"ה ופרטות וכו' מעל הכפורת שם: (ב) ד"ה הכי גרסינן וכו' לאוקמה כב"ש דהא רבי יוסי: (ג) תוס' ד"ה מי איכא וכו' דוקא מעולת תמיד קא מיבעיא ליה: (ד) ד"ה למאי נפקא מינה וכו' גבי אימורי פסחים דאמרינן מאי דהוה הוה ובסנהדרין: (ה) ד"ה שאין וכו' דאילו מדרבנן הא אמר וכו' אין פותחין לפאה אפילו בתבואה לארץ פחות מששים וכו' אין להם שיעור לא למעלה ולא למטה כלומר למטה יוכל לפחות וכו' לכולי עלמא איכא שיעור למטה מדרבנן ומשני וכו' ופריך אמאי לא חשיב תרומה ומשני מפני המחלוקת ואין מחלוקת זה לשון פלוגתא וכו' ששיריה ניכרים כדאמר בפרק בכל וכו' שלא קצר שבולת ראשונה לא נתחייב וכו' ועוד דפליגי נ"ב לפי פירוש זה דקאמר ועוד כו' יהיה מחלוקת זה לשון פלוגתא וק"ל:

גליון הש"ס

תוספות ד"ה יש בשמחה וכו' ולא בשתיהן. עיין פסחים דף ע ע"ב תוספות ד"ה מ"ט:

א הַפֵּאָה, ב וְהַבִּכּוּרִים, ג וְהָרְאָיוֹן, ד וּגְמִילוּת חֲסָדִים, ה וְתַלְמוּד תּוֹרָה. א"ר יוֹחָנָן: כִּסְבוּרִין אָנוּ לוֹמַר הָרְאָיוֹן אֵין לוֹ שִׁיעוּר לְמַעְלָה, אֲבָל יֵשׁ לוֹ שִׁיעוּר לְמַטָּה. עַד שֶׁבָּא ר' אוֹשַׁעְיָא בְּרַבִּי וְלִימֵּד: הָרְאָיוֹן ו אֵין לוֹ שִׁיעוּר לֹא לְמַעְלָה וְלֹא לְמַטָּה. ז אֲבָל (א) חֲכָמִים אוֹמְרִים: הָרְאִיָּיה מָעָה כֶּסֶף, וְהַחֲגִיגָה שְׁתֵּי כֶסֶף. מַאי הָרְאָיוֹן? רַבִּי יוֹחָנָן אָמַר: רְאִיַּית פָּנִים בָּעֲזָרָה, וְרֵישׁ לָקִישׁ אָמַר: רְאִיַּית פָּנִים בְּקָרְבָּן. ח בְּעִיקַּר הָרֶגֶל — כּוּלֵּי עָלְמָא לָא פְּלִיגִי דִּרְאִיַּית פָּנִים בְּקָרְבָּן, כִּי פְּלִיגִי — בִּשְׁאָר יְמוֹת הָרֶגֶל. כָּל הֵיכָא דַּאֲתָא וְאַיְיתֵי — כּוּלֵּי עָלְמָא לָא פְּלִיגִי דִּמְקַבְּלִינַן מִינֵּיהּ, כִּי פְּלִיגִי — דַּאֲתָא וְלָא אַיְיתֵי. דְּר' יוֹחָנָן סָבַר: רְאִיַּית פָּנִים בָּעֲזָרָה דְּכָל אֵימַת דְּאָתֵי לָא צָרִיךְ לְאַתּוּיֵי. רֵישׁ לָקִישׁ אָמַר: רְאִיַּית פָּנִים בְּקָרְבָּן, דְּכָל אֵימַת דְּאָתֵי צָרִיךְ לְאַתּוּיֵי. אֵיתִיבֵיהּ רֵישׁ לָקִישׁ לְרַבִּי יוֹחָנָן: °"וְלֹא יֵרָאוּ פָּנַי רֵיקָם"! אֲמַר לֵיהּ: בְּעִיקַּר הָרֶגֶל. אֵיתִיבֵיהּ: "וְלֹא יֵרָאוּ פָּנַי רֵיקָם" — בִּזְבָחִים, אַתָּה אוֹמֵר בִּזְבָחִים אוֹ אֵינוֹ אֶלָּא בְּעוֹפוֹת וּמְנָחוֹת? וְדִין הוּא: נֶאֶמְרָה חֲגִיגָה לְהֶדְיוֹט וְנֶאֶמְרָה רְאִיָּיה לַגָּבוֹהַּ, מַה חֲגִיגָה הָאֲמוּרָה לְהֶדְיוֹט — זְבָחִים, אַף רְאִיָּיה הָאֲמוּרָה לַגָּבוֹהַּ — זְבָחִים. וּמַה הֵן זְבָחִים — ט עוֹלוֹת. אַתָּה אוֹמֵר עוֹלוֹת, אוֹ אֵינוֹ אֶלָּא שְׁלָמִים? וְדִין הוּא: נֶאֶמְרָה חֲגִיגָה לְהֶדְיוֹט, וְנֶאֶמְרָה רְאִיָּיה לַגָּבוֹהַּ, מַה חֲגִיגָה הָאֲמוּרָה לְהֶדְיוֹט — בָּרָאוּי לוֹ, אַף רְאִיָּיה הָאֲמוּרָה לַגָּבוֹהַּ — בָּרָאוּי לוֹ. *וְכֵן בְּדִין, שֶׁלֹּא יְהֵא שׁוּלְחָנְךָ מָלֵא וְשׁוּלְחָן רַבְּךָ רֵיקָם! אֲמַר לֵיהּ: בְּעִיקַּר הָרֶגֶל. אֵיתִיבֵיהּ, (ב) ר' יוֹסֵי בַּר' יְהוּדָה אוֹמֵר: שָׁלֹשׁ רְגָלִים בַּשָּׁנָה נִצְטַוּוּ יִשְׂרָאֵל לַעֲלוֹת בָּרֶגֶל: בְּחַג הַמַּצּוֹת וּבְחַג הַשָּׁבוּעוֹת, וּבְחַג הַסּוּכּוֹת. וְאֵין נִרְאִין חֲצָאִין — מִשּׁוּם שֶׁנֶּאֱמַר "כָּל זְכוּרְךָ", וְאֵין נִרְאִין רֵיקָנִים — מִשּׁוּם שֶׁנֶּאֱמַר "וְלֹא יֵרָאוּ פָּנַי רֵיקָם!" אֲמַר לֵיהּ: בְּעִיקַּר הָרֶגֶל. אֵיתִיבֵיהּ ר' יוֹחָנָן לְרֵישׁ לָקִישׁ: (ג) "יִרְאֶה" "יֵרָאֶה" — מָה אֲנִי בְּחִנָּם[א] אַף אַתֶּם בְּחִנָּם! *אֶלָּא: כָּל הֵיכָא דַּאֲתָא וְלָא אַיְיתֵי — דְּכוּלֵּי עָלְמָא לָא פְּלִיגִי דְּעָיֵיל, וּמִתְחַזֵי וְנָפֵיק, כִּי פְּלִיגִי — דַּאֲתָא וְאַיְיתֵי. רַבִּי יוֹחָנָן דְּאָמַר רְאִיַּית פָּנִים בָּעֲזָרָה; רְאִיַּית פָּנִים הוּא דְּאֵין לָהּ שִׁיעוּר, הָא לְקָרְבָּן — יֵשׁ לָהּ שִׁיעוּר. וְרֵישׁ לָקִישׁ אָמַר: י רְאִיַּית פָּנִים בְּקָרְבָּן, כ דַּאֲפִילּוּ קָרְבָּן נַמִי אֵין לוֹ שִׁיעוּר. אֵיתִיבֵיהּ: °"הוֹקַר רַגְלְךָ מִבֵּית רֵעֶךָ"! הָתָם בְּחַטָּאוֹת וַאֲשָׁמוֹת, כִּדְרַבִּי לֵוִי, דְּרַבִּי לֵוִי רָמֵי: כְּתִיב "הוֹקַר רַגְלְךָ מִבֵּית רֵעֶךָ" וּכְתִיב °"אָבוֹא בֵיתְךָ בְעוֹלוֹת"! לָא קַשְׁיָא; כָּאן — בְּחַטָּאוֹת וַאֲשָׁמוֹת, כָּאן — בְּעוֹלוֹת וּשְׁלָמִים. תַּנְיָא נַמִי הָכִי: "הוֹקַר רַגְלְךָ מִבֵּית רֵעֶךָ" — בְּחַטָּאוֹת וַאֲשָׁמוֹת הַכָּתוּב מְדַבֵּר, אַתָּה אוֹמֵר בְּחַטָּאוֹת וַאֲשָׁמוֹת אוֹ אֵינוֹ אֶלָּא בְּעוֹלוֹת וּשְׁלָמִים? כְּשֶׁהוּא אוֹמֵר "אָבוֹא בֵיתְךָ בְעוֹלוֹת אֲשַׁלֵּם לְךָ נְדָרָי" — הֲרֵי עוֹלוֹת וּשְׁלָמִים אָמוּר, הָא מָה אֲנִי מְקַיֵּים "הוֹקַר רַגְלְךָ מִבֵּית רֵעֶךָ" — בְּחַטָּאוֹת וַאֲשָׁמוֹת הַכָּתוּב מְדַבֵּר. § "וְאֵין נִרְאִין חֲצָאִין כו'". § סָבַר רַב יוֹסֵף לְמֵימַר: מַאן דְּאִית לֵיהּ עֲשָׂרָה בָּנִים לָא לִיסְקוּ הָאִידָּנָא חֲמִשָּׁה וּלְמָחָר חֲמִשָּׁה. אֲמַר לֵיהּ

(שמות כג) (משלי כה) (תהלים סו)

רש"י

הַפֵּאָה. לֹא נָתְנָה בּוֹ תּוֹרָה שִׁיעוּר (ד). וְאע"פ שֶׁאֵין לַפֵּאָה שִׁיעוּר — נָתְנוּ בּוֹ חֲכָמִים שִׁיעוּר, אַחַת מִשִּׁשִּׁים: וְכֵן הַבִּכּוּרִים. "וְלָקַחְתָּ מֵרֵאשִׁית כָּל פְּרִי הָאֲדָמָה" (דברים כו), וְלֹא נֶאֱמַר כַּמָּה: וְהָרְאָיוֹן. לְקַמָּן מְפָרֵשׁ: אָמַר רַבִּי יוֹחָנָן כִּסְבוּרִין הָיִינוּ לְפָרֵשׁ. הַאי "אֵין לוֹ שִׁיעוּר" דְּקָתָנֵי הָכָא: אֵין לָהֶן שִׁיעוּר לְמַעְלָה. שֶׁיָּבִיא כַּמָּה שֶׁיִּרְצֶה: אֲבָל לְמַטָּה יֵשׁ לוֹ שִׁיעוּר. שֶׁלֹּא לִפְחוֹת מִמָּעָה כֶּסֶף, כְּמוֹ שֶׁשָּׁנִינוּ בְּמִשְׁנָתֵינוּ, וְהָיִינוּ סְבוּרִין דְּשִׁיעוּר דְּאוֹרַיְיתָא הוּא: עַד שֶׁבָּא ר' אוֹשַׁעְיָא בְּרַבִּי וְלִימֵּד. בְּרַבִּי = גָּדוֹל בְּדוֹרוֹ: וְלִימֵּד שֶׁאֵין לוֹ שִׁיעוּר לֹא לְמַטָּה וְלֹא לְמַעְלָה. מִן הַתּוֹרָה: אֲבָל חֲכָמִים כו'. כְּלוֹמַר, שִׁיעוּר מָעָה כֶּסֶף וּשְׁתֵּי כֶסֶף הָאָמוּר בְּמִשְׁנָתֵינוּ בִּרְאִיָּיה וּבַחֲגִיגָה — מִדִּבְרֵי חֲכָמִים הוּא: "אֲבָל אָמְרוּ חֲכָמִים" גָּרְסִינַן: מַאי הָרְאָיוֹן. וְלֹא תָּנָא הָרְאִיָּיה, דְּלֶיהֱוֵי מַשְׁמַע דְּמֵי עוֹלָה. דְּאִלּוּ הַשְׁתָּא לָאו בְּדָמִים מַשְׁמַע אֶלָּא בְּמִצְוַת רְאִיַּית פָּנִים: רַבִּי יוֹחָנָן אָמַר רְאִיַּית פָּנִים בָּעֲזָרָה. כַּמָּה פְּעָמִים שֶׁהוּא חָפֵץ בָּא וּמַרְאֶה עַצְמוֹ בָּעֲזָרָה, וְאֵין צָרִיךְ לְהָבִיא קָרְבָּן בְּכָל רְאִיָּיה וּרְאִיָּיה: רְאִיַּית פָּנִים בְּקָרְבָּן. וְצָרִיךְ לְהָבִיא קָרְבָּן עַל כָּל פַּעַם וָפַעַם: בְּעִיקַּר רֶגֶל. בְּיו"ט רִאשׁוֹן: בִּזְבָחִים. צָרִיךְ לְהָבִיא קָרְבַּן בְּהֵמָה הַזְּבוּחִים בְּסַכִּין, וְלֹא עוֹלַת הָעוֹף שֶׁהִיא נִמְלֶקֶת: נֶאֶמְרָה חֲגִיגָה בָּרֶגֶל. לְמַאֲכַל הֶדְיוֹט: וְנֶאֶמְרָה רְאִיָּיה לַגָּבוֹהַּ. דְּהָא "לֹא יֵרָאוּ פָּנַי" דִּכְתִיב, מַשְׁמַע לְצוֹרְכֵי אֲנִי שׁוֹאֵל: מַה חֲגִיגָה הָאֲמוּרָה לְהֶדְיוֹט זְבָחִים. שֶׁל בְּהֵמָה, דִּכְתִיב: "לֹא יָלִין חֵלֶב חַגִּי עַד בֹּקֶר" (שמות כג), בְּמִידֵי דְּאִית לֵיהּ חֵלֶב הַקָּרֵב לְגָבוֹהַּ קָאָמַר: וְאֵין נִרְאִין חֲצָאִין. מְפָרֵשׁ לְקַמָּן: (ה) בְּחַטָּאוֹת וַאֲשָׁמוֹת. שֶׁלֹּא תֶּחֱטָא וְתִזָּקֵק לְהָבִיא חַטָּאת וְאָשָׁם: מִבֵּית רֵעֶךָ. מִבֵּית אוֹהַבְךָ, הקב"ה, שֶׁקָּרָא יִשְׂרָאֵל רֵעִים, שֶׁנֶּאֱמַר: "לְמַעַן אַחַי וְרֵעָי" (תהלים קכב): סָבַר רַב יוֹסֵף לְמֵימַר כו'. דְּאִי לָאו הָכִי מַאי אֵין נִרְאִין חֲצָאִין דְּיָלֵיף מִ"כָּל זְכוּרְךָ", אִי שֶׁלֹּא יִהְיוּ חֶצְיָין עוֹלִין — מִ"זְּכוּרְךָ" נָפְקָא, שֶׁהֲרֵי כָּל הַזְּכָרִים בִּכְלַל זְכוּרְךָ:
א"ל

תוספות

והבכורים אין לו שיעור לא למעלה ולא למטה. הדר פריך בירושלמי, רבי ברכיה בעי: למה לא תנינן עפר לסוטה, אפר פרה, רוק יבמה, דם לפור של מלורע? א"ר יוסי: לא אייתינן במתני' אלא דברים שהוא מוסיף עליהן ויש בעשייתן מלוה. ואלו, אע"פ שמוסיף עליהן — אין בעשייתן מלוה:

גמילות חסדים. בירושלמי: הדא תימא בגופו, אבל בממונו — יש לו שיעור. ודיקור חולים דאין לו שיעור, כדאיתא בנדרים (דף לט:), הוי בכלל גמילות חסדים:

כסבורין אנו לומר דיש לו שיעור למטה. וסבירא ליה כאידך תנא בירושלמי דחשיב פאה, דיש לה שיעור למטה:

רבי יוחנן אמר ראיית פנים בעזרה. דכיון דאייתי (ו) בראייה חדא זימנא מיפטר בכך אם ירצה, או יביא כמו שירצה. אבל ראיית פנים בקרבן — יש לו שיעור. דסבירא ליה לרבי יוחנן מעה כסף ושתי כסף דאורייתא. והכי איתא בירושלמי דמסכת פאה: מתני' בראייה (ז), אבל בקרבן — יש לו שיעור. דא"ר יוחנן: מעה כסף שתי כסף דאורייתא. ועוד אמר במכילתין: רבי יוחנן כדעתיה, דאמר: כל השיעורים הלכה למשה מסיני. ואמר: מעה כסף ושתי כסף דאורייתא. וריש לקיש, דמוקי לה בראיית פנים בקרבן, סבירא ליה כר' (*יהושע) [ג"ז לוי] דאמר: מעה כסף שתי כסף דרבנן. וכן אמר התם לא יראו פני (ח) כל שהוא, אבל חכמים נתנו להם שיעור: מעה כסף שתי כסף. ומיהו, התלמוד שלנו לא נחית להכי. אלא, להך לישנא קמא משמע דבעי למימר דמתניתין איירי אף במועד, הלכך לא מצי לאוקמי בראיית קרבן, דאז לא מיחייב כלל להביא. אבל בראיית פנים — מיחייב לבוא חדא זימנא, ומשם (זה) והלאה אין לו שיעור. וריש לקיש אמר דמתני' נמי בראיית פנים בקרבן, דמיחייב להביא. ומ"מ לריך לומר דסבירא ליה כרבי יהושע כדפירשתי, כדי שלא יהא שיעור כלל. ולאידך לישנא, דאתא ואייתי בו ביום קאמר דלא מקבלינן (ט) — משום בל תוסיף, כיון דכבר נפיק. אבל למחר וליומא אוחרא — מלי להביא אם ירלה. והא לא פטר ליה קרא מה אני בחנם — רק בחיובא, אבל אי מייתי — שפיר מקבלינן. וכן משמע לישנא דלעיל דאתא ולא אייתי בשאר יומי. ולא פליג רבי יוחנן רק דלא מיחייב לאתויי, אבל אי מייתי — מקבלינן שפיר. וריש לקיש לא איתותב אלא משום דמיחייב ולא מחייב ליה קרא. ולא דמי האי יש לו שיעור להאי דירושלמי, דהתם מלמטה איירי, (*ודחי) [ג"ז ודאי] הקרבן, אבל הכא קיימינן שיעור בהבאתו. ואם נבוא להשוותם יחד — הא לקרבן יש לו שיעור למטה, כדאיתא בירושלמי, וה"נ דין הוא שיש לו שיעור בהבאתו, אי בעי מייתי — אי מקבלינן מיניה או לא. ומיהו, לפי לשון הירושלמי לא ידענא היכי מוקי לה מתני' בראיית פנים בעזרה ולא בקרבן, משום שיש לה שיעור כרבי יוחנן. והא חשיב פאה שיש לה שיעור למטה! ושמא דאיבעי לייתבו למתני' כדברי הכל, אף כתנא דאמר פאה אין לה שיעור לא למעלה ולא למטה, ומתוקמא בראיית פנים לחוד לרבי יוחנן. כן נראה לי הפירוש דהך שמעתתא:

מביאין

רבינו חננאל

דברים שאין להם שיעור הפאה והבכורים והראיון כו'. א"ר יוחנן בא ר' אושעיה ברבי ולימד הראיון אין לו שיעור לא למעלה ולא למטה. אבל חכמים אומרים הראיה מעה כסף וחגיגה שתי כסף. מאי הראיון ר' יוחנן אמר ראיית פנים בעזרה כלומר ביאתו ויציאתו בעזרה כמה פעמים אין לה שיעור. ר"ל אמר ראיית פנים בקרבן. ואמרינן בעיקר הרגל כלומר בתחלת הרגל בעת בואו להקביל פנים בעזרה דברי הכל ראיית [פנים] בקרבן כי פליגי בשאר ימות הרגל וכל עידן דמייתי ועייל כ"ע לא פליגי דמקבלין מיניה כי פליגי היכא דאתא בשאר ימות הרגל ולא אייתי ר' יוחנן אומר עייל דלא צריך לאתויי כל זמן דעייל ור' שמעון בן לקיש [אומר] לא עייל אלא אי מייתי קרבן בהדיה. ומותיב ר"ל והכתיב ולא יראו פני ריקם. ופריק ר' יוחנן ההוא בעיקר הרגל כי קאמרינן דלא צריך היכא דאייתי בעיקר הרגל ולא אייתי בשאר ימות הרגל. איתיביה לא יראו פני ריקם בזבחים אתה אומר בזבחים או אינו אלא בעופות ובמנחות ודין הוא נאמרה חגיגה להדיוט ונאמרה ראיה לגבוה כו' ופריק רבי יוחנן ההיא בעיקר הרגל וכן בהא דר' יוסי ב"ר יהודה והדר ר' יוחנן ומותיב ליה לר"ל כתיב יראה וקרינן יראה מה אני בחנם אף אתם בחנם. ופרקינן אלא לעולם בעו לאתויי דהא כתיב ולא יראו פני ריקם *) וכל היכא דאתא ולא אייתי אע"ג דעבר כ"ע לא פליגי דעייל בעזרה ומתחזי ונפיק כי פליגי דאתא ואייתי בעיקר הרגל. ר' יוחנן אומר תוב לא מייתי דראיית פנים בעזרה הוא דאין לו שיעור וכל אימת דאתי עייל אבל ראיית קרבן יש לה שיעור וכיון דאייתי אי מייתי אחריתי לא מקבלינן מיניה ומותיב ר' יוחנן והכתיב הוקר רגלך מבית רעך כלומר אל תרבה להראות לו פניך ופריק ר"ל התם בחטאות ואשמות כלומר הזהר בעצמך ואל תחטא בכל יום ולהביא חטאת ואשם וכדר' לוי דאמר כתוב אחד אומר אבוא ביתך בעולות וכתוב אחר אומר הוקר רגלך מבית רעך ומשני לא קשיא הא בעולות ושלמים אבוא ביתך והא דכתב הוקר רגלך בחטאות ואשמות. תניא נמי

*) דברי רבינו אלו אינם שלמים לפי סוגיית הגמ' ואולי דגירסא אחרת היה לו וצ"ע.

עין משפט נר מצוה

כז א מיי' פ"א מהל' מתנות עניים הלכה טו סמג לאוין רפד:
כח ב מיי' פ"ב מהל' בכורים הלכה יז סמג עשין קלח:
כט ג מיי' פ"א מהלכות חגיגה הלכה ב סמג עשין רכח:
ל ד מיי' פי"ד מהלכות אבל הלכה א:
לא ה מיי' פ"א מהל' ת"ת הלכה י טוש"ע י"ד סי' רמו סעיף ג:
לב ו ז מיי' פ"א מהל' חגיגה הלכה ב:
לג ח ט מיי' שם הל' ב
לד י כ מיי' שם הל' ב ופ"ב שם הלכה ו:

הגהות הב"ח

(א) גמ' אבל אמרו חכמים הראייה: (ב) שם בעיקר הרגל איתיביה ר"ל לר"י ר' יוסי בר' יהודה: (ג) שם איתיביה ר' יוחנן לריש לקיש יֵרָאֶה יִרְאֶה מה אני: (ד) רש"י ד"ה הפאה וכו' אע"פ שיש לפאה שיעור חכמים נתנו בו שיעור: (ה) ד"ה ואין נראין וכו' לקמן הס"ד ואח"כ מה"ד מבית רעך וכו' אחי ורעי הס"ד ואח"כ מה"ד בחטאות וכו' ואשם הס"ד ואח"כ מה"ד סבר רב: (ו) תוס' ד"ה ר' יוחנן וכו' דכיון דאייתי קרבן בראייה: (ז) בא"ד מתני' בראיית פנים אבל בראיית קרבן יש לו: (ח) בא"ד לא יראו פני ריקם אפילו כל שהוא: (ט) בא"ד דלא מקבלינן מיניה טפי משום בל תוסיף וכו' אם ירלה דהא לא פטר וכו' דלא פליג ר' יוחנן וכו' יש לו שיעור היינו יש לו שיעור למטה כדאיתא בירושלמי וכו' שיעור להבאתו:

[עי' תוספות ב"ב קנד: ד"ה כרס ותוספות בכורות ל: ד"ה אלא]

[ביצה כ:]

גליון הש"ס

גמרא כל היכא דאתא. כעין זה שבת דף ב ע"א ועיין בתוספות שם ד"ה אלא אי אתמר:

הגהות מהר"ב רנשבורג

א] גמרא אף אתם בחנם. נ"ב עי' טורי אבן:

עין משפט
נר מצוה

לה א מיי' פ"ב מהל' חגיגה הלכה י:
לו ב מיי' שם הלכה ח סמג עשין רכט:
לז ג ד מיי' שם פ"א הלכה ח ט:
לח ה מיי' שם הלכה י:
לט ו ז מיי' שם הלכה ח:
מ ח מיי' שם פ"ב הלכה ח סמג עשין רכט:
מא ט מיי' שם הלכה י:
מב י מיי' שם הל' ח:

אֲמַר לֵיהּ אַבַּיֵי: פְּשִׁיטָא, הֵי מִינַּיְיהוּ מְשַׁוֵּית לְהוּ פּוֹשְׁעִים וְהֵי מִינַּיְיהוּ מְשַׁוֵּית לְהוּ זְרִיזִין! אֶלָּא קְרָא לְמַאי אֲתָא — לְכִדְאֲחֵרִים. דְּתַנְיָא, *אֲחֵרִים אוֹמְרִים: הַמְקַמֵּץ, וְהַמְצָרֵף נְחֹשֶׁת, וְהַבּוּרְסִי — פְּטוּרִין מִן הָרְאִיָּה, שֶׁנֶּאֱמַר: °"כָּל זְכוּרְךָ" — מִי שֶׁיָּכוֹל לַעֲלוֹת עִם כָּל זְכוּרְךָ, יָצְאוּ אֵלּוּ שֶׁאֵין יְכוֹלִין לַעֲלוֹת עִם כָּל זְכוּרְךָ.§ **מתני'** עוֹלוֹת בַּמּוֹעֵד בָּאוֹת מִן הַחוּלִּין, וְהַשְּׁלָמִים מִן הַמַּעֲשֵׂר. יוֹם טוֹב הָרִאשׁוֹן שֶׁל פֶּסַח, בֵּית שַׁמַּאי אוֹמְרִים: מִן הַחוּלִּין, וּבֵית הִלֵּל אוֹמְרִים: מִן הַמַּעֲשֵׂר. [א]יִשְׂרָאֵל יוֹצְאִין יְדֵי חוֹבָתָן בִּנְדָרִים וּנְדָבוֹת וּבְמַעְשַׂר בְּהֵמָה, וְהַכֹּהֲנִים בְּחַטָּאוֹת וַאֲשָׁמוֹת וּבִבְכוֹר וּבְחָזֶה וָשׁוֹק, אֲבָל לֹא בָעוֹפוֹת וְלֹא בַמְּנָחוֹת.§ **גמ'** אֶלָּא עוֹלוֹת, בַּמּוֹעֵד הוּא דְּבָאוֹת מִן הַחוּלִּין. הָא בְּיוֹם טוֹב — מִן הַמַּעֲשֵׂר, אַמַּאי? *דָּבָר שֶׁבְּחוֹבָה הִיא, [ב]*וְכָל דָּבָר שֶׁבְּחוֹבָה אֵינוֹ בָּא אֶלָּא מִן הַחוּלִּין! וְכִי תֵּימָא: הָא קָא מַשְׁמַע לָן דְּעוֹלוֹת, בַּמּוֹעֵד — בָּאוֹת, בְּיוֹם טוֹב — אֵינָן בָּאוֹת, כְּמַאן — כְּבֵית שַׁמַּאי?! דְּתְנַן: *בֵּית שַׁמַּאי אוֹמְרִים: מְבִיאִין שְׁלָמִים וְאֵין סוֹמְכִין עֲלֵיהֶן, אֲבָל לֹא עוֹלוֹת. וּבֵית הִלֵּל אוֹמְרִים: [ג]מְבִיאִין שְׁלָמִים וְעוֹלוֹת, [ד]וְסוֹמְכִין עֲלֵיהֶן! חַסּוּרֵי מִיחַסְּרָא וְהָכִי קָתָנֵי: [ה]עוֹלוֹת נְדָרִים וּנְדָבוֹת, בַּמּוֹעֵד — בָּאוֹת, [ו]בְּיוֹם טוֹב — אֵינָן בָּאוֹת, [ז]וְעוֹלַת רְאִיָּה — בָּאָה אֲפִילּוּ בְּיוֹ"ט. [א]וּכְשֶׁהִיא בָּאָה — [ח]אֵינָהּ בָּאָה אֶלָּא מִן הַחוּלִּין. [ט]וְשַׁלְמֵי שִׂמְחָה בָּאִין אַף מִן הַמַּעֲשֵׂר. וַחֲגִיגַת יוֹם טוֹב הָרִאשׁוֹן שֶׁל פֶּסַח, בֵּית שַׁמַּאי אוֹמְרִים: מִן הַחוּלִּין. וּבֵית הִלֵּל אוֹמְרִים: מִן הַמַּעֲשֵׂר. תַּנְיָא נַמִי הָכִי: עוֹלוֹת נְדָרִים וּנְדָבוֹת, בַּמּוֹעֵד — בָּאוֹת, בְּיוֹם טוֹב — אֵינָן בָּאוֹת. וְעוֹלַת רְאִיָּה — בָּאָה אֲפִי' בְּיוֹם טוֹב. [ב]וּכְשֶׁהִיא בָּאָה — אֵינָהּ בָּאָה אֶלָּא מִן הַחוּלִּין. וְשַׁלְמֵי שִׂמְחָה בָּאִין אַף מִן הַמַּעֲשֵׂר. וַחֲגִיגַת יוֹם טוֹב הָרִאשׁוֹן שֶׁל פֶּסַח, בֵּית שַׁמַּאי אוֹמְרִים: מִן הַחוּלִּין, וּבֵית הִלֵּל אוֹמְרִים: מִן הַמַּעֲשֵׂר. מַאי שְׁנָא חֲגִיגַת יוֹם טוֹב הָרִאשׁוֹן שֶׁל פֶּסַח? אָמַר רַב אַשִׁי: הָא קָא מַשְׁמַע לָן, חֲגִיגַת חֲמִשָּׁה עָשָׂר — אִין, חֲגִיגַת אַרְבָּעָה עָשָׂר — לָא.
אַלְמָא

תורה אור
דברים טז

א"ל אַבַּיֵי. הַאי נַמִי לָא תִּיבָּעֵי לָךְ קְרָא, דִּבְלָאו קְרָא נַמִי פְּשִׁיטָא, מֵאַחַר שֶׁחִיֵּיב אֶת כּוּלָּן — אֲנָא יָדַעְנָא דְּכָל אֶחָד צָרִיךְ לְזָרֵז אֶת עַצְמוֹ. דְּהֵיאַךְ יֹאמַר הָאָב לְאֵלּוּ הֱוו זְרִיזִין, וּלְאֵלּוּ הֱווּ עֲצֵלִין: אֶלָּא קְרָא לְכִדְאֲחֵרִים. וְהַיְינוּ נַמִי אֵין נִרְאִין לַחֲצָאִין; דְּמִי שֶׁאֵינוֹ רָאוּי לַעֲלוֹת אֶלָּא בַּחֲבוּרָה מוּעֶטֶת כְּגוֹן אֵלּוּ, שֶׁיַּעֲשׂוּ חֲבוּרָה לְעַצְמָן, כָּךְ נִרְאֶה בְּעֵינַי. וְרַבּוֹתַיי מְפָרְשִׁין דְּלָאו אֵין נִרְאִין לַחֲצָאִין אָתָא אַבַּיֵי לְפָרוּשֵׁי, אֶלָּא לְמֵימְרָא דִּקְרָא לָאו לְהָכִי אָתָא. וְקַשְׁיָא לִי: סוֹף סוֹף הָא דְּאֵין נִרְאִין חֲצָאִין, מַאי קָאָמַר תַּנָּא? וְעוֹד: שֶׁשִּׁיטַת הַתַּלְמוּד כָּל הֵיכָא דְּאִיכָּא סָבַר פְּלוֹנִי לְמֵימַר הָכִי, וְאָמַר לֵיהּ פְּלוֹנִי הָכִי — הַהִיא מִילְּתָא גּוּפָא דַּהֲוָה מָצֵי לְמֵימַר קַמָּא מְתָרֵץ בַּתְרָא, וְאָמַר לֵיהּ דְּלָא תְּפָרְשֵׁיהּ הָכִי אֶלָּא הָכִי: **מתני'** עוֹלוֹת בַּמּוֹעֵד בָּאוֹת מִן הַחוּלִּין. מַשְׁמַע הַשְׁתָּא עוֹלוֹת רְאִיָּה הַבָּאוֹת בְּחוּלּוֹ שֶׁל מוֹעֵד בָּאוֹת מִן הַחוּלִּין, וְלֹא מִמְּעוֹת מַעֲשֵׂר שֵׁנִי. דְּקיי"ל: כָּל דָּבָר שֶׁבְּחוֹבָה אֵינוֹ בָּא אֶלָּא מִן הַחוּלִּין, בְּמַסֶּכֶת מְנָחוֹת (דף כב.). וּלְקַמָּן נַמִי בַּגְּמָרָא (דף ח.) תַּנְיָא: "מִסַּת" — מְלַמֵּד שֶׁאָדָם מֵבִיא חוֹבָתוֹ מִן הַחוּלִּין. וּבַגְּמָ' פָּרֵיךְ: אַמַּאי נָקַט חוּלּוֹ שֶׁל מוֹעֵד? כִּי מַיְיתֵי לָהּ בְּיוֹם טוֹב — נַמִי מִן הַחוּלִּין בָּעֵי לְאַתּוּיֵי! וּשְׁלָמִים מִן הַמַּעֲשֵׂר. בַּגְּמָרָא מְפָרֵשׁ: שַׁלְמֵי שִׂמְחָה, דְּרַבִּינְהוּ קְרָא בְּכָל מִילֵּי: וְיוֹ"ט הָרִאשׁוֹן שֶׁל פֶּסַח. בַּגְּמָרָא מְפָרֵשׁ מַאי הִיא, וּמַאי שְׁנָא פֶּסַח דְּנָקַט: יִשְׂרָאֵל יוֹצְאִין יְדֵי חוֹבָתָן. מִשּׁוּם שִׂמְחָה, בְּכָל עִנְיָן שֶׁיֵּשׁ לָהֶן בָּשָׂר לְשׂוֹבַע, וְאֵין זְקוּקִין לִזְבּוֹחַ שְׁלָמִים לְשֵׁם כָּךְ: בִּנְדָרִים וּנְדָבוֹת. שֶׁהִתְנַדְּבוּ כָּל הַשָּׁנָה, וּכְשֶׁעוֹלִין לִירוּשָׁלַיִם בָּרֶגֶל מְבִיאִין אוֹתָן, וּמַקְרִיבִין אֵימוּרֵיהֶן וְהַבָּשָׂר נֶאֱכָל לִבְעָלִים — יוֹצְאִין בָּהֶן מִשּׁוּם שִׂמְחָה. מִשּׁוּם דְּבָעֵי לְמִיתְנֵי סֵיפָא "וְהַכֹּהֲנִים בְּחַטָּאוֹת" וכו', נָקַט בְּרֵישָׁא יִשְׂרָאֵל: וְהַכֹּהֲנִים. שֶׁבָּאוּ לָהֶן חַטָּאוֹת בָּרֶגֶל, חַטָּאוֹת וַאֲשָׁמוֹת שֶׁהָיוּ עוֹלֵי רְגָלִים מְחוּיָּיבִין, וְיֵשׁ לָהֶן בָּשָׂר לְשׂוֹבַע — יוֹצְאִין בָּהֶן מִשּׁוּם שִׂמְחָה, וְאֵין צְרִיכִין לְהָבִיא שְׁלָמִים לְשֵׁם שִׂמְחָה אֶלָּא בִּזְמַן שֶׁאֵין לָהֶן בָּשָׂר לְשׂוֹבַע: יוֹצְאִין בְּחָזֶה וָשׁוֹק. הַמּוּרָמִים לָהֶן מִשַּׁלְמֵי עוֹלֵי רְגָלִים: אֲבָל לֹא בְּעוֹפוֹת. בְּחַטַּאת הָעוֹף, שֶׁאֵין שׂוֹבֵעַ אֶלָּא בִּבְשַׂר בְּהֵמָה, וּבַגְּמָ' יָלֵיף לָהּ: **גמ'** הָא. אִם הֱבִיאָן בְּיוֹם טוֹב, יְבִיאֵם מִן הַמַּעֲשֵׂר, אִם יִרְצֶה?! בִּתְמִיָּה: וְכִי תֵּימָא. הַאי דְּנָקַט בַּמּוֹעֵד מִשּׁוּם דַּאֲגַב אוֹרְחֵיהּ קָא מַשְׁמַע לָן מִילְּתָא אַחֲרִיתִי: דְּאֵין עוֹלַת רְאִיָּה קְרֵיבָה בְּיוֹם טוֹב, וְאַף עַל פִּי שֶׁהִיא חוֹבַת הָרֶגֶל, הוֹאִיל וְיֵשׁ לָהּ תַּשְׁלוּמִין לְמָחָר: מְבִיאִין שְׁלָמִים. בְּיוֹם טוֹב, לְפִי שֶׁיֵּשׁ בָּהֶם צוֹרֶךְ מַאֲכַל הֶדְיוֹט: וְאֵין סוֹמְכִין עֲלֵיהֶן. שֶׁהַסְּמִיכָה שְׁבוּת הִיא, שֶׁמִּשְׁתַּמֵּשׁ בְּבַעֲלֵי חַיִּים, וּתְנַן: אֵלּוּ הֵן מִשּׁוּם שְׁבוּת: לֹא עוֹלִין בָּאִילָן וְלֹא רוֹכְבִין עַל גַּבֵּי בְהֵמָה (ביצה דף לו:): אֲבָל לֹא עוֹלוֹת. אֵין מְבִיאִין כְּלָל, דִּסְבִירָא לְהוּ לְב"ש "לָכֶם" (שמות יב) — וְלֹא לְגָבוֹהַּ, חוּץ מִתְּמִידִין וּמוּסָפִין שֶׁזְּמַנָּן קָבוּעַ, וְכָל שֶׁזְּמַנָּן קָבוּעַ כְּתִיב בְּהוּ "בְּמוֹעֲדוֹ" וַאֲפִילּוּ בְּשַׁבָּת, וְכָל שֶׁכֵּן בְּיוֹ"ט: וְסוֹמְכִין עֲלֵיהֶן. כֵּיוָן דְּמוּתָּר לַהֲבִיאָן — לֹא גָּזְרוּ שְׁבוּת לְבַטֵּל סְמִיכָתָן: בְּיוֹ"ט אֵינָן בָּאוֹת. וַאֲפִי' לְב"ה, סְבִירָא לֵיהּ לְתַנָּא דְּמַתְנִי' דִּנְדָרִים וּנְדָבוֹת אֵין קְרֵבִין בְּיוֹ"ט. וְכִי שָׁרוּ ב"ה — בְּעוֹלַת רְאִיָּה וְשַׁלְמֵי חֲגִיגָה, אע"פ שֶׁיֵּשׁ לָהֶן תַּשְׁלוּמִין — עִיקַּר מִצְוָתָן בְּיוֹם רִאשׁוֹן, דִּכְתִיב "וְחַגּוֹתֶם אוֹתוֹ" (ויקרא כג) — בְּיוֹם רִאשׁוֹן מַשְׁמַע: וּכְשֶׁהִיא בָּאָה אֵינָהּ בָּאָה אֶלָּא מִן הַחוּלִּין. וְהָכָא לָא מָנוּ לְאִיפְלוּגֵי וּלְמֵימַר טוֹפֵל מְעוֹת מַעֲשֵׂר עִמָּהֶן, דְּכִי אִישְׁתְּרֵי טְפֵילָה — בַּחֲגִיגָה הוּא דְּאִישְׁתְּרֵי(א), לְקַמָּן: מִנַּיִין שֶׁאִם רָצָה לְעָרֵב כו' גַּבֵּי שְׁלָמִים, יֵשׁ אָדָם שֶׁיֵּשׁ לוֹ אוֹכְלִין מְרוּבִּין וּנְכָסִין מוּעָטִים, וְאִי אֶפְשָׁר לְהָבִיא חֲגִיגוֹת כּוּלָּן מִן הַחוּלִּין. אֲבָל עוֹלָה לָמָּה טוֹפְלָהּ? יָבִיא בְּמָעָה כֶּסֶף: אַף מִן הַמַּעֲשֵׂר. דְּלָאו דָּבָר שֶׁבְּחוֹבָה הוּא בְּמָקוֹם שֶׁיֵּשׁ בָּשָׂר, וַהֲרֵי יֵשׁ לוֹ מְעוֹת מַעֲשֵׂר שֵׁנִי שֶׁיֵּשׁ לוֹ לְהוֹצִיא בִּירוּשָׁלַיִם וְיִקְנֶה בָּהֶם שְׁלָמִים, וְרַבֵּי קְרָא לְקַמָּן כָּל מִינֵי שְׂמָחוֹת לְשִׂמְחָה: וַחֲגִיגַת יוֹם טוֹב הָרִאשׁוֹן. שֶׁהוּא וַדַּאי דָּבָר שֶׁבְּחוֹבָה, אֲפִי' יֵשׁ לוֹ בָּשָׂר הַרְבֵּה, דְּיָלְפִינַן לְקַמָּן מִ"וְחַגּוֹתֶם אוֹתוֹ" וגו'. וּלְקַמֵּיהּ פָּרֵיךְ: מַאי שְׁנָא פֶּסַח דְּנָקַט? וב"ה אוֹמְרִים כו'. לְקַמָּן פָּרֵיךְ: הָא וַדַּאי דָּבָר שֶׁבְּחוֹבָה הִיא! וּמוֹקֵי לָהּ בְּטוֹפֵל: חֲגִיגַת י"ד לָא. כְּלוֹמַר, לְהָכִי נָקַט פֶּסַח, לְפִי שֶׁיֵּשׁ עֶרֶב פֶּסַח חֲגִיגָה אַחֶרֶת, כְּשֶׁהָיְתָה חֲבוּרַת פֶּסַח מְרוּבָּה הָיוּ מְבִיאִין עִמּוֹ חֲגִיגָה, כְּדֵי שֶׁיְּהֵא פֶּסַח נֶאֱכָל עַל הַשּׂוֹבַע וְאַשְׁמְעִינַן מַתְנִיתִין דַּחֲגִיגַת יוֹ"ט עַצְמוֹ הוּא דְּאֵינָהּ בָּאָה אֶלָּא מִן הַחוּלִּין, אֲבָל חֲגִיגַת אַרְבָּעָה עָשָׂר — בָּאָה אַף מִן הַמַּעֲשֵׂר:
אָמַר

מביאין שלמים ואין סומכין עליהם. דסבירא להו כשמאי רבם, דאמר לקמן (דף יז.) שלא לסמוך ביום טוב, והלל אומר לסמוך. אבל מעולות לא מצינו פלוגתא דפליגו בה הלל ושמאי, ואמרינן בפרק קמא דשבת (דף טו. ושם) דלא נחלקו רק בשלשה דברים, ומההיא דסמיכה פריך ומשני לה שפיר. אלא התלמידים קבלו מרבם אף עולות(ב), ולא נחלקו בהא. וההיא דפרק שני דביצה (דף כ:): מעשה באחד מתלמידי הלל שהביא עולתו בעזרה כו' ואמר לו אחד מתלמידי שמאי: מה זו סמיכה — הוא הדין דמצי למימר מה זו עולה שהם אומרים שלא להביא. אלא לא הבין שהיה עולה, אבל(ג) הסמיכה שראה לפניו הקפיד. והא דלא הקפיד כמו כן בהלל עצמו, בעובדא דמייתי לעיל מינה — דשמא לא ראו הסמיכה. ועוד, שמא לא היו מוחין אלא לתלמידיו שהיו חולקין, אבל הלל חלק עם רבם ואין בידם למחות:

עולות ונדרים ונדבות במועד באות ולא ביו"ט. דאף בית הלל מודו דאין קריבין ביו"ט. והא דקאמרי' בפ"ק דביצה (דף יב. ושם): השוחט עולת נדבה ביו"ט לוקה, דאמר לך מני — ב"ש היא, ולא מוקי לה כב"ה, דנהי דאיסורא איכא — לאו ליכא, כיון דאית ליה 'מתוך' כדקאמרינן התם. וכן אמרינן התם פ' שני דביצה (דף יט.) בגמרא דהאי משנה: אמר רשב"א לא נחלקו ב"ש וב"ה על עולות שאינם של יו"ט שאין קריבין. [והא] דהתם כי פריך על עולה דאמר מחלוקת ב"ש וב"ה בשלמי חגיגה לסמוך וכו' מברייתא דתני בה פלוגתא על שלמים שאינן של יו"ט כו', ולא אקשי ליה ממתניתין דהכא (ד) — כי היכי דמתרצי לה עולות נדרים ונדבות במועד באות ביו"ט, לא היינו טעמא, דעדיפא ליה לאקשויי מברייתא דמתני בהדיא, ולא ע"י דיוקא וחסורי מיחסרא והכי קתני. והא דלא מייתי להו נדרים ונדבות לעולה, דאמר לב"ה אין קריבין נדרים ונדבות — משום דנפיק בהו משום שלמי שמחה, כדאמרינן בסמוך דאיכא לאוקמי שכבר קרב שמחה כדינו. והרב רבי אלחנן והר"י מתרץ: דלא אמר בסמוך דנפיק בשלמי שמחה בנדרים אלא היינו היכא שהקריבום משום שמחה, אבל הביאום לשם נדרים — לא נפיק רק משום הקדישם:
אלמא

רבינו חננאל

נמי הכי כשנויא דריש לקיש. ואין נראין חצאין פי' כל מי שאינו יכול לעלות בכלל ישראל כולו. כגון המקמץ והמצרף נחשת והבורסקי מפני שריחו רע ומואסין אותו פטורין מן הראייה שנאמר כל זכורך מי שיכול לעלות עם כל זכורך: **מתני'** עולות במועד באות מן החולין כו' ושלמים מן המעשר מעשר שני שאע"פ שהוכנו מעות מעשר שני לשמחת הרגל. שלמים לשמחת הרגל הן באין ומותר תריצנה למתניתין הכי חסורי מחסרא והכי קתני עולות ונדרים ונדבות במועד הן באות אבל לא ביו"ט ועולת ראיה באה אפי' ביו"ט וכשהיא באה אינה באה אלא מן החולין ושלמי שמחה באין אף מן המעשר ממעות מעשר שני וחגיגת יו"ט הראשון של פסח בש"א מן החולין ובה"א מן המעשר. תניא נמי הכי עולות נדרים ונדבות במועד באות ביו"ט אינן באות כו' אסיקנא קסבר ב"ש חגיגת יו"ט הראשון היא מן התורה.

[עי' תוספות לקמן ח. ד"ה אמאי]

מסורת הש"ס

לעיל ז.

[לקמן ח. פסחים עא. ביצה יט: מנחות פב.]

ביצה יט. ולקמן יז. מגילה ה.

הגהות הב"ח

(א) רש"י ד"ה וכשהיא באה וכו' לאישתרי כדתניא לקמן: (ב) תום' ד"ה מביאין וכו' קבלו מרבם אף עולות ונחלקו בה בההוא דפ' שני כצ"ל ותיבת ולא נמחק: (ג) בא"ד אבל על הסמיכה: (ד) ד"ה עולות וכו' ולא אקשי ליה ממתניתין דהכא לבתר דמתרצים לה וכו' ולא ממתניתין ע"י דיוקא וכו' והר"י מתרץ וכו' שמחה בנדרים ונדבות [אלא] היכא שהקריבום:

הגהות הגר"א

[א ב] גמרא אפילו ביו"ט וכשהן באין אינן באין אלא כו' כצ"ל:

אַלְמָא קָסָבַר: *אחֲגִיגַת אַרְבָּעָה עָשָׂר לָאו דְּאוֹרַיְיתָא. אָמַר מָר: בֵּית הִלֵּל אוֹמְרִים: מִן הַמַּעֲשֵׂר. אַמַּאי? דָּבָר שֶׁבְּחוֹבָה הוּא, *בוְכָל דָּבָר שֶׁבְּחוֹבָה אֵינוֹ בָּא אֶלָּא מִן הַחוּלִּין! אָמַר עוּלָּא: גבְּטוֹפֵל. חִזְקִיָּה אָמַר: טוֹפְלִין בְּהֵמָה לִבְהֵמָה וְאֵין טוֹפְלִין מָעוֹת לְמָעוֹת. וְרַבִּי יוֹחָנָן אָמַר: דטוֹפְלִין מָעוֹת לְמָעוֹת וְאֵין טוֹפְלִין בְּהֵמָה לִבְהֵמָה. תַּנְיָא כְּוָותֵיהּ דְּחִזְקִיָּה, תַּנְיָא כְּוָותֵיהּ דְּרַבִּי יוֹחָנָן. תַּנְיָא כְּוָותֵיהּ דְּרַבִּי יוֹחָנָן: דברים טז °"מִסַּת" — *מְלַמֵּד שֶׁאָדָם מֵבִיא חוֹבָתוֹ מִן הַחוּלִּין, וּמִנַּיִן שֶׁאִם רָצָה לְעָרֵב מְעָרֵב — ת"ל: שם °"כַּאֲשֶׁר יְבָרֶכְךָ ה' אֱלֹהֶיךָ", תַּנְיָא כְּוָותֵיהּ דְּחִזְקִיָּה: "מִסַּת" — מְלַמֵּד שֶׁאָדָם מֵבִיא חוֹבָתוֹ מִן הַחוּלִּין, בֵּית שַׁמַּאי אוֹמְרִים: יוֹם רִאשׁוֹן מִן הַחוּלִּין, מִכָּאן וְאֵילָךְ מִן הַמַּעֲשֵׂר. וּבֵית הִלֵּל אוֹמְרִים: האֲכִילָה רִאשׁוֹנָה מִן הַחוּלִּין, מִכָּאן וְאֵילָךְ מִן הַמַּעֲשֵׂר. וּשְׁאָר כָּל יְמוֹת הַפֶּסַח — ואָדָם יוֹצֵא יְדֵי חוֹבָתוֹ בְּמַעְשַׂר בְּהֵמָה. בְּיוֹם טוֹב מ"ט לָא? אָמַר רַב אַשִׁי: זדִּלְמָא אָתֵי לְעַשּׂוּרֵי בְּיו"ט, *וְאִי אֶפְשָׁר לְעַשֵּׂר בְּיוֹם טוֹב מִשּׁוּם סִקְרָתָא. מַאי מַשְׁמַע דְּהַאי "מִסַּת" לִישָּׁנָא אסתר י דְּחוּלִּין הוּא? דִּכְתִיב: °"וַיָּשֶׂם הַמֶּלֶךְ אֲחַשְׁוֵרוֹשׁ מַס עַל הָאָרֶץ". §. "יִשְׂרָאֵל יוֹצְאִין יְדֵי חוֹבָתָן דברים טז בִּנְדָרִים וּנְדָבוֹת". §. ת"ר: °"וְשָׂמַחְתָּ בְּחַגֶּךָ" — לְרַבּוֹת כָּל מִינֵי שְׂמָחוֹת לְשִׂמְחָה. מִכָּאן אָמְרוּ חֲכָמִים: חיִשְׂרָאֵל יוֹצְאִין יְדֵי חוֹבָתָן בִּנְדָרִים וּנְדָבוֹת וּבְמַעְשַׂר בְּהֵמָה, וְהַכֹּהֲנִים בְּחַטָּאת וְאָשָׁם וּבַבְּכוֹר וּבֶחָזֶה וְשׁוֹק. יָכוֹל אַף בְּעוֹפוֹת וּבִמְנָחוֹת — ת"ל: "וְשָׂמַחְתָּ בְּחַגֶּךָ" מִי

תורה אור

אָמַר מָר וּבֵית הִלֵּל אוֹמְרִים אַף מִן הַמַּעֲשֵׂר. וַהֲלֹא דָבָר שֶׁבְּחוֹבָה הוּא: בְּטוֹפֵל. מְחַבֵּר מַעֲשֵׂר עִם הַחוּלִּין וּמֵבִיא, וּפְלִיגִי אָמוֹרָאֵי כֵּיצַד טוֹפְלִין: חִזְקִיָּה אָמַר בְּהֵמָה לִבְהֵמָה. אִם יֵשׁ לוֹ אוֹכְלִין הַרְבֵּה וְאֵין לָהֶן סִיפּוּק בִּבְהֵמָה אַחַת, יָבִיא אַחַת לַחֲגִיגָה מִן הַחוּלִּין וְהַשְּׁאָר מִן הַמַּעֲשֵׂר, וְאע"פ שֶׁכּוּלָּן הַבָּאוֹת בַּיּוֹם רִאשׁוֹן שֵׁם חֲגִיגָה עֲלֵיהֶן, כְּבָר יָצָא יְדֵי חוֹבָה בָּרִאשׁוֹנָה מִן הַחוּלִּין: וְאֵין טוֹפְלִין מָעוֹת לְמָעוֹת. לִקְנוֹת בְּהֵמָה גְּדוֹלָה. וְרַבִּי יוֹחָנָן אָמַר אִיפְּכָא: לְמָר אִתְחֲזֵי לֵיהּ שַׁפִּיר טְפֵי יְצִיאַת יְדֵי חוֹבָתוֹ מִן הַחוּלִּין, כְּשֶׁמֵּבִיא בְּהֵמָה שְׁלֵמָה מִן הַחוּלִּין, וּלְמָר אִתְחֲזֵי לֵיהּ שַׁפִּיר טְפֵי כְּשֶׁחוּלִּין מְעוֹרָבִין עִם כָּל אֲכִילוֹתָיו. וּלְקַמָּן יָלֵיף לָהּ מִקְּרָאֵי דְּמוּתָּר לִהְיוֹת טוֹפֵל: מִסַּת. בְּשָׁבוּעוֹת כְּתִיב: "וְעָשִׂיתָ חַג שָׁבוּעוֹת לַה' אֱלֹהֶיךָ מִסַּת נִדְבַת יָדְךָ", וּלְקַמָּן מְפָרֵשׁ מִסַּת לְשׁוֹן חוּלִּין: מְעָרֵב. אֵין לָשׁוֹן זֶה נוֹפֵל אֶלָּא בְּמָעוֹת שֶׁקּוֹנֶה בָּהֶן בְּהֵמָה, דִּשְׁתֵּי בְּהֵמוֹת — זוֹ נִיכֶּרֶת לְעַצְמָהּ וְזוֹ נִיכֶּרֶת לְעַצְמָהּ: אֲשֶׁר יְבָרֶכְךָ. מִכֹּל אֲשֶׁר יְבָרֶכְךָ: יוֹם רִאשׁוֹן. שֶׁהוּא לְשֵׁם חֲגִיגָה — יְהוּ מִן הַחוּלִּין, וְלֵית לְהוּ לְב"ש טְפֵילָה בְּדָבָר שֶׁבְּחוֹבָה: מִכָּאן וְאֵילָךְ. שֶׁאֵינוֹ אֶלָּא שִׂמְחָה. דְּאִילּוּ בַּחֲגִיגָה כְּתִיב: "וְחַגּוֹתֶם אוֹתוֹ" — יוֹם אֶחָד וְתוּ לֹא, אַף מִן הַמַּעֲשֵׂר: אֲכִילָה רִאשׁוֹנָה. הָשְׁתָּא סָלְקָא דַּעְתָּךְ בְּהֵמָה לְעַצְמָהּ, וִיבִיאֶנָּה עַל שֻׁלְחָן רִאשׁוֹן: מִכָּאן וְאֵילָךְ. אֲפִילּוּ בּוֹ בַּיּוֹם: וּשְׁאָר כָּל יְמוֹת הַפֶּסַח. שֶׁאֵינָן אֶלָּא לְשִׂמְחָה, אָדָם יוֹצֵא בְּמַעֲשַׂר בְּהֵמָה אִם יֵשׁ לוֹ, וְכָל שֶׁכֵּן שֶׁקּוֹנֶה שְׁלָמִים בְּמָעוֹת מַעֲשֵׂר שֵׁנִי: בְּיו"ט מַאי טַעְמָא לֹא. נָפֵיק בְּמַעֲשַׂר בְּהֵמָה בִּשְׁאָר אֲכִילוֹת חוּץ מִן הָרִאשׁוֹנָה, כִּי הֵיכִי דְּשָׁרוּ בְּמַעֲשֵׂר שֵׁנִי: מִשּׁוּם סִקְרָתָא. שֶׁצּוֹבְעוֹ. דִּתְנַן בִּבְכוֹרוֹת (דף נח:): הַיּוֹצֵא בָּעֲשִׂירִי סוֹקְרוֹ בְּסִיקְרָא, וְאוֹמֵר: הֲרֵי זֶה מַעֲשֵׂר. וְהוּא צֶבַע אָדוֹם שֶׁצּוֹבְעִין בּוֹ תְּרִיסִין: וְשָׂמַחְתָּ. כָּל הַשְּׂמָחוֹת בְּמַשְׁמַע, דְּלָא בָּעֵי מִינֵּיהּ אֶלָּא שִׂמְחָה. וְאָמַר מָר: *אֵין שִׂמְחָה אֶלָּא בְּבָשָׂר, וְהַאי בָּשָׂר הוּא: יָצְאוּ

אלמא קסבר חגיגת ארבעה עשר לאו דאורייתא. ואין להקשות: דתניא בפ' "אלו דברים" בפסחים (דף ע. ושם): "לא ילין מן הבשר" – לימד על חגיגת י"ד שנאכלת לשני ימים ולילה אחד כו', אלמא סבירא ליה דהוי דאורייתא! ועוד: אשכחן תנא התם דאינה נאכלת אלא ליום ולילה אחד, משמע דאית ליה דאורייתא, אבל פליג אאידך תנא [דאמר שני ימים ולילה]! ויש לומר: דסבר כתנא דמתני' פרק "אלו דברים" (שם דף סט:), דתנן: אימתי מביאין עמו חגיגה – בזמן שבא בחול בטהרה ובמועט, בזמן שבא בשבת במרובה או בטומאה – אין מביאין. א"כ משמע דלאו חובה, דפעמים לא אתיא, כדקאמר רב אשי התם בגמרא:

אמאי דבר שבחובה הוא. אומר הר"ר אלחנן: הוא הדין דהוה מצי להקשות: עולה היא ואינה נאכלת, ואין נותנין דמי מעשר רק בדבר הנאכל. והכי מוכח בסיפרי פרשת "עשר תעשר": "בכל אשר תאוה נפשך" יכול בעבדים כו', יכול ליקח בהמה למשתה בנו וכו' הרי אתה דן כו', אי מה להלן עולה ושלמים – אף כאן, תלמוד לומר: "ואכלת ושמחת" – שמחה שיש בה אכילה, יצאו עולות שאינן נאכלות. ויש להקשות: דאמר בפ"ק דחולין (דף כא. ושם) בשמעתתא ד"כמשפט": איצטריך "כמשפט" בעולת העוף לומר שאינה באה אלא מן החולין. תיפוק ליה דעולה היא! ומיהו, הא לא קושיא הוא, דהתם נמי פריך (א): ביום – מ"ביום צוותו" נפקא! ומשני: כדי נסבא. והוא הדין דמצי למיפרך עולה היא, ולישני הכי. אבל הר"ר אלחנן מפרש: דכתיב "והקריבו" דהוי חלוק, שמע מינה דמוציא מכלל שאר עולות ולייתי ממעשר, אע"ג דאינה נאכלת. ומיהו, תימה ההיא דמגילה (דף ח.) דאמר אין בין נדרים ונדבות כו', שהקשה הר"ר יעקב מאורליינ"ש: ליתני נמי שהנדרים אינם באים אלא מן החולין דהוה ליה חובה, ונדבות אף ממעשר! *והיה מתרץ הר"ר אלחנן: דמיירי בעולה דבלאו הכי אינה באה *(ב) מן החולין, שאינה נאכלת. כדפרישית:

טופלין בהמה לבהמה. בהמה ראשונה מן החולין, ואידך למעשר. אבל מעות למעות, להצטרף מעות חולין ומעות מעשר לקנות בהמה, (ג)דמשמע ליה דהוי דבר שבחובה ממעשר – לא. וכל אחד ואחד לפי סברתו. מיהו, יש ליתן טעם במילתא דתרוייהו. דחזקיה אמר אין טופלין מעות – סברתו ניכר, כיון שאפשר לו ליטפל בשתי בהמות – הכי עדיף. דסבירא ליה לחזקיה התם: חולק לחובתו לשתי בהמות, הלכך במעות לא איטפל. ור' יוחנן אומר: טופלין למעות, כיון דרבייה קרא טפילה דשרי – על כרחו הכי הוא, דבשתי בהמות לא הוי, דסבירא ליה לר' יוחנן אין אדם חולק חובתו לשתי בהמות. וכן מוכח בירושלמי: אמר רבי אילא בשם רבי אמי: איתפלגון חזקיה ורבי יוחנן, חזקיה אמר: אדם חולק חובתו לשתי בהמות וכו':

מלמד שאדם מביא חובתו מן החולין. ובשילהי פרק "התודה" (מנחות דף פב.) מפקינן ליה מקרא אחרינא, וגם בפרק "דם החטאת" (זבחים דף לח.). וי"ל: דהכא איצטריך, דסלקא דעתך אמינא: כיון דכתיב "אשר יברכך" לטפלה דמעשר – אימא כולי נמי לייתי מן המעשר:

ת"ל אשר יברכך. מיהו, בירושלמי מפקינן ליה דכתיב "מסת" וכתיב "לא תוכל שאתו" (דברים יד) מה להלן מן המעשר כו'. ר' אליעזר אמר: נאמר כאן "שמחה" ונאמר להלן "שמחה", מה להלן מעשר – אף כאן מעשר. רבי עולא בר ישמעאל: נאמר כאן "מסת" ונאמר להלן "ותרב משאת", מה להלן אחת עיקר והשאר טפל – אף כאן: ה"ג ושאר כל ימות הפסח אדם יוצא ידי חובתו במעשר בהמה. אבל יש ספרים שכתוב בהן גירסא אחרת, ואין לְיַשְּׁבָהּ:

משום סקרתא. הקשה הר"ר אלחנן: תיפוק ליה דאין מקדישין ביו"ט, (ד) וכדקאמר בפרק בתרא דבילה (דף לו:)! וי"ל: דשאני הכא דקדושה ועומדת, כיון דחייב מן התורה לקדשו, כדאמרינן בפרק בתרא דבכורות (דף נח.), הלכך לא שייך ביה שום איסור. והר"י תירץ: דצביעה דנקט – לפי שהוא איסור דאורייתא, הלכך גזרו בה. אבל מקדיש, דלא הוי רק דרבנן – לא גזור. וכן משמע התם (ביצה דף לו:) גבי אין רוכבין על גבי בהמה, ומוקי לה משום תחומין. לימא קסבר תחומין דאורייתא? אלא: גזרה שמא יחתוך זמורה. משמע דמשום איסור דרבנן לא גזרו. ורבי אלחנן היה רוצה לתרץ: דלהקדיש לא קאמר, דהא אמרינן בפרק "שואל" (שבת דף קמח:): מקדיש אדם חגיגתו ביו"ט, ופסחו בשבת. א"כ הכא נמי, כיון דנפיק בה ידי שלמי שמחה – מצי להקדיש. אך אין הר"י מודה לו, כיון דלא אתי עיקר משום שלמי שמחה, דאם לא כן – בדין דנדרים ונדבות נמי ליקדשן, כיון דנפיק משום שמחה! ומכל הני שינויי לא יתכן בבכורות פרק בתרא (דף נח.): אמאי נקט סקרתא ולא נקט מקדישין? דהתם לא שייך גזרה, אלא (ה)שינוי ראשון דקדושים ועומדין יתכן התם והכא. ולא דמי להגבהת תרומות ומעשרות דאסור משום מתקן, דהכא לא מתקן הוא, דבלאו הכי שרי למיכל קודם שיעשר בהמותיו:

וישם המלך אחשורוש מס. אבל "יהיו לך למס ועבדוך" (דברים כ) וכן "ויהי למס עובד" (בראשית מט) לא מייתי, דהני לאו מעות משתמעין (ו)אלא לשון עבדות בעלמא: ושמחת בחגך לרבות מיני שמחות לשמחה. גבי חג הסוכות כתיב, ודרשינן ליה מדהדר כתביה הכא, כיון דכתבי' גבי עצרת. ופסח ילפינן מיניה בהיקש. וכן מצא רבי אלחנן בספרי, דמעצרת הוא דרשינן לה, דכתיב: "וזכרת כי עבד היית בארץ מצרים" לימד: כל שנוהג בעצרת נוהג בפסח וחג, או אינו: כל שנוהג בפסח וחג נוהג בעצרת? תלמוד לומר: "אלה" – אלה נוהגין בעצרת כו': מי

אמר טופלין מעות למעות ואין טופלין בהמה לבהמה. תניא כוותיה דר' יוחנן מסת מלמד שאדם מביא חובתו מן החולין ומנא לן שאם רצה לערב מערב ת"ל כאשר יברכך ה' אלהיך אפילו שוורים כלומר מוסיף מעות על מעות החגיגה. תניא כוותיה דחזקיה מסת מלמד שאדם מביא מן החולין בש"א יום ראשון מן החולין מיכן ואילך מן המעשר ובה"א אכילה ראשונה מן החולין מיכן ואילך מן המעשר. פי' אכילה ראשונה בהמה ראשונה שאתה אוכל בחג לא תהא אלא מן החולין ושאר כל ימות הפסח אדם יוצא י"ח במעשר בהמה. אבל ביו"ט לא דלמא אתי לעשורי ואי אפשר לעשר ביו"ט משום סיקרא שסוקר על הבהמה שנמצא כצובע ביו"ט. ומסת מנא לן דלישנא דחולין הוא ואמרינן מסת מלשון מס כדכתיב וישם המלך אחשורוש מס על הארץ: מתני' ישראל יוצאין י"ח בנדרים ונדבות כו'. ת"ר ושמחת בחגך לרבות כל מיני שמחות לשמחה מיכן אמרו ישראל יוצאין י"ח בנדרים ונדבות ובמעשר בהמה. והכהנים בחטאת ואשם ובבכור ובחזה ובשוק יכול אף במנחות ובעופות תלמוד לומר ושמחת בחגך. מי

*) בגמ' ליתא זה וכן משמע מדברי רבינו בסמוך דהולך להביא זה מהירושלמי דהטפלה הוא ממע"ש ודו"ק.

מג א מיי' פ"א מהלכות קרבן פסח הלכה יג ופ"ב מהלכות חגיגה הלכה ז:
מד ב ג ד ה מיי' פ"ב מהל' חגיגה הל' ח:
מה ו ז מיי' שם הל' ט:
מו ח מיי' שם הלכה י:

[פסחים סט:]
[לעיל ז. וש"נ]
[עי' תוספות זבחים נ. ד"ה אם ענו]
[בכורות נח.]
[דף כב.]
[שייך לעיל ז:]
[פסחים קט.]
[עי' תוספות מגילה ח. ד"ה אין בין ותוספות ב"ק סב: ד"ה מי קתני ותוספות תענית יג: ד"ה מאי]

הגהות הב"ח

(א) תוס' ד"ה אמאי וכו' הא לאו קושיא הוא דהתם נמי פריך ידו הימנית מדרבה בר חנה נפקא ומשני כדי נסבא והוא הדין דמצי למימר מן החולין עולה היא ולשני הכי אבל הר"ר אלחנן מפרש דסד"א מדכתיב והקריבו דהוי: (ב) בא"ד אינה באה אלא מן החולין כיון שאינה נאכלת כדפרי': (ג) ד"ה טופלין וכו' משמע ליה לחזקיה דהוי דבר שבחובה ממעשר לא ור' יוחנן משמע ליה שיהא חולין מעורב עם כל אכילותיו וכל אחד ואחד לפי סברתו וכו' לחזקיה דאמר אין טופלין מעות למעות סברתו ניכר דכיון וכו' דסבירא ליה לחזקיה אדם חולק חובתו וכו' ור' יוחנן אומר טופלין מעות למעות דכיון דרבייה: (ד) ד"ה משום וכו' דאין מקדישין ביום טוב כדתנן בפ' בתרא: (ה) בא"ד ולא נקט מקדישין דהתם לא שייך גזירה אלא שינוייא קמא דקדושה ועומדת יתכן התם: (ו) ד"ה וישם וכו' משתמעינן מיניה אלא:

רבינו חננאל

אבל חגיגת ארבעה עשר אינה מן התורה. ובה"א מן המעשר ומקשינן אמאי והא חגיגת ט"ו וודאי היא מן התורה וכל דבר שבא מן החובה אינו בא אלא מן החולין. ופריק עולא בטופל מעשר שני לחולין*). ובאו חזקי' ור' יוחנן לפרש דבריו חזקיה אמר טופלין בהמה לבהמה פי' טופלין בהמה של חגיגה עם בהמות אחרות של מעות מעשר שני או של נדרים ונדבות ומפורש בתלמוד ארץ ישראל שזה שטופל הוא ממעשר שני אבל ביו"ט לא פי' חיישינן משום סקרתא מפני שבשעה שמונה ומעשר סוקר העשירי בסיקרא ואין סוקרין ביו"ט. ואין טופלין מעות למעות פי' אין מוסיפין על מעות של חגיגה מעות של נדרים שעליו או מעות מעשר שני ומביא בהמה שמינה או פר גדול. ור' יוחנן

מז א מיי' פ"א מהל' חגיגה הלכה א:
מח ב מיי' שם פ"ב הלכה י:
מט ג מיי' פ"ו מהל' יו"ט הלכה טז ופ"י מהל' אישות הלכה יד סמג לאוין עה טוש"ע א"ח סימן תקמו סעיף א ב וטור ש"ע א"ה סי' סד סעיף ז:
נ ד מיי' פ"א מהלכות חגיגה הלכה יא:
נא ה מיי' פ"ב שם הלכה ח:
נב ו ז מיי' שם הל' ז:

תורה אור

מי שחגיגה באה מהם, יצאו אלו שאין חגיגה באה מהם. רב אשי אמר: מ"ושמחת" נפקא, יצאו אלו שאין בהן שמחה. ורב אשי, האי "בחגך" מאי עביד ליה? — ההוא לכדרב דניאל בר קטינא. דאמר רב דניאל בר קטינא אמר רב: *מניין שאין נושאין נשים במועד — שנאמר: "ושמחת בחגך" (דברים טז) — ולא באשתך.§

מתני' מי שיש לו אוכלים מרובים ונכסים מועטים — מביא שלמים מרובים ועולות מועטות. נכסים מרובים ואוכלין מועטין — מביא עולות מרובות ושלמים מועטין. זה וזה מועט — על זה נאמר: "מעה כסף" "שתי כסף". זה וזה מרובים — על זה נאמר: "איש (שם) כמתנת ידו כברכת ה' אלהיך אשר נתן לך".§

גמ' שלמים מרובים מהיכא מייתי? הא לית ליה! אמר רב חסדא: טופל ומביא פר גדול. אמר ליה רב ששת: הרי אמרו טופלין בהמה לבהמה! מאי קאמר ליה? אילימא הכי קאמר ליה: הרי אמרו טופלין בהמה לבהמה אבל לא מעות למעות — ולימא ליה: אין טופלין מעות למעות! אלא הכי אמר ליה: הרי אמרו אף טופלין בהמה לבהמה! כמאן — דלא כחזקיה ודלא כרבי יוחנן! וכי תימא אמוראי הוא דפליגי, מתנייתא לא פליגי — והא קתני: אכילה ראשונה מן החולין! מאי אכילה ראשונה — שיעור דמי אכילה ראשונה מן החולין. אמר עולא אמר ריש לקיש: הפריש עשר בהמות לחגיגתו, הקריב חמש ביום טוב ראשון — חוזר ומקריב חמש ביום טוב שני. [נ"ל תמן] רבי יוחנן אמר: כיון שפסק — שוב אינו מקריב. אמר ר' אבא: ולא פליגי: כאן — בסתם, כאן — במפרש. האי סתם היכי דמי? אילימא דליכא שהות ביום לקרב, האי דלא אקרבינהו — (א) דליכא שהות ביום. ואלא דלית ליה אוכלין, האי דלא אקרבינהו — דלית ליה אוכלין! לא צריכא, דאיכא שהות ביום ואית ליה אוכלין. (*מבדקמא) לא אקרבינהו — שמע מינה שיורי שיירינהו. והכי נמי מסתברא, דכי אתא רבין אמר ר' יוחנן: הפריש עשר בהמות לחגיגתו, הקריב חמש ביום טוב ראשון — חוזר ומקריב חמש ביום טוב שני. קשיין אהדדי! אלא לאו שמע מינה: כאן — בסתם, כאן — במפרש, שמע מינה. איתמר נמי, אמר רב שמן בר אבא אמר רבי יוחנן: לא

[נ"ל מדבקמא] [מו"ק ח:]

רש"י

יצאו אלו שאין חגיגה באה מהן. דחגיגה "חלב" כתיב בה, "לא ילין חלב חגי" וגו' (שמות כג): מתני' אוכלין מרובין. בני בית רבים — מביא שלמים רבים, שלמי חגיגה רבים לפי האוכלים, ועולת ראייה מועטת: עולות מרובות. דכתיב: "איש כמתנת ידו": גמ' טופל. מעות חולין ומעשר יחד: אילימא הכי קאמר ליה הרי אמרו בהמה לבהמה (ב) מעות למעות לא. כחזקיה: לימא ליה הרי אמרו אין טופלין מעות למעות. כיון דלמיסר טפילת מעות אתא, ושמעינן לחזקיה בהדיא דאין טופלין — היכי שביק מילתא בהדיא ומותיב מדיוקא? אלא אף טופלין קאמר ליה. דשמעינן לרב חסדא דקאמר בטופל ומביא פר גדול, דוקא מעות למעות, אבל בהמה לבהמה — לא. ואמר ליה איהו: הרי אמרו אף טופלין בהמה לבהמה, כמאן וכו': וכי תימא אמוראי הוא דפליגי. חזקיה ורבי יוחנן הוא דפליגי בבהמה ובמעות: אבל מתנייתא. דאייתינן לעיל תניא כוותיה דמר ודמר: לא פליגי. במעות, אלא בבהמה. דהך דקתני אם רצה לערב — הוא דקאמר מעות דוקא, אבל אידך מתניתא — ס"ל בין מעות בין בהמה, ורב ששת כברייתא בתרייתא סבירא ליה: והא קתני אכילה ראשונה מן החולין. וקא סלקא דעתך דסעודה הבאה ראשונה על השולחן בעי כולה מחולין: דמי אכילה ראשונה. כלומר: אכילה ראשונה סתמא קתני, דאית ליה בין בהמה עצמה, בין מעות שיעור אכילה ראשונה: חוזר ומקריב חמש ביום טוב שני. ולא אמרינן עובר הוא ב"בל תוסיף", (ג) ורחמנא אמר: "וחגותם אותו" — חד יומא ותו לא, דהנך נמי דחד יומא הוא ושני תשלומין דראשון: בסתם. אם הפרישן סתם — אינו חוזר ומקריבן, כדמפרש ואזיל: כאן במפרש. דאמר בהדיא: ליום ראשון אני מפריש את כולן חוזר ומקריבן, שאינו אלא תשלומי ראשון: האי סתם. דאמרת אסור להקריבן, היכי דמי? משום דלא הוה ליה שהות הוא. ומסתמא ליום ראשון הפרישן: שיורי שייר. שהיה בדעתו לחוג שני ימים: ה"נ מסתברא. דמודה ר' יוחנן דמפרש: איתמר נמי. היכא דמוכח מילתא דלא היה בדעתו לחוג שני ימים — מודה ר"י: לא

תוספות

מי שחגיגה באה מהם. פרש"י: דכתיב "לא ילין חלב חגי". ומיהו, לקמן (דף י:) לא מפקינן ליה לפי המסקנא, אלא מגזירה שוה ד"מדבר" "מדבר"! ושמא מכל מקום משמעות המקרא משמע חגיגה. ולקמן מפקינן ליה מ"מדבר" "מדבר" — שמא אלשון ד"ויחוגו" קא סמיך, דמשמע חגיגה. דאי ממדבר — הוה אמינא עולה ושלמים באה מהם. וליכא למימר: אם כן — לא יהו באים שלמי שמחה ממעשר רק על ידי טפילה, כמו חגיגה! דהא בסיפרי ילפינן ליה מגזירה שוה, דכתיב בו "שם" במעשר, וגם ב"התודה" (מנחות פג.) מדכר גזרה שוה 'שם' 'שם' לשלמים. הקשה ה"ר אלחנן: לילף שמחה מהר עיבל, דכתיב (דברים כז): "וזבחת שלמים" ומינה ממעטינן עופות ומנחות. וכן דריש רבי יהודה בן בתירא בפסחים (דף קט.)! ועוד: אמאי לא מוקמינן קרא בבשר חולין, דמיקרי שפיר שמחה! ותירץ: דודאי ילפינן מהר עיבל, מה שמחה דלהלן שלמים — אף כאן שלמים. ובירושלמי איכא: אבל לא בעופות ומנחות, דכתיב "זבח" בהר עיבל:

בחגך ולא באשתך. ות"ק דמפיק לה מדרשה "ושמחת בחגך" מי שחגיגה וכו' — י"ל: דתרוייהו שמעינן מינה, דליכתוב "בחג". ומיהו, מצינו למימר דפליג עליה, ולא משמע ליה. (ד) והא דאין נושאים נשים במועד — מוקי טעמא כאידך דהתם:

מי שיש לו אוכלין מרובין. בירושלמי אמרינן: עני וידו רחבה — קורא אני עליו "איש כמתנת ידו", עשיר וידו מעוטה — על זה נאמר "כברכת ה' אלהיך" עני וידו מעוטה — על זה נאמר: מעה כסף שתי כסף, אין פחות ממעה כסף ואין פחות משתי כסף:

חוזר ומקריב (*הוא) ביו"ט שני. [נ"ל תמן] פרש"י: ואינו עובר משום בל תוסיף, דרחמנא אמר: "וחגותם אותו חג" — חד יומא, והוא חוגג שני ימים — דהוה ליה תשלומין דראשון. אבל בסתם — אסור, כדמפרש ואזיל. ולא שייך לאקשויי: כיון דלא הוי חזי בראשון — איך הוה חזי בשני? הואיל ושמעינן ליה לר' יוחנן בסמוך תשלומין דראשון, דהוה חזי בראשון קרינן ביה, הואיל ואיכא שם הרבה כהנים שיקריבו אותן בבת אחת. ומיהו, ר"ח פירש בענין אחר, וזהו לשונו: אמר ריש לקיש הפריש עשרה בהמות לחגיגתו, הקריב חמשה ביו"ט ראשון — מקריב חמשה ביו"ט אחרון, ואע"ג דאין מקריבין נדרים ונדבות ביו"ט — הואיל והללו תחילת הפרשתן לחגיגה היתה — מותר להקריבן ביום טוב. ורבי יוחנן אמר: כיון שפסק שוב אינו חוזר ומקריב ומביא. א"ר אבא: ולא פליגי, כאן — בסתם, כאן — במפרש. הא דר' יוחנן כגון שהפרישן סתם והקריב, ויש לו שהות ביום לשחוט השאר, וגם יש לו אוכלים, ולא שחטן — שיורי שיירינהו, ונעשו כנדרים ונדבות שלא מחמת יום טוב, שאין קריבין. ודריש לקיש — כגון שפירש שאלו הנשארים יקריבם ביום טוב אחרון, כגון זה — מותר. הכי נמי מסתברא, דכי אתא רבין אמר רבי יוחנן: הפריש עשרה בהמות לחגיגתו הקריב חמשה וכו', חוזר ומקריב וכו' קשיא אהדדי כו', אלא לאו כו', איתמר נמי, אמר רב שמן בר אבא אמר רבי יוחנן: לא שנו דכיון שפסק [שוב אינו מקריב] — אלא שלא גמר היום, דאמרינן: שיורי שיירינהו ונעשו נדרים ונדבות. אבל גמר היום — חוזר ומקריב. כך פירש רבינו חננאל. וראייה לדבריו, משמע בירושלמי דמכילתין: היו לפניו (ה) עשרה בהמות, הקריב חמשה ביום טוב ראשון, והמותר מהו שידחה יום טוב האחרון? רבי קריספא אומר: איתפלגון ר' יוחנן וריש לקיש, חד אומר: דוחה, וחד אומר: אינו דוחה. ולא ידעינן מאן אמר [דא ומאן אמר דא]. אמר רבי זירא: נפרש מליהון דרבנן מן מליהון. דרבי יוחנן דו אמר טופל מעות למעות — דו אמר דוחה, ריש לקיש דו אמר אדם טופל בהמה לבהמה, ואין אדם טופל מעות למעות — דו אמר אינו דוחה. אמר רב שמן בר אבא בשם ר' יוחנן: לעולם הוא מוסיף והולך ודוחה יום טוב, עד שיאמר אין עוד בדעתו להוסיף. משמע — דלענין דחיית יום טוב מיירי:

זה

רבינו חננאל

מי שחגיגה באה מהן יצאו אלו שאין חגיגה באה מהן רב אשי אמר מושמחת יצאו אלו שאין בהן שמחה יצאו עופות ומנחות שאין בהם שמחה. והאי בחגך מיבעי ליה לכדרב דאמר ושמחת בחגך ולא באשתך: [מתני'] מי שיש לו אוכלין מרובין ונכסים מועטין מביא שלמים מרובין ועולות מועטין כו' פי' מי שיש לו בני אדם מרובין וכולן רוצים לאכול בשר במועד ואין לו בהמות אלא מעט אמר רב חסדא טופל ומביא פר גדול. א"ל רב ששת הרי אמרו טופלין בהמה לבהמה ואתינן למידק מאי אמר רב ששת וכי תימא הכי קאמר ליה לרב חסדא אמאי אמרת טופלין מעות למעות חגיגה וקונה פר גדול מכלל שאין טופל בהמה לבהמה הרי אמרו אף טופלין בהמה לבהמה ומקשינן כמאן אמר רב ששת ההיא סברא לא כחזקיה ולא כרבי יוחנן דהא אין אחד מהן אומר טופלין בהמה לבהמה ומעות למעות וכי תימא חזקיה ור' יוחנן הוא דפליגי אבל מתניתא לא פליגי והוא דאמר כבתר מתנייתא והקתני אכילה ראשונה מן החולין כלומר הבהמה הראשונה שאוכל בתחלתה תהיה מן החולין. לאו מכלל שטופלין בהמה לבהמה ואין טופלין מעות וקונה בהמה אחת. מאי אכילה ראשונה דקתני בענין מעות חגיגה כדי שיעור אכילה ראשונה ממעות חולין א"ר שמעון בן לקיש הפריש עשר בהמות לחגיגתו הקריב חמש ליו"ט ראשון חוזר ומקריב חמש ליו"ט האחרון של חג ואע"ג שאין מקריבין נדרים ונדבות במועד הואיל והללו תחלת הפרשתן לחגיגה היתה באה מותר להקריבם ביו"ט ור' יוחנן אמר כיון שפסק שוב אינו מקריב א"ר אבא ולא פליגי כאן בסתם כאן במפרש הא דר' יוחנן כגון שהפרישן בסתם והקריב מהן חמש. ואיכא שהות ביום לשחוט השאר וגם יש לו בני אדם שצריכין לאכלם וכיון שלא שחטם שיורי שיירינהו ונעשו כנדרים ונדבות שלא מחמת יו"ט שאינן קריבין ביו"ט. וריש לקיש כגון שפירש ואמר שאלו הנשארים אקריבם ביו"ט האחרון כגון זה מותר הכי נמי מסתברא דכי אתא רבין

הגהות הב"ח

(א) גמ' האי דלא אקרבינהו משום דליכא שהות ביום ואלא דלית ליה אוכלין לימא האי דלא אקרבינהו משום דלית ליה: (ב) רש"י ד"ה אילימא וכו' לבהמה אבל מעות: (ג) ד"ה חוזר וכו' דרחמנא אמר וכו' דשני תשלומין: (ד) תוס' ד"ה בחגך וכו' ולא משמע ליה בחגך ולא באשתך: (ה) ד"ה חוזר וכו' היו לפניו עשר בהמות והקריב חמש ביום טוב הראשון המותר מהו שידחה יו"ט וכו' יוחנן דאמר אדם טופל מעות למעות ואין אדם טופל בהמה לבהמה הוא דאמר דוחה וריש לקיש דאמר אדם וכו' מעות למעות הוא דאמר אינו דוחה:

תורה אור

לֹא שָׁנוּ אֶלָּא שֶׁלֹּא גָּמַר, אֲבָל גָּמַר – חוֹזֵר וּמַקְרִיב. מַאי גָּמַר? אִילֵימָא גָּמַר קָרְבְּנוֹתָיו – מַאי מַקְרִיב? אֶלָּא שֶׁלֹּא גָּמַר הַיּוֹם, אֲבָל גָּמַר הַיּוֹם – חוֹזֵר וּמַקְרִיב.§ **מתני'** [א]מִי *שֶׁלֹּא חַג בְּיו"ט הָרִאשׁוֹן שֶׁל חָג – חוֹגֵג אֶת כָּל הָרֶגֶל, וְיו"ט הָאַחֲרוֹן שֶׁל חָג. [ב]עָבַר הָרֶגֶל וְלֹא חַג – אֵינוֹ חַיָּיב בְּאַחֲרָיוּתוֹ, עַל זֶה נֶאֱמַר: (קהלת א) °"מְעֻוָּת לֹא יוּכַל לִתְקֹן וְחֶסְרוֹן לֹא יוּכַל לְהִמָּנוֹת". ר' שִׁמְעוֹן בֶּן מְנַסְיָא אוֹמֵר: *אֵיזֶהוּ מְעֻוָּות שֶׁאֵינוֹ יָכוֹל לְהִתָּקֵן – זֶה הַבָּא עַל הָעֶרְוָה וְהוֹלִיד מִמֶּנָּה מַמְזֵר. א"ת בְּגוֹנֵב וְגוֹזֵל – יָכוֹל הוּא לְהַחֲזִירוֹ וִיתַקֵּן. ר"ש בֶּן יוֹחַי אוֹמֵר: אֵין קוֹרִין מְעֻוָּות אֶלָּא לְמִי שֶׁהָיָה מְתוּקָּן בַּתְּחִילָּה וְנִתְעַוֵּות, וְאֵי זֶה? זֶה תַּלְמִיד חָכָם הַפּוֹרֵשׁ מִן הַתּוֹרָה.§ **גמ'** מְנָהָנֵי מִילֵּי? אָמַר רַבִּי יוֹחָנָן מִשּׁוּם רַבִּי יִשְׁמָעֵאל: נֶאֱמַר "עֲצֶרֶת" בַּשְּׁבִיעִי שֶׁל פֶּסַח, וְנֶאֱמַר "עֲצֶרֶת" בַּשְּׁמִינִי שֶׁל חָג, מַה לְהַלָּן לְתַשְׁלוּמִין – אַף כָּאן לְתַשְׁלוּמִין. מוּפְנֶה, דְּאִי לָאו מוּפְנֶה – אִיכָּא לְמִיפְרַךְ: מַה לַשְּׁבִיעִי שֶׁל פֶּסַח – שֶׁכֵּן אֵינוֹ חָלוּק מִשֶּׁלְּפָנָיו, תֹּאמַר בַּשְּׁמִינִי שֶׁל חַג שֶׁחָלוּק מִשֶּׁלְּפָנָיו, לָאֵי, אַפְנוּיֵי מוּפְנֶה. מִכְּדִי, מַאי עֲצֶרֶת – עָצוּר בַּעֲשִׂיַּית מְלָאכָה, הַכְּתִיב: (דברים טז) °"לֹא תַעֲשֶׂה מְלָאכָה", "עֲצֶרֶת" דִּכְתַב רַחֲמָנָא לָמָּה לִי? אֶלָּא שְׁמַע מִינָּהּ לְאַפְנוּיֵי. (ויקרא כג) וְתַנָּא מַיְיתֵי לַהּ מֵהָכָא, דְּתַנְיָא: °"וְחַגּוֹתֶם אוֹתוֹ חַג לַה' שִׁבְעַת יָמִים", יָכוֹל יְהֵא חוֹגֵג וְהוֹלֵךְ כָּל שִׁבְעָה – ת"ל: "אוֹתוֹ" אוֹתוֹ, אַתָּה חוֹגֵג, וְאִי אַתָּה חוֹגֵג כָּל שִׁבְעָה. אִם כֵּן לָמָּה נֶאֱמַר "שִׁבְעָה" – לְתַשְׁלוּמִין. וּמִנַּיִן [ג]שֶׁאִם לֹא חַג יו"ט הָרִאשׁוֹן שֶׁל חַג שֶׁחוֹגֵג וְהוֹלֵךְ אֶת כָּל הָרֶגֶל וְיוֹם טוֹב הָאַחֲרוֹן – ת"ל: (שם) °"בַּחֹדֶשׁ הַשְּׁבִיעִי תָּחֹגּוּ אוֹתוֹ". אִי "בַּחֹדֶשׁ הַשְּׁבִיעִי" – יָכוֹל יְהֵא חוֹגֵג וְהוֹלֵךְ הַחֹדֶשׁ כּוּלּוֹ? ת"ל: "אוֹתוֹ" – אוֹתוֹ אַתָּה חוֹגֵג, וְאִי אַתָּה חוֹגֵג חוּצָה לוֹ. וּמַאי תַּשְׁלוּמִין? ר' יוֹחָנָן אָמַר: *[ד]תַּשְׁלוּמִין לָרִאשׁוֹן, וְר' אוֹשַׁעְיָא אָמַר: תַּשְׁלוּמִין זֶה לָזֶה. מַאי בֵּינַיְיהוּ? א"ר זֵירָא: חִיגֵּר בְּיוֹם רִאשׁוֹן וְנִתְפַּשֵּׁט בְּיוֹם שֵׁנִי אִיכָּא בֵּינַיְיהוּ. רַבִּי יוֹחָנָן אָמַר: תַּשְׁלוּמִין לָרִאשׁוֹן, *[ה]כֵּיוָן דְּלָא חֲזִי בָּרִאשׁוֹן – לָא חֲזִי בַּשֵּׁנִי. וְר' אוֹשַׁעְיָא אָמַר: תַּשְׁלוּמִין זֶה לָזֶה. אַף עַל גַּב דְּלָא חֲזִי בָּרִאשׁוֹן – חֲזִי בַּשֵּׁנִי. וּמִי א"ר יוֹחָנָן הָכִי? וְהָאָמַר חִזְקִיָּה: *נִטְמָא בַּיּוֹם – מֵבִיא, בַּלַּיְלָה – אֵינוֹ מֵבִיא. וְרַבִּי יוֹחָנָן אָמַר: אַף בַּלַּיְלָה נַמִי מֵבִיא! א"ר יִרְמְיָה: שָׁאנֵי טוּמְאָה דְּיֵשׁ לָהּ תַּשְׁלוּמִין בְּפֶסַח שֵׁנִי. מַתְקִיף לָהּ רַב פַּפָּא: הָנִיחָא לְמַאן דְּאָמַר: *פֶּסַח שֵׁנִי

רש"י

לא שנו. הָא דְּתַנְיָא לְקַמָּן: אוֹתוֹ אַתָּה חוֹגֵג וְלֹא יוֹתֵר, אֶלָּא שֶׁלֹּא גָּמַר הַיּוֹם: **אבל גמר היום.** וְלֹא הָיָה לוֹ שְׁהוּת לְהַקְרִיב כָּל חֲגִיגוֹת שֶׁהִפְרִישׁ: **מתני' מי שלא חג.** שֶׁלֹּא הֵבִיא חֲגִיגָתוֹ בַּיּוֹם הָרִאשׁוֹן שֶׁל חַג: **ויו"ט האחרון של חג.** חוֹגֵג שְׁמִינִי עֲצֶרֶת. וְאַע"ג דְּרֶגֶל בִּפְנֵי עַצְמוֹ הוּא – הָוֵי תַּשְׁלוּמִין לָרִאשׁוֹן: **והוליד ממזר.** שֶׁהֵבִיא פְּסוּלִין בְּיִשְׂרָאֵל, וִיהֵא זִכָּרוֹן (א), לְפִיכָךְ אֵין עֲוֹנוֹתָיו נִמְחָקִין בִּתְשׁוּבָה: **יכול להחזיר.** דְּמֵי גְּנֵיבָתוֹ וּגְזֵלָתוֹ לַבְּעָלִים: **ויתקן.** וִיהֵא מְתוּקָּן מִן הַחֵטְא: **מעוות.** מְקוּלְקָל: **גמ' מנהני מילי.** דְּי"ט הָאַחֲרוֹן שֶׁל חַג הַסּוּכּוֹת תַּשְׁלוּמִין לְקָרְבָּנוֹת הֶחָג לִיחִידִים: **עצרת בשביעי של פסח.** בְּפָרָשַׁת "כָּל הַבְּכוֹר" – "שֵׁשֶׁת יָמִים תֹּאכַל מַצּוֹת וּבַיּוֹם הַשְּׁבִיעִי עֲצֶרֶת" (דברים טז): **מה לשביעי של פסח.** תַּשְׁלוּמִין לָרִאשׁוֹן, שֶׁהֲרֵי אֵינוֹ חָלוּק מִשֶּׁלְּפָנָיו – שְׁמִינִי עֲצֶרֶת חָלוּק מִשֶּׁלְּפָנָיו לְעִנְיַן פז"ר קש"ב: **מופנה.** וּצְרִיכָה גְּזֵירָה שָׁוָה זוֹ שֶׁתְּהֵא מוּפְנָה, דְּתוּ לָא פָּרְכִינַן עָלֶיהָ מִידִי. דְּכָל גְּזֵירָה שָׁוָה מוּפְנָה לְמֵידִין וְאֵין מְשִׁיבִין: **לאיי.** בֶּאֱמֶת: **הא כתיב לא תעשה מלאכה.** בְּהַהוּא קְרָא גּוּפֵיהּ "וּבַיּוֹם הַשְּׁבִיעִי עֲצֶרֶת לַה' אֱלֹהֶיךָ, לֹא תַעֲשֶׂה מְלָאכָה": **ותנא מייתי לה מהכא.** מִשּׁוּם דְּר' יוֹחָנָן דְּגָמַר לָהּ כִּדְאָמְרִינַן לְעֵיל אָמוֹרָא הוּא, נָקַט הָכָא הַאי לִישָּׁנָא: **כל שבעה.** כָּל יוֹם וָיוֹם: **בחדש השביעי.** כָּל יְמֵי הֶחָג הָאָמוּר בַּחֹדֶשׁ הַשְּׁבִיעִי: **יכול יהא חוגג והולך כל החדש.** אֵיזֶה יוֹם שֶׁיִּרְצֶה לְתַשְׁלוּמֵי הֶחָג, אִם לֹא הִקְרִיב בֶּחָג: **ת"ל אותו.** בְּסֵיפֵיהּ דִּקְרָא, תְּרֵי "אוֹתוֹ" כְּתִיב בֵּיהּ: **מאי תשלומין.** כֵּיצַד הֵן תַּשְׁלוּמִין: (ב) **כולן תשלומין לראשון.** שֶׁהֲרֵי יוֹם אֶחָד עָשָׂה הַכָּתוּב עִיקָּר בְּכוּלָּן, דִּכְתִיב "אוֹתוֹ", וְשֶׁלְּאַחֲרָיו עָשָׂה תַּשְׁלוּמִין לוֹ: **כולן תשלומין זה לזה.** אֵין לְךָ יוֹם בָּהֶם שֶׁאֵין חוֹבָתוֹ תְּלוּיָה בּוֹ בְּעַצְמוֹ לְמִי שֶׁלֹּא נִרְאָה בַּיָּמִים שֶׁלְּפָנָיו (ג), יוֹם רִאשׁוֹן שֶׁהוּא נִרְאֶה לְהָבִיא עִיקָּר לְדִידֵיהּ, וְיָמָיו שֶׁלְּאַחֲרָיו תַּשְׁלוּמִין לוֹ: **חיגר.** אֵינוֹ רָאוּי לֵירָאוֹת, כִּדְאָמְרִינַן בְּמַתְנִי': **נטמא ביום.** בִּכְרֵיתוֹת (דף ט.) תְּנַן: נָזִיר מֵבִיא קָרְבָּן אֶחָד עַל טוּמְאוֹת הַרְבֵּה. וְאָמַר חִזְקִיָּה: נִטְמָא בְּיוֹם ח', שֶׁהוּא רָאוּי לְהָבִיא קָרְבָּנוֹת וּלְהַתְחִיל מִנְיַן נְזִירוּתָיו, וְיָמִים שְׁמֹנָה קוֹדֶם טוּמְאָה בְּטֵלִין, כְּמוֹ שֶׁנֶּאֱמַר: "וּבַיּוֹם הַשְּׁמִינִי יָבִיא שְׁתֵּי תוֹרִים אוֹ שְׁנֵי בְּנֵי וגו' וְהִזִּיר לַה' כָּל יְמֵי נִזְרוֹ וגו' וְהַיָּמִים הָרִאשׁוֹנִים יִפְּלוּ כִּי טָמֵא נִזְרוֹ" (במדבר ו): **מביא.** קָרְבָּן עַל הַטּוּמְאָה הַשֵּׁנִית, שֶׁכְּבָר נִתְחַיֵּיב בְּקָרְבַּן הַטּוּמְאָה, וְהִתְחִילָּה שְׁנִיָּה – וַהֲרֵי זוֹ טוּמְאָה אַחֶרֶת. אֲבָל נִטְמָא בְּלֵיל שְׁמִינִי – אֵינוֹ מֵבִיא אֶלָּא קָרְבָּן אֶחָד, דְּכֵיוָן דְּלֹא יָצָא מִטּוּמְאָה הָרִאשׁוֹנָה לְשָׁעָה שֶׁהִיא רְאוּיָה לְהָבִיא עָלֶיהָ קָרְבָּן – לֹא נִתְחַיֵּיב בְּקָרְבָּן הָרִאשׁוֹן, וְאֵין לוֹ תַּשְׁלוּמִין: **ורבי יוחנן אמר.** הוֹאִיל וְטָבַל לְטוּמְאָתוֹ רִאשׁוֹנָה וְהֶעֱרִיב שִׁמְשׁוֹ נִתְחַיֵּיב בְּקָרְבָּן, וְאַף עַל פִּי שֶׁאֵין לַיְלָה רָאוּי לְקָרְבָּן. אַלְמָא: אַף עַל גַּב דְּלָא רָאוּי לְקָרְבָּן – יֵשׁ לוֹ תַּשְׁלוּמִין: **שאני טומאה.** קָרְבָּן הַנִּדְחֶה מִפְּנֵי הַטּוּמְאָה, וּלְפִיכָךְ יֵשׁ לוֹ תַּשְׁלוּמִין, וְאַף עַל גַּב דְּלֹא נִרְאָה לְהָבִיא: **הואיל ויש לה תשלומין.** (ד) כְּגוֹן אֵלּוּ בְּפֶסַח שֵׁנִי. שֶׁהֲרֵי מִי שֶׁלֹּא נִרְאָה בָּרִאשׁוֹן יֵשׁ לוֹ תַּשְׁלוּמִין. אֲבָל הַנִּדְחֶה מִפְּנֵי דָּבָר אַחֵר – לֹא מָצִינוּ לוֹ תַּשְׁלוּמִין, אֶלָּא אִם כֵּן נִרְאָה לְהָבִיא: **הניחא למאן דאמר כו'.** פְּלוּגְתָּא הִיא בְּמַסֶּכֶת פְּסָחִים בְּפֶרֶק "מִי שֶׁהָיָה טָמֵא" (דף צג.) אֶלָּא

תוספות

זה הבא על הערוה. דטפי בושתו ניכר, שהממזר נראה לעולם. אבל שאר עבירות, רוצח *וגזלן – אין עדיו לפניו:

נאמר עצרת בפסח. ובירושלמי יליף לה ר' יוחנן בשם ר' ישמעאל: נאמר חמשה עשר בפסח ונאמר חמשה עשר בחג, מה להלן [יו"ט אחרון תשלומין לראשון, אף כאן י"ט אחרון תשלומין לראשון]. ותו ליכא למיפרך כדפריך בתלמוד שלנו, דהא גזרה שוה גמורה, (ה) כדילפינן מינה בסוכה בפ' "הישן" (דף כז.). ועוד, יהודה בר ספרא בשם רבי אושעיא דריש התם: "וחגותם אותו חג לה' שבעת ימים" וכי שבעה הם? והלא שמנה הם! אלא, יצא שבת [מהם] – הרי ז'. ר' יוסי בעי: וכי מכאן למדנו שאין חגיגה דוחה שבת? והלא ממקום אחר התיב רבי יוחנן אחוי דרב ספרא: והתניא: אף בפסח כן, מעתה לא מהן שבת הרי [ששה], הגע עצמך שחל י"ט ראשון ואחרון בשבת [לא מהם שני ימים] – הרי כאן ששה. אתא יהודה בר ספרא בשם ר' אושעיא: "וחגותם אותו חג לה' שבעת ימים" (ו) לא מהן שבת שכבר למדנו שאין חגיגה דוחה שבת, ומה ת"ל "תחגוהו" – לרבות יו"ט האחרון לתשלומין לראשון. וכל אותן דרשות אינן בכאן. אך בפרק "אלו דברים" (פסחים דף ע:) מייתי להיא דיהודה ספרא, ופריך עלה ההיא דחל יו"ט הראשון והאחרון בשבת הרי כאן ששה, ולא מייתי "תחגוהו":

תשלומין זה לזה. וההיא דלקמן (דף יז.) דילפינן תשלומין לחג השבועות מחג המצות כל ז' לא מסתבר למימר תשלומין זה לזה כיון דחול גמור הוא:

כיון דלא חזי בראשון תו לא חזי בשני. וצ"ע: אם היה פשוט בראשון וחגר בשני, מי אמרינן, כיון דחיובא עליה רמיא בראשון – תו לא פקע מיניה, אע"ג דהשתא לא חזי, או דלמא: כיון (ז) דתשלומין זה לזה לר' אושעיא לאו מיחייב? ומיהו, כיון דהשתא לאו בר חיובא הוא – לא מצי מייתי ליה, הואיל ואינו בביאה לא הוי בהבאה:

נטמא ביום מביא. גבי נזיר שנטמא קאי. דע"כ לא פליגי רבי ור' יוסי בר יהודה (נזיר דף יח.) (ח) בנטמא בשמיני, שכן יצא לשעה הראויה להביא קרבן. אבל בליל שמיני, דלא חזי לקרבן – לא. ורבי יוסי בר יהודה דנקט נטמא בשביעי – לאו משום הבאת קרבן הוא, אלא דחשיב ליה כמה טומאות בשביעי:

שאני טומאה הואיל ויש לה תשלומין בפסח שני. היה קשה למורי: א"כ סבירא ליה לר' יוחנן נטמא ביום ראשון וחזי בשני – מייתי חגיגה, אם כן לימא לעיל ריש מכילתין לאתויי טמא בראשון ונטהר בשני! ויש לומר: דאין הכי נמי, אלא משום דלרב פפא דבסמוך לא מצי למימר הכי, נקט מילתא דשוי לתרוייהו:

מסורת הש"ס

[לקמן יז.] ביצה כ. ר"ה ד: מגילה ה. [יומא ג.]

יבמות כב:

[לעיל ב. ערכין ב:]

[פסחים פ.]

[כריתות ח.]

[פסחים צג.]

עין משפט נר מצוה

[עי' מהרש"א ותוס' יו"ט ועי' תוס' ב"ב פח: ד"ה אפשר תמלא סעד גדול למהרש"א ז"ל דבגזל של רבים איירו]

נג א מיי' פ"א מהלכות חגיגה הלכה ד:

נד ב מיי' שם הלכה ו:

נה ג מיי' שם הלכה ז:

נו ד מיי' שם הלכה ד ופ"ב הלכה ה:

נז ה מיי' שם פ"ב הלכה ה:

רבינו חננאל

רבין א"ר יוחנן הפריש עשר בהמות לחגיגתו הקריב חמש ביום טוב ראשון חוזר ומקריב חמש ביו"ט האחרון. קשיין אהדדי אלא לאו ש"מ כאן בסתם כאן במפרש ש"מ אתמר נמי משמיה דר' יוחנן לא שנו כיון שפסק שוב אינו מקריב אלא שלא גמר היום דאמרינן מדלא אקריב שיורי שיירינהו לזמן אחר ונעשו כדין נדרים ונדבות. אבל גמר היום חוזר ומקריב: **מתני'** מי שלא חגג ביו"ט הראשון חוגג והולך את כל הרגל כולו ויו"ט האחרון וגמרינן להו לתשלומין מדכתיב בחג וחגותם אותו חג לה' שבעת ימים בשנה חקת עולם וכתיב בחג המצות ובחג השבועות ובחג הסוכו' אשתכח דאתקוש להו כולהו להדדי. התינח הני יום שמיני של חג מנא ליה. א"ר יוחנן גמרינן ליה בג"ש נאמרה עצרת בשביעי של פסח. ונאמרה עצרת בשמיני של חג. מה שביעי של פסח יש לו תשלומין אף עצרת דחג יש לו תשלומין ואמרינן האי עצרת צריך להיות מופנה ומפורש במס' נדה פרק המפלת שצריך להיות מופנה כדי שתדין ממנו זה הדין שכל ג"ש שהיא מופנה בשני צדדין למידין ואין משיבין. ואע"פ שיש לה פרכא אין משיבין. ואם אינה זו העצרת כתובה בה מופנה. איכא למפרך מה לשביעי של פסח שכן אין חלוק מלפניו פי' כולן שבעת ימי הפסח קרבן אחד לכולן. קרבן של יום ראשון הוא קרבן לכל הימים. אבל שמונת ימי החג. יום הראשון י"ג פרים. ויום השני י"ב פרים הולכין ומתמעטין וביום השמיני פר אחד הנה חלוקים הן זה מזה. ואמרינן לאיי אפנויי מופנה כו'. ותנא מייתי ליה מהכא וחגותם אותו חג לה' שבעת ימים וגו' יכול יהא חוגג והולך כל שבעה ת"ל אותו. אותו כלומר יום ראשון אתה חוגג ואי אתה חוגג כל ז'. א"כ למה נאמר שבעה *) תשלומין זה לזה. פירוש ר' יוחנן סבר מי שנתחייב לחגיגה ביום הראשון ולא חג משלם כל שאר ימות החג ואם לא נתחייב בראשון כגון שהיה חולה וכיוצא בו שאינו מתחייב בחגיגה אע"ג דאתפח בשני פטור הוא. ור' אושעיא סבר כיון דאתפח בשני חייב לשלם בשאר הימים וכן כל ימות החג תשלומין הן זה לזה. א"ר זירא חיגר ביום ראשון ונתפשט בשני איכא בינייהו. ר' יוחנן סבר פטור כיון דלא חזי בראשון לא חזי בשני. ור' אושעיא סבר **) ולא יתכן זה שחלקו לו חזקי' ור' יוחנן כשנטמא בלילה להעמידה בזב ונכוחים הן למבין. ומקשינן מי א"ר יוחנן הכי והאמר חזקיה נטמא ביום מביא. פי' נזיר שנטמא טומאת מת ועוד נטמא ביום שמיני לטומאתו הראשונה טומאת מת אחרת מביא ב' קרבנות נטמא בלילה אינו מביא. ר' יוחנן אמר אף בלילה נמי מביא והאי נזיר בליל שמיני שלו לא חזי לאתויי קרבן וקא"ר יוחנן חייב להביא קרבן אחר בתשלום ח' ימים לטהרתו. ואע"פ שלא נתחייב בעת טומאתו. ופירק ר' ירמיה שאני טומאה הואיל ואית לה תשלומין בפסח שני פירוש הלא מי שנטמא לילי י"ד בניסן או מקודם לכן לא נתחייב עדיין להקריב בפסח בעת טומאתו ואעפ"כ נתחייב באותו פסח להשלימה בי"ד באייר בפסח שני כך זה הנזיר וזה שאמרנו דמיירי בנזיר מפורש בכריתות פ' ארבעה מחוסרי כפרה בגמרא ונזיר שנטמא טומאות הרבה. ואוקימנא התם לר' יוסי ב"ר יהודה. ודלא כר' דתניא וקדש את ראשו ביום ההוא ביום הבאת קרבנותיו דברי רבי ר' יוסי בר"י אומר ביום תגלחתו. דאי ר' לא משתכחת לה נזיר שנטמא טומאות הרבה להיפטר בקרבן אחד ופריש הכי התם כיון דא' ר' נזירות דטהרה עד שמיני לא חיילא עליה אי דנטמא בשביעי וחזר ונטמא בשמיני שלו וחזר ונטמא בשמיני אחר כולה טומאה אריכתא היא ולית הכא טומאות הרבה. ואי דנטמא בשמיני שלו וחזר ונטמא בשמיני אחר וחזר ונטמא בשמיני אחר

*) נראה דחסר כאן וצ"ל שבעה לתשלומין מאי תשלומין ר"י אמר תשלומין לראשון ור"א אומר תשלומין זה לזה וכו'. **) אינו מובן ואולי צ"ל סבר דחייב בשני ומקשינן מי אמר ר"י הכי והאמר חזקיה נטמא ביום מביא. לא יתכן וכו' ונכוחים הם למבין אלא הכי פירושו נזיר שנטמא וכו'.

הגהות הב"ח

(א) רש"י ד"ה והוליד ממזר וכו' זכרון לעונו לפיכך: (ב) ד"ה מאי תשלומין כילד הן תשלומין הס"ד ואח"כ מה"ד הג"ה ומאן דאמר תשלומין לראשון דריש מאותו דראשון וחגותם אותו ומ"ד תשלומין זה לזה דריש מאותו דסיפיה שבעת ימים תחוגו אותו כלומר האי אותו נופל אשבעה דכולן ראויין לו ע"כ הס"ד: (ג) ד"ה כולן תשלומין זה וכו' בימים שלפניו דיום ראשון וכו' תשלומין זה לזה הס"ד: (ד) ד"ה שאני הד"א עם ד"ה הואיל ויש לה תשלומין כגון אילו נטמא בפסח ראשון מביא בפסח שני: (ה) תוס' ד"ה נאמר וכו' גמורה היא דילפינן וכו' אלא לא שבת מהם הרי ז': (ו) בא"ד חג לה' שבעת ימים וכי ז' והלא ח' הם אלא לא מהן שבת: (ז) ד"ה כיון וכו' דהשתא לא חזי או דלמא כיון דהשתא לאו בר חיובא הוא לא מצי מייתי ליה הואיל ואינו בביאה לא הוי בהבאה ומיהו לרבי אושעיא כיון דתשלומין זה לזה לא מחייב הס"ד וכנ"ל: (ח) ד"ה נטמא וכו' דבנטמא בשמיני מביא שכן יצא בשעה הראויה וכו' כמה טומאות בשביעי:

שֵׁנִי תַּשְׁלוּמִין דְּרִאשׁוֹן הוּא. אֶלָּא לְמַאן דְּאָמַר *[א]שֵׁנִי רֶגֶל בִּפְנֵי עַצְמוֹ הוּא — מַאי אִיכָּא לְמֵימַר? אֶלָּא אָמַר רַב פָּפָּא: קָסָבַר רַבִּי יוֹחָנָן *לַיְלָה אֵינוֹ מְחוּסַּר זְמַן. וּמִי א"ר יוֹחָנָן הָכִי? *וְהָאָמַר רַבִּי יוֹחָנָן: [ב]רָאָה אַחַת בַּלַּיְלָה וּשְׁתַּיִם בַּיּוֹם — מֵבִיא, שְׁתַּיִם בַּלַּיְלָה וְאַחַת בַּיּוֹם — אֵינוֹ מֵבִיא. וְאִי ס"ד קָסָבַר רַבִּי יוֹחָנָן לַיְלָה אֵינוֹ מְחוּסַּר זְמַן, אֲפִילּוּ שְׁתַּיִם בַּלַּיְלָה וְאַחַת בַּיּוֹם מֵבִיא! כִּי קא"ר יוֹחָנָן — לְדִבְרֵי הָאוֹמֵר [ג]לַיְלָה מְחוּסַּר זְמַן. לְדִבְרֵי הָאוֹמֵר? פְּשִׁיטָא! שְׁתַּיִם בַּיּוֹם וְאַחַת בַּלַּיְלָה אִצְטְרִיכָא לֵיהּ, סָלְקָא דַּעְתָּךְ אָמִינָא כְּאַתְקַפְתָּא דְּרַב שֵׁישָׁא בְּרֵיהּ דְּרַב אִידִי — קָא מַשְׁמַע לָן כְּדְרַב יוֹסֵף.§ עָבַר הָרֶגֶל וְלֹא חַג אֵינוֹ חַיָּיב בְּאַחֲרָיוּתוֹ, וְעַל זֶה נֶאֱמַר "מְעֻוָּת לֹא יוּכַל לִתְקֹן וְחֶסְרוֹן לֹא יוּכַל לְהִמָּנוֹת".§ אֲמַר לֵיהּ בַּר הֵי הֵי לְהִלֵּל: הַאי "לְהִימָּנוֹת"? לְהִמָּלְאוֹת מִיבָּעֵי לֵיהּ! אֶלָּא זֶה שֶׁמָּנוּהוּ חֲבֵירָיו לִדְבַר מִצְוָה וְהוּא לֹא נִמְנָה עִמָּהֶן. *תַּנְיָא נַמִי הָכִי: "מְעֻוָּת לֹא יוּכַל לִתְקֹן" — זֶה שֶׁבִּיטֵּל קְרִיאַת שְׁמַע שֶׁל שַׁחֲרִית, אוֹ קְרִיאַת שְׁמַע שֶׁל עַרְבִית, אוֹ [ד]שֶׁבִּיטֵּל תְּפִלָּה שֶׁל שַׁחֲרִית, אוֹ תְּפִלָּה שֶׁל עַרְבִית, "וְחֶסְרוֹן לֹא יוּכַל לְהִמָּנוֹת" — זֶה שֶׁנִּמְנוּ חֲבֵירָיו לִדְבַר מִצְוָה וְהוּא לֹא נִמְנָה עִמָּהֶן. אֲמַר לֵיהּ בַּר הֵי הֵי לְהִלֵּל: מַאי דִּכְתִיב: °"וְשַׁבְתֶּם וּרְאִיתֶם בֵּין צַדִּיק לְרָשָׁע בֵּין עֹבֵד אֱלֹהִים לַאֲשֶׁר לֹא עֲבָדוֹ", הַיְינוּ "צַדִּיק" הַיְינוּ "עוֹבֵד אֱלֹהִים", הַיְינוּ "רָשָׁע" הַיְינוּ "אֲשֶׁר לֹא עֲבָדוֹ"! אֲמַר לֵיהּ: "עֲבָדוֹ" וְ"לֹא עֲבָדוֹ" — תַּרְוַיְיהוּ צַדִּיקֵי גְּמוּרֵי נִינְהוּ. וְאֵינוֹ דּוֹמֶה שׁוֹנֶה פִּרְקוֹ *מֵאָה פְּעָמִים לְשׁוֹנֶה פִּרְקוֹ מֵאָה וְאֶחָד. אֲמַר לֵיהּ: וּמִשּׁוּם חַד זִימְנָא קָרֵי לֵיהּ "לֹא עֲבָדוֹ"? אֲמַר לֵיהּ: אִין, צֵא וּלְמַד מִשּׁוּק שֶׁל חַמָּרִין: עֲשָׂרָה פַּרְסֵי — בְּזוּזָא, חַד עֲשַׂר פַּרְסֵי — בִּתְרֵי זוּזֵי. אֲמַר לֵיהּ אֵלִיָּהוּ לְבַר הֵי הֵי וְא"ל לְר' אֶלְעָזָר: מַאי דִּכְתִיב °"הִנֵּה צְרַפְתִּיךְ וְלֹא בְכָסֶף בְּחַרְתִּיךְ בְּכוּר עֹנִי" — מְלַמֵּד שֶׁחָזַר הַקָּדוֹשׁ בָּרוּךְ הוּא עַל כָּל מִדּוֹת טוֹבוֹת לִיתֵּן לְיִשְׂרָאֵל, וְלֹא מָצָא אֶלָּא עֲנִיּוּת. אֲמַר שְׁמוּאֵל וְאִיתֵימָא רַב יוֹסֵף, הַיְינוּ דְּאָמְרִי אֱינָשֵׁי: יָאָה עֲנִיּוּתָא לִיהוּדָאֵי כִּי בַּרְזָא סוּמָּקָא לְסוּסְיָא חִיוָּרָא.§ "ר' שִׁמְעוֹן בֶּן מְנַסְיָא אוֹמֵר: אֵי זֶה הוּא "מְעֻוָּת לֹא יוּכַל לִתְקֹן" — זֶה הַבָּא עַל הָעֶרְוָה וְהוֹלִיד מִמֶּנָּה מַמְזֵר וכו'".§ הוֹלִיד — אִין, לֹא הוֹלִיד — לָא? וְהָא תַּנְיָא, *רַבִּי שִׁמְעוֹן בֶּן מְנַסְיָא אוֹמֵר: גּוֹנֵב אָדָם — אֶפְשָׁר שֶׁיַּחֲזִיר גְּנֵבוֹ וִיתַקֵּן, גּוֹזֵל אָדָם — אֶפְשָׁר שֶׁיַּחֲזִיר גְּזֵלוֹ וִיתַקֵּן, אֲבָל הַבָּא עַל אֵשֶׁת אִישׁ וַאֲסָרָהּ לְבַעְלָהּ — נִטְרָד מִן הָעוֹלָם וְהָלַךְ לוֹ. רַבִּי שִׁמְעוֹן בֶּן יוֹחַי אוֹמֵר: אֵין אוֹמֵר "בַּקְּרוּ גָּמָל", "בַּקְּרוּ חֲזִיר". אֶלָּא: "בַּקְּרוּ טָלֶה". וְאֵי זֶה — זֶה תַּלְמִיד חָכָם שֶׁפֵּירַשׁ מִן הַתּוֹרָה. רַבִּי יְהוּדָה בֶּן לָקִישׁ אָמַר: כָּל תַּלְמִיד חָכָם שֶׁפֵּירַשׁ מִן הַתּוֹרָה עָלָיו הַכָּתוּב אוֹמֵר: °"כְּצִפּוֹר נוֹדֶדֶת מִן קִנָּהּ כֵּן אִישׁ נוֹדֵד מִמְּקוֹמוֹ", וְאוֹמֵר: °"מַה מָּצְאוּ אֲבוֹתֵיכֶם בִּי עָוֶל כִּי רָחֲקוּ מֵעָלָי"?! לָא קַשְׁיָא; כָּאן — בַּאֲחוֹתוֹ פְּנוּיָה, כָּאן — בְּאֵשֶׁת אִישׁ. וְאִי בָּעֵית אֵימָא: הָא וְהָא בְּאֵשֶׁת אִישׁ, וְלָא קַשְׁיָא; כָּאן בְּאוֹנֶס

תורה אור: מלאכי ג; ישעיה מח; משלי כז; ירמיה ב

רש"י

אֶלָּא לְמ"ד רֶגֶל בִּפְנֵי עַצְמוֹ. וְעַכְשָׁיו אֵין לְךָ לִתְלוֹת טַעְמוֹ שֶׁל רַבִּי יוֹחָנָן דְּהוֹאִיל וְיֵשׁ לַטּוּמְאָה תַּשְׁלוּמִין לַשֵּׁנִי: קָסָבַר ר' יוֹחָנָן. אֵין חֶסְרוֹן זְמַן בְּמִי שֶׁהִגִּיעַ לֵילוֹ לְהַקְרִיב קָרְבְּנוֹתָיו מָחָר, הִלְכָּךְ מְחוּיָּיב הוּא בְּקָרְבָּן, אֶלָּא שֶׁהַלַּיְלָה מְעַכְּבוֹ מִלְּהָבִיא אֲבָל חִגֵּר בְּיוֹם רִאשׁוֹן אֵין עָלָיו שׁוּם חוֹבַת רְאִיָּיה לְפִיכָךְ אֵין לוֹ עָלָיו תַּשְׁלוּמִין: וּמִי א"ר יוֹחָנָן. אֵין לַיְלָה מְחוּסַּר זְמַן, וְהא"ר יוֹחָנָן: רָאָה אַחַת בַּלַּיְלָה. זָב שֶׁסָּפַר שִׁבְעָה נְקִיִּים כְּמִשְׁפָּטוֹ וְטָבַל וְהֶעֱרִיב שִׁמְשׁוֹ, וְחָזַר וְרָאָה אַחַת בַּלַּיְלָה וּשְׁתַּיִם לְמָחָר: מֵבִיא. קָרְבָּן עַל טוּמְאָה שְׁנִיָּה זוֹ, לְבַד מִן הַקָּרְבָּן שֶׁיָּבִיא עַל הָרִאשׁוֹנָה. וְיָבִיא שְׁנֵי קָרְבָּנוֹת כְּשֶׁיִּטְהַר, הוֹאִיל וְלֹא רָאָה הַשְּׁנִיָּה עַד שֶׁיָּצָא לְשָׁעָה שֶׁהִיא רְאוּיָה לְהָבִיא קָרְבָּן — יֵשׁ לוֹ תַּשְׁלוּמִין. וְאַף עַל הַשְּׁנִיָּה יָבִיא, אע"פ שֶׁתְּחִילָּתָהּ בְּתוֹךְ זְמַן קָרְבַּן הָרִאשׁוֹנָה — לָא אָמְרִינַן חֲדָא טוּמְאָה הִיא. וּפֵי' רַב יוֹסֵף אֶת הַטַּעַם בְּמַסֶּ' כְּרֵיתוֹת, לְפִי שֶׁהָרְאִיָּיה רִאשׁוֹנָה שֶׁל זָב אֵינָהּ אֶלָּא כְּקֶרִי בְּעָלְמָא, וְכִי חָזֵי אִינָךְ לְמָחָר — מִצְטָרֶפֶת בַּהֲדַיְיהוּ. ה"נ, אע"פ שֶׁהָיְתָה רְאִיָּיה רִאשׁוֹנָה בְּתוֹךְ קָרְבָּן רִאשׁוֹן, כִּי הֲדַר חָזֵי אִינָךְ לְמָחָר — מִצְטָרְפִין בַּהֲדַיְיהוּ: וְאִי סָלְקָא דַּעְתָּךְ לַיְלָה אֵין מְחוּסַּר זְמַן. אֲפִילּוּ רָאָה שְׁלָשְׁתָּן בַּלַּיְלָה זֶה — כְּבָר יָצָא מִזְּמַן רִאשׁוֹן, וּשְׁתֵּי זִיבוֹת הֵן. אִי לָאו דִּסְבִירָא לֵיהּ לַיְלָה מְחוּסַּר זְמַן, הִלְכָּךְ אִם רָאָה שְׁתַּיִם בַּלַּיְלָה — הָוְיָא לָהּ זִיבָה אֲרִיכְתָּא: כִּי א"ר יוֹחָנָן. הַהִיא — לְדִבְרֵי הָאוֹמֵר לַיְלָה מְחוּסַּר זְמַן אֲמָרָהּ, אֲבָל לְדִידֵיהּ סְבִירָא לֵיהּ אֲפִילּוּ רָאָה כּוּלָּן בַּלַּיְלָה מֵבִיא: לְדִבְרֵי הָאוֹמֵר פְּשִׁיטָא. אִי אָמְרַתְּ בִּשְׁלָמָא טַעְמָא דְּנַפְשֵׁיהּ קָאָמַר — אַשְׁמְעִינַן בֵּיהּ דִּסְבִירָא לַיְלָה מְחוּסַּר זְמַן. אֶלָּא אִי לְדִבְרֵי הָאוֹמֵר כו' קָאָמַר — מַאי אַשְׁמְעִינַן בָּהּ? מַהוּ דְּתֵימָא בְּאַתְקַפְתָּא דְּרַב שֵׁישָׁא. דְּאַתְקִיף בִּכְרֵיתוֹת עַל הַטַּעַם שֶׁנָּתַן רַב יוֹסֵף עַל הַדָּבָר, כְּמוֹ שֶׁפֵּירַשְׁתִּי לְמַעְלָה. תֵּדַע, דְּהָא רְאִיָּיה רִאשׁוֹנָה שֶׁל כָּל הַזָּבִים קֶרִי בְּעָלְמָא הוּא, וְכִי הֲדַר חָזֵי תַּרְתֵּי — מִצְטָרְפִין בַּהֲדַיְיהוּ, ה"נ לָא שְׁנָא. וּמַתְקִיף לָהּ רַב שֵׁישָׁא: מִי דָּמֵי? הָתָם — כּוּלְּהוּ בִּזְמַן חִיּוּבָא חֲזִינְהוּ, הָכָא — לָאו בִּזְמַן חִיּוּבָא דְּהַאי קָרְבָּן חַזְיֵיהּ: לְהִמָּלְאוֹת מִיבָּעֵי לֵיהּ. אֲבָל חֶסְרוֹן נוֹפֵל לְשׁוֹן מִילּוּי, שֶׁחִסֵּר מִצְוָה אַחַת — לֹא יִתְמַלֵּא עוֹד חֶסְרוֹן זֶה מִשֶּׁחָסַר: שֶׁמִּינּוּהוּ חֲבֵירָיו לִדְבַר מִצְוָה. שֶׁאָמְרוּ לוֹ בֹּא עִמָּנוּ, וְלֹא הָלַךְ. נִמְצָא שֶׁחִיסֵּר עַצְמוֹ מֵאוֹתוֹ מִנְיָן — לֹא יוּכַל לִימָּנוֹת עוֹד בְּאוֹתוֹ מִנְיָן, שֶׁכְּבָר עָשׂוּ אֶת הַמִּצְוָה: הַיְינוּ צַדִּיק הַיְינוּ עוֹבֵד אֱלֹהִים. מִי הוּא צַדִּיק וּמִי הוּא עוֹבֵד אֱלֹהִים? הֲלֹא אֶחָד הוּא! אֵינוֹ דּוֹמֶה שׁוֹנֶה פִּרְקוֹ כו'. אַף עַל פִּי שֶׁשְּׁנֵיהֶן צַדִּיקִים — לֹא עֲבָדוּהוּ בְּשָׁוֶה, שֶׁזֶּה עֲבָדוֹ יוֹתֵר: עֲשָׂרָה פַּרְסֵי. יַשְׂכִּיר לְךָ אָדָם חֲמוֹרוֹ בְּזוּז אֶחָד, שֶׁכְּבָר נָהֲגוּ כֵּן. וְאִם תֹּאמַר לוֹ לֵילֵךְ פַּרְסָה יוֹתֵר — יִשְׁאָלְךָ שְׁנֵי זוּזִים: צְרַפְתִּיךָ וְלֹא בְכָסֶף. וְלֹא בָּאֵשׁ כְּמוֹ שֶׁצּוֹרְפִים הַכֶּסֶף בָּאֵשׁ, אֶלָּא בְּחַרְתִּיךָ בְּכוּר עוֹנִי לְצוֹרְפוֹ בּוֹ. כּוּר הוּא הַחֶרֶס שֶׁצּוֹרְפִין בּוֹ: גּוֹנֵב אָדָם. גְּנֵיבָה אֶפְשָׁר שֶׁיַּחֲזִירֶנָּה, וִיתַקֵּן: נִטְרָד מִן הָעוֹלָם. אֵין לוֹ עוֹד תְּשׁוּבָה, לְפִי שֶׁעָשָׂה דָּבָר שֶׁאֵין לוֹ רְפוּאָה: אֵין אוֹמֵר בַּקְּרוּ גָּמָל. זֶה לְקָרְבָּן, כְּלוֹמַר: מִי שֶׁהוּא מְעוּוָּת מִתְּחִילָּתוֹ — אֵין זֶה מְעוּוָּת: אֶלָּא בַּקְּרוּ טָלֶה. זֶה לְקָרְבָּן, שֶׁמָּא נָפַל בּוֹ מוּם וְנִתְקַלְקֵל. כָּךְ לְשׁוֹן קִלְקוּל נוֹפֵל בְּאָדָם שֶׁהָיָה טוֹב מִתְּחִילָּה: אֲחוֹתוֹ פְּנוּיָה. הוֹלִיד — אִין, לֹא הוֹלִיד — לָא: בְּאֵשֶׁת אִישׁ. בְּלֹא הוֹלִיד נַמִי יֵשׁ זִכָּרוֹן לַעֲוֹנוֹ, שֶׁאֲסָרָהּ עַל בַּעְלָהּ, לֹא שְׁנָא אֲחוֹתוֹ וְלֹא שְׁנָא נָכְרִית: בְּאוֹנֶס. לֹא אֲסָרָהּ עַל בַּעְלָהּ, לְפִיכָךְ: הוֹלִיד — אִין, לֹא הוֹלִיד — לָא: בְּרָצוֹן

תוספות

שני תשלומין דראשון הוא. היינו ר' נתן. אלא למ"ד שני רגל בפני עצמו הוא היינו רבי. ואע"ג דאית ליה תנא דמסייע ליה – פריך שפיר, דמסתמא לא פליג ארבי דהתם, דקי"ל *הלכה כרבי מחבירו. אבל לא מסתברא למימר דבעי לישנה ככולי עלמא: או תפלה של ערבית. אתיא כמ"ד תפלת ערבית חובה. ואפילו למ"ד רשות – נכנס אין לנו לבטלה, אם לא ע"י אונס קצת, וכן משמע ההיא ד"תפלת השחר" (ברכות דף כו.): שכח ולא התפלל ערבית מתפלל שחרית שתים וכן (שם דף ל:) אם שכח ולא הזכיר של ר"ח בלילה – אין מחזירין אותו, לפי שאין מקדשין החדש בלילה. הא מקדשין – מחזירין, ולא מחלק כלל בין למ"ד רשות או בין למ"ד חובה, דמשמע דליכא מאן דפליג. וההיא דשבת (דף ט: ושם): אי שרא ליה הימייניה לא מטרחינן ליה, וכן בירושלמי: אי עלה למטתו לא ירד – היינו אונס קצת. ולא כפי' ה"ג, שפירש' דאף למ"ד רשות, אי שויה עליה חובה – הויא כחובה. והא ליתא, דמי לא עסקינן בהכי שכבר התפלל בשאר לילות – ואם היינו מפרשים שויה עליה חובה באותה לילה – יתכן ההיא דטעה ולא התפלל ר"ח בלילה. ובברכות הארכתי. *והבאתי ההיא דאמרו (יומא דף פז: ושם) דתפלת נעילה פוטרת של ערבית: **בר** הי הי להלל. יש מפרשים שגר היה, והיינו בן אברהם ושרה שנתוסף ה"א בשמן. וכן בג *בג דכולה הגמרא עולה ה': **כברזא** סומקא. רצועה. ודומה לו: מעיקרא משכא והשתא אברזא (ב"ק דף סו:). ובב"ר *יש: יאי עניותא לברתיה דיעקב כערקתא סומקתא לסוסיא חיורא: **כאן** באחותו פנויה. משמע לישנא דפסיקא ליה, דיש ממזר מחייבי כריתות, מדנקט *אחותו טפי מכל שאר עריות. והיינו כשמעון התימני (*בקדושין בפרק האומר) (דף סח): [עי' קדושין עד:]

אפילו

עין משפט נר מצוה

נח א מיי' פ"ה מהל' קרבן פסח הלכה א סמג עשין רנד: [עירובין מו:]

נט ב מיי' פ"ג מהלכות מחוסרי כפרה הלכה ה:

ס ג מיי' שם הלכה ז:

סא ד מיי' פ"ג מהלכות תפלה הלכה ח טור ש"ע א"ח סי' קח ס"ז: [כריתות ח.]

עיין ברא"ש ברכות פ"ד סי' ב' ובתר"י ד"ה גמ' טעה ולא התפלל ונראה שדברי תוספות ברכות כו. ד"ה טעה חסרים שם וערוכים ביומא שם ד"ה והאמר רב

נראה שצ"ל דעולה הגימטרי' שלו ה'

[ריש פ' בחוקותי ובמ"ר שמיני פ' יג אית' בזה"ל בעזקתיה סומקתא דעל ליבי' דסוסיא חיורא ע"ש]

ר"ל דכתיב בה כרת בהדיא

[נ"ל ביבמות מט.]

מסורת הש"ס

[פסחים צג.]

[יומא כט: נזיר יח: זבחים יב. מנחות ק. כריתות ח.]

ברכות כו.

נראה דצ"ל דר"ת מן עובד אלהים לאשר גימטריא ק"א ור"ת מן לא עבדו גימטרי' מאה הטעתק מחילופי גרסאות

[תוספ' פ"א]

רבינו חננאל

אחר. כיון דנטמא בשעה שהוא ראוי להביא בה קרבן חייב על כל אחת ואחת אלא ש"מ דלא כר' (אליעזר) ומקשה רב פפא אפירוקא דר' ירמיה הניחא לר' נתן דסבר פסח שני תשלומי דראשון הוא איכא לשנויי כדשנינן. אלא לר' דסבר פסח שני רגל בפני עצמו הוא. מאי אית לך למימר דברי ר' ור' נתן מפורשין בפסחים פרק מי שהיה טמא או בדרך רחוקה בתחלתו. (ופריק שאני טומאה דאית לה תשלומין בפסח שני). ונדחה דברי ר' ירמיה ומשני לילי שמיני [שאני דהוי] כאלו נטמא יום שמיני שלו ואמרינן עליה כי כבר נטמא בעת שנתחייב בה קרבן לפיכך משלימין בעת טהרתן. ומקשינן עליה דרב פפא ומי סבר ר' יוחנן לילה אין מחוסר זמן. והא"ר יוחנן בכריתות סוף פרק ראשון זב אם ראה ראייה אחת בלילה ושתים ביום שמיני שלו מביא קרבן אחר. שתים בלילה ואחת ביום שמיני שלו אינו מביא קרבן אחר. ואי ס"ד דר' יוחנן אמר לילה אינו מחוסר זמן אפילו שתים בלילה לילי שמיני ואחת ביום יביא דהא אמרת לר' יוחנן לילי שמיני כיום שמיני הוא ופריק רב פפא כי אמר ר' יוחנן שתים בלילה ואחת ביום אינו מביא לדברי האומר לילה מחוסר זמן ואמרינן הא פשוטה היא מאי אתא ר' יוחנן לאשמעינן. ופריק איצטריך למימר לן ראה ראייה אחת בלילה ושתים ביום מביא. מהו דתימא כיון דלילה מחוסר זמן הוא לא תצטרף הראשונה שראה בלילה בהדיה שתים שראה ביום כאתקפתא דרב ששא בריה דרב אידי התם כיון דלאו בזמן חיובא הוא לא תצטרף. אתא ר' יוחנן לאשמעינן כרב יוסף דאמר תדע דאע"ג דלאו בזמן חיובא חזייה לראשונה מצטרפא דהא ראייה ראשונה של זב שכבת זרע בעלמא הוא וכדחזי אחרנייתא מצטרפא בהדייהו. והא דרב ששא ודרב יוסף מיפרשא בכריתות סוף פרק ראשון ואיפכא התם: עבר הרגל ולא חגג אינו חייב באחריותו על זה נאמר מעוות לא יוכל לתקן וגו' זה שנמנו חביריו לדבר מצוה ולא נמנה עמהם. תניא נמי הכי מעוות לא יוכל לתקן זה שביטל ק"ש של שחרית או של ערבית. וחסרון לא יוכל להמנות זה שנמנו חביריו לדבר מצוה ולא נמנה הוא עמהם. א"ל בר הי הי להלל כתיב ושבתם וראיתם בין צדיק לרשע בין עובד אלהים לאשר לא עבדו היינו צדיק היינו עובד אלהים. א"ל הין. (א"ל) תרווייהו צדיקי נינהו. מיהו צדיק השונה פרקו ק' פעמים ועובד אלהים להשונה פרקו ק"א פעמים. ומשום פעם אחת יתירה היינו נקרא צדיק עובד אלהים. א"ל הין. ואתה למד דבר זה משכירות בהמות י' פרסי משכיר בזוזא. ואם הן י"א פרסי בתרתי זוזי. א' אליהו לבר הי הי מאי דכתיב הנה צרפתיך ולא בכסף בחרתיך בכור עוני. חזר הקב"ה על כל המדות ולא מצא נאה לישראל כעניות כדי שיהא לבם שבור וכוונתם לשמים ועיניהם תלויות לרחמיו וחסדיו. והיינו דאמרי אינשי יאי מסכנותא לישראל כברזא סומקא לסוסיא חוורא שגלוי וידוע לפני הקב"ה כשמרבין עושר בועטין בו שנאמר וישמן ישורון ויבעט וגו'. כרבם כן חטאו לי כבודם בקלון אמיר. הנני מחליף כבודם שהוא עושר. אחליף אותו בעניות שהוא קלון. ר' שמעון בן מנסיא אומר מעוות לא יוכל לתקן זה הבא על הערוה והוליד בן וכו' איני והא איהו דתני כיון שבא על אשת חבירו ואסרה על בעלה אין לו תקנה ואע"פ שלא הוליד. ופרקי' לא קשיא מתני' באחותו פנויה וכיוצא בה שאין ביאתו אוסרה על אחרים ויש לו תקנה בתשובה. אלא אם הוליד ממנה בן כי הוא ממזר לעולם אין לו תקנה.

ועוד

באונס, כאן – ברצון. ואיבעית אימא: הא והא באונס, ול"ק: כאן – באשת כהן, כאן – באשת ישראל. °"וליוצא ולבא אין שלום" (זכריה ח), אמר רב: *כיון שיוצא אדם מדבר הלכה לדבר מקרא – שוב אין לו שלום. ושמואל אמר: זה הפורש מתלמוד למשנה, ור' יוחנן אמר: אפילו מתלמוד לתלמוד.§ **מתני'** *היתר נדרים פורחין באויר ואין להם על מה שיסמכו. הלכות שבת חגיגות והמעילות – הרי הם כהררים התלוין בשערה, שהן מקרא מועט והלכות מרובות. הדינין והעבודות, הטהרות והטמאות, ועריות – יש להן על מה שיסמכו, והן הן גופי תורה.§

גמ' תניא, *רבי אליעזר אומר: יש להם על מה שיסמכו, שנאמר: °"כי יפליא" (ויקרא כז) °"כי יפליא" (במדבר ו) שתי פעמים, אחת הפלאה לאיסור ואחת הפלאה להיתר. רבי יהושע אומר: יש להם על מה שיסמכו, שנאמר: °"אשר נשבעתי באפי" (תהלים צה) – *באפי *) נשבעתי, וחזרתי בי. ר' יצחק אומר: יש להם על מה שיסמכו, שנאמר: °"כל נדיב לבו" (שמות לה). חנניה בן אחי רבי יהושע אומר: יש להם על מה שיסמכו, שנאמר: °"נשבעתי ואקיימה לשמור משפטי צדקך" (תהלים קיט). אמר רב יהודה אמר שמואל: אי הואי התם אמרי להו: דידי עדיפא מדידכו, שנאמר: °"לא יחל דברו" (במדבר ל) *הוא אינו מוחל, אבל אחרים מוחלין לו. אמר רבא: *לכולהו אית להו פירכא, לבר מדשמואל דלית ליה פירכא. דאי מדר' אליעזר – דלמא כדרבי יהודה שאמר משום ר' טרפון. דתניא, רבי יהודה אומר משום רבי טרפון: *לעולם אין אחד מהם נזיר, שלא ניתנה נזירות אלא להפלאה. אי מדר' יהושע – דלמא הכי קאמר: באפי נשבעתי ולא הדרנא בי. אי מדרבי יצחק – דלמא לאפוקי מדשמואל. *דאמר שמואל: [א]גמר בלבו – צריך שיוציא בשפתיו, והא קא משמע לן: דאע"ג דלא הוציא בשפתיו. אי מדחנניה בן אחי רבי יהושע – דלמא כרב גידל אמר רב. *דאמר רב גידל אמר רב: [ב]מנין שנשבעין לקיים את המצוה – שנאמר: "נשבעתי ואקיימה לשמור משפטי צדקך". אלא דשמואל לית ליה פירכא. אמר רבא ואיתימא רב נחמן בר יצחק: היינו דאמרי אינשי: *טבא חדא פלפלתא חריפתא ממלי צנא דקרי.§ "הלכות שבת".§ מיכתב כתיבן! לא צריכא, *לכדר' אבא. דאמר רבי אבא: *החופר [ג]גומא בשבת ואין צריך אלא לעפרה – פטור עליה. כמאן, כרבי שמעון, דאמר: *מלאכה שאינה צריכה לגופה פטור עליה. אפילו תימא לרבי יהודה, התם – מתקן, הכא – מקלקל הוא. מאי כהררין התלויין בשערה? מלאכת

*) [באבות דר"נ פ' לו אמר ר' יהושע בעצמו כן ע"ש]

רש"י

ברצון. אסרה על בעלה: אשת כהן. אפילו באונס אסורה לבעלה, בכתובות (דף נא:*): "והיא לא נתפשה" – אסורה, הא נתפשה – מותרת, ואי זו – זו אשת ישראל. ומדכתיב "היא" – מיעוטא הוי, לומר: יש לך אחרת, שאע"פ שנתפשה אסורה, ואי זו – זו אשת כהן: וליוצא ולבא אין שלום. מקרא הוא בזכריה, ודרשוהו כאן ליוצא מן התורה ובא לו לדברים אחרים: שיוצא אדם מדבר הלכה לדבר מקרא שוב אין לו שלום. שאין הוראה מדבר מקרא, שהמשנה מפרשה סתימת התורה: מתלמוד למשנה. אם שמש את החכמים שהן מדקדקין ליתן טעם משניות, להבין המשניות הסותרות זו את זו ולמצוא טעם לפטור ולחובה, לאיסור ולהיתר. שהמשנה זו קרוי תלמוד, ואם יצא מהן ונתן עסקו לגירסת המשניות – שוב אין לו שלום בדבר הוראה, שאין הוראה נכונה בדבר משנה. שכמה משניות יש שאין דבריהן מכוונין ותירוצם בני התלמוד: הכא במאי עסקינן, חסורי מחסרא, הא מני רבי פלוני היא ואין הלכה כמותו: אפילו מתלמוד לתלמוד. מתלמוד ירושלמי לתלמוד בבלי שהוא עמוק, כדאמרינן בסנהדרין (דף כד.): "במחשכים הושיבני כמתי עולם" – זו התלמוד של בבל: מתני' היתר נדרים פורחים באויר. התרת נדרים שאמרו חכמים, שהחכם מתיר את הנדר – מעט רמז יש במקרא, ואין על מה לסמוך, אלא שכן מסור לחכמים בתורה שבעל פה: הלכות שבת, והלכות חגיגה, הלכות מעילות. יש בהן הלכות שהן תלויות ברמז, מקרא מועט: כהררין התלוים. בשערות ראש: והעבודות. הלכות עבודת קרבן: והעריות. ערוה: הן הן גופי תורה. בגמרא פריך: אטו הנך לאו גופי תורה נינהו?! גמ' כי יפליא שתי פעמים. אחד בערכין ואחד בנזיר: "כי יפליא נדר בערכך", "כי יפליא לנדור נדר נזיר": אחת הפלאה לאיסור. כוליה הפלאה לשון פירוש, כתרגומו (א) "ארי יפריש", ולמה כתב הפלאה בשניהן? אחת כשפירש ונדר ואסר עצמו בנדר, ואחת שחוזר ומפרש לפני החכם, ואומר: כן נדרתי, ולדעת כן נדרתי, אבל לדעת כן לא נדרתי. והרי הוא בא לידי חרטה, ומתוך כך בא לידי היתר: נשבעתי באפי. מדקאמר "באפי" משמע: יכול אני לישאל עליו, לפי שמחמת אפי ולא מדעת מיושבת נשבעתי. יש ללמוד מכאן, שהמוצא פתח לנדרו, לאמר לא לדעת כן נדרתי שיקרני דבר זה שאני רואה הבא לי ע"י נדרי – מתירין לו: כל נדיב לבו הביאו. אם עודנו לבו נודבו עליו – יביאו, ואם מתחרט – יתירו לו: נשבעתי ואקיימה לשמור משפטי צדקך. מדקאמר "ואקיימה", מכלל דאם רצה שלא לקיים – מתירין לו: אי מדרבי אליעזר. דדריש הפלאה יתירתא: דלמא. לכדרבי טרפון אתא: אין אחד מהן נזיר. ג' שהיו יושבין, ובא אחד לפניהם, ואמר אחד: הריני נזיר שזה הבא אלמנו נזיר הוא, וחבירו אומר: הריני נזיר שאינו נזיר, ולבסוף נמצא כאחד מהן – אין אחד מהן נזיר. לפי שלא ניתנה נזירות להיות נזיר בתלייה ובספק, אלא בהפלאה ודאית מפורשת: גמר בלבו. שבועה או נדר או הקדש: שנשבעין לקיים המצוה. כלומר מנין שיהא אדם נשבע לקיים מצוה כדי שיזהר ויזדרז לקיימה: פלפלתא. גרעין אחד של פלפל: מיכתב כתיבן. טובא אזהרות כתיבי בשבת, מאי מקרא מועט דקאמר מתניתין? לא נצרכא כו'. דבר זה וכיוצא בו, רמז מועט יש לו ללמוד מן התורה: חופר גומא. בונה בנין הוא, ואם אינו צריך לה אלא ליטול את העפר, אף על פי שהבנין בנוי – אינו חייב משום בונה: שאינה צריכה לגופה. כגון (ב) זה שאינו צריך לבנין זה. ורבי שמעון אמר מילתיה גבי מוציא את המת במטה לקוברו בשבת (שבת דף צג:), וקאמר רבי שמעון: פטור על הוצאה זו, שבשבילו לא היתה באה אליו, ולא היה צריך לה: אפילו תימא לר' יהודה. דפליג עליה, מודה בהך גומא. דאלו התם הקובר את המת – מתקן הוא, והאי חופר גומא – מקלקל הוא את חצרו: ומאי כהררין. דקאמר במתניתין, דמשמע שיש קצת רמז מן התורה ללמד זה, ומהו הרמז? מלאכת

תוספות

אפילו מתלמוד לתלמוד. מתלמוד ירושלמי לתלמוד בבלי כדפירש רש"י. *וכן אמר בירושלמי: "במחשכים הושיבני כמתי עולם" – אלו תלמוד הבבלי. וכן (*רב כהנא) דהוה לייט דלישתכח מיניה תלמוד הבבלי. ומיהו, אפילו איפכא י"ל, והכי פירושו: שפירש מזה ועדיין לא הבין בזה, שמתוך כך לא יעלה בידו הלכה ברורה: **דלמא** כרבי יהודה. משמע דחשיב ליה פירכא מה שמצריך הכתוב לדרשה אחריתי. ואילו בפ"ק דמגילה (דף ז.) גבי אסתר ברוח הקדש נאמרה, קאמר שמואל, משום דכתיב: "קיימו וקבלו" – קיימו למעלה מה שקבלו למטה. וקאמר התלמוד דלית ליה פירכא ואילו בשבת בפ' "ר' עקיבא" (דף פח. ושם) דרשינן מיניה: קיימו מה שקבלו כבר, דקבלו התורה ברצון בימי אחשורוש! ואמר הר"י: דלאו קושיא היא, דהתם מפיק לה מדשני לה בדבוריה, דליכתוב "קיימו וקיימו" או "קבלו וקבלו", אלא ודאי תרתי שמע מינה: **באפי** נשבעתי ולא הדרנא בי. והקשה הר"ר אלחנן: דעל כרחך קרא בהכי מידריש, מדכתיב: "נשבעתי באפי אם יבואון אל מנוחתי" ודרשינן מינה (ג) גבי דור המדבר שלא באו לארץ! ותירץ לו הר"י: דהאי קרא לאו בביאת ארץ משתעי, אלא בחלק לעולם הבא (ד). ומלינו תנא *) דאמר ב"חלק" (סנהדרין דף קי:): "דור המדבר יש להם חלק לעוה"ב" א"כ איכא למידרש: והדרנא בי: **לאפוקי** מדשמואל דאמר שמואל גמר בלבו צריך שיוציא בשפתיו. לאו משום דלית ליה לשמואל גמר בלבו, דהא קרא כתיב. אלא מוקי לקדשים (ה) (שהביאו) בעזרה הוא דכתיב האי קרא, וגבי קדשים כתיב: "וכל נדיב לב עולות" (דה"ב כט) ושמואל מודה לה שפיר, ומקשי מינה לשמואל מהאי קרא, ומשני לה פרק ג' דשבועות (דף כו: ושם). וכי תימא ניליף מינה – משום דהוה ליה תרומה, ר"ל: תרומת מלאכת המשכן כתיב ביה "כל נדיב לבו" וקדשים שני כתובים הבאין כאחד, ואין מלמדים: **לקיים** מצות. דצריך להזכיר שם שמים, כדי לזרוזי נפשיה: **לשמואל** לית ליה פירכא. והא דדרשינן פ"ב דנדרים (דף טז:): אבל מיחל הוא חפצי שמים – התם מ"דברו" נפקי ליה: **לכדרבי אבא.** ה"ה לשאר מקלקלים דפטורין הוה מצי למימר, אלא רבותא קמ"ל: דאע"ג דצריך לעפר – מיפטר, כיון דלא צריך לגומא: מלאכת

*) [עי' תוס' ב"ב עד. ד"ה ועכשיו]

רבינו חננאל

ועוד אם אנס אשת איש ישראל לא אסרה על בעלה ואם הוליד בן אין לו תקנה אבל אשת כהן אפילו אנסה אסרה על בעלה. רשב"א אין נקרא מעוות אלא מי שהיה מתוקן ונתעוות ואיזה זה ת"ח שפירש מן התורה. אין אומרים בקרו גמל בקרו חזיר אלא בקרו טלה שעיקרו כשר וטהור. כך ת"ח שפירש. וליוצא ולבא אין שלום מן הצר. אמר רב כיון שאדם יוצא מדבר הלכה אין לו שלום. ושמואל אמר זה היוצא מן התלמוד למשנה. ור' יוחנן אמר אפילו יוצא מתלמוד בבלי לתלמוד א"י אין שלום שאין דרכיהן אחת: **ירושלמי** ר' הונא ור' ירמיה בשם שמואל מצאנו שויתר הקב"ה על ע"ז וג"ע וש"ד ועל עזיבת התורה לא ויתר. שנא' על מה אבדה הארץ וגו' ויאמר ה' על עזבם את תורתי וגו'. נמנו וגמרו התלמוד קודם למעשה חדא דאת אמר בשיש מי שיעשה אבל אין שם מי שיעשה המעשה קודם. כי הא דאמר לון ר' אלעזר לר' חייא ולר' יוסי ולר' אמי אן הויתון יומא דין אמרין ליה אזלינן לגמול חסד. אמר לון ולא הוה אחרינין למגמל הדא חסד. אמרו ליה מגור הוה. כלומר אכסנאי הוה: [מתני'] התרת נדרים פורחים באויר ואין להם על מה שיסמכו. תניא ר' אליעזר אומר יש להן. כלומר יש לו ראיה מן התורה שיש לו רשות להתיר נדרים ואינם כעופות הפורחות באויר כאשר שנינו במשנתנו. מנא לן שנא' כי יפליא ב' פעמים אחת הפלאה לאיסור ואחת הפלאה להיתר ר' יהושע אומר מהכא אשר נשבעתי באפי וחזרתי ש"מ שיש היתר לשבועות כו' ודחינן להני כולהו דלמא ההפלאה היתירה לרבויי הא אתאי דתניא ר' יהודה אומר משום ר"ט אין אחד מהן נזיר. לפי שלא נתנה נזירות אלא להפלאה כדכתיב (שמות ח) והפליתי ביום ההוא. כלומר דבר הידוע בודאי ובבירור כך תהיה ההפלאה שמתחייב בה הוא ור' יהושע נמי דלמא לחזוקה לשבועה קאמר אשר נשבעתי באפי מרוב הכעס שהכעיסוני יחרה אפי בהן ואינו להקל כדרך חרטה. והא דר' יצחק נמי אפקוה מכל נדיב לב דאלמא הדבר תלוי בלב וכל דבר שאינו בכוון לב כמי שאינו הוא. דלמא האי קרא לכדשמואל הוא דאתא דאמר גמר בלבו צריך להוציא בשפתיו שאע"פ שכל המצות תלויות בהסכמת לב כדכתיב למען תפוש את ישראל בלבם. שבועה ואיסור אינו תלויה אלא במבטא שפתים. והא דחנניה בן אחי ר' יהושע דדייק מנשבעתי ואקיימה. מכלל שיש דרך שלא לקיים דלמא כדרב גידל אמר רב ולהודיע כי הנשבע לקיים מצוה שבועה חלה עליו שנאמר נשבעתי ואקיימה לשמור משפטי צדקך. מכלל שיש שבועה אחרת שאינו חייב לקיימה כגון הנשבע לבטל את המצוה. אבל הא דאמר שמואל לא יחל דברו. ודייק מכדי כתיב ככל היוצא מפיו יעשה הוה ליה למכתב ולא יעבור דברו. לא יחל דברו למה לי אלא ללמד שכגון זה יש לו חילול והוא לא יחל לעצמו. אבל אחרים מחילין לו. האי מלתא דשמואל לית בה פרכא. ורבינא דהוא בתרא הודה להא דשמואל: **ירושלמי** רבי מניתיה לרב להתיר נדרים ולראות כתמים ולדון יחידי מן דדמך ר' בעא מר"ג בריה למנוייה נמי בראיית מומי בכורות. א"ל איני מוסיף לך על מה שנתן לך אבא ואע"ג דממנין זקנים לדברים יחידים והוא שיהא ראוי לכל הדברים כהדא ריב"ל מני לתלמידוי. והוה מצטער על חד דהוה ולא הוה יכול ממנותיה וממניה לדברים יחידים. כלומר לשאר דברים דגמיר להו הדא אמרה הראוי לכל הדברים ממנין אותו לדברים יחידים ושאינו בקי בכל הדברים אין ממנין אותו אפילו לדברים יחידים. ר' יהודה נשיאה כתב איגרתה דייקר בחוצה לארץ לר' חייא בר אבא וכתב להו הרי שלחנו אליכם אדם גדול. ומה היא גדולתו שאינו בוש לומר לא שמעתי מהו להתעטף בפילונם ולהתיר נדרים ופשטוה מותר במקום שאין טלית: הלכות שבת. ומקשינן הלכות שבת והלא כתוב בתורה שאסור במלאכה. ופרקינן צריכא להלכות להא דאשכחן דאתעבידנא מלאכה דהוא פטור עליה. כדר' אבא. דאמר ר' אבא החופר

עין משפט נר מצוה

[וכן בסנהדרין כד.] [נ"ל רבי זירא ב"מ פה.]

סב א מיי' פ"ב מהל' שבועות הלכה ו ופ"ב מהלכות נדרים הלכה ב טוש"ע י"ד סי' רי סעיף א וסי' רלט סעיף א:

סג ב מיי' פ"א מהלכות שבועות הלכה ג:

סד ג מיי' פ"א מהל' שבת הלכה יז:

מסורת הש"ס

[וביכמות נו:] [סנהדרין לח. נע"ק] [נזיר סב.] [שם] סנהדרין קי: ברכות לב. [יומא פה: מגילה ז.] נזיר לד. סב. סנהדרין כה. ערכין פב. [נדרים יט: כא.] שבועות כו: [נדרים ז: תמורה ג:] יומא פה: מגילה ז. [נ"ל אלא לכדרבי אבא] שבת עג: ביצה ח. [שבת עג: וש"נ]

הגהות הב"ח

(א) רש"י ד"ה אחת הפלאה וכו' כתרגומו אֲרֵי יְפָרֵשׁ: (ב) ד"ה שאינה צריכה לגופה כגון מלאכה זאת שאינו: (ג) תוס' ד"ה באפי וכו' ודרשינן מיניה לדור המדבר כצ"ל ותיבת גבי נמחק: (ד) בא"ד לעולם הבא ותדע דהא מלינו תנא וכו' א"כ צריך למידרש והדרנא בי. נ"ב והכי איתא התם להדיא דר"א דאמר יש להם חלק לעוה"ב דריש נשבעתי וחוזרני בי: (ה) ד"ה לאפוקי וכו' אלא מוקי לה לקדשים דבעזרה הוא דכתיב האי קרא גבי קדשים וכל נדיב לב עולות וכו' ומשני לה הכי פ' ג' דשבועות וקאמר התם ונילף מינה וכו' דכתיב ביה כל נדיב לב הביאו וקדשים. נ"ב וצריך לפרש הא דקאמר הכא לאפוקי מדשמואל משמע דקרא דכל נדיב לב יליף אף בחולין ולאפוקי מדשמואל דאמר [דלא משמע מיניה אלא קדשים]:

*[א]מְלֶאכֶת מַחֲשֶׁבֶת אָסְרָה תּוֹרָה, וּמְלֶאכֶת מַחֲשֶׁבֶת לָא כְּתִיבָא.§ "חֲגִיגוֹת".§ מִיכְתַּב כְּתִיבָן! לָא צְרִיכָא, לְכִדְאָמַר לֵיהּ רַב פָּפָּא לְאַבָּיֵי: מִמַּאי דְּהַאי "וְחַגּוֹתֶם אוֹתוֹ חַג לַה'" זְבִיחָה? דִּלְמָא חוֹגוּ חַגָּא קָאָמַר רַחֲמָנָא! אֶלָּא מֵעַתָּה, דִּכְתִיב: °"וְיָחֹגּוּ לִי בַּמִּדְבָּר" הָכִי נַמִּי דְּחוֹגוּ חַגָּא הוּא? וְכִי תֵּימָא הָכִי נַמִּי — וְהָכְתִיב: °"וַיֹּאמֶר מֹשֶׁה גַּם אַתָּה תִּתֵּן בְּיָדֵינוּ זְבָחִים וְעוֹלוֹת"! דִּלְמָא הָכִי קָאָמַר רַחֲמָנָא: אִכְלוּ וּשְׁתוּ וְחוֹגוּ חַגָּא קַמַּאי. לָא סָלְקָא דַּעְתָּךְ, דִּכְתִיב: °"וְלֹא יָלִין חֵלֶב חַגִּי עַד בֹּקֶר", וְאִי סָלְקָא דַּעְתָּךְ דְּחוּגָּא הוּא — (א) תַּרְבָּא לְחַגָּא אִית לֵיהּ?! וְדִלְמָא הָכִי קָאָמַר רַחֲמָנָא: חֵלֶב הַבָּא בִּזְמַן חַג — לֹא יָלִין? אֶלָּא מֵעַתָּה: הַבָּא בִּזְמַן חַג — הוּא דְּלֹא יָלִין, הָא דְּכָל הַשָּׁנָה כּוּלָּהּ יָלִין? °"כָּל הַלַּיְלָה עַד הַבֹּקֶר" כְּתִיב! דִּלְמָא, אִי מֵהַהוּא הֲוָה אָמִינָא: הַהוּא לַעֲשֵׂה, כָּתַב רַחֲמָנָא הַאי לְלָאו! לְלָאו כָּתַב קְרָא אַחֲרִינָא: °"וְלֹא יָלִין מִן הַבָּשָׂר אֲשֶׁר תִּזְבַּח בָּעֶרֶב בַּיּוֹם הָרִאשׁוֹן לַבֹּקֶר". וְדִלְמָא לַעֲבוֹר עָלָיו בִּשְׁנֵי לָאוִין וַעֲשֵׂה! אֶלָּא: אָתְיָא "מִדְבָּר" "מִדְבָּר". כְּתִיב הָכָא: "וְיָחֹגּוּ לִי בַּמִּדְבָּר", וּכְתִיב הָתָם: °"הַזְּבָחִים וּמִנְחָה הִגַּשְׁתֶּם לִי בַּמִּדְבָּר", מָה לְהַלָּן זְבָחִים — אַף כָּאן זְבָחִים, וּמַאי כַּהֲרָרִין הַתְּלוּיִין בְּשַׂעֲרָה — *דִּבְרֵי תוֹרָה מִדִּבְרֵי קַבָּלָה לָא יָלְפִינַן.§ "מְעִילוֹת".§ מִיכְתַּב כְּתִיבָן! אָמַר רָמִי בַּר חָמָא: לָא נִצְרְכָא אֶלָּא לְכִדְתְנַן: *[ב]הַשָּׁלִיחַ שֶׁעָשָׂה שְׁלִיחוּתוֹ — בַּעַל הַבַּיִת מָעַל, לֹא עָשָׂה שְׁלִיחוּתוֹ — שָׁלִיחַ מָעַל. וְכִי עָשָׂה שְׁלִיחוּתוֹ אַמַּאי מָעַל? וְכִי זֶה חוֹטֵא וְזֶה מִתְחַיֵּיב?! הַיְינוּ כַּהֲרָרִין הַתְּלוּיִין בְּשַׂעֲרָה. אָמַר רָבָא: וּמַאי קוּשְׁיָא? דִּלְמָא שָׁאנֵי מְעִילָה, דְּיָלְפָא "חֵטְא" "חֵטְא" מִתְּרוּמָה, מָה הָתָם *[ג]שְׁלוּחוֹ שֶׁל אָדָם כְּמוֹתוֹ — אַף כָּאן שְׁלוּחוֹ שֶׁל אָדָם כְּמוֹתוֹ? אֶלָּא אָמַר רָבָא: לָא נִצְרְכָא אֶלָּא לְכִדְתַנְיָא*: [ד]נִזְכַּר בַּעַל הַבַּיִת וְלֹא נִזְכַּר שָׁלִיחַ — שָׁלִיחַ מָעַל. שָׁלִיחַ עַנְיָא מַאי קָא עָבֵיד? הַיְינוּ כַּהֲרָרִין הַתְּלוּיִין בְּשַׂעֲרָה. אָמַר רַב אַשִׁי: מַאי קוּשְׁיָא, דִּלְמָא מִידֵּי דַּהֲוָה אַמּוֹצִיא מְעוֹת הֶקְדֵּשׁ לְחוּלִּין? אֶלָּא אָמַר רַב אַשִׁי: לָא נִצְרְכָא אֶלָּא לְכִדְתְנַן: *נָטַל אֶבֶן אוֹ קוֹרָה שֶׁל הֶקְדֵּשׁ — הֲרֵי זֶה לֹא מָעַל, נְתָנָהּ לַחֲבֵירוֹ — הוּא מָעַל, וַחֲבֵירוֹ לֹא מָעַל. מִכְּדִי מִישְׁקַל שְׁקָלָהּ, מַה לִּי הוּא *וּמַה לִּי חֲבֵירוֹ? הַיְינוּ כַּהֲרָרִין הַתְּלוּיִין בְּשַׂעֲרָה. וּמַאי קוּשְׁיָא, דִּלְמָא כִּדְשְׁמוּאֵל, דְּאָמַר שְׁמוּאֵל: *[ה]הַבָּא בְּגִזְבָּר

רש"י

מְלֶאכֶת מַחֲשֶׁבֶת. שֶׁהַמַּחֲשָׁבָה חֲשָׁבָהּ בְּדַעְתּוֹ וְנִתְכַּוֵּון לָהּ, וְזֶה לֹא נִתְכַּוֵּון לָהּ לְבִנְיָן זֶה — לְפִיכָךְ פָּטוּר. וְזֶהוּ רֶמֶז מוּעָט, דְּאִילּוּ מְלֶאכֶת מַחֲשֶׁבֶת בְּשַׁבָּת לֹא כְּתִיבָא, אֶלָּא בַּמִּשְׁכָּן הוּא דִּכְתִיב. וּלְפִי שֶׁסָּמַךְ בְּפָרָשַׁת "וַיַּקְהֵל" פָּרָשַׁת שַׁבָּת לְפָרָשַׁת מִשְׁכָּן — אָנוּ לְמֵדִין מְלֶאכֶת מַחֲשֶׁבֶת לְשַׁבָּת: מִיכְתַּב כְּתִיבָן. כִּדְאָמְרִינַן לְעֵיל מִ"וְחַגּוֹתֶם אוֹתוֹ": חוֹגוּ חַגָּא. לְהַרְבּוֹת שִׂמְחָה: דִּלְמָא הָכִי קָאָמַר רַחֲמָנָא אִכְלוּ וּשְׁתוּ וְחוֹגוּ חַגָּא קַמַּאי. וְהַאי זְבָחִים דִּקְרָא — לָאו שְׁלָמִים נִינְהוּ, אֶלָּא וְזָבַחְתָּ בָּשָׂר לֶאֱכוֹל: חֵלֶב הַבָּא בִּזְמַן הֶחָג. אִם בָּאתָ לְהַקְרִיב קָרְבָּנוֹת צָרִיךְ בָּרֶגֶל — לֹא יָלִינוּ חוּץ לַמִּזְבֵּחַ בַּעֲלוֹת הַשַּׁחַר: הָא כָּל הַשָּׁנָה יָלִינוּ. בִּתְמִיָּה: עַד הַבֹּקֶר כְּתִיב. "הִיא הָעוֹלָה עַל מוֹקְדָהּ עַל הַמִּזְבֵּחַ כָּל הַלַּיְלָה עַד הַבֹּקֶר". מִכָּאן אָנוּ לְמֵדִין, שֶׁמַּעֲלֶה כָּל הַלַּיְלָה אֵבָרִים וּפְדָרִים שֶׁל קָרְבָּנוֹת שֶׁנִּשְׁחֲטוּ הַיּוֹם. אֲבָל לֹא מֵעֲלוֹת הַשַּׁחַר וּלְמַעְלָה, דְּנִפְסְלוּ בְּלִינָה: וּמַאי כַּהֲרָרִין הַתְּלוּיִין. גְּזֵרָה שָׁוָה רְאָיָה גְּדוֹלָה הִיא: דִּבְרֵי תוֹרָה מִקַּבָּלָה לֹא יָלְפִינַן. הִלְכָּךְ רֶמֶז בְּעָלְמָא(ב): הַשָּׁלִיחַ שֶׁעָשָׂה שְׁלִיחוּתוֹ. בַּעַל הַבַּיִת שֶׁהָיוּ בְּיָדוֹ מְעוֹת הֶקְדֵּשׁ, וְנִתְחַלְּפוּ בִּמְעוֹתָיו, וּנְתָנָן בְּשׁוֹגֵג לְשָׁלִיחַ, וְאָמַר לוֹ: קַח לִי מֵהֶם חָלוּק אוֹ טַלִּית, אִם עָשָׂה שְׁלִיחוּתוֹ — בַּעַל הַבַּיִת מָעַל. וְזֶהוּ כַּהֲרָרִין, שֶׁיֵּשׁ לִתְמוֹהַּ וְלוֹמַר: וְכִי שָׁלִיחַ זֶה חָטָא שֶׁהוֹצִיא מְעוֹת הֶקְדֵּשׁ, וּבַעַל הַבַּיִת מִתְחַיֵּיב קֶרֶן וָחוֹמֶשׁ וּלְהָבִיא אָשָׁם מְעִילוֹת? וַהֲרֵי יָדוּעַ לָנוּ בְּכָל הַתַּלְמוּד שֶׁאֵין שָׁלִיחַ לִדְבַר עֲבֵירָה, שֶׁיְּהֵא שׁוֹלֵחַ מִתְחַיֵּיב עַל יְדֵי שְׁלוּחוֹ: מְעִילָה יָלְפִינַן חֵטְא חֵטְא מִתְּרוּמָה. לְכַמָּה דְּבָרִים נֶאֱמַר בְּתוֹרַת כֹּהֲנִים. נֶאֱמַר בִּמְעִילָה: "וְחָטְאָה בִּשְׁגָגָה מִקָּדְשֵׁי ה'" (ויקרא ה), וְנֶאֱמַר בִּתְרוּמָה: "וְלֹא תִשְׂאוּ עָלָיו חֵטְא" (במדבר יח), מַה הָתָם שְׁלוּחוֹ כְּמוֹתוֹ, דִּכְתִיב: "כֵּן תָּרִימוּ גַם אַתֶּם" (שם), וְאָמַר מָר: "גַּם אַתֶּם" — לְרַבּוֹת שְׁלוּחֲכֶם: נִזְכַּר בַּעַל הַבַּיִת כו'. בָּרַיְיתָא הִיא בְּפֶ' בַּתְרָא דִּמְעִילָה. וְהָכִי גָּרְסִינַן: לְכִדְתַנְיָא נִזְכַּר בַּעַל הַבַּיִת שֶׁהֵן שֶׁל הֶקְדֵּשׁ עַד שֶׁלֹּא יַגִּיעַ שָׁלִיחַ אֵצֶל חֶנְוָנִי וְלֹא נִזְכַּר שָׁלִיחַ וְהוֹצִיאָן הַשָּׁלִיחַ חַיָּיב: שָׁלִיחַ עַנְיָא מַאי עֲבַד. נְהִי דְּבַעַל הַבַּיִת פָּטוּר, דְּכֵיוָן דְּנִזְכַּר — אֲנַן סָהֲדֵי דְּתוּ לָא נִיחָא לֵיהּ בִּשְׁלִיחוּתֵיהּ דְּהָהוּא, וּמֵהַשְׁתָּא לָאו שְׁלוּחוֹ הוּא, וּמִיהָא שָׁלִיחַ מַאי עָבֵיד: מִידֵּי דַּהֲוָה. אַשְּׁאָר כָּל מוֹצִיאִין מְעוֹת הֶקְדֵּשׁ לְחוּלִּין בְּשׁוֹגֵג שֶׁיִּמְעֲלוּ — אַף זֶה בְּשׁוֹגֵג הוֹצִיאָן, דְּכֵיוָן שֶׁבִּיטֵּל הַמְשַׁלֵּחַ שְׁלִיחוּתוֹ — הֲוָה לֵיהּ אִיהוּ מוֹצִיא: הוּא מָעַל. דְּכֵיוָן שֶׁנְּתָנָם לוֹ — הוֹצִיאָן מִיַּד הֶקְדֵּשׁ לְחוּלִּין: וַחֲבֵרוֹ לֹא מָעַל. דְּכָל שֶׁיַּעֲשֶׂה הוּא בָּהּ, דְּהָא דִּידֵיהּ הִיא, וַעֲלֵיהּ דְּהָאֵיךְ לְשַׁלּוּמֵי לְהֶקְדֵּשׁ, כִּדְכְתִיב: "וְאֵת אֲשֶׁר חָטָא מִן הַקֹּדֶשׁ יְשַׁלֵּם" (ויקרא ה): דְּכָל

תוספות

מלאכת מחשבת אסרה תורה. פרש"י: שאינה צריכה לגופה במין מלאכה זאת, שברצונו לא היה בנין זה בעולם. ולא יתכן, דאם כן בכל מלאכות נמי, כגון סותר ע"מ לבנות במקומו למה מיחייב(ג)? דהא לא ניחא ליה שהיה הבנין בעולם! וכן בקורע ע"מ לתפור — ג"כ לא ניחא ליה בקרע זה מעולם וקורע הבא באבלו, או מחמת טרדא, וקורע בחמתו למרמי אימתיה. (ד)לכן נראה להר"י לפרש: שאינו צריך לעיקר שורש האיסור, כגון הכא, שאינו צריך לגומא שהיא המלאכה. וכן מוציא מת במטה, והרבה דחשיב פ' "המצניע" (שבת דף צג:). ולא דמו למלאכת המשכן, שהיו צריכים לעיקר המלאכה: מכבה — משום צורך הפחמין, ולידת תחשים וחלזון, וכן כולם כיוצא בהן*:

חוגו חגא. י"מ לשון מחולות, כמו: "יחוגו וינועו כשכור" (תהלים קז):

בזמן חג הוא דלא ילין (והתניא) וכו'. כי מוקמינן קרא בחגיגה לא שייך לאקשויי: בחגיגה הוא דלא ילין, הא כל שאר קרבנות — ילין. הא כתיב: "כל הלילה עד הבקר" ומוקמינן לה לכל העולין על המזבח. דהא איכא למימר דלא הוה מוקמינן קרא רק לעולה, שהיא כולה כליל כמו עולה. אבל שאר קרבנות, כגון שלמים וחגיגות שאינם כליל — לא:

ולא ילין מן הבשר. ואף על גב דמוקמינן לקרא בפרק "אלו דברים" (פסחים דף עא. ושם) בחגיגה שנאכלת לשני ימים ולילה אחד. ועוד: דבשר כתיב — דמשמע אכילת אדם! מ"מ מפקינן מיניה תרתי, מדכתיב: "ביום הראשון לבקר" ולא כתיב ביום השלישי:

לעבור עליו בשני לאוין. ואע"ג דאמרינן בעלמא: *כל היכא דאיכא למידרש — דרשינן, ולא מוקמינן בלאוי יתירי! הכא שאני, שאין להעמידו בקרבן חדש, שלא מצינו כיוצא בו בתורה. ודומה לו כמו שמצינו בריש יבמות (דף ז.) דמוקמינן "לא יגלה" בשומרת יבם של אביו בלאו יתירא, ולא מוקמינן ליה באנוסת אביו:

ויחוגו לי במדבר. "ולא ילין חלב חגי" אתא ללמד על ג"ש, דמיירי בחגיגה ולא בשאר קרבנות:

מעילות מכתב כתיבי וכו' (ה)*מקרא מועט והלכות מרובות. מתוך פרש"י משמע שהוא פירוש: התלויין בשערה — שיש בו הלכות מרובות תלויין ברמז מקרא מועט, כהר התלוי בשיער הראש. וקשה למורי: מאי פריך בגמרא מעילות מכתב כתיבי? ודאי כתיבי, אבל יש בהן הלכות הרבה, והיינו מקרא מועט והלכות מרובות! ומיהו, לפי מה שפירש רש"י תלויות ברמז, משמע דסבירא ליה דבהדיא לא כתיבי, אך גבי שבת פירש: מיכתב כתיבי, פי': טובא אזהרות כתיבי בשבת, מאי מקרא מועט דקאמר מתני'? והכי לא אפשר לי לפרש גבי מעילות. וגם משמע דבהדיא קאמר דכתיבי! ונראה להר"ר אלחנן לפרש דמילתא באפי נפשיה היא: מקרא מועט וקאי לאהלות ויש בהן מקרא מועט, אבל ההלכות מרובות. ובכמה ספרים יש ריוח בין מקרא מועט אדלעיל. א"כ משמע דמילתא באפי נפשיה הוא. אך בתוספתא (פ"א) תנא: מקרא מועט והלכות מרובות כהררין התלויין בשערה, ואין להם על מה שיסמכו. מכאן היה אומר רבי יהושע: לבחר בנבחר. ר"ל: מקרא מועט ותולה ברמז מועט, דמשמע כדפירש רש"י. ופירש כדפרש"י על הא דקאמר מקרא מועט — שברמז נתנו:

נתנה לחברו מעל. ולא דמי להאיא דנתנה לחנוני דלא מעל. דהתם מיירי במזיד ואין מתחלל, וחנוני דלא מעל עד שיוציא — התם משום דלא עבד מעשה:

משקל שקלה מה לי הוא מה לי חברו. יש תימה: דודאי שינה הרבה, כיון שנתנה לחברו — יש לו למעול משום טובת הנאה של שאלה, כדאמרינן פרק "השואל" (ב"מ דף צט.): המשאיל קורדום של הקדש — מעל לפי טובת הנאה של חברו, וחברו מותר לבקע בו לכתחלה. אבל כי לא נתנה — אכתי לא נהנה ממנה כלום! וי"ל: דהכא מיירי שמתכוין להוציא מרשות הקדש, ובמנחות (דף קא.*) פירשתי:

בגזבר

עין משפט נר מצוה

סה א מיי' פ"א מהל' שבת הלכה טו:
סו ב מיי' פ"ז מהלכות מעילה הלכה א:
סז ג מיי' פ"ד מהלכות תרומות הלכה א טוש"ע י"ד סי' שלא סעיף כט:
סח ד מיי' פ"ז מהלכות מעילה הלכה ה:
סט ה מיי' שם פ"ו הלכה ז:

מסורת הש"ס

[ביצה יג: וש"נ]
[וע"ע תוס' שבת לד. ד"ה ר' שמעון]
[ב"ק ב: נדה כג.]
קדושין מב: נדרים עב. מעילה כ. כתובות לח.
[ברכות לד: וש"נ]
מעילה כא. קדושין נ.
מעילה יט: ב"ק כ: ב"מ נט:
מ"ש הכי נטל הוא דלא מעל ומ"ש כי נתנה לחבירו דמעל רש"י במעילה שם
[פסחים כד:]
[שייך לעיל ע"א במשנה]
[מעילה כ.]
[כל"ה אע"ג]

רבינו חננאל

החופר גומא ואין כוונתו לגומא אלא ליטול העפר לכסות לו צואה. וכיוצא בה פטור עליה שנמצא מקלקל לגבי הגומא. דתנן כל המקלקלין פטורין. והן כמו הרים תלויין כחוט השערה. שאין כח בשערה להחזיק ההר אלא נראה כתלוי ועומד באויר. כן הלכות הללו דאי מדאורייתא כל מלאכה אסורה ובבאה ההלכה פירשה מלאכת מחשבת כלומר אינו חייב במלאכה עד שיתכוין לעשות אותה מלאכה: **ירושלמי** כתיב ועליהן ככל הדברים מקרא ומשנה ותלמוד הכל נאמרו לו למשה מסיני. אין מורין לא מן ההלכות ולא מן התוספתות ולא מן האגדות אלא מן התלמוד. ר' חנניא בשם שמואל אמר אין למידין מן ההוראה ולא מן המעשה בההוא דאיכא מאן דפליג אבל בהאי דלא פליג עביד. חגיגות מנא לן דהקרבת זבח היא. דלמא הקפה דרך סיבוב הוא כדכתיב יחוגו וינועו כשכור. ודחינן טובא ודברים פשוטין הן. ואסיקנא אלא בג"ש גמיר לה אתיא מדבר מדבר כתיב הכא ויחוגו לי במדבר. וכתיב הזבחים ומנחה הגשתם לי במדבר. אי הכי אמאי תנינן כהררים תלויין בשערה הן. ופרקינן דדברי תורה מדברי קבלה לא ילפינן. מעילות נמי אוקימנא בהא נזכר בעל הבית ולא נזכר השליח. השליח מעל. שליח מי הוות ליה ידיעא דאינון מעות של הקדש דלמעול. בשלמא מוציא מעות הקדש לחולין אמרינן הות ליה למידק וכיון דלא דק מעל. אבל שליח מי איכא למימר הכי. היינו

הגהות הב"ח

(א) גמ' ואי סלקא דעתך דחוגא חגא הוא תרבא: (ב) רש"י ד"ה דברי תורה וכו' בעלמא הוא הס"ד: (ג) תוס' ד"ה מלאכת וכו' פרש"י כגון מלאכה זאת וכו' ע"מ לבנות במקומו למה מחייב והלא ניחא ליה שלא היה הבנין בעולם וכן בקורע יריעה שנפל בה דרנא ע"מ לתפור ברצונו לא היה טפל בה וכן תופר בגד קרוע גם כן לא ניחא ליה בקרע זה מעולם וקורע באבלו כצ"ל ותיבת הבא נמחק: (ד) בא"ד למרמי אימתיה לחייב התם צריך למלאכה שיהא בעולם ואין לומר דלא ניחא ליה שיצטרך למרמי אימתיה דאם כן מפיס מורסא לעשות לה פה יהא פטור דודאי טוב היה דלא תיהא מורסא לכן נראה להר"י: (ה) ד"ה [מעילות] מכתב וכו' ומאי מקרא מועט:

גמרא

בְּגִזְבָּר הַמְּסוּרוֹת לוֹ אַבְנֵי בִנְיָן עֶסְקִינַן, דְּכָל הֵיכָא דְּמַנְחָה — בִּרְשׁוּתָא דִּידֵיהּ מַנְחָה. אֶלָּא מְסֵיפָא: א"בְּנָאָהּ בְּתוֹךְ בֵּיתוֹ — הֲרֵי זֶה לֹא מָעַל, עַד שֶׁיָּדוּר תַּחְתֶּיהָ בְּשָׁוֶה פְּרוּטָה. מִכְּדִי, שַׁנּוּיֵי שַׁנְּיֵיהּ, מָה לִי דָּר וּמָה לִי לֹא דָּר? הַיְינוּ כַּהֲרָרִין הַתְּלוּיִין בְּשַׂעֲרָה. וּמַאי קוּשְׁיָא, דִּלְמָא לְכִדְרַב, דְּאָמַר רַב: *כְּגוֹן שֶׁהִנִּיחָהּ עַל פִּי אֲרוּבָּה, אִי דָּר בֵּיהּ — אִין, לָא דָּר בֵּיהּ — לָא? אֶלָּא לְעוֹלָם כִּדְרָבָא, וּדְקָא קַשְׁיָא לָךְ מִידֵי דַּהֲוָה אַמּוֹצִיא מְעוֹת הֶקְדֵּשׁ לְחוּלִּין — הָתָם מֵידַע יָדַע דְּאִיכָּא זוּזֵי דְּהֶקְדֵּשׁ, אִיבַּעְיָא לֵיהּ לְעִיּוּנֵי. הָכָא — מִי יָדַע? הַיְינוּ כַּהֲרָרִין הַתְּלוּיִין בְּשַׂעֲרָה.§ "מִקְרָא מוּעָט וַהֲלָכוֹת מְרוּבּוֹת".§ תָּנָא: נְגָעִים וְאֹהָלוֹת — מִקְרָא מוּעָט וַהֲלָכוֹת מְרוּבּוֹת. נְגָעִים מִקְרָא מוּעָט? נְגָעִים מִקְרָא מְרוּבֶּה הוּא! אָמַר רַב פַּפָּא, הָכִי קָאָמַר: נְגָעִים — מִקְרָא מְרוּבֶּה וַהֲלָכוֹת מוּעָטוֹת, אֹהָלוֹת — מִקְרָא מוּעָט וַהֲלָכוֹת מְרוּבּוֹת. וּמַאי נָפְקָא מִינַּהּ? אִי מִסְתַּפְּקָא לָךְ מִילְּתָא בִּנְגָעִים — עַיֵּין בִּקְרָאֵי, וְאִי מִסְתַּפְּקָא לָךְ מִילְּתָא בְּאֹהָלוֹת — עַיֵּין בְּמַתְנִיתִין.§ "דִּינִין".§ מִיכְתַּב כְּתִיבָן! לָא נִצְרְכָא אֶלָּא לְכִדְרַבִּי. דְּתַנְיָא, *רַבִּי אוֹמֵר: °"נֶפֶשׁ תַּחַת נָפֶשׁ" — מָמוֹן. אַתָּה אוֹמֵר מָמוֹן, אוֹ אֵינוֹ אֶלָּא נֶפֶשׁ מַמָּשׁ? נֶאֶמְרָה נְתִינָה לְמַטָּה וְנֶאֶמְרָה נְתִינָה לְמַעְלָה, מָה לְהַלָּן מָמוֹן — אַף כָּאן מָמוֹן.§ "עֲבוֹדוֹת".§ מִיכְתַּב כְּתִיבָן! לָא נִצְרְכָא אֶלָּא לְהוֹלָכַת הַדָּם. דְּתַנְיָא: *°"וְהִקְרִיבוּ" — זוֹ קַבָּלַת הַדָּם. וְאַפְּקַהּ רַחֲמָנָא בִּלְשׁוֹן הוֹלָכָה, דִּכְתִיב: °"וְהִקְרִיב הַכֹּהֵן אֶת הַכֹּל וְהִקְטִיר הַמִּזְבֵּחָה" וְאָמַר מָר: *זוֹ הוֹלָכַת אֵבָרִים לַכֶּבֶשׁ, לְמֵימְרָא דְּהוֹלָכָה לָא תַּפְקַהּ מִכְּלַל קַבָּלָה.§ "טְהָרוֹת".§ מִיכְתַּב כְּתִיבָן! לָא נִצְרְכָא אֶלָּא לְשִׁיעוּר מִקְוֶה, דְּלָא כְּתִיבָא. דְּתַנְיָא: *°"וְרָחַץ (אֶת *בְּשָׂרוֹ) בַּמַּיִם" — בבְּמֵי מִקְוֶה. "אֶת כָּל בְּשָׂרוֹ" — גמַיִם שֶׁכָּל גּוּפוֹ עוֹלֶה בָּהֶן. וְכַמָּה הֵן — אַמָּה עַל אַמָּה בְּרוּם שָׁלֹשׁ אַמּוֹת. וְשִׁיעֲרוּ חֲכָמִים: מֵי מִקְוֶה אַרְבָּעִים סְאָה.§ "טֻמְאוֹת".§ מִיכְתַּב כְּתִיבָן! לָא נִצְרְכָא אֶלָּא לְכַעֲדָשָׁה מִן הַשֶּׁרֶץ, דְּלָא כְּתִיבָא. דְּתַנְיָא: *°"בָּהֶם", יָכוֹל בְּכוּלָּן — תַּלְמוּד לוֹמַר "מֵהֶם". יָכוֹל בְּמִקְצָתָן — ת"ל "בָּהֶם", הָא כֵּיצַד? עַד שֶׁיִּגַּע בְּמִקְצָתוֹ שֶׁהוּא כְּכוּלּוֹ. דשִׁיעֲרוּ חֲכָמִים בְּכַעֲדָשָׁה, שֶׁכֵּן חוֹמֶט תְּחִלָּתוֹ בְּכַעֲדָשָׁה. רַבִּי יוֹסֵי בְּר' יְהוּדָה אוֹמֵר: כִּזְנַב הַלְּטָאָה.§ "עֲרָיוֹת".§ מִיכְתַּב כְּתִיבָן! לָא נִצְרְכָא* לְבִתּוֹ

(שמות כא) (ויקרא ח שם) (שם טו) (שם יא)

רש"י

דְּכָל הֵיכָא דְּמַנְחָה. אֲפִילּוּ מְקַמֵּי הָכִי בִּרְשׁוּתֵיהּ מַנְחָה, הִלְכָּךְ כָּל כַּמָּה שֶׁנְּטָלָהּ — לָא שַׁנְּיֵיהּ מִידֵי דְּתֵיפּוֹק מִיָּדָא דְּהֶקְדֵּשׁ: שַׁנּוּיֵי שַׁנְּיֵיהּ. כְּשֶׁקְּבָעָהּ בַּבִּנְיָן, וְקָנְיֵיהּ בְּשִׁנּוּי שֶׁמְּסַתְּתָהּ וְקוֹבְעָהּ: שֶׁהִנִּיחָהּ ע"פ אֲרוּבָּה. לִפְקוֹק הָאֲרוּבָּה, וְכָל שָׁעָה שֶׁיִּרְצֶה נוֹטְלָהּ, וְלָא שַׁנְּיֵיהּ מִידֵי: כִּדְרָבָא. נִזְכַּר בַּעַל הַבַּיִת כו': הַיְינוּ כַּהֲרָרִין הַתְּלוּיִין בְּשַׂעֲרָה. בִּסְמִיכָה מוּעֶטֶת מְדַמִּינַן לָהּ לְמוֹצִיא מְעוֹת הֶקְדֵּשׁ לְחוּלִּין, שֶׁהֲרֵי קָרוֹב הוּא לְאוֹנֶס יוֹתֵר מִן הַשּׁוֹגֵג: דִּינִין מִיכְתַּב כְּתִיבָן. מְפוֹרָשִׁין יָפֶה. וּמַתְנִיתִין קָתָנֵי יֵשׁ לָהֶן סְמִיכָה מַשְׁמַע שֶׁאֵינָן מְפוֹרָשִׁין: לָא נִצְרְכָא כו'. כְּלוֹמַר: יֵשׁ בָּהֶן דְּבָרִים שֶׁאֵינָן מְפוֹרָשִׁין בְּפֵירוּשׁ, כְּגוֹן זֶה וְכַיּוֹצֵא בּוֹ: דִּכְתִיב נֶפֶשׁ תַּחַת נָפֶשׁ. "אִם אָסוֹן יִהְיֶה" שֶׁמֵּתָה הָאִשָּׁה — יִתֵּן מָמוֹן דְּמֵי הָאִשָּׁה לְיוֹרְשֶׁיהָ, שֶׁאֵין עָלָיו חִיּוּב מִיתָה, שֶׁלֹּא נִתְכַּוֵּון לָהּ אֶלָּא לַחֲבֵרוֹ נִתְכַּוֵּון, דִּכְתִיב "וְכִי יִנָּצוּ אֲנָשִׁים יַחְדָּיו", קָסָבַר רַבִּי: נִתְכַּוֵּון לַהֲרוֹג אֶת זֶה וְהָרַג אֶת זֶה פָּטוּר מִמִּיתָה וּמְשַׁלֵּם מָמוֹן: נְתִינָה לְמַעְלָה. לְעִנְיַן דְּמֵי וְלָדוֹת כְּתִיב, "וְנָתַן בִּפְלִלִים" (שמות כא): נְתִינָה לְמַטָּה. "וְנָתַתָּה נֶפֶשׁ תַּחַת נָפֶשׁ" — מָמוֹן, וּמַאי נֶפֶשׁ — דְּמֵי הַנֶּפֶשׁ: וְהִקְרִיבוּ זוֹ קַבָּלַת הַדָּם. אע"פ שֶׁהוּא לְשׁוֹן הוֹלָכָה — אֵינָהּ אֶלָּא קַבָּלָה, שֶׁהֲרֵי לְאַחַר שְׁחִיטָה נִכְתְּבָה, וְאֵין הוֹלָכָה אֶלָּא אִם כֵּן קִיבֵּל הַדָּם: וְהִקְרִיב הַכֹּהֵן אֶת הַכֹּל. גַּבֵּי אֵבָרִים כְּתִיב, "וְהַקֶּרֶב וְהַכְּרָעַיִם יִרְחַץ בַּמָּיִם, וְהִקְרִיב הַכֹּהֵן אֶת הַכֹּל וְהִקְטִיר הַמִּזְבֵּחָה": זוֹ הוֹלָכַת אֵבָרִים לַכֶּבֶשׁ. דְּאִילּוּ הַקְטָרָה בְּהֶדְיָא כְּתִיב בִּקְרָא: "וְהִקְטִיר הַמִּזְבֵּחָה": לָא תַּפְקֵיהּ מִכְּלַל קַבָּלָה. לְכָל דְּבָרֶיהָ. וְאַע"ג שֶׁהִיא עֲבוֹדָה שֶׁאֶפְשָׁר לְבַטְּלָהּ, שֶׁאִם רָצָה שׁוֹחֵט בְּצַד הַמִּזְבֵּחַ וְזוֹרֵק, הֵיכָא דְּלָא בַּטְלָהּ — עֲבוֹדָה הִיא, וּמְפַגְּלִין אֶת הַקָּרְבָּן בְּמַחְשַׁבְתָּהּ, וּצְרִיכָה כֹּהֵן וּבִגְדֵי כְהוּנָּה, וּפוֹסֵל בָּהּ אוֹנֵן, וְיוֹשֵׁב, וְעָרֵל: בַּמַּיִם. נְקוּדָתוֹ בְּפַתָּח, מַשְׁמַע: מַיִם הַמְיוּחָדִים, לְאַפּוֹקֵי שְׁאוּבִין. וּמִיהוּ, מַיִם חַיִּים לָא צָרִיךְ, מִדִּכְתִיב בְּזָב: "מַיִם חַיִּים" (ויקרא טו) — מִכְּלָל דִּשְׁאָר טְמֵאִין לָאו מַיִם חַיִּים בָּעוּ (א). וּמִיהוּ, "בַּמַּיִם" — בְּמַיִם הַמְיוּחָדִין, בְּמִקְוֶה, אַף עַל פִּי שֶׁהֵן גְּשָׁמִים: בָּהֶם. "כָּל הַנּוֹגֵעַ בָּהֶם": מֵהֶם. "כָּל אֲשֶׁר יִפּוֹל עָלָיו מֵהֶם בְּמוֹתָם יִטְמָא": חוֹמֶט. אוֹמֵר אֲנִי שֶׁהוּא מִין שֶׁרֶץ שֶׁקּוֹרִין לימג"א, הַגָּדֵל בִּקְלִיפָּה הַהוֹלֶכֶת וּמְעַגֶּלֶת תָּמִיד כָּל כַּמָּה שֶׁגָּדֵל, וּתְחִלַּת הִוָּצְרוֹ כִּקְלִיפָּה שֶׁל עֲדָשָׁה הִיא: כִּזְנַב הַלְּטָאָה. לְפִי שֶׁמְּפַרְכֶּסֶת לְאַחַר שֶׁנֶּחְתְּכָה, וְהַיְינוּ מִקְצָתוֹ שֶׁהוּא כְּכוּלּוֹ, שֶׁיֵּשׁ בּוֹ חִיּוּת: לְבִתּוֹ

תוספות

בגזבר המסורות לו. ואפילו למ"ד שליחות יד אין צריכה חסרון — הכא שאני, דכל היכא דאיתא — בי גזא דמלכא קאי:

עד שידור תחתיה בשוה פרוטה. ולא נפקא לחולין רק אותה פרוטה. וכן גרסינן בערכין (דף כא. ושם). וכיון *דדר ביה נפיק (ביה) שכר לחולין. וגם רש"י פירש כן, דדוקא שכר ולא כולא ביתא. וכן פי' הר"י ההיא דהמשאיל קרדום של הֶקדש לחברו, בקע בו וחזר חברו ובקע בו — כולן מעלו. והיכי דמי? הא תנן *אין מועל אחר מועל אלא בהמה וכלי שרת! אלא ודאי בגזבר המסורות לו קרדומות של הקדש, ולא מכוין להוציאן לחולין רק כנגד בקועה, לפיכך כולן מעלו. ובקדושין פ"ב (דף נה. בד"ה אין) ובמנחות פרק "המנחות והנסכים" (דף קא. בד"ה אע"ג) פירשתי:

לא נצרכא אלא לכדרבי דתניא ונתתה נפש תחת נפש ממון. ורבי יוחנן, דאמר: *חייבי מיתות שוגגין פטורין מן התשלומין — מוקי לה לאידך דרבי, דתניא: "ונתת עין תחת עין" דלא פליג אסתם משנה דהכא:

והקריבו זו קבלת הדם. ובהולכה לא מוקמינן ליה כפשטא דקרא, דהא בתר שחיטה כתיב, וקבלה היה מיד — והיינו עבודה ראשונה, כך פרש"י. אך לא משמע לי: דהכי נמי "וזרקו" כתיב בתריה, והולכה מקמי זריקה הוי מיד, לאפוקי קבלה דהולכה בינתיים! ועוד קשה לר"י: דאמרי' שילהי פ"ק דזבחים (דף יג.): "והקריבו" — זו קבלה. אתה אומר זו קבלה, או אינו אלא זריקה? כשהוא אומר "וזרקו" — הרי זריקה אמור, משמע דהוה מוקמינן לה בזריקה אי לאו דכתיב קרא, ואע"ג דלא בתר שחיטה הויא. ומיהו: י"ל דלא ניחא ליה לאוקמי קרא בהולכה לפי שאינה עבודה חשובה, שאפשר לבטלה ויכול לשחוט בראשו של מזבח:

לא נצרכא אלא לשיעור מקוה. לא הוה מצי למימר [לבעלה], דלא כתיב, כדפירש בה"ג דלא נפקא לן אלא בק"ו: דהשתא לטהרות כתיב "ורחץ" לבעלה דכרת — לא כ"ש? דהא לאו מילתא היא, דמהאי ק"ו לא מצי נפיק, דק"ו פריכא הוא. דהא כמה חלילות וכוונה דבפרק ב' דחולין (דף לא.) מלינו לטהרות ולא לבעלה. אלא, מהאי קרא נפקא: דכתיב (ויקרא טו): (*"ותהי נדתה עליו ואחר תטהר") — בנדתה תהא עד שתבא במים. כדדריש ר"ע בפ"ו דשבת (דף סד:). וכן *פר"ת דמהתם נפקא לן טבילת נדה, הלכך הוה ליה כמו כתובה:

במי מקוה. פרש"י: נקודתו בפתח, לאשמועינן מים המיוחדים, לאפוקי מים שאובין. ולא יתכן, דהא מים שאובין לאו מהכא נפקא, אלא מ"אך מעין ובור מקוה מים וגו'" (ויקרא יא) ודרשינן בת"כ: מה מעין בידי שמים — אף מקוה בידי שמים! ועוד: היכי משמע מקוה לאפוקי שאובין? הא עיקר קרא משמע שאובין, אי לאו דסמכיה למעין, כדפי'! ונראה לפרש: מי מקוה — היינו אשבורן, כדאמרינן: *מעין מטהר בזוחלין מקוה באשבורן (שבת דף סה:*):

אמה על אמה. שאדם מחזיק אמה בעובי עם מלבושים, וכן מוכח בשמעתין דכוכין בפ' "הפירות" (ב"ב דף קא.) שאינו מחזיק עם עובי הארון כ"א אמה. והשתא יתכן דלא תקשה היכי טבל אמתא באמתא:

ברום ג' אמות. ואע"ג שאדם מחזיק ד' אמות קומה, כדמוכח בשמעתין דכוכין, *דאורך הכוך ד' אמות — קומת האדם אינו אלא ג' אמות לבד הראש, ומצי להרכין את ראשו מן הצד. והא דנקט ד' אמות — משום עובי צידי הארון. ואע"ג דמצינו בפ"ק דב"ב (דף ג:) גבי היזק ראייה שיעור ראייה ד' אמות — היינו שיכול להגביה עצמו על ראשי אצבעותיו עד שיליך ד' אמות. וכן מוכח בעובדא דבני המן בתרגום של מגילת אסתר שנסדר על פי המדרש, שגובה קומתן ג' אמות לבד הראש, דקחשיב ואזיל על רום חמשים אמות לפי תליית כל העשרה, והיו נהרגים כבר קודם התלייה. וכן משמעי קרא: "בשושן הבירה הרגו היהודים ואבד חמש מאות איש ואת עשרת בני המן" — משמע שבכלל הריגה היו. וגם הפייט יסד בסליחה:* "אדם בקום איש בשלש אמות והרביעית (*וחמישית) אויר מגולה"*:

הא ביצד. פי': איזה מהם שהוא כהם. הקשה הר"ר אליעזר ממיץ: דהכא מוקמינן כוליה קרא בחד ענינא, ואילו בפ' "דם הנדה" (נדה נו.) אמר: כתיב "בהם" — בכולן, וכתיב "מהם" — במקצתן! לא קשיא: כאן — בלח, כאן — ביבש. אלמא בתרי ענייני איירי קרא! ושמא תרתי שמעינן מינה. ולמורי נראה: תרי קראי כתיבי, "כל הנוגע בהם במותם" מהם במותם אשר יפול מהם אל תוכו ואל תטמאו בהם*:

לבתו

עין משפט נר מצוה

ע א מיי' פ"ו מהלכות מעילה הלכה ח:

עא ב מיי' פ"א מהלכות מקואות הלכה ב סמג עשין רמח טוש"ע י"ד סי' רא סעיף א:

עב ג מיי' שם פ"ד הלכה א סמג שם טוש"ע י"ד סי' קצא סעיף א וסי' רא סעיף א:

עג ד מיי' פ"ד מהלכות שאר אבות הטומאה הלכה ב סמג עשין רמו:

[נ"ל דמעל]

[מעילה יט:]

[כתובות לה: ע"ש]

[עי' פסחים קטו.]

[נ"ל והדוה בנדתה]

[עי' תוס' יומא עח. ד"ה מכאן ותוס' יבמות מז. ד"ה במקום]

ע"ש רש"י ותוס'

[ב"ב ק: ושם ד"ה והכוכין]

[בסליחות שלפנינו ליתא]

*) [וע"ע תוס' פסחים קטו: ד"ה ברום]

[ובנדה בד"ה אי בהם תירצו דהכא אסמכתא הוא דשעורין הלכה למשה מסיני]

רבינו חננאל

היינו דתנן מעילות כהררין תלויין בשערה. הדינין דכתב רחמנא ונתת נפש תחת נפש ואמור רבנן ממון. עבודות זו הולכת הדם. טהרות שיעור מי מקוה דלא כתב שיעורו בתורה. ושיערו חכמים אמה על אמה ברום שלש הן מ' סאה. טמאות טומאת שרץ ששיערו חכמים בכעדשה. ר' יוסי אומר כזנב הלטאה. עריות בתו מאנוסתו דלא

מסורת הש"ס

[ב"ק כ: ע"ש מעילה כ.]

הגהות הב"ח

(א) רש"י ד"ה במים וכו' לאו מים חיים בעו ומאי במים:

[סנהדרין עט. פז:]

[קידושין לו:] זבחים יג.

זבחים [ז.] יד: כד: [עירובין קד. פסחים סה. יומא כז. מנחות י.]

עירובין ד: יד: פסחים קט: יומא לא.

[נזיר נב.]

[נ"ל אלא לבתו]

בתורת כהנים פרשה יא

[תענית אסתר]

עין משפט נר מצוה

א א מיי' פ"ד מהלכות יסודי התורה הלכה י:
ב ב מיי' שם הלכה יא:
ג ג מיי' פ"ט מהלכות מלכים הלכה ג:
ד ד מיי' שם הלכה ה:
ה ה מיי' פכ"ב מהלכות איסורי ביאה הלכה יז:

מסורת הש"ס

לְבִתּוֹ מֵאֲנוּסָתוֹ דְּלָא כְּתִיבָא. דְּאִילּוּ בִּתּוֹ מֵאִשְׁתּוֹ כְּתִיבָא: "עֶרְוַת אִשָּׁה וּבִתָּהּ" וגו' (ויקרא יח), מַשְׁמַע: בֵּין שֶׁהַבַּת מִמֶּנּוּ בֵּין מֵאִישׁ אַחֵר, וּכְתִיב קְרָא אַחֲרִינָא: "עֶרְוַת בַּת בִּנְךָ אוֹ בַת בִּתְּךָ" וגו' וּמוֹקְמִינַן לָהּ בִּיבָמוֹת (דף כז.) בְּבִתּוֹ מֵאֲנוּסָתוֹ, מִדְּלָא חָסַר הַכָּתוּב בַּת בִּתָּהּ שֶׁל אִשָּׁה זוֹ אֶלָּא בְּבַת הַבַּת שֶׁנּוֹלְדָה הֵימֶנּוּ. וּבְהַאי קְרָא דַּאֲנוּסָה בַּת בִּתּוֹ וּבַת בְּנוֹ כְּתִיב, בִּתּוֹ – לָא כְּתִיב. וְאִ"ת: ק"ו הוּא! אֵין מַזְהִירִין מִן הַדִּין, וְאֵין עוֹנְשִׁין מִדִּין ק"ו. דִּינֵי מָמוֹנוֹת וּמִצְוֹת עֲשֵׂה וְהִלְכוֹת עֲבוֹדָה וּפְסוּלֵי קָדָשִׁים – אַתָּה לָמֵד בְּק"ו, אֲבָל לֹא אַזְהָרוֹת וְעוֹנָשִׁין. וּמִקְּרָאֵי נָפְקָא לָן בְּמַסֶּ' מַכּוֹת (דף ה:). וּמֵהֵיכָן נָפְקָא לָן לְבִתּוֹ מֵאֲנוּסָתוֹ?

תורה אור

לְבִתּוֹ מֵאֲנוּסָתוֹ דְּלָא כְּתִיבָא. *דְּאָמַר רָבָא, אֲמַר לִי ר' יִצְחָק בַּר אַבְדִּימִי: אָתְיָא "הֵנָּה" "הֵנָּה", אָתְיָא "זִימָּה" "זִימָּה".§ "הֵן הֵן גּוּפֵי תוֹרָה".§ הָנֵי אִין, הָנָךְ לָא?! אֶלָּא, אֵימָא: הֵן וְהֵן גּוּפֵי תוֹרָה.§

הדרן עלך הכל חייבין

אֵין דּוֹרְשִׁין בָּעֲרָיוֹת בִּשְׁלֹשָׁה, וְלֹא בְּמַעֲשֵׂה בְרֵאשִׁית בִּשְׁנַיִם, וְלֹא בַּמֶּרְכָּבָה בְּיָחִיד, אֶלָּא אִם כֵּן הָיָה חָכָם וּמֵבִין מִדַּעְתּוֹ. כָּל הַמִּסְתַּכֵּל בְּאַרְבָּעָה דְּבָרִים רָתוּי לוֹ כְּאִילּוּ לֹא בָּא לָעוֹלָם: *מַה לְּמַעְלָה, מַה לְּמַטָּה, מַה לְּפָנִים, וּמַה לְּאָחוֹר. *וְכָל שֶׁלֹּא חָס עַל כְּבוֹד קוֹנוֹ – רָתוּי לוֹ שֶׁלֹּא בָּא לָעוֹלָם.§ **גמ'** אָמְרַתְּ בְּרֵישָׁא "וְלֹא בַּמֶּרְכָּבָה בְּיָחִיד" וַהֲדַר אָמְרַתְּ: אֶלָּא אִם כֵּן הָיָה חָכָם וּמֵבִין מִדַּעְתּוֹ! הָכִי קָאָמַר: אֵין דּוֹרְשִׁין בָּעֲרָיוֹת לִשְׁלֹשָׁה, וְלֹא [א]בְּמַעֲשֵׂה בְרֵאשִׁית לִשְׁנַיִם, וְלֹא [ב]בַּמֶּרְכָּבָה לְיָחִיד, אֶלָּא אִם כֵּן הָיָה חָכָם וּמֵבִין מִדַּעְתּוֹ.§ "אֵין דּוֹרְשִׁין בָּעֲרָיוֹת בִּשְׁלֹשָׁה".§ מ"ט? אִילֵימָא מִשּׁוּם דִּכְתִיב: °"אִישׁ אִישׁ אֶל כָּל שְׁאֵר בְּשָׂרוֹ" (ויקרא יח) "אִישׁ אִישׁ" – תְּרֵי, "שְׁאֵר בְּשָׂרוֹ" – חַד, וְאָמַר רַחֲמָנָא "לֹא תִקְרְבוּ לְגַלּוֹת עֶרְוָה", אֶלָּא מֵעַתָּה, דִּכְתִיב: °"אִישׁ אִישׁ כִּי יְקַלֵּל אֱלֹהָיו" (שם כד), °"אִישׁ אִישׁ אֲשֶׁר יִתֵּן מִזַּרְעוֹ לַמֹּלֶךְ" (שם כ), הָכִי נָמֵי? אֶלָּא, הָנְהוּ מִיבְּעֵי לֵיהּ [ג]לְרַבּוֹת אֶת הַגּוֹיִם, שֶׁמּוּזְהָרִין עַל בִּרְכַּת הַשֵּׁם וְעַל ע"ז כְּיִשְׂרָאֵל, הַאי נָמֵי מִיבְּעֵי לֵיהּ *לְרַבּוֹת אֶת הַגּוֹיִם, [ד]שֶׁמּוּזְהָרִין עַל הָעֲרָיוֹת כְּיִשְׂרָאֵל! אֶלָּא: מִדִּכְתִיב °"וּשְׁמַרְתֶּם אֶת מִשְׁמַרְתִּי" (שם יח), "וּשְׁמַרְתֶּם" "מִשְׁמַרְתִּי" – תְּרֵי, "מִשְׁמַרְתִּי" – חַד, וְאָמַר רַחֲמָנָא "לְבִלְתִּי עֲשׂוֹת מֵחֻקּוֹת הַתּוֹעֵבֹת". אֶלָּא מֵעַתָּה, דִּכְתִיב: °"וּשְׁמַרְתֶּם אֶת הַשַּׁבָּת" (שמות לא), °"וּשְׁמַרְתֶּם אֶת הַמַּצּוֹת" (שם יב), °"וּשְׁמַרְתֶּם אֶת מִשְׁמֶרֶת הַקֹּדֶשׁ" (במדבר יח), הָכִי נָמֵי?! אֶלָּא אָמַר רַב אַשִׁי: מַאי אֵין דּוֹרְשִׁין בָּעֲרָיוֹת בִּשְׁלֹשָׁה – [ה]אֵין דּוֹרְשִׁין בְּסִתְרֵי עֲרָיוֹת (*בִּשְׁלֹשָׁה). מ"ט – סְבָרָא הוּא: בֵּי תְּרֵי כִּי יָתְבִי קַמֵּי רַבַּיְיהוּ, חַד שָׁקֵיל וְטָרֵי בַּהֲדֵי רַבֵּיהּ, וְאִידָךְ מַצְלֵי אוּדְנֵיהּ לִגְמָרָא. תְּלָתָא, חַד שָׁקֵיל וְטָרֵי בַּהֲדֵי רַבֵּיהּ, וְהָנָךְ תְּרֵי – שָׁקְלוּ וְטָרוּ בַּהֲדֵי הֲדָדֵי, וְלָא יָדְעֵי מַאי קָאָמַר רַבַּיְיהוּ, וְאָתוּ לְמִישְׁרֵי אִיסּוּרָא בָּעֲרָיוֹת. אִי הָכִי כָּל הַתּוֹרָה נָמֵי! עֲרָיוֹת שָׁאנֵי, *דְּאָמַר מָר: גָּזֵל וַעֲרָיוֹת נַפְשׁוֹ שֶׁל אָדָם מִתְאַוָּה לָהֶם וּמְחַמַּדְתָּן. אִי הָכִי גָּזֵל נָמֵי! עֲרָיוֹת, בֵּין בְּפָנָיו בֵּין שֶׁלֹּא בְּפָנָיו נָפֵישׁ יִצְרֵיהּ. גָּזֵל, בְּפָנָיו נָפֵישׁ יִצְרֵיהּ, שֶׁלֹּא בְּפָנָיו – לָא נָפֵישׁ יִצְרֵיהּ.§ "וְלֹא בְּמַעֲשֵׂה בְרֵאשִׁית בִּשְׁנַיִם".§ מְנָא הָנֵי מִילֵּי? דְּתָנוּ רַבָּנַן: °"כִּי שְׁאַל נָא לְיָמִים רִאשֹׁנִים" (דברים ד) – יָחִיד שׁוֹאֵל, וְאֵין שְׁנַיִם שׁוֹאֲלִין. יָכוֹל יִשְׁאַל אָדָם קוֹדֶם שֶׁנִּבְרָא הָעוֹלָם – ת"ל: °"לְמִן הַיּוֹם אֲשֶׁר בָּרָא אֱלֹהִים אָדָם עַל הָאָרֶץ" (שם). יָכוֹל לֹא יִשְׁאַל אָדָם מִשֵּׁשֶׁת יְמֵי בְרֵאשִׁית – ת"ל: "לְיָמִים רִאשֹׁנִים אֲשֶׁר הָיוּ לְפָנֶיךָ". יָכוֹל יִשְׁאַל אָדָם מַה לְּמַעְלָה וּמַה לְּמַטָּה, מַה לְּפָנִים וּמַה לְּאָחוֹר – ת"ל: °"וּלְמִקְצֵה הַשָּׁמַיִם וְעַד קְצֵה הַשָּׁמָיִם" (שם) – מִ"לְּמִקְצֵה הַשָּׁמַיִם וְעַד קְצֵה הַשָּׁמָיִם" אַתָּה שׁוֹאֵל, וְאֵין אַתָּה שׁוֹאֵל מַה לְּמַעְלָה מַה לְּמַטָּה, מַה לְּפָנִים מַה לְּאָחוֹר. הַשְׁתָּא

°) במדבר יח

רש"י

אָמַר רָבָא אָמַר לִי ר' יִצְחָק בַּר אַבְדִּימִי אָתְיָא הֵנָּה הֵנָּה. לְאִיסּוּרָא, אָתְיָא זִימָּה זִימָּה לִשְׂרֵיפָה. כְּתִיב בְּנִישּׂוּאִין: "שַׁאֲרָה הֵנָּה זִימָּה הִיא", וּכְתִיב בְּאוֹנָסִין: "כִּי עֶרְוָתְךָ הֵנָּה", מָה (א) הָאָמוּר בְּנִשּׂוּאִין – עָשָׂה הַכָּתוּב בִּתָּהּ כְּבַת בִּתָּהּ וּכְבַת בְּנָהּ, אַף בְּאוֹנָסִין – עָשָׂה הַכָּתוּב בִּתּוֹ כְּבַת בִּתּוֹ וּכְבַת בְּנוֹ. אָתְיָא זִימָּה זִימָּה לִשְׂרֵיפָה, מֵאַחַר שֶׁלָּמַדְתָּ אֲנוּסָה מִנְּשׂוּאָה, וּבִנְשׂוּאָה כְּתִיב "זִימָּה הִיא", כְּמָה דִּכְתִיב בַּאֲנוּסָה דָּמֵי, וַחֲזוֹר וּלְמוֹד בָּהּ שְׂרֵיפָה מֵ"אִישׁ אֲשֶׁר יִקַּח אֶת אִשָּׁה וְאֶת אִמָּהּ זִימָּה הִיא בָּאֵשׁ יִשְׂרְפוּ אוֹתוֹ וְאֶתְהֶן" (ויקרא כ): הָנֵי אִין הָנָךְ לָא. הָנֵי דְּמִיפָּרְשֵׁי הָווּ גּוּפֵי תוֹרָה, הָנָךְ דְּלָא מִיפָּרְשֵׁי כּוּלֵּי הַאי לָאו גּוּפֵי תוֹרָה?! בִּתְמִיָּה: הֵן וָהֵן. אֵלּוּ וָאֵלּוּ:

הדרן עלך הכל חייבין

אֵין דּוֹרְשִׁין. בִּשְׁלֹשָׁה. שְׁנַיִם וְהוּא: בִּשְׁנַיִם. אֶחָד וְהוּא: בְּיָחִיד. אֵין שָׁם אֶלָּא הוּא לְבַדּוֹ. וּבַגְּמָ' מְפָרֵשׁ לָהּ: אַרְבָּעָה דְּבָרִים. הָנֵי דִּמְפָרֵשׁ וְאָזֵיל: מַה לְּמַעְלָה. מֵרָקִיעַ שֶׁעַל רָאשֵׁי הַחַיּוֹת: וּמַה לְּמַטָּה. מֵהֶן: וּמַה לְּפָנִים. חוּץ לִמְחִיצַּת הָרָקִיעַ לְמִזְרָח: וּמַה לְּאָחוֹר. לְמַעֲרָב: תּוֹסְפוֹת. אֵינוֹ יָכוֹל לִהְיוֹת מַה שֶּׁפֵּירֵשׁ הַמּוֹרֶה, מַה לְּפָנִים חוּץ לִמְחִיצַּת הָרָקִיעַ וּמַה לְּאָחוֹר לְמַעֲרָב, מִדְּפָרֵיךְ בַּגְּמָ': בִּשְׁלָמָא מַה לְּמַעְלָה וּמַה לְּמַטָּה וּמַה לְּאָחוֹר – לַחַיֵּי, אֶלָּא לְפָנִים – מַה דַּהֲוָה הֲוָה! אַלְמָא: מַה לְּפָנִים – קוֹדֶם לָעוֹלָם הוּא. וְעוֹד בַּתּוֹסֶפְתָּא: (ב) מַה לְּפָנִים וּמַה לְּאָחוֹר – מֶה הָיָה וּמֶה עָתִיד לִהְיוֹת. ע"כ תּוֹסָ': כָּל שֶׁלֹּא חָס עַל כְּבוֹד קוֹנוֹ. בַּגְּמָרָא מְפָרֵשׁ מַאי הִיא: רָתוּי הוּא לוֹ. טוֹב וְיָפֶה הָיָה לוֹ אִם לֹא בָּא לָעוֹלָם. וְאוֹמֵר אֲנִי שֶׁהוּא לְשׁוֹן רַחֲמָנוּת, כְּלוֹמַר מְרוּחָם (ג) הוּא אִם לֹא בָּא לָעוֹלָם. וְדוּגְמָתוֹ בְּתוֹרַת כֹּהֲנִים: "אֶל אֶלְעָזָר וְאֶל אִיתָמָר בָּנָיו הַנּוֹתָרִים" (ויקרא י), רְאוּיִין הָיוּ לִישָּׂרֵף, אֶלָּא שֶׁרִיחֲמָה הַכָּתוּב לְאַהֲרֹן: **גמ'** אָמְרַתְּ וְלֹא בַּמֶּרְכָּבָה בְּיָחִיד. וְכֵיוָן דְּיָחִידִי הוּא וְאֵינוֹ שׁוֹמֵעַ מִפִּי הָרַב – עַל כָּרְחָךְ מִדַּעְתּוֹ הוּא מֵבִין, וְקָא אָסְרַתְּ לֵיהּ, וַהֲדַר אָמְרַתְּ: אֶלָּא אִם כֵּן הָיָה חָכָם וּמֵבִין מִדַּעְתּוֹ: לִשְׁלֹשָׁה. לְבַד מִן הַדּוֹרֵשׁ: לֹא בְּמַעֲשֵׂה בְרֵאשִׁית לִשְׁנַיִם. וְכ"שׁ לִשְׁלֹשָׁה: וְלֹא בַּמֶּרְכָּבָה לְיָחִיד. לְתַלְמִיד יָחִיד: אֶלָּא אִם כֵּן הָיָה חָכָם וּמֵבִין מִדַּעְתּוֹ. שֶׁלֹּא יִצְטָרֵךְ לִשְׁאוֹל לָרַב כְּשֶׁיִּסְתַּפֵּק לוֹ, דְּלָאו אוֹרַח אַרְעָא לְפָרוֹשֵׁי בְּהֶדְיָא: וְאָמַר רַחֲמָנָא לֹא תִקְרְבוּ לְגַלּוֹת עֶרְוָה. לֹא תִקְרְבוּ שֶׁלָּשְׁתְּכֶם זֶה אֵצֶל זֶה לְגַלּוֹת טַעֲמֵי פָּרָשַׁת עֲרָיוֹת: בְּסִתְרֵי עֲרָיוֹת. שֶׁאֵינָן מְפוֹרָשׁוֹת, כְּגוֹן בִּתּוֹ מֵאֲנוּסָתוֹ, וְאֵם חָמִיו וְאֵם חֲמוֹתוֹ דְּנָפְקֵי בְּמַסֶּ' סַנְהֶדְרִין (דף עה.) מִדְּרָשָׁא: שָׁקֵיל וְטָרֵי. נוֹשֵׂא וְנוֹתֵן בַּהֲלָכָה עִם רַבּוֹ: מַצְלֵי אוּדְנֵיהּ. מַטֶּה אָזְנוֹ וְשׁוֹמֵעַ דִּבְרֵיהֶן וְהֵן שׁוֹמְעִין אֶת דִּבְרֵי הָרַב, אֲבָל כְּשֶׁהֵן שְׁלֹשָׁה שָׁקְלֵי וְטָרוּ הָנָךְ תְּרֵי זֶה עִם זֶה, וְלֹא שָׁמְעוּ מַאי דְּאָמַר רַבָּן, וְאָתוּ לְמִישְׁרֵי אִיסּוּרָא בָּעֲרָיוֹת עַל יְדֵי שֶׁלֹּא שָׁמְעוּ מִפִּי הָרַב כְּשֶׁדָּרַשׁ בּוֹ אִיסּוּר: דְּאָמַר מָר גָּזֵל וַעֲרָיוֹת כו'. בְּמַתְנִיתִין בַּתְרַיְיתָא דְּמַסֶּכֶת מַכּוֹת (דף כג:): בְּפָנָיו. כְּשֶׁהוּא רוֹאֶה לְפָנָיו שֶׁיָּכוֹל לִגְזוֹל: מְנָא הָנֵי מִילֵּי. דְּאֵין שְׁנַיִם שׁוֹאֲלִין בְּמַעֲשֵׂה בְרֵאשִׁית: יָכוֹל יִשְׁאַל אָדָם. מֶה הָיָה קוֹדֶם שֶׁנִּבְרָא הָעוֹלָם: יָכוֹל לֹא יִדְרוֹשׁ וְלֹא יִשְׁאַל בְּשֵׁשֶׁת יְמֵי בְרֵאשִׁית. דְּהָא לְמִן בְּרִיַּית אָדָם הוּא דְּיָהֵיב רְשׁוּתָא, וְהוּא בְּעֶרֶב שַׁבָּת נִבְרָא: תַּלְמוּד לוֹמַר לְיָמִים רִאשׁוֹנִים. מִיּוֹם רִאשׁוֹן: וְהַשְׁתָּא

תוספות

לבתו מאנוסתו. ההיא ד"ערות בת בנך" מוקמינן לה בריש "נושאין על האנוסה" (יבמות כז.) דמשמע: הא בת בנה דידה – גלי, באנוסתו. ואידך ד"אשה ובתה לא תגלה" – בנישואין, דכתיב בה שאר: **דאמר** רבא אמר לי רב יצחק בר אבדימי. תרי הוו. פי' בפ"ק דיבמות (דף ג. ושם) ובפרק "כל הבשר" (חולין דף קי. *ושם):

הדרן עלך הכל חייבין

אין דורשין. במעשה בראשית. פי' ר"ת: הוא שם מ"ב אותיות, היוצא מבראשית ומפסוק של אחריו: **יכול** ישאל מה למעלה מה למטה. *משמע הכא דלפנים ולאחור הוי מה שיש אחורי הכיפה מזרח ומערב, והוא הדין לפון ודרום. ואילו לקמן (דף טז.) בפירוש משמע מה שהיה קודם שנברא העולם ומה שיהיה לאחר כך. דקאמר: בשלמא מה למעלה מה למטה ומה לאחור – שפיר, אלא לפנים אמאי? מה דהוה הוה! רבי יוחנן ורבי אלעזר אמרי: משל למלך שבנה פלטרין על גבי אשפה כו'. והכי תניא בתוספתא (פ"ב): מה שהיה ומה שעתיד להיות! וי"ל: דאיכא למימר הכי, ואיכא למימר הכי:

מסוף

רבינו חננאל

כתיבא. ורבנן אסקוה מדרשא זמה זמה. וכולהון יש להן אסמכתו' מן התורה בין היתר נדרים בין הלכות שבת בין חגיגות ומעילות כולן הן גופי תורה:

הדרן עלך הכל חייבין

פ"ב אין דורשין בעריות בשלשה כו'. ש"מ כי הרב וב' תלמידים אין דורשין בעריות. מנא לן אי נימא מדכתיב איש איש אל כל שאר בשרו ודרשינן איש איש הרי תרי שאר בשרו חד הרי ג' ואמרה רחמנא לא תקרבו לגלות ערוה. אלא מעתה איש איש כי יקלל אלהיו הכי נמי דלא דרשינן ביה בתרי ודחינן תוב תנינן ולא במרכבה ביחיד דמשמע דאפילו הרב לבדו אסור וקתני סיפא אלא אם היה חכם מבין מדעתו ופירשה רב אשי הכי אין דורשין בעריות בשלשה ומאי ניהו סתרי עריות כגון העראה ונשיקה ואזהרה ועונש *) לדבר הנשכב וכן כמה שנים יהיה ויתחייב השוכב עמו וכיוצא בהן האחד נושא ונותן בהדי רביה והשנים נושאין ונותנין זה עם זה. ואין מקשיבין לדברי הרב. וכיון שהנפש מתאוה להן אין מדקדקין היטב ובאין להתיר האיסור. לפיכך לא התירו לדרוש בסתרי עריות כגון אלו אלא לשנים בלבד. שאפילו אחד מהן נושא ונותן עם הרב השני מטה אוזן ומקשיב ונמצא העיקר שמור בלב שניהן. אבל הא דתנן ולא במעשה בראשית בשנים ממדרש זה הפסוק נשנית: דת"ר כי שאל נא לימים ראשונים מדלא אמר שאלו אלא שאל בלשון יחיד. ש"מ שהיחיד שואל ולא יותר מיכן שאין שואלין יכול ישאל אדם מה היה קודם שנברא העולם. ת"ל לימים ראשונים מששת ימי בראשית ולמטה. יכול לא ישאל מה היה באלו ששת ימי בראשית. ת"ל למן היום אשר ברא אלהים אדם על הארץ. מיום שנברא אדם יש רשות לישאל אבל מקודם לכן אסור לישאל בהן. יכול ישאל אדם מה למעלה מן הרקיע ומה למטה מן הארץ ומה לפנים ומה לאחור ת"ל

*) אולי צ"ל לזכר הנשכב או צ"ל להנשכב:

יבמות כ. סנהדרין נח. עה: פז: כריתות ה.

[תמיד לב.]

[קדושין מ.]

[סנהדרין נו:]

[נ"ל לשלשה]

מכות כג:

[ועי' תוס' מנחות לג. ד"ה רב חסדא ותוס' ב"ב פז. ד"ה מי כלאן ותוס' כתובות נו. ד"ה לאמר ותוס' יבמות ג. ד"ה לאמר ובחולין קי. ד"ה איכא]

[ועי' תוס' מגילה כד: ד"ה מה לפנים]

הגהות הב"ח

(א) רש"י ד"ה אמר רבא וכו' מה הנה האמור בנשואין: (ב) רש"י ד"ה תוספות וכו' בתוספתא תני מה לפנים: (ג) ד"ה רתוי וכו' מרוחם היה אם לא:

גליון הש"ס

רש"י ד"ה לבתו מאנוסתו וכו' ואין עונשין מדין ק"ו ד"מ. עיין ב"ב דף ב ע"א תוס' ד"ה ולא זה ושם ד ע"ב תוס' ד"ה ועדים:

הָשְׁתָּא דְּנָפְקָא לֵיהּ מִ"לְמִקְצֵה הַשָּׁמַיִם וְעַד
קְצֵה הַשָּׁמָיִם", "לְמִן הַיּוֹם אֲשֶׁר בָּרָא אֱלֹהִים
אָדָם עַל הָאָרֶץ" לָמָּה לִי(א)? כִּדְר' אֶלְעָזָר. דְּאָמַר
רַבִּי אֶלְעָזָר: אָדָם הָרִאשׁוֹן מִן הָאָרֶץ עַד לָרָקִיעַ,
שֶׁנֶּאֱמַר: "לְמִן הַיּוֹם אֲשֶׁר בָּרָא אֱלֹהִים אָדָם
עַל הָאָרֶץ", וְכֵיוָן שֶׁסָּרַח — הִנִּיחַ הַקב"ה יָדָיו עָלָיו
תהלים קלט וּמִיעֲטוֹ, שֶׁנֶּאֱמַר: °"אָחוֹר וָקֶדֶם צַרְתָּנִי וַתָּשֶׁת
עָלַי כַּפֶּכָה". אָמַר רַב יְהוּדָה אָמַר רַב: *אָדָם
הָרִאשׁוֹן — מִסּוֹף הָעוֹלָם וְעַד סוֹפוֹ הָיָה, שֶׁנֶּאֱמַר:
"לְמִן הַיּוֹם אֲשֶׁר בָּרָא אֱלֹהִים אָדָם עַל הָאָרֶץ
וּלְמִקְצֵה הַשָּׁמַיִם וְעַד קְצֵה הַשָּׁמָיִם". כֵּיוָן שֶׁסָּרַח
— הִנִּיחַ הַקָּדוֹשׁ בָּרוּךְ הוּא יָדוֹ עָלָיו *וּמִיעֲטוֹ, שֶׁנֶּאֱמַר:
"וַתָּשֶׁת עָלַי כַּפֶּכָה". אִי הָכִי קָשׁוּ קְרָאֵי אַהֲדָדֵי!
אִידִי וְאִידִי חַד שִׁיעוּרָא הוּא. וְאָמַר רַב יְהוּדָה
אָמַר רַב: עֲשָׂרָה דְּבָרִים נִבְרְאוּ בְּיוֹם רִאשׁוֹן,
וְאֵלּוּ הֵן: שָׁמַיִם וָאָרֶץ, תֹּהוּ וָבֹהוּ, אוֹר וָחֹשֶׁךְ,
רוּחַ וּמַיִם, מִדַּת יוֹם וּמִדַּת לַיְלָה. שָׁמַיִם וָאָרֶץ
בראשית א — דִּכְתִיב: °"בְּרֵאשִׁית בָּרָא אֱלֹהִים אֵת הַשָּׁמַיִם
שם וְאֵת הָאָרֶץ", תֹּהוּ וָבֹהוּ — דִּכְתִיב: °"וְהָאָרֶץ הָיְתָה
שם תֹהוּ וָבֹהוּ", אוֹר וָחֹשֶׁךְ, חֹשֶׁךְ דִּכְתִיב: °"וְחֹשֶׁךְ
שם עַל פְּנֵי תְהוֹם", אוֹר — דִּכְתִיב: °"וַיֹּאמֶר אֱלֹהִים יְהִי
שם אוֹר", רוּחַ וּמַיִם — דִּכְתִיב: °"וְרוּחַ אֱלֹהִים מְרַחֶפֶת
עַל פְּנֵי הַמָּיִם". מִדַּת יוֹם וּמִדַּת לַיְלָה — דִּכְתִיב:
שם °"וַיְהִי עֶרֶב וַיְהִי בֹקֶר יוֹם אֶחָד". תָּנָא: תֹּהוּ — קַו יָרוֹק שֶׁמַּקִּיף אֶת כָּל הָעוֹלָם כּוּלּוֹ,
תהלים יח שֶׁמִּמֶּנּוּ יָצָא חֹשֶׁךְ(ב). שֶׁנֶּאֱמַר: °"יָשֶׁת חֹשֶׁךְ סִתְרוֹ סְבִיבוֹתָיו", בֹּהוּ — אֵלּוּ אֲבָנִים
ישעיה לד הַמְפוּלָּמוֹת הַמְשׁוּקָּעוֹת בַּתְּהוֹם, שֶׁמֵּהֶן יוֹצְאִין מַיִם, שֶׁנֶּאֱמַר: °"וְנָטָה עָלֶיהָ קַו
תֹהוּ וְאַבְנֵי בֹהוּ". וְאוֹר בְּיוֹם רִאשׁוֹן אִיבְרִי? וְהָכְתִיב: "וַיִּתֵּן אוֹתָם אֱלֹהִים בִּרְקִיעַ
הַשָּׁמָיִם" וּכְתִיב: "וַיְהִי עֶרֶב וַיְהִי בֹקֶר יוֹם רְבִיעִי(ג)! כִּדְר' אֶלְעָזָר. דא"ר אֶלְעָזָר: אוֹר
שֶׁבָּרָא הַקָּדוֹשׁ בָּרוּךְ הוּא בְּיוֹם רִאשׁוֹן — אָדָם צוֹפֶה בּוֹ מִסּוֹף הָעוֹלָם וְעַד סוֹפוֹ, כֵּיוָן שֶׁנִּסְתַּכֵּל
הַקָּדוֹשׁ בָּרוּךְ הוּא בְּדוֹר הַמַּבּוּל וּבְדוֹר הַפַּלָּגָה וְרָאָה שֶׁמַּעֲשֵׂיהֶם מְקוּלְקָלִים — עָמַד וּגְנָזוֹ
איוב לח מֵהֶן, שֶׁנֶּאֱמַר: °"וְיִמָּנַע מֵרְשָׁעִים אוֹרָם". וּלְמִי גְּנָזוֹ — לַצַּדִּיקִים לֶעָתִיד לָבֹא שֶׁנֶּאֱמַר:
[יומא לח.] "וַיַּרְא אֱלֹהִים אֶת הָאוֹר כִּי טוֹב", *וְאֵין טוֹב אֶלָּא צַדִּיק, שֶׁנֶּאֱמַר: °"אִמְרוּ צַדִּיק ישעיה ג
משלי יג כִּי טוֹב". כֵּיוָן שֶׁרָאָה אוֹר שֶׁגְּנָזוֹ לַצַּדִּיקִים (ד) שָׂמַח, שֶׁנֶּאֱמַר: °"אוֹר צַדִּיקִים יִשְׂמָח".
כְּתַנָּאֵי: אוֹר שֶׁבָּרָא הַקָּדוֹשׁ בָּרוּךְ הוּא בְּיוֹם רִאשׁוֹן אָדָם צוֹפֶה וּמַבִּיט בּוֹ מִסּוֹף הָעוֹלָם
וְעַד סוֹפוֹ, דִּבְרֵי רַבִּי יַעֲקֹב. וַחֲכ"א: הֵן הֵן מְאוֹרוֹת שֶׁנִּבְרְאוּ בְּיוֹם רִאשׁוֹן וְלֹא
נִתְלוּ עַד יוֹם רְבִיעִי. אָמַר רַב זוּטְרָא בַּר טוֹבִיָּא אָמַר רַב: בַּעֲשָׂרָה דְּבָרִים
נִבְרָא הָעוֹלָם: בְּחָכְמָה, וּבִתְבוּנָה, וּבְדַעַת, וּבְכֹחַ, וּבִגְעָרָה, וּבִגְבוּרָה, בְּצֶדֶק,
שם ג וּבְמִשְׁפָּט, בְּחֶסֶד, וּבְרַחֲמִים. בְּחָכְמָה וּבִתְבוּנָה — דִּכְתִיב: °"ה' בְּחָכְמָה יָסַד אֶרֶץ
שם כּוֹנֵן שָׁמַיִם בִּתְבוּנָה". בְּדַעַת — דִּכְתִיב: °"בְּדַעְתּוֹ תְּהוֹמוֹת נִבְקָעוּ". בְּכֹחַ וּגְבוּרָה — דִּכְתִיב: °"מֵכִין הָרִים בְּכֹחוֹ נֶאְזָר
תהלים סה בִּגְבוּרָה". בִּגְעָרָה — דִּכְתִיב: °"עַמּוּדֵי שָׁמַיִם יְרוֹפָפוּ וְיִתְמְהוּ מִגַּעֲרָתוֹ". בְּצֶדֶק וּמִשְׁפָּט — דִּכְתִיב: °"צֶדֶק וּמִשְׁפָּט מְכוֹן
איוב כו / תהלים פט כִּסְאֶךָ". בְּחֶסֶד וְרַחֲמִים — דִּכְתִיב: °"זְכֹר רַחֲמֶיךָ ה' וַחֲסָדֶיךָ כִּי מֵעוֹלָם הֵמָּה". וְאָמַר רַב יְהוּדָה אָמַר רַב: בְּשָׁעָה
שם כה שֶׁבָּרָא הַקָּדוֹשׁ בָּרוּךְ הוּא אֶת הָעוֹלָם הָיָה מַרְחִיב וְהוֹלֵךְ כִּשְׁתֵּי פְקָעִיּוֹת שֶׁל שְׁתִי, עַד שֶׁגָּעַר בּוֹ הַקָּדוֹשׁ בָּרוּךְ הוּא וְהֶעֱמִידוֹ, שֶׁנֶּאֱמַר:
"עַמּוּדֵי שָׁמַיִם יְרוֹפָפוּ וְיִתְמְהוּ מִגַּעֲרָתוֹ". וְהַיְינוּ דְּאָמַר ר"ל, מַאי דִּכְתִיב: °"אֲנִי אֵל שַׁדַּי" אֲנִי הוּא שֶׁאָמַרְתִּי לָעוֹלָם
בראשית לה דַּי. (ה) אָמַר ר"ל: בְּשָׁעָה שֶׁבָּרָא הַקָּדוֹשׁ בָּרוּךְ הוּא אֶת הַיָּם הָיָה מַרְחִיב וְהוֹלֵךְ, עַד שֶׁגָּעַר בּוֹ הַקָּדוֹשׁ בָּרוּךְ הוּא וְיִבְּשׁוֹ, שֶׁנֶּאֱמַר: °"גּוֹעֵר בַּיָּם
נחום א וַיַּבְּשֵׁהוּ וְכָל הַנְּהָרוֹת הֶחֱרִיב". ת"ר: *בֵּית שַׁמַּאי אוֹמְרִים: שָׁמַיִם נִבְרְאוּ תְּחִלָּה וְאַח"כ נִבְרֵאת הָאָרֶץ, שֶׁנֶּאֱמַר: "בְּרֵאשִׁית
[תמיד לב.] בָּרָא אֱלֹהִים אֵת הַשָּׁמַיִם וְאֵת הָאָרֶץ". וּבֵית הִלֵּל אוֹמְרִים: אֶרֶץ נִבְרֵאת תְּחִלָּה וְאַח"כ שָׁמַיִם, שֶׁנֶּאֱמַר: °"בְּיוֹם עֲשׂוֹת ה'
בראשית ב אֱלֹהִים אֶרֶץ וְשָׁמָיִם". אָמַר לָהֶם בֵּית הִלֵּל לְבֵית שַׁמַּאי: לְדִבְרֵיכֶם, אָדָם בּוֹנֶה עֲלִיָּיה וְאַח"כ בּוֹנֶה בַּיִת?! שֶׁנֶּאֱמַר: °"הַבּוֹנֶה בַשָּׁמַיִם
עמוס ט מַעֲלוֹתָיו וַאֲגֻדָּתוֹ עַל אֶרֶץ יְסָדָהּ". אָמְרוּ לָהֶם בֵּית שַׁמַּאי לְב"ה: לְדִבְרֵיכֶם אָדָם עוֹשֶׂה שְׁרַפְרַף וְאַח"כ עוֹשֶׂה כִּסֵּא?! שֶׁנֶּאֱמַר:
ישעיה סו °"כֹּה אָמַר ה' הַשָּׁמַיִם כִּסְאִי וְהָאָרֶץ הֲדֹם רַגְלָי". וַחֲכ"א: זֶה וָזֶה כְּאַחַת נִבְרְאוּ, שֶׁנֶּאֱמַר: °"אַף יָדִי יָסְדָה אֶרֶץ וִימִינִי
שם מח טִפְּחָה שָׁמָיִם קוֹרֵא אֲנִי אֲלֵיהֶם יַעַמְדוּ יַחְדָּו". וְאִידָךְ — מַאי "יַחְדָּו" — דְּלָא מִשְׁתַּלְּפִי מֵהֲדָדֵי(ו). קָשׁוּ קְרָאֵי אַהֲדָדֵי! אָמַר
ר"ל: כְּשֶׁנִּבְרְאוּ — בָּרָא שָׁמַיִם וְאַח"כ בָּרָא הָאָרֶץ, וּכְשֶׁנָּטָה — נָטָה הָאָרֶץ וְאַחַר כָּךְ נָטָה שָׁמַיִם. מַאי שָׁמַיִם? א"ר יוֹסֵי
בַּר חֲנִינָא: שֶׁשָּׁם מַיִם. בְּמַתְנִיתָא תָּנָא: אֵשׁ וּמַיִם. מְלַמֵּד שֶׁהֱבִיאָן הַקָּדוֹשׁ בָּרוּךְ הוּא וּטְרָפָן זֶה בָּזֶה, וְעָשָׂה מֵהֶן רָקִיעַ.
[פסחים כב:] שָׁאַל רַבִּי יִשְׁמָעֵאל אֶת רַבִּי עֲקִיבָא כְּשֶׁהָיוּ מְהַלְּכִין בַּדֶּרֶךְ, אָמַר לֵיהּ: אַתָּה שֶׁשִּׁימַּשְׁתָּ אֶת נַחוּם אִישׁ גַּם זוֹ כ"ב שָׁנָה *שֶׁהָיָה
דּוֹרֵשׁ כָּל אֶתִין שֶׁבַּתּוֹרָה, "אֵת הַשָּׁמַיִם וְאֵת הָאָרֶץ" מָה הָיָה דּוֹרֵשׁ בָּהֶן? אָמַר לֵיהּ: אִילּוּ נֶאֱמַר שָׁמַיִם וָאָרֶץ הָיִיתִי
אוֹמֵר: שָׁמַיִם(ז) — שְׁמוֹ שֶׁל הַקָּדוֹשׁ בָּרוּךְ הוּא, עַכְשָׁיו שֶׁנֶּאֱמַר: "אֵת הַשָּׁמַיִם וְאֵת הָאָרֶץ". שָׁמַיִם — שָׁמַיִם מַמָּשׁ, אָרֶץ — אֶרֶץ מַמָּשׁ,
אֵת

וְהָשְׁתָּא דְּנָפְקָא לָן מִן וּלְמִקְצֵה הַשָּׁמַיִם. דְּאָסוּר לִשְׁאוֹל מַה שֶּׁיֵּשׁ חוּץ לַמְּחִיצוֹת, מִמֵּילָא נָפְקָא לָן דְּאָסוּר לִשְׁאוֹל בְּקוֹדֶם שֶׁנִּבְרָא. דְּהָיָא הִיא, מַה שֶּׁהָיָה קוֹדֶם לִבְרִיָּיתוֹ — הוּא עַכְשָׁיו חוּץ לִמְחִיצָּתוֹ. הִלְכָּךְ, לְמִן הַיּוֹם אֲשֶׁר בָּרָא אָדָם לָמָּה לִי לְמַעוּטֵי מִינֵּיהּ קוֹדֶם שֶׁנִּבְרָא הָעוֹלָם? עַל הָאָרֶץ וּלְמִקְצֵה הַשָּׁמַיִם. **עַל הָאָרֶץ** הָיָה, וּמַגִּיעַ לַשָּׁמַיִם: **אָחוֹר וָקֶדֶם** צַרְתָּנִי. שְׁתֵּי פְעָמִים יְצָרַנִי, תְּחִלָּה גָּבוֹהַּ וּלְבַסּוֹף שָׁפֵל: **מִסּוֹף הָעוֹלָם** וְעַד סוֹפוֹ. כְּשֶׁהָיָה שׁוֹכֵב הָיָה רֹאשׁוֹ לַמִּזְרָח וְרַגְלָיו לַמַּעֲרָב: **תֹּהוּ וָבֹהוּ.** לְקַמָּן מְפָרֵשׁ לְהוּ: **מִדַּת יוֹם וּמִדַּת לַיְלָה.** כ"ד שָׁעוֹת בֵּין שְׁנֵיהֶם: **יָשֶׁת חֹשֶׁךְ סְבִיבוֹתָיו.** לָמַדְתָּ שֶׁקַּו הַחֹשֶׁךְ מַקִּיף אֶת הַשָּׁמַיִם: **מְפוּלָּמוֹת.** לְשׁוֹן לִיחְלוּחַ: **קַו תֹהוּ וְאַבְנֵי בֹהוּ.** לָמַדְתָּ שֶׁהַתֹּהוּ קַו, וְהַבֹּהוּ אֲבָנִים: **חָכְמָה.** יוֹדֵעַ מַה שֶׁלָּמַד: **תְּבוּנָה.** שֶׁהוּא מֵבִין דָּבָר חָדָשׁ מִפִּלְפּוּל חָכְמָתוֹ: **דַּעַת.** יִשּׁוּב: **כֹּחַ.** הוּא כֹּחַ הַזְּרוֹעַ: **גְּבוּרָה.** גְּבוּרַת הַלֵּב: **גְּעָרָה.** נְזִיפָה, כִּדְאָמְרִינַן לְקַמָּן שֶׁגָּעַר בּוֹ וְעָמַד: **פְּקָעִיּוֹת.** לוֹמִישִׁי"ל בְּלַעַ"ז: **שֶׁנֶּאֱמַר הַבּוֹנֶה בַשָּׁמַיִם מַעֲלוֹתָיו.** אַלְמָא: עֲלִיָּיה מִיקְרוּ: **שְׁרַפְרַף.** לְרַגְלָיו, וְכִסֵּא — לֵישֵׁב. עַל כָּרְחֲךָ הַכִּסֵּא עָשׂוּי תְּחִלָּה, וּלְפִי גּוֹבַהּ הַכִּסֵּא הוּא מְתַקֵּן הַשְּׁרַפְרַף: **אַף יָדִי יָסְדָה אֶרֶץ וגו'.** מְסֵיפֵיהּ דִּקְרָא יָלֵיף, דִּכְתִיב: "יַעַמְדוּ יַחְדָּו" כְּשֶׁבְּרָאָן וַעֲשָׂאָן פְּקָעִיּוֹת, כְּמוֹ שֶׁאָמַרְנוּ לְמַעְלָה: **וּטְרָפָן.** עֵירְבָן: לְהַקְדִּים

סנהדרין לח:

[בילקוט איתא והעמידו על מאה אמה ובזה תבין מ"ש הרשב"ם ב"ב עה. ד"ה כשתי קומות וכו' ויותר מבואר ברש"י סנהדרין ק. ד"ה קוממיות ע"ש]

מסוף העולם ועד סופו. מהלך ת"ק שנה (לקמן יג.) שנאמר שדי, שאמר די. שלא להרחיב יותר. שנאמר: "אני אל שדי פרה ורבה" — אני שאמרתי די לעולם. ותימה: מנא לך הא שיש ת"ק שנה ולא יותר ולא פחות? וי"ל: דנפקא לן מן שדי. בשדי יש ג' אותיות שי"ן דל"ת יו"ד, קא י"נ ל"ת ו"ד הנעלם מן שד"י — ויעלה ת"ק. כך שמעתי מר' מנחם ברבי עזריאל. וצ"ע: למ"ד פרק "מי שהיה טמא" (פסחים צד. ושם): כל העולם כולו תחת כוכב אחד עומד, היכי קיימי כל הני כוכבים הנראין ברקיע? וי"מ: שעל ים אוקיינוס הן עומדין, כדאמרינן בפרקי דר"א: כל השיעורים לא נאמרו רק על שאר ימים, אבל ים אוקיינוס — בוראו יודע מדתו. אך במדרש אחר מלינו שלים (ח) ימים, שאמר — הוי בים אוקיינוס, וכן יסד ה"ר בנימין ביוצר שלו: זה הים שליש עולמו *במאה ושמים ושש ועוד סיימו. וצריך למימר שאותו מדרש פליג אההיא דפסחים. ומיהו, יש להעמיד ההיא דהתם — במזלות של גלגל, אבל שאר כוכבים — קטנים הם. ולי נראה: דיש ליישב כל אותן מדרשים, שהם תלוין בכיפת הרקיע והוא גדול הרבה מן הארץ אם היה נמתח עליה זו כזו לפי גדול הארץ. בא וראה: אהל מתוח על הארץ כמין כיפה גבוה באמצע, שתופס כפלי כפלים אם היה נמתח בקו הארץ. אך היה קשה, מדכתיב גבי סיסרא (שופטים ה): "מן שמים נלחמו הכוכבים ממסלותם" ומוכח מינה בנימוקי רש"י. וכן איתא במדרש, שאורך הכוכב מהלך ת"ק שנה, כמן השמים ועד הארץ, שהיה ראש אחד תחוב ברקיע והשני היה בארץ והיכי היה יוצא באויר העולם כיון דכולו תחת כוכב אחד הוא עומד? וצ"ל שהם חולקין יחד, אם לא נחלוק בין מזלות הגלגל לשאר מזלות*:

אידי ואידי חד שיעורא הוא. ופליג אמאן דדריש בתמיד (דף לב.) דמזרח ומערב רחוק טפי, דאי לא תימא הכי — *אדם היכי הוה קם, כיון דכתיב: "מקצה השמים ועד קצה השמים"? וי"ל: שסובר שהיה בגן עדן עד שנתמעט: **ישת** חשך סתרו. מדכתיב: "סביבותיו סוכתו" קדריש:

ואת

כלומר שלש מת"ק שנה הכי הוי וכך ועוד הוא שלש משתי שנים היתרים

[ועי' תוס' פסחים לד. קיח: ד"ה מן]

רבינו חננאל

ת"ל ולמקצה השמים ועד קצה השמים. שיעור מן קצה השמים ועד קצה שמים כשיעור מן הארץ עד לשמים ותרווייהו חדא שיעורא הוא. אמר רב יהודה (ג) [י'] דברים נבראו ביום ראשון. תוהו ובוהו. שמים וארץ. אור וחשך רוח ומים. מדת יום ומדת לילה כו'. תנא תוהו זה קו ירוק שמקיף כל העולם שממנו חושך יוצא. בהו אלו אבנים מפולמות המשוקעות בתהום שמהם מים יוצא שנאמר ונטה עליה קו תוהו ואבני בוהו. וזה האור שנברא ביום ראשון היה בו זיהור שצופין בו ומביטין באורו מסוף העולם ועד סופו. וכיון שנסתכל ברשעים גנזו לצדיקים לעתיד לבא שנא' וימנע מרשעים אורם וכיון שנגנז שמח שנאמר אור צדיקים ישמח. ויש תנא חולק על זה ואומר זה האור נתלה ביום רביעי שנאמר יהי מאורות ברקיע השמים. ופי' יהי אותו האור שנברא ביום ראשון למאורות והן ב' המאורות. אמר רב בעשרה דברים נברא העולם. בחכמה בתבונה. בדעת. בכח. בגבורה. בגערה. בצדק. במשפט. בחסד. ברחמים. וכולהו מקראי. בחכמה ובתבונה שנאמר ה' בחכמה יסד ארץ כונן שמים בתבונה. בדעת כו'. זה שאמר [ר"י אמר רב דבשעה שברא הקב"ה את] העולם. עת שנברא היה מרחיב והולך כשתי פקעיות של שתי כו' עד שגער בו הקב"ה והעמידו שנאמר עמודי שמים ירופפו ויתמהו מגערתו. ר"ל אמר אני אל שדי אני שאמרתי לעולם די. כיוצא בו בים גוער בים ויבשהו אלו כולן מדרשות הן ואין מדקדקין עליהן להשותן למה שהדעת מתקבלת מהן וכן חלוקת ב"ש וב"ה אלו אומרים שמים נבראו תחלה. ואלו אומרים ארץ נבראת תחלה. וכל אחד מביא ראיה לדבריו. וחכמים אומרים שניהם נבראו כאחד אף ידי יסדה ארץ וימיני טפחה שמים קורא אני עליהם יעמדו יחדו. קשו קראי אהדדי. ופריק ר"ל כשבראן ברא שמים ואח"כ הארץ כב"ש [וקשיא דהא דכתיב נוטה שמים על תוהו ותולה ארץ על בלימה הרי תחלה נטה שמים ואח"כ ארץ] כשנטה אותן נטה ארץ ואח"כ שמים כב"ה. וזהו שאמרו חכמים שניהן כאחת עמדו. (טרף) [מאי שמים שטרף] הקב"ה אש ומים ועשה מהן רקיע לפיכך נקראו שמים. אבל דברי נחום איש גם זו פירוש הוא שפירש. אמר אלו נאמר בראשית ברא אלהים שמים *) ואינן שמים דבר ידוע הייתי אומר שמים שם הן וכיון שנאמר את השמים נתברר לנו כי על השמים הידועים לנו הכתוב מדבר. וכיון שכתב את בשמים כתב נמי את בארץ. כי האת שכתב בארץ אינו

הגהות הב"ח

(א) גמ' על הארץ למה לי מיבעי ליה לכדרבי אלעזר וכו' מן הארץ ועד לרקיע היה שנאמר וכו' על הארץ ולמקצה השמים וכיון שסרח וכו' ומיעטו. נ"ב ס"א והעמידו על מאה אמה: (ב) שם יצא חשך לעולם שנאמר ישת: (ג) שם ויהי בקר יום רביעי אלא כלדרבי אלעזר: (ד) שם שגנזו לצדיקים מיד שמח וכו' אדם צופה ורואה ומביט: (ה) שם שאמרתי לעולם די איכא דאמרי אמר ר"ל בשעה שברא הקב"ה את הים הגדול היה מרחיב: (ו) שם דלא משתלפי מהדדי מכל מקום קשו קראי: (ז) שם הייתי אומר שמים וארץ שמותן של הקב"ה: (ח) תוס' ד"ה מסוף וכו' מלינו ששליש עולם הוי מים אוקינוס:

ו א מיי' פ"ג מהלכות יסודי התורה הלכה ה:

רבינו חננאל

אינו צריך לגופו. משל דר' ישמעאל הודיע שהקדים שבחה של ארץ לשבח השמים אבל לא בבריאה. תניא ר' יוסי אומר אוי לבריות שרואות ואינן יודעות כלומר הארץ עומדת על העמודים ועמודי הארץ הן על המים. והמים הן על ההרים. וההרים ברוח. והרוח בסערה וכולה מדרש פסוקים וסערה תלויה בזרועו של הקב"ה שנא' ומתחת זרועות עולם. פי' הדבר שהוא בעולם מתחת הכל תלוי בזרוע גבורתו של הקב"ה. כי הגבורה היא הזרוע כדכתיב לך זרוע עם גבורה. ר' אלעזר אומר על עמוד אחד עומד העולם וצדיק שמו שנאמר וצדיק יסוד עולם זה שאמר ר"ל ז' רקיעין הן. וילון. רקיע. שחקים. זבול. מעון. מכון. ערבות. וכל אחד ואחד פירש מה הן משמשין. אלו כולן קבלה הן הל"מ. וקראי אסמכתא בעלמא הן. ואינם מדרשות. שאינם דברים הנאמרים מן הדעת כלל. אלא דברי קבלה הן. והערבות שהוא רקיע שביעי יש בו צדקה ומשפט. גנזי חיים גנזי שלום גנזי ברכה ונשמת הצדיקי' ונשמות העתידות להבראות. וטל שעתיד הקב"ה להחיות בו את המתים. וכולהו קראי צדק ומשפט שנאמר צדק ומשפט מכון כסאך. גנזי חיים שנאמר כי עמך מקור חיים. גנזי שלום שנאמר ויקרא לו ה' שלום. גנזי ברכה שנא' ישא ברכה מאת ה'. נשמתן של צדיקים שנא' והיתה נפש אדוני צרורה בצרור החיים את ה' אלהיך. רוחות ונשמות העתידו' להבראו' שנא' כי רוח מלפני יעטוף ונשמות אני עשיתי. וטל שעתיד להחיות בו מתים שנאמר גשם נדבות תניף אלהים וגו'. ולמעלה אופנים ושרפים וחיות הקודש ומלאכי השרת וכסא הכבוד ומלך רם ונשא שוכן עליהם. שנאמר סולו לרוכב בערבות ביה שמו. וחושך וענן וערפל מקיפין אותו מבחוץ שנאמר ישת חשך סתרו וגו' ומבפנים אור שנאמר ונהורא עמיה שריה.

תורה אור

"את הארץ" למה לי – להקדים שמים לארץ. "והארץ היתה תהו ובהו" מכדי בשמים אתחיל ברישא, מאי שנא דקא חשיב מעשה ארץ? תנא דבי ר' ישמעאל: משל למלך בשר ודם שאמר לעבדיו: השכימו לפתחי. (א) השכים ומצא נשים ואנשים, למי משבח – למי שאין דרכו להשכים והשכים. תניא, ר' יוסי אומר: אוי להם לבריות שרואות ואינן יודעות (ב) מה רואות, עומדות – ואין יודעות על מה הן עומדות. הארץ על מה עומדת – על העמודים, שנאמר: °"המרגיז ארץ ממקומה ועמודיה יתפלצון". (איוב ט) עמודים – על המים, שנאמר: °"לרוקע הארץ על המים", (תהלים קלו) מים – על ההרים, שנאמר: °"על הרים יעמדו מים", (שם קד) הרים – ברוח, שנאמר: °"כי הנה יוצר הרים ובורא רוח", (עמוס ד) רוח – בסערה, שנאמר: °"רוח סערה עושה דברו", (תהלים קמח) סערה תלויה *בזרועו של הקדוש ברוך הוא, שנאמר: °"ומתחת זרועות עולם". (דברים לג) וחכ"א: על י"ב עמודים עומדת, שנאמר: °"יצב גבולות עמים למספר בני ישראל". (שם לב) וי"א: (ג) ז' עמודים, שנאמר: °"חצבה עמודיה שבעה". (משלי ט) ר"א בן שמוע אומר: על עמוד אחד, וצדיק שמו, שנאמר: °"וצדיק יסוד עולם". (שם י) א"ר יהודה: שני רקיעים הן, שנאמר: °"הן לה' אלהיך השמים ושמי השמים". (דברים י) ר"ל אמר: אשבעה, ואלו הן, וילון, רקיע, שחקים, זבול, מעון, מכון, ערבות. וילון – אינו משמש כלום, אלא נכנס שחרית ויוצא ערבית, ומחדש בכל יום מעשה בראשית, שנאמר °"הנוטה כדוק שמים וימתחם כאהל לשבת". (ישעיה מ) רקיע – שבו חמה ולבנה כוכבים ומזלות קבועין, שנאמר: °"ויתן אותם אלהים ברקיע השמים". (בראשית א) שחקים – שבו רחיים עומדות וטוחנות מן לצדיקים(ד) – שנאמר: °"ויצו שחקים ממעל ודלתי שמים פתח וימטר עליהם מן לאכול וגו'". (תהלים עח) זבול – שבו ירושלים ובית המקדש, *ומזבח בנוי, ומיכאל השר הגדול עומד ומקריב עליו קרבן, (ה) שנאמר: °"בנה בניתי בית זבול לך מכון לשבתך עולמים". (מ"א ח) ומנלן דאיקרי שמים – דכתיב: °"הבט משמים וראה מזבול קדשך ותפארתך". (ישעיה סג) מעון – שבו כיתות של מלאכי השרת, שאומרות שירה בלילה וחשות ביום, מפני כבודן של ישראל, שנאמר: °"יומם יצוה ה' חסדו ובלילה שירה עמי". (תהלים מב) אמר ר"ל: *כל העוסק בתורה בלילה – הקדוש ברוך הוא מושך עליו חוט של חסד ביום, שנאמר: "יומם יצוה ה' חסדו" ומה טעם "יומם יצוה ה' חסדו" – משום "ובלילה שירה עמי". ואיכא דאמרי, אמר ר"ל: כל העוסק בתורה *בעוה"ז, שהוא דומה ללילה – הקדוש ברוך הוא מושך עליו חוט של חסד לעוה"ב, שהוא דומה ליום, שנאמר: "יומם יצוה ה' חסדו ובלילה שירה עמי".

א"ר לוי: *)כל הפוסק מדברי תורה ועוסק בדברי שיחה – מאכילין אותו גחלי רתמים, שנאמר: °"הקוטפים מלוח **)עלי שיח ושרש רתמים לחמם". (איוב ל) ומנלן דאיקרי שמים – שנאמר: °"השקיפה ממעון קדשך מן השמים". (דברים כו) מכון – שבו אוצרות שלג ואוצרות ברד, ועליית טללים רעים, ועליית אגלים,[א] וחדרה של סופה [וסערה], ומערה של קיטור, (ו) ודלתותיהן אש, שנאמר: °"יפתח ה' לך את אוצרו הטוב". (שם כח) הני ברקיעא איתנהו? הני בארעא איתנהו! דכתיב: °"הללו את ה' מן הארץ תנינים וכל תהומות אש וברד שלג וקיטור רוח סערה עושה דברו". (תהלים קמח) אמר רב יהודה אמר רב: דוד ביקש עליהם רחמים, והורידן לארץ. אמר לפניו: רבונו של עולם °"לא אל חפץ רשע אתה לא יגורך (במגורך) רע", (שם ה) *צדיק אתה ה' – לא יגור במגורך רע. [שבת קמט: ע"ש סוטה מב. סנהדרין קג. ע"ש] ומנלן דאיקרי שמים – דכתיב: °"ואתה תשמע השמים מכון שבתך" (מלכים א ח) ערבות – שבו צדק, משפט וצדקה, גנזי חיים וגנזי שלום וגנזי ברכה, ונשמתן של צדיקים, ורוחות ונשמות שעתיד להיבראות, וטל שעתיד הקב"ה להחיות בו מתים. צדק ומשפט – דכתיב: °"צדק ומשפט מכון כסאך", (תהלים פט) צדקה – דכתיב °"וילבש צדקה כשריון", (ישעיה נט) גנזי חיים – דכתיב °"כי עמך מקור חיים", (תהלים לו) וגנזי שלום – דכתיב °"ויקרא לו ה' שלום", (שופטים ו) וגנזי ברכה – דכתיב: °"ישא ברכה מאת ה'", (תהלים כד) נשמתן של צדיקים – דכתיב: °"והיתה נפש אדוני צרורה בצרור החיים את ה' אלהיך", (שמואל א כה) רוחות ונשמות שעתיד להיבראות – דכתיב: °"כי רוח מלפני יעטוף ונשמות אני עשיתי", (ישעיה נז) *וטל שעתיד הקב"ה להחיות בו מתים – דכתיב: °"גשם נדבות תניף אלהים נחלתך ונלאה אתה כוננתה". ([שבת פח:]; תהלים סח) שם אופנים ושרפים וחיות הקדש, ומלאכי השרת, וכסא הכבוד, מלך אל חי רם ונשא שוכן עליהם(ז) בערבות, שנאמר: °"סולו לרוכב בערבות ביה שמו", (שם) ומנלן דאיקרי שמים(ח) – אתיא "רכיבה" "רכיבה"; כתיב הכא: "סולו לרוכב בערבות" וכתיב התם: °"רוכב שמים בעזרך". (דברים לג) וחשך וענן וערפל מקיפין אותו, שנאמר: °"ישת חשך סתרו סביבותיו סוכתו חשכת מים עבי שחקים". (תהלים יח) ומי איכא חשוכא קמי שמיא? והכתיב: °"הוא (*גלי) [נ"ל גלא] עמיקתא ומסתרתא ידע מה בחשוכא ונהורא עמיה שרי"! (דניאל ב) לא קשיא: הא

בבתי

*) ע"ז ג: **) [עי' פרש"י בע"ז]

רש"י

להקדים שמים לארץ. דאי לא כתיב "את", הוה אמינא כאחת נבראו, אלא שאי אפשר לקרות שני שמות כאחת, להכי כתב "את" להקדים: למי שאין דרכו להשכים והשכים. הכא נמי (ט) דקרא לשמים תחלה, ה"ל ארץ אין דרכו להשכים. ועוד: שכל מעשה ארץ מתונים, ומעשה שמים במהירות. וזו השכימה עמה, שנבראו כאחת – לכך התחיל לספר מעשיה תחלה: יוצר הרים ובורא רוח. מה ענין זה אצל זה? אלא ללמדך שההרים עומדין על הרוח: רוח סערה עושה דברו. דבר הרוח, סערה עשאתו: ומתחת. כל היל"ה: זרועות עולם. הסובלות אותו: נכנס שחרית. לתוך תיקו, והאור נראה: ויוצא ערבית. מתיקו, ומתפשט למטה מן האור, והרי העולם חשוך. וזהו חידושו (י) למעשה בראשית בכל יום: כדוק. יריעה, טייל"א בלע"ז. אלמא: יש שמים שאין משמשין אלא תשמיש יריעה פרוסה: מעון. לשון מדור, מקום שמלאכים דרין בו: וחשות. (כ) מפני כבודן של ישראל שמקלסין ביום: יומם יצוה ה' חסדו. יצוה למלאכים לשתוק, כדי לעשות חסד לצריכים חסד, והם התחתונים: ובלילה שירה עמי. (ל) ברקיע עם שיר שלי שקילסתי ביום: ומנלן. דמעון איקרי שמים: מכון. לשון אוצר של פורעניות, כמה דאת אמר: "נכונו ללצים שפטים" (משלי יט): שבו אוצרות שלג כו'. כל אלה לפורעניות: עליית אגלים. לשון (*עוגל) של מים (חולין דף מח.), ולשון אגלי טל (איוב לח), ולשון אגן הסהר (שיר השירים ז) שמתחלפת ל' בנו"ן. והם מים העומדים להלקות פירות: (מ) יפתח ה' לך את אוצרו הטוב. למדת שיש לו אוצר לפורענות: לא יגורך רע. לא יגור אצלך: ורוחות ונשמות. חדא היא. ויש מפרשין: רוח – היא הנשמה העשויה בדמות הגוף, נשמה – נשימה, אליינ"א בלע"ז: מכון כסאך. והכסא בערבות הוא כדמסיק לקמן: וילבש צדקה. למדת שעמו צדקה שרויה: ויקרא לו. קראה אצלו: רוח מלפני. אלמא: לפניו הם: גשם נדבות תניף אלהים וגו'. (נ) והאי קרא במתן תורה כתיב, שיצאתה נשמתן, שנאמר: "נפשי יצאה בדברו" (שיר השירים ה), והניף עליהן טל תחייתו, שנאמר: "גשם נדבות תניף אלהים", והאי קרא משתעי במתן תורה, במזמור "יקום אלהים יפוצו אויביו":

בבתי

[פי' הכל תלוי בגבורות של הקב"ה והגבור' היא זרועו כדכתיב לך זרוע עם גבורה ערוך ע' זרוע]

[עוגה איתא לפנינו וע"ש ברש"י]

[מנחות קי. וע' תוס' שם ד"ה ומיכאל]

ע"ז ג:

[פסחים ב: ב"מ פג:]

הגהות הגר"א

[א] גמ' וחדרה של סופה ומערה של קיטור. כצ"ל:

תוספות

ואת הארץ להקדים שמים לארץ. דאי לאו "ואת", הייתי אומר ששניהם נבראו יחד והכתוב כתבם זה אחר זה שאי אפשר לכתוב שני שמות כאחד כדפירש רש"י. והא דאמרי ב"ה לעיל: ארץ נבראת תחלה דכתיב "ביום עשות ה'" וגו' ולא כתיב "ואת"? התם דריש ליה מדשני קרא בסידריה להסמיך ארץ לעשיה. ומיהו בנימוקי חומש פי' רש"י: "את השמים" לרבות תולדותיהן. ומדרש אחר הוא, ופליג אהא דהכא:

נכנס שחרית. פרש"י: נכנס בתיקו וממילא האור יוצא ונראה, ויוצא ערבית ומכסה האורה ומחשיך העולם. והיה קשה למורי: א"כ היאך נראים כוכבים בשמים (ס) מינה בלילה כיון שהם קבועים בשני, כדמסיק! ומיהו, שמא נראים מתוכו כמו ע"י העננים, אך רוב פעמים שהעננים מחשיכים אותו ומכסין אותו. ונראה למורי לפרש איפכא: נכנס שחרית בעולם וממנה אורה יוצא, ויוצאת ערבית מן העולם [ומסתלק אורה] ולכך הכוכבים נראין:

כל העוסק בתורה. אכתי לא סיים למילתיה דז' רקיעים שהתחיל לפרש:

אוצרות שלג. יש ממנו שמוכן לפורענות (ע) ויש לטובה, כדאמרינן בתענית (דף ג:): טבא תלגא לטורי כחמשה מטרי לארעא. וכן כתיב: "כי כאשר ירד הגשם והשלג כו'" "כי אם הרוה את הארץ וגו'" (ישעיה נה):

דוד ביקש והורידן לארץ. הקשה הרב ר' אלחנן, הא כתיב (ישעיה נה): "כי כאשר ירד הגשם והשלג מן השמים"? ותירץ: דכיון שמן העננים יורד – נראות כיורד מן השמים. ועוד י"ל: דלא הוריד רק המוכנים לפורענות, אבל המרוים את הארץ – נשארו למעלה:

לא יגור במגורך רע. אין זה מקרא אלא "לא יגורך", והכי דריש ליה: (בגמ' שבת קמט: ובסנהדרין קג. איתא שפיר ע"ש)

בן

הגהות הב"ח

(א) גמ' השכימו לפתחי למחר השכים: (ב) שם ואינן יודעות מה הן רואות ומים על ההרים וכו' וההרים על רוח וכו' ורוח בסערה: (ג) שם ויש אומרים על ז': (ד) שם וטוחנות מן לצדיקים לעתיד לבא שנאמר ויצו: (ה) שם ומקריב עליו קרבן בכל יום שנאמר מאי מקריב וכי תעלה על דעתך שיש שם כבשים אלא מקריב נשמתן של צדיקים ומנלן דאיקרי שמים: (ו) שם ודלתותיהן (שנאמר יפתח וכו' הטוב) תא"מ ונ"ב ס"א פח ה' אוצרו ויוציא כלי זעמו: (ז) שם רם ונשא שוכן עליהם בערבות נמחק: (ח) שם ומנלן דאיקרי שמים אמר ר' אבהו אתיא רכיבה: (ט) רש"י ד"ה למי שאין וכו' מקרא לשמים: (י) ד"ה ויוצא ערבית וכו' חידושו של מעשה בראשית: (כ) ד"ה וחשות ביום מפני: (ל) ד"ה ובלילה שירו עמו שירו ברקיע: (מ) ד"ה (יפתח וכו' הטוב) תא"מ ונ"ב ס"א פתח ה' את אוצרו וגו': (נ) ד"ה גשם נדבות וגו' במתן תורה כצ"ל ותיבות והאי קרא נמחק: (ס) תוס' ד"ה נכנס וכו' כוכבים בשמים בלילה כיון שהם קבועים ברקיע השני כצ"ל ותיבת מינה נמחק: (ע) ד"ה אוצרות וכו' לפורענות (ויש לטובה כדאמרינן) תא"מ ונ"ב ס"א היינו שלג מרובה היוצא בשטף מוכן לפורענות אבל שלג היורד בנחת לטובה כדאמרינן:

רש"י

בְּבָתֵּי גַּוָּאֵי. וּנְהוֹרָא עִמֵּיהּ שְׁרָא: בַּמּוּפְלָא מִמְּךָ. בַּמּוּבְדָּל וּמוּפְרָשׁ מִמְּךָ, שֶׁלֹּא רָצָה הַקָּדוֹשׁ בָּרוּךְ הוּא לְגַלּוֹת לְךָ: לְאוֹתוֹ רָשָׁע. נְבוּכַדְנֶצַּר: עָלָיו. לְשׁוֹן נְקִיָּה הִיא, כְּלוֹמַר: עַל עַצְמוֹ, וְלֹא עָלַי: רַגְלֵי הַחַיּוֹת. עוֹדֵי פַּרְסוֹתֵיהֶן: קַרְסוּלֵי. אַסְתְּוִירָא, שֶׁקּוֹרִין קבילי"א בְּלַעַ"ז: שׁוֹק. הוּא עֶצֶם הַנִּמְכָּר עִם (ט) הָרֶגֶל: רְכוּבֵי. הוּא עֶצֶם הַיָּרֵךְ הַסָּמוּךְ לַשּׁוֹק. יָרֵךְ הוּא עֶצֶם הַקּוּלִית הַתָּקוּעַ בַּמָּתְנַיִם: רָאשֵׁי פְּרָקִים. רָאשֵׁי פָּרָשִׁיּוֹת שֶׁבָּהּ: שֶׁלִּבּוֹ דּוֹאֵג. וְאֵינוֹ מֵיקֵל אֶת רֹאשׁוֹ: אִיכָּא דְּאָמְרִי וְהוּא שֶׁלִּבּוֹ דּוֹאֵג בְּקִרְבּוֹ. תַּרְתֵּי בָּעֵינַן: סִתְרֵי תוֹרָה. כְּגוֹן מַעֲשֵׂה הַמֶּרְכָּבָה וְסֵפֶר יְצִירָה וּמַעֲשֵׂה בְרֵאשִׁית, וְהִיא בְּרַיְיתָא: יוֹעֵץ וַחֲכַם חֲרָשִׁים וּנְבוֹן לָחַשׁ. לְקַמָּן מְפָרֵשׁ לְהוּ: לָא קַשָּׁאִי. לֹא זָקַנְתִּי, וּבָעֵינַן לִבּוֹ דּוֹאֵג: מַעֲשֵׂה הַמֶּרְכָּבָה וּמַעֲשֵׂה בְרֵאשִׁית. בְּרַיְיתוֹת הֵן: כִּבְשׁוֹנוֹ שֶׁל עוֹלָם. סִתְרוֹ שֶׁל עוֹלָם, כְּמוֹ: רֵישָׁא בְּכַבְשָׁא (חולין דף נג:), בַּהֲדֵי כַּבְשֵׁי דְרַחֲמָנָא לָמָּה לָךְ (ברכות דף י.), מִמְּנֵי יָלְאוּ כְּבוּשִׁין (מכות דף כג:): תָּנֵינָא עַד וַיֹּאמֶר אֵלַי בֶּן אָדָם. כְּבָר שָׁנִינוּ עַד "וַיֹּאמֶר אֵלַי בֶּן אָדָם עֲמוֹד עַל רַגְלֶיךָ": הֵן הֵן מַעֲשֵׂה הַמֶּרְכָּבָה. אִם עַד כָּאן שְׁנִיתֶם – הַרְבֵּה שְׁנִיתֶם, שֶׁשְּׁנֵי מִקְרָאוֹת הַלָּלוּ שֶׁהֵן "וָאֵרֶא כְּעֵין הַחַשְׁמַל" וגו' "כְּמַרְאֵה הַקֶּשֶׁת" וגו' (י) הֵם שֶׁהִקְפִּידוּ עֲלֵיהֶם חֲכָמִים מִלְּדוֹרְשָׁם, שֶׁהֵן מְדַבְּרִין בְּצוּרַת שְׁכִינָה וּמַרְאֵהוּ: מֵיתִיבֵי. גָּרְסִינַן, וְלָא גָּרְסִינַן: וּמִי הָוֵי מַעֲשֵׂה הַמֶּרְכָּבָה עַד הָכָא: עַד "וָאֵרֶא. כְּעֵין הַחַשְׁמַל", וְלֹא הוּא בִּכְלָל: עַד הַחַשְׁמַל. עַד הַתֵּיבָה הַזּוֹ, וְהִיא בִּכְלָל לִידָּרֵשׁ: עַד וָאֵרֶא מִגְמַר גָּמְרִינַן. כְּלוֹמַר, הָכִי קָאָמַר: עַד הֵיכָן מַעֲשֵׂה מֶרְכָּבָה שֶׁנִּתְּנוּ לִדְרוֹשׁ – עַד וָאֵרֶא אוֹ עַד הַחַשְׁמַל, וּמִשָּׁם עַד "וַיֹּאמֶר" – הֵן הֵן מַעֲשֵׂה מֶרְכָּבָה שֶׁהִקְפִּידוּ עֲלֵיהֶן חֲכָמִים: נִגְנַז סֵפֶר יְחֶזְקֵאל. שֶׁיֵּשׁ בְּסוֹפוֹ דְּבָרִים בַּקָּרְבָּנוֹת שֶׁסּוֹתְרִין דִּבְרֵי תוֹרָה: גַּרְבֵּי שֶׁמֶן. לְהַדְלִיק: וְהָיָה מֵבִין בְּחַשְׁמַל. לִדְרוֹשׁ מַהוּ:

חַיּוֹת

תוספות

בן בנו של נמרוד הרשע. לאו דוקא, שהרי כוש ילד את נמרוד, ולא מצינו אותו רשע מזרע כוש. אלא על שם מעשיו, שמלך גם הוא בשנער*: **שבעים** שנה. לאו משום שלא היה קשיש יותר, שהרי לא וחשוב מימות סנחריב שסמוך למפלתו גבי שליחות שסלח בלאדן לחזקיהו, מלינו שהיה סופר בביתו ומשם זכה למלכות, כדאשכחן באגדות "חלק" (סנהדרין דף נו.) אלא אורחא דמילתא קא חשיב: **ורגלי** החיות כנגד כולם. יש מגיהין בקדושתא שיסד הקליר: וחיות אשר הנה מרובעות לכסא כף רגל חמש מאות וחמש עשרה. ומוחקים הוי"ו, ואומרים כי כן עולה לפי חשבון שבכאן למנין ז' רקיעים *וח' אוירים, הוא ט"ו פעמים ת"ק, והיינו מנין ישרה: ש"ר = ת"ק ו–י"ה לסימנא (כ) שכן עולה ט"ו פעמים כך. ומיהו, בחנם מחקוהו, שיסד דבריו ע"פ הירושלמי "הרואה": א"ר לוי: מארץ ועד לרקיע מהלך ת"ק שנה, אמר ר' ברכיה ור' חלבו בש"ר (בא) סמוקה: גדול מזה רגל אחד *כמנין ישר"ה, ראה כמה (ל) גבוה מעולמו כו'. משמע כמנין שיסד ת"ק ט"ו. וכן היה דרכו שבכמה מקומות היה מניח שיטת התלמוד שלנו כדי לאחוז ◎שיטת התלמוד ירושלמי, שהוא היה תנא, והוא היה ר"א ברבי שמעון דקרי עליה: *"מכל אבקת רוכל": תנא, קרא, קרובץ, ופייטן (ויקרא רבה פ"ל). ובימיו מקדשים ע"פ הראייה, שמעולם לא יסד רק קרובץ מיום (*אחד): **אין** מוסרין דברי תורה לגוי. היה קשה להר"ר אלחנן: תיפוק ליה דגוי העוסק בתורה חייב מיתה, כדאמר בפ' "ד' מיתות" (סנהדרין דף נט. ושם): גוי העוסק בתורה – חייב מיתה, והמלמדו עובר אלפני עור לא תתן מכשול"! וכי תימא (מ) בז' מצות דידהו, דאינו חייב מיתה, כדאמר התלמוד התם – והא *מצוה איכא למוסרם להם, ונפקא לן מהאי קרא: "אשר יעשה אותם האדם וחי בהם" (ויקרא יח) כהן ולוי לא נאמר, אלא אדם, שאפילו גוי ועוסק בתורה וכו'! וי"ל: דהכא איירי אפילו היכא דאיכא גוי אחר שרוצה ללמדו, דליכא "לפני עור" כדאמרינן בע"ז (דף ו:): המושיט כוס יין לנזיר – עובר א"לפני עור", והני מילי – דקאי אתרי עברא דנהרא, שבלאו נתינתו אי אפשר להביאו אליו. אבל אי לאו הכי – אינו עובר א"לפני עור", הכא נמי, אפילו במקום שגוי אחר רוצה ללמדו, דליכא "לפני עור" – מכל מקום אסור משום "מגיד דבריו ליעקב" וכו' (תהלים קמז)*:

והחיות

גמרא

[יחזקאל א] *בְּבָתֵּי גַּוָּאֵי, הָא – בְּבָתֵּי בָּרָאֵי. וְאָמַר רַב אַחָא בַּר יַעֲקֹב: עוֹד רָקִיעַ אֶחָד יֵשׁ לְמַעְלָה מֵרָאשֵׁי הַחַיּוֹת, דִּכְתִיב: °"וּדְמוּת עַל רָאשֵׁי הַחַיָּה רָקִיעַ כְּעֵין הַקֶּרַח הַנּוֹרָא". עַד כָּאן יֵשׁ לְךָ רְשׁוּת לְדַבֵּר, מִכָּאן וְאֵילָךְ – אֵין לְךָ רְשׁוּת לְדַבֵּר, שֶׁכֵּן כָּתוּב בְּסֵפֶר בֶּן סִירָא: בַּמּוּפְלָא מִמְּךָ אַל תִּדְרוֹשׁ וּבַמְכוּסֶּה מִמְּךָ אַל תַּחְקוֹר, בַּמֶּה שֶׁהוּרְשֵׁיתָ הִתְבּוֹנֵן, אֵין לְךָ עֵסֶק בַּנִּסְתָּרוֹת. *תַּנְיָא, אָמַר רַבָּן יוֹחָנָן בֶּן זַכַּאי: מַה תְּשׁוּבָה הֱשִׁיבַתּוּ בַּת קוֹל לְאוֹתוֹ רָשָׁע, בְּשָׁעָה שֶׁאָמַר: [ישעיה יד] °"אֶעֱלֶה עַל בָּמֳתֵי עָב אֶדַּמֶּה לְעֶלְיוֹן" – יָצְתָה בַּת קוֹל וְאָמְרָה לוֹ: רָשָׁע בֶּן רָשָׁע, בֶּן בְּנוֹ שֶׁל נִמְרוֹד הָרָשָׁע, *שֶׁהִמְרִיד (א) כָּל הָעוֹלָם כּוּלּוֹ עָלָיו בְּמַלְכוּתוֹ! כַּמָּה שְׁנוֹתָיו שֶׁל אָדָם – שִׁבְעִים שָׁנָה, שֶׁנֶּאֱמַר: [תהלים צ] °"יְמֵי שְׁנוֹתֵינוּ בָהֶם שִׁבְעִים שָׁנָה וְאִם בִּגְבוּרוֹת שְׁמוֹנִים שָׁנָה". וַהֲלֹא מִן הָאָרֶץ עַד לָרָקִיעַ מַהֲלַךְ חֲמֵשׁ מֵאוֹת שָׁנָה, וְעוֹבְיוֹ שֶׁל רָקִיעַ מַהֲלַךְ חֲמֵשׁ מֵאוֹת שָׁנָה, וְכֵן בֵּין כָּל רָקִיעַ וְרָקִיעַ. לְמַעְלָה מֵהֶן חַיּוֹת הַקֹּדֶשׁ; (ב) רַגְלֵי הַחַיּוֹת כְּנֶגֶד כּוּלָּם. קַרְסוּלֵּי הַחַיּוֹת כְּנֶגֶד כּוּלָּן, שׁוֹקֵי הַחַיּוֹת כְּנֶגֶד כּוּלָּן, רְכוּבֵי הַחַיּוֹת כְּנֶגֶד כּוּלָּן, יַרְכֵי הַחַיּוֹת כְּנֶגֶד כּוּלָּן, גּוּפֵי הַחַיּוֹת כְּנֶגֶד כּוּלָּן, צַוְּארֵי הַחַיּוֹת כְּנֶגֶד כּוּלָּן, רָאשֵׁי הַחַיּוֹת כְּנֶגֶד כּוּלָּן, קַרְנֵי הַחַיּוֹת כְּנֶגֶד כּוּלָּן, לְמַעְלָה מֵהֶן כִּסֵּא כָבוֹד; רַגְלֵי כִּסֵּא הַכָּבוֹד כְּנֶגֶד כּוּלָּן, כִּסֵּא הַכָּבוֹד כְּנֶגֶד כּוּלָּן, מֶלֶךְ אֵל חַי וְקַיָּם רָם וְנִשָּׂא שׁוֹכֵן עֲלֵיהֶם. וְאַתָּה אָמַרְתָּ: "אֶעֱלֶה עַל בָּמֳתֵי עָב אֶדַּמֶּה לְעֶלְיוֹן" – "אַךְ אֶל שְׁאוֹל תּוּרָד אֶל יַרְכְּתֵי בוֹר". § "וְלֹא בַּמֶּרְכָּבָה בְּיָחִיד". תָּנֵי רַבִּי חִיָּיא: [א]אֲבָל מוֹסְרִין לוֹ רָאשֵׁי פְרָקִים. אָמַר רַבִּי זֵירָא: אֵין מוֹסְרִין רָאשֵׁי פְרָקִים אֶלָּא לְאַב ב"ד, וּלְכָל מִי שֶׁלִּבּוֹ דּוֹאֵג בְּקִרְבּוֹ. אִיכָּא דְּאָמְרִי: וְהוּא שֶׁלִּבּוֹ דּוֹאֵג בְּקִרְבּוֹ. אָמַר רַבִּי אַמִי: אֵין מוֹסְרִין סִתְרֵי תוֹרָה אֶלָּא לְמִי שֶׁיֵּשׁ בּוֹ חֲמִשָּׁה דְבָרִים: [ישעיה ג] °"שַׂר חֲמִשִּׁים וּנְשׂוּא פָנִים וְיוֹעֵץ וַחֲכַם חֲרָשִׁים וּנְבוֹן לָחַשׁ" [א]וְאָמַר רַבִּי אַמִי: אֵין מוֹסְרִין דִּבְרֵי תוֹרָה לְגוֹי, שֶׁנֶּאֱמַר: [תהלים קמז] °"לֹא עָשָׂה כֵן לְכָל גּוֹי וּמִשְׁפָּטִים בַּל יְדָעוּם". א"ל רַבִּי יוֹחָנָן לְרַבִּי אֶלְעָזָר: תָּא אַגְמְרָךְ בְּמַעֲשֵׂה הַמֶּרְכָּבָה! אָמַר לֵיהּ: לָא קַשָּׁאִי. כִּי קַשׁ – נָח נַפְשֵׁיהּ דְּרַבִּי יוֹחָנָן. א"ל ר' אַסִי: תָּא וְאַגְמְרָךְ בְּמַעֲשֵׂה מֶרְכָּבָה! א"ל: אִי זְכַאי – גְּמִירְתָּא מַר' יוֹחָנָן רַבָּךְ. רַב יוֹסֵף הֲוָה גְּמִיר מַעֲשֵׂה הַמֶּרְכָּבָה, סָבֵי דְפוּמְבְּדִיתָא הָווּ תָּנוּ בְּמַעֲשֵׂה בְרֵאשִׁית. אָמְרוּ לֵיהּ: לִיגְמוֹר לָן מָר מַעֲשֵׂה מֶרְכָּבָה! אֲמַר לְהוּ: אַגְמְרוּן לִי מַעֲשֵׂה בְרֵאשִׁית! (ג) בָּתַר דְּאַגְמְרוּן אָמְרוּ לֵיהּ: לִיגְמְרוּן מָר בְּמַעֲשֵׂה מֶרְכָּבָה! אָמַר לְהוּ: תָּנֵינָא בְּהוּ: [שיר ד] °"דְּבַשׁ וְחָלָב תַּחַת לְשׁוֹנֵךְ" – [ב]דְּבָרִים הַמְּתוּקִין מִדְּבַשׁ וְחָלָב יְהוּ תַּחַת לְשׁוֹנֵךְ. ר' אַבָּהוּ אָמַר מֵהָכָא: [משלי כז] °[ג]"כְּבָשִׂים לִלְבוּשֶׁךָ" (ד) – דְּבָרִים שֶׁהֵן כִּבְשׁוֹנוֹ שֶׁל עוֹלָם יִהְיוּ תַּחַת לְבוּשְׁךָ. אָמְרוּ לֵיהּ: תָּנֵינַן בְּהוּ עַד [יחזקאל ב] °"וַיֹּאמֶר אֵלַי בֶּן אָדָם". אֲמַר לְהוּ: הֵן הֵן מַעֲשֵׂה הַמֶּרְכָּבָה. מֵיתִיבֵי: עַד הֵיכָן מַעֲשֵׂה הַמֶּרְכָּבָה? רַבִּי אוֹמֵר: עַד [שם א] °"וָאֵרֶא" (ה) בַּתְרָא, ר' יִצְחָק אוֹמֵר, עַד "הַחַשְׁמַל". עַד "וָאֵרֶא" – מַגְמָרִינַן, מִכָּאן וְאֵילָךְ – מָסְרִינַן רָאשֵׁי פְרָקִים. אִיכָּא דְּאָמְרִי: עַד "וָאֵרֶא" – מָסְרִינַן רָאשֵׁי פְרָקִים, מִכָּאן וְאֵילָךְ, אִם הוּא חָכָם מֵבִין מִדַּעְתּוֹ – אִין, אִי לָא – לָא. וּמִי דָּרְשִׁינַן בְּחַשְׁמַל? וְהָא הַהוּא יָנוּקָא דְּדָרֵשׁ בְּחַשְׁמַל (ו) וּנְפַקָא נוּרָא וַאֲכַלְתֵּיהּ! שָׁאנֵי יָנוּקָא דְּלָאו מְטֵי זִימְנֵיהּ. אָמַר רַב יְהוּדָה: [שבת יג. ע"ש מנחות מה.] בְּרַם, *זָכוּר אוֹתוֹ הָאִישׁ לְטוֹב, וַחֲנַנְיָה בֶּן חִזְקִיָּה שְׁמוֹ, אִלְמָלֵא הוּא נִגְנַז סֵפֶר יְחֶזְקֵאל, שֶׁהָיוּ דְּבָרָיו סוֹתְרִין דִּבְרֵי תוֹרָה. מֶה עָשָׂה? הֶעֱלוּ לוֹ ג' מֵאוֹת גַּרְבֵּי שֶׁמֶן, וְיָשַׁב בַּעֲלִיָּיה וּדְרָשׁוֹ. ת"ר: מַעֲשֶׂה בְּתִינוֹק אֶחָד שֶׁהָיָה קוֹרֵא בְּבֵית רַבּוֹ בְּסֵפֶר יְחֶזְקֵאל, וְהָיָה מֵבִין בְּחַשְׁמַל, וְיָצְאָה אֵשׁ מֵחַשְׁמַל וּשְׂרָפַתּוּ. וּבִקְשׁוּ לִגְנוֹז סֵפֶר יְחֶזְקֵאל. (ז) [ב]אָמַר לָהֶם חֲנַנְיָה בֶּן חִזְקִיָּה: אִם זֶה חָכָם – (ח) הַכֹּל חֲכָמִים הֵן?! מַאי חַשְׁמַל? אָמַר רַב יְהוּדָה:

חַיּוֹת

עין משפט נר מצוה

ז א מיי' פ"ב מהלכות יסודי התורה הל' יב ופ"ד שם הלכה יא:

ח ב ג מיי' פ"ב שם הלכה יב:

מסורת הש"ס

[לעיל ה:] [פסחים נ.] [עירובין נג.] [ושלא את ידו בישראל כמו שנמרוד שלח את ידו באברהם] [עי' מהרש"א בח"א] [נ"ל אבא] [שם איתא אף עלפי החיות מהלך ת"ק שנה וחמש עשרה מנין ישרה ע"ש] [בפסיקתא ועי' בהרא"ש ברכות פ"ה סי' כ"א] [נ"ל ראשון] נ"א אמרינן התם דמצוה ללמדם ונפקא [ועי' שמות רבה פרשה ל במעשה לעקילס ולאדריינוס]

גליון הש"ס

תום' ד"ה ורגלי וכו' שיטת הירושלמי שהוא היה תנא. נ"ל וי"א שהוא היה תנא כן הוא ברא"ש בפ"ה דברכות:

הגהות מהר"ב רנשבורג

א] גמ' ואמר רבי אמי אין מוסרין דברי תורה לגוי. נ"ב עיין שו"ת באר שבע בסופו וחלק באר מים חיים סימן י"ד טעם למה השמיטו הפוסקים זה: ב] שם א"ל חנני' אם זה חכם הכל חכמים הן. נ"ב ר"ל אם זה הקטן חכם כל הקטנים חכמים דלגדולים אין לחוש כדאמרינן לעיל שאני ינוקא דלא מטא זימנא עכ"ל מהרש"א בח"א:

רבינו חננאל

עד כאן יש לך רשות לדבר מיכן ואילך אסור. כתוב בספר בן סירא במופלא ממך אל תדרוש ובמכוסה ממך אל תחקור במה שהרשיתה התבונן אין לך עסק בנסתרות והדברים שנאמר מהלך ת"ק שנה דברי קבלה הן. הלא תראה שהן מועתקין מפי ריב"ז שהיה בימי הבית ולא נשאר לו דבר קטן ולא דבר גדול. אלא הכל קיבל בקבלה מרבו ומפורש בו דבר גדול מעשה מרכבה דבר קטן הוויות דאביי ורבא. ואין הדברים הללו באין משיקול הדעת ואין צריך להסתכל בהן שהמסתכל בהן בא בטירוף דעת שאי אפשר לומר יש שם מקום חלל מופנה ואף לא מלא שהכל מתחתיו הן שכשם שאין כח לומר כי קודם יצירת העולם היה חלל או מקום מלא או ריקם אלא אחר שנברא העולם נבראו שמים וארץ ואין ידוע מה למעלה ומה למטה ולפיכך מנעו רבותינו להסתכל מה למעלה ומה למטה מה לפנים ומה לאחור. ויש בגבורתו של הקב"ה לעשות כמה: ולא במרכבה ביחיד תני ר' חייא מוסרין ליחיד ראשי פרקים פי' פותחין לו ראשי דבריו והוא מבין מדעתו *) וזה לבו גם בו כר' אלעזר דאמר ליה ר' יוחנן רביה תא אגמרך מעשה מרכבה א"ל לא קשאי כלומר איני בן חמשים שנה כד נח נפשיה דרבי יוחנן אמר ליה רבי אסי תא אגמרך מעשה מרכבה א"ל אין מוסרין דברי תורה אלא ליועץ חכם חרשים ונבון לחש ואין מוסרין ד"ת לגוי שנאמר מגיד דבריו ליעקב חקיו ומשפטיו לישראל. אלא הא דתניא עד היכן מעשה מרכבה כו' וקיי"ל כלישנא בתרא עד וארא ועד חשמל מסרינן ראשי פרקין כדאמרן מיכן ואילך לא מסרינן אלא אם היה חכם מבין מדעתו מאי חשמל אמר רב יהודה חיות אש ממללות במתניתא תנא חש מל כלומר ב' מלות

*) אולי צ"ל והוא שלא תהא לבו גם בו:

הגהות הב"ח

(א) גמ' שהמריד את כל העולם: (ב) שם ורגלי החיות וכו' וקרסולי וכו' ושוקי וכו' ורכובי וכו' וירכי וכו' וגופי וכו' וצוארי וכו' וראשי וכו' וקרני וכו' ולמעלה מהן כסא כבוד ורגלי וכו' וכסא הכבוד כנגד כולן ולמעלה מהן מלך: (ג) שם מעשה בראשית אגמרוה בתר דאגמרו' אמרו: (ד) שם כבשים ללבושך אל תקרי כבשים אלא כבושים דברים שהן כבשונו: (ה) שם רבי אומר עד וארא כעין חשמל בתרא: (ו) שם ונפיק נורא מחשמל ואכלתיה שאני ינוקא דלא מטי זימנא דלאו אורח ארעא דדריש אמר רב יהודה אמר רב ברם זכור וכו' שאלמלא וכו' מה עשה עלה לעלייה והעלו לו לשם שלש מאות: (ז) שם אמר להם (חנניה בן חזקיה) תא"מ ונ"ב ס"א רשב"ג: (ח) שם אם זה חכם כולם חכמים: (ט) רש"י ד"ה שוק הוא עלם הנמכר עם הרגל הס"ד: (י) ד"ה הן הן וכו' הם הם שהקפידו: (כ) תום' ד"ה ורגלי וכו' לסימנא שיש בו ט"ו פעמים ת"ק ומיהו בחנם מתקוהו: (ל) בא"ד ראה כמה הוא גבוה למעלה מעולמו וכו' כמנין שיסד ת"ק וט"ו וכן וכו' ופייטן ודרשן ובימיו היו מקדשין. נ"ב בויקרא רבה פרשה ל' כל דמך ר"א בר שמעון היה דורו קורא עליו מי זאת עולה כו' מהו מכל אבקת רוכל אלא דהוה קריי ותניי ופייטן ודרשן ובמדרש חזית בפסוק מי זאת עולה גרס קרובץ: (מ) ד"ה אין מוסרין וכו' וכי תימא הכא בז' מצות וכו' וי"ל. נ"ב בספר עין יעקב הירלא תירוץ אחר וז"ל וי"ל דהיינו קודם שניתנה תורה אבל לאחר שניתנה תורה והתירם להם ילפינן מהאי קרא דאף ז' מצות אסור ללמדם:

חַיּוֹת אֵשׁ מְמַלְּלוֹת. בְּמַתְנִיתָא תָּנָא: *עִתִּים חָשׁוֹת עִתִּים מְמַלְּלוֹת. בְּשָׁעָה שֶׁהַדִּיבּוּר יוֹצֵא מִפִּי הַקב"ה — חָשׁוֹת, וּבְשָׁעָה שֶׁאֵין הַדִּיבּוּר יוֹצֵא מִפִּי הַקב"ה — מְמַלְּלוֹת. °"וְהַחַיּוֹת רָצוֹא וָשׁוֹב כְּמַרְאֵה הַבָּזָק". מַאי רָצוֹא וָשׁוֹב? אָמַר רַב יְהוּדָה: כָּאוּר הַיּוֹצֵא מִפִּי הַכִּבְשָׁן. מַאי "כְּמַרְאֵה הַבָּזָק"? אָמַר רַבִּי יוֹסֵי בַּר חֲנִינָא: כָּאוּר הַיּוֹצֵא מִבֵּין הַחֲרָסִים. °"וָאֵרֶא וְהִנֵּה רוּחַ סְעָרָה בָּאָה מִן הַצָּפוֹן עָנָן גָּדוֹל וְאֵשׁ מִתְלַקַּחַת וְנוֹגַהּ לוֹ סָבִיב וּמִתּוֹכָהּ כְּעֵין הַחַשְׁמַל מִתּוֹךְ הָאֵשׁ". (א) לְהֵיכָן אֲזַל? אָמַר רַב יְהוּדָה אָמַר רַב: שֶׁהָלַךְ לִכְבּוֹשׁ אֶת כָּל הָעוֹלָם כּוּלּוֹ תַּחַת נְבוּכַדְנֶצַּר הָרָשָׁע. וְכָל כָּךְ לָמָּה — שֶׁלֹּא יֹאמְרוּ אוּמּוֹת הָעוֹלָם: בְּיַד אוּמָּה שְׁפָלָה מָסַר הַקָּדוֹשׁ בָּרוּךְ הוּא אֶת בָּנָיו. אָמַר הַקָּדוֹשׁ בָּרוּךְ הוּא: מִי גָּרַם לִי שֶׁאֶהְיֶה שַׁמָּשׁ לְעוֹבְדֵי פְסִילִים — עֲוֹנוֹתֵיהֶן שֶׁל יִשְׂרָאֵל הֵן גָּרְמוּ לִי. °"וָאֵרֶא הַחַיּוֹת וְהִנֵּה אוֹפַן אֶחָד בָּאָרֶץ אֵצֶל הַחַיּוֹת", אָמַר ר' אֶלְעָזָר: מַלְאָךְ אֶחָד שֶׁהוּא עוֹמֵד בָּאָרֶץ, וְרֹאשׁוֹ מַגִּיעַ אֵצֶל הַחַיּוֹת. בְּמַתְנִיתָא תָּנָא: סַנְדַּלְפוֹן שְׁמוֹ, (ב) הַגָּבוֹהַּ מֵחֲבֵרוֹ מַהֲלַךְ חֲמֵשׁ מֵאוֹת שָׁנָה, וְעוֹמֵד אֲחוֹרֵי הַמֶּרְכָּבָה, וְקוֹשֵׁר כְּתָרִים לְקוֹנוֹ. אִינִי? וְהָכְתִיב: °"בָּרוּךְ כְּבוֹד ה' מִמְּקוֹמוֹ" מִכְּלָל דִּמְקוֹמוֹ לֵיכָּא דְּיָדַע לֵיהּ! (ג) דְּאָמַר שֵׁם אַתָּגָא, וְאָזֵל וְיָתֵיב בְּרֵישֵׁיהּ. אָמַר רָבָא: כָּל שֶׁרָאָה יְחֶזְקֵאל רָאָה יְשַׁעְיָה. לְמָה יְחֶזְקֵאל דּוֹמֶה — לְבֶן כְּפָר שֶׁרָאָה אֶת הַמֶּלֶךְ, וּלְמָה יְשַׁעְיָה דּוֹמֶה — לְבֶן כְּרַךְ שֶׁרָאָה אֶת הַמֶּלֶךְ. אָמַר רֵישׁ לָקִישׁ: מַאי דִּכְתִיב: °(ד) "אָשִׁירָה לַה' כִּי גָאֹה גָּאָה" שִׁירָה לְמִי שֶׁמִּתְגָּאֶה עַל הַגֵּאִים. דְּאָמַר מָר: מֶלֶךְ שֶׁבַּחַיּוֹת — אֲרִי, מֶלֶךְ שֶׁבַּבְּהֵמוֹת — שׁוֹר, מֶלֶךְ שֶׁבָּעוֹפוֹת — נֶשֶׁר, וְאָדָם מִתְגָּאֶה עֲלֵיהֶן, וְהַקָּדוֹשׁ בָּרוּךְ הוּא מִתְגָּאֶה עַל כּוּלָּן וְעַל כָּל הָעוֹלָם כּוּלּוֹ. כָּתוּב אֶחָד אוֹמֵר: °"וּדְמוּת פְּנֵיהֶם פְּנֵי אָדָם וּפְנֵי אַרְיֵה אֶל הַיָּמִין לְאַרְבַּעְתָּם וּפְנֵי שׁוֹר מֵהַשְּׂמֹאל לְאַרְבַּעְתָּן וגו'" וּכְתִיב: °"וְאַרְבָּעָה פָנִים לְאֶחָד פְּנֵי הָאֶחָד פְּנֵי הַכְּרוּב וּפְנֵי הַשֵּׁנִי פְּנֵי אָדָם וְהַשְּׁלִישִׁי פְּנֵי אַרְיֵה וְהָרְבִיעִי פְּנֵי נֶשֶׁר" וְאִילּוּ שׁוֹר לָא קָא חָשֵׁיב! (ה) אָמַר ר"ל: יְחֶזְקֵאל בִּיקֵּשׁ עָלָיו רַחֲמִים וַהֲפָכוֹ לִכְרוּב. אָמַר לְפָנָיו: רִבּוֹנוֹ שֶׁל עוֹלָם! *קַטֵּיגוֹר יֵעָשֶׂה סַנֵּיגוֹר?! מַאי כְּרוּב? אָמַר רַבִּי אַבָּהוּ: *כְּרַבְיָא, שֶׁכֵּן בְּבָבֶל קוֹרִין לְיָנוּקָא רַבְיָא. א"ל רַב פַּפָּא לְאַבָּיֵי: אֶלָּא מֵעַתָּה, דִּכְתִיב: "פְּנֵי הָאֶחָד פְּנֵי הַכְּרוּב וּפְנֵי הַשֵּׁנִי פְּנֵי אָדָם וְהַשְּׁלִישִׁי פְּנֵי אַרְיֵה וְהָרְבִיעִי פְּנֵי נֶשֶׁר" — הַיְינוּ פְּנֵי כְרוּב הַיְינוּ פְּנֵי אָדָם! (ו) אַפֵּי רַבְרְבֵי וְאַפֵּי זוּטְרֵי. כָּתוּב אֶחָד אוֹמֵר: °"שֵׁשׁ כְּנָפַיִם שֵׁשׁ כְּנָפַיִם לְאֶחָד" וְכָתוּב אֶחָד אוֹמֵר °"וְאַרְבָּעָה פָנִים לְאַחַת וְאַרְבַּע כְּנָפַיִם לְאַחַת לָהֶם"! לָא קַשְׁיָא: כָּאן — בִּזְמַן שֶׁבהמ"ק קַיָּים, כָּאן — בִּזְמַן שֶׁאֵין בֵּית הַמִּקְדָּשׁ קַיָּים, כִּבְיָכוֹל שֶׁנִּתְמַעֲטוּ כַּנְפֵי הַחַיּוֹת. הֵי מִינַּיְיהוּ אִימְעוּט? אָמַר רַב חֲנַנְאֵל אָמַר רַב: אוֹתָן שֶׁאוֹמְרוֹת שִׁירָה בָּהֶן, (ז) כְּתִיב הָכָא: °"וּבִשְׁתַּיִם יְעוֹפֵף וְקָרָא זֶה אֶל זֶה וְאָמַר" וּכְתִיב: °"הֲתָעִיף עֵינֶיךָ בּוֹ וְאֵינֶנּוּ". וְרַבָּנַן אָמְרִי: אוֹתָן שֶׁמְּכַסּוֹת בָּהֶן רַגְלֵיהֶם, שֶׁנֶּאֱמַר: °"וְרַגְלֵיהֶם רֶגֶל יְשָׁרָה" וְאִי לָאו דְּאִימְעוּט — מְנָא (ח) הֲוָה יָדַע? דִּלְמָא דְּאִיגְּלַאי וַחֲזָא לֵיהּ. דְּאִי לָא תֵּימָא הָכִי — "וּדְמוּת פְּנֵיהֶם פְּנֵי אָדָם" הָכִי נַמִי דְּאִימְעוּט? אֶלָּא — דְּאִיגְּלַאי וַחֲזָא לֵיהּ, הָכָא נַמִי — דְּאִיגְּלַאי וַחֲזָא לֵיהּ. הָכִי הַשְׁתָּא! (ט) בִּשְׁלָמָא אַפֵּיהּ — אוֹרַח אַרְעָא לְגַלּוּיֵי קַמֵּיהּ רַבֵּיהּ, כַּרְעֵיהּ — לָאו אוֹרַח אַרְעָא לְגַלּוּיֵי קַמֵּיהּ רַבֵּיהּ. כָּתוּב אֶחָד אוֹמֵר: °"אֶלֶף אַלְפִין יְשַׁמְּשׁוּנֵּיהּ וְרִבּוֹ רִבְבָן קֳדָמוֹהִי יְקוּמוּן" וְכָתוּב אֶחָד אוֹמֵר: °"הֲיֵשׁ מִסְפָּר לִגְדוּדָיו"! לָא קַשְׁיָא: כָּאן — בִּזְמַן שֶׁבֵּית הַמִּקְדָּשׁ קַיָּים, כָּאן — בִּזְמַן שֶׁאֵין בהמ"ק קַיָּים, *כִּבְיָכוֹל שֶׁנִּתְמַעֲטָה פַּמַּלְיָא שֶׁל מַעְלָה. תַּנְיָא, רַבִּי אוֹמֵר מִשּׁוּם אַבָּא יוֹסֵי בֶּן דּוֹסַאי: "אֶלֶף אַלְפִין יְשַׁמְּשׁוּנֵּיהּ" — מִסְפָּר גְּדוּד אֶחָד, "וְלִגְדוּדָיו אֵין מִסְפָּר". וְר' יִרְמְיָה בַּר אַבָּא אָמַר: "אֶלֶף אַלְפִין יְשַׁמְּשׁוּנֵּיהּ" — לִנְהַר דִּינוּר, שֶׁנֶּאֱמַר: °"נְהַר דִּינוּר נָגֵד וְנָפֵק מִן קֳדָמוֹהִי אֶלֶף אַלְפִין יְשַׁמְּשׁוּנֵּיהּ וְרִבּוֹ רִבְבָן קֳדָמוֹהִי יְקוּמוּן". (י) מֵהֵיכָן נָפֵיק — מִזֵּיעָתָן שֶׁל חַיּוֹת. וּלְהֵיכָן שָׁפֵיךְ? — אָמַר רַב זוּטְרָא בַּר טוֹבִיָּה אָמַר רַב: עַל רֹאשׁ רְשָׁעִים בַּגֵּיהִנָּם, שֶׁנֶּאֱמַר: °"הִנֵּה סַעֲרַת ה' חֵמָה יָצְאָה וְסַעַר מִתְחוֹלֵל עַל רֹאשׁ רְשָׁעִים יָחוּל". וְרַב אַחָא בַּר יַעֲקֹב אָמַר: עַל אֲשֶׁר קוּמְּטוּ, שֶׁנֶּאֱמַר: °"אֲשֶׁר קֻמְּטוּ וְלֹא עֵת נָהָר יוּצַק יְסוֹדָם". תַּנְיָא, אָמַר רַבִּי שִׁמְעוֹן הֶחָסִיד: אֵלּוּ תְּשַׁע מֵאוֹת וְשִׁבְעִים וְאַרְבַּע דּוֹרוֹת שֶׁקּוּמְּטוּ לְהִיבָּרְאוֹת קוֹדֶם

קודם

רש"י

חַיּוֹת אֵשׁ מְמַלְּלוֹת. אֵשׁ יוֹצֵא מִדִּיבּוּרָן: רָצוֹא וָשׁוֹב. מוֹצִיאוֹת רָאשָׁן מִתַּחַת הָרָקִיעַ הַנָּטוּי לְמַעְלָה מֵרָאשֵׁיהֶן, וְחוֹזְרוֹת וּמַכְנִיסוֹת אוֹתָן מִמּוֹרָא הַשְּׁכִינָה בִּמְהִירוּת, כְּרִיצָה וְשִׁיבָה שֶׁל לַהַב הַיּוֹצֵא מִפִּי הַכִּבְשָׁן. שֶׁשּׂוֹרְפִין בּוֹ אֲבָנִים לְסִיד. וּבָזָק לְשׁוֹן שִׁבְרֵי *שְׁבָרִים הוּא, שֶׁהָאוּר יוֹצֵא בֵּין אֶבֶן לְאֶבֶן, כִּדְתְנַן בְּעֵירוּבִין (דף קד.): בּוֹזְקִין מֶלַח עַל גַּבֵּי הַכֶּבֶשׁ שֶׁלֹּא יַחֲלִיקוּ הַכֹּהֲנִים: מִבֵּין הַחֲרָסִים. דֶּרֶךְ מְזַקְּקֵי זָהָב לִנְקוֹב כְּלִי חֶרֶס נְקָבִים נְקָבִים, וְכוֹפִין אוֹתוֹ עַל גַּבֵּי גֶּחָלִים שֶׁהַזָּהָב נָתוּן בָּהֵן בְּתוֹךְ כְּתִישַׁת הַחֲרָסִים שֶׁל לְבֵנִים עַל גַּבֵּי חֶרֶס, וְלַהַב יוֹצֵא לְמַעְלָה דֶּרֶךְ נִקְבֵי הַכְּלִי, וְהוּא עָשׂוּי גְּוָונִים גְּוָונִים וְתָמִיד יוֹצֵא וְנִכְנָס: מִן הַצָּפוֹן. מִבָּבֶל, שֶׁהוּא בַּצָּפוֹן, שֶׁנֶּאֱמַר "מִצָּפוֹן תִּפָּתַח הָרָעָה" (ירמיהו א): מַאי בָּעְיָא הָתָם. לָמָּה הָלְכָה לְבָבֶל: רָאָה יְשַׁעְיָה. כְּשֶׁשָּׁרְתָה עָלָיו רוּחַ הַקֹּדֶשׁ, כְּמָה שֶׁנֶּאֱמַר: "וָאֶרְאֶה אֶת ה' יוֹשֵׁב עַל כִּסֵּא רָם וְנִשָּׂא" וגו' (ישעיה ו), אֶלָּא שֶׁלֹּא חָשׁ לְפָרֵשׁ אֶת הַכֹּל, שֶׁהָיָה בֶּן מְלָכִים וְגָדַל בַּפַּלְטִין, וּבֶן כְּרַךְ הָרוֹאֶה אֶת הַמֶּלֶךְ אֵינוֹ נִבְהָל וְאֵינוֹ תָּמֵהַּ, וְאֵינוֹ חָשׁ לְסַפֵּר מֶלֶךְ שֶׁבַּחַיּוֹת אֲרִי כו'. וְאֵלּוּ אַרְבַּעְתָּן בַּכִּסֵּא, וְהוּא לְמַעְלָה מֵהֶן: קַטֵּיגוֹר נַעֲשֶׂה סַנֵּיגוֹר. אָנוּ צְרִיכִין שֶׁיְּבַקְּשׁוּ מֶרְכְּבוֹתֶיךָ עָלֵינוּ רַחֲמִים, וְהַשּׁוֹר קַטֵּיגוֹר הוּא: קַטֵּיגוֹר. שׂוֹנֵא, סַנֵּיגוֹר — אוֹהֵב, מֵלִיץ יוֹשֶׁר: כְּרַבְיָא. פְּנֵי תִּינוֹק: הַיְינוּ פְּנֵי כְרוּב הַיְינוּ פְּנֵי אָדָם. מַה הֵן פְּנֵי כְרוּב, מַה הֵן פְּנֵי אָדָם? וְכִי לֹא אֶחָד הֵן?! אַפֵּי רַבְרְבֵי וְאַפֵּי זוּטְרֵי. הָאֶחָד פְּנֵי גָּדוֹל וְהָאֶחָד פְּנֵי קָטָן: כָּאן בִּזְמַן שֶׁבֵּית הַמִּקְדָּשׁ קַיָּים. בִּימֵי יְשַׁעְיָה הָיָה הַמִּקְדָּשׁ קַיָּים בִּמְכוֹנוֹ. וּבִימֵי יְחֶזְקֵאל כְּבָר הִגִּיעַ זְמַן שֶׁיֵּחָרֵב, וְנִתְמַעֲטָה פַּמַּלְיָא שֶׁל מַעְלָה: וּבִשְׁתַּיִם יְעוֹפֵף. וּסְמִיךְ לֵיהּ: "וְקָרָא זֶה אֶל זֶה". אַלְמָא הָנָךְ נִינְהוּ דְּאָמְרִי בְּהוּ שִׁירָה שֶׁמְּקַשְׁקְשׁוֹת בְּקוֹל כַּנְפֵיהֶם, וּבְהָנָךְ כְּתִיב "וְאֵינֶנּוּ" גַּבֵּי הַתָּעִיף: [כָּאן בִּזְמַן שֶׁאֵין וכו']. בִּימֵי דָּנִיֵּאל כְּבָר חָרַב הַבַּיִת: כִּבְיָכוֹל. אַף כְּלַפֵּי מַעְלָה שְׁכִינָה הוּזְקַקְנוּ לוֹמַר כָּךְ, כְּמוֹ בְּבָשָׂר וָדָם שֶׁיָּכוֹל לוֹמַר בּוֹ מִיעוּט: אֶלֶף אַלְפִין. הוּא מִסְפָּר שֶׁל כָּל גְּדוּד וּגְדוּד, אֲבָל אֵין מִסְפָּר כַּמָּה גְּדוּדִין יֵשׁ: לִנְהַר דִּינוּר. דְּהַאי קְרָא נַמִי גַּבֵּי נְהַר דִּינוּר כְּתִיב: עַל אֲשֶׁר קוּמְּטוּ. עַל תתקע"ד דּוֹרוֹת שֶׁהֶעֱבִיר מִן הָעוֹלָם קוֹדֶם מַתַּן תּוֹרָה וְלֹא בְּרָאָן, כִּדְקָתָנֵי לְקַמָּן, וּנְתָנָן בַּגֵּיהִנָּם, וַעֲלֵיהֶם נוֹפֵל, שֶׁנֶּאֱמַר בָּהֶן: "וְנָהָר יוּצַק יְסוֹדָם", וְהַיְינוּ נְהַר דִּינוּר, שֶׁמּוּצָק עֲלֵיהֶם: קוּמְּטוּ לְהִיבָּרְאוֹת. נִגְזְרוּ לְהִיבָּרְאוֹת, לְשׁוֹן "וַתִּקְמְטֵנִי לְעֵד הָיָה"*: קודם

תוספות

והחיות רצוא ושוב. פר"ח: לפי שהן מגהלים עוממות, ודרכן לדמות לשאר שרפים ולהוליא להבה, והנילוץ חוזר, והיינו רלוא ושוב: **שלא** יאמרו ביד אומה שפלה מסר את בניו. והיינו כפי' דההיא דאמר בגיטין (דף נו:): כל המילר לישראל נעשה ראש. כלומר: כבר נעשה ראש קודם שמילר להם:

וקושר כתרים לקונו. מתפלתן של לדיקים הוא עושה עטרות: **לבן** כפר שראה(כ) המלך. שלריך לו להביא סימנים לאחרים קודם שיאמינוהו, לפי שראהו שלא במקומו, ואין דרכו להתראות שם. וה"נ אמר יחזקאל שראהו על נהר כבר – לפיכך נתמהו שומעיו:

כתוב אחד אומר שש כנפים וכתוב אחד אומר ארבע כנפים. ואע"ג שזה בחיות כתיב וזה בשרפים – מ"מ מסתבר שגם החיות (ל)°בשש כנפים כמו השרפים*:

מזיעתן של חיות. ויולאים ממנו מלאכים, ואומרים שירה, ומיד נטרדים(מ). והכי מלינו במדרש (איכה ג): "חדשים לבקרים" – שבורא מלאכים בכל יום, ואומרים שירה, ונטרדין להן. כדאמר בסמוך, משום שיש אות במלאכים הקבועים *שממתינים זה לזה לומר שירה, ואלו החדשים שאינם יודעים הדת ממהרין לשורר, ונתחייבו כליה. והיינו אשר תקנו ויסדו אנשי כנסת הגדולה ביולר: "ונותנין רשות זה לזה קדושה כולם כאחד עונין ואומרים". וגם למעלה: "יולר משרתים ואשר משרתיו כולם עומדים ברום עולם" כלומר, בכל יום בורא חדשים ונטרדין, אבל משרתיו קבועים ועומדין לעד:

וטרדן

רבינו חננאל

הן עתים חשות עתים ממללות שיר בעוז שנאמר עוז וחדוה במקומו ועתים חשות כשהדבור יוצא מלפני הקב"ה והחיות רצוא ושוב כמראה הבזק. אינה הליכה וחזירה ממש אלא נראות הולכות וחוזרות כמראה הבזק כדכתיב מראיהן כלפידים כברקים ירוצצו כענין האש בעת שמתגברת השלהבת בכבשן נראת כיוצא וחוזרת בפי הכבשן. א"ר יוסי בר' חנינא כאור היוצא מבין החרסין. פי' כשסותמין פי הכבשן בחרסין ויש ביניהם נקבים לשון האש יוצא משם וזהו מראה הבזק. וארא והנה רוח סערה באה מן הצפון וגו' להיכא אזלא אמר רב לכבש העולם תחת נבוכד נצר כו' וארא החיות והנה אופן אחד בארץ. ותני במתניתא סנדלפון שמו וקושר כתרים לקונו. כבר פירשוהו בפירוש משביעו ואזיל ויתיב במקום שחלק לו הקב"ה להושיבו שם וחלילה שיש שם פרחת כל עיקר וראש וגוף כדרך הברואים אלא לקבל מלכותו כדרך שמזכירין בכל יום ישראל בתפלתם כתר יתנו לך המוני כו'. אמר רבה כל שראה יחזקאל ראה כמותו ישעיה. למה יחזקאל תמה מן המראה כי יחזקאל דומה לבן כפר שראה טכסיסי המלך וראה מרכבות וחיילות והתחיל תמה. אבל ישעיה לבן מדינה שראה הטכסיסין הללו בכל יום לפיכך אינו תמה מהן. אשירה לה' כי גאה גאה שירו למי שמתגאה על הגאים כלומר מלך ע"ג המלכים שד' מלכים בעולם אדם בבני אדם אריה בחיות שור בבהמות נשר בעופות והקב"ה ישתבח שמו וכבודו למעלה מכולם. וארבעה פנים לאחד. פני האחד פני הכרוב וגו' הא *) תרגמא דשיתת עשר אנפין לכל ברייתא חדא. שיתין וארבעה אפין לארבעה ברייתא [וארבעה] גפין לכל אנפין שיתין וארבע גפין לברייתא חדא רנ"ו גפין לארבע בריתא. וקיי"ל דכרוב פניו פני אדם ויש לו כנפים כשאר עופות. פני אדם הם גדולים ופני כרוב הם פחותים וכר' אבהו דאמר בבבל קורין לינוקא רביא פי' כגון רבה קשת. וזה שפירש יחזקאל במראה ראשונה שראה המרכבה פני שור מהשמאל לארבעתן ובמראה השניה אמר פני הכרוב לארבעתן ולא הזכיר פני שור כלל. א"ר שמעון בן לקיש יחזקאל בקש רחמים ונהפכו פני השור לפני כרוב ומקשינן וכי בקש יחזקאל להיות שני פני אדם ופרקינן פני אדם פנים גדולים ופני כרוב פנים פחותים ומקשינן ישעיה ראה שש כנפים לאחד ויחזקאל ראה

*) עי' בח"י וכרש"י שם.

גליון הש"ס

תוס' ד"ה כתוב אחד אומר וכו'. בשש כנפים. עי' חולין צב ע"א תד"ה כרוב:

הגהות הב"ח

(א) גמ' החשמל מתוך האש (להיכן אזל) תא"מ ונ"ב מפרש"י נראה שגורס מאי בעיא התם: (ב) שם שמו וגבוה מחבירו מהלך: (ג) שם ליכא דידע ליה (דאמר שם וכו' ברישיה) תא"מ ונ"ב ס"א אלא דקשר ליה לכתר ומשביע בשם המפורש ואזל תגא ויתיב ברישיה: (ד) שם מאי דכתיב שירו לה' כי גאה גאה שירו למי: (ה) שם לא קחשיב ליה אמר ר"ל וכו' רבש"ע אין קטיגור נעשה סניגור: (ו) שם היינו פני אדם והכרוב פני כרוב הוא אפי רברבי: (ז) שם דכתיב הכא ובשתים וכו' וכתיב התם התעיף: (ח) שם מנא הוה ידע [illegible]: (ט) שם [illegible]: (י) שם [illegible]: (כ) תוס' ד"ה לבן כפר שראה [illegible] המלך בכפר שצריך לו וכו' להתראות שם נ"ב צריך הוא לומר ראיתי פ' ופ' השרים עמו ופ' ופ' משרתיו כדי שיאמינו לו וה"נ יחזקאל שראהו על נהר כבר לפיכך נתמהו שומעיו הוצרך לפרש כן סדר המרכבה אבל ישעיהו ראהו יושב על כסא רם ונשא ולא הוצרך לפרש והס"ד: (ל) ד"ה כתוב וכו' שגם החיות יש להם שש כנפים: (מ) ד"ה מזיעתן וכו' ומיד נטרדין כדאמרינן בסמוך [illegible] ונטרדין להן ומשום שיש וכו' לומר שירה כאחד כדכתיב וקרא זה אל זה ואמר גו' ואלו החדשים וכו' עונים ואומרים אבל אלו חדשים שנבראים בכל יום אין אומרים קדושה כסדר אלא נטרדין מיד ועליהם תקנו יוצר משרתים:

ס"א חרסים
[פי' תוס' חולין קח. ד"ה ערוך]
[עי' תוס' חולין צב. ד"ה כרוב]
עי' אבות דרבי נתן פי"ב ד"ה ומניין שיראים זה את זה
[קידושין ה: וש"נ]
סוכה ה:
(איוב כב)
[עי' ברש"י יומא ג:]

קודם שנברא העולם ולא נבראו, עמד הקב"ה ושתלן בכל דור ודור, והן הן עזי פנים שבדור. ורב נחמן בר יצחק אמר: "אשר קומטו" — לברכה הוא דכתיב, אלו תלמידי חכמים שמקמטין (א) עצמן על דברי תורה בעולם הזה, הקב"ה מגלה להם סוד לעולם הבא, שנאמר: "נהר יוצק יסודם". אמר ליה שמואל *לחייא בר רב: בר אריא! תא, אימא לך מילתא מהני מילי מעליותא דהוה אמר אבוך: כל יומא ויומא נבראין מלאכי השרת מנהר דינור, ואמרי שירה ובטלי, שנאמר: "חדשים לבקרים רבה אמונתך". ופליגא דר' שמואל בר נחמני, דאמר ר' שמואל בר נחמני אמר ר' יונתן: כל דיבור ודיבור שיוצא מפי הקב"ה נברא ממנו מלאך אחד, שנאמר: "בדבר ה' שמים נעשו וברוח פיו כל צבאם". כתוב אחד אומר: "לבושיה כתלג חיור ושער (*רישיה) כעמר נקא" וכתיב: "קווצותיו תלתלים שחורות כעורב"! לא קשיא: כאן בישיבה, כאן — במלחמה. דאמר מר: אין לך נאה בישיבה אלא זקן, ואין לך נאה במלחמה אלא בחור. כתוב אחד אומר: "כרסיה שביבין דינור" וכתוב אחד אומר: "עד די כרסון רמיו ועתיק יומין יתיב"! לא קשיא: אחד לו ואחד לדוד. כדתניא: *אחד לו ואחד לדוד, דברי ר' עקיבא. אמר לו ר' יוסי הגלילי: עקיבא! עד מתי אתה עושה שכינה חול! אלא: אחד לדין ואחד לצדקה. קיבלה מיניה או לא קיבלה מיניה? תא שמע: אחד לדין ואחד לצדקה, דברי רבי עקיבא. אמר לו ר"א בן עזריה: *עקיבא! מה לך אצל הגדה? כלך *מדברותיך (ב) אצל נגעים ואהלות. אלא: אחד לכסא ואחד לשרפרף, כסא — לישב עליו, שרפרף — להדום רגליו, שנאמר "השמים כסאי והארץ הדום רגלי". כי אתא רב דימי אמר: שמונה עשרה קללות קילל ישעיה את ישראל, ולא נתקררה דעתו עד שאמר להם המקרא הזה: "ירהבו הנער בזקן והנקלה בנכבד". שמונה עשרה קללות מאי נינהו — דכתיב: "כי הנה האדון ה' צבאות מסיר מירושלים ומיהודה משען ומשענה כל משען לחם וכל משען מים. גבור ואיש מלחמה שופט ונביא וקוסם וזקן. שר חמשים ונשוא פנים ויועץ וחכם חרשים ונבון לחש. ונתתי נערים שריהם ותעלולים ימשלו בם"[א] וגו'. "משען" — אלו בעלי מקרא, "משענה" — אלו בעלי משנה, כגון ר"י בן תימא וחביריו. פליגו בה רב פפא ורבנן, חד אמר: שש מאות סדרי משנה, וחד אמר: שבע מאות סדרי משנה. "כל משען לחם" — אלו בעלי תלמוד, שנאמר: "לכו לחמו בלחמי ושתו ביין מסכתי", "וכל משען מים" — אלו בעלי אגדה, *שמושכין לבו של אדם כמים באגדה. (ג) "גבור" — זה בעל שמועות, "ואיש מלחמה" — זה שיודע לישא וליתן במלחמתה של תורה. "שופט" — זה דיין שדן דין אמת לאמיתו, "נביא" — כמשמעו, "קוסם" — זה מלך, שנאמר: "קסם על שפתי מלך"(ד), "זקן" — זה שראוי לישיבה, "שר חמשים" — אל תקרי "שר חמשים" אלא שר חומשין, זה שיודע לישא וליתן בחמשה חומשי תורה. דבר אחר: "שר חמשים" — כדרבי אבהו. דאמר רבי אבהו: מכאן שאין מעמידין מתורגמן על הצבור פחות מחמשים שנה. "ונשוא פנים" — זה שנושאין פנים לדורו בעבורו, למעלה — כגון רבי חנינא בן דוסא, למטה — כגון רבי אבהו בי קיסר. "יועץ" — *שיודע לעבר שנים ולקבוע חדשים, "וחכם" — זה תלמיד המחכים את רבותיו, "חרשים" — *בשעה שפותח בדברי תורה הכל נעשין כחרשין, "ונבון" — זה המבין דבר מתוך דבר, "לחש" — זה שראוי למסור לו דברי תורה שניתנה *)בלחש. "ונתתי נערים שריהם", מאי "ונתתי נערים שריהם"? א"ר אלעזר: אלו בני אדם שמנוערין מן המצות. "ותעלולים ימשלו בם" אמר רב א) (פפא) בר יעקב: (ה) תעלי בני תעלי. ולא נתקררה דעתו עד שאמר להם "ירהבו הנער בזקן ב) (והנקלה בנכבד)" — אלו בני אדם שמנוערין מן המצות, ירהבו במי שממולא במצות כרמון, "והנקלה בנכבד" — יבא מי שחמורות דומות עליו כקלות וירהבו במי שקלות דומות עליו כחמורות. אמר רב קטינא: *אפי' בשעת כשלונה של ירושלים לא פסקו מהם בעלי אמנה, שנא': "כי יתפש איש באחיו בית אביו (לאמר) שמלה לך קצין תהיה לנו" דברים שבני אדם מתכסין (ו) כשמלה ישנן תחת ידך, "והמכשלה הזאת" ג) מאי "והמכשלה הזאת"? דברים שאין בני אדם עומדין עליהן אא"כ נכשל בהן, ישנן תחת ידך, "ישא ביום ההוא לאמר לא אהיה חובש ובביתי אין לחם ואין שמלה לא תשימוני קצין עם". "ישא", אין ישא אלא לשון שבועה, שנאמר: "לא תשא את שם ה' אלהיך" (ז), "לא אהיה חובש", לא הייתי מחובשי בית המדרש, "ובביתי אין לחם ואין שמלה" — שאין בידי לא מקרא ולא משנה ולא גמרא. ודלמא שאני התם, דאי אמר להו גמירנא — אמרי ליה: אימא לן! הוה ליה למימר גמר ושכח, מאי "לא אהיה חובש" — לא אהיה חובש כלל. איני?! והאמר רבא: *לא חרבה ירושלים עד שפסקו ממנה בעלי אמנה, שנאמר: "שוטטו בחוצות ירושלים וראו נא ודעו ובקשו ברחובותיה אם תמצאו איש אם יש עושה משפט מבקש אמונה ואסלח לה"! לא קשיא: הא

א) [נ"ל אחא וכ"ה בילקוט ובע"י] ב) [מיותר וכ"ה בילקוט] ג) [שבת קיט: גיטין מג.]

קודם שנברא העולם. נגזר עליהם להכרתות להיות קודם מתן תורה, לקיים מה שנאמר: "דבר צוה לאלף דור" (תהלים קה), דראויה היתה תורה להינתן לסוף אלף דור, וכשראה שאין העולם מתקיים בלא תורה – עמד וטרדן, ונתנה לסוף כ"ו דורות מאדם הראשון עד משה רבינו: רבה אמונתך. רבה תהלתך עליהן: (ח) כרסיה. משמע כסא אחד: כרסון רמיו. שני כסאות הוטלו, נתקנו לישב עליהן: שכינה חול. להושיב אדם בצידו: כלך מדברותיך. חדל מדבריך, עד שתגיע אצל נגעים ואהלות, שהן הלכות עמוקות: קילל ישעיה את ישראל. כלומר: נתנבא עליהן י"ח פורעניות: ירהבו. יתגאו: שש מאות סדרי משנה. היו בימיהן: לחם אלו בעלי התלמוד. שיש לסמוך על הוראתן כסמיכת לחם: בעל שמועות. ששמע הלכות פסוקות מרבותיו, ושגורות בפיו: ראוי לישב בישיבה. וליטול ממנו עצה בכל דבר חכמה: כדרבי אבהו. להעמיד לפניו מתורגמן לדרוש ברבים: למעלה נושאין פנים בעבורו לדורו. שהכל ניזונין בזכותו, כגון רבי חנינא בן דוסא, כדאמרינן בעלמא (*תענית דף כד:): כל העולם אינו ניזון אלא בשביל חנינא בני: למטה. מלכי האומות מכבדין אותן בשבילו, כגון ר' אבהו שהיה חשוב בבית המלך, כדאמרינן במסכת סנהדרין (דף יד.*) דהוו נפקי אמהתא דבי קיסר לאפיה כו': שראוי למסור לו כו'. כגון אב"ד ולבו דואג בקרבו: תעלי. שועלים: כי יתפש איש באחיו. הכתוב היה מגנן לומר שלא היו יודעין להשיב לשואלים הלכה: שבני אדם מתכסין בהן. נחבאין שלא ישאלו להן, לפי שאין בקיאין בהן: ישנן תחת ידך. כלומר: אתה בקי בהן: אא"כ נכשל בהם. כשהתלמיד נכשל בשמועתו פעם ראשונה ושניה, הוא נותן לב לעמוד על שמועתו: לא אהיה. איני רגיל להיות: דלמא. האי נמי לאו משום דאנשי אמנה היו, אלא דאי הוה אמר גמירנא, הוו אמרי ליה אימא לן, והוא לא הוה ידע: תקופת

וטרדן. ואיכא למ"ד: ושתלן. פרש"י: לפי לשון ראשון נתן נשמתן בגיהנם, ולא נבראו. ותימה הוא: וכי עביד דינא בלא דינא, כי מה פשעו להיות בגיהנם? ונראה לפרש: וטרדן — שלא נבראו ביחד, כי אם מעט לכל דור ודר, כדי שלא יחריבו העולם. ושני הלשונות בירושלמי שוה, אך הלשון משונה ולכך לא חש למתני "איכא דאמרי לה בהאי לישנא", (ט) כיון שאינו משנה לה רק חדא תיבה: ופליג אר' שמואל בר נחמני. שהוא אומר שמלאכים נבראים בדבור המקום, ולא מנהר דינור: רבי חנינא בן דוסא למעלה. שהיה בעל מעשים יותר מכל בני דורו: ולמטה (י) בבית קיסר. ולאו משום שלא היה חשוב למעלה, אלא משום שגם בדורו היו אנשי מעשה כמותו: נענה

ארבע כנפים ופרקי' ישעיה שראה בזמן שהיה בהמ"ק קיים ראה שש כנפים אבל יחזקאל שראה אחר חרבן ארבע כנפים כביכול שנראה ליחזקאל כאלו נתמעטו מכנפי החיות שתים שתים ואמרינן הי מינייהו אימעוט אמר רב חננאל אמר רב אותן שנאמר בהם ובשתים יעופף וקרא כלומר שמשוררות בהן כדכתיב התעיף עיניך בו ואיננו ורב פי' שאין כתוב בזה הענין בס' שלנו ורבנן באו לגלות דבר זה מדרך אחרת כי ישעיה ראה רגלים מכוסין ויחזקאל ראה רגלים מגולות עד שידע כי הן רגל ישרה ואמר אותן שהיו מכוסין רגליהן בהן הן שנתמעטו ודחינן ודלמא דגלו ואחזו ליה דאי לא תימא הכי אפייהו היכי חזא להו אלא דגלו ואחזו ליה רגליהן נמי דגלו ואחזו ליה ודחינן בשלמא אפיה אורח ארעא לגלויי קמיה רביה אלא כרעא מי אורח ארעא לגלויי קמיה רביה. *) ותוב פרכינן ודלמא במסנא אחוון ליה **) והאי דקאמר ורגליהם רגל ישרה לא אתחזי במסנא מקום גבוה ונמוך ברגל אדם ואף אין בראשה אלכסון כראשי אצבעות רגלי אדם. וכי הכי מתחזי במסנא. ועוד סייענין לרבנן דאמרי כנפים שהיו מכסות בה רגליהן אימעטו וראן מגולות דאי ס"ד מיכסיין הוו רגליהון ואפיהון בשלמא גליין אפיהון כי היכי דלחזינהו יחזקאל דאיכא תמן פני שור וליבעי עלייהו רחמי כריש לקיש אלא רגליהון למה להון לגלינהו אלא אימעיטו גפייהו ואתגליין רגליהון ופרכינן לעולם מיכסיין הוו ולא איגליין אלא לאחוויי יחזקאל דקיימי רגל ישרה לכדריב"ח (ברכות י) ללמד שחייב אדם לכוון את רגליו בתפלתו שנאמר ורגליהן רגל ישרה. נהר דינור נגד ונפק מזיעת החיות ושפיך על ראש רשעים בגיהנם. אשר קומטו בלא עת אלו הרשעים שקומטו קודם שנברא העולם ושתלן הקב"ה בכל דור ודור. והן הן עזי פנים. רב נחמן בר יצחק אמר ברכה היא. אלו ת"ח שמקמטין עצמם משינה בעוה"ז על דברי תורה הקב"ה מגלה להן סוד לעוה"ב. כתוב אחד אומר ושער רישיה כעמר נקי וכתוב אחר אומר קווצותיו תלתלים שחורות כעורב. ל"ק כאן בישיבה פי' במושב הדין כזקן. שאין נאה בישיבה אלא זקן. וכן במלחמה אין נאה אלא בחור פי' יש מי שאומר מראות הללו כדרך חלום נראים כדכתיב אם יהיה נביאכם ה' במראה אליו אתודע בחלום אדבר בו וכתוב ביד הנביאים אדמה. להודיע שמראה לנביאים כעין דמות באובנתא דליבא. אבל הקב"ה ישתבח שמו אין לו דמות. וזה הדבר מוכיח שאין שם דמות שאילו היה תמיד אחד או דמות בחור לעולם או דמות זקן לעולם אלא ללמדך שאין שם דמות כלל. אלא מה שמראה לנביאים כעין דמות מה שיישר לפניו. ויש מי שאמר מלאך הוא זה שנאמר בו ושער רישיה ושחורות כעורב: עד כרסוון רמיו פשטה אחד לכסא ואחד לשרפרף. י"ח קללות קילל ישעיה את ישראל ולא נתקררה דעתו עד שאמר להן ירהבו הנער בזקן והנקלה בנכבד. וחשבון י"ח קללות הא דכתיב כי הנה האדון ה' צבאות מסיר מירושלם ומיהודה משען ומשענה וגו' אלו ת"ר סדרי משנה: לא אהיה חובש כלומר לא הייתי מחובשי ביהמ"ד. ובביתי אין לחם ואין שמלה. אין בידי לא מקרא ולא משנה ולא תלמוד. איני והא אמר רבה לא חרבה ירושלים עד שפסקו ממנה ראשי אמנה שנאמר אם יש איש עושה משפט מבקש אמנה. ומפרקינן

*) מדברי רבינו אלו נראה שנחסר לפניו איזה קושיות ופירוקי בסוגיין ולפני רבינו היה בשלימות. **) אולי צ"ל והיינו דקאמר ורגליהם רגל ישרה דלא אתחזי במסנא.

הגהות הב"ח

(א) גמ' שמקמטין את עצמן משינה על דברי תורה כו' מגלה להם סוד הנהר לעולם הבא: (ב) שם כלך מדברותיך ולך אצל נגעים: (ג) שם גבור זה בעל שמועות. נ"ב ס"א ד"א זה המתגבר ביצרו: (ד) שם קסם על שפתי מלך במשפט לא ימעל פיו זקן זה: (ה) שם אמר רב פפא בר יעקב אלו תעלי וכו' והנקלה בנכבד יבואו בני אדם וכו' במצות כרמון מאי והנקלה: (ו) שם מתכסין בהם כשמלה: (ז) שם ה' אלהיך מאי לא אהיה חובש לא אהיה מחובשי בית המדרש: (ח) רש"י ד"ה כורסיה: (ט) תוס' ד"ה וטרדן וכו' בהאי לישנא ואיכא דאמרי לה בהאי לישנא כיון שאינו משנה רק חדא כצ"ל: (י) ד"ה ולמטה כגון רבי אבהו בבית קיסר:

הגהות הגר"א

[א] גמ' ותעלולים ימשלו בם. נ"ב ונגש העם איש באיש ואיש ברעהו (והוא הי"ח כי וחכם חרשים נחשב לאחד וכן ונבון לחש ומ"ש המהרש"א נ"ל דהוא לענין דרשה ולא לענין מנינא דא"כ י"ט הוויין אף זולת קרא ונגש כו'):

תורה אור

הא — בְּדִבְרֵי תוֹרָה, הָא — בְּמַשָּׂא וּמַתָּן. בְּדִבְרֵי תוֹרָה — הָווּ, בְּמַשָּׂא וּמַתָּן — לָא הָווּ. ת"ר: *מַעֲשֶׂה בְּרַבָּן יוֹחָנָן בֶּן זַכַּאי שֶׁהָיָה רוֹכֵב עַל הַחֲמוֹר, (א) וְהָיָה מְהַלֵּךְ בַּדֶּרֶךְ, וְר' אֶלְעָזָר בֶּן עֲרָךְ מְחַמֵּר אַחֲרָיו. אָמַר לוֹ: רַבִּי! שְׁנֵה לִי פֶּרֶק אֶחָד בְּמַעֲשֵׂה מֶרְכָּבָה! אָמַר לוֹ: לֹא כָּךְ שָׁנִיתִי לָכֶם: וְלֹא בַּמֶּרְכָּבָה בְּיָחִיד אֶלָּא א"כ הָיָה חָכָם מֵבִין מִדַּעְתּוֹ? אָמַר לוֹ: רַבִּי, תַּרְשֵׁינִי לוֹמַר לְפָנֶיךָ דָּבָר אֶחָד שֶׁלִּמַּדְתַּנִי. אָמַר לוֹ: אֱמוֹר. מִיָּד יָרַד רַבָּן יוֹחָנָן בֶּן זַכַּאי מֵעַל הַחֲמוֹר, וְנִתְעַטֵּף וְיָשַׁב עַל הָאֶבֶן תַּחַת הַזַּיִת. אָמַר לוֹ: רַבִּי, מִפְּנֵי מָה יָרַדְתָּ מֵעַל הַחֲמוֹר? אָמַר: אֶפְשָׁר אַתָּה דּוֹרֵשׁ בְּמַעֲשֵׂה מֶרְכָּבָה, וּשְׁכִינָה עִמָּנוּ, וּמַלְאֲכֵי הַשָּׁרֵת מְלַוִּין אוֹתָנוּ, וַאֲנִי אֶרְכַּב עַל הַחֲמוֹר?! מִיָּד פָּתַח ר"א בֶּן עֲרָךְ בְּמַעֲשֵׂה הַמֶּרְכָּבָה וְדָרַשׁ, וְיָרְדָה אֵשׁ מִן הַשָּׁמַיִם *וְסִיבְּבָה כָּל הָאִילָנוֹת שֶׁבַּשָּׂדֶה, פָּתְחוּ (ב) כּוּלָּן וְאָמְרוּ שִׁירָה. מַה שִּׁירָה אָמְרוּ — °"הַלְלוּ אֶת ה' מִן הָאָרֶץ תַּנִּינִים וְכָל תְּהוֹמוֹת" "עֵץ פְּרִי וְכָל אֲרָזִים הַלְלוּיָהּ". נַעֲנָה מַלְאָךְ מִן הָאֵשׁ וְאָמַר: הֵן הֵן מַעֲשֵׂה הַמֶּרְכָּבָה. עָמַד רַבָּן יוֹחָנָן ב"ז, וּנְשָׁקוֹ עַל רֹאשׁוֹ, וְאָמַר: בָּרוּךְ ה' אֱלֹהֵי יִשְׂרָאֵל שֶׁנָּתַן בֵּן לְאַבְרָהָם אָבִינוּ שֶׁיּוֹדֵעַ לְהָבִין וְלַחְקוֹר וְלִדְרוֹשׁ בְּמַעֲשֵׂה מֶרְכָּבָה. (ג) *יֵשׁ נָאֶה דּוֹרֵשׁ וְאֵין נָאֶה מְקַיֵּים, נָאֶה מְקַיֵּים וְאֵין נָאֶה דּוֹרֵשׁ, אַתָּה נָאֶה דּוֹרֵשׁ וְנָאֶה מְקַיֵּים. אַשְׁרֶיךָ אַבְרָהָם אָבִינוּ שֶׁאֶלְעָזָר בֶּן עֲרָךְ יָצָא מֵחֲלָצֶיךָ. וּכְשֶׁנֶּאֶמְרוּ הַדְּבָרִים לִפְנֵי ר' יְהוֹשֻׁעַ הָיָה הוּא וְרַבִּי יוֹסֵי הַכֹּהֵן מְהַלְּכִים בַּדֶּרֶךְ, אָמְרוּ: אַף אָנוּ נִדְרוֹשׁ בְּמַעֲשֵׂה מֶרְכָּבָה. פָּתַח רַבִּי יְהוֹשֻׁעַ וְדָרַשׁ(ד). וְאוֹתוֹ הַיּוֹם תְּקוּפַת תַּמּוּז הָיָה, נִתְקַשְּׁרוּ שָׁמַיִם בְּעָבִים וְנִרְאָה כְּמִין קֶשֶׁת בֶּעָנָן, וְהָיוּ מַלְאֲכֵי הַשָּׁרֵת מִתְקַבְּצִין וּבָאִין לִשְׁמוֹעַ, כִּבְנֵי אָדָם שֶׁמִּתְקַבְּצִין וּבָאִין לִרְאוֹת בְּמִזְמוּטֵי חָתָן וְכַלָּה. הָלַךְ רַבִּי יוֹסֵי הַכֹּהֵן וְסִיפֵּר דְּבָרִים לִפְנֵי רַבָּן יוֹחָנָן בֶּן זַכַּאי, וְאָמַר: אַשְׁרֵיכֶם וְאַשְׁרֵי יוֹלַדְתְּכֶם, אַשְׁרֵי עֵינַי שֶׁכָּךְ רָאוּ. וְאַף אֲנִי וְאַתֶּם בַּחֲלוֹמִי מְסוּבִּין הָיִינוּ עַל הַר סִינַי, וְנִתְּנָה עָלֵינוּ בַּת קוֹל מִן הַשָּׁמַיִם: (ה) עֲלוּ לְכָאן, עֲלוּ לְכָאן! טְרַקְלִין גְּדוֹלִים וּמַצָּעוֹת נָאוֹת מוּצָּעוֹת לָכֶם, אַתֶּם וְתַלְמִידֵיכֶם וְתַלְמִידֵי תַלְמִידֵיכֶם מְזוּמָּנִין לְכַת שְׁלִישִׁית. אִינִי? וְהָתַנְיָא, *ר' יוֹסֵי בְּר' יְהוּדָה אוֹמֵר: שְׁלֹשָׁה הַרְצָאוֹת הֵן: ר' יְהוֹשֻׁעַ הִרְצָה דְּבָרִים לִפְנֵי רַבָּן יוֹחָנָן בֶּן זַכַּאי, רַבִּי עֲקִיבָא הִרְצָה לִפְנֵי ר' יְהוֹשֻׁעַ, חֲנַנְיָא בֶּן חֲכִינַאי הִרְצָה לִפְנֵי רַבִּי עֲקִיבָא. וְאִילּוּ ר"א בֶּן עֲרָךְ לָא קָא חָשֵׁיב? דְּאַרְצִי וְאַרְצוּ קַמֵּיהּ — קָחָשֵׁיב, דְּאַרְצִי וְלָא אַרְצוּ קַמֵּיהּ — לָא קָא חָשֵׁיב. (ו) וְהָא חֲנַנְיָא בֶּן חֲכִינַאי דְּלָא אַרְצוּ קַמֵּיהּ וְקָא חָשֵׁיב! דְּאַרְצִי מִיהָא קַמֵּיהּ מַאן דְּאַרְצִי. ת"ר: אַרְבָּעָה נִכְנְסוּ בַּפַּרְדֵּס, וְאֵלּוּ הֵן: בֶּן עַזַּאי, וּבֶן זוֹמָא, אַחֵר, וְרַבִּי עֲקִיבָא. אָמַר לָהֶם רַבִּי עֲקִיבָא: כְּשֶׁאַתֶּם מַגִּיעִין אֵצֶל אַבְנֵי שַׁיִשׁ טָהוֹר (ז) אַל תֹּאמְרוּ "מַיִם מַיִם"! מִשּׁוּם שֶׁנֶּאֱמַר: °"דּוֹבֵר שְׁקָרִים לֹא יִכּוֹן לְנֶגֶד עֵינָי". בֶּן עַזַּאי הֵצִיץ וָמֵת, עָלָיו הַכָּתוּב אוֹמֵר: °"יָקָר בְּעֵינֵי ה' הַמָּוְתָה לַחֲסִידָיו". בֶּן זוֹמָא הֵצִיץ וְנִפְגַּע, וְעָלָיו הַכָּתוּב אוֹמֵר: °"דְּבַשׁ מָצָאתָ אֱכוֹל דַּיֶּךָּ פֶּן תִּשְׂבָּעֶנּוּ וַהֲקֵאתוֹ". *אַחֵר קִיצֵּץ בַּנְּטִיעוֹת. רַבִּי עֲקִיבָא יָצָא בְּשָׁלוֹם. שָׁאֲלוּ אֶת בֶּן זוֹמָא: מַהוּ לְסָרוּסֵי כַּלְבָּא? אָמַר לָהֶם: °"וּבְאַרְצְכֶם לֹא תַעֲשׂוּ" — *אכָּל שֶׁבְּאַרְצְכֶם *לֹא תַעֲשׂוּ. שָׁאֲלוּ אֶת בֶּן זוֹמָא: בְּתוּלָה שֶׁעִיבְּרָה מַהוּ לְכ"ג? מִי חָיְישִׁינַן לְדִשְׁמוּאֵל, *)דְּאָמַר שְׁמוּאֵל: יָכוֹל

*) נדה סד:

רש"י

תקופת תמוז הוה. דאין דרך להתקשר שמים בעבים: במזומוטי חתן. מיני שחוק שמשחקין לפניהן: סיפר. דברים הללו: לכת שלישית. של כיתות היושבות לפני השכינה: הרצה דברים. דרש במעשה המרכבה: דארצי וארצו קמיה. שהרצה לפני אחרים ואחרים הרצו לפניו: דארצי מיהא קמיה מאן דארצי. אם לא הרצו אחרים לפניו הוא הרצה לפני מי שחזר והרצה לפני אחרים לכך הוזקק להימנות כאן משום דרבי עקיבא, להודיע שהוא הרצה ואחרים הרצו לפניו. אבל ר"א לא אחרים הרצו לפניו ולא הוא הרצה לפני מי שהרצה לפני אחרים: נכנסו לפרדס. עלו לרקיע על ידי שם: שיש טהור. מבהיק כמים צלולין: אל תאמרו מים מים. יש כאן, איך נלך: הציץ. לצד השכינה: ונפגע. נטרפה דעתו: יקר בעיני ה' המותה לחסידיו. הוקשה מיתתו לפניו לפי שמת בחור. ואעפ"כ אי אפשר שלא ימות, משום שנאמר: "כי לא יראני האדם וחי" (שמות לג): שאלו את בן זומא מהו לסרוסי כלבא. הואיל וסירוס כתיב אצל מומי קרבן, וכלב אפילו חליפיו אסור למזבח משום מחיר כלב, אסור לסרסו או לא: בתולה שעיברה מהו לכהן גדול. והיא אומרת שמצאו לה בתולים. אי נמי, כהן גדול נשאה ולא ידע שהיא מעוברת, ומצא לה בתולים, ואחר כך נמצאת מעוברת, מהו לקיימה משום "בתולה מעמיו יקח" (ויקרא כא)? יכול

תוספות

נענה מלאך מתוך האש גרסינן ולא גרסינן מלאך המות. ובירושלמי מייתי קרא: "אז ירננו עלי היער":

במזומוטי חתן וכלה. ובירושלמי גרס: בשמחת חתן, והיא היא:

והתניא שלשה הרצאות יש. פרש"י: דארצי מיהא קמיה מאן דארצי. כלומר, כיון שחנניא בן חכינאי הרצה לפני רבי עקיבא, דארצי לפני ר' יהושע — מיחשב כמו דארצי קמיה. לאפוקי דר"א בן ערך שהרצה לפני רבן יוחנן בן זכאי, שלא הרצה בפני שום אדם. ולא משמע לי כלל: דמנא ליה דחשיב, כיון דארצי קמיה מאן דארצי כמאן דארצי קמיה דמי? ועוד: דלא הוי שיטתו לפי תירוצו דלעיל, דארצי וארצו קמיה דחשיב. והשתא אי הדר ביה — הוה ליה למימר "אלא" כיון דארצי כו'! וגם מה שפי' רש"י בשם רבינו הלוי דמשמע ליה לישנא שאדם אחר הרצה לפני חנניא — לא יתכן, דאם כן ד' הרצאות (ח) בהון. ועוד: מנא ליה הא דהרצה אחר בפני חנניא, ואינו מפורש בשום ברייתא? על כן נראה להר"י כמו שפירש בספר הישר: דארצי וארצו קמיה קחשיב — אותן שהצליחו כל כך להרצות בפני רבם הכי, ר' יהושע בפני רבו רבן יוחנן בן זכאי, ור"ע בפניו שהיה רבו, ורבי חנניא בפני רבי עקיבא רבו. וחשיב שלשה הרצאות שהלכו בענין זה. לאפוקי ר"א בן ערך שלא הרצו בפניו. ואפי' הרצה — לא הרצה מקמי מאן דארצי. ומעיקרא שני ליה כולו, אלא שלא הבין המקשה כל דבריו דפריך ליה. כיון שלא הרצו מקמי חנניא היה לו למנות ר"א בן ערך כמו חנניא! ומשני ליה: דארצי מקמיה מאן דארצו, שהוא הרצה בפני ר"ע רבו, שהצליח בפני ר' יהושע וארצי וארצו קמיה — קרינא ליה בר' עקיבא, לאפוקי ר"א בן ערך שלא הרצו לפניו. (ט) ואפי' הרצו לפניו — רבן יוחנן רבו לא מצינו שהרצה, הלכך לא דמי להאי סידרא. ומיהו, כשנדקדק פרש"י יש לישבו דה"נ קאמר: דארצי מיהא קמיה מאן דארצי, אם לא הרצו אחרים לפניו — הוא הרצה מיהא מקמי מאן דארצי, ומשום ר"ע הוזקק למנותו, דארצי וארצו קמיה. אבל ר"א למה נחשביה? לא הורצו לפניו, ולא הורצו מקמיה מאן דארצי:

נכנסו לפרדס. כגון על ידי שם. ◐ולא עלו למעלה ממש, אלא היה נראה להם כמו שעלו. וכן פי' בערוך*: **לסרוסי** כלבא. משום שאף מחירו אסור לקרבן שאלו לו (י) טפי מאחריני, וכן פרש"י:

בתולה שעיברה מהו לכהן גדול. ופרש"י: (כ) שהיא אומרת בתולה אני, ואי שכיחא דשמואל — מהימנא. וקשה להר"י: דהא פרק קמא דכתובות (דף יג.) תנן: היתה מעוברת, מה טיבו של עובר זה — מאיש פלוני וכהן הוא וכו' רבי יהושע אמר: לא מפיה אנו חיין כו'. והכא משמע דקבעיא אליבא דכ"ע. ◐*ושמא כאן שאף היא בכלל האיסור, כדכתיב: *["והוא אשה בבתוליה יקח"], קרי ביה יקיח — נאמנת. ולהר"י נראה(ל): דטרחינן לבודקה ע"פ חבית כדאיתא בריש כתובות (דף י: ושם). ואי דשמואל לא שכיח — לא טרחינן, ומוקמה בחזקת בעולה. אי נמי: קמיבעיא ליה בהך דבדקוה ע"פ החבית, אי חיישינן שמא לא נבדקה יפה, דשמואל לא שכיח. וכן מסקינן בריש "תינוקת" (נדה דף סד: ושם): שאני שמואל דרב גובריה. אך קשה להר"י: דהא מסקינן בכתובות (דף ו: ושם) בשמעתין דדם מיפקד פקיד, דרוב בקיאין בהטייה! וי"ל: דודאי תחילת ביאה רוב בקיאין בשעת מעשה, (מ) אבל גמר כדי שתתעבר — אי אפשר כי אם לשמואל:

ומחיוהו

רבינו חננאל

ל"ק במשא ומתן לא היו אנשי אמנה אבל בדברי תורה לא היו משקרין אלא היו בעלי אמונה. ג' הרצאות הרצו במעשה מרכבה. ר' יהושע הרצה לפני ריב"ז [חנניא בן חכינאי הרצה] לפני ר' עקיבא הני כולהו ארצו וארצו אחריני קמייהו. אבל ר' אלעזר בן ערך ארצי ולא ארצי אחריני גביה. ת"ר ד' נכנסו לפרדס. אלו הן בן עזאי ובן זומא אחר ור' עקיבא. אמר להם ר' עקיבא כשאתם מגיעים אל אבני שיש טהור אל תאמרו מים מים משום שנאמר דובר שקרים לא יכון לנגד עיני. פי' כינוהו פרדס מעין *) ג"ע שהיא גנוזה לצדיקים כך אותו מקום הוא מקום בערבות שהנשמות של צדיקים צרורות בו ומפורש בהיכלות שהיו החכמים הראוין למדה הזו מתפללין ומנקין עצמן מכל דבר טומאה וצמין ומטבלין ומטהרין והיו משתמשין בשמות וצופין בהיכלות ורואין [היאך] משמרות המלאכים במעמדם והיאך היכל אחרי היכל ולפני' מהיכל וצוה אותם ר"ע כשאתם מגיעין להביט באובנתא דליבא אצל אבני שיש טהור אל תאמרו מים מים שאין שם מים כל עיקר אלא דמות בעולם נראית והאומר מים נהדף שנמצא משקר ובלשון הזה מפורש בהיכלות רבתי מפני ששומרי היכל פתח שיש מטילין ומשליכין אלף אלפי גלי מים ואין שם אפי' טפה אחת. א"ר עקיבא נראה כמי שיש בו גלי מים ואין בו אפילו טפה אחת אלא אויר זיו אבני שיש טהור שהן כלולות בהיכל שהיה זיו פניהם דומים למים והאומר מים הללו מה טיבן נהדף כו' ואינם עולים בשמים אלא צופים ורואים באובנתא דליבא כאדם הרואה ומביט מתוך אספקלריא שאינה מאירה **) ובן עזאי הציץ כלומר הוסיף להזכיר בשמות כדי להביט באספקלריא מאירה ומת בן זומא הציץ ונפגע כלומר נטרפה דעתו אחר קיצץ בנטיעות כיון שכינו המקום ההוא פרדס א' קיצץ בנטיעות. כלומר דיבר כלפי למעלה

*) עי' בערוך ערך אבני שיש טהור ובהכתוב בע"י ד"ה לרב' האי. **) בערוך מסיים בזה"ל ושומעין ואומרין ומדברין כענין הסוכה ברוה"ק זה פירוש רב האי גאון ז"ל.

עין משפט נר מצוה

ט א מיי' פט"ז מהל' איסורי ביאה הל' ט סמג לאוין קכ טוש"ע אה"ע סי' ה סעיף יא:

מסורת הש"ס

[תוספתא פ"ב] — ג"א וסיבבה — תהלים קמח — [יבמות סג:] — [תוספתא פ"ב] — תהלים קטז — שם קטז — [פרש"י ע"ז תמצא לקמן טו. ד"ה אחר] — משלי כה — ויקרא כב — [ב"מ קיח:] — [עי' תוס' שבת קי: ד"ה ת"ל] — [ערך [illegible]] — עי' יבמות פד. — נ"ל אלמנה וגרושה לא יקחו כי אם וגו'

הגהות הב"ח

(א) גמ' שהיה רוכב על החמור ויוצא מירושלים והיה מהלך בדרך וכו' מחמר אחריו ללמוד תורה מפיו אמר לו רבי וכו' אמר לו בני לא כך: (ב) שם פתחו כל האילנות כולן ואמרו שירה וכו' הללויה ויש אומרים שירה זאת אמרו אז ירננו עלי היער (נענה מלאך וכו' המרכבה) תא"מ ונ"ב ס"א ואף מלאך נענה מתוך האש ואמר ודאי הן הן מעשה מרכבה: (ג) שם במעשה מרכבה כר"א בן ערך יש נאה דורש וכו' ואין נאה דורש אבל אתה אב"ע נאה דורש: (ד) שם ר' יהושע ודרש במעשה מרכבה ואותו היום וכו' ונתקשרו שמים וכו' לשמוע מעשה מרכבה כבני אדם: (ה) שם מן השמים ואמר עלו לכאן וכו' טרקלין גדולים מוכנים לכם ומצעות נאות: (ו) שם לא קחשיב איני והא חנניא: (ז) שם אבני שיש טהור הזהרו שלא תאמרו: (ח) תוס' ד"ה והתניא וכו' ד' הרצאות הן ועוד וכו' בפני חנניא לאינו מפורש וכו' בפני רבן כגון הכא ר' יהושע וכו' ור' עקיבא בפני רבי יהושע שהיה רבו ורבי חנניא בפני ר"ע וכו' ופריך ליה כיון: (ט) בא"ד ואפי' הרצו לפניו לא הרצה תלמיד לפני רבו הלכך לא דמי להאי סידרא וכו' ולא הרצה מקמי מאן דארצי רבן יוחנן רבו לא מצינו שהרצה הס"ד: (י) ד"ה לסרוסי וכו' שאלו לו עליו טפי: (כ) ד"ה בתולה וכו' ופרש"י כשהיא אומרת בתולה אני ואי לא שכיחא דשמואל: (ל) בא"ד ולהר"י נראה דקא מיבעיא ליה מי קטרחינן לבודקה על פי חבית כדאיתא בריש כתובות דאי דשמואל לא שכיח טרחינן לבודקה ואי דשמואל שכיח לא טרחינן ומוקמה בחזקת בעולה אי נמי קמבעיא ליה בתר דבדקוה על פי החבית מי חיישינן לדשמואל או דלמא דשמואל לא שכיח והא לא קא מיבעיא ליה אי חיישינן שמא לא נבדקה יפה את"ל דשמואל לא שכיח הס"ד ואח"כ מה"ד דשמואל לא שכיח וכן מסקינן וכו' דרב גובריה וקשה להר"י כצ"ל ותיבת אך נמחק: (מ) בא"ד אבל גמר ביאה כדי:

גליון הש"ס

תוס' ד"ה נכנסו וכו' ולא עלו למעלה ממש. עי' גיטין דף פד ע"א תוס' ד"ה ע"מ שתעלי לרקיע: ד"ה בתולה וכו' ושמא כאן שאף היא בכלל האיסור. עיין נדרים דף ל ע"ב ת"י ד"ה חזרו לומר:

רש"י

יכול אני לבעול. שהיה בקי בהטייה, וזו נמי נבעלת כן: באמבטי. כלי שרוחצין בו כל הגוף. וי"ל שהטיל שם אדם שכבת זרע ונכנס במעיה: מעיקרא. כשיצאת מן האדם: מאין ולאין. מאין תבא ואין לבך טרוד: צופה הייתי. מתבונן הייתי במעשה בראשית: ואין ביניהן. במקום חיבורן, מקום קשרי הרקיע בקרקע: גודא דגמלא. כשמסדרין לוחין של גשר זו אצל זו, אי אפשר שלא תהא ריוח ביניהם, וכן גלימי, וכן כסי: סחופין. כפופין: אחר קיצץ בנטיעות. קלקל ועיוות כשנכנס לפרדס ומקלץ הנטיעות. ולפי שדימה אותן בתחלת הדברים לנכנס לפרדס, נקט לישנא דקיצץ בנטיעות: לא עמידה. לא גרסינן: לא עורף. דכל לדידהו יש להם פנים: עיפוי. פולסי. מכת מקל, בשטונדל"י: פוגלא. צנון: ממישרא. ערוגה: ונוחין לאבדן. על ידי שכחה:

כי

גמרא

תורה אור

יכול אני לבעול כמה בעילות בלא דם, או דלמא דשמואל לא שכיחא? אמר להו: דשמואל לא שכיח, *וחיישינן שמא באמבטי עיברה. והאמר שמואל: *כל שכבת זרע שאינו יורה כחץ אינו מזרעת! (א) מעיקרא נמי יורה כחץ הוה. ת"ר: *מעשה ברבי יהושע בן חנניה שהיה עומד על גב מעלה בהר הבית, וראהו בן זומא ולא עמד מלפניו. אמר לו: מאין ולאין בן זומא? אמר לו: צופה הייתי בין מים העליונים למים התחתונים, ואין בין זה לזה אלא שלש אצבעות בלבד, שנאמר: °"ורוח אלהים מרחפת על פני המים" — כיונה שמרחפת על בניה ואינה נוגעת. אמר להן רבי יהושע לתלמידיו: עדיין בן זומא מבחוץ. מכדי "ורוח אלהים מרחפת על פני המים" אימת הוי — ביום הראשון, הבדלה — ביום שני הוא דהואי, דכתיב: °"ויהי מבדיל בין מים למים". וכמה? אמר רב אחא בר יעקב: כמלא נימא. ורבנן אמרי: כי גודא דגמלא. מר זוטרא ואיתימא רב אסי אמר: כתרי גלימי דפריסי אהדדי, ואמרי לה: כתרי כסי דסחיפי אהדדי. אחר קיצץ בנטיעות, עליו הכתוב אומר: °"אל תתן את פיך לחטיא את בשרך". מאי היא? חזא מיטטרון דאתיהבא ליה רשותא (ב) למיתב למיכתב זכוותא דישראל, אמר: גמירא דלמעלה לא הוי *לא ישיבה ולא תחרות ולא עורף ולא עיפוי, שמא חס ושלום ב' רשויות (ג) הן. אפקוהו למיטטרון ומחיוהו שיתין פולסי דנורא. א"ל: מ"ט כי חזיתיה לא קמת מקמיה? איתיהיבא ליה רשותא למימחק זכוותא דאחר, יצתה בת קול ואמרה: °"שובו בנים שובבים" חוץ מאחר. (ד) אמר: הואיל ואיטריד ההוא גברא מההוא עלמא ליפוק ליתהני בהאי עלמא. נפק אחר לתרבות רעה. נפק אשכח זונה, תבעה. אמרה ליה: ולאו אלישע בן אבויה את? (ה) עקר פוגלא ממישרא בשבת ויהב לה. אמרה: אחר הוא. שאל אחר את ר"מ לאחר שיצא לתרבות רעה, א"ל: מאי דכתיב: °"גם את זה לעומת זה עשה האלהים"? אמר לו: כל מה שברא הקב"ה (ו) — ברא כנגדו, ברא הרים — ברא גבעות, ברא ימים — ברא נהרות. אמר לו: רבי עקיבא רבך לא אמר כך, אלא: ברא צדיקים — ברא רשעים, ברא גן עדן — ברא גיהנם. כל אחד ואחד יש לו ב' חלקים, אחד בגן עדן ואחד בגיהנם, זכה צדיק — נטל חלקו וחלק חברו בגן עדן, נתחייב רשע — נטל חלקו וחלק חברו בגיהנם. אמר רב משרשיא: מאי קראה? גבי צדיקים כתיב: °"לכן בארצם משנה יירשו". גבי רשעים כתיב: °"ומשנה שברון שברם". שאל אחר את ר"מ לאחר שיצא לתרבות רעה: מאי דכתיב: °"לא יערכנה זהב וזכוכית ותמורתה כלי פז"? אמר לו: *אלו דברי תורה, שקשין לקנותן ככלי זהב וכלי פז, *ונוחין לאבדן ככלי זכוכית. (ז) אמר לו: רבי עקיבא רבך לא אמר כך, אלא: מה כלי זהב וכלי זכוכית, (ח) אף על פי שנשברו יש להם תקנה — אף תלמיד חכם, אף על פי שסרח יש לו תקנה. אמר לו: אף אתה חזור בך! אמר לו: (ט) כבר שמעתי מאחורי הפרגוד: שובו בנים שובבים — חוץ מאחר. ת"ר: מעשה באחר שהיה רוכב על הסוס בשבת, והיה רבי מאיר מהלך אחריו ללמוד תורה מפיו. (י) אמר לו: מאיר, חזור לאחריך, שכבר שיערתי בעקבי סוסי עד כאן תחום שבת. א"ל: אף אתה חזור בך. א"ל: ולא כבר אמרתי לך: כבר שמעתי מאחורי הפרגוד "שובו בנים שובבים" — חוץ מאחר. תקפיה, עייליה לבי מדרשא. א"ל לינוקא: פסוק לי פסוקך! אמר לו: °"אין שלום אמר ה' לרשעים". עייליה לבי כנישתא אחריתי, א"ל לינוקא: פסוק לי פסוקך! אמר לו: °"כי אם תכבסי בנתר ותרבי לך בורית נכתם עונך לפני". עייליה לבי כנישתא אחריתי, א"ל

לינוקא

(מראי מקומות בגליון: בראשית א; שם; קהלת ה; ירמיה ג; קהלת ז; ישעיה סא; ירמיה יז; איוב כח; ישעיה מח; ירמיה ב)

תוספות

ומחיוהו שיתין פולסין. להודיע (כ) לו שאין יכולת למטטרון יותר מאחריני: שובו בנים שובבים. בירושלמי מפרש למה אירע לו כך, ואיכא טפי מקראות שדורש והיה הורג (ל) דוכרי דברי תורה. ואמר: כל תלמיד דהוה חמי ליה הוה קטיל, ולא עוד דהוה על לבית ועדא, הוה חמי טליא קמיה סופרא, ואמר: מאן אלו עבדין הכא כו' כיון דהוו שמעין ליה שבקין ואזלין. וקאמר ליה ר"מ, מאי דכתיב: (*"וה' בירך) את כל אשר לאיוב למשנה" (איוב מב) ואמר לו: שכפל לו ממונו. והוא השיב שר"ע דריש ליה בזכות מצות ומעשים טובים ברך מראשיתו. ומייתי ליה "טוב אחרית דבר מראשיתו" ודריש ליה ר"מ לאדם שהוליד בנים בילדותו ומתו, ובזקנותו הוליד ונתקיימו. ואמר לו: ר"ע רבך לא כך דרש, אלא טוב אחרית דבר שהוא טוב מראשיתו. [ובי] הוה המעשה: אבויה אבי הוה מגדולי ירושלים וביום שבא למהולי קרא לכל גדולי ירושלים והושיבן בבית אחד, ולר"א ולר' יהושע במקום אחר. מן דאכלין ושתין, שרין מטפחין ומרקדים, אמרי: עד דאלין עסקין בדידהו נעסוק בדידן. ישבו ונתעסקו בדברי תורה. ירדה אש מן השמים והקיפה אותן. אמר לון אבויה אבא: גברין, מה באתם לשרוף ביתי? אמרו לו: ח"ו, אלא יושבין היינו וחוזרין דברי תורה, מתורה לנביאים ומנביאים לכתובים, והיו הדברים שמחים כנתינתן מסיני, לא באש נתנו? אמר: הואיל וכך כחה של תורה, אם יתקיים הבן הזה — לתורה אני מפרישו. ולפי שלא היתה כונתו לשמים לפיכך לא נתקיימו בו. ובמקום שיש בגמרא שלנו אחורי הפרגוד, יש לשם מאחורי בית קדשי הקדשים. עוד איתא התם שהיה רוכב ביוה"כ שחל להיות בשבת, ושמע כו'. ומייתי ההוא דפרק קמא דקדושין (דף לט:) שראה (מ) אחד שנטל הבנים ושילח את האם, וכי אייתי נפל ומת, ולא היה דורש כר' יעקב, כדמייתי התם. ועוד איתא: שראה לשון רבי יהודה הנחתום נתון בפי כלב, והיינו גברא רבה דקדושין. ורבי נתן אומר: כשהיתה אמו מעוברת ממנו עברה לפני ע"ז, והריחה מאותו המין ואכלה, והיה אותו המין (נ) *מזדעזע בגופה *כעכנא, ולבסוף חלה מתונא, ואמרו לו לר"מ: רבך אבאיש, אזל גביה לבקרתי' וא"ל: חזור בך! אמר: אי הדרנא מתקבלין? אמר ליה, והכתיב (תהלים צ): "תשב אנוש עד דכא ותאמר שובו בני אדם". בכה אלישע ונפטר. א"ר מאיר: דומה שמתוך תשובה נפטר. (ס) וכי מן [דקברוניה] ירדה אש מן השמים ושרפה אותו. וא"ל לר"מ: הא קבר דרבך [אוקיד, אתא] וקא פריס גלימיה עליה, ואמר "ליני (פה) הלילה וגו'" (רות ג), "ליני פה" — בעולם הזה שדומה ללילה, "והיה בבוקר" — לעולם הבא "אם יגאלך טוב יגאל" — זה הקדוש ברוך הוא שנאמר: "טוב ה' לכל" (תהלים קמה), (ע) יגאל, "ואם לא יחפוץ לגאלך וגאלתיך אנכי". אמרו ליה: (פ) אין [אמרין] לך בההיא עלמא למאן את בעי למקרבה קדמייתא לאבוך או לרבך אמר לון מיקרב לרבי קדמוי, ובתר כן לאבא. א"ל: ושמעינן לך? א"ל: ולא כן תנינן: *מצילין תיק הספר עם הספר? מצילין אלישע בזכות תורתו:

הא

רבינו חננאל

דכיון דחזא למטטרון דאתייהבא ליה רשותא הדא שעתא למיתב למכתב זכותא דישראל אמר גמירי דלמעלה באותו מקום אין שם ישיבה שמא שתי רשויות הן. יצתה בת קול ואמרה שובו בנים שובבים חוץ מאלישע אחר שגלוי וידוע לפניו שאינו חוזר בתשובה שלמה לעולם. שאילו היה חוזר לא היה נטרד שאין הפרגוד ננעלת בפני בעלי תשובה מיד מחיוה למטטרון שתין פולסי דנורא. ח"ו שיש עליו דין אלא להראות לאלישע שיש לו אדון שהוא עליו וזה שאמר אחר משום ר' עקיבא כי רשע מתייסר בגיהנם חלקו וחלק הצדיק והצדיק זוכה בג"ע חלקו וחלק הרשע ואסמכוה אקרא זה לכן בארצם משנה יירשו ומשנה שברון שברם. ד"א לאו דסמכא הן וקרא מדרש הוא ולא עיקר. מיהו אית לן למימר שהמחטיא את הרבים אין מספיקין בידו לעשות תשובה ועונו גדול מאד הוא ועליו ועל כיוצא בו נאמר ומשנה שברון

מסורת הש"ס

[וחיישינן נמי אמרינן לקולא רש"י בשבת קנא. ד"ה ושמואל אמר]

[תוספתא פ"ב]

עי' בפי' המשניות להרמב"ם בפ"י דסנהדרין ביסוד השלישי

אדר"נ פכ"ד וע"ש דאיתא בשם אלישע בן אבויה

[עיי' רש"י לסנהדרין לח. ד"ה יש להם וכו']

כארס של חכינה

[שבת קטז:]

גליון הש"ס

גמ' וחיישינן שמא באמבטי עיברה. עיין משנה למלך פט"ו מהל' איסורי ביאה הלכה ד ופ"י מהל' א"ה הל' יג:

הגהות הב"ח

(א) גמ' אינו מזרעת דלמא מעיקרא נמי יורה: (ב) שם דאתיהבא ליה רשותא חדא שעתא ביומא למיתב ולמיכתב זכוותא: (ג) שם שמא חס ושלום שתי רשויות יש בשמים מיד אפקוהו: (ד) שם חוץ מאחר שידע כבודי ומרד בי אמר הואיל ואיטריד כו' לתרבות רעה אשכח כצ"ל ותיבת נפק נמחק: (ה) שם בן אבויה את ששמך יצא בכל הארץ עקר פוגלא: (ו) שם כל מה שברא הקב"ה בעולמו ברא כנגדו: (ז) שם לאבדן ככלי זכוכית נ"ב ס"א א"ל האלהים אפילו ככלי חרס אבל ר"ע כו': (ח) שם וכלי זכוכית הללו אע"פ שנשתברו יש: (ט) שם אמר לו והלא כבר שמעתי: (י) שם ללמוד תורה מפיו כיון שהגיע לתחום שבת אמר לו מאיר: (כ) תום' ד"ה ומחיוהו וכו' להודיע שאין לו יכולת יותר מאחריני כצ"ל: (ל) ד"ה שובו וכו' והיה הורג רבי תורה ואמרינן כל תלמיד דהוה חמי ליה משבח באורייתא הוה קטיל ולא עוד אלא דהוה על וכו' קמי ספרא והוה אמר מאן אלין יתבין עבדין הכא כו' וכיון דהוו שמעין כן הוון שבקין ליה ואזלין לון וקאמר ליה לרבי מאיר וכו' שר' עקיבא דריש ליה וה' ברך את איוב מראשיתו בזכות מצות ומעשים טובים שהיו ביה מראשיתו ומייתי ליה טוב אחרית דבר וכו' אלא טוב אחרית דבר כשהוא טוב מראשיתו ובו הוה המעשה אבויה אביו מגדולי ירושלים היה וביום שבא למהול אותו קרא וכו' אמר ר"א לרבי יהושע עד דאלין עסקין וכו' נעסוק אנן בדידן וכו' אמר לון אבויה רבותי מה באתם לשרוף את ביתי עלי אמרו לו ח"ו אלא יושבין היינו וחוזרין בדברי תורה וכו' הדברים שמחים כנתינתן מסיני והיתה האש מלחך סביבותיו כלחיכתן מסיני נתינתן מסיני לא באש נתנו אמר להן אבויה הואיל וכך: (מ) בא"ד שראה אדם אחד שנטל הבנים: (נ) בא"ד והיה אותו המין מפעפע בגופה כעכנא. נ"ב פירוש כארס של עכנא: (ס) בא"ד דומה שמתוך תשובה נפטר רבי מן דקברוניה ירדה אש מן השמים ושרפה את קברו ואמרו ליה לרבי מאיר הא קיברא דרבך אייקד מה עבד אתא וקא פריס: (ע) בא"ד טוב ה' לכל ואם לא כצ"ל ותיבת יגאל נמחק: (פ) בא"ד אמרו ליה לר"מ אין אמרין וכו' אמר לון אנא מיקרב לרבי קדמי:

י א מיי' פ"ד מהלכות ת"ת הלכה א טוש"ע י"ד סי' רמו סעיף ח:

לְיָנוֹקָא: פְּסוֹק לִי פְּסוּקָךְ! א"ל: °"וְאַתְּ שָׁדוּד מַה תַּעֲשִׂי כִּי תִלְבְּשִׁי שָׁנִי כִּי תַעְדִּי עֲדִי זָהָב כִּי תִקְרְעִי בַפּוּךְ עֵינַיִךְ לַשָּׁוְא תִּתְיַפִּי וגו'". עַיְילֵיהּ לְבֵי כְנִישְׁתָּא אַחֲרִיתִי, עַד דְּעַיְילֵיהּ לִתְלֵיסַר בֵּי כְנִישְׁתָּא, כּוּלְּהוּ פְּסָקוּ לֵיהּ כִּי הַאי גַּוְונָא. (א) לְבַתְרָא א"ל: פְּסוֹק לִי פְּסוּקָךְ! א"ל: °"וְלָרָשָׁע אָמַר אֱלֹהִים מַה לְּךָ לְסַפֵּר חֻקָּי וגו'". הַהוּא יָנוֹקָא הֲוָה מְגַמְגֵּם בְּלִישָּׁנֵיהּ, אִשְׁתַּמַּע כְּמָה דְּאָמַר לֵיהּ "וְלֶאֱלִישָׁע אָמַר אֱלֹהִים". אִיכָּא דְּאָמְרִי: סַכִּינָא הֲוָה בַּהֲדֵיהּ וּקְרָעֵיהּ, וְשַׁדְרֵיהּ לִתְלֵיסַר בֵּי כְנִישְׁתֵּי. וְאִיכָּא דְּאָמְרִי, אֲמַר: אִי הֲוַאי בְּיָדִי סַכִּינָא — הֲוָה קָרַעְנָא לֵיהּ. כִּי נָח נַפְשֵׁיהּ דְּאַחֵר אָמְרִי: לָא מֵידַן לִידַיְינֵיהּ, וְלָא לְעָלְמָא דְּאָתֵי לֵיתֵי. לָא מֵידַן לִידַיְינֵיהּ — מִשּׁוּם דְּעָסַק בְּאוֹרַיְיתָא, וְלָא לְעָלְמָא דְּאָתֵי לֵיתֵי — מִשּׁוּם דְּחָטָא. אָמַר ר"מ: מוּטָב דְּלִידַיְינֵיהּ וְלֵיתֵי לְעָלְמָא דְּאָתֵי, מָתַי אָמוּת וְאַעֲלֶה עָשָׁן מִקִּבְרוֹ. כִּי נָח נַפְשֵׁיהּ דר' מֵאִיר סְלֵיק קוּטְרָא מִקִּבְרֵיהּ דְּאַחֵר. אֲמַר ר' יוֹחָנָן: גְּבוּרְתָּא לְמִיקְלָא רַבֵּיהּ?! (ב) חַד הֲוָה בֵּינָנָא וְלָא מָצֵינַן לְאַצּוֹלֵיהּ. אִי נַקְטֵיהּ בְּיַד — מַאן מְרַמֵּי לֵיהּ, מַאן?! אָמַר: מָתַי אָמוּת וַאֲכַבֶּה עָשָׁן מִקִּבְרוֹ! כִּי נָח נַפְשֵׁיהּ דר' יוֹחָנָן — פְּסַק קוּטְרָא מִקִּבְרֵיהּ דְּאַחֵר. פְּתַח עֲלֵיהּ הַהוּא סַפְדָּנָא: אֲפִילּוּ שׁוֹמֵר הַפֶּתַח לֹא עָמַד לְפָנֶיךָ, רַבֵּינוּ. בִּתּוֹ שֶׁל אַחֵר אֲתְיָא לְקַמֵּיהּ דְּרַבִּי, אָמְרָה לֵיהּ: רַבִּי, פַּרְנְסֵנִי. אָמַר לָהּ: בַּת מִי אַתְּ? אָמְרָה לוֹ: בִּתּוֹ שֶׁל אַחֵר אֲנִי. אָמַר לָהּ: עֲדַיִין יֵשׁ מִזַּרְעוֹ בָּעוֹלָם? וְהָא כְּתִיב: °"לֹא נִין לוֹ וְלֹא נֶכֶד בְּעַמּוֹ וְאֵין שָׂרִיד בִּמְגוּרָיו"! אָמְרָה לוֹ: (ג) זְכוֹר לְתוֹרָתוֹ וְאַל תִּזְכּוֹר מַעֲשָׂיו. מִיָּד יָרְדָה אֵשׁ וְסִכְסְכָה סַפְסָלוֹ שֶׁל רַבִּי. בָּכָה וְאָמַר רַבִּי: וּמַה לַמִּתְגַּנִּין בָּהּ — כָּךְ, לַמִּשְׁתַּבְּחִין בָּהּ — עַל אַחַת כַּמָּה וְכַמָּה. וְר"מ הֵיכִי גָּמַר תּוֹרָה מִפּוּמֵּיהּ דְּאַחֵר? וְהָאָמַר רַבָּה בַּר בַּר חָנָה אָמַר רַבִּי יוֹחָנָן: *מַאי דִּכְתִיב: °"כִּי שִׂפְתֵי כֹהֵן יִשְׁמְרוּ דַעַת וְתוֹרָה יְבַקְשׁוּ מִפִּיהוּ כִּי מַלְאַךְ ה' צְבָאוֹת הוּא", אִם דּוֹמֶה הָרַב לְמַלְאַךְ ה' צְבָאוֹת — יְבַקְשׁוּ תוֹרָה מִפִּיהוּ. וְאִם לָאו — אַל יְבַקְשׁוּ תוֹרָה מִפִּיהוּ! אָמַר ר"ל: ר"מ קְרָא אַשְׁכַּח וְדָרַשׁ: °"הַט אָזְנְךָ וּשְׁמַע דִּבְרֵי חֲכָמִים וְלִבְּךָ תָּשִׁית לְדַעְתִּי". לְדַעְתָּם לֹא נֶאֱמַר, אֶלָּא לְדַעְתִּי. רַב חֲנִינָא אָמַר מֵהָכָא: °"שִׁמְעִי בַת וּרְאִי וְהַטִּי אָזְנֵךְ וְשִׁכְחִי עַמֵּךְ וּבֵית אָבִיךְ וגו'". קַשׁוּ קְרָאֵי אַהֲדָדֵי! לָא קַשְׁיָא, הָא — בְּגָדוֹל, הָא — בְּקָטָן. כִּי אֲתָא רַב דִּימִי אֲמַר, אָמְרִי בְּמַעְרְבָא: ר"מ (ד) אֲכַל תַּחְלָא וּשְׁדָא שִׁיחְלָא לְבָרָא. דָּרַשׁ רָבָא: מַאי דִּכְתִיב: °"אֶל גִּנַּת אֱגוֹז יָרַדְתִּי לִרְאוֹת בְּאִבֵּי הַנָּחַל וגו'" לָמָּה נִמְשְׁלוּ ת"ח לֶאֱגוֹז? לוֹמַר לָךְ: מָה אֱגוֹז זֶה, אַף עַל פִּי שֶׁמְּלוּכְלָךְ בְּטִיט וּבְצוֹאָה — אֵין מַה שֶּׁבְּתוֹכוֹ נִמְאָס, אַף ת"ח, אַף עַל פִּי שֶׁסָּרַח — אֵין תּוֹרָתוֹ נִמְאֶסֶת. אַשְׁכְּחֵיהּ רַבָּה בַּר שֵׁילָא לְאֵלִיָּהוּ, א"ל: מַאי קָא עָבֵיד הקב"ה? א"ל: קָאָמַר שְׁמַעְתָּא מִפּוּמַיְיהוּ דְּכוּלְּהוּ רַבָּנַן, וּמִפּוּמֵיהּ דר"מ לָא קָאָמַר. א"ל: אַמַּאי? מִשּׁוּם דְּקָא גָּמַר שְׁמַעְתָּא מִפּוּמֵיהּ דְּאַחֵר. א"ל: אַמַּאי? ר"מ רִמּוֹן מָצָא, תּוֹכוֹ אָכַל, קְלִיפָּתוֹ זָרַק! א"ל: הַשְׁתָּא קָאָמַר: מֵאִיר בְּנִי (ה) אוֹמֵר: *בִּזְמַן שֶׁאָדָם מִצְטַעֵר שְׁכִינָה מַה לָּשׁוֹן אוֹמֶרֶת — קַלַּנִי מֵרֹאשִׁי, קַלַּנִי מִזְּרוֹעִי. אִם כָּךְ הַקָּדוֹשׁ בָּרוּךְ הוּא מִצְטַעֵר עַל דָּמָן שֶׁל רְשָׁעִים (ו) — ק"ו עַל דָּמָן שֶׁל צַדִּיקִים שֶׁנִּשְׁפַּךְ. אַשְׁכְּחֵיהּ שְׁמוּאֵל לְרַב יְהוּדָה דְּתָלֵי בְּעִיבְרָא דְּדַשָּׁא וְקָא בָּכֵי. א"ל: *) *שִׁינָּנָא, מַאי קָא בָּכֵית? א"ל מִי זוּטְרָא מַאי דִּכְתִיב בְּהוּ בְּרַבָּנַן *°"אַיֵּה סֹפֵר אַיֵּה שֹׁקֵל אַיֵּה סֹפֵר אֶת הַמִּגְדָּלִים". "אַיֵּה סוֹפֵר" — שֶׁהָיוּ סוֹפְרִים כָּל אוֹתִיּוֹת שֶׁבַּתּוֹרָה, אַיֵּה שׁוֹקֵל — שֶׁהָיוּ שׁוֹקְלִים קַלִּין וַחֲמוּרִין שֶׁבַּתּוֹרָה. "אַיֵּה סֹפֵר אֶת הַמִּגְדָּלִים" — שֶׁהָיוּ שׁוֹנִין ג' מֵאוֹת הֲלָכוֹת בְּמִגְדָּל הַפּוֹרֵחַ בָּאֲוִיר. וַאֲמַר רַבִּי אַמִּי: תְּלַת מְאָה בְּעָיֵי בָּעוּ דּוֹאֵג וַאֲחִיתוֹפֶל בְּמִגְדָּל הַפּוֹרֵחַ בָּאֲוִיר. וּתְנַן: *ג' מְלָכִים וְאַרְבָּעָה הֶדְיוֹטוֹת אֵין לָהֶם חֵלֶק לָעוֹלָם הַבָּא, אֲנַן מַה תֶּהֱוֵי עֲלַן?! א"ל: שִׁינָּנָא, טִינָא הָיְתָה בְּלִבָּם. אַחֵר מַאי — זֶמֶר יְוָנִי לָא פָּסַק מִפּוּמֵיהּ. אָמְרוּ עָלָיו עַל אַחֵר, בְּשָׁעָה שֶׁהָיָה עוֹמֵד מִבֵּית הַמִּדְרָשׁ הַרְבֵּה סִפְרֵי מִינִין נוֹשְׁרִין מֵחֵיקוֹ. שָׁאַל נִימוֹס הַגַּרְדִּי אֶת ר"מ: כָּל עֲמַר דְּנָחֵית לְיוֹרָה סָלֵיק? א"ל: כָּל מַאן דַּהֲוָה נָקִי אַגַּב אִימֵּיהּ — סָלֵיק, כָּל דְּלָא הֲוָה נָקִי אַגַּב אִימֵּיהּ — לָא סָלֵיק. רַבִּי עֲקִיבָא עָלָה בְּשָׁלוֹם וְיָרַד בְּשָׁלוֹם, וְעָלָיו הַכָּתוּב אוֹמֵר: °"מָשְׁכֵנִי אַחֲרֶיךָ נָּרוּצָה". וְאַף רַבִּי עֲקִיבָא בִּקְשׁוּ מַלְאֲכֵי הַשָּׁרֵת לְדוֹחֲפוֹ, אָמַר לָהֶם הַקָּדוֹשׁ בָּרוּךְ הוּא: הַנִּיחוּ לְזָקֵן זֶה, שֶׁרָאוּי לְהִשְׁתַּמֵּשׁ בִּכְבוֹדִי. מַאי

*) [בערוך ערך שן פירש שיננא מחודד בתלמוד מלשון חץ שנון וי"א גדול השינים ובשיטה מקובלת כתובות יז. פירש לפי ששיניו גדולות קרי ליה שיננא ע"ש]

ירמיה ד | תהלים נ | איוב יח | מלאכי ב | משלי כב | תהלים מה | שיר ו | ישעיה לג | סנהדרין קו: | קס ל. | שיר א

רש"י

כִּי שְׁכִיב. אַחֵר: אָמְרִי. בְּרָקִיעַ: לָא מֵידַן נִידַיְינֵיהּ כו': חֲדָא הֲוָה בֵּינָנָא. תַּלְמִיד אֶחָד הָיָה בֵּינֵינוּ, וְנִכְשַׁל וְיָצָא לְתַרְבּוּת רָעָה, וְאֵין כֹּחַ בֵּין כּוּלָּנוּ לַהֲבִיאוֹ לָעוֹלָם הַבָּא? אִי נַקְטֵי לֵיהּ בְּיַד מַאן מְרַמֵּי לֵיהּ (ז). אִם אוֹחֵז אֲנִי בְּיָדוֹ לַהֲבִיאוֹ לָעוֹלָם הַבָּא, מִי יִקָּחֶנּוּ מִיָּדִי? מְרַמֵּי לְשׁוֹן נוֹטֵל מִיָּדִי. וְיֵשׁ לוֹ דּוּגְמָא בִּפְסָחִים (דף י:): חֲרַמּוּיֵי חֲרַמְיֵיהּ מִינֵּיהּ, גַּבֵּי כִּכָּר בְּפִי עַכְבָּר: מַאן. כְּמוֹ מִנַּאי, לָשׁוֹן קָצָר הוּא: שׁוֹמֵר הַפֶּתַח. שֶׁל גֵּיהִנָּם, לֹא עָמַד לְפָנֶיךָ, רַבֵּינוּ, כְּשֶׁבָּאתָ לְהוֹצִיא אַחֵר מִשָּׁם: לְדַעְתָּם לֹא נֶאֱמַר. אַלְמָא בִּרְשִׁיעֵי עָסִיקִינַן, וְקָאָמַר: הַט אָזְנְךָ: הַטֵּה אָזְנְךָ לִשְׁמוֹעַ, וְאֶת מַעֲשֵׂיהֶם שְׁכַח וְאַל תִּלְמַד מֵהֶם. וְאֶת מַעֲשֵׂיהֶם שְׁכַח וְאַל תַּלְמִידֵי אוֹתָן: גָּדוֹל. הַיּוֹדֵעַ לִיזָּהֵר [שֶׁלֹּא יִלְמוֹד] מַעֲשָׂיו — יָכוֹל לִלְמוֹד תּוֹרָה מִפִּיו: תַּחְלָא. פְּרִי הַחִיצוֹן הַנֶּאֱכָל בַּתְּמָרָה: שִׁיחְלָא. גַּרְעִינָה הַנִּזְרֶקֶת: [הַשְׁתָּא קָאָמַר]. עַכְשָׁיו שָׁמַע לְקוֹלְךָ וְאָמַר שְׁמוּעָה מִפִּיו: קַלַּנִי מֵרֹאשִׁי. רַבִּי מֵאִיר אֲמָרָהּ בְּמַסֶּכֶת סַנְהֶדְרִין (דף מו.). בַּמִּדְרָשׁ: "כִּי קִלְלַת אֱלֹהִים תָּלוּי" (דברים כא): קַל לֵית, אֵינִי קַל. וְלִישָּׁנָא מְעַלְּיָא כִּינָּה הַדָּבָר כְּלַפֵּי מַעְלָה: קַלַּנִי מִזְּרוֹעִי. כָּבֵד אֲנִי מִזְּרוֹעִי, שֶׁיִּסַּרְתִּי זֶה שֶׁמֵּת בַּעֲוֹנוֹ: וְתָלֵי בְּעִיבְרָא דְּדַשָּׁא. נִשְׁעָן עַל הַבְּרִיחַ: בְּרַבָּנַן. בַּתַּלְמִידִים הַיּוֹצְאִין לְתַרְבּוּת רָעָה: שׁוֹקְלִין. לִדְרוֹשׁ קַל מֵחָמוּר וְחָמוּר מִקַּל, לְפִי הַמִּשְׁקוֹלֶת שֶׁל ק"ו: בְּמִגְדָּל הַפּוֹרֵחַ בָּאֲוִיר. י"מ: שֶׁדּוֹרְשִׁין גּוֹבְהוֹ שֶׁל למ"ד וְדוֹרְשִׁין בּוֹ כָּל זֹאת. וְי"א: מִגְדַּל דּוֹר הַפַּלָּגָה. וְלִי נִרְאֶה: מִגְדָּל הַפָּתוּחַ לָאֲוִיר גָּרְסִינַן, וְהֵן מֵהִלְכוֹת אֳהָלוֹת. מִגְדָּל שֶׁל עֵץ, שֶׁקּוֹרִין משטיי"ר, וְעוֹמֵד בַּפֶּתַח וּפִתְחוֹ פָּתוּחַ לְבִקְעָה אוֹ לְחָצֵר שֶׁהוּא אֲוִיר, בְּמַסֶּכֶת אֳהָלוֹת (פ"ד מ"א) יְשָׁנָהּ מִשְׁנָה: מִגְדָּל הָעוֹמֵד בָּאֲוִיר: ד' הֶדְיוֹטוֹת. בִּלְעָם וְדוֹאֵג וַאֲחִיתוֹפֶל וְגֵחֲזִי, בְּפ' "חֵלֶק": טִינָא הָיְתָה בְּלִבָּם. רְשָׁעִים הָיוּ מִימֵיהֶם: אַחֵר מַאי. מִפְּנֵי מָה בָּא לִידֵי כָּךְ, וְלֹא הֵגִינָה תּוֹרָתוֹ עָלָיו? זֶמֶר יְוָנִי לֹא פָּסַק מִבֵּיתוֹ. וְהָיָה לוֹ לְהַנִּיחַ בִּשְׁבִיל חוּרְבַּן הַבַּיִת, דִּכְתִיב: "בַּשִּׁיר לֹא יִשְׁתּוּ יָיִן" (ישעיה כד): נוֹשְׁרִין מֵחֵיקוֹ. קוֹדֶם שֶׁהִפְקִיר עַצְמוֹ לְתַרְבּוּת רָעָה. אַלְמָא: טִינָא הָוֵות בְּלִבּוֹ: כָּל עֲמַר דְּנָחֵית לְיוֹרָה סָלֵיק. כָּל צֶמֶר שֶׁנִּיתָּן לְיוֹרָה שֶׁל סַמְמָנִין לִצְבּוֹעַ, עוֹלֶה לוֹ צִבְעוֹ, אוֹ אֵינוֹ עוֹלֶה? כְּלוֹמַר: כָּל הַלּוֹמְדִים לִפְנֵי חֲכָמִים, עוֹלָה לָהֶן תּוֹרָתָן לְהָגֵן עֲלֵיהֶן מִן הַחֵטְא (ח)? כָּל דְּנָקִי אַגַּב אִימֵּיהּ (ט). שֶׁלֹּא נִתְלַכְלֵךְ בַּגִּיזָּה — עוֹלֶה לוֹ צִבְעוֹ. כְּלוֹמַר, כָּל שֶׁיִּרְאַת חֶטְאוֹ קוֹדֶמֶת לְחָכְמָתוֹ — עוֹלָה לוֹ, כֵּן נִרְאֶה בְּעֵינַי. וְרַבּוֹתַי מְפָרְשִׁין: כָּל עֲמַר דְּנָחֵית לְיוֹרָה סָלֵיק — כָּל שֶׁיֵּרֵד לִידּוֹן בַּגֵּיהִנָּם עוֹלֶה. אַגַּב אִמּוֹ — לֶאֱמֹר בֶּן יוֹמוֹ שֶׁלֹּא נִרְמַס בְּטִיט עוֹלֶה לוֹ הַצֶּבַע, כְּלוֹמַר: שֶׁיֵּשׁ זְכֻיּוֹת בְּיָדוֹ עוֹלֶה: מַאי

תורה אור

[מו"ק יז. ע"ש] [סנהדרין מו.] [ברכות לו. וש"נ]

תוספות

הא בגדול הא בקטן. והא דריש פ' בתרא דמו"ק (י) (דף יז.) דהוו סנו שומעניה, דשמתיה רב יהודה, איכא למימר דקטנים הוו דגרסי קמיה, וחיישי' דלמא מימשכי. אי נמי: אפילו הוו גדולים נידהו רב יהודה, כיון שמלא מקום לנדותו, ודין היה, כיון דסנו שומעניה. הר"ר אלחנן:

כל עמר דנקי נחית (כ) אגב אימיה. כלומר: מי שיראתו קודמת לחכמתו — חכמתו מתקיימת. ודואג ואחיתופל דלא מגני להו תורתן — לפי שלא היה להם יראה כלל, כדאיתא בסוטה פרק "נוטל" (דף כא.):

כבני

רבינו חננאל

שברם. והאי דבדק אחר בינוקי משום דהוה ר' מאיר מפצר ליה לחזור בתשובה ולא היה לבו חפץ וא"ל שמעתי מאחורי הפרגוד והוא מעיקרא טינא היתה דלא פסק זמר יווני מביתו ובשעה שהיה עומד מבהמ"ד הרבה ספרי מינין היו נושרין מחיקו ויצא לתרבות רעה. זה שאמר ר' מאיר מתי אמות ואעלה עשן מקברו כלומר ידין אותו הקב"ה באש יוקדת מעלה עשן כדי שיתכפרו לו עונותיו ויזכה לעוה"ב וכיון שהגיע ר' מאיר למות ביקש רחמים על זה וקבל תפלתו וכיון שמת עלה עשן מקברו של אחר. ור' יוחנן אמר חד הוה כאן. כלומר אחד מן חכמי [בית] מדרשינו חטא אין בנו זכות לפני הקב"ה להצילו מדינה של גיהנם. מתי אמות ואפסיק עשן מקברו. ור' מאיר היכי הוה גמיר מאחר והכתיב כי שפתי כהן ישמרו דעת ותורה יבקשו מפיהו כי מלאך ה' צבאות הוא וא"ר יוחנן אם דומה הרב למלאך ה' צבאות יבקשו תורה מפיהו ואם לאו אל יבקשו תורה מפיהו. ואע"ג דאמרינן ר' מאיר קרא אחרינא אשכח וסמך עליה דכתיב הט אזנך ושמע דברי חכמים ולבך תשית לדעתי לדעתם לא נאמר אלא לדעתי מכלל שיש לך לקבל תורתו ולא דעתו. ואמרינן קשו קראי אהדדי ושנינן הא דאמרינן אם דומה הרב למלאך ה' צבאות בקשו תורה מפיהו בקטן דעביד כדעתיה דרביה דחיישינן דלמא מפיק ליה לתרבות רעה אבל גדול דכדעתא דנפשיה קא עביד הט אזנך ושמע דברי חכמים וגו' האמר אליהו דאמרי במתיבתא דרקיעא שמעתא מכלהו רבנן. ושמעתתיה דר' מאיר משום דגמר מאחר לא אמרי הלכתא אפילו גדול ללמוד תורה מחבירו ירא שמים טפי עדיף ליה. פי' שיחלא קליפתה שהיא כסותה ותיקה. פי' כמגדל הפורח. משנה ידועה היא. קלני מראשי קלני מזרועי כבר פירשנוה בסנהדרין. פי' בעברא דדשא בבריח הדלת. אף ר' עקיבא ביקשו המלאכים לדחפו אמר הקב"ה הניחו לזקן זה ראוי הוא להסתכל

הגהות הב"ח

(א) גמ' כי האי גוונא לבסוף לבתרא: (ב) שם גבורתא למיקלא רביה בנורא חד הוה וכו' אי נקטי ליה ביד: (ג) שם אמרה לו רבי זכור לתורתו וכו' ירדה אש מן השמים וסכסכה וכו' ומה למתגנין בתורה כך: (ד) שם ר' מאיר אשכח תמרי אכל תחלא: (ה) שם מאיר בני כך הוא אומר: (ו) שם של רשעים שנשפך ק"ו על למן: (ז) רש"י ד"ה אי נקטיה וכו' מאן מרמי ליה מאן אם אוחז: (ח) ד"ה כל עמר וכו' מן החטא או לא והס"ד: (ט) ד"ה כל דנקי אגב אימיה נ"מ בן יומו שלא נתלכלך בטיט בגיזה וכו' כלומר מי שיש זכיות: (י) תוס' ד"ה הא בגדול וכו' והא דריש פ' בתרא דמו"ק בההוא צורבא מרבנן דהוו סנו: (כ) ד"ה כל עמר דנקי אגב כצ"ל ותיבת נחית נמחק:

גליון הש"ס

רש"י ד"ה זמר יוני וכו' דכתיב בשיר. עיין גיטין דף ז ע"א:

יא א טוש"ע א"ח סי' רכט סעיף א:
יב ב מיי' פ"ד מהל' תפלה הל' ז סמג עשין כ טוש"ע א"ח סי' קכח סעיף כג:
יג ג מיי' פ"א מהלכות חגיגה הלכה יב:

מאי דרש? אמר רבה בר בר חנה אמר רבי יוחנן: °"(*ואתא) מרבבות קדש" — אות הוא ברבבה שלו. ורבי אבהו אמר: °"דגול מרבבה" — דוגמא הוא ברבבה שלו. וריש לקיש אמר: °"ה' צבאות שמו" — אדון הוא בצבא שלו. ורבי חייא בר אבא א"ר יוחנן: °"לא ברוח ה' ואחר הרוח רעש לא ברעש ה' ואחר הרעש אש לא באש ה' ואחר האש קול דממה דקה" "והנה ה' עובר". *ת"ר: ששה דברים נאמרו בשדים, שלשה כמלאכי השרת ושלשה כבני אדם. שלשה כמלאכי השרת: יש להם כנפים כמלאכי השרת, וטסין מסוף העולם ועד סופו כמלאכי השרת, ויודעין מה שעתיד להיות כמלאכי השרת. יודעין ס"ד?! אלא: שומעין מאחורי הפרגוד כמלאכי השרת. ושלשה כבני אדם: אוכלין ושותין כבני אדם, פרין ורבין כבני אדם, ומתים כבני אדם. ששה דברים נאמרו בבני אדם, שלשה כמלאכי השרת, שלשה כבהמה. שלשה כמלאכי השרת: יש להם דעת כמלאכי השרת, ומהלכין בקומה זקופה כמלאכי השרת, ומספרים בלשון הקדש כמלאכי השרת. שלשה כבהמה: אוכלין ושותין כבהמה, ופרין ורבין כבהמה, ומוציאין רעי כבהמה.§ "כל המסתכל בד' דברים רתוי לו שלא בא לעולם כו'".§ בשלמא מה למעלה מה למטה מה לאחור — לחיי, אלא לפנים — מה דהוה הוה! ר' יוחנן ור"א דאמרי תרוייהו: (א) משל למלך ב"ו שאמר לעבדיו: בנו לי פלטירין גדולין על האשפה, הלכו ובנו לו, אין רצונו של מלך להזכיר שם אשפה.§ "כל שלא חס על כבוד קונו רתוי לו שלא בא לעולם".§ מאי היא? *ר' אבא אמר: זה המסתכל בקשת, רב יוסף אמר: זה העובר עבירה בסתר. (ב) מסתכל בקשת — דכתיב: °"כמראה הקשת אשר יהיה בענן ביום הגשם כן מראה הנגה סביב הוא מראה דמות כבוד ה'". רב יוסף אמר: זה העובר עבירה בסתר, כדר' יצחק. *דאמר רבי יצחק: כל העובר עבירה בסתר כאילו דוחק רגלי שכינה, שנא': °"כה אמר ה' השמים כסאי והארץ הדום רגלי". איני? (ג) *והאמר ר' אלעא הזקן: אם רואה אדם שיצרו מתגבר עליו — ילך למקום שאין מכירין אותו, וילבש שחורין ויתעטף שחורין, ויעשה מה שלבו חפץ, ואל יחלל שם שמים בפרהסיא! לא קשיא: הא — דמצי כייף ליה ליצריה, הא דלא מצי כייף ליצריה. דרש ר' יהודה ברבי נחמני, מתורגמניה דריש לקיש: כל המסתכל בג' דברים עיניו כהות: [א]בקשת, ובנשיא, [ב]ובכהנים. בקשת — דכתיב: "כמראה הקשת אשר יהיה בענן ביום הגשם הוא מראה דמות כבוד ה'", בנשיא — דכתיב: °"ונתת מהודך עליו". (ד) המסתכל בכהנים בזמן שבהמ"ק קיים, שהיו עומדין על דוכנן ומברכין את ישראל בשם המפורש. דרש ר' יהודה ברבי נחמני מתורגמניה דריש לקיש: מאי דכתיב: °"אל תאמינו ברע אל תבטחו באלוף"? אם יאמר לך יצר הרע חטוא והקב"ה מוחל (ה) — אל תאמן, (שנא'): "אל תאמן ברע" ואין רע אלא יצר הרע, שנאמר: °"כי יצר לב האדם רע" ואין אלוף אלא הקב"ה, שנאמר: °"אלוף נעורי אתה". *)שמא תאמר: מי מעיד בי? אבני ביתו וקורות ביתו של אדם, הם מעידין בו, שנאמר: °"כי אבן מקיר תזעק וכפים מעץ יעננה". (ו) וחכ"א: נשמתו של אדם מעידה בו, שנאמר: °"משכבת חיקך שמור פתחי פיך" אי זו היא דבר ששוכבת בחיקו של אדם — הוי אומר זו נשמה. ר' זריקא אמר: שני מלאכי השרת המלוין אותו הן מעידין בו, שנאמר: °"כי מלאכיו יצוה לך לשמרך בכל דרכיך". (*וחכ"א): אבריו של אדם מעידין בו, שנאמר: °"ואתם עדי נאם ה' ואני אל".§

מתני'

(*יוסי) בן יועזר אומר שלא לסמוך, יוסף בן יוחנן אומר [ג]לסמוך, יהושע בן פרחיה אומר שלא לסמוך. ניתאי הארבלי אומר לסמוך, יהודה בן טבאי אומר שלא לסמוך. שמעון בן שטח אומר לסמוך, שמעיה אומר לסמוך, אבטליון אומר שלא לסמוך. הלל ומנחם לא נחלקו, יצא מנחם נכנס שמאי. *שמאי אומר שלא לסמוך, הלל אומר לסמוך. הראשונים

*) תענית יא:

דברים לג | שיר ה | ישעיה מח | מלכים א יט | יחזקאל א | ישעיה סו | במדבר כז | מיכה ז | בראשית ח | ירמיה ג | חבקוק ב | מיכה ז | תהלים צא | ישעיה מג | שבת טו.

רש"י

מאי דרש. מהיכן הבין מקום השכינה שנזהר שלא הציץ שם. א"נ שלא טעה כמו שטעה אחר: דוגמא. דבר היכר העומד לדוגמא, להראותו, לומר: כזה עשה לי. ואין זה אלא דבר הניכר. אף כאן מקומו ניכר: ומה למטה. והרי אמר: "ומתחת זרועות עולם" (דברים לג), ואם שאל מי סבלן — לא חס על כבוד קונו. לייטי עלה במערבא לא גרסינן לה: כאלו דוחק רגלי השכינה. אומר בלבו: אין השכינה כאן, וכתיב: "והארץ הדום רגלי": למקום שאין מכירין אותו. אין דעתו גסה עליו, ושמא יקל כח יצרו. וגם אם יחטא — אין אדם נותן (ז) לב, לפי שאינו חשוב בעיניהם. וכן בלבוש שחורים: דמצי כייף ליה ליצריה. ובוטח על שהוא נחבא בסתר, כאילו דוחק הרגלים: היכא דלא מצי כייף ליה ליצריה. טוב לו בלינעא מפרהסיא: ומברכין את העם בשם המפורש. שהשכינה שורה על קשרי אצבעותיהם: אל תאמינו ברע. האומר לך חטא: ואל תבטחו באלוף. לומר שימחול: וכפים. חתיכת עץ, כמו כפיסין בבבא בתרא (דף ג.): אתם עדי. הוא מעיד בעצמו בכל עונות שאוכיח בפניו: מתני' יוסי בן יועזר אומר שלא לסמוך. ב"ט, וזו היא מחלוקת ראשונה שהיתה בחכמי ישראל: יהושע בן פרחיה. כולן דור אחר דור: יצא מנחם. בגמרא מפרש להיכן יצא: נכנס שמאי. להיות אב ב"ד תחתיו:

תוספות

כבני אדם. הוה מצי למיחשב ישנים ומוציאין ריעי כבני אדם, כדלקמן גבי דדמי לבהמה. ואיכא למימר דהוי בכלל הני ואף לקמן לא הוה חשיב ליה אלא משום דבעי (ח) אשכחי' שלשה דומין לבהמה. הר"ר אלחנן: ויעשה מה שלבו חפץ. (ט) לגמרי. משמע דמוטב לו לאדם שיעשה חפצו בסתר ולא בפרהסיא. ולא כפר"ח דשילהי פ"ק דקדושין (דף מ. ושם) דפירש דח"ו שהיה מתיר לעשות עבירה, אלא קאמר: ילבש שחורים וילך למקום אחר, דלבישת שחורים ואכסנאות משברין לבו, ולא יבא לידי עבירה, ויוכל לעשות מעכשיו מה שלבו חפץ — דודאי אין יצרו מתגבר עליו. וסוגיא דשמעתא אינו משמע כדבריו הכא ובריש פרק בתרא דמועד קטן (דף יז. ושם):

בכהנים בזמן שבית המקדש קיים. מכאן קשה על פרש"י דפ"ג דמגילה (דף כד:) על ההיא דתנן: *ידיו בוהקניות — לא ישא כפיו, ופי': משום שהעם מסתכלין בו. ואמרינן בחגיגה: המסתכל בכהנים בשעה שנושאין כפיהן — עיניו כהות. והא ליתא, דמסקינן: דוקא בזמן שבית המקדש קיים. ואילו התם בגבולים, מדמקשי מיניה בגמרא מההיא דהוה בשיבבותיה דרב הונא (י) והוה פריס ידיה! ומשני: דלמא דש בעירו הוה, ונראה לפרש דאף בגבולין מיתסר משום היסח הדעת. והכי איתא בירושלמי דהתם, א"ר יוסי: הדא אמרה שאסור להסתכל בכהנים בשעה שהם מברכין את העם, א"ר חגי: כלום אמר אלא משום היסח, אנא מסתכל ולא מסחנא דעתאי:

יוסי בן יועזר כו'. בירושלמי אמר: בראשונה לא היה מחלוקת אלא על הסמיכה בלבד, ועמדו שמאי והלל ועשו ד'. משרבו תלמידי שמאי והלל שלא שמשו כל צרכן — רבו מחלוקות בישראל, ונחלקו לב' כיתות. ויש לתמוה: הרי נחלקו כבר בימי שאול על מלוה ופרוטה (סנהדרין יט.)! ושמא, כיון דשאול ובית דינו הוו סברי דעתו אמלוה, ולא היה אדם חולק עליו, רק לפי סברת דוד — לא מתקרי מחלוקת. ומה שאמר בירושלמי: ועמדו שמאי והלל ועשו ד' — לא מצינו בפ"ק דשבת (דף יד:) רק שלשה דברים שנחלקו בהן:

*שנים מזוגות האחרונים שאמרו לסמוך (כ) נשיאים הוו. ולא תתמה על הא דחשיב שמאי מקמי הלל, והלל נשיא לכ"ע. איכא למימר בהיות כי ג' מזוגות הראשונים אשר אמרו שלא לסמוך היו נשיאים, ושמאי סבר כוותייהו — נקט ליה בראשונה. ואגב דנקט ליה הכא בראשונה — חשיב ליה בכל מקום שמאי מקמי הלל. והכא ליכא למיטעי, לפי שנכנס במקום מנחם דחשיב אחר הלל, וא"כ אב ב"ד היה, וכן שמאי נמי הכי:

רבינו חננאל

בכבודי מאי דרוש אמר ר' יוחנן ואתא מרבבות קודש אות הוא ברבבה שלו [ה' צבאות שמו] אדון הוא בצבא שלו אמר רבי יוחנן לא ברוח ה' ואחר הרוח רעש לא ברעש ה' ואחר הרעש אש לא באש ה' ואחר האש קול דממה דקה [והנה ד' עובר]: ת"ר ו' דברים נאמרו בשדין שלשה כמלאכים יש להן כנפים ושטין מסוף העולם ועד סופו ושומעין מה שעתיד להיות וג' כבני אדם פרין ורבין ואוכלין ושותין ומתין כבני אדם: ו' דברים יש בבני אדם יש בהן דעת ומהלכין בקומה זקופה ומספרין לשון קודש כמלאכים אוכלין ושותין ומוציאין רעי ופרים ורבים כבהמה. א) שאלו את בן זומא בתולה שעיברה מהו. מי חיישינן לדשמואל דאמר יכול אני לבעול כמה בתולות בלא דם. או דלמא הא דשמואל לא שכיחא [כו'] וחיישינן שמא באמבטי עיברה כו', פירוש אשה הרה שנבדקה ונמצאת בתולה מי אמרינן מביאה נתעברה כשמואל והריני קורא בה אשה כי תזריע וילדה זכר ב) וטמאה וחייבת [קרבן] לידה או דלמא אימור באמבטי של מרחץ נתעברה כגון שירד איש באותה האמבטי ופלט ש"ז וירדה אשה וקירבה באותה טיפה של ש"ז ונכנסה בתוך רחמה ונתעברה וזה מעשה נסים הוא ואינה טמאה לידה שאין אני קורא בה אשה כי תזריע. ומקשינן וכי הריון באמבטי כי האי גוונא מי משכחת לה והאמר שמואל כל שכבת זרע שאינו יורה כחץ אינה מזרעת ופרקינן כי אמר שמואל דבעינן יריית כחץ בעת שפולטה האיש וזו הש"ז האיש שפלטה באמבטי יורה כחץ הוה ולא איפשיטא ושמעינן שנמצאת אשה הרה ובעת לידה לא היתה יכולה לילד שאמרו כי היא בתולה וקרעו לה הנשים בדינר של זהב אותם המסוככין המלואין דם בתולין וילדה: מתני' כל המסתכל בד' דברים ראוי לו כאילו לא בא לעולם. פי' טוב ממנו הנפל שלא בא לעולם כי אין לאדם להתעסק אלא [במה] שנצטוה להכיר קונו בעשיית חוקיו ומשפטיו כי עשיית משפט וצדקה הם ידיעתו של הקב"ה כדכתיב בעשיית צדקה ומשפט הלא הוא הדעת אותי נאום ה' ולעשות מצותיו ותורותיו אבל להסתכל לידע מה למעלה ומה למטה מה לפנים ומה לאחור לא. כי לא נתנה רשות לאדם להתעסק אלא בדבר שהוא מן היום אשר ברא אלהים אדם על הארץ ולמקצה השמים ועד קצה השמים ולא בדברים אחרים. בשלמא מה למעלה ומה למטה ומה לאחור יש להימנע דלמא אתי להטיח מילין כלפי למעלה. אלא לפנים מאי איכפת לן [מה] דהוה הוה. ומשני ר' יוחנן ור' אלעזר משל למלך ב"ו כו'. כל שלא חס על כבוד קונו ראוי לו כאלו לא בא לעולם מאי היא רבה אמר זה המסתכל בקשת ואומר כגון זה דמות ה' שנא' כמראה הקשת אשר יהיה בענן וגו' רב יוסף אמר זה העובר עבירה ומסתתר מבני אדם ואינו חושש לכבודו של מקום שנסתרות לפניו כגלויות וכדרבי יצחק [דאמר] העובר עבירה בסתר כו' שנמצא גונב דעת הבריות ואינו חושש לכבודו של מקום ומקשינן איני כי העובר עבירה בסתר יותר הוא רע מן העובר בגלוי. והתניא [ר'] אילעאי הזקן אומר אם רואה אדם שיצרו מתגבר עליו כו' ח"ו שאילעאי הזקן התיר לעבור עבירה כלל אלא כך א' אם ראה אדם שיצרו מתגבר עליו באכילה ובשתיה ובמיני זמר ומתיירא שמא ישתכר ויבא לידי עבירה התיר לו לילך למקום אחר וילבש שחורים כל זה כדי לשבור את יצרו שהאכסניא לבו שבור כדאמרינן כלבא בלא מאתיה שב שנין לא נבח. וכיון שעושה כן לבו נשבר ונמצא נמנע מאליו. אבל לעבור עבירה או אפילו שתיית יין במיני זמר המרגילין לשמחה אסור וכ"ש מה שהוא למעלה מזה והוא דלא מצי כייף ליה ליצריה וההוא צורבא מרבנן [במו"ק יז] דהוו סנו שמעניה היה שותה במיני זמר ופירש שם דעבד כר' אילעאי. דאי ס"ד עבירה ג) הוה רב יהודה בעי אי משמתינן ליה אי לא אלא לא התיר אלעאי אלא כי האי וכיוצא בו דליכא עבירה ואע"פ לצורבא מרבנן חילול שמים הוא כמפורש בפסחים פרק [אלו עוברין דף מט.] כל המסתכל בג' דברים עיניו כהות. בקשת שנאמר כמראה הקשת וגו'

א) שייך לדף יד ע"ב. ב) מדברי רבינו נראה דלא גרס מהו לכה"ג רק בתולה שעיברה מהו סתם ומפ' דמבעיא ליה לענין טומאת לידה וקרבן. ג) נראה דל"ל דאי ס"ד עבירה ממש עבר לא הוי רב יהודא בעי אי משמתינן ליה אי לא וכו'.

הגהות הב"ח

(א) גמ' דאמרי תרוייהו למה"ד משל למלך: (ב) שם רב יוסף אמר זה העובר עבירה בסתר. נ"ב ס"א רבה אמר כל המסתכל בקשת צריך שיפול על פניו דכתיב כמראה הקשת אשר יהיה בענן ביום הגשם וכו' ואראה ואפול על פני וכו' לייטי עליה במערבא משום דמיחזי כמינות אלא לימא ברוך זוכר הברית הרואה את הקשת צריך לברך מאי מברך ברוך זוכר הברית רבי ישמעאל בנו של ר' יוחנן בן ברוקה אומר ברוך זוכר הברית נאמן בבריתו וקיים במאמרו: (ג) שם איני והא תניא רבי אלעא הזקן אומר אם רואה וכו' עליו בכל יום וילך למקום: (ד) שם מהודך עליו בכהנים בזמן שבית המקדש קיים בשעה שהיו כצ"ל ותיבת המסתכל נמחק: (ה) שם מוחל לך אל תאמין וכו' האדם רע מנעוריו ואין אלוף: (ו) שם וכפים מעץ יעננה רבי זריקא אומר נשמתו וכו' זו נשמה תניא רבי שילא אמר שני מלאכי השרת: (ז) רש"י ד"ה למקום וכו' נותן לו לב: (ח) תוס' ד"ה כבני וכו' דבעי לאשכוחי שלשה: (ט) ד"ה ויעשה מה שלבו חפץ משמע דמותר לו לאדם שיעשה לגמרי חפצו וכו' דסוגיא: (י) ד"ה בכהנים וכו' דרב הונא דהוה פריס וכו' נראה לפרש וכו' כלום אמרו אין מסתכלין אלא משום היסח הדעת אנא מסתכל: (כ) ד"ה ושנים וכו' לסמוך היו נשיאים ואל תתמה וכו' בהיות נ"ב ואע"ג דאבטליון נמי סבר שלא לסמוך לא נקיט ליה בראשונה [דאיכא למיטעי דהוה נשיא] משא"כ בשמאי דליכא למיטעי:

אראה בנחמה. לישנא קלילא (ד) הוי, דשבועה בלשון קלר, כלומר: לא יוכל לראות בנחמות ציון אם לא עשה זה*. ודומה לו: אקפח את בני שהלכה זו מקופחת בישראל, דרבי טרפון בשמעתא דמרדעת בפ"ק דשבת (דף יז. ושם). ודוגמא מלינו לשון המקרא: "ואולם חי אני וימלא כבוד ה' וגו' אם יראו וגו'" (במדבר יד)*: **אם** לא הרגתי עד זומם. תימה: אמאי לא מקשינן הכא: השתא בהמתן של לדיקים אין הקב"ה מביא תקלה על ידן – לדיקים עלמן לא כל שכן? כדפריך בגיטין (דף ז. ושם) ובחולין (דף ה: ושם)! וי"ל: דלא שייך לאקשויי רק גבי דבר אכילה, דגנאי הוא ללדיק דאוכל דבר איסור. אבל דבר היתר בשעת האיסור – לא פריך. ולהכי לא פריך בר"ה (דף כא.) דאמר: (ה) כמה בשים תבשילא דבבל בלומא רבא דמערבא. וב"ערבי פסחים" (פסחים קו: ושם) ברב ירמיה בר אבא דאישתלי וטעים קודם הבדלה, אע"ג דמיתתו באסכרא – דאין דבר מגונה כל כך אכילת היתר בשעת האיסור*: **למחר** הוא מת. הא דלא נקט כשאינני שם אין קולו נשמע – משום שהיו אומרים לו דאינו לועק אלא בשעה שישנו שם. אבל השתא, מדנקט מת, שיהא גביה – אז היה לו ללעוק: **אב** ב"ד מי קא מורה בפני נשיא – הוראה לדין. ובירושלמי אמר: מאן דאמר יהודה בן טבאי נשיא – עובדא דאלכסנדריא מסייע ליה(ו). דבני ירושלים בעון מיננא נשיא ולא קבלו עילוי, ערק ואזל לאלכסנדריא. והיו בני ירושלים כותבין: מירושלם הגדולה לאלכסנדריא הקטנה: עד מתי *אחי יושב אללכם ואני יושבת עגומה עליו. ומאן דתני שמעון בן שטח נשיא – עובדא דאשקלון מסייע ליה, ומייתי כולא עובדא שתלה פ' נשים מכשפניות. ובסנהדרין (דף מד:) הביאו רש"י בנימוקו*: **לא** מצטריפנא. לנטות אחרי רבים, כדי לבטל דברי שמעון בן שטח: **דבר** אל בני ישראל וסמך. אבל בשחיטה ליכא למעט נשים מהאי טעמא, אע"ג דסמיך טפי להקרבה מסמיכה, דהא ברים "כל הפסולין" (זבחים לב.) מרבינן נשים לשחיטה. וכן ליכא לאלופי שחיטה בבעלים דומי א דסמיכה, דההוא היקש לא הוי אלא דרבנן*: **לעשות** נחת רוח לנשים. וכגון שהיתה בהמה שלהן, (ז) השתא דומה לסמיכה להיו' בבעלים. בפ"ק דקדושין (דף לא.*) ובפ' בתרא דר"ה (דף לג.*) פירש ר"י: דנשים דידן, אם באות לעשות מלות עשה שהזמן גרמא ולברך עליהן – אין ממחין בידם, אע"ג דפטורות, ולא מיקרי ברכה לבטלה. וכן משמע מהכא, ועוד פירשתי התם [בר"ה] והארכתי*):

*) [וע"ע תוס' עירובין לו. ד"ה דלמא כו']

הראשונים. שהוזכרו ראשון בכל זוג וזוג היו נשיאים: **גמ'** עד זומם. שלא הוזם אלא הוא לבדו: עד שיהרג הנדון. קודם הזמה, ואחר כך הוזמו. שהיו דורשין "נפש בנפש" האמור בעדים זוממין. אמרו להן חכמים, והלא כבר נאמר: "כאשר זמם לעשות לאחיו" ועדיין אחיו קיים, ולמה נאמר: "נפש בנפש" – שאין נהרגים עד שיגמר הדין של נידון קודם שהוזמו: ואין לוקין. אם העידוהו שחייב מלקות. בכולהו גרסי' עד שיזומו שניהן, ובמסכת מכות *יליף לה מקראי: "והנה עד שקר העד", ואמר מר*: כל מקום שנאמר עד – הרי כאן שנים: אלא בפני שמעון. שאם יטעה ילמדהו: היינו דקא מורה הלכה בפני שמעון. דמדקאמר מיד קיבל כו', שמע מינה דעד השתא אורי בפניו: ומאי קיבל. לאו דעד השתא הורה, דודאי לא הורה בפניו מימיו, וכשהרגו לעד זומם לא היה שמעון שם(ב): **לא** מצטריפנא. לישב בדין אלא בהדי שמעון: סיריקון. לבוש בגדי מלכות: אינה אלא משום שבות. דתנן, אלו הן משום שבות: לא עולין באילן, ולא רוכבין על גבי בהמה (ביצה דף לו:). והאי נמי משתמש בבעלי חיים הוא, שסומך עליה בכל כחו, כדאמרינן לקמן: שבות דמצוה. נמי תנינא במתני', ומאי אשמעינן רבי יוחנן: לאפוקי ממאן דאמר. במסכת ביצה (דף כ.): בסמיכה עצמה פליגי, ומאן דאסר – לאו משום שבות אסר, אלא משום דסבירא ליה דשלמי חובה לא בעו סמיכה, דכי כתב "וסמך" – בשלמי נדבה כתיב, וחובה מנדבה לא גמרינן, קא משמע לן רבי יוחנן דטעמא משום שבות הוא, וסמיכתן לעולם מצוה: שמע מינה. מדאוקי ר' יוחנן טעמא משום שבות סמיכה, דקדשים בכל כחו בעינן, והוה ליה משתמש בבעלי חיים: "דבר אל בני ישראל. אדם כי יקריב מכם קרבן לה'", וכתיב בההוא ענינא "וסמך": אבא אלעזר. כך שמו: אקפו ידייכו. לשון וקפא, הקילו ידיכם אקפו לשון דבר הצף ואין מכביד, כדמתרגמינן "ויצף הברזל" – וקפא ברזלא (מלכים ב ו): שמע מינה. מדר' יוחנן, דאוקי טעמא משום שבות, לדדין אסורין. ואע"ג דגבי שבות רכיבה אמרינן – הוא הדין לכל שימוש, ואפילו במקום שאינו עשוי להשתמש, כגון לידי הבהמה, והוא הדין לידי האילן. ופליגי אמוראי בהא מילתא במסכת שבת בפ' בתרא (דף קנד:): (ג) לסמוך. דהא ראש הבהמה כלדדין דמי: דבהדי

תורה אור

הראשונים היו נשיאים, ושניים להם *אב ב"ד.§ **גמ'** *ת"ר: שלשה מזוגות הראשונים שאמרו שלא לסמוך, ושנים מזוגות האחרונים שאמרו לסמוך, (הראשונים) היו נשיאים, ושניים להם אבות ב"ד, דברי רבי מאיר. וחכמים אומרים: יהודה בן טבאי – אב ב"ד, ושמעון בן שטח – נשיא. מאן תנא להא דתנו רבנן: *אמר[א] רבי יהודה בן טבאי: אראה בנחמה אם לא הרגתי עד זומם, להוציא מלבן של צדוקין, שהיו אומרים: "אין עדים זוממין נהרגין עד שיהרג הנידון". אמר לו שמעון בן שטח: אראה בנחמה אם לא שפכת דם נקי, שהרי אמרו חכמים: [א]אין עדים זוממין נהרגין – עד שיזומו שניהם, [ב]ואין לוקין – עד שיזומו שניהם, *[ג]ואין משלמין ממון – עד שיזומו שניהם. מיד קבל עליו יהודה בן טבאי שאינו מורה הלכה אלא בפני שמעון בן שטח. כל ימיו של יהודה בן טבאי היה משתטח על קברו של אותו הרוג, והיה קולו נשמע. כסבורין העם לומר שקולו של הרוג הוא, אמר להם: קולי הוא, תדעו שלמחר הוא מת ואין קולו נשמע. אמר ליה רב אחא בריה דרבא לרב אשי: ודלמא פיוסי פייסיה, או בדינא תבעי'? מני הא? אי אמרת בשלמא רבי מאיר, דאמר: שמעון בן שטח אב ב"ד, ר"י בן טבאי נשיא – היינו דקא מורי הלכה בפני שמעון בן שטח. אלא אי אמרת רבנן, דאמרי: יהודה בן טבאי אב ב"ד, שמעון בן שטח נשיא – אב ב"ד בפני נשיא מי מורה הלכה? לא, מאי קבל עליו דקאמר – לאצטרופי, דאפי' אצטרופי נמי לא מצטריפנא.§ יצא מנחם ונכנס שמאי כו'.§ להיכן יצא? אביי אמר: יצא לתרבות רעה. רבא אמר: יצא לעבודת המלך. תניא נמי הכי: יצא מנחם לעבודת המלך, ויצאו עמו שמונים זוגות תלמידים לבושין סיריקון. אמר רב שמן בר אבא א"ר יוחנן: לעולם אל תהא שבות קלה בעיניך, שהרי סמיכה אינה אלא משום שבות, ונחלקו בה גדולי הדור. פשיטא! שבות מצוה אצטריכא ליה. הא נמי פשיטא! לאפוקי ממאן דאמר בסמיכה גופה פליגי, קא משמע לן בשבות הוא דפליגי. אמר רמי בר חמא: שמע מינה [ד]סמיכה בכל כחו בעינן. דאי ס"ד לא בעינן בכל כחו – מאי קא עביד? ליסמוך! מיתיבי: "דבר (ויקרא א) אל בני ישראל וסמך", *[ה]בני ישראל סומכין ואין בנות ישראל סומכות. רבי יוסי ור'[ב] (*ישמעאל) אומרים: בנות ישראל סומכות רשות. אמר רבי יוסי: סח לי אבא אלעזר: פעם אחת היה לנו עגל של זבחי שלמים, והביאנוהו לעזרת נשים, וסמכו עליו נשים. לא מפני שסמיכה בנשים – אלא כדי לעשות נחת רוח לנשים. ואי ס"ד סמיכה בכל כחו בעינן – משום נחת רוח דנשים עבדינן עבודה בקדשים? אלא לאו שמע מינה: לא בעינן בכל כחו. לעולם אימא לך בעינן בכל כחו. דאמר להו: אקפו ידייכו. אי הכי "לא מפני שסמיכה בנשים"? תיפוק ליה דאינה לסמיכה כלל! א"ר אמי: חדא ועוד קאמר; חדא – דליתא לסמיכה כלל! ועוד: כדי לעשות נחת רוח לנשים. אמר רב פפא: שמע מינה *[ו]צדדין אסורין, דאי ס"ד צדדין מותרין (א) – לסמוך לצדדין, אלא לאו שמע מינה: צדדין אסורין. רב

רבינו חננאל

בנשיא שנאמר ונתת מהידך עליו בכהנים בזמן שבהמ"ק קיים ובשעה שעומדין על הדוכן ומברכין העם בשם המפורש מפני שאלו כולן אתו להרהורי בכבוד השם ולא (יסתכל) [יאמר] האדם כשעובר עבירה בסתר מי מעיד בי ואמרינן אבני ביתו [מעידין אותו] שנאמר כי אבן מקיר תזעק וכפים מעץ יעננה. תניא שני מלאכים המלוין לו לאדם הן מעידין בו שנא' כי מלאכיו יצוה לך לשמרך בכל דרכיך וי"א נשמתו ואבריו הן [מעידין] בו: **מתני'** יוסי בן יועזר אומר שלא לסמוך יוסי בן יוחנן אומר לסמוך כו': ת"ר ג' מזוגות הראשונים שאמרו שלא לסמוך ושנים מזוגות האחרונים שאמרו לסמוך הראשונים נשיאים והשניים אבות ב"ד וכך סידורן יוסי בן יועזר נשיא יוסי בן יוחנן אב ב"ד. יהושע בן פרחיה נשיא נתאי הארבלי אב ב"ד יהודה בן טבאי נשיא שמעון בן שטח אב ב"ד הללו ג' זוגות הנשיאים אמרו שלא לסמוך. ואבות בתי דינים אמרו לסמוך שמעיה והלל נשיאים אמרו לסמוך אבטליון ושמאי אבות בתי דינים אמרו שלא לסמוך אלו דברי הכל הן וחלקו בזה הזוג. ר' מאיר אומר יהודה בן טבאי נשיא ושמעון בן שטח אב ב"ד וחכמים אומרים שמעון בן שטח נשיא ויהודה בן טבאי אב ב"ד ומסתברא כר' מאיר דברייתא מסייעא ליה והאי פירוקא דפרקי לאוקומה לרבנן שנויה היא ולא סמכינן עלה יצא מנחם לעבודת המלך ויצאו עמו שמונים תלמידים לובשי סריקון של זהב א"ר אלעזר לעולם אל תהי שבות קלה בעיניך לזלזל בה שהרי סמיכה על הזבח ביו"ט משום שבות הוא ואע"פ שהוא שבות דמצוה נחלקו עליה גדולי הדור הללו. ולא מצינו שהיתה חלוקה כלל בין החכמים הראשונים אלא בסמיכה בלבד באו הלל ושמאי חלקו בג' דברים אבל תלמידיהן שלא שמשו כל צרכן רבתה חלוקה ביניהן ונעשית תורה כשתי תורות ואמרינן מאי אתא ר' יוחנן לאשמעינן אי משום שבות דמצוה תנינא לא מקדשין ולא מעריכין ולא מחרימין שהיא שבות דמצוה ואינו דוחה. ושנינן לאפוקי ממאן דאמר בסמיכה עצמה פליגי. פי' מי שאומר שלא לסמוך סבר לא בעינן תיכף לסמיכה שחיטה ואפשר לסמוך היום ולשחוט למחר והאומר לסמוך סבר בעינן תיכף לסמיכה שחיטה קמ"ל ר' יוחנן דדברי הכל בעינן תיכף לסמיכה שחיטה וכי פליגי בשבות פליגי הני אסרי והני שרי ואסקה רב אשי אפילו תימא צדדין מותרין כל דלהדי גבאי דרישא כגבא דמו.

עין משפט נר מצוה:

[עי' בפרש"י מכות דף ה:]

יד א ב ג מיי' פ"כ מהל' עדות הלכה א סמג עשין קט טור ח"מ סי' לח:

[עיין תוס' שבת טו: ד"ה אקפח]

טו ד מיי' פ"א מהלכות חגיגה הל' ט ופ"ג מהלכות מעשה קרבנות הלכה יג:

טז ה מיי' שם הלכה ח סמג עשין קפו:

יז ו מיי' שם הל' יג:

[ועי' תוס' שבת יב: ד"ה ר' נתן]

גליון הש"ס

גמ' סמיכה בכל כחו בעינן. עיין לעיל דף ד ע"א תוס' ד"ה אלא טומטום ועיין פסחים קד פע"א תוס' ד"ה ואילו פסח וביבמות דף קה ע"א תוס' ד"ה ואין ב"ד שקול: תוס' ד"ה דבר וכו' בריש כל הפסולין מרבינן נשים לשחיטה. ובעניי לא מלאתי שם רק ילפותא לשחיטה כשרה בזרים אבל על נשים ליכא ראי' וצ"ע:

[ג"ל ארוסי וכ"ה בירושל']

קלת בסיגנון אחר ירושלמי הבלה עיי' עליהם

כדאיתא התם ע"ש ועי' מנחות יט. ול"ע קלת

[בכ"ה דלא]

[בכ"ה האר"י]

מסורת הש"ס:

נ"ל אבות

[תוספתא פ"ב]

[דף ה: בגמרא גופה ליתא אבל בפרש"י ד"ה שהרי איתא]

מכות ה: [תוספתא דסנהדרין פ"ו]

[מכות ג.]

הגהות הב"ח

(א) גמ' לצדדין מותרין נסמוך לצדדין: (ב) רש"י ד"ה מאי קיבל וכו' שמעון שם ולא קיבל הס"ד ואח"כ מה"ד אלא לאצטרופי: (ג) ד"ה לסמוך דהא ראשה: (ד) תוס' ד"ה אראה וכו' קלילא לשבועה הוי בלשון נקר ודוגמא זו מלינו: (ה) ד"ה אם לא וכו' לאמר התם כמה בשים: (ו) ד"ה אב ב"ד כו' מסייע ליה יהודה בן טבאי הוון בני ירושלים בעון ממני יהודה נשיא ולא קביל עילויה ערק לאלכסנדריא וכו' עד מתי ארוסי יושב אללכם: (ז) ד"ה לעשות וכו' דהשתא דומה כו' ובפ' בתרא דר"ה פירשתי דנשים:

הגהות הגר"א

[א] גמ' אמר יהודה כו' כל"ל (וכמ"ש במתני' ובאבות פ"א מ"ח): [ב] שם ישמעאל נ"ל שמעון וכ"ה בעירובין ובר"ה ובחולין:

עירובין צו: ר"ה לג. חולין פה. [קדושין לו.]

[שבת קנה.]

תורה אור

רַב אַשִׁי אָמַר: אֲפִילּוּ תֵּימָא צְדָדִין מוּתָּרִין, כָּל דְּבַהֲדֵי גַּבָּהּ – כְּגַבָּהּ דָּמֵי.§ **מתני'** *בֵּית שַׁמַּאי אוֹמְרִים: מְבִיאִין שְׁלָמִים וְאֵין סוֹמְכִין עֲלֵיהֶם, אֲבָל לֹא עוֹלוֹת. וּבֵית הִלֵּל אוֹמְרִים: אמְבִיאִין שְׁלָמִים וְעוֹלוֹת בוְסוֹמְכִין עֲלֵיהֶם. עֲצֶרֶת שֶׁחָל לִהְיוֹת בְּעֶרֶב שַׁבָּת, בֵּית שַׁמַּאי אוֹמְרִים: יוֹם טְבוֹחַ (א) אַחַר הַשַּׁבָּת, וּבֵית הִלֵּל אוֹמְרִים: *אֵין יוֹם טְבוֹחַ אַחַר הַשַּׁבָּת. *וּמוֹדִים שֶׁאִם חָלָה לִהְיוֹת בַּשַּׁבָּת, שֶׁיּוֹם טְבוֹחַ אַחַר הַשַּׁבָּת. אֵין כֹּהֵן גָּדוֹל מִתְלַבֵּשׁ בְּכֵלָיו, וּמוּתָּרִין בְּהֶסְפֵּד וּבְתַעֲנִית, שֶׁלֹּא לְקַיֵּים דִּבְרֵי הָאוֹמְרִין: עֲצֶרֶת אַחַר הַשַּׁבָּת.§ **גמ'** א"ר אֶלְעָזָר א"ר אוֹשַׁעְיָא: *גמִנַּיִין לַעֲצֶרֶת שֶׁיֵּשׁ לָהּ תַּשְׁלוּמִין כָּל שִׁבְעָה – שֶׁנֶּאֱמַר: °"בְּחַג הַמַּצּוֹת וּבְחַג הַשָּׁבוּעוֹת וּבְחַג הַסּוּכּוֹת" (דברים טז), דמַקִּישׁ חַג הַשָּׁבוּעוֹת לְחַג הַמַּצּוֹת: מַה חַג הַמַּצּוֹת יֵשׁ לָהּ תַּשְׁלוּמִין כָּל שִׁבְעָה, אַף חַג הַשָּׁבוּעוֹת יֵשׁ לָהּ תַּשְׁלוּמִין כָּל שִׁבְעָה. וְאֵימָא: מַקִּישׁ לְחַג הַסּוּכּוֹת, מַה חַג הַסּוּכּוֹת יֵשׁ לָהּ תַּשְׁלוּמִין כָּל שְׁמוֹנָה – אַף חַג הַשָּׁבוּעוֹת יֵשׁ לָהּ תַּשְׁלוּמִין כָּל שְׁמוֹנָה! שְׁמִינִי רֶגֶל בִּפְנֵי עַצְמוֹ הוּא. אֵימוּר דְּאָמְרִי *שְׁמִינִי רֶגֶל בִּפְנֵי עַצְמוֹ הוּא, הָנֵי מִילֵּי *לְעִנְיַן פז"ר קש"ב, אֲבָל לְעִנְיַן תַּשְׁלוּמִין – תַּשְׁלוּמִין דְּרִאשׁוֹן הוּא? *דִּתְנַן: מִי שֶׁלֹּא חָג בְּיוֹם טוֹב הָרִאשׁוֹן שֶׁל חַג – חוֹגֵג אֶת כָּל הָרֶגֶל וְיוֹם טוֹב הָאַחֲרוֹן! *תָּפַשְׂתָּ מְרוּבֶּה – לֹא תָּפַשְׂתָּ, תָּפַשְׂתָּ מוּעָט – תָּפַשְׂתָּ. אֶלָּא (ב) לְמַאי הִלְכְתָא כְּתַבֵיהּ רַחֲמָנָא לְחַג הַסּוּכּוֹת? לְאַקּוּשֵׁי לְחַג הַמַּצּוֹת, מַה חַג הַמַּצּוֹת טָעוּן לִינָה – אַף חַג הַסּוּכּוֹת טָעוּן לִינָה. וְהָתָם מְנָלַן? דִּכְתִיב

רש"י

דְּבַהֲדֵי גַּבָּהּ. שֶׁשָּׁוֶה לְגוּפוֹ הַגַּב שֶׁל בְּהֵמָה: כְּגַבָּהּ שֶׁל בְּהֵמָה דָּמֵי. וְהָרֹאשׁ שָׁוֶה בְּגוּפוֹ לְגַב הַבְּהֵמָה: **מתני'** מְבִיאִין שְׁלָמִים. בְּיו"ט שֶׁהֵן אֲכִילַת הֶדְיוֹט: וְאֵין סוֹמְכִין עֲלֵיהֶן. כִּדְאָמְרִינַן, אֶלָּא סוֹמֵךְ עֲלֵיהֶן מֵעֶרֶב יו"ט, וְשׁוֹחֲטָן בְּיו"ט, דְּלָא בָּעֵינַן תֵּכֶף לִסְמִיכָה שְׁחִיטָה: אֲבָל לֹא מְבִיאִין עוֹלוֹת. בְּאוֹתָן שֶׁיָּכוֹל לַהֲבִיאָן לְאַחַר יו"ט. דִּכְתִיב: "הוּא לְבַדּוֹ יֵעָשֶׂה לָכֶם" (שמות יב) – לָכֶם וְלֹא לְגָבוֹהַּ: יוֹם טְבוֹחַ. שֶׁל קָרְבְּנוֹת רְאִיָּיה וַחֲגִיגָה שֶׁל יו"ט – לְאַחַר הַשַּׁבָּת. שֶׁאֵין קְרֵבִין לֹא בְּיו"ט וְלֹא בְּשַׁבָּת: אֵין לָהּ יוֹם טְבוֹחַ. אֵינָהּ צְרִיכָה יוֹם טְבוֹחַ, שֶׁמּוּתָּר לְהַקְרִיבָן בְּיו"ט: אֵין כֹּהֵן גָּדוֹל מִתְלַבֵּשׁ בְּכֵלִים. נָאִים בְּבֵיתוֹ וּבַשּׁוּק. וְלָאו בִּשְׁעַת עֲבוֹדָה קָאָמַר, וְלֹא בְּבִגְדֵי כְהוּנָּה קָאֵי, אֶלָּא שֶׁלֹּא יִתְנָאֶה בְּאוֹתוֹ הַיּוֹם, שֶׁיּוֹם טְבוֹחַ שֶׁל עֲצֶרֶת אַחַר שַׁבָּת, (ג) שֶׁיָּבִינוּ הַכֹּל שֶׁאֵינוֹ הַיּוֹם יו"ט. מִפְּנֵי הַצְּדוֹקִין שֶׁהָיוּ אוֹמְרִים עֲצֶרֶת אַחַר שַׁבָּת: **גמ'** מַה חַג הַמַּצּוֹת יֵשׁ לָהּ תַּשְׁלוּמִין כָּל שִׁבְעָה. כִּדְדָרְשִׁינַן קְרָאֵי בְּפ"ק (דף ט.) (*בְּחַג הַסּוּכּוֹת. וְה"ה לְחַג הַמַּצּוֹת, שֶׁהֲרֵי אַף הוּא שִׁבְעַת יָמִים: פז"ר קש"ב. פַּיִי"ס זְמַ"ן רֶגֶ"ל קָרְבָּ"ן שִׁי"ר בְּרָכָ"ה פַּיִּיס – לְעִנְיַן פָּרֵי הֶחָג. כָּל שִׁבְעַת יְמֵי הֶחָג אֵין מְפַיְּסִין עֲלֵיהֶן, אֶלָּא לְפִי חֶשְׁבּוֹן הַמִּשְׁמָרוֹת לְפִי סִידְרָן מַקְרִיבִין אוֹתָן, כִּדְתְנַן בְּמַסֶּכֶת סוּכָּה (דף נה:): מִי שֶׁהָיָה מַקְרִיב פָּרִים הַיּוֹם לֹא הָיָה מַקְרִיב לְמָחָר. וּפַר שֶׁל שְׁמִינִי מְפַיְּיסִין עָלָיו אֵיזֶהוּ מִן הַמִּשְׁמָרוֹת יַקְרִיבֶנּוּ. זְמַן – שֶׁהֶחֱיָינוּ. רֶגֶל – שֶׁיֵּשׁ לוֹ שֵׁם רֶגֶל בִּפְנֵי עַצְמוֹ, וְאֵינוֹ קָרוּי סוּכּוֹת. קָרְבָּן – שֶׁאֵין בְּהֵמוֹת קָרְבְּנוֹתָיו כְּסֵדֶר פָּרֵי הֶחָג. שֶׁפָּרֵי הֶחָג מִתְמַעֲטִין וְהוֹלְכִין, וּכְבָשֵׂיהֶן י"ד בְּכָל יוֹם וְאֵילִים שְׁנַיִם, וּבַשְּׁמִינִי – פַּר אֶחָד אַיִל אֶחָד וְשִׁבְעָה כְּבָשִׂים. שִׁיר – אֵין שִׁיר קָרְבְּנוֹתָיו כְּסֵדֶר שִׁיר שֶׁל יְמוֹת הֶחָג, וְאֵינוֹ מְדַבֵּר מֵעִנְיַן פָּרָשִׁיּוֹת שֶׁל הוֹמְבָּה"י (סוכה נה.) שֶׁהוּא סִימָן לַשִּׁיר שֶׁל יְמוֹת הֶחָג. בְּרָכָה – שֶׁהָיוּ מְבָרְכִים אֶת הַמֶּלֶךְ, זֵכֶר לִשְׁלֹמֹה שֶׁנֶּאֱמַר בּוֹ: "בַּיּוֹם הַשְּׁמִינִי שִׁלַּח אֶת הָעָם וַיְבָרְכוּ אֶת הַמֶּלֶךְ" (מלכים א ח): תָּפַשְׂתָּ מְרוּבֶּה לֹא תָּפַשְׂתָּ. כָּל מָקוֹם שֶׁתִּמְצָא שְׁנֵי דְּרָכִים, אֶחָד תּוֹפֵשׂ מְרוּבֶּה וְאֶחָד תּוֹפֵשׂ מוּעָט – טוֹב לְךָ לִתְפּוֹשׂ אֶת הַמּוּעָט. שֶׁאֲפִילוּ הָיָה לְךָ לִתְפּוֹשׂ אֶת הַמְּרוּבֶּה וְתָפַשְׂתָּ אֶת הַמּוּעָט – תְּפִיסָתְךָ תְּפִיסָה, שֶׁיֵּשׁ בִּכְלַל הַמְּרוּבֶּה הַמּוּעָט. אֲבָל אִם תִּתְפּוֹשׂ הַמְּרוּבֶּה, וְהָיָה לְךָ לִתְפּוֹשׂ הַמּוּעָט – נִמְצֵאתָ שֶׁתָּפַשְׂתָּ שֶׁלֹּא כַּדָּת: טָעוּן לִינָה. מוֹצָאֵי י"ט:

וּפָנִיתָ

תוספות

רב אשי אמר, אפילו תימא צדדין מותרין. דיתיה בעלמא, דהא ס"ל לרב אשי בפרק בתרא דשבת (דף קנה. ושם), אמר רב אשי: השתא דאמרינן לצדדין אסורין, אלא הכי קאמר: דמהא ליכא למישמע מינה*: **בית** שמאי אומרים מביאין שלמים. בבילה בפ"ב (דף יט.) מיתניא. והתם עיקר, והכא אגב גררא (ד) נסבה, שמיירי בחגיגה. וכן משמע, שמאריך התם טפי לפרש, ויש להוכיח מינה דבילה מיתניא מקמי מכילתין:

יום טבוח שלו אחר השבת. ולע"ג דלא חזו בראשון – מייתי לה בשני, אפילו למ"ד תשלומין דראשון. (ה) כיון שאין העכבה רק בשביל היום, כדפי' לעיל, חזיא מיהא קרינן ביה:

יום טבוח אחר השבת. פרש"י: קרבנות ראייה וחגיגה, שאין קרבין לא ביו"ט ולא בשבת. ולא יתכן לומר (ו) דחגיגה אמאי לא? ומ"ש משלמים לב"ש? ומיהו, בירושלמי מייתי: *אמרו להם לב"ה: נדרים ונדבות יוכיחו, [שמותרין להדיוט ואסורין לגבוה]. אמרו להם ב"ה: מה לנדרים ונדבות – שאין קבוע להם זמן, תאמרו בחגיגה שזמנה קבוע? אמרו להם ב"ש: חגיגה נמי אין זמנה קבוע, שאם לא חגג בראשון – חוגג והולך כל הרגל. אמרו להם ב"ה: כיון שאם לא חג ברגל אינו יכול לחוג אחר הרגל – היינו זמנו קבוע. משמע דאף בחגיגה פליגי, כדפרישית*: **אין** כהן (ז) מתלבש בכליו. פרש"י: בכלים נאים שלו. ובביתו ובשוק שלא בשעת עבודה, ולא בבגדי כהונה קאמר, אלא שלא יתנאה באותו יום טבוח, שיבינו הכל שאינו יו"ט: וקשה למורי: חדא, דלישנא לא משמע ליה, דה"ל למינקט "בכלים נאין", ועוד: מאי איריא כהן גדול? אפילו שאר אדם נמי! ונראה לו דכ' בגדים איירי, שבימים טובים היה רגיל כהן גדול לעבוד בשביל כבוד היום, אבל ביום טבוח לא היה לובשן כדי לעבוד, שלא יתראה להיות יו"ט. וראיה לדבריו בירושלמי בפירקין: א"ר יוסי בר בון בשם ריב"ל: בכל יום כ"ג מתלבש בכליו והולך ומקריב תמיד של שחר. אם יש שם נדרים ונדבות – מקריב אותן, והולך בביתו, ובא ומקריב תמיד של (ח) ערב. רבי עוקבא בשם ריב"ל אמר: לא היה עושה כן אלא בשבתות וי"ט. כלומר, שלא היה רגיל ומתלבש בכליו ולעבוד אלא אז, מפני כבוד היום. אבל אי בעי – מקריב בכל אות נפשו, כדתנן ביומא(ט) (דף יד.): מקריב בראש. וביום טבוח, אף לכולי עלמא לא היה מתלבש, שלא יכירו שהוא יום טוב:

אף עצרת יש לו תשלומין. *בירושלמי[א], אמר רבי יוסי בר בון: דוד מת בעצרת, והיו כל ישראל אוננין, והקריבו למחר. כלומר: מהתם משמע שהיה לו תשלומין. וקשה לה"ר אלחנן: תיפוק ליה בלאו הכי לא הקריבו בראשון, כיון שהיה שבת, כדמשמע בשבת בפרק "במה מדליקין" (שבת ל.) דבשבת נפטר דוד! ושמא התם לית ליה הכי אלא פליג אהא: **פז"ר** קש"ב. פרש"י: רגל בפני עצמו – שיש לו שם בפני עצמו, ואינו בכלל סוכות. וקשה לר"ת: דהא בפ' "לולב וערבה" (סוכה דף מז. ושם) אמר: כשם שחג טעון שיר קרבן ברכה ולינה – אף שמיני עצרת טעון ברכה וקרבן ושיר ולינה. מאי לאו זמן? לא, ברהמ"ז ותפלה. ועוד: לישנא דנקט ברכה בפני עצמו – משמע דאף בימים אחרים איתיה. והכי איתא בירושלמי: ברכה בפני עצמו מאי היא? א"ל: זמן א"ל זמן כל שבעה מי איכא? משמע דבברכת המזון ותפלה בעי למימר דליכא כל ז', ומפרש לשם מנא ידעינן שהוא רגל, דהא בכולהו כתיב "וביום" וכאן "ביום" ללמד שהוא רגל בפני עצמו. ונראה לר"ת: ברכה – ברכת המזון ותפלה, שמזכירין את שמיני עצרת, ורגל – היינו לינה, שטעון לינה בירושלים. ור"ת מפרש: רגל – לענין אבילות, והכא איתא בפרק בתרא דמועד קטן (דף כד:): הרי עברו עליו ערב החג והחג ושמיני שלו – הרי כאן כ"א. ושניהם יסד ר"ת במעריב שלו(י): לינת שלשים ידחם כשאר אבלים יחם. וברכת המלך לא בעי למימר, משום דנחית לאשר ימים וברכת המלך אינה לשם. ולינה לא בעי למימר לדברי רש"י ור"ת משום דפשיטא ליה. שיר, (כ) פרש"י: לא איתפרש ליה. ור"ת מפרש: דאומר מזמור שלו שלם. דבשאר ימי החג אומר הומבה"י כדמפרש התם, שמתחיל ביום (ל) אחד מזמור ומסיים בשני, וכאן כולו שלם. ורבי עוזיאל מלא *שאמר "למנצח על השמינית", מיהו, אומר ר"י: דהתם לא מדבר רק מה שאומר בפסוקי דזמרה, כמו שמוסיפים מזמורים בשבת – מ"מ משמע שהיו אומרים אותו במקדש, כיון דנתקן לומר: **תפשת** מועט תפשת. לפי שיש בכלל מאתים מנה(מ) ומ"מ חשבון שבידך אמתי. וי"מ: דלמדה מרובה אין קצבה, לעולם תוכל להרבות, אבל למועט יש סוף. ולא יתכן, דבת"כ פליגי תנאי בהא גבי זבה: "ימים" – מיעוט ימים שנים, יכול מרובים? א"ר עקיבא: כל שמשמעו מרובה ומשמעו מועט, תפסת מרובה לא תפסת. א"ר יהודה: שתי מדות, אחת כלה ואחת אינה כלה – מודדין במדה כלה ואין מודדין בשאינה כלה, א"ר נחמיה וכו' למה בא הכתוב לפתוח או לנעול*): **אף** חג הסוכות טעון לינה. אתיא כרשב"י ור"מ. דאילו לת"ק ור"ש ורשב"א בפ"ק דר"ה (דף ה. ושם) נפקא להו מדכתיב: ופנית בבוקר, כל פינות שאתה פונה לא יהו אלא לבקר. והכי נמי מרבה התם בפסחים (דף נה:) פסח שני אין צריכא קרא:

*) [וע"ע תוס' סוכה ה: ד"ה תפסת]

דכתיב

מסורת הש"ס

מגילה ה. לעיל ז: [בילה יט.]

ס"א אין לה יום טבוח

מגילה ה.

ר"ה ד: מו"ק כד:

[נ"ל לחג]

[סוכה מז.]

ר"ה ד: סוכה מח. יומא ג.

[ר"ה ד: יומא פ. סוכה ה. קדושין יז. חולין קלח. ערכין ד:]

[במס' סופרים פי"ט וכ"ה בירושלמי וכ"כ תוס' בסוכה מז. ד"ה שיר ורש"י ר"ה ד: ד"ה פז"ר קש"ב]

עין משפט נר מצוה

יח א ב מיי' פ"א מהל' חגיגה הלכה ח ט:

יט ג ד מיי' שם הלכה ז:

[ועי' תוס' שבת קנה. ד"ה אמר רב פפא וכו']

[וכן הוא בתוספתא פ"ב]

[נ"ל כדפי' רש"י]

לעיל ט. [בילה כ: מגילה ה.]

רבינו חננאל

רב אשי אפילו תימא צדדין מותרין כל דלהדי גבה דרישא כגבה דמו. א"ר אלעזר א"ר אושעיא מניין לעצרת שיש לה תשלומין כל שבעה ת"ל בחג המצות ובחג השבועות ובחג הסוכות כו'. פז"ר קש"ב. פירשנוהו כבר למעלה.

גליון הש"ס

תוס' ד"ה אף עלרת וכו' בירושלמי אר"י. עיין מ"ל פ"ג הלכה ו' מהלכות אבל:

הגהות מהר"י לנדא

א] תוס' ד"ה אף עלרת וכו' בירושלמי. נ"ל פ"ב הלכה ג' ובמס' בילה פ"ב הלכה ד:

הגהות הב"ח

(א) במשנה יום טבוח שלו אחר השבת: (ב) גמ' למאי הלכתא כתביה רחמנא. נ"ב ול"ק דלמא חג השבועות נמי לא כתביה רחמנא אלא לאקושי לחג המצות דטעון לינה דאיכא למימר דאין היקש למחצה וכיון דילפת הקישא מחג המצות לגמרי מקשינן ליה אף דיש לה תשלומין כל ז': (ג) רש"י ד"ה אין כהן וכו' אחר שבת כדי שיבינו הכל שאין היום: (ד) תום' ד"ה בית שמאי וכו' אגב גררא דמיירי בחגיגה נסבה וכן משמע: (ה) ד"ה יום טבוח וכו' תשלומין דראשון דכיון וכו' בשביל היום חזי קרינן ביה כדפי' לעיל הס"ד: (ו) ד"ה יום טבוח אחר וכו' ולא יתכן לומר כן דחגיגה וכו' אמרו להם ב"ש נדרים: (ז) ד"ה אין כהן גדול מתלבש וכו' דלישנא לא משמע הכי דהוה ליה וכו' היה רגיל כהן גדול ללובשן כדי לעבוד בשביל וכו' בירושלמי דפירקין וכו' בכליו ובא ומקריב וכו' נדרים ונדבות הוא מקריבן והולך כצ"ל ותיבת אותן נמחק: (ח) בא"ד תמיד של בין הערבים ובא ולן בלשכת פלהדרין רבי עוקבא בשם: (ט) בא"ד כדתנן ביומא כה"ג מקריב חלק בראש: (י) ד"ה פז"ר קש"ב וכו' ר"ת במעריב שלו קודש ללינה ושלשים ידחם: (כ) בא"ד שיר פרש"י. נ"ב כך הוא בפרש"י דפרק לולב וערבה דף מו סע"א ופ"ק דר"ה דף ד' בסופו: (ל) בא"ד שמתחיל ביום ראשון מזמור ומסיים וכו' ורבי עוזיאל מלא שאומרים למנלא וכו' דניתקן לומר בבית הכנסת הס"ד: (מ) ד"ה תפשת וכו' דמ"מ חשבון וכו' דלמדה מרובה וכו' יש סוף. נ"ב ופ"ק דר"ה כתבו התוס' דהכא ליכא לפרש הכי דהא יש לדבר סוף דטפי משמונה לא ועיין רפ"ק דסוכה דף ה' ובמ"ש התוס' לשם:

[סוטה כז:]

כ א ב מיי' פ"ז מהל' תמידין הלכה כב סמג עשין ר טוש"ע א"ח סי' תפט סעיף א:
[רב אלפס סוף ערבי פסחים דף קא. וברא"ש שם סי' מ]:

ופנית בבקר. שהוא חול המועד, דאילו ביו"ט תחומין אסור: אין לה יום טבוח כלל. אם לא הקריבם ביו"ט, עוד אין להן תשלומין: אבל בהא. בעצרת שחל להיות בערב שבת אימא מודו לב"ה, ויקרבו ביו"ט. דהא מחר שבת היא ולא קרבי, ומתוך שאתה מתייאש מהן אתה בא לפשוע שלא תקריבם עוד: מנה ימים. שלשים יום: וקדש חדש. למוספין: מנה ימים. חמשים יום: וקדש עצרת. בקרבנותיו: מה חדש. קדושתו באחד ממנויו: אף עצרת. קדושתו באחד ממנוייה: האמר אביי. במס' מנחות: מצוה למימני יומי ומצוה למימני שבועי: דבי ר"א בן יעקב תנא. מהכא נפקא לן תשלומין לעצרת: וקראתם בעצם היום הזה. ובחג השבועות כתיב, וסמיך ליה: "ובקצרכם את קציר ארצכם", שאתה קורא מקרא קדש וקוצר: הוי אומר זה עצרת. דהני קראי בעצרת כתיבי: אלא לתשלומין. לאחר יו"ט קאי. וקורא אותן "מקרא קדש" לענין תשלומין, ומותרין במלאכה:

תורה אור

דכתיב: °"ופנית בבקר והלכת לאהליך". (דברים טז) תנן: עצרת שחל להיות ערב שבת, ב"ש אומרים: יום טבוח אחר השבת, וב"ה הלל אומרים: אין לה יום טבוח. מאי לאו — אין לה יום טבוח כלל? — לא, שאינה צריכה יום טבוח. ומאי קמ"ל — דמקרבינן ביומיה, הא איפליגו בה חדא זימנא. דתנן: ב"ש אומרים: מביאין שלמים ואין סומכין עליהם, אבל לא עולות. וב"ה אומרים: מביאין שלמים ועולות וסומכין עליהם! צריכא, דאי אשמעינן בהא — בהא קא אמרי ב"ש, משום דאפשר למחר, אבל (א) הכא, אימא מודו להו לב"ה. ואי אשמעינן בהא — בהא קאמרי בית הלל, משום דלא אפשר למחר, אבל בהא — אימא מודו לב"ש, צריכא. ת"ש: מי שלא חג שבעת ימי הפסח, ושמונת ימי החג, ויו"ט [א]הראשון של עצרת — שוב אינו חוגג. מאי לאו — יו"ט של עצרת! לא, יום טבוח. אי הכי ניפשוט מינה דחד יום טבוח! אימא: ימי טבוח. ת"ש, *דתני רבה בר שמואל: אמרה תורה מנה ימים וקדש חדש, מנה ימים וקדש עצרת. מה חדש למנויו — אף עצרת למנוייה. מאי לאו גמר מחדש, מה חדש יום אחד — אף עצרת יום אחד! אמר רבא: ותסברא? אטו עצרת, יומי מנינן שבועי לא מנינן? והאמר אביי: *אמצוה למימני יומי — דכתיב: °"תספרו חמשים יום", במצוה למימני שבועי — דכתיב: °"שבעה שבועות תספר לך". ועוד: "חג שבועות" כתיב. דבי ר"א בן יעקב תנא: אמר קרא: °"וקראתם" °"ובקצרכם" איזהו חג שאתה קורא וקוצר בו — הוי אומר זה חג עצרת. אימת? אילימא ביו"ט — קצירה ביום טוב מי שרי? אלא לאו — לתשלומין. ואע"ג דאיתמר דר"א א"ר אושעיא, אצטריך דר"א בן יעקב. דאי מדר"א א"ר אושעיא — הוה אמינא: מה תשלומין של חג המצות אסור בעשיית מלאכה — אף תשלומי עצרת נמי אסור בעשיית מלאכה, קמשמע לן דר"א בן יעקב. ואי מדר"א בן יעקב לא

דכתיב ופנית בבקר. פרש"י: בחוש"מ, דאי ביו"ט אסור משום תחומין. ולא יתכן, דהתינח לר"ע, *לרבנן — מאי איכא למימר, דליכא איסור תחומין דאורייתא? וי"מ: די"ב מילין אית להו שפיר לרבנן תחומין. והכי איתא בירושלמי: המחוור מכוון י"ב מילין כנגד מחנה ישראל. והתלמוד שלנו לא ס"ל, (ב) דהא בפ' "כלל גדול" (שבת סט.) גבי שכח עיקר שבת, דבעי: דידע ליה לשבת במאי? דידע לה בתחומין, ואליבא דר"ע. ולא קאמר לדברי הכל. וכן בפ' בתרא דעירובין (דף לו:) גבי אין רוכבין מוקי טעמא בגמרא שמא ילך מחוץ לתחום, ופריך: ש"מ תחומין דאורייתא? אלא: גזירה שמא יחתוך זמורה. אלמא דרבנן לא מודו כלל בתחומין. ובפ"ק דר"ה (ד' ה.) פרש"י: דאי (ג) משום י"ט פשיטא, [שהרי הוא יום] שיתחייב להתראות פנים בעזרה. ור' עזריאל מצא בתוספתא (ד) דתניא: בליל יו"ט האחרון חוזרין לבתיהן, כדכתיב: "ביום השמיני שלח את העם" (מלכים א ח) יכול שאין טעונים לינה — ת"ל: *"וביום עשרים ושלשה לחדש שלח את העם". הא כיצד? נפטרו (ה) והשכימו, והולכי' למחרת יום שמיני, שהוא כ"ג. ועוד הביא הר"י ראיה מהיא דלולב וערבה בשמעתין, דאמר: זמן בשמיני של חג — שהבכורים טעונין לינה. משמע: לינה דומיא דבכורים שהם יום אחד. ועוד, תני בספרי בפרשת "ראה": "והלכת לאהליך" — מלמד שטעונין לינת רגלים, אין לי אלא אלו, מניין לרבות עופות ומנחות יין לבונה ועצים, תלמוד לומר: "ופנית בבוקר" — כל פינות שאתה פונה לא יהיו אלא מן הבקר ואילך. רבי יהודה אומר: יכול יהא פסח קטן כו'. ומשמע מיהא דלינת רגלים אינו רק דומיא דהני, והיינו (ו)יום ולילה. וכי מקשה פ' "לולב וערבה" (סוכה מז:): זמן כל ז' ימים מי איכא? הוה מצי לאקשויי: וליטעמיך, לינה(ז) דלא מקשי כלל. ויש להקשות: דאמרינן בזבחים פרק "דם החטאת" (דף צז.) דרבי טרפון אומר: אם בשל בה מתחלת הרגל כו' — מותר לבשל בה בסוף הרגל, מ"ט — דכתיב: "ופנית בבקר" הכתוב עשאן בקר אחד. אלמא, מדלענין נותר מחשב יום אחד — משמע שטעון לינה כל ז'! ותירץ הר"י: דלפי המסקנא משני התם טעמא אחרינא, משום שכל יום ויום נעשה גיעול לחברו. והר"ר אלחנן תירץ דב' ענייני לינה הם: אחת משום יו"ט, והשנית משום קרבן שטעון לינה, והתם אף בחוש"מ. והכי משמע בההיא דבכורים(ח) לינה וקרבן, משמע שטעונין לינה משום *יו"ט. וכן מצינו בירושלמי גבי ההיא משנה דבכורים: הדא איתמר כשאין עמהן קרבן, אבל יש עמהן קרבן — בלא כך טעונין לינה מחמת הקרבן: **נפשוט** מינה דחד יומא טבוח. וממתני' לא אלימא ליה לאקשויי(ט): ומודים כשחל להיות בשבת שיום טבוח לאחר השבת, ואי אית ליה תשלומין כל שבעה — ימתינו(י) לגיבורא עד תרי בשבת! וי"ל: דהא לא רצו כל כך לאחר: **אמרה** תורה מנה ימים וכו'. היה קשה להרב רבינו משולם: היכן אמרה תורה למנות ימים לקדש חדש? והיה מגיה: מנה שנים וקדש יובל. והכי איתא בתורת כהנים דמצוה למימני שמיטין לקדש יובלות. וכן היה מגיה בפ"ק דר"ה (דף ה.) ובמנחות (דף סה: ושם) בשמעתא דצדוקין שהיו אומרים עצרת לאחר השבת. אך קשה לר"ת למחוק הספרים והגיה גירסא שאינה בשום מקום. ומפרש: דודאי ר"ת נמי דאורייתא הוא למימני ביה יומי, וכדאמרינן בפ"ק דמגילה (דף ה.): מנין שאין מחשבין שעות לחדשים — ת"ל: "עד חדש ימים" — ימים אתה מונה, ואי אתה מונה שעות. ואל תתמה על הלשון, שאע"פ שאין רק דרשה, מצינו כי האי לישנא בפרק בתרא דמגילה, (דף כט.): אמרה תורה חדש והבא קרבן מתרומה חדשה אע"פ (כ) כי אותה דרשה אינה פשוטה, שהרי לדוקין חולקין בה לומר שהיחיד מתנדב ומביא תמיד, הר"ר אלחנן. וכן יש לגרוס כאן: חדש למנויו, שכן מצינו בפ"ק דר"ה (דף י:) בגמרא: ולנטיעה, מה חדש למנויו — אף שנה למנוייה: **אף** עצרת למנוייו. לענין קרבן קאמר, דאי לענין יום טוב — לא צריך קרא: **מצוה** למימני יומי ומצוה למימני שבועי. ותרוייהו איתנהו: יומי לקדש עצרת, שבועי לתשלומין. והקשה הר"ר אלחנן: ליגמר מיובל דלא מקדשין ליה לענין שמיטין רק לשנים, וא"כ לא (ל) נימא כלל הכא מנין שבועי לקדש! ותירץ: דלהכי אצטריך חג השבועות, לומר שמקדשין בו ימים ושבועות. דאי לא תימא הכי — למה לי קרא מדרשה דחג השבועות? דמדרשה דרבה בר שמואל ומנה ימים וקדש חדש לאפוקי מלבן של לדוקין. ועי"ל: דלא גמרינן מיובל דדנין ימים מימים עצרת מחדש, ואל יוכיח יובל דשנים ניניהו. ומהכא שמעינן דמצוה למימני יומי ושבועי בספירת העומר, דקי"ל כאביי: **אלא** לאו לתשלומין. דשרי לקצור ולעשות מלאכה ביום טובו. ומקיים בה בירושלמי, א"ר יוסי ברבי בון: ובלבד שיכלם לעיסתו, כהדא דתנינן לה, (מ) אמר איניש דליהוו עלוואי אעין ובכורים. ואומר הרי עלים למזבח וגיזרין למערכה — אסור בהספד ובתענית ומלעשות מלאכה בו ביום. כלומר, ואע"פ שהתורה התירה מלאכה לתשלומין — לא מצי למיעבד רק לצורך אכילתו, אם כלה עיסתו, כמו שמצינו שאסור לאדם לעשות מלאכה ביום הקריבו את קרבנו. והא דקאמר בסמוך: ואי מדר"א הוה אמינא מה תשלומין בחג המצות אסור בעשיית מלאכה — אף של עצרת (נ) מדאורייתא, ואע"ג דחול המועד אינו אלא מדרבנן, בדבר שאינו אבוד — משום שביעי דאורייתא נקטיה. אבל מ"מ, אף התלמוד שלנו לא פליג בהא דמדרבנן מיהא מיתסר יום טובו, כדפרישית: **ואצטריך** דר"א (ס) ואיצטריך דרבי אושעיא. הקשה הר"ר אלחנן: מברייתא דלעיל ליעבד צריכותא, דתני רבה בר שמואל, ועל ר"א בן יעקב וחג השבועות דאמר ר"א ורבי אושעיא למה לי, דמשמע מיניה שיש לו תשלומין כל ז'! וי"ל: דההיא ברייתא אתיא לסתור דרשת הצדוקין במנחות (דף סה: ושם):

אלא

[ר"ה ה. מנחות סה: ע"ש סו.] | [ד"ה כ ז] | [ר"ה ה. ע"ש מנחות סו.] | ויקרא כג | דברים טז | ויקרא כג שם | [וקרבן יו"ט כצ"ל]

הגהות הגר"א

[א] גמ' תיבת הראשון נמחק:

הגהות הב"ח

(א) גמ' לאפשר למחר אבל בהא אימא מודו: (ב) תום' ד"ה דכתיב וכו' והש"ס שלנו לא סבירא ליה הכי דהא: (ג) בא"ד ובפ"ק דר"ה פרש"י דאי ביום טוב כצ"ל ותיבת משום נמחק: (ד) בא"ד ורבי עזריאל מצא בתוספתא בס"פ בתרא דסוכה דתניא: (ה) בא"ד כילד נפטרו מבע"י והשכימו וכו' בשמעתא דאמר זמן וכו' דומיא דבכורים שהוא לילה אחת ועוד תני: (ו) בא"ד אינו רק דומיא דהני והיינו לילה אחת וכי מקשה כצ"ל ותיבת יום נמחק: (ז) בא"ד הוה מצי לאקשויי וליטעמיך לינה אלא דלא חש לאקושיי כלל ויש להקשות: (ח) בא"ד בההיא דבכורים דתני לינה וכו' הדא דתימר כשאין: (ט) ד"ה נפשוט וכו' לאקשויי דתנן ומודים. נ"ב דלאחר שבת תני אין כ"ג מתלבש בכליו מפני הצדוקין ואי אית ליה תשלומין וכו' ימתינו עד תרי בשבת דאין בו משום צדוקין: (י) בא"ד ימתינו עד תרי בשבת דיש לומר דלא רצו כל כך לאחר לגיבורא הס"ד: (כ) ד"ה אמרה וכו' אע"פ שאותה דרשה כו' בפ"ק דר"ה גמרא דלנטיעה: (ל) ד"ה מצוה וכו' וא"כ לא לימני כלל הכא וכו' למה לי קרא. נ"ב פי' דאי אין מקדשין שבעה לעצרת למה לי קרא דבחג המצות ובחג השבועות ובחג הסוכות הניחא בחג המצות ובחג הסוכות לאקושי לחג המצות דטעון לינה אבל חג השבועות לא אצטריך ולא קשיא נמי השתא דכתיב חה"ש דיש תשלומין שבעה לעצרת הך דתני רבה דמנה ימים כו' למה לי דהלא איצטריך לאפוקי מלבן של צדוקים אבל קשה דלאצטריך קרא דחג השבועות דטעון לינה [והשאר חסר]: (מ) ד"ה אלא וכו' כהדא דתנינן כל אינש דליהוו עלוואי אעין ובכורים פי' האומר הרי עלי עלים וכו' כלומר דאע"פ: (נ) בא"ד אף של עצרת הייתי מדאורייתא: (ס) ד"ה ואצטריך דר' אליעזר ב"י ואצטריך דר"א אמר ר' אושעיא וכו' דתני רבה בר שמואל למה לי הא כתיב חג השבועות דאמר רבי אלעזר א"ר אושעיא דמשמע מיניה כצ"ל ותיבת למה לי נמחק:

לָא יָדְעָנָא כַּמָּה, קָא מַשְׁמַע לָן דְּרַבִּי אֶלְעָזָר א"ר אוֹשַׁעְיָא. וְרֵישׁ לָקִישׁ אָמַר: °"וְחַג הַקָּצִיר" אֵיזֶהוּ חַג שֶׁאַתָּה חוֹגֵג וְקוֹצֵר בּוֹ — הֱוֵי אוֹמֵר זֶה עֲצֶרֶת. אֵימַת? אִילֵימָא בְּיו"ט — קְצִירָה בְּיו"ט מִי שָׁרֵי? אֶלָּא לָאו — לְתַשְׁלוּמִין. *א"ר יוֹחָנָן, אֶלָּא מֵעַתָּה: "חַג הָאָסִיף", אֵי זֶהוּ חַג שֶׁיֵּשׁ בּוֹ אֲסִיפָה — הֱוֵי אוֹמֵר זֶה חַג הַסּוּכּוֹת. אֵימַת? אִילֵימָא בְּיו"ט — מְלָאכָה בְּיו"ט מִי שָׁרֵי אֶלָּא בְּחוּלּוֹ שֶׁל מוֹעֵד. *חוּלּוֹ שֶׁל מוֹעֵד מִי שָׁרֵי, אֶלָּא: חַג הַבָּא בִּזְמַן אֲסִיפָה, הָכָא נַמִי: חַג הַבָּא בִּזְמַן קְצִירָה. מִכְּלָל דְּתַרְוַיְיהוּ סְבִירָא לְהוּ דְּחוּלּוֹ שֶׁל מוֹעֵד אָסוּר בַּעֲשִׂיַּית מְלָאכָה, מְנָהָנֵי מִילֵּי? דְּתָנוּ רַבָּנַן: °"אֶת חַג הַמַּצּוֹת תִּשְׁמוֹר שִׁבְעַת יָמִים" [א]לִימֵּד עַל חוּלּוֹ שֶׁל מוֹעֵד שֶׁאָסוּר בַּעֲשִׂיַּית מְלָאכָה, דִּבְרֵי רַבִּי יֹאשִׁיָּה. רַבִּי יוֹנָתָן אוֹמֵר: אֵינוֹ צָרִיךְ, קַל וָחוֹמֶר: וּמָה רִאשׁוֹן וּשְׁבִיעִי שֶׁאֵין קְדוּשָּׁה לִפְנֵיהֶן וּלְאַחֲרֵיהֶן — אָסוּר בַּעֲשִׂיַּית מְלָאכָה, חוּלּוֹ שֶׁל מוֹעֵד שֶׁיֵּשׁ קְדוּשָּׁה לִפְנֵיהֶן וּלְאַחֲרֵיהֶן — אֵינוֹ דִּין שֶׁיְּהֵא אָסוּר בַּעֲשִׂיַּית מְלָאכָה?! שֵׁשֶׁת יְמֵי בְרֵאשִׁית יוֹכִיחוּ, שֶׁיֵּשׁ קְדוּשָּׁה לִפְנֵיהֶן וּלְאַחֲרֵיהֶן וּמוּתָּרִין בַּעֲשִׂיַּית מְלָאכָה! מַה לְּשֵׁשֶׁת יְמֵי בְרֵאשִׁית — שֶׁאֵין בָּהֶן קָרְבַּן מוּסָף, תֹּאמַר בְּחוּלּוֹ שֶׁל מוֹעֵד — שֶׁיֵּשׁ בּוֹ קָרְבַּן מוּסָף. רֹאשׁ חֹדֶשׁ יוֹכִיחַ, שֶׁיֵּשׁ בּוֹ קָרְבַּן מוּסָף — וּמוּתָּר בַּעֲשִׂיַּית מְלָאכָה! מַה לְּרֹאשׁ חֹדֶשׁ שֶׁאֵין קָרוּי "מִקְרָא קֹדֶשׁ", תֹּאמַר בְּחוּלּוֹ שֶׁל מוֹעֵד שֶׁקָּרוּי "מִקְרָא קֹדֶשׁ", הוֹאִיל וְקָרוּי מִקְרָא קֹדֶשׁ — דִּין הוּא שֶׁאָסוּר בַּעֲשִׂיַּית מְלָאכָה. תַּנְיָא אִידָךְ: °"כָּל מְלֶאכֶת עֲבוֹדָה לֹא תַעֲשׂוּ" לִימֵּד עַל חוּלּוֹ שֶׁל מוֹעֵד שֶׁאָסוּר בַּעֲשִׂיַּית מְלָאכָה, דִּבְרֵי ר' יוֹסֵי הַגְּלִילִי. רַבִּי עֲקִיבָא אוֹמֵר: אֵינוֹ צָרִיךְ, הֲרֵי הוּא אוֹמֵר: °"אֵלֶּה מוֹעֲדֵי ה'" וגו'; בַּמֶּה הַכָּתוּב מְדַבֵּר? אִם בָּרִאשׁוֹן — הֲרֵי כְּבָר נֶאֱמַר שַׁבָּתוֹן, אִם בַּשְּׁבִיעִי — הֲרֵי כְּבָר נֶאֱמַר שַׁבָּתוֹן. הָא אֵין הַכָּתוּב מְדַבֵּר אֶלָּא בְּחוּלּוֹ שֶׁל מוֹעֵד, לְלַמֶּדְךָ שֶׁאָסוּר בַּעֲשִׂיַּית מְלָאכָה. תַּנְיָא אִידָךְ: °"שֵׁשֶׁת יָמִים תֹּאכַל מַצּוֹת וּבַיּוֹם הַשְּׁבִיעִי עֲצֶרֶת לַה'" מַה שְּׁבִיעִי עָצוּר — אַף שֵׁשֶׁת יָמִים עֲצוּרִין, אִי מַה שְּׁבִיעִי עָצוּר בְּכָל מְלָאכָה — אַף שֵׁשֶׁת יָמִים עֲצוּרִין בְּכָל מְלָאכָה? ת"ל: "וּבַיּוֹם הַשְּׁבִיעִי עֲצֶרֶת" — *הַשְּׁבִיעִי עָצוּר בְּכָל מְלָאכָה, וְאֵין שִׁשָּׁה יָמִים עֲצוּרִין בְּכָל מְלָאכָה. הָא *[ב]לֹא מְסָרָן הַכָּתוּב אֶלָּא לַחֲכָמִים, לוֹמַר לְךָ אֵי זֶה יוֹם אָסוּר וְאֵי זֶה יוֹם מוּתָּר, אֵי זוֹ מְלָאכָה אֲסוּרָה וְאֵי זוֹ מְלָאכָה מוּתֶּרֶת.§ "וּמוּתָּרִין בְּהֶסְפֵּד וְתַעֲנִית שֶׁלֹּא לְקַיֵּים אֶת דִּבְרֵי הָאוֹמְרִין עֲצֶרֶת אַחַר הַשַּׁבָּת".§ (*וְהָאִיתְּמַר): מַעֲשֶׂה וּמֵת אֲלֶכְּסָא בְּלוֹד, וְנִכְנְסוּ כָּל יִשְׂרָאֵל לְסוֹפְדוֹ, וְלֹא הִנִּיחָם רַבִּי טַרְפוֹן, מִפְּנֵי שֶׁיּוֹם טוֹב שֶׁל עֲצֶרֶת הָיָה. יו"ט ס"ד?! אִי בְּיוֹם טוֹב, מִי קָאָתוּ? אֶלָּא אֵימָא: מִפְּנֵי שֶׁיּוֹם טְבוֹחַ הָיָה! לָא קַשְׁיָא: כָּאן — בְּיו"ט שֶׁחָל לִהְיוֹת אַחַר הַשַּׁבָּת, כָּאן — בְּיוֹם טוֹב שֶׁחָל לִהְיוֹת בַּשַּׁבָּת.§

מתני'

[שמות כג] [שם] [ויקרא כג] [שם] [דברים טז] [נ"ל א"ל] [מכות כו:]

(רש"י) לָא יָדְעָנָא. כַּמָּה יָמִים יִהְיוּ לְתַשְׁלוּמִין, קָא מַשְׁמַע לָן דְּרַבִּי אֶלְעָזָר, מַה חַג הַמַּצּוֹת שִׁבְעָה אַף כָּאן שִׁבְעָה: וְחַג הַקָּצִיר בִּכּוּרֵי מַעֲשֶׂיךָ. בְּחַג שָׁבוּעוֹת כְּתִיב: ה"נ חַג הַבָּא בִּזְמַן קְצִירָה. קָאָמַר, וְלָאו חוֹגֵג וְקוֹצֵר בּוֹ אָתָא לְאַשְׁמוּעִינַן: מִכְּלָל דְּתַרְוַיְיהוּ כו'. מִדְּקָאָמַר רַבִּי יוֹחָנָן אֲסִיפָה בְּחוּלּוֹ שֶׁל מוֹעֵד מִי שָׁרֵי, וְלָא מְהַדַּר לֵיהּ רֵישׁ לָקִישׁ "אִין", מִכְּלָל דְּתַרְוַיְיהוּ סְבִירָא לְהוּ אָסוּר: אֶת חַג הַמַּצּוֹת תִּשְׁמוֹר שִׁבְעַת יָמִים וגו'. לִימֵּד עַל חוּלּוֹ שֶׁל מוֹעֵד שֶׁאָסוּר בַּעֲשִׂיַּית מְלָאכָה. דָּרוֹשׁ בֵּיהּ: "אֶת חַג הַמַּצּוֹת *תִּשְׁמוֹר" — וְכָל תִּשְׁמוֹר אַזְהָרַת לֹא תַעֲשֶׂה הוּא, שׁוֹמְרֵיהוּ מִן הַמְּלָאכָה: שֵׁשֶׁת יְמֵי בְּרֵאשִׁית. יְמֵי כָּל שָׁבוּעַ וְשָׁבוּעַ בֵּין שְׁתֵּי שַׁבָּתוֹת הֵן יוֹשְׁבִין, הֲרֵי קְדוּשָּׁה לִפְנֵיהֶן וּלְאַחֲרֵיהֶן: רֹאשׁ חֹדֶשׁ יוֹכִיחַ כו'. אַף אַתָּה אַל תִּתְמַהּ עַל חוּלּוֹ שֶׁל מוֹעֵד כו': (א) כָּל מְלֶאכֶת עֲבוֹדָה לֹא תַעֲשׂוּ וכו'. וּסְמִיךְ לֵיהּ: "שִׁבְעַת יָמִים תַּקְרִיבוּ אִשֶּׁה": לִימֵּד עַל חוּלּוֹ שֶׁל מוֹעֵד וכו'. וְהָכִי דָּרֵישׁ בֵּיהּ: "לֹא תַעֲשׂוּ שִׁבְעַת יָמִים". וּבְחַג הַסּוּכּוֹת כְּתִיב, וַעֲלֵיהּ קָיְימָא הַךְ מַתְנִיתָא בְּתוֹרַת כֹּהֲנִים: מִקְרָאֵי קֹדֶשׁ. מַשְׁמַע: קַדְּשֵׁיהוּ בַּעֲשִׂיַּית מְלָאכָה: עָצוּר מִמְּלָאכָה. כִּדְכְתִיב בְּהַאי קְרָא גּוּפֵיהּ: "לֹא תַעֲשֶׂה מְלָאכָה": הָא הֲרֵי לֹא מְסָרָן הַכָּתוּב אֶלָּא לַחֲכָמִים. כְּלוֹמַר: מֵאַחַר שֶׁאָמַר לְךָ הַכָּתוּב שֶׁהֵן עֲצוּרִין מִמְּלָאכָה וְלֹא בְּכוּלָּן, וְלֹא פֵּירֵשׁ אֵי זוֹ הַמּוּתֶּרֶת וְאֵי זוֹ אֲסוּרָה — דַּע וּרְאֵה שֶׁלֹּא מְסָרָן אֶלָּא לַחֲכָמִים, הַיּוֹדְעִים לְהָבִין עַל אֵיזֶהוּ לְהַטִּיל הַהֶיתֵּר וְעַל אֵי זוֹ לְהַטִּיל הָאִיסּוּר, וְהֵם יֹאמְרוּ אֵי זֶהוּ י"ט עַל פִּי קִידּוּשׁ הָרְאִיָּיה וְאָסוּר בְּכָל מְלָאכָה, וְאֵי זֶהוּ חוּלּוֹ שֶׁל מוֹעֵד שֶׁאֵינוֹ אָסוּר בְּכָל מְלָאכָה. וְעַל חוּלּוֹ שֶׁל מוֹעֵד יַגִּידוּ לְךָ אֵי זוֹ מְלָאכָה אֲסוּרָה — דָּבָר שֶׁאֵינוֹ אָבֵד, וְאֵיזוֹ מְלָאכָה מוּתֶּרֶת — דָּבָר הָאָבֵד: וְלֹא הִנִּיחָן ר' טַרְפוֹן. וּמַתְנִי' תָּנֵי שֶׁמּוּתָּרִים בְּהֶסְפֵּד: בְּי"ט שֶׁחָל לִהְיוֹת בַּשַּׁבָּת. שֶׁיּוֹם טְבוֹחַ אַחַר שַׁבָּת מוּתָּר בְּהֶסְפֵּד, מִפְּנֵי הָאוֹמְרִים עֲצֶרֶת אַחַר שַׁבָּת. וְהַאי דַּאֲלֶכְּסָא בְּלוֹד — יו"ט שֶׁחָל לִהְיוֹת בְּחוֹל הוּא, דְּאֵין יוֹם טְבוֹחַ שֶׁלּוֹ בְּא' בַּשַּׁבָּת:

(תוספות) **אלא** חג הבא בזמן אסיפה. הקשה הר"ר אלחנן, דאמר פ"ק דר"ה (דף יג.): א"ל רבי זירא לרבי אסי: ודלמא לא עייל כלל, וקאמר רחמנא תשמט ותיזיל עד חג הסוכות! לא ס"ד, דכתיב "חג האסיף". מאי האסיף? אילימא חג הבא בזמן אסיפה — הכתיב: "באספך את מעשיך", אלא מאי אסיף — קציר. אלמא לא אמרי' חג הסוכות הבא בזמן אסיפה! ותירץ מורי: כיון דמ"באספך" שמעינן חג הבא בזמן אסיפה, ואמר "חג האסיף" — משמע ליקצר. אבל אי לאו האי קרא ["באספך וגו'"] — הוה דרשינן: חג [האסיף] הבא בזמן אסיפה, א"כ גם חג הקציר נימא הכי, הואיל וליכא שום משמעות דמפיק ליה: **חולו** של מועד אסור בעשיית מלאכה. לכאורה משמע דמלאכה דמיתסרא ביה — מדאורייתא, דמפיק ליה מפסוק. וכן בפרק ב' דמו"ק (דף יח: ושם): לא מיבעיא אבל דמדרבנן אלא אפילו חוה"מ דאורייתא. וכן פי' התם בקונטרס. וקשה לר"ת: דא"כ דבר האבד וכמה מלאכות דשרינן התם היכי משתרו? וכי היכן מלינו איסור דאורייתא מקצתו אסור ומקצתו מותר? ועוד, דתנן בפ"ג דמגילה (דף כא.): כל מקום שאין יו"ט ויש מוסף קורין ד' — כגון חוה"מ ור"ח, אלמא: לא מיתסר מלאכה, מדקאמר דאין יו"ט. ועוד: דכייל ליה בהדי ר"ח, דרבנן. כדאמרינן בירושלמי דתענית: ובמקום שנהגו הלין נשיא דרגילין דלא למיעבד עבידתא בריש ירחא — מנהגא הוא. ועוד מלינו בירושלמי בפרק שני דמו"ק: כלום אסרו מלאכה(ב) אלא כדי שיהו אוכלין ושותין ויהיו יגעים בתורה, והם פוחזין ואוכלין ושותין. משמע לישנא דמדרבנן הוא. וכן בפ"ב דמו"ק (דף יב:) גבי ובלבד שלא יכוין מלאכתו במועד. ובעי בגמרא: כיון ומת, מהו שיקנסו בנו אחריו? את"ל גרס אוזן הבכור ומת קנסו בנו אחריו — התם איסורא דאורייתא. משמע דמלאכה במועד הוי דרבנן. ומיהו, יש לדחות דאמכוין מלאכתו במועד קאי. דהשתא מיהא ליכא איסורא דאורייתא, כיון דדבר האבד הוא. מ"מ משמע לפי האמת דלא מיתסר רק מדרבנן. וכי קאמר התם בריש פירקא לא מיבעיא אבל דרבנן אלא אפילו חוה"מ דאורייתא — כעין דאורייתא קאמר, לפי שיש לו סמך(ג) [מקרא דאורייתא. אבל ימי האבל ליכא אסמכתא, אלא] מדברי קבלה, דכתיב: "והפכתי חגיכם לאבל" (עמוס ח). ודקאמר הכא: אלא בחוה"מ מי שרי — א"כ משמע דאסור מן התורה! וי"ל: לאו משום דלא משתרי מדאורייתא, אלא כיון דאקרא סמכינן ליה למיתסר — לא(ד) מסברא ליה לאוקמי קרא דשרי בהדיא בהכי. וכן פירש הריב"ם בשם רבינו יב"א, דמלאכה דמועד מדרבנן. ולא כפירוש רבינו שמואל שפירש ב"ערבי פסחים" (פסחים דף קיח.) גבי כל המבזה את המועדות, כגון: עושה מלאכה בחוה"מ. והא ליתא, דמדרבנן הוי, וכדפי'. והא דאמרינן *גבי כותים ותיפוק ליה משום "לפני עור לא תתן מכשול" במלאכה דחוה"מ — משום דסמך *פשטא דקרא הוי, והוי ליה לדוקין מודין בה: **מה** ראשון ושביעי כו'. הוה מצי למפרך מה להני שכן דבר האבד מיתסר אלא שאין זה ק"ו גמור רק גלוי מילתא בעלמא, לפי מה שפיר' דמלאכה לא מיתסר רק דרבנן: **ראש** חדש יוכיח. דשרי בעשיית מלאכה, שכן אינו קרוי יו"ט(ה) בפ"ג דמגילה (דף כב: ושם), וגם אינו נאסר רק משום מנהג כדפרי'. וכי קאמר בר"ה (דף כג.) משום בטול מלאכה לעם בב' ימים, דר"ח של ראש השנה מיירי, אי נמי: משום נשים דנוהגות שלא לעשות מלאכה, כדאיתא בפירקי דרבי אליעזר, *וכן פרש"י במגילה (דף כב:): **מה** לראש חודש שכן אינו קרוי מקרא קדש. °הוה מצי למימר: מה לחול המועד דאיכא תרתי: מוסף וקדושה לפניו ולאחריו: קשיא

[שם] [ועי' תוס' ע"ז כב. ד"ה תיפוק ליה] [פרק מ"ה]

עין משפט נר מצוה

כא א ב מיי' פ"ז מהל' יו"ט הלכה א טור ש"ע א"ח סי' תקל [רב אלפס ריש מו"ק דף רעח. וברא"ש שם סי' א]:

רבינו חננאל

ת"ר את חג המצות תשמור לימד על חולו של מועד שאסו' בעשיית מלאכה דברי ר' יאשיה כלומר אמרה תורה ושמרתם את המצות עוד את חג המצות תשמור למה לי אלא ללמדך שכל שבעת ימים צריכין שמירה. ר' (יוחנן) [יונתן] אמר ק"ו ומה ראשון ושביעי כו'. תניא אידך כל מלאכת עבודה לא תעשו לימד על חולו של מועד שאסור בעשיית מלאכה דברי ר' יוסי הגלילי. ר"ע אומר [לא] אצטריך הרי הוא אומר אלה מועדי ה' מקראי קודש במה הכתוב מדבר אי ביו"ט ראשון הרי הוא אומר ביום ראשון שבתון אי בשמיני הרי הוא אומר ביום השמיני שבתון הא אין הכתוב מדבר מועדי ה' אלא בחולו של מועד שאסור בעשיית מלאכה. ולא מסרך הכתוב אלא לחכמים לומר איזו מלאכה אסורה [ואיזו מותרת] *) עצרת שחלה להיות ע"ש. בית שמאי אומרים יום טבוח לאחר השבת. וב"ה אומרים אין לה יום טבוח ומודים שאם חלה להיות בשבת כו': **ירושלמי** עצרת שחלה להיות ע"ש ב"ש אומרים יום טבוח לאחר השבת וב"ה אומרים אין לה יום טבוח אלא יומה היא טביחה. ואין כ"ג מתלבש בכליו ומותרין בהספד ובתענית שלא לקיים דברי האומרים עצרת אחר השבת. ומודין שאם חלה בשבת שיום טבוח לאחר השבת. (ומודים שאם חלה בשבת) ומותרין בו ביום בהספד ובתעני'. אבל אם חלה להיות באמצע שבת אסורין בהספד ובתענית:

*) מכאן עד מתני' נוטלין לידים שייך לעיל דף יז ע"א:

רס"א

מסורת הש"ס

[תשמור שבעת ימי' וכל תשמור כצ"ל]

[עי' תוס' מו"ק יב: ד"ה מכניס]

הגהות הב"ח

(א) רש"י ד"ה ראש חדש וכו' של מועד כו' הס"ד ואח"כ מה"ד מקרא קדש וכו' מלאכה הס"ד ואח"כ מה"ד כל מלאכה וכו' אשה לימד וכו' בתורת כהנים הס"ד ואח"כ מה"ד עצור ממלאכה: (ב) תוס' ד"ה חולו וכו' כלום אסרו מלאכה בחוה"מ אלא כדי שיהו אוכלין ושותין ויגעים בתורה והם אוכלים ושותין ופוחזין משמע לישנא כצ"ל: (ג) בא"ד כעין דאורייתא קאמר לפי שיש לו סמך כדמשמע מהאי דרשה אבל תימה אבל נמי לאסור במלאכה קא סמיך לה מדברי קבלה וכו' ודקאמר נמי הכא אלא בחולו של מועד חוה"מ מי שרי משמע כצ"ל ותיבת א"כ נמחק: (ד) בא"ד לא מיסתבר ליה: (ה) ד"ה ראש חדש וכו' פ"ג דמגילה. נ"ב פי' דבפ"ג דמגילה תנן בר"ח ובחוה"מ קורין ארבעה כו' זה הכלל כל שיש בו מוסף ואינו יו"ט קורין ארבעה אלמא דר"ח אינו קרוי יו"ט:

גליון הש"ס

תום' ד"ה מה לר"ח וכו' הוה מצי למימר. עי' תשובת מהר"י בן לב ח"ג סימן י"ג:

[מה"א יתירה קדריש עתוס' מו"ק ב. ד"ה משקין]

[נ"ל והתניא וכוא בתוספתא פ"ב]

מתני' נוטלין לידים [א]לחולין ולמעשר [ב]ולתרומה. [ג]ולקודש – מטבילין, [ד]ולחטאת, *אם נטמאו ידיו – נטמא גופו. טבל *[ה]לחולין – הוחזק לחולין, אסור למעשר. טבל למעשר – הוחזק למעשר, אסור לתרומה. טבל לתרומה – הוחזק לתרומה, אסור לקודש. טבל לקודש – הוחזק לקודש, אסור לחטאת. טבל לחמור – מותר לקל, [ו]טבל ולא הוחזק – כאילו לא טבל. *[ז]בגדי עם הארץ מדרס לפרושין, [ח]בגדי פרושין מדרס לאוכלי תרומה, [ט]בגדי אוכלי תרומה מדרס לקודש, [י]בגדי קודש מדרס לחטאת. יוסף בן יועזר היה חסיד שבכהונה, והיתה מטפחתו מדרס לקודש. [כ]יוחנן בן גודגדא היה אוכל על טהרת הקודש כל ימיו והיתה מטפחתו מדרס לחטאת.§ גמ' חולין ומעשר מי בעו נטילת ידים? ורמינהי: *התרומה והביכורים – *חייבין עליהן [ל]מיתה, [מ]וחומש, [נ]ואסור לזרים, [ס]והן נכסי כהן, [ע]ועולין באחד ומאה, [פ]וטעונין נטילת ידים, [צ]והערב שמש, הרי אלו בתרומה וביכורים – [ק]מה שאין כן במעשר, וכל שכן בחולין. קשיא מעשר אמעשר, קשיא חולין אחולין! בשלמא מעשר אמעשר לא קשיא: הא – ר' מאיר, והא – רבנן. דתנן: *כל הטעון ביאת מים מדברי סופרים מטמא את הקודש, ופוסל את התרומה, ומותר לחולין ולמעשר, דברי רבי מאיר. וחכמים אוסרים במעשר. אלא חולין אחולין קשיא! לא קשיא; כאן – באכילה. כאן – בנגיעה. מתקיף לה רב שימי בר אשי: עד כאן לא פליגי רבנן עליה דרבי מאיר אלא באכילה דמעשר, אבל בנגיעה דמעשר ובאכילה דחולין – לא פליגי! אלא: אידי ואידי באכילה, ולא קשיא: [ר]כאן – באכילה דנהמא, (א) [ש]כאן – באכילה דפירי. *דאמר רב נחמן: [ת]כל הנוטל ידיו לפירות – הרי זה מגסי הרוח. ת"ר: [א]הנוטל ידיו, נתכוון – ידיו טהורות, לא נתכוון – ידיו טמאות. [ב]וכן המטביל ידיו, נתכוון – ידיו טהורות, לא נתכוון – ידיו טמאות. והתניא: בין נתכוון בין לא נתכוון – ידיו טהורות! אמר רב נחמן: לא קשיא; [ג]כאן – לחולין, כאן

[ע"ש ע"ג תוס' ד"ה]

רש"י

מתני' נוטלין לידים לחולין ולמעשר ולתרומה. די להן בנטילה דכלי שאין בו אלא רביעית מים: ולקודש מטבילין. אבל לאכול שלמים או חטאת ואשם לכהנים יש מעלה, שצריך להטביל ידים בארבעים סאה, ואף על פי שאינן אלא סתם ידים שלא נגעו בטומאה דאורייתא המטמאה את כל הגוף: ולחטאת. ליגע במי חטאת, מים המקודשים באפר פרה להזות מהן על טמאי מתים – יש מעלה יתירה, שאם נטמאו ידיו באחת מן הדברים המטמאין את הידים ולא את הגוף, כגון וולד הטומאה, וכגון ספר וכל טומאות שהן מדברי סופרים: נטמא הגוף. וכל הגוף צריך טבילה. וכל מעלות הללו שזה גבוה מזה – מדברי סופרים. והאי דנקט להו הכא גבי הלכות הרגל – לפי שיש בסופן הלכות רגל, שעמי הארץ חשובין טהורים ברגל ולא בשאר ימות השנה, בסוף "חומר בקדש": טבל לחולין הוחזק לחולין. ועוד זו מעלה: טבל לחולין הוחזק לחולין. כלומר, נתכוין לטבול לשם חולין: אסור למעשר. הוחזק – לשון כוונה. כלומר: נתכוין להעמיד גופו בחזקת טהור לחולין: למעשר. למעשר שני הנאכל בירושלים: ולא הוחזק. לא נתכוון לשם טבילת טהרה, אלא לרחיצה בעלמא: מדרס. אב הטומאה לטמא אדם וכלים, כמדרס הזב, שמטמא אדם וכלים, כדכתיב: "ואיש אשר יגע במשכבו יכבס בגדיו" (ויקרא טו): לפרושין. לאוכלי חוליהן בטהרה: לאוכלי תרומה. כהנים. וכל אלו מעלות מדברי סופרים, שאמרו שאין שמירת טהרתן של אלו חשובה שמירה אצל אלו. ומתוך שהן אלו אצל אלו – כאילו לא שמרום. גזרו בהן בבגדיהן שמא ישבה בהן אשתו נדה, והרי הן מדרס הנדה, הכי מפרש לה בפ' "השוחט": גמ' בכורים. קרויין תרומה, דאמר מר: "ותרומת ידך" – אלו הבכורים (מכות דף יז.), לכך הן כתרומה: חייבין עליהן מיתה. זר האוכלן מזיד, דכתיב: "ומתו בו כי יחללוהו", וסמיך ליה: "וכל זר לא יאכל קדש", וכל הענין מדבר בתרומה: וחומש. האוכלן שוגג, דכתיב: "ואיש כי יאכל קדש בשגגה ויסף חמישיתו עליו" (ויקרא כב): ואסור לזרים. בלאו: והן נכסי כהן. לקדש בהן את האשה, וליקח בדמיהן עבדים, וקרקעות, ובהמה טמאה: ועולין באחד ומאה. אבל בפחות אין עולין, אלא כל החולין אסור לזרים: וטעונין רחיצת ידים. לפי שהשני עושה שלישי, וידים גזרו עליהם טומאת שני – לפיכך פוסלות את התרומה, אם לא נטלן: והערב שמש. אם נטמא טומאה דאורייתא וטבל – אינו אוכל בתרומה עד שיעריב שמשו, ביבמות (דף עד:) ילפינן מקראי: מה שאין כן במעשר. אין מיתה, ואין חומש. [ואין] אסור לזרים, שהרי כל עצמו נאכל לזרים. וחומש שמוסיף בפדיונו לא איירי (ב) בחומש הכא כי האי גוונא, דאין בתרומה פדיון. ונכסי הדיוט נמי לא הוי לקנות בו עבדים וקרקעות, דלא ניתן אלא לאכילה ושתיה וסיכה. ואין טעון רחיצת ידים – שאין השני פוסל בו לעשות שלישי. ואינו טעון הערב שמש, דקי"ל: טבל ועלה – אוכל במעשר, ומקראי ילפינן לה ביבמות פרק "הערל": כל הטעון ביאת מים מדברי סופרים. כל שהוא טהור מן התורה, וחכמים גזרו עליו טומאה, (ג) כל הנך דאמרי במסכת שבת בפ"ק (דף יג:): אלו פוסלין את התרומה, האוכל אוכל ראשון ואוכל שני כו': מטמא את הקודש. כלומר: נתנו עליהן טומאת שני לטומאה. והשני מטמא את הקודש להיות קרוי טמא, ופוסל (ד) עליהן עוד את הרביעי: ופוסל את התרומה. להיפסל היא עצמה, אבל אינה פוסלת אחר לעשות רביעי: ומותר לחולין. לאכול חולין. מדלא קתני: ואינו פוסל את החולין, ונקט לישנא דמותר – אפילו לאוכלן משמע: באכילה. מתני' דמצריך נטילה – באכילה קאמר: עד כאן לא פליגי כו'. (ה) דקתני: "אסור במעשר" – לשון אכילה היא, דאי בנגיעת שני – לא פסיל במעשר, דשמעינן לר' מאיר דאמר מותר באכילה ואיפליג עליה באכילה דמעשר. ואילו בחולין כולהו מודו דמותר אפילו באכילה. ומתני' מני? כאן באכילה דפירי. הא דקתני: "מה שאין כן במעשר" – באכילה דפירי קאמר. ומיהו, בתרומה בעי נטילה, שאפילו במגעו הוא [פוסל], דשני פוסל את התרומה: נוטל. בכלי: מטביל. בארבעים סאה: כאן

תוספות

קשיא חולין אחולין. ולא בעי למימר בחולין עד הפרק קאמר, מה שאין כן במעשר – דלישנא לא משמע ליה (ו):

כאן באכילה וכאן בנגיעה. הקשה הר"ר אלחנן: מעשר אמעשר נמי לישני הכי, ולוקמי אפילו כרבנן! ותירץ מורי: דאף (ז) בנגיעה דמעשר נמי פליגי רבנן, ואסרי לה. וכן משמע בסמוך, דקאמר: עד כאן לא פליגי אלא באכילה דמעשר, משמע דמעיקרא סד"א דבכל ענין פליגי. וכן בפ' שני דחולין (דף לג: ושם) דקאמר: ודלמא לא פליגי רבנן אלא באכילה דמעשר כו', משמע לדבר ברור אינו. מיהו, הוי מצי לאקשויי: וליטעמיך, מתניתין *דשבת פ"ק (דף יד) דתנן: ואלו פוסלין את התרומה, לא מיתוקמא כרבנן, דמאי איריא תרומה – אפילו מעשר נמי! אלא לא חש לאקשויי ליה. ומכח דההיא משמע דאמת הוא כי אתקפתא דרב שימי, והא דנקט בפ"ב דחולין (דף לג: ושם) "ודלמא" – לישנא קלילא הוא, דלעולם אמת הוא בנגיעת מעשר. ואכילת חולין לא פליגי, דלכ"ע אין שני עושה שלישי (*בחולין). ואל תתמה: היכי ס"ד דלרבנן לא בעי אכילת חולין נטילה? וי"ל: דאיירי בפירי, דלא בעו נטילה:

הא בנהמא הא בפירי. והשתא לא הוצרך לתרץ תו גבי מעשר הא רבי מאיר והא רבנן. והוא הדין דמצי למימר הא באכילה (ח) הא בנגיעה, אלא כולה באכילה עדיפא ליה:

הנוטל ידיו לפירות. וכי אמר בפ' "כילד מברכין" (ברכות דף מג.*): אורחין שהיו מסובין לשתות אצל בעל הבית – נוטלין כל אחד ידו אחת – התם משום נקיות הוי. וכן משמע לישנא ד"ידו אחת", דקתני:

כאן לחולין כאן למעשר. משמע דאם לא כוון למעשר לא מהני, וכ"ש בתרומה. והקשה הר"ר אלחנן: דאמר בפ' "אלו דברים" בברכות (דף נא:), ב"ש אומרים: נוטלים את הידים, ואח"כ מוזגין את הכוס. שאם ימזגו את הכוס – שמא יגע במשקים שאחורי הכוס. והשתא, אפילו נוטלן נמי, כיון דלא מהניא הך נטילה לתרומה – הויא ליה פוסל את התרומה, ותנן: *)כל הפוסל את התרומה מטמא משקין להיות תחילה! ותירץ: דכיון דנטל ידיו לחולין – לא פסיל תרומה. והכי משמע. דאי לא תימא הכי – אין לך אדם, אף חבר, אוכל חולין בטהרה שלא יטמא משקין:

*) [פרה פ"ח מ"ז פסחים יז:]

נגזור

רבינו חננאל

מתני' נוטלין לידים לחולין ולמעשר כו'. פי' נוטלין לידים ולחולין ולמעשר אבל לתרומה ולקדש מטבילין כך סוגיא דשמעתא. ומקשינן [חולין ומעשר מי] בעו נט"י והתנן. התרומה והבכורים טעונין רחיצת ידים מה שאין כן במעשר ושנינן הא לר' מאיר היא דתני בענין מי שטעון ביאת מים מדברי סופרים כגון רחיצת ידים מותר בחולין ובמעשר ומתניתין דלא כר' מאיר אלא כחכמים דפליגי עליה ואסרי במעשר ומקשינן והא אפילו חכמים דפליגי על ר' מאיר לא פליגי אלא במעשר דתנן וחכמים אוסרין במעשר ושנינן כי תניא ומותר בחולין בנגיעה ולא באכילה *) דחולין אפי' ר' מאיר מודה דצריך נטילה ומתניתין באכילה דחולין דברי הכל וכ"ש למעשר. ודחינן להא שנויה הכי וממאי כדקאמרת דלמא לא פליגי רבנן וחכמים אלא אאכילה דמעשר דר' מאיר מתיר וחכמים אוסרים אבל ואכילה דחולין דברי הכל שרו ושנינן שנוי' אחריתי. מתני' באכילה דנהמא ולדברי הכל בעי נטילה. והא דקתני מותר בחולין ואוקימנה לדברי הכל באכילה דפירי דלא ידים כרב נחמן דאמר בפרק כל הבשר אסור לבשל בחלב. הנוטל ידיו לפירות הרי זה מגסי הרוח: ת"ר הנוטל ידיו נתכוון ידיו טהורות לא נתכוון ידיו טמאות וכן המטביל ידיו כו': ירושלמי. כל הן דתנינן מטבילין במ' סאה. ותניא אידך אע"פ שלא נתכוון ידיו טהורות. קשיין אהדדי ושנינן הא דתניא בעינן כוונה למעשר. ואידך דלא בעי כוונה לחולין מנלן

*) נראה דצ"ל ובאכילה דחולין אפילו ר"מ מודה וכו'.

עין משפט נר מצוה

כב א מיי' פ"ו מהלכות ברכות הלכה א סמג עשין כז טוש"ע א"ח סי' קנח סעיף א:
כג ב מיי' פי"א מהלכות תרומות הלכה ז ופ"ח מהלכות אבות הטומאות הלכה ח ופי"א מהלכות מקוואות הלכה יא:
כד ג מיי' פ"ב מהלכות אבות הטומאות הלכה ז סמג עשין רמז:
כה ד מיי' פי"ג מהלכות פרה אדומה הלכה ד:
[זבחים פ"ה ומייתי לה שבת פ"ק יג: כצ"ל]
כו ה מיי' פי"ג מהלכות אבות הטומאות ה"ב:
כז ו מיי' שם ופי"א מהל' מקוואות הלכה ח ופי"ג הלכה יב:
כח ז מיי' פי"ג מהל' פרה אדומה הלכה ה ופ"ו מהלכות מטמאי משכב ומושב הלכה א:
[נ"ל במעשר]
כט ח מיי' פי"ג מהל' אבות הטומאות שם:
ל ט מיי' שם ופ' י"ב שם הלכה ד:
לא י מיי' פי"ג מהלכות אבות הטומאות שם ופי"א מהלכות פרה אדומה הלכה ב:
לב כ מיי' פי"ג מהל' פרה אדומה שם:
לג ל מיי' פ"ו מהלכות תרומות הלכה ו ופ"ג מהלכות בכורים הלכה א:
[וע"ש תוס' ד"ה כל אחד ותוס' פסחים קטו. ד"ה כל שטיבולו]
לד מ מיי' פ"ו מהל' תרומות שם ופ"י הלכה א:
לה נ מיי' שם הלכה ה ופ"ד מהלכות בכורים הלכה טו:
לו ס מיי' פ"ד מהלכות בכורים הלכה יד:
לז ע מיי' פ"ג מהלכות תרומות הלכה א ופ"ד מהל' בכורים הלכה טו:
לח פ מיי' פי"א מהל' תרומות הלכה ז:
לט צ מיי' שם פ"ז הלכה ב ופ"ג מהלכות מעשר שני הלכה יא:
מ ק מיי' פי"ג מהלכות מעשר שני הלכה א והלכה יז והלכה כד ופ"ז שם הלכה יא:
מא ר ש מיי' פי"א מהל' תרומות הלכה ז ופ"ו מהלכות ברכות הלכה א סמג עשין כז טוש"ע א"ח סי' קנח סעיף א:
מב ת מיי' פ"ו מהלכות ברכות הלכה ג טוש"ע שם סעיף ה:
מג א ב ג מיי' פי"ג מהל' שאר אבות הטומאות הלכה ב (ופ"ט מהלכות מקוואות הלכה יז) טור ש"ע א"ח סי' קנט סעיף יג:

מסורת הש"ס

[פרה פי"ב מ"ז]
חולין לג:
[חולין לג. נדה לג: ועי' תוס' לקמן יט: ד"ה בגדי]
בכורים פ"ב מ"א יבמות עג. ב"מ נב:
פרה פי"א מ"ה סוטה ל. חולין לג:
ברכות מב. חולין קו.

הגהות הב"ח

(א) גמ' באכילה דנהמא כאן. נ"ב (וכרבי מאיר) דכרבנן לא מיתוקמא דאינו (לרבנן אפי' באכילה) דפירי אוסרין: (ב) רש"י ד"ה מה שאין כן וכו' לא איירי הכא בחומש כי האי גוונא: (ג) ד"ה הטעון וכו' טומאה כגון כל הנך: (ד) ד"ה מטמא וכו' ופוסל עוד את הרביעי כצ"ל ותיבת עליהן נמחק: (ה) ד"ה עד כאן לא פליגי כו' בע"כ הא דקתני אסור וכו' מדקמשנינן לר"מ: (ו) תוס' ד"ה קשיא וכו' לא משמע ליה הכי הס"ד: (ז) ד"ה כאן וכו' דבנגיעת למעשר וכו' נטילה דיש לומר דאיירי: (ח) ד"ה הא בנהמא וכו' הא באכילה. נ"ב [פי' מתניתין באכילה] דנהמא נוטלין לחולין [והא דבכורים] בנגיעה דנהמא אין נוטלין לחולין וכר"מ מתוקמא אפילו כי מוקים לה כולה באכילה [לא מתוקמא] אלא לר"מ:

כָּאן — לְמַעֲשֵׂר. וּמְנָא תֵּימְרָא דְּחוּלִּין לָא בָּעוּ כַּוָּונָה, דִּתְנַן: *[א]גַּל שֶׁנִּתְלַשׁ וּבוֹ אַרְבָּעִים סְאָה, וְנָפַל עַל הָאָדָם וְעַל הַכֵּלִים — טְהוֹרִין. קָתָנֵי אָדָם דּוּמְיָא דְּכֵלִים, מַה כֵּלִים דְּלָא מְכַוְּונִי — אַף אָדָם דְּלָא מְכַוֵּין. וּמִמַּאי, דִּלְמָא בְּיוֹשֵׁב וּמְצַפֶּה אֵימָתַי יִתָּלֵשׁ הַגַּל עָסְקִינַן, וְכֵלִים דּוּמְיָא דְּאָדָם, מַה אָדָם דְּבַר כַּוָּונָה — אַף כֵּלִים דִּמְכַוֵּין לְהוּ? וְכִי תֵּימָא: בְּיוֹשֵׁב וּמְצַפֶּה מַאי לְמֵימְרָא — סָלְקָא דַּעְתָּךְ אָמִינָא: לִיגְזוֹר דִּלְמָא אָתֵי לְמִיטְבַּל בְּחַרְדָּלִית שֶׁל גְּשָׁמִים, א"נ נִגְזוֹר רָאשִׁין אַטּוּ כֵּיפִין, קמ"ל דְּלָא גָּזְרִינַן. וּמְנָא תֵּימְרָא דְּלָא מַטְבִּילִין בְּכֵיפִין, דְּתַנְיָא: *[ב]מַטְבִּילִין בְּרָאשִׁין וְאֵין מַטְבִּילִין בְּכֵיפִין, לְפִי שֶׁאֵין מַטְבִּילִין בַּאֲוִיר. אֶלָּא מֵהָא, דִּתְנַן: *[ג]פֵּירוֹת שֶׁנָּפְלוּ לְתוֹךְ אַמַּת הַמַּיִם, וּפָשַׁט מִי שֶׁיָּדָיו טְמֵאוֹת וּנְטָלָן — יָדָיו טְהוֹרוֹת, וּפֵירוֹת אֵינָן בְּ"כִי יוּתַּן". וְאִם בִּשְׁבִיל שֶׁיּוּדְחוּ יָדָיו — יָדָיו טְהוֹרוֹת, וְהַפֵּירוֹת הֲרֵי הֵן בְּ"כִי יוּתַּן". אֵיתִיבֵיהּ רַבָּה לְרַב נַחְמָן: הַטּוֹבֵל לְחוּלִּין וְהוּחְזַק לְחוּלִּין — אָסוּר לְמַעֲשֵׂר, הוּחְזַק — אִין, לֹא הוּחְזַק — לָא! ה"ק: אע"פ שֶׁהוּחְזַק לְחוּלִּין — אָסוּר לְמַעֲשֵׂר. אֵיתִיבֵיהּ: [ד]טָבַל וְלֹא הוּחְזַק — כְּאִילּוּ לֹא טָבַל. מַאי לָאו — כְּאִילּוּ לֹא טָבַל כְּלָל! לֹא, כְּאִילּוּ לֹא טָבַל לְמַעֲשֵׂר, אֲבָל טָבַל לְחוּלִּין. הוּא סָבַר דָּחֵי קָא מַדְחֵי לֵיהּ, נְפַק, דַּק וְאַשְׁכַּח, דְּתַנְיָא: טָבַל וְלֹא הוּחְזַק — אָסוּר לְמַעֲשֵׂר וּמוּתָּר לְחוּלִּין. אר"א: טָבַל וְעָלָה — מַחֲזִיק עַצְמוֹ לְכָל מַה שֶׁיִּרְצֶה. מֵיתִיבִי: עוֹדֵהוּ רַגְלוֹ אַחַת בַּמַּיִם, הוּחְזַק לְדָבָר קַל — מַחֲזִיק עַצְמוֹ לְדָבָר חָמוּר, עָלָה — שׁוּב אֵינוֹ מַחֲזִיק. מַאי לָאו — אֵינוֹ מַחֲזִיק כְּלָל? — לֹא, עוֹדֵהוּ — אע"פ שֶׁהוּחְזַק — מַחֲזִיק, עָלָה — אִם לֹא הוּחְזַק — מַחֲזִיק, וְאִם הוּחְזַק — אֵינוֹ מַחֲזִיק. מַאן תַּנָּא עוֹדֵהוּ רַגְלוֹ אַחַת בַּמַּיִם? א"ר פְּדָת: ר' יְהוּדָה הִיא. דִּתְנַן*: [ה]מִקְוֶה שֶׁנִּמְדַּד וְיֵשׁ בּוֹ אַרְבָּעִים סְאָה מְכוּוָּנוֹת, וְיָרְדוּ שְׁנַיִם וְטָבְלוּ זֶה אַחַר זֶה — הָרִאשׁוֹן טָהוֹר וְהַשֵּׁנִי טָמֵא. אָמַר רַבִּי יְהוּדָה: אִם הָיוּ רַגְלָיו שֶׁל רִאשׁוֹן נוֹגְעוֹת בַּמַּיִם — אַף הַשֵּׁנִי טָהוֹר. אָמַר רַב נַחְמָן אָמַר רַבָּה בַּר אֲבוּהּ: מַחֲלוֹקֶת בְּמַעֲלוֹת דְּרַבָּנַן, אֲבָל מְטוּמְאָה לְטָהֳרָה — דִּבְרֵי הַכֹּל [א](אַף) הַשֵּׁנִי טָמֵא, וְהַיְינוּ דְּרַבִּי פְּדָת. אִיכָּא דְּאָמְרִי, אָמַר רַב נַחְמָן אָמַר רַבָּה בַּר אֲבוּהּ: מַחֲלוֹקֶת מְטוּמְאָה לְטָהֳרָה, אֲבָל בְּמַעֲלוֹת דְּרַבָּנַן — דִּבְרֵי הַכֹּל אַף הַשֵּׁנִי טָהוֹר, וּפְלִיגָא דְּרַבִּי פְּדָת. אֲמַר עוּלָּא, (א) בְּעַי מִינֵּיהּ מֵרַבִּי יוֹחָנָן: לְרַבִּי יְהוּדָה, מַהוּ לְהַטְבִּיל מְחָטִין וְצִינּוֹרִיּוֹת בְּרֹאשׁוֹ שֶׁל רִאשׁוֹן? גּוֹד אַחֵית — אִית לֵיהּ לְרַבִּי יְהוּדָה, גּוֹד אַסֵּיק — לֵית לֵיהּ? אוֹ דִּלְמָא: גּוֹד אַסֵּיק נַמִי אִית לֵיהּ? א"ל תְּנִיתוּהָ: *[ו]שָׁלֹשׁ גְּמָמִיּוֹת בַּנַּחַל: הָעֶלְיוֹנָה, הַתַּחְתּוֹנָה וְהָאֶמְצָעִית. הָעֶלְיוֹנָה וְהַתַּחְתּוֹנָה שֶׁל עֶשְׂרִים עֶשְׂרִים סְאָה, וְהָאֶמְצָעִית שֶׁל אַרְבָּעִים סְאָה, וְחַרְדָּלִית שֶׁל גְּשָׁמִים עוֹבֶרֶת בֵּינֵיהֶן. רַבִּי יְהוּדָה אוֹמֵר, מֵאִיר הָיָה אוֹמֵר: מַטְבִּיל בָּעֶלְיוֹנָה. וְהָתַנְיָא, רַבִּי יְהוּדָה אוֹמֵר, מֵאִיר

רש"י

כָּאן לְמַעֲשֵׂר. בָּעֵי כַּוָּונָה, וְכ"שׁ בִּתְרוּמָה: הָכִי גָּרְסִינַן: מַה כֵּלִים דְּלָא מִיכַּוְּונִי, אַף אָדָם נַמִי דְּלָא מִיכַּוֵּין: חַרְדָּלִית. שֶׁשּׁוֹטֶפֶת וְיוֹרֶדֶת מִמָּקוֹם גָּבוֹהַּ וְיֵשׁ בָּהּ אַרְבָּעִים סְאָה, וְהַטּוֹבֵל בָּהּ לֹא עָלְתָה לוֹ טְבִילָה. מִשּׁוּם דְּמָקוֹם קַטַפְרֵס הוּא — מָקוֹם זָקוּף יוֹתֵר מִדַּאי, וּמ' סְאָה שֶׁבּוֹ אֵינָן בְּמָקוֹם אֶחָד, וּתְנַן: הַנִּצּוֹק וְהַקַּטַפְרֵס אֵינוֹ חִיבּוּר (טהרות פ"ח מ"ט). וְאַף אִם אֵינוֹ קַטַפְרֵס נַמִי אֵין טוֹבְלִין בּוֹ, לְפִי שֶׁאֵין מֵי גְּשָׁמִים מְטַהֲרִים דֶּרֶךְ זְחִילָתָן עַד שֶׁיְּהוּ נִקְוִין דֶּרֶךְ אֲשְׁבּוֹרֶן, דְּתַנְיָא בְּת"כ: אִי מַה מַּעְיָן מְטַהֵר בְּזוֹחֲלִין — אַף מִקְוֶה מְטַהֵר בְּזוֹחֲלִין — ת"ל: "אַךְ מַעְיָן וּבוֹר מִקְוֵה מַיִם יִהְיֶה טָהוֹר" (ויקרא יא), הַמַּעְיָן מְטַהֵר בְּזוֹחֲלִין, וְהַמִּקְוֶה בַּאֲשְׁבּוֹרֶן. וְרַבֵּינוּ הָאי גָּרֵיס: הַרְדָּלִית: רָאשִׁין. אֶחָד מֵרָאשֵׁי הַגַּל כְּשֶׁהוּא מַגִּיעַ לָאָרֶץ: כֵּיפִין. אֶמְצָעִיתוֹ שֶׁל גַּל, שֶׁעוֹמֵד בָּאֲוִיר כְּמִין כִּיפָּה. וְאִם הוֹשִׁיט כֵּלִים לְמַעְלָה וְהִטְבִּילָן בַּכִּיפָּה — אֵינָהּ טְבִילָה, כִּדְמְפָרֵשׁ וְאָזֵיל: שֶׁאֵין מַטְבִּילִין בַּאֲוִיר. שֶׁלֹּא אָמְרָה תּוֹרָה מִקְוֶה שֶׁל אֲוִיר לִטְבִילָה: יָדָיו טְהוֹרוֹת. אַף עַל פִּי שֶׁלֹּא נִתְכַּוֵּון: וּפֵירוֹת אֵינָן בְּכִי יוּתַּן. דְּבָעֵינַן גַּבֵּי הֶכְשֵׁר, יוּתַּן דּוּמְיָא דְּכִי יִתֵּן, דְּנִיחָא לֵיהּ: וְאִם בִּשְׁבִיל שֶׁיּוּדְחוּ יָדָיו. נִתְכַּוֵּון לִיטּוֹל פֵּירוֹת — הֲרֵי הוּא בְּכִי יוּתַּן, וּמְקַבְּלִין טוּמְאָה מֵעַכְשָׁיו. וְכֵיוָן דְּנִתְכַּוֵּון לְהָדִיחַ יָדָיו גָּלֵי דַּעְתֵּיהּ דְּנִיחָא לֵיהּ בְּהַךְ נְפִילָה, שֶׁעַל יָדֶיהָ הֵדִיחַ יָדָיו: הוּחְזַק אִין. אִם נִתְכַּוֵּון הוּא דַּהֲוָיָא טְבִילָה לְחוּלִּין: טָבַל. וְיָצָא וְעָלָה מִן הַמַּיִם: מַחֲזִיק עַצְמוֹ. בַּטְּבִילָה שֶׁטָּבַל כְּבָר, לְכָל מַה שֶּׁיִּרְצֶה: מַאי לָאו אֵינוֹ מַחֲזִיק כְּלָל. כְּלוֹמַר: בֵּין שֶׁהֶחֱזִיק עַצְמוֹ בִּשְׁעַת טְבִילָה בְּדָבָר קַל, בֵּין שֶׁלֹּא הֶחֱזִיק עַצְמוֹ לִכְלוּם — שׁוּב אֵינוֹ מַחֲזִיק: אִם לֹא הוּחְזַק. לְשׁוּם דָּבָר, שֶׁטָּבַל סְתָם — מַחֲזִיק לְכָל מַה שֶּׁיִּרְצֶה. אֲבָל אִם הוּחְזַק לְקַל — אֵינוֹ מוּחְזָק לְחָמוּר, דְּהָא אִינְתִּיק לֵיהּ לְדָבָר קַל: מַאן תַּנָּא. דְּמִשּׁוּם עוֹדֶנּוּ בַּמַּיִם חָשִׁיב לֵיהּ כִּתְחִילַּת טְבִילָה, וְאַף עַל פִּי שֶׁהוּחְזַק — מַחֲזִיק: וְהַשֵּׁנִי טָמֵא. שֶׁהֲרֵי חָסַר הַשִּׁיעוּר בַּמַּיִם שֶׁעַל הָרִאשׁוֹן: מַחֲלוֹקֶת. דְּרַבִּי יְהוּדָה וְרַבָּנַן, כְּשֶׁהָיְתָה טְבִילָתוֹ בִּשְׁבִיל אַחַת מִמַּעֲלוֹת שֶׁל חֲכָמִים, כְּגוֹן הָאוֹנֵן וְהַמְחוּסַּר כִּפּוּרִים שֶׁצְּרִיכִין טְבִילָה לְקוֹדֶשׁ וְאֵינוֹ טָמֵא טוּמְאָה דְּאוֹרַיְיתָא — בְּהַהִיא קָאָמַר רַבִּי יְהוּדָה דְּמַהֲנֵי לֵיהּ רַגְלָיו שֶׁל רִאשׁוֹן נוֹגְעוֹת בַּמַּיִם, דְּאָמְרִינַן: גּוֹד אַחֵית מַיִם שֶׁעָלָיו, כְּאִילּוּ הֵן בַּמִּקְוֶה: וְהַיְינוּ דְּרַבִּי פְּדָת. דְּאוֹקֵי לְעֵיל הָא דְּ"עוֹדֵיהוּ" כְּרַבִּי יְהוּדָה וְלָא כְּרַבָּנַן. אַלְמָא, לְרַבָּנַן אֲפִי' לְגַבֵּי מַעֲלוֹת לָא מְהַנֵּי עוֹדֵיהוּ, דְּהָא חֲזָקָה דְּאָמַר הוּחְזַק לְקַל אָסוּר לְחָמוּר — מַעֲלוֹת נִינְהוּ: אִיכָּא דְּאָמְרִי כו'. הָכָא גָּרְסִי': וּפְלִיגָא דְּר' פְּדָת, דְּאִילּוּ לְרַב נַחְמָן הָא דְּעוֹדֵיהוּ הוּחְזַק לְקַל הוּחְזַק לְחָמוּר דִּבְרֵי הַכֹּל הוּא, דְּהָא לָא פְּלִיגֵי רַבָּנַן עֲלֵיהּ דְּר"י אֶלָּא מְטוּמְאָה דְּאוֹרַיְיתָא לְטָהֳרָה: צִינּוֹרוֹת. שֶׁטּוֹוִין בּוֹ זָהָב, וַעֲשׂוּיִן כְּמִין מַזְלֵג קָטָן מְאֹד: בְּרֹאשׁוֹ שֶׁל רִאשׁוֹן. בְּעוֹדוֹ בַּמַּיִם: גְּמָמִיּוֹת. גּוּמּוֹת בַּנַּחַל, שִׁיפּוּלֵי הָרִים שֶׁקּוֹרִין וולור"א בְּלַעַ"ז, וְכֵן "נַחַל אֵיתָן" "נַחַל אַרְנוֹן". תַּחְתּוֹנָה עֶלְיוֹנָה וְאֶמְצָעִית — שֶׁנַּחַל מִדְרוֹן מְשׁוּפָּע הוּא: עוֹבֶרֶת בֵּינֵיהֶן. וּמְחַבַּרְתָּן:

תוספות

נגזור אטו חרדלית. פרש"י: שיורדת מהר גבוה ויש בה מ' סאה, ולא עלתה שם טבילה, דקטפרס אינו חיבור. והר"י פי', וכן כתוב בכמה פירושים של רש"י: דפסול מטעם דאין מקוה מטהר בזוחלין אלא באשבורן, כדתניא בת"כ. ומיהו, אומר הר"ר אלחנן: ע"כ טעם ראשון עיקר, מדגזרינן בגל של ים. דאי משום זחילה (ב) — אז בשל ים מהני, אי לא מוקמינן לה כר' [מאיר] דאמר במס' מקואות (פ"ה מ"ד): כל הימים כמקוה. והיה קשה למורי: מאי קאמר משום חרדלית של מי גשמים? הא בשל ים נמי לא מהני, כדתנן, ב"ה אומרים: אין מטבילין בחרדלית, ומשמע דבכל חרדלית איירי, מדלא הוזכר ליה בהדיא גשמים! ולפי' ראשון ניחא. ומיהו, אכתי יש להקשות: דקטפרס הוה חיבור לענין מקואות, כדפירש הר"י, ואם כן למה לא מהני! ואי הוה טעמא משום זחילה — יתכן טפי:

לא כאילו לא טבל למעשר. ורבותא דמתני' משום חולין הויא, דמהניא אף בלא כוונה. דאי משום מעשר, אף כי הוחזק לחולין — קתני רישא דלא מהני. הר"ר אלחנן. ועוד י"ל: דאי משום רישא הייתי אומר דטפי עדיף לא הוחזק כלל למעשר מהוחזק לחולין, דהא עקר דעתו לגמרי ממעשר:

טבל ועלה כו'. ועודנו לא. ובכמה ספרים כתיב בהדיא לא:

רבי יהודה אומר מאיר היה אומר מטבילין בעליונה. ל"ג רש"י מכלל דר"י כו'. והכי פירש: מטבילין בעליונה מטעם גוד אסיק, וכ"ש גוד אחית. ולא פליג עליה רבי יהודה, מדלא קתני ליה ואני חולק עליו. והא תניא רבי מאיר אומר בין בעליונה בין בתחתונה ואני אומר בתחתונה ולא בעליונה וכו'. ולשון הכתוב בספרים אין להעמידה, דא"כ מתנייתא קשיין אהדדי ומאי חזית דליית לברייתא? כל זה פרש"י. ומיהו, יש ליישב גירסת הספרים, (ג) וכן היא הלעת הגי' בפר"ח: ר' יהודה אומר ר' מאיר היה אומר בתחתונה ולא בעליונה, דאית ליה גוד אחית ולא גוד אסיק. מכלל דר' יהודה אית ליה גוד אסיק. דמדקאמר רבי מאיר אומר — משמע דאין הוא מודה לו. ופריך: והתניא, ר' יהודה אומר ר"מ אומר בין בתחתונה בין בעליונה, ואני אומר בתחתונה ולא בעליונה. אלמא לית ליה גוד אסיק! ומתני' אהדדי לא קשיין, דקמייתא דר"י אומר מאיר אומר ולא בעליונה — היינו לפי דעתו של רבי יהודה, אבל לסברא של ר"מ — אף בעליונה. בשם מורי: בתחתונה

עין משפט נר מצוה

מד א מיי' פ"ט מהל' מקואות הלכה יז סמג עשין רמח:
מה ב מיי' שם הל' יח סמג שם:
מו ג מיי' פי"ב מהל' טומאת אוכלין הל' י סמג עשין רמו:
מז ד מיי' פ"א מהל' מקואות הלכה יב:
מח ה מיי' שם פ"ח הל' יב טוש"ע י"ד סי' רא סעיף סב:
מט ו מיי' שם הל' ח טוש"ע שם סעיף ס:

מסורת הש"ס

[א] חולין לא. מקואות פ"ה מ"ו
[ב] חולין לא: [תוספתא דמקואות פ"ד]
[ג] חולין שם מכשירין פ"ד מ"ו
[ה] מקואות פ"ז מ"ו גיטין טז. ע"ש
[ו] תוספתא פ"ג דמקואות

הגהות הב"ח

(א) גמ' אמר עולא בעיא מיניה וכו' ואמר לי תניתוה: (ב) תוס' ד"ה נגזור וכו' דאי משום זחילה הא בשל ים וכו' כדתנן פ"ה דמקואות בית הלל: (ג) ד"ה ר' יהודה וכו' היא הגהה וה"ג בפר"ח וכו' לא קשיין דהא דקא מייתי:

הגהות הגר"א

[א] גמ' דברי הכל השני טמא כצ"ל ותיבת אף נמחק:

רבינו חננאל

ומנא לן דלחולין לא בעינן כוונה דתנן גל שנתלש ובו מ' סאה ונפל על האדם ועל הכלים טהורים ואמרינן אדם דומיא דכלים מה כלים לא בעי כוונה אף אדם לא בעי כוונה ונדחת דאית לן לאוקומה במתכוון היכי דמי ביושב ומצפה מתי יתלש הגל. וכי תימא אי הכי מאי למימרא הא קא מיכוון אצטריך סד"א נגזור גל שנתלש ושתי ראשין מעורבין במי הים אטו חרדלית שהן מי גשמים אי נמי מהו דתימא נגזור ראשים אטו כיפים פי' אמצעית הגל העשוי כמין כיפה שחלקתו הרוח מן הים והפריחתו כמו באויר שאין טבילה עולה בהן. כדתנן מטבילין בראשים ואין מטבילין בכיפים קמ"ל דלא גזרינן ראשים אטו כיפים אלא מהא דתנן פירות שנשרו לתוך אמת המים ופשט מי שידיו טמאות ונטלן ידיו טהורות הנה בלא מתכוון כדי להטביל ידיו וקתני טהרו ש"מ לא בעינן כוונה ואסיקנ' מהא דלא בעינן כוונה לחולין דתניא טבל ולא הוחזק מותר בחולין ואסור במעשר. א"ר אלעזר טבל ועלה מחזיק עצמו לכל מה שירצה. ומותבינן עליה והתנינן עודהו רגלו במים הוחזק לדבר הקל מחזיק עצמו לדבר חמור. פי' אם הוחזק למעשר ועודהו רגליו במים מחזיק עצמו בתרומה עלה שוב אינו מחזיק. קשיא לר' אלעזר דאמר אפילו עלה מחזיק עצמו לכל מה שירצה. ופריק הא דתני עלה שוב אינו מחזיק בשכבר הוחזק לדבר ידוע ועודהו במים וכי אמינא אנא דמחזיק עצמו לכל מה שירצה. כשעלה סתם ועדיין לא הוחזק והוחזק עתה. מאן תנא עודהו רגלו במים אע"פ שהוחזק חוזר ומחזיק א"ר פדת ר' יהודה היא דתנן מקוה שיש בו מ' סאה מכוונות וירדו שנים וטבלו זה אחר זה הראשון טהור והשני טמא ר"י אומר אם היו רגליו של ראשון נוגעות במים אף השני טהור אמר רב נחמן אמר רבה בר אבוה מחלוקת ר' יהודה ות"ק דפליג עליה ואמר השני טמא בעולה מטומאה לטהרה. אבל במעלות דרבנן בין חולין למעשר לתרומה לקדש ולחטאת להחזיק עצמו מן הקל לחמור *) ולפיכך תני אף השני טהור ופליגא דר' פדת דאוקמה לר' יהודה במעלות דרבנן מכלל דת"ק פליג עליה דהא דתניא עודהו רגלו במים הוחזק לדבר הקל כו' במעלות דרבנן הוא. איכא דאמרי אמר רב נחמן אמר רבה בר אבוה מחלוקת במעלות דרבנן ור' יהודה מטהר השני אבל מטומאה לטהרה דברי הכל השני טמא והיינו דר' פדת דאוקמה להא ברייתא כר' יהודה. אמר עולא בעאי מיניה דר' יוחנן מהו להטביל אליבא דר' יהודה מחטין וצינורות בראשו של ראשון גוד אחית אית ליה לר' יהודה ורואה כי המים שהן בגופו של ראשון יורדין במקוה וכאילו מעכשיו ישנן בתוך המקוה אבל גוד אסיק לית ליה שאין אומרים ראה כאלו מי המקוה נקוים ועומדים בראשו של ראשון או גוד אסיק נמי אית ליה וא"ל ר' יוחנן ת"ש נחל שיורד ממעלה למטה ויש בו ג' גממיות פי' ג' חפירות כל אחת למטה מחברתה וגומא העליונה והתחתונה של עשרין עשרין סאה ואמצעית של מ' סאה פי' הוצרך לומר והאמצעית של מ' כדי להכשיר חרדלית של גשמים שעוברת ביניהן ומצרפו שכל מקוה שהוא פחות ממ' סאה מי גשמים פוסלין אותו וחרדלית של גשמים עוברת ביניהן. ר' יהודה אומר מאיר היה אומר מטבילין בתחתונה דאלמא אמרינן גוד אחית ולא אמרינן גוד אסיק מדקתני ר' יהודה מאיר היה אומר מטבילין **) בין בתחתונה לאו מכלל דר' יהודה סבר חלופו ואומר מטבילין אף בעליונה אלמא גוד אסיק נמי

ה"ג

*) לכאורה נ"ל דברי הכל אף השני טהור. **) עי' בתוס' בד"ה ר"י גירסת רבינו ככתן.

עין משפט נר מצוה | מסורת הש"ס

מאיר היה אומר: מטביל בעליונה, *ואני אומר: בתחתונה ולא בעליונה! א"ל: *אי תניא — תניא.§ "הטובל לחולין והוחזק לחולין כו'".§ מני מתניתין — רבנן היא, דשני להו בין חולין למעשר. אימא סיפא: בגדי עם הארץ מדרס לפרושין. בגדי פרושין מדרס לאוכלי תרומה. אתאן לר' מאיר, דאמר: חולין ומעשר כהדדי נינהו. רישא רבנן וסיפא ר' מאיר? אין, רישא רבנן וסיפא ר' מאיר. רב אחא בר אדא [א]מתני לה בסיפא חמש מעלות, ומוקי לה כולה כרבנן. אמר רב מרי: שמע מינה, *חולין שנעשו על טהרת הקודש כקודש דמו. ממאי — מדלא

ה"ג: מאיר היה אומר מטבילין בעליונה. ול"ג: מכלל דר' יהודה. וה"פ: ר' יהודה אומר, מאיר היה אומר: מטבילין בעליונה, דאמר גוד אסיק את מי אמצעיתא למעלה ע"י חרדלית של גשמים, להכשיר את העליונה, וכל שכן דמטבילין בתחתונה. דכיון דאית ליה גוד אסיק — כ"ש דאית ליה גוד אחית. ומדלא קתני: ואני חולק עליו לומר כך וכך — שמע מינה דר' יהודה כר"מ ס"ל: והא תניא. דחלוק עליו. וה"ג: מאיר היה אומר מטבילין בעליונה, ואני אומר בתחתונה ולא בעליונה. אלמא: פליג עליה: אמר להו אי תניא. בהדיא דחולקין — תניא, ואלך אחריה, וחוזר אני בי. ובלשון הכתוב בספרים איני יכול להעמידה, דא"כ מתנייתא קשיין אהדדי, ומאי חזית דדיית לבתרייתא? רבנן היא. דפליגי עליה דר"מ בכל הטעון ביאת מים מדברי סופרים, ואסרוהו במעשר: מדרס לאוכלי תרומה. ולא אמר מדרס למעשר: חמש מעלות. פרושים, ואוכלי מעשר, ואוכלי תרומה, ואוכלי קודש, וחטאת: שנעשו על טהרת הקודש. אדם הרגיל לאכול קדשים מקבל עליו לאכול חוליו בטהרת הקודש, כדי שיהו בני ביתו זהירין ובקיאין בטהרת הקודש: מדלא

בתחתונה ולא בעליונה. משמע הכא דקטפרס הוי חיבור, (א) ואנן תנן*, ומייתי לה פ"ב דגיטין (דף טז. ושם): הנצוק והקטפרס ומשקה טופח — אינו חיבור לא לטומאה ולא לטהרה. ועוד: למה לי ג' גממיות? בתרי סגי, בזה כ' ובזה כ', וחרדלית מחברתן? ותירץ ר"ת: דשאני הכא דאיכא מקוה שלם באמצע. וכן משמע בפ' בתרא דע"ז (דף עב. ושם) מתוך פרש"י*, שפי': קטפרס גממיות בזה כ' ובזה כ' וחרדלית מחברתן. ולא נקט ג' כדאיתא הכא. אלמא מסתבר ליה טעמא שיש לחלק. ואל תתמה: היכי מדמה ליה למיפשט מהך דהכא (ב) בעייתו מהו להטביל מחטין וצינורות בראשו של ראשון, כההוא דלעיל, ולא קאמר *דשאני התם משום מקוה שלם. דהתם לעיל איכא טעמא אחרינא, (ג) קטפרס שסופו לירד מה שבראשו של ראשון. ובהכי מתרצינן קושיא אחרינ' דקשיא לר"ת: דמשמע התם בגיטין דנצוק וקטפרס אינו חיבור, ומסיק לענין מקואות ור' יהודה היא. משמע דאף ר' יהודה מודי ליה. ולעיל קאמר: אם היו רגליו של ראשון נוגעות במים אף שני טהור, אלמא קטפרס חיבור. אלא ודאי שאני הכא שסופו לירד. ומיהו, יש לדחות הך דלא מוקי כר' יהודה רק ההיא דטופח ע"מ להטפיח, ולא תניא בהדיא ההוא דנצוק וקטפרס. וההוא דפ' בתרא דע"ז (ד) גבי המערה (ע"ז שם:) יין נסך מחבית לבור, דלא חשיב נצוק חיבור, אע"ג דסופו לירד — יש לחלק בין נצוק לקטפרס. דאין דרך נצוק לבא כי אם דרך אויר, וכי (ה) מדייק התם* מגישתא ובת גישתא דאנח נכרי ידיה עילויה ואסריה רבא — שמע מינה נצוק חיבור, ולא מחשב קטפרס, י"ל: דלא דמי לרגליו של שני נוגעות במים. דהא יין שבתוך הגישתא אין סופו לירד בתוך החבית. ולפי מה שפירש הר"י התם ההיא דנצוק וקטפרס מיתניא לענין השקה במס' טהרות (פ"ח מ"ט). דומיא דרישא דמקל מלא משקין טמאין והשיקו למקוה — אז יתכן שפיר ההיא. דהכא לענין טבילה מהני נצוק וקטפרס, ואפי' לית ביה מ' סאה נמי מטבילין בתחתונה. וכי נקט מ' סאה — לרבותא דעליונה דאין מטבילין בה, ור' יהודה היא. א"נ לאשמעינן דאפ"ה קתני בסיפא בתוספתא וחכ"א אין מטבילין אלא באמצעית (ו) ואע"פ שיש ארבעים באמצעית אין מטבילין בתחתונה, והתם הארכתי, ולא שייך הכא כלל רק לקמן אפרק (בס' חומר בקודש דף כא: בד"ה כעוביה): *בגדי ע"ה מדרס לפרושים. דחיישינן שמא ישבה אשתו נדה עליהן כדאיתא בפ"ב דחולין (דף לה: ושם), אבל משום (ז) עצמו — לא חיישינן. דאינו מטמא בהסיטו. וכן משמע שילהי ד"ניזקין" (גיטין דף סא: ושם) דפריך: וליחוש שמא תסיטם אשתו נדה. וכן תנן פרק שביעי דטהרות (מ"ו): הגנבים שנכנסו לבית אינו טמא אלא מקום רגלי הגנבים. אבל משכבות ומושבות וכלי חרס המוקפים — טהורין. אלמא, דלא מטמא לא משא ולא היסט. וכי תנן התם: (פ"ח מ"א): הדר עם ע"ה בחצר ושכח כלים בחצר אפי' חביות המוקפות צמיד פתיל — טמאים, התם בשביל אשתו שהיא לשם. תדע, מדנקט לישנא דדירה. אך קשיא, דתנן התם לעיל מינה (בפ"ז מ"ה): המניח ע"ה *בחצרו, בזמן שרואה הנכנסין והיוצאין כו'. בזמן שאינו רואה הנכנסין והיוצאין אפי' מוצל, אפי' כפות, כלומר גידם שאינו יכול לילך — הכל טמא. ואין לומר דהתם נמי בשביל אשתו — דהא מניח קתני, לשון אקראי. ועוד: מאי אפילו מוצל? איזה רבותא הוי, כיון דלא הוי טומאה בשביל זה? והיה נראה לי דלאו טעמא משום היסט, אלא משום דטרח ומזייף. וכי רואה את הנכנסין (ח) מרתת דנתפס כגנב. אבל קשיא לי, דתנן התם: (פ"י מ"א): הנועל בית הבד בפני הבדדין והיו שם כלים — טמאים מדרס. משמע דמטמא מדרס, ובסמוך קאמר, א"ר יוסי: וכי מפני מה טמאים — אלא שאין ע"ה בקיאין בהיסט. ועוד: כיון דחכמים גזרו עליהם להיות כזבין לכל דבריהם — אמאי אין מטמאין בהיסט ומדרס כדין זב? ועוד, דגזרו עליהן מעיינות, לקמן* דגזרו על רוקו כדין משקה זב וזבה. ועוד מצינו בפ' "בנות כותים" (נדה דף לג: ושם): הכא בכותי שטבל ודרס על בגדי חבר, דאי משום טומאת ע"ה — הא טביל ליה, אלמא, אי לא טביל מטמא מדרס? ותירץ ר"ת: דודאי אינו מטמא מדרס והיסט, דמשום תקנת השוק נגעו בה. כדאמרינן: (ט) לפי שלעולם לא ימצאו אדם מעביר חבית ממקום למקום, ואין גוזרין גזרה על הצבור אא"כ יכולין לעמוד בה. והכי משמע לקמן בפרקין* שאינו מטמא בהיסט: הרי שהיו חמריו ופועליו טוענין טהרות כו' טהרות טהורות. ואם אמר לכך כו'. ומסיק: מאי שנא רישא ומאי שנא סיפא? ומשני: במטהר חמריו ופועליו לכך. משמע דלא מוקי לה במטהר רק משום דק"ל רישא לסיפא, ולא קשיא ליה דמטמא ליה בהיסט, משום דקים ליה דלא מטמא. וההיא דנדה בלא טבל מטמא ליה במגע, והא דנקט ודרס — משום דבעי למהוי בגד חבר, לתחת רגלו של כותי, דהכי קתני התם במתני': ומטמא משכב תחתון כעליון, ואין להקשות: (י)דלא מוקי לה בשלא טבל, וכשיש דבר חוצץ בין רגלו לבגד — משום דע"כ אצטריך לאוקמי כשטבל, כי היכי דליהוי ספק ספיקא. דאי לא טבל — מה לי בועל בקרוב מה לי בועל ברחוק. והרב רבי משה מפונטוייז"א מפרש: משום דבע"ה אינו מטמא כזב אלא רק מטעם בגדיו, משום שהוא נושא המדרס שהוא לבוש בגדיו שישבה עליהם אשתו נדה. וצינורא שלו טמא משום שנגעה בשפתיו. וקשה: דאמרינן בפ' "בנות כותים" (ג"ז שם): מעשה בכ"ג שהלך בשוק ונתזה צינורא של צדוקי בבגדיו, וקדם אצל אשתו כו'. ופריך: ותיפוק ליה משום צינורא דע"ה! (כ) כלומר, אפילו לא היה טמא בשביל אשתו. אדרבה, הואיל דאם בועל נדה *היה נטמא הוא ובגדיו כנושא רוקו של זב, ואי משום צינורא דע"ה — בגד לחוד הוא דנטמא. ואין לומר דמשום גופו לא היה חש רק משום בגדיו, דאדרבה טומאת גופו חמירא לן. ועוד קשה: דכי מוקי לה בכותי ערום — למה לי טבל? אפי' לא טבל (ל) נמי, כיון דהאידנא לאו נושא המדרס הוי — לא הוי אלא ראשון, ואינו מטמא כלי! ועוד קשה למור"י: דתניא בהדיא בתוספתא (פ"ג): ספק (מ) רשות ע"ה, מדרסו והסיטו ואכילו — טהור לחולין וטמא לתרומה. ע"כ היה נראה לפרש: דלגבי תרומה מטמא כל דבר כְּזָב אבל טהור לחולין. וכל הני דאשכחן דמטמא — מוקמינן בתרומה. וכי קפריך בגיטין (דף סא:): וליחוש שמא תסיטם אשתו נדה. אע"ג דבתרומה קיימא — התם מילתא דפסיקא ליה נקט ואתאי. ועוד: דחייש לטומאה דאורייתא, ולא לשל טומאה דרבנן. וכי קאמר בחולין (דף לה:): שמא תשב עליהם אשתו נדה — משום איך נקטיה. וראיה לדבריו מצינו בירושלמי, דקאמר: בגדי פרושים מדרס לאוכלי תרומה, ובעי: גופו של פרוש מהו שיעשה כזב אצל תרומה? התיב והתנינן: המניח ע"ה בתוך ביתו לשמרו, כיון שהוא רואה את הנכנסין ואת היוצאין — טהורין. אבל משכבות וכלי חרס מוקפין כו'. ואי תימא עשו גופו כזב אצל תרומה — אפי' מוקפין טמאים. א"ר יהודה: תפתר בע"ה אצל פרוש, ולית את כלום. והשתא לא מיבעיא ליה אלא פרוש אצל תרומה, אבל ע"ה אצל תרומה — פשיטא ליה. א"ל ר' מנא: כל מה דאנו קיימין — בתרומה אנו קיימין. תדע לך שכן הוא — דתנינן: אפי' מוצל אפי' כפות הכל טמא. כלום יהיו טמאים אלא משום היסט, ולא כן א"ר יוחנן: ולא אכילות ולא הסיטות ולא רה"י ולא רשות ע"ה אצל תרומה! כלומר, דלא שייך כלל רשות ע"ה אצל תרומה שמטמא בהיסט, ומתני' בע"ה איירי, אבל פרוש אינו מטמא מדרס והיסט. והקשה לו הר"י, דאמר שילהי פ' "הניזקין" (גיטין סב.): אין עושין חלת ע"ה בטהרה, לפי שכבר טימא אותה. אבל עושין עיסתו בטהרה. ונוטל הימנה כדי חלה ומניחה בכפישא או באנחותא, וכשבא ע"ה נוטל שתיהן ואינו חושש, לפי שהכלי אינו מקבל טומאה. ואמאי? כיון שהוא מטמא היסט לתרומה — הא קא מטמא לחלה! וי"ל: דהתם כיון שלא קרא לו שם עדיין הו"ל חולין דפתיכי בהו חלה, דלא מטמאו בהיסט. וכן משמע לישנא דנקט כדי חלה ולא חלה עדיין, ואיהו במגע מטמא ולהכי פריך דלמא נגע:

רבי

[טהרות פ"ח מ"ט]

נ א מיי' פי"ג מהל' אבות הטומאות הל' א:

[כד"ה ולא לטהרה]

נ"ל דשאני הכא. מהרש"א

רבינו חננאל

נמי אית ליה *) ואמר עולא אמרו ליה והתניא בהדיא ר' יהודה אומר מאיר היה אומר מטבילין בין בתחתונה בין בעליונה ואני אומר בתחתונה ולא בעליונה. אלמא לר"י גוד אחית אית ליה גוד אסיק לית ליה א"ל אי תניא הכי בהדיא הא אפשטא בעיא דילך: **מתני'** טבל לחולין הוחזק לחולין אסור למעשר כו'. פי' זה מעשר שני הוא דכתיב ביה ואכלת לפני ה' אלהיך מעשר דגנך וגו' ומתניתין רבנן הוא דאמרי יש מעלה למעשר מן החולין ומקשינן אימא סיפא בגדי עם הארץ מדרס לפרושין פירוש הפרושין שהן חברים האוכלים חוליהן בטהרה וכשנוגעין בבגדי עם הארץ כאילו נטמאו מדרס וצריכין טבילה לאכול חוליהן בטהרה וקתני בתר הא בגדי פירושין מדרס לאוכלי תרומה ודייקינן מדלא קתני מדרס לאוכלי מעשר ש"מ חולין ומעשר שני כי הדדי נינהו לית ביניהו מעלה

*) אולי צ"ל ואמר ליה עולא והתניא וכו'.

הגהות הב"ח

(א) תוס' ד"ה בתחתונה וכו' הוי חיבור ואינו במסכת טהרות פרק שמיני תנן ומייתי לה וכו' שלם באמצע וכן משמע בפ' שני דגיטין מתוך פרש"י. נ"ב אבל בפרק בתרא דמסכת ע"ז פי' בדרך אחר: (ב) בא"ד למפשט מהך דהכא ההיא בעיתו דלעיל מהו להטביל וכו' בראשו של ראשון ולא קאמר דשאני התם משום דאיכא מקוה כנ"ל ותיבות כההיא דלעיל נמחק: (ג) בא"ד דבקטפרס שסופו וכו' של ראשון הוה חיבור ובהכי מתרצינן וכו' התם בגיטין דקטפרס אינו חיבור ומסיק לענין וכו' יש לדחות הך קושיא דלא מוקי וכו' ע"מ להטפיח חיבור ולא ההוא דנצוק כנ"ל ותיבות תניא בהדיא נמחק: (ד) בא"ד גבי המערה מחבית לבור כנ"ל ותיבות יין נסך נמחק: (ה) בא"ד וכי מדמה התם לגישתא ובת גישתא וכו' דלא דמי לרגליו של ראשון נוגעות וכו' הר"י התם דההיא דנצוק וכו' אז יתכן שפיר דהכא כנ"ל ותיבת ההיא נמחק: (ו) בא"ד דאע"פ שיש ארבעים וכו' לקמן אפרק כ"ב בדף כ"א בד"ה כעביה: (ז) ד"ה בגדי עם הארץ וכו' אבל משום ע"ה עצמו לא חיישינן וכו' אבל המשכבות והמושבות וכלי חרס המוקפים צמיד פתיל טהורין אלמא דלא מטמא לא במושב ולא בהיסט וכי תנן וכו' ואפילו חביות המוקפים צמיד פתיל הרי אלו טמאים התם וכו' המניח עם הארץ בתוך ביתו לשומרו בזמן שרואה: (ח) בא"ד וכי רואה את הנכנסין ו... כגנב (אבל קשיא לי וכו' ע"ה בקיאין בהיסט) תא"מ ונ"ב לא מצאתיה לא בתוספתא פ' בנות כותים ולא בהנזקין ולא בפי' ה"ר שמשון פ"ז דטהרות ואין ספק דאיזה תלמיד טועה כתבה בגליון והמדפיסים הכניסוה בפנים תדע שהרי לא נתיישבה לא בתירוצו של ר"ת ולא בפי' ה"ר משה והתלמיד הבין דהכי תנן והיו שם כלים כל אותן הכלים טמאין מדרס ואין זה אלא משום דהבדלין טמאים דמטמאין מדרס וע"ד רבי יוסי הבין נמי הא דקאמר ר' יוסי אלא שאין ע"ה בקיאין בהיסט כלומר ולפ... כן אלא הכי תנן והיו שם כלים טמאים מדרס פי' שכבר נטמאו הכלים טומאת מדרס ופליגי בה תנאי ר"מ אומר בית הבד טמא משום דהבדלין אין חוששין בטומאה ונטמאו בכלים טמאים מדרס דמטמאין אדם וכלים ו... בית הבד טהור דנזהרים על טומאות ודאי הואיל וחבר זה טיהרם לכך ור' יוסי כר"מ ס"ל אלא דסבר דחוששין למגע אבל אין בקיאין ונטמאו על ידי שהסיטו לאותן כלים אע"פ שלא נגעו בהם: (ט) בא"ד דמשום תקנת השוק ... שלעולם וכו' שאינו מטמא בהיסט דתניא הרי שהיו: (י) בא"ד ואין להקשות אמאי לא מוקי לה וכו' מפונטוייז"א מפרש דלשום דבר ע"ה אינו מטמא כזב וכו' של צדוקי בבגדיו וקדם אצל אשתו: (כ) בא"ד כלומר אפילו לא היה טמ... דע"ה ומה הואיל במה שקדם אצל אשתו ומאי פריך הרבה הועיל דאם בועל נדה היה: (ל) בא"ד למה לי טבל אפילו לא טבל. נ"ב קשה הא איצטריך לאוקמיה בטבל כי היכי דליהוי ספק ספיקא כמו בסמוך לפי תירוץ ר"ת [והשאר תמה]: (מ) בא"ד ... סו וכו' התיב רבי חנין והתנינן וכו' ביתו לשמרו בזמן שהוא רואה וכו' אבל המשכבות והמושבות וכלי חרס מוקפים צמיד פתיל טהורין וכו' טמאים משום היסט אמר ר' יהודה תפתר בע"ה אבל פרוש ולית את שמע מינה כלום ... כל מה דאנן קיימין הכא בתרומה אנן קיימין וכו' כלום אמרו יהיו טמאים וכו' אבל פרוש אצל תרומה אינו מטמא וכו' והקשה לו הר"י מהא דאמר וכו' ולהכי פריך התם דלמא נגע:

מסורת הש"ס: שייך מעב"ל | [תוספתא מקואות פ"ג] | [שבת קטו: וש"נ] | ע"כ שייך לע"א | [חולין ב: נדה עא:] | [דף עב:] | [שייך לעיל במשנה יח:] | [נ"ל בתוך ביתו] | [דף כג.] | [דף כ:]

גליון הש"ס

תוס' ד"ה בגדי וכו' היה נטמא הוא ובגדיו כנושא רוקו של זב. עיין בהר"ש פ"א מ"ג דכלים:

מִדְּלָא קָתָנֵי בְּהוּ מַעֲלָה. וְדִלְמָא הַאי דְּלָא קָתָנֵי בְּהוּ מַעֲלָה, דְּאִי דָּמוּ לִתְרוּמָה — הָא תָּנֵי תְּרוּמָה, וְאִי דָּמוּ לְחוּלִּין — הָא תָּנֵי לְחוּלִּין, (*דִּתְנַן): *[א]חוּלִּין שֶׁנַּעֲשׂוּ עַל טָהֳרַת הַקּוֹדֶשׁ הֲרֵי הֵן כְּחוּלִּין, ר' אֶלְעָזָר בְּרַבִּי צָדוֹק אוֹמֵר: הֲרֵי הֵן כִּתְרוּמָה? אֶלָּא מֵסֵיפָא: יוֹסֵי בֶּן יוֹעֶזֶר הָיָה חָסִיד שֶׁבִּכְהוּנָּה, וְהָיְתָה מִטְפַּחְתּוֹ מִדְרָס לַקּוֹדֶשׁ. יוֹחָנָן בֶּן גּוּדְגְּדָא הָיָה אוֹכֵל עַל טָהֳרַת הַקּוֹדֶשׁ כָּל יָמָיו, וְהָיְתָה מִטְפַּחְתּוֹ מִדְרָס לַחַטָּאת, לַחַטָּאת — אִין לַקּוֹדֶשׁ — לָא, אַלְמָא קָסָבַר: חוּלִּין שֶׁנַּעֲשׂוּ עַל טָהֳרַת קוֹדֶשׁ — כְּקוֹדֶשׁ דָּמוּ. א"ר יוֹנָתָן בֶּן אֶלְעָזָר: [ב]נָפְלָה מַעֲפַרְתּוֹ הֵימֶנּוּ, אָמַר לַחֲבֵירוֹ "תְּנָה לִי", וּנְתָנָהּ לוֹ — טְמֵאָה. א"ר יוֹנָתָן בֶּן עַמְרָם: [ג]נִתְחַלְּפוּ לוֹ כֵּלִים שֶׁל שַׁבָּת בְּכֵלִים שֶׁל חוֹל וּלְבָשָׁן — נִטְמְאוּ. א"ר אֶלְעָזָר בַּר צָדוֹק: [ד]מַעֲשֶׂה בִּשְׁתֵּי נָשִׁים חֲבֵירוֹת שֶׁנִּתְחַלְּפוּ לָהֶן כְּלֵיהֶן בְּבֵית הַמֶּרְחָץ, וּבָא מַעֲשֶׂה לִפְנֵי רַבִּי עֲקִיבָא וְטִימְּאָן. מַתְקִיף לַהּ רַבִּי אוֹשַׁעְיָא: אֶלָּא מֵעַתָּה, הוֹשִׁיט יָדוֹ לַסַּל לִיטּוֹל פַּת חִטִּין וְעָלְתָה בְּיָדוֹ פַּת שְׂעוֹרִים — הָכִי נַמִי דְּנִטְמֵאת? וְכִי תֵּימָא הָכִי נַמִי — וְהָתַנְיָא: הַמְשַׁמֵּר אֶת הֶחָבִית בְּחֶזְקַת שֶׁל יַיִן וְנִמְצֵאת שֶׁל שֶׁמֶן — טְהוֹרָה מִלְּטַמֵּא! וּלְטַעֲמִיךְ, אֵימָא סֵיפָא: וַאֲסוּרָה מִלֶּאֱכוֹל, אַמַּאי? א"ר יִרְמְיָה: *בְּאוֹמֵר "שְׁמַרְתִּיהָ מִדָּבָר הַמְטַמְּאָהּ וְלֹא מִדָּבָר הַפּוֹסְלָהּ". וּמִי אִיכָּא נְטִירוּתָא לְפַלְגָּא? אִין. וְהָתַנְיָא: *[ה]הוֹשִׁיט יָדוֹ בַּסַּל, וְהַסַּל עַל כְּתֵיפוֹ, וְהַמַּגְרֵיפָה בְּתוֹךְ הַסַּל, וְהָיָה בְּלִבּוֹ עַל הַסַּל וְלֹא הָיָה בְּלִבּוֹ עַל הַמַּגְרֵיפָה — הַסַּל טָהוֹר וְהַמַּגְרֵיפָה טְמֵאָה. הַסַּל טָהוֹר? תְּטַמֵּא הַמַּגְרֵיפָה לַסַּל! *אֵין כְּלִי מְטַמֵּא כְּלִי. וְלִיטַמֵּא מַה שֶּׁבַּסַּל! אָמַר רָבִינָא, [ו]בְּאוֹמֵר: שְׁמַרְתִּיו מִדָּבָר שֶׁמְּטַמְּאוֹ, וְלֹא מִדָּבָר הַפּוֹסְלוֹ. מִכָּל מָקוֹם קַשְׁיָא. וְעוֹד, מוֹתִיב רַבָּה בַּר אֲבוּהּ: *מַעֲשֶׂה בְּאִשָּׁה אַחַת שֶׁבָּאת לִפְנֵי ר' יִשְׁמָעֵאל, וְאָמְרָה לוֹ: רַבִּי! בֶּגֶד זֶה אֲרַגְתִּיו בְּטָהֳרָה, וְלֹא הָיָה בְּלִבִּי לְשׁוֹמְרוֹ בְּטָהֳרָה. וּמִתּוֹךְ בְּדִיקוֹת שֶׁהָיָה רַבִּי יִשְׁמָעֵאל בּוֹדְקָהּ, אָמְרָה לוֹ: רַבִּי, נִדָּה מָשְׁכָה עִמִּי בַּחֶבֶל. א"ר יִשְׁמָעֵאל: כַּמָּה גְּדוֹלִים דִּבְרֵי חֲכָמִים שֶׁהָיוּ אוֹמְרִים: בְּלִבּוֹ לְשׁוֹמְרוֹ — טָהוֹר, אֵין בְּלִבּוֹ לְשׁוֹמְרוֹ — טָמֵא. שׁוּב מַעֲשֶׂה בְּאִשָּׁה אַחַת שֶׁבָּאת לִפְנֵי ר' יִשְׁמָעֵאל, אָמְרָה לוֹ: רַבִּי, מַפָּה זוֹ אֲרַגְתִּיהָ בְּטָהֳרָה וְלֹא הָיָה בְּלִבִּי לְשׁוֹמְרָהּ. (א) וּמִתּוֹךְ בְּדִיקוֹת שֶׁהָיָה רַבִּי יִשְׁמָעֵאל בּוֹדְקָהּ, אָמְרָה לוֹ: רַבִּי, נִימָא נִפְסְקָה לִי וּקְשַׁרְתִּיהָ בַּפֶּה. אָמַר רַבִּי יִשְׁמָעֵאל: כַּמָּה גְּדוֹלִים דִּבְרֵי חֲכָמִים, שֶׁהָיוּ אוֹמְרִים: בְּלִבּוֹ לְשׁוֹמְרוֹ — טָהוֹר, אֵין בְּלִבּוֹ לְשׁוֹמְרוֹ — טָמֵא. בִּשְׁלָמָא לְרַבִּי אֶלְעָזָר בַּר צָדוֹק — כָּל אַחַת וְאַחַת אוֹמֶרֶת חֲבֶרְתִּי אֵשֶׁת עַם הָאָרֶץ, וּמַסְּחָה דַּעְתָּהּ מִינַּהּ. לְרַבִּי יוֹנָתָן בֶּן עַמְרָם נַמִי, כֵּיוָן דְּכֵלִים דְּשַׁבָּת עָבֵיד לְהוּ שִׁימּוּר טְפֵי — מַסַּח דַּעְתֵּיהּ מִינַּיְיהוּ. אֶלָּא לְרַבִּי יוֹנָתָן בֶּן אֶלְעָזָר — נַעֲבֵיד לְהוּ שִׁימּוּר בִּידֵיהּ דְּחַבְרֵיהּ! — אָמַר רַבִּי יוֹחָנָן: [ז]חֲזָקָה, אֵין אָדָם מְשַׁמֵּר מַה שֶּׁבְּיַד חֲבֵרוֹ. וְלָא?! וְהָתַנְיָא

רש"י

מִדְּלָא קָתָנֵי בְּהוּ מַעֲלָה. לוֹמַר: בִּגְדֵי פְרוּשִׁין הָאוֹכְלִין חוּלֵּיהֶן בְּטָהֳרַת הַקּוֹדֶשׁ מִדְרָס לְאוֹכְלֵי חוּלֵּיהֶן בְּטָהֳרַת הַקּוֹדֶשׁ, שְׁמַע מִינַּהּ: בִּכְלַל קוֹדֶשׁ הֵן, וְהָא תָּנָא לֵיהּ קוֹדֶשׁ: דִּלְמָא. אוֹ כְּחוּלִּין דָּמוּ, דְּלָא מְהַנֵּי בְּהוּ מַאי דְּאָמַר הַאי גַּבְרָא, דְּבָטְלָה דַעְתּוֹ, אוֹ כִּתְרוּמָה דָּמוּ, דְּאִיכָּא תַּנָּאֵי דִּפְלִיגִי בְּמִילְּתָא, כְּדִמְסַיֵּים וְאָזֵיל. הִלְכָּךְ לָא תְּנָא בְּהוּ מַעֲלָה, דְּאִי דָּמוּ לְחוּלִּין – הָא תְּנֵי לֵיהּ חוּלִּין וְאִי דָּמוּ לִתְרוּמָה הָא תְּנַן לֵיהּ בְּמַתְנִיתִין תְּרוּמָה: דִּתְנַן כו'. כְּלוֹמַר: הָא אַשְׁכַּחַן תַּנָּאֵי דִּפְלִיגִי בָּהּ, חַד אָמַר: כְּחוּלִּין, וְחַד אָמַר: כִּתְרוּמָה, אֲבָל כְּקוֹדֶשׁ לָא אָמְרִינַן: מַעֲפַרְתּוֹ. סוּדָר: טְמֵאָה. וַאֲפִילּוּ זֶה טָהוֹר. וּלְקַמָּן מְפָרֵשׁ טַעְמָא: חֲזָקָה אֵין אָדָם מְשַׁמֵּר מַה שֶּׁבְּיַד חֲבֵירוֹ, לְפִיכָךְ הוּא לֹא שְׁמָרָהּ בְּיַד חֲבֵירוֹ, וְגַם זֶה שֶׁנְּתָנָהּ לוֹ לֹא הָיָה חָשׁ לְשׁוֹמְרָהּ, דְּמֵימַר אָמַר: כֵּיוָן שֶׁאָמַר לֵיהּ תְּנָה לִי, וְהוּא אֵינוֹ יוֹדֵעַ אִם טָמֵא אֲנִי אִם טָהוֹר – לֹא חָשׁ לְטָהֳרָתוֹ, וְיֵשׁ כָּאן הֶיסַּח הַדַּעַת, וְלַמַּחְמִירִין בְּטָהֳרוֹת הָוֵי הֶיסַּח הַדַּעַת טוּמְאָה: כֵּלִים שֶׁל שַׁבָּת בְּכֵלִים שֶׁל חוֹל. כִּסָּבוּר לִיטּוֹל בְּגָדָיו שֶׁל חוֹל וְנָטַל שֶׁל שַׁבָּת: נִטְמְאוּ. קָא סָלְקָא דַעְתֵּיהּ הָשְׁתָּא דִּסְבִירָא לֵיהּ מְשַׁמֵּר הַדָּבָר בְּחֶזְקַת שֶׁהוּא דָּבָר זֶה וְנִמְצָא שֶׁהוּא דָּבָר אַחֵר – אֵינוֹ שָׁמוּר: אָמַר רַבִּי יִרְמְיָה. הָא דְּפָרְכַתְּ אֵימָא סֵיפָא (ב) אֲסוּרָה מִלֶּאֱכוֹל – לָא מְסַיֵּיעַ לֵיהּ מִידֵּי: בְּאוֹמֵר שְׁמַרְתִּיהָ מִדָּבָר הַמְטַמְּאָהּ וְלֹא מִדָּבָר הַפּוֹסְלָהּ. אֲבָל בְּמַה שֶּׁמְּשַׁמְּרָהּ הֵימֶנּוּ – הָוְיָא שְׁמִירָתוֹ שְׁמִירָה, וְאַעַ"פ שֶׁאֵינוֹ זֶה: הַסַּל. שֶׁל תְּאֵנִים עַל כְּתֵיפוֹ: וּמַגְרֵיפָה בְּתוֹכָהּ. כְּלִי בַּרְזֶל הוּא, שֶׁקּוֹרִין וודי"ל, שֶׁגּוֹרְפִין בּוֹ אֵפֶר הַכִּירָה, וְגַם מַבְדִּילִין בּוֹ תְּאֵנִים הַמּוּדְבָּקוֹת זוֹ בָּזוֹ: (ג) הַמְטַמֵּא. הַנּוֹתֵן לָהּ טוּמְאָה לְטַמֵּא אֲחֵרִים: (ד) הַפּוֹסְלָהּ. מִלְּהִשְׁתַּמֵּשׁ בָּהּ טְהָרוֹת לְכַתְּחִילָּה. אִי נַמִי: נָפְקָא מִינַּהּ לָאוֹכֶל הַדָּבוּק בָּהּ, שֶׁהוּא פָּסוּל בַּאֲכִילָה. וּמִכָּל מָקוֹם, אִם נָגְעָה בִּטְהָרוֹת – אֵינָהּ פּוֹסַלְתָּן. אַלְמָא: אִיכָּא נְטִירוּתָא לְפַלְגָא. וּבְכִי הַאי גַּוְונָא נַמִי מִיפַּרְקָא מַתְנִיתִין דִּלְעֵיל, וּמִיתַּקְנָא הִיא: קַשְׁיָא. הַךְ דְּקָתָנֵי בָּהּ טְהוֹרָה מִלְּטַמֵּא: אֲרַגְתִּיו בְּטָהֳרָה. יוֹדַעַת אֲנִי שֶׁמִּשָּׁעָה שֶׁנֶּאֱרַג בּוֹ ג' עַל ג' אֶצְבָּעוֹת שֶׁנִּרְאָה לְטוּמְאָה – לֹא נָגְעָה בּוֹ טוּמְאָה, וּמ"מ לֹא הָיָה בְּלִבִּי לְשׁוֹמְרוֹ: וּמִתּוֹךְ בְּדִיקוֹת כו'. הוֹאִיל וְלֹא הָיָה בְּלִבֵּךְ לְשׁוֹמְרוֹ, שֶׁמָּא אֵירַע בּוֹ כָּךְ וְכָךְ וְלֹא נִזְהַרְתְּ? מָשְׁכָה עִמִּי בַּחֶבֶל. שֶׁקְּשָׁרָה בּוֹ הַחֶבֶל בִּכְלֵי הָאֲרִיגָה, וְשֶׁמָּא הֵסִיטַתּוּ: נִפְסְקָה לִי. קוֹדֶם שֶׁאָרַגְתִּי בָּהּ כְּלוּם, (ה) וּקְשַׁרְתִּיהָ בַּפֶּה קוֹדֶם שֶׁאָרַגְתִּי בָּהּ כְּלוּם, שֶׁלֹּא הָיְתָה רְאוּיָה לְטוּמְאָה. וְלֹא נִזְהַרְתִּי בָּהּ וְלֹא הָיִיתִי טְבוּלָה לְנִדָּתִי. וְיֵשׁ לָחוּשׁ שֶׁמָּא כְּשֶׁאָרְגָה בָּהּ שָׁלֹשׁ אֶצְבָּעוֹת עֲדַיִין הָרוֹק לַח, וְרוֹק הַנִּדָּה אַב הַטּוּמְאָה הוּא. כָּךְ נִרְאֶה בְּעֵינַי. וְרַבּוֹתַי מְפָרְשִׁין: מִשּׁוּם לִיגּוּרוֹת עַם הָאָרֶץ, הַמְטַמְּאָה כָּל זְמַן שֶׁהִיא לַחָה. וַאֲנִי אוֹמֵר: ע"כ הָאִשָּׁה זוֹ חֲבֵירָה הָיְתָה, דְּאִי לָא חֲבֵירָה הָיְתָה – מִי אָתְיָא קַמֵּי רַבָּנַן לִישָּׁאֵל עַל הַטְּהָרוֹת? וְעוֹד: מִי מְהֵימְנָא לְמֵימַר אֲרַגְתִּיהָ בְּטָהֳרָה. קָתָנֵי מִיהַת: בְּלִבּוֹ לְשׁוֹמְרָן – טָהוֹר, כְּלוֹמַר: אַחַר כַּוָּונַת הַשְּׁמִירָה הֵן הֵן הַדְּבָרִים: כֵּיוָן דְּכֵלִים שֶׁל שַׁבָּת עָבֵיד לְהוּ שִׁימּוּר טְפֵי. וְזֶה סָבוּר שֶׁאֵלּוּ שֶׁל חוֹל (ו) – אַסְּחָא דַעְתֵּיהּ מִשְּׁמִירָה מַעֲלְיָיתָא שֶׁהָיָה רָגִיל לְשׁוֹמְרָן, וּכְאִילּוּ בְּלִבּוֹ לְשׁוֹמְרָן דָּמֵי: חַמָּרָיו

תוספות

רבי אלעזר בר' צדוק אומר הרי' הוא כתרומה. הקשה הרב ר' אלחנן, (ז) דאמרינן בפרק בתרא דנדה (דף עא:): בראשונה היו אומרים יושבת על דם טהור מערה מים לפסח. ודייק בגמ': מערה – אין, נוגע – לא. אלמא: חולין שנעשו על טהרת הקודש כקודש דמו. ומנליה? דלמא דהוו כתרומה, דטבול יום פוסל תרומה! ונראה למורי: דאי כתרומה הוו – אפי' תגע בה לא הוי אלא פוסל, דלא הוי ליה אלא שלישי, ואין שלישי בתרומה מטמא רביעי בקודש, שאין המים עושין בו רביעי. וקלא משמע כן מתוך פרש"י ור"ת:

שמרתיה מדבר המטמאה ולא מדבר הפוסלה. והיה קשה להר"ר אלחנן: במאי איפסלא הך מגריפה? אי בראשון או בשני – אין אדם וכלים מקבלין טומאה אלא מאב הטומאה, ואי באב הטומאה – האי פסול טמא הוי! ותירץ: שנפסלה במשקין, דמשקין טמאין פוסלין בכלי, כדאמרינן: אחורי כלים שנטמאו במשקין:

נימא נפסקה לי וקשרתיה בפה. פרש"י: קודם (ח) שלא היתה נארגת, שלא היתה ראויה לטומאה, ולא נזהרתי בה ולא הייתי טבולה לנידותי. ויש לחוש שמא כשארגתי בה ג' עדיין הרוק לח בבגד, ואב הטומאה הוי לטמאות. ורבותי הוו מפרשי מטעם ליגורא דע"ה המטמאה כל זמן שהיא לחה. ואני אומר: ע"כ אשה זו חברה היתה, מדקאתיה קמיה דר' ישמעאל לישאל. ועוד: מי מהימנא לומר ארגתיה בטהרה. כל זה פרש"י. ובירושלמי מייתי כל הני עובדי על מתניתין דאידך פרקין (ט) בכלים הנגמרים בטהרה צריכים טבילה לקודש, וקאמר ליה רבי ישמעאל: כמה גדולים מעשה חכמים דאמרי כלים הנגמרים כו'. משמע דבאשה חברה אורגת עסקינן, ובעי טבילה משום דמשמשי בהדיה קודש שנארג כולו, כפרש"י. והקשה הר"ר יוסף לפי' רש"י: היה לו לומר "נדה הייתי", כמו "נדה משכה" באידך עובדא. ונראה לו לפרש: דמתוך שקשרה בפה היה שם רוק לח, ובשעה שארגה נגעה ברוק, וידים שניות הן. ובפרק בתרא דעירובין (דף לט. ושם) משמע דרוק מיחשב משקה, וחזר הרוק ומטמא למפה, כדתנן*: אחורי כלים שנטמאו במשקין. אך לפי שיטת הירושלמי דמדמי לה לכלים הנגמרים, (י) ומוקמי לה לקמן* משום ליגורא דע"ה ומאי איריא משום הכי? אפי' בליגורא דחבר נמי איכא למיחש מטעם מגע ידים. ומיהו, נוכל לומר דלא עיקר טעם נקט לקמן, אלא חדא מינייהו נקט:

עין משפט נר מצוה

נא א מיי' פי"א מהל' אבות הטומאות הל' טו ופי"ב הלכה טז:

נב ב ג ד ה ו מיי' פי"ג מהלכות מטמאי משכב ומושב הלכה ו:

נג ז מיי' שם הלכה א:

רבינו חננאל

מני ר' מאיר היא דקתני כל הטעון ביאת מים מדברי סופרים מטמא קודש ופוסל את התרומה ומותר בחולין ובמעשר דברי ר' מאיר רישא רבנן וסיפא ר' מאיר ומפרקי' אין רישא רבנן וסיפא ר' מאיר. רב אחא בר אדא מתני בסיפא חמש מעלות והכי קתני בגדי עם הארץ מדרס לפרושים לאוכלי חוליהן בטהרה בגדי פרושין מדרס לאוכלי מעשר בגדי אוכלי מעשר לאוכלי תרומה. בגדי אוכלי תרומה מדרס לקודש בגדי אוכלי קודש כגון זבחי שלמים בכור ומעשר שהן קדשים קלים מדרס לאוכלי חטאת שהוא קדש קדשים הרי אלו ה' מעלות מעלות הפרושין אוכלי חוליהן בטהרה על שאר העם שאין אוכלין חוליהן בטהרה. ומעלת מעשר שני על החולין ומעלת טהרת תרומה שהיא חובה שנאמר כל טהור בביתך יאכל אותה וכתיב בה ובא השמש וטהר ואחר יאכל מן הקדשים כי לחמו הוא על המעשר. ומעלת הקדש על התרומה ומעלת החטאת על הקדש ומוקים לה לסיפא כרישא דקתני טבל לחולין אסור במעשר טבל למעשר אסור בתרומה טבל לתרומה אסור בקודש טבל לקודש אסור לחטאת וכולה רבנן היא אמר רב מרי ש"מ חולין שנעשו על טהרת הקודש כקודש דמו ואין בגדיהן מדרס לקודש ממאי מדלא קתני בהו מעלה בהדיא בפני עצמו ודחינן לה וממאי דלמא האי דלא קתני להו מעלה בפ"ע לאו משום דכי קדש דמו אלא משום דפליגי בהו אית תנא דמשוי להו לחולין ואית תנא דמשוי ליה כתרומה דתנן חולין שנעשו על טהרת הקודש הרי הן כחולין ור' אלעזר בר' צדוק אמר הרי הן כתרומה וחזרנו לומר אלא אמר רב מרי מסיפא דמתניתין שמע לה דקתני יוחנן בן גודגדא היה אוכל על טהרת הקדש כל ימיו והיתה מטפחתו מדרס לחטאת ולא לקדש אלמא חולין שנעשו על טהרת הקודש כקדש דמו. א"ר יונתן בן אלעזר נפלה מעפרתו. פי' מצנפתו ממנו וא' לחבירו שהוא פרוש ונאמן כמותו (א"ל) תנה לי ונתנה לו נטמאת. ומקשינן עליה אמאי נטמאת נעביד לה שימור בידא דחבריה. ופריק ר' יוחנן חזקה אין אדם משמר מה שביד חבירו. ומקשינן ולא והתניא הרי שהיו חמריו ופועליו טוענין טהרות אע"פ שהפליגו יתר מכדי מיל טהרותיו טהורות ופריק ר' יצחק במטהר חמריו ופועליו לכך אי הכי סיפא נמי ואוקימנא אין ע"ה מקפיד כו' א"ר יונתן בן עמרם נתחלפו לו כלים של שבת בכלים של חול ולבשם נטמאו. ואקשינן עליה אמאי נטמאו והלא הן בשמירתו וברשותו וכן בשתי נשים חבירות שנתחלפו כליהם וטמאום אמאי הלא מעתה הושיט ידו ליטול פת חטין ועלה בידו פת שעורים וכל הפת היתה טהורה ומשומרת הכי נמי דכיון שנתחלפה לה נטמאת וכי תימא הכי נמי והתניא היה משמר את החבית בחזקת שהיא של יין ונמצאת של שמן טהורה מלטמא ולטעמיך אימא סיפא אסורה מלאכול ואי טהורה היא אמאי אסורה מלאכול ומפרקינן אמר ר'

מסורת הש"ס

[נ"ל דתניא] [חולין לה: ע"ש]

זבחים לט:

ג"ז שם. ע"ש [תוספתא דטהרות פ"ח]

[ברכות נב: פסחים יט:]

[תוספ' דכלים ב"ב פ"א]

[נדה לג: ע"ש] [ע"ש]

[לקמן כב.]

הגהות הב"ח

(א) גמ' לשומרה בטהרה ומתוך בדיקות: (ב) רש"י ד"ה אמר ר' ירמיה וכו' ואסורה מלאכול לא מסייע לך מידי: (ג) ד"ה המטמאו הנותן לו טומאה: (ד) ד"ה הפוסלו וכו' הד"א עם ד"ה וקשיא הך: (ה) ד"ה נפסקה וכו' כלום הס"ד ואח"כ מה"ד וקשרתיה וכו' ורבותי מפרשים משום ליגורא של עם הארץ: (ו) ד"ה כיון דכלים וכו' וזו סבורה שאילו של חול הן אסחא: (ז) תום' ד"ה ר' אלעזר וכו' רבי אלחנן דתנן בפרק: (ח) ד"ה נימא וכו' פרש"י קודם שהיתה כצ"ל ותיבת שלא נמחק: (ט) בא"ד דאידך פירקין דתנן כלים וכו' וקאמר ר' ישמעאל כמה גדולים דברי חכמים וכו' דמשמשי בהדה וקודש שנארג כולו נטמא כפרש"י וכו' ובפ' בתרא דעירובין דף לט ע"א. נ"ב ע"ש בתוספות בד"ה היה אוכל: (י) בא"ד לכלים הנגמרים בטהרה ומוקמי לה לקמן משום ליגורא דע"ה קשה מאי איריא וכו' דנקט לקמן:

גליון הש"ס

תום' ד"ה רבי אלעזר וכו' ואין שלישי בתרומה מטמא רביעי בקודש. עיין פסחים דף יד ע"ב תוספות ד"ה ואילו הכא:

וְהָתַנְיָא: *[א]הֲרֵי שֶׁהָיוּ חַמָּרָיו וּפוֹעֲלָיו טְעוּנִין טְהָרוֹת, אע"פ שֶׁהִפְלִיג מֵהֶן יוֹתֵר מִמִּיל – טָהֳרוֹתָיו טְהוֹרוֹת. וְאִם אָמַר לָהֶם: "לְכוּ וַאֲנִי אָבוֹא אַחֲרֵיכֶם" – כֵּיוָן שֶׁנִּתְעַלְּמוּ עֵינָיו מֵהֶן טָהֳרוֹתָיו טְמֵאוֹת. מַאי שְׁנָא רֵישָׁא וּמַאי שְׁנָא סֵיפָא? א"ר יִצְחָק נַפָּחָא: רֵישָׁא בִּמְטַהֵר חַמָּרָיו וּפוֹעֲלָיו לְכָךְ. אִי הָכִי, סֵיפָא נַמִי! אֵין ע"ה מַקְפִּיד עַל מַגַּע חֲבֵירוֹ. אִי הָכִי רֵישָׁא נַמִי! בְּבָא לָהֶם דֶּרֶךְ עֲקַלָּתוֹן. אִי הָכִי סֵיפָא נַמִי! כֵּיוָן דַּאֲמַר לְהוּ "לְכוּ וַאֲנִי אָבוֹא אַחֲרֵיכֶם" – מִיסְמַךְ סָמְכָא דַּעֲתַיְיהוּ.§

הדרן עלך אין דורשין

חוֹמֶר [ב]בַּקֹּדֶשׁ מִבַּתְּרוּמָה: שֶׁמַּטְבִּילִין כֵּלִים בְּתוֹךְ כֵּלִים לַתְּרוּמָה – אֲבָל לֹא לַקֹּדֶשׁ; אֲחוֹרַיִים וְתוֹךְ וּבֵית הַצְּבִיטָה בַּתְּרוּמָה – אֲבָל לֹא בַּקֹּדֶשׁ; הַנּוֹשֵׂא אֶת הַמִּדְרָס נוֹשֵׂא אֶת הַתְּרוּמָה – אֲבָל לֹא אֶת הַקֹּדֶשׁ; בִּגְדֵי אוֹכְלֵי תְרוּמָה מִדְרָס לַקֹּדֶשׁ. לֹא כְּמִדַּת הַקֹּדֶשׁ מִדַּת הַתְּרוּמָה: שֶׁבַּקֹּדֶשׁ מַתִּיר וּמְנַגֵּב וּמַטְבִּיל וְאח"כ קוֹשֵׁר, וּבִתְרוּמָה קוֹשֵׁר וְאח"כ מַטְבִּיל; כֵּלִים הַנִּגְמָרִים בְּטָהֳרָה צְרִיכִין טְבִילָה לַקֹּדֶשׁ, אֲבָל לֹא לַתְּרוּמָה; *הַכְּלִי מְצָרֵף מַה שֶּׁבְּתוֹכוֹ לַקֹּדֶשׁ – אֲבָל לֹא לַתְּרוּמָה; הָרְבִיעִי בַּקֹּדֶשׁ פָּסוּל, וְהַשְּׁלִישִׁי בַּתְּרוּמָה. וּבַתְּרוּמָה, אִם נִטְמֵאת אַחַת מִיָּדָיו – חֲבֶירְתָּהּ טְהוֹרָה, וּבַקֹּדֶשׁ מַטְבִּיל שְׁתֵּיהֶן, שֶׁהַיָּד מְטַמֵּא אֶת חֲבֶירְתָּהּ בַּקֹּדֶשׁ אֲבָל לֹא בַּתְּרוּמָה; אוֹכְלִין אוֹכָלִים נְגוּבִין בְּיָדַיִם מְסוֹאָבוֹת בַּתְּרוּמָה, אֲבָל לֹא בַּקֹּדֶשׁ; הָאוֹנֵן

רש"י

חַמָּרָיו וּפוֹעֲלָיו. עַמֵּי הָאָרֶץ: טְעוּנִין טְהָרוֹת. כְּגוֹן יַיִן בְּחָבִיּוֹת שֶׁל חֶרֶס. וְהֵן אֵינָן נוֹגְעִין בְּתוֹכָן, וּכְלִי חֶרֶס אֵינוֹ מִיטַּמֵּא מִגַּבּוֹ: טְהָרוֹתָיו טְהוֹרוֹת. וְאֵין חוֹשְׁשִׁין שֶׁמָּא נָגְעוּ. דְּכֵיוָן דְּלֹא הוֹדִיעָן שֶׁהוּא מַפְלִיג – כָּל שַׁעְתָּא סָבְרִי: הַשְׁתָּא אָתֵי. אַלְמָא: אָדָם מְשַׁמֵּר מַה שֶּׁבְּיַד חֲבֵרוֹ: **מַאי שְׁנָא רֵישָׁא וּמַאי שְׁנָא סֵיפָא.** לָא גָּרְסִי' לֵיהּ. וְאִי גָּרְסִי' – הָכִי פֵּירוּשׁוֹ: וְאִי ס"ד אֵין אָדָם מְשַׁמֵּר מַה שֶּׁבְּיַד חֲבֵרוֹ – מַאי שְׁנָא רֵישָׁא מַאי שְׁנָא סֵיפָא? **א"ר יִצְחָק בִּמְטַהֵר חַמָּרָיו וּפוֹעֲלָיו לְכָךְ.** לְעוֹלָם אֵין אָדָם מְשַׁמֵּר מַה שֶּׁבְּיַד חֲבֵרוֹ, וְהָנֵי אֵין צְרִיכִין שִׁימּוּר, דְּאִי נַמִי נָגְעוּ לָא אִיכְפַּת לְהוּ, דִּכְשֶׁהִטְבִּילָן לְכָךְ עָסְקִינַן: **בְּבָא לָהֶן** דֶּרֶךְ עֲקַלָּתוֹן. כְּשֶׁיָּכוֹל לָבוֹא לָהֶם פִּתְאוֹם דֶּרֶךְ עֲקַלָּתוֹן שֶׁלֹּא יָבִינוּ, הִלְכָּךְ דָּחֲלֵי מִינֵּיהּ:

הדרן עלך אין דורשין

חוֹמֶר בַּקֹּדֶשׁ מִבַּתְּרוּמָה כו'. שֶׁמַּטְבִּילִים כְּלִי בְּתוֹךְ כְּלִי שֶׁשְּׁנֵיהֶם(ד) טְמֵאִים: **אֲבָל לֹא לַקֹּדֶשׁ.** בַּגְּמָרָא מְפָרֵשׁ טַעְמָא: **אֲחוֹרַיִים וְתוֹךְ וּבֵית הַצְּבִיטָה לַתְּרוּמָה.** כְּלִי הָרָאוּי לְהִשְׁתַּמֵּשׁ בְּתוֹכוֹ וּמֵאֲחוֹרָיו וּבֵית צְבִיטָתוֹ, כָּל תַּשְׁמִישׁ וְתַשְׁמִישׁ שֶׁבּוֹ חָשׁוּב כְּלִי בִּפְנֵי עַצְמוֹ לְעִנְיַן תְּרוּמָה, שֶׁאִם נִטְמָא זֶה – לֹא נִטְמָא זֶה. וּבְטוּמְאוֹת דְּרַבָּנַן קָאָמַר, כִּדְמְפָרֵשׁ בַּגְּמָ': **אֲבָל לֹא לַקֹּדֶשׁ.** שֶׁאִם נִטְמָא אֶחָד מֵהֶן כּוּלּוֹ טָמֵא לַקֹּדֶשׁ: **הַנּוֹשֵׂא אֶת הַמִּדְרָס.** מִנְעָל שֶׁל זָב: **נוֹשֵׂא אֶת הַתְּרוּמָה.** בְּחָבִית (ה) שֶׁאֵינוֹ נוֹגֵעַ בַּאֲוִירָהּ: **אֲבָל לֹא אֶת הַקֹּדֶשׁ.** בַּגְּמָרָא מְפָרֵשׁ טַעְמָא: **לֹא כְּמִדַּת הַקֹּדֶשׁ.** בַּחֲלִילַת טְבִילוֹתָיו, **מִדַּת הַתְּרוּמָה: שֶׁבַּקֹּדֶשׁ.** אִם יֵשׁ בֶּגֶד טָמֵא וּבָא לְהַטְבִּילוֹ, אִם קָשׁוּר הוּא, מַתִּיר אֶת קִשְׁרוֹ, מִשּׁוּם דְּדָמֵי לַחֲצִיצָה: **וּמְנַגֵּב.** אִם לַח הוּא מְנַגְּבוֹ תְּחִלָּה וְאח"כ מַטְבִּילוֹ. וְכָל זֶה מִשּׁוּם דְּדָמֵי לַחֲצִיצָה הוּא: **וּבִתְרוּמָה.** אִם רָצָה לְקוֹשְׁרוֹ קוֹשֵׁר וְאח"כ מַטְבִּיל: **כֵּלִים הַנִּגְמָרִים בְּטָהֳרָה.** שֶׁנִּזְהַר בָּהֶן מִשֶּׁבָּאוּ סָמוּךְ לִגְמָרָן, שֶׁרְאוּיִין לְקַבֵּל טוּמְאָה: **צְרִיכִין טְבִילָה לַקֹּדֶשׁ.** וּבַגְּמָרָא מְפָרֵשׁ טַעְמָא: **הַכְּלִי מְצָרֵף אֶת מַה שֶּׁבְּתוֹכוֹ.** (ו) אוֹכָלִים חֲתִיכוֹת הַרְבֵּה בִּכְלִי אֶחָד, וְנָגַע טָמֵא בְּאַחַד מֵהֶן הַכְּלִי מְצָרְפָן לִהְיוֹת כּוּלָּן חֲתִיכָה אַחַת, וְנִטְמְאוּ כּוּלָּן: **אֲבָל לֹא לַתְּרוּמָה.** אֶלָּא אוֹתָהּ שֶׁנָּגַע בָּהּ הָוְיָא רִאשׁוֹן, וְהַנּוֹגַעַת בָּהּ הָוְיָא שְׁנִיָּה, וְהַנּוֹגַעַת בַּשְּׁנִיָּה שְׁלִישִׁית, וְהַשְּׁאָר טְהוֹרוֹת: **פָּסוּל.** וְאֵינוֹ פּוֹסֵל עוֹד אַחֵר: **אִם נִטְמֵאת אַחַת מִיָּדָיו.** בְּטוּמְאָה דְּרַבָּנַן, שֶׁאֵינָהּ מְטַמְּאָה אֶלָּא יָדַיִם וְלֹא אֶת הַגּוּף: **נְגוּבִין.** שֶׁהָיוּ נְגוּבִין מֵימֵיהֶן, שֶׁלֹּא הוּכְשְׁרוּ לְטוּמְאָה מֵעוֹלָם: **בְּיָדַיִם מְסוֹאָבוֹת.** שְׁנִיּוֹת לִתְרוּמָה, דְּכֵיוָן דְּלֹא הוּכְשְׁרָה – לֹא מִיפַּסְלָא: **אֲבָל לֹא לַקֹּדֶשׁ.** בַּגְּמָ' מְפָרֵשׁ טַעְמָא: הָאוֹנֵן

תוספות

והתניא וכו'. אלמא: אדם משמר מה שביד חברו. ופי' בתרא דע"ז (דף סט.) פרש"י, גבי מאי שנא רישא ומאי שנא סיפא, דהא(א) חזי ליה דנגע, דקתני: טעונין טהרות. והני לא בחביות מיירי שהיו סתומות, אלא באוכלין מיירי בלא חביות. אך קשה להר"ר אלחנן: לוקמי בחביות, ולא תקשה ליה!
ועוד, דהכא כי אקשי: ור"ל שאדם משמר מה שביד חברו, היכי מלי משמר ליה כיון דאינו בחביות? ותו: למה לי נתעלמו עיניו מהם לטמאותם? תיפוק ליה שהוא נוגע בהם! ועוד: אפי' בלא סיפא נמי תיקשי ליה מ"ט דרישא? ופי' הר"י דהכא בחביות מיירי, ואמנם פתוחות הן. דאי סתומות – לא יטמאו בהעלמת עין(ב). ועוד: לא היה צורך לאוקמי רישא במטהר לכך, כיון שלא הודיעו שהוא מפליג. ומיהו, זה יש לדחות: דאגב דמוקי ליה הכא משום שינויא דשני' ליה – אוקמ' גם התם בע"ז. ופריך מינה מכח ההיא דהכא. דאי לא תימא הכי, אלא אקשי ליה מסברא, כי יש לחוש שמא נגעו בהן ברישא – א"כ הכא בשמעתין, כי פריך: מ"ש רישא משום מה שביד חבירו כו', אכתי תיקשי ליה: ליחוש שמא יגע בהם! אלא ודאי מסברא לא קשיא, דלא נגעו דמרתתי, כיון שלא הודיעום שהוא מפליג. ומיהו, הוה מצי לאקשויי: ולטעמיך רישא גופא, ליחוש שמא נגע. וכן בכמה דוכתי, ולא פריך ליה:

מאי שנא רישא ומאי שנא סיפא א"ר יצחק רישא במטהר חמריו ופועליו לכך. כך כתוב בספרים. ויש פי' כתוב, ולא גרסינן ליה. אך בפי' שלפני מצאתי כתוב. ופירוש: לעולם אין אדם משמר מה שביד חבירו, וכי תימא מאי שנא רישא? במטהר חמריו ופועליו לכך ולפיכך מרתת. ובפי' ישנים כתוב, וכן פי' מורי, דהוי כמו וליטעמיך. כלומר: אדמוכחת מרישא דאדם משמר – תיקשי לסיפא. והיינו מאי שנא רישא ומאי שנא סיפא, דאי אדם משמר – סיפא אמאי לא! אלא במטהר לכך?

בבא להם דרך עקלתון. ואפ"ה בעינן שיטהרם לכך, כדי שיהו מרתתים ליגע בו(ג). ואי לאו הכי לא מירתתי, הואיל ומוסרין להם הטהרות ומחזיקים עצמם כטהורים. ואפי' מזהירין אותן שלא ליגע – סברי דלא קפדי אהן. אבל בגוי סגי בדרך עקלתון לחוד, דלעולם יודע הוא שמקפיד על מגעו – ומרתת:

הדרן עלך אין דורשין

חומר בקדש. י"א מעלות חשיב לרבא, ולרבי אילא י' מעלות. והיה קשה להר"ר אלחנן: ליתני ההיא דלעיל (דף יח:): נוטלין לידים לחולין ולתרומה, ולקדש מטבילין. טבל והוחזק לתרומה – לא הוחזק לקדש! ונראה למורי: דלא קא חשיב במתני' אלא היכא דאיכא דררא דטומאה קצת, ואפי' בבתרייתא נמי. אבל הך – ליכא כלל דררא דטומאה(ז). והכי נמי בפ"ק דנדה (דף ו.) לא חשיב מעת לעת שבנדה – משום דליכא דררא דטומאה. ובגדי אוכלי תרומה מדרס לקדש – איכא דררא דטומאה אף דאורייתא, שמא ישבה עליהן אשתו נדה: **הנושא** את המדרס. מנעל של זב. נושא את התרומה(ח) ובלבד שלא יגע בה רק נושא את החבית. וכי תניא בתורת כהנים: הנושא את המדרס – מטמא שנים ופוסל אחד, פי' מטמא שנים ופוסל אחד – דהוה אב הטומאה, ועושה ראשון ושני בחולין, ופוסל בתרומה – התם בנוגע בה. ועל מה שפרש"י: נושא מדרס שנושא את התרומה בחבית ואינו נוגע באוירה, וקשה לפירושו: דחשיב ליה להאי נושא אב הטומאה לטמא כלי כמו זב, וא"כ ליטמא האי חבית ותרומה שבתוכו בהיסטו! מי לא תניא: משכב ומושב בכף מאזנים, ואוכלין ומשקין בכף שניה, הכריע המשכב – טימא האוכלין! ועוד תניא בת"כ: "הנוגע במשכבו יכבס בגדיו" (ויקרא טו), אין לי אלא בגדים שהוא לבוש, בגדים אחרים מנלן – ת"ל:(ט) "בגד", "בגדיו". א"כ מה ת"ל "בגדיו" – לפרט, פי': לפרט אדם וכלי חרס. אלמא דנושא המדרס לא יטמא כלי אפי' בעת נשאו את המדרס. אלא ודאי, אפי' יגע באוירה אין לחוש:

לא כמדת התרומה מדת הקדש. לפי שמפרש בו הרבה דינים ביניהם, נקט האי לישנא: **הכלי** מצרף מה שבתוכו. הקשה הרב רבי אפרים: דבפ"ק דחולין (דף כד: ושם) דרשינן מ"כל אשר בתוכו יטמא" – לימד על כלי חרס שאפי' מלא חרדל טמא, ומנא ליה דטעמא הכי? דלמא התם מטעמא דצירוף! ותירץ הר"י: דלא מצינו צירוף לחולין*:

כלים הנגמרים וכו'. אומר הר"ר אלחנן: דלהכי נקט נגמרים, ולא נעשים, משום דאין רגילות לשומרם בטהרה בזמן עשייתן עד עת גומרם, לפי שאין מקבלין טומאה עדיין. אבל כי נגמרו, שמקבלין טומאה – נותנין לב(י) להן לשומרם בטהרה:

האונן

עין משפט נר מצוה

נד א מיי' פי"ג מהל' מטמאי משכב ומושב הלכה ה:

א ב הכל במיי' פי"ב מהל' אבות הטומאות מהלכה א עד הלכה ז ומהל' יא עד הל' טו:

רבינו חננאל

ירמיה באומר שמרתיה מדבר המטמאה ולא שמרתיה מדבר הפוסלה וש"מ דאיכא נטירותא לפלגא ואסתייעא מן הסל ומן המגריפה ובמעשה דשתי נשים שארגו בטהרה ואמרו לא היה בלבנו לשמרה וטמאן ר' ישמעאל. פשוטות הן:

הדרן עלך אין דורשין בעריות

פרק ג **חומר** בקדש מבתרומה שמטבילין כלים בתוך כלים לתרומה אבל לא לקדש כו'.

הגהות הב"ח

(א) תוס' ד"ה והתניא וכו' ומאי שנא סיפא דהא קא חזי להו דנגעו דקתני: (ב) בא"ד לא יטמאו בהעלמת עין אלא בכדי שישתום ויסתום ויגוב כדתנן בפ' בתרא דמסכת ע"ז ועוד לא היה צורך לאוקמי בפרק בתרא דמסכת ע"ז רישא במטהר וכו' משום שנויא דשני ליה אין אדם משמר כו' אוקמה גם התם במסכת ע"ז וכו' כי פריך מ"ש רישא משום אין אדם משמר מה שביד חבירו כו' בלאו הכי תיקשי ליה ליחוש שמא יגעו בהם וכו' שמא נגעו וכן: (ג) ד"ה בבא וכו' דאי לאו הכי: (ד) רש"י ד"ה חומר וכו' ששניהם טמאין. נ"ב עי' בדף כ"ב במ"ש התוס' בד"ה מאי איכא: (ה) ד"ה נושא את התרומה בחבית של חרס שאינו נוגע: (ו) ד"ה הכלי מצרף את מה שבתוכו חתיכות אוכלין הרבה: (ז) תוס' ד"ה חומר וכו' ליכא כלל דררא דטומאה והכי נמי לא חשיב מעת לעת שבנדה משום דליכא דררא דטומאה כלל כדאמרינן בפרק קמא דנדה ובגדי אוכלי תרומה: (ח) ד"ה הנושא וכו' את התרומה בכלי חרס ובלבד שלא יגע בה וכו' את התרומה בחבית של חרס ואינו נוגע באוירה קשה לפירושו דכיון דחשיב ליה וכו' לטמא כלי חרס כמו זב אם כן: (ט) בא"ד בגדים אחרים מנלן תלמוד לומר טמא אם כן מה ת"ל בגדיו פרט לאדם וכלי וכו' לא יטמא כלי חרס אפילו כנ"ל ותיבת לפרט פי' נמחק: (י) ד"ה כלים וכו' נותנין לב עליהן לשומרן:

מסורת הש"ס

[תוספתא דטהרות פ"ח] ע"ז סט. ע"ש

פסחים יט. [מנחות כד.]

[ועי' תוספות חולין כד ד"ה התורה]

*האונן ומחוסר כפורים צריכין טבילה לקדש, אבל לא לתרומה.§ **גמ'** בקדש מ"ט לא? א"ר אילא: מפני שכבידו של כלי חוצץ. והא מדסיפא משום חציצה, רישא לאו משום חציצה, דקתני סיפא: ולא כמדת הקדש מדת התרומה, שבקדש מתיר ומנגב ומטביל ואחר כך קושר, ובתרומה קושר ואחר כך מטביל! רישא וסיפא משום חציצה, וצריכא: דאי אשמעינן רישא, הוה אמינא: היינו טעמא דלקדש לא, משום כבידו של כלי דאיכא, אבל סיפא, דליכא כבידו של כלי – אימא לקדש נמי לא הוי חציצה. ואי אשמעינן סיפא, הוה אמינא: היינו טעמא דלקדש לא, משום דקיטרא

זבחים לט. **האונן.** שלא נטמא במתו: **והמחוסר כפורים.** כגון זב שטבל ליום שביעי לספירתו והעריב שמשו, ולמחרת הוא קרוי מחוסר כפורים, שעדיין גמר טהרתו תלויה בקרבנו: **צריכין טבילה.** לאחר שהביא קרבנו, אם רצה לאכול קדש. ובגמרא מפרש טעמא: **גמ' שכבידו של כלי חוצץ.** כבידו של כלי הפנימי, המכביד על החיצון שהוא מונח בתוכו – חוצץ בפני המים, ואין טבילה עולה לא לזה ולא לזה. ולקמן (דף כב.) פריך: אי הכי – אפילו תרומה נמי: **והא מדסיפא.** דמעלה אחריתי דחשיב בסיפא הוה טעמא משום חציצה – רישא לאו משום חציצה. דאי טעמא דתרווייהו משום חציצה, ולאשמעינן דגבי קדש כל דדמי לחציצה פוסל בו, ובתרומה לא פסלה אלא חציצה גמורה דאורייתא – ליתני חדא מינייהו: אהדוקי

האונן ומחוסר כפורים צריכין טבילה לקדש אבל לא לתרומה. משמע לישנא: טבילה(א), אבל הערב שמש – לא, כדדייק לקמן (דף כג.) בכלים הנגמרים. והכי נמי משמע בזבחים בריש "טבול יום" (דף לט.) דקא דייק על הך משנה: משנה היכי דמי? אי דאסח דעתיה מטמא שרץ – טמא מעליא הוי. אם כן משמע דלא הערב שמש בעי. וגם רש"י פי' כן התם, דלא בעי הערב שמש. והא דתנן התם: טבול יום ומחוסר כפורים אין חולקין בקדשים לאכול לערב, משמע דמחוסר כפורים בעי הערב שמש – איכא למימר משום טבול יום נקטיה. אבל קשה לר"י: דאמר בעירובין בפרק בכל מערבין (דף לג.): האשה שהיתה עליה לידה או זיבה – מביאה מעות ונותנת בשופר, טובלת ואוכלת בקדשים לערב, והתם לא תני טבול יום? וי"ל: דלערב דנקט – מיירי שאינה עומדת שם בשעת הקרבה, אלא סומכת לה על חזקת ב"ד – אוכלת לערב, דחזקה אין ב"ד מתעצלין. וק"ל: דלאחר חלות תשתרי, שכן מצינו גבי עומר (מנחות דף סח.): הרחוקים – מחלות ואילך מותרין, לפי שאין ב"ד מתעצלין! ויש לחלק: דהתם בקרבן צבור – ממהר טפי לעשות עד חלות, אבל קרבן יחיד ממתינין כל היום, אבל טפי – לא, כדי שלא יכשל על ידם. וכי תימא: אחר תמיד של ערב תשתרי, דתו לא תשתרי (ב) כיון דכתיבה "עליה העולה", ומינה ילפינן *עשה דהשלמה דאין מקריבין אחרי עולת התמיד בין הערבים כלום! ויש לומר: דאיכא למימר שפעמים מאחרין התמיד עד הערב שמש, כדאמרינן ריש "תפלת השחר" (ברכות דף כו:) שהולך וקרב עד הערב. הלכך, כיון שאין לו זמן קבוע – מספקין לה בכל הספק. אי נמי, כרבי ישמעאל בנו של רבי יוחנן בן ברוקה, שאמר ריש "תמיד נשחט" (פסחים דף נט.) שחטאת העוף קרב אחר תמיד הערב. והכי מפרש הר"י בריש "תמיד נשחט" גבי מחוסר כפורים שטובל ואוכל בקדשים לערב – דלא נקט ערב משום הערב שמש, אלא לפי שאינו עומד לעולם על קרבנו, כדפי', וסומך על חזקת כהנים. וכן יש לפרש ההיא דכריתות בריש פרק "מחוסרי כפרה" (דף ח:): [גר] מעוכב לאכול בקדשים עד שיביא קנו, הביא פרידה אחת שחרית – אוכל בקדשים לערב(ג) – דרבותא נקט, ואע"ג דאם הביאוס שחרית תרוייהו לא יאכל עד הערב, היכא דסומך על חזקה כדפרי', אבל ליכא למימר התם משום הערב שמש דלא צריך כדפרי'. ועוד: דלא מזכיר התם טבילה וגם לא מצינו מחוסר כפרה הצריך טבילה, רק מחוסר כפרה דטומאה. אבל בגר לא מצינו לו. וכן תנן (פרה פי"א מ"ה): כל הטעון ביאת מים מדברי סופרים – מטמא(ד) הקדש וכו'. אחר ביאתו – מותר בכולן. משמע: כל שהוא מדרבנן מותר מיד, בלא הערב שמש. ומההיא דפרישית תירץ הר"ר שמואל מרא"ם הא דתניא בפ"ב דביצה (דף יח. ושם) גבי מתני' דכלי שנטמא בולד הטומאה – מטבילין אותו ביו"ט, ואמאי? והא בעי הערב שמש! ותירץ: דכיון דולד טומאה דרבנן – לא בעי הערב שמש. והכי משמע בירושלמי דתרומות פ"ב גמרא: המטביל כליו בשבת, וכי מתקן מנא לכתחילה? תני: נפל כליו לתוך הבור מערים עליו ומטבילו. כלומר: ביום טוב ובשבת. תרי אמוראי, חד אמר: בכלי שנטמא באב הטומאה, וחד אמר: בכלי שנטמא בולד הטומאה. מתיב מאן דאמר בולד הטומאה למאן דאמר באב הטומאה: אפי' בחול, הא טעון הערב שמש! כלומר, התינח לדידי דאוקימנא ליה בולד הטומאה – שפיר, דלא בעי הערב שמש, אלא לדידך, דמוקמית ליה באב הטומאה – צריך ליה הערב שמש. ולא חזיא לאשתמושי ביה רק בחול, א"כ הוה ליה מטביל משבת לחול! ומוקי לה ברוצה להשתמש (ה) לצורך חולין, דטבול יום שרי בחולין בלא הערב שמש. והשתא לדבריו מוקמי מתני' דביצה (שם) דאין מטבילין כלים שנטמאו באב הטומאה – בכהן מיירי, לאכול תרומה. אי נמי – באוכל חולין על טהרת תרומה. ולא שרי בטומאה דרבנן רק ע"י הערמה. גם שמעתתא דביצה ע"י הערמה מיירי, ובאב הטומאה אפילו על ידי הערמה לא. וכי שרי התם במתני' מדלין בדלי טמא והוא טהור מאליו – הך הערמה עדיפא שפיר מאילו החזירו ריקן. ואותה גירסא שפיר מייתי לה בירושלמי. גם בפ"ב דביצה [ג"ז שם] כתוב בשיבוש בספרים, אמנם הלעת הגירסא כמו שפי'. ועוד היה מביא הר"י סייעתא: דאמר בפרק "האשה" (פסחים דף צ:), אמר רב: אין שוחטין וזורקין על טמא שרץ, דילמא פשע ולא טביל. ואלו במחוסר כפרה אמר התם: שוחטין וזורקין עליו, ולא חיישינן דילמא פשע, דהואיל וטהור מעליא הוי מדאורייתא – לא העמידו חכמים דבריהם במקום כרת לפוטרו בכך מפסח, ושפיר שוחטין וזורקין עליו. ואל תתמה: דאמר בפרק "הוציאו לו" (יומא דף מז.) גבי ר' ישמעאל בן קמחית כהן גדול שסיפר עם נכרי בשוק ונתזה צינורא מפיו, נכנס ישבב אחיו ושימש תחתיו. ואמאי? ליזיל וליטבול. כיון דטומאה דרבנן – הרי לא בעי הערב שמש! התם י"ל: כיון דחכמים שוינהו לנכרים כזבים לכל דבריהם – החמירו בהן והצריכו הערב שמש. ובצינורא דע"ה משמע לקמן (דף כג.) בההיא דשפופרת דבעי הערב שמש. דקאמר: אמאי? יטמא ויטבול. הא מטמא (ו)וקיימא ליה ומאי קאמר הא בטומאה קמייתא לא בעי הערב שמש וליכא היכירא. ואי מטמאין(ז) – בעי הערב שמש ושפיר איכא היכירא לצדוקין! אלא ודאי דאף של ע"ה צריך הערב שמש. ועוד תנן (פרה פ"ג מ"ז) שהיו מטמאין כהן השורף את הפרה. ותניא בתוספתא* [דפרה פ"ב]: שהיו נוגעין בו, כדפירש לעיל דבגדי אוכלי קדש מדרס לחטאת. ואיזה היכירא לצדוקין איכא, כיון דלא בעי הערב שמש כדפרי'! ותירץ הר"ר שמעון: דעשאוהו כטמא מת בשביעי שלו כדלעיל, הלכך אף הערב שמש בעי. אך רש"י לא פירש הכי לקמן, אלא פירש: עשאוהו כטמא מת בז' שלו למימני ביה ראשון ושני, ולא לענין הערב שמש. והשתא קשה: דמשמע דאיכא הערב שמש אף בטומאה דרבנן, ואלו בההיא דכל הטעון ביאת מים משמע דליכא הערב שמש! ואמר הר"י(ח): דמטמא כהן השורף את הפרה מיירי כדי שיהיה טמא לטמא חולין במגעו, וכן בההיא [דצינורא דע"ה ודצינורא דנכרי שנתזה מפיו] שמטמא חולין במגעו, לפיכך בעו הערב שמש, אך לישנא לא משמע שיטמא חולין במגעו בההיא דכהן השורף את הפרה, וכן לקמן גבי שפופרת לא קאמר עשאוהו כטמא מת בז' שלו רק לענין הערב שמש, ולא לענין לטמאות חולין במגעו. והא דבעי הערב שמש – איכא למימר דבפרה החמירו, וגם בשפופרת, טפי מבכלים הנגמרים דסגי להו בטבילה בלא הערב שמש – היינו גבי חולין ותרומה לקדש, ולא לחטאת. וההיא דפסחים פרק "אלו דברים" (דף ע.) דאמר: סכין שנמצא בי"ג שוחט ומטביל אותה, בי"ד – שוחט בה מיד. כלומר, דמסתמא הטבילוה מאתמול כדי לעשות לה הערב שמש. וכ"ת: ליחוש דילמא נטמא בטומאה דרבנן דלא בעי הערב שמש ונטר ליה עד צפרא להטביל, דהא הויא ספק דרבנן – ולקולא! ועוד, דרגילות להטביל מאורתא דלמא מטריד כ"כ ולא טביל כ"כ. וליכא לאתמוהי: האי סכין שנמצא, היכא? אי בירושלים – אפי' בי"ג נמי, ואי חוץ לירושלים – אפי' בי"ד נמי לא, כדאמרינן התם בשלהי פרק קמא דפסחים (דף יט:)! דהא י"ל: דמיירי חוץ מירושלים, אי נמי, בירושלים ובגזייתא שאינו לא דרך ירידה ולא דרך עליה. ובי"ד, דאיכא הוכחא דאטבלה – שריא. והקשה הר"ר אליהו: לפסול האי סכין בהיסח הדעת, כדאמר לעיל שילהי פ"ב (דף כ.) דאמר: לבי על הסל ולא על המגריפה – ופסלינה ליה בהיסח הדעת! ותירץ הר"י: דלא שייך היסח הדעת לפסול רק דומיא דהתם, שהיו בידו ואסח דעתיה הימנה. אבל היכא שאין בידו, כגון שאבד – לא שייך התם היסח הדעת ליפסול. והביא הר"ר אלחנן סעד לדבריו מפרק [ז' דשקלים מ"ג], דאמר התם: נמצא בעזרה, אברים – עולות, חתיכות – חטאות. ומשמע שעולה נקריבה וחטאת *תאכל, ולא מיפסלה בהיסח הדעת. [עי' שם במשנה ובירושלמי] והקשה הר"ר אלחנן: מאי האי דקאמר לישנא דשונה ומטביל, דמשמע שכבר הוטבל! ותירץ לו הר"י: דאפי' הכיר בה שהטבילוה בעלים – נמי מטבילין, דאימא לא נשמרה בטהרה, הואיל ואית ליה שהות כולי יומא. ובההיא דביצה, דאמרינן: כלי שנטמא בולד הטומאה מטבילין, ואקשינן, הא בעי הערב שמש! היה אומר הר"ר אלחנן דביו"ט שחל להיות בע"ש עסקינן, דיו"ט מכין לשבת, הלכך מטבילין אפילו ליומא אחרינא. אך לישנא דמתני' לא משמע ליה, אלא בכל יו"ט מיירי: דקיטרא

[פסחים נח: ע"ש]

רבינו חננאל

ואמרינן מ"ט דמתניתין א"ר אילא משום חציצה פי' חיישינן שמא כבידו של כלי יש בו בקרקעית הכלי החיצון ואין טבילה עולה לו. וה"מ דחיישינן כולי האי לקדש אבל לתרומה לא חיישינן כולי האי. ומקשינן אי משום חציצה הא קתני לה לקמן מדת הקדש מתיר מטביל ומנגב כו' ופרקינן לעולם רישא וסיפא משום חציצה ואצטריך לתרווייהו דאי תנא מטבילין כלים בתוך כלים בלבד היינו אומרים שזה מפני כבידו של כלי אבל התרת חבל אין צריך ואלו תנא מתיר ומטביל בלבד היינו אומרים משום שהקשר במים ואין מים באים לתוכו אבל כלים בתוך כלים אימא המים מצפים אותו ובאין עליו מכל צד קמ"ל דחיישינן בהא

הגהות הב"ח

(א) תוס' ד"ה האונן וכו' משמע לישנא טבילה אין אבל וכו' משמע דלא בעי הערב שמש וגם: (ב) בא"ד אחר תמיד של ערב תשתרי דתו לא ממתינין כיון דכתיב עליה גבי עולה ומינה: (ג) בא"ד ורבותא נקט דאע"ג דהביאוהו שחרית כנ"ל ותיבת דאם נמחק: (ד) בא"ד מטמא את הקדש וכו': (ה) בא"ד להשתמש בהן לצורך חולין וכו' הערמה עדיפא טפי מאילו וכו' מביא הר"י סייעתא מהא דאמר וכו' ואל תתמה מההיא דאמרינן: (ו) בא"ד אמאי יטמא ויטבול הא מיטמא וקאי ומאי קאמר כנ"ל ותיבת וקיימא ליה נמחק: (ז) בא"ד ואי מטמאין ליה בעי הערב שמש וכו' אלא ודאי דאף בצינורא של ע"ה צריך הערב שמש ועוד דקאמר לקמן שהיו מטמאין את הכהן השורף וכו' בשביעי שלו כדלקמן הלכך: (ח) בא"ד ואמר הר"י דההיא דמטמאין לכהן השורף וכו' וכן בההיא דאמר בצינורא מיירי שמטמא חולין וכו' במגעו דבההיא דכהן וכו' וגם בשפופרת החמירו טפי וכו' לא משמע הכי אלא בכל יו"ט מיירי:

גליון הש"ס

תוס' ד"ה האונן וכו' והביא הר"ר אלחנן סעד וכו'. חתיכות חטאת זה וזה תעובר צורתו ויצא לבית השריפה כך היא במתני' פ"ז דשקלים משנה ג' ודברי תוס' צלע"ג:

ב א מיי' פרק יב מהל' אבות הטומאות ה"א:
ג ב מיי' פ"ח מהלכות מקואות הלכה א ה טוש"ע י"ד סימן רא סעיף נב:
ד ג מיי' שם הלכה ו טור וש"ע שם סעיף מ:

(א) דִּקִיטְרָא בְּמַיָּא אַהֲדוּקֵי מִיהֲדַק. אֲבָל רֵישָׁא, דְּמַיָּא אַקְפּוּיֵי מַקְפוּ לֵיהּ לְמָנָא — לָא הַוְיָא חֲצִיצָה, צְרִיכָא. רַבִּי אִילָא לְטַעְמֵיהּ, דְּאָמַר רַבִּי אִילָא א"ר חֲנִינָא בַּר פַּפָּא: עֶשֶׂר מַעֲלוֹת שָׁנוּ כָּאן, חָמֵשׁ רִאשׁוֹנוֹת — בֵּין לַקֹּדֶשׁ בֵּין לַחוּלִּין שֶׁנַּעֲשׂוּ עַל טָהֳרַת הַקֹּדֶשׁ, אַחֲרוֹנוֹת — לַקֹּדֶשׁ אֲבָל לֹא לַחוּלִּין שֶׁנַּעֲשׂוּ עַל טָהֳרַת הַקֹּדֶשׁ, מ"ט? חָמֵשׁ קַמַּיְיתָא דְּאִית לְהוּ דְּרָרָא דְּטוּמְאָה מִדְּאוֹרַיְיתָא — גָּזְרוּ בְּהוּ רַבָּנַן בֵּין לַקֹּדֶשׁ בֵּין לַחוּלִּין שֶׁנַּעֲשׂוּ עַל טָהֳרַת הַקֹּדֶשׁ, בַּתְרַיְיתָא דְּלֵית לְהוּ דְּרָרָא דְּטוּמְאָה *מִדְּאוֹרַיְיתָא — גָּזְרוּ בְּהוּ רַבָּנַן לַקֹּדֶשׁ, לַחוּלִּין שֶׁנַּעֲשׂוּ עַל טָהֳרַת הַקֹּדֶשׁ — לֹא גָּזְרוּ בְּהוּ רַבָּנַן. רָבָא אָמַר: מִדְּסֵיפָא הָוֵי מִשּׁוּם חֲצִיצָה — רֵישָׁא לָאו מִשּׁוּם חֲצִיצָה. וְרֵישָׁא הַיְינוּ טַעְמָא: [א]גְּזֵירָה שֶׁלֹּא יַטְבִּיל מְחָטִין וְצִינּוֹרוֹת בִּכְלִי שֶׁאֵין בְּפִיו כִּשְׁפוֹפֶרֶת הַנּוֹד. (ב) כִּדְתְנַן: *[ב]עֵירוּב מִקְוָאוֹת כִּשְׁפוֹפֶרֶת הַנּוֹד, [ג]כְּעוֹבְיָהּ וְכַחֲלָלָהּ

אַהֲדוּקֵי מִיהֲדַק. וְקָרוֹב הוּא לִהְיוֹת חוֹצֵץ: **אַקְפּוּיֵי מַקְפִּי לֵיהּ לְמָנָא.** מְצִיפוֹת וּמַגְבִּיהוֹת אוֹתוֹ: **רַבִּי אִילָא.** דְּאוּקֵי טַעְמָא דְּרֵישָׁא מִשּׁוּם חֲצִיצָה: לְטַעְמֵיהּ. דְּאָמַר: עֶשֶׂר מַעֲלוֹת שָׁנוּ כָּאן, אֵלּוּ שֶׁבֵּין תְּרוּמָה לַקּוֹדֶשׁ. וַאֲנַן י"א תְּנַן בֵּיהּ, אֶלָּא הָנֵי תַּרְתֵּי דְּחַד טַעְמָא — חָשֵׁיב לְהוּ כַּחֲדָא: בֵּין לַחוּלִּין שֶׁנַּעֲשׂוּ עַל טָהֳרַת הַקֹּדֶשׁ. אַף הֵן נִתְעַלּוּ יוֹתֵר מִן הַתְּרוּמָה בַּמַּעֲלוֹת הַלָּלוּ: **דְּרָרָא דְטוּמְאָה דְּאוֹרַיְיתָא.** חֲשַׁשׁ טוּמְאָה דְּאוֹרַיְיתָא. כְּלִי בְּתוֹךְ כְּלִי, אִי אִיכָּא חֲצִיצָה — טוּמְאָה דְּאוֹרַיְיתָא הִיא, אֲחוֹרַיִים וְתוֹךְ אַף עַל גַּב דִּכְלִים שֶׁנִּטְמְאוּ אֲחוֹרָיו בְּמַשְׁקִין, דְּטוּמְאָה דְּרַבָּנַן הִיא עָסְקִינַן — מִיהוּ הָא דַּאֲמוּר רַבָּנַן: מַשְׁקִין מְטַמְּאִין כְּלִי — מִשּׁוּם גְּזֵרָה דְּמַשְׁקֵה זָב וְזָבָה הוּא, כְּגוֹן רוּקּוֹ וּמֵימֵי רַגְלָיו, וְהָנֵי מְטַמְּאִין כְּלִי מִדְּאוֹרַיְיתָא. וּבְטוּמְאָה דְּאוֹרַיְיתָא אֵין חִילּוּק בִּכְלִי שֶׁטֶף בֵּין אֲחוֹרַיִים לְתוֹכוֹ, שֶׁבְּכָל מָקוֹם שֶׁטּוּמְאָה נוֹגַעַת בּוֹ נִטְמָא כּוּלּוֹ. נוֹשֵׂא אֶת הַמִּדְרָס נַמִי חֲשַׁשׁ טוּמְאָה דְּאוֹרַיְיתָא הִיא, כִּדְמְפָרֵשׁ בַּגְּמָרָא: מַעֲשֶׂה הָיָה שֶׁנָּפְלָה רְצוּעַת הַסַּנְדָּל לַאֲוִיר חָבִית. בִּגְדֵי אוֹכְלֵי תְרוּמָה מִדְרָס לַקֹּדֶשׁ — שֶׁמָּא יָשְׁבָה עֲלֵיהֶן אִשְׁתּוֹ נִדָּה, חֲשַׁשׁ טוּמְאָה דְּאוֹרַיְיתָא הִיא. כֵּלִים הַנִּגְמָרִים כו' — מִשּׁוּם צִינּוֹרָא דְּעַם הָאָרֶץ, שֶׁמָּא זָב הוּא: **בִּכְלִי שֶׁאֵין בְּפִיו כִּשְׁפוֹפֶרֶת הַנּוֹד.** וְהַהִיא לָאו טְבִילָה הִיא, שֶׁאֵין הַמַּיִם הַנִּכְנָסִין לְתוֹכוֹ חִיבּוּר לְמֵי הַמִּקְוֶה, וְלֹא טָבְלוּ הַמְּחָטִין אֶלָּא בְּמִיעוּט מַיִם שֶׁבַּכְּלִי, וּתְנַן כו' דְּלָאו חִיבּוּר הוּא: **עֵירוּב מִקְוָאוֹת.** מִקְוֶה חָסֵר בְּצַד מִקְוֶה שָׁלֵם, וְהַצִּינּוֹר בֵּינֵיהֶן הַמְחַבְּרָן: **אִם יֵשׁ בְּרָחְבּוֹ כִּשְׁפוֹפֶרֶת הַנּוֹד.** כְּקָנֶה שֶׁעוֹשִׂין בְּפִי הַנּוֹד שֶׁל עוֹר (ג): **וְכַחֲלָלָהּ**

[עי' תוספות חולין לה. ד"ה אין לך]

מקוואות פ"ו מ"ז יבמות טו.

דקיטרא במיא אהדוקי מיהדק. ומגגיב דמתניתין הוי משום חלילה, כדפירש רש"י. והא דלא עביד לריכותא ממנגיב – משום דקים ליה (ד) דלא ידעינן מאידך. ויש מפרשים: דמנגיב טעמא אחרינא איכא, משום שהמים חוזרים ומטמאין ליה, ולא סלקא להו השקה משום מעלה דקדש. וקשה למורי: דאם כן – לרבא הוי שנים עשר, ולרבי אילא אחד עשר! וי"ל: רביעי בקדש לא חשיב ליה, או לירוף דאורייתא:

אחרונות לקדש ולא לחולין כו'. תימה להר"ר אלחנן: דמוכח רב מרי לעיל באידך פירקא (דף יט:): ש"מ חולין שנעשו על טהרת הקדש – כקדש דמו, מדלא קתני להו גבי מעלות. כלומר: בגדי אוכלי תרומה מדרס לחולין שנעשו על טהרת הקדש, בגדי חולין (ה) מדרס לקדש. ומאי הוכחא היא? דילמא לאו כקדש דמו בעלמא, ולענין מעלה זו הוו כקדש. שכן מתניתין סבירא גבי ה' ראשונות כקדש דמו. ואפ"ה לא חשיב לה גבי מעלות! ושמא דלא קאמר התלמוד רק לענין הך מעלה לחוד:

בתרייתא דלית בהו דררא דטומאה דאורייתא לקדש גזור, ולא לחולין שנעשו על טהרת הקדש. וקשה לר"י: דאמרינן בפ"ק דנדה (דף ו.): מעת לעת שבנדה – לקדש אבל לא לתרומה. אי הכי – לתנויי גבי מעלות! כי קתני – מילתא דאית ליה דררא כו'. דלית ליה דררא דטומאה דאורייתא – לא קתני. ומאי קא משני ליה? הא גבי בתרייתא חשיב הכא דררא דטומאה דרבנן. והיא דהתם דררא דטומאה דרבנן! (ו) ועו קשה: מאי שנא הני בתרייתא דהכא, דלא הוו לחולין שנעשו על טהרת הקדש. והתם מסקינן דמעת לעת אף לחולין שנעשו על טהרת הקדש! וריב"א היה מפרש: דהתם לא מקשה וליתנייה גבי מעלות רק מקמייתא, דגבי בתרייתא לא דמו. דהתם אף לחולין שנעשו על טהרת הקדש, והכא דוקא לקדש. ולא יתכן להר"י: דאכתי לא קים ליה בהא כי פריך ליה עד דלמסקנא. ועוד: כי משני דלא דמי לקמייתא משום דלית דררא דטומאה – אכתי תקשי ליה מ"ש דהתם לחולין שנעשו עט"ה, והכא דווקא לקדש! להכי נראה להר"י לפרש: וניתנייה גבי מעלות, או קמייתא או בתרייתא. ומשני: דליכא דררא דטומאה כלל אפילו דרבנן, ולא דמי אף לבתרייתא. דהא כי מטמינן לה מעת לעת – קים לן דטהורה היתה. ואל תתמה: היכי מסקינן התם אף לחולין, כיון דליכא דררא דטומאה כלל – לפי שרגילות הוא קלת שנעקר הדם לפני ראייתה, לכך גזרו רבנן אף בחולין שנעשו עט"ה, ומכל מקום לית להו דררא דטומאה התם, כיון דבשעה דעסקה בטהרות אז אין שם ספק טומאה, ואין לה להניח מלעסוק בטהרות, שאינה יודעת מתי תראה אחרי כן:

בתרייתא דלית להו דררא דטומאה דאורייתא. תימה להר"י: הרי רביעי בקדש דקתני, ושלישי בתרומה דהוו דאורייתא, כדאיתא בסוטה פרק "כשם" (דף כט.). ולקמן* אפרש בע"ה, ולא כפי' רש"י שפירש דהוי דרבנן רביעי בקדש! ועוד קשה למורי: דרב נחמן אמר רבה בר אבוה דקתני גבי י"א מעלות לקמייתא כו' אחרונות לקדש דווקא. אם כן סבירא ליה כל אלו דבתרייתא לית להו דררא דטומאה דאורייתא, ואילו לקמן (דף כד.) שמעינן ליה דצירוף סל הוי דאורייתא, דמשני ליה: למימרא דרבי חנין כגון שנשברו על גבי (ז) קטבליא דאורייתא יש לו תוך – מצרף. אלמא הוי דאורייתא בכלי שיש לו תוך! ותירץ הר"י: כיון דלא שייך לחולין – לא חשיב ליה דררא דטומאה, והיינו שייכות דטומאה:

[וכג: ד"ה והא ודף כד. ד"ה מנין]

כעוביה וכחללה. פירש"י: שתי אצבעות חוזרות למקומן. והקשה ר"ת: דתנן*, ומייתי לה פרק שני דגיטין (דף טז. ושם), ובפרק בתרא דע"ז (דף עב.): הנצוק והקטפרס ומשקה טופח – אינן חיבור, הא טופח על מנת להטפיח – חיבור! ואומר ר"ת: דבמים סגי בטופח על מנת להטפיח, אבל בנקב – בעינן ב' אצבעות. אך קשה להר"י: דתנן בפרק חמישי דפרה [מ"ח]: שתי שקתות שבאבן (ח), קדש אחת מהם – מים שבשניה אינן מקודשות. אם היו נקובות זה בתוך זה כשפופרת נוד, או שהיו מים צפין על גביו אפי' כקליפת השום, קדש אחת מהן – מים שבשניה מקודשות. משמע מדקתני סיפא: או שהיו מים צפין על גביו, משמע דבכותל בעינן שפופרת הנוד אפי' ממים, דדוקא בסיפא סגי כקליפת השום! ועו, תנן במסכת מקואות (פ"ו מ"ט): כותל שבין שתי מקוואות שנסדק לְשְׁתִי – מצטרף. לְעֶרֶב – אין מצטרף, עד שיהא במקום אחד כשפופרת הנוד. ר"י אומר חילוף הדברים: נפרצו זה לתוך זה על רוס כקליפת השום ועל רוחב כשפופרת [הנוד], כלומר שתי אצבעות, חוזרות למקומן. וכיון דבעינן חצי הנקב מלא מים – איכא טפי מטופח על מנת להטפיח. ועוד: אי מיתניא ההיא דנצוק וקטפרס לענין מקוואות – מאי האי דקאמר בגיטין (ט) ולענין מקוואות ור"י הוא, מכלל דמעיקרא לא מיתוקמא לענין מקוואות. ונראה לר"י: דלענין השקה מיתניא, דומיא דרישא: [מקל] שהוא מלא משקין טמאין, כיון שהשיקו למקוה טהורה, דברי ר' יהושע, וחכ"א: עד שיטביל את כולה, הנצוק והקטפרס כו'. ובסוף פרק שמיני דטהרות מיתני': אבל לענין מקוואות – מועיל. כדאיתא לעיל (דף יט.) גבי שלש גממיות דטובלין בתחתונה. וכי מוקמינן בגיטין: [דילמא] לענין מקוואות ור"י היא, דאמר גוד אחית – לא מצי לאוקמי כרבנן, דלית להו טופח על מנת להטפיח אפי' בגוד אחית, וכ"ש בקרקע שוה, דלעולם לית להו חיבור עד שיהא כקליפת השום ברוחב שפופרת. והכי משמע ליסנא דידהו דלעולם לא הוי חיבור. ועוד, דאיכא למימר לר"י נמי לית ליה רק היכא דשייך גוד אחית, אבל בקרקע שוה – לא אמרינן. ולעיל (דף יט: בד"ה בתחתונה) פירשתי דנקט ובאמצעית ארבעים לרבותא דר"י, דאע"ג איכא מ' סאה באמצעית – אין טובלין בעליונה. אי נמי רבותא דחכמים, דאפי' הכי קתני (י) סיפא בתוספתא, וחכ"א: אין מטבילין אלו באמצעית. אך תימה להר"ר אלחנן: דסברא הפוכה, דגבי השקה חזינן דקטפרס אינו חיבור בההיא דנצוק וקטפרס, ולענין מקוואות – מהני, כדאיתא לעיל גבי שלשה גממיות (שם) דטובלין בתחתונה דהוי חבור, ואלו טופח על מנת להטפיח – מהני לענין הַשָּׁקָה ולענין מקוואות – בעינן מים צפין על גביו! ותירץ הר"י: דטומאה וטהרה והשקה – הלכתא גמירי לה, ולא בסברא תליא מילתא. ועוד קשיא לו: דגבי טופח על מנת להטפיח הוי חיבור להשקה. ובמקוואות בעינן מים צפין, וכי קאמרינן דילמא לענין מקוואות קאמר – רוצה לומר דלגבי השקה לא הוי חיבור! ויש לומר: דהוא הדין להשקה במקום דאיכא למימר גוד אחית הוי חיבור לרבי יהודה. והא דנקט מקוואות – משום דאיירי ביה נקטיה. ומיהו, יש לחלק מעיקרא וליישב כל המשניות: דבקרקע שוה, היכא דליכא כותל כלל – סגי בטופח על מנת להטפיח, והיכא דאיכא נקב בכותל – בעינן כרוחב שפופרת הנוד, ועל גבי כותל – סגי כקליפת השום ועל רוחב כשפופרת הנוד: [וע' תוס' יבמות טו. ד"ה עירוב]:

טהרות פ"ח מ"ט

מאי

רבינו חננאל

ובהא ור' אילא שפירש זה הפירוש *) לטע' ששם שתיהם לחציצה ומחשב להו חדא לפיכך תני עשר מעלות. ורבא דמוקים לה סיפא משום חציצה דרישא גזרה גזרו שלא להטביל כלים בתוך כלים דחיישינן שמא טבול מחטין וצינורות בכלי שאין בו נקב מרווח כשפופרת הנוד תני אחת עשרה מעלות. כי כל כלי שאין בו נקב מרווח כשפופרת הנוד שיעור כשתי אצבעות שוחקות אין מטבילין בהן כלים אחרים כדתנן במקואות פרק ו' השידה והתיבה שבים אין מטבילין בהם אלא אם כן היו נקובין כשפופרת הנוד. וכשפופרת הנוד תנן בעוביה ובחללה כב' אצבעות חוזרות למקומן עכשיו חיישינן משום הרואה שמטבילין כלים בתוך כלים לקדש שבפיו נקב מרווח כב' אצבעות שוחקות. ואמרינן מפני שהן כלים גדולין כגון סכינין וכיוצא בהן אבל מחטין וצינורות של קדש שהן דקין לא בעי נקב כולי האי ואתי לאטבולי בנקב פחות מב' אצבעות לפיכך גזרו שלא להטביל כלים בתוך כלים לקדש כלל וזה חשבון המעלות מטבילין כלים בתוך כלים לתרומה אבל לא לקדש זו אחת אחוריים ותוך ובית הצביעה לתרומה אבל לא לקדש הרי שתים הנושא את המדרס הוא נושא את התרומה אבל לא את הקדש הרי שלש בגדי אוכלי תרומה מדרס לקדש הרי ד'. מתיר ומטביל ומנגב **) ואחר הנגמרים בטהרה צריכה טבילה לקדש אבל לא לתרומה הרי ו' לדברי רבא ולדברי ר' אילא דתני להו לתרוויהו משום חציצה הוויין להו תרווייהו חדא לפיכך תני להו חמש ואמר דאלו נוהגין בין בקדש בין בחולין שנעשו על טהרת הקדש: כיון דאית להון דררא דטומאה. פי' עיקר טומאה שהנה ודאי יש בהן טומאה ובאין לעלות ממנה וגזרו בהו רבנן אפילו בחולין שנעשו על טהרת הקדש אבל חמש האחרונות שעדיין לא חלה טומאה עליהו לא גזרו בהו. לפיכך אמרנו שנשארו חמש מעלות אחרות שנוהגין בקדש ואין נוהגין בחולין שנעשו על טהרת הקדש ואלו הן הכלי מצרף מה שבתוכו לקדש אבל לא לתרומה. הרביעי בקדש פסול. והשלישי בתרומה היד מטמא את חברתה לקדש אבל לא לתרומה. אוכלין אוכלין נגובים בידים מסואבות בתרומה אבל לא בקדש אונן ומחוסר כפורים צריכין טבילה לקדש אבל לא לתרומה נמצאו מעלות הללו לר' אילא דמשוי להו לתרתי

*) נראה דצ"ל לטעמיה דאמר דעשר מעלות שנו כאן ששם שתיהן וכו'. **) נ"ל ואחר זה כלים הנגמרים כו'.

הגהות הב"ח

(א) גמ' משום דקיטרא אהדוקי כצ"ל ותיבת במיא נמחק: (ב) שם כשפופרת הנוד ותנן עירוב: (ג) רש"י ד"ה עירוב וכו' המחברן הס"ד ואח"כ מה"ד אם יש וכו' של עור כחללה ועוביה והס"ד: (ד) תום' ד"ה דקיטרא וכו' דקים ליה דהלא ידעינן מאידך: (ה) ד"ה אחרונות וכו' הקדש בגדי אוכלי חולין שנעשו עטה"ק מדרס לקדש ומאי הוכחא: (ו) ד"ה בתרייתא וכו' דרבנן היא ותו קשה וכו' דלית ליה דררא דטומאה: (ז) ד"ה בתרייתא וכו' על גבי קרקבלא דאורייתא: (ח) ד"ה כעוביה וכו' שתי שקתות שבאבן אחת קדש אחת מהם המים שבשניה אינן מקודשין ואם היו וכו' המים צפין וכו' וקדש אחת מהן המים שבשניהם מקודשים מדקתני סיפא או שהיו המים כצ"ל ותיבת משמע נמחק: (ט) בא"ד וכיון דבעינן רוחב הנקב מלא מים וכו' דקאמר בגיטין במסקנא דילמא לענין מקוואות: (י) בא"ד קתני בסיפא בתוספתא וכו' דסברא הפוכה היא דגבי:

וְכַחֲלָלָה בִּשְׁתֵּי אֶצְבָּעוֹת חוֹזְרוֹת לִמְקוֹמָן. סָבַר לָהּ כְּהָא דְּאָמַר ר"נ אָמַר רַבָּה בַּר אֲבוּהּ: [א]י"א מַעֲלוֹת שָׁנוּ כָּאן; [ב]שֵׁשׁ רִאשׁוֹנוֹת בֵּין לַקּוֹדֶשׁ בֵּין לַחוּלִּין שֶׁנַּעֲשׂוּ עַל טָהֳרַת הַקּוֹדֶשׁ, אַחֲרוֹנוֹת – לַקּוֹדֶשׁ אֲבָל לֹא לַחוּלִּין שֶׁנַּעֲשׂוּ עַל טָהֳרַת הַקּוֹדֶשׁ. מַאי אִיכָּא בֵּין דְּרָבָא לְדְר' אִילָא? אִיכָּא בֵּינַיְיהוּ סַל וְגַרְגּוּתְנִי שֶׁמִּילְּאָן כֵּלִים וְהִטְבִּילָן. לְמ"ד מִשּׁוּם חֲצִיצָה – אִיכָּא, לְמ"ד מִשּׁוּם גְּזֵירָה שֶׁמָּא יַטְבִּיל מְחָטִין וְצִינּוֹרִיּוֹת בִּכְלִי שֶׁאֵין בְּפִיו כִּשְׁפוֹפֶרֶת הַנּוֹד – סַל וְגַרְגּוּתְנִי שֶׁאֵין בְּפִיהֶן כִּשְׁפוֹפֶרֶת הַנּוֹד לֵיכָּא, וְאָזְדָא רָבָא לְטַעְמֵיהּ, דְּאָמַר רָבָא: סַל וְגַרְגּוּתְנִי שֶׁמִּילְּאָן כֵּלִים וְהִטְבִּילָן – טְהוֹרִין, וּמִקְוֶה שֶׁחִלְּקוֹ בְּסַל וְגַרְגּוּתְנִי – הַטּוֹבֵל שָׁם לֹא עָלְתָה לוֹ טְבִילָה, דְּהָא אַרְעָא כּוּלָּהּ חַלְחוּלֵי מְחַלְחְלָא, וּבָעֵינַן דְּאִיכָּא מ' סְאָה בְּמָקוֹם אֶחָד. [ג]וְהָנֵי מִילֵּי – בִּכְלִי טָהוֹר. אֲבָל בִּכְלִי טָמֵא – מִיגּוֹ דְּסָלְקָא טְבִילָה לְכוּלֵּיהּ גּוּפֵיהּ דְּמָנָא – סָלְקָא לְהוּ נַמִי לְכֵלִים דְּאִית בֵּיהּ. *דִּתְנַן: *כֵּלִים שֶׁמִּילְּאָן כֵּלִים וְהִטְבִּילָן – [ד]הֲרֵי אֵלּוּ טְהוֹרִין, וְאִם לֹא טָבַל, מַיִם הַמְעוֹרָבִים – עַד שֶׁיִּהְיוּ מְעוֹרָבִין כִּשְׁפוֹפֶרֶת הַנּוֹד. מַאי קָאָמַר: "וְאִם לֹא טָבַל"? ה"ק: וְאִם אֵינוֹ צָרִיךְ לְהַטְבִּילוֹ, (א) וּמַיִם הַמְעוֹרָבִין – עַד שֶׁיְּהוּ מְעוֹרָבִין כִּשְׁפוֹפֶרֶת הַנּוֹד. וְהָא דְּרָבָא וּדְר' אִילָא תַּנָּאֵי הִיא. דְּתַנְיָא: *[ה]סַל וְגַרְגּוּתְנִי שֶׁמִּילְּאָן כֵּלִים וְהִטְבִּילָן, בֵּין לַקּוֹדֶשׁ בֵּין לַתְּרוּמָה – טְהוֹרִין, אַבָּא שָׁאוּל אוֹמֵר: לַתְּרוּמָה אֲבָל לֹא לַקּוֹדֶשׁ. אִי הָכִי תְּרוּמָה נַמִי, לְמַאן קָאָמְרִינַן – [ו]חֲבֵרִים, חֲבֵרִים מֵידַע יָדְעִי! א"ה קוֹדֶשׁ נַמִי, חָזֵי לֵיהּ ע"ה וְאָזֵיל מַטְבִּיל, תְּרוּמָה נַמִי חָזֵי לֵיהּ ע"ה וְאָזֵיל מַטְבִּיל! לָא מְקַבְּלִינַן מִינַּיְיהוּ. קוֹדֶשׁ נַמִי לָא נְקַבֵּיל מִינַּיְיהוּ! הָוְיָא לֵיהּ אֵיבָה. – תְּרוּמָה נַמִי הָוְיָא לֵיהּ אֵיבָה! לָא אִיכְפַּת לֵיהּ, דְּאָזֵיל יָהֵיב לֵיהּ לְכֹהֵן עַם הָאָרֶץ חַבְרֵיהּ. וּמַאן תַּנָּא דְּחָיֵישׁ לְאֵיבָה – רַבִּי יוֹסֵי הִיא, דְּתַנְיָא, א"ר יוֹסֵי: מִפְּנֵי מָה [ז]הַכֹּל נֶאֱמָנִין עַל טָהֳרַת יַיִן וְשֶׁמֶן כָּל יְמוֹת הַשָּׁנָה – כְּדֵי °שֶׁלֹּא יְהֵא כָּל אֶחָד וְאֶחָד הוֹלֵךְ וּבוֹנֶה בָּמָה לְעַצְמוֹ, וְשׂוֹרֵף פָּרָה אֲדוּמָּה לְעַצְמוֹ. אָמַר רַב פַּפָּא: [ח]כְּמַאן מְקַבְּלִינַן הָאִידָּנָא סַהֲדוּתָא מֵע"ה, כְּמַאן – כְּרַבִּי יוֹסֵי. וְנֵיחוּשׁ לִשְׁאֵלָה? דִּתְנַן: *כְּלִי חֶרֶס מַצִּיל עַל הַכֹּל, *דִּבְרֵי ב"ה, ב"ש אוֹמְרִים: *[ט]אֵינוֹ מַצִּיל אֶלָּא עַל אוֹכָלִים וְעַל הַמַּשְׁקִים וְעַל כְּלֵי חֶרֶס. אָמְרוּ לָהֶם ב"ה לְב"ש: מִפְּנֵי מָה? *אָמְרוּ ב"ש: [י]מִפְּנֵי שֶׁהוּא טָמֵא ע"ג ע"ה, [כ]וְאֵין כְּלִי טָמֵא חוֹצֵץ. אָמְרוּ לָהֶם ב"ה: וַהֲלֹא טִיהַרְתֶּם אוֹכָלִין וּמַשְׁקִין שֶׁבְּתוֹכוֹ! אָמְרוּ לָהֶם בֵּית שַׁמַּאי: כְּשֶׁטִּיהַרְנוּ אוֹכָלִין וּמַשְׁקִין שֶׁבְּתוֹכוֹ לְעַצְמוֹ

כלים פ"י מ"א

רש"י

וְכַחֲלָלָה וְעוֹבְיָהּ. וְהֵן ב' אֶלְבָּעוֹת חוֹזְרוֹת לִמְקוֹמָן, שֶׁאָדָם יָכוֹל לְגַלְגֵּל בְּתוֹךְ חֲלָלוֹ ב' אֶלְבָּעוֹת לְכָל לַד – הָוֵי עֵירוּב, וּמַטְבִּילִין אַף כֵּלִים. וְהַאי נַמִי חֲשַׁשׁ טוּמְאָה דְּאוֹרַיְיתָא הִיא: גַּרְגּוּתְנִי. סַל גָּדוֹל מְאֹד, שֶׁבּוֹ מְסַנְּנִין הַיַּיִן בְּעֵת הַבָּצִיר, וְנוֹתְנִין אוֹתוֹ תַּחַת קִילוּחַ הַגַּת, וְהַיַּיִן מִסְתַּנֵּן בּוֹ וְיוֹרֵד לַבּוֹר, כִּדְאָמְרִינַן בְּמַסֶּכֶת ע"ז (דף נו:): שֶׁלֹּא הֶחֱזִיר גַּרְגּוּתְנִי לַגַּת: טְהוֹרִין. אַף לַקּוֹדֶשׁ. וְרָבָא לְטַעְמֵיהּ, דְּאוֹקֵי טַעְמָא גְּזֵירָה מִשּׁוּם כְּלִי שֶׁאֵין בְּפִיו כִּשְׁפוֹפֶרֶת הַנּוֹד, וּבְסַל וּבְגַרְגּוּתְנִי לֵיכָּא לְמֵיחַשׁ לְהָכִי: לֹא עָלְתָה לוֹ טְבִילָה. שֶׁעֲשָׂאָן כְּב' מִקְוָאוֹת, וְאֵין שִׁיעוּר לֹא בָּזֶה וְלֹא בָּזֶה. אע"פ שֶׁהַמַּיִם מְחֻבָּרָן בֵּין אֲוִיר הַנְּקָבִים – אֵין זֶה חִיבּוּר: דְּהָא אַרְעָא כּוּלָּא מְחַלְחְלָא. וְהַמַּיִם הַנּוֹבְעִין כָּאן בְּאֵין מַגָּבַר גָּדוֹל, וְלֹא חָשְׁבִינַן כִּמְחוּבָּר, דְּבָעֵינַן מ' סְאָה בְּמָקוֹם אֶחָד: וְהָנֵי מִילֵּי. (ב) דְּאָמְרִינַן: הַמַּטְבִּיל בִּכְלִי שֶׁאֵין בְּפִיו כִּשְׁפוֹפֶרֶת הַנּוֹד טְמֵאִים – בִּכְלִי טָהוֹר, שֶׁלֹּא הָיָה הַכְּלִי הַחִיצוֹן צָרִיךְ לְהַטְבִּיל: אֲבָל. אִם הוּא צָרִיךְ לְהַטְבִּיל: מִיגּוֹ דְּסָלְקָא טְבִילָה לְגוּפוֹ שֶׁל כְּלִי. לִיטָּהֵר תּוֹכוֹ ע"י מַיִם הַנִּכְנָסִין דֶּרֶךְ פִּיו, דִּכְטוּמְאָתוֹ כֵּן טָהֳרָתוֹ – סָלְקָא נַמִי טְבִילָה לְכֵלִים שֶׁבְּתוֹכוֹ: הֲרֵי אֵלּוּ טְהוֹרִין. לִתְרוּמָה, וְלֹא חִלֵּק בֵּין פִּיו רָחָב לְפִיו קָצָר: וְאִם לֹא טָבַל כו'. כִּדְמְפָרֵשׁ לָהּ: וְאִם אֵין צָרִיךְ לְהַטְבִּילוֹ: הַמַּיִם הַמְעוֹרָבִים. לַמִּקְוֶה, וְאַתָּה בָּא לְטַהֵר עַל יְדֵיהֶן כֵּלִים שֶׁבְּתוֹכָם, עַד שֶׁיְּהוּ מְעוֹרָבִין דֶּרֶךְ פֶּה רָחָב כִּשְׁפוֹפֶרֶת הַנּוֹד: וְהָא דְּר' אִילָא. דְּאוֹקֵי טַעְמָא מִשּׁוּם חֲצִיצָה, וְסַל וְגַרְגּוּתְנִי נַמִי כִּשְׁאָר כֵּלִים דָּמוּ, וְהַמַּטְבִּיל כֵּלִים לְתוֹכָן – אֵינָן טְהוֹרִין לַקּוֹדֶשׁ. וְרָבָא דְּאוֹקֵי טַעְמָא דְּמַתְנִי' מִשּׁוּם עֵירוּב מִקְוָאוֹת, וְהָא בְּסַל וְגַרְגּוּתְנִי לֵיכָּא לְמֵיחַשׁ וּטְהוֹרִין – תַּנָּאֵי הִיא: לְמַאן קָאָמְרִינַן חֲבֵרִים. לְמִי אָנוּ אוֹמְרִים הוֹרָאָה זוֹ שֶׁלֹּא יַטְבִּיל כְּלִי בְּתוֹךְ כְּלִי – לְחָבֵר, דְּאִילּוּ עַם הָאָרֶץ לֹא אָתֵי קַמָּן לְמִשְׁאַל. הִלְכָּךְ, לִתְרוּמָה לֵיכָּא לְמֵיחַשׁ, דְּהָא מֵידַע יָדִיעַ שִׁיעוּר עֵירוּב מִקְוָאוֹת, וּלְעִנְיַן כְּבֵידוֹ שֶׁל כְּלִי נַמִי, אִם כָּבֵד הוּא – מַגְבִּיהִין אוֹתוֹ: א"ה קוֹדֶשׁ נַמִי. עַל כָּרְחָךְ מַתְנִי' דְּקָתָנֵי: אֲבָל לֹא לַקּוֹדֶשׁ בְּחָבֵר עָסְקִינַן, דְּאִי ע"ה – מִי קָיֵים לָךְ, וּמִי אָתֵי קַמָּן לְמִשְׁאַל טַעְמָא? תְּרוּמָה נַמִי חָזֵי לֵיהּ. יִשְׂרָאֵל עַם הָאָרֶץ, וּמַטְבִּיל וּמִשְׁתַּמֵּשׁ בּוֹ תְּרוּמָה, וְאַחַ"כ נוֹתְנָהּ לַכֹּהֵן: לֹא מְקַבְּלִינַן. תְּרוּמָה מֵעַם הָאָרֶץ אֶלָּא בִּשְׁעַת הַגִּיתּוֹת וְהַבַּדִּים, שֶׁהַכֹּל מְטַהֲרִים אֶת כְּלֵיהֶן ע"פ חֲכָמִים, כִּדְתְנַן (לקמן דף כו.): עָבְרוּ הַגִּיתּוֹת וְהַבַּדִּים וְהֵבִיאוּ לוֹ חָבִית שֶׁל תְּרוּמָה – לֹא יְקַבְּלֶנָּה מִמֶּנּוּ: עַל טָהֳרַת יַיִן וְשֶׁמֶן. (ג) לְקַבֵּל מִיָּדָם יַיִן לִנְסָכִים וְשֶׁמֶן לִמְנָחוֹת, כִּדְתְנַן בְּמַתְנִיתִין (לקמן דף כד:): חוֹמֶר בִּתְרוּמָה, שֶׁבִּיהוּדָה נֶאֱמָנִין עַל טָהֳרַת יַיִן וָשֶׁמֶן: וּבוֹנֶה בָּמָה. בִּשְׁעַת אִיסּוּר הַבָּמוֹת, וּמַקְטִיר לַשָּׁמַיִם: כְּרַבִּי יוֹסֵי. דְּאִילּוּ לְרַבָּנַן לֹא מְקַבְּלִינַן, כִּדְאָמַר בִּפְסָחִים בְּפֶ' "אֵלּוּ עוֹבְרִין" (דף מט:): וְנֵיחוּשׁ לִשְׁאֵלָה. לֹא נִטְבּוֹל כְּלִי בְּתוֹךְ כְּלִי לִתְרוּמָה, דִּלְמָא חָזֵי עַם הָאָרֶץ וְעָבֵיד הָכִי, וְאָנוּ שׁוֹאֲלִין אֶת כְּלֵיהֶן וּמְשַׁמְּשִׁין בָּהֶן: דִּתְנַן. בְּמַתְנִי' דְּשַׁיְילִינַן מִנַּיְיהוּ: כְּלִי חֶרֶס מַצִּיל עַל הַכֹּל. אִם מוּקָּף צָמִיד פָּתִיל בְּאֹהֶל הַמֵּת. א"נ: הַמֵּת בַּבַּיִת וּטְהָרוֹת בָּעֲלִיָּיה, וַאֲרוּבָּה פְּתוּחָה מִן הַבַּיִת לָעֲלִיָּיה, וְהֹשִׁיבוּ כְּלִי חֶרֶס בִּפְתְחָהּ, וּכְלִי חֶרֶס חוֹצֵץ בִּפְנֵי הַטּוּמְאָה – דְּאֵינוֹ מִטַּמֵּא מִגַּבּוֹ, וּמַצִּיל עַל כָּל מַה שֶּׁבָּעֲלִיָּיה: שֶׁהוּא טָמֵא כו'. הַכְּלִי הַזֶּה הָיָה טָמֵא מִתְּחִילָּתוֹ קוֹדֶם שֶׁנְּתָנוֹ ע"ה עַל פִּי הָאֲרוּבָּה: וַהֲלֹא טִיהַרְתֶּם אוֹכָלִים וּמַשְׁקִין שֶׁבְּתוֹכוֹ. אִם הָיָה מוּקָּף צָמִיד פָּתִיל בְּאֹהֶל הַמֵּת, וְהִיא הִיא:

תוספות

מאי איכא בין רבא לר' אילא. קשיא למורי: איכא בינייהו טובא; כלי חילון כשהטביל כלי בתוך כלי, למאן דמוקי לה משום חצילה – שייך בין בחילון בין בפנימי, ולמאן דמוקי משום גזרה שאין בפיו כשפופרת הנוד – ליכא למגזר רק בפנימי, דבחילון ליכא למגזר, דבכל ענין טהור. והכי משמע לקמן (ד): ה"מ בכלי טהור, אבל בכלי טמא – מגו דמהניא טבילה לחילון, מהני לפנימי! ותירץ לו הר"ר אלחנן: דמתניתין בחילון טהור ופנימי טמא. וכן משמע לישנא, דקתני: מטבילין כלי בתוך כלי. הלכך לא שייך ביה טעמא דכבידו של כלי לגבי חילון, וגם רבא מוקי לה הכי בסמוך, דקאמר: והני מילי בכלי טהור. והיינו מתניתין דמיתוקמא הכי. ומיהו, רש"י מפרש במתניתין: מטבילין כלי בתוך כלי – כששניהם טמאים. ולא נראה, דהא אפי' בכלי שאין בפיו כשפופרת הנוד, אם היו שניהם טמאים – מהני שפיר, דמגו דסלקא לחילון. והשתא לפי סברת רש"י איכא למימר דמצי למימר הכי: איכא בינייהו חילון, אלא כח דהתירא עדיף ליה, דאשכח אף בפנימית סלקא טבילה:

אבא שאול אומר לתרומה וכו'. נ"ע: אמאי לא שרינן בעבר והטביל? והטבילן קאמר, בעבר!

שלא יהא בונה במה לעצמו ושורף פרה לעצמו. דהא לכך נאמנין ע"ה על שמירתה. והכי תניא בתוספתא דחגיגה, ר' יוסי אומר: הכל נאמנין על שמירתה:

לא מקבלין מינייהו. רש"י פירש: דבשעת הגיתות נאמנים, לפי שחבירים מטהרין כליהן. עברו הגיתות והבדים אמרינן דלא מהימן. ול"נ: דפותח בחביתו לא התירו אם לא סופו משום תחילתו, כדקשיא ליה בפרק קמא דבילה (דף יא:). ואם היו טהורים בדין – בלאו הכי נמי משתרי! אלא משמע דחכמים ורבי יהודה שוין בטהורים כל ימות הרגל לחוד, וכן משמע בתלמוד (לקמן דף כו.): "כל ישראל כאיש אחד חברים" – נעשו כולם חברים ברגל. והכי משמע בתוספתא בסיפא:

כמאן מקבלין סהדותא מע"ה כרבי יוסי. הר"ר אלחנן אומר: דקיימא לן כרבי יוסי, וחיישינן לאיבה. לפיכך מזמנין עכשיו בכל ע"ה, אף על גב דאמרינן בברכות (דף מז:): אין מזמנים על ע"ה, וגם רב מנשיא בר תחליפא לא רצה לזמן עליהם. והר"י מפרש דלא כל הרוצה ליטול את השם להחזיק לעצמו כתלמיד חכם, שלא לזמן על ע"ה, בידו ליטול, ואין אנו מחזיקים עצמנו כתלמיד חכם לענין זה:

ניחוש לשאלה. נ"ע: מאי סלקא דעתך דהאי מקשה? פשיטא דבעי טבילה משום מגע עם הארץ:

כלוס

עין משפט נר מצוה

ה א מיי' פי"ב מהלכות אבות הטומאות ה"א:
ו ב מיי' שם הלכה טז:
ז ג ד ה מיי' שם הלכה א ופ"ג מהלכות מקואות הלכה כו ופ"ו הלכה ח טוש"ע י"ד סימן רא סעיף ע:
ח ו מיי' שם פ"ג הלכה כו ופ' יב מהלכות מטמאי משכב ומושב הלכה א:
ט ז מיי' שם פי"א מהלכות מטמאי משכב ומושב הלכה א:
י ח מיי' פי"א מהל' עדות הלכה ב ועי' שם בכ"מ טוש"ע ח"מ סימן לד סעיף יז:
יא ט י כ מיי' פכ"ג מהלכות טומאת מת הלכה א:

[במשנה דמקואות איתא דלי שהוא מלא ולכך כתב הר"ש דהא דאיתא כאן הוא ברייתא ע"ש ולפ"ד הר"ש יש לגרוס הכא דתניא אבל היא גופא נ"ע מ"ט לא הביא הש"ס המשנה]

[תוספתא פ"ג]

מסורת הש"ס

מקואות פ"ו מ"ב [וע"ש בר"ש וברמב"ם ובתוי"ט]

עדיות פ"א מי"ד [במשנה איתא כדברי]

[אמרו להם כצ"ל]

הגהות הב"ח

(א) גמ' ומים המעורבין. נ"ב כלומר או מים המעורבין בשניהם צריך עירוב כשפופרת הנוד: (ב) רש"י ד"ה והני מילי הא דאמרינן: (ג) ד"ה על טהרת יין ושמן ומותר לקבל מידם: (ד) תוס' ד"ה מאי איכא וכו' משמע לקמן דקאמר והני מילי:

גליון הש"ס

גמ' שלא יהא כל אחד ואחד הולך. עי' תוי"ט רפ"ה דפרה:

רבינו חננאל

לתרתי משום מעלה אחת משום חציצה עשר ולרבא אחת עשרה. ואמרינן מאי איכא בין לר' אילא ובין רבא איכא בינייהו סל וגרגותני שמילאן כלים והטבילן שרבי אילא סבר כבידן חוצץ ואין טבילה עולה להן ורבא סבר כי אמרינן אין מטבילין בתוך כלים כגון כוסות בכוסות או כוסות בקערות או קערות בקערות וכיוצא בהן שיש בהן מי שפיהן צר וחיישינן דלמא אתי לאטבולי במי שפיו צר פחות מב' אצבעות שוחקות אבל סל וגרגותני פומייהו רויחן טובא לא חיישינן דהא ליכא סל וגרגותני פחות פומייהו מב' אצבעות ואזדא רבא לטעמיה דאמר סל וגרגותני שמילאן כלים והטבילן טהורין מקוה שחלקה בסל וגרגותני הטובל שם לא עלתה לו טבילה מפני שחולקת את המים ואינן נמצאין מ' סאה במקום אחד. ואי אמרת האיכא נקבים קטנים שהמים מבצבצין בהן כמו נביעת מים לא מטהרין כהאי גוונא דהא ארעא כולה חלחלי מחלחלא ובעינן עד דאיכא מ' סאה במקום אחד וה"מ *) בסל וגרגותני שהן טהורין אבל אם הן טמאין וצריך להטבילן מגו דסלקא להו טבילה סלקא נמי טבילה להני כלין דבגווייהו כמו הדלי דתנן במקואות פ"ו דלי שהוא מלא כלין והטבילן הרי אלו טהורין אם לא טבל המים מעורבין עד שיהא מעורבין כשפופרת הנוד ותריצנה הכי אם לא טבל הכלי אלא הוא טמא וצריך להטבילן כמים מעורבין הן שאין כלי טמא חוצץ ועלתה טבילה לכלי. ואם הדלי טהור שאין צריך טבילה עד שיהו המים מעורבין מה שבמקוה עם המים שבתוך הדלי כשפופרת הנוד. ואם אין שם זה השיעור הדלי כיון שהיה טהור חולק המים כמין כותל בתוך המקוה. ואוקימנא לדר' אילא ודרבא כתנאי. ומקשה מ"ט לא חיישינן לתרומה אלא מטהרינן ובקדש לא מטהרינן דגזרינן בקדש שמא יטבול מחטין וצינוריות בכלי טהור שאין בפיו כשפופרת הנוד בתרומה נמי נגזור ופריק רבא כי מטהרינן בהטבלת כלין בתוך כלין בתרומה לחבירים מטהרינן דידעי ולא אתו לאטבולי בכלי שאין בפיו כשפופרת הנוד. ומקשינן אי הכי קדש נמי נשרי ונימא לחבר שרינן ליה דידע ולא אתי למיטעא. ופרקינן בקדש חיישינן דלמא חזי ליה עם הארץ דטביל כלי בתוך כלי שבפיו כשפופרת הנוד. ומקשינן תרומה נמי נגזור משום עמי הארץ. ופרקינן בכלי שאומר ע"ה אני הטבלתיו בתרומה אין מקבלין הימנו לפיכך לא אכפת לן. אי הכי בקדש נמי לא נקבל מיניה ונטהר כלין הנטבלין בתוך כלי בקדש כמו שמטהרין בתרומה. ופרקינן אם לא נקבל מע"ה טהרת כלין בקדש קושרין איבה על החבירין שיאמרו וכי אנן אין אנו מבני ישראל שאינכם מאמינים אותנו. אי חיישת משום איבת ע"ה אפילו בתרומה ניחוש. ופרקינן בתרומה אין חוששין אם לא יקבלה הכהן חבר ממנו הולך ונותנה לע"ה כהן כמותו אבל הקדש לא יכיל למיהביה אלא לחבר ועלתה משום איבת ע"ה לא מטהרינן כלים בתוך כלים לקדש אפילו לחברים ור' יוסי הוא דחייש לאיבה של ע"ה. וכר' יוסי מקבלין עדותו של ע"ה. ומקשינן ותוב וניחוש לשאלה דלמא שאיל חבר כלי מע"ה לא שאיל. והא מדתנינן כשטיהרת את הכלי טיהרתו לך ולו אלמא שאלו חברים מהם. ופריק רבא כי שאלינן כלים מהם מטבילינן להו אי הכי עד דאמרי ב"ה. והלא טהרתן אוכלין ומשקין שבתוכו לימדו דמטבלינן להו ופריק התם לא יכלי למימר

*) מע"כ רבינו וה"מ בסל וגרגותני נ"ע דהא בסל וגרגותני לעולם יש בהן כשפופרת הנוד ומותר לטבול בהם אף אם הן טהורין ועי' רש"י ד"ה וה"מ ונ"ע.

לְעַצְמוֹ טִהַרְנוּ, אֲבָל נְטַהֵר אֶת הַכְּלִי שֶׁטָּהֳרָתוֹ לְךָ וְלוֹ? תַּנְיָא, *א"ר יְהוֹשֻׁעַ: בּוֹשְׁנִי מִדִּבְרֵיכֶם, ב"ש! אֶפְשָׁר, *אִשָּׁה לָשָׁה בַּעֲרֵיבָה – [א]אִשָּׁה וַעֲרֵיבָה טְמֵאִין שִׁבְעָה וּבָצֵק טָהוֹר?! *[ב]לוֹגִין מָלֵא מַשְׁקִין, – [לוֹגִין] טָמֵא טוּמְאַת שִׁבְעָה וּמַשְׁקִין טְהוֹרִין?! נִטְפַּל לוֹ תַּלְמִיד אֶחָד מִתַּלְמִידֵי ב"ש, אָמַר לוֹ: אוֹמַר לְךָ טַעְמָן שֶׁל ב"ש. אָמַר לוֹ: אֱמוֹר. אָמַר לוֹ: כְּלִי טָמֵא חוֹצֵץ אוֹ אֵינוֹ חוֹצֵץ? א"ל: [ג]אֵינוֹ חוֹצֵץ. כְּלִי שֶׁל עַם הָאָרֶץ טָמֵא אוֹ טָהוֹר? אָמַר לוֹ: טָמֵא. וְאִם אַתָּה אוֹמֵר לוֹ "טָמֵא", כְּלוּם מַשְׁגִּיחַ עָלֶיךָ? וְלֹא עוֹד, אֶלָּא שֶׁאִם אַתָּה אוֹמֵר לוֹ "טָמֵא", אוֹמֵר לְךָ "שֶׁלִּי טָהוֹר וְשֶׁלְּךָ טָמֵא", וְזֶהוּ טַעְמָן שֶׁל ב"ש. מִיָּד הָלַךְ ר' יְהוֹשֻׁעַ וְנִשְׁתַּטַּח עַל קִבְרֵי ב"ש, אָמַר: נַעֲנֵיתִי לָכֶם עַצְמוֹת ב"ש, וּמַה סְתוּמוֹת שֶׁלָּכֶם כָּךְ – מְפוֹרָשׁוֹת עַל אַחַת כַּמָּה וְכַמָּה. אָמְרוּ: כָּל יָמָיו *הוּשְׁחֲרוּ שִׁינָּיו מִפְּנֵי תַּעֲנִיּוֹתָיו. קָתָנֵי מִיהַת: לְךָ וְלוֹ, אַלְמָא: שָׁאֲלִינַן מִינַּיְיהוּ! [ד]כִּי שָׁיְילִינַן מִינַּיְיהוּ – מַטְבְּלִינַן לְהוּ. אִי הָכִי נִיהַדְרוּ לְהוּ ב"ה לְב"ש: כִּי שָׁאֲלִינַן מִינַּיְיהוּ מַטְבְּלִינַן לְהוּ! [ה]טְמֵא מֵת בָּעֵי הַזָּאָה ג' וְז', וּמָנָא לְז' יוֹמֵי לָא מוֹשְׁלֵי אֱינָשֵׁי. וְאַטְבִּילָה לָא מְהֵימְנֵי? וְהָתַנְיָא: [ו]נֶאֱמָנִין עַמֵּי הָאָרֶץ עַל טָהֳרַת טְבִילַת טְמֵא מֵת! אָמַר אַבַּיֵי: ל"ק: הָא – בְּגוּפוֹ, הָא – בְּכֵלָיו. רָבָא אָמַר: אִידִי וְאִידִי בְּכֵלָיו, וְלָא קַשְׁיָא; הָא – דְּאָמַר מֵעוֹלָם לֹא הִטְבַּלְתִּי כְּלִי בְּתוֹךְ כְּלִי וְהָא דְּאָמַר "הִטְבַּלְתִּי אֲבָל לֹא הִטְבַּלְתִּי בִּכְלִי שֶׁאֵין בְּפִיו כִּשְׁפוֹפֶרֶת הַנּוֹד". וְהָתַנְיָא: [ז]נֶאֱמָן עַם הָאָרֶץ לוֹמַר "פֵּירוֹת לֹא הוּכְשְׁרוּ", אֲבָל אֵינוֹ נֶאֱמָן לוֹמַר "פֵּירוֹת הוּכְשְׁרוּ אֲבָל לֹא נִטְמְאוּ". וְאַגּוּפוֹ מִי מְהֵימַן? וְהָתַנְיָא: [ח]חָבֵר שֶׁבָּא לְהַזּוֹת – מַזִּין עָלָיו מִיָּד, עַם הָאָרֶץ שֶׁבָּא לְהַזּוֹת – אֵין מַזִּין עָלָיו עַד שֶׁיֵּעָשֶׂה בְּפָנֵינוּ שְׁלִישִׁי וּשְׁבִיעִי! אֶלָּא אָמַר אַבַּיֵי: מִתּוֹךְ חוֹמֶר שֶׁהֶחְמַרְתָּ עָלָיו בִּתְחִילָּתוֹ – הֵקַלְתָּ עָלָיו בְּסוֹפוֹ. § [ט]"אֲחוֹרַיִם וְתוֹךְ". § מַאי אֲחוֹרַיִם וְתוֹךְ? כִּדְתְנַן: *[י]כְּלִי שֶׁנִּטְמָא אֲחוֹרָיו בְּמַשְׁקִין – אֲחוֹרָיו טְמֵאִין, תּוֹכוֹ אוֹגְנוֹ אָזְנוֹ וְיָדָיו – טְהוֹרִין. נִטְמָא תּוֹכוֹ – כּוּלּוֹ טָמֵא. § "וּבֵית הַצְּבִיטָה וכו'". § מַאי בֵּית הַצְּבִיטָה? א"ר יְהוּדָה אָמַר שְׁמוּאֵל: מָקוֹם שֶׁצּוֹבְטוֹ. וְכֵן הוּא אוֹמֵר: °"וַיִּצְבָּט לָהּ קָלִי". רַבִּי אַסִּי א"ר יוֹחָנָן: מָקוֹם שֶׁנְּקִיֵּי הַדַּעַת *צוֹבְעִין. תָּנֵי רַב בֵּיבָי קַמֵּיהּ דְּר"נ: כָּל הַכֵּלִים אֵין לָהֶם אֲחוֹרַיִם וְתוֹךְ, אֶחָד קָדְשֵׁי הַמִּקְדָּשׁ וְאֶחָד קָדְשֵׁי הַגְּבוּל. א"ל: קָדְשֵׁי הַגְּבוּל מַאי נִינְהוּ – תְּרוּמָה, וְהָתְנַן: אֲחוֹרַיִם וְתוֹךְ וּבֵית הַצְּבִיטָה לַתְּרוּמָה! דִּלְמָא לַחוּלִּין שֶׁנַּעֲשׂוּ עַל טָהֳרַת הַקֹּדֶשׁ קָאָמְרַתְּ. אַדְכַּרְתַּן מִילְּתָא דְּאָמַר רַבָּה בַּר אֲבוּהּ: אַחַת עֶשְׂרֵה מַעֲלוֹת שָׁנוּ כָּאן; שֵׁשׁ רִאשׁוֹנוֹת – בֵּין לַקֹּדֶשׁ בֵּין לַחוּלִּין שֶׁנַּעֲשׂוּ עַל טָהֳרַת הַקֹּדֶשׁ, אַחֲרוֹנוֹת – לַקֹּדֶשׁ, אֲבָל לֹא לַחוּלִּין שֶׁנַּעֲשׂוּ עַל טָהֳרַת הַקֹּדֶשׁ. § [כ]"הַנּוֹשֵׂא אֶת הַמִּדְרָס נוֹשֵׂא אֶת הַתְּרוּמָה אֲבָל לֹא אֶת הַקֹּדֶשׁ". § קֹדֶשׁ מַאי טַעְמָא לָא – [ל]מִשּׁוּם מַעֲשֶׂה שֶׁהָיָה. דְּאָמַר רַב יְהוּדָה אָמַר שְׁמוּאֵל: מַעֲשֶׂה בְּאֶחָד שֶׁהָיָה מַעֲבִיר חָבִית שֶׁל יַיִן קֹדֶשׁ מִמָּקוֹם לְמָקוֹם
וְנִפְסְקָה

רש"י

לְעַצְמוֹ טִהַרְנוּ. הוּא יֹאכְלֵם, שֶׁהֲרֵי הַחֲבֵרִים בְּדֵלִין מֵהֶן וּמִמַּגָּעָן, וּבְלָאו הָכִי מַאֲכָלוֹ טָמֵא: טִהַרְתָּ לְךָ וְלוֹ. שֶׁמָּא תְּשָׁאֲלֶנּוּ וְתִשְׁתַּמֵּשׁ בּוֹ: אִשָּׁה לָשָׁה בַּעֲרֵיבָה. בַּעֲלִיָּיה זוֹ: כְּלוּם מַשְׁגִּיחַ עָלֶיךָ. לְפִיכָךְ טִהֲרוּ לוֹ ב"ש אוֹכָלִין וּמַשְׁקִין וּכְלֵי חֶרֶס. שֶׁאֵין לָהֶן טָהֳרָה אֶלָּא שְׁבִירָתָן, וְאִם בָּאתָ לְאוֹסְרָן עָלָיו לֹא יִשְׁמַע לְךָ. אֲבָל בִּכְלִי שֶׁטֶף – יִשְׁמַע לְךָ, וְיַטְבִּילֶנּוּ: מַטְבִּילִין לְהוּ. שֶׁמָּא הִטְבִּילָם כְּלִי בְּתוֹךְ כְּלִי: וְאַטְבִּילָה לָא מְהֵימְנֵי. דְּקָאָמַר: הַשּׁוֹאֵל מִמֶּנּוּ צָרִיךְ לְהַטְבִּיל: בְּגוּפוֹ. מְהֵימָן: וְהָתַנְיָא. בְּנִיחוּתָא: לֹא הוּכְשְׁרוּ. לֹא נִרְאוּ לְטוּמְאָה: חָבֵר שֶׁבָּא לְהַזּוֹת. וְאָמַר: רָאוּי לְקַבֵּל הַזָּאָה רִאשׁוֹנָה, שֶׁכְּבָר עָבְרוּ ג' יָמִים לְטוּמְאָתוֹ, שֶׁהַיּוֹם יוֹם ג': מִתּוֹךְ חוֹמֶר שֶׁהֶחְמַרְתָּ עָלָיו בַּתְּחִילָּה. כְּשֶׁבָּא לְפָנֶיךָ לְהַזָּאוֹתָיו וְלֹא הֶאֱמַנְתּוֹ – הֵקַלְתָּ עָלָיו בְּסוֹפוֹ לְהַאֲמִינוֹ עַל הַטְּבִילָה, לְפִי שֶׁהוּא נִזְהָר בִּטְבִילָתוֹ שֶׁלֹּא יִצְטָרֵךְ לוֹ עוֹד: כְּלִי שֶׁנִּטְמְאוּ אֲחוֹרָיו. כְּלִי עֵץ אוֹ שֶׁל מַתֶּכֶת קָאָמַר, שֶׁמִּטַּמְּאִין מִגַּבָּן: בְּמַשְׁקִין. דְּטוּמְאָה דְּרַבָּנַן הִיא, דִּמִדְּאוֹרַיְיתָא אֵין אוֹכֶל וּמַשְׁקֶה מְטַמֵּא כְּלִי, שֶׁאֵין כְּלִי מְקַבֵּל טוּמְאָה אֶלָּא מֵאַב הַטּוּמְאָה. וְגָזְרוּ חֲכָמִים שֶׁיְּהוּ מַשְׁקִין מְטַמְּאִין כְּלִי, לְפִי שֶׁיֵּשׁ מַשְׁקֶה שֶׁהוּא אַב הַטּוּמְאָה וּמְטַמֵּא כְּלִי מִן הַתּוֹרָה, כְּגוֹן רוּקּוֹ שֶׁל זָב וּמֵימֵי רַגְלָיו. הִלְכָּךְ, הוֹאִיל וְטוּמְאָה זוֹ מִדִּבְרֵי סוֹפְרִים – אֲחוֹרָיו טְמֵאִין, וּשְׁאָר תַּשְׁמִישִׁין שֶׁבּוֹ טְהוֹרִים, דַּעֲבַדוּ רַבָּנַן הֶיכֵּר לְהוֹדִיעַ שֶׁטּוּמְאָה זוֹ מִדִּבְרֵיהֶם, וְלֹא יִשְׂרְפוּ עָלֶיהָ תְּרוּמָה וְקָדָשִׁים. כָּךְ הִיא מְפוֹרֶשֶׁת בְּמַסֶּכֶת נִדָּה פ"ק: אוֹגְנוֹ. שְׂפָתוֹ הַכְּפוּלָה לְצַד חוּץ, וְרָאוּי לְתַשְׁמִישׁ: אָזְנוֹ. כְּגוֹן אוֹזֶן הֶחָבִית: וְיָדָיו. כְּלִי שֶׁיֵּשׁ לוֹ בֵּית יָד, כְּגוֹן מַחֲבַת: נִטְמָא תּוֹכוֹ. אֲפִילּוּ בְּטוּמְאָה דְּרַבָּנַן, כּוּלּוֹ טָמֵא: שֶׁצּוֹבְטוֹ. שֶׁאוֹחֵז בּוֹ, וּמוֹשִׁיטוֹ לַאֲחֵרִים: וַיִּצְבָּט לָהּ קָלִי. תַּרְגּוּם: וְאוֹשִׁיט לַהּ: נְקִיֵּי הַדַּעַת. אִסְתְּנִיסִים: צוֹבְעִין. מַטְבִּילִין אוֹכָלִין בְּחַרְדָּל אוֹ בְּחוֹמֶץ, שֶׁחוֹקְקִין בְּשׁוּלֵי הַקְּעָרָה בֵּית קִיבּוּל לְעַצְמוֹ וְגוֹבַהּ לוֹ סָבִיב, וְנוֹתְנִין שָׁם חוֹמֶץ וְחַרְדָּל: אֵין לָהֶם אֲחוֹרַיִם. אֵין חִילּוּק (א) לָהֶם שֶׁל אֲחוֹרַיִם וְתוֹךְ, אֶלָּא מִשֶּׁנִּטְמָא אַחַד מֵהֶן – הַכֹּל טָמֵא, בֵּין לְקָדְשֵׁי הַמִּקְדָּשׁ בֵּין לְקָדְשֵׁי הַגְּבוּל: תְּרוּמָה. הַנֶּאֱכֶלֶת בְּכָל גְּבוּל א"י: דִּלְמָא. הַאי קָדְשֵׁי גְּבוּל חוּלִּין שֶׁנַּעֲשׂוּ עַל טָהֳרַת קוֹדֶשׁ קָאָמְרַתְּ וְע"י מִשְׁנָתְךָ זוֹ הוּזְכַּרְתִּי דָּבָר שֶׁשָּׁמַעְתִּי מֵרַבָּה בַּר אֲבוּהּ רַבֵּיהּ דְּרַב נַחְמָן:
וְנִפְסְקָה

תוספות

כלום משגיח בך. פרש"י: אבל כלי שטף – ישמע ספיר ויטבול. ותימה היא: למה ישמע בזה טפי מבאוכלים ומשקין? ואי משום דלית להו טהרה במקוה – משקין מאי איכא למימר? הרי יכול להשיקן! ועוד: כי משקין דמטבלינן להו, ואי לגורכן – למה יטבול להו טפי מכלי חרס! אלא נראה לפרש: כלום משגיח בך? לפיכך לא ישאול לעולם. אבל לא על כלי שטף שישאלם מהם, ולעולם טמאין לחברים:

טמא מת הזאה ג' ושביעי. בהני דלעיל דקאמר כי שיילינן מטבילין, *ודנפלה מעפורת ממנו וב"בנות כותים" (נדה דף לג: ושם) שטבל ודרס אבגדי חבר, דלא טמאו אלא משום עם הארץ ולא חיישינן אטומאת מת – כיון דלא שכיחי לא גזרינן ליה:

ואטבילה לא מהימני והתניא נאמן עם הארץ לומר כו'. פרש"י: כיון דאמר השואל ממנו צריך להטביל – אלמא לא מהימן אטבילה. וקשיא להר"ר אלחנן: מאי פריך ליה ממתני' דנאמן אטומאת מת? הא ע"כ לא קאמר השואל צריך להטביל רק טומאת ערב, אבל טומאת ז' – לא קאמר, דכלי לז' לא מושלי אינשי, כדמסיק. ותירץ מורי, דקאי אהא דקאמר: נהדרו ב"ה לב"ש דמטבילין לכלים. ומסיק דלא דמי, דכיון דמטמא בית שמאי מטעם שאין כלי חרס מציל מטומאת אהל – א"כ בעי הזאה ג' וז', ואם נשתמש בכליהם – נאמן, שהם נאמנים להציל על הכל שלא נטמאו במת. ואמטו להכי פריך אטבילת טמא מת לטהרת כליו בטבילה ממגע טמא מת. דקאמרת שבשאר טומאות מטבילין – לפי שהוא טומאת ערב, אבל הכא – בעי הזאה. לכך לא אהדרי תו ב"ה לב"ש דלא מהני מידי טבילה לדברי ב"ש, דחיישינן בכלים שלא הציל עם הארץ אותו מטומאת אהל. ולהכי פריך: למימרא דלא מהימן לומר שהצילם מאהל, והא תניא נאמן כו'!

מתוך חומר שהחמרת עליו בתחלתו הקלת עליו בסופו. פירש רש"י: תחילתו – הזאתו, סופו – טבילה, ולא יצטרך עוד לחזור ולטבול. ול"ע: דנילף מק"ו; מה כלים שאין נאמן על טבילתן – נאמן על הזאתן, גופו שנאמן על טבילתו – אינו דין שנאמן על הזאתו? ואמר מורי: דעד כאן לא מהימן בהזאת כלים אלא כשבא לפנינו, ואמר שלא נטמאו במת, דלא שכיח. אבל אם בא להזות – אינו נאמן, אפי' בלא גופו. ותניא נמי הכי בתוספתא: ע"ה שבא להזות – מזין עליו ועל כליו אחר ג' ימים. י"מ: תחילתו – בא להזות, סופו – אומר הזיתי. אך היה להם למיגרס: טהרת מת, ואילו בתוספתא תניא: טבילת מת:

כלי שנטמא אחוריו במשקין. דמדאורייתא אין אוכל ומשקה מטמא כלי, ורבנן הוא דגזור משום משקה זב וזבה, כדאיתא בנדה (דף ז:). ועבוד ביה רבנן היכירא לגביה, כי היכי דלא לישרוף עליה תרומה וקדשים, כדאמרינן פרק "אלו מומין" (בכורות דף לח. ושם):

מקום שנקיי הדעת צובעין. פרש"י: חוקקין בשולי הקערה בית קיבול, והגובה סביב, ונותנין בתוך הקיבול חומץ וחרדל. והקשה הר"ר אלחנן: א"כ לתרומה תטמא כולה, כיון דאיטמי החקק? מי גרע מתוך תוכו! וצריך לדחוק ולומר דהכי פי' המתני': אחורים ותוך הצביטה, אם נטמא אחוריו – לא נטמא תוכו ובית הצביטה, נטמא תוכו ובית הצביטה – נטמא אחוריו. א"כ, לפירוש זה, רב יהודה אמר שמואל ורב אסי חלוקין הן בפירוש המשנה, ול"ע:
ונפסקה

רבינו חננאל

למימר דמטבילין להו משום דבטומאת מת פליגי דלאו טבילתו מטהרתו אלא צריך נמי הזאה שלישי ושביעי וכלים לשבעה יומי לא מושלי. זה שהיה רבי יהושע אומר בוש אני מדבריכם ב"ש שהיו אומרים אין כלי ע"ה טהור אלא לגבי אוכלין ומשקין וכלי חרס בלבד אבל כלי ע"ה הנוגע בו טמא מכלל שהכלי עצמו טמא. נמצא אשה שלשה בכלי ע"ה האשה והכלי טמאין והבצק טהור. נמצאו דברים הללו בלא טעם וכשפירש לו אותו תלמיד ב"ש טעם ב"ש ואמר לו כי טעמן של ב"ש מפני שכל כלי ע"ה בחזקת טומאה הן ואע"פ שהן צמיד פתיל וכלי שטף בתוכן כלי מתכת וכיוצא בהן שנמצא זה הכלי כיון שהוא צמיד פתיל חוצץ בפני הטומאה אינו מציל דכיון דבחזקת טומאה הוא קיי"ל אין כלי טמא חוצץ וכי תאמר אי הכי אפילו אוכלים ומשקין נמי ליהוו טמאין. אמר לך ב"ש אוכלין ומשקין דלעצמן הוא מפני שהוא צריך לאכול אתם אם תאמר לו אינם טהורין אינו מקבל ממך שאני (אני) וכליי טהורין מכם הלכך אוכלין ומשקין דלעצמו הן שאין חבר מתארח אצל ע"ה ואינו אוכל ממטעמיו ואם אוכל אתם והם טמאין דינו מסור לשמים אבל בכלים שאנו שואלים מהם חיישנן ומחזקינן להו בחזקת טומאה דע"ה לא מהימן בטהרות. חזר ר' יהושע ואמר נעניתי לכם עצמות ב"ש כו'. ומקשינן וכי ע"ה אם יאמר כי אני הטבלתי הכלים הללו אינו נאמן דאמרת כי שאלינן מינייהו מטבלינן להו. והתנן נאמנים ע"ה על טהרת טבילות טמא מת ופריק אביי כי תניא ההיא דנאמן בגופו וכי אמרינן דאינו נאמן בכליו. רבא אמר הא והא בכליו והא דתניא נאמן בדאמר לא הטבלתי כלי בתוך כלי מעולם וכי האי שאלינן מינייהו לתרומה. אבל אם אמר הין כלי בתוך כלי הטבלתים והוה בפי הכלי רוחב כב' אצבעות שוחקות כי האי גוונא לא מקבלינן מיניה אפילו בתרומה. וכדתניא נאמן ע"ה לומר פירות הללו לא הוכשרו כלל כלומר לא ניתנו עליהן מים מעולם אבל אין נאמנים לומר הוכשרו אבל לא נטמאו הכא נמי נאמן לומר לא הטבלתי כלי בתוך כלי מעולם [אבל] לומר הטבלתי כלי בתוך כלי שפיו רחב כשפופרת הנוד אינו נאמן. ואקשינן ואגופיה מי מהימן. והתניא חבר שבא להזות ואמר היום יום שלישי הוא לטומאתי מזין עליו מיד. ע"ה שבא להזות אין מזין עליו עד שיעשה שלישי ושביעי בפנינו. ופריק אביי מתוך חומר שהחמרת עליו בתחלתו שאין מזין עליו עד שיעשה שלישי ושביעי בפנינו הקלת עליו בסופו כשיאמר טהרתי להיותו נאמן. ועלתה שמועה זו כרבא שאמר אין מטבילין כלי בתוך כלי לקדש מעלה היא לקדש גזירה משום כלי שאין בפיו כשפופרת הנוד. והן אחת עשרה מעלות: מעלה שניה אחורים ותוך [ובית] הצביעה לתרומה אבל לא לקדש. פי' אם נטמא משקין טמאין באחורי הכלים או בבית הצביעה שלהן והוא מקום שתופסו באצבעו תוכו של כלי טהור. ואם יש בתוכו תרומה לא נטמאת ואם יש בתוכו קדש נטמא וזהו שאמרו בכלי שנטמאו אחוריו במשקין אחוריו טמאין. תוכו אוגנו אזנו ידיו טהורין לתרומה אבל לא לקדש נטמא תוכו נטמא כולו. בית הצביעה *) פירש ר' יוחנן מקום שנקיי הדעת שותין בו והוא אצל אזן הכלי שאין אדם ליגע בו כי דרך בני אדם להטות הכלי ולשתות מכנגד אזנו מפני שאוחזין אותו באזניו ונקיי הדעת משנין ואין שותין ממקום שכל אדם שותה בו אלא שותין מאצל אזנו כמו שאמרנו ודרך כ"ה כל הכלים יש להם אחוריים ותוך כגון הכרים והכסתות והשקין והמרצופין כו'. פי' כי הכרים והכסתות משתמשים בהן באחוריהם בשינה שישינים עליהן ומשתמשין עוד בתוכן כדרך אמתחת שמכניסין בתוכן כלים אחרים או תבן וכיוצא בו וישינין עליהן. ותנן נמי כל הכלים יש להן אחוריים ותוך ובית הצביעה ר' טרפון אומר לעריבה גדולה של עץ. ר' עקיבא אומר לכוסות. ר' מאיר אומר לידים טמאות וטהורות. א"ר יוסי לא אמרו אלא לידים הטהורות בלבד. כיצד היו ידיו טהורות ואחורי הכוס טמאין ואחזו בבית צביעתו אינו חושש שמא נטמאו ידיו באחורי הכוס. בכוס שאחוריו טמאין אינו חושש שמא נטמא משקה שבפיו מאחורי הכוס חזר ונטמא את הכוס. קומקומוס שהוא מרתיח אינו חושש שמא יצאו משקין מתוכו ונגעו באחוריו וחזרו לתוכו: כלי הקודש אין להם אחורים ותוך ואין להם בית הצביעה כו' ואסיקנא אמר רבה בר אבוה אחת עשרה מעלות שנו כאן שש ראשונות בין לקדש בין לחולין שנעשו על טהרת הקדש אחרונות לקדש אבל לא לחולין שנעשו על טהרת הקדש: מעלה שלישית הנושא את המדרס נושא את התרומה אבל לא את הקדש. ואמרינן מכדי לא נגע קדש אמאי לא. ואמרינן משום מעשה שהיה שהיה אחד מעביר חבית של יין קדש ממקום למקום
ונפסקה

*) עי' בערוך ערך בית צבע.

עין משפט נר מצוה

יב א ב מיי' פכ"ג מהלכות טומאת מת הלכה ב:
יג ג ד מיי' שם הל' א:
יד ה מיי' פי"א מהלכות פרה הלכה א:
טו ו מיי' פי"א מהלכות מטמאי משכב ומושב הלכה יב:
טז ז מיי' פט"ו מהל' טומאת אוכלין הלכה ב:
[לעיל כ.]
יז ח מיי' פי"א מהל' פרה אדומה הל' ב:
יח ט י מיי' פרק ז מהל' אבות הטומאות הלכה ג ופי"ב שם הל' ב ופי"ג מהלכות כלים הלכה ד:
יט כ ל מיי' פרק י"ב הל' אבות הטומאו' הלכה ג:

מסורת הש"ס

[תוספתא דאהלות פ"ה]
[אהלות פ"ה מ"ד]
[שם במשנה ולקמן כו.]
[נזיר נב:]
ברכות נב. כלים פכ"ה מ"ו נדה ז: בכורות לח.
רות ב
[עי' פירוש נכון בערוך ערך [בית] צבע]

הגהות הב"ח

(א) רש"י ד"ה אין להם וכו' אין חילוק של אחוריים ותוך להם אלא:

ונפסקה רצועה של סנדלו, ונטלה והניחה ע"פ חבית, ונפלה לאויר החבית, ונטמאת. באותה שעה אמרו: הנושא את המדרס נושא את התרומה, אבל לא את הקדש. אי הכי תרומה נמי! [א]הא מני — *ר' חנניה בן עקביא היא, דאמר: לא אסרו אלא בירדן ובספינה, וכמעשה שהיה. מאי היא? דתניא: *[ב]לא ישא אדם מי חטאת ואפר חטאת ויעבירם בירדן ובספינה, ולא יעמוד בצד זה ויזרקם לצד אחר, ולא ישיטם על פני המים, ולא ירכב ע"ג בהמה, ולא על גבי חבירו, אלא אם כן היו רגליו נוגעות בקרקע. אבל מעבירן על גבי הגשר ואינו חושש. אחד הירדן ואחד שאר הנהרות. *ר' חנניה בן עקביא אומר: לא אסרו אלא בירדן, ובספינה, וכמעשה שהיה. *מאי מעשה שהיה? דאמר רב יהודה אמר רב: מעשה באדם אחד שהיה מעביר מי חטאת ואפר חטאת בירדן ובספינה, ונמצא כזית מת תחוב בקרקעיתה של ספינה. באותה שעה אמרו: לא ישא אדם מי חטאת ואפר חטאת ויעבירם בירדן בספינה. איבעיא להו: סנדל טמא, סנדל טהור מהו? חבית פתוחה, חבית סתומה מהו? עבר ונשא מהו? ר' אילא אמר: אם עבר ונשא — טמא, רבי זירא אמר: [ג]עבר ונשא — טהור.§ [ד]"כלים הנגמרים בטהרה כו'".§ דגמרינהו מאן? אילימא דגמרינהו חבר — למה להו טבילה? אלא דגמרינהו עם הארץ — נגמרין בטהרה קרי להו?! אמר רבה בר שילא אמר רב מתנה אמר שמואל: לעולם דגמרינהו חבר, [ה]ומשום צינורא דעם הארץ. דנפל אימת? אילימא מקמי דליגמריה — הא לאו מנא הוא. אלא בתר דגמריה — מיזהר זהיר בהו! — לעולם מקמיה דגמריה, [ו]ודלמא בעידנא דגמריה עדיין לחה היא. טבילה — אין, [ז]הערב שמש — לא. מתני' דלא כר"א. דתנן: *[ח]שפופרת שחתכה לחטאת, ר"א אומר: יטבול מיד, ר' יהושע אומר: יטמא ואחר כך יטבול. והוינן בה: דחתכה מאן? אילימא דחתכה חבר — למה לי טבילה? ואלא דחתכה עם הארץ — בהא לימא ר' יהושע יטמא ויטבול? הא טמא וקאי! ואמר רבה בר שילא אמר רב מתנה אמר שמואל: לעולם דחתכה חבר, ומשום צינורא דעם הארץ דנפל. אימת? אילימא מקמי דליחתכה — הא לאו מנא הוא, ואלא בתר דחתכה — מיזהר זהיר בה! לעולם מקמי דליחתכה, דלמא בעידנא דחתכה עדיין לחה היא. בשלמא לר' יהושע — היינו דאיכא היכירא לצדוקין. דתנן: *[ט]מטמאין היו את הכהן השורף את הפרה, להוציא מלבן של צדוקין, שהיו אומרים: במעורבי שמש היתה נעשית. אלא לר"א, אי אמרת בשלמא בעלמא בעינן הערב שמש — היינו דאיכא היכירא לצדוקין, אלא אי אמרת בעלמא לא בעינן הערב שמש, מאי היכירא לצדוקין איכא! אמר רב: עשאוה

ונפסקה רצועה של סנדלו. מדרס הזב היתה, ונטלה בידו, ומתוך כך נפלה לאויר החבית: ר' חנניה בן עקביא. דאמר: כל מקום שגזרו חכמים על דבר על מעשה שהיה, לא גזרו אלא כדוגמת המעשה, וכאותו דבר. הלכך: בקודש היה מעשה, ובקודש גזרו: ולא יעמוד בצד זה. של נהר: אא"כ רגליו נוגעות בקרקע. משום מעשה שהיה בספינה, כדלקמן. וכל ספינה מהלכת באויר, וגזרו על האוירות כולן: אבל מעבירן על הגשר. הואיל ורגליו נוגעות בו: אלא בירדן. ולא בשאר נהרות. אבל משיטן על פניו, ועומד בצד זה וזורקם לצד אחר: כזית מת תחוב. והאהילו עליו ונטמאו: איבעיא להו סנדל טמא. הא דאמרת דגזרו עליו שלא ישא קודש עמו: סנדל טהור מאי. מי גזור סנדל טהור אטו טמא או לא? חבית פתוחה. ודאי גזור עליו, חבית סתומה מאי? ומשום צינורא דעם הארץ. שמא ניתז עליה רוק מפי עם הארץ כשחבר אוחז בו: הא לאו מנא הוא. ולא ליטמא בכך: עדיין לחה היא. ומטמאה משום שמא זב הוא. ובמסכת נדה (דף נד:) תנן: הזוב והרוק מטמאין לחין ואין מטמאין יבשין: לחטאת. לתת בתוכו אפר פרה: יטבול מיד. שכל תשמישי פרה העשויין בכלי המקבל טומאה טעונין טבילה, וקודם שיעריב שמשו ישתמשו בהן לפרה כדלקמן: [מטמאין היו כו'. נוגעין היו בו שרץ]: להוציא מלבן של צדוקין שהיו אומרים במעורבי שמש היתה נעשית. ולרבנן טבול יום כשר בה, דנפקא להו מריבויא דקרא: "והזה הטהור על הטמא", "טהור" — מכלל שהוא טמא, לימד על טבול יום שכשר בפרה. מכדי בטהור עסקינן ואתי, דכתיב לעיל מיניה: "ולקח אזוב וטבל במים איש טהור" (במדבר יט), למה לי למהדר ולמיכתב "והזה הטהור"? ליכתוב "והזה על הטמא"! אלא: טהור כל דהו. ואשכחן טבול יום דאיקרי טהור, דכתיב: "ורחץ במים וטהר": יטבול מיד. ואין צריך לטמאה טומאה אחרת, שהרי טמאה ועומדת, כדמפרש ואזיל: למה לו טבילה. וכיון דאין לה טומאה — אין היכר לצדוקים בטבול יום שבה: בשלמא לר' יהושע. המצריכה לטמא, היינו דאיכא היכר לצדוקין, שהרי טימאוהו טומאה גמורה הצריכה הערב שמש, וכאן ישתמשו בה טבולת יום — הוי היכר: אלא לרבי אליעזר. שאינו מצריכה אלא טומאה זו: אי אמרת בשלמא בעלמא הצריכו חכמים הערב שמש. בעלמא, בטבילת כלים הנגמרים בטהרה, ודלא כמתני', היינו דהכא לא מצריכין לה — איכא היכירא:

ונפסקה רצועה של סנדלו. אע"ג דגבי טומאה כתיב כלי, והאי רצועה לאו כלי הוא, מדלא שרינן ליה לטלטל בפרק "אלו קשרים" (שבת דף קיב.): אביי *קא אזיל בתר רב יוסף, איפסיק ליה רצועה דסנדלא. ומוכחא דאסור לטלטלה, אלמא לאו מנא הוא! צריך למימר: כגון דנשתייר בהן רצועה, דאיכא מנא דהדיוט יכול להחזירו. ומיהו בירושלמי מלינו*: ונפסקה סנדלו:

לא ישא אדם מי חטאת. ואפילו רבנן דלא בעו כמעשה שהיה, מ"מ לא אחמור מיהא לקדש, רק לחטאת: מת תחוב בקרקעיתה של ספינה. והא דאמר בפרק "דם חטאת" (זבחים דף לג.): מי חטאת שנטמאו, מטהרין, שכן נדה מקבלת הזאה — היינו בשאר טומאות, אבל בטומאת מת נפסלו:

לעולם דגמרינהו חבר. הנוהג לאכול על טהרת קודש משום צינורא דע"ה איכא שאינו אוכל על טהרת הקדש, רק על טהרת תרומה, שטהרתה טומאה היא אצל הקדש. ואי אין צינורא דחבר טמא — מוקמינן ליה בע"ה ממש, והיה קשה למורי: אמאי מוקמינן הכי? לוקמי אפי' בחבר עצמו, וניטמא מחמת הצינורא, דמשקה נינהו, וניטמא הכל מחמת הידים דשניות הן! ונראה לו דידים שניות הן אין להם דרגא דאורייתא רק דרבנן, וידים מטמא כלי ומשקה דרבנן, והוה ליה מעלות בתרייתא ולא קמייתא:

טבילה אין הערב שמש לא. מדלא תנא בהדיא. וכי תימא: א"כ הייתי אומר דלתרומה טבילה מיהא בעיא! וי"ל: דליכא למטעי בהכי, דא"כ לימא בהדיא: צריכין טבילה לתרומה והערב שמש לקדש. הר"ר אלחנן:

שפופרת שחתכה לחטאת. והא דאמרי' (יומא ב.): כל מעשיה היו נעשין בכלי גללים כלי אבנים כלי אדמה, והכא שפופרת של עץ הויא! וכן תנן*: צלוחית שהניחה מגולה ומצאה מכוסה, וסתם צלוחית של חרס! התם דוקא בשעת עשייה בתוך ז' ימים, לפי שהיו מקילים לעשותה במעורבי שמש — היו מחמירין בה שאר חומרות דלא לזלזלו בה, אבל בשאר ימים אין לחושא):

מטמאין היו את הכהן השורף את הפרה. פרש"י: נוגעים היו בו שרץ. אך בתוספתא לא משמע ליה, רק במגע עצמו לחוד. והכי[ב] תניא בתוספתא: כל ז' ימים היו אחיו הכהנים רגילין לפרוש הימנו, וביום השמיני היו נוגעים בו ומטמאין אותו, וחוזרין ומטבילין אותו ונעשית בטבול יום. וז"ל התוספתא*: מעשה בצדוקי הכהן שביקש לשרוף את הפרה, והיה רוצה לשורפה במעורבי שמש. ושמע רבן יוחנן בן זכאי, וסמך ידיו עליו, ואמר לו: אישי כ"ג, כמה נאה לך להיות כהן גדול. ירד וטבל כו'. נהי שאין הצדוקין חוששין אותה טומאה מה שנוגעין בו עכשיו, ולא מעלה של פרה מה שלא נגעו בו כל ז' — מ"מ הכל רואין לדברי חכמים שמגע ע"ה מטמא, ונגעו בו ביום ח' שיש לעשותה בטבול יום:

*עשאוה כטמא מת בז' שלו. כלומר: לבתר הזאה, וכי תימא: א"כ טבילה לא לבעי! איכא למימר: דאף לאחר הזאה בעי טבילה, כדמפרש [ר"ת] *בפ"ג דמגילה, דשתי טבילות יש: אחת לפני הזאה, ואחת לאחר הזאה:

א) [ועיין תוספות יומא ב. ד"ה שכל ותוספות סוכה לז. ד"ה נפל ותוספות חולין ע: ד"ה טמאה ותוספות נדה מט. ד"ה כשר]

ב) [בתוספות יומא ב. ד"ה להוציא הביאו ממשנה דפרה פ"ג מ"ח סמכו כו' נ"ע קצת]

רבינו חננאל

ונפסקה רצועת סנדלו ונטלה והניחה על פי החבית ונפלה לאויר החבית ונטמאת החבית באותה שעה אמרו הנושא את המדרס לא ישא את הקדש ומתניתין רבי חנניה בן עקביא היא דאמר אין גוזרין אלא כמו המעשה שהיה ומעשה שהיה בחבית של הקדש היה ולא בחבית של תרומה לפיכך לא גזרו על התרומה ומאי היא ר' חנניה בן עקביא דתניא [רבי חנניא] בן עקביא אומר לא אסרו אלא בירדן ובספינה כמעשה שהיה מאי היא דאמר רב מעשה באחד שהיה מעביר מי חטאת ואפר חטאת בירדן ובספינה ונמצא כזית מת תחוב בקרקעיתה של ספינה באותה שעה אמרו לא ישא אדם מי חטאת ואפר חטאת ויעבירם בירדן ובספינה. ומיבעיא לן התינח לא ישא אדם סנדל טמאה בידו ובידו האחרת יין קדש. סנדל טהור מאי גזרו טהור אטו טמא אי לא. התינח חבית פתוחה דחיישינן שמא תכנס רצועה באוירה ויטמאנה. חבית סתומה מאי גזרו סתומה אטו פתוחה אי לא. ועוד אמרינן עבר ונשא המדרס והקדש ולא הגיע זה לזה ולא טימא מאי ופשטנא בכולן ר' אילא אומר עבר ונשא טמא. ר' זירא אומר כיון שבריא לן שלא נגע טהור. וכיון דמעלות מדרבנן נינהו קיי"ל כל בדרבנן עבדינן כדברי המיקל: מעלה רביעית בגדי אוכלי תרומה מדרס לקדש. פי' הכהנים הטהורים לאכול התרומה בגדיהם מדרס למי שמבקש לאכול הקדש. ובגדי אוכלי הקדש מדרס לכהן אוכל חטאת כי הקדש קדשים קלים והחטאת קדשי קדשים אלו כולן השנויין בסוף פרק של מעלה מזה כולן מעלה אחת הן חשובין. בגדי ע"ה ובגדי הפרושין ובגדי אוכלי תרומה כולן מדרם לקדש וכ"ש זולתם: מעלה חמישית שבקדש מתיר מטביל ומנגב ואח"כ קושר שהחבל הקשור בכלי חיישינן משום חציצה לקדש אבל בתרומה קושר ואח"כ מטביל. וקיי"ל נימא אחת קשורה חוצצת שלש אינן חוצצות שאינן נהדקות בקשירה והמים באין בהן כ"ש חבל שאינו נהדק כל כך והמים באים ולגבי קדש מעלה בעלמא: מעלה ששית כלים הנגמרין בטהרה צריכין טבילה לקדש אבל לא לתרומה אוקימנא כגון שגמרה חבר ומשום שמא נתזה צינורא של רוק מפי ע"ה קודם שיגמרו ונשאר אותו הרוק לאחר שנגמרו. ואמאי אוקימנא הכי למפשט [משום] דמקמי גמירתן לא מקבלי טומאה ובתר גמירתן חבר מזהר זהיר בהו *) ונתזה צינורא של רוק מפיו עליהן ונשאר הרוק עליהן לח. וצריכין טבילה ולא בעו הערב שמש מדלא מפרש במתניתין הערב שמש אלא טבילה בלבד. ואמרינן נימא מתני' **) דלא כר' יהושע דתנינן שפופרת שחתכה למי חטאת רבי אליעזר אומר יטבול מיד. ר' יהושע אומר יטמא ויטבול. ואוקימנא בשחתכה חבר ומשום צינורא דע"ה דחיישינן דלמא תיכף לחתיכה יגע בה ע"ה ונתן רוק מפיו ונשאר לח על שפופרת זו אחר חתיכה ומשום הכי מצרכינן להטבילה וסבר בעלמא צריכה הערב שמש והכא משום דהוא לגבי מי חטאת אינה צריכה הערב שמש. וכיון דסבר בעלמא כי האי גוונא צריכין הערב שמש נמצאת משנתנו דלא כר' יהושע. ואמרינן בשלמא לר' יהושע היינו דאיכא היכירא לצדוקין דאפילו אם נטמאת אינה צריכה הערב שמש לגבי חטאת ומשום הכי דייקינן מינה דקתני יטמא ויטבול וטהורה מיד ולא בעינן הערב שמש. כדתנן מטמאין היו הכהן השורף את הפרה מפני הצדוקין שלא יהו אומרין במעורבי שמש היתה נעשית. פי' אלא היו מטמאין אותו והיה יורד וטובל ומיד עושה הפרה אלא לר' אליעזר אי אמרת בעלמא נמי לא בעי הערב שמש הכא בשפופרת גבי מי חטאת מאי היכירא לצדוקין

*) אולי צ"ל משו"ה אוקמינן דחיישינן שמא נתזה צינורא של רוק מפיו עליהן קודם שיגמרו ונשאר הרוק וכו'. **) משמע דרבינו גריס נימא מתני' דלא כר"י וכן מסיים בסמוך נמצאת משנתינו דלא כר"י וצ"ע דאינו ראיה כלל וכמו דמסיק בגמ' בסמוך ואולי דט"ס נפל בדברי רבינו וצ"ע.

כ א מיי' פי"ב מהל' אבות הטומאות ה"ג:

[בכ"ד כתוב הוה קאי קמיה]

כא ב מיי' פ"י מהלכות פרה אדומה הל' ב:

[לשון הירושלמי שנקבה חביתו ופקקה בסנדלו]

כב ג מיי' פי"ב מהל' אבות הטומאות הלכה ג:

כג ד ה ו ז מיי' שם הלכה ו:

כד ח מיי' פ"א מהל' פרה אדומה הל' טו:

כה ט מיי' שם הלכה יד:

תוספתא דפרה פ"ח

פרה פ"ט מ"ו יבמות קטז:

[שבת ס:]

יבמות קטז:

נ"א

פרה פ"ה מ"ד

יומא ב. ע"ש זבחים כח. פרה פ"ג מ"ז

שייך לע"ב

[נ"ל בפ"ב דמגילה כ. בד"ה ולא]

גליון הש"ם

תום' ד"ה לעולם וכו' וכ"ל דידים שניות. עיין לעיל דף כ ע"א תוספות ד"ה נימא:

יגא

כו א ב ג מיי' פ"א מהלכות פרה אדומה הלכה טו:
כז ד מיי' פ"ז מהלכות משכב ומושב ה"ח:
כח ה ו מיי' פרק י"ב מהל' אבות הטומאות הלכה ז:
כט ז מיי' פי"ג מהל' פרה אדומה הל' ה:

תורה אור

עֲשָׂאוּהָ כִּטְמֵא שֶׁרֶץ. אֶלָּא מֵעַתָּה לֹא תְּטַמֵּא אָדָם! אַלְמָה תַּנְיָא: [א]חוֹתְכָהּ וּמַטְבִּילָהּ — טָעוּן טְבִילָה. וְאֶלָּא, [ב]עֲשָׂאוּהָ כִּטְמֵא מֵת. אִי הָכִי, תִּיבָּעֵי הַזָּאַת שְׁלִישִׁי וּשְׁבִיעִי! אַלְמָה תַּנְיָא: חוֹתְכָהּ וּמַטְבִּילָהּ — טָעוּן טְבִילָה, טְבִילָה — אִין, [ג]הַזָּאַת שְׁלִישִׁי וּשְׁבִיעִי — לָא! אֶלָּא: עֲשָׂאוּהָ כִּטְמֵא מֵת בַּשְּׁבִיעִי שֶׁלּוֹ. וְהָתַנְיָא: מֵעוֹלָם לֹא חִידְּשׁוּ דָּבָר בְּפָרָה! אָמַר אַבָּיֵי: שֶׁלֹּא אָמְרוּ קוֹרְדוֹם מְטַמֵּא מוֹשָׁב. כִּדְתַנְיָא*: °"וְהַיּוֹשֵׁב עַל (ויקרא טו) הַכְּלִי", [ד]יָכוֹל כָּפָה סְאָה וְיָשַׁב עָלֶיהָ, תַּרְקַב וְיָשַׁב עָלֶיהָ, יְהֵא טָמֵא? ת"ל: "וְהַיּוֹשֵׁב עַל הַכְּלִי אֲשֶׁר יֵשֵׁב עָלָיו יִטְמָא" — מִי שֶׁמְּיוּחָד לִישִׁיבָה, יָצָא זֶה, שֶׁאוֹמְרִים לוֹ עֲמוֹד וְנַעֲשֶׂה מְלַאכְתֵּנוּ.§ [ה]"הַכְּלִי מְצָרֵף מַה שֶּׁבְּתוֹכוֹ לַקֹּדֶשׁ אֲבָל לֹא לַתְּרוּמָה".§ מנה"מ? *א"ר חָנִין, [ו]דְּאָמַר קְרָא: °"כַּף (במדבר ז) אַחַת עֲשָׂרָה זָהָב מְלֵאָה קְטֹרֶת" — הַכָּתוּב עֲשָׂאוֹ לְכָל מַה שֶּׁבַּכַּף אַחַת. מְתִיב רַב *כָּהֲנָא: *הוֹסִיף ר"ע: הַסֹּלֶת וְהַקְּטֹרֶת וְהַלְּבוֹנָה וְהַגֶּחָלִים, שֶׁאִם נָגַע טְבוּל יוֹם בְּמִקְצָתוֹ — פָּסַל אֶת כּוּלּוֹ. וְהָא דְּרַבָּנַן הִיא! מִמַּאי — מִדְּקָתָנֵי רֵישָׁא: הֵעִיד רַבִּי שִׁמְעוֹן בֶּן בְּתֵירָא [ז]עַל אֵפֶר חַטָּאת שֶׁנָּגַע הַטָּמֵא בְּמִקְצָתוֹ, שֶׁטִּימֵּא אֶת כּוּלּוֹ. וְקָתָנֵי: הוֹסִיף ר"ע! אָמַר ר"ל מִשּׁוּם בַּר קַפָּרָא:
לָא

עֲשָׂאוּהָ כִּטְמֵא שֶׁרֶץ. לְעוֹלָם בְּעָלְמָא לָא בָּעֵי הֶעֱרֵב שֶׁמֶשׁ ר"א לְכֵלִים הַנִּגְמָרִים בְּטָהֳרָה, וְאפ"ה אִיכָּא הֶיכֵּירָא. לְפִי שֶׁשְּׁפוֹפֶרֶת שֶׁל חַטָּאת (א) עֲשָׂאָן כְּאִילּוּ נָגְעוּ בְּשֶׁרֶץ לְעִנְיַן מִנְיַן רִאשׁוֹן וְשֵׁנִי, הִלְכָּךְ: אִי לָאו דְּפָרָה נַעֲשֵׂית בִּטְבוּלֵי יוֹם — זוֹ הָיְתָה צְרִיכָה הֶעֱרֵב שֶׁמֶשׁ: אֶלָּא מֵעַתָּה. דְּלָא עֲשָׂאוּהָ אֶלָּא כִּטְמֵא שֶׁרֶץ: לֹא תְּטַמֵּא אָדָם. דְּהָא טְמֵא שֶׁרֶץ לָאו אַב הַטּוּמְאָה הוּא, וְאֵינוֹ מְטַמֵּא אָדָם. שֶׁלֹּא מָצִינוּ טוּמְאָה לְאָדָם וְכֵלִים הַנּוֹגְעִין בְּטָמֵא שֶׁקִּיבֵּל טוּמְאָה מֵאֲחֵרִים חוּץ מִטְּמֵא מֵת, שֶׁנֶּאֱמַר: "וְהַנֶּפֶשׁ הַנּוֹגַעַת תִּטְמָא עַד הָעָרֶב" (במדבר יט): כִּטְמֵא מֵת. כְּאִילּוּ נִטְמָא בְּמֵת שֶׁמְּטַמֵּא אָדָם: לֹא חִידְּשׁוּ דָּבָר בְּפָרָה. אע"פ שֶׁעָשׂוּ בָּהּ מַעֲלוֹת הַרְבֵּה, בִּשְׁבִיל הַזִּלְזוּל הַזֶּה שֶׁהָיוּ מְטַמְּאִין כֹּהֵן הַשּׂוֹרְפָהּ לַעֲשׂוֹתוֹ טְבוּל יוֹם — לֹא חִידְּשׁוּ בִּגְזֵרוֹת מַעֲלוֹתֶיהָ דָּבָר שֶׁאֵינוֹ מָצוּי בְּשׁוּם מָקוֹם. וְאִם כְּשֶׁאָמַרְתָּ שֶׁעָשׂוּ בָּהּ כֵּלִים הַנִּגְמָרִין בְּטָהֳרָה כִּטְמֵא מֵת — הֲרֵי אֵין לְךָ חִדּוּשׁ גָּדוֹל מִזֶּה: שֶׁלֹּא אָמְרוּ קוֹרְדוֹם מְטַמֵּא מוֹשָׁב. כְּלוֹמַר: לֹא נָתְנוּ טוּמְאָה בְּפָרָה לִכְלִי שֶׁאֵינוֹ רָאוּי לְטוּמְאָה, כְּגוֹן לוֹמַר קוֹרְדוֹם שֶׁאֵינוֹ מְיוּחָד לִישִׁיבָה וְאֵינוֹ נַעֲשֶׂה אַב הַטּוּמְאָה בְּמוֹשַׁב הַזָּב (ב) בְּפָרָה. אֲבָל בִּכְלִי הָרָאוּי לְקַבֵּל טוּמְאָה — חִידְּשׁוּ בָּהּ לַעֲשׂוֹת שֶׁאֵינוֹ נוֹגֵעַ בְּמֵת כְּנוֹגֵעַ בְּמֵת: תַּרְקַב. חֲצִי סְאָה: אֲשֶׁר (ג) יֵשֵׁב. מִדְּלָא קָרֵינַן "אֲשֶׁר יָשַׁב" לָמַדְנוּ שֶׁאֵינוֹ מְדַבֵּר אֶלָּא בַּאֲשֶׁר מְיוּחָד לֵישֵׁב שָׁם תָּמִיד: הוֹסִיף ר"ע כו'. רֵישָׁא קָתָנֵי הֵעִיד ר"ש עַל אֵפֶר חַטָּאת שֶׁנָּגַע טָמֵא בְּמִקְצָתוֹ פָּסַל אֶת כּוּלּוֹ: לְבוֹנָה וְגֶחָלִים. אע"ג דְּלָאו אוֹכֶל נִינְהוּ — חִיבַּת הַקֹּדֶשׁ מַכְשַׁרְתָּן לְטוּמְאָה: פָּסַל אֶת כּוּלָּן. לְפִי שֶׁהַכְּלִי מְצָרְפָן יַחַד. וְהַךְ עֵדוּת מִדְּרַבָּנַן הִיא, מִדְּקָתָנֵי רֵישָׁא עַל אֵפֶר חַטָּאת כו'. וְהַהִיא וַדַּאי עַל כָּרְחָךְ דְּרַבָּנַן הִיא, דְּאִי מִקְּרָא דְּרַ' חָנִין — לֵיכָּא לְמֵילַף אֶלָּא קָדְשֵׁי מִזְבֵּחַ, אֲבָל אֵפֶר פָּרָה — לָא:
לא

יצא זה שאומרים לו עמוד ונעשה מלאכתנו. בפרק "ר"ע" (שבת דף פד: ושם) עביד ק"ו: ומה פכין קטנים שטהורים בזב כו', שאין להם תוך הראוי למגע בשר בזב, טמאים במת, מפץ שטמא במדרס – אינו דין שטמא במת. והקשה הר"ר אברהם: מכל הכלים ליעבד ק"ו שאין בני מדרס, כדאמרינן הכא: עמוד ונעשה מלאכתנו – טמאים במת, מפץ כו', ועוד קשה לר"י: ליעבד ק"ו מכלי חרס גדולים, שטהורים אפי' פתוחים במדרס הזב, כדאיתא בפרק "ר"ע" (ג"ז שם) [דיליף מדכתיב (במדבר יט): "וכל כלי פתוח אשר אין צמיד פתיל עליו" בטומאת מת משתעי קרא, מפץ כו'. וי"ל: דלא דמי, דכל הכלים הא דלא מטמאו מדרס – לאו משום דכלי הן, אלא משום דלאו בני מדרס נינהו, דלא שייך שם. וכן כלי חרס גדולים דטהורים במדרס, וטמאים בשאר טומאת הזב – התם משום טומאת מת ושרץ [בתוך] רחמנא תליא, דאיתקש לשק כל כלי עץ. אבל טומאת מדרס – לאו מטעם תוך הוי, אלא מטעם מיוחד לישיבה. הלכך, מפץ שמטמא מדרס, והוא דינו – לא יטמא במת, כיון דלית ליה תוך. אבל השתא עבדינן ק"ו מפכין קטנים, שטהור בהם מגע והיסט, שישנן בכלל גדולים ושייך ביה מטעם תוך, והכא טהור מטעם גזרת הכתוב, דכיון דלא שייך ביה מגע בשר הזב – גם מגע שערו ומעיינו לא שייך ביה, ושוו אפ"ה הן לטומאת מת כגדולים, כ"ש דמפץ שיש שם גם טומאה דזב, כגון מדרס, שיטמא במת. ותו לא שייך לחלק: שכן מיוחד לישיבה, דהואיל ומהני בו יחוד ישיבה, דלא שייך לפכין קטנים מטעם תוך, ואפ"ה יהו טמאים מדרס הזב, הוי הק"ו גמור, הואיל ולית להו טומאת תוך דשייכא בהו. הר"י:

שאם נגע טבול יום במקצתו. הקשה הר"ר נסים גאון: דמשמע הכא דנתקדשו בכלי, מדמהני בהו לרוף, ואילו בשילהי פרק "טרף בקלפי" ביומא (דף מד: ושם): נתפזרו לו קב גחלים – מכבדן לאמה. והיכי מכבדן? הא מפסיד בקדש! ותירץ דבירושלמי דמכילתין מוקמי לה (ד) בשל יום הכפורים ההיא דהכא. וזה לשון ירושלמי: ר' יוסי בר חנינא בשם ר' יוחנן: מפני מה אומרים שְׁיָרֵי מנחות מחברין את עצמן – מפני שנזקקו לכליין, ר' אחא אומר בשם ר"ל: יודעים היו שכלי שרת מחברן, מה באו להעיד – על הסלתות על הלבונה ועל הקטורת ועל הגחלים. ניחא סולת, קטורת ולבונה גחלים מאי? א"ר בון: תיפתר בגחלים של יוה"כ, שבמה שהיה חותה היה מכנים. אבל של כל יום – לא, כההיא דתנן: נתפזר ממנו קב גחלים מכבדו לאמה. ומיהו, הר"י היה מפרש הירושלמי הכי: גחלים מאי? כלומר, למה פוסל את כולם, כיון שיש הרבה שאינו לריך? ומוקי לה בשל יוה"כ, דהכל לריך. וה"ה דמלי לאוקמי במחתה של כל יום, אלא משום דלא פסיק ליה אי מחתה של כסף שחותה בה קדושה אי לא, וכלי שרת מחבלן משמע כל כלי שמכניסין, דומיא דלבונה וקטורת. וכ"ת: הא אמרינן בסמוך דמדרבנן מיהא, אפילו שאינו לריך לכלי – כלי נמי מלרף! איכא למימר: היינו למ"ד לירוף דאורייתא, אבל למ"ד לירוף דרבנן – לא יועיל כלום. והשתא דאתינן להכי, גם מה שהקשה הרב ר' נסים יתכן דכלי אינו מלרף רק הראוי לו, ומה שאין לריך לו בו ביום – אין בכך כלום אם מפסיקו. ור"ת מתרץ: דכלי שרת אין מקדשין אלא לדעת. אך קשה להר"ר אלחנן: דפלוגתא היא שילהי "לולב וערבה" (סוכה דף מט: ושם) וי"א מקדשין! ומיהו, פ"ק דמנחות (דף ז.) וב"התודה" (שם דף עח: ושם) איכא מאן *דמוכח מן "ולקחו את כל כלי השרת" (במדבר ד) דאין מקדשין אלא לדעת. ופלוגתא דאמוראי הוא דהוי, דלא אשכחן פלוגתא דתנאי. וי"מ: מחתה דכסף אינה קדושה כי אם חותה שמערה בה, ונתפזרו לו קב גחלים דמכבדן לאמה – איירי במחתה של כסף. וקשה להר"ר אלחנן: דהא מזבח מקדש את דבר הראוי לו! ולא ידענא מאי תיובתיה, דהא מוריד גחלים מן המזבח לארץ פליגי בה רבי יוחנן ור"ל, משמע דלא שייך בגחלים ראוי למזבח*):

והא דרבנן הוא. משמע: הא לאו הכי – הוה שייך שפיר לירוף דאורייתא, מדלא קדייק רק מ"הוסיף". ועוד: מדקאמר ממאי דהאי לירוף מדרבנן – אלמא דאית ליה דאורייתא. וכן בפ"ב דפסחים (דף לה.): "והבשר כל טהור יאכל בשר" – לרבות עלים ולבונה. וכן בפ"ב דחולין (דף לו:): אלא חיבת הקדש מכשרת דאורייתא מנלן כו', אלא מסיפא: "כל טהור יאכל בשר" – לרבות עלים ולבונה. ובפרק "כל הפסולים" (זבחים דף לד.): טמא שאכל קדש לפני זריקה, חד אומר: לוקה, וחד אומר: אינו לוקה. אבל בטומאת בשר – דברי הכל לוקה, דאמר קרא: "והבשר כו'" ואמר מר: לרבות עלים ולבונה. אלמא: עיקר קרא להכי הוא דאתא. ובפרק "כל שעה" (פסחים דף כד:): "והבשר" למה לי? לרבות עלים ולבונה. בשר למה לי – לרבות אימורין כו'. והא דקאמר בזבחים שילהי "ב"ש" (דף מו.), והאמר מר: "והבשר" – לרבות עלים ולבונה! ומשני: לפסול בעלמא. התם מדאורייתא מיהא הוי פסול להקרבה, ולא קאמר דהוי פסול אלא לאפוקי איכא דאמר התם לוקה. וכי אומרים בפסחים (דף לה.): עלים ולבונה בני קבלת טומאה נינהו וכי אוכלין נינהו? אלא מעלה דאורייתא מיהא הוי, ומעלה דלאו אוכל הוא ושוי ליה אוכל. וכן מייתי התם: הערב שמשו אוכל בתרומה כו'. הביא כפרתו כו' והאי גברא חזי, אלא מעלה. והתם דאורייתא הוא, דהא ב"הערל" (יבמות דף עד:) מפיק ליה מקרא, דקאמר: ג' קראי כתיבי. והשתא משמע דלעולם הוי לירוף דאורייתא גבי עלים ולבונה, וכי קאמר התלמוד בפרק "הקומץ רבה" (מנחות דף כא.) ילאו עלים ולבונה שאין מקבלין טומאה – י"ל דר"ל בלי הכשר, אע"ג דחיבת הקדש מכשרתו דאורייתא, מ"מ לא פסיק ליה כיון דעלי חולין לא מקבלי טומאה דאורייתא אפי' בהכשר, אי לאו יתורא דקרא. א"כ איכא למימר דלא מרבינן אלא בהכשר, וכי קאמר בפסחים (דף יט.): אלמא לירוף דרבנן – דעדותו דר"ע דרבנן, אבל עלים ולבונה – לעולם דאורייתא. ולא כפרש"י דקאמר, דדייק התם לירוף דגבי מעלות דרבנן. ולר"ע דעלים ולבונה לאו בנות קבולי טומאה נינהו דאורייתא, דלאו אוכל הוא – לא יתכן, כדפרישית בכל הני שהבאתי. וגם משמעות דשמעתין לא משמע הכי, אלא דייק דלירוף דרבנן מהא דקתני רישא: העיד רבי שמעון על אפר חטאת וכו' ואפר
חטאת

שבת נט. נדה מט:

[פסחים יט.]

פסחים שם יומא מח. [עדיות פ"ח מ"א]

[עיין תוספות מנחות כד. ד"ה שאין וכו' לירוף דאורייתא]

[הוכחה זו לא מצאתי וכן נשאלתי מהגאב"ד מהר"י זצ"ל]

*) [ועי' תוס' יומא מו: ד"ה כי פליגי]

הגהות הב"ח

(א) רש"י ד"ה עשאוה וכו' של חטאת עשאוהו כאילו נגע בשרץ: (ב) ד"ה שלא אמרו וכו' במושב הזב שיהא טמא בפרה: (ג) ד"ה אשר יֵשֵׁב מדלא קרינן אשר יָשַׁב: (ד) תום' ד"ה שאם וכו' דבירושלמי דמכילתין מוקמי לה ההוא דהכא בשל יום הכפורים וזה לשון ירושלמי:

רבינו חננאל

לצדוקין איכא ופריק ר' זירא עשאוה לשפופרת זו כטמא שרץ חילוף כל הכלים הנגמרין בטהרה וכל טמא שרץ בעי הערב שמש וזו להוציא מן הצדוקין לא הצריכוה הערב שמש. ומקשינן אי הכי דשפופרת זו כטמא שרץ היא לא תטמא אדם אלמא תניא חותכה ומטבילה וטעון טבילה פי' החותכה נמי בעי טבילה. ואסיקנא אלא עשאוה לשפופרת זו כטמא מת ביום שביעי שלו דלא בעי הזאה ובעי הערב שמש. ומקשינן איני דלעלמא כלין הנגמרין בטהרה מטבלינן להו משום חששא דלמא ניתזה צינורא מפי ע"ה עליה ונשארה לחה עד אחר גמירתה ולגבי מי חטאת עשאוה לשפופרת שחתכה למי חטאת כטמא מת בשביעי שלו ומשום הכי מטבלינן לה. והתניא לא חדשו דבר בפרה כלומר לא החמירו בפרה משאר טמאות דעלמא. ופריק אביי מאי לא חדשו שלא אמרו קורדום מטמא מושב משום חומרא דפרה אלא כיון דעלמא לא הוי קרדום מטמא מושב לגבי פרה נמי לא הוי מושב. כדתניא והיושב על הכלי אשר ישב עליו הזב יטמא. אשר ישב מי שמיוחד לישיבה יצא זה שאומרים לו עמוד ונעשה מלאכתנו. אלו שש מעלות נוהגות בקדש ובחולין שנעשו על טהרת הקדש וכדרב נחמן אבל חמש האחרונות נוהגות בקדש ואין נוהגות בחולין שנעשו על טהרת הקדש: מעלה שביעית הכלי מצרף מה שבתוכו לקדש אבל לא לתרומה. וא"ר חנין צירוף זה מן התורה שנאמר כף אחת עשרה זהב וגו' כיון שכתיב כף ידענו שהיא אחת אחת דכתב רחמנא למה לי אלא ללמדך שכל מה שבכף אחת. ומותיב רב כהנא הוסיף ר' עקיבא הסולת והקטרת והלבונה והגחלים שאם נגע טבול יום במקצתו שפסל כולו. והא מדרבנן היא מדקתני רישא העיד ר' שמעון בן בתירא על אפר חטאת שנגע טמא

לָא נְצְרְכָא אֶלָּא לְשְׁיָרֵי מִנְחָה. דְּאוֹרַיְיתָא, *צָרִיךְ לַכְּלִי הַכְּלִי מְצָרְפוֹ, שֶׁאֵ"צ לַכְּלִי — אֵין כְּלִי מְצָרְפוֹ, וְאָתוּ רַבָּנַן וְגָזְרוּ דְּאע"ג דְּאֵינוֹ צָרִיךְ לַכְּלִי — כְּלִי מְצָרְפוֹ. תֵּינַח סֹלֶת, קְטוֹרֶת וּלְבוֹנָה מַאי אִיכָּא לְמֵימַר? אָמַר רַב נַחְמָן אָמַר רַבָּה בַּר אֲבוּהּ: כְּגוֹן שֶׁצְּבָרָן עַל גַּבֵּי קַרְטַבְלָא. דְּאוֹרַיְיתָא, יֵשׁ לוֹ תּוֹךְ מְצָרֵף, אֵין לוֹ תּוֹךְ — אֵינוֹ מְצָרֵף, [א]וְאָתוּ רַבָּנַן וְתִיקְּנוּ דְּאע"ג דְּאֵין לוֹ תּוֹךְ — מְצָרֵף. וּפְלִיגָא דְּר' חָנִין אַדְּר' חִיָּיא בַּר אַבָּא. *דְּא"ר חִיָּיא בַּר אַבָּא א"ר יוֹחָנָן: [ב]מֵעֵדוּתוֹ שֶׁל רַבִּי עֲקִיבָא נִשְׁנֵית מִשְׁנָה זוֹ. § [ג]"הָרְבִיעִי בַּקֹּדֶשׁ פָּסוּל". § תַּנְיָא, א"ר יוֹסֵי: *מִנַּיִן לָרְבִיעִי בַּקֹּדֶשׁ שֶׁהוּא פָּסוּל? וְדִין הוּא: [ד]וּמַה מְחוּסַּר כִּפּוּרִים שֶׁמּוּתָּר בִּתְרוּמָה — פָּסוּל בַּקֹּדֶשׁ, שְׁלִישִׁי שֶׁפָּסוּל בִּתְרוּמָה — אֵינוֹ דִּין שֶׁיֵּעָשֶׂה רְבִיעִי לַקֹּדֶשׁ? וְלָמַדְנוּ שְׁלִישִׁי לַקֹּדֶשׁ מִן הַתּוֹרָה, וּרְבִיעִי בְּק"ו. שְׁלִישִׁי לַקֹּדֶשׁ מִן הַתּוֹרָה [ה]מִנַּיִן? דִּכְתִיב: °"וְהַבָּשָׂר אֲשֶׁר יִגַּע בְּכָל טָמֵא לֹא יֵאָכֵל", מִי לָא עָסְקִינַן דְּנָגַע בְּשֵׁנִי — וְקָאָמַר רַחֲמָנָא: "לֹא יֵאָכֵל". רְבִיעִי מִקַּל וָחוֹמֶר — הָא דַּאֲמָרַן. § [ו]"וּבִתְרוּמָה אִם נִטְמֵאת כו'". § אָמַר רַב שֵׁיזְבִי: בְּחִיבּוּרִין שָׁנוּ, אֲבָל שֶׁלֹּא בְּחִיבּוּרִין — לֹא. אֵיתִיבֵיהּ אַבַּיֵי: יָד נְגוּבָה — מְטַמָּא חֲבֵירְתָּהּ, לְטַמֵּא לַקֹּדֶשׁ, אֲבָל לֹא לִתְרוּמָה, דִּבְרֵי רַבִּי. ר' יוֹסֵי בְּרַבִּי יְהוּדָה אוֹמֵר: [ז]לִפְסוֹל, אֲבָל לֹא לְטַמֵּא. אִי אָמְרַתְּ בִּשְׁלָמָא שֶׁלֹּא בְּחִיבּוּרִין — הַיְינוּ רְבוּתֵיהּ דִּנְגוּבָה. אֶלָּא אִי אָמְרַתְּ בְּחִיבּוּרִין אִין, שֶׁלֹּא בְּחִיבּוּרִין לָא — מַאי רְבוּתָא דִּנְגוּבָה? [א]אִיתְּמַר *)נַמִי, אָמַר רֵישׁ לָקִישׁ: לֹא שָׁנוּ אֶלָּא יָדוֹ אֲבָל

וייקרא ז

רש"י

לא נצרכא. לְהַאי עֵדוּת דְּרַבִּי עֲקִיבָא דְּמִדְּרַבָּנַן אֶלָּא לְסוֹלֶת שֶׁל שְׁיָרֵי מִנְחָה: דְּאִלּוּ מִדְּאוֹרַיְיתָא הַצָּרִיךְ לַכְּלִי. דּוּמְיָא דִּקְטוֹרֶת שֶׁבַּכַּף, דְּאַיְירֵי בֵּהּ קְרָא, כְּלִי מְצָרְפוֹ. וְשֶׁאֵינוֹ צָרִיךְ לַכְּלִי, כְּגוֹן שְׁיָרֵי מִנְחָה שֶׁהֵן אֲכִילַת כֹּהֵן — אֵין הַכְּלִי מְצָרְפָן: מַאי איכא לְמֵימַר. הֲרֵי צְרִיכִין לַכְּלִי: קַרְטַבְלָא. עוֹר שָׁלוּק: ופליגא הא דְּרַבִּי חָנִין. דְּאָמַר לְעֵיל: צֵירוּף דְּאוֹרַיְיתָא, אַדְּר' חִיָּיא בַּר אַבָּא: מחוסר כפורים כָּשֵׁר לִתְרוּמָה וּפָסוּל לַקֹּדֶשׁ. בִּיבָמוֹת יָלְפִינַן לָהּ מִקְּרָאֵי, בְּפֶרֶק "הֶעָרֵל" (דף עד:): שלישי שֶׁפָּסוּל בִּתְרוּמָה. כִּדְנָפְקָא לָן ק"ו בְּמַסֶּכֶת סוֹטָה (דף כט.*): וּמַה טְבוּל יוֹם שֶׁמּוּתָּר בְּמַעֲשֵׂר — אָסוּר בִּתְרוּמָה, שֵׁנִי שֶׁפָּסוּל בְּמַעֲשֵׂר — אֵינוֹ דִּין שֶׁיֵּעָשֶׂה שְׁלִישִׁי בִּתְרוּמָה(א)?! אינו דין שֶׁיֵּעָשֶׂה רביעי לַקֹּדֶשׁ. וְא"ת: דַּיּוֹ לַבָּא מִן הַדִּין לִהְיוֹת כַּנִּדּוֹן! א"כ ק"ו לָא צָרִיךְ, שֶׁהֲרֵי לָמַדְנוּ שְׁלִישִׁי לַקֹּדֶשׁ מִן הַתּוֹרָה, וְהֵיכָא דְּמִיפְרִיךְ ק"ו — לָא אָמְרִינַן דַּיּוֹ לַבָּא מִן הַדִּין לִהְיוֹת כַּנִּדּוֹן, כִּדְאָמְרִינַן בְּבָבָא קַמָּא (דף כה.). וּלְמ"ד נַמִי אָמְרִינַן דַּיּוֹ, הָנֵי מַעֲלוֹת דְּרַבָּנַן נִינְהוּ וְלָאו דְּאוֹרַיְיתָא. וְהַאי דְּנָקַט וְלָמַדְנוּ שְׁלִישִׁי לַקֹּדֶשׁ — מִלְּתָא בְּעָלְמָא הִיא, דְּאַשְׁמָעִינַן דִּשְׁלִישִׁי לַקֹּדֶשׁ מִן הַתּוֹרָה הוּא: מי לא עסקינן כו'. מִי לָא מַשְׁמַע (כו') נַמִי מֵהַאי קְרָא: דנגע בשני. דְּהָא אַשְׁכַּחַן דְּאִיקְרִי שֵׁנִי טָמֵא, דִּכְתִיב: "כֹּל אֲשֶׁר בְּתוֹכוֹ יִטְמָא", וְה"ל הַכְּלִי רִאשׁוֹן וּמַה שֶּׁבְּתוֹכוֹ שֵׁנִי, וְקָרֵי לֵיהּ טָמֵא. וְקָאָמַר רַחֲמָנָא: "וְהַבָּשָׂר אֲשֶׁר יִגַּע בְּכָל טָמֵא" (ב) — בְּשֵׁנִי, וְה"ל שְׁלִישִׁי — "לֹא יֵאָכֵל". וְהַאי קְרָא בִּבְשַׂר שְׁלָמִים כְּתִיב: בחיבורין שנו. מַתְנִיתִין דְּקָתָנֵי: יָד מְטַמְּאָה אֶת חֲבֵירְתָּהּ לַקֹּדֶשׁ — כְּגוֹן שֶׁבְּעוֹד שֶׁהַיָּד הַטְּמֵאָה נוֹגַעַת לַטְּהוֹרָה הָיְתָה טְהוֹרָה נוֹגַעַת בַּקֹּדֶשׁ, דְּגָזוּר רַבָּנַן דִּלְמָא אָתֵי לְמִיגַּע טְמֵאָה בַּקֹּדֶשׁ. וּלְמ"ד (ג) פָּסוּל לְקַמָּן — לִפְסוֹל, דְּמַעֲלָה בְּעָלְמָא הִיא: אבל שלא בחיבורין. שֶׁלְּאַחַר שֶׁפֵּירְשָׁה מִן הַטְּהוֹרָה חָזְרָה טְהוֹרָה וְנָגְעָה בַּקֹּדֶשׁ טָהוֹר, וְאֵין יָד מְטַמְּאָה חֲבֵירְתָּהּ לַעֲשׂוֹתָהּ אֲפִי' שְׁלִישִׁית לִפְסוֹל: יד נגובה. אע"פ שֶׁאֵין בָּהּ מַשְׁקִין: לטמא את הַקֹּדֶשׁ. לַעֲשׂוֹת רְבִיעִי: ר' יהודה אומר. חֲבֵירְתָּהּ פּוֹסֶלֶת אֶת הַקֹּדֶשׁ, אֲבָל לֹא מְטַמְּאָה: אי אמרת בשלמא שלא בחיבורין. קָאָמַר דִּמְטַמְּאָה — הַיְינוּ רְבוּתָא דִּנְגוּבָה(ד), וְאע"ג דִּנְגוּבָה הִיא כְּשֶׁנָּגְעָה בָּזוֹ, וְאֵין לָחוּשׁ שֶׁמָּא נָגְעָה הַיָּד הַטְּהוֹרָה בְּמַשְׁקִין שֶׁבַּטְּמֵאָה שֶׁהֵן רִאשׁוֹנִים, דְּכָל הַפּוֹסֵל אֶת הַתְּרוּמָה מְטַמֵּא מַשְׁקִין לִהְיוֹת תְּחִלָּה, וְהָוְיָא לָהּ הַךְ יָד נַמִי שְׁנִיָּה מֵחֲמַת הַמַּשְׁקִין כְּמוֹ חֲבֵירְתָּהּ, אֲפִילּוּ הָכִי מְטַמְּאָה, דְּמַעֲלָה דְּרַבָּנַן הִיא שֶׁהַיָּד מְטַמְּאָה אֶת חֲבֵירְתָּהּ לְהֵעָשׂוֹת שְׁנִיָּה כְּמוֹתָהּ לַקֹּדֶשׁ. אֶלָּא אִי אָמְרַתְּ לָא אָמְרִינַן אֶלָּא בְּחִיבּוּרִין, וְטַעְמָא מִשּׁוּם דִּלְמָא נָגַע טָמֵא לַקֹּדֶשׁ — מַאי רְבוּתָא דִּנְגוּבָה? הָטוּ יָד קַמַּיְיתָא לָא מְטַמְּיָא לָהּ לַקֹּדֶשׁ בְּלָא מַשְׁקִין?! הֲלֹא שְׁנִיָּה הִיא! אֲבָל

תוספות

חטאת מדרבנן, דאינו קודש אלא חול, כדמוכח ב"התכלת" (מנחות דף נב. ושם) שאין מועלין באפר פרה. וקתני: הוסיף ר"ע, דמשמע דהוי דרבנן כמו רישא, כדדייק הכא. והשתא מתוקמא דרשה דמייתי בכולי התלמוד: "והבשר" — לרבות עצים ולבונה כר"י דפרק "המנחות והנסכים" (שם דף קב: ושם). דאי לרבנן — הא משמע אף בשר בתר שחיטה יש לה פדיון. ומיהו, יכילנא לאוקומי כרבנן, ובהוקדשו בכלי, וכדמוקמינן לה בפסחי', אך איכא לדחות דלא קאי רק אלבונה ולא אעצים. וכן בריש "המנחות והנסכים" פי' בשם הר"י דעיקר קרא לא קאי רק אלבונה, אבל אעצים לא הוי רק אסמכתא בעלמא. והתם הארכתי, ולא שייך הכא. ואין להביא ראיה מהא דלא חשיב עצים בפרק שני דמעילה (דף ט.), כי חשיב אינך הוכשר ליפסל בטבול יום ובמחוסרי כפרה, משום דלא שייך ביה פיגול אף בהולכה ובהקטרה, דלא קרבן גמור הוא*:

דאורייתא יש לו תוך מצרף. הקשה הר"ר אלחנן: אמאי לא קאמר כגון שצברו בכלי חול? דאורייתא כלי שרת מצרף, ולא של חול, דבעינן דומיא דכף, ואע"פ שיש לו תוך! וצ"ע:

מנין לרביעי בקדש שהוא פסול. פרש"י: ולמ"ד דיו — הני מעלות דרבנן נינהו, ולא דאורייתא. והאי דקאמר: ולמדנו שלישי מן התורה — מילתא בעלמא הוא. ולא קאמר נמי מק"ו אלא מלתא בעלמא הוא ובפ"ק דפסחים (דף יט.) פי' רש"י גבי ההיא דר' יוסי ור' שמעון דאין משקה מטמא באוכל, ואין טומאה עושה כיוצא בה, היכי אשכחן רביעי בקדש? אלמא ודאי דרבנן הוא, ומביא ראיה דמכילתין חשיב גבי מעלות דרבנן בתרייתא. וקשה לר"י: לר' חנין, דאית ליה צירוף כלי דאורייתא וקחשיב ליה גבי מעלות דרבנן, ולר' יוחנן דאית ליה צירוף דרבנן הוא, הא מוקי לה כר' עקיבא, ור"ע סבר שלישי בחולין דאורייתא, וא"כ רביעי בקדש נמי דאורייתא, קרי כאן, "והבשר אשר יגע בכל טמא לא יאכל" דמי לא עסקינן דנגע וכו'? ותירץ הר"י: דקרי להו דרבנן — משום דלא משכח לה לחולין שנעשו על טהרת הקדש — [דהוי דאורייתא]. וכן אר"ת: דמשכחת לה לרביעי בקדש [דאורייתא] ע"י עצים ולבונה, דטמאין ע"י חיבת הקדש. וכי מיבעי ליה לר"ל בגריד של מנחות (מנחות דף קב:), אי מונין בו ראשון ושני אי לא, דאי מהני חיבת הקדש למנות בו ראשון ושני — למ"ד אין אוכל מטמא אוכל פשיטא ליה האי. והיה קשה להר"ר אלחנן: לפר"ת דמוקי לה ע"י עצים ולבונה — וכי עדיפא מאוכל גמור דלא אהני חיבת הקדש למימני ביה ראשון ושני?

בחיבורין שנו. פרש"י: שבשעה שהיד טמאה נוגעת לטהורה היתה טהורה נוגעת לקדש. וקשה לפי': דא"כ השניה אינה טמאה כלל, והקדש טמא מחמת גזרה שמא יגע בראשונה הטמאה, ואמאי קאמר ובקדש יטבול שתיהן? יטבול טמאה! ויש ליישבו, דה"ק: הא נטמאה ידו אחת — חבירתה טהורה. ובקדש בתחילתו הצריכו חכמים להטביל שתיהן, שמא נטמאו שתיהן. ועי"ל: בחיבורין שנו — דיד אחת נוגעת בספר הפוסלה, ויד האחרת הנוגעת בה תדון כאילו נגעה בספר, דגזרינן לה שמא תגע. וכן הא דתנן לקמן: יד מטמאה חברתה ועושה אותה שניה בקדש — מוקמינן לה בשמעתין הכי לפי מאי דס"ד לדברי ר' יהושע דיד מטמאה חברתה להיות שניה, ומאיזה טעם לא תהיה שלישית? אלא ודאי דגזרינן שמא נגעה בספר עצמה ואפי' לא נגע ביד השניה — טמאה, שמא נגעה בספר, ותניא בתוספתא: המטביל את ידו אחת מהן כל טהרות שעשה בטהורה עד שלא הטביל את הטמאה — טמאות, שהיד מטמאה חברתה לקדש. משמע דבלא נגיעה מטמאת לה. והשתא יתכן דהוי מעלה לר' יוסי, שאינה אלא בכלל רביעי ליפסול בקדש, אבל לא לתרומה, דבתרומה אין יותר משלישי, לכן אינה מטמאה רק קדש דעושה רביעי. ולית ליה יד מטמאה את חברתה להיות שניה, אלא מטמאה להיות שלישית. והקשה הר"ר אלחנן: אמאי חשיב האי מעלה במתני'? הא הויא בכלל רביעי בקדש! ותירץ: דמ"מ מעלה אחרת היא דיד מטמאה את חברתה, דס"ד כיון דאין גופו נטמא אלא מאב הטומאה — גם ידיו נמי לא, קמ"ל:

אלא אי אמרת בחיבורין אין וכו' מאי רבותא. ואי משום תרומה, דלא מטמאה אף בחיבורין — לא נחית להו רבותא, אלא רבותא דקדש:

אחד* ידו ואחד יד חברו לפסול. דהואיל ומטמא יד חברו — די לנו בכך אם יפסל, אבל לריש לקיש דאמר: דוקא ידו, מוקי טעמא משום איחלופי יד טהורה ביד טמאה. לפיכך, כי היכי דידו טמאה מטמאה קדש, דשניה היא — אף טהורה נמי. וכן משמע בסמוך, כי הדר ביה ריש לקיש פירש לדבריו: לפסול אבל לא לטמא. משמע דמעיקרא סבירא ליה לטמא. בשם רבינו שמואל:

דתנן

רבינו חננאל

טמא במקצתו שטימא את כולו וקתני הוסיף ר' עקיבא אלמא צירוף דרבנן הוא ופריק ר"ל אליבא דרבי חנין לעולם צירוף דאורייתא ור' עקיבא שירי מנחות אתא לאשמעינן דמדאורייתא דבר הצריך לכלי כלי מצרפו שאין צריך לכלי אין כלי מצרפו. ואתו רבנן ועשו מעלה וגזרו אפי' בדבר שאין צריך לכלי ומקשינן תינח דמצרף הכלי הסלת מפני שצריכה כלי קטורת לבונה וגחלים מאי כלי צריכי. ופריק רב נחמן כגון שצברן ע"ג קטבליא מדאורייתא יש לו תוך מצרף. אין לו תוך אינו מצרף. ואתו רבנן תקינו דאע"ג דאין לו תוך מצרף ופליגא דר' חייא בר אבא דאמר משמיה דר' יוחנן מעדותו של ר' עקיבא נשנית משנה זו הכלי מצרף מה שבתוכו לקדש ומסתברא דצירוף כלי מדרבנן היא דהר ר' יוחנן מוקים לה ממתניתין מעדותו של ר' עקיבא ומשנתנו מעלה מדרבנן וכבר פירשנוהו בפסחים בפ' הראשון: מעלה שביעית הרביעי בקדש פסול והשלישי בתרומה פי' טמא מת הוא אבי הטומאה וטומאתו ז' דכתיב וכל אשר יגע על פני השדה בחלל חרב או במת או בעצם אדם או בקבר יטמא שבעת ימים והנוגע בו טמא טומאת ערב שנאמר וכל אשר יגע בו הטמא יטמא והנפש הנוגעת תטמא עד הערב. עוד קדשים הנוגעים בטמא השני שהוא טמא טומאת ערב נטמאו שנאמר והבשר אשר יגע בכל טמא לא יאכל נמצא שלישי לקדש טמא מן התורה כמו שפירשנו. ורביעי מק"ו כדתניא מניין לרביעי בקדש שפסול ודין הוא ומה מחוסר כפורים שמותר בתרומה

שנא' ובא השמש וטהר ואחר יאכל מן הקדשים כי לחמו הוא. ותנן נמי העריב שמשו אוכל בתרומה פסול הוא זה המחוסר כפורים בקדשים כדתנן הביא כפרתו אוכל (בתרומה) [בקדשים] וכתיב וכפר עליה הכהן וטהרה מכלל שעד שלא הביאה כפרתה לא נגמרה טהרתה ובמאי אי לתרומה הא כתיב ובא השמש וטהר ואחר יאכל מן הקדשים כי לחמו הוא והיא התרומה שגם היא נקראת קדשים. אלא לאו בטהרת קדשים הכתוב מדבר עכשיו שלישי שפסול לתרומה אינו דין שיעשה רביעי בקדש וזו היא מעלת הקדש על התרומה: מעלה שמינית שהיד מטמא לחברתה בקדש אבל לא בתרומה אמר רב שיזבי בחבורין שנו. פי' כגון שחיבר ידו לידו האחרת אבל אם לא חיבר היד הטמאה לטהורה לא. ומותיב אביי עלה יד נגובה מטמאה לחברתה לקדש וכו'. ואע"ג דלא פריק רב שיזבי כיון דא"ר יוחנן אחר

עין משפט נר מצוה

ל א ב מיי' פי"ב מהל' אבות הטומאות ה"ז:
לא ג מיי' שם הל' יא ופי"א הלכה ז:
לב ד ה מיי' שם פ"ח הלכה ז:
לג ו ז מיי' שם פ"ב הלכה י"ב ופ"ח שם הלכה ז:

[פסחים יט.]
[ועי' תוספות מנחות כח. ד"ה ולאו]

מסורת הש"ס

[מנחות כד.]
[ע"ש ועיין רש"י פסחים יח: ד"ה שלישי שפסול בתרומה]
פסחים יח: סוטה כט: [תוספתא פ"ג]

הגהות הב"ח

(א) רש"י ד"ה שלישי וכו' שני שפסול במעשר אינו דין שיעשה שלישי בתרומה וכיון דשלישי פסול לתרומה דין הוא שיעשה רביעי בקדש: (ב) ד"ה דנגע בשני וכו' בכל טמא אפילו בשני והוה ליה בשר שלישי: ולמ"ד לקמן פסול לפסול: (ג) ד"ה בחיבורין וכו' (ד) ד"ה אי אמרת וכו' לאחר על גב דנגובה:

*) [עי' בעל המאור ושר תמ"ה שם פי' הגון לכל הסוגיא זו]

הגהות מהר"ב רנשבורג

א] גמ' איתמר נמי אמר ריש לקיש. נ"ב עי' בספר טורי אבן מהו האיתמר נמי:

סייך לעמ"ב

לד א מיי' פי"ב מהל' אבות הטומאות הלכה יב:
לה ב מיי' פ"ח שם הל' ב סמג עשין רמז:
לו ג ד מיי' שם פי"ב הלכה יג:
לז ה ו מיי' שם הל' טו:
לח ז ח ט מיי' פי"א מהל' מטמאי משכב ומושב הלכה א:
לט י מיי' שם הלכה ב:
מ כ מיי' שם הלכה ד:

אֲבָל יַד חֲבֵירוֹ לֹא. וְר' יוֹחָנָן אָמַר: אאֶחָד יָדוֹ וְאֶחָד יַד חֲבֵירוֹ, בְּאוֹתָהּ הַיָּד — לִפְסוֹל אֲבָל לֹא לְטַמֵּא. מִמַּאי — מִדְּקָתָנֵי סֵיפָא: שֶׁהַיָּד מְטַמְּאָה חֲבֵירְתָהּ לַקֹּדֶשׁ, אֲבָל לֹא לַתְּרוּמָה. הָא תּוּ לָמָּה לִי? הָא תָּנָא לֵיהּ רֵישָׁא! אֶלָּא לָאו שְׁמַע מִינָּהּ: לְאַתּוּיֵי יַד חֲבֵירוֹ. וְאַף ר"ל הֲדַר בֵּיהּ, דְּא"ר יוֹנָה א"ר אַמִּי אָמַר ר"ל: אֶחָד יָדוֹ וְאֶחָד יַד חֲבֵירוֹ, בְּאוֹתָהּ הַיָּד — לִפְסוֹל אֲבָל לֹא לְטַמֵּא. וְלִפְסוֹל אֲבָל לֹא לְטַמֵּא תַּנָּאֵי הִיא. דִּתְנַן*: כָּל הַפּוֹסֵל בִּתְרוּמָה — מְטַמֵּא יָדַיִם לִהְיוֹת שְׁנִיּוֹת, וְיָד מְטַמֵּא חֲבֵירְתָהּ, דִּבְרֵי ר' יְהוֹשֻׁעַ. וַחכ"א: ביָדַיִם שְׁנִיּוֹת הֵן, וְאֵין שֵׁנִי עוֹשֶׂה שֵׁנִי (בְּחוּלִּין). מַאי לָאו — שֵׁנִי הוּא דְּלָא עָבֵיד, הָא שְׁלִישִׁי — עָבֵיד! דִּלְמָא לָא שֵׁנִי עָבֵיד, וְלָא שְׁלִישִׁי. אֶלָּא כִּי הָנֵי תַּנָּאֵי, דְּתַנְיָא: יָד נְגוּבָה מְטַמָּא אֶת חֲבֵירְתָהּ לְטַמֵּא בַּקֹּדֶשׁ, אֲבָל לֹא לִתְרוּמָה, דִּבְרֵי רַבִּי. ר' יוֹסֵי בְּר' יְהוּדָה אוֹמֵר: אוֹתָהּ יָד לִפְסוֹל, אֲבָל לֹא לְטַמֵּא.§ ג"אוֹכְלִין אוֹכָלִים נְגוּבִין בְּיָדַיִם מְסוֹאָבוֹת כו'".§ *תַּנְיָא, א"ר חֲנִינָא בֶּן אַנְטִיגְנוֹס: וְכִי יֵשׁ נְגוּבָה לַקֹּדֶשׁ? וַהֲלֹא חִיבַּת הַקֹּדֶשׁ מַכְשַׁרְתָּן! לָא צְרִיכָא דכְּגוֹן שֶׁתָּחַב לוֹ חֲבֵירוֹ לְתוֹךְ פִּיו, אוֹ שֶׁתָּחַב הוּא לְעַצְמוֹ בְּכוּשׁ וּבְכַרְכָּר, וּבִיקֵּשׁ לֶאֱכוֹל צְנוֹן וּבָצָל שֶׁל חוּלִּין עִמָּהֶן. לַקֹּדֶשׁ — גָּזְרוּ בְּהוּ רַבָּנַן, לַתְּרוּמָה — לֹא גָּזְרוּ בְּהוּ רַבָּנַן.§ ה"הָאוֹנֵן וּמְחוּסַּר כִּפּוּרִים כו'".§ מַאי טַעְמָא? וכֵּיוָן דְּעַד הָאִידָּנָא הָווּ אֲסִירֵי — אַצְרְכִינְהוּ רַבָּנַן טְבִילָה.§

מתני' חוֹמֶר בַּתְּרוּמָה, שֶׁבִּיהוּדָה זנֶאֱמָנִין עַל טָהֳרַת יַיִן וָשֶׁמֶן כָּל יְמוֹת הַשָּׁנָה, חוּבִשְׁעַת הַגִּיתּוֹת וְהַבַּדִּים — אַף עַל הַתְּרוּמָה. טעָבְרוּ הַגִּיתּוֹת וְהַבַּדִּים יוְהֵבִיאוּ לוֹ חָבִית שֶׁל יַיִן שֶׁל תְּרוּמָה — לֹא יְקַבְּלֶנָּה מִמֶּנּוּ, אֲבָל מַנִּיחָהּ לַגַּת הַבָּאָה. *כוְאִם אָמַר לוֹ: הִפְרַשְׁתִּי לְתוֹכָהּ רְבִיעִית קֹדֶשׁ — נֶאֱמָן. כַּדֵּי יַיִן וְכַדֵּי שֶׁמֶן הַמְדוּמָּעוֹת

רש"י

אֲבָל יַד חֲבֵירוֹ. אִם נָגְעָה בְּיַד חֲבֵרוֹ לֹא טִימְּאַתָּהּ: בְּאוֹתָהּ הַיָּד. אִם נָגַע בְּיַד הָרִאשׁוֹנָה בְּיַד חֲבֵרוֹ. אֲבָל הַשְּׁנִיָּה אֵינָהּ מְטַמְּאָה יַד חֲבֵרוֹ: וְלִפְסוֹל. אֶת הַקֹּדֶשׁ, הוּא דְּאָמַר יָד מְטַמֵּא חֲבֵירְתָּהּ, אֲבָל לֹא לְטַמֵּא: הָא תָּנָא לֵיהּ רֵישָׁא. וְלַקֹּדֶשׁ מַטְבִּילִין שְׁנֵיהֶן: אֵין שֵׁנִי עוֹשֶׂה שֵׁנִי. אֵין יָד שֶׁהִיא שְׁנִיָּה עוֹשָׂה אֶת חֲבֵירְתָּהּ שְׁנִיָּה. מִכְּלָל דְּשָׁמְעִי' לְר' יְהוֹשֻׁעַ דְּאָמַר הַיָּד מְטַמֵּא אֶת חֲבֵירְתָּהּ לִהְיוֹת כְּמוֹתָהּ: וְדִלְמָא לֹא שֵׁנִי וְלֹא שְׁלִישִׁי. דְּלֵית לְהוּ הַךְ מַעֲלָה דְּמַתְנִי'. אֲבָל מַאן דְּאִית לֵיהּ — אֲפִי' לְטַמֵּא אִית לֵיהּ, לְהָכִי קָאָמַר: יָדַיִם לְעוֹלָם שְׁנִיּוֹת הֵן, לְפִיכָךְ (א) אֵין יָד מְטַמֵּא אֶת חֲבֵירְתָּהּ: וְכִי יֵשׁ נְגוּבָה בַּקֹּדֶשׁ, וַהֲלֹא חִיבַּת הַקֹּדֶשׁ מַכְשֶׁרֶת. אֶלָּא אֵין נְגוּבָה זוֹ לוֹמַר כְּשֶׁלֹּא הוּכְשְׁרוּ, אֶלָּא כְּשֶׁהוּכְשְׁרוּ לְטוּמְאָה וְעַכְשָׁיו הֵן נְגוּבִין, וְטוּמְאָה הֵן מְקַבְּלִין. וְלֹא הוּצְרְכָה מִשְׁנָתֵנוּ לְדַבֵּר בְּאוֹכְלֵי קֹדֶשׁ נְגוּבִין, אֶלָּא בְּאוֹכְלֵי חוּלִּין נְגוּבִין וְאוֹכְלֵי קֹדֶשׁ: תָּחַב לוֹ חֲבֵרוֹ. בְּיָדַיִם טְהוֹרוֹת, וְזֶה הָאוֹכֵל יָדָיו מְסוֹאָבוֹת: אוֹ שֶׁתְּחָבָן הוּא עַצְמוֹ בְּכוּשׁ אוֹ בְּכַרְכַּר. שֶׁהֵן פְּשׁוּטֵי כְּלֵי עֵץ, וְאֵין מְקַבְּלִין טוּמְאָה: וּבִיקֵּשׁ לֶאֱכוֹל צְנוֹן אוֹ בָּצָל שֶׁל חוּלִּין עִמָּהֶן. שֶׁאֵין יָדַיִם מְטַמְּאוֹת אֶת הַחוּלִּין, וְאַפ"ה גָּזוּר רַבָּנַן שֶׁלֹּא יֹאכְלֵם עִם הַקֹּדֶשׁ — פֶּן תִּגַּע יָדוֹ מְסוֹאֶבֶת בְּאוֹכְלֵי קֹדֶשׁ שֶׁבְּפִיו: לְעִנְיַן תְּרוּמָה. אַע"פ שֶׁהַיָּד מְסוֹאֶבֶת פּוֹסַלְתָּהּ — לֹא עָשׂוּ מַעֲלָה, אֶלָּא אָמְרִינַן: זָהִיר וְלֹא נָגַע. וְה"ק מַתְנִיתִין: אוֹכְלִין חוּלִּין בְּיָדַיִם מְסוֹאָבוֹת עִם הַתְּרוּמָה, אֲבָל לֹא עִם הַקֹּדֶשׁ. וּלְהָכִי נָקַט נְגוּבִין, שֶׁאִילּוּ עַכְשָׁיו הָיוּ מַשְׁקִין עֲלֵיהֶם — הָיוּ מַשְׁקִין נַעֲשִׂין רִאשׁוֹנִים מֵחֲמַת הַיָּדַיִם, וְעוֹשִׂין אֶת הַחוּלִּין שְׁנִיִּים, וּכְשֶׁנּוֹגְעִין בַּתְּרוּמָה שֶׁבְּפִיו — פּוֹסְלִין אוֹתָם. א]וְאִית דְּמַסִּיק מִלְּתָא בִּנְגוּבִין שֶׁמֵּעוֹלָם לֹא הוּכְשְׁרוּ, וְקַשְׁיָא לִי: בְּחוּלִּין, מַה לִּי הוּכְשְׁרוּ מַה לִּי לֹא הוּכְשְׁרוּ? הֲלֹא אֵין יָדַיִם מוֹעִילוֹת כְּלוּם לַחוּלִּין: כֵּיוָן דְּעַד הָאִידָּנָא אֲסִירֵי. דִּמְחוּסַּר כִּפּוּרִים מוּתָּר בִּתְרוּמָה וְאָסוּר בְּקֹדֶשׁ, וְכֵן אוֹנֵן. וְאַע"פ שֶׁאֲסוּרִים בְּמַעֲשֵׂר שֵׁנִי — מוּתָּרִין בִּתְרוּמָה, כִּדְאָמְרִינַן בְּמַסֶּכֶת יְבָמוֹת *מ"וְכָל זָר" יְתֵירָה: זָרוּת אָסַרְתִּי לְךָ וְלֹא אֲנִינוּת: **מתני'** שֶׁבִּיהוּדָה נֶאֱמָנִין. עַמֵּי הָאָרֶץ: עַל טָהֳרַת יַיִן וָשֶׁמֶן. שֶׁל קוֹדֶשׁ, אִם הִקְדִּישׁוּהוּ לַמִּזְבֵּחַ בִּשְׁעַת הַגִּיתּוֹת וְהַבַּדִּים — נֶאֱמָנִין עַל שְׁמִירָתָן כָּל יְמוֹת הַשָּׁנָה. וּבַגְּמָ' מְפָרֵשׁ מַאי שְׁנָא יְהוּדָה דְּנָקַט: וּבִשְׁעַת הַגִּיתּוֹת וְהַבַּדִּים. הַכֹּל מְטַהֲרִין אֶת כְּלֵיהֶם: וְהֵבִיאוּ לוֹ. עַמֵּי הָאָרֶץ לְכֹהֵן חָבֵר: אֲבָל מַנִּיחָהּ. עַם הָאָרֶץ לַגַּת הַבָּאָה, וְאָז יִתְּנֶנָּה לַכֹּהֵן: רְבִיעִית לוֹג שֶׁמֶן נֶאֱמָן. דְּמִיגּוֹ דְּנֶאֱמָן אַקֹּדֶשׁ — נֶאֱמָן אַתְּרוּמָה:

הַמְדוּמָּעוֹת

תוספות

דתנן כל הפוסל את התרומה כו'. קשה לר"י: דאמרינן בפ"ק דשבת (דף יד. ושם): אף הידים הבאות מחמת ספר פוסלות את התרומה, משום דר' פרנך דאמר וכו'. מאי קאמר? אפי' כל מילי נמי דפוסל את התרומה מטמא ידים, כדתנן הכא! וי"ל: דספר נגזרה ראשון, ואח"כ של שאר מילי. ועוד יש לומר: דלרבנן איצטריך התם, דפליגי עליה דרבי יהושע. ומיהו, טפי נראה לומר דאף ר' יהושע לא קאמר רק לקדש, כדמשמע כולה שמעתין, אבל לתרומה לא. וכי קאמר בסיפא דמתני', אמר להם רבי יהושע: והלא כתבי הקדש שניים מטמאין את הידים, אמרו ליה: אין למדין דברי תורה כו', ומאי קא מקשי להו? הא איהו מודה דכתבי הקדש מיירי אף לתרומה, והיא דכל הפוסל את התרומה דוקא לקדש! — התם לאו קושיא היא, אלא סיומא דמלתא קמסיק, בא ליתן טעם על דבריו למה שני עושה שני, דה"נ מלינו בתרומה, כ"ש לקדש. אבל קשה להר"ר אלחנן: מאי סייעתא מייתי למילתיה מכתבי הקדש? שאני התם משום דר' פרנך כל האוחז ס"ת ערום כו'! ותירץ הר"י: דבספר נמי היכא דלא שייך דר' פרנך קאמר ליה, כגון רצועות של תפילין עם התפילין. אבל אכתי היה קשה להר"ר אלחנן: בפ"ב דחולין (דף לד.) מלינו לשני עושה שני ע"י משקין, ופריך: תחילה נמי הוה. ואמאי לא קאמר: ביד שמטמאה את חברתה, כי הכא? וי"ל: דאיהו קאמר ליה במס' ידים, לכך לא חש להביא סייעתא ממה שאמר איהו. וגם ע"י ספר לא בעי למימר: מלינו שני עושה שני — דהתם טעמא רבה איכא, משום דר' פרנך. ומיהו, התם לא בעי למימר שני עושה שני משום גזרה דשבת די"ח דבר, דאמרינן: דלמא שדי משקין דתרומה לפיו כי אכיל אוכלין טמאים — דהתם נמי ידע הא טעמא. אלא קמתמה, כיון שלא מלינו טומאה כהאי גוונא היכי *גזרינן? א"ל: הכא והיא דהתם דקאמר שלישי שני לקדש ולא לתרומה בחולין שנעשו עטה"ק. וקשה: אמאי לא חשיב לה גבי מעלות הכא? וי"ל: דהתם מפרש טעמא: שאני תרומה שטהרתה טמאה היא אצל הקדש. א"כ לאו משום מעלה היא, הר"ר אלחנן. ומיהו למאן דלית ליה התם דאהדר ליה הכי ר"א לר' יהושע, ולא קמסיק אף אני לא אמרתי, דקאמר התם אמוראי נינהו ואליבא דר' יוחנן — א"כ אמאי לא חשיב ליה? וי"ל: דאיכא למימר דבתרומה לא גזור משום דזריזין גבי תרומה, אבל לא גבי קדש, הלכך לא שייך למימר בהן מעלה. ודוגמתו מלינו בריש פירקין בירושלמי גבי חומר בקדש, ר' חייא בשם ר' יוחנן: מפני שאוכלי תרומה זריזין הן, ואוכלי קדש אין זריזין. א"ר חנינא קומי ר' מנא: הדא היא מעלה? אילו דבר שבזה ובזה, בזה טהור ובזה טמא — הדא היא מעלה. אלמא לא חשבינן ליה מעלה בדבר התלוי בזריזות:

לא צריכא שתחב לו חבירו בפיו או שתחב כו'. משמע דהוי לישנא דהתלמוד. מיהו, בתוספתא גרסינן ליה: ר' חנינא בן אנטיגנוס אומר: וכי יש נגובה בקודש? אלא: תחב ליה חבריה או שתחב הוא בכוש או בקיסם ואוכל עמה זית או בצל *של תרומה. ולהכי נקט כוש, דהוו ליה פשוטי כלי עץ דלא מקבלי טומאה, ואפי' מדרבנן לא מקבלי טומאה פשוטים קטנים. ודומה לו ההיא דריש חולין (דף ג. ושם): כגון שבדק קרומית של קנה ושחט בה — משום דהוה פשוטי כלי עץ דלא מקבל טומאה. וכי אמרינן ב"המוכר את [הבית]" (ב"ב דף סו.): דף של נחתומין טמא, אע"ג דלית ליה בית קבול כלל — התם טמא משום משמש אדם, ומשתמש ממשמשי אדם. וכן ההיא דטבלא המתהפכת טמאה, דבפרק "שתי הלחם" (מנחות דף נז:) אף למ"ד מסגרתו למטה היתה, אע"ג דלא מחברא לטבלא, כדמשמע בריש סוכה (דף ה.) — אלא מטעם משמשי אדם הוי. והכי איתא בהדיא בת"כ. ובריש סוכה* פירשתי:

לקדש גזור רבנן. שמא יגע בידיו שניות לקדש שבתוך פיו, וכן פירש רש"י. ועוד היינו יכולים לפרש: דלמא נגע ברוק פיו, דחשיב משקה בפרק בתרא דעירובין (דף צט. ושם), גבי אכל דבילה בידים מסואבות:

שביהודה נאמנין על טהרת יין ושמן בכל השנה. פרש"י: אם הקדישו למזבח בשעת הבציר — כל ימות השנה, נאמנין בשמירה. ואמר הר"ר אלחנן: דכן יתכן לפרש, דאי בלא הקדישו בשעת הבציר — ה"ל חולין, ונטמא בטומאת ע"ה. *וכי קדש עליו משום דאקדשיה פקע ליה טומאה מיניה? א"נ: הוה מלינו למימר ביחדו לנסכים נמי, וכגון שידוע לנו שחולין הן שיחדן. וכי אקדשיה — איכא למימר שאימת קדש עליו, ומעיקרא היה נזהר לשומרו בטהרה. וכן מלינו גבי תרומה בסמוך, דע"ה מניח תרומה של כל ימות השנה לשנה הבאה בשעת הגיתות ליתנה לחבר. ותניא בתוספתא: אע"פ שמכירה החבר שהיא היא. ואפי' בחבר עצמו משמע בגמרא שישהנה לשנה הבאה:

שרלועה

רבינו חננאל

אחד ידו ואחד ידו של חבירו לפסול אבל לא לטמא ש"מ מדאשוי ליה לידו ליד חבירו בחיבורין סבירא ליה כרב שיזבי דאי לא תימא הכי יד חבירו שלא בחיבורין איצטריכא ליה למימר דלא מטמאה אלא לאו בחיבורין סבירא ליה. ור"ל נמי הדר ביה ואמר כרבי יוחנן. ואסיקנא לפסול אבל לא לטמא תנאי היא דתניא יד נגובה מטמאה לחברתה לטמא בקדש אבל לא לתרומה דברי ר' רבי יוסי ב"ר יהודה אומר אותה היד לפסול אבל לא לטמא: מעלה תשיעית אוכלין אוכלים נגובין בידים מסואבות לתרומה אבל לא לקדש כיון דבהדיא אמר רחמנא וכי יותן מים על זרע ונפל מנבלתם עליו. פי' אם הוכשרו האוכלין מטמאין ואם לא הוכשרו אין מטמאין ושנינן במשנתנו אוכלין אוכלים נגובין. פי' יבישין שלא הוכשרו ואע"ג שהאוכלין הללו הן תרומה אוכלין אותן בידים מסואבות שכיון שלא הוכשרו אין מקבלין טומאה והני מילי לתרומה אבל לקדש עשו בו מעלה שאע"פ שהם נגובין לא יאכלו לאדם טהור בידים מסואבות. ומתמיה ר' חנניה בן אנטיגנוס וכי יש נגובה לקדש והלא חיבתן מכשרתן. כלומר חיבת הקדש משוה לאוכלין נגובין כאלו הוכשרו והנוגע בהן בידים מסואבות ודאי טימאו כי כמוכשרין הן חשובין למה ליה למתניי' ופרקינן ודאי לנגוע בידים מסואבות לאכלי קדש ואע"פ שהן נגובין לא אצטריכא ליה. כי אצטריך ליה כגון שלא נגען הוא בידו אלא תחב לו אדם טהור וידיו טהורות לתוך פיו של זה שהוא כולו טהור וידיו טמאות שנטמאו בהיסח הדעת או הוא עצמו תחב בכוש או בכרכר והכניסם לתוך פיו וביקש לאכול צנון ובצל של חולין עמהן. אם הן אוכלי קדש גזרו בהן שמא יכנים ידו לתוך פיו להפך המאכל בפיו ויגע בהן ויטמאם אבל באוכלי תרומה לא גזרו בהן. וכן עוד אמרו גבי בשר הקדש האי דכתיב והבשר אשר יגע בכל טמא לא יאכל. האי בשר דאתכשר במאי אי נימא דאתכשר בדם קדשים כו' ואסיקנא אלא דאתכשר בחיבת הקדש ואמרינן אימור דמהניא חיבת [הקדש] לא יפסוליה לטמויי כדי למיניינא ביה ראשון ושני נמי מהניא חיבת הקדש וכבר פירשנוהו בפסחים בפרק ראשון: מעלה עשירית אונן ומחוסר כפורים צריכין טבילה לקדש אבל לא לתרומה זו כבר פרשנוה בפסחים בסוף פרק האשה אונן טובל ואוכל פסחו לערב אבל לא בקדשים מאי טעמא אנינות יום הוא מדאורייתא שנאמר לא אכלתי באוני ממנו אבל לא אנינות לילה אלא מדרבנן הוא בקדשים אפילו בלילה בפסח שהוא עשה שיש בו כרת דכתיב וחדל לעשות הפסח ונכרתה לא העמידו דבריהם במקום כרת כו' ודבריהן פשוטין הן: כבר שלמו המעלות שיש לקדש על מעלות התרומה. וחזרו לברר עוד חומרי התרומה וזו היא ששנינו חומר בתרומה שביהודה נאמנין לקדש על הגתות והבדים מדקתני

מסורת הש"ס

ידים פ"ג מ"ב

[תוספתא פ"ג]

[ועי' תוספות זבחים פח. ד"ה מן ותוספות חולין לג: ד"ה ואם]

[סח: ע: עח.]

בתרומה כצ"ל מהרש"א

[שם בד"ה ומסגרתו]

וכי קדשי מאי הוי משום דאקדשיה כצ"ל

הגהות הב"ח

(א) רש"י ד"ה ודלמא וכו' לפיכך יד מטמאה כצ"ל והיבת אין נמחק:

הגהות מהר"ב רנשבורג

א] רש"י ד"ה לענין תרומה וכו' ואית דמסיק מלתא בנגובים שמעולם לא הוכשרו. נ"ב וכן פרש"י במתניתין ע"ש.

גזרינן ליה הכא כצ"ל

המדומעות – נאמנין עליהם בשעת הגיתות והבדים, וקודם לגיתות שבעים יום.§

גמ' ביהודה – אין, ובגליל – לא. מ"ט? אמר ריש לקיש: מפני שרצועה של כותים מפסקת ביניהן. וניתיב בשידה תיבה ומגדל! הא מני – רבי היא, דאמר: אהל זרוק לאו שמיה אהל. דתניא: *הנכנס לארץ העמים בשידה תיבה ומגדל, רבי [א]מטמא, ור' יוסי בר' יהודה מטהר. ולייתוה בכלי חרס המוקף צמיד פתיל! אמר רבי אליעזר: שונין, [ב]אין הקדש ניצול בצמיד פתיל. *והתניא: *[ג]אין חטאת ניצלת בצמיד פתיל, מאי לאו, הא קדש ניצול! לא, [ד]הא מים שאינן מקודשים ניצולין בצמיד פתיל. והאמר עולא: *חברייא מדכן בגלילא! מניחין, ולכשיבא אליהו ויטהרנה.§ "ובשעת הגיתות נאמנין אף על התרומה".§ ורמינהי: *הגומר זיתיו – ישייר קופה אחת, ויתננה *לעני כהן! אמר רב נחמן: לא קשיא: הא – בחרפי, הא – באפלי. א"ל רב אדא בר אהבה: כגון מאי? כאותן של בית אביך. רב יוסף אמר: בגלילא שנו. איתיביה אביי: עבר הירדן והגליל – הרי הן כיהודה, *נאמנין על היין בשעת היין, ועל השמן בשעת השמן. אבל לא על היין בשעת השמן, ולא על השמן בשעת היין! אלא מחוורתא כדשנין מעיקרא.§ "עברו הגיתות והבדים והביאו לו חבית של יין לא יקבלנה הימנו, אבל מניחה לגת הבאה".§ בעו מיניה מרב ששת: עבר וקיבלה, מהו שיניחנה לגת הבאה? אמר להו: תניתוה,
חבר

רש"י

המדומעות. מפרש בגמרא. והשתא משמע של טבל, תרומה וחולין מעורבין: שבעים יום. מקדימין לטהר את הכלים, גיתות של יין, בדים – של שמן: גמ' רצועה. של ארץ העמים מפסקת בין גליל ליהודה. וירושלים ביהודה היא, וא"א להביאן לירושלים בטהרה, לפי שגזרו חכמים טומאה על ארץ העמים. ואפילו של חברים שמגליל אינו בא לנסכים: אהל זרוק. אהל המיטלטל ונזרק – לאו שמיה אהל להיות מפסיק בין אוירה של ארץ העמים, והם גזרו על אוירה: שונין. תנאים שונין ברייתא שאין הקודש ניצל בצמיד פתיל: אין חטאת. מי אפר פרה: שאינן מקודשין. שלא ניתן האפר עליהן עדיין: ניצולין. וכשירין לקדשן אחר כך: מדכן. מטהרין יינן ושמנן למזבח, ואי רצועה מפסקת למה מטהרין? שמא יבא אליהו. ויראה להן שביל בה שאינו מארץ העמים: הגומר את זיתיו. עם הארץ שבא לגמור את זיתיו: ישייר קופה אחת. לצורך תרומותיו: ויתננה לעני כהן. ויראנה שלא הוכשרו הזיתים, והכהן יעשנה בטהרה. אלמא: בשעת הגיתות והבדים אין נאמנים: באפלי. שכבר עבר זמן הגיתות לרובא דעלמא, קאמר דלא מהימן: כשל בית אביך. אפלי הוו: בגלילא שנו. ומתני' דקא תני דמהימני – ביהודה קאי. דקתני רישא: שביהודה נאמנין על טהרות יין ושמן, ועלה קאי: ובשעת הגיתו' והבדים אף על התרומ': יכול

תוספות

שרצועה של כותים מפסקת. הקשה הר"ר אלחנן: היאך היו מביאין אפר פרה לגליל, דא"א לעשות אלא בירושלים, וא"כ נטמא בהבאת דרך ארץ העמים! וש"מ: דבשביל קטן איכא להביא דרך שם, אבל להביא יין ושמן לנסכים – בעי שביל גדול. א] *אבל ק"ע: היאך עולין לרגל מן הגליל, ב]כיון דאפסקיה ליה רצועה נטמא, ובעי הזאה ג' וז', כדאמר פ' "כ"ג" בנזיר (דף נד.). הקשה הר"ר אלחנן, דתניא בתוספתא: *ארץ העמים טמאה, מקוואותיה ושביליהן טמאין. ארץ הכותים טהורה, ומקוואותיהן טהורין ושביליהן טהורים כו'! ונראה למורי: דהתם נשנית קודם שקלקלו לדמות יונה, כדאיתא פ"ק דחולין (דף ו.). והכי משמע בירושלמי דע"ז פ"ב: בעו כותאי קומי רבי אבהו, אבותיכם היו מסתפקין משלנו, מפני מה אין אתם מסתפקין משלנו? אמר להו: אבותיכם לא קלקלו מעשיהם, אתם קלקלתם מעשיכם, דתנינן תמן: א"י טהורה מקוואותיה טהורים כו'. ולאחר שנתקלקלו, שאף רבי מאיר מצינו שגזר עליהן, בפ"ק דחולין:

אהל זרוק לאו שמיה אהל. בפרק "כ"ג" בנזיר (דף נה. ושם) אמר: כתנאי, הנכנס לארץ העמים בשידה תיבה ומגדל, דרבי מטמא ורבי יוסי בר יהודה מטהר. מאי לאו דרבי סבר משום אוירא גזרו, ורבי יוסי סבר לא גזרו משום אוירא! לא, דכ"ע משום גושא – גזרו, משום אוירא – לא גזרו. מר סבר: אהל זרוק – לא שמיה אהל, ומר סבר: שמיה אהל. והתניא, רבי יוסי בר יהודה אומר: תיבה מלאה *ספרים וזרקה על פני המת באהל – טמאה וכו'. וקשה: מאי קאמר? כיון דס"ל שמיה אהל, אמאי זרק על פני המת טמאה, אהל זרוק הוא, ותולן! וי"מ: "והתניא" לשון קושיא הוי, והכי פריך כדפרשינן ותולן. ואח"כ דמסיק וקאמר: ואי בעית אימא גר', דכ"ע לא שמיה אהל. וגרס דכ"ע – משום אוירא. ומר סבר דלא שכיח, ולא גזרו ביה רבנן. והקשה הר"ר אלחנן: דבשמעתין משמע דפליגי אי שמיה אהל בזרוק אי לא, והכי נמי בפ' "בכל מערבין" (עירובין דף ל: ושם) ודוחק הוא לומר דנקט הכא לישנא דאהל זרוק משום דמעיקרא בעי למימר ליה, ולפי המסקנא אינו. ועוד קשה להר"י: דהתם נמי ל"ל לרבי יוסי בר יהודה דשמיה אהל, כי מוקי פלוגתא בשמא יוצא ראשו ורובו, ולית ליה טעמא דאוירא לא שכיח – ואמאי מטהר רבי יוסי אם לא מטעם דאהל זרוק שמיה אהל? ותהדר קושיין לדוכתה מתיבה מלאה ספרים, אמאי מטמא? ותירץ ר"י: דלעולם אמת הוא דפליגי באהל זרוק שמיה אהל, ודוקא כגון שידה תיבה ומגדל שהולכים. אבל זרק תיבה – לא הוי אהל, וכן משמע במסכת אהלות (פ"ח מ"ה): עוף הפורח או הקופץ וספינה המטרפת – לא הויא אהל. ומייתי סייעתא מזורק תיבה מלאה ספרים, מדקאמר: ואם היתה מונחת – טהורה, והיינו שהולכת בנחת, והיינו אהל זרוק. וזרק דרישא לא חשיב אהל זרוק דומיא דעוף הפורח: שונין אין הקדש ניצול במוקף צמיד פתיל. ל"ע: אמאי לא חשיב ליה גבי מעלות? דתרומה מצינו בשילהי "הניזקין" (גיטין דף סא: ושם) דנילנת בהא, דאמר: מפקידין תרומה אצל ע"ה במוקף צמיד פתיל! הר"ר אלחנן. ויש להקשות על הא דאמר בפ"ק דנדה (דף ה: ושם): ומה כלי חרס המוקף צמיד פתיל הניצול באהל המת – אינו מציל במעת לעת שבנדה. ומאי קאמר, במאי מציל במת – היינו בתרומה ולא בקדש, כדאיתא הכא – בהכי מציל נמי במעת לעת שבנדה, דקאמר התם: מעת לעת שבנדה – לקדש, אבל לא לתרומה! וי"ל: דבהא לא שייך הכלה אי לא מטמא לה. וה"ק: ומה כלי חרס המציל באהל המת במאי שמטמא לה, כגון לתרומה – אינו מציל במעת לעת במאי שמטמא, דהיינו לקדש דוקא: יתננה לעני כהן. פרש"י: ויראה שלא הוכשרו הזיתים. משמע מהכא דבעינן הכשר בזיתים, ולא מכשר ליה בשעת מסיקה. ודלא כפר"ת, שפירש בפ"ק דשבת (דף יז.): אם אתה מקיטני גוזרני על המסיקה, ושוב גזר לה. וכן משמע בכולה תוספתא דטהרות פרק ג', דתני: דבעינן בזיתים הכשר, ויש טעם נכון לדבר, כדפי' ר"י: שמשקה זיתים אינו אלא מוהל בעלמא ולא חשיב משקה. לעיני כהן גר', וכן גרס רש"י. והכי איתא בסדר המשנה דטהרות: הגומר זיתיו יתנה לעיני כהן, דברי רבי מאיר. רבי יהודה אומר: ימסור לו מפתח. ומאן דגרס לעני כהן – שיבוש הוא בידו:

בגלילא שנו. שיש להם רוב שמן ומאחרים בבדים ברוב שמן שיש להם לעשות והכי נמי אמר פרק כירה (שבת דף מז. ושם) גבי מטלטלין כונא אגב קיטמא כלומר מחתה אגב אפרה וכן פירש בערוך, ועדיף טפי מכלכלה ואבן שבתוכה, ואותיב ליה, ושוין שאם יש בה שברי פתילה שאסור לטלטלה, שבטל הכלי והשמן אגב הפתילה, ומוקי לה בגלילא שנו, כלומר: שעשירים הוו מרוב שמן ולא קפדי עליה, בטיל ליה אגב פתילה. ודוגמא לדבר ההוא דפ"ק דסנהדרין (דף יא:): טול אגרתא וכתוב לאחנא בני גלילאה עילאי ותתאי כו' לאפרושי מעשרא ממעטנא דזיתא, ובנזיר פ' "ב"ש" (דף לא:): בגלילא שנו דחמרא עדיף ממשחא, ויין היה מצוי להם הרבה ורוב שתייתן בכך, כדמשמע ב"המוציא יין" (שבת דף עח.), דקתני: מים כדי לשוף את הקילור דחשיב משום דשכיח לרפואה טפי משתיה שלא היו שותין רק יין מתוך עושרם בגליל ואפ"ה הוה עדיף להם היין מן השמן. משמע שהיה להם רוב שמן בזול כדפרי'. ומיהו, פירש רש"י בגלילא שנו דפרק "כירה" (שם דף מז.) שהיו עניים ולא היו להם פתילות מצויות, וב"המוציא" (שם דף עח.) פירש: מתוך שהיו עניים לא היו עושין רפואה רק ממים ולא מיין. ולא משמע כן, דא"כ גם שתיית מים שכיח טפי כיון שלא היה להם יין פורתא לשפות הקילור והיה להם לשער בשתיה! ועוד מצינו בחולין בפ' "אותו ואת בנו" (דף פג.): וערב יום הכפורים בגליל, משמע שהיו עשירים ומרבים בסעודות! ועוד: מה שפי' דלא היו פתילות מצויות – הא אמרינן בשילהי בבא קמא (דף קיט.): מקבלין מן הנשים דבר מועט כלי פשתן בגליל, אלמא שמצוי פשתן ביניהם! וכי קאמר לישנא דאסור לטלטלה דמשמע דקאי אפתילה דשייך בה לשון נקבה, דהא נר לשון זכר, דאיכא למימר דקאי אקערה דמייתי לה לעיל: מותר השמן שבנר ושבקערה מותר וגם מצינו לשון נקבה אנר: נר חנוכה, כבתה אין זקוק לה (שבת דף כא.), כל זה פי' הר"י וגם רבינו מאיר פירש כן. ועוד הוסיף: כי מרוב יין היה להם כאב עינים וטוב המים לרפואה:

חבר

עין משפט נר מצוה

מא א מיי' פי"א מהל' טומאת מת הל' ה:
מב ב מיי' פי"ד מהל' פרה אדומה הל' ז:
מג ג מיי' שם הלכה ג:
מד ד מיי' שם הלכה ז:

[למקוואות פ"ו]

מסורת הש"ס

גיטין ח: עירובין ל: נזיר נה.
[נ"ל והתנן] פרה פי"א מ"א
נדה ו:
טהרות פ"ט מ"ד
[נ"ל לעיני עי' תוס' וכן גרס הערוך ערך עין וכן בתוספתא פ"י דטהרות]
[תוספת' פ"ג]

רבינו חננאל

מדקתני ביהודה נאמנין מכלל דבגליל אין נאמנין מ"ט אמר ר"ל מפני שמפסקת ביניהם מדור הכותים וכיון שצריך לעבור בתוכם חיישינן שמא מטמא טומאת ארץ העמים ומקשינן ויתננה לההיא חבית בשידה תיבה או במגדל דהא לא נטמאה בטומאת ארץ העמים. ופרקינן מתני' רבי היא דאמר אהל זרוק לא הוי אהל דתניא הנכנס בארץ העמים בשידה תיבה ומגדל ר' מטמא ור' יוסי בר' יהודה מטהר וכבר פירשנוה בעירובין פרק בכל מערבין ומקשינן ותוב ולייתוה בכלי חרש המוקף צמיד פתיל. ופרקינן א"ר אלעזר שונין אין קדש ניצל בצמיד פתיל איני והתניא [אין] חטאת ניצלת בצמיד פתיל ומדקתני הכי אין מי חטאת ניצלת בצמיד פתיל הא *) מים שאין מקודשין ניצולין בצמיד פתיל תוב מקשינן וכי לא מצו לאתויי יין ושמן בגליל מפני מדורי הכותים שעוברין בתוכם והא' עולא חבריא מדכו בגלילא פי' חברינו מטהרין האוכלין והמשקין בגליל. ודחי מניחין אותם ואם יבא אליהו ויודיע שלא נטמאו אע"פ שהדרך מפסקת אותה שעה מטהרה **). ובשעת הגיתות והבדים נאמנים אף על התרומה ורמינהו הגומר זיתיו ישייר קופה אחת ויתננה לעיני כהן. ואי מהימן הוא למה לי לעיני כהן. ופריק מתניתין בחרפי. והא דקתני לעיני כהן מכלל הן שאין נאמנין באפלי שכבר עברו הגיתות והבדין ואבותיו של רב נחמן היו להן הרבה והיו מתאחרין הרבה אחרי כל אדם ובא רב יוסף לאוקומה הא דתנא יתננה לעיני כהן בגליל שאינם נאמנים לעולם ומותבינן עליה והא [תניא] עבר הירדן וגליל הרי הן כיהודה נאמנין על היין בשעת היין כו' ואסיקנא אלא מחוורתא באפלי: עברו הגיתות והבדים הביאו לו חבית של יין של תרומה לא יקבלוה כו'. הא דבעו מרב ששת עבר וקיבל מהו שיניחנה לגת הבאה אם לאו פשיט ליה מהא

*) נראה דחסר כאן ונ"ל הא קדש ניצול בצמיד פתיל ומשנינן הא מים וכו'. **) אולי נ"ל שמא יראה שביל שהיא טהורה ועי' רש"י ונ"ע.

גליון הש"ס

תום' ד"ה שרצועה וכו' אבל ק"ע היאך עולין לרגל. עיין ת' שער אפרים סי' לו:

הגהות מהר"ב רנשבורג

א] תום' ד"ה שרצועה כו' אבל ק"ע איך עולין לרגל מן הגליל כו' נ"ב ונלע"ד שהיו עולין ע"י שוורים וע"ג דלתות דהוי אהל מפסיק לכ"ע כמ"ש תוס' בעירובין דף לא ע"א בד"ה ומר סבר וכו' ומה שלא התירו גם הכא עי"כ כמו שהקשה בספר טורי אבן י"ל כמ"ש שם הרש"א בעירובין בתוס' הנ"ל משום דלא שכיח לא התירו אבל לענין עלית רגל דהוי עשה דאורייתא שפיר התירו ודו"ק: ב] שם בא"ד כיון דאפסקי' ליה רצועה נטמא ובעי הזאה ג' וז' וכו' נ"ב עיין שיח יצחק מ"ש בזה:

*[א]חָבֵר וְעַם הָאָרֶץ שֶׁיָּרְשׁוּ אֶת אֲבִיהֶם עַם הָאָרֶץ, יָכוֹל לוֹמַר לוֹ: טוֹל אַתָּה חִטִּין שֶׁבְּמָקוֹם פְּלוֹנִי, וַאֲנִי חִטִּין שֶׁבְּמָקוֹם פְּלוֹנִי. טוֹל אַתָּה יַיִן שֶׁבְּמָקוֹם פְּלוֹנִי, וַאֲנִי יַיִן שֶׁבְּמָקוֹם פְּלוֹנִי. אֲבָל לֹא יֹאמַר לוֹ: טוֹל אַתָּה לַח וַאֲנִי יָבֵשׁ, טוֹל אַתָּה חִטִּין וַאֲנִי שְׂעוֹרִים. וְתָנֵי עֲלָהּ: *אוֹתוֹ חָבֵר שׂוֹרֵף הַלַּח וּמַנִּיחַ אֶת הַיָּבֵשׁ. אַמַּאי? יַנִּיחֶנָּה לַגַּת הַבָּאָה! בְּדָבָר שֶׁאֵין לוֹ גַּת. וְיַנִּיחֶנּוּ לָרֶגֶל! בְּדָבָר שֶׁאֵינוֹ מִשְׁתַּמֵּר לָרֶגֶל.§ "וְאִם אָמַר הִפְרַשְׁתִּי לְתוֹכָהּ רְבִיעִית קֹדֶשׁ נֶאֱמָן".§ *תְּנַן הָתָם: מוֹדִין בֵּית שַׁמַּאי וּבֵית הִלֵּל שֶׁבּוֹדְקִין לְעוֹשֵׂי פֶסַח, וְאֵין בּוֹדְקִין לְאוֹכְלֵי תְרוּמָה. מַאי בּוֹדְקִין? אָמַר רַב יְהוּדָה *אָמַר שְׁמוּאֵל: [ב]מְנַפֵּחַ אָדָם בֵּית הַפְּרָס וְהוֹלֵךְ. *וְר' חִיָּיא בַּר אַבָּא מִשְּׁמֵיהּ דְּעוּלָּא אָמַר: [ג]בֵּית הַפְּרָס שֶׁנִּדַּשׁ טָהוֹר לְעוֹשֵׂי פֶסַח, *לֹא הֶעֱמִידוּ דִּבְרֵיהֶן בִּמְקוֹם כָּרֵת. לְאוֹכְלֵי תְרוּמָה — הֶעֱמִידוּ דִּבְרֵיהֶן בִּמְקוֹם מִיתָה. אִיבַּעְיָא לְהוּ: בָּדַק לְפִסְחוֹ, מַהוּ שֶׁיֹּאכַל בִּתְרוּמָתוֹ? עוּלָּא אָמַר: בָּדַק לְפִסְחוֹ מוּתָּר לֶאֱכוֹל בִּתְרוּמָתוֹ, רַבָּה בַּר עוּלָּא אָמַר: בָּדַק לְפִסְחוֹ — אָסוּר לֶאֱכוֹל בִּתְרוּמָתוֹ. א"ל הַהוּא סָבָא: לָא תִּפְלוֹג עֲלֵיהּ דְּעוּלָּא, דִּתְנַן כְּוָותֵיהּ: וְאִם אָמַר: הִפְרַשְׁתִּי לְתוֹכָהּ רְבִיעִית קֹדֶשׁ — נֶאֱמָן. אַלְמָא: מִדִּמְהֵימַן אַקֹּדֶשׁ — מְהֵימַן נַמִי אַתְּרוּמָה, הָכָא נַמִי: מִדִּמְהֵימַן אַפֶּסַח — מְהֵימַן נַמִי אַתְּרוּמָה.§ [ד]"כַּדֵּי יַיִן וְכַדֵּי שֶׁמֶן כו'".§ [ה]תָּנָא: אֵין נֶאֱמָנִין לֹא עַל הַקַּנְקַנִּים וְלֹא עַל הַתְּרוּמָה. קַנְקַנִּים דְּמַאי? אִי קַנְקַנִּים דְּקֹדֶשׁ — מִיגּוֹ דִּמְהֵימַן אַקֹּדֶשׁ, מְהֵימַן נַמִי אַקַּנְקַנִּים! אֶלָּא קַנְקַנִּים דִּתְרוּמָה — פְּשִׁיטָא; הָשְׁתָּא אַתְּרוּמָה לָא מְהֵימַן — אַקַּנְקַנִּים מְהֵימַן?! אֶלָּא בְּרֵיקָנִים דְּקֹדֶשׁ וּבִשְׁאָר יְמוֹת הַשָּׁנָה, וּבִמְלֵאִין דִּתְרוּמָה וּבִשְׁעַת הַגִּיתּוֹת. תְּנַן: כַּדֵּי יַיִן וְכַדֵּי שֶׁמֶן הַמְדוּמָּעוֹת. מַאי לָאו מְדוּמָּעוֹת דִּתְרוּמָה? אָמְרֵי דְּבֵי ר' חִיָּיא: מְדוּמָּעוֹת דְּקֹדֶשׁ. וּמִי אִיכָּא דִּימּוּעַ לַקֹּדֶשׁ? אָמְרֵי דְּבֵי ר' אֶלְעַאי: [ו]בִּמְטַהֵר אֶת טִבְלוֹ לִיטּוֹל מִמֶּנּוּ נְסָכִים.§ [ח]"קוֹדֶם לַגִּיתּוֹת שִׁבְעִים יוֹם".§ אָמַר אַבָּיֵי, שְׁמַע מִינָּהּ: דִּינָא הוּא דְּעִילָוֵיהּ אָרִיסָא לְמִיטְרַח אַגּוּלְפֵי שִׁבְעִים יוֹמִין מִקַּמֵּי מַעַצַרְתָּא.§

מתני' [ט]מִן הַמּוֹדִיעִים וְלִפְנִים — נֶאֱמָנִין עַל כְּלֵי חֶרֶס, מִן הַמּוֹדִיעִים וְלַחוּץ — אֵין נֶאֱמָנִין. כֵּיצַד? [י]הַקַּדָּר שֶׁהוּא מוֹכֵר הַקְּדֵרוֹת נִכְנַס לִפְנִים מִן הַמּוֹדִיעִים, הוּא הַקַּדָּר וְהֵן הַקְּדֵרוֹת וְהֵן הַלּוֹקְחִין — נֶאֱמָן, יָצָא — אֵינוֹ נֶאֱמָן.§ **גמ'** [כ]תָּנָא: מוֹדִיעִים, פְּעָמִים כְּלִפְנִים, פְּעָמִים כְּלַחוּץ. כֵּיצַד? קַדָּר יוֹצֵא וְחָבֵר נִכְנָס — כְּלִפְנִים, שְׁנֵיהֶן נִכְנָסִין

או

תוספות

חבר ועם הארץ שירשו את אביהם. [*מתני' היא בפ"ו דדמאי]. ופירש רש"י טעם של משנה זו מטעם ברירה, דמעיקרא הוברר הדבר. שאלו לחלקו נפל אבל בשני מינים – לא אמרינן הוברר הדבר וכן פירש הוא עצמו משנה אחרת*: גר ונכרי שירשו את אביהן, יכול לומר: טול אתה ע"ז ואני אטול מעות, דאית ליה ברירה התם. והיה קשה למורי: כיון דסתם משנה אית ליה ברירה – תקשי מיניה לרבי יוחנן דאמר: אחין שחלקו – לקוחות הן, ומחזירין זה לזה ביובל. אלמא אין ברירה! וכן בבכורות פרק "יש בכור" (דף מח.) גבי נתנו עד שלא חלקו מוקי רבא, ר' מאיר ורבי יהודה כרב אסי, דאמר: האחין שחלקו – מחצה יורשין ומחצה לקוחות. אלמא: מספקא להו אי יש ברירה או לא. ומההיא ד"הלוקח יין מן הכותים" (דמאי פ"ז מ"ד) ליכא לאקשויי דשמעינן מינה ברירה, דהתם טעמא אחרינא איכא, שמפרש דבריו בהדיא. אבל ירושה, דממילא הויא – לא. וכן בפ' "בכל מערבין" (עירובין דף לז: ושם) איכא מאן דאית ליה הך סברא. וכי תימא דמדרבנן מודה רבי יוחנן דאית ליה ברירה – הא שמעינן ליה בשילהי בילה (דף לז: ושם) אין ברירה אף בעירובי תחומין. ומיהו, כמה סתמי משניות דמלינו דאין ברירה, ובכמה מקומות פלוגתא דתנאי, ובפרק "בכל מערבין" (עירובין דף לז: ושם) דדחיק לאתויי תנא דברירה – לא מייתי הך, משום דעדיפא ליה לאתויי מילתא דהתנא נזכר בה, וגם מילתא דאיירי בעירובי תחומין דאיירי בה:

מנפח אדם בית הפרס. (א) פירשתי בברכות (דף יט:) כל אורך הדברים מפירשת רבי יהודה נ"ע:

במטהר טבלו ליקח הימנו נסכים. פירש רש"י: דאיכא קדש ותרומה דמהימן. דנאמן אתרומה וקנקנים במיגו דמהימן אקדש, שגנאי הוא לו אם קנקנים שהיה בו הקדישו טמאים. תימה: דא"כ, אמאי נקט שבעים יום קודם? אפילו בשאר ימות השנה נמי, דהא תנן: ואם אמר הפרשתי לתוכה רביעית קדש – נאמן! ותירץ הר"ר אלחנן: דהכא מיירי שייחדו לנסכים כשיצטרך ממנו. אבל התם מיירי – בשכבר הקדישו לכך: הגבאין

רש"י

יָכוֹל לוֹמַר לוֹ טוֹל אַתָּה חִטִּין בְּמָקוֹם פְּלוֹנִי. שֶׁיּוֹדֵעַ בָּהֶן שֶׁהוּכְשְׁרוּ, וַאֲנִי אֶטּוֹל חִטִּים בְּמָקוֹם פְּלוֹנִי שֶׁיּוֹדֵעַ שֶׁלֹּא הוּכְשְׁרוּ. דְּכֵיוָן דְּחַד מִינָא הֵן – אָמְרִי': יֵשׁ בְּרֵירָה, שֶׁאֵלּוּ הֵן חֶלְקוֹ שֶׁל זֶה, וְאֵלּוּ הֵן חֶלְקוֹ שֶׁל זֶה, וְלֹא הֶחֱלִיף לוֹ חָבֵר לְע"ה חֶלְקוֹ שֶׁבַּטְּמֵאִין בִּשְׁבִיל חֶלְקוֹ שֶׁל ע"ה בַּטְּהוֹרִין. אֲבָל בִּשְׁנֵי מִינִין – אֵין לוֹמַר בְּרֵירָה, דִּכְשֶׁמֵּת אֲבִיהֶן נָפַל חֵלֶק לָזֶה וְחֵלֶק לָזֶה בְּכָל הַמִּינִים, וְנִמְצָא חָבֵר זֶה מַחֲלִיפָהּ לוֹ, וְעוֹבֵר בְּ"לִפְנֵי עִוֵּר לֹא תִתֵּן מִכְשׁוֹל" (ויקרא יט): שׂוֹרֵף אֶת הַלַּח. אִם כֹּהֵן הוּא, וְיֵשׁ שֶׁמֶן לִתְרוּמָה – מַדְלִיקוֹ לְנֵרוֹת: בְּדָבָר שֶׁאֵין לוֹ גַּת. כְּגוֹן שֵׁכַר תְּמָרִים שֶׁל תְּרוּמָה, וְהַאי שׂוֹרֵף – לְשׁוֹן אִיבּוּד הוּא: וְיַנִּיחֶנּוּ לָרֶגֶל. שֶׁטּוּמְאַת עַם הָאָרֶץ אֵינָהּ בָּרֶגֶל, וְיִמְכְּרֶנָּה: שֶׁבּוֹדְקִין לְעוֹשֵׂי פֶּסַח. בֵּית הַפְּרָס, כִּדְמְפָרֵשׁ וְאָזֵיל: הָיָה הוֹלֵךְ לַעֲשׂוֹת פִּסְחוֹ, וּבֵית הַפְּרָס שֶׁל שָׂדֶה שֶׁנֶּחְרַשׁ בּוֹ קֶבֶר מַפְסִיקוֹ – בּוֹדְקוֹ בִּנְפִיחָה. וְאִם יֵשׁ עֶצֶם כִּשְׂעוֹרָה – רוֹאֵהוּ וְנִשְׁמָט מִמֶּנּוּ, וְעֶצֶם כִּשְׂעוֹרָה אֵינוֹ מְטַמֵּא בְּאֹהֶל, אֶלָּא בְּמַגָּע וּבְמַשָּׂא. לְפִיכָךְ בּוֹדֵק בִּנְפִיחָה, שֶׁלֹּא יְסִיטֶנּוּ בְּרַגְלוֹ: וְאֵין בּוֹדְקִין לְאוֹכְלֵי תְּרוּמָה. אֵין סוֹמְכִין עַל בְּדִיקָה זוֹ. דְּכֵיוָן דְּאֵין זְמַן קָבוּעַ לַאֲכִילָה – יַמְתִּין שִׁבְעָה יָמִים וְיַזֶּה שְׁלִישִׁי וּשְׁבִיעִי וְיִטְבּוֹל. אֲבָל גַּבֵּי פֶּסַח, הוֹאִיל וּבֵית הַפְּרָס דְּרַבָּנַן – לֹא הֶעֱמִידוּ דִּבְרֵיהֶם בִּמְקוֹם כָּרֵת: שֶׁנִּידַּשׁ. בָּרֶגֶל, וְזוֹ הִיא בְּדִיקָתוֹ: בּוֹדֵק אִם נִידַּשׁ אוֹ לֹא נִידַּשׁ: בְּמָקוֹם שֶׁיֵּשׁ בּוֹ חִיּוּב מִיתָה. כְּגוֹן טָמֵא הָאוֹכֵל תְּרוּמָה: מִיגּוֹ דִּמְהֵימַן אַקֹּדֶשׁ מְהֵימַן אַתְּרוּמָה. שֶׁגְּנַאי הוּא לַמִּזְבֵּחַ שֶׁתְּהֵא תְּרוּמָה הַמְחוּבֶּרֶת לוֹ בְּחֶזְקַת טוּמְאָה, וְהַקֹּדֶשׁ יִקְרַב לַמִּזְבֵּחַ: בְּרֵיקָנִין דְּקֹדֶשׁ. לְאַחַר שֶׁעֵירָה מֵהֶן קוֹדֶשׁ וְהָיָה שׁוֹמְרָן לְקֹדֶשׁ – אֵינוֹ נֶאֱמָן עַל שְׁמִירָתָן: וּבִשְׁאָר כָּל יְמוֹת הַשָּׁנָה. כְּלוֹמַר, כָּל יְמוֹת הַשָּׁנָה. דִּלְקֹדֶשׁ אֵין חִילּוּק בֵּין שְׁעַת הַגִּיתּוֹת לִשְׁאָר יְמוֹת הַשָּׁנָה: וּבִמְלֵאִין דִּתְרוּמָה בִּשְׁעַת הַגִּיתּוֹת. שֶׁאע"פ שֶׁלֹּא גָּזְרוּ עַל תְּרוּמָתָן בִּשְׁעַת הַגִּיתּוֹת מִפְּנֵי הֶפְסֵד כֹּהֲנִים חֲבֵרִים, דְּנִמְלְאָה מַפְסִידָן מֵרוֹב תְּרוּמוֹת אֶרֶץ יִשְׂרָאֵל – עַל הַקַּנְקַנִּים לֹא הֶאֱמִינוּם, וְאֵין הַכֹּהֲנִים חֲבֵרִים מְקַבְּלִין מֵהֶן הַקַּנְקַנִּים עִם הַתְּרוּמָה, אֲבָל מְעָרִין אוֹתָהּ לִכְלֵיהֶן. וְדִכְוָותָהּ אָמְרִינַן לְקַמָּן: אַל תִּתְמַהּ, שֶׁהֲרֵי לָגִין טְמֵאִין טוּמְאַת שִׁבְעָה, וּמַשְׁקִין טְהוֹרִים: מַאי לָאו מְדוּמָּעוֹת דִּתְרוּמָה. וְקָתָנֵי: נֶאֱמָן אַכַּדִּין: – תוס'. וּמִי אִיכָּא דִּימּוּעַ לַקֹּדֶשׁ. טֶבֶל שֶׁלֹּא נִתְקַן מְדוּמָּע בִּתְרוּמָה. אֲבָל קֹדֶשׁ לֹא הוּזְקְקוּ לִפְרוֹשׁ מִתּוֹכָהּ, שֶׁיְּהֵא הַטֶּבֶל מְדוּמָּע בְּתוֹכוֹ. ע"כ: בִּמְטַהֵר אֶת טִבְלוֹ לִנְסָכִים. דְּאִיכָּא חוּלִּין וְקֹדֶשׁ וּתְרוּמָה, מִיגּוֹ דִּמְהֵימַן אַקֹּדֶשׁ – מְהֵימַן נַמִי אַתְּרוּמָה וְאַקַּנְקַנִּים, שֶׁגְּנַאי לַקֹּדֶשׁ שֶׁיְּהוּ הַקַּנְקַנִּים שֶׁעֵירוּהוּ מֵהֶן בְּחֶזְקַת טוּמְאָה וְהוּא קָרֵב: **מתני'** מִן הַמּוֹדִיעִים וְלִפְנִים. מוֹדִיעִים שֵׁם כְּרַךְ רָחוֹק מִירוּשָׁלַיִם ט"ו מִיל, כִּדְאָמַר בְּמַסֶּכֶת פְּסָחִים (דף צג:). מִמֶּנּוּ וְלִפְנִים לְצַד יְרוּשָׁלַיִם – נֶאֱמָנִין קַדָּרִין עַמֵּי הָאָרֶץ לִיקַּח מֵהֶן כְּלֵי חֶרֶס הַדַּקִּין, כְּגוֹן קְדֵרוֹת כּוֹסוֹת וְקִיתוֹנִיּוֹת, שֶׁאִי אֶפְשָׁר בְּלֹא הֵם. וּבִירוּשָׁלַיִם אֵין עוֹשִׂין כִּבְשׁוֹנוֹת מִפְּנֵי הֶעָשָׁן, לֹא לְסִיד וְלֹא לִקְדֵרוֹת, וּלְפִיכָךְ הֶאֱמִינוּם שֶׁלֹּא לִגְזוֹר עֲלֵיהֶן, שֶׁאֵין גּוֹזְרִין גְּזֵירָה עַל הַצִּבּוּר שֶׁאֵין רוֹב הַצִּבּוּר יְכוֹלִין לַעֲמוֹד בָּהּ: הוּא הַקַּדָּר. מִי שֶׁהֱבִיאָן (*חוּץ) לַמּוֹדִיעִים הֶאֱמִינוּהוּ, לְפִי שֶׁא"א. אֲבָל אִם מְסָרָן לְיַד קַדָּר עַם הָאָרֶץ הַיּוֹשֵׁב בְּמוֹדִיעִים אוֹ לִפְנִים – לֹא הֶאֱמִינוּהוּ: וְהֵן הַקְּדֵירוֹת. עַל אוֹתָן הַקְּדֵירוֹת שֶׁהֱבִיא הוּא הֶאֱמִינוּהוּ, וְלֹא לְצָרֵף עִמָּהֶן קְדֵירוֹת שֶׁל קַדָּר אַחֵר הַיּוֹשֵׁב בְּמוֹדִיעִים: וְהֵן הַלּוֹקְחִין. חֲבֵרִים שֶׁרָאוּהוּ שֶׁהֱבִיאָן – נֶאֱמָן הַקַּדָּר אֶצְלָן, וְלֹא אֵצֶל לוֹקְחִים אֲחֵרִים: יָצָא. מִן הַמּוֹדִיעִים לָשׁוּב לַאֲחוֹרָיו – אֵינוֹ נֶאֱמָן: **גמ'** מוֹדִיעִים. הַכְּרַךְ עַצְמוֹ: פְּעָמִים כְּלִפְנִים כו' קַדָּר יוֹצֵא. מִלִּפְנִים מִן הַמּוֹדִיעִים, וְנִכְנָס לַמּוֹדִיעִים: וְחָבֵר. בָּא מִחוּץ לַמּוֹדִיעִים וְנִכְנָס לַמּוֹדִיעִים: כְּלִפְנִים. מוּתָּר לִיקַּח מִמֶּנּוּ, שֶׁהַקַּדָּר לֹא יַחֲזוֹר עוֹד לַאֲחוֹרָיו, וְאִם לֹא עַכְשָׁיו יִקַּח – אֵימָתַי: שְׁנֵיהֶן נִכְנָסִין. מִחוּץ לַמּוֹדִיעִים, וּבָאוּ בְּתוֹךְ הַכְּרַךְ – כְּלַחוּץ. אֶלָּא יַמְתִּין עַד שֶׁיְּהֵא מִן כְּרַךְ וְלִפְנִים:

וְכֵן

עין משפט נר מצוה

מתנייא פ"ו דדמאי כנ"ל

מה א מיי' פי"א מהל' מעשר הלכה ו:

[שם מ"י]

מו ב ג מיי' פ"ו מהל' קרבן פסח הלכה ח:

מז ד ה ו מיי' פי"א מהל' מטמאי משכב ומושב הלכה ד:

מח ז ח מיי' שם הל' ה:

מט ט מיי' שם הלכה ו:

נ י מיי' שם הלכה ז:

נא כ מיי' שם הלכה ו:

[ועיין ברכות יט: מ"ש שם על הגליון]

[עי' תוס' פסחים לב: ד"ה בודקין כו' ותוס' עירובין כו: ד"ה ולכהן]

רבינו חננאל

חבר ועם הארץ שירשו אביהם לא יאמר החבר לעם הארץ טול אתה לח ואני יבש. ותני עלה אותו חבר שורף את הלח ומניח את היבש ואמאי יניחנו לגת הבאה שהוא נאמן בה ופרשי' בדבר שאין לו גת כגון דבש וחלב וכיוצא בהן. ואמרינן יניחנו לרגל וכדבעינן למימר לקמן טומאת עם הארץ ברגל רחמנא טהריה. ודחי' בדבר שאין משתמר לרגל עליה תנינן שורף את הלח: ואם אמר הפרשתי לתוכה רביעית קדש נאמן. ואם בדק לפסחו מותר לאכול בתרומתו כעולא דדייקא מתניתין כוותיה דקתני אם אמר הפרשתי לתוכה רביעית קדש נאמן. מדמהימן אקדש מהימן נמי אתרומה. הכא נמי מדמהימן אפסח מהימן נמי אתרומה. כדי יין וכדי שמן המדומעות כו' אוקימנא להא דתנינן בתוספתא אין נאמנין לא על הקנקנים ולא על התרומה בקנקנים דקדש ריקנים ובשאר ימות השנה במלאין דתרומה [ובשעת הגיתות]. והא דתנן במתניתין כדי יין וכדי שמן המדומעות אוקימנא בקדש. ומקשינן וכי איכא דימוע בקדש. פי' תרומה שנפלה בחולין נדמעו זה נקרא דמע אבל אין לשון דימוע בקדש. ושנינן אין איכא דימוע בקדש כגון דמשמר טבלו להפריש ממנו נסכים לקדש. כי האי גוונא משכחת לה דימוע בקדש: מתני' מן המודיעין ולפנים כו'. מודיעין מקום כדתנא מודיעין רחוקה מירושלים ט"ו מיל. אוקימנא כדתנא מודיעין פעמים כלפנים פעמים כלחוץ כיצד קדר יוצא וחבר נכנס כלפנים שניהן נכנסין או שניהן יוצאין מודיעין עצמה כלחוץ. תנא

מסורת הש"ס

דמאי פ"ו מ"ט

תוספת' דדמאי פ"ה

פסחים לב: אהלות פי"ח מ"ד

ברכות יט: עירובין ל: פסחים לב: מו"ק ה: כתובות כח: בכורות כט. נדה נז.

[נ"ל מחוץ]

הגהות הב"ח

(א) תוס' ד"ה מנפח כו' פירשתי בברכות. נ"ב בש"ס שלנו לא נמצא כלום כי אם בבכורו' דף כט בד"ה היכי אזיל האריך בזה:

אוֹ שְׁנֵיהֶן יוֹצְאִין — כְּלַחוּץ. אָמַר אַבַּיֵי, אַף אֲנַן נַמִּי תָּנֵינָא: הַקַּדָּר שֶׁמָּכַר אֶת הַקְּדֵירוֹת וְנִכְנַס לִפְנִים מִן הַמּוֹדִיעִים. טַעְמָא — דְּלִפְנִים מִן הַמּוֹדִיעִים, הָא מוֹדִיעִים גּוּפָהּ — לָא מְהֵימָן, אֵימָא סֵיפָא: יָצָא — אֵינוֹ נֶאֱמָן, הָא מוֹדִיעִים גּוּפָהּ — נֶאֱמָן! אֶלָּא לָאו ש"מ: כָּאן — בְּקַדָּר יוֹצֵא וְחָבֵר נִכְנָס, כָּאן — כְּשֶׁשְּׁנֵיהֶן יוֹצְאִין אוֹ שְׁנֵיהֶן נִכְנָסִין שְׁמַע מִינַּהּ. *תָּנָא: נֶאֱמָנִין בִּכְלֵי חֶרֶס הַדַּקִּין לַקּוֹדֶשׁ. אָמַר ר"ל: וְהוּא שֶׁנִּיטָּלִין בְּיָדוֹ אַחַת. וְר' יוֹחָנָן אָמַר: אֲפִי' שֶׁאֵין נִיטָּלִין בְּיָדוֹ אַחַת. אָמַר ר"ל: לֹא שָׁנוּ אֶלָּא רֵיקָנִין, אֲבָל מְלֵאִין — לֹא. א]וְרַבִּי יוֹחָנָן אאָמַר: אֲפִי' מְלֵאִים, וַאֲפִילּוּ אַפִּיקַרְסוּתוֹ לְתוֹכוֹ. וְאָמַר רָבָא: בוּמוֹדֶה ר' יוֹחָנָן בְּמַשְׁקִין עַצְמָן שֶׁהֵן טְמֵאִין. וְאַל תִּתְמַהּ, *שֶׁהֲרֵי לָגִין מָלֵא מַשְׁקִין, לָגִין טְמֵאִין טוּמְאַת שִׁבְעָה וּמַשְׁקִין טְהוֹרִין.§ **מתני'** הַגַּבָּאִין שֶׁנִּכְנְסוּ לְתוֹךְ הַבַּיִת, וְכֵן הַגַּנָּבִים שֶׁהֶחְזִירוּ אֶת הַכֵּלִים, נֶאֱמָנִין לוֹמַר "לֹא נָגַעְנוּ", וּבִירוּשָׁלַיִם נֶאֱמָנִין עַל הַקּוֹדֶשׁ, וּבִשְׁעַת הָרֶגֶל אַף עַל הַתְּרוּמָה.§ **גמ'** וּרְמִינְהִי: *הַגַּבָּאִין שֶׁנִּכְנְסוּ לְתוֹךְ הַבַּיִת, הַבַּיִת כּוּלּוֹ טָמֵא! גל"ק: הָא — דְּאִיכָּא גּוֹי בַּהֲדַיְיהוּ, הָא — דְּלֵיכָּא גּוֹי בַּהֲדַיְיהוּ, דִּתְנַן: *אִם יֵשׁ גּוֹי עִמָּהֶן — נֶאֱמָנִין לוֹמַר "לֹא נִכְנַסְנוּ" אֲבָל אֵין נֶאֱמָנִים לוֹמַר "נִכְנַסְנוּ אֲבָל לֹא נָגַעְנוּ". וְכִי אִיכָּא גּוֹי בַּהֲדַיְיהוּ מַאי הָוֵי? ר' יוֹחָנָן וְר' אֶלְעָזָר, חַד אָמַר: דאֵימַת גּוֹי עֲלֵיהֶן, וְחַד אָמַר: אֵימַת מַלְכוּת עֲלֵיהֶן. מַאי בֵּינַיְיהוּ? אִיכָּא בֵּינַיְיהוּ גּוֹי שֶׁאֵינוֹ חָשׁוּב.§ ה"וְכֵן הַגַּנָּבִים שֶׁהֶחְזִירוּ אֶת הַכֵּלִים".§ וּרְמִינְהִי: *הַגַּנָּבִים שֶׁנִּכְנְסוּ לְתוֹךְ הַבַּיִת — אֵינוֹ טָמֵא אֶלָּא מְקוֹם דְּרִיסַת רַגְלֵי הַגַּנָּבִים! *אָמַר רַב פִּנְחָס מִשְּׁמֵיהּ (*דְּרַב): וכְּשֶׁעָשׂוּ תְּשׁוּבָה. דַּיְקָא נַמִּי, דְּקָתָנֵי: "שֶׁהֶחְזִירוּ אֶת הַכֵּלִים", ש"מ.§ ז"וּבִירוּשָׁלַיִם נֶאֱמָנִין עַל הַקּוֹדֶשׁ".§ חתָּנָא: נֶאֱמָנִין עַל כְּלֵי חֶרֶס גַּסִּין לַקּוֹדֶשׁ. וְכָל כָּךְ לָמָּה — *שֶׁאֵין עוֹשִׂין כִּבְשׁוֹנוֹת בִּירוּשָׁלַיִם.§ ט"וּבִשְׁעַת הָרֶגֶל אַף עַל הַתְּרוּמָה".§ מְנָהָנֵי מִילֵּי? אָמַר רַבִּי יְהוֹשֻׁעַ בֶּן לֵוִי: *דְּאָמַר קְרָאךְ ° "וַיֵּאָסֵף כָּל אִישׁ יִשְׂרָאֵל אֶל הָעִיר כְּאִישׁ אֶחָד חֲבֵרִים" — הַכָּתוּב עֲשָׂאָן כּוּלָּן חֲבֵרִים.§ **מתני'** *הַפּוֹתֵחַ אֶת חָבִיתוֹ, וְהַמַּתְחִיל בְּעִיסָּתוֹ עַל גַּב הָרֶגֶל, ר' יְהוּדָה אוֹמֵר: יִגְמוֹר, וַחכ"א: ילֹא יִגְמוֹר.§ **גמ'** יָתֵיב ר' אַמִּי וְרַבִּי יִצְחָק נַפָּחָא אַקִּילְעָא דְּר' יִצְחָק נַפָּחָא. פְּתַח חַד וַאֲמַר: מַהוּ שֶׁיַּנִּיחֶנָּה לְרֶגֶל אַחֵר? א"ל אִידַּךְ: יַד הַכֹּל מְמַשְׁמְשִׁין בָּהּ, וְאַתְּ אָמְרַתְּ יַנִּיחֶנָּה לְרֶגֶל אַחֵר?! א"ל: אַטּוּ עַד הָאִידָּנָא לָאו יַד הַכֹּל מְמַשְׁמְשִׁין בָּהּ? א"ל: הָכִי הַשְׁתָּא! בִּשְׁלָמָא עַד הָאִידָּנָא — טוּמְאַת עַם הָאָרֶץ בָּרֶגֶל רַחֲמָנָא טַהֲרָהּ, אֶלָּא הַשְׁתָּא — טְמֵאָה הִיא. נֵימָא כְּתַנָּאֵי; דְּתָנֵי חֲדָא: יַנִּיחֶנָּה לְרֶגֶל אַחֵר, וְתַנְיָא אִידַּךְ: לֹא יַנִּיחֶנָּה לְרֶגֶל אַחֵר. מַאי לָאו תַּנָּאֵי הִיא! לָא, הָא דְּקָתָנֵי יַנִּיחֶנָּה — ר' יְהוּדָה, וְהָא דְּקָתָנֵי לֹא יַנִּיחֶנָּה — רַבָּנַן. וְתִסְבְּרָא?! (א)הָא רַבִּי יְהוּדָה "יִגְמוֹר" קָאָמַר! אֶלָּא: הָא דְּקָתָנֵי לֹא יַנִּיחֶנָּה — רַבִּי יְהוּדָה, וְהָא דְּקָתָנֵי יַנִּיחֶנָּה — רַבָּנַן. וּמַאי לֹא יַנִּיחֶנָּה — שֶׁאֵין צָרִיךְ לְהַנִּיחָהּ.§ **מתני'** מִשֶּׁעָבַר הָרֶגֶל מַעֲבִירִין עַל טָהֳרַת הָעֲזָרָה. עָבַר הָרֶגֶל לְיוֹם שִׁשִּׁי — לֹא הָיוּ מַעֲבִירִין, מִפְּנֵי כְּבוֹד הַשַּׁבָּת. רַבִּי יְהוּדָה אוֹמֵר: אַף לֹא בְּיוֹם ה', שֶׁאֵין הַכֹּהֲנִים פְּנוּיִין.§ **גמ'** תָּנָא: שֶׁאֵין הַכֹּהֲנִים פְּנוּיִין מִלְּהוֹצִיא בַּדֶּשֶׁן.§ **מתני'** כֵּיצַד מַעֲבִירִין עַל טָהֳרַת עֲזָרָה? כמַטְבִּילִין אֶת הַכֵּלִים שֶׁהָיוּ בַּמִּקְדָּשׁ, וְאוֹמְרִין לָהֶם: הִזָּהֲרוּ

שֶׁלֹּא

וְכֵן שְׁנֵיהֶם יוֹצְאִין. הוֹאִיל וּמְלָאוֹ לִפְנִים וְשָׁם לֹא לָקַח – (*וּמִמֶּנּוּ) לֹא יִקַּח עוֹד. וְכ"ש קַדָּר נִכְנָס וְחָבֵר יוֹצֵא, הוֹאִיל וְסוֹף הַקַּדָּר לִיכָּנֵס לִפְנִים – יַחֲזוֹר הֶחָבֵר הַצָּרִיךְ לִיקַּח, וְיִקַּח: תָּנָא נֶאֱמָנִין עַל כְּלֵי חֶרֶס הַדַּקִּין לַקֹּדֶשׁ. הָא דִּתְנַן: מִן הַמּוֹדִיעִים וְלִפְנִים נֶאֱמָנִין עַל כְּלֵי חֶרֶס – בִּכְלֵי חֶרֶס הַדַּקִּין אָמְרוּ, שֶׁאִ"א בְּלֹא הֵם, כִּדְפָרְשִׁינַן לְעֵיל. אֲבָל גַּסִּין, כְּגוֹן חָבִית לְיַיִן – אֵין נֶאֱמָנִין אֶלָּא בְּתוֹךְ יְרוּשָׁלַיִם, כִּדְלְקַמָּן. וַאֲנִי לֹא כָּךְ שָׁמַעְתִּי, וְלִבִּי מְגַמְגֵּם עַל שְׁמוּעָתִי שֶׁשָּׁמַעְתִּי, כְּשֶׁפִּיהֶן צַר שֶׁאֵין אֶצְבָּעוֹ נִכְנָס לְתוֹכוֹ, וְסוֹפֵינוּ שֶׁשָּׁנוּ מְטַהֲרִין אוֹתָם אֲפִילּוּ מְלֵאִים מַשְׁקִין טְמֵאִין: וַאֲפִי' אַפִּיקַרְסוּתוֹ בְּתוֹכוֹ. אֲפִי' מְלֵאִין מַשְׁקִין שֶׁלּוֹ, שֶׁאֵינָן שֶׁל קֹדֶשׁ: וְאַל תִּתְמַהּ. שֶׁכָּל דִּבְרֵי חֲכָמִי' כָּךְ הֵן, שֶׁהֲרֵי שָׁמַעְתִּי אֵצֶל כְּלֵי חֶרֶס הַמַּצִּיל אֶת הַמַּשְׁקִין שֶׁבְּתוֹכוֹ וְאֵין מַצִּיל כָּל כְּלֵי שֶׁטֶף, שֶׁהַלָּגִין טְמֵאִין טוּמְאַת שִׁבְעָה וְהַמַּשְׁקִין טְהוֹרִין: **מתני'** הַגַּבָּאִין. יִשְׂרָאֵל שֶׁהֵן גַּבָּאִין לְמֶלֶךְ גּוֹי, לִגְבּוֹת מִיַּד יִשְׂרָאֵל גּוּלְגָּלִיּוֹת וּמִסִּין וְאַרְנוֹנִיּוֹת: שֶׁנִּכְנְסוּ לְתוֹךְ הַבַּיִת. לַעֲבוֹט עֲבוֹטוֹ, וְכֵן הַגַּנָּבִים שֶׁגָּנְבוּ כְּלֵי חֶרֶס וְהֶחֱזִירוּם: נֶאֱמָנִים לוֹמַר. שֶׁלֹּא נָגְעוּ לְתוֹכוֹ, לַקֹּדֶשׁ – נֶאֱמָנִין, אֲבָל לֹא לַתְּרוּמָה. דְּכוּלָּהּ מַתְנִי' אַחוֹמֶר בַּקֹּדֶשׁ מִתְּרוּמָה קָיְימָא, וּבְהֶדְיָא שָׁנִינוּ בַּתּוֹסֶפְתָּא*: הַגַּבָּאִין שֶׁנִּכְנְסוּ לְתוֹךְ הַבַּיִת נֶאֱמָנִין עַל טָהֳרַת חַטָּאת וְאֵין נֶאֱמָנִין עַל טָהֳרַת תְּרוּמָה. וְהַאי חַטָּאת – בְּשַׂר קֹדֶשׁ וְלֹא אֵפֶר חַטָּאת, כִּדְמוּכָח הָתָם. אַף אִם עָשׂוּ תְּשׁוּבָה – דָּשִׁין בְּטוּמְאָה הָיוּ: וּבִירוּשָׁלַיִם נֶאֱמָנִין כו'. מְפָרֵשׁ בַּגְּמָרָא: **גמ'** כָּל הַבַּיִת כּוּלּוֹ טָמֵא. כָּל כְּלֵי הַבַּיִת טְמֵאִין, שֶׁחֶזְקָה הַגַּבָּאִין מְמַשְׁמְשִׁין בַּכֵּלִים: אִיכָּא גּוֹי בַּהֲדַיְיהוּ. אֵין נֶאֱמָנִין לוֹמַר לֹא נָגַעְנוּ, דְּמֵרְתִּתוּ אִם לֹא יְחַפְּשׂוּ כָּל הַבַּיִת: אֵימַת גּוֹי עֲלֵיהֶם. פֶּן יַעֲנִישֵׁם בְּגוּף אוֹ בְּמָמוֹן: אֵימַת מַלְכוּת. שֶׁמָּא יַלְשִׁין עֲלֵיהֶן גּוֹי אֵצֶל הַמֶּלֶךְ: גּוֹי שֶׁאֵינוֹ חָשׁוּב. אֵימָתוֹ לֵיכָּא, אֵימַת מַלְכוּת – אִיכָּא: אֶלָּא מְקוֹם דְּרִיסַת רַגְלֵי הַגַּנָּבִים. מ"מ דְּרִיסָתוֹ מִיהָא טָמֵא, וכ"ש כֵּלִים שֶׁגָּנְבוּ וְהֶחֱזִירוּ: כְּשֶׁעָשׂוּ תְּשׁוּבָה. וּמֵחֲמַת תְּשׁוּבָה הֶחֱזִירוּם, הִלְכָּךְ לָא מְשַׁקְּרִי: עַל כְּלֵי חֶרֶס הַגַּסִּין. וכ"ש הַדַּקִּין. וּבְהֶדְיָא תַּנְיָא בִּירוּשַׁלְמִי: נֶאֱמָנִין עַל טָהֳרַת כָּל הַכֵּלִים לַקֹּדֶשׁ: וְכָל כָּךְ לָמָּה. מְהַדֵּר אַף עַל הַדַּקִּים מִן הַמּוֹדִיעִים וְלִפְנִים: שֶׁאֵין עוֹשִׂין כִּבְשׁוֹנוֹת בִּירוּשָׁלַיִם. לֹא לְדַקִּים וְלֹא לְגַסִּין. וּמִיהוּ, בְּדַקִּים הוּצְרַךְ לְאַנְשֵׁי יְרוּשָׁלַיִם, שֶׁכָּל יָחִיד וְיָחִיד נִסְכּוֹ בְּבֵיתוֹ, לְכָךְ הוֹסִיפוּ לָהֶן טָהֳרָה לַיְחִידִים מִגְּבוּל מוֹדִיעִים. אֲבָל בַּעֲלֵי הַלִּשְׁכָּה *הַמּוֹסְרִין נְסָכִים לַצִּבּוּר – דַּי לָהֶם בַּנִּכְנָסִין לְתוֹךְ הָעִיר, וְלָשָׁם בִּלְבַד הָאֱמִינוּם עַל הֶחָבִיּוֹת. א"נ: יְחִידִים צְרִיכִים לְדַקִּים אַף לְבִישּׁוּל שַׁלְמֵיהֶן יוֹם יוֹם: וַיֵּאָסֵף כָּל אִישׁ יִשְׂרָאֵל וגו'. בְּפִלֶגֶשׁ בַּגִּבְעָה כְּתִיב, שֶׁנֶּאֶסְפוּ כָּל יִשְׂרָאֵל בַּגִּבְעָה: הַכָּתוּב עֲשָׂאָן חֲבֵרִים. וְרֶגֶל שְׁעַת אֲסִיפָה הוּא: **מתני'** הַפּוֹתֵחַ אֶת חֲבִיתוֹ. חָבֵר שֶׁפָּתַח אֶת חֲבִיתוֹ לִמְכּוֹר יַיִן בִּירוּשָׁלַיִם בָּרֶגֶל, וְכָל הַבָּא לִיקַּח מְמַשְׁמֵשׁ. וְאַף עַמֵּי הָאָרֶץ מְמַשְׁמְשִׁים: לֹא יִגְמוֹר. אַחַר הָרֶגֶל, אע"פ שֶׁבָּרֶגֶל הֵן טְהוֹרִין. לֹא שֶׁטָּהֳרָתָן טְהוֹרָה, אֶלָּא שֶׁבָּרֶגֶל הַכֹּל חֲבֵרִים. אֲבָל לְאַחַר הָרֶגֶל – מַגָּעוֹ טָמֵא לְמַפְרֵעַ, כִּדְאָמַר בְּמַתְנִי': עָבַר הָרֶגֶל – מַטְבִּילִין כְּלֵי הָעֲזָרָה, מִפְּנֵי שֶׁנָּגְעוּ בָּהֶן ע"ה בָּרֶגֶל: רַבִּי יְהוּדָה אוֹמֵר יִגְמוֹר. וְטַעְמָא מְפָ' בְּמַסֶּכֶת בֵּיצָה (דף יא:): ג' דְּבָרִים הוּתְּרוּ סוֹפָן מִשּׁוּם תְּחִילָּתָם, וְזֶה כְּמוֹ כֵן, שֶׁאִם אַתָּה אוֹמֵר לֹא יִגְמוֹר – אַף הוּא לֹא יַתְחִיל, וְאֵין מָזוֹן מָצוּי לְעוֹלֵי רְגָלִים: **גמ'** מַהוּ שֶׁיַּנִּיחֶנָּה כו'. אַלִּיבָּא דְּרַבָּנַן בָּעֵי לָהּ: אַטּוּ הָאִידָּנָא. כָּל יְמֵי הָרֶגֶל לֹא מְמַשְׁמְשׁוּ בָּהּ הַכֹּל, וְהִתַּרְתָּ בָּרֶגֶל: טְמֵאָה הִיא. לְמַפְרֵעַ, וְחָבֵר אֵינוֹ רַשַּׁאי לִמְכּוֹר דָּבָר שֶׁהוּא טָמֵא לְעוֹלָם. וי"מ אוֹתָהּ בְּע"ה. וְאִי אֶפְשָׁר לוֹמַר בְּע"ה לֹא יִגְמוֹר – דְּמִי לַיְית לָן, וַהֲלֹא אוֹמֵר שֶׁלָּךְ טָמֵא וְשֶׁלִּי טָהוֹר*, וְיִמְלָא לוֹ מֵחֲבֵירָיו הַרְבֵּה שֶׁיִּמְכּוֹר לָהֶם. וְאִם בָּא לֶאֱסוֹר שֶׁלֹּא יִקְחוּ חֲבֵרִים מִמֶּנּוּ – יִקְחוּ וְלֹא יִקְחוּ מִיבְּעֵי לֵיהּ. וְעוֹד: דְּאָמַר בְּמַסֶּכֶת בֵּיצָה שֶׁזּוֹ הִיא אֶחָד מִג' דְּבָרִים שֶׁהוּתְּרוּ סוֹפָן מִשּׁוּם תְּחִילָּתָן, וְאִי בְּע"ה אֲפִי' לֹא שָׁרֵית לֵיהּ לִגְמוֹר – נִיחָא(ב) כְּמַאי דְּמַזְבִּין בָּרֶגֶל: ה"ג: מַאי לָאו תַּנָּאֵי הִיא לֹא הָא דְּקָתָנֵי יַנִּיחֶנָּה ר' יְהוּדָה וְהָא דְּתָנֵי לֹא יַנִּיחֶנָּה רַבָּנַן וְתִסְבְּרָא וְהָא רַבִּי יְהוּדָה יִגְמוֹר קָאָמַר אֶלָּא הָא דְּתַנְיָא יַנִּיחֶנָּה רַבָּנַן וְהָא דְּתַנְיָא לֹא יַנִּיחֶנָּה רַבִּי יְהוּדָה הִיא וּמַאי לֹא יַנִּיחֶנָּה כו'. מַאי לָאו תַּנָּאֵי הִיא וְאַלִּיבָּא דְּרַבָּנַן, וְתִפְשׁוֹט בַּעְיָא דִּלְעֵיל דִּפְלוּגְתָּא דְּתַנָּאֵי הִיא: **מתני'** מַעֲבִירִין עַל טָהֳרַת עֲזָרָה. מַעֲבִירִין אֶת הַכֵּלִים מִמְּקוֹמָן וּלְהַטְבִּילָן, וּלְטַהֵר אֶת הָעֲזָרָה מִטּוּמְאַת ע"ה שֶׁנָּגְעוּ בָּהֶן בָּרֶגֶל. שֶׁאע"פ שֶׁעֲשָׂאָם הַכָּתוּב חֲבֵרִים בָּרֶגֶל – לֹא מִפְּנֵי שֶׁטְּהוֹרִין הֵן, הִלְכָּךְ לְאַחַר הָרֶגֶל מַגָּעָן טָמֵא לְמַפְרֵעַ: מִפְּנֵי כְּבוֹד הַשַּׁבָּת. שֶׁהָיוּ הַכֹּהֲנִים צְרִיכִין לְהִתְעַסֵּק אִישׁ בְּבֵיתוֹ בְּצָרְכֵי שַׁבָּת: אַף לֹא לַיּוֹם הַחֲמִישִׁי. אִם עָבַר הָרֶגֶל לְיוֹם חֲמִישִׁי, אֵין מַטְבִּילִין אוֹתָן עַד לְאַחַר הַשַּׁבָּת: **גמ'** לְפִי שֶׁאֵין הַכֹּהֲנִים פְּנוּיִין. בְּמוֹצָאֵי יוֹם טוֹב לְהַטְבִּילָן, שֶׁטְּרוּדִין לְהוֹצִיא הַדֶּשֶׁן שֶׁעַל הַתַּפּוּחַ שֶׁבְּאֶמְצַע הַמִּזְבֵּחַ, שֶׁקִּיבְּלוּ שָׁם כָּל יְמוֹת הָרֶגֶל כָּל דֶּשֶׁן שֶׁל מַעֲרָכָה: **מתני'** וְאוֹמְרִים לָהֶם. לַכֹּהֲנִים ע"ה בָּרֶגֶל: הִזָּהֲרוּ שֶׁלֹּא תִּגְּעוּ בַּשֻּׁלְחָן. שֶׁלֹּא יוּכְלוּ לְהַטְבִּילוֹ לְאַחַר הָרֶגֶל, שֶׁאִי אֶפְשָׁר לְסַלְּקוֹ מִמְּקוֹמוֹ, דִּכְתִיב בֵּיהּ: "לֶחֶם פָּנִים לְפָנַי תָּמִיד" (שמות כה):

טְעוּנִין

תוספות

הגבאין שנכנסו לבית וכו'. לקדש. ובתרומה קאי, ולא לחטאת. ובהדיא תניא בתוספתא: הגבאים שנכנסו לבית נאמנין לומר לא נגענו על טהרת חטאת ועל טהרת תרומה. והא חטאת הוי קדש כדקתני התם, ולא אפר חטאת, ואפי' עשו תשובה. הר"ר שמעון:

ובירושלים נאמנין על טהרת כלי חרם הגסים. וכ"ש הדקין. וכן תניא בהדיא בירושלמי: נאמנין על טהרת כל הכלים. הר"ר שמעון:

שלא

הגהות הב"ח

(א) גמ' ותסברא והא ר' יהודה: (ב) רש"י ד"ה טמאה הוא וכו' ניחא ליה במאי:

הגהות מהר"ב רנשבורג

א] גמ' ור' יוחנן אמר אפילו מלאים ואפי' אפיקרסותו לתוכו. נ"ב עי' פרש"י ומ"ש בזה בספר טורי אבן בד"ה ואפילו אפיקרסותו וכו':

רבינו חננאל

תנא נאמנין על כלי חרם הדקין לקדש אמר ר"ל והוא שניטלין בידו אחת וריקנין אבל מליאין לא כלומר אינם נאמנים ור' יוחנן אמר אע"פ שאינן ניטלין בידו אחת ובין מליאין ובין ריקנין ואפי' אפיקרסתו לתוכן נאמנין אמר רבה אע"ג *) דר"ל אמר אין נאמנין על כלי חרם מליאין [מודה] היה במשקין עצמן שהן טהורין ואל תתמה שהרי לגין טמא טומאת שבעה ומשקין טהורין. **) קודם לגיתות שבעים יום נאמן אמר אביי ש"מ דיטרח אריסא מקמי הגתות אגולפי שבעים יום: **מתני'** הגבאים שנכנסו לתוך הבית נאמנים לומר לא נגענו. אוקימנא בדאיכא גוי בהדייהו כדתנן אם יש גוי נאמן לומר נכנסנו אבל לא נגענו מ"ט ר' יוחנן ור' אלעזר חד א' אימת גוי עליהן וחד אמר אימת מלכות עליהן. מאי בינייהו איכא בינייהו גוי שאינו חשוב דלית להו אימה. והא דתנינן הגבאין שנכנסו לתוך הבית כולו טמא אוקימנא בדליכא גוי בהדייהו. דכיון דלית אימתה דחד עלייהו נגעו בכל כלים שבבית. וכן הגנבים שהחזירו את הכלים נאמנים לומר לא נגענו פי' לא נגעו זולתם. דווקא שהחזירו הא לא החזירו כל הבית טמא ומקשינן עלה כל הבית טמא ורמינהו הגנבים שנכנסו לתוך הבית אין טמא אלא מקום רגלי גנבים הנה אע"פ שלא החזירו הכלים הבית טהור כלומר אינו טמא. ופריק רב פנחס בגנבים שבאו לגנוב ועשו תשובה ולא גנבו כלום. ואמרינ' כשם שלא גנבו לא נגעו ואין טמא אלא מקום מגע רגליהם ודאי דאי אפשר לעבור אא"כ נגעו ומשום שעשו תשובה אין אנו מחזיקין אותם בזה הדרך וכן נמי גנבים השנוים במשנתנו אינן נאמנים אלא אם עשו תשובה אבל אם לא עשו תשובה בין אלו ובין אלו הבית כולו טמא. דחיישינן דלמא עברי עלייהו ונגעו בהן כדי לגנבן ונטרדו או לקחו טובים מהן והניחו אלו שלא יכלו לעמסן כולן כאחת. ואמרינן דיקא נמי דקתני במתניתין שהחזירו את הכלים ש"מ כשעשו תשובה ש"מ: ובירושלים נאמנים על הקדש תנא נאמנין על כלי חרם הגסין בירושלים. לפי שאין עושין כבשונות בירושלים ומשום הכי מזדהרי ומנטרי להון לפיכך לא גזרו בהו טומאה מספק. ובשעת הרגל נאמנין אף על התרומה מנא הני מילי אריב"ל דאמר קרא ויאסף כל איש ישראל העירה כאיש אחד חברים הכתוב עשה לכל ישראל בשעת אסיפתן כאחד אפי' את עמי הארץ עשה אותן חברים: **מתני'** הפותח את חביתו והמתחיל בעיסתו ברגל פי' כדי למכור ונשאר לו אחר הרגל ר' יהודה אומר יגמור וחכ"א לא יגמור ומיבעיא לן אליבא דחכמים דאמרי לא יגמור מהו שיניחנה לרגל אחר ודחינן יד הכל ממשמשין בה כלומר נגעו בה עמי הארץ ויניחנה לרגל אחר וא"ת אי הכי ברגל עצמו היאך שותין אותה שאני זה הרגל עצמו דהא טומאת עם הארץ ברגל ההיא רחמנא טהריה הא השתא טמאה היא ואתינן לאוקומה כתנאי ודחינן לה ואסיקנא ההיא תנא דתני יניחנה לרגל אחר לרבנן היא והא דתני לא יניחנה לר' יהודה היא ומאי לא יניחנה כלומר אין צריך להניחה אלא יגמור וישתה את כולה: **ירושלמי** ר' חנניה בשם ר' יוחנן התירו סופן משום תחילתן שאם אתה אומר לא יגמור אף הוא אינו פותח ונמצא ממעט בשמחת הרגל: **מתני'** משעבר הרגל

היו

*) גי' רבינו הוא להיפך מגי' דילן דבמשקין הן טהורין אף לר"ל וגירסתו מוכרחת מהרא"ה שהביא רבה מלגין ודו"ק. **) דברי רבינו אלו עד המשנה שייכים לעיל דף כ"ה ע"ב.

מסורת הש"ס: נ"ל ממנו | [תוספתא פ"ג] | [פ"ג] | לעיל כב: אהלות פ"ה מ"ד | טהרות פ"ז מ"ו | [שם ע"ש] | ג"ז שם | יבמות כב: ב"ק לד: ב"מ סב. סנהדרין פה. | [ב"ק פב: זבחים לו.] | נדה לד | ביצה יא: | שופטים כ | [לעיל כב:]

בס"א הגירסא המספקין וכן הוא בכ"מ פי"א מהל' מטמאי משכב ומושב הל' ו

עין משפט נר מצוה:
נב א ב מיי' פי"א מהל' מטמאי משכב ומושב הלכה ה:
נג ג ד מיי' שם פי"ב הלכה יב:
נד ה ו מיי' שם הל' יד:
נה ז ח מיי' שם פי"א הלכה ה:
נו ט מיי' שם הל' ט:
נז י מיי' שם הל' י:
נח כ מיי' שם הל' יא:

עין משפט נר מצוה

נט א מיי' פי"א מהל' מטמאי משכב ומושב הלכה יא:
ס ב מיי' פ"ז מהלכות כלי המקדש הל' יט:
סא ג ד מיי' פי"א מהל' מטמאי משכב ומושב הלכה יא:
סב ה מיי' פ"ג מהל' כלים הלכה א:
סג ו ז ח מיי' שם פ"ו הלכה טו:

גמרא

תורה אור

א שלא תגעו בשלחן. ב כל הכלים שהיו במקדש יש להם שניים ושלישים, שאם נטמאו הראשונים – יביאו שניים תחתיהן. ג כל הכלים שהיו במקדש טעונין טבילה, חוץ ממזבח הזהב, ומזבח הנחשת, מפני שהן כקרקע, דברי ר"א. וחכ"א: ד מפני שהן מצופין.§ **גמ'** תנא: הזהרו שמא תגעו בשולחן, ובמנורה. ותנא דידן, מ"ט לא תני מנורה? שלחן – כתיב ביה "תמיד", מנורה לא כתיב בה "תמיד". ואידך: כיון דכתיב: ° "ואת המנורה נכח השלחן" (שמות כו) כמאן דכתיב בה תמיד דמי. ואידך: ההוא לקבוע לה מקום הוא דאתא. ותיפוק לי דכלי עץ העשוי לנחת הוא, * ה וכל כלי עץ העשוי לנחת לא מטמא, מאי טעמא – * דומיא דשק בעינן, מה שק מיטלטל מלא וריקם – אף כל מיטלטל מלא וריקם? האי נמי מיטלטל מלא וריקם הוא, כדר"ל. * דאמר ר"ל, מאי דכתיב: ° "על השלחן הטהור" (ויקרא כד) – מכלל שהוא טמא. ואמאי? כלי עץ העשוי לנחת הוא, ואינו מקבל טומאה! אלא מלמד שמגביהין אותו, ומראין בו לעולי רגלים לחם הפנים, ואומרים להם: ראו חיבתכם לפני המקום, סילוקו כסידורו. * דא"ר יהושע בן לוי: נס גדול נעשה בלחם הפנים – כסידורו כך סילוקו, שנאמר: ° "לשום לחם חום ביום הלקחו" (שמואל א כא). ותיפוק לי משום ציפוי, דהתנן: ו השלחן והדולפקי שנפחתו או שחיפן בשיש, ושייר בהם מקום הנחת כוסות – טמא. ר' יהודה אומר: מקום הנחת החתיכות. וכי תימא שאני עצי שטים דחשיבי ולא בטלי – הניחא לר"ל, דאמר: לא שנו אלא בכלי אכסלגים הבאין ממדינת הים, אבל בכלי מסמים – לא בטלי, שפיר. אלא לרבי יוחנן, דאמר: ז אפילו בכלי מסמים נמי בטלי, מאי איכא למימר? וכי תימא: כאן – בציפוי עומד, כאן – בציפוי שאינו עומד, הא בעא מיניה ר"ל מרבי יוחנן: בציפוי עומד או בציפוי שאינו עומד, בחופה את לבזבזיו או בשאינו חופה את לבזבזיו, וא"ל: ח לא שנא בציפוי עומד, ולא שנא בציפוי שאינו עומד, לא שנא בחופה את לבזבזיו ולא שנא בשאינו חופה את לבזבזיו! אלא: שאני שלחן

דרחמנא

רש"י

טעונין טבילה. מפני טומאת הרגל: חוץ ממזבח הזהב ומזבח הנחשת מפני שהן כקרקע. שהכתוב קראו "מזבח אדמה", ושלחן – הא אמרן דלא נגעו בו: מפני שהן מצופין. בגמרא מפרש: **גמ'** מנורה לא כתיב בה תמיד. כלומר: תמידין האמורין במנורה לא תמיד יומם ולילה קאמר, אלא תמיד מלילה ללילה, כתמיד האמור בעולת תמיד ובחביתי כ"ג. אבל ביום לא היה דולק, ד"מערב עד בוקר" כתיב (שמות כז): תן לה מדת השמן שיש בה כדי לידלק מערב עד בוקר, לפיכך כל היום אתה יכול לסלקה ולהטבילה. אבל תמיד האמור בשלחן – תמיד יום ולילה הוא, דמשבת לשבת הוא ערוך עליו: נוכח השלחן. כל זמן שהשלחן שם תהא מנורה נוכחו: ותיפוק לי. דאי נמי נגעו בשלחן לא מיטמאו ליה, דהא כלי עץ העשוי לנחת במקום אחד הוא: דומיא דשק בעינן. לענין טומאה הוקשו כלי עץ לשק, דכתיב: "כל אשר יפול עליו מהם במותם יטמא, מכל כלי עץ או בגד או עור או שק" (ויקרא יא): מה שק מיטלטל מלא וריקם. יצא העשוי לנחת דאינו מיטלטל מלא וריקן, יצא כלי עץ המחזיק מ' סאה בלח, שהן כוריים ביבש, אע"פ שמיטלטל ריקן – אינו מיטלטל מלא, שאם יטלטלוהו מלא – ישבר: השלחן הטהור. שאמרתי שיהא טהור, מכלל שהוא ראוי לטומאה. והלא כלי עץ העשוי לנחת הוא: סילוקו כסידורו. שסילוקו לשבת הבאה חם כיום סידורו: חם ביום הלקחו. שיהא חם ביום הלקחו מעל השלחן: ותיפוק לי. דמקבל טומאה, ואפילו הוא עשוי לנחת: משום ציפויו. שהוא מתכת, דכלי מתכת לא איתקש לשק: דהתנן. דבתר ציפוי אזלינן: הדולפקי. כסא המתקפל ומכוסה עור: שחיפהו בשיש. דשוב הוי ככלי אבנים, שאין מקבלין טומאה: ושייר בהן. מן הפחיתה או מן החיפוי, כדי הנחת כוסות: טמא. שעדיין ראוי למלאכתו ראשונה: רבי יהודה אומר. צריך אף הנחת חתיכות לחם ובשר, ואי לא – לאו שלחן הוא. אלמא: ציפויו מבטלו אפילו להקל, וכל שכן להחמיר: לא שנו. הך דקתני ציפויו מבטלו אלא בעצי אכסלגים, שאינו חשוב כ"כ: ציפוי שאינו עומד. שאינו מחוזק במסמרים יפה, ותאמר דההוא דמקדש לאו עומד הוא: לבזבזין. שפה לשלחן סביב:

רחמנא

תוספות

שלא תגעו בשלחן. בכהנים עמי הארץ ההולכין להיכל להשתחוות קאמר. דאילו ישראל – לא היו רשאין לילך אף בין אולם למזבח. וכן פירש רש"י: **מנורה** לא כתיב בה תמיד. פי' רש"י ד"תמיד" דכתיב בה לא דמי לתמיד דשלחן, דהאי "תמיד" – מלילה ללילה הוי, כמו "עולת תמיד" האמור בתמיד. ובחביתי כ"ג. אבל ביום לא היה דולק, ד"מערב ועד בקר" כתיב, תן לה מדתה מערב עד בקר. הלכך, כל היום יכול לסלקה. אבל תמיד האמור בשלחן – כל היום וכל הלילה, דהלחם נסדר עליו משבת לשבת. והקשה הר"ר אלחנן: דהא במסכת תמיד (דף ל:) משמע דנר מערבי דולק כל היום, שממנה היה מדליק ובה היה מסיים, ומסתמא מ"תמיד" נפקא! ועוד קשה להר"ר אלחנן עלה דההיא: דהא כתיב "מערב עד בקר", ושיערו חכמים מדתה לחצי לוג!* וי"ל(א): דמ"מ לא היה בה טפי מבשאר נרות, ומ"מ ממילא מחמת הנס דולק כל היום. ובשעה שלא היה הנס – היו דולקין אותה בבקר כדי להדליק ממנה האחרות:

כלי עץ העשוי לנחת. הקשה הר"ר אלחנן: כל שנים שהיו ישראל במדבר היו מטלטלים אותה, ואם כן אין עשוי לנחת, ואם כן אמאי צריך ראייה מקרא "השלחן הטהור" מכלל דאיכא טמא! ותירץ דלא איצטריך קרא רק לנוב וגבעון ושילה ובית עולמים שלא היתה מטולטלת ושמעינן מקרא שהיו מגביהין אותה. ולא נראה: כיון שהיתה מטולטלת כבר – אף משבאו לבית עולמים נמי לא נפקא מידי קבלת טומאה ראשונה! אלא י"ל דלא מהני טלטולה כיון דלא היתה מטולטלת לבדה כי אם בהדי שאר כלים:

סילוקו כסידורו. לענין שהיה רך. ומה שאמר הפסוק: "חום ביום הלקחו" – לאו דוקא, אלא דחם לא היה. דאיכא מ"ד במנחות (דף נה:) שהיא נאפת מערב שבת, ואי אפשר שישמור החום עד השבת, אם לא שנאמר לדבריו נשאר בתנור לשמור חומו עד השבת בבקר:

בכלי אכסלגים. יתכן לפרש שהיא שם עיר, ושעושים כלים הבאים משם. וקשה: דהכא משמע של עץ היו, והתם בזבחים פרק "דם חטאת" (דף נד.) משמע שהיו של עור, כדפי' רש"י גבי העור טעון כבוס במקו' קדוש! [וע' תוס' מנחות נז. ד"ה כלי]:

כאן בצפוי עומד. ושל מקדש לא היה עומד. דשלש שולחנות היו במקדש כמין שלשה ארונות שעשה בצלאל, והצפוי נוח להסירו. וי"מ בצפוי עומד – צפוי דשיש, כגון שלחן ודולבקי דשייש עב וחזק, וגם בלא עץ נמי עומד מאליו, לכך לא חשיב העץ. אבל שלחן של משה – הזהב היה דק וקלוש, ובלא עץ לא מצי קאי, לפיכך העץ עיקר והצפוי בטל לגביה:

שאני שלחן דרחמנא קרייה עץ. יש להקשות: מזבח נמי איקרי עץ, דכתיב: "המזבח עץ שלש אמות" ותנן ליה במתני' דפליגי ביה משום דלא בטיל הצפוי אגב העץ, אלא העץ בטל. ועוד אמר בסמוך: ואיבעית אימא רבנן לר"א קאמרי: מאי דעתך, משום דמצופין – מיבטל בטל צפוי לגבייהו. אלמא טעמא משום דהצפוי בטל לגבי העץ. ואילו גבי שלחן ודולבקי היכא דלא שייר כלום – בטל העץ אגב הצפוי. ומיהו הך קרא דמזבח של עץ מתרגם יהונתן: פתורא דסמוך למזבח דדהבא, אבל מזבח לא מיקרי של עץ. וגם שלחן לא מלינו דאיקרי עץ כי אם השלחן דסמוך למזבח, מדאפקי' בלשון מזבח. אבל שמא שלחן ודולבקי עץ לא איקרי, לפיכך לא בטיל הצפוי לגבייהו אי לא שייר כלום. והר"ר אלחנן תי': דלא קשה מידי, כדתנן במתני': כל הכלים שהיו במקדש טעונים טבילה, חוץ ממזבח הזהב והנחשת. מזבח הנחשת – דכתיב: "מזבח אבנים תעשה לי", מזבח הזהב – דכתיב: "המנורה והמזבחות" ואיתקוש להדדי. לפיכך נבטל צפוי גבי מזבח הנחשת, הלכך לא מקבלי טומאה. אך צריך עיון: האי קרא ד"מזבח שלש אמות" במאי מיתוקם, אי מזבח הזהב אמתים ותו לא!

שלחנו

רבינו חננאל

היו מעבירין על טהרת העזרה מטבילין הכלים ששמשו בהן במקדש. ואומר להן הזהרו שמא תגעו בשלחן מכלל שאם יגעו בשלחן מטמא ומקשינן וכי שולחן בר קיבולי טומאה הוא והא כלי עץ העשוי לנחת הוא וכל כלי עץ העשוי לנחת לא מקבל טומאה דבעינן כלי עץ דומיא דשק דמיטלטל מלא וריקם אף כלי עץ מיטלטל מלא וריקם ופרקינן שלחן זה שבמקדש נמי מיטלטל ואפי' מלא דהא מגביהין היו הכהנים אותו בעודנו הלחם סדור עליו ומראין אותו לעולי רגלים. ומקשינן ולולי שמיטלטל מלא וריקם שלחן של מקדש לא הוה מטמא. תיפוק לי משום ציפוי דכיון דהוא מצופה זהב הוה ליה ככלי מתכות ומקבל טומאה דהא נפק ליה מתורת כלי עץ דתנן בכלים פרק כ"ב השלחן והדולפקי שנפחתו או שחיפן בשייש כו'. ואסיקנא טעמא דשייר מקום הנחת כוסות שלא חיפהו בשייש אבל לא שייר בו מקום שאינו מחופה טהור שבא החיפוי בשייש שאינו מקבל טומאה כדקי"ל כלי גללין כלי אבנים כלי אדמה אין מקבלין טומאה וביטל העץ ויבא צפוי הזהב ויבטל העץ ויקבל טומאה ככלי מתכות דהא אפי' פשוטין מקבלין. וכי תימא שאני עצי שטים דכיון דחשיבי לא בטלי בציפויין. הניחא לר"ל דאמר לא שנו שלחן שחיפהו בטיל עצו אלא בכלי אכסלגום דזילי. אבל בכלי [מסמים] פי' עצי (אבנים) [מסמים] א) דיקירי לא בטיל אלא לר' יוחנן דאמר כל כלי עץ בטל בציפויין ל"ש כלי אכסלגם ול"ש כלי מסמים ל"ש ציפוי עומד ל"ש ציפוי שאינו עומד ל"ש חופה את לבזבזין ול"ש אינו חופה הכל בטל בצפויו. האי שלחן כיון דמצופה הוא אע"ג דאינו מיטלטל מלא וריקם הרי הוא ככלי מתכות ומקבל טומאה. ופרקי' שאני שלחן של מקדש דהא אע"ג דמצופה זהב הוא

א) וכ"ה בערוך ערך אכסלגס ע"ש.

הגהות הב"ח

(א) תוס' ד"ה מנורה וכו' ויש לומר דנר מערבי לא היה בה שמן טפי:

מסורת הש"ס

[מנחות פט.]
[יומא כא: מגילה כו: מנחות נו:]
[שבת פג: וש"נ]
[מנחות כט: יומא כא.]
מנחות נז:
כלים פכ"ב מ"א [מנחות נו:]

דַּרַחֲמָנָא קַרְיֵיהּ עֵץ, *דִּכְתִיב: °"הַמִּזְבֵּחַ עֵץ שָׁלשׁ אַמּוֹת גָּבוֹהַּ וְאָרְכּוֹ שְׁתַּיִם אַמּוֹת וּמִקְצְעוֹתָיו לוֹ וְאָרְכּוֹ וְקִירוֹתָיו עֵץ וַיְדַבֵּר אֵלַי זֶה הַשֻּׁלְחָן אֲשֶׁר לִפְנֵי ה'". פָּתַח בַּמִּזְבֵּחַ וְסִיֵּים בַּשֻּׁלְחָן. רַבִּי יוֹחָנָן וְרֵישׁ לָקִישׁ דְּאָמְרִי תַּרְוַיְיהוּ: בִּזְמַן שֶׁבֵּית הַמִּקְדָּשׁ קַיָּים מִזְבֵּחַ מְכַפֵּר עַל אָדָם, עַכְשָׁיו — שֻׁלְחָנוֹ שֶׁל אָדָם מְכַפֵּר עָלָיו.§ "כָּל הַכֵּלִים שֶׁבַּמִּקְדָּשׁ יֵשׁ לָהֶם שְׁנַיִים כו'".§ מִזְבַּח הַנְּחוֹשֶׁת — דִּכְתִיב: °"מִזְבַּח אֲדָמָה תַּעֲשֶׂה לִּי" מִזְבַּח הַזָּהָב — דִּכְתִיב: °"הַמְּנוֹרָה וְהַמִּזְבְּחוֹת" אִיתְקוּשׁ מִזְבְּחוֹת זֶה לָזֶה.§ "וַחֲכָמִים אוֹמְרִים מִפְּנֵי שֶׁהֵן מְצוּפִּין".§ אַדְּרַבָּה, כֵּיוָן דִּמְצוּפִּין נִינְהוּ מִיטַּמְּאוּ! אֵימָא: וַחֲכָמִים מְטַמְּאִין מִפְּנֵי שֶׁהֵן מְצוּפִּין. וְאב"א: רַבָּנַן לְר"א קָאָמְרִי: מַאי דַּעְתִּיךְ, מִשּׁוּם דִּמְצוּפִּין — [א]מִיבְטַל בְּטִיל צִפּוּיָין גַּבַּיְיהוּ. א"ר אַבָּהוּ אָמַר ר"א: ת"ח אֵין אוּר שֶׁל גֵּיהִנָּם שׁוֹלֶטֶת בָּהֶן, ק"ו מִסָּלָמַנְדְּרָא; וּמַה סָּלָמַנְדְּרָא שֶׁתּוֹלֶדֶת אֵשׁ הִיא — הַסָּךְ מִדָּמָהּ אֵין אוּר שׁוֹלֶטֶת בּוֹ, ת"ח, שֶׁכָּל גּוּפָן אֵשׁ, דִּכְתִיב: °"הֲלוֹא כֹה דְבָרִי כָּאֵשׁ נְאֻם ה'" — עַל אַחַת כַּמָּה וְכַמָּה. *אָמַר רֵישׁ לָקִישׁ: אֵין אוּר שֶׁל גֵּיהִנָּם שׁוֹלֶטֶת בְּפוֹשְׁעֵי יִשְׂרָאֵל, קַל וָחוֹמֶר מִמִּזְבַּח הַזָּהָב; מַה מִּזְבַּח הַזָּהָב שֶׁאֵין עָלָיו אֶלָּא כְּעוֹבִי דִּינַר זָהָב, כַּמָּה שָׁנִים אֵין הָאוּר שׁוֹלֶטֶת בּוֹ, פּוֹשְׁעֵי יִשְׂרָאֵל שֶׁמְּלֵאִין מִצְוֹת כָּרִמּוֹן, דִּכְתִיב: °"כְּפֶלַח הָרִמּוֹן רַקָּתֵךְ", *אַל תִּקְרֵי "רַקָּתֵךְ" אֶלָּא רֵקָנִין שֶׁבָּךְ — עַל אַחַת כַּמָּה וְכַמָּה.§

הדרן עלך חומר בקודש וסליקא לה מסכת חגיגה

רש"י

רַחֲמָנָא קַרְיֵיהּ עֵץ. אַף כְּשֶׁהוּא מְצוּפֶּה: שׁוּלְחָנוֹ מְכַפֵּר עָלָיו. בְּהַכְנָסַת אוֹרְחִין: הָכִי גָּרְסִינַן: מִזְבַּח הַנְּחוֹשֶׁת דִּכְתִיב "מִזְבַּח אֲדָמָה". הַכָּתוּב קְרָאוֹ אֲדָמָה לַמִּזְבֵּחַ שֶׁמַּעֲלִין עָלָיו הָעוֹלוֹת וְהַשְּׁלָמִים, וְהַיְינוּ מִזְבַּח הַנְּחֹשֶׁת: אַדְּרַבָּה מִשּׁוּם דִּמְצוּפִּין נִינְהוּ נִטְמְאוּ. דְּאִי לָאו מְצוּפֶּה, יֵשׁ לָהֶם לְטַהֲרָם מִשּׁוּם כְּלִי עֵץ הֶעָשׂוּי לְנַחַת: מַאי דַּעְתִּיךְ. דְּיָלְפַתְּ טַעְמָא מִדְּקָרְינְהוּ אֲדָמָה, הָא לָאו הָכִי — טְמֵאִין, אע"ג דַּעֲשׂוּיִן לְנַחַת: מִפְּנֵי שֶׁהֵן מְצוּפִּין. וּבָעֵי לְמֵימַר שֶׁהַצִּיפּוּי מְבַטְּלָן, וְהָוֵי לְהוּ כִּכְלֵי מַתָּכוֹת: מִיבְטַל בָּטֵיל צִיפּוּיָין לְגַבַּיְיהוּ. דְּרַחֲמָנָא קָרָא עֵץ לְכוּלְּהוּ, וּבְלָאו הַאי קְרָא נַמִי לָא מְקַבְּלֵי טוּמְאָה: סָלָמַנְדְּרָא. °חַיָּה הַנִּבְרֵאת מִן הָאוּר, כְּשֶׁבּוֹעֲרִין אֵשׁ בְּמָקוֹם אֶחָד שֶׁבַע שָׁנִים תָּמִיד בְּלִי הֶפְסֵק: כְּעוֹבִי דִּינַר זָהָב. דָּבָר מוּעָט, לֹא חָסַר זְהָבָהּ, דְּנַעֲשָׂה בּוֹ נֵס:

הדרן עלך חומר בקודש וסליקא לה מסכת חגיגה

תוספות

שלחנו של אדם מכפר. דגדול כח הלגימה, כדאיתא בהגדת "חלק" (סנהדרין דף קג.): **מזבח** אדמה תעשה לי. וכי מוקמי לה בזבחים פרק "קדשי קדשים" (דף נח. ושם) גבי מזבח אבנים להאי קרא ד"מזבח אדמה" אמר הר"ר אלחנן דקאי לתרוייהו. ולמורי נראה: לפי שהיה מזבח של משה במקום מזבח של אבנים של בית עולמים, וכי האי גוונא דריש התם (דף נט.): "כי מזבח הנחשת אשר לפני ה' קטן מהכיל" ודריש ליה מזבח אבנים במקום מזבח דנחושת:

ואיבעית אימא רבנן לר"א כו'. וקשה: למה לי השלחן הטהור מכלל שהיה טמא — תיפוק ליה משום ליפוי, דאף במזבחות נמי הוה מטמא [ר"א] משום ליפוי, אי לאו טעמא דכקרקע נינהו ללישנא בתרא, אע"פ דרחמנא קרינהו עץ — אם כן השלחן נמי טמא. אע"ג דאיקרי עץ משום ליפוי! וללישנא קמא דמוקי לה כרבנן דמטמא, ולא בטל הליפוי לגבי עץ! ותירץ הר"ר אלחנן: דאיצטריך שפיר קרא ד"השלחן", דאף במזבחות נמי לא ידעינן ליה שיהיה בטל לגבי הליפוי אלא משום דיליף משלחן, דאף על גב דמיקרי עץ — התורה טמאתו משום ליפוי, ורבנן דאמרי מבטיל בטיל ליפוי לגבייהו אמרי מדאיצטריך לרבויי שלחן, דהא מסברא טמא משום ליפוי — אלא ודאי, לאשמועינן דאע"ג שיש לו ליפוי — צריך קרא לרבויי דמקבל טומאה. ואי לאו הרבוי — הליפוי בטל. א"כ ממילא, גבי מזבח, דליכא רבוי — הצפוי בטל, ללישנא בתרא:

סלמנדרא. החלד והעכבר תרגמם יהונתן כרכושתא וסלמנדרא. ערוך: **פושעי** ישראל אין אור של גיהנם כו'. נראה לי דלאו בפושעי ישראל בגופן, דהא אמרינן בראש השנה (דף יז.): פושעי ישראל בגופן — גיהנם כלה והם אינם כלים. אלא בפושעי קלת קאמר, ומשום דמסיק להו אברהם לכולהו חוץ מבועלי הכותית(א) (*דמבשקר ליה) ערלתיה, כדאמר בריש עושין פסין (עירובין דף יט.). וכי אמרינן בסוף "הזהב" (ב"מ דף נח:) הכל יורדין ועולין חוץ משלשה — לאו בגיהנם איירי, אלא במקום אחד לידון. הן יורדין, ואף הנידון — לאחר שנים עשר חדש עולין, ואין נידונין יותר משנה תמימה*:

שאין בו אלא עובי דינר. בתנחומא יש שהיה משה תמיה על זה: אי אפשר שלא ישרף העץ! ואמר לו המקום: כך דרכי באש של מעלה: אש אוכלה אש, ואינו מכלה, כדכתיב: "והסנה איננו אוכל" (שמות ג):

הדרן עלך חומר בקודש וסליקא לה מסכת חגיגה

מסורת הש"ם

ברכות כה. מנחות לז. ע"ש | יחזקאל מא | שמות כ | במדבר ג | ירמיה כג | עירובין יט. ע"ש | שיר ד [סנהדרין לז. ברכות נז: מגילה ו.] | [נ"ל דלא מבשקר ליה] | [ועיין עדיות פ"ב מ"י]

הגהות הב"ח

(א) תום' ד"ה פושעי וכו' חוץ מבועל כותית דמשכה ליה:

גליון הש"ם

רש"י ד"ה סלמנדרא חיה הנבראת וכו'. עיין חולין ד' קכז ע"א ברש"י ד"ה וסלמנדרא:

עין משפט נר מצוה

סד א מיי' פי"א מהל' מטמאי משכב ומושב הלכה יא [ועי' מה שכתב בזה הכ"מ בפ"ד מהל' כלים הל' ד]:

רבינו חננאל

הוא איקרי עץ שנאמר המזבח עץ שלש אמות גבוה וארכו שתים אמות ומקצועותיו לו וארכו וקירותיו עץ וידבר אלי זה השלחן אשר לפני ה' אלמא דמקרי עץ ומשום הכי בעינן להיותו מטלטל מלא וריקם זו ההלכה כולה ענין השלחן שצפויו אינו מבטל העץ שלו היא במסכת מנחות בפרק שתי הלחם ומפורשת שם כאשר פירשנו והרבה טעו בה דכתיב על השלחן הטהור מכלל דזימנין הוא טמא והשלחן פשוטי כלי עץ הוא ומסגרתו למטה היתה. ותניא (בתוספתא ספ"ג) שלחן שנטמא מטבילין אותו בזמנו אפי' בשבת. משום דמטלטל מלא וריקם. ומעשה שהטבילו המנורה בלילי יום כו'*). חוץ ממזבח הזהב ומזבח הנחושת שהן כקרקע. דכתיב מזבח אדמה וכתיב המנורה והמזבחות [אתקוש מזבחות] להדדי דלהוו כולהו כאדמה דלא מקבלי טומאה. וחכמים מטמאין מפני שהן מצופין. אי בעי תימא לר' אלעזר קאמרי ליה דקאמר טעמא מפני שהן כקרקע דלא מטמו. הא לאו הכי הוו מטמא. והא פשוטי כלי עץ (פשוטי) נינהו ולא מטמו. וכי תימא משום דמצופין. דברי חכמים לר' אליעזר בתימה האי דאמרת דמטמו משום צפויו מיבטיל בטיל ציפויהו והוו להו כלי עץ. אלא בין משום שהן מצופין בין משום שהן בקרקע אפי' הכי טעונין **) טבילה לפי' שנינו כל הכלים טעונין טבילה ואפי' המזבח. א"ר אלעזר תלמידי חכמים אין אור של גיהנם שולטת בהן ק"ו מסלמנדרא ומה סלמנדרא שהוא תולדת אש הסך מדמו אין אור שולט בו. ת"ח (שמשתמשין) שכל גופן אש כדכתיב הלא כה דברי כאש עאכ"ו. אמר ר"ל אפי' פושעי ישראל אין אור של גיהנם שולטת בהן ק"ו ממזבח הזהב ומה מזבח הזהב שאין צפויו אלא כעובי דינר הוה כמה שנים ואין אור שולט בו פושעי ישראל שהן מליאין מצות כרמון. שנאמר כפלח הרמון רקתך. אפי' ריקנין שבך מלאין מצות כרמון עאכ"ו: **הדרן עלך חומר בקודש**

*) נראה שצ"ל בלילי יו"ט ובתוספתא אהגי' שהטבילו המנורה ביו"ט ואפשר שלפני רבינו היה הגי' בלילי יו"ט ובירושלמי איתא סתם הטבילו את המנורה וגי' התוספתא שהביא רבינו נראה העיקר ודו"ק.

**) לכאורה משמע לחכמים נמי ס"ל דלא בעי טבילה ולא פליגי רק בטעמא ודברי רבינו צ"ע.

סליקא ליה מסכת חגיגה, האל יסיר ממנו אף ורוגז וחימה ותוגה

The following paragraph is recited three times:

הַדְרָן עֲלָךְ מַסֶּכֶת חֲגִיגָה וְהַדְרָךְ עֲלָן, דַּעְתָּן עֲלָךְ מַסֶּכֶת חֲגִיגָה וְדַעְתָּךְ עֲלָן, לָא נִתְנְשֵׁי מִנָּךְ מַסֶּכֶת חֲגִיגָה וְלָא תִתְנְשֵׁי מִנַּן, לָא בְּעָלְמָא הָדֵין וְלָא בְּעָלְמָא דְאָתֵי.

יְהִי רָצוֹן מִלְּפָנֶיךָ יהוה אֱלֹהֵינוּ וֵאלֹהֵי אֲבוֹתֵינוּ, שֶׁתְּהֵא תוֹרָתְךָ אֻמָּנוּתֵנוּ בָּעוֹלָם הַזֶּה, וּתְהֵא עִמָּנוּ לָעוֹלָם הַבָּא. חֲנִינָא בַּר פַּפָּא, רָמֵי בַּר פַּפָּא, נַחְמָן בַּר פַּפָּא, אַחַאי בַּר פַּפָּא, אַבָּא מָרִי בַּר פַּפָּא, רָפְרָם בַּר פַּפָּא, רָכִישׁ בַּר פַּפָּא, סוּרְחָב בַּר פַּפָּא, אַדָּא בַּר פַּפָּא, דָּרוּ בַּר פַּפָּא.

הַעֲרֶב נָא יהוה אֱלֹהֵינוּ אֶת דִּבְרֵי תוֹרָתְךָ בְּפִינוּ וּבְפִי
עַמְּךָ בֵּית יִשְׂרָאֵל, וְנִהְיֶה אֲנַחְנוּ וְצֶאֱצָאֵינוּ (וְצֶאֱצָאֵי
צֶאֱצָאֵינוּ) וְצֶאֱצָאֵי עַמְּךָ בֵּית יִשְׂרָאֵל, כֻּלָּנוּ יוֹדְעֵי
שְׁמֶךָ וְלוֹמְדֵי תוֹרָתְךָ לִשְׁמָהּ. מֵאֹיְבַי תְּחַכְּמֵנִי מִצְוֺתֶךָ תהלים קיט
כִּי לְעוֹלָם הִיא־לִי: יְהִי־לִבִּי תָמִים בְּחֻקֶּיךָ לְמַעַן לֹא
אֵבוֹשׁ: לְעוֹלָם לֹא־אֶשְׁכַּח פִּקּוּדֶיךָ כִּי־בָם חִיִּיתָנִי:
בָּרוּךְ אַתָּה יהוה לַמְּדֵנִי חֻקֶּיךָ: אָמֵן אָמֵן אָמֵן סֶלָה
וָעֶד.

מוֹדִים אֲנַחְנוּ לְפָנֶיךָ יהוה אֱלֹהֵינוּ וֵאלֹהֵי אֲבוֹתֵינוּ
שֶׁשַּׂמְתָּ חֶלְקֵנוּ מִיּוֹשְׁבֵי בֵּית הַמִּדְרָשׁ, וְלֹא שַׂמְתָּ חֶלְקֵנוּ
מִיּוֹשְׁבֵי קְרָנוֹת. שֶׁאָנוּ מַשְׁכִּימִים וְהֵם מַשְׁכִּימִים,
אָנוּ מַשְׁכִּימִים לְדִבְרֵי תוֹרָה, וְהֵם מַשְׁכִּימִים לִדְבָרִים
בְּטֵלִים. אָנוּ עֲמֵלִים וְהֵם עֲמֵלִים, אָנוּ עֲמֵלִים וּמְקַבְּלִים
שָׂכָר, וְהֵם עֲמֵלִים וְאֵינָם מְקַבְּלִים שָׂכָר. אָנוּ רָצִים וְהֵם
רָצִים, אָנוּ רָצִים לְחַיֵּי הָעוֹלָם הַבָּא, וְהֵם רָצִים לִבְאֵר
שַׁחַת, שֶׁנֶּאֱמַר: וְאַתָּה אֱלֹהִים תּוֹרִדֵם לִבְאֵר שַׁחַת תהלים נה
אַנְשֵׁי דָמִים וּמִרְמָה לֹא־יֶחֱצוּ יְמֵיהֶם וַאֲנִי אֶבְטַח־בָּךְ:

יְהִי רָצוֹן מִלְּפָנֶיךָ יהוה אֱלֹהַי, כְּשֵׁם שֶׁעֲזַרְתַּנִי לְסַיֵּם
מַסֶּכֶת חֲגִיגָה כֵּן תְּעַזְרֵנִי לְהַתְחִיל מַסֶּכְתּוֹת וּסְפָרִים
אֲחֵרִים וּלְסַיְּמָם, לִלְמֹד וּלְלַמֵּד לִשְׁמֹר וְלַעֲשׂוֹת
וּלְקַיֵּם אֶת כָּל דִּבְרֵי תַלְמוּד תּוֹרָתְךָ בְּאַהֲבָה, וּזְכוּת
כָּל הַתַּנָּאִים וְאָמוֹרָאִים וְתַלְמִידֵי חֲכָמִים יַעֲמֹד לִי
וּלְזַרְעִי שֶׁלֹּא תָמוּשׁ הַתּוֹרָה מִפִּי וּמִפִּי זַרְעִי וְזֶרַע זַרְעִי
עַד עוֹלָם, וְיִתְקַיֵּם בִּי: בְּהִתְהַלֶּכְךָ תַּנְחֶה אֹתָךְ בְּשָׁכְבְּךָ משלי ו
תִּשְׁמֹר עָלֶיךָ וַהֲקִיצוֹתָ הִיא תְשִׂיחֶךָ: כִּי־בִי יִרְבּוּ יָמֶיךָ משלי ט
וְיוֹסִיפוּ לְּךָ שְׁנוֹת חַיִּים: אֹרֶךְ יָמִים בִּימִינָהּ בִּשְׂמֹאולָהּ משלי ג
עֹשֶׁר וְכָבוֹד: יהוה עֹז לְעַמּוֹ יִתֵּן יהוה יְבָרֵךְ אֶת־עַמּוֹ תהלים כט
בַשָּׁלוֹם:

The following paragraph is recited three times:

הַדְרָן We shall return to you, tractate *Ḥagiga,* and your glory is upon us. Our thoughts are upon you, tractate *Ḥagiga,* and your thoughts are upon us. We will not be forgotten from you, tractate *Ḥagiga,* and you will not be forgotten from us; neither in this world nor in the World-to-Come.

יְהִי רָצוֹן May it be Your will, Lord our God and God of our ancestors, that Your Torah will be our avocation in this world and will accompany us to the World-to-Come. Ḥanina bar Pappa, Ramei bar Pappa, Naḥman bar Pappa, Aḥai bar Pappa, Abba Mari bar Pappa, Rafram bar Pappa, Rakhish bar Pappa, Surḥav bar Pappa, Adda bar Pappa, Daru bar Pappa.

הַעֲרֶב נָא Please, Lord our God, make the words of Your
Torah sweet in our mouths and in the mouths of Your
people, the house of Israel, so that we, our descendants
(and their descendants), and the descendants of Your
people, the house of Israel, may all know Your name and
study Your Torah for its own sake. Your commandments *Psalms 119*
make me wiser than my enemies, for they are ever with
me. Let my heart be undivided in Your statutes, in order
that I may not be put to shame. I will never forget Your
precepts, for with them You have quickened me. Blessed
are You, O Lord; teach me Your statutes. Amen, Amen,
Amen, Selah, Forever.

מוֹדִים We give thanks before You, Lord Our God and
God of our ancestors, that You have placed our lot
among those who sit in the study hall and that you have
not given us our portion among those who sit idly on
street corners. We rise early and they rise early. We rise
early to pursue matters of Torah and they rise early to
pursue frivolous matters. We toil and they toil. We toil
and receive a reward and they toil and do not receive a
reward. We run and they run. We run to the life of the
World-to-Come and they run to the pit of destruction,
as it is stated: But You, God, will bring them down into *Psalms 55*
the pit of destruction; men of blood and deceit shall not
live out half their days; but as for me, I will trust in You.

יְהִי רָצוֹן May it be Your will, Lord my God, just as you
have assisted me in completing tractate *Ḥagiga* so assist
me to begin other tractates and books and conclude
them to learn and to teach, to observe and to perform,
and to fulfill all the teachings of Your Torah with love.
And may the merit of all the *tanna'im* and *amora'im* and
Torah scholars stand for me and my descendants so that
the Torah will not move from my mouth and from the
mouths of my descendants and the descendants of my
descendants forever. And may the verse: When you *Proverbs 6*
walk, it shall lead you, when you lie down, it shall watch
over you; and when you awaken, it shall talk with you
be fulfilled in me. For in the Torah your days shall be *Proverbs 9*
multiplied, and the years of your life shall be increased.
Length of days is in her right hand; in her left hand are *Proverbs 3*
riches and honor. May the Lord give strength to His *Psalms 29*
people; the Lord will bless His people with peace.

The following קדיש *requires the presence of a* מנין*.*

יִתְגַּדַּל וְיִתְקַדַּשׁ שְׁמֵהּ רַבָּא
בְּעָלְמָא דְּהוּא עָתִיד לְאִתְחַדָּתָא
וּלְאַחֲיָאָה מֵתַיָּא, וּלְאַסָּקָא יָתְהוֹן לְחַיֵּי עָלְמָא
וּלְמִבְנֵא קַרְתָּא דִירוּשְׁלֵם, וּלְשַׁכְלָלָא הֵיכְלֵהּ בְּגַוַּהּ
וּלְמֶעְקַר פָּלְחָנָא נֻכְרָאָה מֵאַרְעָא
וּלַאֲתָבָא פָּלְחָנָא דִשְׁמַיָּא לְאַתְרֵהּ
וְיַמְלִיךְ קֻדְשָׁא בְּרִיךְ הוּא בְּמַלְכוּתֵהּ וִיקָרֵהּ
(נוסח ספרד: וְיַצְמַח פֻּרְקָנֵהּ וִיקָרֵב מְשִׁיחֵהּ)
בְּחַיֵּיכוֹן וּבְיוֹמֵיכוֹן וּבְחַיֵּי דְכָל בֵּית יִשְׂרָאֵל
בַּעֲגָלָא וּבִזְמַן קָרִיב, וְאִמְרוּ אָמֵן.

יְהֵא שְׁמֵהּ רַבָּא מְבָרַךְ לְעָלַם וּלְעָלְמֵי עָלְמַיָּא.

יִתְבָּרַךְ וְיִשְׁתַּבַּח וְיִתְפָּאַר וְיִתְרוֹמַם וְיִתְנַשֵּׂא
וְיִתְהַדָּר וְיִתְעַלֶּה וְיִתְהַלָּל
שְׁמֵהּ דְּקֻדְשָׁא בְּרִיךְ הוּא
לְעֵלָּא מִן כָּל בִּרְכָתָא
/בעשרת ימי תשובה: לְעֵלָּא לְעֵלָּא מִכָּל בִּרְכָתָא/
וְשִׁירָתָא, תֻּשְׁבְּחָתָא וְנֶחֱמָתָא, דַּאֲמִירָן בְּעָלְמָא
וְאִמְרוּ אָמֵן. (קהל: אָמֵן)

עַל יִשְׂרָאֵל וְעַל רַבָּנָן
וְעַל תַּלְמִידֵיהוֹן וְעַל כָּל תַּלְמִידֵי תַלְמִידֵיהוֹן
וְעַל כָּל מָאן דְּעָסְקִין בְּאוֹרַיְתָא
דִּי בְּאַתְרָא (בארץ ישראל: קַדִּישָׁא) הָדֵין, וְדִי בְּכָל אֲתַר וַאֲתַר
יְהֵא לְהוֹן וּלְכוֹן שְׁלָמָא רַבָּא
חִנָּא וְחִסְדָּא, וְרַחֲמֵי, וְחַיֵּי אֲרִיכֵי, וּמְזוֹנֵי רְוִיחֵי
וּפֻרְקָנָא מִן קֳדָם אֲבוּהוֹן דִּי בִשְׁמַיָּא
וְאִמְרוּ אָמֵן.
יְהֵא שְׁלָמָא רַבָּא מִן שְׁמַיָּא
וְחַיִּים (טוֹבִים) עָלֵינוּ וְעַל כָּל יִשְׂרָאֵל
וְאִמְרוּ אָמֵן.

Bow, take three steps back, as if taking leave of the Divine Presence, then bow, first left, then right, then center, while saying:

עֹשֶׂה שָׁלוֹם/ בעשרת ימי תשובה: הַשָּׁלוֹם/ בִּמְרוֹמָיו
הוּא יַעֲשֶׂה בְרַחֲמָיו שָׁלוֹם, עָלֵינוּ וְעַל כָּל יִשְׂרָאֵל
וְאִמְרוּ אָמֵן.

The following Kaddish requires the presence of a minyan.

Magnified and sanctified may His great name be,
in the world that will in future be renewed,
reviving the dead and raising them up to eternal life.
He will rebuild the city of Jerusalem
and in it re-establish His Temple.
He will remove alien worship from the earth
and restore to its place the worship of Heaven.
Then the Holy One, blessed be He,
will reign in His sovereignty and splendor.
May it be in your lifetime and in your days,
(*Nusaḥ Sepharad:* make His salvation flourish,
and hasten His messiah,)
and in the lifetime of all the House of Israel,
swiftly and soon – and say: Amen.

May His great name be blessed for ever and all time.

Blessed and praised,
glorified and exalted,
raised and honored,
uplifted and lauded
be the name of the Holy One,
blessed be He,
beyond any blessing,
song, praise and consolation uttered in the world –
and say: Amen.

To Israel, to the teachers,
their disciples and their disciples' disciples,
and to all who engage in the study of Torah,
in this (*in Israel add:* holy) place or elsewhere,
may there come to them and you great peace,
grace, kindness and compassion,
long life, ample sustenance and deliverance,
from their Father in Heaven –
and say: Amen.

May there be great peace from heaven,
and (good) life for us and all Israel –
and say: Amen.

Bow, take three steps back, as if taking leave of the Divine Presence, then bow, first left, then right, then center, while saying:

May He who makes peace in His high places,
in His compassion make peace for us and all Israel –
and say: Amen.